Rev'd

ACTS

ACTS

ZONDERVAN
Exegetical
Commentary
ON THE
New Testament

ECKHARD J. SCHNABEL

CLINTON E. ARNOLD
General Editor

ZONDERVAN®

ZONDERVAN.com/
AUTHORTRACKER
follow your favorite authors

For
I. H. Marshall
D. A. Carson

ZONDERVAN

Acts
Copyright © 2012 by Eckhard J. Schnabel

Requests for information should be addressed to:

Zondervan, *Grand Rapids, Michigan 49530*

Library of Congress Cataloging-in-Publication Data

Schnabel, Eckhard J.
    Acts / Eckhard J. Schnabel.
       p. cm — (Zondervan exegetical commentary on the New Testament)
    Includes bibliographical references and indexes.
    ISBN: 978-0-310-24367-0 (hardcover)
    1. Bible N.T. Acts — Commentaries. I. Title.
  BS2625.53.S35 2012
  226.6'07 — dc23   2012002045

Cover design: Tammy Johnson
Interior design: Beth Shagene

Printed in the United States of America

14 15 16 17 18 19 /DCI/ 25 24 23 22 21 20 19 18 17 16 15 14 13 12 11 10 9 8 7 6 5 4 3

Contents

Series Introduction

This generation has been blessed with an abundance of excellent commentaries. Some are technical and do a good job of addressing issues that the critics have raised; other commentaries are long and provide extensive information about word usage and catalog nearly every opinion expressed on the various interpretive issues; still other commentaries focus on providing cultural and historical background information; and then there are those commentaries that endeavor to draw out many applicational insights.

The key question to ask is: What are you looking for in a commentary? This commentary series might be for you if

- you have taken Greek and would like a commentary that helps you apply what you have learned without assuming you are a well-trained scholar.
- you would find it useful to see a concise, one- or two-sentence statement of what the commentator thinks the main point of each passage is.
- you would like help interpreting the words of Scripture without getting bogged down in scholarly issues that seem irrelevant to the life of the church.
- you would like to see a visual representation (a graphical display) of the flow of thought in each passage.
- you would like expert guidance from solid evangelical scholars who set out to explain the meaning of the original text in the clearest way possible and to help you navigate through the main interpretive issues.
- you want to benefit from the results of the latest and best scholarly studies and historical information that help to illuminate the meaning of the text.
- you would find it useful to see a brief summary of the key theological insights that can be gleaned from each passage and some discussion of the relevance of these for Christians today.

These are just some of the features that characterize the new Zondervan Exegetical Commentary on the New Testament series. The idea for this series was refined over time by an editorial board who listened to pastors and teachers express what they wanted to see in a commentary series based on the Greek text. That board consisted of myself, George H. Guthrie, William D. Mounce, Thomas R. Schreiner, and Mark L. Strauss along with Zondervan senior editor at large Verlyn Verbrugge, and former Zondervan senior acquisitions editor Jack Kuhatschek. We also enlisted a board of consulting editors who are active pastors, ministry leaders, and seminary professors to help in the process of designing a commentary series that will be useful to the church. Zondervan senior acquisitions editor Katya Covrett has now been shepherding the process to completion.

We arrived at a design that includes seven components for the treatment of each biblical passage. What follows is a brief orientation to these primary components of the commentary.

Literary Context

In this section, you will find a concise discussion of how the passage functions in the broader literary context of the book. The commentator highlights connections with the preceding and following material in the book and makes observations on the key literary features of this text.

Main Idea

Many readers will find this to be an enormously helpful feature of this series. For each passage, the commentator carefully crafts a one- or two-sentence statement of the big idea or central thrust of the passage.

Translation and Graphical Layout

Another unique feature of this series is the presentation of each commentator's translation of the Greek text in a graphical layout. The purpose of this diagram is to help the reader visualize, and thus better understand, the flow of thought within the text. The translation itself reflects the interpretive decisions made by each commentator in the "Explanation" section of the commentary. Here are a few insights that will help you to understand the way these are put together:

1. On the far left side next to the verse numbers is a series of interpretive labels that indicate the function of each clause or phrase of the biblical text. The corresponding portion of the text is on the same line to the right of the label. We have not used technical linguistic jargon for these, so they should be easily understood.

2. In general, we place every clause (a group of words containing a subject and a predicate) on a separate line and identify how it is supporting the principal assertion of the text (namely, is it saying when the action occurred, how it took place, or why it took place?). We sometimes place longer phrases or a series of items on separate lines as well.

3. Subordinate (or dependent) clauses and phrases are indented and placed directly under the words that they modify. This helps the reader to more easily see the nature of the relationship of clauses and phrases in the flow of the text.

4. Every main clause has been placed in bold print and pushed to the left margin for clear identification.

5. Sometimes when the level of subordination moves too far to the right — as often happens with some of Paul's long, involved sentences! — we reposition the flow to the left of the diagram, but use an arrow to indicate that this has happened.

6. The overall process we have followed has been deeply informed by principles of discourse analysis and narrative criticism (for the Gospels and Acts).

Structure

Immediately following the translation, the commentator describes the flow of thought in the passage and explains how certain interpretive decisions regarding the relationship of the clauses were made in the passage.

Exegetical Outline

The overall structure of the passage is described in a detailed exegetical outline. This will be particularly helpful for those who are looking for a way to concisely explain the flow of thought in the passage in a teaching or preaching setting.

Explanation of the Text

As an exegetical commentary, this work makes use of the Greek language to interpret the meaning of the text. If your Greek is rather rusty (or even somewhat limited), don't be too concerned. All of the Greek words are cited in parentheses following an English translation. We have made every effort to make this commentary as readable and useful as possible even for the nonspecialist.

Those who will benefit the most from this commentary will have had the equivalent of two years of Greek in college or seminary. This would include a semester or two of working through an intermediate grammar (such as Wallace, Porter, Brooks and Winberry, or Dana and Mantey). The authors use the grammatical language that is found in these kinds of grammars. The details of the grammar of the passage, however, are discussed only when it has a bearing on the interpretation of the text.

The emphasis on this section of the text is to convey the meaning. Commentators examine words and images, grammatical details, relevant OT and Jewish background to a particular concept, historical and cultural context, important text-critical issues, and various interpretational issues that surface.

Theology in Application

This, too, is a unique feature for an exegetical commentary series. We felt it was important for each author not only to describe what the text means in its various details, but also to take a moment and reflect on the theological contribution that it makes. In this section, the theological message of the passage is summarized. The authors discuss the theology of the text in terms of its place within the book and in a broader biblical-theological context. Finally, each commentator provides some suggestions on what the message of the passage is for the church today. At the conclusion of each volume in this series is a summary of the whole range of theological themes touched on by this book of the Bible.

Our sincere hope and prayer is that you find this series helpful not only for your own understanding of the text of the New Testament, but as you are actively engaged in teaching and preaching God's Word to people who are hungry to be fed on its truth.

CLINTON E. ARNOLD, general editor

Author's Preface

The writing of a commentary is hard work, but the missionary work of Peter, Stephen, Philip, Barnabas, and Paul was harder. The writing of a commentary on a book of the Scriptures requires prayer, so that readers understand not only the historical details, the literary features, and the theological emphases of Luke's account, but that they will also be able to hear God continue to speak to his church. And the writing of a commentary on the book of Acts is a long journey accompanied, if it seeks to approximate the work of Peter and Paul, by the preaching and teaching of the Word of God before followers of Jesus and before unbelievers. A century ago, the audience for a commentary on the book of Acts would have been located, nearly exclusively, in Europe and in North America. Today, with strong and growing churches in all parts of the world and in nearly every country, with many students and pastors in the Global South reading English, the audience is truly worldwide. While the missionaries, preachers, and teachers whose work Luke reports on took the gospel of Jesus Christ from Jerusalem to Judea, to Samaria, and to the other regions located between Jerusalem and Rome, other missionaries, preachers, and teachers of later centuries took the gospel to all the regions in which people live.

It is my hope that the following explanation of Luke's account of the preaching of the gospel of Jesus Christ and of the life and growth of the church between Jerusalem and Rome encourages and challenges preachers and teachers, evangelists and missionaries, pastors and students, to learn:

- from the commitment of the first missionaries and church leaders
- from their courageous loyalty to Jesus as Israel's Messiah and as the only Savior
- from their unchanging commitment to understand, apply, and teach the will of God as revealed in the Scriptures, in the work of Jesus Christ, and in new revelation that helped them grasp the significance of Jesus Christ
- from their consistent devotion to the task of proclaiming the Word of God to Jews and Gentiles, to believers and unbelievers, irrespective of geographical, cultural, economic, or religious distance

- perhaps most importantly, from their conviction that all achievements in ministry, all conversions, and all new congregations are the work of God, who is active in the life and in the mission of the church through the risen and exalted Jesus and the power of the Holy Spirit.

It has been a privilege to be accompanied on this journey by colleagues, friends, and students. Professors Scott Manetsch and Richard Cook, colleagues at Trinity Evangelical Divinity School, have repeatedly discussed Acts passages with me during long runs on the Des Plaines River Trail. I thank Steve Siebert from Nota Bene, the unfailingly superb word processor for scholars, who reprogrammed the software so that the bibliographic manager could handle the high number of "program calls" when updating the citations in the large manuscript. I thank Christopher Kelleher, David Sloan, Monique Cuany, and Benjamin Snyder, my teaching assistants, who helped in various ways, in particular with the text tables. Pastors Tim Baylor, Ryan Beardsley, Kevin Meek, and Scott Lothery from Arlington Heights Evangelical Free Church (the Orchard) have been kind enough to read and comment on the various chapters as they were being written, with helpful suggestions concerning clarity of expression, precision in argument, and relevance of application.

Dr. Allan Chapple from Trinity Theological College in Perth, Australia, has been reading the manuscript with consistent attentiveness and an amazing eye for detail. He has the rare gift of genuine encouragement. This is also true of my wife, Barbara, who continues to support my work with cheerful devotion, astute humor, and supporting faith. I thank Clint Arnold and the members of the editorial team for their invitation to write the commentary on Acts, for their comments on the manuscript, and for their willingness to work out a solution when the submitted manuscript was twice as long as contracted. While allowing the print edition of the commentary to be longer than originally anticipated, they arranged with Zondervan that the electronic version of the commentary will contain the full manuscript, with a larger number of In Depth sections treating historical and geographical questions, with a more complete discussion of lexical, grammatical, and historical matters, with more extensive documentation of and interaction with the work of other Acts scholars, and with longer Theology in Application sections.

The commentary is dedicated to I. H. Marshall and D. A. Carson, New Testament scholars whose life and work have been an example of academic rigor, dedication to the church, and commitment to mission and evangelism.

As this commentary will be used by pastors and missionaries, evangelists and students, may they be reminded of the priorities of the first witnesses of Jesus in Jerusalem (Acts 6:4), who were joyfully engaged in prayer, who were involved in hard and often dangerous work, and who preached the message of God with faith and courage whenever they had the opportunity. These priorities continue to be the mark of authentic communities of followers of Jesus — *ora et labora et predica verbum Dei.*

ECKHARD J. SCHNABEL
January 25, 2010, the Feast Day of St. Paul's Conversion,
and the Day of Juventinus and Maximinus,
martyrs at Antioch in AD 363

Abbreviations

Abbreviations for books of the Bible, pseudepigrapha, rabbinic works, papyri, classical works, and the like are readily available in sources such as the *SBL Handbook of Style* and are not included here.

AB	Anchor Bible
ABD	*Anchor Bible Dictionary*. Edited by D. N. Freedman. New York, 1972.
ACCS	Ancient Christian Commentary on Scripture
AGJU	Arbeiten zur Geschichte des antiken Judentum und des Urchristentums
AMS	Asia Minor Studien
ANTC	Abingdon New Testament Commentaries
ANRW	*Aufstieg und Niedergang der römischen Welt*. Edited by W. Haase and H. Temporini. Berlin, 1972 –
ANTT	Arbeiten zur neutestamentlichen Textforschung
ASV	American Standard Version
BAR	*Biblical Archaeology Review*
BBR	*Bulletin for Biblical Research*
BDAG	Bauer, W. F. W. Danker, W. F. Arndt, and F. W. Gingrich. *A Greek-English Lexicon of the New Testament and Other Early Christian Literature*. Third Edition. Chicago, 2000.
BDF	Blass, F., A. Debrunner, and R. W. Funk. *A Grammar of the New Testament and Other Early Christian Literature*. Chicago, 1961.
BECNT	Baker Exegetical Commentary on the New Testament
BEThL	Bibliotheca Ephemeridum Theologicarum Lovaniensium
Bib	*Biblica*
BIS	Biblical Interpretation Series
BNP	*Brill's New Pauly*. Edited by H. Cancik and H. Schneider. Leiden, 2002 – 2012.
BNTC	Black's New Testament Commentaries
BSac	*Bibliotheca Sacra*
BT	*Bible Translator*

BWANT	Beiträge zur Wissenschaft vom Alten und Neuen Testament
BZ	*Biblische Zeitschrift*
BZNW	Beihefte zur Zeitschrift für die neutestamentliche Wissenschaft
CBET	Contributions to Biblical Exegesis and Theology
CBQ	*Catholic Biblical Quarterly*
CIJ	*Corpus Inscriptionum Judaicarum*. Edited by J. B. Frey. New York, 1975.
CMRDM	*Corpus Monumentorum Religionis Dei Menis*. Edited by E. N. Lane. Leiden, 1983 – 1989.
CNT	Commentaire du Nouveau Testament
CRINT	Compendium Rerum Iudaicarum ad Novum Testamentum
DDD	*Dictionary of Deities and Demons in the Bible*. Edited by K. van der Toorn, B. Becking, and P. W. van der Horst. Leiden, 1995.
DJD	*Discoveries in the Judaean Desert [of Jordan]*. Oxford, 1955 – 2002.
DJG	*Dictionary of Jesus and the Gospels*. Edited by J. B. Green, S. McKnight, and I. H. Marshall. Downers Grove, 1992.
DLNTD	*Dictionary of the Later New Testament and Its Developments*. Edited by P. H. Davids and R. P. Martin. Downers Grove, 1997.
DNTB	*Dictionary of New Testament Background*. Edited by C. A. Evans and S. E. Porter. Downers Grove, 2000.
DOTP	*Dictionary of the Old Testament: Pentateuch*. Edited by T. Desmond Alexander and David W. Baker. Downers Grove, 2003.
DPL	*Dictionary of Paul and His Letters*. Edited by G. F. Hawthorne, R. P. Martin, and D. G. Reid. Downers Grove, 1993.
DSSSE	*The Dead Sea Scrolls Study Edition*. Edited by F. García Martínez and J. C. E. Tigchelaar. Leiden, 1997 – 1998.
EBC	Expositor's Bible Commentary
EDNT	*Exegetical Dictionary of the New Testament*. Edited by H. Balz and G. Schneider. Grand Rapids, 1990 – 1993.
EDSS	*Encyclopedia of the Dead Sea Scrolls*. Edited by L. H. Schiffman and J. C. VanderKam. Oxford, 2000.
EHS	Europäische Hochschulschriften
EKK	Evangelisch-Katholischer Kommentar
EQ	*Evangelical Quarterly*
ESV	English Standard Version
ETAM	Ergänzungsbände zu den Tituli Asiae Minoris
EBib	Études Bibliques
EpComm	Epworth Commentary
ETL	Ephemerides theologicae lovanienses
FB	Forschung zur Bibel
FilNT	Filología Neotestamentaria

FRLANT	Forschungen zur Religion und Literatur des Alten und Neuen Testaments
FS	Festschrift
FzB	Forschungen zur Bibel
GNB	Good News Bible
HALOT	*The Hebrew and Aramaic Lexicon of the Old Testament in English.* Edited by L. Koehler, W. Baumgartner, and J. J. Stamm. Leiden, 1994 – 2000.
HThKNT	Herders Theologischer Kommentar zum Neuen Testament
HUCA	*Hebrew Union College Annual*
I. Ephesos	*Die Inschriften von Ephesos.* Edited by H. Wankel, R. Merkelbach, and H. Engelmann. Bonn, 1979 – 1984.
I. KorinthKent	*Corinth: Results of Excavations Vol. 8.3: The Inscriptions 1926 – 1950.* Edited by J. H. Kent. Princeton, 1966.
IBD	*The Illustrated Bible Dictionary.* Edited by J. D. Douglas. Downers Grove, 1980.
ICC	International Critical Commentary
IEJ	*Israel Exploration Journal*
IG	*Inscriptiones Graecae*
IGR	*Inscriptiones Graecae ad res Romanas pertinentes.* Edited by E. Leroux. Paris, 1906 – 1927; reprint Chicago, 1975.
IJudO	*Inscriptiones Judaicae Orientis.* Edited by D. Noy, A. Panayotov, H. Bloedhorn, and W. Ameling. Tübingen, 2004.
IK	Inschriften griechischer Städte aus Kleinasien
Int	*Interpretation*
ISBE	*The International Standard Bible Encyclopedia.* Edited by G. W. Bromiley. Grand Rapids, 1979 – 1988.
IThS	International Theological Studies
IVPNTC	InterVarsity Press New Testament Commentaries
JBL	*Journal of Biblical Literature*
JETS	*Journal of the Evangelical Theological Society*
JGRChJ	*Journal of Greco-Roman Christianity and Judaism*
JHS	*Journal of Hellenic Studies*
JJS	*Journal of Jewish Studies*
JPT	*Journal of Pentecostal Theology*
JPTSup	Journal of Pentecostal Theology Supplement series
JSNT	*Journal for the Study of the New Testament*
JSNTSup	Journal for the Study of the New Testament Supplement series
JSPSup	Journal for the Study of the Pseudepigrapha Supplement series
JTS	*Journal of Theological Studies*
KEK	Kritisch-exegetischer Kommentar über das Neue Testament

KJV	King James Version
LCL	Loeb Classical Library
LD	Lectio divina
LEH	Lust, J., E. Eynikel, and K. Hauspie. *A Greek-English Lexicon of the Septuagint*. Stuttgart, 1992 – 1996.
LGPN	*A Lexicon of Greek Personal Names*. Vols. I-VA. Edited by Peter M. Fraser and Elaine Matthews. Oxford, 1987 – 2009 (further volumes to be published).
LN	Louw, J. P., and E. A. Nida. *Greek-English Lexicon of the New Testament Based on Semantic Domains*. New York, 1988.
LNTS	Library of New Testament Studies
LSJ	H. G. Liddell, R. Scott, and H. S. Jones. *A Greek-English Lexikon*. Ninth Edition, with revised supplement edited by Peter G. W. Glare. Oxford, 1996.
LXX	Septuagint; all English translations of LXX passages are taken from Albert Pietersma and Benjamin G. Wright, eds., *A New English Translation of the Septuagint*. Oxford 2007.
Maj.	Majority text (for the Gothic letter "M" used in Nestle-Aland)
MAMA	Monumenta Asiae Minoris Antiqua
MM	J. H. Moulton and G. Milligan. *The Vocabulary of the Greek Testament Illustrated from the Papyri and Other Non-Literary Sources*. Grand Rapids, 1982 [1930].
MT	Masoretic Text
NA[27]	*Novum Testamentum Graece*. Nestle-Aland 27th Edition. Edited by B. Aland, K. Aland, J. Karavidopoulos, C. M. Martini, and B. M. Metzger. Stuttgart, 1993.
NAC	New American Commentary
NCBC	New Century Bible Commentary
NDBT	*New Dictionary of Biblical Theology*. Edited by T. D. Alexander and B. S. Rosner. Downers Grove, 2000.
NEAEHL	*The New Encyclopedia of Archaeological Excavations in the Holy Land*. Edited by E. Stern. Jerusalem and New York, 1993.
NEB	Neue Echter Bibel
NET	New English Translation
NIBC	New International Biblical Commentary
NICNT	New International Commentary on the New Testament
NIDB	*New Interpreter's Dictionary of the Bible*. Edited by K. D. Sakenfeld. Nashville, 2006 – 2009.
NIDNTT	*The New International Dictionary of New Testament Theology*. Edited by C. Brown. Grand Rapids, 1975 – 1978.

NIDOTTE	*New International Dictionary of Old Testament Theology and Exegesis.* Edited by W. A. VanGemeren. Grand Rapids, 1997.
NIGTC	New International Greek Testament Commentary
NIV	New International Version
NJB	New Jerusalem Bible
NLT	New Living Translation
NovT	*Novum Testamentum*
NovTSup	Novum Testamentum Supplements series
NRSV	New Revised Standard Version
NTAbh	Neutestamentliche Abhandlungen
NTD	Das Neue Testament Deutsch
NTS	*New Testament Studies*
NTOA	Novum Testamentum und Orbis Antiquus
OBO	*Orbis biblicus et orientalis*
OCD	*The Oxford Classical Dictionary.* Edited by S. Hornblower and A. Spawforth. Third Edition. Oxford, 1996.
OED	*Oxford English Dictionary.* Second edition (online).
ÖTK	Ökumenischer Taschenbuchkommentar
OTP	*Old Testament Pseudepigrapha.* Edited by James H. Charlesworth. 2 vols. New York, 1983, 1985.
P. Oxy	*Oxyrhynchus Papyri.* Edited by B. P. Grenfell, A. S. Hunt, et al.
PECS	*The Princeton Encyclopedia of Classical Sites.* Edited by R. Stillwell. Princeton, 1976.
PEQ	*Palestine Exploration Quarterly*
PGM	*Papyri graecae magicae*
PNTC	Pillar New Testament Commentary
RB	*Revue Biblique*
RBL	*Review of Biblical Literature*
RdQ	*Revue de Qumran*
REB	Revised English Bible
RivB	*Rivista biblica italiana*
RNT	Regensburger Neues Testament
RPP	*Religion Past and Present: Encyclopedia of Theology and Religion.* Edited by H. D. Betz, D. S. Browning, B . Janowski, and E. Jüngel. Leiden 2007 – 2013.
RSV	Revised Standard Version
RV	Revised Version
SBLDS	Society of Biblical Literature Dissertation Series
SEG	Supplementum Epigraphicum Graecum
SJLA	Studies in Judaism in Late Antiquity
SNTSMS	Society of New Testament Studies Monograph Series

SNTSU	Studien zum Neuen Testament und seiner Umwelt
SP	Sacra Pagina
TAM	Tituli Asiae Minoris
TANZ	Texte und Arbeiten zum neutestamentlichen Zeitalter
TDNT	*Theological Dictionary of the New Testament*. Edited by G. Kittel and G. Friedrich. Grand Rapids, 1964–1976.
TDOT	*Theological Dictionary of the Old Testament*. Edited by G. J. Botterweck, H. Ringgren, and H.-J. Fabry. Grand Rapids, 1974–2006.
THKNT	Theologischer Handkommentar zum Neuen Testament
TLNT	*Theological Lexicon of the New Testament*. Edited by C. Spicq. Peabody, 1995.
TLOT	*Theological Lexicon of the Old Testament*. Edited by E. Jenni and C. Westermann. Peabody, 1997.
TNIV	Today's New International Version
TNTC	Tyndale New Testament Commentary
TRE	*Theologische Realenzyklopädie*. Edited by G. Krause and G. Müller. Berlin, 1977–2007.
TrJ	*Trinity Journal*
TSAJ	Texte und Studien zum antiken Judentum
TSK	*Theologische Studien und Kritiken*
TynBul	*Tyndale Bulletin*
WBC	Word Biblical Commentary
WMANT	Wissenschaftliche Monographien zum Alten und Neuen Testament
WTJ	*Westminster Theological Journal*
WUNT	Wissenschaftliche Untersuchungen zum Neuen Testament
ZBK	Zürcher Bibelkommentare
ZDPV	*Zeitschrift des Deutschen Palästina-Vereins*
ZNT	*Zeitschrift für Neues Testament*
ZNW	*Zeitschrift für die neutestamentliche Wissenschaft*
ZPE	*Zeitschrift für Papyrologie und Epigraphik*

Introduction

Luke and His Readers

The title "Acts of the Apostles" (πράξεις ἀποστόλων) is found in the early Greek manuscripts of the book.[1] If the title goes indeed back to Luke himself, whose work focuses particularly on Peter (Acts 1 – 6; 10 – 12) and on Paul (Acts 9; 13 – 28), the formulation "Acts of the Apostles" may be intended to emphasize that both Peter and Paul are apostles par excellence.[2] Together with the four Gospels, the book of Acts belongs to those New Testament books that are generally called anonymous since the authors do not identify themselves at the beginning of the work (contrast, e.g., Paul's letters). Two comments help us to clarify the matter.

First, neither the Gospels nor the book of Acts were "anonymous" in the first century. It can be reasonably assumed that the early churches knew — on the basis of personal relationships or oral tradition — the identity of the authors of these long books, which were foundational for the life and ministry of the churches.[3] We may note the example of L. Flavius Arrianus of Nicomedia, who did not state his name in the preface of his description of the life of Alexander the Great, published in the first half of the second century AD under the title *Anabasis*; he explains this literary decision with the comment, "I need not write my name, for it is not at all unknown among men, nor my country nor my family."[4]

Second, the anonymity of the historical books of the New Testament is a literary feature that distinguishes them from contemporary Greco-Roman historical books. It has been suggested that this is a specifically Christian phenomenon, which can be explained with the authors' conviction that Jesus Christ is the exclusive authority besides whom any human authority should remain silent.[5] Others assume that the

---

1. In manuscripts ℵ and B (both fourth century); in 𝔓⁷⁴ (seventh century) the title is given at the end of the book. In the Muratorian Canon (ca. AD 180 – 200), the book has the title *Acta omnium apostolorum* ("Acts of All the Apostles"). The term *omnium* ("all") perhaps intends to include Paul as an apostle among the Twelve.

2. Luke calls Paul, together with Barnabas, an "apostle" only in Acts 14:4, 14.

3. Cf. Martin Hengel, *Die Evangelienüberschriften* (Heidel-

berg: Winter, 1984), on the superscriptions of the canonical Gospels.

4. Arrian, *Anabasis* 1.12.5. It should be noted that *Anabasis* was probably published with Arrian's name in the title, cf. A. Brian Bosworth, *A Historical Commentary on Arrian's History of Alexander* (2 vols.; Oxford: Clarendon, 1980/1995), 1:106.

5. Michael Wolter, "Die anonymen Schriften des Neuen Testaments. Annäherungsversuche an ein literarisches Phänomen," *ZNW* 79 (1988): 1 – 16.

anonymity of the historical books of the New Testament emphasizes "the complete dependence of their authors on tradition, rather than on any firsthand experience."[6]

It is important to note that the anonymity of the Gospels and of Acts corresponds to Old Testament historiography, which is rooted in the literary conventions of the ancient Near East — the books from Genesis to Kings do not mention their authors' names (unlike the prophetic and wisdom books). Some of these Old Testament and also later Jewish historical works have been named after their main characters (e.g., Joshua, 1 – 2 Samuel, 1 – 2 Maccabees). A comparison with Greek and Roman historiography shows that in contrast to the motivation of secular authors to earn praise and glory for their literary achievements,[7] the authors of the Gospels, as well as the author of the book of Acts, probably adopted the literary device of anonymity because "they regarded themselves as comparatively insignificant mediators of a subject matter that deserved the full attention of the readers."[8]

Author

From the ninth century on, the author is identified in the title of the book, which is given as "Acts of the Holy Apostles by Luke the Evangelist" (Λουκᾶ εὐαγγελιστοῦ πράξεις τῶν ἁγίων ἀποστόλων).[9] The tradition that Luke, a companion of Paul — the author of the "we passages" in Acts (16:10 – 17; 20:5 – 15; 21:1 – 18; 27:1 – 28:16)[10] — is the author both of the third gospel and of the book of Acts appears already in the second century.[11] In Phlm 24, Luke is described as Paul's "fellow worker;" in Col 4:14 as "our dear friend Luke, the doctor," and 2 Tim 4:11 mentions Luke as Paul's sole companion in his Roman imprisonment. Since Paul mentions other companions in letters that he wrote during his imprisonment in the city of Rome,[12] the consistent and uncontested ascription of the book to Luke is to be taken seriously.[13]

---

6. Alexander J. M. Wedderburn, "The 'We'-Passages in Acts: On the Horns of a Dilemma," *ZNW* 93 (2002): 78 – 98, 96.

7. Josephus, *Ant.* 1.1 mentions several goals that motivate historians to write and publish their works; he begins by pointing out that those who write histories are often "eager to display their literary skill and to win the fame therefrom expected."

8. Armin D. Baum, "The Anonymity of the New Testament History Books: A Stylistic Device in the Context of Greco-Roman and Ancient Near Eastern Literature," *NovT* 50 (2008): 1 – 23, 23.

9. See manuscripts 33, 189, 1891, 2344.

10. Cf. Colin J. Hemer, *The Book of Acts in the Setting of Hellenistic History* (ed. C. H. Gempf; orig. 1989; repr., WUNT 49; Tübingen: Mohr Siebeck, 2001), 308 – 64, who concludes that the use of "we" in Acts is an unobtrusive self-reference of the author, who claims to have been a participant in the events narrated in these sections. See below.

11. Muratorian Canon 34 – 35; Anti-Marcionite Prologue to

the Gospel of Luke; Irenaeus, *Haer.* 3.1.1; 3.14.1 – 4; Clement of Alexandria in *Strom.* 5.12; later Tertullian, *Marc.* 4.2; Eusebius in *Hist. eccl.* 3.4.1; Jerome, *Vir. ill.* 7. For the tradition of the early church cf. C. K. Barrett, *The Acts of the Apostles* (2 vols.; ICC; Edinburgh: T&T Clark, 1994 – 98), 30 – 48; Claus-Jürgen Thornton, *Der Zeuge des Zeugen: Lukas als Historiker der Paulusreisen* (WUNT; Tübingen: Mohr Siebeck, 1991), 8 – 83. The earliest extant manuscript of the third gospel, 𝔓[75] (ca. AD 200), provides at the end of the manuscript the title Εὐαγγέλιον κατὰ Λουκᾶν ("Gospel according to Luke"). Patricia Walters, *The Assumed Authorial Unity of Luke and Acts: A Reassessment of the Evidence* (SNTSMS 145; Cambridge: Cambridge Univ. Press, 2009), challenges the assumed authorial unity of Luke-Acts.

12. See the references in Colossians, Philemon, Ephesians, and Philippians to John Mark, Jesus Justus, Epaphras, Demas, Tychicus, Timothy, Aristarchus, and Epaphroditus.

13. Cf. Joseph A. Fitzmyer, *The Acts of the Apostles* (AB

The name Λουκᾶς is a shortened Greek form of the Latin name, which is either Lucanus, Lucianus, Lucilius, or (most likely) Lucius (Gk. Λούκιος).[14] The use of this name does not tell us whether Luke was a Jew or a Gentile, since many Jews had Greek and Roman names. On the basis of the superior quality of the Greek language, the avoidance of Semitic words, the omission (in the third gospel) of traditions about Jesus' controversies with the Pharisees' understanding of the Mosaic law and about the distinction between what is unclean and what is clean, and other factors, scholars have long assumed that the author was a Gentile Christian.[15] Paul's reference to Luke in Col 4:14, which comes after greetings from Jewish-Christian coworkers in Col 4:10 – 11 (Aristarchus, Mark, Jesus Justus), is often cited in support for the Gentile background of Luke, who is mentioned after Epaphras, a Gentile Christian from Colossae (Col 4:12 – 13).[16]

The substantial influence of the LXX on the language and style of Luke's Greek,[17] the way in which Jesus is described in the book of Acts, the references to Israel as the people of God, the emphasis on the fulfillment of the promises given to Israel, and the depiction of Paul as a missionary to Jews have prompted scholars more recently to regard Luke as a Jewish Christian.[18] If he was indeed born as a Gentile, as many scholars have assumed, he may have been a convert to Judaism, i.e., a proselyte, or he may have belonged to the group of the so-called God-fearers, i.e., Gentiles who had close connections with the local synagogues.[19]

Language

Luke's language is characterized by two factors. First, his Greek is educated standard Koine, the (non-atticizing) linguistic register of the first century that was used in circles "educated to use Greek for administrative, business and professional

31; New York: Doubleday, 1998), 49 – 51; Jacob Jervell, *Die Apostelgeschichte* (KEK 3; Göttingen: Vandenhoeck & Ruprecht, 1998), 79 – 84; Ben Witherington, *The Acts of the Apostles: A Socio-Rhetorical Commentary* (Grand Rapids: Eerdmans, 1998), 51 – 60; Don A. Carson and Douglas J. Moo, *An Introduction to the New Testament* (2nd ed.; Grand Rapids: Zondervan, 2005), 291 – 96; for a refutation of the objections to the traditional identification of the author of Luke-Acts, see ibid.

14. Cf. Joseph A. Fitzmyer, *The Gospel According to Luke* (AB 28; Garden City, NY: Doubleday, 1981 – 85), 1:42 – 43. Cf. Adolf Deissmann, *Light from the Ancient East Illustrated by Recently Discovered Texts of the Graeco-Roman World* (orig. 1927; repr., Grand Rapids: Eerdmans, 1980), 435 – 38, on inscriptional evidence from Pisidian Antioch.

15. François Bovon, *Luke the Theologian: Fifty-Five Years of Research (1950 – 2005)* (2nd rev. ed.; Waco, TX: Baylor Univ. Press, 2006), 490. Cf. Adolf von Harnack, *Luke the Physician: The Author of the Third Gospel and the Acts of the Apostles*

(New York: Putnam, 1907); Robert H. Gundry, *A Survey of the New Testament* (4th ed.; Grand Rapids: Zondervan, 2003), 208; Witherington, *Acts*, 58.

16. Carson and Moo, *Introduction*, 296.

17. Cf. Fitzmyer, *Luke*, 1:114 – 25; see the conclusions of Chang-Wook Jung, *The Original Language of the Lukan Infancy Narrative* (JSNTSup 267; London/New York: T&T Clark, 2004), concerning Luke 1 – 2.

18. Cf. Barrett, *Acts*, 2:xlviii; Jervell, *Apostelgeschichte*, 84 – 85; Loveday C. A. Alexander, *Acts in Its Ancient Literary Context: A Classicist Looks at the Acts of the Apostles* (LNTS 298; London/New York: T&T Clark, 2005), 245 – 46.

19. Cf. Rudolf Pesch, *Die Apostelgeschichte* (2 vols.; EKK 5; Zürich/Neukirchen-Vluyn: Benziger/Neukirchener Verlag, 1986), 1:27; Daniel Marguerat, *Les Actes des Apôtres (1 – 12)* (Commentaire du Nouveau Testament 5a; Geneva: Labor et Fides, 2007), 1:19; cf. François Bovon, *Luke* (3 vols.; Hermeneia; Philadelphia: Fortress, 2002), 1:8.

purposes"; it thus does not belong to "prestige literary registers for which atticizing (or at least classicizing) Greek was fast becoming the norm."[20] This context explains why Luke's style, particularly his figures of speech, can be analyzed in terms of the *progymnasmata* tradition, i.e., the handbooks that introduced students to the fundamental practices of Greek rhetoric in composing speeches and prose texts.[21]

Second, Luke's Greek not only imitates the Greek Bible in terms of quotations, allusions, and echoes, but represents a living variety of Jewish or "biblical" Greek whose range is much wider than the LXX. This distinctive "biblicizing" form of standard educated Greek strongly suggests that Luke belonged to a social context that gave him a grounding in Jewish Greek literature, available in the synagogues of the Jewish diaspora communities.

Luke's Origins

A tradition from the late second century asserts that Luke was a native of Syrian Antioch. The Greek prologue of the third gospel relates that "this Luke is an Antiochene, a Syrian," a tradition that is known to Eusebius (*Eccl. hist.* 3.4.6) and Jerome (*Vir. ill.* 7) as well.[22] Codex Bezae Cantabrigienses (5th cent.) and several Latin manuscripts presuppose the presence of Luke in the church in Antioch in Acts 11:28 (the first "we passage" in the Western text). That Luke came from Antioch remains a distinct possibility, particularly as there was a large Jewish community in the capital of the Roman province of Syria, numbering between 30,000 and 50,000 Jews.[23] Antioch was a city in which Luke would have been able to obtain the level of education that is suggested by his Greek language and style as well as his ability to engage in historical research (Luke 1:1 – 4) and to write extensive biographical and historical monographs.

---

20. Alexander, *Literary Context*, 251; for the following point see ibid. 245 – 49, 251 – 52. On Luke's non-atticizing Greek see also John N. Kazazis, "Atticism," in *A History of Ancient Greek: From the Beginnings to Late Antiquity* (ed. A.-F. Christidis; Cambridge: Cambridge Univ. Press, 2007), 1200 – 1212, 1204 – 5.

21. This is a major emphasis in the commentary of Mikeal C. Parsons, *Acts* (Paideia; Grand Rapids: Baker, 2008). For a translation of *progymnasmata* handbooks, beginning with Theon in the first century AD, cf. George A. Kennedy, *Progymnasmata: Greek Textbooks of Prose Composition and Rhetoric* (Writings from the Greco-Roman World 10; Atlanta: Society of Biblical Literature, 2003). It should be noted that many of the techniques taught in the *progymnasmata* were used in the Old Testament and in Jewish tradition (left unexplored by Parsons); e.g., the rhetorical technique of *synkrisis* (comparison),

defined as "language setting the better or the worse side by side" (Theon, *Prog.* 112) — comparing two persons (or objects) that are similarly noteworthy for the purpose of praise (*synkrisis* in a double encomium, cf. Aphthonius, *Prog.* 31R – 32R), or comparing two persons (or objects) when "we blame one thing completely and praise the other" (Hermogenes, *Prog.* 19; this is a *synkrisis* as an encomium/invective contrast) — can be found in Israel's wisdom tradition: in some psalms the contrast between the wicked and the righteous, in Proverbs the contrast between the wise and the foolish.

22. Cf. Theodor Zahn, *Introduction to the New Testament* (Edinburgh: T&T Clark, 1909), 1:2 – 3; Fitzmyer, *Luke*, 1:38 – 39, 45 – 47.

23. Cf. Eckhard J. Schnabel, *Early Christian Mission* (2 vols.; Downers Grove, IL: InterVarsity Press, 2004), 785.

Luke the Physician

The fact that Luke was a physician (Col 4:14) does not tell us much about his social background since the status of physicians differed from place to place and largely depended on their patients.[24] Physicians treating senators or the imperial family obviously enjoyed a higher prestige than physicians who treated slaves and often were themselves slaves. Some physicians belonged to prominent local families. The level of education that Luke's Greek language, style, and literary activity require suggests a level of rhetorical, philosophical, and medical training that may be compared in general terms to that of Galen of Pergamon.[25]

Galen, born in AD 129, was the son of a prosperous architect. After receiving a wide education that included rhetoric and philosophy, he embarked on a medical career that led him to study not only in Pergamon but also in Smyrna, Corinth, and Alexandria, before being appointed as physician of the gladiators of the high priest of the province of Asia. Later he taught philosophy and practiced medicine in Rome, traveled to find medicinal herbs and to offer his medical services, and wrote extensive medical studies as well as works on philosophical and linguistic matters.[26]

Luke traveled widely in the Mediterranean region, he engaged in historical research consulting documents and records, and he wrote books in educated standard Koine. The conditions that these activities require "excluded all but members of the highest levels of society. Wealth and social contacts were essential to the craft."[27] Indeed

> while Luke may not have been wealthy by some standards, likely he was either a retainer of a wealthy patron or a person of independent means who had the wherewithal to travel and the education to write the sort of account he did. His social status must have been relatively high, at least compared to that of many early Christians.[28]

Luke's travels as Paul's companion need not be interpreted in the sense that Luke was Paul's subordinate. It is not impossible that Luke's travels were motivated, at least in part, as the result of his historical interest in, and investigation of, the origins of the Christian movement. Most scholars agree that Luke's identity as a physician (Col 4:14) cannot be proven from the terminology regarding illnesses in Luke-Acts.[29]

---

24. Cf. Vivian Nutton, "Medicine G. Imperial Period," *BNP*, 8:579 – 80.

25. Cf. Bovon, *Luke*, 1:8, who also argues that Luke must have belonged to the "higher strata of society." The view of Hans Klein, *Lukasstudien* (FRLANT 209; Göttingen: Vandenhoeck & Ruprecht, 2005), 26 – 40, that Luke was a slave who was allowed by his master to attend elementary school and perhaps the *gymnasion*, is hardly plausible.

26. Vivian Nutton, "Galen of Pergamum" *BNP*, 5:654 – 61. Galen's surviving work comprises nearly three million words in Greek.

27. Charles W. Fornara, *The Nature of History in Ancient Greece and Rome* (Eidos; Berkeley: Univ. of California Press, 1983), 49.

28. Witherington, *Acts*, 27.

29. This was the attempt of William Hobart, *The Medical Language of St. Luke* (orig. 1882; repr., Grand Rapids: Baker, 1954), 35; cf. the comments of Kirsopp Lake and Henry J. Cadbury, *The Acts of the Apostles: English Translation and Commentary* (ed. F. J. Foakes-Jackson and K. Lake; The Beginnings of Christianity 1/4; London: Macmillan, 1933), 33 – 34; Barrett, *Acts*, 1:182 – 83. Annette Weissenrieder, *Images of Illness in the Gospel of Luke: Insights of Ancient Medical Texts* (WUNT 2.164; Tübingen: Mohr Siebeck, 2003), 365, establishes that

Luke's Two Volumes

Acts is the second volume of a larger work that begins with a prologue (Luke 1:1 – 4) in which Luke outlines his historiographical principles, which are also relevant for the second volume of Luke's project (Acts 1:1 – 2). Luke comments on the choice of his subject matter, on the nature of the material that he has carefully (ἀκριβῶς) researched, on the organization (καθεξῆς) of the material, and on the purposes of his account, which include objective reliability (ἀσφάλεια). Both content and presentation of the material in the gospel of Luke and in the book of Acts (hence the label "Luke-Acts") display distinct affinities with Greek and Roman historical monographs and biographies.[30] The historical reliability of Acts will be discussed below.

Luke tells his readers that in his first volume, which soon came to be called "the gospel of Luke," he provides a record of "all ... that Jesus began to do and to teach" (Acts 1:1). In the first volume, Luke writes about the life, death, and resurrection of Jesus. In the second volume, he describes the growth of the church and the expansion of Christian communities through the work of the early missionaries, particularly Peter and Paul (Acts). It has been suggested that Luke-Acts could have had the simple title *Ta eis Iēsoun* ("On the matters concerning Jesus") or *Peri Iēsou kai tōn gnōrimōn autou* ("On Jesus and his followers").[31]

Acts shares important themes with Luke's gospel, the central theme being God's purpose to bring salvation to all people through the life and mission of Jesus Christ, his messianic Son, and through the life and mission of his followers. Jesus' life is the fulfillment of God's plan as revealed in the Scriptures (Luke 4:17 – 21; 24:44 – 46; Acts 3:18; 13:27 – 33), in particular his suffering and death leading to his glorification (Luke 9:22; 17:25; 22:37; 24:7, 26, 46; Acts 2:23; 4:28; 17:3). As Jesus had spoken of the future being under God's control (Luke 21:9, 22), so the early church believed that what happens is the result of the will of God (Acts 9:6, 16; 14:22; 27:24), in particular the conversion of people to faith in Jesus (Acts 11:18; 14:27; 15:14).

The gospel emphasizes Jesus' identity as Son of God (Luke 1:32, 35; 3:21 – 22) and as messianic Savior (Luke 1:32 – 33, 68 – 75; 2:11, 26 – 32; 9:20; 4:16 – 21; 18:38 – 39; 22:70 – 71). In Acts, Jesus is present, after his death and resurrection (Acts 1:1 – 3), as the exalted Lord and Messiah (Acts 2:36) whose "name" heals and saves (Acts 2:38 – 41; 3:6, 16; 4:9 – 12, 17, 30; 5:28, 40 – 41; 8:16). In Luke's gospel, salvation is

Luke's particular interest in illness was plausible in the ancient medical context and that his images of illness and healing "far exceed word analogies," comparable to those that can be found in Philo's writings, although it remains uncertain whether Luke (or Philo) were ancient physicians.

30. Hemer, *Acts*, 66 – 70; Claus-Jürgen Thornton, *Zeuge*, 161 – 63; Darryl W. Palmer, "Acts and the Ancient Historical Monograph," in *The Book of Acts in Its Ancient Literary Setting* (ed. B. W. Winter and A. D. Clarke; The Book of Acts

in Its First-Century Setting 1; Grand Rapids: Eerdmans, 1993), 1 – 29; Charles H. Talbert, *Literary Patterns, Theological Themes and the Genre of Luke-Acts* (Missoula, MT: Scholars Press, 1974).

31. Hubert Cancik, "Das Geschichtswerk des Lukas als Institutionsgeschichte: Die Vorbereitung des Zweiten Logos im Ersten," in *Die Apostelgeschichte im Kontext antiker und frühchristlicher Historiographie* (ed. J. Frey, C. K. Rothschild, and J. Schröter; BZNW 162; Berlin: De Gruyter, 2009), 519 – 38, 520.

portrayed as a new, or renewed, relationship with God through repentance and faith and the reception of God's forgiveness (Luke 7:36 – 50; 19:1 – 10).[32] This emphasis is developed in Acts with reference to faith in Jesus as the crucified and risen Lord and the reception of the Holy Spirit, who is, and conveys, God's blessing of salvation (Acts 2:16 – 21, 36 – 40). In addition to the new emphasis on Jesus' death and resurrection and on the Holy Spirit as foundational for salvation, the possibility, and indeed reality, of salvation for the Gentiles (Luke 24:46 – 49; Acts 1:8; 8:4 – 40; 9:15; 10:1 – 11:18; 13:46 – 48; 22:21; 28:25 – 29) is a further development in Acts. For a fuller summary of the theological themes of Acts, see the last chapter of the commentary.

Date

As regards the date of composition, most scholars assume that Luke wrote the book of Acts between AD 80 – 90.[33] This date is predicated on two factors: (1) the dependence of Luke-Acts on the gospel of Mark and (2) the destruction of Jerusalem in AD 70, which is regarded to be presupposed both by Mark 13 and by Luke 19:43 – 44; 21:20. To begin with the second argument: since the description of the fate of Jerusalem by Mark (and Luke) contains many Old Testament and Jewish motifs (Daniel, 1 – 2 Maccabees),[34] and since we should not discount the possibility of genuine prophecy, the date of AD 70 as terminus post quem for the composition of both Mark's gospel and Luke's two volume work is not compelling.

The first argument raises the issue of the reliability of the two-source hypothesis (Mark wrote his gospel first, and both Matthew and Luke depend on Mark as well as on a source that contained mostly sayings of Jesus), which continues to be disputed;[35] and it begs the question when the gospel of Mark was written — some scholars are prepared to date Mark as early as AD 55.[36] If Luke's gospel is indeed dependent on Mark's gospel, and if Luke wrote Acts shortly after having written his gospel, a date

---

32. David G. Peterson, *The Acts of the Apostles* (PNTC; Grand Rapids: Eerdmans, 2009), 68; the following point ibid.

33. Cf. Fitzmyer, *Acts*, 51 – 54; Jervell, *Apostelgeschichte*, 85 – 86; Witherington, *Acts*, 62; James D. G. Dunn, *Beginning from Jerusalem* (Christianity in the Making 2; Grand Rapids: Eerdmans, 2009), 67. For a full and judicious discussion of the date of Acts, cf. Hemer, *Acts*, 365 – 410. A much later date is assumed by Richard I. Pervo, *Dating Acts: Between the Evangelists and the Apologists* (Santa Rosa, CA: Polebridge, 2006), who suggests AD 110 – 120, and Joseph B. Tyson, *Marcion and Luke-Acts: A Defining Struggle* (Columbia: Univ. of South Carolina Press, 2006), who argues that the book of Acts was published, together with the final edition of the third gospel, around AD 120 – 125, when Marcion started to proclaim his version of the Christian gospel (note the critique of D. T. Roth, *RBL* [May 2008]).

34. Cf. Alexander Mittelstaedt, *Lukas als Historiker. Zur Datierung des lukanischen Doppelwerkes* (TANZ 43; Tübingen: Francke, 2006), 49 – 163, who analyzes the evidence for the assumed connection to Mark 13:1 – 2, 14 – 18 and Luke 19:41 – 44; 21:20 – 24 with the events of AD 70; he shows that Luke's version of Jesus' predictions of the destruction of Jerusalem can hardly have been written with the events of AD 70 in mind (ibid. 131 – 59), and that Acts 6:13 – 14 suggests that the temple still existed at the time of Luke's writing his two-volume work (ibid. 159 – 63).

35. Cf. Mark Goodacre, *The Case Against Q: Studies in Markan Priority and the Synoptic Problem* (Harrisburg, PA: Trinity Press International, 2002).

36. Cf. Christopher S. Mann, *Mark: A New Translation with Introduction and Commentary* (AB 27; Garden City, NY: Doubleday, 1986), 72 – 83. Robert H. Gundry, *Mark: A Commentary on His Apology for the Cross* (Grand Rapids: Eerdmans, 1993), 1041 – 43, dates Mark's gospel to AD 60 – 62.

of Mark in the late 50s or even in 60/61 would allow for the completion of Acts certainly before AD 70 and possibly before the date at which Luke's narrative in Acts ends (Paul is a prisoner in Rome from AD 60 – 62). This leaves the possibility that Luke published Acts before he knew the outcome of Paul's trial.[37]

The ending of Acts, which relates Paul's being under house arrest in Rome, preaching the gospel, does not by necessity presuppose that Acts was written before AD 62. If Paul was indeed released from prison, as 2 Tim 4 suggests and *1 Clement* 5:5 – 7 presupposes,[38] Luke may have written Acts soon after Paul's release in AD 62. Luke's silence about Paul's acquittal and about Paul's renewed missionary activity could be explained by his desire not to alert the apostle's enemies about the location of his ministry.[39] Or perhaps Luke took Paul's preaching in Rome to be a more suitable climax for his narrative than a reference to Paul's continuing ministry in the churches of the East.[40] A date not long after AD 62 is suggested not only by the lack of reference to Nero's persecution of Roman Christians between AD 64 – 67 and Paul's (and Peter's) martyrdom, but also by the fact that the Jewish revolt against the Romans in AD 66 and the destruction of Jerusalem in AD 70 are not reflected in Luke's portrayal of the Jews and of Jewish institutions in Jerusalem and in the diaspora.[41] Irenaeus (*Haer.* 3.1.1; 3.14.1) and Eusebius (*Eccl. hist.* 2.22.6) assert that Luke-Acts was written in Rome, which is a good possibility, particularly in view of the historical considerations connected with the date of Acts, but certainty is not possible in this matter.[42]

Luke and His Historical Work

Luke is often considered to be the first historian of the Christian church.[43] While it is certainly correct that Luke writes about historical events that took place in the early years of the history of the church, this assessment needs to be carefully qualified.

---

37. The latter argument has been defended by Adolf von Harnack, *The Date of the Acts and the Synoptic Gospels* (New York: Putnam, 1911), 90 – 116; J. A. T. Robinson, *Redating the New Testament* (Philadelphia: Westminster, 1976), 88 – 92; Gundry, *Mark*, 1042; and more recently Mittelstaedt, *Lukas als Historiker*, 165 – 221.

38. Cf. Jerome Murphy-O'Connor, *Paul: A Critical Life* (Oxford: Oxford Univ. Press, 1996), 359 – 60; Schnabel, *Early Christian Mission,* 2:1270 – 75.

39. Hemer, *Acts*, 406 – 8; Earle E. Ellis, *The Making of the New Testament Documents* (BIS 39; Leiden: Brill, 1999), 391.

40. Carson and Moo, *Introduction*, 300.

41. Cf. Darrell L. Bock, "Luke," in *The Face of New Testament Studies: A Survey of Recent Research* (ed. S. McKnight and G. R. Osborne; Grand Rapids: Baker, 2004), 349 – 72, 370 – 71. Also Mittelstaedt, *Lukas als Historiker*, 251 – 55, who argues

that Luke wrote his gospel in the autumn of AD 59 in Caesarea, and the book of Acts in 62 in Caesarea or in Philippi, after the positive outcome of Paul's trial in Rome, a development concerning which he did not have much information.

42. The Anti-Marcionite Prologues mentioned Achaia, as does Jerome in the preface to his commentary on Matthew.

43. Cf. Hubert Cancik, "The History of Culture, Religion, and Institutions in Ancient Historiography: Philological Observations concerning Luke's History," *JBL* 116 (1997): 673 – 95, who interprets Acts as "institutional history," arguing that Luke traces "the origin and the spread of an institution, the *ekklēsia* or *hairesis* of the Christians" (694). For a critical discussion of Cancik's specific proposal, cf. Mark Reasoner, "The Theme of Acts: Institutional History or Divine Necessity in History?" *JBL* 118 (1999): 635 – 59.

Luke himself acknowledges that other Christian authors wrote about Jesus of Nazareth and his followers: "Many have undertaken to draw up an account of the things that have been fulfilled among us" (Luke 1:1). This statement is usually related to earlier written works on the life and ministry of Jesus, but it may well imply that there were other "histories" of events that took place after Pentecost as well.

Selectivity

Luke is selective in what he reports. He narrates some events in considerable detail (e.g., Paul's journey to Rome, Acts 27:1 – 28:15), while omitting events and developments that would have been considered to be of great importance not only by historians today but also by the early Christians. This is most apparent in Luke's comment after Peter's miraculous escape from prison: "Then he left and traveled to another place" (12:17). Luke must have known where Peter went when he left Jerusalem in AD 42. If Peter indeed died as a martyr in the city of Rome during Nero's persecution in AD 67,[44] he must have been an active leader in the Christian movement for twenty-five years after his departure from Jerusalem — a fact that is reflected in Peter's role during the Apostles' Council in AD 48 (15:7 – 11). But Luke tells us nothing about Peter's travel plans when he left Jerusalem in AD 42, nor does he inform us about his missionary work in the subsequent years. Luke relates events of Peter's ministry for the years AD 30 – 42 (Acts 1 – 12) but is silent about the period AD 42 – 64 (with the exception of one event in AD 48, the Apostles' Council).

Similarly, Luke's report about Paul's ministry focuses on his missionary work from Antioch to Ephesus and on his imprisonment in Jerusalem, Caesarea, and Rome during the years AD 42 – 62 (Acts 13 – 28). While he recounts Paul's conversion, perhaps in AD 31/32 (Acts 9), he is silent about Paul's missionary work in Arabia, Syria, and Cilicia between AD 32 – 42. Also, while Luke provides a list of the apostles in Acts 1:13 in the context of Jesus' missionary commission (1:8), which the apostles take seriously (cf. 1:22; 2:43 – 47), he does not inform his readers about the ministry of John, James, Andrew, Philip, Thomas, Bartholomew, Matthew, James son of Alphaeus, Simon the Zealot, or Judas son of James. Note that Luke provides a list of the Twelve in his gospel (Luke 6:14 – 16); in other words, the list in Acts 1:13 is not really necessary, unless Luke wants to emphasize that the Twelve who followed Jesus in Galilee continued to be his disciples after his death and resurrection and that they indeed fulfilled the commission to engage in international missionary work.

Moreoever, Luke reports the presence of Christians in Damascus and in Rome, but he does not relate how the gospel had reached these cities and who had established churches there. While Luke mentions people from northern Africa (Luke

---

44. Thus the later tradition, cf. *1 Clement* 5:4; 6:1; *Acts of Peter* 35 – 40; Tertullian, *Praescr.* 36; *Marc.* 4.5; Eusebius, *Eccl. theol.* 2.25; 3.1; *Chron.* 2.156 – 57 (ed. Schoene). Cf. Murphy- O'Connor, *Paul*, 370 – 71; Joachim Gnilka, *Petrus und Rom: Das Petrusbild in den ersten zwei Jahrhunderten* (Freiburg: Herder, 2002), 109 – 41.

23:26; Acts 13:1; 18:24), he does not report whether and how the gospel reached the large Jewish communities in Alexandria and in Cyrene.

Luke does not provide us with a full history of all the major events and developments in the early church in Acts, but with a history of the ministries of (mostly) Peter and Paul, with the focus on Jerusalem and on the expansion of the movement of the followers of Jesus beyond Judea and Samaria to the Roman provinces in the eastern Mediterranean.

Luke and Greek Historiography

Luke's prefaces in Luke 1:1 – 4 and Acts 1:1 do not easily fit the genre of classical Greek historiography as represented by Thucydides and Herodotus.[45] While the classical historians use the authorial first person in prefaces, they usually introduce the author (i.e., themselves) in the third person. A dedication (in Luke's case to Theophilus) was not common in historical writing; the attestation of possible dedications is limited to the more "antiquarian" historical writings (Apollodorus) and authors who are outside of the mainstream of Greek culture due to their non-Greek origins (Berossus, Manetho, Josephus) or due to their mostly ethnographic interests (Aristippus, several predecessors of Dionysius of Halicarnassus).

Recapitulations in a preface (i.e., summaries of the contents of the previous book in a series) are not often used by Greek historical writers. While many Greek historians indicate in their prefaces the subject matter of their work, Luke moves, after the opening words of Acts 1:1, to references about Jesus' ascension (1:2), to his passion and resurrection (1:3), to his promise of the Holy Spirit (1:4 – 5), to a conversation about events of the last days (1:6 – 7), before including Jesus' commission of the disciples as his witnesses from Jerusalem to the ends of the earth (1:8), a reference often regarded as a summary of the content of Acts.

A sketch of the work of historians in the Greco-Roman period may help us to understand their research and writing.[46] Lucian of Samosata (ca. AD 125 – 180) describes three steps of the process of writing history.[47] The first step is the collec-

---

45. Cf. Loveday C. A. Alexander, *The Preface to Luke's Gospel: Literary Convention and Social Context in Luke 1.1 – 4 and Acts 1.1* (SNTSMS 78; Cambridge: Cambridge Univ. Press, 1993), who argues that the prefaces in Luke 1:1 – 4 and Acts 1:1 indicate that Luke situates his two-volume work not among the historiographical works of professional historians but among the treatises on technical subjects written by authors of medical, rhetorical, or engineering works. Cf. Alexander, *Literary Context,* 21 – 42; see ibid. for primary evidence relating to the following points.

46. Cf. Baum, "Anonymity of the New Testament History Books," 12 – 13. See A. Brian Bosworth, *From Arrian to Alexander: Studies in Historical Interpretation* (Oxford: Clarendon,

1988); M. Grant, *Greek and Roman Historians: Information and Misinformation* (London: Routledge, 1995); John Marincola, *Authority and Tradition in Ancient Historiography* (Cambridge: Cambridge Univ. Press, 1997); Guido Schepens, "History and Historia: Inquiry in the Greek Historians," in *A Companion to Greek and Roman Historiography* (ed. J. Marincola; Malden: Blackwell, 2007), 39 – 55.

47. Lucian, *De historia conscribenda* (*How to Write History*) 47 – 48. Cf. Aristoula Georgiadou and David H. J. Larmour, "Lucian and Historiography: 'De Historia Conscribenda' and 'Verae Historiae'," *ANRW* II.34.2 (1994): 1449 – 1509; Clare K. Rothschild, "Irony and Truth: The Value of *De Historia Conscribenda* for Understanding Hellenistic and Early Roman

tion of source material. Ideally the author is an eyewitness of the events he seeks to describe. If this is not possible, he consults reliable witnesses. Polybius (2nd cent. BC) emphasizes that contemporary eyewitnesses must be carefully scrutinized; the historian may accept the testimony only of those witnesses who have proven to be reliable.[48] Luke informs his readers in Luke 1:1–4 that he has read and analyzed written source material.

In a second step, the historian produces a stylistically inelegant "series of notes [*hypomnēma ti*], a body of material as yet with no beauty or continuity," which arranges the material in the right order. According to Cicero, Caesar's *Commentarii* supplied merely the (unadorned) material that could be used by another author as the basis for a proper historical work.[49]

The third step involves the transformation of the material in an effort to "give it beauty and enhance it with the charms of expression, figure, and rhythm." Lucian, Josephus, and other historians use the Attic prose writers of the fifth and fourth centuries BC as guides in matters of style, while Polybius writes in educated standard Koine. Luke, as we have seen, uses (non-atticizing) educated standard Koine used by authors who wrote for administrative, business, and professional purposes. In particular Luke writes in the distinctive form of biblicizing Greek, a Jewish version of standard Koine, which lends "a certain solemn and hieratic tone to Luke's diction, dignifying it and raising it above everyday life."[50] Luke's biblicizing Greek would not have made much sense outside the Jewish communities of the diaspora[51] and the Christian communities in which Jewish and Gentile believers continued to read the Jewish Scriptures.

Acts as Historical Monograph

Some suggest that Acts is a short historical monograph,[52] a more specialized category of Hellenistic historiography. The works of Sallust (86–35 BC), comments of Cicero, and Hellenistic Jewish writings (1 Esdras; 1–2 Maccabees) suggest that a historical monograph (a modern term) is a single volume of acceptable length, with a limited historical (chronological) and geographical scope, which focuses on one main figure (or at least on one main figure at a time); in terms of literary components, it includes a prologue, narrative, speeches, dispatches, and letters. The book

---

Period Historiographical Method," in *Die Apostelgeschichte im Kontext antiker und frühchristlicher Historiographie* (ed. J. Frey, C. K. Rothschild, and J. Schröter; BZNW 162; Berlin: De Gruyter, 2009), 277–91.

48. Polybius, *History* 12.4c.5.

49. Cicero, *Brutus* 262.

50. Albert Wifstrand, *Epochs and Styles: Selected Writings on New Testament, Greek Language and Greek Culture in the Post-Classical Era* (ed. L. Rydbeck and S. E. Porter; WUNT

179; Tübingen: Mohr Siebeck, 2005), 30.

51. Alexander, *Literary Context*, 11, 251–52.

52. Cf. Eckhard Plümacher, "Die Apostelgeschichte als historische Monographie 1978," in *Geschichte und Geschichten. Aufsätze zur Apostelgeschichte und zu den Johannesakten* (ed. J. Schröter and R. Brucker; WUNT 170; Tübingen: Mohr Siebeck, 2004), 1–13; Palmer, "Historical Monograph"; cf. ibid., 26–29, for the following description.

of Acts corresponds to this description. It is a single volume of moderate length, covering a limited historical period, with a restricted geographical scope. It has a consistent focus (on the progress of the Christian mission) and portrays one leading figure at a time (Peter, Stephen and Philip, Barnabas, Paul). It includes a prologue, narrative, speeches, and quoted letters.

Since it is difficult to describe a more or less unified genre of "short historical monograph" and since the formal features of Luke's prefaces do not readily fit the varied prefaces of such works, this categorization of Acts is not without problems.[53] Luke's preface in Acts 1:1, particularly the dedication to Theophilus and the recapitulation of events related in the first volume, places Acts on the margins of Greek historiography where the genre is "furthest from epic or rhetorical pretension and closest to the scholarly, scientific side of the Ionian historia-tradition"; and the biblicizing Greek and the biblical subject matter place Acts "closer overall to biblical historiography than to the Greek tradition."[54]

Acts as Apologetic Historiography

Some scholars suggest that Acts represents apologetic historiography, a category that has been defined as "the story of a sub-group of people in an extended prose narrative written by a member of the group who follows the group's own traditions but Hellenizes them in an effort to establish the identity of the group within the setting of the larger world."[55] It is argued that the function of Luke-Acts was "to define Christianity in terms of Rome (politically innocent), Judaism (a continuation), and itself (*traditio apostolica*)."[56]

This analysis, together with other readings of Acts as an *apologia*, fails to convince for several reasons.[57] First, the large number of "apologetic readings" of Acts force us to conclude that if Luke indeed pursued apologetic goals with this work, he has failed. The key elements of audience, charges of accusers, and defendants with their own arguments, which should be easy to grasp from the surface of the text, are evidently not there.

---

53. Cf. Alexander, *Literary Context*, 37 – 40.

54. Cf. ibid., 41, 42. See Detlev Dormeyer, "Die Gattung der Apostelgeschichte," in *Die Apostelgeschichte im Kontext antiker und frühchristlicher Historiographie* (ed. J. Frey, C. K. Rothschild, and J. Schröter), 437 – 75, who classifies Acts as a biographical universal history. Joachim Molthagen, "Geschichtsschreibung und Geschichtsverständnis in der Apostelgeschichte im Vergleich mit Herodot, Thukydides und Polybios," in *Die Apostelgeschichte im Kontext antiker und frühchristlicher Historiographie*, 159 – 81, argues that Acts belongs to ancient historiography, even though it occupies an independent place within the genre.

55. Gregory E. Sterling, *Historiography and Self-Definition: Josephos, Luke-Acts, and Apologetic Historiography* (NovTSup 64; Leiden/New York: Brill, 1992), 17.

56. Sterling, *Historiography*, 386. A sociological version of this perspective is suggested by Philip F. Esler, *Community and Gospel in Luke-Acts: The Social and Political Motivations of Lucan Theology* (SNTSMS 57; Cambridge: Cambridge Univ. Press, 1987).

57. For the following comments cf. Alexander, *Literary Context*, 190 – 93; also Palmer, "Historical Monograph," 15 – 18.

Second, as the apologetic scenario belongs within the framework of forensic rhetoric, we would expect the dominant mode of discourse to be direct speech with a focus on argumentation. Acts, however, is primarily a narrative, as already set up by the preface in Acts 1:1. If an author intends a narrative to have a primary apologetic aim, he needs to inform the reader and provide them with the conclusions that should be drawn from the narrative. Apart from Acts 1:1, however, the narrator never intervenes.

Third, while the encounters with Roman officials indeed end "positively" for Christians, suggesting the political "innocence" of the followers of Jesus (e.g., 18:14 – 15), other texts demonstrate how the reality of the gospel disrupts and challenges pagan values and the pagan way of life (e.g., 16:16 – 24; 19:23 – 41). While some passages in Acts can certainly be used for political apologetic purposes, the latter was not Luke's main goal in writing Luke-Acts.

A more sophisticated attempt to read Acts as "lively political theology in its time" describes Luke as claiming that "the culturally destabilizing power of the Christian mission is not to be construed as sedition or treason but rather as the light and forgiveness of God. The dissolution of patterns basic to Graeco-Roman culture (e.g., sacrifice to the gods) is nothing less than the necessary consequence of forming life-giving communities."[58] It is certainly true that Luke describes the Christian mission, which claims to be a revelation from God and which forms new communities, as a challenge to traditional patterns and practices of pagan life, seen in the incidents in Lystra, Philippi, Athens, and Ephesus.[59] But it is also true that Luke describes the Christian mission as a challenge to Jewish culture, both with regard to the traditional interpretation of Scripture (e.g., as concerning circumcision, the food laws, the place of the Gentiles) and with regard to the "place" of salvation (temple versus Jesus, Israel's Messiah and Savior).

It is certainly correct that Paul's encounters with Gallio, Claudius Lysias, Felix, and Festus allow Luke to portray the Christian mission as innocent of the charge of seditious criminal activity.[60] However, it is also true that Luke does not "solve" the conflict between the Christian mission and the Jewish authorities in Jerusalem and indeed the Jewish opponents "throughout the world" (24:5): he ends his book with Paul in prison in Rome, a twofold "location" that resulted from Jewish charges against his message. Unless Luke is thought to write for Greeks and Romans only, his project of a "political theology" would have to be deemed only partially successful as it arguably fails to address the concerns of the Jewish authorities in Jerusalem and of Jewish leaders in other cities of the eastern Mediterranean.

---

58. C. Kavin Rowe, *World Upside Down: Reading Acts in the Graeco-Roman Age* (Oxford: Oxford Univ. Press, 2009), 6, 7; Rowe acknowledges that Acts cannot be seen as a simple *apologia* articulating the harmlessness of Christianity as far as the Roman Empire was concerned.

59. Ibid., 17 – 51.

60. Ibid., 53 – 89.

Acts as Historical Fiction?

The suggestion that Acts corresponds to the genre of the historical novel is not convincing.[61] The defining condition of fiction is that "it is an untruth which does not intend to deceive. Fiction is neither truth nor lie: both sender and recipient recognize it for what it is"; as regards ancient critics, they are "infuriatingly silent about novels; there is not even a single word to express the concept in either Latin or Greek," although some thinkers allow that "there is a class of untruth whose function is to give pleasure, and that such untruths can even have a legitimate (or at least harmless) place in a text whose principal or ostensible aim is factual information."[62] The purpose of Luke's two-volume work, with long sections about Jesus' suffering and death in the gospel and repeated and long passages about the apostles' persecution and imprisonment, can hardly be described in terms of "giving pleasure," which became a defining feature of fiction.

Acts as Biography

The book of Acts has a biographical interest, but the classification as a biography[63] does not explain the structure and the content of Acts, with the exception perhaps, and in a most general sense, of Acts 9; 13 – 14; 16 – 28, where Luke's narrative focuses on Paul. While the intellectual biography of the Hellenistic period does not explain the literary genre of Acts, it may help us understand how Greek readers who were familiar with the influential moral paradigm of the life of Socrates might have understood Luke-Acts.[64] Biographical features appear in ancient Near Eastern

---

61. Richard I. Pervo, *Profit with Delight: The Literary Genre of the Acts of the Apostles* (Philadelphia: Fortress, 1987), claims that Acts is closer to the Alexander romance than to the Greek historians Thucydides or Polybius. Todd C. Penner, *In Praise of Christian Origins: Stephen and the Hellenists in Lukan Apologetic Historiography* (Emory Studies in Early Christianity 10; New York: T&T Clark, 2004), 6, thinks that as regards the classification of ancient literature, the lines between the three genres of biography, history, and novel are "both fluid and somewhat artificial." For a critique see Steve Walton, "Acts: Many Questions, Many Answers," in *The Face of New Testament Studies* (ed. S. McKnight and G. R. Osborne), 229 – 50, 237.

62. John R. Morgan, "Fiction and History: Historiography and the Novel," in *A Companion to Greek and Roman Historiography* (ed. J. Marincola), 553 – 64, 555, 556. For "giving pleasure" as the defining feature of untrue narrative, see ibid., 557.

63. Talbert, *Literary Patterns*, 125 – 40, who classifies Luke-Acts as "that type of biography which dealt with the lives of philosophers and their successors" (134); also Bernhard Heininger, "Das Paulusbild der Apostelgeschichte und die

antike Biographie," in *Griechische Biographie in hellenistischer Zeit* (ed. M. Erler and S. Schorn; Beiträge zur Altertumskunde 245; Berlin: De Gruyter, 2007), 407 – 29, who compares Luke-Acts with Plutarch's double biographies, with Luke pairing a biography of Jesus with a biography of Jesus' most important disciples, Peter and Paul. For a critical discussion cf. David L. Barr and Judith L. Wentling, "The Conventions of Classical Biography and the Genre of Luke-Acts," in *Luke-Acts: New Perspectives from the Society of Biblical Literature Seminar* (ed. C. H. Talbert; New York: Crossroad, 1984), 63 – 88; Hemer, *Acts*, 91 – 94; Alexander, *Literary Context*, 43 – 62.

64. Alexander, *Literary Context*, 62 – 67. On biography in Greek and Roman historiography see Philip Stadter, "Biography and History," in *A Companion to Greek and Roman Historiography* (ed. J. Marincola), 528 – 40, who discusses Nepos ("biographies for reference and browsing"), Tacitus ("filial piety and imperial politics"), Suetonius ("emperor-watching"), and Plutarch ("character, leadership, and political power"); he concludes that (political) biography "asks what kind of character a historical actor possessed, what motivated his behavior, what he accomplished or failed to achieve. Passing over large-

historiography, which is autonomous from the Greek tradition and which thus can explain its appearance in biblical and Jewish historiography as well as in Luke-Acts.[65]

The Speeches in Acts

Luke follows the model of Greek and Roman historians who invariably include reported speech in their narrative histories.[66] The speeches in classical historical works indicate "the reasons and rationale of the historical characters, why they did what they did and with what aims, goals, and expectations," and they could "provide a more abstract analysis of the underlying issues at stake in actions that were seen as important or distinctive." A speech characterizes the speaker and indicates his or her frame of mind and disposition. Speeches in historical narrative rarely reproduce the actual words that were spoken. However, the speeches were not free inventions but provided an approximation of what was said, even if sometimes imaginative reconstruction was necessary. A speech included in historical narrative "mediates between past and present"[67] and provides an (indirect) opportunity for the author to describe the character of the particular individual.[68]

Even though Acts is relatively short compared with Greek historical works, Luke utilizes the dramatic opportunities for formal speeches provided by the narrated events to express the social location and thus the purpose of his text.[69] The speeches of Luke's characters can be divided into four types of apologetic:

1. Inner-church debate: the dispute between Hebrews and Hellenists (6:1–7); the dispute about Peter's encounter with Cornelius (10:1–11:18); the dispute about the necessity of circumcision for converted Gentiles (15:1–35).
2. Disputes with and speeches before the Jewish community: Peter's and John's hearing before the Sanhedrin (4:1–22); the apostles' hearing before the Sanhedrin (5:17–42); Stephen's hearing before the Sanhedrin (6:8–7:60); Paul's sermon in the synagogue in Pisidian Antioch (13:16–41); Paul's presentation of his message before the Jewish leaders in Rome (28:23–28).

scale movements and consequences, it tends to focus on details and anecdotes. Authorial comments are more frequent than is usual in history, but speeches are rare. Narrative, in particular, is more episodic, or completely excluded."

65. Cf. Alexander, *Literary Context*, 15, who points out that biographical aspects of ancient Near Eastern historiography "appear in the court tales of Herodotus but were rigorously excluded from Thucydides' more democratic conception." For the following comment cf. ibid. 14–15. Also Jervell, *Apostelgeschichte*, 78–79.

66. Cf. John Marincola, "Speeches in Classical Historiography," in *A Companion to Greek and Roman Historiography* (ed. J. Marincola), 118–32; the following quotation, ibid., 119.

67. Ibid., 130.

68. Cf. Luke V. Pitcher, "Characterization in Ancient Historiography," in *A Companion to Greek and Roman Historiography* (ed. J. Marincola), 102–17, 107–8.

69. Cf. Alexander, *Literary Context*, 193–206 for the following comments. On the speeches in Acts see "In Depth: The Speeches in Acts" at 2:14–36. On the trial scenes cf. Allison A. Trites, "The Importance of Legal Scenes and Language in the Book of Acts," *NovT* 16 (1974): 278–84; Saundra Schwartz, "The Trial Scene in the Greek Novel and in Acts," in *Contextualizing Acts: Lukan Narrative and Greco-Roman Discourse* (SBL Symposium 20; ed. T. C. Penner and C. Vander Stichele; Atlanta: Society of Biblical Literature, 2003), 105–37, who briefly analyzes fourteen trial scenes, not all of which contain direct speech.

3. The presentation of the Christian message to a Greek audience: Paul's speech in Lystra (14:11 – 18); Paul's presentation of his message before the Areopagus in Athens (17:16 – 34).

4. Paul's encounters with Roman officials: in Philippi (16:19 – 40); in Thessalonica (17:5 – 9); in Corinth (18:12 – 17); in Ephesus (19:21 – 41); and his self-defense in the Jerusalem temple (21:27 – 22:29), before the Sanhedrin (23:1 – 10), in Caesarea before Felix (24:1 – 23), before Festus (25:1 – 12), before Festus and Agrippa (25:13 – 26:32).

The Purpose of Acts

The role of direct speech, the role of religious convictions and activities, the role of the miraculous, and the exegetical dynamic of Acts correspond to conventions of the historiography of the Greek Bible and the Hellenistic Jewish historians. The above comments have shown, however, that despite similarities to Greek and Roman historical writings and to Hellenized Jewish historiography, the biblicizing Greek, the quotations from and allusions to the Hebrew Scriptures, and the emphasis on fulfillment and promise suggest that Acts would not have been seen by general readers as belonging either to *Roman* historiography or *Greek* biography.[70]

It should be noted that the amount of direct speech — both in the formal speeches and in dialogical material — is rather high, comprising about 9,100 of a total of 18,400 words in Acts.[71] It has thus been suggested that Luke-Acts "demonstrates affinities both to historical monographs and to biographies, but it appears to represent a new type of work, of which it is the only example, in which under the shape of a 'scientific treatise' Luke has produced a work which deals with 'the beginnings of Christianity.'"[72]

The material devoted to inner-church debates and to the presentation of the gospel to a (pagan) Greek audience is relatively limited. Most of the speeches, including those connected with Paul's arrest and imprisonment, are addressed to a Jewish audience.[73] The final explanation of the Christian message and the last comments on the reaction of Jews and of Gentiles to the apostles' preaching are given in connection with Paul's encounter with the leaders of the Jewish community in Rome (28:21 – 22). This suggests that the purpose of Acts has to be understood in the context of the

---

70. Cf. Witherington, *Acts*, 39, who adds, "it would surely, however, have been seen as some sort of Hellenistic historiography, especially by a Gentile audience."

71. Cf. Armin D. Baum, "Paulinismen in den Missionsreden des lukanischen Paulus," *ETL* 82 (2006): 405 – 36, 405; a similar figure of 51 percent for direct speech (*oratio recta*) in Acts is given by Richard I. Pervo, "Direct Speech in Acts and the Question of Genre," *JSNT* 28 (2006): 285 – 307, 288, 304, based on verse count (516 of 1002 verses).

72. I. Howard Marshall, "Acts and the 'Former Treatise,'" in *The Book of Acts in Its Ancient Literary Setting* (ed. B. W. Winter and A. D. Clarke), 163 – 82, 180.

73. This includes Paul's hearings in Caesarea. Even though Paul is presented as innocent of the charges leveled against him in the narrative section (Acts 13 – 19), Luke still leaves the impression that Paul and his preaching cause trouble wherever he goes.

ongoing debate between the followers of Jesus Christ and the Jewish communities both in Palestine and in the diaspora. While Luke traces the rejection of the gospel by Jews, in particular by Jewish leaders, and the inclusion of an increasing number of Gentiles, he seeks to explain

> how a new movement emerging out of Judaism came to incorporate Gentiles into the community of God. At the core of the activity and preaching stands the work of God through the now exalted Jesus, who in turn distributes the Spirit as a sign that the new era and salvation have come to both Jews and Gentiles.[74]

Luke assures Gentiles who had converted to faith in Jesus as Messiah and Savior that being a Gentile in a Jewish movement was part of God's plan. This is true whether Luke's intended audience, and Theophilus in particular, belonged to the group of the God-fearers or not. In this sense Acts is indeed a "work of education"[75] that confirms for its readers the gospel of Jesus Christ (Luke 1:4) and their commitment to the foundations of the Christian faith and to the work of God in Israel and in the world, a work that fulfills God's promises through Jesus Christ as proclaimed by his apostles. It is in this sense that *Acts confirms and consolidates the identity of the church as the community of the followers of Jesus*, presenting the foundational events and the main developments connected with the earliest Christians.[76] Here Luke's emphasis on the Holy Spirit as transforming power present in the lives of the followers of Jesus and their communities[77] is as significant as the miracles that happen in the ministry of Peter and Paul, demonstrating that the life and work of Jesus continues in the life and work of the church.[78]

Luke, however, did not write an analysis of the debates between Jews and Christians, nor did he write a treatise on the identity of the Gentile believers who worship God in the context of a Jewish movement. He advances his theological points in a historical narrative that includes speeches of the main (and of some minor) characters. The main focus of his narrative in two volumes is the life, death, and resurrection of Jesus (gospel of Luke), and the growth of the church and the expansion of Christians communities through the work of the early missionaries, particularly

---

74. Darrell L. Bock, *Acts* (BECNT; Grand Rapids: Baker, 2007), 24.

75. Ernst Haenchen, *The Acts of the Apostles* (Philadelphia: Westminster, 1971), 103.

76. Cf. Frank Thielman, *Theology of the New Testament: A Canonical and Synthetic Approach* (Grand Rapids: Zondervan, 2005), 112, with reference to Sterling, *Historiography*, and Marianne Palmer Bonz, *The Past as Legacy: Luke-Acts and Ancient Epic* (Minneapolis: Fortress, 2000).

77. Cf. Matthias Wenk, *Community-Forming Power: The Socio-Ethical Role of the Spirit in Luke-Acts* (Sheffield: Sheffield Academic Press, 2000); Aaron J. Kuecker, "The Spirit and the 'Other': Social Identity, Ethnicity and Intergroup Reconciliation in Luke-Acts," PhD dissertation (St. Andrews University, 2002). Similarly Rowe, *World Upside Down*, 4, who reads Acts as a "theologically sophisticated political document that aims at nothing less than the construction of an alternative total way of life ... that runs counter to the life-patterns of the Graeco-Roman world."

78. Cf. Friedrich Avemarie, "Acta Jesu Christi. Zum christologischen Sinn der Wundermotive in der Apostelgeschichte," in *Die Apostelgeschichte im Kontext antiker und frühchristlicher Historiographie* (ed. J. Frey, C. K. Rothschild, and J. Schröter), 539 – 62.

Peter and Paul (Acts). Thus, a second major emphasis of Acts is *the mission of the church whose leaders are obedient to the divine commission, charging them to take the gospel to cities and to regions in which the name of Jesus, Messiah and Savior, has not yet been proclaimed.*

It is surely no coincidence that these two major themes — the identity of the church as God's people, and the mission of the church as witnesses of Jesus — are the two themes of the first narrative section in Acts, in which Luke relates the reconstitution of the Twelve after Judas's demise and the emphasis on the task of the Twelve as witnesses of Jesus (Acts 1:15 – 26).

Thus, the book of Acts is a narrative about recent historical events in the movement of the followers of Jesus and about major leaders of the Christian movement who carried the news about Jesus, Israel's Messiah and Savior, to other regions of the Mediterranean world. Acts is a biographical history of important developments in earliest Christianity. Luke-Acts, the two-volume work, is a historical report about "Jesus and his followers."

We do not know for whom Luke wrote his two-volume work. Theophilus (Acts 1:1) is among Luke's intended readers. His appellation as "most excellent" (κράτιστε; Luke 1:3) suggests that he was socially respected, perhaps wealthy. Some have suggested that he was Luke's patron who financed Luke's research and writing as well as the publication of the two-volume work (see commentary on Acts 1:1). Others have suggested that he was a God-fearer, i.e., a Gentile who attended synagogue services learning about Israel's God and Israel's Scriptures before coming to faith in Jesus, reflecting the interest that Luke seems to have in the group of the God-fearers. While this is possible, it cannot be proven, and it certainly does not mean that Luke wrote his two volumes for converted God-fearers. Apart from the fact that there is no evidence to support such an assumption, it is most plausible to assume a wide audience: such a large work is unlikely to have been written for one particular group or one specific church — it was most likely written for all the churches, including the churches that Luke knew personally (Antioch, Philippi, Rome).

Historicity and Sources

The historical reliability of Acts is not necessarily linked to its genre (unless Acts is classified as fiction) — a historical work can contain mistakes. The historical reliability of Luke's narrative depends on Luke's credibility as a historian. While many interpreters have been skeptical,[79] others have concluded that even though Luke has theological and apologetic concerns, he deserves respect as a historian just like other

---

79. In the 19th century F. C. Baur and the Tübingen School; in the 20th century scholars such as H. Conzelmann, M. Dibelius, E. Haenchen, G. Lüdemann, more recently R. I. Pervo and T. C. Penner. Cf. Ferdinand Christian Baur, *Paul, the Apostle* *of Jesus Christ: His Life and Works, His Epistles and Teachings* (orig. 1873; repr., Peabody, MA: Hendrickson, 2003), 1:1 – 14; Haenchen, *Acts*, 98 – 103; Pervo, *Profit with Delight*; Penner, *Christian Origins.*

ancient historians.[80] Classical scholars often defend information provided by Acts against hypercritical New Testament scholars.[81]

An analysis of several areas in which Luke purports to provide information confirms that Luke's account is both conscientious and reliable:[82]

- the chronological connections between information given in Acts with the historical milieu of the middle of the first century
- the geographical information on matters of secondary, often negligible, importance
- information on political, local, and cultural matters that cannot be assumed to have been general knowledge
- the internal correlation of minor details that otherwise assume no leading role in Luke's account
- items that are not significant for Luke's theological intentions, but important enough to be mentioned

The "we passages" suggest that the author of Acts was a contemporary of Paul and an eyewitness to many of the events that he reports.[83]

- The abruptness of the "we passages" can be explained by the unpretentious character of Luke's reference to his legitimacy for writing a reliable historical account (Luke 1:1–4) and of his participation in the missionary movement that he describes.
- The first person account of the "we passages" suggests that Acts was not published anonymously. It is likely that the work was connected with the name of

80. In the 19th century W. M. Ramsay; in the 20th century F. F. Bruce, C. Hemer, R. Riesner, I. H. Marshall, B. Witherington. Cf. William M. Ramsay, *St. Paul the Traveller and the Roman Citizen* (updated and rev. ed.; ed. M. Wilson; Grand Rapids: Baker, 2001); F. F. Bruce, "The Acts of the Apostles: Historical Record or Theological Reconstruction?" *ANRW* II.25.3 (1985): 2569–2603; F. F. Bruce, *The Acts of the Apostles: The Greek Text with Introduction and Commentary* (3rd rev. ed.; Grand Rapids: Eerdmans, 1990), 27–34; I. Howard Marshall, *Luke: Historian and Theologian* (Grand Rapids: Zondervan, 1970), 21–76; Hemer, *Acts*, 1–29 and passim; Witherington, *Acts*, 2–39; Rainer Riesner, "Die historische Zuverlässigkeit der Apostelgeschichte," *ZNT* 18 (2006): 38–43. Scholars such as M. Hengel, C. K. Barrett, and J. A. Fitzmyer seek to steer a middle course between the skeptical approach and the "conservative reaction" (Fitzmyer, *Acts*, 124); cf. Martin Hengel, *Acts and the History of Earliest Christianity* (London: SCM, 1979); Barrett, *Acts*, 2:xxxiii–lxii; similarly Dunn, *Beginning from Jerusalem*, 73–87. See Jörg Frey, "Fragen um Lukas als 'Historiker' und den historiographischen Charakter der Apostelgeschichte," in *Die Apostelgeschichte im Kontext antiker und frühchristlicher Historiographie* (ed. J. Frey,

C. K. Rothschild, and J. Schröter), 1–26.

81. Robin Lane Fox, *Pagans and Christians in the Mediterranean World from the Second Century A.D. to the Conversion of Constantine* (London: Penguin, 1986), 99–100, 293; Helga Botermann, *Das Judenedikt des Kaisers Claudius: Römischer Staat und Christiani im 1. Jahrhundert* (Hermes Einzelschriften 71; Stuttgart: Steiner, 1996), 17–49. See the matter-of-fact treatment of Acts as a historical work by Molthagen, "Geschichtsschreibung"; Cancik, "Geschichtswerk."

82. Cf. Hemer, *Acts*, 101–243, for details concerning the following areas.

83. Cf. ibid., 312–64; Claus-Jürgen Thornton, *Zeuge*, passim; F. Scott Spencer, *The Portrait of Philip in Acts: A Study of Roles and Relations* (JSNTSup 67; Sheffield: JSOT Press, 1992), 246–50; cf. Stanley E. Porter, "The 'We' Passages in Acts as a Source Regarding Paul," in *The Paul of Acts: Essays in Literary Criticism, Rhetoric and Theology* (WUNT 115; Tübingen: Mohr Siebeck, 1999), 10–46. Unconvinced remains Dietrich-Alex Koch, "Kollektenbericht, 'Wir'-Bericht und Itinerar. Neue (?) Überlegungen zu einem alten Problem," *NTS* 45 (1999): 367–90.

an author from the beginning. In the early patristic tradition no alternatives to Luke are ever mentioned.[84]

- It is not plausible to interpret the "we passages" as a stylistic device that seeks to feign *autopsia*, i.e., an eyewitness account.

Luke does not include a self-presentation as the author of the work, which was the standard device for claiming *autopsia*. When Greek and Roman historians emphasize their active participation in the events, in addition to their being eyewitnesses, they do this in a self-reference that is usually formulated in the third person singular. Luke writes part of his report in the first person, which is rare for Greek and Roman authors, in contrast to Jewish tradition. While it is theoretically possible that the "we passages" derive from a source from which the author of Acts copied mechanically, without removing the first person plural, this assumption is not plausible if we consider the customs of Greco-Roman historiography and the literary capabilities of the author of Acts.[85]

The emphasis on the historical reliability of Acts should not be seen as an effort to minimize, or negate, Luke's deliberate shaping of the material in the context of his theological purposes. While a demonstration of the documentary correctness of Luke's historical work is not the same as understanding Luke's text, an exclusive focus on Luke's literary artistry or theological emphasis would leave Luke's readers wondering why a description of God's initiatives and actions in the life and ministry of the new messianic people of God and in the life and ministry of Jesus' witnesses is presented in the form of a historical work. Acknowledging Luke's historical reliability is an integral part of understanding Luke's theological concerns.

As regards the sources of Acts,[86] we have seen the importance of the "we passages" (16:10 – 17; 20:5 – 15; 21:1 – 18; 27:1 – 28:16). If the author of Acts was indeed present at the events connected with Paul's missionary work in Macedonia, Paul's last journey to Jerusalem, Paul's arrest and imprisonment in Caesarea, and Paul's voyage to Rome, he is himself the source of these sections. It is more difficult — some say impossible — to determine what other sources Luke used when he wrote Acts. It is plausible to assume that Luke had access to (written or oral) sources from the Jerusalem community when he wrote Acts 1 – 8; 10 – 12. Assuming that Luke was

---

84. Cf. Claus-Jürgen Thornton, *Zeuge*, 84 – 98, 122, 147, 199; Arthur J. Droge, "Did 'Luke' Write Anonymously? Lingering at the Threshold," in *Die Apostelgeschichte im Kontext antiker und frühchristlicher Historiographie* (ed. J. Frey, C. K. Rothschild, and J. Schröter), 495 – 517. A historical account that includes sections written in the first person plural and does not allow the reader to identify the narrator is a literary absurdity.

85. Cf. Claus-Jürgen Thornton, *Zeuge*, 199, who points out that there was no literary model that would have allowed readers in the first century to understand the "we passages" in this

sense, which "means that the 'we passages' of the Book of Acts must be understood in terms of the author aspiring to mark his personal part in the event."

86. While the early Greek historians relied primarily on oral sources, by the late fourth century BC documents (e.g., inscriptions) became an invaluable source for historians. Josephus includes a large number of documents, which he quotes, in Books 12 – 14 and 16 of his *Antiquities*. Cf. Peter J. Rhodes, "Documents and the Greek Historians," in *A Companion to Greek and Roman Historiography* (ed. J. Marincola), 56 – 66, 64 – 65.

Paul's companion, Paul would have been his source for the account in Acts 9; 13 – 28, perhaps supplemented by local traditions.[87] The events and speeches of Acts 21 – 28 were likely summarized in the official report that the governor Porcius Festus had to send to Rome, a report to which Paul would have had access as the defendant in the case that the Jewish authorities in Jerusalem had initiated against him.[88]

The Greek Text of Acts

The Greek text of Acts is preserved in fourteen papyrus manuscripts dating from the third century to the eighth century,[89] twenty-eight majuscule manuscripts dating from the fourth to the tenth centuries,[90] and hundreds of minuscule manuscripts dating from the ninth to the fifteenth centuries.[91] According to the traditional classification, there are three kinds of texts for Acts: the Alexandrian text, the Western text, and the Byzantine text. The latter represents the result of smoother readings, harmonization, and conflation, and seldom presents readings of the original text. The so-called Western text (which is also attested by manuscripts copied in the East), represented mainly in the bilingual (Greek and Latin) Codex Bezae Cantabrigiensis (manuscript D),[92] is characterized by its fondness for paraphrase, harmonizing difficulties in the text, and adding traditional or apocryphal material. The Greek text of D dates to the fifth century and is almost 10 percent (over 800 words) longer than the Alexandrian text in the extant sections.[93]

---

87. Barrett, *Acts*, 51 – 56, suggests Philip, Caesarea, Antioch, and Paul as possible sources, with an emphasis on Antioch for the accounts of Paul's conversion, his early missionary work, and the Apostles' Council. Martin Hengel, *Between Jesus and Paul: Studies in the Earliest History of Christianity* (London: SCM, 1983), 4, assumes sources about Peter and an Antiochene source for the material in Acts 1 – 15. Fitzmyer, *Acts*, 80 – 88, detects Palestinian, Antiochene, Pauline, and "we section" sources.

88. Cf. Bruce W. Winter, "The Importance of the *Captatio Benevolentiae* in the Speeches of Tertullus and Paul in Acts 24:1 – 21," *JTS* 42 (1991): 505 – 31; Bruce W. Winter, "Official Proceedings and the Forensic Speeches in Acts 24 – 26," in *The Book of Acts in Its Ancient Literary Setting* (ed. B. W. Winter and A. D. Clarke), 305 – 36.

89. Five papyri fragments were copied in the third century ($\mathfrak{P}^{29}$, $\mathfrak{P}^{45}$, $\mathfrak{P}^{48}$, $\mathfrak{P}^{53}$, $\mathfrak{P}^{91}$), one papyrus from the fourth century ($\mathfrak{P}^{8}$), two papyri from the fourth or fifth century ($\mathfrak{P}^{50}$, $\mathfrak{P}^{57}$), and five papyri date from the fifth to the eighty century ($\mathfrak{P}^{33+58}$, $\mathfrak{P}^{41}$, $\mathfrak{P}^{56}$, $\mathfrak{P}^{74}$, $\mathfrak{P}^{112}$).

90. 0189 (3rd century), ℵ, B (4th century), 057 (4th/5th century), A, C, D, 048, 077, 0165, 0166, 0175, 0236, 0244 (5th century), 076 (5th/6th century), E, H, L, P, Ψ, 049, 066, 093, 095+0123, 096, 097, 0120, 0140 (6th to 10th century).

91. 33 (9th century), 1739, 1891, (10th century). For a complete list of the Greek manuscripts of the New Testament, cf. Kurt Aland, *Kurzgefasste Liste der griechischen Handschriften des Neuen Testaments* (2nd ed.; ANTT 1; Berlin: De Gruyter, 1994); this list is updated on the website of the Institute for New Testament Textual Research at Münster University (www.uni-muenster.de/INTF) under *Kurzgefasste Liste*. For the text of most important manuscripts see Reuben J. Swanson, *New Testament Greek Manuscripts: Variant Readings Arranged in Horizontal Lines against Codex Vaticanus: The Acts of the Apostles* (Pasadena: Carey, 1998).

92. For the full evidence cf. Marie-Émile Boismard and Arnaud Lamouille, *Le texte Occidental des Actes des Apôtres. Reconstitution et réhabilitation* (Synthèse 17; Paris: Éditions Recherche sur les Civilisations, 1984), 1:11 – 95.

93. Note that D lacks Acts 8:29 – 10:14; 22:10 – 20; 22:29 – 28:31. Note that one-third of Bruce M. Metzger, *A Textual Commentary on the Greek New Testament* (2nd ed.; Stuttgart: Deutsche Bibelgesellschaft/United Bible Societies, 1994), is devoted to a discussion of variant readings in Acts, mostly in the Western text; see ibid., 222 – 36, for an introduction to the problem of the Western text. Cf. Peter Head, "Acts and the Problem of Its Texts," in *The Book of Acts in Its Ancient Literary Setting* (ed. B. W. Winter and A. D. Clarke), 415 – 44.

Few interpreters have followed scholars who suggest that Luke is responsible for both the Alexandrian and the Western version of the text of Acts — Luke first wrote a rough draft in Rome, a longer and fuller version (represented by the Western text), which he subsequently edited, producing a clearer, more carefully composed version that he sent to Theophilus (represented in the Alexandrian text).[94] Some scholars have attempted to rehabilitate the Western text as the original form of the text of Acts, suggesting that Luke wrote a first redaction of Acts, several years later he produced an altered version, and these two redactions were later fused into one text on which the Alexandrian text form is based.[95] Some have argued that the author of Acts produced a rough draft of Acts and an annotated version of this draft; both versions were published separately in the second half of the second century.[96]

Some scholars argue that since no hypothesis has fully and successfully explained the relation of the Western and the Alexandrian texts of Acts, it cannot be ruled out that the original text may be preserved in the Western group of textual witnesses. These scholars are therefore prepared to "compare the two divergent traditions point by point and in each case select the reading that commends itself in the light of transcriptional and intrinsic probabilities."[97] And many scholars recognize that "some of the information incorporated in certain Western expansions may well be factually accurate, though not deriving from the original author of Acts."[98] Most scholars regard the possibility as unlikely that the readings of the Western text represent original readings.[99]

Despite recent challenges, most textual scholars defend the traditional consensus:[100] the Western text is a later and longer, secondary version of Acts. The text of Luke's second volume is best represented in the Alexandrian tradition. The com-

---

94. Friedrich Blass, "Die Textüberlieferung in der Apostelgeschichte," *TSK* 67 (1894): 86 – 119; Friedrich Blass, *Acta Apostolorum, sive, Lucae ad Theophilum liber alter. Editio Philologica* (Göttingen: Vandenhoeck & Ruprecht, 1895); cf. Theodor Zahn, *Die Urausgabe der Apostelgeschichte des Lucas* (Forschungen zur Geschichte des neutestamentlichen Kanons und der altkirchlichen Literatur; Leipzig: Deichert, 1916); Zahn, *Introduction*, 3:8 – 41; James Maurice Wilson, *The Acts of the Apostles: Translated from the Codex Bezae with an Introduction on its Lucan Origin and Importance* (London: SPCK, 1923).

95. Boismard and Lamouille, *Texte Occidental*; cf. Marie-Émile Boismard and Arnaud Lamouille, *Les Actes des deux Apôtres* (3 vols.; Études bibliques 12 – 14; Paris: Lecoffre, 1990).

96. Will A. Strange, *The Problem of the Text of Acts* (SNTSMS 71; Cambridge: Cambridge Univ. Press, 1992). See also Josep Rius-Camps and Jenny Read-Heimerdinger, *The Message of Acts in Codex Bezae: A Comparison with the Alexandrian Tradition* (4 vols.; London: T&T Clark, 2004 – 2007), whose commentary compares the Codex Bezae version of Acts with the text of Acts in the Alexandrian tradition. For a critique

of Blass and his followers, and of Boismard, Lamouille and Strange, cf. Head, "Acts and the Problem of Its Texts," 420 – 28.

97. Metzger, *Textual Commentary*, 235; Barrett, *Acts*, 1:20 – 29; 2:xix-xxii; cf. Bock, *Acts*, 29.

98. Metzger, *Textual Commentary*, 235.

99. Cf. Frederic G. Kenyon, "The Western Text in the Gospels and Acts," *Proceedings of the British Academy* 24 (1939): 287 – 315; Günther Zuntz, "On the Western Text of the Acts of the Apostles," in *Opuscula selecta: Classica, hellenistica, christiana* (Manchester: Manchester Univ. Press, 1972), 189 – 215; Head, "Acts and the Problem of Its Texts," 443; Fitzmyer, *Acts*, 72; Jervell, *Apostelgeschichte*, 60 – 61. Hemer, *Acts*, 193 – 201, allows for the possibility that Western variant readings may preserve a correct tradition or inference, but finds no Western reading that commends itself to be original.

100. Cf. James Hardy Ropes, *The Text of Acts* (The Beginnings of Christianity, Part. I: The Acts of the Apostles, Vol. III; ed. J. F. Foakes-Jackson and K. Lake; London: Macmillan, 1926), suggesting that the revised, secondary Western text was the "original 'canonical' text" (in the 2nd century) "which was

mentary will mention Western readings only in places where scholars have assumed potential historical significance and where the variant readings illustrate the theological understanding of a later generation.

The Chronology of Early Christian History

The following chart lists key dates for the political history of Judea and the Roman Empire (in italics), and for the history of the early church.[101]

4 BC	*Death of Herod I*
4 BC – AD 39	*Herod Antipas tetrarch in Galilee*
6 – 15	*Annas son of Seth high priest*
14	*Death of Augustus*
14 – 37	*Reign of Tiberius*
15 – 16	*Ishmael son of Phiabi high priest*
16 – 17	*Eleazar son of Annas high priest*
17 – 18	*Simon son of Camith high priest*
18 – 36	*Joseph Caiaphas high priest*
26 – 36	*Pontius Pilate is prefect of Judea*
26/27	Ministry of John the Baptist (cf. Acts 1:5)
27 – 30	Ministry of Jesus (cf. Acts 1:1)
30	Crucifixion and resurrection of Jesus (cf. Acts 1:1 – 11)
30 – 41	Mission of the disciples in Jerusalem and in Judea (Acts 2 – 5)
31/32	Martyrdom of Stephen in Jerusalem (Acts 6 – 7)
	Mission of Philip in Samaria (Acts 8)
	Mission of Peter in Samaria (Acts 8:25)
	Mission of Christians from Jerusalem in Antioch (Syria) (Acts 11:19 – 24)
	Conversion and call of Saul-Paul near Damascus (Acts 9; Gal 1)
32/33	Mission of Paul in Arabia and Damascus (Acts 9:19 – 22; Gal 1:17)
34 – 42	Mission of Peter in Judea, Galilee, Samaria, and the coastal plain (Acts 9:32 – 43)
	Mission of Paul in Syria and Cilicia (Gal 1:21 – 24)
36	*War between Herod Antipas and the Nabatean king Aretas IV*
36 – 37	*Marcellus is new prefect of Judea*
36 – 37	*Jonathan son of Annas high priest*
37 – 41	*Reign of Gaius Caligula*
37 – 44	*Herod Agrippa I (37 – 44) is appointed king*

later supplanted by a 'pre-canonical' text of superior age and merit" (ibid. ccxlv). See Barbara Aland, "Entstehung, Charakter und Herkunft des sog. westlichen Textes untersucht an der Apostelgeschichte," *ETL* 62 (1986): 5 – 65.

101. Cf. Schnabel, *Early Christian Mission*, 1:41 – 52. For a history of the early church, cf. Paul W. Barnett, *Jesus and the Rise of Early Christianity: A History of New Testament Times* (Downers Grove, IL: InterVarsity Press, 1999).

37	*Vitellius, governor of Syria, organizes Judea after Pilate's removal*
37 – 41	*Marullus is new prefect of Judea*
37 – 41	*Theophilus son of Annas high priest*
37	Mission of Peter in Joppa and Caesarea (Acts 10 – 11)
	Conversion of Cornelius, a Roman centurion in Caesarea (Acts 10)
39 – 41	*Petronius is governor in Syria*
39 – 40	*Unrest in Antioch (Syria) between Jews and Gentiles*
	The followers of Jesus are called *christianoi* in Antioch (Acts 11:26)
41 – 54	*Reign of Claudius*
41 – 42	*Simon Cantheras high priest*
41	*Claudius's first edict concerning the Jews, prompted by unrest*
	Herod Agrippa I receives Judea and Samaria
	Persecution of the Jerusalem church by Herod Agrippa I (Acts 12:1 – 4)
	James son of Zebedee, the apostle, is executed in Jerusalem (Acts 12:2)
	Departure of Peter from Jerusalem (goes to Rome in 41/42?) (Acts 12:17)
	Change of leadership in the Jerusalem church (Acts 12:17)
	Departure of the Twelve for international missionary work (?) (*Acts Thom.* 1)
42 – 43	*Matthias son of Annas high priest*
42	James, the brother of Jesus, is the leader of the Jerusalem church (Acts 12:17; 15:2, 13)
	Peter is active in the northeastern regions of Asia Minor (?) (1 Pet 1:1)
	Thomas is active in India (?) (*Acts Thom.* 2 – 29)
42 – 44	Paul is active in Antioch in Syria (42 – 44), together with Barnabas (Acts 11:25 – 26)
43 – 44	*Elioenai son of Cantheras high priest*
44 – 47	*Joseph son of Camei high priest*
44	*Claudius organizes Judea again as a Roman province*
	Death of Herod Agrippa I (Acts 12:19 – 23)
44 – 46	*Cuspius Fadus is procurator of Judea*
44	*Conversion to Judaism of Helena, Queen of Adiabene*
	Church in Antioch organizes famine relief for Jerusalem Christians (Acts 11:27 – 30; 12:25)
	Letter of James (early or mid 40s? or around 55?)
	Consultation of Paul and Peter in Jerusalem (Acts 11:27 – 30; Gal 2:1 – 10)
45 – 47	Mission of Paul and Barnabas on Cyprus and southern Galatia (Acts 13 – 14)

47 – 58	*Ananias son of Nebedaios high priest*
48	Persecution of Jewish Christians in Judea and Jerusalem (Gal 6:12)
	Paul's letter to the Galatians (?)
	Apostles' council in Jerusalem (Acts 15)
49 – 52	Mission of Barnabas and John Mark on Cyprus (Acts 15:39)
	Mission of Paul in Macedonia and Achaia (Acts 16 – 18)
49	Missionary activity of Jewish Christians in Rome; disturbances (Acts 18:2)
50	Paul in Corinth (from February/March 50 to September 51)
	Paul's letter to the Galatians (?)
	Paul's letters to the Thessalonians
	Claudius's expulsion of the Jews from Rome (Suetonius, *Claud.* 25.3 – 4)
52 – 55	Mission of Paul in Ephesus (Acts 19)
	Paul's letter to the Corinthians (1 Cor)
52 – 59	*Antonius Felix is procurator of Judea*
53 – 93	*Herod Agrippa II appointed king, receives territory of Chalcis*
54 – 68	*Reign of Nero*
54	*Herod Agrippa II receives further territories in Galilee and Perea*
55	Paul visits Corinth (May/June?) and returns to Ephesus
	Paul travels from Ephesus to Alexandria Troas
	Paul travels to Macedonia (August?)
	Paul's letter to the Corinthians (2 Cor; written in Philippi?)
	Paul stays in Macedonia over the winter
56	*Revolt of an Egyptian Jew who leads 4,000 Sicarii into the desert*
56	Mission of Paul in Illyricum (Rom 15:19)
	Paul visits Achaia/Corinth (Acts 20:1 – 6)
	Paul's letter to the Romans
57 – 59	Arrest of Paul in Jerusalem, imprisonment in Caesarea (Acts 21 – 26)
59 – 61	*Ishmael son of Phiabi II high priest*
59 – 62	*Porcius Festus is procurator in Judea*
59	*Unrest in Caesarea between Jews and Syrians over citizenship*
	Gospel of Mark (end of the 50s? or 68/69?)
60 – 62	Paul as prisoner in Rome (Acts 28:11 – 31)
	Paul's letters to the Philippians, Colossians, Philemon, Ephesians
61	Peter in Rome (?) (1 Pet 5:13)
62 – 63	*Jesus son of Damnaeus high priest (62 – 63)*
62	James, Jesus' brother, and other Christians are killed in Jerusalem (Josephus, *Ant.* 20.9)
	Luke writes his two-volume work, Luke-Acts (60 – 65?)
	Paul is released from imprisonment in Rome (?)
63/64	Mission of Paul in Spain (?) (*1 Clem.* 5:5 – 7; cf. Rom 15:23 – 28)

Structure and Literary Form

The outline of Acts can be concentrated on the church in Jerusalem (Acts 1 – 7), on the church in Samaria, in Damascus, in Caesarea, and in Antioch (Acts 8 – 12), on the church in Asia Minor and Europe (Acts 13 – 20), and on Paul's trial (Acts 21 – 28). The following outline of Acts reflects Luke's focus on the growth of the church and on the expansion of Christian communities through the work of the early missionaries. The shorter and longer speeches of Peter and Paul are numbered, as are Luke's summaries and his reports of imprisonments.

Structure and Outline

I. Jesus' Exaltation and the Commission of the Apostles (1:1 – 14)

  A. Introduction to the Second Volume of Luke's Work (1:1 – 2)

    1. The Content of Luke's First Volume (1:1 – 2)

      a. The Content of Luke's First Volume (1:1)

      b. The Time Frame of the First Volume (1:2)

  B. The Missionary Commissioning of the Apostles (1:3 – 14)

    2. Jesus' Instructions to Wait in Jerusalem for the Coming of the Spirit (1:3 – 5)

      a. Jesus' Appearances during Forty Days (Flashback) (1:3)

      b. Jesus' Instruction to Stay in Jerusalem and Wait for the Coming of the Spirit (1:4)

      c. Jesus' Promise of the Coming of the Spirit of Prophecy (1:5)

    3. Jesus Commissions the Twelve as His Witnesses (1:6 – 8)

      a. The Disciples' Question about the Restoration of the Kingdom for Israel (1:6)

      b. Jesus Refuses to Engage in Speculations about the Chronology of the Last Days (1:7)

      c. Jesus Promises the Coming of the Empowering Spirit (1:8a-b)

Select Bibliography

Alexander, Loveday C. A. "Acts." Pages 1028–61 in *The Oxford Bible Commentary*. Edited by J. Barton and J. Muddiman. Oxford: Oxford University Press, 2001.

———. *Acts in Its Ancient Literary Context: A Classicist Looks at the Acts of the Apostles*. LNTS 298. London/New York: T&T Clark, 2005.

Anderson, Kevin L. *"But God Raised Him from the Dead": The Theology of Jesus' Resurrection in Luke-Acts*. Paternoster Biblical Monographs. Milton Keynes: Paternoster, 2006.

Aune, David E. *Prophecy in Early Christianity and the Ancient Mediterranean World*. Grand Rapids: Eerdmans, 1983.

———. *Westminster Dictionary of New Testament and Early Christian Literature and Rhetoric*. Philadelphia: Westminster John Knox, 2003.

Avemarie, Friedrich. *Die Tauferzählungen der Apostelgeschichte: Theologie und Geschichte*. WUNT 139. Tübingen: Mohr Siebeck, 2002.

Barrett, C. K. *The Acts of the Apostles*. 2 vols. ICC. Edinburgh: T&T Clark, 1994–1998.

Bauckham, Richard J. "James and the Gentiles (Acts 15.13–21)." Pages 154–84 in *History, Literature, and Society in the Book of Acts*. Edited by B. Witherington III. Cambridge: Cambridge University Press, 1996.

———. "James and the Jerusalem Church." Pages 415–80 in *The Book of Acts in Its Palestinian Setting*. Edited by R. J. Bauckham. The Book of Acts in Its First-Century Setting 4. Grand Rapids: Eerdmans, 1995.

———. "James and the Jerusalem Community." Pages 55–95 in *Jewish Believers in Jesus: The Early Centuries*. Edited by O. Skarsaune and R. Hvalvik. Peabody, MA: Hendrickson, 2007.

———. "James, Peter, and the Gentiles." Pages 91–142 in *The Missions of James, Peter, and Paul: Tensions in Early Christianity*. Edited by B. D. Chilton and C. A. Evans. NovTSup 115. Leiden: Brill, 2005.

Bock, Darrell L. *Acts*. BECNT. Grand Rapids: Baker, 2007.

———. *Proclamation from Prophecy and Pattern: Lucan Old Testament Christology*. JSNTSup 12. Sheffield: JSOT Press, 1987.

Boismard, Marie-Émile, and Arnaud Lamouille. *Les Actes des deux Apôtres*. 3 vols. Études bibliques 12–14. Paris: Lecoffre, 1990.

Bormann, Lukas. *Philippi — Stadt und Christengemeinde zur Zeit des Paulus*. NovTSup 78. Leiden: Brill, 1995.

Breytenbach, Cilliers. *Paulus und Barnabas in der Provinz Galatien*. AGJU 38. Leiden: Brill, 1996.

Brocke, Christoph vom. *Thessaloniki — Stadt der Kassander und Gemeinde des Paulus: Eine frühe christliche Gemeinde in ihrer heidnischen Umwelt*. WUNT 2/125. Tübingen: Mohr Siebeck, 2001.

Bruce, F. F. *The Acts of the Apostles: The Greek Text with Introduction and Commentary*. Third revised and enlarged ed. Grand Rapids: Eerdmans, 1990 [*Acts*].

———. *The Book of the Acts*. Rev. ed. NICNT. Grand Rapids: Eerdmans, 1988 [*Book of Acts*].

Buss, Matthäus F.-J. *Die Missionspredigt des Apostels Paulus im Pisidischen Antiochien*. FB 38. Stuttgart: Katholisches Bibelwerk, 1980.

Conzelmann, Hans. *Acts of the Apostles*. Hermeneia. Philadelphia: Fortress, 1987.

Dibelius, Martin. *Studies in the Acts of the Apostles*. Edited by H. Greeven. New York: Scribner, 1956.

Dobbeler, Axel von. *Der Evangelist Philippus in der Geschichte des Urchristentums: Eine prosopographische Skizze*. TANZ 30. Tübingen/Basel: Francke, 2000.

Dunn, James D. G. *The Acts of the Apostles*. EpComm. London: Epworth, 1996.

———. *Baptism in the Holy Spirit*. London: SCM, 1970.

———. *Beginning from Jerusalem*. Christianity in the Making 2. Grand Rapids: Eerdmans, 2009.

Dupont, Jacques. *Le discours de Milet: testament pastoral de Saint Paul (Actes 20, 18 – 36)*. LD 32. Paris: Cerf, 1962.

———. *The Salvation of the Gentiles: Essays on the Acts of the Apostles*. New York: Paulist, 1979.

Fitzmyer, Joseph A. *The Acts of the Apostles*. AB 31. New York: Doubleday, 1998.

Gaventa, Beverly R. *The Acts of the Apostles*. ANTC. Nashville: Abingdon, 2003.

Haenchen, Ernst. *The Acts of the Apostles*. Philadelphia: Westminster, 1971.

Hanson, Richard P. C. *The Acts*. New Clarendon Bible. Oxford: Clarendon, 1967.

Hemer, Colin J. *The Book of Acts in the Setting of Hellenistic History*. Edited by C. H. Gempf. Orig. 1989. Repr. WUNT 49. Tübingen: Mohr Siebeck, 2001.

Hengel, Martin. *Acts and the History of Earliest Christianity*. London: SCM, 1979.

Hentschel, Anni. *Diakonia im Neuen Testament: Studien zur Semantik unter besonderer Berücksichtigung der Rolle von Frauen*. WUNT 2/226. Tübingen: Mohr Siebeck, 2007.

Horsley, Greg H. R., and Stephen R. Llewelyn, eds. *New Documents Illustrating Early Christianity*. Macquarie University: North Ryde, NSW, Australia, 1981 – 2002.

Ilan, Tal. *Lexicon of Jewish Names in Late Antiquity*. Part 1: *Palestine 330 BCE – 200 CE*. TSAJ 91. Tübingen: Mohr Siebeck, 2002.

Jervell, Jacob. *Die Apostelgeschichte*. KEK 3. Göttingen: Vandenhoeck & Ruprecht, 1998.

———. *The Theology of the Acts of the Apostles*. New Testament Theology. Cambridge: Cambridge University Press, 1996.

Jeska, Joachim. *Die Geschichte Israels in der Sicht des Lukas: Apg 7,25b – 53 und 13,17 – 25 im Kontext antik-jüdischer Summarien der Geschichte Israels*. FRLANT 195. Göttingen: Vandenhoeck & Ruprecht, 2001.

Johnson, Luke Timothy. *The Acts of the Apostles*. SP 5. Collegeville, MN: Liturgical, 1992.

Judge, Edwin A. *Social Distinctives of the Christians in the First Century: Pivotal Essays*. Edited by D. M. Scholer. Peabody, MA: Hendrickson, 2007.

Kee, Howard C. *Good News to the Ends of the Earth: The Theology of Acts*. Philadelphia: Trinity Press International, 1990.

Kennedy, George A. *New Testament Interpretation through Rhetorical Criticism*. Chapel Hill: University of North Carolina Press, 1984.

Kim, Seyoon. *Christ and Caesar: The Gospel and the Roman Empire in the Writings of Paul and Luke*. Grand Rapids: Eerdmans, 2008.

Lake, Kirsopp, and Henry J. Cadbury. *The Acts of the Apostles: English Translation and Commentary*. Edited by F. J. Foakes-Jackson and K. Lake. The Beginnings of Christianity 1/4. London: Macmillan, 1933.

———, eds. *The Beginnings of Christianity, Part 1: The Acts of the Apostles*. Vol. 5: *Additional Notes to the Commentary*. London: Macmillan, 1933.

Larkin, William J. *Acts.* IVPNTC. Leicester: Inter-Varsity Press, 1995.

Lentz, John Clayton. *Luke's Portrait of Paul.* SNTSMS 77. Cambridge: Cambridge University Press, 1993.

Levinskaya, Irina A. *The Book of Acts in Its Diaspora Setting.* The Book of Acts in Its First-Century Setting 5. Grand Rapids: Eerdmans, 1996.

Levinsohn, Stephen H. *Textual Connections in Acts.* SBLMS 31. Atlanta: Scholars Press, 1987.

Lierman, John. *The New Testament Moses: Christian Perceptions of Moses and Israel in the Setting of Jewish Religion.* WUNT 2/173. Tübingen: Mohr Siebeck, 2004.

Litwak, Kenneth D. *Echoes of Scripture in Luke-Acts: Telling the History of God's People Intertextually.* London: T&T Clark, 2005.

Lohfink, Gerhard. *The Conversion of St. Paul: Narrative and History in Acts.* Chicago: Franciscan Herald, 1976.

Longenecker, Richard N. "Acts." Pages 663–1102 in *Expositor's Bible Commentary* (vol. 10). Edited by T. R. Longman III and D. E. Garland. Grand Rapids: Zondervan, 2007.

Maddox, Robert. *The Purpose of Luke-Acts.* Edinburgh: T&T Clark, 1982.

Mallen, Peter. *The Reading and Transformation of Isaiah in Luke-Acts.* LNTS. London: T&T Clark, 2008.

Marguerat, Daniel. *Les Actes des Apôtres (1–12).* Commentaire du Nouveau Testament 5a. Geneva: Labor et Fides, 2007.

——. *The First Christian Historian: Writing the "Acts of the Apostles."* SNTSMS 121. Cambridge: Cambridge University Press, 2002.

Marshall, I. Howard. "Acts." Pages 513–606 in *Commentary on the New Testament Use of the Old Testament.* Edited by G. K. Beale and D. A. Carson. Grand Rapids: Baker, 2007 ["Acts"].

——. *The Acts of the Apostles.* New Testament Guides. Sheffield: Sheffield Academic Press, 1992.

——. *The Acts of the Apostles: An Introduction and Commentary.* TNTC. Leicester: Inter-Varsity Press, 1980 [*Acts*].

Marshall, I. Howard, and David Peterson, eds. *Witness to the Gospel: The Theology of Acts.* Grand Rapids: Eerdmans, 1998.

Martin, Francis, ed. *Acts.* ACCS 5. Downers Grove, IL: InterVarsity Press, 1998.

Matson, David Lertis. *Household Conversion Narratives in Acts: Pattern and Interpretation.* JSNTSup 123. Sheffield: Sheffield Academic Press, 1996.

Menzies, Robert P. *The Development of Early Christian Pneumatology with Special Reference to Luke-Acts.* JSNTSup 54. Sheffield: JSOT Press, 1991.

Metzger, Bruce M. *A Textual Commentary on the Greek New Testament.* Second ed. Stuttgart: United Bible Societies, 1994.

Metzner, Rainer. *Die Prominenten im Neuen Testament: Ein prosopographischer Kommentar.* NTOA 66. Göttingen: Vandenhoeck & Ruprecht, 2008.

Miller, John B. F. *Convinced that God Had Called Us: Dreams, Visions, and the Perception of God's Will in Luke-Acts.* Biblical Interpretation 85. Leiden/Boston: Brill, 2007.

Mitchell, Stephen. *Anatolia: Land, Men, and Gods in Asia Minor.* Oxford: Oxford University Press, 1995.

Miura, Yuzuru. *David in Luke-Acts: His Portrayal in the Light of Early Judaism.* WUNT 2/232. Tübingen: Mohr Siebeck, 2007.

Moule, C.F.D. *An Idiom Book of New Testament Greek.* Orig. 1959. Repr. Cambridge: Cambridge University Press, 1994.

Murphy-O'Connor, Jerome. *Paul: A Critical Life.* Oxford: Oxford University Press, 1996.

——. *St. Paul's Corinth: Texts and Archaeology.* Wilmington, DE: Glazier, 1983.

———. *St. Paul's Ephesus: Texts and Archaeology.* Collegeville, MN: Liturgical, 2008.

Neagoe, Alexandru. *The Trial of the Gospel: An Apologetic Reading of Luke's Trial Narratives.* SNTSMS 116. Cambridge: Cambridge University Press, 2002.

Netzer, Ehud. *The Architecture of Herod, the Great Builder.* Grand Rapids: Baker, 2008.

Omerzu, Heike. *Der Prozess des Paulus: Eine exegetische und rechtshistorische Untersuchung der Apostelgeschichte.* BZNW 115. Berlin: De Gruyter, 2002.

Padilla, Osvaldo. *The Speeches of Outsiders in Acts: Poetics, Theology and Historiography.* SNTSMS 144. Cambridge: Cambridge University Press, 2008.

Pao, David W. *Acts and the Isaianic New Exodus.* WUNT 2/130. Tübingen: Mohr Siebeck, 2000.

Parsons, Mikeal C. *Acts.* Paideia. Grand Rapids: Baker, 2008.

———. *Body and Character in Luke and Acts: The Subversion of Physiognomy in Early Christianity.* Grand Rapids: Baker, 2006.

Pervo, Richard I. *Acts.* Hermeneia. Philadelphia: Fortress, 2008.

Pesch, Rudolf. *Die Apostelgeschichte.* 2 vols. EKK 5. Zürich/Neukirchen-Vluyn: Benziger/Neukirchener Verlag, 1986.

Peterson, David G. *The Acts of the Apostles.* PNTC. Grand Rapids: Eerdmans, 2009.

Pichler, Josef. *Paulusrezeption in der Apostelgeschichte: Untersuchungen zur Rede im pisidischen Antiochien.* IThS 50. Innsbruck: Tyrolia, 1997.

Pilhofer, Peter. *Philippi.* 2 vols. WUNT 87 and 119. Tübingen: Mohr Siebeck, 1995 – 2000.

Pillai, C. A. Joachim. *Early Missionary Preaching: A Study of Luke's Report in Acts 13.* Hicksville, NY: Exposition, 1979.

Pokorný, Petr. *Theologie der lukanischen Schriften.* FRLANT 174. Göttingen: Vandenhoeck & Ruprecht, 1998.

Polhill, John B. *Acts.* NAC 26. Nashville: Broadman, 1992.

Ramsay, William M. *St. Paul the Traveller and the Roman Citizen.* Updated and revised ed. Edited by M. Wilson. Orig. 1896. Repr. Grand Rapids: Baker, 2001.

Rapske, Brian M. *The Book of Acts and Paul in Roman Custody.* The Book of Acts in Its First-Century Setting 3. Grand Rapids: Eerdmans, 1994.

Ravens, David A. S. *Luke and the Restoration of Israel.* JSNTSup 119. Sheffield: Sheffield Academic Press, 1995.

Riesner, Rainer. *Paul's Early Period: Chronology, Mission Strategy, Theology.* Grand Rapids: Eerdmans, 1998.

Rius-Camps, Josep, and Jenny Read-Heimerdinger. *The Message of Acts in Codex Bezae: A Comparison with the Alexandrian Tradition.* 4 vols. London: T&T Clark, 2004 – 2007.

Roloff, Jürgen. *Die Apostelgeschichte.* NTD 5. Göttingen: Vandenhoeck & Ruprecht, 1981.

Rowe, C. Kavin. *World Upside Down: Reading Acts in the Graeco-Roman Age.* Oxford: Oxford University Press, 2009.

Schille, Gottfried. *Die Apostelgeschichte des Lukas.* Third ed. THKNT 5. Berlin: Evangelische Verlagsantalt, 1989.

Schnabel, Eckhard J. *Early Christian Mission.* Downers Grove, IL: InterVarsity Press, 2004.

———. *Paul the Missionary: Realities, Strategies, and Methods.* Downers Grove, IL: InterVarsity Press, 2008.

Schneider, Gerhard. *Die Apostelgeschichte.* 2 vols. HTKNT 5. Freiburg: Herder, 1980 – 1982.

Schürer, Emil. *The History of the Jewish People in the Age of Christ (175 B.C. — A.D. 135).* Revised by G. Vermes, F. Millar, M. Black, and M. Goodman. Edinburgh: T&T Clark, 1973–1987.

Seccombe, David P. *Possessions and the Poor in Luke-Acts*. SNTSU B6. Linz, Austria: Fuchs, 1982.

Seland, Torrey. *Establishment Violence in Philo and Luke: A Study of Non-Conformity to the Torah and Jewish Vigilante Reactions*. Biblical Interpretation 15. Leiden: Brill, 1995.

Sellner, Hans Jörg. *Das Heil Gottes: Studien zur Soteriologie des lukanischen Doppelwerks*. BZNW 152. Berlin: De Gruyter, 2007.

Shauf, Scott. *Theology as History, History as Theology: Paul in Ephesus in Acts 19*. BZNW 133. Berlin: De Gruyter, 2005.

Shelton, James B. *Mighty in Word and Deed: The Role of the Holy Spirit in Luke-Acts*. Peabody, MA: Hendrickson, 1991.

Shepherd, William H. *The Narrative Function of the Holy Spirit as a Character in Luke-Acts*. SBLDS 147. Atlanta: Scholars Press, 1994.

Sherwin-White, Adrian Nicolas. *Roman Society and Roman Law in the New Testament*. Orig. 1963. Repr. Winona Lake, IN: Eisenbrauns, 2000.

Skinner, Matthew L. *Locating Paul: Places of Custody as Narrative Settings in Acts 21–28*. Academia Biblica 13. Atlanta: Society of Biblical Literature, 2003.

Soards, Marion L. *The Speeches in Acts: Their Content, Context, and Concerns*. Louisville: Westminster John Knox, 1994.

Spencer, F. Scott. *Acts*. Readings. Sheffield: Sheffield Academic Press, 1997.

———. *Journeying through Acts: A Literary-Cultural Reading*. Peabody, MA: Hendrickson, 2004.

———. *The Portrait of Philip in Acts: A Study of Roles and Relations*. JSNTSup 67. Sheffield: JSOT Press, 1992.

Squires, John T. *The Plan of God in Luke-Acts*. SNTSMS 76. Cambridge: Cambridge University Press, 1993.

Stenschke, Christoph W. *Luke's Portrait of Gentiles prior to Their Coming to Faith*. WUNT 2/108. Tübingen: Mohr Siebeck, 1999.

Steyn, Gert J. *Septuagint Quotations in the Context of the Petrine and Pauline Speeches of the Acta Apostolorum*. CBET 12. Kampen: Kok, 1995.

Strelan, Richard E. *Paul, Artemis and the Jews in Ephesus*. BZNW 80. Berlin: De Gruyter, 1996.

Tajra, Harry W. *The Trial of St. Paul: A Juridical Exegesis of the Second Half of the Acts of the Apostles*. WUNT 2/35. Tübingen: Mohr Siebeck, 1989.

Talbert, Charles H. *Reading Acts: A Literary and Theological Commentary on the Acts of the Apostles*. Rev. ed. Reading the New Testament. Macon: Smyth, 2005.

Tannehill, Robert C. *The Narrative Unity of Luke-Acts: A Literary Interpretation*. Vol. 2: *The Acts of the Apostles*. Orig. 1990. Repr. Philadelphia: Fortress, 1994.

Thiessen, Werner. *Christen in Ephesus*. TANZ 12. Tübingen/Basel: Francke, 1995.

Thornton, Claus-Jürgen. *Der Zeuge des Zeugen: Lukas als Historiker der Paulusreisen*. WUNT 56. Tübingen: Mohr Siebeck, 1991.

Trebilco, Paul. *The Early Christians in Ephesus from Paul to Ignatius*. Orig. 2004. Repr. Grand Rapids: Eerdmans, 2007.

———. *Jewish Communities in Asia Minor*. SNTSMS 69. Cambridge: Cambridge University Press, 1991.

Turner, Max M. B. *Power from on High: The Spirit in Israel's Restoration and Witness in Luke-Acts*. JPTSup 9. Sheffield: Sheffield Academic Press, 1996.

Turner, Nigel. *A Grammar of New Testament Greek*. Vol. 3: *Syntax*. Edinburgh: T&T Clark, 1963.

Twelftree, Graham H. *In the Name of Jesus: Exorcism among Early Christians*. Grand Rapids: Baker, 2007.

Unnik, Willem C. van. *Sparsa Collecta*. NovTSup 29. Leiden: Brill, 1973.

VanderKam, James C. *From Joshua to Caiaphas: High Priests after the Exile*. Minneapolis: Fortress, 2004.

Walaskay, Paul W. *Acts*. Westminster Bible Companion. Louisville, KY: Westminster John Knox Press, 1998.

———. *"And So We Came to Rome": The Political Perspective of St. Luke*. SNTSMS 49. Cambridge: Cambridge University Press, 1983.

Wall, Robert W. *The Acts of the Apostles*. The New Interpreter's Bible 10. Edited by L. E. Keck. Nashville: Abingdon, 2002.

Wallace, Daniel B. *Greek Grammar beyond the Basics: An Exegetical Syntax of the New Testament*. Grand Rapids: Zondervan, 1996.

Walton, Steve. *Leadership and Lifestyle: The Portrait of Paul in the Miletus Speech and 1 Thessalonians*. SNTSMS 108. Cambridge: Cambridge University Press, 2000.

Wander, Bernd. *Gottesfürchtige und Sympathisanten: Studien zum heidnischen Umfeld von Diasporasynagogen*. WUNT 104. Tübingen: Mohr Siebeck, 1998.

Wasserberg, Günter. *Aus Israels Mitte — Heil für die Welt: Eine narrativ-exegetische Studie zur Theologie des Lukas*. BZNW 92. Berlin: De Gruyter, 1998.

Watson, Alan. *The Trial of Stephen: The First Christian Martyr*. Athens, GA: University of Georgia Press, 1997.

Weatherly, Jon A. *Jewish Responsibility for the Death of Jesus in Luke-Acts*. JSNTSup 106. Sheffield: JSOT Press, 1994.

Weaver, John B. *Plots of Epiphany: Prison-Escape in Acts of the Apostles*. BZNW 131. Berlin: De Gruyter, 2004.

Wehnert, Jürgen. *Die Reinheit des "christlichen Gottesvolkes" aus Juden und Heiden: Studien zum historischen und theologischen Hintergrund des sogenannten Aposteldekrets*. FRLANT 173. Göttingen: Vandenhoeck & Ruprecht, 1997.

Weiser, Alfons. *Die Apostelgeschichte*. 2 vols. ÖTK 5. Gütersloh/Würzburg: Mohn/Echter, 1981 – 1985.

Wendel, Ulrich. *Gemeinde in Kraft: Das Gemeindeverständnis in den Summarien der Apostelgeschichte*. NTD 20. Neukirchen-Vluyn: Neukirchener Verlag, 1998.

Wenk, Matthias. *Community-Forming Power: The Socio-Ethical Role of the Spirit in Luke-Acts*. Sheffield: Sheffield Academic Press, 2000.

Wilckens, Ulrich. *Die Missionsreden der Apostelgeschichte. Form- und traditionsgeschichtliche Untersuchungen*. Third ed. WMANT 5. Neukirchen-Vluyn: Neukirchener Verlag, 1974.

Williams, Charles S. C. *A Commentary on the Acts of the Apostles*. BNTC 5. London: Black, 1969.

Williams, David J. *Acts*. NIBC 5. Peabody, MA: Hendrickson, 1990.

Wilson, Stephen G. *The Gentiles and the Gentile Mission in Luke-Acts*. SNTSMS 23. Cambridge: Cambridge University Press, 1973.

———. *Luke and the Law*. SNTSMS 50. Cambridge: Cambridge University Press, 1983.

Winter, Bruce W. "The Importance of the *Captatio Benevolentiae* in the Speeches of Tertullus and Paul in Acts 24:1 – 21." *JTS* 42 (1991): 505 – 31.

———. "Official Proceedings and the Forensic Speeches in Acts 24 – 26." Pages 305 – 36 in *The Book of Acts in Its Ancient Literary Setting*. Edited by B. W. Winter and A. D. Clarke. The Book of Acts in Its First-Century Setting 1. Grand Rapids: Eerdmans, 1993.

———. "In Public and in Private: Early Christian Interactions with Religious Pluralism." Pages 112 – 34 in *One God, One Lord in a World of Religious Pluralism*. Edited by A. D. Clarke and B. W. Winter. Cambridge: Tyndale House, 1991.

Witherington, Ben III. *The Acts of the Apostles: A Socio-Rhetorical Commentary*. Grand Rapids: Eerdmans, 1998.

Zahn, Theodor. *Die Apostelgeschichte des Lucas*. 2 vols. Kommentar zum Neuen Testament 5. Leipzig: Deichert, 1921 – 1922.

Zangenberg, Jürgen. *Frühes Christentum in Samarien*. TANZ 27. Tübingen/Basel: Francke, 1998.

Zeigan, Holger. *Aposteltreffen in Jerusalem: Eine forschungsgeschichtliche Studie zu Galater 2,1 – 10 und den möglichen lukanischen Parallelen*. Arbeiten zur Bibel und ihrer Geschichte 18. Leipzig: Evangelische Verlagsanstalt, 2005.

Zmijewski, Josef. *Die Apostelgeschichte*. RNT. Regensburg: Pustet, 1994.

Zugmann, Michael. *"Hellenisten" in der Apostelgeschichte: Historische und exegetische Untersuchungen zu Apg 6,1; 9,29; 11,20*. WUNT 2/264. Tübingen: Mohr Siebeck, 2009.

Zwiep, Arie W. *The Ascension of the Messiah in Lukan Christology*. NovTSup 87. Leiden: Brill, 1997.

———. *Judas and the Choice of Matthias: A Study on Context and Concern of Acts 1:15 – 26*. WUNT 2/187. Tübingen: Mohr Siebeck, 2004.

Acts 1:1 – 14

Literary Context

The introduction to the second volume of Luke's work on the life and ministry of Jesus and of his early followers begins with a prologue (1:1 – 2) and continues with a succinct survey of material that Luke had included at the end of his gospel (Luke 24). This introduction to Acts focuses on the reality of Jesus' resurrection and on the missionary commissioning of the apostles (1:3 – 14). The term "missionary" is understood as describing the activity of "mission" (Latin *missio*, from the verb *mittere*, "to send"; Greek *apostolē*, from the verb *apostellō*, "to send"), defined as the activity of individuals who distinguish themselves from the society in which they live both in terms of religious convictions and social behavior; they are convinced of the truth of their belief and actively work to win other people for their convictions and for their way of life, "sent" by God and the risen Jesus Christ to proclaim the gospel.[1]

While 1:1 summarizes the content of Luke's gospel in terms of Jesus' deeds and teaching, 1:2 indicates the end point of Jesus' ministry (the ascension) and the beginning of the apostles' ministry (Jesus' instructions). In 1:3a-c Luke briefly refers to Jesus' suffering (cf. Luke 22 – 23) and resurrection (cf. 24:1 – 12) before summarizing the resurrection appearances (24:13 – 49), providing another account of Jesus' ascension (24:50 – 51), and describing the stay of the disciples in Jerusalem (24:52 – 53) in Acts 1:3d – 14. As 1:1 – 14 links Luke's work on the ministry of the apostles with his early work on the ministry of Jesus, it is not surprising that besides this focus on Jesus' ministry, suffering, resurrection, and ascension, we see a focus on the apostles as witnesses of the risen and exalted Lord Jesus.

Luke makes the following points about the apostles in 1:1 – 14.

1. The apostles have been chosen by Jesus (1:2).

2. They have received instructions from Jesus (1:2); as this statement is part of the prologue of the book, Luke must refer to the missionary commission the

---

1. This broad definition avoids the problem of defining "missionary" as Christians who are called to travel to people who live in different countries and cultures, which the Twelve did not do while they were active in Jerusalem among the Jewish people.

disciples received from Jesus, whose execution is the theme of Luke's second volume; in 1:3 Luke links Jesus' instructions with his message of the kingdom of God.

3. The apostles saw Jesus for forty days after he had risen from the dead (1:3).

4. The disciples, most of whom were Galileans, stayed in Jerusalem as directed by Jesus (1:4, 12 – 14).

5. The apostles' reception of the Holy Spirit, described in Acts 2, is linked with God's promises (1:4) in terms of its significance, with Jerusalem (1:4 – 5) in terms of location, and with Jesus' promises (1:5) in terms of fulfillment.

6. The apostles were concerned about the restoration of the kingdom for Israel (1:6).

7. The apostles had no special insight into the timing of the events of the last days (1:7).

8. The power of the apostles (to carry out Jesus' instructions) was a direct result of their reception of the Holy Spirit (1:8a-b).

9. The apostles were directed by Jesus to be his witnesses in Jerusalem, Judea, Samaria, and to the ends of the earth (1:8c-f).

10. The apostles no longer saw Jesus when his appearances stopped forty days after his resurrection (1:9 – 10).

11. The apostles were waiting for the return of Jesus (1:11).

12. The group of the apostles consisted of Peter, John, James, Andrew, Philip, Thomas, Bartholomew, Matthew, James son of Alphaeus, Simon the Zealot, and Judas son of James (1:13).

13. Besides the apostles, those who witnessed Jesus' ascension included several women, Mary the mother of Jesus, and Jesus' brothers (1:14).

14. As the disciples waited for the coming of the Holy Spirit, they devoted themselves to prayer (1:14).

The introduction, a carefully constructed text,[2] has several functions.

1. It refers the readers to the first volume; this means, from a literary perspective, that the story of Acts cannot be separated from the ministry of Jesus.

2. Cf. Barrett, *Acts*, 63. Max M. B. Turner, *Power from on High: The Spirit in Israel's Restoration and Witness in Luke-Acts* (JPTSup 9; Sheffield: Sheffield Academic Press, 1996), 294 – 95, speaks of "one of the most subtle and concentrated pieces of theological writing in Luke's whole enterprise."

2. It reminds the readers that Jesus' suffering, resurrection, and ascension are of fundamental significance for the ministry of the apostles, for the life of the local church, and for the missionary expansion of the church.

3. It emphasizes the significance of the work of the Holy Spirit for the life and the ministry of the church.

4. It underlines the function of the apostles as witnesses, whose status is due to Jesus' call, whose function is connected with God's promises, and whose effectiveness is prompted by the Holy Spirit.

5. It highlights the fact that the geographical scope of the ministry of the church is universal, extending as far as the ends of the earth.

6. It describes the temporal scope of the life and ministry of the church as extending from Jesus' resurrection and ascension until Jesus' return.

7. It presents the fellowship of the followers of Jesus as consisting of the named eleven apostles (who will be completed to twelve disciples shortly) and others, including Jesus' earthly family and also women.

→ **I. Jesus' Exaltations and the Commission of the Apostles (1:1 – 14)**
   A. Introduction to the Second Volume of Luke's Work (1:1 – 2)
   B. The Missionary Commissioning of the Apostles (1:3 – 14)
   II. The Beginnings of the New People of God (1:15 – 8:3)

Main Idea

In his introduction to the second volume of his work on the ministry of Jesus and the apostles, Luke squarely places Jesus in the center; while the first volume described what Jesus began to do and to teach, the second volume describes what Jesus continues to do and to teach in and through the ministry of the apostles. The missionary work and the pastoral ministry of the apostles depends entirely on Jesus, the risen Lord, who sits at the right hand of the Father and who has granted to his disciples the gift of the Holy Spirit.

Translation

Acts 1:1 – 14

1a	Real reader/Dedication	In the first account, Theophilus,
b	Content	**I wrote about all the things that Jesus began** **to do and**
c		**to teach**
2a	Setting: temporal	until the day when God took him up,
b	Setting: temporal	after he had given instructions
c	Agency	through the Holy Spirit to the apostles
d	Description	whom he had chosen.
3a	Setting: temporal	After he had suffered,
b	Action	**he presented himself alive to them**
c	Means	by many convincing proofs;
d	Action	**he appeared to them**
e	Time	for forty days **and**
f	Action	**spoke about matters concerning the kingdom of God.**
4a	Setting: temporal	When he met with them,
b	Action	**he instructed them**
c	Instruction (negative)	not to leave Jerusalem, but
d	Instruction (positive)	to wait for the promise of the Father —
e	Assertion	*"This,"* **he said**, *"is what you heard from me.*
5a	Contrast	*Because John immersed in water,*
b	Promise	*but you will be washed with the Holy Spirit in a few days."*
6a	Setting: temporal & spatial	As they came together,
b	Question	**they asked him,**
c		*"Lord, is this the time when you will restore the kingdom to Israel?"*
7a	Response	**He said to them,**
b	Assertion (negative)	*"It is not for you to know the times or the seasons*
c	Description	*which the Father has established through his own ↵ authority.*
8a	Assertion (positive)/Promise	*But you will receive power*
b	Time	*when the Holy Spirit comes upon you,*
c	Result/Purpose	*and you will be my witnesses*
d	Place	*in Jerusalem and*
e	Place	*in all Judea and Samaria,*
f	Place	*and even as far as the ends of the earth."*
9a	Setting: time	When he had said this,
b	Setting: time	while they were looking,
c	Event	**he was lifted up**
d	Event	**and a cloud took him up from their sight.**
10a	Setting: circumstance	While they were staring into heaven as he was going,
b	Action: character entrance	**two men … suddenly stood beside them.**
	Description	dressed in white robes

11a	Action	**They said,**
b	Address	*"Men of Galilee,*
c	Question	*why do you stand here looking into heaven?*
d	Assertion/Promise	*This Jesus, … will return in the manner in which you saw him go into heaven."*
e	Description	*who has been taken up from you into heaven,*
12a	Action	Then **they returned to Jerusalem**
b	Place	from the hill known as Mount of Olives,
c	Description	which is near Jerusalem, a Sabbath day's journey away.
13a	Setting: place	When they had entered the city,
b	Action	**they went to the upper room where they were staying,**
c	List	Peter and John and James and Andrew,
d		Philip and Thomas,
e		Bartholomew and Matthew,
f		James son of Alphaeus and Simon the Zealot and Judas son of James.
14a	Action	**They all devoted themselves**
b	Manner	with one mind
c	Action	**to prayer,**
d	Association	together with several women and
e	List	Mary, the mother of Jesus, and
f		his brothers.

Structure and Literary Form

There is no consensus where the prologue and/or the introduction end. If we distinguish between introduction and prologue, the latter naturally comprises 1:1 – 2, the first sentence of the Greek text.[3] The introduction ends at 1:14, since Luke's account of the reconstitution of the Twelve in 1:15 – 26 provides material that has no parallels in Luke 24. The difficulty lies in the fact that the relative clause in Acts 1:2 does not describe the content of Luke's second volume but (like 1:3 – 14) recapitulates material from Luke 24; this means that there is no clear delineation between the prologue in 1:1 – 2 and the rest of the introduction in 1:3 – 14.

The prologue (1:1 – 2) begins with a conventional opening line in which Luke refers to his previous literary work about the life and ministry of Jesus, and in which he repeats the name of one of his main readers (or his patron), Theophilus. Like ancient authors who often used the opening lines of a preface to summarize their subject matter, Luke recapitulates the content of his previous work (1:1); however, he does not summarize the content of his second volume. The second part of the first

---

3. Cf. Fitzmyer, *Acts*, 191 – 92; Jervell, *Apostelgeschichte*, 108 – 9.

sentence (1:2), a relative clause (ἄχρι ἧς ἡμέρας ... ἀνελήμφθη), indicates the temporal setting of the first volume: it ends with Jesus' ascension into heaven.

The introduction (1:3 – 14) is made up four incidents: Jesus' instruction to stay in Jerusalem and wait for the coming of the Spirit (1:3 – 5), the missionary commissioning of the apostles (1:6 – 8), the ascension of Jesus (1:9 – 11), the return of the eleven disciples to Jerusalem (1:12 – 14). The introduction contains *direct speech*. In the first two incidents, Jesus speaks twice (1:4 – 5, 7 – 8), the disciples once (1:6). In the third incident, angels speak (1:11). The fourth incident contains no direct speech.

The first incident (1:3 – 5) is a combination of an *epiphany, instructions*, and a *promise*. After an introductory flashback (1:3) that relates Jesus' repeated appearances after his resurrection to his followers during forty days, during which he explained to them the coming and the reality of the kingdom of God, Luke relates another appearance of Jesus after his resurrection (1:4a), followed by Jesus' instructions to his followers to wait in Jerusalem for the arrival of the Spirit (1:4b-e), with the promise, given in direct discourse, that the disciples will soon be washed through the arrival of the Spirit of prophecy (1:5).

The second incident (1:6 – 8) is a combination of an *epiphany* and a *commission scene*. Luke relates another appearance of Jesus (1:6a), a question of the disciples concerning the time of the restoration of the kingdom to Israel (1:6b-c), and the answer of Jesus in direct discourse (1:7 – 8), which consists of two parts: refusal to engage in speculations about the precise details of the chronology of the last days (1:7), and the commissioning of the apostles to engage in missionary work as his witnesses from Jerusalem to the ends of the earth (1:8).

The third incident (1:9 – 11) is a *narrative* that relates Jesus' ascension into heaven as the apostles are watching, and the explanation of two angels who promise that Jesus will return. Luke emphasizes the visual perception of the disciples who see Jesus disappear, using five different expressions (βλεπόντων, ἀπὸ τῶν ὀφθαλμῶν αὐτῶν; 1:9; ἀτενίζοντες ἦσαν, 1:10; βλέποντες, ἐθεάσασθε, 1:11).

The fourth incident (1:12 – 14) is a *narrative* that relates the apostles' return from the Olive Grove to the city of Jerusalem; it includes a *list* (1:13c-f) of the eleven disciples; and it describes the communal life of the earliest followers of Jesus in Jerusalem in terms of prayer (προσευχή) and unanimity (ὁμοθυμαδόν). Both are characteristics of the early Christians in Jerusalem, which Luke will repeatedly highlight in his subsequent account.

Exegetical Outline

➡ **I. The Missionary Commission of the Apostles (1:1 – 14)**

    A. Introduction to the Second Volume of Luke's Work (1:1 – 2)

        1. The content of Luke's first volume (1:1 – 2)

            a. The content of Luke's first volume (1:1)

            b. The time frame of the first volume (1:2)

    B. Jesus' Missionary Commissioning of the Apostles (1:3 – 14)

        1. Jesus' instructions to wait in Jerusalem for the coming of the Spirit (1:3 – 5)

            a. Jesus' appearances during forty days (flashback) (1:3)

            b. Jesus' instruction to stay in Jerusalem and wait for the coming of the Spirit (1:4)

            c. Jesus' promise of the coming of the Spirit of prophecy (1:5)

        2. Jesus' commissioning of the Twelve as his witnesses (1:6 – 8)

            a. The disciples' question about the restoration of the kingdom for Israel (1:6)

            b. Jesus refuses to engage in speculations about the chronology of the last days (1:7)

            c. Jesus promises the coming of the empowering Spirit (1:8a-b)

            d. Jesus commissions the apostles to witness from Jerusalem to the end of the earth (1:8c-f)

        3. Jesus' ascension (1:9 – 11)

            a. The ascension of Jesus in front of the disciples (1:9)

            b. Appearance of two angels (1:10)

            c. Direct speech (angels): Announcement of Jesus' return (1:11)

        4. The return of the eleven disciples to Jerusalem (1:12 – 14)

            a. The apostles' return to Jerusalem from the Mount of Olives (1:12)

            b. The apostles' sojourn in an upstairs room in the city (1:13a-b)

            c. List of the eleven disciples (1:13c-f)

            d. The apostles' prayers (1:14a-c)

            e. The presence of women and of Jesus' earthly brothers (1:14d-f).

Explanation of the Text

1:1 In the first account, Theophilus, I wrote about all the things that Jesus began to do and to teach (Τὸν μὲν πρῶτον λόγον ἐποιησάμην περὶ πάντων, ὦ Θεόφιλε, ὧν ἤρξατο ὁ Ἰησοῦς ποιεῖν τε καὶ διδάσκειν). This introductory statement establishes Acts as the sequel of Luke's gospel. Luke refers his readers to his account of the ministry of Jesus of Nazareth. Whether he wrote Acts as a separate work or whether Acts was written as the second volume of a unified composition, which seems more likely, there is no doubt that he expected his readers to know the contents of the gospel and to read Acts in the light of the work and the teaching of Jesus. What began in Jerusalem with the outpouring of the Holy Spirit and the proclamation of the apostles really began in Galilee, where Jesus began to preach the good news of the arrival of the kingdom of God and to help people in need.

As in other ancient sources, the word translated "account" (λόγος) designates a literary production, in particular a separate book or treatise of a larger work.[4] Recapitulations of the contents of earlier works have parallels, particularly in Josephus.[5] As Luke's account of Jesus' ministry contained both action (ποιεῖν) and teaching (διδάσκειν), so does his account of the apostles' ministry. Luke's two-volume work relates the basic events on which the Christian movement was founded, as well as the fundamental teachings of the Christian faith. If we link "began" (ἤρξατο) with "until" (ἄχρι) in v. 2, Luke refers to the beginning of Jesus' ministry in Luke 4 until his ascension in Luke 24.[6]

However, since "until" does not refer to Jesus' death or resurrection but to Jesus' ascension and to the instructions of the risen Lord "through the Holy Spirit" (1:2) — instructions explained in 1:8 in terms of the commissioning of the Twelve to missionary work[7] — the meaning of "began" is connected with Jesus the exalted Lord, who promises the gift of the Holy Spirit (vv. 4 – 5) and whose power will enable the apostles to be Jesus' witnesses in Jerusalem, in Judea, in Samaria, and to the ends of the earth (v. 8). This means that "began" should be given its full force: in his first volume, Luke described the beginning of Jesus' work and teaching; in the second volume, he now describes the continuing work of Jesus through the Holy Spirit in the ministry of the Twelve and other believers such as Stephen, Philip, and Paul.

Theophilus (Θεόφιλος), the same person to whom Luke dedicated the first volume (Luke 1:3), is among Luke's intended readers. The fact that the name means "dear to God" or "loved by God" should not be taken to imply that "Theophilus" is a code word for Christian believers.[8] The name Theophilus was common since the third century BC, used by Jews and Greeks, attested both in documentary and literary sources. The adjective "most excellent" (κράτιστε) in Luke 1:3 corresponds to contemporary appellations of real people. Thus, Luke's Theophilus should be regarded as a real person. Whether or not the Greek adjective corresponds to Latin *optimus*, a honorific appellation for officials,[9] it does imply that Theophilus was socially respected and probably wealthy, which may possibly suggest that he was Luke's patron (i.e., who supported, and perhaps financed, Luke's research and writing as well as the publication [or copying] of the two-volume work).[10]

Verse 1 is the only place where Luke directly addresses his readers. In contrast to other ancient texts, we have no further explicit "authorial guide-

---

4. Cf. Philo, *Prob.* 1.1; also Plato, *Parm.* 2.127D; Herodotus, *Hist.* 5.36. LSJ, s.v. λόγος V.3; BDAG, s.v. λόγος 1b. Eventually βίβλος became more common as the designation of a literary work. As regards quotations from BDAG entries, note that abbreviated words will be written out in full without marking the supplemented parts with brackets.

5. In *Ant.* 1.7 Josephus speaks of "hesitation and delay" in beginning the *Antiquities* after the publication of the *J.W.*, and in *Ag. Ap.* 1 he refers to the *Antiquities*.

6. Marguerat, *Actes*, 1:37 n. 7. Cf. NRSV: "In the first book, Theophilus, I wrote about all that Jesus did and taught from the beginning until the day when he was taken up to heaven" (1:1 – 2).

7. Note that in Luke 24:47 – 49, the risen Jesus instructs his disciples between his resurrection and his ascension to engage in missionary outreach to the Jews in Jerusalem and to all nations, as his witnesses and through the power of the promised Holy Spirit ("repentance for the forgiveness of sins will be

preached in his name to all nations, beginning at Jerusalem. You are witnesses of these things. I am going to send you what my Father has promised").

8. This symbolic reading is often traced to Origen.

9. The *optimates* (lit., "best"), as described by Cicero and Livy, are the members of the leadership class of the late Roman republic (cf. Cicero, *Sest.* 97); the term is also used for the ruling classes of foreign cities (Cicero, *Flac.* 54, 63). Cf. L. Bonfante, *BNP*, 10:175 – 77.

10. Cf. Bovon, *Luke*, 1:8; Rainer Metzner, *Die Prominenten im Neuen Testament: Ein prosopographischer Kommentar* (NTOA 66; Göttingen: Vandenhoeck & Ruprecht, 2008), 196 – 201, who suggests that Theophilus could have been a freedman who had become a member of the aristocratic equestrian order (ibid., 197). There is no evidence for dedications to persons who did not exist; cf. Alexander, *Preface to Luke's Gospel*, 188.

posts" either in transitional passages or at the end of the volume. In the "we passages" Luke presents himself as an active participant in the missionary work of the church (cf. 16:10), but he does not proceed to explain the meaning of the events he records. This does not mean that Luke necessarily believed that what he writes is self-explanatory. Given the important role of teachers and of teaching in the church in Jerusalem (2:42; cf. 4:2; 5:21) and in other churches (18:11; 20:20; cf. 21:21, 28; 28:31), Luke probably assumed that as his two-volume work was read in the churches, there would be teachers capable of providing explanations.

1:2 Until the day when God took him up, after he had given instructions through the Holy Spirit to the apostles whom he had chosen (ἄχρι ἧς ἡμέρας ἐντειλάμενος τοῖς ἀποστόλοις διὰ πνεύματος ἁγίου οὓς ἐξελέξατο ἀνελήμφθη). Jesus' earthly ministry ended on the day of his ascension. The passive voice of the verb (lit.) "was taken up" (ἀνελήμφθη) implies that God caused Jesus to be taken up into heaven.[11] The same verb was used for Elijah's ascension (2 Kgs 2:11). For an explanation of the significance of Jesus' ascension, see below on v. 9.

Luke highlights here Jesus' instructions to his disciples as his witnesses between his resurrection and his ascension. This identification of Luke's reference to Jesus' instructions is based on (1) the reference to the Eleven as "apostles," i.e., as people who are sent to others to communicate news and who are thus messengers and representatives; (2) the reference to the Holy Spirit, which anticipates the description of God's Spirit as the power that enables the apostles to proclaim the good news in Jerusalem and to the ends of the earth (v. 8); (3) the reference to the Eleven as a group of people whom Jesus had "chosen" for the task of "fishing for people" (Luke 5:10; cf. 6:13; see in Mark 1:17 the reference to "fish for people").

The term "apostle" (ἀπόστολος) is used here for the first time in Acts.[12] With the exception of 14:4, 14, where Paul and Barnabas are called "apostles," Luke uses the term only for the Twelve as the group of disciples whom Jesus specifically called to follow him, to learn from him, and to carry on his ministry. While Jesus had many followers, he chose twelve as his "apostles" or messengers (Luke 6:13). Understood against the background of the Old Testament, in particular the call and sending of prophets, the term "apostle" is used in the New Testament to denote the sending of a person, or of persons, with a commission to convey news.[13] The concept of the apostle corresponds, at least in a general manner, to the role and function of the envoy (šālîaḥ) in rabbinic tradition — someone who represents the one who sent him and who acts in a manner that is authoritative; he is obligated to strict obedience to his commission, and he has to always act in the interest of the one who sent him.

Verse 2 is the first reference to the Holy Spirit in Acts. Seen in the context of Luke's earlier references to the Spirit of God in his gospel,[14] he envisages here the disciples as having experienced the Holy Spirit as divine presence addressing them, as they had already come under the influence of the Spirit when they accepted Jesus as God's emissary and his teaching as the expression of the presence of God's Spirit on him.[15]

---

11. Several translations add "to heaven" (GNB, NET, NRSV, NIV), which captures the meaning of the expression but is not in the text (cf. 1:11).

12. The term occurs six times in Luke's gospel (6:13; 9:10; 11:49; 17:5; 22:14; 24:10; note that Matthew, Mark, and John use ἀπόστολος only once: Matt 20:2; Mark 6:30 [in 3:14 in variant readings]; John 13:16), and 28 times in Acts.

13. Cf. K. H. Rengstorf, "ἀπόστολος," *TDNT*, 1:407 – 20; J. A. Bühne, "ἀπόστολος," *EDNT*, 1:142 – 46; Andrew C. Clark, "The Role of the Apostles," in *Witness to the Gospel: The Theology of Acts* (ed. I. H. Marshall and D. Peterson; Grand Rapids: Eerdmans, 1998), 167 – 90.

14. Cf. Luke 1:15, 35, 67; 3:16, 22; 4:1, 14, 18; 12:10.

15. Turner, *Power from on High*, 336 – 37.

1:3 After he had suffered, he presented himself alive to them by many convincing proofs; he appeared to them for forty days and spoke about matters concerning the kingdom of God (οἷς καὶ παρέστησεν ἑαυτὸν ζῶντα μετὰ τὸ παθεῖν αὐτὸν ἐν πολλοῖς τεκμηρίοις, δι' ἡμερῶν τεσσεράκοντα ὀπτανόμενος αὐτοῖς καὶ λέγων τὰ περὶ τῆς βασιλείας τοῦ θεοῦ). The subsequent reference to being "alive" indicates that Jesus' suffering includes his death on the cross.[16] Luke had devoted two long chapters to Jesus' suffering and death (Luke 22–23).[17] As Jesus continued to speak and instruct after his suffering and death, Luke reminds his readers that Jesus' role did not come to an end with his death on the cross; Jesus rose from the dead, and he continues to speak, teach, and instruct.

While it is true that Luke, in his account of the apostolic preaching, is surprisingly silent about the atoning significance of Jesus' death on the cross, it is significant that the first sentence after the prologue refers the reader back to Luke's gospel and to Jesus' assertion during his last meal with the Twelve before he was crucified that he was giving up his life for them (ὑπὲρ ὑμῶν, Luke 22:19), and that his violent death, in which he shed his blood for them, would establish the promised new covenant (ἡ καινὴ διαθήκη, 22:20).

Jesus' repeated appearances to his disciples after his death proved convincingly that he had become alive.[18] The term translated as "convincing proofs" (τεκμήρια), which occurs only here in the New Testament, denotes "that which causes something to be known in a convincing and decisive manner."[19] Luke refers to necessary proofs that led the disciples to the conclusion that Jesus was alive after he had been crucified (Luke 23:26–43), after he had died (23:44–49), and after he was buried (23:50–56).

The disciples were not gullible simpletons who were willing to believe anything they wanted to believe. After all, Jewish tradition was not populated by people who had returned from the grave. While Enoch, Elijah, and perhaps Moses (Gen 5:24; 2 Kgs 2:11; Deut 34) were exceptions to the rule that people die and enter afterlife, none of these is reported to have died and then to have risen from the grave to speak and eat with friends. Jews honored their martyrs, but they were not said to have been raised from the dead. Jews expected a general resurrection of all the dead at the end of time, before the day of judgment, not the resurrection of an individual before that day.[20] The empty tomb and the disciples' meetings with Jesus after his death, during which Jesus ate and drank with the disciples (Luke 24:30, 37–39, 41–43; Acts 1:4; 10:41), were proof that Jesus was bodily raised from the dead and was thus alive again.[21]

---

16. Cf. Luke 22:15; 24:26, 46; Mark 8:31; Acts 3:18 — other passages in which παθεῖν denotes Jesus' passion as a whole, including his death; cf. Barrett, *Acts*, 69; Fitzmyer, *Acts*, 202. This is an example of synecdoche, defined as "a figure of speech in which a part represents the whole, the cause the effect, or the effect the cause," David E. Aune, *Westminster Dictionary of New Testament and Early Christian Literature and Rhetoric* (Philadelphia: Westminster John Knox, 2003), 453.

17. From Luke 24:26 on, Jesus' suffering is a key emphasis; cf. Luke 24:46–47; Acts 3:18; 17:3; 26:23.

18. The present tense of the participle ζῶντα underlines the continuous nature of Jesus' repeated postresurrection appearances.

19. BDAG, s.v. τεκμήριον; cf. David L. Mealand, "The Phrase 'Many Proofs' in Acts 1:3 and in Hellenistic Writers," *ZNW* 80 (1989): 134–35.

20. Cf. N. T. Wright, *The Resurrection of the Son of God* (Christian Origins and the Question of God 3; Minneapolis: Fortress, 2003), 85–206.

21. Cf. Robert H. Gundry, "The Essential Physicality of Jesus' Resurrection according to the New Testament," in *Jesus of Nazareth: Lord and Christ* (FS I. H. Marshall; ed. J. B. Green and M. Turner; Grand Rapids: Eerdmans, 1994), 204–19; Gary R. Habermas, "The Resurrection Appearances of Jesus," in *In Defense of Miracles: A Comprehensive Case for God's Action in History* (ed. R. D. Geivett and G. R. Habermas; Downers Grove, IL: InterVarsity Press, 1997), 262–75.

Jesus appeared to his disciples multiple times between his resurrection and the ascension (cf. 1 Cor 15:5 – 8). In 13:31 Luke reports Paul speaking of Jesus appearing "for many days" after his resurrection. Since the "fifty days" of Pentecost in 2:1 establish a chronological link between Pentecost — celebrated fifty days after Passover — and Passover, the date of Jesus' death, there is no reason to regard the "forty days" here as anything other than a chronological marker for the end of Jesus' post-resurrection appearances at his ascension.

Between his resurrection and ascension, Jesus evidently explained to his disciples — who had understood the necessity of his death only after Easter (Luke 24:13 – 49) — the significance of his death and resurrection for his message of "the kingdom of God" (ἡ βασιλεία τοῦ θεοῦ) he had preached. This phrase is linked with the Old Testament and Jewish convictions concerning the sovereignty of Yahweh the Creator, who rules over his people Israel and who will one day rule in an uncontested and visible manner over the whole world.

In his gospel, Luke had described Jesus proclaiming both the future coming and the present reality of God's kingdom, the latter being the focus of Luke's description.[22] Jesus' ministry is the time of fulfillment of God's promises, awaiting consummation in the future. In the proclamation and in the mighty works of Jesus, the kingdom of God becomes a present reality among the Jewish people. The new presence of God's sovereign rule is manifested in the forgiveness of sins extended to sinners by Jesus (Luke 9:23 – 27; 10:9, 11; 13:23 – 30; 18:18 – 30), and in the healings extended to people afflicted by illnesses and demons (11:20). Jesus' words and actions conveyed the claim that God's final intervention in human affairs has presently been initiated.

This connection between the kingdom of God and Jesus' kingship is implied in 1:3 – 8. The connection between the reality of the kingdom of God and the task of the disciples is the subject of vv. 6 – 8 (see below). The reference to the kingdom of God here and in the last sentence of Acts — Paul is in Rome, proclaiming "the kingdom of God and [teaching] about the Lord Jesus Christ" (Acts 28:31) — establishes an *inclusio* that connects the content of Acts, the life of the church and the missionary activity of the apostles, with Jesus and his proclamation of the arrival of God's sovereign and gracious rule.

Luke regularly summarizes the content of the apostolic preaching in terms of the "kingdom of God" (Acts 8:12; 14:22; 19:8; 20:25; 28:23). The teaching "about the Lord Jesus Christ" (28:31b) and the "kingdom of God" (28:31a) are so closely associated (cf. 8:12) that they seem to be interchangeable. In the time between Jesus' ministry (v. 1) and his return (v. 11), God's sovereign reign and the reign of his Messiah have functionally become one, until the final and climactic revelation of God's kingdom (cf. 14:22).

1:4 When he met with them, he instructed them not to leave Jerusalem, but to wait for the promise of the Father — "This," he said, "is what you heard from me" (καὶ συναλιζόμενος παρήγγειλεν αὐτοῖς ἀπὸ Ἰεροσολύμων μὴ χωρίζεσθαι ἀλλὰ περιμένειν τὴν ἐπαγγελίαν τοῦ πατρός ἣν ἠκούσατέ μου). Luke emphasizes again, with another present participle, that Jesus regularly met with the disciples after his resurrection. This verb, translated "when he met with them" (συναλιζόμενος), can mean "to eat at the same table, eat salt with, eat with," or "to assemble, come together."[23] The introductory καί is left untranslated, as often in Acts.[24]

---

22. Cf. Marshall, *Luke: Historian and Theologian*, 128 – 36; Michael Wolter, " 'Reich Gottes' bei Lukas," *NTS* 41 (1995): 541 – 63.

23. Cf. BDAG, s.v. συναλίζω.

24. The coordinating conjunction καί is used in Acts for two different but related reasons: "First, it introduces sentences in which nothing distinctive is presented. Second, it associates distinctive elements, when the information conveyed does not in fact develop the story" (Stephen H. Levinsohn, *Textual Connections in Acts* [SBLMS 31; Atlanta: Scholars Press, 1987], 120; cf. ibid. 96 – 120, 165 – 72).

This is the first of some sixty references to Jerusalem in Acts. Jerusalem, with the temple on Mount Zion, was the center of Israel's life and worship, the place on which Israel's purity and holiness depended.[25] It was the city where Jesus had died on the cross to establish the new covenant (Luke 22:19 – 20) and where Jesus had been raised from the dead. Jesus could have appeared to the disciples in Galilee, where they came from and where they had accompanied Jesus on his travels for three years.[26] But it is in Jerusalem that Jesus instructs them about the connection between the kingdom of God and his death (cf. vv. 6 – 8) and where they are to receive the Holy Spirit, which is why they are to remain in the city (cf. Luke 24:49).

This emphasis on Jerusalem highlights not only the significance of Joel's promise of the Holy Spirit and of salvation "on Mount Zion and in Jerusalem" (Joel 2:32) and the salvation-historical continuity between Israel and the community of the followers of Jesus. More significantly, it underscores that God's sovereign rule and salvation always aimed at the restoration of Zion and Jerusalem, from where it will spread to the nations (v. 8). Jerusalem was and remains the city of salvation for God's people.

Jesus' exposition about the reality of the kingdom of God after his resurrection leads him to speak about the "promise of the Father." His announcement that the promise of the coming of the Holy Spirit would be fulfilled shortly in Jerusalem had already been made on the evening of the day of resurrection (Luke 24:49); this is the reference of the relative clause, "This ... is what you heard from me" (ἣν ἠκούσατέ μου), which abruptly introduces Jesus' words in direct speech. The "promise" (ἐπαγγελία) of God that he would give his people the Holy Spirit (cf. v. 5) is given in Joel 2:28 – 32 (cf. Isa 32:15 – 20; 44:3 – 5). Since Luke in his gospel had not written about the gift of the Holy Spirit as the "promise of the Father,"[27] the statement in v. 4 is anticipatory, pointing forward to Acts 2, where the gift of the Spirit is explicitly connected with Joel's announcement of the fulfillment of God's promise (cf. 2:17). The "promise of the Father" is Jesus' promise of "power from on high" (Luke 24:49).

1:5 "Because John immersed in water, but you will be washed with the Holy Spirit in a few days" (ὅτι Ἰωάννης μὲν ἐβάπτισεν ὕδατι ὑμεῖς δὲ ἐν πνεύματι βαπτισθήσεσθε ἁγίῳ οὐ μετὰ πολλὰς ταύτας ἡμέρας). Luke quotes Jesus' promise given to the disciples. He identifies the "promise of the Father" with John the Baptist's prophecy of the coming Messiah, who would cleanse (i.e., restore) Israel through the gift of the Holy Spirit (Luke 3:16). The normal meaning of the term translated as "immersed" (βαπτίζω) is "dip, plunge, sink,"[28] corresponding to an Aramaic term that means "immerse, dye, wet, wash."[29] Lustrations as rites of repentance were conducted by immersion in "living water," i.e., in water coming from a spring or from rainwater that had flowed into a pool.[30] The dative (ὕδατι) indications location.[31]

---

25. Cf. E. P. Sanders, *Judaism: Practice and Belief 63 BCE — 66 CE* (London: SCM, 1992), 45 – 118, on the function and the significance of the temple for the Jews in the Second Temple period.

26. Cf. Jesus' appearance in Galilee in Matt 28:16 – 20.

27. Note, however, the reference to the Holy Spirit's teaching the disciples in the future (Luke 12:12; cf. 21:15).

28. Cf. LSJ, s.v. βαπτίζω, cf. s.v. βάπτω, "dip, dye, draw water by dipping a vessel." Cf. BDAG, s.v. βαπτίζω for the general meaning in Greek literature: "to put or go under water." See

Eckhard J. Schnabel, "The Meaning of βαπτίζειν in Greek, Jewish, and Patristic Literature" *FilNT* 24 (2011): pp. forthcoming.

29. Cf. *HALOT*, 5:1962 s.v. צבע; cf. Heb. טבל, which means "to dip, immerse, dive, plunge" (*HALOT*, 4:368).

30. Cf. Robert L. Webb, *John the Baptizer and Prophet: A Socio-Historical Study* (JSNTSup 62; Sheffield: JSOT Press, 1991), 179 – 83. Cf. *T. Levi* 2:3; *Sib. Or.* 4:162 – 170; *Apoc. Mos.* 29:11 – 13. For details on Jewish purification practices see the comments on 2:38.

31. The interpretation in terms of a dative of instrument

The traditional translation as "baptized," which merely transliterates the Greek term, obscures both the historical background (particularly in traditions were baptism is performed not by immersion but by affusion or sprinkling) and the significance of the event. In an Old Testament and Jewish context, ritual immersion in water signified repentance, removal of defilement, and purification from sin. John the Baptist expected all Jews to repent (Matt 3:11) — the repentance being demonstrated in immersion in water as a response to his proclamation that the arrival of the promised Messiah is imminent and that all the people of Israel need to prepare themselves to receive him.

Jesus announces here the fulfillment of the expectation that the Messiah, endowed with God's Spirit, would purge and restore the people of God (cf. Isa 11:1 – 4).[32] The literal meaning of "immerse in water" (βαπτίζω) changes to a metaphorical meaning of the term in the second half of the sentence. This can be understood in two ways. First, with direct reference to the literal meaning, the metaphor "you will be immersed in the Holy Spirit" can denote something like "you will be overwhelmed with the Holy Spirit." Jesus announces that the promise of John the Baptist will come true shortly ("in a few days"). John had announced that the Messiah would pour out the "flood" of the Spirit of God, promised for the last days, consuming all evil and transforming creation and the people of God.[33]

Second, if the point of comparison is not so much the physical act of immersing in water, the focus is on the purpose of the "immersion in the Holy Spirit." As John immersed in water, cleansing repentant Israel with water, Jesus the Messiah "washes" with the Spirit and "cleanses" repentant Israel with Spirit (and fire; Luke 3:16; cf. Acts 2:3 – 4) in fulfillment of God's promises.[34] As v. 8 will clarify, the Spirit not only cleanses from uncleanness but also provides power to preach the good news of Jesus in the world.

The verb (βαπτισθήσεσθε) is passive. Readers of the gospel will remember, however, that John had promised that the Messiah, who would be coming soon, would "immerse" (and thus wash) Israel through the Spirit (Luke 3:15 – 17). Implicit in Luke's description here is the expectation that Jesus will somehow bring about the fulfillment of this promise. This fulfillment would constitute a new reality, which is a further climactic manifestation of God's reign through Jesus' messianic rule. John's immersion in water signaled repentance, which prepared Israel for the coming of the Messiah. Jesus' "immersion in the Spirit" signals eschatological salvation and judgment. He cleanses from sin and thus saves from judgment, he brings God's presence into the lives of all who follow him, and he thus enables his followers to live according to God's will and to proclaim the gospel to the ends of the earth.

1:6 As they came together, they asked him, "Lord, is this the time when you will restore the kingdom to Israel?" (οἱ μὲν οὖν συνελθόντες ἠρώτων αὐτὸν λέγοντες· κύριε, εἰ ἐν τῷ χρόνῳ τούτῳ ἀποκαθιστάνεις τὴν βασιλείαν τῷ Ἰσραήλ;). During one of the disciples' meetings with the

---

assumes that John took water and poured it over the people; in the context of Jewish immersion rites, it is more likely that he assisted people as they immersed themselves in water.

32. Cf. *1 En.* 49:2 – 3; 62:1 – 2; *Pss. Sol.* 17:37; 18:7; *4 Ezra* 13:8 – 11; 1QSb V, 24 – 25; 4QpIsa III, 15 – 29. Cf. Turner, *Power from on High*, 183.

33. Cf. I. Howard Marshall, "The Meaning of the Verb 'to

Baptize," *EvQ* 45 (1973): 130 – 40; Turner, *Power from on High*, 181. In this understanding, the preposition ἐν has a local (or "spherical") meaning.

34. Turner, *Power from on High*, 183 – 84. In this interpretation, the preposition ἐν in the phrase ἐν πνεύματι has an instrumental sense.

risen Jesus, they ask for clarification concerning the coming of the promised Holy Spirit.[35] If John's promise of the coming of the Messiah and of the Spirit who cleanses Israel from sin is about to be fulfilled in an even more significant manner than took place in Jesus' ministry, the disciples' question is appropriate. The expected climax of the present and future work of the Messiah is the "restoration" of Israel's kingdom. In the LXX, the verb translated as "restore" (ἀποκαθίστημι)[36] is used repeatedly to refer to the expectation that Israel will be restored to her original condition in the last days.[37]

In the context of Jesus' messianic ministry and in the context of his postresurrection explanations about the kingdom of God, the disciples naturally think that (1) the kingdom is about to be restored *to Israel*, i.e., that Israel's royal rule will be restored in Zion/Jerusalem, and (2) *Jesus* will accomplish this. The disciples evidently assume that once Jesus the Messiah has restored Zion, Israel will finally be supreme among the nations (cf. Isa 49:6 – 7; Dan 7:14, 27 even speak of Israel's rule over the nations). Moreover, they assume that since Jesus is indeed the Messiah and since he saves Israel from her sins, it will be Jesus who grants Israel this exalted status. In the context of AD 30, when Judea was ruled by a Roman governor (Pontius Pilate, prefect from 26 to 36) and Galilee by a ruler who administered only a small part of the former kingdom (Herod Antipas, tetrarch from BC 4 to AD 39), these expectations would entail the elimination of the Roman over-lords and the unification of the ancestral regions of Israel.

1:7 He said to them, "It is not for you to know the times or the seasons which the Father has established through his own authority" (εἶπεν δὲ πρὸς αὐτούς· οὐχ ὑμῶν ἐστιν γνῶναι χρόνους ἢ καιρούς οὓς ὁ πατὴρ ἔθετο ἐν τῇ ἰδίᾳ ἐξουσίᾳ). Jesus begins his answer to the disciples' question about the restoration of the kingdom of God with a comment on chronological matters. The terms "times" (χρόνοι) and "seasons" (καιροί)[38] denote an interval of time. The two terms form a hendiadys, a rhetorical figure in which two nouns connected with "and" express a single idea.

Jesus comments on the chronological and temporal data that the disciples are interested in. His answer to the disciples' question has been interpreted in different ways.

(1) Verse 8 implies that here Luke has "renounced all expectation of an imminent end."[39] However, the disciples' question in v. 6 concerns not the delay of Jesus' return, but Israel's fortunes.

(2) Jesus' answer in vv. 7 – 8 to the disciples' question should be read in terms of a dramatic reinterpretation of the traditional expectations regarding Israel's fortunes.[40] But in view of Jesus' reply in v. 8 with its allusions to Isa 32:15; 43:10 – 12; 49:6, this interpretation is implausible.

(3) Jesus does not answer the disciples' question about the restoration of Israel and its timing, but

---

35. The direct question is introduced with εἰ, which remains untranslated; this use is found in the LXX and is part of Luke's biblicizing Greek, cf. 7:1; cf. BDF §440.

36. The verb ἀποκαθίστημι denotes here "to change to an earlier good state or condition, *restore, reestablish*" (BDAG, s.v. ἀποκαθίστημι).

37. Jer 16:15; 23:8; 24:6; Hos 2:3; 11:11; cf. Hos 6:11; Pss 14:7; 85:2. For the expectation that Israel will be restored in the last days, see also Isa 2:2 – 4; 49:6; Jer 31:27 – 34; Ezek 34 – 37; Amos 9:11 – 15; Tob 13 – 14; *Pss. Sol.* 17 – 18; *1 En.* 24 – 25; Eighteen Benedictions 14. Cf. Bock, *Acts*, 61.

38. Cf. G. Delling, "χρόνος," *TDNT*, 9:591; G. Delling, "καιρός," *TDNT*, 3:459, who defines καιρός as used in the New Testament as "the 'fateful and decisive point,' with strong, though not always explicit, emphasis … on the fact that it is ordained by God."

39. Haenchen, *Acts*, 143.

40. Barrett, *Acts*, 76; Robert Maddox, *The Purpose of Luke-Acts* (Edinburgh: T&T Clark, 1982), 106 – 8, who argues that for Luke, the kingdom will not be restored to national Israel, but will be given to the church.

points them to the fact that the kingdom awaits the missionary movement from Jerusalem to the ends of the earth.[41] While this is certainly correct, the fact that vv. 7 – 8 is one single sentence as well as the ongoing emphasis in Acts suggests that this is not the full answer.

(4) Jesus answers the disciples' question concerning the restoration of the kingdom of God in vv. 7 – 8, albeit in an ambivalent manner: the rise of the community of Jewish believers in Jesus is the locus of the fulfillment of the traditional hope for the restoration of Israel.[42]

Peter's sermon in 3:19 – 25 and the early chapters in Acts look to the future for Israel's restoration; the conversion of many Jews in Jerusalem and beyond to faith in Jesus the Messiah and the life and growth of the community of believers in Jesus evidently suggested to the church's leaders at the Apostles' Council that Israel's restoration is *in principle* complete, as James's speech in 15:13 – 21 and his use of Amos 9:11 – 12 demonstrate.[43]

The first part of Jesus' answer consigns the knowledge about the chronological details of the restoration of God's kingdom to Israel to God's sovereign authority ("which the Father has established through his own authority;" v. 7c). The plurals "times" (χρόνοι) and "seasons" (καιροί) indicate that the question does not concern simply the beginning of the restoration of God's kingdom to Israel, but the specifics of the chronological development of Israel's restoration. The ambivalence in Jesus' answer to the disciples' question is "a change of emphasis from Israel's kingship to her task as servant bringing the light of God's salvation to the nations."[44]

1:8 "But you will receive power when the Holy Spirit comes upon you, and you will be my witnesses in Jerusalem and in all Judea and Samaria, and even as far as the ends of the earth" (ἀλλὰ λήμψεσθε δύναμιν ἐπελθόντος τοῦ ἁγίου πνεύματος ἐφ᾽ ὑμᾶς καὶ ἔσεσθέ μου μάρτυρες ἔν τε Ἰερουσαλὴμ καὶ ἐν πάσῃ τῇ Ἰουδαίᾳ καὶ Σαμαρείᾳ καὶ ἕως ἐσχάτου τῆς γῆς). The second part of Jesus' answer explains the beginning and the reality of the restoration of Israel — the restoration of God's rule in Israel begins with the arrival of the Holy Spirit, who is the "power from on high" (Luke 24:49). It continues with their preaching activity starting in Jerusalem and Judea and extending until the ends of the earth. The genitive absolute translated as "when the Holy Spirit comes upon you" specifies the moment in time when they receive "power" (δύναμις), a term that denotes "potential for functioning in some way"[45] and, particularly when used in the plural (δυνάμεις), "acts of power."

In the Old Testament, the Spirit (πνεῦμα) of God[46] is God's power in the creation of the world (Gen 1:2; Ps 33:6); God's power that sustains all life (Gen 6:17; Ps 104:29 – 30); God's invisible activity in Israel (Num 11:17; Judg 14:6, 19); and, in the majority of passages, God's presence in various types of revelation, charismatic wisdom, and invasive speech (1 Sam 10:10; Isa 48:16; Ezek 11:5 – 25;

---

41. Cf. Wolter, "Reich Gottes," 558 – 63; Fitzmyer, *Acts*, 201, 205; cf. Bock, *Acts*, 62.

42. Jacob Jervell, *The Theology of the Acts of the Apostles* (New Testament Theology; Cambridge: Cambridge Univ. Press, 1996), 18 – 43; Turner, *Power from on High*, 290 – 315, who modifies Jervell's interpretation in important respects.

43. See the commentary for a fuller explanation of these passages. Michael E. Fuller, *The Restoration of Israel: Israel's Re-Gathering and the Fate of the Nations in Early Jewish Literature*

and Luke-Acts (BZNW 138; Berlin: De Gruyter, 2006), interprets Acts 1 – 2 as the climax of Israel's restoration.

44. Turner, *Power from on High*, 301.

45. Cf. BDAG, s.v. δύναμις 1, "power, might, strength, force, capability." Connotations with "dynamite" are not present, which was invented by Alfred Nobel in 1866 and is merely a destructive power.

46. The phrase "Holy Spirit" occurs only in Ps 51:11; Isa 63:10 – 11.

Mic 3:8).[47] Some see here an allusion to Isa 32:15, where the prophet speaks of the desolation of Israel continuing "till the Spirit is poured on us from on high."[48] For Luke's understanding of the Holy Spirit in Acts, see Theology in Application.

The power of the Holy Spirit that Jesus' followers receive helps them in their task as witnesses of God's mighty acts in and through Jesus Christ (vv. 8, 22). A witness (μάρτυς) is a person who testifies in legal matters (cf. 7:58; Matt 18:16), more generally one who affirms or attests something. The apostles are confirmed in their task to attest the life, death, resurrection, and ascension of Jesus. Their witness is based on their being eyewitnesses of these events. As they proclaim the truth about Jesus to people who may not have seen Jesus themselves, they are witnesses in the sense that they help to establish facts on which others can rely.[49]

In the context of Acts 1 – 2, they were witnesses of the life, suffering, and death of Jesus (which has taken place according to Scripture), of his resurrection, and of the message of forgiveness that they will proclaim.[50] Specifically they were witnesses of the resurrection (cf. v. 22) and thus of Jesus' vindication as the messianic Son of Man and Savior. As they saw the risen Jesus, they had proof that Jesus was what he had claimed to be — and this is what

they will proclaim, that Jesus is Lord and Messiah (2:36).

The personal pronoun (μου), emphasized by virtue of being placed before "witnesses" (μάρτυρες), underscores the fact that Jesus is the principal of the apostles' ministry as he mandates what they say and what they do as his witnesses. In the context of a possible allusion to Isa 43:10, 12 ("'You are my witnesses,' declares the LORD"), Jesus does what God does; i.e., he "fulfills the divine function of appointing his own witnesses to the nations."[51]

The apostles are given a "map" of the route that their witness will take.[52] Jesus traveled from Galilee to Jerusalem (Luke 23:5; Acts 10:37); the disciples will travel from Jerusalem via Judea and Samaria to the ends of the earth. Jerusalem is the center of the apostles' mission and their point of departure as witnesses of Jesus. Judea probably includes Galilee — in 9:31 Luke refers to "the church throughout Judea, Galilee, and Samaria," while in 1:8 only Judea and Samaria are mentioned as areas in which the disciples are directed to preach the gospel. One should note that when Luke wrote Acts, Galilee was no longer a separate political entity as it was during Jesus' ministry, but integrated into the Roman province of Judea. Samaria, the region between Judea and Galilee, is the region where descendants of the original Israelite tribes

---

47. In early Judaism, the fourth type was understood as the "Spirit of prophecy," as the Spirit was considered to make known the will and wisdom of God to his people, particularly through oracular speech; cf. Turner, *Power from on High*, 86 – 137.

48. Cf. David W. Pao, *Acts and the Isaianic New Exodus* (WUNT 2/130; Tübingen: Mohr Siebeck, 2000), 92; Peterson, *Acts*, 110 – 11.

49. On the importance of eyewitnesses for the gospel traditions cf. Richard J. Bauckham, *Jesus and the Eyewitnesses: The Gospels as Eyewitness Testimony* (Grand Rapids: Eerdmans, 2006), who concludes, "the Gospels put us in close touch with the eyewitnesses of the history of Jesus. The Gospel writers, in their different ways, present their Gospels as based on and incorporating the testimony of the eyewitnesses. The literary

and theological strategies of these writers are not directed to superseding the testimony of the eyewitnesses but to giving it a permanent literary vehicle" (472).

50. J. Beutler, "μάρτυς," *EDNT*, 2:394 – 5. Cf. Allison A. Trites, *The New Testament Concept of Witness* (SNTSMS 31; Cambridge: Cambridge Univ. Press, 1977).

51. Peterson, *Acts*, 111.

52. While not disputing the significance of the geographical terms in v. 8, many commentators play down or ignore the geographical implications of the phrase "ends of the earth;" cf. Matthew Sleeman, *Geography and the Ascension Narrative in Acts* (SNTSMS 146; Cambridge: Cambridge Univ. Press, 2009), 71, who thinks that the phrase to "the ends of the earth" "signals the earth's outermost margins, not any specific or actual location."

of the north lived, who rejected the Jerusalem-centered history of salvation[53] (see further on 8:5), and with whom the Judeans were "connected" through a long history of hostility. The "map" of v. 8 thus provides both geographical location and a description of "witnessing space" that breaches "the ethnic divides that defined Israel-space."[54]

The phrase "as far as the ends of the earth" alludes to Isa 49:6, where Yahweh says of his Servant: "I will also make you a light for the Gentiles, that my salvation may reach to the ends of the earth" (ἕως ἐσχάτου τῆς γῆς). Since Jerusalem, Judea, and Samaria are geographical terms, "the ends of the earth" should also be given a geographical meaning. It does not refer to Rome, Spain, or Ethiopia,[55] nor to the Jewish diaspora,[56] nor simply to the Gentiles,[57] but literally to the farthest reaches of the inhabited world known at the time.[58]

Some scholars have suggested that since Luke takes his readers from Jerusalem (chs. 1 – 12) to Rome (19:21; 23:11; 25:10; 28:11 – 31), the phrase "ends of the earth" in the "map" of v. 8 refers to Rome (cf. *Pss. Sol.* 8:15). This passage is interpreted as a reference to the invasion of the East by the Roman general Pompey, which began in Rome and ended in Jerusalem. This interpretation is not convincing, however. The phrase "end of the earth"

in *Pss. Sol.* 8:15 is probably an allusion to Jer 6:22, which refers to the invasion of the Babylonians. Moreover, that phrase in *Pss. Sol.* 8:15 could also denote Spain. As the following comments demonstrate, the phrase "end(s) of the earth" had a fixed meaning, referring to the far reaches of the inhabited world, a meaning never applied to the city of Rome, located in the center of the Mediterranean. Note too that in Acts 28, Rome is not portrayed as a goal or fulfillment of the early Christian mission, but as a new starting point from which the gospel was proclaimed "with all boldness and without hindrance" (28:31).

In ancient literature, the phrase "the ends (τὰ ἔσχατα) of the earth" designates the farthest regions of the earth.[59] By the first century, the *western* "end" of the known world was Gaul or Germania on the Atlantic Ocean, as well as Britannia, which emperor Claudius had annexed in AD 43, or, further south, Spain, and particularly the city of Gades (Gadeira, mod. Cadiz) west of the straights of Gibraltar on the Atlantic Ocean. Strabo describes Gades as a city "at the end of the earth."[60]

The *northern* "end" of the world was the Arctic, and in terms of inhabited regions Scythia, whose people lived "at the end of the earth."[61]

---

53. Cf. H. G. M. Williamson, "Samaritans," *DJG*, 724 – 28.

54. Sleeman, *Geography*, 71.

55. Rome is preferred by Hans Conzelmann, *Acts of the Apostles* (Hermeneia; Philadelphia: Fortress, 1987), 7; Fitzmyer, *Acts*, 206 – 7, and others. Barrett, *Acts*, 80, interprets the phrase in terms of Rome as representative of the entire world. Other locales are assumed by Earle E. Ellis, " 'The End of the Earth' (Acts 1:8)," *BBR* 1 (1991): 123 – 32 (Spain); Timothy C. G. Thornton, "To the End of the Earth: Acts 1.8," *ExpTim* 89 (1977 – 78): 374 – 75 (Ethiopia).

56. Jervell, *Apostelgeschichte*, 116.

57. Willem C. van Unnik, "Der Ausdruck ΈΩΣ ΈΣΧΑΤΟΥ ΤΗΣ ΓΗΣ (Apostelgeschichte 1.8) und sein alttestamentlicher Hintergrund," in *Sparsa Collecta* (NovTSup. 29; Leiden: Brill, 1973), 386 – 401; cf. Pao, *New Exodus*, 93 – 94.

58. Schnabel, *Early Christian Mission*, 1:372 – 76; cf. Brian S. Rosner, "The Progress of the Word," in *Witness to*

the Gospel: The Theology of Acts (ed. I. H. Marshall and D. Peterson), 215 – 33.

59. Cf. Strabo, *Geogr.* 1.1.6; 1.2.31; 2.3.5; 2.4.2; Philostratus, *Vit. Apoll.* 6.1.1; Philo, *Cherubim* 99; *Dreams* 1.134; *Migration* 181. James S. Romm, *The Edges of the Earth in Ancient Thought: Geography, Exploration, and Fiction* (Princeton: Princeton Univ. Press, 1992), 11 – 41; James M. Scott, "Luke's Geographical Horizon," in *The Book of Acts in Its Graeco-Roman Setting* (ed. D. W. J. Gill and C. Gempf; The Book of Acts in Its First-Century Setting 2; Grand Rapids: Eerdmans, 1994), 483 – 544, 525 – 57.

60. Strabo, *Geogr.* 3.1.8; cf. 1.2.31; 2.5.14; 3.1.4; cf. Lucanus, *Pharsalia* 3.454; Diodoros Siculus 25.10.1; Juvenal, *Sat.* 10.1 – 2; Silius, *Punica* 17.637. Strabo, *Geogr.* 1.1.5, also knows the Canary Islands, as lying "to the westward of the most western Maurusia [i.e. Morocco]."

61. Propertius 2.7.18.

The *southern* "end" of the world was Ethiopia (mod. Sudan), whose people were said to live "at the ends of the earth on the banks of Oceanus."[62]

The *eastern* "end" of the world was thought to be beyond India and the Seres (silk) people, i.e., China. Procopius, writing in the sixth century, refers to Roman soldiers posted on the eastern border of Persia and India as living "at the ends of the inhabited world."[63]

Even though we have no explicit information about how the apostles understood Jesus' directive, it appears that they took it literally. Note that Luke mentions an Ethiopian (Acts 8:26 – 40), Paul mentions Scythians (Col 3:11) and seeks to go to Spain (Rom 15:24, 28), and India is mentioned in writing in *Acts of Thomas* and in oral traditions as the region where the apostle Thomas engaged in missionary work.[64]

The mission of the apostles is world mission. It begins in Jerusalem, it reaches the surrounding regions of Judea and Samaria, and it extends as far as people live, transcending both geographical and ethnic boundaries.

1:9 When he had said this, while they were looking, he was lifted up and a cloud took him up from their sight (καὶ ταῦτα εἰπὼν βλεπόντων αὐτῶν ἐπήρθη καὶ νεφέλη ὑπέλαβεν αὐτὸν ἀπὸ τῶν ὀφθαλμῶν αὐτῶν). Luke's account of Jesus' ascension begins with a statement that underscores the unique status of the apostles as eyewitnesses. The fact that they see Jesus departing is mentioned several times (cf. vv. 9, 10, 11). Just as Jesus' resurrection was a bodily resurrection, there was something to "see" when he ascended into heaven.[65] Luke repeats in vv. 9 – 11 his report of Jesus' ascension in Luke 24:50 – 51.

The aorist and present participles are significant. With his announcement about the kingdom of God, the coming of the Spirit, and the missionary task of the apostles who will continue his work on earth, Jesus has said all that he has to say to his disciples (εἰπών, aorist participle). The disciples continue to look at him (βλεπόντων, present participle), as they are even now witnesses who see what is happening and as they continue to be dependent on him.

The passive voice expression "he was lifted up" (ἐπήρθη) describes God's action of taking Jesus back into heaven to his right hand (2:33). The cloud is not simply an "apocalyptic stage prop," nor the "vehicle" that transported Jesus into heaven,[66] nor a literary device borrowed from Old Testament passages about the presence of God.[67] As Luke reports a historical event,[68] the cloud should be interpreted as a natural phenomenon that signaled to the apostles that Jesus has just left them — not as he left them during the last forty days, only to appear again for further instruction and fellowship, but in a permanent fashion.[69] This was Jesus' last appear-

---

62. Strabo, *Geogr.* 1.1.6; cf. Homer, *Od.* 1.23; Herodotus 3.25.

63. Procopius, *De bellis* 2.3.52; cf. 6.30.9.

64. For the geographical vision of the apostles, cf. Schnabel, *Early Christian Mission*, 1:444 – 98; on the plausibility of Thomas preaching in India, cf. ibid. 880 – 95.

65. Bock, *Acts*, 67, astutely remarks that "what takes place here illustrates what had already taken place as a result of the resurrection." The New Testament authors do not tell us where Jesus was after his resurrection, between the appearances to his disciples.

66. Fitzmyer, *Acts*, 210; Conzelmann, *Acts*, 7;

67. Cf. Exod 16:10; 19:9; 24:15 – 18; Ezek 10:3 – 4; Ps 18:11.

The Old Testament and Judaism described the raptures of Enoch (Gen 5:24; *1 En.* 39.3; 71:1; *2 En.* 3:1 – 3), Elijah (2 Kgs 2:11; Philo, *QG* 1.86), Moses (Josephus, *Ant.* 4.326), Ezra (*4 Ezra* 14:49), Baruch (*2 Bar.* 76:2).

68. Cf. Witherington, *Acts*, 112, about the historicity of Jesus' ascension. Luke is the only New Testament author who describes Jesus' ascension (although note the brief comment in John 20:17).

69. The verb ὑπολαμβάνω denotes here "to take up by getting under" (LSJ) or "to cause to ascend, *take up*" (BDAG). The idea seems to be that as Jesus was "taken up" into heaven, he disappeared in a cloud. Cf. Sleeman, *Geography*, 77 – 78, who interprets the reference to the cloud as providing "a clear de-

ance after the resurrection before his return some-time in the future (v. 11). At the same time, Luke's narrative demonstrates that Jesus is not absent: "The ascension is *the* moment of spatial realignment in Acts (cf. 1:1 – 2a), and Acts as a narrative whole cannot be understood without ongoing reference to the heavenly Christ."[70]

Note that in comparison to many Jewish stories of ascensions or "translations" into heaven, Luke's description is reserved. It is not a coincidence that Jesus' ascension to God's heavenly throne takes place on the Olive Grove (v. 12), the place where Jesus' triumphal, messianic entry into Jerusalem began (Luke 19:29, 37) and where he announced the destruction of the temple (Matt 24:3, 15 – 28; Luke 19:41 – 44).

1:10 While they were staring into heaven as he was going, two men dressed in white robes suddenly stood beside them (καὶ ὡς ἀτενίζοντες ἦσαν εἰς τὸν οὐρανὸν πορευομένου αὐτοῦ, καὶ ἰδοὺ ἄνδρες δύο παρειστήκεισαν αὐτοῖς ἐν ἐσθήσεσι λευκαῖς). After Jesus' ascension to the Father, the disciples receive divine encouragement. The presence of the angels highlights the supernatural character of what they had just witnessed.[71] The whiteness of the robes speaks, perhaps, not so much of color but of the transcendent glory of the angels. Some have suggested that the two men evoke the motif of two witnesses (Deut 19:15).[72] This is more plau-

sible than the view that they represent Elijah and Moses.[73] Since in Luke's gospel all visions, with the exception of those experienced by Jesus, inspire fear,[74] it is striking that no such reaction is related for the disciples' vision of the two angels, beginning a pattern that continues throughout Luke's narrative: "Like Jesus, believers no longer exhibit fear in visionary encounters."[75]

1:11 They said, "Men of Galilee, why do you stand here looking into heaven? This Jesus, who has been taken up from you into heaven, will return in the manner in which you saw him go into heaven" (οἳ καὶ εἶπαν· ἄνδρες Γαλιλαῖοι, τί ἑστήκατε ἐμβλέποντες εἰς τὸν οὐρανόν; οὗτος ὁ Ἰησοῦς ὁ ἀναλημφθεὶς ἀφ᾽ ὑμῶν εἰς τὸν οὐρανὸν οὕτως ἐλεύσεται ὃν τρόπον ἐθεάσασθε αὐτὸν πορευόμενον εἰς τὸν οὐρανόν). The angels tell the disciples not to stand around, wishing for Jesus to remain with them. They already know what they should be doing in Jesus' absence: to be Jesus' witnesses.

The angels assure the disciples that Jesus' ascension is a guarantee that he will return in the same manner in which he was taken to heaven (see Luke 21:27; cf. Mark 14:62). The reference to Jesus' earlier announcement of his return reminds the disciples, and Luke's readers, of the final sentences of Jesus' discourse about the last days, where he had spoken about the fulfillment of the "times of the

---

marcation between earth and heaven," safeguarding Jesus' "place" in heaven as "sovereignly independent of mortal control" (78).

70. Sleeman, *Geography*, 80.

71. KJV, NKJV, RSV, ESV translate the interjection (ἰδού) as "behold;" the term echoes an idiomatic expression in the Old Testament (cf. LXX) and emphasizes the importance of something; it can be left untranslated (cf. BDAG, s.v. ἰδού 1bα) or rendered with terms expressing emphasis, e.g., "suddenly." Cf. BDF §128.7, 442.7.

72. William J. Larkin, *Acts* (IVPNTC; Leicester: Intervarsity Press, 1995), 43; with caution Bock, *Acts*, 69.

73. Luke Timothy Johnson, *The Acts of the Apostles* (SP 5;

Collegeville, MN: Liturgical, 1992), 31; James D. G. Dunn, *The Acts of the Apostles* (EpComm; London: Epworth, 1996), 14; Robert W. Wall, *The Acts of the Apostles* (The New Interpreter's Bible 10; ed. L. E. Keck; Nashville: Abingdon, 2002), 44.

74. Luke 1:12 – 13 (Zechariah); 1:29 – 30 (Mary); 2:9 – 10 (shepherds); 9:34 (transfiguration); 24:5 (women at the tomb); for Jesus' visions see 4:1 – 13; 10:17 – 20.

75. John B. F. Miller, *Convinced that God Had Called Us: Dreams, Visions, and the Perception of God's Will in Luke-Acts* (Biblical Interpretation 85; Leiden/Boston: Brill, 2007), 169 – 70, notes that "fear is a feature of some of the dream-visions in Acts, but only for those who are not yet followers of 'the Way'" (170).

Gentiles" before the end (Luke 21:24) and about the cosmic signs (21:25 – 26) that mark the time when they should "lift up [their] heads" because their redemption is near (21:28).

The two angels speak about the manner (τρόπος) of Jesus' return, emphasizing the fact of Jesus' return rather than its timing. As Jesus' return is a certainty, the disciples can return to Jerusalem and look forward to fulfilling the task of being Jesus' witnesses in the city and in the regions beyond.

1:12 Then they returned to Jerusalem from the hill known as Mount of Olives, which is near Jerusalem, a Sabbath day's journey away (τότε ὑπέστρεψαν εἰς Ἰερουσαλὴμ ἀπὸ ὄρους τοῦ καλουμένου Ἐλαιῶνος ὅ ἐστιν ἐγγὺς Ἰερουσαλὴμ σαββάτου ἔχον ὁδόν). The disciples return from the Mount of Olives, the location of Jesus' final instructions and of his ascension to heaven. The hill whose name was derived from the presence of an olive grove (ἐλαιών) was "opposite the city to the east, being separated from it by a deep ravine called Kidron," six stadia from Jerusalem, i.e., 1150 meters (Josephus, *J.W.* 5.70).[76] Jesus and the disciples had repeatedly spent time on the Mount of Olives (cf. Luke 21:37; John 8:1). Gethsemane was on its western slope. Observant Jews interpreted the Sabbath law of Exod 16:29 to mean that on Sabbath day, they were allowed to travel on foot no more than 2,000 cubits, i.e., 1,120 meters (3,600 feet).[77] This passage does not allow any inferences concerning the views of the early church regarding Sabbath observance.[78]

1:13a-b When they had entered the city, they went to the upper room where they were staying (καὶ ὅτε εἰσῆλθον εἰς τὸ ὑπερῷον ἀνέβησαν οὗ ἦσαν καταμένοντες). The verb translated as "were staying" (a periphrastic construction of ἦσαν and the present participle καταμένοντες), suggests that the eleven disciples and other followers of Jesus were regularly meeting in the upper room of a certain house. It is unlikely that they all "resided" in one room; this may have been possible for the eleven disciples, but not for the larger group that included women. Since most of the disciples were Galileans (cf. 2:7) and not citizens of Jerusalem, they must have found accommodation with other sympathizers of Jesus, unless they had relatives who lived in the city. Later rabbinic sources attest Pharisaic *haburoth* ("fellowships") that met to study and eat together in the upper rooms of houses.[79]

The "upper room" (τὸ ὑπερῷον) is identified by some with the room where Jesus celebrated his last meal with the disciples (Luke 22:12: ἀνάγαιον also means "room upstairs"), and with a room in the house of Mary, the mother of John Mark, in which followers of Jesus later met (Acts 12:12).[80] But Luke does not specify the location of the "upper room."

1:13c-f Peter and John and James and Andrew, Philip and Thomas, Bartholomew and Matthew, James son of Alphaeus and Simon the Zealot and Judas son of James (ὅ τε Πέτρος καὶ Ἰωάννης καὶ Ἰάκωβος καὶ Ἀνδρέας, Φίλιππος καὶ Θωμᾶς, Βαρθολομαῖος καὶ Μαθθαῖος, Ἰάκωβος Ἁλφαίου καὶ Σίμων ὁ ζηλωτὴς καὶ Ἰούδας Ἰακώβου). Luke organizes the list of Jesus' disciples in three groups of four names.[81]

---

76. A *stadion* measured 192 meters (1/8 mile); cf. BDAG, s.v. στάδιον 1. In *Ant.* 20.169, Josephus states that the Mount of Olives was five stadia (960 meters) from the city; the reference in *J.W.* 5:70 refers to the encampment of Roman troops.

77. Cf. *Mek. Exod.* 16:29 (59a); *Tg. Yer.* on Exod 16:29; *b. ʿErub.* 51a; *b. Ber.* 9a. A cubit is about 56 cm (1.8 feet).

78. Cf. Max M. B. Turner, "The Sabbath, Sunday, and the Law in Luke/Acts," in *From Sabbath to Lord's Day: A Bibli-*

cal, Historical and Theological Investigation (ed. D. A. Carson; Grand Rapids: Zondervan, 1982), 99 – 157, 124.

79. Cf. *m. Šabb.* 1:4; *b. Menaḥ.* 41b; cf. L. M. White, "Christianity: Early Social Life and Organization," *ABD*, 1:927.

80. The article in the phrase τὸ ὑπερῷον could be anaphoric, referring back to Luke 22:12, but this is not certain.

81. The order differs slightly in Luke 6:14 – 16; cf. Mark 3:16 – 19; Matt 10:2 – 4. John's name was brought forward, per-

Peter (Πέτρος), whose Hebrew name was Simon (Luke 6:14), came from Bethsaida. He owned a house in Capernaum, worked as a fisherman on the Sea of Galilee, and was married. Jesus called him "Peter" (meaning "stone"), the Greek equivalent of the Aramaic surname Cephas (Greek Κηφᾶς), which means "rock." This change of name highlights his task and responsibility — he was appointed as the leader and spokesman of the Twelve, the foundation of the new "house" of the messianic community. This is indeed Peter's role in the first half of Acts. He appears with John (as his "silent partner")[82] as spokesman of the Twelve[83] and as a church leader and missionary.[84] On Peter see further on 1:15.

John (Ἰωάννης), one of the sons of Zebedee, was a fisherman from Bethsaida. He is in all probability "the disciple whom Jesus loved" in John's gospel.[85] John was the only disciple among the Twelve who witnessed Jesus' crucifixion (John 19:25 – 27) and the first disciple to see the empty tomb (John 20:2 – 5). Paul describes him as one of those "esteemed as pillars" (Gal 2:9). The early tradition identifies John with the author of the fourth gospel.[86]

James (Ἰάκωβος), John's brother, was executed by Herod Agrippa I in AD 41 (Acts 12:2), the first of the Twelve who was killed on account of his faith. Jesus called James and John "Boanerges" (Βοανηργές), translated by Mark as "sons of thunder" (υἱοὶ βροντῆς, Mark 3:17), presumably be-

cause of their fiery temperament (Luke 9:54; cf. Mark 9:38; 10:35 – 40).

Andrew (Ἀνδρέας), like Simon Peter his brother, had been a disciple of John the Baptist. According to the fourth gospel, Andrew was the first follower of Jesus who is identified by name when he brought Simon Peter to Jesus (John 1:35 – 42). Later he brought the boy with the bread and the fishes to Jesus (John 6:8) and, together with Philip, the Greeks who wanted to see Jesus (John 12:22).

Philip (Φίλιππος) also came from Bethsaida (like the four just mentioned, John 1:44). With Andrew he brought the Greeks who wanted to see Jesus to him (John 12:21 – 22). He is not identical with Philip, who was a member of the Seven (Acts 6:5) and who preached the gospel in Samaria (8:4 – 24).

Thomas (Θωμᾶς), called "the twin" (Δίδυμος; John 11:16; 20:24; 21:2), is mentioned in the fourth gospel as a courageous disciple of Jesus (John 11:16; cf. 14:5) who, after his encounter with Jesus after the resurrection, confessed Jesus as divine Messiah (John 20:28).[87] According to later tradition, he went to India as a missionary.[88]

Bartholomew (Βαρθολομαῖος) is mentioned only in the disciple lists. His Aramaic name may have been Nathanael Bar-Talmai ("son of Talmay"); he has been identified with Nathanael mentioned in John 1:43 – 46; 21:2, though this is uncertain.[89]

Matthew (Μαθθαῖος) is identified in Matt 9:9;

---

haps to underline his association with Peter in the early chapters of Acts (3:1, 3 – 4, 11; 4:13, 19; 8:14); Barrett, *Acts*, 87. On the twelve disciples cf. John P. Meier, *A Marginal Jew: Rethinking the Historical Jesus* (New York: Doubleday, 1991 – 2009), 3:199 – 285; Schnabel, *Early Christian Mission*, 1:265 – 69.

82. Acts 1:15; 2:14; 3:1, 3 – 4, 6, 11 – 12; 4:8, 13, 19; 5:29; 8:14, 20. Cf. Fitzmyer, *Acts*, 213.

83. Acts 2:14; 5:1 – 11, 17 – 39.

84. Acts 1:15 – 25; 9:32 – 43; 10:5 – 46; 11:2 – 13; 15:7.

85. John 13:23; 19:26 – 27; 20:2; 21:7, 20; 21:4 (cf. 1:40; 18:15; 19:35).

86. Explicitly for the first time Theophilus of Antioch around AD 181; cf. Carson and Moo, *Introduction*, 229 – 54.

87. He is often called "doubting Thomas" on account of the fact that he did not believe the reports that Jesus had been raised from the dead (John 20:24 – 29); note, however, that he displayed the same skepticism as the other disciples did.

88. For an evaluation of this tradition cf. Schnabel, *Early Christian Mission*, 2:880 – 95.

89. Cf. Meier, *Marginal Jew*, 3:199 – 200; M. J. Wilkins, "Disciples," *DJG*, 180.

10:3 as Levi the tax collector, whose call by Jesus is described more extensively than the call of any other disciple.[90] Early church tradition credits Matthew/Levi with the authorship of the first gospel.

James son of Alphaeus (Ἰάκωβος Ἀλφαίου) has been identified with "James the younger" (Mark 15:40), the brother of a certain Joses, whose mother was a certain Mary, but this is not certain. Since Levi is also described as "son of Alphaeus" (Mark 2:14), it is possible that James and Matthew/Levi were brothers. However, since the disciple lists in the gospels mention brothers in pairs, which is not the case with regard to James son of Alphaeus, this is not likely.

Simon (Σίμων) "the Zealot" (cf. Luke 6:15) is called "the Cananaean" (ὁ Καναναῖος) in Matt 10:4 and Mark 3:18 (ESV), a term derived from the Aramaic word meaning "the enthusiast, zealot." In the first century AD both the Aramaic and the Greek terms had a broad spectrum of meaning: everybody who stood for a committed fulfillment of the law could be so designated. Whether this Simon formerly belonged to the party of the Zealots, i.e., whether he was at one time a Jewish nationalist prepared to engage in active resistance against the Romans, remains an open question.

Judas (Ἰούδας, Heb. Yehudah) son of James (cf. Luke 6:16) is perhaps identical with the disciple Thaddaeus mentioned in Matt 10:3 and Mark 3:18.[91] Apart from the disciple lists, he is mentioned only indirectly in connection with Jesus' last Passover during which "Judas, not Iscariot" asks: "Lord, why do you intend to show yourself to us and not to the world?" (John 14:22).

1:14 They all devoted themselves with one mind to prayer, together with several women and Mary, the mother of Jesus, and his brothers (οὗτοι πάντες ἦσαν προσκαρτεροῦντες ὁμοθυμαδὸν τῇ προσευχῇ σὺν γυναιξὶν καὶ Μαριὰμ τῇ μητρὶ τοῦ Ἰησοῦ καὶ τοῖς ἀδελφοῖς αὐτοῦ). Luke's first summary of the life and the activities of the followers of Jesus in Jerusalem focuses on prayer. The apostles are not focused on themselves or on their task, but on God, whose power sustains their life and assists them in their mission. The meaning of the verb (προσκαρτερέω), which denotes "to be busily engaged in, be devoted to," and the imperfect periphrastic tense both underscore the persistent and continuous nature of their prayers. In 6:4 the apostles reassert the priority of prayer for the leadership of the Jerusalem church. Before followers of Jesus do anything else, they call on God, whether with praise or petition, thanksgiving or intercession, as they utterly depend on God in whose sovereignty they trust.

The adverb (ὁμοθυμαδόν) means "with one mind, unanimously," although many have argued for the weaker meaning "together." The context indicates that, here, more than physical co-location (mentioned already in v. 13) is meant. Luke describes a shared attitude of heart and mind.[92] The reference to the harmony and unanimity of the disciples is repeatedly stressed in Acts (cf. 2:46; 4:24; 5:12).

The phrase "with several women" (σὺν γυναιξίν) may refer to the wives of the eleven apostles (anarthrous noun),[93] or, which is more likely, to female disciples mentioned among the witnesses of Jesus' ascension. Luke repeatedly mentions women

---

90. Matt 9:9 – 13/Mark 2:13 – 17/Luke 5:27 – 32.

91. Cf. JoAnn F. Watson, "Thaddaeus," *ABD*, 6:435. Meier, *Marginal Jew*, 3:200, rejects this identification. According to the apocryphal *Acts of Thaddaeus*, this disciple later did missionary work in Edessa, a tradition that Eusebius knows (*Hist. eccl.* 1.13; 2.1.6 – 8).

92. Cf. Steve Walton, "Ὁμοθυμαδόν in Acts: Co-location, Common Action, or 'Of One Heart and Mind'?" in *The New Testament in Its First Century Setting: Essays on Context and Background* (FS Bruce W. Winter; ed. P. J. Williams et al.; Grand Rapids: Eerdmans, 2004), 89 – 105, 101.

93. Cf. Luke 4:38, where Peter's wife is mentioned, and

who traveled with Jesus and who were witnesses of Jesus' crucifixion and resurrection.[94] Among these women is Mary, Jesus' mother;[95] also included are Jesus' brothers, whose names are given in Mark 6:3 as James, Joseph, Judas, and Simon.[96] The most natural meaning of "brother" (ἀδελφός) is blood brother. Jesus' "brothers" (ἀδελφοί) were the sons of Joseph and Mary.[97] Mary and Jesus' brothers had been more than skeptical about Jesus' ministry (Mark 3:21, omitted in Luke 8:19 – 21; cf. John 7:5). Luke portrays them as being among those who believe in him. Paul preserves a tradition that included James among those who had seen Jesus after the resurrection (1 Cor 15:7), and points out that "the Lord's brothers" were involved in missionary travels, accompanied by their wives (1 Cor 9:5).

Theology in Application

As Luke refers his readers to the first volume of his work, which was an account of Jesus' life, ministry, death, resurrection, and ascension, and as he again briefly summarizes Jesus' ministry at the beginning of Acts, he underscores the essential and fundamental significance of Jesus. His introduction of Acts emphasizes that the life and work of the church and her leaders depend entirely on the life and work of Jesus, the risen and exalted Lord and Messiah, who rules at God's right hand and who has promised and granted to his disciples the gift of the Holy Spirit, who empowers their life and their ministry.

The themes of the introduction of Acts reappear repeatedly in the first chapters of Acts, which describe the life and work of the Twelve, represented by Peter. Consequently, the emphases highlighted here will be developed further in Acts.

Jesus as Central for the Life of the Church

Jesus remains central for the life of the church, foundational for the teaching in the church, and crucial for the missionary outreach of the church. The ministry of Jesus has not been "overtaken" by the era of the Spirit or by the various concerns of church life. The life and work of the church and of her leaders cannot and must not be separated from the ministry of Jesus. This is why the church has four gospels. Of particular significance are Jesus' suffering (which occupies about a third of the space in all four gospels), resurrection, and exaltation.

---

1 Cor 9:5, where the wives of "the other apostles" are referred to. The Western text in D reads σὺν ταῖς γυναιξίν καὶ τέκνοις ("with the/their wives and children"), which at least shows how an early copyist understood the text; cf. Rius-Camps and Read-Heimerdinger, *Acts*, 1:57, 103 – 4.

94. Cf. Luke 8:1 – 3; 23:49, 55 – 56; 24:1 – 9, 22 – 24.

95. Cf. Luke 1:26 – 56; 2:4 – 7, 19, 34, 51.

96. Sisters of Jesus are mentioned in Mark 6:3/Matt 13:56.

Epiphanius, *Pan.* 78.8.1; 78.9.6 gives their names as Mary and Salome, which may well be authentic information; cf. Richard J. Bauckham, *Jude and the Relatives of Jesus in the Early Church* (Edinburgh: T&T Clark, 1990), 37 – 44.

97. Cf. Barrett, *Acts*, 90; Bauckham, *Relatives*, 19 – 32. Other suggestions for Jesus' "brothers" are the sons of Joseph by his first marriage, or cousins of Jesus, i.e., children of Mary's sister.

Jesus' Ascension

Jesus' ascension to the throne at God's right hand concludes his earthly ministry and inaugurates his "new covenant" ministry, which is carried out by the apostles. Peter will explain in his Pentecost speech the meaning of Jesus' ascension.[98] Three truths are particularly important.

Jesus has been exalted to the eternal throne of David, the throne promised in Psalm 110:1 for David's "Lord" — a throne located not in Jerusalem but at God's right hand (2:33 – 36). Having ascended to God's right hand, Jesus now rules over Israel, fulfilling the announcement made in connection with his birth (Luke 1:32 – 33). His ascension does not remove him from Israel. On the contrary, it has put him into the position of God's chief executive agent, who initiates the promised messianic manifestation of God's reign on earth. God's kingdom is indeed being restored, as God's rule is now, in the days of the Messiah, conveyed through the crucified, risen, and exalted Jesus.[99]

This exalted Jesus, the royal Lord and Messiah, pours out the Holy Spirit of God as the gift of God's own self-manifesting and transformative presence and life (2:33). He acts and speaks through his witnesses as he is the Lord with respect to God's Spirit and his gifts (2:33, 36, 38 – 39).

The Holy Spirit as the Power of God's Presence

The Holy Spirit is the power of God's presence, promised and provided by Jesus the Messiah and Savior, for the life and the ministry of the church and her apostles. As God's effective presence, the Holy Spirit is specifically related in Acts to various realities.

The presence of the Holy Spirit as the power of the almighty God and as the catalyst of the exalted Jesus guarantees that the kingdom is restored to Israel and that God's plan for the world, which includes the Gentiles (who live between Jerusalem and the ends of the earth), will be fulfilled. The context in 1:4 – 7 relates the power of the Holy Spirit to the cleansing and restoring of the messianic people of God, which Jesus and the coming of the Spirit initiated (cf. 11:16; 15:8 – 9, also the allusion to Isa 32:15 in 1:8).

The power of the Holy Spirit sustains and renders effective the missionary witness of the apostles (v. 8). The connection between the gift of the Holy Spirit and the ministry of the apostles explains why apostles are effective. It is not their organiza-

---

98. See 2:33 for a discussion of the relationship between Jesus' resurrection, exaltation, and ascension.

99. Here Dan 7:13 – 14 might be relevant, where "one like a son of man" comes "with the clouds of heaven" before God, to be given "authority, glory and sovereign power; all nations and peoples of every language worshiped him. His dominion is an everlasting dominion that will not pass away, and his kingdom is one that will never be destroyed."

tional or rhetorical gifts that explain the growth of the church, but the presence of God himself and of the risen Jesus Christ in their life and ministry.

In the context of Pentecost, the coming of the Holy Spirit is linked with salvation. It is through the gift of the Spirit, given by the exalted Jesus Messiah, that the promised salvation (Luke 1:32 – 33) is poured out (Acts 2:21, 33, 36, 38 – 39, 40).

The reception of the gift of the Holy Spirit is a fundamental reality of the life of Christians. Conversion involves repentance, faith in Jesus the crucified and risen Messiah, and immersion in water (2:38 – 39).

The new life of believers in Jesus should be understood as the result of the reception of the Spirit. The community of the followers of Jesus and their fellowship, sacrificial service, worship, and evangelism are described as the immediate result of Pentecost (2:42 – 47),

The power of God's Spirit becomes visible in miracles (2:22; 3:12; 4:7; cf. 19:11) and in the proclamation of the Word (4:33; cf. 6:8 – 10; 10:38 – 40).

The Apostles as Jesus Witnesses

The apostles are Jesus' witnesses to unbelievers and to believers. As Jesus' witnesses, the disciples will not testify to their own experiences; they testify to the resurrection of Jesus, who died as Israel's Messiah for the atonement of sins. The Twelve have various roles.[100]

They form the nucleus of a restored Israel (Luke 22:28 – 30). In Acts 3 – 5, Luke describes the political leaders of the Jews as lacking credibility and authority, while the apostles have in a sense become Israel's effective leaders (cf. Acts 3:9 – 10; 4:2, 13, 21; 5:25 – 26) as they are the leaders of the church (cf. 2:26 – 27, 42; 4:35, 37; 5:2; 8:14; 15:2, 4, 6 – 29).

The Twelve are witnesses to Jesus' resurrection (Luke 24:48; Acts 1:8, 21 – 22; 2:32; 3:15; 4:2, 10, 33; 5:32) and to Jesus' deeds more generally (Acts 10:39). Having been called and commissioned by Jesus, they are Jesus' authorized ambassadors, witnesses to his life, death, and resurrection, and expounders of his significance for Israel and for the Gentiles.

The Twelve are authoritative teachers who expound Scripture and who explain the life, death, and resurrection/exaltation of Jesus to Israel and to Gentiles (2:42, 44 – 47; 4:2, 30 – 31; 5:21 – 22, 28, 42). Their main activity is the ministry of God's Word (6:2, 4). They explain the good news about Jesus to unbelievers (4:2, 17; 5:20, 25) and teach the Christian community (2:42; 5:42). As Luke describes the growth of the church as the growth of God's Word (6:7; 12:24; 19:20), the ministry of the apostles is indispensable for the church and her growth.

---

100. For the following comments cf. Clark, "Role of the Apostles," passim.

The Ministry of the Church

The ministry of the church is universal in scope. Authentic communities of Christians never focus all their energies on their own local church. Christian leaders have a comprehensive vision that reaches from their own city to other cities and regions far and wide.

The vision of the church and her leaders extends from the people who live in close proximity (Jerusalem, Judea) to people who live further away (Samaria, to the ends of the earth; 1:8; 2:39). Peter soon reaches people living in Samaria (8:25), in Judea (9:32 – 43), and in Caesarea (10:1 – 48). The churches established in Judea, Galilee, and Samaria continue to grow (9:31). Christian preachers reach and preach in cities in Phoenicia, Cyprus, and Syria (11:19). Paul, after his conversion, preaches in Syria, on Cyprus, and in the provinces of Galatia, Macedonia, Achaia, and Asia (Acts 13 – 20).

The missionary strategy implied in Jesus' geographical directive is simple, although daunting. The apostles are instructed to reach people *wherever they live* with the news about the offer of salvation, whether they are Jews, or Samaritans, or Gentiles. They are certainly directed not to remain "at home" — although when we realize that most disciples were Galileans and that Jerusalem was not their home, they never stayed "at home" as Jesus' witnesses.

The scope of the ministry of the church is universal also in temporal terms. It began at the day of Jesus' return to the Father and will last until Jesus' return to earth. Jesus' reference to God's authority over the chronological details of the life and ministry of his followers (vv. 6 – 7, 11) means that speculations about the periods of salvation history must not be allowed to occupy their theological reflection.

The life of the disciples stands not under the authority of their own personal ideas and hopes. The determination of time with its periods and epochs, and thus the determination of the duration of the last days that have begun, and the knowledge about the duration of their missionary work are the prerogative of the Father, who guides history as Lord of history according to his plan. There are more important things to do than to speculate about the date and the details of Jesus' return to earth.

It is somewhat surprising that self-appointed "end-time specialists" often ignore what Jesus said about not knowing the details and the timing of his return. Apart from earning royalties for best-selling books on these matters, not much good has come of such a misguided focus on the end times. On the contrary, many Christians have been confused about what really matters — waiting joyfully for Christ's return rather than waiting for the antichrist and for a rapture that would deliver them from suffering. Many pastors have been confused as well, so much so that many refrain from preaching through the book of Revelation.

As the disciples have been assured that Jesus' return is a certainty, they can return to Jerusalem and look forward to fulfilling the task of being Jesus' witnesses with joy and anticipation about what Jesus and God's Spirit will do through their ministry. Christians do not wait idly for Jesus' return. They have work to do.

The life of the apostles as witnesses of Jesus who have been given God's Holy Spirit, and the missionary task of the church, which sends the apostles from Jerusalem to the ends of the earth, require prayer — much constant and united prayer (v. 14). In Luke 11:1 the disciples had asked Jesus to teach them how to pray, a request followed by what we call the "Lord's Prayer" (Luke 11:2 – 4; cf. Matt 6:9 – 13). We may assume that in v. 14 the apostles practice what they have learned from Jesus, praying with God's priorities, i.e., without being narrowly introspective.

Followers of Jesus pray that God may act in the world in such a manner, through his people, that others may come to honor him as God (first petition). They pray that God's kingly rule might be manifest and effective in the hearts and minds of people throughout the world (second petition). They pray that God's will might be done by people who do not yet acknowledge and obey that will at present (third petition, in Matt 6). They pray that God may provide for their everyday needs (third petition in Luke 11). They pray that God will forgive their sins, in accordance with the forgiveness they extend to others (fourth petition). They pray with the realization that times of testing will come in which they might respond with unbelief or in which their faith is proven to be genuine, with the admission of human weakness and yet with the unconditional trust in God's will and grace. For church leaders and for the church as a whole, prayer is not a duty — it is a joyful privilege; it is not a chore that can be taken care of by one-liners between praise songs, but a passionate desire for the presence of God.

CHAPTER 2

Acts 1:15 – 26

Literary Context

The second major section of Acts consists of two sections: the first describes the identity and witness of Jesus' followers as God's people (1:15 – 2:47), and the second describes the life, witness, trials, and growth of the church in Jerusalem (3:1 – 8:3).

The first section has three episodes — the reconstitution of the Twelve (1:15 – 26); the coming of the Spirit at Pentecost, with a sermon of Peter and a report concerning the conversion of three thousand Jews (2:1 – 41); and a summary of the life of the Jerusalem community of believers in Jesus (2:42 – 47).

After narrating Jesus' ascension, Luke relates how Matthias was chosen as the twelfth apostle, replacing Judas Iscariot, who had committed suicide (1:15 – 26). The episode consists of four incidents: (1) Peter's initiative regarding the reconstitution of the group of the Twelve (1:15 – 22); (2) the nomination of two candidates (1:23); (3) the prayer of the believers before the decision (1:24 – 25); (4) the decision by the casting of lots and the integration of Matthias into the group of the Twelve (1:26).

This material has no parallels in Luke 24, which makes it the first full narrative section of Acts (acknowledging that 1:1 – 14 includes narrative). After squarely focusing on Jesus, who grants to his disciples the presence and power of the Holy Spirit, who has initiated the restoration of the kingdom to Israel, and who is sending his disciples to be his witnesses in Jerusalem and to the ends of the earth, Luke now turns his focus on the apostles.

The list of apostles in 1:13 had one apostle missing — Jesus had called twelve disciples; when Judas Iscariot had killed himself, there were only eleven. Since Jesus had called the Twelve as an identifiable group (Luke 6:12 – 16) to signal the reorganization and restoration of Israel (Luke 22:29 – 30) that the prophets had predicted for the last days, and since Luke relates in Acts how Jesus restores the kingdom to Israel through his witnesses, the election of Matthias is both a necessity and a key event before the Twelve begin their ministry of preaching and teaching as Jesus' witnesses (which begins in Acts 2).

This reconstitution of the Twelve is not caused by administrative requirements or organizational pressures — such questions become relevant only in Acts 6, when the church of Jerusalem had grown considerably. Rather, this reconstitution, narrated between the commission to missionary ministry as Jesus' witnesses (1:8) and the beginning of missionary proclamation before Israel on the day of Pentecost (2:1 – 42), is part of God's plan (1:16, 20, 22), who is restoring the kingdom to Israel (1:6 – 8); and it is a necessity as the witnesses of Jesus' life, death, and resurrection have been commissioned to proclaim the good news of Jesus from Jerusalem to the ends of the earth (1:8, 22).

The election of Matthias fulfills Scripture (1:16 – 20), is accompanied by prayer (1:24), and is the direct result of the revelation of God's will, as seen in the casting of lots (1:26). The suggestion that Matthias's election was premature since Paul, who was converted later, should have been chosen as the twelfth apostle, misses the point that Paul did not meet the qualifications for witnesses of Jesus' life (1:21 – 22). The argument that Matthias is never again mentioned in Acts ignores the fact that with the exception of Peter, James, and John, none of the other apostles is mentioned in Acts either. Since Luke's narrative in Acts is selective (see the Introduction), he would have omitted the account in 1:15 – 26 if he had found it to be embarrassing.

I. Jesus' Exaltation and the Commission of the Apostles (1:1 – 14)

→ **II. The Beginnings of the New People of God (1:15 – 8:3)**

    A. The Identity and Witness of Jesus' Followers as God's People (1:15 – 2:47)

        6. The reconstitution of the Twelve; Peter's speech (1:15 – 26)

        7. The arrival of the Holy Spirit and the identity of Jesus as Israel's Messiah and Lord (2:1 – 41)

Main Idea

The reconstitution of the Twelve through the election of Matthias underscores the identity of the community of Jesus' followers as the people of God as a manifestation of the restoration of the kingdom to Israel, and it emphasizes the mission of the church, whose leaders are commissioned to be witnesses of Jesus' life, death, and resurrection.

Translation

(See next page.)

Acts 1:15 – 26

15a	Setting: time	During these days
b	Action	**Peter stood up**
c	Social/Place	in the midst of the brothers
d	Action	**and said**
e	Parenthesis	—the group of people gathered together numbered about a hundred ⏎ and twenty—
16a	Address	"Brothers and sisters,
b	Assertion	that Scripture had to be fulfilled
c	Description	which the Holy Spirit spoke in advance through David
d	Character entrance	concerning Judas,
e	Character description	who became the guide of those who ⏎ who arrested Jesus.
17a	Review of history	For he belonged to our number
b	Event	and received a share in our ministry.
18a	Action	He acquired a piece of land with the money paid for his wicked deed,
b	Event	and after having fallen headlong,
c	Event	he burst open in the middle
d	Result	and all his entrails spilled out.
19a	Event	This became known to all the inhabitants of Jerusalem,
b	Result	so that the field came to be called in their own language Akeldama,
c	Translation	which means 'Field of blood.'
20a	Explanation	For it is written in the book of Psalms,
b	Quotation of OT	'Let his homestead become desolate, and
c		let nobody dwell in it,' and
d		'Let someone else take his assignment' (Pss 69:25; 109:8).
21a	Conclusion	Therefore it is necessary that
b	Suggestion	one of the men . . .
c	Association	who accompanied us during the entire time
d	Setting: time	while the Lord Jesus went in and out among us,
22a	Setting: time	from the beginning of the baptism of John
b	Setting: time	until the day when he was taken up from us,
c	Task	. . . becomes with us a witness to his resurrection."
23a	Action	**They nominated two men,**
b	Character entrance	Joseph
	Identification	called Barsabbas,
c	Identification	also known as Justus, and
d	Character entrance	Matthias.
24a	Action	**They prayed,**
b	Prayer/assertion	'Lord, you know the hearts of all people;
c	Petition	show us which one of these two men you have chosen
25a	Purpose	to receive the position of ministry and apostleship
b	Reason	from which Judas deviated to go to his own place."
26a	Action	**They cast lots for them,**
b	Result	**and the lot fell on Matthias;**
c	Action	**and he was added to the eleven apostles.**

Structure and Literary Form

Luke's account of the reconstitution of the Twelve in 1:15 – 26 is made up of four incidents. (1) Peter takes the initiative among the eleven disciples and the 120 followers of Jesus to propose electing a twelfth apostle to replace Judas. His speech (1:15 – 22) outlines three steps: (a) Judas's demise and the fulfillment of Scripture (vv. 16 – 20); (b) scriptural proof, with the quotation of Ps 69:25 and Ps 109:8 (v. 20); (c) the necessity of reconstituting the Twelve (vv. 21 – 22). (2) Two candidates who meet these criteria are nominated: Joseph and Matthias (1:23). (3) The believers pray for God's guidance (1:24 – 25). (4) They cast lots and Matthias is added to the Twelve (1:26).

The passage contains *narrative* (1:15, 23, 26), a *speech* (1:16 – 22), *scriptural interpretation* (1:16, 20), and a *prayer* (1:24 – 25). The speech in 1:16 – 22 is Peter's first speech.

IN DEPTH: Peter's Speeches

Luke relates eleven speeches of Peter. Their audiences, localities, and geographical locations are as follows.

Speech	Passage	Recipient(s)	Location	City
1	1:15 – 22	Believers: 120 people	Upper room	Jerusalem
2	2:14 – 36	Jews: several thousand	Street (Temple complex?)	Jerusalem
3	2:37 – 40	Jews: several thousand	Street (Temple complex?)	Jerusalem
4	3:4 – 6	Jew: beggar	Beautiful Gate of the Temple	Jerusalem
5	3:11 – 26	Jews: crowd	Solomon's Portico in the Temple	Jerusalem
6	4:5 – 22	Jews: aristocrats	Sanhedrin	Jerusalem
7	5:3 – 10	Believers: Ananias, Sapphira	Solomon's Portico (?)	Jerusalem
8	5:27 – 33	Jews: aristocrats	Sanhedrin	Jerusalem
9	10:34 – 43	Gentile God-fearer: Cornelius	Barracks	Caesarea
10	11:1 – 18	Believers	Solomon's Portico (?)	Jerusalem
11	15:7 – 11	Believers	Solomon's Portico (?)	Jerusalem

Exegetical Outline

➡ **I. The Reconstitution of the Twelve (1:15 – 26)**

    A. Peter's Initiative regarding the Reconstitution of the Twelve (1:15 – 22)

        1. Peter's initiative (1:15a-d)

        2. The presence of 120 believers (1:15e)

        3. Peter's speech (1:16 – 22)

            a. Address (1:16a)

            b. Judas's fate and Scripture (1:16b – 19)

                i. The necessity of the fulfillment of Scripture (1:16b-c)

                ii. The involvement of Judas in Jesus' arrest (1:16d-e)

                iii. The inclusion of Judas among the Twelve (1:17)

                iv. The demise of Judas (1:18 – 19)

            c. Scriptural proof (1:20)

                i. Quotation from Ps 69:25 (1:20a-c)

                ii. Quotation from Ps 109:8 (1:20d)

            d. The necessity of the reconstitution of the Twelve (1:21 – 22)

                i. The necessity of replacing Judas (1:21a)

                ii. The criteria for a member of the Twelve (1:21b – 22)

    B. Nomination of Joseph Barsabbas and Matthias (1:23)

        1. Nomination of two men (1:23a)

        2. Nomination of Joseph Barsabbas (1:23b-c)

        3. Nomination of Matthias (1:23d)

    C. Prayer of the Assembled Believers for God's Guidance (1:24 – 25)

        1. Acknowledgment of God's omniscience (1:24a-b)

        2. Petition that God may reveal his choice of the man to be one of the Twelve (1:24c)

        3. Recognition of the purpose of the ministry of the Twelve (1:25)

    D. Election of Matthias by Lot and Reconstitution of the Twelve (1:26)

        1. Casting of lots (1:26a)

        2. Choice of Matthias (1:26b)

        3. Inclusion of Matthias among the Twelve (1:26c)

Explanation of the Text

1:15 During these days Peter stood up in the midst of the brothers and said — the group of people gathered together numbered about a hundred and twenty (καὶ ἐν ταῖς ἡμέραις ταύταις ἀναστὰς Πέτρος ἐν μέσῳ τῶν ἀδελφῶν εἶπεν· ἦν τε ὄχλος ὀνομάτων ἐπὶ τὸ αὐτὸ ὡσεὶ ἑκατὸν εἴκοσι). The "days" that Luke refers to is the period between Jesus' ascension (v. 22) and the coming of the Holy Spirit on the day of Pentecost (2:1). Peter takes the initiative in reconstituting the group of the Twelve. He acts here for the first time as the leader of the apostles and of the community of Jesus' followers. Luke does not relate Jesus' words regarding Peter's role as the "rock" on which he will build his new community (Matt 16:17 – 19; cf. Luke 9:18 – 20), but Peter's initiative and action in 1:15 – 26 indicate that this is exactly the role he fulfills. He plays a leading role in the life of the Jerusalem church and in missionary outreach in Judea and Samaria until he is forced to leave the city in AD 41 (12:17). After having denied Jesus (Luke 22:21 – 31, 54 – 62), he does precisely what Jesus had told him to do (Luke 22:32): he strengthens his brothers.

Luke makes a parenthetical remark to inform the reader that about 120 people[1] were present when Matthias was added to the Twelve. The search for a symbolical meaning of this figure has been unsuccessful. Not convincing either is the suggestion that this figure represents a local sanhedrin[2] — Luke explicitly states this is an approximate number (ὡσεί). These 120 disciples are presumably all who saw Jesus after his resurrection. How many of them belonged to the group of 500 to whom Jesus appeared on one occasion (1 Cor 15:6), we do not know.

IN DEPTH: Peter

Peter is the leading apostle, especially in the first half of Acts. He is mentioned as the first disciple in the apostle list in 1:13, a fact that indicates his leadership position. Peter took the initiative in the matter of the vacancy in the group of the Twelve after Judas's demise (1:15). At Pentecost, Peter was the spokesman of the 120 followers of Jesus, explaining the events connected with the coming of the promised Holy Spirit. He spontaneously called on the listeners to repent and be baptized in the name of Jesus the Messiah (2:14, 37 – 38).

Peter was instrumental in healing a lame man begging at the Beautiful Gate of the temple. When people excitedly congregated in Solomon's Portico, Peter explained the good news about Jesus (3:11 – 26). He was arrested in the temple, together with John; when brought before the Sanhedrin on the next morning, he explained before the "leaders of the people and elders" the message of Jesus the Messiah that he had proclaimed in the temple (4:3, 8 – 12).

---

1. Here, ὄνομα means "person" (BDAG, s.v. ὄνομα); cf. Rev 3:4; 11:13.

2. According to *m. Sanh.* 1:6, 120 residents were required in a town to have a sanhedrin (council).

When Ananias and Sapphira, a Christian couple who belonged to the community of Jesus' followers, wanted to manipulate the church through false information concerning their charitable giving, Peter was the apostle who dealt with this serious matter (5:2, 3, 8). He performed extraordinary miracles in Jerusalem (5:15), so that news about the community of believers in Jesus spread to the surrounding region and towns (5:16). When the apostles were arrested again (5:18), Peter was again the spokesman (5:29).

When the apostles received news of the conversion of large numbers of Samaritans resulting from the missionary work of Philip, the community in Jerusalem sent Peter and John to Samaria to consolidate the new believers (8:14). Peter engaged in missionary work in the cities of the coastal plain (9:32) and in the plain of Sharon, where many people were converted (9:35). During a visit to believers in Lydda, believers in Joppa called Peter after a Christian woman named Dorcas had passed away (9:38).

In Joppa, Peter received a revelation from God, who instructed him that Gentiles who had been converted to believe in Jesus the Messiah should be admitted to the community of the people of God without practicing halakic rules of purity (10:9 – 18). Peter played a major role in the conversion of Cornelius, a Roman centurion in Caesarea (10:24 – 48). When the Jerusalem church asked Peter to explain his conduct in Caesarea, where he had baptized Cornelius and stayed in his house, he defended his behavior and the admission of Gentiles into the church, referring to the revelation he had received from God and to the reception of the Holy Spirit that the converted Gentiles had experienced (11:1 – 18).

Herod Agrippa I arrested Peter in AD 41; Herod wanted to execute him in order to please the Jews in Jerusalem (12:3). After his miraculous escape from prison, Peter left Jerusalem and went to "another place" (12:17), which Luke does not specify. On the occasion of the Apostles' Council (AD 48), when the debate was heating up, Peter took the floor and reminded the believers that God had used him in the early days of the church to take the gospel to the Gentiles, without requiring them to become Jews (15:7).

1:16 "Brothers and sisters, that Scripture had to be fulfilled which the Holy Spirit spoke in advance through David concerning Judas, who became the guide of those who arrested Jesus" (ἄνδρες ἀδελφοί, ἔδει πληρωθῆναι τὴν γραφὴν ἣν προεῖπεν τὸ πνεῦμα τὸ ἅγιον διὰ στόματος Δαυὶδ περὶ Ἰούδα τοῦ γενομένου ὁδηγοῦ τοῖς συλλαβοῦσιν

Ἰησοῦν). Peter begins his speech to the assembled believers about the demise of Judas and the necessity to elect a twelfth apostle with the statement that it was necessary (ἔδει) for Scripture to be fulfilled. This emphasis, supported in v. 20 by the quotation of Ps 69:25 and 109:8, underscores the conviction that Judas's involvement in Jesus' arrest and death was an integral part of God's will and plan.

If Peter's address "brothers" (ἀδελφοί) refers to the entire community of followers of Jesus, which is likely, the women of v. 14 are included (hence "brothers and sisters").[3] When Jews address fellow Jews as "brothers,"[4] they express the conviction that they are all descendants of Abraham and thus belong to the same "family" of people. In Acts, the term "brothers" is often used for fellow Christians, both male and female,[5] expressing the conviction that they belong to the one family of God's reconstituted people.

Scripture[6] represents the words of the Holy Spirit,[7] and that means God's own words. As the Word of God, Scripture reveals God's will for his people for the present and for the future. What God says will certainly happen. The reference to the "speaking" (προεῖπεν) of Scripture should be understood in the context of Scripture being read aloud in the synagogues (and in the Christian communities), so that the assembled people of God "hear" the words of God. As regards the specific texts that Peter will quote, he asserts that the Holy Spirit spoke "through the mouth" (thus lit.) of David, who was traditionally regarded as the author of the Psalms.[8] Peter (and Luke) was convinced that a particular passage in Scripture is

the utterance of the Holy Spirit, who used a human agent to speak the Word of God.

The Scripture passage that Peter refers to here is quoted later in v. 20 (i.e., Pss 69:25 and 109:8). Peter's use of Scripture can be understood in two ways. First, Peter uses the principle of *qal wahomer* (lit., "the light and the heavy"), i.e., the inference from the lighter (less significant) to the weightier (more significant), and vice versa (Lat., *a minori ad maius*).[9] He applies what David said in the Psalms about wrongdoers generally to Judas specifically.[10]

Second, Peter found a specific prophecy about Judas in the Psalms, which was appropriate since David was regarded as a prophet (cf. 2:30 – 31) and since Jesus had applied the psalms to himself.[11] Luke had related in Luke 22:47 how Judas had literally become a "guide" (ὁδηγός)[12] for "the chief priests, the officers of the temple guard, and the elders, who had come for him" (22:52).

1:17 For he belonged to our number and received a share in our ministry (ὅτι κατηριθμημένος ἦν ἐν ἡμῖν καὶ ἔλαχεν τὸν κλῆρον τῆς διακονίας ταύτης). Peter explains how a vacancy came about among the Twelve. Judas had been included in that group (cf. the disciple lists in Matt 10:2 – 4; Mark 3:16 – 19; Luke 6:13 – 16 — always in the last position). Judas Iscariot probably came from a place called Kariot

---

3. Thus NRSV translates ἀδελφοί as "friends." This translation, while materially correct, eliminates the connotation of "family," which the term has here. Note 1:22, where σὺν ἡμῖν refers to the Twelve.

4. Cf. Acts 2:29; 3:17; 7:2, 26; 13:26, 38; 23:1, 5, 6; 28:17.

5. Acts 1:16; 9:30; 10:23; 11:1, 12, 29; 12:17; 14:2; 15:3, 22, 32, 33, 40; 17:6, 10, 14; 18:18, 27; 21:7, 17, 20; 28:14, 15; cf. 15:7, 13, 23.

6. The term translated as "Scripture" (γραφή) refers either to Scripture as a whole (cf. 8:32; the plural αἱ γραφαί is usually used in this sense; cf. Luke 24:27, 32, 45; Acts 17:2, 11; 18:24, 28), or to a particular passage of Scripture (8:35).

7. Cf. Acts 4:25; 28:25; also Heb 3:7; 1 Pet 1:11.

8. Cf. Luke 20:42; Acts 2:24; 4:25; Rom 4:6; Heb 4:7. For "mouth" (στόμα) in the instrumental sense cf. Luke 1:70; Acts

3:18, 21; 4:25; 15:7; cf. Isa 51:16; 59:21; Jer 1:9; Zech 8:9.

9. For Hillel's exegetical rules, among them *qal wahomer*, cf. *t. Sanh.* 7:11; *Abot R. Nat.* 37.10. Cf. Hermann L. Strack and Günter Stemberger, *Introduction to the Talmud and Midrash* (Minneapolis: Fortress, 1992), 16 – 20; David Instone-Brewer, *Techniques and Assumptions in Jewish Exegesis before 70 CE* (TSAJ 30; Tübingen: Mohr Siebeck, 1992), 17 – 23, 226.

10. Richard Longenecker, *Biblical Exegesis in the Apostolic Period* (2nd ed.; Grand Rapids: Eerdmans, 1999), 81.

11. Larkin, *Acts*, 46; cf. Bock, *Acts*, 82, who calls this the "typological-prophetic manner" of applying Scripture.

12. In Luke 22:47 the verb προέρχομαι is used, which means "to precede as a leader/guide, *go before*" (BDAG, s.v. προέρχομαι 2).

(Tell Qirioth in the Negev? or Askaroth near Shechem?).[13] He was the treasurer of the Twelve (John 12:6; 13:29), which means he was regarded as competent in money matters. Like the other eleven disciples, he was called and sent by Jesus "to proclaim the kingdom of God and to heal" (Luke 9:2), and like them he had been given by Jesus a "kingdom" and was appointed as a judge of "the twelve tribes of Israel" (Luke 22:29 – 30). This was the "share" or "lot" (κλῆρος) that the Twelve had received, which is here described as "service" (τῆς διακονίας is partitive genitive), i.e., the task of "functioning in the interest of a larger public."[14]

Luke describes the "ministry" of the Twelve in 6:4 as a "ministry of the word" (διακονία τοῦ λόγου), that is, preaching of the word of God concerning Jesus, Israel's Messiah and Savior. This corresponds to the call of the Twelve as followers of Jesus (Luke 9:2), whose witnesses they are (Acts 1:22). Their "ministry" or "service" is the commission to proclaim the arrival of God's kingdom in Jesus' life, death, resurrection, and exaltation.

Judas finally proved to be dishonest (cf. John 12:4 – 6; 13:19). Luke emphasizes that Judas was under the influence of Satan when he betrayed Jesus (Luke 22:3; cf. John 13:2).[15] This had happened only a few weeks earlier, and despite the explanation that Peter provides, the disciples still might have been in shock that one of their friends had betrayed Jesus and then committed suicide. It is precisely because of these two realities — Judas was numbered among the Twelve, and he had had a share in the ministry — that his place among the Twelve had to be filled after his demise.

1:18 He acquired a piece of land with the money paid for his wicked deed, and after having fallen headlong, he burst open in the middle and all his entrails spilled out (οὗτος μὲν οὖν ἐκτήσατο χωρίον ἐκ μισθοῦ τῆς ἀδικίας καὶ πρηνὴς γενόμενος ἐλάκησεν μέσος καὶ ἐξεχύθη πάντα τὰ σπλάγχνα αὐτοῦ). Luke's description of the outcome of Judas's betrayal in vv. 18 – 19 focuses entirely on Judas. Some regard this description as a parenthetical insertion by Luke into Peter's speech. Matthew's fuller version of the events (Matt 26:14 – 15; 27:3 – 10) focuses on the Jewish leadership and their involvement in the arrest of Jesus; he relates that Judas repented,[16] threw the money (thirty pieces of silver) in the temple before committing suicide by hanging, while the priests used the money to purchase the "field of blood." Luke does not report what the priests were doing; he is mostly interested in Judas's horrible fate. The assertion in v. 18 that Judas acquired a piece of land may simply mean that it was Judas's money that bought the plot of land with the gruesome name (v. 19). Matthew relates that the priests used Judas's money "to buy the potter's field as a burial place for foreigners" (Matt 27:7). To buy a cemetery that is ritually unclean with money that is ritually unclean is rather appropriate.[17]

Luke describes Judas's death in horrific terms. The adjective πρηνής means "forward, head first, headlong" and appears to describe a fall that re-

13. On Judas Iscariot cf. Meier, *Marginal Jew*, 3:141 – 45, 208 – 12.

14. BDAG, s.v. διακονία 3. Cf. Anni Hentschel, *Diakonia im Neuen Testament* (WUNT 2/226; Tübingen: Mohr Siebeck, 2007), 298 – 318.

15. William Klassen, *Judas: Betrayer or Friend of Jesus?* (Minneapolis: Fortress, 1996), suggests that Judas was not a failure — he handed Jesus over to the Jewish authorities, with Jesus' full knowledge and consent, contributing to the final ful-

fillment and realization of Jesus' mission. This view cannot be verified exegetically, nor is it historically plausible.

16. On the possibility that Judas's repentance was genuine, cf. William D. Davies and Dale C. Allison, *The Gospel According to Saint Matthew* (ICC; Edinburgh: T&T Clark, 1988 – 97), 3:561 – 62; John Nolland, *The Gospel of Matthew* (NIGTC; Grand Rapids: Eerdmans, 2005), 1152 – 53.

17. Cf. Nolland, *Matthew*, 1154.

sulted in his body "bursting apart" or "bursting open" (λακάω) in the middle, with all the "inward parts" (τὰ σπλάγχνα), particularly the viscera, spilling out.[18] The gruesome detail is probably meant to elicit in the reader the conclusion that God brought judgment on Judas because of his wicked deed.

1:19 This became known to all the inhabitants of Jerusalem, so that the field came to be called in their own language Akeldama, which means "Field of blood" (καὶ γνωστὸν ἐγένετο πᾶσι τοῖς κατοικοῦσιν Ἰερουσαλήμ ὥστε κληθῆναι τὸ χωρίον ἐκεῖνο τῇ ἰδίᾳ διαλέκτῳ αὐτῶν Ἀκελδαμάχ, τοῦτ᾽ ἔστιν χωρίον αἵματος). The story of Judas's demise was well-known among the citizens of Jerusalem. What precisely was known is unclear: either how Judas died or the purchase of a cemetery with the money from his betrayal.

The field purchased was the one in which his body had burst apart. Whether he had bought the field himself or the priests had bought it with the money Judas returned, Judas, in despair over his betrayal, committed suicide in a field in which foreigners were buried (Matt 27:7).

The name of the field Judas acquired and on which he died was called Akeldama (Ἀκελδαμάχ, transliteration of an Aramaic word), which translates in Greek as "field of blood" (χωρίον αἵματος). Tradition localizes the "field of blood" where the Kidron, Tyropoeon, and Hinnom valleys meet, a location that can be linked with the activity of potters (suitable clay) and had been a place for burial

(2 Kgs 23:6; Jer 26:23).[19] The traditional site is near the Greek Orthodox monastery of St. Onuphrius, built in the nineteenth century at a site where tombs from the Herodian period have been discovered, among them the tomb of the high priest Annas.

1:20 For it is written in the book of Psalms, "Let his homestead become desolate, and let nobody dwell in it," and "Let someone else take his assignment" (γέγραπται γὰρ ἐν βίβλῳ ψαλμῶν· γενηθήτω ἡ ἔπαυλις αὐτοῦ ἔρημος καὶ μὴ ἔστω ὁ κατοικῶν ἐν αὐτῇ, καί· τὴν ἐπισκοπὴν αὐτοῦ λαβέτω ἕτερος). If vv. 18 – 19 is indeed a Lukan parenthesis, Peter's quotation of Pss 69:25 and 109:8 focuses not on Judas's suicide but on the vacancy in the group of the Twelve and on the need to replace him. The first quotation is from Ps 69:25 (LXX 68:26). Psalm 69 is "a psalm of protest and plea" closing with a declaration of trust in Yahweh.[20] The psalmist pleads with God not as a private individual but as representing a community under attack by people with a different spiritual commitment. He prays that God may bring his wrath against these enemies and remove them from the community. John and Paul used the psalm as a typological prediction of Jesus' suffering (John 2:17; 15:25; Rom 15:3), and Paul applies it to the Jews who rejected Jesus (Rom 11:9 – 10).[21]

Since Judas had joined Jesus' enemies, Ps 69 could be applied to him. The term translated "homestead" (ἔπαυλις) can be understood as a

---

18. According to Matt 27:5, Judas "hanged" himself (ἀπάγχω). A long tradition has suggested that Judas hanged himself from a branch that then broke, resulting in a fall into the ravine, with messy results. Cf. Don A. Carson, "Matthew" (ed. F. E. Gaebelein; EBC 8; Grand Rapids: Zondervan, 1984), 562.

19. Yigael Yadin, *The Temple Scroll: The Hidden Law of the Dead Sea Sect* (New York: Random House, 1985), 134, notes that water carrying blood was drained from the temple into this area (11QTemple XXXII; *m. Meʿil.* 3:3; *m. Yoma* 5:6), and

suggests that "field of blood" was an already existing name to which Christian tradition gave a new meaning.

20. John Goldingay, *Psalms* (Baker Commentary on the Old Testament Wisdom and Psalms; Grand Rapids: Baker, 2006 – 2008), 2:338; cf. ibid. for the following comment.

21. Martin C. Albl, *"And Scripture Cannot Be Broken." The Form and Function of the Early Christian Testimonia Collections* (NovTSup 96; Leiden: Brill, 1999), 199, concludes that Psalm 69 may have been part of an early Christian collection of *testimonia* from the Old Testament.

loose reference to the plot of land purchased by Judas. Peter uses the psalm as a scriptural prophecy of what happened when Judas betrayed Jesus and then fell to his death — what he had and what he owned became desolate. The quotation expresses a curse. In the context of Matt 27:7, it can literally refer to the burial place bought with Judas's money. Judas experienced the judgment that falls on the enemies of the righteous sufferer.

The second quotation is from Ps 109:8 (LXX 108:8). Psalm 109 is a prayer for vindication and vengeance. The psalmist describes one of his enemies, a wicked and deceitful man, and formulates a series of curses against him. The term translated "assignment" (ἐπισκοπή) denotes a "position of responsibility." The psalmist prays that the wicked man's days may be few (109:8a), i.e., that his life might be cut short, and that his position of leadership in the community may be given to somebody else (109:8b).

This second quotation expresses Peter's conviction that Judas, who "belonged to our number and received a share in our ministry" (v. 17) and whose life was cut short as he experienced God's judgment, needed to be replaced by another person who would take his place of leadership. In the context of Luke 22:30, Peter (Luke) may think specifically of the role of the Twelve as judges in the community of Israel.

1:21   Therefore it is necessary that one of the men who accompanied us during the entire time while the Lord Jesus went in and out among us (δεῖ οὖν τῶν συνελθόντων ἡμῖν ἀνδρῶν ἐν παντὶ χρόνῳ ᾧ εἰσῆλθεν καὶ ἐξῆλθεν ἐφ᾽ ἡμᾶς ὁ κύριος Ἰησοῦς). To Peter, the two Scripture passages warrant replacing Judas.[22] This statement formulates

the first two criteria for membership in the group of the Twelve: (1) Judas's replacement must be a man (ἀνήρ). (2) He must have been among Jesus' disciples along with the Twelve. According to Luke 6:13, Jesus was surrounded by a larger group of disciples from which he chose the Twelve. Peter clarifies the second criterion: the new member of the Twelve must have been an eyewitness of Jesus' ministry.

1:22   "From the beginning of the baptism of John until the day when he was taken up from us, becomes with us a witness to his resurrection" (ἀρξάμενος ἀπὸ τοῦ βαπτίσματος Ἰωάννου ἕως τῆς ἡμέρας ἧς ἀνελήμφθη ἀφ᾽ ἡμῶν μάρτυρα τῆς ἀναστάσεως αὐτοῦ σὺν ἡμῖν γενέσθαι ἕνα τούτων). The first Christians regarded the ministry of John the Baptist as the beginning of Jesus' work (cf. 10:36 – 41; 13:24 – 31). Note Luke 3:1 – 2, where Luke's only precise date is linked with the ministry of John the Baptist. Luke's formulation probably refers to the activity of John the Baptist in general terms, not specifically to the event of Jesus' baptism in the Jordan River (cf. Luke 3:21). The last event of Jesus' life and ministry was his ascension to the right hand of God, described by Luke in Acts 1:9 – 11.

(3) Peter formulates here the third criterion for membership in the Twelve, which at the same time describes the primary function and task that the Twelve have been given. The twelfth apostle must have encountered Jesus after his death and can thus attest his resurrection. The Twelve are Jesus' witnesses in Jerusalem and to the ends of the earth (1:8) in the sense that they are witnesses of his resurrection, who can testify concerning Jesus' vindication and who can thus explain the meaning of his

---

22. The phrase δεῖ οὖν formulates the necessity of being obedient to Scripture. Bock, *Acts*, 87, points out that while Peter does not exegete the two psalms in a modern sense, he

"takes the principle expressed in the psalm as a summary of how God acts and applies it to an event where God has judged."

life, ministry, death, resurrection, and exaltation. For "witness" (μάρτυς) see 1:8.

1:23 They nominated two men, Joseph called Barsabbas, also known as Justus, and Matthias (καὶ ἔστησαν δύο, Ἰωσὴφ τὸν καλούμενον Βαρσαββᾶν ὃς ἐπεκλήθη Ἰοῦστος, καὶ Μαθθίαν). The assembled followers of Jesus suggest two men, who may represent a short list from a larger group of candidates. The two nominees may have belonged to the seventy (or seventy-two) disciples appointed by Jesus (Luke 10:1).[23] The fact that none of Jesus' brothers, who were present (Acts 1:14), was nominated agrees with the information provided in John 7:5 that Jesus' brothers did not believe in him and thus did not accompany him throughout his ministry.

Two factors underscore the courage of the two candidates willing to be nominated for a place among the Twelve. First, Jesus had been killed only a few weeks earlier, and as the Twelve had been commissioned to be Jesus' witnesses in Jerusalem and beyond, it was a distinct possibility that they might share Jesus' fate. Second, Jesus had tasked the Twelve to be his witnesses in cities and regions beyond Judea and Samaria to the ends of the earth. They were to become involved in missionary ministry for which there were no precedents and no ready models in the first century.[24]

The first nomination was a believer named Joseph. Since Joseph was, like Simon, a popular male name among Palestinian Jews, nicknames were often added to distinguish him from other people with the same name (cf. "Joseph … called Barnabas" in 4:36). This Joseph was known by two other names. Barsabbas (Βαρσαββᾶς) is perhaps the Greek form of the Aramaic name "Son of Sabba," or it means "Son of the Sabbath," i.e., one born on the Sabbath,[25] or it means "son of the old man" (Aram. *sâbayyâ* means "someone with gray hair"), a nickname that suggests his father was already old when Joseph was born.[26] The name Justus (Ἰοῦστος) is the Greek form of the Latin name Iustus, a name used by Gentiles and Jews. The Latin alternative nickname might have been formulated in the Greco-Roman environment of Tiberias. It is also possible that the Latin name, which sounds similar to "Joseph," was adopted "because he became a traveling missionary outside Palestine."[27]

The second nominee was Matthias (Μαθθίας is the shortened form of Ματταθίας, Mattathias), which means "gift of Yahweh."[28]

1:24 They prayed, "Lord, you know the hearts of all people; show us which one of these two men you have chosen" (καὶ προσευξάμενοι εἶπαν· σὺ κύριε καρδιογνῶστα πάντων ἀνάδειξον ὃν ἐξελέξω ἐκ τούτων τῶν δύο ἕνα). The assembled believers turn to God when the time has come to decide between the two candidates for the position of the twelfth apostle. Their ongoing prayers (cf. 1:14) turn to a specific decision that must be made — a decision that in this case they cannot make on their own initiative, relying on their own wisdom.

---

23. This is what Eusebius, *Hist. eccl.* 1.12.3; 2.1.1 says concerning Matthias.

24. Cf. Schnabel, *Early Christian Mission*, 1:536 – 45; as regards the lack of evidence for a Jewish proselyte mission, cf. ibid. 92 – 172.

25. Margaret H. Williams, "Palestinian Jewish Personal Names in Acts," in *The Book of Acts in Its Palestinian Setting* (ed. R. Bauckham; The Book of Acts in Its First-Century Setting 4; Grand Rapids: Eerdmans, 1995), 79 – 113, 101 – 2.

26. Bauckham, *Eyewitnesses*, 81. Cf. Tal Ilan, *Lexicon of Jew-*

ish Names in Late Antiquity, part 1: *Palestine 330 BCE – 200 CE* (TSAJ 91; Tübingen: Mohr Siebeck, 2002), 396.

27. Richard J. Bauckham, "James and the Jerusalem Community," in *Jewish Believers in Jesus: The Early Centuries* (ed. O. Skarsaune and R. Hvalvik; Peabody: Hendrickson, 2007), 55 – 95, 85.

28. An apocryphal gospel was later attributed to him (the "Gospel according to Matthias"), only fragments of which survive. Cf. James K. Elliott, *The Apocryphal New Testament* (Oxford: Oxford Univ. Press, 1993), 19 – 20.

The address "Lord" (κύριε) may refer to Jesus, described in v. 2 as the one who had chosen the apostles and called "Lord Jesus" in v. 21.[29] More likely the believers address their prayer to God,[30] as he is called "God, who knows the human heart" (ὁ καρδιογνώστης) in 15:8, a title that reflects the Old Testament teaching about God's knowledge of the thoughts and motivations of the individual and about his foreknowledge.[31] The choice of who belongs to the Twelve can be made only by God, not by the assembled believers, as the original group of the twelve disciples had been made up not of volunteers but by men selected by Jesus. Thus the believers pray that God will reveal his choice.

1:25 "To receive the position of ministry and apostleship from which Judas deviated to go to his own place" (λαβεῖν τὸν τόπον τῆς διακονίας ταύτης καὶ ἀποστολῆς ἀφ᾽ ἧς παρέβη Ἰούδας πορευθῆναι εἰς τὸν τόπον τὸν ἴδιον). Judas's demise caused a vacancy in the Twelve, an open "place" or "position" (τόπος). The person whom God chooses will receive the "position" Judas has vacated; the aorist infinitive (λαβεῖν) indicates the purpose of God's choice. The phrase "ministry and apostleship" can be interpreted as a hendiadys (see 1:7). Authentic apostleship in the community of the followers of Jesus is ministry for others, and the fundamental service that the Twelve provide is the proclamation of the arrival of God's kingdom in Jesus' life, death, resurrection, and exaltation.

Nevertheless, "ministry" and "apostleship" are not synonyms. While "ministry" (διακονία)

speaks of the commission of the Twelve and of the actual execution of this commission, "apostleship" (ἀποστολή) denotes the sending (out) of the Twelve to people who need to hear the good news of Jesus, in Jerusalem, in Judea and Samaria, and to the ends of the earth. For "apostle" see on 1:2.

Judas had vacated the position of apostolic ministry when he betrayed Jesus and then committed suicide. The term "place" (τόπος) has a different meaning here than in v. 25a; here it describes Judas's destiny. He left the "place" that God through Jesus had chosen for him, to go to a "place" he himself had chosen. This "place" may be a euphemistic reference to Judas's demise, i.e., to the field bought with the money from his betrayal on which he found a horrific death (v. 18). Or the term "place" is a reference to hell, the place of perdition, suffering eternal judgment among the lost.[32] Or the phrase is a symbolic reference to Judas's abandonment of the Twelve symbolized by his purchase of a place with the money from his betrayal.[33]

1:26 They cast lots for them, and the lot fell on Matthias; and he was added to the eleven apostles (καὶ ἔδωκαν κλήρους αὐτοῖς καὶ ἔπεσεν ὁ κλῆρος ἐπὶ Μαθθίαν καὶ συγκατεψηφίσθη μετὰ τῶν ἕνδεκα ἀποστόλων). The ensuing action is narrated with three brief sentences. The syntax of the first sentence is intriguing. Luke does not use the normal word for "casting lots" (βάλλω), a term that reflects the usual method of casting lots — names were written on stones (or on other objects) and placed in a container, and one stone was allowed

---

29. Cf. David J. Williams, *Acts* (NIBC 5; Peabody, MA: Hendrickson, 1990), 34; Barrett, *Acts*, 103; cf. also Luke 6:13; John 6:70; 13:18; 15:16.

30. Barrett, *Acts*, 103; Fitzmyer, *Acts*, 227; Bock, *Acts*, 89.

31. Cf. 1 Sam 16:7, where God is described as "looking at the heart"; cf. Deut 8:2; 1 Kgs 8:39; 1 Chr 28:9; Ps 17:3; 94:11; 139:2; Jer 11:20; 17:10. Luke's use of the term καρδιογνώστης is the earliest attestation of the term in Greek literature; the term became popular in later Christian texts.

32. Cf. Tob 3:6; cf. *Tg. Eccles.* 6:6: on the day of one's death, the soul goes down to Gehinnom, the place where all the guilty go.

33. Johnson, *Acts*, 37. Pesch, *Apostelgeschichte*, 1:90 – 91, interprets it in terms of Judas taking his place among Jesus' enemies. Beverly R. Gaventa, *The Acts of the Apostles* (ANTC; Nashville: Abingdon, 2003), 70, interprets it in terms of apostasy.

to "fall" out (akin to throwing dice).[34] Luke's choice of δίδωμι, which means usually "give," and of the dative "for them" (αὐτοῖς, dative of advantage) has suggested to some that those present "gave their votes for them"; this then explains the verb "he was added" (συγκαταψηφίζομαι) in v. 26c. Luke seems to use loose language to describe the manner by which Judas's replacement was chosen, without indicating the precise method used.

The casting of lots to decide between several options was frequently used in Old Testament times[35] and in Judaism.[36] The lot was used "to reveal God's selection of someone or something out of several possibilities where he kept people in the dark and desired their impartiality in the selection."[37] The purpose of casting lots is expressed in Prov 16:33: "The lot is cast into the lap, but its every decision is from the LORD."[38] It may be argued that Luke's emphasis on the apostles' and believers' unanimity implies that the assembled disciples could have surely decided which candidate was more suited to take his place among the Twelve. If this was the case, the method of casting lots was introduced to ensure that Judas's replacement is decided not by human deliberation but by divine appointment.[39]

Whatever the precise method of casting lots was, Matthias was indicated. This casting of lots is often contrasted with the immediately following account of the coming of the Holy Spirit on the apostles and believers, who thus no longer needed this "mechanistic" manner of determining the will of God.[40] Three factors should be considered, however. (1) The casting of lots was a divinely sanctioned manner of determining God's will used for centuries in Israel. (2) Luke could have omitted the detail of the manner of Matthias's selection if he had regarded casting lots as an inappropriate method for the church. (3) The presence of the Holy Spirit does not necessarily make decisions easier, unless there is a direct prophecy about what action should be taken. In other words, the Jerusalem believers did not act in unbelief but used an entirely proper procedure to ask the Lord to make his choice among the two candidates.

The apostles, together with the assembled believers, accepted the result of the casting of lots as the expression of God's will. Matthias was "chosen together with"[41] the eleven apostles; i.e., he was added to the eleven, so that the group of the Twelve was restored. Thereupon, the apostles again symbolized Jesus' claim and promise to restore the kingdom to Israel, an event and a process in which they were given the task of being Jesus' witnesses to testify to the life, death, resurrection, and exaltation of Jesus.

---

34. Josephus, *Ant.* 6.62; Livy 23.3.7; cf. Barrett, *Acts*, 105.

35. Cf. Lev 16:8; Josh 23:4; 1 Chr 6:65; 25:8 – 9; 26:13 – 14; Neh 10:34; 11:1; Isa 34:17; Jonah 1:7. Cf. the priestly Urim and Thummim, Exod 28:30; Num 27:21; Deut 33:8.

36. 1QS V, 3; VI, 16, 18, 22; *m. Tamid* 1:2; 3:1; *m. Yoma* 3:9; 4:1. For the Greek and Roman practice, see the casting of lots over Jesus' clothes; Matt 27:35; Mark 15:24; Luke 23:34; John 19:24.

37. Bruce K. Waltke, *The Book of Proverbs* (NICOT; Grand Rapids: Eerdmans, 2004/2005), 2:37.

38. T. W. Cartledge, "Lots," *NIDB*, 3:702, suggests that the practice described in Prov 16:33 appears to require a flat object with different markings on each side, "something akin to flipping a coin."

39. John Calvin, *The Acts of the Apostles* (2 vols.; 1965; repr., Calvin's New Testament Commentaries; Grand Rapids: Eerdmans, 1995), 1:45.

40. Barrett, *Acts*, 104; cf. Ajith Fernando, *Acts* (NIVAC; Grand Rapids: Zondervan, 1998), 79.

41. BDAG, s.v. συγκαταψηφίζομαι, translates this rare verb as "be chosen (by a vote) together with," or generally "be added." The term ψῆφος denotes the "pebble" with which people cast their vote.

Theology in Application

The central theme of this passage is the identity and mission of the church. As Jesus initiated the restoration of Israel and her kingdom, a claim and a promise symbolized by the call of twelve disciples, the ministry of the Twelve establishes the new people of God as the people of the Messiah. Just as Jesus commissioned the Twelve to be witnesses of his life, death, resurrection, and exaltation, the ministry of the Twelve consists in proclaiming the good news of Jesus to people in Jerusalem and beyond to the ends of the earth.

The passage is not about apostasy and suicide, or decision making, or the radical nature of forgiveness, although these three themes are present in the text. A discussion about whether Christian believers can fall from grace is more profitably based on other texts (e.g., Rom 8:31 – 39; Heb 6:1 – 12); the eternal fate of Judas is not explicitly expressed in Acts 1.

As regards suicide, the case of Judas Iscariot seems to have been the main reason for the negative moral evaluation of suicide among Christians, in particular the view that suicide is an unforgivable sin. It may thus be impossible to teach this text without commenting on suicide.[42] Taking human life is an attack on God, who created human life. It is not surprising that the Old Testament does not sanction suicide. The earliest surviving condemnation of suicide in Second Temple Judaism comes from Josephus, who rejects Greco-Roman views of the nobility of suicide (*J. W.* 3:369).[43] There is one passage in rabbinic literature in which the suicide of the repentant Alcimus, who had massacred sixty innocent Hasidim (cf. 1 Macc 7:12 – 18), atones for his sins and provides entry into paradise (*Gen. Rab.* on 27:27). Some scholars take Judas's repentance related by Matthew (Matt 27:4) as genuine repentance,[44] no less authentic than the change of heart of Peter, who had denied Jesus (Matt 26:75); they argue that "Judas is not restored in life as are Peter and the other disciples, but, more than likely, Matthew fully expected him to be restored beyond life."[45] But Luke does not include Acts 1:15 – 26 in order to make a statement about suicide.

Neither is the passage about decision making in the church, or more particularly about choosing leaders in church.[46] There are other texts in Scripture that help us formulate principles of decision making, such as the Wisdom literature in the Old Testament or Paul's texts about leaders in the church. Surely prayer, fellowship, con-

---

42. For the modern discussion about suicide see John F. Kilner and C. Ben Mitchell, *Does God Need Our Help? Cloning, Assisted Suicide, and Other Challenges in Bioethics* (Wheaton: Tyndale, 2003).

43. Josephus has a different take on the mass suicide at Masada in AD 73 (*J. W.* 7.325).

44. Judas's suicide may then not be the desperate act of an unrepentant sinner but the act of taking on himself the sort

of punishment that was meted out to people who caused the death of innocent people — a punishment that he may have asked the priests for, who refused his request (which would have implicated them also; see Matt 27:4).

45. Nolland, *Matthew*, 1153.

46. On 1:15 – 26 in terms of decision making, cf. Luke Timothy Johnson, *Scripture and Discernment: Decision Making in the Church* (Nashville: Abingdon, 1996), 83 – 84.

sultation with other Christians, and interpretation of Scripture are necessary and helpful when Christians make decisions. But this is not the point of the text. In vv. 15 – 26, the "one who knows the hearts" is neither Peter nor the interview committee, but God himself. While interviews, recommendations, and personality profiles may be helpful, they still can fail to reveal what is in the heart.[47] The fact that Luke never mentions the casting of lots again in his account of the life and mission of the church does not prove that he denigrates it. He describes the communication of God's will to Christian believers in a multitude of ways, none of which appear to be normative.[48]

When some commentators point out that Christians now have the Holy Spirit to help them make decisions, they generally fail to answer the question of precisely how the Holy Spirit reveals the will of God. Personal impressions, even dreams and visions, are surely not a foolproof manner of determining the course of action that is God's will. Democratic decisions by majority vote can be arbitrary as well. As the casting of lots can be misused in superstitious ways, so can other approaches to establishing God's will. But again, the text in Acts 1:15 – 26 does not focus on decision making in the church.

Peter's leadership role, which is on display in this scene, presupposes Peter's repentance over his denial of Jesus and Jesus' forgiveness. The last time Luke had mentioned Peter in his two-volume work, it was in the connection of discovering the empty tomb (Luke 24:12) and, prior to that, Peter's denial of Jesus in the courtyard of the high priest's house (Luke 22:34, 54, 55, 58, 60, 61). Although Luke does not include a text such as John 21:15 – 19, he clearly implies that Peter had repented of his denial and that Jesus had forgiven him, taking him back as the leader of the apostles. But Acts 1:15 – 26 does not address repentance and forgiveness.

The text is about the identity of the community of the followers of Jesus as God's people, and about the mission of the task that consists in the witness to Jesus' life, death, resurrection, and exaltation.

The Identity of the Church as the People of God

The identity of the church as the people of God is tied to the Twelve as the symbolic representatives of Israel and of God's kingdom, which is now being restored. The identity of the Twelve is unique.[49] The criteria for filling the vacancy among the Twelve are unique qualifications: they were eyewitnesses of the life, death, resurrection, and exaltation of Jesus. The Twelve has a singular role for the church, which cannot be repeated. Once the restoration of the kingdom was well under way, the role of the

---

47. Fernando, *Acts*, 85.

48. Gaventa, *Acts*, 71.

49. Cf. Clark, "Role of the Apostles," 173 – 81; Peter Bolt,

"Mission and Witness," in *Witness to the Gospel: The Theology of Acts* (ed. I. H. Marshall and D. Peterson), 191 – 214, 196 – 202.

Twelve was fulfilled; when James, one of the Twelve, was killed in about AD 41 (12:2), Luke does not describe a replacement.

The church, the community of the followers of Jesus, is the people of God. The church, established by God's revelatory and saving activity in the work of Jesus and through the power of the Holy Spirit, is founded on the ministry and leadership of the Twelve.

The church, as the people of God, represents restored Israel, the fulfillment of the promised restoration of the kingdom of God, which was initiated by Jesus, empowered by the Holy Spirit, and manifested in the testimony of the Twelve.

The church will always seek the salvation of the Jewish people, as the apostles did in Jerusalem and in Judea and as Paul did in the synagogues of the diaspora. The church never gives up on the Jewish people. And the church will always read, study, and observe God's will as revealed in Israel's Scriptures.

The church is dependent on the apostolic Word that records the proclamation of the apostles and in and through which God has revealed himself. The church never moves beyond the normative witness of the apostles. Thus the church will always read, study, and observe the will of God as revealed in what Christians call the New Testament.

The Mission of the Church

The mission of the church is focused on the witness of Jesus. The Twelve speak about the life of the Lord Jesus. The focus on the resurrection in 1:22 is not restrictive, but entails the life, death, and exaltation of Jesus as well. Calvin explained it well:

> He names the resurrection, not because they are to bear witness to that alone, but because, firstly, in that is comprehended the preaching of the death of Christ, and secondly, we have in that the end and completion of our redemption; also it carries with it the heavenly authority of Christ and the power of the Spirit in protecting His own, in establishing justice and equity, in restoring order, in abolishing the tyranny of sin, and in putting to flight all the enemies of the Church.[50]

The life, death, resurrection, and exaltation of Jesus, Lord and Messiah, is the central, the primary, the dominant theme of the followers of Jesus. This is why the church eventually placed four long texts that narrate the life, suffering, death, and resurrection of Jesus at the beginning of the normative list of books to be read and taught in the church.

The material content of the proclamation of the church is Jesus Christ. The good news (*euangelion*) that the Twelve proclaim is the good news of God's revelatory and saving action in and through Jesus, the Lord and the Messiah. Paul passionately

---

agreed with this focus. He reminds the Christians in Corinth that when he preached in their city as a missionary, he did not use the traditional secular strategies of contemporary rhetoric to convince them to accept his message, "for I resolved to know nothing while I was with you except Jesus Christ and him crucified." Streamlined rhetoric and brilliant argumentation cannot convince people of the truth of the gospel; this is possible only if the Holy Spirit works in the hearts and minds of people, whose power can convince them of the truth of the gospel, because Christian faith rests "not on human wisdom, but on God's power" (1 Cor 2:1 – 5).

The formal content of the proclamation of the church is the testimony of the apostles. The Twelve had a unique role; as eyewitnesses of Jesus' life, death, resurrection, and exaltation, they testify to the truth of these foundational events in God's plan of salvation in an authentic and reliable manner. All subsequent generations of Christians are dependent on the testimony of these first witnesses.

The focus of the leaders of the church should not be on strategies, methods, and techniques, but on the person and work of Jesus Christ.

Acts 2:1 – 13

Literary Context

In 1:1 – 14, Luke had reported Jesus' promise that the apostles would receive the promised Holy Spirit in Jerusalem. Jesus, having overcome Satan in the desert, returned to Galilee "in the power of the Spirit" (Luke 4:14) and explained his mission in terms of effecting the fulfillment of God's promises to free Israel from her poverty, captivity, and blindness and to usher in "the year of the Lord's favor" (Luke 4:18 – 21). His proclamation had focused on the arrival of the kingdom of God, Yahweh's royal rule in Israel and in the world, which is being restored through his Messiah.

Before Jesus' promise of the coming of the Holy Spirit could become a reality, with all that this would entail for the restoration of Israel and the establishment of God's kingdom, the group of the Twelve had to be complete after Judas's demise (1:15 – 26). Now the Twelve are ready to do Jesus' work and to continue his mission. Thus, they and the other followers of Jesus are ready to receive God's Spirit and engage in their mission as Jesus' witnesses, a mission in which Jesus would continue to speak, teach, and act (1:1). The coming of the Holy Spirit in Acts 2 (after the introduction in Acts 1) corresponds to the position of Jesus' birth in Luke 2 (after the introduction to his birth in Luke 1).[1]

Luke's report about the coming of the Holy Spirit and the immediate aftermath (2:1 – 41) consists of five incidents: (1) the coming of the Holy Spirit at Pentecost (2:1 – 4); (2) the reaction of diaspora Jews living in Jerusalem (2:5 – 13); (3) Peter's speech on the day of Pentecost (2:14 – 36); (4) Peter's missionary sermon (2:37 – 40); and (5) mass conversions and baptisms (2:41). We will treat these five incidents in three sections, combining the first two and the last two incidents (2:1 – 13; 2:14 – 36; 2:37 – 41).

Luke's narrative is effective in both a dramatic and a theological sense. From a narrative standpoint, the chapter picks up the expectations raised in Acts 1 and

---

1. I. Howard Marshall, *The Acts of the Apostles: An Introduction and Commentary* (TNTC; Leicester: Intervarsity Press, 1980), 67.

shows in what way the apostles continue Jesus' work, which is not yet complete (1:1) since the kingdom still needs to be fully restored to Israel (1:3, 6 – 8). It shows when and how the apostles received the Holy Spirit whom Jesus had promised, a necessary empowerment for the mission of proclamation from Jerusalem to the ends of the earth, to which they have been called (1:8).

The theological focus in Acts 1 was on Jesus the risen and exalted Messiah (cf. Luke 24:46 – 49), on the kingdom of God, on the restoration of the kingdom to Israel, on the coming of the promise of the Holy Spirit, and on the mission of the Twelve from Jerusalem to the ends of the earth. In this context, Acts 2 stresses that Jesus, the crucified and risen Messiah, has assumed the royal position and has received kingly dominion, as David's Lord, at the right hand of God on account of the resurrection and his ascension to the Father (2:33 – 36). He is now able to restore Israel, which happens through the gift of the Holy Spirit (Luke 24:44 – 49; Acts 1:3 – 8; 2:14 – 36),[2] who empowers Peter and the disciples to courageously proclaim Jesus as Israel's Messiah to the Jerusalem crowds gathered to celebrate the day of Pentecost.

While Acts 2 seems to begin abruptly with dramatic events for which there is no immediately discernible cause,[3] the introduction in 1:1 – 14 has alerted the reader to expect startling and extraordinary things to happen when the Holy Spirit arrives in power. As the presence of God's Spirit is evident in visible and audible manifestations and in the eagerness and courage of the apostles to explain who Jesus really is, what he has accomplished, and what he wants to realize in the present and in the future, the stage is set for the rest of Acts. The power of the Holy Spirit, who made the disciples speak in languages they had not learned (2:4 – 11), is only the first of many miracles that happen as the disciples engage in their mission.

Peter's proclamation of Jesus the Messiah at Pentecost (2:14 – 36) is only the first of many speeches and sermons in the book that explain the identity and the significance of Jesus. The transforming power of the Holy Spirit, who leads people to repentance — people coming from many regions of the earth (2:9 – 11, 37 – 42) — creates a congregation of people with diverse backgrounds, united in faith in Jesus as Savior and Lord. This community eventually includes Samaritans, Ethiopians, Romans, Syrians, and many others who come to faith in Jesus and who thus also receive the Holy Spirit.

In this section we will treat the first two incidents of the Pentecost episode: (1) the coming of the Holy Spirit at Pentecost (2:1 – 4), and (2) the reaction of diaspora Jews living in Jerusalem (2:5 – 13), which then leads into Peter's explanatory speech in 2:14 – 36.

2. Turner, *Power from on High*, 315.

3. Robert C. Tannehill, *The Narrative Unity of Luke-Acts:* *A Literary Interpretation*, vol. 2: *The Acts of the Apostles* (orig. 1990; repr., Philadelphia: Fortress, 1994), 26.

Main Idea

With the coming of the Holy Spirit on the day of Pentecost, Jesus, the crucified, risen, and exalted Lord and Messiah, sets in motion the promised restoration of Israel, equipping his disciples with the power of God's presence for their task of witness and mission.

Translation

(See next page.)

Structure and Literary Form

The first two incidents of Luke's report of the events that transpired on Pentecost take place in Jerusalem at nine o'clock in the morning. First, Luke reports the coming of the Holy Spirit upon the believers, who experience audible and visible manifestations (2:1 – 4). As the believers are assembled in Jerusalem on the day of Pentecost (2:1), they hear a sound like a rushing wind (2:2) and see a light above each other's heads, which looks like tongues of fire (2:3). These manifestations signified the coming of the promised Holy Spirit (2:4a), whose presence is further demonstrated in that the believers speak in languages they have not learned (2:4b-c).

Second, Luke relates the reaction of diaspora Jews living in Jerusalem, who can understand what the apostles are saying in various foreign languages (2:5 – 13). After noting the presence of Jews who had come from diaspora communities to visit Jerusalem (2:5), Luke briefly describes their arrival at the scene and their bewilderment (2:6), which is due to the fact that they hear Galilean Jews speaking in the fifteen or so languages spoken in the regions in which these Jews used to reside (2:7 – 11). While some admit that they cannot explain the phenomenon (2:12), others ridicule the believers by suggesting they must be drunk (2:13).

Acts 2:1 – 13

1a	Setting: temporal	When the day of Pentecost arrived,
b	Event	**they were all together in the same place.**
2a	Event	**Suddenly there was a sound from heaven**
b	Comparison	like a violent rushing wind,
c	Event	and **it filled the entire house where they were sitting.**
3a	Event	**There appeared to them tongues**
b	Comparison	as if of fire,
c		which divided up among them
d	Event	and **rested on each one of them.**
4a	Event	**They were all filled with the Holy Spirit,**
b	Result	and **they began to speak in other languages,**
c	Source & means	as the Spirit enabled them to speak out.
5a	Event	Now **there were devout Jews**
b	Geographical	from every nation under heaven
c	Place	living in Jerusalem
6a	Setting: time	When this sound was heard,
b	Event	**a crowd gathered;**
c	Reaction	**they were bewildered**
d	Cause	because each one heard them speaking in their own language.
7a	Cause	Amazed and
b	Cause	astonished,
c	Action	**they asked,**
d	Question	*"Are not all these people who are speaking*
e	Identification	*Galileans?*
8a	Question	*And how is it that each of us hears them speaking*
b	Identification	*in our own native languages?*
9a	Place (List)	*We are Parthians and Medes and Elamites and residents of Mesopotamia,*
b	Place	*Judea, and Cappadocia,*
c	Place	*of Pontus and Asia,*
d	Place	*of Phrygia and Pamphylia,*
10a	Place	*of Egypt and the ☝*
		regions of Libya adjacent to Cyrene,
b	Place	*and visitors from Rome*
11a	Place	*(both Jews and proselytes), Cretans and Arabs,*
b	Contra-expectation	*yet we hear them speaking*
c	Identification	*in our languages*
d	Content	*about the mighty deeds of God."*
12a	Reaction	**They were all bewildered and**
	Reaction	**perplexed,**
b		saying to one another,
c	Question	*"What does this mean?"*
13a	Contrast: reaction	But **others scoffed**
b	Action	and **said,**
c	Accusation	*"They are full of sweet new wine."*

The passage consists mostly of *narrative* (2:1 – 7, 12, 13), with *direct speech* of the diaspora Jews (vv. 7 – 11, 12, 13), containing three questions (vv. 7, 8, 12). In vv. 9 – 11 we have a *list* of fifteen regions and peoples that documents the geographical origins of the diaspora Jews with whom the apostles have contact. The description of visual and audible phenomena in vv. 3 – 4 has been compared with the rhetorical strategy of ekphrasis, which employs "language that appeals as much to the eye as to the ear."[4] The response of the crowd (vv. 9 – 11) is comparable to the rhetorical figure of reasoning by question and answer (*ratiocinatio*).[5] Peter's rejection of the charge of drunkenness corresponds to the common rhetorical strategy of *refutatio*.[6]

Exegetical Outline

➡ **I. The Arrival of the Holy Spirit and the Identity of Jesus as Israel's Messiah and Lord (2:1 – 41)**

    A. The Coming of the Holy Spirit at Pentecost (2:1 – 4)

        1. The assembly of the believers on Pentecost (2:1)

        2. Audible manifestation: Sound like a rushing wind (2:2)

        3. Visible manifestation: Light that looks like tongues of fire (2:3)

        4. The believers are filled with the Holy Spirit (2:4a)

        5. The believers speak in unlearned languages (2:4b-c)

    B. The Reaction of Diaspora Jews Living in Jerusalem (2:5 – 13)

        1. The presence of diaspora Jews living in Jerusalem (2:5)

        2. The arrival of diaspora Jews and their bewilderment (2:6)

        3. The reaction of the diaspora Jews (2:7 – 11)

            a. Rhetorical question: Galilean Jews do not speak foreign languages (2:7)

            b. Fact: These Jews speak in foreign languages (2:8)

            c. List of fifteen regions and peoples (2:9 – 11a)

            d. Fact: These Jews praise God in unlearned foreign languages (2:11b-d)

        4. The perplexity of the diaspora Jews who have no explanation (2:12)

        5. The ridicule of some diaspora Jews (2:13)

---

4. Parsons, *Acts*, 37, with reference to Theon, *Prog.* 118; cf. Kennedy, *Progymnasmata*, 38. The function of ekphrastic language "is often to draw attention to the significance of the event thus described" (Parsons, *Acts*, 38).

5. Parsons, *Acts*, 39, with reference to *Rhet. her.* 4.16.23.

6. Cf. Theon, *Prog.* 93 – 94: students can refute a narrative, a chreia, or a thesis "by demonstrating that the claim was incredible with respect to person, action, place, time, manner, and/or cause" (Parsons, *Acts*, 42).

Explanation of the Text

2:1 When the day of Pentecost arrived, they were all together in the same place (καὶ ἐν τῷ συμπληροῦσθαι τὴν ἡμέραν τῆς πεντηκοστῆς ἦσαν πάντες ὁμοῦ ἐπὶ τὸ αὐτό). Luke begins his report of the coming of the Holy Spirit with a statement about the date when this foundational event took place. The verb translated "arrived" (συμπληρόω) denotes the approach of a certain day or the completion of a certain number of days. The infinitive-with-accusative phrase translated as "when the day of Pentecost arrived" specifies the time of the fulfillment of Jesus' promise in 1:5, 8. It refers to the morning of the full day of the feast, not the evening of the day before, when the feast began. Since Luke usually does not provide firm datings, the sonorous term συμπληροῦσθαι may imply the "complete filling" or fulfillment of God's promises concerning the coming of the Holy Spirit given to the prophets, reaffirmed and announced by Jesus in terms of being fulfilled in the near future in 1:5.

Pentecost (πεντηκοστή, lit., "the fiftieth part") denotes the Festival of New Grain celebrated seven weeks or fifty days after Passover.[7] Pentecost, the "Feast of Weeks," was the second of the three great pilgrimage festivals of Israel. It was essentially a harvest festival, the occasion when the Jews thanked God for the gifts of the grain harvest. Since Israel had arrived at Mount Sinai in the third month after leaving Egypt (Exod 19:1), i.e., in the third month after Passover, the Festival of Pentecost was eventually connected with the celebration

of the giving of the covenant and thus with the gift of the law given at Sinai.

It is unclear when this connection was established. Several early Jewish texts suggest this connection was made by at least some Jews of this period.[8] An analysis of Peter's speech will show that while the individual arguments are clear, the overall pattern — the manifestations reminiscent of a theophany, the assertion that Jesus ascended to God to receive a great gift he bestows on God's people — suggests a connection with Jewish traditions about Moses at Mount Sinai.[9] If this connection is a valid background for Acts 2, Peter (and Luke) suggests that the Holy Spirit of God, poured out by the crucified, risen, and exalted Lord Jesus Christ, is in some way the Spirit of the new covenant, or, more precisely, the Spirit of the life in the renewed covenant and thus in restored Israel.

Luke notes again the regular assemblies of the followers of Jesus in Jerusalem. Luke does not specify who is assembled. However, he likely refers to the 120 believers mentioned in 1:15;[10] among them are the Twelve, several women including Mary, Jesus' mother, and Jesus' brothers. The phrase translated as "in the same place" (ἐπὶ τὸ αὐτό) reinforces "together" (ὁμοῦ): they were together, i.e., in the same place. Luke's readers would assume this was the "upper room" of 1:13.

2:2 Suddenly there was a sound from heaven like a violent rushing wind, and it filled the

---

7. Cf. Exod 23:16; 34:22; Lev 23:15 – 16; Deut 16:9 – 10, 16; 2 Chr 8:13.

8. Cf. *Jub.* 1:1; 6:17 – 19; 14:20; 22:1 – 16; 1QS I, 8 — II, 25; 4Q266 frag. 11, 17 – 18, "And all the inhabitants of the camps shall assemble in the third month and curse those who turn right or left from the Torah."

9. Turner, *Power from on High*, 279 – 89; Miller, *Convinced*, 171 – 72. Other scholars do not see a connection between Pen-

tecost and Moses/Sinai (Darrell L. Bock, *Proclamation from Prophecy and Pattern: Lucan Old Testament Christology* [JSNTSup 12; Sheffield: JSOT Press, 1987], 182 – 83; Robert P. Menzies, *The Development of Early Christian Pneumatology with Special Reference to Luke-Acts* [JSNTSup 54; Sheffield: JSOT Press, 1991], 229 – 44).

10. Note the implication of 2:17 – 18, 33. Thus already Chrysostom; cf. Haenchen, *Acts*, 167 n. 4; Bock, *Acts*, 94.

entire house where they were sitting (καὶ ἐγένετο ἄφνω ἐκ τοῦ οὐρανοῦ ἦχος ὥσπερ φερομένης πνοῆς βιαίας καὶ ἐπλήρωσεν ὅλον τὸν οἶκον οὗ ἦσαν καθήμενοι). The meeting of the Christian believers was "suddenly" (ἄφνω) interrupted by a "sound" (ἦχος) from above. The term οὐρανός can mean "sky," particularly when used in the singular; the reference is thus not necessarily to the dwelling place of God. Nevertheless, there seems to be an obvious correspondence between Jesus ascending "into heaven" (εἰς τὸν οὐρανόν; 1:11) and the sound coming "from heaven" (ἐκ τοῦ οὐρανοῦ). This may be an allusion to the theophany at Mount Sinai, where "a very loud trumpet blast" was heard (Exod 19:16).

The genitive absolute translated as "a violent rushing wind" formulates, after the comparative particle (ὥσπερ), a comparison of the actual phenomenon with meteorological experiences that Luke's readers were familiar with. The sound they heard was like the sound of a strong, violent wind rushing along. This "wind" (πνοή) is not identical with the Spirit — the Greek term (πνεῦμα), which means both "Spirit" and "wind," is not used here; rather, the "wind" signifies the coming of the Spirit. This sound filled the entire house in which the disciples had assembled. The gathering of the crowds mentioned in vv. 5 – 6 is not given a location; they may have heard the sound described in v. 2 and the foreign languages mentioned in v. 4 as passersby on the street.

2:3 There appeared to them tongues as if of fire, which divided up among them and rested on each one of them (καὶ ὤφθησαν αὐτοῖς διαμεριζόμεναι γλῶσσαι ὡσεὶ πυρὸς καὶ ἐκάθισεν ἐφ᾽ ἕνα ἕκαστον αὐτῶν). The second phenomenon of which the believers suddenly became aware was an optical manifestation of an intense, flickering light, compared to tongues of fire. When God appeared on Mount Sinai, there was thunder and lightning (Exod 19:16). Wind and fire often accompany, and symbolize, the presence of God.[11] Based on a messianic interpretation of Isa 4:4; 11:4, the author of *4 Ezra* 13:8 – 11 expected flames and a storm of sparks that come from the mouth of the Man from the sea to destroy the army of the unrighteous. John the Baptist had announced that the one more powerful than he would cleanse Israel "with the Holy Spirit and fire" (ἐν πνεύματι ἁγίῳ καὶ πυρί; Luke 3:16).

The meaning of this prophecy is established in the context of the traditional Jewish expectation of a messianic figure fulfilling Isa 11:1 – 4 (with 4:2 – 6; 9:2 – 7) and Mal 3:2 – 3, purging and restoring Israel "with his decisively authoritative Spirit-imbued command, burning righteousness, and dramatic acts of power, effecting both judgment and salvation."[12] In light of Luke's description of the visible phenomena that the followers of Jesus experienced on the day of Pentecost, it is likely that he regarded the wind and the light shaped like tongues of fire as a fulfillment of the prophecy in Luke 3:16.

This optical phenomenon became rather personal: the manifestation of "tongues" (γλῶσσαι) like fire appeared above each of the believers. This probably points forward to the foreign languages (γλῶσσαι) that each of the believers started to speak (v. 4): the individualized appearance of the "tongues as of fire" symbolize "the diversified power of speech that comes upon them."[13] When we evaluate the experience of the believers who receive the Spirit in the context of an allusion to

---

11. Exod 3:2; 13:21 – 22; 14:20, 24; 1 Kgs 19:11 – 12; Ps 104:4. In Deut 4:24; 9:3 and other passages fire is linked with judgment.

12. Turner, *Power from on High*, 183, with reference to *1 En.* 49:2 – 3; 62:1 – 2; *Pss. Sol.* 17:37; 18:7; *4 Ezra* 13:8 – 11; 1QSb V, 24 – 25; 4QpIsa III, 15 – 29.

13. Fitzmyer, *Acts*, 238.

the Sinai theophany, the different reactions of the people stand out: there is no fear or trembling of the disciples in Jerusalem, unlike the reaction of the Israelites at Mount Sinai (Exod 19:16; 20:18), and unlike their earlier reaction when the risen Jesus had appeared to them (Luke 24:37); instead, they are all filled with God's Spirit and they speak about God's mighty deeds.

2:4 They were all filled with the Holy Spirit, and they began to speak in other languages, as the Spirit enabled them to speak out (καὶ ἐπλήσθησαν πάντες πνεύματος ἁγίου καὶ ἤρξαντο λαλεῖν ἑτέραις γλώσσαις καθὼς τὸ πνεῦμα ἐδίδου ἀποφθέγγεσθαι αὐτοῖς). In addition to the outward manifestations of sound and light, the Holy Spirit came upon the followers of Jesus as an inward, invisible reality. Peter will explain in vv. 33 – 36 that this new and powerful presence of the Holy Spirit is the manifestation and the result of the executive power of Jesus, the risen and exalted Messiah, who reigns at God's right hand to restore Israel. His explanation shows that the Holy Spirit is understood as the "Spirit of prophecy," which the Jews expected would be poured out in the days of the Messiah, affording revelation, wisdom, invasive prophecy, and doxological speech. As fulfillment of Luke 3:16 and Acts 1:5, "filling" (πίμπλημι) with the Holy Spirit is synonymous with "immersion in" or "being washed by" the Holy Spirit.

The verb "fill" (πίμπλημι) is a more intense form (compare with πληρόω). Luke uses the aorist indicative form (ἐπλήσθησαν) with genitive of divine Spirit to designate "short outbursts of spiritual power/inspiration, rather than the inception of long-term endowment of the Spirit,"[14] a fact that

explains why a person might be "filled with the Holy Spirit" on many occasions while at the same time remaining "full" of the Spirit.

The followers of Jesus started to speak in "other languages" (ἕτεραι γλῶσσαι), i.e., in languages other than their own (cf. vv. 6, 8, 11).[15] The phenomenon that the believers experienced and that onlookers observed was xenolalia, the miraculous speaking in unlearned languages — here in the languages spoken in the regions mentioned in vv. 9 – 11, which Galilean Jews would not have spoken either as part of their upbringing (in a multilingual family) or as languages learned later in life (e.g., as traders). The translation "with/in other tongues"[16] is not as clear as "in other languages."

Luke specifies the pronouncements of the believers, who speak under the direct influence of the Holy Spirit, as being uttered clearly, loudly, boldly. The verb translated as "speak out" (ἀποφθέγγομαι) neither describes the disciples as being "ecstatically transported" nor connotes unintelligibility. The words they utter are not of human origin but have been "given" (δίδωμι) by the Spirit. The imperfect (ἐδίδου) does not necessarily imply that the ability to speak in unlearned languages was a permanent gift; it expresses the continuing inspiration of the Spirit during the speaking in unlearned languages on the day of Pentecost.[17]

2:5 Now there were devout Jews from every nation under heaven living in Jerusalem (ἦσαν δὲ εἰς Ἰερουσαλὴμ κατοικοῦντες Ἰουδαῖοι, ἄνδρες εὐλαβεῖς ἀπὸ παντὸς ἔθνους τῶν ὑπὸ τὸν οὐρανόν). The scene changes from the meeting place of the believers to (presumably) the street, where passersby hear multiple languages being spoken. They

---

14. Turner, *Power from on High*, 168.

15. Cf. Christopher B. Forbes, *Prophecy and Inspired Speech in Early Christanity and Its Hellenistic Environment* (WUNT 2/75; Tübingen: Mohr Siebeck, 1995), 44 – 74, who convincingly argues that the phenomenon Paul describes in 1 Cor 14

is also the speaking of unlearned foreign languages.

16. ESV, KJV, NASB, NIV, NKJV, RSV, TNIV.

17. BDF, §327: the imperfect is used here to portray an action as being in progress.

are described as (1) Jews (Ἰουδαῖοι), i.e., members of the Jewish people; (2) "devout men" (ἄνδρες εὐλαβεῖς), i.e., pious Jews who observe the law and the Jewish traditions; (3) Jews "from every nation under heaven," i.e., Jews who lived in Jewish (diaspora) communities in cities in the various Roman provinces and beyond (cf. the list in vv. 9 – 11). It is not entirely clear whether they were diaspora Jews who had returned to Jerusalem to live (or retire) there,[18] or whether they were Jewish pilgrims who had come to stay in Jerusalem during the Feast of Pentecost.[19] If the reference to the day of Pentecost in 2:1 not only provides a chronological reference but also the context for the language miracle, festival pilgrims are likely to be in view as well.[20] Some scholars estimate that one million pilgrims visited Jerusalem for Pentecost.

2:6 When this sound was heard, a crowd gathered; they were bewildered because each one heard them speaking in their own language (γενομένης δὲ τῆς φωνῆς ταύτης συνῆλθεν τὸ πλῆθος καὶ συνεχύθη, ὅτι ἤκουον εἷς ἕκαστος τῇ ἰδίᾳ διαλέκτῳ λαλούντων αὐτῶν). The events described in vv. 2 – 4 attract a large number of people. The genitive absolute phrase translated as "when this sound was heard" (γενομένης δὲ τῆς φωνῆς ταύτης) indicates the time when, or the reason why, a crowd of people approached the believers.

The "sound" was probably not the sound of the wind (v. 2) but the sound of the voices of the believers speaking in different languages (v. 4), as the reaction of the crowd suggests. It should not be assumed, however, that the believers all spoke at the same time; since people in the crowd understood both the languages being spoken and the content of what was being said (v. 11), presumably the believers spoke one after the other.[21]

The effect of the sounds coming from the gathering of the followers of Jesus was utter bewilderment, which Luke describes in vv. 6 – 13 with five verbs denoting strong mental and verbal reactions.[22] (1) The verb used in v. 6 (συγχέω) means "to be amazed, surprised, excited, agitated," and is also used in the story of the confusion of languages at Babel.[23] Since Luke does not say that the "confusion" was brought to an end by the miracle of the disciples speaking in foreign languages, he probably does not want to emphasize that the coming of the Holy Spirit reversed the dispersion of humankind on account of the confusion created by the multiplicity of languages.[24]

(2) The verb used in vv. 7, 12 (ἐξίστημι) denotes "to be out of one's normal state of mind, be amazed, astonished."

(3) The second verb in v. 7 (θαυμάζω) means "to be extraordinarily impressed or disturbed by something, wonder, marvel, be astonished," i.e.,

---

18. Thus Haenchen, *Acts*, 168, and most commentators. This view can be supported with reference to the verb κατοικοῦντες: these "devout Jews" from every nation "resided" in Jerusalem.

19. Cf. BDAG, s.v. κατοικέω, which denotes "to live in a locality for any length of time." Also, note the preposition εἰς indicating direction (εἰς Ἰερουσαλήμ) and the preposition ἀπό indicating origin (ἀπὸ παντὸς ἔθνους). As regards εἰς, note that ἐν is read by B C D and the majority of manuscripts, and that even though εἰς is likely to be original (א‌* A 1175), in Koine Greek εἰς often replaced ἐν.

20. The phrase οἱ ἐπιδημοῦντες Ῥωμαῖοι in 2:10 suggests that at least here pilgrims are in view.

21. The miracle is one of speaking foreign languages, not a

miracle of hearing, as some have assumed, cf. F. F. Bruce, *The Book of the Acts* (rev. ed.; NICNT; Grand Rapids: Eerdmans, 1988), 115.

22. For the following definitions and glosses, cf. BDAG.

23. Gen 11:7 LXX: δεῦτε καὶ καταβάντες συγχέωμεν ἐκεῖ αὐτῶν τὴν γλῶσσαν.

24. Barrett, *Acts*, 119; I. Howard Marshall, "Acts," in *Commentary on the New Testament Use of the Old Testament* (ed. G. K. Beale and D. A. Carson; Grand Rapids: Baker, 2007), 513 – 606, 532. It should be noted that this has been a traditional interpretation of Acts 2; cf. Jaroslav Pelikan, *Acts* (Brazos Theological Commentary on the Bible; Grand Rapids: Brazos, 2005), 52.

their attention is directed to the wondrous, marvelous phenomenon that they are witnessing.

(4) The verb used in v. 12 (διαπορέω) means "to be greatly perplexed, be at a loss" and thus emphasizes the bewilderment over against astonishment and admiration.

(5) In v. 13 a verb is used (διαχλευάζω) that means "to laugh at someone in scorn, jeer."

The amazement and perplexity is triggered by the fact that many people in the crowd hear the Christians speak in their own native language (διάλεκτος; the dative is instrumental or modal); the term denotes the language of a nation or region (and is thus synonymous with γλῶσσα when used for a distinctive language), not the local "dialect" within a language.

2:7 Amazed and astonished, they asked, "Are not all these people who are speaking Galileans?" (ἐξίσταντο δὲ καὶ ἐθαύμαζον λέγοντες· οὐχ ἰδοὺ ἅπαντες οὗτοί εἰσιν οἱ λαλοῦντες Γαλιλαῖοι;). Luke illustrates the perplexity of the crowd with a series of questions. The people in the crowd know that these followers of Jesus are Galileans, and they cannot fathom how they are able to speak in the vernacular languages of cities and regions outside of Galilee. Some people in the crowd, particularly if they are diaspora Jews residing in Jerusalem, may have recognized some of the believers as disciples of Jesus, whom they know to have lived in Galilee; or they may have inquired from citizens living in the same street who these people are. It is not clear whether this question implies the snobbery of diaspora Jews or the stereotyping of Galileans;[25] since the people in the crowd presumably do not belong to the Judean elite, they would have not much reason to look down on Galilean Jews.

The assumption implied in the question would apply to Judean Jews as well: Jews who were born and who lived in Palestine were not expected to speak other languages besides Hebrew, Aramaic, and in many cases also Greek. People who were multilingual usually spoke a local or regional language (such as in the regions listed in vv. 9 – 11), particularly in areas of the Mediterranean that had been under the influence of Hellenism since the conquests of Alexander, where people spoke their traditional vernacular languages as well as Greek, the lingua franca in the region or in the province. In the West, particularly in Spain and Gaul, the situation was similar with regard to the conquests of the Roman army and the establishment of Roman provinces, with people speaking their traditional vernacular languages as well as Latin. Otherwise, bilingualism was mostly limited to merchants and traders whose knowledge of a second language was narrow and practical. While Palestinian Jews were generally multilingual, they would not have been able to speak other languages besides Hebrew, Aramaic, and Greek.

2:8 And how is it that each of us hears them speaking in our own native languages? (καὶ πῶς ἡμεῖς ἀκούομεν ἕκαστος τῇ ἰδίᾳ διαλέκτῳ ἡμῶν ἐν ᾗ ἐγεννήθημεν;). The people on the street outside of the house are surprised that they hear the believers speak in their own language (lit.) "in which we were born," i.e., in their native language, which was spoken in the city in which they grew up. The following list provides names of regions, ethnic groups, and one city whose languages the believers were speaking under the miraculous influence of the Holy Spirit.

2:9 – 10 We are Parthians and Medes and Elamites and residents of Mesopotamia, Judea, and Cappadocia, of Pontus and Asia, of Phrygia and Pamphylia, of Egypt and the regions of Libya adjacent to

---

25. Witherington, *Acts*, 136, with reference to Mark 14:70; Acts 4:13, and to popular opinions about Galileans, described by Geza Vermes, *Jesus the Jew: A Historian's Reading of the Gospel* (London/Philadelphia: Collins/Fortress, 1973), 42 – 57.

Cyrene, and visitors from Rome (Πάρθοι καὶ Μῆδοι
καὶ Ἐλαμῖται καὶ οἱ κατοικοῦντες τὴν Μεσοποταμίαν,
Ἰουδαίαν τε καὶ Καππαδοκίαν, Πόντον καὶ τὴν Ἀσίαν,
Φρυγίαν τε καὶ Παμφυλίαν, Αἴγυπτον καὶ τὰ μέρη
τῆς Λιβύης τῆς κατὰ Κυρήνην καὶ οἱ ἐπιδημοῦντες
Ῥωμαῖοι). The list of fifteen names describes the
ethnic groups and the regions in which the diaspora
Jews who hear the believers speak were born and
where they grew up before going to Jerusalem.

Parthia is the region southeast of the Caspian
Sea in northeastern Iran. Jewish communities have
been attested in Adiabene.

Media, whose borders cannot be precisely determined, is a region in northwestern Iran. Some of
the Israelites who were deported by the Assyrians
lived in Media (2 Kgs 17:6; 18:11). Jews have been
attested in Ecbatana.

Elam was the lowland of Khuzistan and later
included the Iranian highland around Anshan. In
the first century, the Parthians were the one foreign
power that threatened Rome militarily from the
East, while the Medes and the Elamites were former
kingdoms that were no longer politically relevant. A
Jewish community has been attested in Susa.

Mesopotamia is the region between the Tigris
and Euphrates Rivers, in what is now eastern Syria
and northern Iraq; later the term could refer to the
entire region of the two rivers. When Nebuchadnezzar conquered Jerusalem in 586 BC, he deported
the population to Babylonia, i.e., to Mesopotamia.
Jewish communities are attested in Babylon, Cte-
siphon, Dura-Europos, Edessa, Nehardea, Nisibis,
Seleuceia, and Spasinou Charax.

Judea is mentioned in the middle of the list in
agreement with similar Jewish lists, which enumer-
ate the nations of the earth in a counterclockwise
structure.[26] The argument that "Judea" does not
need a language miracle[27] misses the point: most of
these diaspora Jews would have understood either
Aramaic or Greek or both and would thus not have
"needed" a miracle. The miracle consists in the fact
that Galilean Jews speak in unlearned languages
that the diaspora Jews can understand.

For *Cappadocia,* Jews are attested in Caesarea
Mazaca and Tyana. Cappadocia extends from the
Taurus Mountains north of Cilicia to the Black Sea
coast, situated between Paphlagonia in the east and
Phrygia (and later Galatia) in the west, in what is
today eastern Turkey.

In *Pontus* we find Jews in Amisus. If "Pontus" stands for the Roman province of Pontus –
Bithynia, Jewish communities are further attested
in Amastris, Calchedon, Claudiou Polis, Nicaia,
Nicomedia, and Sebastopolis. Pontus is on the
south coast of the Black Sea in northern Anatolia,
between Colchis in the east and Paphlagonia in the
west. Aquila and Priscilla, Christians from Rome
and coworkers of Paul in Corinth and Ephesus,
came from Pontus (18:2).

Asia here may refer to the Greek cities along the
Aegean coast of Asia Minor together with the territory each city controlled, a smaller area than the
Roman province of Asia, which included parts of
Phrygia (the next geographical term mentioned
by Luke).[28] But it is not impossible to take "Asia"
as a reference to the Roman province.[29] The province of Asia was established in 129 BC when Rome
took over the kingdom of Pergamon. It included

---

26. See particularly the "updated" version of the table of nations (Gen 10) in Josephus, *Ant.* 1.122 – 47; cf. James M. Scott,
Paul and the Nations (WUNT 84; Tübingen: Mohr Siebeck,
1995), 166.

27. Jervell, *Apostelgeschichte,* 136; he is correct, however,
when he surmises that "Judea" stands for the center of worldwide Jewry.

28. Cf. Paul R. Trebilco, "Asia," in *The Book of Acts
in Its Graeco-Roman Setting* (ed. D. W. J. Gill and C.
Gempf), 291 – 362, 302.

29. Hemer, *Acts,* 203 – 4; he suggests that in some cases
"Asia" could be used informally "where the great cosmopolitan
centre of Ephesus was mainly in view."

the regions of Caria, Ionia, Mysia, Phrygia, and the Troad. In the province of Asia, Jews are attested in numerous cities including Ephesus, Miletus, Philadelphia, Priene, Sardis, Smyrna, Thyatira, Troas, and on the islands of Chios, Samos, Cos, and Rhodos.

Phrygia, a region whose eastern region was incorporated into the Roman province of Galatia and which in the west belonged to the province of Asia, had Jews living in Aizanoi, Akmonia, Antioch, Apamea, Dokimeion, Dorylaion, Iconium, Hierapolis, Laodicea, and Synnada.

In *Pamphylia,* the coastal region that was also a Roman province (during this time), was located between the province of Asia in the west and Cilicia in the east. Jews lived in Aspendos, Perge, Side, and Sillyon.

As regards *Egypt,* Jewish communities are attested for Lower Egypt in Alexandria, Athribis, Leontopolis, Magdolos, Nitriai, Pelusion, Schedia, Tanis, Thmouis, Xenephrys; for Middle Egypt in Arsinoe, Memphis, Oxyrhynchus, Philadelphia; for Upper Egypt in Apollonopolis Magna (Edfu), Elephantine, Syene, and Thebes. Apollos, a believer from Alexandria, came from Egypt (18:24).

The "regions of Libya adjacent to Cyrene" refer to the region west of Cyrene, which was the Roman province *Africa Proconsularis* since 27 BC. Jewish communities are attested in Carthage, Henchir el-Faouara, Leptis Magna, Naro, Oea, Sabratha, Thaenae, Thagura, and Sullectum. In the region of Cyrene itself, Jews lived in Apollonia, Berenike, Cyrene, Ptolemais, and Teucheira. Simon, who helped carry Jesus' cross, came from Cyrene (Luke 23:26), and Jewish Christians from Jerusalem who established a church in Antioch hailed from Cyrene (11:20; 13:1).

The "*Romans*" (Ῥωμαῖοι) are Jews born in Rome who are in Jerusalem as "foreigners." Their mother tongue may have been Latin, particularly if they were former slaves who received Roman citizenship upon manumission. If we distinguish "visitors" (ἐπιδημοῦντες) from "residents" (κατοικοῦντες, v. 9), at least these Roman Jews were in Jerusalem as festival pilgrims. Aquila and Priscilla were Jewish Christians who lived in Rome before Claudius evicted the Jews from the city (18:2).

Rome, a city of about one million inhabitants in the first century, had a large Jewish community. The estimates for the total number Jews living in Rome vary between ten thousand and sixty thousand. We know of eleven or twelve synagogues in the city of Rome, at least four of which existed in the first century. Rome is the only city mentioned in the list. Luke ends his account of Acts in Rome (28:11 – 31), but he does not report the establishment of the church in the capital of the empire. When Paul arrives, there is already a Christian community in the city (28:15). The reference to Rome in v. 11 could be a hint by Luke that the Jewish Christian community in Rome originated with Jews of Rome who visited Jerusalem on the Feast of Pentecost in AD 30, who heard the message of Jesus the crucified and risen Messiah, who were converted to faith in Jesus, and who took the good news of Jesus back to Rome.[30]

2:11 "(Both Jews and proselytes), Cretans and Arabs, yet we hear them speaking in our languages about the mighty deeds of God" (Ἰουδαῖοί τε καὶ προσήλυτοι, Κρῆτες καὶ Ἄραβες, ἀκούομεν λαλούντων αὐτῶν ταῖς ἡμετέραις γλώσσαις τὰ μεγαλεῖα τοῦ θεοῦ). Luke clarifies that the visiting Jews from Rome included both Jews and proselytes (this clause is in apposition to the previous phrase). This is the first passage in Acts that

---

30. On the history of the Jewish Christian community in Rome, cf. Schnabel, *Early Christian Mission,* 2:800 – 815.

mentions "proselytes," Gentile converts to Judaism who had been circumcised and who kept the Mosaic law.[31]

The *Cretans* lived on Crete, the largest of the Greek islands. Since Augustus, Crete was united with Cyrene in northern Africa to form the senatorial province of *Creta et Cyrenae*. Jews are attested in several epitaphs. Titus, one of Paul's coworkers, preached in the cities of Crete (Titus 1:5).

The *Arabs* are the people living in Nabatea (also called Arabia), the region south of Syria and east of Judea. The Jews regarded the Nabateans as descendants of Ishmael, the son of Abraham. The translators of the LXX identified the Nabateans with Nabaioth, the firstborn of the twelve sons of Ishmael.[32] Kypros, the mother of Herod I, came from a Nabatean family; Salome, the sister of Herod, intended to marry the Nabatean prince Syllaios.[33] Herod Antipas, the tetrarch of Galilee, was married to a daughter of the Nabatean king Aretas IV. Many Nabatean cities had a Jewish population. As Gal 1:17 and 2 Cor 11:32 – 33 indicate, Paul engaged in missionary work in Arabia – Nabatea after his conversion in Damascus.

The connection between Cretans and Arabs, which has puzzled many interpreters, can be explained in the context of the table of nations in Gen 10, a text that provided the basic framework for Jewish geography. Both peoples are descendants of Mizraim (Egypt), who settled in the territories of Palestine (the Caphtorim, giving rise to the Philistines) and Nabatea (the Arabs, descending from Ishmael, the son of Abraham by Hagar the Egyptian).[34]

The second part of v. 11 describes the content of what the believers are saying, miraculously, in the languages of the diaspora Jews who have come to Jerusalem from all corners of the earth. They speak about "the mighty deeds" (τὰ μεγαλεῖα) of God,[35] i.e., they proclaim God's new intervention in history — the powerful salvation through the life, death, resurrection, and ascension of Jesus, Israel's Messiah.

2:12 They were all bewildered and perplexed, saying to one another, "What does this mean?" (ἐξίσταντο δὲ πάντες καὶ διηπόρουν, ἄλλος πρὸς ἄλλον λέγοντες· τί θέλει τοῦτο εἶναι;). While the people understand what the believers are saying, they continue to be bewildered because it is Galileans who speak in languages they cannot have learned. And they are perplexed[36] because they do not understand the significance of this unprecedented, miraculous manifestation of language abilities. The question indicates that the listeners are looking for an answer; this prepares the reader for Peter's speech in vv. 14 – 36.

2:13 But others scoffed and said, "They are full of sweet new wine" (ἕτεροι δὲ διαχλευάζοντες ἔλεγον ὅτι γλεύκους μεμεστωμένοι εἰσίν). Some people in the crowd refuse to be either astonished or perplexed. They have made up their minds about the behavior of the followers of Jesus, that these are people who show the effects of having had too much wine. The "sweet new wine" (γλεύκος) describes wine that is new and thus only partially fermented, and therefore sweet. Some authors compare a passage in Lucian in which this term is contrasted with another term (ἀνθοσμίας) that means "wine with a fine bouquet," which may

---

31. Cf. S. McKnight, "Proselytes and God-fearers," *DNTB*, 835 – 47.

32. Cf. LXX Gen 25:13; 28:9; 36:3; 1 Chr 1:29.

33. Cf. Josephus, *J.W.* 1.181; *Ant.* 14.121; 15.184; 16.220, 225, 322.

34. Scott, *Paul and the Nations*, 166 with n. 149.

35. The term τὰ μεγαλεῖα is used (as a noun) in the LXX for God's interventions in Israel's history, e.g., in the exodus and wilderness events (Deut 11:2; cf. *T. Job* 51:4); cf. Ps 71:19 (LXX 70:19); Sir 17:8; 18:4; 36:7; 42:21; 2 Macc 3:34; 7:17.

36. Cf. Luke 9:7; 24:4 (variant reading); Acts 2:12; 5:24; 10:17.

suggest that the scoffers taunt the followers of Jesus with the suggestion that they have been getting drunk as cheaply as possible.[37]

Since these events take place during the Feast of Pentecost in late May, it has been regarded as a problem that Luke refers to the drinking of sweet new wine several months before the grape harvest, which takes place in August. Some have solved this with reference to contemporary methods that managed to store new wine in such a fashion that the wine was prevented from going sour.[38] A perhaps more plausible explanation takes the reaction of the "scoffers" as a sarcastic insult that does not care whether the accusation can be correct.

The hostile reaction of a minority is not a contradiction to what Luke has said about the people in the crowd who understand the words uttered in their own language.[39] Either these are people who do not recognize any of the languages spoken — perhaps Jews who have always lived in Jerusalem — or their taunts are directed against the exuberant joy of the believers who praise God with loud voices and ostentatious conviction (v. 4).

The events triggered by the coming of the Holy Spirit upon the believers create two opposing groups, one group cautiously open to further inquiry, while the other group is openly skeptical or even hostile. This is a situation that will characterize the missionary ministry of the apostles more often than not.[40]

Theology in Application

Acts 2:1 – 13 is the central text in the New Testament about the coming of the Holy Spirit. In agreement with the main idea of this passage, sermons and lessons on the text should focus on the Holy Spirit as God's own presence, conveyed by Jesus, the crucified, risen, and exalted Lord and Messiah, who has set in motion the promised restoration of Israel and who equips his disciples with the power of God's presence for living their life as God's people and for their task of witness and mission.

The text centers on the coming of the Holy Spirit, on the fulfillment of God's promises that were reiterated and confirmed by John the Baptist and by Jesus, on the tangible presence of God, on the astounding power of God, on the mighty acts of God manifested in Jesus' life, death, and resurrection, and on the reality of the disciples' commission to be Jesus' witnesses from Jerusalem to the ends of the earth. Three major points stand out.

---

37. Barrett, *Acts*, 125, with reference to Lucian, *Sat.* 22.

38. Lake and Cadbury, *Acts*, 20; Bruce, *Book of Acts*, 59 n. 57; cf. Columella, *Rust.* 12; Cato, *Agr.* 120.

39. Thus Barrett, *Acts*, 125.

40. Haenchen, *Acts*, 171, referring to Acts 5:34; 14:4; 17:18; 23:6; 28:24.

The Spirit of Prophecy

The Holy Spirit comes as the Spirit of prophecy, in fulfillment of God's promises for Israel. The prophets in the Old Testament, John the Baptist, and Jesus himself had promised that the Holy Spirit would be poured out in a special way. Luke describes in Acts 2:1 – 13 how these promises have been fulfilled.

This outpouring of the Spirit fulfills the promise of John the Baptist, who announced that the Messiah would cleanse Israel and thus restore the nation, as promised by the prophets — a mission he can accomplish because God would endow him with Spirit and power (Luke 3:16 – 17).

This outpouring of the Spirit fulfills Jesus' promise when he announced that the Spirit would come upon the Twelve in the city of Jerusalem, an event that would continue and extend the restoration of God's reign in Israel (Luke 24:49; Acts 1:5, 8).

In the next section, Peter will explain that the outpouring of the Spirit fulfills the prophecies of Joel, who had announced that in the last days God would send the Spirit of prophecy on all flesh (2:16 – 24, quoting Joel 2:28 – 32).

The outpouring of the Spirit of prophecy on the disciples, manifested in the utterance of unlearned languages, is intimately connected with the believers praising God for his mighty deeds in the life, death, and resurrection of Jesus. While speaking in unlearned languages (glossolalia, xenolalia) was unknown in Judaism, it would have been readily recognized as a special, dramatic form of doxological prophetic speech akin to the "dreams" and "visions" that Joel linked with the promise of the Spirit (Joel 2:28 – 29; cf. Acts 2:17 – 18; 10:46; 19:6).

The reality of the Spirit of prophecy is tied to the promises of salvation and restoration for Israel and for the world, and as such should not be confused with a spirit of personal fulfillment, individual enrichment, or subjective introspection.

Bringing about Israel's Salvation through Jesus

The Holy Spirit comes as the powerful presence of God, who continues to bring about Israel's salvation through Jesus. The coming of the Holy Spirit on Pentecost represents the coming of God, who becomes present among his people. The audible and visible manifestations at Pentecost, the sound and the intense light, are manifestations of the presence of God.

The outpouring of the Holy Spirit continues and completes Jesus' mission. The mission of Jesus consisted in bringing salvation — as announced earlier in Luke's work by Zechariah, by the angels at Jesus' birth, by Simeon at Jesus' presentation in the temple, by Isaiah in a text that John the Baptist used in his proclamation, and by Jesus in his sermon at Nazareth (Luke 1:51 – 53, 74 – 79; 2:14, 30; 3:6; 4:17 – 21). The gift of the Holy Spirit is not an additional reality of something that the disciples had never experienced before.

The outpouring of the Holy Spirit confirms and continues the salvation of the disciples. Even as the coming of the Spirit brings a new experience, manifest in the speaking of unlearned languages, it confirms their previous experience. They had witnessed Jesus bringing salvation to people through liberating miracles of healing and exorcism (Luke 11:20; 10:9, 11). They had become part of the presence of God's reign as followers of Jesus, who ushered in the new sphere of God's blessing that people may enter and enjoy (Luke 4:18 – 19, 21, 43; 14:15 – 24; 16:16). And they had found salvation as followers of Jesus the Messiah, who was on the way to his death and resurrection (Luke 9:20 – 27). The outpouring of the Spirit at Pentecost is thus the continuation and the climax of the ministry of Jesus, who is Israel's Messiah, who had promised that they would receive the Spirit, and who had ascended to the Father's throne.

Extending Israel's Salvation through Jesus

The Holy Spirit comes as the powerful presence of God, who extends Israel's salvation through Jesus. The coming of the Holy Spirit confirms and extends God's restoration of Israel. When the Twelve receive the Spirit (together with other believers), they receive the Spirit as Israel's representatives. And they receive the Spirit in the presence of representatives of Jews from around the world, who (at the end of the chapter) are also offered the gift of the Spirit. If Luke indeed describes the coming of the Holy Spirit against the background of Jewish traditions about the giving of the law at Mount Sinai, remembered at the Feast of Pentecost,[41] several points become important.

(1) The promised second climax of God's revelation has become a reality. After God revealed himself at Mount Sinai, entered into a covenant with Israel, and gave the law, he has *now* poured out of his Spirit on all flesh. He has given to Israel the gracious gift of Jesus, the Messiah and exalted Lord who reigns at the right hand of God. Just as Moses climbed Mount Sinai and received God's law, which he passed on to Israel, accompanied by visible signs of God's presence, Jesus ascended to God's right hand and poured out the gift of God's Spirit on the people of the new covenant. Thus the events of Pentecost belong to the fulfillment and to the renewal of God's covenant with Israel in which the Spirit will have a major role.[42]

(2) The powerful presence of the Holy Spirit is the fundamental power of the renewal of God's covenant in Israel. The Feast of the Firstfruits of the wheat harvest (Exod 34:22) had become the feast when Israel remembered that God gave the law on Mount Sinai. Jewish exegesis concluded from Exod 19:1 – 4 that the day of the

---

41. Cf. Alexander J. M. Wedderburn, "Traditions and Redactions in Acts 2.1 – 13," *JSNT* 55 (1994): 27 – 54, 29 – 39, and others.

42. Cf. Max M. B. Turner, "The 'Spirit of Prophecy' as the Power of Israel's Restoration and Witness," in *Witness to the Gospel: The Theology of Acts* (ed. I. H. Marshall and D. Peterson), 327 – 48.

giving of the law was the same day as the Feast of Weeks; it was, therefore, the feast of covenant renewal. This background receives new significance in the context of the fulfillment of God's covenant with Abraham and the fathers in Jesus the Messiah (Luke 1:73–75; cf. Acts 3:24; 7:8), who ushers in the "new covenant" through his death and resurrection (Luke 22:20).

Jesus' proclamation of God's reign and the presence of the Holy Spirit in Israel — which began with Jesus' ministry and became a new, transforming reality on Pentecost — displace the law from its central, dominant position between God and his people. This means that the gift of the Spirit "constitutes the grounds for the ability to fulfill the Torah, God's social order for his people now interpreted in a definitive way by Jesus who rectifies all distortions, for its translation in the respective social reality of the new society of the church."[43]

The outpouring of the Holy Spirit initiates the proclamation of the good news of God's salvation in a worldwide context. Following Jesus' clarification of the restoration of the kingdom to Israel, the promise of the Holy Spirit, and the commission to proclaim the gospel from Jerusalem to the ends of the earth (Acts 1:3–8), the list of nations in 2:9–11 underlines both the universal scope of the witness of the Twelve and the conversion of Jews who have returned from the dispersion.

The outpouring of the Holy Spirit causes the Galilean disciples to miraculously speak in unlearned languages. Luke's description of this phenomenon in 2:4 should make us cautious not to read into the disciples' experience on Pentecost in Jerusalem a description of normative Christian entry into a permanent state of "fullness of the Spirit." Note that Luke uses the aorist indicative ἐπλήσθησαν + genitive of the divine Spirit to designate "short outbursts of spiritual power/inspiration, rather than the inception of long-term endowment of the Spirit," a fact that explains why a person might be "filled with the Holy Spirit" on many occasions while at the same time remaining "full" of the Spirit.[44]

The criterion for assessing the powerful presence of the Holy Spirit for Luke is, generally speaking, the observable transformation of the lives of Jesus' followers. The disciples speak in unlearned languages; they proclaim God's mighty acts in the life, death, and resurrection of Jesus; and they suddenly have the courage to be Jesus' witnesses in public, in the city where Jesus had been killed a few weeks earlier, in Jerusalem, where they had abandoned and denied Jesus. This means that

in Lukan terms the criterion for judging whether it is appropriate to speak of someone as "full of the Spirit" is not whether he has a baptismal or she a confirmation certificate — nor even whether the person concerned has in the past experienced some "second blessing" — but whether the community of Christians *felt the impact of the Spirit* through that person's life and *saw the Spirit's graces and gifts regularly expressed* through him or her.[45]

43. Pesch, *Apostelgeschichte*, 1:113.
44. Turner, *Power from on High*, 168.
45. Ibid., 169 (emphasis Turner).

The gift of "speaking in tongues" is not a more valuable manifestation of the Holy Spirit than the patience, diligence, and determination of new missionaries who learn to speak the language of a people to whom they seek to proclaim the gospel of Jesus Christ, and who learn the language so well that they no longer sound like foreigners but as people who speak "just like us." It should be noted, however, that the disciples' speaking in unlearned language is not presented by Luke as a means to facilitate the communication of the good news of God's mighty acts; rather, this miracle demonstrated the presence of God's Spirit, whose outpouring had been promised as a reality that would transform God's people. Paul treats the place and function of speaking in unlearned languages in 1 Corinthians 12 – 14.

Acts 2:14 – 36

Literary Context

As the Jews from Jerusalem/Judea and from the Jewish diaspora communities hear the assembled followers of Jesus speak in languages they could not have learned as Galilean Jews, and as they hear and see the audiovisual manifestations of sound and light, they repeatedly inquire as to the significance of these astonishing and bewildering events (2:7, 8, 12).

Luke's narrative of the third incident in the Pentecost episode (2:1 – 41) in 2:14 – 36 relates Peter's speech before the Jews of Jerusalem, Judea, and the diaspora. Peter explains the manifestations as the fulfillment of prophecies in the Scriptures — in particular Joel 2:28 – 32, which explains the phenomenon of speaking in unlearned languages. Peter argues that what they are witnessing is the manifestation of the Spirit of prophecy, who has been poured out by the crucified, risen, and exalted Jesus, who has been made Lord. The positive reaction of Peter's listeners prompts him to give what we might call a missionary sermon (2:38 – 39, 40), in which he argues that they can receive salvation by repenting and calling on the name of Jesus the Messiah. Luke's report of the events on this day ends with mass conversions in Jerusalem (2:41) and a description of the community of the followers of Jesus in Jerusalem (2:42 – 47).

From Luke's perspective, Peter's speech on Pentecost, in which he explains the coming of the Holy Spirit with reference to Jesus' position as exalted Lord and Messiah who has the power to grant salvation, answers (1) the hopes that the angel Gabriel expressed when he announced to Mary the birth of Jesus (Luke 1:32 – 33), (2) the expectation of the coming of "power from on high" that Jesus announced on the day of his resurrection (Luke 24:46 – 49), and (3) the promise of the coming of the Spirit's power that Jesus confirmed before his ascension and exaltation (Acts 1:1 – 11). As the crucified, risen, and exalted Jesus, the Messiah and Lord, has assumed executive power on the eternal throne of David at God's right hand, the kingdom of God manifests itself "in greater than hitherto experienced power and presence in Israel" through the "deepening of the messianic cleansing, restoration and transformation of Israel through the gift of the Spirit."[1]

---

1. Turner, *Power from on High*, 268.

IN DEPTH: The Speeches in Acts

There is general agreement among scholars that the speeches in Acts are not verbatim accounts of what was said on each occasion. The reasons are the following. (1) The speeches in Acts are too short for actual speeches. A straight reading of Peter's speech on Pentecost takes less than three minutes. Luke sometimes indicates that more was said than what he actually recorded (cf. 2:40). (2) Peter's speeches in Jerusalem were presumably delivered in Aramaic, not in Greek. This means that Luke's Greek text is at best a translation of an Aramaic original. (3) Sermons in synagogues certainly took up more than a few minutes. In the synagogues, the Torah was read in a three-year cycle, and many assume that there were also regular readings from the Prophets in the first century.[2] The Scripture readings alone would take up ten or fifteen minutes. We do not know the average length of a synagogue sermon, but presumably it would be at least as long as the Scripture readings.

The historicity of the speeches is connected with the historicity of Acts more generally (see the Introduction). Some scholars have been skeptical concerning the general reliability of the speeches of Acts. They argue that the speeches are Luke's creation, a convention of ancient historiography that asked for speeches interspersed in the historical narrative and a device through which Luke could express his own theological convictions.[3] Other scholars argue that while the speeches have been formulated by Luke, they faithfully summarize what was said on each occasion. Several arguments are important.

    1. As Luke traveled widely and had contact with many of the churches and many

---

2. Cf. Lee I. Levine, *The Ancient Synagogue: The First Thousand Years* (2nd ed.; New Haven: Yale Univ. Press, 2005), 146 – 57.

3. Cf. Martin Dibelius, *Studies in the Acts of the Apostles* (ed. H. Greeven; New York: Scribner, 1956), 138 – 85; Marion L. Soards, *The Speeches in Acts: Their Content, Context, and Concerns* (Louisville: Westminster John Knox, 1994), 1 – 11.

of the main actors of his narrative, he had access to traditions, and documents if they existed, that he could use when he wrote Acts. We know that Greek and Roman orators wrote down their speeches before they memorized them (delivery of the speech was from memory). It is not impossible that some of the speeches that Luke summarizes existed in written form.

2. The content of the speeches and their emphases are diverse enough, despite a basic unity of theological outlook, that it is more likely than not that Luke used traditional material when he summarized the speeches.

3. In many cases the speeches contain material specifically tied to the assumed historical setting, often containing "local color" that is not easy to invent.

4. Acts contains many brief speeches of officials and opponents that are "opaque to the touchstone of Lukan redaction"[4] while they have a clear function in the narrative.

5. The speeches in Acts are considerably shorter than some speeches in Greek historical works. Luke gives more importance to the narrative settings of the speeches that he includes, certainly when compared with Thucydides.

6. Thucydides and other Greek historians do not handle speeches in a radically different fashion than the reporting of historical events. There was no convention that would prompt contemporary historians to freely create speeches; on the contrary, they sometimes criticized authors who did invent speeches.[5] The speeches in Acts can be regarded as abstracts of real addresses.

[Luke] is not just an "edifying writer," but a historian and theologian who needs to be taken seriously. His account always remains within the limits of what was considered reliable by ancient standards of antiquity.... True, the speeches interspersed through Acts also serve to develop Luke's own theological ideas, but as a rule he does this by use of older traditions, and often attempts to give an appropriate characterization of individual speakers.[6]

As regards the *basic pattern* of the missionary speeches, some have assumed a threefold scheme:[7] (1) the kerygma, i.e., a short summary of what God has done in the ministry of Jesus; (2) proof from Scripture, i.e., a demonstration that the events connected with Jesus fulfilled prophecy; (3) exhortation to repentance and faith. Others acknowledge these three elements but analyze the pattern of the speeches in Acts with more sophistication.[8] (1) The age of fulfill-

---

4. Hemer, *Acts*, 424.

5. Ben Witherington III, "Editor's Addendum," in *History, Literature, and Society in the Book of Acts* (ed. B. Witherington III; Oxford: Oxford Univ. Press, 1996), 23–32.

6. Hengel, *Acts and the History of Earliest Christianity*, 61; cf. Dunn, *Beginning from Jerusalem*, 87–98.

7. Based on an analysis of Acts 2:14–36; 3:12–26; 10:34–43; 13:16–41. Cf. Dibelius, *Studies*, 165.

8. Cf. C. H. Dodd, *The Apostolic Preaching and Its Development* (London: Hodder & Stoughton, 1936), 21–24, based on the speeches in 2:14–36; 3:12–26; 4:10–12; 5:30–32; 10:34–43; 13:16–41.

ment has dawned. (2) This has taken place through the ministry, life, death, and resurrection of Jesus, of which a brief account is given. (3) By virtue of the resurrection, Jesus has been exalted at the right hand of God, as messianic head of the new Israel. (4) The Holy Spirit in the church is the sign of Christ's present power and glory. (5) The messianic age will shortly reach its consummation in the return of Christ. (6) The kerygma closes with an appeal for repentance, the offer of forgiveness and of the Holy Spirit, and the promise of salvation.

Others see the following pattern in speeches addressed to Jews and to Gentiles:[9] (1) direct address, adapted to the situation; (2) appeal for attention; (3) misunderstanding of listeners noted; (4) quotation of the Old Testament introducing the body of the speech; (5) christological/theological kerygma; (6) proof from the Old Testament about the kerygma; (7) reply to the problem posed by the misunderstanding; (8) call for repentance and proclamation of salvation; (9) focus of the message on the audience. Recent studies have cast doubt on the suggestion that the speeches in Acts exhibit a common pattern of early Christian preaching.[10]

A different approach analyzes the structure of the speeches in the context of the tradition of the handbooks of Greco-Roman rhetoric.[11] Even here it has been noted that in a particular discourse Luke sometimes uses more than one of the three types of rhetorical speech (judicial, deliberative, epideictic), so that "the definition of the species as a whole can become very difficult."[12]

The list of what is analyzed in terms of speeches or discourses varies considerably. Probably the longest such list[13] distinguishes five missionary speeches addressed to Jews,[14] three missionary sermons addressed to Gentiles,[15] a prophetic indictment,[16] two didactic speeches,[17] two defense speeches,[18] and one debate.[19] On the forensic speeches in Acts 24 – 26 see "In Depth: Reports of Court Proceedings" (in "Structure and Literary Form" on 24:1 – 27).

---

9. Fitzmyer, *Acts*, 107, based on lists of E. Schweizer and H. Conzelmann.

10. Cf. Joachim Jeska, *Die Geschichte Israels in der Sicht des Lukas: Apg 7,25b – 53 und 13,17 – 25 im Kontext antik-jüdischer Summarien der Geschichte Israels* (FRLANT 195; Göttingen: Vandenhoeck & Ruprecht, 2001), 243 – 44.

11. Cf. Philip E. Satterthwaite, "Acts against the Background of Classical Rhetoric," in *The Book of Acts in Its Ancient Literary Setting* (ed. B. W. Winter and A. D. Clarke), 337 – 79, and the commentaries of Witherington and Parsons.

12. Cf. George A. Kennedy, *New Testament Interpretation through Rhetorical Criticism* (Chapel Hill: Univ. of North Carolina Press, 1984), 114 – 40, quotation p. 19.

13. Fitzmyer, *Acts*, 104, lists twenty-eight speeches or discourses; ten are given by Paul, eight by Peter, and one each by the risen Christ, Demetrius, Festus, Gallio, Gamaliel, James, Stephen, Tertullus, the town clerk of Ephesus, and the Twelve.

14. Acts 2:14 – 36, 38 – 39 (Peter); 3:12 – 26 (Peter); 4:8 – 12 (Peter); 5:29 – 32 (Peter); 13:16 – 41 (Paul).

15. Acts 10:34 – 43 (Peter); 14:15 – 17 (Paul); 17:22 – 31 (Paul).

16. Acts 7:2 – 53 (Stephen).

17. Acts 15:7 – 11 (Peter); 15:13 – 21 (James).

18. Acts 22:1, 3 – 21 (Paul); 26:2 – 23, 25 – 27, 29 (Paul).

19. Acts 24:2 – 8 (Tertullus); 24:10 – 21 (Paul).

Main Idea

Peter explains the manifestations of sound and light and the unprecedented speaking in unlearned foreign languages about the mighty acts of God as the fulfillment of Scripture. The Spirit of prophecy has been poured out by the crucified, risen, and exalted Jesus, who is the Messiah and Lord and who reigns on the throne of David at God's right hand.

Translation

Acts 2:14–36

14a	Action	**Peter stood up**
b	Association	with the eleven,
c	Action	**raised his voice, and**
d	Action	**addressed them:**
	Argument I	
e	Address	*"Fellow Jews and*
f	Address & Place	*all who live in Jerusalem!*
g	Call to listen	*Let this be known to you and*
h		*pay attention to my words.*
15a	Assertion	*These people are not drunk,*
b	Character's thoughts	*as you suppose,*
c	Reason	*for it is only nine in the morning.*
16a	Assertion	*Rather, this is what God said*
b	Quotation of OT	*through Joel the prophet:*
17a	Prophecy & Promise	*'It shall happen …*
b	Time	*in the last days,*
c	Source	*says God,*
d	Action	*…. that I will pour out my Spirit*
e	Sphere	*on all people, and*
f	Result	*your sons and your daughters shall prophesy,*
g	Result	*your young men shall see visions, and*
h	Result	*your old men shall dream dreams.*
18a	Contra-expectation	*Indeed, even*
b	Sphere	*on my male slaves and my female slaves*
c	Action	*I shall pour out my Spirit,*
d	Result	*and they shall prophesy.*
19a	Prophecy & Place	*And I will display wonders in the sky above and*
b	Place	*signs on the earth below,*
c	Identification	*blood and fire and a cloud of smoke.*
20a	Example	*The sun shall be turned to darkness*
b	Example	*and the moon to blood,*
c	Time	*before the great and glorious day of the Lord comes.*

21a	Promise (result of 17-20)	*Then everyone …*
b		*who calls on the name of the Lord*
c		*… shall be saved.'* (Joel 2:28–32)
22a	Address	*Fellow Israelites,*
b	Call to listen	*listen to these words.*
c	Assertion	*Jesus of Nazareth was a man accredited to you by God*
d	Verification	*with mighty deeds,*
e	Verification	*wonders, and*
f	Verification	*signs,*
g	Agency	*which God did through him*
h	Place	*in your midst,*
i	Basis	*as you very well know.*
23a	Contra-expectation	*Even though this man was handed over*
b	Basis	*according to the definite plan and*
c		*foreknowledge*
d		*of God,*
e	Action	*you executed him*
f	Manner	*by nailing him to a cross,*
g	Means	*using men outside the law.*
24a	Assertion	*God raised him up,*
b	Manner	*freeing him from the agony of death,*
c	Reason	*because it was impossible for him to be held by it.*

Argument II

25a	Quotation of OT	*For David says about him,*
b	Assertion	*'I see the Lord before me*
c	Time	*always,*
d	Reason	*for he is at my right hand,*
e	Purpose	*so that I may not be shaken;*
26a	Result	*Therefore my heart was glad*
b	Result	*and my tongue rejoiced,*
c	Climax	*and even more,*
d	Result	*my body shall live in hope.*
27a	Reason	*For you will not abandon me to the realm of the dead,*
b	Restatement	*nor will you allow your Holy One to see decay.*
28a	Assertion	*You have made known to me the paths of life;*
b	Restatement	*you will fill me with joy*
c	Sphere	*in your presence.'* (Ps 16:8–11)
29a	Address	*Brothers,*
b	Assertion	*I can speak confidently about David*
c	Identification	*the patriarch:*
d	Event	*he died*
e	Event	*and was buried,*
f	Confirmation	*and his tomb is in our midst*
g	Time	*to this very day.*
30a	Basis	*But because he was a prophet and*
b	Basis	*knew that God had sworn with an oath to him*
c	Promise	*that he would put one of his descendants on his throne,*

Continued on next page.

Continued from previous page.

31a	Assertion	he foresaw
b	Prophecy	*and* spoke of the resurrection of the Messiah,
c	Content	saying that he was not abandoned to the realm of the dead
d	Restatement	nor has his body seen decay.

| 32a | Assertion | This Jesus God has raised up, |
| b | Verification | *and* we are all witnesses of this. |

Argument III

33a	Event	Exalted to God's right hand,
b	Result	he has received …
c	Source	from the Father
d		… the promised Holy Spirit,
e	Action	whom he has poured out.
f	Assertion/Explanation	This is what you now see and hear.

34a	Verification	*For*
b	Negation	it was not David
c	Identification	who ascended into the heavens;
d	Contra-expectation	*yet* he says,
e	Quotation of OT	'The Lord said to my Lord,
f	Call to action	Sit at my right hand,
35	Time & Promise	until I make your enemies a footstool for your feet.' (Ps 110:1)
36a	Inference & Exhortation	*Therefore,* let all the house of Israel know …
b	Manner	with certainty
c	Assertion	… that God has made him both Lord and Messiah,
d		this Jesus
e	Identification	whom you ☙
f		crucified."

Structure and Literary Form

This is the third incident that Luke reports for the Feast of Pentecost in AD 30. Peter gives a *speech* in which he explains the audio-visual manifestations and the speaking in unlearned languages that have bewildered the Jews of Jerusalem. Luke introduces the Pentecost speech with a reference to the Twelve (Peter, standing with the eleven apostles) and with standard indicators that a speech is about to be reported (2:14a-d). This is one of the longest speeches in Acts. Its 429 words in the Greek text can be compared with Paul's first missionary speech in Pisidian Antioch (470 words; the longest speech is Stephen's speech in Acts 7 with 1,014 words). Luke's summary of what Peter said here is certainly longer than his summary of Peter's speech in 1:16 – 25 on the occasion of the reconstitution of the Twelve.

There is no agreement on how to outline the main body of Peter's speech. Some outlines focus on the charge of drunkenness and on indicting the Jews for killing Jesus, assuming that we have an example of forensic rhetoric.[20] Others focus on Peter's explanation of the miraculous manifestations and on the relationship between the coming of the Spirit and Jesus.[21] Some base their outline on what is said about Jesus.[22] Some scholars link their outline with the three Old Testament quotations.[23] This is the most promising approach, particularly if the focus is on the link the scriptural quotations and the explanation for the reality of the coming of the Spirit and for the reality of Jesus as the promised Messiah and Lord.[24]

Exegetical Outline

→ **I. Peter's Speech on the Day of Pentecost (2:14 – 36)**

    A. Introduction (2:14 – 15)

        1. Address (2:14)

        2. Refutation of the charge of drunkenness (2:15)

    B. Argument I: The Spirit of Prophecy Has Arrived in the Ministry of Jesus (2:16 – 24)

        1. The Spirit of prophecy has arrived, as promised in Joel 2:28 – 32 (2:16 – 21)

            a. Assertion that Joel 2:28 – 32 has been fulfilled (2:16)

            b. Joel: God will pour out his Spirit on all flesh in the last days (2:17a-e)

            c. Joel: The result of the Spirit's presence is prophetic speech (2:17f – 18)

            d. Joel: The result of the Spirit's presence is wonders and signs (2:19 – 20)

            e. Joel: All who on this day call on the Lord's name will be saved (2:21)

        2. The prophecy has been fulfilled in Jesus' life, death, and resurrection (2:22 – 24)

            a. Peter calls on Israel to listen to his explanation (2:22a-b)

            b. Assertion that Joel's prophecy was fulfilled in Jesus' ministry (2:22c-i)

            c. Assertion that Jesus' crucifixion was part of God's plan (2:23)

            d. Assertion that God raised Jesus from the dead (2:24)

20. Cf. Witherington, *Acts*, 138; Soards, *Speeches*, 31, who divide into two sections: 2:14 – 21 (judicial rhetoric: refutation of the charge of drunkenness); 2:22 – 36 (indictment of the Jews).

21. Cf. Pesch, *Apostelgeschichte*, 1:116, who divides into three sections: 2:14b – 21 (interpretation of the miracle of Pentecost); 2:22 – 28 (proclamation of Jesus' resurrection); 2:29 – 36 (connection of the miracle of Pentecost with Jesus, the risen and exalted Messiah and Lord).

22. Cf. Ulrich Wilckens, *Die Missionsreden der Apostelgeschichte. Form- und traditionsgeschichtliche Untersuchungen* (3rd ed.; WMANT 5; Neukirchen-Vluyn: Neukirchener Verlag, 1974), 37, who divides into five sections: 2:14 – 21 (reference to the situation and introductory scriptural quotation); 2:22 – 23 (the contrast between the manner in which God and human

beings dealt with Jesus: his miracles and his death); 2:24 – 32 (Jesus' resurrection, with proof from Scripture); 2:33 – 35 (Jesus' exaltation and giving of the Spirit, with proof from Scripture); 2:36 (summary thesis).

23. Cf. Dunn, *Acts*, 27, who divides into three sections: 2:14 – 21 (introduction, answering the charge of drunkenness: Joel 2:28 – 32); 2:22 – 32 (central section on Jesus' resurrection: Ps 16:8 – 11); 22:33 – 36 (climax, linking the Christology to the outpoured Spirit: Ps 110:1). Differently Fitzmyer, *Acts*, 249, who divides into five sections: 2:14b – 15 (introduction); 2:16 – 21 (OT quotation to clarify the situation); 2:22 – 24, 32 – 33 (kerygma); 2:24 – 31, 34 – 35 (OT quotation to relate Jesus to David); 2:36 (climactic conclusion: testimony).

24. Cf. Turner, *Power from on High*, 273 – 76.

C. Argument II: Jesus Is David's Promised Heir by Virtue of His Resurrection (2:25 – 32)

1. David prophesied of a Lord who is Savior, according to Ps 16:8 – 11 (2:25 – 28)

     a. Assertion that Ps 16:8 – 11 applies to Jesus (2:25a)

     b. David: The Lord is at my right hand (2:25b-e)

     c. David: The Lord makes me rejoice (2:26)

     d. David: The Lord will save me from death (2:27)

     e. David: The Lord will give me life and salvation (2:28)

2. The prophecy has been fulfilled in Jesus' resurrection from the dead (2:29 – 32)

     a. Peter calls on Israel to listen to his explanation (2:29a-c)

     b. David has died long ago and is still in his tomb (2:29d-g)

     c. David was a prophet who knew that God had promised an heir (2:30)

     d. David prophesied the resurrection of the Messiah in Ps 16:10 (2:31)

     e. Assertion that this prophecy is fulfilled in Jesus' resurrection (2:32)

D. Argument III: Jesus Has Poured Out the Spirit by Virtue of His Exaltation (2:33 – 36)

1. Jesus is the exalted Lord who reigns and who pours out God's Spirit (2:33 – 35)

     a. Assertion that Jesus has been exalted to God's throne (2:33a)

     b. Result of Jesus' reign: The coming of the Spirit (2:33b-f)

     c. Assertion that Ps 110:1 applies to Jesus (2:34 – 35)

2. Jesus who was crucified is the Lord and the Messiah of prophecy (2:36)

     a. Peter calls on Israel to accept his explanation (2:36a-b)

     b. Jesus is the Davidic Lord and Messiah (2:36c-f)

Explanation of the Text

2:14 Peter stood up with the eleven, raised his voice, and addressed them: "Fellow Jews and all who live in Jerusalem! Let this be known to you and pay attention to my words" (Σταθεὶς δὲ ὁ Πέτρος σὺν τοῖς ἕνδεκα ἐπῆρεν τὴν φωνὴν αὐτοῦ καὶ ἀπεφθέγξατο αὐτοῖς· ἄνδρες Ἰουδαῖοι καὶ οἱ κατοικοῦντες Ἰερουσαλὴμ πάντες, τοῦτο ὑμῖν γνωστὸν ἔστω καὶ ἐνωτίσασθε τὰ ῥήματά μου). Peter, representing the Twelve[25] as their spokesman, explains to the bewildered crowds the reason for and the significance of the audio-visual manifestations and the unprecedented phenomenon of people speaking in foreign languages that they have not learned. The verbs of this statement describe Peter as an orator about to give a speech.

Peter stands, rather than sits down (as in the synagogue), because he is addressing a large number of people, probably in front of the house in which the followers of Jesus had been staying. He raises his voice because he wants to be heard by all the people who are present. He explains the unprecedented phenomena that have bewildered the crowd to his "fellow Jews"[26] and to the diaspora

---

25. Codex D has "ten" instead of eleven apostles, besides Peter, refusing to consider Matthias as fully replacing Judas. Cf. Rius-Camps and Read-Heimerdinger, *Acts*, 1:179.

26. The phrase ἄνδρες Ἰουδαῖοι occurs only here in Acts. On the mode of address, cf. 1:16. The term Ἰουδαῖοι may refer to Judeans proper, i.e., those Jews who live in Jerusalem and the surrounding region (and thus in the Roman province of Judea).

Jews who have come from the regions mentioned in vv. 9 – 11 to live in Jerusalem.

Speeches as well as letters often used the formula "let this be known to you." The call to "pay attention" reinforces Peter's request that those who want an explanation for the unusual phenomena listen carefully to what he has to say (vv. 7, 8, 12).

Against skeptics who believe that the following speech reflects how Luke would have preached or how the church of his day explained the coming of the Holy Spirit, other scholars have argued that this speech "calls for the serious consideration that the early church preserved some recollection about how Peter proclaimed the Christian message on that first occasion, at least that he appealed to Joel and the Davidic Psalter."[27]

2:15 These people are not drunk, as you suppose, for it is only nine in the morning (οὐ γὰρ ὡς ὑμεῖς ὑπολαμβάνετε οὗτοι μεθύουσιν, ἔστιν γὰρ ὥρα τρίτη τῆς ἡμέρας). In order to clarify any misunderstanding right at the start, Peter points out that he and his friends cannot be drunk, as some of the bystanders have suggested. The "third hour of the day," i.e., nine o'clock in the morning, is too early to be intoxicated. The "day" was divided into twelve hours, reckoned from dawn to dark.

2:16 Rather, this is what God said through Joel the prophet (ἀλλὰ τοῦτό ἐστιν τὸ εἰρημένον διὰ τοῦ προφήτου Ἰωήλ). Peters begins his explanation of the manifestations that the crowds had witnessed but not understood with the argument that they are the fulfillment of the prophecy in Joel 2:28 – 32 (LXX 3:1 – 5). The introduction of the scriptural quotation (lit., "what has been said through...") is also attested at Qumran.[28] The pas-

sive participle (εἰρημένον) is a divine passive — it is God who speaks through the words of Joel recorded in Scripture.

2:17 "It shall happen in the last days, says God, that I will pour out my Spirit on all people, and your sons and your daughters shall prophesy, your young men shall see visions, and your old men shall dream dreams" (καὶ ἔσται ἐν ταῖς ἐσχάταις ἡμέραις, λέγει ὁ θεός, ἐκχεῶ ἀπὸ τοῦ πνεύματός μου ἐπὶ πᾶσαν σάρκα, καὶ προφητεύσουσιν οἱ υἱοὶ ὑμῶν καὶ αἱ θυγατέρες ὑμῶν καὶ οἱ νεανίσκοι ὑμῶν ὁράσεις ὄψονται καὶ οἱ πρεσβύτεροι ὑμῶν ἐνυπνίοις ἐνυπνιασθήσονται). The reference to the "last days" establishes how Peter reads the prophets of Scripture: God has begun to fulfill his promises, the last days have begun with Jesus, although the last day will arrive only when Jesus returns (cf. 1:11). As the following verses will show, Peter links the last days not with the coming of the Holy Spirit but with the entire ministry of Jesus. This was a common early Christian conviction that was often expressed: the ministry, death, resurrection, and ascension of Jesus, the Messiah and Savior, with the climax of the coming of the Spirit on Pentecost, constitute the beginning of the final epoch in history when God has acted in a decisive manner to bring salvation through his Son.[29]

The context of Joel 2:28 – 32 is a summons of the prophet who challenges the people of Israel who have suffered an invasion of locusts to truly repent, combined with a warning that worse events will take place on "the ... day of the LORD." The Lord promises to restore the land to abundant prosperity as he is in their midst. The Lord will pour out his Spirit on all flesh, an event that will impact all sectors of society and is accompanied by wonders

---

27. Fitzmyer, *Acts*, 249; cf. Bock, *Proclamation*, 156 – 87.
28. Cf. CD X, 16; XVI, 15; 11QMelch XIV. The translation "what God said" supplies the logical subject of the passive εἰρημένον from the following statement in 2:17.

29. Cf. Rom 13:11; 1 Cor 10:11; Gal 4:4; Eph 1:7 – 10, 20 – 23; 1 Thess 2:19; 3:13; 5:23; Heb 1:1 – 2; 9:26; Jas 5:1 – 9; 1 Pet 1:19 – 21; 2 Pet 3:3; 1 John 2:18; Jude 18.

and signs in the sky and on earth. In those days, before the great and terrible day of the Lord comes, everyone who calls on the name of the Lord will be saved. Peter uses the prophecy that God will pour out his Spirit on his people (see also Isa 32:15; 44:3; Ezek 39:29) to explain the phenomenon of miraculous proclamation of God's mighty works in unlearned languages. The second theme of Joel, that all people who call on the Lord will be saved, eventually becomes dominant in this speech of Peter, who identifies the Lord of Joel's prophecy with the risen and exalted Jesus.[30]

The phrase "in the last days" (ἐν ταῖς ἐσχάταις ἡμέραις)[31] is an addition to the text of Joel, who begins this particular prophecy with the phrase "after this" (μετὰ ταῦτα). Peter clarifies that what follows in Joel's prophecy relates to the last days of God's history of salvation, which is now identified as the new age ushered in by Jesus.

The expression "says God" (λέγει ὁ θεός) is also added to Joel's text. Peter clarifies that the words of Joel's prophecy are the words of God and that God is the one who pours out "his" Spirit. In a Jewish context, this addition is unnecessary — nobody but God himself could pour out his Spirit, who is the personal and effective presence of the transcendent God himself. This change of the text sets up the later point in Peter's speech that it is Jesus, the Messiah, who pours out the Spirit and who has thus, after his exaltation, taken over a divine function.[32] In the Old Testament and in Judaism, "the Spirit is virtually never simply an agent, separable from God, but one of the few ways Judaism reserves

for *God's own* activity *in contrast* to his activity through his agents. Spirit is God's way of being, the 'breath' of his mouth, his own surging 'life,' and so the unmediated extension of his personality and vitality."[33]

God pours his Spirit out "on all people" (lit., "on all flesh"). This means that he distributes the Spirit to not just a few people, on special occasions, and for special tasks, but to everybody. In Joel's context, "all flesh" denotes all the people of Judah whose fortunes will be restored (Joel 3:1, LXX 4:1). Peter will later clarify that "all flesh" are all the people who repent and believe in Jesus as the Messiah (v. 38).[34] And even later he will understand that "all flesh" includes also Gentiles who believe in the Lord Jesus (Acts 11:15–18).

In Joel's prophecy, the effect of the coming of the Spirit is described (1) in terms of gender (sons and daughters), age (young men and old men), and social class (male and female slaves), and (2) in terms of supernatural manifestations in prophecies, visions, and dreams.

Since Joel's prophecy, addressed to his contemporaries, speaks about future events, the expression "your sons and your daughters" refers to all Jews, male and female, who will be alive at "the great and glorious day of the Lord" (v. 20). The pair "young men" and "old men" describes the entire male population above the age of children. In the Greco-Roman world the concept of "young people" (νέοι) was reckoned from eighteen to thirty years, and the age of the "old man" (γέρων/πρεσβύτης) from fifty years and up.[35]

---

30. Cf. Marshall, "Acts," 533; his explanations of Peter's use of Old Testament texts and allusions in Acts 2:14–36 will guide our interpretation.

31. Cf. 2 Tim 3:1; Jas 5:3.

32. Cf. Turner, *Power from on High*, 277–78.

33. Ibid., 277 (emphasis Turner).

34. The preposition ἀπό in 2:17 ("I will pour out from my Spirit" [lit.]) has a partitive meaning and points to the distribution of the Spirit; it fits naturally with the description of the

"pouring out" of the Spirit; cf. Barrett, *Acts*, 136; Bock, *Acts*, 113.

35. G. Binder, "Age(s)," *BNP*, 1:331–36. BDAG, s.v. νεανίας, defines "youth, young man" as "from about the 24th to the 40th year" (with reference to Diogenes Laertius, *Vit. phil.* 8.10 and Philo, *Cherubim* 114). This is only one of many classifications of life's stages in antiquity. Note that the age at marriage for young men in the Roman Empire was between twenty and thirty years of age; cf. J. Wiesehöfer, "Marriage, Age at," *BNP*, 8:394–95. See also R. Larry Overstreet, "The Greek Concept of

The verb translated "prophesy" (προφητεύω) denotes (1) to proclaim an inspired revelation ("prophesy"); (2) to tell about something that is hidden from view ("tell, reveal"); (3) to foretell something that lies in the future ("foretell, prophesy").[36] A helpful definition of prophecy describes this manifestation as

> the reception and subsequent public declaration of (usually) verbal revelation. Such revelation is normally spontaneous ... and the subsequent declaration is normally immediate. Regardless of the novelty or familiarity of its content, the speaker conceives it to be revealed truth, rather than the results of his own thought processes.... Prophecy might include, but was not limited to, the prediction of the future: it might equally be unsolicited guidance, exhortation, or remonstration. It was not normally the basic gospel proclamation itself, but might commonly be some application of its principles to a particular situation.[37]

The New Testament texts repeatedly highlight the significance of prophecy for the church.[38] About sixty prophecies have been identified in the New Testament.[39] In the context of Peter's speech in Acts 2, the verb "prophesy" refers to the proclamation of the mighty acts of God by the 120 disciples in foreign, unlearned languages, spoken under the revelatory inspiration of God and perhaps under some constraint to do so. In Acts, the activity of prophets is attested in 11:27; 13:1; 15:32; 19:6; 21:9–10.

The "visions" (ὁράσεις) and "dreams" (ἐνύπνια) describe experiences that convey, under divine inspiration, supernatural revelation. While these two terms are rare in the New Testament, they frequently occur in the Greek Old Testament to describe the mode of the revelations that the prophets received from God. While the dividing line between visions and dreams is not always clear, one cannot conclude that the Spirit will affect the young and the old in different ways. Visions (ὅραμα) are mentioned in Acts for Old Testament figures such as Moses (7:31), for Peter (10:17, 19; 11:5; cf. 12:9), for Paul (9:12; 16:9, 10; 18:9), for believers in Jesus such as Ananias (9:10), and for devout Gentiles who are being converted, such as Cornelius (10:3). Related is the state of partially (sometimes wholly) suspended consciousness described as trance or ecstasy (ἔκστασις), reported for Peter (10:10; 11:5) and for Paul (22:17).

2:18 Indeed, even on my male slaves and my female slaves I shall pour out my Spirit, and they shall prophesy (καί γε ἐπὶ τοὺς δούλους μου καὶ ἐπὶ τὰς δούλας μου ἐν ταῖς ἡμέραις ἐκείναις ἐκχεῶ ἀπὸ τοῦ πνεύματός μου, καὶ προφητεύσουσιν). Joel's prophecy speaks of male and female slaves receiving God's Spirit and prophesying. This implies that the coming of the Holy Spirit on all people will remove all distinctions of class and caste. In Peter's speech, the possessive pronouns "my" (μου) are added to the Joel text, with the effect that the literal slaves of Joel's day are now understood as a description of God's servants.

2:19–20 And I will display wonders in the sky above and signs on the earth below, blood and fire and a cloud of smoke. The sun shall be turned to darkness and the moon to blood, before the great and glorious day of the Lord comes (καὶ δώσω τέρατα ἐν τῷ οὐρανῷ ἄνω καὶ σημεῖα ἐπὶ τῆς γῆς κάτω, αἷμα καὶ πῦρ καὶ ἀτμίδα καπνοῦ. ὁ ἥλιος μεταστραφήσεται εἰς σκότος καὶ ἡ σελήνη εἰς

---

the 'Seven Stages of Life' and Its New Testament Significance," *BBR* 19 (2009): 537–63.

36. BDAG, s.v. προφητεύω.

37. Forbes, *Prophecy and Inspired Speech*, 229.

38. Paul lists prophecy in his lists of the gifts of the Spirit; cf.

Rom 12:6–8; 1 Cor 12:8–10, 28–29; 14:6, 26.

39. Cf. David E. Aune, *Prophecy in Early Christianity and the Ancient Mediterranean World* (Grand Rapids: Eerdmans, 1983), 247–90, 317–38.

αἷμα πρὶν ἐλθεῖν ἡμέραν κυρίου τὴν μεγάλην καὶ ἐπιφανῆ). The pouring out of God's Spirit on all people will be accompanied by wonders and signs in the sky and on earth. The adverbs "above" (ἄνω) and "below" (κάτω) are added to Joel's text, as is the term "signs" (σημεῖα). This change creates a distinction between "wonders" in the sky and "signs" on earth, with "blood and fire and a cloud of smoke" belonging to the latter.

If these changes are deliberate, of which there can hardly be any doubt, it is unlikely that Peter (and Luke) uses Joel's apocalyptic language to refer to the future judgment. If indeed Peter referred to the future day of judgment, Joel's prophecy in Joel 2:30–31 (LXX 3:3–4) is not fulfilled in the present. Some have therefore argued that Peter cites the entire Joel text even though he needs only the words of Acts 2:21 (Joel 2:32/LXX 3:5).[40] This is not convincing, since Luke can quote Scripture with omissions, if necessary. If Peter only wanted to quote a prophecy that he believed was fulfilled in the phenomena he wants to explain to the crowd, he would not have needed Joel 2:30–32 (LXX 3:3–5). The fact that Peter quotes Joel 2:28–32 (LXX 3:1–5), prefaced with the announcement that this has now been fulfilled (v. 16), suggests that the Joel citation is used to explain more than just the Pentecost phenomena.[41]

(1) Joel's prophecy of "wonders" (τέρατα) and "signs" (σημεῖα) was fulfilled in Jesus' ministry, notably in the miracles Jesus performed, which were signs of the coming of God's kingdom and of Jesus' role in this kingdom. The order "wonders and signs" relates the events that are in view to Jesus' ministry. The usual order in the LXX and in the New Testament, including Acts, is "signs and wonders."[42] The reverse order of the two terms in the phrase "wonders and signs" is used, apart from the reworked quotation from Joel (v. 19), for the miracles of Jesus (v. 22) and for the miracles of the Jerusalem apostles (v. 43).[43]

(2) Joel's prophecy of wonders and signs was fulfilled in the events of Jesus' death, notably in the darkening of the sun, mentioned in v. 20. The order of "wonder" in the sky followed by "sign" on earth corresponds to Luke's account of the darkening of the sun at the time of Jesus' crucifixion (Luke 23:45a) followed by the rending of the curtain in the temple (Luke 23:45b). In Matt 27:51 and Mark 15:38, the rending of the curtain comes after the darkening of the sun and after Jesus' death. Luke does not mention the earthquake that Matt 27:51 reports for the day of Jesus' crucifixion, but it would have been remembered by the people living in Jerusalem.

(3) Joel's prophecy of "wonders in the sky" (τέρατα ἐν τῷ οὐρανῷ) was fulfilled in the ascension of Jesus, who ascended in a cloud (νεφέλη ὑπέλαβεν αὐτόν) into heaven (εἰς τὸν οὐρανόν; 1:9, 11). This prophecy was also fulfilled in the manifestations on Pentecost, which descended "from heaven" (ἐκ τοῦ οὐρανοῦ, v. 2) and which Peter is in the process of explaining.

(4) The reference to "blood and fire and a cloud of smoke" and to the turning of the "moon to blood" cannot easily be linked with Jesus' ministry, death, or ascension. "Blood" (αἷμα) refers in Luke 22:20 to Jesus' shed blood, which inaugurates the new covenant (see also Acts 5:28; 20:28). However, none of these references links Jesus' blood with fire

---

40. Cf. Haenchen, *Acts*, 186.

41. Cf. Martin Rese, *Alttestamentliche Motive in der Christologie des Lukas* (SNT 1; Gütersloh: Mohn, 1969), 45–55; Robert B. Sloan, "'Signs and Wonders': A Rhetorical Clue to the Pentecost Discourse," *EvQ* 63 (1991): 225–40.

42. For the phrase "signs and wonders" cf. Exod 7:3; Deut

4:34; 6:22; 7:19; 26:8; 34:11; Neh 9:10; Ps 135:9; Jer 32:20, 21; Dan 4:2; 6:27; John 4:48; Rom 15:19; 2 Cor 12:12; Heb 2:4; cf. 2 Thess 2:9; and Acts 4:30; 5:12; 14:3; 15:12.

43. Note that in Acts 6:8 and 7:36, the miracles of Stephen and of Moses are described as "wonders and signs."

or smoke or other eschatological signs on earth. Still, some have suggested that "there may be some typology in Jesus' death, as Luke 22:20 combined with the descriptions of Jesus' death might suggest."[44] "Fire" (πῦρ) can be linked with the visual phenomenon mentioned earlier in the chapter, which appeared "as if of fire" (ὡσεὶ πυρός; v. 3).

The "cloud of smoke" (ἀτμὶς καπνοῦ) may allude to either the cloud behind which Jesus disappeared when he ascended to the Father, or to the "tongues" that looked as if they were connected with fire (γλῶσσαι ὡσεὶ πυρός, 2:3), which appeared in the room in which the believers had assembled on Pentecost (v. 3). We should also note that Luke's description of the manifestations on the day of Pentecost in vv. 2 – 4 contained distinct allusions to God's theophany on Mount Sinai; Joel's "cloud of smoke"[45] may denote, in Peter's quotation, God's theophany on the day of Pentecost reminiscent of his appearance on Mount Sinai.

In the context of Joel's prophecy, the manifestations of "blood and fire and a cloud of smoke" (v. 19c) and the prophecy that "the sun shall be turned to darkness and the moon to blood" (v. 20a-b) are connected with God's judgment, which suggests that these "signs" on earth, as Peter portrays them, should be understood as eschatological signs.[46] Peter affirms that the "last days" have already begun in the ministry of Jesus and with his death (and resurrection and ascension, as he will shortly argue); thus, God's judgment that brings the present structure of the cosmos (i.e., sky/heaven and earth) to an end is also drawing close.

The fulfillment of Joel's prophecy in Jesus' ministry and death, in the manifestations on the day of Pentecost, and in future wonders in the sky and signs on the earth will find its climax on the great day of God's judgment and salvation. The conjunction (πρίν, "before") clarifies that the phenomena described in vv. 19c – 20b take place before that last day arrives.

The "day of the Lord" refers to a dramatic intervention of God in history, which is often described by the Old Testament prophets as the decisive day that brings salvation for God's faithful people and destruction for God's enemies, whether they are Israel's enemies or the faithless of Israel.[47] The coming day of the Lord is "great" because it is more decisive, more eminent, more noteworthy than any other day since creation. The day of the Lord is "glorious" (ἐπιφανής) because it is the day on which the Lord appears on earth (ἐπιφάνεια, epiphany).[48]

In v. 20, Peter summarizes his understanding of the divine plan. The followers of Jesus live between Jesus' resurrection and ascension on the one hand, and the return of Jesus on the "day of the Lord" on

---

44. Bock, *Acts*, 116. The suggestion of Colin J. Humphreys and W. Graeme Waddington, "The Jewish Calendar, a Lunar Eclipse and the Date of Christ's Crucifixion," *TynBul* 43 (1992): 331 – 51, that 2:19 refers to a lunar eclipse during which the moon assumes a dull, red color, which was visible in Jerusalem at Passover in AD 33, while intriguing, is unconvincing since the more plausible date for Jesus' crucifixion is the year AD 30; cf. Marshall, "Acts," 535.

45. The term ἀτμίς is mentioned in Gen 19:28 in connection with the destruction of Sodom and Gomorrah. The term καπνός is used for God's theophany on Mount Sinai in Exod 19:18.

46. Cf. Isa 13:10; Ezek 32:7; thus understood in Luke 21:25 (cf. Matt 24:29; Mark 13:24; Rev 6:12) in the context of the end of the present cosmos and the (second) coming of the Son of Man.

47. Cf. Isa 2:6 – 3:15; 13:6 – 9; 34:8 – 12; Jer 46:9 – 12; Ezek 7:19; 10:1 – 9; Joel 1:1 – 2:27; Amos 5:18, 20; 8:9; Obad 15 – 18; Zeph 1:14 – 18; 2:1 – 15; Zech 14:1 – 21; Mal 3:13 – 4:6.

48. BDAG, s.v. ἐπιφανής: "being resplendent, *splendid, glorious, remarkable,* probably suggesting light whose impact is especially striking in its sudden appearance, of the day of God's judgment." Greg H. R. Horsley and Stephen R. Llewelyn, eds., *New Documents Illustrating Early Christianity* (Macquarie University: North Ryde, NSW, Australia, 1981 – 2002), 4:148, compares the expression with the terminology used of Hellenistic rulers and subsequently the Roman emperors in terms of divine status; thus "the implication of the presence of the word in Peter's Pentecost speech is to suggest Jesus' divinity, as the following verses more explicitly indicate (Acts 2.22, 36)."

the other hand. This period is marked by the presence of the Spirit of God and by the presence of the gifts of the Spirit, among which are miraculous speech (prophecy) and signs on earth (cf. v. 43). These signs include portents that take place before the day of Lord — signs connected with the ministry and death of Jesus, with the outpouring of the Spirit, and with the life and work of the apostles. The life of Jesus' followers is thus firmly tied to their origins in the historical ministry and mission of Jesus.

2:21 "Then everyone who calls on the name of the Lord shall be saved" (καὶ ἔσται πᾶς ὃς ἂν ἐπικαλέσηται τὸ ὄνομα κυρίου σωθήσεται). Peter quotes Joel's prophecy not only to explain the audiovisual phenomena and the miraculous speaking of unlearned languages, but primarily to explain the significance of Jesus. In Joel's prophecy, the "Lord" is Yahweh, and salvation is an event that will take place on the great, climactic day of the Lord. For Peter, the "Lord" (κύριος) is Jesus of Nazareth, as the immediately following explanation clarifies (vv. 22–36), underscored by Peter's subsequent evangelistic sermon in vv. 38–39, in which cleansing, forgiveness of sins, and the reception of the Holy Spirit are linked with "the name [τὸ ὄνομα] of Jesus the Messiah."

The phrase "call on the name of the Lord" means to invoke the name of Jesus in faith, with the conviction that he is indeed the crucified Messiah and the risen Lord, exalted to God's right hand. It can be explained as a Hebrew idiom that underscores the fact "that this is not an unknown god, but rather the God whose character and reputation

are known."[49] Peter's statement, quoting from Joel, constitutes both an invitation and a promise of salvation. The term *name* occurs frequently in Acts.[50] In 3:16 Peter emphasizes in a sermon in the temple courts that what saves is not the name but the faith with which Jesus' name is invoked. The "name" of Jesus "represents his divine authority and his continuing power to grant the blessing of salvation."[51]

Salvation is granted by believing in Jesus as Messiah and Lord.[52] In v. 38 salvation is described as cleansing (symbolized in immersion in water), forgiveness of sins, and reception of the Holy Spirit. The passive voice of the verb (σωθήσεται) indicates that it is the Lord, i.e., Jesus, who forgives sins.[53] The fact that salvation is contingent on people calling on and believing in Jesus is expressed with the subjunctive (ἐπικαλέσηται). The identity of those who call on the name of the Lord Jesus is unspecified, as some believe while others do not believe.

"Everyone" (πᾶς) is saved by calling on the name of the Lord — the Jews living in Jerusalem, the diaspora Jews who have returned to Jerusalem, the Jews who continue to live in the regions whose languages the apostles had spoken, and also "all those who are far away" (v. 39), i.e., all human beings, whether they are male or female, young or old, slaves or free (cf. vv. 17–18). We should note that the Joel text added "for on Mount Zion and in Jerusalem there will be deliverance," a line omitted here as salvation moves beyond Jerusalem to Judea, Samaria, and even to the ends of the earth (1:8).

2:22 Fellow Israelites, listen to these words. Jesus of Nazareth was a man accredited to you by God with mighty deeds, wonders, and signs,

---

49. Marshall, "Acts," 536.

50. Acts 2:21, 38; 3:6, 16; 4:7, 10, 12, 17, 18, 30; 5:28, 40, 41; 8:12, 16; 9:14, 15, 16, 21, 27, 28; cf. Rom 10:12–13 (with the same quotation from Joel); 1 Cor 1:2; 2 Tim 2:22.

51. David G. Peterson, "The Worship of the New Community," in *Witness to the Gospel: The Theology of Acts* (ed. I. H.

Marshall and D. Peterson), 373–96, 381.

52. The verb σῴζω is used of Jesus in Acts 4:12; 11:14; 15:1, 11; 16:30–31; cf. 28:28.

53. Cf. Jesus' claim, early in his ministry, to have the authority to forgive sins (Luke 5:17–26; cf. Matt 9:2–8; Mark 2:1–12).

which God did through him in your midst, as you very well know (ἄνδρες Ἰσραηλῖται, ἀκούσατε τοὺς λόγους τούτους· Ἰησοῦν τὸν Ναζωραῖον, ἄνδρα ἀποδεδειγμένον ἀπὸ τοῦ θεοῦ εἰς ὑμᾶς δυνάμεσι καὶ τέρασι καὶ σημείοις οἷς ἐποίησεν δι᾽ αὐτοῦ ὁ θεὸς ἐν μέσῳ ὑμῶν καθὼς αὐτοὶ οἴδατε). Peter addresses his listeners again, after the lengthy quotation from Joel. Instead of "fellow Jews," he now addresses them as "fellow Israelites," using the honorific name of Abraham's descendants, which underscores their status of members of God's people. As people who bear the name that Yahweh gave to Jacob (Gen 32:28), Peter now challenges them to consider the significance of the fulfillment of Joel's prophecy in the present time.

In vv. 22 – 24 Peter applies Joel's prophecy to Jesus' life, death, and resurrection, which constitutes the second part of his first argument that the Spirit of prophecy has arrived in the ministry of Jesus and in the manifestations of Pentecost.

Peter's proclamation focuses on Jesus, as he explains the "name of the Lord" (v. 21). Peter describes him as a historical person, thus "Jesus of Nazareth." As Jews had only one name, the identity of a person was expressed by naming either his father or the town in which he was born and/ or in which he grew up. Nazareth, the town in which Jesus grew up, was a small, unimportant town in western lower Galilee, with perhaps 400 inhabitants.[54]

Jesus is first described as a "man" (ἀνήρ), as a male human being. But he was not an ordinary man; he was "accredited [ἀποδεδειγμένον] by God." This verb emphasizes that God demonstrated who

Jesus is by what he accomplished through him. The prepositional phrase "to you" (εἰς ὑμᾶς) states that the miracles of Jesus happened for the benefit of the Jews, and they happened in public. God's accrediting demonstration of Jesus' identity took place for and among the Israelites, i.e., among God's people. The Jews living in Jerusalem and Judea, along with the festival pilgrims from Galilee who were in town, all knew about Jesus and his ministry, which was a public ministry. His miracles demonstrate what kind of man he was — the multiple and various miracles, the "mighty deeds" (δυνάμεις) and the "wonders" or "portents" (τέρατα), were "signs" (σημεῖα), i.e., events that indicated and confirmed God's intervention in the affairs of human beings and of the cosmos.[55]

Peter emphasizes that through the miracles Jesus performed in the course of his ministry, God showed that Jesus was his special envoy. The miracles were caused by God (ἐποίησεν δι᾽ αὐτοῦ ὁ θεός), and they were public (ἐν μέσῳ ὑμῶν), as the audience knows.

2:23 Even though this man was handed over according to the definite plan and foreknowledge of God, you executed him by nailing him to a cross, using men outside the law (τοῦτον τῇ ὡρισμένῃ βουλῇ καὶ προγνώσει τοῦ θεοῦ ἔκδοτον διὰ χειρὸς ἀνόμων προσπήξαντες ἀνείλατε). Moving from Jesus' life and ministry to Jesus' death, Peter asserts that Jesus died in accordance with God's eternal plan. He makes the following statements about Jesus' death.

(1) Jesus was killed (ἀνείλατε; "executed") by the Jews living in Jerusalem. In vv. 5, 14 Peter identified

---

54. Cf. Jonathan L. Reed, *Archaeology and the Galilean Jesus: A Re-Examination of the Evidence* (Harrisburg, PA: Trinity Press International, 2000), 105 – 6, 115 – 17, 131 – 32; Schnabel, *Early Christian Mission*, 1:184, 228 – 29.

55. Cf. BDAG, s.v. σημεῖον 2. The terms δύναμις and δυνάμεις are regularly used for Jesus' miracles, Luke 4:36; 5:17;

6:19; 8:46; 9:1; 10:13; 19:37; cf. 4:14; it is used for Paul's miracles in Acts 19:11. The phrase τέρατα καὶ σημεῖα occurs in Acts 2:43; 4:30; 5:12; 6:8; 7:36; 14:3; 15:12; in the Old Testament the phrase often describes God's mighty acts on behalf of Israel, Exod 7:3; Deut 4:34; 28:46; 29:3; 34:11; Ps 135:9; Isa 8:18.

the people witnessing the Pentecost manifestations as residents of Jerusalem.[56] In Luke's description of Jesus' trial (Luke 22 – 23), the driving force behind his execution was the Jewish leadership in Jerusalem.[57] Some of those in the crowd listening to Peter's explanation of the strange phenomena that have taken place on Pentecost may have been part of the crowd who, only a few weeks earlier, had shouted, "Crucify him, crucify him!" (Luke 23:18, 21, 23).

(2) Jesus was killed by being fixed (προσπήξαντες) to a cross. Peter does not provide details of the horrific procedure of crucifixion, which was a widespread penalty in the Roman world, inflicted mostly on people from the lower classes (slaves, violent criminals, and political rebels in the provinces), carried out in public as a deterrent, and bringing utter humiliation and shame on the executed criminal.

(3) Jesus was killed after he had been "handed over" (ἔκδοτον)[58] and nailed to a cross by "men outside the law." The Jews used pagans, i.e., Roman officials, to have Jesus executed. The prepositional phrase translated as "using men" (διὰ χειρός, lit., "through the hand of") describes agency. These "(men) outside the law" (ἄνομοι) particularly are not wicked people, but are people who live outside of the Mosaic law, such as Pilate and the Roman soldiers.

(4) Jesus was executed on a cross according to the plan of God. The dative phrase "according to the definite plan and foreknowledge" (τῇ ὡρισμένῃ βουλῇ καὶ προγνώσει) is a dative of cause. What happened to Jesus cannot be fully explained by reference to the intentions of the Jews of Jerusalem or by the involvement of the pagan Romans. Jesus' death was part of God's "plan" (βουλή),[59] which had been determined in advance according to the omniscient wisdom of God's "foreknowledge" (πρόγνωσις). In the Greek text, this statement comes before the reference to those who are guilty of Jesus' death. "What appeared to be a free concerted action by Jews and Gentiles was in fact done because God foreknew it, decided it, planned it."[60]

This is the paradox of Jesus' death: it was engineered and carried out by human beings, while at the same time it was the climax of God's plan of salvation. Jesus' death on the cross was part of his mission. Luke contrasts what wicked people did to Jesus with Jesus' vindication by God, who raised him from the dead (also in 10:39 – 40; 13:28 – 31).

2:24 God raised him up, freeing him from the agony of death, because it was impossible for him to be held by it (ὃν ὁ θεὸς ἀνέστησεν λύσας τὰς ὠδῖνας τοῦ θανάτου καθότι οὐκ ἦν δυνατὸν κρατεῖσθαι αὐτὸν ὑπ' αὐτοῦ). Jesus, killed by the Jews of Jerusalem and by the pagan Romans, was raised from the dead. While nobody doubted that Jesus had performed miracles and then been killed, the assertion that he came back from death is controversial, not only because such an unprecedented event would have to be proven, but also because, if true, such an event would have consequences for the Jews living in Jerusalem and elsewhere. Peter asserts three main points.

(1) Jesus was raised from the dead by God. Luke

---

56. Cf. Jon A. Weatherly, *Jewish Responsibility for the Death of Jesus in Luke-Acts* (JSNTSup 106; Sheffield: JSOT Press, 1994), 83 – 85, who argues against the view that Luke universally indicts all Jews as being responsible for Jesus' death.

57. Cf. Weatherly, *Jewish Responsibility*, 50 – 90. Cf. Acts 2:36; 3:13; 4:10; 5:30; 7:52.

58. From ἐκδίδωμι, "*to give up*, especially something seized and detained unlawfully," or "*to give in charge* to another," or

"*to betray*" (LSJ, s.v. ἐκδίδωμι senses 1, 1, 4, 11). ἔκδοτος is used only here in the NT. It does not describe God's action, but the activity of the Jews of Jerusalem.

59. For the plan (βουλή) of God, cf. Luke 7:30; Acts 4:28; 13:36; 20:27. For the conviction that God planned, or knew, that Jesus would suffer, cf. Luke 9:21 – 22, 44 – 45; 13:33; 17:25; 18:31 – 33; 22:37; 24:46 – 47.

60. Barrett, *Acts*, 142.

mostly uses transitive forms of the verb ἀνίστημι.[61] Jesus' resurrection is the direct result of the powerful action of God. As God made the heavens and the earth (4:24), and as he made from one ancestor all the nations of the earth (17:26), he also raised up Jesus from death.

(2) Death holds captive, and death is agony. The first idea is implied in the verb: God "freed" (λύσας) Jesus from death. Death (θάνατος) is the only option as regards the ultimate future of human beings, and it leaves the dead no option but remaining dead. Nobody escapes death. Jesus, however, escaped death after having died because God raised him up back to life.

The second idea is connected with the term "agony" (ὠδῖνες), a term often used in association with the pain of childbirth ("birth pains, pangs of childbirth").[62] Death is described as a painful experience, as painful as childbirth. In the New Testament, the term "agony" is used metaphorically in this sense for the messianic woes, the birth pangs of the messianic age. The term is used in Ps 18:4–5 (LXX 17:5–6; cf. 2 Sam 22:6), where the phrase "agony of death" (ὠδῖνες θανάτου) translates the Hebrew phrase for "cords of death." The notion of "cords" explains the reference to "freeing" or liberation. Death holds the dead captive. Luke may be using a mixed metaphor, combining the idea of birth pangs (possibly connected with the thought of the messianic woes) with the idea of ropes being loosened and removed: "Death was not able to encircle Jesus and hold him in its painful grip."[63]

(3) Death did not have the power to hold Jesus.

Since God had determined that Jesus had to suffer death on the cross and that he would be raised up to life, death could not keep Jesus captive. The power of death cannot compete with the power of God, who has the power over life and death. The difference between Jesus' resurrection and the resurrection hope of the Jewish people is marked by the fact that the Jews expected a general resurrection of the dead at the end of this age, while Jesus' resurrection was a singular event in which nobody else participated.

2:25 For David says about him, "I see the Lord before me always, for he is at my right hand, so that I may not be shaken" (Δαυὶδ γὰρ λέγει εἰς αὐτόν· προορώμην τὸν κύριον ἐνώπιόν μου διὰ παντός, ὅτι ἐκ δεξιῶν μού ἐστιν ἵνα μὴ σαλευθῶ). Peter explains with a quotation from Ps 16:8–11 (LXX 15:8–11) why death did not have the power to keep Jesus in the realm of the dead. In Psalm 16, an expression of trust in Yahweh, David affirms his commitment to God (16:1–4) and expresses his confidence in him (16:5–11). The psalmist's trust in God is under pressure from people who worship other gods and from the threat of death.[64] Peter quotes from the second part of the psalm.

David "sees" (προορώμην) the Lord before his eyes always; i.e., he is continually aware of God's presence. This encourages reliance on Yahweh and implies that he always seeks to obey God. David acknowledges that Yahweh is at his right hand, the position of support. The psalmist experiences God's help and is therefore encouraged to stay faithful.

---

61. Cf. Acts 2:24, 32; 3:26; 13:34; 17:31; cf. Luke's use of the verb ἐγείρω in 3:15; 4:10; 5:30; 10:40; 13:30, 37. In Luke 24:6, 34, the passive voice is used (lit., "he was raised," divine passive). Intransitive formulations ("he rose from the dead") are used in Acts 10:41; cf. 17:3.

62. Cf. 1 Thess 5:3; in the LXX 1 Sam 4:19.

63. Bock, *Acts*, 122. Kevin L. Anderson, *"But God Raised Him from the Dead": The Theology of Jesus' Resurrection in*

Luke-Acts (Paternoster Biblical Monographs; Milton Keynes: Paternoster, 2006), 203–8, interprets the phrase in the context of Israel's return from exile (Isa 66:7–11; Ezek 37:6, 8) as "an eschatological breakthrough within God's plan to bring salvation to Israel and the world" (207).

64. Goldingay, *Psalms*, 1:228. For the differences between the LXX, which Peter quotes, and the Masoretic text of the psalm, cf. Bock, *Acts*, 138.

As Peter will identify the speaker with Jesus, the Messiah and Lord (vv. 29 – 36), he understands the words of the psalmist as words of Jesus, who expresses his confidence that God will always help him.

2:26 Therefore my heart was glad and my tongue rejoiced, and even more, my body shall live in hope (διὰ τοῦτο ηὐφράνθη ἡ καρδία μου καὶ ἠγαλλιάσατο ἡ γλῶσσά μου, ἔτι δὲ καὶ ἡ σάρξ μου κατασκηνώσει ἐπʼ ἐλπίδι). Yahweh's presence and help provide the basis for joyful confidence regarding the future. This confidence characterizes the entire person: the "heart" (καρδία), the "tongue" (γλῶσσα), and the physical "body" (σάρξ). Since Yahweh is present as his helper, David is not afraid of what can happen to him in the future. In the context of Peter's use of the psalm, Jesus expresses his trust in Yahweh, who raises up the dead back to life.

2:27 For you will not abandon me to the realm of the dead, nor will you allow your Holy One to see decay (ὅτι οὐκ ἐγκαταλείψεις τὴν ψυχήν μου εἰς ᾅδην οὐδὲ δώσεις τὸν ὅσιόν σου ἰδεῖν διαφθοράν). The basis for David's joyful confidence is his certainty that Yahweh will not abandon him[65] to the "realm of the dead" (ᾅδης), where decay reigns.

In the original context, the psalmist is sure that Yahweh will not abandon him to death and thus to the Abyss, perhaps on account of "the possibility that the harvest may fail in fulfillment of the warnings of people who chide those who rely on Yhwh rather than on Baal."[66] The abode in Hades (Sheol) is described here in contrast to being in God's presence. As the psalm is linked with David, readers would be inclined to read the singular "holy one" in terms of David. It is possible, however, to read the psalm in terms of "God's ultimate protection of the kingship of Israel that David's presence and connection to the psalm suggests."[67] The term "decay" (διαφθορά) denotes the decomposition of the body, which was graphically real for Palestinian Jews who reburied the bones of the dead in ossuaries after the body had decomposed.

In the context of Peter's sermon, the Messiah, who is God's Holy One (τὸν ὅσιόν σου),[68] expresses his confidence that God will not allow him to stay in the netherworld of the dead and that his physical body will not be destroyed in the grave. This verse is key to Peter's use of Psalm 16, seen in the fact that it is quoted a second time in v. 31. This quotation implies that when Jesus was seen by his followers after his death, they saw his actual physical body (which means that his tomb was indeed empty). In other words, "what the psalm said is seen to fit what was known about Jesus by actual observation: he came alive after dying, and his body evidently had not decayed."[69]

2:28 "You have made known to me the paths of life; you will fill me with joy in your presence" (ἐγνώρισάς μοι ὁδοὺς ζωῆς, πληρώσεις με εὐφροσύνης μετὰ τοῦ προσώπου σου). The psalmist expresses his assurance that Yahweh will lead him on the "path of life" (the LXX uses the plural, ὁδοὶ ζωῆς, "paths of life"). David rests assured that God will provide an escape from premature death and give him a new lease on life. Not only that, but he knows that God's presence will fill him with rejoicing.

---

65. His "soul" (ψυχή) — the phrase, which refers here to the human person as a whole, can be left untranslated as being implied in the personal pronoun "me."

66. Goldingay, *Psalms*, 1:233.

67. Bock, *Acts*, 124.

68. The term ὅσιος can describe priests (Deut 33:8), but more often is used for the faithful Israelite. In Acts 13:35 the same verse and expression from Ps 16 is used, which suggests that Ps 16 may have been part of a church tradition that explained Jesus' resurrection. Cf. Bock, *Acts*, 124.

69. Marshall, "Acts," 539.

In the context of Peter's identification of the psalmist with the Messiah, Jesus asserts his confidence that God saves him from death, giving him eternal life in his very own presence at his right hand. Peter does not quote the last line of the psalm ("with eternal pleasures at your right hand") — perhaps because the Holy Spirit is one of the "pleasures" (τερπνότητες) who is poured out by Jesus rather than remaining at the right hand of God.

Peter quotes Ps 16:8–11 for a twofold reason. (1) The psalm explains why it was impossible for Jesus to remain in the realm of the dead. Jesus had God's promise that he, the Holy One, would not decay in the grave. (2) Since what happened to Jesus fits what David prophesied in the psalm, Jesus must be the Messiah.

2:29 Brothers, I can speak confidently about David the patriarch: he died and was buried, and his tomb is in our midst to this very day (Ἄνδρες ἀδελφοί, ἐξὸν εἰπεῖν μετὰ παρρησίας πρὸς ὑμᾶς περὶ τοῦ πατριάρχου Δαυὶδ ὅτι καὶ ἐτελεύτησεν καὶ ἐτάφη, καὶ τὸ μνῆμα αὐτοῦ ἔστιν ἐν ἡμῖν ἄχρι τῆς ἡμέρας ταύτης). After quoting Ps 16:8–11, Peter now explains the relevance of the psalm for Jesus' resurrection, which he had asserted as a historical fact in v. 24. Peter explains to his Jewish listeners what David "the patriarch"[70] really meant (vv. 29b–31) and what the significance of his words are as they apply to Jesus (vv. 32–33).

Peter states that it is possible (ἐξόν) to say with great confidence[71] that the psalm is ultimately not about David. Besides the testimony of the Twelve, who are eyewitnesses of Jesus' resurrection from

the dead, Scripture also gives testimony of the necessity and of the reality of his resurrection.

Peter begins his explanation with stating the obvious — David has died,[72] he was put into a grave, and the tomb in which he was buried can still be seen in Jerusalem. In other words, David is still in Hades. The psalm thus cannot refer to David; it must refer to someone else.

According to 1 Kgs 2:10, King David was buried "in the City of David," i.e., on Zion, the hill south of the temple. King Herod attempted to raid David's tomb because he needed money; flames killed two of the guards, which prompted Herod to build a memorial of white marble at the entrance of the tomb.[73] Later Christian tradition identified the western hill of the city with "Zion," hence the localization of "David's tomb" at the site of the Byzantine church Hagia Sion (on the premises of the traditional location of the Upper Room).

2:30 But because he was a prophet and knew that God had sworn with an oath to him that he would put one of his descendants on his throne (προφήτης οὖν ὑπάρχων καὶ εἰδὼς ὅτι ὅρκῳ ὤμοσεν αὐτῷ ὁ θεὸς ἐκ καρποῦ τῆς ὀσφύος αὐτοῦ καθίσαι ἐπὶ τὸν θρόνον αὐτοῦ). Having established that David could not have spoken of himself when he wrote Psalm 16, Peter asserts that he must have spoken about someone else. Since David was a prophet and knew what God had promised him, that "someone" is a person who was to come in the future.

In the Old Testament, David is never called a prophet, but at least in some Jewish circles he was recognized as such, as the Qumran text called

---

70. The term πατριάρχης denotes the "father of a nation"; it is usually reserved for Abraham or one of the twelve sons of Jacob. Cf. 2:29 (David); 7:8 (Jacob's twelve sons); 7:9 (the fathers); Heb 7:4 (Abraham).

71. Cf. BDAG, s.v. παρρησία 1, "a use of speech that conceals nothing and passes over nothing, *outspokenness, frankness,*

plainness," assigning Acts 2:29 to meaning 3, "a state of boldness and confidence, *courage, confidence, boldness, fearlessness.*"

72. According to later rabbinic traditions, David died at Pentecost, on a Sabbath; cf. *y. Ḥag.* 2.78a (41); *y. Beṣah* 2.61c (9); cf. Barrett, *Acts,* 146.

73. Josephus, *Ant.* 16.179–183.

"David's Compositions" (11Q5 XXVII, 2 – 11) demonstrates. This text attributes a total of 4,050 psalms and songs to David's authorship and asserts, "All these he spoke through prophecy that was given to him before the Most High" (line 11). Josephus also refers to David as a prophet.[74] In the context of Peter's argument, the prophetic role of David means that he was able to speak in the psalm about the future event of the resurrection of one of his descendants.

David knew that God had given him a dramatic promise, sworn with an oath. Peter uses the words of Ps 132:11 (LXX 131:11) to refer to the words of the prophet Nathan in 2 Sam 7:12 – 13, spoken in connection with the covenant that Yahweh made with David and his descendants.

The phrase "swear to someone with an oath" (ὅρκῳ ὀμνύειν τινί) has been classified as a Semitism, but there are examples of similar formulations in Greek literature. The dative (ὅρκῳ) is best explained as modal, which in the LXX often translates the Hebrew absolute infinitive.[75] The certainty of God's commitment is expressed by the noun in the dative case: God swore an oath (ὅρκῳ). The specific promise to David was the assurance that God would place one of David's offspring on Israel's throne (2 Sam 7:11 – 14). The Qumran community understood this promise as a prophecy of the appearance of the "sprout of David," who will restore the Davidic dynasty in the last days when Israel would be saved (Amos 9:11; cf. 4Q174 I, 10 – 13).[76]

To Peter, the prophecy of Psalm 132 is now ful-filled — God has indeed put one of David's descendants on the throne from which Israel is ruled, as Jesus has risen from the dead and ascended to the throne at God's right hand, exercising his messianic authority in the distribution of the Holy Spirit upon his followers.

2:31 He foresaw and spoke of the resurrection of the Messiah, saying that he was not abandoned to the realm of the dead, nor has his body seen decay (προϊδὼν ἐλάλησεν περὶ τῆς ἀναστάσεως τοῦ Χριστοῦ ὅτι οὔτε ἐγκατελείφθη εἰς ᾅδην οὔτε ἡ σὰρξ αὐτοῦ εἶδεν διαφθοράν). Peter interprets both Ps 16:8 – 11 and Ps 132:11 as prophecies of the resurrection of the Messiah. Since he was a prophet, David saw in advance that one of his descendants, the Holy One whom God would put on his throne, would experience the miracle of a resurrection (ἀνάστασις) from the dead. And this coming ruler would be the Messiah.

This is the first reference in Acts to the term translated as "the Messiah" (ὁ Χριστός), a Hebrew term that means literally "the Anointed One" (māšîaḥ). The term is used here clearly as a title for "the future ruler in the line of David who will reign in the kingdom of God."[77]

Peter repeats the content of the prophecy from Ps 16:10 that he had quoted earlier (v. 27). He reminds his listeners of the key terms from David's prophecy in the psalm — body/flesh (σάρξ), abandoned (ἐγκατελείφθη), the realm of the dead or Hades (ᾅδης), and decay (διαφθορά). The main verb tenses have been changed from future to aor-

---

74. Josephus, *Ant.* 6.166: "the Deity abandoned Saul and passed over to David, who, when the divine spirit had removed to him, began to prophesy" (ὁ μὲν προφητεύειν ἤρξατο τοῦ θείου πνεύματος εἰς αὐτὸν μετοικισαμένου). Cf. also Philo, *Agriculture* 50.

75. Cf. BDF, §198.6; in the LXX cf. Exod 13:19; Num 30:3; Josh 9:20.

76. 4Q174 I (frags. 1 – 2, 21) quotes both 2 Sam 7:11 – 14 and Amos 9:11. Cf. Johannes Zimmermann, *Messianische Texte*

aus Qumran. Königliche, priesterliche und prophetische Messiasvorstellungen in den Schriftenfunden von Qumran (WUNT 2/104; Tübingen: Mohr Siebeck, 1998), 110 – 13 (using the traditional reference 4Q174 III, 10 – 13).

77. Marshall, "Acts," 540. Cf. Richard N. Longenecker, "Acts" (EBC 10; ed. T. R. Longman and D. E. Garland; Grand Rapids: Zondervan, 2007), 747, who, however, still uses "Christ" as "translation."

ist,[78] underscoring Peter's point that David's prophecy has been fulfilled.

In the context of Peter's sermon, the two parallel statements (οὔτε … οὔτε) assert, again, that Jesus did not disappear into the netherworld, nor did he suffer the usual fate of physical bodies after death. Jesus' "flesh," his physical body, did not decompose after death. Through his resurrection Jesus came back to physical life and his essential person lived on.

Peter has moved through three stages of his argument since he started his quotation from Ps 16:8 – 11 in v. 29: (1) David cannot be the person to whom God's promise of not decaying in the grave applies. (2) The promise of physical life after death that God makes in the psalm is connected with God's oath to David, which assured him of the enthronement of one of his descendants. (3) God's promise will be fulfilled through the resurrection of the Messiah. The movement from the second to the third step of the argument implies that there is a connection between enthronement and resurrection.

2:32 This Jesus God has raised up, and we are all witnesses of this (τοῦτον τὸν Ἰησοῦν ἀνέστησεν ὁ θεός, οὗ πάντες ἡμεῖς ἐσμεν μάρτυρες). Peter identifies Jesus with the Messiah of David's prophecy, and he asserts again the reality of Jesus' resurrection as a result of God's intervention (cf. v. 24). Jesus' resurrection was neither anticipated by the disciples nor immediately believed.[79] When he appeared to disciples for the first time after his crucifixion and burial, "they were startled and frightened, thinking they saw a ghost" (Luke 24:37). Jews did not expect people to be resurrected from the dead before the general resurrection of all the dead at the last day.

Because the Twelve and other followers saw Jesus with their own eyes,[80] touched his body,[81] and ate with him,[82] they are "witnesses" (μάρτυρες) of the reality of his resurrection (Luke 24:48; Acts 1:8). Jesus' resurrection is not a fabricated myth, a symbol or metaphor, or the appearance of a disembodied spirit or ghost. His resurrection was just as real as his death on the cross (Luke 23:33 – 49) and his burial in the tomb of Joseph of Arimathea (Luke 23:50 – 56).

The conclusion of Peter's second argument (vv. 25 – 32) is obvious: since Jesus has been raised from the dead, he must be the Messiah whom David prophesied in Psalm 16. Before Peter spells out this conclusion in v. 36, he begins a third argument, which links Jesus' resurrection with Jesus' exaltation to God's right hand, a connection that explains the significance of the Pentecost manifestations.

2:33 Exalted to God's right hand, he has received from the Father the promised Holy Spirit, whom he has poured out. This is what you now see and hear (τῇ δεξιᾷ οὖν τοῦ θεοῦ ὑψωθεὶς τήν τε ἐπαγγελίαν τοῦ πνεύματος τοῦ ἁγίου λαβὼν παρὰ τοῦ πατρός, ἐξέχεεν τοῦτο ὃ ὑμεῖς καὶ βλέπετε καὶ ἀκούετε).[83] Peter begins his third argument with the assertion that Jesus has been exalted to God's powerful presence in heaven. The aorist participle translated as "exalted" (ὑψωθείς) is temporal, explaining the time when the risen Jesus received the Holy Spirit from God for the purpose of bestowing him on "all flesh" in fulfillment of Joel's promise.

---

78. Acts 2:27 has ἐγκαταλείψεις and δώσεις … ἰδεῖν, while 2:31 has ἐγκατελείφθη and εἶδεν. Cf. Barrett, *Acts*, 148; Bock, *Acts*, 129.

79. The "doubting Thomas" (John 20:24 – 29) was not alone — none of his apostolic colleagues accepted as correct the reports of the women who claimed to have seen Jesus; cf. Luke 24:11, 16, 23 – 24; also Mark 16:11 (in the longer ending of Mark).

80. Luke 24:37 – 41; cf. 24:31; Matt 28:17; John 20:20, 25, 29.

81. Luke 24:39; cf. John 20:20, 27.

82. Luke 24:42 – 43; cf. Luke 24:30 – 31; Mark 16:14; John 21:12 – 13.

83. The controlling verb in 2:33 is ἐξέχεεν ("poured out"), which is connected with Joel's prophecy.

The verb (ὑψόω), which means "to lift up spatially, *lift up, raise high*,"[84] is used here for Jesus' transit to the presence of God after his resurrection from the dead. The passive voice of the participle (ὑψωθείς) refers to God's action, who raised Jesus from the dead and who brought him into his presence. The phrase "to God's right hand" (τῇ δεξιᾷ ... τοῦ θεοῦ) could be understood in an instrumental sense (Jesus was exalted by God's right hand, i.e., by God's power). But in light of Acts 5:31, it is preferable to assume a locative dative — Jesus was exalted by God with the result that he has the privileged status of sitting at God's right hand.[85] The image of "the right hand of God" describes the transcendent God as the source of power, life, and salvation.[86] Jesus' exaltation to God's right hand means that he has done what David, who remained in his tomb, could not achieve — rule on the heavenly throne as the one whom David anticipated and addressed as "my Lord" (Ps 110:1 NASB).

How can Peter conclude that Jesus' resurrection and ascension establish that Jesus is exalted at God's right hand (and not as an angel)? First, the connection between vv. 29–32 and v. 33 is probably established on the basis of the point made in v. 30, that God had promised to David that one of his descendants would sit on his throne, a promise made in Ps 110:1 (LXX 109:1)[87] and quoted in vv. 34–35, a verse that is probably already on Peter's mind; this can be understood to describe the location of this throne — at God's right hand. The connections between vv. 19–32 and vv. 34–36 are all built on God's promises to David.

Second, the reference to Jesus being exalted to the right hand of God combines an allusion to Ps 110:1 with an allusion to Isa 52:13, where the Servant is "lifted up" (LXX ὑψωθήσεται) and "exalted" (LXX δοξασθήσεται) to the heavenly throne of God. "The Servant, both in his humiliation and his exaltation, is therefore not merely a human figure distinguished from God, but, in both his humiliation and his exaltation, belongs to the identity of the unique God."[88]

Peter's second statement describes the result of Jesus' exaltation to the heavenly throne at God's right hand. He received the Spirit of prophecy, which he has now distributed to his followers. The Holy Spirit was promised[89] in passages such as Joel 2:28–32 (quoted in vv. 17–21). It is the promise of new life through the presence of God in the new age of salvation that God would grant to his people.[90] For Luke's readers it refers back to Luke 24:49 and Acts 1:5, 8. The context of Peter's speech excludes a reference to Jesus' baptism when the Holy Spirit descended on Jesus (Luke 3:22). Being in God's presence at God's right hand, Jesus "received" (λαβών) God's Spirit for allocation to all those who believe in him.

Some detect in the term "receive" (λαβών) an allusion to Ps 68:18 (LXX 67:19), which refers to

---

84. Cf. BDAG, s.v. ὑψόω 1; a second meaning, a figurative extension of this definition, is "to cause enhancement in honor, fame, position, power, or fortune, *exalt*."

85. Cf. Fitzmyer, *Acts*, 259; Bock, *Acts*, 132. Cf. Barnabas Lindars, *New Testament Apologetic: The Doctrinal Significance of the Old Testament Quotations* (Philadelphia: Westminster, 1961), 42–44, with reference to the last line of Ps 16:11 (LXX 15:11) as background, which Peter had omitted in his earlier quotation, where the LXX reads ἐν τῇ δεξιᾷ σου.

86. Johnson, *Acts*, 52; cf. Exod 15:6; Pss 18:35; 44:3; 48:10; 60:5; 98:1; 118:15–16; 138:7. On the relationship between Jesus' resurrection, exaltation, and ascension, see on Acts 1:11.

87. Ps 110:1 (LXX 109:1), "The Lord says to my lord, 'Sit at my right hand (κάθου ἐκ δεξιῶν μου) until I make your enemies a footstool for your feet.'"

88. Richard J. Bauckham, *Jesus and the God of Israel: God Crucified and Other Studies on the New Testament's Christology of Divine Identity* (Grand Rapids: Eerdmans, 2008), 36–37.

89. The phrase ἡ ἐπαγγελία τοῦ πνεύματος τοῦ ἁγίου can be rendered "the promise of the Holy Spirit" or, as epexegetical genitive, "the promise that is the Holy Spirit;" cf. Johnson, *Acts*, 52.

90. Cf. Isa 32:15; 44:3; Ezek 11:19; 36:26–27; 37:14.

the Lord ascending to the high mount, leading captives, and receiving gifts from/for people (ἔλαβες δόματα ἐν ἀνθρώπῳ). The Targum understood the psalm to refer to receiving gifts "for" men; i.e., the translators related the text to the words of the law being given to the people of Israel. On this basis some scholars see a (contrasting) parallel between the giving of the law on Mount Sinai, remembered on Pentecost, and Jesus' giving of the Spirit on Pentecost.[91]

The description of Jesus having "poured out" (ἐξέχεεν) the Holy Spirit uses language from Joel 2:28 (LXX 3:1, ἐκχεῶ). Jesus has fulfilled what God had promised through Joel the prophet, establishing the fact that the "last days" (v. 17) have arrived, the new epoch of salvation in which the Messiah mediates salvation from God's side, ruling Israel from the heavenly throne. In bestowing the Spirit, Jesus acts, according to Joel's prophecy, as God acts. This is "high Christology": Jesus, who in the gospel is endowed with the Spirit (Luke 3:22), is now pouring out and thus directing the Spirit (Isa 40:13).

Peter can now explain the audiovisual manifestations of sound and light and the speaking in unlearned, foreign languages. What the assembled people now "see and hear" is the direct result of Jesus' resurrection and exaltation to God's throne and of the coming of the Holy Spirit, whom Jesus has taken from the Father and given to his followers. This assertion of the heavenly exaltation of Jesus, who had been crucified, "in fact puts the

group of his disciples in a completely different situation from that of the other Jewish groups of the time."[92]

2:34 – 35 For it was not David who ascended into the heavens; yet he says, "The Lord said to my Lord, Sit at my right hand, until I make your enemies a footstool for your feet" (οὐ γὰρ Δαυὶδ ἀνέβη εἰς τοὺς οὐρανούς λέγει δὲ αὐτός· εἶπεν ὁ κύριος τῷ κυρίῳ μου· κάθου ἐκ δεξιῶν μου ἕως ἂν θῶ τοὺς ἐχθρούς σου ὑποπόδιον τῶν ποδῶν σου). David died and was buried (v. 29) and never ascended into heaven. This is the reason why the words of Ps 110:1 cannot apply to him. David is not Israel's ruler on God's throne, but Jesus the Messiah is.

Peter's third Old Testament quotation is taken from Ps 110:1 (LXX 109:1). This psalm is a royal psalm, which may have been composed to celebrate David's conquest of Jerusalem and his enthronement as king, and it was used subsequently by kings of his dynasty in a context of enthronement.[93] The "Lord" who speaks is Yahweh (יהוה, LXX ὁ κύριος). The "Lord" who is addressed (אדני, LXX τῷ κυρίῳ μου) is not David himself, nor is it a normal successor of his dynasty, because David recognizes the superiority of this person as his own Lord.

The invitation to "sit" (κάθου) is not made to David but to this greater king. This can only be the Davidic Messiah. The phrase "at my right hand" connects Ps 110:1 with Ps 16:8, quoted earlier (v. 25).[94] Peter's point is that Jesus, as a result of his

---

91. Cf. Lindars, *New Testament Apologetic*, 51 – 59; Mark L. Strauss, *The Davidic Messiah in Luke-Acts: The Promise and Its Fulfilment in Lukan Christology* (JSNTSup 110; Sheffield: Sheffield Academic Press, 1995), 145 – 47. Many remain unconvinced that Luke intended this allusion or that his readers would have recognized the connection (cf. Fitzmyer, *Acts*, 259; Bock, *Proclamation*, 181 – 83, but see now Bock, *Acts*, 131 – 32).

92. Giorgio Jossa, *Jews or Christians? The Followers of Jesus in Search of Their Own Identity* (WUNT 202; Tübingen: Mohr Siebeck, 2006), 68.

93. Leslie C. Allen, *Psalms 101 – 150* (WBC 21; Dallas: Word, 1983), 85. Psalm 110 is also quoted in Matt 22:44/Mark 12:36/Luke 20:42 – 43; 1 Cor 15:25; Heb 1:3, 13.

94. This is the exegetical principle of *gezerah shawah* (lit., "equal ordinance"), which is an argument from analogy: one text is interpreted in the light of another text with which it shares a word or a phrase. This principle is one of Hillel's seven principles that describe the techniques of rabbinic exegesis; cf. Strack and Stemberger, *Introduction to the Talmud and Midrash*, 16 – 20; Instone-Brewer, *Techniques*, 17 – 23.

resurrection and ascension, is sitting at God's right hand, on God's throne, as the Davidic Messiah.[95]

In the original context of the psalm, the new king is promised the subjugation of his enemies. In the El Amarna letters, vassal kings describe themselves as the footstool of Pharaoh.[96] The psalm implies that the king rules not in his own right but as the coregent and representative of Yahweh, who does the fighting and wins the victory. Applied to the risen and exalted Jesus, who is the Messiah reigning at God's right hand, Peter affirms God's victory over death (cf. v. 24) through Jesus' death, resurrection, and exaltation.

2:36 "Therefore, let all the house of Israel know with certainty that God has made him both Lord and Messiah, this Jesus whom you crucified" (ἀσφαλῶς οὖν γινωσκέτω πᾶς οἶκος Ἰσραήλ ὅτι καὶ κύριον αὐτὸν καὶ χριστὸν ἐποίησεν ὁ θεός, τοῦτον τὸν Ἰησοῦν ὃν ὑμεῖς ἐσταυρώσατε). Peter now states the conclusion from his quotations of Joel 2:28 – 32; Ps 16:8 – 11, and Ps 110:1, and from his assertions about Jesus of Nazareth, "whom you crucified": God has made him both Lord and Messiah. Peter is confident that his listeners are able to acknowledge his conclusion. The convictions of Peter and his fellow believers are certain (ἀσφαλῶς) because those convictions are confirmed by Scripture and because the Spirit-filled followers of Jesus are eyewitnesses of his miracles, resurrection, and ascension.

Peter addresses the Jews of Jerusalem as "the house of Israel."[97] The royal status of Jesus, which Peter explains to his listeners, is of utmost significance for all of God's chosen people, for the entire Jewish people. If Jesus is indeed the Messiah, the promised king who is expected to restore Israel and bring salvation, then all Israel must consider the consequences of this truth, acknowledge Jesus' messianic dignity, and find salvation by submitting to his lordship. The prophecies of Joel and David and the events of Jesus' life, resurrection, and exaltation demonstrate several certain truths concerning Jesus of Nazareth, who had been crucified by the Jews of Jerusalem.

(1) Jesus is Lord (κύριος); i.e., he is exalted at God's right hand (Ps 16:8) since his resurrection. He is the Lord of David, sitting on the heavenly throne (Ps 110:1) since his ascension to heaven. He is the Lord in whose name everybody is granted salvation (Joel 2:32), as he has been given the authority to pour out the Spirit of prophecy, the Holy Spirit of God's saving presence (vv. 21, 25, 33, 34).

(2) Jesus is the Messiah (χριστός, *Christos*; Heb. *māšiaḥ*), the king who would save the people of Israel. He is the promised descendant of David (Ps 132:11),[98] who is superior to David as his Lord (vv. 30, 31, 34). It is this conviction that prompted Peter to add "in the last days" to the quotation of Joel's prophecy (v. 17).

(3) Jesus, the Lord and the Messiah, is most closely related to God, sitting at his right hand on his throne (vv. 24, 25, 33, 34). Jesus, the risen and exalted Messiah, has been made the equal of Yahweh, whom Jews address as "Lord." Jesus is identified as (or associated with) the "Lord," where the Old Testament text refers to Yahweh (cf. vv. 20, 21, 25). That "Lord" has become a divine title is evident in the fact that the expression "to call upon the name of the Lord [Yahweh]," which refers to

---

95. Cf. Yuzuru Miura, *David in Luke-Acts: His Portrayal in the Light of Early Judaism* (WUNT 2/232; Tübingen: Mohr Siebeck, 2007), 146 – 49. For the conviction that Jesus sits at God's right hand cf. Luke 20:42 – 44; 22:69; Acts 7:55 – 56; also Rom 8:34; Eph 1:20; Col 3:1; Heb 1:3, 13; 8:1; 10:12 – 13; 12:2; 1 Pet 3:22.

96. Allen, *Psalms 101 – 150*, 80. In the OT cf. Josh 10:24; Isa 51:23; cf. 1 Kgs 5:3.

97. Cf. Lev 10:6; Num 20:29; 1 Sam 7:2; Jer 9:25; Ezek 37:11.

98. In Ps 132:10 (LXX 131:10) King David is called God's "anointed" — Heb. *māšiaḥ*/LXX τοῦ χριστοῦ σου.

the cultic worship of God, was taken over to refer to the acclamation and invocation of Jesus (v. 21, citing Joel 2:32 [LXX 3:5]).[99]

(4) Jesus' death on the cross was a necessary stage in his path to his place at God's right hand, since it was an integral part of God's plan to save and restore Israel through Jesus' victory over death (vv. 21, 23, 24).

(5) Jesus' enemies will eventually be defeated (Ps 110:1) when God's victory will be complete, that is, when Jesus returns (v. 35; cf. 1:11).

(6) The phrase "God has made him" (αὐτὸν ... ἐποίησεν ὁ θεός) does not mean that before his resurrection, Jesus was not the Messiah and Lord. We should note that "the force of the statement is more probably simply to contrast the attitude of those who crucified and rejected Jesus with God's confirmation of his real status by raising him from the dead and exalting him to his right hand."[100] Or, Peter's statement can be understood to mean that the Messiah-designate has now become the Messiah-enthroned.

Theology in Application

Peter's speech on the day of Pentecost is triggered by the manifestations of sound and light and the unprecedented speaking in unlearned foreign languages about the mighty acts of God. He explains to a crowd of Jews living in Jerusalem, among them festival pilgrims, the reason and the significance of this event. He argues that the Spirit of prophecy has been poured out by the crucified, risen, and exalted Jesus, who, as Scripture proves, is the promised Messiah and the Lord at God's right hand who reigns on the eternal throne of David. The Pentecost speech thus focuses on two main themes: (1) the coming of the Holy Spirit and the significance of this event for Israel, and (2) the identity of Jesus of Nazareth as a result of his death, resurrection, and exaltation. In systematic theological terms, the main emphases of Peter's sermon are in the areas of pneumatology and Christology. We will focus on these two themes.

There are several subsidiary themes, the most important of which are (3) the authority of Old Testament Scripture, which is the basis for Peter's argument, and (4) the foundational role of the earliest followers of Jesus, particularly the Twelve, as eyewitnesses of Jesus' life, death, resurrection, and ascension. Other themes are (5) the courage of Peter, who is not afraid to confront the Jews of Jerusalem with their culpability for the death of God's Messiah; (6) the role of visions and dreams; (7) the role of prophecy; (8) the role of glossolalia, i.e., the speaking in unlearned foreign languages; (9) the significance of miracles; (10) evangelistic method; and (11) the nature of the Christian interpretation of the Old Testament Scriptures.[101]

---

99. Cf. Larry W. Hurtado, *Lord Jesus Christ: Devotion to Jesus in Earliest Christianity* (Grand Rapids: Eerdmans, 2003), 179 – 85, who argues that the development from κύριος referring to Jesus as "master" to κύριος being used as a divine title and used in invocations in prayer, happened, as Acts suggests,

in the early Judean circles of Jesus' followers.

100. Marshall, "Acts," 543; cf. C. Kavin Rowe, "Acts 2.36 and the Continuity of Lukan Christology," *NTS* 53 (2007): 37 – 56.

101. For a practical development of several of these themes, cf. Fernando, *Acts*, 110 – 18.

The Holy Spirit as the Transforming Presence of God

The Holy Spirit is the transforming presence of God available to all who are follow-ers of Jesus. Much has already been said about the reality of the Holy Spirit in Acts 2 (see on vv. 1–13). Peter's Pentecost sermon adds the following points.

The transforming power of God's presence is available to "all flesh," i.e., to all people, male or female, old or young, irrespective of social class. Receiving the Holy Spirit is no longer the special privilege given to a few or the temporary privilege given for particular tasks. Peter will clarify in v. 38 that the preconditions for the reception of the Spirit are repentance from opposition to Jesus and baptism in his name; and in 11:15–18 he will emphasize that the reception of the Spirit is possible even for Gentiles who believe in Jesus.

Neither God, whose presence the Spirit represents, nor Jesus, who bestows the Spirit, discriminates between people on the basis of gender or social class. In the congregation of believers in Jesus, who have received the Holy Spirit because of their faith in Jesus Christ, there is no room for racism of any kind, whether it is subtle discrimination or explicit apartheid.

The presence of the Spirit is accompanied by visible manifestations. On the day of Pentecost, this was prophecy, understood as speaking in unlearned foreign languages under the revelatory inspiration of God. The dreams and visions that Joel mentioned were not in evidence on Pentecost, but Luke's account of the apostles and of Paul includes many references to these phenomena. The transforming power of the Spirit is also evident in the fact that Peter, who had denied Jesus only a few weeks earlier, has the courage to explain the significance of Jesus as the crucified and risen Messiah and Lord in front of a crowd of several thousand people.

The message that the presence of the Holy Spirit completely transforms people is provocative, particularly with respect to people who affirm their identity (e.g., as homosexuals) as having been established by the way in which they were born. The power of God's presence effects changes in line with God's holiness and God's revelation.

The presence of the Spirit causes the followers of Jesus to proclaim the mighty acts of God, which are also key elements of Peter's sermon. Prompted by the su-pernatural inspiration of the Holy Spirit, who causes them to speak in unlearned languages, they speak about God's intervention in Israel's history in the life, death, and resurrection of Jesus, whom they worship as Messiah and Lord. The power of the Holy Spirit can be seen, most importantly, in the ministry of Jesus. The presence of God's Spirit visibly descended on Jesus at his baptism; the power of the Spirit was manifest in the miracles he performed; and the signs and wonders Joel proph-esied in connection with the coming of the Spirit were also fulfilled in the events of Jesus' death, resurrection, and ascension. The focus of Christian preaching is Jesus of Nazareth. This is why the first label given by outsiders for the followers of Jesus was "Christians" (Χριστιανοί; 11:26), i.e., people whose one main, primary, and basic subject matter is Jesus and his identity as Israel's Messiah and Savior of the world (see "In Depth: The Self-Understanding of the Church in Jerusalem" at 5:11).

If and when churches focus on emotional experience, on a particular style of (post)modern life, on entertainment, on retaining members, or on attracting seekers, and if and when they minimize the details of the message about Jesus, they underestimate the power of God that accompanies the proclamation of the gospel of Jesus Christ, and they overestimate the power of the particular "model" of "doing church" that they have adopted. An authentic community of Jesus' followers is not a supermarket where customers are always served what they want. The church of Jesus Christ, empowered by the presence of God's Spirit, is focused on Jesus, the Messiah and the Lord.

The arrival of the Spirit of prophecy signifies that the "last days" have begun. The events of Jesus' life, death, and resurrection and of Pentecost mark the beginning of the new age of salvation, the age of the restoration of Israel, the age of the coming of the kingdom of God. Since Joel's prophecy of wonders in the sky and signs on the earth has not yet been completely fulfilled but will be fulfilled on the day of God's judgment, Christians live "between the times" — between the first and second coming of Jesus; between the gift of salvation as forgiveness of sins and the future gift of the removal of all sin; between the experience of God's presence in the midst of ridicule and continued opposition and the experience of God's presence in God's new and perfect world.

We Christians dare not minimize the transforming power and reality of the Spirit, and we dare not minimize the fact that we still live in a fallen world in which trials, sickness, sin, and death are still realities. However, the fact that Jesus has inaugurated the last days means that the Spirit has indeed arrived. The entire messianic era — from Jesus' coming in Bethlehem to Jesus' return at the end of time — is the age of the Spirit, which is the age of "the last days." Followers of Jesus no longer wait for the fulfillment of Joel's prophecy, and they no longer wait for the Holy Spirit — he has come on Pentecost, and he is bestowed on everyone at the moment when he or she acknowledges Jesus as messianic Lord and Savior.

Jesus of Nazareth as the Promised Messiah

Jesus of Nazareth who died on a cross is the promised Messiah and the Lord who reigns at God's right hand. The pivotal explanation of Pentecost is linked with Jesus' life, death, resurrection, and exaltation to God's right hand. This means that Jesus is significant for historical reasons (he lived, he performed miracles, he died on a cross, he rose from the dead, he ascended to the right hand of God), for theological reasons (his life, death, resurrection, and exaltation are part of God's plan to save Israel and the world), and for pastoral and evangelistic reasons (he lives, he bestows salvation, he transforms through the Spirit). The central content of Peter's sermon is christological.

The connection between the coming of the Spirit and the person of Jesus constitutes both an invitation and a promise of salvation. Jesus invites us to "call on the name of the Lord" and thus acknowledge that he, the crucified Jew from Galilee, is indeed the Messiah and the Lord. At the same time his life, death, resurrection, and exaltation are an offer of salvation: those who invoke Jesus' name in acknowledgment of who he was on earth and who he is in heaven will be saved from their sins and from condemnation on the day of judgment.

Jesus is important as a historical person. Peter refers to his origins in Nazareth and to his ministry, which was characterized by the display of divine power in powerful deeds, wonders, and signs. Jesus is neither a symbol nor a theological idea. He was a Jewish man from Galilee, who was eventually executed by Roman soldiers with the help of the Jewish leaders in Jerusalem, and who then rose from the dead.

This focus on Jesus is not unique for Peter or for the book of Acts, but corresponds to the message of the entire New Testament. The name Jesus (Ἰησοῦς) occurs 917 times, Jesus' title "Messiah" (Χριστός) 529 times, while the term "God" (θεός) occurs 1,317 times; in comparison, the name "Peter" occurs 156 times, "Paul" 158 times, and "faith/believe" (πίστις/πιστεύω) occurs 484 times, and "love" (ἀγάπη/ ἀγαπάω) occurs 259 times.[102] More important than these statistics is the fact that the canon of books that became authoritative Scripture for the church begins with four books devoted to a description of the life and ministry of Jesus. The speeches in Acts leave no doubt that the message about Jesus and his significance was the central emphasis of the earliest Christians.

This focus on Jesus of Nazareth is one of the emphases that distinguishes the Christian faith from other religions. Christians proclaim what God has done through Jesus Christ and what Jesus Christ did in his life, death, and resurrection — not what God demands we do or what we think we must do in order to have a fulfilled, complete life.

Jesus' miracles constitute proof that God was revealing himself in Jesus for the salvation of his people. Jesus' ministry happened in the eyes of a public who was able to challenge and critique Jesus' claims. Nobody questioned that extraordinary, miraculous events occurred through Jesus' power. What was debated was the origin of his authority. Jewish leaders argued that he performed his miracles with the help of demonic powers. Jesus argued that such an explanation was logically impossible. While skeptics will never be satisfied with the arguments for the veracity of the accounts of Jesus' miracles, the mighty deeds Jesus performed do form a crucial part of the record that establishes who he was and who he is.

---

102. These figures are based on the text of Nestle-Aland, 27th edition, not considering variant readings (which sometimes add, for example, Χριστός).

Jesus' death on the cross, engineered by the Jewish leaders of Jerusalem and carried out by pagan Roman soldiers, is a crucial part of Peter's sermon as well as of early Christian preaching. While Peter does not provide details of Jesus' crucifixion, he does not gloss over the fact that Jesus suffered this violent penalty that was mostly inflicted on slaves, violent criminals, and political rebels. The next several chapters in Acts show that Peter and the disciples risked their lives as they insisted on proclaiming that Jesus, the crucified man from Nazareth, was the promised Messiah and the Lord on God's heavenly throne.

The apostle Paul knew all too well from personal experience that preaching a crucified Messiah was "a stumbling block to Jews and foolishness to Gentiles" (1 Cor 1:23); in other words, it was a message that could not be made believable by rhetorical brilliance or superior argumentation. Still, he did not "contextualize" the cross, such as by removing it from the core emphases of his preaching, by relegating it to a footnote or to teaching reserved for the more advanced believers, or by reinterpreting it as a symbol of heroic sacrifice. Jews and Gentiles found it impossible to accept that Jesus, the crucified man from Galilee, should be the Savior of the world. This is why believing in Jesus is always a miracle, a result of the powerful intervention of God through his Spirit in the hearts and minds of unbelievers, causing them to come to faith in a crucified Savior who rose from the dead and now rules at the right hand of God. *This* is the "demonstration of the Spirit's power" on which Paul, pastor and missionary, relied for the effectiveness of his preaching (1 Cor 2:4; cf. 1:24, 30; 2:5).

This is the reason why we do not "use" Jesus, or his life, or proofs for his resurrection, in evangelistic preaching. Salvation is possible only by calling in faith on the name of Jesus, by acknowledging his messianic dignity and his power as Lord, and by accepting the effect of his saving faith on the cross. Preaching Jesus *is* the good news, and preaching Jesus involves speaking about his life, death, resurrection, and exaltation. Preaching the good news of Jesus is thus not a method or strategy, but the necessary content of a message that seeks to help people find salvation, which is possible only through faith in Jesus as Messiah and Lord.

Jesus's death on the cross was an integral part of God's plan to bring salvation to Israel and to the world. While the Jewish leaders of Jerusalem were certainly involved in Jesus' death, there is no reason to engage in anti-Jewish, antisemitic tirades, or, worse (but tragically all too often a reality in past history), policies and actions. Those who actually executed Jesus were Roman soldiers, which does not mean that we must despise all Italians or, more logical from a Jewish perspective, all non-Jews! What happened to Jesus cannot be fully explained by reference to the involvement of Jews and Gentiles in his execution. Jesus' death was part of *God's plan of salvation*. Jesus' death on the cross was part of his mission. Good Friday is already implied in Jesus' birth in Bethlehem.

The centrality of Jesus' death as part of God's plan to save Israel and the world explains why the second symbol of the Christian faith (after the water of baptism)

— bread and wine — is linked with Jesus' broken body and his blood shed on the cross. While immersion in water at baptism is celebrated only once in the life of a Christian, remembering Jesus' death in the Lord's Supper is a continuous celebration in Christian worship.

Jesus' resurrection was a historical event, witnessed by his disciples. That fact was controversial in the first century, and it remains so today. People then were not gullible; they did not believe in just about anything that came long. When Paul spoke of Jesus' resurrection before the members of the Council of the Areopagus, many scoffed (17:32). Jesus' resurrection is without parallel in Jewish, Greek, or Roman literature or myth. Peter authenticates the resurrection as a historical reality by appealing to two pieces of evidence: Old Testament prophecy, which Jesus fulfilled, and the eyewitness testimony of the apostles, who saw Jesus after his resurrection.

There are indeed excellent historical reasons why one should accept Jesus' resurrection as a historical fact.[103] If true, however, that resurrection has consequences for how we must understand Jesus' life and death, and thus his identity. If Jesus indeed came back from the dead, it was an act caused by the power of God. If Jesus indeed came back from the dead, it was an event that constitutes triumph over the agonizing power of death. If Jesus indeed came back from the dead, he came back not to earthly life but to life in God's presence at his right hand.

Jesus' exaltation establishes him as messianic king at God's right hand. He is the Messiah whom David prophesied, the expected ruler in the line of David who will reign in the kingdom of God. Jesus' resurrection and exaltation to God's right hand were God's plan to install one of David's descendants on the throne from which Israel is ruled, bringing salvation to Israel and the world. Jesus exercises his messianic authority in the distribution of the Holy Spirit. He has not absconded into heaven. He continues to be present in his gift of the Holy Spirit, whose power transforms lives, empowers for witness, and overcomes death. And he continues to intervene directly in the affairs of the church.

The royal status of Jesus is of utmost significance for the Jewish people. Since Jesus is the promised king who restores Israel and brings salvation, the Jewish people must consider the consequences of this truth, acknowledge Jesus' messianic dignity, and find salvation by submitting to his lordship. This is why the apostles preached the good news of salvation through faith in Jesus Messiah to Jews in Jerusalem, in Judea, and in synagogues in the cities of other regions of the Mediterranean world. Jewish evangelism is not another attempt of (Gentile) Christians to complete the Nazis' Shoah, as some Jews want us to believe. On the contrary, evangelism among the Jewish people is an expression of love — the love of God, who wants to save the

---

103. Cf. William L. Craig, *Assessing the New Testament Evidence for the Historicity of the Resurrection of Jesus* (Studies in the Bible and Early Christianity 16; Lewiston, NY: Mellen, 1989); William Lane Craig and Gerd Lüdemann, *Jesus' Resur-* *rection: Fact or Figment? A Debate between William Lane Craig and Gerd Lüdemann* (ed. P. Copan; Downers Grove, IL: InterVarsity Press, 2000).

Jewish people, and the love of God's people, who want Jews and Gentiles to worship the one true God who revealed himself in Jesus for the salvation of the world.

Jesus, messianic King and Lord at God's right hand, is most closely related to God, sitting on his throne. Jesus is the Lord in whose name people can find salvation and receive the presence of God's Spirit. Jesus is thus due worship, as God is worshiped in the prayers and in the life of his people. Worship services that focus on the subjective experiences of the worshipers serve not God but people. Worship services that deserve the name focus on Jesus, the messianic king and Lord on God's throne, on God, who revealed himself in the life, death, resurrection, and exaltation of Jesus for the salvation of the world, and on the presence of God's Spirit, who manifests himself in the transformation of God's people.

CHAPTER 5

Acts 2:37 – 41

Literary Context

Luke began Acts 2 with an account of the outpouring of the Holy Spirit on the followers of Jesus assembled in Jerusalem (2:1 – 13). Since the arrival of the Spirit was accompanied by audiovisual manifestations, and since the unprecedented phenomenon of people speaking in unlearned foreign languages bewildered Jews living in Jerusalem, Peter gave a speech in which he explained what was happening (2:14 – 36). Peter established that they were witnessing the fulfillment of prophecy — Joel's prophecy of the coming of the Holy Spirit on "all flesh." Moreover, David's prophecies of the coming of the messianic Lord who would rule Israel has been fulfilled, as the manifestations of Jesus' miracles, resurrection, and ascension can be fully explained in terms of his identity as the promised Messiah who has been exalted as ruler on David's throne at God's right hand.

In the fourth and fifth incidents of the Pentecost episode (2:37 – 40 and 2:41), Luke reports the effect of Peter's speech. Many of the listeners were stunned by Peter's explanations, which they evidently accepted as being true. Their inquiry as to the proper course of action prompted Peter to give a missionary sermon, exhorting the listeners to accept and receive the salvation that comes through accepting Jesus as the crucified, risen, and exalted Messiah and Lord, and to demonstrate their repentance through immersion in water. Luke reports that three thousand people were baptized in the name of Jesus on that day.

II. The Beginnings of the New People of God (1:15 – 8:3)
    A. The Identity and Witness of Jesus' Followers as God's People (1:15 – 2:47)
        7. The arrival of the Holy Spirit and the identity of Jesus as Israel's Messiah and Lord (2:1 – 41)
            c. Peter's speech on the day of Pentecost (2:14 – 36)
➡   **d. Peter's missionary sermon (2:37 – 40)**
            e. Mass conversions and baptisms (2:41)
        8. The life of the Jerusalem community of Jesus' followers (2:42 – 47)

Main Idea

As Peter argues before the Jews of Jerusalem for the need to repent, to receive forgiveness of sins, and to accept salvation through acknowledging Jesus as Israel's Messiah and Lord, demonstrated in immersion in water, several thousand people are converted and added to the community of Jesus' followers.

Translation

Acts 2:37 – 41

37a	Setting: time	When they heard this,
b	Event	**they were stunned**
c	Action	**and said to Peter and**
d		**to the other apostles,**
e	Question	*"Brothers, what should we do?"*
38a	Answer	**Peter said to them,**
b	Exhortation	*"Repent,*
c	Exhortation	*and be immersed,*
d	Identification	*every one of you,*
e	Reference	*in the name of Jesus the Messiah,*
f	Cause	*on the basis of the forgiveness of sins,*
g	Result	*and you will receive the gift of the Holy Spirit.*
39a	Basis	*For the promise is*
b	Advantage	*for you and*
c	Advantage	*for your children and*
d	Advantage	*for all those who are far away,*
e	Explanation	*whom the Lord our God will call to himself."*
40a	Action	**He bore witness with many other words**
b	Action	**and exhorted them, saying,**
c	Exhortation	*"Let yourselves be saved from this corrupt generation!"*
41a	Event	**Those ... were baptized.**
b	Identification	who accepted his message
c	(Event)	**About three thousand persons were added that day.**

Structure and Literary Form

The fourth incident that Luke relates for the Feast of Pentecost in AD 30 is the reaction of the people who heard Peter's speech (2:37), prompting Peter to preach a missionary sermon (2:38–40). The fifth incident relates the effect of Peter's missionary proclamation, which is mass conversions and baptisms of three thousand people (2:41).

The text is comprised of *historical narrative* (2:37, 40, 41), a *question* (2:37), and a *speech* (2:38–39, 40). Peter's speech in vv. 38–39, his third in Acts, consists of five parts: call to repentance; call to immersion (baptism) in the name of Jesus, Israel's Messiah; the promise of forgiveness; the promise of the reception of the Holy Spirit; and description of the scope of the promised presence of the Holy Spirit. After a summary statement about Peter's evangelistic efforts (v. 40a-b), Luke relates, again in direct speech, Peter's call to receive salvation (v. 40c).

Exegetical Outline

➡ **I. Peter's Missionary Sermon and Mass Conversions (2:37–41)**

    A. Reaction of the Jews of Jerusalem (2:37)

        1. Stunned reaction of the Jews who had listened to Peter (2:37a-b)

        2. Inquiry of the Jews regarding the proper course of action (2:37c-e)

    B. Missionary Sermon of Peter (2:38–39)

        1. Call to repentance (2:38a-b)

        2. Call to be immersed in the name of Jesus the Messiah (2:38c-e)

        3. Promise of forgiveness of sins (2:38f)

        4. Promise of the reception of the Holy Spirit (2:38g)

        5. The scope of the promised presence of the Holy Spirit (2:39)

    C. Continued Missionary Exhortation of Peter (2:40)

        1. Peter's continued efforts to convince the listeners (2:40a-b)

        2. Call to receive salvation (2:40c)

    D. Mass Conversions and Baptisms (2:41)

        1. The baptism of the new converts (2:41a-b)

        2. The conversion and integration of 3,000 Jews (2:41c)

Explanation of the Text

2:37 When they heard this, they were stunned and said to Peter and to the other apostles, "Brothers, what should we do?" (ἀκούσαντες δὲ κατενύγησαν τὴν καρδίαν εἶπόν τε πρὸς τὸν Πέτρον καὶ τοὺς λοιποὺς ἀποστόλους· τί ποιήσωμεν, ἄνδρες ἀδελφοί;). Involvement in the crucifixion of the Messiah whom God raised from the dead and who shares God's throne is a serious sin against God. As Peter's listeners in Jerusalem — the very city in which Jesus had been crucified — perceive this, they are stunned, pierced in their conscience (καρδία).

It is unclear whether Peter's listeners interrupt his speech, as many assume, or whether Peter had concluded his speech with the explanation of the miraculous manifestations among the followers of Jesus. Since he had demonstrated that Joel's promise of the coming of the Holy Spirit and David's promise of the coming of the Messiah had both been fulfilled in the life, resurrection, and exaltation of Jesus of Nazareth, Peter might have wanted to end his speech at this point, waiting to see what would happen.

Jesus' identity as Messiah sitting on the throne at God's right hand and his crucifixion a few weeks earlier, for which they were in part responsible (cf. vv. 23, 36), prompt people in the crowd to question Peter and the other apostles further. Luke's comment about "the other apostles" suggests that they were involved in the dialogue as well. He clearly assumes that not only Peter but all the disciples of Jesus could explain what was happening.

The address "brothers" identifies the Twelve as fellow Jews.[1] Since the crowd was among those who had rejected Jesus and facilitated his crucifixion, the people find themselves in a situation that seems impossible to resolve. However, since Peter has explained that Jesus' death was part of God's plan (v. 23), there might be the possibility of avoiding God's judgment.

2:38 Peter said to them, "Repent, and be immersed, every one of you, in the name of Jesus the Messiah, on the basis of the forgiveness of sins, and you will receive the gift of the Holy Spirit" (Πέτρος δὲ πρὸς αὐτούς· μετανοήσατε, φησίν, καὶ βαπτισθήτω ἕκαστος ὑμῶν ἐπὶ τῷ ὀνόματι Ἰησοῦ Χριστοῦ εἰς ἄφεσιν τῶν ἁμαρτιῶν ὑμῶν καὶ λήμψεσθε τὴν δωρεὰν τοῦ ἁγίου πνεύματος). Peter's answer involves two exhortations and two promises. The two exhortations are formulated with aorist imperatives: "repent" (μετανοήσατε), and "be immersed" (βαπτισθήτω). The plural of the first imperative concerns the Jews of Jerusalem who are listening.

In Peter's challenge to them, repentance is the precondition for the forgiveness of sins, which in turn is the prerequisite for receiving salvation. The exhortation to repent means, here, that the Jews in Jerusalem regret their (active or passive) involvement in the crucifixion of Jesus, that they confess this tragic sin, that they feel sorrow for their rejection of Jesus, that they turn away from and change their former attitude concerning Jesus, and that they accept Jesus as the promised Messiah and the risen and exalted Lord.

The last emphasis is connected with the second imperative, to be "immersed … in the name of Jesus the Messiah." Peter expects all listeners who repent[2] to go to a pool and let themselves be immersed in water, which signifies the cleansing from their sin and guilt (on βαπτίζω see 1:5). The passive voice (βαπτισθήτω) indicates that they would not

---

1. For the form of the address (ἄνδρες ἀδελφοί), see on 1:16.

2. The genitive ὑμῶν after ἕκαστος is partitive.

be immersing themselves, as Jews were in practice of doing, but would be "baptized" (our modern term), probably by the apostles. This allows them to confess their sorrow for their former rejection of Jesus and to express their new faith in Jesus as Messiah and exalted Lord.

This feature of the immersion Peter demands is not unprecedented: John was called "the Im-merser" ("the Baptist")[3] because people came to him for immersion, accepting that his involvement in the act was important. In contemporary Jewish immersion rites, people effected cleansing from impurity by immersing themselves in water; "there is no clear parallel in any current Jewish immersion rite for someone acting as an immerser alongside the person who is being immersed in the water."[4]

IN DEPTH: Ritual Immersion

Jews regularly practiced immersion in water for purposes of purification from impurities, most of which were contracted during the normal course of living, such as through contact with unclean animals, childbirth, certain skin diseases, bodily discharges, illicit sexual relationships (apart from adultery, which was punished by death), or contact with a corpse.[5] People who were impure could not participate in the temple cult. Since contamination through sources of im-purity was inevitable, law-abiding Jews were required regularly and frequently to immerse themselves for purification.

As water was scarce in Judea and Galilee, having "living water" (i.e., water coming from a spring or rainwater that had flowed into the pool) was a problem. This was solved by the construction of immersion pools — a *miqweh*[6] proper and an adjacent reserve pool (*ʾ ōṣer*) that was filled with "living water," which could be transferred to the *miqweh* by opening a channel.[7] The later rabbinic documents of the Mishnah and Tosefta devote an entire tractate (*Miqwaʾot*) to the discussion of regulations concerning the pools for ritual immersion. The im-portance of immersion for purification explains why numerous *miqwâʾôt* have been discovered in Jerusalem throughout the city as well as on and near the Temple Mount.[8] According to the Mishnah, those who enter a *miqweh* disrobe and completely immerse themselves in the water.

---

3. ὁ βαπτιστής, Luke 9:19; Matt 16:14; Mark 8:28; Josephus, *Ant.* 18.116; or ὁ βαπτίζων, Mark 1:4; 6:14, 24.

4. Joan E. Taylor, *The Immerser: John the Baptist within Sec-ond Temple Judaism* (Grand Rapids: Eerdmans, 1997), 50.

5. See generally Jonathan D. Lawrence, *Washing in Water: Trajectories of Ritual Bathing in the Hebrew Bible and Second Temple Literature* (SBL Academia Biblica 23; Atlanta: Society of Biblical Literature, 2006). For immersion rites in the Old Testament, cf. Exod 29:4; 30:19; 40:12, 30 – 31; cf. 19:10; Lev 8:6; 11:32; 14:8 – 9, 51 – 52; 15:5 – 8, 10 – 13, 16 – 18, 21 – 22, 27; 16:4, 24, 26, 28; 17:15; 22:6.

6. The Hebrew term *miqweh* means "collection" or "gather-ing" (of water).

7. Cf. Shimon Gibson, "The Pool of Bethesda in Jerusalem and Jewish Purification Practices of the Second Temple Pe-riod," *Proche-Orient chrétien* 55 (2005): 270 – 93.

8. Cf. Eyal Regev, "The Ritual Baths near the Temple Mount and Extra-Purification before Entering the Temple Courts," *IEJ* 55 (2005): 194 – 204; Jerome Murphy-O'Connor, *The Holy Land: An Oxford Archaeological Guide from Earliest Times to 1700* (5th ed.; Oxford: Oxford Univ. Press, 2008), 129 – 31.

Among the six large pools of Jerusalem were the Pool of Siloam and the Pool of Bethesda. The Pool of Siloam, discovered in excavations in 2004 at the junction of the Tyropoeon and Kidron Valleys, had a trapezoidal shape and measured 40 by 60 by 70 meters. The Pool of Bethesda was located in the northeast section of the city in the area of the Sheep Gate (on the grounds of the Church of St. Anne); it had two large basins surrounded on four sides by colonnaded halls; the northern pool (53 by 40 meters) served as the upper reservoir (ʾōṣer), the southern pool (47 by 52 meters) was used for immersion, as suggested by the series of steps extending down along the entire western side of the pool, with sets of steps connecting several landings.[9] These landings were capable of accommodating large numbers of people entering and leaving the water on steps.

Peter expected the Jews of Jerusalem who were prepared to repent and accept Jesus as the promised Messiah to be immersed in water — not for purification in preparation for participation in the temple cult, but for purification "in the name of Jesus the Messiah" (ἐπὶ τῷ ὀνόματι Ἰησοῦ Χριστοῦ). This was a completely new, unprecedented feature of immersion for the purpose of purification. Jews who immersed themselves might invoke the name of Yahweh, but not the name of Moses or of prophets such as John the Baptist. In the LXX, the formulation "in the name of the Lord" (ἐν ὀνόματι κυρίου) is used in connection with lifting up one's hand, praising, or blessing Yahweh (κύριος).[10] The formulation "in the name of" names the one on whom people call. The context of these passages justifies "viewing the expression 'in the name' as a reference to the basis, presuppositions, and conditions of the cultus, namely, the work and revelation of God for his people and his presence with them."[11]

In the LXX, the phrase "in the name of" (ἐπὶ τῷ ὀνόματι) generally has the meaning "by commission of, on the authority of." The explanation of the phrase in the context of Hellenistic commercial life, where it denotes the idea of charging to an account over which stands a particular owner — baptism "in the name of Jesus" transfers the person who is baptized to Jesus, who now "owns" the believer — has been disputed. In Acts, the contexts in which the phrase is used do not refer to, or imply, the concept of "being made over" into Jesus' possession. While the notion of being listed in God's "book" is certainly biblical,[12] the connection here with immersion in water introduces a mixing of metaphors that makes sense only if the general meaning of "appropriation" is assumed.[13] The phrase "in the name of Jesus" is often used in Acts in connection with "the power and authorization for apostolic activity."[14]

When the repentant Jews are immersed "in the name of Jesus the Messiah" (ἐπὶ τῷ ὀνόματι Ἰησοῦ

---

9. Cf. Gibson, "Pool of Bethesda," 283–88.

10. Ps 129:8 (LXX 128:8); cf. Pss 63:5 (LXX 62:5); 105:3 (LXX 104:3).

11. L. Hartman, ὄνομα, *EDNT*, 2:521.

12. Cf. Phil 4:3; Heb 12:23; Rev 3:5; 13:8; 17:8.

13. H. Bietenhard, "ὄνομα," *TDNT*, 5:275.

14. Johnson, *Acts*, 57; cf. 3:6, 16; 4:10, 12, 17, 18, 30; 5:28, 40, 41; 8:12; 9:16, 21, 27, 28; 15:26; 16:18; 19:13, 17; 21:13; 22:16; 26:9.

Χριστοῦ), several things happen as they invoke that name.

1. They publicly acknowledge that Jesus is Israel's Messiah and Savior — the crucified, risen, and exalted Lord who rules on David's throne at God's right hand (cf. Peter's sermon).[15]
2. They acknowledge that immersion for cleansing from impurity is *now* fundamentally connected with the person and work of Jesus, the Messiah.
3. They acknowledge their personal need for repentance on account of the fact that Jesus is the Messiah and Savior whom they had rejected.
4. They acknowledge Jesus as the cause of the forgiveness they seek. They publicly confess that Jesus has the authority and power to cleanse them from their sins. They invoke the name of Jesus, who is at God's right hand in heaven, calling on him to be saved (cf. v. 21).
5. They acknowledge Jesus' presence in their lives, Jesus' attention to their needs, and Jesus' intervention for their salvation.

Peter expects immersion in water in the name of Jesus the Messiah not only of those who personally demanded the crucifixion of Jesus, when Pilate gave them the option to choose between Barabbas and Jesus (Luke 23:18 – 25), but of "every one of you" (ἕκαστος ὑμῶν). He asks all Jews to commit themselves to faith in Jesus Christ and to demonstrate, through immersion in water, their acknowledgment of Jesus, the crucified, risen, and exalted Messiah, who cleanses from impurity.

Using the name of Jesus is not a magical formula. This is easily seen in the fact that Luke connects the reception of the Holy Spirit in various ways with immersion "in the name of Jesus" — in v. 38 baptism in the name of Jesus seems to precede the reception of the Spirit (cf. 8:16); in 10:44 – 48 the gift of the Holy Spirit precedes baptism in the name of Jesus; in 19:5 – 6 baptism in the name of the Lord Jesus Christ is accompanied by the laying on of hands and the reception of the Spirit.

Peter makes two promises for those who repent and accept Jesus as the Messiah: they will receive forgiveness and they will receive the Holy Spirit. The verb translated "forgive" (ἀφίημι) means, as often in the LXX, "to release from legal or moral obligation or consequence, *cancel, remit, pardon.*"[16] The image is that of the remission of a debt in a commercial or financial sense (cf. Matt 18:27, 32). The verb "to pardon" is often used in connection with sins, particularly in Luke,[17] who uses the formulation "forgiveness of sins" (ἄφεσις ἁμαρτιῶν) more than any other New Testament author.[18] The Greek term translated "sin" (ἁμαρτία) denotes the entire range of meanings from "involuntary mistake/error to serious offenses against a deity."[19] In the New Testament the term describes "a departure from either human or divine standards of uprightness" (with the context suggesting the level of heinousness), denoting the action itself as well as its result. The term also denotes "special sins," here the sin of having rejected Jesus and being culpable of his crucifixion.

The preposition "for" (εἰς) in the expression "for the forgiveness of sins" raises the question of the relationship between immersion in water (baptism) and the forgiveness of sins. Some interpret the preposition as expressing purpose (the purpose

---

15. Cf. Friedrich Avemarie, *Die Tauferzählungen der Apostelgeschichte. Theologie und Geschichte* (WUNT 139; Tübingen: Mohr Siebeck, 2002), 82 – 87: people are baptized who have heard the proclamation of Jesus Christ and who have come to faith as a result.

16. BDAG, s.v. ἀφίημι.

17. See Matt 6:12, 14, 15; 9:2, 5, 6; 12:31, 32; 18:21, 35; Mark 2:5, 7, 9, 10; 11:25; John 20:23; in Luke, see Luke 5:20, 21, 23, 24; 7:47, 48, 49; 11:4; 12:10; 17:3, 4; 23:34.

18. Luke 24:47; Acts 5:31; 10:43; 13:38; 26:18; cf. Mark 1:4; Matt 26:28; similarly Col 1:14; Eph 1:7. The phrase is not used in the LXX.

19. BDAG, s.v. ἁμαρτία; the following definitions see ibid.

of baptism is the forgiveness of sins),[20] some as expressing result (baptism results in forgiveness).[21] A contextually more plausible interpretation assumes a causal meaning (forgiveness of sins is the cause of baptism)[22]; the Jews who had heard Peter explain that Jesus was the crucified, risen, and exalted Messiah and Lord who saves Israel in the "last days" had repented of their sins and come to faith in Jesus. Otherwise, they would not have been willing to be immersed in water for purification "in the name of Jesus the Messiah"; they were immersed in water for purification "on the basis of the forgiveness of sins," which they had received from Jesus.

Peter does not spell out here the precise relationship between repentance, baptism, and the forgiveness of sins, or how this association "works."[23] However, in the context of Peter's sermon and in view of passages such as Acts 3:19, the connection is obvious: the remission of sins is the direct consequence of the fact that the Jews in Jerusalem repent of their rejection of Jesus and that they turn to Jesus as Messiah, as forgiveness of sins "in the last days" has been achieved by the death, resurrection, and exaltation of Jesus, Israel's Messiah and Lord.

Jews who repent and commit themselves to Jesus the Messiah receive the "gift of the Holy Spirit." The genitive (τοῦ ἁγίου πνεύματος) is epexegetical: the gift consists of the Holy Spirit.[24] Since the coming of God's Spirit is linked with the "last days" (v. 17) for which the Holy Spirit has been promised as a gift for God's people, the new commitment to Jesus includes the new believers in the benefits of the new and final period of God's plan of salvation

through his Messiah. The presence of God's Spirit is the mark of all people who repent and acknowledge that Jesus is the crucified, risen, and exalted Messiah and Lord. After the forgiveness of sins, the transforming and empowering presence of God's Spirit, distributed by Jesus the exalted Lord, is the central offer of the gospel that Peter and the other apostles proclaim.

2:39 "For the promise is for you and for your children and for all those who are far away, whom the Lord our God will call to himself" (ὑμῖν γὰρ ἐστιν ἡ ἐπαγγελία καὶ τοῖς τέκνοις ὑμῶν καὶ πᾶσιν τοῖς εἰς μακρὰν ὅσους ἂν προσκαλέσηται κύριος ὁ θεὸς ἡμῶν). Since the fulfillment of the promise of Joel 2:28–29 has just become a historical reality (Acts 2:16, 33), Jews who repent and commit themselves to Jesus as Israel's Messiah and Lord can be certain that they too will receive the Spirit of prophecy. God's promise (ἡ ἐπαγγελία) of new life through his Spirit in the last days will become a reality in their lives also. The personal pronoun "(for) you" (ὑμῖν) is a dative of advantage.

Since Peter's indictment of the Jews of Jerusalem for Jesus' crucifixion had pierced the hearts of his listeners (v. 37), a second thought may be intended. God's promise of his Spirit's transforming his people in the days of the new covenant remains valid. God has not given up on Israel. His promise remains open for the Jewish people and their descendants.[25] The "children" (τέκνοι) are the offspring, the descendants of the Jews who are listening to Peter. The term does not mean "little

---

20. Fitzmyer, *Acts*, 265; Everett Ferguson, *Baptism in the Early Church: History, Theology, and Liturgy in the First Five Centuries* (Grand Rapids: Eerdmans, 2008), 168.

21. Jervell, *Apostelgeschichte*, 150; Wall, *Acts*, 67.

22. Cf. Nigel Turner, *A Grammar of New Testament Greek*, vol. 3: *Syntax* (Edinburgh: T&T Clark, 1963), 266, s.v. εἰς 5; Daniel B. Wallace, *Greek Grammar beyond the Basics: An Exegetical Syntax of the New Testament* (Grand Rapids: Zondervan, 1996), 369–71; John B. Polhill, *Acts* (NAC 26; Nashville:

Broadman, 1992), 117; Bock, *Acts*, 142.

23. Cf. Dunn, *Acts*, 33, who correctly points out, however, that in view of Luke 24:47 and Acts 3:19; 5:31 "the primary link is between repentance and forgiveness, with baptism as the medium by which the repentance is expressed."

24. Note that the gift (δωρεά) of the Spirit is different from the "gifts" (χαρίσματα) of the Spirit described in 1 Cor 12.

25. Barrett, *Acts*, 155; cf. Rom 11:1–2.

child" but "an offspring of human parents, *child*."[26] The phrase "for your children" (τοῖς τέκνοις ὑμῶν) indicates distance in time: God's promise of forgiveness, of the presence of his Spirit, of new life, remains valid for future generations of Jews.[27]

The phrase "for all those who are far away" (πᾶσιν τοῖς εἰς μακράν) marks distance in space: God's Spirit and his transforming salvation will reach also "those who are far away." The phrase echoes Isa 57:19.[28] Peter expresses a universal vision of salvation in which he and the Twelve will play a major role as Jesus' witnesses (1:8, 22).

Peter concludes with another quotation from Joel, providing an (adapted) citation of Joel 2:32 (LXX 3:5; this line was not included earlier in vv. 17 – 21). Scholars debate whether this clause sets limits on those who receive God's promise (only those who are called by God). This clause certainly asserts that God will "call" people, a call that effectively brings people to repentance, commitment to Jesus as the Messiah and Lord, forgiveness of sins, and reception of the Holy Spirit. This is a theological dialectic that should not be dissolved — people call on the name of the Lord, i.e., Jesus, the Messiah, and thus receive salvation, which includes repentance, forgiveness of sins, and the reception of the Spirit (v. 21 in the context of vv. 33, 36, 38). At the same time it is "the Lord our God" who calls people into his presence.

2:40 He bore witness with many other words and exhorted them, saying, "Let yourselves be saved

from this corrupt generation!" (ἑτέροις τε λόγοις πλείοσιν διεμαρτύρατο καὶ παρεκάλει αὐτοὺς λέγων, σώθητε ἀπὸ τῆς γενεᾶς τῆς σκολιᾶς ταύτης). Peter's missionary sermon consisted not simply of the few lines of vv. 38 – 39, but was an extended explanation (λόγοι) of the significance of Jesus as Israel's Messiah and Lord. The phrase translated as "with many other words" is a dative of instrument. The two verbs of the sentence characterize his proclamation. He gave witness (διεμαρτύρατο) with the authority of an eyewitness who has seen Jesus' miracles, resurrection, and ascension (1:22; 2:32) and who was commissioned by Jesus to be his witness in Jerusalem (1:8). He appealed (παρεκάλει) to them again and again[29] to accept his explanations and arguments, to repent, and to accept Jesus as Messiah and Lord.

Peter's concern is the salvation (σωτηρία, here the verb σῴζω) of the Jews of Jerusalem. The appeal to be saved implies that if they do not repent of their rejection of Jesus, if they do not accept him as the crucified, risen, and exalted Messiah and Lord, they do not have salvation. The aorist imperative passive (σώθητε) has the meaning "allow yourselves to be saved"[30] and denotes the Lord as the one who saves. He is the one on whose name they should call to receive salvation and in whose name they should be immersed (vv. 21, 36, 38). The implied warning not to miss the offer of salvation refers back to Joel's prophecy of judgment on the day of the Lord (vv. 19 – 21). The forgiveness of sins that Peter offers to the Jews of Jerusalem if and

---

26. BDAG, s.v. τέκνον 1. Joachim Jeremias, *Infant Baptism in the First Four Centuries* (Philadelphia: Westminster, 1960), 40 – 41, is therefore wrong when he argues for a reference here to infant baptism. Jewish infants were not immersed for purification; and in Acts, Luke reports baptisms only for people who had been listening and responding to the proclamation of the gospel of Jesus.

27. The phrase echoes passages such as Gen 9:9; 13:15; 17:7 – 10; Ps 18:50.

28. Isa 57:19: "Peace, peace, to the far ones and the near

ones, says the Lord, and I will heal them" (εἰρήνην ἐπ' εἰρήνην τοῖς μακρὰν καὶ τοῖς ἐγγὺς οὖσιν, καὶ εἶπεν κύριος Ἰάσομαι αὐτούς).

29. BDAG, s.v. παρακαλέω 2, "to urge strongly, *appeal to, urge, exhort, encourage;*" note the meaning 1b, "to invite someone." The imperfect παρεκάλει denotes continuous action. The verb παρακαλέω, used 22 times in Acts, is often used to refer to missionary proclamation.

30. Cf. BDF, §314, here with a permissive sense.

when they repent and turn to Jesus delivers from God's judgment.

The present "house of Israel" (v. 36) has proven to be a "corrupt generation" on account of the crucifixion of God's Messiah. Peter's designation of his Jewish contemporaries as a "corrupt generation" (ἡ γενεᾶ τῆς σκολιᾶς ταύτης) refers back to the generation of Israel in the desert.[31] Peter alludes to God's great act of liberation in the history of Israel and to the tragic consequences of unbelief, which resulted in a whole generation perishing in the desert. Peter calls on the Jews of Jerusalem to be rescued from their rejection of God's second great act of liberation and to accept God's salvation, which is now tied to the death, resurrection, and exaltation of Jesus, the Messiah and Lord.

2:41 Those who accepted his message were baptized. About three thousand persons were added that day (οἱ μὲν οὖν ἀποδεξάμενοι τὸν λόγον αὐτοῦ ἐβαπτίσθησαν καὶ προσετέθησαν ἐν τῇ ἡμέρᾳ ἐκείνῃ ψυχαὶ ὡσεὶ τρισχίλιαι). These last two sentences state the effect of Peter's proclamation of the significance of Jesus, the Messiah and Lord, on Pentecost. Jews of Jerusalem accepted his message (λόγος) and were baptized. Public immersion in water for purification followed repentance of their former rejection of Jesus, commitment to Jesus, who, as risen and exalted Lord, forgives sins and sends the Spirit, and the willingness to be immersed "in the name of Jesus the Messiah."

The immersion of Jews of Jerusalem "in the name of Jesus the Messiah" was not a private or secret ceremony but a public demonstration of repentance and a public confession of faith in Jesus.

The baptism of hundreds of people — in the presence of one of the apostles who assisted with the act of immersion, in one of the large immersion pools near the Temple Mount — could not have been kept a private affair.

Luke gives an estimate (ὡσεί) of the number of people who were converted and baptized. The figure of 3,000 converts represents the twenty-five-fold increase in the number of persons added to the initial congregation of 120 people. The figure has no apparent symbolic significance and thus is meant to describe the actual, approximate number of Jews who accepted faith in Jesus as Israel's Messiah and Lord on the day of Pentecost.[32] If we assume 100,000 inhabitants of Jerusalem, 3,000 converts constitute 3 percent of the total population; we do not know how many of the converts belonged to the tens of thousands of festival pilgrims in town for the Feast of Pentecost.

Some scholars object that it would have been impossible to address 3,000 people in the open "without a microphone."[33] In antiquity, large crowds were regularly addressed in the open. The acoustics in theaters were superb; in the theatre in Epidaurus (capacity 14,000), even whispering in the orchestra could be heard in the highest rows of seats.[34] The natural cove of a sloping Galilean hillside near Capernaum allowed 5,000 people or more to clearly hear a speaker.[35] We do not know, however, where Peter addressed the large crowd of Jews.

The immersion of 3,000 Jews in the large public immersion pools of Jerusalem would not have been unique. The thousands of festival pilgrims who were in the city for Pentecost would all have

---

31. Cf. Deut 32:5; Ps 78; cf. *Bam. Rab.* 16.9 (69a); *b. Soṭah* 34b.

32. If Luke understood his figures as expressions of divine blessing, he easily could have used figures with a marked symbolic significance, e.g., 12,000 (12 by 1,000) or 144,000 (12 by 12 by 1,000).

33. Haenchen, *Acts*, 188.

34. F. Krafft, "Acoustics," *BNP*, 1:106.

35. B. Cobbey Crisler, "The Acoustics and Crowd Capacity of Natural Theaters in Palestine," *BA* 39 (1976): 128–41 (136–37).

immersed themselves before entering the gates of the temple complex in the Pool of Siloam or in the Pool of Bethesda. The immense success of John the "Immerser" — Luke emphasizes that "crowds" of people (ὄχλοι) flocked to the site at the Jordan River where he preached (Luke 3:7, 10) — suggests that his immersion activity involved thousands of people. Nevertheless, we must not forget that these were people who publicly pledged allegiance to Jesus — whose message and whose claims had been deemed unacceptable by the Jewish leadership, who had stood trial in Jerusalem only a few weeks earlier, and who had been shouted down by the crowds who demanded his crucifixion.

Several months later, the number of believers had grown to "about five thousand" (4:4), and several years later James mentions the figure of "many thousands" (μυριάδες) of Jewish believers (21:20; this figure could include Jewish believers from Judea and Galilee).

Theology in Application

The central theme of the passage is the proper response to the gospel. After Peter explained in his Pentecost speech the significance of the life, death, resurrection, and exaltation of Jesus, the promised Messiah and the Lord who bestows the Spirit of prophecy, he argues for the need to repent, to receive forgiveness of sins, to commit to Jesus as Israel's Messiah and Lord, and to demonstrate this new commitment by immersion in water in the name of Jesus the Messiah.

Church Growth Methodology

I begin with some comments on the statistical data given in 2:41. Church growth experts may be fascinated by the large figure given for the number of converts who came to faith on the day of Pentecost. Apart from the oral proclamation of the gospel, this passage does not contribute to a "tool kit" of church growth methodology. There is no method that guarantees numerical success. The relatively sparse and general statistical data that Luke provides in Acts for the growth of the church in Jerusalem (and in Judea) suggest two points.[36]

First, the Jewish believers in Jerusalem were evidently not interested in precise statistical data for the growth of the church. The fact that Luke is the only New Testament author who provides any figures suggests that this was true for all early Christians. Luke normally refers to the growth of the church with general formulations without statistical data.[37] As we have seen in the introduction, Luke imitates the style of the Septuagint; this means that he knew the books of Numbers, Ezra, and Nehemiah, which provided models and precedents for giving exact statistical information about the size of the people of God. Luke gives us two rounded figures and a general comment on "many thousands" of believers. The numerical growth of the church is

---

36. Cf. Schnabel, *Early Christian Mission,* 2:733.

37. Acts 5:14; 6:1, 7; 8:6, 12; 9:31, 35, 42; 11:21, 24; 13:43; 14:1, 21; 16:5; 18:8, 10; 21:20.

not of utmost concern to him. Luke would have been bewildered about attempts to "strategize" the growth of a church by statistical projections that are then integrated into a "plan" to tell the "church planters" how to achieve their (statistical) goals. The same is true for Paul, who does not include any statistical data in the letters to his churches and coworkers.

Second, it is nevertheless true that the growth of the church is not a vague, mysterious, or "spiritual" process that cannot be observed. The growth of the church is a visible reality that can be expressed with numbers. The recording of numerical growth shows "how God's blessing accompanies his work and asserts itself even against hostile forces."[38] Clearly, Luke wants to provide specific information to describe the quantitative growth of the Jerusalem church.

Peter and the apostles know that the positive response of listeners who commit their lives to faith in Jesus and who are baptized and added to the church is not the result of good methods of proclaiming the gospel. And they know that rejection, opposition, and persecution are not the result of inferior evangelistic methods. They know that it is God who calls people to salvation (2:39), which means that conversions are always a mystery bound up with the sovereign grace of God, whether they are conversions of a few individuals or mass conversions.

The Universal Need for Repentance

Peter asserts that the Jews of Jerusalem (2:38) as well as all people "who are far away" (2:39) need to repent. If Jesus is indeed the Messiah, Jews must repent of their rejection of Jesus. Peter and the Twelve, and other early Christians such as the apostle Paul, never abandoned evangelism among the Jewish people. Both secular and orthodox Jews today often reject efforts by Christians, including Jewish believers, to lead them to faith in Jesus the Messiah. Sometimes they label such efforts "spiritual genocide," suggesting that Jews who believe that Jesus is the Messiah are no longer Jews. Such attitudes, while understandable, cannot be accepted, and Jewish evangelism cannot be given up, as the "Berlin Declaration on the Uniqueness of Christ and Jewish Evangelism in Europe Today" affirms, a document written by a task force of the Theological Commission of the World Evangelical Alliance in 2008. The declaration affirms that

> Christians everywhere must not look away when Jewish people have the same deep need for forgiveness of sin and true *shalom*, as do people of all nations. Love in action compels all Christians to share the gospel with people everywhere, including the Jewish people of Europe.... We recognize that genocide illustrates the enormity of sin. God is not responsible for genocide; we humans are. God has provided the solution.

---

38. Paul Zingg, *Das Wachsen der Kirche: Beiträge zur Frage der lukanischen Redaktion und Theologie* (OBO 3; Fribourg/ Göttingen: Universitätsverlag/Vandenhoeck & Ruprecht, 1974), 296.

It is often seen as unacceptable to challenge another's religious views. Nevertheless, we regard failure to share the gospel as ignoring the problem of sin. No one should ignore Jesus' assessment of human sin. Everyone needs what God offers by his grace: forgiveness of sin and a transforming divine presence in those who respond. Jesus did not seek to dominate, but gave himself on the cross as sacrifice for sin. His death cleanses from the guilt of sin and provides a new relationship with God. This benefit is neither earned nor entered into by birth. It is received through acknowledging our deep need for God to supply what we lack.[39]

Peter's missionary sermon on Pentecost, in which he appeals to the Jews of Jerusalem to repent, also highlights the need for Gentiles to repent. If being a descendant of Abraham, worshiping and sacrificing in the Jerusalem temple and obeying the law, does not grant salvation now that Jesus the Messiah has arrived, who rules as Lord at God's right hand, the Gentiles who have neither Abraham nor the temple nor the law must repent as well — of their idolatry, their self-centeredness, their greed, their immorality. We see this theme in later passages in Acts.

The Offer of Forgiveness of Sins through Jesus the Messiah

The offer of forgiveness of sins through Jesus is another core belief of Christians. As a result of the life, death, resurrection, and exaltation of Jesus, the former means of atonement for sins — temple sacrifices, immersion for ritual purification, obedience to the law — are no longer effective. As the last days have arrived with the coming of the Messiah, forgiveness comes only through Jesus Christ. Although Peter does not elaborate here on Jesus' atoning death, he emphasizes that the crucifixion was part of God's plan of salvation.

In the context of his Pentecost sermon, which explains the coming of the Holy Spirit, forgiveness of sins and salvation are linked with the transforming and empowering presence of the Holy Spirit and with the acknowledgment of Jesus' lordship on the heavenly throne. Forgiveness of sins is not simply a benefit that I find advantageous. Forgiveness of sins involves acknowledging that Jesus is Lord over my life, that God calls me to himself (2:39), and that the transforming power of the Holy Spirit is at work in my life.

The Appeal to Public Commitment to Jesus

Peter expected the Jews of Jerusalem who repented and who came to faith in Jesus to go to one of the pools in Jerusalem and to have themselves immersed in water — in public, confessing "in the name of Jesus the Messiah" that they regret their

---

39. The declaration is published online at www.worldevangelicals.org/commissions/tc/berlin.htm. See the conference volume, David Parker, ed., *Jesus, Salvation, and the Jewish People* (Milton Keynes: Paternoster, 2010).

former rejection of Jesus and that they have now found salvation through Jesus, the crucified, risen, and exalted Lord. Luke's conception of Christian baptism includes the following elements: "a visible expression of individual conversion, what a person does on coming to faith and at the same time a gift of God that the church cannot deny, performed in the name of the Lord, bringing a consciousness that one receives forgiveness of sins and salvation, bound with outpouring of the Holy Spirit by the laying on of hands [?], reception into the community of all believers, and having consequences for daily life."[40]

Some experts in Muslim evangelism have suggested that the baptism of Muslim converts should be either delayed, or not made public, or refashioned in some "con-textualized" way in order to avoid new converts being persecuted and perhaps killed by members of their families. While such dangers are real and while these concerns are understandable, this text teaches the significance of a public commitment to Jesus. The possibility that an immersion in the pools of Jerusalem with a view to the forgiveness of sins "in the name of Jesus the Messiah" would be regarded as a provo-cation that the Jewish leadership would not tolerate was all too real, as the following chapters in Acts demonstrate. However, commitment to Jesus the Messiah who rules Israel on David's eternal throne on God's right hand could not possibly be a merely private affair. The next section shows that part and parcel of this public commitment to faith in Jesus was integration into the community of local believers in Jesus.

---

40. Ferguson, *Baptism*, 185 n. 53.

Acts 2:42 – 47

Literary Context

This is the last passage in this section of Acts in which Luke explains the identity and witness of Jesus' followers as the new people of God (1:15 – 2:47). In the previous episodes, Luke described the reconstitution of the Twelve as Jesus' witnesses to the people of Israel (1:15 – 26), the coming of the Holy Spirit on Pentecost (2:1 – 13), Peter's explanation of the coming of the Holy Spirit and of the significance of Jesus as the crucified, risen, and exalted Messiah and Lord (2:14 – 36), and Peter's missionary sermon in which he urged his listeners to repent and to commit themselves to Jesus the Messiah (2:37 – 41). In 2:41, Luke had noted that as a result of mass conversions among the Jews living in Jerusalem, about three thousand people who had repented and committed their lives to Jesus were baptized. Luke now describes what effect their conversion to faith in Jesus has for these new followers of Jesus.

II. The Beginnings of the New People of God (1:15 – 8:3)

    A. The Identity and Witness of Jesus' Followers as God's People (1:15 – 2:47)

        7. The arrival of the Holy Spirit and the identity of Jesus as Israel's Messiah and Lord (2:1 – 41)

➡   **8. The life of the Jerusalem community of Jesus' followers (2:42 – 47)**

    B. The Life, Witness, Trials, and Growth of the Community of Believers in Jerusalem (3:1 – 8:3)

Main Idea

The commitment to Jesus, Israel's Messiah and Lord, begins to transform the lives of the followers of Jesus as they worship God in public and in private, as they devote themselves to the teaching of the apostles concerning the significance of Jesus, as they have fellowship with one another in their homes, and as they sacrificially alleviate the needs of fellow believers.

Translation

Acts 2:42 – 47

42a	Action	**They devoted themselves**
b	List	to the teaching of the apostles,
c		to fellowship,
d		to the breaking of bread, and
e		to the prayers.
43a	Event	**Every person felt awe**
b	Cause	on account of the many wonders and
c	Cause	signs
d	Agency	that were being done by the apostles.
44a	Event	**All**
b	Identification	who believed
c		**were together,**
d	Action	and **they held all things in common;**
45a	Means	and **they would sell** **their possessions and**
b	Expansion	**their belongings**
c	Means	and **distribute them**
d	Sphere	among all those who had need.
46a	Event	When they continued to meet
b	Time	each day
c	Manner	unanimously
d	Place	in the temple,
e	Event	and when they broke bread
f	Place	in their homes,
g	Event	**they ate their meals**
h	Manner	with glad and
i	Manner	simple hearts,
47a	Circumstance	praising God
b	Circumstance	and enjoying the respect of all the people.
c	Time	And day by day
d	Action	**the Lord added to their number**
e	Identification	those who were being saved.

Structure and Literary Form

This is the second of Luke's *summary statements* about the life and the activities of the new followers of Jesus. As this is the longest of these statements, a comparison will help us to see the commonalities and the new information that Luke includes.[1]

1:12 – 14	2:42 – 47	4:32 – 37	5:12 – 16	6:7	9:31
	teaching of the apostles	preaching of the apostles			
meetings	fellowship				
	breaking of bread				
prayer	prayers				
	miracles through the apostles		miracles through the apostles		
	unity	unity			
	selling of property	selling of property			
	sharing of possessions	sharing of possessions			
	help for needy believers	help for needy believers			
	meetings in the temple		meetings in the temple		
	breaking of bread in homes				
	common meals				
	praise of God				fear of the Lord
	respect from the people		respect from the people		peace
	church growth		church growth	church growth	church growth

1. The sequence for 2:42 – 47 follows the text, while the items in the other summaries are coordinated with the summary in Acts 2. Some scholars omit 1:12 – 14 from the list of summaries. Some add 2:41 to the summary in Acts 2. Cf. Maria A. Co, "The Major Summaries in Acts: Acts 2.42 – 47; 4.32 – 35; 5.12 – 16. Linguistic and Literary Relationships," *ETL* 68 (1992): 49 – 85.

The purposes of these summaries included in Acts are:

- *historical*, as Luke reports what happened in the early Jerusalem church
- *literary*, as Luke uses them to indicate the passage of time
- *theological*, as they point to the continued presence of the power of God in the community of believers and in the ministry of the apostles, in which miracles continue to happen, and as they illustrate the transformation of the lives of believers
- *ecclesiological*, as they outline the essential characteristic of the communities of Jesus' followers
- *missiological*, as they record the continued growth and expansion of the church

These summaries are located in the early part of Acts, probably because there was a need at the beginning to describe the identity and ministry of the church. The summaries function to generalize and thus make the experience of individuals normative.

The summary in 2:42 – 47 can be analyzed in five parts. (1) Luke provides a summary of the essentials of the life of the Jerusalem church, described with four activities — apostolic teaching, fellowship among the believers, breaking of bread, and prayers (v. 42). (2) Luke comments on the effect that the growth of the church and the miracles of the apostles had on the people of Jerusalem, who felt awe (v. 43). (3) Luke explains the list of the essentials of the life of the church, commenting on the believers' unity, their willingness to sell property in order to help fellow believers in need (fellowship), and their sharing of meals in the temple and in their homes, accompanied by joy and prayers of praise (vv. 44 – 47a). (4) Luke includes another comment on the effect of the life on the people of Jerusalem, who respected the Christians (v. 47b). (5) Luke notes the continued growth of the church (v. 47c-e).

Some have suggested that Luke wanted to remind his readers of the Greco-Roman descriptions of the "golden age": the idyllic conditions that prevailed at the beginning of the history of the human race were realized, for a moment, at the beginning of the history of the church.[2] If this was indeed Luke's intention, he would have also made the theological point that the events in Jerusalem that were initiated by the death, resurrection, and exaltation of Jesus have fundamental significance for the history of the world.

---

2. Brian J. Capper, "Reciprocity and the Ethic of Acts," in *Witness to the Gospel: The Theology of Acts* (ed. I. H. Marshall and D. Peterson), 499 – 518, 504 – 12. Cf. Hesiod, *Op.* 106 – 201; Virgil, *Georg.* 1.125 – 129.

IN DEPTH: The Self-Understanding of the Early Church

The self-understanding of the church in Jerusalem and hence in other cities can be seen in the use of several important designations.[3]

1. "The Way" (ἡ ὁδός; 9:2; 19:9, 23; 22:4; 24:14, 22; cf. 18:25, 26), probably reflecting prophecies such as Isa 40:3 and 30:11, 21; 35:8; 57:14; 62:10. The early Christians believed that they were now traveling on the way on which God was leading his people to salvation.

2. "The holy people" (οἱ ἅγιοι; 9:13, 32, 41; 26:10), a designation probably derived from Dan 7:18, 22, 25, 27, describing the close connection and fellowship between "the holy people of the Most High" and God himself.

3. "The church of God" (ἡ ἐκκλησία τοῦ θεοῦ; 5:11; 8:1, 3; 9:31; etc.),[4] denoting the people who together composed the fellowship of believers in Jesus, whether they were actually gathered or not.

4. "The disciples" (οἱ μαθηταί; 6:1, 2, 7; 9:1; 15:10; etc.), the believers in Jesus who were learning and practicing what Jesus had taught.

5. "The brothers and sisters" (οἱ ἀδελφοί; 6:3), an expression that describes the close bond between those who believed in Jesus and thus belonged to the new community of renewed Israel.

6. "The Nazarenes" (οἱ Ναζωραῖοι; 24:5), the standard designation for believers in Jesus in Semitic languages, a term used by non-Christian Jews in Jerusalem for the believers in Jesus as those who followed the teachings of Jesus of Nazareth.[5] It should be noted that other Jews regarded the "Nazarenes" as a "party" (αἵρεσις; 24:5; 28:22); this Greek term does not have the connotations that the term "sect" has today (it certainly has nothing to do with "heresy"), but is a designation that Luke also uses for the Sadducees and the Pharisees (5:17; 15:5; 26:5; cf. Josephus, *Ant.* 13.171). The "party of the Nazarenes" was thus "one of the parties within Judaism, by no means necessarily one of which the speaker would approve, but not a group outside the accepted parameters of Jewish faith and practice."[6]

---

3. Cf. Bauckham, "James and the Jerusalem Community," 55–60, for the following summary.

4. The expression "church" (ἐκκλησία) is used 21 times for the church in Acts (7:38 refers to the congregation of Israel in the desert). The full designation seems to have been "the church of God," as indicated by 1 Cor 15:9 and 1 Thess 2:14.

5. Christians might have used the term as a self-designation on the basis of the presence of an exegetical pun, designating Jesus as the messianic "shoot" (*nēṣer*) of David (Isa 11:1), a term that was also used of the people of the coming redeemer, "the preserved [*nᵉṣîrê*] of Israel" (Isa 49:6); i.e., the early Christians might have used this term in terms of their conviction that the community of believers in Jesus represented the beginning of the restoration of Israel by the Messiah.

6. Bauckham, "James and the Jerusalem Community," 61.

Exegetical Outline

→ **I. The Life of the Community (2:42 – 47)**

   A. The Essentials of the Life of the Jerusalem Church (2:42)

   1. Teaching of the apostles (2:42a-b)

   2. Fellowship (2:42c)

   3. Breaking of bread (2:42d)

   4. Prayers (2:42e)

   B. The Effect of the Life of the Church on Unbelievers (2:43)

   1. Fearful awe among the people of Jerusalem (2:43a)

   2. Reason: The miracles performed through the apostles (2:43b-d)

   C. The Essentials of the Life of the Church Expanded (2:44 – 47a)

   1. Unity in their meetings (2:44a-c)

   2. Sharing possessions (2:44d – 45d)

      a. Sharing of resources (2:44d)

      b. Sale of possessions (2:45a-b)

      c. Distribution of funds to the needy (2:45c-d)

   3. Sharing meals (2:46a – 47a).

      a. Meetings and meals in the temple (2:46a-d)

      b. Meetings and meals in private homes (2:46e-f)

      c. Eating with glad and simple hearts (2:46g-i)

      d. Praise directed to God (2:47a)

   D. The Effect of the Life of the Church on Unbelievers (2:47b)

   E. The Continued Growth of the Church (2:47c-e)

Explanation of the Text

2:42 They devoted themselves to the teaching of the apostles, to fellowship, to the breaking of bread, and to the prayers (ἦσαν δὲ προσκαρτεροῦντες τῇ διδαχῇ τῶν ἀποστόλων καὶ τῇ κοινωνίᾳ, τῇ κλάσει τοῦ ἄρτου καὶ ταῖς προσευχαῖς). The thousands of new believers (2:41) are persistently and continuously devoted to the essential activities and characteristics of the life of Jesus' followers.

The first essential characteristic is the persistent devotion to the "teaching" (διδαχή) of the apostles.[7]

The phrase "teaching of the apostles" (διδαχῇ τῶν ἀποστόλων) is a subjective genitive: it is the apostles who were teaching the new converts. Luke makes three points. (1) The apostles regarded teaching as one of their main responsibilities (cf. 6:1 – 6). (2) The believers continuously listened to the apostles. (3) The believers practiced what they heard the apostles teach (otherwise they would not "persistently devote" [the meaning of the periphrastic here] themselves to that teaching). Sermons were an integral component of the Sabbath services in

---

7. Cf. Acts 4:2, 18; 5:21, 25, 28, 42; 11:26; 15:35; 18:11; 20:20; 21:21; 28:31; cf. 6:2, 4.

the Jewish synagogues; they usually followed the reading from the Torah and the Prophets and were often related to the latter (cf. Luke 4:16 – 22). The teaching of the apostles followed the same pattern.

The content of this teaching can be gleaned, at least in part, from the sermons in Acts, particularly those of Peter. The apostles' teaching focused on Jesus' life, ministry, death, and resurrection, and on his significance in God's plan.[8] The following themes stand out:

- Jesus as Israel's Messiah and Lord[9]
- the Son of David and God's Servant[10]
- the holy and righteous Savior[11]
- the prophet like Moses and the judge of humankind[12]
- the necessity of repentance in view of God's revelation in the life, death, resurrection, and exaltation of Jesus and in the bestowal of the Spirit of prophecy[13]
- God's offer of salvation through Jesus, who is Israel's Messiah and Lord, available only in personal allegiance to Jesus

As Acts continues, the apostles will teach that God offers his messianic salvation not only to Jews, for whom there is now no other way to salvation open, but also to Gentiles.[14] Salvation means forgiveness of sins through faith in Jesus, Israel's Messiah and Lord;[15] reception of and transformation through the Holy Spirit;[16] integration into the community of the messianic people of God, who worship Jesus and who experience healing from illness,

from demonic oppression, and from material selfishness.[17] Israel's Scriptures (the Old Testament) are read with newly opened eyes concerning the fulfillment of God's promises in Jesus, his Messiah and the Lord of Israel.

Since the Torah reading in the synagogues seems to have been accompanied by the recitation of a *targum*, a translation into the vernacular (i.e., Aramaic or Greek, which evidently existed in both written and oral form in the first century),[18] it is possible that the church in Jerusalem used both Hebrew (for reading) and Aramaic and Greek (for teaching) in their congregational meetings. Note how Acts 6:1 documents the presence of Greek-speaking Jewish believers in the church. Some of the diaspora Jews living in Jerusalem (2:5 – 11), presumably, could not understand Aramaic, which necessitated a translation of both Scripture and teaching.

As the phrase "the teaching of the apostles" describes the entire preaching of the apostles, both the instruction of the followers of Jesus as well as the missionary proclamation before unbelievers may be in view here. Note that Luke uses the expression "the word" (ὁ λόγος) to describe the apostolic preaching of the message of Jesus Christ, and that this expression belongs to the missionary language of the early Christians.[19]

The second characteristic of the church in Jerusalem is "fellowship" (κοινωνία), which should be understood as the personal, fraternal coherence of the individual members of the congregation,[20]

---

8. Cf. Dunn, *Beginning from Jerusalem*, 189 – 96.

9. κύριος: 2:21, 34, 36; 10:36; Χριστός: 2:31, 36, 38; 3:18, 20; 4:10; 10:36.

10. Son of David: 2:29 – 31; Servant of God: 3:13, 26; 4:27, 30.

11. Acts 5:31; holy (and righteous): 3:14; 4:27, 30.

12. Acts 3:22; 10:42.

13. Acts 2:38, 40; 3:19; 5:31; cf. 8:22; 10:42 – 43; 15:8.

14. Acts 2:21, 39; 3:26; 10:34 – 35, 36, 43, 45; 11:18.

15. Acts 2:38; 3:19; 5:31; 10:43; cf. 13:38; 15:9; 22:16; 26:18.

16. Acts 2:38; 9:17; 10:43 – 44; 11:15 – 17; 15:8.

17. Acts 2:1, 44 – 45; 3:1 – 4:12; 4:32 – 5:11; 5:12 – 16; 8:7.

18. The extant manuscripts of Targumim (Onqelos, Jonathan, Pseudo-Jonathan, Neofiti, etc.) date between the seventh and sixteenth centuries.

19. H. Ritt, "λόγος," *EDNT*, 2:359, with reference to Acts 4:31; 6:2, 7; 8:14; 11:1; 13:5, 7, 44, 46; 16:32; 17:13; 18:11; "word of the Lord": 8:25; 13:44, 48, 49; 15:35, 36; 16:32; 19:10.

20. Cf. BDAG, s.v. κοινωνία 1, close association involving mutual interests and sharing, "association, communion, fellowship, close relationship."

the followers of Jesus who live in community "brought into existence by the shared experience of the Spirit."[21] In 2:44 fellowship is explained as "being together." In the context of Luke's summary, the term "fellowship" describes the harmonious unity of the believers and the willingness to sell possessions and give the proceeds to needy fellow believers. We thus can distinguish between attitude and action, between the attitude within the church toward other believers and the actions that result from this attitude. In the first months of the existence of the Jerusalem church, the attitude and the actions of "fellowship" prompted believers to sell their possessions and to share their resources. As Luke had just reported the conversion of thousands of Jews living in Jerusalem (2:41), fellowship was possible only in meetings that took place in private houses (cf. 2:46 – 47).

Some have linked the "fellowship" of the early Christians, focused as it was on the teaching of the apostles and on helping fellow Christians in need, with the "community" (*yaḥad*, derived from the Hebrew word for "one") of the Qumran Essenes. The earliest Christians' emphasis on teaching and on sharing of possessions has been compared with 1QS V, 1 – 2:

> This (is) the rule for the men of the Community who devote themselves to turn away from all evil and hold fast to all which he has commanded as his will: they shall separate themselves from the congregation of the men of deceit, in order to become a Community, with Torah and property, and answerable to the Sons of Zadok, the priests who keep the covenant.

The parallels are obvious: there is a fellowship or community of people; they meet separately from their fellow Jews; they are devoted to Torah (teaching); they have leaders; there is a willingness to share possessions. It should be noted, however, that the Essene community was much more structured than the early church (see further on v. 44).

The third characteristic of the Jerusalem church was "the breaking of bread" (ἡ κλάσις τοῦ ἄρτου). While many scholars suggest the phrase refers to the celebration of the Lord's Supper, i.e., remembering Jesus' last supper with his disciples, and while others argue that this is a reference only to ordinary meals,[22] there is the distinct possibility that it refers to both. The "breaking of bread" is best understood as a reference to the ordinary meals that the believers regularly shared, during which they remembered Jesus' death on the cross for the forgiveness of sins and for the establishment of the new covenant, linked with the command to remember Jesus and his sacrifice during meals (cf. Luke 22:14 – 22).[23]

In the church in Corinth, and probably in other churches as well, the Lord's Supper was commemorated in connection with ordinary, regular meals that the believers shared (1 Cor 11:17 – 34). When the bread was broken at the beginning of the meal, Jesus' words "this is my body, which is for you" would be remembered. After the meal, in connection with wine being served, Jesus' words "this cup is the new covenant in my blood" would be spoken. In Acts 2:46 – 47 Luke clarifies that these meals took place not only in private homes but also in the temple precincts.

The fourth characteristic of the church is the "prayers" (προσευχαί) of the believers. The plural implies regular prayer practices of the Christian believers,[24] perhaps also referring to the traditional prayers that Jews regularly recited. Luke does not clarify whether private or communal prayers are in

---

21. Dunn, *Beginning from Jerusalem*, 196.
22. Jervell, *Apostelgeschichte*, 155; Bock, *Acts*, 150.

23. These meals can be called *agapē* or "love feasts" (Jude 12); see Tertullian, *Apol.* 39.16 – 19.
24. Cf. Acts 1:14 – 15; 3:1; 4:24 – 30; 12:12.

view, but 1:24 and 4:23 – 31 indicate the latter are certainly included.

As regards the Jewish synagogues, the relative absence of explicit evidence concerning communal prayers is conspicuous. Some have suggested that communal prayer played "little or no role in the typical Judaean synagogue."[25] The diaspora synagogues called their buildings προσευχή (*proseuchē*), which literally means "house of prayer." In the temple in Jerusalem, the priests held public prayers every morning, after the slaughter of the morning sacrifice and before the incense offering.[26] Three o'clock in the afternoon was the "hour of prayer" in the temple (3:1), when devout Jews paused to pray.[27] It is a plausible inference from available evidence from Qumran that the priests recited the Decalogue and the *Shema* during the prayers in the temple. The Qumran Essenes had regular communal prayer sessions.[28] The Pharisees seemed to have followed a fixed prayer routine, perhaps communal, at least on holidays. It thus seems that

> the Jewish heritage behind Christian prayer had two distinct patterns: one related to the course of the sun, and the other according to the times of the temple sacrifice. However, there was no central regulation of prayer at this time, and we probably have to reckon with local and personal variations in the actual practices, although of course, the outspoken pious would encourage a maximal approach.[29]

The paucity of evidence makes the inclusion of "prayers" as one of the essential activities of the Christians even more remarkable, especially if reference is made to communal prayers.

Luke points out repeatedly that the prayers of the church were a significant factor in the life and ministry of the earliest Christians.

1. The disciples waited in Jerusalem for the fulfillment of Jesus' promise of the Spirit while praying (1:14).
2. They prayed during the election of a twelfth apostle (1:24 – 25).
3. The healing of a lame man at one of the temple gates happened in connection with the prayer routine of the church leaders (3:1).
4. The reaction of the Jerusalem church to external pressure and to God's intervention was to pray (4:23 – 31).
5. Prayer belonged to the fundamental priorities of the leadership of the church (6:4).
6. The mission in Samaria was accompanied by prayer for the Holy Spirit (8:15).
7. The conversion of Saul was linked with prayer (9:11).

2:43 Every person felt awe on account of the many wonders and signs that were being done by the apostles (ἐγίνετο δὲ πάσῃ ψυχῇ φόβος, πολλά τε τέρατα καὶ σημεῖα διὰ τῶν ἀποστόλων ἐγίνετο). Luke comments here on the effect that the life of the believers and the ministry of the apostles had on the people living in Jerusalem. It appears that the kind of miracles that Jesus performed were now being performed through the apostles; as "wonders and signs" (τέρατα καὶ σημεῖα) validated Jesus as God's promised Messiah (see on 2:22), they now confirm the ministry and the message of the apostles as coming from God.

The result of these miracles, of which Luke will give one example in 3:1 – 10, is "awe" (φόβος),

25. Levine, *Synagogue*, 169; cf. ibid. 162 – 69.

26. Cf. *m. Tamid* 5:1. In the temple, silence accompanied the sacrificial rite; only the Levites sang (occasionally); at the time of the drink offering, regular daily hymns and psalms of praise and thanksgiving were sung; cf. Sir 50:16 – 19; *m. Tamid* 7:3; cf. Daniel K. Falk, "Jewish Prayer Literature and the Jeru-

salem Church in Acts," in *The Book of Acts in Its Palestinian Setting* (ed. R. Bauckham), 267 – 301, 289.

27. Cf. Josephus, *Ant.* 3.237; 14.65; Falk, "Jewish Prayer Literature," 297.

28. CD XI, 21; cf. Philo, *Contempl. Life* 81 – 83.

29. Falk, "Jewish Prayer Literature," 299.

which affected everybody. The term, which can mean "panic, fear, terror," also denotes "reverence, respect, awe." Since Jesus did not perform miracles of judgment, we can assume that the apostles did not perform miracles in which people were harmed; thus the meaning "respect, awe" should be used here.[30] The two imperfect tense verbs (both ἐγίνετο) indicate that this was a continual state of affairs among the population of Jerusalem.

2:44 All who believed were together, and they held all things in common (πάντες δὲ οἱ πιστεύοντες ἦσαν ἐπὶ τὸ αὐτὸ καὶ εἶχον ἅπαντα κοινά). Luke now gives a more extended explanation of the life of the earliest believers in Jerusalem, after his brief statement in 2:42. The nominalized participle "the believers" (οἱ πιστεύοντες) is a designation for the followers of Jesus (for the Greek verb see on 4:4). What sets Jesus' followers off from other Jews is their faith that Jesus is Israel's crucified, risen, and exalted Messiah and Lord.

Luke first comments on the harmonious unity of the followers of Jesus — all believers "were together" (ἦσαν ἐπὶ τὸ αὐτό). This expression should not be understood in a local sense ("all believers were gathered at one place").[31] Rather, it emphasizes the unity of the believers, which is described in 2:46 with the term translated as "unanimously" (ὁμοθυμαδόν).[32]

Second, Luke explains that the unity of the believers expressed itself in practical ways: the believ-

ers shared their possessions. The statement "they held all things in common" (εἶχον ἅπαντα κοινά) can mean that the believers sold everything they owned and pooled the proceeds (as the Essenes required their members to do).[33] Or it can mean that they remained owners of their property while being willing to use their possessions for the common good.[34] In view of the details given in 2:45 and 4:32 – 5:11, the second meaning is preferable.

In Qumran, the surrender of one's property upon entry in the Qumran community was obligatory. The paradox that the members of the Essene community are said to contribute all their wealth, while they still appear to have retained private property, can be explained as follows: Jews in the ancient world did not regard the adjectives "private" and "public," when related to property, as mutually exclusive as we do today. Property that an individual "had" could be understood to "be" both for the individual and for the group. Thus, "the donor offers the right of usufruct to another but retains the right of ownership," a concept that explains the practice of shared property at Qumran.[35]

The fellowship of the Jerusalem believers was anything but shallow. They were willing to use their material possessions for the needs of their fellow believers. This goes way beyond the Hellenistic theme of friendship, expressed in the proverb, "Friends hold all things in common."[36] Theirs was not a utopian vision, but the expression in real life

---

30. Cf. Luke 1:12, 65; 2:9; 8:37; 21:26; Acts 5:5, 11; 9:31, for strong reactions to divine intervention. Cf. Fitzmyer, *Acts*, 271.

31. BDAG, s.v. ἐπί 1cβ; W. Radl, "αὐτός," *EDNT*, 1:179 – 80); cf. NLT ("And all the believers met together in one place").

32. Cf. GNB ("All the believers continued together in close fellowship").

33. Cf. 1QS V, 1 – 3, 14 – 16, 20; VI, 17 – 22, 24 – 25; VII, 242 – 5; VIII, 22 – 23; IX, 3 – 11; CD IX, 10 – 15; X, 18 – 20; XII, 6 – 7; XIII, 14 – 15.

34. Fitzmyer, *Acts*, 272. See also Steve Walton, "Primitive Communism in Acts? Does Acts Present the Community of Goods (2:44 – 45; 4:32 – 35) as Mistaken?" *EvQ* 90

(2008): 99 – 111, who argues that Luke does not present the earliest Christian communities as practicing common ownership.

35. Catherine M. Murphy, *Wealth in the Dead Sea Scrolls and in the Qumran Community* (STDJ 40; Leiden: Brill, 2002) 454. The term "usufruct" is defined by the Oxford English Dictionary as "the right of temporary possession, use, or enjoyment of the advantages of property belonging to another, so far as may be had without causing damage or prejudice to this."

36. Plato, *Resp.* 449C (κοινὰ τὰ φίλων ἔσται); Aristotle, *Eth. nic.* 1168B; *Pol.* 1263A; Plutarch, *Mor.* 767E; Philo, *Abraham* 235. Cf. Johnson, *Acts*, 58 – 59.

of the love and care that believers in Jesus extended in practical terms for one another. The connection of the summary in vv. 42–47 with the account of the coming of the Spirit of prophecy in vv. 1–42 suggests that the reality of the community of believers was the result of the transforming power of the Spirit, who was bringing about the renewed society that the prophet Joel envisioned, as the believers experienced the "year of the Lord's favor" (Luke 4:19) and "times of refreshing" (Acts 3:19).[37]

2:45 And they would sell their possessions and their belongings and distribute them among all those who had need (καὶ τὰ κτήματα καὶ τὰς ὑπάρξεις ἐπίπρασκον καὶ διεμέριζον αὐτὰ πᾶσιν καθότι ἄν τις χρείαν εἶχεν). The verbs in the imperfect tense here signal ongoing activity. Luke describes the believers as holding "all things in common" (v. 44). The Jerusalem believers were in the habit of selling their possessions and their (personal) belongings.[38] Among the possessions and property sold were land and houses (4:34), which indicates that some believers were wealthy. In 4:37 Joseph Barnabas, a Jewish believer from Cyprus, is presented as a positive example of this behavior; in 5:1–11 the couple Ananias and Sapphira are described as a negative example.

The proceeds of the sale of possessions and belongings were distributed among needy believers. The personal pronoun (αὐτά) does not refer to "possessions" (κτήματα) — there was no land distribution — or to "property" (ὑπάρξεις) — they did not give up the right of ownership of personal property. It refers to the money that resulted from the sale of the possessions. In 5:1–11 Luke under-

lines the voluntary nature of the believers' parting with their resources.

Some have suggested that the needy believers were followers of Jesus from Galilee who had moved to Jerusalem and who thus had no means of income in the city. We do not know, however, how many believers were of Galilean origin besides the Twelve (who are not pictured as needy; according to 4:35, 37 the apostles distributed the funds that became available). The fact that Greek-speaking Jewish widows received daily distributions of food (6:1) suggests that at least some of the needy were diaspora Jews who had returned to Jerusalem and who had no income once their spouses had died.

If the history of later Christian missionary work is any indication, it is plausible that many poor Jerusalem Jews were attracted to the followers of Jesus — people like the lame man begging at the Beautiful Gate (3:2–3). Before long, as Christians were persecuted, it can be assumed that social ostracism left many in Jerusalem with a much reduced income. Several years later, there were many poor Christians in Jerusalem as a result of famines, which Agabus prophesied (11:28) and which took place during the reign of Claudius (AD 41–54).

Since the focus is on the sale of possessions, Luke does not describe an early Christian "community of goods" but the renunciation of monetary assets for the sake of the poor.[39] The Jerusalem believers did not share their goods — they sold their goods to support the needy. Luke does not describe a community that denies the appropriateness of private property (as in a monastic order), nor does he propagate a world-denying "communism of

37. Wenk, *Community-Forming Power*, 272.

38. Cf. BDAG, s.v. ὕπαρξις 2 (plural), "that which one has, *property, possession, belongings*." For the distinction between land and personal belongings, cf. Barrett, *Acts*, 169.

39. Ulrich Wendel, *Gemeinde in Kraft. Das Gemeindeverständnis in den Summarien der Apostelgeschichte* (NTD 20; Neukirchen-Vluyn: Neukirchener Verlag, 1998), 134–61; cf. Acts 4:34, 37; 5:1, 4, 8. Cf. Dunn, *Beginning from Jerusalem*, 181–83. For the traditional view see Brian J. Capper, "The Palestinian Cultural Context of Earliest Christian Community of Goods," in *The Book of Acts in Its Palestinian Setting* (ed. R. Bauckham), 323–56.

love."[40] Rather, Luke presents a pragmatic ethics concerning possessions in which the needs of the poor took center stage. The motivation to sell possessions and share the proceeds with believers in need was grounded in their concern for the poor, as well as in Jesus' teaching about not hoarding material possessions (Luke 6:30 – 36) but renouncing them (Luke 12:33 – 34).[41]

2:46 – 47b When they continued to meet each day unanimously in the temple, and when they broke bread in their homes, they ate their meals with glad and simple hearts, praising God and enjoying the respect of all the people (καθ' ἡμέραν τε προσκαρτεροῦντες ὁμοθυμαδὸν ἐν τῷ ἱερῷ κλῶντές τε κατ' οἶκον ἄρτον, μετελάμβανον τροφῆς ἐν ἀγαλλιάσει καὶ ἀφελότητι καρδίας αἰνοῦντες τὸν θεὸν καὶ ἔχοντες χάριν πρὸς ὅλον τὸν λαόν). Luke repeats his earlier comment about the unity of the believers (v. 44), who regularly meet to hear the apostles teach and to have fellowship, including meals (v. 42). The present participle (προσκαρτεροῦντες) is temporal or modal. The believers meet continually in the temple complex, and they meet daily (καθ' ἡμέραν). Some interpret the term ὁμοθυμαδὸν (see on 1:14) as "with one mind, unanimously,"[42] while others prefer the weaker meaning "together" in the sense of physical co-location.[43]

The statement does not necessarily mean that every believer meets every single day. Luke could simply say that every day there were meetings of believers in Solomon's Portico on the Temple Mount. Nevertheless, it is not impossible to assume that all believers do meet daily at a certain time to worship God, to listen to the apostles' teaching, and to have fellowship — perhaps at three o'clock in the afternoon at the "hour of prayer" (3:1). The temple platform that Herod the Great had constructed in order to place the temple building with its inner courts in the middle of a large outer court was surrounded by colonnaded halls. A meeting of three thousand people could be easily arranged in this gigantic complex.

The meetings of the believers took place in Solomon's Portico.[44] Josephus describes the hall as being 400 cubits (ca. 650 ft. or 200 m.) long, with a single nave of 50 feet (15 m.) wide, with two rows of columns that were 43 feet (12.5 m.) high. The portico was constructed "of square stones, completely white," each stone being ca. 33 feet (10 m.) long and 10 feet (3 m.) high.[45] The hall was situated on the eastern side of the temple complex, which dropped steeply to the Kidron Valley (see also on 3:11).

As the believers met in Solomon's Portico, in the eastern part of the outer court,[46] listening to the apostles' teaching, having fellowship, and praising God for his work of salvation, they turned the entire temple complex into a "house of prayer" as Jesus had announced and demanded (Luke 19:45 – 46). Jesus had taught presumably in the same location when he was teaching "every day ... at the temple" the week before his crucifixion, and his listeners "hung on his words" (Luke 19:47 – 48).

The construction of the subordinate sentence in

---

40. Max Weber used the term "communism of love" (Liebeskommunismus) for the practice of the early Christians in Jerusalem. Cf. Max Weber, "Religious Rejections of the World and Their Direction," in *From Max Weber: Essays in Sociology* (ed. H. H. Gerth and C. W. Mills; orig. 1946; repr., Abingdon: Routledge, 1991), 323 – 59, 329 – 30.

41. Note also the parable of the clever manager (Luke 16:1 – 13) and the repentance of Zacchaeus the tax collector (Luke 19:1 – 10).

42. NASB; cf. NET, "gather together by common consent." Cf. Johnson, *Acts*, 59; Wendel, *Gemeinde*, 121 – 24.

43. Walton, "Ὁμοθυμαδόν," 99; cf. NRSV, TNIV, NLT; cf. BDAG, s.v. ὁμοθυμαδόν: "with one mind/purpose/impulse," citing Acts 2:46 for this meaning.

44. Acts 3:11; 5:12; cf. 5:20, 25, 42.

45. Josephus, *Ant.* 20.221; *J.W.* 5.185.

46. The expression "the Court of Gentiles" is a Christian expression; cf. Rev 11:2.

2:46 – 47 suggests that the believers shared meals both in the temple complex and in their private houses: the main clause (v. 46g-i) is preceded by two participial clauses coordinated by the conjunctions "and … and" (τε … τε). The reference to the daily meetings in the temple and the reference to the breaking of bread in their various homes are formulated with modal participles with temporal force — as/while they were meeting in the temple, and as/while they were breaking bread, they always took their meals with glad and simple hearts. This means that "the eating of food is primary as the statement of the main clause. Both the 'sojourn in the Temple' and the 'breaking of bread in houses' are dependent on this statement."[47]

In other words, the believers in Jerusalem shared meals both on the occasion of their daily visits to the temple and in private houses. These communal meals presumably took place in the late afternoon and early evening, the time of the main meal also in Greek and Roman culture. The food that was consumed would have been bread, legumes, eggs, perhaps olives, dates, and figs, and sometimes fish.

The believers regularly met in their various private houses (κατ᾽ οἶκον, with distributive meaning) to share meals and to remember Jesus' death and resurrection (see on 2:42). Since followers of Jesus belong to the same household of faith, sharing common beliefs, values, and purpose, it is a matter of course that they meet in private homes. It was only in such privacy that the new believers could know the other believers, learn about their needs, and have fellowship that included sacrificial giving and sharing.

The communal meals of the believers in Jerusalem were marked by exuberant joy, surely prompted by God's presence through his Spirit, by the assurance of salvation, and by the experience of new friendships and the privilege of giving and receiving. In addition, they were modest ("simple hearts") when they accepted contributions from others. They were not double-minded with envy or with calculation.[48]

As the believers shared meals in the temple and in their homes, they praised God. They glorified God in their prayers; and when they spoke about God's blessings through Jesus, Israel's Messiah and Lord, they cheered God's wisdom in approval and thus recommended him to unbelievers who might be present.

The Christians of Jerusalem "enjoyed the respect" (ἔχοντες χάριν) of all the Jewish people living in Jerusalem. The phrase also shows that the followers of Jesus were recognized as a specific group early on.

2:47c-e And day by day the Lord added to their number those who were being saved (ὁ δὲ κύριος προσετίθει τοὺς σῳζομένους καθ᾽ ἡμέραν ἐπὶ τὸ αὐτό). Luke ends this section with another comment concerning the growth of the church. The fellowship practiced in the private homes of believers had missionary consequences. The meetings of the believers in the temple and in their homes were so attractive that unbelievers started to attend. As individual people came to faith in Jesus Christ, the church grew numerically, at a regular pace. The effect of the proclamation of the gospel and of the life of the church "is related not only to the salvation of many individuals but also to the local congregations as a whole, as they become larger."[49]

Luke's formulation carefully preserves the primacy of God in the "success" of the Jerusalem Christians. It is the Lord who increased the num-

---

47. Wendel, *Gemeinde*, 183.

48. Cf. Johnson, *Acts*, 59, who relates the term to ἁπλότης, which means simplicity and generosity; cf. Luke 11:34; Rom 12:8; 2 Cor 8:2; Eph 6:5; Col 3:22; Jas 1:5.

49. Wendel, *Gemeinde*, 261.

ber of believers. God is the author of the salvation of the new converts (note that "being saved"
[σῳζομένους] is a passive participle).

We know of forty-six people by name who belonged to the community of believers in Jerusalem at any time before AD 70.[50] In addition to the
Twelve (1:13, 26), the Seven (6:5), and the brothers
of Jesus as well as Mary, Jesus' mother (1:14), the
list includes names such as Agabus, the prophet;

John Mark, eventually a missionary who traveled
with Barnabas and Paul; his mother, Mary; Joseph
Barnabas, later a missionary in Syria and in Cyprus;
Joseph of Arimathea, an aristocrat and member of
the Sanhedrin; Nicodemus, another aristocrat and
member of the Sanhedrin; Silas – Silvanus, later a
missionary coworker of Paul; Simon of Cyrene,
who had helped to carry Jesus' cross; and Addai,
the first missionary in Edessa.

Theology in Application

Luke's extensive summary of the life of the Jerusalem church is not only a historical statement about the first months of the Christian movement. It is also a theological statement about God's presence in the community of believers, an ecclesiological
statement about the priorities of an authentic church, and a missiological statement
about the process of church growth.

God Is Present

An authentic church is a church in which God is present. Note the following elements. (1) The teaching of the apostles focused on the fulfillment of God's promises
in Jesus, Israel's Messiah and Lord, and in the coming of the Holy Spirit. (2) The
breaking of bread, when it includes the celebration of the Lord's Supper, reminds
the believers of God's plan of salvation, who sent Jesus to the cross in order that sins
might be forgiven and the promised new covenant might become a reality. (3) The
people experienced the awe-inspiring presence of God in the miracles that happened
through the apostles, which were direct manifestations of the merciful work of God
in their midst. (4) The believers experienced God's presence and invoked prayers of
praise in which they thanked God for his blessings through Jesus. (5) They experienced God's effective presence in new conversions and in the continued growth of
the church.

Proper Priorities

An authentic church is a church whose priorities are set by the gospel. The summary
characteristics in 2:42 do not form an outline of the sequence of the agenda in the

---

50. Bauckham, "James and the Jerusalem Community,"
81 – 92. For Addai see the Syriac Teaching of Addai; Eusebius,
Hist. eccl. 1.13.11 – 21 (where he is called Thaddaeus).

worship services of the Jerusalem church. But it certainly describes the fundamental essentials of the church that experienced God's presence and continued to grow.

The first priority of the church is "teaching." Teaching by the apostles is and always must remain central in the church. Its primary focus is on Jesus, Israel's Messiah and Lord (the New Testament begins with four accounts of Jesus' life!); on God's salvation through Jesus' death, resurrection, and exaltation; on the transforming presence of the Spirit of prophecy; on the integration into the new community of God's messianic people; and on the significance of the Scriptures that are read, explained, and applied to the lives of the believers.[51]

The second priority of the church is "fellowship." The community of believers is exactly that — a community whose members are "one" because they have all accepted Jesus as Israel's messianic Savior and because they have all received God's transforming Spirit. The church is a fellowship in that the believers meet at one place, listen to the teaching of the Word of God, praise God, share meals, love each other, and share resources with fellow believers who are poor. It is the latter that is a most dramatic manifestation of the reality of Christian fellowship, which integrates being together with loving and helping each other. It has been observed that "the ancient world, with its association of κοινωνία and φιλία, accepted the principle; the Christians put it into effect."[52]

The third priority of the church is "the breaking of bread." This includes sharing meals as an expression of belonging to one family, the family of God's people. And it includes the celebration of the death and resurrection of Jesus, Israel's Messiah and Lord. When Christians break bread, they praise God and remember Jesus' sacrifice, and thus they are reminded of the needs of the poor and are challenged to help sacrificially.

The fourth priority of the church is "prayer." Constant and joyful prayer acknowledges the presence of God in the midst of his people. Personal transformation, which produces, for example, the willingness to sell property and give the proceeds to the poor, is possible only when God changes hearts and minds — and hands and feet that carry out the sale of possessions. Constant and joyful prayer acknowledges that only God can lead unbelievers to repentance.

51. Paul Mumo Kisau, "Acts of the Apostles," in *Africa Bible Commentary* (ed. T. Adeyemo; Nairobi and Grand Rapids: WordAlive and Zondervan, 2006), 1297 – 348, 1304, comments that "a faith that is not understood is shaky and has poor foundations, and that is why the new believers had to know what and why they believed. The church in Africa needs to develop the same devotion to teaching. The African church is sometimes described as a mile long and an inch deep, meaning that it has many members but that these members have only a shallow understanding of the word of God. Pastors must be willing to teach, and congregations must be enthusiastic to learn the important tenets of their faith." This assessment of the theological depth of African churches also holds true for churches in the West.

52. Barrett, *Acts*, 169.

Continual Growth

An authentic church is a church that continues to grow. Luke's summary in 2:42 – 47 is preceded by a statement on mass conversions in Jerusalem (2:41), and it ends with the comment that the church in Jerusalem continued to grow at a regular pace (2:47). The growth of a church happens when the church has the right priorities. This is not a question of strategy or method, but a question of reckoning with the power of God.

Churches grow when the gospel is proclaimed. The priority of the "teaching of the apostles" concerns not only pastoral instruction for believers, but also includes evangelistic outreach to unbelievers — this was the primary calling of the Twelve as witnesses of Jesus, commissioned to preach the good news of Jesus from Jerusalem to the ends of the earth.

Churches grow when the church is a fellowship. Luke attributes the continued growth of the church to the believers meeting in the temple and in private homes, listening to teaching, sharing meals, sharing with those in need, and praising God in prayer. These meetings attracted unbelievers, who became willing to repent, to commit themselves to faith in Jesus, the Messiah and Lord of Israel, to be immersed in water, and to join the fellowship of the followers of Jesus.

Churches grow when they acknowledge the power of God. Only God can cause unbelievers to seek salvation through faith in Jesus Christ, and thus only God is able to increase the number of believers. The continued and regular growth of a church is always the result of the work of God — if it is indeed the community of the followers of Jesus that grows, rather than the number of people attending the Christian meetings. It is possible for numerical growth to be nothing more than the attraction of popular entertainment. Numerical growth is authentic church growth only when people find faith in Jesus, the crucified, risen, and exalted Messiah and Savior, and when they receive the Holy Spirit of God, who visibly and powerfully transforms their lives.

CHAPTER 7

Acts 3:1 – 10

Literary Context

In the first section of Luke's description of the beginnings of the new people of God (Acts 1:15 – 8:3), Luke had described the identity and the witness of Jesus' followers as God's people (1:15 – 2:47) in two episodes — the reconstitution of the Twelve (1:15 – 26) and the coming of the Holy Spirit bestowed by the crucified, resurrected, and exalted Messiah and Lord of Israel (2:1 – 41) — and a summary statement (2:42 – 47) after a report of mass conversions among the Jews of Jerusalem (2:41). That summary statement showed how the believing community of Jerusalem enjoyed God's blessings.

In this second section, Luke now describes the life, witness, trials, and growth of the church in Jerusalem in seven episodes (3:1 – 8:3). This first one narrates Peter's miracles, his proclamation of Jesus, and his defense before the Sanhedrin (3:1 – 4:31). It reports the healing of a lame man at the Beautiful Gate of the temple (3:1 – 10), an event that includes a very brief speech of Peter (3:6). The healing of this lame man leads to two speeches of Peter in which he proclaims the gospel (3:12 – 26; 4:8 – 12, 19 – 20) and so advances the gospel.

The description of the lame beggar's healing recalls similar accounts of Jesus' ministry (cf. Luke 5:17 – 26), as does the discussion about what "authority" is at work (Luke 5:21 – 25; Acts 4:7). Luke thus demonstrates that the apostles are "prophetic successors of Jesus."[1] As Jesus did not simply heal bodily ailments but restored the sick so that they could fully participate in the life of God's people, so the apostles heal a person who then accompanies them into the temple, praising God and presumably joining the community of believers (cf. Acts 3:16).

---

1. Johnson, *Acts*, 71; cf. ibid., 72, for the following point.

II. The Beginnings of the New People of God (1:15 – 8:3)

   A. The Identity and Witness of Jesus' Followers as God's People (1:15 – 2:47)

➡   **B. The Life, Witness, Trials, and Growth of the Community of Believers in Jerusalem (3:1 – 8:3)**

     9. Peter's miracles, proclamation of Jesus, and defense before the Sanhedrin (3:1 – 4:31)

       a. The healing of a lame man at the Beautiful Gate of the temple (3:1 – 10)

       b. Peter's sermon in Solomon's Portico (3:11 – 26)

Main Idea

The miracle of the healing of a lame man at a gate of the temple in Jerusalem is an example of the power of Jesus, who continues to heal the sick as the risen and exalted Messiah, a sign that the last days that the prophets predicted have indeed arrived; this miracle also indicates that God's power at work in Jesus is now at work in the apostles as well.

Translation

Acts 3:1 – 10

1a	Setting: temporal	Once,
b	Event	when Peter and John were going up
c	Place	to the temple
d	Time	at the hour of prayer,
e	Time	at three o'clock in the afternoon,
2a	Event & character entrance	**a man crippled from birth was being carried in.**
b	Time	Each day
c	Action	**they would put him**
d	Place	at the gate of the temple
e	Explanation	called the Beautiful Gate
f	Purpose	so that he could ask for alms
g	Source	from the people who entered the temple.
3a	Setting: temporal	When he saw Peter and John
b	Event	about to go into the temple,
c	Action	**he asked them for alms.**
4a	Action	**Peter looked intently at him,**
b	Association	together with John,
c	Action	and **said,**
d	Command	*"Look at us."*

Continued on next page.

Continued from previous page.

5a	Reaction	**He fixed his attention on them,**
b	Character's thoughts	expecting to receive something from them.
6a	Action	Then **Peter said,**
b	Assertion	*"I have neither silver nor gold,*
c	Assertion	*but what I have I give you:*
d	Means	*in the name of Jesus of Nazareth,*
e	Identification	*the Messiah,*
f	Command	*walk!"*
7a	Action	And **he took him by the right hand,**
b	Action	and **helped him**
c	Purpose	to rise up.
d	Time	And immediately
e	Event/Result	**his feet and ankles grew strong.**
8a	Action	**He jumped up,**
b	Action	**he stood,**
c	Action	and **he walked about,**
d	Action	and **he entered the temple**
e	Association	with them,
f	Action	walking about,
g	Action	jumping, and
h	Action	praising God.
9a	Event	When all the people saw him
b	Action	walking about and
c	Action	praising God,
10a	Action	**they recognized him**
b	Identification	as the man
c	Action	who used to sit and
d	Action	ask for alms at the Beautiful Gate of the temple.
e	Reaction	**They were utterly astonished,**
f	Expansion	beside themselves with amazement
g	Cause	on account of what had happened to him.

Structure and Literary Form

The episode is a historical *narrative*. Luke describes the prayer routine of Peter and John (3:1), the presence of a lame beggar at a gate in the temple complex (3:2), the encounter between the two apostles and the beggar, which leads to the beggar being healed (3:3 – 8), and the reaction of the people who see the healed beggar (3:9 – 10). The narrative is a *miracle story*. Its focus is not on Peter and John, or on the lame man and what the healing did for him, but on the continuing effectiveness of the power of Jesus, whom Peter described on Pentecost as the crucified, risen, and exalted Messiah who sits as Lord on the heavenly throne at God's right hand.

The *structure* of the miracle story shares many of the motifs of Jesus' miracles in the Synoptic Gospels:[2] (1) the coming of the miracle worker (3:1); (2) the appearance of the distressed person (3:2); (3) the reason why the sick person approaches the miracle worker (3:3); (4) miracle-working word (3:6);[3] (5) touch (3:7); (6) demonstration of the miracle (3:8); (7) wonder among the people (3:9 – 10); (8) adversaries (4:1 – 22). The focus of the passage is connected with the *direct speech* reported for Peter, "I have neither silver nor gold, but what I have I give you: in the name of Jesus of Nazareth, the Messiah, walk!" (3:6).

Exegetical Outline

→ **I. Peter's Miracles, Proclamation of Jesus, and Defense before the Sanhedrin (3:1 – 4:31)**

    A. The Healing of a Lame Man at the Beautiful Gate of the Temple (3:1 – 10)

        1. The prayer routine of Peter and John, who go to the temple at three o'clock (3:1)

        2. The begging routine of a lame man at the Beautiful Gate of the temple (3:2)

        3. The encounter between the lame beggar and Peter and John (3:3 – 8)

            a. The lame man's request for alms from Peter and John (3:3)

            b. The call for attention by Peter and John (3:4)

            c. The expectation of the beggar (3:5)

            d. Peter's command in the name of Jesus to stand up and walk (3:6)

                i. Assertion that he does not have money (3:6a-b)

                ii. Appeal to the name of Jesus, the Messiah from Nazareth (3:6c-e)

                iii. Command to walk (3:6f)

            e. The miracle (3:7)

            f. The effect of the miracle on the lame man (3:8)

                i. He jumps up, stands, walks (3:8a-c)

                ii. He enters the temple with the apostles (3:8d-g)

                iii. He praises God (3:8h)

        4. The amazement of the people in the temple (3:9 – 10)

            a. The recognition of the healed beggar by the people (3:9 – 10d)

            b. The effect of the miracle on the people in the temple (3:10e-g)

---

2. Cf. Gerd Theissen, *The Miracle Stories of the Early Christian Tradition* (Philadelphia: Fortress, 1983), 47 – 80, who lists thirty-three motifs.

3. Peter's call for attention in 3:4 is not the "pneumatic excitement" of the miracle worker, i.e., the emotional reaction to the distress of the person involved.

Explanation of the Text

3:1 Once, when Peter and John were going up to the temple at the hour of prayer, at three o'clock in the afternoon (Πέτρος δὲ καὶ Ἰωάννης ἀνέβαινον εἰς τὸ ἱερόν ἐπὶ τὴν ὥραν τῆς προσευχῆς τὴν ἐνάτην). The apostles regularly[4] prayed in the temple. The verb "going up" (ἀναβαίνω) corresponds with the fact that the Temple Mount was the highest point in the city. The temple complex was accessed through several stairways on the south, west, east, and north sides. Most likely the apostles used one of the four gates in the western wall, which are, from south to north: the gate associated with Robinson's Arch and the bridge across the Tyropoeon valley; Barclay's Gate, which gave access from the main street to the temple complex and was reached through a flight of stairs; Kipunus (or Coponius) Gate associated with Wilson's Arch and a second bridge across the Tyropoeon valley; Warren's Gate, which also provided access to the Temple Mount from the main street through an underground staircase. John, presumably the son of Zebedee (cf. 1:13) is introduced as the "silent partner" of Peter (cf. also 3:4, 11; 4:13, 19; 8:14).

Luke connects the miracle with the prayer routine of Peter and John. At the "ninth hour"[5] (i.e., three o'clock in the afternoon) the second Tamid was offered, the daily burnt offering that was sacrificed in early morning and in the evening (see Exod 29:38–42; Num 28:3–8). These daily offerings were so important that they were not interrupted even when the Temple Mount was besieged by the Roman army led by Pompey in 63 BC.[6] The time of the evening sacrifice was a time of prayer more generally, as the example of Daniel shows, one of whose daily prayer times coincided with the time of the evening sacrifice (Dan 6:10; 9:21).

Many assert v. 1 reflects "Luke's overall scheme to portray the first Christians as devout and observant Jews, maintaining Jewish practices."[7] Peter and John were certainly devout, they prayed regularly, and they used the temple premises for their prayers. However, the text does not indicate whether they were "observant" in the sense that they observed the burnt offering.[8] If this had been Luke's concern, he could have used words similar to those of Josephus, who underscores the "extreme piety" and "the strict observance" of the laws of the Jews who refused to be prevented from performing "the sacred ceremonies" twice a day. In 3:12 Peter alludes generally to his "piety" (εὐσέβεια), and in v. 1 it is only the "hour of prayer" that is mentioned.

At least Stephen, who is later accused of speaking against the holy temple and against the law, and of teaching that "Jesus of Nazareth will destroy this place and change the customs that Moses handed down to us" (6:14), recognized that believers in Jesus did not need the daily burnt offerings to be reminded of and to prepare for the presence of Yahweh, which was the purpose of the burnt offering.[9] The "glory" (δόξα) of God's presence through

---

4. Cf. the imperfect tense of ἀνέβαινον. On prayer see on 2:42.

5. The first hour began with sunrise, i.e., about six o'clock in the morning.

6. Josephus, *Ant.* 14.65. This is confirmed by *m. Pesaḥ* 5:1, which states that the evening sacrifice was slaughtered about thirty minutes after the eighth hour and offered an hour later.

7. Barrett, *Acts*, 177; Fitzmyer, *Acts*, 277; cf. Witherington, *Acts*, 173, who believes that the Jerusalem believers "probably still offered sacrifices in the Temple," claiming that "the implications of Jesus' death in regard to such Jewish practices was not understood in these earliest days." There is no clear evidence for this view.

8. H.-J. Klauck, "Sacrifice and Sacrificial Offerings: New Testament," *ABD*, 5:888.

9. Cf. James K. Bruckner, *Exodus* (NIBC; Peabody, MA: Hendrickson, 2008), 267.

which the people of God were sanctified (cf. Exod 29:43) was no longer connected with God's presence in the temple nor with the daily burnt offerings; rather, it was connected with Jesus, Israel's Messiah, who is at the right hand of God (Acts 2:33 – 34). Thus, Stephen speaks of the "glory of God" and of Jesus standing "at the right hand of God" (7:55). The purification sacrifices of the Jewish Christians mentioned in 21:26 indicate, however, that some Jewish Christians continued to offer at least some of the prescribed sacrifices.

3:2 A man crippled from birth was being carried in. Each day they would put him at the gate of the temple called the Beautiful Gate so that he could ask for alms from the people who entered the temple (καί τις ἀνὴρ χωλὸς ἐκ κοιλίας μητρὸς αὐτοῦ ὑπάρχων ἐβαστάζετο, ὃν ἐτίθουν καθ᾽ ἡμέραν πρὸς τὴν θύραν τοῦ ἱεροῦ τὴν λεγομένην Ὡραίαν τοῦ αἰτεῖν ἐλεημοσύνην παρὰ τῶν εἰσπορευομένων εἰς τὸ ἱερόν). A "crippled man" is a man who is lame in the feet, who is either limping or who cannot walk at all. In the case of this man, the latter was the case, since he had to be carried to the temple, presumably by relatives who expected him to contribute to his upkeep by begging. He was crippled from birth (ἐκ κοιλίας μητρὸς αὐτοῦ; lit., "from his mother's womb"), which means that this man, now over forty years old (4:22), had never walked and had been a beggar for probably over thirty years. The time of the evening sacrifice would have presented excellent opportunities for encountering a maximum number of people.

Luke's description of the lame man shares important features with the "physiognomic consciousness" of the Greco-Roman world.[10] The crippled man was "carried," they "put him" at a gate, and Peter "took him by the right hand" and "helped him to rise up" because, as a lame man, he had weak feet and ankles (v. 7). Greco-Roman readers would view the condition of the man as an outward physical sign of an inner weak moral character, inferring a soft, timid, or effeminate nature. The fact that the beggar was lame from birth may have been interpreted by some Jews as a sign of some grave sin for which God had punished him (cf. John 9:1 – 2).

The disabled and the lame were often the object of ridicule and cheap humor. Plutarch relates that an insensitive host of a symposium might ask "a stammerer to sing, a bald man to comb his hair, or a lame man to dance on a greased wineskin."[11] Apparently in Jewish society, similar attitudes could be found. The *Apocryphon of Ezekiel* argues for the reunification of body and soul in the resurrection of the dead, making the point that alone, a lame man and a blind man are each only "half a man."[12] In the late first century, a Jewish author urges his readers, "Do not ridicule a lame man" (*4 Ezra* 2:21).

The lame man begged every day at one of the gates leading into the temple. The gate of the temple at which the lame man begged is described as being called "the Beautiful Gate" (ἡ Ὡραίαν; see also v. 10). A gate by this name is mentioned neither by Josephus nor in the Mishnah. Luke's text gives no indication whether this gate was one of the gates that gave access to the Temple Mount, whether it was a gate in the outer court of the temple complex giving access to the inner courts, or whether it was inside the inner courts. Since no certainty can be achieved, we will discuss only two main options.

---

10. Cf. Mikeal C. Parsons, *Body and Character in Luke and Acts: The Subversion of Physiognomy in Early Christianity* (Grand Rapids: Baker, 2006), 109 – 23. When we compare Luke's description with Greco-Roman views, we must keep in mind that for Jews it was not a matter of great concern what the body looked like "provided that the purity of the body was protected" (Martin Goodman, *Rome and Jerusalem: The Clash of Ancient Civilizations* [New York: Vintage, 2007], 279).

11. Plutarch, *Mor.* 621E.

12. Cf. *OTP*, 1:492 – 95.

(1) If Luke did not regard the outer court of the temple complex as the "temple" (ἱερόν), he might imply that the Beautiful Gate was a gate that gave access to the inner courts of the temple proper. The Nicanor Gate, made of Corinthian Bronze and magnificent columns and located at the eastern exit from the Courtyard of the Women, has been suggested as a possibility. Josephus describes this gate as follows, "Of the gates nine were completely overlaid with gold and silver, as were also their door-posts and lintels; but one, that outside the sanctuary, was of Corinthian bronze, and far exceeded in value those plated with silver and set in gold."[13] However, the beauty and renown of the Nicanor Gate constitutes no reason why the lame man should have been begging there, even if it was frequented by a larger number of people, since "a quieter gate might be economically attractive to an individual beggar."[14]

(2) The southernmost gate in the western wall (at Robinson's Arch) is an attractive possibility because of its location. This attractive flight of stairs connected the temple complex, via a bridge over the Tyropoeon Valley, with the center of Jerusalem in the southwest section of the city, providing the most direct access to the Royal Stoa in the southern part of the outer court. Josephus describes this gate as follows: "The last led to the other part of the city, from which it was separated by many steps going down to the ravine and from here up again to the hill.... The fourth front of this (structure), facing south, also had gates in the middle, and had over it the Royal Portico."[15]

The giving of "alms" (ἐλεημοσύνη) was a central feature of Israelite and Jewish piety. The law motivated the people of Israel to help resident aliens, widows, and orphans by reminding them of their slavery in Egypt from which God rescued them.[16] The law contained several stipulations that made sure that the poor and destitute would be cared for. The significance of almsgiving in Judaism can be seen in Tobit 4:6 – 11:

> To all those who practice righteousness give alms from your possessions, and do not let your eye begrudge the gift when you make it. Do not turn your face away from anyone who is poor, and the face of God will not be turned away from you. If you have many possessions, make your gift from them in proportion; if few, do not be afraid to give according to the little you have. So you will be laying up a good treasure for yourself against the day of necessity. For almsgiving delivers from death and keeps you from going into the Darkness. Indeed, almsgiving, for all who practice it, is an excellent offering in the presence of the Most High.

Peter's answer clarifies that in a public urban setting, the alms that perhaps most beggars looked for would have been money, not food.

3:3 – 5 When he saw Peter and John about to go into the temple, he asked them for alms. Peter looked intently at him, together with John, and said, "Look at us." He fixed his attention on them, expecting to receive something from them (ὃς ἰδὼν Πέτρον καὶ Ἰωάννην μέλλοντας εἰσιέναι εἰς τὸ ἱερόν, ἠρώτα ἐλεημοσύνην λαβεῖν· ἀτενίσας δὲ Πέτρος εἰς αὐτὸν σὺν τῷ Ἰωάννῃ εἶπεν· βλέψον εἰς ἡμᾶς. ὁ δὲ ἐπεῖχεν αὐτοῖς προσδοκῶν τι παρ᾽ αὐτῶν λαβεῖν). As the beggar notices Peter and John entering through the gate, he asks them for money, as was his habit as people passed by. There is no indication that he knew Peter and John, although if he sat at the same gate every day and if the apostles always used the same route to enter the temple com-

13. Josephus, *J.W.* 5.201. Cf. J. Jeremias, "θύρα," *TDNT*, 3:173 n. 5; G. Schneider, "θύρα," *EDNT*, 3:508.

14. Christopher J. Cowton, "The Alms Trade: A Note on Identifying the Beautiful Gate of Acts 3.2," *NTS* 42 (1996): 475 – 76.

15. Josephus, *Ant.* 15.410 – 411.

16. Exod 22:21 – 27; Deut 10:18 – 20; 24:17 – 18; 27:19.

plex where they taught the new believers (2:46), he would have seen them before.

Peter returns the expectant stare of the lame man. The command "look at us" (βλέψον εἰς ἡμᾶς) may suggest he is challenging the beggar, being used to casual disregard, to realize that something is about to happen. The beggar looks at Peter and John with the expectation that they will give him money, perhaps a larger sum than he usually receives. The present participle "expecting" (προσδοκῶν) is modal, describing how the beggar looked at the apostles.

3:6 Then Peter said, "I have neither silver or gold, but what I have I give you: in the name of Jesus of Nazareth, the Messiah, walk!" (εἶπεν δὲ Πέτρος· ἀργύριον καὶ χρυσίον οὐχ ὑπάρχει μοι, ὃ δὲ ἔχω τοῦτό σοι δίδωμι· ἐν τῷ ὀνόματι Ἰησοῦ Χριστοῦ τοῦ Ναζωραίου περιπάτει). Peter first disappoints the beggar's expectation — he has no silver or gold coins to give to him.[17] This assertion that he has no money may reflect the practice of the believers to hold all things in common and share possessions with needy fellow believers (2:44–45). Luke portrays the apostles as poor people who have no private funds at their disposal. But Peter does have something more significant to give — the power connected with the name of Jesus. He commands the lame man to "walk" (περιπάτει). The present tense of the imperative implies the healing: he will walk again for the rest of his life.

Interpretations that assume a magical background for the use of the "name" of Jesus miss the point that Luke knows all too well that "powerful names" are used in magic, but that the name of Jesus cannot be used in this sense. In 19:11–17 he relates the story of the seven sons of a Jewish priest called Sceva who worked as exorcists; their

attempt to use the name of Jesus over people who had evil spirits, saying, "I adjure you by the Jesus whom Paul proclaims," backfires when these sons are attacked by a demon, who mauls them. Acts 8:9–11 also demonstrates Luke's rejection of magical practices.

It is not the specific use of the "name" Jesus that heals the lame man. Rather, the source of the power that can and in fact does heal the crippled beggar is Jesus himself. The phrase "in the name of" (ἐν τῷ ὀνόματι) means "by the authority of Jesus" (see on 2:38). The power of Jesus becomes a present reality in his name that has been given so that people believe. The power that healed the lame man is faith in Jesus, which was made possible on account of the proclamation of Jesus' power, as Peter explains in the speech that follows (v. 16).

The name of Jesus stands for Jesus himself, who is the Messiah. The literary parallels with Luke 5:17–26, where Jesus healed a paralyzed man, suggest that Luke deliberately presents the apostles as the "prophetic successors of Jesus," who are thus the leaders over the restored people of Israel who responded to the Messiah.[18]

3:7 And he took him by the right hand, and helped him to rise up. And immediately his feet and ankles grew strong (καὶ πιάσας αὐτὸν τῆς δεξιᾶς χειρὸς ἤγειρεν αὐτόν· παραχρῆμα δὲ ἐστερεώθησαν αἱ βάσεις αὐτοῦ καὶ τὰ σφυδρά). The miracle is reported with two verbs: while Peter "grasps" the lame man's right hand, he "helps him up." The temporal participle (πιάσας) coordinates the action of grasping the man's hand with the action described by the main verb "helped him to rise up" (ἤγειρεν). It was in this moment that the miraculous healing took place, as the next statement indicates.

---

17. The term translated "gold" (χρυσίον) refers either to the raw material or to an object made of gold, such as jewelry or gold coins. The phrase "silver and gold" can generally refer to money, cf. Philo, *On God* 169; Josephus, *Ant.* 15.5; this may be the meaning here.

18. Johnson, *Acts*, 71, followed by Peterson, *Acts*, 170.

The miracle took place "immediately," without delay.[19] The muscles of the feet and ankles of this man that had atrophied decades ago through lack of use suddenly became strong and firm so that they could support the body of a forty-year-old man. The term translated as "feet" (βάσις) is often used for "step" and also denotes "that with which one steps," i.e., a foot; the term translated as "ankles" (σφυδρά) is more clearly a medical term, but not exclusively.[20] Luke's phraseology indicates a fundamental change not only of the life of the beggar but also in the way his contemporaries would have seen him (see on 3:2).

3:8 He jumped up, he stood, and he walked about, and he entered the temple with them, walking about, jumping, and praising God (καὶ ἐξαλλόμενος ἔστη καὶ περιεπάτει καὶ εἰσῆλθεν σὺν αὐτοῖς εἰς τὸ ἱερὸν περιπατῶν καὶ ἁλλόμενος καὶ αἰνῶν τὸν θεόν). The effect of the miracle on the lame man is extraordinary. The man not only walks; he jumps up and down. He cannot contain himself as he experiences complete, unaided freedom of movement. Since he had never expected anything like this to happen, and since he realizes, as a Jew, that this is a powerful miracle that only God the Creator could have caused, he gives praise to God.

Luke describes the effect of the miracle with seven verbs.

1. The present participle translated "he jumped up" (ἐξαλλόμενος) indicates the manner by which the lame man, who had been sitting on the pavement, came to stand.
2. The aorist indicative translated as "he stood" (ἔστη) describes what the man, who never had

been able to stand on his feet, is now able to do for the first time.
3. The imperfect indicative "he walked about" (περιεπάτει) underscores the continuous, uninterrupted activity that the healed man can now engage in, as he can now do what healthy people do everyday.
4. The aorist indicative "he entered" (εἰσῆλθεν) describes the purposeful strides of the healed man, who accompanies the apostles as they enter the temple (ἱερόν).
5. The present participle translated "walking about" (περιπατῶν)[21] underlines the fact that the walking capabilities of the healed man are permanent.
6. The present participle "jumping" (ἁλλόμενος) reinforces the by-now unavoidable impression that this man is really, fully healed. The repetition of the verb (ἅλλομαι, without the prefix) suggests that this is an echo of Isa 35:6, which included in the description of the return of the redeemed to Zion in the last days these lines, "then will the lame leap like a deer [τότε ἀλεῖται ὡς ἔλαφος ὁ χωλός], and the mute tongue shout for joy."
7. The present participle "praising" (αἰνῶν) describes the acknowledgment of the healed man that the new condition of his feet and ankles that allows him to walk and jump is the work of God. Perhaps the healed beggar uses Ps 135:1–2, "Praise the LORD! Praise the name of the LORD; praise him, you servants of the LORD, you who minister in the house of the LORD, in the courts of the house of our God."

The healed man is not moved from "total inactivity"[22] to excessive activity, since he had been

---

19. Luke uses the term παραχρῆμα 16 times, the rest of the New Testament twice; for Acts cf. 3:7; 5:10; 12:23; 13:11; 16:26, 33.

20. On Luke as a physician see the Introduction.

21. The three participles περιπατῶν, ἁλλόμενος, and αἰνῶν

describe the manner in which the healed man accompanied the apostles.

22. Parsons, *Body and Character*, 118; for the following comment cf. ibid.

begging, which involved movement of hands and head and eyes. But his reaction certainly "breaks physiognomic convention" — he does not walk slowly, deliberately, like a man, but jumps up and down, with rapid movements, showing no self-constraint. The healed man leaps in exuberant joy and grateful acknowledgment of God's miraculous intervention.

Luke does not say whether the healed man was converted to faith in Jesus or joined the community of the believers. Peter's comment in v. 16 suggests that the man had come to faith. Luke's readers will certainly link the man's praise given to God on account of the healing with the "name of Jesus," in whose power the miracle had taken place.

3:9 – 10d When all the people saw him walking about and praising God, they recognized him as the man who used to sit and ask for alms at the Beautiful Gate of the temple (καὶ εἶδεν πᾶς ὁ λαὸς αὐτὸν περιπατοῦντα καὶ αἰνοῦντα τὸν θεόν· ἐπεγίνωσκον δὲ αὐτὸν ὅτι αὐτὸς ἦν ὁ πρὸς τὴν ἐλεημοσύνην καθήμενος ἐπὶ τῇ ὡραίᾳ πύλῃ τοῦ ἱεροῦ). The healing of the lame man took place in public, and the onlookers acknowledged it as a bona fide miracle. All those who happened to be in the temple recognize the man as the lame beggar who used to sit at the Beautiful Gate asking for alms. They now see him walking about, and they hear him praising God. The phrase "all the people" (πᾶς ὁ λαός) refers to the crowds present in the temple courts, mostly Jewish inhabitants of Jerusalem. At the same time, the phrase prepares for the formulation in 3:11 – 12 and 4:10, where the entire people of Israel is in view.

3:10e-g They were utterly astonished, beside themselves with amazement on account of what had happened to him (καὶ ἐπλήσθησαν θάμβους καὶ ἐκστάσεως ἐπὶ τῷ συμβεβηκότι αὐτῷ). The miracle produces utter astonishment[23] and complete consternation[24] by the people. The nominalized perfect participle translated as "what had happened" (συμβεβηκότι) underscores again the permanent change that this event has brought about.

People lame from birth were naturally regarded as hopeless cases. Hippocrates, in his book on diseases, lists the condition of being lame among the disorders that disable a person permanently.[25] In his book on the usefulness of body parts, Galen argues that "some things are naturally impossible," and the healing god (Asclepius) "does not attempt these things at all but chooses from among the possible what is best to be done."[26] Little wonder that the onlookers are beside themselves when they realize what has happened. People living in Galilee would have had many opportunities to witness healings of lame people during Jesus' ministry. Most Jews living in Jerusalem probably had only heard about Jesus' miracles. Now a good number of them have finally become witnesses of the power of Jesus.

---

23. Cf. BDAG, s.v. θάμβος, "a state of astonishment brought on by exposure to an unusual event, *amazement, awe*."

24. Cf. BDAG, s.v. ἔκστασις, "a state of consternation or profound emotional experience to the point of being beside oneself, *amazement, astonishment*." Here the Greek term does not refer to a state of a trancelike "ecstasy."

25. Hippocrates, *Morb.* 1.1; cf. J. J. Pilch, "Lame, Lameness," *NIDB*, 3:564; cf. ibid. for the next comment.

26. Galen, *De usu partium* 11.14.

Theology in Application

Luke's focus shifts from the group of the Twelve (1:15–2:41) and the community of believers (Acts 2:42–47) to Peter and John. As they regularly pray in the temple, as they have no personal money on hand, as they perform signs and wonders, and as they stimulate a positive response among the people (3:1, 4, 6–7, 10), they personally exhibit all the qualities that are essential characteristics of the community as a whole.[27] Even though Luke has not included the text in order to cast light on pastoral ministry, highlighting the necessity for leaders to practice what they preach, the challenge of personal encounters with people in need, or the advantage of working as a team, the personal focus is significant. Here as in the subsequent episodes of Acts, Peter is not the great leader and master teacher who makes others do the real work. He is personally involved in prayer, in meeting the needs of others, and in evangelistic proclamation, as the aftermath of the miracle will demonstrate.

Jesus and the Power of God

Jesus the Messiah exercises the power of God the Creator. No physician can heal a person who has been born lame, either in antiquity or today. Only God, who spoke the world into existence, can cause the lame to walk again. Jesus has the power that only God the Creator can exercise, calling into being things that do not exist and causing miracles to happen. Jesus has miracle-working power as the promised Messiah, and thus he performed many miracles during his earthly ministry. Jesus has miracle-working power as the exalted Lord, and thus he continues to perform miracles through his human witnesses.

Ministering to Others with the Power of Jesus

Christian believers minister to others with the power of Jesus. The apostles were called by Jesus to be his witnesses from Jerusalem to the ends of the earth, and the apostles accepted this commission after Jesus' resurrection. In keeping with Jesus' promise of the power of the Holy Spirit (1:8), they carry out their ministry in that power.

Christians live in the power of Jesus, the promised and exalted Messiah. Whether they pray, teach, share, have fellowship, or simply walk through a city, they are connected with the power of Jesus, in whom they have believed for their salvation. As we have experienced the miracle of repentance and salvation ourselves, we trust God that the power of Jesus to save will reach other people through our words and actions.

---

27. Cf. Johnson, *Acts*, 71.

Christians reckon with the power of Jesus to work miracles today. Both a rationalistic attitude that trusts more in physicians than in the miracle-working power of Jesus and an enthusiastic attitude that despises the use of ordinary means to help the sick and the needy are misplaced. As to how Peter knew the lame man would be healed on account of his command in the name of Jesus to stand up and walk, we must reckon with spontaneous prophetic insight.

Christians have never been able to heal all the sick whom they encountered. It is not only naive, but manifestly wrong, to think that if only we had enough faith, we could heal everyone who needs to be healed. It is not the faith of Peter (which is not mentioned in the text) that healed the lame man, nor was it the faith of the lame man (which is mentioned only later in 3:16) that healed him. Authentic Christians always have faith that Jesus' power can work through them to heal others, and they always have faith, if they are sick themselves, that Jesus' power can heal them. But sick people are not always healed.

However, believers in Jesus need to reckon more specifically, more typically, and more fervently that Jesus' power can indeed heal seriously sick people. The power of Jesus continues to heal the sick as he continues to be the risen and exalted Messiah and Lord. At the same time, Jesus' power did not prevent the Jewish leaders from throwing Peter and John into prison, which happened in the evening of the day on which the lame man was healed (4:3).

Christians are actively involved in helping the poor, the sick, the depressed, the challenged. Christians are committed to helping these sorts of people not with stopgap measures, but through seeking real, lasting results. The lame man here was restored to full participation in society after he was healed. Yet even if a healing does not take place, Christians who have lived with, or ministered to, handicapped people know that spending time with them is indeed worth more than silver or gold.

The goal of Christian ministry is ultimately not that the poor, the sick, the depressed, and the challenged are being helped, but that they can fully participate in the community of the people of God, as believers who have found true salvation in the name of Jesus Christ.

Acknowledging the Power of Jesus

People need to acknowledge the power of Jesus. The transforming power of the Holy Spirit was evident in the transformed lives of the community of believers in Jerusalem (2:42 – 47). The miracle-working power of Jesus became manifest in the healing of the lame man, an event that the public could not ignore (3:10).

Christians highlight the people and the places where the effective power of Jesus has become manifest. They need to make sure that onlookers and outsiders realize what is happening, since nobody can afford to ignore God's intervention in the affairs of human beings. In order to do this, Christians must be able to identify the mighty acts that have been caused by the power of Jesus and to distinguish them from eye-catching attractions that provide entertainment but no transformation.

The focus of the attention is not on the miracle workers (who here end up in prison), and not on the healed man (who praises God), but on the power of Jesus as the power of God. In a society where "star power" and celebrity status drive popular culture, the church must refuse to be driven with these secular values. The church celebrates God and Jesus Christ, not human beings.

The challenge that Christians put before unbelievers when they present the powerful deeds caused by Jesus is rendered more acute by the fact that miracles caused by the power of Jesus are a sign that the "last days" prophesied by the prophets have arrived and that they must respond to the presence of the power of Jesus by putting their faith in him.

Acts 3:11 – 26

Literary Context

Luke continues his description of the beginnings of the new people of God (1:15 – 8:3) and his report about the early believers in Jerusalem and their life and work as witnesses of Jesus (3:1 – 8:3). Our text is the second incident of the first episode, which narrates Peter's miracle of the healing of the lame man, his proclamation of Jesus, and his defense before the Sanhedrin (3:1 – 4:31). This healing demonstrated the continued reality of God's power at work in the miracles of Jesus, now active in those of the apostles. Just as Jesus' miracles often gave occasion for teaching about the arrival of the kingdom of God, Peter's miracle prompts the apostle to explain the reason for the miracle here in this section.

The miraculous healing of the lame man causes excitement among the people, since they recognize him as the crippled man who had been begging for years at the gate; they are amazed to see him walking and jumping up and down. As they follow Peter and John into Solomon's Portico, where the Christian believers had been meeting to listen to the teaching of the apostles and to have fellowship (2:46), a crowd assembles who seek an explanation for the miracle. In 3:11 – 26 Luke summarizes the speech Peter gives on that occasion.

This speech is, like Peter's Pentecost speech (2:14 – 36; 429 words), a longer speech (296 words of Greek text) in comparison with the brief summaries of his speeches in 1:16 – 25 and 2:37 – 40. This continues the themes of God's fulfillment of his promises to Abraham's descendants, the significance of Jesus' life, death, and resurrection, and the necessity of repentance and of accepting Jesus as the Messiah who saves Israel. Peter's speech has a consistent focus on Jesus. It contains several titles of Jesus: Servant, Holy and Righteous One, Author of Life, Prophet like Moses, Messiah, and Seed of Abraham.

Main Idea

The Jews of Jerusalem are called to repent and to have faith in Jesus as God's messianic Servant, who forgives sins in fulfillment of God's promises to Israel and on account of the significance of Jesus life, death, and resurrection

Translation

Acts 3:11 – 26

11a	Setting: social	While he was holding on to Peter and John,
b		
c	Event	**all the people rushed over to them**
d	Place	in the colonnade
e	Identification	called Solomon's Portico,
f	Cause	utterly astonished.
12a	Temporal	When Peter saw this,
b	Action	**he addressed the people with these words:**
c	Address	*"Fellow Israelites,*
d	Question	*why are you amazed at this?*
e	Question	*And why do you stare at us,*
f	Negation (cause)	*as though it was our own power or*
g		*piety*
h		*that made him walk?*
13a	Cause	*It is the God of Abraham,*
b	Identification	*the God of Isaac, and*
c	Identification	*the God of Jacob,*
d	Identification	*the God of our fathers,*
e	Action	*who has glorified his Servant Jesus,*
f	Contrast & Action	*whom you handed over and*
g	Contrast & Action	*repudiated in the presence of Pilate*
h	Time	*when he had decided to release him.*

Continued from previous page.

14a	Accusation	*You disowned the Holy and*
b	Identification	*Righteous One*
c	Escalation	*and requested that a man …*
d	Identification	*who was a murderer*
		… be released to you.
15a	Escalation	*You killed the Author of Life,*
b	Identification	*whom God raised from the dead.*
c	Verification	*Of this we are witnesses.*
16a	Cause	*It is because of faith in the name of Jesus,*
b	Event	*that name has made this man strong*
c	Identification	*whom you see and know.*
d	Assertion	*And the faith …*
e	Source	*that comes through Jesus*
f	Result	*… has given him perfect health*
g	Place	*in the presence of all of you.*
17a	Introduction	*Now I know, brothers,*
b	Assertion	*that you acted*
c	Manner	*in ignorance,*
d	Comparison	*as did your leaders.*
18a	Contra-expectation	*But God*
b	Manner	*in this way*
c	Assertion	*fulfilled*
d	Prophecy	*what he announced beforehand*
e		*through all the prophets,*
f		*that his Messiah would suffer.*
19a	Exhortation	*Repent, therefore,*
b	Exhortation	*and turn to God,*
c	Purpose	*so that your sins may be wiped out,*
20a	Purpose	*that times of refreshing may come*
b	Source	*from the presence of the Lord, and*
c	Purpose	*that he may send the Messiah, who has been appointed for you,*
d	Identification	*that is, Jesus,*
21a	Description	*who must remain in heaven*
b	Time	*until the time of restoration of all things,*
c	Prophecy	*about which God spoke*
d		*through his holy prophets*
e		*from time immemorial.*
22a	Quotation of OT	*Moses said,*
b	Prophecy	*'The Lord your God will raise up …*
c	Advantage	*for you,*
d	Sphere	*from your own people,*
e	Identification	*… a prophet like me.*
f	Exhortation	*You must listen to him*
g	Sphere	*in everything*
h	Identification	*that he tells you*

Continued on next page.

Continued from previous page.

23a	Warning	Everyone …
b	Identification	who does not listen to that prophet
c		… shall be utterly rooted out
d	Sphere	from the people.' (Deut. 18:15–20; Lev 23:29)
24a	Verification	And all the prophets who have spoken, …
b	Identification	from Samuel and
c	Identification	his successors onward,
d	Prophecy	… have also predicted these days.
25a	Assertion	You are the children of the prophets and
b	Expansion	of the covenant
c	Identification	that God made with your fathers,
d	Quotation of OT	when he said to Abraham,
e	Means	'Through your offspring
f	Promise	all the families of the earth shall be blessed.' (Gen 12:3; 22:18)
26a	Event	When God raised up his Servant,
b	Assertion	he sent him to you first,
c	Purpose	to bless you
d	Circumstance/	by turning each one of you from your evil ways."
	Condition	

Structure and Literary Form

The passage consists of two parts, the *setting* (3:11 – 12b), which explains why Peter addresses the people in the temple, and *Peter's speech* (3:12c – 26), which explains why the lame man was healed and why all Jews in Jerusalem and people everywhere need to repent and come to faith in Jesus as Israel's Messiah. The introduction sets the stage for Peter's speech (on the speeches in Acts see on 2:14 – 36). Three characters participate: the lame man, who stays with Peter and John; the people in the temple, who run to Solomon's Portico, where they meet the apostles; and Peter, who sees the excitement of the people and proceeds to address them (3:11a-b, 11c, 12a-b).

Peter's speech is best outlined with reference to the twofold direct address of his listeners in 3:12c ("fellow Israelites") and 3:17 ("brothers"), which yields — after introductory remarks that clarify the healing of the lame man (3:12d-h) — two main parts, 3:13 – 16 and 3:17 – 26.[1] The first part is framed by references to the healing miracle and focuses on the proclamation of Jesus' death and resurrection as the suf-

---

1. Cf. Jervell, *Apostelgeschichte*, 171. Fitzmyer, *Acts*, 282, divides the speech into four parts (3:12b – 13b, 13c – 19, 20 – 21, 22 – 26).

fering Servant whom God has vindicated (3:13 – 16). The second part draws the consequences from the reality of God's plan of salvation, of which Jesus' death and resurrection represent the climax in "these days," as Peter appeals to the Jews of Jerusalem to repent, turn to God, and come to faith in Jesus, so that they will experience the times of refreshing and the restoration of all things (3:17 – 25).

Some analyze the speech in terms of ancient rhetoric as a forensic or judicial speech (3:12 – 18) followed by a deliberative speech (3:19 – 26).[2] However, the content of 3:12 – 18 is not "defense and attack" but focuses on the assertion that the miraculous healing of the lame man demonstrates Jesus' vindication by God as the Holy and Righteous One, in whose name Abraham's descendants are to find salvation by faith.[3] Luke utilizes the rhetorical devices of inclusio (vv. 13a-e/15b), antithesis (vv. 13, 14 – 15), escalation (vv. 14 – 15a), and chiasmus (God's action/the Jews' action in vv. 13a-e/13f-g, reversed in vv. 14 – 15a/15b).

Peter's speech in Solomon's Portico has the same general content compared with his Pentecost speech in Acts 2, as well as with his speech before Cornelius in Acts 10: (1) Jesus has been killed by the Jewish and Gentile authorities; (2) Jesus has been raised from the dead by God; (3) God offers forgiveness and blessing for those who repent; (4) Jesus' death and resurrection happened as the fulfillment of Scripture; (5) further fulfillment of God's promises will bring about the consummation of the restoration of Israel.

Special features of the speech in 3:12 – 26 are the following:[4] (1) Jesus is described as the "Servant" of God (παῖς; vv. 13, 26); (2) Pilate wanted to release Jesus (v. 13); (3) Jesus is described as the "Holy and Righteous One" (τὸν ἅγιον καὶ δίκαιον; v. 14); (4) Jesus is described as the "Author of Life" (ἀρχηγὸν τῆς ζωῆς, v. 15); (5) the Jews' rejection of Jesus is explained as ignorance (v. 17); (6) the present time should be understood as "times of refreshing" (καιροὶ ἀναψύξεως; v. 20); (7) Jesus' return will mean the "restoration of all things" (χρόνων ἀποκαταστάσεως; v. 21); (8) Jesus has been appointed as Messiah (v. 20); (9) all who do not listen to Jesus, the promised Prophet (Deut 18:19), are threatened with extirpation (v. 23); (10) Jesus is the promised Seed of Abraham (v. 25).

2. Kennedy, *Rhetorical Criticism*, 118 – 19; Witherington, *Acts*, 176; cf. Bock, *Acts*, 165.

3. Soards, *Speeches*, 40, correctly points out that "the speech is immediately kerygmatic."

4. Josef Zmijewski, *Die Apostelgeschichte* (RNT; Regensburg: Pustet, 1994), 183; Barrett, *Acts*, 189 – 90.

Exegetical Outline

→ **I. Peter's Sermon in Solomon's Portico (3:11 – 26)**

   A. The Reaction of the Excited Crowd to the Miracle (3:11 – 12b)

      1. The lame man stays with Peter and John (3:11a)

      2. The gathering of the people in Solomon's Portico (3:11b-f)

      3. Peter's reaction (3:12a-b)

   B. Peter's Clarification regarding the Origins of the Healing Miracle (3:12c-h)

      1. Address (3:12c)

      2. Correction of a misunderstanding (3:12d-h)

   C. Proclamation of the Significance of Jesus' Death and Resurrection (3:13 – 16)

      1. The death and resurrection of Jesus (3:13 – 15)

         a. The God of Israel has glorified Jesus, his Servant (3:13a-e)

         b. The Jews of Jerusalem are culpable of Jesus' death (3:13f-h)

         c. The Jews of Jerusalem rejected Jesus, the Righteous One (3:14)

         d. The Jews of Jerusalem killed Jesus, the Author of Life (3:15a)

         e. God raised Jesus from the dead (3:15b)

         f. The apostles are witnesses of Jesus' resurrection (3:15c)

      2. Summary: Faith in Jesus and the healing miracle (3:16)

         a. Faith in Jesus has healed the lame man (3:16a-c)

         b. Faith in Jesus has healed the lame man in their presence (3:16d-g)

   D. Exhortation to Repent and Receive Salvation through Faith in Jesus (3:17 – 26)

      1. Jesus' death was the fulfillment of God's plan of salvation (3:17 – 18)

         a. Acknowledgment that the Jews and their leaders acted in ignorance (3:17)

         b. Agreement of the death of Jesus with God's plan of salvation (3:18)

      2. Exhortation to repent, turn to God, and come to faith in Jesus (3:19 – 21)

         a. Appeal to repent and to turn to God for the forgiveness of their sins (3:19)

         b. The promise of times of refreshing from the presence of God (3:20a-b)

         c. The coming of the Messiah, who is Jesus (3:20c-d)

         d. The restoration of all things through the coming of the Messiah (3:21a-b)

         e. The present and future fulfillment of God's promises (3:21c-e)

      3. Proof from Scripture (3:22 – 26)

         a. The necessity of repentance because of the warning of Deut 18:15 – 20 (3:22 – 24)

         b. The necessity of repentance in view of the promised blessing of Gen 22:18 (3:25)

         c. Summary: Jesus, God's risen Servant, seeks to bless Israel (3:26)

Explanation of the Text

3:11 While he was holding on to Peter and John, all the people rushed over to them in the colonnade called Solomon's Portico, utterly astonished (Κρατοῦντος δὲ αὐτοῦ τὸν Πέτρον καὶ τὸν Ἰωάννην συνέδραμεν πᾶς ὁ λαὸς πρὸς αὐτοὺς ἐπὶ τῇ στοᾷ τῇ καλουμένῃ Σολομῶντος ἔκθαμβοι). The amazement caused by the miraculous healing of the lame man, who is holding on to Peter and John with his hand, prompts the Jews in the temple who had not seen the miracle happening to rush over to where Peter and John are standing.

This incident involves a change of location from the Beautiful Gate, where the lame man had been begging and where he was healed (vv. 2 – 10), to Solomon's Portico on the eastern side of the temple complex (v. 11), the location of the daily meetings of the followers of Jesus (2:46; see on 2:46).[5] A portico or stoa (στοά) was an open colonnade with a roof over the hall to a rear wall. Some stoas, like Solomon's Portico, had an additional interior row of columns to support the ridge of the roof. The technical term for a stoa with an extended colonnade is portico (Lat. *porticus*). A stoa provided shade and shelter, served as a social meeting point, and was used for political, religious, and commercial activities.

3:12 When Peter saw this, he addressed the people with these words: "Fellow Israelites, why are you amazed at this? And why do you stare at us, as though it was our own power or piety that made him walk?" (ἰδὼν δὲ ὁ Πέτρος ἀπεκρίνατο πρὸς τὸν λαόν· ἄνδρες Ἰσραηλῖται, τί θαυμάζετε ἐπὶ τούτῳ ἢ ἡμῖν τί ἀτενίζετε ὡς ἰδίᾳ δυνάμει ἢ

εὐσεβείᾳ πεποιηκόσιν τοῦ περιπατεῖν αὐτόν;). As Peter sees a throng of Jews rushing toward him, he takes the initiative to address them. The aorist participle "seeing" (ἰδών) may be temporal or causal. He was probably about to begin his teaching of the assembled Christians. But when these outsiders come into the portico, he turns his attention to them. He uses the occasion presented by the miracle as an opportunity to proclaim the good news of Jesus, the crucified and risen Messiah who saves. The verb translated "he addressed" (ἀπεκρίνατο) means literally "he answered," but it is used here in an absolute sense to introduce direct discourse in reaction to something that has happened or is happening. Alternately, the verb suggests that the people who recognized the lame man have asked about the cause of the healing.

The audience is described with the term "the people" (ὁ λαός, cf. vv. 9, 11), which refers first to the crowds assembled in the outer court of the temple in Solomon's Portico, but also to the entire people of Israel, the people of God (note the address ἄνδρες Ἰσραηλῖται in v. 12).

As on Pentecost, Peter addresses his Jewish audience as "fellow Israelites" (see on 1:16; 2:22). He begins by clarifying that neither he nor John is responsible for the healing. The datives "power" (δυνάμει) and "piety" (εὐσεβείᾳ) are instrumental or causative. Peter emphasizes that the cause of the healing was no power or piety that he and John personally had. The conjunctive perfect participle "made" (πεποιηκόσιν) is the equivalent of a modal clause, expressing the means by which the onlookers surmise the miracle has happened. The verb

---

5. The Western text in D reads, "As Peter and John were coming out together, he came out with them, holding on to them," explicitly stating that the apostles came out of the temple, i.e. out of the inner courts of the temple, with the healed man, moving to Solomon's Portico. This implies that the Beautiful Gate is thought to provide access from the outer court to the inner courts.

"to do" (ποιέω) followed by an articular infinitive construction means "to cause." Luke's formulation of Peter's disclaimer confirms that the invocation of the name of Jesus in the healing (v. 6) had no magical connotations. It did not happen because he had somehow manipulated God, through the power of prayer or the magnitude of his piety, to heal this man.

Peter's question reveals the ignorance of the Jews in the temple who have come here to pray but who evidently are not able to infer that it was God's power alone that could have caused the healing miracle.[6] Later in the speech he ascribes their failure to recognize who Jesus is to their ignorance (v. 17).

3:13 It is the God of Abraham, the God of Isaac, and the God of Jacob, the God of our fathers, who has glorified his Servant Jesus, whom you handed over and repudiated in the presence of Pilate when he had decided to release him (ὁ θεὸς Ἀβραὰμ καὶ ὁ θεὸς Ἰσαὰκ καὶ ὁ θεὸς Ἰακώβ, ὁ θεὸς τῶν πατέρων ἡμῶν, ἐδόξασεν τὸν παῖδα αὐτοῦ Ἰησοῦν ὃν ὑμεῖς μὲν παρεδώκατε καὶ ἠρνήσασθε κατὰ πρόσωπον Πιλάτου, κρίναντος ἐκείνου ἀπολύειν). Peter attributes the healing of the lame man to the power of God, who is the God of the nation of Israel and the God who has given promises to Abraham, Isaac, and Jacob.

Peter's identification with his audience ("*our fathers*") is not an evangelistic ploy to affect commonalities — Peter and the other apostles never stopped being Jewish, worshiping Yahweh, or reading the Hebrew Scriptures as God's revelation. The closest parallel to Peter's designation of God is Exod 3:15 (as in Luke 20:37).[7] That description as-

sured Moses and the Israelites of the identity of this God as their God, so that they would "believe his promises and fulfill his commands."[8] Peter explains the source of the healing of the lame man, first, with a reference to God's covenant faithfulness.

God's initiative is a major theme in Peter's speech: God has glorified his Servant Jesus (v. 13); he raised Jesus from the dead (v. 15); he fulfilled his promises in the death of Jesus, the Messiah (v. 18); he has sent times of refreshing (v. 20a-b); he sent the Messiah (v. 20c); he spoke about the time of restoration (v. 21); he raised up a prophet like Moses (v. 22); he made a covenant with their ancestors (v. 25a-c); he will bless the families of the earth through the seed of Abraham (v. 25e-f); he raised Jesus his Servant and sent them to the Jewish people (v. 26).

Peter asserts that Israel's covenant God has "glorified" (ἐδόξασεν) Jesus, who is "his Servant" (παῖς). While this term may allude to David and Israel as God's chosen servant, it is more plausible to see here an allusion to the first two lines of the fourth Servant Song in Isaiah (Isa 52:13–53:12), as this is the only passage in the LXX in which "servant" (παῖς) and "glorify [exalt]" (δοξάζω) are combined: "See, my *servant* will act wisely; he will be raised and lifted up and highly *exalted*" (Isa 52:13).[9] In this song, the Servant of the Lord experiences great suffering as he is bearing our sins (53:4–6, 10, 12); that suffering, in turn, has brought redemption and healing (53:5); he is then vindicated by God (53:10–12). Peter uses these two key words from this passage to establish who Jesus is and why the miracle of the healing of the lame man has happened. Peter makes two points.

---

6. This assumes that τούτῳ is neuter and refers to the miracle. Others take τούτῳ as masculine and relate it to the healed man.

7. The same description of God is found in the first of the Eighteen Benedictions, the traditional Jewish prayer in the synagogues.

8. Marshall, "Acts," 545.

9. The allusion to Isa 52:13–53:12 is also suggested by the use of Isa 53 in Luke 22:37 and Acts 8:32–33. Cf. Peter Mallen, *The Reading and Transformation of Isaiah in Luke-Acts* (LNTS; London: T&T Clark, 2008), 126.

(1) Jesus is the Servant of Yahweh in Isaiah's prophecy. His suffering and death later in Peter's speech (vv. 13 – 15, 18) corresponds to the suffering and death of the Servant in Isa 53:2 – 10. The forgiveness that God grants in connection with Jesus' suffering and death (vv. 19 – 20) corresponds to the substitutionary atonement for sins that the Servant achieves in these last days (cf. Isa 53:5). Jesus' glorification, i.e., his resurrection on account of God's power (v. 15), corresponds to the glorification of the Servant in Isa 52:13. Jesus is now alive and powerfully at work, as God promised of his messianic Servant.

(2) As God's glorified Servant, Jesus now has the power to do signs and wonders such as the healing of the lame man. That healing demonstrates that Jesus has been glorified by God.

Jesus' glorification by God contrasts sharply with Jesus' rejection by the Jewish people. The Jews listening to Peter in Solomon's Portico merely expected an explanation of the astounding miracle of the healing of the lame man. Now they are suddenly implicated in Jesus' death. Peter uses five verbs in the aorist tense in vv. 13 – 15, stating historical facts that have occurred. They "handed him over" (παρεδώκατε)[10] to the Roman authorities, who tried and executed him. They "repudiated" him (ἠρνήσασθε) when Pilate was prepared to release him. They "disowned" (ἠρνήσασθε) him even though he was the Holy and Righteous One. They "requested" (ᾐτήσασθε) that a murderer be released instead of Jesus. They "killed" (ἀπεκτείνατε) him even though he was the Author of Life.

In Luke's gospel, it is "the council of the elders of the people, both chief priests and the teachers of the law," who interrogated and indicted Jesus and took him to Pilate to stand trial (Luke 22:66 – 23:1). The phrase "in the presence of Pilate" (Acts 3:13) refers to the trial of Jesus before this Roman governor (Luke 23:1 – 5, 13 – 16, 18 – 25). In Luke's account of Jesus' trial, Pilate declared Jesus to be innocent or tried to release him three times (Luke 23:4, 14 – 15, 22). Pontius Pilate was the sixth prefect (Lat. *praefectus*) of Judea, which was part of the province of Syria. He governed from AD 26 – 36. We know little about him. We do not know whether he knew the emperor Tiberius personally or whether he was the creation of Lucius Aelius Sejanus, the powerful prefect of the Praetorian Guard. The latter seems to have been the case.[11] Pilate's two main tasks were to maintain peace in the province and preside as judge over trials that involved the death penalty.

3:14 You disowned the Holy and Righteous One and requested that a man who was a murderer be released to you (ὑμεῖς δὲ τὸν ἅγιον καὶ δίκαιον ἠρνήσασθε καὶ ᾐτήσασθε ἄνδρα φονέα χαρισθῆναι ὑμῖν). The decision of the Jews of Jerusalem to prefer Barabbas[12] over Jesus[13] is ironically pernicious since they do not realize that they favor a murderer over "the Holy and Righteous One" (ὁ ἅγιος καὶ δίκαιος). The use of these two adjectives with an article clearly shows that "holy" and "righteous" function as titles.[14]

In the Old Testament, God is the Holy One. Hannah prays, "There is no one holy like the

---

10. The verb is used for Judas's betrayal (Luke 22:4, 6, 21, 22, 48; 1 Cor 11:23), and it is used for Pilate, who turns Jesus over to the soldiers to carry out Jesus' execution, fulfilling the will of the Jews.

11. Tacitus (*Ann.* 4.2) regarded Pilate as an upstart and protégé of Sejanus.

12. Barabbas (Aramaic meaning "son of Abba," which could mean "son of the father" or "son of the teacher") was a common Jewish name; his full name was possibly "Jesus Barabbas"

(see variant readings for Matt 27:16 – 17). He was a prominent Jew, in all likelihood as a result of his involvement in a rebellion against the Romans, perhaps of merely local significance (which would explain why Josephus does not mention him).

13. Cf. Luke 23:18; also Matt 27:16 – 17, 20 – 21, 26; Mark 15:7, 11, 15; John 18:40.

14. Jesus is called "the Holy One" elsewhere in the New Testament: Luke 4:34/Mark 1:24; John 6:69; cf. 1 John 2:20; Rev 3:7.

LORD; there is no one besides you; there is no Rock [LXX reads δίκαιος] like our God" (1 Sam 2:2).[15] Isaiah often calls God "the Holy One of Israel."[16] Agents of God can also be called "holy ones," such as the high priest (2 Kgs 4:9) or angels (Deut 33:2). In Acts 4:27, 30 the Jerusalem believers call Jesus God's "holy Servant" (τὸν ἅγιον παῖδα).

God is also called "the Righteous One" in the Old Testament.[17] Isaiah links the word "righteous" with the Servant of the Lord and with the work he accomplishes: "my righteous servant will justify many [make many righteous], and he will bear their iniquities" (Isa 53:11).[18] The translators of the LXX describe the coming ruler of God's people as "righteous and victorious [saving]" (Zech 9:9). The centurion who observed Jesus die on the cross acknowledges him as "a righteous man" (οὗτος δίκαιος ἦν; Luke 23:47). Jesus is called "the Righteous One" in Acts 7:52; 22:14 in a manner that indicates that this was an early title he had.[19] The combined title "the Holy and Righteous One" has messianic connotations and describes Jesus as the one who was unreservedly devoted to do God's will, being holy as only God is holy, and that he is the one set apart by God to accomplish his will as his Servant.

3:15 You killed the Author of Life, whom God raised from the dead. Of this we are witnesses (τὸν δὲ ἀρχηγὸν τῆς ζωῆς ἀπεκτείνατε ὃν ὁ θεὸς ἤγειρεν ἐκ νεκρῶν οὗ ἡμεῖς μάρτυρές ἐσμεν). Peter speaks of the action of the Jews of Jerusalem as preferring a murderer over Jesus, whom they killed, even though he was "the Author of Life." This expression is another title of Jesus. The term translated as "author" (ἀρχηγός) could be used in three ways:[20] (1) "one who has a preeminent position" and is thus a "leader, ruler, prince " (used for military leaders and political rulers); (2) "one who begins something that is first in a series, thereby providing impetus for further developments" and who is thus a "pioneer (e.g., Aristotle calls Thales the "pioneer" of philosophy);[21] (3) "one who begins or originates" and who therefore has special esteem, "originator, founder," used of founders of cities, but also of God (often in Plato).

All three uses apply to Jesus (cf. 5:31; Heb 2:10; 12:2). He has a preeminent position as the "prince of life." Jesus is the "pioneer of life," who opened the path to (eternal) life on which others can follow.[22] Jesus is the "founder of life" in the kingdom of God and in the new covenant in which God's people enjoy the fullness of life. In 26:23, Paul later identifies Jesus as "the first to rise from the dead," which suggests that the second meaning may be in view here. At the same time, a connection with the healing that Peter explains in this speech is likely — the new lease of life that the lame man had received "in the name of Jesus" (v. 6) was possible only on account of Jesus, whose power as the messianic Servant of the Lord whom God had exalted after his death healed the lame man (vv. 12 – 13).

Peter connects the title "Author of Life" with Jesus' resurrection. As in his Pentecost speech (2:24, 29 – 32), Peter affirms that God "raised" Jesus

---

15. 2 Kgs 19:22; Job 6:10; Pss 71:22; 78:41; 89:18; Prov 9:10; Jer 2:3; Dan 4:19; Hos 11:9; Hab 1:12; Mal 2:11.

16. Isa 1:4; 5:19, 24; 10:20; 12:6; 17:7; 29:19, 23; 30:11, 12, 15; 31:1; 37:23; 41:14, 16, 20; 43:3, 14, 15; 45:11; 47:4; 48:17; 49:7; 54:5; 55:5; 60:9, 14; 50:29.

17. Cf. Ps 129:4; cf. Zeph 3:5; Dan 9:14 LXX.

18. Cf. Mallen, *Isaiah in Luke-Acts*, 126 – 27. Translation of the LXX from M. Silva, in Albert Pietersma and Benjamin G. Wright, eds., *A New English Translation of the Septuagint* (Ox-

ford: Oxford University Press, 2007), 866.

19. Cf. Hurtado, *Lord Jesus Christ*, 190.

20. The following definitions are from BDAG, s.v. ἀρχηγός; cf. LSJ.

21. Aristotle, *Metaph.* 1.3.983b.20.

22. This is the emphasis of Anderson, *Jesus' Resurrection*, 225, "Jesus is God's appointed originator or champion of resurrection life. The resurrection of Jesus guarantees the resurrection of those who believe in him."

from the dead. His earlier affirmation that God "glorified" Jesus (v. 13) amounts to the same point, as Jesus' resurrection signified that he was "exalted" at the right hand of God (2:33). In 5:31 Peter and the apostles tell the Jewish leaders that God "exalted" Jesus at his right hand "as Leader and Savior" (ἀρχηγὸν καὶ σωτῆρα). Jesus' resurrection and exaltation establish him as the princely pioneer who initiated through his suffering and death the new life of the new covenant (Luke 22:20).

Peter affirms the truth of Jesus' resurrection and of his power to heal the lame man with the fact of his eyewitness testimony. He and the other apostles, together with several hundred other believers (cf. 1 Cor 15:6), have seen Jesus after his death, raised by God to exalted life at God's right hand. They are "witnesses" (μάρτυρες) of the risen Jesus and can thus testify to the fact that he is God's exalted Servant, the Holy and Righteous One, and the Author of Life.

3:16 It is because of faith in the name of Jesus, that name has made this man strong whom you see and know. And the faith that comes through Jesus has given him perfect health in the presence of all of you (καὶ ἐπὶ τῇ πίστει τοῦ ὀνόματος αὐτοῦ τοῦτον ὃν θεωρεῖτε καὶ οἴδατε, ἐστερέωσεν τὸ ὄνομα αὐτοῦ καὶ ἡ πίστις ἡ δι᾽ αὐτοῦ ἔδωκεν αὐτῷ τὴν ὁλοκληρίαν ταύτην ἀπέναντι πάντων ὑμῶν). Commentators acknowledge that the Greek of this verse is cumbersome; it is best understood as a rough synonymous parallelism. There is no need to assume that Luke is struggling "to join the objective power of 'the name' working through the apostles, with the subjective necessity of 'faith'

to make that power operative."[23] Luke's statement makes the following points.

(1) The healing of the lame man has been caused by "the name" of Jesus (τὸ ὄνομα αὐτοῦ). In the healing of the lame man, as a result of which he became strong (cf. v. 7), the name of Jesus was decisive (v. 6; on "the name of Jesus" see on 2:38). Peter emphasizes again the power of the name of Jesus, i.e., of the reality of Jesus, who is present in the ministry of the disciples from the throne of David at God's right hand.

(2) The healing of the lame man has been "because of faith" (ἐπὶ τῇ πίστει). The healing was not the result of the miraculous powers of Peter and John (cf. v. 12), but the result of the trust in and allegiance to the crucified and risen Jesus, the messianic Servant of the Lord. It is unclear whether Peter speaks of his own faith or of the faith of the (formerly) lame beggar. The latter seems more plausible on account of 14:9.[24] The fact that the healed beggar from the Beautiful Gate praises God after his healing (v. 9) suggests that Peter may have spoken to him about faith in Jesus before he commanded him to stand up, after seeing that he believed that Jesus could heal him. The point is that faith in the name of Jesus was the cause of the miraculous healing (the preposition ἐπί expresses the basis or cause of faith). The reference to Jesus as the "object" of faith is bold and provocative since it "further emphasizes that the one through whom seemingly unrelated past and present events are connected stands as the exalted one in close proximity to the 'God of our Ancestors.' "[25]

(3) The faith (of the lame man, or of Peter) that healed the beggar has "come through Jesus"

---

23. Johnson, *Acts*, 68. It is unnecessary to regard 3:16 as parenthetical: it reestablishes the connection with the healing of the lame man.

24. The lame man in Lystra, who was crippled from birth, listens to Paul, who looks at him intently and sees "that he had faith to be saved."

25. Hans F. Bayer, "Christ-Centered Eschatology in Acts 3:17 – 26," in *Jesus of Nazareth: Lord and Christ* (FS I. H. Marshall; ed. J. B. Green and M. Turner), 236 – 50, 243.

(ἡ πίστις ἡ δι' αὐτοῦ), i.e., faith is caused by Jesus himself, as he is proclaimed as the crucified and risen messianic Servant who saves people.

(4) Peter reiterates that the people cannot deny that a miracle has happened. They "know" (οἴδατε) that the man who used to beg at the Beautiful Gate was lame. And they now "see" him walking and jumping up and down. The present tense of this verb indicates that the healed beggar is probably standing next to Peter and John. The miracle has happened in their very presence, i.e., at the Beautiful Gate, only a few steps away, just a few minutes ago. The man who was lame from birth has been restored to perfect health.

The focus on Jesus' name and on faith implies an appeal to the audience. Peter challenges them to come to faith in Jesus, God's crucified and risen Servant, the Holy and Righteous One, the Author of Life. This appeal becomes explicit in vv. 17–21.

3:17 Now I know, brothers, that you acted in ignorance, as did your leaders (καὶ νῦν, ἀδελφοί, οἶδα ὅτι κατὰ ἄγνοιαν ἐπράξατε ὥσπερ καὶ οἱ ἄρχοντες ὑμῶν). Peter begins the second part of his speech by addressing his Jewish listeners as "brothers" (ἀδελφοί; see on 1:16). He now draws the consequences from the reality of Jesus' death and resurrection as God's Servant vindicated as the Holy and Righteous One and as the Author of Life. He appeals to the Jews of Jerusalem who are implicated in Jesus' execution to repent, turn to God, and come to faith in Jesus. His first point is that Jesus' death constituted the fulfillment of God's plan of salvation.

Peter acknowledges that the Jews of Jerusalem and their leaders acted "in ignorance" (κατὰ ἄγνοιαν). The "leaders" are the high priestly families and the members of the Sanhedrin who in-

dicted Jesus of blasphemy and handed him over to Pilate for trial and execution. They did not understand who Jesus really was; they did not grasp that he was God's messianic Servant, the Holy and Righteous One, and the Author of Life, and they were ignorant of the fact that Jesus' death was a central event in God's plan of salvation (v. 18; see also Paul's comment point in 13:27; cf. 17:30 for "ignorance" in a more general sense). Jesus had prayed on the cross, "Father, forgive them, for they do not know what they are doing" (Luke 23:34).

Peter's words should certainly be understood in the sense that "the fact that there were mitigating circumstances for the first rejection of the prophet legitimates the second offering of salvation through his prophetic emissaries."[26] This does not mean, however, that if they reject the second offer of salvation through coming to faith in Jesus again, all hope is then lost for the Jewish people. The apostles never gave up on the Jewish people as they continued to live and preach in Jerusalem and later in the diaspora synagogues.[27]

Equally important, however, ignorance does not eliminate the necessity of repentance and sins being removed (cf. v. 19). Jesus had declared the "house" of Israel to be desolate until they respond to the one who comes in the name of the Lord (Luke 13:33–35). During the last week of his life, he had presented himself to the Jews of Jerusalem as God's emissary to Israel (20:9–16), and as the cornerstone of the new house that God was in the process of building in Israel (20:17–18). This means that the Jews of Jerusalem had been given an opportunity to respond to Jesus' message and claims. Their rejection of Jesus and of his message was based not on a genuine understanding of who he really was and how his message was an integral part of God's plan of salvation as prophesied in

26. Johnson, *Acts*, 68; cf. Wilfried Eckey, *Die Apostelgeschichte: Der Weg des Evangeliums von Jerusalem nach Rom* (2 vols.; Neukirchen-Vluyn: Neukirchener Verlag, 2000), 109.

27. For unintentional sins in the Old Testament; cf. Num 15:22–31; also Lev 22:14.

Scripture. Thus their implication in the execution of Jesus is mitigated by the fact that they failed to perceive what they were truly doing.

3:18 But God in this way fulfilled what he announced beforehand through all the prophets, that his Messiah would suffer (ὁ δὲ θεός, ἃ προκατήγγειλεν διὰ στόματος πάντων τῶν προφητῶν παθεῖν τὸν χριστὸν αὐτοῦ, ἐπλήρωσεν οὕτως). God not only reversed the mistake of the Jews of Jerusalem who arranged for Jesus' execution; he also used it to fulfill his promises and bring about his own purpose. Peter links God's "involvement" in the death of Jesus with the promises of the prophets.[28] The verb translated as "announced beforehand" (προκαταγγέλλω) denotes the announcement of an event before that event takes place. Peter asserts that the prophets announced long ago that God's anointed agent, the Messiah, would suffer (which included death).

Peter and the early church read some of the Psalms as announcing the life, ministry, death, and resurrection of Jesus — in 2:25 – 28 Peter quoted Ps 16:8 – 11, in 2:34 – 35 he quoted Ps 110:1. Both Ps 22 and Ps 69 were probably interpreted as being fulfilled when Jesus died on the cross.[29] In 3:13 Peter had identified Jesus as the Servant of the Lord who was exalted by God and who, in Isa 52:13 – 53:12, suffered and died. The prophecies in Zech 12:10; 13:7 were understood to refer to Jesus,[30] and Jer 11:19 and Dan 9:26 may also have been interpreted as prophecies of the suffering and death of the Messiah.[31] The reference to "all" (πάντων) the prophets seems to be hyperbolic (cf. 1:1, 8, 19; 2:5, 14, 43); Peter's statement in v. 24 ("and all the prophets who have spoken, from Samuel and his successors onward") may imply a limitation of the

"all" in v. 18, since Moses was regarded as a prophet as well.

Peter asserts that God has now fulfilled these promises "in this way" (οὕτως), i.e., through Jesus' death on the cross. Thus that death was not arbitrary and not merely the result of the tragic ignorance of the Jews of Jerusalem. The death of Jesus, the Messiah, represented the fulfillment of prophecies, and it was thus an integral part of God's plan of restoring and saving Israel. Jesus made the same point on the day of his resurrection (Luke 24:25 – 26), as does Paul in his speech before King Herod Agrippa (Acts 26:22 – 23). For Luke, this is an important point, as the Emmaus episode (Luke 24:26, 46) and as Acts 3:18; 17:3; 26:23 demonstrate.

The truth of the claim that Jesus' death is part of God's plan can be seen in the fact that God "raised [him] from the dead" (v. 15). If Jesus had deserved to be executed on the cross or if his death was merely an unfortunate miscarriage of justice, he would have had no significance for the life and faith of the Jews of Jerusalem if he had remained in the grave. The fact that he was raised from the dead — an unprecedented deed that only God can accomplish, and that the apostles can reliably testify to because they saw Jesus alive after his crucifixion (v. 15) — demonstrates that Jesus has a major role in God's plan of salvation.

3:19 Repent, therefore, and turn to God, so that your sins may be wiped out (μετανοήσατε οὖν καὶ ἐπιστρέψατε εἰς τὸ ἐξαλειφθῆναι ὑμῶν τὰς ἁμαρτίας). The call to repentance is the rhetorical center of the speech. The Jews in the temple who merely expected an explanation of the miracle of the healing of the lame man are challenged to

---

28. The expression στόμα τῶν προφητῶν (lit., "mouth of the prophets") is an Old Testament phrase; cf. Deut 18:18; 1 Kgs 17:1; Zech 8:9.

29. Cf. especially Ps 22:1, 7, 15, 18; Ps 69:9, 17, 21.

30. Cf. Luke 21:27; Acts 1:7; Matt 24:30; 26:31; Mark 14:27; John 16:32; 19:37.

31. Marshall, "Acts," 546, commenting that this provides material from Psalms, Isaiah, Jeremiah, and the Minor Prophets (which were regarded as a single "book").

repent of their sins. This call to repentance is formulated with two aorist imperatives, which involve
abandoning previous ways of thinking, believing,
and acting (μετανοήσατε) and adopting new ways
of thinking, believing, and acting (ἐπιστρέψατε).

To "repent" means to turn away from disobedience and wickedness, to confess wrongdoing, and
to give up sin (see on 2:38). The complementary
action is to "turn" (ἐπιστρέφω)[32] to God. This verb
describes the act of turning away from a way of life
that is characterized by disobedience and ignorance and turning to a new way of life controlled by
faith and obedience to God. The Jews of Jerusalem
are going in the wrong direction and need a radical
change of direction — in terms of what they believe
about Jesus, what they think about his death, and
what they assume about the significance of his life
and death for their lives. At the present time they
are walking away from God.

Peter formulates as the result (or purpose) of
repentance and conversion the forgiveness of their
sins. Walking away from God and his revelation is
sin, which deserves punishment if it is not forgiven
and reversed. The sins of the Jews of Jerusalem are
connected with their refusal to recognize and acknowledge Jesus as God's Servant, the Holy and
Righteous One, the Author of Life, and the Messiah, through whom God fulfills his purposes.

If the Jews repent and turn to God, their sins
will be "wiped out" (ἐξαλειφθῆναι). This verb
means "to cause to disappear by wiping away, eras-
ing"; in some texts the term combines these two
connotations, in the meaning "to remove so as to
leave no trace, *remove, destroy, obliterate* … insofar as the removal results from the *blotting out*

of a written record."[33] In Athens, when a citizen
had been sentenced to be executed for a crime,
his name was first erased from the registry of citizens (Dio Chrysostom, *Or.* 31.84). The LXX uses
the verb in Gen 7:4, 23 for the action of God, who
wiped out every living thing from the face of the
earth; in Exod 17:14 it denotes the obliteration of
the "memorial of Amalek from beneath heaven"
(cf. Josephus, *Ant.* 6.133). In the New Testament
the verb is nowhere else used for the blotting out
of sin. The passive voice in v. 19 marks God as the
one who forgives the sins of the Jews of Jerusalem
and removes their guilt, although v. 26 suggests
that Jesus is in view also.

**3:20 That times of refreshing may come from
the presence of the Lord, and that he may send
the Messiah, who has been appointed for you,
that is, Jesus** (ὅπως ἂν ἔλθωσιν καιροὶ ἀναψύξεως
ἀπὸ προσώπου τοῦ κυρίου καὶ ἀποστείλῃ τὸν
προκεχειρισμένον ὑμῖν χριστὸν Ἰησοῦν). The second
result of the repentance and conversion of the Jewish people is that "times of refreshing" will come,
expressed with another purpose clause (ὅπως ἄν).[34]
This expression has no parallels in biblical literature; its meaning can be determined only in the
context of Peter's speech. The noun translated as
"refreshing" (ἀνάψυξις) is defined as "experience of
relief from obligation or trouble" and can be translated as "breathing space, relaxation, relief."

These "times of refreshing" are a gift from the
Lord (ἀπὸ προσώπου τοῦ κυρίου). Some interpret
the phrase in an apocalyptic sense, as "breathing space" before the messianic woes of the end
times.[35] In view of vv. 20c-d, 26, a more positive
and active interpretation seems called for. Others

---

32. Cf. BDAG, s.v. ἐπιστρέφω 4, "to change one's mind or
course of action." Cf. Acts 9:35, 40; 11:21; 14:15; 15:19, 36;
26:18, 20; 28:27.

33. BDAG, s.v. ἐξαλείφω 2; in the papyri the term refers to
washing off the writing on a papyrus so that the sheet could be
reused (MM 221).

34. Cf. BDF, §369(5); purpose clauses generally have the
subjunctive, as here ἔλθωσιν.

35. Cf. Gerhard Lohfink, "Christologie und Geschichtsbild
in Apg 3,19 – 21," *BZ* 13 (1969): 223 – 41, with appeal to *4 Ezra*
11:46; cf. Marguerat, *Actes*, 1:132.

suggest a conceptual link with the "sabbath rest" in Exod 23:12 and in Heb 3:7 – 4:13.[36] The reference to "these days" in v. 24 as the time of the fulfillment of God's promises confirms that the "times" (καιροί; note also the plural!) are not a future event but the present reality of God's restoration of Israel through Jesus, the Messiah.[37] Note the parallel structure of vv. 19 – 20 and 2:38, which suggests that the period of refreshing is the time when the Holy Spirit is bestowed on God's people:

2:38	3:19 – 20
repentance demonstrated in baptism	repentance
forgiveness of sins	forgiveness of sins
bestowal of the Holy Spirit	times of refreshing

In the context of vv. 19, 26, the "times of refreshing" are the lifting of the burden of sin, the "relief" from the knowledge of having been implicated in the execution of God's Messiah, the "relaxation" in the knowledge that the promised new covenant has arrived in God's revelation in and through Jesus, his Servant who is the Author of Life — in short, God's blessing and the realization of the "peace" (Heb. šālôm), promised at Jesus' birth (Luke 2:14). In the context of Acts 2:38, the "times of refreshing" are the age of salvation that has arrived with Jesus, the Messiah, who bestows the transforming presence of God's Spirit on his people.

The third result of the repentance of the Jewish people is the culmination of the "times of refreshing" in the return of Jesus, the Messiah. Peter makes several statements about Jesus. (1) Jesus is the Messiah, the Savior of Israel, whom biblical tradition and the Jews of the Second Temple period

expected for the future (for χριστός see on 2:31, 36).

(2) Jesus "has been appointed" by God as the Messiah. The verb "appointed" (προχειρίζομαι) means "to express preference of someone for a task, *choose for oneself, select, appoint*" (BDAG). The prefix (προ-) should not be interpreted to refer to the time before Jesus' future return, thus implying that Jesus is not *now* the Messiah but will be the Messiah when he returns. Rather, it refers to the time before the time in which Peter is speaking. Jesus had been appointed as Messiah by God in his eternal plan of salvation (v. 18; cf. 2:23), an appointment whose reality has been demonstrated in his resurrection and exaltation (cf. 2:31 – 33, 36). Jesus suffered as the Messiah (v. 18), and he was Messiah already at his birth (Luke 2:11).

(3) Jesus, the Messiah, will come to Israel. Most interpret the reference of the "sending" (ἀποστέλλω) in terms of Jesus' future return at the end of history (cf. 1:11; Luke 21:25 – 28). In view of v. 26, where the same verb is used to describe Jesus' being sent by God to the Jewish people with the purpose of turning them away from their sins and thus bringing them blessing, it is possible that the present "mission" of Jesus is in view.[38] In this view, the "sending" of Jesus Messiah to the Jewish people occurs in the proclamation of the apostles, who announce and explain the significance of Jesus' life, death, resurrection, and exaltation.

3:21 Who must remain in heaven until the time of restoration of all things, about which God spoke through his holy prophets from time immemorial (ὃν δεῖ οὐρανὸν μὲν δέξασθαι ἄχρι χρόνων ἀποκαταστάσεως πάντων ὧν ἐλάλησεν ὁ θεὸς διὰ

---

36. Cf. G. Ferraro, "*Kairoi anapsyxeôs*: Annotazioni su Atti 3,20," *RivB* 23 (1975): 67 – 78.

37. Note the purpose construction ὅπως ἄν. Cf. Anderson, *Jesus' Resurrection*, 229 – 30, who includes the resurrection from the dead. Some commentators interpret the coming of the

"times of refreshment" as coinciding with the return of Jesus at the end; cf. Jervell, *Apostelgeschichte*, 167; Bock, *Acts*, 176; E. Schweizer, "ψυχή κτλ.," *TDNT*, 9:664 – 65 (on ἀνάψυξις).

38. Zmijewski, *Apostelgeschichte*, 195.

στόματος τῶν ἁγίων ἀπ' αἰῶνος αὐτοῦ προφητῶν). God's plan of salvation requires Jesus to remain in heaven, where he went at his exaltation/ascension (1:9 – 11). This period of Jesus' absence from earth will end at the time of the "restoration of all things." The term translated "restoration" (ἀποκατάστασις) denotes "reestablishment,"[39] the "return to an appointed state."[40] There is no consensus as regards the precise reference of this phrase.

The following points should be noted. (1) As applied to Israel, this word implies that the Jewish people have diverged from the condition in which they were intended to be. In other words, the phrase denotes the restoration of the "kingdom to Israel" (1:6, with the verb ἀποκαθιστάνεις).[41] There may be an allusion to Mal 4:5 – 6 (LXX 3:22 – 23), where the prophet conveys God's promise that he will send Elijah before the "great and dreadful day of the Lord," who will "restore [ἀποκαταστήσει] the heart of the father to the son and the heart of a man to his neighbor" (LXX).

(2) If creation is in view,[42] the phrase may allude to Adam's loss of the glory of God in the fall (Gen 3). Reference is then made to the future universal restoration of creation, described by the prophets as the creation of a new heaven and a new earth.[43]

(3) Some link the relative pronoun (ὧν) in v. 21c not with "all" (πάντων) but with "times" (χρόνων), which has Peter speak of the "fulfillment" of all the things that God spoke through the prophets,

culminating in the establishment of God's new world.[44]

(4) It should be noted that as in v. 20 ("times," καιροί), Peter refers to a plurality of events (χρόνοι). This means that, again, Peter has in view "a period of time and a cluster of events."[45] And if χρόνοι is parallel to καιροί, the "times of refreshing" must be parallel to the "time of restoration," suggesting that the two terms materially belong together, so that "the restoration implied in the latter is the mirror image of the liberation implied in the former."[46] In v. 24 Peter declares that all the prophets beginning with Samuel predicted "these days," which is the time in which the nations are blessed through the seed of Abraham (vv. 25 – 26). If this third time reference is correlated with the καιροί of v. 20 and the χρόνοι of v. 21, it becomes apparent that in v. 21 Peter does not speak exclusively of the future but includes the present.[47]

While the "time of restoration" is closely connected to Jesus' future return and the awaited creation of God's new world, it includes events prior to this climax of history. This finds a parallel in Peter's speech on Pentecost, in which he declared Joel's prophecy of the coming of the Spirit and of the coming of the day of the Lord to be fulfilled in the present, while aspects of fulfillment await the future (2:17 – 21). Peter confirms what he has said about the "times of refreshing" and the "time of restoration of all things" (1) with reference to

---

39. LSJ, s.v. ἀποκατάστασις; it can denote the "recovery" from illness, the "reversal" of a movement of military formations, the "return" to an original position (e.g., of a planet), the "restoration" of property.

40. Barrett, *Acts*, 206.

41. Cf. Dennis Hamm, "Acts 3.12 – 26: Peter's Speech and the Healing of the Man Born Lame," *PRSt* 11 (1984): 199 – 217, who sees allusions to Isa 1:26; 61:1 – 2; 49:6; Amos 9:11 – 15. Bayer, "Eschatology," 248, adds Isa 49:6; 66:18 – 21; Ezek 37:21 – 28; Dan 7:27 as expectations that include the Gentiles as participants in the restoration of the people of God.

42. Cf. Bock, *Acts*, 177, with reference to New Testament passages such as Matt 19:28; Rom 8:18 – 23; Heb 2:5 – 8; Rev

19 – 22, which also refer to "the new world and the messianic creation in a final and complete restoration."

43. Isa 62:1 – 5; 65:17; 66:22; cf. *1 En.* 45:4 – 5; 96:3; *4 Ezra* 7:75, 91 – 95; *As. Mos.* 10:10; Fitzmyer, *Acts*, 289.

44. Otto Bauernfeind, *Kommentar und Studien zur Apostelgeschichte* (ed. V. Metelmann; WUNT 22; Tübingen: Mohr Siebeck, 1980), 69; Bruce, *Book of Acts*, 85.

45. Bayer, "Eschatology," 247; this is supported by Luke's use of ἄχρι, which refers to a time span in Acts 20:6.

46. Turner, *Power from on High*, 309 n. 112.

47. Cf. Bayer, "Eschatology," 247 – 48; Turner, *Power from on High*, 309 – 10.

the fact that God has spoken (v. 21), (2) with a quotation from the prophets (vv. 22 – 23, quoting Moses), and (3) with an affirmation of the eternity (ἀπ᾽ αἰῶνος) of God's plan of salvation.

3:22 – 23   Moses said, "The Lord your God will raise up for you, from your own people, a prophet like me. You must listen to him in everything that he tells you. Everyone who does not listen to that prophet shall be utterly rooted out from the people" (Μωϋσῆς μὲν εἶπεν ὅτι προφήτην ὑμῖν ἀναστήσει κύριος ὁ θεὸς ὑμῶν ἐκ τῶν ἀδελφῶν ὑμῶν ὡς ἐμέ· αὐτοῦ ἀκούσεσθε κατὰ πάντα ὅσα ἂν λαλήσῃ πρὸς ὑμᾶς. ἔσται δὲ πᾶσα ψυχὴ ἥτις ἐὰν μὴ ἀκούσῃ τοῦ προφήτου ἐκείνου ἐξολεθρευθήσεται ἐκ τοῦ λαοῦ). Peter underlines the necessity of repentance (v. 19) with a proof from Scripture (vv. 22 – 23). He quotes a portion of Deut 18:15 – 20, combined with Lev 23:29.

Deut 18 belongs to texts that describe the situation Israel will face once the people enter the Promised Land. The nations they are about to dispossess listen to soothsayers and diviners, which Israel must not do. Although Moses will not be there to guide Israel, and since the people had voiced concerns at Mount Sinai about directly facing Yahweh, they are reassured that they will receive guidance from a prophet whom God would raise up, similar to Moses, to act as an intermediary between the people and God — a prophet who would receive direct communication from God, which he would pass on to the people of Israel. God will hold every Israelite accountable who does not listen to this prophet, and any prophet who claims to speak in the name of Yahweh but does not will be punished by death.

The quotation in vv. 22 – 23 removes from Deut

18:15 – 20 the lines that speak of the Israelites' concern for a direct encounter with Yahweh and Yahweh's promise of an intermediary between himself and the people of Israel. The divine judgment on those who do not listen to (obey) the words of the prophets (Deut 18:19, "I myself will call to account") are substituted with words from Lev 23:29 ("shall be utterly rooted out of the people").

The verb "raise up" (ἀνίστημι) describes the appearance of this future prophet in the history of Israel. He would be appointed by "the Lord your God," and he would come "from your own people." While the promise of Deut 18:15 – 20 could be regarded as fulfilled in the succession of prophets whom God appointed in Israel, some Jewish circles interpreted the "prophet like Moses" (προφήτης … ὡς ἐμέ/ὡς Μωϋσῆν)[48] as an ideal prophet whom God would send in the future. In 1 Macc 4:46 (cf. 14:41) a prophet is expected who will decide what should be done with the stones of the altar in front of the temple, which has been defiled. The Qumran texts attest to hopes of a coming "prophet like Moses."

The expectation of an Anointed One is sometimes linked with the end of provisional legal stipulations that will be replaced,[49] evidently, by a new legislative authority, which may be linked with the notion of a "prophet like Moses."[50] In a text called *Moses Apocryphon*, Moses is described as Yahweh's Anointed.[51] This is the only Jewish text from the Second Temple period in which the term "anointed" is applied to Moses. In the text he appears not only as God's counterpart (as the people), but as God's agent and plenipotentiary, as mediator between God and the people. If Moses can be called "the Anointed," the same must apply to the

---

48. The expression ὡς ἐμέ, following after a noun (Μωϋσῆς), is adjectival and used as an attributive to "Moses": "a prophet as I am a prophet"; cf. BDAG, s.v. ὡς 2cβ. If it is interpreted as a comparative clause (with ellipsis of the predicate; BDAG, s.v. ὡς 1bα), the expression could be interpreted as a modal clause,

"he will raise him up like he raised me up." The first alternative seems more likely.
49. 1QS IX, 11; CD XII, 23; XIV, 19.
50. Zimmermann, *Messianische Texte*, 40 – 41.
51. 4Q377 frag. 2, II, 3 – 5.

"prophet like Moses."[52] In the New Testament, this expectation appears in John 1:21, 25 and in Acts 3:22; 7:37.

The future tense translated as "you must listen to him" (ἀκούσεσθε) expresses a strict commandment, and the meaning is an equivalent of "obey." The people of Israel are obligated to listen to this future prophet "in everything that he tells you," i.e., in all matters that he communicates from God, without exception. Israelites who do not listen to this prophet, i.e., who do not accept his words as coming from God and who do not obey what God says through this messenger and leader, are "rooted out" from the people.

The context of Lev 23:29 is a discussion of stipulations for the Day of Atonement (cf. Lev 16); the penalty of destruction is announced for those who do not "deny themselves" (i.e., fast) on that day. In the context of the quotation from Deut 18:15 – 20, this means that obedience to the coming messianic prophet is the criterion by which God decides whether people remain in Israel or are removed from his people. "Continued membership in the people of God is dependent on a positive response to the Messiah."[53] And continued membership in the people of God on account of accepting Jesus as the promised Prophet-Messiah means salvation.

Peter quotes this text from the Torah for three reasons. (1) It was Moses who announced the coming of Jesus as the messianic prophet of the last days. (2) It was Moses who issued a strong warning against Israelites who would refuse to listen to the messianic prophet of the future. (3) Since Jesus is the awaited prophet of the last days, Jews who do not accept his messianic-prophetic authority cease to be members of God's people and no longer enjoy the covenant blessings.

3:24 And all the prophets who have spoken, from Samuel and his successors onward, have also predicted these days (καὶ πάντες δὲ οἱ προφῆται ἀπὸ Σαμουὴλ καὶ τῶν καθεξῆς ὅσοι ἐλάλησαν καὶ κατήγγειλαν τὰς ἡμέρας ταύτας). Peter asserts that not only the law (cited in vv. 22 – 23) but also "all the prophets" from Samuel on spoke of the coming period of messianic refreshing and restoration. Samuel is mentioned either because he is the next prophet after Moses, or because God promised David, in the book of Samuel, that he would establish a future king from David's dynasty as an eternal king in Israel (2 Sam 7:12 – 16).[54]

The phrase "these days" (τὰς ἡμέρας ταύτας) relates the prophecies of the Old Testament prophets concerning the times of refreshing and the times of restoration (vv. 20 – 21) to the present time, which is thus marked as the epoch of salvation that the Law and the Prophets predicted. The plural indicates that Peter is focusing not on a particular event, but on everything that is related to the life, death, resurrection, and exaltation of Jesus. These days are the beginning of the "last days" (2:17) that are characterized by Jesus' rule on the heavenly throne at God's right hand, by the transforming presence of the Holy Spirit, and by the restoration of Israel, the people of God.

3:25 You are the children of the prophets and of the covenant that God made with your fathers when he said to Abraham, "Through your offspring all the families of the earth shall be blessed" (ὑμεῖς ἐστε οἱ υἱοὶ τῶν προφητῶν καὶ τῆς διαθήκης ἧς διέθετο ὁ θεὸς πρὸς τοὺς πατέρας ὑμῶν λέγων πρὸς Ἀβραάμ, καὶ ἐν τῷ σπέρματί σου ἐνευλογηθήσονται πᾶσαι αἱ πατριαὶ τῆς γῆς). Peter makes two assertions about the audience listening to his speech in Solomon's Portico. (1) The Jews

---

52. Zimmermann, *Messianische Texte*, 340.
53. Marshall, "Acts," 548; cf. Barrett, *Acts* 1:210; Bock, *Acts*, 179.

54. Bock, *Acts*, 180, interprets more generally in terms of a messianic allusion as part of a "son of David" Christology, with reference to 1 Sam 13:14; 15:28; 16:13; 28:17.

of Jerusalem (and beyond) are "the children of the prophets" (lit., "the sons of the prophets"). This does not mean that they are prophets themselves.[55] It means that they are heirs of the prophets, indebted to their communication from God and the recipients of their promises. Thus, the people must hear, understand, and obey what the prophets have been saying about "these days" that have seen the fulfillment of God's promises for Israel.

(2) The Jews are "the children ... of the covenant" that God made with the fathers, beginning with Abraham (v. 25b-c).[56] The genitive "of the covenant" (τῆς διαθήκης) is a genitive of possession: the covenant belongs to them, as descendants of Abraham, Isaac, and Jacob. They are members of the covenant that God made with Abraham. As such, they are invited to take their place in "the new covenant" (ἡ καινὴ διαθήκη), which became a reality with Jesus' death on the cross (Luke 22:20). However, their place in the new covenant is contingent on their willingness to listen to and obey the messianic prophet whom God has sent to Israel in "these days." This implies that "Jesus and those who now name his name stand at and as the climax of that unbroken line of divine purpose."[57]

When God established his covenant with Abraham and thus with Israel, promising his blessings to him and to his descendants, he included all "the families" (αἱ πατριαί) of the earth in the promise of blessings (cf. Gen 12:1 – 3). This text speaks of the prominent position that Yahweh gave to Abraham and by implication to Israel: "the promise of blessing for the clans of the earth first of all relates to Abraham and to his descendants. The blessing of Abraham is meant to come true in the blessing for the nations — thus underlining his unique position."[58]

The promise of the blessing of the families of the earth is found in Gen 12:3 (πᾶσαι αἱ φυλαί, "all the peoples [tribes]"); 18:18; and 22:18 (πάντα τὰ ἔθνη); the promise is repeated for Isaac in 26:4 (πάντα τὰ ἔθνη) and for Jacob in 28:14 (πᾶσαι αἱ φυλαί). The formulation here is closest to Gen 22:18 (which includes the phrase ἐν τῷ σπέρματί σου), a passage that is linked with Abraham's willingness to sacrifice his son Isaac. While the meaning of the Hebrew verb translated "shall be blessed" is contested,[59] the passive voice of the Greek verb here (ἐνευλογηθήσονται), which the LXX uses, should be interpreted as a divine passive: God promised Abraham that he would bless all the families of the earth if and when they favor Abraham and his descendants.

In the context of his speech to the Jews in Solomon's Portico, Peter seems to identify Jesus as the "offspring" (σπέρμα) of Abraham through whom God will bless all peoples. The singular "offspring/ seed" (σπέρμα) refers to a specific descendant of Abraham.[60] The "seed" of Abraham is not a generic reference to all the Jewish people, who are Abraham's descendants, but a reference, as v. 26 will show, that Jesus, God's messianic Servant who has been raised from the dead, is the one from whom God's covenant blessings will come to

---

55. The phrase "sons of the prophets" is used in this sense in 1 Kgs 20:35; 2 Kgs 2:3, 5, 7, 15.

56. The expression "sons of the covenant" is also found in Ezek 30:5 LXX; *Pss. Sol.* 17:15.

57. Dunn, *Acts*, 47.

58. Wolfgang Kraus, *Das Volk Gottes: Zur Grundlegung der Ekklesiologie bei Paulus* (WUNT 85; Tübingen: Mohr-Siebeck, 1996), 37 – 38.

59. The niphal could be interpreted as passive (the nations will be blessed through Abraham), reflexive (the nations will bless themselves by Abraham), or middle (the nations will find blessing through Abraham); the last option is preferable, cf. Gordon J. Wenham, *Genesis* (2 vols.; WBC; Waco/Dallas: Word, 1987 – 94), 266, 277 – 78; Paul R. Williamson, *Abraham, Israel and the Nations* (JSOTSup 315; Sheffield: Sheffield Academic Press, 2000), 223 – 28.

60. The translation of singular σπέρμα with the plural "descendants" (GNB, NET, NLT, NRSV, RSV) is misleading. On Jesus as "seed of Abraham," see Paul's exposition of the "seed" of Abraham in Gal 3:8 – 29.

Jewish families and also to the other families of the earth.

Without becoming explicit, this quotation alludes to the later universal mission to the Gentile peoples who become participants in God's covenant as they come to faith in Jesus, the messianic "seed" of Abraham. Peter's statement implies a subtle reference to the expansion of the proclamation of the gospel of Jesus, Israel's Messiah, to the Gentiles.

3:26 When God raised up his Servant, he sent him to you first, to bless you by turning each one of you from your evil ways (ὑμῖν πρῶτον ἀναστήσας ὁ θεὸς τὸν παῖδα αὐτοῦ ἀπέστειλεν αὐτὸν εὐλογοῦντα ὑμᾶς ἐν τῷ ἀποστρέφειν ἕκαστον ἀπὸ τῶν πονηριῶν ὑμῶν). At the end of his speech, summarizing what his Jewish listeners in Solomon's Portico need to hear, Peter asserts that God raised Jesus from the dead, that God sent Jesus first to the Jewish people, that he wants to bless them, and that God's blessings now depend entirely on repentance and conversion to faith in Jesus. Peter makes the following specific points.

(1) Jesus is God's Servant (τὸν παῖδα αὐτοῦ), prophesied by Isaiah, who will forgive Israel's sins through his substitutionary suffering and death in the last days (see on 3:13). As God's Servant, God sent him to Israel. The aorist indicative translated "he sent" (ἀπέστειλεν) describes Jesus as God's emissary.

(2) God has "raised up" Jesus, his Servant. The aorist participle used here has a temporal nuance, referring to Jesus' mission as having taken place. If the participle is related to the entire life, death, resurrection, and exaltation of Jesus, that clause refers to God's bringing Jesus onto the stage of history. If it is limited primarily to Jesus' resurrection (vv. 13,

15), Peter repeats his earlier point that Jesus has been vindicated as God's Servant on account of his resurrection. Interpreted on the background of Isa 49:5–6, where Yahweh's Servant is sent "to restore [raise up] the tribes of Jacob" so that they can be "a light for the Gentiles" and bring God's salvation "to the ends of the earth," the raising up of Jesus may refer to "God sending him as his Servant, to fulfill the divine plan for Israel and the nations."[61]

(3) God sent Jesus, his Servant, "to you [the Jews] first" (ὑμῖν πρῶτον). In the Greek, "to you first" is placed first, in prominent position. The dative in ὑμῖν can be interpreted as a dative of advantage linked with the participle "raised up" (ἀναστήσας), or as the indirect object of the main verb, "sent" (ἀπέστειλεν). The continuity of the fulfillment of God's covenant promises from Abraham to the peoples of the earth is firmly connected with present Israel. The blessing of the nations is tied to Israel. This is why Paul asserts that the gospel is the power of God for salvation to everyone who believes, "first to the Jew, then to the Gentile" (Rom 1:16).

(4) The purpose of Jesus' mission as God's messianic Servant is "to bless." The present participle translated as "to bless you" is final, expressing the purpose of God's sending Jesus to Israel, describing Jesus as the divine agent of blessing. Luke uses the present tense of the participle to express purpose, not the more usual future participle. Here to "bless" means "to bestow a favor, *provide with benefits*."[62] Blessing involves an intimate relationship between the person who blesses and the people who are being blessed. For Israelites it involved the acknowledgment of Israel's covenant God.[63] As God's blessing is now conveyed through Jesus, his messianic Servant, the reception of God's covenant

---

61. Peterson, *Acts*, 185.
62. BDAG, s.v. εὐλογέω 3.

63. J. Scharbert, "ברך," *TDOT*, 2:285.

blessings is connected with, and depends on, the acknowledgment of Jesus and of the significance of his mission.

(5) Participation in God's covenant blessings is tied to conversion. The adverbial phrase beginning with (lit.) "by turning" (ἐν τῷ, with present infinitive) describes the process and content of God's blessings conveyed through Jesus. The modal infinitive clause can be understood either transitively (ἕκαστον as accusative object of ἀποστρέφειν: "in that he turns each one of you away from your wickedness") or intransitively (ἕκαστον as the subject of ἀποστρέφειν: "in that each one of you turns away from your wickedness"). Since v. 26 ends Peter's speech, it is attractive to take the phrase as an implicit summons to repent and turn to God (cf. v. 19). But since God is emphasized throughout Peter's speech as the one who acts, and as he speaks here of a blessing that comes from God, it is preferable to interpret the expression with a transitive meaning — God's purpose in the mission of Jesus consists in turning the Jewish people away from wickedness. This implies at the same time a process and a summons — the Jewish people will not enjoy God's salvation if they do not change direction.

(6) God's blessings consist in the liberation from "evil ways" (αἱ πονηρίαι), a plural that denotes "various kinds of evil-mindedness and individual expressions of it."[64] In the context of Peter's speech, this wickedness is the fact; the Jews of Jerusalem did reject Jesus and became culpable in his execution (vv. 17 – 19). Understood broadly, no Jew would dispute the assertion that the experience of God's covenant blessings depends on the active willingness to do God's will. However, as Jesus is God's messianic Servant who brings salvation, conversion to faith in Jesus has become the new prerequisite for receiving God's blessings. Turning to Jesus means to become a follower of Jesus and to accept him as God's Servant, the Holy and Righteous One, the Author of Life, the Prophet like Moses, the Messiah, and the promised Seed of Abraham. It is only by turning to Jesus that sins are blotted out (v. 19).

The implied warning is obvious. If and when Jewish people do not change direction and accept Jesus, they are far from God (v. 19b), their sins remain unforgiven (v. 19c), they do not experience the times of refreshing (v. 20a), they reject the reality and the presence of the Messiah (v. 20b), and they will not enjoy the blessings of God's covenant promises (v. 25).

Theology in Application

When Peter addresses the people in the temple court who have just heard of the healing of the lame beggar and who are in a state of excitement, he does not present his view of miracles; he does not talk about himself as a follower of Jesus who has been given miraculous powers with which he can heal others; he does not present either himself or the beggar at the Beautiful Gate as examples of miracle-working faith. Rather, he speaks about God, about Jesus, and about the necessity of conversion for the Jewish people. The church receives her identity and her effectiveness not from miracles but from faith in Jesus the Messiah (v. 16).

---

64. BDAG, s.v. πονηρία, defined in the singular as "state or condition of a lack of moral or social values, *wickedness, baseness, maliciousness, sinfulness.*"

God as Lord of History

God is the Lord of history. In agreement with the depiction of God in the Old Testament, Peter describes God as active in history in the sense that he controls the events that create the possibility and the presence of salvation and thus the events that determine the life of his people. God is the Lord of history as he works out his plan of salvation.

History has been governed by God's plan of salvation since the beginning of history (v. 21). The controlling power of history is not some law of natural selection, or the principle of chaos, or chance and senselessness, or an evolutionary process leading to greener pastures and brighter horizons. It is God, the Creator of the universe, who leads a world fallen in sin and wickedness through his covenant with Israel and through his new covenant initiated by Jesus, his messianic Servant, to its ultimate and climactic restoration.

As almighty Creator, God can cause the impossible to happen. The impetus for Peter's speech was the healing of a man lame from birth. What contemporary physicians regarded (and still regard) as humanly impossible, the God of Abraham who intervenes in history can accomplish (vv. 12 – 13). Since the Enlightenment, many in modern society regard true miracles as myth (and label "miracle" anything that is extraordinary or spectacular); as a result, believers in the one true and almighty God need to ask themselves whether they trust the reality of the "laws of nature" more than the reality of the power of God.

God is the God of Abraham, Isaac, and Jacob (v. 13). He is not a philosophical idea or a theological doctrine, but the God of specific, living human beings. All people are accountable to him, and he is Yahweh, who has entered into a covenant with the people of Israel. Before he is the God of the nations, he is the God of the Jewish people. But he is *also* the God of all the families of the earth, whose blessing was part of God's covenant, which is now being fulfilled. The fact that he is not a god of the dead but the God of the living (Luke 20:38) has been demonstrated in the resurrection of Jesus, who has thus become the Author of Life (v. 15).

The Christian church — which was exclusively Jewish for the first years after Pentecost — and Israel, the Jewish people, are positively related to each other as both have been created by God. The reason for this unalienable relationship is not feelings of guilt because of antisemitism or the holocaust (the Shoah), but the history of salvation, which implies a continuity of the old covenant and the new covenant. In the first century, Jews and Christians had more in common than either of the two groups had with Gentiles. Jews and Christians agreed about convictions such as the existence of one true God, the nonexistence of the pagan deities, the significance of God's revelation in the works of creation, the greater significance of God's revelation in the Scriptures and in the history of Israel, the reality of God's future judgment, the need for repentance of sins, the need for obedience to God's will, and the restoration of creation in a new world. In the context of Acts 3, this continuity can be seen in the fact that the apostles prayed and taught in the temple (v. 1, 11), in Peter addressing the Jews of Jerusalem as "brothers" (v. 17), and in the quotations of the Old Testament (vv. 22 – 23, 25).

At the same time, the coming of Jesus, the promised messianic Servant of the Lord, has inaugurated a new phase in God's plan of salvation. The pattern of promise and fulfillment implies that the new epoch of salvation surpasses the former period of God's revelation. Since Jesus, the messianic Servant and the prophet like Moses, fulfilled God's plan of salvation, revealed in the prophecies of the Old Testament Scriptures, the latter are to be read as prophecies and promises concerning Jesus of Nazareth. Since Israel's covenant promises have been fulfilled and are being fulfilled in Jesus Christ, Jews need to convert to faith in Jesus if they want to remain members of God's covenant people who enjoy the times of refreshing that he has brought about through Jesus.

God fulfills all his promises (vv. 18, 24), since nothing is impossible for him. In terms of salvation history, reckoned from postapostolic times, this means that we can be certain that Jesus will return (v. 21a), that the final judgment will take place, and that creation will be restored in a new heaven and a new earth (v. 21b).

Yet when we teach about God's promises, we must not turn every biblical statement into a personal promise. For example, the statement in Prov 11:24, "one person gives freely, yet gains even more," is not a divine promise that if I am actively charitable, I will certainly become rich. The statement in Ps 23:6, "surely your goodness and love will follow me all the days of my life," is not a promise that I will never have a bad day. Wisdom proverbs are not promises; utterances of praise and confidence are not promises either. Differences in genre need to be taken into account.

Also, not every biblical promise is a personal promise from God for my life. When God assures Abraham in Gen 15:5, "so shall your offspring be," I cannot turn this into a promise for a childless couple that they will have biological children, nor is this a promise that their descendants will, one day, be so numerous that they can form their own nation. On the other hand, the "fruit of the Spirit" described in Gal 5:22 – 23 ("love, joy, peace, forebearance, kindness, goodness, faithfulness, gentleness and self-control") is indeed God's promise for the believers in Jesus whose lives are empowered by the transforming presence of the Holy Spirit.

God worked out his plan of salvation in the life, death, and resurrection of Jesus (vv. 13, 15, 18). The culmination of God's plan of salvation in Jesus was prophesied in Scripture; it is not an innovative theological construct. The life and death of the "historical Jesus" must not be confused with the life and death of some famous wisdom teacher, moral leader, social reformer, apocalyptic prophet, or founder of a new religious movement. The life of Jesus — which includes his death, resurrection, and exaltation to God's throne — was and is the incarnated revelation of God, who seeks to save the world from sin and wickedness.

God sends "times of refreshing" (v. 20). He lifts the burden of sin, he gives new life through Jesus who is the Author of Life, he gives peace through Jesus who was born as the bringer of peace. Among the most successful books and programs in Western society are "self-help" publications for everything and anything from depression, anxiety, relationships, wealth, and health, to spirituality and peace. The biblical message, which has not changed in the transition from the old to the new covenant, asserts that human beings cannot help themselves where it really matters — the reality of wicked actions and thoughts, feelings of guilt, separation from God, slavery to sinful patterns of living, alienation from fellow human beings, and the transformation of lifestyles. Sinful human beings need the help of God, who alone is powerful, to remove guilt, cancel sin, bridge the gap between fallen human beings and himself, break the pattern of sinful behavior, bring reconciliation with others, and transform lives.

The context of Peter's speech in Luke's narrative underscores the significance of the new community of the followers of Jesus. Commitment to God, who has revealed himself in Jesus, his Messiah, thus involves a connection between Jesus, the Spirit, the community of those who have come to faith in Jesus, and salvation. Repentance and turning to Jesus, the "prophet like Moses," has at least five parallel effects: (1) times of refreshing (v. 20); (2) the coming of the Messiah and the restoration of all things (vv. 20 – 21); (3) participation in the people of God (cf. v. 23); (4) blessing of the families of the earth (v. 25); (5) blessing for Israel, which manifests itself in turning from wickedness (v. 26).[65]

The sovereign God can bring good out of evil. The Jews of Jerusalem rejected Jesus and helped execute him, while God was working out his purposes in the midst of this human tragedy (vv. 17 – 18).

Jesus as God's Messiah

Jesus is God's Messiah. Jesus is described particularly with regard to his relationship to God and with regard to his significance for salvation. Jesus' mission is integrally connected, here, with his suffering and death (v. 18), his resurrection (vv. 15, 26), his glorification (v. 13), the purpose of bringing God's blessings (vv. 20, 26), and his ultimate return (v. 21). For Christian believers, the entire history of Jesus is important. We cannot pick and choose — focus on his suffering when we are suffering, focus on his resurrection when we are feeling upbeat. The cross is not left behind by the resurrection. At the same time the cross does not cast a shadow over the resurrection. The reality of the risen Christ does not eclipse the significance of his return and the reality of the final judgment (v. 21, 23), a future reality that characterizes all our efforts and actions as preliminary and provisional.

---

65. Kuecker, "Spirit and the 'Other,' " 128 – 29.

Jesus is the Holy and Righteous One (v. 14), God's Servant (v. 13) and thus God's Messiah (v. 18). His relationship to God was unique. His calling and his mission were unique. The uniqueness of Jesus is particularly important in evangelistic sermons. Jesus was not just a good person. He was not just more righteous, by some finite degree, than we are. He did not have a mission as many of us are "on a mission." He was not a servant as Mother Teresa of Calcutta was in serving others. Indeed, he was holy and righteous as only God himself is holy and righteous. He was God's Servant, who took upon himself the sin and suffering of the world, as only he could and was chosen by God as no one else had ever been chosen.

Jesus is "the seed of Abraham" (v. 25) and the Prophet like Moses (vv. 22 – 23). He was Jewish and he came to the Jewish people. He was the fulfillment of prophecies that spoke about the blessings of God's covenant with Abraham reaching all the other nations, and of prophecies that promised a leader of God's people who would again and in a climactic manner reveal the will of God to his people.

Jesus is the Author of Life (v. 15). He not only opened up the path to salvation (cf. 16:17), but he was the first to walk on the path of salvation that characterizes the new life of the new covenant. He is the pioneer of the new covenant, the Savior (5:31; Luke 2:11) in whose name people find salvation, exclusively, as Peter will assert in 4:12.

The Necessity of Conversion

Peter summons his Jewish listeners to repent of their sins, to change direction and turn to God, and to come to faith in Jesus (vv. 16, 19, 26) in order to receive forgiveness of sins, reconciliation with God in "times of refreshing" (v. 20), and God's blessing (v. 26). Conversion involves repentance, a change of direction, and faith in Jesus, who is God's crucified and risen messianic Servant.

All people need to repent. While this is certainly true for pagans who do not know the one true God, and while this is true for Jews who do not care about God's commandments, it is also true for the pious Jews who believed that eliminating Jesus was necessary (vv. 13 – 15). The coming of Jesus has created a new situation in God's plan of salvation. Membership in national Israel, being a biological descendant of Abraham, and keeping the law as revealed to Moses are no longer mechanisms that bestow and maintain the holiness of Israel and the salvation of the individual Jewish person. Everybody must repent — of sins committed, of ignorance perpetuated, *both* with regard to God's will in more general terms *and* with regard to the rejection of Jesus more particularly.

Repentance involves a change of direction (vv. 19, 26). It involves turning away from our own views about God and how he should act, and turning to God and the truth of his revelation in Jesus, the Messiah. It involves turning away from the self-determination and the self-fulfillment that God regards as evil and wickedness, and turning to God and his divine blessing through Jesus, his Servant.

Conversion involves faith in Jesus (v. 16). Faith in Jesus is accepting his identity as God's Servant, as the Holy and Righteous One. Faith in Jesus is trusting in Jesus as God's suffering Servant whose death atones for my sins, as the Author of Life who bestows eternal life, as the Messiah through whom God fulfills his purposes.

Peter uses several motivating arguments for conversion, both positive (vv. 19 – 22, 25 – 26) and negative (v. 23). The reference to the possibility of personal sins being blotted out, the promise of times of refreshing, the prospect of life in fellowship with the promised Messiah, the new divine revelation from the awaited Prophet, the expectation of seeing all the covenant promises given to Abraham being fulfilled, and the assurance of God's blessings are all powerful incentives for conversion, particularly for Jewish people. The threat of judgment (v. 23) constitutes a warning that should make people think and reevaluate their position. At the same time, conversion is the result of the intervention of God himself (v. 26).

Acts 4:1 – 22

Literary Context

In the previous section (3:1 – 26), Peter healed a lame man at the temple and used the opportunity to preach to the people gathered in Solomon's Portico in the outer court of the temple complex. The next incident in this episode relates the arrest of Peter and John by the Jewish authorities (4:1 – 4), where Peter speaks before the Sanhedrin (4:5 – 22).

This arrest is the first such event in Acts; Luke relates two further imprisonments of Peter in Jerusalem: in 5:17 – 42 (together with the apostles) and in 12:3 – 19. Peter's speech in 4:8 – 12 is his sixth speech that Luke relates (see the master outline of Acts in the introduction). On the speeches in Acts see on 2:14 – 36.

II. The Beginnings of the New People of God (1:15 – 8:3)

  B. The Life, Witness, Trials, and Growth of the Community of Believers in Jerusalem (3:1 – 8:3)

   9. Peter's miracles, proclamation of Jesus, and defense before the Sanhedrin (3:1 – 4:31)

→ **c. Arrest of Peter and John (4:1 – 4)**

   d. Peter's defense before the Sanhedrin (4:5 – 22)

   e. The prayer of Jerusalem Christians (4:23 – 31)

Main Idea

The proclamation of Jesus as the Messiah and Savior leads to arrest, imprisonment, and interrogation for Peter and John, which in turn provide the opportunity for explaining with bold assurance the identity and the significance of Jesus.

Translation

Acts 4:1 – 22

1a	Setting: time	While they were speaking to the people,
b	Event:	
	List (Character entrance)	**the priests,**
c	List (Character entrance)	**the captain of the temple, and**
d	List (Character entrance)	**the Sadducees**
e	Event	**approached them**
2a	Cause	annoyed
b	Action	that they were teaching the people
c	Action	and proclaiming …
d	Reference	in Jesus
e	Content	… the resurrection of the dead.
3a	Action	**They seized them**
b	Action	**and put them in prison**
c	Duration	until the next day,
d	Cause	because it was already evening.
4a	Aside/Event	But **many of those**
b	Description	who had heard the word
c	Event	**believed,**
d	Event	**and the number of men who believed was about five thousand.**
5a	Setting: Time	The next day
b	List	**their leaders,**
c	List	**elders,** and
d	List	**scribes**
e	Place	**were gathered in Jerusalem,**
6a	List	with Annas, the high priest,
b	List	and Caiaphas,
c	List	with John and
d	List	Alexander,
e	List	and with all who belonged to the high-priestly class.
7a	Action	**They made them stand in the middle**
b	Action	**and inquired,**
c	Interrogation	
	Agency	*"By what power or*
d	Agency	*by what name,*
e	Action	*have you done this?"*
8a	Action	Then **Peter,**
b	Event (Description)	filled with the Holy Spirit,
c	Action/Speech	**said to them,**
d	Address	*"Leaders of the people and*
e	Address	*elders,*
9a	Argument 1: Explanation (irony)	*if we are examined today,*

b	Event	*because of a good deed*
c	Description	*done to someone who was lame*
d	Event	*and how he was healed*
10a	Answer	
	(address)	*then let it be known to all of you,*
b	(address)	*and to all the people of Israel:*
c	Argument 2: Assertion	*it was in the name of Jesus,*
d	Identification	*the Messiah from Nazareth,*
e	Accusation	*whom you crucified and*
f	Event (contra-expectation)	*whom God raised from the dead,*
g	Explanation	*that this man stands before you healed.*
11a	Verification (Quotation of OT): Assertion	*This Jesus is the stone,*
b	Accusation	*rejected by you builders,*
c	Event (contra-expectation)	*who has become the cornerstone.* (Ps 118:22)
12a	Assertion	*Salvation can be found in no one else,*
b	Reason	*because there is no other name*
c	Sphere	*in the whole world*
d	Event	*given to human beings*
e	Purpose (means)	*through which we are to be saved."*
13a	Cause	When they saw the boldness of Peter and John,
b	Cause	and when they realized
c	Contra-expectation	that they were uneducated amateurs,
d	Reaction	**they were amazed,**
e	Cause	and they recognized
f	Circumstance	that they had been with Jesus.
14a	Cause	When they saw the man who had been cured standing beside them,
b	Result	**they had nothing to say in reply.**
15a	Action	**They ordered them to leave the Sanhedrin**
b	Action	**and conferred among themselves.**
16a	Action (speech)	**They said,**
b	Question	*"What shall we do with these people?*
c	Reason	*Since it is known to all people*
d	Place	*who live in Jerusalem*
e	Event	*that a manifest sign has been performed*
f	Agency	*through them,*
g	(concession)	*and we cannot deny it.*
17a	Purpose	*But that it may spread no further*
b	Place	*among the people,*
c	Action (Plan)	*let us threaten them not to speak in this name to anyone.*
18a	Setting: temporal	After they had called them back in,
b	Action	**they ordered them**
c	Prohibition	never to speak or teach about the name of Jesus.

Continued on next page.

Continued from previous page.

19a	Response	**Peter and John said to them in reply,**
b	Rhetorical question	*"You may decide yourselves*
c		*whether it is right for us in the sight of God*
d	Contrast	*to listen to you rather than*
e		*to God.*
20a	Assertion	*We cannot help but speak of*
b	Content	*what we have seen and heard."*
21a	Setting: action	After they had threatened them further,
b	Action	**they let them go,**
c	Cause	since they could not find a way to punish them
d	Cause	because of the people,
e	Explanation	since they all glorified God for what had happened.
22a	Cause (Aside)	For the man …
b	Identification	on whom this sign of healing
		had been performed
c	Description	… was over forty years old.

Structure and Literary Form

The two incidents recorded here are *historical narratives*. The intervention of the Jewish leaders of Jerusalem after the healing of the lame man provides Peter with another opportunity to proclaim the true identity and the significance of Jesus. Peter and John are arrested in Solomon's Portico in the outer court of the temple in the late afternoon of the day during which these events transpired (4:1 – 3a). Because it is too late for an official examination of these events, the temple police take Peter and John to prison (4:3b-d). In an aside, Luke comments on the numerous conversions of people who heard Peter speak in Solomon's Portico, which brought the number of those who had come to faith in Jesus to about 5,000 believers.

On the following day the Jewish leaders convene the Sanhedrin (4:5), and Peter and John are interrogated (4:7) on account of their teaching about Jesus and his resurrection (4:1 – 2). The *dialogue* between the members of the Sanhedrin (direct speech in v. 7) and the apostles quickly turns into a *speech* of Peter (vv. 8 – 12), which consists of two parts. Peter first responds to the question about the origin of the power through which the lame man was healed (vv. 9 – 10c). The miracle was a good deed that helped a lame man, and good deeds should not be punished. Moreover, the miracle happened through Jesus. The mention of Jesus triggers the second part of the speech (vv. 10d – 12), in which Peter proclaims that Jesus is the Messiah, that he was crucified by the Jewish leaders, that he was raised from the dead by God, and that he is the one who healed the lame man. Peter describes Jesus' significance with a quotation from Ps 118:22, and ends with a confessional commitment to Jesus as the Savior of all people.

The *reaction of the Sanhedrin* to Peter's defense (4:13 – 18, *direct speech* in vv. 16 – 17) is amazement because of the bold assurance with which he speaks. They are in a quandary about what to do. They deliberate without the apostles present, deciding to impose a ban on speaking and teaching about Jesus. Peter and John (4:19 – 20, *direct speech*) challenge the members of the Sanhedrin to decide whether their authority surpasses God's authority, and they flatly reject the ban on speaking. The final reaction of the Sanhedrin is described as motivated by the inability to punish Peter and John because there is no evidence that would warrant a punishment. They are afraid since thousands of citizens have heard of the miracle and praise God for what has happened. Thus all they can do is to intimidate the apostles and release them.

The main strategies for defending the "word" about Jesus and his significance in the trial scene in 4:1 – 12 include the following.[1]

1. Peter and John, who speak as Jesus' witnesses, are characterized as popular with the people (vv. 1 – 2, 4, 21), full of the Holy Spirit (v. 8), having done a good deed (v. 9), persuasive despite being ordinary (vv. 13 – 14), obeying God rather than human beings (vv. 19 – 20), and bold (v. 13).
2. The opponents are characterized as annoyed (v. 2), unable to disprove the apostles' convictions convincingly (vv. 14 – 17), and resorting to threats (v. 18).
3. The section contains appeals to authorities, which the apostles, the Jewish leaders, and Luke's readers share: the Scriptures (v. 11), God's direct verdict (v. 10: Jesus' resurrection), an obvious miracle (v. 10), and witnesses for the authentication of the healing miracle (v. 16).
4. There is logical and theological reasoning based on the cure (or "salvation") of the lame man as a "sign" of salvation (vv. 16, 22).

Exegetical Outline

→ **I. Arrest of Peter and John (4:1 – 4)**

    A. The Arrest of Peter and John by the Jewish Authorities of Jerusalem (4:1 – 3)

        1. Peter and John preach in Solomon's Portico (4:1a)

        2. The approach of the priests and the captain of the temple guard (4:1b-e)

        3. The reason for the intervention of the Jewish authorities (4:2)

        4. The arrest of Peter and John (4:3a)

        5. The imprisonment of Peter and John (4:3b-d)

---

1. Alexandru Neagoe, *The Trial of the Gospel: An Apologetic Reading of Luke's Trial Narratives* (SNTSMS 116; Cambridge: Cambridge Univ. Press, 2002), 144 – 45.

B. The Conversion of Jews in Jerusalem (4:4)

    1. The conversion of many listeners who heard Peter's proclamation (4:4a-c)

    2. The number of male believers rose to 5,000 (4:4d)

II. Peter's Defense before the Sanhedrin (4:5 – 22)

A. The Examination of Peter and John by the Sanhedrin (4:5 – 7)

    1. The assembly of the leaders, elders, and scribes (4:5)

    2. The presence of the high priest and the other chief priests (4:6)

    3. Peter and John are summoned (4:7a)

    4. Interrogation about the power that caused the miraculous healing (4:7b-e)

B. Peter's Defense (4:8 – 12)

    1. Introduction (4:8a-c)

    2. Address (4:8d-e)

    3. Response to the question about the miraculous healing (4:9 – 10c)

        a. Argument 1: The miracle was a good deed that helped a lame man (4:9)

        b. Argument 2: The miracle happened through Jesus, the Messiah (4:10a-c)

    4. Proclamation of Jesus (4:10d – 12)

        a. Jesus of Nazareth is the Messiah (4:10d)

        b. Jesus, the Messiah, has been crucified by the Jewish leaders (4:10e)

        c. Jesus, the Messiah, has been raised from the dead by God (4:10f)

        d. Jesus healed the lame man (4:10g)

        e. Proof from Scripture: Ps 118:22 (4:11)

        f. Commitment to Jesus, the Savior of all people (4:12)

C. The Reaction of the Sanhedrin (4:13 – 18)

    1. Amazement on account of the boldness of Peter and John (4:13)

    2. Quandary on account of the presence of the cured man who was lame (4:14)

    3. Deliberation of the Sanhedrin without Peter and John (4:15 – 17)

        a. Removal of Peter and John (4:15)

        b. The pragmatic question of what action to take (4:16a-b)

        c. Concession that a miracle has happened (4:16c-g)

        d. Decision to prohibit the apostles from proclaiming Jesus to others (4:17)

        e. Command to Peter and John not to speak or teach about Jesus (4:18)

D. The Response of Peter and John (4:19 – 20)

    1. Challenge to acknowledge the authority of God over the Sanhedrin (4:19)

    2. Rejection of the ban on speaking (4:20)

E. The Reaction of the Sanhedrin (4:21 – 22)

    1. Intimidation and release of Peter and John (4:21a-b)

    2. Lack of evidence that would warrant a punishment (4:21c)

    3. Inability to punish Peter and John because they fear the people (4:21d-e)

    4. The reality of the miracle (4:22)

Explanation of the Text

4:1 While they were speaking to the people, the priests, the captain of the temple, and the Sadducees approached them (λαλούντων δὲ αὐτῶν πρὸς τὸν λαὸν ἐπέστησαν αὐτοῖς οἱ ἱερεῖς καὶ ὁ στρατηγὸς τοῦ ἱεροῦ καὶ οἱ Σαδδουκαῖοι). Peter's speech in Solomon's Portico (cf. 3:11 – 12) before the people in the outer court of the temple is interrupted by the Jewish authorities. The plural "they were speaking" includes John as a speaker. Some suggest that "it is easy to complete the picture with the surmise that at the end of Peter's discourse John joined him in conversation with the crowd."[2] The verb translated as "approach" (ἐφίστημι) implies hostile intent. The use of this verb to describe the interruption of Peter and John speaking to the crowds underscores (1) the public nature of the intervention of the Jewish officials; (2) the contrast between the people who listen to Peter and John as they describe the nature of salvation in the messianic days that have arrived, and the Jewish authorities who stood from afar and are only now approaching, with hostile intentions; and (3) the parallel to Jesus' teaching the people in the temple, who was similarly interrupted (Luke 20:1).

Three groups of people are involved in confronting and arresting Peter and John. The "priests" (οἱ ἱερεῖς) are the officials responsible for the temple (particularly for the sacrifices), for other rituals at the Jewish festivals, and matters such as the temple tax. They are mentioned here for the first time in Acts. In 6:7 Luke reports that many priests had come to faith in Jesus as the Messiah.

The "captain of the temple" (ὁ στρατηγὸς τοῦ ἱεροῦ) is the official in charge of all temple affairs, the second in authority in the temple after the high priest, the head of the temple guard (often called temple police), which consisted of 200 priests and Levites. While this term in classical usage describes the "commander of an army" or "general,"[3] it was also used for the chief magistrates of the cities in Asia Minor and for individual consuls and praetors in various cities. The LXX uses the word to translate a Hebrew term that designates a civil leader ("governor, head").[4] According to Josephus and the New Testament, he was the official responsible for maintaining order in and around the temple.[5] The fact that he intervenes here demonstrates that this official took his duties seriously; he regarded the excited crowds listening to Peter and John, if not their message about Jesus as the crucified, risen, and exalted Messiah, to be a threat to the order in the temple.

The "Sadducees" are the members of the priestly families who constitute the aristocracy in Jerusalem, many of whom were members of the Sanhedrin.

4:2 Annoyed that they were teaching the people and proclaiming in Jesus the resurrection of the dead (διαπονούμενοι διὰ τὸ διδάσκειν αὐτοὺς τὸν λαὸν καὶ καταγγέλλειν ἐν τῷ Ἰησοῦ τὴν ἀνάστασιν τὴν ἐκ νεκρῶν). These Jewish leaders are annoyed by the teaching of Peter and John. The activity of Peter and John, who have been explaining the miracle of the healing of the lame man as well as the

---

2. Barrett, *Acts*, 218.

3. LSJ, s.v. στρατηγός I.1 and II.1; for the following usages cf. ibid. II.2 and II.4. Note that in Acts 16:20, 22, 35, 36, 38, the term is used for the magistrates of Philippi (whose official designation in Latin was *duoviri*, the highest officials of a Greco-Roman city).

4. O. Bauernfeind, "στρατεύομαι κτλ.," *TDNT*, 7:706.

5. Cf. Josephus, *Ant.* 20.131, 208; *J. W.* 2.409; 6.294; Acts 4:1; 5:24, 26; cf. Luke 22:4, 52 where the plural στρατηγοί is used. Cf. Oliver Gussmann, *Das Priesterverständnis des Flavius Josephus* (TSAJ 124; Tübingen: Mohr Siebeck, 2008), 100.

identity and significance of Jesus, is described with two verbs: they are teaching (διδάσκω) the people assembled in the temple concerning the cause of the miracle and proclaiming (καταγγέλλω) the significance of Jesus, God's messianic Servant. Three issues prompt the Jewish officials to take action.

(1) The followers of Jesus are teaching the people in Solomon's Portico complex without authorization.

(2) Peter proclaims the resurrection of the dead (τὴν ἀνάστασιν τὴν ἐκ νεκρῶν). This annoys the Sadducees, who denied a future resurrection of the body. Moreover, Peter argues that Jesus' resurrection from the dead[6] took place recently and thus before the day of general resurrection of the dead; as a result, the Pharisees would have been annoyed also.

(3) Peter and John are teaching in the name of Jesus, proclaiming (καταγγέλλω) him publicly to be the promised Messiah, whose crucifixion was engineered by the chief priests. This teaching implies that the Jewish authorities had made a serious mistake and would have provoked the Jewish authorities, irrespective of their theological orientation.

4:3 They seized them and put them in prison until the next day, because it was already evening (καὶ ἐπέβαλον αὐτοῖς τὰς χεῖρας καὶ ἔθεντο εἰς τήρησιν εἰς τὴν αὔριον· ἦν γὰρ ἑσπέρα ἤδη). The temple officials seize Peter and John (lit., "they laid hands on them") and take them into custody. The term translated as "prison" (τήρησις) describes the "act of holding in custody," though it can also describe the place where someone is held under guard. The prepositional phrase "until the next

day" describes both the time period during which Peter and John were imprisoned (overnight) and the reason for the imprisonment — the Jewish authorities responsible to deal with the misconduct of individual Jews could not be convened since it was already evening. In the summer of AD 30, sunset was between 7:00 and 8:00 p.m.

As Peter and John were in the temple since the ninth hour, i.e., since 3:00 p.m. (3:1), the incident of the healing of the lame man and the teaching in Solomon's Portico are pictured as lasting three or four hours. They are now led from Solomon's Portico, across the outer court of the temple, through the Kipunus Gate in the western wall, across the bridge over the Tyropoean Valley; they are presumably taken to the prison of the Sanhedrin, probably located near the Xystos below the western wall of the Temple Mount.[7]

4:4 But many of those who had heard the word believed, and the number of men who believed was about five thousand (πολλοὶ δὲ τῶν ἀκουσάντων τὸν λόγον ἐπίστευσαν καὶ ἐγενήθη ὁ ἀριθμὸς τῶν ἀνδρῶν ὡς χιλιάδες πέντε). Luke interrupts his record of the events to include another summary of the expansion of the community of believers in Jerusalem. The message about Jesus, the crucified, risen, and exalted Messiah and Savior, is described as "the word" (ὁ λόγος, cf. 6:4; 8:4).[8] The good news of God granting salvation through Jesus is proclaimed orally by the apostles as Jesus' witnesses.

Many Jews in Solomon's Portico heard the apostles explain the significance of Jesus, and many of them came to faith ("believed," ἐπίστευσαν, aor-

---

6. The phrase ἐν τῷ Ἰησοῦ can be interpreted as (1) "in the case of Jesus," i.e., the apostles proclaim that "in the case of Jesus, the (ultimate) resurrection — the resurrection expected by Pharisaic faith at the end of history — had taken place;" (2) "by means of," i.e., the apostles proclaim the resurrection of the dead by means of the story of Jesus. These are not mutually exclusive alternatives.

7. Cf. Brian M. Rapske, *The Book of Acts and Paul in Roman Custody* (The Book of Acts in Its First-Century Setting 3; Grand Rapids: Eerdmans, 1994), 137.

8. Luke refers to "the word of God" in 4:31; 6:2, 7; 8:14; 11:1; 13:5, 7, 46; 17:13; 18:11; and to "the word of the Lord" in 8:25; 13:44, 48, 49; 15:35 – 36; 19:10, 20. Cf. Dunn, *Acts*, 50.

ist indicative) in Jesus as the Messiah. In Rom 10:13 – 15, Paul similarly connects hearing the word of God and believing in Jesus. The verb translated as "believed" denotes "to consider something to be true and therefore worthy of one's trust" and, in connection with references to God and Jesus, "to entrust oneself to an entity in complete confidence, *believe (in), trust,* with implication of total commitment to the one who is trusted."[9]

The numerical summary (cf. 1:15; 2:41) for the number of believers is difficult to interpret. It is unclear whether the estimated 5,000 people included only men[10] or also women,[11] and whether the figure includes all believers in Jerusalem up to this time or refers only to new conversions on this occasion. This comment indicates that (1) the opposition of the Jewish authorities cannot prevent the growth of the church, and (2) the process of Israel's restoration is making progress as more and more people turn to God and to his messianic revelation in the last days.[12]

4:5 The next day their leaders, elders, and scribes were gathered in Jerusalem (ἐγένετο δὲ ἐπὶ τὴν αὔριον συναχθῆναι αὐτῶν τοὺς ἄρχοντας καὶ τοὺς πρεσβυτέρους καὶ τοὺς γραμματεῖς ἐν Ἰερουσαλήμ). This next incident narrates the interrogation of Peter and John on the morning of the following day (ἐπὶ τὴν αὔριον), when the Sanhedrin (συνέδριον) convenes (the official term for this body is mentioned in v. 15).[13] Three groups make up the council (the same groups that confronted Jesus as he was teaching in the temple; cf. Luke 9:22; 20:1).

The "leaders" (οἱ ἄρχοντες) are probably identical with the names given in v. 6; they are the leading representatives of the high-priestly class, which consisted of the chief priests and their families. Nicodemus is described in John 3:1 as "a member of the Jewish ruling council" (ἄρχων τῶν Ἰουδαίων). The "chief priests" (οἱ ἀρχιερεῖς) are "the high priest of Jerusalem, his predecessors, and the most distinguished members of the priestly aristocracy (Acts 4:6) who together were the most influential group in the Sanhedrin."[14] Members of this group included the incumbent high priest (still Josephus Caiaphas, who had presided over Jesus' trial), the captain of the temple as the deputy of the high priest, and former high priests.

The "elders" (οἱ πρεσβύτεροι) are senior officials, members of the Jewish elite that presumably included both priests and laymen, among the latter presumably the rich landowners. It is possible that Joseph of Arimathea (Mark 15:43) belonged to this group.

The "scribes" (οἱ γραμματεῖς) are specialists in the law, scholars who are sometimes mentioned together with the priests,[15] sometimes with the Pharisees,[16] which suggests (confirmed by the evidence in other sources) that some Torah scholars belonged to the Pharisees, some to the Sadducees, while some were independent of such party affiliations. The Sanhedrin was the highest assembly in Jerusalem, the supreme legislative, judicial, and executive body of leading citizens meeting in a council chamber at the center of the city, near the temple.[17]

The phrase "in Jerusalem" (ἐν Ἰερουσαλήμ) seems

---

9. Cf. BDAG, s.v. πιστεύω 1, 2.

10. Luke refers to ἄνδρες, which usually describes males. Barrett, *Acts*, 222, points to 5:14; 8:3, 12; 9:2; 17:12; 22:4, where ἄνδρες is coupled with γυναῖκες ("women").

11. Cf. 1:16, where ἄνδρες ἀδελφοί includes women (cf. 1:14); also 17:34 where Damaris, a woman, is included among the ἄνδρες who come to faith as a result of Paul's preaching in Athens.

12. Pao, *New Exodus*, 139.

13. Luke mentions the συνέδριον in Luke 22:66; Acts 4:15; 5:21, 27, 34, 41; 6:12, 15; 22:30; 23:1, 6, 15, 20, 28; 24:20.

14. U. Kellermann, "ἀρχιερεύς," *EDNT*, 1:164.

15. Luke 9:22; 19:47; 20:1, 19; 22:2, 66; 23:10.

16. Luke 5:21, 30; 6:7; 11:53; 15:2.

17. Cf. E. Lohse, "συνέδριον," *TDNT*, 7:860 – 71; E. J. Schnabel, "Sanhedrin," *NIDB*, 5:102 – 6.

redundant — an assembly of the high-priestly rulers, the elders, and leading scribes would only take place in Jerusalem, and Peter and John had been arrested in Solomon's Portico in the temple complex in Jerusalem. Some suggest that "Luke wished to underline the fact that the Gospel was at work, and courageous and effective witness to it was being borne, in the heart of the old religion."[18]

4:6 With Annas, the high priest, and Caiaphas, with John and Alexander, and with all who belonged to the high-priestly class (καὶ Ἄννας ὁ ἀρχιερεὺς καὶ Καϊάφας καὶ Ἰωάννης καὶ Ἀλέξανδρος καὶ ὅσοι ἦσαν ἐκ γένους ἀρχιερατικοῦ). Luke mentions four members of the Sanhedrin by name, linking them with the "high-priestly class" (ἐκ γένους ἀρχιερατικοῦ). The significance of the high priest is reflected in Josephus, who asserts that the high priest, with his priestly colleagues, "will sacrifice to God, safeguard the law, adjudicate in cases of dispute, punish those convicted of crime. Any who disobey him will pay the penalty as for impiety towards God himself" (*Ag. Ap.* 2.194).

Annas (Ἄννας), the son of Sethi, was the first high priest appointed by the Roman governors after they imposed direct Roman rule in Judea after the dismissal of Herod Archelaus in AD 6. Annas served as high priest from AD 6 – 15.[19] In AD 30, Annas was the patriarch of the most powerful high-priestly family in the first century. Josephus describes him as "extremely fortunate. For he had five sons, all of whom, after he himself had previously enjoyed the office for a very long period, became high priests of God — a thing that had never happened to another of our high priests."[20] Annas was high priest at the beginning of John the Baptist's ministry (Luke 3:2). Before Jesus was examined by the Sanhedrin, he was interrogated by Annas (John 18:13, 19 – 24). The fact that Annas is called "the high priest" (ὁ ἀρχιερεύς) underscores his standing in the Sanhedrin. Some believe that his tomb has been located in the area of the Akeldama tombs.[21]

Caiaphas (Καϊάφας), whose full name was Joseph Caiaphas,[22] was the son-in-law of Annas and the high priest during Jesus' trial, during the interrogation of the apostles, and during Stephen's trial (cf. 7:1). He was appointed high priest by the Roman governor Valerius Gratus in AD 15. He was in office under Pontius Pilatus (AD 26 – 36) and was removed from office by Lucius Vitellius, the governor of Syria, in AD 36. Josephus mentions Caiaphas only in connection with his appointment and with his removal as high priest, despite the fact that he held office for eighteen years. His long tenure suggests he was a shrewd diplomat who was acceptable to two Roman governors. John mentions twice that Caiaphas was the high priest in the year of Jesus' crucifixion (John 11:49; 18:13). The burial cave and the ossuary in which Caiaphas was buried have been discovered in Jerusalem.[23]

John (Ἰωάννης) may be Jonathan, son of Annas, who was high priest after Caiaphas[24] (from AD 36 – 37) and who may have been the captain of the temple.[25] This identification depends on the

18. Barrett, *Acts*, 224.

19. Josephus, *Ant.* 18.26. Annas was appointed high priest by Quirinius, the Roman governor in Syria.

20. Josephus, *Ant.* 20.198; cf. 18.34; *J. W.* 5.506.

21. Cf. Leen Ritmeyer and Kathleen Ritmeyer, "Akeldama: Potter's Field or High Priest's Tomb?" *BAR* 20 (1994): 22 – 35, 76, 78.

22. Josephus, *Ant.* 18.35.

23. Zvi Greenhut, "Discovery of the Caiaphas Family Tomb," *Jerusalem Perspective* 4 (1991): 6 – 11; cf. Craig A.

Evans, "Excavating Caiaphas, Pilate, and Simon of Cyrene: Assessing the Literary and Archaeological Evidence," in *Jesus and Archaeology* (ed. J. H. Charlesworth; Grand Rapids: Eerdmans, 2006), 323 – 40, 328 – 29.

24. Josephus, *Ant.* 18.95, 123; 19.313; 20.163; *J. W.* 2.240 – 243, 256.

25. Joachim Jeremias, *Jerusalem in the Time of Jesus* (trans. F. H. and C. H. Cave; Philadelphia: Fortress, 1975), 197; Barrett, *Acts*, 225, remains skeptical.

reading Jonathan (Ἰωναθας) in D and in several old versions. Nothing is known about Alexander (Ἀλέξανδρος); most of the (first-century) individuals with the name Alexander mentioned by Josephus are members of the royal family.[26]

4:7 They made them stand in the middle and inquired, "By what power or by what name have you done this?" (καὶ στήσαντες αὐτοὺς ἐν τῷ μέσῳ ἐπυνθάνοντο· ἐν ποίᾳ δυνάμει ἢ ἐν ποίῳ ὀνόματι ἐποιήσατε τοῦτο ὑμεῖς;). Peter and John, after they were brought into the hall in which the Sanhedrin assembled, were placed "in the middle" — probably literally, as the seats in the Sanhedrin were "arranged like the half of a round threshing-floor so that they all might see one another" (*m. Sanh.* 4:3).

The priests, the captain of the temple, and the Sadducees who arrested Peter and John are annoyed because they have been teaching without authorization and because they taught that Jesus had been raised from the dead (vv. 1 – 2). These topics are hinted at when they ask Peter and John "by what power or by what name" they healed the lame man. They evidently know that Peter and John explained the miraculous healing with reference to Jesus, whom they were proclaiming to be the promised Messiah and Servant through whom God grants salvation to the people of Israel if and when they believe in Jesus (3:12 – 26). Yet they want to hear from Peter and John directly what they were proclaiming in the temple.

The members of the Sanhedrin question Peter and John concerning the "power" (δύναμις) through which "this" (τοῦτο; i.e., the miraculous healing of the lame man) has taken place. They know it takes

a supernatural power to cure a man born lame. For devout Jews, there were only two options for this healing — the power of God, the almighty Creator, or the power of the devil, Beelzebul, the "prince of demons" (ὁ ἄρχων τῶν δαιμονίων).[27]

The term "name" (ὄνομα) links the effect of the miracle-working power (δύναμις) with a particular person whose name was invoked during the healing. Peter and John answer the question in v. 10: the lame man, who is present, was healed "in the name of Jesus, the Messiah from Nazareth." In 3:16 Peter had explained it was not the mere invocation of the name Jesus that had (magically) healed the man; rather, it was faith in Jesus that had caused the healing.

4:8 Then Peter, filled with the Holy Spirit, said to them, "Leaders of the people and elders" (τότε Πέτρος πλησθεὶς πνεύματος ἁγίου εἶπεν πρὸς αὐτούς· ἄρχοντες τοῦ λαοῦ καὶ πρεσβύτεροι). Luke describes Peter's speech to the Jewish leaders in the Sanhedrin with an outburst of spiritual power. The use of the aorist participle (πλησθείς, followed by a genitive) means that "the Spirit was the immediate inspiration of the speech event."[28] Peter speaks for both himself and for John, who reappears in v. 13.

Peter focuses particularly on the "leaders" (ἄρχοντες), the chief priests of Jerusalem, and on the "elders" (πρεσβύτεροι (see on v. 5).[29] The polite address is what one would expect in a situation where the life of Peter and John might be at stake. Jesus had stood at the same spot a few months earlier, with the interrogation resulting in the charge of blasphemy and the transfer to the Roman governor, who was successfully petitioned, and pressured, to

---

26. Williams, "Personal Names," 96 – 97.

27. Cf. Luke 11:15; Matt 9:34; 12:24; Mark 3:22.

28. Turner, *Power from on High*, 167, who argues that these constructions (cf. Luke 1:41, 67; Acts 2:4; 4:8, 31) do not suggest a more enduring endowment. According to Luke's language, "a person might on many occasions be 'filled with Holy Spirit' while nevertheless remaining 'full' of the Spirit; the two

types of metaphor make different but complementary assertions." On being "filled" (πλησθείς) see on 2:4.

29. Manuscripts D E Ψ 33. 1739 Maj as well as Latin and Syriac versions add after πρεσβύτεροι the phrase τοῦ Ἰσραηλ, which created the parallel construction "leaders of the people, elders of Israel," but is certainly secondary.

pronounce a death sentence. Whether the respectful address implies that the apostles, who were all Jews, continued to acknowledge the authorities of the Jewish people is a moot question; living in Jerusalem entailed the acknowledgment of and submission to the governmental authority of the "state," just as Paul accepted and acknowledged the civic powers of the Roman Empire and of the local magistrates who stipulated taxes (Rom 13:1 – 7).

At the same time we should note that the term "leaders" (ἄρχοντες) occurs in Ps 118:9 (LXX 117:9), the psalm Peter will quote in v. 11, in the statement that "it is better to take refuge in the LORD than to trust in princes [ἐπ᾽ ἄρχοντας]," as well as in Ps 2:2, quoted in v. 26 in the prayer in which the Jerusalem Christians express the lament that "the kings of the earth arisen, and the rulers [οἱ ἄρχοντες] band together against the Lord and against his anointed [Messiah]."[30]

4:9 If we are examined today, because of a good deed done to someone who was lame and how he was healed (εἰ ἡμεῖς σήμερον ἀνακρινόμεθα ἐπὶ εὐεργεσίᾳ ἀνθρώπου ἀσθενοῦς ἐν τίνι οὗτος σέσωται). Peter argues, first, that the miracle of the previous day helped a lame man, which implies that the authorities have no real reason to intervene, imprison, and interrogate them. Peter uses irony, although it is hardly likely that he could have hoped to relieve the tension in the assembly hall with this statement. Luke describes the judicial examination before the Sanhedrin with the passive voice of the verb translated "we are examined" (ἀνακρινόμεθα); Peter and John are the objects of the interrogation of the chief priests and other Jewish leaders. The present tense of this verb suggests an extended period of time that the judicial hearing is expected to take, as such examinations are seldom quick affairs.

Peter's repetition of the Sanhedrin's question, formulated as an indirect question, is a clever introduction. The phrase translated as "how he was healed" (ἐν τίνι οὗτος σέσωται) can be understood, on the surface, to refer to the "how" of the healing of the lame man. Or the phrase could refer to the person "through whom" (ἐν τίνι) the lame man was healed. The perfect passive of the verb "was healed" (σέσωται), which describes a continuous state of affairs, can be understood in the sense of being cured from an illness, but it can also be understood in the sense of being saved from eternal death or, positively, of receiving messianic salvation.

The reason for the hearing is a "good deed" (εὐεργεσία) that benefited a crippled man. Actions that benefit others are cause for gratitude, not hostile examination. This Greek term describes a benefit that a person receives from another person, who is in some sense superior (in social status or in wealth). When Herod returned from Rome to Judea in 39 BC, for example, the country folk rallied to him "in return for benefits [εὐεργεσίας] conferred by both father and son" (Josephus, *J. W.* 1.293). Benefaction and the proper response to a favor received was a central phenomenon in Greco-Roman culture. The ethics of reciprocity required a good deed to be answered by corresponding thanks (χάρις, εὐχαριστία), on which the benefactor could count and regarding which he could have social or personal expectations. The social reputation of the person who received the benefaction was dependent on following such rules. Bestowing honor on them would make them more willing to perform further good deeds.[31]

Since no one would dispute that curing a lame

---

30. Marshall, "Acts," 550.

31. Cf. H.-J. Gehrke, "Euergetism," *BNP*, 5:154 – 56; for benefaction in Judea and Galilee, cf. Jonathan S. Marshall, *Jesus, Patrons and Benefactors in Roman Palestine and the Gospel of Luke* (WUNT 2.216; Tübingen: Mohr Siebeck, 2009).

man who had been begging at a gate of the temple all his life was a kind deed that benefited not only the man himself but also society at large (which has one beggar less to support), Peter's ironic statement represents his first argument. He challenges the Jewish authorities to recognize the good deed and to acknowledge the benefaction by expressing gratitude. Not to do so would be shameful. Peter clarifies in the next sentence that he does not expect to receive gratitude and honor personally, as it was not he but Jesus who has healed the lame man.

4:10 Then let it be known to all of you, and to all the people of Israel: it was in the name of Jesus, the Messiah from Nazareth, whom you crucified and whom God raised from the dead, that this man stands before you healed (γνωστὸν ἔστω πᾶσιν ὑμῖν καὶ παντὶ τῷ λαῷ Ἰσραὴλ ὅτι ἐν τῷ ὀνόματι Ἰησοῦ Χριστοῦ τοῦ Ναζωραίου ὃν ὑμεῖς ἐσταυρώσατε, ὃν ὁ θεὸς ἤγειρεν ἐκ νεκρῶν, ἐν τούτῳ οὗτος παρέστηκεν ἐνώπιον ὑμῶν ὑγιής). Peter argues, second, that the healing miracle took place through the power of Jesus of Nazareth, who is the Messiah. He begins his explanation of the facts with the phrase "let it be known" (γνωστὸν ἔστω), emphasizing that what he is about to say is relevant for all members of the Sanhedrin as well as for the entire people of Israel.

Peter addresses the Jewish elite assembled in the Sanhedrin as representatives of the nation of Israel. He speaks as a prophet who proclaims revealed truth through Israel's leaders to the entire nation. He speaks as a witness of Jesus, commissioned to proclaim the good news of God's saving presence in Israel through Jesus the Messiah from Jerusalem and Judea to the ends of the earth. Peter speaks before the Sanhedrin in Jerusalem, but wants the truth about Jesus to be known to all Jews, irrespec-

tive of where they live. As he proclaims publicly, in the very center of the Jewish commonwealth, the significance of Jesus, the Messiah, he asserts that "the authorities are now living in the age when ignorance is no longer an excuse."[32]

This healing miracle took place "in the name of Jesus" (ἐν τῷ ὀνόματι Ἰησοῦ). In other words, the lame man, who is present (οὗτος) and who stands before them "healed" (ὑγιής), i.e., physically sound and well, was able to stand on his feet because of the effective power of Jesus (see on 2:38; 3:6, 16). The perfect indicative (παρέστηκεν) underlines the fact that the cure of the man who was lame from birth and who now "stands" before them is a permanent state of affairs. His healing cannot be disputed.

Peter is not content to attribute the miracle to Jesus of Nazareth (Ἰησοῦ … τοῦ Ναζωραίου). He takes seriously his commission to be a witness of Jesus, and thus he succinctly explains Jesus' significance with three statements — an appositional noun and two relative clauses.

(1) Jesus of Nazareth is the Messiah (χριστός; see on 2:31, 36). He is Israel's Savior, the eschatological agent of God who came to restore the nation and bring salvation. Many scholars state that the phrase "Jesus Christ of Nazareth" employs the full title, with "Christ" being "Jesus' second name."[33] However, Peter is not asserting that Jesus is also called "Christ" — a statement that is nonsensical in a Jewish context. As Peter addresses the Sanhedrin in Hebrew or Aramaic, he would have used the word "Messiah" (māšîaḥ), which is not a Hebrew name but a reference to the promised Messiah. Peter asserts that Jesus is Israel's Messiah.[34]

(2) Peter asserts that the Jewish leaders are responsible for Jesus' crucifixion. There may have

---

32. Witherington, *Acts*, 194; cf. 3:17.

33. Fitzmyer, *Acts*, 300. The English versions transliterate χριστός as "Christ" and thus treat the term as a name, not a title;

cf. ESV, GNB, KJV, NET, NASB, NIV, NKJV, NLT, NRSV, RSV.

34. Johnson, *Acts*, 77; Jervell, *Apostelgeschichte* 178; Hurtado, *Lord Jesus Christ*, 178.

been other Jews living in Nazareth with the name Jesus, but there was only one Jesus of Nazareth whose crucifixion had been engineered by the Jewish authorities in Jerusalem. Peter not only charges the Jewish leaders of being complicit in, and guilty of, Jesus' execution by the Roman authorities. This statement is at the same time a proclamation of the good news of God's granting forgiveness of sins and salvation on account of the suffering and death of Jesus, the Messiah (cf 2:23 – 28; 3:17 – 20).

(3) Jesus has been raised from the dead by God. Jesus is alive and has the power to heal the lame man. In other words, Jesus, the crucified man from Nazareth, is vindicated and indeed confirmed as God's Messiah. The healing miracle proves the reality of his resurrection and the continued power of Jesus, the risen Messiah. That reality should satisfy the curiosity of the Sanhedrin and lead to a swift and positive conclusion of the examination. At the same time, since it was God who has raised Jesus from the dead, the Jewish leaders, who were complicit in Jesus' crucifixion, are indeed guilty of having committed a sacrilege, rejecting God's Anointed (even though it was God's plan that was fulfilled in Jesus' death; cf. 2:23; 3:18).

4:11 This Jesus is the stone, rejected by you builders, who has become the cornerstone (οὗτός ἐστιν ὁ λίθος, ὁ ἐξουθενηθεὶς ὑφ᾽ ὑμῶν τῶν οἰκοδόμων, ὁ γενόμενος εἰς κεφαλὴν γωνίας). Peter verifies his confession of Jesus, the crucified and risen Messiah, with an Old Testament text in which a king celebrates God's intervention in redeeming

him from humiliation and giving him a place of honor.[35] Psalm 118 is the last of the Hallel psalms and thus their climax, "a processional psalm begun outside the gates of the temple and continued inside."[36] Jesus had quoted this psalm in his parable about the vineyard and the wicked tenants who killed the son of the master (Luke 20:9 – 19 par.).

This psalm had an important role in early Christian thinking about Jesus' life, death, and resurrection.[37] This was not surprising given the fact that the psalm had been interpreted in terms of the Messiah in the Targumic tradition that identified the "stone" as David. The citation is unmarked, but most of the members of the Sanhedrin would have been sufficiently biblically literate to recognize the quotation from Ps 118:22. The changes of the LXX text (117:22) are due to the new grammatical context.[38]

The literal meaning of this text is obvious: builders[39] who construct a building reject a stone if they regard is as unsuitable for their purposes, such as if it was cut improperly and did not fit the specific position in the wall where it was projected to fit; another builder may see that stone and recognize its potential as a "cornerstone" (κεφαλὴ γωνίας). The Greek phrase designates "the foundation stone at its farthest (foremost) corner, with which a building is begun — it firmly fixes its site and determines its direction. As a (hewn) squared stone, it had a special quality; in contrast to modern building techniques, it was not sunk deeply into the ground and thus was visible."[40]

---

35. Cf. Allen, *Psalms 101 – 150*, 125, who regards Ps 118:22 as a proverb "which expresses the transition from humiliation to honor."

36. Ibid., 124. Goldingay, *Psalms*, 3:355, cautions that it is "unwise to try to infer a liturgy that was actually taking place as the psalm unfolded."

37. Cf. Luke 19:38 par.; Luke 13:35/Matt 23:39; Acts 2:33; 5:31; 13:27, 41; 1 Pet 2:6 – 8; cf. Albl, *Testimonia Collections*, 265 – 85.

38. For details cf. Marshall, "Acts," 550; for the following cf. ibid. 550 – 51.

39. The noun "builder" (οἰκοδόμος) occurs only here in the New Testament; for the LXX cf. 4 Kgdms 12:12; 22:6; 1 Chr 14:1; 22:15; 2 Chr 34:11; Neh 4:12; Isa 58:12; Ezek 40:3; 1 Esdr 5:57; 6:4. Josephus, *Ant.* 2.66 uses οἰκοδόμος parallel to τέκτων "architect."

40. H. Krämer, "γωνία," *EDNT*, 1:268. The meaning "keystone" or "capstone" crowning the building is to be rejected, despite its popularity among interpreters since J. Jeremias (J. Jeremias, "γωνία, ἀκρογωνιαῖος, κεφαλὴ γωνίας," *TDNT*, 1:791 – 99; NIV). A "capstone" is the most important stone of

The psalmist asserts that the stone rejected by the builders was eventually discovered to be the most important stone in a new building (note that the laying of a cornerstone is the first action in the construction of a building). In the context of Ps 118:22, the statement about the rejected stone that became the cornerstone is used metaphorically, describing people who doubted that the king would be victorious in battle, who eventually, thanks to the help of Yahweh, won an overwhelming victory. Peter applies this statement to Jesus and to the Jewish leaders of Jerusalem, a fact that explains the one significant change from the LXX text — the addition of "you" (ὑμῶν) before "builders," introduced to clarify the interpretation of the psalm in terms of Jesus' rejection by the Jewish leaders. Peter asserts two main points.

(1) Jesus is the "stone" (ὁ λίθος) that was rejected with contempt[41] by the "builders" (οἱ οἰκοδόμοι), i.e., by the Jewish leaders who were responsible for "building" Israel, the nation of the people of God. This assertion corresponds to Peter's indictment in v. 10 that the Jewish leaders of Jerusalem are responsible for Jesus' crucifixion.

(2) Jesus has become the "cornerstone," which determined the location, direction, and size of the building.[42] This application has a fourfold significance. First, Jesus has been vindicated by God. Second, the Jewish leaders have been mistaken in their rejection of Jesus. Third, the fatefully misguided action of the Jewish leaders has been reversed by God, who has raised Jesus from the dead. Fourth, God is building a new building; the reference to a cornerstone suggests a monumental building —

a new (spiritual) temple in which God's presence among his people is based on Jesus' death and resurrection and is thus contingent on the acceptance of God's revelation in Jesus as Israel's Messiah.

4:12a Salvation can be found in no one else (καὶ οὐκ ἔστιν ἐν ἄλλῳ οὐδενὶ ἡ σωτηρία). Peter concludes his speech with the assertion that Jesus is the only means of salvation. The term "salvation" (σωτηρία) occurs here for the first time in Acts.[43] While the New Testament uses this noun and the verb "to save" (σῴζω) also for physical rescue and for physical and mental health and well-being, most passages use the word group to describe spiritual salvation made possible by Jesus' life, death, and resurrection as the fulfillment of the Old Testament promises, the forgiveness of sins, acquittal in the final judgment, lives transformed by the power of God's Spirit, the restoration of Israel, and life in the community of God's new people.[44] Luke's understanding of salvation is summed up in Luke 19:9 – 10, where the mission of the Son of Man is described as seeking and saving the lost, which was Jesus' mission.

In Acts, the content of "salvation" is, repeatedly, the forgiveness of sins,[45] but the term is often a general expression of salvation through faith in Jesus.[46] Here, the meaning of the word is explained by 2:40, 47: salvation means not to share the fate of "this corrupt generation" and to be added to the community of the followers of Jesus. Thus salvation is, negatively, deliverance from God's judgment and deliverance of the individual from sin and guilt and, positively, loyalty to Jesus as God's

---

an *arch*, while the most important stone of a *building* is the cornerstone; see Zmijewski, *Apostelgeschichte*, 218; Bock, *Acts*, 193; ESV, NASB, NET, NLT, NRSV, NIV.

41. Cf. BDAG, s.v. ἐξουθενέω 2, "to have no use for something as being beneath one's consideration, *reject disdainfully*." The LXX has ἀπεδοκίμασαν, which is copied in the other New Testament allusions of Ps 118:22 (LXX 117:22).

42. The size of the building is determined by the weight that

the cornerstone, and thus all stones in the first row of stones, can carry.

43. Cf. Acts 4:12; 7:25; 13:26, 47; 16:17; 27:34; cf. Luke 1:69, 71, 77; 19:9.

44. Acts 2:40, 47; 4:12; 15:1, 11; 11:14; 13:26, 47; 16:17, 30 – 31.

45. Acts 3:19, 26; 5:31; 10:43; 13:38; 22:16; 26:18.

46. Acts 4:12; 13:26; 16:17, 30 – 31.

messianic Servant, rejoicing in the reality of God's presence, transformation through the Holy Spirit, and integration into the (new) people of God. The experience of salvation is the presence of Jesus, the commencement of a new way of life in which the sinner abandons the sinful habits of the past, and the joy of table fellowship.

Peter's statement is perhaps an echo of Ps 146:3 (LXX 145:3), where God's people are asked to praise Yahweh and not to put their trust in "princes" (ἄρχοντας) or in any human beings, who cannot "save" (σωτηρία). Peter declares that Jesus, who is the Messiah, is the only source of salvation. He is the one who was crucified by the Jewish leaders, but has been vindicated by God in his resurrection from the dead and has been set as the foundation of the new "house" God is building (vv. 10 – 11).[47] Here, the emphasis is on the appropriation of salvation, which is now connected with Jesus, the Messiah and Savior.[48]

The negative formulation "in no one else" (οὐκ ἔστιν ἐν ἄλλῳ), placed at the beginning of the sentence for emphasis, expresses the exclusive nature of salvation through Jesus, the Messiah who was crucified and whom God raised from the dead.

4:12b-e "Because there is no other name in the whole world given to human beings through which we are to be saved" (οὐδὲ γὰρ ὄνομά ἐστιν ἕτερον ὑπὸ τὸν οὐρανὸν τὸ δεδομένον ἐν ἀνθρώποις ἐν ᾧ δεῖ σωθῆναι ἡμᾶς). Peter reiterates that Jesus is the only person in the world who can guarantee salvation. The causal clause (γάρ) substantiates the preceding statement with reference to the "name" of Jesus (ὄνομα), i.e., the effective reality of Jesus' life, death, and resurrection granting salvation.

The phrase "in the whole world" (ὑπὸ τὸν οὐρανόν, lit., "under heaven") expresses Peter's con-

viction that there is no other name or place — including the chief priests sitting in front of him, and including the temple and its altar, which are only a few hundred yards to the east of the assembly hall of the Sanhedrin — that could effect salvation. This statement implies "a negation of all religious systems and practices that do not lead people to Christ."[49]

The "name" that alone saves is Jesus, God's Anointed, who has been given to all "human beings" (ἄνθρωποι). The perfect passive participle translated as "given" (δεδομένον) expresses the divine origin of Jesus and of the salvation that he brings (divine passive), and the permanent nature of the significance of Jesus as the only agent of salvation (perfect).

The phrase "through which we are to be saved" (ἐν ᾧ δεῖ σωθῆναι ἡμᾶς) emphasizes that (1) Jesus is the only "place" (spherical meaning of ἐν) or agent of salvation; (2) the granting of salvation exclusively through Jesus is a necessary part of God's plan (δεῖ); (3) God is the one who grants salvation through Jesus (passive infinitive); (4) the salvation that comes through Jesus is an accomplished reality (aorist infinitive).

4:13 When they saw the boldness of Peter and John, and when they realized that they were uneducated amateurs, they were amazed, and they recognized that they had been with Jesus (θεωροῦντες δὲ τὴν τοῦ Πέτρου παρρησίαν καὶ Ἰωάννου καὶ καταλαβόμενοι ὅτι ἄνθρωποι ἀγράμματοί εἰσιν καὶ ἰδιῶται, ἐθαύμαζον ἐπεγίνωσκόν τε αὐτοὺς ὅτι σὺν τῷ Ἰησοῦ ἦσαν). Luke implies that it was not only Peter who spoke; evidently John contributed to the explanation of the origins of the healing miracle and of the significance of Jesus. As the members of the Sanhedrin were observing Peter and John

---

47. Paul clarifies what Jesus has done in order to effect salvation (cf. Rom 3:21 – 31; 5:6, 8; 6:1 – 10; 14:15; 1 Cor 1:18 – 2:5; 15:3; 2 Cor 5:14 – 6:2; Gal 1:4; 2:20).

48. Cf. Acts 2:21; 15:1, 11; 16:31.

49. Peterson, *Acts*, 192 n. 28.

speak over an extended period of time (θεωροῦντες is a present participle), they noticed their "boldness" (παρρησία).

In Greek literature this term has primarily a political meaning, describing the right and the willingness to express one's opinion freely.[50] Since this freedom of speech implies that the speaker testifies to the truth of what he says, the term denotes "candor, straightforwardness." And since such candid speech exposes a person to danger, παρρησία also has the nuance of "hardiness, courage, audacity, confidence."[51] In Acts, "boldness" describes "the *openness* of the mission proclamation" in the sense of "fearlessness, candor, and joyous confidence over against (especially Jewish) critics and adversaries."[52]

The context of v. 8 suggests that the boldness and confidence of Peter and John are the result of the influence of the Holy Spirit. They boldly confess that Jesus is the Messiah, that he was wrongfully accused and executed, that he has been vindicated through his resurrection from the dead, that his continuing power had healed the lame man, and that salvation is possible only through Jesus and through loyalty to him. Such boldness goes so far as to suggest that the Jewish elite in Jerusalem should accept the imperative implied in the exclusive link between salvation, and Jesus, the Messiah.

The reaction of the assembled Jewish leaders is not repentance and faith, but neither do they react with rage and brutality, perhaps because they find Peter's belief in a crucified Messiah absurd and not worthy to be punished; they interpret his talk about "salvation" in a less than theological sense as a reference to healing. At any rate, Luke describes their reaction as one of amazement and perplexed speechlessness.

As Peter and John spoke with complete openness and eloquent confidence, the members of the Sanhedrin realize that these two men are not priests trained to use the law in the context of their ritual duties in the temple, or wealthy aristocrats who have enjoyed the privileges of primary and perhaps secondary education, or law experts schooled in interpreting the Torah in all its minute details. They are "uneducated" (ἀγράμματοι), a term that here does not mean "illiterate"[53] but "uneducated" in terms of scribal education.[54] It is also possible that this evaluation reports the opinion of those who interrogate Peter and John and does not reflect their actual educational background, which must have been rather modest in comparison with the Sanhedrin's own level of education. The Jewish elite here regard them as "amateurs" (ἰδιῶται),[55] as people who have no standing as priestly, political, or scribal experts.

---

50. Cf. Demosthenes, *Or.* 9.3: "If I tell you several truths frankly (μετὰ παρρησίας), I do not see that you have any reason to be angry about it. You want free speech (τὴν παρρησίαν) on every other topic to be the laws for everyone in our city."

51. C. Spicq, "παρρησία," *TLNT*, 3:57.

52. H. Balz, "παρρησία," *EDNT*, 3:46; cf. BDAG, s.v. παρρησία 1, "a use of speech that conceals nothing and passes over nothing, *outspokenness, frankness, plainness*," sense 3, "a state of boldness and confidence, *courage, confidence, boldness, fearlessness*, esp. in the presence of persons of high rank" (with reference to Acts 4:13 under sense 3a, "in association with humans"). Cf. Acts 2:29; 4:13, 29, 31; 28:31; the corresponding verb παρρησιάζομαι is used in Acts 9:27, 28; 13:46; 14:3; 18:26; 19:8; 26:26.

53. Many papyri contain notations at the end of documents pointing out that someone wrote on behalf of someone else; one of the standard formulae was "I wrote for him who is illit-

erate" (ἔγραψα ὑπὲρ αὐτοῦ ἀγραμμάτου ὄντος)." The papyri and other texts thus show that ἀγράμματος had no negative connotations. Cf. Thomas J. Kraus, "'Uneducated,' 'Ignorant,' or even 'Illiterate'? Aspects and Background for an Understanding of ἀγράμματοι and ἰδιῶται in Acts 4.13," *NTS* 45 (1999): 434 – 49.

54. Barrett, *Acts*, 234. The translation "ordinary men of no education" (GNB) implies a complete lack of education, which is not plausible. Better is NLT ("they were ordinary men with no special training in the Scriptures") or The Message ("these two were laymen with no training in Scripture or formal education").

55. Cf. BDAG, s.v. ἰδιώτης 1, "a person who is relatively unskilled or inexperienced in some activity or field of knowledge, *layperson, amateur* in contrast to an expert or specialist of any kind." One should resist the temptation to "translate" ἰδιῶται as "idiots."

This evaluation is reinforced by the fact that they recognize Peter and John as having been companions of Jesus. The phrase "to be with Jesus" can be understood as a basic definition of discipleship in the presence and in the footsteps of Jesus: according to Mark 3:14, Jesus appointed the Twelve to "be with him"[56] and "to be sent out" to proclaim the good news. Here the phrase describes Peter and John as companions of Jesus during his ministry in Galilee.

4:14 When they saw the man who had been cured standing beside them, they had nothing to say in reply (τόν τε ἄνθρωπον βλέποντες σὺν αὐτοῖς ἑστῶτα τὸν τεθεραπευμένον οὐδὲν εἶχον ἀντειπεῖν). The second reaction of the Sanhedrin is speechlessness: they do not know what to "say in reply" (ἀντειπεῖν). They are in a quandary. On the one hand, they know that Peter and John had been teaching in the temple that Jesus was raised from the dead and that he is the Messiah who saves from sin and judgment, and thus they should take severe disciplinary action against them, as they had done with Jesus several weeks earlier. On the other hand, they cannot deny that an astounding miracle has taken place since they see the cured lame man standing right beside Peter and John.

This speechless perplexity fulfills what Jesus had promised his followers when he said, "I will give you words and wisdom that none of your adversaries will be able to resist or contradict [ἀντειπεῖν]" (Luke 21:15). The presence of the healed former beggar who is now standing in front of the Jewish leaders suggests that he may have been locked up with Peter and John during the previous night.

4:15 They ordered them to leave the Sanhedrin and conferred among themselves (κελεύσαντες δὲ αὐτοὺς ἔξω τοῦ συνεδρίου ἀπελθεῖν συνέβαλλον

πρὸς ἀλλήλους). After Peter and John are ordered to leave the assembly hall in which the Sanhedrin is meeting, the Jewish leaders begin to deliberate. The aorist participle (κελεύσαντες) is temporal, indicating the action that took place before the deliberations begin. Peter, John, and the healed man leave the hall, surely under guard. The imperfect of the verb translated as "conferred" (συνέβαλλον) suggests that their deliberations last an extended period of time.

4:16 They said, "What shall we do with these people? Since it is known to all people who live in Jerusalem that a manifest sign has been performed through them, and we cannot deny it" (λέγοντες· τί ποιήσωμεν τοῖς ἀνθρώποις τούτοις; ὅτι μὲν γὰρ γνωστὸν σημεῖον γέγονεν δι᾿ αὐτῶν πᾶσιν τοῖς κατοικοῦσιν Ἰερουσαλὴμ φανερὸν καὶ οὐ δυνάμεθα ἀρνεῖσθαι). In vv. 16–17 Luke provides a summary of the deliberations of the council members. Information about the discussion could have reached the Christians in Jerusalem via Nicodemus, or Joseph of Arimathea, or Saul/Paul if he was indeed a council member. Their concerns are not theological — evidently they quickly dismiss the claim of Peter and John that Jesus of Nazareth is the risen Messiah and that the salvation of the Jewish people now depends on Jesus. Their verdict, which is much more lenient than the treatment Jesus received from the Sanhedrin, contains clues about their deliberation.

If they had taken Peter and John seriously, they would have asked the question, "What shall we do?" They concerns are entirely pragmatic, however; thus they ask the question, "What shall we do with these people?" Their dilemma is obvious. They cannot deny that a miraculous healing had taken place in plain sight of hundreds if not thousands of people in the temple court, and that it had

---

56. The parallels Luke 6:13 and Matt 10:1 do not have this expression.

become the talk of the day in the city. The Sanhedrin must take into account the mood of the people who are praising God for the miraculous healing (v. 21).

Since the Torah experts of the Sanhedrin evidently do not conclude that the miraculous healing had been caused by magic or by Beelzebul, they probably accept it as caused by God.[57] They acknowledge the miracle as a "sign" (σημεῖον), but they do not know what the sign means and what it points to. They are not willing to consider the miracle as evidence for Jesus' vindication by God, nor do they know what this means for Jesus' mission and significance.

4:17 "But that it may spread no further among the people, let us threaten them not to speak in this name to anyone" (ἀλλ᾽ ἵνα μὴ ἐπὶ πλεῖον διανεμηθῇ εἰς τὸν λαὸν ἀπειλησώμεθα αὐτοῖς μηκέτι λαλεῖν ἐπὶ τῷ ὀνόματι τούτῳ μηδενὶ ἀνθρώπων). The Jewish leaders want to do something. They are intent on preventing Peter and John — and presumably the other followers of Jesus in Jerusalem — from continuing to proclaim Jesus and the resurrection. The subject of the aorist passive verb translated "it may spread" (διανεμηθῇ) is probably the publicity for the miraculous healing as a "sign" and thus the message about Jesus' life, death, resurrection, messianic identity, and signification for "salvation" — subjects that Peter and John linked during the examination and which they are probably inclined to continue doing.

The chief priests, elders, and scribes decide on a middle course between conviction and acquittal. They pronounce a ban on speaking. They decide to threaten[58] Peter and John with consequences if

they do not stop proclaiming a message that involves Jesus. The phrase "in this name" (τῷ ὀνόματι τούτῳ) communicates a distancing of the Jewish leaders from Jesus; they refer to him as "this name." They plan to announce a prohibition to speak in the name of Jesus not because they think that the apostles wrongly appeal to divine authority when they speak about Jesus, like the false prophets in the Old Testament, but because they deny that Jesus is a valid authority for beliefs about God and about Israel's salvation. Thus they want to muzzle Peter and John, removing their "freedom of speech" or "boldness" (παρρησία in v. 13), which had caused amazement. They will charge them not to speak to any human being about Jesus.

4:18 After they had called them back in, they ordered them never to speak or teach about the name of Jesus (καὶ καλέσαντες αὐτοὺς παρήγγειλαν τὸ καθόλου μὴ φθέγγεσθαι μηδὲ διδάσκειν ἐπὶ τῷ ὀνόματι τοῦ Ἰησοῦ). After Peter and John are called back into the assembly hall, they inform them about the decision of the Sanhedrin. The decision entails the order[59] "never to speak or teach about the name of Jesus." This ban has a twofold sense. First, Peter and John are "never" allowed to speak to people about Jesus under any circumstances. Second, the ban concerns both "speaking" and "teaching." The Sanhedrin prohibits both the public proclamation about Jesus as well as the regular explanation of the significance of his resurrection. Jesus and his resurrection are to be hushed up.

4:19 Peter and John said to them in reply, "You may decide yourselves whether it is right for us in the sight of God to listen to you rather than to

---

57. They concede that the miracle had happened "through them," i.e., through a higher power, which they do not label demonic, as some of them had done in the case of Jesus' miracles, cf. Luke 11:14 – 23/Mark 3:20 – 30/Matt 12:22 – 32.

58. The only other New Testament occurrence of the verb "threaten" (ἀπειλέω) is 1 Pet 2:23, which speaks of Jesus, who,

"when he suffered, he made no threats."

59. Cf. BDAG, s.v. παραγγέλλω, "to make an announcement about something that must be done, *give orders, command, instruct, direct.*" This term for "command" is common in Acts; cf. 1:4; 4:18; 5:28, 40; 10:42; 15:5; 16:18, 23; 17:30; 23:22, 30.

God" (ὁ δὲ Πέτρος καὶ Ἰωάννης ἀποκριθέντες εἶπον πρὸς αὐτούς· εἰ δίκαιόν ἐστιν ἐνώπιον τοῦ θεοῦ ὑμῶν ἀκούειν μᾶλλον ἢ τοῦ θεοῦ, κρίνατε). The apostles immediately protest against this ban. They advance two arguments, linked with the verb ἀκούω, which is used in the sense of "hear and obey." The first point is a rhetorical question that they explicitly and with emphasis ask the council members to answer themselves: Is it "right [δίκαιον] ... in the sight of God" (i.e., in view of their accountability to God and according to the judgment of God) to listen to them rather than to God? This indirect question implies that Peter and John believe that the Sanhedrin should accept the conclusion that God must be obeyed, that they have been commissioned by God to speak to other people about Jesus, that they cannot possibly accept the ban on speaking that has just been imposed, and that the prohibition to speak about Jesus opposes God's will.

As a principle, every devout Jew acknowledges the statement that in cases where there is a conflict between God's will and the wishes of human beings, God must be obeyed rather than human beings. This principle was known both in the biblical and Jewish tradition[60] as well as among pagans.[61] The apostles force the council members into the role of being judges against themselves.

Peter and John challenge the Jewish leaders to recognize that they must reverse their decision. This consequence can only be avoided if the council members question the disjunction expressed with "rather than" (μᾶλλον ἤ) and argue that God issues commands to the Jewish people through the highest authority in Israel and that Jews thus will obey God by obeying the leaders of God's people who are assembled in the Sanhedrin. It seems that the Sanhedrin is not willing to engage in such an argument, probably because they have been forced to acknowledge that the miracle of healing, which happened through Peter and John and which the whole city is talking about, is a "sign."

4:20 "We cannot help but speak of what we have seen and heard" (οὐ δυνάμεθα γὰρ ἡμεῖς ἃ εἴδαμεν καὶ ἠκούσαμεν μὴ λαλεῖν). The second argument is formulated as an explicit rejection of the Sanhedrin's decision. Peter and John insist that they have no other option but to speak about "what we have seen and heard." The double negative, translated literally as "we cannot ... not speak" (οὐ δυνάμεθα ... μὴ λαλεῖν) has the force of a strong affirmative: the apostles *must* speak about Jesus.

They have seen the risen Jesus after his death with their own eyes, and they have seen him ascend to the glory of God's presence in heaven (1:3 – 10). They are eyewitnesses of his resurrection and glory. They have heard his instructions concerning the restoration of Israel and their commission to be his witnesses in Jerusalem and Judea and to the ends of the earth (1:2 – 3, 6 – 8). The reality of Jesus, the meaning of his life and teaching, and the significance of his death, resurrection, and exaltation must not be hushed up. They cannot allow themselves to be silenced as a result of a gag order issued by human beings, when the exalted Jesus, who sits on David's eternal throne at God's right hand, has bestowed on them God's Spirit, in whose power they speak and teach.

4:21 After they had threatened them further, they let them go, since they could not find a way to punish them because of the people, since they all glorified God for what had hap-

---

60. Cf. 1 Sam 15:22 – 23; Jer 7:22 – 23; 2 Macc 7:2; 4 Macc 5:16 – 21; Josephus, *Ant.* 17.159; 18.268.

61. See the famous response of Socrates to the injunction to stop teaching his philosophy, "Men of Athens, I respect and love you, but I shall obey the god rather than you"; this statement had become a well-known dictum, cf. Plutarch, *Sept. sap. conv.* 152C (7); Epictetus, 1.30.1; Livy, 39.37. Barrett, *Acts*, 237.

pened (οἱ δὲ προσαπειλησάμενοι ἀπέλυσαν αὐτούς μηδὲν εὑρίσκοντες τὸ πῶς κολάσωνται αὐτοὺς διὰ τὸν λαόν, ὅτι πάντες ἐδόξαζον τὸν θεὸν ἐπὶ τῷ γεγονότι). Luke relates two further actions of the Sanhedrin. They issue further threats against Peter and John; they are unwilling to consider whether the followers of Jesus who had been instrumental in the miraculous healing speak for God or not. Second, they release them. They thus acquit them of charges for which they could be punished and let them leave the Sanhedrin without returning them to prison.[62]

The reason for their acquittal is the fact that their examination did not provide the council members with sufficient reasons to punish them. The options for punishment included a beating (forty lashes minus one), a monetary fine, banishment from Jerusalem, or the ultimate punishment of a death sentence. The Jewish leaders have been unable to establish a basis for a criminal indictment and for legally justifiable punishment.

Luke then adds a subjective reason for acquittal. The Jewish leaders surely would have liked to punish Peter and John. While the proclamation of Jesus' resurrection may not be a teaching that could be prosecuted criminally, publicly proclaiming Jesus as the Messiah could well be construed as a seduction of the people, a charge they could take to the Roman governor and ask for a felony indictment for political sedition. But the reaction of the citizens of Jerusalem to the miraculous healing has made this impossible. The people who had heard of the miracle — perhaps the majority of the citizens in Jerusalem — credited God for the miracle of the healing of the lame man who used to beg at the Beautiful Gate. The Jewish leaders are afraid of the people and thus do not dare punish the apostles.

4:22 For the man on whom this sign of healing had been performed was over forty years old (ἐτῶν γὰρ ἦν πλειόνων τεσσεράκοντα ὁ ἄνθρωπος ἐφ᾽ ὃν γεγόνει τὸ σημεῖον τοῦτο τῆς ἰάσεως). Luke ends his report with a statement that underscores both the magnitude of the miracle and the dilemma that the Jewish leaders face on account of the reality of the miracle. The lame man was over forty years old. The genitive "of healing" (ἰάσεως) is epexegetical: the healing was a "sign" (σημεῖον) of the reality of the power of Jesus, who was crucified but who had been raised from the dead.

Theology in Application

To apply this passage, we must keep in mind the main idea: a miracle that happened in the name of Jesus, which led to the proclamation of Jesus as the Messiah and Savior and to arrest, imprisonment, and interrogation of Peter and John, which in turn provides an opportunity for explaining the identity and the significance of Jesus. The main points of this section are the authority to proclaim the gospel, the obligation to proclaim the gospel, the possibility of opposition and persecution, and the opportunity for further witness.

---

62. Cf. BDAG, s.v. ἀπολύω 1, "as legal term, to grant acquittal, *set free, release, pardon*," sense 3, "to permit or cause someone to leave a particular location *let go, send away, dismiss*."

The Authority to Proclaim the Gospel

The proclamation of the gospel of Jesus Christ is a right. Christians have the right to preach the gospel of Jesus, the crucified, risen, and exalted Messiah and Savior. This means, negatively, that the proclamation of the gospel does not constitute an activity that would warrant criminal prosecution (v. 21). This means, positively, that the proclamation of the gospel is an activity that has been authorized by "the name of Jesus Christ" (vv. 7, 10, 12; cf. 1:8; 3:6, 16), who authenticates the witness of his preachers and teachers through "signs" (vv. 16, 22) and through courageous proclamation empowered by the Holy Spirit (v. 8).

The Obligation to Proclaim the Gospel

The proclamation of the gospel of Jesus Christ is a duty. Peter and John assert that they are obligated to speak about Jesus in public and in private. Believers have been commissioned by Jesus Christ to proclaim the gospel locally and to the ends of the earth (1:8), and they must obey that calling. They need to obey Jesus, who commanded them to speak as his witnesses; thus, they cannot obey those who command them to be quiet. Believers have seen the reality of the risen Jesus Christ, the reality of the transforming power of the Holy Spirit, and thus the reality of God's salvation, and they must speak of what they have seen. They have heard the gospel, understood and accepted it, and are under obligation to share the good news of God's salvation through Jesus Christ with others (v. 20).

Most importantly, the obligation to proclaim the gospel of Jesus Christ is grounded in the fact that Jesus is the only Savior in the entire world (v. 12). There are no other paths to salvation. Many religions allow for a variety of journeys that can be traveled to achieve peace and salvation. This was true in antiquity, this was true in the Middle Ages, and it is true today. Some evangelical voices have suggested that v. 12 need not be interpreted in an exclusive sense.[63] It misses the point to claim that the text expresses the incomparable power of the name of Jesus that saves people who hear and who respond, but does not comment on the fate of the Gentiles. While this is correct on the surface of the text, it is obvious that Peter connects salvation, including salvation in God's final judgment, to confessing faith in Jesus Christ.

The Possibility of Opposition and Persecution

Christians who witness to others always face the possibility of opposition. It was not the healing miracle in itself, but the public explanation of the miracle linked with an exposition of the significance of Jesus that got Peter and John arrested, imprisoned,

---

63. Cf. Clark H. Pinnock, "Acts 4:12 — No Other Name under Heaven," in *Through No Fault of Their Own? The Fate of Those Who Have Never Heard* (ed. W. V. Crockett and J. G. Sigountos; Grand Rapids: Baker, 1991), 107 – 15.

and interrogated by the highest Jewish court. Opposition and persecution often increase. The implicit protest in v. 12 against other offers of salvation prompted more opposition and persecution. Peter's rejection of the Sanhedrin's ban on speaking led to further arrests and imprisonments (5:17 – 42; 12:3 – 19; cf. the imprisonments of Paul, 16:19 – 24; 21:33 – 28:31).

Jesus' followers continue the ministry of Jesus as his witnesses, and it is not surprising that they share the fate of the one who was rejected, imprisoned, interrogated, and executed. What Jesus said as a general truth applies specifically here as well, "The student is not above the teacher, but everyone who is fully trained will be like their teacher" (Luke 6:40); and, "If they persecuted me, they will persecute you also" (John 15:20).

The opposition that authentic Christians who witness to Jesus Christ suffer may not be the kind of persecution that entails arrests, trials, and imprisonment. But even in free and open democracies, Christians can easily suffer ostracism and discrimination if they do not "go with the flow," if they are not willing to cut corners, to lie for their boss, or to arrange bribes.

The Opportunity for Further Witness

Christians who face opposition oppose governmental authorities who oppose God. Peter and John emphasize that if there is a conflict between the Word of God and a command of governmental authorities, God's people obey God's Word rather that word of human beings. While such opposition may result in prolonged imprisonment and even martyrdom, Christians have no choice but to obey the clear will of God. Martin Luther's refusal to abandon his convictions concerning the significance of Jesus Christ for salvation (only faith in Jesus Christ saves, rather than praying to the saints or relying on indulgences) and concerning the authority of Scripture (which trumps the authority of church councils and of the pope) is perhaps the most famous, history-changing example.

CHAPTER 10

Acts 4:23–31

Literary Context

Luke's account of Peter's early ministry in 3:1–4:31 told of the healing of a lame man begging at the Beautiful Gate of the temple (3:1–10), of Peter's speech in Solomon's Portico (3:11–26), of the arrest of Peter and John by the Jewish authorities (4:1–4), and of their defense before the Sanhedrin (4:5–22). The fifth incident in this episode is the prayer of the believers in Jerusalem (4:23–31).

The courage of Peter and John as they explained with Spirit-inspired boldness the significance of Jesus the Messiah for the miracle and for salvation (vv. 8, 14) links that incident with this prayer of the believers. They pray not for their own personal safety, but for complete boldness to speak the word of God despite the threats spoken by the Jewish leaders.

Main Idea

The prayer of the believers in Jerusalem is a prayer of thanksgiving for the fulfillment of God's promises, a prayer of praise for God's sovereignty and wisdom, and a prayer of petition for boldness and courage in their efforts to proclaim the gospel as well as for healings and signs and wonders to confirm their message.

Translation

(See next page.)

Acts 4:23 – 31

23a	Setting: Time	After they were released,
b	Action	**they returned to their friends**
c	Action	and **reported**
d	Indirect speech	all that the chief priests and elders had said to them.
24a	Setting: Time	When they heard this,
b	Action	**they raised their voices unanimously to God**
c	Action (restatement)	and **prayed,**
d	Address	"Sovereign Lord,
e	Identification	*who made the heaven and*
	(quotation of OT)	
f	List	*the earth and*
g	List	*the sea and*
h	List	*everything in them,*
25a	Assertion	*it is you who spoke*
b	Agency	*by the Holy Spirit*
c	Agency	*through the mouth of our father David, your servant,*
d	Question/Accusation	*'Why have nations behaved arrogantly,*
e	Question/Accusation	*and why have peoples fixed their minds on vain things?*
26a	Assertion	*The kings of the earth have appeared with hostile intent,*
b	Restatement	*and the rulers have gathered together against the Lord and*
c	Identification	*against his Messiah.'*
		(Ps 2:1-2)
27a	Event (review of history):	*For truly, in this very city,*
	Place	
b	Protagonist	*Herod and*
c	Protagonist	*Pontius Pilate, …*
d	Association	*with the Gentiles and*
e	Association	*the peoples of Israel,*
f	Event	*… gathered together*
	Purpose	*against your holy Servant Jesus,*
g	Identification	*whom you have anointed,*
28a	Fulfillment	*to do what your power and*
b	Fulfillment	*your plan*
c	Fulfillment	*had decided beforehand should happen.*
29a	Address	*And now, Lord,*
b	Petition	*look at their threats*
c	Petition	*and allow your slaves to speak your word,*
d	Manner	*with all boldness*
30a	Petition	*as you stretch out your hand*
b	Purpose	*to heal,*
c	Purpose	*and as signs and wonders happen*
d	Agency	*through the name of your holy Servant Jesus."*
31a	Setting: Time	When they had prayed,
b	Event	**the place in which they were gathered was shaken;**
c	Event	and **they were all filled with the Holy Spirit,**
d	Action	and **they continued to speak the word of God**
e	Manner	with boldness.

Structure and Literary Form

This passage is clearly linked with the preceding incident (vv. 23, 29 – 30), but it forms a distinct unit. Luke relates an incident that takes place as the church gathered in Jerusalem, with the focus on a prayer (quoted verbatim in vv. 24 – 30). The narrative is composed of three parts.

First, in vv. 23 – 24c Peter and John report back to the believers after their release from the Sanhedrin, which had issued a ban on speaking about Jesus. Upon learning of the threats given by the Jewish leaders intent on stopping them from preaching and teaching about Jesus, the believers turn to God in prayer.

Second, Luke provides a summary of the content of the believers' prayer (vv. 24d – 30). The prayer consists of two parts. (1) In the first part, the believers acknowledge God's sovereign power (vv. 24d – 28). The introductory invocation addresses God as the Creator of the heaven, the earth, and the sea, appealing to his sovereign power (v. 24d-h). A second invocation refers to God as the author of David's words speaking through the Holy Spirit (v. 25a-c). Then in vv. 25d – 28 come the quotation and interpretation of Ps 2:1 – 2; the quotation follows the text of the LXX, which is a faithful translation of the Hebrew text. The interpretation in vv. 27 – 28 focuses on the cooperation of Herod and Pilate, who represent the people of Israel and the Gentiles respectively, and who have Jesus killed — an event that was, however, the plan of God.

(2) The second part of the prayer is the petition (vv. 29 – 30). The believers call on God to take notice of the threats issued by the Sanhedrin and to grant the believers boldness in preaching and proclamation and to grant them miracles to confirm their preaching.

Third, Luke records God's answer to the prayer of the Jerusalem believers (v. 31). The building in which the Christians are assembled shakes, the believers are filled with the Holy Spirit, and they continue to preach the word of God with boldness, unafraid of the threats of the Jewish leaders.

This is the second prayer quoted in Acts (cf. 1:24 – 25). It represents the kind of prayer the Jerusalem believers offered during the regular prayer times in the temple and in private homes (2:42). This communal prayer underscores the focus and emphasis of the prayers of the believers: they integrate Old Testament Scripture in their prayers, they read the Scriptures in the light of the life and death of Jesus, they focus on Jesus' death, and they pray for courage and boldness to continue the task Jesus had given to the church and her apostles, namely, to be witnesses for Jesus and his resurrection. There are several verbal connections between the prayer in vv. 24 – 30 and Hezekiah's prayer in Isa 37:16 – 20 (cf. 2 Chr 20:10 – 11).[1]

---

1. Cf. Marshall, "Acts," 551; there is no conclusive evidence to warrant the conclusion that Hezekiah's prayer "served as Luke's model" (Fitzmyer, *Acts*, 306). Zmijewski, *Apostelgeschichte*, 224, compares also with other prayers in the Old Testament: 1 Chr 17:16 – 27; 2 Chr 20:6 – 12; Neh 9:6 – 37; Est 4:16; Jonah 4:2 – 3; cf. Tob 3:2 – 6; 8:5 – 7; 2 Macc 15:22 – 24; 3 Macc 6:2 – 15.

Exegetical Outline

→ **I. The Prayer of the Jerusalem Christians (4:23 – 31)**

    A. The Occasion of the Prayer of the Jerusalem Believers (4:23 – 24c)

        1. The return of Peter and John to their fellow believers (4:23a-b)

        2. The report of the apostles about their interrogation by the Sanhedrin (4:23c-d)

        3. The reaction of the believers, who turn to God in prayer (4:24a-c)

    B. The Prayer (4:24d – 30)

        1. Acknowledgment of God's sovereign power (4:24d – 28)

            a. Invocation of God the Creator, with words from Ps 146:6 (4:24d-h)

            b. Invocation of God as the author of David's words (4:25a-c)

            c. Quotation of Ps 2:1 – 2 (4:25d – 26)

            d. Interpretation of Ps 2:1 – 2 regarding Jesus, Herod, and Pilate (4:27 – 28)

        2. Petition (4:29 – 30)

            a. Invocation of God as Lord (4:29a)

            b. Petition that God may take notice (4:29b)

            c. Petition to be given boldness in their preaching and proclamation (4:29c-d)

            d. Petition to be granted miracles, which give credit to their preaching (4:30)

    C. The Answer to the Prayer (4:31)

        1. The shaking of the building in which the believers are assembled (4:31a-b)

        2. The filling with the Holy Spirit (4:31c)

        3. The continued proclamation of the gospel (4:31d-e)

Explanation of the Text

4:23 After they were released, they returned to their friends and reported all that the chief priests and elders had said to them (ἀπολυθέντες δὲ ἦλθον πρὸς τοὺς ἰδίους καὶ ἀπήγγειλαν ὅσα πρὸς αὐτοὺς οἱ ἀρχιερεῖς καὶ οἱ πρεσβύτεροι εἶπαν). Peter and John return to their friends after they are released and report what happened in the interrogation by the Sanhedrin. The aorist passive participle translated as "after they were released" (ἀπολυθέντες) is temporal and describes the prior action of the Jewish leaders before the two apostles

return to their fellow believers: the leaders permitted them to leave (cf. v. 21).

Peter and John then go "to their friends" (πρὸς τοὺς ἰδίους; lit., "to their own"), a phrase usually interpreted in terms of the community of believers in Jerusalem.[2] Many interpreters assume that what Luke refers to is not the entire church, which had thousands of Jewish believers by now, but a smaller group of believers who met in a room in a private house.[3] However, if the Spirit-inspired boldness of Peter and John characterized larger numbers of

---

2. Some scholars interpret the phrase in terms of the inner circle of the other apostles, i.e., the Twelve; cf. Johnson, *Acts*, 84, 90; Urban C. von Wahlde, "Acts 4,24 – 31: The Prayer of the Apostles in Response to the Persecution of Peter and John; and Its Consequences," *Bib* 77 (1996): 237 – 44, 237.

3. Haenchen, *Acts*, 226; Pesch, *Apostelgeschichte*, 1:175; cf. Bock, *Acts*, 203. Barrett, *Acts*, 242 – 43, suggests a reference "primarily" to the apostles as "leaders in speech and action" without ruling out that "other members of the church" prayed for and with them.

the Jerusalem believers, it is not impossible that the meeting place of these "friends," which Luke does not specify, was Solomon's Portico, where a large number of believers may have continued to assemble at the time of prayer despite the arrest of Peter and John. The nominalized adjective (οἱ ἴδιοι) denotes persons associated with a larger entity and documents the familial relationship of the believers.

Luke relates with two aorists that Peter and Paul report what the chief priests and the elders (see on v. 5) had said. The following prayer suggests that the focus of that report was on the threats that had been made (vv. 17, 21; cf. v. 29), on the ban on speaking (v. 18; cf. v. 29), and on the necessity of continuing to proclaim the gospel (v. 29). While both the report and the prayer would certainly have focused on the danger that the action of the Sanhedrin presented for the believers, it is reasonable to assume that Peter and John gave a full report, including the facts and details of the interrogatory questions and their responses.

4:24 When they heard this, they raised their voices unanimously to God and prayed, "Sovereign Lord, who made the heaven and the earth and the sea and everything in them" (οἱ δὲ ἀκούσαντες ὁμοθυμαδὸν ἦραν φωνὴν πρὸς τὸν θεὸν καὶ εἶπαν· δέσποτα, σὺ ὁ ποιήσας τὸν οὐρανὸν καὶ τὴν γῆν καὶ τὴν θάλασσαν καὶ πάντα τὰ ἐν αὐτοῖς). The believers react with a prayer in which they integrate the most recent events into what Scripture says about opposition to God and his Anointed and in which they ask for boldness to continue the ministry of proclaiming Jesus as the Messiah. They

raise their voices "unanimously" (ὁμοθυμαδόν, see on 1:14), using one voice (φωνήν, singular). In view of Peter's speech before the Sanhedrin (see 4:8 – 12), Peter could be the one who formulated the prayer in vv. 24 – 30, with the other believers expressing their assent with a responsory "Amen."

The believers begin their prayer by invoking God as the Creator of heaven and earth. God is "Sovereign Lord" (δεσπότης),[4] i.e., the omnipotent ruler whose authority extends over all.[5] He is sovereign because he is the Creator of all visible and invisible realities — heaven, earth, and sea, and everything in them (i.e., all heavenly, human, and animal creatures).

The phrase that describes God's activity as Creator (ὁ ποιήσας) corresponds to Ps 146:6 (LXX 145:6). This individual psalm praises Yahweh as Creator of the world, before whom foreign rulers are powerless in the long run and who providentially cares for his people, particularly those who suffer afflictions. As Peter and John have been threatened by the rulers of the Jewish people, the psalm puts their plight in perspective, assuring them of God's sovereign control over these rulers and over future events that they attempt to control.

4:25 It is you who spoke by the Holy Spirit through the mouth of our father David, your servant, 'Why have nations behaved arrogantly, and why have peoples fixed their minds on vain things?' (ὁ τοῦ πατρὸς ἡμῶν διὰ πνεύματος ἁγίου στόματος Δαυὶδ παιδός σου εἰπών· ἱνατί ἐφρύαξαν ἔθνη καὶ λαοὶ ἐμελέτησαν κενά;). God's intervention in history is formulated in a second invocation. The syntax of the participial clause is difficult, but

---

4. Vocative δέσποτα; cf. BDAG, s.v. δεσπότης 1, "one who has legal control and authority over persons, such as subjects or slaves, *lord, master;*" cf. K. H. Rengstorf, "δεσπότης," *TDNT,* 2:44 – 49. While the English word "despot" derives from this Greek term, it has exclusively negative connotations, which is not the case regarding the Greek term.

5. This word often occurs in the LXX (never in the Psalms!), particularly in the Apocrypha, written in Greek; used in prayer in Jer 4:10; Dan 9:8; Jdt 9:12; 2 Macc 15:22. In Josephus, δέσποτα is the most common form of addressing God in prayer (cf. the prayer of Simeon in Luke 2:29 and the prayer of the martyrs in Rev 6:10).

the meaning is sufficiently clear. First, the words of Scripture from Ps 2:1 – 2, quoted in vv. 25d – 26, were spoken by David, who is described as "our father" (τοῦ πατρὸς ἡμῶν), i.e., one of the ancestors of the Jewish people, and as God's "servant" (παιδός σου),[6] i.e., Israel's king who obeyed God. Psalm 2 is not ascribed to David in either the Hebrew or the Greek text; Davidic authorship is assumed in the context of a general attribution of the Psalter to David in Jewish tradition (see on 2:30).

Second, the words of David are the words of God (δέσποτα, σύ … ὁ … εἰπών), which he spoke "by the Holy Spirit" (διὰ πνεύματος ἁγίου). The words of Scripture are the product of God's revelation, who speaks through his Spirit, using human authors; in other words, such words are the very words of God (see on 1:16).

These words from Ps 2:1 – 2 allow the Jerusalem believers to interpret the hostility of the Jewish leaders who have threatened the apostles and who have issued a ban on proclaiming the good news of Jesus, the Messiah. That opposition of these leaders repeats the hostility that both Jewish and pagan rulers turned against Jesus, God's anointed Servant. This psalm can be interpreted in three different contexts — the context of the original composition, the context of the canon of the Hebrew Scriptures, and the context of its use in the New Testament.[7]

Psalm 2 is frequently used in the New Testament as a text that speaks of the Messiah.[8] The psalm is a royal psalm, probably composed for the coronation of a Davidic king (note the parallels between Ps 2 and Nathan's oracle in 2 Sam 7:8 – 16).[9] In the psalm, God promises the king victory over his enemies who plot against the (new) ruler.

In the original context, the opening two lines of Ps 2 pose a rhetorical question that stresses that the attack of hostile nations is futile. The rhetorical question "Why?" (ἱνατί) expresses not lament but a conviction concerning the arrogant and vain designs of hostile peoples. The two aorist indicatives describe the hostility as arrogant, haughty, insolent behavior, and their schemes are "vain," that is, "without content, without any basis, without truth, without power."[10]

4:26 "The kings of the earth have appeared with hostile intent, and the rulers have gathered together against the Lord and against his Messiah" (παρέστησαν οἱ βασιλεῖς τῆς γῆς καὶ οἱ ἄρχοντες συνήχθησαν ἐπὶ τὸ αὐτὸ κατὰ τοῦ κυρίου καὶ κατὰ τοῦ χριστοῦ αὐτοῦ). The hostility of the nations is specified as that of "the kings of the earth" and of "the rulers." These rulers have assembled together to plot against Yahweh and his Messiah. In the original context, the target of the hostile schemes of the kings and rulers is Yahweh (κατὰ τοῦ κυρίου) and his anointed king (κατὰ τοῦ χριστοῦ αὐτοῦ). In view of Yahweh's sovereign and universal power, the scheming of these kings and rulers is extraordinarily stupid,[11] for Yahweh is the Creator of the heavens and the earth, who will not allow his anointed king to be vanquished.

The language of the psalm, unless interpreted in a hyperbolic sense, seems excessive for the Davidic kings, including David and Solomon, who ruled over the neighboring peoples. The reference to "the kings of the earth" suggests not a local rebellion

---

6. Cf. 2 Sam 3:18; 1 Kgs 11:34; Ps 89:3, 20; cf. Luke 1:69.

7. For the following cf. Marshall, "Acts," 552 – 53.

8. Ps 2:1 – 2 is quoted in Acts 4:25d – 26; Ps 2:7 in Acts 13:33; Heb 1:5; 5:5; and Ps 2:7 is alluded to in Luke 3:22; and Ps 2:9 in Rev 2:27; 12:5; 19:15. On the use of Ps 2 in Acts 4, cf. Miura, *David in Luke-Acts*, 160 – 66.

9. Cf. Peter C. Craigie, *Psalms 1 – 50* (WBC 19; Dallas: Word, 1983), 64; Goldingay, *Psalms*, 1:96, is more cautious.

10. BDAG, s.v. κενός 2a; Danker relates the use of the term in v. 25 to κενός 3, "to being without purpose or result, *in vain*."

11. Goldingay, *Psalms*, 1:98.

but a serious threat supported by the whole world. Note that "the Israelites who used this psalm were never a superpower; for most of their history they were a vassal state or a province under some imperial power. The psalm promises that this will not always be how things are."[12]

This, then, raises the question, "To whom does this psalm belong, with its warnings and promises, when there is no individual anointed king to speak it? One possibility is that it belongs to a future king such as one promised in passages like Isa 9:2 – 7 [1 – 6]; 11:1 – 9."[13] Read in this context, the psalm expresses the assurance that the schemes and attacks of the kings and rulers of the world against God and his Messiah are doomed to failure.

4:27   For truly, in this very city, Herod and Pontius Pilate, with the Gentiles and the peoples of Israel, gathered together against your holy Servant Jesus, whom you have anointed (συνήχθησαν γὰρ ἐπ᾽ ἀληθείας ἐν τῇ πόλει ταύτῃ ἐπὶ τὸν ἅγιον παῖδά σου Ἰησοῦν ὃν ἔχρισας, Ἡρῴδης τε καὶ Πόντιος Πιλᾶτος σὺν ἔθνεσιν καὶ λαοῖς Ἰσραήλ). The prayer interprets Psalm 2 in terms of a review of history — the recent history of Herod and Pontius Pilate as those rulers who conspired against Jesus. The phrase "truly" (ἐπ᾽ ἀληθείας) affirms the certainty of what follows. First, there was an assembling of several hostile forces, whose machinations are described with the same verb (συνήχθησαν) that described the "gathering" of the rulers against God and his Anointed One in v. 26.

Second, the conspiracy happened "in this city" (ἐν τῇ πόλει ταύτῃ), i.e., in Jerusalem, the center of Jewish life and faith.

Third, the conspiracy involved Herod and Pontius Pilate. Herod is Herod Antipas, the younger son of Herod I, who became ruler of Galilee and Perea after the death of his father in 4 BC as tetrarch who controlled, by courtesy of Rome, the region in which both John the Baptist and Jesus were active.[14] Luke relates in his gospel that Herod Antipas plotted to kill Jesus, who then moved to another region after being warned by sympathizing Pharisees. Jesus informed the king in a communiqué sent through some Pharisees that he planned to continue his activity, that he would not be intimidated, and that a prophet could die only in Jerusalem (Luke 13:31 – 33). Herod Antipas next encountered Jesus when Pilate interrupted the trial and sent Jesus to the Jewish ruler, who was in Jerusalem for the Feast of Passover (Luke 23:6 – 12, 15). Jesus remained silent during the interrogation, which eventually prompted Antipas to demonstrate his contempt by having his soldiers dress Jesus in a royal robe. Thus, even though his role in Jesus' conviction was limited, he was complicit in Jesus' death.

Pontius Pilate is the Roman prefect (see on 3:13) who tried to release Jesus but who eventually condemned him to death by crucifixion (cf. Luke 23:4, 14 – 15, 22). Both rulers are linked with those whom they represent. Herod Antipas is linked with the "peoples" of Ps 2:1 (λαοί)[15] and thus with the "peoples of Israel" (σὺν ... λαοῖς Ἰσραήλ). For Josephus, King Herod I (and thus his family), who came from Idumean background, was a half-Jew (*Ant.* 14.403). Pilate is linked with "the Gentiles" or "nations" mentioned in Ps 2:1 (ἔθνη), who with his

---

12. Goldingay, *Psalms*, 1:104; the following quotation ibid.

13. Ps 1:1 is quoted in 4Q174 III, 14 (see on 2:30 for the messianic context of 4Q174).

14. Cf. Harold W. Hoehner, *Herod Antipas* (SNTSMS 17; Cambridge: Cambridge Univ. Press, 1972); Morten Hørning Jensen, *Herod Antipas in Galilee: The Literary and Archaeological Sources on the Reign of Herod Antipas and Its Socio-*

Economic Impact on Galilee (WUNT 2/215; Tübingen: Mohr Siebeck, 2006).

15. The plural λαοί comes from Ps 2:1, which Luke evidently did not change into a singular (as the Western text does). Johnson, *Acts*, 85, is certainly correct to say that "the plural also enables Luke to involve *individual* Jews in the death of Jesus."

soldiers carried out the crucifixion. Jesus' execution on the cross is not mentioned, but it is clearly the point of reference since the one meeting between Herod Antipas and Pontius Pilate that Luke relates took place during Jesus' trial, which ended with his crucifixion.

Fourth, the conspiracy of Herod Antipas and Pontius Pilate was directed against Jesus, God's "holy Servant" (ἐπὶ τὸν ἅγιον παῖδα), who is the "Messiah." Just as David, God's servant (v. 25), was attacked by kings and rulers and nations, so Jesus, who is also God's Servant, suffered the hostility of rulers and nations. Seen in the context of Isa 53, the "Servant" is the one who obeys God, suffers, dies, and is eventually vindicated (see on 3:13). The verb of the relative clause "whom you have anointed" (ὃν ἔχρισας) picks up v. 26 ("Messiah," τοῦ χριστοῦ αὐτοῦ) and affirms that Jesus had been anointed and thus commissioned to build a new "house" for the (new) people of God who have been granted salvation through faith in him (vv. 11 – 12). He is "holy" (ἅγιος) because he has been set apart by God to accomplish his purposes.

4:28 To do what your power and your plan had decided beforehand should happen (ποιῆσαι ὅσα ἡ χείρ σου καὶ ἡ βουλή σου προώρισεν γενέσθαι). The Jerusalem believers affirm in this final statement of the first part of the prayer that God had worked out his plan in the history of the opposition to Jesus, which they have just reviewed. The aorist infinitive "to do" (ποιῆσαι) expresses the purpose God accomplished with the conspiracy of Herod Antipas and Pontius Pilate. Jesus' death was an event that happened as the result of what God's

"power" (ἡ χείρ σου, lit., "your hand")[16] and "plan" (ἡ βουλή σου) had decided beforehand.

The aorist indicative verb translated as "decided beforehand" (προώρισεν) refers to what God had decided before it happened. God had predetermined Jesus' death.[17] Herod Antipas and Pilate were instruments in God's hand. The believers assert that the psalm had announced in the past what God had decided should take place regarding Jesus' death by crucifixion.

4:29 And now, Lord, look at their threats and allow your slaves to speak your word with all boldness (καὶ τὰ νῦν, κύριε, ἔπιδε ἐπὶ τὰς ἀπειλὰς αὐτῶν καὶ δὸς τοῖς δούλοις σου μετὰ παρρησίας πάσης λαλεῖν τὸν λόγον σου). In the second part of the prayer, the Jerusalem believers formulate three petitions. The phrase "and now" introduces the petitions they bring before God. Although a phrase that Luke often uses,[18] the adverb "now" (νῦν) signals the interface between the events of the past (the time of David, God's servant) and the events of the present (the interrogation and execution of Jesus, God's Servant), insofar as the Jewish leaders had interrogated Peter and John perhaps an hour or two earlier, threatening them with severe consequences if they continued to speak about Jesus.

The first petition of the Jerusalem believers asks God to look at the threats (cf. vv. 17, 21) that the Jewish leaders had uttered against Peter and John and all the believers in Jerusalem. The petition is formulated with a rare Greek term for "look" (ἔπιδε)[19] that denotes God's concern for their situation. The implication of this petition is that when

---

16. Cf. 4:30; 7:50; 11:21; 13:11. The anthropomorphic language reflects Old Testament usage and denotes, here, power and control.

17. Barrett, *Acts*, 248, is correct to point out that the verb προορίζω does not refer to "a general determinism" but "the special disclosures of God's purpose" in the events of Jesus' trial and death.

18. Cf. Acts 4:29; 5:38; 17:30; 20:32; cf. 24:25; 27:22.

19. Cf. BDAG, s.v. ἐπεῖδον, "to fix one's glance upon, *look at, concern oneself with;*" the term occurs in the New Testament only here and in Luke 1:25. In Greek texts, the verb is often used in connection with the gods, cf. LSJ, s.v. ἐπεῖδον 2.

God turns his attention to the threats of the Sanhedrin, he will intervene on their behalf.

The Jerusalem believers imply, by their use of Ps 2:1 – 2, that the conspiracy of Herod Antipas and Pontius Pilate, of the Gentile nations and the Jewish people, has been defeated, as God's plan involved not only Jesus' death, but also his resurrection and exaltation. The Jewish leaders who had interrogated Peter and John had been implicated in Jesus' interrogation, conviction, and execution (Acts 4:10e). God, however, raised Jesus from the dead (v. 10f), who is thus the cornerstone of the new "house" that God is building (v. 11), in which salvation is dependent entirely and exclusively on Jesus and on faith in him (v. 12).

However, the believers do not use the wording of Psalm 2 for their petitions. They do not pray that God may laugh at the Jewish leaders (cf. Ps 2:4), or terrify them with his wrath (Ps 2:5), or break them with an iron rod or dash them in pieces like a potter's vessel (Ps 2:9) so that they perish (Ps 2:12). They do not pray that the threats of the Sanhedrin may be revoked or may prove harmless. They do not pray that they may be spared opposition, suffering, or execution. They are God's "slaves" (δοῦλοι in v. 29), whose "condition" is entirely in the hand of their sovereign master (v. 24). The believers ask God to be concerned about the threats so that they can face the opposition of the Jewish leaders with courageous faithfulness to their calling: to be witnesses of Jesus and of his resurrection in Jerusalem and Judea and beyond.

The second petition of the Jerusalem believers asks God to grant them the courage to continue to preach and teach the gospel. The petition is formulated with an aorist imperative (δός): "grant" or "allow" us to speak. The apostles in particular and the believers more generally are eager to continue to "speak" (λαλεῖν) about the good news of the significance of the life, death, resurrection, and exaltation of Jesus, who is God's messianic Servant and Savior. The message they preach and teach is God's word. The versatile term translated "word" (λόγος) — it can denote verbal communication, a statement, a message, an assertion, a declaration, a speech, a subject — is frequently used in Acts for the word from God (and about God) and for the word about Jesus (and from Jesus) that communicates publicly and privately the good news of forgiveness of sins and salvation through Jesus, the Messiah.[20]

The believers pray that God will allow them to share the gospel "with all boldness" (μετὰ παρρησίας πάσης; see on 4:13), i.e., with the confident courage that had astonished the Jewish leaders in the Sanhedrin when they realized that Peter and John not only refused to express their convictions in a manner that might be more amenable to general acceptance, but instead explicitly proclaimed their conviction that those leaders had killed Jesus, God's Messiah, that Jesus had risen from the dead, and that he is erecting a new "building" that is the only "place" where God grants salvation. The believers, including the apostles, pray that God will grant them the same courageous boldness in the days, weeks, and months ahead to preach and teach the gospel with clarity, without reservations or modifications, despite the threats and despite the ban on speaking that had been issued. This boldness and confidence are a gift of God and thus more than the courage of the strong personalities of pioneers.

The believers call themselves "slaves" (δοῦλοι). The usual translation as "servant" is a euphemism and historically anachronistic as well as linguistically problematic — there are other Greek terms for

---

20. Cf. 2:41; 4:29, 31; 6:2, 7; 8:14, 25; 11:1; 12:24; 13:5, 7, 44, 46, 48, 49; 15:35, 36; 16:32; 17:13; 18:11; 19:10, 20.

"servant." The Greek term δοῦλος denotes a "male slave as an entity in a socio-economic context" and, as an extension of this meaning, "one who is solely committed to another, *slave, subject*."[21] This self-designation as "slaves" agrees with the invocation of God as "sovereign Lord" (δεσπότης) in v. 24. As used by Christian believers, "slave" occurs only here in Acts for believers[22] but is used frequently throughout the New Testament.[23] As God's subjects the apostles and the other believers are fully committed to doing God's will as stated in the commission given to the Twelve, appointed as Jesus' witnesses in Jerusalem, in Judea, in Samaria, and to the ends of the earth (1:8).

4:30 "As you stretch out your hand to heal, and as signs and wonders happen through the name of your holy Servant Jesus" (ἐν τῷ τὴν χεῖρά σου ἐκτείνειν σε εἰς ἴασιν καὶ σημεῖα καὶ τέρατα γίνεσθαι διὰ τοῦ ὀνόματος τοῦ ἁγίου παιδός σου Ἰησοῦ). This third petition asks God to cause healings and signs and wonders to happen.[24] The believers ask God that as he looks at the threats of the Sanhedrin and grants them boldness to proclaim the good news of Jesus, he causes healings to take place and signs and wonders to happen.

The first part of this petition asks God to demonstrate his power ("hand," χεῖρ, see v. 28) in "heal-ing" (ἴασις). The reference to God's "stretching out his hand" (τὴν χεῖρά σου ἐκτείνειν) occurs only here in the New Testament, but it is used repeatedly in the Old Testament.[25] The healing of the lame man begging at the Beautiful Gate (3:1 – 10) had given Peter and John the opportunity to explain the significance of Jesus, the Messiah, in Solomon's Portico to a large crowd of Jewish listeners (3:11 – 26) and, after a night in prison, to the Jewish leaders assembled in the Sanhedrin (4:1 – 22). They pray for further healings to happen, which will lead to further opportunities to proclaim the good news of Jesus, the Messiah and Savior.

The reference to the "hand of God" implies that the power to do miracles is always God's power, never that of the apostles. The reference to healings in the context of a petition in prayer to the sovereign Lord who made the heavens and the earth (v. 24) means that it is God and God alone who determines whether miraculous healings will take place. Luke relates several healing miracles in Acts (cf. 5:15 – 16; 8:7; 9:33 – 34; 14:8 – 11).

The second part of this petition asks God to cause "signs and wonders" (σημεῖα καὶ τέρατα; see on 2:19, 22) to happen. Acts 5:12 indicates that this prayer for signs and wonders was answered. These further signs and wonders, besides healings, are

---

21. BDAG, s.v. δοῦλος 1, 2; Danker comments that " 'servant' for 'slave' is largely confined to Biblical translations and early American times [s. *OED*, s.v. servant 3a and b]; in normal usage at the present time the two words are carefully distinguished" (BDAG, ibid.). Cf. Murray J. Harris, *Slave of Christ: A New Testament Metaphor for Total Devotion to Christ* (NSBT 8; Downers Grove, IL: InterVarsity Press, 1999). While the history of African slavery in Great Britain and North America complicates a contextually relevant understanding of the Greek term used here, the translation "servant" is too domesticated and fails to communicate what the term "slave" signifies.

22. Cf. Acts 16:17, used by a possessed slave girl for Paul and his coworkers; cf. 2:18 in the Joel quotation.

23. The plural δοῦλοι θεοῦ is used in Acts 2:18; 4:29; 16:17; 1 Pet 2:16; Rev 1:1; 7:3; 10:7; 11:18; 19:2, 5; 22:3, 6; the singular δοῦλος θεοῦ in Luke 1:38, 48 (δούλη); 2:29; Titus 1:1; Jas 1:1;

Rev 1:1; 15:3; the plural δοῦλοι Χριστοῦ in Eph 6:6; Phil 1:1; Rev 2:20; the singular δοῦλος Χριστοῦ in Rom 1:1; Gal 1:10; 1 Cor 7:22; Col 4:12; 2 Tim 2:24; Jas 1:1; 2 Pet 1:1; Jude 1; cf. the terms σύνδουλος/συνδοῦλοι in Col 1:7; 4:7; Rev 6:11; 19:10; 22:9, and verbal expressions using δουλεύω in Matt 6:24; Luke 16:13; Rom 7:6; 1 Thess 1:9. Cf. Harris, *Slave of Christ*, 20 – 24.

24. Differently Bock, *Acts*, 209 (following Larkin, *Acts*, 80), who thinks that "the prayer is not so much a request but an understanding in faith of how God can work." The adverbial clause v. 30 is clearly linked with the two imperatives in v. 29. The adverbial clause which begins with ἐν τῷ (with infinitive) is dependent on the imperatives ἔπιδε and δός in v. 29 and is best interpreted as an imperatival main clause; it is followed by two infinitive clauses (with accusative σε, and coordinated with καί).

25. Cf. Exod 6:8; Num 14:30; Jer 1:9; Zeph 1:4.

not specified. In the light of Jesus' ministry, they would mostly include exorcisms[26] (cf. 5:16; 8:7; 19:12), nature miracles (cf. 28:1 – 6; cf. the miraculous escapes from prison in 5:17 – 26; 12:6 – 17; cf. 16:25 – 26), and raising the dead (cf. 9:36 – 42; cf. 20:9 – 12).

The believers know they cannot cause signs and wonders to take place. Only the power of God the Creator is able to perform miracles — and his holy Servant Jesus (see on v. 27). As the lame man at the Beautiful Gate had been healed "in the name of Jesus of Nazareth, the Messiah" (3:6), the Jerusalem believers expect God to work further signs and wonders "through the name" (διὰ τοῦ ὀνόματος) of Jesus.

In a Jewish context, this prayer for miracles is unusual. Jewish sources do not know of either a movement that was characterized by miracles or of individuals who regularly performed miracles. The traditions about Ḥoni the Circle-Drawer and Ḥanina ben Dosa are often taken as evidence that there were charismatic miracle workers in Palestine in the first century. An analysis of the earliest traditions about these pious men makes this conclusion difficult to uphold.[27] While numerous cures were attributed in antiquity to Asclepius, the healing god,[28] often recorded on tables in temples, "there is no suggestion that the healing had any meaning outside of itself; it is not a pointer to a spiritual transformation or a promise of anything transcendent."[29]

4:31 When they had prayed, the place in which they were gathered was shaken; and they were all filled with the Holy Spirit, and they continued to speak the word of God with boldness (καὶ δεηθέντων αὐτῶν ἐσαλεύθη ὁ τόπος ἐν ᾧ ἦσαν συνηγμένοι καὶ ἐπλήσθησαν ἅπαντες τοῦ ἁγίου πνεύματος καὶ ἐλάλουν τὸν λόγον τοῦ θεοῦ μετὰ παρρησίας). Luke reports an immediate answer to the believers' prayer. The aorist participle (in the genitive absolute phrase δεηθέντων αὐτῶν) has a temporal meaning: "when they had prayed," the place where the believers had assembled "was shaken" (ἐσαλεύθη); i.e., it vibrated. This is an unusual phenomenon as a sign of confirmation that God has heard their prayer.[30]

The second response was another powerful experience of the Spirit (after 2:4; 4:8). Again, the verb "to fill" (πίμπλημι) is a metaphor that denotes "invasive inspiration" of God's Spirit (see on 2:4).[31] As they had prayed for boldness to preach and teach about Jesus despite the threats of the Sanhedrin, this renewed filling with the Spirit is linked with the witness to Jesus, the crucified, risen, and exalted Messiah and Savior, which the Spirit initiates, empowers, and directs.[32] In the context of the trembling of the meeting place, the Spirit represents here the transcendence of God, "the God who cannot be gagged" by the Sanhedrin or any people who want to muzzle the followers of Jesus.

The third response is the continued witness of the believers "with boldness" (μετὰ παρρησίας).

---

26. Cf. 10:38, where Peter describes Jesus' ministry "with power" in terms of "doing good and healing all who were in the power of the devil."

27. Cf. Meier, *Marginal Jew*, 2:581 – 88.

28. For Asclepius, cf. F. Graf, "Asclepius," *OCD*, 187 – 88; F. Graf, "Asclepius," *BNP*, 2:101 – 5.

29. Howard C. Kee, *Miracle in the Early Christian World: A Study in Sociohistorical Method* (New Haven, CT: Yale Univ. Press, 1983), 86 – 87.

30. Cf. Exod 19:18, where Mt. Sinai trembles as a result of God's presence; cf. Ps 18:7 (LXX 17:8); Isa 6:4; *4 Ezra* 6:15, 29; *T. Levi* 3:9; Josephus, *Ant.* 7.76 – 77; see also Virgil, *Aen.* 3.89 – 90; Plutarch, *Publ.* 9.6.

31. Turner, *Power from on High*, 357.

32. Cf. Acts 4:8, 31; 6:10; 8:29, 39; 9:17 – 20, 31; 10:19; 11:12; 13:2, 4; 16:6 – 7; 18:25 – 28. Turner, *Power from on High*, 402, the next quotation ibid., 440.

God answers the prayer for boldness as the believers are willing and eager to continue to preach and teach about Jesus, the Messiah and Savior. While the renewed filling with the Spirit seems to have been a singular experience (in a series of many such experiences), the preaching of the word of God with boldness is a continuous reality ("continued to speak," ἐλάλουν, is imperfect). Despite the ban on speaking and despite the threats made by the Jewish leaders, the Jerusalem believers receive the presence of God's power, which supernaturally emboldens them to preach about Jesus. The "word of God" (see on v. 29) is the message about Jesus, the Messiah and Savior of the world (vv. 10 – 12, 26).

Theology in Application

This is the longest prayer that Luke reports in Acts. In keeping with its main themes — thanksgiving for the fulfillment of God's promises, praise for God's sovereignty and wisdom, petition for boldness and courage in the proclamation of the gospel and for healings, signs, and wonders — the following points are important.

Christians Pray[33]

As created human beings, Christians speak with their Creator. As members of God's people, Christians speak with the God of Abraham, Isaac, and Jacob. As children in God's family, Christians speak with their Father. The universality of prayer in all religions suggests that verbally addressing a higher power is a fundamental concept of being authentically human. Only when God's existence is denied does prayer become superfluous. Contrast this with Luke's account of Jesus' life and ministry in his gospel, which presents a full picture of Jesus engaged in prayer, inculcating regular and consistent prayer upon the disciples.[34]

(1) Prayer is a fundamental activity of the church. When the Jerusalem believers faced the decision which of the two candidates should fill the place among the Twelve that had been vacated by Judas, they prayed (1:24 – 25). When Peter and John are released from arrest and report about the ban on speaking and about the threats that the Jewish leaders in the Sanhedrin made, the believers pray, as a matter of course.

If sustained prayer is eliminated from "worship services" on Sunday mornings because they are deemed unattractive for "seekers" who expect to be entertained, or awkward for churchgoers who expect to be guided through a fast-paced program, the risen Lord may well be knocking at the door — from the outside (Rev 3:20). Many

---

33. On prayer in Luke-Acts, cf. Peter T. O'Brien, "Prayer in Luke-Acts," *TynBul* 24 (1973): 111 – 27; Max M. B. Turner, "Prayer in the Gospels and Acts," in *Teach Us to Pray: Prayer in the Bible and the World* (ed. D. A. Carson; Grand Rapids: Baker, 1990), 58 – 83, 319 – 325; Steven F. Plymale, *The Prayer Texts of Luke-Acts* (American University Studies 7/118; New York: Lang, 1991).

34. Cf. Luke 1:10, 13; 3:21; 5:16; 6:12; 9:18, 28; 11:1 – 13; 18:1 – 8, 9 – 14; 22:32, 39 – 46; 23:34, 46.

churches in the affluent West live in spiritual poverty, as demonstrated by the decline in prayer. Christians who do not pray regularly and consistently are a contradiction in terms — they deny what they profess, that they have been reconciled with God (with whom they do not want to spend time), that they follow in the steps of Jesus (who prayed), and that they have received the Holy Spirit (who is God's presence, which is experienced in prayer).

In the hectic pace of life in modern societies, while it may not lead to a denial of the value of prayer, it easily leads to minimization of time reserved for prayer. As a result, people who profess to be Christians may pray rarely and only in "organized" situations in church. It is telling that one can find churches where people meet to watch a major sports event on television while prayer meetings have been abandoned. Followers of Jesus reserve time for prayer because they yearn to be in the presence of their Father in heaven.

(2) Prayer is an acknowledgment of God's existence. The primary purpose of prayer is not to present God with an agenda that he needs to work on. As God exists in the reality of the world he created and as human beings exist as God's creatures, it is the most "natural" activity in the world that human beings talk to their Creator. This "naturalness" was severely affected when Adam and Eve decided to try and improve their lives by breaking God's commandment — with the result that they hid from the presence of God (Gen 3). God sent Jesus into the world as his Messiah and Savior to finally solve this "sin predicament" of humankind. Consequently, people who have come to faith in Jesus Christ and who thus have been reconciled with God find it again "natural" to pray. As children love to speak with their father, Christians love to spend time in God's presence — which is why they pray.

(3) Prayer is an expression of the unity of believers. When Peter and John were released, they go to "their own" as a matter of course. And it goes without saying that the other believers were interested in their report. Luke takes it for granted that they then pray together. They pray with one voice, united in their loyalty to Jesus, the Messiah, united in their commitment to witness to Jesus, the Savior, and united in their willingness to suffer the consequences of continued missionary work.

Prayer as an Expression of God's Presence

If authentic prayer means speaking with God, praying implies and expresses the presence of God. Prayer marks a time and a place where God is present. As God's presence is mediated through the Holy Spirit, it is not surprising that the prayer of the Jerusalem believers is linked in several ways with the Spirit.

(1) The believers pray with the words of the Spirit as they pray with the words of Scripture, which God has spoken through the Spirit.[35] Living in an age where many

---

35. Jervell, *Apostelgeschichte*, 189.

value originality and creativity above anything else, the prayer in vv. 24 – 30 teaches us that we are well advised if we use the words of Scripture in our prayers.

(2) As the believers pray, they are granted a new experience of being filled with the Spirit. Many Christians seek an experience of the Spirit for their own benefit. Authentic prayer focuses not on personal advantage and emotional advancement — which was the sin of Adam and Eve that drove them from the presence of God. As we pray in God's presence and as we thus acknowledge his sovereignty and our place as his creatures, giving him all the glory while recognizing our need for forgiveness, cleansing, and transformation, we are ready to be filled with a new measure of the presence of God's Spirit.

(3) The presence of God through his Spirit prompts the believers to pray for boldness in missionary witness and causes them to go out and speak God's word with courageous boldness. The presence of God in the Holy Spirit is a reality that the believers experience and enjoy, and they want others to experience and enjoy that realilty also. This will take place only if people come to faith in Jesus, the Messiah and only Savior; that is why the believers are willing and eager to preach the gospel despite the danger this entails.

Prayer as an Expression of Dependence on God

Most people need to ask someone else to fix their car when it breaks down because they are unable to do it themselves. When Christians pray, they express their need for God — for the forgiveness of their sins, for obtaining peace with God, for help with restoring broken relationships, and for guidance in the large and small matters of everyday living.

(1) Christians depend on God, not on themselves. This does not mean that we never know what to do and that every decision that we make as a church or as individuals requires a direct and specific revelation from God. It is significant, however, that the first reaction of the Jerusalem believers to the impending danger that presented itself as a result of the ban on speaking and the threats of the Jewish leaders was prayer, not a strategy discussion.

All too frequently decisions in the church are based on the expertise of specialists who argue pragmatically in terms of "what has worked for others," or on prepackaged programs or plans that have been devised on the basis of sociological or marketing principles. Prayer is "added" because this is what Christian do. The vitality of churches in the global south who rely much more directly on God, as they often have few "modern" resources, raises serious questions for us. There is an immense difference between "what" works and "who" works. The question whether we depend on ourselves or on God — in reality, not in what we say — is a crucial question that must be faced and answered with truthfulness.

(2) Dependence on God is linked with God's revelation in Scripture and in history. This is not just a theological principle; it has a scriptural dimension and a historical dimension. The prayer of the Jerusalem church in vv. 24 – 30 has paradigmatic character with its reference to historical events and with its interpretation of Scripture. The community of believers united in prayer is the place where salvation history is interpreted and where Christians "recognize the structural congruence of the history of the church with Israel's prophecy and with Jesus' history, as thus being under the guidance of God, the Creator, the Lord of history."[36]

(3) It is only God's power that can convince people of the truth of the gospel. This is why prayer is a fundamental reality of churches and of believers who are involved in the task Jesus gave to the apostles — to be his witnesses in Jerusalem, Judea, Samaria, and to the ends of the earth. Because missionary outreach often and regularly faces opposition and hostility, Christians rely on God to give them strength and courage to continue their missionary work.

(4) Miracles have often confirmed the reality of God's presence in the missionary work of the followers of Jesus. The reference to the "hand of God" implies that the power to cause miracles to happen is always God's power, never that of the believers. Christians are entirely dependent on God for miracles to happen. Thus, miracles cannot be used as a "strategy" or "method" in missions and evangelism. The almighty God cannot be manipulated through some formula or scheme — "you must heal because you have promised," or "you must heal because I have faith," or "you must heal because I claim and name the miracle," or "you must heal because I have already given thanks that the miracle will happen." Such attitudes express not dependence on God but arrogance and presumption. Authentic followers of Jesus ask God to grant healings and signs and wonders in his time and according to his sovereign will.

Prayer as an Expression of Obedience to God

God is the sovereign Lord; we are his "slaves," his subjects who seek his glory and do his will. God is the Father; we are his children who are concerned that his will is done on earth as it is in heaven. Christians who pray are not only petitioning God to do things, but they are demonstrating their willingness to do what God asks them to do.

(1) Jesus commissioned the apostles to be his witnesses in Jerusalem and in Judea. They could argue that the ban on speaking and the threats of the Jewish leaders make the fulfillment of this commission impossible, at least temporarily. Or they could argue that the message that has provoked the hostility of the Sanhedrin could be adapted so that they can continue to speak about Jesus, but not about their conviction that he is the Messiah and the only Savior.

36. Pesch, *Apostelgeschichte*, 1:178.

But the Jerusalem believers know that obedience to Jesus' missionary commission does not allow for a suspension of their witness or an adaptation that would make their life easier. They do not want to wait for some day in the future when they will be able to witness for Jesus, and they are not willing to eliminate the fundamental truths about Jesus — his crucifixion and resurrection, his significance as Messiah and as Savior. They want to be joyfully obedient, and thus they pray that God may take note of the situation in which they find themselves and that God may give them courage to continue with their proclamation of God's word.

(2) God graciously confirms the believers' obedience. The shaking of the earth after the prayer and a new filling with the Holy Spirit confirms that the apostles and the believers in the church in Jerusalem are faithful witnesses as they pray for God's help in their continuing proclamation of Jesus. As they do not selfishly ask for personal benefits, but as they pray obediently for boldness and grace to carry out what God had commissioned them to accomplish, God hears their prayer and responds with a manifestation of his presence.

CHAPTER 11

Acts 4:32 – 37

Literary Context

This passage is the second episode in the section that reports the life, witness, and trials of the community of believers in Jerusalem (3:1 – 8:3). The first episode focused on Peter's early ministry in Jerusalem when he healed the lame man at the Beautiful Gate and preached in Solomon's Portico, which led to the arrest of Peter and John and their defense of the message of Jesus before the Jewish leaders in the Sanhedrin (3:1 – 4:31). Luke writes his third summary of the life of the Jerusalem believers (4:32 – 37; cf. 1:14; 2:42 – 47), with a focus on the sharing of material resources in the Christian community.

The example of Barnabas, who sold a field and brought the proceeds to the apostles, sets up the next incident, which narrates the selfish hypocrisy of a married couple in the church (5:1 – 11). This is followed by another summary (5:12 – 16) and second incident of arrest, imprisonment, and courageous defense and explanation of the gospel by the apostles (5:17 – 42).

II. The Beginnings of the New People of God (1:15 – 8:3)
    A. The identity and witness of Jesus' followers as God's people (1:15 – 2:47)
    B. The life, witness, trials, and growth of the community of believers in Jerusalem (3:1 – 8:3)
        9. Peter's miracles, proclamation of Jesus, and defense before the Sanhedrin (3:1 – 4:31)
  ➡   **10. The life of the Jerusalem community (4:32 – 37)**
        11. The demise of Ananias and Sapphira (5:1 – 11)

Main Idea

The commitment to the Lord Jesus generates both power and grace among the believers, who are united not only in heart and mind but also in their willingness to share their material resources with needy people in the community, so much so that the social ideals of the Jewish and Greek traditions are fulfilled.

Translation

Acts 4:32 – 37

32a	Description	**The community of believers was of one heart and mind.**
b	Explanation	**None of them claimed**
c	Description	that any of their possessions was their own,
d	Description	**but they had everything in common.**
33a	Action	**The apostles continued to bear witness**
b	Content	to the resurrection of the Lord Jesus
c	Manner	with great power,
d	(action)	and **great grace was upon them all.**
34a	Assertion	**There was no needy person among them,**
b	Cause	for those who were owners of lands or houses sold them
c	Cause	and brought the proceeds of what was sold,
35a	Cause	and put it at the apostles' feet,
b	Result	and it was distributed to anyone who had need.
36a	Explanation: Character entrance	**There was Joseph,**
b	Identification	whom the apostles called Barnabas
c	Identification (translation)	(which means, when translated, "Son of Exhortation"),
d	Identification	a Levite who had been born in Cyprus,
37a	Action	**who sold a piece of land that he owned;**
b	Action	**he brought the money**
c	Action	and **put it at the feet of the apostles.**

Structure and Literary Form

This summary passage consists of two parts. In the first part Luke describes the life of the Jerusalem community of believers, highlighting three matters: (1) the unity of the believers around a common purpose (4:32); (2) the continuing ministry of the apostles, who proclaim the risen Jesus in Jerusalem and who, together with all other believers, enjoy the blessing of God (4:33); (3) the common ownership of possessions that represents the ideal of a society in which there are no needy persons (4:34 – 35). Individual believers sell their property and share the proceeds by bringing the money to the apostles, who then distribute it to those who are in need.

The summary in 4:32 – 37 shares several elements with the summary in 2:42 – 47 (see the table in "Structure and Literary Form" for 2:42 – 47): a commitment to (1) fellow believers (2:44; 4:32); (2) the teaching of the apostles (2:42; 4:33); and (3) the care for needy members through common ownership of possessions as property is sold and the proceeds are shared (2:44 – 45; 4:32, 34 – 35); here the similarities extend to the exact words that Luke uses:

2:44 εἶχον ἅπαντα κοινά	4:32 ἦν αὐτοῖς ἅπαντα κοινά
2:45 τὰ κτήματα καὶ τὰς ὑπάρξεις ἐπίπρασκον	4:34 ὅσοι ... κτήτορες χωρίων ἢ οἰκιῶν ὑπῆρχον, πωλοῦντες ἔφερον τὰς τιμὰς τῶν πιπρασκομένων
2:45 διεμέριζον αὐτὰ πᾶσιν καθότι ἄν τις χρείαν εἶχεν	4:35 διεδίδετο δὲ ἑκάστῳ καθότι ἄν τις χρείαν εἶχεν

What is missing in this summary is a reference to common meals (2:42, 46) and to common worship (2:42, 46–47).

The second part of the summary describes Joseph Barnabas, a Levite from Cyprus who sold a field and brought the proceeds to the apostles. This is a new feature of Luke's summaries.

The level of self-ascription, commitment to one another, and intimacy represent features that one finds usually only in kinship groups. This means that Luke's summaries describe much more than the religious and moral or social convictions of the followers of Jesus; he describes the community of believers in Jesus as a group (consisting of Jewish members at this point) with a new social identity. This community is consolidated through the conflict with the Jewish leadership, described in the previous sections. Kuecker has observed:

> ...intergroup conflict, especially the perception of external threat directed toward the in-group, intensifies identification with the in-group in three related ways: it causes group members to develop a heightened sense of similarity to their own group (in-group homogeneity), it creates greater differentiation from outgroups (in-group bias), and it cultivates a stronger sense that out-groups have very little social differentiation (out-group homogeneity). Stated simply, intergroup conflict tends to magnify the notions of "we" and "they."[1]

Exegetical Outline

➡ **I. The Life of the Jerusalem Community (4:32–37)**

    A. The Sharing of Resources in the Community of Believers (4:32–35)

        1. The unity of the believers (4:32)

            a. The common purpose of heart and mind (4:32a)

            b. The common ownership of possessions (4:32b-d)

        2. The ministry of the apostles (4:33)

            a. The proclamation of the Lord Jesus in Jerusalem (4:33a-c)

            b. The blessing of God on the believers (4:33d)

---

1. Kuecker, "Spirit and the 'Other,'" 132.

Explanation of the Text

4:32 The community of believers was of one heart and mind. None of them claimed that any of their possessions was their own, but they had everything in common (τοῦ δὲ πλήθους τῶν πιστευσάντων ἦν καρδία καὶ ψυχὴ μία, καὶ οὐδὲ εἷς τι τῶν ὑπαρχόντων αὐτῷ ἔλεγεν ἴδιον εἶναι ἀλλ᾽ ἦν αὐτοῖς ἅπαντα κοινά). The believers are united in their convictions and are committed to witnessing to the life, death, and resurrection of Jesus (v. 33; cf. 2:46). Luke stresses their unity and harmony by placing the numerical term "one" (μία) at the end of the clause.

The term translated as "heart" (καρδία; Heb. *lēb*)[2] describes the heart in terms of (1) personal identity, (2) the vital center of human beings, (3) the affective center for human emotions, (4) the noetic center in terms of the place of "intellectual visualization (cognition and memory), thought, understanding, and attention," (5) the voluntative center in terms of "the driving force behind the voluntative endeavors of the individual," and (6)

the religious and ethical "realm of the relationship between human beings and God."

The term translated as "mind" (ψυχή, Heb. *nepeš*), interpreted in an Old Testament and Jewish context, denotes the vital self of the believers. In the command to "love with all your *nepeš*," the term usually translated as "soul" serves to elevate "the intensity of involvement of the entire being."[3] The phrase "one mind" (ψυχὴ μία) would have reminded educated Gentile readers (listeners) of the Greek idea that "friends are one soul."[4] The collocation "heart and mind" (καρδία καὶ ψυχή) occurs repeatedly in the Old Testament and describes complete and total devotion to God in the context of the commandment to love Yahweh and worship him.[5]

As the assembled believers prayed with one voice (v. 24), they share one faith (in Jesus as Israel's Messiah and Savior), one identity (as the community of the people of God restored by the Spirit), and one purpose (as witnesses of the gospel). It is

---

2. The following definitions are taken from H.-J. Fabry, "לֵב," *TDOT*, 7:412 – 34; for the New Testament evidence cf. F. Baumgärtel and J. Behm, "καρδία," *TDNT*, 3:605 – 14; A. Sand, "καρδία," *EDNT*, 2:249 – 51.

3. H. Seebass, "נֶפֶשׁ," *TDOT*, 9:511; cf. C. Westermann, *TLOT*, 2:750 – 51.

4. Euripides, *Orest.* 1046, quoted as a proverbial sentence by Aristotle, *Eth. nic.* 1168B; cf. Plutarch, *Mor.* 96F.

5. H.-J. Fabry, "לֵב," 7:431; the following ibid. The com-

mandment to love God and worship him "with all your heart and with all our soul" in Deut 6:5; 10:12; 11:13; 13:34 is repeatedly cited paradigmatically (1 Kgs 15:14; 2 Kgs 10:31; 23:3; 2 Chr 15:12, 15, 17; 19:3; 22:9; 34:31; Isa 38:3), as a realized admonition (Josh 22:5; 1 Sam 7:3; 12:20, 24; 1 Kgs 14:8; 1 Chr 22:19; 28:9; 2 Chr 16:9), as a reminder of God's promises (1 Kgs 2:4; 8:23; 2 Kgs 20:3; 2 Chr 6:14), in thanksgiving for assistance (1 Kgs 3:6), and in prayer to God (1 Chr 29:18 – 19; 2 Chr 30:19).

not coincidental that the first occurrence of the concept of "one heart and one soul" is in Deut 6:5, which is part of Israel's daily confession of faith in and love for Yahweh. We should note that even though this description of the harmony and unity of the Jerusalem community of disciples sounds idealistic, Luke does not describe the church as a realm free of conflict, as 5:1 – 11 will show.

Luke describes the community of Jesus' followers with two terms. (1) The term "community" (πλῆθος) describes the Christian community in its entirety (cf. 6:2, 5; 15:12).[6] This term probably relates to the Hebrew term "the many" (rabbîm), a self-designation of the Qumran community.[7] (2) The term translated as "the believers" (οἱ πιστεύσαντες) is a nominalized aorist participle that designates the followers of Jesus in Jerusalem, underscoring the centrality of faith in Jesus as the Messiah and Savior (vv. 10 – 12).

The unity of the Jerusalem believers is demonstrated in their sharing of material resources with the needy. This sentence essentially repeats 2:44 (see comments). None of the believers (οὐδὲ εἷς) said that any of their possessions belonged to them alone. The imperfect tense of the verb "claimed" (ἔλεγεν) suggests a continuous attitude of the believers.

The believers shared their possessions. The term translated "in common" (κοινός, "shared collectively, communal") describes one practical and visible result of their harmony and unity. If the practice of the Qumran community is any guide, we should think here not of "love communism,"

where private property has been abolished and everything is owned by everybody, but of *private ownership* of possessions (what the individual believers "have") linked with *communal use* of possessions.[8] There is thus no tension with 5:4, where Peter asserts that the proceeds of the sale of property that had belonged to Ananias and Sapphira were rightfully theirs.

Gentile readers of Acts who had been recently converted may have been reminded of the ideal of the "community of goods" that Greek philosophers had described.[9] The community of followers of Jesus in Jerusalem is described not as an ideal, but as a reality. The willingness to regard one's own possessions as being at the disposal of the community if needy members needed help is the result of the transforming power of the Holy Spirit. The identity of the Jerusalem community is characterized by "a turn away from pure self-interest or the interests of the in-group and a turn toward the 'other.' "[10]

4:33 The apostles continued to bear witness to the resurrection of the Lord Jesus with great power, and great grace was upon them all (καὶ δυνάμει μεγάλῃ ἀπεδίδουν τὸ μαρτύριον οἱ ἀπόστολοι τῆς ἀναστάσεως τοῦ κυρίου Ἰησοῦ, χάρις τε μεγάλη ἦν ἐπὶ πάντας αὐτούς). This verse describes the ministry of the apostles. The "great power" (δυνάμει μεγάλῃ, modal dative) that is connected with the teaching of the apostles and the "great grace" (χάρις μεγάλη) that is present among the believers describe the fundamental reality and the cause of the life of the community, in which believ-

---

6. Cf. BDAG, s.v. πλῆθος 2bδ, "in the usage of cultic communities as a [technical term] for the whole body of their members, *fellowship, community, congregation*;" cf. J Zmijewski, "πλῆθος," *EDNT*, 3:104.

7. Cf. 1QS VI, 1, 8, 11 – 12, 14 – 21; VII, 10, 13, 16, 19 – 21, 24 – 25; VIII, 19, 26; IX, 2; CD XIII, 7; XIV, 7, 12. Cf. James H. Charlesworth, ed., *Rule of the Community and Related Documents* (The Dead Sea Scrolls 1; Tübingen: Mohr Siebeck, 1994),

27 n. 133; cf. Fitzmyer, *Acts*, 313.

8. Cf. Murphy, *Wealth in the Dead Sea Scrolls*, 454.

9. Aristotle, *Eth. nic.* 1168B; Iamblichus, *Vit. Pyth.* 167.

10. Kuecker, "Spirit and the 'Other,' " 21; cf. ibid. 127, who speaks of "allocentric identity," i.e., an identity focused on the "other" (Gk. *allos*) rather than on oneself (Gk. *ego*, hence "egocentric").

ers are united in faith and purpose and in a willingness to share their possessions. The reference to the "great power" is emphasized by its forefront position in the Greek sentence.

The "power" (δύναμις) is the power of the Holy Spirit, who grants the apostles the boldness to continue to teach about Jesus (vv. 8, 13, 29 – 31), the power through which healings and signs and wonders happen (v. 30), and also, certainly in the context of vv. 32, 34 – 35, the power that transforms the lives of the believers from being egocentric to being willing to share with others. "Grace" (χάρις) is God's enabling care and help as a gift of the Holy Spirit. In 6:8 Stephen is described as one who is "full of grace and power" (πλήρης χάριτος καὶ δυνάμεως).

The activity of the apostles is described as "bearing witness."[11] They bear witness to Jesus' resurrection (cf. 1:22; 3:15; 4:2) as eyewitnesses who saw and spoke with Jesus after his resurrection. Luke singles out this emphasis of their teaching because Jesus' resurrection signifies the beginning of the new creation and thus represents the reality of the new period of salvation in which God's Spirit is present, who transforms the lives of those who have come to faith in Jesus, the Messiah and Savior. The imperfect tense of the verb "continued to bear" (ἀπεδίδουν) highlights the continuity of the apostles' teaching and preaching; the verb perhaps implies here the obligation[12] to be Jesus' witnesses, a task the apostles accepted when they were chosen by Jesus as his disciples.

4:34 – 35 There was no needy person among them, for those who were owners of lands or houses sold them and brought the proceeds of **what was sold, and put it at the apostles' feet, and it was distributed to anyone who had need** (οὐδὲ γὰρ ἐνδεής τις ἦν ἐν αὐτοῖς· ὅσοι γὰρ κτήτορες χωρίων ἢ οἰκιῶν ὑπῆρχον, πωλοῦντες ἔφερον τὰς τιμὰς τῶν πιπρασκομένων καὶ ἐτίθουν παρὰ τοὺς πόδας τῶν ἀποστόλων, διεδίδετο δὲ ἑκάστῳ καθότι ἄν τις χρείαν εἶχεν). As a result of the willingness to share material possessions, any believer with needs received money with which he or she could buy the necessities of everyday life. The Greek term for "needy" (ἐνδεής) means "in want, in need," thus "poor, impoverished"; it occurs only here in the New Testament.

The statement echoes Deut 15:4 (the first occurrence of ἐνδεής in the LXX), where Moses prophesies that once the people of Israel are settled in the Promised Land, "there need be no poor people [ἐνδεής] among you, for in the land the LORD your God is giving you to possess as your inheritance, he will richly bless you."[13] In the context of Deut 15:2, the poor person is "a debtor in the 'hand' of the creditor, who oppresses him by demanding or exacting the debt by force."[14] God's blessing in the Promised Land is connected with the end of poverty.

In view of the life of the Jerusalem believers, who are shaped by the great power that accompanies the preaching and teaching of the apostles, it is perhaps not a coincidence that, in Deut 15:4 – 6, "the prerequisite for Yahweh's blessing, for the inheritance, and for the absence of the poor (ʾebhyôn) is obedience to his voice." If Luke expects his readers to notice this connection, he draws up "a correspondence between, on the one hand, the redemption of the Israelites from Egypt and their prosperous settlement in the land, and, on the other hand, the

---

11. For μαρτύριον see on μαρτύς in 1:8.

12. Cf. BDAG, s.v. ἀποδίδωμι 2, "to meet a contractual or other obligation, *pay, pay out, fulfill.*"

13. In Deut 15:4 and several other Old Testament passages ἐνδεής translates a Heb. term used 61 times in the Old Tes-

tament, designating people who are in need of material and legal assistance and thus, especially in the Psalms, people who expect and receive divine help.

14. Cf. J. Botterweck, "אֶבְיוֹן," *TDOT*, 1:32; the following quotation ibid.

new redemption wrought by Christ and the setting up of the new community."[15]

Luke does not connect this statement with the widows neglected in the daily distribution of food (see 6:1). This does not mean that he paints an ideal picture in v. 34a that never "materialized." Evidently the material support for needy believers grew in complexity as the church became larger, and problems of distribution ensued that required new arrangements.

In vv. 34b – 35 Luke describes a three-step process through which the needy believers were supported so that they were no longer impoverished.

(1) Land owners and owners of houses sold property. The present tense of the temporal participle for "sold" (πωλοῦντες) suggests that the liquidation of property was a regular occurrence and happened over a period of time. In view of vv. 36 – 37 and 5:1 – 11 we may assume that believers who owned land and houses sold them as needs arose. Luke does not say that these believers sold *everything* they had. His words can be taken to mean that "the owners sold some of the properties they possessed and brought the prices of what they sold to the apostles."[16] Nor does Luke say that *all* owners of lands and houses sold everything; according to 12:12 – 13 a believer named Mary still owned a house about ten years later. If all this is correct, v. 34b implies that there were wealthy Jews who owned several houses and who had come to faith in Jesus.[17]

(2) The proceeds of the sale of land and houses were brought to the community to be shared with those in need. The imperfect tense of "brought" (ἔφερον) is probably iterative. Again and again, believers sold property and made the proceeds available for those in need.

(3) The distribution of the resource among the needy believers was organized by the apostles. The two verbs in v. 35 (ἐτίθουν, διεδίδετο) are also iterative imperfects, describing a regular practice. The reference to the apostles' feet (cf. v. 37; 5:2) denotes the authority of the apostles over the funds being brought to the community.[18] Since the selfless giving of believers who sold property was a regular occurrence, it is a plausible assumption that the apostles received the money that the believers brought as they were teaching in Solomon's Portico (cf. 5:12). If so, this would be highly symbolic, demonstrating that Jesus had indeed become the cornerstone of a new "house" or "temple" in which the needy members were supported by selfless and generous contributions.

The apostles were in control of the distribution of the funds, as v. 37 and 6:1 – 6 confirm. This emphasis signals that the generosity of the more well-to-do believers was given without expecting reciprocity, in contrast to the Greek and Roman notion of deriving honor, prestige, and social position through benefaction and patronage.[19] Each believer who was impoverished received funds "to the degree that" (καθότι) he or she needed some-

---

15. Marshall, "Acts," 554.

16. Barrett, *Acts*, 255, who adds that "Luke is not compiling statistics; he means to describe a great movement of generosity." Fitzmyer, *Acts*, 314, thinks that "they gave up 100 percent of the proceeds," but that is not explicitly stated. Acts 5:1 – 11 only implies that the believers expected that the owners who sold property did not claim a more generous gift than they actually brought to the apostles.

17. Cf. David A. Fiensy, "The Composition of the Jerusalem Church," in *The Book of Acts in Its Palestinian Setting* (ed. R. Bauckham), 213 – 36, 226 – 30, for the social status of some of the early believers in Jerusalem.

18. Cf. Johnson, *Acts*, 87, who refers to Josh 10:24; 1 Sam 25:24, 41; 2 Sam 22:39; Pss 8:6; 18:10; 47:4; 99:5; 110:1; 132:7; Luke 7:38, 44 – 46; 8:35, 41; 10:39; 17:16; Acts 10:25; 22:3, for the "body language" of "being at the feet" of another person denoting submission or obedience.

19. Cf. Alan C. Mitchell, "The Social Function of Friendship in Acts 2.44 – 47 and 4.32 – 37," *JBL* 111 (1992): 255 – 72, 266; Kuecker, "Spirit and the 'Other,'" 137 – 38, who points out that the phrase ἐκ τῶν ἰδίων occurs over 1,600 times in Greek honorary inscriptions, a phrase that generally indicates that the bene-

thing.[20] This formulation implies that the apostles assessed the needs of believers when they heard of someone's impoverished situation or when certain believers asked for material support.

4:36 There was Joseph, whom the apostles called Barnabas (which means, when translated, "Son of Exhortation"), a Levite who had been born in Cyprus (Ἰωσὴφ δὲ ὁ ἐπικληθεὶς Βαρναβᾶς ἀπὸ τῶν ἀποστόλων, ὅ ἐστιν μεθερμηνευόμενον υἱὸς παρακλήσεως, Λευίτης, Κύπριος τῷ γένει). The general description of the unity of the Jerusalem believers who cared for needy members through the selfless sharing of material resources is now illustrated with a specific example. Luke introduces Joseph Barnabas here — one of the most frequently mentioned believers in Acts.[21] The apostles called Joseph by the name "Barnabas" (Βαρναβᾶς), a nickname that Luke translates as "Son of Exhortation" (υἱὸς παρακλήσεως). The name is probably connected with the Aramaic expression "son of the prophet." If so, Luke's translation can be understood as a paraphrase for "the one gifted with inspired speech,"[22] a name that fits the emphasis on the Holy Spirit as the Spirit of prophecy. Inter-

preted as "Son of Exhortation," the name describes a "preacher" who urges and encourages believers and unbelievers to accept and live according to the reality of God's revelation in Jesus Christ. Barnabas was a prophet, a teacher (13:1), and an apostle (1 Cor 9:6).

4:37 Who sold a piece of land that he owned; he brought the money and put it at the feet of the apostles (ὑπάρχοντος αὐτῷ ἀγροῦ πωλήσας ἤνεγκεν ὐ χρῆμα καὶ ἔθηκεν πρὸς τοὺς πόδας τῶν ἀποστόλων). While Levites were not allowed to possess the land in Israel in Old Testament times (Num 18:20; Deut 10:9; Josh 21:1 – 41), this had changed by the first century.[23] Barnabas owned a piece of land, perhaps on Cyprus, perhaps in the vicinity of Jerusalem. His action is described with three aorists — he sold (πωλήσας) the land, took (ἤνεγκεν) the money[24] from the sale, and placed (ἔθηκεν) it at the apostles' feet, to be distributed to needy believers. In the historical context of the Jerusalem church, we can assume that he served as a role model for the perhaps 8,000 believers in Jerusalem (1:15; 2:41; 4:4).

---

faction commemorated in the inscription was provided by the named donor, who generously gave from what was "his own."

20. The particle ἄν (with an augmented tense of the indicative, here the imperfect διεδίδετο) describes in Hellenistic Greek in subordinate clauses "repetition in past time" (BDF §367, "the classical iterative optative is thereby avoided").

21. Luke mentions Barnabas 23 times: 4:36; 9:27; 11:22, 25, 30; 12:25; 13:1 – 2, 7, 42 – 43, 46, 50; 14:12, 14, 20; 15:2, 12, 22, 25, 35 – 37, 39. Cf. Schnabel, *Early Christian Mission,* 2:788 – 90.

22. The identification of Joseph Barsabbas, the candidate for the position of the twelfth apostle, with Barnabas, presupposed by the Western Text (Codex D, minuscule 6 suppl.) in a

variant reading in 1:23, is secondary and historically not reliable. The patristic tradition since the end of the second century assumes that he was among the Seventy or Seventy-Two whom Jesus sent on a missionary tour through Galilee (Luke 10:1); cf. Clement of Alexandria, *Strom.* 2.20.112; Eusebius, *Hist. eccl.* 1.12.1; 2.1.4; *Clem. hom..* 1.9.1; *Clem. rec.* 1.7.7.

23. Cf. Josephus, *Life* 68 – 83. Even Jeremiah is said to have owned land; Jer 32:6 – 15. Witherington, *Acts,* 209.

24. The term χρῆμα denotes "property, wealth, means" as well as "any kind of currency, money" (BDAG); it is mostly used in the plural, cf. 8:18, 20; 24:26, only here in the New Testament in the singular.

Theology in Application

Luke stresses here that the transforming power of the Holy Spirit and the grace of God create a community of believers united in a common faith and a common purpose, who selflessly share their material resources with needy members.

Visible Unity

The unity of a local church is real only when it is visible. "The church" is not just a concept but the specific reality of individual believers meeting and worshiping together in a local congregation. In like manner, its unity is not just a theological idea but the concrete reality of believers living and serving together.

(1) The unity of the church becomes visible when believers meet together for prayer and teaching, confirming and consolidating their common convictions, beliefs, and purpose.

(2) The unity of the church becomes visible when the needs of individual believers become known. An important way in which this happens is the sharing of meals (cf. 2:46), where it becomes obvious who has much, who has little, and who has nothing.

(3) The unity of the church becomes visible when believers are willing and eager to help support needy fellow believers.

The Authenticity of Community

We can ascertain the authenticity of a community of believers in their use of material resources. The health of any community can be ascertained by the way in which the weakest members are treated. This is particularly true for the community of Jesus' followers.

(1) Caring for the needy in a selfless manner is an expression of following Jesus. John the Baptist urged the Jewish people who repented and prepared themselves for the coming of the Messiah, "Anyone who has two shirts should share with the one who has none, and anyone who has food should do the same" (Luke 3:11). Jesus, in his first public sermon, explained a text from Isaiah that speaks of Yahweh's Servant, who brings "good news to the poor" (Luke 4:18).

The beatitudes begin with the lines, "Blessed are you who are poor, for yours is the kingdom of God. Blessed are you who hunger now, for you will be satisfied" (Luke 6:20 – 21). Jesus introduced the parable of the rich fool with the warning, "Watch out! Be on your guard against all kinds of greed; life does not consist in an abundance of possessions" (12:15). He had taught his disciples, "Do not be afraid, little flock, for your Father has been pleased to give you the kingdom. Sell your possessions and give to the poor. Provide purses for yourselves that will not wear out, a treasure in heaven that will never fail, where no thief comes near and no moth destroys. For where your treasure is, there your heart will be also" (12:32 – 34).

When Jesus was attending a dinner given by a leading Pharisee, he said, "But when you give a banquet, invite the poor, the crippled, the lame, the blind, and you will be blessed. Although they cannot repay you, you will be repaid at the resurrection of the righteous" (Luke 14:13 – 14). In the parable of the rich man and Lazarus, Jesus emphasized the dangers of riches for the wealthy and the grace that God shows to the poor (16:19 – 31). Jesus challenged a particular rich young ruler, "Sell everything you have and give to the poor, and you will have treasure in heaven. Then come, follow me"; he followed this up by stressing how "hard it is for the rich to enter the kingdom of God! Indeed, it is easier for a camel to go through the eye of a needle than for someone who is rich to enter the kingdom of God" (18:22, 24 – 25). And when Jesus' presence in the house of Zacchaeus changed that man's life, the tax collector volunteered, "Now I give half of my possessions to the poor, and if I have cheated anybody out of anything, I will pay back four times the amount" (Luke 19:8).

(2) Caring for the needy in a voluntary manner is the result of transformation by God's Spirit. When believers voluntarily and selflessly share their resources with others in need, they do this not because they have to or because they are pressured to do so, but because they want to; not because they follow an ideal, but because their focus has been effectively shifted away from their own self-interest to the interest of others who need help.

(3) Caring for the needy needs to be well organized. The "system" that the Jerusalem believers initially used — Christians sold property, took the proceeds to the apostles, who then distributed money to those in need — worked initially, but then it broke down, probably because of the increasing number of believers who needed help. The incident in 6:1 – 7 demonstrates that the apostles were humble enough to admit that the task of caring for the needy had not been handled well, and they were flexible enough to introduce a new structure of organizing the relief efforts in the community.

The Local Church

The local church needs the example of Christian leaders. Churches benefit immensely from the role model of leading Christians. The example of Barnabas, a leading preacher and missionary, was important for Luke to record as a specific illustration of the selfless behavior of Jerusalem believers.

(1) Wealthy Christians need to be challenged to be role models of the proper attitude regarding material possessions.

(2) A local church should never rely on wealthy believers for financial support, as it is a privilege of all believers who are able to help to contribute to the alleviation of the needs of other believers.

Acts 5:1 – 16

Literary Context

The third episode in the section in which Luke presents the life, witness, and trials of the believers in Jerusalem (3:1 – 8:3) describes the case of a wealthy couple who sell property and lie about the proceeds from the sale that they donate for the needy in the church (5:1 – 11). This follows the passage in which Luke has provided a summary description of the life of the Jerusalem believers, focused on the selfless giving of many believers — Joseph Barnabas being a prominent example and role model (4:32 – 37).

The episode of the demise of Ananias and Sapphira leads into another summary statement that emphasizes the miracles that happened in connection with the ministry of the apostles. It also mentions further conversions among the population in Jerusalem and further miracles that attract a continuously increasing number of people (5:12 – 16).

Main Idea

The community of believers in Jerusalem was not perfect. There was temptation inspired by Satan, and the sin of deceit, caused by a selfish concern for a superior reputation, was exposed and judged by God, who knows the hearts of all people. God will not tolerate evil and deception among his people, who must be mindful of the fact that they should fear God as they are accountable to him who is holy, omniscient, and almighty.

Translation

Acts 5:1 – 16

5:1a	Character entrance/ Identification	**A man named Ananias**,
b	Association	together with his wife, Sapphira,
c	Action	**sold a piece of property**
2a	Action	**and put aside for himself some of the proceeds,**
b	Association	his wife being privy to this.
c	Action	**And he brought only a part**
d	Action	**and laid it at the feet of the apostles.**
3a	Action (speech)	**Peter said,**
b	Address	"Ananias,
c	Question: Inference	why has Satan filled your heart
d	Result	that you would lie to the Holy Spirit
e	Result/Action	and put aside for yourself some of the proceeds of the field?
4a	Question	Did it not belong to you
b	Time	before it was sold?
c	Question	And was it not at your disposal
d	Time	after you had sold it?
e	Question	How did you get it into your head
f	Action	to do such a thing?
g	Assertion	You have lied
h	Contrast	not to human beings
i	Clarification	but to God."
5a	Setting: Time	When Ananias heard these words,
b	Event/Result	**he collapsed**
c	Event	**and died.**
d	Event	**All people**
e	Description	who heard what had happened
f	Event	**were gripped with great fear.**
6a	Action	**The young men came forward**
b	Action	**wrapped him up,**
c	Action	**carried him out,**
d	Action	**and buried him.**
7a	Setting: Time (Aside)	**There was an interval of about three hours.**
b	Character entrance	**His wife came in,**
c	Description	who did not know what had happened.
8a	Action	**Peter addressed her,**
b	Question	"Tell me,
c	Inquiry/Question	did you sell the piece of property
d		for such and such an amount?"
e	Answer	**She answered,**
f	Assertion	"Yes, for that amount."

Continued on next page.

Continued from previous page.

9a	Reaction	**Then Peter said to her,**
b	Question/Accusation	*"Why did you agree to test the Spirit of the Lord?*
c	Assertion	*Look, the feet of those who have buried your husband are at the door,*
d	Prophecy	*and they will carry you out."*
10a	Event/Result	**She immediately collapsed at his feet**
b	Event	**and died.**
c	Setting: Time	When the young men came in,
d	Action	**they found her dead;**
e	Action	**they carried her out**
f	Action	**and buried her**
g	Place	next to her husband.
11a	Event/Result	**The whole church and**
b		**all people who heard of these things**
c		**were gripped with great fear.**
12a	Event	**Many signs and wonders**
b	Place	among the people
c		**happened**
d	Agency	at the hands of the apostles.
e	Action	**They were all meeting with one mind**
f	Place	in Solomon's Portico.
13a	Result	**None of the other people dared to join them,**
b	Result/Contrast	**yet the people spoke highly of them.**
14a	Comparison	More than ever,
b	Event	**believers were added to the Lord,**
c	Explanation	great numbers of both men and women.
15a	Result	As a result,
b	Action	**they would carry the sick out into the streets**
c	Action	**and lay them on cots and mats**
d	Purpose	so that
e	Time (cause)	when Peter would pass by,
f	Purpose	his shadow might fall on some of them.
16a	Action	**A large number of people also gathered**
b	Setting	from the towns around Jerusalem;
c	Action	**they brought the sick and**
d	List	the people tormented by unclean spirits,
e	Event	who were all cured.

Structure and Literary Form

The first of two episodes can be divided into five incidents: (1) the deception of Ananias and his wife Sapphira (vv. 1 – 2); (2) Peter's confrontation with Ananias (vv. 3 – 6); (3) developments after Ananias's death (v. 7); (4) Peter's confrontation with Sapphira (vv. 8 – 10); (5) the fear of God that gripped both believers and unbelievers in Jerusalem (5:11).

Many scholars regard this episode as a "miracle of judgment," more specifically, a "rule miracle of punishment" or a rule (violation) miracle.[1] The latter term is not satisfactory, however, for several reasons. (1) Peter is not described as enforcing rules; he does not initiate the judgment, which comes unexpectedly in the case of Ananias and is only prophetically announced in the case of Sapphira. (2) It is usually assumed that the "sacred prescription" violated by Ananias and Sapphira was the rule to donate the full price obtained by the believers when they sold property. But in view of Peter's statement in v. 4a-b, there was no such rule, and the summary in 4:32 – 37 does not state that believers who sold property were expected to donate the entire proceeds. If this is the impression created by Luke's description in 4:34, 37, it is indeed just this, an impression, which is different from a "rule."

There are incidents in the Old Testament that resemble the sudden death of Ananias and Sapphira — the fire that consumed Nadab and Abihu (Lev 10:2); the death of Achan (Josh 7:1, 19 – 26); the death of Abijah (1 Kgs 14:1 – 18). Scholars have especially cited the story of Achan, who had misappropriated material goods from Ai that did not belong to him, as a parallel to our passage.[2] One may point, for example, to the verb "put aside" in 5:2 (νοσφίζομαι), which occurs in the LXX only in Josh 7:1 and in 2 Macc 4:32. But the two passages share no other verbal links or similar motifs; in Acts 5 the sin is deceit, not theft; the wife of Ananias dies with her husband, while Achan dies, perhaps, with his sons and daughters (Josh 7:24 – 25).[3]

More plausible are interpretations in terms of salvation history, where perfect or promising beginnings are followed by accounts of sin.[4] After the perfect harmony of Eden, Adam and Eve fall into sin (Gen 3). After humanity began to spread outside of Eden, the sons of God and the daughters of men intermingle (Gen 6:1 – 4). After God's mighty intervention in the exodus from Egypt, Israel manufactures the golden calf at Mount Sinai (Exod 32). Not long after God had made David king of Israel, he kills Uriah after becoming intimate with his wife (2 Sam 11). Some, therefore, take these episodes as background for our passage: "Now a husband and wife again sin

---

1. Theissen, *Miracle Stories*, 109, who defines "rule miracles" as miracles that "seek to reinforce sacred prescriptions" (ibid., 106).

2. Cf. Bruce, *Book of Acts*, 102; Johnson, *Acts*, 91 – 92.

3. Cf. Marshall, "Acts," 554; Bock, *Acts*, 220.

4. For these other interpretative approaches, cf. Daniel Marguerat, "La mort d'Ananias et Saphira (Ac 5.1 – 11) dans la stratégie de Luc," *NTS* 39 (1993): 209 – 26; Fitzmyer, *Acts*, 318 – 19.

at an early stage of the Christian church and disrupt the idyllic story of the church's beginnings. Satan is said to be at work once again."[5]

It is questionable, however, whether Luke intended to paint an "idyllic" picture of the church in Acts 1–4. Certainly the summary in 4:32–37 sounds idyllic, but the arrest of Peter and John, the ban on speaking, and the threats of the Sanhedrin in 4:1–22 suggest explicitly that the church did not exist in a vacuum. So does the reference to the mocking of the Jerusalem Jews on Pentecost in 2:13 and the description of the suicide of Judas in 1:15–20. As 1 Cor 5–14 demonstrates, there were moral scandals in other churches as well, which Luke does not report; the narrative here in 5:1–11 (and in 8:18–24) is given as an *exemplum* of the challenges that the congregations of Jesus' followers faced.

The passage, which consists largely of *historical narrative*, includes a section of a brief *speech* of Peter (5:3–4, 8–9), which, in Luke's report, consists of a series of questions with a concluding accusatory statement and a prophetic announcement. This is Peter's seventh speech (cf. 1:15–22; 2:14–36; 2:37–40; 3:6; 3:11–26; 4:8–12).

As regards the moral question of how "the harshness of Peter's words" can be reconciled with the manner in which he is portrayed in the earlier episodes and why Peter does not give Ananias and Sapphira a chance to repent, the following points should be noted. In the case of Ananias, Peter begins by asking six questions, evidently giving him an opportunity to respond, before asserting that he has lied to God — none of these questions is harsh. In the case of Sapphira, Peter again begins with a question that gives her the opportunity to admit her wrong and repent, which she refuses to do. Peter does not formulate condemnatory verdicts or utter curses — he asks questions, he states a fact (lying to other people always constitutes lying to God), and he utters a prophecy. It may be said that it is not Peter who is harsh, but God; unless we dispute God's right to judge or we deny the reality of the final judgment, there are no morally offensive elements in the narrative.

The second episode (5:12–16) describes the growth of the church in terms of the effect that "signs and wonders" performed by the apostles have on the population of Jerusalem and other towns in Judea. This is Luke's fourth *summary* statement (cf. 1:14; 2:42–47; 4:32–37). The first part describes the miracles performed by the apostles and their effect on the people. The second part narrates further conversions and miracles in Jerusalem that attract increasing numbers of people from other Judean towns.

---

5. Fitzmyer, *Acts*, 319.

Exegetical Outline

→ **I. The Demise of Ananias and Sapphira (5:1 – 11)**

    A. The Deception of Ananias and Sapphira (5:1 – 2)

        1. Setting: The married couple Ananias and Sapphira (5:1a-b)

        2. Ananias sells a piece of property (5:1c)

        3. Ananias retains part of the proceeds (5:2a-b)

        4. Ananias takes part of the proceeds to the apostles (5:2c-d)

    B. Peter's Confrontation with Ananias (5:3 – 6)

        1. The questioning of Ananias by Peter (5:3 – 4)

            a. Question 1: Why did Satan fill your heart? (5:3a-c)

            b. Question 2: Why did you lie to the Holy Spirit? (5:3d)

            c. Question 3: Why did you keep back part of the proceeds? (5:3e)

            d. Question 4: Why did you not see that you had right of ownership? (5:4a-b)

            e. Question 5: Why did you not exercise control over the proceeds? (5:4c-d)

            f. Question 6: Why did you decide to do such a thing? (5:4e-i)

        2. The reaction of Ananias (5:5a-c)

            a. Ananias hears Peter's questions (5:5a)

            b. Ananias drops dead (5:5b-c)

        3. The reaction of the others: Fear (5:5d-f)

            a. Others hear of Ananias's death (5:5d-e)

            b. People are seized by great fear (5:5f)

        4. The burial of Ananias (5:6)

            a. Young men come, wrap Ananias's body, and carry him out (5:6a-c)

            b. Burial of Ananias (5:6d)

    C. Developments after Ananias's Death (5:7)

        1. Time: Three hours later (5:7a)

        2. Event: Arrival of Sapphira (5:7b)

        3. Circumstances: Sapphira is oblivious of Ananias's death (5:7c)

    D. Peter's Confrontation with Sapphira (5:8 – 10)

        1. The questioning of Sapphira by Peter (5:8 – 9b)

            a. Question 1: Did you sell the property for the specified amount? (5:8a-d)

            b. Answer: Yes (5:8e-f)

            c. Question 2: Why did you conspire to test God's Spirit? (5:9a-b)

        2. Prophetic announcement of Sapphira's death by Peter (5:9c-d)

            a. Disclosure of Ananias's death and burial (5:9c)

            b. Prophecy of Sapphira's burial (5:9d)

         3. The reaction of Sapphira (5:10)

            a. Sapphira drops dead (5:10a-b)

            b. The burial of Sapphira (5:10c-g)

Explanation of the Text

5:1 A man named Ananias, together with his wife, Sapphira, sold a piece of property (Ἀνὴρ δέ τις Ἀνανίας ὀνόματι σὺν Σαπφίρῃ τῇ γυναικὶ αὐτοῦ ἐπώλησεν κτῆμα). After Luke's report of the selfless giving of Barnabas, he relates the machinations of a couple who want to gain prestige in the community of believers. Ananias is a Hebrew name (meaning "Yah[weh] has shown favor"); it was a popular name among Palestinian Jews. Sapphira is an Aramaic name meaning "the beautiful one."

Most think that Ananias and his wife Sapphira were believers in Jesus. Even though in the context of Luke's narrative this seems plausible, matters are not quite as clear-cut. In addition to 5:1, the term translated "man" (ἀνήρ) in Acts repeatedly introduces new characters who are unbelievers when they are introduced (3:2; 8:9, 27; 10:1; 14:8; 16:9). The statement in v. 13a — that people in Jerusalem infer from the fate of Ananias and Sapphira that they should keep a safe distance from the apostles and the congregation — supports, perhaps, the possibility that Ananias and Sapphira are merely sympathizers rather than authentic believers in Jesus.

Ananias, the main protagonist, sold "a piece of property" (κτῆμα), which is identified in v. 3 as a "field." He does what many of the believers had done — sold "possessions and ... belongings" (τὰ κτήματα καὶ τὰς ὑπάρξεις, 2:45), "lands or houses" (4:34), or "a piece of land" (4:37). Ananias's actions are reported with a series of four aorists: he "sold" a piece of property (v. 1c), "put aside" part of the proceeds (v. 2a), "brought" the other part (v. 2c), and "laid" it before the apostles (v. 2d).

5:2 And put aside for himself some of the proceeds, his wife being privy to this. And he brought only a part and laid it at the feet of the apostles (καὶ ἐνοσφίσατο ἀπὸ τῆς τιμῆς, συνειδυίης καὶ τῆς γυναικός καὶ ἐνέγκας μέρος τι παρὰ τοὺς πόδας τῶν ἀποστόλων ἔθηκεν). After Ananias had sold property, he "put aside for himself" (ἐνοσφίσατο) a part of the sale price. The middle voice of this verb is reflexive: what Ananias put aside, he put aside for himself (and his wife). Sapphira had been kept informed about all of her husband's actions. This signals that she will play a role in the narrative later on.

Ananias took the other part of the sale price and brought the sum of money to the apostles. The reference to the "feet" of the apostles indicates that Ananias did exactly what other believers had done, including Barnabas (4:35, 37), carrying out in public an act of selfless giving, possibly in Solomon's Portico, where the believers continued to gather (v. 12; cf. 4:35).

5:3 Peter said, "Ananias, why has Satan filled your heart that you would lie to the Holy Spirit and put aside for yourself some of the proceeds of the field?" (εἶπεν δὲ ὁ Πέτρος· Ἀνανία, διὰ τί ἐπλήρωσεν ὁ σατανᾶς τὴν καρδίαν σου ψεύσασθαί σε τὸ πνεῦμα τὸ ἅγιον καὶ νοσφίσασθαι ἀπὸ τῆς τιμῆς τοῦ χωρίου;). Luke describes Peter as the spokesman of the apostles, who have just received Ananias's gift. He also describes Peter as having the gift of prophecy, which allows him to see into Ananias's heart — something only God can do (cf. Heb 4:13).[6] The scene presupposes that Ananias said something to the apostles. He probably described the sale of his property and asserted that he was now donating all the money from the sale to be used for the needy (cf. in v. 4 the emphasis on the voluntary nature of the sale of personal possessions and of the amount donated to the community of believers).

Peter asks a series of six questions, which unmask Ananias's deception: (1) why he allowed Satan to "fill" his heart (v. 3a-c); (2) why he "lied" to the Spirit (v. 3d); (3) why he "put aside" some of the money for himself (v. 3e); (4) why he did not see that he had the right of ownership (v. 4a-b); (5) why he did not realize he exercised control over the proceeds (4c-d); and (6) why he "got" into his heart

to do such a thing (v. 4e-f). The Greek syntax in vv. 3 – 4 marks only four questions; however, the two aorist infinitives in v. 3 imply questions (2) and (3).

(1) Peter's first question relates Ananias's action to the influence of Satan (ὁ σατανᾶς). Satan is the supernatural power of evil opposed to God and, here, the evil counterpart to the Holy Spirit.[7] Peter confronts Ananias with the query why he allowed Satan to "fill" his heart. The term "heart" (καρδία; see on 4:32) denotes "the driving force behind the voluntative endeavors of the individual."[8] The motivation behind Ananias's action was not the Holy Spirit (v. 3d) and God (v. 4i), but Satan.

The formulation is different from Luke 22:3, where Satan is said to have "entered Judas" and consequently controlled his actions. Here, Satan "filled" Ananias's heart with something — not so much with the desire to lie but, evidently, with the desire to impress the apostles and the community of believers with the selfless sacrifice he and his wife had made. Ananias appears to think in the secular categories of gaining honor, prestige, and influence through benefaction, which impresses people if a real sacrifice has been made and the donation is impressive. The lying (v. 3d) and the setting aside of part of the money (v. 3e) certainly are the consequences of Satan "filling" his heart. They are separate actions, however, for which Peter holds Ananias accountable. Ananias has allowed his heart to function as the seat of human vices (cf. Pss 28:3; 41:7); it has become the seat of hybris, the reason for unrestrained self-aggrandizement (Isa 9:9).[9]

In 4:31 the believers were "all filled" (ἐπλήσθησαν ἅπαντες) with the Spirit. Ananias's heart is "filled" (ἐπλήρωσεν) with inspiration from Satan. The

---

6. Cf. *1 En.* 9:5; 2 Macc 3:34; Philo, *Cherubim* 17; *On God* 29; *Dreams* 1.90 – 91.

7. Luke mentions Satan in Luke 10:18; 11:18: 13:16; 22:3, 31 Acts 5:3; 26:18; and the devil (διάβολος) in Luke 4:2, 3, 6, 13; 8:12; Acts 10:38; 13:10.

8. H.-J. Fabry, "לֵב," *TDOT*, 7:423. In Exod 25:2; 35:5, 21, 22, 29; 1 Chr 29:9, the Heb. term describes the human heart as "instigating voluntary contributions or offerings" (ibid., 7:424).

9. Cf. ibid., 7:427; cf. Pss 10:6, 11; 35:25; Isa 14:13; 47:7, 10; Jer 49:16; Ob 3; Zeph 1:12; 2:15.

contrast is stark and highlights the possibility of serious sinfulness for believers — unless a contrast is being drawn here between believers (who still can fall into sin, but are not filled with Satan) and unbelievers (who can do good, but whose heart is controlled by the driving force of Satan's designs).

(2) Peter's second (implied) question addresses Ananias's attempt to deceive the apostles by lying about the price he had received from the sale of the property and about the amount he was making available to the community. Peter emphasizes that lying to the community of believers is always lying to the Holy Spirit, who is God's presence in the community. The notion that one could deceive the Holy Spirit is ludicrous — no one can deceive God's Spirit, since the almighty and omniscient God cannot be manipulated. The psalmist, drawing on Israel's obduracy after the exodus from Egypt, calls "testing God in the heart" apostasy and rebellion (cf. Ps 78:17 – 18; LXX 77:18).

(3) Peter's third (implied) question addresses the claim that Ananias evidently made, namely, that he was donating the entire proceeds from the sale to the church while in fact hiding some of the money to keep for himself.

5:4 "Did it not belong to you before it was sold? And was it not at your disposal after you had sold it? How did you get it into your heart to do such a thing? You have lied not to human beings but to God" (οὐχὶ μένον σοὶ ἔμενεν καὶ πραθὲν ἐν τῇ σῇ ἐξουσίᾳ ὑπῆρχεν; τί ὅτι ἔθου ἐν τῇ καρδίᾳ σου τὸ πρᾶγμα τοῦτο; οὐκ ἐψεύσω ἀνθρώποις ἀλλὰ τῷ θεῷ). (4) Peter's fourth question reminds Ananias that he had the right of ownership over his piece of land. The sale of personal possessions was clearly voluntary.

(5) Peter's fifth question reminds Ananias that he had personal control over the proceeds of the sale of his property. The donation of money received from the sale of property was voluntary. Selling personal possessions and donating even a part of the money from the sale for the support of impoverished fellow believers is admirable in itself.

(6) Peter's final question essentially repeats the first question: How could Ananias allow his heart to plan such deceit?[10] While the first question ascribes the deception to Satan, the last question asserts the personal culpability of Ananias. This corresponds to Paul's understanding of sin: while sin is the result of Adam's fall in the past, controlling the behavior of all human beings (Rom 5:12 – 21; 7:7 – 24), every human being is personally responsible for his or her sinful actions (Rom 1:18 – 3:20).

After finishing these questions, Peter states Ananias's guilt: he thought that he could deceive the apostles and the community, but in fact he has lied to God. This accusation is a restatement of question (2): lying to human beings is serious enough, because, according to Prov 26:28, "a lying tongue hates those it hurts." God hates lying, which is an abomination: "There are six things the LORD hates, seven that are detestable to him: haughty eyes, a lying tongue, hands that shed innocent blood, a heart that devises wicked schemes, feet that are quick to rush into evil, a false witness who pours out lies and a person who stirs up conflict in a community" (Prov 6:16 – 19). From this list of these seven sins, Ananias (and his wife) committed all but one (he did not shed innocent blood).

5:5 When Ananias heard these words, he collapsed and died. All people who heard what had happened were gripped with great fear (ἀκούων δὲ ὁ Ἀνανίας τοὺς λόγους τούτους πεσὼν ἐξέψυξεν, καὶ ἐγένετο φόβος μέγας ἐπὶ πάντας τοὺς ἀκούοντας). The reaction of Ananias to Peter's questions and

---

10. For the phrase "put something in one's heart" in the sense of "considering something" or "resolving something," cf. 1 Sam 21:12; Jer 12:11; Dan 1:8; Hag 2:18; Mal 2:2; Luke 1:66; 21:14. Fitzmyer, *Acts*, 323.

accusations is sudden, swift, and dramatic. The present participle translated "heard" (ἀκούων) indicates Ananias had been listening to everything Peter said. When he finished his remarks, Ananias "collapsed and died," right next to the money with which he wanted to deceive the apostles.

Peter does not utter a word of judgment, nor do his words condemn Ananias to death, nor does he express a wish that he would die. However, as the apostle has just blamed Ananias for lying against God (v. 4), and as he has unmasked Ananias's heart as being driven by Satan (v. 3), his sudden death must be understood as God's judgment. As Peter laid bare Ananias's heart and stated his rebellion against God, Ananias's heart gives out. Whether he dies of a heart attack, induced by the public exposure of his deceit in front of the apostles and perhaps in front of thousands of believers in Solomon's Portico, or whether his death has supernatural causes, its timing certainly is the result of divine judgment.[11]

Some suggest that as Peter accuses Ananias of having lied to the Holy Spirit (vv. 3, 9), the deception constitutes a blasphemy against the Holy Spirit, which cannot be forgiven (Luke 12:10). However, the issue in vv. 3–4, 9 is deception, not blasphemy, and the statement in Luke 12:10 relates to outsiders, not to the believing community.

The reaction of the people who heard about the sudden death of Ananias—and surely also those who were present and saw what happened—was "great fear" (φόβος μέγας). Here "fear" does not denote reverent awe in view of God's greatness but the frightful apprehension that if such a thing could happen to Ananias, who had been willing, after all, to sell his property and donate a (presumably) large sum to the community, it could happen to anyone. The reference to "great fear" also implies that whatever the cause of Ananias's death, it caused much more than the uneasiness that an expected death often evokes in other people. Ananias's death confronted them with the reality of the holy God who hates sin and judges sinners.

5:6 The young men came forward, wrapped him up, carried him out, and buried him (ἀναστάντες δὲ οἱ νεώτεροι συνέστειλαν αὐτὸν καὶ ἐξενέγκαντες ἔθαψαν). Ananias is buried immediately and quickly. If the phrase translated "the young men" (οἱ νεώτεροι) has a comparative meaning, the "young men" may have been younger than eighteen years, the age for which the term "young men" (οἱ νέοι) was used. The "young men" (νεανίσκοι) in v. 10 (cf. 2:17) presumably refers to the same group. These were young people in the church who were ready to perform various necessary tasks.

Luke describes the removal and burial of Ananias's body with four aorist verbal forms. (1) The young men "came forward" (ἀναστάντες); the participle is temporal and expresses prior action, perhaps in the sense of "after they came to carry out a function" or "after they had gotten ready." (2) They "wrapped him up" (συνέστειλαν) in a piece of cloth so that they could carry the body more easily. (4) They "carried him out" (ἐξενέγκαντες); the participle is again temporal. (5) They "buried" him (ἔθαψαν) in a tomb. The family of Ananias may have owned a tomb with chambers in which he could be buried, or he was buried (temporarily) in another tomb. Without elaborate ceremonies, the burial could be carried out within a couple of hours. The quick and unceremonious burial may be due to the recognition that Ananias had been struck down by God. Demonstrative grief from family members and friends was apparently suspended (Sapphira

---

11. Whether this is "a sort of 'shock therapy' for the community" (Fitzmyer, *Acts*, 324) depends on whether there were other believers who needed such a "therapy." Peterson, *Acts*, 211, speaks of "a divine visitation, anticipating the final judgment of God."

was not even informed, v. 7),[12] as was a procession to the burial site.

5:7 There was an interval of about three hours. His wife came in, who did not know what had happened (ἐγένετο δὲ ὡς ὡρῶν τριῶν διάστημα καὶ ἡ γυνὴ αὐτοῦ μὴ εἰδυῖα τὸ γεγονὸς εἰσῆλθεν). The third incident concerns developments after Ananias's death. Three hours elapse, while the believers and the apostles evidently continue to meet, probably in Solomon's Portico (cf. v. 12). Then Ananias's wife comes into the meeting. She probably knows her husband took money to the apostles and expects to be greeted with gratitude and admiration. But she does not know "what had happened." We do not know what Sapphira was doing during the three-hour interval. Since this was a wealthy couple and since she was involved in the conspiracy concerning the sale of their property and the handling of the proceeds (vv. 1–2), she may have been active in the family business.

This sentence functions as a dramatic introduction to what follows. While Sapphira is ignorant of what has happened, Luke's readers are not, and they wait for the continuation of the narrative, which is bound to confront the woman with her husband's death.

5:8 Peter addressed her, "Tell me, did you sell the piece of property for such and such an amount?" She answered, "Yes, for that amount" (ἀπεκρίθη δὲ πρὸς αὐτὴν Πέτρος· εἰπέ μοι, εἰ τοσούτου τὸ χωρίον ἀπέδοσθε; ἡ δὲ εἶπεν· ναί, τοσούτου). The fourth incident of the episode narrates Peter's confrontation of Sapphira. He asks her a question, with a simple yes or no answer needed. Peter wants Sapphira to confirm the price they had obtained when

they sold their piece of property. Sapphira's answer and Peter's response indicate that the figure Peter confronted her with corresponded to the reduced amount of the sale price that Ananias had brought to the apostles (the silver or gold coins were perhaps still on the floor or on a table).[13] Peter may not know at this point whether Sapphira was part of Ananias's deceit (as distinct from Luke's readers, cf. vv. 1–2). His question is thus not designed to unmask her involvement in the deception, but to give her an opportunity either to corroborate what her husband said or to state the truth.

Some commentators think that Peter provokes Sapphira's lie without giving her an opportunity to state the truth and repent.[14] In Luke's narrative, however, Peter formulates a question that can be answered with either yes or no. Since Sapphira is evidently a capable woman, able to operate independently of her husband — she arrives three hours later, apparently on her own — Peter might well expect his question would make her suspicious of what has happened and prompt her to ask for details.

Sapphira confirms the figure Peter mentions, which is the amount of money the two wanted to donate to the congregation, linked with the claim that this was the entire sale price. This confirms Luke's information in v. 2 that the couple had decided in advance how much money they would donate to the congregation and what they would say about the amount. She misses the opportunity to change their story and tell the truth.

5:9 Then Peter said to her, "Why did you agree to test the Spirit of the Lord? Look, the feet of those who have buried your husband are at the door,

---

12. Compare the many friends and relatives who mourn the death of Lazarus and console his sisters (John 11:17–20).

13. Luke does not relate what happened to the money. Did the apostles keep it and distribute it to the poor, so that some good may still come from this sad and tragic incident? Or did

they regard is as tainted by deception and return it to their family?

14. Cf. Barrett, *Acts*, 269; similarly Jervell, *Apostelgeschichte*, 198, who thinks that v. 9b is not really a question but the promulgation of a verdict.

and they will carry you out" (ὁ δὲ Πέτρος πρὸς αὐτήν· τί ὅτι συνεφωνήθη ὑμῖν πειράσαι τὸ πνεῦμα κυρίου; ἰδοὺ οἱ πόδες τῶν θαψάντων τὸν ἄνδρα σου ἐπὶ τῇ θύρᾳ καὶ ἐξοίσουσίν σε). In an exchange that is abbreviated compared with the queries in vv. 3 – 4, Peter seeks to establish the motivation and the cause for the deceit of the couple. Peter's second question seems to presuppose that he told Sapphira that he knows about the deception. He asks her why she came to an agreement with her husband, assuming that she could have disagreed and perhaps tried to dissuade him from carrying out the deception.

While Peter stated earlier that the deception was a lie against the Holy Spirit (v. 3), he calls it here "testing" (πειράσαι) the Spirit. The use of this verb reminds biblically literate readers of the Israelites in the wilderness who on several occasions "tested" God through rebellion and apostasy, with dire results.[15] Peter asserts that the couple's sin is not only deception, perhaps based on the selfish desire to increase their prestige and standing in the congregation, but arrogance as well. They believed that they could behave in a manner clearly not sanctioned by God and get away with it.

Some claim that Ananias and Sapphira did not conspire to tempt the Spirit but to lie, and that they provoked God unwittingly.[16] Peter's language suggests, however, that they knew what they were doing — not only with their money, but also with the community that was of "one heart and one mind" and in which God's Spirit was present. When God or his Spirit is tested, "the culprit knows that God has issued some command and disobeys it to see if God was really serious about it and will react or not."[17] The couple "challenged the Spirit of the Lord, who searches all things (1 Cor 2:10), whether

He would observe the deception."[18] Peter expects that he will, as the next sentence demonstrates.

Peter announces Sapphira's death. He sees the young men who had buried Ananias return to the congregation, and he prophetically announces God's judgment. Peter first discloses Ananias's death and burial (v. 9c), then announces Sapphira's burial, predicting that the young people who have buried her husband "will carry [her] out" (ἐξοίσουσιν) and bury her also, implying that this will happen instantaneously.

5:10 She immediately collapsed at his feet and died. When the young men came in, they found her dead; they carried her out and buried her next to her husband (ἔπεσεν δὲ παραχρῆμα πρὸς τοὺς πόδας αὐτοῦ καὶ ἐξέψυξεν· εἰσελθόντες δὲ οἱ νεανίσκοι εὗρον αὐτὴν νεκρὰν καὶ ἐξενέγκαντες ἔθαψαν πρὸς τὸν ἄνδρα αὐτῆς). Luke reports what happens next in a dramatic, fast-paced series of six aorists. Sapphira instantly collapses (ἔπεσεν) to the ground at Peter's feet and dies (ἐξέψυξεν). The same young men who buried her husband come in (εἰσελθόντες), find (εὗρον) her dead, carry her out (ἐξενέγκαντες), and bury her (ἔθαψαν) next to her husband. Sapphira, who has shared her husband's deception, shares his fate in sudden death and burial. She may have died of shock — learning of the exposure of their deceit in front of the apostles and the entire congregation, and hearing of her husband's death and burial — or as a result of God supernaturally ending her life, although Luke does not talk about a miracle here.

5:11 The whole church and all people who heard of these things were gripped with great fear (καὶ ἐγένετο φόβος μέγας ἐφ᾽ ὅλην τὴν ἐκκλησίαν καὶ ἐπὶ πάντας τοὺς ἀκούοντας ταῦτα). Luke

---

15. Cf. Exod 17:2; Deut 6:16; 33:8; Num 20:13, 24; cf. Ps 78:18 (77:18 LXX); cf. Ps 106:32 (105:32 LXX); cf. Matt 4:7; Luke 4:12.

16. Conzelmann, *Acts*, 38; Haenchen, *Acts*, 239.

17. Marshall, "Acts," 554.

18. H. Seesemann, "πεῖρα κτλ.," *TDNT*, 6:32.

comments on the effect of the death of both Ananias and Sapphira. He repeats that "all people" who heard of the death of Ananias and Sapphira were gripped with "great fear" (φόβος μέγας). As in v. 5, the "great fear" is more than reverent awe, even for the believers. It involves the distressing apprehension that God has intervened in judgment, the alarming realization that he may do so again in other cases of deception, and the terrifying trepidation that one's own life might be in jeopardy because of sins that one has committed. Luke specifies that not only outsiders are gripped with fear, but also "the whole congregation" (ἐφ᾽ ὅλην τὴν ἐκκλησίαν). Luke uses the term ἐκκλησία here for the first time to designate the congregation of believers in Jesus.

IN DEPTH: The Self-Understanding of the Church in Jerusalem

Luke uses several terms for the Jerusalem church that reflect the self-understanding of the earliest followers of Jesus.[19]

(1) *The brothers and sisters* (οἱ ἀδελφοί; 1:16; 6:3; etc.). Jews used the term "brother" (and "sister") when they addressed each other (cf. 2:29). This terminology has particular significance for the followers of Jesus, however, since Jesus had asserted that those who follow him and do his Father's will are his brothers and sisters (Luke 8:21/Mark 3:35). The term expresses now not the bonds of common kinship and ethnicity, but the bond of the common convictions, values, and goals of those who are followers of Jesus, Israel's Messiah and Savior and thus members of the renewed Israel.

(2) *The believers* (οἱ πιστεύοντες; 2:44; 4:32; 5:14; etc.). This designation describes the central reality that characterizes the new movement among the Jewish people — they are Jews who believe that Jesus is Israel's Messiah and Savior. It is the reality of their faith in Jesus who bestows the Holy Spirit that explains the transformation in their lives as individuals, some of whom are prompted to sell property and share the proceeds with impoverished fellow believers. It is their faith that causes them to be of "one heart and mind" (4:32).

(3) *The congregation* (τὸ πλῆθος; 4:32; 5:16; 6:2, 5; 15:12, 30). The term, which means "large number, multitude," also describes a "meeting" or "assembly." In the context of Luke's description of the followers of Jesus, the term refers to the whole body of the members of the community, i.e., the "congregation" of all the believers in Jesus living in Jerusalem.

(4) *The church of God* (ἐκκλησία; 5:11).[20] For Luke's readers whose first lan-

---

19. Bauckham, "James and the Jerusalem Community," 56 – 59.

20. Luke uses ἐκκλησία 23 times: Acts 5:11; 7:38; 8:1, 3; 9:31; 11:22, 26; 12:1, 5; 13:1; 14:23, 27; 15:3, 4, 22, 41; 16:5; 18:22; 19:32, 39, 40; 20:17, 28. There are only three references to ἐκκλησία in the Gospels (Matt 16:18; 18:17a, 17b); Paul uses

guage is Greek, the meaning of the term translated as "congregation" or "community" is, at least initially, the meaning of the term in the Hellenistic world. In the Greek-speaking cities, the term ἐκκλησία denotes the "regularly summoned legislative body" of the city, i.e., the free men who were eligible to vote.[21] An extended meaning is "people with shared belief, *community, congregation.*"[22] Against this background, ἐκκλησία denotes the followers of Jesus gathering to worship God in the context of his salvific revelation in Jesus' life, death, resurrection, and exaltation, to listen to the teaching of the apostles, and to share meals with one another. The phrase "church of God" (ἐκκλησία τοῦ θεοῦ), used especially by Paul[23] and reflecting earliest Christian usage, is the Greek equivalent for a Hebrew expression (*qᵉhāl-ʾēl*), which is used in early Jewish texts in an eschatological sense for the company of God, i.e., for those among God's people whom he has chosen to serve him during the events of the last days.[24]

Against this background, the expression ἐκκλησία τοῦ θεοῦ denotes the community of people who have come to faith in Jesus as God's Messiah and Savior revealed in the "last days." Thus, the Greek term usually translated "church" denotes the "congregation" or the "congregational assembly" of believers in Jesus as the eschatological people of God, in salvation-historical continuity with Israel. The genitive "of God" describes God as the initiator and owner of the congregation of believers in Jesus — the community of followers of Jesus has been established by God (genitive of authorship) and thus belongs to God (possessive genitive).[25] These people emerge as an ever more clearly identifiable group within first-century Judaism, characterized by the belief that Jesus is Israel's Messiah and Savior.

(5) *The disciples* (οἱ μαθηταί; 6:1, 2, 7; 9:1, 25, 26; 11:26; 15:10 etc.).[26] This term expresses the continuity of the believers in Jesus after Easter with the followers of Jesus during his earthly ministry. It expresses the significance of learning, and thus of teaching, in the earliest Christian community (cf. Acts 6:1–7).[27]

---

the term 62 times (of a total of 114 occurrences in the New Testament).

21. BDAG, s.v. ἐκκλησία 1. The etymological explanation from "to call out" as "the called-out ones" (e.g., William D. Mounce, *Mounce's Complete Expository Dictionary of Old and New Testament Words* [Grand Rapids: Zondervan, 2006], 110) is irrelevant for the meaning of the term both in classical Greek and in the Hellenistic period; the notion of being "called out" from a group that one leaves is never present in the New Testament.

22. BDAG, s.v. ἐκκλησία 2.

23. Acts 20:28; cf. 1 Cor 1:2; 10:32; 11:16, 22; 15:9; 2 Cor 1:1; Gal 1:13; 1 Thess 2:14; 2 Thess 1:4; 1 Tim 3:5, 15.

24. 1QM IV, 10 und 1QSa I, 25. The LXX translates *qhl* with ἐκκλησία, but also with συναγωγή (often in Gen, Lev, Num, Jer, Ezek).

25. Paul in particular emphasizes that the ἐκκλησία belongs to God; cf. 1 Cor 3:23; note the language of election in 1 Thess 1:4; 2:12; 4:7; 5:9, 24.

26. Luke uses the term μαθηταί 28 times in Acts.

27. Cf. BDAG, s.v. μαθητής 1, "one who engages in learning through instruction from another, *pupil, apprentice* (in contrast to the teacher)"; 2, "one who is rather constantly associated with someone who has a pedagogical reputation or a particular set of views, *disciple, adherent.*"

Christians are followers of Jesus who learn from Jesus and who study and (often) memorize Jesus' teaching.

(6) *The Way* (ἡ ὁδός; 9:2; 19:9, 23; 22:4; 24:14, 22). The fuller forms of this designation — "the Way of the Lord" (18:25) and "the Way of God" (18:26) — suggest that this term derives from Isa 40:3 and, more broadly, from other passages in Isaiah[28] that speak of the way on which the Lord will travel when Israel is liberated from exile and restored to Zion. The followers of Jesus in Jerusalem evidently were convinced that the task of preparing the way of the Lord (Isa 40:3), proclaimed by John the Baptist (Matt 3:3/Mark 1:3/Luke 3:4/John 1:23), is complete, and they are now traveling "the Way" of God's renewed people.

(7) *The saints* (οἱ ἅγιοι; 9:13, 32, 41; 26:10).[29] In the Old Testament, the term "holy ones" refers mostly to angels and only rarely to God's people. The use of the term for the believers in Jesus may have developed from the phrase "the holy [ones] of the Most High" in Dan 7:18, 22, 25, 27. This designation expresses the conviction that people who repent and believe in Jesus — the crucified, risen, and exalted Messiah and Savior — have received forgiveness of sins, have been reconciled with God, and thus constitute the people of God, renewed through Israel's Messiah and especially devoted to God.

(8) *The Nazarenes* (οἱ Ναζωραῖοι; 24:5). This is the term the lawyer Tertullus uses to designate the followers of Jesus (Tertullus brings the case of the Jewish authorities against Paul before the Roman governor in Caesarea). While the term "Christians" originated among Latin and Greek speakers (11:26), the term "Nazarenes" was used for the followers of Jesus by speakers of Semitic languages. It appears that this was the only term that non-Christian Jews used to designate Jesus' followers. Since Jesus was a common name in the first century, people called him "Jesus of Nazareth" or "Jesus the Nazarene" to distinguish him from other bearers of the name Jesus, and his followers were then naturally called "the Nazarenes."

This designation may imply the rejection of messianic claims concerning Jesus. Or it may be pun on Jesus' designation as the messianic "shoot" (*nēṣer*) of David (Isa 11:1; cf. 60:21), perhaps with an implied reference to the term "Nazirite" (*nāzîr*), someone consecrated to God (Num 6:1 – 21; Judg 13:5, 7; 16:17). There may be a further pun with the Hebrew term for "to watch, preserve" (*nṣr*) in terms of "the preserved of Israel" whom the Messiah will restore (Isa 49:6).

---

28. Cf. Isa 30:11, 21; 35:8; 42:16; 48:17; 49:11; 57:14; 62:10.

29. The expression "the saints" (NIV has "the Lord's people") is a standard designation of Paul for believers in Jesus; it is used as a term for the Jerusalem church in Rom 15:25, 26, 31; 1 Cor 16:1; 2 Cor 8:4; 9:1, 12.

5:12 Many signs and wonders among the people happened at the hands of the apostles. They were all meeting with one mind in Solomon's Portico (διὰ δὲ τῶν χειρῶν τῶν ἀποστόλων ἐγίνετο σημεῖα καὶ τέρατα πολλὰ ἐν τῷ λαῷ. καὶ ἦσαν ὁμοθυμαδὸν ἅπαντες ἐν τῇ στοᾷ Σολομῶντος). The "many signs and wonders" that happen in Jerusalem indicate that God is answering the prayer of the believers, who asked for signs and wonders (4:30). According to 5:15 – 16, these signs and wonders were miracles of healing and exorcisms.[30] Luke emphasizes that it was "at the hands of the apostles" (placed first for emphasis) that miracles happened, i.e., not only through Peter, but through all the Twelve. The phrase "at the hands of" is probably a Hebrew idiom and not a reference to the laying on of hands during the healing of the sick.

The imperfect translated as "happened" (ἐγίνετο) indicates that the miracles happened over a period of time. The close connection between this sentence and the next suggests that many of these healings took place in the temple court, like the healing of the lame man at the Beautiful Gate in 3:1 – 10. The miracles take place "among the people" (ἐν τῷ λαῷ), i.e., in public, in Israel's center.

Luke notes again that the believers regularly meet in Solomon's Portico (3:11; cf. 2:46; 3:1; 5:20, 42; see on 2:46). The imperfect translated "were meeting" (ἦσαν) suggests that when the believers met as a large group, they met, worshiped, taught, studied, learned, and shared in the temple complex — at Solomon's Portico, located on the east side of the Temple Mount. For ὁμοθυμαδόν see on 1:14.

5:13 None of the other people dared to join them, yet the people spoke highly of them (τῶν δὲ λοιπῶν οὐδεὶς ἐτόλμα κολλᾶσθαι αὐτοῖς ἀλλ' ἐμεγάλυνεν αὐτοὺς ὁ λαός). The "great fear" triggered by the sudden death of Ananias and Sapphira kept "the other people" away from joining the believers meeting in the temple. The identity of "the other people" (οἱ λοιποί) is disputed. They are most plausibly understood as referring to Jewish people in general who do not belong to the congregation of the followers of Jesus.[31] There is no contradiction with vv. 12 or 14 since the Greek term κολλᾶσθαι ("join") is not a technical term denoting conversion[32] but often refers to geographical or personal proximity. Curious people were hesitant to approach the congregation and thus kept themselves at a safe distance.

Nevertheless, these people "spoke highly" of believers. Awe, fear, and the expression of a favorable opinion are not mutually exclusive, but are often connected. If the personal pronoun (αὐτοῖς) refers to the congregation of believers meeting in Solomon's Portico (vv. 11 – 12), the direct object (αὐτούς) refers to the believers in the congregation as well.

5:14 More than ever, believers were added to the Lord, great numbers of both men and women (μᾶλλον δὲ προσετίθεντο πιστεύοντες τῷ κυρίῳ, πλήθη ἀνδρῶν τε καὶ γυναικῶν). The teaching and preaching of the apostles and the meetings of the congregation in Solomon's Portico led to further conversions among the Jewish people. The term "more than" (μᾶλλον) has a comparative meaning: more Jews than ever came to faith in Jesus as Lord (κύριος), as the risen and exalted Messiah and Savior. In view of the numbers given in 2:41 (3,000) and 4:4 (5,000), the plural (πλήθη, "large

---

30. Other types of miracles mentioned later in Acts include miraculous knowledge, raising of the dead, protection from a snake bite. The speaking in unlearned foreign languages (Acts 2) was also a miracle.

31. Thus most interpreters; cf. Polhill, *Acts*, 163; Fitzmyer,

Acts, 328; Jervell, *Apostelgeschichte*, 201; Gaventa, *Acts*, 104.

32. In the LXX it can designate "allegiance to the Lord" (Deut 6:13; 10:20) but also "physical proximity" (Deut 28:60; 29:20). For Luke's use of the term cf. Luke 10:11; 15:15; Acts 8:29; 9:26; 10:28; 17:34.

numbers, multitudes") should be interpreted in terms of many hundreds, if not thousands, of Jews who became believers in Jesus. The present participle translated as "believers" (πιστεύοντες) implies the continuing nature of the faith of these new converts. Luke specifies that both men and women were converted.

The cause of the new conversions may be seen in the miracles (vv. 12a, 15 – 16), a factor, however, that must be "balanced" with the fear that gripped the population (v. 11) and the distance that the people kept from the congregation (v. 13a). The key to resolve this apparent contradiction is the imperfect passive "were added" (προσετίθεντο), which implies God as agent of the action: it was God himself who caused people to overcome their unbelief, their hesitation, and their fear and to come to faith in Jesus as Israel's Messiah and Savior.

5:15 As a result, they would carry the sick out into the streets and lay them on cots and mats so that when Peter would pass by, his shadow might fall on some of them (ὥστε καὶ εἰς τὰς πλατείας ἐκφέρειν τοὺς ἀσθενεῖς καὶ τιθέναι ἐπὶ κλιναρίων καὶ κραβάττων, ἵνα ἐρχομένου Πέτρου κἂν ἡ σκιὰ ἐπισκιάσῃ τινὶ αὐτῶν). The continued growth of the church results in more healings. The connection translated "as a result" (ὥστε) is often regarded as a difficulty, which is resolved if v. 14 is seen as a parenthesis and if the expectation of miracles in v. 15 is connected with the high regard of the population for the believers in v. 13b.[33] Another solution is to interpret ὥστε as indeed linking the faith of the new converts (v. 14) with the expectation and the experience of miraculous healings and exorcisms (vv. 15 – 16).[34]

If this connection is interpreted in a strict sense, the people who expect and experience healings

from illnesses and liberation from demons are believers in Jesus. The crucifixion of Jesus by the Jewish authorities despite the miracles he had performed, their continued opposition to Jesus' followers, whose proclamation of Jesus has been banned (4:17 – 18; 5:28), and the awesome and terrifying presence of God in the congregation of the believers does not make it plausible that unbelieving Jews would want to be healed in the name of Jesus (cf. 3:6; 4:10, 30) by the apostles, who proclaimed that Jesus is the only Savior for the Jewish people (4:12). Certainly people who opposed the apostles and the followers of Jesus would not want to be healed by Peter and his associates. At most they would have to be sympathizers — Jews generally open to consider faith in Jesus. The expectation to be healed through Peter's shadow (5:15) suggests, perhaps, sympathizers rather than authentic believers.

Jews living in Jerusalem carried sick relatives and friends out of their houses and into the streets. It seems that the large number of thousands of believers made it impractical to carry all the sick people up to the temple complex into Solomon's Portico. The term translated "streets" (πλατεία) denotes a "wide road" or "street." In Jerusalem, the main street that ran from northwest to south, leading from the New City via the Tyropoeon Valley to Robinson's Arch at the southwest corner of the Temple Mount, was 10 meters wide, paved with stone slabs measuring 2 by 4 meters (with a sewer beneath the street up to 4 meters deep).[35] Most of the other streets were more narrow and without pavement.

The sick lay on "cots" (κλινάριον) and on "mats" (κράβαττος); the former term is a diminutive and refers to a small bed or cot, while the latter term refers to a mattress or pallet. The sick waited until

---

33. BDF, §465.1; Haenchen, *Acts*, 243 – 44; Gaventa, *Acts*, 104.

34. Cf. Zmijewski, *Apostelgeschichte*, 254.

35. Cf. H. Geva, "Jerusalem: The Temple Mount and Its Environs," *NEAEHL*, 2:739, 741.

Peter (and the other apostles? cf. v. 12d) passed by — perhaps on their way to Solomon's Portico in the temple, where they regularly taught, or on the way to meetings in the houses of believers throughout the city (cf. 2:46). Some evidently believed that Peter's shadow had healing power. The Greek syntax suggests an element of uncertainty in their expectation (particle ἄν), and the indefinite pronoun (τις) indicates that only some, not all, of the sick were healed through Peter's shadow.

Many commentators refer to parallels in Greek, Roman, and (later) Jewish literature that relate the belief that a shadow, being a vital part of a human being (or of an animal), can have a powerful positive or negative effect on another person.[36] However, no exact parallels to v. 15 have been found.[37] Luke does not say whether the apostles encouraged such beliefs, and he does not explicitly state that people who had such beliefs were actually healed (unless the statement in v. 16e should be linked with v. 15).[38] In Luke 8:44, a woman believed that if she touched the fringe of Jesus' robe, she would be healed. The expectation that Paul's handkerchiefs had healing power (19:12) is similarly unusual.

Some suggest that the verb that Luke uses (ἐπισκιάσῃ, "overshadowed"), seen in the context of its use in the LXX and in Luke 1:35; 9:34, points to "the presence and power of God which Peter represents" that effects the cures, rather than the shadow as such.[39] Others suggest that even if popular superstition is involved, God healed in his gracious mercy anyway. Luke does not see these happenings in a critical light. He is convinced that the conver-

sion of thousands of people was accompanied by a mighty display of God's power that healed many people in miraculous ways, and that the reputation of the apostles was linked with the healings that took place during this period. For Luke, it was not the shadow of Peter but God who caused healings to happen when people come to faith in Jesus (3:16; 4:10, 30).

5:16 A large number of people also gathered from the towns around Jerusalem; they brought the sick and the people tormented by unclean spirits, who were all cured (συνήρχετο δὲ καὶ τὸ πλῆθος τῶν πέριξ πόλεων Ἰερουσαλήμ φέροντες ἀσθενεῖς καὶ ὀχλουμένους ὑπὸ πνευμάτων ἀκαθάρτων, οἵτινες ἐθεραπεύοντο ἅπαντες). This is the first notice in Acts that indicates that people from outside Jerusalem were affected by the ministry of the apostles. A large number of people who lived in towns around Jerusalem also gathered. In a Jewish context, the term translated as "towns" (πόλις, singular) was used no longer in the sense of a Greek "city-state" but came to be used for "towns" such as Bethlehem and Nazareth (Luke 2:4, 39), which had less than 400 inhabitants.

Luke does not say where these people gathered. Some assume that they came to Jerusalem.[40] This is far from certain, however. The Twelve had been trained by Jesus to move from town to town and from village to village, they had seen thousands of Jews come to faith in Jesus, and they had been commissioned by Jesus to be his witnesses in Jerusalem and in Judea (1:8). Surely, then, they would start to visit other towns in Judea. If we accept this

36. Peter W. van der Horst, "Peter's Shadow: The Religio-Historical Background of Acts V 15," *NTS* 23 (1977): 204 – 12.

37. Pesch, *Apostelgeschichte*, 1:207; Bock, *Acts*, 232.

38. Graham H. Twelftree, *In the Name of Jesus: Exorcism among Early Christians* (Grand Rapids: Baker, 2007), 143, goes beyond the evidence of the text when he states that healing through Peter's shadow falling on people is accepted by Luke "as a Christian method of exorcism"; the apostles do not seem

to have told the people to wait for their shadow to pass.

39. John Fleter Tipei, *The Laying on of Hands in the New Testament: Its Significance, Techniques, and Effects* (Lanham, MD: Univ. Press of America, 2009), 146 – 47.

40. Fitzmyer, *Acts*, 329. The Western text reads εἰς before Jerusalem (D E Ψ 36 181) and thus assumes that people from the towns around Jerusalem brought the sick "into" the city.

scenario, Luke's comment in v. 16 means that when the apostles, who traveled perhaps in groups of two (cf. Mark 6:7), arrived in a town, people gathered to hear them preach and to heal the sick.

Jews from the towns of Judea, just like those living in Jerusalem, gathered their sick relatives and friends and brought them to the apostles. Luke specifies that some "tormented by unclean spirits" were also "cured" (ἐθεραπεύοντο). The expression "unclean spirits" (πνεύματα ἀκάθαρτα)[41] probably refers to demons. They are "unclean" because they are evil and separated from the purity of God and of his people. The present participle "tormented" (ὀχλουμένους) suggests that these evil spirits affected some of these people as a permanent condition. The particle καί, which separates the sick (ἀσθενεῖς) from those tormented by unclean spirits, indicates that Luke keeps the two categories of afflictions separate. All who wanted to be healed were in fact healed.

Theology in Application

Whether Ananias and Sapphira were authentic believers or not, we should be careful not to portray them as villains. They were willing to sell property and donate part of it — presumably a large sum — to the congregation. Even though their motivation was wrong, their donation in itself was laudable, a reflection of the importance that the Jerusalem church accorded to helping the needy. This fact, however, does not minimize the seriousness of their offense. People who hide something are not salt of the earth and light of the world (Matt 5:13 – 16; cf. Luke 14:34 – 35). If not merely murder is sin, but already anger (Matt 5:21 – 26) is, then the motivation to gain in prestige and reputation through willful misrepresentation is as serious as a power grab with violent means. If our heart is in the place where our possessions are (Luke 12:34), Ananias and Sapphira did not have "a treasure in heaven that will never fail, where no thief comes near and no moth destroys" (Luke 12:33); their hearts were tied to their reputation rather than to their faith in God, who had revealed himself in Jesus, the messianic Savior and the exalted Lord.

This passage does present difficult questions pertaining to the deception and death of Ananias and Sapphira — its suddenness, its harshness, the apparent lack of an opportunity to repent and make amends, and Peter's solitary role. We have attempted to answer most of these questions. Several basic truths are important in this passage.

41. Luke uses the term in Luke 4:33, 36; 6:18; 8:29; 9:42; 11:24; Acts 5:16; 8:7.

The Place of God's Presence

The church is the place of God's presence. Insofar as Ananias and Sapphira wanted to deceive the apostles and the other believers, they were lying to God. When we speak here of "church," we mean the local church, the congregation of believers in Jesus in a specific locality. The congregation of God is not just a human institution where all challenges and problems can be somehow "worked out" with principles and tools derived from the social sciences of schools of business and management. The church is the "temple of the Holy Spirit" and thus the place where God is present.

As such, the believers who make up the congregation live in grateful acceptance and observance of God's will. Their behavior should not be controlled by the values of the society in which they live, but by the revealed will of God, which not infrequently contradicts the secular values of society.

Since the congregation is the place of God's presence, it *is* holy. Paul addresses his letter to the believers in Corinth to "the church of God in Corinth, to those sanctified in Christ Jesus" (1 Cor 1:2). People who have come to faith in Jesus, the Savior, have experienced God's forgiveness of their sins, the removal of their guilt, and their transfer into the status of people who are righteous and holy; thus, they belong to the community of God's holy people.

Since this assembly of people has been made holy, God calls them to live holy lives. The "indicative" of our status and the "imperative" of our obligation must be held together — believers *are* holy because they have been forgiven, justified, and redeemed, and believers are obligated to live according to God's will. All motivations and actions that contradict God's holiness — deception, lies, attempting to gain prestige, and honor — have no place in the life of believers. Sin is always serious; it is always an attack on God. Deceiving the church is not simply deceiving the pastors, or the other members, but God himself, who is present in the church through his Spirit.

The weekly meetings of the congregation thus focus on praise, gratefulness, and obedience to God and his revelation in the Scriptures and in Jesus Christ. Churches that focus on entertaining people have degenerated from places of divine presence to places of human soliloquy. Instead of being in dialogue with God, people have a monologue with themselves.

The reality of the presence of God in the Jerusalem church accounts for the willingness of believers to sell property in order to help the poor, and it accounts for the respect that the population of the city of Jerusalem had for the followers of Jesus during this period. Commitment to Jesus does not always, or not always immediately, lead to opposition and persecution. Authentic, consistent Christian behavior should establish a good reputation for Christian believers in the surrounding culture. Enjoying the favor of the "world" is not automatically worldliness, but may reflect the respect that unbelievers have for the love they see Christians have for each other and for their selfless giving to others.

Grace and Judgment

God's presence brings both grace and judgment. One of the main errors of "liberal" theologies is the notion that God is a gracious Father who forgives and often overlooks the faults of his children. It is impossible for sinful human beings to liberate themselves from God's judgment. If there is no judgment, there is no grace. Grace without judgment is senile bonhomie.

God's merciful *grace* is real. God forgave the disciples who had run away when Jesus was betrayed and arrested. God forgave Peter when he denied on the night of Jesus' trial that he knew Jesus. God forgives sins and transforms believers' lives.

God's eternal *judgment* is also real. Since God's judgment of sinners is a reality, he can punish sinners in the present — through reduced joy in the Lord, illness, and even death. Paul knew, with prophetic insight, that some of the wealthier Corinthian believers were "weak and sick, and a number ... have fallen asleep" because they had despised believers who were poor, neglecting them during the meals and the celebration of the Last Supper (1 Cor 11:30). The possibility of God's judgment on sinners on this side of eternity is also mentioned in 1 Cor 5:5; 1 Tim 1:20; Jas 5:20; 1 John 5:16 – 17. God's temporal judgment on believers does not imply eternal damnation, particularly if Rom 8:31 – 39 and other passages are interpreted in terms of a certain assurance of salvation. If Ananias and Sapphira were believers, remember that the passage makes no statement concerning their eternal salvation or lack thereof.

The story of the deception and death of Ananias and Sapphira will evoke fear in believers and unbelievers alike who are conscious of sins they have committed. This is certainly one of the purposes why Luke included this narrative. Modern audiences can and should be reminded of the sermon entitled "Sinners in the Hands of an Angry God," which Jonathan Edwards preached to the congregation of Enfield, Massachusetts, in July 1741 and which ends with the words, "Therefore, let every one that is out of Christ, now awake and fly from the wrath to come. The wrath of Almighty God is now undoubtedly hanging over a great part of this congregation. Let every one fly out of Sodom: 'Haste and escape for your lives, look not behind you, escape to the mountain, lest you be consumed.' "[42]

---

42. This sermon is widely available on the Internet.

Acts 5:17 – 42

Literary Context

In Acts 1:15 – 8:3, Luke describes the identity, mission, and beginnings of the community of Jesus' followers. The first section (1:15 – 2:47) described the identity and witness of Jesus' followers as God's people. In the longer second section (3:1 – 8:3), Luke shows how the apostles take the news of Jesus, the crucified and risen Messiah and Savior, to the Jewish people living in Jerusalem and in Judea. The present passage is the fifth episode in this section, which relates the second phase of opposition to the apostles in Jerusalem.

Peter, together with John, was arrested once before and put in prison (4:1 – 4), following the miraculous healing of the lame man (3:1 – 10) and their preaching about Jesus in Solomon's Portico (3:11 – 26). In this new episode, triggered by continued growth of the congregation of the believers in Jesus both in Jerusalem and in the surrounding towns in Judea and by numerous miracles (5:12 – 16), the high priest and the leading priests take action and arrest the apostles (5:17 – 18; cf. the similar wording in 4:1 – 3).

The following sequence of events resembles the confrontation between Peter and the Jewish authorities in 4:5 – 22. The interrogation before the Sanhedrin (5:27 – 28) gives Luke another opportunity to include a speech of Peter (5:29 – 32) resembling the speech in 4:8 – 12. Luke also includes a speech of a prominent Pharisee and scribal scholar named Gamaliel (vv. 35 – 39), who seems to be sympathetic to the messianic movement; he later turns out to have been the teacher of Saul-Paul (22:3). The passage confirms the previous reports about the public proclamation of the gospel by the apostles, as Luke makes no fewer than five comments about their public preaching (vv. 20, 21, 25, 28, 42).

Luke uses a pattern of correspondences between 1:12 – 4:23 and 4:24 – 5:42, which contributes to the story of the conflict between the apostles who teach and preach in Jerusalem and the Jewish leaders who seek to halt their activities.[1] In both sections Luke notes that the believers pray (1:14; 4:24 – 30) and are then filled with the Spirit and speak in its power (2:4; 4:31). Then follows a summary description of the life of

---

1. Cf. Talbert, *Literary Patterns*, 35 – 39.

the community (2:42 – 47; 4:32 – 35), and in both sections Luke notes the occurrence of signs and wonders before the arrest of Peter and John and the arrest of the apostles (2:43; 3:1 – 10; 5:12 – 16). This pattern "helps to build suspense as the resolve of both parties to the conflict is tested under increasing pressure. It shows the apostles and the church holding firm under this pressure. That the apostles repeat what they have already said makes the point of their firmness in the face of the threats."[2]

Main Idea

Following Jesus leads into suffering. On this occasion, all the apostles are arrested and interrogated, as the Jewish leaders in the Sanhedrin contemplate their execution. At the same time, following Jesus entails joyful faithfulness, bold proclamation, and divine protection in the midst of suffering.

Translation

(See the next three pages.)

Structure and Literary Form

This episode consists of seven incidents. (1) The apostles are arrested by order of the high priest (vv. 17 – 18). Luke notes that the high priest, not identified by name, collaborated with the Sadducees and comments that the motivation for the arrest was jealousy.

(2) There is a miraculous escape by the apostles (vv. 19 – 21d). An angel of the Lord opens the prison doors and commands them to return to the temple and to continue proclaiming the message of Jesus.

(3) In this third unit (vv. 21e – 26), the high priest convenes the members of the Sanhedrin the next morning and asks the temple police to bring the prisoners, but they find the apostles gone. The report of the temple police leaves the Jewish leaders

---

2. Cf. Tannehill, *Acts*, 64; on the purpose of repetition cf. ibid., 74 – 77.

Acts 5:17 – 42

17a	Action	Then **the high priest and**
b	Association	**all his associates,**
c	Identification	the party of the Sadducees,
d	Action	**took action,**
e	Cause	as they were filled with envy.
18a	Action	**They arrested the apostles**
b	Action	and **put them in the public jail.**
19a	Setting: Time	But during the night
b	Action	**an angel of the Lord opened the doors of the jail,**
c	Action	**led them out,**
d	Action (speech)	and **said,**
20a	Command	"Go,
b	Command	stand and speak
c	Place	in the temple
d	Audience	to the people
e	Content	all the words of this life."
21a	Setting: Cause	As they had been told,
b	Action	**they entered the temple**
c	Time	at dawn
d	Action	and **continued to teach.**
e	Setting: Time	When the high priest and his associates arrived,
f	Action	**they convened the Sanhedrin,**
g	Explanation	the full council of the elders of the Israelites,
h	Action	and **sent to the prison**
i	Purpose	to have the apostles brought in.
22a	Setting: Time	When the officers arrived,
b	Event	**they did not find them**
c	Place	in the jail.
d	Action	**They returned**
e	Action (Report)	and **reported,**
23a	Event	"We found the prison securely locked,
b	Event	and the guards were standing at the doors,
c	Action/Time	but when we opened the doors,
d	Contra-expectation	we found no one inside."
24a	Setting: Time	When the captain of the temple and
b	List (association)	the chief priests
c	Event	heard this report,
d	Result	**they were at a loss concerning this information,**
e	Result	wondering what this might lead to.
25a	Action	Then **someone arrived**
b	Action (report)	and **reported,**

Continued on next page.

Continued from previous page.

c	Address	"Look,
d	Protagonist	the men
e	Identification	whom you put in prison
f	Event	are standing in the temple courts
g	Action	teaching the people."
26a	Action (reaction)	**Then the captain left with his officers**
b	Action	**and brought them in,**
c	Manner	without using force,
d	Reason	because they feared that the people might stone them.

27a	Setting: Time	When they brought the apostles in,
b	Action	**they made them stand before the Sanhedrin.**
c	Action	**The high priest interrogated them, saying,**
28a	Question/Accusation	"Did we not strictly order you
b	Order (Prohibition)	not to teach in that name?
c	Accusation	Yet you have filled Jerusalem with your teaching,
d	Accusation	and you are determined to bring that man's blood upon us."
29a	Identification	**Peter and**
b	Association	**the apostles**
c	Action (response/speech)	**said in reply,**
d	Assertion	"We must obey God
e	Contrast	rather than human beings!
30a	Assertion	The God of our Fathers raised up Jesus,
b	Identification/Accusation	whom you had killed
c	Means	by hanging him on a cross.
31a	Assertion	This man God exalted to his right hand
b	Role	as Leader and
c	Role	Savior
d	Purpose	that he might give to Israel repentance and
e		forgiveness of sins.
32a	Confirmation	We are witnesses of these things,
b	Confirmation	and so is the Holy Spirit,
c	Explanation	whom God has given to those who obey him."

33a	Setting: Time	When they heard this,
b	Reaction	**they were infuriated**
c	Intention (character's thoughts)	**and wanted to kill them.**
34a	Character entrance	**But a Pharisee with the name Gamaliel, . . .**
b	Description	a teacher of the law
c	Description	who was respected by all the people,
d	Action	**. . . stood up in the Sanhedrin**
e	Action	**and ordered the men**
f	Command	to leave the hall
g	Time (Duration)	for a short time.
35a	Action (speech)	**He said to them,**
b	Address	"Fellow Israelites,
c	Exhortation	be careful about what you are going to do with these men.

36a	Setting: Time	*Some time ago*
b	Event/Character entrance	*Theudas arose,*
c	Description	*claiming that he was somebody,*
d	Association	*and about four hundred men joined him.*
e	Event	*But he was killed,*
f	Event	*and all who had been persuaded by him were broken up,*
g	Result	*and they came to nothing.*

37a	Setting: Time	*After him,*
b	Setting: Time	*at the time of the census,*
c	Event/Character entrance	*Judas the Galilean arose*
d	Event	*and caused the people to revolt and to follow him.*
e	Event	*He perished as well,*
f	Result	*and all who had been persuaded by him were dispersed.*

38a	Inference	*Therefore, in the present case*
b	Advice	*I advise you to keep away from these men*
c	Advice	*and to let them alone.*

d	Condition	*For if this plan or activity is of human origin,*
e	Prediction	*it will fail.*
39a	Condition	*But if it is from God,*
b	Prediction	*you will not be able to suppress them;*
c	Warning	*you will only find yourselves fighting against God."*
d	Result	**They were persuaded by him.**
40a	Action	**They called in the apostles**
b	Action	**and had them whipped.**
c	Action	**Then they ordered them**
d	Prohibition	not to speak in the name of Jesus.
e	Action	**Then they let them go.**

41a	Action	**They left the Sanhedrin,**
b	Description (manner)	full of joy
c	Reason	that they had been considered worthy to be insulted
d	Reason	for the sake of ☙ the Name.

42a	Time	Day after day,
b	Place	in the temple courts and
c	Place	in house after house,
d	Action	**they did not stop teaching**
e	Action	**and proclaiming the good news**
f	Content	that Jesus is the Messiah.

perplexed. Someone informs the Sanhedrin that the Twelve are in the temple, where they continue teaching the people. The apostles are arrested again and transferred to the Sanhedrin, albeit without violence as the arresting party fears repercussions from the people in the temple complex.

(4) The Sandredin interrogates the apostles (vv. 27–33) in four parts. First, the apostles are summoned before the Sanhedrin, where the high priest begins the interrogation (v. 27). Second, the high priest makes three accusations: they have ignored the ban on speaking that had been issued by the Sanhedrin, they have filled the entire city with their teaching, and they continue with their preaching because they want to take revenge (v. 28). Third, Peter, who speaks for the Twelve, gives a speech (vv. 29–32). Finally, the high priest and the Sadducees react with outrage, ready to plot the execution of the Twelve (v. 33).

(5) Gamaliel, a respected scribe and Pharisee (vv. 34–39c), asks for a private session of the Sanhedrin without the apostles present. He appeals to the members of the Sanhedrin to proceed with caution. Before he gives his advice, he gives two examples of popular uprisings, both of which failed. He counsels his fellow Jewish leaders to leave the Twelve alone because movements that have a human origin will inevitably fail, and opposition to a movement that is from God is dangerous.

(6) The Sanhedrin makes its decision (vv. 39d–40). The members accept Gamaliel's counsel, punish the Twelve by flogging, issue another ban on speaking, and let them go.

(7) The apostles rejoice because they have been deemed worthy to suffer for the sake of Jesus (vv. 41–42), and they continue their preaching and teaching ministry both in public in the temple and in the private houses of the believers.

The episode, which is a *historical narrative*, relates *direct speech* for the following people: an angel (v. 20), the temple police (v. 23), an anonymous messenger (v. 25), the high priest (v. 28), Peter (vv. 29–32), and Gamaliel (vv. 35–39). Peter's speech in vv. 29–32 has 56 words of Greek text, while Gamaliel's speech in vv. 35–39 is nearly twice as long (103 words).

The narrative is *fast paced*, indicated by the following facts. (1) Of 108 verbal forms in vv. 17–42, there are 67 aorist and 25 present tense forms; for comparison, there are 103 nouns in the passage. (2) More importantly, there are seventeen changes of characters who act and speak. (3) The most hectic geographical movement is connected with the discovery of the apostles' escape from prison: the temple police go to the prison to collect the prisoners (v. 21h-i); the police discover that the prisoners are gone (v. 22a-c); they return to the Sanhedrin (v. 22d) where they give a report (v. 23); when the apostles are located in the temple, the captain and his police force go to the temple (v. 26a); the apostles are rearrested and taken to the Sanhedrin (v. 26b).

Luke highlights almost the same strategies for the defense of the gospel in Peter's speech and its immediate context as in Peter's interrogation in 4:5 – 22.[3] (1) The apostles faithfully preach in the temple (vv. 12, 42), perform miracles (vv. 12, 15 – 16), are well regarded by the people (vv. 13 – 16, 26), are obedient to God rather than to human beings (v. 29), and rejoice in hardships (v. 41). (2) The Jewish leaders are motivated by jealousy (v. 17), are unable to offer convincing arguments against the apostles' beliefs (v. 33b), are willing to use violent means to suppress the apostles' activities (v. 33c), are motivated by a fear of the people (v. 26), and oppose God through their actions (vv. 29, 30, 39). (3) Cautious Gamaliel, held in high esteem by the people (v. 34), is reasonable (vv. 35 – 39) and concerned lest he oppose God (v. 39). (4) Logical and theological reasoning is offered, based on historical precedent and the concern not to fight against God (vv. 35 – 39).

Luke concludes this unit on the identity of the restored people of God and the authority of the Twelve by showing that the leadership of Israel has passed from the old authorities of the Jewish people to the Twelve, who are preaching Jesus as Messiah and Savior in the temple, defying the ban on speaking about Jesus imposed by the Sanhedrin.

Exegetical Outline

→ **I. Renewed Persecution of the Apostles (5:17 – 42)**

    A. The Arrest of the Apostles by the High Priest (5:17 – 18)

        1. Initiative of the high priest (5:17a)

        2. Collaboration of the Sadducees (5:17b-d)

        3. The motivation of jealousy (5:17e)

        4. Arrest and imprisonment of the apostles (5:18)

    B. The Miraculous Escape of the Apostles (5:19 – 21d)

        1. Liberation of the apostles by an angel of the Lord (5:19)

        2. The angel's command to go back to the temple and preach the gospel (5:20)

        3. The apostles enter the temple complex (5:21a-c)

        4. The apostles continue to teach in the temple (5:21d)

    C. The Failed First Session of the Sanhedrin (5:21e – 26)

        1. The high priest convenes a session of the Sanhedrin (5:21e-g)

        2. The attempted transfer of the apostles from the prison to the Sanhedrin (5:21h – 24)

            a. The temple police are dispatched to the prison to get the prisoners (5:21h-i)

            b. The temple police do not find the prisoners in the prison (5:22a-c)

            c. The temple police return to the Sanhedrin (5:22d-e)

            d. The report of the temple police (5:23)

            e. The captain of the temple and the chief priests are perplexed (5:24)

---

3. Cf. Neagoe, *Trial*, 148; for the characterization of the apostles see also Osvaldo Padilla, *The Speeches of Outsiders in Acts: Poetics, Theology and Historiography* (SNTSMS 144; Cambridge: Cambridge Univ. Press, 2008), 111 – 12.

f. The report about the presence of the prisoners in the temple (5:25)

g. The captain of the temple and the officers go to the temple (5:26a)

h. Arrest and transfer of the apostles to the Sanhedrin (5:26b-d)

D. The Interrogation of the Apostles before the Sanhedrin (5:27 – 33)

1. The apostles appear before the assembled members of the Sanhedrin (5:27)

   a. Summons of the Twelve for examination by the Sanhedrin (5:27a-b)

   b. Interrogation by the high priest (5:27c)

2. The accusations of the high priest (5:28)

   a. They have ignored the ban on speaking (5:28a-b)

   b. They have filled Jerusalem with their teaching (5:28c)

   c. Their preaching is an act of revenge (5:28d)

3. Peter's defense, who speaks for the Twelve (5:29 – 32)

   a. Setting: Peter speaks for the apostles (5:29a-c)

   b. Refutation: God's commands have priority over human bans (5:29d-e)

   c. Proclamation of Jesus' resurrection from the dead by God (5:30a)

   d. Accusation that the Jewish leaders have crucified Jesus (5:30b-c)

   e. Proclamation of Jesus' exaltation as Leader and Savior (5:31a-c)

   f. Proclamation of God's offer of forgiveness through Jesus (5:31d-e)

   g. Confirmation through the Twelve, who are eyewitnesses (5:32a)

   h. Confirmation through the Spirit, who is granted to the believers (5:32b-c)

4. The reaction of the high priest and the Sadducees (5:33)

   a. Outrage of the members of the Sanhedrin (5:33a-b)

   b. Scheme to execute the Twelve (5:33c)

E. The Advice of Gamaliel (5:34 – 39c)

1. Intervention of Gamaliel (5:34)

   a. Introduction of Gamaliel as a respected scribe and Pharisee (5:34a-c)

   b. Petition for a session of the Sanhedrin without the Twelve (5:34d-g)

2. Gamaliel's speech (5:35 – 39)

   a. Appeal to proceed with caution (5:35)

   b. Historical example: The popular uprisings of Theudas and Judas (5:36 – 37)

   c. Counsel: Leave the Twelve alone (5:38a-c)

   d. Reason: The fate of movements of human and divine origin (5:38d – 39c)

F. The Decision of the Sanhedrin (5:39d – 40)

1. Acceptance of Gamaliel's counsel (5:39d)

2. Summons of the Twelve (5:40a)

3. Punishment: Flogging of the Twelve (5:40b)

4. Verdict: Ban on speaking about Jesus (5:40c-d)

5. Release of the Twelve (5:40e)

G. The Continued Preaching Ministry of the Apostles (5:41 – 42)

1. The rejoicing of the Twelve (5:41)

2. The continued proclamation and teaching in the temple and in private houses (5:42)

Explanation of the Text

5:17 Then the high priest and all his associates, the party of the Sadducees, took action, as they were filled with envy (ἀναστὰς δὲ ὁ ἀρχιερεὺς καὶ πάντες οἱ σὺν αὐτῷ, ἡ οὖσα αἵρεσις τῶν Σαδδουκαίων, ἐπλήσθησαν ζήλου). The continued growth of the messianic movement connected with Jesus and led by the apostles causes the high priest to take action. Luke provides no information about the timing of this intervention. The aorist participle translated "took action" (ἀναστάς) expresses more than the attendant circumstance of the main verbal idea (ἐπλήσθησαν ζήλου, "they were filled with envy"); it expresses the result of their jealousy.

The high priest who initiates the arrest of the apostles is probably the incumbent high priest Caiaphas (see on 4:6). This is not certain, however, since Annas, the patriarch of the high priestly family, is called "high priest" (ἀρχιερεύς) in 4:6.[4] The intervention of the high priest is linked with his "associates" from the party of the Sadducees. The term translated as "party" (αἵρεσις) denotes "a group that holds tenets distinctive to it" and can thus be translated as "sect, party, school, faction." It is the standard term in references to movements within Judaism, including the followers of Jesus.[5] While in his gospel Luke portrays the Pharisees as the major opponents of Jesus, in Acts it is the Sadducees who are often seen as more hostile against the followers of Jesus. This shift is explained by the move from Galilee to Jerusalem, where the Sadducees seem to have had control of the Sanhedrin.

The motivation for the arrest of the apostles by the high priest and Sadducees is "envy" (ζῆλος).

This Greek term means "zeal, ardor" when intense positive interest in something is in view. Luke may refer to the concerns of the high priest for the political stability of Judea, which was his responsibility as the highest representative of the Jewish population in the Roman province of Judea, and to his concerns for theological orthodoxy, according to which a man deemed dangerous by the religious leadership and then executed by crucifixion could not possibly be the Messiah, let alone the Savior of Israel. If a negative connotation is in view, the term denotes "jealousy" or "envy" in the sense of "intense negative feelings over another's achievements or success,"[6] which seems the more plausible meaning here.

The continued and formidable growth of the believers in Jesus in Jerusalem and in many Judean towns, accompanied by signs and wonders and coupled with the high regard held for the apostles (vv. 12 – 16), causes the chief priests and the Sadducean supporters in the Sanhedrin to resent strongly the reputation and the popularity of the apostles. Since the members in the Sanhedrin were not elected by the people, that increased popularity would not have meant a loss of political power for the Sadducees. Yet they could not afford to tolerate the increasing influence of the apostles, who were leading a movement that believed Jesus of Nazareth was the Messiah and Savior of Israel. They are thus no longer content to move merely against Peter (and John, see 4:1 – 22), but to arrest the entire leadership of the movement.

---

4. The high priest whom Josephus explicitly identifies as a Sadducee (*Ant.* 20.199) is the younger Ananus, not Annas; cf. James C. VanderKam, *From Joshua to Caiaphas: High Priests after the Exile* (Minneapolis: Fortress, 2004), 430 n. 94.

5. The term is used for the Sadducees (Acts 5:17; Josephus,

Ant. 13.171; 20.199), for the Pharisees (Acts 15:5; 26:5; Josephus, *Life* 10, 12, 191), and of the "Nazoreans," i.e., the followers of Jesus of Nazareth (Acts 24:5; cf. 24:14; 28:22).

6. BDAG, s.v. ζῆλος 1 and 2.

5:18 They arrested the apostles and put them in the public jail (καὶ ἐπέβαλον τὰς χεῖρας ἐπὶ τοὺς ἀποστόλους καὶ ἔθεντο αὐτοὺς ἐν τηρήσει δημοσίᾳ). The high priest organizes the arrest of the apostles, presumably carried out by the "officers" mentioned in v. 22. They arrest the apostles, probably as they are teaching in Solomon's Portico on the east side of the temple complex (cf. v. 12), and put them in the "public jail" (τήρησις δημοσία), perhaps a reference to the Jewish "state prison" in Herod's old palace, the praetorium on the west side of the city.[7] In v. 19 the traditional Greek term for jail is used (φυλακή; lit., "guardhouse"), the standard term for the place where prisoners are guarded. In vv. 21, 23 Luke uses yet another Greek term (δεσμωτήριον; lit., "place of binding") to describes a place for prisoners.

5:19 – 20 But during the night an angel of the Lord opened the doors of the jail, led them out, and said, "Go, stand and speak in the temple to the people all the words about this life" (ἄγγελος δὲ κυρίου διὰ νυκτὸς ἀνοίξας τὰς θύρας τῆς φυλακῆς ἐξαγαγών τε αὐτοὺς εἶπεν· πορεύεσθε καὶ σταθέντες λαλεῖτε ἐν τῷ ἱερῷ τῷ λαῷ πάντα τὰ ῥήματα τῆς ζωῆς ταύτης). The second incident relates how the apostles escape during the night with the help of an angel so that they can continue to proclaim the word of God. God's direct intervention with a miracle here is a new development. The angel's rescue demonstrates that God is answering the prayer of the Jerusalem believers to notice the hostility of the Jewish leadership and to grant them boldness to proclaim the gospel despite the ban on speaking (4:29). It also demonstrates that the Sanhedrin is unable to thwart God's will, a point that Gamaliel will make in v. 39.

In the Old Testament the "angel of the Lord" (ἄγγελος κυρίου; Heb. *maPak yhwh*) describes the reality of the presence of Yahweh, who intervenes in history and sends messages.[8] Luke refers to an angel of the Lord repeatedly, as he mentions angels more generally as well.[9] He reports two other miraculous escapes from prison in Acts (12:6 – 11; 16:25 – 26). Since God's intervention in human affairs is, by definition, an expression of his sovereignty and never the result of human manipulation, he can free the apostles whenever he wants, though he does not free Paul in AD 57 when he is imprisoned in Jerusalem (23:10 – 11) and Caesarea (23:35) or in AD 60 when he is imprisoned in Rome (28:16).

The angel opens the doors of the jail (cf. 12:6 – 11). The term "night" (νύξ) denotes the entire period from sundown to sunrise, although the release seems to have taken place in the early hours of the morning.

The angel commands the apostles to continue teaching in the temple. This scene is narrated with the barest essentials. The angel's command communicates four points. (1) The apostles are to stay in Jerusalem despite the danger. After Peter's earlier arrest, the apostles — mostly Galileans — might have considered leaving Jerusalem to preach the gospel elsewhere; note that Jesus was warned on one occasion by sympathetic Pharisees to leave a particular geographical area because they heard that Herod (Antipas) wanted to kill him (Luke 13:31).

(2) The angel tells the apostles to continue preaching and teaching — in the temple, i.e., in public, not merely in the safer environment of private houses in which the believers are also meeting.

---

7. Rapske, *Paul in Roman Custody*, 137.

8. Cf. Gen 16:7 – 11; 21:17; 22:10 – 18; 31:11 – 13; Exod 3:2 – 6; Judg 2:1 – 5.

9. Luke 1:11; 2:9; 12:8 – 9; 15:10; Acts 5:19; 8:26; 12:7, 23.

For angels in general cf. Luke 2:13; 22:43; 24:23; Acts 10:3, 7, 22; 11:13; 27:23. Here the angel of the Lord is not Jesus, who is always mentioned explicitly in Acts when he is present; Bock, *Acts*, 239.

They must return to the one place where they can be most easily found; it is the high priest who controls the temple, after all.

(3) The apostles must continue to focus their preaching and teaching on Jesus. The phrase "the words about this life" (τὰ ῥήματα τῆς ζωῆς ταύτης) describes the message about Jesus. These words form the proclamation of Jesus as "the Author of Life" (ὁ ἀρχηγός τῆς ζωῆς; 3:15). As a result of his resurrection, Jesus is the "prince" of life at God's right hand; he is the "pioneer" of life, who has made eternal life in the presence of God possible for all who believe; he is the "founder" of life in the restored kingdom of God and in the new covenant.

(4) The apostles are told not to hold anything back. They must proclaim "all the words" (πάντα τὰ ῥήματα) about the life and salvation that Jesus alone can provide; they may not omit any part of the message that they had proclaimed earlier and that got them into trouble.

5:21a-d As they had been told, they entered the temple at dawn and continued to teach (ἀκούσαντες δὲ εἰσῆλθον ὑπὸ τὸν ὄρθρον εἰς τὸ ἱερὸν καὶ ἐδίδασκον). The apostles hear the angel's directions and proceed to act as they have been told. They enter the temple complex at dawn, presumably as early as the gates are opened, and continue teaching about Jesus for some period of time, probably in Solomon's Portico (cf. 3:11 – 12; 5:12). They deliberately ignore the speaking ban that the Sanhedrin had issued earlier. But they are obedient to the Lord, who had communicated with them through his angel.

5:21e-i When the high priest and his associates arrived, they convened the Sanhedrin, the full council of the elders of the Israelites, and sent to the prison to have the apostles brought in (παραγενόμενος δὲ ὁ ἀρχιερεὺς καὶ οἱ σὺν αὐτῷ συνεκάλεσαν τὸ συνέδριον καὶ πᾶσαν τὴν γερουσίαν τῶν υἱῶν Ἰσραὴλ καὶ ἀπέστειλαν εἰς τὸ δεσμωτήριον ἀχθῆναι αὐτούς). The third incident relates a failed session of the Sanhedrin. The high priest and his associates from the Sadducees (cf. v. 17) arrive in the hall in which the Sanhedrin convenes (see on 4:5). The aorist participle (παραγενόμενος) is temporal and perhaps indicates simultaneous action: while the apostles enter the temple complex and begin their teaching, the high priest arrives at the council hall, perhaps only 400 meters west of Solomon's Portico.

The high priest summons the members of the Sanhedrin, an institution also called "council of elders" (ἡ γερουσία).[10] The phrase "the full council of the sons of Israel" (lit.) comes from Exod 12:21. This description of the council in Jerusalem probably expresses the self-understanding of the Sanhedrin, whose leaders claimed theological and ethical (halakic) responsibility not only over the Jews in Judea but over the entire Jewish people everywhere. The solemn description indicates that all available leaders of the Jewish people are present, and it underscores their defeat as a result of God's intervention during the previous night.

When the morning session of the Sanhedrin has been convened, the high priest sends officers to the prison (see on v. 19), where the apostles were detained the previous day. They are ordered to transfer the prisoners to the council building. Luke's readers cannot miss the comical aspect of the scene that is building suspense: while the leading priests dispatch officers to the prison, waiting

---

10. The conjunction καί is epexegetical. The term "council" (γερουσία) is used only here in the New Testament; it is used for the Sanhedrin in Jerusalem in Jdt 4:8; 1 Macc 12:6; 2 Macc 1:10; Josephus, *Ant.* 13.166. In Greek sources γερουσία is used for the Roman senate (Plutarch, *Mor.* 789E), city councils (Demosthenes 20.107), and various boards, e.g., the sacred college of priests in temples (IG III 702).

for the prisoners to appear before them, the reader knows that the prisoners have escaped and are preaching again in the temple.

5:22 When the officers arrived, they did not find them in the jail. They returned and reported (οἱ δὲ παραγενόμενοι ὑπηρέται οὐχ εὗρον αὐτοὺς ἐν τῇ φυλακῇ· ἀναστρέψαντες δὲ ἀπήγγειλαν). The officers (οἱ ὑπηρέται, lit., "helpers, assistants")[11] of the captain of the temple (cf. v. 24; 4:1) arrive at the jail. When they open the door of the room in which the leaders of the believers in Jesus had been bound, they find the cell empty. The officers return to the council building and give a report to the assembled leaders of Israel.

5:23 "We found the prison securely locked, and the guards were standing at the doors, but when we opened the doors, we found no one inside" (λέγοντες ὅτι τὸ δεσμωτήριον εὕρομεν κεκλεισμένον ἐν πάσῃ ἀσφαλείᾳ καὶ τοὺς φύλακας ἑστῶτας ἐπὶ τῶν θυρῶν, ἀνοίξαντες δὲ ἔσω οὐδένα εὕρομεν). The report of the officials is succinctly summarized in three points. (1) The prison was "locked." The perfect passive participle (κεκλεισμένον) denotes a state or condition, implying that the prison had been locked all night. The prepositional phrase translated as "securely" (ἐν πάσῃ ἀσφαλείᾳ) underlines that the usual safeguards had been observed.

(2) The guards "were standing" at the doors of the prison. The perfect participle (ἑστῶτας) again describes a state of affairs or condition. Luke does not tell us how the prisoners escaped—whether the guards were blinded and thus did not see the prisoners walk out, or whether they were rendered unconscious and thus missed the departure of the prisoners, who evidently closed and locked the doors as they walked out of the jail.

(3) When they opened the doors of the prisoners' cell,[12] they found "no one inside" (ἔσω οὐδένα). This matter-of-fact report escalates the comical scene. State officials and their officers do not normally have to "look" for prisoners, as prisoners stay in the exact spot where they have been put, bound with ropes or chains to the wall of the cell.

5:24 When the captain of the temple and the chief priests heard this report, they were at a loss concerning this information, wondering what this might lead to (ὡς δὲ ἤκουσαν τοὺς λόγους τούτους ὅ τε στρατηγὸς τοῦ ἱεροῦ καὶ οἱ ἀρχιερεῖς, διηπόρουν περὶ αὐτῶν τί ἂν γένοιτο τοῦτο). The report of the officers left the captain of the temple (see on 4:1) and the chief priests perplexed, which is formulated with an indirect question. The optative (γένοιτο) indicates they do not know the answer to their question. The demonstrative pronoun in the phrase "what this [τοῦτο] might lead to" can refer to the disappearance of the apostles or to the movement of which the apostles are the leaders and which the Sanhedrin does not seem able to control. The possibility that a higher power is involved does not occur to them.

5:25 Then someone arrived and reported, "Look, the men whom you put in prison are standing in the temple courts teaching the people" (παραγενόμενος δέ τις ἀπήγγειλεν αὐτοῖς ὅτι ἰδοὺ οἱ ἄνδρες οὓς ἔθεσθε ἐν τῇ φυλακῇ εἰσὶν ἐν τῷ ἱερῷ ἑστῶτες καὶ διδάσκοντες τὸν λαόν). Someone not identified by Luke arrives in the council hall with new information. The introductory "look" (ἰδού) expresses the surprise of the messenger, who

---

11. Cf. BDAG, s.v. ὑπηρέτης, "one who functions as a helper, frequently in a subordinate capacity, *helper, assistant*," frequently used as a technical term for a governmental or other official.

12. The doors in v. 23b are presumably the doors of the cell in which the Twelve were held in custody. Luke's Greek should not be pressed to indicate that the entire prison was empty, or that the apostles were the only occupants of the prison; Gustav Stählin, *Die Apostelgeschichte* (NTD 5; Göttingen: Vandenhoeck & Ruprecht, 1962), 1:286.

knows that the leaders of the followers of Jesus had been put into prison by the chief priests. He reports that they are now standing in the temple court and teaching the people — which is exactly what the angel of the Lord had told the apostles to do. This piece of news solves the perplexity of the chief priests as least as to the whereabouts of the apostles.

5:26 Then the captain left with his officers and brought them in, without using force, because they feared that the people might stone them (τότε ἀπελθὼν ὁ στρατηγὸς σὺν τοῖς ὑπηρέταις ἦγεν αὐτοὺς οὐ μετὰ βίας, ἐφοβοῦντο γὰρ τὸν λαὸν μὴ λιθασθῶσιν). The captain of the temple leaves the council hall, probably to avoid further complications and delays, accompanies his assistants, and brings the apostles into the Sanhedrin. Luke notes, not without a touch of irony, that the Jewish officials do not dare use force when they rearrest the apostles. The reason given is that they are afraid that if they use force, they might be pelted with stones[13] by the people who have been listening to the apostles.

The support and sympathy of the inhabitants of Jerusalem for the apostles was noted in v. 13. The Sanhedrin officials fear a public lynching if they are not careful in the second arrest of the apostles. Whether some of the believers in Jesus who were undoubtedly present as well would have been willing to use force against the Sanhedrin officials is a possibility, although Luke consistently describes the followers of Jesus in Acts as suffering willingly, on occasion insisting on their rights (cf. 16:37 – 39; 22:25 – 29), but never as using force, in keeping with Jesus' directive in Luke 22:50 – 51.

5:27 When they brought the apostles in, they made them stand before the Sanhedrin. The high priest interrogated them (ἀγαγόντες δὲ αὐτοὺς ἔστησαν ἐν τῷ συνεδρίῳ. καὶ ἐπηρώτησεν αὐτοὺς ὁ ἀρχιερεύς). The fourth incident of this episode narrates the interrogation of the apostles before the Sanhedrin (vv. 27 – 33). The Twelve are taken into the council hall and placed in front of the Sanhedrin. They stand where Peter and John stood several weeks earlier (4:7) and where Jesus stood during his trial (Luke 22:66). The high priest is finally able to question these people who dared defy the ban on speaking that the Jewish leaders had issued when Peter and John were arrested and interrogated (4:1 – 18). The fact that the high priest himself begins the interrogation indicates, from the point of view of the Jewish leaders, the seriousness of the situation that the apostles' preaching and teaching and the numerous miracles have caused.

The high priest does not interrogate the apostles about their means of escape. While Luke may simply not be interested in such details, a plausible historical reason may be found precisely in the popularity of the apostles in Jerusalem. If they had help from "inside" the Sanhedrin, the high priest may prefer not to establish such details at this point. Or, perhaps, he is merely embarrassed that they have managed to escape. As the apostles stand before the Sanhedrin, they face the members of the council sitting in a semicircle before them.

5:28 Saying, "Did we not strictly order you not to teach in that name? Yet you have filled Jerusalem with your teaching, and you are determined to bring that man's blood upon us" (λέγων· οὐ παραγγελίᾳ παρηγγείλαμεν ὑμῖν μὴ διδάσκειν ἐπὶ τῷ ὀνόματι τούτῳ, καὶ ἰδοὺ πεπληρώκατε

---

13. In the Old Testament, execution by stoning was a punishment for criminal offenses such as apostasy (Lev 20:2; Deut 13:10; 17:5), blasphemy (Lev 24:14, 16, 23; 1 Kgs 21:10), sorcery (Lev 20:27), violation of the Sabbath (Num 15:35 – 36), disobedient sons (Deut 21:21), and adultery (Deut 22:21 – 22; John 8:5). While the same verb is used, killing by stoning is obviously not in view in v. 26.

τὴν Ἰερουσαλὴμ τῆς διδαχῆς ὑμῶν καὶ βούλεσθε ἐπαγαγεῖν ἐφ᾽ ἡμᾶς τὸ αἷμα τοῦ ἀνθρώπου τούτου). The high priest charges the apostles with disobeying the ban on speaking that the Sanhedrin had issued (4:18, 21). He asks a rhetorical question: the introductory οὐ expects an affirmative answer.[14] The apostles know, as does probably the entire city, that the Sanhedrin had issued a ban on speaking about Jesus. The solemn formulation translated as "did we (not) strictly order (you)" (παραγγελίᾳ παραγγέλλειν) imitates a Hebrew infinitive absolute, as the modal noun intensifies the meaning of the cognate verb. The high priest reminds the apostles that they have been strictly ordered not to teach about Jesus. As in 4:17, the high priest avoids pronouncing the name of Jesus.

The accusation that follows the rhetorical question, formulated as an assertion, reveals the impotence of the high priest and his associates. They helped execute Jesus, they arrested Peter and issued a ban on speaking about Jesus, yet Jerusalem is "filled" with their teaching about Jesus. In Roman law, offenses subject to public law (crimen) were distinguished from offenses subject to civil law (delictum). Seen against this background, the Twelve are accused not of a transgression but of a crime — they have deliberately defied an earlier sentence by the highest court of the land, whose members had issued a ban on speaking about Jesus. This was a serious charge, which, if conviction followed, could have serious consequences.

In Judea and in the Jewish diaspora, the local synagogues administered justice; they held trials and meted out sentences, which included floggings.[15] We do not know whether in Jerusalem the local synagogues (cf. 6:9) had administrative and juridical functions. The Sanhedrin was the highest court of the land and may not have intervened in minor cases. But they did in the case of Jesus and his claims, and they do so now in the case of the leaders of the movement propagating Jesus' teachings.

The high priest unwittingly becomes a witness for the "success" of the preaching of the gospel by the Twelve in Jerusalem. The perfect indicative translated as "you have filled" (πεπληρώκατε) confirms that the public teaching and its effect on thousands of people in Jerusalem had been a regular feature of "happenings" in the city. This is hyperbole only if we do not trust Luke's earlier reporting and assume that the public teaching of the apostles had had little effect. If indeed thousands of people have become believers in Jesus, who would all have been immersed for purification upon coming to faith in Jesus as the Messiah and Savior in the public pools near the Temple Mount, this would have been news in the city for many months.

In his third accusation, the high priest charges that the apostles are acting out of revenge for the death of Jesus. The present indicative of the verb "you are determined" (βούλεσθε) suggests, from the high priest's point of view, a constant desire on the part of Jesus' followers for vengeance. In the biblical and Jewish tradition (and beyond), spilled human blood cries for revenge (Gen 4:10; Deut 19:10; cf. Heb 12:24; Rev 6:10). If a person has been murdered, the spilled blood causes the death of the murderer.[16] Atonement for murder is possible only through the shedding of the blood of the murderer.

---

14. Early and important manuscripts ($\mathfrak{P}^{74}$ ℵ* A B 1175 pc lat bo) omit the οὐ, thus formulating a rebuke instead of a question (οὐ is included by ℵ² D E Ψ 1739 Maj h p w sy sa mae). Bruce M. Metzger, Textual Commentary, 289, argues that the negation should be omitted (followed by most scholars); this would be the more difficult reading, since the inclusion of οὐ provides a proper link between v. 27 and v. 28. The sense is the same.

15. Cf. Luke 21:12; Acts 22:19; Matt 10:17–18; 23:34; Mark 13:9. Cf. Levine, Synagogue, 143.

16. O. Böcher, "αἷμα," EDNT, 1:37, with reference to Josh 2:19; 2 Sam 3:28–29; m. Sanh. 4:5; cf. Matt 23:30, 35; 27:25; Acts 5:28; for the following points cf. ibid., 1:37–39. For "blood" as a metaphor for (violently) taking life, cf. also Lev 20:9; 2 Sam 1:16; Ezek 33:4 LXX.

If someone was unjustly executed, his spilled blood comes with vengeance over those responsible for the wrongful execution; this is the thought here, as in the action of Pontius Pilate who washed his hands and declared that he was innocent of Jesus' blood (Matt 27:24). Because the Jewish leaders were convinced that Jesus was not innocent and deserved to die, they asserted that his blood may come upon them and their children (Matt 27:25), which thus assumed juridical responsibility for Jesus' death. When the responsibility for a wrongful execution (or murder) of a person is placed on another person, the same juridical assumption is made — as here (cf. 18:6; Matt 27:25). Perhaps the high priest accuses the apostles of seeking divine retribution for Jesus' execution, asking God to inflict punishment on the Jewish leadership. Perhaps the high priest fears a popular uprising, insinuating that the apostles are planning to turn the city against the Jewish leaders in some deliberate, perhaps violent action.

The Twelve have indeed been accusing the Jewish leaders for being responsible for Jesus' crucifixion (2:23, 36; 3:13–15, 17; 4:10–11, 27; cf. 10:39; 13:27). However, there is no trace of a desire for vindictive retaliation. On the contrary, Peter teaches that the Jewish people and their leaders acted out of ignorance, that Jesus' crucifixion and subsequent resurrection was part of God's plan, and that the Jewish people can repent, accept Jesus as God's Messiah, and thus find salvation and times of refreshing (2:23; 3:17–21).

5:29 Peter and the apostles said in reply, "We must obey God rather than human beings!" (ἀποκριθεὶς δὲ Πέτρος καὶ οἱ ἀπόστολοι εἶπαν· πειθαρχεῖν δεῖ θεῷ μᾶλλον ἢ ἀνθρώποις). Peter answers the accusations of the high priest, speaking for the Twelve. He makes seven points in vv. 29–32.

First, the apostles are obligated to obey God,

who commanded them to speak and preach as witnesses of Jesus — most recently the night before through his angel (v. 20). Obedience to God always trumps obedience to human beings whenever there is a conflict between these two demands. The principle of the supreme authority of God is characteristic of the Jewish faith, a principle put to the test with great sacrifice during the reign of Antiochus IV Epiphanes. This ruler sent letters to Jerusalem and the Judean towns forbidding burnt offerings, sacrifices, observance of the Sabbath and the Jewish festivals, and circumcision; he ordered the Jews (under threat of death, 1 Macc 1:50) to build altars and shrines for other gods and to sacrifice pigs and other unclean animals. Many died as martyrs for their faithfulness to God and his law.

Peter's answer repeats what he had already told the Sanhedrin (4:19). He does not deny that he and his colleagues have disobeyed the ban on speaking that the Sanhedrin had imposed. What he denies is the legitimacy of this ban.

5:30 The God of our fathers raised up Jesus, whom you had killed by hanging him on a cross (ὁ θεὸς τῶν πατέρων ἡμῶν ἤγειρεν Ἰησοῦν ὃν ὑμεῖς διεχειρίσασθε κρεμάσαντες ἐπὶ ξύλου). Second, Peter explains the message that he and his friends are proclaiming and teaching in Jerusalem and in the towns of Judea. This explanation provides the reason for their refusal to obey the Sanhedrin's ban on speaking about Jesus. After all, Jesus has been raised from the dead by "the God of our fathers." This means that his death, resurrection, and exaltation are not merely historical events of the recent past, but events that belong to the history of salvation that God initiated with his revelation to Abraham, Isaac, Jacob, Moses, David, and the other prophets (cf. 2:30; 3:13, 18, 21–25). If Jesus has been vindicated by God in his resurrection, the Jewish leaders acted against God when they engineered his death. And they are continuing to work against God by trying to silence the message about God's vindication of Jesus.

Third, Jesus' death is the responsibility of the Jewish leaders, who murdered[17] Jesus by hanging him on a "tree" (ξύλον); this term denotes the wooden pole with crossbeam used for crucifixions. Implying an allusion to Deut 21:22 – 23,[18] Peter accuses the Jewish leaders of having treated Jesus as a dangerous criminal, as someone who is under God's curse and must be eliminated from God's people. In the Second Temple period Jews used the expression "hang on a tree" for crucifixion.[19]

5:31 This man God exalted to his right hand as Leader and Savior that he might give to Israel repentance and forgiveness of sins (τοῦτον ὁ θεὸς ἀρχηγὸν καὶ σωτῆρα ὕψωσεν τῇ δεξιᾷ αὐτοῦ τοῦ δοῦναι μετάνοιαν τῷ Ἰσραὴλ καὶ ἄφεσιν ἁμαρτιῶν). Fourth, Peter explains the significance of Jesus' death and resurrection. Jesus has been exalted in his resurrection and is now Leader and Savior at the right hand of God. This means that Jesus has been welcomed by God to sit with him on his throne as his exalted Servant.[20] Moreover, Jesus has returned to the people of God as Leader and Savior.

Jesus is "Leader" (ἀρχηγός) — Israel's prince who shares God's authority and who initiated the restoration of the kingdom, the pioneer who opened the path to eternal life in the messianic kingdom, the Author of Life in the new covenant in which God's people enjoy the fullness of life (see on 3:15). Jesus is "Savior" (σωτήρ)[21] — the one who delivers from evil, whether national or private, social or moral, physical or emotional, securing life before God and in God's gracious presence.

Fifth, Jesus grants Israel repentance and forgiveness of sins. The purpose of God's resurrection and exaltation of Jesus is an offer to Israel — the offer of "repentance" (μετάνοια) and the "forgiveness of sins" (ἄφεσις ἁμαρτιῶν). God offers salvation, not retribution, for the crucifixion of Jesus. The people of Israel, in particular her leaders, must repent of their sin of rejecting Jesus, God's messianic Leader and Savior. In order to participate in the restoration of the kingdom of God and in the new covenant, the Israelites must come to faith in Jesus as God's Messiah. The opportunity for repentance is God's gift to the people of Israel.

5:32 "We are witnesses of these things, and so is the Holy Spirit, whom God has given to those who obey him" (καὶ ἡμεῖς ἐσμεν μάρτυρες τῶν ῥημάτων τούτων καὶ τὸ πνεῦμα τὸ ἅγιον ὃ ἔδωκεν ὁ θεὸς τοῖς πειθαρχοῦσιν αὐτῷ). Sixth, Peter ends his speech by returning to the role of himself and the other apostles and of the Holy Spirit.[22] He insists that God's offer of repentance and salvation through faith in Jesus is presented to Israel in their preaching and proclamation — which is precisely why they cannot obey the Sanhedrin's ban on speaking about Jesus. The apostles can confirm the truthfulness of Jesus' resurrection and exaltation and thus of his significance as Israel's Leader and Savior because they are eyewitnesses (μάρτυρες).

---

17. Cf. BDAG, s.v. διαχειρίζω (middle), "take hold of someone forcibly with malicious intent and frequently ending in the taking of life, *lay violent hands on, murder, kill*"; this is a stronger word than ἀποκτείνω 1, "to deprive of life, *kill*."

18. A criminal, who was generally stoned to death in Israel, was hanged on a "tree" (ξύλον) after the execution as a deterrent to crime.

19. Cf. 4QpNah frags. 3 – 4 I, 6 – 8; 11QTemple LXIV, 7 – 8, where Deut 21:22 – 23 is quoted. Cf. Joseph A. Fitzmyer, "Crucifixion in Ancient Palestine, Qumran Literature, and the New Testament," *CBQ* 40 (1978): 493 – 513; David W. Chapman, *Ancient Jewish and Christian Perceptions of Crucifixion* (WUNT 2.244; Tübingen: Mohr Siebeck, 2008), 14 – 26, 234. Paul refers to Deut 21:22 – 23 in the context of Jesus' death in Gal 3:13.

20. Note the allusions to Ps 110:1 and Isa 52:13 in the expression "exalted to [the] right hand of God"; see on 2:33.

21. The title σωτήρ occurs here for the first time in Acts; cf. 13:23, the only other time it is used; in Luke 1:47 the term is used for God, as often in the LXX, cf. Isa 45:15, 21; 1 Sam 10:19. On σωτηρία cf. 4:12.

22. Note the same link between the witness of the Twelve and the witness of the Spirit in John 15:26 – 27.

They have seen the risen Jesus and his exaltation to God's right hand (1:1 – 11; cf. 3:15).

Seventh, the ultimate guarantee for the truthfulness of Jesus' role as Leader and Savior is God's Holy Spirit. The Spirit — bestowed on the apostles, indeed on all Jesus' followers — is the second witness who testifies to the truth of Jesus' resurrection, exaltation, and significance. The Spirit affirms about truth of Jesus because he is bestowed on all who come to faith in Jesus (cf. 2:38). The convicting presence of the Holy Spirit, who convinces people of the truth about Jesus and the transforming presence of the Spirit in the lives of Jesus' followers (cf. 4:8), confirms the truth of his significance and thus the truth of the message that the apostles are preaching in Jerusalem and in the towns of Judea (see also 1 John 2:20, 27).

5:33 When they heard this, they were infuriated and wanted to kill them (οἱ δὲ ἀκούσαντες διεπρίοντο καὶ ἐβούλοντο ἀνελεῖν αὐτούς). Luke notes the reception of Peter's speech with a brief sentence that contains four verbs. (1) The Jewish leaders in the Sanhedrin "heard" (ἀκούσαντες, aorist participle) what Peter said. They listened, understood the claims Peter made, rejected their legitimacy, and found them outrageous. (2) Peter's explanations "infuriated" (διεπρίοντο, imperfect) them.[23] This verb, which denotes strong emotion, suggests a visible reaction to Peter's speech, perhaps faces red with fury, raised fists, and insults. (3) They must decide (ἐβούλοντο, imperfect) how to deal with the apostles. This verb suggests that the members of the Sanhedrin discuss the course of action they should be taking. (4) They want to kill (ἀνελεῖν, aorist infinitive) the apostles. They

could kill them for religious reasons, which they might be able to justify before Pontius Pilate (as in the case of Stephen in Acts 7). Or they could take these men to Pilate and accuse them of seducing the people into following a Leader and Savior other than the emperor (cf. Luke 23).[24] The apostles see the hostility of the Jewish leaders and hear their wish to have them killed.

5:34 But a Pharisee with the name Gamaliel, a teacher of the law who was respected by all the people, stood up in the Sanhedrin and ordered the men to leave the hall for a short time (ἀναστὰς δέ τις ἐν τῷ συνεδρίῳ Φαρισαῖος ὀνόματι Γαμαλιήλ, νομοδιδάσκαλος τίμιος παντὶ τῷ λαῷ ἐκέλευσεν ἔξω βραχὺ τοὺς ἀνθρώπους ποιῆσαι). The fifth incident of the present episode relates the intervention of Gamaliel in the deliberations of the Sanhedrin, whose members are about to decide to have the apostles executed. Gamaliel's speech is not a speech in defense of the apostles but in defense of the integrity of the Sanhedrin. If they kill the twelve leaders of a movement that has thousands of followers and it continues to increase in popularity — not in outlying regions of Palestine but in Jerusalem, the center of the Jewish commonwealth — the council might easily and completely discredit itself. Luke introduces Gamaliel as a Pharisee.

Gamaliel is Gamaliel the Elder,[25] who was the son or grandson of the great rabbi Hillel. It is disputed whether he belonged to the more moderate "school" of Hillel or to the stricter school of Shammai. Gamaliel was active in Jerusalem between AD 25 – 50. According to 22:3, Paul was one of Gamaliel's students. Besides Gamaliel's affiliation with the Pharisees, Luke describes him as a "teacher of

---

23. In the NT the term is used here and in 7:54, where it describes the Sanhedrin's reaction to Stephen's speech.

24. Roman emperors were venerated as "savior" (σωτήρ); cf. Simon R. F. Price, "Gods and Emperors: The Greek Language of the Roman Imperial Cult," *JHS* 104 (1984): 79 – 95.

25. To distinguish him from his son R. Simeon ben Gamaliel I, who lived at the time of the Jewish Revolt (Josephus, *Life* 189 – 198), and his grandson R. Gamaliel II, who succeeded R. Johanan ben Zakkai in Yabneh in AD 90 – 110.

the law" (νομοδιδάσκαλος)[26] who was "respected by all the people." His prominence is reflected in the rabbinic comment that "when Rabban Gamaliel the elder died, the glory of the law ceased and purity and abstinence died" (*m. Soṭah* 9:15).

Gamaliel was evidently the first rabbi called Rabban ("our teacher"). Rabbinic traditions indicate that he had authority in establishing the calendar, that he had contacts with the seat of the Roman government in Syria (which also controlled Jerusalem and Judea), and that he had influence in the diaspora.[27] Gamaliel evidently decided questions regarding permissible movement on the Sabbath of witnesses who attested sightings of the sun and moon, essential for establishing details relating to the sacred calendar, a role that indicates Gamaliel's reputation and standing among the chief priests of the temple.[28]

Gamaliel, as a member of the Sanhedrin, has the right to address the council members, which was done standing. But it is his prominence that allows him to call for a session *in camera*. The apostles are escorted out of the hall in which the Sanhedrin meets. Perhaps Gamaliel does not want the apostles to hear that he is willing, at least in theory, to allow for the divine sanction of their message about Jesus. Or he simply assumes that his advice might have a better chance of being taken seriously if his colleagues deliberate their course of action without having the apostles present, whose presentation has caused such an uproar.

5:35 He said to them, "Fellow Israelites, be careful about what you are going to do with these men" (εἶπέν τε πρὸς αὐτούς· ἄνδρες Ἰσραηλῖται, προσέχετε ἑαυτοῖς ἐπὶ τοῖς ἀνθρώποις τούτοις τί μέλλετε πράσσειν). Gamaliel's speech, which begins with a conventional address of the members of the Sanhedrin as fellow Jews (cf. Peter in 2:22), can be divided into four parts.

First, the Sanhedrin should proceed with caution. Gamaliel counsels his colleagues to be careful concerning what they will to do with "these men." In view of their desire to kill them (v. 33), this means that Gamaliel is asking the members of the Sanhedrin to consider the consequences of such action and the problems that the execution of these men might cause for them. In light of the growing numbers of people who have pledged faith in Jesus as Messiah, and in the light of the popularity of the leaders of this messianic movement, it was not difficult to see that the execution of these twelve leaders might provoke a reaction among their supporters that could be anything from angry protests to violent actions.

5:36 Some time ago Theudas arose, claiming that he was somebody, and about four hundred men joined him. But he was killed, and all who had been persuaded by him were broken up, and they came to nothing (πρὸ γὰρ τούτων τῶν ἡμερῶν ἀνέστη Θευδᾶς λέγων εἶναί τινα ἑαυτόν, ᾧ προσεκλίθη ἀνδρῶν ἀριθμὸς ὡς τετρακοσίων· ὃς ἀνῃρέθη, καὶ πάντες ὅσοι ἐπείθοντο αὐτῷ

---

26. This term is used only here and in Luke 5:17 for the Pharisees; differently 1 Tim 1:7. The usual term used for scribes in the New Testament is γραμματεύς, meaning "experts in the Law, scholars versed in the Mosaic Law, scribes"; in non-Jewish sources the term often describes the "chief executive officer of a governmental entity, *secretary (of state), clerk*" (BDAG, s.v. γραμματεύς 1).

27. Jacob Neusner and Bruce D. Chilton, "Paul and Gamaliel," in *In Quest of the Historical Pharisees* (ed. J. Neusner and B. D. Chilton; Waco: Baylor University Press, 2007), 175–223,

211–13, with reference to *m. ʿEd.* 7:7; *t. Sanh.* 2:6, concluding that "Gamaliel clearly emerges from the sources as a force to be reckoned with in Jerusalem and beyond" (212). According to a later tradition preserved in *b. B. Qam.* 83a, Gamaliel had five hundred young men in his "house" studying the Torah and five hundred studying Greek wisdom.

28. According to *m. Roš. Haš.* 2:5. Cf. Jacob Neusner, *The Pharisees: Rabbinic Perspectives* (Hoboken, NJ: Ktav, 1985), 29, 38–43.

διελύθησαν καὶ ἐγένοντο εἰς οὐδέν). Second, Gamaliel appeals to historical precedent as a basis for how to deal with the leaders of the increasingly popular movement of those who follow Jesus. He argues that there were several popular movements that ended in disaster. His first example recounts the rebellion of Theudas, who claimed "that he was somebody," an expression that indicates claims he made about himself.[29] About 400 men whom Theudas was able to "persuade" (ἐπείθοντο)[30] joined him in his rebellion. When Theudas was killed, his supporters were "broken up" and the movement "came to nothing." Gamaliel's point is that as Theudas gathered followers, so do Peter and the Twelve, and just as Theudas's movement came to nothing, the same may happen with the followers of Jesus.

The movement of Theudas is mentioned by Josephus:

> During the period when Fadus was procurator of Judea, a certain impostor named Theudas persuaded (πείθει) the majority of the masses to take up their possessions and to follow him to the Jordan River. He stated that he was a prophet and that at his command the river would be parted and would provide them an easy passage. With this talk he deceived many. Fadus, however, did not permit them to reap the fruit of their folly, but sent against them a squadron of cavalry. These fell upon them unexpectedly, slew many of them and took many prisoners. Theudas himself was captured, whereupon they cut off his head and brought it to Jerusalem. (*Ant.* 20.97 – 98)

Theudas's goals were somewhat nebulous; there are echoes of Israel's exodus from Egypt (Exod 12:29 – 14:30), of the miraculous march across the Jordan River at the beginning of the conquest of the Promised Land (Josh 3 – 4), and of the partition of the Jordan River by Elijah and Elisha (2 Kgs 2:1 – 18). Perhaps Theudas promised his followers a new life east of the Jordan, motivated perhaps by the refusal to pay taxes to the Roman overlords. The intervention of the Roman governor Fadus suggests that Theudas's imminent move across the Jordan River was interpreted as a political rebellion. The fact that Theudas's head was displayed in Jerusalem indicates that Fadus wanted to crush this rebellion in a manner that would serve as a warning for anyone seeking to question Roman rule.

Josephus dates the movement of Theudas the impostor to the governorship of Cuspius Fadus (AD 44 – 46). Since the arrest and interrogation of the apostles and Gamaliel's speech take place at least a decade earlier, scholars have suggested that Luke makes a historical error or that he misread Josephus (who mentions Theudas before Judas, Gamaliel's second example, but dates him clearly to the time of Fadus). There are two other possibilities. First, Josephus may be wrong about dating Theudas to the governorship of Fadus. Scholars who think that Luke may be wrong need to consider that perhaps Josephus made a mistake in dating Theudas.[31]

Second, there may have been an earlier Theudas who led a rebellion before AD 6, when Judas the Galilean led another rebellion.[32] There were several rebellions in Judea after Herod the Great's death in 4 BC — Judas, the son of Ezekias, Simon, slave

---

29. Theudas belonged to the "action prophets" in distinction from the "oracular prophets" such as John the Baptist and Jesus of Nazareth. Cf. Paul W. Barnett, "The Jewish Sign Prophets — AD 40 – 70: Their Intentions and Origin," *NTS* 27 (1981): 679 – 97, 680 – 81.

30. The imperfect tense of πείθω indicates a movement that was sustained over a period of time (the passive voice is used here with the dative).

31. Cf. Shaye J. D. Cohen, *Josephus in Galilee and Rome: His Vita and Development as a Historian* (Columbia Studies in the Classical Tradition 8; Leiden: Brill, 1979), 6 – 7, 32, 232 – 33, for problems in Josephus's accounts.

32. Witherington, *Acts*, 239; Hemer, *Acts*, 162 – 63.

of King Herod, and Athronges.[33] In the decades preceding the outbreak of the Jewish Revolt in AD 66, several "sign prophets" led popular movements, including the movements led by a Samaritan, an Egyptian, and various unnamed individuals.[34] Josephus mentions four persons with the name Simon and three persons named Judas who led rebellions. Theudas is a name that is not as infrequent as some have supposed.[35] Since the name is not uncommon, it is possible, in theory, that there was an earlier Theudas than the prophetic pretender noted above.

5:37 After him, at the time of the census, Judas the Galilean arose and caused the people to revolt and to follow him. He perished as well, and all who had been persuaded by him were dispersed (μετὰ τοῦτον ἀνέστη Ἰούδας ὁ Γαλιλαῖος ἐν ταῖς ἡμέραις τῆς ἀπογραφῆς καὶ ἀπέστησεν λαὸν ὀπίσω αὐτοῦ· κἀκεῖνος ἀπώλετο καὶ πάντες ὅσοι ἐπείθοντο αὐτῷ διεσκορπίσθησαν). The second historical precedent is the movement led by Judas from Galilee who revolted, together with others, during the time of the census. He also managed to persuade (ἐπείθοντο, imperfect) people to follow him. As in the case of Theudas, Judas also perished (though Gamaliel does not say how he died), and all those who had followed him dispersed.

The census (ἀπογραφή) that Gamaliel refers to is generally identified with the census held by P. Sulpicius Quirinius, the governor of the province Syria – Cilicia with the title *legatus pro praetore*. He was commissioned by Augustus "to take a census of property in Syria and to sell the estate of Archelaus," who had been deposed as tetrarch of Judea in

AD 6.[36] Coponius, the new prefect of Judea (which was administered as a district of Syria) organized the census in Judea. Josephus mentions, in connection with this census, Judas of Gamala in the Gaulanitis, whom he also calls "Judas the Galilean," who organized a protest against the census in Judea together with Zaddok, a Pharisee.[37] Josephus calls this the "fourth philosophy" or school of thought in Judaism, which he links with the Zealot movement that caused the first Jewish Revolt in AD 66, which eventually led to the destruction of Jerusalem in AD 70.[38] He describes the convictions of Judas and his followers as in agreement with the Pharisees in all respects "except that they have a passion for liberty that is almost unconquerable, since they are convinced that God alone is their leader and master" (*Ant.* 18.23).

Josephus does not report how the rebellion of Judas the Galilean ended. The sons of Judas followed in the footsteps of their father — two sons, James and Simon, were crucified by the Roman procurator Tiberius Alexander in AD 46/47; Menahem led a rebellion in Jerusalem just before AD 66 and was tortured and killed; after the fall of Jerusalem, Eleazar, probably Judas's grandson, led the defense of the fortress at Masada in AD 73, dying with the other defenders by suicide.[39] If the revolt of Judas the Galilean in AD 6 is indeed connected with the later "Zealots" who fought against Roman oppression, Gamaliel's argument that his movement had come to nothing was unduly optimistic.[40]

5:38 Therefore, in the present case I advise you to keep away from these men and to let them

33. Josephus, *Ant.* 17.271 – 272, 273 – 276, 278 – 285; cf. *J. W.* 2.55 – 65.

34. Josephus, *Ant.* 20.97 – 99, 167 – 168, 169 – 172, 186 – 188; *J. W.* 2.258 – 263; 7.437 – 450; *Life* 424 – 425.

35. See Horsley and Llewelyn, *New Documents*, 4:183 – 85.

36. Josephus, *Ant.* 17.354; he gives a fuller account in 18.1 – 3; cf. *J. W.* 2.117. On the census of Quirinius and the date

of Jesus' birth, cf. Barnett, *Jesus and the Rise of Early Christianity*, 97 – 99.

37. Josephus, *Ant.* 18.4 – 10.

38. Ibid., 18:9, 23 – 25.

39. Ibid., *Ant.* 20.102; *J. W.* 2.433 – 448; 7.253, 320 – 322.

40. Bruce, *Acts*, 177.

alone. For if this plan or activity is of human origin, it will fail (καὶ τὰ νῦν λέγω ὑμῖν, ἀπόστητε ἀπὸ τῶν ἀνθρώπων τούτων καὶ ἄφετε αὐτούς· ὅτι ἐὰν ᾖ ἐξ ἀνθρώπων ἡ βουλὴ αὕτη ἢ τὸ ἔργον τοῦτο, καταλυθήσεται). Third, Gamaliel is ready to propose a course of action that the Sanhedrin should follow with regard to the leaders of the Jesus movement. He proposes that the council should "keep away" from these men and "let them alone." In other words, the council should not deliberate how to have these men killed; rather, they should be tolerated for the time being. As Jesus, the leader of this new messianic movement, had been executed some time ago, one may just have to wait until his followers disperse.

If this is his argument, it has a fundamental flaw from the point of view of the apostles. They are convinced that Jesus himself is the real and effective leader of the movement of "messianic Jews" since he has been raised from the dead and rules on God's throne as the exalted Messiah and Savior.[41]

Gamaliel supports his counsel with a twofold logical reasoning, the first of which is an inference from the historical precedents he has cited. If the plan of the leaders of the Jesus movement and its execution are "of human origin" (ἐξ ἀνθρώπων), it will fail. The Greek construction is a third-class condition (ἐὰν ᾖ), which some interpret as a "less probable condition" indicating Gamaliel's uncertainty whether this is actually the case.[42] Since third class conditions can express a present general condition, a mere hypothetical situation, or a more probable future occurrence,[43] one must conclude

that the sentence does not inform us about Gamaliel's thinking. He simply but powerfully establishes a logical connection between human plans regarding messianic fulfillment and eventual failure.

5:39 "But if it is from God, you will not be able to suppress them; you will only find yourselves fighting against God." They were persuaded by him (εἰ δὲ ἐκ θεοῦ ἐστιν, οὐ δυνήσεσθε καταλῦσαι αὐτούς, μήποτε καὶ θεομάχοι εὑρεθῆτε. ἐπείσθησαν δὲ αὐτῷ). Fourth, Gamaliel argues that the entire matter should be left in God's hands. He argues that the movement of the followers of Jesus could be "from God" (ἐκ θεοῦ). In that case the Sanhedrin will not be able to suppress them and bring the movement to a stop. The Greek formulation as a first class condition (εἰ … ἐστιν) does not illuminate Gamaliel's thinking either, since first class conditions do not express a "much more probable" condition but assume the truth of a statement for the sake of argument.[44] Whether the condition corresponds to reality must be established from the context. His argument is pragmatic rather than pro-Christian. Since the historical examples he has used in his speech are both failed movements, Gamaliel most likely has a negative view of the movement initiated by Jesus.[45]

If the Sanhedrin fights against a movement that is from God, they would be defiling their hands with the blood of these men, and, more seriously, they would be "fighters against God" (θεομάχοι).[46] A movement sanctioned and supported by God cannot be stopped. And those who do battle against God — the primary biblical example is Pharaoh at

---

41. Or, perhaps, Gamaliel argues that the crushing of mass movements that are dangerous should be left to the Romans; cf. Marshall, *Acts*, 123.

42. Witherington, *Acts*, 235; Jervell, *Apostelgeschichte*, 211.

43. Wallace, *Greek Grammar*, 696.

44. BDF, §372.1; cf. Barrett, *Acts*, 296.

45. Padilla, *Speeches*, 128; for a discussion of the "dramatic irony" in Gamaliel's speech, cf. ibid., 128 – 32.

46. The word θεομάχος is used in Greek literature, cf. Euripides, *Bacch.* 45; 2 Macc 7:19; Philostratus, *Vit. Apoll.* 4.44. Cf. John B. Weaver, *Plots of Epiphany: Prison-Escape in Acts of the Apostles* (BZNW 131; Berlin: De Gruyter, 2004), 143 – 44, who points out that the motif of being an enemy of the god(s) is used in contexts that validate a persecuted group vis-à-vis superior authorities who are called θεομάχοι.

the time of Israel's exodus — end up being utterly destroyed.

Gamaliel's point has a material parallel in the test whether a prophet has been sent by God:

> But a prophet who presumes to speak in my name anything I have not commanded, or a prophet who speaks in the name of other gods, is to be put to death.
>
> You may say to yourselves, "How can we know when a message has not been spoken by the LORD?" If what a prophet proclaims in the name of the LORD does not take place or come true, that is a message the LORD has not spoken. That prophet has spoken presumptuously, so do not be alarmed. (Deut 18:20–22)

Relevant too is the following rabbinic dictum: "Any assembling together that is for the sake of heaven will in the end be established; but any that is not for the sake of heaven will in the end not be established" (m. ʾAbot 4:11).

Gamaliel the Pharisee protects the movement of the followers of Jesus for the time being. This confirms that the Christian faith has Jewish roots and a fundamentally Jewish identity. To be a Christian means to be committed to Jesus as Israel's Messiah, who is also the Savior of the world.

The members of the Sanhedrin change their mind. They find Gamaliel's counsel persuasive and abandon their plan to kill the leaders of the Jesus movement. They may have been convinced by the rabbi's reference to historical precedents that the prophetic and messianic movements of the recent past all came to nothing, or they may have been swayed by his logical argument that one should not risk fighting against God. The "persuasion" does not refer to a decision about whether the move-

ment that the apostles represent has a human or a divine origin. It refers to the decision not to plan the execution of these men.

5:40 They called in the apostles and had them whipped. Then they ordered them not to speak in the name of Jesus. Then they let them go (καὶ προσκαλεσάμενοι τοὺς ἀποστόλους δείραντες παρήγγειλαν μὴ λαλεῖν ἐπὶ τῷ ὀνόματι τοῦ Ἰησοῦ καὶ ἀπέλυσαν). The apostles are summoned back to the council hall to be informed about the outcome of the *in camera* session. The final decision of the Sanhedrin has three parts.

(1) The apostles are to be punished by flogging. The verb translated as "whipped" (δέρω) means "to beat, strike, whip." The punishment of flogging is mentioned explicitly only in Deut 25:2–3 as stipulated for the outcome of private litigation, but must have been frequent, as this passage limits the number of lashes to no more than forty. We do not know which offenses were to be punished by flogging. The specific number of strikes to be administered was at the discretion of the court that decided a case.

Luke does not mention Jesus' flogging after his conviction,[47] while the other gospels do.[48] In 16:23 Paul and Silas are flogged as prisoners in Philippi. In 22:24–25 Paul, who is about to be "examined with the whip" by Roman soldiers in the barracks, protests that a Roman citizen cannot be flogged prior to a court sentence. In 2 Cor 11:23–25 Paul says that he was often beaten (NRSV and NIV use "flogged"), that he received "from the Jews the forty lashes minus one" five times,[49] and that he was beaten with rods three times.

We do not know whether the Sanhedrin used

---

47. See, however, the prediction in Luke 18:33, and Pilate's intention of flogging Jesus before releasing him in Luke 23:16, 22.

48. Matt 27:26/Mark 15:15/John 19:1.

49. The subtraction of one lash from the forty lashes described in Deut 25:3 represents the "fence around the law"

that the rabbis built; i.e., it reflects the program of rabbis to describe in more specific detail how a certain commandment needs to be kept in order to avoid breaking it. If the person administering the forty lashes strikes the convicted person once too many, a commandment has been broken. Since the law

the Roman *flagellum*, the scourge consisting of leather thongs, often weighted with pieces of metal or bone to inflict maximum damage, attached to a wooden handle. One could die as a result of this punishment, which was not the intention of the Sanhedrin, and one could end up being crippled for life. Luke does not use the usual terms for the scourge (μάστιξ) or the *flagellum* (φραγέλλιον),[50] but this does not prove much since technical terms were not always used in references to punishments. We do not know how many lashes each of the apostles received, whether they were flogged simultaneously or *ad seriatim*, and whether it occurred in the presence of the council members.

(2) The ban on speaking about Jesus is renewed. The Sanhedrin orders the Twelve not to speak in the name of Jesus. They repeat the ban issued in 4:18, 21 (cf. 5:28). This order had already proven to be ineffective, as the apostles evidently did not mind the consequences for disobeying the Sanhedrin in this matter. Since readers know about the (counter) command of the angel of the Lord given the night before (v. 20), we anticipate that the apostles will continue to defy the Sanhedrin's ban and continue to proclaim Jesus as Israel's Messiah and Savior.

(3) The apostles are released. Their flogging was not so severe that they became incapacitated. As the Sanhedrin renewed the ban on speaking about Jesus, the council members evidently hope that the apostles will return to their hometowns and to their professions. If they cannot speak about Jesus, they have no business staying in Jerusalem, as they are neither priests who work in the temple nor trained Torah scholars who can work and teach in the local synagogues. This means that if the apostles obey the Sanhedrin's ban, the followers of Jesus in Jerusalem and in the Judean towns will disperse, and the movement of people who believe in Jesus as Israel's Messiah and Savior will come to an end.

5:41 They left the Sanhedrin, full of joy that they had been considered worthy to be insulted for the sake of the Name (οἱ μὲν οὖν ἐπορεύοντο χαίροντες ἀπὸ προσώπου τοῦ συνεδρίου, ὅτι κατηξιώθησαν ὑπὲρ τοῦ ὀνόματος ἀτιμασθῆναι). The apostles react to their punishment with joy. As they leave the council building and walk through the streets of Jerusalem — the marks of the beating perhaps visible — they are full of joy. The present participle "full of joy" (χαίροντες) describes not just a brief emotional reaction but a continuous sense of gladness that comes over them as they leave the Sanhedrin. As Peter's boldness to proclaim Jesus as Israel's Messiah and Savior in 4:8 was the result of the invasive presence of the Holy Spirit, so is the reaction of the apostles to the arrest, the night in prison, the interrogation, the beating, and the ban, which they will continue to ignore.

The reason for their joy is expressed with an oxymoron, a figure of speech that links contradictory terms that produces a paradoxical statement. They rejoice because "they had been considered worthy" (κατηξιώθησαν) "to be insulted" (ἀτιμασθῆναι) on account of the name of Jesus. The insult was the ban on speaking and, immediately visible, the beating that they had received. Insults are always intended to wound the self-respect of a person; in honor-shame societies (which Jewish, Greek, and Roman societies were), insults were especially grievous.

The reason for their joy is the blessing that Jesus

does not stipulate that forty lashes must be administered in every case, giving thirty-nine lashes guarantees that the commandment of Deut 25:3 will not be broken (assuming that the mathematical skills of the court attendant who administers the beating and of the witnesses who are present are not so mini-mal that they neglect to count two beatings).

50. The verb φραγελλόω is used for Jesus' flogging before the crucifixion in Matt 27:26; Mark 15:15, while John 19:1 has μαστιγόω.

had pronounced on his followers who are hated, excluded, reviled, and defamed on account of the Son of Man and who thus "rejoice" (χάρητε) and "leap for joy" (σκιρτήσατε) because their reward is great in heaven, "for that is how their ancestors treated the prophets" (Luke 6:22 – 23). The Twelve may have skipped the leaping after their beating, but they rejoice in the fact that they have been treated like the prophets, indeed like Jesus, Israel's Messiah and Savior, because they remained faithful to "the Name" — to Jesus and to his cause.

5:42 Day after day, in the temple courts and in house after house, they did not stop teaching and proclaiming the good news that Jesus is the Messiah (πᾶσάν τε ἡμέραν ἐν τῷ ἱερῷ καὶ κατ᾽ οἶκον οὐκ ἐπαύοντο διδάσκοντες καὶ εὐαγγελιζόμενοι τὸν χριστόν Ἰησοῦν). As expected, the apostles again defy the ban on speaking. Every day they go to the temple and preach, teach, and have fellowship in Solomon's Portico. Every day they also preach in the various houses that believers open for teaching, fellowship, and communal meals (cf. 2:46 – 47). The imperfect "did not stop" (οὐκ ἐπαύοντο) indicates that the refusal to stop speaking about Jesus was a permanent disposition of the apostles. Luke describes their activity with two present participles, underlining again the continuous nature of the "teaching and proclaiming" activity. They teach believers and everyone else who wants to be instructed about Jesus. And they proclaim the good news that Jesus is Israel's Messiah (τὸν χριστόν Ἰησοῦν).

Luke uses the verb "to bring good news"

(εὐαγγελίζομαι) here for the first time in Acts. The term was used in secular Greek for anything from the communication of news about a wedding[51] to the good news of the victory or a benefaction of a monarch or the proclamation of an emperor.[52] In the New Testament the term is mostly used for the good news of God's revelation in Jesus, Israel's Messiah and Savior, who grants forgiveness, salvation, reconciliation, and eternal life to all who come to faith in him; it is the good news of messianic fulfillment, of the beginning and reality of the restoration of Israel and the dawn of God's kingdom, of the inauguration of the new covenant, and of transformation through the Holy Spirit.[53] In view of the reality of this good news and their commission to proclaim it in Jerusalem and in Judea and beyond, defying the ban of the Sanhedrin — with the prospect of further arrests and beatings — was a matter of course for the apostles.

The fact that the apostles defy the Sanhedrin's ban and continue to proclaim Jesus as Israel's Messiah and Savior implies the "parting of the ways" of Jews and followers of Jesus — whether the latter are Jewish believers, as in Jerusalem and Judea in the year AD 30/31, or Gentile believers. As the apostles preach Jesus as Messiah in the temple, despite the ban on speaking imposed by the Jewish leaders in the highest court of the land, Luke "has answered for his readers the question concerning the leadership over Israel. Not the faithless members of the Sanhedrin but the Twelve are truly 'ruling over the twelve tribes of Israel.'"[54]

---

51. Note the papyrus from Oxyrhynchos in which the sentence after the introductory greeting reads: "You filled us with joy when you announced the good news [εὐαγγελισαμένη] of most noble Sarapion's marriage" (P. Oxy XLVI 3313); cf. Horsley and Llewelyn, *New Documents*, 1:10 – 12; with documentary examples of the εὐαγγελ- word group in papyri and inscriptions.

52. Cf. OGIS I 4; SEG I 362; IG XII Sup 168; SB I 421.

53. BDAG, s.v. εὐαγγελίζω 2, "proclaim the divine message of salvation, *proclaim the gospel*," which is a "thin" description of the meaning of the term.

54. Johnson, *Acts*, 103.

Theology in Application

The arrest of the apostles, their hostile interrogation, their beating, and the renewed ban on preaching the gospel continue the theme of suffering we encountered earlier (4:1 – 22). In agreement with the main idea, the present passage underlines several important lessons.

Suffering

Following Jesus leads into suffering. The fact that suffering and persecution for the sake of Jesus are mentioned in the Beatitudes (Matt 5:1 – 12/Luke 6:20 – 26) indicates how fundamental this principle is, despite the fact that Christians in West European countries and in North America have had few opportunities to suffer for the faith in recent times. For Christians in the global South, suffering and persecution are often a reality that is all too real.

Being a Christian does not protect from suffering; on the contrary, it is often the cause for suffering, which may be the distress that comes from discrimination and ostracism, or may consist in arrest and imprisonment, corporal punishments, or even execution. For some, the doctrine of the rapture before the "great tribulation" is motivated not so much by specific passages in the Bible but by the assumption that Christians will be protected when things get really bad. While suffering is unnatural in view of Genesis 1 – 2, it is natural in the light of Genesis 3 and the rest of human history before God creates new heavens and a new earth.

Christian leaders may be persecuted repeatedly. Peter had already been arrested once, and he will be arrested again. Paul was repeatedly detained in synagogues when he received the forty lashes minus one; he was briefly imprisoned in Philippi and then for several years in Caesarea and in Rome. In totalitarian regimes determined to curb the activities of Christians, it is often the pastors, evangelists, and missionaries who suffer the most. This is to be expected.

The difficult question for missionary organizations is how to react when the political situation goes from tense to open hostilities. Most missionary groups have evacuation plans. The decision whether one should stay in a city or region in which persecution is taking place is a difficult one, both for missionaries and local believers, particularly for families with children. Luke later reports several incidents when Paul left the city in which his life was in danger. On other occasions, however, as when he returned from his missionary work in Ephesus via Achaia, he continued on to Jerusalem despite repeated warnings that he would be arrested. There is no simple answer to the question whether Christians should stay in regions in which their lives are in danger.

The apostles are imprisoned together. Serious persecution is seldom directed at individuals but against the entire church and thus often against leaders (still, later, Peter and Paul are imprisoned as individuals). If a pastor or Christian suffers alone, one needs at least to ask the question whether the suffering is self-inflicted.

Christians may experience divine protection in the midst of suffering. The apostles were rescued from prison through an angel of the Lord. Christians will always rely on God, who has not promised, however, that he will always deliver his people from harm in persecutions. A few months after this episode Stephen is killed, and ten years or so later James, one of the Twelve, is executed in another wave of persecution, in the course of which Peter escapes through another miracle involving an angel. Few Christians in prisons and in labor camps in the Soviet Union and in the People's Republic of China have experienced miraculous escapes — but they received divine strength to bear the suffering with patience, faithfulness, and joy.

Christians may receive help from non-Christians. The apostles were rescued here from being executed by the Sanhedrin. Paul was prepared to use his Roman citizenship as an argument that might protect him from imprisonment without trial (Philippi) and beatings (Jerusalem).

Joy

Following Jesus is expressed in joy. The apostles left the Sanhedrin building in which they had been interrogated and beaten with joy, and they continued to preach the good news of Jesus, Israel's Messiah and Savior, in the temple and in private houses despite the ban imposed on them. Joy is a basic need, desire, and goal of being human. Yet the condition of the world and the situation of our individual lives make the experience of joy a fleeting experience that does not last long. The artificial production of joy through drugs, pills, or alcohol is often not much more than merry hilarity, which not infrequently and sometimes with predictable regularity ends in hangovers or addiction.

The joy of believers in Jesus is not a psychological predisposition that some have and some don't, but a disposition granted by the transforming presence of the Holy Spirit. It is an integral part of the fruit of the Holy Spirit (Rom 14:17; Gal 5:22), it is part of the growth in faith (Phil 1:25; Rom 15:13), and it is a "condition" that should characterize all believers all the time (Phil 4:4).

Christians can have joy in the midst of suffering not because they enjoy suffering. Believers in Jesus are not masochists — pain or humiliation is always the result of sin and can therefore never be the cause of pleasure. Christians have joy in suffering because they suffer for the name of Jesus. Christians who suffer for his sake share in God's mission to save the world through his Son Jesus Christ, which is cause for rejoicing. And they have been promised a "reward" in heaven (Luke 6:22 – 23) if and when they suffer in faithful discipleship.

Civil Disobedience

Following Jesus may lead to civil disobedience. The apostles continue to defy the ban on speaking that the highest court of the land had imposed. Peter insists that "we must obey God rather than human beings" (v. 29). Civil disobedience is never easy, but sometimes necessary.[55] Some define civil disobedience as a deliberate, public, nonviolent action that is contrary to law (e.g., blocking a street) and that is designed to draw public attention to some policy of the government (e.g., abortion) in the hope that the policy will be changed. This is not in view here. The apostles do not mobilize the thousands of believers for a "march on the Sanhedrin" in order to pressure them to make faith in Jesus legal. But they do disobey the policy of the Sanhedrin that nobody may teach about Jesus as Israel's Messiah.

If the alternative is between obeying God and obeying a government policy, disobedience to earthly authorities becomes a necessity. While Christians are citizens of an earthly state, they are also citizens of heaven, whose obligations they cannot ignore. Jesus said that we need to give to Caesar what is Caesar's but to give to God what is God's. And if there is a conflict, God's demands have priority. This happens when Christians are required to deny their faith in Jesus as Messiah and Savior, when they are required to commit sinful acts, and when they are required to act contrary to God's specific commands.

While not all believers in Jerusalem were commissioned as Jesus' official witnesses in public and in private, the Twelve had specifically received such a mandate. When disobeying a government becomes a necessity, prudence often suggests various ways in which this may be done. The Twelve hardly had a choice; since the angel of the Lord told them to continue to proclaim the gospel publicly in the temple, they could not now decide that they would teach in safer localities such as private homes (cf. what Christians in Communist countries did). The obligation to obey God rather than human laws that contradict God's will "does not specify which means of disobedience are morally permissible or prudentially advisable."[56]

Divine Authorization

Following Jesus has divine authorization. The counsel of Gamaliel has both historical and theological implications. He suggests that history reveals whether or not

---

55. For brief discussions see John S. Feinberg and Paul D. Feinberg, *Ethics for a Brave New World* (Wheaton, IL: Crossway, 1993), 399–405; D. J. E. Attwood, "Civil Disobedience," in *New Dictionary of Christian Ethics and Pastoral Theology* (ed. D. J. Atkinson and D. H. Field; Downers Grove, IL: InterVarsity Press, 1995), 233–34.

56. Feinberg and Feinberg, *Ethics*, 402, who give the following example: "Many Europeans during World War II refused when told to turn over Jews to the authorities. That decision *per se* did not determine *how* they should disobey. They could have started a revolt, they could have simply said no and tried to protect the Jews by personally fighting the soldiers, they might have tried (like Bonhoeffer) to assassinate Hitler, or they could do what many did — hide the Jewish people in their homes. Morality dictated disobeying the government" (ibid.).

a community or movement comes from God. His counsel is certainly not always a helpful principle to assess whether a movement has divine authorization. Some movements that grew out of the Christian church but must be regarded as unorthodox or outright heretical have managed to survive over long periods of time. The Roman Catholic Church regarded the Protestant church as such a movement without divine sanction, taking legal measures against evangelicals, in some places for hundreds of years.[57] Evangelical churches regard the Church of the Latter Day Saints as a movement without authentic divine authorization, and yet the Mormons have been around since 1827, not only not dying off but growing and expanding.

Still, based on Gamaliel's dictum, the existence of congregations of believers in Jesus who confess allegiance to Jesus as Israel's Messiah and Savior of the world, not only surviving two thousand years but growing in ways that were unimaginable in the Jerusalem of AD 30/31, is an indication that it has the stamp of God's approval.[58] Jesus promised that the gates of Hades will not prevail against the church (Matt 16:18).

The advice to leave a new movement alone and wait to see whether it self-destructs is wise counsel for Christians. Unless new movements in the church radically contradict the church's understanding of the clear teaching of Scripture, they can and should be tolerated with the expectation that they will decline and disappear if they are not of God. Such toleration does not exclude the responsibility of critical dialogue and theological confrontation, but it rejects resorting to the use of force with a view to suppress the new movement.[59]

God is the Lord of history. Gamaliel, a knowledgeable rabbi and Pharisee, correctly and effectively pointed to this biblical truth and thus helped protect the apostles. As Luke reports Gamaliel's "if it is from God" (Acts 5:39), he emphasizes God's agency in the missionary and pastoral work of the apostles, which is the work of God and cannot be stopped by opposition. Christians are committed to this truth. They insist that the message of Jesus as the only Messiah and Savior must be preached, whether it is welcomed or not, because doing so is doing the work of God. Christians are confident that their message and activities, if and when they correspond to God's will, cannot be checked, curtailed, or destroyed by people who eventually turn out to be God's enemies, because God is on their side.

---

57. In Roman Catholic Cologne, the Protestants were allowed to own real estate and to build houses of worship only after the occupation by the French revolutionary troops in October of 1794; cf. Klaus Müller, *Köln von der französischen zur preussischen Herrschaft 1794–1815* (Geschichte der Stadt Köln 8; Köln: Greven, 2005), 303–8.

58. Zmijewski, *Apostelgeschichte*, 275.

59. Embarking on crusades that aim at the physical elimination of people of other faiths contradicts not only Gamaliel's advice but Jesus' commandment to love our neighbor and even our enemies. While the Crusades took place — the first one in 1095–1101, the eighth and last one in 1270 — Christians have not always resisted the temptation to work for the physical elimination of people who held differing convictions.

Acts 6:1 – 7

Literary Context

Up to this point Luke's narrative has focused on Peter's ministry as leader in the community of believers and as preacher and teacher in Jerusalem (1:15 – 5:42). In this new episode the focus is not on Peter, who is not mentioned, but on the apostles. The episode of the seven assistants in 6:1 – 7 is the sixth episode in Luke's description of the life, witness, trials, and growth of the church in Jerusalem (3:1 – 8:3).

Luke narrates a second threat to the unity of the community as it cared for the impoverished members when well-to-do believers willingly shared their possessions by selling property (2:44 – 45; 4:32 – 37). Ananias and Sapphira had injected false motives into this practice (5:1 – 11); now the neglect of Greek-speaking widows among the believers threatens the harmony of the church (6:1 – 7).[1] In both cases the apostles act decisively: Peter's confrontation of the hypocritical and lying couple ends with their quick demise, while the apostles' confrontation of the problem of the neglected widows results in a restructuring of the ministries of the church.

The episode introduces Stephen and Philip and thus prepares the reader for the next episodes, which narrates Stephen's evangelistic work, his defense before the Sanhedrin, and his death and the ensuing persecution (6:8 – 8:3), which then takes Philip to Samaria and to an encounter with an Ethiopian (8:4 – 40). The continuing conflict between the believers in Jerusalem and the Jewish authorities, which inexorably moves toward a first climax in the death of Stephen, cannot prevent the growth of the church.

The episode that narrates the appointment of the Seven is framed by references to the continued expansion of the church (6:1, 7), which the persecution following Stephen's death cannot stop. Churches are being established throughout Judea, Galilee, and Samaria (9:31), and later James informs Paul that there are myriads of Jewish believers (21:20).

---

1. Tannehill, *Acts*, 80.

Main Idea

The growth of the church and increasing numbers of impoverished believers require a restructuring of the community. The Twelve are willing to introduce a new group of leaders with distinct responsibilities, keen to preserve the unity of the community and eager to preserve the priorities of their responsibility as leaders of God's people, namely, prayer and the ministry of the word.

Translation

Acts 6:1 – 7

1a	Setting: Time	In those days,
b	Setting: Event	when the number of disciples was increasing,
c	Conflict	**there was a complaint of the Hellenists against the Hebrews**
d	Cause	that their widows were being neglected
e		in the daily ✍
		distribution of food.
2a	Action/Reaction	So **the Twelve called the community of the disciples together**
b	Action (speech)	and **said,**
c	Assertion	*"It is not right that we should neglect the word of God*
d	Purpose	*to wait on tables.*
3a	Address/Consequence	*Therefore, brothers and sisters,*
b	Call to action	*look for seven men among you*
c	Qualification	*of good reputation,*
d	Qualification	*who are filled with the Spirit and*
e	Qualification	*with wisdom,*
f	Purpose	*whom we may appoint to this task.*
4a	Assertion	*As for us, we will devote ourselves to prayer and*
b	List	*to the ministry of the word."*
5a	Action	**The proposal was approved**
b	Agency	by the whole community,
c	Action (List)/ Character entrance	and **they selected Stephen,**

d	Description	a man full of faith and
e	Description	the Holy Spirit, and
f	List	Philip,
g		Prochorus,
h		Nicanor,
i		Timon,
j		Parmenas, and
k		Nicolaus,
l	Description: geographical	a proselyte from Antioch.
6a	Action	**They presented these men to the apostles,**
b	Action	**who prayed**
c	Action	**and laid their hands on them.**
7a	Event	**The word of God continued to grow.**
b	Event	**The number of disciples increased greatly**
c	Place	**in Jerusalem.**
d	Event	**A large number of the priests became obedient to the faith.**

Structure and Literary Form

This episode is narrated in five incidents. (1) Luke begins by noting the continued growth of the church (v. 1a-b) and the complaint of the Greek-speaking segment of the Jewish believers whose widows are neglected in the distribution of food (v. 1c-e).

(2) The apostles convene a meeting of the entire community of believers in Jerusalem (v. 2a) in which they describe the problem of food distribution, which jeopardizes their focus on preaching and teaching (v. 2b-d). They propose that the Greek-speaking believers should look for seven men (v. 3a-b) who have the necessary qualifications (v. 3c-e) and who can be appointed to distribute food (v. 3f). This solution will preserve the priority of preaching and teaching, which requires much prayer (v. 4). The meeting of the congregation ends with the agreement of the believers that the proposal of the apostles should be accepted (v. 5a-b).

(3) The Greek-speaking Jewish believers select seven men who meet the qualifications (v. 5c-l). Luke's list singles out Stephen for special emphasis (v. 5c-e).

(4) After an unspecified interval the Greek-speaking believers bring the seven men to the apostles (v. 6a), who pray for them and bless them as they begin their ministry (v. 6b-c).

(5) Luke ends the episode with another summary statement regarding the continued growth of the church in Jerusalem (v. 7).

The passage consists mostly of *historical narrative*, into which Luke has integrated a *speech* of the apostles (vv. 2c – 4), a *list* of believers in Jerusalem who are chosen to organize the food distribution (v. 5c-l), and a *summary statement* (v. 7; cf. 1:14; 2:42 – 47; 4:32 – 37; 5:12 – 16). The episode has been called an "appointment history" with parallels in the Old Testament.[2]

Exegetical Outline

→ **I. The Expansion of the Ministry of the Church: The Seven Assistants (6:1 – 7)**

    A. The Neglect of the Greek-Speaking Widows in the Food Distribution (6:1)

        1. The numerical growth of the community of believers (6:1a-b)

        2. The complaint of the Hellenistic Jewish believers (6:1c-e)

           a. The complaint of the Hellenists against the Hebrews (6:1c)

           b. The neglect of the Greek-speaking widows in the food distribution (6:1d-e)

    B. The Meeting of the Community of Believers (6:2 – 5b)

        1. The apostles convene the community of believers in Jerusalem (6:2a)

        2. The solution suggested by the Twelve (6:2b – 4)

           a. The problem: The conflict between teaching and food distribution (6:2b-d)

           b. The proposal: The appointment of seven assistants (6:3)

               i. Suggestion: The Greek-speaking believers should look for seven men (6:3a-b)

               ii. Qualifications: A good reputation and full of the Spirit and wisdom (6:3c-e)

               iii. Solution: These seven men will be appointed to distribute food (6:3f)

           c. Explanation: This will preserve the priority of preaching and prayer (6:4)

           d. Agreement of the community concerning the apostles' proposal (6:5a-b)

    C. The Choice of Seven Candidates (6:5c-l)

        1. The selection of Stephen (6:5c-e)

        2. The selection of Philip, Prochorus, Nicanor, Timon, Parmenas, Nicolaus (6:5f-l)

    D. The Appointment of the Seven Assistants (6:6)

        1. Presentation of the seven men to the apostles (6:6a)

        2. Prayer of the apostles and blessing of the seven assistants (6:6b-c)

    E. The Continued Growth of the Church in Jerusalem (6:7)

        1. The spreading of the word of God (6:7a)

        2. Further numerous conversions in Jerusalem (6:7b-c)

        3. The conversion of many priests (6:7d).

---

2. Charles H. Talbert, *Reading Acts: A Literary and Theological Commentary on the Acts of the Apostles* (rev. ed.; Reading the New Testament; Macon: Smyth, 2005), 73 – 75; Bock, *Acts*, 256; cf. Gen 41:29 – 43; Exod 18:13 – 26; Num 11:1 – 25; 27:12 – 23; Deut 1:9 – 18.

Explanation of the Text

6:1 In those days, when the number of disciples was increasing, there was a complaint of the Hellenists against the Hebrews that their widows were being neglected in the daily distribution of food (ἐν δὲ ταῖς ἡμέραις ταύταις πληθυνόντων τῶν μαθητῶν ἐγένετο γογγυσμὸς τῶν Ἑλληνιστῶν πρὸς τοὺς Ἑβραίους, ὅτι παρεθεωροῦντο ἐν τῇ διακονίᾳ τῇ καθημερινῇ αἱ χῆραι αὐτῶν). The continued growth of the church in Jerusalem leads to problems in the distribution of resources among impoverished believers. The introductory phrase "in those days" links this episode (6:1 – 7) with the preceding one on the arrest, interrogation, and release of the apostles, who continue to preach the gospel despite the renewed ban on speaking (5:17 – 42). This phrase does not allow us to date this episode, which precedes the arrest, interrogation, and killing of Stephen (6:8 – 8:3); presumably it takes place in AD 31/32.

The first comment concerns the continued growth of the church. The present participle "increasing" (πληθυνόντων) is temporal: the difficulties in the Jerusalem community arise *when* the congregation in Jerusalem is growing in number. A causal interpretation is also possible: the difficulties arise *because of* the increasing number of believers. The term "disciples" (μαθηταί) is the self-designation of the believers in Jerusalem (see on 5:11), which emphasizes the continuity with the earthly ministry of Jesus and underscores the significance of learning and thus of teaching in the congregation.

The "complaint" (γογγυσμός)[3] expresses a discontent among the affected believers that even-

tually reached the apostles. Luke describes the problem in terms of "the Hellenists" being pitted against "the Hebrews" in the congregation. "Hellenists" (Ἑλληνισταί) describes Jews whose primary language is Greek while "Hebrews" (Ἑβραῖοι) refers to Aramaic-speaking Jews.[4] These terms describe a linguistic distinction, not ethnic differences — there were no non-Jewish believers in Jerusalem (or anywhere else) at this time. The "Hellenists" were Greek-speaking Jews who had returned from the diaspora to live in Jerusalem, attending their own synagogues (6:9; 9:29).

While it can be assumed that many Jews in Galilee and in Judea understood and spoke Greek, it is not clear whether these "Hellenists" spoke only Greek. If so, there were probably meetings of believers conducted in Aramaic and in Greek. Some if not all of the Twelve would have been able to teach in both groups. Numerous ossuaries found in Jerusalem attest to the fact that Greek was widely used among Jews living in Jerusalem in the first century BC and AD. Perhaps many of diaspora spoke Aramaic before they returned to Jerusalem, and surely many learned to speak some Aramaic after settling down to live there.

While Jews whose primary language was Greek may have had cultural distinctives that distinguished them from Palestinian Jews whose primary language was Aramaic, Luke provides no evidence to suggest social or theological differences between these two sets of believers or two separate congregations. When Luke describes the life of the church, he emphasizes their unity[5] without downplaying the reality and influence of sinful

---

3. Cf. BDAG, s.v. γογγυσμός, "utterance made in a low tone of voice (the context indicates whether the utterance is one of discontent or satisfaction), *behind-the-scenes talk* — Negative aspect: *complaint, displeasure,* expressed in murmuring."

4. In first-century Palestinian Judaism, both Hebrew and

Aramaic were used as languages, with Aramaic being the "first language" used in everyday conversations. Cf. Hengel, *Between Jesus and Paul,* 1 – 29.

5. Acts 1:14; 2:46; 4:24; 5:12; cf. the term "together" (ἐπὶ τὸ αὐτό) in 1:15; 2:1, 44.

behavior in the congregation (5:1 – 11). In 6:2 – 6 Luke pictures the entire congregation in a meeting that seeks to address the problem. Whether the "Hellenists" shared theological views that the "Hebrews" did not share will be discussed under 6:11 – 14. Here, the problem is not deliberate sin or theological differences but the unintentional oversight of widows in the congregation.

The Greek-speaking Jews complain that their widows are neglected in the daily distribution of food. The imperfect tense of the verb translated as "were being neglected" (παρεθεωροῦντο) indicates that this had been a problem for some time. As food was distributed among poor believers, the Aramaic-speaking widows evidently received sufficient help, while the Greek-speaking widows did not. The widows appear in the narrative only as the "object" of the neglect of others; presumably male Greek-speaking Jewish Christians took up their cause and informed the Twelve about the problem. The passive voice leaves the people who did the neglecting unnamed; the action of the apostles in v. 2 implies that distributing food was part of their responsibility (cf. also 4:35, 37; 5:2), though they may not have personally done the work. The passage focuses on a solution proposed by the apostles, not the problem.

The general meaning of the term translated "distribution of food" (διακονία) is "service rendered in an intermediary capacity;" here, in the context of impoverished widows, the term specifically designates the "rendering of specific assistance."[6] In 1:17, 25 the same Greek term is used for the "ministry" that the Twelve received. In the context of food distribution, this term describes an official assignment related to charitable activity. This assignment had been handled in a somewhat

random fashion that served the Hebrew-speaking widows well while the Greek-speaking widows were neglected.

Since in 21:8 Philip is called "one of the Seven," the group of seven men seems to have been known as "the Seven" (οἱ ἑπτά). They are not called "deacons": Luke does not use the term "deacon" (διάκονος) in vv. 1 – 7.[7] The reference to a "daily assistance" (διακονία καθημερινή) suggests that it was not funds but food that was distributed: funds could be distributed once a week, while perishables needed to be distributed daily.

In 4:34 Luke had asserted that the believers in Jerusalem met the needs of all impoverished fellow believers, so much so that no one was in need. In 5:14 Luke noted that more people than ever were converted to faith in Jesus, "great numbers of both men and women" from Jerusalem and from other towns in Judea — an expansion and growth of the church that prompted the high priest to arrest the apostles and issue another ban on speaking about Jesus (5:17 – 40). In 6:1 Luke notes again that the believers are increasing in numbers. Thus, the problem of these Greek-speaking widows reflects a later situation that results from the continuing growth of the church.

These Greek-speaking widows probably had no relatives in Palestine and thus no provisions except for assistance by the church. Greek-speaking Jewish widows in Jerusalem were probably supported by the charitable giving of fellow Jews, perhaps in the synagogues to which they belonged. The rabbinic system of a daily distribution of basic foodstuffs and a weekly distribution of food and clothing for the poor may or may not have been in place in the first century.[8] If a similar system was in

---

6. BDAG, s.v. διακονία 1. In v. 1, the translation "distribution of food" is used in NET, NIV, NLT, NRSV, TNIV; cf. "serving of food" (NASB), "their share of the food" (NCV), "distribution of funds" (GNB), "distribution" (ESV, NKJV, RSV), "ministration" (ASV, KJV).

7. Irenaeus, *Haer.* 1.26.3; 3.12.10; 4.15.1 suggested that this passage describes the origin of the deacons as an office in the church. If this had been Luke's concern, he probably would have used the term διάκονος. Cf. Barrett, *Acts*, 304.

place, the Greek-speaking Jewish Christians either may have chosen not to be assisted by the official Jewish authorities, or they may have been denied such assistance as a result of their faith in Jesus as the Messiah. Note that supporting widows (and orphans) is an Old Testament commandment[9] repeatedly reinforced by the prophets.[10] The neglect of widows is disobedience against God's will.[11]

6:2 So the Twelve called the community of the disciples together and said, "It is not right that we should neglect the word of God to wait on tables" (προσκαλεσάμενοι δὲ οἱ δώδεκα τὸ πλῆθος τῶν μαθητῶν εἶπαν· οὐκ ἀρεστόν ἐστιν ἡμᾶς καταλείψαντας τὸν λόγον τοῦ θεοῦ διακονεῖν τραπέζαις). The apostles take responsibility for the problem of the neglected widows and convene the believers in order to find a solution. The Twelve[12] call the congregation (πλῆθος; see on 4:32; 5:11), whose members are called "disciples" (μαθηταί). The fact that "the Twelve" address the congregation rather than Peter may indicate that on this occasion it was not Peter who speaks for the apostles but another member of the Twelve.

The brief speech of the Twelve (vv. 2–4) consists of two main parts: (1) the statement of the problem as the Twelve see it; (2) the proposal of a solution, which is made in three parts: the Greek-speaking believers should select seven men; these men should meet specific qualifications; once chosen, these men are expected to organize the distribution of food.

(1) The Twelve state the problem from their point of view. They see a conflict between their commission to preach and teach the word of God and the responsibility for food distribution (διακονεῖν τραπέζαις, lit., "to serve tables"). Both tasks are important and represent official assignments (διακονία) — the commission of the Twelve to be witnesses of Jesus' life, death, resurrection, and exaltation (1:17, 25; διακονία), and the commission of believers to care for the needs of impoverished believers through a daily distribution (6:1, διακονία). The "tables" (τράπεζαι) could refer to tables where money is distributed (cf. Mark 11:15; Luke 19:23); in view of the daily distribution (v. 1) the term refers more plausibly to the organization with regard to daily meals.

(2) The Twelve want a solution that remedies the neglect of the widows in the food distribution and, at the same time and more importantly (note v. 2), makes sure that the preaching and teaching the message about Jesus, Israel's Messiah and Savior, and about his ministry, death, resurrection, and exaltation and the presence of the Holy Spirit are not neglected. To prepare for teaching requires time, as does the actual teaching at the regular daily meetings in the temple and in private houses, as well as preaching on evangelistic trips to Judean towns. The phrase "it is not pleasing" or "it is not right" (οὐκ ἀρεστόν ἐστιν) may be read as "it is not acceptable to us, the Twelve" or, in view of the description of their commission in 1:8, 21–22, more probably "to God."[13]

6:3 Therefore, brothers and sisters, look for seven men among you of good reputation, who are filled with the Spirit and with wisdom,

---

8. Cf. *m. Peʾah* 8:7; *t. B. Meṣ* 3:9; *b. B. Bat.* 8b; *b. B. Meṣ* 38a; cf. Jeremias, *Jerusalem*, 131; Barrett, *Acts*, 310.

9. Cf. Deut 10:18; 14:29; 16:11, 14; 24:17, 19–21; 26:12–13; 27:19.

10. Cf. Isa 1:17, 23; 10:2; Jer 5:28; 7:6; 22:3; Ezek 22:7; Mal 3:5; cf. Ps 94:6, and Jas 1:27. Cf. Johnson, *Acts*, 105.

11. Cf. Luke 7:12–14; 20:46–47; and the regulations concerning the assistance for widows in 1 Tim 5:9–13.

12. The "Twelve" are mentioned with this designation only here in Acts, by implication in 1:13, 17, 22; cf. 2:14. They are mentioned as "apostles" in 6:6; 8:1, 14, 18; 9:27; 11:1; 14:4, 14; 15:2, 4, 6, 22, 23; 16:4.

13. Barrett, *Acts*, 311. Since the Greek phrase often translated as "wait on tables" (διακονεῖν τραπέζαις) is not a standard expression for "serving as accountants," there is no "humorous wordplay" here, as BDAG, s.v. τράπεζα 1c suggests.

whom we may appoint to this task (ἐπισκέψασθε δέ, ἀδελφοί, ἄνδρας ἐξ ὑμῶν μαρτυρουμένους ἑπτά, πλήρεις πνεύματος καὶ σοφίας, οὓς καταστήσομεν ἐπὶ τῆς χρείας ταύτης). The Twelve ask the believers to select seven competent men who can be appointed to distribute food among the impoverished believers. They do not impose a solution. Rather, they invite the congregation to be part of the solution by selecting capable candidates who will be responsible for the food distribution.

They stipulate two qualifications. (1) These men must have a "good reputation" (μαρτυρουμένους); i.e., they should be well spoken of in the congregation so that their appointment will meet with the approval of all believers. (2) They must be "filled with the Spirit and with wisdom." There should be evidence that their lives have been transformed by the presence of the Holy Spirit bestowed on them when they became believers in Jesus (cf. 2:38).[14] There should be evidence that they can make good judgments, an important factor in the ministry of daily food distribution.

These qualifications are different from those for the replacement of Judas among the Twelve (see on 1:21 – 22). The Twelve have a different function from the Seven, which does not mean that the Twelve should never be involved in the relief of the needs of the poor, nor that the Seven cannot preach (which Stephen does, cf. vv. 8 – 10, and later, Philip). The term translated as "task" (χρεία) means both "need" in the sense of lack or difficulty, and "office, duty, service" describing the activity that is needed (BDAG).

It is not clear why the Twelve suggest the appointment of seven men (and not twelve, or fifteen).[15] The appointment of the Seven has been

compared to Moses' appointment, following the advice of Jethro, of "officials" over smaller groups of Israelites who decided the "simple cases" so that Moses can be "the people's representative before God" and "teach them decrees and instructions, and show them the way they are to live and how they are to behave" (Exod 18:19 – 22). While the verbal connections between the two passages are not strong, the process of delegating tasks involving less important matters to assistants while the leaders attend to the more serious responsibilities of leading God's people has biblical precedent.

6:4 "As for us, we will devote ourselves to prayer and to the ministry of the word" (ἡμεῖς δὲ τῇ προσευχῇ καὶ τῇ διακονίᾳ τοῦ λόγου προσκαρτερήσομεν). The Twelve explain that the proposed appointment of seven assistants put in charge of the task of food distribution will allow them to devote all their energies to their main responsibilities, which they describe as "prayer" (προσευχή) and "the ministry of the word" (ἡ διακονία τοῦ λόγου). The reference to "prayer" may include the participation in the Jewish prayers in the temple (cf. 3:1). More likely it refers to the prayers in the gatherings of the believers (2:42), both in the temple and in private houses (2:46 – 47), and presumably prayers with and for sick believers.

The "ministry of the word" denotes preaching and teaching of the good news of God's revelation in Jesus, the crucified and risen Messiah and the exalted Lord and Savior (see on 4:4). The focus on preaching the word is not upheld at the expense of caring for the widows. The proposed solution provides for both the primacy of prayers, preaching, and teaching and for the assistance for impov-

---

14. Cf. Turner, *Power from on High*, 167, who argues regarding the phrase "full of" (πλήρης plus defining genitive), "that quality clearly marks the person's life or comes to visible expression in his or her activity."

15. There is some evidence that (some) Jewish cities had

seven judges. Cf. Josephus, *Ant.* 4.214 (with reference to Deut 16:18); 4.287; *J.W.* 2.571. Fitzmyer, *Acts*, 349, comments, "Seven, being a prime number and an odd number (important if decisions had to be made by a vote), is often used for crucial matters in the OT."

erished believers, including the Greek-speaking widows.

6:5 The proposal was approved by the whole community, and they selected Stephen, a man full of faith and the Holy Spirit, and Philip, Prochorus, Nicanor, Timon, Parmenas, and Nicolaus, a proselyte from Antioch (καὶ ἤρεσεν ὁ λόγος ἐνώπιον παντὸς τοῦ πλήθους καὶ ἐξελέξαντο Στέφανον, ἄνδρα πλήρης πίστεως καὶ πνεύματος ἁγίου, καὶ Φίλιππον καὶ Πρόχορον καὶ Νικάνορα καὶ Τίμωνα καὶ Παρμενᾶν καὶ Νικόλαον προσήλυτον Ἀντιοχέα). Luke notes the conclusion of the "whole community" of the Jerusalem church, who approve the proposal of the Twelve. The verb translated "approved" (ἤρεσεν) denotes the "satisfaction produced by the behavior of another."[16]

The third incident of the episode (v. 5c-l) relates the selection of seven men by the congregation, perhaps among a larger number of potential candidates. Luke gives the names of the seven men, with a particular focus on Stephen (in view of his role in the subsequent narrative). He does not tell us by whom and how the seven men were selected.[17] The task of selecting candidates could have been given to those who reported the neglect of the Greek-speaking widows; there may have been a call for volunteers who were then examined, perhaps by believers like Joseph Barsabbas (1:23), who had been among Jesus' disciples and who were among the 120 early believers (1:15); or people like Barnabas, who had been involved in the financial affairs and the assistance efforts for the poor (4:36 – 37).

The seven men have all Greek names, some of whom have not (yet) been attested among Jews living in Palestine, which suggests they were diaspora Jews. Since food needed to be distributed not only among the Greek-speaking widows but among Aramaic-speaking believers (see on v. 1), presumably some of the Seven spoke Aramaic, or perhaps some were bilingual. The latter must be assumed for Philip, who is later described as preaching to audiences in Samaria, who would have required sermons in Aramaic.

Stephen (Στέφανος) was a man "full" of faith and the Holy Spirit, i.e., a man whose life was visibly influenced by his faith in Jesus and by the presence of the Holy Spirit (see on v. 3). The wonders and signs he performed (v. 8) and his powerful teaching and arguing in the local synagogues attest to the Spirit's presence in his life and to his wisdom (v. 10), which were among the qualifications for appointment (v. 3). The emphasis on Stephen's wisdom highlights his role as a preacher and as an interpreter of Israel's history and Scriptures (7:2 – 53).

As Stephen is "full of grace and power" (v. 8) and wisdom (v. 10), so Joseph had the qualities of "favor" and "wisdom" (7:10) while Moses had "wisdom" and was "powerful in words and deeds" (7:22); when Stephen's face shone as he was being interrogated by the Sanhedrin (6:15), he looked like Moses when he came down from Mount Sinai (Exod 34:29 – 35). This characterization establishes Stephen's credentials as sharing the qualities of Jesus, of the apostles, and of leading figures in Scripture.

Philip (Φίλιππος; see on 1:13) is called "the evangelist, one of the Seven" in 21:8, where Luke describes him as residing in Caesarea and having four daughters. He is the evangelist through whose ministry faith in Jesus took hold in Samaria (8:4 – 24), who was instrumental in the conversion of an Ethiopian (8:26 – 39), and who preached in the towns along the Mediterranean coast (8:40)

---

16. BDAG, s.v. ἀρέσκω 2b.

17. Fitzmyer, *Acts*, 350, asserts that "it was not by casting of lots" as in the case of Matthias (1:26), but since Luke refrains from giving details about the selection process, this remains

a possibility. Richard I. Pervo, *Acts* (Hermeneia; Philadelphia: Fortress, 2008), 156, suggests that the Seven were based on house churches.

until he made his base of operations in Caesarea (8:40; 21:8). Philip may well have been a hellenized Jewish believer from Palestine rather than from the diaspora, although the fact that he resided in Caesarea does not prove this possibility.

Nicanor (Νικάνωρ) could have been of Palestinian origin, as his name is attested among Palestinian Jews. Prochorus (Πρόχορος), Timon (Τίμων), and Parmenas (Παρμενᾶς) are Greek names that have not been attested among Palestinian Jews. Nicolaus (Νικόλαος) is described as a proselyte from Antioch, which means that he was a Gentile who had lived in Antioch, the Syrian capital and had converted to Judaism and then to faith in Jesus. He is the first (former) Gentile mentioned in Acts. The fact that he is specifically described as a proselyte suggests that the other six men were all born Jews. This Nicolaus has been regarded in early Christian tradition as the founder of the heretical "Nicolaitans" mentioned in Rev 2:6, 15.[18] Antioch will figure prominently in Luke's subsequent account.

6:6 They presented these men to the apostles, who prayed and laid their hands on them (οὓς ἔστησαν ἐνώπιον τῶν ἀποστόλων, καὶ προσευξάμενοι ἐπέθηκαν αὐτοῖς τὰς χεῖρας). The fourth incident of the episode relates the appointment of these seven assistants. Leading believers of the congregation present these seven men to the apostles. The apostles were responsible for making the final decisions concerning any new developments in the church, which the introduction of seven official assistants certainly represents. They accept the seven men presented to them, "pray" (προσευξάμενοι as modal participle) that the Lord will give them spiritual insight and pragmatic wisdom (v. 3) as they help meet the needs of all the impoverished believers, and then lay their hands on them.

The laying on of hands derives from the Old Testament gesture of laying on hands or hand leaning that accompanies various procedures.[19] Moses transferred his authority to Joshua by laying on both hands (Num 27:23; Deut 34:9).[20] Note that the practical result of the transfer of Moses' sovereignty (Num 27:20) and of the spirit of wisdom (Deut 34:9) to Joshua

> does not seem to happen through the laying on of hands itself, since these blessings do not flow to Joshua "through the hand" of Moses. Rather, here too, the laying on of hands serves to designate Joshua as the recipient of the rite before the priest and congregation. The words accompanying this gesture served the actual transference of the powers of office.[21]

In Acts and the New Testament letters, the laying on of hands is linked with such diverse situations as receiving the Spirit (8:17), healing from blindness (9:17), commissioning for itinerant missionary outreach (13:3), baptism (19:6), receiving a spiritual gift for ministry (1 Tim 4:14; cf. 2 Tim 1:6), and restoring a person to the church (1 Tim 5:22; many see here a reference to the ordination of elders, cf. NRSV, which translates "ordain"). In the

---

18. Thus Irenaeus, *Haer.* 1.26.3.

19. Cf. D. P. Wright and J. Milgrom, "סָמַךְ," *TDOT*, 10:281 – 84, who discuss the various hypotheses (transference, identification, representation, declaration). A basic distinction is the hand leaning carried out with two hands (e.g., Moses transferring authority to Joshua) and the hand leaning carried out with only one hand (as in the sacrificial ritual). Cf. Tipei, *Laying on of Hands*, 44 – 100, for the practice of the laying on of hands in Jewish and Greco-Roman contexts.

20. Num 27:18 speaks of Moses leaning with one hand (sg.)

on Joshua (LXX has pl.); Num 27:23 and Deut 34:9 refer to both hands.

21. Wright and J. Milgrom, "סָמַךְ," 10:282. A similar meaning is present when Jacob blesses Joseph's sons who are appointed sons of Israel (Gen 48:5, 13 – 16). Wright and Milgrom classify the dedication of the Levites in Num 8:10 with the laying on of hands at sacrifice, as the Israelites' signal "that the Levites are *their* gift (instead of the firstborn) to Yahweh" (ibid., 10:284).

context of Acts 6:3, 5, the laying on of hands signifies the apostles' recognition of these men's endowment with the Holy Spirit, their appointment as representatives of the community of believers, and the expectation that God will bless them in their role.[22]

6:7 The word of God continued to grow. The number of disciples increased greatly in Jerusalem. A large number of the priests became obedient to the faith (καὶ ὁ λόγος τοῦ θεοῦ ηὔξανεν καὶ ἐπληθύνετο ὁ ἀριθμὸς τῶν μαθητῶν ἐν Ἰερουσαλὴμ σφόδρα, πολύς τε ὄχλος τῶν ἱερέων ὑπήκουον τῇ πίστει). Luke adds another summary statement that emphasizes the continued growth of the church. It is plausible to see a connection between the continued growth of the church and (1) the renewed focus of the apostles on prayer and on preaching and teaching God's word (vv. 2, 4), and (2) the newly organized care for the needy believers in the church through the daily distribution of food (vv. 1, 3). The summary statement consists of three sentences.

(1) The "word of God" (ὁ λόγος τοῦ θεοῦ) continued to grow.[23] The imperfect indicative (ηὔξανεν) indicates that the growth continued over a longer period of time. The subject of the sentence is the word of God — it is God himself who makes the preaching of the gospel effective and who causes people come to faith in Jesus, the crucified and risen Messiah. The "growth" or "increase"[24] consists in more and more people accepting Jesus as Messiah and Savior. The formulation does not

exclude the possibility that the "increase" of God's word took place within the congregation, in the sense that the believers continued to be transformed by the presence of the Holy Spirit as they listened to and learned from the teaching of the apostles. The metaphor of the "growth" of the word of God echoes Jesus' parable of the growing seed of the sower (Luke 8:4 – 15), which describes the word of God as a dynamic force in the world that will lead to a great harvest despite opposition.[25]

(2) The "number" (ὁ ἀριθμός) of believers increased greatly in Jerusalem. The imperfect of the verb "increase" (ἐπληθύνετο) suggests continuous growth. Luke does not specify here the numerical growth of the congregation in Jerusalem. On Pentecost 3,000 people had come to faith in Jesus (2:41), a figure that includes diaspora Jews visiting Jerusalem; at the time of the healing of the lame man, another 5,000 people had come to faith in Jesus (4:4); after the arrest and release of the apostles, more Jews than ever came to faith (5:14). In 6:1 Luke notes that the number of disciples was increasing. The continued increase noted in 6:7 must have brought the number of Christians in Jerusalem to well over 5,000 believers, perhaps to 10,000, which would be about ten percent of the population if we assume 100,000 inhabitants of Jerusalem (see on 1:4; 2:41). The numerical growth of the church in Jerusalem is the direct result of the power of God's word that the apostles proclaim.

(3) A "large number" of the priests were converted. The imperfect indicative of the verb

---

22. Cf. Tipei, *Laying on of Hands*, 252 – 53, who emphasizes the last point.

23. Cf. 12:24; 19:20, for the same statement. In 7:17 the verbs "grow" (αὐξάνω) and "multiply, increase" (πληθύνω) are used with the single subject of the people of Israel in Egypt (echoing Exod 1:7); here the two verbs have different subjects: the "word of God" grows and "the number of disciples" increases. Cf. Marshall, "Acts," 555, who suggests that "thus there is some parallel between the growth of the people of God at the

time of the exodus and the growth of the number of disciples at the time of the new exodus; the new factor in the latter case is the powerful effects of the preaching."

24. Cf. BDAG, s.v. αὐξάνω 2, "to become greater, *grow, increase.*" The reference to the "growth" of the word of God perhaps echoes Isa 2:3.

25. Cf. Tannehill, *Acts*, 82, who recognized that Luke's version of the parable does not contain the verb αὐξάνω, which is found in Mark 4:8.

"became obedient" (ὑπήκουον) indicates that these were lasting conversions, not brief spurts of interest in the possibility that Jesus was Israel's Messiah. In view of the use of the verb "obey," the term "faith" (πίστις) refers to the content of the faith of the believers, i.e., the message of Jesus and his significance as God's Messiah and Israel's Savior.[26]

The "priests" (ἱερεῖς) are members of the priestly families. Josephus notes that there were 20,000 priests, a figure that some accept as reflecting the situation at the end of the Second Temple period.[27] Others estimate that there were perhaps 8,000 priests besides 10,000 Levites,[28] while some reckon with 2,000 "ordinary Temple priests."[29] Most of the priests worked in a trade, except for two weeks every twelve months when they served in the temple. Josephus relates that during the time of Herod, there were quarrels between the chief priests and the ordinary priests living in the countryside; the chief priests were so shameless that they "send slaves to the threshing floors to receive the tithes that were due to the priests, with the result that the poorer priests starved to death" (*Ant.* 20.181). If similar animosities existed in the 30s, it is perhaps not surprising that many priests came to faith in Jesus and joined the congregation of believers.

Theology in Application

The priorities of the apostles must not be jeopardized by other matters that are indeed important but which can be delegated elsewhere. This passage demonstrates the concern for the poor in the church, for the maintenance of the unity of the various groups in the church, and the willingness of the leadership to be flexible and not only allow but even suggest a restructuring of the ministries of the congregation. The appointment of the Seven is important in the sense that "here for the first time we have an appointment, not through a call of the incarnate or risen Lord, nor through the self-attestation of the charismatic Spirit in a Christian, but by the election of the members of the congregation."[30]

A Focus on Prayer and Proclamation

Authentic church leaders focus on prayer and proclamation. While some may claim that this is a typically Western emphasis, and that in the global South matters related to poverty, corruption, and social reform have priority, the consistent emphasis on teaching throughout the New Testament underscores the probability that Luke included this episode in his account of the life and history of the early church in order

---

26. Paul uses a similar formulation in Rom 1:5. Cf. BDAG, s.v. ὑπακούω 1, "a state of being in compliance, *obedience*;" the dative (τῇ πίστει) expresses the entity "to which one is obedient or which one embraces in full surrender" (ibid.), here the faith in Jesus as Messiah and Savior.

27. Josephus, *Ag. Ap.* 2.108. Cf. Lee I. Levine, *Jerusalem: Portrait of the City in the Second Temple Period (538 B.C.E. — 70 C.E.)* (Philadelphia: The Jewish Publication Society, 2002), 53

n. 26. 1 Chr 9:13 refers to 1,760 priests, Neh 11:10 – 14 to 1,192 priests, Ezra 2:36 – 39 to 4,289 priests.

28. Jeremias, *Jerusalem*, 204; cf. Gerhard Schneider, *Die Apostelgeschichte* (2 vols.; HTKNT 5; Freiburg: Herder, 1980 – 82), 1:430.

29. Fiensy, "Composition," 228.

30. H. W. Beyer, "ἐπισκέπτομαι κτλ.," *TDNT*, 2:604.

to emphasize the priority of prayer and proclamation for an authentic and growing church. Not everything is equally important; some things are more important.

The priority of church leaders is the proclamation of God's word (v. 2). Preaching and teaching are not always pleasing when we confront our listeners, both believers and unbelievers, with the claims of the gospel for their everyday lives. Preaching and teaching the word of God are certainly not a diversion from people's problems; rather, we seek to focus people on the cause of the problems as we preach and teach about God and the world, sin and forgiveness through faith in Jesus Christ, and everyday life and the transforming power of the Holy Spirit. While the Jews attending synagogue services would have been used to the explanation and proclamation of God's word, Greeks and Romans worshiping in pagan temples would not have been used to hearing religious speeches. Paul's preaching and teaching, while reminding Greeks of itinerant philosophers, were not a "contextualized" method of missionary work, evangelism, and pastoral ministry (see "Theology in Application" on 21:18 – 26). But the integrity of God's word is too important to be adapted in such a manner that its priority is diminished or denied.

The priority of church leaders is prayer. Speaking with God, whom one cannot see, is difficult. But prayer is a fundamental priority of church leaders. To refer to the entertainment culture of the West again, it is not surprising that many churches have given up on prayer meetings, and it is not surprising that "worship pastors" who want to have "fast-paced" and "attractive" worship services often deliberately minimize prayer, reducing praying to one-liners between songs. Praying is not entertaining; for those who fail to rejoice in the fact that when we come into God's presence, the presence of God's Spirit helps us in our prayers (Rom 8:26 – 27). And it is not surprising that in countries where many believers are poor or persecuted, the prayers are long and fervent, persistent and extended.

Charitable Assistance

Prayer and proclamation go hand in hand with charitable assistance. The second priority for church leaders is caring for and helping believers in need. The importance that the Old Testament accords the care for widows and orphans underlines this priority. Churches and their leaders should be informed about members who are in financial need and who are needy in other areas (marital, emotional, health, work related). In large churches, the information flow can be a problem, and people who attend services can easily hide themselves; churches must find means of effective communication concerning special needs that people have.

Churches and their leaders need wisdom to know what constitutes the most effective help in the long term. Believers who do not have enough to eat obviously need immediate help. Believers who are impoverished may need to be given monies so that they can pay their rent and buy food. But they may also need advice on how to budget their income. People who are out of work may need immediate assistance, but they also need help finding new employment.

Institutional Flexibility

Authentic priorities imply institutional flexibility. The priorities of the Twelve allowed them to accept the criticism of part of the congregation, to admit that they had failed to see the problem of the neglected Greek-speaking widows, and to solve the shortfall of assistance with the proposal of a restructuring of the ministries of the congregation. Leaders with the right priorities focus not on their prestige in the congregation, but on God's word. As all believers in Jesus are sinners who have repented of failures, churches' leaders should find it easy to admit breakdowns in communication, setbacks in programs, lack of oversight, or one-sided priorities. And they will be prepared to cede authority for the benefit of the congregation.[31]

Leaders with the right priorities are always willing to find flexible solutions that allow them to "stay on message." They will not be defensive, defending the status quo, but offensive, looking for creative solutions. All "offices" and assignments in the church are "services" or "ministries" (διακονία) — the evangelistic preaching of the word as well as the distribution of food, the teaching of believers as well as administration. Paul states that "there are different kinds of service, but the same Lord. There are different kinds of working, but in all of them and in everyone it is the same God at work" (1 Cor 12:5–6).

Shared Governance

Growing churches have shared governance.[32] While "shared governance" may in some instances be merely a sop fed by executives to their underlings with the goal of at least appearing to give their employees a say in the organization, the congregational configuration of the Jerusalem church allowed real participation in the solution of problems in the church and in the decision-making process in particular. Members of the congregation (1) experienced the problem of the uneven distribution of funds and food for the widows, (2) identified the problem as it pertained to the Greek-speaking widows, (3) communicated the problem to the apostles, (4) accepted their proposal for solving the problem, and (5) nominated seven candidates who could resolve the problem. The apostles (1) provided opportunities for the con-

---

31. Cf. Darin H. Land, *The Diffusion of Ecclesiastical Authority: Sociological Dimensions of Leadership in the Book of Acts* (Princeton Theological Monograph; Eugene, OR: Pickwick, 2008), 167: "Whereas functionaries of Greco-Roman religions pursued authority as a means of gaining honor, the Twelve gained honor by eschewing the retention of authority they already possessed."

32. I owe reflection on this point to Kevin Meek, who challenged me to think about congregational polity in the context of 6:1–7. On authority in the churches that Paul established, see Bengt Holmberg, *Paul and Power: The Structure of Authority in the Primitive Church as Reflected in the Pauline Epistles* (Philadelphia: Fortress, 1980).

gregation to voice grievances, (2) accepted the critique and protest of the members, (3) acknowledged the existence of a problem, (4) suggested a solution that would safeguard the priorities of the leadership and properly take care of all needy believers, (5) approved the nomination of the seven candidates, and (6) commissioned the new ministry leaders for their task.

In historical perspective, congregational styles of church polity reflect the configuration of the Jerusalem church better than other approaches to church government. The members of the congregation were not only heard, but they were given a real part in the decision-making process, while neither the role nor the authority of the apostles was undermined. While Luke presents the Jerusalem church as a model to his readers, the minimal information about how other churches in the first century functioned makes us hesitate to take the configuration of that church as a fixed structure that must be adopted by churches today to be "authentic New Testament churches." Such a transfer would, on the one hand, violate the main point of the passage, which emphasizes flexibility more than organizational structure, and, on the other hand, insist on a greater precision in congregational structure than the passage actually conveys. As regards the latter, the new structure of the Jerusalem church was simple.

Acts 6:8 – 7:1

Literary Context

The seventh and last episode of Luke's description of the life, witness, trials, and growth of the church in Jerusalem (3:1 – 8:3) recounts the ministry, trial, and death of Stephen (6:8 – 8:3). Up to this point Luke has focused on the ministry of Peter: his role in the emerging identity and witness of Jesus' followers as God's people in 1:15 – 2:47; his key speech on Pentecost; and his miracles, preaching, two arrests, and two speeches before the Sanhedrin (3:1 – 5:42). Luke narrated the previous episode of the appointment of the Seven (6:1 – 7) without referring to Peter; in the brief description of the seven assistants, Stephen was placed in prominent position at the beginning of the list (6:5c-e).

This episode recounts the conflict between the Greek-speaking Jewish believers engaged in missionary outreach among the Jews of Jerusalem and the Jewish authorities. Luke introduces a new witness of Jesus and new accusations. But it is the same conflict, the one between the believers in Jesus as Israel's Messiah and Savior and the Jewish authorities. The first interrogation by the Sanhedrin ended in a ban on speaking and a warning (4:17, 21); the second interrogation ended in a renewal of the ban on speaking along with a flogging (5:40); this third interrogation now ends in Stephen's being stoned to death (7:60). Thus the conflict is moving toward a climax: Stephen is killed and many believers are forced to flee and leave Jerusalem in a first major persecution of the Christians.

However, even the persecution after Stephen's death cannot stop the growth of the church. Philip takes the gospel to Samaria, to an Ethiopian official, and to the towns on the coast of the Mediterranean (8:4 – 40); Peter preaches in cities on the coastal plain and leads a Roman officer to faith in Jesus (9:31 – 11:18); Paul, who had taken part in the persecution against the Christians and who is miraculously converted, preaches in Damascus and in Jerusalem (9:19 – 30). Other believers take the gospel into the Syrian heartland all the way to Antioch, the capital of the province (11:19 – 26).

The present episode consists of four incidents: (1) the witness of Stephen (6:8 – 7:1); (2) the speech of Stephen before the Sanhedrin (7:2 – 53); (3) the death of Stephen (7:54 – 60); (4) the persecution of the church (8:1 – 3). In this first section, Stephen ministers among the Jews of Jerusalem, accompanied by miracles, and focuses on synagogues in which diaspora Jews have gathered. His teaching is powerful and convincing, which provokes unnamed diaspora Jews living in Jerusalem to conspire against Stephen to accuse him of blasphemy and take him to the Sanhedrin to stand trial. The contours of the episode form the same basic outline as in Acts 3 – 5:[1] Stephen performs signs and wonders, he is arrested, and then he is interrogated by the Sanhedrin. The new elements are: the new opponents (diaspora Jews dispute with and take action against Stephen), and the charges of uttering blasphemy against Moses and against God.

II. The Beginnings of the New People of God (1:15 – 8:3)

   B. The Life, Witness, Trials, and Growth of the Community of Believers in Jerusalem (3:1 – 8:3)

      14. The appointment of the seven assistants (6:1 – 7)

      15. The ministry, trial, and death of Stephen (6:8 – 8:3)

         a. The witness of Stephen (6:8 – 7:1)

         b. The speech of Stephen before the Sanhedrin (7:2 – 56)

Main Idea

The gospel is preached not only by the apostles but also by leaders such as Stephen, to whom God gave "grace and power" and who thus engaged in ministry among diaspora Jews living in Jerusalem. Stephen is an example of a mature Christian leader who is full of faith and wisdom, whose ministry is empowered by the Holy Spirit, and who is not intimidated by increasing opposition that eventually accuses him of blasphemy and drags him into court.

Translation

(See next page.)

Structure and Literary Form

The incident of Stephen's witness in Jerusalem is narrated in four parts. (1) Luke begins with a summary statement concerning Stephen's ministry in Jerusalem (6:8).[2] He is not described as a wise organizer of the distribution of food in the community, but as a believer who has been given "grace and power" and whose ministry is accompanied by miracles.

---

1. Tannehill, *Acts*, 84.

2. This introductory statement needs to be taken seriously; it is a one-sided reading of the passage that leads to headings such as "The Arrest of Stephen" (NRSV) or "Stephen Seized" (TNIV; cf. ESV).

Acts 6:8 – 7:1

8a	Action/Protagonist	**Stephen,**
b	Description	full of grace and power,
c	Action	**was performing great wonders and signs**
d	Sphere	among the people.
9a	Character entrance/Place	**Then some members of the synagogue of freedmen,** as it was called,
b	Place (geographical)	of the Cyrenians, and
c	Place (geographical)	of the Alexandrians, and
d	Place (geographical)	of those from Cilicia and
e	Place (geographical)	Asia,
f	Action	**came forward**
g	Purpose	to debate with Stephen.
10a	Event/Result	**They could not withstand the wisdom** and
b		the Spirit
c	Manner	with which he spoke.
11a	Action/Escalation	**So they instigated some men**
b	Purpose	to say,
c	Accusation	*"We have heard him speak blasphemous words against Moses and*
d	Accusation	*against God."*
12a	Action	**They stirred up the people as well as**
b	List	the elders and
c		the scribes;
d	Action	**they confronted him,**
e	Action	**seized him,**
f	Action	and **took him to the Sanhedrin.**
13a	Action	**They set up false witnesses**
b	Action (speech)	who said,
c	Accusation	*"This man never stops speaking words against this holy place and*
d	Accusation	*against the law.*
14a	Substantiation	*For we have heard him say,*
b	Quotation/accusation	*'Jesus of Nazareth will destroy this place and*
c	Accusation	*change the customs*
d	Description	*that Moses handed down to us.'"*
15a	Action	And **everyone who sat in the Sanhedrin stared at him,**
b	Description	and **they saw that his face was like the face of an angel.**
7:1a	Interrogation	Then **the High Priest asked,**
b	Question	*"Is this so?"*

(2) Luke narrates a dispute between Stephen and diaspora Jews in the local synagogues of Jerusalem, initiated by the latter (6:9 – 10). Stephen proves his "grace and power" by superior argumentation in this dispute.

(3) Luke reports a conspiracy that these diaspora Jews initiate against Stephen (6:11 – 14). It has two stages. First, Stephen's opponents instigate informers who spread the rumor that Stephen has uttered blasphemous words against Moses and against God. They stir up many Jews in the city as well as members of the Sanhedrin (vv. 11 – 12c; *direct speech* in v. 11c-d). Second, Stephen is confronted, probably in

another debate, arrested, and taken to the Sanhedrin (vv. 12d – 14; *direct speech* in vv. 13 – 14).

(4) Luke reports a session of the Sanhedrin in which Stephen is put on trial in three stages (6:13 – 7:1). (a) False witnesses appear who accuse Stephen of speaking against the temple and the law (v. 13) and claim that he said that Jesus of Nazareth will destroy the temple and change the Mosaic law (v. 14). (b) As these charges are brought against Stephen, the members of the Sanhedrin observe his demeanor and note that his face looks like the face of an angel (v. 15). (c) The interrogation by the high priest (7:1) begins with a query that allows Stephen to respond to the charges made against him.

Exegetical Outline

→ **I. The Witness of Stephen (6:8 – 7:1)**

   A. The Ministry of Stephen (6:8)

   1. Characterization of Stephen: He is full of grace and power (6:8a-b)

   2. Miracle-working activity among the people (6:8c-d)

   B. Dispute between Diaspora Jews and Stephen (6:9 – 10)

   1. Identification of the opposing diaspora Jews in local synagogues (6:9a-e)

   2. Initiative of diaspora Jews who debate with Stephen (6:9f-g)

   3. Superiority of Stephen in the debates (6:10)

   C. Conspiracy of Diaspora Jews against Stephen (6:11 – 12)

   1. Conspiracy of diaspora Jews against Stephen (6:11 – 12c)

      a. Instigation of secret informers (6:11a-b)

      b. Accusation: Stephen blasphemed against Moses and God (6:11c-d)

      c. Instigation of the people, the elders, and the scribes (6:12a-c)

   2. Arrest and summons of Stephen before the Sanhedrin (6:12d-f)

      a. Confrontation of Stephen (6:12d)

      b. Arrest of Stephen (6:12e)

      c. Summons of Stephen before the Sanhedrin (6:12f)

   D. Interrogation before the Sanhedrin (6:13 – 7:1)

   1. Appearance of false witnesses (6:13 – 14)

      a. Accusation: Stephen speaks against the temple and the law (6:13)

      b. Substantiation: (Alleged) quotation from Stephen (6:14)

   2. Stephen's appearance in the Sanhedrin (6:15)

      a. Observation of Stephen by the members of the council (6:15a)

      b. Illumination of Stephen's face by God's glory (6:15b)

   3. Interrogation by the high priest (7:1)

      a. Intervention of the high priest (7:1a)

      b. Opportunity of Stephen to address the Sanhedrin (7:1b)

Explanation of the Text

6:8 Stephen, full of grace and power, was performing great wonders and signs among the people (Στέφανος δὲ πλήρης χάριτος καὶ δυνάμεως ἐποίει τέρατα καὶ σημεῖα μεγάλα ἐν τῷ λαῷ). Luke begins by characterizing Stephen's ministry. He is described as being "full of grace and power" and performing miracles.

The fact that Luke does not describe Stephen's involvement in the newly organized food distribution among the impoverished believers (6:1 – 7) should not come as a surprise. He had described the apostles (first and foremost Peter) in their role as Jesus' witnesses who proclaim the significance of his life, death, resurrection, and exaltation. Their role in the charitable ministries to believers in need was mentioned only in summary statements (2:44 – 45; 4:32 – 37) and in a brief comment about the apostles' feet, at which Ananias and Sapphira deposited their hypocritically reduced proceeds from their sale (5:2). The fact that they took responsibility for the neglect of the widows (6:2) suggests that they had been involved in the food distribution program, which they now restructure. It is natural that the Seven focus not only on the distribution of food but on other ministry opportunities that arise. Both the proclamation of the gospel and the serving at tables is designated as "ministry" or "service" (διακονία).

In v. 3 all Seven are believers full of the Holy Spirit and wisdom; in v. 5 Stephen was described as being full of faith and the Holy Spirit; here Stephen is described as full of grace and power. These terms describe Stephen as a mature believer who continues to experience the transforming and empowering presence of the Holy Spirit. "Grace" (χάρις) is God's enabling care and help as a gift of the Holy Spirit (see 4:33). "Power" (δύναμις) is the result of the presence of God's Spirit (see 1:8) and cor-responds to "faith" (πίστις) in v. 5 — both "power" and "faith" cause the miracles to happen (v. 8).

Luke does not specify which "great wonders and signs" happen in Stephen's ministry. As he bears the responsibility for ministering to believers who are in need of food and clothing, he meets people who are ill and who suffer from demonic oppression. Taking food to believers would naturally involve him in conversations about any difficulties and problems the believers have, conversations in which mature believers inevitably explain and confirm the revelation of God in Jesus, the significance of Jesus as Israel's Messiah and Savior, and the reality of the Holy Spirit as the transforming power of God bestowed by Jesus on those who believe. As Stephen meets people who suffer from illnesses and other afflictions, many are miraculously cured. The miracles that happen in Stephen's ministry are characteristic of the ministry of the Twelve (2:43; 5:12); they are God's answer to the prayers of the believers (4:30).

6:9 Then some members of the synagogue of freedmen, as it was called, of the Cyrenians, and of the Alexandrians, and of those from Cilicia and Asia, came forward to debate with Stephen (ἀνέστησαν δέ τινες τῶν ἐκ τῆς συναγωγῆς τῆς λεγομένης Λιβερτίνων καὶ Κυρηναίων καὶ Ἀλεξανδρέων καὶ τῶν ἀπὸ Κιλικίας καὶ Ἀσίας συζητοῦντες τῷ Στεφάνῳ). The ministry of Stephen provokes opposition from diaspora Jews living in Jerusalem. "Some" of the opponents are active in the local synagogues. The Greek syntax is not sufficiently clear to allow a decision regarding the number of synagogues listed here. Luke could refer to one "Synagogue of Freedmen" attended by diaspora Jews from different regions of the Mediterranean world. If the term *freedmen* is to be explained by two clauses, we have two synagogues (one attended by Cyrenian and Alexandrian Jews, the other by Cilician and Asian Jews).[3] If the freedmen, the Cyrenian Jews, and the Alexandrian Jews attend different synagogues, while the Jews from Cilicia and Asia gather in one synagogue, we have a total of four synagogues. If each group met in a different synagogue, we have five.[4] Certainty cannot be achieved. It should be noted that Paul speaks of "synagogues" (plural) in Jerusalem (24:12).

IN DEPTH: Synagogue

A synagogue (συναγωγή) was a meeting place for Jews to discuss community issues, share meals, adjudicate infractions of the law and of tradition, collect and distribute charitable funds for purposes of social welfare, provide elementary education, study Torah, and store the scrolls of the Holy Scriptures and other material; it was also a place of residence for synagogue officials and a hostel for visiting Jews.[5] Not all synagogues had all these functions, but synagogues did not exclusively focus on "worship services" with prayers, readings from the Torah and from the Prophets, and sermons; they also dealt with communal affairs.

The leader of a synagogue was called "president of the synagogue" (ἀρχισυνάγωγος),[6] who was sometimes of priestly descent. He was usually a wealthy person, a leading member of the community who looked after the ritual, administrative, and financial aspects of community life.

The existence of a synagogue in Jerusalem has been confirmed by the discovery of the Theodotos inscription, which honors a certain "Theodotos, son of Vettenos, priest and *archisynagōgos*, son of an *archisynagōgos*, grandson of an *archisynagōgos*," who built the synagogue "for reading the Law and teaching the commandments, and the guest chamber, the rooms, the water installations as an inn for those in need from foreign lands, which his fathers founded together with the elders and Simonides."[7] Since Vettenos is a Latin name, this family probably returned from Rome to live in Jerusalem. It is thus possible, though not certain, that Theodotos was the president of the "synagogue of the freedmen" mentioned by Luke.

The "freedmen" (Λιβερτῖνοι, which is a Greek transliteration of Lat. *libertini*) were Jews who had been manumitted as slaves by their owners or were the descendants of emancipated Jewish slaves. Philo mentions Jews who lived in Rome, most of whom had been taken as captives to Italy (e.g., after Pompey's conquest of Jerusalem in 63 BC) and who continued to live in Rome after their emancipation. Tacitus mentions 4,000 *libertini* who

---

3. Freedmen who were Cyrenians and Alexandrians, and freedmen who were from Cilicia and Asia; cf. Lake and Cadbury, *Acts*, 66; H. Strathmann, "Λιβερτῖνοι," *TDNT*, 4:265.

4. Emil Schürer, *The History of the Jewish People in the Age of Christ (175 B.C. — A.D. 135)* (rev. G. Vermes et al.;. Edinburgh: T&T Clark, 1973 – 1987), 2:428; Levine, *Synagogue*, 56, who argues from the "extensive Diaspora presence in the

city" and "the significant differences between these various communities."

5. Cf. Levine, *Synagogue*, 381 – 411.

6. Luke 8:49; 13:14; Acts 13:15: 18:8, 17.

7. Levine, *Synagogue*, 58; cf. J. S. Kloppenborg Verbin, "Dating Theodotos (*CIJ* II 1404)," *JJS* 51 (2000): 243 – 80, for a defense of a first century AD date.

became Jewish proselytes.[8] Some of these Roman Jews had returned to live in Jerusalem.

Other diaspora Jews who worshiped in the local synagogues were Cyrenians, i.e., Jews who came from the region of the Cyrenaica in northern Africa,[9] and Alexandrians, i.e., Jews from Alexandria in Egypt. Of perhaps 500,000 people living in Alexandria, it is estimated that as many as 100,000 were Jews.[10] A certain Simon of Cyrene, who evidently lived in Jerusalem, is mentioned in connection with Jesus' crucifixion (Matt 27:32/Mark 15:21/ Luke 23:26); it is a plausible assumption that he and his family became members of the Christian community. Cyrenian Jews who had come to faith in Jesus were among the believers who brought the gospel to Antioch (11:20; 13:1). The Christian teacher Apollos came from Alexandria (18:24).

Other diaspora Jews living in Jerusalem came from Cilicia in southeastern Asia Minor, most of which was part of the province of Syria since the end of the first century, and from the province of Asia in western Asia Minor, a senatorial province governed by a proconsul, with its capital in Ephesus. Paul was a diaspora Jew from Tarsus; it is more than likely that he would have had contact with a synagogue in Jerusalem in which Jews from his home region were meeting. Paul later engaged in missionary work in Cilicia and in Asia Minor.

Stephen continued to visit the synagogues in which the diaspora Jews were meeting in Jerusalem (Luke provides no information on Stephen's regional origins). During such visits he would have eagerly spoken about his faith in Jesus as the promised Messiah who was crucified, raised from the dead, and exalted to God's right hand as Israel's Savior. Since diaspora Jews retiring in Jerusalem were undoubtedly devoted to the city and to its temple, it is plausible that the increasing number

of diaspora Jews who came to faith in Jesus — the "Hellenists" mentioned in 6:1 — provoked a strong reaction against the Christian leaders who were particularly active among the Greek-speaking Jewish community in Jerusalem. They would have felt that the ancestral faith that brought them back to the center of the Jewish commonwealth was betrayed by those who believed that Jesus is Israel's Messiah and Savior.

Thus diaspora Jews took the initiative to "debate" with Stephen. The active participle of the verb "debate" (συζητοῦντες) indicates that these debates continued over a period of time, which suggests that these were (initially) not heated discussions but debates in which the pros and cons of the significance of Jesus for the Jewish people were considered.

6:10 They could not withstand the wisdom and the Spirit with which he spoke (καὶ οὐκ ἴσχυον ἀντιστῆναι τῇ σοφίᾳ καὶ τῷ πνεύματι ᾧ ἐλάλει). As Stephen debated with the diaspora Jews with "wisdom" (σοφία) and the power of the Spirit, the Jews were unable to "withstand" (ἀντιστῆναι) his explanation of the gospel. As they, presumably, sought to disprove the belief that Jesus of Nazareth is Israel's Messiah and Savior, Stephen's arguments proved superior.

This does not mean that they were won over for faith in Jesus. Rather, they were silenced by his presentation. If Stephen was among the people who had seen the risen Jesus and thus spoke of his encounter with Jesus after the resurrection, they were unable to dispute his eyewitness testimony. Similarly, if he recounted the testimony of Jesus' resurrection offered by the Twelve and other believers who had seen the risen Jesus, they would not be able to discredit these witnesses, who were nei-

8. Tacitus, *Ann.* 2.85; cf. Philo, *Embassy* 23.155.
9. The region (in modern Libya) formed, together with the island of Crete, a senatorial province ruled by a proconsul.

10. Cf. André Bernand, *Alexandrie la grande* (Nouvelle édition; Paris: Hachette, 1998), 262–64.

ther gullible nor charlatans. He may have pointed as well to the miracles that were happening in his ministry and in the ministry of other believers as evidence for the power of Jesus, who had been exalted to the right hand of God.

As Stephen engaged these diaspora Jews in debate, he experienced the fulfillment of Jesus' promise in Luke 21:15 to give to his disciples "words and wisdom that none of your adversaries will be able to resist or contradict." Stephen also experienced the answer to the prayers of the believers in Acts 4:29 – 30, who asked God for boldness to proclaim his word.

6:11 So they instigated some men to say, "We have heard him speak blasphemous words against Moses and against God" (τότε ὑπέβαλον ἄνδρας λέγοντας ὅτι ἀκηκόαμεν αὐτοῦ λαλοῦντος ῥήματα βλάσφημα εἰς Μωϋσῆν καὶ τὸν θεόν). These diaspora Jews did not want to admit defeat; they believed that the beliefs of Stephen were heretical and that he needed to be eliminated. In Israel, blasphemy deserved the most severe punishment. The perfect of the finite verb "heard" (ἀκηκόαμεν) and the present tense of the participle "speak" (λαλοῦντος) indicate that the diaspora Jews claimed to have heard Stephen speak blasphemous words constantly, over a longer period of time. They start a whisper campaign[11] in the synagogues of Jerusalem, accusing Stephen of uttering words of blasphemy "against Moses and against God." Josephus says of the Essenes that "after God they hold most in awe the name of their lawgiver, and any blasphemer of whom is punished with death" (*J.W.* 2.145).

The term "blasphemy" (βλάσφημα) involves "defaming, denigrating, demeaning" and is linked here not with actions but with verbal speech (ῥήματα). According to Lev 24:11 – 16, blasphemy against "the name of the LORD" was punished by death through stoning, while blasphemy against Moses could be linked with Exod 22:28, which prohibits "curs[ing] the ruler of your people." The term "blasphemy" here is used not in the later "strict" sense of the word in rabbinic law — pronouncing the tetragrammaton YHWH, the name of God (*m. Sanh.* 7:5) — but in a more general sense of defaming Moses and God. The sequence of the two terms suggests that their main focus was the Mosaic law, which they saw denigrated in Stephen's teaching. In v. 13 the charges are related to Stephen's "speaking words against this holy place and against the law," i.e., against the temple and the Mosaic law.

Are these accusations trumped-up charges that have no basis in what Stephen actually said?[12] It has been argued that Stephen was eventually convicted not because of blaspheming by speaking against the temple and the law but because he claimed to see "the Son of Man standing at the right hand of God" (7:56), associating Jesus with God's sovereignty over the world and thus attributing divine status to Jesus.[13] Similarly, in Jesus' trial it was not the charges that Jesus said that he would destroy the temple and rebuild it in three days[14] that prompted the death sentence but Jesus' claim to participate in God's rule over the world.[15] However, the charges that Jesus spoke of the destruction of the temple and of his involvement in replacing the temple with a temple of heavenly origin were not false; Jesus evidently did say something to that effect,[16] although he never claimed that he himself would plot to destroy the temple. The charges, even

---

11. Cf. LSJ, s.v. ὑποβάλλω II.2 "to spread secret rumors *with false suggestions*," sense II.3, "to suborn."

12. Thus Jervell, *Apostelgeschichte*, 226.

13. Bauckham, "James and the Jerusalem Community," 76.

14. Matt 26:60 – 61/Mark 14:57 – 58; omitted in Luke.

15. Matt 26:64/Mark 14:62, with an allusion to Ps 110:1.

16. Cf. Matt 24:1 – 2/Mark 13:1 – 2 /Luke 21:5 – 6/John 2:19; for Jewish traditions concerning the Messiah rebuilding the temple, cf. Zech 6:12; 4QFlor I, 6 – 7; *2 Bar.* 4:3; *Mek.* on Exod 15:17 – 21. Prophecies concerning the destruction of the temple were punishable by death, cf. the story of Jesus ben Ananias and his prophecies in AD 62 in Josephus, *J.W.* 6.300 – 309.

though correct, could not be proven under separate cross-examination of the witnesses and were thus not admissible.

The charges against Stephen, focused as they are on the temple and the law, are similar to those brought against Jesus. If Stephen shared Peter's conviction that "salvation can be found in no one else, because there is no other name in the whole world given to human beings through which we are to be saved" (4:12), the consequences for the temple and the law are not difficult to see. The interface between the temple and the law are the sacrifices. The focus there was on the sin- and guilt-offerings and on the ritual of the Day of Atonement. Believing in Jesus as the only one who saves from sins implies that the sins of Israel are no longer atoned for through animal sacrifices, and that purity and holiness are no longer established by rituals prescribed by the law, but, rather, on account of Jesus' life, death, resurrection, and exaltation.

While it is conceivable that believers with a diaspora background grasped the consequences of Jesus for the temple cult sooner than other believers, Luke never implies that they were more "liberal" than their Palestinian fellow believers; as regards the latter, it was the indisputable reality of the lame man who was healed and standing next to Peter and John that silenced their accusers in the interrogation of 4:5 – 22, which may have been a sufficient reason not to charge them with blasphemy.

Luke does not comment on the motivation of the diaspora Jews who accuse Stephen of blasphemy. If they had heard of Gamaliel's counsel suggesting caution (5:35 – 39), they were not convinced that this was the proper course of action. After Stephen's death, Saul/Paul "continued to cause harm to the church" in Jerusalem by "entering house after house," dragging male and female

believers off to prison (8:3; cf. 9:2 – 3; 22:5; 26:12). He seems to have been among the diaspora Jews who unsuccessfully tried to disprove Stephen's beliefs in theological debates. Luke notes in 8:1 that he approved of Stephen's being killed. He evidently shared the concerns of other diaspora Jews concerning the serious consequences of Stephen's beliefs for Jewish faith and life.

Saul regarded the proclamation of Jesus as Israel's Messiah and Savior as so utterly despicable, in view of the fact that Jesus had been convicted by the highest Jewish court and executed by crucifixion, that he became convinced that the adherents of this new movement must not be tolerated but that active measures had be taken to stop their activities. Jews who rejected the claims of the believers in Jesus evidently were convinced that faith in Jesus as Messiah and in the atoning efficacy of his death on the cross put into question the very foundations of their obedience to the law as the basis of salvation bestowed by God.

6:12 They stirred up the people as well as the elders and the scribes; they confronted him, seized him, and took him to the Sanhedrin (συνεκίνησάν τε τὸν λαὸν καὶ τοὺς πρεσβυτέρους καὶ τοὺς γραμματεῖς καὶ ἐπιστάντες συνήρπασαν αὐτὸν καὶ ἤγαγον εἰς τὸ συνέδριον). After instigating informers in the local synagogues who accuse Stephen of blaspheming by speaking against the Mosaic law and thus against God, the diaspora Jews expand their campaign to eliminate Stephen. Luke describes their activities with four verbs in the aorist tense. (1) They "stirred up" (συνεκίνησαν) the people, i.e., citizens of Jerusalem who had resisted becoming believers or sympathizers of the apostles,[17] perhaps more specifically the people in the synagogues in which diaspora Jews were

---

17. According to 2:47; 4:21; 5:13 the "people" (λαός) held the believers in high esteem. This may have changed as a result of the agitation of the diaspora Jews.

meeting, and members of the Sanhedrin — elders (πρεσβύτεροι) and Torah experts (γραμματεῖς; see on 4:5). The verb translated as "stirred up" means "to excite" or "move" with a focus on emotions.

(2) They "confronted" him (ἐπιστάντες); i.e., they approached him, probably as he was speaking in one of the synagogues, without Stephen being aware of what they planned to do.

(3) They "seized" (συνήρπασαν) him with force; i.e., they arrested him.

(4) They "took him" (ἤγαγον) to the Sanhedrin, the highest court in the land (see on 4:5), where he was to stand trial for charges of blasphemy. This happened perhaps on the next day, which would mean that Stephen was first taken into prison (cf. 4:1 – 3; 5:17 – 18), unless a session of the Sanhedrin was organized specifically with the goal of putting Stephen on trial.

6:13 They set up false witnesses who said, "This man never stops speaking words against this holy place and against the law" (ἔστησάν τε μάρτυρας ψευδεῖς λέγοντας· ὁ ἄνθρωπος οὗτος οὐ παύεται λαλῶν ῥήματα κατὰ τοῦ τόπου τοῦ ἁγίου τούτου καὶ τοῦ νόμου). As in Jesus' trial before the Sanhedrin, "false witnesses" (μάρτυρες ψευδεῖς)[18] appear. To give false testimony is prohibited in the Decalogue (Exod 20:16; Deut 19:16 – 18).[19] Since the charges against Stephen probably did contain some truth (see on v. 11), these witnesses are "false" because they could not get their testimony to agree under cross-examination. Or, from Luke's perspective they are "false witnesses" because they spoke against God's spokesman.[20] The reference to Stephen as "this man" is derogatory. The formulation he "never stops" (οὐ παύεται, present tense) indi-

cates that Stephen had expressed his convictions for a sustained period of time.

The charges of v. 11 are here reformulated in terms of speaking "against this holy place and against the law." The expression "this holy place" refers to the temple in Jerusalem, which represented God's presence in Israel. The "law" stands for "Moses" in v. 11.[21] The interface between the Mosaic law, the temple, and God is the presence of the holy God among the people of Israel, which is possible only if Israel's sins are atoned for regularly and consistently. If the believers in Jesus teach that salvation is found, for everyone, in Jesus and in Jesus alone, this view can easily be presented as blasphemy against the Most Holy Place, where the sins of the people of Israel had been atoned for since the days of Moses; as blasphemy against the Mosaic law, which stipulated that sins were forgiven and access to God restored through sacrifices and other ritual procedures such as those carried out on the Day of Atonement; and as blasphemy against God, who had given the law and who was present in the temple cult.

Some point to Luke's positive portrayal of the temple in 2:46; 3:1; 5:12, 20 – 21, 42, disputing that Stephen argues against the temple itself.[22] A discussion of the passages in Acts 7 will have to wait; suffice it to say at this point that Stephen concludes his argument in 7:49 – 50 by quoting Isa 66:1 – 2. In the context of Isaiah 66, the prophet confronted Israel with the danger of restricting the presence of God to the temple and in taking the offering of sacrifices as Yahweh's only or final demand of his people. This attitude turned the temple into an idol.[23] Isaiah also censured Israel for not paying

---

18. Cf. Matt 26:60 (ψευδομάρτυρες); also Mark 14:56, 57.

19. Several Old Testament passages lament that false testimony is often brought against the righteous, cf. Pss 27:12; 35:11; Prov 14:5; 24:28.

20. Bock, *Acts*, 273.

21. This is the first reference to the Mosaic law in Acts;

cf. 7:52 – 53; 13:15, 38 – 39, etc.

22. Mallen, *Isaiah in Luke-Acts*, 114, following Gaventa, *Acts*, 129.

23. Gregory K. Beale, *The Temple and the Church's Mission: A Biblical Theology of the Dwelling Place of God* (NSBT 17; Downers Grove, IL: InterVarsity Press, 2004), 224 – 25.

attention to the word of God (Isa 66:2, 4 – 5; cf. 65:12; 58:1 – 12). Similarly Stephen accuses his audience of having uncircumcised ears and opposing what the Holy Spirit spoke through the prophets. "Hence Stephen's audience are guilty of the same charge as the wicked in Isaiah's day. They too have failed to listen to God's word, spoken in their time concerning Jesus, the promised prophet like Moses."[24]

6:14 "For we have heard him say, 'Jesus of Nazareth will destroy this place and change the customs that Moses handed down to us'" (ἀκηκόαμεν γὰρ αὐτοῦ λέγοντος ὅτι Ἰησοῦς ὁ Ναζωραῖος οὗτος καταλύσει τὸν τόπον τοῦτον καὶ ἀλλάξει τὰ ἔθη ἃ παρέδωκεν ἡμῖν Μωϋσῆς). Luke explains the charges of v. 13 with a direct quotation. The witnesses claim to have heard Stephen say that Jesus will destroy the temple and change the Mosaic law.

The first part of the charge was used in Jesus' trial (Matt 26:60 – 61/Mark 14:57 – 58). Jesus had prophesied the destruction of the temple (Matt 24:1 – 2/Mark 13:1 – 2/Luke 21:5 – 6); according to John 2:19 Jesus challenged the Jews, who asked for a sign, that if the temple were destroyed, he would rebuild it in three days, a statement John explains by saying that the "temple … was his body," which would be raised from the dead (John 2:21 – 22). Nothing is said in this charge that Jesus himself wanted to destroy or replace the temple.

The second part of the statement charges Stephen of announcing changes in the law as a result of Jesus' life and significance. He is not charged of wanting to abolish the law as such but of changing the customs that the law stipulated for Israel. The most thoroughgoing change in the Mosaic law is found in Jesus' teaching about food: "Nothing outside a person can defile them by going into them.

Rather, it is what comes out of a person that defiles them" (Mark 7:15; cf. 7:19; cf. Matt 15:17 – 20). The statement formulates a basic principle that abrogates the concept of ritual defilement through unclean food, changing the food laws in Lev 11 and 17. The food laws were of fundamental importance, since "together with the rite of circumcision and their observance of the Sabbath, the literal adherence to these dietary laws served to mark out the Jews as the distinctive people of God, and to separate them socially from other people."[25] Jesus' behavior on the Sabbath and his statements about the Sabbath[26] might have been relevant as well.

For Jesus (and for the early Christians), such changes did not constitute an abolishment of the law but its fulfillment (Matt 5:17). Luke does not tell his readers what Stephen specifically taught regarding Jesus' statements about the temple and the law or what Stephen himself taught. It is plausible, however, to assume that Stephen spoke about the consequences of Jesus' life, death, resurrection, and exaltation for the validity of the law in terms of the sacrificial cult, the atonement for sin, and the establishment and maintenance of holiness (see on v. 11). An implied charge may relate to Stephen's being associated with a condemned deceiver of the Jewish people who has been sentenced to death by the Sanhedrin.

6:15 And everyone who sat in the Sanhedrin stared at him, and they saw that his face was like the face of an angel (καὶ ἀτενίσαντες εἰς αὐτὸν πάντες οἱ καθεζόμενοι ἐν τῷ συνεδρίῳ εἶδον τὸ πρόσωπον αὐτοῦ ὡσεὶ πρόσωπον ἀγγέλου). As the witnesses are questioned about their claims concerning Stephen's teaching, the members of the Sanhedrin look at him intently. Perhaps Luke indicates that the testimony of the witnesses could not

---

24. Mallen, *Isaiah in Luke-Acts*, 115.

25. R. T. France, *The Gospel of Mark* (NIGTC; Eerdmans: Grand Rapids, 2002), 277.

26. Cf. Luke 6:1 – 11; 13:10 – 17; 14:1 – 6, with parallels in Mark and Matthew.

be corroborated in the cross-examination, so that the outcome of the trial depends now entirely on what Stephen will say — as in Jesus' trial, when the high priest intervenes with a direct question posed to Jesus after the testimony of the witnesses does not agree (Mark 14:59 – 61).

The members of the Sanhedrin see a change in the appearance of Stephen's face. The description of Stephen's face looking like "the face of an angel" (πρόσωπον ἀγγέλου), unique in the New Testament, emphasizes the presence of God in Stephen's witness.[27] It implies that Stephen is filled with God's Holy Spirit (cf. 4:8) and that his speech

(7:2 – 53) should be regarded as that of an authoritative witness of God inspired by the Spirit.

7:1 Then the High Priest asked, "Is this so?" (εἶπεν δὲ ὁ ἀρχιερεύς· εἰ ταῦτα οὕτως ἔχει;). The high priest, i.e., Joseph Caiaphas (see on 4:6), intervenes in the legal proceedings. After the cross-examination of the witnesses, which was presumably inconclusive because of contradictory explanations of what Stephen actually said, he addresses Stephen directly, asking him to comment on the charge that he has uttered words of blasphemy against the temple and against the Mosaic law. Much of chapter 7 is Stephen's response.

Theology in Application

This passage emphasizes that the gospel should be preached by mature believers as well as by the main leaders of the church. Moreover, authentic ministry is linked with faith and wisdom and may be accompanied by signs and wonders. Finally, Christians should refuse to be intimidated by threats, hostile campaigns, or legal action.

Comprehensive Ministry

Effective ministry is comprehensive ministry. Stephen's ministry was not limited to organizing and carrying out the charitable support for impoverished believers, including the Greek-speaking widows, but included signs and wonders (v. 8), the defense of the gospel in discussions initiated by others (v. 9), and the proclamation and explanation of the message about Jesus (vv. 10 – 11, 13 – 14). In other words, his ministry resembled the ministry of the Twelve, who also preached, were involved in caring for the needy, and demonstrated their concern for the latter by restructuring the church so that food distribution could be organized more fairly and more effectively.

While specialization is unavoidable, Christian ministries need to be careful not to focus in a one-sided manner either on charitable relief work only or on preaching

---

27. Cf. in the Old Testament, particularly Moses returning from Mount Sinai, where he had been in God's presence, Exod 34:29 – 35; cf. Gen 33:10; 1 Sam 29:9; 2 Sam 14:17; Dan 3:92 LXX. See also *Jos. Asen.* 5:5 – 6; 6:1 – 3; 1Q28b IV, 4 – 24 – 27; *Targum* on Song of Songs 1:5; *Rab. Deut.* 11 (207d); *Pirqe R.*

El. 2 ("Then Eliezer sat down and expounded. His face shone like the light of the sun and his radiance beamed like that of Moses, so that no one knew whether it was day or night"). In the New Testament cf. the change of the appearance of Jesus' face during the transfiguration (Luke 9:29).

the gospel only. While a single person may not be able to do both in a competent fashion — e.g., the apostles — it is often possible, even necessary, to combine the two, certainly in a team context where Christians work together. It is true that relief work without an explanation of the gospel is a worthwhile venture, but it is not particularly Christian. And Christian ministries that only preach the gospel but ignore the practical needs of people are not particularly Christian either. Stephen served at tables, but he also explained the gospel.

Grace, Power, and Wisdom

Effective ministry is based on grace, power, and wisdom. Stephen's ministry is characterized by grace and power (v. 8), and by wisdom and the presence of the Holy Spirit (v. 10). As God bestows grace on people who come to faith in Jesus, it is God's Spirit who bestows wisdom and empowers ministry. Christians living in the West are in danger of being too thoroughly influenced by a culture that values technical skills, management strategies, and methodical planning. While expertise in these areas is not unimportant, it can easily obscure the fact that ministries, particularly mission and evangelism, are not rendered effective by techniques but by the power of God, who empowers his witnesses through his Spirit.[28] Luke describes the reason for Stephen's powerful ministry with reference to God's grace and the empowering presence of the Holy Spirit.

While signs and wonders may and do accompany Christian ministry, they are not the explanation for the effectiveness of Stephen's ministry. The diaspora Jews were apparently aware of the miracles performed by Stephen; they were even more impressed by "the wisdom and the Spirit with which he spoke" (v. 10). Signs and wonders cannot be "used" as a strategic or tactical means of making ministry effective. By definition they are divine interventions in history, which cannot be controlled and must not be manipulated by human beings. At the same time, the secular worldview of Western culture must not be allowed to minimize or doubt God's ability and gracious willingness to miraculously heal and help believers in need.

Facing Opposition and Persecution

The church may repeatedly face opposition and persecution. Peter and John had been arrested and interrogated by the Sanhedrin earlier (4:1 – 22), as were all the apostles together (5:17 – 42). Stephen's arrest and interrogation is the third incident of determined opposition against the church. Stephen will lose his life, and there will be more opposition to come. Christians should not be surprised if their oppo-

---

28. Cf. Eckhard J. Schnabel, *Paul the Missionary: Realities, Strategies, and Methods* (Downers Grove, IL: InterVarsity Press, 2008), 400 – 419.

nents use all means possible, from intimidation and smear campaigns to legal action. Christian preachers must refuse to be cowed by opposition. Sometimes missionaries and evangelists may have to leave a city or a region if there is danger for life and limb. Sometimes evasive measures are not possible.

Stephen, with persistence and courage, explained the gospel in the synagogues of the diaspora Jews and then before the Sanhedrin, experiencing the fulfillment of Jesus' promise that times of opposition, persecution, and suffering provide new opportunities for witness (Luke 21:13), and of the promise that he will be present and give his witnesses words and wisdom as they testify to the truth of God's word (Luke 21:15). The fact that the trial of Stephen shares many similarities with that of Jesus expresses the truth that Jesus' witnesses who suffer on account of their proclamation of the gospel are particularly close to Jesus.

CHAPTER 16

Acts 7:2 – 8:3

Literary Context

The last episode in Luke's description of the beginnings of the new people of God (1:15 – 8:3), the second part of which focused on the life, witness, trials, and growth of the church in Jerusalem (3:1 – 8:3), narrates the ministry, trial, and death of Stephen (6:8 – 8:3). Stephen caused opposition in the synagogues in Jerusalem in which diaspora Jews were meeting, who eventually arrested him and took him to trial before the Sanhedrin (6:8 – 7:1). The first incident contains Stephen's speech before the Sanhedrin (7:2 – 56). Then the passage narrates Stephen's killing in a location outside the city walls (7:57 – 60), and the final incident reports the aftermath of Stephen's martyrdom as the believers in Jerusalem suffer a time of intense persecution (8:1 – 3). I am treating all these incidents together, since all pertain to Stephen's speech. Stephen is the first follower of Jesus to share Jesus' fate of being killed by the Jewish leaders.

This sequence of three incidents constitutes the final climax of this first major section in Acts and at the same time prepares the reader for the continuation of the narrative that will take the reader to regions outside of Jerusalem, the city from which the believers were driven out in the great persecution that followed after Stephen's death.

II. The Beginnings of the New People of God (1:15 – 8:3)

    B. The Life, Witness, Trials, and Growth of the Community of Believers in Jerusalem (3:1 – 8:3)

        14. The appointment of the seven assistants (6:1 – 7)

        15. The ministry, trial, and death of Stephen (6:8 – 8:3)

            a. The witness of Stephen (6:8 – 7:1)

➡   **b. The speech of Stephen before the Sanhedrin (7:2 – 56)**

            c. The end of the session in the Sanhedrin and the death of Stephen (7:57 – 60)

            d. The persecution of the church in Jerusalem (8:1 – 3)

  III. The Beginnings of the Mission to Gentiles (8:4 – 12:25)

Main Idea

Luke narrates Stephen's defense and proclamation with a threefold focus: the story of Israel is a story of God's raising up leaders of his people whom Israel repeatedly failed to recognize; God has fulfilled his promises to the fathers as he gave them the land and the law and eventually the temple, but Israel repeatedly turned away from God to idolatry and did not realize that God cannot be contained in a temple built by human beings; Israel's behavior in the past and the behavior of Jewish leaders in the present demonstrates their need for salvation. Stephen's martyrdom and the ensuing persecution take place because of the irreconcilable differences between the followers of Jesus and the Jews over the identity of Jesus.

Translation

(See pages 356 – 61.)

Structure and Literary Form

The first incident is Stephen's *speech* in 7:2 – 53; with 1014 words in the Greek text, it is the longest speech in Acts.[1] Attempts to analyze Stephen's speech in classical rhetorical terms have limited value, since few scholars agree on its structure. Some scholars suggest the speech is based on geography or on chronology.[2] Most scholars structure it using the biographical focus on Abraham (vv. 2b – 8), Joseph (vv. 9 – 16), Moses (vv. 17 – 43), and the temple (vv. 44 – 50).

When we analyze the participants in the speech as expressed in the syntax of the Greek text, the following picture emerges.[3] Abraham never appears as an explicit subject in vv. 2 – 8,[4] while God is ten times the explicit subject of the sentences in this section. Joseph appears three times as subject and five times as nonsubject participant in vv. 9 – 16, with the focus on the jealousy of his brothers. Moses is thirty times the subject and fifteen times the participant in vv. 20 – 40 (and v. 44), with the focus on his rejection by the Israelites and his being chosen and blessed by God. The Moses section is divided into three forty-year periods and thus has a chronological structure.

Luke interrupts Stephen's speech by describing the reaction of the members of the

---

1. Paul's speech in Pisidian Antioch has 470 words (Acts 13:16 – 41), Peter's speech on Pentecost has 429 words of Greek text (Acts 2:14 – 36). On the speeches in Acts see on 2:14 – 36.

2. For example Sleeman, *Geography*, 138 – 73, who is too narrowly focused on a "spatial reading" of the speech.

3. Cf. Gustavo Martín-Asensio, "Participant Reference and Foregrounded Syntax in the Stephen Episode," in *Discourse Analysis and the New Testament: Approaches and Results* (ed. S. E. Porter and J. T. Reed; JSNTSup 170; Sheffield: Sheffield Academic Press, 1999), 235 – 57.

4. Abraham is five times the nonexplicit subject and seven times a nonsubject participant.

Acts 7:2 – 8:3

2a	Action (speech)	**Stephen replied,**
b	Address	*"Brothers and fathers,*
c	Call to listen	*listen.*
d	Event (review of history)	*The God of glory appeared to our father Abraham*
e	Place	*when he was in Mesopotamia*
f	Time	*before he settled in Haran.*
3a	Action	*He said to him,*
b	Command (OT quotation)	*'Leave your land and your relatives*
c	Command	*and go to the land that I shall show you'* (Gen 12:1).
4a	Action/Result (geographical)	*So he left the land of the Chaldeans*
b	Action/Result (geographical)	*and settled in Haran.*
c	Time/Place	*From there, after his father died,*
d	Event	*God made him move to this land*
e	Description	*in which you are now living.*
5a	Negation/Contra-expectation	*He did not give him any of it as his inheritance,*
b		*not even a foot's length,*
c	Promise (contra-expectation)	*yet he promised to give it to him and*
d	Advantage	*to his descendants after him*
e	Description	*as his possession,*
f	Concession	*even though he had no child.*
6a	Action	*God spoke to him in this way,*
b	Prophecy (OT quotation)	*'His descendants will be resident aliens in a foreign land,*
c	Prophecy	*and they will enslave them and mistreat them for four hundred years.*
7a	Promise	*But I will judge the nation that they serve as slaves'*
b	Reminder	*God said,*
c	Promise (OT quotation)	*'and after that they shall come out'* (Gen 15:13-14)
d	Result/Purpose	*and worship me in this place'* (Exod 3:12).
8a	Action	*He gave him the covenant of circumcision.*
b	Event	*And so he became the father of Isaac*
c	Action	*and he circumcised him on the eighth day.*
d	Event	*And Isaac became the father of Jacob,*
e	Event	*and Jacob became the father of the twelve patriarchs.*
9a	Cause	*Because the patriarchs were jealous of Joseph,*
b	Action	*they sold him as a slave into Egypt.*
c	Cause	*Yet God was with him*
10a	Action	*and rescued him from all his afflictions.*
b	Action	*He granted him favor and*
c		*wisdom*
d	Sphere	*before Pharaoh,*
e	Description	*the king of Egypt, who appointed him governor*
f	Sphere	*over Egypt and*
g	Sphere	*over his entire household.*
11a	Event	*Then a famine and great suffering came upon all Egypt and*
b	Place	*Canaan,*
c	Result	*and our fathers could find no food.*

12a	Time	When Jacob heard that there was grain in Egypt,
b	Action	he sent our fathers there for the first time.
13a	Time	On the second visit
b	Action	Joseph made himself known to his brothers,
c	Event	*and* Joseph's family became known to Pharaoh.
14a	Action	*Then* Joseph sent and summoned his father Jacob and
b	Association	all his relatives,
c	Description	seventy-five people in all.
15a	Action	*So* Jacob went down to Egypt.
b	Event	He himself died there as well as our fathers.
16a	Event	They were brought back to Shechem
b	Event	*and* laid in the tomb
c	Description	that Abraham had bought for a sum of money from the sons ↵
		of Hemor
d	Place	in Shechem.
17a	Time	When the time approached for the fulfillment of the promise
b	Description	that God had made to Abraham,
c	Event	the people grew and multiplied
d	Place	in Egypt
18a	Event/Time (OT quotation)	*until a different king came to power in Egypt,*
b	Identification	*who did not know Joseph* (Exod 1:8).
19a	Event	He took advantage of our people
b	Event	*and* mistreated our fathers
c	Means	by forcing them to expose their infants
d	Purpose	so that they would not remain alive.
20a	Time	At this time
b	Event	Moses was born,
c	Description	well-bred in God's sight.
d	Event	He was cared for in his father's house
e	Duration	for three months.
21a	Time	When he was exposed,
b	Event	he was claimed by Pharaoh's daughter,
c	Description	who brought him up as her own son.
22a	Character description	Moses was educated in all the wisdom of the Egyptians.
b		He was powerful in words and
c		deeds.
23a	Time	When he was forty years old,
b	Character's thoughts	he decided that he should visit his brothers,
c	Character description	the sons of Israel.
24a	Time/Cause	When he saw one of them being mistreated,
b	Action	he came to his aid
c	Action	*and* avenged the man who was being wronged
d	Means	by striking down the Egyptian.

Continued on next page.

Continued from previous page.

25a	Character's thoughts	He thought that his brothers would understand
b	Event	that God was offering them salvation
c	Means	through him,
d	Contrast	but they did not understand.

26a	Time	The next day
b	Action	he appeared to some of them
c	Cause	who were fighting.
d	Action	He tried to reconcile them
e	Purpose	so that they would be peaceful.
f	Question/Interrogation	He said,
g	Assertion	'Men, you are brothers.
h	Question	Why do you do wrong to each other?'
27a	Action	But the man who was mistreating his neighbor pushed him aside
b		and said,
c	Question (OT quotation)	'Who appointed you ruler and judge over us?
28a	Question	Do you want to kill me
b	Comparison	just as you killed the Egyptian yesterday?' (Exod 2:14).

29a	Time/Cause	When Moses heard this,
b	Action	he fled
c	Result	and became a resident alien
d	Place	in the land of Midian,
e	Event	where he became the father of two sons.

30a	Time	When forty years had passed,
b	Event	an angel appeared to him
c	Place	in the desert of Mount Sinai
d	Place	in the flame of a burning bush (Exod 3:2).

31a	Time	When Moses saw it,
b	Reaction	he was amazed at the sight.
c	Time	When he came closer to look at it,
d	Event	the voice of the Lord was heard:
32a	Identification (OT quotation)	'I am the God of your fathers,
b	Identification	the God of Abraham, Isaac, and Jacob' (Exod 3:6).
c	Reaction	Moses trembled
d	Reaction	and did not dare to look.
33a	Action	Then the Lord said to him,
b	Command (OT quotation)	'Remove the sandals from your feet,
c	Cause	because the place where you are standing is holy ground (Exod 3:5).
34a	Assertion	I have surely seen the mistreatment of my people in Egypt,
b	Assertion	I have heard their groaning,
c	Action	and I have come down
d	Purpose	to set them free.
e	(command)	Now come, I shall send you to Egypt' (Exod 3:7-8, 10).
35a	Assertion	It was this Moses,
b	Identification	whom they rejected when they said,

c	Flashback (OT quotation)	*'Who appointed you ruler and judge?'* (Exod 2:14),
d	Event/Contra-expectation	*whom God sent as ruler and*
e		*redeemer*
f	Means	*through the angel*
g	Identification	*who appeared to him in the bush.*
36a	Action	*He led them out,*
b	Means	*performing wonders and*
c		*signs*
d	Place	*in the land of Egypt,*
e	Place	*at the Red Sea, and*
f	Place	*in the desert*
g	Duration	*for forty years.*
37a	Identification	*This is the Moses*
b	Flashback	*who said to the Israelites,*
c	Prophecy (OT quotation)	*'A prophet like me God will raise up*
d	Advantage	*for you*
e	Source/Sphere	*from among your brothers'* (Deut 18:15).
38a	Identification	*He is the one*
b	Place	*who was in the congregation in the desert*
c	Association	*with the angel*
d	Event	*who spoke to him*
e	Place	*at Mount Sinai,*
f	Association	*and who was with our fathers,*
g	Event	*and who received living words*
h	Purpose	*to give to you.*
39a	Event	*Our fathers were unwilling to obey him.*
b	Action	*They pushed him aside*
c	Action	*and turned in their hearts back*
d	Place	*to Egypt.*
40a	Action	*They said to Aaron,*
b	Request (OT quotation)	*'Make gods for us*
c	Purpose	*who will go before us.*
d	Reference	*As for this Moses,*
e	Character description	*who led us out from the land of Egypt,*
f	Assertion	*we do not know what has happened to him'* (Exod 32:1, 23).
41a	Action	*So they manufactured a calf in those days,*
b	Action	*offered a sacrifice to the idol,*
c	Action	*and celebrated over the works of their own hands.*
42a	Reaction	*But God turned away*
b	Reaction	*and handed them over to worship the host of heaven,*
c	Verification (OT quotation)	*as it is written in the book of the prophets,*
d	Question	*'Did you bring me sacrifices and offerings*
e	Duration	*forty years*
f	Place	*in the desert,*
g	Address	*O house of Israel?*
43a	Action/Accusation	*You took along the tent of Moloch and*
b	List	*the star of your god Rephan,*

Continued on next page.

Continued from previous page.

c		*the images that you made to worship.*
d	Prophecy (consequence)	*Therefore I will deport you*
e	Place	*beyond Babylon* (Amos 5:25-27).

44a	Assertion	*Our fathers had the tent of testimony*
b	Place	*in the desert,*
c	Flashback	*as the One who had spoken to Moses had ordered him to make it,*
d	Basis	*according to the model that he had seen.*
45a	Action	*Our fathers who received it brought it in*
b	Association	*with Joshua*
c	Time	*when they took possession of the land of the nations,*
d	Event	*whom God drove out before our fathers,*
e	Time	*until the time of David.*

46a	Description	*He found favor with God*
b	Request	*and asked that he might find a habitation*
c	Advantage	*for the house of Jacob.*
47a	Identification	*It was Solomon*
b	Action	*who built a house for him.*
48a	Assertion	*Yet the Most High does not dwell in structures*
b	Manner	*made by human hands,*
c	Verification (OT quotation)	*as the prophet says,*
49a	Assertion	'*Heaven is my throne,*
b	Assertion	*the earth is my footstool.*
c	Rhetorical question	*What kind of a house will you build for me,*
d	Reminder	*says the Lord,*
e	Rhetorical question	*or what is my place of rest?*
50	Rhetorical question	*Did not my hand make all these things?*' (Isa 66:1-2a).

51a	Accusation	*You stubborn people,*
b	Character description	*uncircumcised in hearts and ears,*
c	Accusation	*you are always resisting the Holy Spirit;*
d	Comparison	*just as your fathers did,*
e	Assertion	*so do you.*

52a	Rhetorical question	*Which of the prophets did your fathers not persecute?*
b	Accusation (Flashback)	*They killed those who predicted the coming of the Righteous One.*
c	Accusation	*Now you have become his betrayers and*
d		*murderers.*
53a	Assertion	*You are the people*
b	Identification	*who received the law*
c	Agency	*as transmitted by angels,*
d	Accusation	*but you have not observed it.*"

54a	Time	*When they heard this,*
b	Reaction	**they were infuriated**
c	Action	**and gnashed their teeth at him.**

55a	Action	But **he,**
b	Character description	full of the Holy Spirit,
c		**looked intently into heaven**
d	Action	and **saw the glory of God and Jesus**
e	Character description	standing at the right hand of God.
56a	Action (speech)	**He said,**
b	Command	*"Look,*
c	Assertion	*I see the heavens opened and*
d	Assertion	*the Son of Man*
e	Place	*standing at the right hand of God!"*

57a	Escalation	**They shouted with a loud voice,**
b	Action	**stopped their ears,**
c	Action	and **rushed at him together.**
58a	Action	**They dragged him out of the city**
b	Action	and **began to throw stones.**
c	Action	**The witnesses laid their robes**
d	Place	at the feet of a young man
e	Character entrance	named Saul.

59a	Time	As they kept stoning Stephen,
b	Action	**he called out**
c	Action	and **prayed,**
d	Prayer	*"Lord Jesus, receive my spirit."*
60a	Action	**He knelt down**
b	Action	and **shouted with a loud voice,**
c	Prayer/Address	*"Lord,*
d	Prayer/Intercession	*do not hold this sin against them."*
e	Time	When he had said this,
f	Event	**he passed away.**

8:1a	(foreshadowing)	**Saul approved of this killing.**
b	Setting: Time	On that day
c	Event	**a great persecution began**
d	Disadvantage	against the church
e	Place	in Jerusalem.
f	Event	**All were scattered**
g	Place	throughout the countryside of Judea and
h	Place	Samaria,
i	Exception	except the apostles.

2a	Action	**Devout men buried Stephen**
b	Action	and **mourned him publicly.**
3a	Action	**Saul continued to cause harm to the church,**
b	Means/Place	entering house after house and
c	Means/Social	dragging out both men and
d		women,
e	Action	whom he put into prison.

Sanhedrin (who did not interrupt Stephen at this point) in v. 54. Stephen's statement about Jesus' identity as the Son of Man at the right hand of God (v. 56) is part of his speech, the intended climax that was interrupted by the Jewish leaders no longer willing to listen (v. 57). This connection is missed if a break is inserted between v. 53 and v. 54, which unfortunately has become an established tradition (cf. the translations that insert a heading).[5]

The speech thus has six major parts: (1) God and Abraham (vv. 2b – 8); (2) God and Joseph (vv. 9 – 16); (3) God and Moses (vv. 17 – 43); (4) God, the tabernacle, and the temple (vv. 44 – 50); (5) an indictment of Israel and the reality of Israel's need for salvation (7:51 – 53); (6) an explication of Jesus' identity (v. 56). In terms of rhetoric, Stephen's speech has been classified as a judicial speech.[6] It is, however, not a defense (or *apologia*) since Stephen goes on the offensive, employing the strategy of *refutation*, which involves "an overturning of something that has been proposed."[7]

Most of the speech is a *summary review of Israel's history*, similar to historical summaries in the Old Testament and in later Jewish texts that demonstrate the relevance of the narrated history for the presence of the speaker and hearers/readers.[8] The difference between Paul's review of Israel's history in 13:16 – 41 and Stephen's speech is the critique of Israel's behavior in the latter, corresponding to the "Deuteronomistic" perspective of several Old Testament summaries critiquing Israel's rebellious behavior in view of God's gracious sovereignty in the history of his people.[9] The speech contains "one of the densest webs of OT material in the NT,"[10] as Stephen speaks with "wisdom and the Spirit" (6:10). We find direct quotations from Genesis, Exodus, Deuteronomy, Amos, and Isaiah, and allusions to these and other Old Testament books, including Leviticus, Numbers, Joshua, 1 Kings, 1 – 2 Chronicles, Nehemiah, Psalms, Jeremiah, and Hosea. The speech concludes with a *vision* (v. 56).

The actualizing remarks in 7:4 ("this land in which you are now living"); v. 7 ("worship me in this place"); and v. 38 ("who received living words to give to you") demonstrate that the speech indeed takes up the charges of 6:13 – 14 in which the law plays an important role. Stephen shows in his account of Israel's history that the

5. Thus ESV, NASB, NET, NIV, NKJV, NRSV, GNB, TNIV. The statement in v. 54 is not an "epilogue to the main address" (Soards, *Speeches*, 58), but the last part and climax of Stephen's address, which ends only when he is prevented from continuing his speech, which happens in v. 57. Typical is the statement of Tannehill, *Acts*, 86, that the audience's angry reaction in v. 54 "does not permit Stephen to continue" — when in fact he does continue to speak, in the same location, in v. 56. See the arguments in Sleeman, *Geography*, 141, for v. 56 as part of Stephen's speech.

6. Kennedy, *Rhetorical Criticism*, 121.

7. Theon, *Prog.* 11; cf. Parsons, *Acts*, 89 – 90.

8. Cf. Deut 6:20 – 24; 26:5 – 10; Josh 24:2 – 13; 1 Sam 12:8 – 13; Neh 9:6 – 31; Pss 78:5 – 72; 105:7 – 44; 106:7 – 46;

135:5 – 12; 136:4 – 25; Ezek 20:5 – 29; and Jdt 5:6 – 19; 1 Macc 2:52 – 60; Wis 10:1 – 11:1; Sir 44:3 – 50:21; *3 Macc.* 2:4 – 12; 6:4 – 8; *1 En.* 85:3 – 90:38; 93:3 – 10; 91:11 – 17; *2 Bar.* 56:2 – 74:4; *4 Ezra* 3:4 – 36; 14:29 – 33; *L.A.B.* 32:1 – 11; 23: 4 – 11; *Sib. Or.* 3:248 – 294; CD II, 17 — IV, 12; Josephus, *J.W.* 5.379 – 412; *Ant.* 3.86 – 87; 4.40 – 49.

9. Cf. 2 Kgs 17:7 – 20; Neh 9:26; 2 Chr 36:14 – 16. Bock, *Acts*, 277.

10. Marshall, "Acts," 556, who rejects the suggestion of John W. Bowker, "Speeches in Acts: A Study in Proem and Yelammedenu Form," *NTS* 14 (1967 – 68): 96 – 111; 107, that Stephen's speech is a proem type of homily based on readings of Exod 33:12 – 34:9 and Isa 65:22 – 66:5 with Gen 12:1 as the proem text.

death of Jesus by the Jewish leaders corresponds to the pattern of rejecting God and his messengers that has characterized Israel's history. In fact, whereas the fathers killed God's messengers, the Jewish leaders whom Stephen addresses killed the One whom God's messengers had predicted (7:52). Listening to the prophets is tantamount to keeping the law, which should have resulted in the acknowledgment of the Righteous One (v. 53).

At the same time, Stephen describes Israelites who are worthy of praise as they fulfilled their mission as God's emissaries despite being rejected. Those who rejected God's servants include Egyptians (vv. 6 – 7), the patriarchs (i.e., Joseph's brothers, vv. 9 – 10), the Israelites in the desert (vv. 35 – 41), the ancestors who killed the prophets (v. 52), and Jewish leaders who killed Jesus (v. 52). Among those who accepted God's revelation and envoys are Abraham (vv. 2 – 8), Joseph (vv. 9 – 14), Moses (vv. 30 – 39), the prophets (v. 52), and Jesus (v. 52).

While Stephen's review of Israel's history is presented as common history, two distancing remarks introduce a polemical note: in v. 4 Stephen refers to the Promised Land "in which you (ὑμεῖς) are now living," and in v. 38 he refers to the law as containing the living oracles that God gave "to you" (ὑμεῖς) — the distancing personal pronoun "you" (instead of "us") signals Stephen's point that the Jewish leaders who have killed Jesus are not worthy of God's gifts of land and the law since they have not acknowledged the Righteous One whom the prophets had announced.[11] A major emphasis of the speech is the universal relevance of God's promises, irrespective of the land of Canaan: the Abraham section highlights the primacy of the promise over the possession of land, the Joseph section shows that God himself calls Abraham's descendants into a foreign country, while the Moses section shows that the "brothers" reject the message of salvation.

The incident narrating Stephen's death (7:57 – 60) is a *historical narrative* and includes two *prayers* (7:59d, 60c-d). The final incident, which reports the persecution of the church after Stephen's death (8:1 – 3), is again a *historical narrative*.

Stephen was characterized in Acts 6 as full of grace and power, performing miracles, (6:8), and speaking with wisdom and empowered by the Holy Spirit (6:10); now he is characterized as being filled with the Holy Spirit (7:55b), being granted a vision of the glory of God (v. 55c-d) and of the glory of the exalted Jesus (v. 55d-e), praying for his enemies (v. 60), dying with courage, faith, and piety (vv. 59 – 60), and lamented by devout Jews (8:2). The characterization of the Jewish leaders as enraged and grinding their teeth (7:54), shouting, covering their ears, rushing at the accused (v. 57), and dragging Stephen out of the city (v. 58a) tell the reader that "due to their inability to produce credible accusations, the opponents consistently have to resort 'to noise, anger, and violence; their weapon is heat, not light.'"[12]

---

11. Jeska, *Geschichte Israels*, 151 – 53; for the following observation cf. ibid. 214 – 20.

12. Neagoe, *Trial*, 169.

Exegetical Outline

→ **I. The Speech of Stephen before the Sanhedrin (7:2 – 56)**

    A. Introduction (7:2a-c)

        1. Address (7:2a-b)

        2. Appeal for a hearing (7:2c)

    B. God and Abraham (7:2d – 8)

        1. God's revelation to Abraham in Mesopotamia (Gen 12:1) (7:2d – 3)

        2. Abraham's move from Mesopotamia to Haran and to Judea (7:4)

        3. God's revelation to Abraham in Judea (7:5 – 7)

            a. God's promise of land and descendants (Gen 17:8) (7:5)

            b. God's prophecy of Israel's slavery and deliverance (Gen 15:13 – 14/Exod 3:12) (7:6 – 7)

            c. God's covenant of circumcision with Abraham (7:8a)

        4. Abraham's descendants (7:8b-e)

    C. God and Joseph (7:9 – 16)

        1. Joseph's adversity: The betrayal by his brothers and his slavery in Egypt (7:9a-b)

        2. God's blessing (7:9c – 10)

            a. God's presence and deliverance (7:9c – 10a)

            b. God's bestowal of favor, wisdom, and position in Egypt (7:10b-g)

        3. Israel's adversity: The famine and the visit of the twelve patriarchs in Egypt (7:11 – 12)

        4. God's blessing (7:13 – 16)

            a. The patriarchs' acceptance by Joseph and by Pharaoh (7:13)

            b. Jacob's move to and deliverance in Egypt (7:14 – 15)

            c. The patriarchs' death and transfer back to Judea (7:16)

    D. God and Moses (7:17 – 43)

        1. Moses' birth and protection in Egypt (7:17 – 29)

            a. God's promise of land made to Abraham and the growth of Israel in Egypt (7:17)

            b. Israel's oppression by Pharaoh (Exod 1:8) (7:18 – 19)

            c. Moses' birth and God's blessing (7:20)

            d. Moses' upbringing: The first forty years (7:21 – 22)

            e. Moses' rejection and flight to Midian (7:23 – 29)

        2. God's commissioning of Moses near Mount Sinai (7:30 – 34)

            a. Time and place: After forty years in Midian, near Mount Sinai (7:30a-c)

            b. Description of the epiphany: The angel in the burning bush (Exod 3:2) (7:30d)

            c. Reaction and approach of Moses (7:31)

            d. God's self-introduction as God of the fathers (Exod 3:6) (7:32a-b)

            e. Moses' reaction (7:32c-d)

            f. God's commission of Moses as his envoy to rescue Israel (Exod 3:5, 7 – 8, 10) (7:33 – 34)

        3. Moses and Israel (7:35 – 43)

            a. Moses was rejected by Israel although God had sent him as redeemer (Exod 2:14) (7:35)

            b. Moses was the miracle worker who led Israel out of Egypt (7:36)

       c. Moses was the prophet who predicted a prophet like him (Deut 18:15) (7:37)

       d. Moses was the mediator of God's law at Mount Sinai (7:38)

       e. Israel refused to obey Moses, who was pushed aside (7:39)

       f. Israel fell into idolatry sacrificing to a manufactured calf (Exod 32:1, 23) (7:40 – 41)

       g. God gave Israel up into her self-chosen idolatry (7:42a-b)

       h. Israel's indictment by the prophets for her idolatry (Amos 5:25 – 27) (7:42c – 43)

E. God, the Tabernacle, and the Temple (7:44 – 50)

    1. Israel worshiped God in the tabernacle (7:44 – 45)

       a. Israel worshiped God in the tabernacle built by Moses in the desert (7:44)

       b. Israel worshiped God in the tabernacle during the conquest (7:45a-d)

       c. Israel worshiped God in the tabernacle until the time of David (7:45e)

    2. David, Solomon, and the temple (7:46 – 47)

       a. David found favor with God (7:46)

       b. Solomon was the one who built the temple (7:47)

    3. God, the tabernacle, and the temple (7:48 – 50)

       a. God does not dwell in buildings made by human hands (7:48)

       b. Confirmation through Scripture (Isa 66:1 – 2a) (7:49 – 50)

F. Indictment of the Jewish People for Not Recognizing Jesus as the Promised Messiah (7:51 – 53)

    1. General indictment of the people of Israel (7:51)

       a. The people of Israel are stubborn (7:51a)

       b. The people of Israel are uncircumcised in hearts and ears (7:51b)

       c. The people of Israel oppose the Holy Spirit (7:51c)

       d. The people of Israel have always resisted God (7:51d-e)

    2. Specific indictment of the people of Israel (7:52 – 53)

       a. The people of Israel persecuted the prophets (7:52a)

       b. The people of Israel killed those who prophesied the Messiah (7:52b)

       c. The Jewish leaders have killed the Messiah (7:52c-d)

       d. The Jewish leaders have the law but they have not kept it (7:53)

G. Aside: Description of the Members of the Sanhedrin and of Stephen (7:54 – 55)

    1. The members of the Sanhedrin are audibly infuriated (7:54)

    2. Stephen is visibly filled with the Holy Spirit (7:55a-b)

    3. Stephen has a vision of the glory of God and of Jesus (7:55c-e)

H. Climax: Jesus' Identity (7:56)

    1. The heavens are opened (7:56a-c)

    2. Jesus is the heavenly Son of Man standing at the right hand of God (7:56d-e)

II. The End of the Session in the Sanhedrin and the Death of Stephen (7:57 – 60)

A. The End of Stephen's Interrogation in the Sanhedrin (7:57)

    1. The termination of Stephen's interrogation (7:57a-b)

    2. The Jewish leaders rush at Stephen (7:57c)

B. The Stoning of Stephen (7:58 – 60)

    1. Transfer of Stephen to outside the city walls (7:58a)

2. The stoning of Stephen (7:58b – 60)

    a. The stoning begins (7:58b – 59a)

    b. Stephen's prayer to Jesus for himself (7:59b-d)

    c. Stephen kneels and calls out with a loud voice (7:60a-b)

    d. Stephen's prayer to Jesus for the Jewish leaders (7:60c-d)

    e. Stephen's death (7:60e-f)

III. The Persecution of the Church in Jerusalem (8:1 – 3)

A. The Persecution of the Believers in Jerusalem (8:1 – 2)

1. Saul's approval of Stephen's killing (8:1a)

2. The beginning of a severe persecution on the day of Stephen's death (8:1b-e)

3. The believers of Jerusalem have to flee to Judea and Samaria (8:1f-h)

4. The Twelve are not as much affected by the persecution (8:1i)

5. The burial of Stephen (8:2)

B. The Involvement of Saul in the Persecution (8:3)

1. Saul goes door to door to find believers (8:3a-b)

2. Saul arrests men and women and puts them into prison (8:3c-e)

Explanation of the Text

7:2 – 3 Stephen replied, "Brothers and fathers, listen. The God of glory appeared to our father Abraham when he was in Mesopotamia before he settled in Haran. He said to him, 'Leave your land and your relatives and go to the land that I shall show you'" (ὁ δὲ ἔφη· Ἄνδρες ἀδελφοὶ καὶ πατέρες, ἀκούσατε. Ὁ θεὸς τῆς δόξης ὤφθη τῷ πατρὶ ἡμῶν Ἀβραὰμ ὄντι ἐν τῇ Μεσοποταμίᾳ πρὶν ἢ κατοικῆσαι αὐτὸν ἐν Χαρρὰν καὶ εἶπεν πρὸς αὐτόν· ἔξελθε ἐκ τῆς γῆς σου καὶ ἐκ τῆς συγγενείας σου, καὶ δεῦρο εἰς τὴν γῆν ἣν ἄν σοι δείξω). Stephen, who stands accused as having uttered blasphemous opinions about the law and the temple and thus about God, politely asks the members of the Sanhedrin to hear him out. He is prepared and willing to explain his convictions about Israel and about God (the law embodies God's revelation to Israel and the criteria for Israel's behavior, and the temple stands, literally, for God's presence), and his convictions about Jesus, whose witness he is.

Stephen's speech ends in v. 56 with the members of the Sanhedrin covering their ears, refusing to listen any longer. As "brothers" (ἀδελφοί), which here means "fellow Jews," these members of the Sanhedrin are respectfully addressed as "fathers" (πατέρες), and they are children of "our father" (ὁ πατὴρ ἡμῶν) Abraham.

Stephen begins his speech by recounting God's revelation to Abraham (vv. 2d – 8). He characterizes Abraham's call as a revelatory event — God "appeared" to Abraham and spoke to him. The subject of the main verbs in this section is God; that is, the focus is on God rather than on Abraham, which suggests that Stephen is speaking about the worship of God and thus about the temple. He uses the expression "the God of glory" (ὁ θεὸς τῆς δόξης), a title that otherwise occurs only in Ps 29:3 (LXX 28:3); it is a majestic description of God that may echo the glorious theophanies during Israel's desert wanderings.[13] The God of glory is the God of Israel, whom Israel does, and must, worship.

God appeared to Abraham while he lived in Mesopotamia, before his move to Haran. According to Gen 11:28 – 32, Terah took Abram and Nahor from Ur to Haran, where he settled and eventually died. Then God appeared to Abram, calling him to leave Haran (Gen 12:1, 7). Stephen's reference to God's directive to Abraham is taken from Gen 12:1 (cf. Gen 15:7), in accordance with early Jewish traditions that also focused on Abraham leaving Ur in Chaldea.[14] God called Abraham to leave his land and relatives and to go to a land that would be revealed later. God's initial revelation to Abraham occurred not in the Holy Land but beyond Canaan.

7:4 So he left the land of the Chaldeans and settled in Haran. From there, after his father died, God made him move to this land in which you are now living (τότε ἐξελθὼν ἐκ γῆς Χαλδαίων κατῴκησεν ἐν Χαρράν. κἀκεῖθεν μετὰ τὸ ἀποθανεῖν τὸν πατέρα αὐτοῦ μετῴκισεν αὐτὸν εἰς τὴν γῆν ταύτην εἰς ἣν ὑμεῖς νῦν κατοικεῖτε). Abraham was obedient to God's call: he left the land in which he had lived[15] and settled in Haran;[16] eventually God moved him to "this land" (εἰς τὴν γῆν ταύτην), i.e., to Canaan.

Abraham's settlement in Canaan was not his own choice but the result of the revelation of God, who made him move to the land in which the Jewish people and its leaders now live. Stephen asserts, by implication, that God's promise to Abraham of a land to live in was fulfilled in later centuries when the people of Israel moved into the Promised Land under the leadership of Joshua — with the consequence that the Jewish people, who are Abraham's descendants and who continue to live in the Promised Land, should understand the entire history of God's revelation in and salvation of his people.

7:5 He did not give him any of it as his inheritance, not even a foot's length, yet he promised to give it to him and to his descendants after him as his possession, even though he had no child (καὶ οὐκ ἔδωκεν αὐτῷ κληρονομίαν ἐν αὐτῇ οὐδὲ βῆμα ποδὸς καὶ ἐπηγγείλατο δοῦναι αὐτῷ εἰς κατάσχεσιν αὐτὴν καὶ τῷ σπέρματι αὐτοῦ μετ᾽ αὐτόν, οὐκ ὄντος αὐτῷ τέκνου). God gave to Abraham not the land but a promise. Abraham never owned the land that God led him to dwell in, as it was inhabited by the Canaanites (Gen 12:6). The word translated as "inheritance" (κληρονομία), which can denote "possession, property" received during one's lifetime, is often used in the Old Testament to refer to the land that God promised to give to his people.[17] Abraham himself never saw the fulfillment of this promise. He received "not even a foot's length" of the Promised Land.

The second part of this verse contrasts (adversative καί) the reality of Abraham's life with God's promise of land to Abraham and to his descendants as "possession" (εἰς κατάσχεσιν). This statement alludes to Gen 17:8 or 48:4 (see also 12:7; 13:15). The genitive absolute translated as "even though

---

13. Fitzmyer, *Acts*, 369, with reference to Exod 16:10; 24:16 – 17.

14. Philo, *Abraham* 62; Josephus, *Ant.* 1.154.

15. The kings of the last dynasty that ruled Babylonia between 626 – 539 BC were called "Chaldeans" — from Nabopolassar and Nebuchadrezzar II to Nabonidus, the last Babylonian king.

16. As regards the chronological problem concerning Abraham's departure from Haran (Gen 11:26, 32; 12:4), Stephen/Luke again follows a Jewish tradition — Philo, *Migration* 177,

has Terah die at age 145, with Abraham leaving after Terah's death, as Stephen does; cf. the Samaritan Pentateuch and the Pentateuch Targum, which also give Terah's age as 145 when he died; see also Josephus, *Ant.* 1.151 – 154; Fitzmyer, *Acts*, 370, comments that this Jewish tradition "did not want to admit that Abraham had abandoned his elderly father."

17. Words of the κληρονομία family occur in Gen 15:7; Exod 6:8; 15:17; Josh 11:23; cf. Isa 49:8. For the promise of land cf. Gen 17:8; 48:4; also 12:7; 13:15; 15:18 – 20; 24:7.

he had no child" is concessive — God's promise to Abraham was given at a time when he was married to Sarah but had no child; it was a promise that explicitly included descendants (cf. 15:1 – 6; 17:2 – 6). The omission of the characterization of the possession of the land as "everlasting" in 17:8; 48:4, if deliberate, underscores the point that the "everlasting" possession of the land is no longer an important factor.

Since Stephen emphasizes that Abraham was not "at home" in the land that God had promised and in which the Jewish people now live, he implies that being a descendant of Abraham does not depend on geographical location, since it is not tied to living in the Promised Land. This implication, if intended, corresponds to the self-understanding of Hellenistic Judaism in the diaspora, to which Stephen probably belonged. And it fits the concern of Luke, who assures his Christian readers that Israel's privileges, among which the Promised Land figures prominently, while God-given, are not as pivotal as Jews traditionally believe. God's history of salvation is dependent on God's promise rather than on human realities, a fact that characterizes Abraham as the exemplar of a person who believes in God's word and intervention while not having anything that would guarantee the fulfillment of that promise.

7:6 – 7 God spoke to him in this way, "His descendants will be resident aliens in a foreign land, and they will enslave them and mistreat them for four hundred years. But I will judge the nation that they serve as slaves." God said, "And after that they shall come out and worship

me in this place" (ἐλάλησεν δὲ οὕτως ὁ θεὸς ὅτι ἔσται τὸ σπέρμα αὐτοῦ πάροικον ἐν γῇ ἀλλοτρίᾳ καὶ δουλώσουσιν αὐτὸ καὶ κακώσουσιν ἔτη τετρακόσια· καὶ τὸ ἔθνος ᾧ ἐὰν δουλεύσουσιν κρινῶ ἐγώ, ὁ θεὸς εἶπεν, καὶ μετὰ ταῦτα ἐξελεύσονται καὶ λατρεύσουσίν μοι ἐν τῷ τόπῳ τούτῳ).

In a further message God informed Abraham that it would take a long time for his descendants to possess the land they had been promised — a time in which his descendants would live as "resident aliens"[18] in a foreign land whose inhabitants would enslave and mistreat them. The first statement in vv. 6 – 7c quotes Gen 15:13 – 14. While Exod 12:40 specifies 430 years of Israel's sojourn in Egypt (cf. Gal 3:17), a rabbinic tradition speaks of 400 years from the birth of Isaac to the exodus. The 400 years should probably be understood as a rounded number. The fulfillment of God's promise to Abraham took place through Israel's suffering in Egypt, God's judgment of the Egyptians, and Israel's exodus from Egypt.

The second statement in v. 7d is a paraphrase of Exod 3:12, which reads "on this mountain" (referring to Mount Horeb) and which Luke replaces by the phrase "in this place" (ἐν τῷ τόπῳ τούτῳ, referring to Canaan); in this context Luke probably means more specifically Jerusalem and/or the temple on Mount Zion.[19] Stephen began his speech with Abraham's movement from Mesopotamia through Canaan and Egypt. He now shifts to an account of the history of Israel (i.e., Abraham's descendants), which begins with their sojourn in Egypt, the crisis of enslavement and mistreatment, the intervention of God in the exodus, and their entry into the Promised Land, where they would

---

18. Cf. BDAG, s.v. πάροικος, "stranger, alien, one who lives in a place that is not one's home"; the term is often used in inscriptions for people who lived in a certain city without being citizens, having been born somewhere else and not having obtained citizenship.

19. Sleeman, Geography, 145 – 46. Others suggest a reference to Jerusalem and/or to the temple, cf. John J. Kilgallen, The Stephen Speech: A Literary and Redactional Study of Acts 7,2 – 53 (AnBib 67; Rome: Biblical Institute Press, 1976), 37 – 39. Pervo, Acts, 181 n. 69, sees a reference both to the land (cf. vv. 4 – 5) and to the temple (cf. 6:13 – 14).

worship the God who rescued them from bondage in Egypt. The decisive verb in v. 7 is "worship" (λατρεύσουσιν, future indicative), which serves as the basic description of the purpose of Israel's existence and of the life of the nation in the Promised Land.

7:8 He gave him the covenant of circumcision. And so he became the father of Isaac and he circumcised him on the eighth day. And Isaac became the father of Jacob, and Jacob became the father of the twelve patriarchs (καὶ ἔδωκεν αὐτῷ διαθήκην περιτομῆς· καὶ οὕτως ἐγέννησεν τὸν Ἰσαὰκ καὶ περιέτεμεν αὐτὸν τῇ ἡμέρᾳ τῇ ὀγδόῃ, καὶ Ἰσαὰκ τὸν Ἰακώβ, καὶ Ἰακὼβ τοὺς δώδεκα πατριάρχας). The climax of God's revelation to Abraham in Judea is the covenant God granted to Abraham (Gen 17:2, 9 – 14), a covenant of which circumcision — the removal of the foreskin of the males — was the visible sign (Gen 17:11). The interpretation of this construction as an epexegetical genitive ("a covenant consisting of circumcision") is too narrow since God's covenant with Abraham focused on land and descendants, not merely on circumcision. It is preferable to interpret the phrase "covenant of circumcision" (διαθήκη περιτομῆς) as an objective genitive: the covenant between God and Abraham and his (promised) descendants has circumcision as a sign that renders the covenant visible.[20]

The continuation with "and so" (καὶ οὕτως) indicates that when Abraham fathered Isaac and circumcised him on the eighth day (Gen 21:1 – 5), he obeyed God's covenant, who promised him children and who stipulated circumcision on the eighth day as the sign of the covenant (Gen 17:12). Stephen passes over the stories of Isaac and Jacob and of the birth of Jacob's twelve sons[21] as he is focused on relating the fulfillment of God's promises in the birth of further descendants of Abraham.[22] The view that Stephen (Luke) does not criticize circumcision[23] is only superficially correct. Note that the focus is not on the "possession" of circumcision but on Abraham's obedience in circumcising Isaac, and that the Jews who are addressed are described as "uncircumcised in hearts and ears" (v. 51) at the end of the speech. This implies that what matters is not the external sign of circumcision but God's promise and obedience to God and his revelatory word.

7:9 – 10 Because the patriarchs were jealous of Joseph, they sold him as a slave into Egypt. Yet God was with him and rescued him from all his afflictions. He granted him favor and wisdom before Pharaoh, the king of Egypt, who appointed him governor over Egypt and over his entire household (καὶ οἱ πατριάρχαι ζηλώσαντες τὸν Ἰωσὴφ ἀπέδοντο εἰς Αἴγυπτον. καὶ ἦν ὁ θεὸς μετ' αὐτοῦ καὶ ἐξείλατο αὐτὸν ἐκ πασῶν τῶν θλίψεων αὐτοῦ καὶ ἔδωκεν αὐτῷ χάριν καὶ σοφίαν ἐναντίον Φαραὼ βασιλέως Αἰγύπτου καὶ κατέστησεν αὐτὸν ἡγούμενον ἐπ' Αἴγυπτον καὶ ἐφ' ὅλον τὸν οἶκον αὐτοῦ).

Now Stephen relates, in greater detail, the story of Joseph.[24] After having emphasized God's initiative and the primacy of God's promise over the possession of the land of Israel in his account of

---

20. Marguerat, *Actes*, 1:242.

21. Cf. Gen 25:19 – 26; 29:31 – 30:24; 35:16 – 18. The limited role of Isaac and Jacob as connecting links corresponds to the summaries of Israel's history in Josh 24:3 – 4; Sir 44:22 – 23; *4 Ezra* 3:15 – 16; *L.A.B.* 23:8 – 9. Cf. Jeska, *Geschichte Israels*, 159.

22. The term "twelve patriarchs" (δώδεκα πατριάρχαι) occurs here for the first time in biblical literature; the term "patriarchs" (lit., "father of a nation") does not occur in the OT

but occurs in 4 Macc 7:19; 16:25 and other Greek texts of early Judaism (in 1 Chr 24:31; 27:22; 2 Chr 19:8; 23:20; 26:12, it denotes chiefs of families or chief of tribes, not Israel's "founding fathers").

23. Jervell, *Apostelgeschichte*, 234; cf. Fitzmyer, *Acts*, 372.

24. Cf. Gen 37 – 50; cf. Ps 105:16 – 22 and *1 En.* 89:12 – 14 for a similar summary account of Joseph's career.

the story of Abraham in vv. 2c – 8, Stephen now focuses on the adversity of Joseph and Israel and on God's blessing for both Joseph and Israel in Egypt (vv. 9 – 16).[25] The theme of adversity and blessing suggests that this section consists of four parts:[26] (1) Joseph's adversity as he is betrayed by his brothers and sold as a slave to Egypt (v. 9a-b); (2) God's blessing of Joseph in Egypt (vv. 9c – 10); (3) Israel's adversity in the Promised Land as the result of a famine (vv. 11 – 12); (4) God's blessing of Israel as the nation is delivered from the famine by moving to Egypt (vv. 13 – 16).

The patriarchs (i.e., the sons of Jacob), who possess Abraham's promise, cause a crisis in God's history with Abraham and his descendants. Stephen characterizes them as having a problematic character (they were "jealous") and committing a serious sin (they sold their brother to foreigners, who took him as a slave to Egypt). The verb translated "they sold him as slave" (ἀπέδοντο) means, in the middle voice, "to sell, trade"; people who are sold to others are by definition slaves. The jealousy of Joseph's brothers is mentioned in Gen 37:11; the selling of Joseph and his transport to Egypt are related in Gen 37:12 – 36 (cf. 45:4). Even though Stephen (Luke) does not make such connections explicit, the jealous patriarchs can be seen as prototypes of the contemporary Jewish leaders who plotted to eliminate Jesus (Acts 2:23, 36; 3:13 – 15; 4:10 – 11; 5:30), and Joseph as a prototype of Jesus' followers, whom the Jewish leaders oppose out of jealousy (5:17; cf. 13:45; 17:5).

God's blessing of Joseph in Egypt (vv. 9c – 10) is the major emphasis in this section. The blessing is, first, God's presence with Joseph when he suffered as a slave in Egypt — God was "with him" (v. 9c) — and God's deliverance of Joseph — God "rescued him" (v. 10a) from oppressive slavery (cf. Gen 39:2) and imprisonment (cf. Gen 41:14). Note again that God's blessing was revealed beyond the Holy Land.

Second, God's blessing manifested itself in granting "favor and wisdom" before Pharaoh and in Joseph's appointment as governor over Egypt and over Pharaoh's household.[27] Joseph is a prototype of the righteous and wise person who suffers and is thus a prototype of Stephen (cf. Acts 6:3, 8, 10); being eventually vindicated, Joseph becomes a prototype of Jesus, who was vindicated by God (2:24, 36; 3:15; 4:10 – 11; 5:31) because "God was with him" (10:38; cf. Luke 2:40). "The one who saves is the one who has been rejected, he saves those who rejected him precisely through their having rejected him."[28]

7:11 – 12 Then a famine and great suffering came upon all Egypt and Canaan, and our fathers could find no food. When Jacob heard that there was grain in Egypt, he sent our fathers there for the first time (ἦλθεν δὲ λιμὸς ἐφ᾽ ὅλην τὴν Αἴγυπτον καὶ Χανάαν καὶ θλῖψις μεγάλη, καὶ οὐχ ηὕρισκον χορτάσματα οἱ πατέρες ἡμῶν. ἀκούσας δὲ Ἰακὼβ ὄντα σιτία εἰς Αἴγυπτον ἐξαπέστειλεν τοὺς πατέρας ἡμῶν πρῶτον). The second period of adversity came as the result of a famine that brought "great suffering" over Egypt and Canaan.[29] The term translated as "food" (χορτάσματα) often denotes "fodder for domesticated animals" and is perhaps used to indicate the severity of the famine in which even the fodder for cattle was not sufficient to alleviate the hunger of the patriarchs in

---

25. Jeska, *Geschichte Israels*, 161 – 64, points out that in most summaries of Israel's history an existence of the people of God outside of Canaan rarely comes into view (e.g., Neh 9!). The emphasis of Acts 7:9 – 16 on the possibility of a good life in a foreign country is singular.

26. Cf. Martín-Asensio, "Participant Reference," 245 – 46.

27. Cf. Gen 39:4 – 6, 21; 41:37 – 45.

28. Kilgallen, *The Stephen Speech*, 186. The rejected-yet-redeemed theme is prominent in Acts, cf. 2:23 – 24, 31 – 33; 3:15 – 16; 4:10 – 12; 5:30 – 31; 10:39 – 40; 13:27 – 31; 26:23. Cf. Parsons, *Acts*, 94.

29. Cf. Gen 41:54 – 57; 42:5; cf. Pss 37:19; 105:16 – 22.

Canaan. The first visit of "our fathers," i.e., of ten of Jacob's sons, to Egypt to buy grain (v. 12) is recounted at length in Gen 42:3 – 38.

7:13 – 15 On the second visit Joseph made himself known to his brothers, and Joseph's family became known to Pharaoh. Then Joseph sent and summoned his father Jacob and all his relatives, seventy-five people in all. So Jacob went down to Egypt. He himself died there as well as our fathers (καὶ ἐν τῷ δευτέρῳ ἀνεγνωρίσθη Ἰωσὴφ τοῖς ἀδελφοῖς αὐτοῦ καὶ φανερὸν ἐγένετο τῷ Φαραὼ τὸ γένος τοῦ Ἰωσήφ. ἀποστείλας δὲ Ἰωσὴφ μετεκαλέσατο Ἰακὼβ τὸν πατέρα αὐτοῦ καὶ πᾶσαν τὴν συγγένειαν ἐν ψυχαῖς ἑβδομήκοντα πέντε. καὶ κατέβη Ἰακὼβ εἰς Αἴγυπτον καὶ ἐτελεύτησεν αὐτὸς καὶ οἱ πατέρες ἡμῶν).

God's blessing of Israel, who suffered in the famine in Canaan, is linked with the second visit of Jacob's sons, who now included Benjamin (Gen 43 – 45). On that visit Joseph revealed himself to his brothers, an event that came to Pharaoh's attention (v. 13; cf. Gen 45:1 – 2, 16). Stephen's biblically literate audience would remember Joseph's dramatic explanation that it was God's sovereign providence that caused him to be sold into slavery in Egypt: "It was to save lives that God sent me ahead of you" (Gen 45:5; cf. vv. 7 – 8). Joseph invited Jacob and all his relatives to come to Egypt (vv.13 – 14). According to Gen 46:26, sixty-six persons emigrated from Canaan to Egypt; Stephen follows the tradition of the LXX, which includes in the number of seventy-five the nine sons of Joseph (omitting Jacob and Joseph).[30] Jacob accepted Joseph's invitation and emigrated to Egypt, where he and his sons died (v. 15).[31]

The patriarchs' emigration to Egypt partici-

pates in the dual aspect of the fulfillment of God's promise and of the typological foreshadowing of the story of Jesus, which characterizes in particular the Joseph section of Stephen's speech. The emigration to Egypt fulfills the first part of God's promise in Gen 15:13 – 14 that Abraham's descendants "will be strangers in a country not their own." The role of Joseph, who rescues Israel from affliction, corresponds to the role of Moses (cf. v. 36) and especially of Jesus.

7:16 They were brought back to Shechem and laid in the tomb that Abraham had bought for a sum of money from the sons of Hemor in Shechem (καὶ μετετέθησαν εἰς Συχὲμ καὶ ἐτέθησαν ἐν τῷ μνήματι ᾧ ὠνήσατο Ἀβραὰμ τιμῆς ἀργυρίου παρὰ τῶν υἱῶν Ἐμμὼρ ἐν Συχέμ). Stephen concludes his summary of the story of Joseph with the reminder that even though Jacob and his sons lived and died in Egypt, they were buried in the Promised Land. The Greek term translated as "tomb" (μνῆμα, lit., "sign of remembrance") is the standard term for "grave," which is thus a place where the dead are remembered.

According to Gen 50:12 – 14 (cf. 49:29 – 32), Jacob was buried at Machpelah near Hebron in a plot of land that Abraham had purchased (Gen 23) and where Abraham was buried (Gen 27:8 – 10). While the Old Testament does not specify where the sons of Jacob were buried, Jewish tradition asserts they were buried with their father at Hebron.[32] According to Josh 24:32 Joseph was buried at Shechem on land Jacob had purchased from the sons of Hemor (Gen 33:18 – 20). While many commentators assume that Stephen (Luke) has confused several Old Testament traditions, some

---

30. Cf. Gen 46:26 – 27 LXX; Exod 1:5 LXX; cf. 4Q13; Philo, *Migration* 199. The figure of seventy persons (Gen 46:27; cf. Exod 1:5; Deut 10:22) includes Jacob and Joseph and his two sons who were already in Egypt.

31. Cf. Gen 45:9 – 11; 46:1 – 7, 28 – 29; for Jacob's death cf.

Gen 49:33; Stephen's summary is based on Exod 1:6.

32. Josephus, *Ant.* 1.237; 2.193 – 199; according to *Jub.* 45:15; 46:9 – 10, Joseph was buried in Egypt while his brothers were buried at Hebron.

suggest that Machpelah near Hebron and Shechem have been telescoped into one site and that the two transactions have been run together into one, with such a procedure being "on a par with other instances of telescoping in this speech."[33]

The reference to Shechem, mentioned twice, is significant since it is a Samaritan city at the foot of Mount Gerizim. Shechem as the burial site of the patriarchs seems to underline the point that God's fulfillment of his promises is not focused exclusively on Jerusalem or Judea; rather, the place where the Samaritans live is part of God's history with his people. Luke's readers know from 1:8 that the good news must also be proclaimed in Samaria. There may be a "negative" typology at work as well: while the patriarchs died and were buried in a grave whose location is known, Jesus died and was buried but did not remain in the grave.[34]

7:17 When the time approached for the fulfillment of the promise that God had made to Abraham, the people grew and multiplied in Egypt (καθὼς δὲ ἤγγιζεν ὁ χρόνος τῆς ἐπαγγελίας ἧς ὡμολόγησεν ὁ θεὸς τῷ Ἀβραάμ, ηὔξησεν ὁ λαὸς καὶ ἐπληθύνθη ἐν Αἰγύπτῳ). Stephen begins his account of the story of Moses (vv. 17 – 43), which focuses on Moses' rejection by the Israelites and on Moses' being chosen and blessed by God, with a reference to God's promise to Abraham that his descendants would inherit the land of Canaan (cf. vv. 5 – 7). As Joseph played a decisive role in God's plan of salvation when he rescued Abraham's descendants from perishing in the famine by inviting them to stay in Egypt, so Moses is an instrument of God's sovereign providence in leading Abraham's descendants from Egypt back to Canaan.

Moses' life is divided into three forty-year periods (vv. 17 – 29, 30 – 34, 35 – 43), probably based on the tradition that Moses lived 120 years (Deut 34:7). Compared with other summaries of Israel's history, Stephen emphasizes the activity of Moses, particularly in the sections describing the exodus and Israel in the desert (vv. 35 – 39).

While Egypt and Egyptians are characterized in a negative manner (vv. 17 – 19, 24, 34), Stephen (Luke) provides also a positive characterization for the action of Pharaoh's daughter (v. 21) and for the wisdom of the Egyptians (v. 22). Note that Moses' flight to Midian is caused in v. 29 by the Israelites and not by Pharaoh (as in Exod 2:15), and that the account of the theophany in vv. 33 – 34 omits the explicit references to Israel's oppression by the Egyptians in Exod 3:7; also their role during the exodus is omitted in vv. 36, 40. The destruction of the Egyptians (cf. Exod 14 – 15), which figures prominently in many of the summaries of Israel's history (e.g., Josh 24; Neh 9; Ps 106; 136; Wis 10; *3 Macc.* 2; 6; *L.A.B.* 23), is also omitted.

While the pagan Egyptians are thus somewhat exonerated and while Moses is characterized positively throughout as savior sent by God, the "sons of Israel" (v. 23) are presented in a negative light: they fail to understand the salvation that God offers them through Moses (v. 25), they push him aside (vv. 27 – 28), they cause him to flee to Midian (v. 29), they reject him as ruler and redeemer sent by God (v. 35), they were unwilling to obey him (v. 39), and they manufacture and then worship a golden calf (vv. 40 – 41).

The expression translated "the time ... for the fulfillment of the promise" (ὁ χρόνος τῆς ἐπαγγελίας, lit., "the time of the promise") is a

---

33. Bruce, *Acts*, 196; cf. Marshall, "Acts," 560; Bock, *Acts*, 289.

34. Many commentators suggest that the reference to Samaritan Shechem prepares Luke's readers for the expansion of the church to Samaria (Acts 8). This is not as certain as some

seem to think — the gospel does not follow the "movement" of Jacob and his sons, Luke does not include an explicit reference to Samaria in Acts 7, and in Acts 8 he does not refer to Shechem.

genitive of respect. Luke ties the fulfillment of the promise of land that God had made to Abraham to the prosperity of Jacob's descendants in Egypt, which he had described in the Joseph section. The first phase of the fulfillment of God's promise made to Abraham is the growth of the people, i.e., of Jacob's descendants, in the foreign country of Egypt (cf. Exod 1:7).

7:18 – 19 Until a different king came to power in Egypt, who did not know Joseph. He took advantage of our people and mistreated our fathers by forcing them to expose their infants so that they would not remain alive (ἄχρι οὗ ἀνέστη βασιλεὺς ἕτερος ἐπ᾽ Αἴγυπτον ὃς οὐκ ᾔδει τὸν Ἰωσήφ. οὗτος κατασοφισάμενος τὸ γένος ἡμῶν ἐκάκωσεν τοὺς πατέρας ἡμῶν τοῦ ποιεῖν τὰ βρέφη ἔκθετα αὐτῶν εἰς τὸ μὴ ζῳογονεῖσθαι). The second phase of the fulfillment of God's promise of land is the oppression of the Israelites by the new "king" who came to power in Egypt after Joseph's death (Exod 1:7 – 22; v. 18 quotes Exod 1:8, v. 19 alludes to Exod 1:10 – 14). The pharaoh in question is likely Ramesses II (1290 – 1224 BC), who built the vast city Pi-Ramesse A-nakhtu, abbreviated as "Ra(a)mses" in Hebrew.[35]

Among the numerous surveys of Israel's history in the Old Testament outside of Exodus and in Jewish tradition, only *1 En.* 89:15 includes a reference to the killing of the Israelite newborn babies, a passage that takes up the motif of fear as the reason for this measure from Exod 1:12. But here in vv. 18 – 19 the Egyptian king, although he is characterized negatively, is not described as a despot who acted out of fear of the Israelites.[36] Stephen's description of the era of Joseph and of Israel in Egypt underscores the fact that the welfare of Israel in a land ruled by a foreign king depends on the personal attitude of the individual ruler.

In v. 19, the modal participle translated as "he took advantage of" (κατασοφισάμενος) and the main verb "mistreated" (ἐκάκωσεν) refer to the forced labor that the pharaoh imposed on the Israelites as he built the cities of Raamses and Pithom. The epexegetical infinitive translated "by forcing them" (τοῦ ποιεῖν) explains the cunning mistreatment of the Israelites by the Egyptian king in terms of forcing them to "abandon" or "expose" (ἔκθετα) their infants so that they would die, making the parents complicit in the infanticide.

If the expression "the people grew and multiplied" in v. 17 reminds Luke's readers of the growth of the church (cf. 6:7; 12:24), Stephen's reference to Israel's oppression in Egypt implies a typological link with the persecution by the Jewish leaders of the followers of Jesus, who represent the ultimate fulfillment of God's promises to Abraham.

7:20 – 22 At this time Moses was born, well-bred in God's sight. He was cared for in his father's house for three months. When he was exposed, he was claimed by Pharaoh's daughter, who brought him up as her own son. Moses was educated in all the wisdom of the Egyptians. He was powerful in words and deeds (ἐν ᾧ καιρῷ ἐγεννήθη Μωϋσῆς καὶ ἦν ἀστεῖος τῷ θεῷ· ὃς ἀνετράφη μῆνας τρεῖς ἐν τῷ οἴκῳ τοῦ πατρός, ἐκτεθέντος δὲ αὐτοῦ ἀνείλατο αὐτὸν ἡ θυγάτηρ Φαραὼ καὶ ἀνεθρέψατο αὐτὸν ἑαυτῇ εἰς υἱόν. καὶ ἐπαιδεύθη Μωϋσῆς ἐν πάσῃ σοφίᾳ Αἰγυπτίων, ἦν δὲ δυνατὸς ἐν λόγοις καὶ ἔργοις αὐτοῦ). The brief biographical sketch of Moses birth (v. 20), forced exposure (v. 21a), adoption by Pharaoh's daughter (v. 21b), and education (vv. 21c, 22) summarizes Exod 2:2 – 10.[37]

---

35. Cf. Kenneth A. Kitchen, *On the Reliability of the Old Testament* (Grand Rapids: Eerdmans, 2003), 255 – 56.

36. As in Ps 105:24 – 25; Philo, *Moses* 1.8; Josephus, *Ant.* 2.201 – 202. Cf. Jeska, *Geschichte Israels*, 165.

37. The only summaries of Israel's history that give more space to the story of Moses are Sir 44:23 – 45:5; *2 Bar.* 59:1 – 12; *1 En.* 89:16 – 38, the closest parallel being the latter text; cf. Jeska, *Geschichte Israels*, 166.

Stephen's description here underscores Moses' role as savior figure, who typologically prefigures Jesus as the Savior of the people of Israel. (1) Moses was born "at this time" (ἐν ᾧ καιρῷ), i.e., at the right time (cf. Luke 2:1 – 2). (2) Moses was "well-bred in God's sight," a physical beauty that results from God's providence and is "a sign of his vocation."[38] (3) Moses was educated "in all the wisdom" of the Egyptians,[39] a wisdom he needed for the mission to which God would commission him (cf. Luke 2:40, 52, which speaks of Jesus' growth in "wisdom" and "in favor with God and man"). (4) Moses was "powerful in words and deeds" (δυνατὸς ἐν λόγοις καὶ ἔργοις), a phrase not found in Exod 2[40] but occurs in Luke 24:19 as a description of Jesus as "a prophet, powerful in word and deed [δυνατὸς ἐν ἔργῳ καὶ λόγῳ] before God" (cf. Acts 2:22: "a man accredited to you by God with mighty deeds").

The summary description of Moses in vv. 20 – 22 is followed by two narrative episodes: Moses' killing of an Egyptian (vv. 23 – 29) and God's theophany in the burning bush (vv. 30 – 34). These episodes are not only significant for Moses' life, but they also have a paradigmatic character, confirmed by the second summary description of Moses in vv. 35 – 38.

7:23 – 24 When he was forty years old, he decided that he should visit his brothers, the sons of Israel. When he saw one of them being mistreated, he came to his aid and avenged the man who was being wronged by striking down the Egyptian (ὡς δὲ ἐπληροῦτο αὐτῷ τεσσερακονταετὴς χρόνος, ἀνέβη ἐπὶ τὴν καρδίαν αὐτοῦ ἐπισκέψασθαι τοὺς ἀδελφοὺς αὐτοῦ τοὺς υἱοὺς Ἰσραήλ. καὶ ἰδών τινα ἀδικούμενον ἠμύνατο καὶ ἐποίησεν ἐκδίκησιν τῷ

καταπονουμένῳ πατάξας τὸν Αἰγύπτιον). Even though Moses was educated at Pharaoh's court as an Egyptian, he never forgot that the "sons of Israel" (οἱ υἱοὶ Ἰσραήλ) were his "brothers," i.e., his family, the people among whom he was born and to whom he belonged.[41]

The statement that Moses was forty years old when he "visit[ed]" the Israelites oppressed by Pharaoh derives from the division of Moses' life of 120 years (Deut 34:7) into three periods of forty years (vv. 23, 30, 36). Exodus 2:11 dates Moses' visit to the people of Israel to the time "after Moses had grown up." The phrase translated as "he decided" describes not a spur of the moment choice but a conscious decision to reconnect with the people of Israel.

In v. 24 Stephen paraphrases Exod 2:11 – 12, which provides clearer details about an Egyptian attacking an Israelite man and Moses taking precautions before he killed the Egyptian in his effort to help the Israelite man. Going beyond the biblical text, Stephen characterizes Moses' action as just punishment on the Egyptians for wrongdoing and thus as fulfillment of God's promise in Gen 15:14, where God had promised that he would "punish the nation they serve as slaves." Moses is thus portrayed as God's instrument for the salvation of Israel.

7:25 He thought that his brothers would understand that God was offering them salvation through him, but they did not understand (ἐνόμιζεν δὲ συνιέναι τοὺς ἀδελφοὺς αὐτοῦ ὅτι ὁ θεὸς διὰ χειρὸς αὐτοῦ δίδωσιν σωτηρίαν αὐτοῖς· οἱ δὲ οὐ συνῆκαν). The "brothers" of the Israelites failed to understand the role of Moses as God's in-

---

38. Fitzmyer, *Acts*, 375, who compares with Heb 11:23; Philo, *Moses* 1.9, 18.

39. The proverbial wisdom of the Egyptians is not mentioned in Exod 2, but see 1 Kgs 4:30.

40. Moses describes himself as "slow of speech and tongue"

(Exod 4:10); cf. Philo, *Moses* 1.80; Josephus, *Ant.* 2.271.

41. NLT and NRSV translate the term "brothers" (ἀδελφοί) as "relatives," TNIV as "his own people," NET as "his fellow countrymen."

strument offering them "salvation" (σωτηρία), i.e., liberation from the oppression by Pharaoh and the Egyptian people. While Moses is characterized positively as a savior sent by God, the people of Israel are described negatively as those who fail to understand that divine salvation (see v. 17). This comment has no counterpart in the Exodus narrative and thus underscores the typological link with the fate of Jesus, who was rejected out of "ignorance" (3:17) even though he offered salvation (4:12; 5:31), and with the opposition against Jesus' emissaries in Jerusalem. The problem of Israel was, and continues to be, that "they did not understand."

7:26 The next day he appeared to some of them who were fighting. He tried to reconcile them so that they would be peaceful. He said, "Men, you are brothers. Why do you do wrong to each other?" (τῇ τε ἐπιούσῃ ἡμέρᾳ ὤφθη αὐτοῖς μαχομένοις καὶ συνήλλασσεν αὐτοὺς εἰς εἰρήνην εἰπών· ἄνδρες, ἀδελφοί ἐστε· ἱνατί ἀδικεῖτε ἀλλήλους;). Stephen describes Moses as peacemaker among the Israelites. The passive voice of the verb translated "he appeared" (ὤφθη), used for God's theophany in v. 2 and for the appearance of the angel of the Lord in v. 30, hints that Moses is a divine messenger. Moses tries to reconcile (συνήλλασσεν, conative imperfect) two Israelites fighting. The description of Moses pointing out that they are "brothers" reinforces the negative characterization of the "sons of Israel" in the speech.

7:27 – 28 But the man who was mistreating his neighbor pushed him aside and said, "Who appointed you ruler and judge over us? Do you want to kill me just as you killed the Egyptian yesterday?" (ὁ δὲ ἀδικῶν τὸν πλησίον ἀπώσατο αὐτὸν εἰπών· τίς σε κατέστησεν ἄρχοντα καὶ δικαστὴν ἐφ' ἡμῶν; μὴ ἀνελεῖν με σὺ θέλεις ὃν τρόπον ἀνεῖλες

ἐχθὲς τὸν Αἰγύπτιον;). The Israelite man who was mistreating another Israelite challenges Moses, rejects his efforts to reconcile, and pushes him away, disputing both his jurisdiction and his loyalty to the people of Israel. The "brother" (v. 26) refuses to answer the rhetorical question that he poses — he should either know that Moses, adopted by Pharaoh's daughter and educated at Pharaoh's court, might indeed have administrative jurisdiction that gave him the right to intervene when Israelite workers fought against each other. Or he should know that God had appointed Moses "ruler" (ἄρχων) and "judge" (δικαστής) to rescue Israel (v. 25).[42] Instead, he accuses Moses of presumptuous arrogance and imperious despotism. At least from the point of view of Stephen's listeners, the Israelite man repudiates the divinely appointed leader who would rescue Israel from bondage in Egypt.

The comment that Moses is "pushed aside" by a brother goes beyond the account in Exod 2:13 – 14 and again reinforces the negative characterization of the Israelites. Disobeying a ruler and judge is serious indeed. The typological connection between Moses and Jesus is again obvious. Just as Moses was sent by God to Israel as "ruler and judge" to save Israel, so God exalted Jesus as "Leader and Savior" (5:31); and as Moses was pushed away by an Israelite brother, so Jesus was rejected by the Jewish people.

7:29 When Moses heard this, he fled and became a resident alien in the land of Midian, where he became the father of two sons (ἔφυγεν δὲ Μωϋσῆς ἐν τῷ λόγῳ τούτῳ καὶ ἐγένετο πάροικος ἐν γῇ Μαδιάμ, οὗ ἐγέννησεν υἱοὺς δύο). Moses' rejection by the Israelite brother causes his flight to Midian. Stephen abbreviates Exod 2:14 – 15, where Moses flees Egypt because his killing of the Egyptian man

---

42. On "ruler" (ἄρχων) see 4:5; the term δικαστής (which occurs in the New Testament here and in v. 35) means "judge"

in the sense of "one who presides over and decides cases in court, *judge*" (BDAG).

has come to the attention of Pharaoh, who wants to take action against Moses. Here it is the word of a fellow Israelite (ἐν τῷ λόγῳ) that prompts Moses to abandon, for the time being, his rescue mission of the people of Israel.

Moses goes to the region in which the Midianites lived, located somewhere in the Sinai Peninsula or in northwest Arabia on the east coast of the Gulf of Aqaba. The continuation of the Moses story indicates that his flight was not motivated by fear pure and simple, but served to preserve the life of the savior of Israel whom God had appointed (v. 25) and whom God would send back to Egypt to rescue Israel in due time. While Moses lived in Midian as a "resident alien," he married Zipporah, the daughter of a priest, who bore him two sons, Gershom and Eliezer (Exod 2:21 – 22; 18:3 – 4). The reference to Moses' family in Midian perhaps serves to underline the importance of God's call described in vv. 30 – 34, without which Moses "would have good reason to remain in Midian."[43] The fact that Moses, the divinely appointed ruler, flees to a foreign land because he is rejected by the sons of Israel continues the negative characterization of the Israelites; the fulfillment of God's promise is, at least initially, postponed by Israel's ignorant behavior.

7:30 – 31 When forty years had passed, an angel appeared to him in the desert of Mount Sinai, in the flame of a burning bush. When Moses saw it, he was amazed at the sight. When he came closer to look at it, the voice of the Lord was heard (Καὶ πληρωθέντων ἐτῶν τεσσεράκοντα ὤφθη αὐτῷ ἐν τῇ ἐρήμῳ τοῦ ὄρους Σινᾶ ἄγγελος ἐν φλογὶ πυρὸς βάτου. ὁ δὲ Μωϋσῆς ἰδὼν ἐθαύμαζεν τὸ ὅραμα, προσερχομένου δὲ αὐτοῦ κατανοῆσαι ἐγένετο φωνὴ κυρίου). The second (forty-year) period of Moses'

life constitutes the next narrative episode Stephen includes in order to describe the mission of Moses. The episode of God's theophany in the burning bush (vv. 30 – 34; Exod 3:1 – 10) is made up of six parts.

First, Stephen notes the time and place of God's revelation to and call of Moses (v. 30a-c). God appeared to Moses when he was eighty years old (cf. v. 23; Exod 7:7). The revelation took place in the desert of Mount Sinai. In the Old Testament the mountain is called Horeb (Exod 3:1; 17:6; 33:6; Deut 1:2, 6); here it is called Sinai, the mountain at which God revealed his law to Israel.[44] The later rabbis interpreted God's revelation in the desert with the comment that no place is too desolate for the presence of God (*Exod. Rab.* 2.86c). While the desert at Mount Sinai was not in dispute with regard to God's revelation to Moses, Stephen, who is accused of speaking against the temple, underlines the point that the revelation that triggered the saving events of the exodus took place not in Jerusalem but in the desert.

Second, God spoke to Moses through an angel who appeared in the flame of a burning bush (v. 30d). While Exod 3:2 refers to the "angel of the Lord" (ἄγγελος κυρίου), Stephen simply refers to the "angel" in whose voice Moses hears the "voice of the Lord" (φωνὴ κυρίου; v. 31). Stephen intensifies the transcendent manifestation: first the angel appears (v. 30), then the voice of God is heard (vv. 31 – 32), then the Lord speaks (v. 33). In Philo's interpretation of this episode, the angel is a "symbol of God's providence which all silently brings relief to the greatest dangers, exceeding in every hope" (Philo, *Moses* 1.67). The suggestion that the angel is the preexistent Jesus Christ[45] is doubtful; Stephen gives his listeners in the Sanhedrin no clue that he intends such an identification.

---

43. Barrett, *Acts*, 360.
44. Exod 19:1 – 2, 11, 18, 20, 23; 24:16; 31:18; Lev 7:38; 25:1. The Old Testament tradition assimilates the two place-names,

cf. Exod 3:12; 19:11; cf. *Jub.* 48:2; Marguerat, *Actes*, 1:250.
45. Calvin, *Acts*, 190, on the basis of 1 Cor 10:4.

Third, the psychological reaction of Moses to the "vision," which is introduced into the description of Exod 3:3 – 4, underlines the reality of the theophany. While Moses has been rejected by the Israelites, he approaches the God of Israel.

7:32 "I am the God of your fathers, the God of Abraham, Isaac, and Jacob." Moses trembled and did not dare to look (ἐγὼ ὁ θεὸς τῶν πατέρων σου, ὁ θεὸς Ἀβραὰμ καὶ Ἰσαὰκ καὶ Ἰακώβ. ἔντρομος δὲ γενόμενος Μωϋσῆς οὐκ ἐτόλμα κατανοῆσαι). Fourth, God introduces himself as "the God of your fathers" (ὁ θεὸς τῶν πατέρων σου, v. 32a-b; Exod 3:6). Stephen reverses the sequence of God's command to Moses to remove his shoes and of God's self-revelation in Exod 3:5 – 6, placing God's self-revelation as the God of the fathers Abraham, Isaac, and Jacob at the front. He thus emphasizes the faithfulness of God and of his promise given to Abraham — a promise that will be fulfilled, "notwithstanding the patriarch's treatment of Joseph and the Israelites' rejection of Moses."[46] In the context of the typological links of the speech, Stephen (Luke) emphasizes that Christians worship the same God, notwithstanding Jesus' rejection by the Jewish leaders.

Fifth, Moses' reaction to hearing the voice of the Lord (7:32c-d) underscores the reality and thus the authority of God's revelation to Moses.

7:33 – 34 Then the Lord said to him, "Remove the sandals from your feet, because the place where you are standing is holy ground. I have surely seen the mistreatment of my people in Egypt, I have heard their groaning, and I have come down to set them free. Now come, I shall send you to Egypt" (εἶπεν δὲ αὐτῷ ὁ κύριος· λῦσον τὸ ὑπόδημα τῶν ποδῶν σου, ὁ γὰρ τόπος ἐφ' ᾧ ἕστηκας γῆ ἁγία ἐστίν. ἰδὼν εἶδον τὴν κάκωσιν τοῦ λαοῦ μου τοῦ ἐν Αἰγύπτῳ καὶ τοῦ στεναγμοῦ αὐτῶν ἤκουσα, καὶ κατέβην ἐξελέσθαι αὐτούς· καὶ νῦν δεῦρο ἀποστείλω σε εἰς Αἴγυπτον).

Sixth, Stephen recounts God's commission of Moses as his envoy to rescue Israel (Exod 3:5, 7 – 8). The spot in the desert in front of the burning bush where Moses stands is "holy ground" (γῆ ἁγία). While this is an exact quotation of Exod 3:5 LXX, Stephen (Luke) would naturally be keen to cite this divine assertion since it can be used to relativize the claims of the Jewish leaders concerning "this holy place" that Stephen is charged to speak against (Acts 6:13). Stephen makes the point that holy ground is where God is, which implies that the temple in Jerusalem is not the only holy place.

God's commission of Moses to go to Egypt as his envoy is the result of God's gracious intervention for the benefit of the people of Israel whose mistreatment he has seen and whose groaning he has heard. Fulfilling the promise given to Abraham (vv. 6 – 7), God will personally come to the people of Israel in order to rescue them (ἐξελέσθαι, infinitive of purpose). He commissions Moses to this task.

The formulation of the commission ("now come, I shall send you to Egypt") abbreviates Exod 3:10 LXX ("And now come, let me send you to Pharaoh, king of Egypt, and you will bring my people, the sons of Israel, out of the land of Egypt" [lit. trans.]). The verb translated as "I shall send" in Acts 7:34 (ἀποστείλω) means "to dispatch someone for the achievement of some objective" (BDAG). In the context of the typological links between Moses and Jesus and his envoys, Stephen implies that as Moses was sent by God to the children of Israel to lead, judge, and save the nation even though they had rejected him earlier, so Jesus was sent by God to the people of Israel to save the nation — God's "com[ing]" to Israel in Jesus' mission and in

---

46. Barrett, *Acts*, 361; cf. ibid. for the following point.

the preaching of his followers, despite the earlier rejection.

7:35 It was this Moses, whom they rejected when they said, "Who appointed you ruler and judge?" whom God sent as ruler and redeemer through the angel who appeared to him in the bush (τοῦτον τὸν Μωϋσῆν ὃν ἠρνήσαντο εἰπόντες· τίς σε κατέστησεν ἄρχοντα καὶ δικαστήν; τοῦτον ὁ θεὸς καὶ ἄρχοντα καὶ λυτρωτὴν ἀπέσταλκεν σὺν χειρὶ ἀγγέλου τοῦ ὀφθέντος αὐτῷ ἐν τῇ βάτῳ). The third part of the Moses story summarizes briefly the third forty-year period (v. 36) of Moses' life and mission. The description of the exodus and Israel's time in the desert (vv. 35 – 43) begins with a second summary description of Moses in vv. 35 – 38. These four sentences make the following assertions about Moses.

First, Moses was rejected by Israel even though God had appointed and sent him as their ruler and redeemer (v. 35). The first part of v. 35 alludes to Exod 2:14, which was quoted in vv. 27 – 28. Despite the fact that the people of Israel had repudiated Moses, God "sent" (ἀπέσταλκεν) him to Israel as "ruler" (ἄρχων) and "redeemer" (λυτρωτής).[47] The statement in v. 35d-e is the answer to the rhetorical question in v. 35c: since God sent Moses as "ruler and redeemer" to Israel, Moses was indeed the "ruler and judge" (ἄρχων καὶ δικαστής) whom God had "appointed" (κατέστησεν) for Israel. Stephen presents Moses' divine call and commission as being established by God's appearance to Moses in the burning bush.

This first and basic statement concerning Moses

reminds the listeners of the preaching of the apostles, whose convictions Stephen shares, who proclaimed that even though Jesus had been rejected and repudiated by the Jewish people (3:13),[48] he was, like Moses, sent by God for the "redemption" (λύτρωσις) of the people of Israel (Luke 2:38; cf. 1:68) and exalted as "Leader and Savior" (ἀρχηγὸς καὶ σωτήρ; 5:31). While the statement in v. 35 indirectly repudiates the charge that Stephen utters blasphemous words against Moses (6:11), it establishes — equally implicitly — a link between Moses and Jesus in terms both of being rejected by the people of Israel and of being commissioned as ruler and redeemer of Israel.

7:36 He led them out, performing wonders and signs in the land of Egypt, at the Red Sea, and in the desert for forty years (οὗτος ἐξήγαγεν αὐτοὺς ποιήσας τέρατα καὶ σημεῖα ἐν γῇ Αἰγύπτῳ καὶ ἐν ἐρυθρᾷ θαλάσσῃ καὶ ἐν τῇ ἐρήμῳ ἔτη τεσσεράκοντα). Second, Stephen summarizes the events of the exodus and of Israel's desert wanderings in a few brief sentences[49] that focus on the role of Moses and thus continue the encomium.

Moses was the miracle worker who led Israel out of Egypt. He performed "wonders and signs" (τέρατα καὶ σημεῖα) in Egypt leading up to the exodus, at the Red Sea during the exodus, and in the desert after the exodus. Those miracles confirm that he was indeed the "ruler" God had appointed over Israel, and the fact that he "led" the people of Israel out of Egypt confirms that he was the "redeemer" whom God had sent to Israel. This reference to Moses' role as Israel's redeemer being

---

47. On "ruler" (ἄρχων) see v. 27 and 4:5; the term "redeemer" (λυτρωτής) occurs only here in the New Testament; it is not used in nonbiblical writings; in the LXX it describes God in Pss 19:14 (LXX 18:15); 78:35 (LXX 77:35). Cf. John Lierman, *The New Testament Moses: Christian Perceptions of Moses and Israel in the Setting of Jewish Religion* (WUNT 2/173; Tübingen: Mohr Siebeck, 2004), 113 – 18.

48. Cf. 2:23, 36; 3:13 – 15; 4:10 – 11; 5:30.

49. Verse 36b-c alludes to Exod 3:12; the reference to the "wonders and signs" alludes to Exod 7:3, 9; 11:9 – 10; Deut 4:34 (cf. Deut 34:11). For the miracles of the ten plagues, cf. Exod 7:8 – 11:10 (cf. Ps 105:27 – 36); for the miracles at the Red Sea, cf. Exod 14:21 – 31 (cf. Ps 106:9, 22); for the miracles in the desert, cf. Exod 16:35; Num 14:33; Deut 2:7 (Ps 95:10). The "forty years" in the desert are first mentioned in Num 14:33; cf. Ps 95:10 (LXX 94:10).

confirmed by miracles has typological significance — Jesus' ministry was accompanied by miracles attesting to his divine calling as well (2:22), as was the ministry of his followers (2:43).

7:37 This is the Moses who said to the Israelites, "A prophet like me God will raise up for you from among your brothers" (οὗτός ἐστιν ὁ Μωϋσῆς ὁ εἴπας τοῖς υἱοῖς Ἰσραήλ· προφήτην ὑμῖν ἀναστήσει ὁ θεὸς ἐκ τῶν ἀδελφῶν ὑμῶν ὡς ἐμέ). Third, Stephen moves from the exodus events to the end of Moses' life, quoting Deut 18:15 in order to emphasize that Moses was more than a ruler and redeemer, and more than God's instrument in performing miracles.

Moses was the prophet who predicted that God would send a prophet who would be "like" (ὡς) him, i.e., who also would be Israel's ruler and redeemer and through whom God would intervene in the history of his people performing "wonders and signs." As the apostles' preaching included references to Moses' prophecy in Deut 18:15 (cf. 3:22; see comment there), Stephen's listeners may have recognized the typological link between Moses and Jesus here, a link made explicit at the end of the speech in v. 52. Moses, the prophet, is the prototype of Jesus, who is, like Moses, not only a redeemer and a miracle worker but also God's messenger who brings God's revelation to the "sons of Israel" (lit.).

7:38 He is the one who was in the congregation in the desert with the angel who spoke to him at Mount Sinai, and who was with our fathers, and who received living words to give to you (οὗτός ἐστιν ὁ γενόμενος ἐν τῇ ἐκκλησίᾳ ἐν τῇ ἐρήμῳ μετὰ τοῦ ἀγγέλου τοῦ λαλοῦντος αὐτῷ ἐν τῷ ὄρει Σινᾶ καὶ τῶν πατέρων ἡμῶν, ὃς ἐδέξατο λόγια ζῶντα δοῦναι ὑμῖν). Fourth, this last statement begins with an emphatic "he is the one" (οὗτός ἐστιν), which focuses on Moses as the mediator of the law, a role that is formulated with the help of three prepositional phrases, a relative clause, and an infinitive clause.

Moses is the mediator of the law given at Mount Sinai. This statement is carefully formulated. (1) Moses was "in the congregation" (ἐν τῇ ἐκκλησίᾳ); i.e., he was the leader of the assembly of the people of God.[50] The term "congregation" (ἐκκλησία) became a standard designation of the "assembly" or "church" of the followers of Jesus.

(2) This happened "in the desert" (ἐν τῇ ἐρήμῳ). Moses mediated between God, who revealed himself on Mount Sinai, and the assembly of the people of Israel.

(3) Moses was "with the angel" (μετὰ τοῦ ἀγγέλου) who spoke to him at Mount Sinai. The theophany was described above as the appearance of an angel who communicated the voice of the Lord, with God himself speaking to Moses (vv. 30 – 32). Here, now, the giving of the law of God is attributed to an angel (cf. v. 53; Gal 3:19; Heb 2:2).[51] The reference to an angel signals Stephen's reverence that "puts God at a further remove from earthly affairs."[52]

---

50. Cf. Deut 23:1 (LXX 23:2) "the assembly of the Lord" (ἐκκλησία κυρίου); cf. the phrase "the day of the assembly" (ἡμέρα τῆς ἐκκλησίας) in Deut 4:10; 9:10; 18:16, which refers to the day when the people of Israel were assembled at Mount Sinai "when — it might be said — the Israelites became the people of the Lord, constituted as such by the Law" (Barrett, *Acts*, 365).

51. The tradition of angels being involved in the giving of the law derives from Deut 33:2, whose last line was translated in the LXX as "from his right hand angels with him." Cf. *Jub.* 1.27 – 29; *T. Dan* 6:2; Josephus, *Ant.* 15.136; Philo, *Dreams* 1.140 – 144; *Apoc. Mos.* 1; *Pesiq. Rab.* 21:7 – 10; *Targum Neofiti* Deut 33:2; cf. the "angel of his presence" in Isa 63:9. In Gal 3:19 the description of the giving of the law via angels is meant as a disparagement; this is not the case in the other passages. Neither Exod 19 nor Deut 4 mentions the presence of angels on Mount Sinai.

52. Barrett, *Acts*, 366.

(4) Moses received "living words," i.e., the law God gave to Israel to preserve life for his chosen people.[53] This expression confirms that the accusation against Stephen that he utters blasphemous words against Moses (6:11) misunderstands Stephen's teaching. He acknowledges that the words of the law that God revealed to Moses are words of life.

(5) God revealed life-giving words to Moses so that he would give them to the people of Israel. This statement underlines Moses' role as mediator. The expression "to you" (ὑμῖν), which is more likely the original reading,[54] communicates a distancing of Stephen from his Jewish listeners — they have received the law, but they have not grasped its significance, both in the past (vv. 39 – 43) when the people of Israel were disobedient in the desert, and in the present (vv. 51 – 53) when the Jewish leaders failed to recognize Jesus as God's Righteous One.

7:39 Our fathers were unwilling to obey him. They pushed him aside and turned in their hearts back to Egypt (ᾧ οὐκ ἠθέλησαν ὑπήκοοι γενέσθαι οἱ πατέρες ἡμῶν, ἀλλὰ ἀπώσαντο καὶ ἐστράφησαν ἐν ταῖς καρδίαις αὐτῶν εἰς Αἴγυπτον). Stephen ends the story of Moses by pointing out that the people of Israel were unwilling to obey Moses, and by implication God's law given through Moses. The phrase "our fathers" establishes a connection between Stephen's Jewish listeners and the disobedience of the people of Israel at the time of Moses. They "pushed him aside" and wanted to "turn back" to Egypt. Stephen alludes here to the events described in Num 14:2 – 3 (cf. Exod 16:3). This is the second rejection of Moses (cf. v. 27).

Instead of relying on God's promise of the land of Canaan and trusting in Moses as leader and redeemer, the "fathers" wanted to return to Egypt. The reference to the "hearts" of the fathers underscores the radical nature of their repudiation of Moses, and the timing — after the giving of the "living words" at Mount Sinai — marks their rejection of Moses as a repudiation of God's offer of salvation. A typological link with the present connects the second rejection of Moses with the rejection of the preaching of the apostles and of Stephen, who proclaim Jesus as Leader and Redeemer of the people.

7:40 – 41 They said to Aaron, 'Make gods for us who will go before us. As for this Moses, who led us out from the land of Egypt, we do not know what has happened to him.' So they manufactured a calf in those days, offered a sacrifice to the idol, and celebrated over the works of their own hands (εἰπόντες τῷ Ἀαρών· ποίησον ἡμῖν θεοὺς οἳ προπορεύσονται ἡμῶν· ὁ γὰρ Μωϋσῆς οὗτος, ὃς ἐξήγαγεν ἡμᾶς ἐκ γῆς Αἰγύπτου, οὐκ οἴδαμεν τί ἐγένετο αὐτῷ. καὶ ἐμοσχοποίησαν ἐν ταῖς ἡμέραις ἐκείναις καὶ ἀνήγαγον θυσίαν τῷ εἰδώλῳ καὶ εὐφραίνοντο ἐν τοῖς ἔργοις τῶν χειρῶν αὐτῶν). Israel's willingness to "turn back" led to idolatry. The participle translated "they said" (εἰπόντες) is modal: as they wished to return to Egypt, they asked Aaron to manufacture an idol.

The rejection of Moses and his leadership on the way to the Promised Land was a repudiation of Israel's covenant God, which resulted in their apostasy from worshiping the one true God, who had been part of the covenant with Abraham (v. 7).

---

53. Cf. Lev 18:5; Deut 4:1, 33; 5:26; 16:20; 30:15; cf. Ps 119:25, 50, 154 (LXX 118:25, 50, 154). The phrase "living words" (λόγια ζῶντα) does not occur in the Old Testament; the closest parallel is Ps 119:50 (LXX 118:50); cf. in Rom 3:2 the reference to τὰ λόγια τοῦ θεοῦ; cf. Num 24:4; Deut 33:9; Ps 119.

54. The second person plural ὑμῖν is read by 𝔓[74] ℵ B 36 453 al p co, while the first person plural ἡμῖν is read by A C D E

Ψ 33. 1739 Maj lat sy. The second person (NA[25]) is better attested and supported by the similar distancing from the Jewish listeners in connection with the giving of the law in v. 53; cf. NASB, NET; Jeska, *Geschichte Israels*, 152 – 53. The first person is preferred by NA[27] and most English versions; cf. Metzger, *Textual Commentary*, 307.

Stephen quotes Exod 32:1 (cf. 32:23). The rejection of Moses is expressed (1) in the contemptuous expression "this Moses" (ὁ Μωϋσῆς οὗτος); (2) in the fact that they regarded his role as leader and redeemer from slavery in Egypt as irrelevant; (3) in their lack of interest in Moses, who had gone up Mount Sinai to receive the law and the commandments (Exod 24:12 – 18); and (4) in their decision to manufacture deities.

Stephen describes the outcome of Israel's rejection of Moses with three brief sentences.

(1) They manufactured an image of a calf.

(2) They brought an offering to the image of a calf, which is disparagingly described as an "idol" (εἴδωλον). The Greeks used the term "image" (ἄγαλμα) for the representation of their deities in wood, stone, or bronze. The term translated as "idol," derived from the verb "to see" (ἰδεῖν), denotes "form" or "image" but was used already in Homer with the meaning "shadow," "phantom," or "vision" (in the sense of lack or loss of existence). The term is used in the LXX for the images and statues of pagan deities; in other words, those deities had no reality and no power since they were the products of fantasy,[55] and they were manufactured by human hands. Insofar as the pagan deities represented demonic realities, they were subject to God as fallen creatures and thus should not be worshiped.[56]

(3) The Israelites celebrated a product of their own hands. The account in Exod 32:6 details that the celebration included eating, drinking, and playing before the golden calf — a description that Paul includes in his citation of the passage in 1 Cor 10:7. Stephen emphasizes not the impious revelry but the fact that they celebrated an idol they had manufactured.

7:42 – 43 But God turned away and handed them over to worship the host of heaven, as it is written in the book of the prophets, "Did you bring me sacrifices and offerings forty years in the desert, O house of Israel? You took along the tent of Moloch and the star of your god Rephan, the images that you made to worship. Therefore I will deport you beyond Babylon" (ἔστρεψεν δὲ ὁ θεὸς καὶ παρέδωκεν αὐτοὺς λατρεύειν τῇ στρατιᾷ τοῦ οὐρανοῦ καθὼς γέγραπται ἐν βίβλῳ τῶν προφητῶν· μὴ σφάγια καὶ θυσίας προσηνέγκατέ μοι ἔτη τεσσεράκοντα ἐν τῇ ἐρήμῳ, οἶκος Ἰσραήλ; καὶ ἀνελάβετε τὴν σκηνὴν τοῦ Μόλοχ καὶ τὸ ἄστρον τοῦ θεοῦ ὑμῶν Ῥαιφάν, τοὺς τύπους οὓς ἐποιήσατε προσκυνεῖν αὐτοῖς, καὶ μετοικιῶ ὑμᾶς ἐπέκεινα Βαβυλῶνος).

Israel's willingness to "turn back" resulted in God's turning his back on Israel. Despite the wonders and signs that Moses performed during and after the exodus, and despite God's giving the law at Mount Sinai, the forty years Israel wandered in the desert are fundamentally a time of apostasy and of divine judgment. God allowed the people of Israel "to become captive to the consequences of their own evil choices."[57] Stephen asserts that Israel worshiped not only the golden calf but "the host of heaven" (ἡ στρατιὰ τοῦ οὐρανοῦ), i.e., sun, moon, and stars.[58]

The statement that God "handed over" (παρέδωκεν) the people of Israel corresponds to the statement in Wis 11:15 – 6 that God forced Israel, which had been led astray, to worship

55. Cf. 1 Kgs 18:27; Isa 41:29; 44:9 – 17; Jer 10:3 – 11; 16:19 – 20; Ep Jer 2 – 73; *Let. Aris.* 135 – 137; Josephus, *Ant.* 10.50; Philo, *Alleg. Interp.* 1.5.28; *Decalogue* 52 – 82.

56. Cf. Deut 4:19; 32:17; 1 Chr 16:26 LXX; Ps 106:36 – 37; Isa 8:19; *Jub.* 1:11; 11:4 – 6; *1 En.* 19:1; 99:6 – 10; *T. Naph.* 3:3 – 4.

57. Johnson, *Acts*, 131, with reference to Lev 26:25; Num

21:3; Deut 1:27; Pss 10:14 (LXX 9:35); 27:12 (LXX 26:12); 41:1 (LXX 40:2); 63:9 (LXX 62:10).

58. Thus the translation of the TNIV. The expression "host of heaven" (cf. in the LXX 1 Kgs 22:19; Jer 7:18; 19:13; Neh 9:6) also refers to the spirits or angels that are thought to rule the movement of the stars.

"irrational serpents and worthless animals" so that "they might learn that one is punished by the very things by which one sins."[59] Since Amos 5:25 refers to the forty years of Israel's sojourn in the desert and to Israel's idolatry, Stephen proceeds to quote Amos 5:25 – 27 to validate his statement, a text that condemns Israel's worship "because it was contaminated with idolatry and because it was not accompanied by moral obedience to the commandments of Yahweh."[60]

Stephen uses the Amos text to make several points. (1) The people of Israel offered sacrifices not to their God, who had rescued them from Egypt but to idols, like the calf they had manufactured.[61]

(2) Israel worshiped Moloch, the Canaanite-Phoenician god of sky and sun to whom some people in Judah offered infants as sacrifices,[62] as well as Rephan, perhaps the Egyptian sun god Repa.[63] Amos (and Stephen) perhaps refers to Israel's apostasy to the worship of Baal of Peor (Num 25:1 – 9). Instead of worshiping the true God in the "tent of testimony" (v. 44), Israel chose to worship foreign gods in the "tent of Moloch."

(3) Israel made "images" in order to worship them (προσκυνεῖν, infinitive of purpose). Their idolatry was a deliberate act of apostasy from the one true God, and it was a foolish act of worship since they worshiped what they themselves had manufactured.

(4) God punished his people for their idolatry through deportation "beyond Babylon," i.e., to Assyria, which was east Babylon. The reference to the Babylonian captivity reminds Stephen's listeners

of the lowest point of Israel's history, when God punished the people of Israel for their idolatry and apostasy by deporting them to Babylonia, and when the temple in Jerusalem was destroyed. Idolatry was a pattern of Israel's behavior; the reality of God's punishment of Israel in the past is a stark reminder that disobedience to God's redemptive intervention in Israel's history has consequences.

7:44 – 45 Our fathers had the tent of testimony in the desert, as the One who had spoken to Moses had ordered him to make it, according to the model that he had seen. Our fathers who received it brought it in with Joshua when they took possession of the land of the nations, whom God drove out before our fathers, until the time of David (ἡ σκηνὴ τοῦ μαρτυρίου ἦν τοῖς πατράσιν ἡμῶν ἐν τῇ ἐρήμῳ καθὼς διετάξατο ὁ λαλῶν τῷ Μωϋσῇ ποιῆσαι αὐτὴν κατὰ τὸν τύπον ὃν ἑωράκει· ἦν καὶ εἰσήγαγον διαδεξάμενοι οἱ πατέρες ἡμῶν μετὰ Ἰησοῦ ἐν τῇ κατασχέσει τῶν ἐθνῶν, ὧν ἐξῶσεν ὁ θεὸς ἀπὸ προσώπου τῶν πατέρων ἡμῶν ἕως τῶν ἡμερῶν Δαυίδ). The fifth section of Stephen's speech (vv. 44 – 50) focuses on God and his relationship with the tabernacle and the temple. In the first of three parts in this section, Stephen describes Israel's worship in the tabernacle (vv. 44 – 45) with the following facts.

(1) After the exodus, the Israelites had "the tent of testimony" (ἡ σκηνὴ τοῦ μαρτυρίου; v. 44a). This expression is used in Exod 27:21[64] for the Hebrew phrase "tent of meeting," which refers to the meeting place between God and the Israelites. The LXX

---

59. Paul asserts the same truth concerning the consequences of idolatry in Rom 1:24, 26, 28; cf. Deut 4:19; Lev 26:25; Ps 106:41.

60. Marshall, "Acts," 565. Note that CD VII, 14 – 17 also quotes Am 5:25 – 27.

61. The answer to the rhetorical question in v. 42d-g is no; other interpretations suggest that Amos thought that Israel did not offer sacrifices in the desert, or that they offered not only sacrifices but also the obedience of their hearts.

62. Cf. Lev 18:21; 20:2, 3, 4, 5; 1 Kgs 11:7; 2 Kgs 23:10; Jer 32:35. The reference to "tent" (σκηνή) in the LXX and Acts 7:43 understands the Hebrew consonants *skt* as denoting "tent" rather than as (the intended) reference to Sikkut, i.e., Sakkuth, an Assyrian astral god of war.

63. The Hebrew text refers to Kaiwan(u), an Assyrian astral deity (the planet Saturn).

64. Cf. also Exod 28:43; 33:7; Num 1:50; 12:4; Deut 31:14.

translators incorrectly believed that the Hebrew term translated "meeting" was derived from the root for "witness." While the LXX translation "tent of testimony" is "linguistically inexact, it is materially appropriate" if we understand "testimony" (μαρτύριον) to have the sense of the revelation of God's commandments through Moses. In the tabernacle "the attestation of God takes place through the directions there imparted to Moses for Israel."[65] Stephen emphasizes that God revealed himself to Israel in the tabernacle.

(2) The tabernacle was built "in the desert" according to the instructions God gave to Moses, who saw a model (τύπος) on Mount Sinai (v. 44b-d; Exod 25:8 – 9, 40).[66] The phrase "the One who had spoken to Moses" describes God, who revealed himself and his law to Israel, including laws concerning the place of worship and its construction. Stephen underlines the fact that God took the initiative and revealed the details about the construction of the tabernacle. In the desert, the tabernacle was a divinely ordained and therefore fully adequate place of worship.

(3) The tabernacle was a portable tent used in the desert (v. 44a-b) and was eventually brought into Canaan when Joshua[67] led the Israelites into the Promised Land (v. 45a-b). Joshua 3:10 – 4:18 relates how the ark of the covenant crossed the Jordan, and Josh 18:1 reports that the "tent of the meeting" was set up at Shiloh, about 35 kilometers (22 miles) north of Jerusalem. The tent, a temporary structure that could be easily dismantled and that could not compete in terms of durability and

aesthetic beauty with the temples of the pagans, remained the divinely ordained place of Israel's worship after the conquest, after God had driven out the nations (τὰ ἐθνή),[68] i.e., even after God had fulfilled the promise to Abraham that his descendants would inherit the land of Canaan. The tabernacle continued to be Israel's place of worship until the time of David (v. 45e), i.e., for about 300 years.[69] In other words, Stephen emphasizes that the temporary tent remained as Israel's place of worship for a long time.

7:46 – 47 He found favor with God and asked that he might find a habitation for the house of Jacob. It was Solomon who built a house for him (ὃς εὗρεν χάριν ἐνώπιον τοῦ θεοῦ καὶ ᾐτήσατο εὑρεῖν σκήνωμα τῷ οἴκῳ Ἰακώβ. Σολομὼν δὲ οἰκοδόμησεν αὐτῷ οἶκον). The second part of vv. 44 – 50 focuses on David, Solomon, and the temple in Jerusalem (vv. 46 – 47). David brought the tabernacle from Shiloh to Jerusalem (2 Sam 6:1 – 17) and expressed the desire to build a proper "habitation" (2 Sam 7:2). Stephen alludes to Ps 132:5 (LXX 131:5). This psalm speaks about God's promise to David that he would establish his descendants on the throne forever and about God's choice of Zion to be his dwelling place; the psalmist asks God to fulfill his promises, to be present in the temple, and to bless the priests and the people.

The verb "find" refers to the provision of a location for the temple, acquiring the site and building the sanctuary. The term translated as "habitation" (σκήνωμα) is related to "tent" (σκηνή) and does not

---

65. H. Strathmann, "μάρτυς κτλ.," *TDNT*, 4:482, 485, with reference to Exod 25:22.

66. Heb 8:5 posits a heavenly sanctuary of which the tabernacle was a copy. For the concept of a heavenly temple, see also Rev 15:5.

67. Since the Greek term for Joshua (Ἰησοῦς) is identical with the name of Jesus of Nazareth, one could establish a typological link between Joshua's role of fulfilling God's promise to Abraham that his descendants would inherit the land of Ca-

naan. Stephen's listeners would only have heard a reference to Joshua and the conquest of Canaan.

68. Cf. the list given by Joshua in Josh 3:10: the Canaanites, Hittites, Hivites, Perizzites, Girgashites, Amorites, and Jebusites.

69. From the time of the exodus in ca. 1270 BC to David's death in 970 BC. Cf. K. A. Kitchen and T. C. Mitchell, *NBD*, 190 – 92.

specifically refer to a permanent temple built of stone. It is perhaps significant that Stephen does not specifically say that David wanted to "build" (οἰκοδομέω) a temple.[70] Even though his listeners in the Sanhedrin, meeting only a stone's throw away from the temple, would have understood the statement in v. 46 in terms of David's desire to build a permanent temple, Stephen uses the words of Ps 132:5 to formulate a more general wish to provide a dwelling place for God that would be an improvement over the tent of the wilderness.

The dative phrase "for the house of Jacob" (τῷ οἴκῳ Ἰακώβ, v. 46) has been regarded as difficult;[71] however, the concept of a "habitation" within the "house of Jacob" (i.e., Israel) as a dwelling for God to be used as a temple for God's people is not ambiguous. David's desire to provide a permanent sanctuary was initially approved by Nathan, but subsequently denied when the prophet announced that not he but his son would build a house for God's name (2 Sam 7:3, 4 – 17). Stephen emphasizes that God was with David[72] and that David's desire to secure a permanent dwelling place for the worship of the people of Israel had divine sanction.

Verse 47 implies that God denied David's desire to build a temple, although Stephen does not explicitly state this. The introductory "but" (δέ, left untranslated) should be interpreted as a coordinating conjunction, not as adversative.[73] Luke does *not* portray the temple as a misunderstanding of God.[74] Stephen states that Solomon built (οἰκοδόμησεν) a "house" (οἶκος) for the house of Jacob, i.e., for the people of Israel.[75] The fact that King David wanted to build the temple but was not allowed to build it intimates that the temple in Jerusalem is not as important for Israel's worship as the Jewish people seem to think.

At the same time it is obvious that Luke, who summarizes Stephen's speech, does not intend to disparage the temple — after all, the temple continued to be a house of prayer and a place of proclamation (Luke 19:46 – 47; 24:53; Acts 2:46 – 47; 3:1; 5:20, 25).[76] Solomon himself recognized that God's presence is not limited to the temple that he had built when he said in his prayer on the occasion of the dedication of the temple, "But will God really dwell on earth? The heavens, even the highest heaven, cannot contain you. How much less this temple I have built!" (1 Kgs 8:27). However, the laconic statement of the five Greek words in v. 47 does imply that the significance of the temple of Jerusalem is relativized.

7:48 – 50 Yet the Most High does not dwell in structures made by human hands, as the prophet says, "Heaven is my throne, the earth is my footstool. What kind of a house will you build for me, says the Lord, or what is my place of rest? Did

---

70. Craig A. Evans, "Prophecy and Polemic: Jews in Luke's Scriptural Apologetic," in *Luke and Scripture: The Function of Sacred Tradition in Luke-Acts* (ed. C. A. Evans and J. A. Sanders; Minneapolis: Fortress, 1993), 172 – 211, 197.

71. Note that manuscripts ℵ[2] A C E Ψ 33 1739 Maj lat sy co read "for the God (θεῷ) of Jacob," probably in assimilation to Ps 132:5 (LXX 131:5). Johnson, *Acts*, 132 – 33, decides to "overturn" the rules of textual criticism here, opting for the reading θεῷ.

72. For the expression "he found favor with God," see 2 Sam 15:25.

73. Dennis D. Sylva, "The Meaning and Function of Acts 7.46 – 50," *JBL* 106 (1987): 261 – 75, 264 – 65; Jervell, *Apostelgeschichte*, 244 n. 717.

74. Cf. Kilgallen, *The Stephen Speech*, 88 – 89.

75. For Solomon building the temple in Jerusalem cf. 1 Kgs 5:2 – 6; 6:1 – 38; 2 Chr 3:1 – 14. There is no implied contrast between the "house" that Solomon built and the "dwelling" that David wished to find.

76. Cf. Peter Doble, "Something Greater Than Solomon: An Approach to Stephen's Speech," in *The Old Testament in the New Testament* (FS J. L. North; ed. S. Moyise; JSNTSup 189; Sheffield: Sheffield Academic Press, 2000), 181 – 207, 196, who insists that the temple is not the primary issue in vv. 47 – 50 but, rather, Solomon, whose subsequent disobedience disqualified him from being the son of David in whom God's promises were fulfilled.

not my hand make all these things?" (ἀλλ᾽ οὐχ ὁ ὕψιστος ἐν χειροποιήτοις κατοικεῖ, καθὼς ὁ προφήτης λέγει· ὁ οὐρανός μοι θρόνος, ἡ δὲ γῆ ὑποπόδιον τῶν ποδῶν μου· ποῖον οἶκον οἰκοδομήσετέ μοι, λέγει κύριος, ἢ τίς τόπος τῆς καταπαύσεώς μου; οὐχὶ ἡ χείρ μου ἐποίησεν ταῦτα πάντα;). The third part of vv. 44 – 50 addresses the relationship between God, the tabernacle, and the temple in Jerusalem (vv. 48 – 50), against which Stephen has allegedly uttered blasphemous words (6:11, 14).

While many interpret the introductory conjunction translated as "yet" (ἀλλά) as expressing a critique of the temple built by Solomon mentioned in the previous verse,[77] this interpretation is problematic for the following reasons. (1) Luke has a positive view of the temple in Jerusalem, for the apostles continued to meet there (see on vv. 46 – 47). (2) Solomon himself expressed the conviction that God's presence cannot be confined to the temple (1 Kgs 8:27). (3) Solomon recognized that God hears prayers from heaven, where he dwells (1 Kgs 8:30). (4) Structures "made by human hands" (χειροποίητοι) include not only temples but also the tabernacle. Both in the description of Bezalel and Oholiab, who were chosen to build the tabernacle (Exod 35:30 – 35), and in the description of the building of the tabernacle (Exod 36:1 – 38), the verb "to make" (ποιέω) is used numerous times, always implying "making with hands." (5) The Greek verb translated as "dwell" (κατοικεῖ) can be used both with regard to permanent buildings made of stone and with temporary structures such as tents.[78]

As regards the phrase "made by human hands" (χειροποίητοι), the fact that most English versions translate the Greek nominalized adjective with "houses made by (with) human hands" prejudices the interpretation in terms of a reference to the temple (a house) in contrast to the tabernacle (a tent). The nominalized adjective can refer to any structure that human beings have made, including the tabernacle. The fact that the term occurs in the LXX most often as a derogatory expression used for idols and their temples[79] does not mean that the Greek term used by Luke automatically has this negative connotation for his Greek-speaking readers (who would use the term in many other contexts).[80]

This is particularly true for Stephen, who would have used an Aramaic expression; note that in the LXX the term χειροποίητοι often translates the Hebrew term for "idols," which does not have the connotation "handmade." Note too that Luke reports on the "rage" of the audience in v. 54, not after v. 48 but after Stephen's charge that they oppose the Holy Spirit (v. 51), that they are just like those Jews who killed the prophets (v. 52), and that they have not kept the law (v. 53). Stephen's point is not that Solomon made a mistake in building the temple "but that those people are wrong who think that God dwells there and is confined to this one place."[81] The problem is not the temple in Jerusalem as such "but Israel's false perception that the temple somehow renders God manageable."[82] The description of God as "the Most High"[83] underlines his transcendence and sovereign rule over all things, which cannot be contained in a structure made by human beings.

---

77. Cf. most recently Pervo, *Acts*, 191, who asserts that "on the bases [*sic*] of vv. 48 – 50, Solomon's action must be judged a mistake."

78. E.g., Gen 9:27; 13:6; 13:12.

79. Cf. Lev 26:1, 30; Isa 2:18; 10:11; 16:12; 19:1; 21:9; 31:7; 46:6; Dan 5:4, 23; 6:28; Jdt 8:18; Wis 14:8; Philo, *Moses* 1.303; 2.88, 165, 168.

80. Cf. Josephus, *J. W.* 1.419; 7.294; *Ant.* 15.324; Philo, *Moses* 2.51.

81. Marshall, "Acts," 568, correcting his earlier view (Marshall, *Acts*, 146). Cf. Evans, "Prophecy and Polemic," 197.

82. Gaventa, *Acts*, 129.

83. Cf. Gen 14:18, 19, 22 and in other Old Testament texts. Luke uses the term often, cf. Luke 1:32, 35, 76; 6:35; 8:28; Acts 16:17.

Stephen's statement that God cannot and must not be confined to one particular structure built by humans rests not only on Solomon's words during the dedication of the temple (1 Kgs 8:27, 30) but also on the words of Isaiah in Isa 66:1 – 2, where God emphasizes, as the context in Isa 66 indicates, that he wants "humble obedience from his people rather than the building of an elaborate temple and the offering of sacrifices that are no better than the abominable practices of other people if unaccompanied by full obedience to him."[84] Note the continuation of v. 2 in Isa 66: "These are the ones I look on with favor: those who are humble and contrite in spirit, and who tremble at my word" (Isa 66:2b). Stephen does not accuse Israel of wrongly worshiping God in a temple of wood and stone. He emphasizes that the people of Israel misunderstand worship as taking place in a man-made structure while failing to see that God has created everything and thus demands full obedience expressed in repentance and in humble acceptance of God's revelation.

Stephen emphasizes that it is not he who denigrates the temple but the Jewish leaders, who abase the temple by thinking they have God at their command. They fail to use the temple as a place for a dynamic encounter with the living God. He is not the one who speaks against God but the Jewish leaders, who offend God by failing to understand his transcendence of which the temple is only a sign, and by failing to grasp the full extent of what God demands from them — which now includes, most critically, believing in Jesus as the one who rules on David's throne at God's right hand and who fulfills God's promises for the last days. This is Stephen's point, the main point of his speech, as the following verses demonstrate.

7:51 You stubborn people, uncircumcised in hearts and ears, you are always resisting the Holy Spirit; just as your fathers did, so do you (σκληροτράχηλοι καὶ ἀπερίτμητοι καρδίαις καὶ τοῖς ὠσίν, ὑμεῖς ἀεὶ τῷ πνεύματι τῷ ἁγίῳ ἀντιπίπτετε ὡς οἱ πατέρες ὑμῶν καὶ ὑμεῖς). The sixth section of Stephen's speech formulates an indictment of the Jewish people for not recognizing that Jesus is the promised Messiah (vv. 51 – 53). True worship means acceptance of God's revelation and obedience to God's words — communicated through Moses (v. 38), through the prophets (vv. 49 – 50, 51 – 52a-b), and now through Jesus (v. 52c-d).

Throughout his review of Israel's history, Stephen has noted the resistance of the people of Israel to Yahweh — Joseph was sold into Egypt by the patriarchs (v. 9), Moses was pushed aside by the Israelites before the exodus (vv. 27 – 28, 35) and after the exodus (v. 39), and God was abandoned by the Israelites who worshiped other gods (vv. 40 – 43). This recalcitrant condition continues to characterize the behavior of the Jewish people in the present. Stephen employs Old Testament language used in critiques of Israel's behavior from the time of Moses to the later prophets as he formulates the following accusations against the Jewish leaders and the Jewish people as a whole, who resist God's new revelation in Jesus, the promised Righteous One, just as their "fathers" had done.

First, the members of the Sanhedrin and the Jewish people whom they represent are "stubborn" or "stiff-necked people," (σκληροτράχηλοι), a characteristic they share with the Israelites during the exodus and the wilderness wanderings.[85] Stephen points out that they refuse to yield to the presence of God beyond the temple, in the Righteous One (cf. v. 52).

---

84. Marshall, "Acts," 569.

85. The Greek term σκληροτράχηλος reproduces the Hebrew phrase meaning "hard in neck," which describes "people who refuse to attend or yield" (M. Zipor, "קָשָׁה," TDOT, 13:192); all occurrences of the Hebrew phrase occur in the context of the episode of the golden calf, cf. Exod 32:9; 33:3, 5; 34:9; Deut 9:6, 13.

Second, the Jewish leaders are "uncircumcised" people with regard to their hearts and ears,[86] i.e., they are disobedient to Israel's covenant God, who fulfills his promises in the coming of Jesus, the Righteous One. In contrast to Abraham, who obeyed God's revelation (vv. 2 – 8) and received the covenant of circumcision (v. 8), the Jewish leaders have repudiated God's new revelation. They have failed to truly hear and accept God's word, whose promise of the coming Redeemer and Prophet like Moses (cf. vv. 35, 37) has been fulfilled in Jesus (v. 52).

Third, the Jewish leaders "resist" (ἀντιπίπτετε) the Holy Spirit. This point alludes to Isa 63:10 ("they rebelled and grieved his Holy Spirit") and echoes Num 27:14 ("the community rebelled [ἀντιπίπτειν] at the waters in the Desert of Zin"). Since Isa 63:10 is the only passage in the Old Testament (besides Ps 51:10 – 11) that refers to God's Spirit as the "Holy Spirit," Stephen seems to allude to this passage, even though he uses a different verb. In Isa 63:9 – 14 the prophet recounts the gracious deeds of the Lord, who became Israel's Savior. He points out that "in all their distress he too was distressed, and the angel of his presence saved them. In his love and mercy he redeemed them" (63:9). He challenges the people to remember the days of Moses when God "set his Holy Spirit among them" (63:11). Despite God's presence and despite the experience of God's salvation in the past, they rebelled against him and acted against his Holy Spirit. Stephen asserts that the behavior of the Jewish people in the present corresponds with Israel's behavior at the time of Moses and at the time of Isaiah, who "always" (ἀεί) disobeyed God. Not resisting the Spirit would have meant repentance, along with faith in and obedience to God's new revelation.

7:52 – 53 "Which of the prophets did your fathers not persecute? They killed those who predicted the coming of the Righteous One. Now you have become his betrayers and murderers. You are the people who received the law as transmitted by angels, but you have not observed it" (τίνα τῶν προφητῶν οὐκ ἐδίωξαν οἱ πατέρες ὑμῶν; καὶ ἀπέκτειναν τοὺς προκαταγγείλαντας περὶ τῆς ἐλεύσεως τοῦ δικαίου, οὗ νῦν ὑμεῖς προδόται καὶ φονεῖς ἐγένεσθε, οἵτινες ἐλάβετε τὸν νόμον εἰς διαταγὰς ἀγγέλων καὶ οὐκ ἐφυλάξατε). Stephen continues his indictment of the Jewish leaders with a rhetorical question, formulated in a hyperbolic manner to drive home the point.

Fourth, the people of Israel persecuted and even killed the prophets whom God sent to them (v. 52a-b). This motif is frequently found in the Old Testament;[87] Jesus mentions it as well.[88] Stephen's account of how Joseph and Moses were treated by the "fathers" prepared his listeners for this statement, which is formulated in a climactic manner to suggest that it appears to be normal for God's people to oppose the prophets whom he sent to help Israel deal with the sins of the people and their leaders. Stephen pinpoints the fate of those prophets "who predicted the coming of the Righteous One" (ὁ δίκαιος), i.e., of the Messiah (cf. 3:14).

One view suggests that since all prophets foretold in one way or another the ultimate revelation of God's salvation through the Messiah, any persecution of the prophets was always a persecution of the Messiah.[89] Stephen (Luke) probably thinks more specifically of Isaiah, who was especially remembered for having been murdered;[90] Isaiah had

---

86. Cf. Lev 26:41; Jer 4:4; 6:10; 9:26 (LXX 9:25); Ezek 44:7, 9; cf. 1QS V, 5; 1QpHab XI, 13; *Jub.* 1:7, 23.

87. Cf. 1 Kgs 18:4, 13; 19:10, 14; Jer 2:30; 26:20 – 24; 2 Chr 24:20 – 21; 36:16; Neh 9:26.

88. Cf. Matt 5:12/Luke 6:23; Matt 23:29 – 36/Luke 11:47 – 51; Matt 23:37/Luke 13:34; cf. also 1 Thess 2:15; Heb 11:36 – 38.

89. Jervell, *Apostelgeschichte*, 247.

90. See the text *Martyrdom and Ascension of Isaiah*.

predicted the suffering of the "Righteous One" as God's Servant, who would give his life as an offering for sin, who bore the sins of the many, and who thus made many righteous (Isa 53:10 – 12).

Fifth, the Jewish leaders have betrayed and murdered the Righteous One whom the prophets had announced and who had arrived in the person of Jesus (v. 52c-d). Peter earlier made a similar accusation before the Sanhedrin (3:14). The Jewish leaders are betrayers of Jesus, the Messiah, as they handed him over to Pilate, a pagan. As they convicted Jesus of blasphemy, as they took him to Pilate with the charge of being a seducer of the people, and as they demanded Jesus' execution by crucifixion, they are the "murderers" of the Messiah.

Sixth, the Jewish leaders have failed to "observe" the law that God had given them through angels (v. 53).[91] The Jewish leaders assembled in the Sanhedrin — chief priests, Sadducees, leading Pharisees, and Torah scholars — would naturally be convinced that they are paragons of Torah obedience. Stephen, however, accuses them of belonging to a people who habitually disobey God and his law. And he accuses them of having betrayed and killed Jesus, the Righteous One who came to redeem the people — an action that represents the ultimate failure to obey the law and the "living words" (v. 38) that Moses and now Jesus brought to the people. Rejection of Jesus as God's righteous Servant is tantamount to a failure to keep the law.

7:54 When they heard this, they were infuriated and gnashed their teeth at him (ἀκούοντες δὲ ταῦτα διεπρίοντο ταῖς καρδίαις αὐτῶν καὶ ἔβρυχον τοὺς ὀδόντας ἐπ᾽ αὐτόν). Before Luke recounts the end of Stephen's speech, he includes a note concerning the reaction of the members to the San-

hedrin to the accusations that Stephen has just formulated, indicting them for failing to act in accordance with God's covenant and with God's law and of having murdered the Righteous One, whose arrival the prophets had foretold. They were "infuriated," a rage that manifested itself in that they "gnashed their teeth" at Stephen. This expression describes "the enraged baring of the teeth of the mortal enemy."[92]

The members of the Sanhedrin are outraged about Stephen's accusations and, presumably, about what they would have regarded as a one-sided account of Israel's history focusing on the sins, disobedience, apostasy, pushing aside, and persecution of God's envoys. They did not interrupt his speech (it is Luke who interrupts his account of Stephen's speech with the comment in v. 54), but they want Stephen to come to a close.

7:55 – 56 But he, full of the Holy Spirit, looked intently into heaven and saw the glory of God and Jesus standing at the right hand of God. He said, "Look, I see the heavens opened and the Son of Man standing at the right hand of God!" (ὑπάρχων δὲ πλήρης πνεύματος ἁγίου ἀτενίσας εἰς τὸν οὐρανὸν εἶδεν δόξαν θεοῦ καὶ Ἰησοῦν ἑστῶτα ἐκ δεξιῶν τοῦ θεοῦ καὶ εἶπεν· ἰδοὺ θεωρῶ τοὺς οὐρανοὺς διηνοιγμένους καὶ τὸν υἱὸν τοῦ ἀνθρώπου ἐκ δεξιῶν ἑστῶτα τοῦ θεοῦ). Stephen's vision of Jesus, exalted at the right hand of God, is the conclusion of his speech. Luke's description in v. 55 is a natural inference from Stephen's concluding statement. Luke's report of Stephen's vision (v. 55) and Stephen's own description of that vision (v. 56) are in substantial agreement despite differences in formulation.

The effect is a twofold reference to the identity and role of Jesus that emphasize the significance of

---

91. On the role of the angels at the giving of the law at Mt. Sinai, see on v. 38.

92. V. Hasler, "βρύχω," *EDNT*, 1:227, with reference to Acts 7:54; Job 16:9; Pss 35:16 (LXX 34:16); 37:12 (LXX 36:12); Lam 2:16.

the content of the vision. The fact that Stephen proclaims what he sees underlines his role as a faithful witness, which is confirmed by the reference to his empowerment by the Holy Spirit (v. 55a-b). Stephen could have proclaimed the basic content of the vision — Jesus of Nazareth is the messianic Son of Man, who, after his death, was raised from the dead and exalted to the right hand of God (as Peter proclaimed on the day of Pentecost, 2:34 – 36). The fact that the fundamental assertion that Jesus had been raised from the dead and exalted to God's presence is communicated in a vision underscores its divinely vindicated validity. The report and the content of the vision emphasize the following points.

First, Jesus' identity as the exalted Son of Man is of immediate significance. This point is suggested by the introductory "look" (ἰδού, v. 56b), which corresponds to Luke's report that Stephen "looked intently into heaven" (v. 55c). During his speech, Stephen presumably looked at the members of the Sanhedrin. Now he looks upward, beyond the walls and the ceiling of the hall in which the Sanhedrin is meeting, being granted by the Holy Spirit a view of the reality of God — and he invites his listeners to look with him and acknowledge the presence of Jesus at God's right hand.

Second, Jesus is present in the reality of God's heavenly transcendence (vv. 55d, 56c). Luke reports that Stephen is granted a view into heaven (εἰς τὸν οὐρανόν), where he sees the "glory of God" (δόξαν θεοῦ), and Stephen describes his vision in terms of seeing "the heavens opened" (τοὺς οὐρανοὺς διηνοιγμένους). The "opening" of the heavens describes the event of a divine revelation (cf. 10:11) or the entry into heaven (Rev 4:1).[93] This means that the description of Jesus' position at the right hand of God is a revelation granted by God, not an inference devised by Stephen or the apostles. And it means that "the God of glory" (ὁ θεὸς τῆς δόξης), who revealed himself to Abraham and throughout Israel's history, now reveals his presence to Stephen and invites the Jewish leaders to acknowledge his glory, as it has been revealed in and through Jesus' life, death, resurrection, and exaltation.

The reference to Jesus of Nazareth in the accusations made against Stephen (6:14) and the reaction of the Jewish leaders indicate that they can recognize the reference to "the Son of Man" as a reference to Jesus. Since Jesus had been condemned by the members of the Sanhedrin and taken to Pilate, the Roman governor, with the request to execute him by crucifixion only a short time ago, the Jewish leaders would have regarded as blasphemy the proposition that Jesus can be seen in God's presence sharing the glory of God. If the Jewish leaders understood Stephen's statement as a claim that he has had a vision of God (which is not entirely clear, because the focus of Luke's summary is on Jesus), they could accuse him of claiming to see him whom not even Moses was allowed to see (Exod 33:18 – 23).

Third, Jesus is the messianic Son of Man, the exalted figure of Daniel's prophecy (Dan 7:13 – 14), "standing" at the right hand of God (vv. 55e, 56e).[94] The expression "Son of Man" (ὁ υἱὸς τοῦ ἀνθρώπου), frequent in the Gospels as a self-designation of Jesus,[95] occurs only here in Acts. The sayings about the earthly activity of the Son of Man in the Gospels emphasize Jesus' claim to full authority and majesty.[96] The link with Dan 7:13 – 14 is significant since early Jewish tradition

---

93. Cf. Marshall, "Acts," 571. On "glory" (δόξα) in connection with revelations see Luke 2:9, 14; Acts 22:11; for the "opened heavens" cf. Luke 3:21 – 22 (Jesus' baptism); Acts 10:11.

94. On the expression "at the right hand of God" see 2:25, 33.

95. The expression "Son of Man" occurs 82 times — 14 times in Mark, 30 times in Matthew, 25 times in Luke, 12 times in John, and here in Acts.

96. E.g., Matt 9:6/Mark 2:10/Luke 5:24; Luke 6:22; Matt 11:18 – 19/Luke 7:33 – 34.

attests "a figure of a heavenly man whose primary function is one of judgment and salvation, and which in isolated instances is also integrated with inner-worldly or personal expectations."[97]

At the end of his ministry, Jesus used the expression to refer to the one who has judicial authority from the right hand of God.[98] The description of Jesus as "standing" rather than as sitting at the right hand of God (cf. Ps 110:1) suggests impending action, perhaps as judge who receives Stephen's witness and vindicates his claims (cf. Luke 12:8); it implies that any rejection of Stephen's witness will be subject to the judgment of God.[99] Stephen insists that Jesus is alive, that he fulfills God's purposes for his people in his exalted position at the right hand of God, and that he marks the space of true worship.[100]

7:57 They shouted with a loud voice, stopped their ears, and rushed at him together (κράξαντες δὲ φωνῇ μεγάλῃ συνέσχον τὰ ὦτα αὐτῶν καὶ ὥρμησαν ὁμοθυμαδὸν ἐπ᾽ αὐτόν). The members of the Sanhedrin interrupt Stephen as he describes his vision of the risen and exalted Jesus standing in the presence of God. Luke describes their reaction with three verbs in the aorist tense: they "shouted" (κράξαντες), they "stopped" or "covered" (συνέσχον) their ears,[101] and they "rushed" (ὥρμησαν) at him. This marks the end of the interrogation.

The fact that they cover their ears suggests that in their view a blasphemy has been uttered, for to them no human being has the right to share the glory of God at God's right hand.[102] According to Philo, blasphemy was an insult to the pious, "who immediately feel an indescribable and irreconcilable affliction, which enters in at their ears and pervades the whole soul" (Philo, *Decalogue* 63). For Stephen, however, the fact that the Jewish leaders cover their ears would confirm his earlier point that they are uncircumcised in their ears (v. 51) — they refuse to listen to and acknowledge the truth about the revelation of Jesus.

Since the Jewish leaders reject the claims of the Twelve and of preachers like Stephen concerning Jesus' identity, status, and significance, their reaction is understandable. But Luke's characterization of these leaders signals that they have no convincing arguments with which to rebut Stephen's explanations. People who shout and who put their hands over their ears look more like children than experienced lawmakers and judges. As before, Luke shows his readers that the Jewish leaders who oppose the followers of Jesus are unable to produce convincing counterarguments, let alone plausible accusations; they resort again "to noise, anger, and violence; their weapon is heat, not light."[103]

Many scholars interpret the end of Stephen's interrogation at this point as an indication that the Sanhedrin did not proceed to an ordinary conclusion of the trial with a proper verdict followed by an announced execution (which the Sanhedrin could not carry out at this time), and that Stephen's death was a lynch killing.[104] This interpretation seems to require that the subject of the expression

---

97. F. Hahn, "υἱός," *EDNT*, 3:388.

98. Cf. Matt 26:64; Mark 14:62; Luke 22:69. As regards the authenticity of these passages, cf. Darrell L. Bock, *Blasphemy and Exaltation in Judaism: The Charge against Jesus in Mark 14:53 – 56* (orig. 1998; repr., Grand Rapids: Baker, 2000), 220 – 30.

99. Cf. Witherington, *Acts*, 275; Bock, *Acts*, 311 – 12. Some suggest that the "standing" of the Son of Man means his readiness to receive Stephen, or his role as witness of Stephen's martyrdom.

100. Cf. Sleeman, *Geography*, 165.

101. The verb translated as "stopped" (συνέχω) can be understood literally (they cover their ears with their hands) or metaphorically (they refuse to listen).

102. Cf. Alan F. Segal, *Two Powers in Heaven: Early Rabbinic Reports about Christianity and Gnosticism* (SJLA 25; Leiden: Brill, 1977), 94 – 95.

103. Neagoe, *Trial*, 169.

104. Recently Schwartz, "Trial Scene," 122, assuming that "the trial ends with a shocking form of mass violence."

translated as "rushed at him" is an uncontrollable mob, a point that is seldom discussed. It is difficult to imagine that the members of the Sanhedrin would turn into an uncontrollable mob — after having successfully tried Jesus and after heeding Gamaliel's counsel at an earlier hearing.

It is preferable, therefore, to interpret Luke's description in the sense that the Sanhedrin trial was not interrupted but ended "in a violent killing of Stephen in an act of establishment violence" as a "legally legitimate killing of an irregular nature by those present."[105] Even though capital punishments were the prerogative of the governor in a Roman province (cf. John 18:31), the law was not always followed, particularly if the provincial elites could argue (if held accountable for their action) that they were maintaining order in the province threatened by teachings that violated the ancestral laws in the most serious manner.

7:58 They dragged him out of the city and began to throw stones. The witnesses laid their robes at the feet of a young man named Saul (καὶ ἐκβαλόντες ἔξω τῆς πόλεως ἐλιθοβόλουν. καὶ οἱ μάρτυρες ἀπέθεντο τὰ ἱμάτια αὐτῶν παρὰ τοὺς πόδας νεανίου καλουμένου Σαύλου). The members of the Sanhedrin proceed to execute Stephen (7:58 – 8:1). Luke's report of Stephen's death has two parts.

First, Stephen is transferred from the hall in which the Sanhedrin held its meeting to a place outside the city, probably by the temple police mentioned in 5:22, perhaps by the captain of the temple mentioned in 5:26 in connection with the arrest of the apostles. Executions by stoning were carried out outside the city (Lev 24:14; Num 15:35;

cf. *m. Sanh.* 6:1). Stephen might have been taken from the Sanhedrin building adjacent to the western wall of the Temple Mount (near Wilson's Arch) along the main street in the Tyropoeon Valley past the Pool of Siloam to the gate in the southern wall of the city to the Hinnom or Kidron Valley. Or he could have been taken across the Upper City past Herod's palace (the Praetorium) through a gate in the western city wall, perhaps to the site where executions took place — perhaps to the very location of Jesus' crucifixion.

Second, Stephen is stoned (ἐλιθοβόλουν, vv. 58b – 59a).[106] The imperfect tense of this verb, repeated twice, indicates that the throwing of stones (λίθοι) went on for some time. In the law, stoning was prescribed as the death penalty for the following offenses: worshiping pagan gods (Lev 20:2 – 5; Deut 17:2 – 7), prophesying in the name of a pagan god (Deut 13:2 – 6), divination (Lev 20:27), blasphemy (Lev 24:14 – 16), violation of the Sabbath (Num 15:32 – 36), adultery (Deut 22:22), and refusal to submit to one's parents (Deut 21:18 – 21). Since Stephen had been accused of uttering blasphemous words against Moses (the law) and God (the temple), he is stoned on account of the perceived blasphemy (6:11, 14).

"The witnesses" (οἱ μάρτυρες) who had heard Stephen utter words they deemed blasphemous — members of the Sanhedrin — execute him, throwing the first stones (cf. Deut 17:7). The comment about the witnesses removing their robes probably means nothing more than that they prepare themselves for a strenuous activity during which their outer garments might get soiled with the blood of the victim. According to *m. Sanh.* 6:4 it is the

---

105. Torrey Seland, *Establishment Violence in Philo and Luke: A Study of Non-Conformity to the Torah and Jewish Vigilante Reactions* (Biblical Interpretation 15; Leiden: Brill, 1995), 241, 242, who regards this as a variant of a lynching or vigilante killing, the latter being carried out by a mob, the former being

carried out by the establishment in a legal context.

106. The verb λιθοβολέω is also used in Matt 23:37/Luke 13:34; Matt 21:35; Heb 12:20. The synonymous term λιθάζω is used in Acts 5:26; 14:19; cf. John 8:5; 10:31, 32, 33; 11:8; 2 Cor 11:25; Heb 11:37.

person to be stoned who has to remove his clothes; this may well have happened here too, although Luke does not mention it.

The fact that Luke mentions the name of the person who guards the clothes of the executioners indicates that he will have much more to say about Saul (Σαῦλος). He is described as a "young man" (νεανίας), a term that covers the age from about eighteen to thirty years (see on 2:17). If Stephen was executed in AD 31, Paul would have probably been born in the first decade of the first century AD.[107] His description as a young man is not meant to absolve him from participation in Stephen's execution. Even though he evidently did not throw stones, he accompanied the executioners, either as one of the witnesses or as the assistant of one of the members of the Sanhedrin, and he agreed with those who argued for and carried out Stephen's execution (8:1). In Acts 9:1 – 2 Luke emphasizes Saul's proactive initiatives in the persecution and execution of the followers of Jesus.[108]

7:59 As they kept stoning Stephen, he called out and prayed, "Lord Jesus, receive my spirit" (καὶ ἐλιθοβόλουν τὸν Στέφανον ἐπικαλούμενον καὶ λέγοντα· κύριε Ἰησοῦ, δέξαι τὸ πνεῦμά μου). Luke describes the dying of Stephen in some detail. As members of the Sanhedrin kept pelting Stephen with stones, he "called out." The verb does not connote crying out in pain, but calling on someone for a particular purpose. Stephen calls on the Lord and thus assures himself of his presence, as he is about to die. Then he prays, addressing his prayer to the "Lord Jesus" (κύριε Ἰησοῦ), the risen and exalted Jesus standing at the right hand of God in heaven.[109] He prays that Jesus may receive his

spirit, similar to Jesus' prayer, who had committed his spirit to the Father (Luke 23:46).

Stephen, who had proclaimed Jesus in the synagogues of Jerusalem and before the Jewish leaders in the Sanhedrin, affirms his faith in Jesus as the risen and exalted Savior one final time before he dies. Jesus' prayer cites and Stephen's prayer echoes Ps 31:5 (LXX 30:6), where a person who is oppressed and who suffers expresses his confidence that God will preserve his life; it is "not a statement that simply accepts the end of life, but one that also works with the fact that God can and will continue to give us life."[110] Stephen affirms that even though he is about to die, his life will continue in the presence of the Lord Jesus.

7:60 He knelt down and shouted with a loud voice, "Lord, do not hold this sin against them." When he had said this, he passed away (θεὶς δὲ τὰ γόνατα ἔκραξεν φωνῇ μεγάλῃ· κύριε, μὴ στήσῃς αὐτοῖς ταύτην τὴν ἁμαρτίαν. καὶ τοῦτο εἰπὼν ἐκοιμήθη). After he has affirmed his faith in Jesus, confidently committing the continuation of his life after his imminent death to Jesus, he "kneels down," having managed to stand upright up to this point. Bending his knees is here not a sign of respect for the members of the Sanhedrin. It is either a posture in prayer, or, in the final stages of the execution, the result of injuries sustained in the course of the stoning.

Kneeling, Stephen "shouted" with a loud voice, praying. His last words formulate a petition to the Lord (probably Jesus, as in v. 59), asking him to pardon those stoning him. The "sin" (ἁμαρτία) is the sin of executing a witness of Jesus who has spoken the truth about Jesus' resurrection and exaltation.

---

107. In Phlm 9, written in the Roman imprisonment between AD 60 – 62, Paul calls himself an "old man" (πρεσβύτης), i.e., fifty years and older.

108. Cf. Paul's own references to his activity as a persecutor of the followers of Jesus in Gal 1:13, 23; cf. 1 Cor 15:9; Phil 3:6.

109. Bauckham, *Jesus and the God of Israel*, 128 – 29, points out that "since Jesus was understood as the active mediator of grace from God ... and as the Lord for whose service Christians lived, prayer addressed to him was natural."

110. Goldingay, *Psalms*, 1:450.

The verb translated as "hold" refers either to legal enforcement (of the penalty for their sin of executing an innocent man), or to the record or balance sheet (in which their sin will be entered). In praying for the Lord's forgiveness for his executioners, Stephen follows Jesus' command to pray for those who abuse you (Luke 6:27 – 28), and he follows Jesus' example on the cross (Luke 23:34). Since Saul, guarding the clothes of the executioners, was later converted to faith in Jesus, Stephen's prayer was answered. Stephen's death is described with a verb (ἐκοιμήθη) that means literally "to fall asleep," an expression often used for the sleep of death.[111]

8:1 Saul approved of this killing. On that day a great persecution began against the church in Jerusalem. All were scattered throughout the countryside of Judea and Samaria, except the apostles (Σαῦλος δὲ ἦν συνευδοκῶν τῇ ἀναιρέσει αὐτοῦ. ἐγένετο δὲ ἐν ἐκείνῃ τῇ ἡμέρᾳ διωγμὸς μέγας ἐπὶ τὴν ἐκκλησίαν τὴν ἐν Ἱεροσολύμοις, πάντες δὲ διεσπάρησαν κατὰ τὰς χώρας τῆς Ἰουδαίας καὶ Σαμαρείας πλὴν τῶν ἀποστόλων). Stephen's interrogation and execution results in a persecution of the followers of Jesus in Jerusalem with far-reaching consequences, reported in the fourth and final incident (8:1 – 3) of Luke's account of the ministry, trial, and death of Stephen (6:8 – 8:3).[112] After the brief introduction of Saul in 7:58 as a participant in Steven's execution, Luke notes Saul's ongoing approval of what had happened (v. 1a), which explains why Saul is actively and fiercely involved in the persecution of the followers of Jesus in Jerusalem and beyond (v. 3; 9:1 – 2).

Luke gives a summary account of the persecu-

tion in 8:1b-c. The following details are important. (1) The term "persecution" (διωγμός) refers to "a program or process designed to harass and oppress someone" (BDAG).

(2) It was a "severe" or "great" (μέγας) persecution that affected the entire Jerusalem church. This means, in the context of Acts 4 – 5, that the persecution went beyond the arrests and interrogations of which the apostles had so far been the target.

(3) The persecution "began" on the day that Stephen was executed, and it continued for some time (cf. v. 3).

(4) The program of suppressing the activities of the followers of Jesus was directed against the entire congregation of believers living in Jerusalem. Luke states that "all" (πάντες) believers were affected; v. 3 suggests that the persecution went on for some time.

(5) The Jerusalem believers were "scattered," i.e., the congregation was broken up as the individual believers were driven out of Jerusalem in all directions in random fashion.

(6) The believers from Jerusalem sought refuge in towns and villages in the countryside of Judea and of Samaria — perhaps staying with other believers or with relatives. Luke does not address the question of what happened to the impoverished believers of the Jerusalem congregation, especially the widows from a diaspora background.

(7) The statement "except the apostles" (πλὴν τῶν ἀποστόλων, v. 1i) should not be taken to mean that only the Greek-speaking believers (such as Philip and the believers mentioned and implied in 6:1 – 6) were affected by the persecution, while

111. Cf. Acts 13:36; 1 Cor 7:39; 11:30; 15:6, 51; 2 Pet 3:4; also in the LXX: Gen 47:30; Deut 31:16; Isa 14:8, and in secular Greek, cf. Homer, *Il.* 11.241. The expression is perhaps not merely a euphemism but describes, from a human standpoint, what deceased people "do" before the day of the resurrection.

112. Most scholars, and English translations, link 8:1a with the preceding section, which narrates Stephen's death. While

this is certainly correct, matters are complicated by the fact that 8:2, which relates Stephen's burial, should then be included in the previous section as well. The reference to Saul in 8:3 links this brief comment on the persecution of Christians in Jerusalem with the execution of Stephen, in which Saul played a role (7:58); it thus seems preferable to include 8:1 – 3 in the aftermath of Stephen's death.

the Hebrew/Aramaic-speaking Christians were spared.[113] This is historically unlikely, given the leadership role of the Twelve and the common theological convictions in the one "congregation" in Jerusalem. Luke does not state that the apostles were exempt from the persecution, nor does he assert that they were not attacked or put under pressure by the Jewish authorities.

Luke's subsequent report indicates that many prominent members of the Jerusalem church, particularly Greek-speaking believers, permanently settled in other regions of the country — such as Philip, who moved to Samaria (8:5) and later settled in Caesarea (8:40), and the unnamed believers who settled in Phoenicia, Cyprus, and Antioch (11:19 – 20). The Twelve, however, remained the leaders of the Jerusalem church, for the time being (see on 12:17). The formulation of v. 1i allows for the possibility that the Twelve left Jerusalem for a short time and returned later, or that they were arrested just like other believers (v. 3) but were eventually released. One can thus conclude that "all that Luke maintains is that the persecution did not bring their leadership of the Jerusalem church to an end."[114]

8:2 Devout men buried Stephen and mourned him publicly (συνεκόμισαν δὲ τὸν Στέφανον ἄνδρες εὐλαβεῖς καὶ ἐποίησαν κοπετὸν μέγαν ἐπ᾽ αὐτῷ). Stephen received a proper burial. It is unclear who the "devout men" (ἄνδρες εὐλαβεῖς) were who buried Stephen. Had they been believers, Luke would have said so, referring to "brothers." The term may refer to Jews who sympathized with the Christian message.[115] Some suggest that the expression could refer to friends of Stephen among the Essene community living in Jerusalem.[116] We do not know if the rabbinic stipulations that prescribed limited funeral rites for executed criminals — prohibiting public lamentation (often accompanied by breast-beating) for a person executed by stoning (*m. Sanh.* 6:5 – 6) — were in force in the first half of the first century. If so, the "great lamentation" (lit. trans. of κοπετὸν μέγαν) may have been a public protest by the people who buried Stephen and who disagreed with what the Jewish authorities had done.

8:3 Saul continued to cause harm to the church, entering house after house and dragging out both men and women, whom he put into prison (Σαῦλος δὲ ἐλυμαίνετο τὴν ἐκκλησίαν κατὰ τοὺς οἴκους εἰσπορευόμενος, σύρων τε ἄνδρας καὶ γυναῖκας παρεδίδου εἰς φυλακήν). Saul became actively and vigorously involved in attempts to suppress the followers of Jesus. Having witnessed Stephen's execution and agreeing that he needed to be eliminated, Saul "continued to cause harm" to the congregation of believers in Jesus.[117] In his letters Paul confirms that he persecuted the church (Gal 1:13; Phil 3:6).

Two present participles, which underline the persistent nature of his activities, describe how

---

113. Thus Martin Hengel and Anna Maria Schwemer, *Paul between Damascus and Antioch: The Unknown Years* (London/Louisville: SCM/Westminster John Knox, 1997), 137.

114. Richard J. Bauckham, "James and the Jerusalem Church," in *The Book of Acts in Its Palestinian Setting* (ed. R. J. Bauckham), 415 – 80, 429.

115. Barrett, *Acts*, 392, "'good' Jews who if not already Christians are ready to be persuaded." Note that according to Luke 23:50, Joseph of Arimathea, who arranged Jesus' burial, is described as "a good and upright man" (ἀνὴρ ἀγαθὸς καὶ δίκαιος).

116. Cf. Rainer Riesner, "Das Jerusalemer Essenerviertel und die Urgemeinde," *ANRW* II.26.2 (1995): 1775 – 1922, 1862 – 63.

117. The imperfect of the verb λυμαίνω ("to cause harm to, injure, damage, spoil, ruin, destroy") emphasizes the ongoing activity of Saul as persecutor of the believers; if translated as "to destroy," the tense should be understood as a conative imperfect, which denotes the attempt to achieve a goal — he "tried" or "began to destroy" (NIV, TNIV) or "began ravaging" (NASB) the church. The translation offered in BDAG, "Saul was making it hard for the [Christian] community" is an understatement — Paul sought to eliminate Christians from "circulation" by arresting them (v. 3; 9:13) and by trying to have them executed (9:1; 26:10).

Saul caused harm among the believers. He "entered" one house after another in which the believers were meeting, the "houses" (οἶκοι) being the private residences of believers in which a group of believers met (cf. 5:42; 12:12). And he "dragged" away believers, irrespective of their gender, by force. The concluding phrase "he put them into prison" (παρεδίδου εἰς φυλακήν), formulated in the imperfect tense to emphasize an ongoing activity, was in preparation for an interrogation and a sentence. Since the ban on speaking issued earlier (4:18; 5:40) had proven ineffective, the juridical sentence that Saul and his associates had in mind probably ranged from flogging (the forty lashes minus one; see on 5:40) to the death sentence.

The description of Saul's activity as a persecutor suggests two things. First, the house churches in Jerusalem were not only meeting places for believers who kept to themselves, but centers of teaching and evangelism where believers actively proclaimed the gospel and attracted new converts. Second, the persecution that followed Stephen's execution was organized. Jews connected with the Sanhedrin moved against the believers with a specific plan, tracking down their meeting places and arresting believers in their private residences with the aim of forcing them to abandon their religious convictions or of eliminating them altogether by throwing them into prison, by having them executed, or by forcing them to leave the city.

Why did Saul persecute the followers of Jesus? The most plausible explanation recognizes that Saul would have regarded the proclamation of a crucified Messiah as utterly despicable, indeed blasphemous. He was convinced that believing Jews — who devoted their lives to Jesus, who believed that the crucified man from Nazareth had come back to life, and who taught that he had been exalted into heaven as Lord and Savior at the right hand of God — could not be allowed to proclaim these convictions to others. He was convinced that Jesus was under God's curse: according to Deut 21:22 – 23, "If someone guilty of a capital offense is put to death and their body is exposed on a pole," that person is under God's curse (cf. Gal 3:13).

Paul obviously disagreed with Gamaliel's advice (5:34 – 39), convinced that active and decisive measures needed to be taken to stop the activities of these people. Pious and educated Jews who rejected the claims of the followers of Jesus were convinced that belief in Jesus as Messiah and in the atoning efficacy of his death on the cross put into question the foundations of Torah obedience as the basis of salvation of God's people.

Theology in Application

The long section in which Luke describes Stephen's interrogation, defense, conviction, and execution and the aftermath of the persecution of the believers in Jerusalem (7:2 – 8:3) provides an opportunity to probe several important matters: the continuity of the church with Israel, the continuity of the Jewish people with the people of Israel in past times who disobeyed God and who pushed aside God's envoys, the continuity of the church with a people whose history is marked by the tension of obedience and disobedience, and, last but not least, the life, the courage, and the death of true witnesses of Jesus and the reality of persecution.

The Continuity of the Church with Israel

As Stephen is interrogated about his convictions, he responds with a long review of the history of Israel. This could be regarded as a response that fits the context, since Stephen stands before the Jewish leaders in the Sanhedrin. However, from the fact that the early Christians relied on the Old Testament as their Scriptures, and from the fact that many foundational terms, metaphors, and convictions are used in the New Testament to describe the transformative salvation that has become a reality through Jesus Christ, there is an obviously fundamental continuity between Israel and the church. When we relate this continuity to the history of Israel that Stephen summarizes in Acts 7, three basic points emerge.

(1) The revelation and salvation that characterized the history of God's people since Abraham explain God's revelation and salvation through Jesus and thus characterize the history of God's people ever since. Stephen recounts Israel's history in order to explain, among other things, the climactic fulfillment of God's promises in Jesus, the messianic Son of Man who is the Prophet-Redeemer like Moses. The life, death, resurrection, and exaltation of Jesus is the new foundation and center of the life of God's people — since the promises given to Abraham have been fulfilled, since the redemption effected by his death supersedes the redemption that God provided at the time of Joseph and Moses, and since the function of the tabernacle and of the temple as places of God's presence has been absorbed by Jesus, the exalted Son of Man who works on behalf of his people from his position at the right hand of God.

But Jesus' significance cannot be properly understood if we do not understand God's promises to Abraham, God's intervention at the time of Joseph, God's redemption at the time of Moses through the exodus from Egypt, God's revelation at Mount Sinai, and God's worship in the tabernacle and in the temple. Since Jesus has a dramatically increasing number of people who follow him and who constitute the "congregation" of God's people in the present time (both in the first century and today), they claim Israel's history as their own history. Paul's arguments in Rom 4 indicate that this is true even for Gentile Christians — Abraham is their "father" also, and God's promises to Abraham and his redemption in the exodus inform their self-understanding as the people of God just as in the case of Jewish Christians.

(2) Stephen's review of Israel's behavior in the past and his indictment of the behavior of the Jewish leaders in his own time demonstrate Israel's need for salvation. Despite repeated arrests of the apostles, the Jerusalem believers never gave up on the Jewish people. As God never abandoned Israel despite the repeated disobedience, idolatry, and apostasy of his people, and as the earliest followers of Jesus in Jerusalem did not give up on their fellow Jews despite the persecution, so Christians today need to persist in their witness to the Jewish people.

(3) If Israel's history is the history of the church, written in the Scriptures for our instruction (Rom 15:4; cf. 1 Cor 10:1 – 10), then Israel's disobedience, apostasy,

and rejection of God's envoys serve as a warning for Christians. The fact that the patriarchs were capable of selling their brother into slavery, that the Israelites pushed Moses away and worshiped a golden calf, and that the Jewish leaders misunderstood the reality of God's presence forces us to reflect on the sins that Christians and churches have committed, on the rejection or marginalization of leaders who called the church to repentance and reform, and on the attempt to manipulate God through various programs. As Stephen could tell Israel's history as the ambiguous reality of blessing and curse, of salvation and judgment, so the history of the church is the history of God's glorious intervention and, at the same time, of abject human failure.

The Persecution of the Jerusalem Believers

Stephen is the first witness (μάρτυς) in the church who died for his confession of faith in Jesus, the crucified, risen, and exalted Lord and Savior. An authentic witness of Jesus is a person full of the Holy Spirit willing to serve at tables (6:1 – 6), active in proclaiming Jesus Christ (6:8 – 10), unfazed by opposition (6:11 – 14), capable of explaining the significance and meaning of the gospel (7:2 – 56), unwilling to compromise his convictions (7:51 – 53), willing to die for his faith (which he regards as more precious than his own life, 7:57 – 60), and loving people who have not yet accepted the gospel, including his enemies (7:60). What Luke emphasizes is not Stephen's courage but the presence of the Holy Spirit in his life (6:10; 7:55).

CHAPTER 17

Acts 8:4 – 25

Literary Context

In the first main section of Acts (1:15 – 8:3), Luke wrote about the beginnings of the new people of God. He described the identity and the witness of Jesus' followers as God's people (1:15 – 2:47) and the life, witness, trials, and growth of the church in Jerusalem, focusing on the ministry of Peter (3:1 – 8:3). The last part of this section dealt with the ministry, trial, and death of Stephen (6:8 – 8:3), one of the seven Greek-speaking Jewish believers chosen to assist the needy widows of the church, who actively proclaimed the gospel of Jesus, the crucified, risen, and exalted Messiah and his significance for the faith and life of the people of Israel. While Luke briefly noted that the activities of the apostles reached beyond Jerusalem (5:16), he had not described any missionary travels of the apostles or of other believers beyond Jerusalem.

This should not be interpreted as disobedience on the part of the apostles, who had been commissioned by Jesus to go from Jerusalem to Judea, Samaria, and the ends of the earth (1:8). Three points are important. (1) The evidence shows that the Twelve received, understood, planned, organized, and carried out Jesus' commission to "international" missionary work.[1]

(2) It was presumably the immense and continuous growth of the congregation in Jerusalem, numbering in the thousands, that kept them initially in the capital. The note in 5:16 suggests that the apostles traveled to other towns at least in Judea. Since Luke's reporting is selective and he does not comment on the activities of any of the apostles besides Peter, we have no way of knowing whether some of the apostles left Jerusalem to travel to Galilee and preach there, organizing the earlier followers of Jesus into local congregations. While this possibility is hypothetical, we should not assume that what Luke does not report did not happen. Also, we should not forget that if Stephen's death dates to the year 32, the leadership of the Jerusalem church focused their outreach on the Jewish capital for two years before they had to leave the city, some of them perhaps permanently.

---

1. Cf. Schnabel, *Early Christian Mission*, 2:519 – 33, 670 – 72, 729 – 910. On missionary work in Galilee, see ibid., 747 – 64.

(3) From a literary point of view, there is no doubt that Luke commences his report about the beginnings of the mission to the Gentiles (8:4 – 12:25) in connection with the persecution that scattered believers in Jerusalem. However, since his characterization of the apostles and of other leading believers such as Stephen was consistently and thoroughly positive, it is a mistake to censure the leaders of the Jerusalem church for not engaging in missionary outreach to areas outside of Jerusalem and Judea. Thus, it is incorrect from both a literary and a historical point of view to assume that it was the persecution after Stephen's execution that forced the Jerusalem believers to leave the city and take the gospel elsewhere.

While the Samaritans are not Gentiles, the episode that reports their conversion (8:4 – 25) belongs to the second major section entitled "The Beginning of the Mission to Gentiles" (8:4 – 12:25). The persecution after Stephen's execution and the dispersal of Jerusalem believers to regions outside of Judea mark a break in Luke's narrative and signal a new phase of missionary outreach. After the gospel was preached in Jerusalem (1:15 – 8:3) and in Judea (5:16),[2] Luke narrates the move of the gospel to regions outside of Jerusalem, from Samaria to Syria. The major section 8:4 – 12:25 consists of five sections:

- the mission of Philip to Samaritans and the conversion of an Ethiopian (8:4 – 40)
- the conversion of Saul, who is called to preach to Jews and Gentiles (9:1 – 30)
- the mission of Peter in Judea and in Caesarea, where a Gentile officer of the Roman army is converted (9:31 – 11:18)
- the mission in Antioch, the capital of the Roman province of Syria (11:19 – 30)
- the persecution by Herod Agrippa I, which forces Peter to leave Jerusalem permanently (12:1 – 25)

The message of Jesus Christ thus moves from Jerusalem and Judea to Samaria and to Gentiles in Caesarea and Antioch. The concurrence of opposition and persecution on the one hand, and of missionary activity in new areas on the other hand, constitutes a pattern that frequently characterizes Luke's subsequent narrative. Opposition does not stop the missionary work of the followers of Jesus, but prompts them to move to regions and towns in which the gospel of Jesus Christ has not yet been proclaimed.

The section that relates the mission of Philip to the Samaritans and the conversion of an Ethiopian (8:4 – 40) consists of two episodes. Luke first reports on Philip's mission in Samaria (8:4 – 25) and then his encounter with an Ethiopian official (8:26 – 40).

---

2. On two occasions Paul mentions, in passing, that there were "churches" (ἐκκλησίαι) in Judea (Gal 1:22; 1 Thess 2:14). On missionary work in Judea, cf. Schnabel, *Early Christian Mission*, 2:738 – 47.

Main Idea

In his report about Philip's mission among the Samaritans, Luke emphasizes that missionaries are willing to preach in areas where they cannot expect sympathy, that they are not intimidated by local celebrities or magical practices, that confessions of faith do not preclude serious theological misunderstanding, that the gift of the Holy Spirit is linked (at this stage) with the apostles and cannot be manipulated, and that conversions result in the reconciliation of previously hostile groups and (in this case) in the revitalization of Israel.

Translation

(See next two pages.)

Structure and Literary Form

The four incidents that make up the bulk of the episode of Philip's missionary work among the Samaritans (8:4 – 25) describe the proclamation of the gospel by Philip among the Samaritans (8:5 – 11), the conversion of Samaritan people, including Simon (8:12 – 13), the arrival of Peter and John and the gift of the Holy Spirit (8:14 – 17), and the confrontation between Peter and Simon (8:18 – 24).

The episode is another *historical narrative*. It begins and ends with a *summary statement* that, in each case, emphasizes the expanding missionary work of the church in areas outside of Jerusalem, namely, in Judea and in Samaria (vv. 1, 4, 25). There is a summary report of *miracles* (v. 7), but Luke does not include a miracle story. In v. 4 Luke reports the missionary work of believers who flee Jerusalem and proclaim the word of God as they travel from place to place.[3] In v. 25 Luke reports the missionary work of Peter and John in many Samaritan villages as they travel back to

---

3. The expression μὲν οὖν marks 8:4 as the beginning of a
new section; cf. Barrett, *Acts*, 400.

Acts 8:4 – 25

4a	Action	**Those who were scattered traveled from place to place**
b	Action	and **proclaimed the word.**
5a	Action/Place	
	(Character entrance)	**Philip went to a city of Samaria**
b	Action	and **proclaimed the Messiah**
c		to the people.
6a	Action	**The crowds paid close attention**
b	Object	to what Philip said
c	Circumstance	as they listened and
d	Circumstance	as they saw the signs
e	Agency	that he performed.
7a	Event	**Unclean spirits came out of many that were possessed,**
b	Manner	shrieking loudly.
c	Event	**Many who were paralyzed or**
d	List	**crippled**
e		**were cured.**
8	Event/Result	So **there was great joy in that city.**
9a	Character entrance	Now **a man named Simon had been practicing magic**
b	Place	in that city
c	Description	and **amazed the people of Samaria,**
d	Indirect speech	saying that he was someone great.
10a	Description	**All the people,**
b	Sphere	from the least to the greatest,
c	Acclamation	**paid attention to him,** saying,
d	Assertion	*"This man is the Power of God called Great."*
11a	Description	**They paid attention to him**
b	Explanation	because he had amazed them
c	Duration	for a long time
d	Means	with his magic.
12a	Setting: Time (Contrast)	But when they believed Philip,
b	Description	who proclaimed the good news about the kingdom of God and
c	Description	the name of Jesus the Messiah,
d	Action	**they were baptized,**
e	Sphere	both men and women.
13a	Action	Even **Simon himself came to faith**
b	Action	and **was baptized.**
c	Action	**He attached himself to Philip**
d	Description	and **was amazed**
e	Cause	when he saw the signs and great miracles that took place.
14a	Setting: Time	When the apostles in Jerusalem heard
b	Report	that Samaria had accepted the word of God,
c	Action	**they sent Peter and**
d	List	**John**
e	Social/Place	**to the people there.**

Continued on next page.

Continued from previous page.

15a	Setting: Time		When they arrived,
b	Action		**they prayed for them**
c	Purpose		that they might receive the Holy Spirit,
16a	Cause		because the Spirit had not yet come upon any of them,
b	Cause		as they had only been baptized in the 🕊 name of the Lord Jesus.
17a	Action		**Then Peter and John laid their hands on them,**
b	Result		**and they received the Holy Spirit**.
18a	Setting: Time/Event		When Simon saw that the Spirit was given
b	Means		through the laying on of the apostles' hands,
c	Action		**he offered them money**
19a	Action		**and said,**
b	Entreaty		*"Give me that power too*
c	Sphere		*so that anyone …*
d	Means		*on whom I lay my hands*
e	Result		*… may receive the Holy Spirit."*
20a	Reaction		**But Peter said to him,**
b	Prophecy/Warning		*"May your money perish with you,*
c	Cause		*because you thought*
d	Character's thoughts		*you could buy the gift of God*
e	Means		*with money!*
21a	Assertion		*You have no part or share in this matter,*
b	Cause		*for your heart is not right in God's sight.*
22a	Command		*Repent of this wickedness*
b	Command		*and ask the Lord*
c	Purpose		*that he may possibly forgive you the intention of your heart.*
23a	Assertion		*For I see that you are full of poison and*
b	Assertion		*captive to unrighteousness."*
24a	Reaction		**Simon responded,**
b	Entreaty		*"Pray for me to the Lord*
c	Purpose		*that nothing of what you have said may happen to me."*
25a	Setting: Time		After they had borne witness
b	Action		and preached the word of the Lord,
c	Action		**they returned to Jerusalem,**
d	Action		proclaiming the good news
e	Place		in many of the villages of the Samaritans.

Jerusalem; this summary statement contains the only reference to "villages" (κῶμαι) in the New Testament outside of the Gospels,[4] a social location in which Jesus often proclaimed the arrival of the kingdom of God. Since the Twelve accompanied Jesus during his travels, they had experience in interacting with village people. As Jesus trained the Twelve to "fish for people" (Mark 1:17/Luke 5:10), and as Jesus spent most of his time in the villages of Galilee, we would expect a preaching activity of the Twelve in villages as well. It is thus surprising that Acts 8:25 is the only explicit reference to missionary preaching in villages in Acts.[5] Since Luke reports selectively, we should not read too much into this silence concerning these villages.

Luke reports *direct speech* for Simon, a Samaritan magician (v. 10d concerning his claims, v. 19 concerning his attempt to buy the ability to convey the gift of the Holy Spirit, v. 24 his request for prayer for himself), and for Peter, who rebukes the magician and calls him to repent (v. 20 – 23). The direct speech segments for Simon (vv. 10, 19, 24) contribute to the negative characterization with which he is introduced (v. 9).

Exegetical Outline

→ **I. The Mission of Philip in Samaria (8:4 – 25)**

    A. Summary Statement regarding the Missionary Work of Jerusalem Believers (8:4)

    B. The Proclamation of the Gospel by Philip among the Samaritans (8:5 – 11)

        1. Philip's arrival in Samaria (8:5a)

        2. Philip's proclamation of Jesus as the Messiah (8:5b-c)

        3. The attention of the crowds, who listen and observe (8:6)

        4. The performance of miracles by Philip and the joy of the crowds (8:7 – 9)

        5. The activity of Simon the magician in Samaria (8:9 – 11)

    C. The Conversion of the Samaritans (8:12 – 13)

        1. The conversion and baptism of Samaritan men and women (8:12)

        2. The conversion and baptism of Simon the magician (8:13)

    D. The Arrival of Peter and John and the Gift of the Holy Spirit (8:14 – 17)

        1. The apostles in Jerusalem hear the news from Samaria (8:14a-b)

        2. Peter and John are sent to Samaria (8:14c – 15a)

        3. Peter and John pray for the gift of the Spirit for the Samaritans (8:15b – 16)

        4. The Samaritan believers receive the gift of the Holy Spirit (8:17)

    E. The Confrontation between Peter and Simon (8:18 – 24)

        1. Simon's offer of money in exchange for spiritual power (8:18 – 19)

---

4. Matthew refers to a village (κώμη) or villages (κῶμαι) four times, Mark seven times, Luke twelve times (5:17; 8:1; 9:6, 12, 52, 56; 10:38; 13:22; 17:12; 19:30; 24:13, 28), and John three times.

5. The reference in 19:10 to "all ... who lived in the province of Asia" hearing the gospel while Paul was based in Ephesus for two years may imply outreach to other towns and perhaps villages.

    2. Peter's rejection of Simon's offer (8:20 – 23)

        a. Threat of a curse as punishment for Simon's offer (8:20)

        b. Assertion that Simon's faith is defective (8:21)

        c. Advice to repent and pray for forgiveness (8:22)

        d. Assertion that Simon's attitude is poisonous and unrighteous (8:23)

    3. Simon's repentance and plea (8:24)

F. Summary Statement regarding the Missionary Work of Peter and John in Samaria (8:25)

    1. Peter and John preach and teach in the city in which Philip had worked (8:25a-b)

    2. Peter and John proclaim the gospel in numerous Samaritan villages (8:25c-e)

Explanation of the Text

8:4 Those who were scattered traveled from place to place and proclaimed the word (οἱ μὲν οὖν διασπαρέντες διῆλθον εὐαγγελιζόμενοι τὸν λόγον). The believers impacted by the persecution that the Jewish authorities organized after Stephen's execution (v. 1) were forced, if they managed to escape imprisonment (v. 3), to leave Jerusalem. The grammatical focus of this summary statement is Luke's reference to the fact that the scattered believers "traveled from place to place" (διῆλθον). The present participle translated "proclaimed" (εὐαγγελιζόμενοι) is modal, underscoring the fact that as they traveled in the regions of Judea and Samaria, they kept proclaiming the good news of the word of God concerning Jesus, the promised Messiah and Savior. Presumably if these believers preached the gospel in towns outside of Jerusalem, they had been actively sharing the message about Jesus in the city.

The following description of the preaching activity of Philip in Samaria (vv. 5 – 13) and Luke's later comment about scattered Jerusalem believers reaching Antioch, the capital of the province of Syria (11:19), are but two examples of what was

happening after Stephen's execution.[6] In fact, the material between 8:4 and 11:19 can be regarded as illustrations of the "traveling from place to place" that took place at this time — Philip traveling to Samaria (8:5 – 13), Peter and John traveling through Samaria (8:14 – 25), Philip traveling toward Gaza (8:26 – 39) and along the coast from Azotus to Caesarea (8:40), Saul being converted in Damascus and encountering believers (9:1 – 22), Saul traveling to Jerusalem (9:23 – 29) and to Tarsus (9:30), Peter traveling through the Plain of Sharon to Lydda and Joppa (9:32 – 43), and to Caesarea (10:1 – 48) and back to Jerusalem (11:1 – 18).

8:5 Philip went to a city of Samaria and proclaimed the Messiah to the people (Φίλιππος δὲ κατελθὼν εἰς πόλιν τῆς Σαμαρείας ἐκήρυσσεν αὐτοῖς τὸν Χριστόν). Philip, one of the Seven (cf. 6:1 – 6),[7] arrived in Samaria and proclaimed Jesus as the Messiah. The distance from Jerusalem to Shechem at the foot of Mount Gerizim is only thirty-seven miles (sixty km) and could thus be reached in two or three days. According to John 4:19 – 26, 39 – 42, Jesus had sympathizers in Samaria. In local synagogues Philip may have encountered disciples of

---

6. The translation of 8:5 in NLT ("Philip, for example, went to the city of Samaria") is thus correct.

7. The Philip of 8:5 could be the member of the Twelve mentioned in 1:13 or the member of the Seven mentioned in

6:5; since the latter reference is closer to 8:5, and since Luke distinguishes Philip from the apostles in Jerusalem in 8:14, the conclusion seems obvious that the evangelist who brought the gospel to Samaria is Philip, one of the Seven.

John the Baptist who had baptized in the border region of Samaria.[8] If the congregation in Jerusalem maintained regular contacts with Jesus' supporters in Galilee, believers would have regularly traveled through Samaria. Thus there were several points of contact that would have helped Philip in his preaching activities.

At the same time we should not forget that Jesus and his disciples had not only positive experiences in Samaria; on one occasion a Samaritan town refused to provide Jesus and his disciples with hospitality (Luke 9:52 – 56).[9] It is not entirely clear where Philip preached the gospel. The phrase translated "to a city of Samaria" (εἰς πόλιν τῆς Σαμαρείας) assumes the textual-critical decision that the Greek text does not include the article.[10] The phrase "of Samaria" thus refers not to the city (called Sebaste since Herod I) but to the district.

Luke provides no specific information about the town in which Philip preaches. Even if the indeterminate reading "a city" is preferred, Sebaste is mentioned by some as a possible location. Other suggested locations are Qedumim, Umm Rihan, and Sychar. Justin Martyr suggested the city of Geth (Gitta), about six miles (ten km) northwest of Sebaste, the birthplace of Simon Magus (Justin, *1 Apol.* 26); this identification cannot be confirmed, however. In v. 9, Luke refers to "the people of Samaria" (τὸ ἔθνος τῆς Σαμαρείας) who had been under the spell of Simon Magus. In view of similar formulations and in the context of 1:8, the phrase "the people of Samaria" is most plausibly interpreted as the population of the geographical region of Samaria, which evidently belongs, in Luke's perspective, to the twelve tribes of Israel.[11]

> [The Samaritans] were at best among the "lost sheep" of Israel. The evangelization of them by Philip therefore continues the work of Jesus in reaching out to the marginal and outcast among the people and inviting them to a full participation in the restored people of God forming around the Prophet whom God raised up.[12]

The term translated "proclaim" (κηρύσσω) is not a technical term. Its use in the New Testament, when applied to Jesus and the apostles, corresponds to the ministry of the Old Testament prophets, who were God's spokesmen, proclaiming with authority the will of God, with the expectation that the listeners would react to the message, absorb its meaning, and follow God's will. Thus the verb frequently designates the oral proclamation of the gospel of Jesus Christ — a message entrusted to the Twelve and to other messengers such as Philip, Paul, and other early Christian missionaries, a message that they thus convey with divine authority and with courageous confidence.[13]

---

8. In Aenon near Salem, twelve kilometers south of Scythopolis (thus Eusebius); cf. Rainer Riesner, "Bethany Beyond the Jordan (John 1.28): Topography, Theology and History in the Fourth Gospel," *TynBul* 38 (1987): 29 – 63.

9. It should be noted that apart from John 4:4 – 42, it is Luke who has a particular interest in the people of Samaria; apart from Luke 9:52 – 56, note the parable of the good Samaritan (10:30 – 37) and the Samaritan leper who thanks Jesus for healing him (17:11 – 19).

10. The reading εἰς τὴν πόλιν ("in the city") is found in 𝔓74 ℵ A B 1175 *pc* (ESV, GNB, NASB, NET, NLT, NRSV); if correct, the reference would likely refer to Sebaste – Samaria. The reading εἰς πόλιν ("in a city") is attested by C D E Ψ 33 1739 Maj (NIV, TNIV). While the manuscript evidence favors the inclusion of the article, internal considerations (e.g., note the

reference in v. 8) favor the omission of the article; see the full discussion by Martina Böhm, *Samarien und die Samaritai bei Lukas* (WUNT 2/111; Tübingen: Mohr Siebeck, 1999), 281 – 89, who decides that the article should be omitted.

11. Cf. Böhm, *Samarien*, 192. In Sir 50:25 – 26 a similar phrase seems to describe the population of the city of Samaria, polemically identified with the Gentiles. Josephus uses the phrase "the people of the Samaritans" for the members of the Garizim community, probably with the connotation of "a foreign race" or "proselytes."

12. Johnson, *Acts*, 151.

13. The verb κηρύσσω, which occurs 61 times in the New Testament, is found eight times in Acts (8:5; 9:20; 10:37, 42; 15:21; 19:13; 20:25; 28:31) and nineteen times in Paul's letters.

The content of Philip's proclamation is summarized with the term "Messiah" (τὸν Χριστόν; see on 2:31, 36); according to 8:12 he "proclaimed the good news about the kingdom of God and the name of Jesus the Messiah." He preached what the Jerusalem apostles had been preaching — that Jesus of Nazareth, who had been crucified, was raised from the dead and exalted to the right hand of God, and that he is thus the promised Savior of Israel. Assuming that Philip as familiar with Samaritan views, he would have known that they did not share many of the messianic expectations found among the Jews, since they regarded only the Pentateuch as Holy Scripture. He undoubtedly focused his message about Jesus on the Samaritans' expectation of the coming of a "prophet like Moses" (Deut 18:15, 18; see on 3:22), whom they called "Taheb" (probably from an Aramaic verb meaning "the Returning One").

8:6 The crowds paid close attention to what Philip said as they listened and as they saw the signs that he performed (προσεῖχον δὲ οἱ ὄχλοι τοῖς λεγομένοις ὑπὸ τοῦ Φιλίππου ὁμοθυμαδὸν ἐν τῷ ἀκούειν αὐτοὺς καὶ βλέπειν τὰ σημεῖα ἃ ἐποίει). The Samaritans listened to Philip's preaching. Luke notes that Philip spoke before "crowds," that the people paid attention over an extended period of time (note the imperfect tense προσεῖχον), that they were of "one mind" (ὁμοθυμαδόν) as they listened, and that they saw the miraculous signs (τὰ σημεῖα; see on 2:19, 22) that Philip performed. Just as the proclamation of the apostles in Jerusalem was accompanied by miracles,[14] so was Philip's, which certainly boosted the eagerness of the people to listen to what he had to say. Luke does not say, however, that the Samaritans believed (v. 12) merely because they witnessed miracles.

8:7–8 Unclean spirits came out of many that were possessed, shrieking loudly. Many who were paralyzed or crippled were cured. So there was great joy in that city (πολλοὶ γὰρ τῶν ἐχόντων πνεύματα ἀκάθαρτα βοῶντα φωνῇ μεγάλῃ ἐξήρχοντο, πολλοὶ δὲ παραλελυμένοι καὶ χωλοὶ ἐθεραπεύθησαν· ἐγένετο δὲ πολλὴ χαρὰ ἐν τῇ πόλει ἐκείνῃ). Luke specifies what kind of miracles happened among the Samaritan population (v. 7). People were liberated from unclean spirits, and people who were paralyzed or crippled were healed. The "loud shrieks"[15] confirmed that a miraculous liberation from evil spirits had taken place, rendering the miracles of exorcism audible, as healings of paralyzed and crippled people are visible miracles. The passive voice of the verb "cured" (ἐθεραπεύθησαν) could point to Philip as the one who "performed" miracles (v. 6), but more likely implies God as the one who caused the miracles to happen. The repetition of the word "many" (πολλοί) indicates that miraculous healings were not isolated events but frequent occurrences.

Since the miracles resulted in a large number of people experiencing relief from ailments that had afflicted them, presumably, for many years, there was "great joy" (πολλὴ χαρά) among the inhabitants of the city in which Philip was staying. It is natural, and theologically plausible (cf. 2:46; 3:8; 5:41), to link the joy of the Samaritans with their faith (v. 12). The "interruption" that many scholars see in vv. 9–11 is not really an interruption of the narrative but a further illustration of the effect of Philip's ministry — the crowds listened (v. 6), miracles happened (v. 7), and people rejoiced (v. 8), having been liberated not only from evil spirits and illnesses but from the magic of Simon (v. 9), to whom everybody had listened (v. 10) and who had amazed the people with his magic tricks

---

14. Acts 2:42–43; 3:1–10; 4:33; 5:12–16.

15. Cf. Luke 4:41; Acts 16:17. Luke reports exorcisms performed by Jesus in Luke 4:33, 36; 6:18; 8:2, 29; 9:1, 6, 42; 11:24.

(v. 11). Thus, even though the joy (v. 8) of the Samaritans is separated in the biblical text from their faith (v. 12), joy and faith belong together since the "experience of gladness"[16] is a fundamental characteristic of people who have repented of their sins and come to faith in Jesus as Messiah and Savior.

8:9 Now a man named Simon had been practicing magic in that city and amazed the people of Samaria, saying that he was someone great (ἀνὴρ δέ τις ὀνόματι Σίμων προϋπῆρχεν ἐν τῇ πόλει μαγεύων καὶ ἐξιστάνων τὸ ἔθνος τῆς Σαμαρείας, λέγων εἶναί τινα ἑαυτὸν μέγαν). Luke now introduces Simon in order to highlight the changes taking place among the Samaritan population. Instead of listening to Simon, a celebrity on account of his effectiveness in the art of magic (vv. 10 – 11), they listen to Philip (v. 6); instead of being amazed by what Simon did through his magic (vv. 9, 11), they are amazed at the miracles Philip is performing (vv. 6 – 7); instead of acknowledging Simon's claims to divine power (v. 10), they believe in the message about Jesus the Messiah and the kingdom of God (v. 12).

Simon is evidently a Samaritan, as he is active in the Samaritan town in which "people of Samaria" (τὸ ἔθνος τῆς Σαμαρείας) were living. The term translated as "people" here denotes "a body of persons united by kinship, culture, and common traditions" (BDAG). Linked with the geographical term "Samaria," the first (geographical) meaning of "Samaritans" (cf. v. 25) may be in view. At the same time, the term "people" (ἔθνος) suggests an ethnic meaning that, in the New Testament references to the Samaritans, also implies a religious sense. Simon belonged to the people who claimed to be the descendants of the Israelite tribes of Ephraim and Manasseh and who worshiped Yahweh on Mount Gerizim.

Simon had been "practicing magic" for an extended but unspecified period of time. In the ancient world, magic — what today we would call witchcraft, sorcery, or the occult — was based on the view that human beings, gods, demons, and the visible world are all connected by sympathies and antipathies in ways that can be influenced by rituals involving incantations and the manipulation of objects. Its purpose was to overcome public or private problems. Usually magic was defensive, harnessing the powers of gods or spirits in order to gain protection against diseases and demons. Active forms of magic sought victory in a race or success in sexual liaisons; the offensive use of magic against personal enemies, involving curses, was feared and often punished.

The term translated "magic" (αἱ μαγεῖαι) denotes "rites ordinarily using incantations designed to influence/control transcendent powers" (BDAG). According to the Mosaic law, all forms of magic were forbidden,[17] though this did not prevent Jews from engaging in magical practices. The fact that Simon practiced magic probably implies that he earned money from the sale of magic spells, but it does not necessarily mean that "magician" was his profession.

Simon claimed "that he was someone great" (εἶναί τινα ἑαυτὸν μέγαν). In view of v. 10 and the formulation there with a passive participle (καλουμένη), Simon evidently used a title that included the term "great" (μέγας). He practiced not only magic but made claims concerning himself, which perhaps implied divine status of some sort (see on v. 10). Justin Martyr (ca. AD 100 – 165) says that Simon declared that he was "God above all power and authority and might" (*Dial.* 120.6), that "he was thought to be a god," and that the Samaritans "confess this man as their first God"

16. Thus the definition of "joy" (χαρά) in BDAG.
17. Exod 22:18; Lev 19:26, 31; 20:6, 27; Deut 18:10 – 11.

These prohibitions remained in place; cf. the later rabbinic stipulations in *m. Sanh.* 7:4, 11.

(*1 Apol.* 26). Since Justin Martyr was himself a Samaritan, born in Neapolis (ancient Shechem), he may have had additional information about Simon.

Simon gained a large following among the Samaritan people who were "amazed" (ἐξιστάνων, vv. 9, 11) about what he was able to do through his magic. Luke does not report what Simon was capable of accomplishing. The apocryphal *Acts of Peter* 4:32 claims that Simon was able to "fly" (levitate), a feat that made him famous in Rome. It is among these people excited by the magic activity of Simon that Philip is preaching the message of Jesus.[18]

8:10 – 11 All the people, from the least to the greatest, paid attention to him, saying, "This man is the Power of God called Great." They paid attention to him because he had amazed them for a long time with his magic (ᾧ προσεῖχον πάντες ἀπὸ μικροῦ ἕως μεγάλου λέγοντες· οὗτός ἐστιν ἡ δύναμις τοῦ θεοῦ ἡ καλουμένη μεγάλη. προσεῖχον δὲ αὐτῷ διὰ τὸ ἱκανῷ χρόνῳ ταῖς μαγείαις ἐξεστακέναι αὐτούς). The entire population was enthralled by Simon's activities and claims. All the people, from the uneducated to the influential, paid attention to what he was doing. Luke notes that the people accepted Simon's claims concerning himself (cf. v. 9d). It is likely that the expression "the Power of God" (ἡ δύναμις τοῦ θεοῦ), explained with the word "Great" (μεγάλη), should be understood as a title reflecting Simon's claims.

In the context of the ancient world, this formulation is ambiguous. The expression can be read as a claim to be the highest of the supernatural powers or as an explicit claim to divinity. If Simon claimed to have divine status, we would expect Luke to challenge such a claim. He has been described as

a charismatic figure adept in the traditions of the Magoi, who exercised considerable ability, authority, and influence. A self-proclaimed expert in divine things, Simon would not have rejected the notion of being a "Gnostic," at least not in the original classical sense of the word. He taught a source of truth and salvation that differed from mainstream Jewish thought and practice; he claimed the preeminent role of "Standing One" — some called him the "first God," Christians viewed him as a "Christ pretender" — and he enjoyed public favor and widespread respect from Samaria to Rome.[19]

8:12 But when they believed Philip, who proclaimed the good news about the kingdom of God and the name of Jesus the Messiah, they were baptized, both men and women (ὅτε δὲ ἐπίστευσαν τῷ Φιλίππῳ εὐαγγελιζομένῳ περὶ τῆς βασιλείας τοῦ θεοῦ καὶ τοῦ ὀνόματος Ἰησοῦ Χριστοῦ, ἐβαπτίζοντο ἄνδρες τε καὶ γυναῖκες). The Samaritan people of the town in which Simon had been active and in which Philip was preaching responded to the evangelist's message. The report about the conversion of Samaritan people in vv. 12 – 13 is the second incident of this episode. Samaritans "believed" (ἐπίστευσαν) and "were baptized" (ἐβαπτίζοντο) as a sign of their commitment to faith in Jesus; the passive voice of the verb suggests that it was Philip who immersed the new believers.[20]

Luke's report about conversions among the Samaritan people includes another brief summary (cf. vv. 4 – 5) of Philip's message, formulated with a present tense participle clause: he "proclaimed the good news" (εὐαγγελιζομένῳ; see on 5:42) regard-

---

18. Böhm, *Samarien*, 307, notes that Luke does not describe the Samaritans as syncretistic, "only as people seduced by Simon. There are no traces of a general polemic or of religious defamation."

19. Stephen C. Haar, *Simon Magus: The First Gnostic?*

(BZNW 119; Berlin: De Gruyter, 2003), 306 – 7; for the early view of Simon as divine pretender and the originator of heresies; cf. Irenaeus, *Haer.* 1.23.

20. On the meaning of the verb translated as "baptize" (βαπτίζω) see 1:5; 2:38.

ing the kingdom of God and Jesus the Messiah. As Philip explains the arrival of the kingdom of God, a present reality that became visible in his miracles (vv. 6 – 7), he continues the ministry of Jesus and the apostles.[21] And as he explains "the name of Jesus the Messiah," he stands in continuity with the proclamation of the Twelve in Jerusalem.[22]

8:13 Even Simon himself came to faith and was baptized. He attached himself to Philip and was amazed when he saw the signs and great miracles that took place (ὁ δὲ Σίμων καὶ αὐτὸς ἐπίστευσεν καὶ βαπτισθεὶς ἦν προσκαρτερῶν τῷ Φιλίππῳ, θεωρῶν τε σημεῖα καὶ δυνάμεις μεγάλας γινομένας ἐξίστατο). Simon was converted as well. In vv. 9 – 11 Luke had commented on Simon's influence on the Samaritan population in order to underscore the power of the gospel that turned the people away from Simon to believing in Philip and his message about Jesus (vv. 6 – 8, 12). In this verse Luke emphasizes that same power of the gospel by highlighting the fact that even Simon, who had practiced magic to great effect, came to faith.

In view of Simon's subsequent behavior, some have doubted whether he experienced a genuine conversion.[23] Luke's description leaves little room for debate, however. He states that Simon "believed" or (if the tense of the verb ἐπίστευσεν is interpreted as an ingressive aorist) "came to faith," and he was immersed (βαπτισθεὶς) as an expression of his repentance and his profession of faith in Jesus as the Messiah and Savior. There is no reason to doubt that Philip would have followed the practice of the Jerusalem church regarding baptism as linked with the acceptance of the message about

the need for repentance and about faith in Jesus as Messiah and Savior (2:38, 41).

While the Samaritans had been amazed by Simon's works of magic, Simon himself is now amazed as he follows Philip around and sees the "signs and great miracles" (σημεῖα καὶ δυνάμεις μεγάλας; cf. vv. 6 – 7) being done. The present tense of the participles translated "he attached himself" (προσκαρτερῶν) and "he saw" (θεωρῶν), having semantic prominence, imply that Simon's conversion had ongoing consequences for his behavior in initial discipleship, which again indicates there is no reason to doubt the genuine nature of his faith commitment. There is no hint that Philip baptized Simon prematurely.

8:14 When the apostles in Jerusalem heard that Samaria had accepted the word of God, they sent Peter and John to the people there (ἀκούσαντες δὲ οἱ ἐν Ἱεροσολύμοις ἀπόστολοι ὅτι δέδεκται ἡ Σαμάρεια τὸν λόγον τοῦ θεοῦ, ἀπέστειλαν πρὸς αὐτοὺς Πέτρον καὶ Ἰωάννην). The third incident of this unit relates the arrival of Peter and John in Samaria and their involvement in the reception of the Holy Spirit by the Samaritans (vv. 14 – 17). The localization of the apostles "in Jerusalem" confirms the comment in 8:1 that the persecution that followed after Stephen's execution had not permanently driven the apostles from Jerusalem. The fact that this prepositional phrase is embedded in the reference to the apostles (οἱ ... ἀπόστολοι) indicates, perhaps, that not all apostles were present in Jerusalem when the report about conversions in Samaria reached them.

The fact that the apostles in Jerusalem heard about the conversion of people in Samaria and

---

21. Cf. Luke 4:43; 6:20; 8:1; 9:2, 11; 16:16; 17:21; Acts 1:3. See on 1:3.

22. Cf. Acts 2:38; 3:6, 16; 4:10, 17, 30; 5:28, 40; see on 2:31, 36, 38; 3:6, 16. Cf. Johnson, *Acts*, 148, 151.

23. So already Irenaeus, *Haer.* 1.23.1; Eusebius, *Hist. eccl.*

2.1.11 (Simon "feigned and counterfeited faith in Christ, even going so far as to receive baptism"); cf. Jervell, *Apostelgeschichte*, 262. Differently Barrett, *Acts*, 409; Avemarie, *Tauferzählungen*, 53 – 54.

sent Peter and John there indicates that the Twelve naturally acted as the group responsible for the proclamation of the gospel in regions beyond Jerusalem (cf. 1:8). The phrase "accepted" or "received the word of God" (δέδεκται ... τὸν λόγον τοῦ θεοῦ) confirms that at least in the report that reached Jerusalem, the conversions of the Samaritans resulting from Philip's preaching were described as genuine (cf. 2:41; 11:1). Luke does not say why the apostles sent Peter and John to Samaria, but since vv. 14 – 16 is one single sentence, the report likely contained the information that the Samaritan believers had not received the Holy Spirit.

8:15 – 16 When they arrived, they prayed for them that they might receive the Holy Spirit, because the Spirit had not yet come upon any of them, as they had only been baptized in the name of the Lord Jesus (οἵτινες καταβάντες προσηύξαντο περὶ αὐτῶν ὅπως λάβωσιν πνεῦμα ἅγιον· οὐδέπω γὰρ ἦν ἐπ᾽ οὐδενὶ αὐτῶν ἐπιπεπτωκός, μόνον δὲ βεβαπτισμένοι ὑπῆρχον εἰς τὸ ὄνομα τοῦ κυρίου Ἰησοῦ). Peter and John arrive in the Samaritan town in which Philip has been preaching the gospel. They pray (προσηύξαντο) that God may cause the Samaritan converts to receive the Holy Spirit (v. 15). That Peter and John pray for the reception of the Holy Spirit rather than explain the gospel in more detail confirms that they accept the faith of the Samaritans as authentic.[24] Luke marks the delay of the reception of the Holy Spirit in v. 16 as extraordinary, stating that the Spirit had "not yet" (οὐδέπω) come upon any of them. This explanation would be superfluous if Luke or his readers regarded an interval between baptism and the reception of the Spirit as normal. The Samaritans had believed (v. 12) and been immersed on account of their confession of faith, passing "into the sphere in which Jesus is acknowledged as Lord, becoming (so to speak) Jesus' property."[25]

IN DEPTH: The Reception of the Holy Spirit and the Samaritan Believers

[The Holy Spirit] performs important soteriological functions and so Spirit-reception normally attaches to the complex of conversion-initiation itself. In that case, however, the believer's responsive faith to the message, and submission to baptism, would generally be more than enough "initial evidence" that the convert had joined the Israel of fulfillment, the people of the Spirit ... one might anticipate that for many, if not most, the actual moment of Spirit-reception passed relatively unnoticed as one in the whole series of experiences involved in the titanic upheaval of conversion-initiation.[26]

---

24. Turner, *Power from on High*, 367; cf. Spencer, *Portrait of Philip*, 48 – 53.

25. Bruce, *Acts*, 221, interpreting the phrase "in the name of" (εἰς τὸ ὄνομα) against a commercial background "as when a sum of money or the like is paid or transferred 'into the name' of someone, i.e. into his account." This expression occurs here and in 19:5; otherwise Luke uses the propositions ἐν or ἐπί (2:38; 10:48) in connection with baptism. On the verb translated as "baptize" (βαπτίζω), see on 1:5; 2:38.

26. Turner, *Power from on High*, 448; the following quotation ibid., 449.

Luke regularly describes the conversion of both Jews and Gentiles, which includes the acceptance of the gospel as preached and explained, repentance of sins, coming to faith in Jesus as Israel's Messiah and Savior, and immersion as a sign of commitment to Jesus. In these descriptions he often does not specify the moment of reception of the Spirit or any initial manifestation, such as speaking in unlearned languages (cf. 8:36 – 39; 9:1 – 19; 16:14 – 15; 16:30 – 34). Realities such as rejoicing (8:39; 16:34) or missionary ministry (9:20 – 22) are taken as adequate ongoing evidence of the presence of the Holy Spirit. For the majority of conversions, "initial evidence" beyond baptism itself and, for example, joy in the gospel "would not have been an issue. It would only *become* an issue were there no *ongoing* evidence of the Spirit's presence and manifestation," as apparently is true for the Samaritan believers.

This raises the question of how the apostles in Jerusalem concluded that the Samaritan believers had not received the Holy Spirit — or how Philip himself reached this conclusion, if the report taken from Samaria to Jerusalem originated with Philip. In view of v. 18, where Simon "sees" the effects of the reception of the Spirit, the most plausible explanation is that "the 'Spirit of prophecy' had not yet been manifest among the disciples in the kinds of charismata the writer expected to characterize possession of this gift (and which apparently did become manifest when the apostles prayed and laid their hands on the Samaritans, 8.18)."[27]

Luke himself provides no explanation for the delay of the Holy Spirit in Samaria. Perhaps God withheld the Spirit in his sovereignty in order to establish a connection between the Samaritan believers and the Jewish believers in Jerusalem through the apostles Peter and John. Because of several hundred years of alienation between Jews and Samaritans, the latter would naturally be prone to reject the authority of the Jewish leaders of the church in Jerusalem. At the same time, Jewish believers in Jerusalem might have been easily skeptical regarding Samaritans being granted salvation, despite Jesus' command in Acts 1:8. The delay of the Spirit's reception by the Samaritans and the involvement of Peter and John teach these new believers that they need the mother church in Jerusalem, and it demonstrates to the Jewish believers that God granted Samaritans who came to faith in Jesus the same messianic salvation that they had been granted. The delay of the Holy Spirit thus may find its explanation in the fact that this was the first significant extension of salvation beyond Judaism (understood as focused on Jerusalem).

---

27. Ibid., 373 – 74; also Ferguson, *Baptism*, 171.

8:17 Then Peter and John laid their hands on them, and they received the Holy Spirit (τότε ἐπετίθεσαν τὰς χεῖρας ἐπ᾿ αὐτοὺς καὶ ἐλάμβανον πνεῦμα ἅγιον). The Samaritan believers receive the Holy Spirit as Peter and John lay their hands on them. Here the laying on of hands (see on 6:6) signifies the transfer of power,[28] specifically the power of the Holy Spirit, and accompanies a prayer of invocation asking for God's blessing,[29] i.e., the granting of his promise of the Holy Spirit.

There must have been a visible or audible manifestation of the coming of the Spirit that prompted Simon to think that he might acquire the ability to convey the Spirit from the apostles through money (vv. 18 – 19). It is a plausible assumption that the Samaritan Christians spoke in unlearned foreign languages (glossolalia) when they received the Holy Spirit; when Luke introduces a new group of people who accepted the gospel of Jesus Christ, he links the reception of the Spirit with glossolalia (in 2:4 – 12 the Jews; in 10:46; 11:15, 17 the Gentiles; and in 19:6 the disciples of John the Baptist). These four groups (including the Samaritans) represent people who are distinct from a salvation-historical perspective.

The conversion of the Samaritans is particularly significant as the gospel for the first time reaches people who are not unambiguously members of the people of Israel. It also should be noted that in these four cases, the manifestations linked with the reception of the Holy Spirit, whether it included speaking in tongues or laying on of hands, constituted corporate rather than individual experiences. When Luke reports the conversion of individuals such as Lydia or the jailer in Philippi (16:11 – 15,

25 – 34), he does not describe a two-stage experience of conversion/baptism followed at a later date by the reception of the Spirit.

8:18 – 19 When Simon saw that the Spirit was given through the laying on of the apostles' hands, he offered them money and said, "Give me that power too so that anyone on whom I lay my hands may receive the Holy Spirit" (ἰδὼν δὲ ὁ Σίμων ὅτι διὰ τῆς ἐπιθέσεως τῶν χειρῶν τῶν ἀποστόλων δίδοται τὸ πνεῦμα, προσήνεγκεν αὐτοῖς χρήματα λέγων· δότε κἀμοὶ τὴν ἐξουσίαν ταύτην ἵνα ᾧ ἐὰν ἐπιθῶ τὰς χεῖρας λαμβάνῃ πνεῦμα ἅγιον). Simon, the former expert in the magical arts, is presented as committing a serious sin. The fourth incident of the Samaria unit concludes with the confrontation between Peter and Simon (vv. 18 – 24) over the latter's suggestion that if he gave the apostles money, they would give him in return the power to convey the Holy Spirit. The offer of money is motivated by Simon's observation of the manifestations caused by the Holy Spirit, whom the Samaritans receive as Peter and John lay their hands on them (v. 18).

Simon evidently saw dramatic effects of the arrival of the Holy Spirit, best understood in terms of invasive prophecy and doxological speech (see on 2:4 and 8:17). The verb translated "offered" (προσήνεγκεν) implies that Simon brought money to the apostles for them to grant his request to receive the "power" (ἐξουσία) to confer the gift of the Holy Spirit by the laying on of hands (v. 19). Simon's offer to purchase such spiritual power gave rise to the term *simony*, which Thomas Aquinas defines as "a deliberate design of selling or buying

---

28. Cf. Luke 4:40; Acts 9:12, 17; see also Matt 9:18; Mark 5:23; 6:5.

29. Cf. Matt 19:13, 15; Mark 10:16. Cf. Tipei, *Laying on of Hands*, 203, who argues that the laying on of hands here "is not *the* rite which conveys the Spirit on a regular basis" but "is to

be understood as an *ad hoc* taken by the two apostles in order to 'correct' an usual situation." The later ecclesial practice of laying on of hands at baptism developed from the comment in Acts 8:17; Fitzmyer, *Acts*, 406, with reference to Tertullian, *Bapt.* 1.1 – 2.

for a temporal price something spiritual or annexed to the spiritual."[30]

8:20 But Peter said to him, "May your money perish with you, because you thought you could buy the gift of God with money!" (Πέτρος δὲ εἶπεν πρὸς αὐτόν· τὸ ἀργύριόν σου σὺν σοὶ εἴη εἰς ἀπώλειαν ὅτι τὴν δωρεὰν τοῦ θεοῦ ἐνόμισας διὰ χρημάτων κτᾶσθαι). Peter's response to Simon is also reported in direct speech, making the narrative more vivid and, more important, underlining the significance of Peter's rejection of Simon's offer to buy spiritual power. Peter's response has four components. In this first one, Peter formulates a threat that implies a curse as punishment for Simon's offer: "May your money perish with you" (v. 20b). The noun translated as "perish" (ἀπώλεια) refers in the Old Testament to the destruction that God brings on human beings as a result of their rebellion against him (Deut 8:19; Job 11:20; Isa 57:4; Dan 2:5; 3:96). Peter threatens that God will destroy Simon and the money that has been offered.

The present optative (εἴη) expresses a wish. The threat of judgment is often interpreted as representing a curse.[31] Peter's words imply at least the threat of curse,[32] which in view of the call to repentance (v. 22) is a warning of serious consequences if Simon persists in the mind-set with which he has approached the apostles. Since Peter calls Simon to repentance, the translation of v. 20b as "To hell with your and your money!" (Phillips; cf. GNB) is therefore not appropriate, unless it is understood

as a colloquial idiom that expresses disgusted rejection and thus is not taken literally.

Simon's sin is the notion that the power to convey the gift of the Holy Spirit can be bought with money (v. 20c-e). Two things are important here. First, it is not only the action of buying (and then selling)[33] spiritual power that provokes God's judgment, but already the thought that this is possible. Both actions and attitudes constitute sin that God judges when and if they stand in opposition to God's demands and standards.[34] Second, the Holy Spirit and his manifestations are a "gift" (δωρεά) that God gives and that thus cannot be acquired by money. The attempt to buy (and sell) the gift of conveying the Spirit of God amounts to an attempt to manipulate God himself, which is not only impossible but a most serious sin. God's good gifts can only be received with thankful hearts.

8:21 You have no part or share in this matter, for your heart is not right in God's sight (οὐκ ἔστιν σοι μερὶς οὐδὲ κλῆρος ἐν τῷ λόγῳ τούτῳ, ἡ γὰρ καρδία σου οὐκ ἔστιν εὐθεῖα ἔναντι τοῦ θεοῦ). The second part of Peter's response is the assertion that Simon's faith is defective. His heart is not right in the sight of God.[35] The term translated as "right" (εὐθεῖα) means in a literal sense "in a straight or direct line"; used figuratively it refers to the heart being (or not being) "proper, honest, right." Here "heart" (καρδία; see on 4:32) refers to (1) Simon's intellectual understanding of spiritual realities, (2) the voluntative driving force of his actions, which

---

30. Aquinas, *Summa theologica*, II. II, q. 100, a. 1. The *OED* defines simony as "the act or practice of buying or selling ecclesiastical preferments, benefices, or emoluments; traffic in sacred things."

31. Cf. J.D.M. Derrett, "Simon Magus (Act 8.9 – 24)," *ZNW* 73 (1982): 52 – 68; Susan R. Garrett, *The Demise of the Devil: Magic and the Demonic in Luke's Writings* (Minneapolis: Fortress, 1989), 70 – 72.

32. Barrett, *Acts*, 414; Bock, *Acts*, 333.

33. Simon's previous activities would have involved receiving remuneration for his services in the arts of magic. He

evidently wants to buy the ability to convey the Spirit so that when he practices this spiritual power himself, he can benefit financially by charging for his services in conveying manifestations of the Spirit.

34. Cf. Matt 5:21 – 30, where Jesus explains that sin that provokes God's judgment must be seen not only in actual murder and adultery but also in anger and in lustful thoughts.

35. The comment echoes Ps 78:37 (LXX 77:37), where the wilderness generation is described in terms of "their hearts" not being "loyal" to God.

continue to be focused on power and prestige, and (3) his relationship with God, which is defective both in theological and ethical respects since he has misunderstood the nature of God's Spirit and his conscience still cannot distinguish between vice and virtue.

The key word for the interpretation of v. 21a is the term translated as "matter" (λόγος); the demonstrative pronoun "this" indicates that λόγος here does not mean "word" in terms of the Christian message[36] but refers to the "matter" of the bestowal of the gift of the Spirit, which is the substance of Simon's request. Peter asserts that Simon has no "part" (μερίς) or, what amounts to the same, "share" (κλῆρος) in conveying the Spirit. His point is not that Simon is not an apostle; rather, he points to Simon's defective relationship with God. Luke's words do not take back the force of his description of Simon's conversion in v. 13. While it is true that if believers are not on guard about their actions or attitudes, they may still end in "perish[ing]" (ἀπώλεια), such perdition does not necessarily mean the loss of salvation but could refer to the kind of instantaneous death that Ananias and Sapphira suffered (5:1–11).

8:22 Repent of this wickedness and ask the Lord that he may possibly forgive you the intention of your heart (μετανόησον οὖν ἀπὸ τῆς κακίας σου ταύτης καὶ δεήθητι τοῦ κυρίου, εἰ ἄρα ἀφεθήσεταί σοι ἡ ἐπίνοια τῆς καρδίας σου). The third component of Peter's response is the advice to repent. Simon must "repent" (μετανόησον) and "ask" (δεήθητι) the Lord for forgiveness. These two aorist imperatives imply Peter's authority and underline the seriousness of Simon's situation.

Peter does not make suggestions but formulates commands. The "wickedness" from which Simon must turn away is the "intention of [his] heart" (ἡ ἐπίνοια τῆς καρδίας), i.e., the specific sin of attempting to buy the power of conveying the gift of the Spirit. Here repentance means a change of heart — a change exhibited in proper intentions and in right behavior. The formulation of the conditional clause with the future indicative (first class condition) indicates that the repentance of Simon is a real possibility.[37]

8:23 "For I see that you are full of poison and captive to unrighteousness" (εἰς γὰρ χολὴν πικρίας καὶ σύνδεσμον ἀδικίας ὁρῶ σε ὄντα). The final component of Peter's response is the assertion that Simon's attitude is poisonous and unrighteous. The phrase translated as "full of poison" consists of a genitive construction whose first noun (χολή) denotes a substance with an unpleasant taste ("gall, bile") and, figuratively, bitter anger. The LXX uses the term to translate Hebrew words that mean "gall" (Job 16:13), "wormwood" (Prov 5:4; Lam 3:15 NRSV), "poison" (Ps 69:21 [LXX 68:22] NRSV), and "venom" (Job 20:14). The second noun (πικρία) means "bitterness," either literally (of a bitter taste) or figuratively ("bitterness, animosity, anger, harshness" in an affective sense).

This expression probably does not describe Simon's emotional attitude in terms of "bitterness at the success of Philip's preaching and the ability of the apostles to confer the Spirit,"[38] i.e., in terms of envy,[39] but in terms of Simon being destined for "bitter anger" in the sense of his experiencing the wrath of God,[40] or in terms of "bitter poison" in the sense of Simon's experiencing the bitter results of

---

36. As in Acts 4:31; 8:14, 25.

37. The possibility of Simon's repentance is also indicated by the conjunction ἄρα (cf. BDAG, s.v. εἰ 8aα: "εἰ ἄρα expressing possibility *if, indeed; if, in fact; whether (perhaps)*.")

38. Fitzmyer, *Acts*, 407.

39. Thus GNB ("full of bitter envy"), NET ("bitterly envious"), NLT ("full of bitter jealousy").

40. Barrett, *Acts*, 416, who recognizes that this interpretation presupposes that Simon will not repent.

his sinful attitude.[41] The latter interpretation does not require the assumption that Simon will not repent and can also accommodate a divine punishment such as Ananias and Sapphira suffered. The second expression asserts that Simon is still in the bond that holds his desires captive to unrighteousness. Despite his faith in Jesus expressed in baptism (v. 13), his intentions are still wicked, at least as far as his attempt to buy the power for conveying the Spirit is concerned.

8:24 Simon responded, "Pray for me to the Lord that nothing of what you have said may happen to me" (ἀποκριθεὶς δὲ ὁ Σίμων εἶπεν· δεήθητε ὑμεῖς ὑπὲρ ἐμοῦ πρὸς τὸν κύριον ὅπως μηδὲν ἐπέλθῃ ἐπ᾽ ἐμὲ ὧν εἰρήκατε). Simon's reaction to Peter's indictment indicates that he has repented. His plea that Peter should pray for him is best understood as showing remorse.[42] The fact that he does not pray himself may indicate that he has come to realize that his former way of handling supernatural power is no longer adequate and is afraid that what he might say to the Lord would again be manipulative. Thus he asks Peter to intercede for him.

8:25 After they had borne witness and preached the word of the Lord, they returned to Jerusalem, proclaiming the good news in many of the villages of the Samaritans (οἱ μὲν οὖν διαμαρτυράμενοι καὶ λαλήσαντες τὸν λόγον τοῦ κυρίου ὑπέστρεφον εἰς Ἰεροσόλυμα, πολλάς τε κώμας τῶν Σαμαριτῶν εὐηγγελίζοντο). Luke brings this episode to an end with a second summary statement, creating an *inclusio* that places the conversion of the Samaritans through the missionary work of Philip in the broader context of the missionary work of other believers from Jerusalem (vv. 4, 25). The expression translated "they" (οἱ μέν) could refer not only to Peter and John, but also include Philip. However, since Peter and John are the nearest antecedents of the definite article (vv. 14, 15, 17, 18; Philip is mentioned for the last time in v. 13), it is more plausible that only Peter and John are in view.

As the two apostles return to Jerusalem, they preach the gospel in many villages of the Samaritans. The focus is on the activity (rather than on the success) of Peter and John, which is described with two aorist participles and a finite verb in the imperfect tense indicating the process of their preaching over time — they "bear witness" (διαμαρτυράμενοι) to Jesus, they "preach" (λαλήσαντες) the word of the Lord, and they "proclaim the good news" (εὐηγγελίζοντο). As they preach among the population living in the Samaritan villages, they may have covered the entire region of Samaria south of the town in which Philip had been preaching. We know of 140 settlements in Samaria in the Hellenistic period and of 146 villages in the early Roman period.[43] The comment in v. 25 could indicate "a broad and persistent success of the Christian mission in the region."[44]

41. BDAG, s.v. χολή 2; Marshall, "Acts," 572. Translations such as ESV, NASB, NRSV ("in the gall of bitterness"), "literal" as they are, do not make sense to the modern English reader.

42. Barrett, *Acts*, 418; Fitzmyer, *Acts*, 407; Haar, *Simon Magus*, 190–91. Others read Simon's plea for prayer as dismissive in terms of his refusal to pray himself; cf. Bock, *Acts*, 335; Pervo, *Acts*, 216; Garrett, *Demise of the Devil*, 72.

43. Adam Zertal, "Mount Manasseh Survey," *NEAEHL*, 4:1312; cf. Schnabel, *Early Christian Mission*, 2:765–69.

44. Böhm, *Samarien*, 307.

Theology in Application

This passage focuses on missionary work among the Samaritan people, whom the Jews of Judea (and of Galilee) despised, if not hated. The emphasis here is on conversion, both in terms of mass conversions and the conversion of an individual, a local celebrity, a man who was an expert in the occult. Another issue touched on here is the manipulation of spiritual power and the implied emphasis that God and his Spirit cannot be manipulated and certainly not influenced through money.[45]

While the passage is neither the only nor the most important passage that describes, illustrates, and models missionary work in Acts, it teaches us several important lessons about preaching in areas in which the people have not heard the gospel.

Opportunities for evangelistic work are not always the result of deliberate planning. They sometimes come as the result of accidental developments, or even the corollary of external pressure and persecution. Philip arrives in Samaria because persecution in Jerusalem forces him to leave the city. As important as strategizing and planning are, Christians need to take care lest they overlook opportunities for sharing their faith that present themselves or, rather, which God presents in his sovereignty.

Missionaries are willing to go to and settle in regions in which they cannot expect sympathies since the population is hostile — here on account of historical and cultural factors. The Samaritans were no friends of the Jews. When Jesus sent the apostles beyond Jerusalem and Judea to the Samaritans, he left the leaders of the church no alternative but to engage in outreach to people whom many Jews were glad to avoid. This requires courage.

Philip preached Jesus as the Messiah (8:5) — not the Samaritan Taheb, but the Savior promised in those parts of the Scriptures the Samaritans rejected. While v. 5 gives us an all-too-brief summary of the content of Philip's preaching, we cannot be sure whether and how Philip "contextualized" the gospel, i.e., adapted it to Samaritan traditions and expectations. However, as Jesus had explained to a Samaritan woman outside the town of Sychar that "salvation is from the Jews" (John 4:22), there is no reason to expect that Philip removed what would have been for Samaritan ears the "Jewish" aspects of the message about Jesus, who was not a Samaritan but from the royal line of Davidic kings from the tribe of Judah.

While missionaries do adapt their preaching and teaching to regional and local circumstances and "become all things to all people" (1 Cor 9:22), a Greek to the Greeks and a Jew to the Jews, they do this "for the sake of the gospel" (1 Cor 9:23) and not for the sake of a principle or for the sake of "maximizing" the response. Missionaries who preach the gospel of Jesus Christ must reject the temptation to preach a

---

45. On this issue of "traps relating to money and power," see Fernando, *Acts*, 280 – 81.

watered-down version of the gospel that represents the lowest common denominator of what is acceptable. The message of Jesus, the crucified, risen, and exalted Messiah, Savior, and Lord, will always be a stumbling block for some and nonsense for others (1 Cor 1:18 – 2:5). And it is always, and only, the power of God who convinces people of the truth of the gospel (1 Cor 1:24, 30; 2:5).

Missionaries should not be intimidated by magical practices or demonic phenomena. Philip had no qualms about contacts with Simon, a recognized and probably feared expert in the arts of the occult. Missionaries who worked on the island of Java in Indonesia report encounters with witch doctors who challenged them to a duel of spiritual powers, killing chickens on the other side of the street with a curse as preparation for the real showdown and a demonstration of what they were capable of.[46] Even in such extreme circumstances, where one's life might be in danger, followers of Jesus do not have to be afraid of the supernatural powers that sorcerers may be able to conjure up, since the power of the one true God is greater than the power of any spirit, curse, or spell. At the same time we should note that Luke's narrative shows no fascination with magic or with magic practices.

Missionaries are not intimidated by celebrities. Philip was evidently not afraid to acquaint Simon with the gospel of Jesus Christ, reckoning with the possibility that even this man who seemed to have had immense influence in the community might be converted to faith in Jesus. At the same time, note that converted celebrities do not automatically become the leaders of newly emerging churches. Simon is a case in point.

Missionaries reckon with the possibility of mass conversions, i.e., with the possibility that a large number of people come to faith in Jesus Christ over a short period of time. This had happened in Jerusalem; now it was happening in Samaria. This does not mean that mass conversions are the norm of missionary work; neither Luke nor Paul report conversions or large numbers of people for Paul's missionary ministry (although note Luke's account of Paul's work in Ephesus in Acts 19:8 – 20, where the value of the magic books and the reaction of the guild of silversmiths suggest conversions of Gentiles on a large scale).

Missionary work results in the reconciliation of hostile groups. Jewish and Samaritan believers have fellowship with each other. Note that in 9:31 the presence of Samaritans in "the church" is taken for granted: "the church throughout Judea, Galilee, and Samaria had peace."

Extraordinary missionary success may be accompanied by instances of believers who have a defective faith. Thus missionary work and pastoral ministry go hand in hand. There will always be people who misunderstand aspects of the gospel,

---

46. Cf. Detmar Scheunemann, *The Ministries of the Holy Spirit: Studied against the Background of the Indonesian Revival* (Malang, Indonesia: Indonesian Missionary Fellowship, 1984).

sometimes fundamental truths. Simon, an expert in magic, evidently thought it natural that spiritual powers could be acquired at will and be purchased. As Paul later takes the gospel to people who have grown up in the Greco-Roman culture, he deals with people who think nothing of engaging in immoral sexual behavior, such as visiting prostitutes, behavior that carried over into the church (cf. 1 Cor 6:12 – 20; note the lists of vices in which immorality often stands at the top).[47]

47. Cf. Mark 7:21; 1 Cor 5:11; 6:9; Gal 5:19; Eph 5:3, 5; Col 3:5; 1 Tim 1:10; cf. Matt 5:19; 1 Thess 4:3; Rev 22:15.

Acts 8:26 – 40

Literary Context

The second episode of Luke's report on Philip's ministry narrates his encounter with an Ethiopian official. In the immediate aftermath of Stephen's execution and the persecution that scattered the Jerusalem believers, Philip had traveled north to Samaria, where he preached the gospel to the people living in an unnamed town (8:4 – 25). His missionary outreach in Samaria had considerable success as crowds of people paid attention to the proclamation of the gospel and large numbers of Samaritans came to faith in Jesus and were baptized; this included a local celebrity who had been an expert in the arts of magic. The delay of the bestowal of the Holy Spirit on the Samaritan believers allowed the Jerusalem apostles to visit Samaria and pray for the new believers, who then received the Holy Spirit, an event that was evidently accompanied by visible and audible manifestations, confirming the integration of the Samaritan believers into the congregation of the followers of Jesus (cf. 9:31).

As Peter and John return to Jerusalem, Philip is told by an angel to go to the road that leads south to the city of Gaza, where he encounters an Ethiopian official. The episode in 8:26 – 40 describes that event and the Ethiopian's conversion, illustrating again how the gospel reached members of the aristocratic classes.

Main Idea

Luke's report of Philip's encounter with the Ethiopian official who comes to faith in Jesus emphasizes that the church is involved in taking the gospel to the ends of the earth; that the mission of the church is directed by the Spirit of God, who calls missionaries to proclaim the gospel to people in different geographical locations and with different cultural and social identities; that not only large crowds of people but also single individuals need to hear the gospel; and that instruction from the Scriptures is an important element in the proclamation of the good news of Jesus, whose life and death fulfill Scripture.

Translation

Acts 8:26–40

26a	Event	Then **the angel of the Lord said to Philip,**
b	Command	*"Go south*
c	Place	*on the road that goes from Jerusalem to Gaza,*
d	Identification	*the desert route."*
27a	Action	So **he started out.**
b	Character entrance	**There was an Ethiopian eunuch,**
c	Description	*a court official of Candace,*
d	Identification	*the queen of the Ethiopians,*
e	Description	*who was in charge of her entire treasury.*
f	Action (Flashback)	**He had visited Jerusalem**
g	Purpose	*to worship*
28a	Action	and **was returning home.**
b	Circumstance	*Seated in his chariot*
c	Action	**he was reading the prophet Isaiah.**
29a	Action	**The Spirit said to Philip,**
b	Command	*"Go and stick to this chariot."*
30a	Action/Response	**Philip ran up**
b	Event	and **heard him reading the prophet Isaiah.**
c	Action	**He said to him,**
d	Question	*"Do you understand what you are reading?"*
31a	Response	**He replied,**
b	Question	*"How can I, unless someone guides me?"*
c	Action	Then **he invited Philip to get in**
d	Action	and **sit beside him.**
32a	Description	**This is the passage of Scripture that he was reading:**
b	Quotation of OT	*"He was led like a sheep to the slaughter, and*
c	Comparison	*like a lamb before its shearer is silent,*

d	Event	*so he did not open his mouth.*
33a	Event	*He was deprived of justice*
b	Sphere	*in his humiliation*
c	Question	*Who can speak of his descendants?*
d	Explanation	*For his life is taken away from the earth."* (Isa 53:7-8)
34a	Action	**Then the official said to Philip,**
b	Question	*"May I ask about whom the prophet says this?*
c	Alternative	*About himself or*
d	Alternative	*about someone else?"*
35a	Answer/Action	**Then Philip began with this passage of Scripture**
b	Action	**and proclaimed the good news about Jesus.**
36a	Setting: Place	As they traveled along the road,
b	Event	**they came to some water.**
c	Action	**The official said,**
d	Exclamation	*"Look, here is water!*
e	Rhetorical question	*What prevents me from being baptized?"*
38a	Action	**He ordered the chariot to stop,**
b	Action	**and both of them, Philip and the official, went down into the water,**
c	Action	**and he immersed him.**
39a	Setting: Time	When they came up out of the water,
b	Event	**the Spirit of the Lord took Philip away.**
c	Event	**The official saw him no more,**
d	Action	**but continued on his way**
e	Manner	rejoicing.
40a	Event	**Philip found himself**
b	Place	at Azotus.
c	Action	As he continued his travels,
d	Action	**he proclaimed the good news**
e	Place	in all the towns
f	Time	until he reached Caesarea.

Structure and Literary Form

The episode of Philip's encounter with the Ethiopian official is another *historical narrative* that includes geographical movement (vv. 26–28, 39–40), introduction of characters (v. 27), dialogue (vv. 30–36), and a *conversion report* (vv. 30–38, with the following elements: explanation of Old Testament Scripture, vv. 30–35a; proclamation of the good news about Jesus, v. 35b; baptism, vv. 36–38). The passage contains several short pieces of *direct speech* (of the angel in vv. 26b-d; of the Spirit in 29b; of Philip in v. 30d; of the Ethiopian official in vv. 31b, 34, 36d-e); the second part of the narrative is driven by the three questions that the Ethiopian is asking.

The episode is narrated with vivid detail: Philip is instructed by an angel to walk to Gaza via the desert route (v. 26); an Ethiopian official who is sufficiently wealthy to afford a chariot journeys to Jerusalem, purchases an Isaiah scroll, sits in his chariot, and reads aloud Isaiah's prophecies about a suffering servant (vv. 27–28, 30–33); Philip approaches the chariot and hears the Ethiopian murmur the words of Isaiah 53 and asks him whether he understands (v. 30); the Ethiopian confesses that he does not understand the meaning of the prophet's words and invites Philip to join him (vv. 31, 34); after he understands and accepts the gospel of Jesus Christ and the necessity of a faith commitment that involves immersion, the Ethiopian commands his driver to stop the chariot and enters the water together with Philip, who immerses him (v. 38). The Holy Spirit then takes Philip to the cities on the Palestinian coast, where he proclaims the good news until he reaches Caesarea (vv. 39–40).

The context of this episode in Acts raises the question of the religious identity of the Ethiopian official. Eusebius regarded the Ethiopian as the first Gentile to be converted.[1] This view agrees with the interpretation of "eunuch" (εὐνοῦχος; vv. 27, 34, 36, 38, 39) in terms of a physically castrated man who was excluded from admission to the people of Israel (Lev 21:17–21; Deut 23:1). By contrast, Cornelius, the Roman officer in Caesarea converted through the preaching of Peter (Acts 10:1–11:18), seems to have been the first Gentile to come to faith in Jesus (note Peter's comment in 15:7). Thus many scholars see the Ethiopian as a representative of proselytes in the Jewish diaspora (see on v. 27).[2]

The narrative so far in Acts has reported the conversions of Palestinian Jews in Jerusalem (2:41; 5:14) and in Judea (5:16), of diaspora Jews in Jerusalem (6:1), and of Samaritans (8:12). A culturally consistent story line makes it plausible to assume that the Ethiopian official converted in 8:35–39 is a proselyte, followed by the conversion of Cornelius, a Gentile God-fearer living in Caesarea (10:1–48). That episode, then, is followed by the conversion of a number of Greeks in Antioch (11:20–21). In terms of Luke's concerns, the broad and detailed narrative of the conversion of Cornelius through Peter's preaching in 10:1–11:18, with the threefold telling of the divine revelation that instructed Peter not to treat Gentiles as impure, does not make much sense unless Luke wants his readers to understand that the conversion of Cornelius represents a fundamentally new step in the movement of the gospel of Jesus Christ from Jerusalem via Judea and Samaria to the ends of the earth (1:8).

Some have suggested that the present episode has been shaped as a fulfillment of Zeph 2:4, 11–12; 3:4, 10, where we find references to Gaza, desert, worship by all the nations, Ethiopians, prophets borne by the wind, and God's scattered people from beyond the rivers of Ethiopia bringing sacrifices. There are also references to the worship of Ethiopians in Ps 68:31 (LXX 67:32), and in Isa 11:11; 18:1–7; 45:14, and

---

1. Eusebius, *Hist. eccl.* 2.1.13, asserting that the Ethiopian official "first among the Gentiles, received of the mysteries of the divine word from Philip in consequence of a revelation, and having become the first-fruits of believers throughout the world." Cf. Christoph W. Stenschke, *Luke's Portrait of Gentiles prior to Their Coming to Faith* (WUNT 2/108; Tübingen: Mohr Siebeck, 1999), 147–48.

2. Cf. Johnson, *Acts*, 159.

there are references to foreigners from distant lands praying in Solomon's temple in 1 Kgs 8:41 – 43 and promises to foreigners and eunuchs in Isa 56:3 – 8. Some suggest the main focus of the episode is not that the official is an Ethiopian but a eunuch, in whom the promise of Isa 56:3 – 8 has been fulfilled.[3] While there are no obvious allusions to any of these passages, "we do have the phenomenon of echoes, intended or otherwise, that might be picked up by the alert reader; what is promised in the OT now finds fulfillment."[4] A different explanation of this episode suggests that the conversion of the Ethiopian official represents the movement of the gospel to the second of the three geographical regions in the Jewish "table of nations" (Gen 10), i.e., the mission to Ham.[5]

Exegetical Outline

→ **I. The Conversion of an Ethiopian Official (8:26 – 40)**

    A. Introduction: Philip and an Ethiopian Official (8:26 – 28)

        1. Philip's travels prompted by a heavenly revelation (8:26 – 27a)

        2. Introduction of the Ethiopian official (8:27b – 28)

    B. The Encounter of Philip and the Ethiopian (8:29 – 31)

        1. Philip's approach to the Ethiopian's chariot (8:29 – 30a)

        2. Philip hears the Ethiopian read from the prophet Isaiah (8:30b)

        3. Philip asks the Ethiopian whether he understands the prophet's words (8:30c-d)

        4. The Ethiopian confesses his lack of understanding (8:31a-b)

        5. The Ethiopian invites Philip into the chariot (8:31c-d)

    C. The Proclamation of the Gospel of Jesus by Philip (8:32 – 35)

        1. The Ethiopian was reading Isa 53:7 – 8 (8:32a)

        2. The Servant who is willingly killed: quotation of Isa 53:7 – 8 (8:32b – 33)

        3. The Ethiopian inquires about the identity of the one who died (8:34)

        4. Philip explains the fulfillment of Isaiah's prophecy in the good news of Jesus (8:35)

    D. The Conversion and Baptism of the Ethiopian (8:36 – 38)

        1. The Ethiopian requests to be baptized (8:36)

        2. The Ethiopian stops the chariot (8:38a)

        3. The Ethiopian goes with Philip into the water (8:38b)

        4. Philip immerses the Ethiopian (8:38c)

    E. Philip and the Ethiopian Believer Continue Their Travels (8:39 – 40)

        1. Philip is removed by the Spirit (8:39a-b)

        2. The Ethiopian convert continues his journey (8:39c-e)

        3. Philip preaches in the cities on the Palestinian coast (8:40)

---

3. Cf. Pao, *New Exodus*, 140 – 42.

4. Marshall, "Acts," 573.

5. Scott, "Luke's Geographical Horizon," 533 – 38; according to Scott, the mission to Shem is described in Acts 2:1 – 8:25, the mission to Ham in 8:26 – 40, and the mission to Japheth in 9:1 – 28:31; for a critical discussion of the description of Paul's mission as "mission to Japheth," cf. Schnabel, *Early Christian Mission*, 2:1297 – 99.

Explanation of the Text

8:26 Then the angel of the Lord said to Philip, "Go south on the road that goes from Jerusalem to Gaza, the desert route" (ἄγγελος δὲ κυρίου ἐλάλησεν πρὸς Φίλιππον λέγων· ἀνάστηθι καὶ πορεύου κατὰ μεσημβρίαν ἐπὶ τὴν ὁδὸν τὴν καταβαίνουσαν ἀπὸ Ἰερουσαλὴμ εἰς Γάζαν, αὕτη ἐστὶν ἔρημος). Philip's encounter with the Ethiopian official is the result of the initiative of "the angel of the Lord" (ἄγγελος κυρίου), a divine intervention that is not uncommon in Acts.[6] In v. 29 the directive to approach the chariot of the Ethiopian is given by the Holy Spirit; here (as in 10:3, 19) there is no appreciable difference between the source of the heavenly intervention. Philip is the same person as the evangelist among the Samaritans (8:4 – 25), the Greek-speaking Jewish believer who belonged to the group of the Seven (6:1 – 6). He is directed to "go south." The phrase translated "south" (κατὰ μεσημβρίαν) could also be interpreted as a temporal marker meaning "at noon";[7] since the following directive concerns geographical location, the meaning "south" is more likely.

The "desert route" from Jerusalem to Gaza passes through Beth-Ther via Beth Guvrin (Begabris) and Lachish. Gaza was a major center on the caravan route leading to Egypt. The city of Gaza, the old city of the Philistines in the southern coastal plain, was destroyed by Alexander the Great in 332 BC and sacked by Alexander Jannaeus in 98 BC. It became famous as a center of trade with Arabia, which extended as far east as India. After the death of Herod I, the city became a semiautonomous

polis under the control of the Roman governor in Syria. By the middle of the first century, Gaza is described as an important city with numerous pagan temples. When the new Gaza was built, the site of the old city remained "desolate" (ἔρημος; Strabo, 16.2.30); thus understood, Luke's comment may mean, "I refer to the old deserted Gaza."[8]

8:27 So he started out. There was an Ethiopian eunuch, a court official of Candace, the queen of the Ethiopians, who was in charge of her entire treasury. He had visited Jerusalem to worship (καὶ ἀναστὰς ἐπορεύθη. καὶ ἰδοὺ ἀνὴρ Αἰθίοψ εὐνοῦχος δυνάστης Κανδάκης βασιλίσσης Αἰθιόπων, ὃς ἦν ἐπὶ πάσης τῆς γάζης αὐτῆς, ὃς ἐληλύθει προσκυνήσων εἰς Ἰερουσαλήμ). Philip instantly follows the angel's instructions, which allows him to meet, as part of God's sovereign plan, a high Ethiopian official. Luke provides detailed information about the individual whom Philip is directed to meet.

1. He is an "Ethiopian man" (ἀνὴρ Αἰθίοψ), i.e., he comes from Nubia, the kingdom south of Egypt in which dark-skinned people live.

2. He is a "eunuch" (εὐνοῦχος), a term that denotes a male rendered infertile through castration.[9] Many eunuchs were slaves, and they were stigmatized for life because of their castration. While they were ridiculed, they could achieve high office, particularly in oriental courts as the officials responsible for the harem and raising the children. The term can also denote a person who abstains from sexual activity.[10] The use of

---

6. Cf. 5:19; 10:3, 7, 22; 11:13; 12:7 – 11, 23; 27:23; in the Old Testament cf. Gen 16:9; 2 Kgs 1:3, 15.

7. The meaning "south" reflects the position of the sun at midday; cf. BDAG, s.v. μεσημβρία 2.

8. Barrett, *Acts*, 423. In this context, the term ἔρημος does not refer to a desert but to a deserted or desolate site.

9. The Greek term is derived from the phrase ὁ τὴν εὐνὴν

ἔχων ("the one who supervises the bed"). The LXX uses the term εὐνοῦχος (Gen 39:1; 40:2, 7; 1 Sam 8:15) or σπάδων (from σπάω "to tear out"; cf. Gen 37:36; Isa 39:7).

10. Cf. Matt 19:12, where εὐνοῦχος refers to a castrated male person, to an impotent male person (without having had a physical operation), and a male person who abstains from marriage (without being impotent); cf. BDAG.

εὐνοῦχος in the LXX does not necessarily imply emasculation.[11] In Esther and Daniel it denotes officers of the royal household. According to Deut 23:1 (MT 23:2) castrates were not permitted to enter the sanctuary.[12] Precisely what Luke intends here is debated. If the Ethiopian has been castrated, Luke presumably uses the episode to demonstrate that the promise of Isa 56:3 – 8, which removes the ban of Deut 23:1, finds fulfillment in the mission of the early church.

3. He was a "court official" (δυνάστης) of "Candace, the queen of the Ethiopians." Candace was the title of the Ethiopian queens, who sometimes ruled for their sons. A queen Nawidemak ruled Nubia in the first half of the first century AD, attested as *qore*; she could be the Candace of Luke's account.[13]

4. He was "in charge of her entire treasury," i.e., he was the official responsible for the financial affairs of the queen and thus probably of the Ethiopian state. The fact that he undertook the long journey from Nubia to Judea suggests he was a person of means.

5. He had been visiting Jerusalem in order to worship (προσκυνήσων, future participle expressing purpose). This piece of information makes sense if he was a diaspora Jew or a proselyte, although a visit to the temple in Jerusalem would also be appealing for a sympathizer of the Jews and even for a Gentile. In view of the long and detailed exposition of the conversion of Cornelius in 10:1 – 11:18, the assumption seems plausible that Luke would take note if a Gentile had been converted earlier. This implies that the Ethiopian was either a diaspora Jew (who may

have been castrated at some point, perhaps as a slave), a proselyte (described as "eunuch" on account of his position at the royal court), or a Gentile firmly tied to Judaism — he visits Jerusalem in order to worship Yahweh and he reads Isaiah.

If he was literally a eunuch, he probably would have been prohibited from entering the inner courts of the temple. It is unclear, however, whether a proselyte or God-fearer knew about the prohibition of Deut 23:1, and it is unclear how the prohibition would have been enforced. Also, he could have worshiped the God of Israel by praying in the outer court, which anyone could visit (see on 2:46). If he did enter the court of the Israelites, his worship would have involved the offering of sacrifices.

8:28 And was returning home. Seated in his chariot he was reading the prophet Isaiah (ἦν τε ὑποστρέφων καὶ καθήμενος ἐπὶ τοῦ ἅρματος αὐτοῦ καὶ ἀνεγίνωσκεν τὸν προφήτην Ἠσαΐαν). The Ethiopian official returns via Gaza and Alexandria to Ethiopia, traveling in a "chariot" (ἅρμα), a term that denotes both a war chariot and a traveling carriage. The comment in v. 38 implies that the Ethiopian was using a carriage, which needed at least a driver, if not also a man at the bridle. As a court official he would not have traveled alone, which means that he used one of the larger carriages and was accompanied by one or presumably two people.

As he was sitting in his carriage, he was reading in the book of Isaiah. The imperfect tense of the verb for reading (ἀνεγίνωσκεν) suggests that he was involved in reading over an extended period of time. Since he had probably bought the scroll

---

11. Cf. Jer 52:25; Neh 1:11 (= LXX 2 Esdr 11:11).

12. Deut 23:2 MT is usually interpreted in the sense that Gentiles who had been castrated could not become proselytes. The rabbinic tradition interprets the text with regard to Jews (!) who have been castrated and who are prohibited from marrying an Israelite woman; they were allowed to marry a proselyte

woman or a Gentile female slave who had been manumitted by her owner. Cf. *Sipre Deut.* 247; *y. Yebam.* 8:2; *b. Yebam.* 76a-b; cf. Avemarie, *Tauferzählungen*, 57 – 61.

13. Edwin M. Yamauchi, *Africa and the Bible* (Grand Rapids: Baker, 2004), 172; Craig S. Keener, "Novels' 'Exotic' Places and Luke's African Official (Acts 8:27)," *AUSS* 46 (2008): 5 – 20, 18.

he was reading in Jerusalem, he would have presumably started reading from the beginning. By the time he met Philip, he had progressed to the section we call Isaiah 53.[14] If he was a diaspora Jew, he could have bought a Hebrew scroll. If he was a proselyte, we can assume that his Isaiah scroll was written in Greek. It is perhaps no coincidence that the verses quoted from Isa 53 in Acts 8:32 – 33 correspond exactly to the LXX, which diverges significantly from the Masoretic text. The comment in v. 30 indicates that the Ethiopian was reading aloud, as was the custom in antiquity. The book of Isaiah was often copied and read by Jews, as the twenty-one Isaiah manuscripts and the six Isaiah commentaries (*pesharim*) discovered at Qumran indicate.[15]

8:29 – 30 The Spirit said to Philip, "Go and stick to this chariot." Philip ran up and heard him reading the prophet Isaiah. He said to him, "Do you understand what you are reading?" (εἶπεν δὲ τὸ πνεῦμα τῷ Φιλίππῳ· πρόσελθε καὶ κολλήθητι τῷ ἅρματι τούτῳ. προσδραμὼν δὲ ὁ Φίλιππος ἤκουσεν αὐτοῦ ἀναγινώσκοντος Ἡσαΐαν τὸν προφήτην καὶ εἶπεν· ἆρά γε γινώσκεις ἃ ἀναγινώσκεις;). God's Spirit directs Philip to approach the carriage driving along at some distance from him and join it. Philip obeys the twofold command and runs toward and then alongside the carriage, which allows him to hear what the traveler is reading. He asks him whether he understands what he is reading (v. 30). Reading does not guarantee understanding, irrespective of whether "understanding" (γινώσκω) should be understood here in terms of "arriving at a knowledge of something," "acquiring information," or "grasping the significance or meaning of something."[16]

The Ethiopian official has reached a passage whose significance Philip is eager to explain, as it would allow the traveler to understand the reference of the Isaiah text to the life and death of Jesus. While Philip's question is not rhetorical in the strict sense, it is certainly leading, as he is not likely to encounter a wealthy foreign traveler on the road to Gaza who reads Isaiah in the light of the events of Jesus' life, death, and resurrection.

8:31 He replied, "How can I, unless someone guides me?" Then he invited Philip to get in and sit beside him (ὁ δὲ εἶπεν· πῶς γὰρ ἂν δυναίμην ἐὰν μή τις ὁδηγήσει με; παρεκάλεσέν τε τὸν Φίλιππον ἀναβάντα καθίσαι σὺν αὐτῷ). The Ethiopian official replies that he cannot understand the meaning of what he is reading unless somebody "guides" him to the correct meaning. The official's reply does not communicate literary incompetence: he is able to read Isaiah's words, and he understands what the words mean, but he does not know the reference of the text. He does not discern whether Isaiah describes his own life and death or the affliction of another person (v. 34). Since the Ethiopian is looking for guidance, he invites Philip to get into the carriage and sit beside him. Philip accepts the invitation.

8:32 – 33 This is the passage of Scripture that he was reading: "He was led like a sheep to the slaughter, and like a lamb before its shearer is silent, so he did not open his mouth. He was deprived of justice in his humiliation. Who can speak of his descendants? For his life is taken away from the earth" (ἡ δὲ περιοχὴ τῆς γραφῆς ἣν ἀνεγίνωσκεν ἦν αὕτη· ὡς πρόβατον ἐπὶ σφαγὴν ἤχθη καὶ ὡς ἀμνὸς ἐναντίον τοῦ κείραντος αὐτὸν ἄφωνος, οὕτως οὐκ ἀνοίγει τὸ στόμα αὐτοῦ. Ἐν τῇ ταπεινώσει αὐτοῦ ἡ κρίσις αὐτοῦ ἤρθη· τὴν γενεὰν

---

14. The modern chapter divisions were created by Stephan Langdon for the University of Paris around 1203, revised by Hugh of St. Cher around 1240.

15. L. H. Schiffman, "Isaiah, Book of," *EDSS*, 1:384 – 85.

16. Cf. BDAG, s.v. γινώσκω 1 – 3, with v. 30 linked with the third meaning.

αὐτοῦ τίς διηγήσεται; ὅτι αἴρεται ἀπὸ τῆς γῆς ἡ ζωὴ αὐτοῦ).

The next part of the episode narrates the proclamation of the gospel by Philip (vv. 32 – 35). The portion that the Ethiopian was reading is Isa 53:7 – 8, quoted here following the Greek translation. These lines belong to the larger context of Isa 52:13 – 53:12, which speaks of a servant of Yahweh who suffers intense humiliation and affliction, who is deprived of justice and is treated like an outcast. He suffers willingly, silent like a lamb about to be slaughtered, without complaint. He is killed before he can have descendants, and he is buried. However, he is eventually vindicated by God and exalted and honored even by kings.

Luke does not quote the statement in Isa 53:12, which speaks of the Servant's vindication, nor Isa 53:5 – 6 or the last line of 53:8, which describe the purpose of the Servant's suffering and death as being "pierced for our transgressions," "crushed for our iniquities," "cut off from the land of the living," and punished "for the transgression of my people," with the result that "the punishment that brought us peace was on him, and by his wounds we are healed." The fact that the effects of the servant's suffering are not mentioned agrees with Luke's tendency in Acts: he does not focus on the significance of Jesus' death in terms of a vicarious sacrifice that creates the possibility of forgiveness and salvation for sinners who repent (but see 20:28). Rather, he uses Scripture here to emphasize that Jesus is God's agent and that his suffering and death do not negate the fact that he was the promised Messiah since they were an essential part of his divinely ordained mission as expressed in Scripture.[17]

8:34 Then the official said to Philip, "May I ask about whom the prophet says this? About himself or about someone else?" (ἀποκριθεὶς δὲ ὁ εὐνοῦχος τῷ Φιλίππῳ εἶπεν· δέομαί σου, περὶ τίνος ὁ προφήτης λέγει τοῦτο; περὶ ἑαυτοῦ ἢ περὶ ἑτέρου τινός;). The fundamental question that the Ethiopian asks was the same question that Isaiah's contemporaries, and Jews ever since, have been asking, namely, who is the servant described not only in Isa 52:13 – 53:12 but in other passages? The people of Israel themselves (as in Isa 41:8 – 9; 43:10; 44:1 – 2)? Rulers such as David (Isa 37:35)? God's messengers (Isa 44:26)? Someone who has a mission to Israel, like a prophet (Isa 49:5 – 7; 50:10)? Perhaps Isaiah himself? Who is the servant who establishes justice on earth and who is a light to the nations (Isa 42:1 – 7)? Who is the servant sent as God's messenger who is accused of being blind and deaf (Isa 42:18 – 20)?

One could indeed be excused "for being uncertain whether by the time we get to chapter 53 the reference is to the people or to an individual messenger and servant of God, perhaps even the author himself, whose message was not always acceptable to his audience."[18] The exaltation of the servant was applied to the true Israel in Dan 11 – 12; the elect and righteous Servant is identified with the Son of Man in Dan 7:13 and with the Messiah of Isa 11 and thus understood as Savior and Judge in the Similitudes of *1 Enoch* 37 – 71. Some Qumran texts seem to have interpreted the text messianically in terms of the end-time high priest, with the motif of a vicarious atoning death perhaps present in 4Q541, a motif that is clearly retained from the Hebrew text in the Greek translation of the LXX.[19]

---

17. Marshall, "Acts," 575, who points out that this emphasis "is of a piece with the emphasis both in the Gospels and in the evangelistic and apologetic speeches in Acts"; he rejects the suggestion that Luke deliberately avoided the concept of atonement as unlikely, arguing that "more probably he is relating how the church at this early stage dealt with the offense of the crucifixion by emphasizing that it was willed by God."

18. Marshall, "Acts," 574.

19. Martin Hengel, "The Effective History of Isaiah 53 in the Pre-Christian Period," in *The Suffering Servant: Isaiah 53 in Jewish and Christian Sources* (ed. B. Janowski and P. Stuhlmacher; Grand Rapids: Eerdmans, 2004), 75 – 146. On 4Q541 see Zimmermann, *Messianische Texte*, 247 – 77.

8:35 Then Philip began with this passage of Scripture and proclaimed the good news about Jesus (ἀνοίξας δὲ ὁ Φίλιππος τὸ στόμα αὐτοῦ καὶ ἀρξάμενος ἀπὸ τῆς γραφῆς ταύτης εὐηγγελίσατο αὐτῷ τὸν Ἰησοῦν). Philip uses this Scripture passage to "proclaim the good news" (εὐηγγελίσατο) about Jesus. Rather than explicitly asserting that Philip explained Isaiah's words as fulfilled in the life and death of Jesus,[20] Luke points out that Philip "began" (ἀρξάμενος)[21] with the Isaiah text and uses it to explain the life, suffering, and death of the Servant in Isaiah before proceeding to explain the connections with the life, suffering, and death of Jesus in terms of being "good news" (εὐαγγέλιον).

Since Jesus himself had described the purpose of his life and death in terms of the Servant of Isa 53 (cf. Mark 10:45), the connection between Isaiah's Servant and the life and death of Jesus was recognized in the early church right from the beginning. Luke does not tell us how Philip proclaimed the good news of Jesus on the basis of Isa 53. The description of v. 32 (Isa 53:7) could be used to present Jesus' suffering as the humble acceptance of God's will and his death as in some sense sacrificial; v. 33a-b (Isa 54:8a) continues the theme of suffering and could be linked to Jesus' humiliation as the right to a fair trial was taken away from him. The reference to descendants in v. 33c (Isa 54:8b) is ambiguous, unless it is understood as a reference to Jesus' followers, who are described as becom-

ing so numerous that they cannot be counted. The statement in v. 33d (Isa 54:8c) refers either to Jesus being killed or to his ascension, which removed him from the earth. The earlier speeches in Acts suggest that Philip would have spoken about the need for repentance, God's offer of forgiveness of sins and salvation through faith in Jesus, the crucified, risen, and exalted Messiah and Savior — expressed as personal commitment through immersion in water (cf. 2:22 – 36, 38 – 40).

8:36 As they traveled along the road, they came to some water. The official said, "Look, here is water! What prevents me from being baptized?" (ὡς δὲ ἐπορεύοντο κατὰ τὴν ὁδόν, ἦλθον ἐπί τι ὕδωρ, καί φησιν ὁ εὐνοῦχος· ἰδοὺ ὕδωρ, τί κωλύει με βαπτισθῆναι;). As the carriage of the Ethiopian official continues to travel on the road to Gaza, he sees "some water" (τι ὕδωρ), an expression that may refer to a stream or a pool. The phrase "what prevents me" may simply mean something like "why not?" and should not be interpreted in terms of liturgical requirements for a valid baptism. Philip's explanation of the good news of Jesus included instruction about repentance and faith in Jesus as Messiah and Savior, expressed in immersion in water "in the name of Jesus the Messiah" (cf. 2:38). The official's request to be baptized implies that he wants to express his faith in Jesus and become a follower of Jesus.[22]

---

20. Cf. Acts 1:16; 3:18; 7:17; 13:32 – 33.

21. The phrase that ESV, KJV, NASB, RSV, translate with "(Philip) opened his mouth" (ἀνοίξας … τὸ στόμα αὐτοῦ) reflects a Hebrew expression, translated literally in the LXX, that signals the beginning of a verbal statement; the same expression occurs in 10:34; 18:14; cf. also 1:16; 3:18; 4:25. The phrase has no equivalent in idiomatic English and should be left untranslated (as here, since the Greek word for "begin" also occurs in v. 35), or rendered with "he began to speak."

22. Since Irenaeus (*Haer.* 3.12.8) in the second century, the tradition of Acts 8 knows of a confession of faith of the Ethiopian official; since the eighth century (codex E) several ancient manuscripts and quotations in the church fathers include all or

parts of the sentence, "And Philip said, 'If you believe with all your heart, you may.' And he replied, 'I believe that Jesus Christ is the Son of God.'" The most important early manuscripts do not have v. 37 ($\mathfrak{P}^{45}$ $\mathfrak{P}^{74}$ ℵ A B C etc.). The verse does not appear in manuscript 2 (12th century), which Erasmus used for Acts and the Pauline epistles; he copied it from the margin of manuscript 4 (13th century) because he "judged that it had been omitted by the carelessness of scribes;" cf. Metzger, *Textual Commentary*, 315 – 16. Since Erasmus's Greek New Testament, v. 37 has been included in the translations of the Bible (in English versions since William Tyndale); today most English translations omit v. 37; NASB includes it in brackets.

8:38 He ordered the chariot to stop, and both of them, Philip and the official, went down into the water, and he immersed him (καὶ ἐκέλευσεν στῆναι τὸ ἅρμα καὶ κατέβησαν ἀμφότεροι εἰς τὸ ὕδωρ, ὅ τε Φίλιππος καὶ ὁ εὐνοῦχος, καὶ ἐβάπτισεν αὐτόν). Luke records the Ethiopian's baptism, not Philip's answer to his suggestion that he might be baptized. The details of the verse are vivid; four verbs in the aorist tense describe what happened. The official "ordered" (ἐκέλευσεν) the driver "to stop" (στῆναι) the carriage. This allowed the occupants to step out of the carriage and walk to the water. Then Philip and the official "went down" (κατέβησαν) into the water, and standing in the water, Philip "immersed" (ἐβάπτισεν) him.[23]

8:39 When they came up out of the water, the Spirit of the Lord took Philip away. The official saw him no more, but continued on his way rejoicing (ὅτε δὲ ἀνέβησαν ἐκ τοῦ ὕδατος, πνεῦμα κυρίου ἥρπασεν τὸν Φίλιππον καὶ οὐκ εἶδεν αὐτὸν οὐκέτι ὁ εὐνοῦχος, ἐπορεύετο γὰρ τὴν ὁδὸν αὐτοῦ χαίρων). The Spirit continues to direct Philip's movement (cf. vv. 26, 29). After the Ethiopian official has committed himself to faith in Jesus and been baptized, the Spirit takes Philip away, disappearing from view. Although the verb translated "took away" (ἥρπασεν) does not necessarily imply a supernatural event, this is evidently meant here.[24] Philip suddenly disappears, carried away by the Spirit of the Lord.[25]

The Ethiopian official continues his journey "rejoicing," a remark that reflects the reality of his faith in Jesus as Israel's Messiah and the Savior from sins, implying that he had received the Holy Spirit;[26] the present participle "rejoicing" (χαίρων) suggests a permanent reality of his commitment to Jesus. Irenaeus and Eusebius relate that the converted eunuch was the first missionary to Ethiopia.[27]

8:40 Philip found himself at Azotus. As he continued his travels, he proclaimed the good news in all the towns until he reached Caesarea (Φίλιππος δὲ εὑρέθη εἰς Ἄζωτον· καὶ διερχόμενος εὐηγγελίζετο τὰς πόλεις πάσας ἕως τοῦ ἐλθεῖν αὐτὸν εἰς Καισάρειαν). The Spirit takes Philip to Azotus, the ancient Philistine capital of Ashdod, about twenty-two miles (35 km) north of Gaza. Luke does not report that Philip preached in Azotus, but this seems to be implied from the following statement. Evidently Philip had become one of the early itinerant missionaries who "traveled from place to place" (continuously, note the present participle διερχόμενος) and "proclaimed the good news" (continuously, note the imperfect εὐηγγελίζετο).

The comment that he preached "in all the towns" implies the tactical (or "strategic") decision by Philip to cover an entire region — in this case the cities in the coastal plain between Azotus and Caesarea. In 21:8 Philip is described as an "evangelist" (εὐαγγελιστής) living in Caesarea, which may suggest that at this later point in time he was no longer an itinerant missionary but a leader in the local church responsible for proclaiming the gospel.

---

23. This is the most likely scenario. If the body of water was an intermittent stream resulting from recent rains, there may not have been sufficient water for immersion; note that the *Didache* states that immersion is not necessary (7:3) while asserting that baptism should take place in running water if possible (7:1).

24. As in 2 Cor 12:2, 4; 1 Thess 4:17; Rev 12:5.

25. Scholars mention 1 Kgs 18:12; 2 Kgs 2:16; Ezek 3:14 as parallels; note that the verbs used in these passage is different (αἴρω, ἐξαίρω).

26. Cf. Acts 2:46; 5:41; 13:52; 15:3; 16:34.

27. Irenaeus, *Haer.* 4.23.2; Eusebius, *Hist. eccl.* 2.1.13.

Theology in Application

This passage about Philip's evangelism of the Ethiopian suggests several elements about the mission of the church.

Taking the Gospel to the Ends of the Earth

The mission of the church involves taking the gospel to the ends of the earth. Jesus had commanded the Twelve to take the gospel to "all nations" (Matt 28:19), from Jerusalem, Judea, and Samaria to "the ends of the earth" (Acts 1:8). Since the Twelve represent the church, it is the task of the church to preach the good news of Jesus in cities and towns in every region of the earth. Philip had been preaching in Samaria (8:4 – 25); now he explains the gospel to an Ethiopian official, who is converted to faith in Jesus (8:26 – 39). Philip then continues to preach in the territory of Judea in the cities of the coastal plain from Azotus to Caesarea (8:40). Since Ethiopia was regarded as being located at the southern end of the earth (see on 1:8; 8:27), our passage implies that the church takes Jesus' commission seriously in terms of a "global" perspective, although it must be emphasized that the contact with the Ethiopian official was not the result of Philip's planning but the result of the supernatural guidance of the Holy Spirit.

The church in Jerusalem was under immense pressure during this period, suffering persecution by the Jewish authorities. However, the leaders of the church, among whom Philip has to be counted as a member of the group of Seven, continued to focus on missionary work. Modern management methods may suggest that in order to achieve a goal — such as raising sufficient money for a church building — the leaders of a congregation must "stay on message," which means that they should allow neither themselves nor the congregation to be "distracted" by other matters, such as the implementation of a small groups program or new church planting initiatives. The early church had to deal with many issues simultaneously; missionary outreach and evangelism always seem to have been a key component of their "program."

Directed by the Spirit of God

The mission of the church is directed by the Spirit of God. Luke repeatedly emphasizes God's initiative (vv. 26, 29, 39), making the theological point that the church and her missionaries reckon with and follow divine guidance. Here, the Spirit specifically calls Philip to proclaim the gospel to a person in a different geographical location and with a different cultural and social identity — an educated and politically influential man who lives in another country in a society with different values and traditions. While the emphasis on crossing cultural, social, and religious boundaries is stronger and more explicit in the narrative of Peter's vision and visit to the pagan Cornelius in 10:1 – 11:18, it cannot be missed here either.

There are no intrinsic communication problems in Philip's encounter with this Ethiopian high court official, who has just embarked on a long journey back to his home country. Philip takes advantage of the opportunity that presents itself — or, rather, that God's Spirit presents to him — for explaining the good news of Jesus. As important and as helpful as strategies, methods, and planning are in the task of missionary proclamation and evangelistic outreach, Christians must not miss the promptings of God's Spirit to initiate spontaneous conversations in unforeseen circumstances that some might deem even inappropriate. At the same time, we should note that the direction by the Spirit did not absolve Philip from being obedient to God's call to witness to the traveler in the carriage on the road to Gaza.

Individuals and Groups

The mission of the church is directed to individuals as well as to larger groups of people. While Luke has recounted the preaching and teaching of the apostles in Jerusalem and of Philip in Samaria before larger groups of people, Philip's encounter with the Ethiopian official is an example of evangelistic conversations with individuals. Evangelism before larger groups of people involves preaching; evangelism of individuals is never preaching in the formal sense of the word but involves a conversation with questions and comments by the person who is willing to hear the gospel.

Not every non-Christian is asking questions while reading the Bible. Some conversations about the Christian faith with unbelievers are easy, others are difficult. Some training for "personal evangelism" has involved specific, streamlined principles or truths that are to be communicated in a particular sequence, perhaps using memorized lines. Such approaches may work, for the Holy Spirit does not wait to speak to people through our words until we have the "perfect" method. But we may miss the more important point that followers of Jesus who have truly understood the gospel and who love and care for those who are not believers in Jesus may have a way of speaking about the gospel that is in tune with the particular occasion. If Christians can talk about the weather, or baseball, or their children, or their dog, they should be able to find words to talk about what they claim is their first love and their most important priority. It is in personal conversations that people can ask questions — both the person who has not yet heard or understood the gospel and the evangelist sharing the gospel — questions that can then be used to explain the meaning of the God's Word and the significance of Jesus Christ.

The Study of Scripture and the Proclamation of Jesus

The mission of the church is focused on the study of Scripture and on the proclamation of Jesus. Philip helps the Ethiopian official to understand a passage of Scripture that can be used to explain the life, death, resurrection, and exaltation of Jesus Christ. Instruction from the Scriptures is an important element in the proclamation of the good news of Jesus, whose life and mission fulfill Scripture. The question "do you understand what you are reading?" (v. 30) is the most fundamental question of biblical hermeneutics. A true understanding of Scripture that comprehends not only the meaning of words and phrases but the significance of its connection with God's plan of salvation requires somebody who can explain. While skits, pantomimes, music, and video clips may help in communicating the gospel, the most basic process is explaining the meaning of the Bible.

We deplored earlier the disappearance of prayer meetings in many churches. Equally deplorable is the disappearance of regular Bible study opportunities, the emphasis on entertainment rather than on learning, and the depreciation of scriptural content in sermons in some churches. The good news of Jesus Christ cannot be truly proclaimed if Scripture has not been understood, since the gospel does not consist of philosophical or religious truths and ethical maxims but of the historical reality of God's intervention in the history of humankind in Jesus, the Messiah and Savior. This explains the second part of this point: authentic missionary work and evangelism focuses on Jesus, the messianic Servant of God, who was willing to suffer and die so that sinners can have their sins forgiven and find a new life transformed by the Holy Spirit, who gives them joy.

Acts 9:1 – 30

Literary Context

The second major section in Acts relates the beginnings of the mission to the Gentiles (8:4 – 12:25), describing (in five parts) Philip's mission to the Samaritans and his encounter with an Ethiopian official (8:4 – 40); Saul's conversion and mission in Damascus and Jerusalem (9:1 – 30); Peter's mission in Judea and in Caesarea, where a pagan officer is converted (9:31 – 11:18); the mission of Jerusalem believers in Antioch in Syria (11:19 – 30), and the persecution initiated by the newly appointed Jewish king Herod Agrippa (12:1 – 25). The next three main sections focus on Paul's missionary outreach to Jews and Gentiles in Asia Minor (13:1 – 15:33), in Europe (15:35 – 18:22), and in Ephesus, again in Asia Minor (18:23 – 21:17), before Luke concludes with a long section on Paul's imprisonment in Jerusalem, Caesarea, and Rome (21:18 – 28:31).

The fact that Luke shifts the central character of his narrative from Peter (Acts 1 – 5) to Stephen (Acts 6 – 7), to Philip (Acts 8), to Saul (Acts 9), then back to Peter (Acts 10 – 12), then again to Paul (Acts 13 – 28) could rupture the unity of the narrative. However, it should be noted that Luke "stresses the similarity of the mission that central characters share, calling this similarity to our attention through similar descriptive phrases. This procedure unifies the narrative and gives this mission central thematic significance."[1]

Here we combine two episodes: the conversion of Saul (9:1 – 19b) and the beginning of his missionary work in Damascus and in Jerusalem (9:19c – 30). These two episodes constitute the second main section of Luke's report on the beginnings of the mission to the Gentiles, sandwiched by his report on Philip's mission among the Samaritans and the conversion of an Ethiopian official (8:4 – 40), and then Peter's mission among Judeans and among Gentiles living in Caesarea (9:31 – 11:18). Jesus' initiative in the conversion of Saul, who is called to preach the gospel among Gentiles as well as Jews (9:15), points forward to the later extensive description of his missionary work in synagogues and among Gentiles outside of Judea. Even though Peter's role in the conversion of Cornelius, the first pagan to come to faith in Jesus, is a major factor in the move of the gospel from Jerusalem toward the ends of the

---

1. Tannehill, *Acts*, 115.

earth, the mission of Philip and the conversion of Saul are important developments as the gospel moves into new regions.

Saul's conversion illustrates the power of the risen Jesus and the gospel as it moves from Jerusalem and Judea to the ends of the earth. The importance of that conversion is apparent since Luke narrates it three times (9:1 – 19; 22:1 – 16; 26:9 – 18).[2] In 9:1 – 19 Luke speaks; in the next two narratives Paul speaks. In 9:1 – 19 the audience is the implied reader; in 22:1 – 16 the Jews of Jerusalem are added, and in 26:9 – 18 the Roman governor Festus, King Agrippa and his wife Bernice, and other notables are there. The different contexts are responsible for the emphasis on the Jewish character of the Christian faith in 22:1 – 16 and 26:9 – 18.

III. The Beginnings of the Mission to Gentiles (8:4 – 12:25)
    A. The Mission of Philip to the Samaritans and the Conversion of an Ethiopian (8:4 – 40)
➡   **B. The Conversion of Saul-Paul and the Beginning of His Missionary Work (9:1 – 30)**
        18. The conversion of Saul of Tarsus (9:1 – 19b)
        19. The mission of Saul in Damascus and in Jerusalem (9:19c – 30)
    C. The Mission of Peter in Palestine (9:31 – 11:18)
    D. The Mission in Antioch (11:19 – 30)

Main Idea

The narrative of the sudden conversion of Saul, who had vigorously persecuted the followers of Jesus, presents this and every conversion as the result of the direct intervention in history of the risen and exalted Jesus as the Lord of the church and as the Lord of the church's mission, in which Saul is called to play a major role.

Translation

Acts 9:1 – 30

1a	Protagonist	But **Saul,**
b	Description	still breathing threats and murder against the disciples of the Lord,
c	Action	**went to the high priest**
2a	Action	and **asked him for letters**
b	Place	to the synagogues
c	Place	in Damascus,

2. Differences in the accounts will be mostly discussed in the commentary on 22:1 – 16 and 26:9 – 18. For Paul's own description of his conversion cf. Gal 1:11 – 16; 1 Cor 9:1; 15:8 – 10; Phil 3:6 – 8; 1 Tim 1:12 – 16.

d	Purpose	so that …
e	Condition	if he found any men or women there belonging to the Way,
f	Purpose	… he might bring them bound
g	Place	to Jerusalem
h	Manner	as prisoners.
3a	Setting: Time	As he approached Damascus on his journey,
b	Event	**a light from heaven suddenly flashed around him.**
4a	Setting: Action	As he fell to the ground,
b	Event	**he heard a voice saying to him,**
c	Address	*"Saul, Saul,*
d	Question	*why do you persecute me?"*
5a	Response	**He asked,**
b	Question	*"Who are you, Lord?"*
c	Response	**The reply was,**
d	Identification	*"I am Jesus,*
e		*whom you are persecuting.*
6a	Command	*Get up*
b	Command	*and go into the city*
c	Promise	*and you will be told what you must do."*
7a	Event	**The men who were traveling with him stood speechless**
b	Cause	because they heard the voice but
c	Contrast	saw no one.
8a	Action	**Saul got up from the ground,**
b	Concession	and although his eyes were open,
c	Contra-expectation	**he could see nothing.**
d	Action	**They led him by the hand**
e	Action	**and brought him**
f	Place	to Damascus.
9a	Setting: Time	For three days
b	Event	**he could not see,**
c	Event	**and he neither ate nor drank.**
10a	Character entrance	**There was a certain disciple in Damascus**
b	Identification	whose name was Ananias.
c	Action (speech)	**The Lord said to him**
d	Means	in a vision,
e	Address	*"Ananias!"*
f	Response	*"Here I am, Lord,"*
g	Action	**he answered.**
11a	Action (speech)	**The Lord said to him,**
b	Command	*"Go at once to the street*
c	Identification	*called Straight,*
d	Identification	*and at the house of Judas*
e	Command	*look for a man from Tarsus*
f	Identification	*whose name is Saul.*
g	Description	*He is there praying.*

Continued on next page.

Continued from previous page.

12a	Means/Flashback	*In a vision*
b	Event	*he has seen a man named Ananias come in*
c	Event	*and lay his hands on him*
d	Purpose	*that he may recover his sight."*
13a	Response	**Ananias answered,**
b	Address	*"Lord,*
c	Assertion	*I have heard from many people about this man,*
d	Assertion	*and how much harm he has done to your holy people*
e	Place	*in Jerusalem.*
14a	Assertion	*And he has come here*
b	Manner	*with authority from the chief priests*
c	Purpose	*to arrest all those who call upon your name."*

15a	Action	**The Lord said to him,**
b	Command	*"Go,*
c	Cause	*for he is my chosen instrument*
d	Purpose	*to carry my name*
e	Sphere/List	*before Gentiles and*
f	List	*kings, and*
g	List	*the people of Israel.*
16a	Promise	*I will show him how much he will have to suffer*
b	Cause	*for the sake of my name."*

17a	Action	**So Ananias went**
b	Action	**and entered the house.**
c	Action	**He laid his hands on him**
d	Action	**and said,**
e	Address	*"Saul,*
f	Identification	*my brother,*
g	Assertion	*the Lord Jesus,*
h	Identification	*whom you saw on the road as you were coming here,*
i	Assertion	*has sent me*
j	Purpose	*so that you may regain your sight and*
k	Purpose	*be filled with the Holy Spirit."*

18a	Time	*Immediately*
b	Event	**something like scales fell from his eyes**
c	Event	**and he regained his sight,**
d	Event	**and he was baptized,**
19a	Time	*and after taking some food,*
b	Event	**he regained his strength.**
c	Action	**He stayed with the disciples**
d	Place	in Damascus
e	Time	several days.

20a	Time	At once
b	Action	**he proclaimed Jesus**
c	Place	in the synagogues,
d	Assertion	that he is the Son of God.
21a	Reaction	**All who heard him were bewildered**
b	Action (speech)	and **said,**
c	Rhetorical question	*"Is not this the man who caused such havoc*
d	Place	*in Jerusalem*
e	Social	*among those who invoke his name?*
f	Rhetorical question	*And has he not come here*
g	Purpose	*in order to arrest them and*
h	Purpose	*take them to the chief priests?"*
22a	Time	As Saul grew steadily stronger,
b	Action	**he continued to confound the Jews**
c	Place	who lived in Damascus
d	Means	by proving that Jesus was the Messiah.
23a	Time	After considerable time had passed,
b	Action (conflict)	**the Jews conspired to kill Saul,**
c	Event	but **their plot became known to him.**
24a	Action Place	**They stood guard at the city gates**
b	Time	day and night
c	Purpose	in order to kill him.
25a	Action (resolution)	But **his disciples took him one night**
b	Action	and **let him down over the wall**
c	Means	by lowering him in a basket.
26a	Setting: Place	When he came to Jerusalem,
b	Action	**he tried to associate with the disciples,**
c	Reaction	but **they were all afraid of him,**
d	Cause	for they did not believe that he was a disciple.
27a	Action	But **Barnabas took him**
b	Action	and **brought him to the apostles.**
c	Action/Review of history	**He explained to them**
d	Report	how he had seen the Lord on the road,
e	Report	that the Lord had spoken to him,
f	Report	and how he had spoken boldly in the name of Jesus
g	Place	in Damascus.
28a	Action	So **he stayed with them**
b	Action/Place	and **moved about freely in Jerusalem,**
c	Description	preaching boldly in the name of the Lord.
29a	Action	**He conversed**
b	Action	and **debated**
c	Sphere	with the Greek-speaking Jews,
d	Reaction (conflict)	who kept attempting to kill him.
30a	Time	When the believers learned of this,
b	Action/Place (resolution)	**they took him to Caesarea**
c	Action/Place	and **sent him off to Tarsus.**

Structure and Literary Form

The two episodes that narrate the conversion of Saul of Tarsus (9:1 – 19b) and his mission in Damascus and in Jerusalem (9:19c – 30) are distinct in that his encounter with the living Jesus is the cause for the about-face of his life's mission, changing his occupation, his message, and his geographical movements. They belong closely together since Saul's missionary work in Damascus is the direct result of Jesus' call and commission to proclaim the gospel to Gentiles and to Jews (v. 15).

The first episode (the conversion of Saul) consists of four incidents. Luke first recapitulates and thus emphasizes Saul's involvement in the persecution of Jesus' followers (vv. 1 – 2) before he reports Saul's encounter with the risen and exalted Jesus on the road to Damascus (vv. 3 – 9). The third incident involves a change of scene: Jesus appears to Ananias, a follower of Jesus in Damascus, directing him to visit Saul and convey to him Jesus' call to proclaim Jesus before Gentiles and Jews, to both kings and ordinary people (vv. 10 – 16). Finally, Luke relates the evidence of Saul's conversion resulting from Jesus' revelation, Ananias's visit, and the reception of the Holy Spirit (vv. 17 – 19b).

The second episode has two incidents. Luke describes Saul's missionary activity in the synagogues of Damascus and his escape over the city walls (vv. 19c – 25); then he relates Saul's stay in Jerusalem, which includes his encounter with the local believers, his missionary activity among the Greek-speaking Jews of Jerusalem, and his forced relocation to Tarsus (vv. 26 – 30).

Both episodes are *historical narratives*. The first one, described more specifically as a *conversion narrative* and a *commissioning narrative*, takes Saul from Jerusalem to Damascus. The (active and passive) participants in the narrative are, besides Saul, the believers in Jerusalem (v. 1), the high priest (v. 1), Saul's travel companions (v. 7), Jesus (vv. 4 – 6, 10 – 12, 15 – 16), and Ananias (vv. 10 – 17). The narrative contains extensive *direct speech* (146 of 331 words in the Greek text, i.e., 44 percent), mostly of the risen and exalted Jesus (90 words) and Ananias (53 words); Saul's direct speech is limited to the question, "Who are you, Lord?" (v. 5b), merely three words of Greek text (τίς εἶ, κύριε;). The narrative includes (not a theophany in the strict sense but) a *christophany*, i.e., a manifestation of the risen and exalted Jesus (vv. 3 – 7), and a *revelation* of Jesus, who gives Ananias words of instruction and explanation (vv. 10 – 16).

The active verbs connected with Saul concern his activity as a persecutor of the followers of Jesus (vv. 1, 2, 3, 13); most of the time he is passive — he receives a command by the risen Jesus (v. 6); he is led by his companions into Damascus (v. 8); he is being spoken of by Jesus (vv. 11 – 12, 15 – 16) and by Ananias (vv. 13 – 14), and he receives a message from Ananias (v. 17). The focus on Saul's conversion (rather than on his call as a missionary) fits the context in Acts 8 – 12 with the focus on persecution (8:1 – 3; 11:19; 12:1 – 19) and on conversion (of the Samaritans, of the Ethiopian official, of Cornelius and his friends). Finally, the narrative includes a *miracle story* as Saul is healed from blindness.

The second episode takes Saul from Damascus to Jerusalem and from there to Caesarea and to Tarsus. The two occasions that Luke uses *direct speech* are linked with Saul's missionary activity in Damascus: while Saul's proclamation of Jesus as the Son of God in the synagogues is not reported in direct speech (v. 20), the reaction of the Jews of Damascus is (v. 21, two rhetorical questions). By contrast to the first episode, most of the active verbs are connected with Saul: he is with the disciples in Damascus (v. 19), he proclaims Jesus (v. 20), he increases in strength (v. 22), he confounds the Jews with his arguments (v. 22), he attempts to join the believers in Jerusalem (v. 26), he has seen the Lord on the road to Damascus (v. 27), he spoke boldly about Jesus in Damascus (v. 27), he speaks with the Greek-speaking Jews in Jerusalem (v. 28), he argues with the Jews (v. 28) — all of which demonstrate the reality of Saul's conversion to faith in Jesus as well as his obedience to Jesus' call and commission.

Exegetical Outline

➡ **I. The Conversion of Saul of Tarsus (9:1 – 19b)**

    A. Saul's Involvement in the Persecution of the Followers of Jesus (9:1 – 2)

        1. Saul and the persecution of the followers of Jesus in Judea (9:1a-b)

        2. Saul's request for letters of introduction to the Jews in Damascus (9:1c – 2c)

        3. Saul and the persecution of the followers of Jesus outside of Judea (9:2d-h)

    B. Saul's Encounter with the Risen and Exalted Jesus (9:3 – 9)

        1. Setting: Saul's travel to Damascus (9:3a)

        2. Vision: A light from heaven (9:3b)

        3. Saul's reaction: He falls to the ground (9:4a)

        4. Audition: Dialogue with the risen and exalted Jesus (9:4b – 6)

            a. Address by a voice from heaven (9:4b-c)

            b. Question of Jesus regarding the reason for Saul's activities (9:4d)

            c. Question of Saul regarding the identity of the heavenly speaker (9:5a-b)

            d. Reply of Jesus: Self-identification and identification with the believers (9:5c-e)

            e. Directive of Jesus to go into Damascus and wait for instructions (9:6)

        5. Effect on Saul's travel companions: speechless puzzlement (9:7)

        6. Effect on Saul: Blindness, travel to Damascus, and fasting (9:8 – 9)

    C. Ananias's Assignment by the Risen Jesus (9:10 – 16)

        1. Setting: Ananias is a follower of Jesus in Damascus (9:10a-b)

        2. Vision and audition (9:10c – 16)

            a. Address by the Lord (9:10c-e)

            b. Reply of Ananias, who recognizes the Lord (9:10f-g)

    c. Directive of Jesus to go to Saul (9:11 – 12)

    d. Objection of Ananias (9:13 – 14)

    e. Directive of Jesus repeated as Jesus has chosen Saul as his instrument (9:15 – 16)

D. The Evidence of Saul's Conversion (9:17 – 19b)

    1. Setting: Ananias goes to Saul and lays his hands on Saul (9:17a-c)

    2. Ananias's message (9:17d-k)

        a. Jesus speaks through Ananias (9:17d-i)

        b. Jesus will cure Saul of his blindness (9:17j)

        c. Jesus will fill him with the Holy Spirit (9:17k)

    3. Effect on Saul: He is cured of his blindness (9:18a-c)

    4. Saul's baptism (9:18d)

    5. Saul's recovery (9:19a-b)

II. The Mission of Saul in Damascus and in Jerusalem (9:19c – 30)

A. Saul's Mission in Damascus (9:19c – 25)

    1. Saul's integration into the congregation of the believers in Damascus (9:19c-e)

    2. Saul's proclamation of Jesus as the Son of God in the synagogues (9:20)

    3. Surprised reaction of the Jews of Damascus (9:21)

    4. Saul's increasing strength (9:22a)

    5. Saul's proclamation of Jesus as the Messiah (9:22b-d)

    6. Plot of the Jews of Damascus to kill Saul (9:23)

    7. Saul's escape from Damascus (9:24 – 25)

B. Saul's Visit in Jerusalem and the Departure for Tarsus (9:26 – 30)

    1. Saul's arrival in Jerusalem (9:26a)

    2. Saul's difficulties in joining the congregation in Jerusalem (9:26b-d)

    3. Saul's introduction to the believers through Barnabas (9:27)

    4. Saul's integration into the congregation and its ministry (9:28)

    5. Saul's proclamation of the gospel among the Greek-speaking Jews (9:29a-c)

    6. Plot of the Jews of Jerusalem to kill Saul (9:29d)

    7. Saul's escape from Damascus and relocation to Tarsus (9:30)

Explanation of the Text

9:1 – 2 But Saul, still breathing threats and murder against the disciples of the Lord, went to the high priest and asked him for letters to the synagogues in Damascus, so that if he found any men or women there belonging to the Way, he might bring them bound to Jerusalem as prisoners (ὁ δὲ Σαῦλος ἔτι ἐμπνέων ἀπειλῆς καὶ φόνου εἰς τοὺς μαθητὰς τοῦ κυρίου, προσελθὼν τῷ ἀρχιερεῖ ἠτήσατο παρ᾽ αὐτοῦ ἐπιστολὰς εἰς Δαμασκὸν πρὸς τὰς συναγωγάς, ὅπως ἐάν τινας εὕρῃ τῆς ὁδοῦ ὄντας, ἄνδρας τε καὶ γυναῖκας, δεδεμένους ἀγάγῃ εἰς Ἰερουσαλήμ). Saul had been involved in the attempt of the Jewish leaders to suppress the followers of Jesus since the execution of Stephen (7:58; 8:1, 3). In the introductory comments of Luke's narrative of Saul's conversion, he reiterates that Saul continued to participate in the persecution of the "disciples" (μαθηταί; see on 5:11), i.e., of those who acknowledge Jesus as Lord.

The present participle "breathing" (ἐμπνέων) indicates that Saul was involved over an extended period of time in uttering "threats" and "murder" against the believers. The interpretation that takes the phrase "threats and murder" as a hendyadis ("murderous threats;" TNIV, cf. NET) weakens the sense of Luke's statement. The threats are described in 26:11 ("by punishing them often in all the synagogues I tried to force them to blaspheme"), and in 26:10 ("I locked up many of the saints in prison with the authority that I received from the chief priests. And when they were condemned to death, I cast my vote against them"). On the reasons for Saul's violent persecution of the followers of Jesus, see on 8:3.

IN DEPTH: Saul of Tarsus, Also Called Paul

Saul was born in Tarsus (Acts 21:39; 22:3), the metropolis of Cilicia, which was administered by the Roman governor of the province of Syria throughout much of the first century. The Jewish family into which he was born was devout.[3] He was, in his own words, "circumcised on the eighth day, of the people of Israel, of the tribe of Benjamin, a Hebrew of Hebrews; in regard to the law, a Pharisee" (Phil 3:5; cf. Acts 26:5). His parents were evidently able and interested in tracing their lineage to the tribe of Benjamin. The description of being a "Hebrew of Hebrews" indicates that Saul was brought up speaking Hebrew and Aramaic and that the family adhered to the Jewish way of life regulated by the stipulations of the law, avoiding as much as possible assimilation to Gentile customs and maintaining contact with the Jewish community in Palestine.

An expression of the family's dedication to Israel's God and his law was the fact that they belonged to the Pharisaic movement (Acts 23:6). Saul had been given the name of Israel's first king, Saul (see on 7:58).[4] His Roman (or Greek) name was Paul (Lat. *Paulus* or *Paullus*, Greek Παῦλος). Since Saul/Paul was a Roman citizen (16:37), he would have had three official names (*tria nomina*); "Paul" was either the *cognomen* of his family, i.e., the official element of his name as a Roman citizen, which his family may have received after manumission by the Roman who had owned and eventually released an ancestor (Saul's father?) from slavery;[5] or it was the *signum* or *supernomen*, i.e., the Roman surname that the family used. Roman citizenship did not mean Roman ethnicity, nor does it not prove competency in using Latin. Luke transitions from using the name

---

3. Acts 22:3; Rom 11:1; 2 Cor 11:22 – 23; Gal 1:13 – 14; Phil 3:5 – 6.

4. Luke uses the Old Testament form Σαούλ in his accounts of Saul's conversion, cf. 9:4, 17; 22:7, 13; 26:14.

5. Several church fathers claim to know that Paul's father had lived in Gischala in Galilee, that he became a prisoner of war, perhaps in connection with Pompey's conquest of Palestine in 63 BC, and that he was sold as a slave; cf. Jerome, *Comm. Phlm.* 23; *Vir. ill.* 3.5.

"Saul" to "Paul" in connection with the missionary work of Saul and Barnabas on Cyprus (13:9: "Saul, also known as Paul").[6]

Saul's native language was probably Greek, because of his early years living in Tarsus, where he and his family held citizenship (Acts 21:39).[7] Growing up in Cilicia, he may even have understood the Cilician dialect, and he possibly spoke some Latin.

We do not know when Saul moved from Tarsus, his hometown, to Jerusalem. Paul's excellent Greek and his sovereign use of the Greek translation of the Hebrew Bible indicates that his upbringing in Tarsus must have played a major role in his education, even though it took second place after Jerusalem in Paul's biography. The fact that young Saul/Paul came to Jerusalem for rabbinical studies under Rabbi Gamaliel suggests that his parents were well-to-do. This, combined with his Roman citizenship, may explain why Paul had access to the elites in the Greek and Roman cities where he preached the gospel (cf. Acts 13:4 – 12; 19:31).

Saul's eagerness to help oppress the followers of Jesus comes to expression in the fact that he took the initiative to expand the persecution beyond Jerusalem and Judea. He went to the high priest, Joseph Caiaphas (see on 4:6), and asked for letters to give him the authority (v. 14) to arrest the followers of Jesus in Damascus, both men and women, and to take them to Jerusalem for interrogation and punishment. Saul's active persecution of believers in Jesus contradicts the advice that his teacher Gamaliel had given earlier to the Sanhedrin (5:34 – 39). Gamaliel may have changed his mind as he observed the continued growth and expansion of the Jesus movement. Or Saul regarded Gamaliel's position as too soft in view of the threat that the teaching of the followers of Jesus posed.

Commentators and English Bible translations assume that the letters Saul procured from the high priest were written to the synagogues in Damascus. While this is historically plausible, it is not the only possibility to understand the Greek expression here. The letters could have been written "to Damascus," i.e., to the city magistrates in Damascus "concerning the synagogues." The Mishnah preserves a report about Gamaliel going to Damascus "to ask for permission from the government in Syria" (m. 'Ed. 7:7), presumably in connection with one of the great feasts whose date depended on details of the Jewish calendar established by the Jewish authorities in Jerusalem, for which the Romans provided security. The Mishnah text "reflects a time when Gamaliel was a go-between who negotiated the interests of the Temple with the government, demonstrating his role in international Judaism as well as in Jerusalem proper."[8]

Saul, Gamaliel's student, may have used Gama-

---

6. Saul did not receive the name "Paul" at his baptism after his conversion, as is popularly assumed — there was never any dramatic change "from Saul to Paul" since the apostle had both names from his childhood onward; depending on the situation, either "Saul" or "Paul" would be used.

7. Paul's family seems to have held dual citizenship. Cf. Rainer Riesner, *Paul's Early Period: Chronology, Mission Strategy, Theology* (Grand Rapids: Eerdmans, 1998), 148 – 49.

8. Neusner and Chilton, "Paul and Gamaliel," 211.

liel's connections both in Jerusalem and in Damascus to obtain official political cover for the arrest of followers of Jesus in Syria and for their transfer to Jerusalem. Since the believers in Jerusalem could be found in the temple and in the local synagogues (2:46; 3:1; 4:1 – 2; 6:8 – 10), Saul assumes that the followers of Jesus were active in the synagogues in Damascus and could be located there. Since Ananias has heard about Saul's involvement in persecuting Christians (v. 13), he and probably most of the believers in Damascus were locals, although it is possible that some of the believers of Jerusalem who fled after Stephen's execution (8:1) made their way to Damascus.

The term "the Way" (ἡ ὁδός),[9] derived from Isa 40:3 and other passages in Isaiah that speak of the "way" on which the Lord would travel when he came to restore Israel, is used in Acts as a designation for the believers in Jesus and their teaching that God was restoring Israel through Jesus, the crucified and risen Messiah and exalted Lord and Savior, and that the community of the followers of Jesus is now the renewed people of God.

9:3 As he approached Damascus on his journey, a light from heaven suddenly flashed around him (ἐν δὲ τῷ πορεύεσθαι ἐγένετο αὐτὸν ἐγγίζειν τῇ Δαμασκῷ, ἐξαίφνης τε αὐτὸν περιήστραψεν φῶς ἐκ τοῦ οὐρανοῦ). The conversion of Saul, who travels to Damascus in order to arrest the followers of Jesus, is initiated by a vision. Luke describes what happened with two expressions. First, there was a "light from heaven" (φῶς ἐκ τοῦ οὐρανοῦ) that

"flashed around" him; i.e., it was a divine manifestation. Second, the light appeared "suddenly," without Saul having expected anything unusual to happen. The term underscores God's sovereignty in this event and links the appearance of the exalted Jesus (v. 5) with the appearances of God (theophanies) in the Old Testament.[10]

However, it is not God who appears to Saul but the crucified, risen, and exalted Jesus. The description in v. 3 describes a vision, while vv. 4 – 7 describe an audition: Saul and also his companions hear a voice, while only Saul sees the "light from heaven." Paul asserts in 1 Cor 9:1 that he has "seen" (ἑόρακα) the Lord in terms of "a real, 'objective' seeing of a supernatural reality in divine splendor of light, which makes itself known as the 'Lord' and is recognized by him as such."[11] In 1 Cor 15:5 – 8 he argues that he is an apostle because he has seen the Lord just as the Twelve have seen him, i.e., in a real ("tangible") encounter with the risen Jesus. The statement in v. 7 that Saul's travel companions "saw no one" implies that Saul saw somebody, namely, the risen Jesus.

9:4 As he fell to the ground, he heard a voice saying to him, "Saul, Saul, why do you persecute me?" (καὶ πεσὼν ἐπὶ τὴν γῆν ἤκουσεν φωνὴν λέγουσαν αὐτῷ· Σαοὺλ Σαούλ, τί με διώκεις;). Saul's reaction is typical for human encounters with visible manifestations of God's reality, an expression of the alarm and fear caused by that appearance.[12] Then Saul hears a voice coming from the light, recalling God's revelation to Moses at the

---

9. See "In Depth: The Self-Understanding of the Church in Jerusalem" at 5:11. Cf. 19:9, 23; 22:4; 24:14, 22.

10. Cf. Exod 24:15 – 17; Pss 29:7; 97:1 – 5; Isa 9:2; 42:16; 60:1; Ezek 1:4 – 14; Mic 7:8.

11. Hengel and Schwemer, *Paul*, 39. It is difficult, if not impossible, to provide a historically cogent answer to the question how the audio-vision of Paul on the road to Damascus compared with the bodily appearances of the risen Jesus among the disciples after Easter.

12. Cf. Ezek 1:28; Dan 8:17; 10:9; Rev 1:17. Painters often depict this scene in terms of Paul falling from a horse; the same is true for many children's Bibles and dramatizations of the life of Paul on video. While it is not impossible that Saul's party included horses, as he was on an official mission sanctioned by the Sanhedrin in Jerusalem, the horse is in the imagination of those who retell and illustrate the story of Saul's conversion, not in Luke's text.

burning bush (Exod 3:3) and on Mount Sinai (Exod 19:16 – 20). The dialogue that ensues has five elements.

(1) The heavenly voice addresses Saul (in Hebrew, as we learn in 22:2). This is reflected here in the fact that the name Saul (Σαούλ) represents a Hebrew name, which is usually rendered in Greek as *Saulos* (Σαῦλος). The repetition of the name shows the significance of the divine communication and underlines the solemnity of the event. In Old Testament theophanies, it is God who begins the conversation and addresses the human person with his or her name.

(2) The heavenly voice asks Saul why he is persecuting him. The present tense of the verb "persecute" (διώκεις) shows that Saul lies on the ground not because he has submitted to Jesus but because the divine manifestation has forced him to the ground. The heavenly voice abruptly interrupts Saul, whose heart and soul are in persecuting the followers of Jesus. The question of the voice implies the equivalence of "me" and "the Way" (ἡ ὁδός), i.e., the identity of the risen and the exalted Jesus (cf. v. 5) and his followers, indicating that as Saul persecutes the followers of Jesus, he is persecuting Jesus himself.[13] Thus, the question is not simply the opening of the conversation but an accusation that throws Saul's life in question.

9:5 – 6 He asked, "Who are you, Lord?" The reply was, "I am Jesus, whom you are persecuting. Get up and go into the city and you will be told what you must do" (εἶπεν δέ· τίς εἶ, κύριε; ὁ δέ· ἐγώ εἰμι Ἰησοῦς ὃν σὺ διώκεις· ἀλλὰ ἀνάστηθι καὶ εἴσελθε εἰς τὴν πόλιν καὶ λαληθήσεταί σοι ὅ τί σε δεῖ ποιεῖν). Saul is aware that something extraordinary, super-

natural is happening. He responds to the question and receives an answer.

(3) Saul responds to the question with a counterquestion. An explanation of the reason and the motivation for his involvement in persecuting the followers of Jesus depends on who is asking the question. Thus Saul asks the person who speaks from the heavenly light to identify himself (v. 5b). The context of the flashing light, the fall to the ground, the heavenly voice, and the question regarding the reason for his activities as a persecutor of believers in Jesus indicates that the term "Lord" (κύριε) is more than a polite address used in encounters with a person. While he does not yet know with whom he is dealing, he would assume, as a devout Jew who knows the Old Testament theophanies, that he is being addressed either by an angel or by God himself. If he saw Jesus in the heavenly light (see on v. 3), he would probably not have recognized him (since he evidently never met Jesus of Nazareth during his earthly ministry).

(4) Jesus replies by identifying himself with the statement "I am Jesus" (ἐγώ εἰμι Ἰησοῦς) and repeating his identification with his followers whom Saul is persecuting (v. 5d-e). The use of the name "Jesus" underlines the identity of Jesus, who speaks from the reality of God's heavenly light as Jesus of Nazareth, who had been executed by crucifixion and whose followers Saul is persecuting. Jesus has died, but he is now alive and active as the risen and exalted Son of God (cf. Gal 1:16), intervening in the mission of the church, which Saul seeks to oppress.

(5) Jesus directs Saul to go into Damascus and wait for instructions (v. 6).[14] This directive underlines the authority of the risen Jesus, who expects

---

13. Cf. Luke 10:16; Matt 10:40; 25:35 – 40, 42 – 45.

14. Some manuscripts add here or in v. 4 Jesus' statement from 26:14, "It is hard for you to kick against the goad," and from 22:10 Saul's question, "What am I to do?" These are har-

monizations with the later accounts of Saul's conversion and are not included in the best Greek manuscripts; cf. Metzger, *Textual Commentary*, 317 – 18.

immediate and full obedience. While Saul had actively taken the initiative in persecuting Christians outside of Jerusalem, he is told to wait passively for someone to take the initiative and speak to him about what he "must do" (δεῖ ποιεῖν). Since the risen Jesus had twice made Saul's involvement in the persecution of his followers an issue, identifying himself with those who believe in him, Saul can expect that his future doings will be connected with Jesus and his followers, who were proclaiming Jesus as Israel's Messiah and Savior.

9:7 The men who were traveling with him stood speechless because they heard the voice but saw no one (οἱ δὲ ἄνδρες οἱ συνοδεύοντες αὐτῷ εἱστήκεισαν ἐνεοί, ἀκούοντες μὲν τῆς φωνῆς μηδένα δὲ θεωροῦντες). The event that Luke described in vv. 3 – 6 was not a subjective, psychological, or mystical experience of Saul; it had an effect on Saul's travel companions, who stood speechless.[15] The people with Saul could have been fellow travelers en route from Judea or Galilee to Damascus. In antiquity travelers on foot avoided walking between cities alone, preferring to travel in groups for security reasons. It is more likely, however, that they were assistants, perhaps members of the temple police. After all, Saul wanted to arrest Christians in Damascus and transport them back as prisoners to Jerusalem, an action for which he would certainly need enforcers and guards.

Whoever his travel companions were, they were speechless because they heard the heavenly voice but saw "no one," a comment that implies Saul saw somebody in the manifestation of the heavenly light (cf. v. 3).[16] As they, in contrast to Saul, did not

see anyone, they would not have understood the meaning and significance of what was happening.

9:8 – 9 Saul got up from the ground, and although his eyes were open, he could see nothing. They led him by the hand and brought him to Damascus. For three days he could not see, and he neither ate nor drank (ἠγέρθη δὲ Σαῦλος ἀπὸ τῆς γῆς, ἀνεῳγμένων δὲ τῶν ὀφθαλμῶν αὐτοῦ οὐδὲν ἔβλεπεν· χειραγωγοῦντες δὲ αὐτὸν εἰσήγαγον εἰς Δαμασκόν. καὶ ἦν ἡμέρας τρεῖς μὴ βλέπων καὶ οὐκ ἔφαγεν οὐδὲ ἔπιεν). After describing the effect of the audiovisual revelation from heaven on the other travelers, Luke describes the effect of the heavenly light and of Jesus' communication on Saul. He gets up from the ground. He cannot see anything despite his eyes being open. He needs his fellow travelers to lead him into Damascus, taking him by the hand. He cannot see for three days, during which he neither eats nor drinks.

Saul had anticipated a different arrival in Damascus: contacting the local authorities, collaborating with the synagogues, gathering names and addresses of the followers of Jesus (cf. 8:3), beginning with arrests, and organizing the transport back to Jerusalem. Although he was seeking to persecute those who described themselves as "the Way," he is now unable to find his own way. He arrives in Damascus physically blinded by the heavenly light[17] and spiritually shaken by his encounter with the risen and exalted Jesus. Saul will be called by the risen Lord to be a light to the nations; but before he can fulfill this commission, "he must be converted from his condition of embodying Israel's blind resistance to the straight way of God."[18]

---

15. According to 26:14 they had fallen to the ground as well; Witherington, *Acts*, 312, explains the "we" in 26:14 as a generalizing statement that indicates that "this experience involved more than one person."

16. There is precedent for seeing but not hearing in theophanies, cf. Deut 4:12; Dan 10:7; Wis 18:1. For the discrepancy

regarding 22:9 see the comments there.

17. The blindness is not explicitly portrayed as divine punishment.

18. Dennis Hamm, "Paul's Blindness and Its Healing: Clues to Symbolic Intent (Acts 9, 22, and 26)," *Bib* 71 (1990): 53 – 72, 70.

9:10 There was a certain disciple in Damascus whose name was Ananias. The Lord said to him in a vision, "Ananias!" "Here I am, Lord," he answered (ἦν δέ τις μαθητὴς ἐν Δαμασκῷ ὀνόματι Ἀνανίας, καὶ εἶπεν πρὸς αὐτὸν ἐν ὁράματι ὁ κύριος· Ἀνανία. ὁ δὲ εἶπεν· ἰδοὺ ἐγώ, κύριε). The third incident relates the vision of Ananias, a follower of Jesus in Damascus, whom Jesus sends to Saul with the instructions that he was promised on the road (vv. 10 – 16). The first statement introduces Ananias. He is a "disciple" (μαθητής; see on 5:11) of Jesus who lives in Damascus. Luke's comment in v. 19 indicates that there was a group of disciples in the city. Since the Lord chooses Ananias as the recipient both of a vision and of the commission to go to Saul and help him in his coming to faith, we may assume that Ananias is one of the leading believers in Damascus whom Saul would have arrested and taken to Jerusalem for interrogation and punishment, had he been able to successfully carry out his original mission. In 22:12 Ananias is described as "a devout man according to the law" with a good reputation among the Jews of Damascus. The report of Ananias's vision is narrated in five steps.

First, Ananias recognizes Jesus, who appears to him in a "vision" and who speaks to him. His reply ("Here I am, Lord") indicates his readiness to carry out the Lord's will (v. 10f). While the identity of the "Lord" (κύριος) is unclear at this point in the narrative, the continuation of the dialogue in v. 15 will clarify that the Lord whom he sees and hears is the risen Jesus.

9:11 – 12 The Lord said to him, "Go at once to the street called Straight, and at the house of Judas look for a man from Tarsus whose name is Saul. He is there praying. In a vision he has seen a man named Ananias come in and lay his hands on him that he may recover his sight" (ὁ δὲ κύριος πρὸς αὐτόν· ἀναστὰς πορεύθητι ἐπὶ τὴν ῥύμην τὴν καλουμένην Εὐθεῖαν καὶ ζήτησον ἐν οἰκίᾳ Ἰούδα Σαῦλον ὀνόματι Ταρσέα· ἰδοὺ γὰρ προσεύχεται καὶ εἶδεν ἄνδρα ἐν ὁράματι Ἀνανίαν ὀνόματι εἰσελθόντα καὶ ἐπιθέντα αὐτῷ τὰς χεῖρας ὅπως ἀναβλέψῃ). The content and purpose of appearances of God in the Old Testament are never to entertain the person experiencing the theophany. God appears to individuals in order to convey a directive or commission. The same is true for appearances of the risen Jesus, as vv. 3 – 9 (Saul) and vv. 10 – 16 (Ananias) and the two visions in 10:3 – 6 (Cornelius) and 10:10 – 16 (Peter) demonstrate.

Second, Jesus directs Ananias to go to Saul and help him recover his eyesight (vv. 11 – 12). The directive is formulated with the imperative "go" (πορεύθητι). The modal participle (ἀναστάς; often translated as "get up," NASB, NRSV), signals the initiation of an action; it is here translated "at once." The Lord's directive consists of the following elements.

(1) Ananias is given an address. He is to go to "Straight Street" (ἡ Εὐθεῖα), the main east-west street in Damascus, which is still called "Straight Street" (Derb el-Mustaqim, also Souk et-Tawil or Midhat Pasha Street), located in the eastern part of the Old City, leading to the East Gate. This street was nearly 40 feet wide, with colonnaded halls for commercial activities on both sides with two rows of Corinthian columns.

(2) Ananias must go to the house that belongs to a man named Judas, evidently a well-to-do Jew who owns a house in "downtown" Damascus. If Saul had begun to grasp the significance of his encounter with the risen Jesus while being led into the city, and if he knew the address of a leading follower of Jesus in the city, it is not impossible that this Judas with whom Saul was staying was a believer in Jesus.[19] However, Ananias's fears

19. Barrett, *Acts*, 453.

(vv. 13 – 14) suggest that Saul does not yet have contact with followers of Jesus in Damascus.

(3) With Jesus' second imperative, Ananias must "look for" Saul. The verb probably indicates that Saul is staying at the house of Judas. Or, the verb may suggest that Ananias can find out there about Saul's whereabouts, implying that he is staying somewhere else; however, v. 17 makes the first option more plausible.

(4) Then, Ananias receives the name of the person Jesus directs him to visit: he is Saul, a "man from Tarsus." People living in the eastern regions of the Mediterranean world (but also in Greece) had only one name; if it became necessary to identify a person more specifically, details of origin may be indicated by adding the city of birth. As Saul was born in Tarsus (cf. 22:3; cf. 21:39), the formulation "Saul from Tarsus" (Σαῦλος Ταρσεύς) corresponds to Hellenistic custom. Luke continues to introduce Saul gradually; here he adds the detail that Saul is a diaspora Jew born in Tarsus.

The information that Saul is now praying (προσεύχεται, present tense) suggests to Ananias that it is safe to visit the man who was planning to arrest him and his fellow believers. As regards Saul, his prayers might have conveyed to God expressions of remorse for working against Jesus, whom he encountered in the light of divine glory; of repentance for fighting against God (cf. Gamaliel's warning in 5:39); and of regret for having been involved in the arrest, punishment, and execution of followers of Jesus. Saul also probably asks for guidance concerning his life, which the risen Lord had promised in the vision on the road to Damascus.

Since v. 18 relates Saul's immersion in water, a sign of cleansing that implied confession of sin, immediately after Ananias's visit during which

he regains his eyesight, Luke clearly implies that Saul's praying and fasting for three days was the time when he was converted to faith in Jesus, the crucified, risen, and exalted Messiah and Savior, whom he proclaims "at once" in the synagogues in Damascus (v. 20).

(5) Ananias is informed about a second vision (v. 12) in which this Saul saw a man named Ananias doing two things: he would visit him, and he would lay his hands on him with the purpose of his eyesight being restored. This information should be additional motivation for Ananias to go to Saul, as God has been working in this man's life, granting him a vision and wanting to use Ananias as the person through whom he will bring healing to Saul.

9:13 – 14 Ananias answered, "Lord, I have heard from many people about this man, and how much harm he has done to your holy people in Jerusalem. And he has come here with authority from the chief priests to arrest all those who call upon your name" (ἀπεκρίθη δὲ Ἀνανίας· κύριε, ἤκουσα ἀπὸ πολλῶν περὶ τοῦ ἀνδρὸς τούτου ὅσα κακὰ τοῖς ἁγίοις σου ἐποίησεν ἐν Ἰερουσαλήμ· καὶ ὧδε ἔχει ἐξουσίαν παρὰ τῶν ἀρχιερέων δῆσαι πάντας τοὺς ἐπικαλουμένους τὸ ὄνομά σου). A frequent element in commissioning theophanies is the expression of an objection to the call, mission, or task that God has just given.[20] Ananias is no exception.

Third, therefore, Ananias objects to Jesus' directive that he should visit Saul. Despite the fact that Ananias acknowledges the lordship of Jesus in his address (κύριε), he dares object, a fact that highlights the fear that the believers had of Saul. While followers of Jesus can be courageous in the face of danger (note the apostles in Acts 5 and Stephen

---

20. Cf. Exod 3:11, 13; 4:1, 10, 13 (Moses); Isa 6:5 (Isaiah); Jer 1:6 (Jeremiah); Luke 1:18 (Zechariah). Miller, *Convinced*, 192, notes that in contrast to Zechariah's punishment for his objections to the angel Gabriel (Luke 1:20), Ananias is not punished.

in Acts 7), there is no need to walk voluntarily into the lair of a notorious henchman sent by the opposition.

The objection Ananias gives focuses on the purpose of Saul's visit to Damascus. He has heard "about this man" (v. 13c). This information came "from many people" (ἀπὸ πολλῶν) — followers of Jesus who may have fled from Jerusalem to Damascus, perhaps also local Jews who had visited Jerusalem and who were informed about the crackdown of the Jewish authorities on the followers of Jesus, with Saul playing a prominent role. The information that Ananias has received is both general and specific. He has heard that Saul has harmed the followers of Jesus in Jerusalem (v. 13d-e). The word translated as "harm" (κακά) denotes people or conditions that are socially bad and morally evil, or that are harmful and injurious and thus dangerous and pernicious. And he has heard, more specifically, that Saul has come "here" (ὧδε), i.e., to Damascus, with the explicit "authority" from the chief priests to "arrest" the followers of Jesus.

Ananias calls the believers in Jesus "your holy people" (οἱ ἅγιοί σου, v. 13d; see on 5:11), i.e., the people of God. The term is used here not for the Jewish people as a whole[21] but for the limited group of the followers of Jesus. This expression communicates the conviction that "the people of God" are "the people of the Lord Jesus," with the relationship to the Lord Jesus being decisive. God's holy people form the community of the believers in Jesus. This is a conviction that implies that the restoration of Israel has been fulfilled through Jesus, Israel's Messiah, and it implies that the concept of the people of God has been spiritualized.

Fourth, Ananias calls the followers of Jesus "those

who call upon your name" (οἱ ἐπικαλούμενοι τὸ ὄνομά σου; v. 14c), i.e., the people who invoke Jesus' name in prayer. This language (cf. v. 21; 22:16),[22] which in the Old Testament regularly describes the worship of God,[23] is drawn from Joel 2:32 into early Christian usage, where it "indicates a cultic practice of confessing Jesus as Lord that was regarded as the defining characteristic of Christians."[24]

9:15–16 The Lord said to him, "Go, for he is my chosen instrument to carry my name before Gentiles and kings, and the people of Israel. I will show him how much he will have to suffer for the sake of my name" (εἶπεν δὲ πρὸς αὐτὸν ὁ κύριος· πορεύου, ὅτι σκεῦος ἐκλογῆς ἐστίν μοι οὗτος τοῦ βαστάσαι τὸ ὄνομά μου ἐνώπιον ἐθνῶν τε καὶ βασιλέων υἱῶν τε Ἰσραηλ· ἐγὼ γὰρ ὑποδείξω αὐτῷ ὅσα δεῖ αὐτὸν ὑπὲρ τοῦ ὀνόματός μου παθεῖν). Objections voiced in theophanies and commission narratives are never accepted by God in the sense that he withdraws his commission. The same is true in the case of Ananias's objection, which Jesus overrules.

Fifth, the risen Jesus repeats his directive here. Ananias must indeed visit Saul and convey Jesus' instructions, which are now spelled out in more detail. The imperative of v. 11 is repeated: Ananias is commanded to "go" (πορεύου; v. 15; cf. v. 11) to the address previously given, find Saul of Tarsus, who is praying, and lay his hands on him so that he will regain his eyesight. The content of the earlier commission (vv. 11–12) is not repeated, but further details of Jesus' plans for Saul's life are provided, which explain why he overrules Ananias's objections. The risen Jesus makes three statements that formulate Saul's missionary commission.

(1) Saul is Jesus' "chosen instrument" (σκεῦος ἐκλογῆς; v. 15c). The term translated "instrument"

---

21. Cf. the use of the expression in Isa 62:12; see Exod 19:6; Deut 7:6; Ps 16:3; Dan 7:18, 22, 25, 27.

22. Cf. in Paul's letters also Rom 10:12–14; 1 Cor 1:2; 2 Tim 2:22.

23. Cf. Gen 4:26; 12:8; 13:4; Ps 105:1; cf. Ralph P. Martin,

Worship in the Early Church (London: Marshall, Morgan & Scott, 1964), 31.

24. Bauckham, *Jesus and the God of Israel*, 129, with further reference to Rom 10:9; 1 Cor 12:3; Phil 2:11.

denotes Saul as a person "exercising a particular function."[25] He is an "instrument" in Jesus' hands, to be used for Jesus' purposes. God's "choice" or "selection" (ἐκλογῆς) of Saul for the task described in the next statement establishes him, in the context of Saul's encounter with the risen Jesus on the road to Damascus, as an "instrument" of Jesus, in analogy to the Twelve, who were chosen and sent by Jesus (cf. Rom 1:1; 1 Cor 15:3–11).[26]

(2) The purpose of Saul's life and work is to proclaim the message of Jesus (v. 15d-g). The expression "my name" (τὸ ὄνομά μου) stands for "Jesus" (cf. 4:12, 30) and for the proclamation of the good news of Jesus as Israel's Messiah and the Savior (8:12). The word "carry" (βαστάσαι) means here "to confess" in a missionary context; Saul will acknowledge and proclaim Jesus as risen and exalted Messiah, Savior, and Lord "before" or "in front of" (ἐνώπιον) people who have not heard this message. Ananias must convey to Saul the life-changing fact that the risen Lord has called him, Saul, to missionary ministry. To confess Jesus before Gentiles and Jews means, at the same time, to go to them and introduce to them the message of Jesus.

As Jesus' instrument who takes his message and thus Jesus himself to Gentiles and Jews, Saul is his "envoy" or "apostle" (ἀπόστολος), just like the Twelve. In Gal 1:1 Paul formulates his self-understanding as Jesus' envoy in precisely this manner: "Paul, an apostle [Παῦλος ἀπόστολος] — sent not from men nor by a man, but by Jesus Christ [διὰ Ἰησοῦ Χριστοῦ] and God the Father, who raised him from the dead." Saul, who persecuted those who called on Jesus' name (v. 14), is called to confess Jesus' name. The focus of his proclamation of Jesus is the Gentiles (ἔθνη), i.e., polytheists, people who worship other gods. Luke will report Saul's

proclamation of the gospel among Gentiles in his subsequent account.[27]

But Saul is also sent to the people of Israel (υἱοὶ Ἰσραήλ, lit., "sons" or "children of Israel"). Saul's commissioning as a missionary to Gentiles (Rom 11:13; 15:15–16) does not preclude the proclamation of Jesus among the Jewish people. Paul preaches the gospel to the uncircumcised and to the circumcised (1 Cor 9:19–23). Luke will report on Saul's preaching in synagogues in his subsequent narrative.[28] And Saul will proclaim Jesus "before … kings" (ἐνώπιον … βασιλέων), a prophecy that will come to pass when he explains the message of Jesus before King Agrippa II (25:23–26:29) and perhaps before the emperor in Rome (25:12).

(3) Saul will suffer (παθεῖν) as he confesses Jesus before Gentiles and Jews. Saul, who has made those who called on Jesus' name suffer by arresting, interrogating, and punishing them, will himself suffer as Jesus' representative.[29] As Saul will take the message of Jesus to the people of Damascus (vv. 20–22), Jerusalem (vv. 28–29), Tarsus (v. 30), Antioch (11:25–26), and then Galatia, Macedonia, Achaia, and the province of Asia (Acts 13–20), the impression of "triumphalism" that some scholars see is negated both by the constant opposition Paul endures and by this announcement that his suffering is an integral part of his missionary commission.[30]

9:17 So Ananias went and entered the house. He laid his hands on him and said, "Saul, my brother, the Lord Jesus, whom who saw on the road as you were coming here, has sent me so that you may regain your sight and be filled with the Holy Spirit" (ἀπῆλθεν δὲ Ἀνανίας καὶ εἰσῆλθεν εἰς τὴν οἰκίαν καὶ ἐπιθεὶς ἐπ᾽ αὐτὸν τὰς χεῖρας εἶπεν· Σαοὺλ ἀδελφέ, ὁ κύριος ἀπέσταλκέν με, Ἰησοῦς ὁ ὀφθείς

---

25. Cf. BDAG, s.v. σκεῦος 3.

26. Cf. Matt 28:19–20; Mark 1:17; Luke 5:10; 6:13; Acts 1:8.

27. Acts 13:45–49; 14:8–20; 15:3; 17:4, 12, 17, 19 34; 18:4, 7–8; 19:9–10.

28. Acts 13:5, 15–41; 14:1; 17:2–4, 10–12, 17; 18:4–5; 19:8.

29. Cf. Luke 6:22; 21:12, 17; Acts 5:41; Johnson, *Acts*, 165.

30. For details of Paul's suffering see 1 Cor 4:11–13; 2 Cor 4:7–12; 6:4–10; 11:23–33; 12:10; cf. Rom 8:35; Phil 4:12–13.

σοι ἐν τῇ ὁδῷ ᾗ ἤρχου, ὅπως ἀναβλέψῃς καὶ πλησθῇς πνεύματος ἁγίου). The fourth incident relates the evidence of Saul's conversion (vv. 17 – 19b). Ananias departs for the house of Judas on Straight Street, enters, finds Saul, lays his hands on him, and explains why he has come.

Ananias addresses Saul as "brother" (ἀδελφέ). This may simply be the term that a Jew uses to address another Jew.[31] But since Ananias has been informed by Jesus in his vision that Saul has been blinded but will be healed, and that Jesus has chosen Saul to confess him as Messiah and Savior before Jews and Gentiles, he may have concluded that Saul has already come to faith in Jesus. Further, since Ananias would have spoken to Judas, in whose house Saul has been staying and refusing to eat as he was praying, he may have concluded from Judas's report that Saul had come to understand the truth about Jesus as the promised Messiah and Savior. Thus, the term "brother" probably suggests that Ananias greets Saul as a fellow believer who belongs to the group of followers of Jesus.

Ananias tells Saul, first, that "the Lord" (ὁ κύριος) has sent him. Since the Hebrew and Greek terms for "Lord" (see on 2:36), if they are not used for human beings, refer for Jews to Israel's God, Ananias clarifies that he is speaking of "Jesus, whom you saw" (Ἰησοῦς ὁ ὀφθείς σοι) on the road as he came to Damascus. Since Luke's report of Ananias's vision in vv. 10 – 16 did not include the information that Saul had actually seen the risen Jesus as he was traveling to Damascus, the reader must infer

that Ananias had been given fuller information about the vision than what Luke provided to his readers. The passive form of the verb translated as "saw" (ὀφθείς σοι), which occurs prominently in Paul's enumeration of the eyewitnesses of Jesus' bodily resurrection,[32] can be interpreted as passive ("he was seen by you," i.e., "you saw") or as passive with intransitive meaning ("he appeared;" thus most English translations in v. 17).

The interpretation in terms of a transitive meaning is often linked with the interpretation of the Easter events and of Saul's experience on the road to Damascus in terms of a vision, which is then sometimes interpreted as a psychological experience in which Jesus "appeared" to the disciples and to Saul in a dream, i.e., without having objective reality. But this interpretation is not inevitable if the verb is understood in a transitive sense; that is, the objectivity of the "appearance" of Jesus after his crucifixion is not tied to the grammar of the verb but is established by other elements in the text. The interpretation of the verbal form as a passive[33] emphasizes the objectivity of Jesus' appearance: he "was seen" by Saul (in the same manner as the disciples had seen the risen Jesus). Since Jesus, whom Saul saw on the road, has "sent" (ἀπέσταλκεν) Ananias to Saul, he comes with the authority of the risen Jesus, the exalted Lord.

The purpose of Ananias's visit is to heal Saul — Jesus wants Saul to be able to see again — and to have him receive the Holy Spirit. To accomplish this, Ananias lays his hands on Saul;[34] this laying on

---

31. Cf. 2:29, 37; 7:2, 26; 22:1.

32. See 1 Cor 15:5 – 8, with the third person aorist passive indicative ὤφθη, repeated in vv. 5, 6, 7, 8; in Acts 9:17 the aorist passive participle ὀφθείς is used.

33. This interpretation understands ὀφθείς as the aorist passive (participle) of ὤφθη ("he was seen") with the dative σοι ("by you") instead of ὑπό + genitive. A variation of this interpretation takes the passive ὀφθείς as a divine passive ("God has made Jesus visible to you"). The interpretation of ὀφθείς (and of ὤφθη in 1 Cor 15:5 – 8) is supported by Luke 24:34 and

Mark 9:4; cf. also the formulations in Gen 12:7 and Exod 3:2 in the LXX. In the papyri, the term ὤφθη is usually used in the literal meaning of "to be seen;" cf. Peter Arzt-Grabner, et al., *1. Korinther* (Papyrologische Kommentare zum Neuen Testament 2; Göttingen: Vandenhoeck & Ruprecht, 2006), 476.

34. For the laying on of hands for healing see, e.g., Mark 5:23; 6:5; Luke 4:40; Acts 9:12; for the laying on of hands for conveying a blessing see Matt 19:13, 15; Mark 10:16, specifically for the conveying of the Spirit in Acts 8:16 – 19; 19:6.

of hands here is not a commissioning ceremony or ordination for ministry.[35] While it is surprising that Luke reports direct speech of Ananias but not of Saul, the focus on Ananias's message underscores Saul's passive reception of Jesus' revelation, of Jesus' healing, and of Jesus' gift of the Holy Spirit. Saul will be active soon enough.

9:18 – 19b Immediately something like scales fell from his eyes and he regained his sight, and he was baptized, and after taking some food, he regained his strength (καὶ εὐθέως ἀπέπεσαν αὐτοῦ ἀπὸ τῶν ὀφθαλμῶν ὡς λεπίδες, ἀνέβλεψέν τε καὶ ἀναστὰς ἐβαπτίσθη καὶ λαβὼν τροφὴν ἐνίσχυσεν). The effect of Ananias's blessing is immediate. Luke mentions three actions of Saul (formulated with three verbs in the aorist tense).[36] First, he regains his eyesight (ἀνέβλεψεν). The term translated as "scales" (λεπίδες) refers in Greek literature not only to the scales of fish and snakes, but also the coat of an onion, the shell of a nut, the blade of a saw, or snowflakes.[37] The proverbial expression denoting the scale of scab of an injury refers to the eye problem that caused Saul's blindness. As Ananias lays his hands on Saul and conveys Jesus' promise and blessing, Saul is instantly healed of his blindness.

Second, Saul is immersed in water (ἐβαπτίσθη; see on 1:5; 2:38). The passive voice suggests that Ananias baptized Saul. It must be assumed that Saul's baptism was performed "in the name of Jesus Christ" (2:38; 10:48) or "in the name of the Lord Jesus" (8:16; 19:5), which means that Saul confessed his faith in Jesus as Israel's Messiah and as the risen and exalted Lord. The immersion in water symbolized his cleansing from sin, particularly the sins he committed as a persecutor of Jesus' followers (cf. v. 5). While acknowledging the crucified Jesus as risen Lord and Israel's Savior represents the

removal of the blindness of unbelief, Luke himself does not connect Saul's recovery of eyesight symbolically with his coming to faith in Jesus. Paul's conversion was fully complete when he called on Jesus as Messiah and Lord, when he was filled with the Holy Spirit, and when he had submitted to immersion in water for the washing away of his sins. Paul's baptism presumably took place in one of the *miqwaʾot* of the Jewish community in Damascus (see "In Depth: Ritual Immersion" at 2:38).

Third, Saul regains his strength (ἐνίσχυσεν) as he ends his fast and eats food (v. 19a-b), presumably served by Judas, his host, possibly by Ananias if Saul is transferred to the house of his new brother in Christ. Bread was a staple, usually supplemented by legumes, eggs, perhaps olives, dates, and figs, and perhaps fish or meat, depending on the prosperity of the host.

9:19c – 20 He stayed with the disciples in Damascus several days. At once he proclaimed Jesus in the synagogues, that he is the Son of God (ἐγένετο δὲ μετὰ τῶν ἐν Δαμασκῷ μαθητῶν ἡμέρας τινὰς καὶ εὐθέως ἐν ταῖς συναγωγαῖς ἐκήρυσσεν τὸν Ἰησοῦν ὅτι οὗτός ἐστιν ὁ υἱὸς τοῦ θεοῦ). The next episode after Luke's report on Saul's conversion in 9:1 – 19b narrates two incidents: the beginning of Saul's missionary work in Damascus (vv. 19c – 25) and then in Jerusalem, with his subsequent departure for Tarsus (vv. 26 – 30).

Saul joined the "disciples" (μαθηταί, see on 5:11) in Damascus, whom he had wanted to arrest and take to Jerusalem for interrogation and punishment (see vv. 1 – 2). The statement does not indicate where Saul lived during this time. If Judas was a believer, a sympathizer, or a tolerant Jew, Saul would have stayed in his house on Straight Street; otherwise, he would have stayed in the house of

---

35. Turner, *Power from on High*, 376 – 77.

36. The participle ἀναστάς before "he was baptizcd" is left untranslated.

37. Cf. LSJ, s.v. λεπίς. For the formulation cf. Tob 3:17; 11:13.

one of the believers in Damascus, perhaps in the house of Ananias (if he owned one). The expression "the disciples in Damascus" (οἱ ἐν Δαμασκῷ μαθηταί) could be a designation for a formally constituted congregation of the followers of Jesus in the city, but it may simply describe the local Christians as a group, whom Saul joins.

The phrase "several days" (ἡμέρας τινάς) is vague. According to Gal 1:17, Saul went to Arabia, the Nabatean kingdom located south of Syria, ruled at the time by King Aretas IV, extending from the Hauran Mountains in the north to the regions east and west of the Gulf of Aqaba. The Jewish people regarded the Nabateans as descendants of Ishmael, the son of Abraham, and thus as kindred tribes. The Nabateans would thus be a natural first "step" for the newly commissioned envoy sent by Jesus to the Gentiles.

According to 2 Cor 11:32 – 33, the ethnarch of King Aretas wanted to arrest Paul in Damascus, a fact that suggests two things. First, Paul was active as a missionary in the towns of Arabia, evidently provoking unrest among the population in line with the regular corollary of his ministry as described by Luke in Acts 13 – 19 (people who meditate in the desert — an assumption that is made with respect to the newly converted Saul — are harmless and would not have come to the attention of the king). Second, since the escape from Damascus in 2 Cor 11:32 – 33 corresponds to Acts 9:23 – 25, the "several days" in v. 19e may refer to the time that Saul stayed in Damascus before he embarked on his first missionary project in the towns of Arabia/Nabatea.[38] He may have used the church in Damascus as his base to which he returned periodically (cf. Gal 1:17: "I went into Arabia. Later I returned to Damascus"). The phrase

"after considerable time had passed" in v. 23 refers to the three years that Saul mentions as the interval between his conversion and stay in Damascus and his return to Jerusalem (Gal 1:18).

With a second "at once" (εὐθέως; v. 20) Luke reports the beginning of Saul's missionary activity. In Gal 1:16 – 17 Paul maintains that after God had revealed "his Son" to him and called him to proclaim the good news of Jesus among the Gentiles, he complied "immediate[ly]" (εὐθέως), without consulting with anyone, going to Arabia. How could Saul proclaim the good news of Jesus without first learning about Jesus, being instructed by other Christians? The fact that Saul was forcefully involved in the persecution of the followers of Jesus in Jerusalem and Judea[39] presupposes that he was fully informed about their views concerning Jesus — which he then rejected as serious theological error and blasphemy, but now acknowledged as true and confessed as his own beliefs as a result of his encounter with the risen Jesus.

Since Saul had arrested followers of Jesus and was presumably involved in their interrogations, he would have witnessed not only the courageous commitment of the believers to these convictions, but learned more details about Jesus' life and teaching. And as a trained Torah expert who had probably memorized the Scriptures, he quickly would have linked relevant passages in Scripture with Jesus' life, death, resurrection, and exaltation, and he would soon have been able to formulate the implications and consequences of Jesus' identity.

Saul confesses his faith in Jesus in the synagogues in Damascus. The plural indicates that there were several synagogues that Saul visited. He was making the rounds of the Jewish places of learning as he "proclaimed Jesus" (ἐκήρυσσεν τὸν Ἰησοῦν).[40] This

---

38. Cf. Jerome Murphy-O'Connor, "Paul in Arabia," *CBQ* 55 (1993): 732 – 37; Schnabel, *Early Christian Mission*, 2:1032 – 45.

39. Acts 8:1, 3; Gal 1:22 – 23; cf. 1 Thess 2:14.

40. On the verb "proclaim" (κηρύσσω) see on 8:5. The im-

perfect tense of the verb is usually interpreted as an inceptive or ingressive imperfect (Wallace, *Greek Grammar*, 544 – 45); most English translations have something like "he began to proclaim" (NASB, NET, NRSV; cf. GNB, NLT, TNIV).

means that he explained that Jesus, the man from Nazareth who was executed by crucifixion during the Passover feast two (or three) years earlier, had been raised from the dead, that he had been exalted into the light of God's glorious presence, where he had seen him while traveling to Damascus in order to arrest his followers, and that he is the Son of God. The title "the Son of God" (ὁ υἱὸς τοῦ θεοῦ) here is not simply synonymous with the title "Messiah" (ὁ χριστός; v. 22) but expresses "Jesus' unique standing and intimate favor with God, and God's direct involvement in Jesus' redemptive work."[41] The imperfect tense of the verb "proclaimed" emphasizes that Paul's preaching in the synagogues was going on for some time.

9:21 All who heard him were bewildered and said, "Is not this the man who caused such havoc in Jerusalem among those who invoke his name? And has he not come here in order to arrest them and take them to the chief priests?" (ἐξίσταντο δὲ πάντες οἱ ἀκούοντες καὶ ἔλεγον· οὐχ οὗτός ἐστιν ὁ πορθήσας εἰς Ἰερουσαλὴμ τοὺς ἐπικαλουμένους τὸ ὄνομα τοῦτο, καὶ ὧδε εἰς τοῦτο ἐληλύθει ἵνα δεδεμένους αὐτοὺς ἀγάγῃ ἐπὶ τοὺς ἀρχιερεῖς;). Luke notes the surprised reaction of the Jews of Damascus who hear Saul speak in the synagogues, explaining the significance of Jesus' true identity as Son of God and as Israel's Messiah (cf. v. 22). They are naturally perplexed (ἐξίσταντο; see on 2:6). Their reaction is given in direct speech to underline the significance of the new and completely unexpected development that has taken place.

Their bewilderment is expressed with two rhetorical questions, and the answer to each is obvious: yes, Saul is the man who had "caused such havoc" (cf. Gal 1:13, 23) among the followers of Jesus in

Jerusalem, and yes, Saul had come to Damascus to "arrest" Jesus' followers in the city and "take them" to Jerusalem to the chief priests. Just as Ananias was skeptical concerning Saul (vv. 13 – 14), the Jews in the synagogues are perplexed since they know about Saul's plans to arrest the followers of Jesus in Damascus and transport them to Jerusalem for interrogation and punishment (vv. 1 – 2). They know that these people whom Saul wanted to arrest "invoke" (ἐπικαλουμένους, present participle) the name of Jesus in their worship, calling on him as they call on Israel's God (see v. 14).

9:22 As Saul grew steadily stronger, he continued to confound the Jews who lived in Damascus by proving that Jesus was the Messiah (Σαῦλος δὲ μᾶλλον ἐνεδυναμοῦτο καὶ συνέχυννεν τοὺς Ἰουδαίους τοὺς κατοικοῦντας ἐν Δαμασκῷ συμβιβάζων ὅτι οὗτός ἐστιν ὁ χριστός). Luke's second summary description of Saul's preaching in the local synagogues (cf. v. 20) emphasizes that he is not intimidated by the perplexed and increasingly hostile reaction of the Jews of Damascus (cf. v. 23). The verb translated "grew stronger" (ἐνεδυναμοῦτο) may refer to Saul regaining his physical strength after his traumatic conversion and the three days of fasting (cf. v. 19);[42] most interpreters and many translators follow a manuscript of the fifth century that adds after "grew stronger" the phrase "in the word,"[43] thus relating Saul's increasing strength to his preaching. The expression could refer to both Saul's physical recovery and to his increasing confidence and ability of proclaiming Jesus as Messiah.

The imperfect tense of the verb translated as "confound" (συνέχυννεν) indicates that Saul's preaching in the synagogues of Damascus went on for some time. What threw his Jewish listeners into

41. Hurtado, *Lord Jesus Christ*, 104; cf. ibid. 101 – 8 for a discussion of Jesus' divine sonship in Paul's letters.

42. Thus the suggestion in BDAG, s.v. ἐνδυναμόω 2a.

43. Manuscript C, also Johnson, *Acts*, 171, sees "biblical as-

sociations" in the verb that he relates to Judg 6:34 (the Spirit takes possession of Gideon) and 1 Chr 12:18 (the Spirit comes upon the prophet Amisai); cf. Parsons, *Acts*, 133.

consternation was the fact that he "proved" that Jesus was the Messiah (οὗτός ἐστιν ὁ χριστός).[44] The verb "prov[ed]" (συμβιβάζων) denotes here the presentation of a logical conclusion. The present tense of the participle suggests again that this was happening over an extended period of time. Paul knows quite well, as he later writes to the believers in Corinth, that faith in Jesus as Israel's Messiah and Savior who has been crucified and raised from the dead is not the result of logical argumentation or rhetorical brilliance (1 Cor 1:18–2:5). For Jews, the center of the Christian message is a stumbling block, and for pagans it is nonsense.

This does not mean, however, that Paul does not argue. It means that he does not rely on his rhetorical and argumentative capabilities but on the power of God and his Spirit to move Jews and Gentiles from unbelief to faith. Saul is "effective" not because of his persuasive argumentation or brilliant rhetoric, but because of the reality of the power of God present in the proclamation of the gospel. The arguments of Saul by which he seeks to convince the Jews in Damascus that Jesus is the Messiah rest on three sets of facts: (1) God's promises and the prophets' prophecies in the Scriptures,[45] (2) the bestowal of the Spirit of prophecy, and (3) his own encounter with Jesus on the road to Damascus. These arguments show that Jesus is Israel's promised Messiah — executed on a cross for our sins, buried, but risen on the third day, and exalted to God's right hand, from where he appeared to his followers (cf. 1 Cor 15:3–6). Saul's proclamation in Damascus is his first missionary effort (see on 13:1–12, "In Depth: Paul's Missionary Work").[46]

9:23–25 After considerable time had passed, the Jews conspired to kill Saul, but their plot became known to him. They stood guard at the city gates day and night in order to kill him. But his disciples took him one night and let him down over the wall by lowering him in a basket (ὡς δὲ ἐπληροῦντο ἡμέραι ἱκαναί, συνεβουλεύσαντο οἱ Ἰουδαῖοι ἀνελεῖν αὐτόν· ἐγνώσθη δὲ τῷ Σαύλῳ ἡ ἐπιβουλὴ αὐτῶν. παρετηροῦντο δὲ καὶ τὰς πύλας ἡμέρας τε καὶ νυκτὸς ὅπως αὐτὸν ἀνέλωσιν· λαβόντες δὲ οἱ μαθηταὶ αὐτοῦ νυκτὸς διὰ τοῦ τείχους καθῆκαν αὐτὸν χαλάσαντες ἐν σπυρίδι). The perplexity of the Jews in Damascus eventually morph into a hostility so intense that they plot to kill Saul.

Luke provides the following pieces of information concerning the attempt on Saul's life. (1) It happens "after considerable time had passed" (v. 23a), i.e., probably after three years, during which Saul proclaimed the gospel in Damascus and in Arabia/Nabatea (see on v. 19).

(2) The Jews of Damascus "conspire" to kill Saul; this verb (συνεβουλεύσαντο) signifies "to be involved with others in plotting a course of action" (v. 23b). In other words, a group of Jews has made plans to eliminate Saul. In v. 24 a term is used (ἐπιβουλή) that characterizes the plot as "a secret plan to cause harm" (BDAG). The apostle's comment in 2 Cor 11:32 suggests that the Jews of Damascus evidently have the support of the ethnarch of the Nabatean king Aretas, whose agents are supposed to make the arrest.

(3) Saul hears of the plot; the passive voice of the verb "became known" (ἐγνώσθη) does not reveal how Saul obtained the information. In languages which have no passive voice, v. 23c has to be translated "someone told Saul of their plot." Either believers in Damascus hear of the plot and tell Saul, or sympathetic Jews who want to avoid bloodshed inform him.

(4) Saul receives a piece of information that some people are constantly ("day and night") guarding

---

44. On the Greek term for "Messiah" (χριστός) see on 2:31, 36.

45. See on 2:17, 36, 42; 3:13; 4:27; 8:5, 32–33, 35.

46. His proclamation of the gospel in Arabia/Nabatea is his second missionary effort.

the city gates (v. 24). Planning for Saul's arrest has evidently progressed to the point where a specific period of time was determined to be favorable for such an arrest. The guarding of the city gates suggests that Saul was warned for some time and kept his whereabouts in the city secret; it also implies that Saul was no longer preaching publicly in the synagogues (unless the conspirators did not dare to touch Saul in public because of his popularity).

The Christians of Damascus help Saul escape (v. 25). The phrase "his disciples" (οἱ μαθηταὶ αὐτοῦ) was regarded as difficult early on, as seen in the manuscript tradition.[47] The expression probably refers to the believers in Damascus "who owed their faith to Paul and stood particularly close to him."[48] The escape "in a basket from a window in the wall" is also mentioned in 2 Cor 11:33 (where a different word is used for the basket).

9:26 When he came to Jerusalem, he tried to associate with the disciples, but they were all afraid of him, for they did not believe that he was a disciple (παραγενόμενος δὲ εἰς Ἰερουσαλὴμ ἐπείραζεν κολλᾶσθαι τοῖς μαθηταῖς, καὶ πάντες ἐφοβοῦντο αὐτὸν μὴ πιστεύοντες ὅτι ἐστὶν μαθητής). While the first incident of the episode reported Saul's evangelistic ministry in Damascus (vv. 19c – 25), the second incident relates Saul's visit in Jerusalem and his departure for Tarsus (vv. 26 – 30). Three years after Saul had left Jerusalem and traveled to Damascus to arrest the followers of Jesus (cf. v. 19; Gal 1:18), he returns — not only a believer in Jesus himself but as a witness who has encountered Jesus and who has been commissioned to proclaim the good news of Jesus among Jews and Gentiles. If Saul's conversion can be dated to AD 31/32, this visit to Jerusalem dates to AD 33/34.

In Depth: Paul's Visits to Jerusalem

The following table shows the dates and the historical context of Paul's postconversion visits to Jerusalem in the context of his other chronology.[49]

31/32	Conversion of Paul		49 – 51	Missionary work in Macedonia and Achaia
32 – 34	Missionary work in Arabia and in Damascus		51	**Fourth visit** (Acts 18:22), three years after the third visit
33/34	**First visit** (Acts 9:26 – 29), three years after Paul's conversion		52 – 56	Missionary work in the Province of Asia and visit to Achaia
34 – 44	Missionary work in Syria and Cilicia (eleven years)		57	**Fifth visit** (Acts 21:15 – 17): collection visit, six years after the fourth visit
44	**Second visit** (Acts 11:27 – 30): taking gifts to the poor, eleven years after the first visit		57 – 61	Arrest in Jerusalem and imprisonment in Caesarea and in Rome
45 – 47	Missionary work on Cyprus and in Galatia			
48	**Third visit** (Acts 15:1 – 29): Apostles' Council, three years after the second visit			

47. Some copyists omit the personal pronoun, some change the genitive (αὐτοῦ) to an accusative (αὐτόν), which functions as the object of the verb ("they took *him*"); for details see the technical commentaries. Some scholars regard the genitive αὐτοῦ as a scribal error (Metzger, *Textual Commentary*, 321 – 22). As the more difficult reading that is also much better attested (𝔓[74] ℵ A B C 81. 1739), the genitive should be regarded as the original reading.

48. Barrett, *Acts*, 457. More specifically K. H. Rengstorf, "μαθητής," *TDNT*, 4:459, who argues for Paul's travel companions on the road to Damascus who had later come to faith in Jesus; this seems overly hypothetical.

49. Cf. Schnabel, *Early Christian Mission*, 2:1019 – 20; for a full discussion of the contacts of Paul with the Jerusalem apostles, cf. ibid., 983 – 1030.

Luke does not explain why Saul returns to Jerusalem. While Paul emphasizes in Gal 1:15–17 his independence of the Jerusalem apostles, there is nothing in Luke's narrative that suggests that Saul is seeking authorization from the Twelve. In Gal 1:18 Paul asserts that he went to Jerusalem "to get acquainted with Cephas," an expression that should be understood not merely in terms of a courtesy call but as implying an element of respect for his role as the leading disciple during Jesus' ministry in Galilee and in the Jerusalem church.

Saul's initial attempts to associate with the Jerusalem disciples meet with suspicion as the local believers are afraid of him. They have heard what happened when he traveled to Damascus, but they do not believe he has truly become a disciple (see on 5:11) of Jesus. Since presumably many of the Jerusalem believers had been personally arrested, imprisoned, and interrogated by Saul in the dangerous persecution in which Saul was actively involved (8:1, 3), their suspicions are understandable. The period of three years between Saul's conversion and his first visit to Jerusalem, rather than being a historical problem, may have increased the wariness of some of the believers in Jerusalem; if his conversion was genuine, why not return to Jerusalem immediately, apologize to the believers, and join their suffering?

9:27 But Barnabas took him and brought him to the apostles. He explained to them how he had seen the Lord on the road, that the Lord had spoken to him, and how he had spoken boldly in the name of Jesus in Damascus (Βαρναβᾶς δὲ ἐπιλαβόμενος αὐτὸν ἤγαγεν πρὸς τοὺς ἀποστόλους καὶ διηγήσατο αὐτοῖς πῶς ἐν τῇ ὁδῷ εἶδεν τὸν κύριον καὶ ὅτι ἐλάλησεν αὐτῷ καὶ πῶς ἐν Δαμασκῷ ἐπαρρησιάσατο ἐν τῷ ὀνόματι τοῦ Ἰησοῦ). Barnabas introduces Saul to the apostles, which results in Saul's integration in the worship and the ministry of the Jerusalem church (vv. 27–28; on Barnabas see on 4:36).

Luke describes Barnabas's intervention in the awkward situation between Saul and the suspicious believers in the city with three aorist verbs: he "took" (ἐπιλαβόμενος) Saul, taking hold of him in order to help him out of care and concern; he "brought" (ἤγαγεν) him to the apostles, physically accompanying him; and he "explained" (διηγήσατο) the integrity of Saul's conversion. Luke does not indicate why Barnabas takes this initiative to vouch for Saul. The suggestion that he was, like Saul, a diaspora Jew is not convincing, since it is not clear how Saul's status as a Jew born in the diaspora should raise suspicions, particularly if there were many bilingual believers in the church (see on 6:1, 5).

The definite article in the formulation "to the apostles" (πρὸς τοὺς ἀποστόλους) should not be pressed to mean that all twelve apostles are present in Jerusalem at this time and meet Saul in a meeting arranged by Barnabas. According to Gal 1:18–19, Saul saw only Peter and James during this period; the other ten apostles are evidently involved in missionary work elsewhere during Saul's brief stay in the city.

Barnabas's account, which is meant to vouchsafe Saul's integrity as a believer called to proclaim the gospel, consists of three parts. (1) He points out that Saul "has seen the Lord," i.e., that he has had an encounter with the risen Jesus on the road to Damascus, perhaps pointing out that Saul was thus one of Jesus' followers who had seen him after his resurrection (cf. 1 Cor 15:5–9). (2) He explains that the risen Jesus had "spoken to him" (cf. vv. 5–6; 22:7–8, 10; 26:14–18). The reference to the conversation between the risen Jesus and Saul validates the previous point and prepares for the next comment. (3) He points out how Saul had "spoken boldly" (ἐπαρρησιάσατο) in the name of Jesus[50] in Damascus; Saul's commitment to Jesus was confirmed by his open and courageous proclamation of the significance of Jesus' life, death, resurrection, and exaltation among the Jews of Damascus.

9:28 So he stayed with them and moved about freely in Jerusalem, preaching boldly in the name of the Lord (καὶ ἦν μετ᾽ αὐτῶν εἰσπορευόμενος καὶ ἐκπορευόμενος εἰς Ἰερουσαλήμ, παρρησιαζόμενος ἐν τῷ ὀνόματι τοῦ κυρίου). The result of Barnabas's intervention is described with four verbs. Saul "stayed with them," i.e., he was accepted by the apostles. He "moved about freely" (lit., "going in and going out"); i.e., he lived in close fellowship with them, participating in their activities.[51] He was "preaching boldly" as he had done in Damascus (cf. v. 27). Saul's bold preaching in v. 28c can be linked (1) with a teaching ministry among the believers in Jerusalem, and (2) with the evangelistic ministry that the apostles were perhaps able to carry out again in public (in Solomon's Portico in the temple complex?) after the persecution following Stephen's execution (8:1 – 3) had subsided. Paul's statement in Gal 1:22 that he was "personally unknown to the churches of Judea" suggests that he limited his activities during this visit to Jerusalem, so that the followers of Jesus living in other towns of Judea did not meet him.

9:29 He conversed and debated with the Greek-speaking Jews, who kept attempting to kill him (ἐλάλει τε καὶ συνεζήτει πρὸς τοὺς Ἑλληνιστάς, οἱ δὲ ἐπεχείρουν ἀνελεῖν αὐτόν). Luke emphasizes Saul's evangelistic activity in Jerusalem. His con-

versations with the Greek-speaking Jews were presumably the same diaspora Jews in the synagogues of the Jews from Rome, Cyrene, Alexandria, Cilicia, and Asia (6:9) who had debated with Stephen three years earlier and who were unable to "withstand the wisdom and the Spirit with which he spoke" (6:10). The imperfect tense of the verbs used here again underlines that Saul explained, argued for, and defended the good news of Jesus habitually, not just occasionally. Saul had been called by the risen Lord Jesus to proclaim the gospel to Jews and Gentiles. After preaching in Damascus and in Arabia, the time in Jerusalem was his third missionary effort (see on 13:1 – 12, "In Depth: Paul's Missionary Work").

Since the diaspora Jews in Jerusalem who opposed Stephen had had success in eliminating a vigorous proponent of the beliefs concerning Jesus that they regarded as blasphemy (6:11 – 13), they attempt to kill Saul. The imperfect tense of the verb "attempting" (ἐπεχείρουν) suggests that they made plans over some period of time, determined to arrest him and have him interrogated, perhaps by a session of the Sanhedrin (cf. 6:15; 7:1), unless the political situation made it prudent to eliminate Saul "privately" without a trial on blasphemy charges.

9:30 When the believers learned of this, they took him to Caesarea and sent him off to Tarsus (ἐπιγνόντες δὲ οἱ ἀδελφοὶ κατήγαγον αὐτὸν εἰς Καισάρειαν καὶ ἐξαπέστειλαν αὐτὸν εἰς Ταρσόν). The Jerusalem believers[52] learn of the plot against Saul's life and bring him to Caesarea Maritima, the harbor city northwest of Jerusalem, which was also

---

50. See 2:38; 3:6, 16 for the expression "in the name of Jesus." The verb παρρησιάζομαι means "express oneself freely, *speak freely, openly, fearlessly.*" Luke often uses the verb and the associated noun παρρησία ("a use of speech that conceals nothing and passes over nothing, *outspokenness, frankness, plainness* . . . a state of boldness and confidence, *courage, confidence, bold-*

ness, fearlessness;" BDAG, s.v. 1, 3) in connection with the proclamation of the gospel; cf. 2:29; 4:13; 9:28; 18:26; 19:8; 26:26; cf. 2 Cor 3:12; 7:4; Phil 1:20.

51. Cf. 1:21; Marguerat, *Actes* 1:343.

52. Here called "brothers and sisters"; see on 1:16; 5:11.

the seat of the governor of the province of Judea (see on 10:1); this was a journey of about seventy miles (100 km).[53] Then they "sent him off" to Tarsus, the capital of Cilicia, Saul's hometown. It is safe to assume that Saul traveled to Tarsus by ship, perhaps with funds provided by the believers of Jerusalem.

There is no hint in the text that allows us to conclude that the Jerusalem believers wanted Saul out of the picture "because he was stirring up trouble among Jews there, with whom they had come to some amicable understanding."[54] The verb translated "when [they] learned of this" (ἐπιγνόντες) refers not to Saul's conversations and discussions about the gospel in the local synagogues but to the efforts to have him killed. The next incident in Saul's life that Luke reports is linked with Barnabas's ministry in Antioch, the capital of the province of Syria, who recruited Saul to work with him there since Gentiles were coming to faith in Jesus in increasing numbers (11:20 – 26), probably in AD 42. Saul's statement in Gal 1:18 – 24 indicates that he was involved in missionary work in Cilicia and Syria after leaving Jerusalem (i.e., from AD 34 – 44), together with Barnabas, in AD 44 (Acts 11:30; 12:25; Gal 2:1).[55]

Theology in Application

Luke's account of the conversion of Saul invites us to explore further (after Acts 8) the reality and the meaning of conversion. In several respects, his conversion is certainly not typical for all conversions. He was a Jewish rabbi, he had persecuted Christians, he saw Jesus and heard him speak in a real encounter, and his conversion coincided with Jesus' missionary commission. But the following points are certainly fundamental aspects of conversion.

Conversion: The Result of Jesus' Initiative

Saul had vigorously persecuted the followers of Jesus and was on his way to Damascus, where he wanted to arrest more Christians. His conversion happened unexpectedly, with no psychological or emotional preparation for the dramatic and drastic turnaround that resulted from his encounter with the risen Jesus. If we interpret Saul's blindness not only literally in a physical sense but metaphorically, we may say that conversion implies the realization that I am utterly helpless and need divine, indeed miraculous help. This is why the coming to faith in Jesus and the experience of salvation are *sola gratia*, "by grace" alone — the result of nothing but the gracious power of God working in the lives of people.

Sometimes conversions are "prepared" as unbelievers find themselves with friends who become Christians and who share their faith; or they experience pain

---

53. An average person could travel between 15 and 20 Roman miles (22 to 29 kilometers, i.e., 14 to 18 miles) per day, by walking. People who traveled to a court date were expected to travel 20 Roman miles (29 kilometers or 18 miles) per day. The journey from Caesarea to Jerusalem thus takes three days.

54. Fitzmyer, *Acts*, 440.

55. The fourteen years mentioned in Gal 2:1 seem to be reckoned from the time of Paul's conversion in 31/32, not from his first postconversion visit to Jerusalem in AD 33/34.

and suffering from broken relationships or from chronic disease or from incurable cancers and look for answers; or they read literature or hear something in the news that makes them wonder about the truth claims of the Christian faith. But not all conversions have a psychological "lead time." It is both a challenge and a relief for Christians to know that conversion can happen in surprising and unexpected ways — a challenge because we can never give up on even the most ardent opponent of the Christian faith, and a relief because we can rest assured that it is not our efforts at witnessing to unbelievers but the sovereign power of God, who draws people to himself. Conversion is not a human choice but a divine choice.

Conversion: An Encounter with Jesus

While Saul's encounter with the risen Jesus involved an actual seeing and an audible conversation, this one was the last such resurrection appearance of Jesus according to 1 Cor 15:8. The typical aspect of Saul's encounter is the fact that conversion is never simply the regret for past misdeeds, or the learning of truths about God, or the emotional experience of God's Spirit working in our heart. Conversion involves the conscious acceptance of the claims concerning the life and identity of Jesus as crucified, risen, and exalted Lord who is Israel's Messiah and the Savior of the world. It is in this comprehensive sense that authentic conversion always involves an encounter with Jesus. For Saul it was a real, physical encounter.

As missionaries among Muslims report, many conversions involve visions of Jesus (which are not the same as Saul's encounter with Jesus on the road to Damascus). For most of us who have been born at a time when Jesus' resurrection appearances have ended, the encounter with Jesus is still real, but not physical — it is a spiritual encounter, i.e., an encounter mediated by the Spirit, who allows us to grasp the significance of Jesus' life, death, resurrection, and exaltation. It is no coincidence that the missionary sermons in Acts tell the story of Jesus, and it is no coincidence either that the church eventually placed four books that recount the life, ministry, death, and resurrection of Jesus at the beginning of their authoritative list of books to be read in their meetings. This is again both a challenge and a relief — a challenge because churches, missionaries, evangelists, and every Christian must make sure that unbelievers can encounter Jesus (rather than us, or our method, or our denomination) when they hear the gospel, and a relief because it is Jesus himself, through his Spirit, who convinces people of the truth of the gospel.

Conversion: A Change from Enemy to Servant

While not many Christian converts resemble Saul in that they ardently persecuted followers of Jesus before their conversion, all human beings, prior to coming to faith in Jesus, are God's enemies exposed to and threatened by God's wrath and judgment (Rom 1:18–3:20). It is always true that "while we were God's enemies, we were reconciled to him through the death of his Son" (Rom 5:10). And while not many Christian converts resemble Saul in that they are called to missionary ministry at the time of their conversion (although some are!), all believers in Jesus confess him as "Lord" and are thus his servants or "slaves" totally devoted to him.[56] This new commitment to Jesus is expressed in baptism — which, in the first century, was usually a public act of one's confession of faith in Jesus as Israel's Messiah, Savior, and Lord. This aspect of conversion is both a relief and a challenge — a relief because nobody is outside the realm of God's reach since enemies both big and small can be transformed by the power of the gospel, and a challenge as conversion means total commitment to and consistent loyalty for Jesus throughout our lives as people who claim to have experienced a conversion.

Conversion and Other Believers

The process of Saul's conversion was only complete when Ananias conveyed to him the healing, the blessing, and the commission of Jesus. While some people (e.g., in communist countries) have been converted to faith in Jesus as the result of radio broadcasts, without contacts with other Christians, this is not the norm. Conversions are connected with the personal involvement of believers. Even supernatural phenomena surrounding missionary situations do not absolve Christians from the necessity of personal witnessing. Jesus certainly could have continued to speak to Saul directly, particularly when Ananias initially objected to getting involved. But he insisted that Ananias visit Saul.

Some interpreters express surprise and find it "noteworthy that Saul received the Spirit when an otherwise unknown believer laid his hands on him and welcomed him into the new fellowship."[57] Such statements fail to see that Luke knows much more than he includes in his narrative in Acts (he probably has much fuller information about Ananias and his ministry in Damascus and perhaps in other regions). And such statements sometimes presuppose a hierarchical structure of the church, which says more about the ecclesiological location of the interpreter than about the early church. The Jerusalem apostles did not claim the prerogative that they alone could convey the Holy Spirit or commission new leaders and missionaries, despite the responsibility for the international mission and expansion of the church that they had been given and were carrying out. The fact that conversion involves other believers represents again both a challenge and a relief — the challenge that believers may not remain at a distance or leave the involvement in the lives of unbelievers to the "professionals," but also a relief as "otherwise unknown" believers can be confident that if they witness to others in obedience to Jesus' call and prompting, people will listen and conversions will take place.

---

56. Cf. Harris, *Slave of Christ*, 87 – 125, 139 – 56.   57. Bruce, *Acts*, 239.

Conversion and Integration into the Fellowship of Believers

This integration is usually mediated by another believer, in this case Ananias (later, in Jerusalem, by Barnabas). Jesus asserts that when Saul persecuted the Christian believers, Saul was persecuting him. This identification between Jesus and the community of his followers implies that "joining this community is the sign of obedience to his presence."[58] When Paul emphasizes in his letters the independence of his missionary commission (e.g., Gal 1:15), he defends himself against charges that he depends on the other apostles and that the gospel he preaches is not the authentic version for developing faith in Jesus. Paul does not try to defend his independence as an apostle but the integrity of the gospel, which he has not "learned" secondhand but received from Jesus himself. His arguments in 1 Cor 12 and his project of the collection for the poor believers in Jerusalem (2 Cor 8 – 9) underline how important and fundamental the unity of the church and the integration of every believer in the church were for Paul.

---

58. Johnson, *Acts*, 168.

Acts 9:31 – 43

Literary Context

The main theme that unites the five sections of Luke's report on the beginnings of the mission to the Gentiles (8:4 – 12:25) is the missionary work of Jerusalem believers among new groups of people. Philip preaches the good news of Jesus among Samaritans and before an Ethiopian who seems to be a proselyte (8:4 – 40); Saul is converted, a main persecutor of the church and the foremost missionary to the Gentiles in the years to come (9:1 – 30); Peter preaches in the cities on the coastal plain and before Gentiles in Caesarea (9:31 – 11:18); Jerusalem believers take the gospel to Antioch, the capital of the province of Syria, where more Gentiles are converted (11:19 – 30); the church continues to grow despite the new persecution under Herod Agrippa I, which leads to Peter's departure from Jerusalem (12:1 – 25). Our passage is the first of two episodes in the third section of this sequence, namely, the mission of Peter in Lydda and Joppa, two cities on the coastal plain (9:31 – 43); the second episode will describe Peter's mission in Caesarea (10:1 – 11:18).

Main Idea

The miracles that happen in Lydda and Joppa in the context of Peter's missionary work confirm that the apostles are Jesus' representatives whose missionary ministry is evidence for the ongoing restoration of Israel, the visible presence of the time of salvation, and the effective reality of God's power.

Translation

Acts 9:31 – 43

31a	Event/Place	**Meanwhile the church throughout Judea,**
b	Place	Galilee, and
c	Place	Samaria
d	Event	**had peace.**
e	Event	**It continued to be built up**
f	Event	and **advanced in the fear of the Lord,**
g	Event	and **it increased in numbers**
h	Cause (Agency)	through the encouragement of the Holy Spirit.
32a	Setting: Place	As Peter traveled throughout the country,
b	Action	**he also came to the Lord's people**
c	Place	living in Lydda.
33a	Event/Character entrance	**There he came upon a man named Aeneas,**
b	Character description	who had been bedridden for eight years,
c	Cause	for he was paralyzed.
34a	Action	**Peter said to him,**
b	Address	*"Aeneas,*
c	Prophecy/Assertion	*Jesus Christ heals you!*
d	Command	*Get up*
e	Command	*and make your bed!"*
f	Response	**Immediately he got up.**
35a	Event/Place	**All the inhabitants of Lydda and**
b	Place	Sharon
c	Identification	who saw him
d	Event	**turned to the Lord.**
36a	Setting: Place	In Joppa
b	Event	**there was a disciple**
c	Identification	whose name was Tabitha,
d	Explanation	which in Greek is Dorcas.
e	Description	**She was devoted to doing good works and**
f		charitable giving.
37a	Setting: Time	At that time
b	Event	**she became ill**
c	Event (Crisis)	and **died.**
d	Time/Action	After washing her,
e	Action/Place	**they laid her out in an upstairs room.**
38a	Cause	Since Lydda was near Joppa,
b	Action	**the disciples who had heard that Peter was there sent two men to him**
c		with the request,
d	Entreaty	*"Please come to us without delay."*
39a	Action	So **Peter went with them.**

Continued on next page.

Continued from previous page.

b	Setting: Time	When he arrived,
c	Action	**they took him to the room upstairs.**
d	Action	**All the widows stood beside him,**
e	Manner	weeping and
f	Action	showing him the tunics and robes
g	Description	that Dorcas had made
h	Time	while she was with them.
40a	Action	**Peter asked them all**
b	Request	to leave the room.
c	Action	Then **he knelt down**
d	Action	and **prayed.**
e	Action	**He turned to the body**
f	Action	and **said,**
g	Address	*"Tabitha,*
h	Command	*get up!"*
i	Response	**She opened her eyes,**
j	Response	**looked at Peter,**
k	Response	and **sat up.**
41a	Action	**He gave her his hand**
b	Action	and **helped her up.**
c	Action	**Then he called in the believers and**
d	List	the widows
e	Action (Resolution)	and **presented her to them alive.**
42a	Result	**This became known**
b	Place	all over Joppa,
c	Result	and **many people came to faith in the Lord.**
43a	Event	**Peter stayed in Joppa**
b	Time	for some time
c	Association	with Simon
d	Character description	the tanner.

Structure and Literary Form

The first episode of Luke's report on Peter's mission in Palestine (9:31 – 11:18) relates his mission in the cities of the coastal plain. Luke begins with a summary statement on the growth of the church in Judea, Galilee, and Samaria (9:31), which places the two incidents that follow into the context of Peter's missionary work — the healing of the lame Aeneas in Lydda (vv. 32 – 35) and the raising of the dead Tabitha in Joppa (vv. 36 – 42). The second miracle reminds us of Jesus' resurrection of the widow's son in Nain and of Jairus's daughter (Luke 7:11 – 17; 8:41 – 42, 49 – 56).[1] In Acts 20:7 – 12 Luke relates a similar miracle for Paul.

---

1. See Talbert, *Acts*, 126 – 27, for a discussion of the parallels, including similarities with the Old Testament narratives of people being raised from the dead by Elijah (1 Kgs 17:17 – 24) and Elisha (2 Kgs 4:18 – 37).

The *summary statement* in v. 31 (the eighth in Acts)[2] notes the geographical and numerical growth and consolidation of the church in Judea, Galilee, and Samaria.

The two *miracle stories* follow the same structure. The main difference is the introduction: the healing of Aeneas is introduced with a reference to Peter's ministry in Judea (v. 32), while the raising of Tabitha begins with a description of Tabitha and her reputation in Joppa, then her death and the request for help from Peter by the local believers (vv. 36 – 38). Beginning with Peter's arrival (vv. 32/39), the two narratives are parallel: (1) encounter (vv. 33a/39c); (2) report of illness/life (vv. 33b-c/39f-h); (3) the healing/resuscitation (vv. 34/40 – 41), narrated in four parts — address/attention (vv. 34b/40g); word of healing (vv. 34c-e/40h); report of healing (vv. 34f/40i – 41b); confirmation of the healing (vv. 35a-c, 41c – 42b); (4) report of further conversions (vv. 35d/42c). *Direct speech* is limited, mostly to Peter's words of healing: spoken to Aeneas involving two imperatives (v. 34b-e), and to Tabitha involving one imperative (v. 40g-h);[3] the request of the believers in Joppa for Peter to come and help them is also reported in direct speech (v. 38d).

Exegetical Outline

→ **I. The Mission of Peter in Cities on the Coastal Plain (9:31 – 43)**

   A. The Growth of the Church in Judea, Galilee, and Samaria (9:31)

   1. The geographical consolidation of the church (9:31a-c)

   2. The theological and numerical growth of the church (9:31d-h)

   B. The Healing of the Lame Aeneas in Lydda (9:32 – 35)

   1. Peter's ministry in Palestine (9:32a)

   2. Peter's arrival at the church in Lydda (9:32b-c)

   3. Peter heals Aeneas (9:33 – 34)

      a. Peter's encounter with Aeneas (9:33a)

      b. Aeneas's chronic illness reported (9:33b-c)

      c. Aeneas's healing (9:34 – 35c)

         i. Peter's address of Aeneas (9:34a-b)

         ii. Word of healing (9:34c-e)

         iii. Report of the healing (9:34f)

         iv. Confirmation of the healing (9:35a-c)

   4. Further conversions in Lydda and other towns (9:35d)

   C. The Resuscitation of the Dead Tabitha in Joppa (9:36 – 43)

   1. Introduction of Tabitha/Dorcas (9:36 – 38)

      a. Tabitha's good works in Joppa (9:36)

      b. Tabitha's illness and death (9:37)

      c. Request for help from Peter by the local believers (9:38)

---

2. Acts 1:12 – 14; 2:42 – 47; 4:32 – 37; 5:12 – 16; 6:7; 8:4; 8:25.

3. The first imperative for Aeneas and the imperative for Tabitha are identical: "Get up!" (ἀνάστηθι).

Explanation of the Text

9:31 Meanwhile the church throughout Judea, Galilee, and Samaria had peace. It continued to be built up and advanced in the fear of the Lord, and it increased in numbers through the encouragement of the Holy Spirit (ἡ μὲν οὖν ἐκκλησία καθ' ὅλης τῆς Ἰουδαίας καὶ Γαλιλαίας καὶ Σαμαρείας εἶχεν εἰρήνην οἰκοδομουμένη καὶ πορευομένη τῷ φόβῳ τοῦ κυρίου καὶ τῇ παρακλήσει τοῦ ἁγίου πνεύματος ἐπληθύνετο). Luke transitions from his report of Saul's conversion on the road to Damascus and his missionary activity in Damascus and in Jerusalem (vv. 1 – 30) to Peter's ministry in two Judean towns on the coastal plain (vv. 32 – 43) with a summary statement on the status of the church.

Luke has been using the singular term translated as "the church" (ἡ ἐκκλησία; see on 5:11) for local congregations of believers,[4] but he appears to use it here in the theological sense of the "universal" church, i.e., for the one community of believers that has local congregations in many regions. Earlier references had reported believers in Judea and Samaria (5:16; 8:4 – 25). Here we learn that there are communities of believers in Galilee as well.[5]

In other words, there are believers in all Jewish regions. We see again that Luke knows more than he tells his readers.

Luke makes three statements about the church in Palestine during this period. (1) The church had "peace" (εἰρήνη), which means in the context of 8:1 – 3 and 9:26 that the persecution following Stephen's execution has come to an end and the followers of Jesus are no longer harassed by the Jewish authorities. In the context of the following statement, "peace" probably refers to the combination of political peace and personal contentment "in the land of promise" that the Hebrew term šālôm often entails (cf. Lev 26:6), to the joy and satisfaction resulting from their acceptance of the gospel and their relationship with Jesus, Israel's Messiah and Savior. The believers in the Jewish homeland enjoy God's blessing.

(2) The church is being "built up" (οἰκοδομουμένη) and "advanc[ing]" (πορευομένη) in the fear of the Lord. These two modal participles in the present tense describe the circumstances of the peace that the church enjoys. The ongoing consolidation of

---

4. Acts 5:11; 8:1; cf. 11:22; 13:1; 14:23, 27; etc.

5. This is the second of only four references to Galilee in Acts (cf. 1:11; and the speeches of Peter and Paul referring to

Jesus' ministry in Galilee in 10:37; 13:31). For Judea see on 1:8; 5:16; for Samaria on 1:8; 8:5.

the church is described with two metaphors. The image of the church as a "building" in the process of being constructed speaks, in Paul's letters,[6] about the importance of the foundation, about the responsibility of the leaders, and about the identity of all believers, who are "stones" in this building, which is the temple of the Holy Spirit and thus the place of God's presence, the "house" that Stephen had redefined (7:47, 49). The passive voice of the first verb (οἰκοδομουμένη) refers to the activity of God and of the risen and exalted Jesus.

The image of "advanc[ing]" is related to the description of the believers as people who are (on) "the Way" (see on 5:11). The way of life of the followers of Jesus, in which they make progress, is "the fear of the Lord," which denotes reverence for the God who has revealed himself in the Lord Jesus, the knowledge of God's revelation in Jesus, Israel's Messiah, and obedience to Jesus, whose followers they are; the fear of the Lord characterizes their entire life.

(3) The church "increased in numbers" (ἐπληθύνετο); there was not only internal consolidation but also numerical growth. The phrase "through the encouragement of the Holy Spirit" (τῇ παρακλήσει τοῦ ἁγίου πνεύματος) is an instrumental dative that describes the cause of the church's growth; it was the "encouragement" (παράκλησις) given by the Holy Spirit to the followers of Jesus throughout Judea, Galilee, and Samaria that made the witness of the believers effective, resulting in new conversions.

9:32 As Peter traveled throughout the country, he also came to the Lord's people living in Lydda (ἐγένετο δὲ Πέτρον διερχόμενον διὰ πάντων κατελθεῖν καὶ πρὸς τοὺς ἁγίους τοὺς κατοικοῦντας Λύδδα). Peter is involved in a ministry that was geographically wide-ranging, as indicated both by the verb "traveled" (διερχόμενον) and the prepositional phrase (διὰ πάντων). The translation of the latter is disputed; "throughout the country" assumes a reference back to the regions mentioned in v. 31, i.e., to Judea, Galilee, and Samaria, which seems most plausible.[7] Since Peter was mentioned last in 8:25 (explicitly in 8:20) with a reference to missionary preaching in the Samaritan villages, the expression may describe here missionary activity in all the towns of the regions mentioned in v. 31.

If the description of Peter's ministry thus far in Acts is any indication, his travels in v. 32a have a dual purpose — to preach the gospel before Jews (and Samaritans) who have not yet heard or believed, and to teach the believers living in the towns and villages of these regions. Verses 31–32 together suggest that the consolidation and the numerical growth of the church is due, apart from the transforming power of the Holy Spirit (v. 31), to Peter's work. During his travels he visits believers who live in Lydda.

9:33 There he came upon a man named Aeneas, who had been bedridden for eight years, for he was paralyzed (εὗρεν δὲ ἐκεῖ ἄνθρωπόν τινα ὀνόματι Αἰνέαν ἐξ ἐτῶν ὀκτὼ κατακείμενον ἐπὶ κραβάττου, ὃς ἦν παραλελυμένος). In Lydda Peter encounters a man for whom Luke has a name (Aeneas) and an illness: he "was paralyzed" (ἦν παραλελυμένος) and, because he could not walk, he was confined to his bed (ἐπὶ κραβάττου). The reference to "eight years" suggests Aeneas had a stroke that paralyzed him, or he had suffered a fall from which he had not recovered. If the main verb "came upon" (εὗρεν) is linked with the last verbal clause in v. 32b-c ("the Lord's people living in Lydda"),

---

6. For the image of the church as a "building under construction" in Paul's letters, cf. Rom 14:19; 15:2; 1 Cor 8:1; 10:23; 14:4, 17; 2 Cor 10:8; 12:19; 1 Thess 5:11.

7. Some link the prepositional phrase (διὰ πάντων) with

"the Lord's people" (πρὸς τοὺς ἁγίους, lit., "the saints") in v. 32b (cf. NRSV: "now as Peter went here and there among all the believers"), which is less likely since Peter did not limit his ministry to believers only.

Aeneas is a believer.[8] Unlike the second miracle account, Luke does not indicate where this encounter takes place — either his friends bring him to the place where Peter is staying or to a house in which the believers meet (cf. Luke 5:18 – 19), or Peter goes to Aeneas's house (cf. Luke 4:38; 8:51).

9:34 Peter said to him, "Aeneas, Jesus Christ heals you! Get up and make your bed!" Immediately he got up (καὶ εἶπεν αὐτῷ ὁ Πέτρος· Αἰνέα, ἰαταί σε Ἰησοῦς Χριστός· ἀνάστηθι καὶ στρῶσον σεαυτῷ. καὶ εὐθέως ἀνέστη). Peter addresses the paralyzed man with his name. His word of healing has three parts. (1) Peter announces with a verb in the present tense (ἰαταί) that Jesus, Israel's Messiah, is at this very moment healing him. (2) He commands Aeneas with an imperative to "get up" (ἀνάστηθι), ordering him to do something that only divine power can make possible. (3) He commands Aeneas with a second imperative to "make your bed" (στρῶσον σεαυτῷ), an order that spells out the consequences of his healing: from now on he will be able to spread his sleeping mat on the floor, no longer needing others to do this for him. Peter's healing command is followed by the report of the healing: Aeneas "got up" (ἀνέστη) and was instantly capable of standing on his feet.[9]

9:35 All the inhabitants of Lydda and Sharon who saw him turned to the Lord (καὶ εἶδαν αὐτὸν πάντες οἱ κατοικοῦντες Λύδδα καὶ τὸν Σαρῶνα, οἵτινες ἐπέστρεψαν ἐπὶ τὸν κύριον). The fact that Aeneas is miraculously healed is confirmed by the inhabitants of Lydda, as they see him walking in the streets. The reference to the inhabitants of towns in the Plain of Sharon north of Lydda suggests either that they see him when they visit Lydda, perhaps on market days, or that Aeneas visits these towns

— perhaps supporting the believers in their missionary witness in the towns of the Sharon. All the inhabitants of Lydda and the Sharon region "turn" (ἐπέστρεψαν) to the Lord, i.e., come to faith in Jesus as Israel's Messiah and Lord. The term "all" is hyperbolic, implying that a large number of people are converted.

9:36 In Joppa there was a disciple whose name was Tabitha, which in Greek is Dorcas. She was devoted to doing good works and charitable giving (ἐν Ἰόππῃ δέ τις ἦν μαθήτρια ὀνόματι Ταβιθά, ἣ διερμηνευομένη λέγεται Δορκάς· αὕτη ἦν πλήρης ἔργων ἀγαθῶν καὶ ἐλεημοσυνῶν ὧν ἐποίει). The second miracle (vv. 36 – 43) involves a woman who lives in Joppa. This woman is the object of one of the most astounding miracles in Acts. Luke introduces her with great care. She is a "disciple" (μαθήτρια) named Tabitha, which translates into Greek as "Dorcas" (Δορκάς) (both mean "gazelle"). This Christian woman is devoted to "good works" (ἔργα ἀγαθά), among which is the practice of "charitable giving" (ἐλεημοσύναι), i.e., donations of (presumably) food, clothing, and/or money to the needy.

In the context of the reference to the paralyzed Aeneas, bedridden for eight years (v. 33), the good works that Tabitha continuously engages in perhaps include, besides sewing clothing for widows (v. 39), visiting and caring for the sick and the chronically ill. This description probably implies that Tabitha is a prosperous woman and an indispensable pillar of the congregation. Since no husband is mentioned, she may have been a widow.

9:37 – 38 At that time she became ill and died. After washing her, they laid her out in an upstairs room. Since Lydda was near Joppa, the

---

8. Cf. Barrett, *Acts*, 480; Gaventa, *Acts*, 158. If the verb is linked with the preceding geographical term, Aeneas may not have been a believer; cf. Fitzmyer, *Acts*, 444.

9. Similar healings are found in Luke 5:17 – 26 (Jesus); Acts 3:1 – 10 (Peter); 14:8 – 12 (Paul).

disciples who had heard that Peter was there sent two men to him with the request, "Please come to us without delay" (ἐγένετο δὲ ἐν ταῖς ἡμέραις ἐκείναις ἀσθενήσασαν αὐτὴν ἀποθανεῖν· λούσαντες δὲ ἔθηκαν αὐτὴν ἐν ὑπερῴῳ. ἐγγὺς δὲ οὔσης Λύδδας τῇ Ἰόππῃ οἱ μαθηταὶ ἀκούσαντες ὅτι Πέτρος ἐστὶν ἐν αὐτῇ ἀπέστειλαν δύο ἄνδρας πρὸς αὐτὸν παρακαλοῦντες· μὴ ὀκνήσῃς διελθεῖν ἕως ἡμῶν). Tabitha dies "at that time," i.e., during the time when the church in Judea has peace (v. 31) and when Peter is involved in missionary and pastoral ministry in the towns of Judea (v. 32).

The illness from which Dorcas suffers and eventually dies is not specified (v. 37b-c). Family members wash her body, suggesting preparation for the burial (see on 5:6), and lay her out in a room on the second floor of the house, which may have been the only room where the laying out of the body was possible. The believers of Lydda know that Peter is in nearby Joppa (v. 38a-b); they send two men to ask Peter to come "without delay" (μὴ ὀκνήσῃς; v. 38d).[10] It is not entirely clear whether they expect Peter to be able to bring Tabitha back from the dead. Parallels to similar episodes in the Old Testament (1 Kgs 17:19 – 22; 2 Kgs 4:20 – 37) do not prove such an expectation. The laying out of her body in an upstairs room indicates at any rate that they do not want to proceed with the burial until Peter has arrived (or denies their request to come, if this is implied in the verb).[11]

9:39 So Peter went with them. When he arrived, they took him to the room upstairs. All the widows stood beside him, weeping and showing him the tunics and robes that Dorcas had made while she was with them (ἀναστὰς δὲ Πέτρος συνῆλθεν αὐτοῖς· ὃν παραγενόμενον ἀνήγαγον εἰς τὸ ὑπερῷον

καὶ παρέστησαν αὐτῷ πᾶσαι αἱ χῆραι κλαίουσαι καὶ ἐπιδεικνύμεναι χιτῶνας καὶ ἱμάτια ὅσα ἐποίει μετ' αὐτῶν οὖσα ἡ Δορκάς). Peter's arrival in Joppa (v. 39a-b) is specified as in the previous incident when he arrived in Lydda (v. 32b) with three verbs, highlighting Peter's role in the miracle.

The account of Tabitha's resuscitation (vv. 39b – 42a) begins with Peter being taken by the believers to the room on the second floor where Tabitha is laid out (v. 39c). The next statement serves to remind the audience of Tabitha's charitable works (v. 39d-h). Next to Tabitha's body are "all the widows" who have benefited from Tabitha, who has sewn "tunics" and "robes" for them, i.e., inner and outer garments. The fact that they are "weeping" demonstrates their sense of loss and underlines the significant role that Tabitha has had.

9:40 – 41b Peter asked them all to leave the room. Then he knelt down and prayed. He turned to the body and said, "Tabitha, get up!" She opened her eyes, looked at Peter, and sat up. He gave her his hand and helped her up (ἐκβαλὼν δὲ ἔξω πάντας ὁ Πέτρος καὶ θεὶς τὰ γόνατα προσηύξατο καὶ ἐπιστρέψας πρὸς τὸ σῶμα εἶπεν· Ταβιθά, ἀνάστηθι. ἡ δὲ ἤνοιξεν τοὺς ὀφθαλμοὺς αὐτῆς, καὶ ἰδοῦσα τὸν Πέτρον ἀνεκάθισεν. δοὺς δὲ αὐτῇ χεῖρα ἀνέστησεν αὐτήν). Seven verbs describe Peter's involvement in the resuscitation of Tabitha.

(1) Peter asks everyone to leave the room (v. 40a-b), as Jesus did when he brought Jairus's daughter back to life;[12] the masculine form of "all" (πάντας) indicates that besides the widows, there were also men in the upstairs room (cf. v. 41c-d). (2) He gets down on his knees (θεὶς τὰ γόνατα), expressing his submission to God. (3) He prays (προσηύξατο);

---

10. The journey from Lydda to Joppa would have taken half a day; i.e., Peter would have arrived on the following day after Tabitha's death.

11. Cf. Barrett, *Acts*, 484; differently Bock, *Acts*, 378, who

suggests that the expression represents a formal request that "simply reflects respect."

12. Mark 5:40; this detail is omitted in the parallel narrative in Luke 8:49 – 55.

the following pronouncement of a command to Tabitha indicates that Peter prays for God's power to bring the dead woman back to life, and presumably for the assurance that this will happen right at this moment, allowing him to speak the command. (4) He "turns" (ἐπιστρέψας) to the body of Tabitha, who has died at least a day earlier and who has been washed for burial.

(5) Peter then speaks to Tabitha, addressing her with her Aramaic name and ordering her to "get up" (Ταβιθά, ἀνάστηθι).[13] The miracle, which happens instantly, is described with three verbs. Tabitha "opened" (ἤνοιξεν) her eyes; she "looked" (ἰδοῦσα) at Peter, the only person in the room, kneeling beside the bed (or the mattress) on which she had been placed; she "sat up" (ἀνεκάθισεν), probably as a result of seeing a man in the room. (6) Peter's sixth action brings him into physical contact with Tabitha: he "gave her his hand" (δοὺς δὲ αὐτῇ χεῖρα) as she was sitting on the bed. (7) Finally, Peter "helped her up" (ἀνέστησεν), to stand on her feet, proof that she is alive.

9:41c – 42 Then he called in the believers and the widows and presented her to them alive. This became known all over Joppa, and many people came to faith in the Lord (φωνήσας δὲ τοὺς ἁγίους καὶ τὰς χήρας παρέστησεν αὐτὴν ζῶσαν. γνωστὸν δὲ ἐγένετο καθ᾽ ὅλης τῆς Ἰόππης καὶ ἐπίστευσαν πολλοὶ ἐπὶ τὸν κύριον). The reality of Tabitha's miraculous resuscitation is immediately confirmed. Peter calls the believers and the widows back into the room and presents Tabitha to them

alive (v. 41e). The present participle "alive" (ζῶσαν) underlines the fact that Tabitha has been fully restored to life. It is not only the believers, but also the residents living in Joppa who hear about the miracle (v. 42a-b). With Tabitha back on her feet, they would have encountered her in the city.

Luke's statement that "many people" (πολλοί) come to faith in the Lord, i.e., in Jesus as Israel's Messiah and Savior, may be a standard feature of healing narratives, but the reality of such an astonishing miracle would surely lead many to recognize the power of God and acknowledge the truth of the message about Jesus that the believers in Joppa had been committed to and in whose name Peter had prayed (cf. 3:6).

9:43 Peter stayed in Joppa for some time with Simon the tanner (ἐγένετο δὲ ἡμέρας ἱκανὰς μεῖναι ἐν Ἰόππῃ παρά τινι Σίμωνι βυρσεῖ). This remark concludes this episode and prepares the audience for the next one in which Peter is called from Joppa to Caesarea up the coast. Peter lodges with a certain Simon, presumably a believer, whose profession was that of a tanner. Since tanning involved bad smells, it was usually done outside of town or near a body of water; it is no coincidence that Simon's house is located "by the sea" (10:6). Depending on the use to which the owner decides to put the leather, it is capable of ritual defilement: "It takes on the qualities of the object which it is to become. But it is not yet subject to the laws of defilement while in the possession of the tanner, since he is not the final owner."[14]

---

13. Many commentators point out that the words Ταβιθά, ἀνάστηθι recall Jesus' words to the dead daughter of Jairus as recorded, in Aramaic, by Mark — ταλιθα κουμ, which means "Little girl ... get up" (Mark 5:41). Luke's audience would have seen a parallel only if they knew Mark's gospel quite well (the words in Luke 8:54 — ἡ παῖς, ἔγειρε — are different from Mark's), if they did not mind the difference between Ταβιθά and ταλιθα (words that sound close in a language that is not one's mother language), and if they were willing to ignore that

one term is the name of a mature woman and the other a term meaning "little girl." The verb (ἀνίστημι) is used several times for resuscitation of the dead or for resurrection, cf. 2:24, 32; 3:26; 13:33, 34.

14. R. Meyer, "καθαρός κτλ.," *TDNT*, 3:420, with reference to *m. Kelim* 26:8. For negative comments on tanners in rabbinic literature cf. *m. Šabb.* 1:2; *m. Meg.* 3:2; *b. Pesaḥ.* 65a. It seems doubtful whether rabbinic texts can be used to establish for the first century that tanners were suspected of immorality.

While tanners were often scorned, it seems doubtful that they were regarded as unclean. Moreover, it seems doubtful that Luke's comment on Simon's profession is meant to convey that Peter disregarded social or ritual boundaries, having overcome traditional Jewish scruples against contact with what was ceremonially unclean — which thus minimizes the main point of the following episode of Peter's encounter with Cornelius, a pagan officer in the Roman army.

Theology in Application

This episode focuses on Jesus' power to work miracles and on the role of Peter in particular or the apostles (or pastors, evangelists, and missionaries) in general.

The Power of Jesus

The power of Jesus to work miracles. The focus of Luke's narrative here, which reports the healing of Aeneas, a lame man, and the resuscitation of Tabitha, a dead woman, is entirely on Jesus, the risen Messiah, who is active as the Lord (see Theology in Application for 3:1 – 10). This is particularly evident in the incident of Aeneas's healing, in which the word of healing begins by an affirmation that Jesus, Israel's Messiah, is about to heal miraculously. After Aeneas's healing, people turn to Jesus (not to Peter, the miracle worker). In the second incident, the rare reference to kneeling in v. 40[15] emphasizes Peter's submission to God and to Jesus as he prays. While Peter pronounces the word of healing with an imperative, the authority that renders the imperative immediately effective is Jesus' authority, not Peter's. The attention that Christian faith healers solicit, and receive, stands in stark contrast to Peter's attitude and his demeanor. Before he prays for Tabitha's resuscitation, he clears the room of all who are present (while contemporary faith healers "perform" on a stage and in front of television cameras!).

Because of this consistent focus on Jesus and his power, the link between miracles and conversions and church growth (vv. 35, 42) is the power of Jesus the Lord. There is no automatic link between the two. Miracles do not automatically lead to conversions and church growth (see Paul's experience in Lystra, 14:8 – 18, and 19), and the lack of miracles does not hinder or prevent conversions and church growth (see Paul's experience in Pisidian Antioch, 13:14 – 49). Miracles are caused by Jesus' power, and conversions are caused by Jesus' power. Sometimes Jesus chooses to heal miraculously; sometimes he does not heal despite the believers' prayers and their faith in the Lord. Tabitha is brought back to life not because she was devoted to good works, but because this was the will of the Lord.

---

15. In 7:60 Stephen kneels, praying, as he is about to die; in 20:36 Paul and the Ephesian elders kneel to pray, likewise in 21:5 Paul and the believers in Tyre.

Sometimes Jesus chooses to lead larger numbers of people to come to faith in him, resulting in dramatic church growth; sometimes it is only an individual here and there who comes to faith, resulting in slow church growth. It is not the faith of the pastor, evangelist, or missionary, nor is it the method used, that accounts for either rapid or slow church growth, but the sovereign and inscrutable will of Jesus, who is Lord in both cases.

The miracle of Tabitha's resuscitation demonstrates that indeed nothing is impossible for Jesus, who reigns at God's right hand. At the same time such miracles as the raising of the dead are rare in Scripture. While Tabitha's healing provides a precedent for asking Jesus to intervene even in cases of death, we should not forget that many leaders, such as Stephen and (later) James, died untimely deaths without being brought back to life. More important, we should never forget that as a result of Jesus' victory, death has lost its sting (1 Cor 15:54–55) and believers look forward to depart from this earth to "be with Christ" (Phil 1:23).

The Role of Pastors and Missionaries

The role of Peter emerges from the two miracle stories as Jesus' representative,[16] as missionary,[17] and as pastor.[18] The miracles that happen in Lydda and Joppa in the context of Peter's missionary work confirm that the apostles are Jesus' representatives, whose missionary ministry is evidence for the ongoing restoration of Israel, for the visible presence of the time of salvation, and for the effective reality of God's power.

While Peter was committed to devoting his time to prayer and to preaching and teaching the Word (6:2–4), we see him here visiting a paralyzed man and traveling to another town in order to help believers in a situation where somebody had died. There is a lesson here for all pastors, evangelists, and missionaries. While we may (and in the West usually we do) have specialized callings and ministries, the primary devotion to Jesus Christ and a love for his people will prompt us to help people in need. The centrality of Jesus in ministry always entails the centrality of people in need; followers of Jesus, after all, are following a Lord who "did not come to be served, but to serve, and to give his life as a ransom for many" (Mark 10:45).[19]

---

16. Cf. v. 34, and the raising of Tabitha paralleling the raising of Jairus's daughter.

17. Cf. vv. 32, 35, 42 in the context of v. 31.

18. Cf. vv. 32, 38–39, 41.

19. Fernando, *Acts*, 314–15, has a helpful section on "the blessings of staying in homes," although this is not the reason why Luke included the comment in v. 43.

Acts 10:1 – 11:18

Literary Context

In the first main section of Acts (1:15 – 8:3), Luke described the beginnings of the new people of God with a nearly exclusive focus on the life, the witness, the trials, and the growth of the congregation in Jerusalem, with the apostle Peter being the central character. The second main section (8:4 – 12:25) describes the beginning of the mission to the Gentiles. The first two sections reported the mission of Philip to the Samaritans and the conversion of an Ethiopian (8:4 – 40), and the conversion of Saul of Tarsus (9:1 – 30). This third section narrates the mission of Peter in Palestine (9:31 – 11:18) — in the towns of the coastal plain (9:31 – 43) and in Caesarea (10:1 – 11:18, the subject of this unit).

Peter's preaching in Caesarea leads to the conversion of a Roman officer. This is one of the longest episodes in Acts since the context and details of Peter's vision, in which the Lord calls him to eat unclean animals, are repeated three times, signaling the central importance of the inclusion of Gentiles in the new people of God. The basic point of the narrative is the acceptance of uncircumcised Gentiles who become believers in Jesus into the fellowship of God's people. The normative function of this new reality is stated twice by the Jerusalem leadership in connection with Cornelius's conversion — in 11:18 they acknowledge after Peter's report that "the Gentiles" have been granted "the repentance that leads to life," and in 15:8 – 9 Peter reminds the Apostles' Council of the circumstances under which Cornelius and his family and friends were accepted into God's people, without mentioning Cornelius's name. Such universalizing tendencies can be seen in the entire narrative.[1]

Luke provides no chronological data that dates Peter's mission in Caesarea. A terminus ad quem is the (brief) rule of Herod Agrippa I (AD 41 – 44), who initiated another persecution of the believers in Jerusalem (12:1 – 4); some scholars regard it as unlikely that Roman troops (mentioned in 10:1) were stationed in Caesarea during Agrippa's rule.[2] The conversion of Cornelius is thus most plausibly dated before AD 41 to the reign of Caligula. Since Saul/Paul, probably converted in AD 31/32, was active as a missionary in Cilicia since about AD 34, there may have been earlier

---

1. Avemarie, *Tauferzählungen*, 340 – 41.   2. Mittelstaedt, *Lukas als Historiker*, 229.

conversions among Gentiles before Cornelius — but outside of Palestine, without the Jerusalem congregation having personal contact with Saul during this time. Luke does not actually claim that Cornelius was the first Gentile to be converted, although in the narrative of Acts he is the first pagan to come to faith in Jesus.

Main Idea

The divine revelation to Peter clarifies that God now grants salvation to all people irrespective of ethnic or religious background. Peter's reaction to the Lord's directive underlines the importance of obedience to God's word, resulting in a fuller understanding of the gospel and in the courage to explain and defend this new understanding. The conversion of Cornelius emphasizes the significance of prayer, of obedience to God's directives, and of the proclamation of the good news of Jesus.

Translation

Acts 10:1 – 11:18

1a	Description (Character entrance)	**There was a man**
b	Place	in Caesarea
c	Identification	with the name Cornelius,
d	Character description	a centurion in what was known as the Italian Cohort.
2a	Description	**He was a devout man**
b	Explanation	who feared God with his entire household;
c	Description	**he used to give alms generously to the people,**
d	Description	**and he prayed to God constantly.**
e		
3a	Setting: Time	One afternoon
b	Specific	at about three o'clock,
c	Event	**he had a vision**

d	Description	in which he clearly saw an angel of God come to him and
e	Action	say,
f	Address	"Cornelius!"
4a	Reaction	**He stared at him in fear**
b	Action	**and said,**
c	Question	"What is it, Lord?"
d	Response	**He said to him,**
e	Assurance	"Your prayers and
f		your alms
g		have ascended as a memorial offering before God.
5a	Command	Now send men to Joppa
b	Command	and summon a certain Simon
c	Identification: Name	who is called Peter;
6a	Identification: Place	he is staying with Simon the tanner,
b	Identification: Place	whose house is by the sea."
7a	Time	When the angel who spoke to him had left,
b	Action	**he called** two of his slaves and
c	List (Association)	a devout soldier from his staff.
8a	Action	**He told them everything**
b	Action	**and sent them to Joppa.**
9a	Setting: Time	The next day,
b	Setting: Place	as they were traveling and approaching the city,
c	Action	**Peter went up on the roof to pray**
d	Time	at about noon.
10a	Event	**He became hungry**
b	Event	**and wanted something to eat.**
c	Time	While they were making preparations,
d	Event	**he fell into a trance.**
11a	Event	**He saw** the heaven opened, and
b	Event	an object resembling a big sheet
c	Event	being lowered by its four corners came down to the ground.
12a	Description/List	**In it were all the quadrupeds and**
b	List	**reptiles of the earth and**
c	List	**birds of the air.**
13a	Event	**A voice said to him,**
b	Address	"Peter,
c	Command	get up!
d	Command	Slaughter
e	Command	and eat!"
14a	Action/Response	**Peter said,**
b	Assertion (rejection)	"Certainly not,
c	Address	Lord,
d	Cause	for I have never eaten anything that is profane or
e		unclean."

Continued on next page.

Continued from previous page.

15a	Response	**The voice said to him again,**
b	Repetition	a second time,
c	Assertion	*"What God has made clean,*
d	Exhortation	*you must not call profane."*
16a	Event/Repetition	**This happened three times,**
b	Event	**and the object was suddenly lifted up to heaven.**
17a	Setting: Character's thoughts	While Peter was at a loss in his mind
b	Reference	concerning the meaning of this vision,
c	Event	**the men sent by Cornelius suddenly stood at the gate,**
d		having found Simon's house.
18a	Action	**They called out,**
b	Indirect question	asking whether Simon called Peter was staying there.
19a	Setting: Time	While Peter was still pondering on the vision,
b	Action	**the Spirit said to him,**
c	Address	*"Simon,*
d	Event	*three men are looking for you.*
20a	Command	*Get up,*
b	Command	*go downstairs,*
c	Command	*and go with them,*
d	Manner	*not making a distinction,*
e	Cause	*for I have sent them."*
21a	Action	**Peter went down**
b	Action	**and said to the men,**
c	Identification	*"I am the man you are looking for.*
d	Question	*What is the reason for your coming?"*
22a	Response	**They answered,**
b	Event (Report)	*"Cornelius, …*
c	Identification	*a centurion,*
d	Character description	*an upright and God-fearing man,*
e	Character description	*who is well spoken of among all the Jewish people,*
f	Event	*… was directed*
g	Agency	*by a holy angel*
h	Command	*to send for you*
i	Purpose	*to come to his house and*
j	Purpose	*to hear what you have to say."*
23a	Action	**Then Peter invited them in**
b	Action	**and entertained them as guests.**
c	Setting: Time	The next day
d	Action	**Peter left with them,**
e	Action (Association)	**and some of the brothers from Joppa accompanied him.**
24a	Setting: Time	The following day
b	Event	**they arrived in Caesarea.**
c	Event	**Cornelius was expecting them**

d	Action	and **had called together his relatives and**
e		**close friends**.
25a	Setting: Time	As Peter entered the house,
b	Event	**Cornelius met him;**
c	Action	**he fell at his feet**
d	Action	and **paid him homage.**
26a	Action/Reaction	But **Peter pulled him up**
b	Action	and **said,**
c	Command/Exhortation	"Stand up!
d	Explanation	I am only a human being myself."
27a	Setting: Time	As he continued to talk to him,
b	Action	**he went in**
c	Action	and **found that many people had gathered there.**
28a	Action	**He said to them,**
b	Assertion	"You are well aware that it is not allowed for a Jew
c	Explanation of law	to associate with or
d		to visit …
e		… a Gentile.
f	Pronouncement	But God has shown me
g	Content	that I should not call anyone profane or
h		unclean.
29a	Basis	For this reason
b	Assertion	I came without raising any objection
c	Time	when I was sent for.
d	Question	May I ask why you sent for me?"
30a	Report (speech)	
	(flashback)	**Cornelius said,**
b	Time	"Four days ago,
c	Time	at this very hour,
d	Time	at three o'clock,
e	Action	I was praying in my house
f	Event	when a man in a brightly shining garment suddenly stood before me.
31a	Action	He said,
b	Address	'Cornelius,
c	Assertion	your prayer has been heard
d	Assertion	and your alms have been remembered before God.
32a	Command	Send someone to Joppa
b	Command	and invite Simon
c	Identification	who is called Peter;
d	Description	he is staying at the house of Simon
e	Identification	the tanner by the sea.'
33a	Response/Action	Thus I sent for you immediately,
b	Event	and you have been kind enough to come.
c	Result	Now we are all here in the presence of God
d	Purpose	to hear all the instructions
e		that the Lord has given you."

Continued on next page.

Continued from previous page.

34a	Action (speech)	**Then Peter began to speak:**
b	Assertion	*"I truly understand that God shows no partiality,*
35a	Assertion	*but accepts those in every nation who fear him and*
b		*do what is right.*
36a	Assertion/Review of history	*God sent the message to the people of Israel,*
b	Manner	*proclaiming the good news of peace*
c	Agency	*through Jesus Christ,*
d	Identification	*who is Lord of all.*
37a	Event (Assertion)	*You know what has happened*
b	Place	*throughout Judea,*
c	Place	*beginning in Galilee*
d	Time	*after the baptism that John preached —*
38a	Event	*how God anointed Jesus of Nazareth with the Holy Spirit and*
b	Expansion (Means)	*with power,*
c	Event	*how he traveled from place to place doing good and*
d	Expansion	*healing all who were in the power of ☙*
		the devil,
e	Cause	*because God was with him.*
39a	Verification	*We are witnesses of everything that he did*
b	Place	*in the country of the Jews and*
c	Place	*in Jerusalem.*
d	Event	*They executed him*
e	Manner	*by hanging him on a cross.*
40a	Event	*God raised him from the dead*
b	Time	*on the third day*
c	Verification	*and caused him to be seen,*
41a	Clarification	*not by all people but*
b	Agency	*by witnesses whom God had chosen beforehand, and*
c	Character description	*who ate and drank with him*
d	Time	*after he rose from the dead.*
42a	Command	*He commanded us to preach to the people and*
b	Command	*to bear witness*
c	Content	*that he is the one appointed by God as judge of the living and*
d		*the dead.*
43a	Verification	*All the prophets bear witness to him,*
b	Assertion (Content)	*that everyone who believes in him receives forgiveness of sins*
c	Agency	*through his name."*
44a	Setting: Time	While Peter was still speaking these words,
b	Event	**the Holy Spirit fell upon all the people**
c	Description	who were listening to the word.
45a	Reaction	**The circumcised believers**
b	Description	who had accompanied Peter
c		**were astonished that the gift of the Holy Spirit had been poured out**
d	Sphere	on the Gentiles as well,
46a	Cause	for **they heard them** **speaking in other languages and**
b	Cause	**exalting God.**
c	Action (speech)	**Then Peter said,**

47a	Assertion	*"Surely no one can stand in the way of these people being immersed in water;*
b	Basis	*they have received the Holy Spirit*
c	Comparison	*just as we have."*
48a	Action	**He gave instructions**
b	Command	*that they be immersed*
c	Reference	*in the name of Jesus Christ.*
d	Action	**Then they invited him to stay**
e	Time (Duration)	*for a few days.*

11:1a	Event	**The apostles and**
b	List (Association)	**the believers throughout Judea**
c	Event	**heard that the Gentiles had also accepted the word of God.**

2a	Setting: Time	When Peter went up to Jerusalem,
b	Event	**the circumcised believers took issue with him**
3a	Action (speech)	and **said,**
b	Accusation	*"You went into the house of uncircumcised men*
c	Accusation	*and ate with them."*

4a	Response	Starting from the beginning,
b	Action (speech) (review of history/report)	**Peter explained it to them**
c	Manner	step by step.
5a	Event (10:9-10)/Place	*"I was in the city of Joppa*
b	Action	*praying,*
c	Event (Vision)	*when I saw a vision in a trance.*
d	Event (10:11)/Description	*I saw an object resembling a big sheet*
e	Description	*being lowered by its four corners from heaven,*
f	Description (Event)	*and it came right up to me.*

6a	Event (10:12)/Manner (Time)	*As I looked intently into it,*
b	Assertion (Event)/List	*I noticed quadrupeds of the earth,*
c	List	*wild animals,*
d	List	*reptiles, and*
e	List	*birds of the air.*
7a	Event (10:13)/Event	*Then I heard a voice say to me,*
b	Command	*'Peter, get up!*
c	Command	*Slaughter*
d	Command	*and eat!'*
8a	Event (10:14)/Response	*But I replied,*
b	Rejection	*'Certainly not, Lord,*
c	Cause	*for nothing profane or*
d	Cause	*unclean …*
e	Assertion	*… has ever entered my mouth.'*
9a	Event (10:15)/Event (Repetition)	*The voice from heaven spoke a second time,*
b	Command	*'What God has made clean, you must not call profane.'*

Continued on next page.

Continued from previous page.

| 10a | Event (10:16)/Event (Repetition) | This happened three times, |
| b | Description (Event) | *then* everything was lifted up again to heaven. |

11a	Event (10:17)/Time	At that very moment
b	Event	three men
c	Description	who had been sent to me from Caesarea
d		arrived at the house where we were staying.
12a	Event (10:20-23)/Command	The Spirit told me to go with them
b	Manner	without making a distinction.
c	Event (Action)	These six brothers accompanied me,
d	Event (Action)	*and* we entered that man's house.
13a	Event (10:30-33)/Report (speech)	He reported
b	Vision	how he had seen the angel standing in his house
c	Action	and saying,
d	Command	'Send to Joppa
e	Command	*and* summon Simon who is called Peter;
14a	Promise	he will bring a message
b	Promise	through which you and your entire household will be saved.'

15a	Event (10:44, 47)/Event (Time)	As I began to speak,
b	Event	the Holy Spirit fell upon them
c	Comparison	just as he had fallen upon us at the beginning.
16a	Flashback (1:5)	*And* I remembered the word of the Lord,
b	Report	how he had said,
c	Flashback	'John immersed in water,
d	Promise	*but* you will be immersed in the Holy Spirit.'
17a	Cause	*So* if God gave them the same gift that he gave us
b	Time	when we believed in the Lord ⤶ Jesus Christ,
c	(Rhetorical) Question/ Conclusion	who was I that I could stand in God's way?"

18a	Time	When they heard this,
b	Reaction	**they remained silent.**
c	Action	**And they praised God,**
d	Action	saying,
e	Assertion	"So God has granted even to the Gentiles the repentance
f	Result	that leads to life."

Structure and Literary Form

A structural analysis shows Luke's emphasis on Peter's vision. The encounter of Peter and Cornelius is prepared in each case by two visions — Cornelius is directed by God to send for Peter (vv. 3 – 6), while Peter is prepared to accept Cornelius's invitation (vv. 9 – 16), a vision in which the Lord repeats three times that he must no longer distinguish between ritually pure and profane food, allowing him to eat with and thus to accept Gentiles. The episode can be divided into seven incidents or scenes:

1. The vision of Cornelius (10:1 – 8)
2. The vision of Peter (10:9 – 16)
3. The messengers of Cornelius and Peter (10:17 – 23b)
4. The encounter of Peter and Cornelius (10:23c – 33)
5. Peter's sermon (10:34 – 43)
6. The conversion of the first Gentiles (10:44 – 48)
7. Peter's justification in Jerusalem of his acceptance of Gentile believers (11:1 – 18)

Luke "slows" the narrative by including a host of details, and the repetition of both Peter's vision and the conversion of Cornelius and his Gentile friends underlines the importance of this section for Luke.

Scenes 1 – 3 prepare for the encounter of Peter and Cornelius in Caesarea and its aftermath, narrated in scenes 4 – 6. Scene 7 moves Peter from Caesarea to Jerusalem and repeats the events that had transpired in Caesarea, focusing on Peter's vision (11:5 – 17) and recapitulating in summary form much of Acts 10. The main point of the entire episode is how the Lord forces Peter to acknowledge God's granting of salvation through Jesus with no required obedience to the law; the people of Israel no longer need to separate pure and profane foods, and pure and profane people. Now Gentiles who have come to faith in Jesus, Israel's Messiah and Savior, and who have received the Holy Spirit must be accepted as members of God's people, just as the apostles and all the other (Jewish) believers in Jerusalem belong to that community that is in the process of being restored in the last days.

IN DEPTH: Peter's Vision

The dream-vision in which the Lord shows Peter the importance of changing his views concerning the distinction between clean and profane food (and clean and profane people) is repeated several times; the central portions of the versions in Acts are verbatim.[3]

10:9 – 16	10:28	11:5 – 10
The next day, as they were traveling and approaching the city, Peter went up on the roof <u>to pray</u> at about noon. He became hungry and wanted something to eat. While they were making preparations, he fell <u>into a trance</u>. He saw the heaven opened, and **an object resembling a big sheet being lowered by its four corners** came down to the ground.		I was in the city of Joppa <u>praying</u>, when I saw a vision <u>in a trance</u>. I saw **an object resembling a big sheet being lowered by its four corners,** from heaven and it came right up to me. As I looked intently into it,
In it were all the **quadrupeds**		I noticed **quadrupeds** of the earth, wild animals,
and **reptiles** of the earth and **birds of the air**. <u>A voice said to him,</u> **"Peter, get up! Slaughter and eat!"** <u>Peter said,</u> **"Certainly not, Lord,** for I have never eaten **anything that is profane or unclean."** <u>The voice said to him again, a second time,</u> **"What God has made clean, you must not call profane." This happened three times,** and the object was suddenly lifted up **to heaven**.	He said to them, "You are well aware that it not allowed for a Jew to associate with or to visit a Gentile. But God has shown me that I should not call anyone profane or unclean.	**reptiles**, and **birds of the air**. <u>Then I heard a voice say to me,</u> **"Peter, get up! Slaughter and eat!"** <u>But I replied,</u> **"Certainly not, Lord,** for nothing profane or unclean** has ever entered my mouth." <u>The voice from heaven spoke a second time,</u> **"What God has made clean, you must not call profane." This happened three times,** then everything was lifted up again **to heaven**.

The episode is a *historical narrative*. It includes *vision reports* in 10:3 – 6, 22, 30 – 32; 11:13 – 14 (Cornelius) and in 10:10 – 16; 11:5 – 10 (Peter). Over 60 percent of the episode is *direct speech*, which is reported for God's angel (10:3, 4 – 6), Jesus (10:13, 15), the Spirit (10:19 – 20), Cornelius (10:4, 30 – 33), Cornelius's men (10:22), most importantly, Peter (10:14, 21, 26, 28 – 29, 34 – 43, 47; 11:5 – 17),[4] and believers in Jerusalem (11:3, 18). The narrative is driven by divine intervention, initiating

---

3. Bold underlining: verbatim agreement (in the Greek text); underlining: near verbatim agreement.

4. Of the 703 Greek words that are in direct speect, over 60 percent of them are Peter's (441 words).

visions[5] and giving directions for specific behavior.[6] The designation as a *conversion story*,[7] while not wrong, overlooks that the emphasis is less on Cornelius's conversion than on his being accepted by Peter despite Cornelius's being a pagan.

Note that while Cornelius is mentioned by name in 10:1, 3, 17, 22, 24, 25, 30, 31, he is not mentioned again after Peter begins his sermon. The references to the reception of the Spirit (vv. 44 – 46) and the immersion in water (vv. 48) are connected with "all the people who were listening to the word" (v. 44). Moreover, as Peter retells the events in Caesarea in 11:18, Cornelius is not mentioned. Note that the question raised in 11:1 – 18 is not the Gentile mission as such, but the question whether converted Gentiles should follow (specifically) the food laws of the Torah and whether Jewish believers can have table fellowship with uncircumcised Gentiles. The subsequent discussion in Jerusalem in 11:1 – 18 prepares for the Apostles' Council, where the Jerusalem congregation and the apostles address the question whether converted Gentiles must be circumcised and made to obey all stipulations of the law (15:1 – 29).

Exegetical Outline

→ **I. The Mission of Peter in Caesarea and the Conversion of Cornelius (10:1 – 11:18)**

    A. The Vision of Cornelius (10:1 – 8)

        1. Setting: Cornelius, a God-fearing Roman centurion in Caesarea (10:1 – 2)

        2. Cornelius's vision (10:3 – 6)

            a. The circumstances of Cornelius's vision (10:3a-e)

            b. Address by the angel (10:3f)

            c. Response of Cornelius (10:4a-c)

            d. Angel assures Cornelius that God has heard his prayers (10:4d-g)

            e. Angel directs Cornelius to send for Simon in Joppa (10:5 – 6)

        3. Cornelius's response (10:7 – 8)

    B. The Vision of Peter (10:9 – 16)

        1. Setting: Peter in Joppa on a roof waiting for dinner (10:9 – 10)

        2. Peter's vision (10:11 – 16)

            a. Peter has a vision of a large sheet containing unclean animals (10:11 – 12)

            b. Address by a voice commanding him to slaughter and eat the animals (10:13)

            c. Response of Peter, who refuses to obey the directive (10:14)

            d. Repetition of the command to slaughter and eat the animals (10:15)

            e. Report of a third repetition, and the end of the vision (10:16)

    C. The Messengers of Cornelius and Peter (10:17 – 23b)

        1. Peter is puzzled (10:17a)

---

5. Acts 10:3, 13, 22, 30; 11:13.

6. Acts 10:5, 13, 15, 19 – 20, 28, 32; 11:7 – 9, 12, 13; cf. 10:47; 11:16.

7. Cf. David Lertis Matson, *Household Conversion Narratives in Acts: Pattern and Interpretation* (JSNTSup 123; Sheffield: Sheffield Academic Press, 1996), 86 – 134.

    2. Cornelius's messengers arrive (10:17b – 18)

    3. Peter continues to think about the vision (10:19a)

    4. The Spirit directs Peter to go with the men who are looking for him (10:19b – 20)

    5. Peter asks the men for the purpose of their visit (10:21)

    6. Cornelius's messengers report the vision and invite Peter to come (10:22)

    7. Peter invites the messengers in, who stay overnight (10:23a-b)

D. The Encounter of Peter and Cornelius (10:23c – 33)

    1. Peter and believers from Joppa arrive in Caesarea (10:23c – 24b)

    2. Cornelius, with relatives and friends, welcomes Peter (10:24c – 25)

    3. Peter prevents Cornelius from worshiping him (10:26)

    4. Peter meets Cornelius's Gentile relatives and friends (10:27)

    5. Peter explains that he is visiting them because of God's directive (10:28 – 29)

    6. Cornelius explains that God has directed him in a vision to invite Peter (10:30 – 33)

E. Peter's Sermon (10:34 – 43)

    1. Introduction: Comment about God's nonpartiality, related to the context (10:34 – 35)

    2. Proclamation of Jesus (10:36 – 41)

       a. God's fulfillment of his promise of salvation for all people through Jesus (10:36)

       b. Jesus' ministry of proclamation and healing (10:37 – 39c)

       c. Jesus' death and resurrection (10:39d – 41)

    3. Offer of salvation (10:42 – 43)

       a. The proclamation of the eyewitnesses (10:42)

       b. The possibility of forgiveness of sins through faith in Jesus (10:43)

F. The Conversion of the First Gentiles (10:44 – 48)

    1. Reception of the Holy Spirit by the Gentiles who hear the word of God (10:44)

    2. Astonishment of the Jews who hear the Gentiles speak in unlearned languages (10:45 – 46b)

    3. Peter's conclusion that the Gentiles should be baptized (10:46c – 47)

    4. Baptism of the Gentile believers in the name of Jesus, the Messiah (10:48a-c)

    5. Peter stays with the Gentile believers for several days (10:48d-e)

G. Peter's Justification of the Acceptance of Gentile Believers (11:1 – 18)

    1. News of the conversion of Gentiles reaches the Jerusalem congregation (11:1)

    2. The Jewish believers in Jerusalem challenge Peter for having eaten with Gentiles (11:2 – 3)

    3. Peter's explanation (11:4 – 17)

       a. Report of the vision in Joppa (11:4 – 10)

       b. Report of God's directive to go to Caesarea (11:11 – 12)

       c. Report of Cornelius's vision from God (11:13 – 14)

       d. Report of his proclamation and of the Gentiles' reception of the Spirit (11:15)

       e. Reference to Jesus' promise of the coming of the Holy Spirit (11:16)

       f. Conclusion: God has given the Gentiles the Spirit, thus they were baptized (11:17)

    4. The Jewish believers in Jerusalem are won over and praise God (11:18)

Explanation of the Text

10:1 – 2 There was a man in Caesarea with the name Cornelius, a centurion in what was known as the Italian Cohort. He was a devout man who feared God with his entire household; he used to give alms generously to the people, and he prayed to God constantly (ἀνὴρ δέ τις ἐν Καισαρείᾳ ὀνόματι Κορνήλιος, ἑκατοντάρχης ἐκ σπείρης τῆς καλουμένης Ἰταλικῆς, εὐσεβὴς καὶ φοβούμενος τὸν θεὸν σὺν παντὶ τῷ οἴκῳ αὐτοῦ, ποιῶν ἐλεημοσύνας πολλὰς τῷ λαῷ καὶ δεόμενος τοῦ θεοῦ διὰ παντός). Luke introduces his report of Peter's mission in Caesarea with a description of one of the two main protagonists. Cornelius (Κορνήλιος) is a centurion (ἑκατοντάρχης) living in Caesarea.

A centurion was responsible for eighty men; Cornelius's unit was called the Italian Cohort. Several Italian cohorts are attested for the Roman army. The one in which Cornelius served was probably the *Cohors II Italica civium romanorum voluntariorum miliaria*, a regiment attested by a funerary inscription from Carnuntum.[8] We have little information about the military units stationed in Palestine before Herod Agrippa I.[9] When Judea became a Roman province in AD 6, the Roman governors commanded auxiliary forces stationed in Caesarea (Roman troops were not stationed in Judea before AD 70).[10] The Romans maintained six or seven auxiliary units in Judea, with five of the infantry units and the one cavalry unit recruited locally, primarily from the non-Jewish cities of Sebaste and Caesarea, together about three thousand men.[11] Cornelius's name, profession, and rank of centurion imply that he was a Roman citizen and a Gentile.

Cornelius's religious commitment is described in v. 2 with five phrases. (1) He was "a devout man" (εὐσεβής); i.e., he was recognizably religious.

(2) He was a God-fearer (φοβούμενος τὸν θεόν); i.e., he worshiped Israel's God. Since Cornelius is later described as having an excellent reputation among the Jewish people (v. 22), and since Luke's use of the expression "God-fearer" often describes Gentiles who sympathized with the Jewish faith (see on v. 22), Luke describes Cornelius as a Roman officer who worshiped the God of the Jews.

(3) Cornelius practiced his piety with his entire household (οἶκος), which suggests that his wife and children also worshiped Yahweh.

(4) He generously gave alms (ποιῶν ἐλεημοσύνας) to people, which is often taken in terms of the Jewish people. It is possible, however, that his generosity extended to the soldiers in his unit and to the Greeks living in the city.

(5) He prayed (δεόμενος) to God constantly, which probably means that he observed regular prayer times. Prayer and almsgiving are described in a Jewish text as the ideal of piety: "Prayer with fasting is good, but better than both is almsgiving with righteousness. A little with righteousness is better than wealth with wrongdoing. It is better to give alms than to lay up gold. For almsgiving saves

---

8. ILS III.2 9168 (AD 69). Cf. Dennis B. Saddington, "Roman Military and Administrative Personnel in the New Testament," *ANRW* II.26.3 (1996): 2409 – 35, 2415 – 16.

9. Cf. Michael P. Speidel, "The Roman Army in Judea under the Procurators: The Italian and the Augustan Cohort in the Acts of the Apostles [1982 – 1983]," in *Roman Army Studies II* (Stuttgart: Steiner, 1992), 224 – 32.

10. Roman legions moved into Judea when the Roman governor of the province of Syria had to intervene in Jewish mat-

ters, as was necessary under Vitellius (AD 35 – 39), Petronius (AD 39 – 42), and Quadratus (AD 51 – 60).

11. Josephus, *J.W.* 3.66; *Ant.* 19.365. The sixth infantry unit was the "Italian cohort" mentioned in Acts 10:1. Note 25:23, where Luke mentions multiple military commanders. Cf. E. Mary Smallwood, *The Jews under Roman Rule: From Pompey to Diocletian: A Study in Political Relations* (orig. 1976; repr., SJLA 20; Leiden: Brill, 2001), 146 – 47.

from death and purges away every sin. Those who give alms will enjoy a full life" (Tob 12:8 – 9; cf. 1:3).

Cornelius is not said to have attended synagogue services[12] or to have obeyed some of the laws of the Torah. This may be due to the selectivity of Luke's reporting, or it may indicate that Cornelius was a God-fearer in more general terms as a sympathizer. It would not have been easy for a leading Roman military officer in Caesarea to demonstrate publicly his sympathies for the Jewish people and their faith. In Luke's portrayal Cornelius is "as Jewish as a Gentile can be without ceasing to be a Gentile."[13]

10:3 One afternoon at about three o'clock, he had a vision in which he clearly saw an angel of God come to him and say, "Cornelius!" (εἶδεν ἐν ὁράματι φανερῶς ὡσεὶ περὶ ὥραν ἐνάτην τῆς ἡμέρας ἄγγελον τοῦ θεοῦ εἰσελθόντα πρὸς αὐτὸν καὶ εἰπόντα αὐτῷ· Κορνήλιε). Cornelius has a vision in which God gives him directions (vv. 3 – 6). This vision leads to Peter's visit to Caesarea and eventually to the conversion of Cornelius. The description of the angel of God appearing to Cornelius (see 10:22, 30; 11:13) underscores God's initiative in the conversion of the first Gentile that Luke records.

Cornelius's vision contains five elements. (1) He notes the circumstances of the vision (ὅραμα): it happened in the afternoon, at about three o'clock.[14] This time reference assures the reader that Cornelius was not asleep or dreaming; he was wide awake. Luke does not actually say that Cornelius was praying when he had the vision, but this would provide a plausible context for thoughts focused on God. Cornelius "clearly" (φανερῶς) saw an angel of God as he came toward him; i.e., he was not mistaken when he identified the angel's appearance in

the vision as "a man in a brightly shining garment" (v. 30).

(2) The angel of God initiates a conversation with Cornelius, addressing him by name.

10:4 He stared at him in fear and said, "What is it, Lord?" He said to him, "Your prayers and your alms have ascended as a memorial offering before God" (ὁ δὲ ἀτενίσας αὐτῷ καὶ ἔμφοβος γενόμενος εἶπεν· τί ἐστιν, κύριε; εἶπεν δὲ αὐτῷ· αἱ προσευχαί σου καὶ αἱ ἐλεημοσύναι σου ἀνέβησαν εἰς μνημόσυνον ἔμπροσθεν τοῦ θεοῦ). (3) Cornelius responds to the appearance of the heavenly being with taut attention, fear,[15] and incomprehension, expressed in the question, "What is it, Lord?" Cornelius does not know whom he is seeing and what the appearance of the heavenly being means. The address "Lord" (κύριε) is more than a polite address: it reflects the willingness to obey any instructions that he might be given.

(4) The angel assures Cornelius that God has heard his prayers and taken notice of his piety, evidenced by his almsgiving. The Greek term translated "memorial offering" (μνημόσυνον) reflects the LXX's translation of a Hebrew term referring to the portion of the grain offering that consisted of a handful of flour mixed with oil to which incense was added (Lev 2:2, 9, 16), which was then burned on the altar. As the sacrificial portion set aside for Yahweh, it was consecrated by the invocation of Yahweh's name. The angel assures Cornelius that God has noticed his devotion to him and is about to bless him.

Luke's repeated description of Cornelius's piety (vv. 2, 4, 22, 31, 35) does not mean that he and his "house" deserve God's grace as a result of his devotion and charity.[16] It means, rather, that the pagan

---

12. Cf. 13:16, 26; 17:4, 17 (cf. 16:14) for God-fearers attending synagogue services.

13. Stenschke, *Luke's Portrait of Gentiles*, 150.

14. Lit., "the ninth hour of the day," described as the Jewish time of prayer (3:1).

15. This is the first time in Acts that Luke explicitly ascribes fear to the recipient of a vision, explained by the fact that Cornelius is the first Gentile to see a vision in the narrative; cf. Miller, *Convinced*, 204.

16. As Barrett, *Acts*, 503, assumes.

God-fearer is as close to God through this charity and his prayers as the Jews are. He is brought within reach of the gospel of Jesus, Israel's Savior, not because of his past devotion to God as a pagan God-fearer but because of his willingness to obey the instructions of the angel, which follow (vv. 5 – 6), and because of his willingness to listen to Peter, the Jewish preacher (vv. 30 – 33).

10:5 – 6 "Now send men to Joppa and summon a certain Simon who is called Peter; he is staying with Simon the tanner, whose house is by the sea" (καὶ νῦν πέμψον ἄνδρας εἰς Ἰόππην καὶ μετάπεμψαι Σίμωνά τινα ὃς ἐπικαλεῖται Πέτρος· οὗτος ξενίζεται παρά τινι Σίμωνι βυρσεῖ, ᾧ ἐστιν οἰκία παρὰ θάλασσαν). (5) The angel directs Cornelius to send for Simon in Joppa (vv. 5 – 6; cf. 9:36). The angel provides Cornelius with details that will help him find Simon: the name of the city (Joppa), the Greek (Peter) and Hebrew name (Simon) of the person he is to contact, the name of the person with whom Peter is staying (Simon the tanner; cf. 9:43), and the location of Simon's house. Cornelius must send some of his people to Joppa and "summon" Peter to come to Caesarea. The implication from v. 4 is that Cornelius will receive God's blessing if he follows the angel's directions.

10:7 – 8 When the angel who spoke to him had left, he called two of his slaves and a devout soldier from his staff. He told them everything and sent them to Joppa (ὡς δὲ ἀπῆλθεν ὁ ἄγγελος ὁ λαλῶν αὐτῷ, φωνήσας δύο τῶν οἰκετῶν καὶ στρατιώτην εὐσεβῆ τῶν προσκαρτερούντων αὐτῷ καὶ ἐξηγησάμενος ἅπαντα αὐτοῖς ἀπέστειλεν αὐτοὺς εἰς τὴν Ἰόππην). Cornelius's response is swift. As soon as the vision of the angel ends, he calls two of his trusted domestic slaves (οἰκέτης)[17] and a soldier (στρατιώτης) who belonged to his staff and

who evidently was also a God-fearer (εὐσεβῆ; v. 7; see "In Depth: God-Fearers" at v. 22). Cornelius informs these three men of "everything," i.e., the appearance of the angel and the angel's instruction to send for a certain Simon Peter, including the address in Joppa where they could find him.

Then he sends them off to Joppa, about thirty-seven miles (60 km.) to the south. According to v. 9 (cf. v. 17), they arrive at Simon the tanner's house in Joppa on the next day around noon. If they left within an hour of Cornelius's vision, which happened at three o'clock in the afternoon (v. 3), they had twenty-one hours to cover this distance — for military men a performance on the road that was not easy to accomplish but possible.

10:9 – 10 The next day, as they were traveling and approaching the city, Peter went up on the roof to pray at about noon. He became hungry and wanted something to eat. While they were making preparations, he fell into a trance (τῇ δὲ ἐπαύριον, ὁδοιπορούντων ἐκείνων καὶ τῇ πόλει ἐγγιζόντων, ἀνέβη Πέτρος ἐπὶ τὸ δῶμα προσεύξασθαι περὶ ὥραν ἕκτην. ἐγένετο δὲ πρόσπεινος καὶ ἤθελεν γεύσασθαι. παρασκευαζόντων δὲ αὐτῶν ἐγένετο ἐπ᾽ αὐτὸν ἔκστασις). After relating Cornelius's vision of an angel (vv. 1 – 8), Luke reports a vision of Peter (vv. 9 – 16), involving a change of scene from Caesarea to Joppa (second incident of this episode).

Luke provides four temporal markers for the time at which Peter's vision takes place: it happens "on the next day" (ἐπαύριον), i.e., a day after Cornelius had his vision; it takes place as Cornelius's envoys are traveling on the road from Caesarea to Joppa; it happens as they are approaching the city; it happens at noon (περὶ ὥραν ἕκτην, lit., "at the sixth hour"). This focus on the timing of the vision emphasizes God's sovereignty in the events that transpire on that day — Peter's vision

---

17. The term οἰκέτης means literally "member of the household" and is often used for household slaves.

ends just as Cornelius's envoys arrive at the house in which Peter is staying, a fact that presumably helps Peter to grasp the provocative meaning of the vision.

The four chronological markers are complemented by further information: the vision occurs when Peter goes up on the roof[18] (i.e., on the roof terrace of the house where he has more privacy, even though he would be exposed to the hot midday sun); it takes place as he is praying; it happens at a time when he is hungry and as his host is preparing for the midday meal (see also on 2:46; 9:19). Peter's hunger and the preparations in the house for a meal, whose appetizing odors he may have savored on the roof, make the "food content" of the vision all the more apropos and provocative.

The fact that Peter is hungry could mean that the anticipated meal is his first meal of the day. That Peter's hunger is the reason for the trance is unlikely, as this would not have been the first time he was famished. At the same time, the reference to Peter's hunger serves, perhaps, to help Luke's audience share Peter's perplexity, wondering whether Peter imagines the "vision" on account of his hunger. The next revelation by the Spirit, who informs Peter that he has visitors (vv. 19 – 20), clarifies that the vision is real. The term "trance" (ἔκστασις) denotes here "a state of being in which consciousness is wholly or partially suspended."[19]

10:11 – 12 He saw the heaven opened, and an object resembling a big sheet being lowered by its four corners came down to the ground. In it were all the quadrupeds and reptiles of the earth and birds of the air (καὶ θεωρεῖ τὸν οὐρανὸν ἀνεῳγμένον καὶ καταβαῖνον σκεῦός τι ὡς ὀθόνην μεγάλην τέσσαρσιν ἀρχαῖς καθιέμενον ἐπὶ τῆς γῆς, ἐν ᾧ ὑπῆρχεν πάντα τὰ τετράποδα καὶ ἑρπετὰ τῆς γῆς καὶ πετεινὰ τοῦ οὐρανοῦ). The report of Peter's vision has five elements. (1) Peter sees heaven being opened[20] and an object that resembled a large sheet coming down, being lowered by its four corners (v. 11). The sheet descended all the way "to the ground" (ἐπὶ τῆς γῆς) so that Peter could see its content: quadrupeds, reptiles, and birds. The adjective "all" means that specimens of the entire fauna were in the sheet, which thus would have included profane (unclean) animals that the law prohibited with regard to the diet of Israel (Lev 11; Deut 14). Devout Jews observed Lev 11:47 to "distinguish between the unclean and the clean, between living creatures that may be eaten and those that may not be eaten."

IN DEPTH: Pure and Profane Animals

Israel's dietary laws can only be understood in the context of the Old Testament concept of holiness, which was an extension of God's nature.[21] In Old Testament thought, persons and objects can exist in four possible states: holy, common

---

18. On roofs as places of worship and prayer, cf. 2 Kgs 23:12; Jer 19:13; Zeph 1:5. Roofs were accessible through exterior or interior stairways.

19. BDAG, s.v. ἔκστασις 2; the same meaning is present in 11:5; 22:17. The LXX uses the term in Gen 2:21 and 15:12 for the "deep sleep" that fell on Adam and Abraham. In Acts 3:10 and Luke 5:26 Luke uses ἔκστασις for the emotional reaction of crowds to healings.

20. The perfect passive participle (ἀνεῳγμένον) implies that God had opened the heaven, which remained open as the object resembling a sheet was being lowered three times. For heaven being opened cf. Luke 3:21; Acts 7:56.

21. The following summary is based on Jacob Milgrom, *Leviticus* (3 vols.; AB 3; New York: Doubleday, 1991 – 2001), 1:615 – 17, 718 – 36.

(profane), pure (clean), and impure (unclean). While the common (people, animal, objects) can be pure or impure, the holy (e.g., the temple) can never be impure. Persons are divided into three categories (which can be represented as concentric circles): priests (holy), Israel (pure), and mankind (profane). The three human divisions correspond to three animal divisions: sacrifices to God (God accepts as sacrifices only those pure animals that are domesticated and unblemished), pure animals (Israel eats only animals deemed to be pure), and all animals (Gentiles eat all animals, including from the profane categories). These tripartite divisions have a spatial dimension as well: sanctuary (priests, sacrifices), the land (Israel, eating only pure animals), and the earth (mankind, eating profane animals).

As the sanctuary and the land must remain separate entities, so the priests and the laity are deliberately set apart. Correspondingly, as God has chosen Israel as his people from among all the nations (the middle of the "person circles"), so Israel must restrict its choice of animals for their diet to the few animals that God has sanctioned (the middle of the "animal circles"). This connection is clearly spelled out in Lev 20:24 – 26: Israel's attainment and preservation of holiness depends on setting itself apart from all other nations and refusing to eat the prohibited animals. This means that the dietary laws are not arbitrary rules but "a reflection and reinforcement of Israel's election."[22] The criteria for the animals that Israel is permitted to eat are generally explained by the basic principle that "each species must exhibit the locomotion that fits its medium."[23] The law limits Israel's diet to only a few of the animals that other nations eat, as a reminder that Israel, as God's people, must separate itself from the nations — which affected their buying habits in the food markets.

The basic rationale for the distinction between pure and profane animals is the concept of holiness.[24] The distinction between holy and pure on the one hand and impure (as forbidden to Jews) and profane (as permitted for Gentiles) on the other hand needs to be understood on the background of the three sources of ritual impurity: carcasses/corpses, genital discharges, and scale disease (Lev 11; 12; 13 – 14; 15), the common denominator being death — carcasses/corpses embody death, the emission of blood or semen means loss of life, and the wasting of flesh (producing scale) is compared with a corpse (Num 12:12). Interpreted against this background, Israel's severely restricted choice of animal food (cattle, sheep, goats, several kinds of fish, pigeons, turtledoves,

---

22. Ibid., 1:725.

23. Ibid., 1:726, following Mary Douglas, *Purity and Danger: An Analysis of the Concepts of Pollution and Taboo* (London: Routledge, 1966).

24. Cf. Exod 22:29 – 31; Lev 11:44 – 45; 20:22 – 26; Deut 14:4 – 21.

several other birds, and locusts) taught God's people to revere life (which was in the blood, Lev 17:11) and to prevent wanton killing of animals.

It should be noted that in the Second Temple period, Gentiles were not regarded as ritually impure since the rules of purity applied only to Jews, not to Gentiles.[25] Gentiles were morally impure — the defiling offenses of which the law accuses the Canaanites (idolatry, sexual sins, perhaps eating blood; Lev 18:24 – 25, 27) were common among Gentiles.[26] They were inherently profane, which is the ontological opposite of sacred (or holy).[27] This is why Gentiles may never enter the temple, "not because they are impure, but because they are profane: they do not belong to the holy people of Israel."[28] Gentiles who had repented of idolatry and immorality typical of Gentiles, without having become Jews through circumcision, would be both ritually pure and morally pure — but they would still be profane. In the diaspora, such God-fearers or "righteous Gentiles" could worship with Jews in synagogues, without their "anomaly" (being ritually and morally pure, but not circumcised) creating too many difficulties. But this anomaly, as noted above, prohibited them from entering the temple.

10:13 – 14 A voice said to him, "Peter, get up! Slaughter and eat!" Peter said, "Certainly not, Lord, for I have never eaten anything that is profane or unclean" (καὶ ἐγένετο φωνὴ πρὸς αὐτόν· ἀναστάς, Πέτρε, θῦσον καὶ φάγε. ὁ δὲ Πέτρος εἶπεν· μηδαμῶς, κύριε, ὅτι οὐδέποτε ἔφαγον πᾶν κοινὸν καὶ ἀκάθαρτον). (2) A voice addresses Peter with the command to slaughter the animals in the big sheet and to eat their meat (v. 13), evidently without distinguishing between clean and unclean animals. It is conceivable that the majority or even all of the animals in the sheet were unclean.

(3) Peter simply refuses to slaughter and eat the animals he has seen in the large sheet (v. 14). The adverb translated as "certainly not" (μηδαμῶς), which occurs in the New Testament only here and in 11:8, states a decisive negative reaction. The reason for Peter's refusal to obey the voice is obvious: Israel had been commanded by God never to eat anything that is profane or unclean. The terms "profane" (κοινόν) and "unclean" (ἀκάθαρτον) are often regarded as forming a hendiadys (see on 1:7), expressing a single idea. On the terms *pure* (*clean*) and *sacred* (*holy*) and *impure* (*unclean*) and *com-*

---

25. Cf. Jonathan Klawans, *Impurity and Sin in Ancient Judaism* (New York: Oxford Univ. Press, 2000). Differently Sanders, *Judaism*, 72 – 76. An exception may have been the Essenes, who regarded Gentiles as ritually impure and bathed after physical contact with them; Josephus, *J.W.* 2.150.

26. Cf. Wis 11 – 15; *2 En.* 10:4 – 6; *Sib. Or.* 3:8 – 45; *T. Abr.* A 10.

27. The tabernacle and the temple is defiled by impurity, but profaned by profaneness: Lev 21:23; Ezek 44:6 – 7; cf. Acts 21:28; 24:6.

28. Richard J. Bauckham, "James, Peter, and the Gentiles," in *The Missions of James, Peter, and Paul: Tensions in Early Christianity* (ed. B. D. Chilton and C. A. Evans; NovTSup 115; Leiden: Brill, 2005), 91 – 142, 100; for the following point cf. ibid. 101 – 2, commenting that the anomaly of the non-Jew regarded as morally pure "may have been intolerable to zealous Jews, especially in the land" because they would regard the blurring of the line between Jews and Gentiles to be the greatest threat.

mon (*profane*), see "In Depth: Pure and Profane Animals." For Peter, forbidden animals and Gentiles are both impure and profane.

If Peter acknowledges the voice as being the voice of God, he would have regarded the command to slaughter and eat from all of the animals presented to him as a test of his obedience, assuming that he would hardly reject a direct command from God. Alternately, Peter's strong negative reply and the third-person reference to God in v. 15 can be taken as an indication that the voice from heaven is Jesus' voice, which would fit with Peter's previous interactions with Jesus, who once more corrects a position put forward by Peter. Nevertheless, as the origin of the voice and the identity of the speaker remain vague at this point, and since the term "Lord" (κύριε) may simply be a polite address, Peter may refuse the command coming from an unknown source as a temptation to engage in unlawful behavior that must be resisted.

10:15 – 16 The voice said to him again, a second time, "What God has made clean, you must not call profane." This happened three times, and the object was suddenly lifted up to heaven (καὶ φωνὴ πάλιν ἐκ δευτέρου πρὸς αὐτόν· ἃ ὁ θεὸς ἐκαθάρισεν, σὺ μὴ κοίνου. τοῦτο δὲ ἐγένετο ἐπὶ τρίς καὶ εὐθὺς ἀνελήμφθη τὸ σκεῦος εἰς τὸν οὐρανόν). (4) The next element of Peter's vision is a rebuke from the Lord. It asserts that God has made clean all the animals he had been told to slaughter and eat. The verb "made clean" (ἐκαθάρισεν) is used in the LXX for the pronouncements of the priests concerning persons who had been impure and who, after the appropriate purification, were then declared clean (cf. Lev 13:6, 13, 17).[29]

This is the main point of the vision: God has declared all animals to be clean, an assertion that implies the abolishment of the dietary laws.[30] In view of Luke's earlier reports about Peter's convictions concerning the significance of Jesus and his life, death, resurrection, and exaltation, there can be little doubt that this cleansing refers to Jesus' death and its effects. If this is indeed the meaning of the vision, Peter must change his behavior in obedience to the heavenly voice. Peter must not consider as profane animals that God has declared ritually clean (pure). In other words, Peter must refrain from discriminating between pure animals that can be eaten and impure (profane) animals that cannot be eaten (cf. Mark 7:19).

(5) The final element of Peter's vision is the report of a threefold repetition of the command to slaughter and eat the animals in the sheet (v. 16). This repetition underscores both the novelty of the practice that Peter is to adopt and the importance of the divine revelation for Peter — and for the narrative of the Cornelius episode as well as for the Gentile mission in the book of Acts. The subsequent narrative indicates that once Peter places his vision in the context of the vision granted to the pagan Cornelius and of his imminent encounter with Cornelius, he recognizes that God had taken the initiative to change his behavior about ritual stipulations of the law, which includes their applicability to encounters between Jewish believers and Gentiles.

The last descriptive remark of Peter's vision — the object is lifted back up to heaven — confirms that the sheet did not contain anything that could not have been eaten by Peter, since the holy God would not take anything profane into the presence in heaven.

While it is true that Luke has no parallel to Mark 7:19 and that Luke nowhere explicitly asserts

---

29. Cf. Luke 4:27; 5:12 – 13; 7:22; 17:14, 17, concerning the healing of people with leprosy; cf. Johnson, *Acts*, 184.

30. Cf. Milgrom, *Leviticus*, 1:726.

that the work of Jesus included the abrogation of the dietary laws, it does not follow that "what is being given in the vision is a revelation of what eternally is the mind of God, rather than a statement of a new order of things that God has now initiated."[31] First, the interpretation of the vision in 10:28 makes sense only if it is related to food that Gentiles ate but was prohibited for Jews and that made intimate encounters between Jews and Gentiles difficult.

Second, the heavenly voice in the vision speaks of eating all the animals (v. 13), including those whom God has declared clean (v. 15), which implies in the context of Peter's refusal to eat impure (profane) animals (v. 14) that God is indeed revealing a new order.

Third, this is confirmed by the criticism of the Jerusalem believers (11:3), which focuses precisely on eating with uncircumcised Gentiles. This means that the distinction between "them" and "us" that Peter learns no longer to make (11:12) is at the same time the distinction between pure and impure animals (11:7 – 9). If Jews and Gentiles come together in close fellowship, the dietary laws that restricted intimate encounters had to be rescinded, as "Israel's restrictive diet is a daily reminder to be apart from the nations."[32] This apartness was mandated by the law that sees the distinction between pure and impure animals as representing the distinction between Israel and the Gentiles (Lev 20:22 – 26): "just as Israelites are to avoid defilement from the ritually impure animals, so they are to remain separated from the Gentiles lest they be morally contaminated by the moral impurities of the Gentiles."[33]

10:17 – 18 While Peter was at a loss in his mind concerning the meaning of this vision, the men sent by Cornelius suddenly stood at the gate, having found Simon's house. They called out, asking whether Simon called Peter was staying there (ὡς δὲ ἐν ἑαυτῷ διηπόρει ὁ Πέτρος τί ἂν εἴη τὸ ὅραμα ὃ εἶδεν, ἰδοὺ οἱ ἄνδρες οἱ ἀπεσταλμένοι ὑπὸ τοῦ Κορνηλίου διερωτήσαντες τὴν οἰκίαν τοῦ Σίμωνος ἐπέστησαν ἐπὶ τὸν πυλῶνα, καὶ φωνήσαντες ἐπυνθάνοντο εἰ Σίμων ὁ ἐπικαλούμενος Πέτρος ἐνθάδε ξενίζεται). In the third incident of the episode, Luke relates the encounter of Cornelius's envoys and Peter, merging the vision of Cornelius with the vision of Peter (vv. 17 – 23b).

(1) Luke begins by noting that the vision of the unclean animals combined with the directive to "slaughter and eat" leaves Peter puzzled. Peter has been reflecting on the meaning of his vision. He recognizes the clean and unclean animals presented to him, and he understands the divine directive to eat the animals, but he cannot grasp the significance of the vision,[34] particularly of the declaration that God has declared all animals to be clean and fit to be eaten. Peter presumably wonders whether he should take both the directive and the declaration literally, which would be a momentous step because it would abolish the apartness (and the implied inequality) of Israel and the nations.

(2) Luke notes the arrival of Cornelius's messengers at precisely this moment (vv. 17c – 18). The description is vivid, expressed with four verbal forms (three aorists and one imperfect). They had found Simon's house by inquiry and suddenly[35] stand at the gate of the house;[36] they call out to the people inside the house beyond the gate and the

---

31. Barrett, *Acts*, 509.

32. Milgrom, *Leviticus*, 726.

33. Bauckham, "James, Peter, and the Gentiles," 104 – 5. Cf. *Let. Aris.* 139: Moses "surrounded us with unbroken palisades and iron walls to prevent our mixing with any of the other peoples in any matter."

34. Both the optative of the verb (εἴη) and the particle ἂν add to the emphasis on uncertainty.

35. On ἰδού cf. 1:10.

36. The fact that Simon's house had a gate (πυλών), which needs to be distinguished from the door (θύρα), suggests that this was an elegant residence rather than a simple house.

courtyard and inquire whether Simon Peter is staying in Simon the tanner's house as a guest. This was the man Cornelius had been directed to contact (vv. 5 – 6).

10:19 – 20 While Peter was still pondering on the vision, the Spirit said to him, "Simon, three men are looking for you. Get up, go downstairs, and go with them, not making a distinction, for I have sent them" (τοῦ δὲ Πέτρου διενθυμουμένου περὶ τοῦ ὁράματος εἶπεν αὐτῷ τὸ πνεῦμα· ἰδοὺ ἄνδρες τρεῖς ζητοῦντές σε, ἀλλὰ ἀναστὰς κατάβηθι καὶ πορεύου σὺν αὐτοῖς μηδὲν διακρινόμενος ὅτι ἐγὼ ἀπέσταλκα αὐτούς). (3) Luke's report about the arrival of Cornelius's messengers repeats the first element: Peter continues to give serious thought to the meaning of the vision, which has left him puzzled.

(4) Luke reports another supernatural message and directive, attributed to the Holy Spirit, emphasizing again the divine initiative throughout the episode. The Spirit informs Simon Peter about the arrival of three men looking for him (v. 19b-d) and directs him to go downstairs, meet these men, and go with them (v. 20a-c). The Spirit does not explain who the men are or what they want, nor does the Spirit reveal the meaning of the vision. But he tells Simon to accompany the men "not making a distinction" (μηδὲν διακρινόμενος; v. 20d).

This expression is usually translated "without hesitation," in the sense of "without entertaining doubts."[37] While this somewhat trivial meaning is not impossible, it is unlikely in the context of the vision. As Peter has just been directed by the heavenly voice three times not to treat pure animals differently from impure animals but to slaughter and eat animals that only profane Gentiles eat (vv. 12 – 15), the Spirit now directs Peter not to make a distinction that he would normally make

between pure Jews and morally impure and profane Gentiles.

The reason why Simon should go with the three men is God's initiative that brought these men from Caesarea to Joppa (v. 20e). It was God's Spirit[38] who has sent them to find Simon. Since the Spirit does not provide further details, Simon does not yet know that these men are Gentiles and want to take him to the house of a Gentile officer in the Roman army.

10:21 – 22 Peter went down and said to the men, "I am the man you are looking for. What is the reason for your coming?" They answered, "Cornelius, a centurion, an upright and God-fearing man, who is well spoken of among all the Jewish people, was directed by a holy angel to send for you to come to his house and to hear what you have to say" (καταβὰς δὲ Πέτρος πρὸς τοὺς ἄνδρας εἶπεν· ἰδοὺ ἐγώ εἰμι ὃν ζητεῖτε· τίς ἡ αἰτία δι᾿ ἣν πάρεστε; οἱ δὲ εἶπαν· Κορνήλιος ἑκατοντάρχης, ἀνὴρ δίκαιος καὶ φοβούμενος τὸν θεόν, μαρτυρούμενός τε ὑπὸ ὅλου τοῦ ἔθνους τῶν Ἰουδαίων, ἐχρηματίσθη ὑπὸ ἀγγέλου ἁγίου μεταπέμψασθαί σε εἰς τὸν οἶκον αὐτοῦ καὶ ἀκοῦσαι ῥήματα παρὰ σοῦ).

(5) Simon is obedient to the Spirit's directive. He leaves the roof of the house and enters (presumably) the courtyard, where he identifies himself to the men looking for him (v. 21). The conversation that ensues is narrated with direct speech. Simon inquires why they have come to Joppa looking for him — information that the Spirit had not provided when Simon was directed to go and meet the three men.

(6) In his report of the men's answer to Simon's question, Luke relates for the second time Cornelius's vision (cf. vv. 3 – 6; a third telling of the vision is implied in v. 8). The report, given presumably by the God-fearing soldier mentioned in v. 7, mentions five matters that are particularly important.

---

37. ESV, GNB, NET, NIV, NLT, TNIV, NRSV; cf. NASB "without misgivings." Also suggested by BDAG, s.v. διακρίνω 6.

38. In v. 3 it was an angel of God.

(a) The men come from Cornelius, who is a centurion (cf. v. 1), i.e., a Gentile. (b) Cornelius is "an upright and God-fearing man"; i.e., he worships Israel's God and lives in many respects like a Jew, a fact that has resulted in a good reputation among the Jewish people. (c) Cornelius received a visit from an angel of God who told him to invite Simon; i.e., he received a divine directive just as he, Simon, received a divine directive. (d) God's angel wants Simon to go to Cornelius's "house," i.e., the house of a Gentile, which was a potential source for defilement (see on v. 28). (e) God's angel directed Cornelius to hear what Simon has to say (ῥήματα παρὰ σοῦ, lit., "words from you"); i.e. Cornelius is waiting to hear the message about Jesus, Israel's Messiah and the Savior of the world, the message that Peter has been proclaiming in Jerusalem, Judea, and Samaria.

IN DEPTH: God-Fearers

Most scholars agree that the term "God-fearers" (σεβόμενοι τὸν θεόν,[39] φοβούμενοι τὸν θεόν,[40] θεοσεβεῖς[41]) should be regarded as designating a distinct group between Gentiles on the one hand and Jews and proselytes on the other hand. In the New Testament and in other Jewish texts, God-fearers are Gentiles who are attracted by the Jewish faith, who worship Israel's God, who attend synagogue services, and who (probably) adhere to some of the Jewish laws, but who have not (yet) been circumcised and who do not follow all the stipulations of the Torah. This term is used for Jews whose Torah obedience is emphasized, but also for uncircumcised Gentiles who have certain functions in the synagogue, for Gentiles who are honored by Jews because they participated in charitable activities.[42]

In Akmonia in Phrygia (Asia Minor), a Gentile woman with the name Julia Severa, who was the high priestess of the imperial cult in the city, supported the local synagogue of the Jews and was consequently honored, together with Jewish officials of the synagogue, in an inscription.[43] The description of Cornelius in Acts 10:2, 22 emphasizes not his status in the local Jewish community but his piety; his almsgiving, his prayers to Israel's God, and his good reputation among the Jewish people indicate that he had taken over some Jewish views and practices. The fact that he is not circumcised (10:28, 45; 11:3) means that he is not a member of the local Jewish community.

---

39. Cf. 13:50; 16:14; 17:4, 17; 18:7; cf. 18:13; 19:27.

40. Cf. Acts 10:2, 22, 35; 13:16, 26.

41. The term θεοσεβεῖς occurs in the Aphrodisias inscription; cf. Walter Ameling, *Inscriptiones Judaicae Orientis. Band II: Kleinasien* (TSAJ 99; Tübingen: Mohr Siebeck, 2004), no. 14. It is used in a somewhat different sense in John 9:31.

42. Bernd Wander, *Gottesfürchtige und Sympathisanten: Studien zum heidnischen Umfeld von Diasporasynagogen* (WUNT 104; Tübingen: Mohr Siebeck, 1998), 232–33. Besides God-fearers, Wander finds "sympathizers" in the broadest sense for Gentiles who are attracted to Judaism and who demonstrate their sympathy in some way: they may be "interested persons," i.e., Gentiles who simply attend synagogue services; or they are "imitators," i.e., Gentiles who adopt certain Jewish views and ways of behavior but who have no social contact with Jewish communities.

43. Ameling, *Inscriptiones Judaicae Orientis II*, no. 168. Julia Severa, who is also attested on coins, was active between AD 60–80.

10:23 – 24 Then Peter invited them in and entertained them as guests. The next day Peter left with them, and some of the brothers from Joppa accompanied him. The following day they arrived in Caesarea. Cornelius was expecting them and had called together his relatives and his closest friends (εἰσκαλεσάμενος οὖν αὐτοὺς ἐξένισεν. τῇ δὲ ἐπαύριον ἀναστὰς ἐξῆλθεν σὺν αὐτοῖς καί τινες τῶν ἀδελφῶν τῶν ἀπὸ Ἰόππης συνῆλθον αὐτῷ. τῇ δὲ ἐπαύριον εἰσῆλθεν εἰς τὴν Καισάρειαν. ὁ δὲ Κορνήλιος ἦν προσδοκῶν αὐτοὺς συγκαλεσάμενος τοὺς συγγενεῖς αὐτοῦ καὶ τοὺς ἀναγκαίους φίλους). Luke's account of the encounter of Cornelius's messengers and Peter ends with a note on Peter's reaction to their report about Cornelius and the vision that the Gentile centurion had had of an angel of God. Peter invites the three men into the house and entertains them as guests.

The fourth incident in this episode narrates the encounter of Peter and Cornelius (vv. 23c – 33). Since Cornelius's messengers had arrived at Simon the tanner's house in the early afternoon (v. 9), it was too late to set out immediately; thus, they stay overnight. Peter leaves with the three men on the next day, taking with him "some of the brothers," i.e., fellow believers from Joppa (v. 23e). In 11:12 Luke specifies "six brothers" (i.e., fellow believers). Peter's later comment that the three men from Caesarea arrived at the place where "we were staying" (11:11) may suggest that the group included coworkers of Peter who also were guests of Simon the tanner. These brothers will play an important role as witnesses of what happened in Caesarea (10:45). With Peter and the three emissaries, the party that traveled about thirty-seven miles (ca. 60 km.) north to Caesarea consisted of ten people. They arrive a day after their departure (v. 24a-b),

evidently staying overnight somewhere between Joppa and the capital.

Cornelius had been waiting for Peter since he dispatched his messengers; if one of the slaves whom he had sent along (v. 7) was a runner and capable of covering the distance between the two cities faster than the larger party, he would have given Cornelius the opportunity to gather his relatives and friends before Peter arrived (v. 24c-e). The term translated as "relatives" (συγγενεῖς) denotes family members — in this case, presumably Cornelius's wife and children; the term "close friends" (ἀναγκαίοι φίλοι) refers to the most intimate friends, perhaps soldiers from his unit who were also God-fearers (cf. v. 7).[44] Cornelius was evidently convinced that the divine message he hoped to receive from Peter was relevant not only for himself but for others as well. Luke suggests that Cornelius and his relatives and close friends are ready to hear Peter speak as soon as he arrives. Cornelius's encounter with God's angel has made him eager to hear from Peter God's words (vv. 5, 22).

10:25 – 26 As Peter entered the house, Cornelius met him; he fell at his feet and paid him homage. But Peter pulled him up and said, "Stand up! I am only a human being myself" (ὡς δὲ ἐγένετο τοῦ εἰσελθεῖν τὸν Πέτρον, συναντήσας αὐτῷ ὁ Κορνήλιος πεσὼν ἐπὶ τοὺς πόδας προσεκύνησεν. ὁ δὲ Πέτρος ἤγειρεν αὐτὸν λέγων· ἀνάστηθι· καὶ ἐγὼ αὐτὸς ἄνθρωπός εἰμι). Luke underlines Cornelius's anticipation for Peter's arrival with the notice that the centurion met Peter as soon as the latter entered his house. He describes Cornelius's reaction to the presence of Peter in terms of two actions: he prostrates himself before Peter and pays him homage. Presumably as a result of his vision, the centurion believes that Peter is more than an average human

---

44. Luke's subsequent narrative in vv. 28, 45 suggests that these close friends were Gentiles; while Cornelius had a good reputation among the local Jews (v. 22), it is hardly plausible

that Luke would describe them as being among the "most intimate friends" of Cornelius.

being. The homage of the Roman centurion is a pagan element that Luke did not eliminate from his story despite his otherwise positive description of Cornelius.

Peter swiftly rejects the officer's obeisance and homage. Peter does indeed bring a message from God, but he is not superhuman. The fact that the first word Peter says in the presence of Cornelius, a commanding officer in the Roman army, is a command formulated as an imperative (ἀνάστηθι, "stand up") is not so much irony but an expression of Peter's abhorrence of being mistaken for a divine being, robbing the one true God of his glory.[45] He clarifies that he is only a human being (ἄνθρωπος). Later Paul and Barnabas similarly reject an attempt by the people in Lystra to worship them as divine messengers (14:15).

10:27 – 29 As he continued to talk to him, he went in and found that many people had gathered there. He said to them, "You are well aware that it is not allowed for a Jew to associate with or to visit a Gentile. But God has shown me that I should not call anyone profane or unclean. For this reason I came without raising any objection when I was sent for. May I ask why you sent for me?" (καὶ συνομιλῶν αὐτῷ εἰσῆλθεν καὶ εὑρίσκει συνεληλυθότας πολλούς, ἔφη τε πρὸς αὐτούς· ὑμεῖς ἐπίστασθε ὡς ἀθέμιτόν ἐστιν ἀνδρὶ Ἰουδαίῳ κολλᾶσθαι ἢ προσέρχεσθαι ἀλλοφύλῳ· κἀμοὶ ὁ θεὸς ἔδειξεν μηδένα κοινὸν ἢ ἀκάθαρτον λέγειν ἄνθρωπον· διὸ καὶ ἀναντιρρήτως ἦλθον μεταπεμφθείς. πυνθάνομαι οὖν τίνι λόγῳ μετεπέμψασθέ με;). Peter meets Cornelius's relatives and friends (v. 27) and explains how he has come to be there (vv. 28 – 29). This explanation may be the content of a conversation that Peter has with Cornelius as they walk toward the room where the people whom Cornelius has invited are gathered.

Peter begins by making a deliberate, interpretive move from the vision that had puzzled him two days before (vv. 11, 19) to the events in which God has involved him by sending him to Gentiles. Peter sees clearly that the issue at stake was not just food but people. Peter voices the concerns that will be raised later by the Jewish believers in Jerusalem (11:3): since a Jew cannot associate with Gentiles (v. 28a-e), it is highly unusual for him to come to Cornelius's house. Luke characterizes the problem that Peter says his visit poses for him with two verbs — a Jew should not "associate with" (κολλᾶσθαι) or "visit" (προσέρχεσθαι) a pagan. Both verbal forms are present infinitives and thus indicate a continuous, extensive association.

The term translated as "not allowed" (ἀθέμιτος) refers to behavior that is forbidden. Most English versions translate as "unlawful";[46] a better rendering is "against our laws" (NLT) because it leaves the question open which specific laws Peter was afraid to violate; helpful is GNB, "a Jew is not allowed by his religion." The Mosaic law did not forbid Israelites from eating with Gentiles. Jews were only forbidden from eating impure food, which they could do by eating only the vegetables at a meal with Gentiles. Nor did later Jewish tradition uniformly and unanimously stipulate a prohibition concerning Jews visiting Gentiles.

But contact with Gentiles was always a potential source of moral defilement for Jews (see on vv. 15 – 16). A Jewish text exhorts its readers, "Keep yourself separate from the nations, and do not eat with them; and do not imitate their rites, nor as-

---

45. Cf. Luke 4:8, where Jesus said to the devil who wants to be worshiped, "It is written, 'Worship the Lord your God and serve only him'" (quoting Deut 6:13).

46. ESV, KJV, NKJV, NASB, NET, NRSV, RSV; even more

strongly related with the Jewish law is the translation "against our law" (NIV, TNIV), which most readers would associate with the Mosaic law.

sociate yourself with them" (*Jub.* 22:16).[47] A devout Jew had the following options when invited by a Gentile:[48] he could refuse to enter the house of a Gentile and disapprove of all table fellowship with Gentiles; he could accept the invitation and bring his own food; he could eat at the table of Gentiles with the explicit or implicit understanding that the food served was not prohibited in the Torah and was not tainted by idolatry; he could eat only certain foods provided by the Gentile host. Some argue that a strict position was the norm, probably among both Palestinian and diaspora Jews.[49] Others regard the situation as more fluid, particularly in the diaspora, allowing for the possibility that Jews could eat with Gentiles without transgressing the Jewish law.[50]

As Peter refers in his explanation to his vision, he anticipates that his visit to Cornelius would involve eating food that Gentiles prepared for him. The fact that he had been informed by Cornelius's envoys that their master was a God-fearer respected by the Jewish community (v. 22) might imply that Cornelius knew how to provide hospitality to a devout Jew without requiring the latter to compromise his convictions concerning food. Nevertheless, Peter knew that Cornelius was a Roman officer (v. 22), a position in which regular contacts with pagan deities and pagan rites could not be avoided. Thus, Peter's point that since he is a practicing Jew he should not really be associating with a "Gentile" (v. 28e)[51] may be a polite way of saying that he should not be consorting with an officer of the Roman army and his friends, who would likely be defiled by idolatry, despite their piety and their good reputation among local Jews. Peter acknowledges that those present are "well aware" (ἐπίστασθε) of such matters.

Peter explains to the assembled group of Gentiles that God had shown him not to call anyone "profane or unclean" (κοινὸν ἢ ἀκάθαρτον; v. 28f–h). He has now understood the meaning of his vision and the significance of the heavenly voice that had told him not to call anything profane that "God has made clean" (ἐκαθάρισεν; v. 15). Gentiles who come to faith in Jesus as Israel's Messiah and Savior are neither impure nor profane. They should not be avoided out of fear that they might exert a morally corrupting influence. As Peter has recognized the significance of the vision for food and for people, he has become willing to change his behavior in two fundamental ways.

First, he can now associate with pagans and visit their houses, for he knows that contact with Gentiles will not defile him. God has shown him that a Jew who associates with Gentiles is thereby not rendered profane. Second, he can eat the food offered by a Gentile (cf. 11:3) without fearing defilement, because he has come to understand — as he will explain to the Jewish believers in Jerusalem (11:9) — that God has "cleansed" the Gentiles, i.e.,

---

47. Josephus relates that the Essenes bathed after contact with foreigners (*J.W.* 2.150).

48. Cf. Markus Bockmuehl, *Jewish Law in Gentile Churches: Halakhah and the Beginning of Christian Public Ethics* (Grand Rapids: Baker, 2003), 58; he mentions as another option for the association of Jews and Gentiles that a Jew can invite a Gentile into his own house and prepare a Jewish meal. Bockmuehl considers Peter's attitude expressed in v. 28 as belonging to the "clearly hard-line views about Gentile intentions that would most obviously include conservative Palestinian Jews to enter a Gentile's house 'unlawful'" (ibid. 59).

49. Cf. Gedalyahu Alon, *Jews, Judaism and the Classical World: Studies in Jewish History in the Times of the Second Temple and Talmud* (Jerusalem: Magnes, 1977), 146 – 89; Esler, *Community and Gospel*, 71 – 86.

50. John M. G. Barclay, *Jews in the Mediterranean Diaspora* (Edinburgh: T&T Clark, 1996), 434 – 37; Goodman, *Rome and Jerusalem*, 111 – 12, who points out that Tacitus's statement that Jews stay "separate in their meals and apart in their beds" was a caricature "that was largely, but not totally, true" (111); cf. Tacitus, *Hist.* 5.5.

51. The term translated as "Gentile" (ἀλλόφυλος) describes foreigners (lit., people "from another tribe"); from a Jewish perspective "foreigners" are Gentiles (BDAG).

removed their status of being unclean on account of their diet and idolatry.

The second conviction can be interpreted, on the one hand, as amounting to an abolition of the dietary regulations of the law, prompted and sanctioned by the divine revelation Peter had received in Joppa. On the other hand, since defilement can come not only from food but also from idolatry, it is possible that Peter's willingness to eat with Gentiles may not amount to a full abrogation of all food laws of the Torah. The first conviction, as expressed in v. 28f-h, could be understood as an abolition of the distinction between Jews and Gentiles. But since the vision's focus was on food, the application to human beings can be understood as focusing on sources of defilement rather than on larger questions related to Jews belonging to God's chosen people. The later disputes about these matters (cf. 15:1 – 33; Gal 2:1 – 14) show that the Jewish Christians came to different conclusions about what Gentile believers must do and what Jewish believers can do.

Because God was the one who had taken the initiative in overcoming Peter's rightful resistance regarding associating with Gentiles, Peter has been willing to come "without raising any objection" when Cornelius sent for him (v. 29a-c). As Peter had asked Cornelius's envoys why they had come (v. 21), he now asks Cornelius why he had sent for him (v. 29d). Cornelius's envoys had informed Peter about their master's encounter with an angel of God and the latter's directive to invite Peter and listen to what he has to say (v. 22) — which can only refer to the message about Jesus, Israel's Messiah and Savior, that Peter proclaimed wherever he went. Peter's question is thus a cue for Cornelius to recount his encounter with the angel and to state personally his eagerness to hear Peter speak.

10:30 – 32 Cornelius said, "Four days ago, at this very hour, at three o'clock, I was praying in my house when a man in a brightly shining garment suddenly stood before me. He said, 'Cornelius, your prayer has been heard and your alms have been remembered before God. Send someone to Joppa and invite Simon who is called Peter; he is staying at the house of Simon the tanner by the sea'" (καὶ ὁ Κορνήλιος ἔφη· ἀπὸ τετάρτης ἡμέρας μέχρι ταύτης τῆς ὥρας ἤμην τὴν ἐνάτην προσευχόμενος ἐν τῷ οἴκῳ μου, καὶ ἰδοὺ ἀνὴρ ἔστη ἐνώπιόν μου ἐν ἐσθῆτι λαμπρᾷ καὶ φησίν· Κορνήλιε, εἰσηκούσθη σου ἡ προσευχὴ καὶ αἱ ἐλεημοσύναι σου ἐμνήσθησαν ἐνώπιον τοῦ θεοῦ. πέμψον οὖν εἰς Ἰόππην καὶ μετακάλεσαι Σίμωνα ὃς ἐπικαλεῖται Πέτρος, οὗτος ξενίζεται ἐν οἰκίᾳ Σίμωνος βυρσέως παρὰ θάλασσαν).

Cornelius's explanation of inviting Peter (vv. 30 – 33) is the final element of this incident that relates the encounter of Peter and Cornelius (vv. 23c – 33). Cornelius begins with a precise time reference (v. 30b-d), a fact that highlights the dramatic impact that his vision of the angel of God has had on him. Luke allows Cornelius to tell the events in his own words. The differences fit the context of the retelling before the Jewish visitors: Cornelius does not presume, as a Gentile, to be able to identity an angel of Israel's God and thus describes him as "a man in a brightly shining garment" (v. 30f). The formulation "your alms have been remembered before God" (v. 31d) omits the sacrificial language used earlier (v. 4) while emphasizing God's response to his almsgiving. The retelling of the directive given by the heavenly visitor in v. 32 is nearly identical with the report in vv. 5 – 6, a fact that focuses the attention on the words of the angel, thus highlighting the divine initiative.

10:33 "Thus I sent for you immediately, and you have been kind enough to come. Now we are all here in the presence of God to hear all the instructions that the Lord has given you" (ἐξαυτῆς οὖν ἔπεμψα πρὸς σέ, σύ τε καλῶς ἐποίησας παραγενόμενος. νῦν οὖν πάντες ἡμεῖς ἐνώπιον τοῦ θεοῦ πάρεσμεν ἀκοῦσαι πάντα τὰ προστεταγμένα σοι ὑπὸ τοῦ κυρίου). Cornelius emphasizes his instant obedience to the angel's directive. He expresses his gratefulness for Peter's willingness to accept his invitation and to come to Caesarea, and he describes the situation in which he and his relatives and friends find themselves as a solemn occasion. It is solemn because they are gathered "in the presence of God" (ἐνώπιον τοῦ θεοῦ) to hear God speak through Peter. The nominalized participle translated as "instructions" (προστεταγμένα) connotes an official directive or command.[52] Cornelius is prepared to respond to everything that "the Lord"[53] gives through Peter, his earthly messenger.

10:34 – 35 Then Peter began to speak: "I truly understand that God shows no partiality, but accepts those in every nation who fear him and do what is right" (ἀνοίξας δὲ Πέτρος τὸ στόμα εἶπεν· ἐπ᾽ ἀληθείας καταλαμβάνομαι ὅτι οὐκ ἔστιν προσωπολήμπτης ὁ θεός, ἀλλ᾽ ἐν παντὶ ἔθνει ὁ φοβούμενος αὐτὸν καὶ ἐργαζόμενος δικαιοσύνην δεκτὸς αὐτῷ ἐστιν). The fifth incident of the Caesarea episode is Peter's speech (vv. 34 – 43), which has three parts: an introduction (vv. 34 – 35), the proclamation of Jesus (vv. 36 – 41), and the concluding offer of salvation (vv. 42 – 43). This is the final missionary speech of Peter in Acts and formulates the proclamation of the gospel of Jesus Christ to Gentile sympathizers with Judaism.

Peter begins his speech with a comment on the impartiality of God (v. 34), an emphasis that links the following proclamation of the gospel of Jesus Christ with Peter's earlier reference to his new insight regarding Gentiles, whom God no longer wants to be called impure or unclean (v. 28). The position of the negation (οὐκ) and of the predicate

"one who shows partiality" (προσωπολήμπτης) before the subject "God" (ὁ θεός) underlines the point that Peter presents as a newly won conviction — the understanding, which is in accordance with truth, that God's nonpartiality is relevant not only within Israel (cf. Deut 10:17; 2 Chr 19:7) but now applies to Gentiles as well.[54] God shows his favor not only to Jews who fear him and who live accordingly, but to Gentiles who fear him and do what is right as well.

The result of God's impartiality is his acceptance of people "in every nation" (ἐν παντὶ ἔθνει), a phrase that is emphasized by being placed at the beginning of the clause. Whether a person was born a Jew or a Roman, a Greek or a Syrian, all are accepted by God if and when they "fear him and do what is right." Peter does not declare all nations or all Gentiles to be acceptable before God, irrespective of their religious beliefs and practices, but speaks of individuals who fear God and who "do what is right" (ἐργαζόμενος δικαιοσύνην, lit., "practice righteousness"). Cornelius qualifies on both counts: he fears and prays to Israel's God (vv. 2, 4, 22), and he gives alms (vv. 2, 4), which Jews regard as the practice of righteousness.

The basic requirement to fear God corresponds to the first of the Ten Commandments (Exod 20:3). Fearing God and doing what is right forms the essence of the law; in Deut 10:12 the question "And now, Israel, what does the LORD your God ask of you?" is answered, in first place, with the assertion "to fear the LORD your God, to walk in obedience to him, to love him, to serve the LORD your God with all your heart and with all your soul."

Cornelius's practice of doing what is right does

---

52. The related term προστάγματα refers in inscriptions and papyri to official edicts, cf. Horsley and Llewelyn, *New Documents*, 6:91. In religious inscriptions and literary texts discussing the gods, the term is used for divine precepts; in Tobit 1:6 the term refers to what is "prescribed for all Israel by an everlasting decree."

53. The term κύριος refers here presumably to the God of Israel, as Cornelius has not yet heard Peter's message about Jesus, whom Peter will identify as Messiah and Lord in v. 36.

54. Cf. Jouette M. Bassler, "Luke and Paul on Impartiality," *Bib* 66 (1985): 546 – 52.

not mean obedience to the Jewish law (he is neither a Jew nor a proselyte). This may refer to Cornelius's observance of the Noahic commandments, as some have suggested,[55] or more generally to his almsgiving, which in later rabbinic tradition was called "righteousness" (cf. Matt 6:1). When Peter asserts that Cornelius is "accept[ed]" by God, he does not describe him as having earned salvation on account of his fear of God and his righteous behavior (see 11:14), for salvation comes only through hearing and accepting Peter's message about Jesus, Israel's Messiah and Savior — which Peter emphasizes at the end of his sermon (10:43). Note also that the Jerusalem church eventually acknowledges that the Gentiles in Caesarea have repented and received from God "life" (11:18).

10:36 God sent the message to the people of Israel, proclaiming the good news of peace through Jesus Christ, who is Lord of all (τὸν λόγον ὃν ἀπέστειλεν τοῖς υἱοῖς Ἰσραὴλ εὐαγγελιζόμενος εἰρήνην διὰ Ἰησοῦ Χριστοῦ, οὗτός ἐστιν πάντων κύριος). The central part of Peter's speech, which explains the significance of Jesus' person and ministry (vv. 36 – 41), consists of three parts: God's fulfillment of his promise of salvation for all people through Jesus (v. 36), Jesus' ministry of proclama-

tion and healing (vv. 37 – 39c), and Jesus' death and resurrection (vv. 39d – 41).

Peter begins with two statements about God. First, God has fulfilled his promise of salvation to the people of Israel through Jesus, Israel's Messiah (v. 36a-c). The term translated as "message" (λόγος) is the good news that the peace the Messiah was expected to bring has arrived with Jesus. Jesus is the one through whom God sent his message to Israel (v. 36a; cf. Luke 4:18), a phrase that echoes Ps 107:20 (LXX 106:20) and refers, perhaps, to the effective presence of God, whose words achieve what he intends.[56] Note again the close association of God and Jesus: God proclaimed the good news "through Jesus Christ." Jesus proclaimed "the good news of peace" (v. 36b-c; cf. Luke 1:79; 4:18), a phrase that echoes Isa 52:7 (cf. Nah 1:15) and thus evokes the prophetic hopes for the eschatological era.[57] This peace "corresponds to the Hebrew concept of 'well-being' associated particularly with the messianic age (cf. Luke 2:14; 10:5; 19:42) and with the freedom from hostile powers, whether spiritual or temporal, that his state involves (cf. Luke 1:78, 71)."[58] God sent the message and the reality of messianic salvation through Jesus to Israel first, implying that the new mode of salvation in which

55. Barrett, *Acts*, 520. It is unclear which specific commandments traced back to the time of Noah were regarded as normative for humanity as a whole, and it is unclear which Jewish groups thought in these terms. The so-called Noahic commandments have been attested for the second part of the second century AD at the earliest, and the available sources are not unanimous regarding which specific commandments Gentiles can be expected to observe. The pre-Christian text *Jub.* 7:20 mentions the prohibition of nudity and immorality and speaks more generally of observing righteousness, blessing God as Creator, honoring father and mother, loving the neighbor, and avoiding all iniquity. Later rabbinic texts mention seven commandments that all human beings should observe: the prohibitions of idolatry, blasphemy, murder, incest, stealing, perverting justice, and eating flesh containing blood (*t. ʿAbod. Zar.* 8.4 – 6; *y. ʿAbod. Zar.* 2.1 (40c); *b. ʿAbod. Zar.* 64b). Cf. David Novak, *The Image of the Non-Jew in Judaism:*

An Historical and Constructive Study of the Noahide Laws (TST 14; New York: Mellen, 1983), 3 – 41.

56. Marshall, "Acts," 579, with reference to Pss 107:20 (LXX 106:20); 147:15, 18 [LXX 147:4, 7], which the expression "God sent the message [word]" echoes, although he points out that this nuance "may be somewhat muted here."

57. For Luke 1:79 see David Pao and Eckhard J. Schnabel, "Luke," in *Commentary on the New Testament Use of the Old Testament* (ed. G. K. Beale and D. A. Carson; Grand Rapids: Baker, 2007), 251 – 414, 265, with reference to Isa 11:6 – 9; 65:17 – 25; 59:8. The echo of Isa 52:7 should be related to the echo of Isa 61:1 in Acts 10:38, and it should be noted that the proclamation of peace in Isa 52:7 is linked with Isa 61:2 – 3 in 11Q13 II, 15 – 25, evidence that here Isaiah's new exodus is the last days is in view; cf. Pao, *New Exodus*, 75.

58. Turner, *Power from on High*, 262. Fitzmyer, *Acts*, 463, refers to Isa 48:18; 54:10; Ezek 34:25 – 29; Pss 29:11; 85:8 – 10.

God accepts people from every nation does not invalidate the salvation-historical priority of the people of Israel.

The second point Peter emphasizes — for Luke, in the context of the Caesarea episode, perhaps the crucial statement — is the fact that God's salvation through Jesus is offered to all people (v. 36d). Jesus, Israel's Messiah, is "Lord of all" (οὗτός ἐστιν πάντων κύριος). While the adjective "all" (πάντων) could be neuter and refer to the entire creation, it is preferable to take it as masculine and relate it to people. This means here that he is Lord not only of the Jewish people but also of the Gentiles.[59]

10:37 You know what has happened throughout Judea, beginning in Galilee after the baptism that John preached (ὑμεῖς οἴδατε τὸ γενόμενον ῥῆμα καθ' ὅλης τῆς Ἰουδαίας, ἀρξάμενος ἀπὸ τῆς Γαλιλαίας μετὰ τὸ βάπτισμα ὃ ἐκήρυξεν Ἰωάννης). Next, Peter explains the ministry of Jesus (vv. 37 – 38). He presumes that Cornelius and his friends have basic information about what happened during Jesus' public ministry. A Jewish preacher who performs miracles and draws large crowds would certainly not have escaped the notice of the Roman governor and his troops stationed in Caesarea, only about sixty-two miles (100 km.) from Capernaum. The term "Judea" (Ἰουδαία; see on 1:8) includes here Galilee, as the formulation "beginning in Galilee" demonstrates. The reference to John the Baptist highlights the importance of this prophet who prepared the Jewish people for the one who would come after him to immerse them into the reality of the Spirit of God.[60]

10:38 How God anointed Jesus of Nazareth with the Holy Spirit and with power, how he trav- **eled from place to place doing good and healing all who were in the power of the devil, because God was with him** (Ἰησοῦν τὸν ἀπὸ Ναζαρέθ, ὡς ἔχρισεν αὐτὸν ὁ θεὸς πνεύματι ἁγίῳ καὶ δυνάμει, ὃς διῆλθεν εὐεργετῶν καὶ ἰώμενος πάντας τοὺς καταδυναστευομένους ὑπὸ τοῦ διαβόλου, ὅτι ὁ θεὸς ἦν μετ' αὐτοῦ). Luke's account of what happened begins with the ministry of Jesus of Nazareth in Galilee (v. 38). He highlights the following points.

(1) Jesus is God's Anointed One (ἔχρισεν αὐτὸν ὁ θεός), i.e., the Messiah who was set apart, commissioned, and empowered by God to usher in the fulfillment of the promises concerning the coming of God and of his rule, bringing comprehensive peace and salvation to Israel and to the world.[61] The definite subject of the clause ("God," ὁ θεός) emphasizes that the key element in Jesus' ministry was God's initiative. This reality is reemphasized with the phrase "because God was with him" (ὅτι ὁ θεὸς ἦν μετ' αὐτοῦ) at the end of the sentence.

(2) Jesus was endowed with the Holy Spirit (πνεύματι ἁγίῳ), a statement that echoes Luke 4:14, 18. As the Holy Spirit represents the reality of God's powerful presence, the presence of the Spirit in Jesus has made the saving and transforming power of God a reality in Jesus' ministry.

(3) Jesus is the locus of God's "power" (δυνάμει). The syntactical connection between "with the Holy Spirit" and the phrase "and with power," understood as a hendiadys, identifies God's Spirit with the power in Jesus' ministry. Jesus' identity and role as Messiah anointed with the Holy Spirit is expressed in the manifestation of God's power.

(4) Jesus' ministry took him from place to place, beginning in Galilee and eventually throughout Judea. As the promised Messiah, Jesus confined

---

59. On the title "Lord" (κύριος) see on 2:36.

60. Cf. Luke 3:1 – 18; 7:18 – 28; 9:19; 11:1; 16:16; 20:4 – 6; Acts 1:5, 22; 10:37; 11:16; 13:24 – 25; 19:4.

61. If the reference to God's anointing of Jesus in v. 38a is linked with the reference to John's baptism in v. 37d (e.g.,

Fitzmyer, *Acts*, 465), this should be taken to mean that Jesus was Israel's Messiah only after his baptism by John; one should note that the reference to God's "anointing" (ἔχρισεν) of Jesus is metaphorical — Jesus literally anointed with oil. According to Luke 2:11, Jesus was God's Anointed One already at his birth.

his ministry of proclaiming "peace" (v. 36) not to one locality; rather, he reached the entire Jewish people.

(5) Jesus' proclamation of "peace" was accompanied by actions that demonstrated the arrival of the kingdom of God. The verb translated "doing good" (εὐεργετῶν) means "to render exceptional service, especially to a community, *do good to, benefit*" (BDAG). In Acts 4:9 Luke uses the related noun (εὐεργεσία) for the healing of the lame man at the Beautiful Gate. The words "and healing all who were in the power of the devil" can be understood either (a) epexegetically (as another hendiadys): Jesus' works of beneficence were exorcisms of demons through which the devil had controlled, and made sick, people in Galilee and in Judea; or (b) as examples of how God's power overcame the tyrannical power of the devil through healing and exorcisms.[62] Jesus, empowered by God through his Spirit, effected the liberation of people "from the realm of satanic affliction into a sphere of salvation."[63]

10:39a-c We are witnesses of everything that he did in the country of the Jews and in Jerusalem (καὶ ἡμεῖς μάρτυρες πάντων ὧν ἐποίησεν ἔν τε τῇ χώρᾳ τῶν Ἰουδαίων καὶ ἐν Ἰερουσαλήμ). Peter transitions from his account of Jesus' ministry (vv. 37 – 38) to Jesus' death and resurrection (vv. 39d – 40) with a comment on the disciples as eyewitnesses of "everything" Jesus did (v. 39a). The role of the apostles as "witnesses" (μάρτυρες) is focused here on Jesus' earthly ministry of proclamation and healing in "the country of the Jews," i.e., in Galilee and in Judea, including Jerusalem.[64] The apostles witnessed his proclamation of the message of the arrival of God's kingdom before small and large crowds; they saw the miracles of healing and exorcism; they were present when Jesus was challenged by the Pharisees, scribes, and Sadducees; they accompanied Jesus during his triumphal entry into Jerusalem; they witnessed his prophetic demonstration in the temple.

10:39d – 40b They executed him by hanging him on a cross. God raised him from the dead on the third day (ὃν καὶ ἀνεῖλαν κρεμάσαντες ἐπὶ ξύλου, τοῦτον ὁ θεὸς ἤγειρεν ἐν τῇ τρίτῃ ἡμέρᾳ). Luke's report of Peter's reference to Jesus' death and resurrection is succinct (only fourteen Greek words). We can assume that Peter spoke at greater length about these events, which already played a fundamental role in his earlier speeches.[65] As regards Jesus' death (v. 39d-e), Peter mentions the people who are responsible for Jesus' execution (the Jews)[66] and the method by which Jesus was executed (crucifixion). The expression "hanging him on a cross" alludes to Deut 21:22 – 23 and thus to God's curse on executed people who are hanged on a tree (see on 5:30), the significance of which Peter may have explained to Cornelius.

---

62. Jesus' victory over the devil stands at the beginning of his ministry (Luke 4:1 – 13, with διάβολος mentioned in vv. 2, 3, 6, 13). In the LXX, "devil" (διάβολος) translates the Hebrew term *haśśāṭān* ("Satan"; cf. Job 1:6 – 9, 12; 2:1 – 7; 1 Chr 21:1; Zech 3:1 – 2; the English term "devil" is derived from the Greek term διάβολος via the Latin term *diabolus*). The term διάβολος means "slanderous, backbiting" (LSJ) and describes the supreme adversary of God and of his people, the highest sovereign of the demons; cf. O. Böcher, "διάβολος," *EDNT*, 1:297 – 98.

63. Turner, *Power from on High*, 264.

64. Luke's account of Jesus' ministry in Jerusalem in Luke 19:28 – 21:38 is more extensive than Matthew's and Mark's;

Fitzmyer, *Acts*, 465. On the Twelve as "witnesses" commissioned by Jesus to give testimony about him and his ministry, see Luke 24:48; Acts 1:8, 22; 2:32; 3:15; 5:32; 10:41; 13:31; 22:15; 26:16.

65. For Jesus' death cf. 2:23, 36; 3:14 – 15; 4:10; 5:30; for his resurrection cf. 2:24 – 28; 3:15; 4:10; cf. 5:31.

66. The subject of the sentence (implied in the verb ἀνεῖλαν) is the Jews in whose territory Jesus had been active (v. 39a-c), in particular the Jews and the Jewish leaders in Jerusalem who were directly charged with the responsibility for Jesus' death in 2:23, 36; 3:14 – 15; 4:10; 5:30. In his address before the Roman centurion, Peter places the responsibility on the Jews more generally.

As regards Jesus' resurrection (v. 40a-b), Peter mentions God as the one who is responsible (ὁ θεὸς ἤγειρεν) and reports the chronological detail of the "third day" (ἐν τῇ τρίτῃ ἡμέρᾳ) on which Jesus was raised from the dead. Jesus was crucified on a Friday, and the empty tomb was discovered on Sunday morning, the third day after Friday. Jesus' resurrection was a space-time event that happened in a specific place (Jerusalem) and on a specific day, observed by eyewitnesses, as the next comment insists.

10:40c – 41 And caused him to be seen, not by all people but by witnesses whom God had chosen beforehand, and who ate and drank with him after he rose from the dead (καὶ ἔδωκεν αὐτὸν ἐμφανῆ γενέσθαι, οὐ παντὶ τῷ λαῷ, ἀλλὰ μάρτυσιν τοῖς προκεχειροτονημένοις ὑπὸ τοῦ θεοῦ, ἡμῖν, οἵτινες συνεφάγομεν καὶ συνεπίομεν αὐτῷ μετὰ τὸ ἀναστῆναι αὐτὸν ἐκ νεκρῶν). Peter's reference to eyewitnesses who saw Jesus after his death and resurrection is longer than his reference to Jesus' death and resurrection, which reflects either Luke's editorial decision in reporting Peter's speech before Cornelius or Peter's careful attention to the arguments for Jesus' resurrection.

While Jews (with the exception of the Sadducees) believed in the bodily resurrection of the dead, Greeks and Romans did not, requiring more detailed arguments. Peter emphasizes four points. (1) It was God who caused Jesus to be seen after his crucifixion, just as it was God who had raised Jesus from the dead. (2) Jesus was "seen" (ἐμφανῆ): people saw him after he had come back to life. (3) The risen Jesus was seen not by all Jews in Jerusalem and in Judea or Galilee, but only by those whom God had appointed as witnesses before these events transpired — not only the eleven apostles but other followers of Jesus as well (Luke 24:33; cf. 1 Cor 15:5 – 9), who were granted, by God's providence, an encounter with Jesus in which they saw him. (4) The encounters of witnesses who saw Jesus after his return from the dead involved meals at which they ate with him and drank with him (e.g., Luke 24:30 – 35, the Emmaus disciples; 24:36 – 43, the eleven disciples and their companions; cf. Acts 1:3 – 4) and underlines the physical nature of Jesus' resurrection (cf. 1 Cor 15).

10:42 He commanded us to preach to the people and to bear witness that he is the one appointed by God as judge of the living and the dead (καὶ παρήγγειλεν ἡμῖν κηρύξαι τῷ λαῷ καὶ διαμαρτύρασθαι ὅτι οὗτός ἐστιν ὁ ὡρισμένος ὑπὸ τοῦ θεοῦ κριτὴς ζώντων καὶ νεκρῶν). Peter ends his proclamation of Jesus before Cornelius and his friends with an (implicit) offer of salvation. He relates Jesus' command to the apostles ("us") to preach the good news of the significance of Jesus' death and resurrection. Their activity is described as "preach[ing]" and "bear[ing] witness."[67] Their audience is described as "the people" (τῷ λαῷ), i.e., the Jewish people (v. 37)[68] — a proclamation that now also is reaching the Gentiles.

The content of the proclamation is "the good news of peace through Jesus Christ" (v. 36) and Jesus' role as "judge" (κριτής) of "the living and the dead" (v. 42c-d), i.e., of all people.[69] This is the role of the heavenly Son of Man of Daniel's vision, to whom God gave the authority to execute judgment (Dan 7:13 – 14; Luke 12:8).[70] Presiding at the last judgment is a divine function. The reference to

---

67. On "preaching" (κηρύσσω), see on 8:5; for "bearing witness" (διαμαρτύρομαι), cf. 8:25.

68. Thus most interpreters; differently Bock, *Acts*, 399, who sees a reference to "people of all nations."

69. In 13:20; 18:15; 24:10 the term κριτής is used of human judges. The expression "the living and the dead" became a standard formula in many creeds; Barrett, *Acts*, 527.

70. For Jesus' role as judge cf. 17:31; see also 1 Thess 1:10; 2 Tim 4:1; 1 Pet 4:5; Heb 6:1 – 2.

Jesus' role as judge may at first sight seem surprising, but note the connection with the beginning of Peter's speech (which began with a reference to God's impartiality, v. 34) and with its center (in which Jesus was described as "Lord of all," v. 36). The universal scope of Jesus' role as judge is tied to the universal scope of his status as Lord, which in turn is connected with the fact that forgiveness of sins — the decisive factor for the divine verdict on the day of judgment — is found only through Jesus Christ. This is the emphasis of the next verse.

10:43 "All the prophets bear witness to him, that everyone who believes in him receives forgiveness of sins through his name" (τούτῳ πάντες οἱ προφῆται μαρτυροῦσιν ἄφεσιν ἁμαρτιῶν λαβεῖν διὰ τοῦ ὀνόματος αὐτοῦ πάντα τὸν πιστεύοντα εἰς αὐτόν). At the end of his explanation of the message of Jesus and its significance, Peter emphasizes that forgiveness can be obtained by everyone who believes in Jesus. God grants forgiveness of sins "through" (διά) Jesus (cf. 2:38), God's appointed judge of all people (v. 42). If the Judge himself is involved in forgiving sins, the accused will certainly go free since the sins that have been committed will not affect the outcome of the trial.

However, people must receive (λαβεῖν) forgiveness of sins; it is not simply "declared" as a reality that affects all people. It can and will be received by "all people," whether they are Jews, Greeks, or Romans (note the context of the speech), who believe in Jesus (πιστεύοντα εἰς αὐτόν), i.e., who acknowledge Jesus as Lord of all and as Judge of all and as the one through whom God makes forgiveness of sins possible.

This message of the forgiveness of sins through Jesus, Israel's Messiah and the Lord of the world, has been announced by "all the prophets." This is either a general reference to the Old Testament[71]

or to passages such as Isa 33:17 – 24, where the prophet Isaiah speaks of a future when Israel will see with her eyes God, her king, in his beauty, when the unrighteous will be judged, when Jerusalem will be safe forever, and when God the Lord, who is Judge, Ruler, and King, will save Israel and forgive her sins. Or it may refer to the prophet Jeremiah, who announced the forgiveness of sins for the new covenant (Jer 31:34), or to the prophet Joel, who announced a time when God would pour out his Spirit on all people so that all who call on the name of the Lord will be saved (Joel 2:32; Acts 2:21).

10:44 While Peter was still speaking these words, the Holy Spirit fell upon all the people who were listening to the word (ἔτι λαλοῦντος τοῦ Πέτρου τὰ ῥήματα ταῦτα ἐπέπεσεν τὸ πνεῦμα τὸ ἅγιον ἐπὶ πάντας τοὺς ἀκούοντας τὸν λόγον). The sixth incident of the Caesarea episode relates the conversion of Cornelius and his family and friends. If we understand vv. 42 – 43 as the offer of forgiveness, then indeed "there was nothing else for Peter to say."[72] Peter's later retelling of the incident clarifies that through "listening" (ἀκούοντας) to the word of the gospel, Cornelius and his friends came to faith in Jesus as Messiah and Lord (cf. 11:17). Luke's concern here is not the sequence of repentance, faith, and reception of the Holy Spirit, but the initiative of the Spirit and the dramatic nature of what happened. "Heaven itself points the way to the admission of the 'Gentiles.'"[73] The description of the arrival of the Spirit as "falling" (ἐπέπεσεν) is "Luke's way of distinguishing abnormally dramatic irruptions of the Spirit."[74]

10:45 – 46b The circumcised believers who had accompanied Peter were astonished that the gift of the Holy Spirit had been poured out on the Gentiles as well. For they heard them speaking in

---

71. Cf. Luke 24:25 – 27, 44; Acts 3:17 – 18, 24; 8:35.
72. Barrett, *Acts*, 529.
73. Conzelmann, *Acts*, 84.
74. Turner, *Power from on High*, 357.

other languages and exalting God (καὶ ἐξέστησαν οἱ ἐκ περιτομῆς πιστοὶ ὅσοι συνῆλθαν τῷ Πέτρῳ, ὅτι καὶ ἐπὶ τὰ ἔθνη ἡ δωρεὰ τοῦ ἁγίου πνεύματος ἐκκέχυται· ἤκουον γὰρ αὐτῶν λαλούντων γλώσσαις καὶ μεγαλυνόντων τὸν θεόν). The outpouring of the gift of the Spirit on this group of people was dramatic in the sense that it was perceived immediately as an indisputable reality, as in the case of the apostles on Pentecost (2:1 – 13;[75] see later the Ephesian disciples in 19:6); i.e., they spoke "in other languages."

The reference to "the circumcised believers" from Joppa who accompanied Peter (v. 23) underlines the unexpectedness of this event. The Spirit of prophecy that Joel had promised for the last days — a promise that had become a reality on the day of Pentecost when the apostles and other followers of Jesus in Jerusalem had received the Holy Spirit — had until now come only on Jewish and Samaritan believers. Now the Spirit of prophecy was poured out by the Lord on Gentiles, a new development that leaves the Jewish believers "astonished" (ἐξέστησαν; see on 2:6).

The fact that Cornelius and his household had received the Holy Spirit as a gift from the Lord could not be doubted since they suddenly spoke in unlearned languages, praising God. The last comment suggests that Hebrew or Aramaic was among the languages being spoken — languages that Cornelius or some of his friends may not have been able to speak but languages that Peter and his friends from Joppa would have understood. Luke does not say that all the assembled Gentiles spoke in tongues; it is possible some spoke in unlearned languages while others experienced invasive praise.[76]

In the context of Peter's sermon, the praise directed to God would have acknowledged and celebrated God's mighty acts in Jesus' ministry (vv. 36 – 39), Jesus' death and resurrection (vv. 39 – 41), the possibility of salvation through Jesus, and the reality of the divine forgiveness of sins and justification in view of the day of judgment (vv. 42 – 43) — available not only to Jews but to people in every nation who fear God (v. 35) and believe in Jesus (v. 43).

10:46c – 47 Then Peter said, "Surely no one can stand in the way of these people being immersed in water; they have received the Holy Spirit just as we have" (τότε ἀπεκρίθη Πέτρος· μήτι τὸ ὕδωρ δύναται κωλῦσαί τις τοῦ μὴ βαπτισθῆναι τούτους, οἵτινες τὸ πνεῦμα τὸ ἅγιον ἔλαβον ὡς καὶ ἡμεῖς). Peter acknowledges that Cornelius and his Gentile household "have received the Holy Spirit" (τὸ πνεῦμα τὸ ἅγιον ἔλαβον). In 15:9 Peter explains his reasoning: since these Gentiles who had come to faith in Jesus had unquestionably received the Holy Spirit, it follows that God had cleansed their hearts, making "no distinction" between profane Gentile sinners and ritually pure Jewish sinners.

Ezekiel had prophesied that when God restored Israel, he would pour out his Spirit on his people (Ezek 39:29) and effect a transformation of the heart that would enable them to keep his commandments (Ezek 11:17 – 21: 36:25 – 27) and would purify them from the moral impurities with which they had polluted the land: "I will sprinkle clean water on you, and you will be clean; I will cleanse you from all your impurities and from all your idols " (Ezek 36:25; cf. 36:17 – 19, 29, 33; Zech 13:1). Thus, "Peter's reasoning is that if this blessing of the Spirit has now been given to Gentiles as well as to Jews who believe in Christ, it must mean that God has purified these Gentiles of their

---

75. The parallel between the reception of the Spirit by the Jerusalem believers and by Cornelius and his household is emphasized in v. 47; 11:15; 15:8.

76. Turner, *Power from on High*, 395; this does not offset the fact that Luke viewed glossolalia as a special form of doxological prophetic speech (ibid., 271).

moral impurity and that he is including them in his people as it is being reconstituted by the Spirit in the last days."[77]

Peter acknowledges more specifically that the manner in which they received the Spirit corresponds to the events of Pentecost.[78] His conclusion that these Gentiles should be "immersed in water" (βαπτισθῆναι) in the name of Jesus Christ (v. 48) certifies that they have come to faith in Jesus, that they are ready to pledge allegiance to Israel's Messiah, and that resistance to Gentiles being admitted to the people of God should be abandoned. Peter's statement confirms the norm of 2:38 – 39, which stated the association between baptism and the reception of the Holy Spirit. The dramatic outpouring of the Spirit (v. 44) commits Peter and the believers from Joppa (vv. 45, 47), and eventually the church in Jerusalem (11:15 – 18), to accepting Cornelius and his Gentile household into the congregation of the followers of Jesus immediately, without demanding circumcision and full submission to the Torah.

Baptism (i.e., immersion in water that signals cleansing through the power of God's Spirit, who is bestowed by the risen Lord Jesus) is also now available for Gentiles who have received forgiveness of their sins through Jesus (v. 43) and who are ready to commit themselves to the name of Jesus, Israel's Messiah, in public (v. 48). God is no longer partial to Jews (v. 34) since the purity laws related to food no longer separate Jews and Gentiles (vv. 15, 28). Peter's instant willingness to baptize Cornelius and his household is impressive, given his earlier insistence that he did not cross the boundary between clean and impure things (v. 14).

The decisive factors in the conversion of Cornelius and his household are (1) Peter's sermon with its offer of forgiveness of sins through Jesus Christ; (2) Cornelius's listening to and acceptance of Peter's proclamation and his believing in Jesus as Israel's Messiah, demonstrated in his willingness to be immersed in water in the name of Jesus; and (3) the reception of the Holy Spirit. The positive portrayal of Cornelius (vv. 2, 4, 22, 31, 33) and the divine revelation to Peter not to call anyone profane or unclean (v. 28) does not mean that Cornelius is righteous and thus not in need of conversion since he worships already the one true God. Note how Peter emphasized in his sermon the need to receive forgiveness of sins (v. 43). Note too that the later retellings of the Cornelius episode do not mention his piety; rather, Cornelius received salvation only through the message Peter preached (11:14), he was saved when he repented (11:18), and he received cleansing through faith (15:9).[79]

10:48 He gave instructions that they be immersed in the name of Jesus Christ. Then they invited him to stay for a few days (προσέταξεν δὲ αὐτοὺς ἐν τῷ ὀνόματι Ἰησοῦ Χριστοῦ βαπτισθῆναι. τότε ἠρώτησαν αὐτὸν ἐπιμεῖναι ἡμέρας τινάς). Peter now follows through on God's acceptance of these Gentiles with arrangements for their baptism. The formulation "he gave instructions" (προσέταξεν) suggests that he asked his companions from Joppa to baptize Cornelius and his gathering.[80] Peter and the believers from Joppa accept the Roman centurion and his Gentile family members and friends, who have come to faith and who have received forgiveness of sins, as fellow believers in Jesus Christ.

Luke portrays the events following the conversion of Cornelius and his household as the found-

---

77. Bauckham, "James, Peter, and the Gentiles," 115.

78. Note (1) the common language of 10:45; 11:17 / 2:38 – 39 ("the gift of the Holy Spirit") that is distinct from other passages; (2) the common experience of glossolalia and invasive praise (10:44, 46 / 2:4 – 11); (3) the comparison expressed ex-plicitly by the apostles (11:15, 17; 15:8).

79. For details cf. Turner, *Power from on High*, 385 – 86.

80. For "immerse" (βαπτίζω) see on 1:5; 2:38; for the expression "in the name of" (ἐν τῷ ὀνόματι) see 2:38; 3:6, 16.

ing of a congregation in Caesarea. Peter and the believers from Joppa encounter not only Cornelius but a larger group of Gentiles who hear Peter explain the gospel, who come to faith in Jesus, who are baptized, and who invite him to stay.[81] Luke's report in 11:3 shows that Peter accepted the invitation, staying with the Gentile converts "for a few days."

11:1 – 3 The apostles and the believers throughout Judea heard that the Gentiles had also accepted the word of God. When Peter went up to Jerusalem, the circumcised believers took issue with him and said, "You went into the house of uncircumcised men and ate with them" (ἤκουσαν δὲ οἱ ἀπόστολοι καὶ οἱ ἀδελφοὶ οἱ ὄντες κατὰ τὴν Ἰουδαίαν ὅτι καὶ τὰ ἔθνη ἐδέξαντο τὸν λόγον τοῦ θεοῦ. Ὅτε δὲ ἀνέβη Πέτρος εἰς Ἰερουσαλήμ, διεκρίνοντο πρὸς αὐτὸν οἱ ἐκ περιτομῆς λέγοντες ὅτι εἰσῆλθες πρὸς ἄνδρας ἀκροβυστίαν ἔχοντας καὶ συνέφαγες αὐτοῖς). In the final incident of the Cornelius episode, Luke reports Peter's justification of his acceptance of Gentile converts after his return to Jerusalem (11:1 – 18).

Some think that Luke's retelling of the visions of Cornelius and of Peter and of Cornelius's conversion and reception of the Holy Spirit can be explained by the obtuseness of Luke's readers, who are not yet ready to draw the conclusion from the events in Caesarea that these Gentiles belong fully to the messianic community. However, other explanations of the repetition of what had transpired in Caesarea are preferable. One reason is the historically plausible scenario that Peter's unprecedented behavior would be challenged in Jerusalem by Jewish believers who continued to live according to the purity stipulations of the law revealed on Mount Sinai. Since Peter himself had voiced objections in three consecutive visions concerning the sugges-

tion that he should eat impure and unclean animals, it is to be expected that the Jewish believers in Jerusalem would voice the same protest. The fact that Peter was the spokesman of the Twelve and the leader of the Jerusalem church does not mean that his decisions were automatically accepted by the other apostles and the Jerusalem congregation.

A second reason for this retelling is the importance of the events of the "Gentile Pentecost" for the missionary work of the early church. The readers of Acts cannot fail to notice that the repeated retelling of the Cornelius episode and of Paul's conversion constitute landmark events for the expansion of the messianic people of God beyond Jerusalem and Judea, as the good news of Jesus is proclaimed among all nations to the ends of the earth.

Luke begins his account of Peter's explanation of his behavior in Caesarea with the comment that the news of the conversion of Cornelius and his household had reached "the apostles" in the Jerusalem church and "the believers" in the congregations in other towns throughout Judea (v. 1). Instead of speaking of the conversion of Cornelius and his friends, Luke speaks generally of "the Gentiles" (τὰ ἔθνη), underlining the significance of the events in Caesarea for the mission of the church that is now "also" (καί) reaching Gentiles. Their coming to faith (10:43) in the crucified and risen Jesus (10:39 – 40) and their willingness to become followers of Jesus as Israel's Messiah through baptism (10:48) is described here as "accept[ing]" the word of God. The proclamation of Jesus' life, death, resurrection, and exaltation as Lord who imparts the Holy Spirit is the word that comes from God.

When Peter returned to Jerusalem, the circumcised believers (οἱ ἐκ περιτομῆς, lit., "those from

---

81. The singular personal pronoun (αὐτόν) refers to Peter, as does the discussion in 11:3; it can be assumed, however, that the believers from Joppa stayed in Caesarea as well.

the circumcision") criticized[82] his behavior. Since their critique does not mention the need to circumcise the converted Gentiles, they are evidently not identical with the "circumcision group" of Gal 2:12 (οἱ ἐκ περιτομῆς), nor are they identical with the minority group in the Jerusalem church consisting of converted Pharisees who later demanded that Gentile converts be circumcised (Acts 15:5). The expression "the circumcised believers" thus describes Jewish believers who, as Jews, obviously were circumcised, in contrast to the converted Gentiles (τὰ ἔθνη, v. 1), who were not.

Luke relates the critique of the Jewish believers in direct speech, focusing on their opposition to the table fellowship that Peter had enjoyed in the house of Gentiles (v. 3). The fact that they do not refer to Cornelius and his household as believers, as people who have received the Holy Spirit, or at least as God-fearers, but as "uncircumcised men" (ἄνδρες ἀκροβυστίαν ἔχοντες, lit., "men having foreskins"),[83] may suggest that they made other demands as well — such as the full observance of the law including the food laws, and perhaps circumcision — but this is not clear. Their statement is an accusation: Peter went into the house of pagans and ate with them. One could assume that Cornelius, being a God-fearer who had a good reputation in the Jewish community (10:2, 22), would have offered Peter and the Jewish believers from Joppa only kosher food that observant Jews are able to eat, such as bread, legumes, vegetables, and fruit. However, observant Jews suspected that Gentiles were most likely unclean and thus a source of defilement.

If Peter stayed for several days (10:48) in the house of Cornelius — who was, after all, a Roman centurion whose duties brought him in regular contact with pagan deities — Peter evidently did not care about becoming unclean. If the report about his behavior had come from the believers in Joppa, the Jerusalem believers would know about Peter's newly found conviction that he should no longer call anyone impure or unclean (10:28) and that God no longer shows partiality when it comes to Gentiles (10:34). The believers do not object to Peter's preaching to Gentiles, and they do not explicitly accuse him of having eaten unclean food. But they do criticize Peter for having associated with Gentiles in the course of his ministry without regard for the purity laws of Scripture, which suggests, perhaps, that a ministry that risks involvement in forbidden practices cannot be authentic ministry in the service of Israel's Messiah.

11:4 – 6 Starting from the beginning, Peter explained it to them step by step. "I was in the city of Joppa praying, when I saw a vision in a trance. I saw an object resembling a big sheet being lowered by its four corners from heaven, and it came right up to me. As I looked intently into it, I noticed quadrupeds of the earth, wild animals, reptiles, and birds of the air" (ἀρξάμενος δὲ Πέτρος ἐξετίθετο αὐτοῖς καθεξῆς λέγων· ἐγὼ ἤμην ἐν πόλει Ἰόππῃ προσευχόμενος καὶ εἶδον ἐν ἐκστάσει ὅραμα, καταβαῖνον σκεῦός τι ὡς ὀθόνην μεγάλην τέσσαρσιν ἀρχαῖς καθιεμένην ἐκ τοῦ οὐρανοῦ, καὶ ἦλθεν ἄχρι ἐμοῦ. εἰς ἣν ἀτενίσας κατενόουν καὶ εἶδον τὰ τετράποδα τῆς γῆς καὶ τὰ θηρία καὶ τὰ ἑρπετὰ καὶ τὰ πετεινὰ τοῦ οὐρανοῦ).

Peter's response to the critique of the believers in Jerusalem consists of a straightforward account of the events that had transpired in Caesarea (vv. 4 – 17). The bulk of the report is devoted to his vision in Joppa (vv. 4 – 10), a fact that again underlines that the central concern of Luke in the

---

82. Cf. BDAG, s.v. διακρίνω 5a, "to be at variance with someone by maintaining a firm opposing position or adverse judgment, *take issue*" (Ezek 20:35 – 36; "took issue" in Acts 11:2).

83. The phrase "have a foreskin" (ἔχει ἀκροβυστίαν) is used in Gen 34:14 LXX to describe the uncircumcised inhabitants of Shechem.

Cornelius episode is the breakdown of the "purity boundary" between Jews and Gentiles. Peter's retelling of the earlier vision (10:11 – 16) adds details that underline God's role in this event.

Luke's introductory statement in v. 4 emphasizes Peter's concern to report everything that had happened to explain its meaning. He starts "from the beginning" and "explain[s]" what has happened "step by step" (καθεξῆς), i.e., carefully drawing out the significance of the events.[84] The report of the vision in vv. 5 – 6 repeats 10:9 – 12. Peter begins in 11:5 with an emphatic "I" (ἐγώ). He omits mentioning he was on the roof of the house in which he was staying, the hour of prayer, his hunger, and the preparation of a meal while he was praying. He comments that the large sheet was lowered "from heaven" (ἐκ τοῦ οὐρανοῦ), a detail that highlights God's intervention. Where 10:11 reported that the sheet "came down to the ground" Peter states here that the sheet "came right up to me" (ἦλθεν ἄχρι ἐμοῦ), highlighting the inevitability of his personal involvement. In v. 6 Peter adds the comment that he "looked intently" into the sheet, and he adds "wild animals" (τὰ θηρία) to the list of 10:12.

11:7 – 10 Then I heard a voice say to me, "Peter, get up! Slaughter and eat!" But I replied, "Certainly not, Lord, for nothing profane or unclean has ever entered my mouth." The voice from heaven spoke a second time, "What God has made clean, you must not call profane." This happened three times; then everything was lifted up again to heaven (ἤκουσα δὲ καὶ φωνῆς λεγούσης μοι· ἀναστάς, Πέτρε, θῦσον καὶ φάγε. εἶπον δέ· μηδαμῶς, κύριε, ὅτι κοινὸν ἢ ἀκάθαρτον οὐδέποτε

εἰσῆλθεν εἰς τὸ στόμα μου. ἀπεκρίθη δὲ φωνὴ ἐκ δευτέρου ἐκ τοῦ οὐρανοῦ· ἃ ὁ θεὸς ἐκαθάρισεν, σὺ μὴ κοίνου. τοῦτο δὲ ἐγένετο ἐπὶ τρίς, καὶ ἀνεσπάσθη πάλιν ἅπαντα εἰς τὸν οὐρανόν).

The report of the dialogue with the heavenly voice in vv. 7 – 10 recounts 10:13 – 16. The command from heaven (v. 7) and Peter's protest of "certainly not, Lord" (μηδαμῶς, κύριε; v. 8) repeats verbatim the earlier report. Instead of saying that he has "never eaten anything that is profane or unclean" (10:14), Peter says here, more dramatically, that "nothing profane or unclean has ever entered my mouth." This rare expression, which does not occur anywhere else in Acts or in Luke's gospel, echoes Matt 15:11.[85] The second command from heaven not to call anything profane that God has made clean (v. 9b) repeats 10:15a word for word, highlighting again the fundamental importance of the words of the heavenly voice.

11:11 – 12 At that very moment three men who had been sent to me from Caesarea arrived at the house where we were staying. The Spirit told me to go with them without making a distinction. These six brothers accompanied me, and we entered that man's house (καὶ ἰδοὺ ἐξαυτῆς τρεῖς ἄνδρες ἐπέστησαν ἐπὶ τὴν οἰκίαν ἐν ᾗ ἦμεν, ἀπεσταλμένοι ἀπὸ Καισαρείας πρός με. εἶπεν δὲ τὸ πνεῦμά μοι συνελθεῖν αὐτοῖς μηδὲν διακρίναντα. ἦλθον δὲ σὺν ἐμοὶ καὶ οἱ ἓξ ἀδελφοὶ οὗτοι καὶ εἰσήλθομεν εἰς τὸν οἶκον τοῦ ἀνδρός). The second part of Peter's report to the Jerusalem believers relates God's directive to go to Caesarea (vv. 11 – 12), recounting 10:17 – 24. Since Peter reports the events from his point of view, he omits the inquiry

---

84. The term καθεξῆς here does not denote chronological order, which would require Peter to begin with Cornelius's vision; his audience would certainly be more interested in a vision that Peter had than in an experience of a Gentile, which is the reason for the reversal of the chronological order of the events.

85. On Matt 15:11 cf. R. T. France, *The Gospel of Matthew*

(NICNT; Grand Rapids: Eerdmans, 2007), 583 – 84, who argues against interpretations that see only a relative negation that "the principle of externally contracted defilement," which is the basis for the Levitical food laws (Lev 11; 17:10 – 16), is here set aside by Jesus. The parallel passage Mark 7:15 is worded differently.

of Cornelius's envoys for the house of Simon the tanner.

He begins with the arrival of three men who "had been sent" (ἀπεσταλμένοι) from Caesarea to the house in which he was staying (v. 11). He does not mention the name of Cornelius in his account in vv. 4 – 17 because he does not focus on a particular individual (whose reception of the Spirit as an uncircumcised pagan may be an exception) but on the universal lesson that God taught him through the vision. Peter omits the invitation to the pagan messengers to stay overnight in Simon the tanner's house as his guests.

The command of the Spirit to go with the three men to Caesarea (v. 12) is given in indirect speech. The Greek phrase translated "without making a distinction" (μηδὲν διακρίναντα), formulated with the active voice of the verb, expresses the conclusions that Peter had drawn from the vision of the animals as it applied to the traditional distinctions that Jews made between themselves and the Gentiles.[86] Peter specifies that he was accompanied by six fellow believers (adding a number to the report in 10:23). He admits the first part of the accusation in v. 3: he indeed entered the house of a pagan.

11:13 – 14 He reported how he had seen the angel standing in his house and saying, "Send to Joppa and summon Simon who is called Peter; he will bring a message through which you and your entire household will be saved" (ἀπήγγειλεν δὲ ἡμῖν πῶς εἶδεν τὸν ἄγγελον ἐν τῷ οἴκῳ αὐτοῦ σταθέντα καὶ εἰπόντα· ἀπόστειλον εἰς Ἰόππην καὶ μετάπεμψαι Σίμωνα τὸν ἐπικαλούμενον Πέτρον, ὃς λαλήσει ῥήματα πρὸς σὲ ἐν οἷς σωθήσῃ σὺ καὶ πᾶς ὁ οἶκός σου). The third part of Peter's speech in

Jerusalem recounts Cornelius's vision, again without mentioning his name. Peter omits references to Cornelius's prayers and his almsgiving, which allows Peter to focus on the divine initiative that brought him to Caesarea into the house of these Gentiles.

The main difference to the previous reports of Cornelius's vision (10:3 – 6, 30 – 33) is the addition of the phrase "through which you and your entire household will be saved" (v. 14). The passive voice of the verb "will be saved" (σωθήσῃ) describes the salvation of Cornelius and his family and friends as the action of God, who has been taking the initiative in preparing Peter for the encounter with these Gentiles and who has taken the initiative in prompting these Gentiles to invite Peter and listen to his message.[87] In other words, the issue in this debate is not food or ceremonial defilement contracted from the association with Gentiles, but the salvation of people — the purpose of Jesus' ministry (Luke 19:10) and of the proclamation of the apostles (2:21, 40). Salvation is given by God, it comes through listening to the message about Jesus, and it involves the reception of the Holy Spirit (v. 15) and baptism (v. 16).

11:15 As I began to speak, the Holy Spirit fell upon them just as he had fallen upon us at the beginning (ἐν δὲ τῷ ἄρξασθαί με λαλεῖν ἐπέπεσεν τὸ πνεῦμα τὸ ἅγιον ἐπ᾽ αὐτοὺς ὥσπερ καὶ ἐφ᾽ ἡμᾶς ἐν ἀρχῇ). The fourth part of Peter's speech reports his proclamation of the gospel and the Gentiles' reception of the Holy Spirit, recounting in a concise manner Luke's report in 10:44 – 46. The temporal articular infinitive translated "as I began" underscores again God's initiative in the salvation of the

---

86. See on 10:20. Cf. BDAG, s.v. διακρίνω 2, "to conclude that there is a difference, *make a distinction, differentiate.*" In 11:2 the verb means "to take issue with, criticize" (BDAG, s.v. 5b). GNB, NET, NIV, TNIV translate 11:12 as in 10:20 ("without hesitation"), while NRSV translates "not to make a distinction" (cf. RSV, ESV; cf. NLT "not to worry that they were Gentiles").

87. On the verb "save" (σῴζω) see on 4:9, 12; on "salvation" (σωτηρία) see on 4:12; on Jesus as "Savior" (σωτήρ) see on 5:31.

Gentiles in Caesarea. Peter had not finished his proclamation of the good news of Jesus when the Holy Spirit "fell," i.e., came in dramatic and recognizable fashion upon the Gentiles. The comparative particle "just as" (ὥσπερ) relates the coming of the Spirit on Cornelius and his household to the coming of the Spirit on the apostles (ἐφ᾽ ἡμᾶς) "at the beginning" (ἐν ἀρχῇ), i.e., on Pentecost. The apostles had suddenly spoken in unlearned languages (2:4), as did Cornelius and his friends (10:46).

11:16   And I remembered the word of the Lord, how he had said, "John immersed in water, but you will be immersed in the Holy Spirit." (ἐμνήσθην δὲ τοῦ ῥήματος τοῦ κυρίου ὡς ἔλεγεν· Ἰωάννης μὲν ἐβάπτισεν ὕδατι, ὑμεῖς δὲ βαπτισθήσεσθε ἐν πνεύματι ἁγίῳ). Next, Peter explains that he remembered Jesus' promise of the coming of the Holy Spirit, quoting Jesus' words from 1:5 (and recalling the words of John the Baptist in Luke 3:16). The point of the saying is not that in contrast to the followers of John the Baptist, believers in Jesus are not immersed in water, but rather, that Jesus brings the fulfillment of God's promises regarding the Spirit of prophecy, which was to fall on all human beings and effect salvation (Joel 2:28 – 32, quoted by Peter in Acts 2:17 – 21).

What Peter's statement does assert is the primacy of being immersed "in the Holy Spirit" (ἐν πνεύματι ἁγίῳ) over being immersed in water. While followers of Jesus continued to practice the latter when people came to faith in Jesus as Israel's Messiah, the decisive event is that God[88] grants to new believers the gift of the Spirit, who

has cleansed them from sin. Jesus and now Peter (as earlier John the Baptist) compare John's role of cleansing Israel through immersion in water with the Messiah's cleansing of Israel because he was endowed by God with the power of the Holy Spirit. The followers of Jesus are granted "immersion in the Holy Spirit" because Jesus, Israel's Messiah, is the agent of God who cleanses sinners through the presence of God's Spirit.[89]

Peter learned from his vision that God's impartiality (10:15, 28) means his willingness to accept both Jews and Gentiles (without distinction) into the messianic congregation of "the Israel of fulfillment," since the Gentiles have become "clean" through their faith in the word about Jesus.[90] Peter remembers John's promise (Luke 3:16) that Jesus reiterated in Acts 1:5 because it speaks of the work of the Messiah cleansing and restoring Israel through the power of the Spirit of God, which he as the crucified, risen, and exalted Lord who sits at God's right hand pours out. Jesus' promise of "immersion in the Holy Spirit" implies that the Gentiles, who had come to faith in Jesus and who had incontrovertibly received the Holy Spirit, should be considered "clean" since it is God's Spirit who cleanses and restores "Israel" in the last days, as God had promised through the prophets.

The vision God granted to Peter announced the removal of defilement from Gentiles who come to faith in Jesus and who receive the Spirit who cleanses them. Thus, Peter was justified to associate with Gentiles who had come to faith in Jesus and upon whom the Holy Spirit had fallen. Moreover, Peter was also justified to incorporate them into the congregation of "Israel" by immersion in water

---

88. The passive of the verb "will be immersed" (βαπτισθήσεσθε) is a divine passive: Jesus spoke about what God will do.

89. Cf. Turner, *Power from on High*, 183 – 84 n. 44, who explains the metaphor implied in the term "immerse" (βαπτίζω) in Luke 3:16. For βαπτίζω see on 1:5; 2:38.

90. Turner, *Power from on High*, 385. Turner points out that the fact that Peter only "remembers" the saying of Jesus (and from John) means that the expression "baptism in the Holy Spirit" was not widely current in the church of Luke's or Peter's day (ibid. 386 – 87); for the following points see ibid.

and by eating with them. All people, both Jews and Gentiles, without distinction, upon whom the Messiah bestows the Holy Spirit, are part of God's restoration of Israel and belong to the people of God.

11:17 "So if God gave them the same gift that he gave us when we believed in the Lord Jesus Christ, who was I that I could stand in God's way?" (εἰ οὖν τὴν ἴσην δωρεὰν ἔδωκεν αὐτοῖς ὁ θεὸς ὡς καὶ ἡμῖν πιστεύσασιν ἐπὶ τὸν κύριον Ἰησοῦν Χριστόν, ἐγὼ τίς ἤμην δυνατὸς κωλῦσαι τὸν θεόν;). Peter ends his report with a conclusion (formulated as a question). Since[91] God granted the Gentiles "the same gift" of the Holy Spirit that he had granted to the Jewish believers who acknowledged Jesus as Messiah and Lord, it follows that he could certainly not oppose God by refusing to baptize Gentiles in the name of Jesus (10:48a-c), accept their hospitality (10:48d-e), and eat with them (11:3). Luke repeats this statement when he summarizes Peter's speech at the Apostles' Council (15:8 – 9). It is one of the central theological statements both of Peter and of Luke.

11:18 When they heard this, they remained silent. And they praised God, saying, "So God has granted even to the Gentiles the repentance that leads to life" (ἀκούσαντες δὲ ταῦτα ἡσύχασαν καὶ ἐδόξασαν τὸν θεὸν λέγοντες· ἄρα καὶ τοῖς ἔθνεσιν ὁ θεὸς τὴν μετάνοιαν εἰς ζωὴν ἔδωκεν). Luke ends his narrative of the Cornelius episode with a brief but important report about the reaction of the Jerusalem believers to Peter's account of what happened in Caesarea. The Greek term translated "they remained silent" (ἡσύχασαν) means that they abandoned their objections (v. 3).[92] They were convinced by Peter's report and by his conclusions, agreeing that God's bestowal of the Holy Spirit on the Gentiles means that they are part of the salvation that God has brought to Israel through Jesus, the crucified, risen, and exalted Messiah and Lord. While repentance (μετάνοια) is an action required of sinners (2:38), it is also, and fundamentally, God's gracious gift to sinners (ὁ θεὸς ... ἔδωκεν). As repentance had been granted to Israel by Jesus (5:31), it has now also been granted to the Gentiles by God.

The "life" (ζωή) that the repentance of sinners leads to is the reality of salvation (11:14), a reality that includes the forgiveness of sins (10:43) and the reception of the Holy Spirit (10:44 – 47; 11:15 – 17). The fact that the uncircumcised Gentiles in Caesarea were granted repentance, salvation, and the gift of the Holy Spirit means that God accepted them into the "Israel of fulfillment." When the Jewish believers in Jerusalem came to realize this truth, they "praised" God for this new development in God's plan of salvation.

---

91. The conditional clause is a first-class conditional, here expressing a fact — the protasis restates v. 15.

92. NIV, TNIV translate the term "they had no further objections;" similarly GNB, NET, NLT.

Theology in Application

After Luke showed to his audience that God's promises to Israel have been fulfilled in and through Jesus, Israel's Messiah and exalted Lord, by describing the faith and life of the followers of Jesus in Jerusalem (Acts 1 – 7), and after he reported on the spreading of the good news of Israel's restoration through Israel's Messiah, despite persecution, across geographical and demographic boundaries to the Samaritans, an Ethiopian proselyte, Jews living in Damascus, and Jews living in the coastal cities of Judea (Acts 8 – 9), he describes in 10:1 – 11:18 how the good news of salvation through Jesus overcame the greatest divide of all, the apartheid of Jews and pagans. The central point of the Caesarea episode is the gradually but decisively emerging conviction that the messianic movement of Jesus' followers is not limited to a particular ethnic group but is open to all people, irrespective of their ethnic and religious background, provided that they come to faith in Jesus and receive God's Holy Spirit. The text underscores several historical and theological points.

God's Revelation and the Obedience of Believers

A major emphasis in this passage is on God's initiative in the various stages of the narrative. Even though God took the initiative in granting Peter a vision meant to teach him the changed status of Gentiles in the divine plan of salvation, there was a process of human decision-making as Peter and the Jerusalem church had to catch up to God's new initiative. As Acts 15 demonstrates, the learning process concerning the status of Gentile believers in the messianic movement was a long and painful process, in which Peter and the Jewish believers in Jerusalem needed to acknowledge and accept the modification of the law in the context of the new covenant (Luke 22:20). God's will concerning the Gentiles was communicated to Peter through a vision, but it needed to be interpreted for Peter. This interpretation included obedience to the heavenly voice (11:12a), understanding the significance of the vision (11:12b), remembering the words Jesus had spoken (11:16), noting historical precedents and parallels (11:17a-b), and logical reasoning that linked the heavenly voice in the vision with Jesus' words and with the experience of the apostles (11:17c).

Understanding and following divine revelation often require courage. Peter had to overcome previously held convictions that had made contacts with Gentiles difficult and a more intimate association with Gentiles impossible. In addition, Peter had to overcome the resistance of believers in Jerusalem, who questioned his behavior. The critical discussion in Jerusalem shows that Peter was willing to risk the peace in the congregation, perhaps even friendships, in his endeavor to explain God's new initiative. Christian leaders, and Christians in general, if confronted with God's claims, cannot simply point to traditional positions of law and convention in the attempt to avoid what might be uncomfortable changes in outlook and behavior. Martin

Luther's behavior in 1517 is comparable: he was willing to risk the peace of his monastic order and of the church in Germany and Europe since he was convinced that his newfound conviction of forgiveness and salvation being granted by faith in Jesus Christ alone apart from works (including indulgences) was the only authentic understanding of God's revelation in Scripture.

God's Impartiality and the Church of Jews and Gentiles

This was a painful lesson for Peter and for the Jerusalem believers to learn — that not only Samaritans and God-fearing proselytes can be welcomed in the messianic people of God, but also uncircumcised Gentiles who come to faith in Jesus. The international and multiethnic composition of the church is God's intention. This is evident in the promise that Jesus would be "a light for revelation to the Gentiles" (Luke 2:32), and this is evident in the divine intervention in the life of Cornelius, a centurion in Roman auxiliary troops, and in the life of Peter. God set up their encounter in Caesarea and demonstrated indisputable bestowal of the Holy Spirit on the Gentiles assembled in Cornelius's house. The inclusion of the Gentiles is the fulfillment of God's promise to Abraham that through him and his descendants all the families of the earth would be blessed (Acts 3:25 – 26; cf. Gen 12:1 – 3).

The multiethnic composition of God's people was the ultimate goal of Jesus' ministry. The preaching of John the Baptist, who stands at the beginning of the messianic movement of Jesus and his followers, was accompanied by Isaiah's promise that "all people will see God's salvation" (Luke 3:6; cf. Isa 40:5). Jesus told his disciples after his death and resurrection that repentance and forgiveness of sins "will be preached in his name to all nations" (Luke 24:47), and the arrival of the Holy Spirit empowered them to be his witnesses "as far as the ends of the earth" (Acts 1:8).

The multiethnic identity of the church means that no one may be regarded as a second class member of God's people. Christians must be willing to give up prejudices concerning people with other ethnic and cultural backgrounds. Cornelius and his friends received the Holy Spirit and were thus integrated into the messianic people of God on account of their faith and through baptism, without first becoming Jews (proselytes) through circumcision and full submission to the law. While we should not accuse Peter of being "xenophobic" and "prejudiced" against Gentiles or as having (unnecessary) "scruples," the truth of God's acceptance of Gentiles is a truth that Christians in all contexts need to grasp and live out in their encounters with people from other ethnic or social backgrounds. Salvation is not limited to particular groups of people, as God seeks the salvation of all people, including Gentiles, polytheists, and Romans, since Jesus "is Lord of all" (10:36).

Acts 11:19 – 30

Literary Context

This relatively short text is the fourth of five sections in Luke's narrative that describe the beginnings of the mission to the Gentiles (8:4 – 12:25). After describing Philip's mission to the Samaritans and the conversion of an Ethiopian eunuch (8:4 – 40), the conversion of Saul of Tarsus, who preaches in Damascus, in Jerusalem, and then in the province of Cilicia (9:1 – 30), and the mission of Peter in Palestine in the cities of the coastal plain (9:31 – 43) in the course of which the first Gentiles come to faith in Jesus (10:1 – 11:18), Luke now describes the mission of Jerusalem believers in Antioch, the capital of the province of Syria (11:19 – 30). The following section (12:1 – 25) shifts the focus again to events in Jerusalem.

The fact that in Antioch Gentiles come to faith in Jesus shows that the expansion of the new messianic movement to include Gentiles was not an exception but became the rule as the good news of Jesus is taken from Jerusalem, Judea, and Samaria to the ends of the earth (1:8). This passage reports the third appearance of Barnabas in Acts. He was introduced as a dedicated follower of Jesus who sold his property (4:36 – 37); he was described as a perceptive and courageous believer who introduced Saul, the former persecutor, to the other apostles in Jerusalem (9:27). Now he is portrayed as the envoy of the Jerusalem congregation sent to support and consolidate the new congregation in Antioch. As Barnabas establishes a firm link between Jerusalem and Antioch and as he recruits Saul for the ministry in the capital of Syria, Luke shows that there is "continuity between the restored people of God in Jerusalem, and the ever extending messianic people, now including great new areas and entire new races."[1]

---

1. Johnson, *Acts*, 207.

III. The Beginnings of the Mission to Gentiles (8:4 – 12:25)

    B. The Conversion of Saul-Paul and the Beginning of His Missionary Work (9:1 – 30)

    C. The Mission of Peter in Palestine (9:31 – 11:18)

        20. The mission of Peter in cities on the coastal plain (9:31 – 43)

        21. The mission of Peter in Caesarea and the conversion of Cornelius (10:1 – 11:18)

➡   **D. The Mission in Antioch (11:19 – 30)**

        22. The mission of Jerusalem believers, Barnabas, and Saul in Antioch (11:19 – 26)

        23. The famine relief of the congregation in Antioch for the Jerusalem believers (11:27 – 30)

    E. The Departure of Peter from Jerusalem in the Persecution under Herod Agrippa I (12:1 – 25)

Main Idea

The missionary proclamation of the church is empowered by God, driven by outreach across cultural boundaries, consolidated by competent preachers, supported by teamwork, and assisted by the solidarity of believers and churches.

Translation

Acts 11:19 – 30

19a	Action	Now **those who had been scattered by the persecution**
b	Description	that took place over Stephen
c	Action/Place	**traveled as far as Phoenicia,**
d	List	**Cyprus, and**
e	List	**Antioch,**
f	Action	speaking the word only to Jews.
20a	Action/Contrast	**Some of them, however,**
b	Identification (Place)	men from Cyprus and
c	Identification (Place)	Cyrene
d	Identification (Place)	who reached Antioch,
e	Action	**also spoke to the Greeks,**
f	Specific	proclaiming the good news about the Lord Jesus.
21a	Event	**The hand of the Lord was with them,**
b	Result	and **a great number of people believed**
c	Result	and **turned to the Lord.**
22a	Event	**News of this came to the ears of the church**
b	Place	in Jerusalem.

c	Response	**They sent Barnabas to travel**
d	Place	to Antioch.
23a	Setting: Time	When he arrived
b	Setting: Event	and saw the grace of God,
c	Action/Result	**he rejoiced**
d	Action	and **encouraged them all**
e	Exhortation	to remain steadfast in their devotion to the Lord.
24a	Character description	**He was a good man,**
b		full of the Holy Spirit and
c		faith.
d	Event/Result	**And a large number of people were brought to the Lord.**
25a	Action/Place	Then **Barnabas went to Tarsus**
b	Purpose	to look for Saul.
26a	Setting: Time	When he found him,
b	Action	**he brought him to Antioch.**
c	Setting: Time	For a whole year
d	Action	**they met with the congregation**
e	Action	and **taught a large number of people.**
f	Event/Place (Aside)	**It was in Antioch**
g	Identification	that the disciples were first called Christians.
27a	Setting: Time	During this time
b	Event	**prophets came from Jerusalem to Antioch.**
28a	Event	**One of them,**
b	Identification	named Agabus,
c	Action	**stood up**
d	Action	and **predicted**
e	Agency	through the Spirit
f	Prophecy	that there would be a severe famine
g	Place	throughout the world;
h	Event/Fulfillment	**this happened**
i	Time	during the reign of Claudius.
29a	Action	**The disciples determined that …**
b	Explanation	according to their ability,
c	Advantage	**… each would send something for the support of** ↵
		the believers
d	Place	living in Judea.
30a	Action	**This they did,**
b	Action (Manner)	sending it to the elders
c	Agency	by Barnabas and
d	Agency	Saul.

Structure and Literary Form

These two episodes (11:16–26 and 11:27–30) are closely linked. Both take place in Antioch, the capital of the province of Syria, and both narrate events related to the early phase of the history of the congregation of believers there. Both episodes refer to the close connection that the new believers had to the church in Jerusalem (the location of the narratives in 11:1–18 and 12:1–25). The first episode ties the foundation of the church in Antioch with the believers from Jerusalem who had to leave the city after the killing of Stephen (11:19–21; cf. 8:1–4). And it links the consolidation of their missionary efforts with Barnabas, sent from Jerusalem to Antioch. The second episode ties the financial support from the Antioch congregation to the believers in Jerusalem with Christian prophets who had traveled from Jerusalem to Antioch (11:27–28), and it reports a journey of Barnabas and Saul from Antioch to Jerusalem (11:29–30).

In both episodes Barnabas and Saul are the main characters. There is thus a geographical connection with the immediate context in 11:1–18 and 12:1–24 (Jerusalem) and a personal connection with the wider context in 9:26–30 and 12:25 (Barnabas and Saul). Together with 12:1–25, these two episodes link the first part of Acts, focused on Peter's ministry in Jerusalem and Judea (1:1–11:18), with the second part of Acts, focused on Paul's ministry in Asia Minor and in Europe and his imprisonment in Jerusalem, Caesarea, and Rome (13:1–28:31).

Both episodes are *historical narrative* — more specifically a missionary report (11:19–26), a report about the activity of Christian prophets (11:27–28), and a report about famine relief ministries of the Antiochene church (11:29–30). There is no direct speech in these two episodes. They contain seven geographical names — Phoenicia (v. 19), Cyprus (vv. 19, 20), Antioch (vv. 19, 20, 22, 26b, 26f, 27), Cyrene (v. 20), Jerusalem (vv. 22, 27), Tarsus (v. 25), and Judea (v. 29). There are multiple references to travel (vv. 19. 20, 23, 25, 26, 27, 30), to sending (vv. 22, 29, 30), to missionary activity (vv. 19, 20, 23, 26), and to the success of missionary work (vv. 21, 24, 26). Elements that stand out are the statement that "the hand of the Lord was with them" (v. 21, i.e., with the Jewish Christian missionaries), the characterization of Barnabas (v. 24), and the prophecy of Christian prophets from Jerusalem (v. 28) with the reaction taken by the church in Antioch (vv. 29–30).

The first episode consists of three incidents, corresponding to three phases of the history of the foundation of the church in Antioch: the mission of Jewish-Hellenistic Christians from Jerusalem (11:19–21), the mission of Barnabas (11:22–24), and the mission of Barnabas and Saul (11:25–26). The second episode recounts the prophecy of Agabus, a Christian prophet from Jerusalem (11:27–28), and the relief efforts of the believers in Antioch for the believers in Jerusalem (11:29–30).

Exegetical Outline

→ **I. The Mission of Jerusalem Believers, Barnabas, and Saul in Antioch (11:19 – 26)**

    A. The Mission of Jewish-Hellenistic Christians from Jerusalem in Antioch (11:19 – 21)

        1. The missionary work of Jerusalem believers among diaspora Jews (11:19)

        2. The missionary work in Antioch among Greeks (11:20)

        3. The conversion of large numbers of Jews and Greeks in Antioch (11:21)

    B. The Mission of Barnabas in Antioch (11:22 – 24)

        1. The dispatch of Barnabas to Antioch by the congregation in Jerusalem (11:22)

        2. The missionary work of Barnabas in Antioch (11:23 – 24)

    C. The Mission of Barnabas and Saul in Antioch (11:25 – 26)

        1. The recruitment of Saul by Barnabas (11:25 – 26b)

        2. The work of Barnabas and Saul in Antioch (11:26c-e)

        3. The designation of the followers of Jesus as "Christians" (11:26f-g)

II. The Famine Relief of the Congregation in Antioch for the Jerusalem Believers (11:27 – 30)

    A. The Prophecy of Agabus (11:27 – 28)

        1. The arrival of Christian prophets from Jerusalem in Antioch (11:27)

        2. The prophecy of Agabus of a severe famine (11:28)

    B. The Relief Efforts of the Antioch Christians through Barnabas and Paul (11:29 – 30)

        1. The decision of the believers in Antioch to support the believers in Judea (11:29)

        2. The dispatch of Barnabas and Saul to Jerusalem (11:30)

Explanation of the Text

11:19 Now those who had been scattered by the persecution that took place over Stephen traveled as far as Phoenicia, Cyprus, and Antioch, speaking the word only to Jews (οἱ μὲν οὖν διασπαρέντες ἀπὸ τῆς θλίψεως τῆς γενομένης ἐπὶ Στεφάνῳ διῆλθον ἕως Φοινίκης καὶ Κύπρου καὶ Ἀντιοχείας μηδενὶ λαλοῦντες τὸν λόγον εἰ μὴ μόνον Ἰουδαίοις). The report in vv. 19 – 26 begins with a brief description of the missionary work of Jewish Christians from Jerusalem, who preach the good news of Jesus among Jews living outside of Judea. Luke ties their activity with the persecution of the followers of Jesus in Jerusalem that ensued after the execution of Stephen (8:1 – 4). He thus makes the theological point that God continues to empower Jesus' followers for witness and prompts people to come to faith

in Jesus as Israel's Messiah and Savior, causing the church to grow and expand.

Whether there is a causal connection between the persecution in Jerusalem and the expansion of the church through missionary activity seems doubtful. The Twelve preached the gospel of Jesus Christ in Jerusalem, defying an official ban on speaking about Jesus, facing repeated imprisonments and interrogations, and risking their lives, as the fate of Stephen demonstrates. Also, Peter did not need the pressure of a persecution to be active in the cities of the coastal plain (9:32 – 43; 10:1 – 48). The apostles and other leading believers such as Stephen, Philip, and Barnabas were not timid disciples who needed to be forced by the Lord, through a persecution, to finally embark on missionary journeys in the direction of the ends of the earth.

Luke mentions three regions in which these unnamed Jerusalem believers preached the gospel. Phoenicia is the territory of the city states on the Levant coast north of Mount Carmel, which belonged to the province of Syria. Jewish communities are attested in Byblos, Berytus, Dora, Ptolemais, Sidon, and Tyre.[2] Cyprus (see on 13:3, 4), the third largest island in the Mediterranean, is only about sixty miles (100 km.) from the Syrian coast; the cities on the southern coast of Cyprus — Salamis, Kition, Amathus, Kourion, Paphos — could easily be reached from Caesarea or from any of the ports on the Phoenician coast. Antioch (see on 11:20), the capital of the Roman province of Syria and the congregation of followers of Jesus established there, will figure more prominently in the subsequent narrative. The term translated "as far as" (ἕως, v. 19) may suggest that the Jerusalem believers preached not only in the city of Antioch, but in the cities south of Antioch that belonged to the province of Syria.

The comment in v. 21 suggests that Jews who lived in Phoenician and Cypriot cities came to faith in Jesus as Israel's Messiah. A later comment in 15:3 attests the existence of Christian congregations in Phoenicia (see also 21:3–6; 27:3). Luke's brief description indicates that he knows more than what he includes in his narrative. The statement in 11:19 that the Jerusalem believers proclaimed the gospel "only to Jews" (εἰ μὴ μόνον Ἰουδαίοις) indicates either that their mission took place before the events of 10:1–11:18 and the "official" opening of the church and her mission to Gentiles, or it reflects the missionary tactics of these believers who focused exclusively on the Jewish people whom they encountered.

11:20 Some of them, however, men from Cyprus and Cyrene who reached Antioch, also spoke to the Greeks, proclaiming the good news about the Lord Jesus (ἦσαν δέ τινες ἐξ αὐτῶν ἄνδρες Κύπριοι καὶ Κυρηναῖοι, οἵτινες ἐλθόντες εἰς Ἀντιόχειαν ἐλάλουν καὶ πρὸς τοὺς Ἑλληνιστὰς εὐαγγελιζόμενοι τὸν κύριον Ἰησοῦν). From the large-scale mission of the Jerusalem believers after Stephen's execution, Luke singles out the missionary work of those who reached Antioch, a city with about 250,000 inhabitants, including perhaps as many as 25,000 Jews.

The Jerusalem believers who proclaimed the good news about Jesus in Antioch were diaspora Jews who originally came from Cyprus and from Cyrene,[3] a Roman province in North Africa that had thriving Jewish communities. Jews from Cyrene are mentioned in the New Testament several times: a certain Simon of Cyrene carried Jesus' cross to Golgotha,[4] Jews from Cyrene were present at Pentecost (2:10), and Jews from Cyrene who had returned to Jerusalem worshiped in their own synagogue (6:9). As diaspora Jews, they were able to speak Greek. Luke relates that "they proclaim[ed] the good news" (εὐαγγελιζόμενοι) of Jesus also "to the Greeks" living in the city. If the comment in v. 19 that many Jerusalem believers preached the gospel "only to Jews" is relevant for v. 20e, we can assume that the Jewish believers from Cyprus and Cyrene preached to both Jews and Greeks — presumably in the numerous local synagogues, in which they would meet not only Jews but also proselytes and God-fearers.

---

2. Cf. Schnabel, *Early Christian Mission*, 2:774–80, for these and other cities on the Phoenician coast.

3. On the Jewish community in Cyrene cf. Barclay, *Jews in the Mediterranean Diaspora*, 232–42.

4. Luke 23:26; Matt 27:32; the fact that Mark 15:21 describes this Simon as "the father of Alexander and Rufus" suggests that at least his sons were known to Mark's readers and thus in all probability were believers in Jesus; cf. Bauckham, *Eyewitnesses*, 51–52.

11:21 The hand of the Lord was with them, and a great number of people believed and turned to the Lord (καὶ ἦν χεὶρ κυρίου μετ᾽ αὐτῶν, πολύς τε ἀριθμὸς ὁ πιστεύσας ἐπέστρεψεν ἐπὶ τὸν κύριον). The missionary work of the believers from Jerusalem led to the conversion of "a great number of people." The reason for their missionary success was the presence of "the hand of the Lord," i.e., of Jesus (v. 20) and/or of God.[5] This may refer to "signs and wonders" that these believers performed.[6] The presence of divine power is not so much a "validation" of their testimony as the effective cause of the conversion of people in Antioch.

The goal of missionary work and the central process of conversion are people coming to faith as they "turn" (ἐπέστρεψεν; see on 3:19) to the Lord. While "Lord" (κύριος) can refer to God — polytheistic Greeks in Antioch coming to faith in Israel's God — it is more plausible that it refers to the proclamation of Jesus (cf. "the Lord Jesus" in v. 20). Jews and Greeks in Antioch come to faith in Jesus as Israel's Messiah and as the crucified, risen, and exalted Lord. Apparently the Jerusalem believers did not ask the converted Greeks to be circumcised.

11:22 News of this came to the ears of the church in Jerusalem. They sent Barnabas to travel to Antioch (ἠκούσθη δὲ ὁ λόγος εἰς τὰ ὦτα τῆς ἐκκλησίας τῆς οὔσης ἐν Ἰερουσαλὴμ περὶ αὐτῶν καὶ ἐξαπέστειλαν Βαρναβᾶν διελθεῖν ἕως Ἀντιοχείας). This second incident recounts the mission of Barnabas in Antioch (vv. 22 – 24). The news of conversions of both Jews and Greeks in Antioch reached the church in Jerusalem. Presumably the believers

from Jerusalem who were preaching the gospel in the cities of the Phoenician coast, on Cyprus, and in Syria kept in contact with the church in Jerusalem. Since the same happened when Philip preached in Samaria (see 8:14), it seems plausible that the early Christian missionaries regarded the apostles (not mentioned here specifically) as responsible for the missionary expansion of the congregations of believers in Jesus — a responsibility they accepted, as their dispatch of Barnabas to Antioch demonstrates.

Barnabas was not just an "inspector" of the work done by others, as many commentators assume.[7] The leaders of the Jerusalem church "sent" (ἐξαπέστειλαν) Barnabas as an experienced missionary leader, theological teacher, and church organizer, who consolidated the growing congregation of believers in Jesus and who continued the evangelistic outreach to Jews and Greeks in the city (see vv. 23 – 26). Luke consistently portrays Barnabas as a bridge-builder between people (see 4:36 – 37; 9:27; 11:25, 30; 15:2; 15:36 – 39).

11:23 When he arrived and saw the grace of God, he rejoiced and encouraged them all to remain steadfast in their devotion to the Lord (ὃς παραγενόμενος καὶ ἰδὼν τὴν χάριν τὴν τοῦ θεοῦ, ἐχάρη καὶ παρεκάλει πάντας τῇ προθέσει τῆς καρδίας προσμένειν τῷ κυρίῳ). This verse describes Barnabas's ministry in Antioch with four verbs. The reference to Barnabas's arrival reflects the importance of a missionary's entrance into a new city. He "saw" the grace of God; i.e., he recognized that the conversions of Jews and Greeks to

---

5. The phrase "the hand of the Lord" as an anthropomorphic description of God's effective power, used by Luke in Luke 1:66, occurs in 1 Sam 5:3, 6, 9 LXX; 2 Sam 3:12 LXX; 1 Chr 28:19; 4:10; Isa 66:2.

6. Cf. Acts 2:43; 4:30; 5:12; 6:8; cf. 2:22, where Jesus is described as "a man accredited to you by God with mighty deeds, wonders, and signs, which God did through him in your midst."

7. More helpful is Marguerat, *Actes*, 1:412, who points out that Barnabas's mission was not an attempt by the Jerusalem church to assure their control over the new congregation, or to legalize the missionary operation of the new missionaries who had reached Antioch, but the effort to verify the spiritual legitimacy of the new believers and to ensure a link between them and the "church of origin" (*l'église des origines*).

faith in Jesus (v. 20) and the effect of God's grace in the conduct of the new believers were the result of God's power.[8]

The third verb notes Barnabas's reaction to the visible reality of God's favor bestowed on Jews and Gentiles in Antioch: he "rejoiced" (ἐχάρη); i.e., he was filled with joy that God had blessed the missionary work of the Cypriot and Cyrenian believers in Antioch, diaspora Jews like himself, whom he knew from the Jerusalem congregation.

Finally, Barnabas "encouraged" (παρεκάλει, imperfect tense) the new believers to be steadfast in their association with the Lord, i.e., to remain true to their faith in Jesus Christ. The Greek expression translated as "devotion" (τῇ προθέσει τῆς καρδίας) describes the purpose of one's will, the resolve to believe in the crucified, risen, and exalted Jesus as Israel's Messiah, Lord, and Savior of the world, to rely on God for the atonement of sins through Jesus' death, to count on Jesus for reconciliation with God, and to depend on the Holy Spirit for the transformation of one's life and behavior. Barnabas thus consolidates and strengthens the work of the Jerusalem missionaries. The imperfect tense of "encouraged" describes ongoing activity, probably with an iterative nuance — new converts (and older believers as well) need repeated reminders of the importance of being firm, resolute, and consistent in faith and practice.

11:24 He was a good man, full of the Holy Spirit and faith. And a large number of people were brought to the Lord (ὅτι ἦν ἀνὴρ ἀγαθὸς καὶ πλήρης πνεύματος ἁγίου καὶ πίστεως. καὶ προσετέθη ὄχλος ἱκανὸς τῷ κυρίῳ). This descrip-

tion of Barnabas, consisting of three comments, is similar to Stephen's.[9] (1) Barnabas is a "good man" (ἀνὴρ ἀγαθός), i.e., a person of impeccable character whose work is beneficial for the community.[10] (2) He is "full" (πλήρης) of the Holy Spirit, a description that suggests that he experienced "notable continuing prophetic experience of the Spirit,"[11] which means, in the context of vv. 23–25, that the Spirit helped Barnabas give direction and encouragement to the church. This resulted in continuing evangelistic outreach and further conversions. (3) Barnabas is full of "faith," a term that describes "a dynamic and motivating way of understanding the relation of God to one's own world … fuelled by God's self-revealing presence and charismatic wisdom."

Barnabas's teaching of the new believers in the emerging congregation in Antioch resulted in further conversions, caused by God and his grace (vv. 21, 23), who made effective the continuing evangelistic outreach of the believers from Jerusalem (vv. 20–21). Luke notes that "a large number of people" (ὄχλος ἱκανός) "were brought" (or "added") to the Lord. The dative "to the Lord" (τῷ κυρίῳ) can be taken as an instrumental dative; that is, it was the Lord who added new converts to the congregation.[12]

11:25–26 Then Barnabas went to Tarsus to look for Saul. When he found him, he brought him to Antioch. For a whole year they met with the congregation and taught a large number of people. It was in Antioch that the disciples were first called Christians (ἐξῆλθεν δὲ εἰς Ταρσὸν ἀναζητῆσαι Σαῦλον, καὶ εὑρὼν ἤγαγεν εἰς Ἀντιόχειαν. ἐγένετο

---

8. Luke does not state whether the "gift" of God's favor was tangible in signs and wonders, or in glossolalia.

9. Cf. Acts 6:5, 8; 7:55. On Barnabas, see on 4:36.

10. Cf. BDAG, s.v. ἀγαθός 2aα. In Luke 23:50 Joseph of Arimathea was called "a good and upright man." Josephus, *Ant.* 18.117, calls John the Baptist "a good man."

11. Turner, *Power from on High*, 150; the following quotation ibid. 351.

12. A similar comment on the expansion of the church is found in 5:14. Dunn, *Beginning from Jerusalem*, 156, points out that the close succession of the summaries in 11:21, 24 "is a reminder of just how compressed Luke's account of this major breakthrough is."

δὲ αὐτοῖς καὶ ἐνιαυτὸν ὅλον συναχθῆναι ἐν τῇ ἐκκλησίᾳ καὶ διδάξαι ὄχλον ἱκανόν, χρηματίσαι τε πρώτως ἐν Ἀντιοχείᾳ τοὺς μαθητὰς Χριστιανούς). The third incident narrates Barnabas's recruitment of Saul to work in the church at Antioch (vv. 25–26). Saul, who was born in Tarsus and held Tarsian citizenship,[13] had gone to Tarsus when he left Jerusalem, where he had been preaching the gospel (see on 9:30).

What was Saul doing in Tarsus? Why did Barnabas ask him to join in his work in Antioch? The context of 9:30 and 11:19–26, combined with other passages, allows us to answer these questions. Saul had been called to preach the good news of Jesus as Israel's Messiah and Savior by the risen Lord himself—both among Jews and Gentiles (9:6, 15; 22:14–15; 26:16–17). He had proclaimed the gospel in Damascus (9:20–22, 27), in Arabia/Nabatea (9:23; Gal 1:17; 2 Cor 11:32–33), in Jerusalem (9:28–29), and in the regions of Syria and Cilicia (Gal 1:21–24).[14] Thus, Barnabas recruited Saul for the pastoral ministry and the evangelistic outreach of the believers in Antioch because he was a trained theologian (as a student of Gamaliel) and an experienced missionary (for about six years), who could reach out to Jews and Greeks. Since the activities of the followers of Jesus came to the attention of the Roman authorities in Antioch (cf. v. 26f-g), the fact that Saul held Roman citizenship may have also been a factor in asking him to relocate to Antioch, the capital of the Roman province of Syria.

Luke gives a detailed description of Barnabas's effort to recruit Saul for ministry in Antioch. Barnabas left Antioch and traveled 130 miles (210 km.) to Tarsus overland, an eight-day journey. He had to "look for" (ἀναζητῆσαι) Saul, a comment that suggests two things. Barnabas knew that Saul was based in Tarsus, and he knew how to contact Saul's family; the latter could be easily located through the Jewish community of Tarsus, particularly in view of the fact that Saul's family, holding both Tarsian and Roman citizenship, would be among the most prominent Jewish families in the city.

Saul was evidently not in Tarsus since Barnabas had to "look for" him, which suggests he was engaged in missionary outreach in other cities and towns of Cilicia. Eventually Barnabas "found" him (v. 26a), possibly in one of the Cilician cities in which he was preaching the gospel. From there he "brought" him to Antioch, having secured Saul's willingness to leave his ministry in Cilicia behind and to relocate in Antioch.

The combined missionary work of Barnabas and Saul in Antioch (dated between AD 42–44) is narrated concisely (v. 26c-e). Luke begins with a chronological comment: they worked together in Antioch for "a whole year." Then he mentions two main activities of Barnabas and Saul. First, they "met with the congregation" (ἐκκλησία, see on 5:11), a term Luke has used only for the congregations in Jerusalem, Judea, Galilee, and Samaria up to this point.[15] The use of ἐκκλησία indicates that the congregation of the followers of Jesus in Antioch, consisting of Jewish and Gentile believers, was just as much the people of God as the congregation in Jerusalem.

These meetings with the church—if the model of the Jerusalem church is any indication of what followers of Jesus did in their meetings (2:42–47)—consisted of (1) instruction in the teachings of Jesus and in the significance of his life, death,

---

13. Cf. 21:39; 22:3; see on 9:1–2.

14. For Saul's missionary work in Damascus, Arabia, Jerusalem, Syria, and Cilicia, cf. Schnabel, *Early Christian Mission,* 2:1030–69.

15. Acts 5:11; 8:1, 3; 9:31; 11:22.

resurrection, and exaltation in the context of the Hebrew Scriptures and the teaching of the apostles; (2) fellowship, including shared meals; (3) celebration of the Lord's Supper during meals; (4) prayers of praise and intercession. The fact that the believers are called "disciples" (μαθηταί; see on 5:11) in v. 26g places the focus on teaching and on learning.

In their second activity, Barnabas and Saul "taught [διδάξαι] a large number of people." This can hardly refer to the teaching of the congregation, mentioned in the preceding comment. The "large number of people" (ὄχλος ἱκανός) refers to unbelieving Jews and Greeks (cf. v. 24), who perhaps attended the (open) meetings of the congregation. In other words, Barnabas and Saul instructed the believers in the church and they engaged in evangelistic outreach, teaching Jews and Greeks about the good news of Jesus, Israel's Messiah and the Savior of the world.

Luke's final comment here about the origins and the early years of the congregation in Antioch notes that it was in Antioch that the disciples, i.e., the followers of Jesus, were first called "Christians" (Χριστιανοί). This term occurs in the New Testament only on the lips of outsiders.[16] Josephus, Pliny, and Tacitus use the term as well.[17] The first Christian usage of the term as a self-designation comes from the second century,[18] which suggests that the term "Christian" was not a self-designation of the followers of Jesus as early as the 30s.

The verb translated as "were called" (χρηματίσαι) is not necessarily a reflexive ("they called themselves Christians") but can be treated as a passive, which suggests that the term "Christians" was introduced by others.[19] The followers of Jesus called themselves "disciples," "believers," "brothers," "slaves" or "servants of Jesus Christ," and perhaps also "those who are in Christ Jesus." The form of the Greek expression — in particular the ending (-ιανοί; singular -ιανός) — also suggests an origin outside of the church, pointing to Latin-speaking circles.[20] In Rome we hear of the *Caesariani* and *Augustiani*; in Judea we encounter the *Herodiani* (the relatives, clients, and the supporters of the Herodian court, who are also mentioned in the New Testament, cf. Mark 3:6; 12:13). The term "Christians" (Χριστιανοί) was evidently an official designation coined by the Roman authorities in Antioch for the new religious group.[21] The designation was probably applied to the followers of Jesus by outsiders "when, not least as a result of their missionary activity to the Greeks, they began to separate themselves from the synagogue congregations and acquire an identity as a separate group."[22]

It is possible that the followers of Jesus who proclaimed the good news of Jesus, Israel's Messiah, Lord, and Savior, in the synagogues, in private houses, and perhaps in the marketplace had come to the attention of the Roman authorities — perhaps as early as AD 39, in connection with the unrest among the Jews provoked by Emperor Caligula's directive to have his statue erected in

---

16. Herod Agrippa in 26:28, opponents in 1 Pet 4:16.

17. Josephus, *Ant.* 18.64; Pliny, *Ep.* 10.96–97; Tacitus, *Ann.* 15.44 (Lat. "Christianos"). In a graffito in Pompeii (CIL IV 679), dated before AD 79, the term seems to be used as well.

18. Cf. Ignatius, *Rom.* 3:2; cf. *Eph.* 11:2; *Magn.* 10:3; *Pol.* 7:3). See also *Did.* 12:1, 4.

19. The verb (χρηματίσαι) here means "to take/bear a name/title (as so and so), to go under the name of" (active); in English translation, the verb is frequently rendered as a passive, "be called/named, be identified as" (BDAG, s.v. χρηματίζω 2). Cf. Fitzmyer, *Acts*, 478.

20. Greek speakers would use terms such as Χρίστειοι or Χριστικοί; cf. Hengel and Schwemer, *Paul*, 453 n. 1171. Jews usually called the followers of Jesus "Nazarenes" (Greek Ναζωραῖοι), cf. Acts 26:9. Unbelieving Jews would hardly have called the believers in Jesus "followers of the Messiah."

21. Justin Taylor, "Why Were the Disciples First Called 'Christians' at Antioch? (Acts 11,26)," *RB* 101 (1994): 75–94.

22. G. Schneider, "Χριστιανός," *EDNT*, 3:478.

the Jerusalem temple. The followers of Jesus were probably recognized by the Roman authorities in Antioch as a group of people who publicly proclaimed their loyalty to a Jew named Jesus as Messiah (Χριστός), who grew in numbers and who thus had to be watched.

11:27 – 28 During this time prophets came from Jerusalem to Antioch. One of them, named Agabus, stood up and predicted through the Spirit that there would be a severe famine throughout the world; this happened during the reign of Claudius (ἐν ταύταις δὲ ταῖς ἡμέραις κατῆλθον ἀπὸ Ἱεροσολύμων προφῆται εἰς Ἀντιόχειαν. ἀναστὰς δὲ εἷς ἐξ αὐτῶν ὀνόματι Ἅγαβος ἐσήμανεν διὰ τοῦ πνεύματος λιμὸν μεγάλην μέλλειν ἔσεσθαι ἐφ᾽ ὅλην τὴν οἰκουμένην, ἥτις ἐγένετο ἐπὶ Κλαυδίου). The episode of the famine relief that the congregation in Antioch organized for the believers in Jerusalem begins with a report on the prophecy of a Christian prophet named Agabus, who predicted a famine (vv. 27 – 28; see also 21:10).

Luke dates the arrival of Agabus, one of the Christian prophets (προφῆται)[23] who traveled from the congregation in Jerusalem to Antioch, to "this time" (ἐν ταύταις δὲ ταῖς ἡμέραις, lit., "in these days"). This comment can be linked with the year during which Barnabas and Saul worked together in Antioch (between AD 42 and 44). It could also be linked more generally with the early years of the

church in Antioch that had its origins in the aftermath of the persecution after Stephen's execution in AD 31. Or it could be linked with the comment in v. 26 about the designation of the believers of Jesus as "Christians," which could be a note referring to a different period.

The reference to Agabus standing up assumes a meeting of the congregation in which he actively participated.[24] His prophecy is a prediction attributed to the Holy Spirit. The content of the prophecy has two elements: (1) a future event: a famine that would be severe; (2) the place where this event will take place: throughout the world. Famines during which people go hungry and starve to death are caused by extended grain shortages caused by local or provincial harvest failures.[25] The phrase "throughout the world" (ἐφ᾽ ὅλην τὴν οἰκουμένην) is often used in ancient literature and can refer to the entire inhabited world, to the Roman Empire, a much larger area than a specific region, and to a particular region.

Luke notes the time when the famine actually occurred: "during the reign of Claudius" (AD 41 – 54). There were indeed food crises in Egypt, Syria, Judea, and Greece during AD 45 – 47,[26] a year (at the latest) after Agabus visited Antioch. The fact that Egypt was affected was particularly dire, since Egypt was one of the most important grain-growing regions of the empire. Josephus

---

23. Christian prophets are also mentioned in 13:1; 15:32; 21:10; see also 1 Cor 12:28 – 29; 14:29, 32, 37; Eph 2:20; 3:5; 4:11. In the Old Testament, a prophet was God's mouthpiece through whom Israel received exhortation, instruction, critique, encouragement, and revelations about future events. In the New Testament, the role of prophets is similar, although it is not always easy to describe their precise function. Luke mentions Old Testament prophets over twenty times (e.g., Luke 1:70; 3:4; 10:24; 24:25, 27, 44; Acts 2:16, 30; 3:18, 21, 24); he uses the term for John the Baptist (Luke 1:76; 7:26; 20:6) and for Jesus (Luke 7:16, 39; 13:33 – 34; 24:19; Acts 3:22 – 23; 7:37).

24. The Western text expands, inserting comments that constitute the first "we passage" in this textual tradition: "There

was much rejoicing. When we were gathered together, one of them whose name was Agabus spoke." Cf. Barrett, *Acts*, 564, for the discussion of whether the text of Codex Bezae is original (proposed by R. Bultmann) or not.

25. Cf. Bruce W. Winter, "Acts and Food Shortages," in *The Book of Acts in Its Graeco-Roman Setting* (ed. David W. J. Gill and Conrad Gempf), 59 – 78; for the following points see ibid. 65 – 69.

26. Suetonius, *Claud.* 18; Tacitus, *Ann.* 12.43; Dio Cassius, *Rom. Hist.* 40.11; Josephus, *Ant.* 3.320 – 21; 20.101. Cf. Peter Garnsey, *Famine and Food Supply in the Graeco-Roman World: Responses to Risk and Crisis* (Cambridge: Cambridge Univ. Press, 1988), 21.

attests a famine in Syria-Palestine during which Queen Helena of Adiabene, who had converted to Judaism, organized a relief mission for Jerusalem by buying Egyptian grain and dried figs from Cyprus for the poor in Judea, an event that Josephus dates to the time when Tiberius Julius Alexander was procurator in Judea (AD 45 – 48).[27] If Agabus's prophecy was given in AD 44,[28] resulting in the relief mission of the church in Antioch in the same year, the believers in the congregation in Jerusalem would have received help at least a year earlier than the Jews of Jerusalem received aid through the action of Helena.

11:29 – 30 The disciples determined that according to their ability, each would send something for the support of the believers living in Judea. This they did, sending it to the elders by Barnabas and Saul (τῶν δὲ μαθητῶν, καθὼς εὐπορεῖτό τις, ὥρισαν ἕκαστος αὐτῶν εἰς διακονίαν πέμψαι τοῖς κατοικοῦσιν ἐν τῇ Ἰουδαίᾳ ἀδελφοῖς· ὃ καὶ ἐποίησαν ἀποστείλαντες πρὸς τοὺς πρεσβυτέρους διὰ χειρὸς Βαρναβᾶ καὶ Σαύλου). Luke ends the episode with a report on the reaction of the believers ("disciples") in Antioch to Agabus's prophecy.

(1) They made a decision to act to "support" their fellow "believers" (ἀδελφοῖς) living in Judea. Both Barnabas and the Cypriot and Cyrenian believers who had established the church in Antioch came from Jerusalem, but Saul had lived there for many years as well. However, since all believers belong to God's family, a truth expressed in the term "brothers (and sisters)" (ἀδελφοί, see on

1:16; 5:11), all believers in Antioch, whether Jews or Greeks, would have wanted to help their "relatives" in Judea.

(2) They decided to send money to buy grain and other food, regularly priced out of the reach of the poor during food shortages, or food stuffs, which would have to be transported to Judea. If the expression "by the hand" (lit. trans. of διὰ χειρός) of Barnabas and Saul is meant literally, Luke undoubtedly has the sending of silver and gold coins in mind.

(3) "Each" believer contributed, according to their ability. Each one was free to decide how much of what they owned would be contributed to the relief mission. When Paul organized a collection for the believers in Jerusalem between AD 50 and 57, he followed the same practice (1 Cor 16:1 – 2; 2 Cor 9:7).

(4) The believers sent their collected support through Barnabas and Saul to Judea. This was Saul's second postconversion visit to Jerusalem, ten years after his visit in AD 34 (see 9:26 – 30). The direct, initial recipients were the "elders" (πρεσβύτεροι; see on 14:23), who were obviously expected to organize the distribution of the material support among the needy believers. Most interpreters assume that the reference to the "elders" relates to the leadership of the congregation in Jerusalem.[29] If the congregations that existed in other cities and towns in Judea had elders,[30] they could be in view as well. The return of Barnabas and Saul from Jerusalem to Antioch, accompanied by John Mark, is noted in 12:25.

---

27. Josephus, *Ant.* 20.51 – 53, 101.

28. Riesner, *Paul's Early Period*, 132, 135, dates Agabus's prophecy earlier, to AD 39 – 42.

29. Acts 15:2, 4, 6, 22, 23; 16:4; 21:18. If the elders of the congregation in Jerusalem are in view, this presupposes the departure of Peter, and perhaps of the other apostles, from Jerusalem on account of the persecution organized by Herod Agrippa I (12:1 – 17); see on 12:17. Fitzmyer, *Acts*, 483, correctly speaks of "officials of Christian communities in Judea."

30. Cf. in 14:23 the elders in the newly established congregations in southern Galatia.

Theology in Application

These two episodes that Luke relates in connection with the early phase of the congregation in Antioch teach three lessons about the mission of the church.

Empowered by God

The mission of the church is empowered by God. This truth, which Luke has repeatedly emphasized in his narrative, is an important focus in his report of the foundation and growth of the church in Antioch. It is the "hand of the Lord" that made the preaching of the Jerusalem witnesses effective, resulting in conversions (11:21). Barnabas attributes the establishment of a congregation to the "grace of God" (11:23). The continued growth of the church is the result of Barnabas's ministry, who is "full of the Holy Spirit" (11:24).

The fact that Luke does not link the establishment of the church in the Syrian capital of Antioch (11:19 – 26) with the conversion of Cornelius (10:1 – 11:18) in terms of a cause-and-effect relationship underscores that "those who preach in Antioch do so, not because the Jerusalem leaders had devised a missionary strategy, but because they have fled Jerusalem during persecution" and that "the emergence of the church in Antioch is God's doing through the Holy Spirit, not that of any individual or group."[31]

This emphasis does not mean that strategies and tactical plans are unnecessary, but it does mean that they must never form the basis of the confidence of missionaries and pastors. They rely on God, not on programs or plans. In a society in which the "can-do spirit" is part of the national psyche, ministers of the gospel constantly need to remind themselves that they can do nothing unless God himself is at work, through his Spirit, in the hearts and minds of people.

Godly Preachers

The mission of the church is carried out by godly preachers. The emphasis on God as the effective cause of the foundation and growth of churches should not obscure the fact that God works through human beings who carry the message of the gospel as Jesus' witnesses to people living in other cities and towns. The fact that the Jerusalem believers who engaged in missionary work in the cities of Phoenicia and Cyprus and in Antioch are not named does not mean that they are not important. It is true that Luke focuses on Peter and on Paul, and he names a few other missionaries and evangelists (Stephen, Philip, Barnabas). But the famous are "not necessarily the most significant or most important people in the church."[32]

---

31. Gaventa, *Acts*, 181.

32. Fernando, *Acts*, 353, who goes on to comment on the fact that many Christians today spend much effort in making an event newsworthy by associating it with "big names" of famous people: "all this is unnecessary, for our task is to be faithful to what God calls us to do" (354).

In the first episode of this text, Luke underlines the significance of the charismatic personality and ministry of Barnabas, whose instruction of believers and whose teaching of unbelievers contributes to the internal consolidation and the external growth of the church. The addition of Saul to the ministry team in Antioch leads to further church growth. The competency of Barnabas is linked, again, not with an effective strategy or plan, but with the integrity of his character, the transforming power of the Spirit, and faith (11:24).

> There are many things that we can do in ministry without godliness and the fullness of the Spirit. We can lead meetings, prepare and deliver messages, organize and implement programs, win elections, and head committees. But we cannot help people abide in the Lord. To produce godly people we too must be godly. To produce people of prayer we too must be people of prayer. To produce people who walk close to God we too must walk close to God.[33]

The one activity of these missionaries that Luke emphasizes is their preaching (not their organizing): the Jerusalem believers "spoke" to the Greeks in Antioch and "proclaim[ed]" the good news about the Lord Jesus (11:20); Barnabas "encouraged" the believers to be steadfast (11:23). The name "Christians" that was given to the followers of Jesus reflects the focus of the preaching and teaching of the Jerusalem believers, of Barnabas, and of Saul: they proclaimed Jesus as Israel's Messiah (Christ), Lord, and Savior.

The Solidarity of Believers and Churches

The mission of the church is assisted by the solidarity of believers and churches. The material support of the church in Antioch for the believers in Judea, who are "brothers and sisters," demonstrates that followers of Jesus are linked with each other in a community whose members act in solidarity, concerned for the welfare of those who are less fortunate. In this community some give and some receive, depending on present or future needs. The partnership between the church in Antioch and the churches in Jerusalem and in Judea thrived because the believers in Antioch did not feel inferior to the believers in the "mother church" and because the believers in Jerusalem were poorer than the believers in the "daughter church."

If relationships between rich American churches and poor churches in the global South are true partnerships, the former will share their material resources so that the real and urgent needs of the poor churches are alleviated. At the same time, the latter will share their prayers, their experience of suffering, their spiritual integrity, and their willingness to sacrifice so that the materially rich churches can also become spiritually rich.

33. Fernando, *Acts*, 357.

CHAPTER 23

Acts 12:1 – 25

Literary Context

Luke began his second volume on the work that Jesus, the crucified, risen, and exalted Messiah of Israel, continues to do and teach through the apostles and through the church (1:1 – 14) by focusing on the life and mission of the congregation of Jesus' followers in Jerusalem (1:15 – 8:3) and then in Samaria, in Judea, and on the coastal plain and as far as Antioch (8:4 – 11:30). Beginning in 13:1, the focus will be nearly entirely on Paul and his missionary work. Luke places the report on the persecution initiated by Herod Agrippa I that forced Peter to leave Jerusalem between the shift of his focus from Peter and Jerusalem to Paul and Roman provinces in the eastern Mediterranean — a shift he started to make in 11:19 – 30, when Barnabas moved from Jerusalem to Antioch and Paul from Tarsus to Antioch.

The famine relief that the congregation in Antioch sent to the believers in Jerusalem and Judea was presented by Barnabas and Paul to "the elders," a new group of leaders who are neither the Seven (6:5 – 6) nor the apostles, whom they evidently replaced. The report in 12:1 – 24 explains the transition of leadership in the Jerusalem congregation, as indicated by the fact that this report is framed by comments on the famine relief mission in AD 44 by Barnabas and Saul (11:30; 12:25). The persecution that Herod Agrippa I organized against the leaders of the congregation in Jerusalem is best dated to AD 41, i.e., to the beginning of his tenure as king of Judea (AD 41 – 44; see on 12:1).

Peter's departure from Jerusalem is not simply an escape; it is not a defeat for the church, nor does it slow down the expansion of the congregations of Jesus' followers. On the contrary, Luke notes the continued growth and expansion of the church (12:24), connected with Peter's departure. Luke certainly knew to which "another place" (12:17) Peter traveled, but he does not tell his readers that story as he shifts his attention to Paul. Peter's departure from Jerusalem in AD 41 brings to an end the first phase of the church in Jerusalem and thus also the first phase of the missionary expansion of the church, which had been initiated and organized by Jewish Christian missionaries from the Jerusalem congregation.

Main Idea

Luke's report of Peter's imprisonment, miraculous escape, and departure from Jerusalem informs us about a major transition of leadership in the early history of the church, reveals the power of God at work in the messianic movement of Jesus' followers, and illustrates the dangers of being a believer in Jesus and of opposing God's work.

Translation

(See next three pages.)

Structure and Literary Form

This section consists of two episodes. The first episode, featuring the persecution of the church in Jerusalem (12:1 – 23), is narrated in three incidents: a report on persecution organized by Herod Agrippa and on the execution of James, one of the Twelve (vv. 1 – 2); the arrest and miraculous liberation of Peter by an angel of the Lord (vv. 3 – 19); and the circumstances of Herod Agrippa's death in Caesarea (vv. 20 – 23). The second episode consists of a *summary statement* concerning the continued growth of the church in Jerusalem, Judea, and beyond (v. 24), and a *historical note* concerning the return of Barnabas and Saul to Antioch (v. 25).

The first episode (12:1 – 23) is a *narrative* about historical events in Jerusalem (vv. 1 – 19) and in Caesarea (vv. 20 – 23) affecting the church and King Agrippa, respectively. The second incident of this episode includes a *miracle story* (vv. 6 – 11), with the following traditional elements present:[1] (1) the coming of the miracle worker — here the angel of the Lord (v. 7); (2) the appearance of the distressed person (v. 6); (3) the miracle-working word: "Get up quickly" (v. 7); (4) touch: the angel

---

1. On the structure of miracles stories see on 3:1 – 10 (Structure and Literary Form).

Acts 12:1 – 25

1a	Setting: Time	At that time
b	Action (Character entrance)	**King Herod arrested some**
c	Identification	who belonged to the church,
d	Purpose	intending to mistreat them.
2a	Action	**He had James,**
b	Identification	the brother of John,
c		**executed with the sword.**
3a	Setting: Time (Cause)	When he saw that this pleased the Judeans,
b	Action	**he proceeded to arrest Peter also.**
c	Time	**This happened during the Festival of Unleavened Bread.**
4a	Action	**He had him seized**
b	Action	**and put into prison**
c	Manner	with four detachments of soldiers to guard him,
d	Purpose	intending to bring him before the people
e	Time	after Passover.
5a	Setting: Time	While Peter was kept in prison,
b	Action	**the church prayed earnestly to God for him.**
6a	Setting: Time	During the very night
b	Setting: Time	before Herod was going to summon him,
c	Event	**Peter was sleeping between two soldiers,**
d	Circumstance	bound with two chains,
e	Circumstance	while sentries in front of the door guarded the prison.
7a	Manner	Suddenly
b	Action (Character entrance)	**an angel of the Lord appeared**
c	Description	**and a light gleamed**
d	Place	in the cell.
e	Action	**He tapped Peter on the side**
f	Action	**and woke him**
g	Manner	with the words,
h	Command	*"Get up*
i	Manner	*quickly."*
j	Event/Result	**And the chains fell off his wrists.**
8a	Action	**Then the angel said to him,**
b	Command	*"Fasten your belt*
c	Command	*and put on your sandals."*
d	Action/Response	**This he did.**
e	Action	**Then the angel said to him,**
f	Command	*"Put on your cloak*
g	Command	*and follow me."*
9a	Action	**He went out**
b	Manner	following the angel,
c	Irony	not knowing what was really happening
d	Agency	with the angel's help;
e	Character's thoughts	**he thought he was seeing a vision.**

Continued on next page.

Continued from previous page.

10a	Setting: Place	After they had passed the first and
b		the second guard,
c	Action	**they came to the iron gate**
d	Identification	leading to the city.
e	Event	**It opened for them**
f	Manner	by itself.
g	Action	**They went out**
h	Action	and **walked along one street.**
i	Manner	Then, suddenly,
j	Action	**the angel left him.**
11a	Event	Then **Peter came to himself**
b	Action	and **said,**
c	Character's thoughts	*"Now I know for sure that the Lord has sent his angel*
d	Assertion	*and rescued me from the hand of Herod and*
e		*from all that the Jewish people were expecting."*
12a	Setting: Time	When this dawned on him,
b	Action/Place	**he went to the house of Mary,**
c	Identification	the mother of John
d	Identification	who is called Mark,
e	Description	where many people had gathered and
f	Action	were praying.
13a	Setting: Time	When he knocked at the door of the gate,
b	Action	**a female slave**
c	Identification	named Rhoda
d		**came to answer the door.**
14a	Setting: Time	When she recognized Peter's voice,
b	Reaction	**she was so overjoyed**
c	Result	that instead of opening the gate,
d	Action	**she ran inside**
e	Action	and **reported**
f	Indirect speech	that Peter was standing
g	Place	at the gate.
15a	Dialogue (Response)	**They said to her,**
b	Accusation	*"You are out of your mind."*
c	Reaction	**She insisted that it was so.**
d	Response	Then **they said,**
e	Assertion	*"It is his angel."*
16a	Action	**Peter continued to knock.**
b	Setting: Time	When they finally opened the gate,
c	Action	**they saw him**
d	Reaction	and **were astonished.**
17a	Action	**He motioned to them**
b	Purpose	to be quiet,

c	Action	then **he explained to them**
d	Indirect speech	how the Lord had brought him out of the prison.
e	Action	Then **he said,**
f	Request	*"Report this to James and*
g		*the brothers."*
h	Action	Then **he left**
i	Action	and **traveled to another place.**

18a	Setting: Time	In the morning
b	Event	**there was no small commotion**
c	Sphere	among the soldiers
d	Cause	over what had become of Peter.

19a	Setting: Time	After Herod had organized a search for him
b	Setting: Cause	and did not find him,
c	Action	**he interrogated the guards**
d	Action/Command	and **ordered their execution.**
e	Action (Place)	Then **he went down from Judea to Caesarea**
f	Action	and **stayed there.**

20a	Event (Flashback)	**He had been infuriated with the people of Tyre and**
b	Place	**Sidon.**
c	Action	**They joined together**
d	Action	and **presented themselves in an audience with him.**
e	Event (flashback)	**They had secured the support of Blastus,**
f	Identification	the chamberlain of the king,
g	Action	and **asked for peace,**
h	Cause	because their region depended on the king's territory for food.

21a	Setting: Time	On the appointed day,
b	Action	**Herod put on his royal robes,**
c	Action	**took his seat on the platform,**
d	Action	and **addressed them.**
22a	Action	**The assembly shouted,**
b	Acclamation	*"This is the voice of a god, not of a human being!"*

23a	Manner/Time	Immediately
b	Action (Character entrance)	**an angel of the Lord struck him down,**
c	Cause	because he did not give the honor to God.
d	Event	**He was eaten by worms**
e	Event	and **expired.**

24a	Event (Summary)	**The word of God continued to advance**
b	Event	and **gain converts.**

25a	Action	**Barnabas and Saul returned**
b	Time	after they had completed their ministry to Jerusalem.
c	Action/Character entrance	**They brought John with them,**
d	Identification	who was also called Mark.

tapped Peter on the side (v. 7); (5) demonstration of the miracle: they pass through the guards and through the gate of the prison and walk down a street (v. 10); (6) wonder among the people (v. 16); (7) adversaries: Herod Agrippa searches for Peter, without success, and then has the guards executed (vv. 18 – 19).

Exegetical Outline

➡ **I. The Persecution of the Church in Jerusalem by Herod Agrippa I (12:1 – 23)**

　A. The Execution of James son of Zebedee (12:1 – 2)

　　1. The persecution organized by Herod Agrippa (12:1)

　　2. The execution of James (12:2)

　B. The Arrest and Miraculous Liberation of Peter (12:3 – 19)

　　1. The arrest and imprisonment of Peter (12:3 – 5)

　　　a. Peter's arrest (12:3)

　　　b. Peter's imprisonment and impending execution (12:4)

　　　c. The prayers of the church (12:5)

　　2. The miraculous escape of Peter (12:6 – 11)

　　　a. The conditions of Peter's detention during the night before his execution (12:6)

　　　b. The appearance of an angel in Peter's cell (12:7a-d)

　　　c. The angel's command to Peter to get up (12:7e-i)

　　　d. Peter's liberation from his chains (12:7j)

　　　e. The angel's command to Peter to get ready to leave the prison (12:8)

　　　f. The escape from the cell and from the prison (12:9 – 10)

　　　g. Peter's realization of what has happened (12:11)

　　3. The aftermath of Peter's escape (12:12 – 19)

　　　a. Peter's contact with the believers assembled in Mary's house (12:12 – 17g)

　　　b. Peter's departure from Jerusalem (12:17h-i)

　　　c. The commotion among the soldiers over Peter's disappearance (12:18)

　　　d. The unsuccessful search for Peter (12:19a-c)

　　　e. The execution of the prison guards (12:19d)

　　　f. King Agrippa's relocation to Caesarea (12:19e-f)

　C. The Death of Herod Agrippa I (12:20 – 23)

　　1. The delegations from Tyre and Sidon and Agrippa's public speech (12:20 – 21)

　　2. The acclamation of Agrippa as divine (12:22)

　　3. Agrippa's death (12:23)

II. The Growth of the Church (12:24 – 25)

　A. The Growth of the Church in Jerusalem, Judea, and Beyond (12:24)

　B. The Return of Barnabas and Saul to Antioch (12:25)

　　1. Barnabas and Saul return from Jerusalem to Antioch (12:25a-b)

　　2. John Mark accompanies Barnabas and Saul (12:25c-d)

Explanation of the Text

12:1   At that time King Herod arrested some who belonged to the church, intending to mistreat them (κατ᾿ ἐκεῖνον δὲ τὸν καιρὸν ἐπέβαλεν Ἡρῴδης ὁ βασιλεὺς τὰς χεῖρας κακῶσαί τινας τῶν ἀπὸ τῆς ἐκκλησίας). Luke begins his account of the persecution of the Jerusalem church (vv. 1 – 23) with a general chronological reference that introduces the first incident (vv. 1 – 2), the execution of James. The ruler called "King Herod" (Ἡρῴδης ὁ βασιλεύς) is Agrippa I. The vague time reference "at that time" (κατ᾿ ἐκεῖνον δὲ τὸν καιρόν) refers, perhaps, in summary fashion to the rule of Agrippa from AD 41 – 44. The persecution organized by the new Jewish king took place in AD 41, immediately after his return from Rome. The famine relief mission of Barnabas and Saul to Jerusalem (11:30) took place in AD 44. At that time the apostles had left Jerusalem (see comment on 12:17); this is why they take the famine relief to the "elders" of the Jerusalem church. This reference to the elders indicates that the apostles had had to leave Jerusalem, with a new set of leaders responsible for the congregation (see on 12:17).

King Agrippa arrested several who belonged to the church, Jewish followers of Jesus whom he planned to mistreat, i.e., interrogate and punish by beatings and executions (see v. 2). Agrippa undoubtedly occupied the palace of Herod on the west side of the city, which had been used by the Roman governors and evidently included a prison.[2] The conditions in the prison — in which James stayed before his execution (v. 2), and presumably also Peter (v. 4) — were harsh. When Silas,

the commander of the army under Agrippa I, was thrown into prison for being presumptuous, he complained to the king that all that he received as a reward for his loyalty was "chains and a gloomy dungeon" (Josephus, *Ant.* 19.324).

12:2 He had James, the brother of John, executed with the sword (ἀνεῖλεν δὲ Ἰάκωβον τὸν ἀδελφὸν Ἰωάννου μαχαίρῃ). Among the first believers to be arrested and mistreated was James, the brother of John, i.e., one of the Twelve (Luke 6:14; Acts 1:13) and one of the earliest followers of Jesus (Luke 5:10) who belonged to the inner circle of disciples.[3] James's execution with the sword,[4] i.e., probably through beheading, may indicate that a political charge was advanced against James, suggesting that due to their large numbers in Jerusalem the Christians were regarded as "more than a religious nuisance; they threatened the security of the state."[5] Others have suggested, based on (later) Mishnaic law that calls beheading the most shameful of deaths and stipulates beheading for murderers and for the people of an apostate city who have no share in the world to come, that the new king sided with the Jewish leaders who regarded the followers of Jesus as apostates and idolaters, or that James's execution was the result of a lawless and arbitrary course of action.

Since our knowledge of criminal law in Palestine in the first century is limited, particularly as it was administrated during the brief reign of Agrippa I, any suggestion must remain hypothetical. James's execution demonstrates that Agrippa's measures against the church were severe and violent, ending

---

2. Cf. Rapske, *Paul in Roman Custody*, 137.

3. Cf. Luke 8:51; 9:28, 54. James son of Zebedee needs to be distinguished from James son of Alphaeus, another member of the Twelve (Luke 6:15), and James, the brother of Jesus (Matt 13:55; Mark 6:3; Gal 1:19; Acts 12:17; 15:13 – 21; 21:18).

4. The fact that Agrippa ordered an execution by sword indicates that he had been given the authority for capital punishment (*ius gladii*).

5. Barrett, *Acts*, 575; cf. J. Duncan M. Derrett, *Law in the New Testament* (London: Darton, Longman & Todd, 1970), 340.

the period of tranquility of about ten years since the persecution that ensued after Stephen's execution in AD 31.

12:3 When he saw that this pleased the Judeans, he proceeded to arrest Peter also. This happened during the Festival of Unleavened Bread (ἰδὼν δὲ ὅτι ἀρεστόν ἐστιν τοῖς Ἰουδαίοις, προσέθετο συλλαβεῖν καὶ Πέτρον – ἦσαν δὲ αἱ ἡμέραι τῶν ἀζύμων). The second incident of the episode narrates the arrest and miraculous liberation of Peter (vv. 3 – 19). After James was arrested, imprisoned, perhaps tried in legal proceedings, and executed (v. 2), Agrippa continues to attempt to eliminate the leadership of the church in Jerusalem. The arrest of Peter is the next phase of his persecution of the followers of Jesus. Agrippa had evidently carefully gauged the reaction among the Jewish population,[6] which was positive. While Luke does not explain the change of mood in Jerusalem concerning the followers of Jesus (compare with 2:47; 5:14), his comment implies that despite the phenomenal growth of the church, the believers in Jesus continued to be a minority.

Peter is arrested during the Festival of Unleavened Bread (τὰ ἄζυμα), which began with the Passover meal (τὸ πάσχα, v. 4) on Nisan 14 and lasted seven days.[7] In AD 41, Passover (Nisan 14) fell on April 5, which means that Agrippa wanted to try Peter on April 12 (Nisan 22) and execute him presumably on the next day. The date given for Peter's arrest underlines the significance of his imprisonment and his subsequent departure from Jerusalem for the history of the church.

12:4 He had him seized and put into prison with four detachments of four soldiers to guard him, intending to bring him before the people after Passover (ὃν καὶ πιάσας ἔθετο εἰς φυλακὴν παραδοὺς τέσσαρσιν τετραδίοις στρατιωτῶν φυλάσσειν αὐτόν, βουλόμενος μετὰ τὸ πάσχα ἀναγαγεῖν αὐτὸν τῷ λαῷ). Agrippa's action and intention is described with four phrases. (1) Peter is arrested. (2) He is put in prison, presumably the prison located in Herod's palace on the west side of the city. (3) He is guarded by four detachments of four soldiers[8] during the seven days of the festival. Details regarding the placement of the guards are given in v. 6 for the night hours: Peter sleeps between two soldiers, to whom he is tied with chains, while two soldiers guard the door of the cell in which he is imprisoned; the four soldiers would have been relieved after three hours by the next detachment of four soldiers. The heavy guard is meant to make an escape (such as in 5:21 – 26) impossible. (4) Agrippa intends to "bring him before" the people, presumably for a public trial whose outcome he can control.

12:5 While Peter was kept in prison, the church prayed earnestly to God for him (ὁ μὲν οὖν Πέτρος ἐτηρεῖτο ἐν τῇ φυλακῇ· προσευχὴ δὲ ἦν ἐκτενῶς γινομένη ὑπὸ τῆς ἐκκλησίας πρὸς τὸν θεὸν περὶ αὐτοῦ). Luke does not record Peter's reaction to his arrest and imprisonment, but he does relate the believers' reaction — they pray "earnestly" (ἐκτενῶς), with zeal and anticipation of God's intervention. Some think the content of the church's prayer is Peter's liberation, which would have to

---

6. The term Ἰουδαῖοι, probably a reference to the Jewish leadership, is used here negatively for the first time in Acts (cf. Jervell, *Apostelgeschichte*, 332) and is thus translated as "Judeans" (cf. BDAG, s.v. Ἰουδαῖος 1).

7. For Passover and the Festival of Unleavened Bread, see Exod 12:1 – 13:10. In v. 4 the term "Passover" stands for the two consecutive festivals, seen as one holiday. On Nisan 13 (the first month of the Jewish calendar, in earlier times called Abib),

all leavened foodstuffs were removed from the house before the Passover lamb was slaughtered in the evening when Nisan 14 began; unleavened bread was eaten for the next seven days (Deut 16:3 – 4).

8. The term τετράδιον denotes a detachment or squad of four soldiers, one soldier for each of the four night watches (BDAG).

be miraculous; but since vv. 14 – 15 suggests that they do not anticipate Peter's escape, they may have prayed for a positive outcome of the trial that will soon take place (in 4:21 Peter and John were let go), for a lesser punishment than execution (in 5:40 the apostles were not executed, but flogged), or for courage and strength to endure the interrogation and execution (as Jesus had endured both).

12:6 During the very night before Herod was going to summon him, Peter was sleeping between two soldiers, bound with two chains, while sentries in front of the door guarded the prison (ὅτε δὲ ἤμελλεν προαγαγεῖν αὐτὸν ὁ Ἡρῴδης, τῇ νυκτὶ ἐκείνῃ ἦν ὁ Πέτρος κοιμώμενος μεταξὺ δύο στρατιωτῶν δεδεμένος ἁλύσεσιν δυσὶν φύλακές τε πρὸ τῆς θύρας ἐτήρουν τὴν φυλακήν). Luke here describes the conditions of Peter's detention. The day Agrippa planned to summon Peter was the day after the Festival of Unleavened Bread. Peter's miraculous escape happens during the night before his trial, when Peter is sleeping, chained by the wrists (cf. v. 7) to two soldiers, with two further soldiers guarding his prison cell. Peter's miraculous rescue takes place at the last possible moment, evidently during the third night watch (cf. v. 18), i.e., between 4:00 and 6:00 a.m. The fact that Peter is fast asleep the night before his trial demonstrates his trust in the Lord; he does not know whether he will be rescued again, as before, or he will stand trial and be executed, as happened to Jesus and Stephen.

12:7 – 8 Suddenly an angel of the Lord appeared and a light gleamed in the cell. He tapped Peter on the side and woke him with the words, "Get up quickly." And the chains fell off his wrists. Then the angel said to him, "Fasten your belt and put on your sandals." This he did. Then the angel said to him, "Put on your cloak and follow me" (καὶ ἰδοὺ ἄγγελος κυρίου ἐπέστη καὶ φῶς ἔλαμψεν ἐν τῷ οἰκήματι· πατάξας δὲ τὴν πλευρὰν τοῦ Πέτρου ἤγειρεν αὐτὸν λέγων· ἀνάστα ἐν τάχει. καὶ ἐξέπεσαν αὐτοῦ αἱ ἁλύσεις ἐκ τῶν χειρῶν. εἶπεν δὲ ὁ ἄγγελος πρὸς αὐτόν· ζῶσαι καὶ ὑπόδησαι τὰ σανδάλιά σου. ἐποίησεν δὲ οὕτως. καὶ λέγει αὐτῷ· περιβαλοῦ τὸ ἱμάτιόν σου καὶ ἀκολούθει μοι). Luke narrates Peter's rescue from prison in vivid detail, focusing on the appearance, words, and actions of an angel.

(1) An angel sent by the Lord (ἄγγελος κυρίου) appears in the cell in which Peter is kept as prisoner (v. 7). The suddenness of his appearance is highlighted by the introductory "suddenly" (ἰδού) and the aorist tense of the verb "appeared" (ἐπέστη), which follows the imperfect verbal forms of vv. 5 – 6 that described the ongoing conditions of Peter's incarceration. The "Lord" may refer to God, but could also refer to Jesus as the risen Lord, who continues to intervene in the life of the church and of his witnesses. The angel who stands over Peter is accompanied by "light" (φῶς), which signals divine presence.[9]

(2) The angel touches[10] Peter on his side, wakes him up, and commands him to get up (ἀνάστα, imperative).

(3) The chains with which Peter's wrists were tied to the soldiers who guard him fall off, which allows him to obey the angel's command.

(4) The angel issues two further commands, again related in direct speech (v. 8). He directs Peter to fasten his belt and to put on his sandals. Luke notes Peter's compliance with another verb in the aorist tense.

(5) The angel issues two more commands. He

---

9. As in the Lord's appearance to Saul on the road to Damascus; cf. 9:3; 22:6, 9 – 11; 26:13. See the appearance of the angels at Jesus' birth (Luke 2:9).

10. The verb often describes a heavy blow; evidently Peter is fast asleep.

directs Peter to put on his cloak[11] and to "follow" (ἀκολούθει) him; the last imperative is a present tense imperative; Peter should stay right behind the angel on the way out of the prison.

This sequence of events presumes that the guards are fast asleep, not noticing the angel, the chains falling to the ground, or Peter getting dressed. This dramatic description emphasizes that Peter's escape from prison is a divine rescue mission.

12:9 – 10   He went out following the angel, not knowing what was really happening with the angel's help; he thought he was seeing a vision. After they had passed the first and the second guard, they came to the iron gate leading to the city. It opened for them by itself. They went out and walked along one street. Then, suddenly, the angel left him (καὶ ἐξελθὼν ἠκολούθει καὶ οὐκ ᾔδει ὅτι ἀληθές ἐστιν τὸ γινόμενον διὰ τοῦ ἀγγέλου· ἐδόκει δὲ ὅραμα βλέπειν. διελθόντες δὲ πρώτην φυλακὴν καὶ δευτέραν ἦλθαν ἐπὶ τὴν πύλην τὴν σιδηρᾶν τὴν φέρουσαν εἰς τὴν πόλιν, ἥτις αὐτομάτη ἠνοίγη αὐτοῖς καὶ ἐξελθόντες προῆλθον ῥύμην μίαν, καὶ εὐθέως ἀπέστη ὁ ἄγγελος ἀπ᾽ αὐτοῦ). Luke highlights Peter's passive role in his escape by remarking that though Peter follows behind the angel, he does not realize that what is happening is real (ἀληθές; "true"). Having been fast asleep and evidently not anticipating an escape from a heavily guarded prison cell, he thinks that he may be seeing a "vision" (ὅραμα). He will soon realize, however, that the appearance of the angel is more real than the appearance of the unclean animals on the roof in Simon's house in Joppa (10:9 – 16).

Luke's narrative of Peter's escape from the

prison cell and building focuses, naturally and realistically, on the guards outside the cell mentioned in v. 6 and on the iron gate that leads into the city, which opens "by itself," i.e., miraculously.[12] After leaving the prison, the angel and Peter proceed for "one street," i.e., probably one block,[13] at which point the angel "suddenly" (εὐθέως) disappears.

12:11   Then Peter came to himself and said, "Now I know for sure that the Lord has sent his angel and rescued me from the hand of Herod and from all that the Jewish people were expecting" (καὶ ὁ Πέτρος ἐν ἑαυτῷ γενόμενος εἶπεν· νῦν οἶδα ἀληθῶς ὅτι ἐξαπέστειλεν ὁ κύριος τὸν ἄγγελον αὐτοῦ καὶ ἐξείλατό με ἐκ χειρὸς Ἡρῴδου καὶ πάσης τῆς προσδοκίας τοῦ λαοῦ τῶν Ἰουδαίων). Only when Peter is alone, on a street corner one block from the prison, does he come to his senses and recognize the true reality of what has just happened. The Lord has sent his angel, who rescued him from the king and from the hostile expectations of the Jewish people, who undoubtedly count on a conviction and execution as with James (vv. 2 – 3).

Luke relates Peter's realization in a brief monologue of direct speech, as he often does, to make the narrative vivid and to underline a central insight. Since, for Luke, the expression "the people" (ὁ λαός) usually suffices to denote the Jewish people, the emphatic "the people of the Jews [τῶν Ἰουδαίων]" presents Peter as separated from the unbelieving Jews in Jerusalem. God, who sent his angel to rescue Peter, is on the side of the followers of Jesus, whereas the Jewish king turns out to be God's opponent, together with those of the Jewish

---

11. Presumably Peter had lain on his cloak while sleeping; Pesch, *Apostelgeschichte*, 1:365.

12. The term translated as "by itself" (αὐτόματος) is defined in BDAG, as pertaining to "something that happens without visible cause."

13. The term translated as "street" (ῥύμη) means "narrow street, lane, alley;" construed as direct object of the verb, with the numeral "one" (μία); the meaning of the construction seems to be "they went one block further" (BDAG, s.v. προέρχομαι 1; cf. Barrett, *Acts*, 582).

people who welcome the violent oppression of those who believe in Jesus as the Jewish Messiah.

12:12 When this dawned on him, he went to the house of Mary, the mother of John who is called Mark, where many people had gathered and were praying (συνιδών τε ἦλθεν ἐπὶ τὴν οἰκίαν τῆς Μαρίας τῆς μητρὸς Ἰωάννου τοῦ ἐπικαλουμένου Μάρκου, οὗ ἦσαν ἱκανοὶ συνηθροισμένοι καὶ προσευχόμενοι). In vv. 12 – 19 Luke narrates the aftermath of Peter's escape from prison. After realizing what has just happened, Peter is able to act on his own initiative again. He decides to go to a house where he knows he will meet other believers and then leave the city. So he goes to the house of Mary, who is identified as the mother of John Mark.

Mary (Μαρία)[14] is a follower of Jesus and an evidently wealthy woman who placed her house — a substantial house with an outer gate (v. 13) — at the disposal of the believers in Jerusalem. As she is mentioned without a reference to her husband, she is presumably a widow, unless her husband tolerated Christian meetings in his house despite not being a follower of Jesus himself, which seems less likely. John Mark, her son, is mentioned on account of his role in the subsequent missionary work of Barnabas and Paul in the cities of Cyprus and southern Galatia (12:25; 13:5, 13; 15:37 – 39). Paul describes him in Col 4:10 as the cousin of Barnabas.[15] The gathering of believers in Mary's house is one of the regular meetings held in private houses during which the Christians spent time in prayer (2:46 – 47), praying here for Peter during the early days of this new wave of persecution; it is also possible that this meeting is specifically convened to pray for Peter. On the content of their prayers, see v. 5.

12:13 – 14 When he knocked at the door of the gate, a female slave named Rhoda came to answer the door. When she recognized Peter's voice, she was so overjoyed that instead of opening the gate, she ran inside and reported that Peter was standing at the gate (κρούσαντος δὲ αὐτοῦ τὴν θύραν τοῦ πυλῶνος προσῆλθεν παιδίσκη ὑπακοῦσαι ὀνόματι Ῥόδη, καὶ ἐπιγνοῦσα τὴν φωνὴν τοῦ Πέτρου ἀπὸ τῆς χαρᾶς οὐκ ἤνοιξεν τὸν πυλῶνα, εἰσδραμοῦσα δὲ ἀπήγγειλεν ἑστάναι τὸν Πέτρον πρὸ τοῦ πυλῶνος). The reference to a "gate" (πυλών), as distinct from a door (θύρα), describes the house of Mary as an apparently elegant residence that consisted of a house (οἰκία) separated from the street by an inner courtyard and a gateway. When Peter knocks at the door of the gate, a woman named Rhoda, evidently a "female slave" (παιδίσκη) working in Mary's household, comes to the gate to answer.

As Peter stands in the street in front of the house and hears someone coming to the gate, he presumably asks for the door to be opened. The joy that grips Rhoda when she recognizes the voice of Peter (v. 14) indicates that she recognizes Peter, that she is herself a believer, and that she does not expect to see Peter that night. Rather than opening the gate, her emotional response moves her to run back inside and report to Mary and the believers gathered in her house that Peter is standing at the gate.

---

14. The NT mentions six women with the name of Mary: (1) the mother of Jesus; (2) Mary Magdalene, a disciple of Jesus; (3) Mary of Bethany, the sister of Martha, a disciple of Jesus; (4) the mother of James and Joseph, a disciple of Jesus who was at the tomb on Easter morning; (5) the wife of Clopas, a disciple of Jesus who witnessed Jesus' crucifixion; (6) the mother of John Mark. The Jewish name was also used later by Christians.

15. The Mark mentioned in 2 Tim 4:11; Phlm 24; 1 Pet 5:13, is likely the same person, since Paul and Peter refer to him as "Mark" without further specification (which would be otherwise required for a name as common as Mark); cf. Bauckham, *Eyewitnesses*, 206 n. 10. The tradition of the early church identifies John Mark as the author of the gospel of Mark; the earliest evidence is that of Papias, preserved in Eusebius, *Hist. eccl.* 3.39.15; cf. Bauckham, cf. ibid., 202 – 39, for Papias's testimony concerning Mark and the gospel of Mark.

12:15 – 16 They said to her, "You are out of your mind." She insisted that it was so. Then they said, "It is his angel." Peter continued to knock. When they finally opened the gate, they saw him and were astonished (οἱ δὲ πρὸς αὐτὴν εἶπαν· μαίνῃ. ἡ δὲ διϊσχυρίζετο οὕτως ἔχειν. οἱ δὲ ἔλεγον· ὁ ἄγγελός ἐστιν αὐτοῦ. ὁ δὲ Πέτρος ἐπέμενεν κρούων· ἀνοίξαντες δὲ εἶδαν αὐτὸν καὶ ἐξέστησαν). Luke narrates what follows in a brief dialogue. The believers do not believe Rhoda, suggesting that she is crazy. Rather than going back to the gate, letting Peter into the house and thus proving that she is right, she argues that her report is true. The believers are thoroughly incredulous and suggest she has encountered Peter's "angel" (ἄγγελος, v. 15e), a term usually understood here in terms of "guardian angel" and considered as "the double of the person guarded."[16] The believers gathered in Mary's house evidently are not praying for a miraculous escape of Peter from prison on the night before his trial and execution.

Only after Peter's knocks on the door continue do they open the gate (v. 16). When they see Peter, they realize that he is not an angel but Peter himself, a fact that astonishes them (see on 2:6). This reaction demonstrates the reality of the miracle of Peter's escape.[17]

12:17 He motioned to them to be quiet, then he explained to them how the Lord had brought him out of the prison. Then he said, "Report this to James and the brothers." Then he left and traveled to another place (κατασείσας δὲ αὐτοῖς τῇ χειρὶ σιγᾶν διηγήσατο αὐτοῖς πῶς ὁ κύριος αὐτὸν ἐξήγαγεν ἐκ τῆς φυλακῆς εἶπέν τε· ἀπαγγείλατε Ἰακώβῳ καὶ τοῖς ἀδελφοῖς ταῦτα. καὶ ἐξελθὼν ἐπορεύθη εἰς ἕτερον τόπον). The necessity of a manual signal, meant to silence the believers, suggests that they are all talking at the same time, trying to make sense of Peter's sudden appearance. Luke summarizes the report that Peter gives to the believers and tells them "how" (πῶς) he escaped. The fact that "the Lord" (ὁ κύριος) is the subject of the sentence of Peter's report indicates that he focuses on God's initiative and intervention in his rescue from prison, although κύριος can also refer to the risen Jesus who continues to intervene in human affairs from God's throne.

Luke relates in direct speech Peter's request that the believers assembled in Mary's house should report his miraculous escape from prison "to James and the brothers" (v. 17f-g). Since James cannot be the apostle James, the brother of John, who had been executed by Agrippa (v. 2), and since James is not more closely identified — which suggests a well-known person and, in the present context, a person of authority — he is most plausibly identified with James, the brother of Jesus (Mark 6:3), who surfaces in 15:13 – 21 and 21:18 as the leader of the Jerusalem church (cf. Gal 1:19; 2:9, 12; see on 15:13). Eusebius describes James as the first bishop of Jerusalem (*Hist. eccl.* 2.23.1). The "brothers" (οἱ ἀδελφοί) are either other believers in general or the elders who appear in 11:30 as the leadership of the Jerusalem church.[18]

Luke does not relate why Peter leaves the congregation and Jerusalem (v. 17h), but the reason is obvious: his life is in danger, more so than ever before, and thus he leaves to be active elsewhere. Luke does not identify the "another place" (ἕτερον τόπον) to which Peter travels (v. 17i), reflecting perhaps the necessity of keeping Peter's where-

---

16. Fitzmyer, *Acts*, 489, with reference to Ps 91:11; Matt 18:10; Heb 1:14. Note that none of these passages speaks of a "guardian angel" appearing to people on earth. The later rabbinic text *Gen. Rab.* 78, on Gen 33:10, mentions a personal angel whose look matches that of the person he protects; cf.

Bock, *Acts*, 429, who also refers to *L.A.B.* 59:4; *T. Jac.* 1:10, and the later Christian text *Herm. Mand.* 6.2.2. See on Acts 23:8.

17. See on 3:1 – 10 (Structure and Literary Form).

18. See also 11:30; 15:2, 4, 6, 22, 23; 16:4; 21:18, in the last reference together with James.

abouts secret.[19] Read against the background of Gal 2:11 – 15 and 1 Cor 9:5, Luke's comment should be interpreted in terms of intensive and extensive missionary work undertaken by Peter after his departure.

12:18 – 19 In the morning there was no small commotion among the soldiers over what had become of Peter. After Herod had organized a search for him and did not find him, he interrogated the guards and ordered their execution. Then he went down from Judea to Caesarea and stayed there (γενομένης δὲ ἡμέρας ἦν τάραχος οὐκ ὀλίγος ἐν τοῖς στρατιώταις τί ἄρα ὁ Πέτρος ἐγένετο. Ἡρῴδης δὲ ἐπιζητήσας αὐτὸν καὶ μὴ εὑρών, ἀνακρίνας τοὺς φύλακας ἐκέλευσεν ἀπαχθῆναι, καὶ κατελθὼν ἀπὸ τῆς Ἰουδαίας εἰς Καισάρειαν διέτριβεν). When daylight comes and the soldiers wake up from their sleep, they are in "a state of mental agitation."[20] They cannot understand "what had become of Peter," i.e., how he could have disappeared (v. 18). Peter's escape becomes public knowledge when Agrippa asks for Peter to be brought out to stand trial (cf. v. 4).

The next three comments in v. 19, all formulated in the aorist tense, follow as a matter of course. The king "organized a search" (ἐπιζητήσας), which is unsuccessful (v. 19a-b) since Peter had left Jerusalem several hours earlier, perhaps hiding among the thousands of Passover pilgrims leaving Jerusalem in all directions. The king has the guards "interrogated" (ἀνακρίνας), probably under torture, about their conduct while on guard duty, their whereabouts during the night, perhaps their potential complicity in Peter's escape. Eventually Agrippa "ordered their execution" (ἐκέλευσεν ἀπαχθῆναι) for dereliction of duty and probably out of fury that Peter was nowhere to be found.

Luke ends the narrative of Peter's escape from prison by commenting on Agrippa's relocation from Jerusalem to Caesarea (see on 10:1), where he stayed, presumably in the luxurious palace built by Herod I that Marullus, the last Roman governor before Agrippa was given Judea, had used as a praetorium.

12:20 He had been infuriated with the people of Tyre and Sidon. They joined together and presented themselves in an audience with him. They had secured the support of Blastus, the chamberlain of the king, and asked for peace, because their region depended on the king's territory for food (ἦν δὲ θυμομαχῶν Τυρίοις καὶ Σιδωνίοις· ὁμοθυμαδὸν δὲ παρῆσαν πρὸς αὐτὸν καὶ πείσαντες Βλάστον, τὸν ἐπὶ τοῦ κοιτῶνος τοῦ βασιλέως, ᾐτοῦντο εἰρήνην διὰ τὸ τρέφεσθαι αὐτῶν τὴν χώραν ἀπὸ τῆς βασιλικῆς). Luke concludes his narrative of Agrippa's persecution of the church in Jerusalem with a third incident that relates the king's death (vv. 20 – 23), emphasizing the truth that God is more powerful than the earthly powers that seek to destroy the church. Luke relates the events leading up to Agrippa's death (v. 20), the cause of his death (vv. 21 – 22), and the manner of his death (v. 23). Josephus's account of Agrippa's demise (*Ant.* 19.343 – 350) corresponds with Luke's account in many of the details and in the interpretation of Agrippa's death as punishment for the blasphemous hubris he displayed in Caesarea.[21]

There was a dispute between the citizens of Tyre (see on 21:3 – 6) and Sidon (see on 27:3) and Agrippa. The controversy is not mentioned in other sources and cannot be reconstructed in detail, but it concerned food. The form of the verb used here (τρέφεσθαι) is either middle ("because their country supported itself") or passive ("because their

---

19. Dunn, *Beginning from Jerusalem*, 410.
20. BDAG, s.v. τάραχος.

21. As to differences, in Josephus's account, the divine messenger is an owl (not an angel of the Lord), and Agrippa seems to regret accepting the acclamation as god (*Ant.* 19.346 – 347).

country was supported [by importing grain] from the king's country," BDAG). Tyre and Sidon, free cities on the Phoenician coast in southern Syria, had done something that made Agrippa furious so that he had blocked shipments of food, perhaps grain from Galilee exported to southern Syria.[22]

The city magistrates of Tyre and Sidon collaborated in trying to resolve the dispute; they sent a delegation to Caesarea whose members presented themselves in an audience with the king after they had secured the support of Blastus, a court official described as "the chamberlain" (ὁ ἐπὶ τοῦ κοιτῶνος, lit. "the one in charge of the bed chamber") of the king. They petitioned Agrippa to make peace, with the argument that their region depended on the king's territory for food supply.

12:21 – 22 On the appointed day, Herod put on his royal robes, took his seat on the platform, and addressed them. The assembly shouted, "This is the voice of a god, not of a human being!" (τακτῇ δὲ ἡμέρᾳ ὁ Ἡρῴδης ἐνδυσάμενος ἐσθῆτα βασιλικὴν καὶ καθίσας ἐπὶ τοῦ βήματος ἐδημηγόρει πρὸς αὐτούς. ὁ δὲ δῆμος ἐπεφώνει· θεοῦ φωνὴ καὶ οὐκ ἀνθρώπου). The delegation of Tyre and Sidon evidently succeeded in achieving their goals. The peace agreement was to be publicly announced on an "appointed day" (v. 21). Josephus, who does not mention a delegation from Tyre and Sidon, describes "spectacles in honor of Caesar" held in the theater of Caesarea. These games were probably the quadrennial games founded by Herod the Great in 10 BC in honor of Augustus.[23]

On the appointed day Agrippa entered the theater at daybreak, "clad in a garment woven completely of silver so that its texture was indeed wondrous" (Josephus, *Ant.* 19.344). Luke refers to "royal robes" (ἐσθὴς βασιλική) when he sat on the platform, a term that describes here a "throne-like speaker's platform."[24] The term "assembly" (ὁ δῆμος) in v. 22 suggests that the occasion was larger than the meeting with the delegation. Agrippa seems to have addressed the officials of the court, the delegation from the two cities, and the citizens of Caesarea.

Josephus relates that when Agrippa appeared in the theater, "the silver, illumined by the touch of the first rays of the sun, was wondrously radiant and by its glitter inspired fear and awe in those who gazed intently upon it" (*Ant.* 19.344). Both Josephus and Luke relate that the people assembled acclaimed him as a god. Luke reports their reaction in direct speech. They shouted that Agrippa's voice was "the voice of a god" (θεοῦ φωνή), not the voice of a human being (v. 22).[25] This was the reaction of a Gentile crowd who failed to distinguish a human from a divine being. The imperial cult understood the emperor as a "god present in the world," i.e., like one of the traditional gods, though "located in an ambivalent position, higher than mortals but not fully the equal of the gods."[26]

12:23 Immediately an angel of the Lord struck him down, because he did not give the honor to God. He was eaten by worms and expired (παραχρῆμα δὲ ἐπάταξεν αὐτὸν ἄγγελος κυρίου ἀνθ᾽ ὧν οὐκ ἔδωκεν τὴν δόξαν τῷ θεῷ, καὶ γενόμενος σκωληκόβρωτος ἐξέψυξεν). Apparently Agrippa accepted, perhaps even welcomed, the acclamation as a god.[27] He did not give "the honor" (τὴν δόξαν) to

---

22. Trade between Judea and Tyre and Sidon is mentioned from the time of Solomon (1 Kgs 5:9 – 11); cf. Ezek 27:17.

23. Josephus, *J.W.* 1.415. Others have suggested that these were games founded by Agrippa I in honor of Claudius, who conquered Britain in AD 44.

24. BDAG, s.v. βῆμα 3.

25. Josephus also relates the reaction of the crowd in direct

speech, after he states that they were "addressing him as a god": "May you be propitious to us, and if we have hitherto feared you as a man, yet henceforth we agree that you are more than mortal in your being."

26. Price, "Gods and Emperors," 94.

27. Josephus, *Ant.* 19.346, relates that "the king did not rebuke them nor did he reject their flattery as impious." It is only

the one true God, thus committing the most fundamental sin that a Jew can commit, violating the first commandment. Divine retribution followed swiftly. An angel of the Lord "struck him down," a phrase that may signal sudden pain. Luke describes Agrippa's death as the result of being eaten by worms, a Greek expression that is not a medical technical term, although the term appears to describe a form of phthiriasis as a terminal illness.[28] Josephus relates that apart from a stab of pain in the heart, "he was also gripped in his stomach by an ache that he felt everywhere at once and that was intense from the start" (*Ant.* 19.346), a condition that has been identified with appendicitis.[29] Luke's description of Agrippa's death identifies him as villain, a bad character whose death was deserved.

12:24 The word of God continued to advance and gain converts (ὁ δὲ λόγος τοῦ θεοῦ ηὔξανεν καὶ ἐπληθύνετο). This next episode describes the growth of the church (vv. 24–25). First, Luke provides another summary statement,[30] noting the continued expansion of the church as more people accepted the preaching of "the word of God," i.e., of the good news of Jesus, Israel's Messiah and the Savior of the world. Despite the persecution that King Agrippa initiated against the church, despite the execution of James and the departure of Peter from Jerusalem, the movement of the followers of Jesus grew and continued to gain new converts.

Placed after the long narrative of the persecution of Agrippa against the apostles, this verse may indicate continued church growth in Jerusalem. Placed after the events related to Agrippa's death

in Caesarea, the brief comment may have a wider geographical perspective, encompassing the realm of Agrippa's rule over Judea, Samaria, Galilee, and other adjacent areas. Placed at the transition from Peter's ministry in Jerusalem, Judea, and Samaria (Acts 1–12) to Paul's ministry in Syria, Cyprus, Asia Minor, and Europe (Acts 13–28), the comment may be intended to communicate the fact that Jews and Gentiles continued to be converted in large numbers in the 40s. Luke emphasizes, again, that nothing can stop the advance of God's word proclaimed by Jesus' witnesses (see the introduction to this section).

12:25 Barnabas and Saul returned after they had completed their ministry to Jerusalem. They brought John with them, who was also called Mark (Βαρναβᾶς δὲ καὶ Σαῦλος ὑπέστρεψαν εἰς Ἰερουσαλὴμ πληρώσαντες τὴν διακονίαν, συμπαραλαβόντες Ἰωάννην τὸν ἐπικληθέντα Μᾶρκον). Luke's second remark picks up his narrative in 11:30, where he had related the famine relief visit of Barnabas and Saul from Antioch to Jerusalem to deliver the collection from the believers in the Syrian capital to the believers in Jerusalem and Judea. The fact that they encounter "elders" (11:30; see on 12:17) rather than apostles confirms that their famine relief visit to Jerusalem took place after Peter's departure from Jerusalem in AD 41, probably AD 44. After completing their "ministry" (διακονία) to Jerusalem, they return to Antioch, taking with them John Mark (see on v. 12). He will accompany Barnabas and Saul during their missionary work on Cyprus (13:5).

---

when he saw an owl perched on a rope over his head, which he recognized as "a harbinger of woes," and when he was gripped by pain in his heart and stomach, that he seemed to regret his action (ibid., 346–347).

28. Thomas Africa, "Worms and the Death of Kings: A Cautionary Note on Disease and History," *Classical Antiquity* 1 (1982): 1–17, 1–2.

29. Smallwood, *Jews under Roman Rule*, 198. Nikos Kokkinos, *The Herodian Dynasty: Origins, Role in Society and Eclipse* (JSPSup 26; Sheffield: Sheffield Academic Press, 1997), 303–4, suggests that Agrippa I was poisoned.

30. Cf. 1:14; 2:42–47; 4:32–37; 5:12–16; 6:7; 8:4, 25; 9:31.

Theology in Application

The main theme of the persecution of the Jerusalem church by Agrippa I informs readers about a major transition of leadership in the early history of the church caused by dramatic events that transpired in Jerusalem. At the same time, the passage reveals the power of God at work in the messianic movement of Jesus' followers, and it illustrates the dangers of being a believer in Jesus, particularly being a leader of the church, and the danger of opposing God's work. This passage has several emphases.

Leaders Prepared for Persecution

Leaders of the church are prepared for persecution. The persecution organized by Agrippa I was not the first time that the apostles had come under pressure. They had been imprisoned, threatened, and beaten before, repeatedly. They were ready and willing to face new attempts to suppress the followers of Jesus. Enemies of the Christian faith who want to silence Christians generally choose the leaders of local congregations, of regional organizations, and of national denominations as their first targets of violent persecutions. Luke's narrative of James's execution and of Peter's near-execution challenges Christian leaders to examine their priorities and motivations. It is obvious, in contexts of political danger, that only believers with the right priorities and motivations will accept calls to lead churches; motivations focused on prestige, position, comfort, and salary will not survive the fire of arrest, legal (sham) trials, imprisonment, and potential execution.

Changes in Leadership

Churches are prepared for changes in leadership. The apostles had led the Jerusalem church for twelve years after Jesus' death, resurrection, and ascension. Then James was killed, Peter had to leave Jerusalem in the early morning hours after his escape from prison, and it appears that the other apostles left as well. The leadership of the church shifted from the apostles, whose names we know (Acts 1:13, 26), to elders, whose names Luke does not record (with the exception of James, the brother of the Lord). Since Luke's focus shifts from Peter to Paul and thus from Jerusalem to the Roman provinces beyond Palestine, we do not know much about the history of the Jerusalem church after this transition of leadership. Luke's narrative of Peter's departure demonstrates, however, that all leaders can be replaced. The itinerant missionary ministry (on which Peter embarked) is not inferior to local pastoral ministry, and the growth of the church (12:24) does not depend on one person nor on a particular group of leaders; rather, it depends always, and only, on the power of the word of God.

God's Intervention

Believers reckon with the possibility of God's intervention. Luke does not report whether the imprisoned Peter prayed for a miraculous escape; his report of the reaction of the believers assembled in Mary's house to Rhoda's excited news of Peter standing at the door suggests that they did not reckon with a miraculous escape in the night before his trial and execution. But they did pray, and God answered their prayer, perhaps in ways they had not anticipated. God intervened by rescuing Peter from prison with the assistance of an angel in the middle of the night. But God did not intervene in the case of James, who was arrested, imprisoned, and executed (12:1 – 2).

Believers trust in God, which means that they know that they cannot manipulate him into getting him to fulfill what they wish for. Trust in God implies the confidence that God will give strength to endure suffering, courage to endure execution, and boldness to be a witness of God's power and grace right to the end. This is precisely what Daniel's friends said to Nebuchadnezzar, who had demanded that all people should fall down and worship the golden statue that King Nebuchadnezzar had set up: "King Nebuchadnezzar, we do not need to defend ourselves before you in this matter. If we are thrown into the blazing furnace, the God we serve is able to deliver us from it, and he will deliver us from Your Majesty's hand. But even if he does not, we want you to know, Your Majesty, that we will not serve your gods or worship the image of gold you have set up" (Dan 3:16 – 18). They give witness of their faith in the one true God, they are prepared to die for their faith, and they express their conviction that God can rescue them. Believers do not "name and claim" outcomes they expect God to bring about; authentic believers express their faith, they formulate their hopes and wishes in prayers, they acknowledge God's sovereignty to do as he sees fit, and they leave their fate in his hands.

God's Enemies and Judgment

God's enemies face God's judgment. Agrippa died after only three or four years on the throne, punished by God on account of his acceptance of divine acclamation, and — in the context of Acts 12 — on account of his persecution of the church. Not all political leaders who persecute the church, and not all individuals who belong to a mob burning churches and killing Christians, die instantly or suffer horrible deaths. But all of God's enemies will face God's judgment. It is certainly true that from Luke's account "many an early Christian will have drawn comfort and strength in the face of political pressure and persecution."[31] Believers in Jesus knew that they would participate in God's judgment of the world (1 Cor 6:2), a fact that helped them

---

31. Dunn, *Beginning from Jerusalem,* 413.

to stand with courage before God's enemies. John Stott comments, "Tyrants may be permitted for a time to boast and bluster, oppressing the church and hindering the spread of the gospel, but they will not last. In the end, their empire will be broken and their pride abased."[32]

32. John R.W. Stott, *The Message of Acts: The Spirit, the Church and the World* (Bible Speaks Today; Leicester: Inter-Varsity Press, 1990), 213.

Acts 13:1 – 12

Literary Context

In the first part of his account of Jesus' continuing work through the apostles who are his witnesses, Luke focused on Peter and on the life and work of the Jerusalem church, showing how God fulfilled his promises, how Jesus continues at work as Israel's crucified, risen, and exalted Messiah and Savior, and how he is restoring Israel in Jerusalem, Judea, and Samaria even as the messianic people of God have begun to move into the Gentile world. In the second part, which begins in Acts 13, Luke's focus shifts to Paul, showing how the good news of Jesus spreads through new regions of the eastern Mediterranean world and how Gentile believers are accepted as full participants in the restored people of God.[1]

In this second half, Luke relates in four major sections the missionary work of Paul in the cities of Cyprus and southern Galatia (13:1 – 15:33), his work in Macedonia and Achaia (15:35 – 18:22), his work in Ephesus (18:23 – 20:38), and his imprisonment in Jerusalem, Caesarea, and Rome (21:17 – 28:31). The present text is the first major section, consisting of five episodes that comprise period 7 of Paul's missionary work (see below, "In Depth: Paul's Missionary Work"): Paul and Barnabas proclaim the gospel in Salamis and Paphos (13:1 – 12), Pisidian Antioch (13:13 – 52), Iconium (14:1 – 7), Lystra (14:8 – 20), and in Derbe and Perge (14:21 – 28).

Up until now, Luke has referred to Paul by his Hebrew name, Saul. He was mentioned first as among those who executed Stephen (7:58; 8:1) and who persecuted the followers of Jesus, both in Jerusalem (8:3) and in other cities (9:1 – 2). In 9:3 – 30 Luke related Paul's conversion to faith in Jesus as the crucified, risen, and exalted Messiah and Lord and his commissioning as Jesus' witness to Jews and Gentiles. Luke briefly mentioned Saul's missionary preaching in Damascus (9:20 – 22) and in Jerusalem (9:28 – 29). He then took Saul from Jerusalem to Tarsus (9:30), implying that he was preaching there as well, and then from Tarsus to Antioch in Syria (11:25 – 26), where he preached and taught alongside Barnabas.

Together with Barnabas, Saul took the famine relief that the Antiochene believers

---

1. Johnson, *Acts*, 225.

had organized for the believers in Judea to the elders of the congregation in Jerusalem (11:30), and they returned to Antioch (12:25). In 13:1–14:28 Luke relates the missionary work of Saul and Barnabas on Cyprus and in southern Galatia. In 13:9, introducing Saul's first words in his narrative, given in direct speech, Luke transitions from using "Saul" to using his Latin name "Paul," which he will use in the remainder of his narrative, a change in nomenclature that signifies the transition from missionary outreach to the Jewish people to missionary work among both Jews and Gentiles in areas outside of Palestine.

In terms of chronology, the previous episode, which focused on the persecution led by King Agrippa against the church in Jerusalem with the subsequent departure of Peter, and perhaps all the remaining apostles, from Jerusalem, was a flashback to events that probably transpired in AD 41. Barnabas invited Saul/Paul to join the missionary and pastoral ministry in Antioch perhaps in AD 42. The two of them brought the famine relief from the church in Antioch to the believers in Judea in Jerusalem probably in AD 44. The mission to Cyprus took place in AD 45, the immediately following missionary work in the cities of southern Galatia in AD 45–47 (or 46–47; we don't know how long Barnabas and Paul stayed on Cyprus).

IN DEPTH: Paul's Missionary Work

It is customary to describe Paul's work in terms of "three missionary journeys," which are so labeled in Bible translations and commentaries and so marked in the maps reproduced in Bibles, Bible atlases, and Bible dictionaries. The so-called "first missionary journey" takes Paul to Cyprus and Galatia (Acts 13–14), the "second missionary journey" takes him to Macedonia and Achaia (Acts 16–18), and the "third missionary journey" has Paul preaching in Ephesus and returning to Jerusalem via Macedonia and Achaia (Acts 19–20). Our analysis of Paul's missionary activity after his conversion has him preaching in Damascus, Arabia, Jerusalem, Syria/Cilicia, and Antioch prior to going to Cyprus. In other words, to talk of his "missionary journeys" wrongly creates the impression that

Paul's missionary work was limited to these journeys. Of course, those journeys[2] played an important role in Paul's work as a missionary. The table below specifies the individual phases of Paul's missionary work as they emerge from a study not only of Luke's narrative in Acts but also from Paul's letters.[3]

Period 1	Damascus	Acts 9:19 – 25; Gal 1:17	AD 32/33
Period 2	Arabia/Nabatea	Gal 1:17; 2 Cor 11:32	32 – 33
Period 3	Jerusalem	Acts 9:26 – 29; Rom 1:16	33/34
Period 4	Syria/Cilicia Tarsus	Acts 9:30; 11:25 – 26; Gal 1:21	34 – 42
Period 5	Syria Antioch	Acts 11:26 – 30; 13:1	42 – 44
Period 6	Cyprus (Salamis; Paphos)	Acts 13:4 – 12	45
Period 7	Galatia (Pisidian Antioch; Iconium; Lystra; Derbe) Pamphylia (Perge)	Acts 13:14 – 14:23 Acts 14:24 – 26	45 – 47 47
Period 8	Macedonia (Philippi; Thessalonica; Berea)	Acts 16:6 – 17:15	49 – 50
Period 9	Achaia (Athens; Corinth)	Acts 17:16 – 18:28	50 – 51
Period 10	Asia (Ephesus)	Acts 19:1 – 41	52 – 55
Period 11	Illyricum	Rom 15:19	56
Period 12	Judea (Caesarea)	Acts 21:27 – 26:32	57 – 59
Period 13	Rome	Acts 28:17 – 28	60 – 62
Period 14	Spain	1 Clement 5:5 – 7	63 – 64?
Period 15	Crete	Titus 1:5	64 – 65?

Main Idea

The missionary work of Paul and Barnabas is authenticated by the Holy Spirit, supported by the church in Antioch, characterized by geographical movement, and focused on proclaiming the word of God.

---

2. Cf. Schnabel, *Early Christian Mission*, 1287 – 88, for statistics. A conservative estimate of the distances that Paul covered during his missionary work between AD 32 – 65 indicates that he traveled at least 15,500 miles (25,000 km.), of which about 8,700 miles (14,000 km.) represent journeys by land, in all probability on foot.

3. Cf. Schnabel, *Paul the Missionary*, 58 – 122.

Translation

Acts 13:1 – 12

1a	Setting: Place	In the church in Antioch
b	Description	**there were prophets and**
c		**teachers:**
d	List (1)	Barnabas,
e	(2) (Identification)	Simeon called Niger,
f	(3) (Identification)	Lucius of Cyrene,
g	(4) (Identification)	Manaen, who had been brought up with Herod the tetrarch, and
h	(5)	Saul.
2a	Setting: Time	While they were worshiping the Lord and
b		fasting,
c	Action (Character entrance)	**the Holy Spirit said,**
d	Command	*"Appoint Barnabas and*
e		*Saul*
f	Purpose	*for the work to which I have called them."*
3a	Setting: Time/Action	So, after they had fasted and
b	Action	prayed,
c	Action	**they laid hands on them**
d	Action	and **they let them go.**
4a	Setting: Cause	Thus sent out by the Holy Spirit,
b	Action (Place)	**they went down to Seleucia**
c	Action (Place)	and **from there they sailed to Cyprus.**
5a	Setting: Time/Place	When they arrived in Salamis,
b	Action	**they proclaimed the word of God**
c	Place	in the synagogues of the Jews.
d	Association	**John was with them as their helper.**
6a	Setting: Time	After they had traveled from place to place
b	Place	through the whole island
c	Place	and reached Paphos,
d	Character entrance	**they met a certain man,**
e	Character description	a magician,
f	Character description	a false prophet
g	Character description	who was a Jew,
h	Identification	whose name was Bar-Jesus.
7a	Character entrance	**He was in the service of the proconsul Sergius Paulus,**
b	Character description	an intelligent man,
c	Action	who had summoned Barnabas and Saul
d	Cause	as he wished to hear the word of God.
8a	Antagonist	But **the magician Elymas**
b	Aside/Explanation	(for this is what his name means)
c	Action (Conflict)	**opposed them**

d	Description	as he tried to turn the proconsul away from the faith.
9a	Protagonist	But **Saul,**
b	Identification	also known as Paul,
c	Description/Cause	who was filled with the Holy Spirit,
d	Action	**looked intently at him**
10a	Action (speech)	and **said,**
b	Assertion/Accusation	*"You are full of all kinds of deceit and*
c		*fraud,*
d	Accusation	*you son of the devil and*
e	Accusation	*enemy of all that is right;*
f	Rhetorical question	*will you not stop making crooked the straight paths of the Lord?*
11a	Assertion	*Look, the hand of the Lord is now against you:*
b	Prophecy	*you shall be blind,*
c	Explanation	*unable to see the sun,*
d	Time	*for a while."*
e	Setting: Manner	Immediately
f	Event	**a dark mist came over him,**
g	Action	and **he went groping about for someone to lead him**
h	Means	by the hand.
12a	Setting: Time	When the proconsul saw what had happened,
b	Action (Result)	**he believed,**
c	Cause	amazed at the teaching about the Lord.

Structure and Literary Form

The fourth major section of Acts (13:1 – 15:33), which begins Luke's narrative of Paul's missionary work, has two parts. In the first part, Luke reports on the missionary work of Paul and Barnabas on Cyprus, in southern Galatia, and in Pamphylia (13:1 – 14:28). The second part narrates the background, the proceedings, and the outcome of the Apostles' Council in Jerusalem, confirming existing policies for missionary work among Gentiles (15:1 – 33). The first episode of the fourth major section, which focuses on the mission to Cyprus (13:1 – 12), consists of four incidents. (1) Luke begins by explaining the departure of Paul and Barnabas from Syrian Antioch, who embark on a new missionary initiative (vv. 1 – 3). (2) Luke briefly narrates the proclamation of the gospel in cities on the southern coast of Cyprus (vv. 4 – 5). (3) The narrative shifts to Paphos, the seat of the governor of the province, and to Paul's encounter with Bar-Jesus, a Jewish magician (vv. 6 – 11). (4) Luke reports the conversion of Sergius Paulus, the proconsul (v. 12).

The episode is a *narrative* that includes a *list* of names (v. 1), a *revelation* by the Holy Spirit related in direct speech (v. 2), *travel notices* (vv. 4 – 5, 6), a *miracle story* (a punitive miracle; vv. 9 – 11) with a *speech* by Paul (vv. 10 – 11), as well as a *conversion story* (vv. 7 – 12). Paul's speech in vv. 10 – 11 is the first of several Pauline speeches in Acts, most of which are considerably longer. Some have identified vv. 4 – 12 as a *missionary narrative.*[4]

IN DEPTH: Paul's Speeches

Luke relates twelve speeches of Paul. Their audiences, localities, and geographical locations can be listed as follows.

Speech	In Acts	Recipient	Place	Location
1	13:6 – 11	Jew: Bar-Jesus	Governor's praetorium (?)	Paphos (Cyprus)
2	13:16 – 41	Jews, proselytes, God-fearers	Synagogue	Antioch (Pisidia)
3	14:15 – 18	Gentiles: polytheists	In front of temple of Zeus	Lystra (Galatia)
4	17:22 – 31	Gentiles: aristocrats	Areopagus	Athens (Achaia)
5	20:17 – 38	Christians: elders	Meeting place of church	Miletus (Asia)
6	22:1 – 21	Jews	Outer court of the temple	Jerusalem (Judea)
7	23:1 – 6	Jews: aristocrats	Sanhedrin	Jerusalem (Judea)
8	24:10 – 21	Gentiles: Governor Felix	Governor's praetorium	Caesarea (Judea)
9	25:8 – 11	Gentiles: Governor Festus	Governor's praetorium	Caesarea (Judea)
10	26:1 – 23	Gentiles, Jews: Festus, Agrippa	Governor's praetorium	Caesarea (Judea)
11	28:17 – 20	Jews: Jewish leaders	Prison	Rome (Italy)
12	28:25 – 28	Jews: Jewish leaders	Prison	Rome (Italy)

Exegetical Outline

➡ **I. The Mission on Cyprus (13:1 – 12)**

    A. The New Missionary Initiative of Barnabas and Paul (13:1 – 3)

        1. The prophets and teachers of the church in Antioch (13:1)

        2. The worship of the Antioch church (13:2a-b)

        3. The revelation of the Holy Spirit commissioning Barnabas and Saul (13:2c-f)

        4. The invocation of God's blessing for the missionary work of Barnabas and Saul (13:3)

---

4. Cilliers Breytenbach, *Paulus und Barnabas in der Provinz Galatien* (AGJU 38; Leiden: Brill, 1996), 24. Other missionary narratives that Luke includes in his account of Paul's mission have essentially the same elements, although there is no stereotypical uniformity.

Explanation of the Text

13:1 In the church in Antioch there were prophets and teachers: Barnabas, Simeon called Niger, Lucius of Cyrene, Manaen, who had been brought up with Herod the tetrarch, and Saul (ἦσαν δὲ ἐν Ἀντιοχείᾳ κατὰ τὴν οὖσαν ἐκκλησίαν προφῆται καὶ διδάσκαλοι ὅ τε Βαρναβᾶς καὶ Συμεὼν ὁ καλούμενος Νίγερ καὶ Λούκιος ὁ Κυρηναῖος, Μαναήν τε Ἡρῴδου τοῦ τετραάρχου σύντροφος καὶ Σαῦλος). Luke begins his account of the missionary work of Saul/Paul with a brief description of the life of the congregation in Antioch (vv. 1 – 2), in whose ministry and leadership Saul and Barnabas were fully integrated.

The church in Antioch, the capital of the Roman province of Syria (see on 11:20), was led by two groups of people: "prophets" (προφῆται) and "teachers" (διδάσκαλοι). Christian prophets (see on 11:27) would have conveyed, as did the prophets in Israel's history, God's revelation, expressed in terms of exhortation, instruction, critique, encouragement, and at times disclosure about future events. Teachers are mentioned only here in Acts, but the central importance of teaching God's word — revealed in Israel's Scriptures, in Jesus' ministry, and in the apostles' preaching — is evident in Luke's frequent references to teaching activity[5] and

---

5. The verb "to teach" (διδάσκω) is used in Acts 1:1; 4:2, 18; 5:21, 25, 28, 42; 11:26; 15:1, 35; 18:11, 25; 20:20; 21:21, 28;

28:31. Luke describes both Paul's missionary proclamation as well as the instruction of believers with the verb "teach."

to the body of teaching that is passed on.[6] Luke's favorite term for the leaders of local congregations is "elder" (see on 11:30; 14:23).[7]

In 1 Cor 12:28 – 29 (cf. Rom 12:6 – 7; Eph 4:11) prophets and teachers are also mentioned prominently as the leaders of the local churches. The roles of prophets and teachers together "imply a balance necessary to the life of any church — an openness to new insight and development inspired by the Spirit (the role of the prophet), balanced by a loyalty to the tradition taught and interpreted (the role of the teacher)."[8] We should not assume, however, that the boundaries between the roles and functions of apostles, prophets, and teachers were well defined in the first-century church. Peter, Paul, and Barnabas seem to have been apostles, prophets, and teachers at the same time.

The diversity of the group of five "prophets and teachers" is noteworthy. Barnabas (see on 4:36) was a Greek-speaking Jew from Cyprus who had lived in Jerusalem and who guaranteed the continuity of the growing church in Antioch with the church in Jerusalem. He is mentioned first because of his leading role in the church in Antioch (cf. 11:23 – 26), possibly also because of his age.

Simeon may have been a black man of African origin as his grecized Latin name "Niger" (Νίγερ) suggests, a term that means "dark-complexioned" or "black."

Lucius originally came from Cyrene in North Africa. He may have belonged to the synagogue of the Cyrenians in Jerusalem (6:9) but came to Antioch fleeing from Jerusalem after Stephen's execution.[9]

Manaen had been "brought up" with Herod An-

tipas, the son of Herod I who ruled as tetrarch over Galilee during the ministries of John the Baptist and Jesus (Luke 3:1). Some have linked him with Chuza, a steward of Herod Antipas (perhaps a manager of one of his estates), whose wife Joanna was among the women who accompanied Jesus (Luke 8:3). This connection must remain hypothetical, however. Manaen evidently belonged to a noble Jewish family with connections to Herod's court. Since Herod I made sure his sons had a good Greek education, the same can be assumed for Manaen. Since "brought up" (σύντροφος) was used as a title, Manaen, before his conversion, may have held an influential position at the court of Herod Antipas.[10]

Saul (see on 9:1 – 2) was a diaspora Jew from Tarsus who had studied under Gamaliel in Jerusalem, was present when Stephen was executed, had persecuted the believers in Judea, and had been a missionary in Damascus, Nabatea, and Cilicia before coming to Antioch (cf. 7:58; 9:20 – 22, 30; 11:25 – 26).

13:2 While they were worshiping the Lord and fasting, the Holy Spirit said, "Appoint Barnabas and Saul for the work to which I have called them" (λειτουργούντων δὲ αὐτῶν τῷ κυρίῳ καὶ νηστευόντων εἶπεν τὸ πνεῦμα τὸ ἅγιον· ἀφορίσατε δή μοι τὸν Βαρναβᾶν καὶ Σαῦλον εἰς τὸ ἔργον ὃ προσκέκλημαι αὐτούς). The worship of the church in Antioch would have included prayers (v. 3) as well as teaching and the breaking of bread (2:42). It also included the practice of fasting (νηστευόντων, present participle), evidently a regular part of the devotional discipline of the congregation.

---

6. The noun "teaching" (διδαχή) is used in Acts 2:42; 5:28; 13:12; 17:19.

7. The term "elder" (πρεσβύτερος) is used in Acts 11:30; 14:23; 15:2, 4, 6, 22, 23; 16:4; 20:17; 21:18. In 20:28 they are called "overseers" (ἐπίσκοποι). It is unclear whether the "prophets" and "teachers" of the Antioch church constituted

the leading "elders" or whether Luke's terminology in 13:1 reflects the local organization of the church in Antioch.

8. Dunn, *Beginning from Jerusalem*, 320.

9. He is not identical with the Lucius mentioned in Rom 16:21 or with Luke, the author of the book of Acts.

10. Cf. Metzner, *Die Prominenten*, 406.

During one of the regular worship times that included fasting, one of the leaders of the church receives a specific prophetic utterance. The Holy Spirit directs them to appoint Barnabas and Saul for the work to which he has called (or summoned) them. The term "work" (τὸ ἔργον) refers to the missionary work that they will jointly undertake in the cities of Cyprus and southern Galatia, described in the next two chapters. The exalted Jesus had called Saul to proclaim the good news to Jews and Gentiles (9:15; cf. 22:15; 26:16 – 18; Gal 1:15 – 16), a missionary commission that Saul obeyed immediately after his conversion twelve years or so earlier. Barnabas had earlier been commissioned by the leaders of the Jerusalem church to go to Antioch and assist the missionary work and the pastoral ministry in the church there (11:22).

Now God's Spirit commissions these two preachers and teachers to leave Antioch and proclaim the gospel in new regions. The fact that Luke relates the words of the Holy Spirit in direct speech, placed between his comment on the worship of the church (v. 2a-b) and the sending off of Barnabas and Saul by the church (v. 3), underscores Luke's emphasis that the initiative for the missionary work comes from God's Spirit. In Acts this is the only direct imperative that the Spirit gives to a church — which is all the more significant since it inaugurates Paul's missionary work after his ministry in Antioch.[11]

13:3 So, after they had fasted and prayed, they laid hands on them and they let them go (τότε νηστεύσαντες καὶ προσευξάμενοι καὶ ἐπιθέντες τὰς χεῖρας αὐτοῖς ἀπέλυσαν). The congregation responds to the prophetic directive of the Spirit with four actions. They call for another period of fasting (νηστεύσαντες). They pray (προσευξάμενοι),

surely for wisdom, guidance, courage, and protection for Barnabas and Saul as they embark on a new missionary initiative. They lay hands on them (ἐπιθέντες τὰς χεῖρας αὐτοῖς), probably as they pray for Barnabas and Saul, invoking God's presence, blessing, and empowerment (see on 6:6). Then they send them on their way (ἀπέλυσαν), acting in obedience to the directive of the Spirit.

While in human terms the church in Antioch is the "sending agency" of Barnabas and Saul, in theological terms it is the Holy Spirit who sets apart, calls, commissions, and empowers the two missionaries. The commissioning by the church in Antioch does not mark the beginning of the missionary work of either Barnabas or Saul/Paul, but should be seen as confirming their missionary calling and as inaugurating a new phase of missionary work.

Luke does not explain why Barnabas and Saul go to Cyprus (v. 4); this destination is not mentioned in the prophetic utterance of v. 2. Barnabas and Saul may have planned a new missionary initiative with the goal of reaching Cyprus for some time. Two factors may have been decisive. (1) Barnabas was a native of Cyprus (4:36); as he had recruited Saul as a coworker for the evangelistic and pastoral ministry in Antioch (11:25 – 26), he may well have taken the initiative in suggesting Cyprus as the next geographical area for the gospel. (2) Some of the Greek-speaking Jewish believers who had to leave Jerusalem in AD 31/32 engaged in missionary work in cities on the Phoenician coast, in Antioch, and on Cyprus (11:19); since Barnabas would have known these believers, he may well have felt responsible not only for the consolidation of the work that Jerusalem believers had initiated in Antioch but also for their work in the cities of Cyprus. Barnabas, together with Saul and the other

---

11. For the Spirit directing actions of individuals see 8:29; 10:19 – 20; 21:11; 28:25, 27.

leaders of the church in Antioch, would surely have asked God for a confirmation of these plans to engage in missionary outreach in other regions.

13:4 Thus sent out by the Holy Spirit, they went down to Seleucia, and from there they sailed to Cyprus (αὐτοὶ μὲν οὖν ἐκπεμφθέντες ὑπὸ τοῦ ἁγίου πνεύματος κατῆλθον εἰς Σελεύκειαν, ἐκεῖθέν τε ἀπέπλευσαν εἰς Κύπρον). Luke once again emphasizes God's initiative: it is the Holy Spirit who has sent out the two missionaries. They travel 16 miles (25 km.) from Antioch to Seleucia, where they embark on a ship and sail to Cyprus, a distance of about 62 miles (100 km.). Seleucia was one of the most important harbor cities on the Syrian coast, with an artificial inner and an outer harbor that served as a base of the imperial fleet.

13:5 When they arrived in Salamis, they proclaimed the word of God in the synagogues of the Jews. John was with them as their helper (καὶ γενόμενοι ἐν Σαλαμῖνι κατήγγελλον τὸν λόγον τοῦ θεοῦ ἐν ταῖς συναγωγαῖς τῶν Ἰουδαίων. εἶχον δὲ καὶ Ἰωάννην ὑπηρέτην). The missionaries arrive in Salamis, a harbor city on the east coast of Cyprus. Salamis was the seat of the Ptolemaic governors in the second century BC, rebuilt with help from Augustus after the devastating earthquake of 15 BC. Luke's brief account of the activities of Barnabas and Saul/Paul reflects a pattern that characterizes all missionary work reported by Luke in the rest of Acts: the missionaries first establish contact with the Jewish community.[12]

The plural "synagogues" (see on 6:9) indicates that the Jewish community was large, meeting regularly in several locations. Barnabas and Saul preach "the word of God" (see on 4:29, 31), i.e., the good news of Jesus, Israel's Messiah and Savior. As they had been important leaders of the ministry

connected with the believers in Antioch through which a large number of Greeks came to faith in Jesus (11:20–26), it can be assumed that they also reach out to Gentiles, at least to God-fearers attending the synagogue services, in which Barnabas and Saul are able to explain the word of God as it relates to Jesus. Luke does not report the success, or lack thereof, of the missionaries' preaching in Salamis. However, the reference to the proclamation of God's word implies, in Acts, the coming to faith of people who hear Jesus' witnesses preach the good news.

The two missionaries are assisted[13] by John Mark, whom they brought along from Jerusalem to Antioch (12:25). This comment can be taken in the sense that they not only preached in synagogues, an activity for which they would not need the help of John Mark, but also helped people come to faith, who were then baptized and integrated into the new community of believers in Jesus, Israel's Messiah and Savior — a series of activities for which Barnabas and Saul would indeed benefit from the assistance of a coworker.

13:6 After they had traveled from place to place through the whole island and reached Paphos, they met a certain man, a magician, a false prophet who was a Jew, whose name was Bar-Jesus (διελθόντες δὲ ὅλην τὴν νῆσον ἄχρι Πάφου εὗρον ἄνδρα τινὰ μάγον ψευδοπροφήτην Ἰουδαῖον ᾧ ὄνομα Βαριησοῦ). The comment in v. 6a-c summarizes the missionary work of Barnabas and Saul in the cities on the southern coast of Cyprus — Kition, Amathos, Neapolis, Kourion, and Paphos. The verb translated as "traveled from place to place" and the phrase "the whole island" suggest missionary work: in 8:4 the same verb conveys missionary activity. The distance from Salamis to Paphos is about 112

---

12. Cf. 13:14; 14:1; 16:13; 17:1–2, 10, 17; 18:4–6; 18:19; 19:8; cf. 9:20.

13. On the term "helper" (ὑπηρέτης) see on 5:22.

miles (180 km.). Assuming that private travelers walked about 15 to 20 miles (25 to 30 km.) per day,[14] the journey from Salamis to Paphos involved seven days of walking — a period that does not include longer stays in the cities through which they passed. Whether Paul, who traveled by foot, always carried all of his provisions of clothing (in addition to food) is doubtful. He and his companions would have traveled with little baggage: "they would only have taken with them as much as they could carry with ease."[15]

We do not know how long they spent in the cities they visited. The fact that Luke provides no details and reports no conversions does not mean that the proclamation of the gospel in these cities was not successful. The return of Barnabas and John Mark in AD 49 to Cyprus (15:39) indicates, perhaps, that there were churches on Cyprus that they wanted to visit and assist in their ministry, just as Barnabas had gone from Jerusalem to Antioch to assist the newly founded church there.

In vv. 6d – 11 Luke describes the encounter in Paphos of Barnabas and Saul with the Jewish astrologer Bar-Jesus, who advised the Roman governor Sergius Paulus. The capital city of the province since 15 BC, Paphos was a typical Greco-Roman city with the usual infrastructure that included numerous temples, a theater, an amphitheater, a *gymnasion*, baths, and also a mint. The temple of Aphrodite in Old Paphos, about 10 miles (16 km.) southwest of the new city, was famous during the early Roman imperial period.

This is the second time in Acts that Luke reports a confrontation with a magician: Peter confronted Simon in Samaria (8:9 – 11, 18 – 24); now Paul confronts Bar-Jesus in Paphos. Luke introduces Bar-Jesus with a lengthy description that strings together five descriptors: (1) "a certain man"; (2) a "magician" (μάγος), i.e., a person skilled in the use of incantations with the goal of influencing or controling transcendent powers to overcome public or private problems (see on 8:9); (3) a "false prophet," i.e., a person who appealed to divine authority for his pronouncements but whose claims are rejected as false,[16] an evaluation of his status that may come from the Jewish community in Paphos or that may be the result of Saul's confrontation; (4) a "Jew," i.e., of Jewish descent, but not necessarily a member in good standing of the local Jewish community, who probably would not have approved of his involvement in magic; (5) a man named Bar-Jesus, Aramaic for "son of Jesus" or "son of Joshua";[17] in v. 8 the "meaning" (μεθερμηνεύεται) of his name is given as "Elymas."[18]

---

14. Cf. Lionel Casson, *Travel in the Ancient World* (orig. 1974; repr., Baltimore: Johns Hopkins Univ. Press, 1994), 189, who adds that ambitious travelers could cover 40 to 45 miles (65 to 72 km.), "but it meant an exhaustingly long and hard day's travel." The *mansiones*, more or less well-equipped roadside inns, were 25 to 35 miles (40 to 55 km.) apart (ibid., 184 – 85).

15. S. R. Llewelyn, in Horsley and Llewelyn, *New Documents*, 7:89.

16. The term occurs 10 times in the LXX (Jer 6:13; 33:7, 8, 11, 16; 34:9; 35:1; 36:1, 8; Zech 13:2) and 11 times in the NT (Matt 7:15; 24:11, 24; Mark 13:22; Luke 6:26; 2 Pet 2:1; 1 John 4:1; Rev 16:13; 19:20; 20:10, and in the present passage.

17. There is no reason to call the name Bar-Jesus ("son of Jesus") "provocative" (Johnson, *Acts*, 222), or to surmise that the man claimed to be a disciple of Jesus (Richard E. Strelan,

"Who was Bar Jesus [Acts 13,6 – 12]?" *Bib* 85 [2004]: 65 – 81, 74), since "Jesus" was a not uncommonly used Jewish name in the first century.

18. The term "Elymas" is not attested as a Greek name. Several explanations of the obscure "Elymas" deserve to be mentioned. (1) "Elymas" derives from a Semitic root akin to Arabic ʾalim ("wise, learned"). (2) "Elymas" derives from the Aramaic term haloma ("dreamer"). (3) The reading of Codex D should be preferred, which has "Hetoimas" (Ἑτοιμας), a term that can denote a person who has "that dexterity and rapidity of speech and action which are acquired by practice, qualities indispensable to a sorcerer or conjuror"; this Hetoimas/Bar-Jesus has been identified with Atomos, a Cypriot Jew who was a magician during the time when Felix was proconsul (Josephus, *Ant.* 20.142). (4) The verb in v. 8 (μεθερμηνεύεται) should be taken in a nontechnical sense.

13:7 He was in the service of the proconsul Sergius Paulus, an intelligent man, who had summoned Barnabas and Saul as he wished to hear the word of God (ὃς ἦν σὺν τῷ ἀνθυπάτῳ Σεργίῳ Παύλῳ, ἀνδρὶ συνετῷ. οὗτος προσκαλεσάμενος Βαρναβᾶν καὶ Σαῦλον ἐπεζήτησεν ἀκοῦσαι τὸν λόγον τοῦ θεοῦ). It appears that Bar-Jesus was "in the service of" (σύν, lit., "with") the Roman proconsul; i.e., he probably was his court astrologer. The Greek term translated with the Latin *proconsul* (ἀνθύπατος) is the standard term for "the head of the government in a senatorial province."[19]

When Barnabas and Saul arrived in Paphos, Sergius Paulus was the proconsul of the Roman province of Cyprus. Luke characterizes him with three comments. (1) He was an "intelligent man" (ἀνὴρ συνετός). The Greek term generally denotes human intelligence, discernment, the ability to judge — not a prerequisite for becoming proconsul of a senatorial province, but certainly an advantage for a man in such a position. He was evidently a pagan, the first reported polytheist with whom Christian missionaries have contact in Acts. Some interpret the term in a religious sense: Sergius Paulus was "a man of understanding" because "he proves receptive to the Christian message."[20]

(2) He had taken the initiative in contacting Barnabas and Saul: he "summoned" (προσκαλεσάμενος) them, i.e., called for the missionaries to appear before him. He may have heard of the arrival of the two Jewish teachers from Bar-Jesus.

(3) He "wished" (ἐπεζήτησεν) to hear the "word of God," i.e., wanted to be informed about the message that Barnabas and Saul were proclaiming in the synagogue of Paphos.

13:8 But the magician Elymas (for this is what his name means) opposed them, as he tried to turn the proconsul away from the faith (ἀνθίστατο δὲ αὐτοῖς Ἐλύμας ὁ μάγος, οὕτως γὰρ μεθερμηνεύεται τὸ ὄνομα αὐτοῦ, ζητῶν διαστρέψαι τὸν ἀνθύπατον ἀπὸ τῆς πίστεως). Bar-Jesus/Elymas intervenes, apparently when Barnabas and Saul appear before the proconsul. He "opposes" them — he argues against the truth of the "faith" (πίστις) in Jesus as Israel's Messiah and Savior, whom the missionaries proclaim. He makes the sustained attempt (ζητῶν, present participle) to "turn away" (διαστρέψαι)[21] the proconsul away from accepting the missionaries' message and coming to faith in Jesus. If preaching the gospel in Paphos had already led to conversions, the Jewish magician presumably knows that accepting faith in Jesus as Israel's Messiah will bring the proconsul's willingness, perhaps eagerness, to receive guidance through magical incantations and rituals to an end.

13:9 – 11d But Saul, also known as Paul, who was filled with the Holy Spirit, looked intently at him and said, "You are full of all kinds of deceit and fraud, you son of the devil and enemy of all that is right; will you not stop making crooked the straight paths of the Lord? Look, the hand of the Lord is now against you: you will be blind, unable to see the sun, for a while" (Σαῦλος δέ, ὁ καὶ Παῦλος, πλησθεὶς πνεύματος ἁγίου ἀτενίσας εἰς αὐτὸν εἶπεν· ὦ πλήρης παντὸς δόλου καὶ πάσης ῥαδιουργίας, υἱὲ διαβόλου, ἐχθρὲ πάσης δικαιοσύνης, οὐ παύσῃ διαστρέφων τὰς ὁδοὺς τοῦ κυρίου τὰς εὐθείας; καὶ νῦν ἰδοὺ χεὶρ κυρίου ἐπὶ σὲ καὶ ἔσῃ τυφλὸς μὴ βλέπων τὸν ἥλιον ἄχρι καιροῦ). In these verses Luke relates Saul's announcement of the

---

19. BDAG, s.v. ἀνθύπατος. Cf. W. Kierdorf, "Proconsul," *BNP*, 11:919 – 20. Both Sergius Paulus and Gallio (18:12) were ex-praetors who had not yet risen to the rank of consul. The imperial provinces were governed by military prefects (ἡγεμών), such as Pontius Pilate (cf. Luke 2:2; 3:1), Felix (Acts 23:24, 26), and Festus (24:27) in Judea.

20. Haenchen, *Acts*, 398; cf. Zmijewski, *Apostelgeschichte*, 488.

21. The term is often used in the LXX for distorting the truth and perverting the people; Johnson, *Acts*, 223.

divine punishment of Bar-Jesus. He also uses this confrontation with the Jewish magician and the subsequent conversion of the Roman proconsul to introduce Saul's Roman name.

Having used his Hebrew name "Saul" (Σαῦλος) until now, Luke henceforth employs his Roman name "Paul" (Παῦλος; see on 9:1 – 2) as he relates the missionary work of Saul/Paul in various cities of the Greco-Roman world.[22] The fact that his Roman name is the same as that of the proconsul is coincidental; Luke did not borrow the name from Paul's "first convert" (the first convert mentioned explicitly in his narrative), nor is there any evidence that a family connection existed between Paul's family, who lived in Tarsus, and the family of the proconsul, who came from Rome. Paul would have introduced himself to Sergius Paulus, the proconsul of the Roman province of Cyprus, not with his Jewish name but with his Latin name, which he had as a result of being a Roman citizen.

The comment that Paul "was filled" (πλησθείς) with the Holy Spirit suggests that the Spirit was the immediate inspiration for evaluating Bar-Jesus' spiritual state in v. 10 and the oracle of judgment in v. 11.[23] Paul's intent look focuses the attention of Bar-Jesus, and of Luke's readers, on the following indictment. Paul's statement consists of five elements.

(1) Paul accuses Bar-Jesus of being "full" (πλήρης) of all kinds of deceit and fraud. Luke's readers will contrast this description with Paul, "filled" with God's Holy Spirit (v. 9) and proclaiming God's word (v. 7).

(2) Paul denounces Bar-Jesus as being a "son of the devil" (υἱὸς διαβόλου) and an "enemy" (ἐχθρός) of everything that is right.[24] Since Bar-Jesus is a magician and a false prophet (v. 6), he is obviously not inspired by God and his Spirit but by the devil, which renders him an enemy of God and his will. This is strong language[25] that already implies divine judgment. The term translated "devil" (διάβολος) describes in secular Greek "one who engages in slander" and hence "the adversary." The LXX uses this term to translate the Hebrew term for "adversary" (haśśāṭān),[26] in particular for the principal adversary of God, a transcendent evil being that is the lord of the demons. According to Luke 10:19, Jesus had spoken of his disciples who proclaim the message of the kingdom of God as having authority over "all the power of the enemy," a promise being fulfilled here in Paul's confrontation with this magician.

(3) Using the device of a rhetorical question, which reinforces the significance of the statement, Paul asserts that Bar-Jesus "makes crooked" the "straight paths" of the Lord.[27] He accuses him of attempting to manipulate the guidance of God, who is leading the Roman governor and other people in Paphos to faith in Jesus.

(4) Paul announces God's judgment when he

---

22. An additional reason for the switch from Saul to Paul may have been the fact that the term σαῦλος, in Greek, denotes the "straddling" or "waddling" gait of a tortoise, of prostitutes, or of a prancing horse (LSJ, s.v. σαῦλος); cf. Tim J. Leary, "Paul's Improper Name," *NTS* 38 (1992): 467 – 69.

23. Cf. Turner, *Power from on High*, 167, 350. Johnson, *Acts*, 223, thinks that the comment serves to identify Paul as a prophet; Parsons, *Acts*, 189, sees a contrast between Paul, a true prophet, and Bar-Jesus, the false prophet.

24. NIV, TNIV; lit., "of all righteousness" (NASB, NRSV); GNB and NLT translated "of all that is good." The term (δικαιοσύνη) probably has an ethical meaning here (Barrett,

Acts, 617); it is not impossible, however, that Paul (followed by Luke) thinks of God's righteousness revealed in the death and resurrection of Jesus as the central content of God's word that he has been proclaiming in the synagogue in Paphos.

25. Cf. 1 John 3:10, with the stark contrast of "the children of God" and "the children of the devil."

26. Cf. Job 1:6 – 8, 12; 2:1 – 7; Zech 3:1, 2, etc.

27. Similar expressions are found in Prov 10:9; Hos 14:9 [LXX 14:10]. Cf. Pao, *New Exodus*, 201 – 2, who points to the contrast with Isa 40:3 (cited in Luke 3:4 – 5), which speaks of making "straight in the desert a highway for our God."

states that "the hand of the Lord,"[28] i.e., the power of God, is set "against" (ἐπί) the Jewish magician. As Bar-Jesus is the enemy of the Lord's straight paths (to salvation through Jesus), so God is the enemy of Bar-Jesus and his attempts to pervert God's will.

(5) Paul announces God's punishment for Bar-Jesus: he will be blind, which means he will be "unable to see the sun"; i.e., he will not see anything; he will be completely blind. The punishment will be limited in time: "for a while." This qualification may imply the hope that Bar-Jesus will give up his opposition to the proclamation of the gospel by Paul and Barnabas, and perhaps expresses the possibility that Bar-Jesus may begin to walk on the "straight paths" of the Lord, repent, and come to faith in Jesus.

13:11e-h Immediately a dark mist came over him, and he went groping about for someone to lead him by the hand (παραχρῆμά τε ἔπεσεν ἐπ᾽ αὐτὸν ἀχλὺς καὶ σκότος καὶ περιάγων ἐζήτει χειραγωγούς). The divine punishment that Paul announces takes effect "immediately" (παραχρῆμα).

The proconsul's astrologer is enveloped in a "dark mist" that causes him to lose his eyesight and thus his orientation. As a result, he "groped about" looking for people who would lead him by the hand, which demonstrates that the punitive miracle Paul announced has actually taken place.[29] The dramatic divine judgment that falls on Bar-Jesus can be seen, in the context of the reference to the Holy Spirit in v. 9, as the "purgative fire of the Spirit" that John the Baptist expected.[30]

13:12 When the proconsul saw what had happened, he believed, amazed at the teaching about the Lord (τότε ἰδὼν ὁ ἀνθύπατος τὸ γεγονὸς ἐπίστευσεν ἐκπλησσόμενος ἐπὶ τῇ διδαχῇ τοῦ κυρίου). Luke ends the episode with the conversion of Sergius Paulus, who "believed" (ἐπίστευσεν), i.e., who came to faith in Jesus whose life, death, and resurrection Paul and Barnabas proclaimed as the word of God (cf. vv. 5, 7). The proconsul's conversion is initially connected with the punitive miracle that had blinded his court astrologer, but is then related to his reaction to the "teaching" (διδαχή) about the Lord that caused him to be amazed.

---

28. The anthropomorphic phrase "the hand of the Lord" (χεὶρ κυρίου) denotes God's powerful activity in the world; cf. Judg 2:15 (LXX) and 1 Sam 12:15 where the "hand of the Lord" is "against" people who oppose his will.

29. Helplessness is a common feature of the *topos* of blindness; cf. Chad Hartsock, *Sight and Blindness in Luke-Acts: The*

Use of Physical Features in Characterization (Biblical Interpretation 94; Leiden: Brill, 2008), 197.

30. Turner, *Power from on High*, 407, with reference to William H. Shepherd, *The Narrative Function of the Holy Spirit as a Character in Luke-Acts* (SBLDS 147; Atlanta: Scholars Press, 1994), 211.

Theology in Application

The narrative of Paul and Barnabas, commissioned by the church in Antioch to engage in a new missionary effort and to proclaim the gospel on the island of Cyprus, emphasizes that missionary work is authenticated by the Holy Spirit, supported by the local church in Antioch, characterized by geographical movement, and focused on proclaiming the word of God.

Authenticated by the Holy Spirit

Missionary work is authenticated by the Holy Spirit. The primary cause of the missionary work of Paul and Barnabas and the primary cause of the effectiveness of their proclamation of the gospel is the Holy Spirit as the transforming power of God's powerful presence. The reference to prophets in the church in Antioch (v. 1) suggests the presence of the Holy Spirit, who reveals his will to the congregation during a time of worship and fasting, prompting the church to commission Barnabas and Saul for a new missionary initiative (v. 2), and who sends the two missionaries out to Cyprus (v. 4). In addition, the Holy Spirit reveals God's indictment and punishment of the magician Bar-Jesus to Paul (v. 9). The Holy Spirit thus authenticates Paul's earlier commission as an envoy of Jesus Christ (9:15), Paul's call to engage in missionary work on Cyprus (vv. 2, 4), and Paul's confrontation with the Jewish astrologer of the proconsul (vv. 9, 11). The missionary work of the early church — indeed of any church — can be adequately understood only if one grasps the reality, the power, and the work of the Holy Spirit as the effective reality, power, and work of God himself.

Confrontation with the Forces of Evil and Their Representatives

Missionary work involves confrontation with the forces of evil and their representatives. The supernatural events of the episode have several functions. The miracle of Elymas's blindness is punitive; he is being punished for his deceit and his active involvement in perverting the will of God. Note that the punishment is not final, as in the case of Ananias and Sapphira (5:1 – 10), but temporary (13:11), leaving open the possibility of a future conversion of the opponent. At the same time the miracle calls the witnesses of Elymas's punishment to a decision concerning their own reaction to the message of the gospel; the governor Sergius Paulus is converted after he sees the effect that Paul's words have on Elymas.

Paul's evaluation of the spiritual status of Bar-Jesus, Paul's announcement of God's punishment on Bar-Jesus, the punitive miracle of blindness inflicted on Bar-Jesus, and the conversion of the proconsul subsequent to the sudden blindness of his astrologer are all manifestations of the power of the Holy Spirit. For Luke's readers, whether in the first century or today, the Elymas episode warns against involvement in occult practices of any kind. People involved in magic or sorcery may not become literally blind when they encounter the gospel, but they are metaphorically blind, groping about in darkness. Missionaries, evangelists, and pastors can be assured that the power of the one true God who works through his Spirit, conveyed through Jesus' witnesses who proclaim the gospel, is stronger than any magic.[31]

The Local Church

Missionary work is supported by the local church. Luke's report of the new missionary initiative begins with worship and prayer in the church at Antioch. Paul did not operate as a missionary independent of the church but as a missionary who belonged to a local congregation, who was recommissioned by a local congregation to new missionary initiative, and who regarded himself as accountable to the congregations in Antioch and in Jerusalem — two churches he regularly visited after the conclusion of each phase of missionary work.

It should be noted, however, that the church in Antioch was not the "sending church" of Paul; Barnabas and Saul were commissioned and sent by the Holy Spirit (vv. 2, 4). Barnabas had ten years of missionary experience before he left Antioch for Cyprus, and Paul had nearly fifteen years of missionary experience before they evangelized on Cyprus. It was neither the church in Jerusalem nor the church in Antioch that decided on the details of the missionary work of Barnabas and Paul in the cities of Cyprus. The two missionaries evidently made the relevant decisions regarding the cities in which they would proclaim the gospel, and presumably regarding the recruitment of John Mark as an assistant.

However, the "preface" of vv. 1 – 3 underlines the significance of local congregations for missionary work in general and for new missionary initiatives in particular. The "support" of the church in Antioch for the new missionary initiative was the release of their most senior pastor and teacher (Barnabas, from Jerusalem) and the release of their presumably most experienced missionary among Gentiles and their most astute theologian (Paul, from Tarsus, student of Gamaliel). The challenge of missionary work requires that the most gifted and experienced Christians are commissioned for missionary work.

Geographical Movement

Missionary work is characterized by geographical movement. While authentic missionary work is always the work of the Holy Spirit, it is at the same time an endeavor that is visible, so visible that it can be traced on a map. The missionaries move from

---

31. See F. Mussner, *Apostelgeschichte* (Würzburg: Echter, 1984), 78; Pesch, *Apostelgeschichte*, 2:26 – 27; Zmijewski, *Apostelgeschichte*, 491 – 92.

Antioch to the port city of Seleucia (v. 4b), they sail from there to Cyprus (v. 4c), they arrive at Salamis in the eastern region of the island (v. 5a), they travel along the south coast of Cyprus (v. 6a-b), and they arrive in Paphos, the capital of the province (v. 6c). Since the term "mission" is derived from the Latin verb "to send" (*mittere*), missionary work implies geographical movement to regions, to cities, and to people who have not yet heard the good news of Jesus Christ.

"Mission" is not simply Christian existence or "everything that the church does," but the deliberate activity of a community of faith that distinguishes itself from its environment both in terms of religious belief (theology) and social behavior (ethics). Those going out are convinced of the truth claims of the Christian faith, and they actively work to win other people for the content of faith and the way of life espoused by that community. Intentionality and geographical movement are an integral part of authentic missionary work.

Proclamation of God's Word

Missionary work is focused on the proclamation of God's word. Paul and Barnabas proclaim God's word in the synagogues of Salamis (v. 5), and they proclaim it in Paphos, apparently so effectively that their presence and message come to the attention of the proconsul (v. 7). The brief reference concerning the conversion of Sergius Paulus demonstrates that the "word of God" they proclaim is the "teaching about the Lord" (v. 12), i.e., the proclamation of the fulfillment of God's promises in Jesus and of salvation through faith in Jesus as Israel's Messiah and Savior of the world. This focus is confirmed by Luke's extensive summary of Paul's sermon in the synagogue in Pisidian Antioch (vv. 16 – 41) in the next episode.

CHAPTER 25

Acts 13:13 – 52

Literary Context

The second episode of Luke's report on the missionary work of Paul and Barnabas in the cities of Cyprus, south Galatia, and Pamphylia (13:1 – 14:28) describes their proclamation of the gospel in Pisidian Antioch (13:13 – 52). In 13:1 – 12, Paul and Barnabas traveled from Antioch to Cyprus, preaching the gospel in Salamis and other cities on the southern coast of Cyprus before they reached Paphos, the capital of the province, where they encountered a Jewish magician and were instrumental in leading the Roman proconsul, Sergius Paulus, to faith in Jesus. In this first episode Saul/Paul is initially called by his Jewish name Saul (13:7), but Luke transitions to calling him by his Latin name Paul (13:9). That episode also has Barnabas's name before Saul/Paul (13:7), a fact that would have suggested to some readers that Barnabas was the lead missionary, with Saul as his coworker. Now in the second episode, Luke speaks of "Paul and his companions" (13:13), and he mentions Paul before Barnabas (13:43, 46, 50).

While the content of Paul's preaching was summarized with the phrases "the word of God" (13:5, 7) and "the teaching about the Lord" (13:12) in the first episode, Luke now provides a long summary of Paul's preaching in the synagogue of Antioch (13:16 – 41), with further direct speech explaining the move from preaching before a Jewish audience to preaching to Gentiles (13:46 – 47). The central place of this episode in Acts 13 – 14 underlines the importance of the events in Pisidian Antioch for Luke. Paul's sermon in the synagogue of Antioch is the first, and the last, missionary sermon that Luke relates for Paul.[1] Also, Luke gives a detailed report about the positive and the negative reactions of Jews and Gentiles to Paul's preaching (13:42 – 45, 48 – 52. This second episode thus provides extensive evidence for three areas: (1) the content of Paul's missionary proclamation among the Jewish people; (2) the rationale of Paul's missionary methods in terms of preaching both to Jews and to Gentiles; (3) the reactions to Paul's preaching among Jews and Gentiles.

---

1. Paul's speech before the Areopagus has a different function (see on 17:16 – 34).

Main Idea

The realities of missionary work involve reaching out to Jews and Gentiles, interpreting the Scriptures, explaining the significance of Jesus, instructing new believers, and encountering opposition; the content of missionary preaching focuses on the fulfillment of God's promises in the salvation that results from the death and resurrection of Jesus, Israel's messianic Savior.

Translation

Acts 13:13 – 52

13a	Place	From Paphos
b	Identification	**Paul and**
c	Association	**his companions**
d	Action	**set sail,**
e	Action/Place	and **they came to Perge**
f	Geographical	in Pamphylia.
g	Action	But **John left them**
h	Action/Place	and **returned to Jerusalem.**
14a	Action/Place	**They went on from Perge**
b	Place	and **reached Pisidian Antioch.**
c	Setting: Time	On the Sabbath
d	Action	**they went into the synagogue**
e	Action	and **sat down.**
15a	Setting: Time	After the reading of the Law and
b		the Prophets,
c	Action/Character entrance	**the presidents of the synagogue sent word to them,**
d	Action (speech)	saying,
e	Address	"Brothers,
f	Condition	if you have a word of encouragement for the people,
g	Entreaty	please speak."

Continued on next page.

Continued from previous page.

16a	Action (Response)	So **Paul stood up,**
b	Action	**motioned with his hand,**
c	Action (speech)	and **said:**
d	Address	"People of Israel and
e	Address	you who are God-fearers,
f	Call to listen	listen to me.
17a	Review of history	The God of the people of Israel chose our ancestors,
b	Action	and he made the people great
c	Time	during their stay in Egypt,
d	Action	and with mighty power he led them out of that country.
18a	Setting: Time (Duration)	For about forty years
b	Event/Place	he put up with them in the desert.
19a	Action/Place	He overpowered seven nations in Canaan,
b	Result	giving their land
c	Description	as an inheritance
d	Advantage	to his people
20a	Time (Duration)	for about four hundred and fifty years.
b	Setting: Time	After that
c	Action	God gave them judges
d	Time	until the time of Samuel
e	Identification	the prophet.
21a	Event	Then they asked for a king,
b	Action (Character entrance)	and he gave them Saul,
c	Identification	the son of Kish,
d	Character description	a man of the tribe of Benjamin,
e	Character description	who ruled for forty years.
22a	Setting: Time	When he had removed him,
b	Action (Character entrance)	he gave them David as their king,
c	Character description	about whom he testified,
d	Assertion	'I have found David
e	Identification	son of Jesse
f	Character description	a man after my heart,
g	Declaration (Prophecy)	who will do everything I want him to do.'
23a	Setting: Social	From this man's descendants
b	Action	God brought Jesus
c	Identification	as Savior
d	Advantage	to Israel,
e	Reference	according to his promise.
24a	Setting: Time	Before his coming,
b	Event (Character entrance)	John had proclaimed a baptism of repentance
c	Sphere	to all the people of Israel.

25a	Setting: Time	As John was completing his mission,
b	Action (speech)	he said,
c	Question	'What do you suppose me to be?
d	Assertion (Denial)	I am not the one.
e	Assertion	But there is one
f	Character description	who will come after me
g	Character description	the sandals of whose feet I am not worthy to untie.'
26a	Address	Brothers,
b	Description	descendants of Abraham's family and
c	Description	you who are God-fearers,
d	Assertion/Reminder	the message of this salvation has been sent to us.
27a	Character entrance	The residents of Jerusalem and
b	Character entrance	their leaders
c	Assertion	failed to recognize him;
d	Action	and when they condemned him,
e	Fulfillment	they fulfilled the oracles of the prophets
f	Description	that are read every Sabbath.
28a	Concession	Even though they found no basis for a death sentence,
b	Contra-expectation	they asked Pilate
c	Wish	to have him executed.
29a	Setting: Time/Action	When they had carried out everything
b	Prophecy/Fulfillment	that was written about him,
c	Action	they took him down from the cross
d	Action	and laid him in a tomb.
30	Action	But God raised him from the dead,
31a	Time (Duration)	and for many days
b	Event	he was seen
c	Identification (Agency)	by those who had come with him
d	Place	from Galilee to Jerusalem,
e	Character description	who are now his witnesses
f	Sphere	before the people.
32a	Assertion	And we proclaim to you the good news
b	Indirect speech	that God's promise to our ancestors has been realized;
33a	Assertion	God has fulfilled this promise for us,
b	Character description	their children,
c	Means	by raising up Jesus,
d	OT Quotation	as it is written in the second psalm:
e	Assertion	'You are my Son;
f	Assertion	today I have begotten you.' (Ps 2:7)
34a	Action	He raised him from the dead
b	Result	so that he will not return to corruption.
c	OT Quotation	As God has said,
d	Promise	'I will grant you the unfailing assurances
e		made to David.' (Isa 55:3)

Continued on next page.

Continued from previous page.

35a	OT Quotation	So he also said in another passage:
b	Promise	'You will not let your Holy One see corruption.' (Ps 16:10)

36a Time   For when David had served God's purpose
  b   Sphere   in his own generation,
  c   Event   he fell asleep
  d   Event   *and* was gathered to his ancestors,
  e   Event   *and* experienced corruption.

35a	OT Quotation	So he also said in another passage:
b	Promise	'You will not let your Holy One see corruption.' (Ps 16:10)
36a	Time	For when David had served God's purpose
b	Sphere	in his own generation,
c	Event	he fell asleep
d	Event	*and* was gathered to his ancestors,
e	Event	*and* experienced corruption.
37a	Protagonist (Contrast)	*But* the One
b	Identification	whom God raised from the dead
c	Event	did not experience corruption.
38a	Inference	*Therefore* I want you to know,
b	Address	brothers,
c	Content	that
d	Agency	through him
e	Event	forgiveness of sins is proclaimed to you and
f	Content	that
g	Separation	from all those things
h	Description	from which you could not be justified by the law of Moses,
39a	Agency	by this man
b	Assertion/Promise	everyone who believes is justified.
40a	Exhortation	Beware, then,
b	Warning	that what the prophets said does not happen to you:
41a	Appeal	'Look,
b	Address/Accusation	you scoffers,
c	Exhortation	be alarmed
d	Exhortation	*and* perish,
e	Cause	for I am doing a deed in your days,
f	Accusation	a deed which you will not believe
g	Contra-expectation	even if someone told you.'"
		(Hab 1:5)
42a	Setting: Time	As they were leaving,
b	Action	**the people requested**
c	Request	that they speak further about these matters
d	Time	on the following Sabbath.
43a	Setting: Time	After the meeting of the synagogue had broken up,
b	Event	**many of the Jews and**
c	Association	devout proselytes
d	Event	**followed Paul and**
e	Association	**Barnabas,**
f	Description	who continued to speak to them,
g	Action	urging them
h	Exhortation	to continue in the grace of God.

44a	Setting: Time		On the next Sabbath
b	Event	**almost the whole city gathered**	
c	Purpose		to hear the word of the Lord.
45a	Setting: Cause		When the Jews saw the crowds,
b	Event	**they were filled with zeal**	
c	Action (Conflict)	and **contradicted what Paul said,**	
d	Means		slandering him.

46a	Protagonist	Then both **Paul and**	
b	Association		**Barnabas**
c	Action	**spoke out fearlessly:**	
d	Assertion		*"It was necessary*
e			*that the word of God should be proclaimed*
f	Sphere/Advantage		*to you first.*
g	Cause		*Because you reject it*
h	Cause		*and do not consider yourselves worthy of eternal life,*
i	Assertion/Announcement	*we now turn to the Gentiles.*	
47a	OT Quotation	For *so the Lord instructed us:*	
b	Assertion		*'I have made you a light*
c	Sphere		*for the Gentiles,*
d	Purpose		*that you may bring salvation*
e	Sphere		*to the ends of the earth.'"* (Isa 49:6)

48a	Setting: Time		When the Gentiles heard this,
b	Reaction	**they were glad**	
c	Reaction	and **honored the word of the Lord,**	
d		and **all**	
e	Character description		who were destined for eternal life
f	Response	**believed.**	
49a	Event	**The word of the Lord spread**	
b	Place		through the entire region.

50a	Action/Sphere	**The Jews, however, incited** **prominent women among the God-fearers and**	
b	Association		the leading men of the city
c	Action (Conflict)	and **started a persecution against** **Paul and**	
d			**Barnabas,**
e	Action		whom they forced
f	Result		to leave their district.
51a	Action	So **they shook the dust off their feet**	
b	Reference		in protest against them
c	Action (Place)	and **went to Iconium.**	
52a	Event	**The disciples were filled with** **joy and**	
b			the Holy Spirit.

Structure and Literary Form

This episode is made up of five incidents. Luke first narrates the missionaries' travel from Paphos to Pisidian Antioch (13:13–15). He then provides a summary of Paul's sermon in the synagogue of Antioch (vv. 16–41), followed by a report of the beginnings of the church comprised of Jewish and Gentile believers (vv. 42–49). After a detailed report on the opposition of the Jews and the local elite (v. 50), Luke ends with comments on the departure of Paul and Barnabas and the reaction of the believers in Antioch to these events (vv. 51–52).

The episode is a *narrative* that can be analyzed in terms of a *missionary narrative* that includes a *travel narrative* (vv. 13–14), a *sermon (speech)* (vv. 16–41), and *reports* on a variety of topics: the reaction of the Jewish audience and of Gentiles living in Antioch (vv. 42–45), the missionaries' reaction to opposition in the synagogue (vv. 46–47), conversions among the people in Antioch (v. 48), conversions in the region (v. 49 — the tenth summary statement in Acts), opposition in Antioch (which forces Paul and Barnabas to leave the city, vv. 50–51), and the reaction of the believers in Antioch (v. 52). *Direct speech* is given for the officials of the synagogue (v. 15), for Paul (vv. 16–41), and for Paul and Barnabas (vv. 46–47). Unlike 13:1–12, Luke does not mention the name or names of converts, nor does he mention miracles.

Paul's sermon in vv. 16–41 resembles Peter's speeches before Jews with his proclamation of Jesus as the Davidic Messiah (2:22–36; 3:12–26) and Stephen's speech with its review of salvation history (7:2–53). The threefold address of the audience (13:16d-e, 26a-c, 38b) divides the speech into three main parts, which can be linked with the traditional rhetorical parts of (1) the brief *exordium* (introduction, v. 16d-f), followed by the *narratio* (statement of the facts) that reviews salvation history (vv. 17–25), (2) the *argumentatio* (proofs), the proclamation of the significance of Jesus as Messiah (vv. 26–37), and (3) the *peroratio* (conclusion), which calls the listeners to repent (vv. 38–41).[2] Paul's sermon would have been based on the reading of the Law and the Prophets (v. 15). The two texts read on this occasion may have been Deut 4:25–46 (the reading from the Law) and 2 Sam 7:6–16 (the reading from the Prophets).[3]

Paul's speech, while formulated by Luke as a summary, contains several important conceptual parallels in Paul's letters.[4]

1. A reference to the leaders (in Jerusalem) who did not acknowledge Jesus and who thus killed him (vv. 27–28) is (only) found in 1 Cor 2:8.
2. Prophecies in Scripture for Jesus' lying in a tomb and being raised by God

2. Cf. Josef Pichler, *Paulusrezeption in der Apostelgeschichte: Untersuchungen zur Rede im pisidischen Antiochien* (IThS 50; Innsbruck: Tyrolia, 1997), 124–31; Fitzmyer, *Acts*, 507–8. Parsons, *Acts*, 192, correctly recognizes that Paul's speech "does not fit the specific pattern of a forensic, deliberative, or epideictic speech."

3. Bowker, "Speeches in Acts," 101–4.

4. Cf. Baum, "Paulinismen," 414–24.

from the dead, Jesus' appearances before numerous disciples, and a reference to eyewitnesses (vv. 29 – 31, 34 – 35) are (only) found in 1 Cor 15:3 – 7.

3. A reference to the fathers to whom God gave a promise and the fulfillment of that promise among the fathers' descendants who believe in Jesus (vv. 32 – 33) is found in Rom 4:13 – 16 and Gal 3:14 – 16.

4. Jesus' recognition as Son of God as the fulfillment of Scripture (v. 33) is found in Rom 1:2, 4.

5. The combination of justification, the law, and faith (vv. 38 – 39) is found in Rom 3:28; Gal 2:16; Phil 3:9.

6. The combination of closed eyes, blind eyes, deaf ears, rejection of the gospel by Jews, and the gospel addressed to the Gentiles (v. 46) is found in Rom 11:8 – 11.

Exegetical Outline

➡ I. The Mission in Pisidian Antioch (13:13 – 52)

    A. Travel from Paphos to Antioch (13:13 – 14b)

        1. The journey from Paphos to Perge (13:13a-e)

        2. The departure of John Mark for Jerusalem (13:13g-h)

        3. The journey from Perge to Pisidian Antioch (13:14a-b)

    B. Paul's Sermon in the Synagogue of Antioch (13:14c – 41)

        1. The visit to the synagogue on the Sabbath (13:14c-e)

        2. The invitation by the synagogue officials to give the homily (13:15)

        3. Paul's acceptance of the invitation (13:16a-c)

        4. Paul's sermon (13:16d – 41)

            a. Review of salvation history (13:16d – 25)

                i. Address to the Jews and God-fearers (13:16d-f)

                ii. The history of Israel from the patriarchs to David (13:17 – 22)

                    (a) The election of the patriarchs (13:17a)

                    (b) Israel in Egypt and the exodus (13:17b-d)

                    (c) Israel in the wilderness (13:18)

                    (d) Israel in Canaan (13:19)

                    (e) Israel during the time of the judges (13:20)

                    (f) Israel during the reign of Saul (13:21)

                    (g) The appointment of King David (13:22)

                iii. The fulfillment of God's promises in Jesus (13:23)

                iv. The proclamation of John the Baptist (13:24 – 25)

            b. Proclamation of the significance of Jesus (13:26 – 37)

                i. The relevance of the gospel for the audience (13:26)

                ii. The execution of Jesus (13:27 – 29)

iii. The resurrection of Jesus (13:30 – 37)

    (a) The fact of Jesus' resurrection (13:30 – 31)

    (b) The fulfillment of God's promises in Jesus' resurrection (13:32 – 33c)

    (c) Proof from Scripture (Ps 2:7; Isa 55:3; Ps 16:10) (13:33d – 37)

  c. Call to repentance (13:38 – 41)

    i. The offer of the forgiveness of sins through Jesus (13:38 – 39)

    ii. Warning not to ignore the work of God (Hab 1:5) (13:40 – 41)

C. The Beginnings of the Church Comprised of Jewish and Gentile Believers (13:42 – 49)

  1. The desire of Jews and God-fearers to receive further instruction (13:42)

  2. The conversion of Jews and God-fearers (13:43)

  3. The meeting of a large crowd on the following Sabbath (13:44)

  4. The opposition of zealous Jews (13:45)

  5. The reaction of Paul and Barnabas (13:46 – 47)

    a. The courageous response of the missionaries (13:46a-c)

    b. The priority of the missionaries' proclamation before the Jews (13:46d-f)

    c. The turn to the Gentiles on account of the Jews' rejection of the gospel (13:46g-i)

    d. The missionaries' obedience to God's commission (13:47a)

    e. Confirmation from Scripture (Isa 49:6) (13:47b-e)

  6. The conversion of Gentiles (13:48)

  7. The conversion of Gentiles in the region beyond Antioch (13:49)

D. The Opposition of the Jews and the Local Elite (13:50)

  1. The incitement of aristocratic women among the God-fearers (13:50a)

  2. The mobilization of members of the elite in the city against the missionaries (13:50b)

  3. The persecution of Paul and Barnabas (13:50c-f)

E. The Departure of Paul and Barnabas (13:51 – 52)

  1. The departure of the missionaries from Antioch (13:51a-b)

  2. The journey from Antioch to Iconium (13:51c)

  3. The joy of the disciples resulting from the presence of the Holy Spirit (13:52)

Explanation of the Text

13:13 From Paphos Paul and his companions set sail, and they came to Perge in Pamphylia. But John left them and returned to Jerusalem (ἀναχθέντες δὲ ἀπὸ τῆς Πάφου οἱ περὶ Παῦλον ἦλθον εἰς Πέργην τῆς Παμφυλίας, Ἰωάννης δὲ ἀποχωρήσας ἀπ᾽ αὐτῶν ὑπέστρεψεν εἰς Ἱεροσόλυμα). The episode begins with a travel narrative (vv. 13 – 14b)

that relates the missionaries' journey from Paphos on Cyprus to Pisidian Antioch in the province of Galatia. The journey by ship (ἀναχθέντες)[5] from Paphos to Perge was about 150 miles (280 km.). In the first century, Perge (see on 14:25) could be reached directly by ship traveling up the River Cestrus (mod. Aksu), which was navigable in an-

---

5. Cf. BDAG, s.v. ἀνάγω 4, as a nautical technical term, middle or passive, denoting "to begin to go by boat, *put out to* sea" or "to set sail." See also 16:11; 18:21; 20:3, 13; 21:1 – 2; 27:2; 27:4, 12, 21; 28:10; also Luke 8:22.

tiquity, with the city lying about three miles west of the river. At Perge the missionaries could access the Roman road called Via Sebaste, the most direct route into the interior.

After arriving at Perge, John Mark left Paul and Barnabas and returned to Jerusalem to his mother, Mary (cf. 12:25). The reasons for his departure remain unclear. Some have suggested that John Mark loathed the fact that Paul had become the leader of the missionary venture "replacing" Barnabas, that he objected to the continuation of the missionary journey beyond Cyprus through Pamphylia to southern Galatia, or that he had lost enthusiasm or courage for missionary work. We do know, however, that at least Paul did not approve of John Mark's departure (cf. 15:37 – 39, where John Mark is back in Antioch). Luke does not report any missionary activity for Paul and Barnabas in Perge at this time, although this may be implied in the formulation "they came to Perge … they went on from Perge." He does point out that the missionaries preached the gospel in Perge after they returned from southern Galatia (14:25).

The fact that Paul and Barnabas evidently traveled on the Via Sebaste through the province of Pamphylia/Lycia and the region of Pisidia — bypassing cities such as Attalia, Termessos, Ariassos, and Komama — raises the question of their missionary strategy (or, rather, tactics) at this point. One explanation is the possibility that Paul had contracted malaria and wanted to reach the higher elevations of central Anatolia to find relief.[6] Another suggestion points to the connections of Sergius Paulus, the governor of Cyprus, with the family of the Sergii Paullii, who owned estates in southern Galatia.[7] Sergius Paulus may have suggested missionary work in Pisidian Antioch, "no doubt providing [Paul] with letters of introduction to aid his passage and his stay."[8]

13:14 They went on from Perge and reached Pisidian Antioch. On the Sabbath they went into the synagogue and sat down (αὐτοὶ δὲ διελθόντες ἀπὸ τῆς Πέργης παρεγένοντο εἰς Ἀντιόχειαν τὴν Πισιδίαν, καὶ εἰσελθόντες εἰς τὴν συναγωγὴν τῇ ἡμέρᾳ τῶν σαββάτων ἐκάθισαν). The first city for which Luke reports missionary activity of Paul and Barnabas in central Asia Minor is Pisidian Antioch. The appellation "Pisidian" distinguishes this Antioch from Antioch on the Maeander River (also located in Phrygia). Antioch belonged to the Roman province of Galatia, as did all the other cities in which Paul and Barnabas preached the gospel during the following year.

As they had done in Salamis on Cyprus (v. 5) and as it was Paul's regular practice,[9] the missionaries go to the synagogue (see on 6:9) at the first Sabbath after their arrival in Antioch in order to worship. Luke's description of what happened when Paul and Barnabas visit the synagogue in Antioch is, together with Luke 4:16 – 27, the oldest historical depiction of central elements of a synagogue service.

Paul and Barnabas "sat down" (ἐκάθισαν), perhaps on one of the stone benches built against two or three sides of the wall, perhaps on wooden benches in the middle of the room. Paul, a Jewish-Christian teacher, would naturally begin missionary work in the local synagogue, where he would encounter Jews and Gentiles: proselytes, God-fearers, and sympathizers attracted by the ethical monotheism of the Jewish faith.

---

6. Cf. Gal 4:13, where Paul asserts that he came to Galatia and preached the gospel there "because of an illness." Cf. William M. Ramsay, *St. Paul the Traveller and the Roman Citizen* (London: Hodder & Stoughton, 1896), 92 – 97.

7. Cf. Schnabel, *Early Christian Mission*, 2:1085 – 86.

8. Stephen Mitchell, *Anatolia: Land, Men, and Gods in Asia Minor* (Oxford: Oxford Univ. Press, 1995), 2:7.

9. Cf. 14:1 (Iconium); 17:17 (Athens); 18:4 (Corinth); 18:19; 19:8 (Ephesus).

13:15 – 16 After the reading of the Law and the Prophets, the presidents of the synagogue sent word to them, saying, "Brothers, if you have a word of encouragement for the people, please speak." So Paul stood up, motioned with his hand, and said: "People of Israel and you who are God-fearers, listen to me" (μετὰ δὲ τὴν ἀνάγνωσιν τοῦ νόμου καὶ τῶν προφητῶν ἀπέστειλαν οἱ ἀρχισυνάγωγοι πρὸς αὐτοὺς λέγοντες· ἄνδρες ἀδελφοί, εἴ τίς ἐστιν ἐν ὑμῖν λόγος παρακλήσεως πρὸς τὸν λαόν, λέγετε. ἀναστὰς δὲ Παῦλος καὶ κατασείσας τῇ χειρὶ εἶπεν· ἄνδρες Ἰσραηλῖται καὶ οἱ φοβούμενοι τὸν θεόν, ἀκούσατε). In vv. 15 – 16 Luke relates the invitation of the synagogue officials to Paul and Barnabas to address the congregation. The reading of the Law and the Prophets, perhaps accompanied by a translation, was a regular and central part of the Jewish worship services.[10]

The two texts read on this occasion may have been Deut 4:25 – 46 (the Torah reading) and 2 Sam 7:6 – 16 (the Haftara, the reading from the Prophets). The "presidents of the synagogue" (οἱ ἀρχισυνάγωγοι) were leading members of the community who supervised the religious, financial, administrative, and political aspects of the life of the Jewish community, including matters related to the synagogue.[11] In diaspora synagogues, the president of the synagogue could be a non-Jewish benefactor of the local Jewish community who donated or renovated the synagogue building or who, for example, financed a mosaic floor.

Paul and Barnabas, both being Jews, are addressed as "brothers" (ἄνδρες ἀδελφοί). They are politely asked to say a "word of encouragement,"

i.e., a hortatory discourse or sermon.[12] As Paul and Barnabas would have introduced themselves to the leaders of the Jewish community, perhaps earlier in the week, the synagogue officials would have known that Paul was a trained rabbi who had studied under the famous Gamaliel.

Paul accepts the invitation, a fact that Luke gives careful attention using three verbs (v. 16): he "stood up" (ἀναστάς) in order to be seen and heard; he "motioned with his hand" (κατασείσας τῇ χειρί), a sign for silence and attention; then he spoke. He addresses both the Jews in the audience (ἄνδρες Ἰσραηλῖται) and the "God-fearers" (οἱ φοβούμενοι τὸν θεόν; see on 10:21 – 22), asking them to listen to what he has to say.

13:17 – 18 The God of the people of Israel chose our ancestors, and he made the people great during their stay in Egypt, and with mighty power he led them out of that country. For about forty years he put up with them in the desert (ὁ θεὸς τοῦ λαοῦ τούτου Ἰσραὴλ ἐξελέξατο τοὺς πατέρας ἡμῶν καὶ τὸν λαὸν ὕψωσεν ἐν τῇ παροικίᾳ ἐν γῇ Αἰγύπτου καὶ μετὰ βραχίονος ὑψηλοῦ ἐξήγαγεν αὐτοὺς ἐξ αὐτῆς, καὶ ὡς τεσσερακονταετῆ χρόνον ἐτροποφόρησεν αὐτοὺς ἐν τῇ ἐρήμῳ). The first part of the sermon, after the address, consists of three elements. Paul begins by reviewing the history of Israel from the election of the patriarchs to the appointment of King David (vv. 17 – 22). In his review of Israel's history, Paul focuses on seven periods and events (see the Exegetical Outline), which he describes with a series of verbs in the aorist tense.

---

10. Later Jewish evidence suggests that the service in the synagogue began with the recitation of the Jewish confession of faith (the *Shema*), followed by the recitation of the Eighteen Blessings (the *Shemoneh Esreh* or *Tephillah*), a priestly blessing, a reading from the Torah and a reading from the Prophets, followed by a sermon.

11. Levine, *Synagogue*, 415 – 27. In secular Greek, the term

ἀρχισυνάγωγος is often used for benefactors who were conspicuous in their contributions to an association; cf. Horsley and Llewelyn, *New Documents*, 4:213 – 20.

12. The same expression occurs in Heb 12:23; it is sometimes interpreted as having "something of a technical flavor for a sermon based on the lections" (Johnson, *Acts*, 230).

Alluding to Exod 6:6 – 7 and Deut 4:37, Paul first indicates that Israel is God's chosen people not because of their innate goodness or superior spirituality, but because God freely "chose [ἐξελέξατο] our ancestors." Although Luke does not have Paul recite God's promise to Abraham that all the families of the earth would be blessed through him (Gen 12:3; 18:18; 22:18), his later reference to Jesus as the fulfillment of God's promise that Israel will bring salvation to the ends of the earth (v. 47) ultimately rests on the divine election of the patriarchs.

Next, Paul highlights the fact that God "made the people great" (ὕψωσεν) while they lived in Egypt, both in numbers and in power, and he "led them out" (ἐξήγαγεν) of Egypt.[13] The reference to God's mighty power[14] alludes to the captivity of the Israelites in Egypt, who had to do forced labor and whose exodus from Egypt was initially blocked by Pharaoh. And it points forward to the power of God, who raised Jesus from the dead (v. 30), thus fulfilling the promises that God had given to the fathers (vv. 32 – 33).

The third period that Paul highlights is the time when God "put up with" (ἐτροποφόρησεν) the Israelites in the wilderness for about forty years (v. 18). As God acted despite the grumbling and trespasses of the Israelites during this period, so God carried his purposes connected with the life, death, and resurrection of Jesus despite the lack of understanding and the opposition of the Jewish leaders who asked Pilate for Jesus' execution (vv. 27 – 29).

13:19 – 20 He overpowered seven nations in Canaan, giving their land as an inheritance to his people for about four hundred and fifty years. After that God gave them judges until the time of Samuel the prophet (καὶ καθελὼν ἔθνη ἑπτὰ ἐν γῇ Χανάαν κατεκληρονόμησεν τὴν γῆν αὐτῶν ὡς ἔτεσιν τετρακοσίοις καὶ πεντήκοντα. καὶ μετὰ ταῦτα ἔδωκεν κριτὰς ἕως Σαμουὴλ τοῦ προφήτου). The fourth period of Israel's history that Paul accentuates is the conquest of Canaan, presented as an action of God.[15] God "overpowered" seven nations in the land of Canaan, an allusion to Deut 7:1.[16] And God "[gave] ... as an inheritance" (κατεκληρονόμησεν) the land of these seven nations to Israel (cf. Josh 14:1 – 2).

If the 450 years in v. 20a are taken with v. 18, they combine 400 years in Egypt, 40 years in the desert, and 10 years of the conquest before the rule of the judges.[17] If the 450 years in v. 20a are linked with what follows in v. 20b-e, they refer to the length of the period of the judges, a figure that seems to agree with Josephus's chronology.[18] The review of the conquest by which Israel received the fulfillment of God's promises of land to the fathers prepares Paul's subsequent emphasis on God's fulfillment of his promises in and through Jesus.

The fifth period is the time when God "gave" (ἔδωκεν), i.e., appointed, judges (v. 20). The judges were charismatic military leaders who liberated Israel from her enemies and provided guidance for the people, as did the prophets, the first of whom

---

13. Cf. Exod 6:1, 6, 8; 12:51; Deut 4:34; 5:15; 9:29.

14. The phrase translated as "with mighty power" (μετὰ βραχίονος ὑψηλοῦ) means literally "with uplifted arm." The term "arm" (βραχίων) is an anthropomorphic symbol of God's power (BDAG).

15. Cf. Jeska, *Geschichte Israels*, 223, who suggests that this is the reason why Moses is not mentioned (ibid., 224); the stress on God's activity in the conquest of Canaan is the traditional emphasis of summaries of Israel's history (not emphasized in Acts 7).

16. Deut 7:1 singles out "the Hittites, Girgashites, Amorites, Canaanites, Perizzites, Hivites and Jebusites" as the "seven nations larger and stronger than you."

17. Cf. Gen 15:13; cf. Acts 7:6 (400 years in Egypt); Num 14:33 – 34 (40 years in the desert); Josh 14 (conquest).

18. See *Ant.* 8.61. Note that 1 Kgs 6:1 mentions 480 years (the LXX has 440 years) for the period between the exodus and the beginning of the building of the temple in Jerusalem by Solomon. Cf. Eugene H. Merrill, "Paul's Use of 'About 450 Years' in Acts 13.20," *BSac* 138 (1981): 246 – 57.

was Samuel.[19] It is probably relevant that in Jdg 3:9, 15 the judges are described as saviors (σωτήρ). This prepares Paul's emphasis on Jesus as Israel's ultimate Savior (v. 23), in whom the promises of the prophets were fulfilled (vv. 23, 32 – 33). Among the judges was Samuel, who prophesied the events of Jesus' death and resurrection (3:24).

13:21 Then they asked for a king, and he gave them Saul, the son of Kish, a man of the tribe of Benjamin, who ruled for forty years (κἀκεῖθεν ᾐτήσαντο βασιλέα καὶ ἔδωκεν αὐτοῖς ὁ θεὸς τὸν Σαοὺλ υἱὸν Κίς, ἄνδρα ἐκ φυλῆς Βενιαμίν, ἔτη τεσσεράκοντα). The sixth period of Israel's history under review is the reign of Saul. Because the Israelites asked for a king,[20] God "gave [ἔδωκεν] them Saul," the first king of Israel, who ruled for forty years.[21] Another reason why Saul is mentioned may be connected with the way he is described: Saul is "the son of Kish" and "a man of the tribe of Benjamin,"[22] which reminds the readers that Paul's Jewish name is Saul, who also belongs to the tribe of Benjamin.[23]

It is unclear, however, whether Paul's audience in Antioch or Luke's readers would necessarily have known about Paul's affiliation with the tribe of Benjamin. Saul is contrasted with David in v. 22a-b, which suggests that Saul is mentioned as Israel's first king who was "removed" by God. That removal was due to Saul's disobedience, a point that may allude again to the disobedience of the Jewish leaders who engineered Jesus' elimination (vv. 27 – 29). Or the removal was due to the demand of the people of Israel for a king (whose disobedience is not mentioned here), suggesting that Paul criticizes not the behavior of Saul but of Israel (similar to 1 Sam 12). Neither the people of Israel who demanded a king nor the leaders of God's people, once they have been appointed, are immune to serious error. Human behavior (whether Saul's or Israel's) thwarts God's initiative.

13:22 When he had removed him, he gave them David as their king, about whom he testified, "I have found David son of Jesse a man after my heart, who will do everything I want him to do" (καὶ μεταστήσας αὐτὸν ἤγειρεν τὸν Δαυὶδ αὐτοῖς εἰς βασιλέα ᾧ καὶ εἶπεν μαρτυρήσας· εὗρον Δαυὶδ τὸν τοῦ Ἰεσσαί, ἄνδρα κατὰ τὴν καρδίαν μου, ὃς ποιήσει πάντα τὰ θελήματά μου). The seventh period of Israel's history is the appointment of King David. After God removed Saul,[24] he "gave" them David as the new king.[25] The verb "gave" (ἤγειρεν) is the same as the term used for Jesus' resurrection (vv. 30, 37), a fact that underlines David's role as the model (or type) of a ruler sent by God and faithful to his divine calling. The latter point is confirmed by a composite quotation from Scripture that combines three texts.

In Ps 89:20 (LXX 88:21) God says "I have found David my servant; with my sacred oil I have anointed him." That psalm is the longest presentation of David in the Psalter. It describes David's anointing and God's promise to David, i.e., the establishment of the Davidic dynasty based on God's covenant with David. The psalm calls on God to honor his covenant with David in a situation where God's wrath has been revealed against David's de-

---

19. 1 Sam 3:20. In Acts 3:24 Samuel is described as the first of the prophets. Only six summaries of Israel's history mention individual judges; cf. 1 Sam 12:11; Neh 9:27 – 28; Sir 46:11 – 12; *L.A.B.* 32; *1 En.* 89:39, 41; cf. 1 Macc 2:55. Cf. Jeska, *Geschichte Israels*, 225.

20. Cf. 1 Sam 8:5 – 10:25; 12:13.

21. The OT does not clearly specify the length of Saul's reign. Josephus, *Ant.* 6.378, asserts that Saul reigned for eigh-

teen years during the time of Samuel and twenty-two years after Samuel (in *Ant.* 10.143 he speaks of a twenty-year reign of Saul).

22. Cf. 1 Sam 9:3; 10:21; and 9:1; 10:20 – 21.

23. Cf. 9:4, 17; 22:7, 13; 26:14; and Rom 11:1; Phil 3:5.

24. Cf. 1 Sam 15:23, 26; 16:1.

25. Cf. 1 Sam 16:11 – 13.

scendants. The designation of David as "son of Jesse" occurs in several Old Testament passages.[26] Note that "son of Jesse" may not be only a title for David, as the historical David can be fused with the eschatological David in terms of the Davidic Messiah.[27]

In 1 Sam 13:14 God announced to Saul, who had disobeyed God's directive, that he would seek out a man after his own heart, who would be appointed ruler over his people.[28]

In Isa 44:28 the prophet describes King Cyrus as God's "shepherd," who will rebuild Jerusalem, with the phrase who "will accomplish all that I please" (cf. v. 22g). This task of King Cyrus can be understood in the context of Isaiah's new exodus motif: in Isa 40 – 55, a new deliverer is described who will deliver Israel from spiritual captivity. Cyrus is the only person whom Isaiah calls "anointed one" (Gk. χριστός; Isa 45:1). Thus, "Luke's Paul seems to have the image of the Davidic Messiah, who is the Isaianic New Exodus deliverer like Cyrus, in mind when using 'who will carry out all my will' for David."[29]

13:23 From this man's descendants God brought Jesus as Savior to Israel, according to his promise (τούτου ὁ θεὸς ἀπὸ τοῦ σπέρματος κατ᾽ ἐπαγγελίαν ἤγαγεν τῷ Ἰσραὴλ σωτῆρα Ἰησοῦν). The next element of Paul's sermon (vv. 16d – 25) consists of a brief statement concerning God's fulfillment of his promise in Jesus (v. 23). Paul ends his historical survey with David (around 1000 BC) and moves to Jesus, whom God "brought" as Savior to Israel

"according to [the] promise" (κατ᾽ ἐπαγγελίαν). The specific promise is not mentioned, but can hardly be any other text than 2 Sam 7:12, where God said to King David, "I will raise up your offspring to succeed you, your own flesh and blood, and I will establish his kingdom." Israel's prophets interpreted Nathan's oracle in terms of a future "David,"[30] an expectation understood in terms of a coming messianic king who would save and restore Israel.[31] The reference to Israel in v. 23 (and in v. 24) creates an inclusio with v. 17: Jesus and John the Baptist are part and parcel of God's intervention in the history of Israel in which God acts for the salvation of his people.

In the Old Testament it is God himself who is repeatedly described as "savior" (σωτήρ).[32] When Paul describes Jesus as Savior, he emphasizes that Jesus does what God does, that Jesus carries out God's will as the Servant of the Lord,[33] and that Jesus is the climax of salvation history fulfilling God's promises to his people. The connection between David and Jesus in vv. 22 – 23 involves two elements of Davidic messianism: Jesus came as the Davidic Messiah[34] who was a descendant of David, and he was typologically prefigured in David, God's chosen and righteous king who carried out God's will. Paul proclaims to the Jews and God-fearers in the synagogue in Pisidian Antioch that the promised messianic Savior has arrived, and that his name is Jesus.

13:24 – 25 Before his coming, John had proclaimed a baptism of repentance to all the people

---

26. 1 Chr 10:14; 29:26; Ps 72:20.

27. Cf. 2 Sam 23:1; 11QPsᵃ XXVII:2; XXVIII:3.

28. Cf. Miura, *David in Luke-Acts*, 179, who suggests that since David's "heart" in its relation to God is "fully reflected in the Psalms rather than in Samuel," the second phrase connotes the righteous sufferer of David in the psalm.

29. Miura, *David in Luke-Acts*, 181.

30. Cf. Jer 30:9; Hos 3:5; Ezek 37:24 – 25.

31. Cf. Dan 9:25; *Pss. Sol.* 17:21 – 34; Fitzmyer, *Acts*, 511.

32. Isa 45:15, 21. Cf. related words in 2 Sam 22:3; Pss 17:7; 106:21; Isa 43:3, 11; 60:16; Hos 13:4. Note Isa 43:11, "I, even I, am the Lord, and part from me there is no savior."

33. Cf. Isa 49:6, where the Servant of the Lord restores the tribes of Jacob and is "a light for the Gentiles," carrying God's "salvation … to the ends of the earth."

34. For Jesus' Davidic descent cf. Matt 1:1; Mark 12:35; Luke 3:23, 31; Rom 1:3; 2 Tim 2:8.

of Israel. **As John was completing his mission, he said, "What do you suppose me to be? I am not the one. But there is one who will come after me the sandals of whose feet I am not worthy to untie"** (προκηρύξαντος Ἰωάννου πρὸ προσώπου τῆς εἰσόδου αὐτοῦ βάπτισμα μετανοίας παντὶ τῷ λαῷ Ἰσραήλ. ὡς δὲ ἐπλήρου Ἰωάννης τὸν δρόμον, ἔλεγεν· τί ἐμὲ ὑπονοεῖτε εἶναι; οὐκ εἰμὶ ἐγώ· ἀλλ᾽ ἰδοὺ ἔρχεται μετ᾽ ἐμὲ οὗ οὐκ εἰμὶ ἄξιος τὸ ὑπόδημα τῶν ποδῶν λῦσαι). The fourth element of the first part of Paul's sermon explains the proclamation of John the Baptist, who was active before Jesus came (vv. 24 – 25).

(1) John's ministry took place "before his coming," i.e., before Jesus' entry into his public ministry. John was Jesus' forerunner, who preached at the transition from God's history of salvation linked with Israel to God's history of salvation linked with Jesus, in and through whom he fulfilled his promises given to Israel. His "mission" or "course of life" (δρόμος, v. 25a) consisted of announcing Jesus' "coming" (εἴσοδος) on the stage of history.[35]

(2) John's proclaimed a "baptism of repentance" (βάπτισμα μετανοίας). The genitive is, in a Jewish context, a subjective genitive: John called people to repent and be immersed in water as an expression of their repentance. He summoned the Jewish people to turn away from ignorance and guilt, to confess sin, and to give up wickedness and evil (see on 2:38).

(3) John addressed his message of repentance to "all the people of Israel," to the devout and law-abiding Jews as well as those who did not care about God's will as revealed in the law.

(4) John asked all people to demonstrate their repentance through public immersion in water (βάπτισμα) that proclaimed the admission of sin, a change of mind and heart, and a willingness to live a life in accordance to God's will.

(5) John preached that the promised Messiah was about to appear (v. 25). He rejected the suggestion that he was the Messiah.[36] At the same time he clarified that his ministry was connected with the coming of the Savior. John emphasized the fact (ἰδού) that a person would come after him who was infinitely superior, so much so that he, John, the acclaimed prophet, was "not worthy" (οὐκ ... ἄξιος) even to perform the menial task of untying Jesus' sandals.[37]

13:26 Brothers, descendants of Abraham's family and you who are God-fearers, the message of this salvation has been sent to us (ἄνδρες ἀδελφοί, υἱοὶ γένους Ἀβραὰμ καὶ οἱ ἐν ὑμῖν φοβούμενοι τὸν θεόν, ἡμῖν ὁ λόγος τῆς σωτηρίας ταύτης ἐξαπεστάλη). Moving now to the second part of his sermon (vv. 26 – 37), Paul explains the significance of Jesus in three steps. He begins this new section with a new direct address of the listeners, an address that modifies the address of v. 16d-e. Instead of addressing them as "people of Israel and you who are God-fearers," he addresses the audience more intimately as "brothers" (ἄνδρες ἀδελφοί; see on 1:16), among whom are "descendants of Abraham's family" and "God-fearers" (v. 26a-c). The connection between the Jewish listeners in the synagogue and Abraham links the following explanation of the significance of Jesus with the history of salvation that began with God's election of and promises to Abraham, and it emphasizes the responsibility of the listeners

---

35. Note that Luke describes Jesus' ministry as a "way" (ὁδός), Luke 3:4; 7:27, a term that he also uses to describe the faith and life of the followers of Jesus, Acts 9:2; 19:9, 23; 22:4; 24:14, 22. Cf. Fitzmyer, *Acts*, 513.

36. Cf. John 1:19 – 23. On the variant readings and the grammar of Acts 13:25, which do not alter the meaning,

cf. Barrett, *Acts*, 638.

37. Cf. Luke 3:16, where the wording is slightly different; cf. Mark 1:7; John 1:27. Note the later text *b. Ketub.* 96a, where R. Joshua b. Levi says, "A disciple should do for his teacher anything a slave would do — except take off his shoes."

to ascertain that they are worthy representatives of the history of salvation.

Paul explains the significance of Jesus by underlining the relevance of the gospel of Jesus Christ for the audience (v. 26d). The "message" (ὁ λόγος) that Paul is about to proclaim "has been sent" by God (ἐξαπεστάλη; divine passive). Its content is "this salvation" (τῆς σωτηρίας ταύτης), i.e., the salvation mentioned in v. 23 — the fulfillment of God's promises to Israel through Jesus, who is Israel's Savior. In vv. 38 – 39 Paul will explain "this salvation" in more detail as being set free from sins, even those that could not be forgiven by the law. Paul mentions the addressees of this message in emphasized position at the beginning of the clause: God sent the message of salvation "to us" (ἡμῖν), i.e., to the Jews and to all who worship the one true God.

13:27 – 29 The residents of Jerusalem and their leaders failed to recognize him; and when they condemned him, they fulfilled the oracles of the prophets that are read every Sabbath. Even though they found no basis for a death sentence, they asked Pilate to have him executed. When they had carried out everything that was written about him, they took him down from the cross and laid him in a tomb (οἱ γὰρ κατοικοῦντες ἐν Ἰερουσαλὴμ καὶ οἱ ἄρχοντες αὐτῶν τοῦτον ἀγνοήσαντες καὶ τὰς φωνὰς τῶν προφητῶν τὰς κατὰ πᾶν σάββατον ἀναγινωσκομένας κρίναντες ἐπλήρωσαν, καὶ μηδεμίαν αἰτίαν θανάτου εὑρόντες ᾐτήσαντο Πιλᾶτον ἀναιρεθῆναι αὐτόν. ὡς δὲ ἐτέλεσαν πάντα τὰ περὶ αὐτοῦ γεγραμμένα, καθελόντες ἀπὸ τοῦ ξύλου ἔθηκαν εἰς μνημεῖον). The second step of Paul's explanation of the

significance of Jesus focuses on Jesus' execution (vv. 27 – 29). While his ministry was focused on Galilee, Paul indicts the Jerusalem Jews for Jesus' death — in particular the Jewish leaders, i.e., the high priest, the chief priests, and the members of the Sanhedrin.[38] Paul explains Jesus' execution as follows.

(1) The Jews "failed to recognize" (ἀγνοήσαντες) Jesus (v. 27a-c); i.e., they failed to understand that Jesus was Israel's Savior through whom God fulfilled his promises to their fathers.

(2) They "condemned" Jesus; i.e., they convicted him in the trial before the Sanhedrin and sentenced him to death (v. 27d). According to the gospel accounts, Jesus was condemned in the Jewish trial as a blasphemer.[39]

(3) Their condemnation of Jesus "fulfilled [ἐπλήρωσαν] the oracles of the prophets" (v. 27e-f) — unwittingly, since they heard the Prophets read in the synagogue every Sabbath (cf. v. 15). Despite their reading and hearing of the Scriptures, they did not recognize how their prophecies related to Jesus as Israel's Savior. Paul probably thinks of texts such as Isa 53:3 and Ps 118:22. The rejection and execution of Jesus fulfilled Scripture.[40]

(4) The Jewish leaders did not "find" any basis for a death sentence (v. 28a).[41] The gospel accounts suggest that the Jewish leaders accused Jesus before Pilate as being a seducer of the people, who proclaimed heretical teachings, and as a demagogue, who led the masses astray.[42] Even though Pilate concluded in the Roman trial that Jesus was not guilty of a crime,[43] the Jewish leaders still asked him for Jesus to be executed (v. 28b-c). Luke relates that when Pilate announced his conclusion

---

38. Cf. 4:5, 8, 23.

39. Cf. Matt 26:62 – 66; Mark 14:60 – 64; cf. Luke 22:66 – 71, where the term "blasphemy" is not used.

40. Cf. 1:16; Luke 18:31; 22:37.

41. Cf. BDAG, s.v. αἰτία 3, "a basis for legal action" (legal terminus technicus); sense 3a, "charge, ground for complaint":

the expression αἰτία θανάτου corresponds to Latin *causa capitalis*, "reason/grounds for capital punishment."

42. Cf. *m. Sanh.* 7:1 – 10; *y. Sanh.* 25d (5 – 10).

43. Cf. Luke 23:4, 14 – 15, 22, Pilate's threefold declaration of Jesus' innocence. Cf. John 18:38; 19:4, 6.

that Jesus was innocent, the Jews kept shouting, "Crucify him! Crucify him!" (Luke 23:21).

(5) The execution of Jesus, initiated by the Jews of Jerusalem and carried out by Pilate, the Roman governor, was not an unfortunate miscarriage of justice but the fulfillment of "everything" that the prophets had written about him (v. 29a-b).

(6) They took Jesus down from the cross[44] and placed him in a tomb (v. 29c-d).[45]

13:30 – 31 But God raised him from the dead, and for many days he was seen by those who had come with him from Galilee to Jerusalem, who are now his witnesses before the people (ὁ δὲ θεὸς ἤγειρεν αὐτὸν ἐκ νεκρῶν, ὃς ὤφθη ἐπὶ ἡμέρας πλείους τοῖς συναναβᾶσιν αὐτῷ ἀπὸ τῆς Γαλιλαίας εἰς Ἰερουσαλήμ, οἵτινες νῦν εἰσιν μάρτυρες αὐτοῦ πρὸς τὸν λαόν). The third step of Paul's explanation of the significance of Jesus highlights his resurrection (vv. 31 – 37). Paul first explains the fact of Jesus' resurrection (vv. 30 – 31). The following points are central.

(1) God "raised him" (ἤγειρεν) from the dead (v. 30).[46] Just as God had revealed himself during the history of salvation in mighty acts that repeatedly saved Israel from her enemies, he has now sent a Savior to his people, Jesus, (v. 23), whom he raised "from the dead," implying that the basic problem of the reality of sin and its nexus with death has been solved. The same contrast is emphasized in 2:24; 10:39 – 40.

(2) Jesus "was seen" (ὤφθη; see on 9:17) for many days (v. 31a-d).[47] The reality of Jesus' resurrection was such that his disciples and others who

had come with him from Galilee to Jerusalem[48] saw him alive with their own eyes after his crucifixion and burial. These were the witnesses who knew that Jesus, who proclaimed the kingdom of God in Galilee, was the Jesus who was crucified in Jerusalem, buried, and raised from the dead. In 1 Cor 15:8 Paul describes his own encounter with the risen Jesus on the road to Damascus[49] with the same verbal form (ὤφθη): he is one of those who have seen Jesus and who can speak of his resurrection with the authority of an eyewitness.

(3) The reality of Jesus' resurrection is proclaimed by these "witnesses" (μάρτυρες) who have seen the crucified and risen Jesus (v. 31e-f).[50] This proclamation is taking place "now" (νῦν), "before the people" of Israel.

13:32 – 33 And we proclaim to you the good news that God's promise to our ancestors has been realized; God has fulfilled this promise for us, their children, by raising up Jesus, as it is written in the second psalm: "You are my Son; today I have begotten you" (καὶ ἡμεῖς ὑμᾶς εὐαγγελιζόμεθα τὴν πρὸς τοὺς πατέρας ἐπαγγελίαν γενομένην, ὅτι ταύτην ὁ θεὸς ἐκπεπλήρωκεν τοῖς τέκνοις αὐτῶν ἡμῖν ἀναστήσας Ἰησοῦν ὡς καὶ ἐν τῷ ψαλμῷ γέγραπται τῷ δευτέρῳ· υἱός μου εἶ σύ, ἐγὼ σήμερον γεγέννηκά σε). Paul next emphasizes that Jesus' resurrection represents the fulfillment of God's promises in Psalm 2, a fact that confirms Jesus as God's Son.

(1) Paul and Barnabas "proclaim ... the good news" (εὐαγγελιζόμεθα; v. 32a).[51] The news of Jesus'

---

44. For the use of "tree" (ξύλον) for "cross," see 5:30; 10:39; Gal 3:13; cf. Deut 21:22. Cf. BDAG, s.v. ξύλον 2c. In the present context, "they" refers to the Jews as Jesus' enemies (although a reference to Pilate mentioned in v. 28 is possible, as his soldiers carried out the execution mentioned in v. 29). According to Luke 23:50 – 52; John 19:38 it was Joseph of Arimathea who took Jesus' body down from the cross.

45. Cf. Luke 23:53; John 19:41 – 42.

46. Cf. 3:15; 4:10; 10:40.

47. Cf. 1:3, where Luke asserts that Jesus was seen after his resurrection for "forty days."

48. Cf. Luke 9:51; 18:31; 19:28; 23:49; Acts 1:21 – 22; 10:39, 41. Cf. Jervell, *Apostelgeschichte*, 358.

49. Cf. 9:3 – 5; 22:6 – 9; 26:13 – 16.

50. Cf. Luke 24:48; Acts 1:8; 2:32; 3:15; 5:32; 10:39, 41.

51. For the verb "proclaim good news" (εὐαγγελίζομαι) see on 5:42.

death and resurrection is "good news" because it conveys the fulfillment of God's promises to the fathers — the climax of the history of salvation has arrived with Jesus, Israel's Savior (v. 23).

(2) This good news is proclaimed "to you" (v. 32a), i.e., to the Jews and the God-fearers in the synagogue of Antioch (vv. 16, 26), and, as will become obvious before long, to the Gentiles living in Antioch as well (vv. 46 – 47).

(3) God's "promise" (ἐπαγγελία) to the fathers "has been realized" (v. 32b). This "promise" is the promise God made to David, namely, that one of his descendants would be raised up to become Israel's Savior. Paul asserts that this promise has become a reality in and through the death and resurrection of Jesus.

(4) Paul presents Jesus as the fulfillment of Ps 2:7 (v. 33). The first of three quotations from Scripture is given a precise location (the only such instance in the New Testament): the resurrection of Jesus "fulfills" what is written "in the second psalm." Paul quotes Ps 2:7, where God says, "You are my son [υἱός μου]; today I have begotten [γεγέννηκα] you" (NRSV). This text is linked with 2 Sam 7:14 via the expression "my son" (ἔσται μοι εἰς υἱόν).[52] Psalm 2 describes the opposition of the nations and their rulers against the Anointed of the Lord, i.e., against the ruler of God's people; in this context Ps 2:7 refers to the legitimacy of Israel's king as "son of God," as ruler who is given the assurance of God's care and protection.

The interpretation is complicated by the fact that the term "begotten" (γεγέννηκα) denotes, understood in a strict sense, procreation, which makes the term "today" (σήμερον), addressed to the child,

difficult. This can be resolved if the statement is understood in the sense "[I declare to you] today [I begat you]," which could be associated with the enthronement of the king or with the renewal of God's promise to the monarch.[53]

In some traditions of Second Temple Judaism, Psalm 2 was interpreted in terms of the Messiah.[54] Some interpreters refer this statement to God's voice heard at Jesus' baptism (Luke 3:22), suggesting that it was at his baptism that Jesus was "begotten" or "adopted" by God. This interpretation can be ruled out since the occasion on which Jesus, the Son, was "begotten" (γεγέννηκα) by God is linked in v. 33 with Jesus being "raised up" (ἀναστήσας) by God, an expression that fits either Jesus' resurrection or Jesus' being raised up as Messiah at his birth.

Other scholars interpret the application of Ps 2:7 to Jesus in terms of the resurrection (described in v. 34 with ἀνέστησεν) as the event in which Jesus was "begotten" by God: Jesus' divine sonship was made evident by Jesus' resurrection from the dead.[55] More likely is the interpretation of "begotten" in terms of Jesus' being raised up as Messiah at his birth (parallel to the raising up of David as king, described in v. 22 with ἤγειρεν, which is a synonym of ἀναστήσας).[56] Paul asserts that Jesus is the Son of David and the Son of God — the Messiah and Savior of Israel, whom God promised in Scripture.

13:34 He raised him from the dead so that he will not return to corruption. As God has said, "I will grant you the unfailing assurances made to David" (ὅτι δὲ ἀνέστησεν αὐτὸν ἐκ νεκρῶν μηκέτι μέλλοντα ὑποστρέφειν εἰς διαφθοράν, οὕτως

---

52. For the exegetical method of *gezerah shawah*, see on 2:34.

53. Marshall, "Acts," 585; cf. ibid. for the following discussion.

54. Cf. *Pss. Sol.* 17:26.

55. Cf. Fitzmyer, *Acts*, 517; Bock, *Acts*, 456. Cf. Rom 1:3 – 4

and Heb 1:5; 5:5, which associate Jesus' sonship with his resurrection.

56. Barrett, *Acts*, 645 – 46; Marshall, "Acts," 585. Strauss, *Davidic Messiah*, 162 – 66, interprets v. 33 in terms of the entire ministry of Jesus from his birth to his resurrection and exaltation.

εἴρηκεν ὅτι δώσω ὑμῖν τὰ ὅσια Δαυὶδ τὰ πιστά). After confirming Jesus' messianic status as Son of David and Son of God from Scripture, Paul turns to Jesus' resurrection. He explains that when God "raised" (ἀνέστησεν) Jesus from the dead, Jesus was not simply brought back to life (like the son of the widow in Nain, Luke 7:11 – 17, who would have died later), but in such a manner that he "will not return" to a state where his body could decay. When God raised Jesus from the dead, he received incorruptible, everlasting life — the prerequisite for his being the Savior of the present generation of Israelites, God-fearers, and Gentiles for all time.

Paul substantiates this point with a quotation from Isa 55:3: God promises to exiled Israel that he will grant them the "assurances made to David" (τὰ ὅσια Δαυὶδ), which are "unfailing" (τὰ πιστά). In Hebrew, Isa 55:3 is linked via the expression "faithful love to David" with 2 Sam 7:15, where the same term is related to David, and with 2 Sam 7:16, where the verb "to show oneself faithful" is used. In the context of Isa 55:3, the people of Israel are invited to receive God's gifts and live. The divine promises to David include an eternal covenant with the people of Israel, a covenant that consists of acts of faithful love, as well as David's role as witness among the nations.

Paul emphasizes with the quotation of Isa 55:3 that Jesus, the messianic Son of David (2 Sam 7:14 – 16) and Son of God (Ps 2:7), whom God raised from the dead, has been granted everlasting dominion that is relevant for "you" (ὑμῖν), i.e., for the Jewish people whom he addresses. In other words, "the faithfulness of God to David will continue to be shown to a later generation by God's raising up of Jesus to be the author of forgiveness and justification."[57] The "holy things" or "assurances" (τὰ ὅσια) — in Isaiah, the covenant with David — refer to "the larger complex of salvation blessings (i.e., life in the kingdom of God) which includes God's 'raising up' a promised heir to David and the establishment of an eternal kingship and dominion and inheritance for the people of God, as was promised to Israel's ancestral leaders."[58]

13:35 – 37 So he also said in another passage: "You will not let your Holy One see corruption." For when David had served God's purpose in his own generation, he fell asleep and was gathered to his ancestors, and experienced corruption. But the one whom God raised from the dead did not experience corruption (διότι καὶ ἐν ἑτέρῳ λέγει· οὐ δώσεις τὸν ὅσιόν σου ἰδεῖν διαφθοράν. Δαυὶδ μὲν γὰρ ἰδίᾳ γενεᾷ ὑπηρετήσας τῇ τοῦ θεοῦ βουλῇ ἐκοιμήθη καὶ προσετέθη πρὸς τοὺς πατέρας αὐτοῦ καὶ εἶδεν διαφθοράν· ὃν δὲ ὁ θεὸς ἤγειρεν, οὐκ εἶδεν διαφθοράν). Paul's third quotation is from Ps 16:10 (LXX 15:10),[59] a text connected with Isa 55:3 via the word "the Holy One" (τὸν ὅσιόν; Isa 55:3 has τὰ ὅσια), and via the expression translated as "you will not let" (οὐ δώσεις; the reformulated quotation of Isa 55:3 in v. 34 has δώσω).

Psalm 16 is also connected with 2 Sam 7:12: "when your days are over and you rest with your ancestors, I will raise up your offspring [σπέρμα] to succeed you, your own flesh and blood, and I will establish his kingdom." These texts emphasize the eternal dominion of Jesus the Messiah, who has been raised from the dead. Paul interprets the promise to David (2 Sam 7:12 – 16), whose reliability God himself confirmed (Isa 55:3) — the promise that God will not let his Holy One, i.e., the

---

57. Marshall, "Acts," 586. Cf. Mallen, *Isaiah in Luke-Acts*, 110.

58. Anderson, *Jesus' Resurrection*, 254; cf. ibid. 249 – 54 for a discussion of other interpretations. See also Bock, *Proclamation*, 252 – 54.

59. Ps 16:10 has already been quoted at 2:27; see there for details.

messianic "seed" of David, see corruption — with reference to Jesus' resurrection.

Paul interprets Ps 16:10 in terms of its application. He argues, similarly to Peter's argument in 2:27 – 31, that "the Holy One" whose body did not decay cannot be David. Paul makes four statements about David in v. 36. (1) He "served" God's purpose; i.e., he obediently and faithfully carried out the will of God in his own generation. (2) When David had completed his life during which he served God's purpose, he "fell asleep," i.e., he died (see on 7:60). (3) When he had died, he was "gathered to his ancestors,"[60] which means either that he joined his ancestors in the grave; i.e., he was buried, or that he died and joined his ancestors in Sheol. (4) David's body "experienced corruption," i.e., decayed in the grave.

Since the words of Ps 16:10 cannot refer to David, they must refer to someone else. Paul argues that God's announcement in this passage refers to "the one whom God raised from the dead," i.e., Jesus (vv. 30, 34). Jesus died and was buried (vv. 28 – 29), but God raised him from the dead with the result that he did not experience corruption; i.e., Jesus' body did not decay in the grave — which means that he is alive and is thus indeed Israel's promised Savior (v. 23), a point that Paul emphasizes in the next sentence.

13:38 – 39 Therefore I want you to know, brothers, that through him forgiveness of sins is proclaimed to you and that from all those things from which you could not be justified by the law of Moses, by this man everyone who believes is justified (γνωστὸν οὖν ἔστω ὑμῖν, ἄνδρες ἀδελφοί, ὅτι διὰ τούτου ὑμῖν ἄφεσις ἁμαρτιῶν καταγγέλλεται, καὶ ἀπὸ πάντων ὧν οὐκ ἠδυνήθητε ἐν νόμῳ Μωϋσέως δικαιωθῆναι, ἐν τούτῳ πᾶς ὁ πιστεύων δικαιοῦται). In the third unit of his ser-

mon, marked by another direct address of the audience as "brothers," Paul draws his conclusion from the significance of Jesus that he has just explained, calling the Jews and God-fearers in the synagogue to repentance (vv. 38 – 41). This is the climax of Paul's sermon, whom the Lord had chosen as his instrument to take the news of Jesus, Israel's Messiah and the Savior of the world, to Jews and Gentiles (9:15). The introductory phrase "therefore I want you to know" takes Jesus' resurrection as the basis for the assertion that God now forgives sins through Jesus. Luke summarizes the content (introduced by ὅτι) of Paul's exhortation by emphasizing several elements.

(1) The good news that Paul and Barnabas "proclaim" in the synagogue in Antioch is the result of God's climactic intervention in the history of Israel (vv. 16 – 25) in the death and resurrection of Jesus (vv. 27 – 37), who is Israel's Savior (v. 23). It is a message that is relevant for them, a message they need to know (v. 38a). This is the first imperative in Paul's "word of exhortation" that he was invited to give to the congregation (v. 15). Linked with the subsequent reference to God's offer of forgiveness of sins, the "supply [of] the hearers with the necessary information" is an implicit call to repentance.[61]

(2) God offers "forgiveness of sins" (ἄφεσις ἁμαρτιῶν; see on 2:38) through Jesus — through the one (διὰ τούτου, in emphatic position in v. 38c-d) who was executed by Pilate with the help of the Jews of Jerusalem by crucifixion and who was raised from the dead (vv. 27 – 37). Whereas the forgiveness of sins was tied in Israel's history to the tabernacle and then to Jerusalem and to the sacrificial system connected with the temple, God's pardon for human sin is now linked with the crucified and risen Jesus, who is thus Israel's Savior (v. 23). God extends this offer of forgiveness of

---

60. The expression is often used in the Old Testament; cf. Judg 2:10; 2 Kgs 22:20; cf. 1 Kgs 2:10.

61. Soards, *Speeches*, 87.

sins through Paul, who is one of Jesus' witnesses (cf. v. 31).

(3) God's offer of forgiveness through Jesus pertains to "all those things" from which people could not be acquitted by the Mosaic law (v. 38g-h). This formulation suggests to some that according to Paul, the Mosaic law could provide for the forgiveness for some sins, but not for others.[62] It is more likely that Paul asserts that while the law may provide for the atonement of sins through sacrifice, it could not bring complete forgiveness and was thus inadequate. Paul's main point is clear: the forgiveness that God provides through Jesus is total forgiveness, an acquittal from everything, without exception, that separates sinners from a righteous God.

(4) God's offer of forgiveness through Jesus means that God "declares righteous" or "justifies" (δικαιοῦται) everyone who believes (v. 39). Luke does not elaborate on this theme of justification. In the context of Paul's letters to the Christians in Galatia and in Rome, in which this word group plays a central role,[63] the meaning of the verb is sufficiently clear: to "declare righteous" or "justify"[64] means to acquit someone in a trial in which accusations of being guilty of wrongdoing have been made, to pronounce and treat the accused person as righteous. If an accused person is declared righteous, they are vindicated, not punished. The image that the Greek terms present speaks of a forensic or legal setting in which all human beings, who are all sinners, stand before the tribunal of the divine Judge. Paul emphasizes that God acquits sinners of their sin and guilt as a result of Jesus' death and resurrection.

(5) The basis of God's forgiveness of sins is two-fold: the acquittal of the sinner has been made possible "by this man" (ἐν τούτῳ, v. 39), i.e., by the crucified and risen Jesus (vv. 27 – 37); and the forgiveness of sins is open to "everyone who believes" (πᾶς ὁ πιστεύων, v. 39). In other words, the basis of God's forgiveness now is the death and resurrection of Jesus, and it is through the faith of sinners who place their confidence in Jesus for the forgiveness of sins that they are justified. That is, God forgives sinners their sins and acquits them of their guilt if and when they believe that the crucified and risen Jesus is the promised Savior, the messianic Son of David and Son of God. The present active participle of the verb "believes" indicates that this "faith" involves a continuous, ongoing commitment to Jesus as Savior. The scope of the forgiveness of sins and the acquittal of the sinner through Jesus is "everyone" (v. 39) — Jews and God-fearers, and Gentiles as well (vv. 46 – 47).

13:40 – 41 Beware, then, that what the prophets said does not happen to you: "Look, you scoffers, be alarmed and perish, for I am doing a deed in your days, a deed which you will not believe even if someone told you" (βλέπετε οὖν μὴ ἐπέλθῃ τὸ εἰρημένον ἐν τοῖς προφήταις· ἴδετε, οἱ καταφρονηταί, καὶ θαυμάσατε καὶ ἀφανίσθητε, ὅτι ἔργον ἐργάζομαι ἐγὼ ἐν ταῖς ἡμέραις ὑμῶν, ἔργον ὃ οὐ μὴ πιστεύσητε ἐάν τις ἐκδιηγῆται ὑμῖν). Paul concludes with the warning not to ignore the work of God, who offers forgiveness of sins through Jesus, the crucified and risen Savior. The second imperative in Paul's "word of exhortation" ("beware," βλέπετε) implies the warning to make sure that listeners do not fail to learn the lesson of Hab 1:5, namely, that the consequence of refusing God's

---

62. In theory the law could provide forgiveness only for sins committed unwittingly, not for sins committed deliberately; cf. Marshall, "Acts," 587, who comments that "the practical situation must have been different."

63. Cf. Rom 2:13; 3:4, 20, 24, 26, 28, 30; 4:2, 5; 5:1, 9; 6:7;

8:30, 33; Gal 2:16, 17; 3:8, 11, 24; 5:4.

64. The English translations render the verb (δικαιοῦται) as follows: "is declared right with God" (NLT); "is justified" (NET, NIV 1984); "is set free" (GNB, NRSV, NIV, cf. NASB, ESV). Cf. BDAG, s.v. δικαιόω 2bβ.

gracious offer is a disaster. If they do not come to faith in Jesus and accept God's offer of forgiveness linked with Jesus' death and resurrection, "what the prophets said" will "happen" to them.

The quotation from Hab 1:5 (LXX) in v. 41 underlines the urgency of Paul's message, and it anticipates the rejection that follows. In the Hebrew context, Habakkuk formulates a warning to the Jewish people of his time that God will "perform a work" that they will find hard to believe: he will cause the Babylonians to invade their country as an instrument of God's judgment. The prophet "does not offer the usual comfort but announces an attack by a cruel nation which will set Israel's wickedness right by a devastating judgment."[65] The point is that

> God is already at work. Habakkuk and his hearers would be surprised at the Lord's answer. Who could expect that the Lord would use such a wicked instrument to judge a nation more righteous than they?... The Lord's answer indicates his sovereignty. He is not bound by the listener's whims or by their standards of "fairness." He responds according to his sovereign will. He is the Lord of history who works in history to accomplish his purpose.[66]

The interpretation of Hab 1:5 in Qumran (in 1QpHab II, 1 – 10) applies the divine judgment to the apostates refusing to follow the Teacher of Righteousness, who issued warnings concerning events in the future carried out by the Kittim.

Paul warns his audience — "look" (ἴδετε) is the third imperative in his sermon — not to be "scoffers," i.e., not to treat God's warning and God's work with contempt. If they do not accept God's work, they will be "alarmed" to find that they will "per-ish" — the fourth and fifth imperatives in Paul's sermon express the urgent warning directed against people who refuse to believe (v. 39) the work that God is doing. This "work" (ἔργον) that God has accomplished is Jesus' resurrection, which is

> the goal of God's saving purpose for Israel. It is the fulfilment of the promises to Israel's ancestors that have been summed up in God's covenant with David that he would enthrone one of his descendants as head of an eternal kingdom. Consequently, belief in "this one" (i.e., the risen Jesus) will result in forgiveness of sins and justification apart from the Law of Moses. Rejection will result in eschatological destruction.[67]

Paul calls on the audience in the synagogue not to rebuff the offer of salvation that God is making through him and Barnabas, but to come to faith in Jesus as Israel's Savior.

13:42 As they were leaving, the people requested that they speak further about these matters on the following Sabbath (ἐξιόντων δὲ αὐτῶν παρεκάλουν εἰς τὸ μεταξὺ σάββατον λαληθῆναι αὐτοῖς τὰ ῥήματα ταῦτα). The third incident of the Pisidian Antioch episode relates the consolidation and expansion of missionary work in seven phases (vv. 42 – 49). Luke begins by noting the desire of the Jews and God-fearers who heard Paul's word of exhortation to receive further instruction. His description is again vivid: as Paul and Barnabas "were leaving" the room or building in which the congregation was meeting, the listeners "requested" that they speak about "these matters" (τὰ ῥήματα ταῦτα) on the following Sabbath. This request suggests that the invitation to speak in the next synagogue service was expressed by the officials of the synagogue (cf. v. 15).

---

65. Brevard S. Childs, *Introduction to the Old Testament as Scripture* (Philadelphia: Fortress, 1977), 451.

66. Waylon Bailey, "Nahum, Habakkuk, Zephaniah," in *Micah, Nahum, Habakkuk, Zephaniah* (Kenneth L. Barker and Waylon Bailey; NAC 20; Nashville: Broadman & Holman, 1999), 302.

67. Anderson, *Jesus' Resurrection*, 258.

13:43 After the meeting of the synagogue had broken up, many of the Jews and devout proselytes followed Paul and Barnabas, who continued to speak to them, urging them to continue in the grace of God (λυθείσης δὲ τῆς συναγωγῆς ἠκολούθησαν πολλοὶ τῶν Ἰουδαίων καὶ τῶν σεβομένων προσηλύτων τῷ Παύλῳ καὶ τῷ Βαρναβᾷ, οἵτινες προσλαλοῦντες αὐτοῖς ἔπειθον αὐτοὺς προσμένειν τῇ χάριτι τοῦ θεοῦ). Luke reports a second, different reaction from those present in the synagogue. When the meeting ended, many Jews and proselytes were attracted by Paul's explanation of the significance of Jesus as Savior. They "followed" the missionaries; i.e., they accompanied them (literally) to the place where they were staying, where they received further instruction. The present participle translated as "continued to speak" (προσλαλοῦντες) and the imperfect "urging" (ἔπειθον) describe the ongoing process of oral instruction.

The comment in v. 43b-c indicates that "many" do come to faith in Jesus, either as a direct result of Paul's first sermon or as a result of further instruction. The missionaries urge the Jews and proselytes following them to "continue in the grace of God." The latter expression refers to the "favor" (χάρις; see on 4:33) of God, who forgives sins and justifies sinners who believe in Jesus (vv. 38 – 39) as Israel's crucified and risen Savior (vv. 26 – 37). The Jews and proselytes who accept Paul's message about the fulfillment of God's promises through the resurrection of the crucified Jesus receive God's grace. A new community of believers is emerging.

13:44 On the next Sabbath almost the whole city gathered to hear the word of the Lord (τῷ δὲ ἐρχομένῳ σαββάτῳ σχεδὸν πᾶσα ἡ πόλις συνήχθη ἀκοῦσαι τὸν λόγον τοῦ κυρίου). The next phase of Paul's missionary work in Pisidian Antioch is a large gathering on the second Sabbath that the missionaries are in town. Luke relates a large gathering of people who want to hear Paul explain further the significance of Jesus as Savior, a message that is again described as "the word of the Lord" (cf. 8:25; 11:16). Besides the Jews, proselytes, and God-fearers who had been in the synagogue the week before (vv. 16, 26, 43), "almost the whole city" comes together, i.e., a crowd that includes many Gentiles.

Most scholars interpret the phrase "almost the whole city" as a hyperbolic comment that is meant to show that the missionaries have a large audience. The qualification "almost" (σχεδόν) and the description of the initially ambiguous reaction of the listeners suggest that Luke has a mass gathering in mind with probably several thousand people wanting to hear Paul speak. It should be noted that Luke does not claim that the large crowd gathers in the synagogue. Obviously the synagogue in Antioch could not have accommodated thousands of people. The crowd could have gathered in front of the synagogue (whose location has not been established), or perhaps in the large open space of the *Tiberia Platea* in front of the temple of Augustus, or in the square called *Augusta Platea* at the northern end of the main street (the *cardo maximus*), or in the theater. If indeed Paul arrived in the city with a letter of introduction from the governor of Cyprus, and if he was able to establish contact with the leading aristocratic families in the city during the first days of his visit, it is not impossible that several thousand people gather to hear Paul speak.

13:45 When the Jews saw the crowds, they were filled with zeal and contradicted what Paul said, slandering him (ἰδόντες δὲ οἱ Ἰουδαῖοι τοὺς ὄχλους ἐπλήσθησαν ζήλου καὶ ἀντέλεγον τοῖς ὑπὸ Παύλου λαλουμένοις βλασφημοῦντες). The reaction of Jews that Luke describes could be related to the large "crowds" of mostly Gentile listeners; more plausibly it may describe the reaction of Jews after the large gathering that results in the conversion of an unspecified number of Gentiles (v. 48).

Luke describes a threefold reaction of "the Jews," i.e., Jews who had not come to faith in Jesus (v. 43), possibly especially the officials of the synagogue. They were "filled with zeal" (ἐπλήσθησαν ζήλου), they "contradicted" (ἀντέλεγον) what Paul said, and they "slandered" (βλασφημοῦντες) Paul. The fact that the verb translated as "filled" is formulated with the aorist, and the two subsequent verbal forms with the imperfect indicative and the present participle respectively, suggests that their "zeal" was the basis for the ongoing reaction of contradiction and slander. Because they were "zealous," they spoke against Paul's message (presumably in future synagogue services) and slandered him[68] (both in the synagogue and in public before Gentiles). The slander may have involved the utterance of blasphemies, probably against Jesus, presumably pronouncing the curse of the Torah (Deut 21:22 – 23) upon the crucified Jesus.

The term translated as "zeal" (ζῆλος) has been interpreted in terms of the Jews' zeal for the law or in terms of their envy or jealousy regarding the missionary success of Paul and Barnabas; some interpreters combine the theological and the psychological explanations. The social situation of the Jewish diaspora communities in the historical context of the first century must have played a role as well. The Jews of Pisidian Antioch certainly opposed Paul and Barnabas because they disagreed with their teaching.

However, there are reasons to believe that the significance of maintaining their religious and ethnic identity also played an important role in their forceful and sometimes violent reaction. The Jews of Asia Minor were surely concerned to preserve the social and political rights and privileges they had enjoyed since Julius Caesar and which had come under pressure in different places at different times — rights and privileges that might be jeopardized if the movement of the followers of Jesus were ignored. That man, after all, had been executed by the Roman governor of Judea (v. 28). Also, the Jews of Asia Minor might have been motivated by concerns regarding the financial strength of their community, and they were probably also concerned to avoid actions or to tolerate developments that contravened decisions made by the leadership of the Jewish commonwealth in Judea.[69]

13:46 Then both Paul and Barnabas spoke out fearlessly: "It was necessary that the word of God should be proclaimed to you first. Because you reject it and do not consider yourselves worthy of eternal life, we now turn to the Gentiles" (παρρησιασάμενοί τε ὁ Παῦλος καὶ ὁ Βαρναβᾶς εἶπαν· ὑμῖν ἦν ἀναγκαῖον πρῶτον λαληθῆναι τὸν λόγον τοῦ θεοῦ· ἐπειδὴ ἀπωθεῖσθε αὐτὸν καὶ οὐκ ἀξίους κρίνετε ἑαυτοὺς τῆς αἰωνίου ζωῆς, ἰδοὺ στρεφόμεθα εἰς τὰ ἔθνη). Luke describes the reaction of Paul and Barnabas to the opposition, the contradiction, and the defamation by some of the Jews in Pisidian Antioch in five comments.

(1) They "spoke out fearlessly" (παρρησιασάμενοι; see on 4:13); i.e., they reaffirm their message with courage and boldness and formulate their conclusion to the opposition of the Jewish community with openness and clarity. Luke relates their words in direct speech.

(2) They affirm their commitment to the priority of proclaiming the message of Jesus, Israel's Savior, before Jewish audiences. The necessity of proclaiming the "word of God" about the fulfillment of his promises in Jesus "to you first" (ὑμῖν ... πρῶτον) arises from God's plan. The people of the

---

68. Cf. BDAG, s.v. βλασφημέω, "primarily 'to demean through speech,' an especially sensitive matter in an honor-shame oriented society; *to speak in a disrespectful way that demeans, denigrates, maligns*," i.e., "to slander, revile, defame."

69. Cf. Eckhard J. Schnabel, "Jewish Opposition to Christians in Asia Minor in the First Century," *BBR* 18 (2008): 233 – 70.

promise must be the first to hear about the fulfill-ment of God's promises to the fathers, a fact that confirms that God is faithful to his promises. In Rom 1:16 Paul asserts that the gospel "is the power of God that brings salvation to everyone who be-lieves: first to the Jew, then to the Gentile." This priority of the Jews is, for Paul, both a chronologi-cal and a theological priority. Whenever he enters a city, he seeks out the Jews first because he will be able, as a Jew with rabbinical training, to get a hearing in the meetings of the synagogue (chrono-logical priority). And he seeks out the Jews first be-cause they are descendants of Abraham, members of God's covenant people who deserve to hear the good news of the arrival of the Messiah and his sal-vation before this message is proclaimed to pagans.

(3) The missionaries note that (evidently lead-ing) members of the Jewish community "reject" the word of God about Jesus, Israel's Messiah, with the result that they do not consider themselves "worthy [ἀξίους] of eternal life." The expression "eternal life" (ζωὴ αἰώνιος)[70] occurs in Dan 12:2 (cf. Isa 65:17–25) and in Second Temple Jewish texts,[71] where it de-notes life that overcomes death, granted by God to the righteous, linked with the notion of exaltation to the heavenly realm and bodily resurrection in the time of final consummation. In the context of Paul's sermon, eternal life is the result of the resurrection of Jesus (vv. 30–37), of the divine forgiveness of sins, of the justification of the sinner, and of faith in Jesus (vv. 38–39), and is tantamount to God's grace (v. 43) and salvation (vv. 23, 26, 47). The rejection of the message about Jesus, Israel's messianic Savior, amounts to a rejection of eternal life.

Paul and Barnabas affirm that the rejection of God's word about Jesus Messiah by members of the Jewish community means that they will now evangelize the Gentiles (v. 46i). Paul has not given up on the Jewish people, of course. He continues to proclaim the good news of Jesus as Israel's Mes-siah to Jewish audiences.[72] His missionary work among Gentiles is not motivated by the rejection of the gospel by fellow Jews but by his divine call and commission (v. 47); he has preached before Gentiles audiences before.[73] Rather, Paul and Barn-abas state that if it becomes impossible to preach before the Jewish congregation in a city, they will by necessity have to turn to the Gentiles and look for other venues in which to preach and teach. The "Gentiles" (τὰ ἔθνη) are those people who do not profess faith in Israel's God, i.e., polytheists who worship other gods.

13:47 For so the Lord instructed us: "I have made you a light for the Gentiles, that you may bring salvation to the ends of the earth" (οὕτως γὰρ ἐντέταλται ἡμῖν ὁ κύριος· τέθεικά σε εἰς φῶς ἐθνῶν τοῦ εἶναί σε εἰς σωτηρίαν ἕως ἐσχάτου τῆς γῆς). (4) Paul and Barnabas explain that their proc-lamation about Jesus Messiah before Jewish audi-ences and their willingness now to focus on Gentile audiences reflects their obedience to God's com-mission. They do what the Lord has "instructed" them to do. The order to preach among the Gen-tiles should not be linked with Paul's conversion and call on the road to Damascus (9:15) alone: the instruction to go "to the ends of the earth" (ἕως ἐσχάτου τῆς γῆς, echoing 1:8), i.e., to "all nations" (Matt 28:19), was given to the Twelve and by exten-sion to the entire community of Jesus' followers, as the reaction of the Jerusalem church to Peter's ex-perience in Joppa and Caesarea indicates (11:18).

---

70. The expression "eternal life" occurs only here and in v. 48 in Acts; cf. Luke 10:25; 18:18, 30; note 17 occurrences in the gospel of John; for Paul cf. Rom 2:7; 5:21; 6:22, 23; Gal 6:8; 1 Tim 1:16; 6:12; Titus 1:2; 3:7.

71. Cf. Sir 37:26; 4Q181 frag. 1 II, 4.6; 1 QS IV, 7; CD III,

20; 4Q511 frag. 2 II, 4.

72. Cf. 14:1: Iconium; 16:13: Philippi; 17:1–4: Thessalonica; 17:10–12: Berea; 17:17: Athens; 18:4: Corinth; 18:19–21; 19:8–10: Ephesus. Cf. Rom 9:1–2.

73. See on 9:20–22, 30; 11:25–26.

(5) Paul and Barnabas confirm their turning to the Gentiles to proclaim the good news of God's forgiveness of sins and justification of sinners through faith in Jesus as Savior with a scriptural quotation (v. 47b-e). Their proclamation of good news among the Gentiles fulfills God's commission to his Servant in Isa 49:6, who was expected to restore Israel, to return the exiles to the land of Israel, and to bring salvation to the nations. In Luke 2:32 Luke used similar language for Jesus and his mission: Jesus is the Servant who brings God's salvation as "a light for revelation to the Gentiles, and the glory of your people Israel" (see also Luke 4:16 – 21).

Now Paul and the other missionaries have been given the role of the servant. Their mission fulfills Scripture, particularly Isa 49:6. The reference in that passage to Israel, to Jews living in exile, and to the nations matches the movement in Acts from the proclamation of the good news about Jesus as Israel's Messiah and Savior of the world among Jews in Jerusalem, among Jews in the diaspora (Damascus, Antioch, Cyprus, and now in southern Galatia), and among Gentiles (in Caesarea, now in Pisidian Antioch). The phrase "light for the Gentiles" (φῶς ἐθνῶν; objective genitive) describes the messengers of the good news — here, Paul and Barnabas as carriers of "light," symbolizing "salvation" (σωτηρία), to the nations.

13:48 When the Gentiles heard this, they were glad and honored the word of the Lord, and all who were destined for eternal life believed (ἀκούοντα δὲ τὰ ἔθνη ἔχαιρον καὶ ἐδόξαζον τὸν λόγον τοῦ κυρίου καὶ ἐπίστευσαν ὅσοι ἦσαν τεταγμένοι εἰς ζωὴν αἰώνιον). The Gentiles, whose reaction to Paul's explanation of these details of their missionary initiative Luke relates, are evidently Gentiles who have come to faith in Jesus. Their response is described with verbs in the imperfect tense, indicating an ongoing reality: they "were glad" (ἔχαιρον) and they "honored" (ἐδόξαζον), i.e., praised and extolled the word of the Lord. They rejoice because God is offering Gentiles forgiveness of their sins upon coming to faith in Jesus. Thus God's plan of salvation is being realized.

Not all Gentiles in Pisidian Antioch come to faith in Jesus and thus receive salvation. Rather, the Gentiles who believe in Jesus are "all who were destined for eternal life." The word translated as "all" (ὅσος) denotes "as many as," with the following clause indicating the quantitative scope of those who come to faith — people whom God "destined" (τεταγμένοι) for eternal life, i.e., for forgiveness of sins, for justification before his tribunal, for salvation. The verb from which this form comes (τάσσω) means "to assign someone to a certain classification, to be classed among those possessing."[74] The expression stresses God's sovereign work in moving people to come to faith in Jesus, the crucified and risen Messiah and Savior.

In 1 Cor 1:18 – 2:5 Paul similarly emphasizes that it is only the power of God (not rhetorical brilliance or effective argumentation) that convinces Jews or Gentiles of the truth of the gospel. It is God who "assigns" people to the group of people who inherit eternal life (ζωὴ αἰώνιος; see on v. 46). The idea of being "assigned to a certain classification" may echo the Old Testament concept of being recorded in the "book of life," in which God's people are listed.[75]

13:49 The word of the Lord spread through the entire region (διεφέρετο δὲ ὁ λόγος τοῦ κυρίου δι' ὅλης τῆς χώρας). The next phase of Paul's missionary

---

74. BDAG, s.v. τάσσω 1b, citing Plato, *Resp.* 2.371C, *Pol.* 289E, as parallels.

75. Cf. Exod 32:32 – 33; Ps 69:28; Dan 12:1; see the Jewish texts *Jub.* 30:18 – 23; *1 En.* 47:3; 104:1; 108:3. In the New Testament see Rev 13:8; 17:8.

campaign in Pisidian Antioch consists in the expansion of the community of followers of Jesus beyond Pisidian Antioch to "the entire region." As Jews, proselytes, God-fearers, and polytheists are converted in the city of Antioch, people living in the towns and villages of the territory controlled by Antioch[76] also accept the word of the Lord, i.e., the good news about Jesus the Savior. These people would have been polytheists, since Jews normally lived in the cities, not in the smaller towns and villages. The subject of the verb "spread" (διεφέρετο) is "the word of the Lord." Since the gospel is given a voice by Jesus' witnesses, it appears that Paul and Barnabas "carry" the word of the Lord to the towns and villages of the region, following Jesus' example, who had proclaimed the dawn of the kingdom of God in the villages of Galilee.

13:50 The Jews, however, incited prominent women among the God-fearers and the leading men of the city and started a persecution against Paul and Barnabas, whom they forced to leave their district (οἱ δὲ Ἰουδαῖοι παρώτρυναν τὰς σεβομένας γυναῖκας τὰς εὐσχήμονας καὶ τοὺς πρώτους τῆς πόλεως καὶ ἐπήγειραν διωγμὸν ἐπὶ τὸν Παῦλον καὶ Βαρναβᾶν καὶ ἐξέβαλον αὐτοὺς ἀπὸ τῶν ὁρίων αὐτῶν). The fourth incident of the Pisidian Antioch episode relates the continuing opposition of the Jewish community and the local elite (v. 50). Luke does not specify who "the Jews" include; they are certainly Jews who have contacts with the local elites, perhaps the officials of the synagogue. In their effort to get rid of Paul and Barnabas, they succeed in mobilizing the support of two groups: the "prominent women" who attend the synagogue services and thus belong to the group of the God-fearers, as well as the "leading men of the city," i.e., influential members of the local aristocracy, per-

haps including the *duoviri*, the highest municipal magistrates.

The prominent Gentile women may have been benefactors of the local synagogue. They had influence among the highest circles of the city and could thus be mobilized against the missionaries. Either the prominent women were the wives of the "leading men" who influenced their husbands to take action against Paul and Barnabas, or the prominent women who were God-fearers and the husbands whom they influenced are a separate group from the "leading men," who were contacted directly by representatives of the Jewish community. They argued, perhaps, that the activities of Paul and Barnabas jeopardized the position of the main deity of the city, a development that was unavoidable if worshipers of the god Men (an Anatolian deity who had a major temple on a hill outside of Antioch) accepted the message of Jesus Christ and followed the missionaries.[77] And they may have argued that the activities of Paul and Barnabas violated the social and political privileges that the emperors had granted the Jews, allowing them to live according to their ancestral rights, which could be threatened if Jews and Gentiles, becoming followers of Jesus, whom they worship as Savior, are integrated in a new community of believers.

The action of some members of the Jewish community in Pisidian Antioch is described with three verbs in the aorist tense: they "incited" (παρώτρυναν) the prominent women and the leading men of the city; i.e., they provoked a strong emotional reaction against the two Jewish Christian missionaries. They "started a persecution" (ἐπήγειραν διωγμόν; see on 8:1) against Paul and Barnabas; i.e., they initiated a process that was aimed at making their lives and ministry as difficult as possible. And they "forced [them] to leave"

---

76. Cf. Schnabel, *Early Christian Mission*, 2:1107. Antioch controlled over fifty villages.

77. Cf. Horsley and Llewelyn, *New Documents*, 3:30–31, followed by Barrett, *Acts*, 660.

(ἐξέβαλον) the district; i.e., they expelled them from Antioch and the territory controlled by the city.

The persecution that caused the departure of Paul and Barnabas presumably presupposes that the evangelistic and pastoral ministry of the missionaries had considerable success, with a large number of Jews and Gentiles becoming believers in Jesus, receiving regular instruction in the word of God, and forming a new community of God's people. When Paul and Barnabas revisit the city several months later, Luke relates that they strengthen the disciples, encourage them to continue in the faith, and appoint elders (14:22 – 23).

13:51 So they shook the dust off their feet in protest against them and went to Iconium (οἱ δὲ ἐκτιναξάμενοι τὸν κονιορτὸν τῶν ποδῶν ἐπ᾿ αὐτοὺς ἦλθον εἰς Ἰκόνιον). The final incident of this episode in Pisidian Antioch relates the departure of Paul and Barnabas from the city. As they leave, they "shake the dust off their feet," an action that

expresses protest "against them" (ἐπ᾿ αὐτούς), i.e., against the Jews and the members of the elite who forced them to leave. This action symbolizes that they leave behind defilement and that the responsibility for bringing the proclamation of the gospel to a premature end lies with the leading Jews and the officials of the city.[78] They then travel from Pisidian Antioch to Iconium (see on 14:1), walking in an easterly direction via Neapolis and Pappa along the Via Sebaste, a distance of about 93 miles (150 km.).

13:52 The disciples were filled with joy and the Holy Spirit (οἵ τε μαθηταὶ ἐπληροῦντο χαρᾶς καὶ πνεύματος ἁγίου). The reaction of "the disciples" (see on 5:11), i.e., of Paul and Barnabas, is linked with the work of the Holy Spirit. Since they are filled with joy even though they have been rejected, they have a deepened sense of God's self-revealing presence and they experience supernatural joyfulness, refreshed for a new missionary initiative in the next city.

Theology in Application

This passage describes the realities of missionary work and the content of missionary preaching.

The Realities of Missionary Work

Luke's detailed and vivid description of the missionary work of Paul and Barnabas in Pisidian Antioch allows us to describe and explain important aspects of the missionary work of the early church and in our own time.

Reaching out to Jews and Gentiles, to average citizens and the elites. Paul and Barnabas were Jews and thus attended the synagogue service, a tactical decision motivated not by convenience (Jews like to speak with Jews) but by the primary relevance of God's promises in the Scriptures for the Jewish people as the descendants of Abraham. Paul always established contacts with Jews first, before preaching to Gentiles.

---

78. Bock, *Acts*, 466. Jesus had commanded that his disciples perform this action; cf. Luke 9:5; 10:11; Matt 10:14.

When he took a seat in the synagogue of Pisidian Antioch (v. 14), agreed to address the congregation (v. 16), and surveyed the history of Israel (vv. 17 – 25), he was a Jew for Jews in order "to win the Jews" (1 Cor 9:20).

For Jewish Christians, the principle of "Jews first" is a natural standard to follow — if unbelieving Jews are willing to give them a hearing. For Gentile Christians, this often is more problematic on account of the tragic history of anti-Semitism, pogroms, and the Shoah (the holocaust). It is precisely because of this history that Gentile Christians cannot afford *not* to engage Jewish neighbors and friends regarding their conviction that Jesus of Nazareth is Israel's Messiah who forgives sins, justifies sinners, and gives eternal live.

Paul also preached to Gentiles, with greater focus once the leaders of the Jewish community made further synagogue visits impossible (vv. 46 – 49; Rom 15:16; 1 Cor 9:21). It should be noted, however, that the Gentile mission was not grounded in the rejection of the gospel by the Jews but in God's plan, announced in Scripture, to bring salvation to the Gentiles (v. 47; 1:8).

Most of the Jews in Pisidian Antioch and many of the Romans and Greeks living in the city where Paul and Barnabas preached the gospel were average citizens. As all Greek cities had a large number of slaves, most likely the large crowd to which Paul spoke on the second Sabbath (v. 44) included slaves. The presidents of the synagogue (v. 15) probably were wealthy, as were the Gentile women of high standing (v. 50) who heard Paul preach in the synagogue. The representatives of the local elite (v. 50) who eventually drove the missionaries out of the city may have been contacted by Paul after his arrival in Antioch, who may have had letters of introduction from Sergius Paulus, the governor of Cyprus. Paul did not pick "specialized" audiences but proclaimed the gospel to anyone who was willing to listen, whether educated or uneducated, powerful or disenfranchised, freeborn or slaves, men or women.[79] While "specialized" ministries to specific groups have advantages, missionaries and evangelists, pastors, and teachers should never forget that the good news of Jesus Christ needs to be proclaimed and explained to everyone who is willing to listen, without exception.

Interpreting the Scriptures. Paul read and explained Scripture in the synagogue. In terms of Luke's emphases in his two-volume work, reading and interpreting Scripture is a foundational reality not only in the church but also in missionary work. Paul used traditional Jewish methods of interpretation (e.g., *gezerah shawah*) with which his Jewish audience was familiar. He developed his explanation of the significance of Jesus not from the life of Jesus (which he could have done) but from the Scriptures, which the Jews acknowledged as authoritative.

For Christians today, the four Gospels, Paul's letters, and the other texts in the

---

79. Cf. Rom 1:14 – 16; 1 Cor 1:26 – 29; 9:22; Gal 3:28; Col 3:11.

New Testament belong to Scripture, which continues to include Israel's Scriptures (the Old Testament). The lesson here is that truth about God, about sinners, about salvation, and about Jesus as Savior is not deduced logically or experientially from first principles and from contemporary social or philosophical thinking, but from Scripture as the revealed word of God. The reading and explanation of Scripture must remain a central element of missionary work.

Explaining the significance of Jesus. Paul's explanation of God's promises given to Israel and recorded in Scripture focused on the good news about Jesus and the blessings that God bestows on Jews and Gentiles as a result of his death and resurrection. Since faith in Jesus leads to salvation, rejection of Jesus as Israel's Messiah and Savior of the world results in exclusion from eternal life (v. 48). Authentic missionary preaching is always christocentric, focusing on the life, death, resurrection, and exaltation of Jesus as Savior.

The power of God. Luke asserts that the "success" of Paul's sermon was due to the sovereignty of God, who caused people to come to faith in Jesus (v. 48). This is a major emphasis of Paul in his letters.[80] The "scandal" and the "nonsense" of the cross cannot be resolved logically, religiously, aesthetically, or ethically, neither for Jews nor for Gentiles. Missionaries and evangelists do not rely on rhetorical brilliance or on convincing argumentation but on God, who is present in the proclamation of his word and who convinces people of the truth of the gospel through the power of his Spirit.

It should be noted that although the people who listened, understood, and responded to Paul's proclamation of the gospel by putting their faith in Jesus were "all who were destined for eternal life" (v. 48), Paul did not attempt to establish who these "elect" were. Irrespective of our position in the discussion about God's election (predestination), preachers and missionaries never know who will respond and come to faith in Jesus. Missionaries who rely on the power of God do not look for people who might be responsive and then tailor their methods or their rhetoric accordingly; they proclaim the gospel to all people, to anyone who is willing to listen.

Instructing new believers. Missionary work and evangelism include instruction of new believers (v. 43). Paul's letters show that such instruction had a theological focus and an ethical orientation. He explained God's revelation in Israel's history and, climactically, in the life, death, and resurrection of Jesus. He explained the significance of Jesus as the crucified and risen Messiah and Savior, the utter sinfulness of mankind, the role and function of the Mosaic law, and the reality of the life of believers in Jesus, whom God's Spirit transforms. And he explained the relevance of these truths for the everyday life of the believers who lived in cities, in which hedonistic lifestyles were tolerated and propagated by the cultural and social elites.

---

80. Cf. 1 Cor 3:5 – 9; 2 Cor 5:18 – 21; 1 Thess 2:13.

Encountering opposition. At least for Paul's missionary work, opposition and persecution were a constant experience. In Pisidian Antioch he was forced to leave the city as members of the local aristocracy declared him *persona non grata* (vv. 45, 50 – 51). This was part of God's plan (v. 48). While it is tragic when people reject God's offer of salvation through Jesus (cf. the stern warning in vv. 40 – 41), rejection of the gospel and opposition against missionaries and evangelists must never be allowed to lead to personal disappointment or to moralistic attacks against recalcitrant listeners. The reasons for rejection and opposition (v. 45), here, include jealousy, zeal for the law, and the effort to protect rights and privileges. The methods that the opposition uses (vv. 45, 50), here, include contradictory argumentation, slander, and the mobilization of the secular authorities in the city.

With some variation, the same reasons and methods have been used throughout history in efforts to oppress or eliminate the church. Communities of believers in Jesus continue to exist, in ever-increasing numbers, while violent persecution, official anti-Christian measures, insults, and hate speech also continue to be a reality. Sometimes missionaries and believers can leave, as Paul and Barnabas did (v. 51), while most often believers must stay and endure difficult circumstances, as was the case with the Jewish and Gentile believers in Pisidian Antioch. The proper reaction of Christians to opposition and persecution is joy, which the Holy Spirit makes possible even in the midst of suffering.[81]

The Content of Missionary Preaching

While Paul spent a lot of time reviewing and explaining the history of Israel from the fathers to King Saul and King David and to John the Baptist (vv. 17 – 25), his focus is on Jesus and on his significance for the Jews and God-fearers sitting in the synagogue of Pisidian Antioch.

The fulfillment of God's promises. Paul explained God's promises to Israel, recorded in Scripture, and their fulfillment in Jesus. The main themes here are the authority of Scripture, God's faithfulness, God's covenant with Abraham, God's promise to David, God's intervention in Israel's history, and God's revelation in the life, death, and resurrection of Jesus.

The death and resurrection of Jesus. As important as the concept of God's fulfillment of his promises in Jesus is, Paul's focus on Jesus was connected with his death and resurrection. Paul evidently explained the details of Jesus' trial before the Jewish Sanhedrin and before the Roman governor (v. 28), of Jesus' crucifixion and burial (v. 29), of Jesus' resurrection from the dead, and of the appearances of the risen Jesus

---

81. Note the joyful expression of triumph and glory in Rom 8:31 – 39 in the context of suffering (8:35 – 36, 38 – 39).

to various people who are witnesses of his resurrection (vv. 30 – 31). Indeed, "Paul did not preach theological abstractions or credal formulae, but the story of Jesus."[82]

The identity of Jesus as Israel's messianic Savior and as light for the nations. Paul explained what Jesus' death and resurrection meant in terms of who he is (vv. 32 – 39). He argued from Scripture and from the facts of his death and resurrection that Jesus is the messianic Son of David and Son of God — Israel's Savior (v. 23) and the Servant of the Lord, who is a light for the nations and who brings salvation to the ends of the earth (v. 47).

The forgiveness of sins and the justification of the sinner. Paul explained what Jesus' death and resurrection accomplished. Since Jesus is the promised Savior, both of Israel and of the Gentiles, God now offers, exclusively through Jesus (no longer through the law, v. 38), forgiveness of sins, justification of sinners, salvation, and eternal life (vv. 26 – 37, 46 – 48) for Jews as well as for Gentiles.

---

82. David Wenham, "From Jesus to Paul — via Luke," in *The Gospel to the Nations: Perspectives on Paul's Mission* (FS P. O'Brien; ed. P. Bolt and M. Thompson; Leicester: InterVarsity Press, 2000), 83 – 97, 90.

26

Acts 14:1 – 28

Literary Context

The third, fourth, and fifth episodes of Luke's report on the missionary work of Paul and Barnabas in the cities of Cyprus, South Galatia, and Pamphylia (13:1 – 14:28) describe the missionaries' proclamation of the gospel in Iconium (14:1 – 7), in Lystra (14:8 – 20), and in Derbe and Perge (14:21 – 28). The latter episode includes the return journey to Antioch in Syria (vv. 26b – 28). Since the missionaries' experience in Iconium and Lystra is similar, their work in Derbe is related in only a few words, and the Lystra episode contains a speech to pagans narrated in direct speech (vv. 15 – 17), I will treat these three episodes together. The next episode narrates the events of the Apostles' Council (15:1 – 33), which clarifies the modalities of Paul's missionary work among Gentiles, whom he does not require to submit to circumcision and to the entire Mosaic law, a practice that the other apostles and the Jerusalem church under the leadership of James confirm.

Main Idea

The missionary work of Paul and Barnabas takes place in a context of opposition and persecution; it is accompanied by signs and wonders; it challenges religious ideas that confuse God and the world; it proclaims the living God and his grace; and it nurtures new churches through structural consolidation and sending churches through missionary information.

Translation

Acts 14:1–28

1a	Setting: Place	In Iconium
b	Action	**Paul and**
c	Association	**Barnabas**
d	Place	**went as usual into the synagogue of the Jews.**
e	Action	**They spoke in such a manner**
f	Result	that a large number of Jews and
g		Greeks …
h		… believed.
2a	Protagonist	**The Jews, however,**
b	Character description	who did not believe,
c	Action (Conflict)	**stirred up the Gentiles**
d	Action	and **poisoned their minds**
e	Disadvantage	against the brothers.
3a	Action	Nevertheless **they stayed there**
b	Time (Duration)	for a considerable time,
c	Action	speaking fearlessly for the Lord,
d	Verification	who confirmed the message about his grace
e	Means	by enabling them to perform signs and wonders.
4a	Event	**The people of the city were divided;**
b	Action	**some sided with the Jews**
c	Contrast	while **some sided with the apostles.**
5a	Setting: Time	When an attempt was made by Gentiles and
b	Antagonists	Jews,
c	Association	together with their leaders,
d	Purpose	to mistreat and
e	Purpose	stone them,
6a	Action	**they found out about it**
b	Action/Place	and **fled to Lystra and**
c	Place	**Derbe,**
d	Identification	cities in Lycaonia,
e	Geographical	**and to the surrounding region,**
7	Action	where they continued to proclaim the ☙ gospel.
8a	Setting: Place	In Lystra
b	Character entrance	**there sat a man**
c	Character description	who could not use his feet;
d	Character description	**he was lame from birth**
e	Character description	and **had never walked.**

Continued on next page.

Continued from previous page.

9a   Action   **He listened to Paul**
  b   Circumstance   as he was speaking.

  c   Setting: Time   When Paul looked directly at him
  d   Action   and saw that he had faith
  e   Result   to be saved,
10a   Action   **he said**
  b   Manner   in a loud voice,
  c   Command   *"Stand up on your feet!"*
  d   Action (Result)   And **the man leaped up**
  e   Action   and **walked around.**

11a   Setting: Time   When the crowds saw
  b   Event/Cause   what Paul had done,
  c   Action   **they shouted**
  d   Manner   in the Lycaonian language,
  e   Exclamation   *"The gods have come down to us*
  f   Manner   *in human form!"*
12a   Action   **Barnabas they called Zeus,**
  b   Action   and **Paul they called Hermes**
  c   Explanation   because he was the leading speaker.
13a   Character entrance   **The priest of Zeus,**
  b   Social/Place   whose temple was just outside the city,
  c   Action   **brought   bulls and**
  d   List   **garlands**
  e   Place   to the gates
  f   Cause   because he and the crowd wanted to offer sacrifices.

14a   Setting: Time   When the apostles Barnabas and Paul heard of this,
  b   Action   **they tore their clothes**
  c   Action   and **rushed out into the crowd,**
  d   Action (speech)   shouting,
15a   Address   *"Friends,*
  b   Question   *why do you do this?*
  c   Assertion   *We are human beings*
  d   Comparison   *like you,*
  e   Action   *bringing you the good news*
  f   Exhortation   *that you should turn from these worthless things*
  g   Alternative   *to the living God,*
  h   Identification   *who made   the heavens and*
  i   List   *the earth and*
  j   List   *the sea and*
  k   List   *all that is in them.*
16a   Time   *In past generations*
  b   Review of history   *he let all the nations go their own ways.*
17a   Assertion   *Yet he has not left himself without witness,*
  b   Explanation: general   *for he has conferred benefits—*

c	Action List (Specific)	*he gave you rains from heaven and*
d	List	*fruitbearing seasons,*
e	Action	*he filled you with food*
f	Action	*and your hearts with gladness."*
18a	Manner	Even with these words
b	Action	**they dissuaded the crowds from offering sacrifices to them**
c	Manner	only with difficulty.
19a	Event/Place	Then **Jews came from Antioch and**
b	Place	**Iconium**
c	Action	**who won over the crowds.**
d	Action	**They stoned Paul**
e	Action	and **dragged him outside the city,**
f	Character's thoughts	thinking that he was dead.
20a	Action	But **the disciples formed a circle around him,**
b	Action	and **he got up**
c	Action	and **went into the city.**
d	Time	The next day
e	Action	**he and Barnabas left**
f	Place	for Derbe.
21a	Action	**They proclaimed the gospel**
b	Place	in that city
c	Action	and **won many disciples.**
d	Action/Place	**They returned to Lystra,**
e	Place	**Iconium, and**
f	Place	**Antioch.**
22a	Action	**They strengthened the disciples**
b	Action	and **encouraged them**
c	Purpose/Exhortation	to persevere in the faith,
d	Cause	because, they said,
e	Assertion	*"We must endure many hardships*
f	Purpose	*to enter the kingdom of God."*
23a	Setting: Place	In each congregation
b	Action	**they appointed elders for them,**
c	Means	and with prayer and
d	Means	fasting
e	Action	**they committed them to the Lord**
f		in whom they had come to believe.
24a	Action/Place	Then **they traveled through Pisidia**
b	Action/Place	and **came to Pamphylia.**
25a	Action/Place	**They preached the word in Perge**
b	Action/Place	and **then went to Attalia.**

Continued on next page.

Continued from previous page.

26a	Place	From there
b	Action	**they sailed back to Antioch,**
c	Flashback	where they had been committed to the grace of God
d	Purpose	for the work they had now ↵ completed.
27a	Setting: Time	When they arrived,
b	Action	**they called the congregation together**
c	Action	and **reported everything**
d	Agency	that God had done
e	Agency	through them,
f	Action	and **how he had opened a door of faith**
g	Sphere/Advantage	to the Gentiles.
28a	Action	And **they stayed there with the disciples**
b	Time (Duration)	for some time.

Structure and Literary Form

The *Iconium episode* (14:1–7) consists of two brief incidents. Luke narrates the proclamation of the gospel in Iconium (vv. 1–4) in summary fashion with six elements: the proclamation of the gospel in the synagogue (v. 1a-d); the conversion of a large number of Jews and Gentiles (v. 1e-h); the opposition of local Jews against the believers (v. 2); the continued missionary work of Paul and Barnabas (v. 3a-c); the occurrence of signs and wonders (v. 3d-e); the divided reaction of the citizens of Iconium (v. 4). The second incident reports on the opposition and persecution of local Jews and Gentile city officials who force Paul and Barnabas to leave the city (vv. 5–7), narrated in three steps: the plan to stone Paul and Barnabas (v. 5); the flight of Paul and Barnabas to Lycaonia (v. 6); the proclamation of the gospel in Lycaonia (v. 7).

The experiences of Paul and Barnabas parallel their experiences in Pisidian Antioch: preaching in the synagogue leads to conversions of Jews and Gentiles, unbelieving Jews oppose the missionaries, who continue to preach and teach until the situation becomes too dangerous and they are forced to leave the city. The episode is a *narrative*, with statements that could be regarded as *summaries* (vv. 1, 3, 7), and a brief comment on *travel* (v. 6).

The *Lystra episode* (14:8–20) consists of three incidents: Paul heals a lame man in Lystra (14:8–14, the third such healing in Acts);[1] Paul speaks at the temple of Zeus (14:15–18, his third speech in Acts);[2] the local Jews persecute the missionaries (14:19–20). The episode is a *narrative* that includes a *miracle story* (vv. 8–12), *direct*

---

1. Cf. 3:1–10 (lame man at the Beautiful Gate in Jerusalem); 9:32–35 (Aeneas in Lydda).

2. After 13:7–11 (Paphos); 13:16–41 (Pisidian Antioch).

speech (of the citizens of Lystra, who speak Lycaonian; v. 11), a *speech* (vv. 15 – 17), and a brief *travel notice* (v. 20).

The episode that narrates the *mission in Derbe and Perge* (vv. 21 – 28) consists of four incidents. First, Luke briefly narrates the missionary work of Paul and Barnabas in Derbe (v. 21a-c). The second incident relates the consolidation of the churches in Lystra, Iconium, and Antioch (vv. 21d – 23), which includes the appointment of elders. Third, Luke gives a brief report on missionary work in Perge (vv. 24 – 25). The fourth incident relates the return journey of Paul and Barnabas to Antioch in Syria, where they report on their missionary work (vv. 26 – 28). This episode is a *narrative*, a brief report on *church organization* (v. 23), brief *direct speech* (v. 22), and several *travel notices* (vv. 21, 24, 25, 26).

Exegetical Outline

→ **I. The Mission in Iconium (14:1 – 7)**

    A. The Proclamation of the Gospel in Iconium (14:1 – 4)

        1. The proclamation of the gospel in the synagogue (14:1a-e)

        2. The conversion of a large number of Jews and Gentiles (14:1f-h)

        3. The opposition of local Jews against the believers (14:2)

        4. The continued missionary work of Paul and Barnabas (14:3a-c)

        5. The occurrence of signs and wonders (14:3d-e)

        6. The divided reaction of the citizens of Iconium (14:4)

    B. The Persecution by Local Jews and Gentile Officials (14:5 – 7)

        1. The plan to stone Paul and Barnabas (14:5)

        2. The flight of Paul and Barnabas to Lycaonia (14:6)

        3. The proclamation of the gospel in Lycaonia (14:7)

II. The Mission in Lystra (14:8 – 20)

    A. The Healing of a Lame Man in Lystra (14:8 – 14)

        1. Description of a lame man in Lystra who has been crippled since birth (14:8)

        2. Paul's proclamation of the gospel in the presence of the lame man (14:9a-b)

        3. The faith of the lame man and Paul's reaction (14:9c-e)

        4. Paul's command to stand up (14:10a-c)

        5. The miracle (14:10d-e)

        6. The effect of the miracle on the crowds (14:11 – 13)

            a. The acknowledgment of the miracle (14:11a-b)

            b. Acclamation of Paul and Barnabas as gods in human form (14:11c-f)

            c. Admiration of Barnabas and Paul as Zeus and Hermes (14:12)

            d. The plan of the priest of Zeus to offer sacrifices for Paul and Barnabas (14:13)

        7. The refusal of Barnabas and Paul to have sacrifices offered in their honor (14:14)

    B. Paul's Speech in Front of the Temple of Zeus (14:15 – 18)

        1. Address: "Friends" (14:15a)

2. The human identity of Paul and Barnabas (14:15b-d)

3. The purpose of their visit (14:15e)

4. The content of the good news that they proclaim (14:15f – 17)

    a. Call to turn from worthless idols to the living God (14:15f-g)

    b. God's sovereignty as the Creator (14:15h-k)

    c. God's forbearance of the nations' behavior (14:16)

    d. God's goodness in providing rain, fruit, and food (14:17)

5. The difficulty of preventing the crowds' sacrifice (14:18)

C. The Persecution by Local Jews and the Citizens of Lystra (14:19 – 20)

1. The arrival and activity of Jews from Pisidian Antioch and Iconium (14:19a-c)

2. The stoning of Paul (14:19d-f)

3. The recovery of Paul (14:20a-c)

4. The departure of Paul and Barnabas, who travel to Derbe (14:20d-f)

III. The Mission in Derbe and Perge (14:21 – 28)

A. Missionary Work in Derbe (14:21a-c)

1. The proclamation of the gospel in Derbe (14:21a-b)

2. The conversion of people in Derbe (14:21c)

B. Consolidation of the Congregations in Lystra, Iconium, and Antioch (14:21d – 23)

1. The visitation of the churches in Lystra, Iconium, and Pisidian Antioch (14:21d-f)

2. The encouragement of the believers and the appointment of elders (14:22 – 23)

C. Missionary Work in Perge (14:24 – 25)

1. The journey through Pisidia to Pamphylia (14:24)

2. The proclamation of the gospel in Perge (14:25a)

3. The journey from Perge to Attalia (14:25b)

D. Return Journey to Antioch in Syria (14:26 – 28)

1. The journey from Attalia to Antioch (14:26)

2. The report of Paul and Barnabas to the church in Antioch (14:27)

3. The sojourn of Paul and Barnabas in Antioch (14:28)

Explanation of the Text

14:1 In Iconium Paul and Barnabas went as usual into the synagogue of the Jews. They spoke in such a manner that a large number of Jews and Greeks believed (ἐγένετο δὲ ἐν Ἰκονίῳ κατὰ τὸ αὐτὸ εἰσελθεῖν αὐτοὺς εἰς τὴν συναγωγὴν τῶν Ἰουδαίων καὶ λαλῆσαι οὕτως ὥστε πιστεῦσαι Ἰουδαίων τε καὶ Ἑλλήνων πολὺ πλῆθος). This first incident (vv. 1 – 4) of the Iconium episode narrates the proclamation of the gospel by Paul and Barnabas. As in Salamis (13:5), evidently in Paphos (13:6), and in Pisidian Antioch (13:14), they attend "as usual"[3] the synagogue service (see on

3. Thus Barrett, *Acts*, 667, for the phrase κατὰ τὸ αὐτό, with the argument that "together" does not make much sense; cf. NIV, TNIV, also GNB, NET, NLT, NRSV ("the same thing happened"). BDAG, s.v. κατά 5bα suggests "together" (cf. ESV, NASB; Fitzmyer, *Acts*, 527) on account of the singular instead of the plural (κατὰ τὰ αὐτά).

6:9) with the goal of proclaiming the good news of Jesus, Israel's Messiah, to the Jews gathered there. Iconium (mod. Konya), located at the juncture of several important roads, was the most important assize center where the governors regularly heard legal cases. Augustus established a Roman colony besides which the old Greek city continued to exist. Pliny describes Iconium as a "most famous city" of a tetrarchy (*Nat.* 5.25.95).

Without giving further details, Luke relates that the missionaries "spoke," obviously with the understanding that Paul and Barnabas preached a message similar to that presented in Pisidian Antioch (13:16 – 41). The results of their preaching are similar as well: Jews "believed" (πιστεῦσαι); i.e., they came to faith in Jesus as Israel's Messiah and Savior, as did "Greeks," a reference either to God-fearers or, more plausibly, to Greek citizens of Iconium who heard the gospel preached in other venues in the city. Luke's account is compressed and omits references to other locations, but he is concerned to note that "a large number" of people were converted.

14:2 The Jews, however, who did not believe, stirred up the Gentiles and poisoned their minds against the brothers (οἱ δὲ ἀπειθήσαντες Ἰουδαῖοι ἐπήγειραν καὶ ἐκάκωσαν τὰς ψυχὰς τῶν ἐθνῶν κατὰ τῶν ἀδελφῶν). Once again Jews opposed Paul and Barnabas. Luke relates three actions, expressed with verbs in aorist tenses: they "did not believe" the proclamation about the fulfillment of God's promises in Jesus Messiah. They "stirred up" the Gentiles, i.e., the unbelieving Greeks in the city, and "poisoned" their minds against the brothers; i.e., they caused the population of Iconium to think badly about the Christians. The "brothers" are either Paul and Barnabas, or, more likely, the new be-

lievers in the emerging congregation, which would have included men and women.

14:3 Nevertheless they stayed there for a considerable time, speaking fearlessly for the Lord, who confirmed the message about his grace by enabling them to perform signs and wonders (ἱκανὸν μὲν οὖν χρόνον διέτριψαν παρρησιαζόμενοι ἐπὶ τῷ κυρίῳ τῷ μαρτυροῦντι ἐπὶ τῷ λόγῳ τῆς χάριτος αὐτοῦ, διδόντι σημεῖα καὶ τέρατα γίνεσθαι διὰ τῶν χειρῶν αὐτῶν). While many commentators find the transition from v. 2 to v. 3 harsh and the narrative logic "very obscure,"[4] even generally skeptical exegetes see Luke's point, particularly if the expression translated as "nevertheless" (μὲν οὖν) is taken to be adversative ("rather") and not as expressing result. Luke affirms that "opposition did not daunt the two, who dug in their heels"[5] since "the brothers needed their support, and the greater the opposition the bolder they became."[6]

Paul and Barnabas stayed "for a considerable time," a general time reference that could imply several months. They "spoke fearlessly" (παρρησιαζόμενοι; see on 4:13; 9:27) for the Lord, despite the opposition; the present tense of the participle fits the missionaries' preaching over a considerable period of time. The content of their proclamation is described as "the message about his grace" (ὁ λόγος τῆς χάριτος αὐτοῦ), i.e., the proclamation of God's grace (see on 4:33) revealed and made possible through the life, death, and resurrection of Jesus, Messiah and Savior, a message they proclaimed to everyone who was willing to listen, both Jews and Gentiles.

The fact that the Lord "confirmed" the proclamation of the gospel through "signs and wonders" (σημεῖα καὶ τέρατα; see on 2:19, 22) may have been the reason why Paul and Barnabas were able to stay

---

4. Johnson, *Acts*, 246.
5. Pervo, *Acts*, 350.

6. Barrett, *Acts*, 669.

in Iconium for some time. The miracles that happened must have caused people to be in awe of the missionaries, as had happened in Jerusalem (2:43; 5:12 – 13) and in Samaria (8:6 – 7), minimizing for the time being the influence of the hate campaign initiated by some of the Jews. God's intervention, mediated through the missionaries (διὰ τῶν χειρῶν αὐτῶν, lit., "by their hands"), was expressed (presumably) in healings and exorcisms. Note that the subject of the phrase that describes confirmation of the missionaries' message through miracles is not the missionaries but "the Lord." It is God, not human beings, who initiates authentic miracles, which means that they cannot be "used" in evangelism as "tools" to provoke faith.

14:4 The people of the city were divided; some sided with the Jews while some sided with the apostles (ἐσχίσθη δὲ τὸ πλῆθος τῆς πόλεως, καὶ οἱ μὲν ἦσαν σὺν τοῖς Ἰουδαίοις, οἱ δὲ σὺν τοῖς ἀποστόλοις). Luke notes the divided reaction of the population of the city to the presence of Paul and Barnabas and their message, accompanied by miracles. Some sided with the unbelieving members of the Jewish community in Iconium, while others sided with the missionaries. In other words, some citizens were impressed with their activities and were willing to let them be active in the city, while others wanted to get rid of them; the division of opinion may have been voiced in a meeting of the popular assembly of the citizens. Or Luke could be describing more conversions: the preaching of Paul and Barnabas, accompanied by miracles, made some people willing to side with those Jews who opposed the missionaries, while other citizens believed their message and joined the emerging congregation.

Paul and Barnabas are called "apostles" here and in v. 14. Paul is otherwise never described with this term in Acts, as Luke reserves the term "apostles" (ἀπόστολοι; see on 1:2) for the Twelve. Since Luke is the only evangelist who traces the designation of the Twelve as "apostles" to Jesus himself (Luke 6:13; see Matt 10:2 and Mark 3:14; 6:30 for the term "apostles" used by the gospel writers), he evidently wants to be consistent and use that title for the Twelve only, even though he knows that there were other missionaries who used that designation (see vv. 4, 14). Luke surely would have known that Paul had to insist on his right to be called an apostle,[7] yet he did not use the second volume of his work to bolster Paul's apostolic credentials.

Paul and Barnabas are "apostles" not in the sense of the Twelve, who had accompanied Jesus during his ministry in Galilee, "from the beginning of the baptism of John until the day when he was taken up from us" (1:22). However, both Paul and Barnabas had been "sent" out by the risen Lord (Paul, 9:15), by the church in Jerusalem (Barnabas, 11:22), and by the church in Syrian Antioch (Barnabas and Paul, 13:3, 4) to which they reported back (14:26 – 27). Thus, Luke's use of the term "apostle" in v. 4 is a hint that he saw Paul and Barnabas as having a role similar to that of the twelve apostles.

14:5 – 7 When an attempt was made by Gentiles and Jews, together with their leaders, to mistreat and stone them, they found out about it and fled to Lystra and Derbe, cities in Lycaonia, and to the surrounding region, where they continued to proclaim the gospel (ὡς δὲ ἐγένετο ὁρμὴ τῶν ἐθνῶν τε καὶ Ἰουδαίων σὺν τοῖς ἄρχουσιν αὐτῶν ὑβρίσαι καὶ λιθοβολῆσαι αὐτούς, συνιδόντες κατέφυγον εἰς τὰς πόλεις τῆς Λυκαονίας Λύστραν καὶ Δέρβην καὶ τὴν περίχωρον, κἀκεῖ εὐαγγελιζόμενοι ἦσαν). The second incident (vv. 5 – 7) of the Iconium episode relates the persecution of Peter and Barnabas by local Jews and Gentile officials, with the subse-

7. Cf. 1 Cor 9:1 – 2; 2 Cor 11:5 – 33; Gal 1:1 – 17.

quent departure of the missionaries. The Gentiles and the Jews rejecting the proclamation of Paul and Barnabas conspire with their "leaders" in their common desire to mistreat[8] and stone the two missionaries (v. 5). The city officials involved probably include descendants of the Roman colonists, as Iconium had been refounded as a Roman colony.

In a Jewish context, death by stoning was done to false teachers for teaching blasphemy. Since officials of the city are involved, it seems obvious that Luke does not refer to a synagogue punishment — the death penalty cases had to be tried by the governors of Roman provinces. It appears that some Jewish, Greek, and Roman citizens of Iconium wanted to harass the missionaries and pelt them with stones as a deterrent to further activities, probably accepting the possibility that they would be seriously injured or even killed.

Paul and Barnabas receive information about the plot to mistreat and stone them (v. 6a). They decide that the collaboration of their Jewish and Gentile enemies with city officials has created a situation so dangerous that they must leave the city in a hurry (v. 6b). Luke's reference to disciples and to elders appointed by Paul and Barnabas during their return journey (vv. 21 – 23) implies that a church was established. Luke then notes that Paul and Barnabas go to Lystra and Derbe and the territory controlled by these two cities in Lycaonia (v. 6b-e; for Lystra and Derbe, see on 14:8, 20). Lystra was about 20 miles (34 km.) southwest of Iconium, and Derbe was 93 miles (150 km.) east of Lystra.

Luke concludes the Iconium episode by noting in summary fashion that Paul and Barnabas continue to proclaim the gospel (εὐαγγελιζόμενοι, present participle; see on 5:42) in Lycaonia (v. 7a),

the region to which Iconium, Lystra, and Derbe belonged. Since the conjunction translated "where" (κἀκεῖ) comes after the phrase that refers to the territories controlled by Lystra and Derbe, it is possible that the missionaries preach in other Lycaonian towns besides these two cities. Traveling from Lystra to Derbe on the Via Sebaste, Paul and Barnabas would have passed through Dalisandos, Kodylessos, Posala, Ilistra, and Laranda.[9]

14:8 In Lystra there sat a man who could not use his feet; he was lame from birth and had never walked (καί τις ἀνὴρ ἀδύνατος ἐν Λύστροις τοῖς ποσὶν ἐκάθητο, χωλὸς ἐκ κοιλίας μητρὸς αὐτοῦ ὃς οὐδέποτε περιεπάτησεν). Luke now focuses on a sequence of events that take place in Lystra (vv. 8 – 20). He provides few details concerning the missionary activity of Paul and Barnabas in Lystra; instead, he concentrates entirely on the healing of a lame man and on the nearly fatal consequences for the missionaries.

Lystra (near mod. Hatunsaray), an older town in which Augustus established a military colony, was the "sister" city of Pisidian Antioch, perhaps because the Roman colonies were founded at the same time. Research has shown that Lystra was a prosperous city that was not as insignificant as earlier scholars assumed. The fact that the inhabitants of Lystra spoke Lycaonian (v. 11) does not mean that they were "rustics";[10] many of the people living in Asia Minor, particularly those in the cities, were bilingual, speaking their native, indigenous languages as well as Greek.

Luke begins with the healing of a lame man.[11] He introduces the unnamed man with four descriptions: (1) he "sat," probably in the central

---

8. The term ὑβρίζω denotes "to treat in an insolent or spiteful manner" (BDAG) and can describe committing a personal injury (LSJ II.1).

9. For details on these towns cf. Schnabel, *Early Christian Mission*, 2:1120 – 21.

10. Johnson, *Acts*, 251.

11. On the structure of miracle accounts see on 3:1 – 10 (Structure and Literary Form).

plaza, earning his living as a beggar (cf. v. 9); (2) he "could not use his feet," i.e., he was crippled, which was the reason why he was sitting on the ground; (3) he was "lame from birth"; (4) he had thus "never walked" in his life.

14:9 – 10 He listened to Paul as he was speaking. When Paul looked directly at him and saw that he had faith to be saved, he said in a loud voice, "Stand up on your feet!" And the man leaped up and walked around (οὗτος ἤκουσεν τοῦ Παύλου λαλοῦντος· ὃς ἀτενίσας αὐτῷ καὶ ἰδὼν ὅτι ἔχει πίστιν τοῦ σωθῆναι, εἶπεν μεγάλῃ φωνῇ· ἀνάστηθι ἐπὶ τοὺς πόδας σου ὀρθός. καὶ ἥλατο καὶ περιεπάτει). Luke relates that the lame man was in Paul's audience, listening as Paul proclaimed the good news of God's offer of forgiveness and justification through faith in Jesus, the Lord and Savior. While Luke does not indicate whether the man was Jewish (who could have heard Paul speak in the synagogue, although Luke does not mention a synagogue in the Lystra episode), or a Greek or a Roman, the presence of the crowd (v. 11) suggests that Paul was speaking in public, probably in the agora, the central plaza of Lystra. The present tense of the participle (λαλοῦντος) suggests that the lame man listened to Paul over a period of time.

Luke highlights three details at the beginning of the miracle account. (1) When Paul sees the lame man among the people listening to his message, he "looks directly at him." The stare, together with the loud voice mentioned subsequently, may help explain how the citizens of Lystra come to the conclusion that "the gods have come down to us" in Paul and Barnabas (v. 11). In Greco-Roman texts as well as in Jewish literature, the stare and the loud voice are indicators of the action or presence of the gods (or God) who mingle with human beings.

(2) Paul perceives that the man has "faith" to be saved. In the context of the description of the lame man's illness and Luke's earlier accounts of the healing of lame men (3:1 – 10; 9:32 – 35) and of other miracles (4:30; 5:12; 6:8; 8:13; 14:3), the man's hope to be "saved" (σωθῆναι; see on 4:9) should be understood in terms of an expectation to be cured. Since Luke's readers know that Paul's message connects faith with Jesus the Savior, with forgiveness of sins, and with eternal life (13:12, 39, 48), the faith of the lame man probably includes all of these. The expectation that the power of the God of the Jews whom Paul proclaims, a power that brought Jesus back from the dead, would bring him onto his feet and heal him from his birth defect and also grant him forgiveness of sins and eternal life.

(3) Paul addresses the lame man "in a loud voice," which is appropriate for the following command: "Stand up on your feet!" (v. 10c). He commands him to do what he cannot do by himself, never having stood on his feet without people supporting him.[12] Paul knows, supernaturally, that God will heal this lame man and thus he issues the command, with the expectation that God will grant healing instantaneously.

Luke's next comment formulates the demonstration of the miracle: the man "leaped up" (ἥλατο) and "walked around" (περιεπάτει; v. 10d-e). The tenses of the verbs (first aorist, then imperfect) underline in the first instance the immediate and total effectiveness of the healing, demonstrated in the fast motion of the leap, and, in the second instance, the permanent effects of the healing: the man who has never walked before is now able to walk around.

14:11 – 12 When the crowds saw what Paul had done, they shouted in the Lycaonian language,

---

12. The additions of Codex Bezae ("I say to you in the name of the Lord Jesus Christ, stand up on your feet and walk") adapt Paul's command to the command of Peter in 3:6.

"The gods have come down to us in human form!" Barnabas they called Zeus, and Paul they called Hermes because he was the leading speaker (οἵ τε ὄχλοι ἰδόντες ὃ ἐποίησεν Παῦλος ἐπῆραν τὴν φωνὴν αὐτῶν Λυκαονιστὶ λέγοντες· οἱ θεοὶ ὁμοιωθέντες ἀνθρώποις κατέβησαν πρὸς ἡμᾶς, ἐκάλουν τε τὸν Βαρναβᾶν Δία, τὸν δὲ Παῦλον Ἑρμῆν, ἐπειδὴ αὐτὸς ἦν ὁ ἡγούμενος τοῦ λόγου). The narrative continues with a description of the effect of the miracle on the people who witness the healing (wonder among the people is a regular element in miracle accounts). Luke describes four phases of the effect that the healing miracle has on the people.

(1) The crowds acknowledge that a miracle has taken place (v. 11a-b). The people who saw what happened conclude that it was Paul who had caused the miracle to happen — which was correct on the surface but not in reality, for only God the Creator can do the impossible.

(2) The crowds respond with an acclamation, hailing Paul and Barnabas as gods in human form (v. 11c-f). Luke relates the response of the crowds in direct speech, in Greek, although he notes that they spoke in their native Lycaonian language. This is Luke's only comment about a language other than Greek (21:37) or Hebrew/Aramaic (21:40; 22:2; 26:14). While Greek had become the main language of Asia Minor since the conquest of Alexander in 334/333 BC, remaining the *lingua franca* until the eleventh century, the indigenous languages had not vanished. The geographer Strabo (died in AD 21) states that four indigenous languages could be heard in the border areas of the provinces of Asia and Lycia (Pisidian, Solymian, Greek, and Lydian), that the Carian language was still spoken in the region around Kaunos, and that

in the region of Kibyra one could still hear the Lydian language.[13]

Since the lame man was listening to Paul's preaching (v. 9), he was evidently able to understand Greek besides his native Lycaonian. Luke's comment about the language used by the citizens of Lystra signals that Paul did not preach only to Greeks but also to "barbarians" (cf. Rom 1:14), and that he was not only active in major centers like Antioch, Corinth, Athens, or Ephesus but also in rural regions such as the hinterland of Lycaonia. Some have suggested that the use of the Lycaonian language accounts for the fact that "Paul and Barnabas are slow to pick up on the populace's intentions."[14] This inference goes beyond the text.

As the citizens hail Paul and Barnabas as deities, they would have made sure that the two "gods in human form" understand that they have recognized them. The fact that they evidently do not prevent any preparations from being made could be explained in various ways; e.g., Paul and Barnabas may have continued to preach in the agora while citizens of Lystra leave in order to contact the priest of Zeus, who then starts preparations for a procession and sacrifice. In any case, the Lystrans conclude from the healing miracle that Paul and Barnabas are "gods" (θεοί) who have "come down" appearing "in human form." The definite article (οἱ θεοί) probably points forward to v. 12, as the Lycaonians certainly would not have believed that only two gods existed. Thus, their acclamation can be understood in the sense that "the gods whom we particularly associate with our region have come down."[15] The verb "come down" suggests that the gods live in heaven.

(3) The people admire Barnabas as Zeus (Διός or Ζεύς; v. 12), perhaps because he had a more impressive appearance, but more probably because he

---

13. Strabo, *Geogr.* 13.1.65; 14.2.3; 14.2.8.
14. Johnson, *Acts*, 248; cf. Bock, *Acts* 476.
15. Barrett, *Acts*, 676.

is the older of the two. Paul is identified as Hermes (Ἑρμῆς) because he was the leading speaker. Zeus is the Sky Father, the highest god, the gatherer of clouds who sends rain and thunder and lightning, the god who presides over the dealings of the community, the savior, the god of the universe. Hermes is, as Zeus's son, the swift messenger sent by Zeus, the emissary (with staff in hand) who crosses the boundary between the living and the dead, and thus the god of transition and the mediator between the gods and humans.[16]

The reaction of the Lystrans can be understood in the context of local traditions. A legend connected with neighboring Phrygia relates that two local gods, perhaps Tarchunt and Runt (or Pappas and Men), wandered through the region as human beings. Nobody provided them with hospitality until Philemon and Baucis, an older couple, shared their supplies with the unrecognized gods. The gods rewarded the couple, making them priests in the temple of Zeus, eventually transforming them into sacred trees, while inflicting judgment on the other people.[17] Several scholars suggest that Luke consciously alludes to this legend, which does not preclude the possibility that the citizens of Lystra, thinking of this myth, indeed reacted as Luke describes because they do not want to make the same mistake again.[18]

14:13 The priest of Zeus, whose temple was just outside the city, brought bulls and garlands to the gates because he and the crowd wanted to offer sacrifices (ὅ τε ἱερεὺς τοῦ Διὸς τοῦ ὄντος πρὸ τῆς πόλεως ταύρους καὶ στέμματα ἐπὶ τοὺς πυλῶνας ἐνέγκας σὺν τοῖς ὄχλοις ἤθελεν θύειν). The final effect of the healing miracle is the plan of the priest

of Zeus and of the crowd to organize a spontaneous procession from the city to the temple and to kill bulls as sacrifices. Apparently the preaching of Paul and Barnabas has "failed to affect these Gentiles."[19]

"Bulls," the noblest sacrificial animal, were often sacrificed to Zeus, the strongest of the gods. "Garlands" woven from twigs were worn on the head by people participating in the procession from the city to the temple, which, often in Greek cities, was located outside the city walls. Garlands were brought into the city for Paul and Barnabas to wear as participants in the procession from the city to the altar of Zeus situated in front of the temple where the bulls (adorned with ribbons and gilded horns) would be sacrificed. Other participants in the procession would have carried a basket with the knife for the sacrifice, a vessel containing water, and an incense burner; musicians played the flute. The ritualized slaughter of the bull would be followed by a meal. The "gates" to which the priest brought the bulls and garlands were the gates of the city; from there a procession could be organized to the temple.

14:14 – 15 When the apostles Barnabas and Paul heard of this, they tore their clothes and rushed out into the crowd, shouting, "Friends, why do you do this? We are human beings like you, bringing you the good news that you should turn from these worthless things to the living God, who made the heavens and the earth and the sea and all that is in them" (ἀκούσαντες δὲ οἱ ἀπόστολοι Βαρναβᾶς καὶ Παῦλος διαρρήξαντες τὰ ἱμάτια αὐτῶν ἐξεπήδησαν εἰς τὸν ὄχλον κράζοντες καὶ λέγοντες· ἄνδρες, τί ταῦτα ποιεῖτε; καὶ ἡμεῖς ὁμοιοπαθεῖς ἐσμεν ὑμῖν ἄνθρωποι εὐαγγελιζόμενοι

---

16. Cf. F. Graf, "Zeus," *DDD*, 934 – 40; L. H. Martin, "Hermes," *DDD*, 405 – 11; Walter Burkert, *Greek Religion* (Cambridge: Harvard Univ. Press, 1985), 125 – 31, 156 – 69.

17. Ovid, *Metam.* 8.626 – 724.

18. Cf. Dean Philip Béchard, *Paul outside the Walls: A Study*

of Luke's Socio-Geographical Universalism in Acts 14:8 – 20 (AnBib 143; Rome: Editrice Pontificio Istituto Biblico, 2000), 49 – 50, 292 – 301.

19. Stenschke, *Luke's Portrait of Gentiles*, 183.

ὑμᾶς ἀπὸ τούτων τῶν ματαίων ἐπιστρέφειν ἐπὶ θεὸν ζῶντα, ὃς ἐποίησεν τὸν οὐρανὸν καὶ τὴν γῆν καὶ τὴν θάλασσαν καὶ πάντα τὰ ἐν αὐτοῖς).

As soon as Paul and Barnabas, again called "apostles" (cf. v. 4), hear of the plan to organize a procession to the temple of Zeus and to offer sacrifices, they express their refusal to participate in the strongest terms. They tear their clothes as a sign of grief and horror;[20] they rush out into the crowd, moving quickly in order to stop the proceedings; they shout with a loud voice so that their protests are clearly and unambiguously heard. They protest because they cannot "retranslate" the healing and the reaction of the crowds into Christian terms.[21]

The speech that follows (vv. 15 – 18) is attributed in v. 14 to both Paul and Barnabas, though it is usually treated as a speech of Paul. It begins with a brief address as "friends" (ἄνδρες, lit., "men"). Its first part (v. 15a-d) relates the assertion of Paul and Barnabas that they are "human beings" (ἄνθρωποι), just like the citizens of Lystra; the personal pronoun "we" is emphatic (καὶ ἡμεῖς, at the beginning of the clause). Since they are humans, the Lystrans should not be "doing this"; they should not organize a procession, a sacrifice, and a communal meal in their honor. Paul and Barnabas want to make sure that only the one true God is honored.

In the second part of the speech, Paul explains the purpose of their visit (v. 15e). He and Barnabas have come to Lystra "bringing ... the good news" (εὐαγγελιζόμενοι). This means they are not the message, only the messengers. The present tense of the participle expresses an action in progress: they have been preaching the good news of Jesus the Savior since they arrived in Lystra, and this is

what they intend to continue to do while they are in the city.

Next, Paul explains the content of the good news that they proclaim (vv. 15f – 17). Luke summarizes four assertions of Paul's explanation of the gospel, which is adapted to this particular situation — face-to-face with a priest of Zeus, with people about to honor them as gods, and with a bull to be sacrificed on an altar in front of a temple erected in honor of Zeus. This situation explains why the speech is not christological or kerygmatic as earlier speeches in Acts, but theological, explaining the sovereignty of the one true God in whom they believe and whose reality is part of the message of Jesus the Savior, which they proclaim in Lystra.

(1) The first assertion (v. 15f-g) is a call to turn from worthless idols to the living God. Paul asserts that the gods that have been mentioned, Zeus and Hermes, together with the sacrificial bulls, the garland, the procession, the altar of sacrifice, and the temple, are "worthless things" (μάταια, a Greek word that describes persons or things that are "of no use" and thus "idle, empty, fruitless, useless, powerless, lacking truth").[22] This is Old Testament language, where the LXX uses the same derogatory term to condemn the pagan worship of other gods.[23] In nonbiblical Greek, the term refers to vain and foolish persons or empty talk, and would thus be understandable for polytheists who do not know the Jewish use of the term.

The fact that the traditional gods are "worthless" means that they have no power, e.g., no power to heal the lame man, since these gods do not intervene in human affairs. This is why they should "turn" away from from their traditional gods and

---

20. Cf. LXX (using the same verb): Gen 37:29, 34; 44:13; Lev 10:6; Num 14:6; Josh 7:6; Judg 11:35; 2 Sam 1:11; 3:31; 1 Kgs 20:27; 2 Kgs 22:19; Ezra 9:3; Esth 4:1; in Jdt 14:16 – 17 the same actions are described with the same verbs. See also Cassius Dio 48.37.7; Arrian, *Anab.* 7.24.3; Diodoros 17.35.5.

21. Mark S. Smith, *God in Translation: Deities in Cross-Cul-*

tural Discourse in the Biblical World (FAT 57; Tübingen: Mohr Siebeck, 2008), 307.

22. BDAG, s.v. μάταια.

23. Cf. Lev 17:7; 1 Kgs 16:13, 26; 2 Kgs 17:15; Isa 2:20; 30:7, 15, 28; 31:2; 44:9; Jer 2:5; 8:19; Ezek 8:10.

worship rituals, which means stopping their preparations for a procession to the temple of Zeus and for offering sacrifices. This first assertion is first negative before it makes a positive point: the citizens of Lystra must stop practicing their ancestral religions and turn away from their ineffective gods and temples and sacrifices, and they must turn to to the "living God" (θεὸς ζῶν), an expression used in the Old Testament to describe the one true God who created heaven and earth, who has revealed himself to Israel, and who intervened in Israel's history.[24] The adjective "living" expresses the biblical and Jewish conviction that Israel's God is the source of life.[25]

(2) God is the sovereign Creator God. The living God whom Paul and Barnabas proclaim has made the heavens, the earth, and the sea, and all animate beings and inanimate objects that exist in the heavens, on the earth, and in the sea.[26] This God has the power to heal the lame man. A fuller explanation of this point would have led to a critique of the religiosity of the pagans, who divinized individual forces of nature — including Zeus, venerated as weather god. And it would have provided the opportunity to critique pagan cosmology, which claimed that "Zeus is aether, Zeus is earth, Zeus is sky, Zeus is everything" (Aeschylus), which expresses "the philosophical speculation which culminated in the pantheism of the Stoics."[27]

Biblical revelation offers a clear distinction between the living God and heaven, earth, the sea, and all creatures therein as God's creation. It is certainly correct to assert that "the first step required in non-Jewish hearers of the Gospel is that they should recognize that there is but one God, and take him and his requirements seriously."[28] Since Paul and Barnabas have been preaching for some time in Lystra, they would have made this point earlier; thus, they either reiterate their earlier emphasis, or they express convictions that are immediately relevant for the specific situation of the attempted procession and sacrifice.

14:16 In past generations he let all the nations go their own ways (ὃς ἐν ταῖς παρῳχημέναις γενεαῖς εἴασεν πάντα τὰ ἔθνη πορεύεσθαι ταῖς ὁδοῖς αὐτῶν). (3) Paul's third assertion emphasizes God's forbearance of the nations' behavior. In past generations God allowed the nations to "go their own ways," i.e., to worship their own gods, organize processions to temples, and sacrifice animals. The Jews believed that God the Creator had revealed himself to them; the history of Israel is proof that God did not allow Abraham's descendants to "go their own ways" and worship whomever they wanted to worship. The first part of the Decalogue formulates this conviction (Exod 20:2 – 6). Since the Gentiles were ignorant of the one true God and thus worshiped gods that were not alive and behaved in ways that contradicted the will of God the Creator, God has overlooked their errors. He did not intervene in their affairs. But God will now no longer tolerate their useless worship of idols.

14:17 "Yet he has not left himself without witness, for he has conferred benefits — he gave you rains from heaven and fruitbearing seasons, he filled you with food and your hearts with gladness" (καίτοι οὐκ ἀμάρτυρον αὐτὸν

---

24. Cf. Hos 1:10 (MT/LXX 2:1); 4:15; Isa 37:4; Dan 5:23; see also Deut 5:26; Josh 3:10; 1 Sam 17:36; 2 Kgs 19:4, 16; Ps 84:2 (LXX 83:3), where the description of God as "living" is contrasted with dead idols; cf. Marshall, "Acts," 588. In the New Testament see 2 Cor 3:3; 6:16; 1 Thess 1:9; 1 Tim 3:15; Heb 3:12.

25. Ps 36:9 (LXX 35:10); cf. Ps 42:1 (LXX 41:2); Jer 2:13; 17:13.

26. Paul uses biblical language; cf. Exod 20:11; Ps 146:6 (LXX 145:6).

27. Burkert, *Greek Religion*, 131.

28. Barrett, *Acts*, 680. Similarly Calvin, *Acts*, 2:11, "Since Paul and Barnabas were preaching to Gentiles, it would have been useless for them to attempt to bring them to Christ at once."

ἀφῆκεν ἀγαθουργῶν, οὐρανόθεν ὑμῖν ὑετοὺς διδοὺς καὶ καιροὺς καρποφόρους, ἐμπιπλῶν τροφῆς καὶ εὐφροσύνης τὰς καρδίας ὑμῶν). (4) Paul's final assertion emphasizes God's goodness in providing rain, fruit, and food. God the Creator was never without a witness. He plainly revealed himself in creation as he "conferred benefits" on mankind; he gave the nations rains that watered the fields, and through the rains came "fruitful seasons" (i.e., harvest times that provided "food"), which filled their hearts with "gladness."

The reference to regular harvest seasons echoes God's promise to Noah after the flood that "as long as the earth endures, seedtime and harvest, cold and heat, summer and winter, day and night will never cease" (Gen 8:22).[29] In the context of Lycaonian and Greek traditions, Paul argues that it is the living God, the Creator of the universe, who grants fertility, not the local fertility gods who came to be associated with Zeus, worshiped as weather god and given epithets that communicated the conviction that he provided the harvest and fruit on which human beings depend.[30] These blessings should have prompted the nations to inquire concerning their source.

Paul's fuller argumentation in Rom 1:19 – 21 indicates his conviction that the nations failed to worship the one true and living God not because of the inadequacy of God's self-revelation in creation (natural revelation), but because of their own inadequacy in failing to "read" correctly creation in terms of the one Creator. He argues in Rom 1:18 – 3:20 that this failure to recognize and worship God the Creator brings the Gentiles under God's judgment. In view of the useless, powerless, fruitless gods that the citizens of Lystra worshiped, "the mere existence of a *living* God, who over a long period of time has demonstrated his goodness and care through manifold provisions, is good news for the Gentiles."[31] The ultimate, and new, good news is the message of God's grace revealed through Jesus the Savior, who grants forgiveness of sins and eternal life — a message that Paul had been preaching in Lystra.

14:18 Even with these words they dissuaded the crowds from offering sacrifices to them only with difficulty (καὶ ταῦτα λέγοντες μόλις κατέπαυσαν τοὺς ὄχλους τοῦ μὴ θύειν αὐτοῖς). Luke ends this particular incident in the two apostles' missionary ministry in Lystra with a brief description of the reaction of the crowd. Despite the energetic protest of Paul and Barnabas against the planned procession and sacrifice in their honor, and despite Paul's speech in which he explained the foolishness of such honors in view of the reality of the one true and living God, the Lystrans continue to insist on offering sacrifices. It is "only with difficulty" that they manage to dissuade the crowds from carrying out their plans. Luke's report is realistic. Paul's words do not convince these people to turn away from their traditional gods, they do not cause them to accept the reality of the one true and living God, and they just barely succeed in preventing the idolatrous sacrifice in front of the temple of Zeus.

14:19 Then Jews came from Antioch and Iconium who won over the crowds. They stoned Paul and dragged him outside the city, thinking that he was dead (ἐπῆλθαν δὲ ἀπὸ Ἀντιοχείας καὶ Ἰκονίου Ἰουδαῖοι καὶ πείσαντες τοὺς ὄχλους καὶ λιθάσαντες τὸν Παῦλον ἔσυρον ἔξω τῆς πόλεως νομίζοντες αὐτὸν τεθνηκέναι). The last incident of the Lystra episode (vv. 19 – 20) relates the persecution of Paul and Barnabas by Jews and the citizens

---

29. For similar promises specifically to Israel, cf. Lev 26:4; Jer 5:24. For general descriptions of God's goodness in sending rains and providing harvests, see Pss 145:15 – 16; 147:8 – 9.

30. Cf. Cilliers Breytenbach, "Zeus und der lebendige Gott: Anmerkungen zu Apg 14.11 – 17," *NTS* 39 (1993): 396 – 413.

31. Stenschke, *Luke's Portrait of Gentiles*, 190.

of Lystra. Luke does not indicate how much time elapsed between the enthusiastic response to the healing of the lame man among the population and their attack on Paul. The initiative to harass the missionaries comes not from the citizens of Lystra but from Jews who lived in Pisidian Antioch and in Iconium. They have traveled to Lystra and convince the crowds that the activities of Paul and Barnabas should not be tolerated in the city.

Perhaps these visiting Jews convince the people of Lystra that Paul is turning the world upside down, that they act contrary to the decrees of the emperor in proclaiming another king, namely, Jesus (see the accusation of Jews in Thessalonica; 17:6 – 7); or perhaps they argue that Paul is proclaiming ways of worshiping gods that are contrary to the law (as did the Jews in Corinth; 18:13). Luke leaves open the possibility that the Jews from Pisidian Antioch and Iconium have come to Lystra for personal reasons, perhaps to visit relatives or to attend to business interests. The fact that they manage to get a hearing in Lystra points to the existence of a Jewish community in the city; Gentiles living in a city without a Jewish community would hardly be impressed by complaints against Jewish preachers made by Jews from other cities.

The citizens of Lystra stone Paul, perhaps the same citizens who earlier identified him with the god Hermes. They have evidently accepted Paul's insistence that he and Barnabas are mere mortals and not gods. Thus, being mere human beings, they can be attacked and killed. The depiction of the scene suggests mob violence. Paul relates in 2 Cor 11:25 that he was stoned once, evidently referring to the incident in Lystra. Paul, perhaps severely wounded and probably unconscious, is dragged outside the city, where his body is left for dead. This is the raw side of popular piety; evidently convinced by the visiting Jews that Paul and Barnabas are politically dangerous agitators, their enthusiasm about the healing miracle has morphed into the excitement for a stoning.

14:20 But the disciples formed a circle around him, and he got up and went into the city. The next day he and Barnabas left for Derbe (κυκλωσάντων δὲ τῶν μαθητῶν αὐτὸν ἀναστὰς εἰσῆλθεν εἰς τὴν πόλιν. καὶ τῇ ἐπαύριον ἐξῆλθεν σὺν τῷ Βαρναβᾷ εἰς Δέρβην). Luke's report of the aftermath of Paul's stoning briefly notes his recovery and the apostles' departure from Lystra. The "disciples" are citizens of Lystra who have become followers of Jesus as a result of the missionary activity of Paul and Barnabas in the city. Since Luke has consistently focused on the healing of the lame man and on the pagan "translation" of this event into local religious traditions, he has not yet reported conversions among the population.

Luke's brief statement can be interpreted as a healing miracle. As the believers of Lystra stand in a circle around Paul, who is lying on the ground, bleeding and perhaps unconscious, they undoubtedly pray for him. God answers their prayers in terms of granting Paul a miraculous recovery. Or, the believers stand around Paul, wait for him to slowly recover his senses, and then help him to get up, supporting the injured apostle as he walks back into the city. Since the situation in Lystra has become perilous, Paul and Barnabas leave on the following day, traveling to Derbe. This city had been the center of a vassal kingdom ruled by Antipater son of Perilaus, taken over by the Galatian king Amyntas in 31 BC and incorporated into the province of Galatia in 25 BC. Derbe seems to have had a special relationship with the emperor Claudius, as it was renamed Claudioderbe.

14:21a-c They proclaimed the gospel in that city and won many disciples (εὐαγγελισάμενοί τε τὴν πόλιν ἐκείνην καὶ μαθητεύσαντες ἱκανούς). In a new episode, Luke briefly narrates the missionary work of Paul and Barnabas in Derbe and in Perge and their return to Antioch in Syria (14:21 – 28). The first incident reports the apostles' missionary work in Derbe with a mere eight Greek words (v. 21a-c). Derbe was 93 miles (150 km.) east of Lystra. Traveling on the main Roman road (the Via Sebaste), they would pass through Dalisandos, Kodylessos, Posala, Ilistra, and Laranda, cities in which they may also have preached the gospel (see on 14:7).

Luke mentions the fundamental activity of missionary work. Paul and Barnabas "proclaim the gospel" (εὐαγγελισάμενοι) in the city (v. 21a-b). He also relates the fundamental goal of missionary work: to "win disciples" (μαθητεύσαντες; v. 21c).[32] This term connotes teaching, which implies the two missionaries spend an extended period of time there that lasts longer than the brief reference suggests. A considerable number of people become believers.

14:21d – 22 They returned to Lystra, Iconium, and Antioch. They strengthened the disciples and encouraged them to persevere in the faith, because, they said, "We must endure many hardships to enter the kingdom of God" (ὑπέστρεψαν εἰς τὴν Λύστραν καὶ εἰς Ἰκόνιον καὶ εἰς Ἀντιόχειαν ἐπιστηρίζοντες τὰς ψυχὰς τῶν μαθητῶν, παρακαλοῦντες ἐμμένειν τῇ πίστει καὶ ὅτι διὰ πολλῶν θλίψεων δεῖ ἡμᾶς εἰσελθεῖν εἰς τὴν βασιλείαν τοῦ θεοῦ). The second incident narrates the consolidation of the churches established in Lystra, Iconium, and Pisidian Antioch (vv. 21d – 28). Luke briefly notes the journey from Derbe in a westerly direction to Lystra, Iconium, and Antioch (v. 21d-f), a distance of about 200 miles (330 km.), or thirteen days of walking. Luke's

report of Paul and Barnabas's visitation of the churches in these three cities (vv. 22 – 23) stresses four elements.

(1) The two missionaries "strengthen" (ἐπιστηρίζοντες) the disciples (v. 22a); i.e., they help the Jewish and Gentile believers to become stronger in their commitment to Jesus, Israel's Messiah and Savior. The present participle used here suggests a sustained effort, certainly carried out through teaching the congregation and counseling individuals.

(2) They "encourage" (παρακαλοῦντες) the believers to persevere in the faith (v. 22b-c), urging them to remain loyal to Jesus and to persist in the confidence they have placed in the grace of God revealed in the crucified and risen Jesus. The present participle again indicates sustained teaching by the two apostles. Luke records the theological explanation for the encouragement to persevere. Paul and Barnabas affirm that "we" (i.e., all believers in Jesus) must endure "many hardships" (πολλοὶ θλίψεις) before they enter "the kingdom of God."

The expression "kingdom of God" (ἡ βασιλεία τοῦ θεοῦ) is used in the Synoptic Gospels to summarize Jesus' message of God's salvific revelation that is intimately connected with his own ministry. It is sometimes used in Acts to summarize the truth about God and Jesus that the apostles proclaim (cf. 1:3). Here the expression refers to the final vindication after death in the consummation of salvation.[33] The "hardships" are the afflictions that Old Testament and Jewish texts announce for the messianic age,[34] paralleled in Jesus' announcements about signs of the end of the present age[35] that began with Jesus' first coming and will end

---

32. The only other passage where the verb (μαθητεύω) has the meaning "to cause one to be a pupil, *teach, make a disciple of*" (BDAG) is Matt 28:19.

33. On the notion of "entering" (εἰσελθεῖν) the kingdom of God cf. Mark 9:47; 10:23 – 25; Luke 18:25; 23:42; John 3:5. Cf. Barrett, *Acts*, 686.

34. Cf. Dan 9:20 – 27; 12:1 – 4; *1 En.* 80:2 – 8; 99:4 – 9; 100; *Jub.* 23:11 – 25; *4 Ezra* 5:1 – 13; 6:17 – 28; 7:10 – 35; *Sib. Or.* 3:538 – 44, 633 – 51, 796 – 807; *2 Bar.* 25 – 27; *T. Mos.* 8; 10:1 – 10.

35. Matt 24:7 – 29; Mark 13:7 – 24; Luke 21:9 – 26; see also Rev 6:1 – 17; 7:9 – 9:21; 11:1 – 14; 16:1 – 21.

with his return. Such afflictions are part of God's plan ("we must [δεῖ] endure").[36]

14:23 In each congregation they appointed elders for them, and with prayer and fasting they committed them to the Lord in whom they had come to believe (χειροτονήσαντες δὲ αὐτοῖς κατ᾽ ἐκκλησίαν πρεσβυτέρους, προσευξάμενοι μετὰ νηστειῶν παρέθεντο αὐτοὺς τῷ κυρίῳ εἰς ὃν πεπιστεύκεισαν). (3) The third element of the two apostles' visitation in the churches of Lystra, Iconium, and Pisidian Antioch is the appointment of elders. The verb that Luke uses (χειροτονέω) denotes the election or appointment of people for specific tasks. The term translated as "elders" (πρεσβυτέροι) often describes an older person, but here it describes an "official," i.e., a leader in the local congregation. Since the appointment of officials is made by an authority, it follows that Luke implies here the apostolic authority of Paul and Barnabas.

They appoint elders "in each congregation"; i.e., each church had its own basic organizational structure of leaders. The personal pronoun translated as "for them" (αὐτοῖς) is a dative of advantage. The purpose of appointing elders is not the opportunity for better control of the churches by Paul and Barnabas (or by Syrian Antioch, or by Jerusalem), but the well-being of each local congregation. Understood in the immediate context, the task includes helping the other believers in the hardships they will encounter.

(4) They "commit" the believers to the care and protection of the Lord Jesus in whom the Jewish and Gentile Christians in Lystra, Iconium, and Pisidian Antioch have placed their trust. This is accompanied by prayer and fasting.

14:24 – 25 Then they traveled through Pisidia and came to Pamphylia. They preached the word in Perge and then went to Attalia (καὶ διελθόντες τὴν Πισιδίαν ἦλθον εἰς τὴν Παμφυλίαν καὶ λαλήσαντες ἐν Πέργῃ τὸν λόγον κατέβησαν εἰς Ἀττάλειαν). The third incident of 14:21 – 28 narrates the missionary work of Paul and Barnabas in Perge (vv. 24 – 25). The missionaries travel from Pisidian Antioch through the region of Pisidia in a southerly direction to the region of Pamphylia (see on 13:13 – 14). This journey was 175 miles (280 km.) long — about eleven days of travel. Perge was the capital of the newly constituted province of Pamphylia; with a theater seating 14,000 spectators, it was the largest city since Syrian Antioch in which Paul proclaimed the gospel. Perge's sophisticated culture is demonstrated by inscriptions that document the presence of physicians, philosophers, philologists, athletes, actors, poets, singers, mimes, musicians, and dancers.

Paul's preaching in Perge is related in six Greek words (v. 25a), summarized in this manner: "they preached the word" (λαλήσαντες ... τὸν λόγον). They proclaim the good news of God's gracious offer of forgiveness of sins and eternal life through faith in the crucified and risen Jesus, available for both Jews and Gentiles — the same message they had proclaimed in Salamis and in Paphos, in Pisidian Antioch and in Iconium, in Lystra and in Derbe.

The incident ends with a brief travel notice (v. 25b). Paul and Barnabas go "down" to Attalia, a port city only 9 miles (15 km.) from Perge. Since they want to return to Syria as quickly as possible, they look for and find a ship in Attalia, a proper seaport.

---

36. Cf. 20:23; cf. Rom 8:17; 1 Thess 3:3, 7; 2 Thess 1:5. Bock, *Acts*, 482, rejects the alternative of future ("eschatological") tribulation and present affliction, emphasizing that Paul

regards all events between Jesus' first coming and his return at the end as "eschatological" and as part of the birth pangs (Rom 8:12 – 25).

14:26 From there they sailed back to Antioch, where they had been committed to the grace of God for the work they had now completed (κἀκεῖθεν ἀπέπλευσαν εἰς Ἀντιόχειαν, ὅθεν ἦσαν παραδεδομένοι τῇ χάριτι τοῦ θεοῦ εἰς τὸ ἔργον ὃ ἐπλήρωσαν). The fourth and final incident of the episode on the missionary work in Derbe and Perge consists of three comments (vv. 26–28). First, Luke notes the return journey from Attalia to Antioch in Syria (v. 26). After weeks of travel by foot, the missionaries travel by ship from Attalia to Antioch (v. 26a-b), a journey of about 300 miles (480 km.). Luke comments that Antioch was the place where Paul and Barnabas had been commissioned by the church to embark on the new missionary initiative that had taken them to Salamis, Paphos, Pisidian Antioch, Iconium, Lystra, Derbe, Perge, and other cities along the way.

This reminder (cf. 13:1–3) marks the end of the section that has narrated the mission of Paul and Barnabas on Cyprus and in southern Galatia. The comment reminds Luke's readers of at least three truths. (1) The two missionaries have faithfully carried out their mission, so they return to the church that had sent them on the way. (2) The proclamation of the gospel is "work" (ἔργον), i.e., deeds and actions such as walking, sailing, contacting strangers, speaking with Jews and with Gentiles, entering synagogues, explaining Scripture, proclaiming Jesus as Savior, teaching new believers, and deciding how to react to opposition and persecution. (3) The conversions of Jews and Gentiles and the establishment of new congregations was the result of the "grace of God" (χάρις τοῦ θεοῦ; 13:2, 4 referred to the initiative of the Holy Spirit) into whose care they had been committed, who had caused people to believe in the message about

Jesus the Savior, and who had protected them in difficult and dangerous situations.

14:27 When they arrived, they called the congregation together and reported everything that God had done through them, and how he had opened a door of faith to the Gentiles (παραγενόμενοι δὲ καὶ συναγαγόντες τὴν ἐκκλησίαν ἀνήγγελλον ὅσα ἐποίησεν ὁ θεὸς μετ᾽ αὐτῶν καὶ ὅτι ἤνοιξεν τοῖς ἔθνεσιν θύραν πίστεως). Luke's second comment concerns the report that Paul and Barnabas deliver to the church in Antioch. The fact that they call the congregation together suggests that the believers in Antioch are able to assemble in one place; this may mean that the church is sufficiently small that they can gather in a large house, but it may also mean that they can hold larger gatherings in a public place.

The verb translated as "reported" (ἀνήγγελλον) can be defined as "to carry back information" (BDAG). This is precisely what Paul and Barnabas do; they report the events that happened during the last weeks and months when they proclaimed the gospel in the cities of Cyprus, in south Galatia, and in Pamphylia. Luke emphasizes three elements of their report, in which they provide a theological explanation of the events that had transpired.

(1) They report "everything" that had happened, which would have included many more events than Luke has included in 13:4–14:26. They mention details about missionary work in cities not recorded by Luke, such as Derbe and Perge. Perhaps they give the number of Jews and Gentiles who were converted, the names and the stories of specific individuals,[37] the names of the elders appointed in Derbe, Lystra, Iconium, and Pisidian Antioch (and perhaps in Perge), and the names of

---

37. The only personal name of a convert that Luke includes in 13:4–14:26 is that of Sergius Paulus, the governor of Cyprus (13:7).

those who organized the opposition in the cities of southern Galatia.

(2) They emphasize that everything they had accomplished was God's doing. God had worked "through them," but he was the one who did the work. In 10:38 Peter had explained the activity of Jesus who "traveled from place to place doing good and healing all who were in the power of the devil" with a nearly identical phrase: "God was with him." The miracles that happened in Paphos and in Lystra (and perhaps in other cities) certainly were caused by the power of God. Paul and Barnabas emphasize that everything they did — their travels as much as their quick getaways, their preaching as well as their teaching — was God's work.

(3) They emphasize that Gentiles had come to faith in the one true God and in Jesus the Savior in significant numbers, a development for which God "opened a door." Paul repeatedly refers to "a door" (i.e., a favorable opportunity for missionary work) through which the message of Jesus entered the hearts and minds of people. While Paul usually refers to a door that has been given to *him*,[38] here God has opened a "door of faith" for the Gentiles (τοῖς ἔθνεσιν, dative of advantage). In this context the genitive translated "of faith" (πίστεως) is best understood as an objective genitive: God has given the Gentiles the opportunity to believe in the one true God and in Jesus as the Savior, thus providing a way into the messianic people of God through repentance (13:24), into eternal life (13:46), into salvation (13:47), into the kingdom of God (14:22).

This last statement on the conversion of Gentiles reminds the readers of the conclusion that the Jerusalem church had reached after hearing Peter's report about the conversion of Cornelius and his family and friends: "So God has granted even to the Gentiles the repentance that leads to life" (11:18). Thus, Luke does not assert here that the mission of Paul and Barnabas in the cities of Cyprus, Galatia, and Pamphylia has inaugurated the time of mission to the Gentiles; that had happened several years earlier, when Peter preached the gospel in Caesarea, which led to the conversion of Cornelius (10:45; 11:1, 18). The breakthrough that Paul and Barnabas report when they speak of "a door" that God has opened is the *mass conversion* of Gentiles.

14:28 And they stayed there with the disciples for some time (διέτριβον δὲ χρόνον οὐκ ὀλίγον σὺν τοῖς μαθηταῖς). Luke's final comment relates to the sojourn of Paul and Barnabas in Antioch. The imperfect of the verb (διέτριβον) indicates that their stay in the Syrian capital is indefinite, lasting "for some time" (χρόνον οὐκ ὀλίγον, lit., "no little time"). They stay "with the disciples"; i.e., the two missionaries join and participate in the life of the church in Antioch.

---

38. 1 Cor 16:9; 2 Cor 2:12; Col 4:3. Cf. J. Jeremias, "θύρα," *TDNT*, 3:173, for Jewish and Hellenistic parallels.

Theology in Application

In agreement with the main idea formulated above, the three episodes of the mission in Iconium, in Lystra, and in Derbe and Perge emphasize a number of points.

A Context of Opposition and Persecution

Missionary work takes place in a context of opposition and persecution. Luke reports opposition for Iconium, where citizens want to stone Paul and Barnabas (14:5), and for Lystra, where citizens do manage to stone Paul (14:19). God's opening of a door should not be confused with the elimination of all perils, dangers, and ordeals. Since believers are followers of Jesus, who suffered and died, this should not come as a surprise. While missionary strategies that seek to minimize personal risk for the missionary are certainly valid — Paul and Barnabas did not stay in Lystra after Paul had been stoned but left, although they returned a few weeks later — risks will remain, if it is indeed the gospel that is being preached rather than the lowest common denominator of some religious or ethical consensus that nobody finds objectionable.

Signs and Wonders

Missionary work is accompanied by signs and wonders. Luke records the occurrence of signs and wonders for the ministry of Paul and Barnabas in Iconium (14:3), and the focus of the Lystra episode is the healing of a lame man (14:8 – 14). The occurrence of miracles cannot be "factored in" when missionaries plan strategies or write "to-do lists" for successful church-planting ministries. The supernatural power of God cannot be reduced to a mere "factor" that we can plan, use, or execute in order to achieve preformulated goals. Miracles, should God grant them, do not make church planting automatically successful. The end result of the healing of the lame man was the Lystrans' stoning of Paul. Miracles are easily misunderstood if their cause and meaning are not seen in the context of the proclamation of the word of God.

Religious Ideas That Confuse God and the World

Missionary work challenges religious ideas that confuse God and the world. The belief of the people in Lystra that Paul and Barnabas are the gods Zeus and Hermes visiting their town is the first encounter of Christians with "pure" pagans in Acts. Luke's account, which follows the healing of the lame man, illustrates the difficulties of such an encounter, the potential for misunderstanding, and the importance of penetrating theological analysis and decisive action.

The difficulty is caused by several factors. Pagans believe in many gods. They also confuse God and the world in that tangible objects (such as idol images) are venerated as possessing divine power, human beings can acquire divine status (such as heroes and the emperor worshiped in many Greek towns), and divine entities can come down in the guise of human beings (such as Zeus and Hermes). Such misunderstandings result from the fact that the citizens of Lystra, who presumably have heard Paul preach, do not grasp his conviction that there is only one true God, that God's envoys (Paul and Barnabas) are not divine themselves, and that Paul is calling their entire system of worship into question.

The importance of penetrating theological analysis is evident in the fact that Paul, when he realizes what the citizens of Lystra are planning, immediately relates their actions with the truth about the one true God; in so doing, he communicates the gospel in a manner that is intelligible for Lystrans. The integrity of missionary work and the integrity of the gospel are maintained by penetrating theological analysis. Missionaries do not simply tell stories; rather, they communicate theology in the proper sense of the word. That is, they proclaim God's word, which is the truth about the reality of God and of his salvation in the life, death, and resurrection of Jesus, Israel's Messiah and the Savior of the world.

The importance of decisive action is seen in the vehement protest of Paul and Barnabas against the planned sacrifice and in the speech in which they explain to the people of Lystra why such a sacrifice would be a sacrilege. Paul and Barnabas refuse to utilize the superstitious, uncritical piety of the Lycaonians for missionary purposes. For example, they could have argued that even though the sacrifice itself was problematic, the community that it created among the participants would help them to become more acceptable in the city, a strategically important development.

Proclaiming the Living God and His Grace

Missionary work proclaims the living God and his grace. The proclamation of the gospel includes "monotheistic propaedeutics"[39] in terms of a biblical theology of the one true God, of the world as his creation, and of his revelation in creation. The monotheistic focus implies a criticism of human religion, performed not as a philosophical critique but as a theological analysis, based on the Scriptures. Paul proclaims the one true living God, who demands to be recognized. Paul draws inferences concerning the identity of the pagan deities that he calls "worthless things," and he emphasizes the distinction between God and mere mortals such as himself and Barnabas — all in the desire to lead the people of Lystra to faith in the one true God and in Jesus the Savior.

While Paul shows understanding for the traditional ways of the Lystrans, he does not play down their guilt. Instead, he challenges them to turn away from their ances-

---

39. Jürgen Roloff, *Die Apostelgeschichte* (NTD 5; Göttingen: Vandenhoeck & Ruprecht, 1981), 215.

tral forms of worship and to turn to the living God. The Lystra episode underlines again that salvation depends on faith, and faith comes from hearing the word of God (14:9). At the same time, the missionary work in Lystra underlines the universality of authentic missionary work. Paul and Barnabas evangelize not only among the educated in the cities but also among people who live in a more rural setting. They contact not only Greeks but also "barbarians," who speak another language; they travel not only to the centers of Greek culture, but also to the politically unimportant hinterland of Lycaonia.

Nurturing New Churches and Sending Churches

Missionary work nurtures both new churches and sending churches. When Paul and Barnabas have completed their mission in Derbe, they could have reached Tarsus traveling further east for only about 140 miles (220 km.) and then reaching Antioch in Syria after a further 140 miles. Instead, they backtrack their earlier route through the cities in which they encountered severe opposition that put their lives in dangers, walking 195 miles (330 km.) back in a westerly direction. Paul and Barnabas felt it was important to nurture the new believers in Lystra, Iconium, and Pisidian Antioch, strengthening them through further teaching and structural consolidation. When they eventually do return to Antioch in Syria, they give a report to the church, which nurtures the involvement of the Antioch believers in missionary outreach and strengthens their trust in the Lord, who had opened doors to the Gentile world.

Acts 15:1 – 33

Literary Context

Luke's narrative of the missionary work of Paul and Barnabas in Asia Minor (13:1 – 15:33) consists of two sections: the report of the two apostles' mission in the provinces of Cyprus, Galatia, and Pamphylia (13:1 – 14:28), and the report of the Apostles' Council in Jerusalem (15:1 – 33). While some commentators treat 15:1 – 33 as a separate major section,[1] it is preferable to treat the passage as an episode connected with the missionary work of Paul and Barnabas.[2] The dispute about the policies for the mission among Gentiles broke out in Antioch (14:28; 15:1), and it was the debate between the Jewish Christians from Jerusalem (who taught that Gentile believers must be circumcised) and Paul and Barnabas (15:1 – 2b) that triggered the plan of a conference in Jerusalem where this matter would be discussed with the apostles and the elders (15:2c-j).

The Apostles' Council in Jerusalem (15:1 – 33) completes Luke's shift from his focus on Peter's mission (chs. 1 – 12) to Paul's mission (chs. 13 – 14; 16 – 20). However, while Peter disappears from Luke's narrative after Acts 15, Jerusalem does not: Paul's last journey to Jerusalem is narrated in great detail (21:1 – 16), and it is Paul's contact with the Jerusalem church and his willingness to counter rumors that he teaches Jews to abandon the law (21:17 – 25) that lead to his arrest (21:27 – 22:21) and imprisonment (22:22 – 23:35) in Jerusalem and then Caesarea.

The interpretation of the Apostles' Council in Acts 15 has been complicated by chronological questions that arise from the correlation of Acts 15 with Gal 2. The view that Acts 15 and Gal 2:1 – 10 describe the same event has been the majority view. However, problems with this identification have prompted a significant minority to identify the meeting that Paul describes in Gal 2 with the famine relief visit of Paul and Barnabas (Acts 11:27 – 30) and to interpret Acts 15 without correlation to Paul's report in Gal 2.[3] The following sequence of events appears to be the most plausible:

---

1. Cf. Barrett, *Acts*, 695; Fitzmyer, *Acts*, 538.
2. Cf. Pesch, *Apostelgeschichte*, 2:68 – 71; Bock, *Acts*, 486.

3. Cf. Bauckham, "James, Peter, and the Gentiles," 135 – 39; Schnabel, *Early Christian Mission*, 2:987 – 92.

32	Damascus	Paul's conversion
32 – 34	Arabia	Paul's missionary work in Damascus and in Arabia (Acts 9:20 – 24; Gal 1:15 – 17)
34	Jerusalem	Paul visits Jerusalem for the first time after his conversion, meeting Barnabas, Peter, and James (Acts 9:26 – 28; Gal 1:18 – 19)
34 – 43	Cilicia/Syria	Paul's missionary work in Cilicia and Syria (Acts 9:30; Gal 1:21 – 24)
44	Jerusalem	Consultation: Paul visits Jerusalem for the second time after his conversion, sent by the church in Antioch on the occasion of the famine relief for the believers in Jerusalem (Acts 11:27 – 30), accompanied by Barnabas; they consult with Peter, John, and James concerning the gospel that he preaches among the Gentiles (Gal 2:1 – 10)
45 – 47	Cyprus/Galatia	Paul's missionary work in Cyprus, Galatia, and Pamphylia
48	Antioch	Antioch Incident: Paul clashes with Peter in Antioch over the question of table fellowship between Jewish Christians and Gentile Christians (Gal 2:11 – 14); the Antioch incident probably takes place in the summer of AD 48
48	Antioch	Paul writes his letter to the Galatians
48	Jerusalem	Apostles' Council: Paul visits Jerusalem for the third time after his conversion, accompanied by Barnabas, to discuss with the apostles and the elders of the Jerusalem church the question of circumcision of Gentile believers and other matters related to the Mosaic law (Acts 15:1 – 33); the Apostles' Council probably takes place in the fall of AD 48

Main Idea

Luke relates in this episode how the early church reached a consensus decision regarding the disputed question of whether Gentile Christians should submit to circumcision and to wholesale obedience to the Mosaic law. The passage states (with Peter) that faith in Jesus and the grace of the Lord are the basis for salvation. It states (with Paul and Barnabas) that God has authenticated the Gentile mission in which Gentiles are not told to become Jewish proselytes. And it states (with James) that Gentile Christians are members of God's people *as Gentiles*, worshiping God in the temple of "restored Israel," which is the messianic community of the last days, and

that Gentile Christians need to comply only with some fundamental regulations that
the law stipulated for Gentiles living among Jews.

Translation

Acts 15:1–33

15:1a	Event/Antagonist	**Certain people came from Judea to Antioch**
b	Action	**and taught the believers:**
c	Condition	*"Unless you are circumcised*
d	Reason	*because of the custom of Moses,*
e	Assertion	*you cannot be saved."*
2a	Event	After Paul and Barnabas engaged in sharp dispute and
b		controversy with them,
c	Action	**it was decided** that
d	Protagonist	Paul,
e	Protagonist	Barnabas, and
f	Protagonist	some of the others
g	Action	should go to Jerusalem
h	Purpose	to discuss this controversial matter
i	Protagonist	with the apostles and
j	Protagonist	the elders.
3a	Action	**The congregation sent them on their way,**
b	Place	and as they traveled through Phoenicia
c	Place	and Samaria,
d	Action	**they informed the believers about the conversion of the Gentiles**
e	Action	**and brought great joy to all the believers.**
4a	Setting: time & geographical	When they arrived in Jerusalem,
b	Event	**they were welcomed by the congregation and by**
c		**the apostles and**
d		**elders,**
e	Action	**and they reported all that God had accomplished**
f	Agency	through them.
5a	Action	**Then some**
b	Description	who belonged to the party of the Pharisees,
c	Description	who had become believers,
d	Action	**stood up and said:**
e	Demand	*"They must be circumcised*
f	Demand	*and ordered to keep the law of Moses."*
6a	Event/Protagonist	**The apostles and the elders met together**
b	Purpose	to look into this matter.
7a	Event	After much discussion,
b	Action/Protagonist	**Peter stood up and said to them:**

c	Address	"Brothers,
d	Reminder	you know that
e	Setting: time	in the early days
f	Action	God chose me from among you
g	Purpose	to be the one
h	Agency	from whose lips the Gentiles should hear the word of the gospel
i	Result	and believe.
8a	Action	And God,
b	Description	who knows the human heart,
c	Action	confirmed that he accepted them
d	Means	by giving them the Holy Spirit,
e	Comparison	just as he did to us.
9a	Action	He made no distinction between us and them
b	Action	when he cleansed their hearts
c	Means	by faith.
10a	Question	Why then are you now testing God
b	Means	by placing a yoke on the neck of the disciples
c	Assertion	that neither your ancestors nor we have ☞ been able to bear?
11a	Assertion	Rather, we believe that
b	Means	it is through the grace of the Lord Jesus
c	Assertion	that we are saved,
d	Comparison	just as they are."
12a	Result/Event	**The whole assembly kept silent.**
b	Event/Protagonist	**And they listened to Barnabas and Paul**
c	Action	as they described the signs and wonders
d	Agency	that God had performed
e	Agency	through them
f	Setting: geographical	among the Gentiles.
13a	Setting: time	After they finished,
b	Action/Protagonist	**James spoke up:**
c	Address	"Brothers,
d	Exhortation	listen to me.
14a	Reminder	Simeon has described
b	Action	how God first intervened to acquire a people
c	Setting: social	from among the Gentiles
d	Purpose	for his name.
15a	Assertion	The words of the prophets agree with this,
b	Quotation of OT	as it is written, (Amos 9:11-12)
16a	Setting: time	'After this (Hos 3:5)
b	Action	I will return, (Jer 12:15-16)
c	Action	and I will rebuild the fallen tent of David;
d	Restatement	from its ruins I will rebuild it,
e	Action	and I will restore it,

Continued on next page.

Continued from previous page.

17a	Purpose	so that the rest of humanity may seek the Lord,
b	Setting: social	even all the Gentiles
c	Description	over whom my name is invoked,
d	Confirmation	says the Lord,
e	Assertion	who does these things,
18	Expansion	things known from long ago.' (Isa 45:21)
19a	Conclusion	Therefore it is my judgment that
b	Suggestion	we should stop causing trouble for the Gentiles
c	Description	who are turning to God.
20a	Suggestion	We should instruct them
b	Means	in a letter
c	Command	to abstain
d	Instruction	from food polluted by idols,
e	Instruction	from sexual immorality,
f	Instruction	from the meat of strangled animals, and
g	Instruction	from blood.
21a	Reminder	For Moses has had those who proclaim him
b	Setting: geographical	in every city,
c	Setting: social	for generations,
d	Reminder	and he is read in the synagogues
e	Setting: time	every Sabbath."
22a	Action/Protagonist	**Then the apostles**
b	Protagonist	**and elders**
c		**decided,**
d	Protagonist	together with the entire congregation,
e	Action	to choose some of their own men
f	Action	and send them to Antioch
g	Protagonist	with Paul and Barnabas.
h	Action Protagonist	**They chose Judas called Barsabbas and**
i	Protagonist	**Silas,**
j	Description	leading men among the brothers.
23a	Action	**They were to deliver the following letter:**
b	Prescript Sender	"The apostles and elders,
c	Description	your brothers,
d	Address Setting: social	to the believers of Gentile origin in
e	Setting: geographical	Antioch,
f	Setting: geographical	Syria, and
g	Setting: geographical	Cilicia,
h	Greeting	greetings!
24a	Reason	Since we have heard that
b	Antagonist	some people
c	Description	who have gone out from us without any orders from us
d	Action	have thrown you into confusion
e	Means	with their talk,
f	Result	causing you inward distress,

25a	Action	we decided
b	Manner	unanimously
c	Action	to choose some men
d	Action	and send them to you
e	Association	with our dear friends Barnabas and Paul,
26	Description	who have devoted their lives to the name of our Lord ↺ Jesus Christ.
27a	Action	Thus we send Judas and
b		Silas,
c	Action	who themselves will convey to you the same message
d	Means	by word of mouth:
28a	Assertion	It is the decision of the Holy Spirit,
b	Assertion	and ours as well,
c	Decision	not to burden you beyond these essentials:
29a	Command	to abstain
b	Instruction	from food sacrificed to idols,
c	Instruction	from blood,
d	Instruction	from the meat of strangled animals, and
e	Instruction	from sexual immorality.
f	Exhortation	If you keep away from these things,
g		you will do well.
h	Greeting	Farewell."
30a	Action	**So they were sent off**
b	Action	**and traveled to Antioch,**
c	Action	where they gathered the congregation together
d	Action	and delivered the letter.
31a	Action	When they read it,
b	Result	they were delighted at the encouragement.
32a	Action	**Judas and Silas,**
b	Description	who were themselves prophets,
c	Action	**encouraged and strengthened the believers**
d	Means	with many words.
33a	Setting: time	After spending some time there,
b	Action	**they were sent off by the believers**
c	Means	with a blessing of peace
d	Setting: social	to those who had sent them.

Structure and Literary Form

The episode of the Apostles' Council (15:1 – 33) is made up of eight incidents.

1. Luke relates the prehistory of the meeting in Jerusalem, namely, the dispute in Antioch about the necessity for Gentile believers to be circumcised and keep the Mosaic law (vv. 1 – 3).

2. The Antioch delegation arrives, with a report of Paul and Barnabas about what happened in their missionary work; this brings to light the controversy over the status of Gentile Christians (vv. 4 – 5).

3. The apostles and elders convene a council meeting to discuss the status of the converted Gentiles (vv. 6 – 7a).

4. Peter gives a speech (vv. 7b – 11) in which he reminds the assembly of the events in Caesarea when Gentiles who believed in Jesus were converted and received the Holy Spirit.

5. Briefly and without direct speech, Paul and Barnabas report about their missionary work, authenticated by God through signs and wonders (v. 12).

6. James gives a speech (vv. 13 – 21) that confirms the theological consensus of the apostles and elders, as well as of Paul and Barnabas.

7. The decision of the assembly (the "apostolic decree") is recorded in a letter addressed to the Gentile Christians (vv. 22 – 29).

8. Luke ends the narrative of the Apostles' Council where he started it — in Antioch, where the outcome of the deliberations are being made known (vv. 30 – 33).

The episode is a *historical narrative* that includes *direct speech* (v. 1c-e: the Jewish Christians who demand that Gentile believers be circumcised; v. 5e-f: Pharisaic believers who demand that Gentile believers be circumcised; vv. 7c – 11: Peter's speech;[4] vv. 13 – 21: James's speech), a *quotation* from the Old Testament (vv. 15 – 18), a *letter* quoted verbatim (vv. 23 – 29), an *official decree* (vv. 25 – 29), brief *missionary reports* (vv. 3d-e, 4e-f, 12), and brief *travel notices* (vv. 3b-c, 30a-b).

Exegetical Outline

➡ **I. The Council of the Apostles, Elders, as well as Paul and Barnabas (15:1 – 33)**

    A. Prehistory: The Dispute in Antioch about Circumcision and the Role of the Mosaic Law (15:1 – 3)

        1. Arrival of Judean Christians who demand that Gentile Christians become proselytes (15:1)

---

4. Peter's speech in 15:7b – 11 is the eleventh (and last) speech of Peter that Luke includes in his narrative; cf. 1:15 – 22; 2:14 – 36; 2:37 – 40; 3:1 – 10; 3:11 – 26; 4:5 – 22; 5:3 – 6, 8 – 10; 5:27 – 33; 10:34 – 43; 11:1 – 18.

2. Debate between these Judean Christians and Paul and Barnabas (15:2a-b)

3. Preparations for a conference with the apostles and elders in Jerusalem (15:2c-j)

4. Travel through Phoenicia and Syria contacting existing churches (15:3)

B. Reception of the Antioch Delegation in Jerusalem (15:4 – 5)

1. Arrival and welcome in the Jerusalem church (15:4a-d)

2. Report of Paul and Barnabas about their missionary work (15:4e-f)

3. Protest and demands of Jewish Christians belonging to the Pharisees (15:5)

C. Council of the Apostles and Elders (15:6 – 7a)

1. Convocation of the apostles and elders (15:6)

2. Debate about the status of the Gentile converts (15:7a)

D. Peter's speech (15:7b – 12a)

1. Address (15:7b-c)

2. Argument from God's gift of the Holy Spirit in the conversion of Cornelius (15:7d – 9)

3. Inference: Faith and the grace of the Lord Jesus as the basis of salvation (15:10 – 11)

4. Reaction of the audience (15:12a)

E. Barnabas's and Paul's report (15:12b-f)

1. The attention of the audience (15:12b)

2. The report of Paul and Barnabas (15:12c)

3. The authentication of the Gentiles' faith through miracles (15:12d-f)

F. James's speech (15:13 – 21)

1. Address (15:13)

2. Argument from God's initiative: Circumcision is not necessary for Gentiles (15:14)

3. Argument from Scripture (Amos 9:11 – 12; with Hos 3:5; Jer 12:15 – 16; Isa 45:21) (15:15 – 18)

4. Inference: Gentile believers do not have to become Jews in order to have salvation (15:19)

5. Suggestion: Gentile believers should keep certain Jewish regulations (15:20)

6. Rationale of the four stipulations (15:21)

G. Decision of the Assembly and Letter to the Gentile Christians (15:22 – 29)

1. Appointment of envoys from the apostles and elders to the church in Antioch (15:22)

2. Letter of the apostles and elders (15:23 – 29)

H. Aftermath: The Explanation of the Decision in Antioch (15:30 – 33)

1. Paul and Barnabas as well as Judas and Silas travel to Antioch (15:30a-b)

2. Convocation of the Antioch church and delivery of the apostolic letter (15:30c-d)

3. Reading of the letter of the apostles and Jerusalem elders (15:31a)

4. Reaction of the believers in Antioch, who rejoice over the decision in Jerusalem (15:31b)

5. Judas's and Silas's involvement in the ministry in the church in Antioch (15:32)

6. Judas and Silas depart for Jerusalem (15:33)

Explanation of the Text

15:1 Certain people came from Judea to Antioch and taught the believers: "Unless you are circumcised because of the custom of Moses, you cannot be saved" (καί τινες κατελθόντες ἀπὸ τῆς Ἰουδαίας ἐδίδασκον τοὺς ἀδελφοὺς ὅτι, ἐὰν μὴ περιτμηθῆτε τῷ ἔθει τῷ Μωϋσέως, οὐ δύνασθε σωθῆναι). While Paul and Barnabas are involved in teaching and preaching in Antioch after their return from Galatia (14:28), Jewish Christians arrive and raise demands regarding the Gentile Christians. Luke identifies the new arrivals vaguely as "certain people" (τινες) who came "from Judea" (see on 1:8; 5:16).

In v. 5 Luke describes Jewish Christians who want to formulate new requirements for Gentile Christians as belonging to the movement of the Pharisees, centered in Jerusalem. While the reference to "Judea" may simply be a stylistic variant for "Jerusalem," it is possible the Jewish Christians who make these demands belong to churches both in Jerusalem and in other towns of Judea.[5] These people are probably identical with the "men ... from James" (Gal 2:12) who belong to the group of Jewish Christians who insist that Gentile Christians should be circumcised and keep the Mosaic law, including the food laws. Luke does not explain why these Jewish Christians traveled 335 miles (540 km.) from Jerusalem to Antioch. They may have had private reasons for visiting the Syrian capital, or they were concerned about the status of the Gentile converts in the church in Antioch, which was proving to become a key center for missionary work.

The reference to "the believers" (οἱ ἀδελφοί)[6] should not be limited to the Gentile Christians. The teaching activity of the Judean Christians *also* targets Jewish Christians such as Paul, Barnabas, and Peter (see on v. 2), who have been teaching Jewish believers and Gentile believers in Antioch that they do *not* have to keep the requirements that the Judean Christians are now emphasizing.

The significance of their teaching is emphasized by relating its content in direct speech (introduced by ὅτι). When we analyze the demands that these Judean Christians raise in the light of v. 5, two related matters are emphasized: Gentile Christians must be circumcised,[7] and they must observe the Mosaic law. While the syntax of the Greek formulation focuses on the demand for circumcision, it should be noted that while the Mosaic law stipulates that newborn (male) members of God's people must be circumcised (Lev 12:3); Jewish tradition connects circumcision with Abraham (Gen 17:9–14) rather than with Moses.[8] The reference to "the custom of Moses" (τὸ ἔθος τὸ Μωϋσέως) does not describe a mere "habit" but the long-established "practice" of the Jewish people, whose lives were determined by the Mosaic law.

These Judean Christians are teaching that a Gentile must be circumcised and keep the stipulations of the Mosaic law in order to "be saved." The passive voice of the verb (σωθῆναι) denotes God

---

5. Cf. 1:8; 2:14; 8:1, where Luke distinguishes between Jerusalem and Judea.

6. GNB, NLT, TNIV; most English versions translate "brothers" (ESV, NET, NIV 1984, NRSV; cf. NASB, RSV "brethren"). While circumcision would have affected the male Gentile Christians (thus the "brothers"), the insistence on keeping the food laws would have affected the female Gentile Christians as well (thus the "believers").

7. On circumcision see 7:8.

8. Codex D clarifies the ambiguity, reading in v. 1: "unless you are circumcised and walk according to the custom of Moses"; cf. Rius-Camps and Read-Heimerdinger, *Acts*, 3:176–77. This is a theological, ritual, ceremonial, and ethical condition — the Mosaic law regulates all areas of life.

as the author of salvation. These Judeans hold that before the one true God can accept Gentiles as genuine members of his holy people, saved from the consequences of their idolatry and other sins, and bestow on them all the benefits of his mercy and grace, they must become proselytes. Circumcision was the sign of belonging to God's people since the time of Abraham,[9] the first "convert" from paganism according to Jewish tradition. Moreover, obeying the law was the sine qua non of belonging to God's people since the time of Moses, the leader who secured salvation for Israel in the exodus from Egypt. Thus, the position of the Judean Christians is logically consistent.

This position assumes that the life, death, resurrection, and exaltation of Jesus, Israel's Messiah and Savior, affect the *quality* of what constitutes the life of the people of God (full forgiveness of all sins through faith in Jesus), but not the *quantity* of what constitutes the boundaries of the elect people of God (full membership through circumcision and obedience to the law). And since full membership in the people of God is required for being granted full salvation, bona fide members of God's people must have *both* faith (Lat. *fides*) in Jesus *and* circumcision and obedience to the law. The discussion at the Apostles' Council was "not merely post-conversion behavior but what constitutes true conversion in the first place."[10]

15:2 After Paul and Barnabas engaged in sharp dispute and controversy with them, it was decided that Paul, Barnabas, and some of the others should go to Jerusalem to discuss this controversial matter with the apostles and the elders

(γενομένης δὲ στάσεως καὶ ζητήσεως οὐκ ὀλίγης τῷ Παύλῳ καὶ τῷ Βαρναβᾷ πρὸς αὐτούς, ἔταξαν ἀναβαίνειν Παῦλον καὶ Βαρναβᾶν καί τινας ἄλλους ἐξ αὐτῶν πρὸς τοὺς ἀποστόλους καὶ πρεσβυτέρους εἰς Ἰερουσαλὴμ περὶ τοῦ ζητήματος τούτου). Paul and Barnabas strongly disagree with the position and the teaching of these Judean Christians. Luke describes the ensuing debate in the church in Antioch with two nouns: there was a "dispute" (στάσις), i.e., "a lack of agreement respecting policy" and thus "strife, discord, disunion" (BDAG), and a "controversy" (ζήτησις), i.e., a controversial discussion, an argumentative debate about the merits of the teaching of these Judean Christians on the one hand and of the teaching and practice of Peter and Barnabas on the other.

The vehemence of the discussion (οὐκ ὀλίγης, lit., "not a little," a litotes, i.e., a deliberate understatement) was due to the fact — if the above historical reconstruction is correct — that the activity of these Judean Christians had caused Peter, who was visiting Antioch, to abandon his practice of having table fellowship with the Gentile Christians (Gal 2:12), which in turn prompted other Jewish believers in the Antioch congregation, including Barnabas, to withdraw from full fellowship with the Gentile believers (Gal 2:13).

In Gal 2:13 Paul calls this behavior of Peter and Barnabas "hypocrisy," i.e., behavior that contradicts their views about this matter. They hold that Gentiles who come to faith in Jesus are saved and thus members of God's people without submitting to circumcision and to all the other stipulations of the Mosaic law,[11] and yet they now pull away from the Gentile believers because certain Christians

---

9. Abandonment of circumcision by Jews was regarded as apostasy, cf. 1 Macc 1:11 – 15; Philo, *Abraham* 89 – 92. There are virtually no exceptions to the requirement of circumcision: the advice of the Jewish Ananias to the Gentile Izates, king of Adiabene, not to be circumcised as this may place his position as king in jeopardy, is only a partial exception: Eleazar from

Galilee advised circumcision, to which Izates then submitted (Josephus, *Ant.* 20.38 – 48).

10. Wilson, *Luke and the Law* (SNTSMS 50; Cambridge: Cambridge Univ. Press, 1983), 72; Barrett, *Acts*, 700.

11. For Peter, see Acts 11:1 – 17; for Barnabas, see his collaboration with Paul in Acts 13 – 14.

from Jerusalem (Gal 2:12) demand that Gentile believers should be circumcised and keep the law. The Antioch church sends Paul and Barnabas as well as other church members to Jerusalem so that this "controversial matter" (ζήτημα) can be considered and decided in a meeting with the apostles and elders.

15:3 The congregation sent them on their way, and as they traveled through Phoenicia and Samaria, they informed the believers about the conversion of the Gentiles and brought great joy to all the believers (οἱ μὲν οὖν προπεμφθέντες ὑπὸ τῆς ἐκκλησίας διήρχοντο τήν τε Φοινίκην καὶ Σαμάρειαν ἐκδιηγούμενοι τὴν ἐπιστροφὴν τῶν ἐθνῶν καὶ ἐποίουν χαρὰν μεγάλην πᾶσιν τοῖς ἀδελφοῖς). Luke ends his report of the prehistory of the Apostles' Council with a travel notice. The congregation in Antioch sends Paul, Barnabas, and other believers on their way. The group travels through Phoenicia (see on 11:19) and Samaria (see on 1:8; 8:5). The reference to "believers" (ἀδελφοί) in these regions implies the existence of congregations of followers of Jesus in several cities and towns of Phoenicia and Samaria (cf. 11:19; 8:5), documented later for Tyre (21:3 – 4) and Sidon (27:3).

The Antioch delegation informs the believers in the churches in Phoenicia and Samaria about the conversion of the Gentiles. This is the only occurrence of the noun "conversion" (ἐπιστροφή) in the New Testament, describing the turning of Gentiles from idols to the one true and living God, trusting in the life, death, and resurrection of Jesus, Israel's Messiah and Savior, for forgiveness of sins, rescue from God's wrath, and eternal life (cf. 1 Thess 1:9 – 10). Since it can be assumed that the conversion of Greeks in Antioch (11:21), the capital of the province, was already common knowledge, the report evidently concerns the establishment of congregations of followers of Jesus in the cities of Cyprus, Galatia, and Pamphylia (13:1 – 14:25).

The report that Paul and Barnabas had presented to the church in Antioch (14:27) is now given to the churches in Phoenicia and Samaria.

As Paul and Barnabas provide details about the conversion of Gentiles, they cause "great joy" (χαρὰν μεγάλην) among "all" the believers. This means that the believers in these churches of Phoenicia and Samaria — whether they were Jews, Samaritans, Phoenicians, Syrians, or Greeks — approve of their mission among the Gentiles. In other words, there is widespread public support for the missionary work of Paul and Barnabas, who did not require converted Gentiles to be circumcised and keep the full law.

15:4 When they arrived in Jerusalem, they were welcomed by the congregation and by the apostles and elders, and they reported all that God had accomplished through them (παραγενόμενοι δὲ εἰς Ἰερουσαλὴμ παρεδέχθησαν ἀπὸ τῆς ἐκκλησίας καὶ τῶν ἀποστόλων καὶ τῶν πρεσβυτέρων, ἀνήγγειλάν τε ὅσα ὁ θεὸς ἐποίησεν μετ' αὐτῶν). Luke uses the second incident of the Apostles' Council narrative to describe the controversy in Jerusalem over the status of the Gentile Christians (vv. 4 – 5).

Luke first notes the arrival of the Antioch delegation in Jerusalem. The group, which includes Paul and Barnabas, is "welcomed" by the three groups that participate in the conference: (1) "the congregation" (ἡ ἐκκλησία), i.e., the community of the followers of Jesus in Jerusalem; (2) "the apostles" (οἱ ἀπόστολοι), i.e., the Twelve, Jesus' closest group of disciples — at least those of the Twelve who had returned to Jerusalem after the persecution under King Agrippa I (see on 12:1, 17), perhaps with the specific aim of attending the conference on the status of the Gentile believers; (3) the "elders" (οἱ πρεσβύτεροι), i.e., the present leaders of the Jerusalem church — among them James, Jesus' brother (v. 13; cf. 12:17). The location of the meeting and of the subsequent deliberations may have been Solomon's Portico, which is particularly plausible if a large part of the Jerusalem congregation was present.

After their arrival and welcome, the Antioch delegation "reports" the missionary initiatives and successes that they have been involved in. If Luke intends his readers to distinguish between their report in the churches in Phoenicia and Samaria (v. 3), where the Antioch delegation specifically recounts the conversions of Gentiles, and their report in the church in Jerusalem (v. 4), the expression "all" (ὅσα) refers more generally to the conversion of both Jews and Gentiles to faith in Jesus as Israel's Messiah and Savior. This included the Roman proconsul Sergius Paulus in the city of Paphos (13:12). Local congregations were established and elders had been appointed (14:23).

Paul and Barnabas emphasize that the conversions of people and the establishment of communities of believers had been accomplished by God, who had worked "through them"; i.e., God had been active in their preaching and teaching (cf. 14:27). Paul and Barnabas will repeat this report during the meeting of the apostles and elders (v. 12). The emphasis on God as the causative agent in the conversion of Jews and Gentiles is not a "tactical" move to preempt the discussion about the status of the Gentiles believers, suggesting that any argument against their practice of not circumcising the Gentile converts is tantamount to questioning God himself. Rather, Paul is *always* convinced that only God's power can move either Jews or Gentiles to faith in Jesus, the crucified and risen Messiah and Savior (cf. 1 Cor 1:18 – 2:5).

15:5 Then some who belonged to the party of the Pharisees, who had become believers, stood up and said: "They must be circumcised and ordered to keep the law of Moses" (ἐξανέστησαν δέ τινες τῶν ἀπὸ τῆς αἱρέσεως τῶν Φαρισαίων πεπιστευκότες λέγοντες ὅτι δεῖ περιτέμνειν αὐτοὺς παραγγέλλειν τε τηρεῖν τὸν νόμον Μωϋσέως). In contrast to the reaction of the believers in the churches in Phoenicia and Samaria, who had rejoiced when they heard the report of the Antioch delegation (v. 3), the report before the Jerusalem congregation provokes the protest of some Jewish Christians who belonged to the "party" (αἵρεσις; see on 5:17) of the Pharisees and who had come to faith (πεπιστευκότες)[12] in Jesus as Israel's Messiah.

While Luke provides no further details about the circumstances of the conversion of Pharisees, the comment in v. 5b is significant in documenting the fact that there were Pharisees (besides Saul/Paul, 26:5) who had responded to the proclamation of Jesus as Israel's Messiah and Savior by faith. Since the Pharisees were arguably the Jews most devoted to Israel's God and his will as revealed in the law, it was hardly surprising that they were the main dialogue partners of Jesus. Thus, it is hardly surprising that an (unknown) number of Pharisees have become Christians.

The Pharisaic Jewish Christians stand up in the first meeting of the Jerusalem congregation with the Antioch delegation to protest against the status accorded to the Gentiles who had been converted and accepted as members of God's people without circumcision and full commitment to the Mosaic law. While they may not be identical with the Judean Christians mentioned in v. 1 (who seemed to have moved on to southern Galatia), they also want to mandate for Gentile converts circumcision and the keeping of the law as a condition for salvation.

---

12. The perfect tense of the participle indicates that they had indeed become believers. It is thus incorrect when Johnson, *Acts*, 260, states at this point that "Luke never portrays the Pharisees in positive terms" — to become a believer in Jesus is certainly and always "positive"! Also, Luke does not set all Christian Pharisees in opposition to Paul and Barnabas: only "some" (τινες) were critical of their missionary theology and practice.

To underline the significance of their demands, Luke reports in direct speech the robust rigor of their demand: Gentile believers "must [δεῖ] be circumcised" and "must" (δεῖ) be ordered to "keep" (τηρεῖν) the law of Moses; this is the will of God.

For these Jews, these two demands constitute one single reality: people who are circumcised and who are thus members of God's people, enjoying the privileges of God's covenant with Abraham and with Israel, will keep the stipulations of the law, the duties of God's covenant with Israel; and people who keep the law of Moses are, naturally, people who have been circumcised. This had been true since the time of Abraham and Moses, and since Jesus had not abrogated the law (they could have pointed to Matt 5:17 – 20 or Luke 16:17), this foundational principle is still in effect. The Pharisaic Jewish Christians argue that Gentile converts must first become Jewish proselytes if they want to be members of God's people.

15:6 The apostles and the elders met together to look into this matter (συνήχθησάν τε οἱ ἀπόστολοι καὶ οἱ πρεσβύτεροι ἰδεῖν περὶ τοῦ λόγου τούτου). The third incident relates the convocation of the apostles and elders and the ensuing debate (vv. 6 – 7a). After the initial meeting with the Antioch delegation, the apostles and elders convene an assembly in order "to look into this matter [λόγος]," i.e., to deliberate about the status of converted Gentiles and the necessity of circumcision and their obligation to keep the Mosaic law. While some commentators assume only one plenary assembly, the sequence of v. 4 and v. 6 suggests two meetings: a full assembly of the entire Jerusalem congregation with the apostles, elders, and the Antioch delegation (v. 4), and then a council meeting of the apostles, the elders of the Jerusalem congregation, and the Antioch delegation.

15:7 After much discussion, Peter stood up and said to them: "Brothers, you know that in the early days God chose me from among you to be the one from whose lips the Gentiles should hear the word of the gospel and believe"** (πολλῆς δὲ ζητήσεως γενομένης ἀναστὰς Πέτρος εἶπεν πρὸς αὐτούς· ἄνδρες ἀδελφοί, ὑμεῖς ἐπίστασθε ὅτι ἀφ᾿ ἡμερῶν ἀρχαίων ἐν ὑμῖν ἐξελέξατο ὁ θεὸς διὰ τοῦ στόματός μου ἀκοῦσαι τὰ ἔθνη τὸν λόγον τοῦ εὐαγγελίου καὶ πιστεῦσαι). Luke notes the debate about the status of the converted Gentiles with three words (v. 7a). The "discussion" (ζητήσεως) that ensues is extensive and profound (πολλῆς). This brief comment implies that many more than the four people mentioned in vv. 7b – 21 contribute to the discussion. The next three incidents narrate speeches of Peter (vv. 7b – 11), of Paul and Barnabas (v. 12), and of James (vv. 13 – 21), informing the reader about their main contributions, and they determine the outcome of the conference. The council of apostles and elders focuses on establishing a theological solution (vv. 7b – 19) before providing practical guidance for Gentile believers and their interaction with Jewish believers (vv. 20 – 21), expressed in a pastoral letter to the churches outside Palestine (vv. 22 – 29).

Part of the lively and wide-ranging debate is Peter's speech, which Luke summarizes first (vv. 7b – 11). Luke underlines the importance of Peter's speech by noting that he "stood up," a comment that implies that the other apostles and the elders are sitting. Peter begins by reviewing developments in the past in which God established a precedent regarding the status of Gentile believers in Jesus (vv. 7c – 9). Addressing the apostles and elders as "brothers," Peter appeals to events that were common knowledge (ὑμεῖς ἐπίστασθε, "you know") in the Jerusalem church and among other missionaries such as Paul.

Peter reminds the audience of the time when he lived among them, i.e., before his departure as leader of the church in Jerusalem (12:17) seven years earlier. In those "early days"[13] God had chosen Peter to be the missionary who would proclaim the gospel to the Gentiles. Peter thus has a special right to be heard in the deliberations of the council — not because of his status among the Twelve but because God had chosen him to be the first apostle to reach the Gentiles with the good news of salvation through faith in Jesus. The expression "the Gentiles" (τὰ ἔθνη) refers to Cornelius, a centurion in the Roman army, and his relatives and close friends, all uncircumcised (albeit God-fearing) Gentiles (10:1 – 2, 24, 28 – 29, 45; 11:3).

The phrase "the word of the gospel" (ὁ λόγος τοῦ εὐαγγελίου) is singular; it denotes the fact that the good news about God's granting salvation to sinners on account of the life, death, and resurrection of Jesus, Israel's Messiah and Savior of the world, is a "word" or "message" that is proclaimed orally (διὰ τοῦ στόματος).[14] The term "gospel" (τὸ εὐαγγέλιον) occurs in Acts only here and in 20:24;[15] the Greek word denotes "good news," specifically God's good news for uncircumcised Gentiles — sinners par excellence and by definition — concerning the possibility of their receiving forgiveness of sins through faith in Jesus (10:43) and thus justification on the day of God's final judgment (10:42), the gift of the Holy Spirit and thus of God's transforming presence (11:15 – 17), and eternal life (11:18).

In v. 7 Peter describes the process of conversion. He reminds the apostles and elders in the assembly that (1) as a result of God's initiative, (2) he proclaimed the good news of divine salvation through Jesus to Cornelius and his Gentile relatives and friends (10:34 – 43). (3) They heard the message, and (4) they believed. That is, they accepted Peter's message to be true, and they committed themselves to Jesus as Savior.[16]

15:8 And God, who knows the human heart, confirmed that he accepted them by giving them the Holy Spirit, just as he did to us (καὶ ὁ καρδιογνώστης θεὸς ἐμαρτύρησεν αὐτοῖς δοὺς τὸ πνεῦμα τὸ ἅγιον καθὼς καὶ ἡμῖν). Peter emphasizes that God accepted the Gentiles as Gentiles, without prior circumcision and submission to the Mosaic law. Peter underscores that this was not an oversight on God's part by describing God as he "who knows the human heart" (ὁ καρδιογνώστης; see on 1:24). The all-knowing God, who knew what was in the heart of Cornelius and his relatives and friends, "confirmed that he accepted them"[17] by giving them the Holy Spirit "just as" (καθώς) he had bestowed the Spirit on the apostles "in the early days."

Peter is referring to instantly recognizable manifestations of the Holy Spirit, who had "fallen" on Cornelius and his friends (cf. 10:44 – 47; 11:15 – 17). The conjunction (καθώς), which compares Cornelius's experience with the experience of the apostles (καὶ ἡμῖν; 2:4; cf. 11:17), suggests that Cornelius and his relatives and friends, after hearing and believing the gospel, also spoke in unlearned languages. God had shown Peter in a revelation repeated three times that he no longer shows partiality as regards Gentiles (10:34); he has now cleansed them (10:15; 15:9) as they have received the Holy Spirit in a manner that is indisputable

---

13. The Greek phase (ἀφ᾽ ἡμερῶν ἀρχαίων) can also be translated as "some time ago" (NET, NIV, NLT, TNIV) or "a long time ago" (GNB; cf. BDAG, s.v. ἀρχαῖος 2).

14. Here, as in other passages (Luke 4:22; 11:54; Acts 1:16; 3:18), the "mouth" (στόμα) is the organ of speech (thus "lips").

15. The corresponding verb (εὐαγγελίζω) occurs in Acts fifteen times: 5:42; 8:4, 12, 25, 35, 40; 10:36; 11:20; 13:32; 14:7, 15, 21; 15:35; 16:10; 17:18.

16. The connection between hearing and believing (cf.

8:11 – 18) is also emphasized by Paul; cf. Rom 10:14, 17; Gal 3:2, 5.

17. Cf. NLT; NIV ("God ... showed that he accepted them"), GNB ("God ... showed his approval"). The Greek verb (μαρτυρέω) denotes "to confirm or attest something on the basis of personal knowledge or belief" (BDAG, s.v. μαρτυρέω 1); the dative of the personal pronoun that follows as direct object (αὐτοῖς) is a dative of advantage, indicating the person(s) for whose benefit the testimony is given.

(10:47). God's giving the Holy Spirit to Cornelius and his relatives and friends is his testimony, which the Jewish believers need to accept, that he has accepted the Gentile believers.

15:9 He made no distinction between us and them when he cleansed their hearts by faith (καὶ οὐθὲν διέκρινεν μεταξὺ ἡμῶν τε καὶ αὐτῶν τῇ πίστει καθαρίσας τὰς καρδίας αὐτῶν). When God gave the Spirit of his holy presence to the Gentiles in exactly the same way in which he had given his Spirit to Peter and the other apostles, he made no distinction between Jewish believers in Jesus and Gentile believers in Jesus (cf. 10:20; 11:12). God is the subject of the participial clause: God "cleansed" (καθαρίσας) the hearts of the Gentiles[18] by removing the impurity of the Gentile sinners, forgiving their sins, and granting them purity (see on 10:47).

Such purity and thus salvation and membership in God's people depends on faith (τῇ πίστει) — faith in Jesus as crucified and risen Messiah and Savior — and not on circumcision and submission to the Mosaic law. The dative case used here is instrumental or causal. While vv. 8 – 9 link the reception of the Spirit with the cleansing of the heart, the Cornelius episode links the reception of the Spirit with immersion in water (10:47 – 48). Since baptism, practiced as immersion in water, symbolizes cleansing, it connects the reality of receiving God's Spirit, who cleanses from impurity, with faith in Jesus as the grounds for God's grace granting forgiveness of sins. The emphasis is on God as the source of saving faith. Peter's conclusion is direct and clear: distinction between ritually pure Jews and morally impure Gentiles has been abolished.

15:10 Why then are you now testing God by placing a yoke on the neck of the disciples that

neither your ancestors nor we have been able to bear? (νῦν οὖν τί πειράζετε τὸν θεὸν ἐπιθεῖναι ζυγὸν ἐπὶ τὸν τράχηλον τῶν μαθητῶν ὃν οὔτε οἱ πατέρες ἡμῶν οὔτε ἡμεῖς ἰσχύσαμεν βαστάσαι;). In this second part of his speech, Peter reaffirms the conclusion (οὖν) that faith and the grace of the Lord Jesus are the basis of salvation, not circumcision and obedience to the Mosaic law (vv. 10 – 11). The question in v. 10 is addressed to the Jewish Christians about the conviction of the Pharisees, who are demanding that Gentile believers be circumcised and obey the Mosaic law (v. 5). In the Old Testament, "testing" God often meant that Israelites wanted to discover whether God noticed sin and would really punish it.[19]

Testing God usually came as the result of unbelief and mistrust by God's people. Peter therefore asks the Pharisaic Christians why they are challenging the consequences that God's initiative has for the present. Their demands for the Gentile believers represent a challenge directed against God, for they refuse to believe the revelation God had given to Peter in Caesarea and the fact that the Holy Spirit had truly been given to Cornelius and his friends. By "testing God" they resemble Satan, who tested Jesus in the wilderness (Luke 4:2); they resemble Jesus' opponents, who suggested that he cast out demons by Beelzebul (Luke 11:15 – 16); and they resemble Ananias and Sapphira, who tested the Spirit of God and perished (Acts 5:9). To test God is to provoke him, with potentially serious results. Their refusal to understand and accept that God has cleansed the hearts of Gentiles on account of their faith in Jesus, without circumcision and apart from the law, is a provocation directed against God, challenging him to reverse his deci-

---

18. A related formulation is the metaphor of the "circumcision of the heart," cf. 7:51; Rom 2:29; Col 2:11; see Deut 30:6; Jer 4:4.

19. Cf. Exod 15:22 – 27; 17:2, 7; Num 14:22; Isa 7:12; Ps 78:18, 41, 56.

sion to grant Gentiles his Spirit and to welcome them into his people.

The Pharisaic Christians are attempting to place the "yoke" (ζυγός) of the law on the neck of the Gentile disciples (v. 10b).[20] A yoke linked two animals together, enabling them to do the will of the farmer. As a symbol of Israel's obedience, the image of the "yoke" linked together Yahweh and Israel in the Sinaitic covenant.[21] In rabbinic literature, the expression "yoke of the law" denotes the rule of the law that demands and enforces specific human behavior as stipulated by the Mosaic law. Together with similar expressions, such as "the yoke of the commandments," "the yoke of the Holy One," "the yoke of Heaven," and "the yoke of God," the focus is on submission to the will of God.[22] While the metaphorical use of the term "yoke" as related to the law is generally positive, the reference to the "neck" on which the yoke has been placed suggests a negative meaning,[23] as does the statement in v. 10c that the Jewish people have not been able to bear the yoke of the law.

A long history of Christian interpretation posits that the Mosaic law could not be kept and was regarded (or should have been regarded) as a burden. This view clashes with Israel's conviction that the law was a good and precious gift from God, and that the obligation to obey the law was a privilege, a joy, and a blessing.[24] Jesus stated categorically that he had come to fulfill the Law and the Prophets, not to abolish them (Matt 5:17).[25] Paul asserts that he does not abolish the law (Rom 3:31), that "the

law is holy, and the commandment is holy, righteous and good" (Rom 7:12), and that he himself has indeed fulfilled the law (Phil 3:6). Christian discussions about the law all too often forget that the Mosaic law includes burnt offerings, sin offerings, guilt offerings, and other rituals through which God provided for the atonement of the sins of the people of Israel, maintaining the holiness of his people.[26]

It should be noted that the statement in v. 10c is linked with v. 11 in terms of a contrast (ἀλλά, "rather"). This suggests that Peter's emphasis about the yoke of the law in v. 10c falls not on the particular commandments of the Mosaic law that Jews found difficult or impossible to fulfill, but on the conviction that salvation is granted by God on account of Jesus Christ, not achieved through obedience to the law. The life, death, resurrection, and ascension of Jesus have created a new situation that distances the messianic community of believers in Jesus from the experience of the fathers and of all Jews. In the messianic age God's grace is received through Jesus rather than through the law; the cleansing of the heart (vv. 8 – 9) is effected through God's Holy Spirit rather than through full and consistent submission to the law with its stipulations concerning, for example, circumcision and clean and unclean food.

15:11 "Rather, we believe that it is through the grace of the Lord Jesus that we are saved, just as they are" (ἀλλὰ διὰ τῆς χάριτος τοῦ κυρίου Ἰησοῦ

---

20. The infinitive translated as "by placing" (ἐπιθεῖναι) expresses the means by which the Pharisaic Christians "test" God.

21. Cf. Fitzmyer, *Acts*, 548, with reference to Exod 19:5; 34:10 (where the term "yoke" is not used).

22. K. H. Rengstorf, "ζυγός," *TDNT*, 2:900. Cf. Sir 51:26; *m. ʾAbot* 3:5; *m. Ber.* 2:2, 5. In the Old Testament, the term "yoke" (ʿōl), used metaphorically, denotes forced labor and foreign domination; it is used as a positive symbol in Jer 2:20 (Yahweh's tutelage) and Lam 3:27 (ennobling hardship); cf. H. Schmoldt, "עֹל," *TDOT*, 11:72 – 76.

23. Note Old Testament passages where Israel's refusal to listen to God's words and to do his will is described in terms of "stiffening their necks," cf. Exod 32:9; 33:3, 5; 34:9; Jer 7:26; 17:23; 19:15. Cf. John Nolland, "A Fresh Look at Acts 15:10," *NTS* 27 (1980): 105 – 15.

24. Cf. Ex 19:5; 24:7 – 8; Lev 18:1 – 5; Deut 4:7 – 18, 32 – 40; Ps 19.

25. On Jesus' assertion that his yoke is "easy" and his burden is "light" (Matt 11:30) see the Theology in Application section.

26. Cf. Lev 1:4; 4:20, 26, 31, 35; 5:6, 10, 13, 16, 18; 6:7; 7:7.

πιστεύομεν σωθῆναι καθ᾽ ὃν τρόπον κἀκεῖνοι). Peter formulates the basic conviction of Jewish Christians: God grants salvation[27] to human beings through the grace that has been effected by Jesus, i.e., by his death and resurrection, and that continues to be available on account of Jesus being the risen Lord. "Grace" (χάρις) denotes "that which one grants to another, the action of one who volunteers to do something not otherwise obligatory."[28] The author of salvation is God, the source of salvation is Jesus, and the means of salvation is free grace.

The need for salvation implies that people are sinners. Since the first person plural verb translated as "we believe" (πιστεύομεν) refers to Jewish believers in Jesus, Peter implies by this statement that the provisions of the Mosaic law through which Israelites and Jews could receive atonement and forgiveness of their sins are no longer in force; rather, salvation[29] is through divine grace by the work of Jesus. This is true for Jews as it is for Gentiles. In other words, Peter fundamentally agrees with Paul (as v. 12 implies): salvation comes not from circumcision and obedience to the law but is freely granted by God on account of the sinners' faith in Jesus, Israel's Messiah and Savior (cf. Gal 2:15 – 16).

If the Antioch incident during which Paul confronted Peter on account of his withdrawal from table fellowship with Gentile Christians (Gal 2:11 – 14) indeed took place before the Apostles' Council (see Chronological Table, p. 621), the *theological* agreement between Peter and Paul in Acts 15 presents less of a problem than the *behavior* of Peter in Gal 2, who, according to Paul, failed to live up to his theological convictions (which is "hypocrisy," Paul's charge against Peter). Peter may have come to realize that his behavior in Antioch was wrong. Or he may have waited for the assembly of the apostles and elders for a final clarification regarding the validity of the stipulations of the Mosaic law for Gentile Christians.

15:12 The whole assembly kept silent. And they listened to Barnabas and Paul as they described the signs and wonders that God had performed through them among the Gentiles (ἐσίγησεν δὲ πᾶν τὸ πλῆθος καὶ ἤκουον Βαρναβᾶ καὶ Παύλου ἐξηγουμένων ὅσα ἐποίησεν ὁ θεὸς σημεῖα καὶ τέρατα ἐν τοῖς ἔθνεσιν δι᾽ αὐτῶν). Luke briefly comments on the reaction of the assembly (v. 12a): the apostles and elders "kept silent." They say nothing, evidently because they realize that the debate (v. 7) has been effectively decided by Peter's speech. If God now grants salvation through the "grace of the Lord Jesus," it makes no sense to demand circumcision and obedience to the Mosaic law from the Gentiles, since they are saved by faith in Jesus as well, as God had made clear to Peter in connection with the conversion of Cornelius.

The fifth incident of Luke's account of the Apostles' Council is the report of Barnabas and Paul. He begins by noting that the apostles and elders listen as Barnabas and Paul speak (v. 12b-c). Their report is narrated without direct speech (cf. also 14:27). Since their report concerned their missionary work in the cities of the provinces of Cyprus (at least Salamis, Paphos), Galatia (Pisidian Antioch, Iconium, Lystra, Derbe), and Pamphylia (Perge), which Luke has narrated extensively in 13:4 – 14:26, there was no need to provide details at this point.

Luke highlights one aspect of their report: the miraculous events that happened in the course of their missionary work (v. 12d-e). "Signs and wonders" (see on 2:19) took place in Paphos (punish-

---

27. The logical subject of the passive infinitive translated as "that we are saved" (σωθῆναι) is God (divine passive).

28. BDAG, s.v. χάρις 2a.

29. For the verb "to save" (σῴζω) see on 4:9; for "salvation" (σωτηρία) cf. 4:12. For the designation of Jesus as "Savior" (σωτήρ) see on 5:31.

ment of Bar-Jesus with blindness; 13:11), in Iconium (unspecified signs and wonders; 14:3), in Lystra (healing of a lame man; 14:8 – 10), and perhaps in other cities as well. These mighty deeds were not the work of the missionaries but work that "God had performed" (v. 12e). These signs and wonders were done "among the Gentiles," which means that God authenticated the Gentile mission of Barnabas and Paul, who did not require Gentile believers in Jesus to first be circumcised and become Jewish proselytes. The fact that God expressed his approval of the Gentile mission of the two apostles constitutes at the same time a validation of what Peter had said, namely, that Gentile believers in Jesus should not be circumcised and be made to submit to the Mosaic law in all its details.

15:13 After they finished, James spoke up: "Brothers, listen to me" (μετὰ δὲ τὸ σιγῆσαι αὐτοὺς ἀπεκρίθη Ἰάκωβος λέγων· ἄνδρες ἀδελφοί, ἀκούσατέ μου). The sixth incident of the Apostles' Council relates the speech of James (vv. 13 – 21), in Luke's narrative the longest and thus the decisive contribution to the deliberations of the assembly of apostles and elders. After Barnabas and Paul finish their report, James, the brother of Jesus,[30] takes the floor, addresses the apostles and elders as "brothers" (ἄνδρες ἀδελφοί; see on 1:16), and asks them to listen to him.

15:14 Simeon has described how God first intervened to acquire a people from among the Gentiles for his name (Συμεὼν ἐξηγήσατο καθὼς πρῶτον ὁ θεὸς ἐπεσκέψατο λαβεῖν ἐξ ἐθνῶν λαὸν τῷ ὀνόματι αὐτοῦ). James begins by arguing from God's initiative in Peter's Gentile mission, affirm-

ing that circumcision is not necessary for Gentile believers (v. 14). Probably speaking in Aramaic, he uses the grecized form (Συμεών) of the Hebrew name Simon (see "In Depth: Peter," at 1:15). He agrees that God himself was active in the conversion of Gentiles (Cornelius and friends). Thus, Gentile believers in Jesus do not need to be circumcised or be asked to submit wholesale to the law. James characterizes the events in Caesarea with three comments.

(1) When Cornelius and his relatives and friends were converted to faith in Jesus and received the Holy Spirit, this was an event in which God "intervened" (ἐπεσκέψατο) in history.[31] In other words, if God accepted uncircumcised Gentiles who believed in Jesus, bestowing on them the Spirit of his holy presence, the Pharisaic Christians should accept them as well without demanding circumcision and the wholesale obedience to the law before the Gentile believers can be regarded as having salvation.

(2) When Cornelius and his relatives and friends believed in Jesus and received the Holy Spirit, God accepted them as members of his "people" (λαός). This term is almost always as a reference to Israel as the people of God.[32] The application of this term to Gentile believers in Jesus has a threefold significance. (a) Gentiles are "acquired" (λαβεῖν) by God as his people just as Israel had been chosen by God as his people. This statement probably alludes to passages in the Pentateuch that refer to Israel as God's special possession (λαὸς περιούσιος) chosen by God from among the nations to be a people for himself.[33]

---

30. Matt 12:46 – 50; Mark 3:31 – 35; Luke 8:19 – 21. Paul may allude to James's conversion in 1 Cor 15:7.

31. This verb often refers to God's (sometimes miraculous) intervention in history; in the LXX see Gen 21:1; 50:24 – 25; Exod 3:16; 4:31; cf. Luke 1:68, 78; 7:16; *T. Levi* 16:5; *1 En.* 25:3. Cf. BDAG, s.v. ἐπισκέπτομαι 3, "to exercise oversight in behalf of, *look after, make an appearance to help,* of divine oversight."

32. Luke 1:17, 68, 77; 2:32; 7:16, 29; 20:1; 22:66; 24:19; Acts 2:47; 3:23; 4:10; 5:12; 7:17, 34; 13:17. In the LXX see Deut 26:18 – 19; 32:8 – 9; Ps 134:12 (LXX 135:12).

33. Exod 19:5; 23:22 (LXX); Deut 7:6; 14:2; 26:18 – 19. Cf. Deut 14:2 LXX: "the Lord your God has chosen you to be a people set apart from all the nations."

(b) The meaning of the phrase "the people of God" now includes uncircumcised Gentiles who believe in Jesus. Thus, "Israel" can now no longer be defined in terms of ethnicity or ritual practice, but in terms of faith in Jesus as Israel's crucified, risen, and exalted Messiah and Savior. God takes Gentile believers in Jesus "from among the Gentiles" (ἐξ ἐθνῶν) and makes them his "people," i.e., integrates them into the messianic people of God that Jesus and the Twelve have been bringing into existence. According to John 10:16, Jesus said, "I have other sheep that are not of this sheep pen. I must bring them also. They too will listen to my voice, and there shall be one flock and one shepherd."

(c) The Gentile mission and the inclusion of Gentiles in the people of God can claim continuity with biblical history, while it is at the same time "an innovation of the new era that Jesus and the distribution of the Spirit on Gentiles have brought."[34]

(3) Converted Gentiles belong to God, just as Israel belonged to God. This notion is expressed with the phrase "for his name" (τῷ ὀνόματι αὐτοῦ); the term "name" refers to God himself, and the dative is best understood as a dative of possession. James's statement may echo Zech 2:11: "Many nations will be joined with the LORD in that day and will become my people" (the Targum uses the phrase "a people for his name").

15:15 The words of the prophets agree with this, as it is written (καὶ τούτῳ συμφωνοῦσιν οἱ λόγοι τῶν προφητῶν καθὼς γέγραπται). James confirms from Scripture that Gentile believers in Jesus are indeed bona fide members of God's people. The demonstrative pronoun "this" (τούτῳ) refers to God's intervention in the conversion of Gentiles in Caesarea and their reception of the Holy Spirit (vv. 7 – 9), which James has accepted as such (v. 14).

What the prophets have written — their words and thus their teaching — "agrees" (συμφωνοῦσιν) with this interpretation of God's intervention in the conversion of Gentiles. In other words, the following quotation of Amos 9:11 – 12 reflects what the prophets teach and confirms the conviction of Peter, Paul, and James that uncircumcised Gentiles can become members of God's people, marking it as fulfillment of God's promises.[35]

15:16 – 18 "After this I will return, and I will rebuild the fallen tent of David; from its ruins I will rebuild it, and I will restore it, so that the rest of humanity may seek the Lord, even all the Gentiles over whom my name is invoked, says the Lord, who does these things, things known from long ago" (μετὰ ταῦτα ἀναστρέψω καὶ ἀνοικοδομήσω τὴν σκηνὴν Δαυὶδ τὴν πεπτωκυῖαν καὶ τὰ κατεσκαμμένα αὐτῆς ἀνοικοδομήσω καὶ ἀνορθώσω αὐτήν, ὅπως ἂν ἐκζητήσωσιν οἱ κατάλοιποι τῶν ἀνθρώπων τὸν κύριον καὶ πάντα τὰ ἔθνη ἐφ᾽ οὓς ἐπικέκληται τὸ ὄνομά μου ἐπ᾽ αὐτούς, λέγει κύριος ποιῶν ταῦτα γνωστὰ ἀπ᾽ αἰῶνος). The citation from Amos 9:11 – 12 comes from the last chapter of Amos's prophecy. God had sent judgment on Israel, but there would be a restoration in the future, a restoration particularly of "the tent of David," presumably a reference to the "house" or dynasty of David that had come to an end when Jehoiachin and Zedekiah were forced into exile in Babylon (2 Kgs 24:15 – 25:7).[36] At this time nations that have been invaded and conquered will be called by God's name.

The Qumran community alludes to Amos 9:11 – 12 as a prophecy fulfilled when God established the law, i.e., the proper study and observance of the law, within their Essene community, and as a prophecy that will be fulfilled when the Messiah

---

34. Bock, *Acts*, 502.
35. See also Isa 2:2; 45:20 – 23; Jer 12:15 – 16; Zech 8:22.

36. Amos's ministry is dated to 786 – 742 BC (Amos 1:1). Zedekiah was the last reigning king of Judah (597 – 586 BC). And

restores the Davidic dynasty in the last days.[37] The LXX diverges from the Hebrew text in the second part of the quotation; the prophecy that Israel will possess "the remnant of Edom" (MT) becomes a prophecy that "the rest of humanity" will seek the Lord. In the present context, the LXX text has been modified, resulting from competent exegetical work that draws on other Old Testament texts through similar content and wording (*gezerah shawah*; see on 2:34). The variations belong to a consistent interpretation of Amos 9:11 – 12 with the help of related texts that refer to the building of the eschatological temple (Jer 12:15 – 16; Hos 3:4 – 5) and the conversion of the Gentile nations (Isa 45:20 – 23; Zech 8:22) in the messianic age.

> The modified and conflated text expresses the close connection between these two themes: In the messianic age, when Davidic rule is restored to Israel, God will build the eschatological temple, as the place of his presence on earth, *so that* (ὅπως) all the Gentile nations may seek his presence there, as he has purposed and predicted throughout history.[38]

The quotation of Amos 9:11 – 12 is prefaced in Acts 15:16a with the prepositional phrase "after this" (μετὰ ταῦτα; the LXX has "in that day"), which probably comes from Hos 3:5, where the restoration of the temple and seeking the Lord in the restored temple is also linked with the restoration of Davidic rule. The verb "I will return"

(ἀναστρέψω), which is added to the MT/LXX text, probably comes from Jer 12:15 – 16, a passage that follows a prophecy that God will abandon the temple and judge his people, and predicts that God will "return" and have mercy on the Gentile nations, who "shall be built in the midst of my people" (pers. trans.). The reference to the conversion of the nations in the last days and the metaphor of a building can easily be understood that in the messianic period Gentiles will form together with Israel a community (the "temple" of the last days) where God is worshiped — both ideas to which Amos 9:11 refers.

The expression "tent of David" (ἡ σκηνὴ Δαυίδ) in v. 16c can refer to the Jerusalem temple[39] or to the city of Jerusalem,[40] both of which were destroyed in 587 BC. While the LXX text speaks of the "tent of David" being "raised up" (ἀναστήσω), Luke twice uses the verb "I will rebuild" (ἀνοικοδομήσω). While this is an acceptable translation of the Hebrew verb ʾqym, it suggests specifically the restoration of a building, i.e., of the eschatological "temple."[41] The "tent of David" is the (metaphorical) "temple" of the messianic age.[42] If James echoes Jesus' prophecy in Mark 14:58, he could have understood the "tent of David" to refer to God's building the temple of the messianic age miraculously ("not made with hands") through the agency of Jesus, the Davidic Messiah. The statement in v. 16d restates v. 16c: God will rebuild the "ruins" of the "tent of David." The statement in v. 16e is a second

---

37. CD VII, 12 – 18; 4Q174 frag. 1 III,10 – 13. Cf. Zimmermann, *Messianische Texte*, 96 – 97, 110 – 11; Evans, "Prophecy and Polemic," 207 – 8.

38. Richard J. Bauckham, "James and the Gentiles (Acts 15.13 – 21)," in *History, Literature, and Society in the Book of Acts* (ed. B. Witherington; Cambridge: Cambridge Univ. Press, 1996), 154 – 84, 165.

39. Cf. Pss 27:5; 31:20; 42:5.

40. Cf. Isa 1:8; 16:5.

41. Cf. Bauckham, "James and the Gentiles," 158; he argues that the change of verbs clarifies that James does not refer to

the resurrection of Jesus or to the restoration of the Davidic dynasty to the throne in Jesus' messianic rule. Differently Strauss, *Davidic Messiah*, 187 – 92; cf. Miura, *David in Luke-Acts*, 187 – 94, who argues that v. 16 refers to "the restoration of the Davidic kingdom which commenced through the events of the Davidic Messiah/Jesus (life-death-resurrection-exaltation)" (194).

42. Cf. Tobit 13:11, which speaks of the temple (σκηνή) that will be built in Jerusalem in the last days. *Sib. Or.* 5.414 – 434 speaks of the building of a temple built in the last days by God and by the Messiah (who acts as God's agent).

restatement of v. 16c: God will "restore"[43] the tent of David.

The purpose of God's rebuilding of the tent of David is expressed in v. 17a-c (note the introductory "so that," ὅπως). God's rebuilding of the eschatological temple in the messianic age will prompt "the rest of humanity," i.e., the Gentiles, to "seek" the Lord. The LXX differs from the Hebrew text of Amos 9 in two important points: the expression "that they may possess" is replaced by "[they] may seek" (ἐκζητήσωσιν); and "Edom" is replaced by "humanity" (τῶν ἀνθρώπων; in Hebrew both words have the same consonants, ʾdm). In order to clarify the object of the verb "seek," Luke adds "the Lord" (τὸν κύριον); this change may be an allusion to Zech 8:22 LXX,[44] a text that prophesies that after Yahweh's return to Zion (8:3) and after the laying of the foundation for the rebuilding of the temple (8:9), Gentiles will seek God's presence in the temple. James asserts that once the rebuilding of the "temple" of the messianic age has begun, the "rest of humanity," i.e., not only Jews but also Gentiles, will seek the Lord.

In v. 17b-c the prophecy of Amos 9:12 predicts that there will be Gentiles "over whom my name is invoked." This expression, which is frequently used in the Old Testament to express ownership,[45] is often used for Israel as the people "over whom the name of Yahweh has been invoked."[46] Gen-

tiles are people who "have not been called by your name" (Isa 63:19). When this expression describes the covenant status of the people of Israel as God's chosen people, it is equivalent to the description of Israel as God's "treasured possession" (λαὸς περιούσιος).[47]

James, in other words, understands Amos as prophesying that the covenant status and the privileges of Israel will be extended to the Gentile nations who will belong to Yahweh as Gentiles, i.e., without being circumcised and becoming proselytes. If the expression "who have not been called by your name" alludes to the words spoken at Christian baptism, it "indicates the incorporation of the Gentiles into the eschatological people of God with no requirements for admission other than baptism in the name of the Lord Jesus."[48]

In vv. 17d-e and 18, the reference to the Lord "who does these things" (ποιῶν ταῦτα) that are "known from long ago" (γνωστὰ ἀπ᾽ αἰῶνος) — the latter phrase is an addition to Amos 9:12 — probably echoes Isa 45:21, which is part of a prophecy that predicts that the nations will turn to God and be saved. Isa 45:21 is another prophecy that the nations will turn to the God of Israel and receive salvation. James uses this allusion to show that God's intention to integrate Gentiles into his eschatological people is older than these prophecies.

In sum, James uses the quotation from Amos

---

43. The Greek verb translated as "restore" (ἀνορθώσω) also means "to rebuild" (BDAG); it replaces the verb "rebuild" (ἀνοικοδομήσω) of the LXX text, which has already been used twice in v. 16c and in v. 16d. James omits from Amos 9:11d the phrase "as in the days of old" probably because it conflicts with the traditional expectation that the temple of the last days will be superior to the temple of the present age; Bauckham, "James and the Gentiles," 160, with reference to 1 En. 90:29; Sib. Or. 5.422–425; 2 Bar. 32:4; 4 Ezra 10:55.

44. Zech 8:22 LXX: "And many peoples (λαοί) and many nations (ἔθνη) shall come to seek the face of the Lord (ἐκζητῆσαι τὸ πρόσωπον κυρίου) Almighty in Jerusalem." The link between Zech 8:22 and Amos 9:12 is established via the verb "seek" (ἐκζητέω).

45. With regard to Yahweh's "owning" the ark of covenant, the temple, the city of Jerusalem, and the people of Israel.

46. Cf. Deut 28:10; 2 Chr 7:14; Jer 14:9; Dan 9:19. The expression is often used in Second Temple texts; cf. Sir 36:17; 2 Macc 8:15; Bar 2:15; Pss Sol. 9:9; L.A.B. 28:4; 49:7; 4 Ezra 4:15; 10:22. The expression "over whom the name of Yahweh has been invoked" is often explicitly connected with the temple in Jerusalem; cf. 2 Chr 7:14; Isa 63:18–19; Dan 9:17–19; Sir 36:17, 18–19; 4 Ezra 10:22.

47. Exod 19:5; Deut 7:6; 14:2; 26:18; Ps 135:4; Mal 3:17.

48. Bauckham, "James and the Gentiles," 170.

9:11–12, interpreted with other Old Testament texts that refer to the building of the temple of the messianic age, in order to provide the exegetical foundation for the theological position that Peter, Barnabas and Paul, and he himself are advocating. God's plan includes the integration of the Gentiles into his people *as Gentiles*, without having to become Jewish proselytes. The messianic temple, the restored "tent of David," is the community of all people who believe in Jesus as Israel's Messiah and Savior, people who as a result of their faith in Jesus belong to Yahweh. The messianic community, the promised temple of the last days, has been established, initiated by Jesus and led by the Twelve (!), with a large number of Jews turning to God as they have believed in Jesus as Israel's Messiah and Savior.[49] If James is taken to mean that the fallen "tent of David" has been restored in the conversion of thousands of Jews to faith in Jesus as Israel's Messiah and Savior, and that therefore Gentile believers may now be added, one may conclude that for Luke, Israel's restoration is *in principle* complete by Acts 15, where Peter, Barnabas, Paul, and James make the argument for the inclusion of the Gentiles in God's people.[50]

15:19 Therefore it is my judgment that we should stop causing trouble for the Gentiles who are turning to God (διὸ ἐγὼ κρίνω μὴ παρενοχλεῖν τοῖς ἀπὸ τῶν ἐθνῶν ἐπιστρέφουσιν ἐπὶ τὸν θεόν). James concludes that Gentiles who come to faith should not be bothered with unnecessary "trouble." The basis for the conclusion is (1) Peter's report about God's intervention when he bestowed the Holy Spirit on believing Gentiles (vv. 7–11), (2) the report of Barnabas and Paul, which included God's authentication of their missionary work among the Gentiles, and (3) the meaning of the prophecy of

Amos 9:11–12. This conclusion concerns Gentiles who are "turning" (ἐπιστρέφουσιν; see on 3:19) to God, i.e., who repent of their idolatry, worship the one true God, and believe in Jesus as Israel's Messiah and Savior.

The "trouble" that the Pharisaic Christians are advocating is not commands of the law in addition to the stipulations of the decree formulated in vv. 20, 29 (cf. 21:25); there are, after all, further elements of the law that will be binding for Gentile Christians, such as not using the name of the one true God in a wrongful manner, honoring father and mother, not stealing, not giving false witness, or not coveting other people's possessions (Exod 20:7, 12, 15–17; cf. Rom 13:8–10). The "trouble" is the demands for circumcision and wholesale submission to the Mosaic law as preconditions for salvation and acceptance into God's people (vv. 1, 5). James agrees with Peter, Barnabas, and Paul that Gentile believers should not be forced to be circumcised and to become proselytes who must keep all the commandments of the law. Clearly James does not regard the stipulations that he formulates in v. 20 as contradictory to that fundamental position. This means that the main issue for which the assembly of the council of the apostles and elders was called has been resolved.

15:20 We should instruct them in a letter to abstain from food polluted by idols, from sexual immorality, from the meat of strangled animals, and from blood (ἀλλὰ ἐπιστεῖλαι αὐτοῖς τοῦ ἀπέχεσθαι τῶν ἀλισγημάτων τῶν εἰδώλων καὶ τῆς πορνείας καὶ τοῦ πνικτοῦ καὶ τοῦ αἵματος). James suggests that the assembly formulate a formal rejection of the demands of the Pharisaic Christians, written up in a letter, in which their decision would be communicated to the Gentile Christians.

---

49. The same understanding of the church as "temple" is the background for Paul's description of Peter, John, and James as "pillar apostles" in Gal 2:9.

50. Cf. Turner, *Power from on High*, 419–20.

In addition to the decision *not* to demand circumcision and wholesale submission to the Mosaic law, one request should be made of the Gentile believers.[51] They should be asked to "abstain" (ἀπέχεσθαι) from four things. This verb means "to avoid contact with or use of something" and can be translated as "keep away, abstain, refrain from."[52]

The first item is "food polluted by idols" (τὰ ἀλισγήματα τῶν εἰδώλων). The term "the polluted things" (τὰ ἀλισγήματα) is rare; the verb (ἀλισγέω) means in the LXX "to make ceremonially impure."[53] In v. 29 the term "food sacrificed to idols" (τὰ εἰδωλόθυτα) is used, denoting anything sacrificed to the cult image of a pagan deity (usually food; see on v. 29). The genitive "by idols" (τῶν εἰδώλων) indicates the source of the pollution: contact with pagan deities defile God's people. The Greek term translated as "idol" was used in secular Greek literature to denote a form, an image, a shadow, or a phantom.[54] In a Jewish context (including the LXX), the term was used for the deities of the polytheists (or pagans, Gentiles) that have no reality; they are the products of fantasy, they have been manufactured by human hands.

The term "idol" reflects the Old Testament critique of pagan religiosity according to which the deities that the pagans manufacture and worship are an "image," i.e., a copy, distinct from reality.[55] The Decalogue prohibits images: God may not be depicted as an "image/idol" (εἴδωλον).[56] The people of Israel "knew that Yahweh was never so ready to hand as the deity in the ritual forms of the ancient Near East, in which the image of the god was waited on."[57] And the law prohibited offering sacrifices to idols (Lev 17:7). Some New Testament scholars assume that most if not all of the meat one could buy in Greek and Roman cities came from animals that had been sacrificed in local temples to honor pagan deities. This is incorrect. Paul's discussion in 1 Cor 10:25, 28 indicates that it was possible, at least in Corinth, to buy meat that did not come from animals that had been slaughtered in a cult ceremony in a pagan temple. Food polluted by pagan idol worship was consumed in connection with the sacrifice, on the premises of a temple.

James's first prohibition thus concerns idolatry: the Gentile believers are to refrain from attending sacrificial ceremonies in pagan temples and from attending banquets held in pagan temples where they would be eating meat from animals slaughtered on altars devoted to pagan deities. This prohibition corresponds to the first commandment of the Decalogue not to have any other God besides Israel's God (Exod 20:3), and to the commandment of Exod 34:15 that stipulated, "Be careful not to make a treaty with those who live in the land; for when they prostitute themselves to their gods and sacrifice to them, they will invite you and you will

---

51. Several manuscripts (including Codex D) add after "blood" a form of the Golden Rule ("and whatever they do not wish to be done to them, they should not do to others"), which is a secondary expansion.

52. BDAG, s.v. ἀπέχω 4.

53. Cf. Dan 1:8: "Daniel resolved not to defile himself with the royal food and wine, and he asked the chief official for permission not to defile himself this way." Cf. Mal 1:7, 12.

54. The Greeks called the statues representing their deities with a term (ἄγαλμα) denoting "glory, delight, honor, pleasing gift" or simply "image," in this case translated as "statue" (in honor of a God). The often voiced view that the term εἴδωλον is never used in nonbiblical Greek to denote "cult statues" is incorrect; see Polybius 30.25.13, and the papyri, e.g., P.Stras. II 91,10–11 (87 BC); PSI VIII 901 (46 BC). Cf. Arzt-Grabner, et al., *1. Korinther*, 329.

55. Cf. F. Büchsel, "εἴδωλον," *TDNT*, 2:376. Cf. Isa 41:29; 44:9–17; Jer 10:3–11; 16:19–20; Ep Jer 2–73; *Let. Aris.* 135–137; Josephus, *Ant.* 10.50; Philo, *Spec. Laws* 1.5.28; *Decalogue* 52–82.

56. Cf. Exod 20:4–6; Deut 5:8.

57. Walther Zimmerli, *Old Testament Theology in Outline* (Atlanta: John Knox, 1978), 121; cf. H.Hübner, "εἴδωλον," *EDNT* 1:387. Cf. Gen 31:19, 34, 35; Exod 20:4; Lev 19:4; 1 Chr 16:26; Ps 113:12 LXX; Josephus, *Ant.* 9.273; *T. Reu.* 4:6; *T. Jos.* 4:5.

eat their sacrifices." The consistent commitment to this commandment had prompted Paul and Barnabas to refuse the honor of being treated like deities by the citizens of Lystra (14:12 – 18).

For the Jewish people, the refusal to eat meat from animals that had been sacrificed to pagan deities, tantamount to the refusal to be involved in idol worship, was so fundamental that they were willing to die as martyrs rather than commit this sin.[58] Paul agrees that Gentile believers should not attend banquets in pagan temples and eat meat from animals sacrificed to idols (1 Cor 10:1 – 11:1). John warns of false teachers who were telling the believers in Pergamon and Thyatira that they could eat meat sacrificed to idols (Rev 2:14, 20). This first provision prohibits either buying meat that may have been used in an idol offering or participation in idolatry, including attendance at social functions in pagan temples — or both.

The second prohibition concerns "sexual immorality" (πορνεία), a term that refers to any kind of unsanctioned sexual immorality. From an Old Testament and Jewish perspective, this included prostitution, extramarital sex (fornication), incest, bestiality, homosexual relationships, and marriage within close degrees of kinship prohibited by the law. Adultery (Gk. μοιχεία), i.e., intercourse with a married partner other than one's spouse, certainly also constitutes sexual immorality, since the law prohibited adultery on pain of death (Lev 20:10; Deut 22:22); since adultery was a criminal offense in Greco-Roman societies as well, it did not have to be mentioned.

Prostitution, fornication, and homosexual relationships were acceptable or at least tolerated behavior in Greco-Roman society but were viewed negatively in the Old Testament and Jewish society; the last of these was punishable by death.[59] These sexual activities are certainly in view here. If the origin of the four stipulations is Lev 17 – 18 (see below), the primary reference of "sexual immorality" would be intrafamilial sexual relationships that the Mosaic law prohibits in Lev 18:6 – 18.[60] In the Old Testament and in Jewish tradition, sexual immorality was often linked with idolatry.[61] If the focus of the prohibitions here is on meal preparation, the reference to sexual immorality could refer either to the provision of prostitutes that a Roman host might provide for postmeal activities, or to the impurity of the women who prepared the meal due to menstrual uncleanness (Lev 18:19).[62]

The third item is "what has been strangled" (τὸ πνικτόν), a rare term usually understood to mean "meat of strangled animals," i.e., meat from animals

---

58. Antiochus IV "ordered the guards seize each and every Hebrew and to compel them to eat pork and food sacrificed to idols [εἰδωλοθύτων]. If any were not willing to eat defiling food, they were to be broken on the wheel and killed" (4 Macc 5:2 – 3). Cf. Dan 1:8; Tob 1:10 – 11; Esth 4:17 LXX; *Jos. Asen.* 8:5; *Let. Aris.* 142; *t. Ḥul.* 2:18; *m. ʿAbod. Zar.* 2:3.

59. Prostitution is prohibited according to Lev 19:29; Deut 23:18, but was apparently tolerated (Lev 21:7, 14; 1 Kgs 3:16), although with a great degree of contempt (1 Kgs 22:38; Jer 3:3; Amos 7:17). Sexual intercourse with an unbetrothed virgin (fornication) was against Israelite law but not a capital offense; the offender has to pay punitive damages (Exod 22:16; Deut 22:28 – 29). Incest is prohibited in Lev 18:6 – 18; 20:11 – 21; homosexuality is outlawed in Lev 18:22; bestiality is outlawed in Exod 22:19; Lev 18:23; 20:11 – 16; all three offenses are punishable by death.

60. Cf. Fitzmyer, *Acts*, 557; it should be noted that the term "sexual immorality" (πορνεία) does not occur in Lev 18:6 – 18. The Essene text CD IV, 12 – V, 14 speaks of three "nets of Belial" in which Israel has become ensnared: unchastity, arrogance, and defilement of the sanctuary; "unchastity" is explained as "taking two wives in their lives" (polygamy and divorce, a contravention of Gen 1:27; 7:9; Deut 17:17), and "marry each one his brother's daughter or sister's daughter" (contravention of Lev 18:13).

61. Cf. Jer 3:6 – 8; Ezek 16:15 – 46; 23:7 – 35; Hos 5:4; 6:10; cf. Wis 14:12: "For the idea of making idols was the beginning of fornication, and the invention of them was the corruption of life."

62. David Instone-Brewer, "Infanticide and the Apostolic Decree in Acts 15," *JETS* 52 (2009): 301 – 21, 306, 318.

that were improperly butchered, with the result that the blood has not been drained from them. The Mosaic law prohibits eating such meat.[63] An alternative translation is "what has been smothered," as the term is used to denote the smothering of very young animals for tender meat and to the gentle cooking of very tender food. If the decree refers to moral matters, the term could refer to infanticide (or abortion), which was used in ancient societies for birth control.[64]

The fourth prohibition concerns "blood" (αἷμα), a term that could refer to murder, i.e., the spilling of blood, but refers more plausibly to eating food made from the blood of animals, which the Mosaic law prohibits.[65]

The rationale for these four particular stipulations is disputed. Six main interpretations have been suggested, the last two being the most likely.

(1) The four stipulations are practical measures meant to facilitate the (table) fellowship between Jewish Christians and Gentile Christians as "*ad hoc* advice on how not to offend certain Jews."[66] This explanation is not convincing since the stipulation that forbids idolatry does not fit the assumed concern for harmony between Jewish Christians and Gentile Christians; rather, abandonment of idolatry was a fundamental part of the conversion of Gentiles. Also, the matters related to idolatry, immorality, and the ingestion of blood are not mere intrapersonal offenses for Jews (which the Gentile believers should take into account), but offenses against God prohibited in the law. James does not ask the Gentile believers to "respect" the Jewish believers, nor does he ask the Jewish believers not to "force" themselves on the Gentile believers. Had this "ethos" been James's main concern, he would have had other linguistic means to make his point.

(2) The stipulations correspond to the Noahide commandments that the Jews regarded as normative for humanity.[67] The parallel is not striking, since the concrete specifications of the Noahide commandments in the rabbinic sources prohibit idolatry, blasphemy, murder, incest, stealing, perverting justice, and eating meat containing blood. The stipulations of v. 20 have only the first, third, fourth and seventh command (if "sexual immorality" is understood as incest, and "blood" as reference to murder).

(3) The stipulations correspond to the cardinal sins that a Jew was not supposed to commit under any circumstances — idolatry, fornication, and murder (blood).[68] This explanation cannot account for the prohibition of eating "what is strangled."

(4) The stipulations come from the catalogues of vices and virtues that Jews used in teaching Gentiles when they became proselytes. The apostles' decision removed circumcision from such a list, but kept the other requirements.[69] While intriguing, this explanation cannot explain the phrase "what has been strangled," and it fails to see that

---

63. Cf. Lev 17:14; cf. Gen 9:4; Exod 22:31. The Greek term used in v. 20 is not used in the LXX translation of these passages.

64. Cf. Instone-Brewer, "Infanticide," 301 – 4, 310 – 12, 317, who acknowledges the fact that other Greek terms were used to describe infanticide (e.g., ἐκβάλλω, "to throw out," or ἐκτίθημι, "to set outside"). However, note the Jewish text *Sib. Or.* 3.762 – 766, which describes a law that will apply to both Jews and Gentiles and that prohibits idolatry, adultery and homosexuality, and infanticide.

65. Cf. Lev 17:10 – 11; cf. Lev 3:17; 7:26 – 27. Cf. Milgrom, *Leviticus,* 1:704 – 13.

66. Turner, "Sabbath," 114 – 19; Craig L. Blomberg, "The Law in Luke-Acts," *JSNT* 22 (1984): 53 – 80, 65 – 66.

67. Bockmuehl, *Jewish Law in Gentile Churches,* 145 – 73. The earliest form of the Noahide commandments is *Jub.* 7:20 – 21; cf. *t. ʿAbod. Zar.* 8:4; *b. Sanh.* 56a.

68. This was a decision of rabbinic authorities in Lydda around AD 120; cf. *Sipre Deut.* 41.85; *b. Qidd.* 40b; *b. Sanh.* 74a; *y. Sanh.* 3.21b; 4.35a.

69. Peder Borgen, "Catalogues of Vices, the Apostolic Decree, and the Jerusalem Meeting [1988]," in *Early Christianity and Hellenistic Judaism* (Edinburgh: T&T Clark, 1996), 233 – 51.

by the removal of the requirement of circumcision, the Gentile converts were thus exempted from the necessity of becoming proselytes.

(5) The stipulations should be interpreted in the context of the Jewish diaspora on the background of the Old Testament polemic against idolatry; they direct the Gentile believers to refrain from participating in pagan cultic and other practices.[70] This interpretation suggests that the first stipulation concerns matters related to pagan idols; the term "sexual immorality" refers to prostitution linked with pagan temples; the references to strangled animals and to blood refer to cultic practices of pagans. This interpretation is valid in a general sense. The first stipulation concerns idolatry, and as Paul's discussion in 1 Cor 8 – 10 shows, Gentile believers were tempted to continue to attend banquets in pagan temples. However, by itself this explanation is insufficient. If the four stipulations only wanted to direct Gentile Christians to give up their former pagan practices and to worship the one true God, concerns regarding idolatry could have been formulated more clearly and without recourse to rare Greek words. Also, the decree would not have said anything new and would therefore have been redundant, since the renunciation of pagan religious practices was a fundamental part of the message that missionaries preached among Gentiles.

(6) The four stipulations should be interpreted in terms of the regulations that Lev 17 – 18 formulates for Gentiles who live in Israel as resident aliens.[71] Prohibited are sacrifices that are not offered on the altar at the tabernacle, which means that consumption of meat sacrificed in other places to idols is prohibited (Lev 17:8 – 9); immorality, specifically sexual relations between blood relatives (18:10 – 18); eating meat from animals that have been strangled (17:13); and eating blood (17:14; cf. 18:26). Understood against this background, these four stipulations have been explained as a (cultic-ritual) compromise aimed at facilitating the communal fellowship of Jewish Christians and Gentile Christians in "mixed churches."[72]

However, the pragmatic desire to facilitate fellowship between Jewish Christians and Gentile Christians alone does not suffice to explain the selection of the four stipulations, particularly since other stipulations of the law for the resident alien are missing, as, for example, the Sabbath commandment.[73] It seems that the four stipulations in v. 20 are requested of Gentile Christians not only because they occur in Lev 17 – 18 but also because they are linked with the phrase "in the midst of them" (Heb. $b^e t \hat{o} k \bar{a} m$; Lev 17:8 – 9, 10 – 14; 18:26), and that these stipulations for the resident alien living in Israel are connected via this catchphrase with the prophecies in Jer 12:16 and Zech 2:11 (MT 2:15) concerning the Gentiles joining the people of God and living in the midst of them.

Thus, the provision in v. 20 is not an arbitrary qualification of the decision to admit Gentile believers into the people of God without requiring them to become Jewish proselytes. Rather, the prohibitions follow with exegetical logic from vv. 16 – 18: "If Gentile Christians are the Gentiles to whom the prophecies conflated in Acts 15.16 – 18 refer, then they are also the Gentiles of Jer 12.16;

---

70. Wilson, *Luke and the Law*, 94 – 102; Witherington, *Acts*, 461 – 67; Peterson, *Acts*, 433 – 36.

71. Cf. Jürgen Wehnert, *Die Reinheit des 'christlichen Gottesvolkes' aus Juden und Heiden: Studien zum historischen und theologischen Hintergrund des sogenannten Aposteldekrets* (FRLANT 173; Göttingen: Vandenhoeck & Ruprecht, 1997), 209 – 38; Jervell, *Apostelgeschichte*, 397 – 98.

72. Cf. Nicholas Taylor, *Paul, Antioch and Jerusalem: A Study in Relationships and Authority in Earliest Christianity* (JSNTSup 66; Sheffield: JSOT Press, 1992), 140 – 42.

73. Exod 20:10; Deut 5:14; for further legal stipulations for the resident alien, cf. Exod 23:12; Lev 16:29; 20:2; 22:10, 18; Num 15:30; Deut 16:11, 14; 26:11.

Zech 2.11/15, and therefore the part of the Law of Moses which applies to them is Leviticus 17 – 18."[74] In other words, James's exegetical argument created a link between the prophecy of Amos 9:11 – 12, quoted in vv. 16 – 18, and Lev 17 – 18, quoted in v. 20, by alluding to prophecies that announced the integration of Gentiles into the people of God (Jer 12:16; Zech 2:11). James established that the law contains these commandments that explicitly apply to Gentiles living among Israel.

15:21 "For Moses has had those who proclaim him in every city, for generations, and he is read in the synagogues every Sabbath" (Μωϋσῆς γὰρ ἐκ γενεῶν ἀρχαίων κατὰ πόλιν τοὺς κηρύσσοντας αὐτὸν ἔχει ἐν ταῖς συναγωγαῖς κατὰ πᾶν σάββατον ἀναγινωσκόμενος). The last element of James's speech is the rationale[75] for the stipulations in v. 20. These regulations are scriptural, a fact that is common knowledge to the Gentiles who have contact with synagogues in which the Mosaic law "is read" and "proclaimed." The statement that the law is read and explained "in every city" every Sabbath obviously refers to cities that had a Jewish community. James argues that just as the conversion of the Gentiles and their admission into the people of God has been made known in the prophecy of Scripture a long time ago (vv. 17b – 18, referring to Amos 9:12 and alluding to Isa 45:21), so the regulations that the Gentile believers should keep are not new inventions but an integral part of the Mosaic law that has been explained in the synagogues for generations.

Many assume that the last two stipulations would have been a burden — refraining from eating the meat of strangled animals and from consuming blood. The fact that the publication of the decision of the Apostles' Council in the Antioch church was greeted with joy (v. 31) makes this assumption doubtful. If Jews were able to buy meat from animals that had been slaughtered appropriately, with the blood drained, so could Gentiles.[76] Thus the third stipulation of the apostolic decree would have been easy to comply with. Since only well-to-do people were able to buy and consume meat, many if not most of the Gentile believers would not have been affected by this regulation anyway. As regards the consumption of blood, this was untypical among pagans and could be easily avoided.[77]

15:22 Then the apostles and elders decided, together with the entire congregation, to choose some of their own men and send them to Antioch with Paul and Barnabas. They chose Judas called Barsabbas and Silas, leading men among the brothers (τότε ἔδοξε τοῖς ἀποστόλοις καὶ τοῖς πρεσβυτέροις σὺν ὅλη τῇ ἐκκλησίᾳ ἐκλεξαμένους ἄνδρας ἐξ αὐτῶν πέμψαι εἰς Ἀντιόχειαν σὺν τῷ Παύλῳ καὶ Βαρναβᾷ, Ἰούδαν τὸν καλούμενον Βαρσαββᾶν καὶ Σιλᾶν, ἄνδρας ἡγουμένους ἐν τοῖς ἀδελφοῖς). The seventh incident of the episode of the Apostles' Council relates the decision of the assembly and reproduces the letter that was drafted (vv. 22 – 29). Luke first records what was "decided" (ἔδοξε) by the assembled apostles and

---

74. Bauckham, "James and the Gentiles," 174 – 78 (quotation 177). Cf. Dunn, *Beginning from Jerusalem*, 466 – 67.

75. Note the introductory "for" (γάρ).

76. The city of Sardis issued a decree in 47 BC formally recognizing three specific rights for which the Jews had asked so that they could live according to their laws and customs: the permission to assemble on the Sabbath and on their feast days, the permission to build and use a building for meetings, and the request to have the market officials of the city "be charged

with the duty of having suitable food for them brought in" (Josephus, *Ant.* 14.259 – 261). Cf. Miriam Pucci Ben Zeev, *Jewish Rights in the Roman World: The Greek and Roman Documents Quoted by Josephus Flavius* (TSAJ 74; Tübingen: Mohr Siebeck, 1998), 216 – 25 (No. 20).

77. Bockmuehl, *Jewish Law in Gentile Churches*, 170, who points out that black pudding (Lat. *sanguiculus*) had to be bought at specialist butchers.

elders (vv. 6 – 7) who had debated the demands of the Pharisaic Christians (v. 5). The prepositional phrase "with the entire congregation" (v. 22d) suggests that the apostles and elders of the Jerusalem church — with Barnabas and Paul among the former, James probably among the latter — present their decision to the entire congregation in Jerusalem. This would have included the Pharisaic believers, although Luke does not state that these "conservative" Jewish believers are all convinced by the arguments advanced by Peter, Barnabas, Paul, and James. It is indeed the whole body of believers in Jerusalem, as well as leading missionaries such as Barnabas and Paul, who are involved in the debate and its outcome.

The decision is made to choose believers from the Jerusalem church and to send them to the church in Antioch (v. 22c-f). They will accompany Paul and Barnabas, who were sent by the Antioch church to discuss the activity of Jewish believers from Judea who demanded that Gentile believers be circumcised and become Jewish proselytes who obey the entire law (vv. 2 – 3). The letter is addressed to more churches (v. 23) and was disseminated in other churches as well (16:4), but Antioch is singled out here because it was in this congregation that the debate about the application of the Mosaic law to Gentile believers had erupted in public discussions.

The apostles and the Jerusalem congregation with its elders chose two of the "leading men" (ἄνδρας ἡγουμένους; v. 22j), i.e., prominent Jewish believers involved in the ministry and outreach of the Jerusalem church. In v. 32 they are both described as "prophets," Christian leaders who con-veyed new insights from God and who explained God's revelation in Scripture and in Jesus and his teaching, as understood and applied by the apostles (see on 11:27; 13:1). The first and perhaps more prominent representative is Judas Barsabbas.[78] The second envoy is Silas (Σίλας), who becomes Paul's fellow missionary.[79] He is a Roman citizen like Paul (16:37 – 38); in Paul's letters he is identified by his Latin cognomen Silvanus (Σιλουανός), which sounded like his Semitic name Silas.[80] He was, together with Timothy, the cosender of Paul's two letters to the church in Thessalonica, written in Corinth not long after the three missionaries had proclaimed the gospel in Macedonia, who joined Paul in his missionary work in Corinth. Later Silas appeared in Rome with Peter and John Mark, other former members of the Jerusalem church (1 Pet 5:12).

15:23 They were to deliver the following letter: "The apostles and elders, your brothers, to the believers of Gentile origin in Antioch, Syria, and Cilicia, greetings!" (γράψαντες διὰ χειρὸς αὐτῶν· Οἱ ἀπόστολοι καὶ οἱ πρεσβύτεροι ἀδελφοὶ τοῖς κατὰ τὴν Ἀντιόχειαν καὶ Συρίαν καὶ Κιλικίαν ἀδελφοῖς τοῖς ἐξ ἐθνῶν χαίρειν). Luke quotes the letter that Paul and Barnabas as well as Judas Barsabbas and Silas are to deliver verbatim (vv. 23 – 29).[81] As the letter is sent to several locations, it can be classified as an encyclical letter. The letter has a prescript (v. 23b-h) and a closing (v. 29h).

As is typical in Hellenistic letters, the prescript has three parts (X to Y, greetings). First, the sender is mentioned (v. 23b-c; nominative): the letter is written by the apostles and elders, who identify

---

78. One of the earliest followers of Jesus, Joseph, was also called Barsabbas; he is mentioned in 1:23 as one of the two candidates for the replacement of Judas Iscariot.

79. See 15:40; 16:19, 25, 29 (Philippi); 17:1, 4 (Thessalonica); 17:10, 14 (Berea); 17:15 (Athens); 18:5 (Corinth).

80. 2 Cor 1:19; 1 Thess 1:1; 2 Thess 1:1. He seems to be identified as an apostle in 1 Thess 2:7.

81. Cf. E. A. Judge, in Horsley and Llewelyn, *New Documents*, 1:78 (no. 26), who comments that Luke expects his readers to take the letter of vv. 23 – 29 as well as the letter of 23:26 – 30 "as the direct citation of transcripts available to him."

with the recipients as "brothers" (ἀδελφοί). Second, the recipients are listed (v. 23d-g; dative): the brothers (τοῖς … ἀδελφοῖς), i.e., fellow believers. They are more specifically described as being of Gentile origin; i.e., they are Gentile Christians, which would include converted God-fearers (see on 10:22) and converted polytheists born from non-Jewish parents. The recipients are further identified with a geographical address: they live in the city of Antioch, in other cities in Syria, and in cities in Cilicia.

Syria, the region between the Taurus Mountains in the north and Judea in the south, was a Roman province since 64 BC; the seat of the governor was Antioch on the river Orontes. Cilicia, the region in Asia Minor between Pamphylia in the west and Syria in the east, had become a Roman province in 102 BC but was ruled by native vassal rulers after Caesar's death, then administered as a part of Syria after AD 17 until it became again a separate province in AD 72.[82]

This address confirms that there were churches in other Syrian cities besides Antioch, established by the preaching of Jewish believers from Jerusalem after Stephen's execution (11:19), for sure in the cities of Tyre and Sidon (21:3 – 6; 27:3). The address is also the first explicit indication that there were churches in Cilician cities, established by the missionary work of Paul (9:30; 11:25 – 26; 15:41; Gal 1:21 – 24).

Third, the salutation (v. 23h) is formulated with the traditional Greek word that is usually translated as "greetings" (χαίρειν).

15:24 Since we have heard that some people who have gone out from us without any orders from us have thrown you into confusion with **their talk, causing you inward distress** (ἐπειδὴ ἠκούσαμεν ὅτι τινὲς ἐξ ἡμῶν ἐξελθόντες ἐτάραξαν ὑμᾶς λόγοις ἀνασκευάζοντες τὰς ψυχὰς ὑμῶν οἷς οὐ διεστειλάμεθα). The apostles and elders first outline the prehistory of the letter. They write because (ἐπειδὴ) they want to clarify that the Jewish Christians "who have gone out from us," i.e., who came from Jerusalem to Antioch (and evidently to other churches in Syria and Cilicia), did not have their backing. They traveled and taught "without any orders from us," i.e., neither the apostles nor the elders had told them what to do or what to teach. It was the fact that they came from Jerusalem that evidently gave them their authority in the eyes of the Gentile believers in Antioch, an authority that would have been enhanced if the Jewish Christians in Antioch agreed with their teaching.

If the Antioch incident (Gal 2:11 – 14) took place before the Apostles' Council (see pp. 620 – 21), the impact of their teaching was so effective that even Peter and Barnabas were affected, withdrawing from fellowship with Gentile Christians. The apostles and elders assert that they had only heard about the activities of these people, whose names are not given (in contrast to Judas Barsabbas and Silas, the authorized envoys of the Jerusalem church, who are mentioned twice by name; vv. 22, 27). It was Paul and Barnabas who informed the apostles and the Jerusalem elders about these Jewish Christian teachers who had come north (vv. 2 – 4).

Their teaching is described with the bland term "words" (λόγοι), which can be translated with the derogatory term "talk" (Fitzmyer); it could also be taken to denote "speeches" or "instructions."[83] The content is not specified, only the effect: their speeches created "confusion" (ἐτάραξαν) and "distress" (ἀνασκευάζοντες). The first verb carries the

---

82. Syria is mentioned here for the first time in Acts; cf. 15:41; 18:18; 20:3; 21:3. Cilicia has been mentioned in 6:9 and is mentioned again in 15:41; 21:39; 22:3; 23:34; 27:5. For Syria

and Cilicia see on 5:37; 6:9; 9:1, 30.
83. BDAG, s.v. λόγος 1aδ.

emphasis (aorist tense of the finite verb); it denotes "to cause inward turmoil" and can be translated as "disturb, unsettle, throw into confusion" (BDAG). The second verb (present tense participle) shows the ongoing distress of the confusion these teachers have brought;[84] the term is used by logicians in the sense of "demolishing" someone's arguments. The deeply unsettling teaching of these troublemakers was the insistence that Gentile Christians must be circumcised and keep the Mosaic law in a wholesale fashion in order to be saved (v. 1).

15:25 – 26 We decided unanimously to choose some men and send them to you with our dear friends Barnabas and Paul, who have devoted their lives to the name of our Lord Jesus Christ (ἔδοξεν ἡμῖν γενομένοις ὁμοθυμαδὸν ἐκλεξαμένοις ἄνδρας πέμψαι πρὸς ὑμᾶς σὺν τοῖς ἀγαπητοῖς ἡμῶν Βαρναβᾷ καὶ Παύλῳ, ἀνθρώποις παραδεδωκόσι τὰς ψυχὰς αὐτῶν ὑπὲρ τοῦ ὀνόματος τοῦ κυρίου ἡμῶν Ἰησοῦ Χριστοῦ). The report that the apostles and the Jerusalem elders had received from Antioch about the activities of the troublemakers has led to a decision in Jerusalem (v. 25a-b), which was unanimous (ὁμοθυμαδόν; see on 1:14).

The phrase translated "we decided" (ἔδοξεν ἡμῖν) is frequently used to introduce official decrees. Greek inscriptions contain over three thousand examples of the verbal forms ἔδοξε/ἔδοξεν, mostly in formulas such as "Decision of the Council and the People" (ἔδοξεν τῆι βολῆι καὶ τῶι δήμωι), indicating the official decision of the magistrates and the people of a city. What follows in v. 25 is not the personal opinion of Jerusalem Christians but an official decree resulting from a decision made in the full assembly of the apostles and elders.[85] One

element of the decision is to send representatives together along with Barnabas and Paul to Antioch to convey the agreement of the Jerusalem assembly.

The two missionaries are characterized as "our dear friends" (οἱ ἀγαπητοὶ ἡμῶν; v. 25e) and as men (ἄνθρωποι) who have "devoted" (παραδεδωκόσι) their lives to "the name of our Lord Jesus Christ" (v. 26). Most English translations render the verb as "risked (their lives)," evidently on the basis of the standard Greek dictionaries, which give this meaning for this passage (and only for this passage); this is not the standard meaning of the verb.[86] Even though Luke's account of the missionary work of Paul and Barnabas in the cities of southern Galatia certainly included situations where their lives were at risk (cf. 14:19), the phrase describes more generally the constant (perfect tense participle) dedication of the two missionaries to Jesus and to the proclamation of the good news about Jesus as Israel's Messiah and Lord.

15:27 Thus we send Judas and Silas, who themselves will convey to you the same message by word of mouth (ἀπεστάλκαμεν οὖν Ἰούδαν καὶ Σιλᾶν καὶ αὐτοὺς διὰ λόγου ἀπαγγέλλοντας τὰ αὐτά). The decision to send Judas and Silas (cf. v. 22) will enable the believers in the churches in Syria and Cilicia to hear an oral report that will confirm the contents of the letter. It was a common function of ancient letter carriers to affirm the content of what the sender had written in his letter. The fact that Judas Barsabbas and Silas are sent together with Barnabas and Paul is a visible demonstration that there is no division between the apostles, the Jerusalem elders, and the missionaries based in Antioch.

---

84. The direct object "your minds" (NRSV, RSV, TNIV; NASB as "your souls") is translated as "inward"; GNB, NLT leave it untranslated.

85. Note in 16:4 the term "decisions" or "decrees" (δόγματα) used to describe the demands of the Apostles' Council.

86. ESV, GNB, NASB, NET, NIV, NLT, NRSV, RSV, TNIV; differently NEB ("have devoted themselves to"). Cf. BDAG, s.v. παραδίδωμι 1a.

15:28 It is the decision of the Holy Spirit, and ours as well, not to burden you beyond these essentials (ἔδοξεν γὰρ τῷ πνεύματι τῷ ἁγίῳ καὶ ἡμῖν μηδὲν πλέον ἐπιτίθεσθαι ὑμῖν βάρος πλὴν τούτων τῶν ἐπάναγκες). The terms of the apostolic decree are formulated in vv. 28 – 29. The decision (ἔδοξεν; see on v. 25) of the Apostles' Council has a twofold origin (v. 28a-b). It was "our" (ἡμῖν) decision, i.e., the decision of the apostles and the Jerusalem elders, including Peter, Barnabas, Paul, and James, whose speeches Luke has reported (vv. 7 – 11, 12, 13 – 21). More importantly (note the emphatic first position), it is the decision of the Holy Spirit; this decision has divine sanction. In his report of the proceedings of the assembly, Luke has not indicated how the Holy Spirit provided direction to the church. The emphasis on the active role of the Spirit suggests revelatory words or guidance that prompted the final decision, perhaps through a revelatory word of one of the Christians prophets present (cf. v. 32), perhaps in unexpectedly bringing about unanimity among the apostles and elders and the congregation.

The content of the decision has two parts. First, it was decided "not to burden" Gentile Christians (v. 28c). In the context of the demands of the Pharisaic Jewish Christians (vv. 1 – 2, 5) and in the context of the speeches of Peter, Barnabas, Paul, and James, the decision "not to burden" Gentile Christians means that they are accepted as having received salvation and are admitted into the people of God without circumcision and wholesale obedience to the Mosaic law. At least for Peter, Barnabas, Paul, and James, this is not a new decision. They

have not changed their mind regarding this question — after the events in Caesarea in the case of Peter, and after the circumcision-free missionary work among Gentiles in the case of Paul — nor do they need to adopt a new practice that results from their conviction and from this decision.

Second, Gentile Christians shall adhere to certain regulations that are "essentials" (τὰ ἐπάναγκες; v. 28c), i.e., matters that they must adhere to because they are compulsory.[87] The particle translated with "beyond" (πλήν) indicates an exception.[88] No burden is placed on the Gentile Christians, but there are obligations that they need to keep (which thus are not a burden). These "necessary things" are not necessary for salvation, but necessary nevertheless since the law requires it (cf. v. 20).

15:29 "To abstain from food sacrificed to idols, from blood, from the meat of strangled animals, and from sexual immorality. If you keep away from these things, you will do well. Farewell" (ἀπέχεσθαι εἰδωλοθύτων καὶ αἵματος καὶ πνικτῶν καὶ πορνείας ἐξ ὧν διατηροῦντες ἑαυτοὺς εὖ πράξετε. Ἔρρωσθε). The essentials that Gentile Christians shall adhere to, listed in v. 29, correspond to the four stipulations that James had suggested (v. 20). The first essential is "food sacrificed to idols" (εἰδωλόθυτα), corresponding to "food polluted by idols" (τὰ ἀλισγήματα τῶν εἰδώλων) in v. 20. The Greek term occurs only in Jewish[89] and in Christian texts. Paul's use of the term (1 Cor 8:1, 4, 7, 10; 10:19) is the earliest attested use in Greek literature. The term designates things that have been sacrificed (θύω) to an "idol" (εἴδωλον; see on

---

87. Cf. LSJ, s.v. ἐπάναγκες, "it is compulsory, necessary." Cf. Bock, *Acts*, 513. The stipulations of the decree are thus more than "desirable customs" (Craig L. Blomberg, "The Christian and the Law of Moses," in *Witness to the Gospel: The Theology of Acts* [ed. I. H. Marshall and D. Peterson; Grand Rapids: Eerdmans, 1998], 397 – 416, 409).

88. Thus BDF, §216.2; BDAG, s.v. πλήν 2.

89. See 4 Macc 5:2; ; *Sib. Or.* 2:96; *Ps.-Phoc.* 31. The first of these speaks specifically of "meat sacrificed to idols" (κρέα … εἰδωλόθυτα). The term is also used in Rev 2:14, 20 in the prophetic oracles addressed to the church in Pergamon and in Thyatira, referring to Christians who advocate that Christian believers can eat meat sacrificed to idols and tolerate sexual immorality.

15:20). People who were not Jewish spoke of "what has been devoted," i.e., "what has been sacrificed to a god" (τὸ ἱερόθυτον; thus, τὰ ἱερόθυτα, "sacrifices"), or of "what has been sacrificed to a god" (τὸ θεόθυτον). Since other things besides animals were brought as offerings, the Greek term translated as "food sacrificed to idols" could refer to other items of sacrifice as well, such as cakes and wine.

The second, third, and fourth stipulations are the same as in v. 20, although the order is different, which follows here the order of their prescription in Lev 17 – 18: food sacrificed to idols is followed by "blood," "meat of strangled animals" (the reference to meat is again implied), and "sexual immorality."

The enumeration of the four essential requirements for Gentile Christians ends with the concluding exhortation to "keep away" (διατηροῦντες), i.e., to make sure that they do not practice (πράξετε) "these things" listed in the previous sentence.[90] The letter ends in with the standard greeting "farewell" (ἔρρωσθε), which often occurs at the end of Greek letters.[91]

15:30 So they were sent off and traveled to Antioch, where they gathered the congregation together and delivered the letter (οἱ μὲν οὖν ἀπολυθέντες κατῆλθον εἰς Ἀντιόχειαν, καὶ συναγαγόντες τὸ πλῆθος ἐπέδωκαν τὴν ἐπιστολήν). The last incident of the episode of the Apostles' Council (vv. 30 – 33) relates the aftermath of the decision of the assembly of the apostles and elders. Luke notes first the travel of Barnabas and Paul as well as Judas Barsabbas and Silas from Jerusalem to Antioch, where they deliver the letter recorded in vv. 23 – 39 to the congregation. The four verbal forms in the aorist tense emphasize the actions of the Jerusalem believers and of these four Christian leaders: they were "sent off" by the apostles, the elders, and the congregation in Jerusalem; they "traveled" to Antioch; they "gathered" the congregation; and they "delivered" the letter.

15:31 When they read it, they were delighted at the encouragement (ἀναγνόντες δὲ ἐχάρησαν ἐπὶ τῇ παρακλήσει). One of the Antioch believers read the letter aloud before the congregation, with the result that the believers "were delighted." The cause of rejoicing is indicated with the word "encouragement" (παράκλησις). They were glad that the issues raised by Jewish Christians who demanded that Gentile believers be circumcised and subjected to the Mosaic law had been resolved by the apostles and elders, and unanimously at that (vv. 24 – 25).

The Gentile believers rejoiced that they did not have to be circumcised and they did not have to become Jewish proselytes. The Jewish believers in the congregation probably rejoiced that the apostles and elders were able to come to a unanimous decision. The fact that the entire congregation (τὸ πλῆθος, v. 30) rejoiced confirms that the four stipulations were not regarded as a burden by the Gentile Christians, but as regulations to which they had already committed themselves (avoiding contact with idolatry and abstaining from sexual immorality) or that were easy to comply with (buying meat without blood, and not eating food made of blood). See further Theology in Application.

15:32 Judas and Silas, who were themselves prophets, encouraged and strengthened the believers with many words (Ἰούδας τε καὶ Σιλᾶς καὶ αὐτοὶ προφῆται ὄντες διὰ λόγου πολλοῦ παρεκάλεσαν τοὺς ἀδελφοὺς καὶ ἐπεστήριξαν). The two envoys from Jerusalem fulfilled their

---

90. The formulation in v. 29b does not make the four regulations of the decree "optional" (Blomberg, "Law of Moses," 409): "doing right" is never optional for God's people. Also, the verb (διατηροῦντες, a conditional participle) is used in the LXX

"in contexts of fidelity to the covenant and commandments" (Johnson, *Acts*, 277, with reference to Gen 17:10; 37:11; Num 18:7; Deut 7:8; 33:9; Sir 1:26).
91. Cf. 2 Macc 9:27; 11:21, 33; 3 Macc 3:12; 7:1, 9.

responsibilities given to them by the apostles and elders. They "encouraged" (παρεκάλεσαν) the Antioch believers by confirming the decision of the Apostles' Council; a word from the same word group is used in v. 31 describing the effect on the Antioch congregation when the letter with the apostolic decree was read.

The fact that Judas Barsabbas and Silas are described as "prophets" (προφῆται; see on 11:27; 13:1; for prophecy see on 2:17) serves two purposes. (1) It confirms again the divine sanction and origin of the decision of the apostles and elders (cf. v. 28, the reference to the Holy Spirit). (2) It explains why their speaking and teaching in the Antioch church contributed to the believers being encouraged and strengthened.[92] As Christian prophets, they conveyed God's revelation through exhortation, instruction, critique, encouragement, and at times disclosure about future events.

15:33 After spending some time there, they were sent off by the believers with a blessing of peace to those who had sent them (ποιήσαντες δὲ χρόνον ἀπελύθησαν μετ᾽ εἰρήνης ἀπὸ τῶν ἀδελφῶν πρὸς τοὺς ἀποστείλαντας αὐτούς). The final comment on the episode of the Apostles' Council confirms that a harmonious resolution of the debate about the necessity of circumcision and wholesale obedience to the law, introduced and described in the first two incidents of the episode (vv. 1–5), has been achieved. The two envoys from Jerusalem,

leading Jewish Christian believers, spend some time in Antioch, involved in the pastoral ministry of the congregation. They are accepted both by the Jewish Christians and by the Gentile Christians, a fact underscored by the manner of their departure. When they embark on their journey back to Jerusalem, they are sent off with "a blessing of peace" (μετ᾽ εἰρήνης).[93] In the present context, this expression is more than a farewell greeting ("keep well"): they have played a role in helping to (re-) establish peace between Gentile Christians and Jewish Christians. They are sent off with a blessing of peace not just by the leadership of the Antioch church but by the believers (ἀδελφῶν), including the Gentile Christians who had been unsettled by the Jewish Christians from Judea (vv. 1–2, 24).

The believers in Antioch acknowledge that peace has been established — both in the Antioch congregation where the two Jerusalem envoys had arrived several weeks earlier, as well as in the church in Jerusalem to which they will return. The specific reference to "those who had sent them" confirms, yet again, that the Christians in Antioch acknowledge and accept the decision of the apostles and elders that the assembly in Jerusalem had formulated. Unity and peace have been restored. As Judas Barsabbas and Silas were on an official mission, returning to those who had sent them as envoys and reporting back on the outcome was part and parcel of their mission.[94]

---

92. On the verb translated as "strengthened" (ἐπεστήριξαν) see on 14:22, where Paul and Barnabas strengthen and encourage the believers in Lystra, Iconium, and Pisidian Antioch. The use of the same two verbs in 15:32 confirms for the careful reader the unity of ministry of the two Jewish Christians from Jerusalem and the two Jewish Christian missionaries.

93. Cf. NIV, NLT, TNIV, Fitzmyer. See BDAG, s.v. εἰρήνη 2a, with the suggested translation "send someone away with a greeting of peace." Cf. Gen 26:29; Josephus, *Ant.* 1.179, where similar expressions are used.

94. Older translations (KJV) included a v. 34 (included by NASB in brackets) — "But it seemed good to Silas to stay there" (C 33. 36. 323 etc.), "it seemed good to Silas to stay with them" (D³), "it seemed good to Silas that they should stay, and Judas journeyed alone" (D* gig l w vg^cl). This is probably an improvement intended to explain the presence of Silas in v. 40. Cf. Metzger, *Textual Commentary*, 388; Barrett, *Acts*, 750.

Theology in Application

The episode of the Apostles' Council relates how the early church reached a consensus regarding the disputed question of whether Gentile Christians should submit to circumcision and to wholesale obedience to the Mosaic law. In keeping with the main idea formulated above, the following emphases are important.

Grace and Faith

Gentiles are saved on account of the grace of the Lord and their faith in Jesus. This is the emphasis of Peter's speech (vv. 7 – 11), and presumably of the speech(es) of Paul and Barnabas as well (cf. v. 12), and James confirms the validity of Peter's arguments. Gentiles are saved on the same grounds as Jews: God grants both the Holy Spirit and thus the gracious gift of his holy presence when they become believers in Jesus, Israel's crucified, risen, and exalted Messiah and the Savior of the world. This has been the central emphasis of the speeches of Peter and Paul earlier in Acts, an emphasis that is confirmed as valid by the apostles and elders at the Apostles' Council in Jerusalem.

While the specific demands of the Jewish Christian troublemakers have rarely been made in the later church history, plenty of Christian teachers have argued, or implied, that faith in Jesus needs to be supplemented by other convictions and practices in order for sinners to "find salvation." The latter phrase is precisely the problem with such demands. Once people think that people need to "find" salvation, with the emphasis placed on what people need to do, the list can easily get longer and longer. If we recognize that salvation is God's free gift to sinners, then it is God who determines the grounds of salvation. In AD 48, the apostles and elders confirmed and agreed that the only ground for receiving God's gift of salvation is faith in Jesus. In AD 1517 it was Martin Luther who reemphasized this truth, against both official and popular church teaching that Christian discipline or a righteous life conveys salvation.

Not Becoming Jewish Proselytes

Gentile believers are saved without having to become Jewish proselytes. It follows from the first emphasis that Gentiles who believe in Jesus as Israel's Messiah and Savior, who receive the Holy Spirit as God's gracious gift, and who thus have salvation do not have to submit to circumcision and to wholesale obedience to the law as a prerequisite for salvation. The demands of the Jewish Christians from Judea who had traveled to Antioch (v. 1) and of the Pharisaic Jewish Christians in Jerusalem (v. 5) are rejected. The introduction to the apostolic decree in v. 25 suggests that at least the Jewish Christians in Jerusalem with Pharisaic connections were convinced by the arguments advanced by Peter, Barnabas and Paul, and James. Gentiles are saved as Gentiles, not as Gentiles who first become Jewish proselytes. Christians who do not have a Jewish background must not be envious of Jewish Christians as if the latter have a deeper grasp or greater experience of salvation. Conversely, Jewish believers must not look down on non-Jewish believers as if they were somehow deficient.

Bona Fide Members of God's People

Gentile believers are bona fide members of God's people. The apostles and elders clarified that it is not people who determine who is an authentic member of the people of God, but God himself. And God's decision about who is "in" is bound up solely with people's faith in Jesus, whether Jew or Gentile. James argued from Scripture that Gentile Christians are members of God's people *as Gentiles*, that Gentile Christians worship God in the temple of "restored Israel," which is the messianic community of the last days. The result of this recognition is the unity of the local congregation, consisting of Jewish believers and Gentile believers.

Gentile Believers and Regulations of the Law

Gentile believers must keep some fundamental regulations of the law. This point arises from the fact that the stipulations of the apostolic decree are derived from scriptural passages (Lev 17–18; see on v. 20). At the same time this point raises questions that are disputed. Some exegetes and theologians contrast law and gospel in such a manner that the Mosaic law is regarded as having been valid in the period before the coming of Jesus Christ. While the law holds significance for Christians in terms of prophecies of the messianic period and may have value in showing sinners their sinfulness and as a foundation for political and civil order, the Mosaic law is no longer directly applicable to believers. Proponents of this position interpret Luke's narrative of the stipulations of the apostolic decree either as a paradigm, i.e., as a model for the church, and/or in terms of principles that can be applied to other contexts — Christians should take into account the scruples of other believers.

There is a wealth of evidence that indicates that it is preferable to view the stages of salvation history as organically related to each other, with some elements of the old covenant (such as circumcision, atonement of sin and forgiveness through sacrifices) having become obsolete because of the fundamental fulfillment of God's promises given to Adam, Abraham, and Israel, while other elements of the old covenant continue to be valid in the new covenant (such as the sinfulness of humankind, the necessity of repentance, the worship of the one true God, the sanctity of life, the prohibition of sexual immorality, the concern for the poor and needy). There is both discontinuity and continuity. The law/gospel alternative creates confusion if it is taken as an absolute either/or alternative.

Both Jesus and Paul assert that the law has not been abolished in the newly inaugurated messianic period (Matt 5:17–18; Rom 3:31). The prohibitions of idolatry and of sexual immorality belong to the fundamental commandments of the law, of which neither Jewish nor Gentile Christians are "free." Believers in Jesus are "free" from the law as the "context" that provides and maintains salvation through God's grace mediated via circumcision, membership in Israel, and obedience to God's Old Testament ritual regulations. But Gentile Christians are not free from the law in the sense that they can ignore all of the commandments. The law continues to be the revelation of God's will. The believer encounters the law as someone who belongs to Jesus Christ and thus as the "law of Christ" (Gal 6:2). Jesus Christ "owns" the Torah as a result of his atoning death, replacing the ownership of the Torah over the sinner, with the result that the believer lives "under Christ's law" (1 Cor 9:21).

As far as stipulations of the apostolic decree are concerned, the prohibition of idolatry and sexual immorality (the first and second stipulation) corresponds to Paul's prohibitions of sexual immorality[95] and idolatry (1 Cor 8 – 10; 1 Thess 1:9), and to John's censure of the churches in Pergamon and in Thyatira who tolerated people who advocated that Christian believers can eat meat sacrificed to idols and tolerate sexual immorality (Rev 2:14, 20). Christians may not be involved in any manner in idolatrous practices that assume the existence of other gods beside the one true God the Creator, the Father of Jesus Christ.

The prohibition of consuming blood (the third and fourth stipulation) is also a basic requirement of the law that Gentile Christians must adhere to if they live in fellowship with Jewish Christians. Some might argue that since the rationale for the prohibition of consuming blood as food is scriptural exegesis, it applies to all Christians irrespective of the presence of Jewish believers in their midst. This is a theological "pure" position that can surely be maintained: Christians must order steaks "well done" rather than rare, and they must refrain from eating blood sausage (depending on the culture known as drisheen, moronga, black pudding, Blutwurst, etc.), blood soup (czernina, dinuguan, haejangguk, etc.), and blood pancakes (blod-plättar, etc.). Others argue, with greater contextual justification, that the discussion of the Apostolic Council became necessary because the fellowship of Jewish believers and Gentiles believers in the same congregation had become a problem, and that the stipulations of the council addressed the issue of the validity of the Mosaic law in this particular context.

This means that the first two stipulations are always normative for Christian behavior, since they are directly related to idolatry. They "reinforce the danger of polytheism even for Gentile believers.... These strictures against anything that might reek of the gods in the context of the church's earliest community offer a powerful reminder of the need for distinguishing God from the gods."[96] And this means that the second two stipulations, the prohibition to consume blood, are normative when Gentile Christians have (table) fellowship with Jewish Christians, but not necessarily when the congregation has no Jewish believers as members.

---

95. Rom 1:26 – 27; 13:9; 1 Cor 5:1 – 13; 6:9, 12 – 20; 7:2; 10:8; 2 Cor 12:21; 1 Thess 4:1 – 8; 1 Tim 1:9.

96. Gaventa, *Acts*, 223.

CHAPTER 28

Acts 15:35 – 16:10

Literary Context

The fifth major section in the book of Acts (15:35 – 18:22) describes Paul's missionary work in Europe, in particular in the Roman provinces of Macedonia and Achaia, focused on five cities: Philippi, Thessalonica, Berea, Athens, and Corinth. In the first major section (1:1 – 14) Luke reported Jesus' exaltation and the commissioning of the Twelve for international missionary work beginning in Jerusalem, continuing in Judea and Samaria, and moving toward the ends of the earth. In the second major section (1:15 – 8:3) he described the beginnings of the new, messianic people of God and their witness of Jesus, Israel's crucified, risen, and exalted Messiah and Savior, in Jerusalem and Judea. In the third major section (8:4 – 12:25) Luke narrated the beginnings of the mission to the Gentiles; the focus was on Philip's witnessing to Samaritans and to an Ethiopian official, Saul's being converted to faith in Jesus and being commissioned as witness among Jews and Gentiles, and Peter's proclaiming the gospel in Caesarea on the coastal plain and before Gentile God-fearers in the city of Joppa. In the fourth major section (13:1 – 15:33) Luke shifted the focus to the missionary work of Paul and Barnabas, who preached the gospel in the cities of Cyprus, south Galatia, and Pamphylia. The increasing number of Gentiles coming to faith without becoming Jewish proselytes triggered a reaction among "conservative" Jewish Christians, who insisted that Gentile converts had to be circumcised and obey the Mosaic law. These questions were settled at the Apostles' Council, where the apostles and the elders of the Jerusalem church — with major contributions in the deliberation by Peter, Barnabas and Paul, and James — confirmed the decision not to require Gentile Christians to be circumcised and to obey the entire law.

This new major section consists of three sections: the beginnings of a new missionary initiative, as Paul sets out from Antioch (15:35 – 16:10), Paul's missionary work in Macedonia (16:11 – 17:15), and Paul's missionary work in Achaia (17:16 – 18:22). In this unit, we combine two episodes: (1) the disagreement between Paul and Barnabas, new missionary plans, and Paul's travels from Antioch to south Galatia (15:35 – 16:5), and (2) Paul's travels from south Galatia to Troas (16:6 – 10). These travels are to be dated to the spring of AD 49.

Main Idea

The core process of the proclamation of God's word is the teaching of believers in local congregations and the preaching to unbelievers in unreached areas; while the latter is closely connected with the church, personal initiative is a key factor, but this can cause disagreements and separation resulting from different opinions regarding the most effective missionary strategies whose details are ultimately dependent on God's guidance.

Translation

(See next two pages.)

Structure and Literary Form

The first of the two episodes of this passage narrates disagreements between Paul and Barnabas and Paul's travel from Antioch to south Galatia (15:35 – 16:5). This episode consists of four incidents. (1) Luke reports on the cooperation of Paul and Barnabas in Antioch, followed by disagreement regarding the suitability of John Mark for missionary work and the separation of these two leading missionaries (15:35 – 40). (2) Luke briefly narrates Paul's visit along with Silas to the churches in Syria and in Cilicia (v. 41). (3) Luke narrates their travel to south Galatia and Paul's recruitment of Timothy from Lystra as a new coworker (16:1 – 3). (4) The episode ends with a report on Paul's visit to the churches in south Galatia (vv. 4 – 5).

The second episode narrates the travels of Paul, Silas, and Timothy from south Galatia to Troas (16:6 – 8) in two brief incidents: the travel from south Galatia to Alexandria Troas (vv. 6 – 8), and Paul's dream in which he is called to cross over to Macedonia and proclaim the gospel there (vv. 9 – 10).

The two episodes are *narratives* that include *direct speech* (15:36: Paul; 16:9: a Macedonian man), several *travel notices* (15:39, 41; 16:1, 4, 6 – 8, 10), a *summary statement* (16:5), and a *vision report* (16:9).

Acts 15:35 – 16:10

35a	Event	**Paul and Barnabas remained in Antioch,**
b	Action	teaching and
c	Action	preaching,
d	Association	along with many others,
e	Content	… the goods news of the word of the Lord.
36a	Setting: temporal	Some time later
b	Event	**Paul said to Barnabas,**
c	Call to action	*"Let us go back*
d	Call to action	*and visit the believers*
e	Place	*in every city where we have proclaimed the word of the Lord,*
f	Call to action	*and see how they are doing."*
37a	Event	**Barnabas wanted to take John,**
b	Description	also called Mark,
c	Association	along with them.
38a	Event	**But Paul insisted**
b	Assertion	that he should not be taken along
c	Reason	since he had deserted them
d	Place	in Pamphylia
e	Reason	and had not accompanied them in the work.
39a	Event	**They had such a sharp disagreement that they decided**
b	Result	to separate from each other.
c	Action	**Barnabas took Mark**
d	Action	**and sailed**
e	Place	to Cyprus,
40a	Action	**while Paul chose Silas**
b	Action	**and departed,**
c	Event	after the believers had commended him to the grace of the Lord.
41a	Action	**He traveled**
b	Place	through Syria and
c	Place	Cilicia
d	Action	**and strengthened the congregations.**
16:1a	Action & Place	**Paul came to Derbe and**
b	Place	**to Lystra,**
c	Character entrance	where a disciple named Timothy lived,
d	Character entrance	the son of a Jewish woman
e	Description	who was a believer and
f	Character entrance	of a father
g	Description	who was a Greek.
2a	Description	**This disciple had a good reputation**
b	Place	**among the believers in Lystra and Iconium.**

3a	Character's thoughts	**Paul wanted to take him along**
b	Time	when he continued his journey;
c	Action	**so he circumcised him**
d	Reason	on account of the Jews
e	Identification	who lived in these cities,
f	Reason	for they all knew that his father was Greek.

4a	Setting: geographical	As they traveled from city to city,
b	Action	**they delivered the decisions**
c	Description	that the apostles and elders in Jerusalem had reached
d	Purpose	for the believers to obey.
5a	Result	**So the congregations were strengthened**
b	Sphere	in the faith and
c	Result	**grew daily**
d	Sphere	in numbers.

6a	Action & Place	**They traveled through the region of Phrygia** and
b	Place	**Galatia,**
c	Circumstance	after the Holy Spirit had prevented them from speaking the word
d	Place	in the province of Asia.

7a	Setting: geographical	When they came to the border of Mysia,
b	Action & Place	**they attempted to travel to Bithynia,**
c	Prohibition	but **the Spirit of Jesus did not permit them to do so.**
8a	Action & Place	**They passed through Mysia**
b	Action & Place	**and went down to Troas.**

9a	Setting: time	During the night
b	Event	**Paul had a vision of a Macedonian man**
c	Action	who stood there and
d	Action	invited him,
e		saying,
f	Entreaty	*"Come over to Macedonia*
g	Entreaty	*and help us!"*

10a	Setting: temporal	After Paul had seen the vision,
b	Reaction	**we sought to leave immediately for Macedonia,**
c	Reason	as we came to the conclusion that
d	Assertion	God had called us
e	Purpose	to preach the good news to them.

Exegetical Outline

→ **I. Disagreements, Travels, and Missionary Plans (15:35 – 16:5)**

   A. Paul and Barnabas in Antioch: Cooperation, Disagreement, Separation (15:35 – 40)

      1. The cooperation of Paul and Barnabas in the teaching ministry in Antioch (15:35)

      2. Paul's suggestion to visit the congregations that they had established (15:36)

      3. The disagreement about John Mark (15:37 – 39c)

         a. Barnabas's plan to take John Mark along as a coworker (15:37)

         b. Paul's refusal to accept John Mark as coworker (15:38)

         c. The separation of Paul and Barnabas (15:39a-b)

      4. Barnabas travels with John Mark to Cyprus (15:39c-e)

      5. Paul travels with Silas and the blessing of the Antioch church (15:40)

   B. Paul's Visit of the Churches in Syria and in Cilicia (15:41)

      1. Travel through Syria and Cilicia (15:41a-c)

      2. Paul strengthens the congregations (15:41d)

   C. The Recruitment of Timothy from Lystra as Coworker (16:1 – 3)

      1. Travel to Derbe and Lystra (16:1a-b)

      2. The recruitment of Timothy in Lystra (16:1c – 3)

         a. Biographical introduction of Timothy (16:1c-g)

         b. Character witnesses for Timothy (16:2)

         c. Paul's plan to take Timothy along as coworker (16:3a-b)

         d. The circumcision of Timothy (16:3c-f)

   D. The Visitation of the Churches in South Galatia (16:4 – 5)

      1. Visit of the congregations in south Galatia (16:4a)

      2. Notification of the decisions of the Apostles' Council (16:4b-d)

      3. The edification and the growth of the congregations (16:5)

II. Travels from South Galatia to Troas (16:6 – 10)

   A. The Travels from South Galatia to Alexandrian Troas (16:6 – 8)

      1. Travel through the regions of Phrygia and Galatia (16:6a-b)

      2. Intervention of the Spirit, who prevents travel to the province of Asia (16:6c-d)

      3. Travel to Mysia (16:7a)

      4. Intervention of the Spirit, who prevents travel to the province of Bithynia (16:7b-c)

      5. Travel to Alexandria Troas (16:8)

   B. The Call to Macedonia in a Vision (16:9 – 10)

      1. Paul's vision of a man who invites him to come to Macedonia (16:9)

      2. Decision to travel to Macedonia (16:10)

Explanation of the Text

15:35 Paul and Barnabas remained in Antioch, teaching and preaching, along with many others, the goods news of the word of the Lord (Παῦλος δὲ καὶ Βαρναβᾶς διέτριβον ἐν Ἀντιοχείᾳ διδάσκοντες καὶ εὐαγγελιζόμενοι μετὰ καὶ ἑτέρων πολλῶν τὸν λόγον τοῦ κυρίου). Paul and Barnabas continue their ministry in Antioch (cf. 14:28), which had been interrupted by the debates caused by the demands of Jewish Christians concerning circumcision and obedience to the law for Gentile Christians.[1] Most commentators link this verse with the previous incident, some treat it as a transitional unit, while others link it with the new episode of Paul's missionary ministry.

The latter seems to be most plausible: Luke's focus has shifted to the work of Paul and Barnabas.[2] They stay in Antioch; the imperfect tense of the verb "remained" (διέτριβον) suggests an extended period of time. Their activity is described with two present tense participles, which again suggests sustained action: "teaching" (διδάσκοντες) the believers in the congregation and "preaching ... the good news" (εὐαγγελιζόμενοι) to unbelievers. They are involved in the pastoral and missionary (evangelistic) ministry of the Antioch church. The reference to "many others" (ἑτέρων πολλῶν) who teach and preach the good news describes the Antioch church as engaged in proclaiming the "word of the Lord" (see on 4:29) both to believers and to nonbelievers; they would have included Simon Niger, Lucius of Cyrene, and Manaen (cf. 13:1), but evidently other teachers and preachers who had

assumed leadership functions when Barnabas and Paul had been sent off by the church (13:2 – 3) to do missionary work in the cities of Cyprus, Galatia, and Pamphylia.

15:36 Some time later Paul said to Barnabas, "Let us go back and visit the believers in every city where we have proclaimed the word of the Lord, and see how they are doing" (μετὰ δέ τινας ἡμέρας εἶπεν πρὸς Βαρναβᾶν Παῦλος· ἐπιστρέψαντες δὴ ἐπισκεψώμεθα τοὺς ἀδελφοὺς κατὰ πόλιν πᾶσαν ἐν αἷς κατηγγείλαμεν τὸν λόγον τοῦ κυρίου πῶς ἔχουσιν). The length of their stay in Antioch is not specified; "some time" (τινας ἡμέρας, lit., "some days") could mean a few weeks or a few months. If Silas returned from Antioch to Jerusalem, as 15:33 suggests, Paul and Barnabas stayed in Antioch at least two months,[3] allowing Silas to travel the 335 miles (540 km.) twice: from Antioch to Jerusalem and back.

Paul suggests another journey to Barnabas, to visit the churches "in every city" (κατὰ πόλιν πᾶσαν)[4] they had established during their missionary work recorded in chs. 13 – 14, and then to go to cities in the province of Asia (16:6). Paul wants to know how the believers are doing, i.e., whether they are continuing in the faith, strengthened and encouraged by the elders whom Paul and Barnabas had appointed (14:22 – 23). The reference to the "word of the Lord" (ὁ λόγος τοῦ κυρίου) illustrates Paul's focus on Jesus, Israel's crucified, risen, and exalted Messiah and Savior about whom

---

1. These discussions had taken place at Antioch (15:1 – 2b), and had prompted the Antioch church to send Paul and Barnabas to Jerusalem to meet with the apostles and elders for a decision on these matters (15:2c-j). The previous episode records the discussion and decision of the apostles and elders in Jerusalem (15:4 – 29).

2. The conjunction (δέ) is not necessarily a marker of con-

trast, but often indicates a new narrative segment (BDAG, s.v. δέ 2; cf. 1:7).

3. On the speed of travel see on 13:6.

4. Cf. 13:5 – 6, 14, 51; 14:1, 8, 20, 25. See Barrett, *Acts*, 753, who concludes from the distributive preposition (κατά) and the emphatic "every" (πᾶσαν) that Paul proposes "a comprehensive visitation."

he preaches (objective genitive) and who is the source of the message that he proclaims (subjective genitive).

15:37 – 38 Barnabas wanted to take John, also called Mark, along with them. But Paul insisted that he should not be taken along since he had deserted them in Pamphylia and had not accompanied them in the work (Βαρναβᾶς δὲ ἐβούλετο συμπαραλαβεῖν καὶ τὸν Ἰωάννην τὸν καλούμενον Μᾶρκον· Παῦλος δὲ ἠξίου, τὸν ἀποστάντα ἀπ᾽ αὐτῶν ἀπὸ Παμφυλίας καὶ μὴ συνελθόντα αὐτοῖς εἰς τὸ ἔργον μὴ συμπαραλαμβάνειν τοῦτον). Barnabas agrees to embark on another missionary journey. But a disagreement ensues when he wishes to take along with them John Mark, his cousin (Col 4:10). Paul rejects Barnabas's suggestion and insists that John Mark should not come along. The reason Paul gives is that Mark had "deserted them in Pamphylia" and refused to accompany them when they traveled to the cities in south Galatia (13:13).[5] The term "the work" (τὸ ἔργον) denotes missionary work, i.e., the proclamation of the good news of Jesus to Jews and Greeks and the teaching of new converts, and it includes the travels and the travails of missionaries.

Some have suggested that the real reason for the disagreement between Barnabas and Paul was the theological position of the "Antiochene majority," which had withdrawn from fellowship with the Gentile Christians and had opposed Paul (Gal 2:13), a position Barnabas shared — a fact that prompted the dissolution of the missionary partnership between the two missionaries.[6] This reconstruction is implausible. First, apart from the

question of the date of the Antioch incident, Paul accuses Peter and Barnabas not of maintaining an erroneous theological position but of hypocrisy (Gal 2:13), i.e., of acting contrary to their convictions. Second, there is no evidence for a permanent split between Paul and Antioch or between Paul and Barnabas.[7] Third, from Luke's perspective, Paul's behavior during this period is characterized in a positive manner: Paul and Silas leave Antioch with the blessing of the Antioch congregation (15:40), Paul complies with the wishes of the Apostles' Council when he visits the churches in Syria and Cilicia (15:23, 41), and Paul strengthens the churches in Syria and Cilicia (15:41) — all activities that have no counterpart in Luke's description of Barnabas in this passage.

15:39 They had such a sharp disagreement that they decided to separate from each other. Barnabas took Mark and sailed to Cyprus (ἐγένετο δὲ παροξυσμὸς ὥστε ἀποχωρισθῆναι αὐτοὺς ἀπ᾽ ἀλλήλων, τόν τε Βαρναβᾶν παραλαβόντα τὸν Μᾶρκον ἐκπλεῦσαι εἰς Κύπρον). Barnabas insists that John Mark deserves a second chance, and Paul insists that he should not be taken along as coworker. Barnabas may have argued out of pastoral concern, while Paul may have focused on the requirements of missionary work. Luke does not comment on the motivations of Paul and Barnabas, but he notes that the "sharp disagreement" (παροξυσμός) could not be resolved; the Greek term implies the strong emotional involvement of both parties.[8] They decide to "separate" from each other and pursue independent itineraries. Barnabas takes John Mark with him as coworker and

---

5. The reasons for John Mark's return to Jerusalem are unknown; the suggestion that he resisted the Gentile mission has no basis in the text.

6. Recently Alexander J. M. Wedderburn, "Paul and Barnabas: The Anatomy and Chronology of a Parting of the Ways," in *Fair Play Diversity and Conflicts in Early Christianity* (FS Heikki Räisänen; ed. I. Dunderberg, C. M. Tuckett, and K.

Syreeni; NovTSup 103; Leiden: Brill, 2002), 291 – 310.

7. Cf. 1 Cor 9:6, where Paul speaks positively of Barnabas in connection with a description of his missionary praxis.

8. Cf. BDAG, s.v. παροξυσμός 2, "a state of irritation expressed in argument, *sharp disagreement* ('irritation, exasperation')."

sails to Cyprus (see on 13:4) to visit the churches that had been established in Salamis and Paphos and perhaps in other cities.

15:40   While Paul chose Silas and departed, after the believers had commended him to the grace of the Lord (Παῦλος δὲ ἐπιλεξάμενος Σιλᾶν ἐξῆλθεν παραδοθεὶς τῇ χάριτι τοῦ κυρίου ὑπὸ τῶν ἀδελφῶν). Paul chooses Silas as coworker, a leading Jewish Christian from Jerusalem (v. 22), who was a Roman citizen (16:37 – 38). The fact that the first "we passage" (see on 16:10) is connected with Paul's travels from Antioch via Syria, Cilicia, Galatia, Phrygia, and Mysia to Troas (15:41 – 16:10), is most plausibly interpreted to indicate that Luke was among Paul's associates as an eyewitness during this period (see the Introduction to Acts, "Luke's Origins"). Silas would have the support of the Jerusalem church and could testify to the outcome of the Apostles' Council. Since the letter of the apostles and elders was addressed not only to the church in Antioch but also to the churches in Syria and Cilicia (v. 23), and since the letter had been entrusted to Silas alongside Judas Barsabbas, the presence of Silas among Paul's missionary associates signals the unity of the church consisting of Jewish believers and Gentile believers.

Luke notes the approval of Paul's travel to Syria and Cilicia as well as of his choice of Silas as coworker by the Antioch church. The Antioch believers "commended" (παραδοθείς) Paul to the grace of the Lord; i.e., they pray that the Lord may bless Paul's journey and the pastoral ministry in south Galatia and the new missionary work planned for cities in the province of Asia (16:6). The fact that Paul takes along not only Silas, the Jerusalem envoy, but also Luke, and the fact that he recruits Timothy in Lystra as a fourth associate (16:3), indicates that Paul has made plans for missionary work in new areas. Thus begins the eighth and ninth periods of Paul's missionary work (mission

in Macedonia and in Achaia; see on 13:1), lasting three years from AD 49 to 51.

15:41   He traveled through Syria and Cilicia and strengthened the congregations (διήρχετο δὲ τὴν Συρίαν καὶ τὴν Κιλικίαν ἐπιστηρίζων τὰς ἐκκλησίας). Setting out from Antioch, Paul and company travel through Syria and Cilicia, visiting the congregations he had established during the fourth period of his missionary work in the eight years between AD 34 – 44 (see on 9:30; cf. 11:25 – 26; Gal 1:21). Luke's brief reference to "the congregations" (αἱ ἐκκλησίαι) confirms that Paul's earlier missionary work in these areas had resulted in the conversion of people — presumably Jews, God-fearers, and Gentiles — who gathered in local congregations. It is these believers whom Paul, Silas, and Luke visit. They "strengthened" (ἐπιστηρίζων; see on 14:22) the churches; i.e., they helped the believers to become stronger in their commitment to Jesus, Israel's Messiah and Savior. The present tense of the participle emphasizes the importance of this aspect of Paul's ministry.

16:1   Paul came to Derbe and to Lystra, where a disciple named Timothy lived, the son of a Jewish woman who was a believer and of a father who was a Greek (κατήντησεν δὲ καὶ εἰς Δέρβην καὶ εἰς Λύστραν. καὶ ἰδοὺ μαθητής τις ἦν ἐκεῖ ὀνόματι Τιμόθεος, υἱὸς γυναικὸς Ἰουδαίας πιστῆς, πατρὸς δὲ Ἕλληνος). Luke takes Paul and his coworkers from Cilicia to south Galatia, where the apostle recruits another coworker (16:1 – 3). Paul would be traveling from Tarsus north, crossing the Taurus mountains on the road through the Cilician Gates, then traveling westward on the major Roman road called Via Sebaste, passing through Podandos, Tynna, and Kybistra in Cappadocia, and Sidamaria, before reaching Derbe and Lystra (see on 14:8, 21) in southern Galatia, two cities in which congregations existed (14:8 – 20, 21). As

Paul travels in a westerly direction, he arrives first in Derbe before reaching Lystra.[9]

The reference to Timothy (Τιμόθεος) is explained by Paul's intention to take him on as his coworker (v. 3), and by Timothy's importance for Paul's ministry. The biographical details that Luke provides focus on his ethnicity, the reason of which will become evident in v. 3: he has a Jewish mother and a Greek father. Eunice, the name of his mother (2 Tim 1:5), is the name of various figures in Greek mythology. The Greek name of Timothy's Jewish mother is consistent with the fact that her family allowed her to marry a Greek man — a mixed marriage that was highly problematic according to Old Testament law and precedent;[10] this fact suggests that her family had assimilated to Greek culture.

Children born to mixed marriages in which the mother was Jewish and the father a Gentile were considered Gentile according to Old Testament law (patrilinear principle), but Jewish according to Mishnaic law (matrilinear principle, which may have been followed as early as the first century). See further on v. 3. According to 2 Tim 3:15 Timothy had been instructed in the Scriptures since childhood, which suggests that the assimilation of the family to Greek culture was not complete; he had relatives who took him to the synagogue, perhaps his mother or the brothers of his mother.

The mother of Timothy is characterized as being "a believer" (πιστῆς), who evidently was converted to faith in Jesus two years earlier, in AD 46/47, when Paul and Barnabas had proclaimed the gospel in Lystra (14:8 – 20). According to 2 Tim 1:5 both his mother Eunice and his grandmother Lois were Christian believers. Timothy is described

as a "disciple" (μαθητής), i.e., also as a believer in Jesus,[11] converted either during Paul's missionary work in Lystra or in the following months on account of the witness of the emerging congregations of Christian believers in the region.

16:2   This disciple had a good reputation among the believers in Lystra and Iconium (ὃς ἐμαρτυρεῖτο ὑπὸ τῶν ἐν Λύστροις καὶ Ἰκονίῳ ἀδελφῶν). Paul's decision to take on Timothy as a coworker (v. 3) is supported by the affirmation of Timothy's reputation by the "believers" (ἀδελφοί) in the congregations of Lystra and Iconium. The two towns were only 22 miles (35 km.) apart. Luke's comment indicates that there were at least personal connections between the believers in neighboring congregations.

16:3   Paul wanted to take him along when he continued his journey; so he circumcised him on account of the Jews who lived in these cities, for they all knew that his father was Greek (τοῦτον ἠθέλησεν ὁ Παῦλος σὺν αὐτῷ ἐξελθεῖν, καὶ λαβὼν περιέτεμεν αὐτὸν διὰ τοὺς Ἰουδαίους τοὺς ὄντας ἐν τοῖς τόποις ἐκείνοις· ᾔδεισαν γὰρ ἅπαντες ὅτι Ἕλλην ὁ πατὴρ αὐτοῦ ὑπῆρχεν). Paul wanted to take Timothy along once he left the region. The reason for the decision to recruit Timothy as a missionary associate is connected with the good reputation Timothy enjoyed in the churches of the region (v. 2), but motivated, evidently, by the potential that Paul saw in Timothy, demonstrated perhaps in Timothy's involvement in the teaching of Scripture (cf. 2 Tim 3:15) in the new congregations in Lystra and Iconium.

Luke then relates that Paul took Timothy and

---

9. Barrett, *Acts*, 759, suggests that Timothy and his mother lived in Derbe; this is not indicated by the wording of v. 1, however, which renders it more plausible to link Timothy's family with Lystra, particularly in the light of v. 2.

10. Exod 34:15 – 16; Deut 7:3 – 4; 23:2 – 9; cf. Josh 23:12 – 13; Judg 3:5 – 11; Neh 13; Ezra 9 – 10; Mal 2:10 – 16; cf. *Jub.*

30:7 – 17. Cf. Shaye J. D. Cohen, *The Beginnings of Jewishness: Boundaries, Varieties, Uncertainties* (Hellenistic Culture and Society 31; Berkeley: Univ. of California Press, 1999), 241 – 62, on the prohibition of intermarriage.

11. Cf. 6:1; 9:36, 38.

"circumcised him."[12] In addition to Paul's intention to invite Timothy to serve on his missionary team, the second reason that Luke provides for Paul's action is the fact that the Jews who lived in these cities knew that Timothy's father was a Greek[13] and that he was not circumcised. They also knew he had a Jewish mother; otherwise his not being circumcised would not have been surprising.

The phrase "they all knew" (ᾔδεισαν ἅπαντες) may not be Lukan hyperbole but can be taken literally: if his father was an uncircumcised God-fearer attending synagogue services, they would have known him. Since fathers had authority over their children, it was evidently the pagan father who had prevented Timothy's circumcision after birth; he may have thought that looser contacts with the Jewish community such as God-fearers had was sufficient for both himself and for his son(s). "The Jews who lived in these cities" are presumably non-Christian Jews; if Luke wanted to indicate Jewish Christians he would have referred to "Jewish brothers."

Paul's initiative to circumcise Timothy, motivated by the opinions of unbelieving Jews, seems surprising, following Paul's rejection of the demand that Gentile believers should be circumcised (15:1 – 2),[14] a position that was confirmed by the apostles and elders in Jerusalem (15:5 – 21) and by the letter that reported the apostolic decree, delivered by Paul to the churches, including Lystra and Iconium (16:4). Some scholars question the historicity of v. 3.[15] Several arguments and scenarios plausibly explain Timothy's circumcision by Paul. (1) Luke portrays Paul as a flexible missionary who

was prepared to become a Jew to the Jews (1 Cor 9:20) and circumcised Timothy for the benefit of his continuing missionary work among Jewish communities, without according salvific value to Timothy's circumcision.

(2) While Paul consistently objected to Gentile believers being circumcised in order to have full salvation, he never argued that Jews should no longer circumcise their children. Paul's loyalty to the Mosaic law expressed in Timothy's circumcision does not contradict his basic theological position regarding the salvation-historical role of the law in view of the death, resurrection, and exaltation of Jesus as Israel's Messiah and Savior, but remedies the ambiguous ethnic and social status of Timothy. If his Jewish mother made him legally Jewish (matrilinear principle), Timothy is an uncircumcised Jew, a status that was untenable for Jews, constituting a violation of the covenant, and strange for Gentiles, who knew that Jews were circumcised. The belated circumcision thus becomes plausible. If his Gentile father made him legally a Gentile (patrilinear principle), his Jewish upbringing in the context of a synagogue (2 Tim 3:15) suggests a quasi-Jewish identity in social terms, a situation that would be clarified by circumcision.

Paul's circumcision of Timothy shows two concerns of Luke (Paul). (1) The apostolic mission, whose terms had been confirmed at the Apostles' Council (Acts 15), does not require Jews to abandon their traditions since "everything appropriate to that tradition could still be practiced, so long as it was understood to have cultural rather than soteriological significance."[16] (2) Paul's focus on the

12. On circumcision cf. 7:8.

13. The verb translated as "was" (ὑπῆρχεν) denotes "to be in a state or circumstance" (BDAG, s.v. ὑπάρχω 2) and adds emphasis to the ethnic status of Timothy's father, which is expressed in v. 1 with an implied form of εἰμί. The imperfect tense does not necessarily imply that his father had died (contra Barrett, *Acts*, 761).

14. Cf. Gal 5:2; 1 Cor 7:18.

15. Cf. Baur, *Paul*, 1:135, who deems v. 3 "simply incredible"; Haenchen, *Acts*, 480 – 82; Barrett, *Acts*, 760 – 61.

16. Johnson, *Acts*, 289; for the following point ibid., 289 – 90.

proclamation of the gospel among Gentiles does not mean that he has abandoned the Jewish people, whom he continues to introduce to the good news of Jesus, Israel's Messiah and Savior.

16:4 As they traveled from city to city, they delivered the decisions that the apostles and elders in Jerusalem had reached for the believers to obey (ὡς δὲ διεπορεύοντο τὰς πόλεις, παρεδίδοσαν αὐτοῖς φυλάσσειν τὰ δόγματα τὰ κεκριμένα ὑπὸ τῶν ἀποστόλων καὶ πρεσβυτέρων τῶν ἐν Ἰεροσολύμοις). Luke's report about the visitation of the churches in south Galatia in vv. 4 – 5 begins with the comment that Paul and his associates — Silas, Luke, and Timothy — traveled to the cities in which Christian communities existed. After Derbe (v. 1), this included Lystra and Iconium (v. 2), and presumably Pisidian Antioch. It is curious that Luke reported extensively about Paul's missionary work in Pisidian Antioch (13:14 – 50), mentioning his pastoral visit on the return journey (14:21), but does not mention the city and its congregation here. Paul's subsequent travels (v. 6) leave little doubt that he visited Pisidian Antioch.

Paul "delivered" (παρεδίδοσαν), i.e., passed on the decisions of the Apostles' Council. The transmission of the decisions would have happened orally, through reports given by Paul and Silas, who had attended the Jerusalem Council. At the same time it is plausible that Silas, one of the two envoys that the apostles and elders had sent to Syria and Cilicia, had made copies of the apostolic letter (15:23 – 29), one of which he carried with him to the churches in south Galatia. The term translated "decisions" (δόγματα) denotes "a formal statement concerning rules or regulations that are to be observed" (BDAG); this can be a formalized set of rules by any person of political body ("ordinance, decision, command"), including decrees of the emperor promulgated in imperial "edicts" (cf. 17:7) that are not to be disobeyed; the translation

"decrees" (NASB, NET; cf. GNB "rules") is thus appropriate.

These decisions had been "reached" (κεκριμένα); i.e., these decrees had been decided by the apostles and elders in Jerusalem (see 15:1 – 29). Their decision is meant to be obeyed (φυλάσσειν; infinitive of purpose); i.e., they are to observe the two decisions that were made — Gentile Christians should not be circumcised and subjected to wholesale obedience to the Mosaic law (which means that Jewish Christians should not make these demands), and Gentile believers should follow those stipulations of the law that applied to them, in particular regarding idolatry, sexual immorality, and the consumption of blood.

If Paul indeed wrote his letter to the Galatian churches a year or so earlier (before the Apostles' Council) — a letter in which he warned the Gentile believers in the strongest term to refuse to be subjected to circumcision and the law (suggested by Jewish Christian teachers as necessary for salvation) — he would have introduced the decisions of the Apostles' Council as confirming his teaching: Gentile Christians have salvation and are members of God's messianic people without circumcision and obedience to the entire Mosaic law. The fact that Paul makes the decisions of the Apostolic Council known in the churches in south Galatia, which were not included in the address of the apostolic letter (which mentioned only Antioch, Syria, and Cilicia), underscores the general validity of the decisions, which were to be followed wherever Jewish and Gentile believers met in community.

16:5 So the congregations were strengthened in the faith and grew daily in numbers (αἱ μὲν οὖν ἐκκλησίαι ἐστερεοῦντο τῇ πίστει καὶ ἐπερίσσευον τῷ ἀριθμῷ καθ' ἡμέραν). Paul's visit and the notification of the decisions of the Apostles' Council resulted in the continued growth of the local congregations, both internally with regard to their "faith" (πίστις) and externally in terms of their "number" (ἀριθμός). Believers became firmer in their commitment to Jesus, and the congregations became larger as more and more people were converted.

The growth of the churches was presumably the result of renewed missionary preaching of Paul and his coworkers.[17] In the context of the promulgation of the decisions of the Apostles' Council in v. 4, Luke's reference to new church growth in v. 5 demonstrates, at the same time, that the solution of the conflict about circumcision and the Gentiles' obedience to the Mosaic law proved successful; congregations in which Jewish believers and Gentile believers quarrel about circumcision and obedience to the law will hardly serve to strengthen the believers' faith in Jesus or witness the influx of new converts.

16:6 They traveled through the region of Phrygia and Galatia, after the Holy Spirit had prevented them from speaking the word in the province of Asia (διῆλθον δὲ τὴν Φρυγίαν καὶ Γαλατικὴν χώραν κωλυθέντες ὑπὸ τοῦ ἁγίου πνεύματος λαλῆσαι τὸν λόγον ἐν τῇ Ἀσίᾳ). In a new episode, Luke narrates Paul's travels from south Galatia to Troas, where the missionary team is called to go to Macedonia (vv. 6 – 10). The travel from south Galatia in central Anatolia to Troas on the west coast of Asia Minor (vv. 6 – 8) results from Paul's being forced twice to change his plans. His initial plan was to "speak the word" (λαλῆσαι τὸν λόγον), i.e., to preach the good news of Jesus Christ, in the province of Asia (see on 2:9 – 10).[18]

This notice is usually interpreted in terms of Paul's plan to preach the gospel in Ephesus, the principal city of Asia.[19] While this is certainly plausible, this is not a foregone conclusion, since Paul had not set his sights on large metropolitan centers so far in his missionary work; Syrian Antioch was the only exception, although he had worked there not on his own initiative but as a result of Barnabas's invitation (11:25 – 26).[20] There were other cities in the province of Asia with thriving Jewish communities, the first point of contact for Paul's missionary work: Laodicea, Hierapolis, Colossae, Tripolis on the Maeander, Antioch on the Maeander, Nysa, Tralles, Magnesia, Priene, Miletus, Philadelphia, Sardis, Thyatira, Pergamon, and Smyrna.

Paul had to abandon his plan to engage in missionary work in Asia because the Holy Spirit "prevented" (κωλυθέντες) his team from beginning missionary work there, perhaps through a dream, a vision, or a prophetic message.[21] Luke's comment indicates that Paul's mission is directed by the Holy Spirit, as was the missionary work of Peter and the Jerusalem church. The reason for the intervention of the Spirit may be connected with public and official hostility in the old royal cities of Sardis and Pergamon or in the capital city of Ephesus, the kind of hostility and persecution that Paul had encountered earlier in Pisidian Antioch, Iconium, and Lystra, causing major difficulties for his missionary work.[22]

As v. 7 indicates, Paul then decides to travel to the province of Bithynia. The verb translated as "they traveled" (διῆλθον) indicates missionary

---

17. The expansion of Codex D in v. 4 makes this point explicit: "they passed through the cities and preached and presented the Lord Jesus with all boldness."

18. The Roman province of Asia, located in western Asia Minor, must not be confused with the modern geographical term "Asia."

19. Recently Dunn, *Beginning from Jerusalem*, 666, referring to Paul's "city-centred mission tactic."

20. For this and the following comments cf. Schnabel, *Paul the Missionary*, 267 – 70.

21. According to 15:32, Silas was a prophet.

22. Thus David H. French, "Acts and the Roman Roads of Asia Minor," in *The Book of Acts in its Graeco-Roman Setting* (ed. D. W. J. Gill and C. Gempf; Grand Rapids: Eerdmans, 1994), 49 – 68, 57 – 58. The route that Paul and his associates took avoided the large Roman roads.

work in 8:4 and 13:6, but not necessarily here; i.e., it is possible but not certain that Paul and his associates preach the gospel in the cities through which they pass. The route north passes through "the region of Phrygia and Galatia," a phrase that refers to the region of *Phrygia Paroreius*, i.e., to the region on both sides of the Sultan Dağ Mountains whose inhabitants were ethnically Phrygian; parts of *Phrygia Paroreius* belonged to the province of Galatia while other parts belonged to the province of Asia.[23]

16:7 – 8 When they came to the border of Mysia, they attempted to travel to Bithynia, but the Spirit of Jesus did not permit them to do so. They passed through Mysia and went down to Troas (ἐλθόντες δὲ κατὰ τὴν Μυσίαν ἐπείραζον εἰς τὴν Βιθυνίαν πορευθῆναι, καὶ οὐκ εἴασεν αὐτοὺς τὸ πνεῦμα Ἰησοῦ· παρελθόντες δὲ τὴν Μυσίαν κατέβησαν εἰς Τρῳάδα). After Paul abandons the prospect of preaching the gospel in cities in the province of Asia, he decides to travel to Bithynia, evidently with the goal of starting missionary work in the cities of Nicea, Nicomedia, and Chalcedon. The plan to travel to Bithynia suggests the continuation of the journey on the road leading to the north, passing via Synnada to Prymnessos. If Paul intends to reach Bithynia in Nikaia or Nikomedia, he presumably travels as far as Kotiaeion (Cotiaeum), located on the northwestern border between the regions of Phrygia and Mysia; perhaps he reaches Dorylaion, an important crossroads northeast of Cotiaeum.[24]

Again, due to divine intervention by the Holy Spirit, Paul is not permitted (οὐκ εἴασεν) to proceed. He cannot preach the gospel in Bithynia.[25] This is the only time that the Holy Spirit is called "the Spirit of Jesus," appropriate in the light of 2:33, where Peter asserts that Jesus, the risen and exalted messianic Son of David, has brought about the fulfillment of the promise of the Spirit of prophecy, bestowing God's Spirit upon his disciples. For Luke, Jesus continues to be involved in the life and ministry of his witnesses (cf. 7:56; 9:5). The expression "the Spirit of Jesus," referring to the Holy Spirit, is another example of Luke's "high" Christology.

Since the plan to travel north to Bithynia cannot be realized, Paul travels through Mysia. Mysia, which never formed a geographical, economic, or administrative unity, is the region in the northwest of Asia Minor; main cities were Pergamon and the ports of Apollonia, Cyzicus, Priapus, and Parium. Coming from Cotiaeum, Paul presumably passed through Kadoi, traveling along the upper reaches of the Makestus River (mod. Simav) in a westerly direction via Synaos, Hadrianothera, and the port city of Adramyttium, then along the coast via Antandros, Gargara and Skamandreia to Troas (Alexandria Troas).

Why does Paul travel from eastern Mysia to Troas? If he wanted to reach the closest port in order to sail back to Judea or to Syria, he could have reached Adramyttium on a more westerly route, or he could have traveled straight south to Perge or to Attalia in Pamphylia. A more plausible suggestion surmises that Paul did not arrive in Troas as a clueless missionary uncertain about his

---

23. Stephen Mitchell, *Anatolia*, 2:3 – 4. The assumption that Paul visited the cities of the Celtic tribes (the ethnic Galatians) in northern Galatia, is unconvincing; on Paul's travel route and on the north Galatian theory cf. Schnabel, *Early Christian Mission*, 2:1131 – 37.

24. Cf. Robert Jewett, "Mapping the Route of Paul's 'Second Missionary Journey' from Dorylaeum to Troas," *TynBul* 48 (1997): 1 – 22, 5 – 6.

25. Christians in Bithynia are attested in 1 Pet 1:1 — the fruit of the missionary work of unnamed missionaries in the region (possibly Peter's?) — and rapidly growing Christian communities are attested by Pliny, the Roman governor in the early second century, who complains in a letter to the emperor Trajan that the Christian "superstition" had penetrated not only the cities but also the villages and the rural areas (Pliny, *Ep. Tra.* 10.96.9 – 10).

future movements. As the provinces of Asia and Bithynia had been ruled out at this time as areas for missionary work, and since Paul evidently did not want to return to Syria, he traveled to Troas with the purpose of taking a ship to Europe.[26] This suggestion is not contradicted by the dream-vision in which Paul is called by a Macedonian man to "come over to Macedonia and help us" (16:9); Luke perhaps wants to assert in 16:9 that the new plans of missionary outreach to Macedonia receive divine confirmation when they arrive in Troas.

16:9 During the night Paul had a vision of a Macedonian man who stood there and invited him, saying, "Come over to Macedonia and help us!" (καὶ ὅραμα διὰ τῆς νυκτὸς τῷ Παύλῳ ὤφθη, ἀνὴρ Μακεδών τις ἦν ἑστὼς καὶ παρακαλῶν αὐτὸν καὶ λέγων· διαβὰς εἰς Μακεδονίαν βοήθησον ἡμῖν). The episode of Paul's travels from south Galatia to Macedonia concludes with the narrative of the apostle's call to come to Macedonia (vv. 9 – 10). Paul has a "vision" (ὅραμα)[27] during the night, i.e., either a dream or, if he had woken up, a vision proper. The references to the Spirit's direction in vv. 6 – 7 suggest that it is the Spirit who has caused Paul to have a dream-vision with visual and audio elements. Paul sees a Macedonian man who stands there and invites him. Paul hears what the man says, narrated by Luke in direct speech, thus underlining the significance of the invitation.

The words of the man in the vision are focused on the imperative "help us" (βοήθησον); the verb denotes "to render assistance to someone in need" (BDAG). Its general meaning fits the vision of a man who does not know the gospel and who does not perceive how Paul may be able to provide aid. Paul can only help if he crosses over to Macedonia.

16:10 After Paul had seen the vision, we sought to leave immediately for Macedonia, as we came to the conclusion that God had called us to preach the good news to them (ὡς δὲ τὸ ὅραμα εἶδεν, εὐθέως ἐζητήσαμεν ἐξελθεῖν εἰς Μακεδονίαν συμβιβάζοντες ὅτι προσκέκληται ἡμᾶς ὁ θεὸς εὐαγγελίσασθαι αὐτούς). Paul and his associates decide to travel to Macedonia. Paul had seen the vision, but he did not make the decision to act on what he had seen and heard by himself: he evidently presented the content of the vision to his coworkers, and together they "came to the conclusion" (συμβιβάζοντες) that the vision represented God's guidance. This verb denotes rational reflection and inference, the plural indicates the involvement of others, and the participle signals cause: because Paul and his associates have concluded that God had revealed his will through the vision, they seek to leave Troas and sail to Macedonia.

The first person plural of the verb marks the beginning of the first "we passage" in Acts (16:10 – 17),[28] which is most naturally interpreted in terms of the author being involved as an eyewitness. Paul involved Silas and Luke (perhaps even young Timothy?) in the interpretation of the vision. Once they concluded that it was God who had called them, they attempt to leave "immediately," i.e., without delay. They knew that God's call concerned the proclamation of "the good news" of Jesus (εὐαγγελίσασθαι; see on 5:42), Israel's Messiah and Savior of humankind. And they now understand that the "negative" guidance of the Spirit regarding missionary work in the provinces of Asia and Bithynia (vv. 6 – 7) was meant to prepare them for the "positive" guidance through the vision, so they accept the challenge of a new missionary initiative — the evangelization of Europe.

---

26. W. Paul Bowers, "Paul's Route through Mysia: A Note on Acts XVI.8," *JTS* 30 (1979): 507 – 11; see ibid. for the following comment.

27. Cf. 7:31; 9:10, 12; 10:3, 17, 19; 11:5; 12:9; 18:9.

28. The other "we passages" are 20:5 – 15; 21:1 – 18; 27:1 – 28:16.

Theology in Application

In agreement with the main idea formulated above, this passage emphasizes several points.

A Twofold Responsibility

The church has a twofold responsibility concerning the proclamation of God's Word: teaching believers in local congregations and preaching to unbelievers in unreached areas. Paul and Barnabas do both: they teach in the congregation in Antioch (15:35), and they initiate new missionary ventures (15:36, 39 – 40). Churches do not need to "discover" what their "mission" is — the task of missionary outreach is an integral part of the DNA of an authentic church. An exclusive focus of pastoral activities and financial resources on one's own local congregation is not only selfish, but a denial of the good news of Jesus that needs to be carried to regions, cities, neighborhoods, and people who have not yet heard, or understood, the gospel.

Both teaching in the churches and proclaiming the gospel in missionary outreach get their bearings from the "decisions" of the leaders of the church. Such decrees are not meant to be shackles that restrict the believers; nevertheless, Christian freedom is not to be confused with a laissez-faire attitude where anything goes and where personal preferences carry the day. There is wisdom in the decisions of church leaders and missionary leaders, meant to help churches and ministries grow and thrive.

Personal Initiative

Personal initiative is a key factor in the proclamation of the gospel. This is true for teachers in local congregations who have to discern the theological, pastoral, and personal needs of the members of the congregation. And this is particularly true for missionaries who move into new regions and who open up new phases of evangelism. The experience of Paul and his associates, who are prohibited by God's Spirit from evangelizing in the provinces of Asia and Macedonia and who are directed in a vision to travel to Macedonia, demonstrates that human initiative and divine initiative are not mutually exclusive.

Any biography of a contemporary missionary illustrates this point. It is important to note that Paul's missionary drive did not make him immune to hearing God speak to him. He did not force his plans to evangelize in cities in the province of Asia, nor did he push through his new plan to start missionary work in cities in the province of Bithynia. Instead, he willingly followed God's guidance communicated through the Holy Spirit. Authentic preachers of the gospel are not "movers and shakers" motivated by action for its own sake or by programs they push through at all cost. Rather, they are and remain believers who follow Jesus, who have been given God's Spirit and who are willing to modify, change, or abandon plans if and when God reveals it as his will. God's guidance may come through supernatural means such as visions, dreams, and prophecies (which must be evaluated by other believers, see 1 Cor 14:29), through subsequent evaluation of earlier plans (see 2 Cor 1:12 – 2:4), or through circumstances (see Rom 1:8 – 15).

Disagreements Are Unavoidable

Disagreements are unavoidable. Since personal initiatives involve subjective evaluations of facts and factors that are relevant for both pastoral ministry and missionary work, disagreements are the natural result of different opinions regarding the most effective missionary strategies. Potential disagreements should not be short-circuited, with the senior pastor or the senior missionary making all the decisions. Effectiveness in pastoral and missionary work is so important that all relevant viewpoints need to be communicated and discussed. Paul and Barnabas found a solution that served the advance of the gospel, recognizing the need for distinct ministries in different geographical locations. While disagreements may be painful and the resulting separation less than ideal, God's sovereign plan can still be at work, provided that the reasons for the separation are not personal prestige and power but considerations connected with the proclamation of the gospel.

Theological Discernment

Missionary accommodation requires theological discernment. Since Paul's circumcision of Timothy (16:3) is narrated in the context of several divine initiatives (16:6 – 7, 9 – 10), it can be seen as part of God's guidance. Interpreted in terms of missionary accommodation — once the ethnic-social status of Timothy is clarified, missionary work in synagogues had one problem less to deal with — the fact remains important that Paul did not compromise fundamental theological principles. As he conveyed the decisions of the Apostles' Council to the churches in south Galatia, he did not circumcise here a Gentile believer whose salvation he regarded as incomplete, but a Christian whose ethnic-social status was ambiguous.

Missionary accommodation for Paul is not a rigid principle that needs to be employed at all costs in order to achieve missionary success — a stance that itself would be nothing more than the enslavement to a law — but is closely tied to the truth of the gospel, which cannot be compromised, and is tied to the freedom of faith and to the love among believers in Jesus. Some principles are worth standing up for, while others are opinions of lesser importance; to know the difference between the two is "a sign of discernment and leadership."[29]

---

29. Bock, *Acts*, 524.

Acts 16:11 – 40

Literary Context

The second half of Acts narrates the missionary work of Paul (Acts 13 – 28). It began with Paul and Barnabas preaching the good news of Jesus, Israel's Messiah and Savior of the Gentiles, in Asia Minor in the provinces of Cyprus, Galatia, and Pamphylia (13:1 – 14:28). The increasing number of Gentile conversions raised concerns among a vocal group of Jewish Christians who taught that in order to be fully saved, Gentile Christians had to be circumcised and committed to obey the entire Mosaic law. This issue was resolved by the Apostles' Council (15:1 – 33).

The next major section relates Paul's missionary work in Europe (15:35 – 18:22). Paul and a new partner, Silas, visit the existing churches in Syria, Cilicia, and south Galatia, explaining the decisions of the Apostles' Council. Plans to establish new centers of missionary work in cities in the province of Asia were thwarted by divine intervention, as were plans to move north to cities in the province of Bithynia. Then, as the result of a dream-vision, Paul and his associates perceive that God wants them to travel to Macedonia and preach the gospel in Macedonian cities. This new section narrates the implementation of this new missionary initiative in Macedonia (16:11 – 17:15). This section is made up of three episodes: Paul's missionary work in Philippi (16:11 – 40), in Thessalonica (17:1 – 9), and in Berea (17:10 – 15). Paul's mission in Philippi probably takes place from August to October in AD 49.

Main Idea

The events connected with Paul's work in Philippi demonstrate how God directs the mission of the church, aiding the missionaries to overcome social, cultural, demonic, political, and legal difficulties and rendering successful their efforts to lead people to saving faith and to establish a community of followers of Jesus.

Translation

Acts 16:11 – 40

11a	Action	**We put out to sea**
b	Setting: geographical	from Troas
c	Action & Place	and **took a straight course to Samothrace;**
d	Action & Place	**the next day we went on to Neapolis.**
12a	Setting: geographical	From there
b	Action & Place	**we traveled to Philippi,**
c	Description	a leading city of that district of Macedonia and
d	Description	a Roman colony.
e	Action & Time	**We stayed several days in that city.**
13a	Setting: temporal	On the Sabbath
b	Action	**we went outside the city gate**
c	Place	by the river,
d	Reason	where we expected to find a synagogue.
e	Action	**We sat down**
f	Action	and **spoke to the women**
g	Identification	who had gathered there.
14a	Character entrance	**One of the women who listened was Lydia,**
b	Description	a merchant dealing in purple cloth,
c	Description	from the city of Thyatira,
d	Description	a God-fearer.
e	Action	**The Lord opened her heart**
f	Result	so that she followed what Paul said.
15a	Event	When she and the members of her household were baptized,
b	Action	**she invited us,**
c		saying,
d	Condition	*"If you consider me to be faithful to the Lord,*
e	Entreaty	*come and stay at my house."*
f	Action	**And she strongly urged us.**
16a	Setting: temporal & spatial	Once when we were going to the synagogue,
b	Character entrance	**we met a slave girl**

Continued on next page.

Continued from previous page.

c	Description	who had a spirit of divination and
d	Description	who brought great profit to her owners
e	Means	by giving oracles.
17a	Action	**She followed Paul and the rest of us,**
b		shouting:
c	Assertion	*"These men are slaves of the Most High God*
d		*who proclaim to you a way to salvation."*
18a	Action	**She kept doing this**
b	Duration	**for many days.**
c	Action	**Then Paul,**
d	Reason	who was greatly disturbed by this,
e	Action	**turned around and said to the spirit:**
f	Command	*I order you*
g	Means	*in the name of Jesus Christ*
h	Result	*to come out of her!"*
i	Action	**And the spirit came out of her**
j	Time	that very hour.
19a	Reason	When her owners saw
b	Reason	that their prospects of financial profit were gone,
c	Action	**they seized Paul and**
d		**Silas and**
e	Action	**dragged them into the agora**
f	Purpose	to face the city officials.
20a	Action	**They brought them before the chief magistrates**
b	Action	and **said:**
c	Assertion	*"These men throw our city into confusion.*
d	Description	*They are Jews*
21a	Assertion	*and they are proclaiming customs*
b	Description	*that are unlawful for us Romans to adopt or practice."*
22a	Action	**The crowd joined in attacking them,**
b	Action	and **the magistrates had them stripped of their clothes and**
c	Action	**ordered that they be beaten with rods.**
23a	Setting: temporal	After they had been severely beaten,
b	Action	**they threw them into prison.**
c	Action	**They ordered the jailer**
d	Command	to guard them
e	Manner	securely.
24a	Setting: temporal	Following these orders,
b	Action	**he put them in the inner cell and**
c	Action	**secured their feet in the stocks.**
25a	Setting: temporal	About midnight
b	Action	**Paul and Silas were praying and**
c	Action	**singing hymns to God,**
d	Action	and **the other prisoners listened to them.**

26a	Event	**Suddenly there was a large earthquake,**
b	Result	which shook the foundations of the prison.
c	Event	**Immediately all the doors were opened,**
d	Event	**and everyone's chains came loose.**
27a	Event	**The jailer woke up and**
b	Event	**saw the prison doors open;**
c	Action	**he drew his sword and**
d	Intention	**was about to kill himself**
e	Reason	because he assumed that the prisoners had escaped.
28a	Action	**But Paul shouted**
b		with a loud voice,
c	Exhortation	*"Do not harm yourself!*
d	Assertion	*We are all here!"*
29a	Action	**The jailer called for lights,**
b	Action	**rushed in, and**
c	Action	**fell down trembling before Paul and Silas.**
30a	Action	**Then he brought them outside**
b	Action	**and said,**
c	Question	*"Gentlemen, what must I do to be saved?"*
31a	Response	**They answered,**
b	Exhortation	*"Believe in the Lord Jesus,*
c	Result	*and you will be saved —*
d	Identification	*you and*
e	Identification	*your household."*
32a	Action	**They spoke the word of the Lord to him and**
b		**to all the people in his household.**
33a	Action & Time	**The jailer took them at that hour of the night and**
b	Action	**washed their wounds.**
c	Event & Participant	**Then he and**
d	Participant	**his entire household**
e		**were baptized**
f	Time	at once.
34a	Action	**He brought them into his house and**
b	Action	**set food before them.**
c	Event	**He and his entire household were overjoyed**
d	Reason	because he had come to faith in God.
35a	Time	When morning came,
b	Action	**the magistrates sent the lictors with the order:**
c	Command	*"Let these men go!"*
36a	Action	**The jailer reported these words to Paul,**
b		saying:
c	Report	*"The magistrates sent word*
d		*to let you go.*
e	Permission	*Now you can leave.*
f	Instruction	*Go in peace."*
37a	Action	**But Paul said to them:**
b	Accusation	*"They beat us in public,*
c	Complaint	*without due process,*

Continued on next page.

Continued from previous page.

d	Identification & Reason	*men who are Roman citizens,*
e	Accusation	*and they threw us into prison.*
f	Rhetorical question	*And now they are releasing us in secret?*
g	Rejection	*No!*
h	Demand	*Let them come themselves and*
i	Demand	*escort us out."*
38a	Action	**The lictors reported these words to the magistrates.**
b	Reason	When they heard that they were Roman citizens,
c	Action	**they became frightened.**
39a	Action	**They came,**
b	Action	**and they placated them,**
c	Action	**and they escorted them from the prison,**
d	Entreaty	asking them to leave the city.
40a	Setting: temporal	After they left the prison,
b	Action & Place	**they went to Lydia's house,**
c	Action	where they met and encouraged the believers.
d	Action	**Then they departed.**

Structure and Literary Form

The episode of Paul's missionary work in Philippi is narrated in five incidents. (1) Luke reports the conversion of Lydia, a wealthy purple merchant who was a God-fearer (vv. 11 – 15). Paul and his associates travel to Philippi, visit the synagogue by the river, and proclaim the gospel to women in the synagogue. Lydia becomes a believer and is baptized along with her family, and she invites the missionaries to stay in her house.

(2) The next incident is the exorcism of a spirit of divination from a slave girl (vv. 16 – 18), which corresponds to Peter's confrontation with Ananias and Sapphira in Jerusalem (5:1 – 11) and with Simon Magus in Samaria (8:17 – 24), as well as Paul's confrontation with Bar-Jesus in Paphos (13:6 – 11). It is narrated in three parts: a biographical introduction of the slave girl, followed by the girl's prophetic utterance concerning the missionaries on the streets of Philippi, which prompts Paul to exorcise the demonic spirit from the girl.

(3) Luke then narrates the arrest of Paul and Silas (vv. 19 – 24) by the owners of the slave girl, the accusation of the missionaries before the city magistrates, and their imprisonment in a secure cell in the local prison.

(4) In vv. 25 – 34, Paul and Silas pray and sing songs at night in prison. An earthquake happens, which opens the prison and moves prisoners' chains. The ensuing encounter with the jailer is narrated in great detail (vv. 27 – 34), focusing on his conversion.

(5) The final incident relates the discharge of the missionaries (vv. 35 – 40) in six stages: the magistrates' order of release of Paul and Silas, the jailer's communication of the release order to Paul and Silas, Paul's protest by appeal to his Roman citizenship, the magistrates' apology, Paul's encouragement of the new believers in Lydia's house, and the missionaries' departure from Philippi.

The episode is a *historical narrative* with two *conversion stories* (Lydia, vv. 14 – 15; the jailer and his family, vv. 29 – 34), two *miracle stories* (the exorcism of the slave girl, vv. 16 – 18; the earthquake that opens the prison doors, v. 26), and a *travel notice* (vv. 11 – 12). Luke uses *direct speech* to create a vivid account of the events; six different people speak: Lydia (v. 15); the slave girl and her spirit of divination (v. 17); the owners of the slave girl (vv. 20 – 21); the jailer, who inquires about salvation and later communicates the magistrates' decision to Paul and Silas (vv. 30, 36); the local police, who tell the jailer to release the missionaries (v. 35); Paul, who commands the spirit to leave the girl, commands the jailer not to harm himself, explains salvation, and requests public rehabilitation (vv. 18, 28, 31, 37).

Exegetical Outline

→ **I. The Mission in Philippi (16:11 – 40)**

  A. The Conversion of the Purple-Merchant Lydia (16:11 – 15)

    1. Travel from Troas to Philippi (16:11 – 12b)

    2. The city of Philippi (16:12c-e)

    3. Visit to the synagogue of Philippi (16:13a-d)

    4. Proclamation of the gospel to women in the synagogue (16:13e-g)

    5. The conversion of Lydia (16:14)

    6. The baptism of Lydia and her family (16:15a)

    7. Lydia's invitation of the missionaries to stay in her house (16:15b-f)

  B. The Exorcism of a Spirit of Divination from a Slave Girl (16:16 – 18)

    1. Biographical introduction of the slave girl (16:16)

    2. The slave girl's prophetic utterance concerning the missionaries (16:17 – 18b)

    3. The exorcism of the demonic spirit (16:18c-j)

  C. The Arrest of Paul and Silas (16:19 – 24)

    1. The arrest of Paul and Silas by the owners of the slave girl (16:19)

    2. The accusation of Paul and Silas before the city magistrates (16:20 – 23)

      a. The accusation by the owners of the slave girl of illegal activities (16:20 – 21)

      b. The attack of the citizens (16:22a)

      c. The magistrates order the flogging of Paul and Silas (16:22b-c)

      d. Paul and Silas are flogged (16:23a)

      e. The magistrates order the imprisonment of Paul and Silas (16:23b-e)

    3. The imprisonment of Paul and Silas in a secure cell (16:24)

D. **The Conversion of the Jailer (16:25 – 34)**

    1. The prayers and the singing of Paul and Silas in prison (16:25)

    2. The earthquake (16:26a-b)

    3. The opening of the prison and of the chains (16:26c-d)

    4. The encounter with the jailer (16:27 – 34)

        a. The jailer's attempted suicide (16:27)

        b. Paul saves the jailer from suicide (16:28)

        c. The jailer's acknowledgment of Paul's superior status (16:29)

        d. The removal of the prisoners from their cell (16:30a)

        e. The jailer's question about salvation (16:30b-c)

        f. Paul proclaims the gospel to the jailer and his family (16:31 – 32)

        g. The jailer's care for the missionaries (16:33a-b)

        h. The baptism of the jailer and his family (16:33c-f)

        i. The jailer's care for the missionaries (16:34a-b)

        j. The jailer's joy about his faith in God (16:34c-d)

E. **The Discharge of the Missionaries (16:35 – 40)**

    1. The magistrates' order of release of Paul and Silas (16:35)

    2. The jailer's communication of the release order to Paul and Silas (16:36)

    3. Paul's protest by appeal to his Roman citizenship (16:37)

    4. The magistrates' apology (16:38 – 39)

    5. Paul's encouragement of the new believers in Lydia's house (16:40a-c)

    6. The departure from Philippi (16:40d)

Explanation of the Text

16:11 We put out to sea from Troas and took a straight course to Samothrace; the next day we went on to Neapolis (ἀναχθέντες δὲ ἀπὸ Τρῳάδος εὐθυδρομήσαμεν εἰς Σαμοθρᾴκην, τῇ δὲ ἐπιούσῃ εἰς Νέαν πόλιν). Luke begins the episode with a note on Paul's travel from Troas in the province of Asia to Philippi in the province of Macedonia (vv. 11 – 12a).[1] Paul and his associates "put out to sea" from the harbor in Troas on a ship that sailed across the Mare Macedonicum, the northern part of the Aegean Sea, past the island of Iambros, taking a straight course to Samothrace, a town on the northern end of the island with the same name, which was dominated by a high mountain. The ship anchored for the night and sailed the following day to Neapolis on the coast of Macedonia.

16:12 From there we traveled to Philippi, a leading city of that district of Macedonia and a Roman colony. We stayed several days in that city (κἀκεῖθεν εἰς Φιλίππους, ἥτις ἐστὶν πρώτη τῆς μερίδος τῆς Μακεδονίας πόλις, κολωνία. ἦμεν δὲ ἐν ταύτῃ τῇ πόλει διατρίβοντες ἡμέρας τινάς). Paul and his coworkers travel the from harbor city of

---

1. The sea passage from Alexandria Troas to Neapolis covered 119 nautical miles (220 km.), the journey from Neapolis to Philippi was a mere 10 miles (16 km.).

Neapolis on the Roman road called *Via Egnatia* to Philippi, where they stay for "several days" (ἡμέρας τινάς), a rather vague indication of time. The imperfect tense of the auxiliary verb "stayed" (ἦμεν) suggests a continuous stay; perhaps the phrase refers to the time they stay in the city before the next Sabbath, when they establish contact with the Jewish community.

Luke describes the city of Philippi with two phrases. (1) It was "a leading city" (πρώτη πόλις) of the Macedonian district to which it belonged. The term translated as "district" (μερίς) designates a region or an administrative district. Since 148 BC the four districts of Macedonia were retained as judicial districts only, having lost administrative independence. The chief city of the district to which Philippi belonged was Amphipolis. The term translated as "leading" (πρώτη) often refers to the capital city in administrative contexts. But this cannot be the meaning here. Thus, this term is best understood to reflect the civic pride of the citizens of Philippi, who regarded their city as the "leading" city of the region — "foremost," or "most honored" city.[2] (2) Philippi was a Roman colony (κολωνία) with between 5,000 and 10,000 inhabitants.

16:13 On the Sabbath we went outside the city gate by the river, where we expected to find a synagogue. We sat down and spoke to the women who had gathered there (τῇ τε ἡμέρᾳ τῶν σαββάτων ἐξήλθομεν ἔξω τῆς πύλης παρὰ ποταμὸν οὗ ἐνομίζομεν προσευχὴν εἶναι, καὶ καθίσαντες ἐλαλοῦμεν ταῖς συνελθούσαις γυναιξίν). Luke's narrative of the missionary activity of Paul in Philippi is selective. He merely relates that Paul established contact with the Jewish community on the Sabbath, as was his custom,[3] without specifically indicating that Paul proclaimed the good news of Jesus, Israel's Messiah, to the assembled Jews, which is surely what he did. Paul knew that the Jews of Philippi assemble "outside the city gate" next to the river. The river can hardly be the Gangites (or Bounarbachi) river, which is 1.5 miles (2.4 km.) from the city and thus too far for a journey on the Sabbath day (see 1:12). A better alternative is the river west of the city that was close to the city, flowing parallel to the city walls at a distance of about fifty yards at one point in the vicinity of the third gate.[4]

Instead of the usual term "synagogue" (συναγωγή), Luke uses the term "place of prayer" (προσευχή), a Greek term that means "Jewish prayer house"[5] and can thus be translated with the more common term "synagogue." Some surmise that the use of the expression "place of prayer" indicates that the Jews of Philippi were meeting "al fresco" in the open air.[6] This is not necessarily so: if the local Jews lived within the city walls, they could have met in a private house situated near the river, which would have not been unusual for a Jewish diaspora community. Note that the weather in Macedonia does not permit outdoor meetings throughout the entire year. The fact that the "place of prayer" was outside the city walls does not preclude that they were meeting in a building. Some

---

2. Cf. Richard S. Ascough, "Civic Pride at Philippi: The Text-Critical Problem of Acts 16.12," *NTS* 44 (1998): 93 – 103, 96 – 100, for examples of cities competing for the honor of carrying the term "first" or "most honored" (πρώτη) in their title, claims that were meant to distinguish one city as greater than all the others in a region.

3. Cf. 13:14; 14:1; 17:1 – 2, 10, 17; 18:4, 19, 26; 19:8.

4. Cf. Peter Pilhofer, *Philippi* (2 vols.; WUNT 87.119; Tübingen: Mohr Siebeck, 1995 – 2000), 1:165 – 74. The third gate, called the Gate in the Marshes, is located 925 feet (300 m.)

south of the Krenides Gate (or Amphipolis Gate) on the west side of the city. Pilhofer connects the phrase "by the river" with the city gate rather than with the synagogue.

5. Cf. Irina A. Levinskaya, *The Book of Acts in Its Diaspora Setting* (The Book of Acts in Its First-Century Setting 5; Grand Rapids: Eerdmans, 1996), 207 – 15; Horsley and Llewelyn, *New Documents*, 3:121 – 22; 4:219 – 20.

6. H. Balz, "προσεύχομαι, προσευχή," *EDNT*, 3:169; Pervo, *Acts*, 402.

diaspora Jewish communities preferred to build their meeting places outside the city near a body of water.[7] The river could be used for ceremonial immersion.

The reference to women who had gathered (συνελθούσαις), presumably in the synagogue, could mean that the Jewish men and the women met at different times; or it could mean that only the women were willing to speak with Paul and his friends. The women would have included Jews by birth, perhaps proselytes, and Gentile God-fearers who sympathized with the Jewish religion and prayed to Israel's God. As Paul and his friends sat and "spoke" (ἐλαλοῦμεν) with the women, they would have explained their reason for visiting Philippi: to proclaim the good news of Israel's Messiah and Savior. Sitting is a natural posture for teaching. The imperfect tense of this verb may indicate teaching over an extended period of time.

16:14 One of the women who listened was Lydia, a merchant dealing in purple cloth, from the city of Thyatira, a God-fearer. The Lord opened her heart so that she followed what Paul said (καί τις γυνὴ ὀνόματι Λυδία, πορφυρόπωλις πόλεως Θυατείρων σεβομένη τὸν θεόν, ἤκουεν, ἧς ὁ κύριος διήνοιξεν τὴν καρδίαν προσέχειν τοῖς λαλουμένοις ὑπὸ τοῦ Παύλου). Luke now singles out one particular person, Lydia, not only to illustrate Paul's missionary work but to explain the origins of the congregation in Philippi, which met in Lydia's house (v. 40). Lydia is introduced (like Cornelius) with her name, profession, provenance, and religious status as a God-fearer. Since Thyatira, the city from which she came and in which she probably held citizenship, was located in Lydia, her name has sometimes been explained as that of a freed-woman whose name as a slave was "the Lydian woman," the latinized form of the name indicating that her former master was a Roman.[8]

Lydia is a "merchant dealing in purple cloth" (πορφυρόπωλις). A Latin inscription from Philippi refers to dealers in purple, an inscription from Thessalonica documents a guild of purple dyers, and an inscription from Philippi mentions purple dyers from Thyatira.[9] The purple dye was extracted from the purple fish (πορφύρα, "purple-fish," Lat. *Murex trunculus, Purpura haemastoma*). The purple industry had a long history in the cities of the Phoenician coast, particularly Tyre, but played an important role in Lydia and Phrygia in Asia Minor as well. Contrary to the opinion of many, "the use of purple was not restricted to the wealthy, for the majority of purple dyes was manufactured and readily accessible, in different grades of quality and color variation," although colorfast purple extracted from the *Murex* was expensive.[10] Purple could also be derived from *rubia*, the madder plant, the so-called "Turkey red," which was used in Asia Minor. As a dealer in purple products (garments, blankets, carpets), Lydia would have been well-to-do.

Lydia's hometown was Thyatira, for which the dye industry is attested. Lydia may have lived in Thyatira while owning a retail shop in Philippi that she occasionally visited, or she may have settled in Philippi permanently. Her professional status as a merchant — evidently working on her own initiative and independently of a husband — suggests that she was widowed or divorced. If she was a freeborn woman with three children, or a freedwoman with four children, she would have been given a range of legal privileges according to Roman law,

---

7. Cf. Levine, *Synagogue*, 132, 316. Note Josephus, *Ant.* 14.258, who quotes a decree from Halicarnassus that specifically allowed the Jewish community to gather near the sea for prayer.

8. Cf. Horsley and Llewelyn, *New Documents*, 2:27 – 28.

9. Pilhofer, *Philippi*, 1:174 – 82.

10. Horsley and Llewelyn, *New Documents*, 2:25; for the following point see ibid. 3:53 – 55.

including "the right to undertake legal transactions without the necessity to obtain the consent" of her legal guardian (*kyrios*).[11] The fact that she owned a house in which she evidently could accommodate Paul and his coworkers as well as the meetings of the emerging church (vv. 15, 40) confirms that she is a woman of means.

Lydia is a "God-fearer" (σεβομένη τὸν θεόν); the Greek term replaces the expression "those who fear God" (φοβούμενοι τὸν θεόν; see on 10:22) that Luke used earlier. She attends the Jewish synagogue; i.e., she is a Gentile who sympathizes with the Jewish faith and prays to Israel's God. Luke describes her as hospitable, gracious, and humble (v. 15); like Cornelius, she is the ideal God-fearer.

Luke notes that Lydia "listened" (ἤκουεν); the imperfect may indicate that she listened for an extended period of time. Luke does not state that she was baptized (v. 15) on the very day that she met Paul and his coworkers. Paul spoke, Lydia listened, but it was the Lord who "opened" (διήνοιξεν)[12] Lydia's heart, causing her to understand and accept the gospel. On account of the Lord's initiative, Lydia "followed" closely the words spoken by Paul and turned to the proclamation of the good news of Jesus, Israel's Messiah, whose death, resurrection, and exaltation provides for the forgiveness of sins and eternal life to those who put their trust in Jesus. According to Rom 10:9, the "heart" is the "organ" of faith whose cause is Jesus, the Messiah, whose word is proclaimed, who has sent the apos-

tle, and who opens the hearts of those who believe (Rom 10:14 – 17).

16:15 When she and the members of her household were baptized, she invited us, saying, "If you consider me to be faithful to the Lord, come and stay at my house." And she strongly urged us (ὡς δὲ ἐβαπτίσθη καὶ ὁ οἶκος αὐτῆς, παρεκάλεσεν λέγουσα· εἰ κεκρίκατέ με πιστὴν τῷ κυρίῳ εἶναι, εἰσελθόντες εἰς τὸν οἶκόν μου μένετε· καὶ παρεβιάσατο ἡμᾶς). The conversion of Lydia leads to her baptism (ἐβαπτίσθη; see on 2:38).[13] In the context of the Jewish synagogue, she would have been immersed in water, presumably in the river nearby. Luke notes that "the members of her household," i.e., the people who live in her house,[14] are also baptized. Since Luke is not more specific, it is impossible to say whether Lydia's household included children, slaves, or other dependents.

The authenticity of Lydia's faith is indicated in her eagerness to provide hospitality to Paul and his coworkers (note the parallel to the Cornelius episode; 10:48). Lydia "invited" Paul and his missionary team to come into her house and stay there, i.e., to sleep and eat in her house and to use it as the basis for their activities in the city. Perhaps the current accommodations of Paul and his friends were inadequate in her eyes, which would be particularly true if they stayed in a hostel for travelers (ξενοδοχεῖον).[15]

The formulation of her invitation as a conditional clause ("if you consider me to be faithful")

---

11. Ibid., 2:29, 32.

12. The verb is used in Luke 24:32 for the "opening" of the Scriptures by Jesus, in Luke 24:31 for the opening of the disciples' eyes when they recognize the risen Jesus, and in Luke 24:45 for the opening of the disciples' minds by the risen Lord Jesus.

13. According to 1 Cor 1:14 – 17, Paul did not baptized all of the new converts, since he did not think that it mattered who performed the baptism.

14. BDAG, s.v. οἶκος 1a, "house, dwelling," and sense 2, "household, family." In Greek culture, a "house" in the sense

of "household" or "family" consisted of husband, wife, children, and slaves and included all possessions (Aristotle, *Pol.* 1252A – 1254A); the group of persons included in a "house" could be expanded to include dependent relatives as well as other dependents. Cf. G. Thür, "Oikos," *BNP*, 10:69 – 71.

15. In a Greek context, both simple hostels (πανδοχεῖον) and larger hostels (καταγώγιον) existed. Such buildings had a saloon with a bar, a dining room, and lockable guest rooms in a residential wing with separate access to the road; cf. B. Wagner-Hasel, "Hospitality III," *BNP*, 6:529 – 32; idem, "Inn II," *BNP*, 6:818 – 21.

should not be taken to imply that perhaps she is not yet a believer.[16] Lydia extends a polite invitation — which is repeated — to Paul, presenting her faith in the Lord as evidence that her new allegiance to Jesus has made her willing to share her house and thus her possessions with Paul and his associates — and with other believers in Jesus (v. 40). Lydia's house becomes not only the basis for the subsequent missionary work of Paul in Philippi (vv. 16 – 17), but also the place where the emerging congregation of Philippi meets (v. 40).

Luke reports no further missionary activity of Paul and his associates in Philippi. This does not necessarily mean, however, that they proclaim the gospel only in the synagogue outside the city or that only Lydia and later the prison official are converted. The action of the city magistrates suggests a longer stay and a more extensive evangelistic activity in Philippi.

16:16 Once when we were going to the synagogue, we met a slave girl who had a spirit of divination and who brought great profit to her owners by giving oracles (ἐγένετο δὲ πορευομένων ἡμῶν εἰς τὴν προσευχὴν παιδίσκην τινὰ ἔχουσαν πνεῦμα πύθωνα ὑπαντῆσαι ἡμῖν, ἥτις ἐργασίαν πολλὴν παρεῖχεν τοῖς κυρίοις αὐτῆς μαντευομένη). The second incident of the Philippi episode narrates the exorcism of a spirit of divination from a slave girl (vv. 16 – 18). Luke first notes that Paul and his coworkers regularly visit the synagogue, surely to preach to Jews and God-fearers about Jesus and to teach the new converts. On one occasion, as they

are walking through the city, they meet a slave girl who is possessed by a demon. Luke specifies that she has "a spirit of divination" (πνεῦμα πύθωνα); the term translated as "spirit" denotes here an evil spirit, a demon.

The term *pythōn* (πύθων) refers to the enormous female dragon (or snake) called Python, which Apollo killed near Delphi; the town and the god were given the nickname Pytho.[17] The Greek term *pythōn* (πύθων) came to designate a "spirit of divination" and was then also used of ventriloquists, who were believed to have such a spirit dwelling in their belly.[18] The syntax of the Greek expression can be read in two ways: the slave girl had a spirit named Python, or she had a pythonic spirit, i.e., a spirit that produced oracles. The latter is certainly what was happening: the girl was "giving oracles" (μαντευομένη), perhaps speaking with her belly. She foretold the future or used her abilities to inform clients how to protect themselves from misfortune or how to harm their enemies — psychic gifts that attracted people who paid for her services and that consequently brought "great profit" for her "owners" (κύριοι αὐτῆς).

It is possible, but not necessary, that the disclosure of oracles took place in a local temple rather than in a private home. For Luke, the implied reference to clairvoyants speaking in a way that appears to be ventriloquism would have had strongly evil connotations; in the LXX the term "belly-talkers" (ἐγγαστρίμυθοι) is regularly used for mediums — such as the witch of Endor — whose activities are condemned.[19]

---

16. Cf. Avemarie, *Tauferzählungen*, 91 – 92, who argues that this curious proviso indicates that the missionaries sought to ascertain the faith of the people whom they baptized.

17. Cf. T. Junk, "Python I," *BNP*, 12:298. The earliest version of the myth is found in *Hymni Homerici* 3.300 – 374.

18. For the latter see Plutarch, *Mor.* 414E, who describes Apollo, the Pythian god, inspiring *pythones* (πύθωνες) or "belly-talkers" (ἐγγαστρίμυθοι), i.e., ventriloquists, persons

who speak from their belly; cf. Pollianus 2.168.

19. Lev 19:31; 20:6, 27; Deut 18:11; 2 Chr 33:6; 35:19; Isa 8:19; 19:3; 44:25. For the witch of Endor cf. 1 Sam 28:7; 1 Chr 10:13. Cf. Twelftree, *Exorcism*, 146, who also notes the strong negative connotations of the verb μαντεύομαι (used only here in the New Testament) relating to false prophets in the LXX; cf. Deut 18:10; 1 Sam 28:8; 2 Kgs 17:17; Jer 34:9; Ezek 12:24.

16:17 She followed Paul and the rest of us, shouting: "These men are slaves of the Most High God who proclaim to you a way to salvation" (αὕτη κατακολουθοῦσα τῷ Παύλῳ καὶ ἡμῖν ἔκραζεν λέγουσα· οὗτοι οἱ ἄνθρωποι δοῦλοι τοῦ θεοῦ τοῦ ὑψίστου εἰσίν, οἵτινες καταγγέλλουσιν ὑμῖν ὁδὸν σωτηρίας). Since the first time that the psychic slave girl met Paul (v. 16), she follows him and his associates around whenever he walks through the city. As she does so, she shouts in a prophecy that "these men are slaves of the Most High God who proclaim to you a way to salvation." Inspired by the spirit of divination, her prophecy is ambiguous at least in three respects.

(1) While the term "the Most High God" (ὁ θεὸς ὁ ὕψιστος) may refer to Israel's God,[20] it could also refer to Zeus as the highest deity of the Greek pantheon, the god on the highest mountain (Mount Olympus), who is the lord of heaven. Numerous inscriptions document that the worship of Zeus as Zeus Hypsistos (Ζεὺς ὕψιστος) and Theos Hypsistos (Θεὸς ὕψιστος) was alive and well.[21] Of particular interest are inscriptions that link the "Most High God" with the epithet "listening" (ἐπήκοος), which was virtually the same as "savior" (σωτήρ), since "the god who hears was great or the greatest, and vice versa."[22] Note that Luke uses the expression "the Most High God" elsewhere only as the appellation from a demon-possessed man (Luke 8:28). While the Jews living in Philippi would think of the God of Israel as the only true God, the Greek and Roman citizens of Philippi would take the reference to refer to Zeus or another "listening god" whom they already worship and from whom they expect salvation.[23]

(2) While the term "slaves" (δοῦλοι) is also used in nonbiblical Greek for the relationship of human beings to a god in the sense of being subservient to that god,[24] the early Christian notion of being "slaves of God"[25] has nothing to do with "cringing servility, fear of displeasing the master and particularly fear of the punishment that may follow,"[26] but has everything to do with total devotion to God, who has given his Son to die for the sins of the world.

(3) The phrase "way to salvation" (ὁδὸς σωτηρίας), with no definite article, could be understood by pagans in Philippi in terms of Paul proclaiming one path to salvation among many possibilities of finding salvation.[27]

16:18 She kept doing this for many days. Then Paul, who was greatly disturbed by this, turned around and said to the spirit: "I order you in the name of Jesus Christ to come out of her!" And the spirit came out of her that very hour (τοῦτο δὲ ἐποίει ἐπὶ πολλὰς ἡμέρας. διαπονηθεὶς δὲ Παῦλος καὶ ἐπιστρέψας τῷ πνεύματι εἶπεν· παραγγέλλω σοι ἐν ὀνόματι Ἰησοῦ Χριστοῦ ἐξελθεῖν ἀπ' αὐτῆς· καὶ ἐξῆλθεν αὐτῇ τῇ ὥρᾳ). The spectacle of the psychic slave girl following Paul and his fellow missionaries, shouting about God the Most High and a path

---

20. In the LXX, the term "Most High" denotes "the powerful status of the God enthroned in Heaven" (*TLOT*, 892); e.g., Num 24:16; Deut 32:8; 2 Sam 22:14; Pss 9:3; 21:8 (LXX 20:8); Isa 14:14. For the following point see Pindar, *Nem.* 1.60; 11.2; Aeschylus, *Eum.* 28.

21. Cf. C. Breytenbach, "Hypsistos," *DDD*, 822 – 30; F. Graf, "Hypsistos," *BNP*, 6:650 – 52.

22. Hendrik S. Versnel, "Religious Mentality in Ancient Prayer," in *Faith, Hope and Worship: Aspects of Religious Mentality in the Ancient World* (ed. H. S. Versnel; Studies in Greek

and Roman Religion 2; Leiden: Brill, 1981), 1 – 64, 35.

23. Cf. Pilhofer, *Philippi*, 1:182 – 87.

24. Cf. Euripides, *Ion* 309; Dio Cassius 63.5.2. In the magical papyri, people are called "slaves of the Most High God" (*PGM* 12.71).

25. Cf. Luke 1:38, 48; 2:29; Acts 4:29; 1 Pet 2:16; Rev 1:1; 7:3; 10:7; 11:18; 19:2, 5; 22:3, 6.

26. Harris, *Slave of Christ*, 142, a view he criticizes.

27. Cf. Twelftree, *Exorcism*, 146 – 47.

to salvation that these visitors proclaim, occurred in the streets of Philippi for "many days" (note the imperfect tense of "kept doing," ἐποίει). Paul may have tolerated her shouting for a period of time because he was aware of the anti-Jewish sentiments of the Roman population and the possible consequences in a conflict.

Paul's response is narrated with three aorist verbs. First, he was "greatly disturbed" (διαπονηθείς), annoyed because he perceived it was a demonic spirit speaking from the slave girl, a psychic whose messages were exploited by her owners as a source of financial gain. The girl is thus doubly unqualified to proclaim the truth of the good news of Jesus. Second, he "turned around" (ἐπιστρέψας); i.e., he confronted the spirit that spoke from the girl. Third, he spoke (εἶπεν) to the spirit, commanding him to come out of the girl. The verb "order" (παραγγέλλω) denotes a directive from an authoritative source.[28] The command "in the name of Jesus Christ" (ἐν ὀνόματι Ἰησοῦ Χριστοῦ) establishes for the citizens of Philippi (and for Luke's readers) that the source of salvation is Jesus, Israel's Messiah and Savior (cf. 2:21, 40). An order "in the name of Jesus" is a command of Jesus himself.[29]

Luke narrates the reaction of the spirit in stark, dramatic terms: the spirit obeys by coming out of the girl in "that very hour" (αὐτῇ τῇ ὥρᾳ), i.e., immediately. Paul removes not only the ambiguity from the psychic girl's proclamation in the streets of Philippi, he also removes the source of her gift of clairvoyance. Luke does not tell us whether the girl becomes a believer in Jesus, finding the one way to true salvation that Paul was preaching, but he narrates the reaction of the girl's owners, who find that a major source of their income is gone.

16:19 When her owners saw that their prospects of financial profit were gone, they seized Paul and Silas and dragged them into the agora to face the city officials (ἰδόντες δὲ οἱ κύριοι αὐτῆς ὅτι ἐξῆλθεν ἡ ἐλπὶς τῆς ἐργασίας αὐτῶν, ἐπιλαβόμενοι τὸν Παῦλον καὶ τὸν Σιλᾶν εἵλκυσαν εἰς τὴν ἀγορὰν ἐπὶ τοὺς ἄρχοντας). The third incident of the Philippi episode narrates the arrest of Paul and Silas (vv. 19–24). The reaction of the slave girl's owners to the removal of the spirit of divination is reported with three verbs in the aorist tense. (1) They "saw" that their prospects for financial gain had vanished; i.e., they had evidence that led them to conclude that the slave girl could no longer provide oracles for which their customers paid them. Thus, their "prospects" (ἐλπίς) for continued financial gain from their psychic slave left as well. Presumably Paul would have anticipated the economic ramifications of the exorcism; if so, he clearly is more concerned about the authenticity of his message than about the fate of the slave girl or her owners.

(2) They "seized" (ἐπιλαβόμενοι) Paul and Silas; i.e., they grabbed them by their arms, forcing them to accompany them to the authorities. Their action might be described as a semiofficial arrest, the channeling of private revenge in the context of the obligation to conduct a judicial procedure.

(3) They "dragged" them into the agora (ἀγορά), in the Roman colony of Philippi the Forum, the central public square whose buildings reflected the political, religious, social, and economic focus of the city, where they wanted them to face[30] the authorities. The term translated as "officials" (οἱ ἄρχοντες) denotes here "rulers" who have administrative authority in Philippi;[31] among them are the

---

28. F. Hauck, "παραγγέλλω," *TDNT*, 5:763. In Luke 8:29 (Mark 5:8), Jesus also "commands" an evil spirit.

29. See on 2:38; 3:6, 16. Cf. Twelftree, *Exorcism*, 147–48.

30. The preposition ἐπί is here a "marker of legal proceeding, *before*" in the language of the law courts (BDAG, s.v. ἐπί 10).

31. Cf. P. J. Rhodes, "Archontes I. Office," *BNP*, 1:1028–30: "In general, the term applied to all holders of *archai* [i.e. offices]."

"chief magistrates" mentioned in v. 20. The following scene may have taken place on the northwest side of the agora, the probable site of the *bema* or *rostrum*, the raised podium where hearings and trials took place.

16:20–21 They brought them before the chief magistrates and said: "These men throw our city into confusion. They are Jews and they are proclaiming customs that are unlawful for us Romans to adopt or practice" (καὶ προσαγόντες αὐτοὺς τοῖς στρατηγοῖς εἶπαν· οὗτοι οἱ ἄνθρωποι ἐκταράσσουσιν ἡμῶν τὴν πόλιν, Ἰουδαῖοι ὑπάρχοντες, καὶ καταγγέλλουσιν ἔθη ἃ οὐκ ἔξεστιν ἡμῖν παραδέχεσθαι οὐδὲ ποιεῖν Ῥωμαίοις οὖσιν). The owners of the girl bring[32] Paul and Silas to the "chief magistrates" (οἱ στρατηγοί); the Greek term corresponds to the Latin term *duoviri iure dicundo*,[33] the officers of record who had jurisdiction (below the praetor of the province), which means that they could judge cases personally and serve as public prosecutors in criminal and in civil cases in the colony; they convened the city council (*ordo decurionum*) and the popular assembly of the citizens, they conducted the election of other officials, and they represented the city before the emperor and before the official authorities of other cities.

Luke relates the accusation of the psychic slave's owners against Paul and Silas in direct speech, highlighting the significance of the charges and the potentially disastrous consequences for the two missionaries. The owners of the girl formulate their accusation in political terms, utilizing slogans of Roman patriotism, the xenophobia of a Roman colony, and latent pagan anti-Judaism. In doing so, they mask the real reason for the legal initiative (the loss of revenue resulting from the exorcism of the Python spirit), which is consistent with Roman law in that loss of profit was not relevant to criminal law.[34]

Their accusation consists of two elements. (1) The accused are agitators causing an uproar in the city. The Greek verb "throw … into confusion" (ἐκταράσσουσιν) denotes the action of causing an uproar: "agitate, cause trouble to, throw into confusion" (BDAG). Causing a disturbance in the city would have to be punished by the authorities, whose main responsibility — particularly in a Roman colony — was to maintain order. The punishment depended on the kind of disturbance. Roman law distinguished different kinds of disturbances that were sanctioned as *crimen*. There was the *tumultus*, the disturbance of the peace, and the public brawl or assault, which was closely related to the charge of *turba*, both punishable by the payment of damages. More serious was the charge of *seditio*, understood as a serious disturbance of public order, a breach of the public peace, particularly in connection with larger groups banding together, i.e., a rebellion, punished by exile (*exilium*), loss of citizenship and all assets, and even death.[35]

The charge of causing a disturbance, directed against the missionaries, is new in Luke's account, which has so far described only Jews as causing

---

32. This verb (προσάγω) is used sometimes used in the context of a defendant (or a witness) "brought" into a law court (LSJ, s.v. προσάγω I.8a).

33. Pilhofer, *Philippi*, 1:195–97; Heike Omerzu, *Der Prozess des Paulus: Eine exegetische und rechtshistorische Untersuchung der Apostelgeschichte* (BZNW 115; Berlin: De Gruyter, 2002), 142–43. The "chief magistrates" (στρατηγοί) should not be identified with the *praetores*, as suggested by Ramsay, *St. Paul the Traveller*, 174–76.

34. Omerzu, *Prozess*, 124.

35. Cf. J. von Ungern-Sternberg, "Seditio," *BNP*, 13:195–96; R. Gamauf, "Exilium," *BNP*, 5:268–29; Z. Végh, "Relegatio," *BNP*, 12:454. Luke distinguishes different kinds of disturbances: he speaks of rebellion (στάσις, Luke 23:19, 25; Acts 19:40; 24:5; ἀναστατόω, Acts 17:6; 21:38; this corresponds to Lat. *seditio*) and tumults (θόρυβος, 20:1; 21:34; 24:18; θορυβέω, 17:5; 20:10); the terms τάραχος and (ἐκ)ταράσσω (12:18; 15:24; 17:8; 19:23) designate tumults as well, but could overlap with *turba*.

disturbances.[36] The reference to "these men" (οὗτοι οἱ ἄνθρωποι) has a derogatory connotation, as is their description as "Jews" (Ἰουδαῖοι) — being Jewish, they can be expected to cause trouble. Anti-Jewish bigotry was found among both Greeks and Romans, in views and actions of government officials and as popular prejudice.[37] Since Paul and Silas are Jews visiting their city, they are aliens (*peregrini*) who possess neither influence (*potentia*) nor favor (*gratia*) among the citizens of Philippi — in contrast to the accusers, who are "Romans" and thus legally and socially superior. The self-designation "us Romans" (ἡμῖν ... Ῥωμαίοις) reflects the Latin character of the city and the civic pride of its citizens. Since Paul and Silas have (presumably) no money, their poverty would be regarded with suspicion, easily connected with criminal behavior.

(2) The accused have introduced new "customs" (ἔθη) that are "unlawful" (ἃ οὐκ ἔξεστιν) for Roman citizens. The syndicate who controlled the psychic woman argue, in other words, that the two Jewish men are seeking to alter the ancestral customs (*mores*) of the Roman colony of Philippi, altering the way of life of the Romans living in Philippi, as these visitors teach the Philippians to live like Jews (e.g., by refusing to worship in pagan temples), which in Roman eyes amounts to revolution. Roman custom, understood as *mos maiorum* ("custom of the fathers"), was "the core concept of Roman traditionalism."[38]

The Roman citizens of Philippi were proud of their place in history, their colony being the site of the decisive battle between those who wanted to avenge the murder of Julius Caesar and his murderers. Since Philippi participated in "the most im-portant historical roots of the constitution of the Roman state, the principate of the Julian-Claudian dynasty," it was a city "in which the Roman self-consciousness is formed as trust in the divine right and the inspired ability of the Julian-Claudian family."[39] Public teaching about a Jewish Savior and a public exorcism performed by invoking the Messiah of the Jewish people (v. 18) could easily be construed as undermining the Roman identity and the civic distinctiveness of Philippi and its citizens. Since the accusation is directed against Paul and Silas as Jewish teachers, whose message the accusers may not have known let alone understood, the charge of introducing new "customs" that Romans may not adopt or practice could refer to circumcision, the observance of the Sabbath, and the Jewish dietary laws — the three practices of the Jews most often attacked by pagans.

If the Roman citizens in Philippi were aware of recent developments in Rome, the charges of Paul's accusers may be linked with the fact that this was a critical time for Jews. Seneca, the anti-Jewish adviser of the imperial court, returned from exile, and Claudius intensified his program of restoring the ancient Roman religion while at the same time (but for other reasons; see on 18:2) expelling the Jews from the city of Rome because "men of foreign birth" had caused disturbances at the instigation of a certain Chrestus.[40] In such a political climate, the public teaching of "Jewish customs" was an invitation, from the Roman perspective, of promoting what the emperor was restricting.

16:22 The crowd joined in attacking them, and the magistrates had them stripped of their clothes and ordered that they be beaten with rods

---

36. Cf. 13:50; 14:5, 19. The characterization of Paul and Silas as "they are Jews" is thus, for Luke's readers, ironic.

37. Cf. Louis H. Feldman, *Jew and Gentile in the Ancient World: Attitudes and Interactions from Alexander to Justinian* (Princeton: Princeton Univ. Press, 1993), 107 – 76; for the following comment cf. ibid. 125 – 26.

38. W. Kierdorf, "Mos maiorum," *BNP*, 9:216 – 17.

39. Lukas Bormann, *Philippi — Stadt und Christengemeinde zur Zeit des Paulus* (NovTSup 78; Leiden: Brill, 1995), 83 – 84.

40. Suetonius, *Claud.* 25.3 – 4 (many scholars think this "Chrestus" was *Christos*, i.e., Christ; see on 18:2). Cf. Riesner, *Paul's Early Period*, 194.

(καὶ συνεπέστη ὁ ὄχλος κατ᾽ αὐτῶν καὶ οἱ στρατηγοὶ περιρήξαντες αὐτῶν τὰ ἱμάτια ἐκέλευον ῥαβδίζειν). Before Luke narrates the action taken by the chief magistrates, he comments on the reaction of the crowd in the agora who has witnessed the accusations leveled by the owners of the clairvoyant woman against Paul and Silas. The verb translated "joined in attacking [them]" (συνεπέστη) does not denote a mob riot but the spontaneous participation of the citizens of Philippi in the legal proceedings. The prefix (συν-) that accounts for the notion of "joining" correlates the behavior of the crowd with the behavior of the accusers, and these had articulated their complaints against Paul and Silas in legal terms and in an orderly fashion. Had their intervention resembled a "riot," they would have bludgeoned the two visitors and not taken them to the magistrates in the agora. The crowd's concerted opposition to accuse Paul and Silas "might dash any hopes of favour from the magistrates and effectively silence the accused who might otherwise claimed what protections Roman citizenship could afford."[41]

Paul does not appeal to his Roman citizenship at this point (see later v. 37), a fact that can be explained with reference to practical, religious, and missionary reasons. Such an appeal may have caused legal complications that would have required time to resolve, causing unwanted delays.[42] Since the accusers had linked their charges with judaeophobic sentiments, an appeal to Roman citizenship could have been interpreted as a negative qualification of Jewish identity, which Paul would not have wanted to happen, since he wanted to maintain contacts with local synagogues and since he proclaimed the God of the Jews and a Jewish Savior. In addition, an appeal to Roman citizenship in the context of the accusers' appeal to the civic pride of the Roman citizens of Philippi would have implied the endorsement of Roman *civitas* as the magistrates of Philippi would have described it, thus putting his proclamation of the good news of Jesus, Israel's Messiah and the Savior of humankind, at risk. Thus, Paul's silence concerning his citizenship at this point "reflects a carefully considered choice rather than a novelistic dramatization or the expression of Luke's juridical naivete."[43] And we should not forget that Paul at times deliberately refrained from insisting on all his rights (1 Cor 9:12).

The chief magistrates ordered the lictors (bailiffs of the magistrates whose responsibility was often to inflict punishment) to strip Paul and Silas of their clothes as preparation for the flogging, which was administered on the bare skin. Then they beat them with rods (ῥαβδίζειν). Flogging and beating occur in the Roman legal system as concomitant punishment combined with other penalties, e.g., the death penalty or the removal of citizenship. During the imperial period beatings were also administered as independent penalty. Flogging was also used during interrogation to extort a confession. The beating was severe; v. 23a speaks of "many blows" (πολλάς πληγάς, translated as "severely beaten"), and v. 33 speaks of "wounds" (τῶν πληγῶν) that needed to be cleaned. Their punishment is consistent with the fact that the chief magistrates treated them as low-status individuals who

---

41. Rapske, *Paul in Roman Custody*, 122; for the following comments see ibid. 130 – 34.

42. Since Paul was accused as a Jewish visitor in the city, he would have been asked to prove his citizenship had he protested with reference to his status of being a legal Roman citizen. Births of Roman citizens were registered in the *tabularium publicum* in one's hometown. A Roman citizen could carry with him a copy of his birth certificate, usually attested by seven witnesses; at the end of such a *testatio* the letters *c. r. e.* were inscribed, signifying *c(ivem) r(omanum) e(sse)* — "he is a Roman." Paul could have been required to prove the correctness of such a *testatio*, assuming that he carried one with him, which would have required sending envoys to Tarsus, which would have been both time-consuming and costly.

43. Rapske, *Paul in Roman Custody*, 134.

could be assumed to be guilty of criminal behavior by accusation alone. Paul relates in 2 Cor 11:25 that he was beaten with rods three times; the beating in Philippi was one such occasion.

16:23–24 After they had been severely beaten, they threw them into prison. They ordered the jailer to guard them securely. Following these orders, he put them in the inner cell and secured their feet in the stocks (πολλάς τε ἐπιθέντες αὐτοῖς πληγὰς ἔβαλον εἰς φυλακὴν παραγγείλαντες τῷ δεσμοφύλακι ἀσφαλῶς τηρεῖν αὐτούς. ὃς παραγγελίαν τοιαύτην λαβὼν ἔβαλεν αὐτοὺς εἰς τὴν ἐσωτέραν φυλακὴν καὶ τοὺς πόδας ἠσφαλίσατο αὐτῶν εἰς τὸ ξύλον). The severe beating was followed by a further punishment: Paul and Silas are thrown into prison. The magistrates employ incarceration as a police measure for the short-term penalty of misbehaving individuals in the context of their *coercitio*, i.e., "the authority of Roman magistrates to intervene when they judged the public order had been violated by citizens and non-citizens, restricting their rights and exercising sovereign power."[44] Since Luke does not suggest that the magistrates want to put Paul and Silas on trial at a later date, the imprisonment is not a pretrial detention.

The magistrates order the jailer to guard the two men "securely" (ἀσφαλῶς), i.e., in a manner that ensures continuing detention. Consequently, the jailer puts Paul and Silas in "the inner prison," i.e., in an inner maximum security cell, where he secures their feet in the stocks made of wood.[45] The

prison would be located near the court and thus near the agora of the city. The jailer was neither a Roman official nor a Roman soldier with the rank of a centurion or a veteran,[46] but probably a public slave, i.e., a slave owned by the city whom the magistrates had put in charge of the city jail, responsible for securing the prisoners with the help of junior slaves.[47] He would be familiar with the reasons why the two Jewish teachers are incarcerated: prisoners and their crimes are entered into a log. Eighteen years earlier, Paul himself had thrown followers of Jesus into prison (8:3). Now he sits in a jail himself.

16:25 About midnight Paul and Silas were praying and singing hymns to God, and the other prisoners listened to them (κατὰ δὲ τὸ μεσονύκτιον Παῦλος καὶ Σιλᾶς προσευχόμενοι ὕμνουν τὸν θεόν, ἐπηκροῶντο δὲ αὐτῶν οἱ δέσμιοι). The fourth incident of the Philippi episode narrates the conversion of the jailer (vv. 25–34). Luke begins with the reaction of Paul and Silas to the events that have transpired — the first statement about their behavior since Paul's command to the Python spirit to leave the slave girl (v. 18). Since then, the two missionaries have been portrayed as the passive "recipients" of the actions of others (vv. 19–24). The description of their deportment in the maximum security cell confirms what the reader expects: their spirit has not been extinguished, despite the fact that they have been in prison for probably over twelve hours,[48] that they are sitting on the floor in a most uncomfortable position with their feet se-

---

44. C. Gizewski, "Coercitio," *BNP* 3:508.

45. Cf. BDAG, s.v. ξύλον 2b, "a device for confining the extremities of a prisoner, *stocks*." These contraptions often consisted of "wood pierced at regular intervals with notches or holes and split along the length so that the feet of the prisoner could be set in a secured way" (Rapske, *Paul in Roman Custody*, 127).

46. Thus Bruce, *Book of Acts*, 315; Matson, *Household Conversion Narratives*, 156–57.

47. Civil administrations tended to recruit the personnel in charge of the municipal prison from among the public slaves (*servi publici*). Several public slaves are documented for Philippi; cf. Pilhofer, *Philippi*, 2:228–29. The fact that the jailer occupied a senior civic post explains indications of wealth, e.g., the reference to his "household" in vv. 31–33, which may have included slaves.

48. The accusation before the chief magistrates presumably took place before noon.

cured in the stocks, that the open wounds and the dried blood would make them grimace with pain, that they are confined in utter darkness (in the innermost cell), and that they evidently cannot sleep — they are still awake around midnight.

Paul and Silas have been singing hymns (ὕμνουν) to God; the imperfect of the tense of this verb indicates continuous action over a period of time. A "hymn" (ὕμνος) to God is a song in praise of God that proclaims the virtues and deeds of God before others, or it is a song of praise to God, i.e., the reiteration of the virtues and deeds of God formulated as a prayer that is sung to a tune. The present tense of the participle translated as "(they) were praying" (προσευχόμενοι) is either circumstantial (while they were praying, they were singing hymns of praise) or modal (through their prayers they sang praises to God). Since the term ὕμνος is sometimes used to describe the psalms (ψαλμοί) of David, Paul and Silas may have been singing Old Testament psalms of thanksgiving and praise, particularly those that praise God for his help in times of distress. Or they are singing new, Christian compositions that would have included praise for God's sending of his Son Jesus, Israel's Messiah and Savior. Jews who know the psalms of David have ample material from which they can draw in times of acute physical suffering; examples include the imprisoned Joseph, Daniel's three friends, the martyrs of the Maccabean period, and, of course, the example of Jesus.

The prayers of Paul and Silas are not silent prayers, and their songs are not whispered in the darkness of the night. They pray and sing sotto voce, in the stale air and the stench of the maximum security cell, in the middle of the night, in complete darkness. The fact that the other pris-

oners are able to listen to Paul and Silas praying and singing hymns of praise suggests that they are accommodated in the same cell. There is some evidence in ancient literature that a jailer took prisoners from other rooms in the prison, or from the prison yard, and crammed them into the most secure part of the prison overnight.[49]

16:26 Suddenly there was a large earthquake, which shook the foundations of the prison. Immediately all the doors were opened, and everyone's chains came loose (ἄφνω δὲ σεισμὸς ἐγένετο μέγας ὥστε σαλευθῆναι τὰ θεμέλια τοῦ δεσμωτηρίου· ἠνεῴχθησαν δὲ παραχρῆμα αἱ θύραι πᾶσαι καὶ πάντων τὰ δεσμὰ ἀνέθη). Luke's narrative of the missionaries' deliverance begins with the report of a "large earthquake" (σεισμὸς μέγας). While earthquakes were not uncommon in Macedonia, an earthquake at this particular time and place implies divine intervention, although it is not narrated as directly and as personally as in the prison escapes of Peter.[50] The strong tremors of the earthquake affect the foundations of the prison, which are shaken; the doors are all opened, and the chains come loose from their moorings in the prison walls. As the earthquake happens suddenly, so its effects are felt both immediately and pervasively: "all the doors" are opened and "everyone's chains" are released.

16:27 The jailer woke up and saw the prison doors open; he drew his sword and was about to kill himself because he assumed that the prisoners had escaped (ἔξυπνος δὲ γενόμενος ὁ δεσμοφύλαξ καὶ ἰδὼν ἀνεῳγμένας τὰς θύρας τῆς φυλακῆς, σπασάμενος τὴν μάχαιραν ἤμελλεν ἑαυτὸν ἀναιρεῖν νομίζων ἐκπεφευγέναι τοὺς δεσμίους). Rather than commenting on the reaction of the

---

49. Rapske, *Paul in Roman Custody*, 200 – 204, with reference to Lucian, *Toxaris* 150 – 51: to be put in stocks overnight was a normal security precaution. Paul's shout to the jailer that he and the other prisoners were still "here" (v. 28) and the

jailer's headlong rush into the inner cell (rather than the prison generally) can be readily explained by such an arrangement.

50. Cf. 5:19; 12:7 – 10.

prisoners, which the reader would expect after the reference to Paul and Silas praying and singing hymns of praise in v. 25, Luke relates the reaction of the jailer, whose living quarters are on the premises of the city jail. After being awaked by the tremors of the earthquake and, probably, by the falling masonry, he notices the doors of the prison stand open. Assuming (νομίζων) that the prisoners have escaped, he draws his sword in preparation for killing himself. In view of the punishment for allowing the prisoners to escape, he considers suicide a better alternative. As a slave, he may well have anticipated execution by crucifixion.[51]

16:28 But Paul shouted with a loud voice, "Do not harm yourself! We are all here!" (ἐφώνησεν δὲ μεγάλῃ φωνῇ ὁ Παῦλος λέγων· μηδὲν πράξῃς σεαυτῷ κακόν, ἅπαντες γάρ ἐσμεν ἐνθάδε). The first reference to Paul's speech after the command to the Python spirit to leave the slave girl (v. 18) is his intervention in the life of the jailer, who is about to commit suicide. Luke does not indicate how Paul became aware of the jailer's resolution to kill himself.[52] But Paul interrupts the suicide in progress with a loud shout, exhorting the jailer not to harm himself, reassuring him that none of the prisoners has left the premises; they are all (ἅπαντες) still "here" (ἐνθάδε). If indeed all prisoners were kept overnight in the inner maximum security cell of

the jail, Paul would have known why none of the prisoners had left.[53]

Luke's readers would realize at this point that the accusations of the owners of the slave girl are indeed unfounded. By not fleeing, Paul demonstrates his commitment to civic order.[54] Paul is concerned for the well-being of the jailer, just as Stephen was concerned for the men who were stoning him (7:60).

16:29 The jailer called for lights, rushed in, and fell down trembling before Paul and Silas (αἰτήσας δὲ φῶτα εἰσεπήδησεν καὶ ἔντρομος γενόμενος προσέπεσεν τῷ Παύλῳ καὶ τῷ Σιλᾷ). The jailer's reaction to Paul's reassuring shout is narrated with four verbs. He "called for lights," i.e., asked his servants to bring torches, as the inside of the prison would have been in total darkness around midnight. He "rushed" into the maximum security cell. He was "trembling" as he presumably made a head count to ascertain the veracity of Paul's reassuring shout, shaken not only by the earthquake but by the experience of his interrupted suicide. Then he "fell down" before Paul and Silas.

This reaction is presumably due to two factors. Since pagans associated earthquakes with the action of a god, particularly Poseidon,[55] the jailer would have thought that prostration before the prisoners who saved his life is the appropriate reac-

---

51. The problem that commentators have with the behavior of the jailer, which is sometimes explained as not being entirely rational, are resolved, at least in part, by the recognition that the jailer was a slave of the city, not a Roman soldier or a veteran of the Roman army. Even if the jailer could have recaptured the prisoners (assuming that they had escaped), he could still be facing the most severe punishment for the dereliction of his duties.

52. Various scenarios are possible: Paul may have seen, through the now open door, the jailer's preparation for suicide from the maximum security cell; the distress of the jailer reached a climax when he passed through the open doors of the prison, and he realized that this most important door (to the maximum security area) was open as well.

53. The reason why the prisoners did not escape and leave

the prison may be explained by two considerations: first, they may have realized that the door of the maximum security cell was open, but they may not have known that all doors of the prison were open; second, since they were detained for shorter periods waiting for trial (rather than spending long years locked up in prison), running away would require leaving the city and the region permanently, an option that might be less attractive than waiting in prison for the conclusion of the ongoing legal proceedings. The total number of prisoners in the city jail was surely small, considering that Philippi had only 5,000 to 10,000 inhabitants.

54. Pervo, *Acts*, 412 n. 108.

55. Homer, *Il.* 20.57 – 58 calls Poseidon the "Earth-shaker." Poseidon's anger was considered to be the cause of earthquakes; cf. J. N. Bremmer, "Poseidon," *BNP* 11:674.

tion. Moreover, since the jailer would have known about the religious crimes in the service of the Most High God of the Jews that Paul and Silas had been accused of, he certainly could have construed a causal connection between the earthquake, the opening of the prison doors, the dropping off of the chains, the potential for the escape of the prisoners, and the commanding and calming voice of Paul.

16:30   Then he brought them outside and said, "Gentlemen, what must I do to be saved?" (καὶ προαγαγὼν αὐτοὺς ἔξω ἔφη· κύριοι, τί με δεῖ ποιεῖν ἵνα σωθῶ;). The last point also helps to explain the question of the jailer that he puts to Paul and Silas after he has let them out of the maximum security cell.[56] He addresses them as "gentlemen" (κύριοι), using a Greek term that may be nothing more than a polite address of the two men who have saved his life, but which also may indicate his perception that something extraordinary has happened that is somehow linked with these two prisoners. His question may reflect "religious terror" caused by the recognition that his abuse of the prisoners "had aroused the ire of the apostles' gods"[57]; he asks the two men how he can be saved from the consequences of the wrath of the gods, perhaps from the wrath of the Most High God whom they have been proclaiming in the city.[58]

If he had information about the message about Jesus, whom Paul and Silas proclaimed in the city as Israel's Messiah and Savior of humankind, his question might inquire about the salvation and the forgiveness of sins that Jesus brings. It is impossible to assess the jailer's knowledge of the content of Paul's proclamation, however. In any case, the jailer formulates his readiness to religious action with a typically pagan perspective: he wants to know what he "must do" (δεῖ ποιεῖν). In a pagan context, the answer would point the jailer to sacrifices that he should offer to the gods in order to appease their wrath.

16:31   They answered, "Believe in the Lord Jesus, and you will be saved — you and your household" (οἱ δὲ εἶπαν· πίστευσον ἐπὶ τὸν κύριον Ἰησοῦν καὶ σωθήσῃ σὺ καὶ ὁ οἶκός σου). The opportunity that Paul and Silas have been given to proclaim the gospel confirms that the earthquake did not rescue the missionaries but did save the jailer and his household. The answer of Paul and Silas succinctly summarizes the "way to salvation" (v. 17).[59] They inform the jailer that only faith "in the Lord Jesus" and an acknowledgment that he is Lord (κύριος) can save him. If Paul, in his surely more elaborate answer to the jailer's question, referred to Jesus' death on the cross as the event in which God atoned the sins of sinners, Jesus' acknowledgment as Lord presupposes the belief that God raised Jesus from the dead, as otherwise the crucified Jesus could not be Lord.

The conversation between the jailer and Paul and Silas takes place outside of the maximum security cell (v. 30), perhaps in the prison yard where

---

56. Codex D adds that after the jailer had let Paul and Silas out of the cell, he secured the other prisoners; Rius-Camps and Read-Heimerdinger, *Acts*, 3:274, 292.

57. Rapske, *Paul in Roman Custody*, 264. The cruelty of jailers is attested by Philo: "Everyone knows well how jailers are filled with inhumanity and savagery. For by nature they are unmerciful, and by practice they are trained daily toward fierceness, as to become wild beasts. They see, say, and do nothing good, not even by change, but instead the most violent and cruel things.... Jailers, therefore, spend time with robbers, thieves, burglars, the wanton, the violent, corrupters, murder-

ers, adulterers, and the sacrilegious. From each of these they draw and collect depravity, producing from that diverse blend a single mixture of thoroughly abominable evil" (*Joseph* 81, 84).

58. Less plausible is the interpretation of the word translated as "saved" (σωθῶ) in a purely secular sense, that the jailer asks what he can do to be "rescued" from the consequences of the possible escape of the prisoners (thus Barrett, *Acts*, 796 – 97); while the Greek verb certainly can have this "secular" meaning, it is less clear how Paul and Silas could be of any help to the jailer.

59. Cf. 2:38; 5:14; 9:42; 11:17; 13:38 – 39; 15:11.

others may have gathered after the earthquake and listened to the exchange between Paul and Silas and the jailer. This probably includes the household (οἶκος) of the latter, to whom the missionaries also extend the offer of salvation. The jailer's household would have included any slaves who assisted him in his duties as the official in charge of the municipal jail (see on v. 24).

16:32 They spoke the word of the Lord to him and to all the people in his household (καὶ ἐλάλησαν αὐτῷ τὸν λόγον τοῦ κυρίου σὺν πᾶσιν τοῖς ἐν τῇ οἰκίᾳ αὐτοῦ). The brief answer of Paul and Silas to the jailer's question summarized in v. 31 leads to a more extended proclamation of the "word of the Lord" (ὁ λόγος τοῦ κυρίου; see on 4:29), i.e., the good news of Jesus. Luke's readers can supply further content from his more extended presentations of the message of the followers of Jesus earlier in this book.

Luke's comment also confirms that the gospel of the Lord Jesus is presented not only to the jailer but also to "all" the people in his household (οἰκία, which has the same meaning here as οἶκος in v. 31). The members of the "household" are saved (v. 31) not because the jailer hears the gospel and believes, but because they also hear the word of the Lord "spoken," i.e., proclaimed and explained with the exhortation to believe in the Lord Jesus and thus be saved.[60]

16:33 – 34 The jailer took them at that hour of the night and washed their wounds. Then he and his entire household were baptized at once. He brought them into his house and set food before them. He and his entire household were overjoyed because he had come to faith in God (καὶ παραλαβὼν αὐτοὺς ἐν ἐκείνῃ τῇ ὥρᾳ τῆς νυκτὸς ἔλουσεν ἀπὸ τῶν πληγῶν, καὶ ἐβαπτίσθη αὐτὸς καὶ οἱ αὐτοῦ πάντες παραχρῆμα, ἀναγαγών τε αὐτοὺς εἰς τὸν οἶκον παρέθηκεν τράπεζαν καὶ ἠγαλλιάσατο πανοικεὶ πεπιστευκὼς τῷ θεῷ). The jailer's reaction to the presentation of the good news of the Lord Jesus is described not in terms of faith or conversion but in terms of providing for the prisoners. His behavior is described with four actions: he "took" them to a place where there was water, presumably in the prison yard; he "washed" their wounds; he "brought" them into his house; he "set food" before them.

Understanding prison culture in antiquity helps one to appreciate the impropriety or even illegality of the jailer's reaction, who was evidently more concerned for Paul and Silas and their message of salvation than for the potential consequences of his highly unusual behavior. Jailers faced punishment when they relaxed the confinement of their prisoners, especially if they had been ordered to lock up the prisoners in a maximum security cell (vv. 23 – 24). Jailers did not feed their prisoners: this was the responsibility of the prisoners' relatives and friends. And dining with a prisoner may have been a punishable offense. While the jailer had been obedient to the commands of the chief magistrates, devoted to his responsibilities as prison warden, he now "casts caution and concern for legal niceties aside in his zeal to help the prisoners who have converted him."[61] His eagerness to alleviate the suffering of Paul and Silas in the middle of the night, his courage in view of the potential consequences of his behavior, and his generosity to share his own food are all indications of his acceptance of the gospel.

The water source from which the jailer washes the wounds of Paul and Silas — perhaps a fountain

---

60. Barrett, *Acts*, 797 – 98, astutely observes that the "household" (οἰκία) could hardly have included infants, "since not only were οἱ αὐτοῦ πάντες baptized (v. 33), all heard the word of the Lord spoken by Paul and Silas (v. 32) and as a result the whole household rejoiced (ἠγαλλιάσατο πανοικεί)."

61. Rapske, *Paul in Roman Custody*, 392.

in the prison yard — is presumably the location of the baptism of the jailer and the members of his household. Their jailer's baptism follows the explanation of the word of the Lord Jesus as the way to salvation. This sequence indicates that all those baptized had accepted the gospel and were willing and eager to be immersed in water, demonstrating their purification from sins and their acceptance of the authority of Jesus, in whose name they were baptized.

The reference to the meal that Paul and Silas are served is the first explicit reference to food after the deliberations of the Apostles' Council (15:20, 29). The two missionaries evidently feel free to consume whatever food the jailer offers to them.

Luke concludes the incident of Paul's imprisonment with the explicit comment that both the jailer and the members of his household rejoice because they have "come to faith" in God. The perfect tense of the causal participle (πεπιστευκώς) indicates a state of affairs: they have become believers. The reference to God ties the message of the Lord Jesus as the way to salvation with the one true God, the God of Israel, whom Paul and Silas have been proclaiming. Joy is a sign of the presence of both salvation and faith.[62] Faith in Jesus, the Lord who saves, triggers joy at the presence of the Lord — in the middle of the night, in the house of a jailer.

16:35 – 36 When morning came, the magistrates sent the lictors with the order: "Let these men go!" The jailer reported these words to Paul, saying: "The magistrates sent word to let you go. Now you can leave. Go in peace" (ἡμέρας δὲ γενομένης ἀπέστειλαν οἱ στρατηγοὶ τοὺς ῥαβδούχους λέγοντες· ἀπόλυσον τοὺς ἀνθρώπους ἐκείνους. ἀπήγγειλεν δὲ ὁ δεσμοφύλαξ τοὺς λόγους τούτους πρὸς τὸν Παῦλον ὅτι ἀπέσταλκαν οἱ στρατηγοὶ ἵνα ἀπολυθῆτε· νῦν οὖν ἐξελθόντες πορεύεσθε ἐν εἰρήνῃ). The fifth and last incident of the Philippi episode narrates the discharge of Paul and Silas (vv. 35 – 40). The next morning after the earthquake, the magistrates send the lictors (ῥαβδοῦχοι) to the city jail, ordering the prison warden to let "these men" (τοὺς ἀνθρώπους ἐκείνους) go free.[63]

Luke provides no motive for the decision of the magistrates. One explanation relates their action to the earthquake, assuming that the latter was connected by the magistrates with the beating and the imprisonment of two Jewish teachers of the Most High God; they concluded that to continue to keep the two men in prison would invite the wrath of the god(s) and they decided that the safest course of action was to release them and move them out of the city as quickly as possible.[64] Or, the magistrates simply concluded that the two Jewish teachers had been sufficiently punished for what was a minor offense.[65] From their perspective, "the punishment showed the accused their proper place, appeased the injured parties and gratified the offended populace."[66]

---

62. Cf. Luke 15:24; Acts 8:39; 13:48.

63. For ἀπολύω in the sense of "set free, release from prison" see 5:40 (the Twelve); 17:9 (Jason); and 26:32; 28:18 (Paul), otherwise frequently in the gospel accounts of Jesus' arrest and trial; cf. Luke 23:16, 18, 20, 22, 25 (with parallels in Matt and Mark). There is no reason to think that Luke wanted to evoke the connotation of Jesus' trial.

64. This is the explanation in the addition in D: "when it was day, the magistrates came together in the agora. And because they remembered the earthquake that had occurred they grew frightened."

65. Cf. Tannehill, *Acts*, 199, who adds that the omission of an explanation by Luke is not "a major disturbance to the integrity of the narrative." Luke's major interest is Paul's behavior in response to the Roman city officials, while "the character and motives of these officials is a matter of slight interest." The punishment of *relegatio* could be imposed only after a regular trial, which had to be conducted by the governor of the province.

66. Rapske, *Paul in Roman Custody*, 129, who continues, "it seems clear that the Philippian magistrates did not consciously pervert the law" (Paul had not asserted his Roman citizenship when he was arrested).

In Luke's account, the jailer's report of the magistrates' orders that he conveyed to Paul (v. 36) is fuller than the account of the magistrates' orders to the jailer through their lictors (v. 35). While again not providing a motive, Luke indicates that the magistrates' release order included the charge (or condition) to leave the city.

16:37 But Paul said to them: "They beat us in public, without due process, men who are Roman citizens, and they threw us into prison. And now they are releasing us in secret? No! Let them come themselves and escort us out" (ὁ δὲ Παῦλος ἔφη πρὸς αὐτούς· δείραντες ἡμᾶς δημοσίᾳ ἀκατακρίτους, ἀνθρώπους Ῥωμαίους ὑπάρχοντας, ἔβαλαν εἰς φυλακήν, καὶ νῦν λάθρᾳ ἡμᾶς ἐκβάλλουσιν; οὐ γάρ, ἀλλὰ ἐλθόντες αὐτοὶ ἡμᾶς ἐξαγαγέτωσαν). Paul's reaction to the magistrates' release order and to the charge to leave the city contains two accusations, the rejection of the release conditions, and two demands.

The two accusations focus on the illegal beating and on the imprisonment. (1) Paul points out that the magistrates had beaten them in public without a proper legal process (ἀκατακρίτους), despite the fact that they were Roman citizens. Roman citizens asserted their status with the statement, "I am a Roman citizen" (Lat. *civis Romanus sum*).[67] Paul refers to the public beating not so much because of the pain it caused, but because of the shame that was associated with a public beating. In 1 Thess 2:2 he explains that he, Silas, and Timothy (cf. 1 Thess 1:1) were "treated outrageously at Philippi." The fact that there was no legal process before the beating was a serious matter because he and apparently Silas were Roman citizens. While slaves and non-Romans could be interrogated under torture,[68] the law pro-

tected Roman citizens from flogging and imprisonment as measures of *coercitio* (see on v. 23).[69]

(2) He was thrown into prison — the second part of his punishment — with bleeding wounds, secured in the stocks in the maximum security cell, left in the jail overnight without food — all without establishing the necessity of the imprisonment through a legal process.

After Paul accuses the magistrates of an illegal beating and an illegal imprisonment, he rejects the magistrates' release conditions. They have beaten him in public, bringing shame on him, but they want to release him "in secret" (λάθρᾳ), without the public knowing, to avoid the shame of having to admit their illegal behavior. Paul rejects the magistrates' desire to get rid of him with a vehement "No!" (οὐ γάρ).

Paul ends his response with two demands: he wants the magistrates to come themselves to the prison, and he demands that they escort him and Silas out of the prison personally. Paul wants public rehabilitation — presumably not for his own sake but for the sake of the new community of followers of Jesus in the city, whose safety and legal standing he cannot guarantee, but who at least would not be ridiculed on account of their founder who was beaten bloody in public with impunity.

16:38 – 39 The lictors reported these words to the magistrates. When they heard that they were Roman citizens, they became frightened. They came, and they placated them, and they escorted them from the prison, asking them to leave the city (ἀπήγγειλαν δὲ τοῖς στρατηγοῖς οἱ ῥαβδοῦχοι τὰ ῥήματα ταῦτα. ἐφοβήθησαν δὲ ἀκούσαντες ὅτι Ῥωμαῖοί εἰσιν, καὶ ἐλθόντες παρεκάλεσαν αὐτοὺς καὶ ἐξαγαγόντες ἠρώτων ἀπελθεῖν ἀπὸ τῆς πόλεως). Luke reports the magistrates' reaction to the lic-

---

67. Cicero, *Verr.* 2.5.57 (147).

68. Cf. Juvenal, 6.474 – 485; cf. Rapske, *Paul in Roman Custody*, 139.

69. When Paul is arrested in Jerusalem and about to be interrogated under torture, he points out to the centurion that he is a Roman citizen from birth (22:25, 28).

tors' report of Paul's response to their release order with six verbs, all construed in the aorist tense apart from the last verb. The magistrates "heard" that Paul and Silas were Roman citizens. As a result they "became frightened," suddenly aware that they were liable for punishment for contravening laws that protected Roman citizens from being flogged. They "came" to the city jail and met Paul and Silas; they "placated" (παρεκάλεσαν) them; i.e., they sought to assuage what they assumed were very angry Roman citizens whom they had treated badly. They "escorted" (ἐξαγαγόντες) them from the prison.[70]

Finally, the magistrates "asked" (ἠρώτων) them to leave the city. The imperfect of the last verb carries emphasis, suggesting the possibility that Paul and Silas asserted their right to stay in the city, prompting the magistrates to beg them repeatedly to leave; they are keen to get rid of the two Jewish visitors. By asking Paul and Silas to leave, they risk that they will travel to Thessalonica, the provincial capital, where they might lodge a complaint with the governor of the province. Their wish that they leave Philippi thus seems to be motivated by the desire not to alienate the syndicate that owned the slave girl by reversing their earlier "verdict" — perhaps an indication of the social status and prominence of the owners of the psychic woman who had lost her Python spirit. This end of the incident of the imprisonment of Paul and Silas marks an astonishing reversal, as the two Jewish preachers are "emerging as social victors in their honor contest with Philippi's elite *duumviri*."[71]

16:40 After they left the prison, they went to Lydia's house, where they met and encouraged

the believers. Then they departed (ἐξελθόντες δὲ ἀπὸ τῆς φυλακῆς εἰσῆλθον πρὸς τὴν Λυδίαν καὶ ἰδόντες παρεκάλεσαν τοὺς ἀδελφοὺς καὶ ἐξῆλθαν). The response of Paul and Silas consists in general compliance with the magistrates' wishes. They leave the prison and then go to Lydia's house, where they had stayed and where the new converts had been meeting. They meet and speak with the believers assembled there. They encourage them in their faith (see on 14:22), and then they leave Philippi. Luke does not indicate how long Paul and his associates stayed in Philippi. The fact that the first "we passage" ends with the departure of Paul and Silas and resumes in Philippi when Paul travels back to Jerusalem eight years later (in the spring of AD 57) suggests that Luke remains in Philippi.[72]

The reference to "the believers" (οἱ ἀδελφοί) is evidence that the missionary work of Paul and Silas in Philippi resulted in the founding of a church. The two missionaries evidently had been proclaiming the gospel in Philippi for some time before the incident of the attack of the syndicate that owned the psychic woman. There had been several conversions beyond that of Lydia and her household (vv. 14–15) and of the official in charge of the city jail with his household (vv. 30–34). The emerging community of believers met in Lydia's house.

Apart from Lydia, several members of the church are known from Paul's letter to the Philippian believers: Epaphroditus (Phil 2:25–30; 4:18), Euodia (4:2), Syntyche (4:2), and Clement (4:3); the name of the jailer is not known. Luke does not relate how long Paul and Silas, together with Timothy and Luke, stayed in Lydia's house teaching the new believers. Paul's protest to the chief magistrates of the city and their compliance with his

---

70. The phrase "from the prison" is not in the Greek text, but is implied in the prefix ἐξ- of the verb; cf. GNB, NIV, TNIV. In view of Paul's location in the jailer's house in v. 34, the verb in v. 39 suggests that Paul and Silas were taken back into the prison; this is confirmed by v. 40.

71. Joseph H. Hellerman, *Reconstructing Honor in Roman Philippi: Carmen Christi as Cursus Pudorum* (SNTSMS 132; Cambridge: Cambridge Univ. Press, 2005), 116.

72. Cf. Dunn, *Beginning from Jerusalem*, 676.

request may have prompted him to stay some time before they departed.

We learn from Paul's letter to the Christians in Philippi that the Philippian believers had entered into a "partnership in the gospel" from the first day until five or six years later (Phil 1:5), supporting Paul and his missionary work right after he had left the city, when he was active in Thessalonica (Phil 4:16) and then when he left Macedonia and traveled to Achaia (Phil 4:15; cf. 2 Cor 11:8 – 9). The Christians in Philippi evidently "followed Paul's travels closely and contributed occasional gifts to the apostle, gifts which enabled Paul not to burden other churches as he preached the gospel to them."[73]

Theology in Application

Luke's narrative of Paul's missionary work in Philippi illustrates various elements about God, about missionary work, and about missionaries.

Empowerment for Mission

The mission of the church is empowered by God and Jesus Christ. The willingness of Lydia to listen to Paul's explanation of the gospel and her coming to faith is connected with God's initiative and activity: it was God who opened her heart (v. 14). The Python spirit was driven out of the slave women when Paul confronted it in the name of Jesus Christ (v. 18). The possibility of a conversation between the jailer and Paul in the course of which Paul was able to explain the gospel was triggered by an earthquake, which may have had natural causes but whose timing seems to have been directed by God (v. 26).

Reaching All People

Missionary work reaches all people. Luke describes Paul and Silas speaking of Jesus to Jews and God-fearers in the synagogue of Philippi, to a woman who is probably a wealthy purple merchant from the province of Asia but who resides in Philippi and who attends synagogue services, to a woman who is a slave and possessed by a spirit of divination and consequently a money-maker for her owners, and to a man who is (probably) a public slave owned by the city and who has been put in charge of the local prison. They may also have taken advantage of the opportunity to speak of Jesus with the chief magistrates when they come to escort them out of the jail.

The mission of Paul, Silas, Timothy, and Luke in Philippi illustrates how the word of God, which is the good news of Jesus, the crucified and risen Lord, overcomes social, cultural, and ethnic differences. Paul, the educated Jewish rabbi from Tarsus who is a Roman citizen, shares a meal with a jailer who is a public slave, and he

73. John P. Dickson, *Mission-Commitment in Ancient Judaism and in the Pauline Communities: The Shape, Extent and* *Background of Early Christian Mission* (WUNT 159; Tübingen: Mohr Siebeck, 2003), 207.

shares his joy over his conversion (v. 34). The community of believers that meets in Lydia's house (v. 40) includes the God-fearing businesswoman, who deals in purple, and members of her household, Jews who have (presumably) come to faith in Jesus, the pagan jailer and other slaves from his household who have come to faith, and, perhaps, the slave girl who used to be successful as a psychic. These people are ethnically, socially, legally, and psychologically "worlds apart,"[74] but they are all transformed by the word of the Lord, so much so that they share the joy of conversion, meals, and continued instruction.

Flexible and Courageous

Missionaries are both flexible and courageous as they proclaim the word of God. While Luke's selective narrative needs to be interpreted with caution in terms of details that may or may not be implied, it appears that when Paul and his friends proclaimed the gospel in the synagogue, it was a group of women who were willing to listen — an opportunity Paul did not pass up (v. 13). He was flexible when he and Silas were accosted by a clairvoyant slave girl with a rather ambiguous message that she conveyed on the streets of Philippi (vv. 16 – 18); he confronted her with reference to Jesus, Israel's Messiah. A third opportunity that required an instant willingness to explain the gospel presented itself after an earthquake that led to a conversation with the jailer and to an encounter with other members of his household (vv. 30 – 33).

Paul did not follow some streamlined method in his evangelistic activities. Even the strategic decision to first visit synagogues was handled flexibly — if women were more willing to listen, he stayed with them rather than giving up on the synagogue altogether. Authentic evangelism and true missionary work are motivated by love for people who need to hear the word of God. As a result, evangelists and missionaries are willing to speak to anybody, at any time — flexible in terms of audience, timing, and words used to convey the gospel.

Missionary flexibility ends, however, when the integrity of God's word as the gospel of Jesus Christ is concerned. Paul is unwilling to have a psychic slave girl promote their message, because she speaks under the inspiration of a supernatural spirit, her message is ambiguous, and she is not a Christian believer. Paul is not amenable to tolerate any "method" if only the "word" about God and salvation "gets out." While perhaps not always true, the phrase "the medium is the message" (Marshall McLuhan) aptly explains why Paul cannot "use" the slave girl for his purposes; a psychic medium cannot be a channel for the message about the way of salvation. Not all methods are suitable for the proclamation of the gospel, even if they may "work" from a secular point of view. The proclamation of the gospel requires integrity and authenticity of both messenger and message.

---

74. Stott, *Acts*, 268.

The courage of Paul and his coworkers is an integral part of their missionary work. They are willing, as Jewish men, to speak with women (v. 14), risking ridicule and gossip. They are willing, as devout Jews, to have contact with a psychic through whom a Python spirit communicates with the citizens of Philippi (vv. 17–18), risking misunderstanding and suspicion. They exorcise the Python spirit (v. 18), risking the ire of those who profited financially from her activity. They stand their ground when the syndicate that owns the psychic slave accosts them and drags them to the agora, where they are severely beaten (vv. 19–23), risking permanent disability and potentially death on account of the flogging.

Paul and his coworkers are willing, as freeborn citizens, to engage in conversation and to share a meal with the jailer and his staff (vv. 28–34), risking further ridicule and shame. They are willing to confront the chief magistrates of Philippi with their illegal behavior (vv. 35–39), risking delays (if the magistrates ask for proof of their status as Roman citizens) and further mistreatment in the prison in which they would be locked up until their case has been settled. The missionaries' courage is motivated by their sense of obligation to the commission they had received to proclaim the word of God and by their love for people — for sinners who need to hear the gospel and for believers whose fellowship they enjoy.

Acts 17:1 – 15

Literary Context

This passage, made up of two episodes, belongs to the section that narrates Paul's missionary work in Macedonia (16:11 – 17:15), which is the middle section of Luke's report on the mission of Paul in the provinces of Macedonia and Achaia (15:35 – 18:22). Having recounted the proclamation of the gospel in Philippi (16:11 – 40), Luke now reports on Paul's mission in Thessalonica (17:1 – 9) and in Berea (17:10 – 15). The next section narrates his mission in Achaia in the cities of Athens and Corinth (17:16 – 18:22).

Luke's report on Paul's work in Thessalonica and his movements before and after his stay in the city corresponds with information given by Paul himself in 1 Thessalonians, a letter written from Corinth within a few months of the foundation of the church. He writes that his proclamation of the gospel in Thessalonica was carried out with full conviction and was accompanied by miracles (1 Thess 1:5), that he suffered and was shamefully treated in Philippi before coming to Thessalonica (2:2), that he encountered opposition in Thessalonica as well (2:2), that Jewish opponents were instrumental in forcing him to leave the city (2:15 – 16), that the believers in Thessalonica accepted the gospel "in the midst of severe suffering" (1:6), that Paul went to Athens after leaving Thessalonica (3:1), and that Paul sent Timothy back to encourage and strengthen the believers (3:2). While Luke's narrative focuses on Paul's preaching in the synagogue of Thessalonica and on the accusations of Jews before the politarchs, the chief magistrates of the city, Paul's first letter to the Thessalonian believers suggests that the congregation consisted of a large number of Gentile believers. The Thessalonian mission probably took place from October to December in AD 49, the mission in Berea in December and January of AD 49/50.

Main Idea

These two episodes emphasize the significance of the authority of the Scriptures, the invariability of the gospel of Jesus as the crucified and risen Messiah, the constancy of opposition to the gospel, and the reality of solidarity among the followers of Jesus.

Translation

Acts 17:1 – 15

1a	Event/Place	**They traveled through Amphipolis and Apollonia and**
b	Action/Place	**came to Thessalonica,**
c	Setting: social	where there was a synagogue of the Jews.
2a	Comparison	As was his custom,
b	Action	**Paul went into the synagogue and**
c	Action	**engaged** them
d	Time	on three Sabbaths
e	Content	about the Scriptures,
3a	Means	explaining and
b	Means	demonstrating
c	Content	that the Messiah had to suffer and
d	Content	rise from the dead,
e	Action (speech)	saying:
f	Identification/Assertion	*"This Jesus I am proclaiming to you is the Messiah."*
4a	Result	**Some of them were persuaded and**
b	Result	**associated with Paul and Silas,**
c	Identification	as did a large number of the Greek God-fearers and
d	Identification	not a few prominent women.
5a	Reaction	**But the Jews became jealous;**
b	Action	**they organized some bad characters from the rabble in the agora,**
c	Action	**formed a mob,**
d	Action	**and started a riot in the city.**

e	Action	**They attacked Jason's house**
f	Reason	as they were looking for Paul and Silas,
g	Purpose	whom they wanted to bring before the ↵
		assembly.
6a	Setting: Time	When they did not find them,
b	Action/Character entrance	**they dragged Jason and several other believers**
c	Place	before the city officials,
d	Action (speech)	shouting,
e	Identification	*"These people*
f	Identification	*who have upset the stability of the world*
g	Event	*have now come here,*
7a	Action	*and Jason has entertained them as guests;*
b	Accusation	*they are all acting contrary to the emperor's decrees,*
c	Explanation	*saying that there is another king,*
d	Identification	*named Jesus."*
8a	Result	**They unsettled** **the people and**
b	List	**the city officials**
c	Time	when they heard this.
9a	Action	**They took bail from Jason and the others and**
b	Action	**let them go.**
10a	Setting: Time	That very night
b	Action	**the believers sent Paul and Silas away**
c	Place	to Berea.
d	Setting: Time	When they arrived,
e	Action	**they went to the synagogue of the Jews.**
11a	Event	**These Jews were more open-minded**
b	Comparison	than those in Thessalonica;
c	Action	**they received the message with much goodwill,**
d	Event	examining the Scriptures daily
e	Reason	to see if these things were true.
12a	Result	**Many of them came to faith,**
b	Identification	including prominent Greek women and many men.
13a	Setting: Time	When the Jews in Thessalonica learned
b	Setting: Place	that Paul proclaimed the word of ↵
		God in Berea,
c	Action	**they came there too,**
d	Action	inciting and
e	Action	unsettling the crowds.
14a	Setting: Time	Immediately thereafter
b	Reaction	**the believers sent Paul away to the coast,**
c	Event	while Silas and Timothy stayed there.
15a	Action	**Those who accompanied Paul brought him to Athens and**
b	Action	**left with instructions for Silas and Timothy**
c	Purpose	to join him
d	Time	as soon as possible.

Structure and Literary Form

Paul's missionary work in Thessalonica (17:1 – 9) consists of two incidents. Luke first describes the proclamation of the gospel in the synagogue for three consecutive weeks, resulting in the conversion of Jews, God-fearers, and sympathizers among the women of the local elite (vv. 1 – 4). The second incident reports on the persecution of Paul and his associates, organized by Jews of the city who mobilize citizens to cause a disturbance in the city; several believers are dragged before the city magistrates as hosts of the missionaries, and they are accused of preaching revolution and a rival king in defiance of the emperor (vv. 5 – 9).

Paul's missionary work in Berea (17:10 – 15) follows the same structure: the first incident relates the proclamation of the gospel in the synagogue leading to conversions among those Jews who verify their teaching through the study of the Scriptures (vv. 10 – 12). The second incident reports the persecution and eviction of Paul (vv. 13 – 15).

Both episodes are *narratives*, with several *travel notices* (17:1, 10, 14 – 15). The first episode contains *direct speech*: a brief summary of Paul's proclamation in the synagogue of Thessalonica (v. 3), and a longer summary of the accusation of citizens of Thessalonica before the magistrates (vv. 6 – 7).

Exegetical Outline

2. Paul's teaching in the synagogue (17:10d-e)

3. The receptivity of the Jews who consult the Scriptures (17:11)

4. The conversion of Jews, aristocratic women, and men (17:12)

B. Opposition and Eviction of the Missionaries (17:13 – 15)

1. The opposition of Jews coming from Thessalonica (17:13)

2. The departure of Paul, who travels to the coast (17:14a-b)

3. Silas and Timothy stay in Berea (17:14c)

4. Paul travels from the coast to Athens (17:15a)

5. Paul sends instructions to Silas and Timothy to join him in Athens (17:15b-d)

Explanation of the Text

17:1 They traveled through Amphipolis and Apollonia and came to Thessalonica, where there was a synagogue of the Jews (διοδεύσαντες δὲ τὴν Ἀμφίπολιν καὶ τὴν Ἀπολλωνίαν ἦλθον εἰς Θεσσαλονίκην ὅπου ἦν συναγωγὴ τῶν Ἰουδαίων). The Thessalonica episode begins with a travel notice: Paul and his missionary associates, Silas and Timothy (cf. vv. 4, 10, 14),[1] travel from Philippi along the Via Egnatia via Amphipolis and Apollonia to Thessalonica, a journey of about 102 miles (165 km.). Roman Thessalonica was the capital of the province of Macedonia, which Claudius had reorganized in AD 44. The city, which had between 40,000 to 65,000 inhabitants, was governed by a group of five or six magistrate officials called politarchs (πολιτάρχαι), mentioned in 17:6.[2]

17:2 As was his custom, Paul went into the synagogue and engaged them on three Sabbaths about the Scriptures (κατὰ δὲ τὸ εἰωθὸς τῷ

Παύλῳ εἰσῆλθεν πρὸς αὐτοὺς καὶ ἐπὶ σάββατα τρία διελέξατο αὐτοῖς ἀπὸ τῶν γραφῶν). Luke describes Paul's attendance of synagogue services as being his custom.[3] The first verb refers to Paul's visit in the synagogue, where he teaches and preaches to all the people — Jews, proselytes, God-fearers, sympathizers — present in the meetings. The verb "engaged" (διελέξατο) describes Paul's activity and can be defined either as "engage in speech interchange" and translated "converse, discuss, argue," or as "instruct about something" and translated as "inform, instruct."[4] The prepositional phrase that follows the verb (ἀπὸ τῶν γραφῶν, "about the Scriptures") makes the first meaning more plausible: Paul engaged those present in the synagogue in conversations about Scripture, specifically about those passages that speak about the coming Redeemer and Savior of Israel, as the next verse shows.

The basis for Paul's explanation of the good

---

1. Luke seems to have stayed in Philippi: the first "we passage" ended in 16:17 in Philippi, and the next "we passage" begins in 20:5 – 6, with "we" sailing from Philippi to Troas.

2. Cf. Greg H. R. Horsley, "The Politarchs," in *The Book of Acts in Its Graeco-Roman Setting* (ed. D. W. J. Gill and C. Gempf; The Book of Acts in Its First-Century Setting 2; Grand Rapids: Eerdmans, 1994), 419 – 31.

3. See 13:5, 14; 14:1; 16:13; also 17:10, 17; 18:4, 19; 19:8; 28:17, 23. BDAG, s.v. εἴωθα, "to maintain a custom or tradition, *be accustomed*."

4. BDAG, s.v. διαλέγομαι 1, "to engage in speech interchange, *converse, discuss, argue*," especially "of instructional discourse that frequently includes exchange of opinion"; sense 2, "to instruct about something, *inform, instruct*." Cf. LSJ, s.v. διαλέγομαι B1, "converse with, discuss, discourse, reason"; sense 2, "in Philosophy, *practise dialectic, elicit conclusions by discussion*"; sense 3, "later, *discourse, lecture*."

news of Jesus was the Scriptures. If Luke intends his readers to compare Paul's activity in the synagogue in Thessalonica with his description of Paul's preaching in the synagogue in Pisidian Antioch, where the synagogue officials invited him to address the congregation (13:15), it appears that in Thessalonica Paul was not invited to teach the congregation, although he was clearly allowed to participate in discussions about the Scriptures, an opportunity that he would have used to introduce his convictions about Jesus.

The temporal phrase "on three Sabbaths" can also mean "for three weeks" since the term "Sabbath" (σάββατον) means either the seventh day of the Jewish week or a period of seven days. Since we have no information about the meeting schedule of the synagogue in Thessalonica, both meanings are possible. Paul's letter to the Thessalonian believers and his reference to the recurring support he received from the Philippian believers while in Thessalonica (Phil 4:16) suggest that he spent more than three weeks in the city.

Paul's missionary activity focuses on the synagogue for three weeks. He is then forced to reduce or abandon meeting there because of growing opposition from members of the Jewish community. At that time he relocates the base of his activities probably to the house of Jason, one of the new converts (vv. 5, 7).

17:3 Explaining and demonstrating that the Messiah had to suffer and rise from the dead, saying: "This Jesus I am proclaiming to you is the Messiah" (διανοίγων καὶ παρατιθέμενος ὅτι τὸν χριστὸν ἔδει παθεῖν καὶ ἀναστῆναι ἐκ νεκρῶν καὶ ὅτι οὗτός ἐστιν ὁ χριστὸς ὁ Ἰησοῦς ὃν ἐγὼ καταγγέλλω ὑμῖν). Luke further describes Paul's activity in the synagogue with two modal present participles that specify the manner of Paul's discussions in the synagogue and emphasize his continued focus on the Jewish community. The basic meaning of the first verb (διανοίγων) is to "open" or "reveal" — Paul opens the Scriptures by showing how they anticipate and teach about Israel's Redeemer.[5] The second meaning is to "explain, interpret" — Paul engages the Jews and God-fearers about the Scriptures by explaining relevant texts that speak about Israel's Redeemer. The second verb (παρατιθέμενος) means to "lay something before someone," often in the sense of "explain"; its middle forms can also mean to "cite as evidence or authority." Both meanings make sense here: Paul explains the Scriptures in the sense that he cites them as evidence for his message.

The following clause describes the content of Paul's conversations, explanations, and proofs. He speaks about Jesus, Israel's Messiah, who has arrived on the scene, in particular about the necessity and the significance of his suffering, death, and resurrection. The identification of the Messiah (whom the Jews expected as Israel's Redeemer) with Jesus is related in direct speech, underscoring the significance of this identification. In other words, Paul publicly proclaims (καταγγέλλω, see on 4:2) that Jesus is Israel's Messiah, the promised Redeemer, who suffered and died[6] and whom God raised from the dead[7] — events that are part of God's plan, as anticipated and revealed in the Scriptures. Verse 7 indicates that Paul described Jesus also as the royal Messiah, who is Israel's king. The insistence that Jesus the Messiah had to suffer and die and that God raised him from the dead is a key theological theme for Luke.

17:4 Some of them were persuaded and associated with Paul and Silas, as did a large number of the Greek God-fearers and not a few prominent women (καί τινες ἐξ αὐτῶν ἐπείσθησαν καὶ

---

5. Cf. 2:23; 3:18; see also Luke 9:22; 17:25; 24:26, 32, 46.
6. Cf. Luke 22:15; 24:26, 46; Acts 1:3; 2:23; 3:18; 26:22–23.

7. Cf. Luke 24:46; Acts 2:22–24; 10:41; 13:32–36.

προσεκληρώθησαν τῷ Παύλῳ καὶ τῷ Σιλᾷ, τῶν τε σεβομένων Ἑλλήνων πλῆθος πολύ, γυναικῶν τε τῶν πρώτων οὐκ ὀλίγαι). After listening to Paul's proclamation of Jesus as the suffering and risen Messiah, some people in the audience "were persuaded" (ἐπείσθησαν); i.e., they accepted the point of view that Paul presented when he explained the meaning of scriptural texts regarding Israel's coming Redeemer and his arrival in the coming of Jesus, who suffered, died, and rose from the dead. They also accepted the course of action that Paul put forward — believing in Jesus for the forgiveness of their sins, the bestowal of the Spirit of prophecy who would transform their lives, and the certain hope of eternal life.[8] The passive voice of this verb points to God and his Spirit as the one who convinced the people to become followers of Jesus (rather than Paul's exposition of Scripture or the cogency of his arguments; cf. 1 Cor 1:18 – 2:5).

The second verb, "associated with" (προσεκληρώθησαν), describes the emergence of a community of believers in Jesus. The people who became believers in Jesus joined with Paul and Silas. The verb can also be translated as "were assigned to" (LSJ), which underscores more explicitly God's initiative (indicated again in the passive voice of the verb) not only in the conversion of the new believers but also in the foundation of the new community.

Luke notes three groups who respond to Paul's proclamation of the gospel: Jews in the synagogue; Greeks attending the synagogue meetings as God-fearers, i.e., Gentile sympathizers with an interest in the Jewish faith; and "prominent women" (γυναικῶν τῶν πρώτων; the phrase can also be understood to refer to the "women/wives of the leading men"). While Luke does not provide specific numbers, he gives some indication about the conversions: the new believers include "some" (τινες) Jews, "a large number" (πλῆθος πολύ) of Greeks who were God-fearers, and many (i.e., "not a few," οὐκ ὀλίγαι) women.

Paul's letter to the Thessalonian believers, written within a few months of the establishment of the church in Thessalonica, reminds the believers that they had turned away from idols (1 Thess 1:9), which suggests that Paul's ministry was probably not limited to the synagogue and to Jewish audiences while he stayed in the city; the majority of the new Christian community consisted of former polytheists.[9] This is confirmed by the reason that Luke gives for the Jewish opposition against Paul and Barnabas in v. 5. Note that two believers in Thessalonica were Aristarchus and Secundus, who accompanied Paul on his final journey to Jerusalem (Acts 20:4; 27:2). There is the intriguing possibility that this Aristarchus might be identical with the "Aristarchos son of Aristarchos" mentioned as a politarch in several inscriptions.

17:5 But the Jews became jealous; they organized some bad characters from the rabble in the agora, formed a mob, and started a riot in the city. They attacked Jason's house as they were looking for Paul and Silas, whom they wanted to bring before the assembly (ζηλώσαντες δὲ οἱ Ἰουδαῖοι καὶ προσλαβόμενοι τῶν ἀγοραίων ἄνδρας τινὰς πονηροὺς καὶ ὀχλοποιήσαντες ἐθορύβουν τὴν πόλιν καὶ ἐπιστάντες τῇ οἰκίᾳ Ἰάσονος ἐζήτουν αὐτοὺς προαγαγεῖν εἰς τὸν δῆμον). The second incident of the Thessalonica episode relates the opposition that the missionaries encounter and their eviction from the city (vv. 5 – 9).

Luke first reports on the opposition of Jews, who mobilize other citizens to take action against

---

8. Cf. 13:38 – 39, 46, 48, 52.

9. Cf. Christoph vom Brocke, *Thessaloniki — Stadt der Kassander und Gemeinde des Paulus: Eine frühe christliche Ge-*

meinde in ihrer heidnischen Umwelt (WUNT 2/125; Tübingen: Mohr Siebeck, 2001), 114.

Paul and Silas (v. 5a-d).[10] The motivation of the Jews who oppose the missionaries is described, as in Pisidian Antioch, with reference to "jealousy," a term that probably refers not only to their jealousy over the conversion of Jews and of a large number of Gentiles including God-fearers, but also to their "zeal" for the traditional understanding of the Mosaic law. The Thessalonian Jews want to maintain their Jewish identity and its religious distinctives in the capital city of the province of Macedonia and to preserve the rights and privileges they have enjoyed in the cities of the Roman provinces (see on 13:45). Since several women of high social status who apparently had been attending the synagogue were converted to faith in Jesus, unbelieving Jews would have feared the loss of influential patrons in the city.

These Jews from the synagogue had heard Paul expound his convictions about Jesus as Israel's Messiah; they have not been convinced and decide to take steps to silence Paul and his associates. Luke describes their actions with two aorist circumstantial participles and a finite verb (imperfect) that carries the weight of the description. (1) They "organized" (προσλαβόμενοι) bad characters[11] from the rabble in the agora, the central square of the city.[12] (2) They "formed a mob" (ὀχλοποιήσαντες); i.e., they used these ruffians to gather a crowd (ὄχλος). (3) They "started a riot" (ἐθορύβουν); i.e., they threw the city into disorder, causing disturbances among the citizens. This can be interpreted as an unofficial but organized demonstration, a feature of Hellenistic city life: "if not constitution-

ally valid, they often gained their point in a rough and ready way. The mass chanting of a crowd was difficult to resist."[13]

Luke next relates the opposition of the citizens whom the Jewish agitators managed to organize (v. 5e – 6d). He again reports three actions. (1) "They were looking for" (ἐζήτουν) Paul and Silas, i.e., trying to find the visiting teachers; the imperfect tense of the verb suggests a persistent effort to locate them. Their intention was to bring Paul and Silas before the "assembly" (δῆμος), i.e., the popular assembly of the (free) citizens of Thessalonica, which had the rights of a free city (*civitas libera*) and is mentioned in numerous inscriptions of the city. They evidently hoped that the assembly would indict Paul and Silas and pass sentence on them.

(2) They "attacked" (ἐπιστάντες) the house of Jason. Since they evidently knew that Paul and Silas had received hospitality from Jason, they figured they would find the two missionaries there. This Jason is likely identical with the Jason of Rom 16:21, where Paul describes him as a fellow Jew, mentioned next to Sopater, who was from Berea (Acts 20:4). The third action is described in the next verse.

17:6 – 7 When they did not find them, they dragged Jason and several other believers before the city officials, shouting: "These people who have upset the stability of the world have now come here, and Jason has entertained them as guests; they are all acting contrary to the emperor's decrees, saying that there is another

10. For Paul's reference to the Jewish opposition cf. 1 Thess 1:6; 2:13 – 16. Riesner, *Paul's Early Period*, 352 – 54, argues that Luke's account makes Paul's "shockingly harsh manner of expression" in 1 Thess historically comprehensible.

11. The phrase translated as "bad characters" (ἄνδρας ... πονηρούς; NIV, TNIV) is also translated as "wicked fellows" (RSV; Johnson), "ruffians" (NRSV), "wicked men" (ESV, NASB), "evil men" (Barrett), "worthless loafers" (GNB; Fitzmyer), "worthless men" (NET).

12. The expression translated as "the rabble in the agora" (τῶν ἀγοραίων) refers to "the market people" (BDAG), a term that can have a neutral meaning ("the traders," Aelianus, *Tact.* 2.2), but here has a pejorative meaning such as "the common sort, low fellows, agitators" (LSJ, s.v. ἀγοραῖος II.1).

13. Edwin A. Judge, *Social Distinctives of the Christians in the First Century: Pivotal Essays* (ed. D. M. Scholer; Peabody, MA: Hendrickson, 2007), 18; cf. Riesner, *Paul's Early Period*, 355.

king, named Jesus" (μὴ εὑρόντες δὲ αὐτοὺς ἔσυρον Ἰάσονα καί τινας ἀδελφοὺς ἐπὶ τοὺς πολιτάρχας βοῶντες ὅτι οἱ τὴν οἰκουμένην ἀναστατώσαντες οὗτοι καὶ ἐνθάδε πάρεισιν, οὓς ὑποδέδεκται Ἰάσων· καὶ οὗτοι πάντες ἀπέναντι τῶν δογμάτων Καίσαρος πράσσουσιν βασιλέα ἕτερον λέγοντες εἶναι Ἰησοῦν). The failure to locate Paul and Silas prompted the crowds, together with the Jews opposing the two missionaries, to take further action.

(3) They "dragged" (ἔσυρον) Jason and several other believers before the "city officials" (οἱ πολιτάρχαι). The politarchs, a group of five or six senior magistrates, were responsible for convening both the assembly of the people (ἐκκλησία) and the city council (βουλή), introducing motions and confirming its decisions. They were responsible to act for the people, carrying out the wishes of the assembly of the citizens. They possessed judicial authority, and they were responsible to maintain peace and order to ensure that the Roman authorities would not be forced to intervene in the affairs of the city.[14] The location of the following scene would undoubtedly have been the Roman forum in the center of Thessalonica.

The accusation against Paul and Silas (in absentia) and against Jason and the other believers is presented as an acclamation, indicated by the verb translated as "shouting" (βοῶντες). The accusation consists of two different allegations. (1) Paul and Silas are accused as agitators who have upset the stability of "the world" (τὴν οἰκουμένην; see on 11:28) in other regions of the Roman Empire and who "have now come here" (καὶ ἐνθάδε πάρεισιν; the present tense means that they have come and are now here). This charge is much more serious than translations such as "these men who have upset the world" (NASB) or even "these men who

have turned the world upside down" (RSV, ESV, cf. NRSV) suggest, even though the last rendering of the Greek expression captures the hyperbolic, exaggerated sense of the crowd's accusation.

By AD 50 Paul had preached the gospel only in Damascus, Jerusalem, Tarsus, Antioch, and Perge, as far as larger cities in the Roman Empire were concerned. He had not (yet) been in Ephesus, Corinth, or Rome, nor had he been active in Alexandria. The charge of the missionaries' opponents was not founded in reality as far as the term "the world" or the motivation of Paul was concerned. But the charge was not completely invented either, if indeed the Jews of Thessalonica had heard of Paul's activities in other provinces through contacts with the Jewish communities in Palestine and Syria, or through contacts with the Jewish community in Philippi, a few days travel northeast of Thessalonica. Wherever Paul proclaimed his message, trouble ensued both in the local Jewish communities and among the citizens of the cities — as a result of the disputes that arose in the Jewish communities, of the conversion of Jews and Gentiles, and of the emergence of a new group whose members adopted new practices in worship and behavior.

The fact that Paul and his associates more often than not were forced by magistrates to leave the city in which they had been teaching indicates, certainly, that they caused disturbances that the officials in these cities were not willing to tolerate. The accusation of threatening the stability of the world, designed to portray Paul and Silas as criminals, uses allegations from the traditional arsenal of polemics, slander, and defamation, while being rooted to some degree in the reality of the effects of Paul's missionary ministry. Such accusations

---

14. Horsley, "The Politarchs," 425, 430. The politarchs were not officials of the Roman provincial administration, although in the first century many holders of the annual office

(which could be held more than once) would have had Roman citizenship.

of causing disturbances had been leveled against Jewish communities before. Jason, who has entertained Paul and Silas as guests, is implicated in the charges. Since he has provided hospitality to the two visitors and perhaps because he hosts the meetings of the new group of followers of Jesus, he is also guilty of upsetting the stability of the peace and order of Thessalonica.

(2) Paul and Silas, together with Jason and the other believers, are accused of acting "contrary to the emperor's decrees." The more general charge of upsetting the stability of society and of the empire is specified in terms of an explicit political charge: they contravene the decrees of the emperor. The Greek term translated "decrees" (τὰ δόγματα) denotes formal statements "concerning rules or regulations that are to be observed" — here more specifically the imperial declarations of the emperor.

The term "emperor" (lit., "Caesar," Καῖσαρ) was originally the cognomen of the *gens Iulia*, one of the old Roman families. It was linked with Julius Caesar, the general and politician who brought the Roman republic to an end and established the Roman Empire; when he adopted Octavian and designated him as his successor in his last will, the senate recognized Octavian as Gaius Julius Caesar Octavianus (later given the title Augustus). Thus "Caesar" was used as a title for subsequent Roman emperors. At this time, the emperor was Tiberius Claudius, who ruled from AD 41 to 54. His main claim to fame was the conquest of Britain in AD 43.

The specific accusation made here is substantiated by a reference to the beliefs and teachings of the accused: they are "saying that there is another king," whose name is Jesus; the term translated "king" (βασιλεύς) is used in Greek texts to denote the Roman emperors.[15] In other words, Paul and his associates are charged with advocating loyalty to a certain Jesus rather than to the emperor in Rome. The proclamation that Jesus is Israel's Messiah (v. 3) is construed in a political sense; Jesus is a king — not only king of the Jews (which would suffice to constitute sedition, since Claudius had appointed Agrippa as king of Judea in AD 41), but also of the Greeks and Romans in Thessalonica, whom Paul invites to become followers of Jesus. Christians could hardly deny they were loyal to Jesus, the King of the Jews and the Savior of the world.

Luke's reference to the "decrees" (plural) of Caesar that Paul and Silas and the Thessalonian believers are accused of violating have been interpreted in two ways. (1) They are accused of committing the crime of treason, i.e., of violating the Roman law of treason (*maiestas*, short for *maiestas populi romani minuta*, "diminishing the majesty of the Roman people").[16] (2) They are accused of violating the legislation of Augustus and Tiberius prohibiting astrology and predictions of the change of rulers,[17] and more specifically the oath of allegiance to the emperor that provinces and cities swore, pledging reverence and obedience to the emperor, with the local magistrates being responsible for administering the oath. Since the citizens of Thessalonica were aware of their dependence on

---

15. LSJ, s.v. βασιλεύς III.3. English versions generally translated "king" in v. 7, although the translation "saying that there is another emperor named Jesus" is also possible. Fitzmyer, *Acts*, 596, cautions that the title "emperor" did not exist in Roman history then.

16. Cf. Harry W. Tajra, *The Trial of St. Paul: A Juridical Exegesis of the Second Half of the Acts of the Apostles* (WUNT 2/35; Tübingen: Mohr Siebeck, 1989), 36 – 42; Omerzu, *Prozess*, 190, 200 – 207.

17. Note Paul's proclamation concerning the returning Lord Jesus, the Messiah (cf. 1 Thess 4:16; 5:2 – 3; 2 Thess 2:1 – 12), which could be construed to refer to a prediction of a change of ruler. Cf. Edwin A. Judge, "The Decrees of Caesar at Thessalonica [1971]" in *The First Christians in the Roman World: Augustan and New Testament Essays* (ed. J. R. Harrison; WUNT 229; Tübingen: Mohr Siebeck, 2008), 456 – 62, 457 – 61.

imperial benefaction, "it would be quite surprising if such expressions of loyalty were not performed enthusiastically."[18] Since the charges were brought by a demagogic mob and were objectively false, both explanations may have played a role.

The second accusation, then, charges Paul and Silas and the Thessalonian believers that they accept and promulgate a pretender king, Jesus, which constitutes treason and violates the oath of allegiance to the emperor. In the second century, Christians were executed because they refused to swear an oath of allegiance to the emperor. In the *Acts of the Scillitan Martyrs*, the earliest dated document from the Latin church, which relates the hearing, judgment, and execution of twelve martyrs on July 17, 180, the proconsul Saturninus says: "We too are a religious people, and our religion is a simple one: we swear by the genius of our lord the emperor and we offer prayers for his health — as you also ought to do."[19]

17:8 – 9 They unsettled the people and the city officials when they heard this. They took bail from Jason and the others and let them go (ἐτάραξαν δὲ τὸν ὄχλον καὶ τοὺς πολιτάρχας ἀκούοντας ταῦτα, καὶ λαβόντες τὸ ἱκανὸν παρὰ τοῦ Ἰάσονος καὶ τῶν λοιπῶν ἀπέλυσαν αὐτούς). Luke relates the reaction of the people and the magistrates with three verbs. (1) The accusers "unsettled" (ἐτάραξαν) the people and the politarchs (v. 8); i.e., the citizens of Thessalonica and their highest officials were agitated on account of the potential consequences of the presence and teaching of Paul and Silas for the city, given the gathering of crowds of people and the ensuing disturbances in the city (v. 5). The citizens of autonomous Thessalonica would not want the Roman governor to intervene to restore the peace.

(2) The magistrates "took bail" (λαβόντες τὸ ἱκανόν; cf. the Latin expression *satis accipere*, "to receive bail, bond, security") from Jason and from other believers (v. 9), who either are forced or volunteer to give security for Paul and Silas, guaranteeing their good behavior and/or their departure.[20] Presumably the charges of disturbing the peace and of disloyalty to the emperor were successfully deflected by Jason (whose argumentation Luke does not report), which would imply "that Jason had some standing in the city or friends in high places."[21]

(3) They "let them go" (ἀπέλυσαν), which implies that they dismissed the charges of the accusers, perhaps content that they satisfied the accusers and the mob by requiring Jason and his friends to post bail, while putting pressure on the new group at the same time.

17:10　That very night the believers sent Paul and Silas away to Berea. When they arrived, they went to the synagogue of the Jews (οἱ δὲ ἀδελφοὶ εὐθέως διὰ νυκτὸς ἐξέπεμψαν τόν τε Παῦλον καὶ τὸν Σιλᾶν εἰς Βέροιαν, οἵτινες παραγενόμενοι εἰς τὴν συναγωγὴν τῶν Ἰουδαίων ἀπῄεσαν). The Berea episode begins with a travel notice and a report on the proclamation of the gospel by Paul and Silas in that city (vv. 10 – 12). The Thessalonian believers,

---

18. Craig S. de Vos, *Church and Community Conflicts: The Relationships of the Thessalonian, Corinthian and Philippian Churches with Their Wider Civic Communities* (SBLDS 168; Atlanta: Scholars Press, 1999), 156 – 57.

19. Herbert Musurillo, ed., *The Acts of the Christian Martyrs II* (orig. 1972; repr., Oxford: Clarendon, 2000), 86 – 87.

20. Adrian Nicolas Sherwin-White, *Roman Society and Roman Law in the New Testament* (orig. 1963; repr., Winona Lake, IN: Eisenbrauns, 2000), 95 – 97. The passive voice of the verb "we were orphaned" in 1 Thess 2:17 confirms that Paul's departure from Thessalonica was forced on him; cf. Abraham J. Malherbe, *The Letters to the Thessalonians* (AB 32B; New York: Doubleday, 2000), 61. In 1 Thess 2:18 Paul attributes his inability to return to Thessalonica to the supernatural force of Satan, which may allude to the actions of the politarchs.

21. Dunn, *Beginning from Jerusalem*, 680 n. 105; cf. Malherbe, *Thessalonians*, 63.

who evidently knew all along where Paul and Silas were, send them away to Berea. Thus, Paul and Silas leave Thessalonica, acknowledging the danger that the activities of their Jewish and Gentile opponents constitute both for themselves and for the new community of believers, who might find life in the city easier once the two visitors have left. Note the circumstances of their departure: they leave immediately, during the night.

As was his custom (v. 2), Paul attends the meetings of the synagogue in Berea. The temporal participle (παραγενόμενοι) suggests that the synagogue service, which Paul and Silas go to after their arrival in the city, is the very next meeting of the Jews of Berea.

17:11 These Jews were more open-minded than those in Thessalonica; they received the message with much goodwill, examining the Scriptures daily to see if these things were true (οὗτοι δὲ ἦσαν εὐγενέστεροι τῶν ἐν Θεσσαλονίκῃ, οἵτινες ἐδέξαντο τὸν λόγον μετὰ πάσης προθυμίας καθ᾽ ἡμέραν ἀνακρίνοντες τὰς γραφὰς εἰ ἔχοι ταῦτα οὕτως). Luke describes the Jews of Berea with three verbs, comparing them with the Jews of Thessalonica: they were more "open-minded" (εὐγενέστεροι) and thus more ready to listen;[22] they "received" (ἐδέξαντο) the word of God[23] with much goodwill, i.e., without prejudice; they were "examining" (ἀνακρίνοντες)[24] the Scriptures to establish the plausibility, or truth, of Paul's message.

The temporal phrase "daily" does not describe the frequency of the regular meetings in the synagogue of the entire Jewish community but the frequency of Paul's interaction with Berean Jews. Their interest was such that every day some Jewish people were willing and eager to discuss with Paul the content of his message. The synagogue (see on 6:9) was a place of study where the scrolls with "the Scriptures" (αἱ γραφαί) were kept — either in Hebrew, or in Greek translation, or both — and where members of the Jewish community as well as visiting Jewish teachers could consult the texts. Since Paul explained from the Scriptures that Jesus was the Messiah whose death and resurrection must be understood as an integral part of God's plan, it was only appropriate that the Berean Jews would examine the scriptural proofs adduced by Paul in order to ascertain whether "these things" (ταῦτα), i.e., Paul's assertions, "were true."

17:12 Many of them came to faith, including prominent Greek women and many men (πολλοὶ μὲν οὖν ἐξ αὐτῶν ἐπίστευσαν καὶ τῶν Ἑλληνίδων γυναικῶν τῶν εὐσχημόνων καὶ ἀνδρῶν οὐκ ὀλίγοι). Luke notes the conversion of "many" (πολλοί) of them, i.e., a large number of Jews[25] and a large number[26] of Greeks, both men and "prominent Greek women." The conversion of many Greeks suggests that Paul proclaimed the gospel not only in the synagogue but in other venues as well, such as in the marketplace (as in Athens, cf. v. 17), unless all Greek converts were God-fearers and other sympathizers with the Jewish faith whom he en-

---

22. The term εὐγενής here does not denote "being of high status, *well-born, high-born*, but "having the type of attitude ordinarily associated with well-bred persons, *noble-minded, open-minded*" (BDAG). The translation "(these Jews were) more noble" (ESV, RSV) is ambiguous; the translation "of more noble character" (TNIV, NIV) suggests that moral virtues are in view, which is not likely. The focus is on their behavior in the meetings of the synagogue; cf. GNB, NET, NLT, "more open-minded;" NRSV, "more receptive;" Fitzmyer: "better disposed;" Johnson: "more refined."

23. For "word" (λόγος) as referring to the message of the

gospel about Jesus as Israel's Messiah and Savior, see on 4:29.

24. Here the term ἀνακρίνω does not denote "conduct a judicial hearing, *hear a case, question*" (as in 4:9; 12:19, 24:8; 28:18), but "engage in a careful study of a question, *question, examine*" (BDAG; cf. LSJ, s.v. ἀνακρίνω II.3).

25. Contrast v. 4: in Thessalonica only "some of them" (τινες ἐξ αὐτῶν); i.e., only a few Jews came to faith.

26. The literal expression "not a few" (οὐκ ὀλίγοι; cf. ESV, RSV) is a litotes that means "many" (thus most English versions; cf. also 1:5).

countered in the synagogue meetings. Both Jews and Gentiles, men and women, ordinary people as well as members of the elite, came to faith in Jesus as Israel's Messiah and Savior of humankind.

17:13 When the Jews in Thessalonica learned that Paul proclaimed the word of God in Berea, they came there too, inciting and unsettling the crowds (ὡς δὲ ἔγνωσαν οἱ ἀπὸ τῆς Θεσσαλονίκης Ἰουδαῖοι ὅτι καὶ ἐν τῇ Βεροίᾳ κατηγγέλη ὑπὸ τοῦ Παύλου ὁ λόγος τοῦ θεοῦ, ἦλθον κἀκεῖ σαλεύοντες καὶ ταράσσοντες τοὺς ὄχλους). Luke narrates the opposition that the missionaries encounter and their eviction from the city (vv. 13 – 15) at greater length than the missionary work in Berea (vv. 10d – 12). Luke first notes the arrival of Jews from Thessalonica, who had heard — evidently through their contacts in the city — that Paul was now active in Berea. Since they had successfully accused Paul, his associates, and his followers as acting in violation of imperial decrees and had him evicted from Thessalonica, they are bound to be confident that they can rid Berea of Paul as well. What Paul proclaimed as "the word of God," they believed to be both contrary to the Scriptures and positively dangerous for the Jewish community and for society more generally. What happened in Thessalonica happens in Berea — the Jewish opponents of the missionaries incite and unsettle (cf. v. 8) the crowds in the city. The present tense of the participles here indicates that their efforts to disrupt and terminate the preaching of Paul in Berea took some time to be successful.

17:14 Immediately thereafter the believers sent Paul away to the coast, while Silas and Timothy stayed there (εὐθέως δὲ τότε τὸν Παῦλον ἐξαπέστειλαν οἱ ἀδελφοὶ πορεύεσθαι ἕως ἐπὶ τὴν θάλασσαν, ὑπέμεινάν τε ὅ τε Σιλᾶς καὶ ὁ Τιμόθεος ἐκεῖ). The Berean "believers" (οἱ ἀδελφοί) who intervened were either Jewish Christians who re-

ceived information about the plans of the visiting Thessalonian Jews, or the prominent Greek female converts who may have learned from their husbands that Berean citizens were planning legal action against Paul, or more generally the believers who realized that the situation was getting too dangerous for Paul. The adverb translated "immediately" (εὐθέως) should not be related to the coming of the Jews from Thessalonica but to the events following their arrival, i.e., to their success, after some time of agitating the crowds, in mobilizing people living in Berea (whether official citizens or freedmen) to move against Paul, who seems to have been the main target of the growing opposition.

Silas and Timothy are able to "stay" (ὑπέμειναν) in the city, while the Berean believers send Paul away to the coast, accompanied by several believers (v. 15). The journey to the sea suggests that they plan to take Paul to safety by ship. The closest harbors were in Methone and Pydna on the Thermaic Gulf in the Plain of Katerini, reached by a two-day journey along the southern end of the Plain of Bottiaia, skirting Mount Titarion.

In 20:4 Luke mentions a Berean believer named Sopater son of Pyrrhus as a member of the party that accompanied Paul on his final journey back to Jerusalem. If Paul was accompanied from Berea to the coast and on to Athens by one of the leading believers, it is not impossible that it was this Sopater who helped lead Paul to safety. If he is identical with Sosipater mentioned in Rom 16:21, he would have been a Jewish believer — a possibility that might explain why Paul was taken to Athens, where his first activity is to proclaim the gospel in the synagogue (17:17). As the Jewish believers of Thessalonica had (probably) introduced Paul to the Jews of Berea, the Jewish believers of Berea may have introduced Paul to the Jews of Athens.

17:15 Those who accompanied Paul brought him to Athens and left with instructions for

Silas and Timothy to join him as soon as possible (οἱ δὲ καθιστάνοντες τὸν Παῦλον ἤγαγον ἕως Ἀθηνῶν, καὶ λαβόντες ἐντολὴν πρὸς τὸν Σιλᾶν καὶ τὸν Τιμόθεον ἵνα ὡς τάχιστα ἔλθωσιν πρὸς αὐτὸν ἐξῄεσαν). The believers who take Paul to the Macedonian coast bring him to Athens in the province of Achaia. Since Paul wants to continue his missionary work with the help of Silas and Timothy, who have stayed behind in Berea (v. 14), he sends the Berean believers back with the instruction that Silas and Timothy "join him as soon as possible," i.e., as soon as they think that the consolidation of the emerging community of followers of Jesus have made sufficient progress that they can function on their own.

It is unclear where Paul wants his associates to join him. If Athens was the next objective of Paul's missionary work, he would be asking them to join him there. If Athens is only a stopover on the way to Corinth as the next major center of missionary activity, he would have instructed them to travel to Corinth. It is in fact in Corinth that Silas and Timothy join him again (18:5), which does not prove, however, that Athens was not intended as a location for missionary work. Silas and Timothy could have traveled to Athens in the hope of meeting up with Paul there, only to be informed by Athenian believers (cf. 17:34) that Paul had moved on to Corinth. The instructions of Paul and the ministry and travel of Silas and Timothy and of the Berean believers foreshadow the correspondence between Paul and the Thessalonian believers and more generally "the network of communication Paul was soon to establish for his churches."[27]

Theology in Application

With the two episodes of Paul's missionary work in Thessalonica and in Berea, Luke emphasizes several points that remain significant for pastors and teachers in local churches as well as for evangelists and missionaries.

The Invariability of the Gospel

Peter proclaimed Jesus as Israel's Messiah who had to die and whom God raised from the dead in Jerusalem. Paul proclaimed the same message in Antioch (13:23–30), and he preached the same message in Thessalonica (17:3). The good news that the church proclaims is always the good news of Jesus, the crucified and risen Messiah and Savior, who died and rose from the dead so that sinners can have forgiveness of their sins, find salvation, receive God's Spirit, and be granted eternal life. This good news is proclaimed to, and believed by, both Jews and Gentiles, ordinary people and members of the aristocracy.

While the manner of presentation of the gospel may differ — Paul engages in conversation, proclamation, discussion, argumentation, and exposition of Scripture (17:2–3, 11) — the content of the message invariably remains the same: it is the good news of God's revelation in and through Jesus, Israel's Messiah and Savior. The "word of the Lord" (16:32) is proclaimed as the "word of God" (17:13). Authentic contextualization of the gospel does not mean that the content of the gospel message is changed.

The Authority of the Scriptures

Luke emphasizes Paul's argumentation as being based on the Scriptures in connection with his mission in Thessalonica and by implication with his mission in Berea (17:2, 11). While it is a matter of course that Jews who teach in a synagogue setting read, explain, and argue with the Scriptures, Luke's report underlines the importance of tying the preaching of the gospel with convictions that the listeners have, and in particular with what they regard as normative authority. In a Jewish context, this authority is Scripture, whose books pious Jews accept as words from God.

At the same time one must not forget that Paul's argumentation with Scripture was much more than a tactical move. He was himself utterly convinced that the Scriptures are God's Word. They not only inform us about Israel's past and announce God's plan of redemption to remove the curse that resulted from the fall of Adam and Eve, a hope that became reality in and through Jesus, the promised Messiah and Savior, but also the authority of Scripture is confirmed by Jesus (Matt 5:17 – 20; Luke 24:32, 45 – 46) and by the apostles (Acts 2:22; 3:18, 21 – 25; 10:43). The proclamation of Jesus as Messiah and Savior receives its integrity not from the pathos of the preacher but from its agreement with the Scriptures as God's Word.[28]

The Constancy of Opposition

While Jews and Gentiles, ordinary people and members of the elite, are being converted in the cities in which Paul preaches, the reaction to the gospel is always mixed. Sometimes only a few Jews come to faith in Jesus as Messiah; sometimes many Jews become believers, although it is never *all* Jews who accept the gospel as God's truth confirmed by the Scriptures. Sometimes only a few Greeks believe; sometimes a large number of Greeks believe, although it is never *all* Gentiles in a city who come to faith. The mixed response is not due to the more or less successful application of specific methods of evangelism, but to the unpredictability of the hardness of the listeners' hearts.

In Thessalonica and Berea the mixed reaction was not faith on the one hand and indifference on the other, but conversions of some listeners and opposition by others — just as in Paul's earlier missionary ministry in Damascus, Jerusalem, Pisidian Antioch, Lystra, Iconium, and Philippi. In Thessalonica and Berea certain Jews remained unconvinced by Paul's message and organized the opposition against Paul,

28. Cf. Andrew T. B. McGowan, *The Divine Authenticity of Scripture: Retrieving an Evangelical Heritage* (Downers Grove, IL: InterVarsity Press, 2008). For a study of the significance of Scripture for Paul's ethical and pastoral teaching cf. Brian S. Rosner, *Paul, Scripture and Ethics: A Study of 1 Corinthians 5 – 7* (Grand Rapids: Baker, 1999).

succeeding in starting riots and legal maneuvers to force him to leave, with other believers fearing for his safety. The opposition can come from Paul's coreligionists, and
it can come from civic and political authorities and institutions. The charges against
the missionaries may be grounded in reality to some degree — Paul's proclamation
of Jesus as Messiah and of his kingdom can be construed as presenting a rival to the
emperor in Rome and his demands for loyalty — or they may be exaggerated and
extreme, drawing on stereotypes.

These charges were effective for Paul's enemies and harmful for missionaries
and for the church. But a gospel proclamation that is never offensive is, perhaps,
never authentic. In churches in the Western world, where greed is part and parcel
of the inner workings of capitalist societies, it may be impolitic to emphasize Paul's
insistence that greed amounts to idolatry (Eph 5:5; Col 3:5) because it contradicts
the character of God, the love of Jesus Christ, and the new life of those who have
committed themselves to Jesus Christ (Eph 5:1 – 2; Col 3:1 – 4).[29]

The Reality of Solidarity

In Thessalonica, Jason extends hospitality to Paul and his associates (17:7). He
and other believers share the consequences of the opposition directed against Paul,
suffering for the gospel by being dragged before the authorities, being identified with
the accused troublemakers, and being forced to post bail for Paul (17:6, 9). Both in
Thessalonica and in Berea the local believers are concerned for the safety of the missionaries whom they send to other cities (17:10, 14) — in the latter case providing
escorts across provincial boundaries (17:15). The church is a community based on
the principle of solidarity, the solidarity of brothers and sisters in the same family; it
is not merely a community of common interests but a community with a common
life and a common destiny. As Paul asserts in 1 Cor 12:26, "If one part suffers, every
part suffers with it; if one part is honored, every part rejoices with it."

---

29. Cf. Brian S. Rosner, *Greed as Idolatry: The Origin and
Meaning of a Pauline Metaphor* (Grand Rapids: Eerdmans,
2007), passim.

Acts 17:16 – 34

Literary Context

The Athens episode (17:16 – 34) is the first episode of Luke's report of Paul's missionary work in Achaia, with the Corinth episode (18:1 – 22) as the second episode one, which ends Luke's narrative of Paul's mission in Europe (15:35 – 18:22). After Paul attempted, unsuccessfully, to reach cities in the province of Asia and in the province of Pontus-Bithynia (15:35 – 16:10), he received a divine call to travel to Macedonia, where he proclaimed the gospel of Jesus Christ in Philippi, Thessalonica, and Berea (16:11 – 17:15). In each of these cities, Paul and his associates were forced by local opposition to leave and to find other locations for missionary work. Berean Christians had taken Paul to Athens, probably in the spring of AD 50, presumably connecting him with local contacts in the synagogue.

Many scholars claim that Paul did not intend to proclaim the gospel in Athens or establish a church there; his preaching was an ad hoc reaction to the idols on display in the city. While not impossible, this interpretation does not seem likely, given the length of Luke's account of Paul's stay in Athens (17:16 – 34),[1] Paul's teaching in the local synagogue, his preaching in the agora (17:17), and the long summary of his speech to the Areopagus Council (17:22 – 31). Paul's missionary work in Athens was not unsuccessful, as many have claimed.[2] Luke mentions two converts by name (Dionysius, a member of the Areopagus Council, and a certain woman named Damaris), and he refers to "others" who came to faith in Jesus Christ (17:34).[3]

---

1. The Athens episode comprises 372 words of Greek text; compare (also in words of Greek text) Luke's narrative of Paul's missionary work in Ephesus (775), Pisidian Antioch (705), Philippi (544), Corinth (391), Lystra (241), Cyprus (230), Thessalonica (167), Berea (136), Iconium (116), Derbe (17), and Perge (14).

2. Cf. Ramsay, *St. Paul the Traveller*, 252; Dunn, *Beginning from Jerusalem*, 692.

3. The fact that Luke mentions the names of two converts is significant since he specifies only one convert by name for Paphos (Sergius Paullus; 13:7, 12), for Philippi (Lydia; 16:14), for Thessalonica (Jason; 17:6), and for Corinth (Crispus; 18:8), and he mentions no names of converts for Pisidian Antioch, Iconium, Lystra, Derbe, Perge, Berea, or Ephesus.

Main Idea

The Athens episode emphasizes that preachers of the gospel approach people wherever they can be found and whatever their social identity, that the proclamation of the gospel involves seeking points of agreement and stating points of disagreement, and that Christian beliefs involve truths about God, about human beings, about the world, and about Jesus.

Translation

Acts 17:16 – 34

16a	Setting: Time	While Paul was waiting for them
b	Setting: Place	in Athens,
c	Event	**his spirit was provoked**
d	Cause	when he saw
e	Explanation	that the city was full of cult images.
17a	Action	**So he argued**
b	Place	in the synagogue
c	Sphere	with the Jews and
d	Sphere	the God-fearers and
e	Place	in the agora
f	Time	day by day
g	Sphere	with those who happened to be there.
18a	Character entrance	**Some Epicurean and**
b	Character entrance	**Stoic philosophers**
c	Action	**debated with him;**
d	Action	**some said,**
e	Question	*"What is this scavenger trying to say?"*
f	Action/Contrast	**Others said,**
g	Assertion	*"He seems to be a preacher of foreign deities."*

h	Explanation	**They said this**
i	Cause	because he was preaching the good news about Jesus and
j		the resurrection.
19a	Action	**So they took him**
b	Action	**and brought him**
c	Place	to the Areopagus,
d	Action	where they said,
e	Question	*"May we know*
f		*what this new teaching is*
g		*that you are presenting?*
20a	Assertion	*For you are introducing foreign ideas to our ears,*
b	Request	*and so we would like to know*
c	Indirect question	*what they mean."*
21a	Aside	*Now* **all the Athenians and**
b	List	**the foreigners who lived there**
c	Description	**spent their time doing nothing but talking and**
d	Description	**listening to new ideas.**
22a	Action	*So* **Paul stood up**
b	Place	**in the midst of the Council of the Areopagus**
c	Action (speech)	**and said,**
d	Address	*"People of Athens,*
e	Assertion	*I recognize*
f	Content	*that you are most religious in every way.*
23a	Setting: Time	*For as I walked around*
b	Setting: Action	*and looked carefully at the objects of your worship,*
c	Event	*I even found an altar*
d	Description	*on which was inscribed,*
e	Quotation (inscription)	*'To an unknown god.'*
f	Description	*What you worship as unknown,*
g	Assertion	*this I am proclaiming to you.*
24a	Assertion	*The God*
b	Description	*who created the world and*
c	List	*everything in it,*
d	Description	*he who is the Lord of heaven and*
e	List	*earth,*
f	Assertion	*does not live in temples*
g	Description	*built by human hands.*
25a	Assertion	*Nor is he served by human hands,*
b	Condition	*as if he needed anything.*
c	Action	*Rather, he himself gives everyone life and*
d	List	*breath and*
e	List	*everything else.*
26a	Action (Review of history)	*From one man he made all the nations*
b	Purpose	*to inhabit the earth;*
c	Action	*he determined fixed times and*
d	List	*the boundaries of their lands*

Continued on next page.

Continued from previous page.

27a	Purpose	so that they would seek God
b	Purpose	and perhaps feel around for him
c	Purpose	and find him,
d	Concession	even though he is not far from any one of us.
28a	Assertion	For in him we live and
b	Restatement	move and
c	Restatement	have our being,
d	Verification	as some of your own poets have said,
e	Quotation	'We too are his offspring.'

29a	Cause	Since we are God's offspring,
b	Inference	we should not think
c	Negation	that the divine being is like gold or
d	List	silver or
e	List	stone,
f	Restatement	an image carved with human skill and
g	Means	imagination.
30a	Time/Concession	While God has overlooked the times of ignorance,
b	Action	now he commands all people
c	Place	everywhere
d	Purpose	to repent.
31a	Action (Prophecy)	For he has set a day
b	Time/Action	when he will pass judgment
c	Sphere	on the world
d	Means	with justice
e	Agency	by the man
f	Identification	whom he has appointed.
g	Verification	He has given proof of this to everyone
h	Assertion (Means)	in that he raised him from the dead."

32a	Setting: Time	When they heard of the resurrection of the dead,
b	Action	**some scoffed,**
c	Action/Contrast	while **others said,**
d	Assertion	"We will hear you again about this subject."
33	Action	**At that point Paul left them.**
34a	Action	**Some men joined Paul**
b	Action	and **came to faith,**
c	Description	including Dionysos,
d	Identification	a member of the Council of the Areopagus,
e	Description	and a woman
f	Identification	named Damaris,
g	Description	and others with them.

Structure and Literary Form

The Athens episode consists of five incidents. (1) Luke reports Paul's missionary activity in the synagogue and in the agora (17:16 – 17). While preaching and teaching in the local synagogue was Paul's custom (see on 17:2), and while he had proclaimed the gospel before Gentile audiences before, the specific reference to the agora of Athens in which Paul established contact with Athenians is a new feature of Luke's narrative, as is his reference to the fact that Paul here engages in missionary work alone, without coworkers (v. 16). (2) Luke relates an encounter with Epicurean and Stoic philosophers in the agora (v. 18), a section that could be combined with vv. 16 – 17 but is better viewed as a separate incident marking the transition from the ongoing missionary ministry of Paul in the city to the appearance before the Areopagus Council. (3) The next incident is the invitation extended to Paul to appear before the Areopagus Council (vv. 19 – 21). (4) This is followed by Paul's speech before the Areopagus Council (vv. 22 – 31). (5) The final incident relates the aftermath of the speech and the conversions of several individuals (vv. 32 – 34).

The episode is a *narrative* reporting missionary work, with a *summary* of missionary activity in the synagogue and in the agora (v. 16 – 17), the report of a speech that Paul is invited to give before one of the venerated councils of the city of Athens (vv. 22 – 31), and a reference to conversions (v. 34). The narrative includes *direct speech* for Epicurean and Stoic philosophers (v. 18), for members of the Areopagus Council (vv. 19 – 20, 32), and for Paul (vv. 22 – 31). While Luke relates that Paul's exposition of his beliefs was met with ridicule (v. 32), there is no reference to Jewish or Gentile opposition that forces him to leave the city. While there is no specific reference to the establishment of a church, Luke mentions the names of two converts, which is rare and thus significant.

The Areopagus speech (vv. 22 – 31) is the fourth speech of Paul narrated by Luke.[4] It resembles his speech before pagans in Lystra (14:15 – 17). However, the brevity of Luke's summary of the Lystra speech and the different context — in Lystra, Paul argues that he and Barnabas should not be accorded divine honors, whereas in Athens Paul explains that he is not introducing new deities into Athens — makes the comparison of the two speeches difficult. The Areopagus speech is best divided into three parts: (1) introduction (*exordium*, vv. 22 – 23), with a commendation of the audience (*captatio benevolentiae*) and a summary of the subject matter (*propositio*); (2) proofs (*argumentatio* or *probatio*, vv. 24 – 29), with an exposition of Paul's views concerning God as the Creator of the human race and concerning God on whom all human life depends; (3) conclusion (*peroratio*, vv. 30 – 31), with the emphasis that God the Creator commands all people everywhere to repent.

---

4. Cf. 13:7 – 11 (Paphos); 13:16 – 41 (Pisidian Antioch); 14:15 – 18 (Lystra).

Parallels in Paul's letters are found in the following statements of the speech.[5]

1. Some of the statements about God (vv. 23 – 25) are similar to Rom 1:4, 19 – 20, 23; 2:5, 16.
2. The reference to God's revelation in creation (vv. 26 – 27) has a parallel in Rom 1:19.
3. The accusation that Gentiles have abandoned the worship of the true God by venerating images (v. 29) is found in the New Testament only here and in Rom 1:23.
4. The references to repentance and to God's forbearance on account of the Gentiles' ignorance (v. 30) are found in Rom 3:25 – 26; 1 Cor 15:15, 34; 1 Thess 1:9.
5. The reference to a coming day of judgment, for which God has appointed a man on account of the fact that he rose from the dead (v. 31), has a parallel in Rom 1:4; 2:5, 16.

Orators who were invited by the magistrates of a city to demonstrate their rhetorical abilities and their philosophical orientation were usually given a day's notice to prepare their declamation on a predetermined topic. They would compose the declamation, write it down, memorize it, and present it without reliance on notes to the audience. Since such declamations were often copied and circulated in the city in the early imperial period, it is not impossible that the speech of 17:22 – 31 is the summary of a written source.[6]

Exegetical Outline

→ **I. The Mission in Athens (17:16 – 34)**

    A. The Proclamation of the Gospel in the Synagogue and in the Market (17:16 – 17)

        1. The provocation of the idols in Athens (17:16)

        2. Paul's teaching in the synagogue before Jews and God-fearers (17:17a-d)

        3. Paul's teaching in the agora before the people of Athens (17:17e-g)

    B. The Discussion with Athenian Philosophers (17:18)

        1. The encounter with Epicurean and Stoic philosophers (17:18a-c)

        2. The irritated reaction of some intellectuals (17:18d-e)

        3. The assumption that Paul is introducing new deities (17:18:f-g)

        4. Paul's teaching of the news about Jesus, the crucified and risen Savior (17:18h-i)

    C. The Invitation to Appear before the Areopagus Council (17:19 – 22c)

        1. Paul's invitation to the Areopagus Council (17:19a-c)

        2. Query concerning the foreign deities that Paul is introducing to Athens (17:19d – 20)

        3. Comment on the Athenians' quest for new things (17:21)

---

5. Baum, "Paulinismen," 424 – 33.

6. Cf. Bruce W. Winter, *Philo and Paul among the Soph-* ists (SNTSMS 96; Cambridge: Cambridge Univ. Press, 1997), 149 – 51.

4. Paul's presentation before the council (17:22a-c)

D. Paul's Speech before the Council of the Areopagus (17:22d – 31)

1. Introduction (17:22d – 23)

   a. Address: "People of Athens" (17:22d)

   b. Opening commendation of the audience: The Athenians' religiosity (17:22e-f)

   c. Summary of Paul's exposition (17:23)

      i. Existence in Athens of an altar dedicated to "an unknown god" (17:23a-e)

      ii. The fact that he proclaims no foreign deity (17:23f-g)

2. The truth about God the Creator, the human race, and the presence of God (17:24 – 29)

   a. Description of God the Creator (17:24 – 25)

      i. The Creator God made the universe and is Lord of heaven and earth (17:24a-e)

      ii. The Creator God does not live in man-made temples (17:24f-g)

      iii. The Creator God does not need sacrifices (17:25a-b)

      iv. The Creator God gives and sustains life (17:25c-e)

   b. Description of God the Creator, who created the human race (17:26 – 27)

      i. The human race is one due to its origins (17:26a-b)

      ii. The human race was created to inhabit the earth in its diversity (17:26c-d)

      iii. The human race was created to be in fellowship with God (17:27)

   c. Description of God the Creator, on whom all human life depends (17:28 – 29)

      i. Human existence is rooted in God (17:28)

      ii. Human worship must not confuse God with images (17:29)

3. The truth about God the Creator, who commands all to repent (17:30 – 31)

   a. Recapitulation: God overlooks the times of ignorance (17:30a)

   b. Assertion: God commands all people to repent (17:30b-d)

   c. Grounds: God will judge the world (17:31)

      i. God has determined the day of judgment (17:31a-d)

      ii. God has appointed the judge (17:31e-f)

      iii. This judge is qualified due to his resurrection from the dead (17:31g-h)

E. The Aftermath of the Speech and Conversions (17:32 – 34)

1. The reaction of the members of the Areopagus Council (17:32)

   a. The ridicule of some members of the council (17:32a-b)

   b. The interest of some members of the council (17:32c-d)

2. Paul's departure from the Areopagus Council (17:33)

3. Conversions in Athens (17:34)

   a. The conversion of some Athenians (17:34a-b)

   b. The conversion of Dionysos, a member of the Areopagus Council (17:34c-d)

   c. The conversion of Damaris (17:34e-f)

   d. The conversion of other Athenians (17:34g)

Explanation of the Text

17:16 While Paul was waiting for them in Athens, his spirit was provoked when he saw that the city was full of cult images (ἐν δὲ ταῖς Ἀθήναις ἐκδεχομένου αὐτοὺς τοῦ Παύλου παρωξύνετο τὸ πνεῦμα αὐτοῦ ἐν αὐτῷ θεωροῦντος κατείδωλον οὖσαν τὴν πόλιν). The city of Athens was five hundred years past its prime when Paul arrived in AD 50. The golden age of Athens was the so-called Pentekontaetia, the Great Fifty Years from the end of the campaign of Xerxes (479 BC), who burned the Acropolis and almost completely destroyed the lower city, to the beginning of the Pelopponesian War (431 BC). After Augustus emerged victorious from his civil war, he visited Athens repeatedly and helped finance the rebuilding of temples and civic buildings. In gratitude, the Athenians erected a temple of Roma and Augustus on the Acropolis between 27 – 17 BC, honoring the emperor with an inscription that describes Augustus as "Savior and Benefactor." Some estimate the size of the population of Athens in the first century at 30,000 people. Jews lived in Athens since the fourth century BC.

Luke's report about Paul's missionary work in Athens begins with a comment on Paul's thoughts regarding the statues representing deities that the Athenians worshiped: he "was provoked" (παρωξύνετο) when he saw that the city was full of cult images.[7] This verb can be understood in terms of becoming irritated or angry, which leads to translations such as "distressed" (NRSV, TNIV), "greatly upset" (GNB, NET), or "annoyed" (Fitzmyer). The definition "cause a state of inward arousal" implies a possible positive meaning: Paul's "spirit" (πνεῦμα) may not have been simply stimulated by the emotion of anger because of the idolatry of the Athenians and of grief concerning the people who did not know or worship the one true God, but — at the same time — by a desire to convert them.

Since Athens was one of the oldest cities Paul visited, the number and the diversity of cult images may have exceeded anything he had seen. If the theater of Ephesus alone displayed twenty-nine gold statues of Artemis and 120 statues of Nike and Eros, the temples and the public spaces of Athens would certainly have been endowed with many more visualizations of the deities that the Athenians worshiped. Pliny reckons that in his day the city of Rhodes had 73,000 statues, with "no fewer" in Athens and in the temple cities of Olympia and Delphi.[8] Obviously, a Jewish teacher would not be counting the number of statues of gods and goddesses on display, but he would be provoked by even a single act of devotion to a god he knew did not exist.

The context and thus the cause and purpose of Paul's reaction to the cult statues on display in Athens depend on the interpretation of the genitive absolute phrase at the beginning of v. 16: the "waiting" (ἐκδεχομένου) in Athens for Timothy and Silas to arrive from Macedonia, where they were consolidating the new churches in Thessalonica and Berea.[9] This is often used to prove that the following events that Luke relates "were the result of accident rather than a set missionary plan."[10] As

---

7. The adjective translated "full of cult images" (κατείδωλον) occurs only in Christian texts. LSJ suggests as an alternative translation "given to idolatry." For "cult image" or "idol" (εἴδωλον) see on 15:20.

8. Pliny, *Nat.* 34.36; cf. Mary Beard and John Henderson, *Classical Art: From Greece to Rome* (Oxford: Oxford Univ. Press, 2001), 83.

9. See the introduction to this section; cf. 17:14 – 15; 1 Thess 3:1 – 2. Luke relates in 18:5 that Silas and Timothy joined Paul in Corinth, arriving from Macedonia.

10. Johnson, *Acts*, 312.

we have noted in the introduction to this episode, this view, while not impossible, is not plausible. Luke's report of Paul's activities in Athens begins with a summary reference to his teaching in the local synagogue (v. 17), which indicates that v. 16 is not written to explain Paul's activities in Athens but serves as a backdrop for Luke's focus on the question of the Areopagus Council, whether Paul will add other deities to the pantheon of gods whose temples, altars, and images dominated the skyline and infrastructure of the city.

17:17 So he argued in the synagogue with the Jews and the God-fearers and in the agora day by day with those who happened to be there (διελέγετο μὲν οὖν ἐν τῇ συναγωγῇ τοῖς Ἰουδαίοις καὶ τοῖς σεβομένοις καὶ ἐν τῇ ἀγορᾷ κατὰ πᾶσαν ἡμέραν πρὸς τοὺς παρατυγχάνοντας). Luke summarizes Paul's missionary activity in Athens. The coordinating conjunction translated "so" (μὲν οὖν) denotes continuation; here, as often in Acts, it introduces a development in the narrative[11] and thus is not necessarily the result of the provocation of the cult images mentioned in v. 16. Whatever Paul's original intentions were, the fact that he engaged Jews and God-fearers in the synagogue and Greeks in the agora demonstrates that he did what he had been doing in every city he visited: explaining to Jews and Gentiles the gospel of Jesus Christ (v. 18).

Luke mentions two locations where Paul taught — the synagogue and the agora — and three groups of people whom he engaged regarding the message about Jesus — Jews, God-fearers, and Greeks. Paul customarily began his outreach in the synagogue (see 17:2) on the Sabbath.[12] As he had done in other synagogues — Damascus (9:20 – 22), Pisidian Antioch (13:16 – 41), and Thessalonica (17:2 – 3)

— he sought to convince the Jews and the "God-fearers" (οἱ σεβόμενοι)[13] present that Jesus is Israel's Messiah and Savior, crucified and raised from the dead according to God's plan of salvation revealed in the Scriptures.

Luke does not record the reaction of the Jews of Athens to Paul's proclamation of the message about Jesus. His narrative focuses instead on his missionary teaching in front of Greek audiences in the agora, which eventually results in an invitation to appear before the Areopagus Council (vv. 19 – 21), an invitation he accepts and engages in (vv. 22 – 31).

The second location of Paul's activity, then, is the agora, the central plaza of Athens (i.e., the forum of Roman Athens rather than the new Roman market). Paul's discussions with Epicurean and Stoic philosophers presumably took place in the Stoa Poikile, the "Painted Stoa" built in the 470s BC, a true public building that was a popular meeting place used, among others, by philosophers.[14] Looking south across the agora, Paul would have seen a large number of temples with their cult images and altars dedicated to the worship of Zeus, Athena, Aphrodite, Apollo, Ares, Hephaistos, the Mother of the gods, Nike, the twelve gods, mystery religions, and the emperor Augustus — for a missionary an intense stimulus not for touristic excitement but for evangelistic urgency and zeal (v. 16). The comment in v. 18 indicates that Paul proclaimed the death and resurrection of Jesus, the Savior who bestows eternal life, as "good news" for the Greek population of Athens (cf. 13:46 – 47).

Luke describes Paul's teaching before Jewish audiences in the synagogue and before Greek audiences in the agora with the same term: "he

---

11. BDAG, s.v. μέν 2e; cf. Barrett, *Acts*, 828. See Gaventa, *Acts*, 248, who correctly points out that the "so" that NRSV (and other translations) have at the beginning of v. 17 should not be allowed to "misleadingly suggest that Paul goes to the synagogue in reaction to Athenian idolatry."

12. See 13:5, 14; 14:1; 16:13; 17:10, 17; 18:4, 19; 19:8; 28:17, 23.

13. Cf. 10:2; 13:43; see 10:21 – 22 on the God-fearers.

14. John M. Camp, *The Archaeology of Athens* (New Haven: Yale Univ. Press, 2001), 68 – 69.

argued" (διελέγετο; see on 17:2), which suggests a dialogical style of teaching, instructional discourses that allowed the audience to ask questions and make comments, although it could also denote a discourse or lecture. The imperfect tense of this verb suggests an extended missionary activity in the Jewish community and among the Athenian population. The prepositional phrase translated as "day by day" (κατὰ πᾶσαν ἡμέραν) marks Paul's teaching in the agora as a habit, which is reinforced by the present participle that describes his audiences as "those who happened to be there" (παρατυγχάνοντας).

17:18 Some Epicurean and Stoic philosophers debated with him; some said, "What is this scavenger trying to say?" Others said, "He seems to be a preacher of foreign deities." They said this because he was preaching the good news about Jesus and the resurrection (τινὲς δὲ καὶ τῶν Ἐπικουρείων καὶ Στοϊκῶν φιλοσόφων συνέβαλλον αὐτῷ, καί τινες ἔλεγον· τί ἂν θέλοι ὁ σπερμολόγος οὗτος λέγειν; οἱ δέ· ξένων δαιμονίων δοκεῖ καταγγελεὺς εἶναι, ὅτι τὸν Ἰησοῦν καὶ τὴν ἀνάστασιν εὐηγγελίζετο). Luke's narrative focuses on Paul's teaching, particularly on Paul's encounter with Epicurean and Stoic philosophers.

The verb Luke uses to describe this encounter ("debated" [συνέβαλλον]) is not a technical term for a philosophical discussion; initially this verb meant to "throw together" and thus often designated "bring together, unite, collect, contribute"; in the last sense it can mean to "contribute one's opinion to a discussion," which fits the context here. The philosophers contribute their views to Paul's teaching about God's revelation and the necessary response of human beings; thus they "converse" with him, which is another meaning of the term. Used in a negative sense, the term also denotes to "bring people together in a hostile sense," thus "pit against each other, join in a fight, come to blows," and thus could describe the philosophers' contentious challenges to Paul's teaching. Most commentators assume a positive meaning here ("debate, converse"), although some suggest the negative meaning of "challenge."[15]

IN DEPTH: Epicureans and Stoics[16]

The Epicureans believed that the cosmos is the result of accident, that the gods are atomic compounds like every other object, and that the gods live an undisturbed life of happiness without interfering in the affairs of the world through providence. Purpose in the structure of living beings can be explained with the natural movement of the atoms and the survival of the fittest. Moreover, the criterion of the good life of mortal human beings is pleasure, which can be achieved by avoiding the competitive life (with the distress of jealousy and failure) and by avoiding intense emotional commitments (with the pain of emotional turmoil).

---

15. For the latter interpretation cf. Theodor Zahn, *Die Apostelgeschichte des Lucas* (2 vols.; Kommentar zum Neuen Testament 5; Leipzig: Deichert, 1921–22), 602.

16. Cf. John M. Rist, *Epicurus: An Introduction* (Cambridge: Cambridge Univ. Press, 1977); Howard Jones, *The Epicurean Tradition* (London: Routledge, 1989); John M. Rist, *Stoic Philosophy* (Cambridge: Cambridge Univ. Press, 1969); Robert W. Sharples, *Stoics, Epicureans and Sceptics: An Introduction to Hellenistic Philosophy* (London: Routledge, 1996).

Stoic logic was consistently empiricist, tracing knowledge from the impact that "appearances" from the outer world make on the human mind. Stoic physics explain the world in materialistic and deterministic ways. The world consists of material objects whose interactions are controlled by always valid laws or fate. God is present in the material world as the active principle (λόγος) acting on matter (the passive principle) and is thus physically present in all matter as "designing fire" (πῦρ τεχνικόν) or as "spirit" (πνεῦμα). Nothing has existence outside the material world and its principles. There is no spiritual world (as in popular superstitions) and no world of ideas (as in Plato). Everything happens according to providence (which is identified with fate) for the good of the world, which means that evil does not exist (illness and disasters are part of fate and are providential for the well-being of the cosmos). Despite fate, human beings are free in their actions, for which they are thus morally responsible.

Stoic ethics insist that virtue is sufficient for human happiness; virtue is the skill of putting other things and other people to correct use. They insist that nothing except virtue is good and that emotions are always bad. Stoics appeal both to nature and to reason: human beings find happiness when they live in agreement with nature, which is the same as living in agreement with reason. Happiness does not depend on attaining to things that are good (such as health and wealth), but on making the right choices that we have the power to make, applying reason to our judgments. Negative emotions such as fear or grief are false judgments about the world. Happiness is found in being without passions (ἀπάθεια), which can be achieved by accepting matters that are out of our control as being part of nature and thus being self-sufficient.

Luke notes two reactions of Paul's audience. The subject of the phrase translated "some said" could be related in a general sense to people in the audience, or it more likely refers to the Epicurean and the Stoic philosophers mentioned earlier in v. 18. It is not impossible that the first reaction comes from the Epicurean philosophers, who, as materialists and practical atheists, ridicule Paul as a "babbler," and that the second one comes from the Stoic philosophers, who recognize that Paul presents a religious message that is new.

The first reaction is disparaging; note the word "this" (οὗτος), which is often derogatory when used for a person who is present; also note the optative in "trying [to say]" (θέλοι). Some call Paul a "scavenger" (σπερμολόγος).[17] This Greek term, which denotes birds picking up seeds, is used metaphorically for someone "who wanders about the market and collects the scraps and debris scattered here and there."[18] It also describes someone "who is always hunting for news and spreading it everywhere, running his mouth carelessly, who pretends

---

17. BDAG, s.v. σπερμολόγος, "in pejorative imagery of persons whose communication lacks sophistication and seems to pick up scraps of information here and there," suggesting

"scrapmonger, scavenger" as translation.
18. C. Spicq, "σπερμολόγος," *TLNT*, 3:268; see ibid. for the following definition.

to be in the know but actually spouts his gossip without understanding it: an ignoramus" — thus a person "who picks up and retails scraps of knowledge."[19] Most English versions translate the term as "babbler,"[20] which misses the image of unsystematic gathering.[21] In the context of a philosophical discussion about God, the world, and human beings, the interpretation "a third-rate intellectual devoid of method" seems appropriate.[22] Some conclude from Paul's presentation of his convictions about Jesus as Israel's Messiah and Savior of the world that he is a charlatan, an unsystematic collector of the ideas of others.

The second reaction suggests that Paul wants to introduce gods. The term "preacher" (καταγγελεύς) denotes a person who proclaims or announces something. The "foreign deities" (ξένα δαιμόνια) would be gods that are not worshiped in Athens, i.e., gods not represented in Athens with a temple or at least with an altar, whose names would be known from inscriptions on the bases of cult statues, on the architrave of a temple, or on an altar. The word for "deity" (δαιμόνιον) denotes "divine manifestation" or "divine power" and was used to describe lesser divine beings, independent transcendent beings distinguished from a more personal god (θεός).[23]

The plural in "foreign deities" is probably explained by Luke's comment that some voiced this assumption because Paul proclaimed the good news about "Jesus and the resurrection." Some Athenians evidently assumed that this Jewish orator from Tarsus wanted to add two divine beings to the pantheon of deities that Athenians worship: Jesus, a deceased person and thus a "spirit" (the term δαιμόνιον was used of the spirit of the departed),[24] and Anastasis, "The Resurrection" (ἡ ἀνάστασις), perhaps understood as the personification of the afterlife.[25]

Personifications of abstract concepts appeared first in Greek poetry and then found their way into actual cults. Zeus has Themis (Order) and Metis (Wisdom) as consorts, and his daughter is Dike (Justice); Athena carries Nike (Victory) in her hand; Ares, the god of war, is accompanied by Phobos (Fear) and Deimos (Terror), Aphrodite by Eros (Love), Himeros (Yearning), and Peitho (Persuasion).[26] When Paul spoke of Israel's God — of Yahweh, the God of the Jews — this was not a "foreign deity" since he was already worshiped by the Jews living in Athens.

---

19. LSJ, s.v. σπερμολόγος III, suggesting "idle babbler, gossip" as translation.

20. ESV, NIV, NLT, NRSV, TNIV; cf. NASB ("idle babbler"), NET ("foolish babbler"); NJB ("parrot"); cf. Fitzmyer ("chatterer").

21. Thus the critique in BDAG. GNB has "ignorant showoff;" Johnson, Acts, "busybody."

22. Barrett, Acts, 830, suggests "third-rate journalist," where the term "journalist" does not fit the first century. Pervo, Acts, 427, suggests "a bird-brain devoid of method" (referring to Spicq, "σπερμολόγος," 3:268 – 29).

23. Cf. LSJ, s.v. δαιμόνιον I-II. The negative connotation "demon" derives from the application of the Greek term to transcendent powers that are hostile ("evil spirit"). Cf. Burkert, Greek Religion, 179 – 81. Daimon is used for transcendent powers that cannot be named: "Daimon is the veiled countenance of divine activity. There is no image of a daimon, and there is no cult" (ibid. 180).

24. On the cult of the heroized dead in Athens, cf. Homer A. Thompson and Richard E. Wycherley, The Athenian Agora, vol. 14: The Agora of Athens: The History, Shape and Uses of an Ancient City Center (Princeton: American School of Classical Studies at Athens, 1972), 119 – 21.

25. Cf. Bruce, Acts, 377; Richard N. Longenecker, Acts, 981. Critical is Bock, Acts, 562, who argues that "Paul would not be that unclear about a reference to a goddess;" Barrett, Acts, 831, states that Paul would not have referred to "Resurrection" in quasi-personal terms but more probably used verbs ("Jesus was raised from the dead" or "whom God raised from the dead"). This critique misses the possibility that while Paul's teaching regarding resurrection may have been clear for Jews, it may not have been at all clear for Greeks, especially if they thought in abstracts terms of a personification.

26. Burkert, Greek Religion, 184 – 85. In Roman religion, personifications of abstract concepts played a major role; note the cults of Aequitas (Equanimity), Concordia (Harmony),

IN DEPTH: Introducing Foreign Deities

While the population in Greek and Roman cities worshiped many gods and while both cultural and religious tolerance were a significant reality during the Hellenistic period, the proclamation and introduction of foreign gods and cults was not a minor matter, because "in both classical and Hellenistic times the introduction of foreign cults and rites required the official authorization of the state."[27] An Athenian decree stipulated: "The king archon shall fix the boundaries of the sanctuaries/sacred precincts in the Pelargikon, and in the future no one shall found altars, cut the stones from the Pelargikon or take out earth or stones without (the authorization of) the council and the demos." Socrates was accused not only of corrupting the youth but also of introducing alien deities.[28] Isocrates praised the Athenians for guarding "against the elimination of any of the ancestral sacrifices and against the addition of any sacrifices outside the traditional ones."[29] Josephus writes that the Athenians severely punished those who initiated people into the mysteries of foreign gods; this was "forbidden by their law, and the penalty decreed for any who introduced a foreign god was death."[30]

The request to be allowed to introduce a new deity into a city would prompt the magistrates to ascertain the novelty of a cult, the desirability of allowing the cult, and the requirements of the cult, such as the need for a temple, an altar, sacrifices, festivals, priests, and processions. When the Citians wanted to establish a temple of Aphrodite in Athens, a decree was passed that recorded the name of the person who made the motion (a certain Antidodos son of Apollodoros), the decision by the council to have the assembly of the people discuss this matter, the name of the person who put this matter to a vote (Phanastratos), the name of the person who made the motion to decide the matter (Lycurgus son of Lycophron), the request of the Citian merchants to obtain "a plot of land on which they might build a temple of Aphrodite," and finally the decision of the council to give to the merchants of the Citians the use of a plot of land; they cited the precedent of the Egyptians, who were allowed to build a temple of Isis.[31]

Fortuna (Good Fortune), Honos (Fame), Libertas (Freedom), Mens (Understanding), Pietas (Reverence), Salus (Well-Being), Spes (Hope), Victoria (Victory), Virtus (Virtue), and the personification of the city of Rome (Dea Roma).

27. Hendrik S. Versnel, *Ter Unus: Isis, Dionysos, Hermes: Three Studies in Henotheism* (Leiden: Brill, 1990), 122; for the following see ibid., 102 – 31.

28. Xenophon, *Mem.* 1.1.1: "The indictment against him was to this effect: Socrates is guilty of rejecting the gods acknowledged by the state and of bringing in strange deities; he is also guilty of corrupting the youth." Cf. Plato, *Apol.* 11.24B.

29. Isocrates, *Areop.* 30.

30. Josephus, *Ag. Ap.* 2.262 – 268, the quotation ibid. 267. Cf. Euripides, *Bacch.* 255 – 56.

31. Cf. Stephen D. Lambert, "Athenian State Laws and Decrees, 352/1 — 322/1: II Religious Regulations," *ZPE* 154 (2005): 125 – 59, 153.

17:19 – 20 So they took him and brought him to the Areopagus, where they said, "May we know what this new teaching is that you are presenting? For you are introducing foreign ideas to our ears, and so we would like to know what they mean" (ἐπιλαβόμενοί τε αὐτοῦ ἐπὶ τὸν Ἄρειον πάγον ἤγαγον λέγοντες· δυνάμεθα γνῶναι τίς ἡ καινὴ αὕτη ἡ ὑπὸ σοῦ λαλουμένη διδαχή; ξενίζοντα γάρ τινα εἰσφέρεις εἰς τὰς ἀκοὰς ἡμῶν· βουλόμεθα οὖν γνῶναι τίνα θέλει ταῦτα εἶναι). Since Luke does not specify the subject of the verbs translated as "they took him" (ἐπιλαβόμενοι) and "[they] brought him" (ἤγαγον), the reference could be either to the Epicurean and Stoic philosophers mentioned in v. 18, or, which seems more likely, to members of the audience in the agora mentioned in v. 17 who were members of the Areopagus Council or who had contact with members of the council.

While the first verb can denote an arrest, it often has the meaning "take hold of" without the connotation of violence. As the Council questions Paul about the "new teaching" (ἡ καινὴ … διδαχή; v. 19) concerning "foreign ideas" (ξενίζοντα; v. 20) that he was presenting to the Athenians, it seems apparent that he was not arrested. Rather, he is being investigated concerning the foreign gods that he seems to be introducing to the population, an endeavor for which he may need official permission (but which they may refuse to grant). Both the first and the second verbal phrase with which the speaker of the council describes their request (δυνάμεθα γνῶναι; "may we know" v. 19; and βουλόμεθα γνῶναι; "we would like to know" v. 20) express a polite, but certainly forceful request for information and explanation.[32]

17:21 Now all the Athenians and the foreigners who lived there spent their time doing nothing but talking and listening to new ideas (Ἀθηναῖοι δὲ πάντες καὶ οἱ ἐπιδημοῦντες ξένοι εἰς οὐδὲν ἕτερον ηὐκαίρουν ἢ λέγειν τι ἢ ἀκούειν τι καινότερον). Luke's comment on the Athenians' quest for new things is a parenthetical remark to his readers (rare in Acts). The curiosity of "all the Athenians" and of "the foreigners who live there" should not be identified, pure and simple, with the reasons for the request of the Areopagus Council that Paul explain his new teaching. The suggestion that Luke's reference to the Athenians' proverbial curiosity[33] "gives the impression that little at all is at stake" and that Paul is merely invited to appear before the Areopagus "to make his case before a cultured, sophisticated audience"[34] is not plausible. The change of location (vv. 19, 22), the verbs denoting the action of getting Paul to the Areopagus (v. 19), the description of Dionysos as a member of the Areopagus Council (v. 34), and the potential consequences of introducing foreign deities to the Athenians, which Paul seems to be doing (vv. 18, 20), render it unlikely that Paul is merely "sharing the new thought of the day on the hill with those who are there."[35]

Rather, Paul is being asked to explain his "new teaching" concerning "foreign deities" before the guardians of Athenian traditions. The reference to the proverbial curiosity of the Athenians is not necessarily a critique of the people of Athens, accused

---

32. Bruce W. Winter, "In Public and in Private: Early Christian Interactions with Religious Pluralism," in *One God, One Lord in a World of Religious Pluralism* (ed. A. D. Clarke and B. W. Winter; Cambridge: Tyndale House, 1991), 112 – 34, 114 – 15, suggests that the council invited Paul to demonstrate his competence as an orator besides presenting the content of his teaching.

33. Cf. Demosthenes, *Or.* 4.10.43: "Or do you want … to run around and ask one another, 'Is anything new being said? Could there be anything newer?" See also Aristophanes, *Eq.* 1260 – 1263; Thucydides, *Hist.* 3.38.4 – 7. For a negative interpretation of the Athenians' curiosity, cf. Patrick Gray, "Athenian Curiosity (Acts 17:21)," *NovT* 47 (2005): 109 – 16.

34. Gaventa, *Acts*, 250, 249.

35. Bock, *Acts*, 563.

of wasting their time by listening to and talking about the latest fads. Rather, it is morely likely an explanation why the Areopagus Council wishes to hear Paul's new teaching about foreign gods. If the "new ideas"[36] are found to be incompatible with the customs and traditions of the Athenians, then the "talking" and "listening" can easily result in "rejecting" (ἀθετεῖν) and "condemning" (δικάζειν, καταγινώσκειν, κατακρίνειν). The parenthetical remark also allows Luke to establish the rhetorical situation for the following speech, "in which Luke cleverly reverses the expectation of his readers by allowing Paul to demonstrate that in proclaiming the true identity of the 'unknown God' he presents something far from new."[37]

17:22 So Paul stood up in the midst of the Council of the Areopagus and said, "People of Athens, I recognize that you are most religious in every way" (σταθεὶς δὲ ὁ Παῦλος ἐν μέσῳ τοῦ Ἀρείου πάγου ἔφη· ἄνδρες Ἀθηναῖοι, κατὰ πάντα ὡς δεισιδαιμονεστέρους ὑμᾶς θεωρῶ). Standing while speaking was appropriate in an official setting. Paul, having been invited to explain his new teaching about foreign gods, stands "in the midst" (ἐν μέσῳ) of the Areopagus, i.e., in front of the members of the Areopagus Council, who sit in a half circle.

The introduction of Paul's speech (vv. 22d – 23) begins with the address of the members of the council: they are "people of Athens" (ἄνδρες Ἀθηναῖοι) — Athenian men who represent the people of Athens.[38] What follows is the customary opening commendation of the audience (*captatio benevolentiae*): Paul acknowledges the Athenians' religiosity with an expression translated "most religious" (ὡς δεισιδαιμονεστέρους). The Greek term means "fearing the gods"; it can be used positively in the sense of "pious, religious," or in the negative sense of "superstitious."[39] Used in the opening line of an address before the council, it can hardly have the denigrating sense of "superstitious." Luke underlines the proverbial piety of the Athenians[40] with the comparative form of the adjective (used for the elative or superlative), and with the prepositional phrase translated as "in every way" (κατὰ πάντα). Paul mentions the basis for what he "recognizes" concerning the religious devotion of the Athenian people in the next verse.

17:23 For as I walked around and looked carefully at the objects of your worship, I even found an altar on which was inscribed, "To an unknown god." What you worship as unknown, this I am proclaiming to you (διερχόμενος γὰρ καὶ ἀναθεωρῶν τὰ σεβάσματα ὑμῶν εὗρον καὶ βωμὸν ἐν ᾧ ἐπεγέγραπτο· Ἀγνώστῳ θεῷ. ὃ οὖν ἀγνοοῦντες εὐσεβεῖτε, τοῦτο ἐγὼ καταγγέλλω ὑμῖν). Paul states the theme and argument of his speech (*propositio*) with a historical comment derived from personal observation and with a succinct assertion.

First, Paul points out that he has seen the objects of worship — statues, altars, shrines, and temples — that express the Athenians' piety; he notes in

---

36. The adjective translated as "new ideas" (καινότερον), which is a comparative, is taken as a positive; understood as a superlative, it would mean "the latest news." BDAG, s.v. καινός 2, suggests "something quite new" (= "the latest thing").

37. Béchard, *Paul outside the Walls*, 383; cf. Parsons, *Acts*, 245.

38. For the mode of address cf. 1:16. NRSV translates "Athenians"; NIV, "people of Athens"; most versions have "men of Athens." Barrett suggests "gentlemen of Athens."

39. LSJ, s.v. δεισιδαίμων. Cf. C. Spicq, "δεισιδαίμων," *TLNT*,

1:305 – 8: the favorable meaning is "religion and reverence toward the deity" while the pejorative meaning is "superstitious and punctilious," the latter being much more commonly attested.

40. Josephus calls the Athenians "the most pious [εὐσεβεστάτους] of the Greeks" (*Ag. Ap.* 2.130). Pausanias writes in the second century, "and they are conspicuous not only for their humanity but also for their devotion to religion [θεοὺς εὐσεβοῦσιν]" (*Descr.* 1.17.1).

particular that he saw the altar dedicated to the worship of "an unknown god." Read against the notion that he is proclaiming foreign deities (vv. 18, 19 – 20), Paul is careful to point out that he "walked around" (διερχόμενος) the city and "looked carefully" (ἀναθεωρῶν)[41] at the objects that were part of the cultus of the Athenians, suggesting, perhaps, that he knows which gods the Athenians worship and which temples, shrines, and altars are part of the religious and social infrastructure of the city. During his tour through the streets and plazas of the city, including the structures on the Acropolis, he found an altar on which two Greek words were inscribed: "To an unknown god" (Ἀγνώστῳ θεῷ).

Second, Paul asserts that this god whom the Athenians "worship" (εὐσεβεῖτε)[42] as "unknown" (ἀγνοοῦντες) is the God he proclaims[43] in the agora. In other words, he is not introducing a "foreign deity" (v. 18) or a "foreign idea" (v. 20); rather, he is declaring and explaining a divine being that is already present in the city and worshiped by the Athenians, a deity whose name, spheres of influence, power, and forms of appearance are unknown to them.

Luke's summary of Paul's speech before a philosophically, historically, and rhetorically trained audience exhibits what can be called points of connection (agreement, contextualization) and points of contradiction (disagreement, decontextualization). While Luke's language is remarkably reminiscent of Epicurean and especially Stoic philosophy, he is not simply providing a "Greek interpretation" of biblical revelation, presenting orthodox Stoicism. While there are indeed points of contact with Stoic and Epicurean philosophy, Paul also critiques the orthodoxy of contemporary popular philosophy on the basis of Scripture. Paul clearly distinguishes philosophical religion (or religious philosophy) and biblical revelation, referring to common notions and contradicting the elements that are contradicted by the revelation of Scripture.[44]

Epicurus believed that knowledge of the divinity is a function of human reason: it is "according to the notion of God indicated by the common sense of mankind … for there are gods, and the knowledge of them is manifest."[45] The Epicurean philosophers in Paul's audience would have understood his argument that the "unknown god" can be known.

This point of agreement, apparent on the surface of Paul's point, is contradicted by biblical revelation. If biblically literate Jews could have heard Paul address the members of the Areopagus Council with these words, the reference to the "unknown god" would have reminded them of the dialogue between the one true God and the nations who do not know Israel's God, described by the prophet Isaiah (Isa 45:15, 18 – 25). After repeating Israel's monotheistic confession, "Truly you are a God who has been hiding himself, the God and Savior of Israel" (Isa 45:15), Isaiah narrates a speech in which Yahweh seeks to convert the peoples to worshiping the one true God. If Israel's God appears to be hidden and thus an unknown God, Yahweh's works as Creator prove that he is not in hiding at all:

> Thus says the Lord who created the heaven, he is the God who formed the earth and made it; he established it, he did not create it without purpose, rather he formed it to be inhabited: I am the Lord, and there is no other [ἐγώ εἰμι, καὶ οὐκ ἔστιν ἔτι]. I did not speak in secret, in a land of darkness; I did

---

41. The two present participles emphasize Paul's deliberate inspection of the religious objects in the city.

42. The verb εὐσεβέω denotes acts and attitudes of pious reverence toward the gods (LSJ); BDAG, s.v. εὐσεβέω, defines the verb this way: "to show uncommon reverence or respect, *show profound respect for someone*."

43. For καταγγέλλω see 4:2; the term denotes "to declare, proclaim" something.

44. Cf. Schnabel, *Early Christian Mission*, 2:1392 – 404.

45. Epicurus, *Ep.* 3.123.

not say to the offspring of Jacob, "You have sought me in vain." I am the Lord, I speak the truth, I declare what is right. (Isa 45:18 – 19 LXX)

Yahweh goes on to state that the nations "have no knowledge" and that "those who carry about their wooden idols" are praying to "gods that cannot save" (πρὸς θεοὺς οἳ οὐ σῴζουσιν), since "I am God, and there is no other god besides me [ἐγὼ ὁ θεός, καὶ οὐκ ἔστιν ἄλλος πλὴν ἐμοῦ], a righteous God and a Savior; there is no one besides me" (Isa 45:20 – 21 LXX). This truth leads to an invitation: "Turn to me and you will be saved, all [people] from the ends of the earth! For I am God, and there is no other [ἐγώ εἰμι ὁ θεός, καὶ οὐκ ἔστιν ἄλλος]. By myself I have sworn, from my mouth has gone forth in righteousness a word that shall not return: 'To me every knee shall bow, every tongue shall swear'" (Isa 45:22 – 23 LXX). Read in the light of this dialogue between Yahweh and the nations, Jewish listeners would recognize that the reference to Athenian religiosity and to the altar of an "unknown god" was intended as a commendation on the surface only.

17:24 The God who created the world and everything in it, he who is the Lord of heaven and earth, does not live in temples built by human hands (ὁ θεὸς ὁ ποιήσας τὸν κόσμον καὶ πάντα τὰ ἐν αὐτῷ, οὗτος οὐρανοῦ καὶ γῆς ὑπάρχων κύριος οὐκ ἐν χειροποιήτοις ναοῖς κατοικεῖ). The main body of Paul's speech (vv. 24 – 29) begins, in a first line of argument, with a description of God the Creator as the God whom Paul proclaims in the city (vv. 24 – 25). The existence in the city of an altar dedicated to the worship of an unknown god (or unknown gods) provides an opening for the explanation of the God whom Paul proclaims in Athens — a God who is already present and a God who is the one (and only) God who created the world.

First, Paul insists that he proclaims the one God who created the universe. The term translated "the world" (ὁ κόσμος) denotes the universe, the sum total of everything that exists. The reference to "everything" that the world contains (πάντα τὰ ἐν αὐτῷ) — all inanimate objects such as the stars, mountains, rivers, seas, and all animate objects such as plants, animals, human beings, spirits — removes any exceptions from the scope of the creational activity of the God Paul proclaims. This truly cosmic dimension is reinforced by a description of "world": both heaven (οὐρανός) and earth (γῆ), i.e., the sun, the moon, the stars, and the spirits as well as animals, plants, and human beings. Since the one God created everything without exception, he "is" (ὑπάρχων) the "Lord" (κύριος) of the entire cosmos.

The Stoics apparently followed a fixed order in their discussions of reality: first they prove that the gods exist; then they discuss their nature and show how they order the world before they explain how they care for the well-being of mankind.[46] Paul argues similarly: as the creator, God is the Lord of heaven and of the earth (v. 24), he gives to human beings life and everything they need to live (v. 25), and he cares for people as he determines the times of their existence and the boundaries of the places where they live (v. 26). While the Stoics spoke of the gods in their plurality and diversity, they were also able to speak of "god" (θεός) in the singular. Cleanthes, the successor of Zenon, begins his hymn to Zeus with these lines:

> Noblest of immortals, many-named, always all-powerful Zeus, first cause and ruler of nature, governing everything with your law, greetings! For it is right for all mortals to address you: for we have our origin in you, bearing a likeness to God, we, alone of all that live and move as mortal creatures

---

46. Thus Quintus Lucilius Balbus, a Stoic philosopher, according to Cicero, *Nat. d.* 2.3.

on earth. Therefore I shall praise you constantly; indeed I always sing of your rule.[47]

The Stoic philosophers in Paul's audience would not have been bothered by Paul's use of the articular noun "the God" (ὁ θεός). Moreover, the Stoics believed in divine providence; they argued that the gods rule the world by their providence, demonstrated by the divine wisdom and power, the nature of the world, the miracles of nature, and the care of the gods for human beings. Paul could agree with these convictions, as the description of "the God" as "Lord" suggests (see also Paul's statements in vv. 25–26). However, Paul would have been concerned with the Stoics' easy transition from "god" to the "gods." As his reference to the one ancestor of the human race (v. 26) clarifies, Paul does not proclaim a philosophical concept of divine reality and divine providence; rather, he teaches about the one true God of biblical revelation who created the heavens and the earth.[48]

Second, Paul insists that because the one God who created the universe is the Lord of the heavens and the earth, he does not live (οὐκ … κατοικεῖ) in temples built "by human hands" (χειροποιήτοις), i.e., by human beings. The infinitely powerful Creator of the universe cannot be confined by walls and columns constructed by finite human beings. The point of contact with the Stoic philosophers was their conviction that the gods do not live in temples that human beings had built. Plutarch writes that "it is Zenon's teaching that one should not build temples of the gods."[49] The Epicureans rejected what they called "the superstitions" of their contemporaries; they spoke of the psychological effects of false faith in deities, mocking the demean-

ing practices in the cults that one could observe in the temples. Paul similarly criticizes the notion that God lives in temples that human beings have erected for their gods.[50]

The implicit point of contradiction is the fact that Paul derives this conviction not from a philosophical critique of the religious convictions and practices of his contemporaries but from the teaching of Scripture, particularly the critique of pagan religious belief and practice by Isaiah. This prophet refers to God as insisting: "'Heaven is my throne, and the earth is my footstool. Where is the house that you will build for me? Where will my resting place be? Has not my hand made all these things, and so they came into being?' declares the LORD" (Isa 66:1–2).

17:25 Nor is he served by human hands, as if he needed anything. Rather, he himself gives everyone life and breath and everything else (οὐδὲ ὑπὸ χειρῶν ἀνθρωπίνων θεραπεύεται προσδεόμενός τινος, αὐτὸς διδοὺς πᾶσι ζωὴν καὶ πνοὴν καὶ τὰ πάντα). Paul continues his exposition of the God whom he proclaims in Athens — the one God who is already present in Athens as the unknown God whom the Athenians acknowledge — with two further assertions.

Third, Paul asserts that God the Creator does not need sacrifices. God the Creator is "not served [οὐδὲ … θεραπεύεται] by human hands." This verb has the basic meaning of "be an attendant to, do service" and often denotes "do service to the gods." The most basic and most frequent service provided "by human hands" for the gods was the offering of sacrifices; details of what was expected were often

---

47. Johan Carl Thom, *Cleanthes' Hymn to Zeus: Text, Translation, and Commentary* (Studien und Texte zu Antike und Christentum 33; Tübingen: Mohr Siebeck, 2005), 40.

48. Cf. Gen 1:1; 14:19, 22; Exod 20:11; Ps 146:6 (LXX 145:6); Isa 42:5; in Jewish texts cf. Wis 9:1, 9; 11:17; 2 Macc 7:23, 28; 4 Macc 5:25; 1QH I, 13–15; Philo, *Creation*; Josephus, *Ant.* 1.27.

49. Plutarch, *Mor.* 1034B; cf. Euripides, frag. 968: "What house fashioned by builders can contain the divine form within enclosing walls?" Lucian, *Sacr.* 11, ridicules the idea that the gods require shelter.

50. Compare the same point made by Stephen in 7:48.

inscribed on the walls of the sanctuary (which specific animals, with or without wine or incense, etc., were to be offered). Other "services" that worshipers rendered to the gods included the payment for and erection of cult statues, altars, dedicatory inscriptions honoring a specific deity, bas-reliefs, and painted frescoes; the bathing of cult images in water; carrying images on parades through the city; and dressing cult images in rich clothes.

The reason, Paul argues, why the one God the Creator does not need sacrifices or any other services is the fact that he does not need anything. There is nothing that human beings have or can do that God the Creator needs. Paul agrees with the Epicureans, who rejected the offering of sacrifices to the gods with the argument that a deity does not need human things.[51] Paul also agreed with the Stoics, such as Seneca:

> Let us forbid men to offer morning salutation and to throng the doors of temples; mortal ambitions are attracted by such ceremonies, but god is worshipped by those who truly know him. Let us forbid bringing towels and flesh-scrapers to Jupiter, and proffering mirrors to Juno; for god seeks no servants. Of course not; he himself does service to mankind.[52]

At the same time, Paul's critique of pagan sacrifices and other devotional acts is again biblically informed. In Israel's worship, the people of the one true God were regularly reminded of God's sovereign independence of human beings: "If I were hungry I would not tell you, for the world is mine, and all that is in it. Do I eat the flesh of bulls or drink the blood of goats?" (Ps 50:12–13).[53] When Josephus recounts Solomon's prayer on the occasion of the dedication of the temple in Jerusalem, he prays, "Not by deeds is it possible for men to

return thanks to God for the benefits they have received, for the Deity stands in need of nothing and is above any such recompense" (*Ant.* 8.111). Human beings need to be served (including those who built temples, sculpture statues, and offer sacrifices), not the one God who created the heavens and the earth.

Fourth, Paul asserts that God the Creator gives and sustains life. He not only created the world, but continues to give (διδούς; present active participle) to everyone "life" (ζωή, i.e., existence), "breath" (πνοή, i.e., continued existence), and "everything else" (τὰ πάντα) that human beings need for their existence. Paul agreed with the Stoics who affirmed that God is the source of all life. The quotation of Seneca noted above continues:

> Everywhere and to all he is at hand to help. Although a man hear what limit he should observe in sacrifice, and how far he should recoil from burdensome superstitions, he will never make sufficient progress until he has conceived a right idea of god — regarding him as one who possesses all things, and allots all things, and bestows them without price.

At the same time, Paul has derived his conviction of God's sustaining all life from the creation narrative at the beginning of the first book of the Scriptures, which speaks about God's forming the first human being from the dust of the ground, breathing into him "the breath of life" (πνοὴν ζωῆς), with the result that he became "a living being" (ψυχὴ ζῶσα; Gen 2:7). In addition, Paul knows what the prophet Isaiah proclaims: "This is what God the LORD says — the Creator of the heavens, who stretches them out, who spreads out the earth with all that springs from it, who gives breath to its people, and life [LXX πνεῦμα, spirit] to those who

---

51. Euripides, *Herc. fur.* 1345–46: "For God, if indeed God he be, is in need of nothing." Cf. Philodemus, *Piet.*, frag. 38; Plutarch, *Mor.* 1052A.

52. Seneca, *Ep.* 95.48–49.
53. Cf. 2 Macc 14:35.

walk on it" (Isa 42:5). The implication of Paul's assertion is that human beings understand the nature and identity of the human race only when they understand "its fundamental dependence upon God, with the corollary that such an understanding calls for appropriate worship."[54]

17:26 From one man he made all the nations to inhabit the earth; he determined fixed times and the boundaries of their lands (ἐποίησέν τε ἐξ ἑνὸς πᾶν ἔθνος ἀνθρώπων κατοικεῖν ἐπὶ παντὸς προσώπου τῆς γῆς, ὁρίσας προστεταγμένους καιροὺς καὶ τὰς ὁροθεσίας τῆς κατοικίας αὐτῶν). The second line of argument (vv. 26 – 27) in the main part of Paul's speech before the Areopagus Council focuses on the description of God as the Creator of the human race. In the Greek text, vv. 26 – 27 from one single sentence. Paul advances three points.

First, Paul asserts that the human race is one on account of its origins. God "made" (ἐποίησεν), i.e., created,[55] the whole human race. The prepositional phrase translated as "from one man" describes the origins of mankind; all human beings, to whatever nation they may belong, have one common ancestor. Without specifically referring to Adam or citing Gen 1:27 – 28 or 2:7, Paul clearly alludes to the biblical creation account (cf. Rom 5:12): God created all the nations of the earth from one man, Adam, the father of all human beings. The fact that all human beings have one common origin signifies the unity of "all the nations."

General references to "Greek philosophical thinking about the one and the many"[56] do not constitute a point of agreement with the Stoic or Epicurean philosophers in the audience; there is no parallel for the notion of a common ancestor of the entire human race in Greek or Roman mythology. If we assume that the educated listeners in the Areopagus Council, who were certainly aware of the presence of a Jewish community in Athens, had some knowledge of Jewish cosmology, they would have realized at this point of Paul's speech that the God whom Paul proclaims in Athens is indeed not a foreign deity but the God of the Jews, whose holy Scriptures claim that the human race began with the creation of Adam, the first human being, brought into existence by God. This human race inhabits, as one, the earth.[57]

Second, Paul asserts that the human race was created by God to inhabit the earth in all its diversity. God "determined" not only the existence of human beings but also the conditions of their existence. The terms translated "seasons" (καιροί) and "boundaries" (ὁροθεσίαι) can have a philosophical or a historical meaning. Interpreted in terms of a natural philosophy, the "fixed times" denote the seasons of the year,[58] while the "boundaries of their lands" refers to the inhabitable zones of the earth.[59] If this is Paul's meaning, then he agrees here with Cicero, who regarded the seasons and the zones of the earth as evidence of the existence of god; in the Stoics' exposition of divine providence, they argued that "the revolutions of the sun and moon and other heavenly bodies" contribute to "the maintenance of the structure of the world," including the seasons.[60]

However, the context does not speak of proofs of God from nature; rather, the adjectival passive

---

54. Dunn, *Beginning from Jerusalem*, 687.

55. In Gen 1:1 LXX, ἐποίησεν translates the Hebrew term *bārāʾ*, "to create."

56. Fitzmyer, *Acts*, 609.

57. The phrase "on the face of the earth" (lit.; ἐπὶ παντὸς προσώπου τῆς γῆς) imitates LXX Greek (cf. Gen 1:28; 2:6; Jdt 2:7, 19).

58. See 14:17; Gen 1:14 LXX; Wis 7:18; 1QM X, 12 – 16;

Philo, *Creation* 59; Plutarch, *Mor.* 378 – 79; IG XIV 1018. Cf. LSJ, καιρός III.2a.

59. Walter Eltester, "Gott und die Natur in der Areopagrede," in *Neutestamentliche Forschungen für R. Bultmann* (ed. W. Eltester; BZNW 21; Berlin: Töpelmann, 1954), 202 – 27, 209 – 12, suggests the boundaries of the land against the sea; cf. Gen 1:9 – 10; Pss 74:17; 104:9; Job 38:8 – 11; Prov 8:28 – 29.

60. Cicero, *Tusc.* 1.28.68 – 69 and *Nat. d.* 2.155.

participle (προστεταγμένους) better fits the meaning "times" in the sense of "periods of history," and Luke is closer to historians than to philosophers, which means that a historical interpretation of v. 26c-d is more plausible. Thus, the "fixed times" are the various epochs in the history of the nations,[61] and the "boundaries of their lands" are the political boundaries between the places where people live — whether cities, regions, provinces, or continents.[62] Paul argues that cities, countries, and empires rise and fall during the course of history, both in terms of their political power and in terms of their political boundaries. The God whom Paul proclaims is the Creator of the world and of the human race, and he is the Lord of the history of the human race. This argument would have been recognized and accepted as valid by the Stoics, who argued that the gods rule the world by their providence (see on v. 24).

17:27 So that they would seek God and perhaps feel around for him and find him, even though he is not far from any one of us (ζητεῖν τὸν θεόν, εἰ ἄρα γε ψηλαφήσειαν αὐτὸν καὶ εὕροιεν, καί γε οὐ μακρὰν ἀπὸ ἑνὸς ἑκάστου ἡμῶν ὑπάρχοντα). Paul continues his argument that he does not proclaim a foreign god, a deity that would need to be formally introduced to the Athenians, because he is already "here."

Third, Paul asserts that the human race was created by God so that people are in fellowship with him. Beyond the (physical and) historical existence of the human race, God created human beings so that they would "seek" (ζητεῖν) him, i.e., that they would try to find him. The use of this verb here implies that human beings do not know God and do not know how or where to find God, but it also implies that they desire to find him and have a relationship with him.[63] The introduction of the speech (vv. 22 – 23) reflects Paul's acknowledgment that the Athenians, including the educated members of the Areopagus Council, are searching for God.

The verb translated as "find" (εὕροιεν) indicates "confidence in the possibility of successful seeking."[64] The conditional clause it is in, however, signals uncertainty concerning the outcome of humankind's search for God. (1) The verb translated "feel around" (ψηλαφήσειαν), which denotes "to look for something in uncertain fashion," is sometimes used for the groping around of a blind man who has difficulties finding the object that he seeks to touch or hold. (2) The optative of the verbs "feel around" (ψηλαφήσειαν) and "find" (εὕροιεν), combined with the conditional conjunction (εἰ),[65] strengthened with a marker (here) of indirect questions (ἄρα) — translated "and perhaps" — implies an element of questioning and expectation that may or may not be answered.[66]

Paul adds a participial clause that is either concessive[67] or intensive[68] in which he states that God

---

61. Cf. 1:7; 3:20; Luke 21:24. Note Dan 2:21: "He changes times and seasons; he deposes kings and raises up others." Cf. NRSV ("he allotted the times of their existence"); NIV ("their appointed times in history"), NLT ("he decided beforehand when they should rise and fall").

62. Gen 10; Job 12:23; Dan 2:21; Deut 32. Cf. NIV 1984, "the exact places where they should live;" the translation "the boundaries of their lands" (NIV) seems to focus on geographical (or even agricultural) units, whereas the Greek term (κατοικία) denotes the place(s) where people live; the verb denotes "to live in a locality for any length of time, *live, dwell, reside, settle (down)*" (BDAG, s.v. κατοικέω 1).

63. Cf. Deut 4:29; Pss 14:2; 53:2; Isa 55:6; 65:1; Wis 13:6. See Rom 1:19 – 25.

64. Barrett, *Acts*, 844.

65. Fourth class conditionals express "a possible condition in the future, usually a remote possibility" (Wallace, *Greek Grammar*, 699).

66. Wis 13:5 – 9 voices similar doubts.

67. BDF §425 n. 1. Cf. NASB, NET, NIV, NLT, NRSV, TNIV ("though").

68. BDAG, s.v. καί 2iβ. Cf. ESV, RSV ("yet"); also Martin M. Culy and Mikeal C. Parsons, *Acts: A Handbook on the Greek Text* (Waco: Baylor University Press, 2003), 340: "who seek God, who is really not far from any one of us."

is "not far" from any human being. The present active participle (ὑπάρχοντα) expresses the continued presence of God in his creation, indeed among the human race. This statement establishes a further point of contact with members of the Areopagus Council versed in Stoic philosophy, which asserted the presence of the divine in the world. Seneca formulated that "god is near you, with you, in you."[69] At the same time, Jewish listeners would have recognized the implied conviction that even though the pagans search for God, they have not found him, and even though God is "near" to them, they have not encountered him — they do not hear his voice, he does not save them. This is the implication of Moses' rhetorical question in Deut 4:7 ("What other nation is so great as to have their gods near them the way the LORD our God is near us whenever we pray to him?"), and of the statement in Ps 145:18 – 20:

> The LORD is near to all who call on him,
>   to all who call on him in truth.
> He fulfills the desire of those who fear him;
>   he hears their cry and saves them.
> The LORD watches over all who love him,
>   but all the wicked he will destroy.[70]

17:28 For in him we live and move and have our being, as some of your own poets have said, "We too are his offspring" (ἐν αὐτῷ γὰρ ζῶμεν καὶ κινούμεθα καὶ ἐσμέν, ὡς καί τινες τῶν καθ' ὑμᾶς ποιητῶν εἰρήκασιν· τοῦ γὰρ καὶ γένος ἐσμέν). After Paul has explained that the God whom he proclaims in Athens is the God who has created the world and who thus needs neither temples nor sacrifices (vv. 24 – 25), and that God created the human race with the purpose that human beings would live in fellowship with him (vv. 26 – 27), his third line of argument (vv. 28 – 29) presents two statements about God the Creator, on whom all human life depends.

First, Paul asserts that the existence of the human race is rooted in God (v. 28). He describes human existence with three verbs. We human beings "live" (ζῶμεν); i.e., we are alive physically; we "move" (κινούμεθα); i.e., we are living beings who are in motion, not stationary objects; we "have our being" (ἐσμέν); i.e., we exist. This sentence is often regarded as a quotation[71] from a hymn to Zeus composed by Epimenides of Crete (ca. 600 BC)[72] or from Posidonius.[73] These suggestions are not convincing; the triadic formulation that emphasizes the complete dependence of human beings on God for their existence and their lives "is not a veiled poetic quotation, but a combination that must be ascribed to Paul or Luke."[74]

The members of the Areopagus Council, knowledgeable as they certainly were regarding Stoic philosophy, probably would have understood the

---

69. Seneca, *Ep.* 41.1; cf. Dio Chrysostom, *Or.* 12.27 – 28; 30.26.

70. On the nearness of Yahweh see also Pss 34:18; 139:5 – 10; Jer 23:23 – 24.

71. Most English translations mark both v. 28a-c and v. 28e as a quotation (ESV, NIV, NRSV, RSV, TNIV); NIV in a footnotes notes this is from "the Cretan philosopher Epimenides"; GNB is most consistent in adding the phrase "It is as some of your poets have said" before the (alleged) quotation in v. 28a-c. Exceptions are NASB, NET, NLT.

72. Cf. Bruce, *Acts*, 384 – 85; cf. Lynn A. Kauppi, *Foreign but Familiar Gods: Greco-Romans Read Religion in Acts* (JSNTSup 277; London: T&T Clark, 2006), 83 – 93, who sees an allusion to Aeschylus's *Eumenides*.

73. Hildebrecht Hommel, "Neue Forschungen zur Areopagrede Acts 17," *ZNW* 46 (1955): 145 – 78, sees Plato, *Tim.* 37C as the source of the sentence, mediated through Posidonius.

74. Bertil Gärtner, *The Areopagus Speech and Natural Revelation* (Lund: Gleerup, 1955), 195; cf. Barrett, *Acts*, 846 – 47; similarly Fitzmyer, *Acts*, 610, who regards the suggested Greek parallels as "farfetched" and asserts that this tricolon reflects "an old and frequent pattern in the Greek language, with nothing particularly philosophical about it, even through the tricolon was also used in Greek philosophical writing (Plato, *Soph.* 248E – 249A; Aristotle, *De an.* 414A 12 – 13). This Lucan tricolon is an echo of neither Platonic nor Stoic philosophy."

initial prepositional phrase translated "in him" (ἐν αὐτῷ) in a spatial sense and related it to god, the active principle (λόγος) physically present in all matter as spirit (πνεῦμα). They would thus understand the triadic formulation in terms of the life, the movement, and the existence of humankind "in god" in a pantheistic (or panentheistic) sense, i.e., in terms of the immanence of all human beings in the all-pervasive divine principle.[75] While Stoics in the audience may have seen a point of agreement, Paul likely understood the prepositional phrase in an instrumental sense ("by him"), in which case the triadic formulation is not an argument for humankind's ontological connectedness with deity but a biblical reference to God's act of creation through which human beings came into existence, who are thus both dependent on him and close to him — expressed in Hellenistic philosophical terminology.

Paul does use a quotation from Aratus of Soli in Cilicia (ca. 300 BC) to emphasize that human beings are not only close to God, but related to him as his kin. The statement "we too are his offspring" (τοῦ γὰρ καὶ γένος ἐσμέν) is taken from Aratus's astronomical poem *Phaenomena* (line 5). Stoics would have agreed with Paul's assertion, understanding the statement in the pantheistic sense that god and human beings are one in the creative power of nature. But in the context of an address in which Paul explains the God whom he proclaims, the quotation from Aratus must be interpreted in the context of his reference to Adam in v. 26. For Paul, the line from Aratus is not an accommodation to the philosophical convictions of his audience but

very aptly chosen since the statement that human-

kind is god's offspring can again be placed within the context of a biblical theology of creation: people are God's offspring since he has created "the one ancestor" from whom he made humankind (v. 26) as the "image of God" (Gen 1:26 – 27; cf. Ps 8:5 – 6). The attempt to integrate the "ignorant" knowledge of the poets into the truth of revelation proves possible on the basis of the theology of creation (v. 24).[76]

17:29 Since we are God's offspring, we should not think that the divine being is like gold or silver or stone, an image carved with human skill and imagination (γένος οὖν ὑπάρχοντες τοῦ θεοῦ οὐκ ὀφείλομεν νομίζειν χρυσῷ ἢ ἀργύρῳ ἢ λίθῳ, χαράγματι τέχνης καὶ ἐνθυμήσεως ἀνθρώπου, τὸ θεῖον εἶναι ὅμοιον). The conclusion from the Aratus quotation introduces the last point of Paul's exposition concerning the God that he proclaims in Athens.

Second, Paul asserts that the worship of the human race must not confuse God with images (v. 29). The fact that human beings are God's offspring — a conviction with which Greeks can agree (v. 28) — leads to the conclusion that we human beings are not under the obligation (οὐκ ὀφείλομεν) to think that the divine being[77] is like a manufactured object. Since human beings have been brought into existence by God, human beings cannot bring a god into existence by their "skill and imagination." The "carved" work of sculptors, bronze artists, and wood carvers who imagine what a divine being looks like and then produce an image made of gold, silver, or stone[78] that is displayed in a temple, in one of the plazas of the city, or in a private house cannot possibly be the God who created human

---

75. The Stoics argued that the substance of god is "the entire world and the heavens" (Diogenes Laertius 7.14, referring to Zeno).

76. Pesch, *Apostelgeschichte*, 2:139.

77. The expression τὸ θεῖον means "divine being, divinity,"

also in the sense of "the numinous" (BDAG, s.v. θεῖος 1b; LSJ, s.v. II).

78. Sculptures were also made of marble, wood, bronze, ivory, and terra-cotta.

beings, including the idol manufacturers. If human beings live and move and exist as a result of being God's offspring, images who exist but who neither live nor move cannot be God — the divine nature cannot be of a lower order.[79]

Imagination and artistic skill can produce works of art but not God. The God who created the universe and the human race — the God whom Paul proclaims to the Athenians — is not "like" (ὅμοιον) these human productions — and certainly not identical with them. Paul's reference to cult images carved with human skill and imagination would have prompted the members of the Areopagus Council to think in particular of the most famous statue of the city, the forty-foot-high, gold-ivory statue of Athena Parthenos by Phidias, made between 447 – 439 BC of gold from the Athenian state treasury, understood as "a self-representation of Athens."[80]

Paul's critique of the manufacture of representations of divine beings and thus of idol images is an indictment of popular piety in the cities of the Greco-Roman world, a piety with which the Stoic and Epicurean philosophers disagreed in theory,[81] but which they accommodated in practice. Both schools had integrated their philosophical convictions with contemporary religiosity with its statues of deities and temples, altars and sacrifices. Epicurus was convinced that popular piety was misguided, but he did not tell his followers to refrain from participating in the local cults.[82] Plutarch accuses the Stoics of contradicting themselves

as they visit the mysteries in the temples and ascend the Acropolis to honor the idol statues and lay down wreaths in the sanctuaries despite their convictions.[83]

If Paul's educated audience in the Areopagus Council agrees with what he asserted in vv. 27 – 28, they are now confronted with a critique of the philosophers' rapprochement with the plurality and diversity of the religious cults (there is only one God, the Creator of the universe and of the human race) and with the reality of the religious cults (the images that are housed in the temples and are the target of the sacrifices offered on the altars do not represent the one true God). This critique of idols is not merely a philosophical argument, however. Paul takes up the biblical and Jewish condemnation of idol makers and of idolatry; images manufactured by human beings are "all false! Their deeds amount to nothing; their images are but wind and confusion" (Isa 41:29). When people turn to their collection of images, they cannot deliver them in a time of need: "The wind will carry all of them off, a mere breath will blow them away" (57:13).[84]

Paul asserts, in other words, that God who created the universe and the human race — the God whom he has been proclaiming in Athens — is incompatible with the religious pluralism and the diversity of gods and idol images on display in Athens (vv. 22 – 23). This demonstrates their religiosity but also their lack of knowledge as regards the one God, the Creator, who is the Lord of heaven and earth (v. 24).

---

79. Barrett, *Acts*, 849.

80. A. Ley, "Athena," *BNP*, 2:239. For a description see Pausanias, *Descr.* 1.24.5 – 7.

81. Cf. David L. Balch, "The Areopagus Speech: An Appeal to the Stoic Historian Posidonius against Later Stoics and the Epicureans," in *Greeks, Romans, and Christians* (FS Abraham Malherbe; ed. D. L. Balch, E. Ferguson, and W. A. Meeks; Minneapolis: Fortress, 1990), 52 – 79, 67 – 72.

82. An Epicurean text asserts that piety cannot be proved by the offering of sacrifices, but then goes on to argue that of-

fering to the gods is permitted since it is in agreement with religious traditions (see P. Oxy II 215; dated ca. AD 50). Cf. André J. Festugière, *Epicurus and his Gods* (orig. 1955; repr., New York: Russell & Russell, 1969), 64 – 65; Winter, "Religious Pluralism," 126.

83. Plutarch, *Moralia* 1034B-C; cf. Seneca, *Ep.* 31.11; Lucretius 1.63 – 80.

84. Cf. Deut 4:28; Isa 40:18 – 20; 41:7; 44:9 – 17; 46:5 – 6; Jer 1:16; 2:26 – 28; 10:2 – 5, 8 – 9; Ps 115:4; Wis 13:10 – 14:11; *Sib. Or.* 3:8 – 45.

17:30 While God has overlooked the times of ignorance, now he commands all people everywhere to repent (τοὺς μὲν οὖν χρόνους τῆς ἀγνοίας ὑπεριδὼν ὁ θεός, τὰ νῦν παραγγέλλει τοῖς ἀνθρώποις πάντας πανταχοῦ μετανοεῖν). In the second main section of his address before the Areopagus Council (vv. 30 – 31), Paul expounds on the truth that God the Creator commands all people to repent — an exhortation that is part of Paul's proclamation in the city of which he has been invited to give an account before this council. The conclusion has three parts: Paul recapitulates his address, he asserts that God commands all people to repent, and he explains that God has already made preparations for the day when he will sit in judgment of the human race.

In view of the question that the Areopagus Council has asked Paul to clarify — whether he is introducing new, foreign deities to the Athenians — it is noteworthy that Paul's concluding remarks do not seek to reassure the council members that they do not need to take action allowing (or prohibiting) the establishment of a new "cult" in the city. Paul ends with a report of God's summons for all people to repent. He does not explicitly apply this summons to repent to the council members, but he formulates it as a report of what God the Creator, whom he proclaims in Athens, orders all people to do. This allows Paul to present a significant element of his message to the council members, albeit indirectly: while God has the right, the authority, and the power to judge people for their failure to know, acknowledge, and worship him, he gives them the opportunity to repent, an opportunity that is connected with the risen Jesus.

First, Paul summarizes the content of his speech. Despite the fact that God the Creator had made the heaven and the earth, creating all living human beings, who should have perceived, acknowledged, and worshiped him, people everywhere have produced images that they worship, imagining that they represent the divine reality. The error of this way of thinking is displayed in Athens as well — observable in the temples, plazas, streets, and private houses of people where homage is paid to thousands of cult images (vv. 22 – 23). Paul's reference to "times of ignorance" (χρόνοι τῆς ἀγνοίας) reminds the audience of the fact that there is an altar in the city where people worship in ignorance (ἀγνοοῦντες) an "unknown god" (v. 23). The identification of this divine being — God the Creator, who made the heaven and the earth and who gives to human beings physical existence — with works of art produced by sculptors, confining them to temples and altars, is an act of ignorance (ἀγνοία).

The assertion that God has "overlooked" (ὑπεριδών) the pluralism of their gods and cults, of their temples and mysteries, of their altars and statues, means that he has so far disregarded the consequences of their thinking and behavior. Even though such ignorance concerning the reality of God the Creator is culpable, God has left it unpunished. Paul regularly spoke about God's merciful willingness not to punish the ignorant, false worship of people. In Lystra, he had made a nearly identical statement: "In past generations he let all the nations go their own ways" (14:16).[85] The description of the proud history of Athens as "times of ignorance" is a bold move that might just be acceptable before the Areopagus Council, whose members were educated and probably philosophically sophisticated enough to concede Paul's point, since it focused not on the role of Athens in the development of democracy but on the religious

---

85. Cf. Rom 3:25; 1 Cor 1:19 – 22. Cf. Barrett, *Acts*, 850 – 51, who states that "from nature the Greeks have evolved not natural theology but natural idolatry."

pluralism of the city that was shared with all cities of the Greco-Roman world. Stoics and Epicureans had been criticizing this pluralism of gods and cults as well, albeit not trying to move people to worship only the one true God who made heaven and earth.

Second, Paul asserts that God the Creator now commands all people to repent. The divine tolerance of "times of ignorance" has come to an end; God "now" commands repentance. The call to repentance signals that their ignorance of the true God whom they acknowledge as the "unknown God" indeed establishes their guilt before God. The present tense of the verb "he commands" (παραγγέλλει) underlines the new reality of God's expectations. All human beings without exception must repent — a divine announcement proclaimed by Paul in the Jewish synagogue and in the agora of Athens and a conviction he does not suppress in his speech before the Areopagus Council. "All people" includes both Jews who worship in synagogues and Gentiles who worship in the multitude of temples in the city, as well as the Stoic and Epicurean philosophers and the educated members of the Areopagus Council.

God directs all people to "repent" (μετανοεῖν; see on 2:38), which means for Gentiles that they recognize their production of cult images, altars, and temples and their worship of these same cult images as mistaken, that they stop producing and worshiping the cult images of the sculptors, that they turn to the one true God, the Creator of heaven and earth, and that they worship only the one whose offspring they are. This call to repentance demonstrates that Paul's ultimate concern was not to advance a philosophical argument that

will compel people to abandon religious pluralism. In view of the fact that God is no longer prepared to tolerate the ignorance of people who do not acknowledge and worship him as the one true God, Paul wants to make people see the need to change religious convictions and behavior. God demands the conversion of all people in the entire world because he is no longer an unknown God — Paul (and other preachers) are now proclaiming the reality of the Creator of heaven and earth.

17:31 "For he has set a day when he will pass judgment on the world with justice by the man whom he has appointed. He has given proof of this to everyone in that he raised him from the dead" (καθότι ἔστησεν ἡμέραν ἐν ᾗ μέλλει κρίνειν τὴν οἰκουμένην ἐν δικαιοσύνῃ, ἐν ἀνδρὶ ᾧ ὥρισεν, πίστιν παρασχὼν πᾶσιν ἀναστήσας αὐτὸν ἐκ νεκρῶν). Paul ends his address by stating the reason[86] for the need to repent. Since the day of judgment on which God will hold all human beings accountable as regards their knowledge and worship of the one, true divine being is approaching, everyone must repent of ignorant and false worship and turn to the one true and living God. Paul presents three facts.

First, God has determined the date when he will sit in judgment over all human beings. The verb translated "he has set" (ἔστησεν) denotes "specify contractually, set/fix a time."[87] The day (ἡμέρα) whose date God has set is the day of judgment. The verb translated as "will" (μέλλει) indicates that the date of this day is at a future point of time. The verb translated "pass judgment" (κρίνειν) is used here as a technical legal term that denotes "engage in a judicial process" and can be translated as "judge, decide, hale before a court" — the court in question

---

86. The conjunction translated as "for" (καθότι) denotes the rationale for something (BDAG, s.v. καθότι 2, "in view of the fact that").

87. BDAG, s.v. ἵστημι 6 and 6a, with reference to Acts 17:31; for the next definition cf. BDAG, s.v. ἡμέρα 3 and 3b (where BDAG fails to list Acts 17:31 in 3bβ, "the day of God's final judgment").

being the divine tribunal occupied by God. On that day "the world" (ἡ οἰκουμένη; see on 11:28), i.e., the inhabited world of human beings who are God's offspring (vv. 26 – 29), will be judged.

It goes without saying that the judgment of the one true God who created heaven and earth will be "with justice" (ἐν δικαιοσύνῃ); i.e., it will be fair. The subject of divine judgment was not alien to the Greeks, who believed in and feared the Erinyes, also called the Eumenides (the "Well-Meaning Ones") and the Semnai Theai ("Honored Goddesses"); the Romans call these divine beings the Furiae, conceived of as goddesses (Megaera or "Envious One," Tisiphone or "Avenger of Murder," Allecto or "Irreconcilable One") and as "the angry dead who return in order to punish the living."[88] In Athens, the Erinyes had a temple near the Areopagus. Their vengeance was a fate from which there was no escape. At the same time, the expectation of God's judging the world was an integral part of Israel's faith and Jewish theology.[89] What Paul proclaims is the opportunity of repentance and thus of salvation from the fate of eternal death.

Second, God "has appointed" (ὥρισεν) the judge. This verb is a general term denoting the appointment or designation of a person for a particular task. The "man" (ἀνήρ) who is God's agent of judgment is a reference to Jesus. If indeed Paul avoided mentioning the name of Jesus, he may have wanted to avoid the impression that he proclaimed "foreign deities" (v. 18). If Paul was invited to speak specifically about the question whether he

introduces Jesus and personified Resurrection as new, foreign deities (cf. vv. 18 – 20), then the reference to a "man" is "not a cryptic reference to Jesus, but deliberate correction of the previous Athenian syncretising apprehension of him — failing to appreciate his significance — as a pagan deity to be treated in this frame of reference."[90] The setting of a court date and the appointment of a judge indicated in the cities of the Greek and Roman world that unless there was some intervention where the parties concerned come to an agreement, the case would be taken up in the near future.

Third, the qualification of this "man" for the task of judging the human race has been established on account of his resurrection from the dead. This is the only passage in the New Testament where the word πίστις, usually translated as "faith," means "proof" in the sense of "a token offered as a guarantee of something promised."[91] God proved to all human beings that the judge whom he has appointed to judge the world is fully and uniquely qualified for this responsibility. Human beings can judge other human beings, but not the entire human race; a universal judge needs special proof that he has the necessary credentials. The fact that God raised (ἀναστήσας) Jesus "from the dead" (ἐκ νεκρῶν) means, first, that God has power over the dead; second, that God has the authority to appoint a judge over the living; and third, that the one raised from the dead can legitimately receive the authority to judge the living and the dead.[92] The notion of a (bodily) resurrection from

---

88. S. I. Johnston, "Erynis," *BNP*, 5:34, 35; also Sarah Iles Johnston, *Restless Dead: Encounters between the Living and the Dead in Ancient Greece* (Berkeley/London: Univ. of California Press, 1999), 250 – 87.

89. Cf. Pss 95:11; 98:9; Isa 2:12; 34:8; Dan 7:9 – 11; Joel 2:1 – 2; Amos 5:18; Zeph 1:14 – 2:3; 3:8; Mal 4:1; for Luke see Luke 10:12; 12:46; 17:24, 30; Acts 2:20; for Paul see Rom 2:5, 16; 1 Cor 1:8; Phil 1:6, 10; 1 Thess 5:2 – 4; 2 Thess 1:10; 2:2; 2 Tim 1:18; for other NT writers, see Heb 6:11; 2 Pet 3:10; Rev 20:11 – 15.

90. Stenschke, *Luke's Portrait of Gentiles*, 220.

91. BDAG, s.v. πίστις 1c. For the combination with the verb παρέχω, see Polybius 2.52.4; Josephus, *Ant.* 2.218; 15.260.

92. For the belief that Jesus is the judge of the living and the dead cf. 10:40 – 42. Note the importance of Jesus' designation as "the Son of Man" against the background of Dan 7:13 – 14, where the Son of Man receives judgment and authority from God. Cf. Bock, *Acts*, 570; Bauckham, *Jesus and the God of Israel*, 172 – 73.

the dead was a Jewish conception that the Greeks would have rejected, for they regarded the road to the underworld as a one-way street.

Thus, at the end of his address before the Areopagus Council, Paul expresses his conviction that people who approach the one true God should also approach Jesus: "When one looks to God, Paul says, one will find Jesus."[93] Since God stipulates that all people of the entire world — including the Athenians — will be tried in God's judgment on the court day whose date God has already fixed, before his appointed judge, Jesus, it is ultimately impossible to distinguish between God's action and the action of Jesus. Paul ends his speech with an emphasis on the significance of Jesus. As Paul provides an exposition of the God whom he proclaims — the God acknowledged in Athen as an "unknown god" — he speaks of the one true God and he speaks of Jesus (cf. 1 Cor 8:5 – 6).

17:32 When they heard of the resurrection of the dead, some scoffed, while others said, "We will hear you again about this subject" (ἀκούσαντες δὲ ἀνάστασιν νεκρῶν οἱ μὲν ἐχλεύαζον, οἱ δὲ εἶπαν· ἀκουσόμεθά σου περὶ τούτου καὶ πάλιν). Luke notes the reaction of the members of the Areopagus Council in a brief comment. The reference to the resurrection of the dead in the report of the council's reaction does not indicate that Paul's speech is interrupted as soon as he speaks about the resurrection from the dead or the judge of the world appointed by God (v. 31) — Paul's address is complete. The earlier reaction of ridicule and misunderstanding (vv. 18 – 19) gives way to derision and interest.[94] The cause for the mocking is Paul's

brief but explicit reference to the resurrection of Jesus from the dead. Greeks did not believe in a "standing up" (ἀνάστασις) of the dead.[95]

The concept of a bodily resurrection from the dead[96] — implied in Paul's reference to Jesus as the judge in God's day of judgment — was alien to the Greeks, who believed in the immortality of the soul. Only a small number of the thousands of epigraphs that survive from antiquity expresses any hope in an afterlife; rather, hope was usually expressed in terms of the immortality of the soul, which lives in the heavens or is identified with the stars. The most widely held opinion concerning the afterlife was that "death is nothingness, eternal sleep."[97] People often joked about annihilation at death; many wrote the letters *n.f.n.s.n.c.* on their gravestones, an abbreviation for the phrase *non fui, non sum, non curo* ("I was not, I am not, I care not"). The philosophers taught the "art of dying" in the sense that they taught people to accept their mortality. But other council members express cautious interest, wanting to hear Paul further.

17:33 At that point Paul left them (οὕτως ὁ Παῦλος ἐξῆλθεν ἐκ μέσου αὐτῶν). The divided response of the members of the Areopagus Council marks the end of Paul's presentation. He exits the place where the council meeting took place. Luke does not record a decision of the council concerning Paul and his activities in the city. Since no official reaction by magistrates or opposition from citizens is related, Luke seems to signal to his readers that Paul's address before the Areopagus Council was successful in the sense that he was able to convince them that they need not take any official

---

93. Darrell L. Bock, "Athenians Who Have Never Heard," in *Through No Fault of Their Own? The Fate of Those Who Have Never Heard* (ed. W. V. Crockett and J. G. Sigountos; Grand Rapids: Baker, 1991), 117 – 24, 120 – 21.

94. Cf. Stenschke, *Luke's Portrait of Gentiles*, 222.

95. Cf. Aeschylus, *Eum.* 647 – 648, where Apollo says, "When the dust has soaked up the blood of a man, once he has

died, there is no resurrection (οὔτις ἔστ᾽ ἀνάστασις)"; see also Homer, *Il.* 24.551; Sophocles, *El.* 137 – 139.

96. See Paul's discussion in 1 Cor 15.

97. Paul Veyne, "The Roman Empire," in *A History of Private Life*, vol.1: *From Pagan Rome to Byzantium* (ed. P. Veyne; 2003; repr., Cambridge: Harvard Univ. Press, 1987), 5 – 234, 219.

action against Paul's religious teaching in the agora. They can leave him and any new converts alone, as no Athenian laws are affected by his teaching.

17:34 Some men joined Paul and came to faith, including Dionysos, a member of the Council of the Areopagus, and a woman named Damaris, and others with them (τινὲς δὲ ἄνδρες κολληθέντες αὐτῷ ἐπίστευσαν, ἐν οἷς καὶ Διονύσιος ὁ Ἀρεοπαγίτης καὶ γυνὴ ὀνόματι Δάμαρις καὶ ἕτεροι σὺν αὐτοῖς). Luke ends the Athens episode with a report on conversions in the city. This note should not be related in a narrow fashion to Paul's address before the Areopagus Council but more broadly to his preaching in the synagogue and in the agora (v. 17). The report has four parts.

First, Luke notes that "some men" were converted, presumably both Jews and Gentiles, the two audiences of his preaching. Luke describes their reaction to Paul's preaching with two verbs: they "came to faith" (ἐπίστευσαν, see on 4:4); that is, they put their trust in Jesus, the crucified and risen Savior, for the forgiveness of their sins and for eternal life. And they "joined" (κολληθέντες; see on 5:13) Paul by associating themselves with him, becoming disciples who continued to listen to Paul's teaching and began to form a community of believers.

Second, Luke singles out the conversion of a certain Dionysos, a member of the Areopagus Council (ὁ Ἀρεοπαγίτης), who came to faith and joined Paul. His membership in the Areopagus Council implies that he had been an Archon, one of the highest offices in Athens. Luke does not indicate whether he was converted to faith in Jesus immediately after Paul's presentation before the council or after further listening to Paul (cf. v. 32). According to a bishop of Corinth in the second century who happens to have the same name, Dionysos was the first *episkopos* of the church in Athens.[98]

Third, a woman named Damaris was also converted. Luke mentions neither her ethnic background nor her social status. The fact that she is mentioned by name may indicate that she played an important role in the church of Athens (or in the churches of Achaia).[99]

Fourth, "others" (ἕτεροι) were converted as well. Luke's comment in v. 34 thus reports the conversion of at least one prominent Athenian, of at least one woman, and of other citizens.

The fact that Paul describes the Corinthian believer Stephanas and his household as "the first converts in Achaia" (1 Cor 16:15) does not prove that the first conversions in Achaia happened in Corinth and that Luke's comment in v. 34 is therefore erroneous as Paul's missionary work in Athens was evidently unsuccessful. The description of Stephanas and his family as "first converts" (lit., "firstfruits") in Achaia can be understood in several ways. The first church in Achaia was established in Corinth, while the conversion of several individuals in Athens did not lead to the foundation of a church; the term "Achaia" describes Corinth as capital of Achaia;[100] the term "firstfruits" in 1 Cor 16:15 describes not exclusively and perhaps not even primarily a temporal priority but means "first" in the sense of "model," "pledge," or "promise" of further fruit, i.e., of further conversions.

---

98. Eusebius, *Hist. eccl.* 3.4.10; 4.23.3.

99. There is no evidence for the suggestion of John Chrysostom, *Sac.* 4.7, that Damaris was the spouse of Dionysos. Zahn, *Apostelgeschichte*, 2:608–9, suggests that Damaris could have been the spouse or wife of one of the philosophers with whom Paul had contact. Metzner, *Die Prominenten*, 434, suggests in the context of Luke's tendency to mention prominent women that Damaris belonged to the aristocratic circles of Athens.

100. Anthony C. Thiselton, *The First Epistle to the Corinthians* (NIGTC; Grand Rapids: Eerdmans, 2000), 1338; the next comment ibid.

Theology in Application

Paul's Address before the Areopagus Council

Some interpreters regard Paul's address before the Areopagus Council as barely Christian.[101] Others regard Paul's speech as an evangelistic sermon that provides a model for contextualized preaching.[102] A recent helpful and informed example of the latter approach to Paul's Areopagus speech points to the persuasive features of Paul's rhetoric; the initial point of contact is seen in the fact that Paul "begins where his audience is and builds on as much common territory as possible," refusing to demean their belief system or to condemn their religiosity while recognizing that "there is something genuine in their religious aspirations and felt needs." He first addresses them "at the level of their basic worldview assumptions, creating a necessary context and foundation" for proclaiming Christ; he takes advantage of "similarities between the Jewish Scriptures and Hellenistic thought in order to construct apologetic bridges to his listeners." At the same time his "deeper purpose is to confront and correct their understanding of God at a fundamental level," achieved "not by overtly attacking pagan doctrines, but rather by positively confessing the God of the Scriptures." The "genius of Paul's context-sensitive preaching" is seen in the fact that

> he intentionally uses the philosophical language of his audience, not simply to stake out common ground but in order to transform their worldview. Behind this strategy stands a deep conviction that the pagan world was capable of being redeemed. Familiar terminology is, therefore, co-opted and infused with new meaning in light of biblical revelation and the Christ event.[103]

As the commentary on the text of Paul's speech has shown, the view that the Areopagus address is barely Christian is unwarranted, while the view that it provides a model for a sensitive, contextualized presentation of the gospel of Jesus Christ, while plausible in the most general sense, is an overinterpretation. As far as the latter is concerned, it is telling that one finds qualifications such as "the speech is *basically* a call to repentance."[104] Paul's speech, as related by Luke, speaks of Jesus' resurrection and of God's day of judgment, but *not* of how people are saved on judgment day; Paul speaks of the Gentiles groping for God but *not* of how to find God through faith in Jesus; Paul speaks of God's command to people everywhere to repent but he does *not* exhort his listeners to repent. As Paul's speech before governor Festus and King

---

101. Cf. Mark S. Smith, *God in Translation*, 308 – 9.

102. Cf. Stephen Rost, "Paul's Areopagus Speech in Acts 17: A Paradigm for Applying Apologetics and Missions to Non-Christian Religious Movements," in *Encountering New Religious Movements: A Holistic Evangelical Approach* (ed. I. Hexham, S. Rost, and J. Morehead; Grand Rapids: Kregel, 2004), 113 – 36.

103. Dean E. Flemming, *Contextualization in the New Testament: Patterns for Theology and Mission* (Downers Grove, IL: InterVarsity Press, 2005), 75 – 79.

104. Tannehill, *Acts*, 218 (italics mine), quoted by Flemming, *Contextualization*, 80.

Agrippa demonstrates, Luke has no difficulties in reporting a direct evangelistic appeal by Paul to people of high social standing (26:27 – 29).

The fact that such an evangelistic appeal is made only indirectly suggests that Paul's speech before the Areopagus Council is not missionary proclamation. When we take the historical context seriously — the query whether Paul is introducing foreign gods into Athens, and the corollary that a positive answer would have for the Areopagus Council, whose members would have to approve, or disapprove, the introduction of a new cult — we recognize that Paul gives an address before civic leaders who have the authority to regulate all public activities in Athens. It is in their power to regulate, prohibit, or punish his proclamation in the agora if they think that he is introducing foreign deities. Most interpreters seem to assume that since the pagan world in general and the Hellenistic period in particular was tolerant of many different gods and cults, the introduction of a new faith and the establishment of a new community of believers would have raised no eyebrows. As we have seen, this was not the case, especially not in the city of Athens.

In a context where Paul is invited by one of the most venerated law courts of Athens to explain whether or not he is introducing new deities, it is a priori unlikely that Paul "has been given a forum to proclaim the gospel in order to convince the philosophers to repent and turn to Jesus." Moreover, it goes beyond the evidence of the text of the speech to assert that Paul uses the acknowledged existence of general revelation "as the basis for an evangelistic appeal."[105] The realization that Paul's Areopagus speech does not include either an explicit exhortation to repent of false beliefs and false behavior and to believe in Jesus, or an exposition on or even reference to Jesus as Savior, has prompted some to describe the speech not as "evangelism" but as "pre-evangelism"; that is, Paul explains the framework of his message about Jesus as the Savior of all people in terms of a biblical theology of God the Creator of the world before whom all human beings are accountable for their beliefs and actions. While this interpretation is more helpful, it still misses both the historical context in which Paul finds himself as a result of his preaching in the agora and the function of the Areopagus Council in the first century.

Points of Agreement

As the above interpretation of Paul's speech has demonstrated, Paul formulated his address in such a manner that points of agreement concerning views about the divine being, about the world, and about human beings would stand out. In the following nine points of agreement, the first five concern Stoic philosophy, while the last four would have been accepted by council members with Epicurean leanings.

---

105. Lynn A. Losie, "Paul's Speech on the Areopagus: A Model of Cross-Cultural Evangelism: Acts 17:16 – 34," in *Mission in Acts: Ancient Narratives in Contemporary Context* (ed. R. L. Gallagher and P. Hertig; American Society of Missiology Series 34; Maryknoll, NY: Orbis, 2004), 220 – 38, 226, 232.

1. God is immortal, Lord of heaven and earth, who gives life and existence to human beings.
2. There is a unity of one divine being.
3. God is immanent in the world and is proximate to human beings.
4. In his sovereign providence, God rules the world.
5. Human beings are accountable before the divine being.
6. Animated nature, the immortality of the soul, and the bliss of the divine truly do exist.
7. The knowledge of God is apparent, a function of human reason.
8. God does not live in man-made temples.
9. God does not need sacrifices or other services from human beings.

Missionary sermons and evangelistic preaching certainly emphasize points of agreement with the audience, risking to sound vague and incomplete for Christian ears. This is particularly important in a civic address before political authorities in a situation in which legal issues of the continued work of the church are at stake. Not every situation presents Christian preachers with a *status confessionis* in which they must bear witness to the full truth of the gospel of Jesus Christ. In some situations it is necessary to speak about particular aspects of Christian convictions. Such a focused exposition of Christian beliefs is not a betrayal of the gospel, if the preacher does not deny what Christians believe. Usually there will be other opportunities to explain those areas of Christian belief that have not been addressed in the first encounter (note the later conversion of Dionysus the Areopagite).

Paul's knowledge of Stoic and Epicurean philosophical concepts and his ability to use their formulations and quote a Cilician poet implies prior study of and interest in Greek and Roman traditions. Christian preachers and missionaries who neither know nor understand the intellectual and material culture in which they seek to proclaim the gospel cannot possibly know which ideas and formulations constitute points of contact and agreement that can help listeners to understand the new content of the gospel message.

Points of Contradiction

While Paul seeks understanding through agreement, he does not accommodate his convictions to the philosophical convictions of the Athenian intellectuals. He "displays courtesy and sensitivity, but there is restraint in his tactical alignments, lest he jeopardize the gospel."[106] While Paul uses terminology that was readily understood in Athens, and while many of his statements are acceptable at least for some

---

106. Don A. Carson, *The Gagging of God: Christianity Confronts Pluralism* (Grand Rapids: Zondervan, 1995), 499; Carson goes on to conclude that "Paul will never compromise the gospel so as to make it pleasantly compatible with the culture he is evangelizing."

members of the council, he leaves no doubt that he rejects the plurality of gods and cults and the proliferation of temples, altars, and statues. Paul disputes the Athenians' understanding of the divine and thus their worldview[107] in the following respects.

1. The reference to the "unknown god" (v. 23), understood in the context of Isa 45:15 – 25, implies a censure of the religious convictions of the Athenians.

2. The reference to "fixed times and the boundaries of their lands" (v. 26), understood in the context of Deut 32:8, implies that as the one true God whom the Athenians do not know crosses national boundaries, he is also working against polytheism, which means that there are no more concessions to human fallenness or "times of ignorance" (v. 30).[108]

3. Paul acknowledges that Gentiles seek God (v. 27), but his formulation shows that he is skeptical concerning the actual outcome of this search.

4. The statement that God "is not far from any one of us" (v. 27) makes careful listeners wonder whether this is a reference to Stoic notions of the presence of the divine in everything that exists or, rather, a critical comment on the Athenians' unsuccessful attempts to find God, who is "near" but not quite present.

5. The statement that the one God created the one ancestor from whom he made all human beings (v. 26) reveals that the knowledge of the Greek poets is partial.

6. Paul's critique of the notion that God lives in man-made shrines and that God needs sacrifices is reminiscent not only of Epicurean arguments but more pointedly and more consistently of the anti-idol polemic of Isaiah. Paul's critique of idol production and of idol worship is an indictment of popular Greco-Roman piety with which the Stoic and the Epicurean philosophers had come to an arrangement.

7. Paul's reference to "times of ignorance" (v. 30) expresses his conviction that the religious beliefs and practices of the Athenians make them guilty before God. One cannot ignore truth for too long without being responsible for one's behavior.

8. Paul's report of God's command that all people everywhere repent shows that his ultimate concern is not to advance philosophical arguments with which his audience — in the agora, and perhaps even in the Areopagus Council — agrees but to make people realize the need to change their religious convictions and behavior.

9. Paul's reference to a day of judgment whose date God has fixed not only speaks of a personal God (judges are always persons, not ideas) but also of a situation that is potentially dangerous for human beings — certainly dangerous for

---

107. For this focus see Don A. Carson, "Athens Revisited," in *Telling the Truth: Evangelizing Postmoderns* (ed. D.A. Carson; Grand Rapids: Zondervan, 2000), 384 – 98.

108. Witherington, *Acts*, 527.

people who have an altar to an unknown God because they do not know God, the Creator of heaven and earth. Paul asserts that the religious activities of the Athenians are evidence of ignorance, and he clearly implies that none of the deities and none of the cults of the city are able to guarantee a verdict of "innocent" on the day of universal judgment.

10. Paul's reference to the resurrection from the dead of a man whom God has appointed as judge of the world flies in the face of Greek and Roman notions about what happens at death and about the afterlife. Paul is unafraid to point to the resurrection of the dead, even though he knows that the idea of a bodily resurrection is a laughable concept for the dualistically thinking Greeks.

Authentic evangelism never emphasizes only points of agreement with the audience, but also expresses disagreement and contradiction. God's salvific revelation in and through Jesus Christ, requiring acknowledgment of false thinking and false behavior, contains by necessity claims, emphases, and exhortations that contradict the values, traditions, and practices of unbelievers. Whether points of contradiction are expressed implicitly or explicitly depend on the situation. Christian preaching will not be taken seriously if the preacher merely reformulates the beliefs of the general public or of a particular audience. If there was general agreement concerning beliefs about God and the world, and about human existence and the accountability of human beings, there would be no need for Christian preaching. Confrontation of pluralistic religious beliefs and secular convictions remains a fundamental process of missionary work and evangelistic preaching.

A Civic Speech with Risky Assertions

Paul's address is a civic speech in which he does not directly aim at changing the convictions of the audience but instead emphasizes common ground concerning the belief in a divine being. At the same time, his rejection of the religious beliefs and practices of the Athenians — both implicit and explicit — might have real and potentially dangerous consequences. No Athenian would welcome abandoning the temples for which Athens had been famous for hundreds of years, discontinuing the sacrifices that ensured the goodwill of the gods who were thought to be responsible for the prosperity of the city, or missing the opportunity to officiate in the cults of the city, thereby consolidating one's superior social status. It was dangerous to imply that the cultic veneration of the deceased emperors — an essential and an increasingly important element of Roman culture in the larger cities — should be stopped. Paul's unqualified rejection of the Athenians' religious pluralism was ill-advised from the point of view of the principle of accommodation, detrimental for his missionary project in Athens, and potentially dangerous to himself and to future followers of Jesus Christ in the city.

Acts 18:1 – 22

Literary Context

Paul's proclamation of the gospel and the establishment of a church in Corinth (18:1 – 22) is the final episode of the fifth major section of Acts, in which Luke narrates the mission of Paul in Europe (15:35 – 18:22). After the change of initial plans to evangelize in cities in the province of Asia or in Pontus-Bithynia (15:35 – 16:10), Paul established churches in the province of Macedonia in Philippi, Thessalonica, and Berea (16:11 – 17:15), and in the province of Achaia in Athens and now in Corinth (17:16 – 18:22).

Luke's account of Paul's missionary work in Corinth agrees with what we learn from Paul's first letter to the Corinthian believers in several points:

- Paul's preaching in Corinth to both Jews and Gentiles (18:4; 1 Cor 1:22 – 25; 9:19 – 23)
- Aquila and Priscilla known to Paul and to the Corinthians (18:2; 1 Cor 16:19)
- Paul's working for a living through manual labor (18:3; 1 Cor 9:12, 15 – 18)
- Paul's involvement in the conversion and baptism of Crispus (18:8; 1 Cor 1:14)
- Paul's association with Sosthenes (18:17; 1 Cor 1:1)
- Paul's experiencing difficult situations with "fear and trembling" (18:9; 1 Cor 2:3)
- Timothy's involvement in Paul's Corinthian ministry (18:5; 1 Cor 4:17; 16:10 – 11)

The mission in Corinth took place from February or March AD 50 to September AD 51.

Main Idea

The Corinth episode highlights the reality of God's presence in missionary work and points of contact between missionary work and wider political realities.

Translation

Acts 18:1 – 22

1a	Setting: time	After these events
b	Action	**Paul left Athens**
c	Action	**and went to Corinth.**
2a	Event: character entrance	**There he met a Jew**
b	Identification	named Aquila,
c	Geographical	a native of Pontus,
d	Geographical	who had recently come from Italy
e	Association	with his wife, Priscilla,
f	Cause	because Claudius had ordered all Jews to ☾ leave Rome.
g	Action	**Paul approached them**
3a	Cause	and because he practiced the same trade,
b	Action	**he stayed with them**
c	Action	**and worked,**
d	Explanation	for they were tentmakers by trade.
4a	Action	**Paul led discussions**
b	Place	in the synagogue
c	Time	every Sabbath
d	Action	**and persuaded Jews and**
e		**Greeks.**
5a	Setting: time	When Silas and Timothy arrived
b	Place	from Macedonia,
c	Event	**Paul was wholly absorbed with the proclamation of the word,**
d	Action	bearing witness to the Jews
e	Content	that Jesus was the Messiah.

6a	Conflict/Cause	When they opposed and
b	Conflict/Cause	defamed him,
c	Reaction	**he shook out his clothes in protest**
d	Response	**and said to them,**
e	Exclamation (curse)	*"Your blood be on your own heads!*
f	Assertion	*I am innocent.*
g	Time	*From now on*
h	Assertion	*I will go to the Gentiles."*
7a	Resolution of conflict	**So Paul left the synagogue**
b	Action	**and went to the house of a man named Titius Justus,**
c	Character description	a God-fearer,
d	Place	whose house was next door to the ✡ synagogue.
8a	Character entrance	**Crispus,**
b	Character description	the president of the synagogue,
c	Action	**came to faith in the Lord**
d	Association	together with his entire household.
e	Character entrance	**And many Corinthians**
f	Character description	who heard Paul
g	Action	**believed and**
h	Action	**were baptized.**
9a	Setting: time	One night
b	Event	**the Lord said to Paul**
c	Means	in a vision,
d	Command (exhortation)	*"Do not be afraid!*
e	Command	*Speak out and*
f	Command	*do not be silent,*
10a	Cause (promise)	*for I am with you,*
b	Result	*and nobody will lay a hand on you*
c	Purpose	*in order to harm you,*
d	Cause	*because there are many of my people*
e	Place	*in this city."*
11a	Action	**So he stayed there**
b	Duration	for a year and six months,
c	Action	teaching the word of God among them.
12a	Setting: time	When Gallio was proconsul of Achaia,
b	Event	**the Jews rose up**
c	Manner	with one mind
d	Conflict	against Paul
e	Action	**and brought him before the judicial bench,**
13a	Accusation	saying, *"This man is inducing people to worship God*
b	Manner	*in ways that are against the law."*
14a	Attempted action	As Paul was about to speak,
b	Character entrance: response	**Gallio said to the Jews:**

Continued on next page.

Continued from previous page.

c	Address	*"Jews,*
d	Condition	*if it were a matter of crime or*
e	Condition	*some serious case of deception,*
f	Inference	*I would be justified in accepting your complaint.*

15a	Contrast & cause	*But since this is a matter of controversial questions about teaching and*
b	List	*names and*
c	List	*your own law,*
d	Command	*see to it yourselves.*
e	Decision (assertion)	*I refuse to be the judge of such matters."*
16a	Action	So **he drove them away**
b	Place	**from the judicial bench.**
17a	Escalation: action	**Then they all seized Sosthenes,**
b	Character description	the president of the synagogue,
c	Action	and **beat him in front of the judicial bench.**
d	Contrast	But **none of this was of concern to Gallio.**

18a	Action	**Paul stayed in Corinth**
b	Duration	for many days.
c	Action	**Eventually he took leave of the believers**
d	Action	and **sailed for Syria,**
e	Association	accompanied by Priscilla and
f	Association	Aquila.
g	Setting: place	At Cenchreae
h	Action	**he had his hair cut**
i	Cause	because he had made a vow.

19a	Setting: place	When they reached Ephesus,
b	Action	**he left them there.**
c	Action	**He went into the synagogue,**
d	Action	where he held discussions with the Jews.

20a	Question	When they asked him to stay for a longer period of time,
b	Response	**he declined.**

21a	Simultaneous	As he took his leave,
b	Promise	**he said,**
		"I will come back to you,
c	Condition	*if God wills."*
d	Action	**Then he set sail**
e	Place	from Ephesus.

22a	Setting: place	When he had landed at Caesarea,
b	Action	**he went up to Jerusalem and**
c	Action	**visited the congregation.**
d	Action	**Then he went to Antioch.**

Structure and Literary Form

The Corinth episode consists of six incidents. (1) Luke relates Paul's proclamation of the gospel in the synagogue while he was earning money as a leatherworker and living with Aquila and Priscilla (18:1 – 4). (2) Luke describes Paul's preaching of Jesus as Messiah and opposition in the synagogue, prompting him to move to the house of Titius Justus, a God-fearer (vv. 5 – 8). (3) God encourages Paul in a vision, assuring him that the opponents will not be able to harm him; as a result Paul was active in Corinth for a year and six months (vv. 9 – 11). (4) Corinthian Jews attempt to initiate legal proceedings against Paul before Gallio, the governor of Achaia, who refuses to hear the case because of the religious nature of the complaint of the Jews (vv. 12 – 17). (5) Paul continues missionary work in Corinth (v. 18a-b). (6) Finally, Paul returns, via Cenchreae, Ephesus, and Caesarea, to Jerusalem and Antioch (vv. 18c – 22).

The episode is a *historical narrative*, with *travel notices* (vv. 1, 18 – 19, 21, 22); *reports* of missionary work (vv. 4, 5, 11), including a report on the conversion of the president of the synagogue (v. 8); *direct speech* of Paul (vv. 6, 21), of the Lord (vv. 9 – 10), of Jews bringing charges against Paul (v. 13), and of the Roman governor Gallio (vv. 14 – 15); and a *vision report* (vv. 9 – 10). Luke mentions six personal names of local people: Aquila and Priscilla, Jews from Rome; Titius Justus, a God-fearer; Crispus, president of the synagogue; Gallio, the Roman governor of Achaia; Sosthenes, the new president of the synagogue.[1] The brief speech of Gallio conveys his judicial decision not to hear the case brought against Paul; it can be analyzed in terms of a short *exordium* (v. 14c), a *narratio* (vv. 14d – 15c), and a *peroratio* (v. 15d-e).

Exegetical Outline

→ **I. The Mission in Corinth (18:1 – 22)**

    A. The Proclamation of the Gospel in the Synagogue (18:1 – 4)

        1. Departure from Athens (18:1a-b)

        2. Arrival in Corinth (18:1c)

        3. Encounter with Aquila and Priscilla (18:2 – 3)

           a. Geographical origins: Pontus and Italy (18:2a-e)

           b. The edict of Claudius evicting the Jews from Rome (18:2f)

           c. Paul initiates contact with Aquila and Priscilla (18:2g)

           d. Paul lives and works with Aquila and Priscilla (18:3)

        4. Paul's teaching in the synagogue before Jews and Greeks (18:4)

---

1. For comparison: the Cyprus episode (13:4 – 12) mentions two individuals: Elymas/Bar-Jesus, Sergius Paulus; the Antioch episode (13:13 – 52), the Iconium episode (14:1 – 7) and the Lystra episode (14:8 – 20) none; the Philippi episode (16:11 – 40) one: Lydia; the Thessalonica episode (17:1 – 9) one: Jason; the Berea episode (17:10 – 15) none; the Athens episode (17:16 – 34) two: Dionysius, Damaris; only the Ephesus episode (18:23 – 20:1) mentions more names (if we include Aquila, Priscilla, and Apollos), namely, seven: Apollos, Aquila, Priscilla, Tyrannus, Sceva, Demetrius, and Alexander.

B. The Proclamation of Jesus as Messiah and Opposition in the Synagogue (18:5 – 8)

1. The arrival of Silas and Timothy from Macedonia (18:5a-b)
2. Paul's proclamation of Jesus as Israel's Messiah among the Jews (18:5c-e)
3. Opposition from Corinthian Jews (18:6a-b)
4. Paul's reaction (18:6c-h)
5. Paul's relocation to the house of Titius Justus (18:7)
6. Conversions in Corinth (18:8)
   a. The conversion of Crispus, the president of the synagogue (18:8a-c)
   b. The conversion of Crispus's family (18:8d)
   c. The conversion and baptism of many Corinthians (18:8e-h)

C. Divine Encouragement in a Vision (18:9 – 11)

1. Epiphany of the Lord in a vision (18:9 – 10)
   a. Appearance of the Lord in a night vision (18:9a-c)
   b. Exhortation not to be afraid (18:9d)
   c. Exhortation to continue to preach (18:9e-f)
   d. Assurance of the Lord's presence (18:10a)
   e. Assurance of the Lord's protection (18:10b-c)
   f. Assurance of missionary success (18:10d-e)
2. Paul's ministry in Corinth for a year and six months (18:11)

D. The Accusation of Paul before Gallio (18:12 – 17)

1. The opposition of the Corinthian Jews (18:12)
2. The court case before Gallio, the Roman governor (18:13 – 16)
   a. Accusation that Paul conveys illegal religious teaching (18:13)
   b. Paul's willingness to defend himself (18:14a)
   c. Gallio's legal ruling (18:14b – 15d)
      i. Address: "Jews" (18:14b-c)
      ii. The proconsul and the Jewish community (18:14d – 15)
      iii. Dismissal of the case (18:15e)
   d. Dismissal of the Jews from the tribunal (18:16)
3. Beating of Sosthenes, the president of the synagogue, by the Jews (18:17)

E. Continued Missionary Work (18:18a-b)

F. Return to Jerusalem and Antioch (18:18c – 22)

1. Departure for Syria with Aquila and Priscilla (18:18c-f)
2. Haircut in Cenchreae on account of a vow (18:18g-i)
3. Stopover in Ephesus (18:19 – 21)
   a. Arrival in Ephesus (18:19a-b)
   b. Paul's teaching in the synagogue (18:19c-d)
   c. Invitation of the Jews to stay in Ephesus (18:20a)
   d. Postponement of a stay in Ephesus to a later time (18:20b – 21c)
   e. Departure from Ephesus (18:21d-e)
4. Arrival in Caesarea (18:22a)
5. Arrival in Jerusalem and visit of the church (18:22b-c)
6. Travel to Antioch (18:22d)

Explanation of the Text

18:1 After these events Paul left Athens and went to Corinth (μετὰ ταῦτα χωρισθεὶς ἐκ τῶν Ἀθηνῶν ἦλθεν εἰς Κόρινθον). Luke begins the Corinth episode with brief comments on Paul's departure from Athens and his travel to Corinth. The prepositional phrase translated "after these events" (μετὰ ταῦτα) is vague and does not allow us to specify the amount of time Paul spent in Athens. The journey to Corinth was about 50 miles (85 km.), a three-day journey that would have taken Paul to the cities of Eleusis and Megara before reaching Corinth.

IN DEPTH: Corinth

The city of Corinth, situated strategically at the southwest end of the isthmus separating the Peloponnese and Attica, minted coins since 600 BC. The city was known for its pottery industry (Corinthian vases), metal manufacture (an alloy known as Corinthian Bronze), and carpet weaving. Because Corinth was the center of the resistance of the Greek cities against Rome, the Roman Senate decreed that the city must be destroyed, a decision carried out in 146 BC. The city remained virtually deserted for a century. In 44 BC Julius Caesar refounded the city as a Roman colony (*Colonia Laus Iulia Corinthus*), settling 3,000 freed slaves and veterans in the city. Many of the destroyed buildings were restored and new buildings erected. When Achaia was organized as a senatorial province separately from Macedonia in AD 44, Corinth became the provincial capital. Strabo describes Corinth as wealthy "because of its commerce" (8.6.20). It is estimated that Roman Corinth had about 80,000 inhabitants; if we include the towns and villages that Corinth controlled, another 20,000 people should be added. The theater could seat 15,000 spectators. The moral depravity of the Corinthian population is exaggerated by ancient authors, whose assertions owe more to Athens' propaganda against a rival city than to the realities of everyday life in Corinth.

18:2 There he met a Jew named Aquila, a native of Pontus, who had recently come from Italy with his wife, Priscilla, because Claudius had ordered all Jews to leave Rome. Paul approached them (καὶ εὑρών τινα Ἰουδαῖον ὀνόματι Ἀκύλαν, Ποντικὸν τῷ γένει προσφάτως ἐληλυθότα ἀπὸ τῆς Ἰταλίας καὶ Πρίσκιλλαν γυναῖκα αὐτοῦ, διὰ τὸ διατεταχέναι Κλαύδιον χωρίζεσθαι πάντας τοὺς Ἰουδαίους ἀπὸ τῆς Ῥώμης, προσῆλθεν αὐτοῖς). Luke's readers know from earlier reports of Paul's missionary practice that he would have visited the synagogue in Corinth upon his arrival (see on v. 4). Before noting Paul's contact with the Jewish community (v. 4), Luke relates his encounter with Aquila and Priscilla,[2] a Jewish couple whom he would have met in the synagogue. The verb translated

---

2. She is called Prisca in Rom 16:3; 1 Cor 16:19; 2 Tim 4:19.

"met" (εὑρών) denotes "to come upon something either through purposeful search or accidentally" (BDAG).

Aquila was born into a Jewish diaspora family living in Pontus, the region in northern Asia Minor on the southern coast of the Black Sea, which had been combined with Bithynia into a Roman province (see on 2:9; 16:7). The geographical origins of Priscilla are not mentioned; if Aquila moved to Rome in connection with his profession of a tentmaker (v. 3), he presumably met and married Priscilla in Pontus. Luke reports that the couple had "recently" come from Italy. They had relocated to Corinth because Emperor Claudius had issued an edict ordering all Jews to leave Rome. Estimates put the number of Jews living in Rome between 40,000 and 50,000. Only Jews who were resident aliens would have been affected by the edict.

Roman sources report two edicts of Claudius affecting the Jewish community in Rome.[3] Dio Cassius reports with regard to the first year of Claudius's principate (AD 41) that the emperor commanded the Jews to adhere to their ancestral way of life and not to conduct meetings (Cassius Dio 60.6.6). This edict seems to have been a reaction to the missionary activity of Jewish Christians, which had provoked disturbances in the synagogues, prompting Jewish leaders to register complaints at the imperial court.

In a second edict, issued in AD 49, Claudius ordered Jews expelled from Rome. The Roman historian Suetonius relates measures that Claudius initiated against "men of foreign birth" who are mentioned in connection with the Jews who "constantly made disturbances at the instigation of Chrestus," with the result that "he expelled them

from Rome."[4] Most scholars see the name "Chrestus" here as a misunderstanding and interpret the text as referring to Jesus Christ: the disturbances were provoked by the missionary outreach of Jewish Christians who preached Jesus as Messiah ("Christos") in the synagogues of Rome.

When Paul arrived in Corinth, probably in February or March of the year AD 50, Claudius's edict of AD 49 was indeed a recent event that had forced Aquila and Priscilla to leave Rome and move to Corinth. Luke's account gives the impression that Aquila and Priscilla were believers when Paul met them in Corinth. If they had been involved in missionary outreach to other Jews in Rome, it is not impossible to assume that they were "independent" missionaries who had engaged in missionary work in Corinth even before Paul's arrival. Nevertheless, Paul implies in 1 Cor 2:1 – 5 that he founded the church in Corinth. It is possible that "the couple decided after they experienced the difficulties in Rome resulting from the edict of Claudius to live in peace in their new home" while setting up their workshop.[5]

18:3 And because he practiced the same trade, he stayed with them and worked, for they were tentmakers by trade (καὶ διὰ τὸ ὁμότεχνον εἶναι ἔμενεν παρ' αὐτοῖς, καὶ ἠργάζετο· ἦσαν γὰρ σκηνοποιοὶ τῇ τέχνῃ). The reason why Paul came into contact with Aquila and Priscilla was the fact that they "practiced the same trade": they were "leatherworkers" (σκηνοποιοί). This Greek term has traditionally been understood as referring to tentmakers,[6] i.e., weavers of tent fabric or craftsmen sewing together "sun awnings of linen for private customers seeking protection from the hot

---

3. Cf. Riesner, *Paul's Early Period*, 157 – 201; Schnabel, *Early Christian Mission,* 2:806 – 9.

4. Suetonius, *Claud.* 25.3 – 4.

5. David Alvarez Cineira, *Die Religionspolitik des Kaisers*

Claudius und die paulinische Mission (Herders biblische Studien 19; Freiburg: Herder, 1999), 221.

6. Cf. ESV, GNB, NASB, NET, NIV, NLT, NRSV, TNIV. Cf. Hemer, *Acts*, 119; Barrett, *Acts*, 86.

Roman sun."[7] Paul "stayed" with them, living in their house, where he also "worked." Aquila and Priscilla gave Paul the opportunity to support himself financially by working in his trade.[8] It is possible that the emerging church met in their house.

Thus Paul moved from intellectual debate with philosophers and giving a speech before the Areopagus Council members in Athens to manual work among Corinthian artisans. The shops in the North Market, completed shortly before Paul's arrival, have been suggested as illustrating the conditions under which Aquila, Priscilla, and Paul lived and worked.

> The shops gave on to a wide, covered gallery running round all four sides of the square. They had a uniform height and depth of 4 m. (13 feet). The width varied from 2.8 m. (8 feet) to 4 m. (13 feet). There was no running water or toilet facilities. In one of the back corners, a series of steps in stone or brick was continued by a wooden ladder to a loft lit by an unglazed window centred above the shop entrance, which at night was closed by wooden shutters. Prisca and Aquila had their home in the loft, while Paul slept below amid the tool-strewn work-benches and the rolls of leather and canvas.[9]

Luke and Paul repeatedly mention Aquila and Priscilla.[10] When Paul left Corinth in early fall of AD 51, the couple accompanied him to Ephesus (18:18 – 19), where a church eventually met in their house (1 Cor 16:19). Luke relates in 18:26 that Aquila and particularly Priscilla (who is mentioned before her husband) taught Apollos from Alexandria. Paul writes that they "risked their lives for me. Not only I but all the churches of the Gentiles are grateful to them" (Rom 16:4); this presumably refers to a dangerous situation during his missionary work in Ephesus in which their intervention contributed to Paul's being rescued from harm. By AD 56 Aquila and Priscilla are back in Rome, with a church meeting in their house (Rom 16:3, 5).

18:4 Paul led discussions in the synagogue every Sabbath and persuaded Jews and Greeks (διελέγετο δὲ ἐν τῇ συναγωγῇ κατὰ πᾶν σάββατον ἔπειθέν τε Ἰουδαίους καὶ Ἕλληνας). Luke describes Paul's missionary work in Corinth with a summary statement whose terms, activities, and location are known from the previous narrative. Paul "led discussions" (διελέγετο; see on 17:2) in the synagogue[11] every Sabbath,[12] a comment that implies a teaching ministry in the Jewish community that lasted for several weeks. Luke does not indicate whether Paul was invited by the synagogue officials to speak to the congregation (as in Pisidian Antioch, cf. 13:15). Besides opportunities for preaching and teaching in the weekly meetings, Paul would have had the opportunity to converse with Jews and God-fearers who attended the meetings.

Paul "persuaded" (ἔπειθεν) Jews and Greeks; the imperfect tense of the verb is usually interpreted as having a conative sense ("he tried to persuade").[13] The fact that Paul's preaching was effective — so successful, in fact, that members of the Jewish community became convinced that Paul's activities should be curbed by legal action before the governor of the province — indicates that there is no

---

7. Peter Lampe, *From Paul to Valentinus: Christians at Rome in the First Two Centuries* (Minneapolis: Fortress, 2003), 188 – 89, who suggests that Aquila was an independent craftsman whose social status was that of "the lower and poorer folk."

8. Cf. 20:34; see also Paul's references to manual work with which he supported himself (thereby avoiding the obligations of patron-client relationships) in 1 Cor 4:12; 2 Cor 11:7; 1 Thess 2:9.

9. Murphy-O'Connor, *Paul*, 263.

10. Acts 18:2 – 3, 18, 26; Rom 16:3 – 5; 1 Cor 16:19; 2 Tim 4:19.

11. Cf. 13:5, 14; 14:1; 16:13; 17:2, 10, 17.

12. Cf. 13:14, 42, 44; 16:13; 17:2.

13. Thus ESV, GNB, NASB, NET, NIV, NLT, NRSV, TNIV; Barrett, *Acts*, 864; Fitzmyer, *Acts*, 626; Bock, *Acts*, 578.

good reason why the verb cannot have an ongoing sense: Paul indeed "persuaded" Jews and Gentiles of the truth of the gospel.[14]

The location of Paul's encounter with "Greeks" (Ἕλληνες) is disputed. While most commentators regard the "Greeks" as Gentiles connected with the synagogue (as God-fearers, or more generally as sympathizers), it seems more plausible to regard v. 4 as a summary statement on Paul's missionary work in Corinth, in which case Paul sought encounters with Jews in the local synagogues and with Greeks in the agora or other places where Gentiles gathered. If Paul worked during the day in his trade as tentmaker (v. 3), he would have encountered Greeks in the workshop of Aquila and Priscilla.

18:5 When Silas and Timothy arrived from Macedonia, Paul was wholly absorbed with the proclamation of the word, bearing witness to the Jews that Jesus was the Messiah (ὡς δὲ κατῆλθον ἀπὸ τῆς Μακεδονίας ὅ τε Σιλᾶς καὶ ὁ Τιμόθεος, συνείχετο τῷ λόγῳ ὁ Παῦλος διαμαρτυρόμενος τοῖς Ἰουδαίοις εἶναι τὸν χριστὸν Ἰησοῦν). The second incident of the Corinth episode begins with the arrival of Silas and Timothy, who had stayed in Berea in Macedonia (17:14–16).[15] Paul's comments in 2 Cor 11:8–9 and Phil 4:15 explain why the arrival of his two associates allowed him to be "wholly absorbed" (συνείχετο) with proclaiming the gospel. Since they brought financial support for his work from the Macedonian churches, he was able to devote more of his time and energy to preaching and teaching.[16] The term "word" (λόγος) stands for the proclamation of the good news of Jesus.[17] Paul was "bearing witness" (διαμαρτυρόμενος), i.e., declaring and explaining before Jewish audiences that Jesus was the promised Messiah.

18:6 When they opposed and defamed him, he shook out his clothes in protest and said to them, "Your blood be on your own heads! I am innocent. From now on I will go to the Gentiles" (ἀντιτασσομένων δὲ αὐτῶν καὶ βλασφημούντων ἐκτιναξάμενος τὰ ἱμάτια εἶπεν πρὸς αὐτούς· τὸ αἷμα ὑμῶν ἐπὶ τὴν κεφαλὴν ὑμῶν· καθαρὸς ἐγὼ ἀπὸ τοῦ νῦν εἰς τὰ ἔθνη πορεύσομαι). At some point the opposition in the Jewish community became sufficiently intense that Paul was no longer allowed to speak in the synagogue, though we do not know what transpired. The opponents evidently made a continued ministry in the synagogue impossible, and they seem to have had access to the courts and to the Roman governor (v. 12), a fact that suggests that they may have been Jews who held Roman citizenship or belonged to the Corinthian elite.

Luke describes their resistance with two verbs: they "opposed" (ἀντιτασσομένων), i.e., resisted him face-to-face; and they "defamed" (βλασφημούντων; see on 6:11) him; i.e., they slandered and reviled him.[18] We can assume that the attack on Paul that the second verb implies was directed against his proclamation that Jesus was the Messiah. The Jews saw it as impossible that a crucified person could be the Messiah. Some Jews in Corinth believed (as evidently Paul did before his conversion) that the crucified Jesus was a criminal cursed by God (cf. 13:45; 26:11), a belief that would have constituted

---

14. Thus RSV; Johnson, *Acts*, 321; Jervell, *Apostelgeschichte*, 458.

15. Paul mentions the participation of Silvanus/Silas and Timothy in the proclamation of the gospel in Corinth in 2 Cor 1:19.

16. Thus many commentators; the imperfect tense of συνείχετο suggests, however, that when Silas and Timothy arrived (κατῆλθον; aorist) from Macedonia, they found Paul oc-

cupied with preaching; cf. Barrett, *Acts*, 866.

17. Cf. 4:29, 31; 6:2, 4; 8:4.

18. The two participles can be interpreted in a temporal ("when they opposed him") or causal sense ("because they opposed him"); the present tense of the participles indicates that the opposition of Corinthian Jews to which Paul reacts in v. 6c-h was not manifested in one particular event but had been building up over a period of time.

blasphemy.[19] What made the continuation of Paul's teaching in the synagogue impossible was not only the slanderous accusations but also, presumably, the repeated interruption of Paul's teaching with charges of blasphemy and moves to block Paul from participation in the Jewish meetings.

Paul reacted to the intense and increasing opposition by Corinthian Jews with a symbolic action accompanied by an explanation, a declaration, and an announcement. Paul "shook out his clothes" as a protest against being slandered and expressed his rejection toward those in the Jewish community who had rejected him.[20] He declared that he was not responsible for their refusal to accept Jesus as Israel's Messiah. The statement "your blood be on your own heads"[21] assigns the blame for the consequences that would result from their rejection of Jesus Messiah to the Jews who made his teaching in the synagogue impossible, and the declaration "I am innocent" states that Paul felt free of responsibility for the loss they would suffer (cf. 20:26).

The announcement that "from now on" he will go to the Gentiles does not mean that he has not yet proclaimed the gospel to Gentiles in Corinth (cf. v. 4), nor does it mean that he will no longer explain the good news of Jesus to Jews (note v. 19); rather, he announces that since he can no longer teach in the synagogue, he will focus his ministry on the non-Jewish people living in Corinth (see also this pattern Pisidian Antioch, 13:46).

18:7 So Paul left the synagogue and went to the house of a man named Titius Justus, a God-fearer, whose house was next door to the synagogue (καὶ μεταβὰς ἐκεῖθεν εἰσῆλθεν εἰς οἰκίαν τινὸς ὀνόματι Τιτίου Ἰούστου σεβομένου τὸν θεόν, οὗ ἡ οἰκία ἦν συνομοροῦσα τῇ συναγωγῇ). The opposition in the synagogue forces Paul to transfer (μεταβάς)[22] his teaching activity from there to the house of a certain Titius Justus, a God-fearer who had heard Paul preach and teach in the synagogue, had evidently come to faith in Jesus, and made his house available as a new center of preaching and teaching. The suggestion that his full Roman name was Gaius Titius Justus and that he was Paul's host in Corinth when he wrote his letter to the Romans (Rom 16:23; cf. 1 Cor 1:14) is possible, but must remain hypothetical.

Luke may have included the comment that the house of Titius Justus was "next door" (συνομοροῦσα) to indicate that Paul remained close to the synagogue. Since we do not know the location of the synagogue, we do not know whether it was convenient that Paul began to teach in the house next door to the synagogue. The Jews who opposed Paul probably regarded the proximity of the meeting place of the followers of Jesus as a provocation.

18:8 Crispus, the president of the synagogue, came to faith in the Lord together with his entire household. And many Corinthians who heard Paul believed and were baptized (Κρίσπος δὲ ὁ ἀρχισυνάγωγος ἐπίστευσεν τῷ κυρίῳ σὺν ὅλῳ τῷ οἴκῳ αὐτοῦ, καὶ πολλοὶ τῶν Κορινθίων ἀκούοντες ἐπίστευον καὶ ἐβαπτίζοντο). Luke ends

---

19. O. Hofius, "βλασφημία, βλασφημέω, *EDNT*, 1:221, with reference to Deut 21:22 – 23.

20. A parallel may be seen in Neh 5:13: "I also shook out the folds of my robe and said, 'In this way may God shake out of their house and possessions anyone who does not keep this promise. So may such a person be shaken out and emptied!'"

21. For the formula see Lev 20:9; Deut 21:5; 2 Sam 1:16; 3:28 – 29; 14:9; 1 Kgs 2:31 – 33, 44 – 45; *As. Mos.* 9:7; *T. Levi* 16:3; *m. Sanh.* 4.5; cf. Ezek 33:1 – 9; Matt 27:25; Acts 5:28; 20:26.

22. Cf. BDAG, s.v. μεταβαίνω 1, "to transfer from one place to another." The Western text adds "from Aquila" and assumes that Paul has relocated his place of lodging from Aquila's house to the house of Titius Justus. Fitzmyer, *Acts*, 627, assumes that this is the logic of the narrative (without reference to the Western text). It is more plausible to connect ἐκεῖθεν with the synagogue rather than with the house of Titius Justus; cf. Hemer, *Acts*, 197.

this second incident with a comment on conversions. (1) Crispus, the president of the synagogue (ὁ ἀρχισυνάγωγος; see on 13:15) who coordinated the religious, administrative, and political affairs of the Jewish community, came to faith in Jesus as Israel's Messiah (v. 5) and as the crucified, risen, and exalted Lord. Paul mentions baptizing Crispus in 1 Cor 1:14. As president of the synagogue, he would have been the official who granted Paul permission to address the congregation.

(2) The entire household of Crispus, i.e., family members and any relatives and slaves who belonged to his household, were converted to faith in Jesus as well.

(3) "Many Corinthians" (πολλοὶ τῶν Κορινθίων), Jews and Greeks who heard Paul preach the good news of Jesus (v. 4), also believed. These people had listened, understood, and accepted Paul's proclamation of the gospel. All who believed were immersed in water (ἐβαπτίζοντο; see on 1:5; 2:38) as a symbol of their acknowledging sin and need for forgiveness, and as a sign that God forgave their sins on account of Jesus' death, resurrection, and exaltation as they put their trust in Jesus for their salvation and for eternal life.

18:9 – 10 One night the Lord said to Paul in a vision, "Do not be afraid! Speak out and do not be silent, for I am with you, and nobody will lay a hand on you in order to harm you, because there are many of my people in this city" (εἶπεν δὲ ὁ κύριος ἐν νυκτὶ δι᾽ ὁράματος τῷ Παύλῳ· μὴ φοβοῦ, ἀλλὰ λάλει καὶ μὴ σιωπήσῃς, διότι ἐγώ εἰμι μετὰ σοῦ καὶ οὐδεὶς ἐπιθήσεταί σοι τοῦ κακῶσαί σε, διότι λαός ἐστί μοι πολὺς ἐν τῇ πόλει ταύτῃ). In a third incident Luke relates a vision in which the Lord encourages Paul to continue his missionary work in Corinth, which he does for eighteen months (v. 11). The epiphany has six parts.

(1) The Lord appears to Paul in a vision (ὅραμα) during one night. This suggests that the vision of the Lord happens in a dream.[23] The "Lord" should be understood as referring to the risen and exalted Jesus, whose words are given in direct speech,[24] a fact that highlights their significance. The revelation can be described as an oracle of assurance.[25]

(2) Jesus exhorts Paul not to be afraid (μὴ φοβοῦ). The reason for being afraid is not the supernatural epiphany of the Lord (as in other vision reports) but the opponents, who are slandering him and who before long will take legal proceedings against him (vv. 12 – 17).

(3) Jesus exhorts Paul to continue to preach. The imperative "speak out!" (λάλει) and the prohibition "do not be silent!" (μὴ σιωπήσῃς) formulate the divine charge positively and negatively. Paul must continue to proclaim the gospel of Jesus Christ in Corinth.

(4) Jesus assures Paul of his continued presence. The statement "I am with you" (ἐγώ εἰμι μετὰ σοῦ) underwrites the charge to continue to preach despite the mounting opposition. In the Old Testament, the phrase "being with" often describes Yahweh's active assistance to his chosen instruments and his people.[26]

(5) Jesus assures Paul of protection. He promises that "nobody will lay a hand on you"; i.e., nobody will attack Paul or harm him.

(6) Jesus assures Paul that more people in

---

23. The term "vision" (ὅραμα) also occurs in 7:31; 9:10, 12; 10:3, 17, 19; 11:5; 12:9; 16:9, 10; otherwise in the New Testament only at Matt 17:9. Paul refers to visions (ὀπτασίαι) that he received only once (2 Cor 12:1), recounting one particular vision.

24. Cf. 9:4 – 6, 10 – 16; 10:13, 15; 11:7, 9; 22:18, 21; 23:11.

25. Aune, *Prophecy*, 266 – 67. The two other oracles of assurance (23:11; 27:23 – 24) are also given to Paul "under circumstances of great stress, though none are explicit responses to a prayer of lament or distress" (ibid. 267).

26. Cf. Gen 21:22; 26:3; 31:3; Exod 3:12; Josh 1:5. Fitzmyer, *Acts*, also compares Josh 1:9; Isa 41:10; Jer 1:8; Matt 28:20.

Corinth will come to faith and join the new community of disciples. Jesus' assertion that "many of my people" are in Corinth refers to Jews and Gentiles who will be converted in the course of Paul's continuing ministry in the city, thus becoming "Jesus' people." The statement implies divine foreknowledge of future conversions.

18:11 So he stayed there for a year and six months, teaching the word of God among them (ἐκάθισεν δὲ ἐνιαυτὸν καὶ μῆνας ἓξ διδάσκων ἐν αὐτοῖς τὸν λόγον τοῦ θεοῦ). The effect of the epiphany and of Jesus' assurances is Paul's decision to remain in Corinth, refusing to let the opposition drive him out of the city. Luke notes that Paul stays for a year and six months (from February or March AD 50 to early autumn of AD 51), a long period of time compared to his missionary work since he left Antioch in Syria in AD 45 to begin his missionary work (13:1 – 4). The eighteen months probably relate to the entire time that Paul worked in Corinth,[27] evidently referring to the greater part of his time in Corinth before the Gallio incident (cf. v. 12).

18:12 When Gallio was proconsul of Achaia, the Jews rose up with one mind against Paul and brought him before the judicial bench (Γαλλίωνος δὲ ἀνθυπάτου ὄντος τῆς Ἀχαΐας κατεπέστησαν ὁμοθυμαδὸν οἱ Ἰουδαῖοι τῷ Παύλῳ καὶ ἤγαγον αὐτὸν ἐπὶ τὸ βῆμα). The fourth incident of the Corinth episode relates the effort by members of the Jewish community to initiate a court case against Paul before the governor of the province. While Luke does not link this incident with his previous comment on the length of Paul's stay in Corinth, the context seems to indicate that Gallio's arrival as the new proconsul (ἀνθύπατος)[28] of Achaia prompted the Corinthian Jews who opposed Paul to assume that the new governor would be favorably disposed to a legal case brought against Paul. An inscription from the temple of Apollo in Delphi allows us to date Gallio's proconsulship in the province of Achaia from July 1, AD 51, to June 30, AD 52.[29] Most likely the legal proceedings against Paul before Gallio took place early in that time span — in the summer of AD 51, perhaps in July or August.

Luke describes the initiative of the unbelieving Jews, who were of "one mind" (ὁμοθυμαδόν; see on 1:14) to accuse Paul before the Roman governor, with two verbs. They "rose up" (κατεπέστησαν) to take decisive action against Paul, and they "brought" (ἤγαγον) him to the judicial bench (βῆμα, Latin *rostra*; see on 12:21), the platform in the forum,[30] although the permanent tribunal in one of the basilicas or in the praetorium of the governor are possibilities as well. In the center of the *bēma* was a broad platform about 2.3 meters high rising on two blue marble steps; it had an elaborate superstructure that enclosed the platform on the back and partially along the sides, with benches in the corners and white marble piers that formed three doors in the rear.

The Jews initiated trial proceedings by forcing Paul to appear before the governor, where they introduced the complaint for which they hoped to achieve an *actio* of the provincial court, leading to the appointment of a trial (*iudicium*) in which they hoped to convince the court to issue a guilty verdict (*condemno*). This was the first time Paul had

---

27. Hemer, *Acts*, 119 n. 48; cf. Riesner, *Paul's Early Period*, 208 – 9.

28. On "proconsul" (ἀνθύπατος) see on 13:7.

29. Cf. Riesner, *Paul's Early Period*, 203 – 7; for the following comment see ibid. 209 – 10.

30. The βῆμα of v. 12 is most likely identical with the building whose foundations can still be seen slightly east of the center of the central terrace in the forum (agora) of Corinth. Cf. Mary E. H. Walbank, "The Foundation and Planning of Early Roman Corinth," *JRA* 10 (1997): 95 – 130, 121 – 22.

to defend himself before an official of the central Roman government, a proconsul who had full judicial authority.

18:13 Saying, "This man is inducing people to worship God in ways that are against the law" (λέγοντες ὅτι παρὰ τὸν νόμον ἀναπείθει οὗτος τοὺς ἀνθρώπους σέβεσθαι τὸν θεόν). The court case scene (vv. 13 – 16) begins with the accusation of Paul by some Corinthian Jews. Even though the charge echoes the charges brought against Stephen (6:13), the location, the audience, and the focus of the charge are different. Scholarly discussion has focused on what "the law" (ὁ νόμος) refers to. Some see a reference to the Mosaic Torah,[31] some to Roman law,[32] and some take the charge to be deliberately ambiguous.[33]

From a narrative and historical perspective, a reference to Roman law makes most sense. Roman governors were not responsible for coercing Jews to keep Jewish laws. Moreover, deliberately ambiguous accusations in a legal case before a provincial governor could hardly hope to have the intended effect of curbing Paul's activities. But a breach of Roman law is precisely the point, where the highest administrator of a province can be expected to intervene. Paul is accused of violating the laws of the Roman Empire (not the laws of the city of Corinth, for which the local magistrates would be responsible).

In Philippi and Thessalonica, Paul had also been accused before civil authorities (16:20 – 21; 17:6 – 7), but there it involved causing an upheaval in the city, a charge not leveled against Paul in Corinth. As in Thessalonica, the charge in Corinth includes a comment on the problematic nature of Paul's teaching activity. Since the effect of Paul's teaching on the population in the city is not mentioned, the focus is on his actual message, which is regarded as dangerous not primarily because it prompts unrest but because it is "against the law"; i.e., its very content is dangerous.

In Thessalonica, Paul had been accused on account of his proclamation of Jesus as Messiah-King (17:7), implying that Paul was instigating a rebellion against the emperor and his rule over the world. Luke's account of the charges against Paul in Corinth is not specified beyond breaking the law. Perhaps similar charges as those in Thessalonica are in the background. Or, the Jews may have appealed to an earlier edict of Claudius that guaranteed that the Jews were allowed to practice their customs without interference, arguing that Paul disturbed the peace of their community with his religious teaching before "people," a term that includes both Jews and Gentiles.[34] Or, the Jews wanted to signal to the governor that the new congregation that Paul had started and that was meeting in the house of Titius Justus was not a rival synagogue (which would be exempted from the imperial ban on weekly meetings of associations) but a new cult that was meeting contrary to the law.

The proconsul was responsible primarily for maintaining public order in "his" province. The legal bases for his governorship were specifically formulated directives (*mandata*) for his term of office. The vaguely formulated charge of the Corinthian Jews who accuse Paul makes sense if we take v. 13 to be the beginning of the pretrial hearing in which the charges would be summarized, with the prospect that the actual trial would bring the fuller charges to light.[35]

---

31. Bock, *Acts*, 581; Peterson, *Acts*, 516 – 17.

32. Fitzmyer, *Acts*, 629; Omerzu, *Prozess*, 254.

33. Cf. Tajra, *Trial*, 56; Dunn, *Beginning from Jerusalem*, 701.

34. The Jews were allowed by various imperial edicts, sent to individual cities, to live according to their ancestral beliefs and customs; cf. Josephus, *Ant.* 14.185 – 222, 256, 267; 19.280 – 91.

35. Omerzu, *Prozess*, 257.

18:14 As Paul was about to speak, Gallio said to the Jews: "Jews, if it were a matter of crime or some serious case of deception, I would be justified in accepting your complaint (μέλλοντος δὲ τοῦ Παύλου ἀνοίγειν τὸ στόμα εἶπεν ὁ Γαλλίων πρὸς τοὺς Ἰουδαίους· εἰ μὲν ἦν ἀδίκημά τι ἢ ῥᾳδιούργημα πονηρόν, ὦ Ἰουδαῖοι, κατὰ λόγον ἂν ἀνεσχόμην ὑμῶν). Paul is ready to defend himself against the charges of the Corinthian Jews, but he is cut short by the Roman proconsul, who dismisses the case and thus does not need to hear Paul's arguments. Luke's account implies that Gallio, probably accompanied by his legal advisers, dispenses with the customary recess after the preliminary hearing. He immediately renders his judgment on the legal merits of the case.[36] Gallio's actions confirm that Luke's narrative of the legal case against Paul can be interpreted in terms of the *cognitio extra ordinem*, in which "cases are heard by the holder of imperium in person on his tribunal" and in which "it is within the competence of the judge to decide whether to accept a novel charge or not."[37]

Gallio notes two areas in which he has to intervene in his responsibility as governor of the province: when a "crime" (ἀδίκημα) has been committed and when a "serious case of deception" (ῥᾳδιούργημα πονηρόν) has been brought to light. The term translated "accepting your complaint" (ἀνεσχόμην) is a technical legal term for proceeding with a legal case. The formulation as a second class conditional sentence (with ἄν in the apodosis) implies neither of these applies, which means that there are no legal grounds for him to proceed with the case.

18:15 "But since this is a matter of controversial questions about teaching and names and your own law, see to it yourselves. I refuse to be the judge of such matters" (εἰ δὲ ζητήματά ἐστιν περὶ λόγου καὶ ὀνομάτων καὶ νόμου τοῦ καθ᾽ ὑμᾶς, ὄψεσθε αὐτοί· κριτὴς ἐγὼ τούτων οὐ βούλομαι εἶναι). Gallio considers that the legal case before him concerns "controversial questions" (ζητήματα), i.e., matters of dispute or claims.[38] He identifies the nature of the legal case with three expressions, formulated with a first class conditional clause that expresses what the governor believes to be true.

(1) The dispute is about "teaching" (λόγος). This Greek word can also mean "argument" (concerning the necessity of faith in Jesus), "rule of conduct" (determined no longer by Jewish tradition), "tale, story" (about Jesus' resurrection), "rumor" (about matters that happened in Galilee and in Judea twenty years ago), or "declaration of legal immunity."[39] In the context of the latter meaning, the Corinthian Jews may have argued that Paul's new group did not qualify for the imperial exemption from the ban of weekly meetings of associations or for the immunity from having to sacrifice to the emperor.[40]

(2) The dispute is about "names" (ὀνόματα), a word that can refer to "names" in contrast to "actions" (Roman law holds people responsible for their actions, not for names they profess), to particular "persons" (Moses or Jesus), or to "terms" (the meaning of words such as "savior," "righteousness," or "resurrection").

(3) The dispute concerns "your own law" (νόμος

---

36. Bruce W. Winter, "Rehabilitating Gallio and His Judgement in Acts 18:14 – 15," *TynBul* 57 (2006): 291 – 308, 307, who suggests that this "may be a reflection of his legal competence."

37. Sherwin-White, *Roman Society*, 99 – 100.

38. The term has been used by Luke in 15:2; cf. also 23:29; 25:19; 26:3.

39. For these senses of λόγος cf. LSJ, s.v. λόγος III.2, III.3, V.3, VI.2b, VII.6.

40. Cf. Bruce W. Winter, "Gallio's Ruling on the Legal Status of Early Christianity (Acts 18:14 – 15)," *TynBul* 50 (1999): 213 – 24, 219; the Jews were granted immunity from observing the imperial cult, in acknowledgment of the fact that sacrifices were offered in Jerusalem for the emperor (although not to the emperor).

ὁ καθ᾽ ὑμᾶς), i.e., the Mosaic law. The Corinthian Jews could have argued that since Paul wants to invite Gentiles into the synagogue as full members of the community, with all the rights and privileges that the Jews enjoy, without requiring of them circumcision or submission to the law, he is changing the Mosaic law. Or the Jews could have argued that Paul's message about Jesus being the Jewish Messiah contradicted the Jewish law on account of the fact that Jesus had been crucified and was thus subjected to the curse of the law (Deut 21:23), which means that he cannot possibly be a savior. Since Gallio emphasizes the distinction between "your own" law and Roman law, he rejects the charge that Paul has violated Roman law. This means, at the same time, that Gallio sees no distinction between Jews who live according to the Jewish law and the followers of Jesus.

This was an immensely important verdict, not only because it protected the Christians in the province of Achaia from legal cases against their beliefs and against the existence of their new congregations, but also because this was the first time that a Roman official issued a legal verdict concerning the followers of Jesus. This verdict declared that they should be regarded as a Jewish group, with the corollary that they would have the right to the same legal privileges that the Jews had been granted by the emperors.[41]

The Corinthian Jews end up securing for Paul and the Christians in Achaia a ruling that is the opposite of what they hoped. They wanted a legal conviction of Paul and a suppression of the new group of Jewish and Gentile followers of Jesus as Messiah as an illegal association; what they get instead is an official acknowledgment by the Roman governor that the new community of followers of Jesus is a group within Judaism and therefore a legal association of people against which no legal action can be taken. To be a Christian is not a criminal offense. It should be noted that Paul in his later legal defense before Roman authorities emphasizes that he is being accused on matters related to Jewish questions, not for breaking Roman law.[42]

Gallio reiterates that he does not intend to be the "judge" of the disputes in the three areas he outlines. Since he will not get involved in their disputes, he advises the Jews to solve these matters among themselves, i.e., in the court of the synagogue. The Greek phrase translated "see to it yourselves" is a Latinism — perhaps reflecting Gallio's formulation of his verdict, which would have been in Latin. The Jews need to deal with these questions themselves.

Luke does not report whether the Corinthian Jews ever try to put Paul on trial for the synagogue court. In order to do so, Paul would have to visit the synagogue again, where they could hold him and adjudicate his case. Or they could invite Paul to stand trial before the synagogue court (giving him another opportunity to explain his message about Jesus). Or they could seize him on the street, perhaps when he entered the house of Titius Justus, and forcibly take him to the synagogue next door and put him on trial. Paul states in 2 Cor 11:24 that he received five times from the Jews "the forty lashes minus one" — the official punishment of the synagogues based on Deut 25:2 – 3.[43] It is not im-

---

41. Note in Philippi (16:22 – 23) and in Thessalonica (17:8 – 9) the behavior of the magistrates: they released Paul and his associates from prison, they even apologized, but they did not issue an official legal verdict. Cf. Omerzu, *Prozess*, 262 – 63.

42. Cf. Padilla, *Speeches*, 160, with reference to 21:40; 22:3, 14; 23:6; 24:14, 21; 26:2 – 3.

43. Jewish sources acknowledge that a person could die during or after receiving thirty-nine lashes (*m. Mak.* 3.14, stipulating that in this case "the scourger is not culpable"). Josephus, *Ant.* 4.238 calls this punishment "most ignominious" for a free man.

possible that one of the occasions for this serious penalty was the aftermath of the Gallio episode.

18:16 So he drove them away from the judicial bench (καὶ ἀπήλασεν αὐτοὺς ἀπὸ τοῦ βήματος). Gallio expels the plaintiffs from the judicial bench (βῆμα, see on 18:12; 12:21). The Greek verb expresses the fact that Gallio "had no patience with the Jews," judging that "they were wasting the time of his court."[44] The governor presumably directs the lictors to remove the Jews from the *rostra*.

18:17 Then they all seized Sosthenes, the president of the synagogue, and beat him in front of the judicial bench. But none of this was of concern to Gallio (ἐπιλαβόμενοι δὲ πάντες Σωσθένην τὸν ἀρχισυνάγωγον ἔτυπτον ἔμπροσθεν τοῦ βήματος· καὶ οὐδὲν τούτων τῷ Γαλλίωνι ἔμελεν). In the context of the previous verse, the substantival adjective "all" (πάντες) refers to the Jews who brought the legal case against Paul before the governor in v. 12, who spoke in v. 13, to whom Gallio's words in vv. 14–15 were spoken, and who were dismissed in v. 16. As the Corinthian Jews realize that their legal case has been disallowed and that Paul and his group have been given, by implication, official legal sanction, they beat up Sosthenes in front of the *rostra*, inflicting revenge on him.

Sosthenes evidently replaced Crispus, who had become a Christian (v. 8), as "president of the synagogue" (ὁ ἀρχισυνάγωγος; see on 13:15). He was presumably the point person of the delegation that brought the legal case against Paul before the governor, whose disappointed members took out their frustration against Sosthenes for the way he had handled the legal case. Alternately, many assume that it was the Greek and Roman citizens of the city who beat up Sosthenes, perhaps due to

the casual anti-Semitism among the population in Greek and Roman cities, perhaps as a penalty for an attempted prosecution based on slander aimed at prejudicing the court. If this is correct, the turn of events is rather ironic: while the Jews wanted to harm Paul, "the Roman patrons and clients present in the forum turned the tables against Sosthenes."[45]

A third option sees both Romans (Greeks) and Jews to be the referent of "all"; the dismissal of the case leads to a fracas in which the Romans beat Sosthenes, perhaps to demonstrate their support of the emperor's recent anti-Jewish edict (v. 2), while the Jews clobber him because he made the Jewish community and their case against Paul and his group a laughingstock in the city. Gallio ignores the beating of Sosthenes, despite the fact that he would have been a prominent citizen of Corinth. If the identification with Sosthenes in 1 Cor 1:1 is plausible,[46] Crispus' successor (or colleague) as president of the synagogue also becomes a Christian.

18:18 Paul stayed in Corinth for many days. Eventually he took leave of the believers and sailed for Syria, accompanied by Priscilla and Aquila. At Cenchreae he had his hair cut because he had made a vow (ὁ δὲ Παῦλος ἔτι προσμείνας ἡμέρας ἱκανὰς τοῖς ἀδελφοῖς ἀποταξάμενος ἐξέπλει εἰς τὴν Συρίαν, καὶ σὺν αὐτῷ Πρίσκιλλα καὶ Ἀκύλας, κειράμενος ἐν Κεγχρεαῖς τὴν κεφαλήν, εἶχεν γὰρ εὐχήν). The fifth incident of the Corinth episode (v. 18a-b) relates Paul's continued missionary work in the city. Gallio's decision in vv. 12–17 is the reason why Paul can stay in Corinth. The phrase translated "for many days" (ἡμέρας ἱκανάς) does not allow us to ascertain the time of the Gallio incident. If the attempt of the Jews to have Gallio try and indict Paul took place in July or August AD

---

44. Barrett, *Acts*, 875. Fitzmyer, *Acts*, 630, translates in terms of a more polite evaluation of Gallio's action: "he dismissed the case from the court"; for the following comment see ibid.

45. Winter, "Rehabilitating Gallio," 305.

46. This identification, assumed by many (cf. Murphy-O'Connor, *Paul*, 264), is not entirely certain because Sosthenes was a not uncommon name.

51, and if Paul left for Syria in September before the end of navigation on the Mediterranean,[47] the "many days" should be reckoned in days (cf. 27:7) rather than weeks.

We know more about the Corinthian congregation than about any other church Paul established, mostly because of the correspondence preserved in the New Testament. The church included Jews (Acts 18:4, 8; 1 Cor 7:18), proselytes, God-fearers (Acts 18:4, 7), and Gentiles, i.e., former polytheists (1 Cor 8:7). Some believers were members of the local elite, belonging to the powerful, the educated, and the wealthy aristocracy (1 Cor 1:26): Crispus (and Sosthenes), presidents of the synagogue (Acts 18:8, 17; 1 Cor 1:14); Titius Justus, who had a house (Acts 18:7); Gaius, who owned a house (Rom 16:23); Stephanas, who also owned a house (1 Cor 1:16; 16:15, 17); perhaps Chloe, who seems to have had slaves (1 Cor 1:11); and Erastus, the city treasurer (see on 19:22; cf. Rom 16:23; 2 Tim 4:20). Erastus would have been a Roman citizen; other educated and wealthy Christians in Corinth probably held Roman citizenship too. It seems that most of the problems that Paul deals with in 1 Corinthians were caused by this elite group.

Most of the Christians, however, were at the bottom of the social pyramid. The majority of the believers were poor, with little, if any, education. The people of "Chloe's hosehold" (1 Cor 1:11) were probably slaves or perhaps freedmen; Corinthian believers who had names often attested for slaves were Achaicus, Fortunatus, and Quartus (1 Cor 16:17; Rom 16:23), perhaps Tertius, who was a secretary in the household of Gaius (Rom 16:22), and other slaves (1 Cor 7:21 – 22), including the members of the household of Stephanas and Crispus. Aquila and Priscilla, as well as probably Phoebe, were merchants (Acts 18:2 – 3; Rom 16:1 – 2).

When Paul eventually leaves Corinth, it is his own decision. He is confident that the new congregation can continue the work of teaching and preaching without his presence, a fact that allows him to start a new missionary initiative. For some, the difficulties that arise in the church in Corinth within two or three years suggest that Paul's departure was premature. While we do not know whether Paul later regretted leaving Corinth too early, we should not forget that he was confident that the presence of God's grace and the manifestation of the gifts of the Holy Spirit would strengthen the Corithians believers even in the midst of the difficulties that had arisen (1 Cor 1:4 – 8). Paul trusted God's faithfulness, manifested in Jesus, Messiah and Lord (1 Cor 1:9), more than he trusted in the necessity of his continued presence in Corinth.

The sixth and final incident of the Corinth episode relates Paul's return to Antioch via Cenchreae, Ephesus, Caesarea, and Jerusalem (vv. 18c – 22). Paul returned to Syria (see on 15:23), specifically to Antioch (18:22), from where he had set out together with Silas (15:40). Luke does not name Paul's travel companions on the journey back to Antioch (apart from Aquila and Priscilla, who accompany him as far as Ephesus); it is unlikely that Paul traveled alone. When Paul had set out from Antioch, he originally planned to proclaim the gospel and establish congregations in the province of Asia (16:6). As this had proven impossible at the time, he traveled to Macedonia and Achaia, where he established churches in Philippi, Thessalonica, Berea, Athens, and Corinth. If the stopover in Ephesus during the journey back to Antioch (vv. 19 – 21) was not caused by the itinerary of the ship or by the itinerary of Aquila and Priscilla, who wanted to move to Ephesus, Paul may have decided to try again a mission to Asia.

---

47. Riesner, *Paul's Early Period*, 210. The term *mare clausum* ("closed sea") referred to the time between November 11 and March 5, according to the theory of Vegetius, *Rei militaris* *instituta.* 4.39, who wrote in the fourth century AD. Cf. E. Olshausen, "Mare Nostrum," *BNP*, 8:336.

After Paul took leave of the Corinthian believers, he embarked on a ship headed to Syria. The fact that Priscilla and Aquila (see on v. 2) accompanied him does not indicate that they have replaced Silas and Timothy as Paul's primary travel companions. They are mentioned here in order to explain how the couple came to live and work in Ephesus (vv. 19, 26). Traveling east, Paul went to Cenchreae, Corinth's harbor on the Saronic Gulf, about seven miles (11 km.) southeast of the city center. Cenchreae had perhaps 4,400 inhabitants; the harbor was enlarged by artificial breakwaters, with one of the piers extending 390 feet (120 m.) into the sea. It appears that during Paul's work in Corinth, a church was established in Cenchreae as well,[48] with Phoebe as a patron of the congregation, a woman with means who, five years later, traveled to Rome taking Paul's letter from Corinth to the Roman Christians (Rom 16:1 – 2).

Before Paul embarked on the ship to Syria, he had his hair cut "because he had made a vow."[49] Since Luke provides no details concerning the vow, several questions must remain unanswered. Was this a Nazirite vow (Num 6:1 – 21)?[50] Most scholars assume so. If this is correct, Paul had asked God for some kind of intervention, promising something in return.[51] Assuming that Paul fulfilled the requirements set out in Num 6:2 – 8 for the duration of the Nazirite vow, he would not have imbibed

any intoxicating drink, or cut his hair, or defiled himself by touching a dead body. The reference to Paul's having his hair cut can be understood either in terms of Paul's final haircut before the vow took effect, or in terms of the completion of the vow (which would also have required, according to Num 6:13 – 21, the offering of sacrifices and other ceremonies).[52]

What did Paul hope to achieve with a Nazirite vow? One suggestion has been that Paul wanted to demonstrate his "willingness to follow the Torah in matters of personal spiritual discipline" and thus his "good faith" to the conservative Jewish Christians in Antioch and in Jerusalem, hoping that this gesture "would heal any continuing rift."[53] While not impossible, nothing in the context specifically indicates that Paul wanted (or needed) to demonstrate his willingness to become a Jew to the Jews (1 Cor 9:20). The vow could be related to God's promise of protection in vv. 9 – 10 and to Paul's subsequent willingness to stay in Corinth for an extended period of time; in this case, the vow would presumably have been made in thankfulness for God's protection (i.e., for past blessings).[54]

Or was the vow a private religious exercise in which Paul thanked God for his protection during his mission in Corinth?[55] This suggestion posits a non-Jewish background: Paul's vow and the decision to cut his hair may be "a standard Greek

---

48. Note that according to 2 Cor 1:1 there were other churches in the province of Achaia besides Corinth.

49. Since Aquila is the nearest noun and in the nominative, he could be the antecedent of the participle (κειράμενος) and the main verb (εἶχεν); however, since Paul is the central figure of the narrative, he is probably intended, as most commentators assume.

50. See also Judg 13:7, 13 – 14; 16:17; Amos 2:11 – 12; cf. 1 Sam 1:11; 1 Macc 3:49; Josephus, J.W. 2.313; Ant. 4.72; 19.293 – 294.

51. Note the definition in BDAG, s.v. εὐχή 2, "a solemn promise with the understanding that one is subject to penalty for failure to discharge the obligation." See further on 21:23 – 24.

52. According to (later) Mishnaic law, the hair could be cut

someplace else, while the sacrifices and other ceremonies had to take place in Jerusalem, requiring a stay there of thirty days (m. Naz. 6:8).

53. Dunn, Beginning from Jerusalem, 752; cf. Bart J. Koet, "Why Did Paul Shave His Hair (Acts 18:18)? Nazirite and Temple in the Book of Acts," in The Centrality of Jerusalem: Historical Perspectives (ed. M. Poorthuis and C. Safrai; Kampen: Kok Pharos, 1996), 128 – 42, 140.

54. Marshall, Acts, 300; Witherington, Acts, 557.

55. Bruce, Acts, 398, who argues that a Nazirite vow "could not be observed outside of the land of Israel, because of the constant exposure to defilement in a Gentile environment" (m. Naz. 7.3). For regulations concerning general vows cf. Deut 23:21 – 22.

cultural reaction to some dream through which came divine guidance."[56] Or, if it was a Nazirite vow, it could have involved a petition that God will protect him during the upcoming dangerous sea voyage and during his visit to Jerusalem and to Antioch (i.e., a vow in connection with future blessings).[57] Certainty is impossible. Luke makes nothing of Paul's vow in his subsequent narrative.

18:19 When they reached Ephesus, he left them there. He went into the synagogue, where he held discussions with the Jews (κατήντησαν δὲ εἰς Ἔφεσον κἀκείνους κατέλιπεν αὐτοῦ, αὐτὸς δὲ εἰσελθὼν εἰς τὴν συναγωγὴν διελέξατο τοῖς Ἰουδαίοις). The ship that took Paul and Aquila and Priscilla from Cenchreae to Ephesus sailed straight east, past Cape Sounion, passing between the Cyclades islands of Andros and Tenos, sailing north of the island of Samos before reaching Ephesus.[58]

Luke relates the stopover in Ephesus in some detail (vv. 19 – 21). When the travel party arrives in Ephesus (see on 18:24), Aquila and Priscilla stay in the city while Paul continues to travel to Syria. The formulation translated "he went into the synagogue" introduces vv. 19c – 21. This should not be taken to mean that Aquila and Priscilla stay in the city while Paul visits the synagogue outside of the city, or that only Paul visits the synagogue while Aquila and Priscilla stay away. The Jewish couple evidently own a house in Ephesus, the location of a future house church (1 Cor 16:19).

Paul's visit to the synagogue in Ephesus may be because the ship taking him to Syria docked in the harbor for a few days, allowing him to attend a synagogue service. Or, if Paul is planning his next missionary initiative with a base in Ephesus, his visit to the synagogue may be a deliberate attempt to establish contact with the Jewish community. Whatever Paul's intentions, he "held discussions" (διελέξατο; see on 17:2) with the Jews, explaining the Scriptures in terms of the fulfillment of God's promises in the death and resurrection of Jesus Christ.

18:20 – 21 When they asked him to stay for a longer period of time, he declined. As he took his leave, he said, "I will come back to you, if God wills." Then he set sail from Ephesus (ἐρωτώντων δὲ αὐτῶν ἐπὶ πλείονα χρόνον μεῖναι οὐκ ἐπένευσεν, ἀλλὰ ἀποταξάμενος καὶ εἰπών· πάλιν ἀνακάμψω πρὸς ὑμᾶς τοῦ θεοῦ θέλοντος, ἀνήχθη ἀπὸ τῆς Ἐφέσου). Paul's explanation of his views concerning the Scriptures and Jesus Christ do not lead to controversy. On the contrary, the Ephesian Jews invite Paul to stay "for a longer period of time" when they realize that he is only visiting the city. Paul declines their invitation since he wants to reach Syria (v. 18).

Since Luke does not report any particular activity of Paul in Jerusalem and Antioch (vv. 22 – 23), the reasons for his departure despite the open door in Ephesus remain unclear. Perhaps Paul is determined, after an absence of three years, to return to Jerusalem and Antioch, both for a time of rest and to give a report about the new congregations established in various cities in Macedonia and Achaia.[59] Or he wants to visit Jerusalem in connection with his (Nazirite) vow and its fulfillment, which required residence in Israel and involvement in various ceremonies in Jerusalem.[60] Or, Paul regards it

---

56. Horsley and Llewelyn, *New Documents*, 1:24, referring to dedications set up in fulfillment of a vow. See ibid., 4:114 – 15, for a reference to Juvenal, *Sat.* 12.25 – 28, 81, with literary evidence for vows and dedications regarding near-shipwrecks, and for sailors who return safely in the harbor and who shave their heads, probably in fulfillment of vows.

57. Cf. Barrett, *Acts*, 877.

58. The 220 mile (350 km.) journey would have taken, assuming normal wind conditions, three or four days.

59. Johnson, *Acts*, 334 – 35; Paul wanted "to assert his continuing fidelity to the original apostolic community."

60. Cf. Witherington, *Acts*, 557, 558.

as strategically important to maintain good links between the Gentile churches and the Jerusalem church.[61]

More specifically, perhaps Paul wants to strengthen and consolidate (and, if necessary, rehabilitate) his relationship with the churches in Jerusalem and Antioch, which had come under pressure on account of Jewish believers from Jerusalem visiting the churches in Syria, Cilicia, and Galatia and demanding that Gentile believers should be circumcised and commit totally to the Mosaic law (see 15:1 – 35).[62] All of these reasons are not mutually exclusive.

Paul expresses his willingness to return to Ephesus. The phrase translated "if God wills" (τοῦ θεοῦ θέλοντος; Lat. *Deo volente*) was common in antiquity.[63] For Jews, the concern was not so much the avoidance of the suspicion of pride but an expression of dependence on God, who alone knows the future. It derives from the Old Testament principle that "many are the plans in a person's heart, but it is the LORD's purpose that prevails" (Prov 19:21).

Paul then sets sail, leaving Ephesus when the ship on which he had booked the passage to Syria departs. It is safe to assume that the ship would not have traveled straight from Ephesus to Caesarea;[64] it probably put in at various harbors — perhaps in Cnidos, Rhodos, and Paphos (on Cyprus) — to take on supplies and to engage in trade.

18:22   When he had landed at Caesarea, he went up to Jerusalem and visited the congregation. Then he went to Antioch (καὶ κατελθὼν εἰς Καισάρειαν, ἀναβὰς καὶ ἀσπασάμενος τὴν ἐκκλησίαν κατέβη εἰς Ἀντιόχειαν). Luke relates the events following the end of Paul's sea voyage with four verbs (all construed in the aorist, the first three being participles). Paul "landed" (κατελθὼν)[65] in Caesarea, he "went up" (ἀναβάς) to Jerusalem, he "visited" (ἀσπασάμενος) the congregation, and he "went" (κατέβη) to Antioch. The participle translated "he went up" (ἀναβάς) does not have an object in the Greek text; there can be little doubt, considering the combination with the verb translated "going down" (καταβαίνω), which often connotes going away from Jerusalem (in the hill country) or from Palestine, that a visit to Jerusalem is in view. This visit in the fall of AD 51 was Paul's fourth visit in Jerusalem after his conversion (others visits: AD 33/34, Acts 9:26 – 29; Gal 1:18; AD 44, Acts 11:27 – 30; Gal 2:1), and AD 48, Acts 15:1 – 29). The journey from Jerusalem to Antioch, the capital of Syria, would have taken Paul over three weeks on foot 335 miles (540 km.).

---

61. Cf. Peterson, *Acts*, 522.

62. Cf. Barrett, *Acts*, 880 – 81; cf. Dunn, *Beginning from Jerusalem*, 753 – 54.

63. Cf. Josephus, *Ant.* 2.333, 347; 7.373; in the NT: 1 Cor 4:19; 16:7; Heb 6:3; Jas 4:15; cf. Rom 1:10; also Plato, *Alc. maj.* 135D; *Phaedo* 80D; Epictetus 1.1.17; also in a papyrus from the second century AD (BGU II 423).

64. The distance from Ephesus to Caesarea is about 650 miles (1040 km.), for which a ship would need five to ten days, given normal weather conditions.

65. Cf. BDAG, s.v. κατέρχομαι 2: nautical technical term "of ships and those who sail in them, who 'come down' from the 'high seas.'"

Theology in Application

There are several features of the Corinth episode that are familiar from Luke's account in the earlier sections of Acts, particularly Paul's preaching in synagogues, which eventually leads to conflict (18:4 – 7; cf. 13:45; 17:5). New elements are the emphasis on teamwork (18:2 – 3, 5, 18), a divine revelation admonishing and encouraging Paul to stay in Corinth (18:9 – 10), and the legal case before the Roman governor of Achaia (18:12 – 17). Thus, in keeping with the main idea formulated above, the following emphases are important.

Missionary Work and God's Presence

God granted Paul a visionary experience in which he reassured him concerning the power of his presence. At the beginning of this phase of his missionary work there was another visionary experience, the vision of a Macedonian man pleading for Paul to move from Asia Minor to Macedonia (16:9). Such experiences do not eliminate problems — the vision in 16:9 happened after weeks of uncertainty about a new location for missionary work (16:6 – 8), and the vision in 18:9 – 10 was a response to Jewish opposition (v. 6) that over time only intensified (vv. 12 – 13). The Lord reassured Paul of his presence and of his protection, which reflects Jesus' promise that he will be with his witnesses until the end of the age (Matt 28:20).

Without denigrating the specific reality of hearing the Lord speak in a vision, Jesus' words to Thomas continue to have fundamental significance for missionaries, pastors, preachers, and indeed all Christians: "Because you have seen me, you have believed; blessed are those who have not seen and yet have believed" (John 20:29). This blessing is significant precisely in the context of the promise of the risen Jesus Christ that he is present every single day, always, whether in a vision or in the everyday life and work as his witness. The reality of the Lord's presence not only reassures us that we do not have to be afraid, but, more importantly, makes the proclamation of the gospel effective (cf. 1 Cor 2:1 – 5).

Missionary Work and Political Realities

The Corinth episode relates three "intersections" of Paul's mission with contemporary political realities: the arrival of Aquila and Priscilla as a result of the eviction of the Jews from Rome by imperial edict (v. 2), the opposition of Jews in the synagogue (v. 6), and the attempt of Corinthian Jews to have Paul tried and convicted before the Roman governor (vv. 12 – 13).

The first episode has positive consequences for Paul. He finds in Aquila and Priscilla fellow Jews who provide accommodation, work, and practical support in his missionary work.

The second incident has a negative outcome for Paul, at least on the surface. Further ministry in the synagogue becomes impossible, and Paul has to find a new location for his work and congregation (v. 7). At the same time, the president of the synagogue is converted, and it might be precisely the new location of the believers in the house of a (Gentile) God-fearer that contributes to the numerous conversions among the Corinthian population (v. 8).

The third incident has a positive outcome for Paul. The Roman governor refuses to let the legal case go forward and dismisses the case by affirming that Paul and his group are part of the Jewish community. This has not only theological ramifications (followers of Jesus are God's people who believe in Israel's Messiah), but also political consequences: the new group enjoys, for the time being, the same privileges as the Jewish community, including the right to organize weekly meetings.

All three occasions are examples of Paul's dictum that "in all things God works for the good of those who love him" (Rom 8:28). Christians recognize God's guidance in the midst of personal difficulties. Even forced relocations to other places can serve a higher purpose. Missionaries and pastors should refuse to be intimidated by opposition and be confident in God's presence and care. Churches rejoice in political protection when they receive it. The gospel does not threaten city, regional, or national governments since Christians are not lawbreakers, even though their message may provoke the status quo of sinners and sinful traditions and structures.

CHAPTER 33

Acts 18:23 – 20:1

Literary Context

This section, made up of two episodes, is the first of two sections in Luke's report about Paul's ministry in Ephesus (18:23 – 21:17). Having described Paul's missionary work in Cyprus, Galatia, and Pamphylia in Asia Minor (13:1 – 15:33), and in Macedonia and Achaia (15:35 – 18:22), Luke now describes Paul's work in the province of Asia. He first describes Paul's mission in Ephesus (18:23 – 20:1) before he relates his visits to the churches in Europe and his return to Jerusalem (20:2 – 21:17). The first of the two episodes of this section narrates Paul's departure from Antioch, his visit to the churches in Galatia and Phrygia, and the ministry of Apollos in Ephesus and then Achaia before Paul's arrival (18:23 – 28). The second episode describes in detail Paul's missionary work in Ephesus in AD 52 – 55 (19:1 – 20:1).

Paul's farewell speech to the elders of the Ephesus congregation (20:18 – 35) relates additional details about his mission there. It was during that ministry that he wrote 1 Corinthians (AD 54), a letter that contains, however, no information about events in Ephesus.[1] Paul's letter "To the Ephesians" seems to have been written not to the Ephesian believers exclusively (the address "in Ephesus" in Eph 1:1 is missing in the best manuscripts), but more generally to Christians living in Asia Minor; that letter provides no specific information on Paul's ministry in Ephesus either. Paul's work in Ephesus and, more widely, in the province of Asia during AD 52 – 55 is the tenth phase of Paul's missionary work.[2]

---

1. Some scholars think that the letters to the Christians in Galatia and in Philippi were also written during Paul's ministry in Ephesus, but this is not certain. The letter to the Galatian Christians may have been written as early as AD 48 in Syrian Antioch, shortly after his return from his Galatia mission, or in AD 50 in Corinth. The letter to the Philippian Christians was perhaps written during Paul's imprisonment in Caesarea (AD 57 – 59) or, more likely, during his imprisonment in Rome (AD 60 – 62).

2. See "In Depth: Paul's Missionary Work," in Literary Context on 13:1 – 12. This phase of Paul's missionary work is traditionally referred to as Paul's "third missionary *journey*" — rather obviously a mistaken term when we consider the fact that Paul worked in Ephesus for about three years.

Main Idea

Luke depicts Aquila and Priscilla as ideal believers, Apollos as an ideal preacher, and Paul as the ideal missionary who corrects deficient theology, preaches boldly, and overcomes opposition, and whose ministry is accompanied by miracles and characterized by impact on society at large.

Translation

Acts 18:23 – 20:1

23a	Setting: Time	After spending some time there,
b	Action	**he departed**
c	Action	**and traveled from place to place**
d	Place	through the region of Galatia and
e	Place	Phrygia,
f	Purpose	strengthening all the disciples.
24a	Character entrance	**Meanwhile a Jew named Apollos,**
b	Geographical	a native of Alexandria,
c	Event	**arrived in Ephesus.**
d	Character description	**He was a learned man,**
e	Character description	well-versed in the Scriptures.
25a	Character description	**He had been instructed in the Way of the Lord;**
b	Character description	**he spoke being fervent in the Spirit,**
c	Character description	**and he taught about Jesus accurately,**
d	Concession	even though he knew only the baptism of John.
26a	Action	**He began to speak boldly in the synagogue.**
b	Time	When Priscilla and Aquila heard him,
c	Action	**they took him aside**
d	Action	**and explained to him the Way of God**
e	Manner	more accurately.

Continued on next page.

Continued from previous page.

27a	Setting: time	When he wanted to go to Achaia,
b	Action	**the believers encouraged him**
c	Action	**and wrote to the disciples there**
d	Purpose	to welcome him.
e	Setting: time	On his arrival
f	Action	**he was of great assistance to those**
g	Character description	who through grace had become believers,
28a	Cause	for he vigorously refuted the Jews
b	Place	in public,
c	Means	demonstrating
d	Source	from the Scriptures
e	Content	that Jesus was the Messiah.
19:1a	Setting: time	While Apollos was in Corinth,
b	Action	**Paul passed through the interior regions**
c	Place	**and came to Ephesus,**
d	Event	where he found some disciples.
2a	Dialogue	**He said to them,**
b	Question	*"Did you receive the Holy Spirit*
c	Time	*when you came to faith?"*
d	Response	**They replied,**
e	Assertion	*"We have not heard*
f	Content	*that there is a Holy Spirit."*
3a		**He said,**
b	Question	*"Then how were you baptized?"*
c	Response	**They said,**
d	Means	*"With the baptism of John."*
4a	Instruction	**Paul said,**
b	Event (review of history)	*"John immersed*
c	Means	*with a baptism of repentance,*
d	Circumstance	*telling the people*
e	Content	*that they should believe*
f	Content	*in the one who would come after him,*
g	Identification	*that is, in Jesus."*
5a	Time	When they heard this,
b	Action	**they were immersed**
c	Association	in the name of the Lord Jesus,
6a	Time	and when Paul laid his hands on them,
b	Event	**the Holy Spirit came upon them;**
c	Action	**they spoke in unlearned languages and**
d	Action	**prophesied.**
7	Measure (Aside)	**In all, there were about twelve men.**
8a	Action (Place)	**Paul went into the synagogue**
b	Action	**and spoke freely**

c	Duration	for three months,
d	Purpose	informing and
e	Purpose	seeking to convince them
f	Content	about the reality of the kingdom of God.

9a	Setting: Time	When some became hardened and
b	Conflict	refused to believe, and
c	Action	insulted the Way
d	Place	before the assembly,
e	Reaction	**he left them**
f	Action	and **took the disciples with him.**

g	Setting: Time	Day after day
h	Action	**he lectured**
i	Place	in the hall of Tyrannus.
10a	Duration	**This continued for two years,**
b	Result	with the result that all people
c	Geographical	who lived in the province of Asia,
d	Ethnic	both Jews and
e	Ethnic	Greeks,
f	Result	heard the word of the Lord.

11a	Event	**God continued to perform extraordinary miracles**
b	Means	through Paul,
12a	Event	so that when handkerchiefs and aprons had touched his skin and
b	Event	were taken to the sick,
c	Result	their diseases left them and
d	Result	the evil spirits departed.

13a	Action	**Some of the itinerant Jewish exorcists tried to evoke the name of the Lord Jesus**
b	Sphere	over people possessed by evil ↵ spirits,
c	Assertion	saying,
d	Command	*"I adjure you*
e	Means	*by the Jesus*
f	Identification	*whom Paul proclaims."*
14a	Character entrance	**Seven sons of a Jewish chief priest**
b	Identification	named Sceva
c	Action	**were doing this.**
15a	Response	But **the evil spirit answered them,**
b	Assertion	*"I know Jesus, and*
c	Assertion	*I am acquainted with Paul,*
d	Question	*but who are you?"*
16a	Action	**Then the person with the evil spirit jumped on them;**
b	Action	**he subdued all of them and**
c	Action	**overpowered them**
d	Result	so that they fled from the house
e	Manner	naked and
f	Manner	wounded.

Continued on next page.

Continued from previous page.

17a	Event	**This became known to all the Jews and**
b	Ethnic	**Greeks**
c	Geographical	living in Ephesus.
d	Event	**Fear came over all of them,**
e	Event	and **the name of the Lord Jesus was glorified.**
18a	Character description/ Action	**Many of those who had come to faith came forward**
b	Purpose	to confess and
c	Purpose	admit their practices.
19a	Character entrance	**Quite a few of those**
b	Character description	who practiced magic
c	Action	**gathered their books together**
d	Action	and **burned them**
e	Place	in public.
f	Measure (Aside)	**The value of these books was assessed to be 50,000 silver coins.**
20a	Summary	**So the word spread and**
b		**grew**
c	Means	in power
d	Cause	on account of the power of the Lord.
21a	Setting: time	After these events had happened,
b	Character's thoughts	**Paul resolved**
c	Sphere	in the Spirit
d	Geographical	to travel through Macedonia and
e	Geographical	Achaia before going to Jerusalem.
f	Assertion	**He said,**
g	Time	*"After I have been there,*
h	Assertion	*I must visit Rome."*
22a	Action	**He sent two of his assistants,**
b	Identification	Timothy and
c	Identification	Erastus,
d	Place	to Macedonia,
e	Time	while he stayed for some time longer
f	Place	in the province of Asia.
23a	Time	**It was about this time**
b	Event	that a great commotion erupted about the Way.
24a	Character entrance	**A silversmith**
b	Identification	with the name Demetrius,
c	Character description	who made silver shrines of Artemis,
d	Action	**provided much profit for the artisans.**
25a	Action	**He called a meeting of these artisans and**
b		**of the workers in related crafts,**
c	Speech	and **said,**
d	Address	*"Gentlemen,*
e	Assertion	*you know*
f	Content	*that we get our prosperity from this business.*

26a	Assertion	You observe and
b	Assertion	you hear that …
c	Geographical	not only here in Ephesus but
d	Geographical	in almost the entire province of Asia
e	Report	… this Paul has persuaded and
f	Accusation	misled
g	Sphere	a considerable number of people.
h	Report	He says
i	Content	that gods made with hands are not gods.
27a	Warning	There is danger
b	Content	not only that our line of business is discredited,
c	Content	but also that the temple of the great goddess Artemis may be looked upon
d	Manner	as nothing,
e	Result	and she,
f	Geographical	whom the entire province of Asia and
g	Geographical	indeed the entire world worships,
h	Result	will suffer the loss of her grandeur."

28a	Time	When they heard this,
b	Result	**they became very angry.**
c	Action	**They shouted,**
d	Exclamation	"Great is Artemis of the Ephesians!"
29a	Event	**The city was in chaos.**

b	Cause	Prompted by the same impulse,
c	Action	**people rushed**
d	Place	to the theater,
e	Action: character entrance	dragging with them Gaius and
f	Character entrance	Aristarchus,
g	Character description	Paul's Macedonian travel companions.
30a	Character's thoughts	**Paul wanted to go into the popular assembly,**
b	Contrast: action	**but the disciples did not allow him to do so.**
31a	Character entrance	**Some of the Asiarchs**
b	Character description	who were kindly disposed to him
c	Action	**sent him a message,**
d	Content	urging him
e	Instruction	not to venture into the theater.

32a	Time	Meanwhile,
b	Action	**some people were shouting one thing,**
c	Action	**others another;**
d	Result	**the assembly was confused,**
e	Event	**most of the people did not know**
f	Indirect question	why they had come together.
33a	Action: character entrance	**Some people in the crowd advised Alexander,**
b	Character description	whom the Jews pushed forward.
c	Action	**Alexander motioned for silence,**
d	Purpose	wanting to make a defense before the people.

Continued on next page.

Continued from previous page.

34a	Time	When they recognized
b	Content (ethnic)	that he was a Jew,
c	Reaction	**they all roared in unison**
d	Duration	for about two hours,
e	Exclamation	shouting,
f		*"Great is Artemis of the Ephesians!"*
35a	Character entrance & time	When the city clerk had quieted the crowd,
b	Action: speech	**he said,**
c	Address	*"People of Ephesus,*
d	Rhetorical question	*who does not know*
e	Content	*that the city of the Ephesians is the guardian of the temple of the great Artemis and*
f	Content	*of her image*
g	Description	*that fell from heaven?*
36a	Reason	*Since this is undeniable,*
b	Instruction (command)	*you must be calm*
c	Instruction (command)	*and do nothing reckless.*
37a	Review of history (flashback)	*You have brought these men here*
b	Character description	*who are neither temple robbers*
c	Character description	*nor blasphemers of our goddess.*
38a	Condition	*If Demetrius and*
b		*his fellow artisans*
c		*have a complaint against anyone,*
d	Inference: place	*there are courts in session*
e	Inference: place	*and there are proconsuls.*
f	Command	*Let them file their claims against one another.*
39a	Condition	*If there is anything further that you want to know,*
b	Inference	*it will have to be settled*
c	Place	*in the regular assembly.*
40a	Warning	*As it is, we are in danger of being accused of rioting*
b	Cause	*because of what happened today;*
c	Assertion	*there is no reason for it,*
d	Assertion	*and we cannot explain this disorderly gathering."*
41	Resolution: action	**With these words he dismissed the assembly.**
20:1a	Time	After the turmoil had ceased,
b	Action	**Paul sent for the disciples**
c	Action	and **encouraged them.**
d	Action	**Then he said farewell**
e	Action: geographical	and **set out for Macedonia.**

Structure and Literary Form

The first episode (Paul's departure for the province of Asia, 18:23 – 28), consists of two incidents. First, Luke relates Paul's departure from Antioch and his visit to the churches in Galatia and Phrygia (18:23). Then he narrates events that transpired in Ephesus after Paul's earlier visit (18:19 – 20) and before his arrival in the city (19:1): the ministry of Apollos, a Christian believer from Alexandria whose deficient theology is corrected by Priscilla and Aquila and who eventually relocates from Ephesus to Corinth (18:24 – 28).

This episode is a *narrative* that includes *travel notices* related to Paul's movements (v. 23). Apollos, who appears in Acts for the first time, is characterized in some detail (vv. 24 – 25). The ministry of Paul and Apollos is briefly summarized (vv. 23, 28). The succinct report about the evangelistic work of Apollos in Ephesus (v. 26) and then in Corinth (v. 28) illustrates the significance of the network of churches as well as the reality of the ongoing and expanding missionary work of Jewish Christians beyond the circle of the Twelve and beyond the team of Paul and his associates.

The second episode that narrates Paul's mission in Ephesus (19:1 – 20:1) consists of nine incidents. (1) Paul arrives in Ephesus and encounters followers of John the Baptist (vv. 1 – 7). (2) Paul proclaims the gospel in the synagogue in Ephesus (vv. 8 – 9f). (3) He relocates his preaching and teaching activity to the lecture hall of Tyrannus (vv. 9g – 10). (4) Luke relates the effect of miracles that happened in Paul's ministry there (vv. 11 – 12). (5) The fiasco involving Jewish exorcists has an immense impact on the population of Ephesus (vv. 13 – 16). (6) There are further conversions among the Jews and Greeks in the city, and the church consolidates as believers confess their sins and burn magic texts (vv. 17 – 20). (7) Paul decides to visit Macedonia, Achaia, Jerusalem, and Rome (vv. 21 – 22). (8) This incident (vv. 23 – 41) is the longest of the episode: Luke reports in detail the riot that the silversmiths of Ephesus instigate in three dramatic scenes: the genesis of the riot (vv. 23 – 28), the riot of the pagan population and the assembly in the theater (vv. 29 – 34), and the resolution by the city clerk (vv. 35 – 41). (9) Paul then departs from Ephesus (20:1).

This episode is again a *narrative* that includes *travel notices* (vv. 1, 21, 22; 20:1), a *conversion narrative* (vv. 1 – 7), *reports of conversions* and baptisms (vv. 5, 10, 18), *reports of missionary success* (vv. 10, 20), *reports of miracles* (vv. 11 – 12, 16), *reports of opposition* (vv. 9, 23 – 41), information about locations where Paul preached (vv. 8 – 9), *plans* of further travels (vv. 21 – 22), and *summary statements* (vv. 10, 11, 20).[3] There is also *direct speech* by Paul (vv. 2, 3, 4, 21), by disciples of John the Baptist (vv. 2, 3), by Jewish exorcists (v. 13), by an evil spirit (v. 15), by Demetrius the silversmith (vv. 25 – 27), by the excited pagan population (vv. 28, 34), and by the city clerk

---

3. See the earlier summaries in 1:14; 2:42 – 47; 4:32 – 37; 5:12 – 16; 6:7; 8:4; 8:25; 9:31; 12:24; 13:42 – 49; 16:4 – 5.

(vv. 35 – 40). These focus not on Paul's preaching (as earlier) but on the opposition and on the successful attempt of the local magistrates to quell turmoil in the city.

The two episodes contain elements familiar from Luke's earlier account of Paul's missionary work: concern about and care for believers in congregations established earlier,[4] preaching in synagogues resulting in conflict,[5] miracles,[6] and confrontation with magic.[7]

Exegetical Outline

→ **I. The Departure for the Province of Asia (18:23 – 28)**

    A. The Visit to the Churches in Galatia and Phrygia (18:23)

        1. Paul's stay in Antioch (18:23a)

        2. Paul's departure from Antioch (18:23b)

        3. Paul's visit to the churches in Galatia and Phrygia (18:23c-f)

    B. The Ministry of Apollos from Alexandria in Ephesus (18:24 – 28)

        1. The arrival of Apollos in Ephesus (18:24a-c)

        2. Description of Apollos (18:24d – 25)

        3. Apollos's preaching in the synagogue (18:26a)

        4. Apollos's instruction by Priscilla and Aquila (18:26b-e)

        5. The support of the Ephesian believers for Apollos's move to Achaia (18:27a-d)

        6. Apollos's teaching in the churches of Achaia (18:27e-g)

        7. Apollos's preaching in the synagogues of Achaia (18:28)

II. The Mission of Paul in Ephesus (19:1 – 20:1)

    A. Paul's Arrival in Ephesus and the Disciples of John the Baptist (19:1 – 7)

        1. Paul's arrival in Ephesus (19:1a-c)

        2. Paul's encounter with disciples of John the Baptist (19:1d)

        3. Dialogue between Paul and John's disciples (19:2 – 4)

            a. Paul's question regarding their reception of the Spirit (19:2a-c)

            b. Answer: They have not heard of the Spirit given as a gift (19:2d-f)

            c. Paul's question regarding the association of their baptism (19:3a-b)

            d. Answer: They were baptized in association with John (19:3c-d)

            e. Paul's explanation of John's baptism regarding repentance and faith in Jesus (19:4)

        4. The conversion of John's disciples (19:5 – 7)

            a. John's disciples hear the news about Jesus (19:5a)

            b. The baptism of John's disciples in the name of Jesus the Lord (19:5b-c)

            c. The reception of the Holy Spirit (19:6)

            d. The number of John's disciples who became believers in Jesus (19:7)

---

4. See 18:23; cf. 14:22; 15:32, 41; 16:5.

5. See 19:8 – 10; cf. 13:45; 17:5; also 18:19.

6. See 19:11 – 12; cf. 14:8 – 10; 15:12; see also 3:1 – 10; 5:15 – 16.

7. See 19:13 – 20; cf. 13:4 – 12; also 8:9 – 24.

B. The Proclamation of the Gospel in the Synagogue (19:8 – 9f)

1. Paul's preaching in the synagogue for three months (19:8)

2. Opposition of Ephesian Jews (19:9a-d)

3. Paul's departure from the synagogue (19:9e-f)

C. The Proclamation of the Gospel in the Hall of Tyrannus (19:9g – 10)

1. Paul's preaching in the lecture hall of Tyrannus (19:9g-i)

2. Paul's two-year ministry in Ephesus (19:10a)

3. The conversion of Jews and Greeks in the province of Asia (19:10b-f)

D. The Miracles (19:11 – 12)

1. The occurrence of miracles in Paul's ministry (19:11)

2. Miracles resulting from touching handkerchiefs and aprons (19:12)

E. The Fiasco involving an Encounter with Itinerant Jewish Exorcists (19:13 – 16)

1. Jewish exorcists use the name of Jesus and Paul in their work (19:13)

2. Description of the exorcists (19:14)

3. Rebuff by the evil spirit (19:15)

4. Subjugation of the exorcists by the evil spirit (19:16)

F. Further Conversions and Consolidation of the Church (19:17 – 20)

1. Dissemination of the news of the incident in the city (19:17a-c)

2. Awe among the citizens who recognize the power of Jesus (19:17d-e)

3. Confessions of believers concerning their involvement in magic (19:18)

4. The burning of magic texts (19:19)

5. The conversion of people through the power of Jesus the Lord (19:20)

G. The Decision to Visit Macedonia, Achaia, Jerusalem, and Rome (19:21 – 22)

1. Paul's decision to travel to Macedonia and Achaia before visiting Jerusalem (19:21a-e)

2. Paul's decision to travel to Rome (19:21f-h)

3. Paul sends Timothy and Erastus to Macedonia (19:22a-d)

4. Paul stays in the province of Asia (19:22e-f)

H. The Riot of the Silversmiths in Ephesus (19:23 – 41)

1. The origins of the riot (19:23 – 28)

   a. The time of the riot (19:23)

   b. Description of Demetrius the silversmith (19:24)

   c. The meeting of the members of the guild of silversmiths (19:25a-c)

   d. Demetrius's speech (19:25d – 27)

      i. The prosperity of the guild of silversmiths in Ephesus (19:25d-f)

      ii. The impact of Paul's activity in Ephesus and in the province (19:26a-g)

      iii. Paul's damaging teaching concerning the gods (19:26h-i)

      iv. The potential damage of Paul's activity for silversmiths (19:27a-b)

      v. The potential damage for the temple of Artemis (19:27c-d)

      vi. The potential damage for the cult of Artemis (19:27e-h)

Explanation of the Text

18:23 After spending some time there, he departed and traveled from place to place through the region of Galatia and Phrygia, strengthening all the disciples (καὶ ποιήσας χρόνον τινὰ ἐξῆλθεν διερχόμενος καθεξῆς τὴν Γαλατικὴν χώραν καὶ Φρυγίαν, ἐπιστηρίζων πάντας τοὺς μαθητάς). Luke begins his narrative of Paul's missionary work in the province of Asia with a brief comment on Paul's departure from Antioch, where he had been "spending some time" (see on 15:33), and on his travels before reaching Ephesus (19:1).

After leaving Antioch, Paul traveled north, visiting the churches in Syria and Cilicia (15:41), reaching the Anatolian highland via the Cilician Gates. The expression "from place to place" and the reference to "disciples" indicate that Paul visited churches that he had established in these areas. Read in this context, the phrase translated as "the region [χώρα] of Galatia and Phrygia" suggests that Paul traveled through the regions of Lycaonia and Phrygia that were incorporated into the province of Galatia, as well as through the region of Phrygia that belonged to the province of Asia. Thus, when he strengthened "all the disciples" in this region, he evidently visited the churches in Derbe, Lystra, Iconium, and Pisidian Antioch.

The later comment in 19:1 that Paul "passed through the interior regions" before reaching Ephesus seems to indicate that he traveled from Pisidian Antioch to Apamea (cf. 16:6) and continued on the traverse of the hill road running from Apamea to the valley of the Kaystros River north of the Messogis Mountains and to Ephesus. The journey from Antioch, the capital of Syria, to Ephesus, the capital of Asia Minor, was about 800 miles (1,300 km.), requiring nine weeks of walking if we assume one day of rest per week. The fact that Paul did not sail from Antioch to Ephesus but walked via an arduous inland route confirms his concern for the consolidation of the churches he had established. If he indeed passed through Derbe, Lystra, Iconium, and Pisidian Antioch, this would have been his third visit after establishing the churches in these cities (cf. 14:21 – 28; 15:36; 16:1 – 5).

18:24 Meanwhile a Jew named Apollos, a native of Alexandria, arrived in Ephesus. He was a learned man, well-versed in the Scriptures (Ἰουδαῖος δέ τις Ἀπολλῶς ὀνόματι, Ἀλεξανδρεὺς τῷ γένει, ἀνὴρ λόγιος, κατήντησεν εἰς Ἔφεσον, δυνατὸς ὢν ἐν ταῖς γραφαῖς). Before Luke reports on Paul's missionary work in Ephesus, he relates a development in Ephesus that transpired between his earlier, brief visit to the city (18:19 – 20) and his arrival after leaving Antioch (18:23; 19:1).

IN DEPTH: Ephesus

When Rome established the province of Asia Minor in 133 BC, Ephesus was granted the status of a free city. In 30 – 29 BC, Augustus made Ephesus the seat of the provincial governor (*proconsul*). A new governmental quarter was built, which included a Sebasteion (temple of Augustus) and a Bouleuterion (council building). The political status of the city and its harbor, the largest in Asia Minor, contributed to the economic growth of Ephesus. With 200,000 inhabitants in the first century, Ephesus was one of the largest cities of the empire. The theater could hold 24,000 spectators, who were seated according to civic status, association, and guild.

The worship of Artemis Ephesia was the dominant cult of the city. Traditionally connected with hunting, Artemis's central function was connected with female (and also male) initiation, which turned girls into women, and with childbirth. She was worshiped privately as a helper in need and addressed in magical papyri. The temple of Artemis, about one and a half miles east of the city center, was four times larger than the Parthenon in Athens. The giant marble temple belonged to the seven wonders of the ancient world. The double circular hall, measuring 69 by 154 feet (21 by 47 m.), was constructed with 127 columns, each 60 feet (20 m.) high. The cult statue of Artemis Ephesia was a wooden image equipped with clothes, a headdress (sometimes a crown), two or four Nike (Lat. Victoria) figures depicted on her upper garment, adorned with necklaces made of pearls and amber, round protuberances[8] between the necklaces and the waistband, and a tight, ankle-length skirt filled with animal motifs. The Artemisia, the festival in honor of the goddess, was celebrated in the month Artemision (March/April) with banquets, processions, sacrifices, athletic games, and competitions in drama. A second festival that celebrated the Artemis mysteries was celebrated on the birthday of Artemis and Apollo on the sixth day of the month Thargelion (May/June).

An Egyptian Jew from Alexandria named Apollos arrives in Ephesus. Luke describes Apollos with eight pieces of information. (1) He is a Jew, born into a Jewish family.

(2) He is a native of Alexandria; he was born in that Egyptian city and spent his formative years there. Jews had been settling in Egypt for several centuries, numbering several hundred thousand in the first century; synagogues are attested as early as the third century BC. It is estimated that 100,000 Jews lived in Alexandria, a city founded by Alexander the Great.[9] The Greek term does not imply Apollos held Alexandrian citizenship, although this is possible.

(3) He was "learned" (λόγιος); i.e., he had received formal education — perhaps in Greek schools, certainly in Jewish schools located in the synagogues, as the next comment indicates. He was both eloquent and cultured (the two meanings of the Greek term that suggest rhetorical training,[10] which was an integral part of Greek and Roman education).

(4) He was "well-versed" and competent in the Scriptures, powerful in explaining them in sermons and effective in using biblical texts in debates.

18:25 He had been instructed in the Way of the Lord; he spoke being fervent in the Spirit, and he taught about Jesus accurately, even though he knew only the baptism of John (οὗτος ἦν κατηχημένος τὴν ὁδὸν τοῦ κυρίου καὶ ζέων τῷ πνεύματι ἐλάλει καὶ ἐδίδασκεν ἀκριβῶς τὰ περὶ τοῦ Ἰησοῦ, ἐπιστάμενος μόνον τὸ βάπτισμα Ἰωάννου). (5) Apollos had been "instructed" (κατηχημένος) in the "Way of the Lord,"[11] learning about the life, death, resurrection, and exaltation of Jesus as Israel's Messiah and Savior. Luke thus portrays him as a believer in Jesus. The Western text reads, "he had been instructed in his homeland in the word of the Lord," which presupposes that Apollos was converted to faith in Jesus in Alexandria (a Christian community seems to have existed in Alexandria in the late 40s). However, we have no proof that Apollos became a Christian in Alexandria. Some take the reference to the baptism of John to indicate that he had relocated to Judea, where he came in contact with John himself or with John's disciples, that he subsequently became a Christian, and that he "worked as an independent Jewish-Christian missionary" who eventually reached Ephesus.[12]

(6) He spoke "being fervent in the Spirit" (ζέων

---

8. The older interpretation as breasts should be abandoned: the protuberances represent a removable piece of Artemis's clothing; cf. Robert Fleischer, *Artemis von Ephesos und verwandte Kultstatuen aus Anatolien und Syrien* (EPRO 35; Brill: Leiden, 1973), 74 – 88.

9. Cf. Smallwood, *Jews under Roman Rule*, 224 – 42.

10. Cf. Winter, *Philo and Paul*, 174 – 76.

11. On the expression of "the Way" (ἡ ὁδός; cf. 9:2; 19:9, 23; 22:4; 24:14, 22), see "In Depth: The Self-Understanding of the Church in Jerusalem" at 5:11.

12. Reidar Hvalvik, "Named Jewish Believers Connected with the Pauline Mission," in *Jewish Believers in Jesus: The Early Centuries* (ed. O. Skarsaune and R. Hvalvik; Peabody, MA: Hendrickson, 2007), 154 – 78, 158.

τῷ πνεύματι).[13] Since this comment is placed between the description of Apollos's having been instructed in the "Way of the Lord" and his teaching about Jesus, the reference to "spirit/Spirit" (πνεῦμα) should be understood as a reference to the Holy Spirit.[14] Apollos's witness was empowered by God's Spirit.

(7) Apollos taught about Jesus "accurately" (ἀκριβῶς); i.e., he proclaimed, with accurate information, Jesus' words and deeds, and his death, resurrection, and exaltation.[15]

(8) He knew only "the baptism of John,"[16] i.e., the ritual immersion in water administered by John the Baptist (and his disciples). Discussion about this deficiency of Apollos who knows "only" (μόνον) John's baptism is hampered by the fact that Luke provides no details concerning the instruction he received from Priscilla and Aquila (v. 26), which seems to have remedied his lack of accuracy here. But note that, unlike the "disciples" of 19:1 – 7, Apollos is not baptized "in the name of the Lord Jesus" (cf. 19:5), a fact that suggests he was thought to have saving faith in Jesus. Whenever Apollos was immersed by John or one of John's disciples (cf. Luke 3:3), after repentance and reception of forgiveness of sins, he had accepted John's witness about the Coming One, who would "immerse" people in the Spirit as promised by the prophets; he had recognized Jesus as the promised Messiah and Savior of Israel; and he evidently received the gift of God's Spirit (he was "fervent in the Spirit") and taught about Jesus accurately.

Perhaps Apollos's teaching about baptism was deficient. He may have baptized people with an emphasis on repentance and forgiveness of sins,

without explaining the association of immersion in water with the life, death, and resurrection of Jesus. This would certainly have been confusing for new converts and would have to be rectified. Since his teaching about Jesus was accurate and since the presence of God's Spirit in his life and ministry was evident, John's own baptism of repentance for the forgiveness of sins was sufficient (cf. 1:5). What matters in baptism is not the precise formula being pronounced at the moment of immersion, but repentance, faith in Jesus, forgiveness of sins, and reception of the Spirit (2:38) — all realities present in Apollos's life.

18:26 He began to speak boldly in the synagogue. When Priscilla and Aquila heard him, they took him aside and explained to him the Way of God more accurately (οὗτός τε ἤρξατο παρρησιάζεσθαι ἐν τῇ συναγωγῇ. ἀκούσαντες δὲ αὐτοῦ Πρίσκιλλα καὶ Ἀκύλας προσελάβοντο αὐτὸν καὶ ἀκριβέστερον αὐτῷ ἐξέθεντο τὴν ὁδὸν τοῦ θεοῦ). When Apollos arrives in Ephesus, he begins to "speak boldly" (παρρησιάζεσθαι; see 4:13 on παρρησία) about Jesus to the Jewish community meeting in the synagogue. The welcome that the Ephesian Jews had extended to Paul, whom they asked to stay for a longer period of time (18:19 – 20), reflected an openness to the message about Jesus as Israel's Messiah and Savior that is extended also to Apollos — as well as to Priscilla and Aquila, active Christian believers attending the synagogue services since Paul's departure.

When Priscilla and Aquila hear Apollos speak in the synagogue, they recognize that his teaching is incomplete and requires further instruction, at least with regard to the significance of repentance

---

13. Compare the similar expression in Rom 12:11.

14. Cf. James D. G. Dunn, *Baptism in the Holy Spirit* (London: SCM, 1970), 88 – 89; Turner, *Power from on High*, 389. Most English translations interpret in terms of the human spirit: NASB, RSV/ESV ("being fervent in spirit"); NET, GNB ("with great enthusiasm"), NRSV ("with burning enthusiasm"),

NLT ("with an enthusiastic spirit"), NIV/TNIV ("with great fervor").

15. The phrase "the things about Jesus" (τὰ περὶ … τοῦ Ἰησοῦ) occurs in 28:31 as an expression describing Paul's proclamation in Rome.

16. On the baptism of John cf. 1:22; 10:37; cf. 19:3.

and immersion and its relation to Jesus. They are eager and able to explain "the Way of God," the revelation of God's path to salvation for Israel and for the world through Jesus — in particular his death and resurrection. The comparative "more accurately" indicates that his teaching about Jesus, which is accurate (ἀκριβῶς, v. 25), is incomplete, and is now rounded out by Paul's coworkers from Rome and Corinth, perhaps with Priscilla taking the lead.

18:27 – 28 When he wanted to go to Achaia, the believers encouraged him and wrote to the disciples there to welcome him. On his arrival he was of great assistance to those who through grace had become believers, for he vigorously refuted the Jews in public, demonstrating from the Scriptures that Jesus was the Messiah (βουλομένου δὲ αὐτοῦ διελθεῖν εἰς τὴν Ἀχαΐαν, προτρεψάμενοι οἱ ἀδελφοὶ ἔγραψαν τοῖς μαθηταῖς ἀποδέξασθαι αὐτόν, ὃς παραγενόμενος συνεβάλετο πολὺ τοῖς πεπιστευκόσιν διὰ τῆς χάριτος· εὐτόνως γὰρ τοῖς Ἰουδαίοις διακατηλέγχετο δημοσίᾳ ἐπιδεικνὺς διὰ τῶν γραφῶν εἶναι τὸν χριστὸν Ἰησοῦν).

Apollos wants to go to Achaia in order to continue his ministry of teaching about Jesus and the "Way of the Lord" (see v. 25). Luke does not relate the reason for Apollos's desire to leave Ephesus and travel to another province.[17] Luke speaks generally of "Achaia," not of Corinth: Apollos may have planned to proclaim the gospel not only in Corinth but also in other cities in Achaia that had Jewish communities.[18]

The reference to "believers" (οἱ ἀδελφοί, see on 1:16; 5:11) in Ephesus who encourage Apollos indicates that some Jews have come to faith in Jesus as the result of Apollos's preaching, and perhaps of Paul's preaching (vv. 19 – 20) and of the activity of Priscilla and Aquila (v. 26). They encourage Apollos in his plans, surely because they have observed his ministry and are confident that his preaching will be effective in Achaia as well. Thus they write a letter of recommendation[19] in which they ask the disciples (τοῖς μαθηταῖς) in Achaia "to welcome him," i.e., to receive him favorably and assist him in his mission (perhaps by providing lodging and other material support).

Luke's report of Apollos's ministry in Achaia focuses on three matters. (1) Apollos "was of great assistance" to those who had come to faith earlier. Luke clarifies that it was God's grace (διὰ τῆς χάριτος) that brought people to faith in Jesus and sustained them in remaining faithful to Jesus even in the midst of attacks and hostilities. Grammatically the prepositional phrase translated "through grace" can also be related to Apollos's assisting the Achaian believers, which would make the same point: growth and perseverance in the faith are possible only on account of God's sovereign initiative, which makes effective all human efforts to proclaim the gospel and to encourage believers.

(2) Apollos refutes the Jews in public; i.e., in discussions about the validity of the claims concerning Jesus he overwhelms them with his arguments. In the context of the description of Apollos as a

---

17. Manuscripts 𝔓³⁸ D provide a reason, adding at the beginning of v. 27, "And some Corinthians who were on a visit to Ephesus and had heard him invited him to cross over with them to their native place." This scenario is not impossible (despite Metzger, *Textual Commentary*, 414 – 15; see Barrett, *Acts*, 890 – 91), although the addition is not likely to preserve the original reading. Another scenario would point to Paul's expected return to Ephesus and to the practice of both Paul — and perhaps Apollos — to engage in missionary work with

associates but not with other prominent missionaries.

18. For references to Apollos's ministry in Corinth, see 1 Cor 1:12; 3:4 – 6, 22; 4:6. The fact that Paul at one point urged Apollos to return to Corinth (1 Cor 16:12) demonstrates that Paul fully supported Apollos's ministry.

19. Letters of recommendation were common in antiquity; for the practice see Rom 16:1; 2 Cor 3:1; Col 4:10; for examples see Horsley and Llewelyn, *New Documents*, 1:62 – 66; 4:71 – 72; 5:136; 8:125.

learned Jew, well-versed in the Scriptures (v. 24), Luke's readers know that Apollos's arguments are derived from Scripture, as outlined in the earlier speeches of Peter and Paul. Apollos's argumentation was about Jesus' life and ministry accompanied by miracles, his death as an integral part of God's plan of salvation, his resurrection as his vindication as Israel's Messiah, and his exaltation as the reality that fulfilled the prophets' expectation that God would pour out his Spirit on his people.

Luke characterizes Apollos's powerful argumentation with two adverbs: "vigorously" (εὐτόνως), i.e., with visible energy, and "in public" (δημοσίᾳ), i.e., in the synagogues of the Jewish community that were open not only to Jews and proselytes but also to God-fearers and Greek and Roman polytheists.

(3) Apollos was "demonstrating" (ἐπιδεικνύς) from the Scriptures that Jesus is the Messiah (ὁ χριστός).[20] The present tense of the participle indicates that this is the focus of his proclamation and argumentation: the identity of Jesus, who died on the cross and rose from the dead, as Israel's Messiah. For the Scriptures as basis for the proclamation of Jesus as Messiah and Savior see 3:18; 7:52; 8:31; 10:43; 13:27; 17:2.

19:1 While Apollos was in Corinth, Paul passed through the interior regions and came to Ephesus, where he found some disciples (ἐγένετο δὲ ἐν τῷ τὸν Ἀπολλῶ εἶναι ἐν Κορίνθῳ Παῦλον διελθόντα τὰ ἀνωτερικὰ μέρη κατελθεῖν εἰς Ἔφεσον καὶ εὑρεῖν

τινας μαθητάς). The Ephesus episode (19:1 – 20:1) begins with a note on Paul's arrival in Ephesus. The reference to his travel "through the interior regions," i.e., through the mountainous region of southern Galatia and Phrygia (see on 18:23), and to the timing of his arrival — after Apollos's relocation from Ephesus to Corinth — forms a transition with the preceding episode (cf. 18:23, 27 – 28). Paul arrives in Ephesus in the late summer of AD 52.

The first incident of Paul's extended ministry in Ephesus relates his encounter with certain "disciples" (vv. 1 – 7). The identity of these disciples, reconstructed on the basis of the answers they give to Paul's questions in vv. 2 – 3, is contested. Some argue that they were disciples won by the preaching of Apollos before he received instruction from Priscilla and Aquila — Gentile converts to faith in Israel's God and in Jesus who had not heard of the Holy Spirit (cf. 18:25).[21] Others argue that they were (Jewish) followers of John the Baptist,[22] perhaps immersed by John himself in the Jordan River twenty-five years earlier, or by one of John's disciples at a later time. Some suggest that they were disciples of John who had come in contact with the pre-Easter Jesus movement.[23] Others suggest that Luke reports from Paul's perspective; Paul initially believed that these "disciples" were Christian believers, only to discover this was not the case.[24] Still others argue that since the term "disciple" is used exclusively for Christians in Acts, they must be taken as Christian believers — either

---

20. In the phrase εἶναι τὸν χριστὸν Ἰησοῦν, the noun with the article is the subject: Apollos proved from Scripture that the expected Anointed One of God, the Messiah, "had appeared in the person of Jesus" (Barrett, *Acts*, 891). The resistance of translators to use the term "Messiah," preferring "Christ" (which for most readers is a name, a meaning that makes no sense in v. 28), can be seen even here, cf. ESV, NASB, NET, NIV, RSV. For the translation as "Messiah" cf. NLT, NRSV, NIV, GNB. For the assertion that "Jesus is the Messiah" see 9:22; 17:3, 7. See on 2:31, 36.

21. Dunn, *Beginning from Jerusalem*, 760; cf. Joan E. Taylor, *John the Baptist*, 73 – 76.

22. Paul R. Trebilco, *The Early Christians in Ephesus from Paul to Ignatius* (orig. 2004; repr., Grand Rapids: Eerdmans, 2007), 128 – 29.

23. Knut Backhaus, *Die 'Jüngerkreise' des Täufers Johannes: Eine Studie zu den religionsgeschichtlichen Ursprüngen des Christentums* (Paderborner Theologische Studien 19; Paderborn/München: Schöningh, 1991), 209 – 12.

24. Marshall, *Acts*, 305 – 6; Polhill, *Acts*, 398.

as genuine but "fringe Christians"[25] or as "incomplete" Christians.[26]

Since Apollos is described as fervent in the Spirit (18:25) while these disciples do not know the Spirit (v. 2), and since Apollos is not baptized (again) while these disciples are baptized in the name of Jesus (v. 5), Luke seems to be contrasting these disciples with Apollos, which makes it unlikely that they were converts of Apollos. While Luke does not call them "disciples of John the Baptist," the fact that they have been baptized with the baptism of John (v. 3) suggests a connection between these disciples and John, whether directly or indirectly. Luke probably did not regard these disciples as Christians.[27]

The "coming to faith" (πιστεύσαντες) that Paul's question in v. 2 assumes for these disciples likely reflects his initial assumption, which is then modified. The disciples' answer to Paul's questions (vv. 2 – 3) prompts him to lead them to faith in the Coming One, i.e., in Jesus as the Messiah (v. 5). These disciples hear from Paul that Jesus is Messiah and Lord. Since faith in Jesus as Messiah and Lord is the prerequisite for being a Christian believer, it seems obvious that these disciples were not Christians before their encounter with Paul.

19:2 He said to them, "Did you receive the Holy Spirit when you came to faith?" They replied, "We have not heard that there is a Holy Spirit" (εἶπέν τε πρὸς αὐτούς· εἰ πνεῦμα ἅγιον ἐλάβετε πιστεύσαντες; οἱ δὲ πρὸς αὐτόν· ἀλλ' οὐδ' εἰ πνεῦμα ἅγιον ἔστιν ἠκούσαμεν). Since Paul believed and taught that being a Christian and receiving God's Spirit is one and the same reality,[28] his opening question expresses suspicion, designed to reveal

whether they are Christians or not. He has his doubts; presumably Paul has deduced from their behavior or their talk that the Holy Spirit is not present in their lives. Paul's question addresses the point of what it means to be a Christian: a genuine believer in Jesus is not someone who is immersed with the correct formula, but who has faith combined with the Holy Spirit, whose presence is evident in their lives (whether through prophetic manifestations or through transformed behavior).

The disciples' answer confirms Paul's suspicions: they have not heard that "there is a Holy Spirit." Unless these disciples are Gentiles who received, perhaps, "garbled reports" of John's teaching propagated in Asia Minor,[29] which omitted John's reference to the Coming One who would immerse people in the Spirit (Luke 3:16), we must assume that they (as Jewish disciples of John) have not heard that the Holy Spirit, promised by the prophets, was bestowed on the day of Pentecost, or they had not connected their baptism with the Holy Spirit.

19:3 He said, "Then how were you baptized?" They said, "With the baptism of John" (εἶπέν τε· εἰς τί οὖν ἐβαπτίσθητε; οἱ δὲ εἶπαν· εἰς τὸ Ἰωάννου βάπτισμα). The disciples' ignorance of the Holy Spirit prompts a second question from Paul aimed at uncovering their claims to discipleship: if they have not heard of the Spirit and his coming, they have a confused understanding of John's message and, unlike Apollos, they seem to have no knowledge of Jesus. Paul's question assumes that baptism is part of a conversion event in which people come to faith in Jesus as Messiah and Lord and in which God's Spirit is received (see on 2:38 – 39). The

---

25. Fitzmyer, *Acts*, 642; Pervo, *Acts*, 468 ("'Christians' of a sort").

26. Bruce, *Book of Acts*, 363; Avemarie, *Tauferzählungen*, 70 – 73.

27. Cf. Witherington, *Acts*, 569 – 71; Dunn, *Baptism*,

83 – 89; Turner, *Power from on High*, 390 – 92.

28. Rom 8:9; 1 Cor 12:3; Gal 3:2 – 3; 1 Thess 1:5 – 6; Titus 3:5. This is also Peter's conviction, cf. Acts 11:17; 1 Pet 1:2.

29. Marshall, *Acts*, 306.

Greek expression translated as "how"[30] reproduces a prepositional phrase (εἰς τί) that is usually translated "into what."[31] The context of v. 5 suggests that the expression is derived from the concept of being immersed into the reality of Jesus as Messiah and Savior.

In Paul's letters, the expression "to be immersed into" is followed by a reference to either Jesus Christ (Rom 6:3; Gal 3:27) or the body of Christ (1 Cor 12:13). The phrase is perhaps, but not necessarily, a "baptismal formula" that Paul used when he immersed people who had come to faith in Jesus in water. Paul's question reveals that these disciples had been baptized merely "with the baptism of John" without receiving the Holy Spirit. Their lack of the Holy Spirit reveals their lack of faith in Jesus and thus confirms that they are not Christian believers.

19:4 Paul said, "John immersed with a baptism of repentance, telling the people that they should believe in the one who would come after him, that is, in Jesus" (εἶπεν δὲ Παῦλος· Ἰωάννης ἐβάπτισεν βάπτισμα μετανοίας τῷ λαῷ λέγων εἰς τὸν ἐρχόμενον μετ᾽ αὐτὸν ἵνα πιστεύσωσιν, τοῦτ᾽ ἔστιν εἰς τὸν Ἰησοῦν). Paul reminds these disciples that when John immersed people in water (ἐβάπτισεν), it was an immersion that expressed "repentance" (μετάνοια) of sins and faith (πιστεύσωσιν) in the coming Messiah. If these men were disciples of John, they would have known this much. Since they have not received the Holy Spirit, they have evidently not come to faith in Jesus, since Jesus bestows the Spirit on his followers who believe in him.[32] This is Paul's new information: that the Coming One in whom they were to believe, according to John's message, is Jesus. In other words,

as disciples of John who do what John told them to do, they must now believe in Jesus. If they do, they will receive the Holy Spirit (cf. Luke 3:16).

19:5 When they heard this, they were immersed in the name of the Lord Jesus (ἀκούσαντες δὲ ἐβαπτίσθησαν εἰς τὸ ὄνομα τοῦ κυρίου Ἰησοῦ). The disciples respond positively to Paul's proclamation of Jesus as the Messiah who fulfills God's promises concerning Israel's salvation and who bestows God's Spirit. Paul would not have baptized[33] these disciples if they had not professed such faith in Jesus. They are immersed in water "in the name of the Lord Jesus"; i.e., they invoke the name of Jesus, acknowledging him as Lord (κύριος; see on 2:36), who has the power to cleanse them from sin and to convey the presence of God's Holy Spirit.

19:6 And when Paul laid his hands on them, the Holy Spirit came upon them; they spoke in unlearned languages and prophesied (καὶ ἐπιθέντος αὐτοῖς τοῦ Παύλου τὰς χεῖρας ἦλθε τὸ πνεῦμα τὸ ἅγιον ἐπ᾽ αὐτούς, ἐλάλουν τε γλώσσαις καὶ ἐπροφήτευον). When Paul baptizes these disciples of John, he lays his hands on them (which may have been his practice) and they receive the Holy Spirit. Luke describes that reception of the Spirit in terms parallel to the reception of the Spirit by Jesus' followers on Pentecost (see on 2:1 – 4).

This manifestation corresponds to the expectation that the reception of the Spirit would be "a matter of immediate perception; the Ephesians are expected to know whether they did in fact receive the Spirit when they 'believed' (19:2), whether from 'initial' charismata or following experience."[34] Their commitment to the Lord Jesus, expressed in their invocation of the name of Jesus as they were immersed in water, and their reception of the Spirit

---

30. NJB, Fitzmyer; NEB: "what baptism were you given?"

31. NET, NRSV; cf. NIV, NLT, TNIV.

32. Cf. Luke 24:49; Acts 1:4 – 5; 2:16 – 36; 11:15 – 16; 13:25; 15:8.

33. On the verb translated "immersed" (βαπτίζω, usually transliterated "baptized"), see on 1:5; 2:38.

34. Turner, *Power from on High*, 392 – 93.

constitute their conversion: they are now Christian believers.

19:7 In all, there were about twelve men (ἦσαν δὲ οἱ πάντες ἄνδρες ὡσεὶ δώδεκα). Luke concludes this incident by noting that the manifestations mentioned in v. 6 take place in a group of twelve disciples of John. While it is probable (but not certain) that each of the twelve experiences the "charismatic" manifestations, some may have spoken in unlearned languages (glossolalia) while others experienced invasive prophecy/praise. It is also possible that these twelve men (ἄνδρες) had family members who also needed to be brought to faith in Jesus.

19:8 Paul went into the synagogue and spoke freely for three months, informing and seeking to convince them about the reality of the kingdom of God (εἰσελθὼν δὲ εἰς τὴν συναγωγὴν ἐπαρρησιάζετο ἐπὶ μῆνας τρεῖς διαλεγόμενος καὶ πείθων τὰ περὶ τῆς βασιλείας τοῦ θεοῦ). The second incident of the Ephesus episode relates Paul's proclamation of the gospel in the synagogue of Ephesus (vv. 8 – 9f). Luke emphasizes three facts. First, Paul attended the synagogue services and proclaimed the gospel for three months, perhaps on twelve Sabbath days and an unknown number of meetings held during the week in the synagogue building.

His activity there is described with a finite verb and two participles: he "spoke freely" (ἐπαρρησιάζετο),[35] i.e., openly, without fear; he "informed" them (διαλεγόμενος; see on 17:2); i.e., he taught instructional discourses on the gospel with question and answer sessions; he sought to "convince" (πείθων) them concerning the truth of the gospel. The imperfect tense of "spoke freely"

emphasizes the continuous preaching activity in the synagogue for the duration of three months, while the consistent focus on information and on his effort to persuade his audience is highlighted by the two present participles. In his discussions, Paul reasons with the Jews, proselytes, and God-fearers attending the synagogue services. Among his listeners would have been the disciples of John who had been converted (19:1 – 7) as well as Priscilla and Aquila.

Luke describes the content of Paul's teaching as "the reality of the kingdom of God" (τὰ περὶ τῆς βασιλείας τοῦ θεοῦ; see on 1:3). Most translations leave the article (τά)[36] untranslated; if it is taken as nominalizing the prepositional phrase, the expression can be translated in a general sense as "the things concerning the kingdom of God," or, more specifically, as "the reality of the kingdom of God." In Jesus' teaching and consequently in the proclamation of the apostles, the "kingdom of God" is the reality of the fulfillment of God's promises concerning Israel's restoration and the salvation of the world—a reality brought about by the life, death, resurrection, and exaltation of Jesus, Israel's Messiah and Savior of the world, and a reality that grows as a result of the Spirit-empowered work of the apostles and the churches. Paul does not teach general scriptural truths but specifically about Jesus, about his royal rule as the exalted Savior and Lord, and about coming to faith in Jesus in order to share in God's kingdom.[37]

19:9 When some became hardened and refused to believe, and insulted the Way before the assembly, he left them and took the disciples with him. Day after day he lectured in the hall of Tyrannus (ὡς δέ τινες ἐσκληρύνοντο καὶ ἠπείθουν

---

35. Cf. 9:27, 28; 13:46; 14:3; 18:26; 26:26. On the noun παρρησία see on 4:13.

36. The article is read in manuscripts ℵ A E 33. 1739 Maj, while it is omitted in B D Ψ 1175. 1891ᶜ *pc*.

37. Cf. 8:12; 14:22; 20:25; 28:23, 31; in Paul's letters cf. Rom 14:17; 1 Cor 6:9 – 10; 15:24, 50; Gal 5:21; 1 Thess 2:12.

κακολογοῦντες τὴν ὁδὸν ἐνώπιον τοῦ πλήθους, ἀποστὰς ἀπ᾽ αὐτῶν ἀφώρισεν τοὺς μαθητὰς καθ᾽ ἡμέραν διαλεγόμενος ἐν τῇ σχολῇ Τυράννου). Opposition developed in the synagogue. Certain Jews "became hardened" (ἐσκληρύνοντο) or unyielding in their resistance to Paul's teaching.[38] They "refused to believe" (ἠπείθουν), i.e., were disobedient to what Paul proclaimed as the word of God,[39] refusing to accept that the kingdom of God has become a reality through Jesus, the crucified and risen Messiah.

These opponents also "insulted" (κακολογοῦντες) the believers; i.e., they spoke evil of them, presumably slandering their character with misrepresentations of their teaching and their intentions. They slandered the "Way" (ἡ ὁδός; see on 9:2); i.e., those who believed that God has come to Israel and to the world through Jesus. These verbal attacks on Paul and believers in Jesus took place "before the assembly." This could refer to the synagogue community or to the general public of the city; the former seems more likely. The two verbs in the imperfect tense and the present participle indicate that opposition to Paul's teaching and preaching did not suddenly erupt in a particular synagogue service but was an ongoing reality for some time.

Luke then relates Paul's departure from the synagogue. The details of what triggered this development are obscure. Either the verbal attacks became stronger, forcing Paul again and again to talk about matters that distracted from his exposition of the Scriptures and the explanation of the good news of Jesus as Messiah and Savior. Or the attacks prompted the officials of the synagogue to ask Paul to refrain from teaching there, perhaps because they wanted to conduct the synagogue services in a peaceful and dignified manner, which was being threatened by hecklers who interrupted Paul's teaching, or perhaps because they had been won over by those who refused to believe in Paul's message.

Paul then left the synagogue, which implies that he distanced himself from the unbelieving Jews who insulted the Christian faith and who made his continued ministry there impossible. When he left, he took (ἀφώρισεν)[40] with him "the disciples" (οἱ μαθηταί) — the Jews, proselytes, God-fearers, and Gentile sympathizers who had come to faith in Jesus during the three months when Paul had proclaimed and explained the gospel in the synagogue. The fact that only "some" refused to believe and insulted Paul and the other believers does not automatically prove that Paul had great success in the synagogue; some may have remained skeptical without insulting Paul and without following him to the new location.

Luke does not tell us how many Jews and God-fearers of the Jewish community were converted and followed Paul, but the following incidents indeed suggest that a large number of Jews had come to faith in Jesus. Luke also does not tell us where Paul took the new believers; the grammar of the Greek sentence appears to suggest that he took them to the "hall of Tyrannus," where he lectured, but the main verb (ἀφώρισεν, "to separate, take away") is not linked with a geographical term or a building. The new community of followers of Jesus could have met in the private house of one of the believers (1 Cor 16:19 mentions a house church meeting in the home of Priscilla and Aquila).

38. If the verb is taken as a middle, these Jews are themselves hardening their hearts.

39. Cf. LSJ, s.v. ἀπειθέω, "to be disobedient, refuse compliance."

40. The definition of BDAG, s.v. ἀφορίζω 1, "to remove one party from other parties so as to discourage or eliminate con-

tact, *separate, take away*" is helpful only if the elimination of contact is related not to the entire Jewish community or to all unbelieving Jews in Ephesus, but to the few (τινες) who forced the Jewish believers out of the synagogue on account of their continuous and public insults.

The third incident of the Ephesus episode relates Paul's proclamation of the gospel in the hall of Tyrannus (vv. 9g – 10). After Paul left the synagogue, he moved his teaching activities to the hall of Tyrannus. Most translations assume that the term translated "hall" (σχολή) refers to a "lecture hall." The Greek term can indeed refer to a building, but its primary meaning is "leisure, rest"[41] and refers, by extension, to "a group to whom lectures were given."[42] If the primary meaning of the term is assumed, Luke relates that Paul now lectures among "a group of people to whom addresses were given during their leisure hours" in the sense that

> Paul embarks on his daily discussions and debate … among those meeting under the aegis of Tyrannos. Paul was rubbing his shoulders with others who have their own philosophies and *modus vivendi* to espouse. Each was competing for the attention of the same crowd, who by late morning or early afternoon were free of their other commitments and had time to relax and talk.[43]

However, it seems most likely that since Paul's entering the synagogue (v. 8) refers to a building, the reference to the σχολή of Tyrannus also refers to a building. The name "Tyrannus" is attested in Ephesus. If the "hall" was a lecture hall, Tyrannus may have been the customary lecturer, who allowed Paul to use his hall when he did not need it; if it was a guild hall,[44] he may have been the owner of the building who leased it to Paul.

While final certainty regarding the meaning of σχολή is elusive, Paul's activities are not. Once he left the synagogue, he "lectured" (διαλεγόμενος; see on 17:2) "day after day,"[45] in a public space that would have been more accessible to non-Jewish citizens than the synagogue.

19:10 This continued for two years, with the result that all people who lived in the province of Asia, both Jews and Greeks, heard the word of the Lord (τοῦτο δὲ ἐγένετο ἐπὶ ἔτη δύο, ὥστε πάντας τοὺς κατοικοῦντας τὴν Ἀσίαν ἀκοῦσαι τὸν λόγον τοῦ κυρίου, Ἰουδαίους τε καὶ Ἕλληνας). The two years that Paul taught in the hall of Tyrannus should be reckoned from the end of the three-month ministry in the synagogue (v. 8), perhaps also the period described as "some time longer" (v. 22), which explains the reference to a three-year ministry in Ephesus in 20:31 (from late summer AD 52 to the spring or summer of AD 55). These two years were eventful, as the evidence of Acts and of Paul's letters demonstrate.[46]

Date	Events	Passage
Winter 51 – 52	Paul in Antioch Apollos in Ephesus	Acts 18:22 Acts 18:23 – 26
Spring/Summer 52	Paul in Galatia and Phrygia Apollos to Corinth	Acts 18:22; 19:1; cf. 1 Cor 16:1 Acts 18:27; 19:1; 1 Cor 3:6

41. LSJ, s.v. σχολή I.

42. Ibid., II.2. The translation of NASB ("school") can be understood in this sense.

43. Horsley and Llewelyn, *New Documents*, 130; for the following comment see ibid.

44. Cf. Abraham J. Malherbe, *Social Aspects of Early Christianity* (2nd ed.; Philadelphia: Fortress, 1983), 89 – 91.

45. Manuscript D (614 gig sy^h) adds "from the fifth hour to the tenth" (ἀπὸ ὥρας εʹ ἕως δεκάτης), i.e., from 11 a.m. to 4 p.m., which was the siesta period — even though this addition is surely secondary (no copyist would omit such specific information), it may reflect a correct observation, as many commentators assume, since during this time the lecture hall "would not normally be in use" (Barrett, *Acts*, 905).

46. The chart is adapted from Jerome Murphy-O'Connor, *St. Paul's Ephesus: Texts and Archaeology* (Collegeville, MN: Liturgical, 2008), 201 – 2.

Date	Events	Passage
Late summer 52	Paul arrives in Ephesus Three-month ministry in the synagogue Conversion of disciples of John the Baptist Teaching in the hall of Tyrannus, for two years	Acts 19:1 Acts 19:8 Acts 19:1 – 7 Acts 19:9 – 10
Winter 52 – 53	Consolidation and growth of the church in Ephesus Mission to other cities in the province of Asia	Acts 19:20 Acts 19:10
Spring 53	Epaphras establishes churches in Colossae, Hierapolis, Laodicea	Col 1:7; 4:12
Summer 53	Apollos from Corinth to Ephesus Paul writes "Previous Letter" to Corinth	1 Cor 16:12 1 Cor 5:9
Spring 54	Chloe's people from Corinth to Ephesus Timothy from Ephesus to Corinth Stephanas, Fortunatus, and Achaicus from Corinth to Ephesus with letter Paul writes 1 Corinthians, plans to stay in Ephesus until Pentecost (2 June), then go to Macedonia and Corinth and Jerusalem	1 Cor 1:11 1 Cor 4:17 1 Cor 16:17; 7:1 1 Cor 16:8 1 Cor 16:3, 5 – 6; Acts 19:21
Early Summer 54	Timothy returns from Corinth to Ephesus, Timothy and Erastus to Macedonia	Acts 19:22
Summer 54	Paul's second visit to Corinth, returns to Ephesus Titus to Corinth with "Severe Letter" Riot in Ephesus caused by the guild of the silversmiths Paul suffers afflictions in the province of Asia	2 Cor 13:2 2 Cor 2:4, 13 Acts 19:23 – 41 2 Cor 1:8
Spring 55	Paul to Troas Paul to Macedonia	2 Cor 2:12 Acts 20:1; 2 Cor 2:13

The significance of Paul's being able to teach uninterrupted for two years cannot be emphasized enough. Being a trained rabbi and an experienced missionary, this period allows us

> to envisage a large syllabus covering exposition of many Scriptures, instruction in Jesus tradition, and elaboration of the characteristic Pauline themes that we know of from his letters.... This picture in turn involves the recognition that his letters should not be seen as simply off-the-cuff compositions in response to particular questions;

rather he was able to draw on many expositions and arguments already well honed by such presentations and by discussions and arguments which they presumably sparked off.[47]

Luke concludes his reference to Paul's proclamation and exposition of the gospel in the hall of Tyrannus with a summary statement regarding the impact of his missionary work in Ephesus. During these two years, Paul preached the gospel unhindered, with the result that (ὥστε) people who lived in other cities of the province also hear the gospel.

---

47. Dunn, *Beginning from Jerusalem*, 769, with reference to Hengel, *Acts and the History of Earliest Christianity*, 11.

Luke's statement that all people in the province of Asia heard the gospel is unique: we do not find a corresponding claim regarding Paul's ministry in the provinces of Cilicia, Syria, Galatia, Pamphylia, Macedonia, or Achaia. This statement not only suggests its historical veracity but also underlines that this period was perhaps the most fruitful of Paul's missionary ministry. Paul informs the Corinthian Christians in a letter written during this period that God has opened "a great door for effective work" (1 Cor 16:8 – 9).

The assertion that "all" (πάντας) people who lived in the province of Asia (see on 2:9 – 10) heard the gospel does not imply the claim that Paul personally spoke to every single person in the province, or that he personally proclaimed the gospel in every city of the province. Rather, the gospel reached the entire province. Luke does not specify how this took place, e.g., by Paul's preaching or through missionary associates who proclaimed the gospel in the Lycus Valley in Laodicea, Hierapolis, and Colossae (Col 1:3 – 8; 4:13). Note Paul's many coworkers during this period: Aquila and Priscilla (Acts 18:24 – 26), Timothy (1 Cor 16:10), Epaphras (Col 1:3 – 8; 4:13) and Philemon (Phlm 1 – 2) from Colossae, Aristarchus from Macedonia (Acts 19:29; 20:4; 27:2; Phlm 23), Gaius from Corinth (Acts 19:29), Tychicus and Trophimus (Acts 20:4; Col 4:7), perhaps also Stephanas, Fortunatus, and Achaicus from Corinth (1 Cor 16:17)

In his letter to the Christians in Corinth, Paul conveys greetings from "the churches in the province of Asia" (αἱ ἐκκλησίαι τῆς Ἀσίας, 1 Cor 16:19), which implies various congregations in the province established during this period. It is not impossible that the churches mentioned in Rev 2 – 3, in addition to the churches in Ephesus and Laodicea, were established during this period — Smyrna, Pergamon, Thyatira, Sardis, and Philadelphia — either through Paul or through missionary coworkers. There also seems to have been a church in Troas (20:5, 7 – 11; 2 Cor 2:12), perhaps in Miletus (20:17) and in Magnesia and Tralles.[48]

Luke emphasizes that both Jews and Greeks heard "the word of the Lord" (v. 10; see on 4:29), i.e., the gospel of Jesus, Israel's Messiah and the Savior of the world. The fact that Paul was no longer able to proclaim the gospel in the synagogue of Ephesus did not mean that his ministry no longer reached Jews. On the contrary, Paul himself and his missionary associates continued to present and explain the good news of Jesus Christ to the Jewish communities in other cities of the province.

19:11 – 12 God continued to perform extraordinary miracles through Paul, so that when handkerchiefs and aprons had touched his skin and were taken to the sick, their diseases left them and the evil spirits departed (δυνάμεις τε οὐ τὰς τυχούσας ὁ θεὸς ἐποίει διὰ τῶν χειρῶν Παύλου, ὥστε καὶ ἐπὶ τοὺς ἀσθενοῦντας ἀποφέρεσθαι ἀπὸ τοῦ χρωτὸς αὐτοῦ σουδάρια ἢ σιμικίνθια καὶ ἀπαλλάσσεσθαι ἀπ᾽ αὐτῶν τὰς νόσους, τά τε πνεύματα τὰ πονηρὰ ἐκπορεύεσθαι). The fourth incident of Paul's ministry in Ephesus reports miracles (vv. 11 – 12). Luke begins with another summary statement about "extraordinary miracles" (δυνάμεις; see on 2:22). Luke clarifies that these were not performed by Paul but by God (ὁ θεὸς ἐποίει), whose power worked "through Paul" (διὰ τῶν χειρῶν Παύλου, lit. "through the hands of Paul").[49]

---

48. The letters of Ignatius of Antioch document the existence of churches in Magnesia and Tralles at the end of the first century.

49. Note the same emphasis concerning the miracles for Peter's ministry in 3:6; 5:15 – 16. The phrase "by the hands" is an expression of agency (cf. Luke 4:11; Acts 5:12; 7:41; 11:30; 17:25; 19:26; cf. Matt 4:6; Heb 1:10; Rev 9:20; cf. Twelftree, *Exorcism*, 148), although healing through laying on of hands, or touching with the hands, is attested as well (Luke 4:40; 5:13; 13:13; cf. Matt 8:3, 15; Mark 1:41; 6:5; 8:23, 25). Twelftree points out

In the context of the role of miracles that Luke reports for Jesus and for Peter, it is correct to say that these extraordinary miracles authenticated Paul's preaching as God's work,[50] but Luke does not emphasize this aspect. While Paul regarded miracles as an authenticating sign of his apostleship (Rom 15:18 – 19; 2 Cor 12:12), he knew that miracles by themselves do not convince unbelievers of the truth of the gospel (1 Cor 1:22 – 23). Rather, it is only God's power, who works in and through the proclamation of Jesus as the crucified Messiah and Savior (1 Cor 1:24 – 25, 27 – 28; 2:4 – 5).

The extraordinary miracles are specified in v. 12. Spiritual power was transmitted through handkerchiefs and aprons that mediated physical contact between Paul's body[51] and the body of the sick and demon-possessed. The term translated as "handkerchiefs" (σουδάρια, a loanword from Latin *sudarium*) denotes a facecloth for wiping perspiration.[52] "Aprons" (σιμικίνθια, a loanword from Latin *semicinctium*), a term that refers to protective pieces of cloth worn by workers, could also denote cloths used "for general mopping up."[53] These pieces of cloth could be related to Paul's tentmaking work; they can also represent the "accepted dress of an orator."[54]

Contact with pieces of cloth that had touched Paul's skin sufficed to cause miracles. Sick people were healed as diseases that had made their lives miserable left them, and people who were demon-possessed were liberated as "evil spirits departed." The use of handkerchiefs and aprons for healings and exorcisms can be interpreted as representing a serious misunderstanding among the population in the context of their traditional magical views and practices, where pieces of cloth functioned as amulets or talismans.[55] These people thought of miraculous power "in material terms, so that it can be 'tapped' from the person of the wonder-worker and stored for subsequent use," an understanding that is "located in dangerous border territory, and Luke intends to direct it into correct theological channels by means of his reference to God's working (v. 11), which presents the human messenger only as an instrument."[56]

While Luke does not describe Paul as giving his approval or encouragement to this activity, Luke certainly presents it as both possible and acceptable. It was God who performed these miracles (v. 11), described as "extraordinary" precisely because miracles of this kind did not commonly happen in the ministry of Jesus or the apostles. If read in the context of the following incident of the failure of Jewish exorcists (vv. 13 – 17), Luke emphasizes God's powerful presence in Paul's ministry — indeed, in Paul's person — resulting in "effortless, successful, and numerous healings and exorcisms."[57]

---

that even though laying on of hands was part of the techniques of exorcising evil spirits in the Greek and Roman world, Luke seems to avoid referring to the laying on of hands in connection with exorcism (note δὲ καί in Luke 4:41; ibid. 148 n. 120).

50. Fitzmyer, *Acts*, 648.

51. The term translated "skin" (χρώς) is defined in BDAG, as "surface of the body." The term, frequent in Greek literature, occurs only here in the New Testament.

52. P. G. W. Glare, *Oxford Latin Dictionary* (Oxford: Oxford Univ. Press, 1976), 1859. BDAG, s.v. σουδάριον; LSJ offers "towel, napkin"; Barrett, *Acts*, 900, 907, suggests "sweatbands," which were "worn on the head to prevent the sweat from running into the eyes." English translations generally use "handkerchiefs."

53. Barrett, *Acts*, 907. Tim J. Leary, "The 'Aprons' of St Paul — Acts 19.12," *JTS* 41 (1990): 527 – 29, suggests "belts."

54. Richard E. Strelan, "Acts 19:12: Paul's 'Aprons' Again," *JTS* 54 (2003): 154 – 57, 157.

55. Note that no speech or command by Paul is mentioned, which explains why the evil spirits come out rather than are driven out; cf. Twelftree, *Exorcism*, 149. It also should be noted that, contrary to pagan practices, Paul did not accept money for providing these cloths.

56. Hans-Josef Klauck, *Magic and Paganism in Early Christianity: The World of the Acts of the Apostles* (orig. 2000; repr., Minneapolis: Fortress, 2003), 98.

57. Twelftree, *Exorcism*, 150; similarly Jervell, *Apostelgeschichte*, 481.

The parallels with Jesus' ministry, where some people were healed through touching him (Luke 6:18 – 19), and with the ministry of Peter, where people were healed through his shadow (Acts 5:12, 15 – 16), combined with the fact that Paul did not promote himself as a miracle worker, unlike Simon Magus (8:9 – 10) and the sons of Sceva (19:13 – 15), allow the conclusion that "this was not a manipulative human process, designed to capture attention and win disciples," but represents "the unique role and status of Peter and Paul in God's purposes" and helps "his readers to differentiate their activity from captivating and misleading alternatives."[58]

19:13 Some of the itinerant Jewish exorcists tried to evoke the name of the Lord Jesus over people possessed by evil spirits, saying, "I adjure you by the Jesus whom Paul proclaims" (ἐπεχείρησαν δέ τινες καὶ τῶν περιερχομένων Ἰουδαίων ἐξορκιστῶν ὀνομάζειν ἐπὶ τοὺς ἔχοντας τὰ πνεύματα τὰ πονηρὰ τὸ ὄνομα τοῦ κυρίου Ἰησοῦ λέγοντες· ὁρκίζω ὑμᾶς τὸν Ἰησοῦν ὃν Παῦλος κηρύσσει). The fifth incident of the Ephesus episode relates attempts of itinerant Jewish exorcists to drive out evil spirits with the help of the name of Jesus (vv. 13 – 16). Jews who were active as exorcists[59] in various cities, traveling from place to place,[60] perhaps in the province of Asia (cf. v. 10),[61] attempt to pronounce the name of Jesus when they address the evil spirits that they seek to drive out of people possessed by them.

The existence of Jewish exorcists is implied in Luke 11:19 (Matt 12:27). Josephus asserts that Solomon had been granted knowledge of "the art used against demons for the benefit and healing of men" and that he left behind "forms of exorcisms with which those possessed by demons drive them out," establishing a tradition that was still alive in his own day, in the first century.[62] The expression translated "evoke the name" (ὀνομάζειν ... τὸ ὄνομα) refers to the incantation of a formula that includes a name regarded as having the power to drive out evil spirits from people. The belief that names have magical potency, that a higher power resides in the knowledge of the name of a person or a god, is attested in numerous pagan texts.

These Jewish exorcists have heard of Paul who proclaimed Jesus in Ephesus and of the extraordinary miracles that happened in his ministry, which evidently included exorcisms done in the name of Jesus Christ (cf. 16:18). They may have believed that the mere use of the name of Jesus would allow them to drive out demons, without having to use more complicated forms of exorcisms requiring the use of objects and elaborate incantations.[63] Luke relates their brief incantation in direct speech: when they addressed evil spirits, they adjured them "by the Jesus" (τὸν Ἰησοῦν) proclaimed by Paul and whose power was manifested in the extraordinary miracles taking place in his ministry.

---

58. Peterson, *Acts*, 537, 538; cf. Clinton E. Arnold, *Ephesians: Power and Magic: The Concept of Power in Ephesians in Light of its Historical Setting* (1989; repr., Grand Rapids: Baker, 1992), 19.

59. BDAG, s.v. ἐξορκιστής, "one who drives out evil spirits by invocation of transcendent entities."

60. The present tense of the participle translated as "itinerant" (περιερχομένων) indicates that they had been active as exorcists for some time.

61. Since the last geographical location in the episode is the province of Asia (v. 10), the comment in v. 17 that the following events became known in Ephesus leaves open the possibility that this incident took place not in Ephesus but in another city of the province.

62. Josephus, *Ant.* 8.45 – 49; he tells the story of a certain Eleazar, who "put to the nose of the possessed man a ring which had under its seal one of the roots prescribed by Solomon, and then, as the man smelled it, drew out the demon through his nostrils."

63. According to Israel's Scriptures, magical practices were forbidden; cf. Deut 18:9 – 14 listing different kinds of magicians and magical practices. The Mishnah cites Deut 18 in its reaffirmation of the prohibition of magic, stipulating for magicians the death penalty of stoning (*m. Sanh.* 10:1). The rabbis distinguished between prayer for healing, which was permitted, and magical practices such as whispering secret words and divine names over a wound.

19:14 Seven sons of a Jewish chief priest named Sceva were doing this (ἦσαν δέ τινος Σκευᾶ Ἰουδαίου ἀρχιερέως ἑπτὰ υἱοὶ τοῦτο ποιοῦντες). Luke identifies the Jewish exorcists in terms of number ("seven") and origin — all the sons of a man named Sceva, a Jew who was a "chief priest" (ἀρχιερεύς), i.e., a member of one of the families in Jerusalem from which high priests were appointed. The name Sceva is neither Semitic nor Greek; it is a Latin cognomen (Scaeva), attested for gladiators who were evidently "left-handed."[64] The Latin name means, perhaps, that the man was left-handed, "or his name expressed a secondary, metaphorical sense of the word as 'favorable omen.' "[65]

Some suggest that the term "chief priest" refers not to the chief priest(s) in Jerusalem but to the "chief priest" (also designated ἀρχιερεύς) of the cult of "Roma and Augustus" in Ephesus. Sceva may have been a renegade Jew who served in the imperial cult as "chief priest."[66] This is not likely since Luke specifically identifies him as a "Jewish" chief priest. Others suggest that the description of Sceva as "chief priest" or "high priest" was a (false) claim with which the exorcists advertised their services.[67] However, Luke does not indicate that the "dignity" of belonging to a (high) priestly family was merely a claim. Others suggest that he may have belonged to one of the families from which the high priests of Jerusalem were appointed, or the title may reflect the fact that he belonged to the Jewish priestly aristocracy in Ephesus or Asia Minor.[68]

19:15 But the evil spirit answered them, "I know Jesus, and I am acquainted with Paul, but who are you?" (ἀποκριθὲν δὲ τὸ πνεῦμα τὸ πονηρὸν εἶπεν αὐτοῖς· τὸν μὲν Ἰησοῦν γινώσκω καὶ τὸν Παῦλον ἐπίσταμαι, ὑμεῖς δὲ τίνες ἐστέ;). Luke now relates a specific example of the sons of Sceva. They had entered a house (v. 16) and use the incantation quoted in v. 13 in the attempt to expel an evil spirit from a person. When they address the evil spirit in the name of Jesus, the spirit answers back, asserting that he knows Jesus and Paul but not the sons of Sceva.

The question "Who are you?" (ὑμεῖς δὲ τίνες ἐστέ;) clarifies that it is not a formula (in which the name of Jesus is used) that is powerful in the spirit world, but the identity of the exorcist. Jesus had the power to drive out evil spirits since he was Israel's Messiah and Lord, and Paul has the power to expel evil spirits because God works directly through him (v. 11), while the sons of Sceva must rely on a thirdhand source of power and are thus not known in the spirit world.[69] The name of Jesus is not a magical device;[70] only those empowered by God can liberate people from evil spirits. What is important about Paul is not his name or that Paul uses the name of Jesus in exorcisms, but the fact that Paul acknowledges the power of Jesus as the Lord and thus drives out evil spirits in the name of Jesus — a fact known in the spirit world.

19:16 Then the person with the evil spirit jumped on them; he subdued all of them and overpowered them so that they fled from the house naked and wounded (καὶ ἐφαλόμενος ὁ ἄνθρωπος ἐπ᾽ αὐτοὺς ἐν ᾧ ἦν τὸ πνεῦμα τὸ πονηρόν, κατακυριεύσας ἀμφοτέρων ἴσχυσεν κατ᾽ αὐτῶν ὥστε γυμνοὺς καὶ τετραυματισμένους ἐκφυγεῖν ἐκ τοῦ οἴκου ἐκείνου). The subject changes from the evil

---

64. Cf. LSJ, s.v. σκεῦας, "gladiator fighting with his left hand." The name is attested for a Jew in Cyrene (Gert Lüderitz, *Corpus jüdischer Zeugnisse aus der Cyrenaika* [Wiesbaden: Reichert, 1983], no. 43c).

65. Hemer, *Acts*, 234.

66. Fitzmyer, *Acts*, 650.

67. Bruce, *Acts*, 411.

68. Metzner, *Die Prominenten*, 453.

69. Twelftree, *Exorcism*, 151.

70. Note the critique of magical practices in 8:9 – 24 (Simon in Samaria), 13:6 – 11 (Elymas in Paphos), and 16:16 – 18 (the slave girl in Philippi).

spirit (v. 15) to the person who was controlled by the spirit. The former challenges the Jewish exorcists verbally, the latter attacks them physically.

The action of the demon-possessed man is described with three verbs in the aorist to signal completed action. He "jumped" on the men (i.e., attacked them physically), resulting in their togas being torn so that they are naked and the men are wounded — visible perhaps in black eyes, bleeding noses, and scratch marks. He "subdues" all seven men, gaining power over them, which means that the demon acting through the man proves stronger than the would-be exorcists. Finally, he "overpowers" them; he is able to control them, with the result (ὥστε) that they flee from the house in a hurry, leaving behind their torn-off clothes.

19:17 This became known to all the Jews and Greeks living in Ephesus. Fear came over all of them, and the name of the Lord Jesus was glorified (τοῦτο δὲ ἐγένετο γνωστὸν πᾶσιν Ἰουδαίοις τε καὶ Ἕλλησιν τοῖς κατοικοῦσιν τὴν Ἔφεσον καὶ ἐπέπεσεν φόβος ἐπὶ πάντας αὐτοὺς καὶ ἐμεγαλύνετο τὸ ὄνομα τοῦ κυρίου Ἰησοῦ). In the sixth incident of the Ephesus episode, Luke relates further conversions and the ongoing consolidation of the church (vv. 17 – 20), both as a result of the incident of the Jewish exorcists. While some might regard the events of v. 16 as comical,[71] neither the demon-possessed man nor the Jewish exorcists or their contemporaries in Ephesus — nor Luke's readers still involved in magical practices — would have regarded the outcome of the attempt at exorcism as being funny. The man is still afflicted by a powerful demon. The seven exorcists are in physical pain and, more significantly, suffer the shame of having been proved powerless.

The first reaction mentioned by Luke is that the Jews and Greeks living in Ephesus who hear of these events are gripped with fear, alarmed that evil spirits might attack them as well. Next comes praise of "the name of the Lord Jesus." The passive of "was glorified" (ἐμεγαλύνετο) is best linked with the Jews and Greeks living in Ephesus: as they hear of the failed attempt to drive out an evil spirit by the invocation of the name of Jesus by those who do not believe in Jesus, they realize there is indeed supernatural power connected with the name of Jesus, and this power cannot be manipulated. While it is certainly possible that unbelieving Jews and Greeks spoke highly of Jesus and of the power of his name (cf. 5:13), the comment in v. 20 suggests that "was glorified" indicates further conversions among the Jews and Greeks in the city.

19:18 Many of those who had come to faith came forward to confess and admit their practices (πολλοί τε τῶν πεπιστευκότων ἤρχοντο ἐξομολογούμενοι καὶ ἀναγγέλλοντες τὰς πράξεις αὐτῶν). The third reaction to the surprising and awe-inspiring events described in v. 16 is the admission of magical practices by Christian believers — probably the new believers whose conversions are suggested in v. 17. The imperfect tense of the verb "came forward" (ἤρχοντο) suggests that believers come to Paul and before the congregation, over an extended period of time, with the desire to confess their sins.

The syntax of the Greek sentence can be understood in two ways. (1) The two participles form a hendiadys[72] expressing the frank confession of sins, which is either sinful behavior in general or magical spells more particularly. (2) Luke describes two reactions of Ephesian believers: some come forward to confess (ἐξομολογούμενοι) their sins, admitting wrongdoing, and others come forward to admit (ἀναγγέλλοντες) their "practices," i.e., to disclose their use of magical spells. Since

---

71. Pervo, *Acts*, 478, who asserts that "the boisterous climax is worthy of New Comedy."

72. Cf. BDF §442.16: "the co-ordination of two ideas, one of which is dependent on the other."

magic was part of everyday life in Ephesus (as in any other city of the Greco-Roman world), it is not surprising that new converts would disclose their involvement in magical practices perhaps not immediately, but some time after their conversion.[73]

19:19 Quite a few of those who practiced magic gathered their books together and burned them in public. The value of these books was assessed to be 50,000 silver coins (ἱκανοὶ δὲ τῶν τὰ περίεργα πραξάντων συνενέγκαντες τὰς βίβλους κατέκαιον ἐνώπιον πάντων, καὶ συνεψήφισαν τὰς τιμὰς αὐτῶν καὶ εὗρον ἀργυρίου μυριάδας πέντε). The new believers who confess their involvement in magical practices take practical steps that show their repentance and determination to change their behavior. Numerous believers practicing "magic" take a twofold action: they gather together magical texts and "burn them in public."[74] They remove these magical texts not only from their homes and from their own private use; they make sure that no one else will be able to read and use them.

The term translated as "books" (βίβλοι)[75] denotes scrolls that contained magical spells and formulae. The fact that these magical texts are brought out into the public can be interpreted in terms of the desire of the new believers to render the spells recorded in these texts inoperative, since "according to magical theory, the potency of a spell is bound up with its secrecy; if it is divulged, it becomes ineffective."[76]

Someone evidently computed the value of these books: 50,000 silver coins (ἀργύρια; here, Attic silver drachmas), which amounts to the yearly wage (with no days off) of 137 workers.[77] Book burnings are attested in antiquity. Often rulers ordered books to be burned in order to repudiate their content regarded as offensive, seditious, or dangerous.[78] Here the books that are burned are not forcibly seized (by Paul or the leaders of the congregation) but brought voluntarily and burned at great personal loss. The immense value of these magical texts indicates that the church had grown considerably, with perhaps hundreds of people, both poor and rich, having come to faith in Jesus and now publicly renouncing their involvement in magical practices.

19:20 So the word spread and grew in power on account of the power of the Lord (οὕτως κατὰ κράτος τοῦ κυρίου ὁ λόγος ηὔξανεν καὶ ἴσχυεν). Luke ends this incident with another summary statement that records further conversions in Ephesus (v. 17) and in other cities of the province of Asia (v. 10). The "word" (λόγος; see on 4:29) is the word of God, i.e., the proclamation of the good news of Jesus as Israel's Messiah and Savior of humankind.[79]

---

73. Cf. Polhill, *Acts*, 405, who comments: "Salvation involves a process of growth, of increasing sanctification. And after all, the Ephesian spells were not that remote from the horoscopes and board games that supposedly communicate telepathic messages with which many Christians dabble in our own day."

74. The expression translated "in public" (ἐνώπιον πάντων; lit., "before all") can refer to the people of Ephesus, who all had heard of the power of the name of Jesus (v. 17), or to the congregation of all the believers.

75. The definite article (τάς) functions here as possessive pronoun: they bring the books that they had acquired in the past.

76. Bruce, *Book of Acts*, 369; cf. Trebilco, *Early Christians in Ephesus*, 151.

77. Cf. BDAG, s.v. ἀργύριον 2c. Polhill, *Acts*, 405, computes that 50,000 silver coins "would come to about $35,000 in current silver value" (adding that "the Attic drachma contained 67.5 grains of silver, or approximately 14 percent of a troy ounce. With silver at $5 a troy ounce, the drachma would contain about 70 cents in silver value"). In September 2009, a troy ounce of silver sold at $14, which translates into $98,000 for the value of the magical texts — an example for the notorious unreliability of the computation of biblical currency figures.

78. Suetonius, *Aug.* 31; Livy 39.16; 40.29.3 – 14; Pliny, *Nat.* 13.84 – 88; Diogenes Laertius, *Vit. phil.* 9.52; Lucian of Samosata, *Alex.* 47; cf. Jer 36:20 – 27; 1 Macc 1:56.

79. Cf. 4:4; 6:4; 8:4; 10:36, 44; 11:19; 14:25; 16:6; 17:11.

Luke makes three statements. (1) The word "spread" (ηὔξανεν; cf. 6:7; 12:24); i.e., the gospel was accepted by more and more people, resulting in the numerical growth of the church(es). (2) The word "grew in power" (ἴσχυεν); i.e., the proclamation of the gospel was accompanied by events such as those narrated in vv. 11 – 12 (extraordinary miracles), vv. 13 – 16 (the defeat of the Jewish exorcists), and vv. 18 – 19 (public renunciation of magic), which demonstrated the power of Jesus manifested in the gospel message. (3) The growth of the church and the visibility of the impact of the truth of the gospel were caused by the "power" (κράτος) of the Lord[80] — not by Paul's rhetoric, not by the faith of the believers, and certainly not by magic, but by Jesus' sovereign power manifested in the effects of Paul's proclamation of the gospel. Thus, an ever-increasing number of people who confessed their sins and publicly renounced their involvement in magic were converted; moreover, miracles and exorcisms occurred.

19:21 After these events had happened, Paul resolved in the Spirit to travel through Macedonia and Achaia before going to Jerusalem. He said, "After I have been there, I must visit Rome" (ὡς δὲ ἐπληρώθη ταῦτα, ἔθετο ὁ Παῦλος ἐν τῷ πνεύματι διελθὼν τὴν Μακεδονίαν καὶ Ἀχαΐαν πορεύεσθαι εἰς Ἱεροσόλυμα εἰπὼν ὅτι μετὰ τὸ γενέσθαι με ἐκεῖ δεῖ με καὶ Ῥώμην ἰδεῖν). Luke now signals the end of

Paul's missionary work in Ephesus, which is at the same time the end of Paul's missionary travels — his return to Jerusalem will end in his imprisonment.

The reference to "these events" (ταῦτα), i.e., to the growth and consolidation of the church described in vv. 17 – 20, marks the end of Luke's report about the missionary work of Paul in Ephesus. Paul's decision to leave Ephesus is described either as a personal decision[81] or as a decision guided by the Holy Spirit.[82] The latter is more plausible. Paul's "prophetic sense" that he "must" (δεῖ) see Rome implies a reference to the will of God. In 20:22 – 23 Paul asserts that his journey to Jerusalem is the result of the guidance of the Spirit.[83] It is unlikely that Luke suggests that Paul came up with the idea of his final journey to Jerusalem on his own. The reference to the Spirit accords with numerous other passages in which the Spirit takes the initiative and directs the movements of missionaries.[84]

What we know about Paul's plans and movements in AD 55 – 56 suggests that the plan to travel to Macedonia and Achaia did not involve new missionary work in cities that Paul had not visited before,[85] but visits to the churches that he had established: in Philippi, Thessalonica, Berea, Athens, and Corinth. Note that Luke uses the name of Roman provinces rather than of regions or cities (unlike in his earlier accounts, but corresponding to Paul's practice). Paul had announced a visit to the

---

80. Assuming that the genitive "of the Lord" (τοῦ κυρίου) is dependent on "power" (κράτος) rather than on "the word" (ὁ λόγος); the latter is assumed by most English translations (note the changed word order in 𝔓⁷⁴ ℵ² 33. 1739 Maj, which read ὁ λόγος τοῦ κυρίου; e.g., NIV: "In this way the word of the Lord spread widely and grew in power").

81. BDAG, s.v. τίθημι 1bα. "have (in mind)," in Acts 19:21 "Paul resolved." Cf. NIV, TNIV: "Paul decided," NET: "Paul resolved," NJB, GNB: "Paul made up his mind." In this case, "spirit" (πνεῦμα) is Paul's human spirit.

82. Cf. ESV, NASB, NLT, NRSV, RSV. Cf. Gaventa, *Acts*, 268; Peterson, *Acts*, 543.

83. Many see an echo of Jesus' decision, made under divine necessity, to go to Jerusalem, where he would suffer (Luke 9:51;

13:31 – 35). See David P. Moessner, "'The Christ Must Suffer': New Light on the Jesus-Peter, Stephen, Paul Parallels in Luke-Acts," *NovT* 28 (1986): 220 – 56.

84. See 8:29; 10:19 – 20; 11:12; 13:2, 4; 16:6 – 7; 21:4. Bock, *Acts*, 605, suggests that the middle voice of the verb and the presence of the term "must" (δεῖ) "suggests a combination of wills. It appears that Paul has a resolve that he lays before God to see if it is from the Spirit."

85. There is a possibility that between his visit to the churches in Macedonia and Achaia, Paul traveled to the province of Illyricum and preached the gospel there (cf. Rom 15:19), perhaps testing his ability to work in Latin-speaking cities (through a translator?) before moving to Spain. Cf. Schnabel, *Early Christian Mission*, 2:1260 – 57.

Christians in Corinth in 1 Cor 16:5 – 9, a passage that mentions a prior visit to Macedonia. The plan to travel to Macedonia first and then to Achaia was later changed (see 2 Cor 1:15 – 16, where Paul announces that he wanted to visit Corinth [in Achaia] first before traveling to Macedonia, and then to return again to Corinth). This plan was also changed, as 2 Cor 1:23 indicates. If we follow Luke's account in Acts 20:1 – 6, Paul reverted to his original plan and traveled to Macedonia first (where he wrote 2 Corinthians), then visited Greece.

The goal of Paul's next initiative is Rome, highlighted by the use of direct speech. The fact that Luke uses a verb that generally means "see" and which should be translated here as "visit"[86] indicates that Paul's plans are specific. In Rom 15:23 – 33, written a few months later from Corinth, the last stage of Paul's travels before reaching Jerusalem, Paul explains that he wants to come to Rome in order to organize and initiate a planned mission to Spain. Luke does not mention Paul's plans for a mission to Spain, nor does he mention the collection that Paul was in the process of organizing for the believers in the Jerusalem congregation.[87]

19:22 He sent two of his assistants, Timothy and Erastus, to Macedonia, while he stayed for some time longer in the province of Asia (ἀποστείλας δὲ εἰς τὴν Μακεδονίαν δύο τῶν διακονούντων αὐτῷ, Τιμόθεον καὶ Ἔραστον, αὐτὸς ἐπέσχεν χρόνον εἰς τὴν Ἀσίαν). Paul sends Timothy and Erastus ahead to Macedonia. Timothy is one of Paul's most

trusted and effective missionary associates (see 16:1). Erastus was at one point the city treasurer of Corinth.[88] He is probably identical with the Erastus mentioned in an inscription discovered in the paved square east of the theater of Corinth. The text of the inscription states that Erastus donated the pavement in gratitude for being appointed aedile: "Erastus in return for his aedileship laid [the pavement] at his own expense."[89] The dedication records

> Erastus's dedication in exchange for, or as an obligation of, his office. As an aedile he was an important, annually elected civic official responsible for the maintenance of civic property, the revenue from such properties, and for judging commercial and financial litigation. The inscription indicates that the benefaction was made for the purpose of self-advancement in his career.[90]

Erastus, evidently free from municipal obligations in Corinth at this time, had come to Ephesus to assist Paul in his missionary work, both in Ephesus and elsewhere.

Timothy and Erastus are "assistants"[91] (διακονούντων, a participle), a term that should not be interpreted in terms of menial service but in terms of official duties as assistants alongside Paul; their duties would have included the task of preparing the congregations in Macedonia for Paul's farewell visit.[92] While Paul does use the term "service" (διακονία) to describe his collection for the saints,[93] the related Greek verb does not

---

86. BDAG, s.v. εἶδον 5, "to show an interest in, *look after, visit*." Cf. NIV, TNIV; most English translation have "see" (NASB, NET, RSV, NRSV), which could be misunderstood as describing Paul as a tourist who wants to see the sights of the capital of the empire.

87. See on Acts 20:3 – 4; 21:18. For the collection cf. Rom 15:25 – 28; 1 Cor 16:1 – 4; 2 Cor 8 – 9.

88. Rom 16:23; in 2 Tim 4:20 he is also in Corinth; also see on 18:18.

89. Latin text: ERASTUS*PRO*AEDILIT[AT]E / S(UA)*P(ECUNIA)*STRAVIT. Cf. David W. J. Gill, "Erastus

the Aedile," *TynBul* 40 (1989): 293 – 301.

90. Mary C. Sturgeon, *Corinth IX, iii: Sculpture: The Assemblage from the Theater* (Princeton: American School of Classical Studies at Athens, 2004), 48.

91. Cf. NET, NLT, Barrett, Fitzmyer. Most English versions translate with "helpers" (ESV, GNB, NIV, NRSV, RSV, TNIV).

92. Hentschel, *Diakonia*, 350 – 53.

93. Rom 15:31; 2 Cor 8:4; 9:1, where Paul uses διακονία for the collection of the church in Antioch for the believers in Jerusalem (cf. Acts 11:29; 12:25).

automatically suggest that the main task of Timothy and Erastus was related to the collection (see on 19:21), although presumably they would have promoted this important project of Paul in the Macedonian churches.

Luke does not explain why Paul sends his two assistants ahead while he stays "for some time longer" in the province of Asia. Either Paul's travel is delayed by unspecified developments, perhaps in cities in the province other than Ephesus, that require his presence, or there are other reasons for Paul's change of plans. In Luke's account, Paul's journey to Macedonia and Achaia and eventually Jerusalem (and Rome) begins at 20:1, i.e., after the riot of the silversmiths of Ephesus (vv. 23 – 41), which happens toward the end of Paul's missionary work in Asia (v. 23).

19:23 It was about this time that a great commotion erupted about the Way (ἐγένετο δὲ κατὰ τὸν καιρὸν ἐκεῖνον τάραχος οὐκ ὀλίγος περὶ τῆς ὁδοῦ). The eighth incident of the Ephesus episode recounts the riot of the silversmiths (vv. 23 – 41). Luke begins his description of the origins of the riot (vv. 23 – 28) by noting the time when it took place.[94] The "Way" (ὁδός; see on 5:11; 9:2), i.e., the followers of Jesus, became the reason for a commotion in Ephesus at the conclusion of Paul's ministry in the province of Asia, when he had decided to travel to Macedonia and Achaia before visiting Jerusalem and Rome (v. 21). Since Paul wanted to stay in Ephesus until the Feast of Pentecost (1 Cor 16:8), celebrated in early June, and since the main Artemis festival was celebrated in March/April, it is possible that the initiative of the silversmiths' guild that argued for the grandeur of Artemis Ephesia occurred in the spring of AD 55.

19:24 A silversmith with the name Demetrius, who made silver shrines of Artemis, provided much profit for the artisans (Δημήτριος γάρ τις ὀνόματι, ἀργυροκόπος, ποιῶν ναοὺς ἀργυροῦς Ἀρτέμιδος παρείχετο τοῖς τεχνίταις οὐκ ὀλίγην ἐργασίαν). The instigator of the "great commotion" was a particular silversmith named Demetrius. Silversmiths (ἀργυροκόποι) are attested in inscriptions found at Ephesus, as is a guild of silversmiths. Demetrius, or rather his "artisans" or craftsmen (τεχνίται), produced miniature replicas of the great temple of Artemis.

While no silver replicas of the temple of Artemis have been discovered (yet), the archaeological evidence shows that various industries participated in the production of devotional objects related to the cult of Artemis. A figure of Artemis made of lead and a miniature marble temple of Artemis have been discovered.[95] Demetrius's business had been thriving; the significance of the cult of Artemis for the large Ephesian population and the attraction of Artemis Ephesia and the various festivals connected with her cult guaranteed the manufacturers of devotional objects a good deal of profit.

19:25 He called a meeting of these artisans and of the workers in related crafts, and said, "Gentlemen, you know that we get our prosperity from this business" (οὓς συναθροίσας καὶ τοὺς περὶ τὰ τοιαῦτα ἐργάτας εἶπεν· ἄνδρες, ἐπίστασθε ὅτι ἐκ ταύτης τῆς ἐργασίας ἡ εὐπορία ἡμῖν ἐστιν). The convocation of the silversmiths and other workers involved in the production of devotional Artemis objects, initiated by Demetrius, suggests either that Demetrius was the dominating manufacturer of Artemis miniatures[96] or, more likely, that he was

---

94. The term translated "commotion" (τάραχος, synonymous with ἡ ταραχή) is used "especially for disorders, social disturbances, political agitation, and riots" (C. Spicq, "ταράσσω, τάραχος," *TLNT*, 3:372, who calls the noun "a technical term for insurrections").

95. Horsley and Llewelyn, *New Documents*, 4:9.

96. Peter Lampe, "Acta 19 im Spiegel der ephesischen Inschriften," *BZ* 36 (1992): 59 – 76, 19.

the master of the guild of the silversmiths.[97] His speech indicates that he is acting not on the basis of private financial interests but in the context of the statues of associations or guilds.

The speech of Demetrius (vv. 25 – 27) can be divided into six parts.[98] First, he begins by attracting the attention of his colleagues to their wealth (v. 25d-f). The term translated "prosperity" (εὐπορία) denotes resources in terms of being wealthy, "an ease that allows the free use of one's possessions."[99] Demetrius reminds the men who belong to the guild of silversmiths that their prosperity derives from the manufacture and sale of devotional Artemis objects.

19:26 You observe and you hear that not only here in Ephesus but in almost the entire province of Asia this Paul has persuaded and misled a considerable number of people. He says that gods made with hands are not gods (καὶ θεωρεῖτε καὶ ἀκούετε ὅτι οὐ μόνον Ἐφέσου ἀλλὰ σχεδὸν πάσης τῆς Ἀσίας ὁ Παῦλος οὗτος πείσας μετέστησεν ἱκανὸν ὄχλον λέγων ὅτι οὐκ εἰσὶν θεοὶ οἱ διὰ χειρῶν γινόμενοι). Second, Demetrius describes the impact of Paul's activity in Ephesus and in the province of Asia (v. 26a-g). Luke uses two present tense verbs to describe the artisans' awareness of what is happening: they "observe" (θεωρεῖτε) and "hear" (ἀκούετε) the activity of "this Paul,"[100] which is described with two verbs in the aorist tense: by "persuading" (πείσας, modal participle) people not only in Ephesus but in "almost" the entire province of Asia to accept his teaching, he has "misled" (μετέστησεν) many people.

The term ὄχλος reflects the effect of Paul's

preaching and teaching: a large "crowd" of people was converted to faith in Jesus. Luke's previous description in vv. 10, 20 suggests that Demetrius is not exaggerating. The charge that Paul has misled many people indicates that Demetrius refers to pagans who have been moved from worshiping Artemis and buying miniatures that reminded them of their devotion to the goddess to worshiping another deity, prompting them to cease their worship of Artemis and to stop buying devotional objects.

Third, Demetrius describes Paul's teaching concerning the gods (v. 26h-i). He proclaims that "gods made with hands" are "not gods" (οὐκ εἰσὶν θεοί). Luke relates this emphasis of Paul's missionary proclamation before pagan audiences as an accusation by Demetrius rather than in a report about Paul's preaching activity. While the philosophers of Athens would have agreed with Paul (see on 17:29), popular piety identified the images of deities with the deities they represented. According to Demetrius, Paul's deceitful activity consists in his efforts to convince the people to give up worshiping the traditional gods. Once people refrain from doing so, they will also refrain from buying replicas of a deity such as Artemis (and replicas of her temple).

19:27 "There is danger not only that our line of business is discredited, but also that the temple of the great goddess Artemis may be looked upon as nothing, and she, whom the entire province of Asia and indeed the entire world worships, will suffer the loss of her grandeur" (οὐ μόνον δὲ τοῦτο κινδυνεύει ἡμῖν τὸ μέρος εἰς ἀπελεγμὸν ἐλθεῖν ἀλλὰ καὶ τὸ τῆς μεγάλης θεᾶς Ἀρτέμιδος ἱερὸν εἰς

---

97. Reinhard Selinger, "Die Demetriosunruhen (Apg 19,23 – 40): Eine Fallstudie aus rechtshistorischer Perspektive," ZNW 88 (1997): 242 – 59, 245.

98. Padilla, *Speeches*, 178, describes the speech as "an unpolished address (in terms of modelling clear, separate parts) which contained mostly epideictic qualities," which are visible in Demetrius's point of presenting Paul's preaching "as an activ-

ity that was having an effect up to the time of speaking."

99. C. Spicq, "εὐπορέω, εὐπορία," *TLNT*, 2:135; cf. LSJ, s.v. εὐπορία I.1, "ease, facility of doing something, easy means of providing"; sense 2, "plenty abundance, welfare, wealth."

100. The demonstrative pronoun (οὗτος) is used here in a contemptuous sense (BDF §290.6: "of a person present": Paul is pictured as present in the city of Ephesus).

οὐθὲν λογισθῆναι, μέλλειν τε καὶ καθαιρεῖσθαι τῆς μεγαλειότητος αὐτῆς ἣν ὅλη ἡ Ἀσία καὶ ἡ οἰκουμένη σέβεται). Fourth, Demetrius warns of the damage that Paul's activities might inflict on the guild of silversmiths. There is the present risk that the silversmiths' line of business might be discredited. If people no longer believe that the statues of the gods worshiped in Ephesus are indeed gods and if their allegiance to Artemis is withdrawn, they will criticize the manufacture of devotional objects that have provided the silversmiths a steady stream of income.

Fifth, Demetrius warns of the damage that Paul's successful preaching might have for the temple of Artemis. It "may be looked upon as nothing" (εἰς οὐθὲν λογισθῆναι).[101] If the people "deceived" by Paul accept his teaching that gods made with hands are not gods, the temple of Artemis (see on 18:24) will no longer be one of the main reasons for the fame of Ephesus — the grand structure in which the famous image of "the great goddess Artemis" (ἡ μεγάλη θεὰ Ἄρτεμις)[102] awed thousands of visitors to the temple, the sanctuary famous for its size and antiquity and for its beauty and works of art, the "common bank of Asia" and the "refuge of necessity"[103] granting asylum to people unjustly accused of murder or facing imprisonment.

About fifty-five years after Paul's ministry in Ephesus, Pliny the Younger, governor of the province of Bithynia, warned the emperor Trajan that what he called the "superstition" of the followers of Jesus — which has been "not confined to the cities only, but has spread through the villages and rural districts" — posed a threat to the economy of the region since people were buying fewer sacrificial animals. In his letter Pliny assured the emperor that his forceful measures against the Christians was resulting in the revival of the sacred festivals.[104]

Sixth, Demetrius warns of the damage that the success of Paul's activities will inflict on the cult of Artemis. The great goddess Artemis will "suffer the loss of her grandeur." This grandeur was connected with her numerous palpable manifestations (*epiphaneia*) — physical appearances reported in myth, novels, inscriptions, and revelations in response to prayers for safety and healing.[105] The grandeur of Artemis is also reflected in that she was worshiped not only in Ephesus but by "the entire province of Asia," and indeed by "the entire world."

The sphere of influence of Artemis Ephesia is attested by sanctuaries for the goddess in other cities throughout the Roman world (e.g., elsewhere in Asia Minor as well as in Greece, Gaul, and Spain), and by over fifty cities in Asia Minor that minted coins of the Artemis Ephesia type. Ephesus was not permitted to erect a temple to Tiberius and Gaius Caligula on the grounds that it had already the distinction of the temple of Artemis.[106] The suggestion that Paul's activities jeopardize the cult of Artemis is thus most incendiary and dangerous for Paul and for the increasing number of new believers in Jesus who have abandoned the worship of Artemis; once the cult of Artemis declines, the city itself will suffer. Demetrius assumes, correctly, that if her cult is threatened, the city will quickly come to her defense. As the citizens of Ephesus venerate Artemis as the "leader of our city" and as they believe that Ephesus is "the nurturer of its own

---

101. For the Greek phrase see Isa 40:17; Wis 3:17; 9:6 (without reference to a pagan deity).

102. Xenophon, *Ephesiaca* 1.11.15 speaks of "our ancestral goddess, the great Artemis of the Ephesians." Both the masculine form (θεός) and the feminine form (θεά) are used for Artemis; in v. 37 the town clerk speaks of τὴν θεὸν ἡμῶν.

103. Aelius Aristides, *Or.* 23.24.

104. See Pliny, *Ep.* 10.96.

105. Cf. R. Oster, in Horsley and Llewelyn, *New Documents*, 4:80 – 81. Note the epithet ἐπιφανεστάτῃ used for Artemis (I. Ephesos Ia 27, 385).

106. Tacitus, *Ann.* 4.55 – 56; Dio Cassius 59.28.1. Cf. Murphy-O'Connor, *St. Paul's Ephesus*, 62.

Ephesian goddess,"[107] they will have to take action against Paul and his converts.

19:28   When they heard this, they became very angry. They shouted, "Great is Artemis of the Ephesians!" (ἀκούσαντες δὲ καὶ γενόμενοι πλήρεις θυμοῦ ἔκραζον λέγοντες· μεγάλη ἡ Ἄρτεμις Ἐφεσίων). Luke reports the effect of Demetrius's speech with two statements: the members of the guild of silversmiths become furious, and they start to chant an acclamation of Artemis as the great goddess of the Ephesians.[108] This acclamation does not necessarily mean that the economic interest that was the primary concern of Demetrius (vv. 25d-f, 27a-b) has been lost; rather, the excited invocation of the greatness of Artemis Ephesia serves to mobilize the city to defend the integrity of the worship of the goddess and thus to safeguard the prosperity of the manufacturers of devotional objects.

19:29   The city was in chaos. Prompted by the same impulse, people rushed to the theater, dragging with them Gaius and Aristarchus, Paul's Macedonian travel companions (καὶ ἐπλήσθη ἡ πόλις τῆς συγχύσεως, ὥρμησάν τε ὁμοθυμαδὸν εἰς τὸ θέατρον συναρπάσαντες Γάϊον καὶ Ἀρίσταρχον Μακεδόνας, συνεκδήμους Παύλου). Luke presents the riot that ensues, triggered by the guild of silversmiths and Demetrius's speech, with dramatic vividness in nine scenes (vv. 29 – 34; see Exegetical

Outline). Demetrius and the guild, cleverly combining religious, patriotic, and commercial factors in support of the cult of Artemis Ephesia, somehow manage to get the citizens of Ephesus excited about the clear and present danger that the cult of the great goddess of the city of Ephesus and of the entire world is facing.[109]

Demetrius and his guild do not take legal action against Paul and his activities before the courts, the proconsuls, or the regular assembly (as eventually suggested by the city clerk, vv. 38 – 39),[110] perhaps because they suspect that they would stand little chance before the authorities to have Paul expelled from the city. They may have aimed from the start to create "chaos" among the population, triggering a civil disturbance that would scare Paul away. The confusion fills the city; i.e., the silversmiths succeed in getting a substantial portion of the citizenry to talk about Paul and his converts being a threat to the majesty of Artemis Ephesia and thus to the fame and welfare of Ephesus.

The people rush to the theater, "prompted by the same impulse" (ὁμοθυμαδόν), namely, to defend the grandeur of Artemis Ephesia, the integrity of her celebrated cult, the prominence of her famous temple, and thus the fame and welfare of the city of Ephesus. The theater of Ephesus, which could seat 24,000 people, was the natural location for the people to gather. It was used not only for the performance of plays but also for the meeting

---

107. These descriptions of Artemis Ephesia are used in an inscription dated to AD 162 – 64; cf. Horsley and Llewelyn, *New Documents*, 74 – 76.

108. For parallels to such an acclamation cf. Bel 1:41; Pss 86:10; 99:2; 135:5. The Western text adds, between the anger and the shouting of the silversmiths, the phrase "they ran into the street" (δραμόντες εἰς τὸ ἄμφοδον), which explains the connection between what happened in the guild hall where Demetrius spoke (vv. 25 – 28b) and what happened on the streets of the city (v. 29).

109. Alexander Weiss, "Der Aufruhr der Silberschmiede (Apg 19,23 – 40) und das Edikt des Paullus Fabius Persicus (I.

Ephesos 17 – 19)," *BZ* 53 (2009): 69 – 81, suggests that the reason for the riot is linked with the sensitivity of the Ephesians regarding Artemis and her temple at this time, heightened on account of the events of AD 44 (only ten years before Paul was in Ephesus) when the proconsul of the province, Paullus Fabius Persicus, intervened in the affairs of the city in reaction to financial problems connected with the temple of Artemis; local officials sold priestly offices to fellow members who were free to determine the financial benefit they derived from the Artemision.

110. Compare the legal action taken by Paul's opponents in Philippi (16:19 – 21) and in Corinth (18:12).

of the popular assembly, for events of the guilds, and for the Artemis processions. The Salutarius inscription relates that during processions, thirty-one gold and silver statues and images, including nine statues of Artemis, were carried from the temple of Artemis into the theater, where they were placed on inscribed bases during the assembly, and were brought back after the proceedings.[111]

Two of Paul's coworkers are seized and taken to the theater, perhaps by the silversmiths' guild. Gaius and Aristarchus are Macedonians who were Paul's "travel companions." Luke mentions a Gaius from Derbe in Lycaonia as a later travel companion of Paul (20:4). He might be called a "Macedonian travel companion" if he accompanied Paul from someplace in Macedonia. The same may hold true for Gaius of Corinth, who had been baptized by Paul and who was Paul's host in Corinth (1 Cor 1:14; Rom 16:23); alternately, this Gaius is an unknown assistant of Paul during his mission in Ephesus. Aristarchus is a Macedonian from Thessalonica.[112] The two missionaries are probably displayed on the stage of the theater as delinquents.

19:30 Paul wanted to go into the popular assembly, but the disciples did not allow him to do so (Παύλου δὲ βουλομένου εἰσελθεῖν εἰς τὸν δῆμον οὐκ εἴων αὐτὸν οἱ μαθηταί). Paul decides to attend the meeting of the popular assembly[113] in the theater, presumably to calm the citizens and to extricate his two assistants from a sticky and potentially dangerous situation. The "disciples" (οἱ μαθηταί), i.e.,

the local believers, do not allow him to go into the theater. Evidently they fear for his life.

19:31 Some of the Asiarchs who were kindly disposed to him sent him a message, urging him not to venture into the theater (τινὲς δὲ καὶ τῶν Ἀσιαρχῶν, ὄντες αὐτῷ φίλοι, πέμψαντες πρὸς αὐτὸν παρεκάλουν μὴ δοῦναι ἑαυτὸν εἰς τὸ θέατρον). It takes a second intervention to prevent Paul from going into the theater; some of the Asiarchs warn him not to go. The Asiarchs, over a hundred of whom are attested in inscriptions in over forty cities of the province of Asia, were municipal magistrates who introduced motions in the assemblies of the city council, dedicated buildings, commissioned statues, and organized festivals and games.[114]

Luke relates that some Asiarchs were "kindly disposed" (φίλοι) to Paul. The Greek term φίλοι may imply that some of these municipal officials had become believers and were thus "devoted" to Paul (which might help account for the lengthy period of Paul's ministry in the city); or it may mean more generally that Paul became acquainted with high city officials who liked him, perhaps because he was a Roman citizen with "international" contacts in many Roman provinces. Paul's contact with these officials certainly allows the assumption that he would have explained to them his message about Jesus, Israel's Messiah and the Savior of the world.

Whether or not they are believers, they want to protect Paul in a riot. If a Roman citizen such as

---

111. Cf. Trebilco, "Asia," 340 – 50 n. 257.

112. Acts 20:4; 27:2; cf. Col 4:10; Phlm 24.

113. The term translated "popular assembly" (δῆμος) is the technical term for the "convocation of citizens called together for the purpose of transacting official business" (BDAG). Political decisions in many (city) states were "issued by the council and the people"; cf. P. J. Rhodes, "Demos 1," *BNP*, 4:288. While the assembly of the people in v. 30 was evidently not called by the magistrates, it would not have been a "official" meeting of the *demos*, but it was an assembly of the citizens of Ephesus nonetheless.

114. Cf. R. A. Kearsley, in Horsley and Llewelyn, *New Documents*, 4:46 – 55. Steven J. Friesen, "Asiarchs," *ZPE* 126 (1999): 275 – 90, argues that the office of the *Asiarch* was a special category of *agōnothetēs* (official in charge of games), i.e., an official associated with games put on by cities that had regional significance. The view that the *Asiarchs* were delegates of the provincial assembly of the province of Asia (G. Schneider, "Ἀσιάρχης," *EDNT*, 1:172, and many commentators) needs to be abandoned.

Paul came to harm in civil disturbances, the city of Ephesus and its officials would risk the intervention of the Roman proconsul in the affairs of the city. Luke's description of the events that transpire in the theater implies that Paul accepted the advice of the believers and of some municipal magistrates, refraining from going into the theater.

19:32 Meanwhile, some people were shouting one thing, others another; the assembly was confused, most of the people did not know why they had come together (ἄλλοι μὲν οὖν ἄλλο τι ἔκραζον· ἦν γὰρ ἡ ἐκκλησία συγκεχυμένη καὶ οἱ πλείους οὐκ ᾔδεισαν τίνος ἕνεκα συνεληλύθεισαν). The confusion on the streets of Ephesus concerning the alleged attack of Paul and his converts on the grandeur of Artemis (v. 29) has moved into the theater. Luke's description of the confusion contains the following elements. (1) People are shouting (ἔκραζον; the imperfect tense indicates a sustained period of yelling). Some people shout one thing while others shout something else, presumably demanding that the city officials take measures against Paul and his associates, two of whom are standing on the stage of the theater. (2) People seem confused and agitated (συγκεχυμένη; the perfect tense suggests a prolonged state of affairs), a result of the danger that some visiting foreigners allegedly pose for Artemis as well as from the fact that nobody is taking charge of the meeting in the theater. (3) Most of the people in the theater are oblivious to the reasons for the assembly; they have been carried along by the rush of people walking excitedly to the theater.

The expression translated "the assembly" (ἡ ἐκκλησία), if it does not denote "people with shared belief, community, congregation," usually means "a

regularly summoned legislative body,"[115] a meaning that fits v. 39, where the city clerk suggests that Demetrius and the silversmiths should either use the courts or discuss their complaints in the "regular assembly" (ἐν τῇ ἐννόμῳ ἐκκλησίᾳ). This suggests that the assembly in v. 32 is not a duly constituted, official assembly of the citizens (the δῆμος, a term used in vv. 30, 33 for the gathering in the theater; in vv. 33, 35 Luke uses ὄχλος, "a casual gathering of large numbers of people without reference to classification"[116]). The term ἐκκλησία thus has a more general meaning here.[117] The fact that Paul expected to have an opportunity to speak (v. 30), that some Jews assumed that one of their leaders would be allowed to address the assembled people (v. 33), and that eventually the city clerk manages to conclude the meeting (vv. 35–41) suggests that some process is being followed.

19:33 Some people in the crowd advised Alexander, whom the Jews pushed forward. Alexander motioned for silence, wanting to make a defense before the people (ἐκ δὲ τοῦ ὄχλου συνεβίβασαν Ἀλέξανδρον, προβαλόντων αὐτὸν τῶν Ἰουδαίων· ὁ δὲ Ἀλέξανδρος κατασείσας τὴν χεῖρα ἤθελεν ἀπολογεῖσθαι τῷ δήμῳ). A certain Alexander is put forward by the Jews, perhaps to defend the Jews from being implicated in the threat to the grandeur of Artemis Ephesia that Paul and his associates, as visiting Jewish teachers, allegedly pose.[118] The initiative of "the Jews" suggests that Alexander is himself a Jew, probably a prominent leader of the Jewish community who can represent them in public. Alexander is pushed to the front stage of the theater, from where he can address the assembly.

The role of "some people in the crowd" is unclear

---

115. BDAG, s.v. ἐκκλησία 3 and 1.

116. BDAG, s.v. ὄχλος 1a.

117. BDAG, s.v. ἐκκλησία 2, "a casual gathering of people, *an assemblage, gathering*," suggested for vv. 32, 40, with reference to 1 Sam 19:20 LXX; 1 Macc 3:13; Sir 26:5.

118. The reason for the inclusion of the Alexander intermezzo remains obscure, as it does not advance the narrative. Perhaps he was known to Luke's readers on account of the fact that he later became a Christian; cf. Barrett, *Acts*, 934.

because of the syntax of the Greek sentence. While the meaning of the verb "advised" (συνεβίβασαν) here is "advise by giving instructions,"[119] the prepositional phrase (ἐκ τοῦ ὄχλου) can be taken either as adverbial description ("they instructed Alexander to come forward out of the crowd"),[120] or as the subject of the verb ([τινες] ἐκ τοῦ ὄχλου, "some people in the crowd gave instructions to Alexander").[121] In view of the sequence of the phrases in the Greek text, the latter seems more likely: people in the crowd give instructions to Alexander after the Jews have pushed him to the front (temporal genitive absolute).[122]

The Jews want Alexander to "make a defense" (ἀπολογεῖσθαι) of the Jewish community, while people in the crowd presumably advise him what to say regarding Gaius and Aristarchus (v. 29) and regarding Paul and his converts. Luke relates that Alexander is willing to speak. He "motioned for silence" (lit., "waved his hand"; κατασείσας τὴν χεῖρα), seeking to gain the attention of the agitated crowd. Since Alexander is asked to speak as a representative of the Jewish community, the implication of this scene is that the crowd has lumped Paul and his associates together with the local Jews. This was not surprising, given the focus of Demetrius's speech on Paul's opposition to the worship of images representing gods.[123]

19:34 When they recognized that he was a Jew, they all roared in unison for about two hours, shouting, "Great is Artemis of the Ephesians!" (ἐπιγνόντες δὲ ὅτι Ἰουδαῖός ἐστιν, φωνὴ ἐγένετο μία ἐκ πάντων ὡς ἐπὶ ὥρας δύο κραζόντων· μεγάλη ἡ Ἄρτεμις Ἐφεσίων). Alexander's attempt to gain a hearing in the theater proves unsuccessful. Once they recognize he is a Jew, they shout him down. Presumably the crowd has not distinguished between the Jewish community and the Jewish followers of Jesus and thus assume Alexander is connected with the activities of Paul and his converts, or (2) they are unwilling to listen to someone who was not a worshiper of Artemis Ephesia.

Neither Gaius nor Aristarchus, the representatives of the followers of Jesus (v. 29), nor Alexander, the representative of the Jewish community, is given a chance to present their case. The crowd fills the theater with the acclamation "Great is Artemis of the Ephesians!" — a cry that is unanimous, taken up by all the Gentiles in the theater. It resounds for two hours from the theater all the way to the harbor and in the entire city. Public feeling was often expressed during religious festivals and in political assemblies with rhythmic acclamations, "with friendly or disapprobatory shouts, clapping, hissing, whistling."[124] In Greek popular assemblies and in cult gatherings, the *acclamatio* is known to have accompanied decisions.

The citizens of Ephesus leave no doubt where their sympathies lie. While the formulation of an acclamation was often secondary, both the wording and the effect of the cry are important: the Ephesians are proud of Artemis Ephesia, willing to defend her grandeur, and they have contempt for

---

119. BDAG, s.v. συμβιβάζω 4; cf. Culy and Parsons, *Acts*, 377. Differently NET: "Some of the crowd concluded it was about Alexander because the Jews had pushed him to the front"; similarly NASB, GNB; this is less likely in view of the fact that συνεβίβασαν has a direct object.

120. Cf. NIV: "The Jews in the crowd pushed Alexander to the front, and they shouted instructions to him;" similarly NLT: "The Jews in the crowd pushed Alexander forward and told him to explain the situation."

121. Cf. NRSV: "Some of the crowd gave instructions to

Alexander, whom the Jews had pushed forward." Thus also RSV=ESV: "Some of the crowd prompted Alexander, whom the Jews had put forward."

122. Or because the Jews had pushed him to the front (causal genitive absolute).

123. Cf. Scott Shauf, *Theology as History, History as Theology: Paul in Ephesus in Acts 19* (BZNW 133; Berlin: De Gruyter, 2005), 251 – 53.

124. Cf. R. Hurschmann, "Acclamatio," *BNP*, 1:64.

citizens and visitors who refuse to acknowledge her majesty.

19:35 **When the city clerk had quieted the crowd, he said, "People of Ephesus, who does not know that the city of the Ephesians is the guardian of the temple of the great Artemis and of her image that fell from heaven?"** (καταστείλας δὲ ὁ γραμματεὺς τὸν ὄχλον φησίν· ἄνδρες Ἐφέσιοι, τίς γὰρ ἐστιν ἀνθρώπων ὃς οὐ γινώσκει τὴν Ἐφεσίων πόλιν νεωκόρον οὖσαν τῆς μεγάλης Ἀρτέμιδος καὶ τοῦ διοπετοῦς;). The intervention of the "city clerk" (γραμματεύς) changes the situation and brings the riot to an end (vv. 35 – 41). This person had become, in the early imperial period, the chief executive officer of the city. The secretary of the *demos* was the most powerful official of the city administration. He supervises municipal building projects, coordinates the erection of statues, and facilitates consecrations to the emperor. He is the contact person in the city administration for the imperial administrators living in Ephesus and thus the direct link between the citizens of Ephesus and the imperial government.[125]

The fact that the executive office of the secretary of the *demos* had strong links with the office of the Asiarchs explains why both some of the Asiarchs (v. 31) and the city clerk intervene. The appearance of the city clerk, presumably on the stage of the theater, silences the crowd. His speech aims at diffusing their anger, ending the riot, and maintaining order in the city; it can thus be categorized as a deliberative speech, "in which the speaker recommends or advises against an action belonging to the future."[126] The city clerk advises the crowd in the theater not to act in a rash manner concerning the people whom the silversmiths have targeted. The speech can be divided into four parts.

The city clerk begins by appeasing the crowd, seeking to win their attention and goodwill (*exordium*).[127] He addresses the assembled crowd as "people of Ephesus" (ἄνδρες Ἐφέσιοι) and reminds them of the special relationship that the city of Ephesus has with Artemis. The fact that the reminder is formulated as a rhetorical question reinforces the general knowledge as regards the fame of the temple of Artemis in Ephesus. The city clerk praises the Ephesians and their city as the guardian of the temple of Artemis, whose greatness he underlines.

The term translated as "guardian" (νεωκόρος) refers to Ephesus as the city "responsible for the maintenance and security of a temple."[128] A statue base of white marble carrying an inscription honoring Androkles, the mythical founder of Ephesus, describes the citizens of Ephesus as "the most holy people of the foremost of all and greatest and most highly esteemed metropolis of Asia and temple-warden of Artemis (νεωκόρου τῆς Ἀρτέμιδος)."[129] The term means that "the temple belonged to the κοινόν, the assembly of the Greek cities in the province of Asia, and that Ephesos hosted the temple on behalf of the κοινόν and provided the necessary infrastructure — and participated in its splendor and prominence."[130]

The term translated "her image that fell from

125. Cf. Claudia Schulte, *Die Grammateis von Ephesos: Schreiberamt und Sozialstruktur in einer Provinzhauptstadt des römischen Kaiserreiches* (Stuttgart: Steiner, 1994), 130 – 31.

126. Heinrich Lausberg, *Handbook of Literary Rhetoric: A Foundation for Literary Study* (Leiden: Brill, 1998), 97.

127. Cf. Quintilian 4.1.5: "The sole purpose of the exordium is to prepare our audience in such a way that they will be disposed to lend a ready ear to the rest of our speech." Cf. Aune, *Dictionary*, 175 – 76.

128. BDAG, s.v. νεωκόρος; cf. J. Williams, "Neokoros," *BNP*, 9:639 – 40: "In the Roman period, Greek cities were given the by-name *neōkóros* in their capacity as the special 'patron' of a cult of their particular tutelary deities."

129. R. A. Kearsley, in Horsley and Llewelyn, *New Documents*, 6:203 – 6 (no. 30).

130. Stephan Witetschek, "Artemis and Asiarchs: Some Remarks on Ephesian Local Color in Acts 19," *Bib* 90 (2009): 334 – 55, 349.

heaven" (διοπέτης)[131] describes the cult image of Artemis, standing in her temple outside the city, as having a divine origin. The Greek term implies perhaps a meteorite, an object from the sky that was honored in some cults, or it denotes "a neolithic implement which was kept in the temple-like shrine on top of the head of the Artemis image."[132] This description was a clever response to the accusation leveled by Demetrius against Paul and his converts who say that gods made with hands are not gods (v. 26), and it is a clever response to the Jews (who are also the target of the tumult) who believe that the images worshiped in the temples of the Greek and Roman cities are the work of human hands. The city clerk argues that given the special relationship between Ephesus and Artemis and given the divine origin of the image of Artemis in her Ephesian temple, there is no reason why they should be concerned about people who claim otherwise, let alone start a riot.

19:36 Since this is undeniable, you must be calm and do nothing reckless (ἀναντιρρήτων οὖν ὄντων τούτων δέον ἐστὶν ὑμᾶς κατεσταλμένους ὑπάρχειν καὶ μηδὲν προπετὲς πράσσειν). The *exordium* is followed by the *propositio*, in which the speaker formulates his suggestions concerning the course of action to be taken.

The city clerk counsels the excited crowd to stop their disorderly behavior and warns them to do nothing rash. These two suggestions characterize his speech as deliberative rhetoric, whose purpose is to dissuade the audience from a future course of action. The basis for this twofold suggestion is the undeniable fact of the exalted status of Ephesus, the guardian of the temple of Artemis and of the

heavenly origin of the image of Artemis that stands in her temple. There is therefore no reason for the frenzied mayhem in the city.

This proposition of the city clerk is forceful: the people must (δέον ἐστίν) be "calm,"[133] i.e., show restraint and be quiet, and end the chanting of acclamations. They must do nothing "reckless," i.e., impetuous, rash, thoughtless. This is not merely a plea for civil behavior but also a warning not to kill the people who have been the cause of the silversmiths' displeasure — Paul, who has been active in the city for some time, and his associates Gaius and Aristarchus, who have been brought to the theater.

19:37 You have brought these men here who are neither temple robbers nor blasphemers of our goddess (ἠγάγετε γὰρ τοὺς ἄνδρας τούτους οὔτε ἱεροσύλους οὔτε βλασφημοῦντας τὴν θεὸν ἡμῶν). The *propositio* is followed by the *probatio* (or *argumentatio*), the proofs that a speaker offers to persuade the audience (vv. 37 – 39).

The city clerk supports his call for calm with several arguments (note the introductory γάρ). He begins by pointing out that "these men" (τοὺς ἄνδρας τούτους) whom they have brought to the theater have committed no crime against Artemis. They have not removed objects from the temple of Artemis (or any other temple) by force or stealth. The robbing of temples, repeatedly mentioned in Greek and Roman sources, was regarded as a serious offense. In classical Athens, prosecution for temple robbing, like legal action for impiety and for harm to sacred olive trees, could be set in motion by information provided by slaves (who were granted such power over their masters only in relation to religious offenses). People convicted of

---

131. BDAG, s.v. διοπέτης, lit. "fallen from Zeus" or "fallen from the sky"; originally "of meteorites viewed as heaven-sent cult objects *fallen from heaven* (of images of deities)." The image of Artemis of Tauris is described as having fallen from the sky (Euripides, *Iph. taur.* 85 – 88, 1381 – 85).

132. Richard E. Strelan, *Paul, Artemis and the Jews in Ephesus* (BZNW 80; Berlin: De Gruyter, 1996), 151.

133. For καταστέλλω; see its use in v. 35. The use of the perfect tense reflects the concern of the city clerk that permanent calm should be restored.

temple robbery suffered the severest penalty that the city could inflict — death or exile (the latter accompanied by confiscation of property and denial of the right of burial in Attica).[134]

Moreover, the city clerk points out, these men are not blasphemers (βλασφημοῦντας) of "our goddess." They have not spoken in a disrespectful manner about Artemis that demeans, denigrates, or maligns Artemis Ephesia. Slandering one of the deities worshiped in a city, in particular the tutelary god (such as Artemis in Ephesus), could have been prosecuted under the rubric of impiety (ἀσέβεια), an offense that had no defined content but was serious. Socrates was executed on account of this charge: "not acknowledging the gods the city acknowledges, and introducing other, new powers. He also does wrong by corrupting the young."[135] In an inscription dated AD 180 – 192, Ephesus decreed that anyone attempting to alter the arrangements for the religious festivals of the city will be "indictable on charges both of impiety [ἀσέβεια] and of sacrilege [ἱεροσυλία]."[136]

The basis for the city clerk's assertion that Gaius and Aristarchus have neither robbed the temple of Artemis nor spoken in disrespectful terms of the goddess may be an inference from Demetrius's complaint, which focused on potential economic loss due to the teaching of Paul (vv. 24 – 27). Or the city clerk is personally acquainted with Paul's teaching, and he and the Asiarchs apparently regard it as unobjectionable and inoffensive as far as Artemis is concerned. It is true that Paul's teaching about the one true God who cannot be confined to temples made by human hands or to images that are served by human hands (cf. 17:24 – 25) could have been construed as a denigration of Artemis.[137]

However, the city clerk's argument in v. 37 is not necessarily merely generous, "putting the best possible appearance on the matter so as to quieten the crowd."[138] The diaspora Jews had learned to speak about Israel's God as the one and only true God without insulting the local deities in the cities in which they lived.[139] There is no evidence that Paul had slandered Artemis or any other local deity when he proclaimed the good news of Israel's God who had revealed himself in Jesus, the promised Savior. The city clerk must have been sure that neither of these two charges could be leveled against Paul and his associates, and that a violent assault on Gaius and Aristarchus, or on Paul (who was a Roman citizen), by the crowd could have serious consequences, triggering an intervention by the Roman governor.

19:38 If Demetrius and his fellow artisans have a complaint against anyone, there are courts in session and there are proconsuls. Let them file their claims against one another (εἰ μὲν οὖν Δημήτριος καὶ οἱ σὺν αὐτῷ τεχνῖται ἔχουσι πρός τινα λόγον, ἀγοραῖοι ἄγονται καὶ ἀνθύπατοί εἰσιν, ἐγκαλείτωσαν ἀλλήλοις). The next argument that the city clerk cites in support of his call for calm is the point that the silversmiths must initiate legal action at the local courts with the proconsuls, not instigate wild disturbances in the city. While the city clerk had not mentioned Gaius and Aristarchus by name, he refers specifically to Demetrius, thereby implying that he will be culpable if the disturbance gets out of hand. Any complaint that Demetrius

---

134. Robert Parker, "Law and Religion," in *The Cambridge Companion to Ancient Greek Law* (ed. M. Gagarin and D. Cohen; Cambridge: Cambridge Univ. Press, 2005), 61 – 81, 64 – 65, with reference to Xenophon, *Hell.* 1.7.22.

135. Parker, "Law and Religion," 67.

136. Trebilco, "Asia," 354. The term ἱεροσυλία denotes both temple robbery and sacrilege.

137. Padilla, *Speeches*, 184 – 85.

138. Barrett, *Acts*, 936.

139. Cf. Strelan, *Paul*, 151, with reference to Philo, *Mos.* 2.205; Josephus, *Ant.* 1.310, 322. See also Josephus, *Ag. Ap.* 2.237: "Our legislator has expressly forbidden us to deride or blaspheme the gods recognized by others, out of respect for the word 'God.' "

and his fellow artisans have against Paul or anyone else must be taken to the courts, where they
can "file their claims" (ἐγκαλείτωσαν).[140] The term
translated "courts" (ἀγοραῖοι) refers to the practice of the Roman proconsul or his deputy holding court sessions in the main seats of the assize
districts on fixed days.

As to "proconsuls," the province of Asia had one
proconsul; the plural may be a generalizing statement ("there are such people as proconsuls"), may
refer to the fact that there was a constant change of
proconsuls who held the position for one or two
years, or may allude to the interregnum after the
murder of Julius Silanus, proconsul of the province, after Nero's accession in October AD 54.[141]
Proconsuls were responsible for the administration of justice and the maintenance of security, and
they could help members of the local aristocracy
advance their careers and secure advantages for
the city. The city clerk "would not want to jeopardize this relationship, either personally, or as far
as Ephesus was concerned, by getting off-side with
the proconsul."[142] The city clerk refers Demetrius
and the guild of silversmiths to the court sessions
of the proconsul before whom they can file charges
against Paul and his associates.

**19:39 If there is anything further that you want
to know, it will have to be settled in the regular
assembly** (εἰ δέ τι περαιτέρω ἐπιζητεῖτε, ἐν τῇ
ἐννόμῳ ἐκκλησίᾳ ἐπιλυθήσεται). If Demetrius does
not want to involve the proconsul and the courts,
he and his colleagues can take up the subject of the
activities of Paul and his associates in a meeting of
the regular assembly, which can pass a resolution
concerning the conduct of resident aliens (such as

Paul, Gaius, and Aristarchus), who are not citizens
of Ephesus.

**19:40 "As it is, we are in danger of being accused
of rioting because of what happened today;
there is no reason for it, and we cannot explain
this disorderly gathering"** (καὶ γὰρ κινδυνεύομεν
ἐγκαλεῖσθαι στάσεως περὶ τῆς σήμερον, μηδενὸς
αἰτίου ὑπάρχοντος περὶ οὗ οὐ δυνησόμεθα
ἀποδοῦναι λόγον περὶ τῆς συστροφῆς ταύτης).
The speech ends with a *peroratio*, the conclusion
in which a speaker either refreshes the memory of
the audience by summarizing the main arguments
of the speech (*recapitulatio*) or aims at influencing
the emotions of the audience (*affectus*).[143] Here the
city clerk summarizes his main argument and in-
stills fear. He describes what has been happening in
the city as (1) a "riot" (στάσις), a term that denotes
uprisings, revolts, and rebellions — the opposite of
civil harmony and peaceful conduct; and as (2) a
"disorderly gathering" (συστροφή), a term that describes a tumultuous gathering of people.

The principal emotion that the city clerk wants
to generate among the audience in the theater is
fear, as the phrase "we are in danger" (κινδυνεύομεν)
indicates; the present tense heightens the danger
that exists right now for the city of Ephesus. The
riot and the disorderly gathering, none of which
can be explained with good reason, may prompt
the intervention of the Roman proconsul, who will
"accuse" the city of tolerating a revolt and a seditious commotion. The charge of riotous behavior
was serious indeed for a city in the Roman Empire.
A city could lose not only the respect of the emperor or the proconsuls, but local officials could be
punished, guilds could be disbanded, and the city

---

140. Cf. BDAG, s.v. ἐγκαλέω: a legal technical term, "bring
charges against, *accuse*."

141. Cf. Trebilco, *Early Christians in Ephesus*, 163, with n.
33; cf. Hemer, *Acts*, 123, 169.

142. Trebilco, "Asia," 355; cf. Stephen Mitchell, *Anatolia*,

1:64 – 67; Peter Garnsey, "The Criminal Jurisdiction of Governors," *JRS* 58 (1968): 51 – 59.

143. Cf. Lausberg, *Handbook*, 204 – 8; Aune, *Dictionary*,
347.

could lose its autonomy. When the city of Cyzicus allowed some Roman citizens to be put to death in 20 BC, evidently in connection with a riot, the autonomy (freedom) of the city was rescinded.[144]

The danger that the city clerk perceives is aggravated by the fact that it was caused by a guild, a group with (perhaps only embryonic) internal organization, "considered more threatening to the peace of the provinces by the Roman administration."[145] The call for calm, the insistence that complaints should be taken up before the court sessions of the proconsul and the popular assembly, and the reference to a potential intervention of the Roman authorities in the affairs of the city characterize the city clerk as an informed and capable official.

19:41 With these words he dismissed the assembly (καὶ ταῦτα εἰπὼν ἀπέλυσεν τὴν ἐκκλησίαν). The city clerk's dismissal of the assembly implies that Gaius and Aristarchus are set free and that no official measures will be undertaken against Paul, the original target of Demetrius's and the silversmiths' actions, unless they take their complaint to court. Paul, his associates, and his converts do not pose a threat for the civic order of the city of Ephesus.

20:1 After the turmoil had ceased, Paul sent for the disciples and encouraged them. Then he said farewell and set out for Macedonia (Μετὰ δὲ τὸ παύσασθαι τὸν θόρυβον μεταπεμψάμενος ὁ Παῦλος τοὺς μαθητὰς καὶ παρακαλέσας, ἀσπασάμενος ἐξῆλθεν πορεύεσθαι εἰς Μακεδονίαν). In the last incident of this Ephesus episode, Luke relates Paul's departure from Ephesus. He leaves the city with the goal of visiting Macedonia, Achaia, and Jerusalem before going to Rome (v. 21). This comment indicates that the city clerk's speech was successful: Paul and his associates, including Gaius and Aristarchus (cf. 20:4), are able to safely leave Ephesus.

The comment that Paul sends for the believers in the city seems to suggest that he leaves Ephesus immediately after the end of the riot, perhaps seeking to preempt a legal case before the proconsul or an official complaint before the popular assembly, both possibilities that the city clerk has suggested. As his departure was planned (v. 21), the sudden necessity of leaving the city does not allow Paul to wait for the next regular meeting of the local believers. He summons them, perhaps to the hall of Tyrannus (vv. 9 – 10), in order to "encourage" them in the faith, presumably counseling them on how to deal with attacks in the future.

After Paul says his good-byes, he leaves Ephesus and goes to Macedonia. Luke provides no details concerning the travel route; Paul may have left by ship, heading straight for the Macedonian port of Neapolis, or he may have taken the road along the coast, visiting churches north of Ephesus (e.g., in Troas) before crossing the Aegean Sea.

---

144. Cf. Trebilco, "Asia," 344 – 47. See Dio Chrysostom *Or.* 34.33, 39; Plutarch, *Praec. ger. rei publ.* 813E-F.

145. Ilias N. Arnaoutoglou, "Roman Law and *collegia* in Asia Minor," *RIDA* 49 (2002): 27 – 44, 42.

Theology in Application

The two episodes in which Luke relates the establishment of the church in Ephesus advance his description of the missionary work of the early church in several ways: Aquila and Priscilla are depicted as ideal believers, Apollos is an example of an ideal preacher, and Paul is the ideal missionary. In all three areas, theological competence is fundamental.

Theological Competence and Pastoral Sensitivity of Ideal Believers

Luke's portrayal of Aquila and Priscilla reminds the readers of Acts of the behavior of responsible believers.

(1) Whether Aquila and Priscilla relocate from Corinth (18:2 – 3) to Ephesus (18:18 – 19) as missionary workers or as business people, they readily grasp the opportunity of explaining the word of God whenever it presents itself (18:26). The question is not so much whether Aquila and Priscilla are "tentmakers," i.e., missionaries who use the opportunities of their profession to share the gospel; there is no evidence that their "tentmaking" was a missionary tactic. Rather, and more importantly, this Christian couple is a paradigm for believers who know the gospel and who support and promote the truthful proclamation of the gospel no matter where they reside.

(2) Aquila and Priscilla — evidently Priscilla in particular — are theologically competent believers capable of detecting defective teaching and competent to correct it (18:26). They know the content of the gospel, they care about the accuracy and integrity of the gospel, and they are willing to speak up when they detect deficiencies in preachers. They make sure that the message of Jesus is preached and practiced according to the teaching and practice of the apostles. Thus, they insist that correct information about Jesus is insufficient if potential converts are not instructed about the association of immersion in water (baptism) with the life, death, and resurrection of Jesus.

The fact that Luke mentions Priscilla before Aquila underlines the integral role of women in the proclamation of God's word. The task of evaluating, verifying, and even correcting one-sided, defective, or erroneous theology or practice is not only the responsibility of pastors, teachers, and missionaries, but indeed of all believers. The basis for such evaluation and correction is not the feelings, the personal experience, or the ecclesiastical tradition of a believer, but a sound knowledge of the Scriptures (which now includes the apostolic preaching in the New Testament), a fact that highlights the importance of solid teaching in the church.

(3) Aquila and Priscilla are sensitive enough not to expose the deficiencies of Apollos's teaching in public; they correct him in private (18:26). While sometimes public confrontation is necessary (see the Antioch incident in Gal 2:11 – 14), often correction is more readily accepted when it is passed on in private.

(4) The fact that the reception of the Holy Spirit by the disciples of John in baptism was accompanied by speaking in unlearned languages (19:6) does not mean that Luke presents "speaking in tongues" here as a normative experience of Christian believers who receive the Holy Spirit. These disciples are a special case, even if not as strongly as the other groups of believers who spoke in unlearned languages (the Jewish believers in Jerusalem at Pentecost, 2:1 – 4; the Samaritan believers, 8:17 – 19; the first Gentile believers, 10:46).[146]

Note the following points. (a) The conversion of disciples of John the Baptist in Ephesus concludes Luke's description of John the Baptist, who anticipated the coming of the Messiah as one who would immerse people in the Holy Spirit and fire (Luke 3:16 – 17; Acts 1:8; 11:16). The "out of the ordinary" manifestations they exhibit underline the reality of disciples taught by John as at last coming into the community established by Jesus and his disciples. (b) Since Paul had been forbidden by the Spirit to speak the word of God in the province of Asia (16:6), and since Paul had been uncertain whether God would allow him to preach the gospel in Ephesus (18:21), the presence of supernatural phenomena manifested by Paul's first converts in Ephesus confirms for him God's will that he should continue his missionary ministry in capital of that province. (c) The parallels of vv. 1 – 7 with the speech and the actions of Peter on Pentecost and with the Samaria episode where the Spirit was granted through the laying on of hands (8:17) underline the fact that the same Spirit that was active in the ministry of Peter and John also works through Paul.

Theological Competence and Spiritual Integrity of Ideal Preachers

Despite, or perhaps precisely because of, the fact that he was willing to accept correction, Apollos is portrayed by Luke as the ideal preacher.[147]

(1) Apollos had received a thorough education, probably in Alexandria in the context of the synagogue and of Greek culture. He was both eloquent and cultured, he had a thorough knowledge and understanding of the Scriptures, he had a commanding presence in his sermons, and he was effective in the use of biblical texts in debates (18:24 – 26, 28). Authentic preaching is always based on biblical competence, resulting from a comprehensive study of the Scriptures.

(2) Eloquence in preaching must always be subordinate to the reality of the power of God's Spirit in the life and ministry of the preacher. Apollos was "fervent in the Spirit," which means that his witness was empowered by the Spirit of God rather than by his rhetorical eloquence or his personal charisma. It is the power of God himself that makes preaching powerful and effective (cf. 1 Cor 1:18 – 2:5). The conscious recognition of the reality of God's Spirit sustains the spiritual integrity of the preacher.

(3) Authentic Christian preaching is always focused on Jesus. Luke's description

---

146. Turner, *Power from on High*, 395 – 97, with reference to Shepherd, *Narrative Function of the Holy Spirit*, 229.

147. Cf. Zmijewski, *Apostelgeschichte*, 678 – 79.

of Apollos's teaching "accurately" about Jesus (18:25) emphasizes the fundamental importance of accurate information about Jesus' words and deeds and about his death, resurrection, and exaltation. It is no coincidence that the New Testament begins with four books on the life of Jesus, all of which focus in the last third of their narrative on Jesus' suffering, death, and resurrection. Preaching without this focus on Jesus may be helpful sermonizing about ethical questions, but it is not Christian preaching.

(4) The authentic Christian preacher is in agreement with the apostolic tradition. Priscilla and Aquila correct Apollos's deficient view of baptism, which showed a lack of focus on Jesus. The effective power of the Spirit in Christian preaching depends on the elimination of heresy and the correction of theological error. Here, tradition, rightly understood, is important. Note that it is Priscilla and Aquila who mediate a robust understanding of the gospel from Christian teachers in Rome and from Paul in Corinth to Apollos in Ephesus.

Theological Competence and Courageous Engagement of Ideal Missionaries

The nine incidents that make up Luke's narrative of Paul's mission in Ephesus depict the focus, the work, and the character of authentic missionaries.

(1) Paul corrects deficient theology. He does not take the identification of Ephesian Jews as disciples of Jesus at face value. He questions them regarding their experience of the reality of the Holy Spirit and their understanding of the significance of Jesus, he instructs them in areas where they lack understanding, he leads them through his teaching to true conversion, and he helps them complete their integration into the messianic people of God through immersion in water and the laying on of hands (19:1 – 7). Thus, theological competence plays a fundamental role in the encounter between Paul and some disciples of John the Baptist. Paul's theological competence is based on his study of the Scriptures, on his encounter with the crucified, risen, and exalted Jesus Christ, and on his experience in evangelistic preaching, missionary work, and pastoral ministry. True Christians are people who have come to faith in Jesus, the crucified and risen Messiah of Israel and the exalted Savior of the world; they are people who have pledged allegiance to Jesus and who have received the gift of the Holy Spirit, whose presence is evident in the transformed reality of their lives.

(2) Paul preaches boldly. He knows from repeated experience that teaching in synagogues can be risky and dangerous, but that does not prevent him from explaining the connection between God's rule and God's purposes with Jesus, Israel's Messiah, as the word of the Lord in the synagogue in Ephesus and (evidently) in other cities of the province as well (19:8 – 10). Paul's boldness is also evident in his willingness to go into the theater after a crowd, stirred up by the guild of silversmiths,

had arrested two of his associates (19:30). Paul knows that facing an angry crowd can easily lead to being stoned to death (14:19).

Missionaries do not seek to become martyrs. They are prepared to evacuate an area that has become dangerous — too dangerous perhaps to try to rescue fellow missionaries who have been arrested, or local Christians who might not be able to flee. At the same time they will to do all they can to assist other believers, circumstances permitting, even if it means risking their lives.

(3) Paul overcomes opposition. His teaching in the synagogue eventually meets strong opposition (19:9). Paul is not cowed by potential antagonism. He argues for the truth of the gospel publicly in the synagogue when he is given the opportunity to address the assembled Jews, proselytes, and God-fearers. When opposition arises, when people challenge him in public, slandering him and the message that he presents, he is readily willing to move to another location where he can continue to preach the gospel. When missionaries and evangelists face opposition, they do not pack up and go home; they look for other venues where they can continue their ministry. The same holds true for each individual believer; when they meet ridicule and antagonism from the people they witness to, they look for other opportunities and for other people to whom they can introduce the gospel.

(4) Paul's ministry is accompanied by miracles. While Luke does not provide details for the extraordinary miracles that happened while Paul engaged in missionary work in Ephesus (19:11), he reports the effect that they have on the population at large: people believe that the mere contact with pieces of clothing touched by Paul have healing powers (19:12), and Jewish exorcists believe that the use of the name of Jesus and of Paul in magical formulas guarantees victory in battles against evil spirits (19:13 – 14). Luke's anti-magical corrective in v. 11 is crucial. In theological terms, it needs to be emphasized that authentic miracles are always caused by God himself. In anthropological terms, authentic miracles caused by God do not happen on account of *some thing* but are mediated through God's servants, who announce liberation through Jesus, the Savior of humankind.

The story of the sons of Sceva (19:13 – 16) demonstrates that the name of Jesus is not a magical formula. That name is powerful only when it is spoken in the awareness of Jesus' presence, thus presupposing faith in the resurrection of the crucified Messiah who has been exalted to God's right hand and who is actively involved in the mission of the church. This truth has consequences far beyond miracles and exorcisms. The line "in Jesus' name" spoken at the end of prayers does not guarantee that God answers our petitions, particularly if its content is self-serving. Saying "Lord, Lord" to Jesus in and of itself is ultimately futile if we are not willing to submit to the will of Jesus (cf. Luke 6:46).

(5) Paul's ministry impacts society at large. This is seen at several levels. (a) The effect of Paul's missionary work is seen not only in Ephesus but in other cities of the province of Asia, with local Jewish communities and with Gentiles (19:10). In

Ephesus, Paul's influence reaches the Asiarchs, high local officials with whom he has contact and who support him during the riot caused by the silversmiths (19:31).

(b) Paul's preaching and the events connected with the punishment of the sons of Sceva cause believers to confess their sins, admit magical practices, and burn magical texts despite their monetary value (19:18 – 19). While this incident demonstrates that (both new and older!) believers can still be tied to secular, pagan, unbiblical views and practices, the main point of Luke's summary report in vv. 18 – 19 is the liberating and contagious reality of an authentic faith in Jesus, a faith that is "seen" in public acts of confession and commitment.

(c) The commitment of the new believers to faith in the one true God and in Jesus and the growth of the church threaten the commercial interests of local trades linked with the worship of Artemis (19:23 – 28). This leads to a massive protest not only of the silversmiths but of thousands of Ephesians who congregate in the theater and who arrest two of Paul's coworkers (19:29 – 41). An authentic proclamation of the gospel threatens the fusion of religious and commercial interests, a combination that has sometimes characterized Christian churches and ministries as well. Authentic faith in Jesus must be kept free from commercial interests.

(d) The intervention of the Asiarchs (19:31) and the speech of the city clerk (19:37) demonstrates that missionaries, Christians, and churches operate with the principle of legality. They focus on the gospel and do not deliberately aim at undermining the loyalty of the population to the political authorities. The associates of Paul, and Paul himself, are spared persecution because the local authorities recognize that these people do not threaten the civil order in Ephesus. They have not robbed temples and have not slandered Artemis. Missionaries and pastors do not attack the places of worship of people of other faiths, nor do they insult the gods that other people worship.

While Paul proclaims the gospel with uncompromising conviction, he does not target local religious traditions or the silversmiths, nor does he seek to displace the city magistrates with Christians (which would have been a utopian goal in the first century). Persecution results from the violence of people who oppose the gospel; persecution should never be the reaction of people to the violent behavior of Christians. The notion that Christians "upset the stability of the world" (17:6) is an accusation made against Christians, not a "mission statement" formulated by Christians — even though the growth of the church in a region may indeed lead to a change of government and to the transformation of a particular culture at some point in time. What triggered the hostility of the silversmiths was not a program to stamp out magic or idolatry, but the faithful proclamation of the gospel by the missionaries and the changed lifestyle of a growing number of believers.[148]

---

148. Bock, *Acts*, 614.

Acts 20:2 – 21:17

Literary Context

This passage treats the three episodes that make up the second part of Luke's report on Paul's mission in Ephesus (18:23 – 21:17). The first part described his missionary work in that city (18:23 – 20:1); the second part narrates his visits to the churches in Europe and his return to Jerusalem (20:2 – 21:17). The first episode of the second part relates Paul's visits to the believers in Macedonia, Achaia, and Asia (20:2 – 12). The second episode reports his travel from Troas to Miletus and his meeting with the elders of the church in Ephesus (20:13 – 38). The third episode relates his travels from Miletus to Jerusalem, with reports on visits to the believers in Tyre, Ptolemais, and Caesarea (21:1 – 17).

These travels constitute the realization of Paul's plan (19:21; cf. 1 Cor 16:5) to visit the churches in Macedonia before visiting Achaia, in particular Corinth (2 Cor 2:13), where he spends three months during the winter of AD 56 – 57 (20:3). During his stay there he writes the letter to the Christians in Rome (cf. Rom 16:23). Because of a plot of the Corinthian Jews he is unable to sail from Corinth to Syria (and Jerusalem); instead he travels overland north to Macedonia, where he spends Passover in Philippi (April 15, AD 57; 20:3 – 6). The journey via Troas, Miletus, Tyre, Ptolemais, and Caesarea — cities in which he meets with the local church — takes Paul finally to Jerusalem, which he reaches in time for the Feast of Pentecost (May 29, AD 57).

Main Idea

Luke's report of Paul's final visits to churches in the provinces of Macedonia, Achaia, and Asia emphasizes the importance of encouragement that invigorates and comforts believers, of exhortation that warns and advises Christian leaders, of pastoral ministries that support and safeguard believers, and of exemplary behavior that motivates believers. The narrative highlights again the importance of teamwork, of flexibility in carrying out one's plans, and of the significance of God's will in view of the possibility and the reality of suffering.

Translation

Acts 20:2 – 21:17

2a	Setting: time	After he had traveled through those regions [of Macedonia]
b	Setting: action	and encouraged the believers
c	Means	with much preaching,
d	Action: geographical	**he came to Greece.**
3a	Action	**He stayed there**
b	Duration	for three months.
c	Setting: social	When some Jews plotted
d	Conflict	to cause him harm
e	Time	just as he was about to sail for Syria,
f	Reaction	**he decided**
g	Action: geographical	to return through Macedonia.
4a	Association (list)	**He was accompanied by**
b		Sopater
c	Description: familial	son of Pyrrhus
d	Description: geographical	from Berea,
e		Aristarchus and
f		Secundus
g	Description: geographical	from Thessalonica,
h		Gaius
i	Description: geographical	from Derbe,
j		Timothy, and
k		Tychicus and
l		Trophimus
m	Description: geographical	from the province of Asia.
5a	Action	**These men went on ahead**
b	Action	and **waited for us**
c	Place	in Troas;

6a	Action: geographical	**we sailed from Philippi**
b	Time	after the Feast of Unleavened Bread,
c	Time	and five days later
d	Action: geographical	**we joined them in Troas,**
e	Action	where we stayed
f	Duration	for seven days.

7a	Setting: Time	On the first day of the week,
b	Setting: Social	when we came together
c	Purpose	to break bread,
d	Action	**Paul instructed the believers.**

e	Cause	Because he intended
f	Character's thoughts	to leave the next day,
g	Action	**he extended his speech**
h	Time	until midnight.
8a	Measure	**There were many lamps**
b	Place	in the upstairs room
c	Place	where we were meeting.
9a	Character entrance	**A young man**
b	Identification	named Eutychus,
c	Place	who had been sitting at the window,
d	Event	**sank into a deep sleep**
e	Cause	as Paul spoke at length.

f	Time	When he was sound asleep,
g	Event	**he fell**
h	Place	from the third story
i	Place	to the ground below,
j	Event	and **was picked up dead.**
10a	Action	**Paul went down,**
b	Action	**threw himself upon him,**
c	Action	**put his arms around him,**
d	Action	and **said,**
e	Exhortation	*"Do not be alarmed!*
f	Assertion	*There is life in him."*
11a	Action	Then **he went upstairs**
b	Action	and **broke bread**
c	Action	and **ate.**

d	Setting: time	After he conversed with them
e	Duration	for a long time
f	Duration	until dawn,
g	Action	**he departed.**
12a	Action	**They took the boy**
b	Place	home
c	Manner	alive
d	Event	and **were greatly comforted.**

Continued on next page.

Continued from previous page.

13a	Action	**We went ahead**
b	Place	to the ship
c	Action: geographical	**and set sail for Assos,**
d	Purpose	where we planned to take Paul on board.
e	Flashback: action	**He had arranged this**
f	Cause	because he wanted to travel
g	Manner	overland.
14a	Time & Place	When he met us at Assos,
b	Action	**we took him on board**
c	Action: geographical	**and sailed to Mitylene.**
15a	Time	The next day
b	Action	**we sailed from there**
c	Action: geographical	**and arrived off Chios.**
d	Time	On the next day
e	Action: geographical	**we crossed over to Samos,**
f	Time	and on the following day
g	Action: geographical	**we arrived at Miletus.**
16a	Person's thought	**Paul had decided**
b	Content	to sail
c	Place	past Ephesus
d	Purpose	so that he would not lose time
e	Place	in the province of Asia,
f	Cause	because he was in a hurry
g	Purpose	to reach Jerusalem
h	Time	by the Feast of Pentecost,
i	Condition	if possible.
17a	Setting: geographical	From Miletus
b	Action	**he sent a message**
c	Place	to Ephesus
d	Action	**and called for the elders of the church**
e	Purpose	to meet him.
18a	Setting: time	When they arrived,
b	Speech	**he said to them:**
c	Call to remember	*"You know*
d	Action	*how I have lived with you*
e	Duration	*the whole time*
f	Time	*from the day*
g	Action	*that I set foot*
h	Place	*in the province of Asia.*
19a	Action	*I served the Lord as his slave*
b	Manner	*with all humility and*
c	Manner	*with tears, and*
d	Sphere	*in the midst of the trials*
e	Description	*that happened to me*

f	Cause	because of the plots of the Jews.
20a	Event	I have not kept silent
b	Content	about anything
c	Description	that is profitable
d	Advantage	for you;
e	Action	I have proclaimed
f	Content	everything
g	Advantage	to you,
h	Means	as I taught you
i	Place	publicly and
j	Place	from house to house.
21a	Action	I was bearing witness
b	Sphere	to both Jews and
c	Sphere	Greeks
d	Content	about repentance
e	Object	toward God and
f	Content	about faith
g	Object	in our Lord Jesus.
22a	Time	And now,
b	Manner	compelled by the Spirit,
c	Action	I am going
d	Place	to Jerusalem
e	Manner	without knowing
f	Content	what will happen to me there.
23a	Assertion	I only know
b	Content (prophecy)	that the Holy Spirit testifies to me
c	Place	in city after city
d	Content	that imprisonment and hardships await me.
24a	Contrast	However, I do not count my life
b	Manner	as having any value for myself;
c	Assertion	my only aim is
d	Purpose	to finish the course and
e	Purpose	the ministry
f	Identification	that I received from the Lord Jesus —
g	Description	the ministry of bearing witness
h	Object	to the good news of God's grace.
25a	Assertion	And now I know
b	Content	that none of you
c	Sphere	among whom I went about proclaiming the kingdom
d	Prediction	will ever see me again.
26a	Assertion	Therefore, I declare to you today
b	Content	that I am not responsible
c	Content	for the blood of anyone;
27a	Explanation	for I have not hesitated
b	Action	to proclaim to you
c	Content	the whole will of God.
28a	Command	Keep watch
b	Sphere	over yourselves and

Continued on next page.

Continued from previous page.

c	Sphere	over the whole flock,
d	Action	in which the Holy Spirit has appointed you
e	Result	as overseers
f	Purpose	with the task of shepherding the church of God,
g	Description	which he has acquired
h	Means	with his own blood.
29a	Assertion	I know that
b	Time	after my departure
c	Prediction	fierce wolves will come in among you,
d	Prediction	who will not spare the flock.
30a	Sphere	From among yourselves
b	Prediction	men will rise up
c	Prediction	and teach perversions of the truth
d	Purpose	in order to draw the disciples away as their followers.
31a	Warning	Therefore, be vigilant,
b	Call to remember	remembering that …
c	Duration	for three years
d	Flashback: action	… I never stopped instructing each of you
e	Time	night and
f	Time	day
g	Manner	with tears.
32a	Action	Now I commend you
b	Sphere	to God and
c	Sphere	to the message
d	Content	about his grace,
e	Assertion	who is able
f	Result	to build you up and
g	Result	to give you the inheritance
h	Sphere	among all those who are sanctified.
33a	Assertion	I have never desired anyone's silver or
b	List	gold or
c	List	clothing.
34a	Call to remember	You yourselves know
b	Flashback: action	that these hands of mine served
c	Purpose/Result	my own needs as well as
d	Association	the needs of those who were with me.
35a	Action	I showed you at every opportunity
b	Content	that we must support the weak
c	Means	by such hard work,
d	Means	remembering the word of the Lord Jesus,
e	Explanation (quotation)	for he said, 'It is more blessed to give
f	Contrast	than to receive.'"
36a	Setting: time	When he had finished speaking,
b	Action	**he knelt down**
c	Association	with all of them
d	Action	and **prayed.**

37a	Action	**They all wept loudly**
b	Time (simultaneous)	as they embraced Paul
c	Time (simultaneous)	and kissed him.
38a	Description	**They were especially pained**
b	Cause	on account of his statement
c	Content	that they would never see him again.
d	Action	**Then they accompanied him**
e	Place	to the ship.

21:1a	Setting: time	After we had torn ourselves away from them,
b	Action	**we set sail,**
c	Action	**ran a straight course,**
d	Action: geographical	and **came to Cos.**

e	Setting: time	The next day
f	Action: geographical	**we sailed to Rhodes**
g	Action: geographical	and from there to Patara.

2a	Setting: time	When we found a ship there
b	Geographical	bound for Phoenicia,
c	Action	**we went on board**
d	Action	and **set sail.**

3a	Setting: geographical	When we caught sight of Cyprus,
b	Action	**we passed to the south of it,**
c	Action: geographical	**sailed to Syria,**
d	Action: geographical	**and landed at Tyre,**
e	Cause	because the ship had to unload its cargo there.

4a	Action	**We looked up the disciples**
b	Action	and **stayed there**
c	Duration	for seven days.
d	Event	**They told Paul**
e	Means	through the Spirit
f	Content: Warning	not to go to Jerusalem.

5a	Setting: time	When our time was up,
b	Action	**we left**
c	Action	**and continued on our way.**
d	Character entrance	**All the disciples,**
e	Association	including their wives and
f	Association	children,
g	Action	**escorted us**
h	Place	outside the city,
i	Action	where we knelt down on the beach
j	Action	and prayed.
6a	Action	**We said our good-byes**
b	Action	and **went aboard the ship,**
c	Time: action	while they returned home.

Continued on next page.

Continued from previous page.

7a	Action: geographical	**We continued our voyage from Tyre**
b	Action: geographical	**and arrived at Ptolemais,**
c	Action	where we greeted the believers
d	Action	and stayed with them
e	Duration	for one day.
8a	Setting: time	The next day
b	Action	**we left**
c	Action: geographical	**and came to Caesarea,**
d	Action: place	where we went into the house of Philip
e	Identification	the evangelist,
f	Identification	one of the Seven,
g	Action	**and stayed with him.**
9a	Description	**He had four unmarried daughters**
b	Identification	who had the gift of prophecy.
10a	Setting: time	After we had stayed there
b	Duration	for several days,
c	Character entrance	**a prophet**
d	Identification	named Agabus
e	Event	**arrived from Judea.**
11a	Action	**He came to us,**
b	Action	**took Paul's belt,**
c	Action	**and tied his own feet and hands with it,**
d	Speech	**and said,**
e	Prophecy	"Thus says the Holy Spirit,
f	Manner	'In this way the Jews in Jerusalem will bind the man who owns this belt
g	Protagonist	and hand him over to the Gentiles.'"
12a	Setting: time	When we heard this,
b	Reaction	**we and**
c	Association	**the local believers**
d	Entreaty	**urged Paul**
e	Warning	not to go to Jerusalem.
13a	Response	**Then Paul answered,**
b	Rhetorical question	"What are you doing,
c	Manner	weeping and
d	Manner	breaking my heart?
e	Assertion	I am ready
f	Assertion	not only to be bound,
g	Escalation	but even to die
h	Place	in Jerusalem
i	Circumstance	for the name of the Lord Jesus."
14a	Cause	Since Paul would not be persuaded,
b	Reaction	**we refrained from saying anything more, except ,**
c	Exclamation	"The Lord's will may be done!"

15a	Setting: time	After these days
b	Action	**we got ready**
c	Action	**and started to travel**
d	Place	to Jerusalem.
16a	Character entrance	**Some of the disciples**
b	Geographical	from Caesarea
c	Association	**accompanied us**
d	Action	**and took us to the house of Mnason**
e	Character description	of Cyprus,
f	Character description	one of the early disciples,
g	Action	who would entertain us as guests.
17a	Setting: time	When we arrived
b	Setting: place	in Jerusalem,
c	Character entrance/Action	**the believers welcomed us**
d	Manner	warmly.

Structure and Literary Form

The three episodes relate five scenes of community life: (1) in Troas, (2) in Miletus, where Paul meets the Ephesian elders, and (3) in Tyre, Ptolemais, and Caesarea. These three episodes alternate with six accounts of travel that take Paul from Ephesus to Jerusalem.[1]

20:2 – 6	Travel report (Ephesus – Macedonia – Achaia – Philippi – Troas)
20:7 – 12	*Meeting with believers in Troas*
20:13 – 16	Travel report (Troas – Assos – Mitylene – Chios – Samos – Miletus)
20:17 – 38	*Meeting with the Ephesian elders in Miletus*
21:1 – 3	Travel report (Miletus – Cos – Rhodes – Patara – Tyre)
21:4 – 6	*Meeting with the believers in Tyre*
21:7a-b	Travel report (Tyre – Ptolemais)
21:7c-e	*Meeting with the believers in Ptolemais*
21:8a-c	Travel report (Ptolemais – Caesarea)
21:8d – 14	*Meeting with believers in Caesarea*
21:14 – 17	Travel report (Caesarea – Jerusalem)

1. Adapted from Beverly R. Gaventa, "Theology and Eschatology in the Miletus Speech: Reflections on Content and Context," *NTS* 50 (2004): 36 – 52, 37 – 43, who analyzes the text in terms of three community scenes (Troas, Miletus, Caesarea) and four accounts of travel. This analysis downplays Paul's meeting with the believers in Tyre (21:4 – 6) and Ptolemais (21:7). Since the latter two meetings are recounted more briefly than Paul's meetings with the believers in Troas and Miletus, as is Paul's meeting with believers in Caesarea, we are integrating the meetings with the believers in Tyre, Ptolemais, and Caesarea into one episode (21:1 – 17).

The community scenes emphasize the gathering of believers for worship (20:7 – 12), instruction (20:18 – 35), listening to the word of God (21:4, 7 – 14), fellowship (21:7), and providing hospitality for missionaries (21:4, 8). As regards the travel reports, Luke provides far more detail than in his previous narrative of Paul's work (see below). When interpreted in the context of the community scenes, the details of the travel reports highlight the fact that Paul brings together the Christian communities in Troas, Miletus, Tyre, Ptolemais, and Caesarea.

These three episodes, with their combination of travel reports and community scenes, provide a portrait of the life of the churches, established by Paul (Troas, Ephesus) and other missionaries (Tyre, Ptolemais, Caesarea), that shares fundamental characteristics with the church in Jerusalem as summarized in 2:42: instruction (20:7 – 12, 17 – 38), the breaking of bread (20:7, 11), prayer (20:36; 21:5), sharing of possessions (20:34 – 35), the anticipation of opposition (20:23; 21:4, 11).

The first episode, which relates Paul's visits to the believers in Macedonia, Achaia, and Asia (20:2 – 12), consists of two incidents. (1) Luke relates Paul's visit to the believers in Macedonia (v. 2a-c) and then in Achaia (vv. 2d – 3b), the decision to travel overland due to a Jewish plot (v. 3c-g), the travel companions of Paul for his journey to Jerusalem (v. 4), and Paul's travel from Corinth via Philippi to Troas in the province of Asia (vv. 5 – 6). (2) Luke describes Paul's meeting with the believers in Troas, where the accident and resuscitation of Eutychus occur (vv. 7 – 12). The episode is a *narrative* with *travel notices* (vv. 2 – 3, 5 – 6) with five different geographical terms: Macedonia, Greece, Syria, Troas, Philippi, with *reports* of Paul's preaching and teaching in Troas (vv. 7 – 11), and with a *miracle story* (vv. 9 – 12). There is a brief line of *direct speech* in v. 10 in connection with Eutychus's restoration to life. The *list* in v. 4 itemizes seven associates of Paul (Sopater, Aristarchus, Secundus, Gaius, Timothy, Tychicus, Trophimus) and four geographical terms (Berea, Thessalonica, Derbe, Asia).

The second episode narrates Paul's meeting with the Ephesian elders in Miletus (20:13 – 38) in two incidents: Paul's travel from Troas to Miletus (vv. 13 – 16), and Paul's speech before the elders of the church from Ephesus (vv. 17 – 38). The episode is a *narrative* with *travel notices* (vv. 13 – 16), with eight geographical terms (Assos, Mitylene, Chios, Samos, Miletus, Ephesus, Asia, Jerusalem), and a long *speech* by Paul (vv. 18 – 35).

The speech before the Ephesian elders is the fifth speech of Paul in Acts.[2] It is the only extended speech of Paul before Christians, and it is the only speech that is a general speech addressing matters relating to the past, present, and future. There are many similarities with Paul's letters: the reminder of Paul's way of living (v. 18; cf. 1 Thess 1:5 – 6; 2:1 – 12; Phil 4:10 – 15); missionary work described as serving the Lord (v. 19; cf. Rom 1:1; 12:11; Phil 2:22); the emphasis on humility (v. 19; cf. 2 Cor

---

2. Cf. 13:7 – 11 (Paphos); 13:16 – 41 (Pisidian Antioch); 14:15 – 18 (Lystra); 17:22 – 31 (Athens).

10:1; 11:7; 1 Thess 2:6); reference to tears, i.e., personal concern (v. 19; cf. Rom 9:2; 2 Cor 2:4; Phil 3:18); opposition by Jews (v. 19; cf. 2 Cor 11:24, 26; 1 Thess 2:14 – 16); visiting from house to house (v. 20; cf. Rom 16:5; Col 4:15; Phlm 22); profitable teaching (v. 20; cf. Gal 4:16; 2 Cor 4:2); preaching to both Jews and Gentiles (v. 21; cf. Rom 1:16; 1 Cor 9:20); faith in the Lord Jesus (v. 21; cf. Rom 10:9 – 13); uncertainty about the future (v. 22; cf. Rom 15:30 – 32); lack of concern to preserve his own life (v. 24; cf. 2 Cor 4:7 – 5:10; 6:4 – 10; Phil 1:19 – 26; 2:17; 3:8); Paul's task of preaching the gospel of God's grace (v. 24; cf. Gal 1:15 – 16; 2 Cor 6:1); and the point that he is innocent of his converts' blood (v. 26; cf. 1 Thess 2:10).

This speech to the Ephesian elders is a *farewell address*. It takes place at a scene of leave-taking (departure or death), with family or friends (here the latter) assembled; it has a strong hortatory (paraenetic) emphasis, with examples drawn from Paul's earlier ministry; it contains a prediction of future events.[3] The classification as farewell address has prompted some scholars to discuss the speech as reflecting epideictic rhetoric;[4] the epideictic and apologetic elements of the speech serve its focus on the future (i.e., the speech is deliberative). The structure of the speech has been much debated; an analysis in terms of five sections seems most plausible:[5] introductory retrospect on Paul's ministry in Ephesus (vv. 18 – 21); prospects of Paul in Jerusalem (vv. 22 – 24); retrospect on Paul's ministry in Ephesus (vv. 25 – 27); exhortation of the elders regarding their present and future task (vv. 28 – 31); conclusion, with blessing, a final charge to the elders, and a final retrospect on Paul's ministry (vv. 32 – 35).

The third episode describes Paul's visits to believers in Tyre, Ptolemais, and Caesarea (21:1 – 17), narrated in four incidents: Paul's meeting with the believers in Tyre (vv. 1 – 6); his meeting with the believers in Ptolemais (v. 7); his meeting with the believers in Caesarea (vv. 8 – 14); and the journey from Caesarea to Jerusalem (vv. 15 – 17). The episode is a *narrative* with *travel notices* (vv. 1 – 3, 5 – 6, 7, 15 – 17) with ten different geographical terms (Cos, Rhodes, Patara, Phoenicia, Cyprus, Syria, Tyre, Ptolemais, Caesarea, Jerusalem) and three personal names (in addition to Paul's: Philip, Agabus, Mnason). *Direct speech* is used for the prophecy of Agabus, who announces Paul's imprisonment in Jerusalem (v. 11), for Paul's words of comfort to his travel companions and to the Caesarean believers (v. 13), and for the believers' acquiescence to the will of the Lord (v. 14).

On both a literary and a historical level, the contrast between the Saul who had persecuted Christians and the Paul who is welcomed by Christians who warn him of persecution is striking.[6] According to 8:3, Saul entered house after house, dragged

---

3. Cf. Aune, *Dictionary*, 182 – 83.

4. Latin *genus demonstrativum*, the rhetoric of praise or blame. Cf. Duane F. Watson, "Paul's Speech to the Ephesian Elders (Acts 20.17 – 38): Epideictic Rhetoric of Farewell," in *Persuasive Artistry: Studies in New Testament Rhetoric* (FS George A. Kennedy; ed. D. F. Watson; JSNTSup 50; Sheffield: JSOT Press, 1991), 184 – 208.

5. Steve Walton, *Leadership and Lifestyle: The Portrait of Paul in the Miletus Speech and 1 Thessalonians* (SNTSMS 108; Cambridge: Cambridge Univ. Press, 2000), 66 – 75. Some divide the speech into three, some into four parts; some argue for a chiastic structure.

6. Spencer, *Portrait of Philip*, 258 – 60.

both men and women off, and committed them to prison. Now, as Paul returns to Jerusalem and visits the believers in Tyre, Ptolemais, and Caesarea, he enters the houses of believers to stay there (21:4, 7, 8); he is embraced by husbands and wives (21:5 – 6); and he is welcomed by fathers and daughters (21:8 – 9), who plead with him not to go to Jerusalem, where he will face imprisonment (21:4, 11 – 12) — in churches established by the Greek-speaking believers who had been driven out of Jerusalem after the execution of Stephen (8:1, 4; 11:19).

Exegetical Outline

→ **I. Paul Visits Believers in Macedonia, Achaia, and Asia (20:2 – 12)**

    A. Paul's Travels in Macedonia, Achaia, Macedonia, and to Troas (20:2 – 6)

        1. Visits to believers in Macedonia (20:2a-c)

        2. Visits to believers in Greece (Corinth, in Achaia) (20:2d – 3b)

        3. Plot of the Jews against Paul (20:3c-e)

        4. Decision to return to Jerusalem via Macedonia (20:3f-g)

        5. Paul's seven travel companions (20:4)

        6. The travel companions sail from Corinth to Troas (20:5)

        7. Paul travels from Corinth to Philippi and from there to Troas (20:6)

    B. Paul's Meeting with the Believers in Troas and the Accident of Eutychus (20:7 – 12)

        1. Meeting with the believers on the first day of the week in an upstairs room (20:7 – 8)

        2. The fall of Eutychus from the third floor (20:9)

        3. Paul's intervention (20:10)

        4. Meal and further teaching (20:11a-f)

        5. Paul's departure from Troas (20:11g)

        6. The recovery of Eutychus (20:12)

II. Paul Meets with the Ephesian Elders in Miletus (20:13 – 38)

    A. Paul's Travel from Troas to Miletus (20:13 – 16)

        1. The travel companions sail from Troas to Assos (20:13a-d)

        2. Paul's overland travel to Assos (20:13e-g)

        3. Sea journey from Assos via Mitylene, Chios, and Samos to Miletus (20:14 – 15)

        4. Paul's decision not to visit Ephesus (20:16)

    B. Paul's Meeting with the Elders of the Church in Ephesus (20:17 – 38)

        1. Paul's invitation to the Ephesian elders to meet him in Miletus (20:17)

        2. The arrival of the Ephesian elders in Miletus (20:18a-b)

        3. Paul's address (20:18c – 35)

            a. Retrospect on Paul's ministry in Ephesus (20:18c – 21)

                i. Paul's service for the Lord (20:18c – 19)

                ii. Paul's proclamation (20:20 – 21)

            b. Prospects of Paul in Jerusalem (20:22 – 24)

                i. Paul's apprehensions about what will happen in Jerusalem (20:22 – 23)

                ii. Paul's willingness to die and his dedication to his ministry (20:24)

  c. Retrospect on Paul's ministry in Ephesus (20:25 – 27)

   i. Paul's awareness that this is the last encounter with the Ephesians (20:25)

   ii. Paul's faithful discharge of his responsibilities in Ephesus (20:26 – 27)

  d. Exhortation regarding the present and future tasks of the elders (20:28 – 31)

   i. Exhortation to keep watch over both themselves and the church (20:28)

   ii. Exhortation to be vigilant about false teachers (20:29 – 31)

  e. Conclusion (20:32 – 35)

   i. Blessing: Paul entrusts the elders to God and to his grace (20:32)

   ii. Paul's integrity in financial matters (20:33 – 34)

   iii. Exhortation to support the weak, supported by a word of Jesus (20:35)

 4. Paul's farewell to the Ephesian elders (20:36 – 38)

  a. Paul and the elders kneel and pray (20:36)

  b. The elders weep, and embrace and kiss Paul (20:37)

  c. The grief of the elders (20:38a-c)

  d. The elders accompany Paul to the ship (20:38d-e)

III. Paul Visits Believers in Tyre, Ptolemais, and Caesarea (21:1 – 17)

A. Paul's Meeting with the Believers in Tyre (21:1 – 6)

 1. Travel from Miletus via Cos, Rhodes, and Patara to Tyre (21:1 – 3)

 2. The meeting with the believers in Tyre (21:4 – 6)

  a. Paul stays for seven days (21:4a-c)

  b. The warning of the Spirit not to go to Jerusalem (21:4d-f)

  c. The prayer and farewell on the beach (21:5 – 6)

B. Paul's Meeting with the Believers in Ptolemais (21:7)

 1. Travel from Tyre to Ptolemais (21:7a-b)

 2. The meeting with the believers in Ptolemais (21:7c-e)

C. Paul's Meeting with the Believers in Caesarea (21:8 – 14)

 1. Travel from Ptolemais to Caesarea (21:8a-c)

 2. The meeting with the believers in Caesarea (21:8d – 14)

  a. The hospitality of Philip the evangelist (21:8d-g)

  b. The daughters of Philip with the gift of prophecy (21:9)

  c. The arrival of Agabus (21:10)

  d. The prophecy of Agabus concerning Paul's imprisonment in Jerusalem (21:11)

  e. The advice of the believers not to go to Jerusalem (21:12)

  f. Paul's willingness to die in Jerusalem for the Lord Jesus (21:13)

  g. The acquiescence of the believers regarding Paul's plan to go to Jerusalem (21:14)

D. Paul's Travel from Caesarea to Jerusalem (21:15 – 17)

 1. The journey from Caesarea to Jerusalem (21:15)

 2. The escort of Caesarean believers (21:16a-c)

 3. The hospitality of Mnason (21:16d-g)

 4. The welcome of the brothers in Jerusalem (21:17)

Explanation of the Text

20:2 After he had traveled through those regions [of Macedonia] and encouraged the believers with much preaching, he came to Greece (διελθὼν δὲ τὰ μέρη ἐκεῖνα καὶ παρακαλέσας αὐτοὺς λόγῳ πολλῷ ἦλθεν εἰς τὴν Ἑλλάδα). The first travel report of Paul's return journey from Ephesus to Jerusalem via Macedonia and Achaia (19:21) takes him from Miletus to Macedonia, and then to Achaia, where he spends the winter. From there Paul goes back to Macedonia, then to Troas (vv. 2 – 6). The visit to the churches in Macedonia (see on 16:11 – 12), which was important for Paul, as his repeated comments in the Corinthian correspondence demonstrates,[7] is narrated briefly. Luke merely mentions the fact that Paul traveled, that he "encouraged" (παρακαλέσας; see on 2:40) the believers, and that he engaged in much preaching (λόγῳ πολλῷ).[8] Luke emphasizes that exhortation and encouragement are key elements in Christian preaching.[9]

Paul's comment in 2 Cor 2:12 – 13 suggests that he traveled from Ephesus north to Troas, where he had remarkable opportunities for proclaiming the gospel. When he entered Macedonia, he certainly would have visited the churches he had established in Philippi (16:11 – 40), Thessalonica (17:1 – 9), and Berea (17:10 – 15). Paul's comment in Rom 15:19 suggests that he traveled from Macedonia to Illyricum,[10] the next province to the west, perhaps to test his ability to function in a Latin-speaking environment before embarking on his mission to Spain (cf. Rom 15:24, 28). In Greece (Ἑλλάς), churches existed in Athens (17:16 – 17, 32 – 34), Cenchreae (Rom 16:1; cf. Acts 18:18), and Corinth (18:1 – 22).

20:3 He stayed there for three months. When some Jews plotted to cause him harm just as he was about to sail for Syria, he decided to return through Macedonia (ποιήσας τε μῆνας τρεῖς· γενομένης ἐπιβουλῆς αὐτῷ ὑπὸ τῶν Ἰουδαίων μέλλοντι ἀνάγεσθαι εἰς τὴν Συρίαν, ἐγένετο γνώμης τοῦ ὑποστρέφειν διὰ Μακεδονίας). The three months that Paul spent in "Greece," i.e., in Achaia, is to be connected with his extended stay in Corinth over the winter (of AD 56 – 57), when travel stopped and navigation on the Mediterranean was closed.[11] According to Rom 16:23, Gaius was his host in Corinth, where he wrote the letter to the Christians in Rome on the eve of his departure for Jerusalem (Rom 15:25) and where he finalized the arrangements for the collection that he put together for the church in Jerusalem (cf. 1 Cor 16:3) — details that Luke does not mention (see on 19:21; 21:18; 24:17).

Luke provides no details for the "plot" (ἐπιβουλή) by local Jews against Paul. Perhaps the Jews, who had unsuccessfully hoped to obtain Paul's punishment in the legal case they brought before Gallio, the Roman governor (18:12 – 17), recognized the significance of Paul's activities not only for Corinth but for other Jewish communities, causing them to take the desperate action of eliminating Paul outside of the Roman court system. It has been plausibly suggested that Jews who planned to travel to Jerusalem as pilgrims for the

---

7. See 1 Cor 16:5; 2 Cor 1:16; 2:12 – 13; 7:5, 13 – 16; 8:1 – 5. For a reconstruction of the events, cf. Hemer, *Acts*, 256 – 61.

8. If the Greek phrase refers to a single occasion, it would denote "a long speech" (cf. BDAG, s.v. λόγος 1aβ with reference to 15:32). As Paul preached in churches in various areas, the sense here is "much speaking" or "much preaching"; cf. Barrett, *Acts*, 946.

9. Cf. παρακαλέω in 2:40; 8:31; 9:38; 11:23; 13:42; 14:22; 15:32; 16:9, 15, 39, 40; 19:31; 20:1, 2, 12; 21:12; 24:4; 25:2; 28:14, 20.

10. Cf. Schnabel, *Early Christian Mission*, 2:1250 – 57; also Hemer, *Acts*, 260.

11. See on 18:18; 27:9.

Passover Festival, taking the same ship that Paul would take, hoped to kill him en route to Judea.[12] When Paul was informed of the plot, he abandoned his plan to travel from Greece to Syria by taking a ship from Corinth across the Aegean Sea. Instead, he decided to return to Syria and Jerusalem by first traveling overland to Macedonia.

20:4 He was accompanied by Sopater son of Pyrrhus from Berea, Aristarchus and Secundus from Thessalonica, Gaius from Derbe, Timothy, and Tychicus and Trophimus from the province of Asia (συνείπετο δὲ αὐτῷ Σώπατρος Πύρρου Βεροιαῖος, Θεσσαλονικέων δὲ Ἀρίσταρχος καὶ Σεκοῦνδος, καὶ Γάϊος Δερβαῖος καὶ Τιμόθεος, Ἀσιανοὶ δὲ Τύχικος καὶ Τρόφιμος). The list of seven men who accompany Paul is not explained; Luke evidently assumes that his readers know why Christians from various regions in which Paul had established churches had assembled in Greece with the goal of traveling with Paul to Jerusalem. Most scholars interpret the names in the list in terms of representatives of the churches that contributed to the collection Paul had organized for the church in Jerusalem (24:17; cf. 1 Cor 16:1 – 2; 2 Cor 8 – 9; cf. Rom 15:25, 31). The Macedonian churches are represented by Sopater (Berea) and Aristarchus and Secundus (Thessalonica), the Galatian churches by Gaius (Derbe) and Timothy (Lystra), and the Asian churches by Tychicus and Trophimus (Ephesus).[13]

Sopater, identified as "son of Pyrrhus," may be identical with the Sosipater mentioned in Rom 16:21.[14] Aristarchus, who had been arrested in Ephesus (19:29), is also mentioned in 27:2 (ac-companying Paul on his journey as prisoner from Caesarea to Rome), in Col 4:10 (as Paul's fellow prisoner), and in Phlm 24 (as Paul's coworker); he is described here as being a Christian from Thes-salonica. A second "delegate" from the church in the Macedonian capital is Secundus,[15] who is mentioned only here in the New Testament. Gaius may be the second of Paul's associates arrested in Ephesus (19:29); he is described as a believer "from Derbe," a city in Lycaonia that had been incorpo-rated into the province of Galatia. Timothy was Paul's trusted coworker from Lystra in Lycaonia. Tychicus, from the province of Asia, is probably identical with the Tychicus mentioned in several of Paul's letters as a "dear brother, a faithful min-ister."[16] Trophimus is described as an Ephesian in 21:29, which suggests he was a Gentile believer; he is mentioned in 2 Tim 4:20 as being left behind in Miletus because he became ill.

If these seven men represent churches contrib-uting to Paul's collection for the church in Jerusa-lem, the fact that Luke mentions no representatives from Corinth and from Philippi is striking. Paul gave specific instructions to the Corinthian church on how to participate in the collection (2 Cor 8 – 9), and the Philippian church had supported Paul financially in the past (Phil 4:10 – 20). Some suggest that the representatives from Corinth and Philippi belonged, just like Timothy, to the group that did not travel by ship to Troas ahead of Paul but joined Paul on his overland journey through Macedonia, celebrating Passover in Philippi. If we add to the group mentioned in v. 4 in terms

---

12. Ramsay, *St. Paul the Traveller*, 220; cf. Bruce, *Book of Acts*, 382 n. 15.

13. Some have suggested that any of these delegates could be the two unnamed delegates mentioned in 2 Cor 8:16 – 24 who accompany Titus to Corinth to facilitate arrangements there for the completion of the collection for Jerusalem. Cer-tainty is impossible. Cf. Margaret E. Thrall, *The Second Epistle to the Corinthians* (ICC; Edinburgh: T&T Clark, 1994 – 2000),

560 – 62; Murray J. Harris, *The Second Epistle to the Corinthians* (NIGTC; Grand Rapids: Eerdmans, 2005), 601 – 2.

14. Cf. Hemer, *Acts*, 236, for evidence for the names Sopa-ter, Sosipater, and Pyrrhus from Macedonian sources.

15. Brocke, *Thessaloniki*, 243 – 44, 249, assumes that Secun-dus was a Roman citizen.

16. Col 4:7; Eph 6:21; also 2 Tim 4:12; Titus 3:12.

of two delegates from Corinth and two delegates from Philippi (perhaps Lucius and Jason, who are mentioned in Rom 16:21 between Timothy and Sosipater), we would have twelve representatives of seven churches. Some suggest that Luke (whose presence seems implied by the first person plural in vv. 5 – 6) was the representative of the church in Philippi; Paul may have regarded himself as the representative of the church in Corinth.

20:5 – 6 These men went on ahead and waited for us in Troas; we sailed from Philippi after the Feast of Unleavened Bread, and five days later we joined them in Troas, where we stayed for seven days (οὗτοι δὲ προελθόντες ἔμενον ἡμᾶς ἐν Τρῳάδι, ἡμεῖς δὲ ἐξεπλεύσαμεν μετὰ τὰς ἡμέρας τῶν ἀζύμων ἀπὸ Φιλίππων καὶ ἤλθομεν πρὸς αὐτοὺς εἰς τὴν Τρῳάδα ἄχρι ἡμερῶν πέντε, ὅπου διετρίψαμεν ἡμέρας ἑπτά). The seven believers mentioned in v. 4 sailed from Corinth across the Aegean Sea to Troas, where they waited for Paul to arrive. It is unclear why they sailed to Troas rather than to Ephesus; time may have been a factor (cf. v. 16). Paul and several companions traveled overland from Corinth to Philippi, a journey of about 450 miles (730 km.), which took about five weeks.

The departure of Paul's travel party includes Luke (note "we," ἡμεῖς, in v. 6). The comments in vv. 5 – 6 resume the "we passages" abandoned after Acts 16, suggesting that Luke has remained in Philippi during Paul's missionary work in Athens, Corinth, and Ephesus. Paul's departure from Philippi — i.e., from Neapolis, the port of Philippi (cf. 16:11 – 12) — is dated with reference to the Feast of Unleavened Bread, which was connected with the Feast of Passover (τὸ πάσχα; cf. Luke 22:1).[17] Passover (the 14th day of Nisan) was celebrated in AD 57 on April 7, which left five weeks

for the journey from Philippi via Troas, Miletus, Tyre, and Caesarea to Jerusalem, which Paul wants to reach in time for Pentecost (May 29, AD 57; cf. 20:16). The comment in v. 6 suggests that Paul celebrated the Feast of Passover and Unleavened Bread with the Jewish Christians of Philippi.

The preposition "later" (ἄχρι), used in connection with "five days," means either that Paul and his party sailed "within" five days, or, more plausibly in the context, that the sea voyage from Philippi/Neapolis to Troas lasted five days, a plausible time since the ship would be sailing against the wind in the springtime. Given Paul's hurry to reach Jerusalem (cf. v. 16), the fact that Paul and his associates spend seven days in Troas appears to be due to the schedule of the ship that Paul must board for his journey to Syria, rather than to the "open door" that Paul had (presumably on an earlier occasion) in Troas (2 Cor 2:12 – 13).

20:7 – 8 On the first day of the week, when we came together to break bread, Paul instructed the believers. Because he intended to leave the next day, he extended his speech until midnight. There were many lamps in the upstairs room where we were meeting (ἐν δὲ τῇ μιᾷ τῶν σαββάτων συνηγμένων ἡμῶν κλάσαι ἄρτον, ὁ Παῦλος διελέγετο αὐτοῖς μέλλων ἐξιέναι τῇ ἐπαύριον, παρέτεινέν τε τὸν λόγον μέχρι μεσονυκτίου. ἦσαν δὲ λαμπάδες ἱκαναὶ ἐν τῷ ὑπερῴῳ οὗ ἦμεν συνηγμένοι). The second incident of this episode (20:2 – 12) relates Paul's meeting with the believers in Troas (vv. 7 – 12). Luke provides the following details about the meeting of the Christians in Troas.

(1) The community of believers gathered "on the first day of the week," with Paul planning to leave after sunrise the next day. This was probably a regular meeting of the community rather than

---

17. Cf. BDAG, s.v. πάσχα 1, commenting that Passover, celebrated on the 14th day of Nisan, "was followed immediately by the Feast of Unleavened Bread (Mazzoth; ἄζυμος 2) on the 15th to 21st. Popular usage merged the two festivals and treated them as a unity, as they were for practical purposes."

an ad hoc gathering because of Paul's presence in the city. If Jewish reckoning is used, the day of the meeting was Saturday evening; if the Roman week is used, the first day of the week was Sunday. However, the overlay of Jewish, Roman, and Greek practices of reckoning the beginning of the day from sunset, from midnight, or from sunrise, respectively, creates difficulties for understanding what Luke's readers would have assumed; the meeting could have taken place on Saturday night and early Sunday morning,[18] or on Sunday evening and Monday morning.[19] There are too many variables to be certain on this issue, although a meeting on Sunday seems most plausible.[20]

(2) The community of believers met in the evening, with lamps illuminating the room (v. 8). Paul taught until midnight (v. 7). Paul's stated intention of leaving Troas the next day suggests that the meetings of the church usually did not last that late. The timing of the meeting in the evening is probably because most believers would have had to work from morning until evening; only the rich were free in the afternoons. Eutychus's drowsiness is not explained by the "many lamps"[21] but by the fact that this meeting lasted well into the night. The many lamps were probably brought to the upper room by the believers traveling from their houses to the meeting place through the (unlit) streets of the city.

(3) The community of believers came together in order to "break bread," i.e., to share a meal, as was the practice in the community of Jesus' followers in Jerusalem (cf. 2:42, 46) and of the Christian communities established by Paul (cf. 1 Cor 11:17 – 34). If 1 Cor 11 is any indication, Jesus'

death (the Lord's Supper) would have been remembered at the beginning and end of the meal. Most likely the meeting began with the meal, followed by the teaching.

(4) The community gathered for teaching. Paul "instructed" (διελέγετο; see on 17:2) the believers; the Greek term describes either a discussion of a topic or a series of topics by one person (sermon, lecture), or a conversation about a topic or topics between two or more persons (dialogue, discussion). On the importance of teaching see on 2:42. Paul had recently written a long letter to the Christians in Rome as a summary of the gospel he had preached and defended since his conversion; it is not implausible to think that in this long meeting Paul explained the gospel and the life of believers in Jesus along the same lines.

(5) The meeting took place in an "upstairs room" of a house that had three stories, i.e., the second story above ground level (v. 9). This location suggests that the church met in a large house, perhaps a tenement building, in the center of Troas, rather than in a villa belonging to a rich person (which would have had one story only, or two if built on a slope).

20:9 A young man named Eutychus, who had been sitting at the window, sank into a deep sleep as Paul spoke at length. When he was sound asleep, he fell from the third story to the ground below, and was picked up dead (καθεζόμενος δέ τις νεανίας ὀνόματι Εὔτυχος ἐπὶ τῆς θυρίδος, καταφερόμενος ὕπνῳ βαθεῖ διαλεγομένου τοῦ Παύλου ἐπὶ πλεῖον, κατενεχθεὶς ἀπὸ τοῦ ὕπνου ἔπεσεν ἀπὸ τοῦ τριστέγου κάτω καὶ ἤρθη νεκρός).

---

18. Fitzmyer, *Acts*, 668 – 69.

19. Bock, *Acts*, 619; cf. Turner, "Sabbath," 128 – 30.

20. Hemer, *Acts*, 270, dates the Eutychus incident to "the night of Sunday 24th April AD 57." Note how Paul advised putting aside money for the collection "on the first day of every week" (1 Cor 16:2). "The Lord's Day" (κυριακὴ ἡμέρα) men-

tioned in Rev 1:10 (cf. *Did.* 14:1) is also related to Sunday, the day of Jesus' resurrection.

21. As assumed by many scholars; cf. Fitzmyer, *Acts*, 669; Pervo, *Acts*, 510. Eutychus could have fallen asleep despite the lamps.

The meeting of the congregation with Paul teaching was interrupted by the commotion that resulted from Eutychus's fall from the third story to the street. Eutychus was a common Greek name; the fact that it means "Lucky One" is a coincidence.

The narrative is told with vivid detail. Eutychus was a young man (νεανίας), i.e., between eighteen and thirty years old (see on 2:17; in v. 12 he is described as παῖς ["boy"], which suggests a youth below the age of puberty). He was sitting "at the window" while Paul was speaking "at length."[22] Eutychus sank into a "deep sleep," with the passive tense of the verb "sank" (καταφερόμενος) suggesting that a force stronger than his will pulled him down into a profound slumber, a fact mentioned twice.[23] As Eutychus lost control over his posture, he "fell" out of the window "to the ground below"; some believers who noticed what had happened rushed outside and picked him up; his lifeless body on the pavement looked "dead" (νεκρός). There is no reason to assume that the young man only appeared to be dead and that the miracle consisted in Eutychus's surviving the fall.

20:10 Paul went down, threw himself upon him, put his arms around him, and said, "Do not be alarmed! There is life in him" (καταβὰς δὲ ὁ Παῦλος ἐπέπεσεν αὐτῷ καὶ συμπεριλαβὼν εἶπεν· μὴ θορυβεῖσθε, ἡ γὰρ ψυχὴ αὐτοῦ ἐν αὐτῷ ἐστιν). Paul's intervention is narrated with four verbs formulated in the aorist tense, suggesting completed actions: he "went down" (καταβάς) from the meeting room on the third floor to the street; he "threw" (ἐπέπεσεν) himself on top of the lifeless body of Eutychus; he "put his arms around him"

(συμπεριλαβών); he spoke (εἶπεν) to the other believers, commanding them not to be agitated. The reason for his quiet confidence is his prophetic insight that "there is life in him," a statement that is performative: "he was dead, but now there is life in him as a result of my action."

Biblically literate readers would be reminded of resuscitations of dead people by Elijah and Elisha (1 Kings 17:19 – 22; 2 Kings 4:34 – 35); Christian readers would be reminded of resuscitations effected by Jesus (Luke 7:11 – 15, the son of the widow of Nain; 8:49 – 56, the daughter of Jairus; John 11:38 – 44, Lazarus); readers of Acts would be reminded of a resuscitation in the ministry of Peter (9:36 – 41, Dorcas). The resuscitation of Eutychus places Paul in the line of the prophets from the Old Testament to Jesus and to Peter, demonstrating that the life-giving power of God (cf. Rom 4:17) was present in Paul's ministry in similar ways.

20:11 – 12 Then he went upstairs and broke bread and ate. After he conversed with them for a long time until dawn, he departed. They took the boy home alive and were greatly comforted (ἀναβὰς δὲ καὶ κλάσας τὸν ἄρτον καὶ γευσάμενος ἐφ᾽ ἱκανόν τε ὁμιλήσας ἄχρι αὐγῆς, οὕτως ἐξῆλθεν. ἤγαγον δὲ τὸν παῖδα ζῶντα καὶ παρεκλήθησαν οὐ μετρίως). Paul's actions after the miracle are narrated succinctly with five verbs, all formulated in the aorist tense: he "went upstairs" (ἀναβάς), i.e., back to the meeting room on the third story; he "broke bread" (κλάσας τὸν ἄρτον), perhaps commencing another meal in the small hours of the night; he "ate" (γευσάμενος); i.e., he consumed the meal, presumably with the other believers; he "con-

---

22. Cf. BDAG, s.v. πολύς 2bβ. The translation "as Paul talked on and on" (NIV, TNIV; also NLT) suggests a speaker who forgets both time and his audience, whose delivery is monotonous, and whose content is probably pompous and boring. The Greek term does not have such connotations. More appropriate is NET: "Paul continued to speak for a long time."

23. Note the progression from the present passive participle (καταφερόμενος ὕπνῳ βαθεῖ), suggesting the progressive sinking into sleep, to the aorist passive participle (κατενεχθεὶς ἀπὸ τοῦ ὕπνου, "when he was sound asleep"), noting the fait accompli of the deep slumber. In the Qumran community, falling asleep during an assembly was punished by a thirty-day exclusion (1QS VII 10).

versed" (ὁμιλήσας) with the believers, an activity emphasized by two temporal qualifications ("for a long time" and "until dawn"); then Paul "departed" (ἐξῆλθεν), either to catch a few hours of sleep or to embark on his overland journey to Assos.

The reality of the miracle that brought Eutychus back to life is demonstrated by the remarks in v. 12: the believers "took" the boy who was "alive"; i.e., he was probably able to walk, led by members of the congregation. It seems that after Eutychus had been restored to life, they had brought him back to the meeting room upstairs before Paul ate and continued his teaching. Rather than stating that the believers were astounded by the miracle, Luke asserts that they were "comforted" (παρεκλήθησαν).

20:13 We went ahead to the ship and set sail for Assos, where we planned to take Paul on board. He had arranged this because he wanted to travel overland (ἡμεῖς δὲ προελθόντες ἐπὶ τὸ πλοῖον ἀνήχθημεν ἐπὶ τὴν Ασσον ἐκεῖθεν μέλλοντες ἀναλαμβάνειν τὸν Παῦλον· οὕτως γὰρ διατεταγμένος ἦν μέλλων αὐτὸς πεζεύειν). The second episode, which narrates Paul's meeting with the Ephesian elders in Miletus (20:13 – 38), also begins with a travel report (vv. 13 – 16). Some of Paul's associates, including the narrator of the "we passages" (Luke), boarded a ship in Troas and sailed south, then east, passing between the island of Lesbos and the mainland around Cape Lekton to Assos, a distance of perhaps 43 miles (70 km.), which could be covered in eight to seventeen hours. Paul had arranged, presumably with the ship's captain, to be taken on board in Assos because he wanted to travel on foot. The distance overland from Troas to Assos was about 30 miles (50 km.), which would have taken two days. Luke does not explain why Paul decided to travel overland.[24]

20:14 – 15 When he met us at Assos, we took him on board and sailed to Mitylene. The next day we sailed from there and arrived off Chios. On the next day we crossed over to Samos, and on the following day we arrived at Miletus (ὡς δὲ συνέβαλλεν ἡμῖν εἰς τὴν Ασσον, ἀναλαβόντες αὐτὸν ἤλθομεν εἰς Μιτυλήνην, κἀκεῖθεν ἀποπλεύσαντες τῇ ἐπιούσῃ κατηντήσαμεν ἄντικρυς Χίου, τῇ δὲ ἑτέρᾳ παρεβάλομεν εἰς Σάμον, τῇ δὲ ἐχομένῃ ἤλθομεν εἰς Μίλητον). The ship that took Paul and his associates from Assos to Miletus — a distance of about 125 miles (200 km.), covered in four days of travel — sailed south to Mitylene, the chief town on the eastern coast of the island of Lesbos. The next day the ship continued on a southerly course, rounding Cape Malia, sailing between the peninsula of Chalkitis west of Smyrna and the island of Chios, presumably putting into the chief town on the eastern coast also called Chios.

The next day the ship continued south, sailing through the straights between the island of Chios and Cape Argennon on the mainland toward the west coast of the island of Samos, arriving in the chief town also called Samos. The trip from Samos to Miletus was only 20 miles (35 km.), which would have taken nine hours of sailing against headwinds. Miletus was a major port south of Ephesus.

20:16 Paul had decided to sail past Ephesus so that he would not lose time in the province of Asia, because he was in a hurry to reach Jerusalem by the Feast of Pentecost, if possible (κεκρίκει γὰρ ὁ Παῦλος παραπλεῦσαι τὴν Ἔφεσον, ὅπως μὴ γένηται αὐτῷ χρονοτριβῆσαι ἐν τῇ Ἀσίᾳ· ἔσπευδεν γὰρ εἰ δυνατὸν εἴη αὐτῷ τὴν ἡμέραν τῆς πεντηκοστῆς γενέσθαι εἰς Ἱεροσόλυμα). The decision to bypass Ephesus was probably made in Troas when Paul arranged for a passage on a ship; ships

---

24. Fitzmyer, *Acts*, 671, suggests that Paul may have wanted to avoid the treacherous coast, which begs the question why his travel companions travel by ship. If there were churches in the

towns that he would have passed through — Kolonai, Larisa, Hamaxitos, Smintheion — this might explain his decision not to take the ship.

that wanted to reach the eastern Mediterranean as fast as possible "may have deliberately avoided entering the gulf of Ephesus, especially if the silting there was already causing delays."[25]

Apart from the need to travel "in a hurry" since he wanted to reach Jerusalem in time for the Feast of Pentecost (see on 2:1),[26] another reason to avoid Ephesus may have been the possibility of becoming entangled in legal matters linked with the guild of silversmiths, who possibly brought Paul's situation to the local courts and to the Roman governor (see 19:35 – 40). Since the congregation in Ephesus was large, Paul could anticipate a prolonged visit of a week or two, which would delay the journey to Syria. Paul wants to reach Jerusalem by Pentecost (May 29, AD 57) and then travel to Rome, presumably in early summer, before moving to Spain in the fall of AD 57 or in the spring of AD 58.

20:17 – 18b From Miletus he sent a message to Ephesus and called for the elders of the church to meet him. When they arrived, he said to them (ἀπὸ δὲ τῆς Μιλήτου πέμψας εἰς Ἔφεσον μετεκαλέσατο τοὺς πρεσβυτέρους τῆς ἐκκλησίας. ὡς δὲ παρεγένοντο πρὸς αὐτὸν εἶπεν αὐτοῖς). The second incident of this episode relates Paul's meeting with the elders of the church in Ephesus (vv. 17 – 38). It begins with Paul's invitation to the Ephesian elders to come to meet him in Miletus. The journey of Paul's emissary — one of his associates who conveyed Paul's message to Ephesus — and the return journey of the elders would have taken four days each.[27] The "elders" (πρεσβύτεροι), i.e., the official leaders of the congregation, presumably had been appointed by Paul when he

established the church, a fact that implies the apostolic authority of Paul with regard to both the elders and the congregation (cf. 11:30; 14:23). Paul speaks to the elders of the church in Ephesus as soon as they arrive.

20:18c – 19 "You know how I have lived with you the whole time from the day that I set foot in the province of Asia. I served the Lord as his slave with all humility and with tears, and in the midst of the trials that happened to me because of the plots of the Jews (ὑμεῖς ἐπίστασθε, ἀπὸ πρώτης ἡμέρας ἀφ᾽ ἧς ἐπέβην εἰς τὴν Ἀσίαν, πῶς μεθ᾽ ὑμῶν τὸν πάντα χρόνον ἐγενόμην, δουλεύων τῷ κυρίῳ μετὰ πάσης ταπεινοφροσύνης καὶ δακρύων καὶ πειρασμῶν τῶν συμβάντων μοι ἐν ταῖς ἐπιβουλαῖς τῶν Ἰουδαίων). This address before the Ephesian elders is the only speech of Paul in Acts presented to Christian believers. As Paul reviews his past ministry in Ephesus (vv. 18 – 21, 24, 25, 27, 31, 33 – 35), anticipates events that might transpire in Jerusalem (vv. 22 – 24), and reminds the elders of their tasks (vv. 28 – 31), he focuses not so much on himself but on the identity of the church, whose survival does not depend on him but on adhering to the gospel and understanding its origin in God, Jesus, and the Holy Spirit.

The first section of the speech (vv. 18c – 21) reviews Paul's ministry in Ephesus with a strong focus on the gospel. Paul begins by describing his service for the Lord (vv. 18c – 19). (1) His ministry was public ministry. The elders personally knew Paul and his ministry when he lived in Ephesus. He is no stranger to them. He is the missionary through whose teaching they came to faith in Jesus;

---

25. Hemer, _Acts_, 125.

26. The optative of the verb (εἴη) indicates Paul's awareness of the fact that not all plans can be carried out with certainty.

27. Bock, _Acts_, 621, posits 30 miles between Ephesus and Miletus, which is correct for a crow that can fly. Actual travelers on foot had to cross over the spur between the Thorax

Mountains and the Mycale Mountains, travel southwest upon reaching Magnesia on the Maeander River, reaching the coast via Priene, then turn east along the northern shore of the Gulf of Latmos, turning west at Heraclea, continuing along the southern shore of the Gulf of Latmos, reaching Miletus after about 62 miles (100 km.).

he is the pastor who helped them understand the consequences of the truth of the gospel for their lives; and, even more important, he is a former colleague in the ministry of the gospel in the city of Ephesus and thus their brother and friend.

(2) Paul's ministry was corporate ministry. He lived with them, not in the splendid isolation of some missionary headquarters but in the same environment in which they lived.

(3) Paul's ministry was exemplary ministry. They understand how (πῶς) he lived, they observed his missionary and pastoral practices, they noted his lifestyle, and they saw his courage in the face of potentially deadly opposition.

(4) Paul's ministry was subservient ministry. He "served [δουλεύων] the Lord as his slave"; i.e., he consented to and carried out the will of Jesus, Israel's crucified and risen Messiah and Lord.[28] Most English translations downplay the significance of the strong term δουλεύω, which does not simply mean "serve" but "to be owned by another, *be a slave*" and "to act or conduct oneself as one in total service to another, *perform the duties of a slave.*"[29] Paul repeatedly and prominently describes himself as a (lit.) "slave of Jesus the Messiah" (Rom 1:1; 1 Cor 7:22; Gal 1:10; Phil 1:1; Titus 1:1).

(5) Paul's ministry was selfless ministry. He worked "with all humility" (μετὰ πάσης ταπεινοφροσύνης) — not for selfish reasons but with selfless devotion to the Lord, an attitude fitting a slave. Humility (or "modesty") means, negatively, renouncing any will to rule, and, positively, serving with goodness and understanding.[30] Interpreted in the context of Phil 2:3, humility is the opposite of selfish striving for advantage (ἐριθεία) and of exaggerated self-evaluation (κενοδοξία).[31]

(6) Paul's ministry was embattled ministry. There were "tears," the result of deep-seated anguish, profound distress, and heartfelt sorrow caused by the unbelief of many Jews in Ephesus who hatched "plots" to cause him harm.[32] This opposition resulted in situations that Paul endured as "trials" (πειρασμοί), i.e., as afflictions that tested his love for the Jews (more so than his commitment to his missionary commission that the Lord had given him).[33]

20:20 – 21 I have not kept silent about anything that is profitable for you; I have proclaimed everything to you, as I taught you publicly and from house to house. I was bearing witness to both Jews and Greeks about repentance toward God and about faith in our Lord Jesus (ὡς οὐδὲν ὑπεστειλάμην τῶν συμφερόντων τοῦ μὴ ἀναγγεῖλαι ὑμῖν καὶ διδάξαι ὑμᾶς δημοσίᾳ καὶ κατ' οἴκους, διαμαρτυρόμενος Ἰουδαίοις τε καὶ Ἕλλησιν τὴν εἰς θεὸν μετάνοιαν καὶ πίστιν εἰς τὸν κύριον ἡμῶν Ἰησοῦν). Paul now describes his preaching (vv. 20 – 21). What he emphasizes is not only characteristic of his own missionary and pastoral activity, but also the ministry of all witnesses of the gospel. Paul describes the means, process, venue, audience, and content of the witness of the church.

(1) Christian witness involves oral proclamation.

---

28. In the context of vv. 21, 24, 35, "Lord" (κύριος) here clearly refers to Jesus Christ.

29. BDAG, s.v. δουλεύω 1 and 2, adding under 2aβ, "especially in expressions relating to God or Jesus Christ as recipients of undivided allegiance" because "a slave can take orders from only one master." See Rom 12:11; 14:18; 16:18. See Harris, *Slave of Christ*, 154, on v. 18, with the translation adopted above.

30. H. Giesen, "ταπεινοφροσύνη," *EDNT*, 3:334.

31. See also Rom 9:2; 1 Cor 2:3; 2 Cor 1:8; 2:4; Phil 3:18.

32. The term used here (ἐπιβουλή) occurs in 9:24; 20:3, 19; 23:30 for the opposition of Jews to Paul. In Acts see the events reported in 13:50; 14:2 – 7, 19; 17:5 – 9, 13; 18:6, 12 – 17; 19:9; 20:3; see also 1 Thess 2:15; Titus 1:10, 14. For opposition in Ephesus cf. 1 Cor 15:32; 16:9. On shedding tears cf. 2 Cor 2:4. Note that in Acts 21:27 – 29 it is Jews from the province of Asia who lead the action in the Jerusalem temple that prompts Paul's arrest.

33. See Paul's lists of hardships: 1 Cor 4:9 – 13; 2 Cor 4:8 – 9; 6:4 – 10; 11:23 – 33; 12:10.

Paul has "not kept silent"; i.e., he did not avoid speaking to people about Jesus. This verb (ὑποστέλλω) emphasizes the boldness and frankness of Paul's preaching. Or the verb can denote here "to withhold, to hold back," which would mean that Paul emphasizes the completeness of his preaching in which he did not withhold the truth. There is no reason why both meanings could not be intended. The point is that Paul has spoken about the gospel with the result that people heard what was spoken, always with a reaction — some accepting his message while others opposed it.

(2) Christian witness communicates critical information. Paul emphasizes that he "proclaimed" (ἀναγγεῖλαι) everthing to them; i.e., he provided information about God's new revelation, he announced Jesus as Israel's Messiah, and he taught about the significance of Jesus' death, resurrection, and exaltation.[34] Paul also "taught" (διδάξαι); i.e., he provided a structured explanation of the gospel, with the goal that the Ephesians would remember the content of the teaching. And Paul asserts that he was "bearing witness" (διαμαρτυρόμενος); i.e., he was eager to "make a solemn declaration about the truth" of the message that he proclaimed and to "exhort with authority in matters of extraordinary importance."[35] Christian preaching is not a rhetorical event for the promotion of the fame of the speaker and for the entertainment of the audience. It is more consequential than the education of the youth taught by knowledgeable teachers, and more serious than the situation in a court of law where witnesses relate what they have seen and heard.

Christian preaching is critical because it informs about the revelation of God's grace and God's judgment in the coming of his Messiah.

(3) Christian witness happens in public and private venues. Paul preached and taught the gospel "publicly": in the synagogues,[36] in the lecture hall of Tyrannus, and in the agora (forum), the center of Greco-Roman cities.[37] And he preached and taught "from house to house" (κατ᾽ οἴκους), i.e., in private homes, particularly of believers in whose houses new converts and the curious gathered.[38] Paul's greetings in 1 Cor 16:19 – 20 document the existence of several house churches in Ephesus. Both his message and his mode of life were consistent, whether he appeared in public or spoke in private.[39]

(4) Christian witness addresses any audience (v. 21). Paul preached and taught both Jews and Greeks.[40] He spoke before his fellow Jews, members of God's people who knew the Scriptures and were waiting for the Messiah. He spoke before Greeks — in the synagogue, where he encountered God-fearers (Gentiles who sympathized with the beliefs and practices of the Jewish people), and in the forum, where he encountered anybody who happened to be in there — including philosophers (17:17 – 18), rich and poor, men and women. Paul proclaimed the gospel to all human beings, without ethnic, religious, social, or gender distinctions.

(5) Christian witness proclaims "repentance" (μετάνοιαν; see on 2:38) toward God and "faith" (πίστις; see on 4:4) in Jesus Christ. Repentance is necessary because all people, both Jews and Gen-

---

34. The term "everything" in the translation is derived from the negative phrase (οὐδὲν ὑπεστειλάμην): as Paul did not hold back anything, it follows that he proclaimed everything.

35. Thus the two definitions given in BDAG, s.v. διαμαρτύρομαι.

36. Cf. 9:20; 13:5, 14 – 15; 14:1; 17:1, 10, 17; 18:4; 19:8.

37. Cf. 19:8 – 9 (Tyrannus's hall in Corinth); 17:17 (the forum in Athens).

38. Cf. 18:7 – 8 (Titius's house in Corinth); 20:7 – 11 (upper room in Troas); cf. 1 Cor 14:23.

39. For the corresponding practice of the church in Jerusalem cf. 5:18, 42.

40. Cf. 13:44 – 48; 14:1, 15, 27; 16:31; 17:4, 11 – 12, 17; 18:4 – 6, 28; 19:10, 17; also Rom 1:16; 2:9 – 10; 3:9; 10:12; 4:6; 1 Cor 1:24; 10:32; 12:13; Gal 3:28; 1 Thess 1:9 – 10.

tiles, have sinned and face God's wrath of judgment (Rom 1:18 – 3:20). The position of the phrase "toward God" highlights Paul's focus on God. People must acknowledge and express regret for their rebellion against God the Creator — rebellion expressed in perverted thinking about God and the world and themselves as well in perverted lifestyles — and turn to the one true and living God to serve him on his own terms.[41] The positive side of repentance is faith in the Lord Jesus. All people must acknowledge Jesus as Israel's crucified Messiah and risen Lord, who is the only Savior from God's impending judgment.[42]

On some occasions Paul stressed the need to turn away from worshiping images made by human hands;[43] on other occasions he emphasized the need for faith in Jesus as Israel's crucified and risen Messiah.[44] Thus both repentance and faith are related to God as well as to Jesus: repentance before God involves coming to faith in Jesus,[45] and believing in Jesus involves turning away from everything that displeases God.[46] In v. 20 Paul's message is described as what "is profitable." The gospel benefits those who come to faith in Jesus (the forgiveness of sins, the reconciliation with God), it brings an advantage to the believers (acquittal on the day of judgment), and it is profitable and useful for the everyday life of the believers (providing knowledge of God's will concerning holy living in an unholy world).

20:22 – 23 And now, compelled by the Spirit, I am going to Jerusalem without knowing what will happen to me there. I only know that the Holy Spirit testifies to me in city after city that imprisonment and hardships await me (καὶ νῦν ἰδοὺ δεδεμένος ἐγὼ τῷ πνεύματι πορεύομαι εἰς Ἰερουσαλὴμ τὰ ἐν αὐτῇ συναντήσοντά μοι μὴ εἰδώς, πλὴν ὅτι τὸ πνεῦμα τὸ ἅγιον κατὰ πόλιν διαμαρτύρεταί μοι λέγον ὅτι δεσμὰ καὶ θλίψεις με μένουσιν). In the second part of his speech,[47] Paul describes his prospects in Jerusalem, the city he plans to reach in a few weeks (vv. 22 – 24).

Paul begins by asserting that he does not know what will happen when he arrives in Jerusalem. He is going to Jerusalem "compelled" by the Spirit, i.e., under divine constraint.[48] In the context of passages that emphasize the guidance of the Holy Spirit in Paul's missionary work (13:2, 4, 9; 16:6 – 7; 19:21), and in the context of the reference to the Holy Spirit in v. 23 in connection with imprisonment and dangers waiting for him (cf. 21:6), the phrase "by the Spirit" (τῷ πνεύματι, instrumental dative) refers not to Paul's human spirit deciding to go to Jerusalem, but to God's Spirit, who imposed on him the necessity of visiting Jerusalem again.

The assertion that he does not know what will happen once he arrives in the city is qualified by the assertion that the Holy Spirit informs him that "imprisonment" (δεσμά; "bonds, fetters") and "hardships" (θλίψεις) await him there. Paul does not know the sequence of events or the outcome. He had been imprisoned in Philippi but was released (16:19 – 40), and he had been arrested and brought before the governor of the province of Achaia but was let go (18:12 – 17). He does not know all the

---

41. Cf. 2:38; 3:19; 14:15; 17:30 – 31; cf. Peterson, *Acts*, 565; cf. ibid. for the next comments.

42. Cf. 4:11 – 12; 10:42 – 43; 13:38 – 41; 15:11.

43. Cf. 14:15 (Lystra); 17:30 – 31 (Athens).

44. Cf. 13:38 – 41 (Pisidian Antioch); 16:31 (Philippi); 17:2 – 3 (Thessalonica).

45. Cf. 2 Cor 3:14 – 16 (Jews); 1 Thess 1:9 – 10 (Gentiles).

46. Cf. Rom 2:4; 2 Cor 7:9 – 10; 12:21; 2 Tim 2:25 – 26.

47. Note the introductory "and now" (καὶ νῦν ἰδού).

48. The basic meaning of the verb δέω is "to confine a person or thing by various kinds of restraint, *bind, tie*" (BDAG) and is often used for imprisonment (as in 9:2, 14, 21; 12:6: 21:11, 13, 33; 22:5, 29; 24:27). Here the term is used figuratively for inward constraint and compulsion. The participle (δεδεμένος) is modal or causal, explaining Paul's going to Jerusalem; the perfect tense of the participle indicates that the need to go to Jerusalem had been fixed in his mind for some time (cf. 19:21).

details, but he knows he will be imprisoned. The association of being constrained by the Holy Spirit in his missionary work and travels with a lack of knowledge is not really surprising. While God guides Paul's movements and even gives him supernatural, revelatory insight into what he should do (cf. 16:6 – 7; 18:9 – 10), the sequence and nature of events are either the result of his own decisions or of powers he cannot control. As it turns out, the imprisonment and trials he faces in Jerusalem do in fact not lead to his execution. Rather, he reaches the city of Rome, as he had planned, albeit as a prisoner.

20:24 However, I do not count my life as having any value for myself; my only aim is to finish the course and the ministry that I received from the Lord Jesus — the ministry of bearing witness to the good news of God's grace (ἀλλ' οὐδενὸς λόγου ποιοῦμαι τὴν ψυχὴν τιμίαν ἐμαυτῷ ὡς τελειῶσαι τὸν δρόμον μου καὶ τὴν διακονίαν ἣν ἔλαβον παρὰ τοῦ κυρίου Ἰησοῦ, διαμαρτύρασθαι τὸ εὐαγγέλιον τῆς χάριτος τοῦ θεοῦ). As Paul relates his anticipation of imprisonment in Jerusalem, he is willing to die in fulfilling his ministry. He has two basic convictions. First, he does not consider his life to be (lit.) "worth a single word";[49] i.e., his life has value less for himself than for the Lord. If the imprisonment in Jerusalem leads to his execution, he is willing to suffer the loss of his life, since that visit is not his own idea but part of God's plan. Second, he is fully and immovably dedicated to the task given to him by Jesus. Paul describes his self-understanding as preacher of the gospel as follows.

(1) Paul's life is a "course" (δρόμος) that has a definite purpose. The Greek term describes a run in a stadium from one end to the other and the race course itself, which, depending on the stadium, was between 175 and 208 yards (160 and 190 m.). The metaphor of the athlete running, as used by Paul, communicates goal-oriented behavior, arduous effort, and proclamation of the gospel.[50] The term δρόμος thus connotes Paul's total life commitment to his task, an absolute dedication of all aspects of his ministry, a resolute concentration of mind and will to his task, and a determined willingness to bear pain and suffering.[51]

(2) Paul's life is "ministry" (διακονία). The Greek term does not automatically denote the menial service of social-ethical support ministries, but emphasizes an official commissioning for a particular task as well as the responsibility and obligation necessary for the person who received the assignment (see on 1:25; 6:1). Paul's ministry is his task of proclaiming, teaching, explaining, and defending the gospel.[52] That his missionary and pastoral work is described as διακονία places him on the same level as the Twelve (cf. 1:25).

(3) Paul wants to "finish" the course well; i.e., he wants to keep running to the end and accomplish what he can. He wants to proclaim and explain the gospel in Jerusalem yet again, as the Spirit requires him to do, even if it results in suffering. He refuses to give up, which means that impending imprisonment in Jerusalem will not keep him from going there. He travels constrained by God's Spirit, and he will continue on this course, even if it means losing his life.

(4) Paul received his ministry from "the Lord Jesus." His life and work as a missionary were not

---

49. Thus the suggestion of BDAG, s.v. λόγος 1aα for the difficult construction οὐδενὸς λόγου ποιοῦμαι τὴν ψυχὴν τιμίαν.

50. Martin Brändl, *Der Agon bei Paulus: Herkunft und Profil paulinischer Agonmetaphorik* (WUNT 2.222; Tübingen: Mohr Siebeck, 2006), 279.

51. Cf. 1 Cor 9:24; Phil 3:14; 2 Tim 4:7, where Paul uses related athletic metaphors. The point in Paul's use of athletic metaphors is not the effort that is required to reach moral perfection, but his full engagement in the task of preaching the gospel. Cf. ibid., 409 – 22.

52. Cf. Rom 11:13; 2 Cor 4:1; 5:18; 6:3.

his own choice, but a commission he "received" (ἔλαβον) from Christ. The position of "Lord" (κυρίος) before Jesus underscores the authority of Jesus as the crucified, risen, and exalted Messiah who spoke to Paul from the heavenly reality of God's glory and who commissioned him as his "chosen instrument to carry my name before Gentiles and kings, and the people of Israel" (9:15).[53]

(5) Paul is a witness. His task and ministry is "bearing witness" (διαμαρτύρασθαι; see on 8:25). As a witness (μάρτυς; see on 1:8) he attests to what he has seen and heard — the life, death, and resurrection of Jesus, Israel's Messiah and Savior of the world. While he was not an eyewitness of these events, he has personally seen the risen Jesus. He is a witness in the sense that he testifies to realities that will allow others to accept the truth about Jesus.

(6) Paul proclaims "the good news of God's grace." The "good news" (τὸ εὐαγγέλιον), the gospel, is about the "grace" (χάρις) given by God to those who repent of their sins, who turn from false gods and from preconceived ideas about how Israel's God has to act, and who come to faith in Jesus as Messiah and Savior whose life, death, resurrection, and exaltation as Lord atones for sin and gives new life.[54] Paul's preaching is summarized in vv. 25, 27, 28, 32 with the terms "kingdom" (βασιλεία), "the whole will of God" (πᾶσα ἡ βουλὴ τοῦ θεοῦ), God's acquiring a covenant people through Jesus' blood shed on the cross; and, again, "grace."

20:25 And now I know that none of you among whom I went about proclaiming the kingdom will ever see me again (καὶ νῦν ἰδοὺ ἐγὼ οἶδα ὅτι οὐκέτι ὄψεσθε τὸ πρόσωπόν μου ὑμεῖς πάντες ἐν οἷς διῆλθον κηρύσσων τὴν βασιλείαν). In the third section of his speech, Paul again reviews his ministry in Ephesus (vv. 25 – 27). He begins by making a point about the future: this will be his last encounter with Ephesian believers (cf. v. 38). Paul is traveling to Jerusalem (v. 16) and then plans to go to Rome (19:21), where he hopes to receive support and help for the next phase of his missionary work in Spain (Rom 15:24 – 28). Paul's arrest in Jerusalem and his captivity in Caesarea (21:18 – 26:32) delays his plans of visiting Rome, which he eventually reaches, albeit as a prisoner (27:1 – 28:31).

It appears that Paul was released after two years of imprisonment in Rome, engaged in missionary work in Spain, and returned to the east, spending time on Crete (Titus 1:5), in Nicopolis in the province of Epirus (Titus 3:12), in Macedonia (1 Tim 1:3), and in Troas in the province of Asia (2 Tim 4:13).[55] If he did not return to Ephesus during his last journeys in the Aegean regions, his premonition in v. 25 proved to be correct; if he did visit Ephesus, his premonition would have been premature.

Paul describes his ministry in Ephesus in terms of proclamation (κηρύσσων), whose content he summarizes with the term "kingdom" (βασιλεία; see on 1:3), a term that underlines the continuity between the preaching of Jesus (Luke 4:43; 8:1; 9:11; Acts 1:3), of the Twelve (Luke 8:10), and of the Jerusalem church (cf. Acts 8:12). Paul's preaching is summarized in terms of the "kingdom of God" in 19:8; 28:23, 31 (cf. 14:22) as well.

---

53. Cf. 26:16; see Rom 1:1; 11:13; 15:15 – 16; 1 Cor 1:17; 2 Cor 5:18; Gal 1:1, 12.

54. On the "grace of God" cf. 11:23; 13:43; 14:26; and Rom 5:15; 1 Cor 1:4; 3:10; 15:10; 2 Cor 1:12; 6:1; 9:14; Gal 2:21; for the term "gospel of God" (εὐαγγέλιον τοῦ θεοῦ) cf. Rom 1:1; 15:16; 2 Cor 11:7; 1 Thess 2:2, 8 – 9.

55. Note the confident comment in Phil 1:25, the changed content and tone of 2 Timothy, and the early traditions about Paul preaching the gospel in Spain (e.g., *1 Clem.* 5:5 – 7; Muratorian Canon lines 35 – 39; *Acts of Peter* 1); cf. Murphy-O'Connor, *Paul*, 359 – 60; Schnabel, *Early Christian Mission*, 2:1270 – 87.

20:26 – 27 Therefore, I declare to you today that I am not responsible for the blood of anyone; for I have not hesitated to proclaim to you the whole will of God (διότι μαρτύρομαι ὑμῖν ἐν τῇ σήμερον ἡμέρᾳ ὅτι καθαρός εἰμι ἀπὸ τοῦ αἵματος πάντων· οὐ γὰρ ὑπεστειλάμην τοῦ μὴ ἀναγγεῖλαι πᾶσαν τὴν βουλὴν τοῦ θεοῦ ὑμῖν). Paul's next point asserts the faithful discharge of his ministry during his time in Ephesus. The strong verb "declare" (μαρτύρομαι),[56] denoting a solemn declaration, and the emphatic "today" mark Paul's statement as essential for his self-understanding as a preacher of the gospel. Paul is "not responsible for the blood of anyone"; he is "pure," i.e., free and thus innocent of the (eternal) death of anyone in Ephesus.

Paul makes the same assertion in 18:6 concerning the Jews in Corinth (see there for Old Testament parallels). He has fulfilled the responsibility that the prophet Ezekiel had been given as "a watchman for the people of Israel," whom God had commissioned to warn the wicked from their wicked ways in order to save their lives (Ezek 3:17 – 21). The conjunction at the beginning of Paul's statement (διότι) explains why he can depart from Ephesus and the province of Asia without planning a return visit and further preaching. He has made sure that all people were warned of God's judgment and heard the gospel. If people reject the gospel, he is not responsible for their condemnation.

The contrast of Paul's statement with his involvement in the stoning of Stephen (7:58) and the interrogation and imprisonment of followers of Jesus (8:3) is not "strange"[57] but an indication of the radical nature of God's forgiveness and of Paul's conversion. He was indeed responsible for the blood that Christians shed when he persecuted them, but this sin was forgiven when he received God's grace and Jesus' commission to bring about obedience to God and to Jesus Christ the Lord (Rom 1:5) — a commission he consistently and faithfully discharged since his encounter with the risen Lord on the road to Damascus.

Paul never "hesitated" (ὑπεστειλάμην; see on v. 20) to preach; i.e., he never held back or avoided proclaiming[58] the whole purpose and will of God[59] concerning the salvation of Jews and Gentiles through Jesus, Israel's crucified, risen, and exalted Messiah, Savior, and Lord. If Jews and Gentiles have refused to turn from their wicked ways and come to faith in Jesus as Savior (cf. 3:26; 13:38 – 41; 14:15; 17:30 – 31), they alone are responsible for the consequences of their condemnation: they have heard from Paul everything that they needed to hear in order to receive salvation. This is why Paul can leave, never to return.

20:28 Keep watch over yourselves and over the whole flock, in which the Holy Spirit has appointed you as overseers with the task of shepherding the church of God, which he has acquired with his own blood (προσέχετε ἑαυτοῖς καὶ παντὶ τῷ ποιμνίῳ, ἐν ᾧ ὑμᾶς τὸ πνεῦμα τὸ ἅγιον ἔθετο ἐπισκόπους ποιμαίνειν τὴν ἐκκλησίαν τοῦ θεοῦ, ἣν περιεποιήσατο διὰ τοῦ αἵματος τοῦ ἰδίου). In the fourth section of his address, Paul exhorts the Ephesian elders concerning the present and future tasks and responsibilities in the church (vv. 28 – 31), more particularly concerning their own and the community's spiritual integrity (v. 28) and concerning false teachers from outside and from inside the church (vv. 29 – 31).

The "elders" (πρεσβύτεροι) of v. 17 are described

---

56. Cf. BDAG, s.v. μαρτύρομαι 1, "to affirm something with solemnity, *testify, bear witness;*" cf. 26:22; Paul uses the verb in Gal 5:3; Eph 4:17; 1 Thess 2:12 as well; διαμαρτύρομαι is more frequent: 2:40; 8:25; 10:42; 18:5; 20:21, 23, 24; 23:11; 28:23.

57. Fitzmyer, *Acts*, 678.

58. For the verb ἀναγγέλλω see v. 20; also 14:27; 15:4; 19:18.

59. GNB, NASB, NET, NRSV; similarly KJV, RSV, ESV ("the whole counsel of God"); NLT "all that God wants you to know" is flat.

here as "overseers" (ἐπίσκοποι), a term that generally denotes "one who has the responsibility of safeguarding or seeing to it that something is done in the correct way, *guardian*"; in the Greco-Roman world, an ἐπίσκοπος is "one who has a definite function or fixed office of guardianship and related activity within a group" and who is thus an "overseer," a term that is a better rendering of the Greek than the loanword "bishop," which is "too technical and loaded with late historical baggage for precise signification of usage of ἐπίσκοπος" (BDAG).[60] This term is used in the LXX for God as judge of the ungodly (Job 20:29), for military leaders (Num 31:14; Judg 9:28; 2 Kgs 11:15), for rulers of the people (Isa 60:17), and for supervisors in the temple (Num 4:16; 2 Kgs 11:18; 12:12; 2 Chr 34:12, 17; Neh 11:22). In Greek texts, the term can be used for the gods who watch over people or objects given to them, for the captain of a ship, for various offices, particularly local officials and officers of clubs or associations, and for religious officials in temples.[61]

While some link the origin of the use of the term in the New Testament with the temple overseers in Judaism or with the officials in Greek associations, others suggest a connection with the *mebaqqer* of Qumran, a figure who has responsibility for teaching, judging the members of the community, handling money, assigning work, and examin-

ing candidates for membership.[62] The tradition-historical origin of the term is less important than its use in the New Testament (cf. Phil 1:1; 1 Tim 3:2; Titus 1:7; 1 Pet 2:25). In the context of Luke's narrative of Paul's ministry (vv. 17, 28 cf. 14:23), as supported by the evidence of Paul's letters, including the Pastoral Epistles, the two designations of "elder" and "overseer" refer to the same office.[63] While "elder" connotes the age, experience, and wisdom of the leaders of the Christian communities, "overseer" underlines "the more active side of their work in managing affairs, guarding the group, and directing activities."[64] The plural of both terms connotes plural leadership. Paul describes their tasks and responsibilities as follows.[65]

Elders/overseers watch over the community, the "flock," as shepherds (ποιμένες; cf. Eph 4:11) — people who care for their flock by nurturing (providing pasture and water) and by protecting (against dangers). The image of the shepherd is used in both Jewish and Greek sources for leaders and rulers.[66] As shepherds are concerned about their flock, so the elders/overseers must "keep watch" (προσέχετε), i.e., be in a state of alertness in terms of what the flock needs. The present tense of the imperative underscores the permanent nature of the responsibility of being vigilant.

These elders/overseers have two tasks. They must keep watch over themselves, taking care of

---

60. Most English translations use "overseer;" differently NJB ("guardians"), and NLT, which has "elders" and thus obliterates the different connotation of the term ἐπίσκοπος compared with πρεσβύτερος; GNB translates with a verbal phrase ("the flock which the Holy Spirit has placed in your care"). Everett Ferguson, *The Church of Christ: A Biblical Ecclesiology for Today* (Grand Rapids: Eerdmans, 1996), 318 – 27, retains "bishop." In the New Testament, ἐπίσκοπος is not a title but the description of a function.

61. Cf. Benjamin L. Merkle, *The Elder and Overseer: One Office in the Early Church* (Studies in Biblical Literature 57; New York: Lang, 2003), 59 – 61, for evidence.

62. Cf. Barbara E. Thiering, "*Mebaqqer* and *Episkopos* in

the Light of the Temple Scroll," *JBL* 100 (1981): 59 – 74; see the discussion in Ferguson, *Biblical Ecclesiology*, 319 – 23.

63. Cf. Merkle, *Elder and Overseer*, 67 – 160; Trebilco, *Early Christians in Ephesus*, 187.

64. Ferguson, *Biblical Ecclesiology*, 323.

65. The qualifications for the office of elder/overseers are described in 1 Tim 3:1 – 7; Titus 1:5 – 9, most having to do with character.

66. For the metaphor of shepherding God's flock, see Ps 100:3; Isa 40:11; Jer 13:17; Ezek 34; for God as shepherd see in particular Ps 23. For the image of shepherding in the New Testament, cf. John 10; 21:15 – 17; 1 Pet 2:25; 5:2; Heb 13:20; Jude 12.

their own theological, spiritual, and ethical integrity. If they do not nurture themselves, they cannot take care of others. They must also keep watch over "the whole flock" ($\pi\alpha\nu\tau\grave{\iota}$ $\tau\hat{\omega}$ $\pi o\iota\mu\nu\acute{\iota}\omega$), caring for all members of the church — Jewish and Gentile believers, slaves and freeborn, rich and poor, men and women, and old and young.[67]

While the overseers lead the flock, they are at the same time part of the flock. They are not set over against the church but are an integral part of it. The care for the church is a task to which the Holy Spirit has "appointed" ($\check{\epsilon}\theta\epsilon\tau o$) them. When Paul and his coworkers appointed elders (14:23, with the verb $\chi\epsilon\iota\rhoo\tau ov\acute{\epsilon}\omega$, "appoint, install"), they acted with the authority of the Holy Spirit. The leaders of the church are neither chosen "from below" in a "democratic" election, nor imposed "from above" by a decision of apostles, but "from within" as the Holy Spirit is present and active in the church as God's holy temple, "choosing and preparing by his gifts those who are to be ministers."[68]

The congregation ($\check{\epsilon}\kappa\kappa\lambda\eta\sigma\acute{\iota}\alpha$; see on 5:11) belongs to God ($\tauo\hat{\upsilon}$ $\theta\epsilon o\hat{\upsilon}$; genitive of possession),[69] not to the overseers. While shepherds may own the flock for which they care, it is God who "owns" the church, and it is his will (v. 27) that is to be proclaimed and explained when the gospel is preached. Thus, the elders/overseers/shepherds must focus on the welfare of the believers, not on any benefits they themselves may have (see also vv. 33 – 35).

The church is described as having been "acquired with his own blood." The verb used here

($\pi\epsilon\rho\iota\epsilon\pi o\iota\acute{\eta}\sigma\alpha\tau o$) denotes "to gain possession of something" and can be translated as "acquire, obtain, gain for oneself." It describes the action by which God has acquired the community of believers as his people. The statement stands in continuity with Isa 43:21,[70] where Yahweh speaks of his people "I formed [$\pi\epsilon\rho\iota\epsilon\pi o\iota\eta\sigma\acute{\alpha}\mu\eta\nu$] for myself that they may proclaim my praise" because he is the only Savior (43:11). The verb emphasizes that the church is not a human institution.

The phrase "with his own blood" ($\delta\iota\grave{\alpha}$ $\tauo\hat{\upsilon}$ $\alpha\check{\iota}\mu\alpha\tauo\varsigma$ $\tauo\hat{\upsilon}$ $\grave{\iota}\delta\acute{\iota}o\upsilon$) is difficult, at first sight, when seen in the context of the reference to "God" in the previous clause. Six main suggestions for understanding the phrase have been made.[71] (1) The blood is God's own blood. This would mean that "when Jesus Christ shed his blood on the cross he was acting as the representative of God; he was God's way of giving life, blood, for the world."[72] (2) The blood is the "heart blood" of Jesus the Son, understood at the same time as the blood of God the Father, in the context of the conviction that the Father and the Son are one in thought and action. (3) The blood is Jesus' blood: Luke moves from a statement about God (acquiring the church) to a statement about Jesus (shedding his blood), without providing a transition; or he combines a statement about the church (of God) with a traditional statement about Jesus' death. (4) The blood is Paul's blood. Luke asserts that it is Paul and his blood as martyr, shed in the service of establishing the church. (5) The Greek term should be understood as "blood relative." God preserved ($\pi\epsilon\rho\iota\epsilon\pi o\iota\acute{\eta}\sigma\alpha\tau o$)

---

67. See the so-called "household codes" in Col 3:18 – 4:1; Eph 5:22 – 6:9; 1 Tim 2:8 – 15; 6:1 – 2; Titus 2:1 – 10.

68. Barrett, *Acts*, 974 – 75; he asserts that "there is no suggestion of any succession in episcopal office; there is no need for succession (in the commonly understood sense); the Holy Spirit will provide ministers as they are required" (976).

69. Cf. 1 Cor 1:2; 10:32; 11:22; 15:9; 2 Cor 1:1; Gal 1:13; 1 Tim 3:5, 15; the plural "churches of God" occurs in 1 Cor 11:16; 1 Thess 2:14; 2 Thess 1:4.

70. Marshall, "Acts," 596. See also Mal 3:17.

71. Cf. Murray J. Harris, *Jesus as God: The New Testament Use of Theos in Reference to Jesus* (Grand Rapids: Baker, 1992), 137 – 41; Walton, *Leadership*, 96 – 98.

72. Barrett, *Acts*, 977, with reference to Calvin, who points to the figure of speech of the *communicatio idiomatum*: "the property of one nature is applied to the other" (Calvin, *Acts*, 184).

his congregation by means of the one nearest to him. (6) The blood is the blood of Jesus, who is described as God's "own." The term "his own" (ὁ ἴδιος), while unique as a christological title in the New Testament, corresponds to titles such "the beloved" (ὁ ἀγαπητός).[73]

The first suggestion is usually regarded as unlikely since the phrase "the blood of God" does not occur in Christian literature before the second century,[74] though, since there are other unique statements in the speech, this interpretation cannot be ruled out. Luke is evidently "less concerned to assign precise roles to God and Jesus than to locate the church's origin in their actions."[75] The second suggestion downplays the fact that the Greek term αἷμα refers to real blood, signifying death, and is closer to John than to Luke.[76] The third proposal ignores the fact that there is no explicit change of subject in the Greek sentence. The problem of the fourth proposal is the aorist tense of the verb (rather than the future tense), and the question how Paul's martyrdom was instrumental in acquiring the Ephesian church for God. The fifth proposal is unlikely since it ignores the meaning of "blood" in the LXX. While the sixth proposal assumes a unique christological title, it can be defended on the grounds that there are other unique features in the speech.[77]

The reference to Jesus' blood describes his death as a sacrificial, vicarious death that brought the messianic people of God into existence.[78] This phrase reminds Luke's readers of the Last Supper, where Jesus spoke about God's establishing the new covenant through Jesus' blood (Luke 22:20).[79] By Jesus' death (διά is instrumental), God fulfilled the promises given to Abraham, establishing a universal covenant people consisting of Jews and Gentiles[80] — which is the "church of God," in which the Holy Spirit has appointed the elders as shepherds (note references to God, to the Spirit, and to "blood," which implies the Son).

20:29   I know that after my departure fierce wolves will come in among you, who will not spare the flock (ἐγὼ οἶδα ὅτι εἰσελεύσονται μετὰ τὴν ἄφιξίν μου λύκοι βαρεῖς εἰς ὑμᾶς μὴ φειδόμενοι τοῦ ποιμνίου). After the exhortation to the elders to keep watch over themselves and over the congregation, Paul exhorts them to be vigilant about false teachers (vv. 29 – 31).

First, he warns the elders of the danger from false teachers who infiltrate the church from outside. The reference to "fierce wolves" continues the metaphor of the flock.[81] In biblical and Jewish tradition, the wolf is a predator, a fierce and vicious animal that tears its prey to pieces.[82] In Greek literature, people who are "faithless, treacherous, pestilent" are compared with wolves (Epictetus 1.3.7). The wolf is described as "bold, treacherous, vicious, plundering, greedy, harmful, deceitful, offering help in order to harm" (Polemo, *Physiogn.*

---

73. Cf. Mark 1:11; 9:7; 2 Pet 1:17 (ὁ ἀγαπητός); Eph 1:6 (ὁ ἠγαπημένος).

74. Ignatius, *Eph.* 1.1.

75. Gaventa, "Miletus Speech," 48 – 49.

76. Cf. John 14:7 – 11; 17:21 – 23.

77. Walton, *Leadership*, 97.

78. For references to the blood of Christ (on the cross) in Paul's letters, cf. Rom 3:25; 5:9; 1 Cor 10:16; 11:25, 27; Col 1:20. Bock, *Acts*, 630, compares with Abraham's willingness to sacrifice Isaac, his only son (Gen 22), "only here God does carry out the offering so that others can benefit from the sacrifice."

79. Cf. Hans Jörg Sellner, *Das Heil Gottes: Studien zur So-*teriologie des lukanischen Doppelwerks (BZNW 152; Berlin: De Gruyter, 2007), 475. Note that in Luke 22:19 – 20, the allusion to the Passover lamb is explicit.

80. Cf. Luke 1:73 – 75; Acts 3:24; 7:8.

81. In Matt 10:16 / Luke 10:3 Jesus sends the Twelve "like sheep among wolves," i.e., as messengers who are in danger of being devoured. In contrast, Paul in v. 29 does not refer to persecution by unbelievers.

82. Cf. Jer 5:6; Hab 1:8; Zeph 3:3; *Jos. Asen.* 12:9 – 10. Isaiah 11:1 – 6; 65:25 describes the coming kingdom of God as an era of peace when lambs and wolves will live and feed together.

172).[83] Paul predicts that dangerous people — people whose behavior is bad, treacherous, impious — will come into the congregation, presumably from other churches, who will not spare the believers. The metaphor of the wolves shows that "the error is not a minor evil but represents a mortal threat to the community which has to be averted."[84]

The seriousness of the activity of these infiltrating teachers is also highlighted by the reference to the enormous value of the congregation that has been obtained with the price of God's own Son (v. 28). The comparison with the current elders in v. 30 suggests that they are teachers with their own brand of theological and ethical emphasis, teachers who "pursue their own ends regardless of what becomes of the church."[85] Paul's subsequent point in vv. 33 – 35 that he did not live at the expense of the Ephesian believers and his challenge to the elders that they should be focusing on giving rather than on receiving suggest that the traveling teachers who will reach Ephesus must be measured by this norm as well.

Paul's letter to the Christians in the Galatian churches deals with the impact of false teachers who confuse believers and who pervert the gospel of Jesus Christ (Gal 1:7; 3:1). In his follow-up letter to the Corinthian Christians, which he had recently written, he says with regard to false teachers that "if someone comes to you and preaches a Jesus other than the Jesus we preached, or if you receive a different spirit from the Spirit you received, or a different gospel from the one you accepted, you put up with it easily enough"; Paul goes on to describe them as boasters who are "false apostles, deceitful workers, masquerading as apostles of Christ" (2 Cor 11:4, 13). In his letters to the believers in

Philippi and Colossae, the dangerous influence of false teachers from outside is also underscored (Phil 3:2 – 4; Col 2:4, 8).

According to John 10:11, Jesus described himself as the true shepherd who protects against the wolves who, like thieves, want to snatch away sheep and devour them. Paul exhorts the Ephesian elders to recognize the danger that false teachers from outside pose and to prevent such people having any influence in the congregation. The reference to "many deceivers" who have "gone out into the world" and who want to infiltrate and influence more churches in 2 John 7 – 11 indicates that Paul's prophecy was indeed fulfilled, thirty or forty years after his farewell from the Ephesian elders (the letters 1 – 3 John are traditionally linked with Ephesus).

20:30 From among yourselves men will rise up and teach perversions of the truth in order to draw the disciples away as their followers (καὶ ἐξ ὑμῶν αὐτῶν ἀναστήσονται ἄνδρες λαλοῦντες διεστραμμένα τοῦ ἀποσπᾶν τοὺς μαθητὰς ὀπίσω αὐτῶν). Second, Paul warns of the danger from false teachers who exert influence from within the church. These men will rise up from among the believers in Ephesus themselves, perhaps even from among the group of overseers. They will speak perversions (διεστραμμένα),[86] i.e., teachings that deviate from the truth of the gospel. They "draw the disciples away" after them as their followers, which means their activity will result in a schism of the church. Depending on the number and influence of these teachers, they split the church into two, or three, or four congregations, each with a different teaching that strays from the truth.

In his first letter to Corinthians, Paul had to ad-

---

83. Cf. Parsons, *Body and Character*, 73.

84. G. Bornkamm, "λύκος," *TDNT* 4:310.

85. Barrett, *Acts*, 978. Note that according to Matt 7:15 Jesus warned of false prophets who come in sheep's clothing but who are inwardly "ferocious wolves" (λύκοι ἅρπαγες).

86. The nominalized perfect passive participle describes the content of their teaching: "perverse things" (cf. BDAG, s.v. διαστρέφω 2, "to cause to depart from an accepted standard of moral or spiritual values, *make crooked, pervert*").

dress divisions within the church, which evidently resulted not so much from false theology but from secular values that caused believers to admire brilliant rhetoric and clever arguments more than the message of Jesus, the crucified Messiah (1 Cor 1 – 4), and which caused them to shame the poor believers during common meals in the congregation (1 Cor 11:18 – 19). In his letter to the Christians in Rome, which he had just written, Paul exhorts the believers "watch out for those who cause divisions and put obstacles in your way that are contrary to the teaching you have learned. Keep away from them. For such people are not serving our Lord Christ, but their own appetites. By smooth talk and flattery they deceive the minds of naive people" (Rom 16:17 – 18). In Rom 15:30 – 32 he expected trouble both from unbelievers in Judea and from Jewish believers in Jerusalem who might oppose him.

Here, Paul exhorts the Ephesian elders to recognize the danger that false teachers who are members of the church will pose for the congregation and to prevent them from teaching and from creating subgroups within the church. The evidence of 1 John indicates that Paul's prophecy of internal heresy leading to divisions was fulfilled a generation later.[87] The message to the church in Ephesus in Rev 2:1 – 7 praises the congregation for hating "the practices of the Nicolaitans" (Rev 2:6), a group present in Ephesus; they taught that "it was acceptable for Christians to eat food which had been offered to idols and to be involved in some undefined way in pagan worship, perhaps including the imperial cult" in the effort to avoid persecution and enjoy more harmonious relations with non-Christians.[88]

20:31 Therefore, be vigilant, remembering that for three years I never stopped instructing each of you night and day with tears (διὸ γρηγορεῖτε μνημονεύοντες ὅτι τριετίαν νύκτα καὶ ἡμέραν οὐκ ἐπαυσάμην μετὰ δακρύων νουθετῶν ἕνα ἕκαστον). Third, Paul repeats the exhortation to be vigilant, reminding the Ephesian elders of his ministry among them. This exhortation applies both to the need to keep watch over themselves and over the congregation as overseers (v. 28), and to the need to inhibit false teachers from the outside (v. 29) and on the inside of the church (v. 30). The present imperative "be vigilant" (γρηγορεῖτε) corresponds to the present imperative "keep watch" (προσέχετε) in v. 28.

Paul then references his behavior during the three years (cf. 19:8, 10) when he was active in Ephesus. As he watched over the believers in the congregation, so they must be alert as they fulfill their responsibilities. Paul describes his Ephesian ministry succinctly as follows. (1) He "instructed" (νουθετῶν) the believers; i.e., he counseled them "about avoidance or cessation of an improper course of conduct."[89] (2) He instructed "each" of the elders and the members of the congregation without exception. (3) He "never stopped" (οὐκ ἐπαυσάμην) instructing them during his three years in Ephesus, a statement that is reinforced by the phrase "night and day" (νύκτα καὶ ἡμέραν; accusatives of time). Paul's manual labor by which he supported himself (v. 34) was part of his ceaseless

---

87. Cf. Robert W. Yarbrough, *1 – 3 John* (BECNT; Grand Rapids: Baker, 2008), 52, suggesting that 1 John 1:6 – 10 possibly "reflects the situation in Asia Minor that Paul feared and projected might arise (Acts 20:30), with treacherous leaders betraying apostolic teaching and leading Christians astray."

88. Trebilco, *Early Christians in Ephesus*, 320. See particularly the description in Rev 2:14 – 16, 20. John calls idolatry (spiritual) "sexual immorality."

89. BDAG, s.v. νουθετέω, suggesting "admonish, warn, instruct" as translations. Most English translations use "warn" (NET, NIV, NRSV, TNIV) or "admonish" (ESV, NASB, RSV). The verb is used elsewhere in the New Testament only in Paul's letters: Rom 15:14; 1 Cor 4:14; Col 1:28; 3:16; 1 Thess 5:12, 14; 2 Thess 3:15; Titus 1:11; the noun (νουθεσία) is used in 1 Cor 10:11; Eph 6:4; Titus 3:10.

endeavors. (4) He taught the believers "with tears" (μετὰ δακρύων; see on v. 19), i.e., with intense personal involvement. This persistence and integrity of Paul's teaching in the church of Ephesus should serve as an example for the elders.[90]

20:32 Now I commend you to God and to the message about his grace, who is able to build you up and to give you the inheritance among all those who are sanctified (καὶ τὰ νῦν παρατίθεμαι ὑμᾶς τῷ θεῷ καὶ τῷ λόγῳ τῆς χάριτος αὐτοῦ, τῷ δυναμένῳ οἰκοδομῆσαι καὶ δοῦναι τὴν κληρονομίαν ἐν τοῖς ἡγιασμένοις πᾶσιν). In his conclusion (vv. 32 – 35)[91] Paul entrusts the elders to God's grace, before a final reminder of his ministry in Ephesus and an exhortation to support the weak. The conclusion begins with a blessing: he "commends" them to God; i.e., he entrusts them for safekeeping to God's care and protection. Paul's departure does not leave them helplessly alone, since it is (and always has been) God himself who is active in and among believers in Jesus who are committed to the gospel. The future of the congregation "belongs neither with the 'wolves' nor with the 'shepherds,' but with God."[92]

The phrase "and to the message about his grace" is a hendiadys (see on 1:7), explaining the one concept that it is God who is active in the "message" or word (λόγος)[93] about God's grace that Paul has proclaimed in Ephesus and which the Ephesian elders continue to preach and to live by. The gospel of Jesus Christ is the word of saving "grace" (χάρις; see on 4:33; 15:11),[94] granted by God to those who come to faith in Jesus.

Since God is active in the proclamation of the gospel, the Ephesians can have confidence that the congregation will be "built up" (οἰκοδομῆσαι). For the metaphor of the congregation as a building see on 9:31.[95] The good news of God's gracious, salvific revelation through Jesus, Israel's crucified and risen Messiah and the Savior and Lord of all humankind, is the foundation of the (spiritual) building being constructed by God. This is an ongoing "project" in which the Ephesian elders have important responsibilities as they help all believers in the congregation to be living "stones" in this building in which God is present through his Spirit. The power to upbuild the congregation rests with God and his word — with God who is active in his word and who sustains, develops, and expands the life of the congregation.

The second effect of God's powerful presence through the proclamation of the word of his saving grace is that the believers will receive the "inheritance" (κληρονομία), i.e., the blessings, of God's consummated salvation in the destiny of all believers in the age to come.[96] The reference to the "inheritance" that "all those who are sanctified" (ἡγιασμένοις)[97] will receive echoes Deut 33:3 – 4 LXX ("And he spared his people, and all of the sanctified ones [πάντες οἱ ἡγιασμένοι] were under your hands — even these are under you,

---

90. The present tense of the participle "remembering" reinforces the exhortation that Paul's behavior continues to be a model for their own responsibilities. The verb (μνημονεύω) means "remember, keep in mind, think of" (BDAG).

91. Note again the phrase "now" (καὶ [τὰ] νῦν), after vv. 22, 25.

92. Gaventa, *Acts*, 289.

93. For λόγος as the message of the gospel see 1 Cor 1:18; 14:36; 15:2; 2 Cor 2:17; 5:19; Gal 6:6; 1 Thess 1:8; 2:13.

94. Cf. Rom 3:24; 4:16; 5:2, 15, 20 – 21; 6:14; 2 Cor 4:15; 6:1; 8:9; Gal 1:6, 15; 2:21.

95. In Paul's letters, the metaphor is used in Rom 14:19;

15:2; 1 Cor 3:9; 8:1; 10:23; 14:3 – 5, 12, 17, 26; 2 Cor 10:8; 12:19; 13:10; Eph 4:12, 29; 1 Thess 5:11.

96. For the symbol of the "inheritance" in Paul's letters, cf. 1 Cor 6:9 – 10; 15:50; Gal 3:18, 29; 4:30; 5:21; Eph 1:14, 18; 5:5; Col 3:24; Titus 3:7. On the link with the concept of the promised land as an inheritance in Gen 15:7; Exod 6:8; 15:17; Josh 11:23; Isa 49:8, see Pao, *New Exodus*, 174 – 76.

97. The passive voice of the nominalized participle (ἡγιασμένοις) implies God as the one who made the believers holy; the perfect tense underlines that the holiness of the believers is a present and future state, or status, they have received.

and it [i.e. the people] accepted from his words a law, which Moses commanded us, an inheritance [κληρονομίαν] for the congregation of Jacob"; cf. also Ps 16:5/LXX 15:5). Paul asserts that God makes sure that the Ephesian elders and all the believers in Ephesus will be "given a share in the blessings of God's salvation in and with the whole of God's new people."[98]

20:33 – 34 I have never desired anyone's silver or gold or clothing. You yourselves know that these hands of mine served my own needs as well as the needs of those who were with me (ἀργυρίου ἢ χρυσίου ἢ ἱματισμοῦ οὐδενὸς ἐπεθύμησα· αὐτοὶ γινώσκετε ὅτι ταῖς χρείαις μου καὶ τοῖς οὖσιν μετ᾽ ἐμοῦ ὑπηρέτησαν αἱ χεῖρες αὗται). In a final retrospect on his missionary work in Ephesus, Paul asserts his integrity in financial matters. He never desired to secure "silver or gold" (i.e., money in the form of silver or gold coins). Nor did Paul expect material compensation in the form of "clothing." Paul never expected to be paid for his missionary and pastoral work; he was not interested in personal gain, nor was he motivated by greed.[99]

Paul did accept gifts from other churches after he had left them (2 Cor 11:8 – 9; Phil 4:15 – 16), but not from the people among whom he was preaching the gospel.[100] Paul reminds the Ephesian elders that he provided for his own needs as well for the needs of his coworkers.[101] The demonstrative pronoun (αὗται) at the end of v. 34 implies that Paul

showed his hands to the Ephesian elders as he was speaking.

20:35 "I showed you at every opportunity that we must support the weak by such hard work, remembering the word of the Lord Jesus, for he said, 'It is more blessed to give than to receive'" (πάντα ὑπέδειξα ὑμῖν ὅτι οὕτως κοπιῶντας δεῖ ἀντιλαμβάνεσθαι τῶν ἀσθενούντων, μνημονεύειν τε τῶν λόγων τοῦ κυρίου Ἰησοῦ ὅτι αὐτὸς εἶπεν· μακάριόν ἐστιν μᾶλλον διδόναι ἢ λαμβάνειν). Paul's care for his coworkers is a model that the Ephesian elders should emulate. He focused his selfless and supportive behavior on the people in Ephesus rather than on himself; "at every opportunity" he showed them that Christians — in particular, leaders of the church — must support the weak by hard work.

The verb translated as "I showed" (ὑπέδειξα) often means "to direct someone's attention to something, indicate, point out," with the extended sense "to give instruction or moral direction" with the translation "show, give direction, prove, set forth" (BDAG), and in some contexts, as here, denotes more specifically "to set a pattern or example." Paul engaged in "hard work" (κοπιῶντας); the present tense of the verb, which denotes not simply "work" but "to exert oneself physically, mentally, or spiritually,"[102] underscores the constant necessity of working hard in order to be able to help the weak.[103] The term "the weak" (οἱ ἀσθενοῦντες) describes here

---

98. Marshall, "Acts," 597.

99. Cf. 1 Cor 9:12 – 15; 2 Cor 7:2; 11:8 – 9; Phil 4:10 – 11. The language of v. 34 is similar to that of the prophet Samuel at the end of his life, cf. 1 Sam 12:3 – 4; cf. Fitzmyer, *Acts*, 681.

100. 1 Cor 9:12 – 15. He did not want to become dependent on patrons; cf. John K. Chow, *Patronage and Power: A Study of Social Networks at Corinth* (JSNTSup 75; Sheffield: Sheffield Academic Press, 1992), 106 – 7. In 1 Cor 9:4 – 12 Paul defends the right of missionaries to be supported by churches.

101. In 18:3, Paul was working as a tentmaker in the shop of Aquila and Priscilla (cf. 1 Cor 4:12; 9:15 – 18; 1 Thess 2:9; 2 Thess 3:6 – 10).

102. BDAG, s.v. κοπιάω 2, with the translation options "work hard, toil, strive, struggle." The verb is used only here in Acts; cf. Luke 5:5; 12:27; in Paul's letters it often includes missionary work, cf. Rom 16:6, 12; 1 Cor 4:12; 15:10; 16:16; Gal 4:11; Eph 4:28; Phil 2:16; Col 1:29; 1 Thess 5:12; 1 Tim 4:10; 5:17; 2 Tim 2:6.

103. On the care for the weak, see Rom 14:1 – 2, 21; 1 Cor 1:27; 4:10; 8:11 – 12; 9:22; 12:22; see also Rom 15:1; Gal 6:2; Eph 4:28; 1 Thess 4:10 – 11; 5:14. On the care for widows see 1 Tim 5:3 – 10; cf. Acts 6:1 – 6.

not the physically ill, but people who "experience some personal incapacity or limitation" causing a lack of material necessities.[104]

The verb translated as "support" (ἀντιλαμβάνεσθαι) describes the assistance that the elders must provide for those who need help. Such support is grounded in the mandate given in a "word" (λόγος) or saying of Jesus, whose instructions they must remember (μνημονεύειν; cf. v. 31) and obey since he is "Lord" (κύριος). If God's displeasure with the church in Ephesus revealed in the prophetic word of Rev 2:4 — the church had abandoned the love they had at first — includes active love for those in the congregation who need it most, i.e., for the weak,[105] later leaders of the Ephesian church did not live up to Paul's example.

Paul quotes a word of Jesus not found in the gospel tradition, but a word that they know and must remember: Those who "give" to others, rather than thinking about "receiving" from others, enjoy God's blessing (μακάριον). The term μακάριος describes in the Greco-Roman world those on whom fortune smiles ("being fortunate or happy because of circumstances," thus "fortunate, happy" or "privileged, blessed" [BDAG]; from a transcendent perspective it denotes people who are "especially favored," thus "blessed, fortunate, happy, privileged"). The New Testament beatitudes (cf. Matt 5:3–12) use a Greek term that translates the Hebrew (ʾašrē),[106] which denotes a state of true well-being. In the beatitudes, as here, the focus is

on being truly content, living the good life among God's people and thus in God's presence.

The logic of the comparative translated as "more" (μᾶλλον) should not be pressed.[107] Those who can give to those in need are morally obligated to do so, and, more importantly, they will be truly content and blessed if they use their resources for the benefit of others who are not as fortunate. Paul's reminder of Jesus' word about giving[108] breaks the cycle of the Greco-Roman principle of reciprocity, which describes the practice of voluntary requital. Following Jesus' word on selfless giving will protect the Ephesian elders from misusing their position in the church in selfish ways. As Paul ends his address to the elders, he pronounces a final blessing, spoken by Jesus himself, promised to those who serve the "sheep" of God's flock as Jesus served those in need of help (cf. Luke 15:4).

20:36–37 When he had finished speaking, he knelt down with all of them and prayed. They all wept loudly as they embraced Paul and kissed him (καὶ ταῦτα εἰπὼν θεὶς τὰ γόνατα αὐτοῦ σὺν πᾶσιν αὐτοῖς προσηύξατο. ἱκανὸς δὲ κλαυθμὸς ἐγένετο πάντων καὶ ἐπιπεσόντες ἐπὶ τὸν τράχηλον τοῦ Παύλου κατεφίλουν αὐτόν). Luke's report of the meeting of Paul and the Ephesian elders ends with a farewell scene (vv. 36–38). The sentence begins with two temporal participles: after Paul had spoken (εἰπών) and after he and the elders knelt down (θεὶς τὰ γόνατα), he prays (προσηύξατο). On prayer see on 2:42.

---

104. BDAG, s.v. ἀσθενέω, lists v. 35 under meaning 3 ("to experience lack of material necessities, *be in need*"), which does not need to be distinguished from meaning 2 ("to experience some personal incapacity or limitation, *be weak* of weakness in general").

105. See the discussion in Grant R. Osborne, *Revelation* (BECNT; Grand Rapids: Baker Academic, 2002), 115–16.

106. *HALOT*, s.v. אַשְׁרֵי, "the formal introduction of a blessing" with the translation options "happy, blessed is he who."

107. Both the exclusive interpretation (giving is blessed, not receiving) and the strictly logical comparative interpretation (those who give are more blessed than those who receive) are hardly correct. The saying addresses those for whom both giving and receiving is an option, and they are told that they will be more content when they give than when they receive; cf. Barrett, *Acts*, 983. The saying does not assert that people who have no choice but to receive do not receive God's blessing.

108. The essence of Jesus' saying can be found in Luke 6:35–36. There are parallels in Greek literature (Plutarch, *Mor.* 173D, 181F; Seneca, *Ep.* 81.17; Thucydides, *Hist.* 2.97.4).

The phrase "with all of them" is most plausibly construed with the kneeling[109] and then by implication with the prayer. They all kneel, probably Paul taking the initiative, and Paul prays. Kneeling (or "bending the knee," e.g., Isa 45:23; Phil 2:10) is a gesture of humility before a superior, and at the same time a gesture of reverence before God. The prayer presumably contained intercession for the Ephesian elders in their tasks as leaders of the congregation, a blessing for the elders, and a petition for a safe journey for Paul.

Luke reports a threefold reaction of the elders to Paul's address and prayer. They "weep," they "embrace" Paul, and they "kiss" him.[110] The public kiss among Christians signals the freedom of the Christians "to express without inhibition to all people of whatever background, rank or gender, the ardour of ἀγάπη in any context."[111] The scene is clearly emotional, hardly surprising given Paul's final farewell.

20:38 They were especially pained on account of his statement that they would never see him again. Then they accompanied him to the ship (ὀδυνώμενοι μάλιστα ἐπὶ τῷ λόγῳ ᾧ εἰρήκει, ὅτι οὐκέτι μέλλουσιν τὸ πρόσωπον αὐτοῦ θεωρεῖν. προέπεμπον δὲ αὐτὸν εἰς τὸ πλοῖον). Luke explains the elders' grief with Paul's "statement" (λόγος) that he is leaving Ephesus and the province of Asia permanently, never to return. The episode ends with the comment that the elders accompany Paul from their meeting place in the city to the harbor of Miletus and to the ship booked for the journey to Syria.

21:1 After we had torn ourselves away from them, we set sail, ran a straight course, and came to Cos. The next day we sailed to Rhodes and from there to Patara (ὡς δὲ ἐγένετο ἀναχθῆναι ἡμᾶς ἀποσπασθέντας ἀπ᾽ αὐτῶν, εὐθυδρομήσαντες ἤλθομεν εἰς τὴν Κῶ, τῇ δὲ ἑξῆς εἰς τὴν Ῥόδον κἀκεῖθεν εἰς Πάταρα). The third episode narrates Paul's journey from Miletus to Jerusalem and his visits to the believers in Tyre, Ptolemais, and Caesarea (21:1 – 17). The sea journey from Miletus to Caesarea was 578 nautical miles (1070 km.), the land journey from Caesarea to Jerusalem 63 miles (100 km.).

The first incident relates Paul's journey from Miletus via Cos, Rhodes, and Patara to Tyre[112] and his meeting with the believers in Tyre (vv. 1 – 6). The departure of Paul and his associates is related with two verbs: the "we" narrator reports that "we tore ourselves away" (ἀποσπασθέντας; temporal participle) and "set sail" (ἀναχθῆναι ἡμᾶς). The sea journey from Miletus to Tyre has two parts, as the travel party needs to book passage on two ships. The first leg takes them from Miletus in a straight course south, passing between the mainland and the islands of Kalymna and Pserimos, heading to Cos, the chief city of the island with the same name, famous for its export of wine and olive oil, fine weaving products, and ointments.

After staying overnight, they sailed the next day between the island of Nisyros and the Chersonesus peninsula and arrived at Rhodes, an important commercial center for trade in the Mediterranean, located on the northern end of the island of Rhodes. The ship evidently anchored for the night,

---

109. Thus most English versions; ESV, RSV, and NASB link the prepositional phrase with the following verb ("he knelt down and prayed with them all"), similarly NLT.

110. In Jewish society, the kiss was a form of greeting between relatives or hosts and guests upon arrival (Gen 29:11 – 13; 45:15; Exod 4:27; 18:7; Luke 7:36 – 46) or departure (Gen 31:28; Ruth 1:14).

111. William Klassen, "The Sacred Kiss in the New Testament: An Example of Social Boundary Lines," *NTS* 39 (1993): 122 – 35, 130.

112. With favorable winds, this distance could be covered in a week of sailing, assuming overnight stays in Cos and Rhodes.

then continued to Patara, a port city in western Lycia. Patara's harbor was used by the grain ships that sailed between Egypt (Alexandria) and Italy (Rome) (see on 27:6), which enabled Paul and his associates to find a ship to take them further east.

21:2 – 3 When we found a ship there bound for Phoenicia, we went on board and set sail. When we caught sight of Cyprus, we passed to the south of it, sailed to Syria, and landed at Tyre, because the ship had to unload its cargo there (καὶ εὑρόντες πλοῖον διαπερῶν εἰς Φοινίκην ἐπιβάντες ἀνήχθημεν. ἀναφάναντες δὲ τὴν Κύπρον καὶ καταλιπόντες αὐτὴν εὐώνυμον ἐπλέομεν εἰς Συρίαν καὶ κατήλθομεν εἰς Τύρον· ἐκεῖσε γὰρ τὸ πλοῖον ἦν ἀποφορτιζόμενον τὸν γόμον). The second leg of Paul's voyage, on another ship they found in Patara, took them from southern Asia Minor to the coast of Phoenicia (see on 11:19). Leaving the port of Patara, they sailed in a southeasterly direction past Cyprus to the coast of Syria and landed at Tyre. The ship had sailed into the harbor of Tyre because it needed to unload[113] its cargo.

21:4 We looked up the disciples and stayed there for seven days. They told Paul through the Spirit not to go to Jerusalem (ἀνευρόντες δὲ τοὺς μαθητὰς ἐπεμείναμεν αὐτοῦ ἡμέρας ἑπτά, οἵτινες τῷ Παύλῳ ἔλεγον διὰ τοῦ πνεύματος μὴ ἐπιβαίνειν εἰς Ἱεροσόλυμα). The second part of this incident relates Paul's meeting with the believers in Tyre (vv. 4 – 6).

Luke's brief account has three parts. (1) Paul met with the Christians for a week. The temporal participle translated "we looked up" (ἀνευρόντες) im-

plies that Paul and his associates expected to find followers of Jesus in Tyre, without knowing where they would find them; thus they had to search for where they were meeting. Paul and Barnabas and other Christians from Antioch had visited believers in Phoenicia on their journey from Antioch to Jerusalem (15:3), presumably including believers in Tyre; perhaps their meeting place had changed.

Since Jesus' teaching and healing activity attracted people from the region around Tyre and since Jesus had spent time in the region of Tyre,[114] it is possible that some of the "disciples" had been followers of Jesus. Other Tyrians — Jews, God-fearers, as well as Syrophoenician and Greek residents — were converted to faith in Jesus as a result of the preaching of the Jerusalem believers who, after leaving the Jewish capital after the execution of Stephen, reached Phoenicia (11:19). They stayed with the disciples for seven days, which may suggest that Paul and his fellow travelers met daily for preaching and worship with the believers of Tyre, who presumably welcomed them in their houses and provided food.

(2) Luke relates a warning not to go to Jerusalem, inspired by the Holy Spirit and conveyed by the Tyrian believers.[115] The statement is not entirely clear in view of the fact that Paul does continue his journey to Jerusalem (v. 7). Perhaps Paul questioned the inspiration of the Tyrian Christians.[116] Others suggest that the Spirit's revelation disclosed to the believers the tribulations and the imprisonment that Paul would face and so they warned Paul not to go to Jerusalem.[117] The best interpretation takes the text at face value; what

---

113. The verb (ἀποφορτίζομαι) is a nautical technical term, denoting "discharge one's cargo" (LSJ; also "jettisoning cargo in a storm," BDAG).

114. Cf. Mark 3:8/Luke 6:17 and Matt 15:21/Mark 7:24.

115. For earlier revelatory words, instructions, or guidance given by the Spirit, cf. 1:2, 16; 4:25; 7:51; 8:29; 10:19; 11:12, 28; 13:2, 4; 15:28; 16:6 – 7; 19:21; 20:22, 23.

116. John Chrysostom, *Hom. Act.* 45.2; Lake and Cadbury, *Acts*, 266.

117. Cf. Calvin, *Acts*, 2:193; Barrett, *Acts*, 990; Bock, *Acts*, 637. Here the plural subject (οἵτινες) can be interpreted in the sense that one believer received a revelation from the Spirit, which the Tyrian believers interpreted to mean that Paul should not go to Jerusalem.

is identified as an utterance of the Spirit (διὰ τοῦ πνεύματος) is the word not to go to Jerusalem. Paul hears that warning and receives it as a revelatory word; yet without doubting the Spirit's inspiration, he concludes in his assessment[118] that it does not invalidate the earlier revelation of the Spirit that he must go to Jerusalem even though it would mean imprisonment and persecution (20:22 – 23).

21:5 – 6 When our time was up, we left and continued on our way. All the disciples, including their wives and children, escorted us outside the city, where we knelt down on the beach and prayed. We said our good-byes and went aboard the ship, while they returned home (ὅτε δὲ ἐγένετο ἡμᾶς ἐξαρτίσαι τὰς ἡμέρας, ἐξελθόντες ἐπορευόμεθα προπεμπόντων ἡμᾶς πάντων σὺν γυναιξὶ καὶ τέκνοις ἕως ἔξω τῆς πόλεως, καὶ θέντες τὰ γόνατα ἐπὶ τὸν αἰγιαλὸν προσευξάμενοι ἀπησπασάμεθα ἀλλήλους καὶ ἀνέβημεν εἰς τὸ πλοῖον, ἐκεῖνοι δὲ ὑπέστρεψαν εἰς τὰ ἴδια). (3) Luke relates the departure of Paul and his associates and the farewell from the Tyrian believers. When the seven days are completed, Paul and his companions leave the city and continue their travel. Luke draws a vivid picture of the farewell scene: all the disciples assemble with the travel party and escort them from the city to the harbor. The wives and children come along as well, highlighting the close bonds that developed between Paul, his companions, believers from Asia Minor, Greece, and Macedonia, and the families of believers in Tyre during the seven days.

As in Miletus, Paul and the believers kneel down (see on 20:36) and pray, surely for a good outcome of the journey to Jerusalem, for strength in view of the trials that lie ahead, and for God's blessings for the Tyrian believers. After they say good-bye to

each other, Paul and his companions board the ship while the Tyrian believers return to their homes.

21:7 We continued our voyage from Tyre and arrived at Ptolemais, where we greeted the believers and stayed with them for one day (ἡμεῖς δὲ τὸν πλοῦν διανύσαντες ἀπὸ Τύρου κατηντήσαμεν εἰς Πτολεμαΐδα καὶ ἀσπασάμενοι τοὺς ἀδελφοὺς ἐμείναμεν ἡμέραν μίαν παρ' αὐτοῖς). The second incident relates Paul's meeting with the believers in Ptolemais. Luke first describes the voyage from Tyre to Ptolemais, about 27 nautical miles (50 km.) down the coast, where they arrive after a journey of perhaps ten hours of sailing.

Luke then indicates that a meeting between Paul and the believers in Ptolemais takes place. These Christians are called "brothers" (ἀδελφοί; see on 1:16; 5:11); the standard designation of the members of the community of Jesus' followers are called "brothers (and sisters)" in other congregations as well. Paul and his companions "greet" (ἀσπασάμενοι) the believers[119] and are welcomed into their houses. Perhaps the largest house serves as the meeting place of the congregation. They stay overnight, assuming an arrival on the late afternoon of the day when they set sail from Tyre; they eat together, probably exchange news about the growth of the gospel in various regions, and presumably engage in teaching and worshiping.

21:8 – 9 The next day we left and came to Caesarea, where we went into the house of Philip the evangelist, one of the Seven, and stayed with him. He had four unmarried daughters who had the gift of prophecy (τῇ δὲ ἐπαύριον ἐξελθόντες ἤλθομεν εἰς Καισάρειαν καὶ εἰσελθόντες εἰς τὸν οἶκον Φιλίππου τοῦ εὐαγγελιστοῦ, ὄντος ἐκ τῶν ἑπτά, ἐμείναμεν παρ' αὐτῷ. τούτῳ δὲ ἦσαν

---

118. Note that in 1 Cor 14:29 Paul insists that the prophecies of Christian prophets need to be evaluated (διακρίνω), i.e., judged as to the meaning of the prophecy and its significance for specific behavior.

119. Cf. BDAG, s.v. ἀσπάζομαι 1, "to engage in hospitable recognition of another (with varying degrees of intimacy), *greet, welcome;*" v. 7 is listed (with 18:22; 25:13) under sense 1b, "of short friendly visits, 'look in on.'"

θυγατέρες τέσσαρες παρθένοι προφητεύουσαι). In this third incident, Paul meets with the believers in Caesarea (vv. 8 – 14). Luke first mentions the journey from Ptolemais to Caesarea (the same distance as from Tyre to Ptolemias), which could be covered in a good day of sailing. The departure "on the next day" (τῇ ἐπαύριον [ἡμέρᾳ]; temporal dative) suggests that Paul and his party are bound by the sailing schedule of the ship.

Paul then meets with the believers in Caesarea. After arriving in the large harbor of that city, they go into the house of Philip. Philip is identified (1) as the evangelist, i.e., as a preacher of the good news of Jesus as Israel's Messiah and Savior, which recalls his earlier missionary work in Samaria (8:4 – 9) and on the road to Gaza (8:25 – 40); and (2) as a member of the Seven, who had been appointed by the Jerusalem church to organize the support ministry for the widows of the congregation.[120] Luke had "left" Philip in Caesarea in 8:40, after he had preached the gospel in Samaria and explained it to the Ethiopian official. Philip evidently settled in Caesarea, the seat of the Roman governor, bought a house, and preached the gospel before Jews and, presumably, Gentiles in Caesarea and the surrounding areas. Paul and his companions stay at his house "for several days" (v. 10).

The term "evangelist" (εὐαγγελιστής) is used in the New Testament only here and in Eph 4:11 and 2 Tim 4:5 (Timothy). In Eph 4:11, evangelists are mentioned after the supraregional ministries

of apostles and prophets[121] and before the local ministry of pastors and teachers, which suggests a regional ministry for "evangelists," with a basis in a particular local congregation.[122] The term εὐαγγελιστής is rare in Greek; the only potentially non-Christian occurrence is in an (undated) inscription from Rhodes, where it possibly describes a "proclaimer of oracular messages."[123]

The reference to Philip's four unmarried daughters reinforces the community setting of the incident, which has been indicated by the theme of hospitality (the house of Philip) and the description of Philip as an evangelist. There is no good reason why Luke mentions the fact that Philip's daughters were unmarried (παρθένοι, "virgins") unless he wants to indicate that they were of marriageable age. There is no connection between prophecy and virginity. While the prophetess Anna was a widow (Luke 2:36 – 37) and thus not engaging in sexual intercourse, the women in Corinth who prophesied (1 Cor 11:5) included married women (cf. 1 Cor 14:35 in the context of 14:29 – 37). The role of Philip's daughters as prophets — the present participle (προφητεύουσαι) implies the habitual character of their exercise of the gift of prophecy — is presumably mentioned by Luke to highlight their involvement in the community of believers in Caesarea with whom Paul and his companions meet and interact.[124]

21:10 – 11 After we had stayed there for several days, a prophet named Agabus arrived from

---

120. He is thus distinguished from Philip, one of the Twelve (1:14).

121. Note that Agabus is a Christian prophet from Jerusalem who travels to Antioch in Syria (11:28) and to Caesarea (21:10).

122. The distinction between supraregional, regional, and local ministries should not be understood in a rigid sense. Both the Twelve and Paul engaged in regional and local ministry at times, and the "local" Seven traveled to other regions after Stephen's execution.

123. IG XII 1, 675 (line 6); cf. LSJ, s.v. εὐαγγελιστής 705 (II); MM 259 ("proclaimer of oracular messages"); BDAG ("title of polytheistic priests"); Horsley and Llewelyn, *New Documents*, 3:14. For the meaning of the verb εὐαγγελίζομαι see on 5:42.

124. For prophecy in the churches established by Paul, see 1 Cor 11:2 – 6; 14:1 – 25. The fact that Luke does not relate a prophecy of Philip's daughters but does report a prophecy of Agabus, does not mean that Luke elevates a male prophet over the four women: "Prophetic groups and individuals are not competing for honors in this scene" (Gaventa, *Acts*, 294).

Judea. He came to us, took Paul's belt, and tied his own feet and hands with it, and said, "Thus says the Holy Spirit, 'In this way the Jews in Jerusalem will bind the man who owns this belt and hand him over to the Gentiles'" (ἐπιμενόντων δὲ ἡμέρας πλείους κατῆλθέν τις ἀπὸ τῆς Ἰουδαίας προφήτης ὀνόματι Ἅγαβος, καὶ ἐλθὼν πρὸς ἡμᾶς καὶ ἄρας τὴν ζώνην τοῦ Παύλου, δήσας ἑαυτοῦ τοὺς πόδας καὶ τὰς χεῖρας εἶπεν· τάδε λέγει τὸ πνεῦμα τὸ ἅγιον· τὸν ἄνδρα οὗ ἐστιν ἡ ζώνη αὕτη, οὕτως δήσουσιν ἐν Ἰερουσαλὴμ οἱ Ἰουδαῖοι καὶ παραδώσουσιν εἰς χεῖρας ἐθνῶν). The repeated reference to Paul and his companions' staying in Caesarea highlights again the community setting, underscored by the present tense of the participle and the temporal notice "several days" (ἡμέρας πλείους; temporal accusative).

The link between the arrival of Agabus, a prophet from Jerusalem (see on 11:27 – 28), and "us" invokes the community setting. Agabus's prophecy was before both Paul and his companions and the local believers (cf. v. 12). Agabus is described as coming from Judea, the region that includes Jerusalem but not Caesarea, which was, in Jewish geographical perspective, part of Samaria.

The following incident presumably took place in a meeting of Paul with the local believers. Agabus stood up, approached Paul, took his belt, sat down again, tied first his own feet with the belt, then his hands, tying the knot with his teeth while crouching in a hog-tie position, and then uttered (εἶπεν) a prophecy.[125] Acted parables as prophetic signs were a feature of several Old Testament prophets.[126] Paul's belt (ζώνη) is taken to symbolize the chains with which Paul as prisoner will be bound.

The verbal prophecy is introduced by a formula that asserts divine authority for the following prediction; the phrase "thus says the Holy Spirit" replaces the customary "thus says the Lord."[127] The connection between the symbolic action and the prophecy is established with the modal adverb οὕτως ("in this way"), placed in the middle of the prophecy. The Greek sentence places the person to whom the symbolic action applies — the person who will be bound — at the beginning: "the man who owns this belt." As it is Paul's belt with which Agabus has tied himself up, the prophecy is given for Paul. Agabus predicts that the Jews "will bind" (δήσουσιν) Paul, i.e., imprison him, and "hand him over" (παραδώσουσιν) to the Gentiles,[128] presumably to be tried and sentenced to death.

The Jews could imprison people and inflict the punishment of forty lashes minus one (cf. the flogging of the Twelve by the Sanhedrin; 5:40), but it was only the Gentiles (specifically the Roman governor), who could impose the death penalty. Luke's narrative in 21:27 – 33 relates the fulfillment of the prophecy, albeit in a general sense: the Jews "seize" (ἐπέβαλον, 21:27) Paul in the temple; then they drag him out of the temple precinct and try to kill him (21:30 – 31). They hand him over to the Roman authorities only when a Roman officer intervenes, who arrests Paul and orders him to be bound (δεθῆναι) by two chains (21:33).

21:12 – 13 When we heard this, we and the local believers urged Paul not to go to Jerusalem. Then Paul answered, "What are you doing, weeping and breaking my heart? I am ready not only to

---

125. The aorist participles here function as temporal adverbials modifying the main verb (εἶπεν), which carries the main force of the sentence. Agabus's actions serve to underscore the verbal prophecy.

126. Ahijah (1 Kgs 11:29 – 39); Isaiah (Isa 8:1 – 4; 20:1 – 6), Jeremiah (Jer 19:1 – 13; 27:2 – 15), Ezekiel (Ezek 4:1 – 17; 5:1 – 12).

127. The phrase "thus says the Lord" occurs in Isaiah 26 times, in Jeremiah 64 times, and in Ezekiel 126 times. The phrase occurs a total of 322 times in the Old Testament.

128. Note the parallel in Jesus' prediction of his arrest in Luke 24:7.

be bound, but even to die in Jerusalem for the name of the Lord Jesus" (ὡς δὲ ἠκούσαμεν ταῦτα, παρεκαλοῦμεν ἡμεῖς τε καὶ οἱ ἐντόπιοι τοῦ μὴ ἀναβαίνειν αὐτὸν εἰς Ἰερουσαλήμ. τότε ἀπεκρίθη ὁ Παῦλος· τί ποιεῖτε κλαίοντες καὶ συνθρύπτοντές μου τὴν καρδίαν; ἐγὼ γὰρ οὐ μόνον δεθῆναι ἀλλὰ καὶ ἀποθανεῖν εἰς Ἰερουσαλὴμ ἑτοίμως ἔχω ὑπὲρ τοῦ ὀνόματος τοῦ κυρίου Ἰησοῦ). Paul's companions and the local believers evidently conclude from Agabus's prophecy that God does not want Paul to go to Jerusalem, and so they urge Paul "not to go." The first person plural of the main verb "we ... urged" (παρεκαλοῦμεν) includes Paul's coworkers in the group of Christians, who advise him not to go to Jerusalem.

In Miletus it was the Ephesian elders who had wept (20:37), in Tyre it was the local believers who told Paul not to go to Jerusalem (21:4), and now Paul's close associates try to stop him from continuing his journey.[129] The imperfect tense of "we ... urged" suggests that they pleaded with Paul for some time. Paul's reply v. 13 indicates that they are weeping (κλαίοντες), the present tense of the participle also suggesting continuous action.

Luke narrates Paul's answer in direct speech, underscoring the importance of his statement. Paul's question "What are you doing?" (τί ποιεῖτε) shows that the entreaty of his friends and of the believers has an emotional impact on him: they are "breaking [his] heart" (συνθρύπτοντες). This rare verb can be rendered as "soften, wear down" and interpreted in the sense that they are pressuring Paul hard for a decision, or it can be rendered as "break" and interpreted in the sense that they break Paul's heart through their grief.[130] Paul affirms in Caesarea, the last stop before reaching Jerusalem,

his decision to go on, as he had done in Miletus (20:22) and in Tyre (21:4 – 6). He is determined to go to Jerusalem, despite the prophecy of Agabus (who had not included in the prophecy a directive not to go there).

Paul asserts emphatically (ἐγώ) that he is "ready" and willing to be arrested in Jerusalem, and even to die, if it should come to that. Paul knows that if he is arrested, tried, and executed in Jerusalem, it will be "for the name of the Lord Jesus" — for the risen Lord who revealed himself to Paul on the road to Damascus, who commissioned him to preach before Gentiles and kings and Jews (9:5), and who showed him right at the beginning of his ministry as a follower of Jesus that he would suffer "for the sake of my name" (9:15 – 16). The Twelve had suffered "for the sake of the Name" and rejoiced (5:41),[131] as they experienced the reality of Jesus' words, who pronounced a blessing on his disciples who are hated, excluded, reviled, and defamed on account of him (Luke 6:22 – 23), and who predicted that they would be arrested, imprisoned, and brought before kings and governors "on account of my name" (Luke 21:12).

If Jesus' followers experience the reality of the power of Jesus' presence when they preach and heal in Jesus' name (2:21, 38; 3:6, 16; 4:7), they are ready to suffer and die for him. The fact that the witnesses of Jesus are willing to die and thus face the consequences of their preaching demonstrates both the consistency of their convictions and the seriousness of their proclamation. Thus, Paul suffers for the name of Jesus since he proclaims and teaches that the resurrection hope of Israel is fulfilled — only — through Jesus, Israel's Messiah and Savior (cf. 23:6; 24:15; 26:6 – 7; 28:20).[132]

---

129. Cf. Gaventa, *Acts*, 295, who sees v. 12 as the climax of foreboding that surrounds Paul's journey to Jerusalem. Note the parallel with Peter, who rebukes Jesus, who is on the way to Jerusalem to be arrested and killed, arguing that this must not happen (Matt 16:22/Mark 8:32).

130. G. Schneider, "συνθρύπτω," *EDNT*, 3:306 – 7.

131. Cf. 4:7, 10 – 12, 17 – 18, 30.

132. Cf. Scott Cunningham, *"Through Many Tribulations": The Theology of Persecution in Luke-Acts* (JSNTSup 142; Sheffield: Sheffield Academic Press, 1997), 277 – 81.

21:14 Since Paul would not be persuaded, we refrained from saying anything more, except, "The Lord's will may be done!" (μὴ πειθομένου δὲ αὐτοῦ ἡσυχάσαμεν εἰπόντες· τοῦ κυρίου τὸ θέλημα γινέσθω). Finally, Luke narrates the acquiescence of the believers regarding Paul's determination to go to Jerusalem. The comment that Paul would not be persuaded makes the point that Paul's companions and the Caesarean believers have repeatedly attempted to dissuade Paul from continuing his journey (note the present tense of the participle πειθομένου). They fall eventually silent, refraining from repeating their appeals to turn around.

Luke relates the final reaction of the community of believers in direct speech. They accept "the Lord's will" (τοῦ κυρίου is placed in emphasized initial position), who will do what he will do in his wisdom and grace. They respond to Paul's determination not with resignation but with acknowledgment that it is the Lord's will that Paul be arrested in Jerusalem. Their submission to God's will agrees with the conviction of the early Christians, reflected throughout Luke's narrative in Acts, that it is the crucified, risen, and exalted Lord who directs the mission of his followers, who empowers their witness, and who gives them courage to suffer.

21:15 – 16 After these days we got ready and started to travel to Jerusalem. Some of the disciples from Caesarea accompanied us and took us to the house of Mnason of Cyprus, one of the early disciples, who would entertain us as guests (μετὰ δὲ τὰς ἡμέρας ταύτας ἐπισκευασάμενοι ἀνεβαίνομεν εἰς Ἱεροσόλυμα· συνῆλθον δὲ καὶ τῶν μαθητῶν ἀπὸ Καισαρείας σὺν ἡμῖν, ἄγοντες παρ᾽ ᾧ ξενισθῶμεν Μνάσωνί τινι Κυπρίῳ, ἀρχαίῳ μαθητῇ). Paul now travels from Caesarea to Jerusalem (vv. 15 – 17). Luke describes the departure from Caesarea with two verbs: they "got ready"; i.e., they prepared for the final leg of the journey up into the hill country of Judea, and they "started to travel" to Jerusalem. The distance from Caesarea to Jerusalem is about 62 miles (100 km.), which required four days of walking.[133]

Some of the disciples "accompanied" (συνῆλθον) Paul and his companions to Jerusalem (v. 16).[134] They took them to the house of a certain Mnason, a native of Cyprus, who would "entertain [them] as guests" (ξενισθῶμεν). Mnason was probably a Cypriot Jew who had lived in Jerusalem. He is described as "one of the early disciples"; this description suggests that he may have been among the followers of Jesus before the crucifixion, or he came to faith in the early months after the resurrection. It is not impossible that he was among the early Cypriot believers who were forced to leave Jerusalem after Stephen's execution and who preached the gospel in Antioch (11:20). This would explain why Paul and his travel companions stayed with him in Jerusalem.

21:17 When we arrived in Jerusalem, the believers welcomed us warmly (γενομένων δὲ ἡμῶν εἰς Ἱεροσόλυμα ἀσμένως ἀπεδέξαντο ἡμᾶς οἱ ἀδελφοί).

---

133. Commentators who assume that the journey took two days have to assume that the travel party rode on horseback (e.g., Marshall, *Acts*, 341; cf. Peterson, *Acts*, 582 n. 35, without reference to Marshall's horses). This is unlikely. The party consisted of at least twelve people (Paul, the seven companions mentioned in 20:4, and presumably Luke, as well as an unspecified number of Caesarean believers). It is doubtful that the believers in Caesarea owned, or were likely to hire, twelve horses for the journey to Jerusalem.

134. The Western text apparently assumes that the journey took two days and that the travel party spent the night in the house of Mnason, in a village en route to Jerusalem: "*And these* brought us to those with whom we were to lodge; *and when we arrived at a certain village, we stayed* with Mnason of Cyrene, a disciple of long standing. *And when we had departed from there we arrived in Jerusalem*" (D^vid). Cf. Metzger, *Textual Commentary*, 428; Barrett, *Acts*, 1004.

Luke concludes[135] his narrative of Paul's travels after his departure from Ephesus — travels that took him through Macedonia and Achaia and back to the east with the goal of visiting Jerusalem before traveling to Rome (19:21) — with the comment that when they arrived in Jerusalem, "the believers welcomed [them] warmly." The adverb translated "warmly" (ἀσμένως), used only here in the New Testament, signals that the believers were "well pleased, glad, and ready" to see Paul and his companions.

Theology in Application

The three episodes that make up this section relate in some detail Paul's geographical movements (six travel reports), but they focus on his visits to the believers in Macedonia and Achaia and on his meetings with the believers in Troas, Miletus/Ephesus, Tyre, Ptolemais, and Caesarea. The significance of the latter focus is confirmed by the numerous occurrences of direct speech for Paul's encounters with local believers and congregations. Paul's address to the elders of the church in Ephesus summarizes his missionary work and his concerns for the churches. The following emphases, both implicit and explicit, are important here.

Missionary Work Focuses on People

Neither Paul's missionary work nor Luke's report of Paul's ministry is fixated on strategies, geographical location, or the missionaries themselves, as relevant as these matters are. Paul's ministry is focused on *people* — in these three episodes, on Christian believers — and on their commitment to the gospel.

Luke explicitly mentions the believers in Macedonian churches (20:2) and in Troas (20:7 – 12), Ephesus (20:17), Tyre (21:4 – 6), Ptolemais (21:7), and Caesarea (21:12, 16); he implicitly refers to believers in Philippi (20:6) and Miletus (20:38). Luke also highlights how long Paul stayed with believers: three months in Greece (20:2 – 3), seven days in Troas (20:6), seven days in Tyre (21:4), one day in Ptolemais (21:7), and several days in Caesarea (21:8 – 14). He mentions several believers by name (20:4, 9; 21:8, 10, 16). Missionaries and pastors should be known for their commitment to people: churches are made up of people, whose commitment to the Lord takes precedence over plans, programs, strategies, and structures.

Paul's address to the Ephesian elders reflects this focus on people as well. Paul taught what is helpful for people (20:20); he taught in private homes (20:20); he preached before Jews and Greeks (20:21); he is concerned that he will never see the Ephesian elders again (20:25). Paul is also concerned to teach the whole counsel of

---

135. The headings in many translations, and many commentators (e.g., Bruce, *Acts*, 442 – 43; Fitzmyer, *Acts*, 692; Peterson, *Acts*, 583), take v. 17 as the beginning of a new section. It is preferable, however, to take v. 17 as the end of the section: the welcome in Jerusalem marks the end of the journey; the next section begins with Paul's visit to James in v. 18. Cf. Gaventa, "Miletus Speech," 39; Pervo, *Acts*, 541.

God so that he will not be held accountable for the condemnation of people on the day of judgment (20:26 – 27). He shows concern for the elders — both for their well-being and for their commitment to their responsibilities (20:28); he is concerned about members of the flock being influenced by false teachers (20:29 – 30); he speaks about his pastoral care that kept him busy for three years, night or day, and cost him many tears (20:31); and he arranges for the care of the weak in the congregation (20:35).

Missionary Commitment Involves Suffering

Paul suffered trials during his ministry in Ephesus, as when local Jews plotted against him; he endured that suffering with tears (20:19). Paul knows that he will be imprisoned and that he will suffer once he arrives in Jerusalem (20:23) — knowledge that is reinforced by prophecies in Tyre (21:4) and Caesarea (21:11). Since Paul knows it is God's will to suffer in Jerusalem (20:22), he is prepared not to change plans but willingly, with open eyes, to go into a dangerous situation that may cost him his life (21:13). The Lord had told him at his conversion, through Ananias from Damascus, that he would suffer (9:15 – 16). Paul is willing to suffer and even to die if this is part of God's plan; he knows it will be suffering for the name of the Lord Jesus (21:13), in fulfillment of his task of preaching the gospel before Jews and Gentiles. Paul asserts that his life is less important than the ministry that the Lord has given to him, which involves proclaiming the good news of God's grace revealed in Jesus (20:24).

Paul's journey from Ephesus via Achaia and Macedonia back to Jerusalem is accompanied by continual references to Paul's imprisonment and suffering in Jerusalem, and nearly the last quarter of Luke's material in Acts (266 of a total of 1006 verses) narrates Paul's imprisonment first in Jerusalem, then in Caesarea, then in Rome. Neither personal motives (avoiding the pain of suffering, escaping the possibility of a martyr's death) nor pragmatic considerations (further years of missionary ministry, the opening up of a new missionary field in Spain) trump obedience to God's will. While suffering is always an expression of the fallenness of God's good creation that was once perfect, it may be an integral part of God's will, not in a masochistic sense of regarding suffering as something good, but as prompting submission to the good will of God, who may want missionaries, evangelists, and pastors to carry out tasks that are more important than the preservation of one's personal life (cf. 20:24).

Pastoral Encouragement Strengthens Believers

Paul encourages the believers in the Macedonian churches (20:2), he encourages the Ephesian elders by commending them to God and to the power of his grace (20:32), and he encourages the churches in Achaia (Corinth), Troas, Tyre, Ptolemais, and Caesarea by meeting with the believers over extended or shorter periods of time. Paul's travel route after leaving Ephesus — heading west to Achaia and Macedonia rather than going straight to Jerusalem before traveling on to Rome — may have been necessary on account of the collection,[136] but it was surely also motivated by Paul's desire to see the churches in Macedonia and Achaia one last time before beginning missionary work in Spain.

In his address to the Ephesian elders, the metaphor of the shepherd and the sheep (20:28) underscores the importance of pastors caring for the members of the congregation, nurturing their commitment to Jesus, strengthening their faith by teaching, and explaining the whole counsel of God (20:27). Pastors pass on what is profitable and helpful (20:20) and thus contribute to the building up of the church, which is God's temple in which sinners gather who have been made holy (20:32). The main task of pastoral ministry, according to Paul's address to the Ephesian elders, is not the quantitative growth of the church, but the maturity of the believers. Pastors serve the Lord (20:19), not a plan; they serve with humility (20:19), not with their own reputation in mind; they do not hesitate to do any task that is helpful for believers (20:20), rather than seeking to stay away from situations in which they will get their hands dirty; they teach in any location and at any time of the day that facilitates effective ministry (20:20); they do not exclude anybody from the reach of their ministry (20:21); they teach the whole counsel of God (20:27), not focusing on subject areas selected on the basis of personal preference or prescribed by some program; they have the functions of shepherds who care for the sheep by leading them to good pastures and by protecting them from the dangers presented by wild animals (20:28 – 29); they ensure that only the truth of the gospel is being taught (20:30); they care for the weak in the congregation (20:35).

Pastoral Exhortation Advises Christian Leaders

Churches that deserve the title "church of God" (20:28) — churches that care about the salvation of Jews and Greeks (20:21); churches that are committed to preaching and teaching about repentance toward God, faith in the Lord Jesus, the kingdom of God, the whole counsel of God, the grace of God (20:21, 25, 27, 32) — have hardworking elders and pastors who are committed to evangelism, to preaching and teaching characterized by theological integrity, and to the care for the weak in the congregation. Paul's concern for the personal integrity of the Ephesian elders (20:28), for the theological integrity of the congregation (20:28 – 30), and for the social integrity of the leaders in their selfless care for the helpless (20:32 – 35) describes fundamental characteristics of healthy, mature churches.

(1) Authentic churches have leaders committed to safeguarding their personal

---

136. 1 Cor 16:1 – 2; 2 Cor 8 – 9; cf. Rom 15:25, 31.

integrity in all areas of doctrine (the whole counsel of God) and in terms of their commitment to selfless service (day and night, with tears, without greed), seeking to give rather than to receive.

(2) Missionaries and pastors consolidate the church. In order to be able to do this with theological competence and pastoral sensitivity, missionaries and evangelists, pastors and elders must understand the nature of the church. Paul's address at Miletus, while not aiming at presenting a fully rounded description of the nature and function of the church, nevertheless provides fundamental truths about what a Christian congregation is.

The identity of the church is fundamentally linked with God, with Jesus, and with the Holy Spirit. The church is "the church of God" (20:28); i.e., the church has been established by God and the church belongs to God. The church is the church of God on account of Jesus' death on the cross (20:28); i.e., it constitutes the messianic people of God whose members are committed to Jesus as Israel's Messiah and as the Savior who died for the forgiveness of sins and to give them eternal life in the presence of God. The church is the church of God as the Holy Spirit is active in the church (20:22 – 23, 28); i.e., the church is the place of the presence of the holy God — thus the temple of the Holy Spirit.

The church is God's flock (20:28). This means, again, that the church belongs to God and that the church needs "shepherds" through whom God, Jesus, and the Spirit provide care and nurture. The church is a building in progress (20:32), God's building (1 Cor 3:9). This means that there needs to be a firm foundation — which is the reality of Jesus, Israel's crucified, risen, and exalted Messiah who is proclaimed in the gospel (1 Cor 3:10 – 11). This means that there must be "builders" through whom God builds up his people.

The church consists of saints (20:32) — people who have been purified on account of God's grace (20:24) made available through the blood that Jesus Christ shed on the cross (20:28) and appropriated through repentance toward God and faith in the Lord Jesus (20:21).

The church is built up and nurtured through the "good news of God's grace" (20:24, 32), i.e., through the teaching of the gospel; through proclaiming "the whole will of God" (20:27), i.e., through teaching the entire Scriptures beginning with the first Adam and ending with the last Adam; and through commitment to the truth in teaching (20:30), i.e., through unmasking false teachers and staying committed to the truth.[137]

The church is led by "shepherds" (20:28). These shepherds are leaders who stand under the authority of the owner of the flock (God). They have the responsibility of "overseers" (20:28); i.e., they have real authority in the congregation — an authority

---

137. On Paul's theology of ministry and proclamation, developed through a discussion of 2 Corinthians, cf. Michael P. Knowles, *We Preach Not Ourselves: Paul on Proclamation* (Grand Rapids: Brazos, 2007).

that is focused on caring for the believers through preaching the word of grace, through safeguarding the theological integrity of the church by exposing false teachers (20:29 – 30), and through selfless service for the benefit of all, especially of the weak (20:33 – 35).

(3) Authentic church leaders are committed to safeguarding the truth of the gospel in their churches. They resist the temptation to adapt the gospel to cultural values in such a manner that the gospel is "good news" for sinners only in the sense that they do not really have to change ways of behavior and ways of thinking that are contrary to the revealed will of God. They "keep the faith" (see 2 Tim 4:7). The history of the church is full of church leaders introducing teaching that detracts from the reality of God's wrath toward sinners, from the significance of Jesus' death on the cross as securing the salvation of sinners, from the power of the Holy Spirit (cf. 20:28) in favor of management stratagems for "doing church," and from the authority of God's word (cf. 20:35) in favor of tradition.[138]

(4) Authentic church leaders serve their congregations with unchecked love and commitment, dedicated to the spiritual, personal, and even financial well-being of the believers, and willing to sacrifice from their own resources. As there will always be some church members who are wealthy, and as collections and gifts of money to the church provide a constant stream of income, pastors need to take care not to think that they have the right to benefit financially to such an extent that "greed" is the only valid term describing their intentions or their practices.[139] True leaders of true churches are committed to serve, not to be served. The fact that this reality is established by Paul with a rare quotation of a saying of Jesus (20:35) underlines the importance of selfless service with tears and with humility.

(5) Paul reminds the Ephesian elders of his personal conduct when he was working in Ephesus. Personal example motivates not only elders but believers in general. While church growth does not originate in the actions of the missionary and the pastor — as "church of God" each Christian congregation is ultimately called into being by God himself, whose power is present and active in the proclamation of the gospel of Jesus Christ — bad behavior of missionaries, pastors, and elders certainly neither promotes confidence in the gospel on the part of unbelievers nor is it conducive to encourage maturity in believers.[140]

---

138. For a recent prophetic indictment of contemporary North American evangelicalism see David F. Wells, *The Courage to Be Protestant: Truth-Lovers, Marketers and Emergents in the Postmodern World* (Grand Rapids: Eerdmans, 2008), summarizing his earlier work. See also Don A. Carson, *Evangelicalism: What Is It and Is It Worth Keeping?* (Wheaton: Crossway, 2009).

139. Cf. Peterson, *Acts*, 573: "Covetousness spoils relationships and hinders the work of the gospel, since those who are seeking to advance themselves materially will be tempted to evaluate their contacts and ministry opportunities in economic terms."

140. Cf. Joe E. Trull and James E. Carter, *Ministerial Ethics: Moral Formation for Church Leaders* (2nd ed.; Grand Rapids: Baker, 2004).

Authentic Missionary Work and Pastoral Ministry
Submit to God, Jesus, and the Spirit

Luke refers here repeatedly to God, to Jesus Christ, and to the Spirit. In this way he highlights yet again his concern to show that the missionary work of the early church was directed by God himself, active in his witnesses through the risen and exalted Jesus Christ, revealing himself through the Spirit. Luke refers to the need for sinners to repent before *God the Father* (20:21), to the good news of God's grace that Paul proclaimed before Jews and Greeks and taught in the congregation (20:24), to the whole counsel of God that Paul preached in the church in Ephesus (20:27), to the congregation in Ephesus as the church of God (20:28), and to the God whose sovereign power will take care of the Ephesian elders (20:32).

Luke also speaks of faith in the *Lord Jesus* as the basic content of his message (20:21), to Jesus as the source of his missionary ministry (20:24), to Jesus' blessing on those who give rather than want to receive (20:35), to Paul's willingness to suffer and die in Jerusalem in the name of Jesus (21:13), and to the believers' submission to the Lord's will (21:14).

He also speaks of the *Holy Spirit* when he explains that his journey to Jerusalem is undertaken as constrained by the Spirit (20:22); the Spirit testifies in city after city that Paul will suffer and be imprisoned (20:23); it is the Spirit who made the Ephesian elders overseers in the congregation (20:28); the believers in Tyre receive a revelation from the Spirit to warn Paul not to go to Jerusalem (21:4); and the Spirit predicts through the prophet Agabus Paul's imprisonment in Jerusalem (21:11).

Submission to God, to Jesus, and to the Spirit often takes place in the midst of tensions. In our text there is the tension between the revelation of God's will through the Spirit, who wants Paul to go to Jerusalem despite the prospect of imprisonment and suffering (20:22), which Paul accepts, and the human reaction on the part of the Ephesian elders and the believers in Caesarea as well as the delegates from several churches who accompany Paul (20:36 – 38; 21:12 – 13). There is also tension between the will of God and human freedom: God does not impose his plan on Paul; rather, Paul accepts God's plan of God willingly, despite warnings not to go to Jerusalem. Indeed, "Paul 'must' go, but he freely affirms his destiny."[141]

These repeated references to God, Jesus, and the Spirit signal to the reader that even though Paul will indeed be imprisoned in Jerusalem,[142] the identity and the continued ministry of the church has little to do with Paul since "its survival never depended on Paul or any other 'hero.' The example offered in the Miletus speech, then, is not that of doing what Paul did but of adhering to the gospel and understanding its origin in God, Jesus, and the Holy Spirit."[143]

---

141. Conzelmann, *Acts*, 178.

142. There are essentially no references to believers once Paul is arrested in 21:26 – 36.

143. Gaventa, "Miletus Speech," 51 – 52. For practical application see Stephen Seamands, *Ministry in the Image of God: The Trinitarian Shape of Christian Service* (Downers Grove, IL: InterVarsity Press, 2005).

Acts 21:18 – 26

Literary Context

This episode of Paul's encounter with the Jerusalem church begins the last major section in the book of Acts, which relates events during Paul's imprisonment in Jerusalem, Caesarea, and Rome (21:18 – 28:31). The first three major sections were devoted to the beginning of the life and ministry of the followers of Jesus as the new messianic people of God. After the foundational report of the missionary commission of the apostles by the crucified and risen Jesus Christ (1:1 – 14), Luke described the beginnings of the new messianic people of God who lived, worshiped, and evangelized in obedience to Jesus' commission and with the power of the Holy Spirit (1:15 – 8:3); and he described the beginnings of the mission to the Gentiles when followers of Jesus preached the gospel in Samaria, before an Ethiopian, in coastal towns, in Phoenicia and Syria, when Saul the persecutor was converted, and when a new wave of persecution during the reign of King Agrippa I led to the death of James and to the departure of Peter (8:4 – 12:25).

The next three major sections described the missionary work of Paul. Luke first narrated Paul's mission in Asia Minor, together with Barnabas, focusing on his proclamation of the gospel and the establishment of churches in cities on Cyprus, in south Galatia, and in Pamphylia; subsequent to that was the report of the Apostles' Council in Jerusalem, which confirmed and consolidated the policies for the mission among Gentiles (13:1 – 15:33). The next section described Paul's missionary work in the provinces of Macedonia and Achaia, with churches being established in Philippi, Thessalonica, Berea, Athens, and Corinth (15:35 – 18:22). The following section narrated Paul's mission in Asia Minor in the city of Ephesus, detailing the great success of the gospel as the conversion of a large number of Ephesians had a noticeable impact on public life in the city (18:23 – 21:17). This section ended with a report of Paul's journey from Ephesus to Macedonia and Achaia and from there via Macedonia, Asia, and Syria back to Jerusalem, with particular attention paid to Paul's meetings with believers in Macedonia, Achaia, Troas, Miletus, Tyre, Ptolemais, and Caesarea (20:2 – 21:17).

Now Paul has arrived in Jerusalem, in time for the Feast of Pentecost (May 29, AD 57) — his fifth visit after his conversion. Luke begins his report of Paul's stay in Jerusalem with an account of his meeting with James and the elders of the Jerusalem church, who ask Paul to demonstrate that rumors are baseless that allege Paul teaches a wholesale abandonment of the Mosaic law. Paul does so, but certain events lead to his arrest in the temple.

This episode demonstrates, on the one hand, that Paul had a reputation among diaspora Jews who lived in the cities of the Roman provinces in which he had established churches (21:28 – 29), and it shows, on the other hand, a tension between Paul and Jewish believers who were zealous for the Mosaic law (21:20 – 21). The report and the suggestion of the elders of the Jerusalem church (21:20 – 25) is the last time that the word "church" appears in Acts. That is, the church as a fellowship of disciples "virtually disappears after Paul's arrest in Jerusalem."[1] The narrative reflects the importance of missionary work for the early church, linked as usual with the acknowledgment that it is God who leads Gentiles to faith in Jesus (21:19 – 20a). It reflects earlier concerns of the church leaders to maintain the unity of the church by addressing tensions that continue to exist concerning matters related to the Mosaic law and its validity among God's new messianic people (21:20b – 25), and it reflects Paul's efforts to vindicate the gospel.

Main Idea

Luke's report of Paul's meeting with James and the elders of the Jerusalem church highlights the significance of missionary work as God's mission. It demonstrates the importance of efforts to maintain the unity of the church by addressing existing tensions, and it underlines the importance of efforts to vindicate the gospel against false accusations.

---

1. Gaventa, "Miletus Speech," 50, who points out that the term "church" (ἐκκλησία) occurs for the last time in Paul's address to the Ephesian elders in 20:28.

Translation

Acts 21:18 – 26

18a	Setting: time	The next day
b	Protagonist	**Paul and**
c	Association	**the rest of us**
d	Action	**went to see James.**
e	Character entrance	**All the elders were present.**
19a	Setting: time	After greeting them,
b	Action	**Paul described in detail**
c	Report	all that God had done
d	Sphere	among the Gentiles
e	Means	through his ministry.
20a	Reaction	**All who heard it praised God.**
b	Speech	**They said to him,**
c	Address	"Brother,
d	Report	you see how many thousands of Jews have come to faith,
e	Description	and they are all zealous for the law.
21a	Report	They have been informed
b	Reference	concerning you
c	Action	that you teach all the Jews
d	Description	who live among the Gentiles
e	Accusation	to abandon Moses,
f	Accusation	and that you tell them not to circumcise their children
g	Accusation	or live according to our customs.
22a	Rhetorical question	What is to be done?
b	Assertion (prediction)	They will certainly hear that you have come.
23a	Entreaty	So, do what we tell you.
b	Character entrance	There are four men among us
c	Character description	who are under a vow.
24a	Instruction	Take these men,
b	Instruction	purify yourself along with them, and
c	Instruction	pay the expenses for them
d	Purpose	so that they may have their heads shaved.
e	Result (prediction)	Then all will know
f	Content	that there is nothing to the reports
g	Description	that they have been given about you,
h	Content	but that you too conform to the observance of the law.
25a	Reference	As regards the Gentile believers,
b	Flashback (action)	we have instructed them
c	Means	by letter
d	Reference	concerning our decision

e	Instruction		that they must abstain from food sacrificed to idols,
f	Instruction		from blood,
g	Instruction		from the meat of strangled animals, and
h	Instruction		from sexual immorality."

26a	Setting: time		On the following day
b	Action		**Paul took the men**
c	Action		**and purified himself**
d	Association		**together with them.**
e	Action		**Then he went into the temple**
f	Purpose		to give notice of the fulfillment of the days of purification,
g	Time		when the offering would be made for each of them.

Structure and Literary Form

Paul's encounter with the Jerusalem church (21:18 – 26) consists of three incidents. (1) Paul visits the leaders of the Jerusalem church; he meets James and all the elders of the congregation and gives a detailed report of the events of his missionary work since their last meeting, and the elders praise God for what has been accomplished through Paul's missionary work (vv. 18 – 20a). (2) Luke relates the concerns of James and the elders regarding rumors that Paul allegedly encourages Jewish believers in Jesus in the diaspora to neglect the Mosaic law. They suggest that Paul counteract these rumors by undergoing purification rites in the temple and paying for the sacrifices required for the purification of four Jewish Christians who are under a vow (vv. 20b – 25). (3) Paul agrees with the elders' suggestion and accompanies these four Jewish believers on the next day to the temple (v. 26).

The episode is a *historical narrative* with time references ("the next day;" vv. 18, 26), implied geographical references (the meeting place of the leadership of the Jerusalem church [v. 18] and the temple [v. 26]), a missionary report (v. 19), and worship and praise (v. 20a). The *speech* by the elders — perhaps given by James, although this is not clear — is narrated in *direct speech* (vv. 20b – 25). That speech reports the conversion of thousands of Jews in Jerusalem and Judea who are zealous for the Mosaic law (v. 20d-e); they report the rumors concerning Paul and his teaching that have created problems (v. 21); they propose a course of action — for Paul to submit to a rite of purification and pay for the shaving of four Jewish believers who are under an oath (vv. 22 – 24); finally, they remind Paul of the decision of the Apostles' Council in Acts 15 (v. 25).

Exegetical Outline

→ **I. Paul's Encounter with the Jerusalem Church (21:18 – 26)**

    A. Paul's Visit to James and the Elders of the Jerusalem Church (21:18 – 20a)

        1. The visit to James (21:18a-d)

        2. The presence of all the elders (21:18e)

        3. Paul's detailed report of his missionary work (21:19)

        4. James and the elders' approval of Paul's mission as they praise God (21:20a)

    B. The Speech of the Elders: Concerns about Paul's Reputation (21:20b – 25)

        1. Address (21:20b-c)

        2. Report about the conversion of thousands of Jews in Jerusalem and Judea (21:20d-e)

            a. The conversion of thousands of Jews (21:20d)

            b. The zeal of these Jewish believers for the law (21:20e)

        3. Rumors that Paul encourages Jewish believers to neglect the Mosaic law (21:21)

            a. The existence of rumors in Jerusalem and Judea (21:21a-b)

            b. The rumors about Paul's teaching before Jewish diaspora audiences (21:21c-d)

            c. The charges against Paul (21:21e-g)

                i. Paul teaches apostasy from the Mosaic law (21:21e)

                ii. Paul abolishes circumcision (21:21f)

                iii. Paul abolishes the Jewish customs (21:21g)

        4. The elders' suggested course of action (21:22 – 24)

            a. Rhetorical question introducing the proposal (21:22a)

            b. The urgency of disowning the rumors due to Paul's arrival (21:22b)

            c. Proposal: Paul submits to a rite of purification (21:23 – 24)

                i. Request to accept their suggestion (21:23a)

                ii. The opportunity provided by four Jewish believers under a vow (21:23b-c)

                iii. Paul's demonstration of his obedience to the law (21:24a-d)

                iv. The expected results of Paul's action (21:24e-h)

        5. Reminder: The decision about the requirements for Gentile believers (21:25)

            a. The decision concerning the Gentile believers recorded in a letter (21:25a-d)

            b. The stipulations of the apostolic decree (21:25e-h)

                i. Abstention from idolatry (21:25e)

                ii. Abstention from consuming blood (21:25f)

                iii. Abstention from the meat of strangled animals (21:25g)

                iv. Abstention from sexual immorality (21:25h)

    C. Paul's Demonstration of His Obedience to the Law (21:26)

        1. Paul joins the four men (21:26a-b)

        2. Paul submits to a rite of purification (21:26c-d)

        3. Paul enters the temple to arrange his payment for the four men's sacrifices (21:26e-g)

Explanation of the Text

21:18 The next day Paul and the rest of us went to see James. All the elders were present (τῇ δὲ ἐπιούσῃ εἰσῄει ὁ Παῦλος σὺν ἡμῖν πρὸς Ἰάκωβον, πάντες τε παρεγένοντο οἱ πρεσβύτεροι). Luke states with succinct brevity the purpose of Paul's visit to Jerusalem: he wants to see James and the Jerusalem church, here represented by the elders. Paul is accompanied by "the rest of us" (σὺν ἡμῖν), i.e., by the seven delegates from churches in Asia Minor and in Europe, as well as by Luke (the narrator behind the "us").

Paul's letters indicate that from the apostle's point of view, the main purpose of his visit to Jerusalem was to deliver the collection he had organized in the churches of Macedonia, Achaia, and Asia Minor.[2] The reason why Luke omits a reference to the collection[3] is hardly the refusal of the Jerusalem leaders to accept financial help from the churches Paul had established, fearing being compromised by an association with Paul.[4] Nor is Luke's silence explained by the suggestion that the Jerusalem leadership accepted the collection on the condition that Paul must follow the proposal of the elders demonstrating his obedience to the Mosaic law.[5] More plausible is the suggestion that when Luke wrote his account, the significance of Paul's arrest and long imprisonment completely overshadowed the collection.[6]

Luke points out that "all the elders" (πάντες ... οἱ πρεσβύτεροι) were present, representing the en-

tire church. Their presence may suggest that the meeting took place on the occasion of one of the larger congregational gatherings of the Jerusalem believers — perhaps one of the assemblies in Solomon's Portico in the temple precincts (cf. 3:11; 5:12). The notice that the meeting took place on "the next day" underscores the eagerness of Paul and his companions to meet the Jerusalem believers. The urgency may be explained by his desire to reach Rome (19:21), which he probably hoped to do before the end of the seafaring season on the Mediterranean in the fall. His desire to hand over the collection of funds to the leaders of the Jerusalem church would explain the speed with which the meeting is arranged.

21:19 – 20a After greeting them, Paul described in detail all that God had done among the Gentiles through his ministry. All who heard it praised God (καὶ ἀσπασάμενος αὐτοὺς ἐξηγεῖτο καθ' ἓν ἕκαστον, ὧν ἐποίησεν ὁ θεὸς ἐν τοῖς ἔθνεσιν διὰ τῆς διακονίας αὐτοῦ. οἱ δὲ ἀκούσαντες ἐδόξαζον τὸν θεόν). Paul's agenda with the leaders of the Jerusalem church was his missionary work. The last opportunity to inform the Jerusalem church about his work was four years earlier, when he had returned from Macedonia and Achaia (18:18 – 22) and the planting of churches in Philippi, Thessalonica, Berea, Athens, and Corinth (AD 49 – 52; see "In Depth: Paul's Visits to Jerusalem" at 9:26).[7]

---

2. Cf. 1 Cor 16:1 – 2; 2 Cor 8 – 9; cf. Rom 15:25, 31; see Acts 24:17.

3. Note the reference to alms and sacrifices in 24:17, and the reference to Trophimos, one of the delegates of the churches established by Paul in 21:29 (cf. 20:4). On Paul's collection see 19:21; 20:3 – 4.

4. Cf. Dunn, *Beginning from Jerusalem*, 970 – 72, concluding that "it is hard to shake off the suspicion that the collection was *not* welcomed and possibly not even received by the Jerusalem church" (972).

5. Haenchen, *Acts*, 613 – 14; Dieter Georgi, *Remembering the Poor: The History of Paul's Collection for Jerusalem* (Nashville: Abingdon, 1992), 125 – 26.

6. Marshall, *Acts*, 313. Bruce, *Acts*, 481, and Witherington, *Acts*, 644, explain Luke's silence with "the failure of the collection to accomplish the ends intended by Paul," without clarifying whether James and the elders accepted the collection.

7. Note Luke's explicit reference to Paul and Barnabas giving a full report to the Jerusalem church and the assembled elders and apostles in 15:4 and 15:12; Paul also "visited" the Jerusalem congregation in 18:22.

During the past five years (AD 52 – 56) Paul had been proclaiming the gospel and planting churches in the province of Asia, based in Ephesus (19:1 – 20:1) but impacting other cities in the province as well (19:10, 22, 26; also 20:16; 21:27). Since Paul now plans to move to the city of Rome (19:21) and eventually to Spain (Rom 15:24 – 28), he would have used this perhaps last opportunity[8] to give a full account of his missionary work in Ephesus and other cities in Asia Minor, and a report about the churches in Macedonia and Achaia that he had just visited. Paul undoubtedly reported the conversion of many Jews and Gentiles and the establishment of local congregations, as well as his contacts with high officials (the Asiarchs) and the opposition that he had encountered. While Luke does not mention the presence of the delegates of the congregations in Berea, Thessalonica, Derbe, Lystra, Ephesus, and other cities, his reading audience would naturally assume that these Christian leaders, who were prominently mentioned in 20:4, would have provided, or confirmed, some of the details in Paul's report.

The verb translated as "described" (ἐξηγεῖτο) means "narrate, describe, recount," often with interpretative comment.[9] The phrase "in detail" suggests a full report with cities, converts, congregations, contacts, and opponents mentioned by name. Luke emphasizes again that it was God (ὁ θεός) who "had done" (ἐποίησεν) in Paul's ministry.[10] The phrase translated "among the Gentiles" could describe the focus of Paul's report, detailing the conversion of non-Jews in the province of Asia. However, as Luke regularly reported Paul's preaching in synagogues and the conversion of Jews resulting from Paul's missionary work (for Ephesus, see 19:8 – 9; for the province of Asia, see 19:10), it is preferable to interpret the phrase as describing the lands outside of Judea, i.e., the diaspora, where the majority of the people are Gentiles. At the same time, the phrase sets up the following scene in which James and the elders report rumors about Paul's teaching before "Jews who live among the Gentiles."

James and the elders, hearing Paul's report, "praise God" (ἐδόξαζον τὸν θεόν); i.e., they recognize and acknowledge God's presence in Paul's ministry as the one who caused people to come to faith and mighty acts to occur (for Ephesus, see 19:9, 10, 11 – 17, 20). Note that they will address Paul as "brother" (21:20c). The imperfect tense of ἐδόξαζον implies the durative aspect of their acknowledgment, which renders it likely that the collection of the "Pauline" congregations was indeed accepted — coming from congregations that are acknowledged as the work of God.[11]

21:20b-e They said to him, "Brother, you see how many thousands of Jews have come to faith, and they are all zealous for the law" (εἶπόν τε αὐτῷ· θεωρεῖς, ἀδελφέ, πόσαι μυριάδες εἰσὶν ἐν τοῖς Ἰουδαίοις τῶν πεπιστευκότων καὶ πάντες ζηλωταὶ τοῦ νόμου ὑπάρχουσιν). The second incident of the episode relates the speech of the elders (vv. 20b – 25). The fact that Luke does not mention James as the one who conveys the concerns of the Jerusalem leadership possibly indicates that he does not want to link James directly with the proposal put to Paul, which soon leads to his arrest.

---

8. Paul's statement to the Ephesian elders in 20:25 probably implies that as he plans to move to the western Mediterranean, he will leave the eastern provinces for good, presumably including Syria and Judea.

9. Cf. Spicq, "ἐξηγέομαι," *TLNT*, 2:21 – 23.

10. For "ministry" (διακονία) see on 1:25; 6:1. There is no linguistic reason to see the collection alluded to in the Greek term (as Johnson suggests, *Acts*, 374).

11. The attestation of a "frosty reception of Paul" by James and the elders (Dunn, *Beginning from Jerusalem*, 959), despite their praise of God, underestimates the significance of praise for Luke and for the early church (cf. 4:21; 11:18; 13:48; 19:17). See Jervell, *Apostelgeschichte*, 527.

Luke does not relate in direct speech the praise of James and the elders after hearing Paul's missionary report (v. 20a). Rather, he relates the second portion of their response: their concerns regarding Paul's reputation and the impact this may have on the Jewish believers in Jerusalem. In the first part of this speech (vv. 20d-e) Jerusalem leaders report new developments in their missionary work in Jerusalem and Judea. Paul had met the Jewish believers during his visit to Jerusalem six years earlier, among them some (τινες; cf. 15:1, 5, 24) who had argued that Gentile converts to faith in Jesus should be circumcised and ordered to keep the entire Mosaic law. There is no reason to doubt that Luke's earlier report about the unanimous agreement (15:25) of the meeting of the Apostles' Council about the Gentile mission (15:1–33) was correct.

The elders of the Jerusalem church do not ask Paul to require that the new Gentile converts be circumcised and be ordered to a wholesale submission to the Mosaic law. But there is every reason to assume a large-scale success of the Jewish mission in Judea, leading to the conversion of many "thousands" (μυριάδες)[12] of Jews who have accepted Jesus as Israel's Messiah. The perfect tense of the participle "have come to faith" (πεπιστευκότων) underlines that large numbers of Jews have believed and continue to be committed to faith in Jesus.

In 2:41 Luke had recorded the conversion of three thousand Jews, among them evidently a large number of Jews from the diaspora who traveled back to their cities. In 2:47 Luke had noted more daily conversions. In 4:4 a total of five thousand male believers is given, evidently a figure for the size of the church in Jerusalem. In 5:16 Luke mentions healing of "a large number of people" from towns around Jerusalem; in 9:31 he mentions in general terms the church "throughout Judea, Galilee, and Samaria," implying believers and congregations in various towns. In 11:1 Luke refers to believers "throughout Judea," i.e., from congregations in the towns in Judea, believers who needed and received help from those in Antioch (11:29). The "thousands" of believers now mentioned in 21:20 and described as "zealous for the law" are either new believers who have come to faith during Paul's absence, or Jewish believers in general who have been influenced more recently by teachers who have promoted rigorous adherence to the law.

The term translated as "zealous" (ζηλωταί) does not refer to the members of the militant "Zealot party" that came to power in the mid-60s of the first century AD. Josephus uses the term in the sense of "someone who is ardent for a cause" (*Life* 11) and designates a political, revolutionary party as "Zealots" only when he describes the outbreak of the Jewish rebellion against Rome in AD 66 (*J.W.* 4:160–161). In a later speech before the Jews of Jerusalem, Paul describes himself as a "zealot" for God (ζηλωτὴς τοῦ θεοῦ) as a result of his education at the feet of Gamaliel (22:3), a zeal that led him to persecute and arrest the followers of Jesus (22:4–5). The elders speak of Jewish believers who were ardent in their commitment to Mosaic law, including the rites of purification that figure prominently in the elders' proposal. Their report confirms the numerical strength of the Jerusalem church, numbering in the thousands.

21:21 They have been informed concerning you that you teach all the Jews who live among the Gentiles to abandon Moses, and that you tell them not to circumcise their children or live according to our customs (κατηχήθησαν δὲ περὶ σοῦ ὅτι ἀποστασίαν διδάσκεις ἀπὸ Μωϋσέως τοὺς κατὰ τὰ ἔθνη πάντας Ἰουδαίους λέγων μὴ περιτέμνειν

---

12. The term μυριάς describes a group of 10,000, but also "a very large number, not precisely defined" (BDAG, s.v. μυριάς 2).

αὐτοὺς τὰ τέκνα μηδὲ τοῖς ἔθεσιν περιπατεῖν). The second part of the elders' speech cites rumors among Jewish Christians that Paul encourages Jewish believers who live in the cities of the diaspora to neglect the Mosaic law (v. 21).

The elders first note the existence of rumors. The reference in "they have been informed" is the thousands of Jewish believers in Jerusalem and in Judea. The passive voice does not specify who has provided the information about Paul — they could be Jewish Christian missionaries who had traveled to the cities in which Paul had been preaching in the local synagogues; or they could be unbelieving diaspora Jews who visited Jerusalem for one of the festivals, informing the synagogues in Jerusalem about the activities of Paul. The latter possibility is made likely by Luke's reference to Jews from the province of Asia visiting Jerusalem, who assume that the presence of the uncircumcised Trophimus from Ephesus as Paul's companion can only mean that Paul had taken a Gentile into the inner courts of the temple — evidently a logical assumption of hostile diaspora Jews who clearly believe that Paul has no regard for the law.

These rumors concern Paul's teaching before Jews who live "among the Gentiles" (κατὰ τὰ ἔθνη), i.e., in the synagogues of the diaspora communities; in other words, the rumors are that whenever Paul speaks to Jewish audiences, he promotes the same teaching. The present tense of the verb translated "you teach" (διδάσκεις) underlines that this is not a problem of past behavior but a present, ongoing activity that Paul is accused of.

Luke details three charges against Paul. (1) He teaches apostasy from the Mosaic law. The term translated "abandon" (ἀποστασία) is a noun that denotes "defiance of an established system or authority" (BDAG), used here not in the sense of a political rebellion but in the sense of teaching Jews to abandon their commitment to the Mosaic law.[13] A Jew who stops keeping the commandments of the law lives like a Gentile and thus has become a Gentile.

(2) The next charge is that Paul abolishes circumcision. Since circumcision is one of central commandments of the Mosaic law, a defining mark of God's covenant with Israel that was kept presumably even by those Jews who otherwise were willing to compromise in their commitment to the law, this is a serious charge.

(3) He abolishes the Jewish customs. Paul is accused of teaching diaspora Jews that they no longer need to live according to the long-established customs (τὰ ἔθη),[14] i.e., that they should stop keeping the commandments of the law that stipulate how Jews were to conduct themselves in everyday life (περιπατεῖν).[15] The implication of these charges is that Jewish Christians should retain their Jewish identity by wholesale obedience to the law.

These charges are false. Paul argues against circumcision with regard to Gentile believers, but there is no evidence that he discouraged Jewish believers from circumcising their children. Note Paul's statement in 1 Cor 9:20 that when he preaches among Jews, he "became like a Jew, to win the Jews. To those under the law I became like one under the law (though I myself am not under the law), so as to win those under the law." Note too that Luke reported in 16:3 Paul's circumcision of Timothy.

At the same time, these rumors were not entirely without foundation. Paul could speak and write

13. For ἀποστασία referring to religious apostasy cf. in the LXX Josh 21:22; 2 Chr 29:19; 1 Macc 2:15.

14. Cf. BDAG, s.v. ἔθος 1, "a usual or customary manner of behavior, habit, usage," sense 2, "long-established usage or practice common to a group, custom."

15. Here περιπατέω means not "to go about, walk around" (as in 3:6, 8, 9, 12; 14:8, 10), but denotes "to conduct one's life, comport oneself, behave, live as habit of conduct" (BDAG, s.v. περιπατέω 2), as often in Paul's letters (e.g. Rom 6:4; 8:4; 13:13; 1 Cor 3:3; Gal 5:16).

about the believers' freedom from the law in terms that could be misunderstood to imply the removal of any obligation to keep the law, as the parenthetical qualification in 1 Cor 9:20 suggests; see Paul's teaching that Christian believers — both Jews and Gentiles — are no longer "under the law" (Rom 6:14 – 15; Gal 3:23; 4:5; cf. Gal 4:21 – 5:1) and that "circumcision is nothing" (1 Cor 7:19; Gal 6:15).[16] If Paul had indeed taught Jews to abandon the law, he would be a "seducer of the people," a person who seduces an entire town to apostasy and thus is subject to the death penalty (Deut 13:13; *m. Sanh.* 7:4). Paul is aware that this is his reputation among unbelieving Jews in Jerusalem, and he knows that they may pose a danger to him (Rom 15:31).

21:22 What is to be done? They will certainly hear that you have come (τί οὖν ἐστιν; πάντως ἀκούσονται ὅτι ἐλήλυθας). The third part of the elders' speech contains a proposal for Paul that will allow him to counteract the false rumors being spread about his teaching. This proposal is introduced by a rhetorical question (τί οὖν ἐστιν;): the elders know what action Paul should take to minimize the danger to himself and to those associated with him (such as the leadership of the Jerusalem church). The fact that the Jewish believers who are zealous for the law will certainly hear that Paul has arrived in Jerusalem underscores the urgency of action.

21:23 So, do what we tell you. There are four men among us who are under a vow (τοῦτο οὖν ποίησον ὅ σοι λέγομεν· εἰσὶν ἡμῖν ἄνδρες τέσσαρες εὐχὴν ἔχοντες ἐφ᾽ ἑαυτῶν). The proposal has four parts. The elders first request that Paul accept the course of action that they propose. The use of the aorist imperative (ποίησον) indicates that translations such as "our suggestion is"[17] are too weak;

while perhaps not an outright command, it clearly expresses a request.

Next, the elders describe the opportunity that presents itself by four Jewish believers who are under a vow. The reference to the shaving of heads in v. 24 indicates that the "vow" (εὐχή) that these four men had sworn was a Nazirite vow. They had asked God for some kind of intervention and promised something in return, while they refrained from intoxicating drink, from cutting their hair, and from defiling themselves through touching a dead body (Num 6:1 – 21; see on 18:18). Since they had completed the period of the vow, which now allowed them to shave (v. 24) and required sacrifices (v. 26), Paul is presented with an opportunity to publicly demonstrate his own observance of the law, his willingness to encourage others to be devoted to the law, and his refutation of the rumors about his teaching concerning the law as baseless.

21:24 Take these men, purify yourself along with them, and pay the expenses for them so that they may have their heads shaved. Then all will know that there is nothing to the reports that they have been given about you, but that you too conform to the observance of the law (τούτους παραλαβὼν ἁγνίσθητι σὺν αὐτοῖς καὶ δαπάνησον ἐπ᾽ αὐτοῖς ἵνα ξυρήσονται τὴν κεφαλήν, καὶ γνώσονται πάντες ὅτι ὧν κατήχηνται περὶ σοῦ οὐδέν ἐστιν ἀλλὰ στοιχεῖς καὶ αὐτὸς φυλάσσων τὸν νόμον). Next, the elders make a specific proposal how Paul can demonstrate his obedience to the law, consisting in three steps.

(1) Paul should join the four men in a portion of their actions; i.e., he should associate with them as they complete the period of their vow. (2) Paul should "purify" (ἁγνίσθητι; imperative) himself, i.e., undergo a rite of purification. (3) Paul should "pay the expenses" (δαπάνησον; imperative) for the

---

16. Also note the critical questions of Paul's dialogue partner in Rom 3:1 – 8.

17. Fitzmyer, *Acts*, 694.

men.[18] The shaving of the head had to take place at the entrance of the temple (cf. Num 6:19). The reference to a seven-day period in v. 27 renders it impossible that the elders suggest that Paul should make a Nazirite vow (which would last for at least thirty days).[19] The following explanations have been suggested.

(a) The four men are about to terminate their Nazirite vow. According to Num 6:14 – 15, Nazirites who end the period of their vow must sacrifice "a year-old male lamb without defect for a burnt offering, a year-old ewe lamb without defect for a sin offering, a ram without defect for a fellowship offering, together with their grain offerings and drink offerings." The expenses are thus considerable. In this case the elders ask Paul to join the four men in a purification rite (of unspecified significance; purification was not part of the regular termination of a Nazirite vow in Num 6) and pay the expenses that the four men have incurred.

(b) The four men had contracted uncleanness during the period of their Nazirite vow and are thus required to purify themselves after a period of seven days by bringing "two doves or two young pigeons to the priest at the entrance of the tent of meeting" (Num 6:9 – 10). The elders ask Paul to participate in *their* purification rites (without implying that Paul needed purification from defilement) and pay their expenses.

(c) The reason for the purification of Paul is *unrelated* to the vow of the four men. While the four men undergo the purification rites that have become necessary, evidently because they had con-

tracted uncleanness, fulfilling the mandated ritual law of Num 6:9 – 10, Paul will purify himself from the defilement caused by travel in Gentile areas.[20] The purification of the four men coincides in terms of time with Paul's purification.

The third scenario appears to be the most likely explanation.[21] Any Jew who visited the temple in order to offer sacrifices and partake of hallowed foodstuffs had to immerse himself in water so as not to defile, through mere physical contact, any of the consecrated vessels, clothing, or foodstuffs. Persons defiled by ritual impurities such as eating or drinking ritually impure foodstuffs or liquids, washing or bathing in any bath other than a valid *miqweh*, or having any form of physical contact with a Gentile, and who wanted to enter the inner courts of the temple, were deemed completely pure after ritual immersion without having to wait until sunset. The expenses that Paul is asked to pay would be large if the four men are terminating their Nazirite vow. It would be much less if they needed to restore their state of cleanness after contracting impurity in order to continue the period of their vow.

(4) Whatever the precise background of the proposal, the elders hope — this is the fourth part of their proposal — that such an action undertaken by Paul will have a twofold result. All the Jewish believers "will know" that there is "nothing" to the reports that people have been spreading about Paul. And they will know that Paul "conforms" (στοιχεῖς) to the "observance" of the law. The present tense of both the finite verb and the participle

---

18. Josephus, *Ant.* 19.294 relates that King Agrippa "shouldered the expense for the offering of poor Nazirites," an act that was meant to underscore his piety.

19. The expression "as long as they remain under their Nazirite vow" (Num 6:4) was later interpreted in terms of a period of thirty days (*m. Naz.* 1:3).

20. Note *m. ʾOhal.* 2:3 for defilement by "earth from a foreign country."

21. Cf. Reidar Hvalvik, "Paul as a Jewish Believer — According to the Book of Acts," in *Jewish Believers in Jesus: The Early Centuries* (ed. O. Skarsaune and R. Hvalvik; Peabody, MA: Hendrickson, 2007), 121 – 53, 142. The suggestion that Paul used funds from the collection for the cost of the expenses remains hypothetical; while it is true that the collection money goes to the Jerusalem church (Bock, *Acts*, 648), the elders could have made some of such funds available.

underline the point that Paul's action is not a tactical maneuver at one particular point in time but a reflection of his continuous, constant commitment to the law — a fact that the elders know and that the zealous among the Jewish believers should know as well. The proposed action "implies a public association between Paul and the Jerusalem Christian community."[22]

The elders are confident that Paul can counteract the unjustified reputation that he has among the Jewish diaspora communities and that he can lay to rest the rumors making the rounds in the Jerusalem church by proving that he is law-observant. On the question whether Paul could have indeed accepted this proposal, see below.

21:25 "As regards the Gentile believers, we have instructed them by letter concerning our decision that they must abstain from food sacrificed to idols, from blood, from the meat of strangled animals, and from sexual immorality" (περὶ δὲ τῶν πεπιστευκότων ἐθνῶν ἡμεῖς ἐπεστείλαμεν κρίναντες φυλάσσεσθαι αὐτοὺς τό τε εἰδωλόθυτον καὶ αἷμα καὶ πνικτὸν καὶ πορνείαν). The fourth part of the elders' proposal consists of a reminder about the decisions of the Apostles' Council and the letter the apostles and elders had written to the Gentile believers (15:23 – 29). Paul, of course, knows the content of the letter: he had accompanied it to Antioch and had made its contents known to the congregations in Syria and Cilicia (15:22, 31, 41; 16:4).

The point of the reference to the stipulations of the apostolic decree (see on 15:20) is to articulate the distinction between the behavior of the Gentile believers and the behavior of the Jewish believers. The former had been addressed by the apostolic letter, while the latter needed to be addressed by Paul. Gentile Christians do not need to be concerned about circumcision and many other matters

of the law, although they had been instructed of the decision to abstain from food sacrificed to idols (i.e., from participating in idolatry), from blood and from the meat of strangled animals (i.e., from consuming food products containing blood), and from sexual immorality (i.e., from adultery, visits to prostitutes, and homosexual acts).[23]

The elders and the Jewish Christians in Jerusalem and Judea are not asking the Gentile Christians to become Jews — that was precisely the unanimous decision at the council. They are asking that Jewish Christians should not be made Gentile Christians, which would happen if they were asked to abandon circumcision and renounce other ritual stipulations of the law.

21:26 On the following day Paul took the men and purified himself together with them. Then he went into the temple to give notice of the fulfillment of the days of purification, when the offering would be made for each of them (τότε ὁ Παῦλος παραλαβὼν τοὺς ἄνδρας τῇ ἐχομένῃ ἡμέρᾳ σὺν αὐτοῖς ἁγνισθείς, εἰσῄει εἰς τὸ ἱερὸν διαγγέλλων τὴν ἐκπλήρωσιν τῶν ἡμερῶν τοῦ ἁγνισμοῦ ἕως οὗ προσηνέχθη ὑπὲρ ἑνὸς ἑκάστου αὐτῶν ἡ προσφορά). The third and final incident of the episode that narrates Paul's encounter with the elders of the Jerusalem church relates Paul's demonstration of his obedience to the law. The incident takes place on the day immediately after the meeting with the elders.

Two aorist participles describe Paul's compliance with the elders' request in v. 24: Paul took (παραλαβών) the four men and purified (ἁγνισθείς) himself with them. It can be assumed that one of the large immersion pools (*miqwaot*) was the site where the five men immersed themselves for purification — perhaps in the Pool of Siloam at the junction of the Tyropoeon and Kidron Valleys, or

---

22. Bauckham, "James and the Jerusalem Church," 479.

23. The order of the four stipulations corresponds to the order in the letter (15:23 – 29), not the order that James spoke in his speech (15:19 – 21).

in the Pool of Bethesda near the Sheep Gate (see on 2:38). Then Paul went into the inner temple courts in order to give notice, presumably to one of the priests, about the terms of the completion of the seven (v. 27) days of purification, with specific information concerning the offering that would be offered at the end of this period. If the purification

of the four Jewish believers is explained by Num 6:9 — they renew their vow after having become defiled — the offering would have required two turtledoves or young pigeons for each man.[24] This would probably mean that the phrase "for each of them" refers to the four men and does not include Paul, whose purification, then, is a more private matter.

Theology in Application

Luke's account of Paul's meeting with James and the elders of the Jerusalem church raises the question whether Paul could have accepted the elders' proposal. Scholars who think that Paul advocated the abrogation of the Mosaic law regard v. 26 as not credible. Often quoted is the rebuttal, expressed in vivid terms, that "all this is about as likely as that Luther in his old age should have made a pilgrimage on peas to a hermitage, or that Calvin on his death-bed vowed a golden coat to the Holy Mother of God."[25] However, an act of personal piety, symbolizing purification through immersion in water (see on 2:38) — a regular Jewish practice — would not have contradicted Paul's conviction that full purification of both Jewish and Gentile sinners has been achieved by the sacrificial and atoning death of Jesus (Rom 3:25), cleansing sinners who believe in Jesus from their sin.[26] Paul knows that sinners justified by Jesus' death still need cleansing; note 2 Cor 7:1: "Since we have these promises, dear friends, let us purify ourselves from everything that contaminates body and spirit, perfecting holiness out of reverence for God." The notion that Paul would express repentance and renewed commitment to God through the symbolic action of immersion in water is not at all impossible.

Missionary Tactics or Expression of a Consistent Theological Position?

Was Paul's agreement only a tactical move? Some suggest that Paul could adopt Jewish customs when it served missionary purposes, pointing to 1 Cor 9:20 as Paul's principle of "contextualized" ministry: among Jews he lives as a Jew, among Gentiles he lives as a Gentile.[27] While not impossible, there are two problems with this expla-

---

24. The reference to the completion of the Nazirite vow in Num 6:5, 13 does not refer to purification.

25. Adolf Hausrath, *A History of the New Testament Times* (4 vols.; London: Williams & Norgate, 1895), 4:112. Cf. Marshall, *Acts*, 346. Few quote Hausrath's earlier, rather anti-Jewish sounding (and quite anachronistic) view regarding the Jerusalem leaders who want Paul to submit to "all the liturgical pedantries of ritual as then established at the hands of the unbelieving Levites and priests" (ibid., 4:111). Peterson, *Acts*, 588,

speaks of a "minefield of ritual requirements and prohibitions," which seems more a reflection of his views concerning how the Nazirite vow was handled in the first century than of alleged complexities of the Mosaic law.

26. Cf. Rom 6:17–19; 14:20; Phil 1:10–11; Eph 5:25–26; and the passages that call the believers "holy" or "saints" (e.g., Rom 1:7; 11:16; 12:1; 1 Cor 1:17; 6:19).

27. Cf. Günther Bornkamm, "The Missionary Stance of Paul in I Corinthians 9 and in Acts," in *Studies in Luke-Acts*

nation. First, Paul's point in 1 Cor 9:19 – 23 is that he does not exclude anybody from his preaching and that he does not set limits on his identification with the people whom he seeks to win for faith in Jesus — which is his commission and desire as an apostle.[28] His concern in this passage (in the context of 1 Cor 8 – 10) is not to advocate a particular position regarding the law, but to underline the necessity of focusing on other people rather than on our own rights and privileges. Paul states that he is no longer "under the law" (1 Cor 9:20), which means that he does not follow all stipulations of the Mosaic law, particularly the laws that distinguish between Jews and Gentiles, such as the commandments that regulate food.

But Paul is quick to point out that his "freedom" is not lawlessness (antinomianism). He does not advocate the abrogation of the law: as far as the law is the law of God "in Christ," i.e., modified by Jesus, Israel's Messiah and Savior, it remains valid, which means that he continues to live "under Christ's law" (ἔννομος Χριστοῦ; 1 Cor 9:21). At the same time Paul maintains the freedom that is given with Jesus Christ in his contacts with Gentiles. He does not require them to keep the stipulations of the Torah; he eats what they eat. He does not transform them to Jews (which would require circumcision) before they can become full members of the people of God.

Paul's accommodation is not absolute. With regard to the Gentiles, accommodation is decisively limited by the religious convictions and ethical values of the pagans (Paul never says that he becomes "a pagan to the pagans"). Paul cannot "live like a Gentile" and worship in a pagan temple or visit prostitutes or despise the slaves, and this is what he teaches the Gentile converts. With regard to the Jews, accommodation is decisively constrained by his faith in Jesus as Israel's Messiah and Savior: Paul cannot "live like a Jew" and treat the temple as the central place of God's presence (and continue to bring sin and guilt offerings), or regard the Jewish people as the only place where salvation is possible (and require Gentiles to become Jews if they want forgiveness). The religious relativism and polytheism of Gentile society make it impossible for Paul — or any other Christian — to live "as a Gentile" in every respect. And the reality of Jesus as Israel's crucified, risen, and exalted Messiah and Savior, and the significance of God's calling together a new people among whom he is present, consisting of Jewish and Gentile believers in Jesus, make it impossible for Paul to live "as a Jew" in every respect.

Not a few commentators think that "undoubtedly the plan, as described in Acts, misfired."[29] The fact that Paul was arrested when Jews from the province of Asia claim they saw him in the temple with Trophimus (21:27 – 29) does not prove that the elders' proposal was problematic. If the Jerusalem congregation continued to meet in Solomon's Portico in the outer temple courts, and if Paul attended their meetings

(FS Paul Schubert; ed. L. E. Keck and J. L. Martyn; Nashville: Abingdon, 1966), 194 – 207; Bruce, *Book of Acts*, 407 – 8, who suggests that "the wisdom of Paul's complying with the elders' plan may well be doubted."

28. For a discussion of 1 Cor 9:19 – 23, see Schnabel, *Early Christian Mission*, 2:953 – 60; for the following comments see ibid., 955.

29. Barrett, *Acts*, 1013.

there, he still would have been spotted by diaspora Jews. There is no indication that the elders' proposal was meant to preempt attacks on Paul by Jews from Asia Minor. Since Luke is silent about the reaction of the Jewish believers in Jerusalem and Judea who had heard rumors about Paul's teaching, it is mute to speculate on the success, or lack thereof, of Paul's willingness to respond positively to the elders' proposal.

The Significance of Missionary Work as God's Mission

The beginning of the episode recalls again, and not for the last time, Luke's conviction that it is God himself who is active in the proclamation of the gospel and in the expansion of the church. God, not Paul, caused the things to happen that Paul relates in his report before James and the elders of the Jerusalem church (21:19) — the conversion of people, the establishment of new churches, the encouragement of the believers. Because missionary work is God's work, the question is not so much how we, today, "do" church but whether we allow God to do his work or whether we think that the key to "success" in missionary work and church growth lies with anthropological analysis, social-scientific exploration, business management methods, or the use of modern media. The adulation of "stars" in evangelicalism who are famous because they have large churches or because they have founded large ministries contrasts with the praise that James and the elders gave *to God* when they heard Paul report how God had worked in his ministry.

The Importance of Concrete Efforts to Maintain the Unity of the Church

Since Luke is silent about the collection as an important factor in Paul's decision to visit Jerusalem, despite multiple warnings concerning the danger of visiting Jerusalem, the purpose of the collection in expressing and consolidating the unity between the mixed congregations in which Jewish believers and Gentiles believers worship is not explicitly addressed in the text. Paul's willingness to accept and act on the elders' proposal makes this point just as strongly, however. Whether or not Paul regularly immersed himself in water, following Jewish custom stipulated in the Mosaic law (and regulated in Jewish tradition), as a symbolic expression of repentance and purification of sin, his willingness to comply with the wishes of the leadership of the Jerusalem church underscores Paul's concern for unity.

While rumors may be unavoidable, Paul does not want them to come between himself and the Jewish believers of Judea and Jerusalem. The text also demonstrates the importance of identifying existing tensions. Neither the church nor its leaders are helped if they gloss over friction in the church. James and the elders who want to help Paul (re-)gain the trust of the Jewish believers model effective church leadership. Truth and people are crucial and must be protected — here the truth of the continued validity of God's revelation in the Scriptures, and Paul as a missionary who must not be sidelined or left to fend for himself.

Acts 21:27 – 22:21

Literary Context

The second episode in Luke's report of Paul's last stay in Jerusalem (21:18 – 23:35) narrates his arrest (21:27 – 22:21), an event whose consequences determine all subsequent episodes of Acts: Paul never regains his freedom; he remains a prisoner in Jerusalem and is then transferred to Caesarea and eventually to Rome. Paul's arrest is triggered by Jews from the province of Asia, who see Paul both in the city and in the inner courts of the temple. They assume he had taken one of his associates, Trophimus from Ephesus (whom they believe to be a Gentile) into the inner courts, which would defile the temple. While it seems that Paul's enemies are about to triumph, Paul is rescued by a commander in the Roman army who allows him to address a large crowd of Jews.

Further opportunities to speak about his encounter with Jesus and to confess his faith in Jesus as Israel's Messiah and Savior arise in later episodes: in front of two Roman governors and the Jewish king, and eventually before the leaders of the Jewish community in Rome. While there are no more miraculous escapes from prison,[1] Luke portrays Paul as continuing to explain the gospel of God's revelation in and through Jesus; and he presents Paul as reaching Rome, which has been his goal since Ephesus (19:21). The fact that Paul is a prisoner is thus less important than the reality of his commitment to the name of the Lord Jesus (21:13) and the fact that he is bound with chains for the sake of the hope of Israel (28:20), Jesus Christ, who continues to direct and empower the mission of the church.

This episode, with the first of four defensive speeches of Paul (22:1 – 21; 24:10 – 21; 25:8 – 11; 26:1 – 23), introduces the major themes that Luke presents in the last major section of Acts, which is as long as Luke's narrative that relates Paul's missionary work (13:1 – 21:26). The main legal issue is the alleged anti-Jewish teaching and behavior of Paul, whose mission is impugned as an attack on the Jewish people and its ancestral faith and who is accused as having defiled the temple and creating disturbances. At contention is Paul's personal behavior, teaching, and missionary work among Jews and Gentiles, and thus the gospel itself is at stake.

---

1. Cf. 5:17 – 21; 12:1 – 17; 16:25 – 30.

Paul's defense before Jews in the outer court of the temple in 22:1 – 21 contains the second retelling of his conversion (the third account is in 26:1 – 23). The fact that Paul's conversion is told three times is significant. Luke repeats what he wants to impress upon his readers: Paul, an active witness of Jesus for many years, is a prime witness of Jesus' resurrection, having encountered him in person on the road to Damascus. It is no coincidence that the first and the last defense speeches Paul gives are both addressed to Jewish audiences (here in 22:1 – 21, the Jews in the temple court; in 26:1 – 23, King Agrippa II). Only the second speech is a trial scene proper, set in Caesarea before the Roman governor Festus, with Paul refuting the charges of the Jews point by point (24:10 – 21). The third speech does not present arguments for Paul's innocence but describes his appeal to the emperor before the new governor Festus (25:8 – 11), a legal move that effectively removes Paul from Jewish jurisdiction (cf. 25:9).

The concern of Paul — and thus of Luke — is essentially negative: Roman officials need not be concerned about the Jews' opposition to the missionary work of Paul (nor that of the followers of Jesus in general). Neither the content of Paul's teaching nor the specifics of his behavior warrant legal intervention by Roman authorities, let alone a guilty verdict. The real issue is the conviction of Paul, and of all followers of Jesus, that Jesus is Israel's Messiah and that God wants both Jews and Gentiles to come to faith in Jesus as Savior. The events reported in 21:27 – 22:21 take place in May AD 57, shortly before the Feast of Pentecost.

Main Idea

Witnesses of Jesus who are arrested and are in danger of being killed share in Jesus' suffering; if Jesus chooses to save his witnesses, they will be rescued, even if the instruments of divine intervention are pagans. Believers in Jesus, even in dangerous situations, profess God who reveals himself in Jesus, and they give testimony of Jesus of Nazareth, who is alive, who saves, and who directs the life of the restored people of God consisting of Jews and Gentiles.

Translation

Acts 21:27 – 22:21

27a	Setting: time	When the seven days were almost completed,
b	Character entrance	**Jews**
c	Description: geographical	from the province of Asia
d	Event	who saw Paul
e	Place	in the temple
f	Action	**stirred up the whole crowd**
g	Action	and **seized him.**
28a	Action	**They shouted,**
b	Exclamation	"Fellow Israelites, help!
c	Identification (accusation)	This is the man
d	Character description	who is teaching
e	Sphere (hyperbole)	everyone
f	Place (hyperbole)	everywhere
g	Conflict	against our people,
h	Conflict	against the law, and
i	Conflict	against this place.
j	Report: action	Besides, he has even brought Greeks
k	Place	into the temple
l	Result	and defiled this holy place."
29a	Flashback: explanation	**They had earlier seen Trophimus**
b	Description: geographical	the Ephesian
c	Place	in the city
d	Association	with Paul
e	Character's thought	and **assumed**
f	Content	that he had brought him
g	Place	into the temple.
30a	Event	**The whole city was in turmoil,**
b	Action	and **people rushed together.**
c	Action	**They seized Paul**
d	Action	and **dragged him out of the temple,**
e	Action	and **immediately the gates were shut.**
31a	Setting: time	While they were trying to kill him,
b	Event	**it was reported**
c	Character entrance	to the commander of the cohort
d	Report	that the entire city of Jerusalem was in chaos.
32a	Action	**He at once took his soldiers and**
b		**centurions**
c	Action	and **ran down to them.**
d	Setting: time	When they saw the commander and
e		the soldiers,
f	Reaction	**they stopped beating Paul.**
33a	Action	**The commander approached them,**
b	Action	**arrested Paul,**

Continued on next page.

Continued from previous page.

c	Action	and **ordered him to be bound**
d	Means	with two chains.
e	Question	Then **he asked**
f	Indirect question	who he was and
g	Indirect question	what he had done.
34a	Action	**Some people in the crowd shouted one thing, some another.**
b	Cause	Since he could not get to the truth
c	Cause	because of the noise,
d	Action	**he ordered him to be taken into the barracks.**
35a	Setting: time	When Paul reached the flight of stairs,
b	Action	**he had to be carried by the soldiers**
c	Cause	because of the violence of the crowd.
36a	Action	**The crowd of people kept following,**
b	Exclamation	shouting, *"Take him away!"*
37a	Setting: time	As Paul was about to be taken into the barracks,
b	Action	**he said to the commander,**
c	Question	*"May I be permitted to say something to you?"*
d	Response	**He replied,**
e	Question	*"Do you speak Greek?*
38a	Question: identification	*Are you not the Egyptian*
b	Character description	*who instigated a revolt*
c	Time	*some time ago*
d	Action	*and led four thousand terrorists*
e	Place	*into the desert?"*
39a	Response	**Paul replied,**
b	Identification	*"I am a Jew,*
c	Geographical	*from Tarsus in Cilicia,*
d	Character description	*the citizen of an important city.*
e	Entreaty	*I beg you,*
f		*allow me to speak to the people."*
40a	Setting: time	When he had received his permission,
b	Action	**Paul stood on the steps**
c	Action	and **motioned to the people with his hand.**
d	Setting: time	When all were silent,
e	Action	**he addressed them**
f	Manner	in Hebrew.
22:1a	Address	*"Brothers and fathers,*
b	Exhortation	*listen to my defense*
c	Description	*that I now present before you."*
2a	Setting: time	When they heard him addressing them
b	Manner	in Hebrew,
c	Action	**they became even more quiet.**
d	Action: speech	Then **Paul said:**

3a	Identification	"I am a Jew,
b	Geographical	born in Tarsus in Cilicia,
c	Geographical (contrast)	but brought up in this city.
d	Action	I studied under Gamaliel
e	Manner	in strict conformity to the standard of our ancestral law.
f	Action	I was as zealous for God
g	Comparison	as all of you are today.
4a	Action	I persecuted this Way to the point of death,
b	Means	arresting and imprisoning men and women,
5a	Verification	as the high priest and
b	Verification	the whole council of elders
c	Verification	can testify about me.
d	Action	I even obtained letters
e	Source	from them
f	Object	to our Jewish brothers in Damascus,
g	Action	and I went there
h	Purpose	in order to bring these people as prisoners back
i	Place	to Jerusalem
j	Purpose	for punishment.
6a	Setting: geographical	As I was on my way
b	Setting: geographical	and approached Damascus,
c	Setting: time	about noon
d	Event	a great light
e	Manner	suddenly
f		flashed around me.
7a	Reaction	I fell to the ground
b	Event (character entrance)	and heard a voice say to me,
c	Address	'Saul, Saul,
d	Question	why are you persecuting me?'
8a	Response	I replied,
b	Question	'Who are you, Lord?'
c	Response	Then he said to me,
d	Identification	'I am Jesus of Nazareth,
e	Identification	whom you are persecuting.'
9a	Description	The men who were with me saw the light,
b	Contrast	but they did not hear the voice of him who was speaking to me.
10a	Reaction	I asked,
b	Question	'What am I to do, Lord?'
c	Response	The Lord replied,
d	Command	'Get up
e	Command: geographical	and go to Damascus.
f	Pronouncement	There you will be told everything
g	Description	that you have been ordered to do.'
11a	Cause	Since I could not see
b	Cause	because of the brightness of the light,
c	Action	the men who were with me led me by the hand
d	Place	to Damascus.

Continued on next page.

Continued from previous page.

12a	Character entrance	A certain Ananias,
b	Character description	a devout man according to the law
c	Character description	who was well spoken of by all the Jews living there,
13a	Action	came to me.
b	Action	He stood beside me
c	Action: speech	and said,
d	Address	'Brother Saul,
e	Command	regain your sight!'
f	Time (simultaneous)	At that very moment
g	Event	I regained my sight
h	Action	and looked at him.
14a	Action: speech	Then he said,
b	Pronouncement	'The God of our ancestors has chosen you
c	Purpose	to know his will,
d	Purpose	to see the Righteous One, and
e	Purpose	to hear his own voice.
15a	Pronouncement/Commission	You will be his witness
b	Sphere	before all people,
c	Means	bearing witness
d	Content	to what you have seen and
e	Content	heard.
16a	Rhetorical question	And now, what are you waiting for?
b	Command	Get up,
c	Command	be immersed, and
d	Command	wash your sins away
e	Means	by calling on his name.'
17a	Setting: time	When I returned to Jerusalem
b	Setting: place	and was praying in the temple,
c	Event	I fell into a trance
18a	Vision	and saw the Lord speaking to me,
b	Command	'Hurry,
c	Command	leave Jerusalem
d	Time	immediately,
e	Cause	because they will not accept your testimony
f	Content	about me.'
19a	Response	I answered,
b	Assertion	'Lord, they know that I went from one synagogue to another
c	Purpose	to imprison and
d	Purpose	beat those who believed in you.
20a	Event	While the blood of Stephen,
b	Character description	your witness,
c	Event	was being shed,
d	Action	I stood there,
e	Cause	giving my approval and
f	Purpose	guarding the clothes of those who were killing him.'
21a	Response	Then he said to me,
b	Command	'Go!
c	Commission	I am sending you far away to the Gentiles.'"

Structure and Literary Form

The episode is made up of five incidents. (1) Luke narrates the riot in the temple instigated by Jews from the province of Asia, who recognize Paul in the inner courts (21:27 – 29). (2) People then hear about an alleged defilement of the temple caused by Paul, who is reported to have taken a Gentile into the temple; they rush into the temple and try to kill Paul (vv. 30 – 31). (3) The Roman commander of the troops stationed in the Antonia Fortress, which overlooks the temple complex, intervenes and rescues Paul (vv. 32 – 36). (4) On the steps from the outer temple court up to the Antonia Fortress Paul protests his innocence before the Roman commander (vv. 37 – 40). (5) Paul then speaks before the Jews assembled in the temple (22:1 – 21). In the first, second, and third incidents Paul is entirely passive, while the crowd is active (21:27 – 36). In the fourth and fifth incidents Paul's actions drive the narrative: he speaks with the Roman commander (21:37 – 40) and then addresses the Jews assembled in the temple (22:1 – 21).

The first four incidents of the episode are *narratives* that relate events in the inner temple courts (21:27 – 28), in the city (21:30), in the outer temple courts (21:31, 32 – 36), and on the steps from the outer temple courts up into the barracks in the Antonia Fortress (21:37 – 40). The last incident consists largely of narrative as well, as Paul recounts his life before and after his conversion. Involved in these events are Jews from the province of Asia, the Jews of Jerusalem, Paul, Trophimus, the priests who shut the temple doors, the commander of the Roman troops stationed in the Antonia Fortress, the soldiers who bind Paul with chains and take him across the outer temple court in the northern part of the temple complex, where Paul speaks.

Several sections of *direct speech*, some of them substantial, make the narrative vivid, drawing the reading and listening audience into the story: the rallying cry of the Jews from the province of Asia (21:28), the shouts of the crowd demanding Paul's death (21:36), the dialogue between Paul (21:37c, 39) and the Roman commander (21:37e – 38), and Paul's extensive speech (22:1, 3 – 21), which contains *reports of direct speech* from Jesus (22:7c-d, 8d-e, 10d-g, 18, 21), from Paul (22:8b, 10b, 19 – 20), and from Ananias (22:13d-e, 14 – 16), as well as a *missionary commission* (22:15, 21).

The speech on the steps before the Jews in the outer temple court (22:1 – 21) is Paul's sixth speech.[2] In a formal defense speech,[3] the *exordium* and *narratio* is followed by the *probatio* (the presentation of the proofs), the *refutatio* (the rebuttal of the case of the opponent), and the *peroratio* (the conclusion that summarizes the

---

2. Cf. 13:9 – 11 (Paphos); 13:16 – 41 (Pisidian Antioch); 14:15 – 18 (Lystra); 17:22 – 31 (Athens); 20:18 – 35 (Miletus). For the following analysis see Witherington, *Acts*, 666 – 68, following Kennedy, *Rhetorical Criticism*, 134.

3. Paul calls his speech ἀπολογία (22:1). It should be noted

that the setting is not that of a formal trial. The noun ἀπολογία is also used in 25:16, while the verb ἀπολογέομαι is used in 24:10; 25:8; 26:1, 2, 24 — evidence that suggests Luke wants Paul's speech in 22:1 – 21 to be understood as defense speech. Cf. Omerzu, *Prozess*, 372.

case and calls for a specific course of action).[4] Here we have only the introduction (*exordium*) and the statement of the facts (*narratio*); the crowd interrupts Paul before the *peroratio*, i.e., before he can answer the charge that he teaches against the Jewish people, the Mosaic law, and the temple, as well as against the more specific charge that he brought a Gentile into the inner temple courts (21:28). As a result, Paul's speech consists of his presenting the facts of the case, which demonstrate that he is not a Jewish apostate who teaches other Jews to become apostates. New material in the story of Paul's conversion not recorded in 9:1 – 19 is his vision in the temple (22:17 – 21), which took place after he had returned from Damascus to Jerusalem a few years after his conversion, which underscores the divine authorization to be active in Gentile regions outside of Judea.

Exegetical Outline

→ **I. Paul's Arrest in the Temple (21:27 – 22:21)**

    A. The Riot in the Temple Instigated by Jews from the Province of Asia (21:27 – 29)

        1. The time of Paul's arrest (21:27a)

        2. The riot caused by Jews from the province of Asia (21:27b-g)

        3. The cause of concern of the Jews from the province of Asia (21:28)

            a. Call to action (21:28a-b)

            b. Identification of Paul as the infamous Jewish teacher (21:28c-f)

            c. The charges against Paul (21:28g-i)

                i. Paul teaches against the Jewish people (21:28g)

                ii. Paul teaches against the law (21:28h)

                iii. Paul teaches against the temple (21:28i)

                iv. Paul has brought Greeks into the temple (21:28j-k)

                v. Paul has defiled the temple (21:28l)

        4. The reason for the action of the Jews from the province of Asia (21:29)

            a. They had seen the Ephesian Trophimus with Paul (21:29a-d)

            b. They had concluded that Paul had brought him into the temple (21:29e-g)

    B. The Attempted Killing of Paul in the Outer Court of the Temple (21:30 – 31)

        1. The riot in the city (21:30a-b)

        2. Paul's arrest in the inner courts (21:30c-e)

        3. The attempt to kill Paul in the Outer Court (21:31a)

        4. The report given to the Roman commander about the riot (21:31b-d)

---

4. For the rhetorical terms see Structure and Literary Form on 13:13 – 52. Cf. Jerome H. Neyrey, "The Forensic Defense Speech and Paul's Trial Speeches in Acts 22 – 26," in *Luke-Acts: New Perspectives from the Society of Biblical Literature Seminar* (ed. C. H. Talbert; New York: Crossroad, 1984), 210 – 24, 210 – 11.

C. The Intervention of Claudius Lysias (21:32 – 36)

    1. Appearance of the Roman commander and his soldiers in the Outer Court (21:32a-c)

    2. The end of the Jews' assault on Paul (21:32d-f)

    3. Paul's arrest by the Roman commander (21:33a-d)

    4. The commander's query (21:33e-g)

        a. Questions concerning Paul's identity (21:33e-f)

        b. Questions concerning Paul's actions (21:33g)

    5. The confusion among the Jewish crowd (21:34a)

    6. The commander's order to take Paul into the barracks (21:34b-d)

    7. Paul's transfer to the barracks through the outer temple court (21:35)

    8. The Jews' demand for Paul's execution (21:36)

D. Paul Asks for Permission to Address the Jewish Crowd (21:37 – 40)

    1. The arrival of the soldiers at the steps leading up into the Antonia Fortress (21:37a)

    2. Paul's request to speak with the Roman commander (21:37b-c)

    3. The commander's inquiry concerning Paul's identity (21:37d – 38)

    4. Paul's clarification of his identity as a Jew from Tarsus (21:39a-d)

    5. Paul's request to be allowed to address the assembled Jews (21:39e-f)

    6. The commander's permission (21:40a)

    7. The commencement of Paul's speech, given in Hebrew (21:40b-f)

E. Paul's Speech to the Jews Assembled in the Outer Temple Courts (22:1 – 21)

    1. Address (*exordium*) (22:1)

    2. Narrator's aside: The attentiveness of the crowd (22:2)

    3. The facts of the case (*narratio*) (22:3 – 21)

        a. Paul's life before his conversion (22:3 – 5)

            i. Paul's Jewish credentials (22:3)

            ii. Paul's activity as a persecutor of the followers of Jesus (22:4 – 5)

        b. Paul's conversion (22:6 – 16)

            i. Paul's encounter with Jesus of Nazareth on the road to Damascus (22:6 – 11)

            ii. Paul's commission by God to be a witness of Jesus to the world (22:12 – 16)

        c. Paul's vision in the temple after his return to Jerusalem (22:17 – 21)

            i. Paul's return to Jerusalem and his vision (22:17)

            ii. Jesus' directive to leave Jerusalem because of the Jews' unbelief (22:18)

            iii. Paul's protest that he can be an effective witness in Jerusalem (22:19 – 20)

            iv. Jesus' directive to Paul to go far away to the Gentiles (22:21)

Explanation of the Text

21:27　When the seven days were almost completed, Jews from the province of Asia who saw Paul in the temple stirred up the whole crowd and seized him (ὡς δὲ ἔμελλον αἱ ἑπτὰ ἡμέραι συντελεῖσθαι, οἱ ἀπὸ τῆς Ἀσίας Ἰουδαῖοι θεασάμενοι αὐτὸν ἐν τῷ ἱερῷ συνέχεον πάντα τὸν ὄχλον καὶ ἐπέβαλον ἐπ᾽ αὐτὸν τὰς χεῖρας). This first incident of the episode that narrates Paul's arrest in the temple (21:27 – 22:21) relates a riot caused by Jews from the province of Asia. A week after Paul's initial meeting with James and the elders of the Jerusalem church, he visits the temple when the seven days of purification were almost completed — presumably to immerse himself, which would allow him to enter the temple courts and participate in the purification of the four Jewish believers who had taken a Nazirite vow (see on v. 24).

Luke connects the cause of Paul's arrest and subsequent imprisonment with Jews from the province of Asia. They may be identical with the people who spread the rumors concerning Paul's annulment of the Mosaic law (v. 21), although Luke does not explicitly identify the two groups. The Jews from Asia may include those from Ephesus who had forced Paul to relocate his teaching from the synagogue to the lecture hall of Tyrannus (19:9). This is a plausible assumption since they know Trophimus (v. 29), a Christian from Ephesus who had come with Paul to Jerusalem (20:4). Since Luke mentions the impact of Paul's ministry on "all people who lived in the province of Asia, both Jews and Greeks" (19:10; cf. 19:22, 26; 20:16, 18), Jews of other cities may be in view as well.

These Jews from the province of Asia, who are in Jerusalem as pilgrims attending the Feast of Pentecost (cf. 20:16), see Paul, stir up the crowd, and seize him (cf. 5:18). The imperfect tense of the second verb (συνέχεον, "stirred up"), framed by two verbal forms in the aorist tense, places the emphasis on the process of the deliberate fomentation of trouble.

Paul's arrest takes place in one of the inner courts of the temple. The reference to the "gates" of the temple in v. 30 could refer to (1) the gates that connected the temple complex with the city; (2) the seven gates of the Inner Enclosure: there were three gates on the northern side, three gates on the southern side, and one gate on the east (the Nicanor Gate); (3) the three gates that connected the Court of Women to the court within the outer court.[5] The first possibility is unlikely because the reported movements of the Roman commander, who arrests Paul in the outer court (vv. 31 – 35), and because of the charge against Paul that he has defiled the temple (v. 28), which makes sense only if he was in the inner courts.

The second and third options are both possible. Paul could have been in the Place of the Hearth (*bet hammoked*), one of the gatehouses located in the Inner Enclosure, which functions as a "supervision center" for all activities carried out in the temple:

> It was used not only by the priests and Levites on duty, but also by Jewish males bringing sacrifices, who were allowed to enter its northern half in order to obtain the token needed for bringing their sacrifices ... from *bet hamoked* access could also be gained to the three offices attached to it and to the stairwell leading to a ritual bath and lavatory via the corridor below the *chel*.[6]

---

5. Cf. Ehud Netzer, *The Architecture of Herod, the Great Builder* (Grand Rapids: Baker, 2008), 141 (fig. 32), 154 – 60, 171 – 75.

6. Ibid., 158; for further details see ibid., 155 – 56, 158.

Or Paul was in the Court of the Women: one of its enclosures, called *liškat hann^ezirîm*, served the Nazirites who burnt their offerings here. The movements of the Roman commander implied in vv. 31 – 34 make it most likely that the place "in the temple" (ἐν τῷ ἱερῷ, v. 27) where Paul was spotted and arrested was either of these two places.

Dragged outside either of these courts (v. 30), Paul is taken across the court into the outer court to which the Roman commander has direct access (v. 32) through two external staircases that connected the northern and western colonnades of the outer court with the Antonia Fortress. The commanding officer arrests Paul in the outer court and eventually takes him up the staircase into the barracks in the Antonia (vv. 33 – 35).

In v. 27 Luke conveys to his readers the ominous feeling that Paul's life is about to end: he stands in the middle of a hostile crowd whose anger has been stirred up by Jews from the province of Asia, unable to leave because he is restrained by these diaspora Jews.

21:28 They shouted, "Fellow Israelites, help! This is the man who is teaching everyone everywhere against our people, against the law, and against this place. Besides, he has even brought Greeks into the temple and defiled this holy place" (κράζοντες· ἄνδρες Ἰσραηλῖται, βοηθεῖτε· οὗτός ἐστιν ὁ ἄνθρωπος ὁ κατὰ τοῦ λαοῦ καὶ τοῦ νόμου καὶ τοῦ τόπου τούτου πάντας πανταχῇ διδάσκων, ἔτι τε καὶ Ἕλληνας εἰσήγαγεν εἰς τὸ ἱερὸν καὶ κεκοίνωκεν τὸν ἅγιον τόπον τοῦτον). The Jews from Asia seize Paul because they disagree with the theological content of his teaching and because they believe that he has defiled the temple.

Luke begins by describing their call to action — with loud and continuous shouts (κράζοντες,

present participle). They summon other Jews to assist them in dealing with Paul. As v. 30 indicates, their cries for help on the Temple Mount are carried by onlookers into the city, so that other Jews rush into the temple courts toward the commotion. They identify Paul to the Jews in the outer court, who have been attracted by their shouts, as a teacher who is teaching "everyone," i.e., both Jews and Greeks (as the subsequent specific charges indicate), and who is teaching "everywhere," i.e., in the cities of the province of Asia and beyond. This description, unwittingly, confirms that Paul is a prominent, famous teacher with an international scope of influence and reputation known in most Jewish communities of Asia Minor and beyond. The present tense of the participle "teaching" (διδάσκων) reflects that the Jews from Asia Minor regard Paul's teaching activities as a clear and imminent danger for the Jewish commonwealth.

The Jews from the province of Asia bring five charges against Paul.[7] The first three are described in terms of Paul's opposition to (κατά), or attack against, the foundations of the Jewish commonwealth, while the last two charges are linked with the accusation that he teaches against the temple, which makes this accusation the central charge. Thus the accusation resembles the charges against Stephen (6:11, 13 – 14), who, the reader will remember, was executed. The Jews from the province of Asia allege the following.

(1) Paul teaches "against our people" (κατὰ τοῦ λαοῦ), i.e., against Israel, the people of God. Luke's description of Paul's teaching never reported that Paul spoke against the Jewish people; on the contrary, he always preached in synagogues before he preached before Gentile audiences, and he left the local synagogues only when he was forced

---

7. In terms of the syntax of the Greek, one could speak of two charges: an accusation against his teaching (ὁ κατὰ … διδάσκων) and an accusation against his defilement of the

temple (ἔτι τε καὶ … καὶ κεκοίνωκεν). In terms of content, five charges can be distinguished.

to relocate his activities due to opposition from members of the Jewish communities. Still, Paul's teaching that Jews are sinners just like the Gentiles despite their circumcision (Rom 1:18 – 3:20), and that Jews are ignorant of the righteousness that comes from God (Rom 10:1 – 3), could be construed as teaching *against* the Jewish people if interpreted in isolation. The irony is that these diaspora Jews initiate with Paul's arrest an action that eventually forces the Roman authorities to take action that has ever larger repercussions (vv. 34 – 36; 22:22 – 24; 23:12 – 33); the governor Festus concludes that Paul has done nothing to deserve imprisonment and should have been set free (26:30 – 31). The secretary of Ephesus had managed to calm the excited crowds in the theater with the argument that their behavior could lead to the charge of rioting by the Roman authorities (19:40). Paul's Jewish opponents care more about the elimination of Paul than about Roman intervention.

(2) Paul teaches "against the law" (κατὰ ... τοῦ νόμου). Teaching against Israel is tantamount to teaching against the Mosaic law, which describes Israel's identity as God's people and whose commandments maintain Israel's status as God's people. He who attacks Israel attacks the law. This charge corresponds to the accusations circulating as rumors among recently converted Jewish Christians in Jerusalem who are told that Paul teaches diaspora Jews to abandon Moses, such as teaching Jews not to circumcise their children or observe the ancestral customs stipulated by the law (cf. v. 21).

(3) Paul teaches "against this place" (κατὰ ... τοῦ τόπου τούτου), i.e., against the temple, looming above the Jews who hold on to Paul in the outer court. The Jerusalem temple was the place of God's holy presence, whose holiness was the effective foundation of Israel's holiness, the only place where Jews could offer sacrifices and receive forgiveness of sins and restore purity. Since Paul taught that Jesus was sent by God as Israel's Messiah, whose death and resurrection procures forgiveness of sins and eternal life (13:37 – 38, 46) — as the new place of God's atoning presence, a sacrifice that forgives sins and procures righteousness for all who believe in Jesus (Rom 3:25 – 26) — the temple is no longer the exclusive and effective place of God's atoning presence among his people.

While there is ample evidence for Paul's teaching about Jesus as the Messiah who saves us from God's wrath, there is no evidence that Paul explicitly taught that the Jerusalem temple had become redundant.[8] In Stephen's case the accusation that he spoke against the temple came before the accusation that he spoke against the law (6:13); the reversed sequence here is explained by the next two charges, which refer to an alleged recent crime Paul has committed.

(4) Paul has "brought Greeks into the temple" (εἰσήγαγεν εἰς τὸ ἱερόν). The basis for this charge is explained in v. 29. Non-Jews were strictly forbidden to enter the inner part of the temple. Latin and Greek inscriptions were inscribed on the balustrade that surrounded the court within the outer court and thus the Court of the Women, the Inner Enclosure, and the temple building proper; they prohibited, under penalty of death, non-Jews from accessing the inner courts. It is ironic that the Jews from the province of Asia, who attacked Paul and instigated the Jewish crowd, create a disturbance that promptly causes a Roman military commander and his soldiers to appear in the outer court of the temple — which was accessible to Gentiles, but in which a Gentile who worshiped the God of Israel

---

8. On Jesus' statements that were critical of the temple — plausibly part of the explanation for Paul's position — see Luke 13:34 – 35; 19:45 – 46; 21:5 – 6 (with parallels in Matt and Mark); also Matt 26:61; Mark 13:1 – 2; 14:58; 15:29; John 2:19; Acts 6:14.

(Trophimus) was surely more welcome than members of the Roman military.

(5) Paul "has defiled" (κεκοίνωκεν) the holiness of the temple. This charge follows from the accusation that Paul has taken a Gentile into the inner courts of the temple. The verb means "to make common or impure, defile."[9] The perfect tense of this verb denotes a state of affairs that affects the status of the temple. This accusation implies that Paul does not care about maintaining the purity of the temple, since he has allegedly brought a Gentile into the temple courts with full knowledge of what would happen to the temple.

If the Jews from Asia were aware of Paul's teaching that "nothing is unclean in itself" (Rom 14:14),[10] they could have construed grounds for the accusation that Paul did not respect the distinction between ritual purity and impurity and thus would have no qualms about bringing an unclean Gentile into the holy inner courts of the temple. This charge is even more serious than the accusation of heretical teaching: defiling the temple carried the death sentence. Such defilement would necessitate purification rites and a rededication of the temple by means of legitimate sacrifices, perhaps similar to the rededication of the temple by Judas Maccabeus in 164 BC, three years after Antiochus IV had defiled the temple by offering pagan sacrifices.[11]

21:29 They had earlier seen Trophimus the Ephesian in the city with Paul and assumed that he had brought him into the temple (ἦσαν γὰρ προεωρακότες Τρόφιμον τὸν Ἐφέσιον ἐν τῇ πόλει σὺν αὐτῷ, ὃν ἐνόμιζον ὅτι εἰς τὸ ἱερὸν εἰσήγαγεν

ὁ Παῦλος). Luke now states the basis for these charges against Paul. The Jews from the province of Asia had seen Trophimus, an Ephesian (20:4), in the city with Paul, walking in the street or, perhaps, in one of the meetings of the Jerusalem Christians open to the public. In the context of their accusations against Paul, the Asian Jews' conclusion was not unnatural, but it was in fact false since there was no proof that this had happened. In his defense before the Roman governor Felix, Paul asserts that his opponents cannot prove their accusation (24:13; cf. 25:7).

The explanation of the charge that Paul defiled the temple means that the alleged crime of Paul was a special case. He is accused, as a Jew, to have brought a Gentile into the temple. By not preventing his Gentile friend from entering the inner courts, Paul has contributed to the temple's defilement. Luke's subsequent account suggests that there may have been special provisions for Roman citizens in Jewish capital punishment trials. The Sanhedrin was involved in the legal proceedings (24:1 – 9; 25:5), but the Jewish leaders here never file a legal claim with the Roman authorities for Paul's extradition. Rather, they attempt to "solve" the case by extrajudicial means (23:12 – 15; 25:2 – 3).[12]

While Luke's account does not help us to verify Josephus's comment about Jewish jurisdiction in capital cases in connection with the defilement of the Jerusalem temple (J.W. 6.126), the later proceedings of Paul's trial seem suggest that the original crime of profaning the temple could not

---

9. BDAG, s.v. κοινόω 2.

10. Note Peter's new insight, "God has shown me that I should not call anyone profane or unclean" (Acts 10:28; cf. 10:14 – 15; 11:8), and Jesus' teaching that locates defilement in the human heart rather than in external sources of defilement (Mark 7:14 – 23).

11. Cf. 1 Macc 4:36 – 59; 2 Macc 10:1 – 8. The Feast of Hanukkah commemorates the day when Judas rededicated the

temple. The historical model for the purification of the temple was the cleansing of the temple by King Hezekiah (2 Chr 29:3 – 36). The rededication ceremonies could have been based on King Solomon's dedication of the temple (1 Kgs 8:62 – 65) and on the dedication of the second temple in 515 BC under Ezra (Ezra 6:16 – 18).

12. Cf. Omerzu, *Prozess*, 354, 395 – 96.

be prosecuted because of a lack of evidence. This changed the legal situation; in the course of the trial, Paul is primarily accused of sedition (24:5).

21:30 The whole city was in turmoil, and people rushed together. They seized Paul and dragged him out of the temple, and immediately the gates were shut (ἐκινήθη τε ἡ πόλις ὅλη καὶ ἐγένετο συνδρομὴ τοῦ λαοῦ, καὶ ἐπιλαβόμενοι τοῦ Παύλου εἷλκον αὐτὸν ἔξω τοῦ ἱεροῦ καὶ εὐθέως ἐκλείσθησαν αἱ θύραι). The second incident of the episode of Paul's arrest relates the attempted killing of Paul in the outer court (vv. 30 – 31). Luke describes the result of the shouts of the Asian Jews in the inner courts of the temple with four verbal phrases: the entire city "was in turmoil" and the people "rushed together," moving from the city into the temple complex, where they "seized" Paul and "dragged" (εἷλκον) him out of the inner courts. The imperfect tense of the fourth verb (the first three are aorists) emphasizes that Paul is forcibly moved out of the temple.

The phrase "out of the temple" refers to the inner courts of the temple, which comprised the Inner Enclosure, the Court of Women, and the court within the outer court. The Roman officer had no access to the court within the outer court and must have encountered Paul (v. 33) in the outer court (see v. 27). As v. 31 will show, the purpose of Paul's removal from the inner courts is the attempted killing: stoning was impossible in the inner courts of the temple because of the resultant defilement, whereas it was possible in the outer court.

The juxtaposition of the two geographical phrases is ironic: "the whole city" moves from their "secular" activities in the city into the inner courts of the temple (potentially rendering the inner courts impure), while Paul, who is engaged

in "holy" activities in the temple in a state of ritual purity, is moved "out of the temple." There is no reason for the suggestion that the reference to turmoil in the whole city should be treated as a Lukan exaggeration: defiling the temple was a serious offense, and the presence of thousands of pilgrims in town for the Feast of Pentecost contributed to the volatility of the situation. Even "a perceived slight against the ancestral customs could quickly generate a riot that required suppression by the military authorities," as Josephus frequently attests.[13]

The "gates" (αἱ θύραι) of the Inner Enclosure and the Court of the Women were shut, perhaps by the captain of the temple, the official in charge of all temple affairs (see on 4:1). This prevents Paul from seeking refuge in the Inner Enclosure.

21:31 While they were trying to kill him, it was reported to the commander of the cohort that the entire city of Jerusalem was in chaos (ζητούντων τε αὐτὸν ἀποκτεῖναι ἀνέβη φάσις τῷ χιλιάρχῳ τῆς σπείρης ὅτι ὅλη συγχύννεται Ἰερουσαλήμ). The commotion in the outer court brings the commander of the Roman troops stationed in Jerusalem on the scene. The subject of the genitive absolute (ζητούντων) is the mass of Jews from the city and those present in the temple complex, including the Jews from Asia, who had alerted the crowds of Paul's presence. Since Luke does not specify the presence of members of the Sanhedrin, who would be responsible for conducting a trial and investigating the charge that Paul had defiled the temple, he apparently describes an attempted lynch killing. In a Jewish context, such a killing would have been carried out by stoning or by beating; the latter is suggested by v. 32.

After Paul had been seized and dragged out of the inner courts and while throngs of Jews were

---

13. Johnson, *Acts*, 381, with reference to Josephus, *J. W.* 1.88 – 89; 2:8 – 13, 42 – 48, 169 – 174, 223 – 227, 229 – 231, 314 – 320, 406 – 407, 449 – 456.

coming from the city up to the Temple Mount via the four gates and two bridges to the temple complex (see on 3:1), those closest to Paul began beating him and pelting him with stones. News about the commotion reaches the Roman commander of the garrison stationed in the Antonia Fortress. The commander's name is Claudius Lysias, as we learn in 23:26.

21:32 – 33 He at once took his soldiers and centurions and ran down to them. When they saw the commander and the soldiers, they stopped beating Paul. The commander approached them, arrested Paul, and ordered him to be bound with two chains. Then he asked who he was and what he had done (ὃς ἐξαυτῆς παραλαβὼν στρατιώτας καὶ ἑκατοντάρχας κατέδραμεν ἐπ᾽ αὐτούς, οἱ δὲ ἰδόντες τὸν χιλίαρχον καὶ τοὺς στρατιώτας ἐπαύσαντο τύπτοντες τὸν Παῦλον. τότε ἐγγίσας ὁ χιλίαρχος ἐπελάβετο αὐτοῦ καὶ ἐκέλευσεν δεθῆναι ἁλύσεσι δυσί, καὶ ἐπυνθάνετο τίς καὶ τί ἐστιν πεποιηκώς). Luke's account of the intervention of the Roman commander (vv. 32 – 36) reflects topographical and historical realities.

Since the commander was responsible for order in Jerusalem,[14] he took action immediately, which Luke describes with six verbs. (1) He "took" (παραλαβών) the solders and their officers — probably including the soldiers who had been patrolling on the walkway between the Antonia and the wall surrounding the fortress and who had seen the commotion below. Since he wanted to quell the disturbance in the outer court, which involved a large crowd of angry, shouting Jews who were in the process of killing Paul, he may have organized two centurions[15] and their two hundred men in order to restore peace.

(2) He "ran down" (κατέδραμεν) the steps that led from the Antonia Fortress into the outer court

of the temple complex. Since the coming of the Roman soldiers and their officers could not be anything but conspicuous, the Jews in the outer court promptly stopped beating Paul. The commander did not come to save Paul but to restore order.

(3) He "approached" (ἐγγίσας) the people who had been beating Paul, creating the commotion that prompted his intervention.

(4) He "arrested" (ἐπελάβετο) Paul; i.e., he took him into custody. The violence of the crowd and the shouts that a capital offense has been committed (v. 36) suggested to the commander that the man at the center of the commotion must be arrested immediately, even before he obtained more concrete information.

(5) He "ordered" (ἐκέλευσεν) his soldiers to bind Paul with two iron chains. If they were manacles, Paul was bound to two soldiers.

(6) He "asked" (ἐπυνθάνετο) the Jews beating Paul for more information. While the first five verbal forms were all aorists, ἐπυνθάνετο is imperfect, emphasizing the efforts of the military tribune to gather information. The first question ("Who might the person be?"), formulated with an optative (εἴη), indicates uncertainty about his identity; perhaps he is an insurrectionist from Egypt (v. 38). The second question ("What has he done?"), formulated with the indicative periphrastic (ἐστιν πεποιηκώς), suggests certainty that a crime has been committed.

21:34 Some people in the crowd shouted one thing, some another. Since he could not get to the truth because of the noise, he ordered him to be taken into the barracks (ἄλλοι δὲ ἄλλο τι ἐπεφώνουν ἐν τῷ ὄχλῳ. μὴ δυναμένου δὲ αὐτοῦ γνῶναι τὸ ἀσφαλὲς διὰ τὸν θόρυβον ἐκέλευσεν ἄγεσθαι αὐτὸν εἰς τὴν παρεμβολήν). The Jews who had seized and beaten Paul could not agree either

---

14. On legal matters regarding revolt see on 16:20 – 21.

15. The plural "centurions" (ἑκατοντάρχας) suggests at least two centurions.

on Paul's identity or on his alleged crime. Or, perhaps, some bellowed bits of personal information about Paul while others hollered accusations about the alleged defilement of the temple. The result was "noise" (θόρυβος), a term that describes the result of people raising their voices; the term also denotes confusion, unrest, turmoil, uproar. Paul will later deny that he had caused a "disturbance" (θόρυβος) in the temple (24:18).

The cacophony of voices and the confusion did not allow the military tribune to obtain factual and definite information about Paul. Therefore he decided that Paul should be brought into the Antonia Fortress for further interrogation (cf. 22:24). He ordered his soldiers, with Paul being bound with chains, to take the prisoner into the "barracks," a term that describes a fortified camp but here refers to the barracks of the Roman troops stationed in the Antonia Fortress.

21:35 – 36 When Paul reached the flight of stairs, he had to be carried by the soldiers because of the violence of the crowd. The crowd of people kept following, shouting, "Take him away!" (ὅτε δὲ ἐγένετο ἐπὶ τοὺς ἀναβαθμούς, συνέβη βαστάζεσθαι αὐτὸν ὑπὸ τῶν στρατιωτῶν διὰ τὴν βίαν τοῦ ὄχλου, ἠκολούθει γὰρ τὸ πλῆθος τοῦ λαοῦ κράζοντες· αἶρε αὐτόν). The transfer of Paul from the northern part of the outer court into the barracks of the Antonia Fortress was impeded by the crowd's violence. When Paul reached the flight of stairs that connected the outer court with the Antonia, he had to be carried by the soldiers to whom he was chained because the "violence" of the crowd threatened

Paul's safety.[16] Evidently people are reaching out to seize his arms or legs, yanking at his clothes.

As they see Paul about to vanish into the interior of the Roman barracks, they find a unified voice. They demand that the Roman commander finish what they have started: Paul's execution. The phrase translated "Take him away!" (αἶρε αὐτόν) is tantamount to the demand, "Kill him!" (cf. 22:22). The shouts of the crowd echo the shouts of the Jews in Herod's palace who demanded Jesus' execution as he stood trial before Pilate (αἶρε τοῦτον; Luke 23:18).[17]

21:37 – 38 As Paul was about to be taken into the barracks, he said to the commander, "May I be permitted to say something to you?" He replied, "Do you speak Greek? Are you not the Egyptian who instigated a revolt some time ago and led four thousand terrorists into the desert?" (Μέλλων τε εἰσάγεσθαι εἰς τὴν παρεμβολὴν ὁ Παῦλος λέγει τῷ χιλιάρχῳ· εἰ ἔξεστίν μοι εἰπεῖν τι πρὸς σέ; ὁ δὲ ἔφη· Ἑλληνιστὶ γινώσκεις; οὐκ ἄρα σὺ εἶ ὁ Αἰγύπτιος ὁ πρὸ τούτων τῶν ἡμερῶν ἀναστατώσας καὶ ἐξαγαγὼν εἰς τὴν ἔρημον τοὺς τετρακισχιλίους ἄνδρας τῶν σικαρίων;). As Paul is about to be taken as a prisoner into Roman custody, he first asks for permission to speak to the military tribune, then asks the military tribune for permission to address the Jewish crowd (vv. 37 – 40). This is the fourth incident of the episode that relates Paul's arrest in the temple.

Paul asks the tribune for authorization to say something to him. He addresses the tribune in Greek, which surprises[18] the latter, who evidently

---

16. The text does not indicate whether or to what extent Paul was injured; the fact that the soldiers had to carry him is explained not by Paul's weakness due to injuries as is often assumed (e.g. Haenchen, *Acts*, 618; Omerzu, *Prozess*, 366), but by the violent pressure of the crowd.

17. Cf. John 19:15: ἆρον ἆρον, σταύρωσον αὐτόν ("Take him away! Crucify him!").

18. The particle ἄρα here expresses astonishment ("You speak Greek: are you not the Egyptian?"); cf. BDF §440.2(2); Barrett, *Acts*, 1024; NIV, NLT, TNIV. Others assume that ἄρα expresses an inference ("You speak Greek: then you are not the Egyptian?"), cf. Haenchen, *Acts*, 619; Johnson, *Acts*, 383; GNB, NASB, NET, NRSV. Since Egyptians generally spoke Greek, the tribune would hardly infer from Paul's use of Greek that he cannot be an Egyptian.

had not heard Paul speak. Paul would not have expected a military tribune of the Roman army to speak Aramaic let alone Hebrew. Greek was the language used by Roman officials in the cities of the eastern Mediterranean, and thus it is in Greek that Paul addressed the tribune. Paul's upbringing in Tarsus had taught him Greek, besides his knowledge of Hebrew and Aramaic.[19]

The tribune thinks that Paul is the Egyptian who was active as a political insurrectionist. He either does not know that many Egyptians spoke Greek, the language preferred by the Jews living in Egypt, or he has information that the Egyptian insurrectionist he has in mind does not speak Greek. The tribune has four pieces of information about this Egyptian: (1) He instigated a revolt by leading a group of terrorists into disturbing the peace. (2) This took place "some time ago." (3) He had led 4,000 terrorists.[20] (4) He led his terrorists out into the desert.

This characterization corresponds to an event related by Josephus.[21] A false prophet from Egypt came into the country and gathered 30,000 people, whom he led through the desert to the Mount of Olives with the promise that the walls of Jerusalem would collapse, allowing them to enter the city, defeat the Roman occupiers, and establish himself as ruler over the people. But the Romans captured 200 and killed 400 of the Egyptian's followers, though he himself managed to escape.[22] The reference to the Mount of Olives suggests messianic aspira-

tions of this Egyptian impostor (cf. Zech 14:1 – 5). The tribune evidently believed, not unreasonably, that the Egyptian was now renewing his efforts at a political revolt.[23] Since "the entire people" of Jerusalem had assisted the Romans in repulsing the Egyptian, the assault of an excited crowd in the outer court against Paul, demanding his execution, would make sense. The tribune thought at first that "he had captured a real prize — the Egyptian revolutionary who had recently slipped Felix's grasp."[24]

21:39 Paul replied, "I am a Jew, from Tarsus in Cilicia, the citizen of an important city. I beg you, allow me to speak to the people" (εἶπεν δὲ ὁ Παῦλος· ἐγὼ ἄνθρωπος μέν εἰμι Ἰουδαῖος, Ταρσεὺς τῆς Κιλικίας, οὐκ ἀσήμου πόλεως πολίτης· δέομαι δέ σου, ἐπίτρεψόν μοι λαλῆσαι πρὸς τὸν λαόν). Paul quickly clarifies the tribune's misunderstanding, beginning with his identity. He does not provide all the details that are relevant (e.g., he does not reveal his Roman citizenship at this point; see on 22:25). Paul first identifies himself as a Jew from Tarsus in Cilicia. This proves that he is not the Egyptian and that he would not defile the temple. Paul, the Christian missionary, never ceases to identify himself as a Jew.[25]

Second, Paul identifies himself as a "citizen" (πολίτης) of Tarsus. Paul and his family evidently possessed both Tarsian and Roman citizenship.[26] Greek cities made citizenship dependent on the fulfillment of specific conditions, often financial contributions or involvement in public building

---

19. See "In Depth: Saul of Tarsus, Also Called Paul" at 9:1 – 2.

20. The Greek term translated as "terrorists" (σικάριοι; from Lat. *sica*, "dagger;" thus also GNB, NIV, TNIV, Fitzmyer; most English translations have "assassins") denotes "one who is intent on killing someone as part of an organized subversive political program, *dagger man, assassin, terrorist* (BDAG, s.v. σικάριος). The "party" of the Sicarii is assumed by translations that capitalize "Assassins" (ESV, NASB, NET, NLT, RSV).

21. The episode occurred two years before Felix's recall as governor; cf. Smallwood, *Jews under Roman Rule*, 269 n. 40.

22. Josephus, *Ant.* 20.169 – 172; *J.W.* 2.261 – 263.

23. The more militant version of the event in *J.W.* 2.263 uses the term "attack, invasion"; for the following comment see ibid.

24. Rapske, *Paul in Roman Custody*, 136.

25. Cf. 22:3; and in his letters Rom 11:1; 2 Cor 11:22; Phil 3:5.

26. Paul's Tarsian citizenship is mentioned only here; for his Roman citizenship cf. 16:37 – 38; 22:25 – 29; 23:27; cf. 25:10 – 11; 28:19. Cf. Rapske, *Paul in Roman Custody*, 72 – 83; Riesner, *Paul's Early Period*, 147 – 56.

projects. Paul's assertion that he was a Tarsian is made with pride — Tarsus is (lit.) "a not unimportant city"; this reflects the municipal patriotism of the citizens of Greek cities whose identity always remained associated with their native city. The Roman commander may have known that Mark Antony and then Augustus had rewarded Tarsus because its citizens had remained faithful to Caesar in the battle against Brutus and Cassius, Caesar's killers, granting Tarsus the status of a free city and tax exemption. Paul's insistence that he is a Tarsian citizen can be understood as a rebuttal of someone who resents being mistaken for an Egyptian.[27]

Paul asks with considered politeness whether the tribune will allow him to speak to the people, i.e., to the agitated crowd of Jews who stand menacingly at the staircase leading up into the Antonia Fortress. They are Jews like himself, and he wants to address them, perhaps his last chance to defend himself before the Jewish people and, more importantly, to explain his faith in Jesus as Israel's Messiah.

21:40 When he had received his permission, Paul stood on the steps and motioned to the people with his hand. When all were silent, he addressed them in Hebrew (ἐπιτρέψαντος δὲ αὐτοῦ ὁ Παῦλος ἑστὼς ἐπὶ τῶν ἀναβαθμῶν κατέσεισεν τῇ χειρὶ τῷ λαῷ. πολλῆς δὲ σιγῆς γενομένης προσεφώνησεν τῇ Ἑβραΐδι διαλέκτῳ λέγων). The Roman commander gives Paul permission to address the Jews assembled in the outer court of the temple complex, perhaps impressed with Paul's credentials. He evidently hopes that Paul might himself clarify the incident. If so, he is disappointed: Paul speaks in Hebrew (or Aramaic), which the centurion does not understand; if one of his soldiers gives an im-

promptu translation, he would have heard religious issues addressed.

Luke describes the beginning of Paul's speech with three verbs that vividly depict the dramatic scene. Paul, who had just escaped with his life by the skin of his teeth, "stood" on the steps leading into the Antonia Fortress, looking out over the throngs of Jews toward the temple. Paul, bound with chains to Roman soldiers, "motioned" with his hand to the people, the traditional gesture of an orator,[28] made perhaps in agony and with difficulty, but to eventual effect: a great hush ensued. Then Paul called out to them in Hebrew (cf. 22:2). The term "Hebrew" (Ἑβραΐς) can denote the Aramaic language (διαλέκτος), the main language spoken by the Jews of Palestine. While Paul likely spoke to the crowd in Aramaic, it is not impossible that he spoke in Hebrew, a language still in use, as the Dead Sea Scrolls have demonstrated.

22:1 – 2 "Brothers and fathers, listen to my defense that I now present before you." When they heard him addressing them in Hebrew, they became even more quiet. Then Paul said (ἄνδρες ἀδελφοὶ καὶ πατέρες, ἀκούσατέ μου τῆς πρὸς ὑμᾶς νυνὶ ἀπολογίας. ἀκούσαντες δὲ ὅτι τῇ Ἑβραΐδι διαλέκτῳ προσεφώνει αὐτοῖς, μᾶλλον παρέσχον ἡσυχίαν. καὶ φησίν). Paul's speech to the Jewish crowd (22:1 – 21) begins with a brief introduction (*exordium*). The address "brothers and fathers" (see on 1:16) was also used by Stephen (7:2). "Fathers" (πατέρες), which is added to the usual combination of two nouns (ἄνδρες ἀδελφοί), adds a note of respect, acknowledging the presence of those who are his seniors, perhaps even members of the Sanhedrin.

---

27. John Clayton Lentz, *Luke's Portrait of Paul* (SNTSMS 77; Cambridge: Cambridge Univ. Press, 1993), 28 – 30, who points out that Alexandrian Jews resented being identified as Egyptians.

28. Cf. 12:17; 13:16; 19:33; 21:40; 26:1. Quintilian, *Inst.* 11.3.98, advises the orator to extend the thumb, the index finger, and the middle finger while closing the remaining two fingers into the palm (also Apuleius, *Metam.* 2.21; and portrayals of speakers in Greek art).

The imperative "listen" (ἀκούσατε) expresses not a command but a request; he asks his listeners for their favorable attention.[29] The fact that Paul gives his speech in Hebrew (v. 2; cf. 21:40) renders his request for attention effective: the silence beomes even more pronounced. Paul characterizes the content of his speech as "defense" (ἀπολογία), a term used in Greek rhetoric for speeches of the defense, even though the setting is here not a court of law. Jews in the crowd who do not know Paul but who have heard that he has been charged with defiling the temple may have been surprised when Paul addresses them in Hebrew. This is the first of six defense speeches of Paul.[30] He defends not only himself (on a personal or biographical level) as a messenger of the gospel, but, more importantly, he defends the message he proclaims.[31]

22:3 "I am a Jew, born in Tarsus in Cilicia, but brought up in this city. I studied under Gamaliel in strict conformity to the standard of our ancestral law. I was as zealous for God as all of you are today" (ἐγώ εἰμι ἀνὴρ Ἰουδαῖος, γεγεννημένος ἐν Ταρσῷ τῆς Κιλικίας, ἀνατεθραμμένος δὲ ἐν τῇ πόλει ταύτῃ, παρὰ τοὺς πόδας Γαμαλιὴλ πεπαιδευμένος κατὰ ἀκρίβειαν τοῦ πατρῴου νόμου, ζηλωτὴς ὑπάρχων τοῦ θεοῦ καθὼς πάντες ὑμεῖς ἐστε σήμερον). Paul begins his statement of the facts of the case (*narratio*) with an autobiographical narrative (vv. 3 – 5). He chooses to speak about himself because he has been charged with teaching against the law, against Israel, and against the temple. In forensic rhetoric, the character of a person (*ethos*) is of particular importance,[32] but "an exposition of the good qualities of a person or thing, in general or individually,"[33] called *encomium*, could occur in many rhetorical genres.

Paul begins with topics regarded as essential when describing the life of a person: origins, nurture, training, deeds and virtues, and comparison.[34] As he sketches his life, he focuses on his Jewish credentials. Luke's point of including this *encomium* is not the praise of Paul per se. Paul's reputation is important not only for his defense in a legal setting, but also in terms of Paul's function as missionary to the Gentiles and thus in terms of what the early church preaches, which is not a betrayal of its Jewish roots but the fulfillment of God's promises given for Israel — and for the world.

Luke's original account of Paul's conversion in 9:1 – 19 omits a biographical sketch of Paul's background for obvious reasons. He introduces Paul (Saul) here as a persecutor of the church, who is a bona fide diaspora Jew from a prominent city, a well-trained rabbi, and committed to the law. In his third account of Paul's conversion in 26:1 – 32 the *encomium* is more fully developed than in 22:3, which makes sense in a setting where the Roman governor and the Jewish king and other notables are the main audience.

Paul's comments on his *origins* are succinct. He

---

29. Paul thus chooses the "direct approach" in his *exordium*, which in a forensic speech aimed at gaining the favorable attention of the audience (*Rhet. Her.* 1.7; Cicero, *Inv.* 1.20); cf. Parsons, *Acts*, 308.

30. Cf. also 23:1 – 6 (Sanhedrin); 24:10 – 21 (Felix, in Caesarea); 25:8 – 11 (Festus); 26:1 – 23 (Festus and Agrippa); 28:17 – 20 (Jewish leaders in Rome).

31. The latter is particularly evident in the detailed reports of Paul's encounter with the risen Jesus on the road to Damascus (vv. 6 – 11) and of the divine commission given to Paul that he will be a witness of Jesus (vv. 14 – 15, 18 – 21). Cf. Neagoe, *Trial*, 196 – 97.

32. Cf. Quintilian, *Inst.* 4.1.7: if the person who is defended "is believed to be a good man, this consideration will exercise the strongest influence at every point in the case."

33. Hermogenes, *Prog.* 14 (Kennedy, *Progymnasmata*, 81).

34. Cf. Michael W. Martin, "Progymnastic Topic Lists: A Compositional Template for Luke and Other Bioi?" *NTS* 54 (2008): 18 – 41. Cf. Hermogenes, *Prog.* 14 – 16; Aphthonius, *Prog.* 35 – 40; Nicolaus, *Prog.* 47 – 53 (Kennedy, *Progymnasmata*, 81 – 82, 108, 156 – 58).

is a "Jew," a fact that explains his ethnic or "national" origins (cf. 21:39). And he was "born" in Tarsus in Cilicia, a fact that highlights his city of birth — an important part of the identity of people in the ancient world (cf. 21:39).

Paul's information about *nurture and training* relates his growing up "in this city," i.e., in Jerusalem, the city where he also received his training as he "studied" (πεπαιδευμένος) under Gamaliel, the famous rabbi. His studies had taken place "in strict conformity" to the Mosaic law and its interpretation and application in the ancestral customs. His teacher, Gamaliel (see on 5:34), had guided him in his studies of the Scriptures and of the law, so that he would be able to recognize, adhere to, interpret, and apply God's law with exactness and precision.

It is unclear when Paul moved from Tarsus to Jerusalem. Some argue that the three participles in v. 3c-d reflect a biographical pattern that ancient authors followed, detailing three stages of development (cf. 26:4 – 5): birth (mother); childhood, with upbringing in the parental home and elementary education (father); higher education (teachers).[35] Since the verb translated "brought up" (ἀνατρέφω) denotes physical and mental nurture and upbringing in general terms,[36] and since the stages of biographical development cannot be definitely linked with specific ages, we cannot be certain that Paul moved from Tarsus to Jerusalem as a child.[37] But the suggestion that Paul moved to Jerusalem at an early period in his life agrees with his statement that he was "a Hebrew of Hebrews" (Phil 3:5) — Paul's Palestinian Jewish roots must be taken seriously.

At the same time it is also true that Paul was not a "pure" Palestinian Jew such as Peter or James. His excellent knowledge and use of the Greek language, his familiarity with the LXX, and his emphasis on Tarsus (here before a Jewish audience) indicate that Tarsus cannot be pushed aside as having had a formative influence on Paul. While Tarsus is less important than Jerusalem in his biography, his early years and upbringing in Tarsus — presumably into his early teenage years — most plausibly explain the fact that he was bilingual and bicultural, moving with ease between Jewish culture and Gentile culture.[38]

Paul's reference to *deeds and virtues* focuses on his devotion to God: he was "zealous" (ζηλωτής) for God. This statement resembles James's description of the Jewish believers who were "zealous for the law" and whose concerns about Paul are the direct reason why Paul had come to the temple. In Gal 1:14 Paul describes himself as having been "zealous" (ζηλωτής) for the ancestral traditions. Paul emphasizes that during his studies under Gamaliel and in his subsequent life he was firmly committed to God's cause. In the *encomium* in 26:4 – 6 Paul further mentions his affiliation with the Pharisees and the fact that the caliber and the vigor of his studies was well-known among his contemporaries.

Paul's *comparison* with his audience is the last el-

---

35. Willem C. van Unnik, "Tarsus or Jerusalem: The City of Paul's Youth [1952]" in *Sparsa Collecta* (NovTSup 29; Leiden: Brill, 1973), 259 – 320, who believes that Paul's family moved from Tarsus to Jerusalem when Paul was still a toddler, "apparently before he could peep round the corner of the door and certainly before he went roaming on the street" (301).

36. It also denotes "to educate" and "to convalesce" after an illness (LSJ, s.v. ἀνατρέφω). Note C. Spicq, "ἀνατρέφω," *TLNT*, 1:115 – 16, who asserts that the verb "encompasses the entire life of the child until his maturity, including feeding and physical care, the formation of the mind and character, in which case

it is synonymous with *paideuō* … (it) designates by preference the education received at home, almost always in relation with family members."

37. Since Paul's sister lived in Jerusalem with her family (23:16), this early move to Jerusalem has been suggested as a likely possibility; cf. Zahn, *Apostelgeschichte*, 751.

38. Cf. Martin Hengel, *The Pre-Christian Paul* (Philadelphia: Trinity Press International, 1991), with a critical investigation into van Unnik's theory; he suggests that Paul may have been moving back and forth between Tarsus and Jerusalem multiple times.

ement in his introduction, which serves to explain who he is. He emphasizes that his zeal for God can be compared with the zeal for God to which all the Jews who are in the outer court of the temple are committed.

22:4 – 5 I persecuted this Way to the point of death, arresting and imprisoning men and women, as the high priest and the whole council of elders can testify about me. I even obtained letters from them to our Jewish brothers in Damascus, and I went there in order to bring these people as prisoners back to Jerusalem for punishment (ὃς ταύτην τὴν ὁδὸν ἐδίωξα ἄχρι θανάτου δεσμεύων καὶ παραδιδοὺς εἰς φυλακὰς ἄνδρας τε καὶ γυναῖκας, ὡς καὶ ὁ ἀρχιερεὺς μαρτυρεῖ μοι καὶ πᾶν τὸ πρεσβυτέριον, παρ᾽ ὧν καὶ ἐπιστολὰς δεξάμενος πρὸς τοὺς ἀδελφοὺς εἰς Δαμασκὸν ἐπορευόμην, ἄξων καὶ τοὺς ἐκεῖσε ὄντας δεδεμένους εἰς Ἰερουσαλὴμ ἵνα τιμωρηθῶσιν). In the second part of his biographical narrative, Paul describes his activities as a persecutor of the followers of Jesus.

He begins by stating that he arrested and imprisoned believers in Jesus, collaborating with the high priest and the Sanhedrin. Paul's goal here is not to appease the crowd, which stands literally between Paul and the temple, presumably with many priests in the audience, but to underline Paul's Jewish credentials and to demonstrate that he did not begin as a partisan of the movement of the followers of Jesus. He is not an assimilated diaspora Jew who does not care about the law or the temple, but an educated rabbi who personally knew the leaders of the Jewish commonwealth. And he has not always been an advocate of Jesus of Nazareth. Rather, he

was once a fierce opponent to the Jesus movement (see also 7:58; 8:1, 3; 9:1 – 2, 21; 26:9 – 11).[39] Here Luke has Paul describe his actions, in the first person singular, with six verbal forms.

(1) Paul "persecuted" (ἐδίωξα) "this Way" (αὕτη ἡ ὁδός; see on 5:11; 9:2); i.e., he sought out Christians in order to prevent them from continuing to spread their convictions. He was willing to help inflict the death penalty, at least in some cases (cf. 9:1; 26:10).[40]

(2) Paul arrested (δεσμεύων) followers of Jesus; i.e., he bound them with chains (cf. 8:3). The present tense of this and the following participle underline that these activities took place over some period of time.

(3) Paul imprisoned (παραδιδοὺς εἰς φυλακάς) believers, both men and women. The reference to women (cf. 9:2) underlines Paul's consistent and ruthless dedication to the task of eradicating believers in Jesus. The Christians arrested in Jerusalem would be taken to the prison of the Sanhedrin, probably located near the Xystos below the western wall.[41] Christians arrested in other towns of Judea and of regions further away may also have been taken to Jerusalem for trial and punishment. Paul asserts that he was acting with the full knowledge of the high priest at the time (Joseph Caiaphas) and the entire council of the elders (see on 4:5).

This point underscores his agreement with the leadership of the Jewish commonwealth. He was familiar with and had access to the highest levels of Jewish leadership. Thus, the listeners could verify Paul's account, since many of the members of the Sanhedrin who had supported his efforts were still

---

39. Cf. also 1 Cor 15:9; Gal 1:13; Phil 3:6; 1 Tim 1:13.

40. If Paul wanted Christians to be executed, this would require a trial before the Sanhedrin (if he could accuse Christians of violating the sanctity of the temple in Jerusalem) and ultimately before the Roman governor. Since the Sanhedrin's judicial proceedings against Jesus were successful (from the Jewish leaders' perspective) in obtaining the death penalty from Pon-

tius Pilate, "follow-up trials" against followers of Jesus were probably regarded as an effective means of eliminating leaders of the new movement. Some see a conflict with v. 19 and with 26:11, where Paul inflicts only synagogue punishments. Note, however, that the synagogue punishment of forty lashes minus one (see on 4:21; 5:40) could result in injuries that were fatal.

41. Cf. Rapske, *Paul in Roman Custody*, 137. See on 4:3.

alive: their testimony would confirm his account. While Caiaphas, the high priest from AD 18 – 36, was no longer in office — the incumbent high priest was Ananias son of Nebedaios (AD 47 – 58; cf. 23:2, 5; 24:1) — Caiaphas may still have been alive in AD 57.

(4) Paul obtained (δεξάμενος) letters from the high priest and the Sanhedrin. He acted as an official agent of the Sanhedrin, expanding the actions taken against the followers of Jesus into cities in regions farther away from Jerusalem and Judea. While 9:1 – 2 emphasized the initiative of Paul in obtaining letters of authorization, the formulation "I obtained … from them" may imply the initiative of the high priest and the Sanhedrin who wanted Paul to go to Damascus. The latter is not made explicit by Luke, however. In any case, Paul was officially authorized to persecute Christian believers. The "brothers in Damascus" are fellow Jews ("Jewish brothers").

(5) Paul traveled (ἐπορευόμην) to Damascus from Jerusalem — about 170 miles (270 km.) — with the goal of arresting "these people" who belonged to "this Way."

(6) Paul would bring (ἄξων) the followers of Jesus back to Jerusalem for punishment. The term "punishment" (τιμωρηθῶσιν) does not include the imprisonment and the interrogation but refers to the penalty after the trial, which could range from flogging with forty lashes minus one (see on 5:40) to execution.

22:6 As I was on my way and approached Damascus, about noon a great light suddenly flashed around me (ἐγένετο δέ μοι πορευομένῳ καὶ ἐγγίζοντι τῇ Δαμασκῷ περὶ μεσημβρίαν ἐξαίφνης ἐκ τοῦ οὐρανοῦ περιαστράψαι φῶς ἱκανὸν περὶ ἐμέ). The second part of Paul's statement of the facts relates his conversion to faith in Jesus (vv. 6 – 16). This is the central element of the *narratio* and its longest part. Many of the differences that distinguish Paul's account here with Luke's account in 9:1 – 19 can be

explained by the fact that Paul describes events as they unfolded for him, while the earlier account is given by an "omniscient" narrator.

Paul begins with an account of his encounter with Jesus of Nazareth on the road to Damascus (vv. 6 – 11). In v. 6 Luke adds two details to the third person account in 9:3. Both the time reference ("about noon") and the characterization of the light as "great" provide precise and vivid details appropriate for an eyewitness account in the first person. The temporal specification underscores the fact that this was an objective event, not a dream during sleep at night.

22:7 – 8 I fell to the ground and heard a voice say to me, "Saul, Saul, why are you persecuting me?" I replied, "Who are you, Lord?" Then he said to me, "I am Jesus of Nazareth, whom you are persecuting" (ἔπεσά τε εἰς τὸ ἔδαφος καὶ ἤκουσα φωνῆς λεγούσης μοι· Σαοὺλ Σαούλ, τί με διώκεις; ἐγὼ δὲ ἀπεκρίθην· τίς εἶ, κύριε; εἶπέν τε πρός με· ἐγώ εἰμι Ἰησοῦς ὁ Ναζωραῖος, ὃν σὺ διώκεις). Paul's description of his reaction to the bright light — he fell to the ground — and the dialogue in direct speech agree with Luke's account in 9:4 – 5 and with Paul's defense in 26:14 – 15. The words of the heavenly voice and Paul's response were so memorable that they are repeated verbatim: the question, "Saul, Saul, why are you persecuting me?" and the response, "Who are you, Lord?" occur in all three accounts of Paul's conversion.

In the reply of the heavenly voice to Paul's question there is a slight variation in v. 8: while 9:5 and 26:15 have "I am Jesus, whom you are persecuting" (ἐγώ εἰμι Ἰησοῦς ὃν σὺ διώκεις), here the speaker from heaven identifies himself as "Jesus of Nazareth" (Ἰησοῦς ὁ Ναζωραῖος; see on 2:22), an addition that is appropriate for the setting of the speech before a Jewish audience. At the same time Paul's listeners may have noted that Jesus did not come from a famous city such as Tarsus (cf. v. 3), nor from Jerusalem, the center of the world for Jews, where they expected the Messiah to rule. Nevertheless, the fact that Nazareth is a quintessential Jewish town emphasizes the Jewishness of Paul's loyalties and convictions. Paul informs the Jews standing in front of him that he has personally met Jesus of Nazareth — after he had been executed and while his followers were being persecuted for proclaiming his resurrection.

22:9 The men who were with me saw the light, but they did not hear the voice of him who was speaking to me (οἱ δὲ σὺν ἐμοὶ ὄντες τὸ μὲν φῶς ἐθεάσαντο τὴν δὲ φωνὴν οὐκ ἤκουσαν τοῦ λαλοῦντός μοι). There is a major discrepancy between this description of the reaction of the Jews who accompanied Paul from Jerusalem to Damascus and that in 9:7: here Paul's travel companions saw the light (φῶς) but did not hear the voice (φωνή) of Jesus, while according to 9:7 they "stood speechless because they heard the voice but saw no one."

These differences can be explained in two ways. Luke followed classical usage, using the verb "hear" (ἀκούω) with a genitive object in the sense that someone has heard someone or something, probably without understanding; ἀκούω with a direct object in the accusative is connected with understanding. In other words, in 9:7 Luke reports that Paul's travel companions heard (ἀκούοντες) the sound of the heavenly voice (τῆς φωνῆς), while Paul reports in 22:9 that they did not hear (οὐκ ἤκουσαν) the intelligible words of the voice (τὴν φωνήν) that Paul himself understood.[42] A second explanation emphasizes the import of the qualifying participial phrase in v. 9 (τοῦ λαλοῦντός μοι): Paul relates that

the companions heard a "voice" (φωνή) that "was speaking to me," while Luke relates in 9:7 that the men heard a "sound" (φωνή), i.e., "heard a noise but did not comprehend the conversation."[43]

22:10 I asked, "What am I to do, Lord?" The Lord replied, "Get up and go to Damascus. There you will be told everything that you have been ordered to do" (εἶπον δέ· τί ποιήσω, κύριε; ὁ δὲ κύριος εἶπεν πρός με· ἀναστὰς πορεύου εἰς Δαμασκὸν κἀκεῖ σοι λαληθήσεται περὶ πάντων ὧν τέτακταί σοι ποιῆσαι). Paul's question acknowledges the authority of Jesus of Nazareth, who has risen from the dead and who is alive in the light of God's heavenly existence, and it implies his willingness to accept any task that Jesus the Lord will assign to him. Thus he asks what he should do (ποιήσω). The question "What am I to do, Lord?" (τί ποιήσω, κύριε;) has no parallel in Acts 9 or Acts 26.

Jesus' answer focuses on the next step: Paul should "get up" from the ground and "go" into Damascus. As the crucified and risen Lord, Jesus has the authority to issue an imperative. According to Paul's account in v. 10, Jesus revealed to him only the next step — the short journey into the city of Damascus, where he would receive further instruction. This focus and the directive to wait there for further instructions correspond to 9:6,[44] with two additions: in Damascus he will be told "everything" of what he has "been ordered" (τέτακται) to do by God. With these additions Paul underlines two facts: the full scope of what he has been doing in his ministry, without exception, has been assigned to him, and his activities are divine orders,[45] not his subjective, individualistic choice.

---

42. This explanation has been rejected on the grounds that writers of Hellenistic Greek, including Luke, do not consistently make such a distinction in the meaning of ἀκούω. Cf. Horst R. Moehring, "The Verb AKOYEIN in Acts ix 7 and xxii 9," *NovT* 3 (1959): 80 – 99.

43. Polhill, *Acts*, 235 n. 15; cf. Witherington, *Acts*, 313.

44. Paul's explanation of his conversion before King Agrippa inserts at this point a lengthy description of his divine call to proclaim Jesus among Jews and Gentiles (26:16 – 20; see there for an explanation).

45. Cf. BDAG, s.v. τάσσω 2, "to give instructions as to what must be done."

22:11 Since I could not see because of the brightness of the light, the men who were with me led me by the hand to Damascus (ὡς δὲ οὐκ ἐνέβλεπον ἀπὸ τῆς δόξης τοῦ φωτὸς ἐκείνου, χειραγωγούμενος ὑπὸ τῶν συνόντων μοι ἦλθον εἰς Δαμασκόν). Paul's account of the blinding effect of the bright light, which left him blind and unable to walk unaided to Damascus, parallels 9:8. While 9:8 acknowledges that Paul got up from the ground in obedience to the heavenly voice, his focus here is on the "brightness" or "glory" (δόξα) of the light that he saw, as he does in 2 Cor 4:4, where he describes his (and all believers') experience of conversion to faith in Jesus as seeing "the light of the gospel that displays the glory of Christ [τῆς δόξης τοῦ Χριστοῦ], who is the image of God."

22:12 – 13 A certain Ananias, a devout man according to the law who was well spoken of by all the Jews living there, came to me. He stood beside me and said, "Brother Saul, regain your sight!" At that very moment I regained my sight and looked at him (Ἀνανίας δέ τις, ἀνὴρ εὐλαβὴς κατὰ τὸν νόμον, μαρτυρούμενος ὑπὸ πάντων τῶν κατοικούντων Ἰουδαίων, ἐλθὼν πρός με καὶ ἐπιστὰς εἶπέν μοι· Σαοὺλ ἀδελφέ, ἀνάβλεψον. κἀγὼ αὐτῇ τῇ ὥρᾳ ἀνέβλεψα εἰς αὐτόν). Paul now turns to his commission by God to be a witness of Jesus to the world (vv. 12 – 16). He introduces Ananias, with a new description that has no parallels in 9:10, where he is merely described as "a certain disciple in Damascus." Befitting the context of his defense before the Jews in the outer court who charge him with being disloyal to the Jewish people and the law, Paul characterizes Ananias as "a devout man," whose piety conformed to the standard of the law (κατὰ τὸν νόμον); i.e., he was an observant Jew who followed the commandments, a fact confirmed by

the entire Jewish community in Damascus. This description possibly suggests that Ananias was a leader in one of the local synagogues.

Paul does not describe Ananias's objections to the risen Jesus' instructions and the dialogue that ensues (9:10 – 16). Rather, Paul moves straight to their encounter that restored his eyesight (cf. 9:17 – 18). Paul omits the fact that Ananias laid his hands on Saul and that Ananias was instrumental in his receiving the Holy Spirit.

Here as in 9:17 Ananias begins with the words, "Brother Saul" (Σαοὺλ ἀδελφέ), which underlines in the present setting that Paul was acknowledged by a devout Jew in Damascus as a fellow (devout) Jew.[46] The command "regain your sight!" (ἀνάβλεψον) corresponds to a purpose clause in 9:17. Paul's report of the miracle through which he instantly regained his eyesight parallels 9:18, with the addition that Paul looked at Ananias, a detail that confirms that a miracle had indeed taken place.

22:14 – 15 Then he said, "The God of our ancestors has chosen you to know his will, to see the Righteous One, and to hear his own voice. You will be his witness before all people, bearing witness to what you have seen and heard" (ὁ δὲ εἶπεν· ὁ θεὸς τῶν πατέρων ἡμῶν προεχειρίσατό σε γνῶναι τὸ θέλημα αὐτοῦ καὶ ἰδεῖν τὸν δίκαιον καὶ ἀκοῦσαι φωνὴν ἐκ τοῦ στόματος αὐτοῦ, ὅτι ἔσῃ μάρτυς αὐτῷ πρὸς πάντας ἀνθρώπους ὧν ἑώρακας καὶ ἤκουσας). Paul's report of Ananias's explanation of the revelation he had received on the road to Damascus in v. 14 expands the first phrase of the risen Lord's explanation to Ananias in 9:15, presenting the words of Jesus to Ananias as words of God. This change is fitting in terms of Paul's attempt to explain to hostile Jews in Jerusalem how God himself had initi-

---

46. For Luke's Christian readers, the term "brother" may imply that Ananias greeted Paul as Christian brother (Barrett, *Acts*, 1040); but in the setting of the speech in the temple's outer court, the address as "brother" by Ananias acknowledges Paul as a fellow Jew.

ated his ministry as a teacher who proclaims Jesus. The phrase "the God of our ancestors" (ὁ θεὸς τῶν πατέρων ἡμῶν) confirms Paul's identity as a Jew (proselytes do not address God as "God of our fathers"), and it highlights God's powerful initiative in his life. At the same time, this change reflects Paul's tendency to link the crucified and risen Jesus with God in the closest of terms (cf. 1 Cor 8:6).

God appeared to Paul because he, Paul, is God's "chosen instrument" (σκεῦος ἐκλογῆς; 9:15); this means four things. (1) God has "chosen" (προεχειρίσατό)[47] Paul; his encounter with the risen Lord and his conversion to faith in Jesus as Israel's Messiah and Savior are the result of God's choosing him and mobilizing him for his task of teaching. (2) God has revealed to Paul his "will" (θέλημα), i.e., his plan of salvation involving Jesus' crucifixion, resurrection, and exaltation. (3) God has allowed Paul to "see" (ἰδεῖν) with his own eyes "the Righteous One" (ὁ δίκαιος); i.e., Paul has seen Jesus the Messiah, who was unconditionally devoted to the will of God (see on 3:14; 7:52 – 53; cf. Rom 3:21 – 26). (4) God has allowed Paul to "hear" (ἀκοῦσαι) the "voice" of Jesus, the crucified, risen, and exalted Messiah of his people, who spoke to him from the realm of heavenly glory.

Paul's report of Ananias's communication of God's commission in v. 15 is a reformulation of the clause in 9:15. Paul describes the commission that he received through Ananias. (1) He has been appointed by God as a "witness" (μάρτυς; see on 1:8) of Jesus. The subject matter of his teaching is Jesus of Nazareth (v. 8), who was crucified in Jerusalem, rose from the dead, and is now exalted into the presence of God's glory. (2) He has been chosen as a witness "before all people," i.e., before Jews and Gentiles, which is explicitly specified in 9:15. (3) He has been commissioned to speak of what he has "seen" and "heard," i.e., of his encounter with Jesus as the crucified, risen, and exalted Messiah and Lord. The perfect tense of the verb "seen" (ἑώρακας) underlines Paul's calling as a bona fide eyewitness of the risen Lord (1 Cor 9:1; 15:8 – 10).[48] As the Twelve focused their preaching on the resurrection of the crucified Jesus as Israel's Messiah and Savior,[49] so does Paul (cf. 13:31; 17:31).

22:16 "And now, what are you waiting for? Get up, be immersed, and wash your sins away by calling on his name" (καὶ νῦν τί μέλλεις; ἀναστὰς βάπτισαι καὶ ἀπόλουσαι τὰς ἁμαρτίας σου ἐπικαλεσάμενος τὸ ὄνομα αὐτοῦ). What Luke relates in 9:18 in narrative form, Paul reports as instructions from Ananias. The rhetorical question prompts Paul to respond to the divine message conveyed by Ananias, i.e., to acknowledge that his encounter with Jesus on the road to Damascus was God's initiative, that the crucified Jesus of Nazareth is indeed the Righteous One, the exalted Lord whose voice he has heard and whose reality he has seen, and that God has given him the task of proclaiming the risen Jesus to all people.

Ananias asks Paul to complete four actions. (1) Paul must "get up" (v. 10), i.e., take action in obedience to God's directives. (2) He must "be immersed" in water (βάπτισαι), i.e., express repentance of sins, the need for cleansing, and confidence in God's provision of forgiveness by immersion in water (see 1:5; 2:38). (3) He must "wash away" (ἀπόλουσαι) his sins; i.e., he is in need of God's forgiveness, in particular of his rejection of Jesus and his actions as persecutor of Jesus' followers. The

---

47. Cf. BDAG, s.v. προχειρίζω, "to express preference of someone for a task, *choose for oneself, select, appoint;*" cf. LSJ, s.v. προχειρίζω II, middle: "make ready for oneself, mobilize," or "choose, select."

48. Note that neither Luke in 9:15 nor Paul in 22:15 speak of

Paul's commissioning as an apostle, a title that Luke uses for the Twelve, who have accompanied Jesus throughout his ministry (1:21 – 22), and only rarely for Paul (14:4, 14).

49. Cf. 1:8, 22; 2:32; 3:15; 5:32; 10:39.

metaphor of "washing away" connects with the reference to immersion, for in Jewish culture, immersion in water symbolized the cleansing from sins. (4) He must "call on" (ἐπικαλεσάμενος) the name of Jesus, i.e., invoke the name of Jesus as he is immersed in water, trusting that God now forgives sins through Jesus, his Righteous One (see on 2:38; 3:6, 16).

22:17 – 18 When I returned to Jerusalem and was praying in the temple, I fell into a trance and saw the Lord speaking to me, "Hurry, leave Jerusalem immediately, because they will not accept your testimony about me" (ἐγένετο δέ μοι ὑποστρέψαντι εἰς Ἰερουσαλὴμ καὶ προσευχομένου μου ἐν τῷ ἱερῷ γενέσθαι με ἐν ἐκστάσει καὶ ἰδεῖν αὐτὸν λέγοντά μοι· σπεῦσον καὶ ἔξελθε ἐν τάχει ἐξ Ἰερουσαλήμ, διότι οὐ παραδέξονταί σου μαρτυρίαν περὶ ἐμοῦ). The third and last section of Paul's statement of the facts of his case relates a vision he had during a visit to the temple in Jerusalem (vv. 17 – 21). Luke's account of Paul's conversion and postconversion activities in Acts 9 does not refer to this incident, which must have taken place after Paul's missionary preaching in Damascus and in Arabia/Nabatea (9:20 – 25; Gal 1:17) during his visit to Jerusalem three years after his conversion (cf. 9:26 – 29; Gal 1:18; i.e., AD 33/34).

When Paul tells his audience that he visited the temple in order to pray when he returned to Jerusalem after his encounter with the crucified and risen Jesus of Nazareth on the road to Damascus, he counters the accusation that he is teaching against the temple (21:26). During his prayers he fell into a trance (see on 10:10), a state of consciousness in which he saw Jesus and Jesus spoke to him. It is possible that Paul received this vision of Jesus during one of the meetings of the church in Jerusalem in Solomon's Portico.

Note that according to 9:28, when Paul visited Jerusalem for the first time after his conversion, he

stayed with the believers and "moved about freely in Jerusalem." The report of his vision in the temple is not a recasting of the missionary commission of 9:15 but a confirmation of that commission received at the time of his conversion (22:15).

Paul tells his audience that in this vision, Jesus directed him to leave Jerusalem (v. 18). The two imperatives underline the urgency of the command: Paul is told to "hurry" (σπεῦσον) and "leave" (ἔξελθε) immediately because of the unbelief of the Jews in Jerusalem: they will not accept his "testimony" (μαρτυρία). This statement implies several points. (1) Paul was obedient to Jesus' commission conveyed through Ananias; he had become a witness of Jesus, speaking about what he had seen and heard. (2) Paul was preaching the good news of Jesus as Israel's risen Messiah and Savior "boldly" before Jewish audiences in Jerusalem, both among the Hebrew-speaking population as well as among the Greek-speaking Jews, as Luke reported in 9:28 – 29. (3) It confirms Paul's assertion in Rom 15:19 that he had preached the gospel "from Jerusalem all the way around to Illyricum."

Paul presumably made contact with the rabbis, his former fellow students, and the members of the synagogue of the Cilician Jews (6:9), which he probably had attended before his conversion. The fact that he had to leave in a hurry corresponds to Paul's assertion in Gal 1:18 that his first visit to Jerusalem after his conversion lasted only for fifteen days; it also fits the information given in 9:29, where Paul left Jerusalem as the result of a plot of Greek-speaking Jews who wanted to kill him. Jesus had commissioned Paul to be his witness, but not for the people living in Jerusalem.

22:19 – 20 I answered, "Lord, they know that I went from one synagogue to another to imprison and beat those who believed in you. While the blood of Stephen, your witness, was being shed, I stood there, giving my approval and guard-

ing the clothes of those who were killing him"
(κἀγὼ εἶπον· κύριε, αὐτοὶ ἐπίστανται ὅτι ἐγὼ
ἤμην φυλακίζων καὶ δέρων κατὰ τὰς συναγωγὰς
τοὺς πιστεύοντας ἐπὶ σέ, καὶ ὅτε ἐξεχύννετο τὸ
αἷμα Στεφάνου τοῦ μάρτυρός σου, καὶ αὐτὸς ἤμην
ἐφεστὼς καὶ συνευδοκῶν καὶ φυλάσσων τὰ ἱμάτια
τῶν ἀναιρούντων αὐτόν). In his vision, Paul responded to the Lord's directive to leave Jerusalem
by protesting that he could be an effective witness
in Jerusalem (vv. 19 – 20). Paul reminded the Lord
that he was known in Jerusalem, and that the Jews
in the Jerusalem synagogues knew him as someone
who was actively involved in arresting and beating
believers in Jesus — one specific example being the
execution of Stephen. The fact that they knew his
past as a persecutor of the followers of Jesus should
trigger the conclusion that the reason why he was
now himself a believer in Jesus must be incontro-
vertible evidence that Jesus is Israel's Messiah and
Savior.

The reference to the synagogues in which
the believers worshiped refers to Luke's report
concerning Stephen's preaching activity in the
synagogue of freedmen, of the Cyrenians, of the
Alexandrians, and of those from Cilicia and Asia
(6:9). Paul's involvement in the persecution of the
followers of Jesus was mentioned in 9:2, his participation in the execution of Stephen in 7:58 – 8:1.
The periphrastic construction (ἤμην φυλακίζων καὶ
δέρων) in v. 19 underscores that Paul's initiative in
imprisoning and beating the Christians was not a
onetime action but a long-term engagement. The
periphrastic construction in v. 20 (ἤμην ἐφεστὼς
καὶ συνευδοκῶν καὶ φυλάσσων) likewise highlights
his participation in Stephen's killing by standing
by, approving, and guarding the clothes of the
executioners. The reference to the shed blood of

Stephen, underlines the violent death of Stephen
through stoning. The term "witness" (μάρτυς) describes Stephen as a believer in Jesus who publicly
attested to the truth of Jesus' identity as Israel's crucified, risen, and exalted Messiah and Savior (see
on 1:8); the term as used here does not yet have the
technical meaning of "martyr."[50]

Paul probably thinks that since the Jews in Jerusalem remember his sincerity as persecutor of
the Christians, they should be willing to accept
his sincerity as someone who has himself become
a Christian believer. And if the audience remembers the charges against Stephen, who was accused
of speaking against the law and against the temple
(6:13 – 14), that may prompt them to consider that
he, Paul, must have convincing reasons to now profess faith in Jesus.

**22:21 Then he said to me, "Go! I am sending
you far away to the Gentiles"** (καὶ εἶπεν πρός με·
πορεύου, ὅτι ἐγὼ εἰς ἔθνη μακρὰν ἐξαποστελῶ σε).
The vision ends with the Lord directing Paul to go
to the Gentiles. Jesus repeats the command of v. 18
to leave Jerusalem: the imperative "Go!" (πορεύου)
corresponds to "Leave!" (ἔξελθε). In this vision,
Paul receives a confirmation of the commission to
go to the Gentiles (εἰς ἔθνη) that the risen Jesus had
given to him in Damascus through Ananias when
Jesus chose him "to carry my name before Gentiles
[ἐνώπιον ἐθνῶν] and kings, and the people of Israel" (9:15), thus making him "a light for the Gentiles" (φῶς ἐθνῶν; 13:47). Similarly, in Gal 1:16 Paul
describes his commission in terms of proclaiming
Jesus "among the Gentiles" (ἐν τοῖς ἔθνεσιν).

The verb translated "I am sending" (ἐξαποστελῶ)
is not a technical term for apostolic sending (or
"mission," to use the Latin term), but its use here

---

50. This is the assumption in the translation of NIV ("your
martyr Stephen," though see text note "witness"). The reference
to Polycarp in *Mart. Pol.* 14:2 is usually credited to be the first

attested meaning of μάρτυς in terms of "martyr" (Polycarp died
ca. AD 155).

may reflect Paul's apostolic self-understanding (cf. Gal 1:1; Rom 1:1). The geographical reference "far away" refers to areas and populations outside of Jerusalem and Judea. Luke's readers know that the term translated as "Gentiles" (ἔθνη) does not refer exclusively to non-Jews: Paul preached before both Jewish and Gentile audiences, as he reminds the Ephesians elders at the end of his ministry (20:20 – 21). The term ἔθνη is used here not in an ethnic but in a geographical sense, denoting the

"nations" outside of Palestine, among them the Jewish people living in the diaspora.[51] Paul is an "apostle to the Gentiles" (Rom 11:13), a witness among non-Jewish people but also among the Jewish people. Paul, accused of having defiled the temple, hopes that he can convince the Jews listening to his defense that his proclamation of Jesus among the diaspora Jews was the result of the divine revelation and commission that he received in the very temple where they are standing.

Theology in Application

The five incidents that make up Luke's account of the arrest of Paul in Jerusalem portray Paul as a witness of Jesus who shares in Jesus' suffering: he is arrested and in danger of being killed. He is rescued from the Jewish crowds by the intervention of a Roman army commander. As Luke's subsequent narrative shows, Paul continues to be protected by the actions of Roman officials. The "interface" between local, national, and imperial politics is one area of theological reflection and application occasioned by this episode. Paul never has to stand trial before the Sanhedrin, where he presumably would be condemned to death for the alleged crime of teaching against the Jewish people, against the Mosaic law, and against the temple, and the specific crime of bringing a Gentile into the inner courts of the temple, thus defiling the place of the presence of Israel's God — accusations that are voiced in the episode of Paul's arrest in the temple.

Luke's retelling of Paul's conversion, the central part of Paul's defense speech before the Jews in the temple complex, emphasizes his Jewish identity as well as the identity of Jesus as risen Lord, who vindicates the faith of the followers of Jesus as he brings Paul the persecutor to the acknowledgment that Jesus is alive and that Jesus is Lord.

Christians Do Not Cause Political Uprisings

The opposition of Jews against Paul's ministry[52] comes to a climax in the attempt of Jews from the province of Asia to kill Paul after they have arrested him in the temple (21:27 – 31). Paul is rescued by the intervention of a representative of the imperial power of Rome. Paul accepts protective custody from the commander of the Roman

---

51. Note that while Luke uses ἔθνος mostly for non-Jews, he uses the term also for Israel, cf. 10:22; later in 24:10, 17; 26:4; 19:28.

52. Cf. 13:50; 14:2, 5, 19; 17:5 – 9; 18:12 – 17.

army unit stationed in Jerusalem, but he protests against the suspicion that he is the Egyptian insurrectionist who had instigated a rebellion against Roman rule in Judea. Christians do not start revolutions. Even though the Christian message has visible consequences and dramatic effects on a society at large if enough people come to faith in Jesus (as the Ephesus episode demonstrated), Christians do not preach revolution. They are witnesses of Jesus, the crucified, risen, and exalted Messiah of Israel and Savior of the world in and through whom God fulfills his promises — forgiving sins and reconciling Jews and Gentiles as the restored people of God (overcoming the apartheid of Jews and Gentiles that Jews had been practicing).

While Paul's opponents can be accused of "a traditionalism that ends up distorting the genuine tradition" that takes place as his opponents denied "the messianic hope that God has confirmed through Jesus' resurrection,"[53] Paul did not preach "against" Jewish tradition as expressed in the Mosaic law, as practiced in Israel, and as based on the temple. He proclaimed the fulfillment of God's prior revelation in Jesus, the Messiah and Savior, and in the new people of God consisting of believing Jews and believing Gentiles. Christians know that their convictions change society because they change what people value and how they behave, but they do not aim at provoking social and political upheavals. It is not Paul who starts a riot; rather, the Jews from the province of Asia trigger a disturbance that calls Roman soldiers on the scene. Paul's interaction with the Roman commander here and his interactions with Roman governors in the subsequent narrative demonstrate that the imperial system of Rome has nothing to fear from Paul and the message he proclaims. Authentic Christians are people of integrity, who do not threaten the right of states or legal systems that maintain and promote law and order.

Christians Are Witnesses of Jesus

Believers in Jesus profess God who reveals himself in Jesus, even in dangerous situations, and they give witness of Jesus of Nazareth, who is alive, who saves, and who directs the lives of God's people. Paul defends himself in his speech before the Jews in the outer court of the temple, but he does so by speaking about Jesus. Paul speaks not only about Jesus of Nazareth, but also, and more extensively, about his encounter with the crucified, risen, and exalted Jesus, who spoke to him from the glory of God's reality. Paul is a witness of Jesus' resurrection, and as difficult as this might be for the Jews in the temple to accept, it is a reality that Paul wants to proclaim, not only because it changed his own life but because it demonstrates that Jesus is indeed the Lord, Israel's Messiah and Savior, whom God has sent to Israel and to the world.

---

53. Bock, *Acts*, 665; he continues to argue that a traditionalism that fails to "to consider how God's recent activity relates to God's promise and program" makes the Jews "unwilling and unable to respond to a hope designed for them" and thus ends up being a "tradition gone bad. It creates blindness and stubbornness, a deadly combination."

Believers in Jesus who are witnesses of Jesus have been chosen by God (22:14); they have been sent by Jesus, Israel's Messiah (22:10, 14 – 15, 17 – 21); and they are obedient to the commission they have received (22:10, 19 – 20). Paul's commission was a particular event (note the directive to leave Jerusalem, and the directive to go to the Gentiles who live "far away"), but the theological basis of his commission and the christological content of his proclamation remain fundamental necessities for authentic witnesses of Jesus.

Acts 22:22 – 23:35

Literary Context

The first two episodes of Luke's report about Paul's last visit to Jerusalem (21:18 – 23:35) related Paul's encounter with James and the elders of the Jerusalem church (21:18 – 26) and Paul's arrest in the inner courts of the temple and his address to the Jews who wanted to kill him in the outer court (21:27 – 22:21). The third and last episode of this section relates Paul's imprisonment in Jerusalem (22:22 – 23:35). It begins with Paul's custody in the Antonia Fortress (22:22 – 29) and ends with his transfer to Caesarea (23:23 – 35). Paul will remain a prisoner for the remainder of Luke's narrative in Acts: the last two sections report Paul's imprisonment in Caesarea (24:1 – 26:32) and Paul's transfer to and imprisonment in Rome (27:1 – 28:31). The events reported in this episode took place in May AD 57.

Main Idea

In the midst of fanaticism that is willing to kill, pragmatism that is willing to torture, and unscrupulousness that is willing to manipulate, Christians will defend themselves with prophetic zeal, with continued focus on the crucified and risen Jesus Christ, and with individuals who are willing to help in dangerous situations.

Translation

Acts 22:22 – 23:35

22a	Action	**They listened to him until he made this statement.**
b	Action	**Then they raised their voices**
c	Action	**and shouted,**
d	Exclamation	*"Rid the earth of this fellow!*
e	Explanation	*He should not be allowed to live."*
23a	Setting: time	As they were shouting and
b	Action	taking off their robes and
c	Action	throwing dust into the air,
24a	Action	**the commander ordered**
b	Command	that Paul be taken into the barracks,
c	Assertion	saying that he would be examined
d	Means	with the whip
e	Purpose	in order to find the cause
f	Cause	why they were shouting at him like this.
25a	Setting: time	As they stretched him out
b	Purpose	for the whips,
c	Action	**Paul said to the centurion**
d	Character description	who was standing by,
e	Question	*"Do you regard it as legal*
f	Content	*to flog a Roman citizen*
g	Manner	*without due process?"*
26a	Setting: time	When the centurion heard this,
b	Reaction	**he went to the commander**
c	Action	**and reported it;**
d	Action: report	**he said,**
e	Question	*"What will you do?*
f	Identification	*This man is a Roman citizen."*
27a	Reaction	**The commander came**
b	Action	**and asked,**
c	Question	*"Tell me,*
d	Content	*are you a Roman citizen?"*
e	Response	**He said,**
f	Assertion	*"Yes."*
28a	Response	**The commander responded,**
b	Assertion (flashback)	*"I acquired citizenship*
c	Means	*for a large sum of money."*
d	Response	**Paul said,**
e	Contrast	*"I was indeed born a citizen."*
29a	Setting: time	Immediately
b	Action	**the soldiers**
c	Intention	who were about to interrogate him
d		**backed away from him,**

e	Event	**and the commander became alarmed**
f	Time	when he realized
g	Cause	that Paul was a Roman citizen and
h	Cause	that he had put him in chains.
30a	Setting: time	The next day,
b	Time: character's thoughts	when he wanted to find out exactly
c	Content	what charges were brought against Paul
d	Agency	by the Jews,
e	Action	**he released him**
f	Action	**and ordered the chief priests and**
g	Association	**the entire Sanhedrin**
h	Command	**to assemble.**
i	Action	**He brought Paul down**
j	Action	**and had him stand**
k	Place	before them.
23:1a	Action	**Paul looked intently at the Sanhedrin**
b	Action: speech	**and said,**
c	Address	*"Brothers,*
d	Review of history	*I have lived my life*
e	Manner	*with a perfectly clear conscience*
f	Sphere	*before God*
g	Time	*up to this day."*
2a	Character entrance	**But the high priest**
b	Identification	Ananias
c	Action	**ordered those standing near him**
d	Command	to strike Paul
e	Place	on the mouth.
3a	Reaction	**Then Paul said to him,**
b	Pronouncement	*"God will strike you,*
c	Exclamation	*you whitewashed wall!*
d	Rhetorical question	*You, do you sit here*
e	Purpose	*to judge me*
f	Means	*according to the law,*
g	Contra-expectation	*and yet in violation of the law*
h	Accusation	*you order me*
i	Content	*to be struck?"*
4a	Character entrance	**Those who stood nearby said,**
b	Question	*"Do you insult God's high priest?"*
5a	Response	**Paul responded,**
b	Address	*"Brothers,*
c	Assertion	*I did not know*
d	Content	*that he was the high priest.*
e	Quotation	*It is written,*
f	Command	*'Do not speak evil about a ruler of your people.'"*
6a	Setting: character's thought	As Paul knew
b	Content	that some were Sadducees
c	Content	and some were Pharisees,

Continued on next page.

Continued from previous page.

d	Action	**he called out**
e	Place	in the Sanhedrin,
f	Address	*"Brothers,*
g	Identification (social)	*I am a Pharisee,*
h	Description: familial	*the son of Pharisees.*
i	Assertion	*I am on trial*
j	Cause	*because of the hope of the resurrection of the dead!"*

7a	Setting: time	When he said this,
b	Reaction: conflict	**a dispute broke out between the Pharisees and**
c		**the Sadducees,**
d	Result	and **the assembly became divided.**
8a	Explanation	**For the Sadducees say**
b	Content	that there is no resurrection,
c	Specification	neither as an angel,
d	Specification	nor as a spirit,
e	Contrast	**whereas the Pharisees confess belief in them both.**
9a	Event	**A loud uproar arose.**
b	Action	**Some scribes**
c	Identification	who belonged to the party of the Pharisees
d		**stood up**
e	Action: speech	and **contended,**
f	Assertion	*"We find nothing wrong in this man.*
g	Question (hypothesis)	*What if a spirit*
h	(hypothesis)	*or an angel*
i	(hypothesis)	*has spoken to him?"*

10a	Setting: time	When the dispute became so heated
b	Consequence	that the commander feared
c	Content	that Paul would be torn into pieces
d	Agency	by them,
e	Action	**he ordered his troops**
f	Command	to go down,
g	Command	to remove him, and
h	Command	to bring him into the barracks.

11a	Setting: time	The following night
b	Event	**the Lord stood**
c	Place	at Paul's side
d	Action	and **said,**
e	Encouragement	*"Keep up your courage!*
f	Comparison	*As you have borne witness to me*
g	Place	*here in Jerusalem,*
h	Comparison	*so you must bear witness*
i	Place	*also in Rome."*

12a	Setting: time	In the morning
b	Action	**the Jews organized a conspiracy**
c	Action	**and bound themselves with an oath,**
d	Content	saying that they would not eat
e	Content	or drink
f	Duration	until they had killed Paul.
13a	Aside: Measure	**There were more than forty men**
b	Identification	who were involved in this plot.
14a	Action	**They went to the chief priests and**
b		elders
c	Action	**and said,**
d	Report	"We have bound ourselves
e	Means	by a solemn oath
f	Content	to take no food
g	Duration	until we have killed Paul.
15a	Call to action	Now then, you and
b	Association	the Sanhedrin
c	Instruction	must report to the commander
d	Content	that he should bring Paul down to you,
e	Means	on the pretext
f	Content	that you want to conduct a more thorough examination
g	Description	of his case.
h	Assertion	We are ready to kill him
i	Time	before he arrives here."
16a	Setting: time	When the son of Paul's sister heard of the arrangement
b	Purpose	for the ambush,
c		**he went**
d	Action	**and entered into the barracks**
e	Action	**and told Paul.**
17a	Reaction	**Paul called one of the centurions**
b	Action	**and said,**
c	Command	"Take this young man
d	Place	to the commander.
e	Explanation	He has something to report to him."
18a	Reaction	**The centurion took him**
b	Action	**and brought him to the commander,**
c	Action	**and said,**
d	Report	"The prisoner Paul called me
e	Report	and asked me
f	Content	to bring this young man to you
g	Cause	because he has something to tell you."
19a	Reaction	**The commander took him**
b	Manner	by the hand,
c	Action	**drew him aside**
d	Manner	privately,
e	Question	**and asked him,**
f	Question	"What do you have to report to me?"

Continued on next page.

Continued from previous page.

20a	Response	**He answered,**
b	Report	"The Jews have agreed
c	Content	to ask you
d	Content	to bring Paul down
e	Place	to the Sanhedrin
f	Time	tomorrow,
g	Basis	on the pretext
h	Content	that they want to inquire more thoroughly into his case.

21a	Warning	But do not be persuaded by them,
b	Cause	because more than forty of their men are lying in ambush for him.
c	Explanation	They have bound themselves
d	Means	by an oath
e	Content	not to eat or
f	Content	drink
g	Duration	until they kill him.
h	Assertion	They are ready now,
i	Assertion	*and* they are waiting for your consent."
22a	Reaction	**The commander dismissed the young man,**
b	Instruction	ordering him,
c	Command	"Tell no one
d	Content	that you have reported this to me."

23a	Action	**Then he called two of the centurions**
b	Action	**and said,**
c	Command	"Get two hundred soldiers ready
d	Purpose	to leave for Caesarea
e	Time	by nine o'clock
f	Time	tonight,
g	Association	together with seventy cavalrymen
h	Association	and two hundred bowmen.
24a	Command	Provide horses for Paul
b	Purpose	to ride,
c	Command: character	*and* bring him safely to Felix,
d	Identification	the governor."
25a	Action	**He wrote a letter,**
b	Identification	which had the following text:

26a	Author	"Claudius Lysias
b	Addressee	to His Excellency,
c	Identification	Felix,
d	Identification	the governor:
e	Salutation	Greetings!
27a	Report	This man was seized
b	Agency	by the Jews
c	Action	*and* they were about to kill him.
d	Action	I came with my troops
e	Action	*and* rescued him

| f | Time (cause) | *when I learned* |
| g | Content (identification) | *that he was a Roman citizen.* |

28a	Cause	*Because I wanted to know*
b	Content	*the cause of their charges against him,*
c	Action	*I brought him*
d	Place	*before their Sanhedrin.*
29a	Action	*I found*
b	Content	*that he was accused of controversial questions*
c	Sphere	*of their law,*
d	Contrast	*but that there was no charge*
e	Result	*deserving death or*
f	Result	*chains.*
30a	Time	*When I was informed*
b	Content	*that there would be a plot against the man,*
c	Action	*I sent him to you*
d	Time	*at once,*
e	Action: command	*and I also ordered his accusers*
f	Content	*to state their case against him*
g	Place	*before you."*
31a	Action	**So the soldiers,**
b	Manner	in accordance with their orders,
c	Action	**took Paul**
d	Action	**and brought him**
e	Time	during the night
f	Place	to Antipatris.

32a	Setting: time	The next morning
b	Action	**they let the cavalrymen go on with him,**
c	Time	while they returned
d	Place	to the barracks.

33a	Setting: time	When they arrived
b	Place	in Caesarea,
c	Action	**they delivered the letter to the governor**
d	Action	**and handed Paul over to him.**
34a	Action	**He read the letter**
b	Question	**and asked Paul**
c	Geographical	what province he was from.

d	Time	When he learned
e	Geographical	that he was from Cilicia,
35a	Reaction	**he said,**
b	Affirmation	*"I will hear your case*
c	Time	*when your accusers get here."*
d	Action: command	**Then he ordered**
e	Content	that he be kept under guard
f	Place	in Herod's praetorium.

Structure and Literary Form

This episode is made up of four incidents focused on four different locations. Luke relates Paul's interrogation in the Antonia Fortress (22:22 – 29), Paul's interrogation before the Sanhedrin (22:30 – 23:11), the plot of Jews in Jerusalem to kill Paul (23:12 – 22), and Paul's transfer from Jerusalem to Caesarea (23:23 – 35). As in the previous episode, Luke gives a defense of Paul and of the gospel message, both for Jews and for the Roman world: Paul is a law-abiding Jew (23:6), and the real reason of the dispute between Paul and the Jews is his faith in the hope of the resurrection of the dead (23:6). Paul's identity as a Roman citizen spares him from torture during interrogation (22:24 – 29) while the investigation by the Roman commander Claudius Lysias into Paul's culpability results in his rescue from a plot of Jerusalem Jews (23:12 – 35) and his description as innocent of any accusations that would warrant imprisonment or a death sentence (23:29).

The four incidents of the episode consist of *narrative* with precise chronological markers: the second incident happened "the next day" (τῇ δὲ ἐπαύριον) after Paul's imprisonment in the Antonia Fortress narrated in the first incident (22:30), and ends with the night (τῇ ἐπιούσῃ νυκτί) of that day (23:11); the third incident is dated to the morning (γενομένης δὲ ἡμέρας) of the next day (23:12). While there is no chronological information concerning the planning of the plot against Paul narrated in the third incident or for its discovery by Paul's nephew, the fourth incident follows within a few hours of the disclosure of the plot to the Roman commander in Jerusalem, who orders two centurions and their troops to leave Jerusalem by "nine o'clock tonight" (ἀπὸ τρίτης ὥρας τῆς νυκτός; 23:23); Luke notes the departure during the night (διὰ νυκτός) and the second day of the journey (τῇ δὲ ἐπαύριον; 23:31, 32).

Luke includes twenty-two examples of *direct speech*, narrated in the first incident for the Jerusalem Jews (22:22), Paul (vv. 25, 27, 38), a Roman centurion (v. 26), and the Roman commander (vv. 27, 28); in the second incident for Paul (23:1, 3, 5, 6), members of the Sanhedrin (v. 4), Pharisees in the Sanhedrin (v. 9), and the Lord (v. 11); in the third incident for Jews of Jerusalem (vv. 14 – 15), Paul (v. 17), a centurion (v. 18), the Roman commander (v. 19, 22), Paul's nephew (vv. 20 – 21); in the fourth incident for the Roman commander (vv. 23 – 24) and Felix the Roman governor (v. 35). Paul's *speech* in 23:6, narrated succinctly with fourteen words of Greek text, is Paul's seventh speech in Acts.[1] The fourth incident includes the text of the *letter* that the Roman commander in Jerusalem wrote and sent to Felix (vv. 26 – 30).

---

1. Cf. 13:7 – 11 (Paphos); 13:16 – 41 (Pisidian Antioch); 14:15 – 18 (Lystra); 17:22 – 31 (Athens); 20:18 – 35 (Miletus); 22:1 – 21 (outer court of the temple in Jerusalem).

Exegetical Outline

➡ **I. Paul's Imprisonment in Jerusalem (22:22 – 23:35)**

A. Paul's Interrogation in the Antonia Fortress (22:22 – 29)

1. The interruption of Paul's speech by the Jews in the Outer Court (22:22 – 23)

   a. The Jews' interruption of Paul's speech (22:22a-c)

   b. The Jews' demand for Paul's execution (22:22d-e)

   c. The Jews' expression of disgust and outrage against Paul (22:23)

2. Paul's transfer into the Antonia Fortress (22:24)

   a. The Roman commander's order to take Paul into the barracks (22:24a-b)

   b. The Roman commander's order to interrogate Paul under torture (22:24c-d)

   c. The Roman commander's goal of establishing Paul's crimes (22:24e-f)

3. The cancellation of Paul's interrogation (22:25 – 29)

   a. The preparations for Paul's interrogation under torture (22:25a-b)

   b. Paul's protest against flogging with reference to his Roman citizenship (22:25c-g)

   c. The centurion's report to the commander regarding Paul's citizenship status (22:26)

   d. The commander's interview of Paul regarding his citizenship status (22:27 – 28)

      i. The commander's query as to Paul's Roman citizenship (22:27a-d)

      ii. Paul's self-identification as a Roman citizen (22:27e-f)

      iii. The commander's explanation of the origin of his citizenship (22:28a-c)

      iv. Paul's assertion that he was born a Roman citizen (22:28d-e)

   e. The cancellation of Paul's interrogation (22:29)

B. Paul's Interrogation before the Sanhedrin (22:30 – 23:11)

1. The commander's summons of a meeting of the Sanhedrin (22:30)

   a. The commander's determination to establish charges against Paul (22:30a-d)

   b. The release of Paul from custody (22:30e)

   c. The summons of the Sanhedrin (22:30f-h)

   d. Paul's transfer from the Antonia to the hall of the Sanhedrin (22:30i-k)

2. Paul's appearance before the Sanhedrin (23:1 – 9)

   a. Paul's courage (23:1a)

   b. Paul's assertion that he is a law-abiding Jew (23:1b-g)

   c. The high priest's attempt to brand Paul as a liar, with blows (23:2 – 5)

      i. Ananias's order that Paul be struck on the mouth (23:2)

      ii. Paul's protest against the blows (23:3)

      iii. Ananias's dignity asserted by his associates (23:4)

      iv. Paul's apology for his choice of words (23:5)

   d. Paul's defense (23:6)

      i. Paul's consideration of the composition of the Sanhedrin (23:6a-e)

      ii. Paul's declaration that he is a Pharisee (23:6f-h)

      iii. Paul's assertion that the dispute is about the resurrection (23:6i-j)

     e. The disagreement among the members of the Sanhedrin (23:7 – 9a)

         i. The dispute between the Pharisees and the Sadducees (23:7)

         ii. The disagreement concerning the resurrection (23:8)

         iii. The dispute becomes an uproar (23:9a)

     f. The judgment of Pharisaic scribes concerning Paul's innocence (23:9b-i)

     3. The commander's termination of the Sanhedrin hearing (23:10 – 11)

         a. The tumult in the Sanhedrin (23:10a)

         b. The commander's order to have Paul placed in protective custody (23:10b-h)

         c. The Lord's assurance that Paul will be kept safe and travel to Rome (23:11)

C. The Plot of Jerusalem Jews to Kill Paul (23:12 – 22)

     1. The plan of Jews who want to kill Paul (23:12 – 15)

         a. The beginning of the conspiracy (23:12a-b)

         b. The oath of the conspirators (23:12c-f)

         c. The size of the conspiracy (23:13)

         d. The official support of the conspirators (23:14a-b)

         e. The conspirators' oath (23:14c-g)

         f. The conspirators' plans (23:15)

     2. The disclosure of the plot to kill Paul (23:16 – 22)

         a. Paul's nephew informs Paul (23:16)

         b. Paul asks a centurion to take his nephew to the commander (23:17)

         c. The centurion complies with Paul's request (23:18)

         d. Paul's nephew informs the commander (23:19 – 21)

         e. The commander orders Paul's nephew to tell no one (23:22)

D. Paul's Transfer to Caesarea (23:23 – 35)

     1. The commander's instructions to two of his centurions (23:23 – 24)

         a. Instructions concerning troop strengths for the escort (23:23)

         b. Instructions concerning horses for Paul (23:24a-b)

         c. Instructions concerning Paul's transfer to Felix, the governor (23:24c-d)

     2. The commander's letter to Felix, the governor (23:25 – 30)

         a. The commander's composition of a letter (23:25)

         b. The letter (23:26 – 30)

             i. Prescript (23:26)

             ii. Report of Paul's arrest (23:27)

             iii. Report of the Sanhedrin hearing (23:28)

             iv. Preliminary conclusion concerning Paul's innocence (23:29)

             v. Explanation of Paul's transfer to the governor (23:30)

     3. The journey to Caesarea (23:31 – 33)

         a. The night journey from Jerusalem to Antipatris (23:31)

         b. The journey from Antipatris to Caesarea (23:32)

         c. The arrival in Caesarea and the handover of Paul (23:33)

4. Paul's first encounter with Felix, the governor (23:34 – 35)

    a. The governor's reading of the commander's letter (23:34a)

    b. Query concerning Paul's home province (23:34b-e)

    c. The decision to hear Paul's case (23:35a-c)

    d. The order to keep Paul under guard in the governor's residence (23:35d-f)

Explanation of the Text

22:22 They listened to him until he made this statement. Then they raised their voices and shouted, "Rid the earth of this fellow! He should not be allowed to live" (ἤκουον δὲ αὐτοῦ ἄχρι τούτου τοῦ λόγου καὶ ἐπῆραν τὴν φωνὴν αὐτῶν λέγοντες· αἶρε ἀπὸ τῆς γῆς τὸν τοιοῦτον, οὐ γὰρ καθῆκεν αὐτὸν ζῆν). Paul's imprisonment in Jerusalem ensues from the tumult caused by the Jews in the outer court of the temple who listened to Paul's defense (22:1 – 21). Luke begins the episode by noting the Jews' interruption of Paul's speech.

When Paul makes the statement about the crucified and risen Lord, who sent him away from Jerusalem to the Gentiles (v. 21), they stopped listening and began to shout: "Rid the earth of this fellow!" (αἶρε ἀπὸ τῆς γῆς τὸν τοιοῦτον). This cry takes up their earlier demand that Paul should be killed, expressed with the shout "Take him away!" (αἶρε αὐτόν; see on 21:36). This first phrase of the crowd's direct speech is not rhetorical hyperbole but a demand for Paul's execution; their second cry confirms this, that Paul should not be allowed to live. They demand that the Roman commander order his execution.

22:23 – 24 As they were shouting and taking off their robes and throwing dust into the air, the commander ordered that Paul be taken into the barracks, saying that he would be examined with the whip in order to find the cause why they were

shouting at him like this (κραυγαζόντων τε αὐτῶν καὶ ῥιπτούντων τὰ ἱμάτια καὶ κονιορτὸν βαλλόντων εἰς τὸν ἀέρα, ἐκέλευσεν ὁ χιλίαρχος εἰσάγεσθαι αὐτὸν εἰς τὴν παρεμβολήν, εἴπας μάστιξιν ἀνετάζεσθαι αὐτὸν ἵνα ἐπιγνῷ δι᾽ ἣν αἰτίαν οὕτως ἐπεφώνουν αὐτῷ). Luke uses three more verbs to describe the reaction of the Jewish crowd: "they were shouting" (κραυγαζόντων); i.e., they screamed excitedly. They were "taking off" (ῥιπτούντων) their robes, presumably shaking them out as a gesture of protest and indignation, similar to the gesture of shaking the dust off one's feet, or perhaps as preparation for Paul's execution by stoning (cf. 7:58; 22:20).[2] And they were "throwing" (βαλλόντων) dust into the air, an expression of frenzied rage. The present tense of the three participles underlines that the tumult in the outer court went on for some time.

The Roman commander orders Paul to be taken into the barracks in the Antonia Fortress (v. 24). He evidently has not understood Paul's speech, given in Hebrew or Aramaic. When he hears the enraged Jews demand Paul's execution — the Jews from the province of Asia (cf. 21:27) would have shouted in Greek — he orders Paul to be taken into the barracks for interrogation under torture. Claudius Lysias informs the shouting Jews that Paul will be interrogated "with the whip" (μάστιξιν; instrumental dative). He wants to use the *flagellum* to extract information from Paul (see on 5:40). People who

---

2. Cf. Omerzu, *Prozess*, 374, who points out that while the removal of robes before a stoning is not mentioned in Jewish

law, *m. Sanh.* 6:3 indicates that those condemned to death by stoning were disrobed.

were scourged could die as a result of this method of interrogation and punishment, or one could end up being crippled for life.

Since the Jewish crowd does not provide Lysias with coherent grounds for granting their request for Paul's execution (21:34), and since Paul's speech has provided no clarification either, he wants to extract from Paul his identity and crime. The fact that Paul has declared that he is a citizen of Tarsus does not make him exempt from being tortured. Lysias proceeds within his rights: all other forms of inquiry have been exhausted, and the situation suggests that Paul has committed a serious crime. But Lysias makes his second mistake: having wrongly believed that Paul was an Egyptian, he now believes that he is only a Jew, i.e., a Jew who is no different from most other Jews and who can thus be interrogated under torture.

22:25 As they stretched him out for the whips, Paul said to the centurion who was standing by, "Do you regard it as legal to flog a Roman citizen without due process?" (ὡς δὲ προέτειναν αὐτὸν τοῖς ἱμᾶσιν, εἶπεν πρὸς τὸν ἑστῶτα ἑκατόνταρχον ὁ Παῦλος· εἰ ἄνθρωπον Ῥωμαῖον καὶ ἀκατάκριτον ἔξεστιν ὑμῖν μαστίζειν;). Luke vividly describes the preparation for the interrogation of Paul under torture. The soldiers stretch him out; i.e., they spread him in a forward position creating a tense posture of his upper body so that the blows will inflict maximum damage on the naked skin. Paul then suggests to the centurion (ἑκατοντάρχης; see on 10:1) that he should not be flogged because he is a Roman citizen; Paul uses a rhetorical question to point out that it is illegal to be flogged "without due process" (ἀκατάκριτος), i.e., without a trial and a sentence stipulating flogging.

Roman law allowed "enhanced methods" in the examination of slaves and non-Romans, but it protected people who held Roman citizenship from being flogged as a measure of *coercitio* (for details see on 16:37). While most commentators assume that Paul appeals to or invokes his status as a Roman citizen, the Greek syntax indicates that Paul only insinuates his Roman citizenship: note the hypothetical conditional clause (εἰ) and the rhetorical question regarding trial procedure. The fact that Paul insinuates rather than stridently asserts his privileged status as a Roman citizen indicates that he does not want "to undercut his religious commitment to Judaism before Roman eyes" and that he "is still prepared to suffer or even die without complaint (cf. Acts 21:13) if it is disregarded."[3]

The question as to why did Paul not disclose his Roman citizenship earlier, in the court of the temple when the commander bound him with chains, must be answered in the context of the situation Paul faced in the outer court: the Jews who excitedly accused him of teaching everyone everywhere against the Jewish people and of bringing Greeks into the inner courts of the temple (21:28), and who would hear Paul's declaration of being a Roman citizen, surely would respond by declaring that Paul had just conceded the truth of their charge; they would become further enraged by Paul's proclaiming, in their eyes, his distance from the Jews.[4]

22:26 When the centurion heard this, he went to the commander and reported it; he said, "What will you do? This man is a Roman citizen" (ἀκούσας δὲ ὁ ἑκατοντάρχης προσελθὼν τῷ χιλιάρχῳ ἀπήγγειλεν λέγων· τί μέλλεις ποιεῖν;

---

3. Rapske, *Paul in Roman Custody*, 143; for the following point see ibid., 142.

4. Much less convincing is the suggestion that the timing of Paul's disclosure of his Roman citizenship is a literary device that allows Luke to portray Paul's rescue from flogging as

a "last-second rescue" (Pervo, *Acts*, 568). While Paul's remark may reflect, in literary terms, "a flair for the dramatic" (Parsons, *Acts*, 313), the situation Paul found himself in would not have been perceived by him as an occasion to demonstrate his enthusiasm for dramatic gestures.

ὁ γὰρ ἄνθρωπος οὗτος Ῥωμαῖός ἐστιν). The centurion grasps the implication of Paul's question concerning the identity of the prisoner on which he is about to inflict the scourge. Luke describes the actions of the centurion succinctly with four verbs: he "heard" and understood what Paul said; he "went" to Claudius Lysias, the commanding officer; he "reported" what he had learned by "speaking" with Paul.

Luke relates the centurion's report in direct speech ("this man is a Roman citizen"), which is preceded by the decisive question that ensues from Paul's comment, which the centurion (correctly) interprets as an assertion of Roman citizenship and thus as a protest. His status as a Roman citizen requires a different treatment than if he were merely a Jew, irrespective of the crime he may have committed. The centurion now knows that he cannot examine Paul under torture and asks for new instructions.

22:27 – 28 The commander came and asked, "Tell me, are you a Roman citizen?" He said, "Yes." The commander responded, "I acquired citizenship for a large sum of money." Paul said, "I was indeed born a citizen" (προσελθὼν δὲ ὁ χιλίαρχος εἶπεν αὐτῷ· λέγε μοι, σὺ Ῥωμαῖος εἶ; ὁ δὲ ἔφη· ναί. ἀπεκρίθη δὲ ὁ χιλίαρχος· ἐγὼ πολλοῦ κεφαλαίου τὴν πολιτείαν ταύτην ἐκτησάμην. ὁ δὲ Παῦλος ἔφη· ἐγὼ δὲ καὶ γεγέννημαι). The centurion's report forces Lysias to interview Paul regarding his legal status. Paul answers Lysias' question whether he is indeed a Roman citizen with a succinct "Yes" (ναί).

The commander's response is an attempt at "juridical damage assessment" as he seeks to draw Paul into disclosing the origins of his citizenship status, hoping that the prisoner's citizenship was more recently granted under inferior circumstances than his own.

Claudius Lysias discloses that he had to purchase Roman citizenship (πολιτεία) "for a large sum of money," which "may indicate that he was a person of considerable status before his entry into the army."[5] His name suggests he was a Greek who acquired citizenship during the reign of Claudius (AD 41 – 54). If he had purchased Roman citizenship before entering the army "as a means of reaching a better position than that of an ordinary auxiliary,"[6] his advancement to the rank of commander (or tribune) suggests he had realized his ambitions. Military tribunes were usually appointed by the emperor himself, and the rank allowed for a greater degree of independence than the corresponding rank in a legion. Lysias was the highest ranking officer in Jerusalem. Afraid that he might be charged for having mistreated a fellow Roman citizen, he would have hoped that if Paul turned out to be his social inferior, he might be punished only lightly or even be forgiven, if Paul should seek legal redress.

Paul responds that in contrast to Lysias, he was born a Roman citizen (ἐγὼ ... γεγέννημαι).[7] Paul's protest is not an exercise in social one-upmanship to the tribune's purchase of citizenship.[8] Rather, Paul uses all means at his disposal to avoid being

---

5. Horsley and Llewelyn, *New Documents*, 6:153. Cf. Sherwin-White, *Roman Society*, 154 – 55: the great sum that Lysias paid "was the bribe given to the intermediaries in the imperial secretariat or the provincial administration who put his name on the list of candidates for enfranchisement."

6. Dennis B. Saddington, *The Development of the Roman Auxiliary Forces from Caesar to Vespasian* (Harare: Univ. of Zimbabwe, 1982), 190; for the following comment see Horsley and Llewelyn, *New Documents*, 6:154.

7. Cf. Cicero, *Fam.* 10.32.3: "civis Romanus natus sum."

Fritz Schulz, "Roman Registers of Births and Birth Certificates," *JRS* 32 (1942): 78 – 91, 63 – 64, asserts that when Paul affirmed his Roman citizenship before the Roman tribune, "he must have produced his birth certificate for corroboration. As he was Roman born, he was in possession of such a document which he doubtless carried with him wherever he travelled."

8. Lentz, *Portrait of Paul*, 44 – 45, 93; Paul W. Walaskay, *Acts* (Westminster Bible Companion; Louisville: Westminster John Knox, 1998), 205.

interrogated under torture. More importantly, he asserts his legal privileges, hoping that his status as a Roman citizen, combined with the fact that he has not broken any Roman or Jewish law, will secure his freedom. The fact that Lysias had to purchase Roman citizenship at high cost and that Paul was born a Roman citizen suggested to Lysias that even though his status as the Roman commander in Jerusalem is higher, this is true only locally — his status with Roman citizenship purchased by money was lower than Paul's. This fact complicates matters immensely for Lysias. He cannot only be accused of having broken the law that prohibited the binding and torture of Roman citizens, but he had abused a Roman citizen with higher status. This realization explains the commander's reaction to Paul's disclosure in the next verse.

22:29 Immediately the soldiers who were about to interrogate him backed away from him, and the commander became alarmed when he realized that Paul was a Roman citizen and that he had put him in chains (εὐθέως οὖν ἀπέστησαν ἀπ᾽ αὐτοῦ οἱ μέλλοντες αὐτὸν ἀνετάζειν, καὶ ὁ χιλίαρχος δὲ ἐφοβήθη ἐπιγνοὺς ὅτι Ῥωμαῖός ἐστιν καὶ ὅτι αὐτὸν ἦν δεδεκώς). The soldiers who prepared Paul for interrogation (cf. v. 24) under torture back away from Paul, perhaps following a command by Lysias, who "became alarmed" (ἐφοβήθη) because of his actions to someone with a superior status as a fellow Roman. The *lex Julia de vi publica* stipulated that liable is "anyone who, while holding *imperium* or office, puts to death or flogs a Roman citizen contrary to his right of appeal, or order any of the above mentioned things to be done, or puts (a yoke) on his neck so that he may be tortured" (*Dig.* 48.6.7; see on 16:37). The commander removes Paul's chains. Since the specific charges against him are yet unknown, he keeps him in custody in the Antonia Fortress overnight.

The commander's reaction is evidence of the key role of Paul's Roman citizenship for the subsequent account of Paul's trial. Without Roman citizenship, Paul would have been interrogated under torture and probably handed over to the Jewish authorities, without any legal or physical protection; and the Jewish authorities presumably would have condemned him, or they would have permitted a plot hatched by Jews to lynch Paul (cf. 23:12).

22:30 The next day, when he wanted to find out exactly what charges were brought against Paul by the Jews, he released him and ordered the chief priests and the entire Sanhedrin to assemble. He brought Paul down and had him stand before them (τῇ δὲ ἐπαύριον βουλόμενος γνῶναι τὸ ἀσφαλές, τὸ τί κατηγορεῖται ὑπὸ τῶν Ἰουδαίων, ἔλυσεν αὐτὸν καὶ ἐκέλευσεν συνελθεῖν τοὺς ἀρχιερεῖς καὶ πᾶν τὸ συνέδριον, καὶ καταγαγὼν τὸν Παῦλον ἔστησεν εἰς αὐτούς). The second incident of the episode narrating Paul's imprisonment in Jerusalem relates Paul's appearance before the Sanhedrin (22:30 – 23:11). The incident has four parts: the Roman commander summons a meeting of the Sanhedrin (22:30), Paul appears before the Sanhedrin (23:1 – 9), the commander terminates the hearing (23:10), and the Lord assures Paul that he will be safe and travel to Rome (23:11). The incident begins with a change of location and of the protagonists (Sanhedrin) in 22:30, and it ends with Paul's return to the original location in the Antonia Fortress and the reappearance of the commander (23:10).

Lysias summons a meeting of the Sanhedrin to deal with Paul's case. The Roman commander does not hand Paul over to Jewish jurisdiction, which would be a violation of his status as a Roman citizen. Lysias's subsequent actions to having become aware of Paul's Roman citizenship indicate that he is acting out of self-preservation, which precludes handing Paul over to the Jewish authorities. He convenes the Sanhedrin for a hearing because he was determined to ascertain the accusations against Paul.

Since Lysias expects the Sanhedrin to level accusations (κατηγορεῖται; note the present tense) against Paul,[9] we can assume that he had seen leading priests in the crowd demanding Paul's execution. In order to decide on further proceedings, he wants to find out with certainty what accusations are being raised. Since Paul's appearance before the Sanhedrin is not a formal judicial trial but a preliminary hearing (cf. 23:28), there is no reason to doubt the historical possibility that Lysias could summon the chief priests and the Sanhedrin in an advisory role.[10]

Lysias releases Paul; i.e., he further slackens the custodial arrangements, perhaps removing all bonds before taking him to the Sanhedrin. He orders that the chief priests and the entire Sanhedrin convene. He then brings Paul down from the Antonia Fortress to the meeting hall of the Sanhedrin, located below the western wall of the Temple Mount. Paul stands before the assembly of the council members. The purpose of the meeting is not to allow the Sanhedrin to arrive at a judgment concerning Paul, but to allow the commander to determine the exact nature of the accusations against Paul.

The fact that Lysias has to order his troops to go to the council hall and take Paul back to the Antonia Fortress once trouble erupts in the Sanhedrin session (23:10) suggests that the Roman commander has respected the sensibilities of the Sanhedrin by not insisting on a military presence during the hearing. It appears that he "stood at a distance but had also temporarily given up Paul to his own recognisances."[11] However, this fact, together with the physical abuse by the high priest, accounts for Paul's perception that he is tried by the Sanhedrin (κρίνομαι; 23:6).

23:1 Paul looked intently at the Sanhedrin and said, "Brothers, I have lived my life with a perfectly clear conscience before God up to this day"

(ἀτενίσας δὲ ὁ Παῦλος τῷ συνεδρίῳ εἶπεν· ἄνδρες ἀδελφοί, ἐγὼ πάσῃ συνειδήσει ἀγαθῇ πεπολίτευμαι τῷ θεῷ ἄχρι ταύτης τῆς ἡμέρας). Luke's account of Paul's appearance before the Sanhedrin (23:1 – 9) begins with a reference to Paul's courage. He "looked intently" at the members of the Sanhedrin sitting on the benches of the council hall in front of him, returning their stares — particularly those of the senior members sitting in the front row — without showing any fear, ready to begin his defense.

Paul addresses the Sanhedrin with the traditional phrase "brothers" (ἄνδρες ἀδελφοί; see on 1:16). He begins by asserting that he is a law-abiding Jew. The verb translated "I have lived my life" (πεπολίτευμαι) means, here, not "to be a citizen" but "to conduct one's life." Paul makes four assertions about his conduct in everyday life. (1) He has lived his life "before God," i.e., in conformity with God's will as revealed in the law. (2) He has lived "with a clear ... conscience," (συνειδήσει ἀγαθῇ), i.e., with a self-awareness that resulted from the knowledge that his behavior in thought, word, and deed consistently followed the standard of God's laws.[12] (3) He has lived with a "perfectly" (πάσῃ)

---

9. The term translated "bring charges" here is a technical legal term denoting "bring legal charges in court"; cf. BDAG, s.v. κατηγορέω 1. Cf. 24:2, 8, 13, 19; 25:5, 11, 16; 28:19.

10. Papyrus evidence indicates that a judicial body could be summoned in Ptolemaic Egypt to serve as an advisory council.

11. Rapske, *Paul in Roman Custody*, 147. Note the liberty of the high priest to strike Paul (23:2) without the Roman commander intervening. The references to Claudius Lysias in 22:30 and 23:10 show that "the Romans" are not simply "extras" who stand in the background (thus Jervell, *Apostelgeschichte*, 553),

but the crucial, active authority in the trial proceedings.

12. Hans-Joachim Eckstein, *Der Begriff Syneidesis bei Paulus* (WUNT 2/10; Tübingen: Mohr Siebeck, 1983), 304. The term "good conscience" (συνείδησις ἀγαθή; also 1 Tim 1:5, 19; 1 Pet 3:16, 21; cf. συνείδησις καλή in Heb 13:18) is synonymous with "pure conscience" (συνείδησις καθαρά; 1 Tim 3:9; 2 Tim 1:3) and "clear conscience" (συνείδησις ἀπρόσκοπος; Acts 24:16). For references of Paul to his conscience in his letters see Rom 9:1; 13:5; 1 Cor 4:4; 10:25 – 29; 2 Cor 1:12; 2:17; 4:2; 5:11; cf. also 1 Cor 8:7 – 13 (the conscience of the weak).

clear conscience, i.e., with consistent conformity to the will of God in all his behavior. This included his activity as a persecutor of the Christians (cf. 22:4 – 5) from the perspective of his theological convictions before his conversion to Jesus as Israel's Messiah. (4) He has lived in conformity to the will of God "up to this day," a phrase that adds a temporal element to the assertion that his conduct followed the standard of God's laws consistently.[13]

This opening statement is a direct response to the charge that he teaches everyone everywhere against the people of God, against the law, and against the temple (21:28). A Jew who lives in consistent and constant conformity to God's will cannot, by definition, teach against the Jewish people, whose history is determined by God's repeated intervention, against the law that records God's revealed will, or against the temple, the place of God's presence.

23:2 But the high priest Ananias ordered those standing near him to strike Paul on the mouth (ὁ δὲ ἀρχιερεὺς Ἀνανίας ἐπέταξεν τοῖς παρεστῶσιν αὐτῷ τύπτειν αὐτοῦ τὸ στόμα). The high priest responds to Paul's assertion of being innocent of the charges against him with an attempt to brand Paul as a liar.[14] He orders "those standing near him," i.e., probably subordinates whom he can compel to carry out his orders, to strike Paul on the mouth because of what he has said. If he had been informed about Paul's citizenship status, he may have concluded that a Jew with Tarsian and Roman citizenship could not possibly claim, with a straight face, to have lived in conformity to God's laws with a perfectly clear conscience.

23:3 Then Paul said to him, "God will strike you, you whitewashed wall! You, do you sit here to judge me according to the law, and yet in violation of the law you order me to be struck?" (τότε ὁ Παῦλος πρὸς αὐτὸν εἶπεν· τύπτειν σε μέλλει ὁ θεός, τοῖχε κεκονιαμένε· καὶ σὺ κάθῃ κρίνων με κατὰ τὸν νόμον καὶ παρανομῶν κελεύεις με τύπτεσθαι;). Luke relates Paul's response in direct speech, countering a physical assault with a verbal assault. The statement "God will strike you" can be understood in two ways, which are not mutually exclusive. Paul makes a prediction of God's judgment: God will judge such flagrant injustice as Ananias's order represents on the future day of judgment. And he utters an imprecation that invokes divine intervention against those who disobey God's commandments. The text Deut 28:22 LXX announces God's judgment for disobedience with these words: "May the Lord strike you with difficulty and fever and cold and irritation and murder and with blight and paleness, and they shall pursue you until they destroy you." According to later rabbinic tradition discussed in the tractate on "oaths," the statement "God smite thee" or "Thus may God smite thee" is permissible because "this is the adjuration that is written in the Law" (*m. Šeb.* 4:13).[15]

The expression "whitewashed wall" possibly echoes Ezek 13:8 – 15, where false prophets are denounced who mislead God's people, saying "peace, peace" when there is no peace and who build a "wall" and then "cover it with whitewash," making the wall look solid although it will fall down. While Ananias's words appear strong, they are deceptive and will eventually fall when it is recognized that he is violating the law. Or the expression insinuates hypocrisy: "he is supposed to be a just judge and yet is acting contrary to the law in defiance of the requirement of justice in Lev 19:15."[16] According to

---

13. Note that in his brief autobiographical statement in Phil 3:1 – 11, Paul asserts that "as for righteousness based on the law" he was "faultless" (Phil 3:6).

14. Another explanation of Ananias's order may be that Paul addressed the council without having been given permission to speak; cf. VanderKam, *From Joshua to Caiaphas*, 457.

15. The biblical passage is either Lev 5:1 or Deut 28:22.

16. Marshall, "Acts," 598. Compare Matt 23:27. Note that Luke 11:44 omits the reference to whitewash.

this passage, "Do not pervert justice; do not show partiality to the poor or favoritism to the great, but judge your neighbor fairly."

Paul's rhetorical question (introduced with καί) expresses indignation.[17] He accuses the council member who is sitting as his judge and who is thus obligated to comply with the standards of the law, yet who has ordered him to be struck, of having violated the law himself. Since the Mosaic law treats people who are accused of breaking the law as innocent until proven guilty, this has not (yet) happened, so Paul accuses Ananias of not adhering to the principle of impartiality. The fact that Lysias, the commander of the Roman cohort in the city, left Paul in the council hall of the Sanhedrin, giving Ananias the liberty to order Paul to be beaten on the face without intervening, explains the difference in perception. While Lysias did not regard the meeting of the Sanhedrin as a trial but rather as a preliminary hearing (22:30; 23:28), Paul perceives that he is being tried by the council members (vv. 3, 6; cf. 24:20 – 21).

23:4 – 5 **Those who stood nearby said, "Do you insult God's high priest?" Paul responded, "Brothers, I did not know that he was the high priest. It is written, 'Do not speak evil about a ruler of your people'"** (οἱ δὲ παρεστῶτες εἶπαν· τὸν ἀρχιερέα τοῦ θεοῦ λοιδορεῖς; ἔφη τε ὁ Παῦλος· οὐκ ᾔδειν, ἀδελφοί, ὅτι ἐστὶν ἀρχιερεύς· γέγραπται γὰρ ὅτι ἄρχοντα τοῦ λαοῦ σου οὐκ ἐρεῖς κακῶς). Ananias's associates, perhaps members of the Sanhedrin, scold Paul for insulting Ananias by asserting his dignity as high priest, which is underscored with reference to his appointment by and service for God.

Paul responds by stating that he "did not know" that the man who ordered that he be struck on the mouth was the high priest (v. 5). Many interpreters have regarded this statement as unthinkable or disingenuous. The argument is that Paul must have known that the person presiding over the proceedings of the Sanhedrin was the high priest. This is far from certain, however, if it is granted that the later rabbinic regulations do not reflect the historical situation in the first century. Some have suggested that Paul merely said that he did not know who had given the order to strike him. Others suggest that Paul apologizes by allowing that he had not remembered that Ananias was the high priest. Some suggest that Paul was speaking ironically: "I did not think that a man who could give such an order could be the high priest."[18]

This last interpretation is made plausible by the subsequent quotation of Exod 22:28 (LXX 22:27): since a "ruler" of Israel who sits as judge would comply with the law of impartiality (Lev 19:15, alluded to in v. 3), he, Paul, does not recognize him as high priest because he was not acting like a ruler of God's people who deserves to be spoken of with respect. This means that "far from an 'apology' for a mistake, Paul's statement is another prophetic criticism of the chief priest, whose behavior makes him 'unrecognizable.'"[19] At the same time it is not impossible that Paul in fact did not know Ananias personally: the last time he was in Jerusalem (in AD 51, i.e., six years earlier) likely was the time when Ummidius Quadratus, recently appointed as governor of Syria, had sent Ananias in chains to Rome.[20]

The attempt of Ananias the high priest to brand Paul as a liar by having him struck on the

---

17. BDAG, s.v. καί 1bθ, "to introduce an abrupt question, which may often express wonder, ill-will, incredulity." Cf. BDF §442.8.

18. Marshall, *Acts*, 364; thus already Augustine, *Ep.* 138; Calvin, *Acts*, 2:229.

19. Johnson, *Acts*, 397; also Parsons, *Acts*, 315.

20. Hemer, *Acts*, 171. The reference to the high priest in 22:5 is not necessarily an appeal to Ananias, the incumbent high priest in AD 57; see on 22:5.

mouth, requiring Paul to cite the law twice — once to remind the council members of the basic legal principle that a defendant is guaranteed fair and impartial legal proceedings, with punishments administered only after guilt has been established, and once to remind the council members that the one person who is protected against being reviled is the ruler of the people of God — shows that Paul cannot expect to receive justice from this body. This recognition convinces Paul that he must avoid having his case tried by the Sanhedrin in Jerusalem — a recognition that will eventually prompt him to appeal to the emperor for trial in Rome (25:8 – 11).

23:6 As Paul knew that some were Sadducees and some were Pharisees, he called out in the Sanhedrin, "Brothers, I am a Pharisee, the son of Pharisees. I am on trial because of the hope of the resurrection of the dead!" (γνοὺς δὲ ὁ Παῦλος ὅτι τὸ ἓν μέρος ἐστὶν Σαδδουκαίων τὸ δὲ ἕτερον Φαρισαίων ἔκραζεν ἐν τῷ συνεδρίῳ· ἄνδρες ἀδελφοί, ἐγὼ Φαρισαῖός εἰμι, υἱὸς Φαρισαίων, περὶ ἐλπίδος καὶ ἀναστάσεως νεκρῶν ἐγὼ κρίνομαι). Paul focuses his defense in the Sanhedrin hearing on Jesus and his resurrection from the dead. The fact that Luke points out that Paul knew that some members of the Sanhedrin were Sadducees while other members were Pharisees has led commentators to interpret Paul's assertion of the hope of resurrection as a tactical move to "divide and conquer" the members of the Sanhedrin.[21] While the effect of Paul's assertion indeed divides the audience, the consequence of his stated belief in the resurrection of the dead is the support that he receives from the Pharisees (v. 9).

Paul's statement is not a clever legal tactic but the succinct formulation of the "main question" of the case against him; in a formal legal defense speech, the assertion would have been part of the *narratio* or "statement of facts" segment.[22] For Paul, the belief in the resurrection is not a game but the central truth of his witness (cf. 22:6 – 10, 14 – 15, 18 – 21). Luke refers to Paul's knowledge of the Sadducees and Pharisees and their beliefs (v. 8) because his Jewish readers would certainly know that Paul might be able to gain some sympathy for his convictions only from the Pharisees.

Luke does not indicate how he views Paul's defense strategy. Paul may have eventually introduced the subject of Jesus' resurrection, which vindicated him as the Son of God, i.e., as the promised Messiah and Savior in and through whom God has fulfilled his promises given to the fathers (cf. 13:33 – 39).[23] It would have been prudent to begin with a general statement about the truth and reality of the resurrection of the dead that the Pharisaic members of the Sanhedrin would accept. Thus Paul begins his "statement of faith" with the assertion that he is a Pharisee and the son of Pharisees (cf. 26:5; Phil 3:5).

The formulation in the present tense (εἰμί) may imply that Paul still regarded himself as a Pharisee in some sense, although most certainly not in the "party" sense of the word (i.e., as αἵρεσις, as described by Josephus) but in terms of their belief in the resurrection, in angels and spirits, and in their devotion to God's revelation of his will in the law, transmitted, preserved, and developed (!) in written and oral tradition. In Phil 3:5 Paul focuses his affiliation with the Pharisees on the law, i.e., on the

---

21. The principle of "divide et impera" is often invoked as an explanation by interpreters; e.g., Pervo, *Acts*, 574, suggesting that Paul's admirers would have labeled this "a deft political maneuver" while his detractors would have called it "a cheap lawyer's stunt."

22. F. Scott Spencer, *Journeying through Acts: A Literary-*

Cultural Reading (Peabody, MA: Hendrickson, 2004), 223; for the following observation see ibid.; also Jervell, *Apostelgeschichte*, 555.

23. Cf. Neyrey, "Defense Speech," 214 – 15, who states that the "main question" that Paul introduces is the resurrection of Jesus.

interpretation and application and perhaps "development" of the law. The statement that he comes from a (long?) line of Pharisees cannot be verified, although there is no reason to doubt its veracity. The fact that no Pharisees have been documented for the Jewish communities in the diaspora does not prove that they did not exist. More importantly, we do not know when Paul's ancestors moved to Tarsus and when Paul's family moved from Tarsus back to Jerusalem (see on 22:3).

23:7 – 8 When he said this, a dispute broke out between the Pharisees and the Sadducees, and the assembly became divided. For the Sadducees say that there is no resurrection, neither as an angel nor as a spirit, whereas the Pharisees confess belief in them both (τοῦτο δὲ αὐτοῦ εἰπόντος ἐγένετο στάσις τῶν Φαρισαίων καὶ Σαδδουκαίων καὶ ἐσχίσθη τὸ πλῆθος. Σαδδουκαῖοι μὲν γὰρ λέγουσιν μὴ εἶναι ἀνάστασιν μήτε ἄγγελον μήτε πνεῦμα, Φαρισαῖοι δὲ ὁμολογοῦσιν τὰ ἀμφότερα). The dispute that ensues when Paul mentions his belief in the resurrection is explained by the fact that the resurrection of the dead is not explicitly taught in the Mosaic law, which the Sadducees accepted as authority. While a few passages in the Hebrew Scriptures could be interpreted in terms of the resurrection of the dead,[24] it was only later passages such as Ezek 37:1 – 14 and Dan 12:1 – 3 that explicitly spoke about the resurrection of the dead, a fact that made the interpretation of these passages a point of contention.

While many Jews believed in a future bodily resurrection when "the King of the universe will raise us up to an everlasting renewal of life, because we have died for his laws" (2 Macc 7:9),[25] others ac-

cepted the Greek (and Roman) concept of the immortality of the soul as the proper way of thinking about "life after death."[26] This difference of interpretation and belief regarding the question of the hope beyond death divided Sadducees and Pharisees and thus caused a "dispute" (cf. v. 10) in the council hall when Paul expressed and defended his belief in the resurrection of the dead, introduced as a conviction that the Pharisees share. The members of the Sanhedrin "became divided" (ἐσχίσθη); i.e., the difference of belief was clearly and loudly (v. 9) expressed by the Pharisaic and Saducean members of the council.

The fact that Luke describes the event in the Sanhedrin as a "dispute" — the Greek term (στάσις) also means "uprising, revolt" — is ironic in that this is what Ananias and the elders accuse Paul of causing among the Jewish people when they bring official charges before Felix (24:5). Paul's opponents thus discredit themselves and unwittingly demonstrate Paul's innocence.

In v. 8 Luke includes a comment that clarifies the reason for the dispute. The Sadducees believe and teach that there is no resurrection of the dead. This agrees with Matt 22:23/Luke 20:27, and with Josephus's description in *Ant.* 18.16: "The Sadducees hold that the soul perishes along with the body" (also *J.W.* 2.164 – 165). The next phrase ("neither as an angel nor as a spirit") is usually understood to describe further denials of the Sadducees: they do not believe in the bodily resurrection of the dead, nor do they believe in the existence of angels or spirits. This interpretation conflicts with the expression "both" at the end of the verse, but also with the fact that angels and spirits are frequently mentioned in the Pentateuch, accepted by

---

24. Fitzmyer, *Acts*, 718, refers to Ps 49:15; Isa 26:19; Hos 6:1 – 3; 13:14; see also Pss 16:8 – 11; 22:15, 22 – 31; 73:18 – 20, 23 – 27; 104:29 – 30; Job 33:15 – 30; cf. Wright, *Resurrection*, 85 – 128, on resurrection in the Old Testament.

25. Cf. 2 Macc 7:11, 14, 22 – 23, 29; 12:43; 14:46.

26. Cf. Wis 3:4: "For though in the sight of others they were punished, their hope is full of immortality;" cf. Wis 4:1; 8:13, 17; 15:3; 4 Macc 14:5; 16:13. On the hope beyond death in Second Temple Judaism cf. Wright, *Resurrection*, 129 – 206.

the Sadducees as authority.[27] A denial of angels and spirits, which Josephus does not mention for the Sadducees, could be explained only if Luke refers to members of the Sadducean party who had become Hellenistic "free-thinkers" or skeptic rationalists who denied the existence of transcendent beings such as angels or spirits (demons).

A more plausible interpretation posits that the Sadducees did not deny the existence of angels and spirits per se. Rather, since they denied the resurrection of the dead (on the day of the future resurrection, which is also the day of judgment), they denied the existence of an interim state between death and the day of resurrection during which the people who have died exist as angels or spirits,[28] the latter being more or less synonymous.[29] Another suggestion is that the Sadducees rejected the existence of angels and spirits for two reasons: angels were part of the apocalyptic world view that they rejected, and they often served as God's servants to administer providence, which they rejected as well.

This means that "although the Sadducees might not have objected to the notion of angels carrying out the will of God in some general sense, they would have objected to their doing so in the fulfillment of a preordained eschatological program and to their interfering with the will of an autonomous human being."[30] In contrast to the Sadducees, who believed in no positive form of life beyond death, the Pharisees "confess belief in them both," i.e., both in the resurrection of the dead[31] and in the intermediate state for those who have died existing as angels and spirits.[32]

23:9 A loud uproar arose. Some scribes who belonged to the party of the Pharisees stood up and contended, "We find nothing wrong in this man. What if a spirit or an angel has spoken to him?" (ἐγένετο δὲ κραυγὴ μεγάλη, καὶ ἀναστάντες τινὲς τῶν γραμματέων τοῦ μέρους τῶν Φαρισαίων διεμάχοντο λέγοντες· οὐδὲν κακὸν εὑρίσκομεν ἐν τῷ ἀνθρώπῳ τούτῳ· εἰ δὲ πνεῦμα ἐλάλησεν αὐτῷ ἢ ἄγγελος;). Luke picks up his reference to the dispute and division that arose in the assembly of the Sanhedrin when Paul started to speak about the resurrection of the dead, characterizing the development in the proceedings of the council with the expression "load uproar." The council members become more and more excited, behaving like the crowd in the city the day before, which had created chaos (21:31) and which had noisily bawled one thing or another in the outer court of the temple (21:34).

Eventually some council members who were scribes (γραμματεῖς) and supported Pharisaic positions stood up and addressed the assembly. They "contended" (διεμάχοντο); i.e., they fought for the opinion, that since spirits and angels (of deceased persons) exist, and since it is possible that when Paul claims to have heard the crucified and risen Jesus speak to him, as he had claimed in his address in the outer court of the temple the day before

---

27. Cf. Gen 16:7 – 11; 19:1, 15; 21:17; 22:11, 15; 24:7; Exod 3:2; 14:19; 23:20; for πνεύματα see Num 16:22; 27:16.

28. Cf. *1 En.* 22:3, 7; 45:4 – 5; Matt 22:30; Mark 12:25; Luke 20:36.

29. David Daube, "On Acts 23: Sadducees and Angels," *JBL* 109 (1990): 493 – 97; Barrett, *Acts*, 1065 – 66; Witherington, *Acts*, 692.

30. Floyd O. Parker, "The Terms 'Angel' and 'Spirit' in Acts 23:8," *Bib* 84 (2003): 344 – 65, 364; Bock, *Acts*, 672.

31. Cf. Josephus, *Ant.* 18.14; *J.W.* 2.163. Cf. *m. Sanh.* 10:1:

"these are they that have no share in the world to come: he that says there is no resurrection of the dead prescribed in the Law, and [he that says] that the Law is not from Heaven, and an Epicurean."

32. Note that when Jesus appears to his disciples after the resurrection, they think he is "a ghost" (Luke 24:36 – 43), and note that when the believers in Jerusalem find it difficult to believe that Peter, whom they know to be in prison, is at the gate of the house in which they are assembled, they think that it is his "angel" (Acts 12:15). See also 23:9.

(22:7 – 10, 18, 21),[33] he heard the "spirit" (πνεῦμα) or the "angel" (ἄγγελος) of Jesus speak (cf. Luke 24:36 – 43; John 12:29; Acts 12:15). Given this possibility, the Pharisees "would not have been shocked that God might send a messenger to enforce his plan, since they believed in predestination to some extent."[34] Thus, they come to the conclusion that Paul is not saying anything "wrong" — nothing that is contrary to the law as they interpret it.

True, they would not have contended for Paul's claim that since this voice from heaven belonged to the crucified Jesus, and since he saw Jesus in the splendor of God's glory, Jesus has been raised from the dead and exalted to the right hand of God and is thus Israel's Messiah, Savior, and Lord. Luke's language and the brevity of v. 9f-i does not allow us to answer the question whether the Pharisaic scribes would have conceded that this was Paul's personal interpretation of his experiences, which, while misguided, did not contradict the law to the degree that the Sanhedrin was forced to sentence him and demand punishment.[35]

23:10 When the dispute became so heated that the commander feared that Paul would be torn into pieces by them, he ordered his troops to go down, to remove him, and to bring him into the barracks (πολλῆς δὲ γινομένης στάσεως φοβηθεὶς ὁ χιλίαρχος μὴ διασπασθῇ ὁ Παῦλος ὑπ᾽ αὐτῶν ἐκέλευσεν τὸ στράτευμα καταβὰν ἁρπάσαι αὐτὸν ἐκ μέσου αὐτῶν ἄγειν τε εἰς τὴν παρεμβολήν). Since

the dispute was becoming more and more heated, with the noise level increasing in a crescendo, Lysias, who apparently was within earshot, fears that Paul will be lynched.[36] As he cannot allow a Roman citizen to be killed in a hearing by an excited and angry crowd, he is forced to intervene and to terminate the meeting of the Sanhedrin. He gives his troops an order consisting of three elements: "go down" into the council hall, "remove" Paul from the Sanhedrin, and "bring him" into the Antonia Fortress.

Thus ends Paul's appearance before the Sanhedrin — with a different outcome than the hearings of Jesus and of Stephen, who had both been executed. Paul is still a prisoner. The chaos in Sanhedrin made it impossible to arrive at a decision that would have allowed the Roman commander to release Paul, even though he has come to recognize that Paul had done nothing to warrant the death sentence (v. 29) — the serious charges relating to the defilement of the temple evidently had not played a role in the Sanhedrin hearing.

As Paul is taken back into the barracks in the Antonia Fortress, he does not seem to have been chained (cf. v. 29). He seems to have been granted some dignity in the Antonia: his nephew has access to him, a scenario that suggests that "Paul is neither manacled to a soldier nor attended so closely that he and his nephew cannot communicate privately."[37] But he certainly remains a prisoner (cf. v. 18). He is not simply in protective custody, as

---

33. Luke implies either that the council members were aware of Paul's address in the outer court (22:1 – 21), or that Paul repeated the report of his encounter with Jesus on the road to Damascus in the Sanhedrin meeting, omitted by Luke after 23:6, relating only the initial assertion of belief in the resurrection.

34. Parker, "Angel," 364 – 65.

35. The statement "we find nothing wrong in this man" is similar to Pilate's assertion to the chief priests in the trial of Jesus that he finds "no basis for a charge against this man"

(Luke 23:4; also 23:14, 22; cf. Matt 27:23). Paul's innocence is similarly asserted again in 23:29 (Claudius Lysias) and in 25:25 (Festus). The verbal similarity has prompted scholars to conclude that Luke seems to "draw attention to the similarity between the innocent suffering of Paul and that of Jesus" (Barrett, *Acts*, 1067). While possible, it should be noted that it is not surprising in judicial settings that the innocence of defendants tends to be described in similar terms.

36. The Greek term (διασπάω) means "to tear apart, tear up."

37. Rapske, *Paul in Roman Custody*, 148.

the continuation of the examination of Paul's case in Caesarea demonstrates.

23:11 The following night the Lord stood at Paul's side and said, "Keep up your courage! As you have borne witness to me here in Jerusalem, so you must bear witness also in Rome"

(τῇ δὲ ἐπιούσῃ νυκτὶ ἐπιστὰς αὐτῷ ὁ κύριος εἶπεν· θάρσει· ὡς γὰρ διεμαρτύρω τὰ περὶ ἐμοῦ εἰς Ἰερουσαλήμ, οὕτω σε δεῖ καὶ εἰς Ῥώμην μαρτυρῆσαι). The day of the confrontation in the Sanhedrin ends with a vision of the Lord, who assures Paul that he will be kept safe and that he will reach Rome. The Lord (ὁ κύριος), i.e., the risen Lord whose resurrection is the center of Paul's proclamation and the main reason for the dispute with the Jewish opponents, appears to Paul in a vision and speaks to him, as he had spoken to him before (e.g., 18:9 – 10).

The Lord encourages Paul with the exhortation, "Keep up your courage!" (θάρσει). This encouragement implies the Lord's commendation of Paul's past witness in Jerusalem to the Sanhedrin, and it expresses the Lord's promise of protection for Paul's future "witness" (μαρτυρῆσαι) in Rome. The focus of Paul's witness to the Lord Jesus is highlighted again, as is Paul's goal of reaching Rome. While the plan to reach Rome was described in 19:21 as Paul's desire, the Lord now confirms that such a visit to Rome is an integral part of God's own plan. The prophecy does not clarify whether Paul will be released from Roman custody and travel to Rome as a free man or whether he will be taken to Rome as a prisoner, and it certainly promises no miraculous deliverance. But his next assignment is to witness for Jesus in Rome, the center of the empire that controls large parts of the Gentile world.

23:12 – 13 In the morning the Jews organized a conspiracy and bound themselves with an oath, saying that they would not eat or drink until they had killed Paul. There were more than forty

men who were involved in this plot (γενομένης δὲ ἡμέρας ποιήσαντες συστροφὴν οἱ Ἰουδαῖοι ἀνεθεμάτισαν ἑαυτοὺς λέγοντες μήτε φαγεῖν μήτε πιεῖν ἕως οὗ ἀποκτείνωσιν τὸν Παῦλον. ἦσαν δὲ πλείους τεσσεράκοντα οἱ ταύτην τὴν συνωμοσίαν ποιησάμενοι). The third incident of Luke's report of Paul's imprisonment in Jerusalem relates a plot against Paul (vv. 12 – 22).

Luke explains the plan of the Jews who want to kill Paul (vv. 12 – 15) and discloses their plot (vv. 16 – 22) in vivid detail. The origin of the "conspiracy" is traced to the morning after the Sanhedrin hearing and is linked with Jews who clearly are not divided in their opinion about Paul and what should be done with him (cf. v. 7). The fact that Pharisees supported Paul in the assembly of the Sanhedrin (v. 9), making an official Jewish demand for a severe punishment of Paul impossible, does not prove that the Jews who organize this conspiracy are all Sadducees. The very fact that the conspirators seek the support of the chief priests and the elders (vv. 14 – 15) suggests that not all of them are members of the Sanhedrin.

Some have suggested that the conspirators belonged to the party of the Zealots or Sicarii, which is theoretically possible but not likely: the chief priests and the Sanhedrin, which they controlled, were generally friendly to Rome. The determination of the conspirators is indicated by two actions. (1) They bind themselves "with an oath" (ἀνεθεμάτισαν ἑαυτούς); i.e., they invoke God's curse (ἀνάθεμα) if they fail to carry out their plans. (2) They resolve not to eat any food or drink any liquids until they have killed Paul. Luke does not indicate which punishment they ask God to punish them with in the case that they fail to kill Paul. The resolve not to eat or drink anything suggests that they are determined to kill Paul within a day or two.

The severity of the oath may suggest that the conspirators are willing to risk their lives in the attempt to kill Paul right under the nose of the Roman troops stationed in the city. Luke comments on the size of the conspiracy in v. 13: more than forty men are involved.[38] Paul had been in danger of his life before (2 Cor 11:24 – 26), but the determination and the size of this attempt to kill him is, presumably, the most serious situation he has faced.

23:14 – 15   They went to the chief priests and elders and said, "We have bound ourselves by a solemn oath to take no food until we have killed Paul. Now then, you and the Sanhedrin must report to the commander that he should bring Paul down to you, on the pretext that you want to conduct a more thorough examination of his case. We are ready to kill him before he arrives here" (οἵτινες προσελθόντες τοῖς ἀρχιερεῦσιν καὶ τοῖς πρεσβυτέροις εἶπαν· ἀναθέματι ἀνεθεματίσαμεν ἑαυτοὺς μηδενὸς γεύσασθαι ἕως οὗ ἀποκτείνωμεν τὸν Παῦλον. νῦν οὖν ὑμεῖς ἐμφανίσατε τῷ χιλιάρχῳ σὺν τῷ συνεδρίῳ ὅπως καταγάγῃ αὐτὸν εἰς ὑμᾶς ὡς μέλλοντας διαγινώσκειν ἀκριβέστερον τὰ περὶ αὐτοῦ· ἡμεῖς δὲ πρὸ τοῦ ἐγγίσαι αὐτὸν ἕτοιμοί ἐσμεν τοῦ ἀνελεῖν αὐτόν). The plan to eliminate Paul includes securing the official support of the Sanhedrin (v. 14a-b).

If members of the Sanhedrin are among the conspirators, they would have used their contacts with "the chief priests" and the "elders" (see on 4:5). Luke repeats, in direct speech, the fact that they have sworn an oath (ἀναθέματι ἀνεθεματίσαμεν),[39] that they have pledged not to take food, and that they are planning to kill Paul.

The plan of the conspirators is simple (v. 15): since they cannot get at Paul inside the Antonia Fortress, they need to create a scenario that causes the Roman commander to take his prisoner into the city, where they can ambush Paul. The plan has the following elements. (1) The chief priests and the elders will contact other members of the Sanhedrin and request a meeting of the council. (2) The Sanhedrin will send a report to Lysias, requesting another hearing before the Jewish council for a more thorough examination. (3) The hearing requires the presence of Paul. (4) This request will force Lysias to bring Paul down from the Antonia Fortress to the council hall of the Sanhedrin, either across the outer court of the temple to one of the gates in the western boundary of the Temple Mount that gave access to the road below, or via the direct access from the Antonia into the city. (5) The conspirators will be posted along the route traveled by the detachment of Roman soldiers taking Paul to the council hall, perhaps hiding in crowds. They will be ready to kill Paul — presumably with a dagger — before he arrives.[40]

In vv. 12, 14, the verb ἀποκτείνω is the usual term denoting "to deprive of life, kill"; here the verb ἀναιρέω is used, which means "to do away with, destroy," denoting "killing by violence, in battle, by execution, murder, or assassination." Luke does not relate the response of the chief priests and the elders, but the following narrative implies that they have accepted the plot against Paul's life.

23:16   When the son of Paul's sister heard of the arrangement for the ambush, he went and entered into the barracks and told Paul (ἀκούσας δὲ ὁ υἱὸς τῆς ἀδελφῆς Παύλου τὴν ἐνέδραν, παραγενόμενος καὶ εἰσελθὼν εἰς τὴν παρεμβολὴν

---

38. Seland, *Establishment Violence*, 292 – 93, compares the plot of the forty Jews against Paul with a plot of ten men against King Herod, who also swore an oath and whose plot was also related to the authorities (i.e., Herod) by an informant; Josephus, *Ant.* 15.281 – 291.

39. The repetition of the noun ἀνάθεμα, denoted already by

the verb ἀνεθεματίζω, underscores the seriousness of the conspiracy for whose success the conspirators invoke God's help by putting themselves under God's curse in the case that they abandon their plans.

40. For political murders in Jerusalem during the time of Felix see Josephus, *J. W.* 2.254 – 255.

ἀπήγγειλεν τῷ Παύλῳ). Luke narrates the disclosure of the plot (vv. 16 – 22) in vivid detail. Without explanation he introduces relatives of Paul: a married sister and her son live in Jerusalem, perhaps his hosts when he came to Jerusalem to study (see 22:3). The fact that the nephew warns Paul of the plot may suggest that he was a follower of Jesus, although it is conceivable that he merely wants to rescue his famous uncle from being assassinated because relatives remain relatives.

If Paul was in his late fifties, his nephew would have been in his late twenties or early thirties. In v. 17 he is called a "young man" (νεανίας), a term that describes the age of a person from about eighteen to thirty years (see on 2:17; 7:58). We are not told how the nephew has heard of the conspiracy. Several possibilities exist: since too many people were involved in the plot, it could not be kept secret; if Paul's early "career" as an ardent persecutor of the followers of Jesus was characteristic of his relatives, his sister's family could have had contacts with Jerusalem Jews who believed that the followers of Jesus should be prosecuted and punished; if Paul's family attended the Jerusalem synagogue in which Jews from Cilicia and Asia assembled (6:9), whose members were well informed about Paul's proclamation (9:29), they may have had contact with the Jews from the province of Asia who accused Paul of having defiled the temple (21:27 – 28; cf. 24:19) and who may have been involved in the plot to kill Paul.

The involvement of Paul's nephew is narrated with four verbs: he "heard" about the arrangements for the ambush; he "went" to the Antonia Fortress; he "entered" the barracks where Paul was kept in custody; he "told" Paul what he knew. Paul was evidently not manacled (cf. v. 10) and since he was allowed to receive visitors, the conversation with his nephew probably took place in private.[41]

23:17 Paul called one of the centurions and said, "Take this young man to the commander. He has something to report to him" (προσκαλεσάμενος δὲ ὁ Παῦλος ἕνα τῶν ἑκατονταρχῶν ἔφη· τὸν νεανίαν τοῦτον ἀπάγαγε πρὸς τὸν χιλίαρχον, ἔχει γὰρ ἀπαγγεῖλαί τι αὐτῷ). Paul's reaction is swift and, considering the protection that his status as Roman citizen gave him, logical. He summons one of the centurions (see on 10:1), who would not have been a Roman citizen; such a person had direct access to the commander. Luke relates Paul's request in direct speech: the centurion is to take his nephew to the commander to report something (τι).

Paul wants to maintain as direct as possible a channel of communication with the highest representative of the Roman authorities. Also, since there was corruption among the tribune's officers, the information that Paul's nephew had was "a virtual gold mine for anyone who leaked it to the right parties," which means that Paul's caution of neither identifying his nephew nor relating the information that he had uncovered to the centurion reflects the fact that the Roman garrison in the Antonia "was still a hostile and potentially life-threatening place" for Paul.[42]

23:18 The centurion took him and brought him to the commander, and said, "The prisoner Paul called me and asked me to bring this young man to you because he has something to tell you" (ὁ μὲν οὖν παραλαβὼν αὐτὸν ἤγαγεν πρὸς τὸν χιλίαρχον καὶ φησίν· ὁ δέσμιος Παῦλος προσκαλεσάμενός με ἠρώτησεν τοῦτον τὸν νεανίσκον ἀγαγεῖν πρὸς σὲ ἔχοντά τι λαλῆσαί σοι). Luke continues to describe what happens next in direct speech, giving voice to

---

41. For similar accounts of relatives, friends, or servants having access to a prisoner cf. Josephus, *Ant.* 18.203 – 204; Cicero, *Verr.* 2.5.118; Lucian, *Peregr.* 12 – 13; *Tox.* 30; Matt 11:2

(John the Baptist); Phil 2:25; 2 Tim 1:16 – 17. Cf. Rapske, *Paul in Roman Custody*, 381 – 85.

42. Rapske, *Paul in Roman Custody*, 266.

the words of the centurion (v. 18), the commander (vv. 19, 22), and Paul's nephew (vv. 20 – 21).

The centurion takes Paul's nephew to the commander of the garrison. Paul is called "the prisoner" (ὁ δέσμιος), which confirms that Paul is not in protective custody but kept as a prisoner until the serious charges against him are more fully examined and either dismissed or confirmed. The centurion reports that Paul asked him to take the young man to him; he understood Paul's statement in v. 17 as a request, not a command.

23:19 The commander took him by the hand, drew him aside privately, and asked him, "What do you have to report to me?" (ἐπιλαβόμενος δὲ τῆς χειρὸς αὐτοῦ ὁ χιλίαρχος καὶ ἀναχωρήσας κατ᾽ ἰδίαν ἐπυνθάνετο, τί ἐστιν ὃ ἔχεις ἀπαγγεῖλαί μοι;). Luke narrates the commander's reaction to the report of the centurion with three verbs: he "took" Paul's nephew by the hand; he "drew him aside" privately; he "asked him" (ἐπυνθάνετο) him a question about the information that he allegedly has to convey — perhaps secret information about the prisoner whose guilt in a crime, or lack thereof, still has to be established.

23:20 – 21 He answered, "The Jews have agreed to ask you to bring Paul down to the Sanhedrin tomorrow, on the pretext that they want to inquire more thoroughly into his case. But do not be persuaded by them, because more than forty of their men are lying in ambush for him. They have bound themselves by an oath not to eat or drink until they kill him. They are ready now, and they are waiting for your consent" (εἶπεν δὲ ὅτι οἱ Ἰουδαῖοι συνέθεντο τοῦ ἐρωτῆσαί σε ὅπως αὔριον τὸν Παῦλον καταγάγῃς εἰς τὸ συνέδριον ὡς μέλλον τι ἀκριβέστερον πυνθάνεσθαι περὶ αὐτοῦ. σὺ οὖν μὴ πεισθῇς αὐτοῖς· ἐνεδρεύουσιν γὰρ αὐτὸν ἐξ αὐτῶν ἄνδρες πλείους τεσσεράκοντα, οἵτινες ἀνεθεμάτισαν ἑαυτοὺς μήτε φαγεῖν μήτε πιεῖν ἕως οὗ ἀνέλωσιν αὐτόν, καὶ νῦν εἰσιν ἕτοιμοι προσδεχόμενοι τὴν ἀπὸ

σοῦ ἐπαγγελίαν). Paul's nephew reports to the commander information about the conspiracy against Paul's life.

That report contains the following details: (1) The Jews have reached an agreement. (2) They will approach the commander with a petition. (3) The petition involves a meeting of the Sanhedrin on the next day. (4) They expect the commander to bring Paul down to the council hall in which the Sanhedrin meets. (5) They will tell the commander that they want to examine the case of Paul more thoroughly, but this is a pretext. (6) The conspiracy involves over forty Jews. (7) These men will lie in ambush, waiting for an opportunity to kill Paul. (8) They have bound themselves with an oath. (9) They have resolved not to eat or drink. (10) They are ready now; i.e., they have made all the necessary arrangements. (11) They are merely waiting for the commander's consent to the petition, to be made the next morning, to bring Paul again from the Antonia Fortress into the council hall of the Sanhedrin.

Paul's nephew pleads with the commander not to be persuaded by the Jews when they come to him the next morning with their petition to bring Paul again before a meeting of the Sanhedrin (v. 21a). The negated subjunctive "Do not be persuaded" (σὺ οὖν μὴ πεισθῇς), which usually expresses a prohibition, here formulates a request or plea, which is intensified by the inclusion of the personal pronoun in emphatic position.

23:22 The commander dismissed the young man, ordering him, "Tell no one that you have reported this to me" (ὁ μὲν οὖν χιλίαρχος ἀπέλυσε τὸν νεανίσκον παραγγείλας μηδενὶ ἐκλαλῆσαι ὅτι ταῦτα ἐνεφάνισας πρός με). Luke relates the commander's reaction, again in direct speech. (1) He dismisses Paul's nephew with the order not to reveal to anybody that he has informed the commander of the conspiracy.

**23:23 – 24 Then he called two of the centuri-
ons and said, "Get two hundred soldiers ready
to leave for Caesarea by nine o'clock tonight,
together with seventy cavalrymen and two hundred bowmen. Provide horses for Paul to ride,
and bring him safely to Felix, the governor"** (καὶ
προσκαλεσάμενος δύο τινὰς τῶν ἑκατονταρχῶν
εἶπεν· ἑτοιμάσατε στρατιώτας διακοσίους, ὅπως
πορευθῶσιν ἕως Καισαρείας, καὶ ἱππεῖς ἑβδομήκοντα
καὶ δεξιολάβους διακοσίους ἀπὸ τρίτης ὥρας τῆς
νυκτός, κτήνη τε παραστῆσαι ἵνα ἐπιβιβάσαντες
τὸν Παῦλον διασώσωσι πρὸς Φήλικα τὸν ἡγεμόνα).
(2) Lysias then organizes Paul's immediate transfer
from Jerusalem to Caesarea (vv. 23 – 35). He asks
two of his centurions to get soldiers and cavalry
ready for a ride to Caesarea (vv.23 – 24); he writes
a letter to Felix, the governor (vv. 24 – 30); he dispatches the solders who will guard Paul on the
journey to Caesarea (v. 31).

Claudius Lysias summons two "centurions" (see
on 10:1), officers normally responsible for eighty
men, and directs them to organize an expedition-
ary force of two hundred foot soldiers, seventy cavalrymen, and two hundred bowmen.[43] The size of
the contingent of 470 soldiers to guard Paul is often
called fantastic, meant to convey the importance of
the prisoner or the enormity of the danger. However, the growing unrest in Judea during this period "suggests that the numbers are realistic" since
a wise senior officer "who heeded trustworthy

warnings and anticipated the level of popular animosity toward a prisoner in his care" would have
taken swift and effective measures.[44]

The size of the troop contingent and the presence of seventy cavalry on horseback does not indicate that Paul is escorted "like a king";[45] rather,
Lysias does not want to be accused of military
incompetence. He orders his officers with their
troops to leave for Caesarea the same day, after
dark, at 9:00 p.m. (v. 23e-f),[46] to provide horses for
Paul to ride on (v. 24a-b), and to bring him safely to
Felix, the Roman governor (AD 52 – 59; Paul's imprisonment in Caesarea dates to the last two years
of Felix's governorship).

**23:25 He wrote a letter, which had the follow-
ing text** (γράψας ἐπιστολὴν ἔχουσαν τὸν τύπον
τοῦτον). The second action of Claudius Lysias is
to compose a letter to Felix in which he explains
why he is sending Paul to Caesarea. Luke introduces the letter with an expression ("text," τύπος)
that suggests to his readers that he is providing a
direct citation of a transcript of the letter,[47] not a
rhetorical approximation of what the Roman commander might have written.[48] The letter contains a
high number of legal terms.

How would Luke have obtained a copy of Lysias'
letter? Two possibilities exist: the letter was likely
read in court, where Paul, who was Luke's source,
became familiar with the text;[49] or the letter likely
became part of the official documentation of Paul's

---

43. The term translated as "bowmen" is not otherwise at-
tested. See BDAG, s.v. δεξιολάβος, with reference to Joannes
Lydus in the sixth century. Cf. Saddington, *Roman Auxiliary
Forces*, 210, who suggests "archers."

44. Rapske, *Paul in Roman Custody*, 154, with reference to
Josephus, who reports "a number of acts by individuals which
touched off explosive and devastating general uprisings calling
for military intervention" (*Ant.* 20.108 – 112/*J. W.* 2.224 – 227;
Ant. 20.113 – 116/*J. W.* 2.228 – 231).

45. Thus Chrysostom, *Hom.* 50.417, quoted by Pervo, *Acts*,
583 n. 27.

46. The expression ἀπὸ τρίτης ὥρας τῆς νυκτός means (lit.)
"at the third hour of the night," i.e., three hours after nightfall
at about 6:00 p.m.

47. E. A. Judge, in Horsley and Llewelyn, *New Documents*,
1:77 – 78. The translation "he wrote a letter as follows" (NIV,
TNIV) is adequate, better is NLT, "he wrote this letter."

48. Cf. BDAG, s.v. τύπος 4 for Acts 23:25: "somewhat as
follows, after this manner, to this effect"; thus GNB, NET (he
"wrote a letter that went like this"), RSV, NRSV, ESV ("he wrote
a letter to this effect"), suggesting that Luke summarizes the
gist of the letter.

49. Hemer, *Acts*, 207, 348.

legal case and would thus have been available to the defendant.[50] The letter has five parts: prescript (v. 26); report of Paul's arrest (v. 27); report of the Sanhedrin hearing (v. 28); preliminary conclusion concerning Paul's innocence (v. 29); explanation of Paul's transfer to the governor (v. 30). The summary of a legal case and of juridical decisions in the form of a report was called *elogium*.[51] As *litterae dimissoriae* ("letters of report") they summarized the facts of the case and the status of the proceedings when a legal case was transferred to the higher court.[52]

23:26 "Claudius Lysias to His Excellency, Felix, the governor: Greetings!" (Κλαύδιος Λυσίας τῷ κρατίστῳ ἡγεμόνι Φήλικι χαίρειν). The epistolary prescript mentions, in agreement with standard letter openings, the sender (*superscriptio*), the addressee (*adscriptio*), and a greeting (*salutatio*). Since the sender of the letter mentions himself by name, Luke relates the name of the commander of the Roman cohort stationed in Jerusalem — Claudius Lysias (Κλαύδιος Λυσίας). The name is mentioned here for the first time (on Claudius Lysias see on 21:31 – 38; 22:28). The addressee is Felix, who is addressed as "Excellency" (κράτιστος),[53] and "governor" (ἡγεμών), the Greek term used for "leaders" such as the emperor or the head of an imperial province in the Roman Empire, including the *praefectus* and the *procurator* of the province of Judea. The term translated "greetings!" (χαίρειν) is the standard, formalized greeting in Greek letters wishing the addressees well (see 15:23).

23:27 This man was seized by the Jews and they were about to kill him. I came with my troops and rescued him when I learned that he was a Roman citizen (τὸν ἄνδρα τοῦτον συλλημφθέντα ὑπὸ τῶν Ἰουδαίων καὶ μέλλοντα ἀναιρεῖσθαι ὑπ᾽ αὐτῶν ἐπιστὰς σὺν τῷ στρατεύματι ἐξειλάμην μαθὼν ὅτι Ῥωμαῖός ἐστιν). Lysias's account of Paul's arrest has two parts. He first relates the events that led to Paul's arrest: he was "seized" by the Jews, who wanted to kill him. This report corresponds to the events as Luke has described them in 21:30 – 31. Next he informs the governor of his involvement in the case, describing his role in a more favorable light than the actual course of events as narrated in 21:31 – 22:29 warrant.

The information that Claudius Lysias intervened with his troops and rescued Paul, who was about to be killed by the Jews, is correct, as far as it goes. But Lysias fails to mention the tumult of Jewish crowds (which may have called his precautions to prevent turbulences in Jerusalem in question), the location of these events in the temple courts (which were right under the nose of his troops stationed in the Antonia Fortress), his suspicion that he was the Jewish-Egyptian insurrectionist, as well as the fact that he chained Paul and called for his interrogation under torture without establishing his identity. Lysias did not rescue Paul because he had learned that he was a Roman citizen, but because there was an attempted lynching taking place in the outer court in the temple. He was informed about the citizenship status of the man who was nearly killed subsequent to the rescue, not before.

---

50. Winter, "Official Proceedings," 309, who points to P. Oxy. II 237 (AD 186), a petition in which a woman quotes official correspondence and official proceedings between the governor of Egypt and the *strategos*.

51. G. Schiemann, "Elogium," *BNP*, 4:929: "In the context of police and criminal law, *elogium* refers predominantly to written record, e.g., of an illegal or criminal offense or a criminal procedure, including the sentence passed."

52. This was particularly true in the case of appeal (*provocatio*), see *Digesta* 49.6.1. The letter that Festus speaks about in 25:26 – 27 belongs to this category. Cf. Tajra, *Trial*, 106; Omerzu, *Prozess*, 407.

53. BDAG, s.v. κράτιστος, "strongly affirmative honorary form of address, *most noble, most excellent*." This term corresponds to the Latin honorary address *egregius*. This address is also used in 24:3 and 26:25.

Rather than accusing Lysias of "improving on the facts for the benefit of his superior,"[54] he can be excused for summarizing the events in a concise report to the provincial governor in such a fashion that he omits the embarrassing fact that he was about to flog a prisoner who turned out to be a Roman citizen. He portrays himself as the protector of a Roman citizen who had been attacked by Jews in Jerusalem.

23:28 Because I wanted to know the cause of their charges against him, I brought him before their Sanhedrin (βουλόμενός τε ἐπιγνῶναι τὴν αἰτίαν δι᾽ ἣν ἐνεκάλουν αὐτῷ, κατήγαγον εἰς τὸ συνέδριον αὐτῶν). Lysias's report of the Sanhedrin meeting corresponds to Luke's account of the events in 22:30. Lysias emphasizes his plan to establish the cause of the charges[55] against Paul and his initiative in calling a meeting of the Sanhedrin.

23:29 I found that he was accused of controversial questions of their law, but that there was no charge deserving death or chains (ὃν εὗρον ἐγκαλούμενον περὶ ζητημάτων τοῦ νόμου αὐτῶν, μηδὲν δὲ ἄξιον θανάτου ἢ δεσμῶν ἔχοντα ἔγκλημα). Lysias continues to highlight his role in the affair by formulating preliminary conclusions that he was able to draw from the meeting of the Sanhedrin. The report of his findings has two parts. (1) Lysias asserts that he was able to establish that the prisoner was accused of "controversial questions" (ζητήματα)[56] concerning the "law" (νόμος) of the Jews. This is an adequate summary of the Sanhe-

drin hearing in 23:1 – 9, in which Paul had emphasized the consistent morality of his conduct before God, i.e., the God of the Jewish people (23:1), his insistence that he be treated in accordance with the Jewish law (23:3), his willingness to be corrected with reference to the law (23:5), his commitment to the party of the Pharisees who were known for their obedience to the law (23:6), and his hope regarding the resurrection of the dead (23:6).

(2) Lysias asserts that he has come to the conclusion that Paul is not guilty of any criminal charge (ἔγκλημα)[57] that warrants a death sentence. This is the important statement, which exonerates Paul from having violated the criminal law of Rome in a matter for which Roman citizens must be punished with execution. Lysias further asserts that he has come to the conclusion that Paul does not "deserve … chains." He recommends that as Paul's case is further investigated by the governor, Paul's custody should be honorable, i.e., without chains.[58]

23:30 "When I was informed that there would be a plot against the man, I sent him to you at once, and I also ordered his accusers to state their case against him before you" (μηνυθείσης δέ μοι ἐπιβουλῆς εἰς τὸν ἄνδρα ἔσεσθαι ἐξαυτῆς ἔπεμψα πρὸς σὲ παραγγείλας καὶ τοῖς κατηγόροις λέγειν τὰ πρὸς αὐτὸν ἐπὶ σοῦ). Finally, Lysias explains why he is transferring Paul to Caesarea. When he was informed of a conspiracy against Paul (cf. 23:19 – 22), he acted immediately, securing the safety of the detained Roman citizen. The connec-

---

54. Barrett, *Acts*, 1083.

55. The verb ἐγκαλέω ("bring charges against, accuse") is a legal technical term; in 22:30 Luke used the verb κατηγορέω ("bring charges [in court]"), also a legal term.

56. The same term is used in 18:15 for the conclusion of Gallio, the governor of Achaia, concerning the accusation of the Jews of Corinth against Paul.

57. The term ἔγκλημα is a legal technical term that denotes "an indictment or charge brought against someone through judicial proceedings, *charge, accusation*" (BDAG).

58. English translations uniformly render δεσμῶν as "imprisonment." If this had been Lysias' conclusion, he would not have been able to justify sending Paul as a prisoner to Felix under heavy guard, using resources of the empire that were unnecessary if Paul did not deserve to be a prisoner. The meaning must be the literal "chains;" cf. Rapske, *Paul in Roman Custody*, 148, 152. This also means that Lysias does not declare Paul's innocence, as is often assumed; there may be other charges deserving the death sentence that Paul might be guilty of.

tion between Lysias's reference to the plot against Paul's life and the fact that he sent him to Felix in Caesarea is likely the recognition that Lysias is unable to bring Paul's case to a successful conclusion in Jerusalem, where the prisoner's life is in danger.

Lysias's second action, after sending Paul to Felix (which has not yet happened as Lysias pens his letter on the evening of Paul's secret transfer to Caesarea), is his order (παραγγείλας; see on 5:28) given to the Jews, the "accusers" (κατήγοροι) of Paul, to appear before Felix and to state their case against Paul. This can be interpreted as an additional favor to Paul (after the suggestion of an honorable custody); the Jews who make accusations against Paul have been ordered to go to Felix rather than await a summons, a fact that "would presumably pre-empt the governor's trial calendar" and save Paul from a delayed date for a judicial hearing.[59]

23:31 – 32 So the soldiers, in accordance with their orders, took Paul and brought him during the night to Antipatris. The next morning they let the cavalrymen go on with him, while they returned to the barracks (οἱ μὲν οὖν στρατιῶται κατὰ τὸ διατεταγμένον αὐτοῖς ἀναλαβόντες τὸν Παῦλον ἤγαγον διὰ νυκτὸς εἰς τὴν Ἀντιπατρίδα, τῇ δὲ ἐπαύριον ἐάσαντες τοὺς ἱππεῖς ἀπέρχεσθαι σὺν αὐτῷ ὑπέστρεψαν εἰς τὴν παρεμβολήν). The journey to Caesarea (vv. 31 – 33) is narrated in some detail. The focus is on the travel during the night and on the presence of soldiers and cavalrymen. The Roman troops, which must include the two centurions of v. 23, are the active protagonists: the infantry carry out their orders by taking Paul and bringing him from Jerusalem to Antipatris. Then they allow the cavalry to escort Paul to Caesarea while they return to their barracks in Jerusalem. Paul, since he is a prisoner, is passive.

Antipatris was located in the coastal plain, about 37 miles (60 km.) northwest of Jerusalem and 31 miles (50 km.) south of Caesarea. It would have been impossible for the infantry to reach Antipatris in one day. They either accompany the cavalry escort of Paul only during the night hours (perhaps as far as Bethoron), or there is a full day of marching between the night during which they leave Jerusalem and their arrival in Antipatris. The reference to "the next morning" (τῇ δὲ ἐπαύριον) thus refers either to the departure of the infantry escort before the company reaches Antipatris, or to the morning after their arrival in Antipatris on the second day of travel. In Antipatris, the troops and their prisoner would have stayed in the fortress that Herod I had built on the acropolis. Since the region between Antipatris and Caesarea was largely Gentile, the regular soldiers could return to their barracks in Jerusalem, while Paul is taken with the lighter cavalry escort to the provincial capital.

23:33 When they arrived in Caesarea, they delivered the letter to the governor and handed Paul over to him (οἵτινες εἰσελθόντες εἰς τὴν Καισάρειαν καὶ ἀναδόντες τὴν ἐπιστολὴν τῷ ἡγεμόνι παρέστησαν καὶ τὸν Παῦλον αὐτῷ). The events connected with Paul's arrival in Caesarea are recounted in rapid sequence with three verbs: the cavalry escort together with Paul "arrives" in Caesarea; they "deliver" the letter of Claudius Lysias to the governor, and they "hand over" Paul to the governor. That Paul is immediately presented to the governor for a preliminary hearing is historically plausible.[60]

23:34 – 35 He read the letter and asked Paul what province he was from. When he learned that he was from Cilicia, he said, "I will hear your case when your accusers get here." Then he ordered that he be kept under guard in Herod's praetorium (ἀναγνοὺς δὲ καὶ ἐπερωτήσας ἐκ ποίας

59. Rapske, *Paul in Roman Custody*, 153.

60. Cf. Omerzu, *Prozess*, 413.

ἐπαρχείας ἐστίν, καὶ πυθόμενος ὅτι ἀπὸ Κιλικίας, διακούσομαί σου, ἔφη, ὅταν καὶ οἱ κατήγοροί σου παραγένωνται· κελεύσας ἐν τῷ πραιτωρίῳ τοῦ Ἡρῴδου φυλάσσεσθαι αὐτόν). Luke's report of Paul's first encounter with Felix, the Roman governor of the province of Judea (vv. 34–35), has four elements. (1) Felix reads the letter written by the commander of his troops stationed in Jerusalem (v. 34a), perhaps aloud, with Paul and his guards listening.

(2) Felix queries Paul concerning his home province (v. 34b-e), which suggests he may have tried to avoid accepting jurisdiction for the case.[61] A defendant in a criminal case could be transferred to the court of his home province (*forum domicilii*), although this was not required in the early imperial period.[62] Felix learns from Paul's answer that his new prisoner is from Cilicia.

(3) Felix accepts Paul's case, probably because at this time Cilicia, together with Tarsus where Paul held citizenship, belonged (like Judea) to the provincial complex subordinate to the Roman governor of Syria and therefore to the same ultimate jurisdiction.[63] Presumably he does not want to bother the Syrian governor with a relatively minor case.[64] Felix will hear Paul's case when "his accusers," i.e., the Jews who had brought charges against Paul in Jerusalem, arrive in Caesarea, where they have been ordered by his commander in the Antonia Fortress to appear.

(4) Felix orders Paul to be kept under guard in "Herod's praetorium," i.e., the official residence of the governor built by Herod as his palace. Luke's comment suggests that Herod's palace was able to hold prisoners.[65] The term used for Felix's order that Paul be "kept under guard" suggests, in the light of 24:23 (where he grants him "some liberty"), that "the guards' constraints on Paul during the first five days of his Caesarean custody would have been severe. Paul would be closely watched and virtually immobile," in isolation from friends.[66] Felix does not seem impressed either by the letter of his military commander in Jerusalem or by Paul himself.

---

61. Cf. Rapske, *Paul in Roman Custody*, 155.

62. Cf. Sherwin-White, *Roman Society*, 28–31, 55–57; Erika Heusler, *Kapitalprozesse im lukanischen Doppelwerk: Die Verfahren gegen Jesus und Paulus in exegetischer und rechtshistorischer Analyse* (NTAbh 38; Münster: Aschendorff, 2000), 222.

63. Hemer, *Acts*, 172, 180. Cf. Sherwin-White, *Roman Society*, 55–57. Cf. Acts 15:23. Cilicia became a separate province under Vespasian in AD 72. The term ἐπαρχεία (v. 34) generally means "subject territory" but is most often used in the sense of "the government of an ἔπαρχος, or the district governed by him = Lat. *provincia*" (LSJ); BDAG: "a Roman administrative area ruled by an ἔπαρχος or prefect, *province*."

64. Cf. Omerzu, *Prozess*, 414, who also points out that Tarsus, an autonomous city (*civitas libera*), might have been exempt from the usual jurisdiction of the province.

65. Prisoners in Caesarea are mentioned frequently by Josephus, cf. *J.W.* 2.273; 7.20, 37–40; Josephus himself was held in Caesarea as a prisoner, cf. *J.W.* 3.410; 4.622–629; *Life* 414; for the civil magistrates of Caesarea holding prisoners cf. *J.W.* 2.269; *Ant.* 17.175, 178.

66. Rapske, *Paul in Roman Custody*, 157, who points out that since there were no centurions among the cavalry with whom Paul had arrived, the command to guard Paul "is probably fulfilled by military personnel below the grade of centurion" (ibid., 158).

Theology in Application

Paul is in Roman custody because the Jerusalem Jews were eager to kill him on the Temple Mount, accusing him of defiling the sanctity of the temple and of promulgating teachings that violated the Mosaic law and damaged the Jewish people. Paul faces Roman soldiers ordered to interrogate him under torture, and Jewish conspirators who plan to manipulate the authorities so that they get a chance to assassinate Paul. While few Christians will find themselves in similar circumstances, Luke's narrative and Paul's behavior point us to the following truths.

Fanaticism Warrants a Prophetic Response

When Paul is taken to the Sanhedrin, aware that some of its members want to kill him, he takes the initiative by protesting his innocence (22:1). He takes further initiative when he challenges a leading member of the Sanhedrin who orders him to be beaten in the face, accusing him of deceptive hollowness and hypocrisy and of not adhering to the scriptural principle of impartiality. The "whitewashed wall" statement is certainly not meant to convey to Luke's Christian audience how to salute unbelievers. It demonstrates, however, that Christians can, in extraordinary circumstances, use strong words to counter attacks on their physical or moral integrity. Such strong speech is justified if and when it is prophetic speech.

This means that such forceful words are not everyday parlance to be used in circumstances that we may find to be difficult, but the trenchant words of prophetic speech uttered in crisis situations. The point is not to insult the other person (even if the "recipient" of such drastic prophetic speech might indeed feel insulted), but to protest illegal behavior that contradicts God's will. Paul did not know that the culprit who ordered him to be struck on the mouth was the incumbent high priest: had he known that, he evidently would have chosen different words (23:5), but surely with undiminished prophetic zeal, demanding treatment that is in agreement with the law. While Christians will always seek to be polite, they are willing, if the circumstances demand it, to forgo political correctness and unmask hypocrisy, condemn unlawfulness, and threaten divine judgment.

A Renewed Focus on Jesus Christ

Opposition requires a renewed focus on Jesus Christ. In his speech before the Sanhedrin, Paul defends his personal integrity and his theologically conservative commitments, but more importantly he confesses his faith in the crucified and risen Jesus Christ (23:6). His statement about the resurrection of the dead was not a tactical maneuver. Rather, it pinpoints the cause for his conversion from being a persecutor of Christians to becoming a follower of Jesus, and it summarizes his fundamental conviction that Jesus is the crucified, risen, and exalted Messiah of Israel, who saves from sin and to whose lordship Jews and Gentiles need to submit.

Paul knows that the Sadducean members of the Sanhedrin will not consider the truth of his theological statement concerning the bodily resurrection of the dead; he knows too that the Pharisaic members of the Sanhedrin will accept that theological statement as correct in theory and with reference to the future day of the resurrection of all flesh, but hardly as a statement that explains his encounter with Jesus of Nazareth weeks and months after his crucifixion. While his statement about the resurrection leads to a breakdown of the proceedings in the Sanhedrin, forcing the Roman commander to intervene, it had a missionary purpose. Opposition to the gospel cannot be countered by keeping quiet about the gospel. Opposition to the gospel requires renewed efforts to explain the gospel as the message of Jesus as exalted Savior and Lord.

Danger Necessitates Outside Help

Paul accepts the help of the Roman commander of the foreign troops stationed in Jerusalem in the outer court of the temple (21:30–35; 22:22–24); faced with being lynched, he welcomes even military intervention, although he does not solicit it. Paul uses his status as Roman citizen to avoid being tortured (22:24–29); facing military pragmatism whose representatives are willing to torture, he insists on being treated in accordance with the political-social status that he has as a Roman citizen. Paul accepts the intervention of the Roman commander in the Sanhedrin hearing (23:10); faced with another mob scene, he is willing to be led away by military escorts. Paul solicits the help of the Roman commander when he hears about a plot of over forty Jews planning to kill him (23:12–22). Paul allows himself to be transported to Caesarea on horseback, escorted by a large contingent of infantry and cavalry out of Jerusalem in the middle of the night (23:23–24, 31–33).

While Paul knows that the Lord has pledged deliverance from the hands of the Jews with the promise that he will reach Rome (23:11), he is actively involved in escaping dangerous situations. While followers of Jesus are willing to die for the faith, they do not seek martyrdom. They accept help from outsiders, even from rather unlikely quarters, if it allows them to live another day — as witnesses of the Lord.

Acts 24:1 – 27

Literary Context

The two episodes on Paul's imprisonment in Caesarea during the governorship of Antonius Felix report Paul's trial before Felix (24:1 – 23) and his continued custody during Felix's administration (24:24 – 27). The next episode reports Paul's trial before Festus (25:1 – 26:32). These three episodes stand between three episodes that relate events during Paul's visit to Jerusalem, which led to his arrest and imprisonment (21:18 – 23:35), and two episodes on Paul's transport to Rome and his imprisonment there as he waits for his case to be heard by the emperor (27:1 – 28:31). Caesarea, the seat of the Roman governors in the province of Judea, is thus the link between Jerusalem and Rome.

Since the Sanhedrin in Jerusalem did not have full jurisdiction for an independent criminal prosecution of a case that could lead to a death sentence, the Jews needed the cooperation of the Roman governor.[1] A legal death sentence was indeed the goal of the Jewish authorities, after their attempt to kill Paul in the temple courts by lynching had failed (21:27 – 36). Since Paul was in Roman custody after the tumult in the temple, the Jewish authorities knew they would have to convince the governor to convict Paul in a Roman trial. Moreover, they had to take the initiative; according to Roman law, it was not the state but private individuals who prosecuted criminal cases. Since Paul had been transferred from Jerusalem to Caesarea because of the failed plot to ambush Paul, they knew that the trial before the Roman authorities would take place in Caesarea. They knew also that the Roman authorities were not competent to judge the religious charges against Paul: profanation of the temple and apostasy from the Mosaic law and Jewish traditions — charges for which the Roman governor may choose to decline jurisdiction.

Thus they transpose the religious accusations into political charges, in particular the charge of *seditio*, which, if accepted, would force the governor to issue a sentence against Paul. That charge diminishes the role of the Jews in the case against Paul,

---

1. For the following comments, see Omerzu, *Prozess*, 394, 456 – 57.

since it was a crime that only the provincial governor had the right to examine. While this is positive for Paul, the charge of sedition is difficult to defend against, since cause and effect are difficult to distinguish; there *was* a tumult in the temple courts in connection with Paul's visit there. The events reported in these two episodes take place between May AD 57, the time of Paul's defense before Felix, and AD 59, when Festus replaced Felix as governor of Judea.

VII. Paul in Jerusalem, Caesarea, and Rome (21:18 – 28:31)

    A. Paul in Jerusalem (21:18 – 23:35)

    B. Paul in Caesarea (24:1 – 26:32)

➡   **47. The trial before Governor Antonius Felix (24:1 – 23)**

       48. The imprisonment in Caesarea during the governorship of Felix (24:24 – 27)

       49. The imprisonment in Caesarea during the governorship of Porcius Festus (25:1 – 26:32)

Main Idea

Accused by a rhetorically gifted and politically shrewd lawyer, and facing a powerful career politician who subordinated justice to the effort to keep his options open, Paul remains a faithful witness, speaking about the fulfillment of the Scriptures in Jesus Christ, about the resurrection of the dead and the last judgment, and about the ethical consequences of authentic faith in the areas of justice and self-control, which results in a clear conscience.

Translation

Acts 24:1 – 27

1a	Setting: time	Five days later
b	Character entrance: action	**the high priest Ananias came down**
c	Association	with some of the elders and
d	Association	an attorney,
e	Identification	a certain Tertullus,
f	Action	and **they brought formal charges against Paul**
g	Place	before the governor.
2a	Setting: time	After Paul had been summoned,
b	Action (speech)	**Tertullus began to accuse him as follows:**
c	Review of history	*"We have enjoyed a long period of peace*
d	Agency	*through your governorship,*

e	Action	*and reforms have been carried out*
f	Advantage	*for this nation*
g	Means	*through your foresight.*
3a	Assertion	*We accept this in every way and*
b	Place	*everywhere,*
c	Address	*most excellent Felix,*
d	Manner	*with utmost gratitude.*
4a	Cause	*Since I do not want to impose on you any longer,*
b	Entreaty	*I beg you to hear us briefly*
c	Manner	*with your customary graciousness.*
5a	Report	*We have, in fact, found this man to be*
b	Accusation	*a public enemy,*
c	Accusation	*one who causes riots*
d	Sphere: ethnic	*among all the Jews*
e	Sphere: geographical	*throughout the world, and*
f	Accusation	*a ringleader of the sect of the Nazarenes.*
6a	Accusation	*He even tried to desecrate the temple,*
b	Result	*and so we arrested him.*
8a	Time	*When you examine him yourself,*
b	Prediction	*you will be able to ascertain the charges*
c	Description	*that we are bringing against him."*
9a	Action	**The Jews also joined in the attack,**
b	Means	*asserting that all this was true.*
10a	Time	*When the governor motioned to him to speak,*
b	Action (response)	**Paul replied:**
c	Cause	*"Knowing that you have been a judge*
d	Sphere	*over this nation*
e	Duration	*for many years,*
f	Assertion	*I cheerfully defend myself against these charges.*
11a	Assertion	*You can ascertain*
b	Time	*that it is not more than twelve days*
c	Place	*since I went to Jerusalem*
d	Purpose	*in order to worship.*
12a	Assertion (negation)	*They did not find me*
b	Action	*arguing with anyone*
c	Place	*in the temple*
d	Action	*or organizing a crowd*
e	Place	*either in the synagogues*
f	Place	*or in the city.*
13a	Assertion (negation)	*Neither can they prove to you the charges*
b	Description	*that they now bring against me.*
14a	Assertion (admission)	*But I admit to you*
b	Action	*that I worship the God of our fathers*
c	Manner	*according to the Way,*
d	Description	*which they call a sect;*

Continued on next page.

Continued from previous page.

e	Assertion	*I believe everything laid down*
f	Means	*by the Law*
g	Sphere	*or written in the Prophets.*
15a	Assertion	*I have a hope in God,*
b	Description	*a hope that they themselves also accept,*
c	Content	*that there will be a resurrection of both the righteous and*
d	Contrast	*the unrighteous.*
16a	Consequence	*Therefore always I do my best*
b	Purpose	*to have a clear conscience*
c	Sphere	*before God and*
d	Sphere	*before people.*

17a	Time	*After an absence of several years,*
b	Report	*I came to bring alms to my nation*
c	Purpose	*and to present offerings.*

18a	Time	*While I was doing this,*
b	Report	*they found me in the temple,*
c	Manner	*ritually pure,*
d	Manner	*without any crowd or*
e		*disturbance.*
19a	Request	*There are some Jews*
b	Geographical	*from the province of Asia,*
c		*however,*
d	Demand	*who ought to be here before you*
e		*and bring charges,*
f	Condition	*if they have anything against me.*

20a	Request	*Or else let these men here tell*
b	Content	*what crime they had found*
c	Time	*when I stood before the Sanhedrin,*
21a	Concession	*unless it was this one declaration*
b	Description	*that I called out*
c	Time	*when I stood before them,*
d	Cause	*'It is on account of the resurrection of the dead*
e	Description	*that I am on trial before you today.'"*

22a	Action	**Then Felix,**
b	Character description	*who was well-informed about the Way,*
c		**adjourned the proceedings.**
d	Time: Character entrance	*"When Lysias*
e	Character description	*the commander*
f	Action	*comes down,"*
g		**he said,**
h	Announcement	*"I will decide your case."*

23a	Action	**Then he ordered the centurion**
b	Command	*to keep him under guard,*

c	Command	but to let him have some freedom
d	Command	and not to prevent any of his friends
e		from taking care of his needs.
24a	Event	**Several days later Felix came**
b	Association	with his wife, Drusilla,
c	Character description	who was Jewish;
d	Action	**he sent for Paul**
e	Action	and **heard him**
f	Action	speak about faith in the Messiah Jesus.
25a	Action (list)	As Paul discussed righteousness,
b	(list)	self-control, and
c	(list)	the coming judgment,
d	Result	**Felix became alarmed**
e	Action	and **said,**
f	Command	*"Leave for now.*
g	Time	*When I find an opportunity,*
h	Prediction	*I will send for you."*
26a	Expectation	**At the same time he hoped**
b	Content	that Paul would give him money,
c	Action	and **so he sent for him**
d	Time	frequently
e	Action	and **conversed with him.**
27a	Time	After two years had passed,
b	Event: Character entrance	**Felix was succeeded by Porcius Festus**.
c	Cause	Since he wanted to grant the Jews a favor,
d	Action	**Felix left Paul**
e	Place	in prison.

Structure and Literary Form

The episode of Paul's trial before governor Antonius Felix (24:1 – 23) is narrated in five incidents, three of which are short compared with the speeches of the lawyer Tertullus and of Paul. Luke begins by relating the arrival of Ananias, the high priest, and other members of the Sanhedrin in Caesarea (vv. 1 – 2c). The next four incidents make up Luke's report about Paul's trial: Tertullus' speech for the prosecution (vv. 2d – 8), the Jewish leaders' confirmation of the charges against Paul (v. 9), Paul's defense before Felix (vv. 10 – 21), and the adjournment of the trial by Felix, with a reference to the terms of Paul's imprisonment (vv. 22 – 23).

The episode of Paul's imprisonment in Caesarea during the governorship of Felix (24:24 – 27) is made up of two incidents. Luke begins with a report on the private conversations between Paul and Felix (vv. 24 – 26) before briefly commenting on Paul's two-year imprisonment (v. 27).

Both episodes are *historical narrative* with chronological information (vv. 1, 24, 27) and personal names (vv. 1, 2, 22, 24, 27), most of which are attested in extrabiblical historical sources (Ananias, Festus, Drusilla, Felix). Paul's trial before Felix contains mostly *direct speech*: by Tertullus, who speaks for the prosecution (vv. 2c – 8), and by Paul, who defends himself (vv. 10 – 21); Felix's decision is narrated in a brief sentence in direct speech as well (v. 22). The second episode includes a brief direct speech from Felix as well (v. 25). A comparison of the legal speeches of Tertullus and Paul with official protocols of court proceedings extant in papyri documents establishes the possibility that they are based on legal documents and summaries of official proceedings that Luke used when he wrote his narrative.[2]

The speech of Tertullus in 24:2d – 8 has four parts, as recommended in the rhetorical handbooks. (1) In the artful *exordium* (or *captatio benevolentiae*, the commendation of the audience), Tertullus affirms Felix's success as governor of Judea, expresses his gratitude on the behalf of the Jewish people, promises his speech will be brief, and appeals to Felix's graciousness (vv. 2d – 4). (2) In his statement of the facts of the case (*narratio*), Tertullus brings two charges against Paul: he is an agitator among Jews all over the world, and he is a ringleader of the sect of the Nazarenes (v. 5). Tertullus focuses on political charges, in particular on the charge of sedition (στάσις, Lat. *seditio*), which, if proven, was serious and would warrant a death sentence. (3) The confirmation of the charges (*confirmatio* or *probatio*) is seen in Paul's desecration of the temple in Jerusalem and in his arrest by the Jewish authorities (v. 6). Thus, while Tertullus's charges were political, his supporting evidence was theological. (4) In the conclusion of his speech (*peroratio*), Tertullus appeals to Felix to examine Paul himself and expresses confidence that Felix will confirm the veracity of the charges (v. 8). While the *exordium* is of standard length, the *narratio* and the *confirmatio* are summaries.

Paul's *speech* in 24:10 – 21, his seventh, also consists of four parts. (1) In the *exordium*, Paul acknowledges Felix's judicial experience in Judea and expresses his eagerness to defend himself before Felix (v. 10). (2) In the succinct *narratio*, Paul describes his visit to Jerusalem twelve days earlier, whose purpose was to worship God (v. 11). (3) The *confirmatio* (*probatio*) advances three proofs for Paul's innocence: he was not involved in any disputes, he did not organize crowds, and the charges brought against him have not been proven (vv. 12 – 13). (4) The refutation (*refutatio*), the longest section of the speech, specifically answers the charges that Tertullus, the high priest, and the members of the Sanhedrin have brought against him (vv. 14 – 21). While Tertullus brought two political charges against Paul, which rested on theological evidence, Paul reduces the charges to a theological one: his affirmation of the resurrection, an issue that divided the members of the Sanhedrin.

2. Winter, "*Captatio Benevolentiae*," 529 – 31; Winter, "Official Proceedings," 334.

IN DEPTH: Reports of Court Proceedings

Over 250 papyri dated to the period of the early Roman Empire containing official court proceedings make it possible to ascertain how court proceedings described in literary sources and how forensic speeches outlined in rhetorical handbooks "worked" in actual practice.[3] Speeches given during court proceedings were recorded by an official in the form of direct discourse (*oratio recta*), taken down in shorthand in the courtroom and summarized by the scribe as *oratio recta* after the proceedings. This practice explains the approximately similar length of the speeches in Acts 24 – 26, which are summaries. Such records were regarded as accurate reports of what had been said in court.

Defendants had access to certified copies of official documents, including the legal petition that initiated the court proceedings, records of the proceedings that had been resumed, and the verdict. Legal assistants to the rhetor prepared briefs, called "N"-documents,[4] which presented a summary of the facts of the case (*narratio*) and sometimes included the name of the clients, the proofs (*confirmatio*), and the conclusion (*peroratio*). The absence of the introduction (the *captatio benevolentiae* in the *exordium*) suggests that this part of the speech was composed by the rhetor himself.

Exegetical Outline

→ **I. The Trial before Governor Antonius Felix (24:1 – 23)**

    A. The Initiation of Trial Proceedings by Ananias the High Priest (24:1 – 2b)

        1. The arrival of Paul's accusers (24:1a-e)

        2. The filing of charges against Paul (24:1f)

        3. The summons of Paul (24:2a)

        4. The prosecution by Tertullus (24:2b)

    B. Tertullus's Speech for the Prosecution (24:2c – 8)

        1. Address (*exordium*) (24:2c – 4)

            a. Affirmation of Felix's success as governor of Judea (24:2d-h)

            b. Expression of gratitude on the behalf of the Jewish people (24:3)

            c. Promise of brevity (24:4a-b)

            d. Appeal to Felix's graciousness (24:4c)

---

3. The following summary depends on Winter, "*Captatio Benevolentiae*," 508 – 14, 526 – 28; Winter, "Official Proceedings," 306 – 14.

4. The term "N"-document is derived either from *narratio* or, which seems more likely (since the documents contain more than the *narratio* of the speech), from the term νομικός ("advocate, jurisprudent"). These documents, which have a crossed "N" at the beginning, have wide left-hand margins that often contain notes.

2. The facts of the case: The charges against Paul (*narratio*) (24:5)

    a. The accused is an agitator among Jews all over the world (24:5a-e)

    b. The accused is a ringleader of the sect of the Nazarenes (24:5f)

3. The confirmation of the charges (*confirmatio*) (24:6)

    a. The accused has desecrated the temple (24:6a)

    b. The arrest of the accused by the Jewish authorities in Jerusalem (24:6b)

4. Conclusion (*peroratio*) (24:8)

    a. Appeal to Felix to examine Paul himself (24:8a)

    b. Expression of confidence that Felix will confirm the veracity of the charges (24:8b-c)

C. The Confirmation of Tertullus's Charges by the Jewish Leaders (24:9)

1. The public appearance of the Jewish authorities (24:9a)

2. The confirmation of Tertullus's charges by the Jewish authorities (24:9b)

D. Paul's Defense before Felix (24:10 – 21)

1. Felix's permission that Paul begins his defense (24:10a)

2. Paul begins his defense (24:10b)

3. Paul's defense speech (24:10c – 21)

    a. Address (*exordium*) (24:10c-f)

        i. Acknowledgment of Felix's judicial experience in Judea (24:10c-e)

        ii. Expression of eagerness to defend himself before Felix (24:10f)

    b. The facts of the case (*narratio*) (24:11)

        i. Paul's visit to Jerusalem twelve days earlier (24:11a-c)

        ii. The purpose of that visit (24:11d)

    c. Proofs of Paul's innocence (*confirmatio*) (24:12 – 13)

        i. He was not involved in any disputes (24:12a-c)

        ii. He did not organize crowds (24:12d-f)

        iii. The charges brought against him have not been proven (24:13)

    d. Refutation of the charges (*refutatio*) (24:14 – 18)

        i. Refutation of the charge of being a ringleader of the Nazarenes (24:14 – 16)

        ii. Refutation of the charge of having desecrated the temple (24:17 – 18)

    e. Conclusion (*peroratio*) (24:19 – 21)

        i. Protest concerning the absence of the Jews from Asia (24:19)

        ii. Protest concerning the absence of proof of a crime committed in Jerusalem (24:20)

        iii. Assertion of one possible charge against him: Belief in the resurrection (24:21)

E. The Adjournment of the Trial by Felix (24:22)

1. The adjournment of the trial proceedings (24:22a-c)

2. Promise of a decision at the time of the arrival of Claudius Lysias (24:22e-h)

F. The Terms of Paul's Imprisonment in Caesarea (24:23)

1. Paul kept in custody (24:23a-b)

2. Paul granted freedom while in custody (24:23c-e)

    a. Paul can receive friends (24:23c-d)

    b. Paul can receive provisions (24:23e)

II. **The Imprisonment in Caesarea during the Governorship of Felix (24:24 – 27)**

   A. **The Private Conversations between Paul and Felix (24:24 – 26)**

      1. The arrival of Felix and his wife, Drusilla (24:24a-c)

      2. Felix's summons to hear Paul (24:24d-e)

      3. Paul's discourse (24:24f – 25c)

         a. Faith in Jesus the Messiah (24:24f)

         b. Righteousness granted by God through Jesus (24:25a)

         c. Self-control demanded by God (24:25b)

         d. Judgment at the resurrection of the righteous and the unrighteous (24:25c)

      4. Felix's uneasiness (24:25d)

      5. Felix's promise of further conversation (24:25e-h)

      6. Felix's expectation of receiving a bribe (24:26a-b)

      7. Felix's frequent conversations with Paul (24:26c-e)

   B. **The Confinement of Paul for Two Years until Felix Is Replaced by Festus (24:27)**

      1. The passing of two years (24:27a)

      2. Felix's replacement by Festus (24:27b)

      3. Felix's desire to please the Jews (24:27c)

      4. Paul's continued custody (24:27d-e)

Explanation of the Text

24:1 – 2c Five days later the high priest Ananias came down with some of the elders and an attorney, a certain Tertullus, and they brought formal charges against Paul before the governor. After Paul had been summoned, Tertullus began to accuse him as follows (μετὰ δὲ πέντε ἡμέρας κατέβη ὁ ἀρχιερεὺς Ἀνανίας μετὰ πρεσβυτέρων τινῶν καὶ ῥήτορος Τερτύλλου τινός, οἵτινες ἐνεφάνισαν τῷ ἡγεμόνι κατὰ τοῦ Παύλου. κληθέντος δὲ αὐτοῦ ἤρξατο κατηγορεῖν ὁ Τέρτυλλος λέγων). Luke sets the scene of Paul's trial before Felix with chronological and geographical comments that tie the episode of Paul's trial in Caesarea before the Roman governor to the previous episode. The high priest Ananias and "some of the elders"[5] arrive in Caesarea "five days later," i.e., five days after Paul's arrival; they travel down from Jerusalem in the Judean hills to Caesarea on the coast.

After removing Paul from Jerusalem in a hastily arranged ride during the night, Claudius Lysias, the commander of the garrison, had informed the Jewish authorities that they would have to present their charges against Paul before the governor in Caesarea. Luke's comment implies that Ananias and the Jewish officials left Jerusalem more or less immediately after Paul's transfer, traveling the 60 miles (100 km.) to Caesarea either on foot (four days) or on horses (two days). They would have needed as least one full day in Caesarea to arrange for a meeting with the governor and to lodge the petition to initiate trial proceedings against Paul.

The high priest and the Jewish officials arrived with Tertullus, described as an "attorney" (ῥήτορος), a term that designates the "public speaker" or "orator" and can thus describe, in a court setting, both

---

5. Senior officials who were members of the Jewish elite, presumably members of the Sanhedrin in Jerusalem, cf. 4:5.

the judge and the advocate — the latter speaking either as prosecutor or as lawyer for the defense.[6] The participation of legal counsel who knew the law and who had rhetorical expertise was not obligatory in the Roman legal system, but it was permitted. Thus, Ananias and the elders present their charges with the help of Tertullus, an otherwise unknown advocate. Tertullus possibly had represented members of the Jewish elite before Felix in the past. The presence of a legal and rhetorical expert underlines the importance of the case for Ananias and the Sanhedrin, who perhaps sense that they are at a disadvantage in prosecuting a Roman citizen in front of a Roman governor.[7] The absence of legal counsel for Paul implies that he is able, and willing, to defend himself.

Ananias and members of the lay aristocracy, together with Tertullus, have met with the governor to formulate "formal charges" against Paul (v. 1f). If extant documentary evidence is any guide, it can be assumed that this petition, which aimed at initiating legal proceedings, follows the normal divisions of a courtroom speech, with an introduction (*exordium*), a statement of the facts of the case (*narratio*), the proofs (*confirmatio*), and a conclusion (*peroratio*).[8] This formal deposition is made in Paul's absence. Since the high priest, the highest representative of the Jewish population of the province, is bringing charges against Paul, the governor probably does not have much choice in accepting the case, even if the letter from Lysias in Jerusalem (23:26 – 30) alerted him to the fact that the dispute is about questions of the Jewish law (in which he is not competent) and that no crime has been committed to warrant a capital charge.

After Felix has accepted the petition to initi-ate legal proceedings, Paul is summoned from the place of his custody in the praetorium (cf. 23:35) to stand trial (v. 2a), which takes place perhaps on the same day that the charges were officially introduced by Ananias and accepted by Felix, although the trial may have taken place a few days later.

24:2d-h "We have enjoyed a long period of peace through your governorship, and reforms have been carried out for this nation through your foresight" (πολλῆς εἰρήνης τυγχάνοντες διὰ σοῦ καὶ διορθωμάτων γινομένων τῷ ἔθνει τούτῳ διὰ τῆς σῆς προνοίας). Tertullus begins his speech (vv. 2c – 8) with the customary *exordium* (vv. 2c – 4), which consists mostly of a *captatio benevolentiae*, an introduction in papyrus petitions that seeks "to win the goodwill of the prefect by drawing his attention to an aspect of his own judicial and administrative competence which made him highly suited to hear a particular case, rather than have it referred to a subordinate official for a jury trial."[9] Tertullus praises Felix for the manner in which he has carried out his *imperium* in the province of Judea.

First, Tertullus acknowledges that Felix has established "peace" (εἰρήνη), i.e., law and order, which the Jews have enjoyed for "a long period." Maintaining law and order was the most basic and the most important task of a Roman governor. While there is evidence suggesting that the enmity and hatred of the Jews in Judea against the Romans increased during Felix's governorship, resulting in internal unrest and a deteriorating political situation,[10] Tertullus's statement is not mere flattery. Felix had recently suppressed a rebellion of an Egyptian prophet who had threatened Jerusalem with thousands of supporters,[11] and he had

---

6. The translation "spokesman" (RSV, ESV) is too anemic.

7. Rapske, *Paul in Roman Custody*, 159.

8. Cf. Winter, "Official Proceedings," 312 – 14.

9. Winter, "*Captatio Benevolentiae*," 507 – 8; cf. Quintilian, *Inst.* 4.1.16, 26.

10. Josephus, *Ant.* 20.160 – 181; *J.W.* 2.252 – 270.

11. Josephus, *Ant.* 20.169 – 172; *J.W.* 2.261 – 263; see on Acts 21:38.

captured Eleazar, the leader of the "dagger bearers," crucifying many of his followers. While many ordinary Jews were less than excited about Felix's governorship, the Jewish leaders in Jerusalem certainly appreciated that he had saved their capital. Tertullus thus acknowledges Felix's maintaining law and order.

Second, Tertullus acknowledges that Felix has demonstrated "foresight" (πρόνοια), i.e., thoughtful planning and management, when he carried out "reforms" of legal ordinances that benefited the Jewish nation (ἔθνος), perhaps as regards the cooperation between the Jewish authorities in the Sanhedrin and the Roman provincial government, or with regard to the administration of the temple. The virtue of foresight or providence is repeatedly mentioned in legal papyri and in descriptions of rulers. While the background of Tertullus's statement in specific legal reforms during Felix's tenure as governor of Judea remains unclear, his comment seems to have been justified, for Ummidius Quadratus, the governor of Syria, had appointed Felix to assist Claudius in deciding a legal matter regarding the Samaritans, which had resulted in Jonathan, the high priest in AD 36 – 37, asking Claudius to appoint Felix as governor of Judea.[12]

Besides praising Felix for his competent governorship, this opening point is a clever choice since the two virtues of "peace" and "foresight" through legal reforms take up points that are intimately related to Paul's case, who is accused of disturbing the peace among the Jewish people — the very peace that Felix has managed to establish (v. 5).

24:3 We accept this in every way and everywhere, most excellent Felix, with utmost gratitude (πάντη τε καὶ πανταχοῦ ἀποδεχόμεθα, κράτιστε Φῆλιξ, μετὰ πάσης εὐχαριστίας). Tertullus asserts that Felix's competent administration of the province was a source of genuine gratitude that was absolute (πάντη; "in every way"), universal (πανταχοῦ; "everywhere"), and complete (πάσης; "utmost"). The "we" implied in the verb, whose present tense underlines the ongoing, current appreciation of Felix's governorship, should be connected with the aristocratic elite, who had come to accept the Roman imperial government and who were grateful for governors with whom they could work together. Laudatory titles such as "most excellent" (κράτιστε) are customary in the introduction of legal petitions addressing government officials.

24:4 Since I do not want to impose on you any longer, I beg you to hear us briefly with your customary graciousness (ἵνα δὲ μὴ ἐπὶ πλεῖόν σε ἐγκόπτω, παρακαλῶ ἀκοῦσαί σε ἡμῶν συντόμως τῇ σῇ ἐπιεικείᾳ). Tertullus concludes his introduction with the promise of brevity. He assures the governor that he does not want to "impose"[13] on his time and promises to speak "briefly." Brevity (*brevitas*) was an ideal of rhetoric,[14] which was apparently "an ideal more often praised than practiced."[15] Since references to self-imposed brevity could function as a form of *insinuatio*, implying that one could provide further information, rhetorically informed readers of Luke may see here "the hint of an

---

12. Cf. Tacitus, *Ann.* 12.54; Josephus, *Ant.* 20.162.

13. The verb (ἐγκόπτω) denotes "to make progress slow or difficult, *hinder, thwart*" (BDAG), i.e., Tertullus might say that he does not want to prevent Felix from attending to other business. Some translate "detain" (RSV, ESV, NRSV), others as "weary" (NASB, NIV, TNIV); NLT has "bore," NET "delay," GNB "take up too much of your time." BDAG, suggests "weary" and regards "impose" or "detain" as possibilities.

14. Quintilian, *Inst.* 8.3.82; note 4.1.34: "We shall also find it a useful device to create the impression that we shall not keep them long and intend to stick closely to the point." In cases where the issue involved was complex, requiring a lengthy introduction, Quintilian suggests that the advocate apologize to the jury or judge (4.1.79).

15. Johnson, *Acts*, 410. The speeches of advocates in courts of law were timed by the use of a water clock; cf. Lucian, *Bis acc.* 15, 19.

incipient attack against Paul."[16] The last phrase of the *exordium* again compliments Felix, as Tertullus appeals to his "customary graciousness."

24:5 We have, in fact, found this man to be a public enemy, one who causes riots among all the Jews throughout the world, and a ringleader of the sect of the Nazarenes (εὑρόντες γὰρ τὸν ἄνδρα τοῦτον λοιμὸν καὶ κινοῦντα στάσεις πᾶσιν τοῖς Ἰουδαίοις τοῖς κατὰ τὴν οἰκουμένην πρωτοστάτην τε τῆς τῶν Ναζωραίων αἱρέσεως).

The statement of the facts of the case (*narratio*) in v. 5 focuses on two charges that Ananias and the Jewish elite, through their advocate Tertullus, bring against Paul.[17] The first charge asserts that Paul is a "public enemy" (λοιμός); the Greek term means "being diseased" or "pestilential" when used for birds of prey; when used of human beings, the term means "public menace" or "public enemy."[18] This description implies that Paul has exerted a pernicious, destructive influence, infecting like a pest the Jewish people with his dangerous activities.

Tertullus then explains the metaphor: Paul has caused riots among "all the Jews throughout the world." The term used for Paul's activities — "riots" (στάσεις) — denotes uprisings, revolts, and rebellions that threaten the civil harmony and peaceful conduct that Roman governors are responsible for maintaining. The transposition of the religious charges (21:28; also 23:29 in Lysias' letter) into political charges is not necessarily a clever tactical move or an intentional distortion of the facts. The religious accusations are present in the background, as the second charge (v. 5f) demonstrates.

Moreover, Paul's missionary work in numerous cities of the Jewish diaspora had regularly provoked controversies that disturbed the harmony and peace not only of the various local Jewish communities but also of the cities themselves, as Luke's readers know all too well (who, however, would regard the charge as spurious since it was local Jews who triggered the tumults, such as recently in the Jerusalem temple). The comparison of a riot (στάσις; Lat. *tumultus*) with a disease is a common theme of Greco-Roman legal language.

The charge of *seditio* diminishes the possibility that the Jews can influence the course of the trial, since causing riots is a crime that only the governor can examine. At the same time the charge of *seditio* puts Paul in the awkward situation of having to defend himself against a charge that on the surface seems plausible. Wherever he went, dissension (at least in the Jewish communities) followed, and it would be difficult to explain to the governor that his preaching and teaching did not result in the tumults. While the charge that Paul acted contrary to the law, which the Corinthian Jews brought against Paul before Gallio, the governor of Achaia, could be interpreted either in political or in religious terms (18:13), the charge of *seditio* was exclusively political and could not simply be dismissed by Felix, particularly as Tertullus had praised him in the *captatio benevolentiae* for his maintenance of law and order (v. 2c-d).

The second charge accuses Paul of being a "ringleader" (πρωτοστάτης) of the sect of the Nazarenes.[19] The Greek term literally means "one who

---

16. Craig S. Keener, "Some Rhetorical Techniques in Acts 24:2 – 21," in *Paul's World* (ed. S. E. Porter; Pauline Studies 4; Leiden: Brill, 2008), 221 – 51, 228.

17. The verb translated "we have found" (εὑρόντες) insinuates legal discovery and due diligence (cf. BDAG, s.v. εὑρίσκω 2, "to discover intellectually through reflection, observation, examination, or investigation, *find, discover*"). The brevity of the *narratio* is explained by Winter, "Official Proceedings," 307,

312 – 14, with the protocols for recording legal proceedings.

18. Cf. BDAG, s.v. II λοιμός. The author of 1 Macc 10:61; 15:21 uses the term for wanted criminals; Demosthenes for people who are dangerous to the welfare of the public (*Or.* 25.80).

19. Keener, "Rhetorical Techniques," 232, argues that Tertullus accuses Paul of being a leader of the Nazarenes because "the leader of sedition can do little damage without followers,"

stands first"; in a military context it designates "the first man on the right of a line," a right-hand man or a man who stands in the front rank (LSJ). Used metaphorically, the term describes a person who is the chief or leader of a group.

The term translated as "sect" (αἵρεσις) has a neutral sense denoting "a group that holds tenets distinctive to it" and thus a "party, school, faction."[20] The followers of Jesus did not use the term as a self-designation (cf. 24:14). This fact, and the context in which Tertullus uses the term, suggests here a derogatory meaning: Paul is accused of leading a faction from which the religious and political leadership of the Jews distance themselves. While establishing local assemblies with regular meetings was a potential problem given the suspicious attitude of some emperors concerning voluntary associations, the connection between Paul's group, labeled here as "Nazarenes" (Ναζωραῖοι),[21] and Jesus of Nazareth, who was crucified by the Roman governor twenty-seven years earlier, explains the seriousness of the second charge.

In other words, Tertullus charges Paul with leading a party that pledges devotion to a man executed by the Roman authorities as a teacher who (allegedly) seduced the people and falsely claimed to be the king of the Jews.[22] Whether or not Tertullus is alluding directly to the charges against Jesus brought by the Jewish authorities to Pontius Pilate that led to Jesus "the Nazarene" being executed, the fact of Paul's leadership of this troublesome

group is presented as a crime that needs to be punished.

24:6 He even tried to desecrate the temple, and so we arrested him (ὃς καὶ τὸ ἱερὸν ἐπείρασεν βεβηλῶσαι ὃν καὶ ἐκρατήσαμεν). The proofs (*confirmatio*) for the high priest's case against Paul, conveyed through Tertullus, seem to be given in v. 6. The first proof for establishing the veracity of the charge that Paul is a ringleader of the Nazarenes is the "fact" that he tried to profane the temple. Tertullus argues that Paul has brought his activities from the Jewish communities "throughout the world" to Jerusalem. If accepted as fact, Felix would have to take the Jewish demand for Paul's summary execution seriously, particularly if he feared Claudius's wrath that had been communicated to the governor in Egypt (cf. v. 5).

As noted earlier, Tertullus asserts not that Paul actually defiled the temple (cf. 21:28), but that he "tried" (ἐπείρασεν) to desecrate the temple. A desecrated temple can no longer be used for sacrifices and worship until the temple has again been sanctified. While this seems a "milder form of the accusation,"[23] it does not improve Paul's legal position since the Jews can present their intervention as a preventive measure taken just in time.[24] Also, Paul now has to prove not only that he had not actually desecrated the temple but that he had harbored no intentions of profaning the temple, a subjective charge difficult to rebut.

---

thereby unwittingly attributing to Paul significant political influence "that complicates the political convenience of simply handing Paul over to his politically influential accusers."

20. BDAG, s.v. αἵρεσις 1. In 5:17 the term describes the Sadducees, in 15:5 and 26:5 the Pharisees; cf. Josephus, *Ant.* 13.171; 20.199; *Life* 10, 12, 191.

21. The designation of the Christians as "Nazarenes" was probably coined by opposing Jews, as a derogatory term reflecting the insignificance of the town/village of Nazareth. For the singular Ναζωραῖος see on 2:22; cf. 3:6; 4:10; 6:14; 22:8; 26:9.

22. Note the *titulus* at the cross, which included the des-

ignation Ναζωραῖος: "Jesus of Nazareth, the King of the Jews" (Ἰησοῦς ὁ Ναζωραῖος ὁ βασιλεὺς τῶν Ἰουδαίων), John 19:19; cf. Luke 23:1, 38 (without the term Ναζωραῖος). Notwithstanding parallels between Jesus' trial (Luke 23:2) and Paul's trial (Acts 24:5 – 6), including the transposition of religious charges to political charges, they are outweighed by the differences, particularly the fact that Jesus is accused of claiming to be king (*crimen maiestatis*) while Paul is accused of fomenting riots (*seditio*); cf. Omerzu, *Prozess*, 428 – 30.

23. Witherington, *Acts*, 708.

24. Omerzu, *Prozess*, 437; cf. Bruce, *Book of Acts*, 441.

The second proof Tertullus offers is the intervention of the Jewish authorities: Paul's attempt to desecrate the temple is proven by the fact that he was arrested. Considering the situation of the trial and his role in the legal proceedings before the governor, it is understandable (from the Jewish leaders' point of view) that Tertullus omits any mention that Paul was arrested in the middle of a tumult caused by Jews from the province of Asia, and that Paul's life was saved by the intervention of the Roman commander of the garrison in the Antonia Fortress.

There is no criticism of Roman behavior in Tertullus's speech, as some assume.[25] The suggestion that Tertullus asserts Jewish legal jurisdiction ignores the legal strategy of Tertullus, who asserts that Paul is guilty of a serious crime that demands summary execution rather than merely Paul's extradition to the Jewish authorities. Also, if Acts 24 indeed reports a trial rather than a preliminary hearing, Tertullus's legal strategy has to be evaluated in the context of the proceedings of a court in session in which the governor has to pronounce a verdict on the case as presented to him. Tertullus, true to his role as advocate of the accusers, does everything in his power to make it more difficult for Paul to defend himself.

24:8 "When you examine him yourself, you will be able to ascertain the charges that we are bringing against him" (παρ᾽ οὗ δυνήσῃ αὐτὸς ἀνακρίνας περὶ πάντων τούτων ἐπιγνῶναι ὧν ἡμεῖς κατηγοροῦμεν αὐτοῦ). Tertullus concludes his speech (*peroratio*) with an appeal to Felix to examine Paul himself; he is confident that Felix will confirm the charges against Paul. He expects, in agreement with Roman criminal law, that the accused will admit his guilt in cross-examination by

the judge, and that his guilt will be established by witnesses. The latter is the point of the next verse.

24:9 The Jews also joined in the attack, asserting that all this was true (συνεπέθεντο δὲ καὶ οἱ Ἰουδαῖοι φάσκοντες ταῦτα οὕτως ἔχειν). The term "the Jews" refers to the high priest, Ananias, and the representatives of the lay aristocracy who have come to Caesarea as Paul's accusers (v. 1). They join in the attack; i.e., they provide testimony for the charges that Paul has caused riots among Jews all over the world and that he is a ringleader of the Nazarenes. While Luke provides no details, there is no doubt that the Jewish authorities are seeking to confirm Tertullus's assertion that Paul desecrated the temple and that the Jewish leadership was instrumental in arresting him (cf. vv. 5 – 6).

24:10 When the governor motioned to him to speak, Paul replied: "Knowing that you have been a judge over this nation for many years, I cheerfully defend myself against these charges" (ἀπεκρίθη τε ὁ Παῦλος νεύσαντος αὐτῷ τοῦ ἡγεμόνος λέγειν· ἐκ πολλῶν ἐτῶν ὄντα σε κριτὴν τῷ ἔθνει τούτῳ ἐπιστάμενος εὐθύμως τὰ περὶ ἐμαυτοῦ ἀπολογοῦμαι). Luke's report of Paul's defense (vv. 10 – 21) begins with Felix's signaling to Paul that he may now speak in his own defense. The *exordium* (v. 10c-f) is succinct. (1) Paul acknowledges in a *captatio benevolentiae* Felix's expertise as a judge (κριτής) with respect to the Jewish nation. Governors had judicial responsibilities and experience, and Felix was no exception. The assertion that Felix has had judicial experience "for many years" is not merely "flowery language."[26] While Felix was governor of Judea only since AD 52, i.e., since five years at the time of Paul's trial in May AD 57, he had earlier ruled Samaria under Cumanus and thus

---

25. Tajra, *Trial*, 123, thinks that Paul is described by Tertullus as "a temple-prisoner snatched away illegally by the tribune"; similarly Witherington, *Acts*, 708, who thinks that

Tertullus wants "to claim jurisdictional rights to judge Paul under Jewish law by Jewish authorities."

26. Conzelmann, *Acts*, 199.

held office in the region for eight or nine years, and his marriage to Drusilla, the youngest daughter of King Agrippa I, would have given him "an unusual degree of knowledge of Jewish affairs."[27]

(2) Paul expresses his eagerness to defend himself before Felix against the charges that Tertullus, Ananias, and the members of the Jewish aristocracy have presented, precisely because Felix has experience and expertise in Jewish affairs. This point hints that Paul will present the charges leveled against him as a religious dispute over matters of the Jewish faith. Paul is much less flattering in his introduction than Tertullus. At the same time he displays the confidence that an orator was encouraged to adopt,[28] that Felix will understand the arguments presented in Paul's defense (ἀπολογοῦμαι) and will pronounce a just verdict as the judge overseeing the trial.

24:11 You can ascertain that it is not more than twelve days since I went to Jerusalem in order to worship (δυναμένου σου ἐπιγνῶναι ὅτι οὐ πλείους εἰσίν μοι ἡμέραι δώδεκα ἀφ᾽ ἧς ἀνέβην προσκυνήσων εἰς Ἰερουσαλήμ). Paul's *narratio* is brief and to the point.[29] He arrived in Jerusalem not more than twelve days ago, and the purpose of his visit was to worship. The temporal reference suggests to Felix that it should be easy for him to "ascertain" (ἐπιγνῶναι) the truth about what happened since it was so recent. The reference to twelve days may also imply that this was hardly a sufficient time period in which one can organize a rebellion.

The reckoning of the "twelve days" has gener-

ated some discussion. Luke's narrative provides the following chronology:

1st day	Paul's arrival in Jerusalem	21:17
2nd day	visit of James	21:18
3rd to 9th day	seven days of purification	21:26
9th day (+ X)[30]	arrest	21:33
10th day (+ X)	hearing in the Sanhedrin	22:30
11th day (+ X)	plot against Paul	23:12
12th day (+ X)	arrival in Caesarea	23:32 – 33
17th day (+ X)	trial before Felix	24:1

Three suggestions for reckoning the twelve days have been made. (1) The twelve days are the result of the addition of the figures given in 21:27 and 24:1.[31] (2) The twelve days refer to the time Paul spent in Jerusalem; the twelfth day is the day he was transferred to Caesarea.[32] (3) The twelve days relate to the time between Paul's arrival in Jerusalem and his arrest in the temple.[33] The last suggestion seems most plausible: Paul's visit to Jerusalem was motivated by the desire to worship in the temple (not to organize a rebellion), an activity that was interrupted when the Roman authorities took him into custody.

Paul does not refer to the charge that his allegedly criminal activities have taken place all over the world. He speaks only of his visit to Jerusalem, presumably because events in other provinces are outside of Felix's jurisdiction, and because Felix can only investigate events that took place in the Jewish

27. Dunn, *Beginning from Jerusalem*, 980.

28. Cf. Winter, "*Captatio Benevolentiae*," 523; cf. Quintilian, *Inst.* 5.21.51.

29. Differently Parsons, *Acts*, 326 – 27, who sees a long *narratio* (vv. 11 – 18a) composed as a ring structure (vv. 11 – 12/17 – 18a, v. 13/16, and a central section in vv. 14 – 15 interpreted as a concession).

30. This event (and the following) event took place at the earliest on the day indicated. Omerzu, *Prozess*, 444.

31. Conzelmann, *Acts*, 199; Fitzmyer, *Acts*, 735. This is un-

likely since it would render Paul's defense implausible on the narrative level.

32. Haenchen, *Acts*, 654 with n. 2; Bruce, *Acts*, 478; Witherington, *Acts*, 710. Here Paul's statement becomes imprecise and not logical since "after his arrest Paul could hardly have fomented sedition" (Gerhard A. Krodel, *Acts* [Minneapolis: Augsburg, 1986], 438).

33. Lake and Cadbury, *Acts*, 300; Krodel, *Acts*, 438; Omerzu, *Prozess*, 445.

capital.[34] Paul resists the broadening of the charges to all Jewish communities in the "world," which would be unfavorable for his case. Paul affirms that his visit to Jerusalem was innocent: he went to Jerusalem in order to worship (προσκυνήσων); i.e., he came as a pilgrim for purely religious reasons when he went to the temple (cf. 21:26).

24:12 – 13 They did not find me arguing with anyone in the temple or organizing a crowd either in the synagogues or in the city. Neither can they prove to you the charges that they now bring against me (καὶ οὔτε ἐν τῷ ἱερῷ εὗρόν με πρός τινα διαλεγόμενον ἢ ἐπίστασιν ποιοῦντα ὄχλου οὔτε ἐν ταῖς συναγωγαῖς οὔτε κατὰ τὴν πόλιν, οὐδὲ παραστῆσαι δύνανταί σοι περὶ ὧν νυνὶ κατηγοροῦσίν μου). Paul proves his innocence in the *confirmatio* (or *probatio*) with three points. (1) He was not involved in any disputes when he was in Jerusalem. When the Jewish authorities came upon Paul in the temple, he was not "arguing" (διαλεγόμενον) with anyone on political or theological issues. Since the verb "arguing" is a standard one Paul uses to describe his preaching and teaching,[35] his assertion can be interpreted as stating that during the twelve days he was in Jerusalem before he was detained, he did not teach anywhere in the city.

(2) Paul was not "organizing" a crowd in the synagogues of Jerusalem (cf. 6:9) or anywhere else in the city. Thus, he is not guilty of sedition (στάσις). The reference to multiple locations — the temple, the synagogues, the city — responds to Tertullus's charge that Paul is a contagious disease and causes riots among the Jewish people (v. 5). The emphasis on the temple, mentioned first, corresponds to the charge that he was trying to desecrate the temple (v. 6).

(3) The evidence given by his accusers before Felix have not proven the charges they brought against him.[36] Despite the fact that he was in Jerusalem for twelve days before his arrest by the Jewish authorities, they have failed to provide proof for their charges. At the same time it should be noted that the legal strategy of Paul's accusers is successful: their rather general accusations are difficult to prove, but they are also difficult to disprove; despite Paul insistence that he is innocent, he is not officially declared innocent and released by Felix.[37]

24:14 But I admit to you that I worship the God of our fathers according to the Way, which they call a sect; I believe everything laid down by the Law or written in the Prophets (ὁμολογῶ δὲ τοῦτό σοι ὅτι κατὰ τὴν ὁδὸν ἣν λέγουσιν αἵρεσιν, οὕτως λατρεύω τῷ πατρῴῳ θεῷ πιστεύων πᾶσι τοῖς κατὰ τὸν νόμον καὶ τοῖς ἐν τοῖς προφήταις γεγραμμένοις). Paul begins his *refutatio* (vv. 14 – 18) with Tertullus's second charge, namely, that he is a criminal ringleader of the party of the Nazarenes (v. 5f). Paul readily admits that he indeed belongs to the followers of Jesus, thus taking the wind out of his accuser's sails.[38] He confesses that he worships God "according to the Way" (κατὰ τὴν ὁδόν), which the Jews call "a sect" (αἵρεσις; see on v. 5). For Paul, as for the other followers of Jesus, the worship (λατρεύω) of God is now fundamentally and irrevocably connected with Jesus, Israel's Messiah, whose life, death, resurrection, and exaltation constitute the only "way" to salvation, and who is thus Savior and Lord.

The placement of this statement at the beginning of the ὅτι clause emphasizes the significance of Paul's "admission" (τοῦτο is also emphatic).

---

34. Cf. Winter, "*Captatio Benevolentiae*," 524; Omerzu, *Prozess*, 443; cf. ibid. for the following comment.

35. Cf. 17:2 (Thessalonica); 17:17 (Athens); 18:4 (Corinth); 18:19; 19:8, 9 (Ephesus); 20:7, 9 (Troas).

36. The demand for proof "rhetorically presupposed one's innocence by appearing confident that no such proof could be

offered" (Keener, "Rhetorical Techniques," 238, with reference to Lysias, *Or.* 24.24.170; 25.14.172; also John 8:46).

37. Omerzu, *Prozess*, 445.

38. Keener, "Rhetorical Techniques," 242, suggests that "admitting" one matter, which was not a crime, was a clever rhetorical strategy.

Paul begins his defense by defining the real issue at stake in the case that the Jewish leaders bring against him. He rejects the negative connotations of the term "sect" because he believes that the group of Jesus' followers is more than just another Jewish party such as the Pharisees and Sadducees (each of which Josephus describes as a αἵρεσις): the followers of Jesus *are* the true people of God pure and simple, "and its way is the halakah for all Israel."[39] At the same time Paul insists that the "Way" to worship and to salvation — the "Way" on which Jesus' followers walk — does not lead him outside of Judaism. He has not abandoned Jewish monotheism; he continues to worship "the God of our fathers," i.e., the God of Abraham, Isaac, and Jacob (Exod 3:16), albeit in a new way.

Paul's next argument to disprove he is the criminal ringleader of a Jewish party points to his commitment to the Scriptures. He believes everything that is laid down by the Law (the Torah) and everything written in the Prophets (προφῆται), i.e., in these two sections of the Hebrew Scriptures. The Old Testament continues to be normative for Paul, as it is for his accusers. He is not an enemy of the Jewish people, advancing teachings that lead the people astray and cause riots. This argument begins a section in which Paul insists he has been leading a blameless life as a conservative Jew (vv. 14e–18c), which is in rhetorical terms an appeal to *ethos*, i.e., character. Appeal to one's past character belonged to the arguments from probability: Paul argues that being who he is, it is unlikely that he is guilty of sedition.[40]

24:15 I have a hope in God, a hope that they themselves also accept, that there will be a resurrection of both the righteous and the unrigh- teous (ἐλπίδα ἔχων εἰς τὸν θεὸν ἣν καὶ αὐτοὶ οὗτοι προσδέχονται, ἀνάστασιν μέλλειν ἔσεσθαι δικαίων τε καὶ ἀδίκων). Paul's third argument in refuting the charge that he is a criminal ringleader is an affirmation of his belief in the resurrection of the dead. A foundational belief of his faith in Israel's God, which he shares with the Jewish people, is the hope that the dead will rise. The term translated "hope" (ἐλπίς) denotes "the looking forward to something with some reason for confidence respecting fulfillment."[41] The basis for the expectation of a resurrection of the dead is a set of passages in Scripture.[42]

Paul goes on to claim that his accusers share his belief in and expectation of the resurrection of the dead. If Ananias or any of the other accusers shared the Sadducean rejection of the belief in the (literal) resurrection of the dead, Paul might be challenging them with his assertion in v. 15b to enter into a theological debate (as in the Sanhedrin, cf. 23:6–10). This would demonstrate beyond doubt to the governor that the dispute was indeed about theological matters and questions related to the interpretation of the Scriptures.

Belief in the resurrection of the righteous and the unrighteous implies belief in the day of judgment, when God will reward the righteous (δίκαιοι) and punish the unrighteous (ἄδικοι; cf. Dan 12:2).[43] This description of the judgment day implies a warning to his accusers, whose charges Paul regards as false: Exod 23:1 LXX stipulates that one must "not accept a groundless report" and "not consent with the unjust person to be an unjust witness [μάρτυς ἄδικος]"; Lev 19:15 warns not to act unjustly (ἄδικον) in matters of judgment, demanding to judge fellow Israelites with justice (ἐν

---

39. Barrett, *Acts*, 1104.
40. Cf. Keener, "Rhetorical Techniques," 240–41.
41. BDAG, s.v. ἐλπίς 1.
42. Cf. Ps 49:15; Hos 6:1–3; 13:14; Isa 26:19; Ezek 37:1–14;

Dan 12:1–3; see also Pss 16:8–11; 22:15, 22–31; 73:18–20, 23–27; 104:29–30; Job 33:15–30.
43. In the New Testament see John 5:28–29; Rev 20:12–13.

δικαιοσύνη); and Deut 19:15 – 21 stipulates that an "malicious witness" (μάρτυς ἄδικος; 19:16, 18) shall be executed.

Paul's affirmation of the hope of the resurrection of the dead, which disproves the accusation that he is the leader of a new sect whose teachings contradict the faith of the fathers, provides at the same time a transition to the refutation of Tertullus's first charge, that Paul is an enemy of the Jewish people fomenting rebellion. Paul believes there is a difference between right and wrong, just and unjust, and he will not do anything that would render the day of resurrection of the dead, for him, a day of judgment for having acted against God's people.

24:16 Therefore always I do my best to have a clear conscience before God and before people (ἐν τούτῳ καὶ αὐτὸς ἀσκῶ ἀπρόσκοπον συνείδησιν ἔχειν πρὸς τὸν θεὸν καὶ τοὺς ἀνθρώπους διὰ παντός). The refutation of Tertullus's first charge (vv. 16 – 18) begins with Paul's affirmation that he docs his best to have a clear conscience. The adjective translated as "clear" (ἀπρόσκοπον) can denote "not causing offense," in which case is Paul asserting that the purpose of his consistent endeavor to live his life before God and the people consists in his effort to make sure that his conscience (συνείδησις; see on 23:1) will not accuse him of transgressing God's commands or sinning against the people. The adjective can also denote "being without fault because of not giving offense, undamaged, blameless," which suggests the point that Paul's conscience guides him unfailingly in his relationships with God and people.

The reference to both God and "people"[44] underlines the seriousness of Paul's affirmation: because of the reality of the resurrection of the dead

and of the coming day of judgment, he is absolutely honest as regards his past behavior. The expression "always" demonstrates the consistency of his behavior. His faith in the God of the fathers (v. 14b), his commitment to the Law and the Prophets (v. 14e-g), and his belief in the resurrection (v. 15) do not allow for any exceptions in which God's will or the welfare of the people are not the criterion of his behavior — nor does the fact that he is a follower of Jesus (v. 14c).

24:17 After an absence of several years, I came to bring alms to my nation and to present offerings (δι᾽ ἐτῶν δὲ πλειόνων ἐλεημοσύνας ποιήσων εἰς τὸ ἔθνος μου παρεγενόμην καὶ προσφοράς). The second point of Paul's refutation of Tertullus's charge that Paul is an enemy of the Jewish people and a man who foments rebellion addresses the purpose of his visit to Jerusalem. Paul asserts that he was absent from Jerusalem for several years, implying perhaps that his activities over many years were outside of the jurisdiction of either the Sanhedrin or the governor of Judea. The period between his last visit to Jerusalem (18:22) in AD 51 and his most recent visit (21:17) in AD 57 lasted six years, or in Jewish reckoning seven years, if the years of these two visits are both counted as full years.[45]

Paul came to Jerusalem not to organize a riot but in order to offer alms.[46] The term translated as "alms" (ἐλεημοσύναι) refers to benevolent giving, generally of money, to meet a specific or a general need. The recipient of the alms is "my nation" (τὸ ἔθνος μου), i.e., for the benefit of the Jewish people. Most commentators see this statement as a veiled reference to the collection Paul had organized in the churches he had established.[47] If so, the expression "my nation" refers specifically to the Jewish

---

44. NRSV and TNIV translate "all people," which goes beyond the formulation of the text but fits the intended meaning.

45. Seven years are indeed "many" years in the life of a person, in antiquity more so than today.

46. The future participle (ποιήσων) expresses purpose.

47. Cf. 1 Cor 16:1 – 4; 2 Cor 8 – 9; Rom 15:25 – 28, 31; cf. Gal 2:10 (the famine relief visit described in Acts 11:27 – 30, completed in Acts 12:25, is unrelated to v. 17).

believers in the Jerusalem church. Luke's reticence in including a fuller description of the collection may find its explanation in the possibility "that at Paul's trial it was misrepresented as an improper diversion of money that ought to have swelled the Jerusalem temple tax, and Luke judged it wise to refer to it only in the most general terms."[48] The bringing of alms to Jerusalem was not a crime;[49] rather, it demonstrated Paul's loyalty to the Jewish people.

The third argument of Paul's refutation of Tertullus's first charge addresses more specifically the purpose of his visit to the temple in whose outer court he had been arrested. Paul explains that he came to present (sacrificial) offerings (προσφοραί) in connection with the purification of the four Jewish Christian men (21:26, where the singular ἡ προσφορά is used); i.e., he paid the expenses for the sacrifices that the four men had to offer (21:23 – 24). Neither the purpose of his visit to the temple nor his activities there posed any threat to anybody.

24:18 While I was doing this, they found me in the temple, ritually pure, without any crowd or disturbance (ἐν αἷς εὗρόν με ἡγνισμένον ἐν τῷ ἱερῷ οὐ μετὰ ὄχλου οὐδὲ μετὰ θορύβου). Paul's fourth argument in refuting Tertullus's charge that Paul was an enemy of the Jewish people and a man causing riots affirms that when he was in the temple presenting offerings, he was in a state of ritual purity (ἡγνισμένον; perfect participle). Purification rites, which generally consisted in ritual immersion in an immersion pool (*miqweh*), were necessary not only for Jewish pilgrims coming from abroad but for any Jew who had attracted various kinds of im-

purity. For the ritual purity in view here see 21:24, 26. Paul cannot be accused of profaning the temple or even of having attempted to desecrate the temple, as his accusers allege (v. 6).

Paul's fifth and final argument is the affirmation that he was quite innocuous when he was involved in presenting offerings in a state of purity. When the Jews "found" him in the temple, he was neither surrounded by "any crowd" nor stationed close to a "disturbance." The fact that there was both a crowd and a disturbance (cf. 21:34) was a subsequent development that had nothing to do with his activities in the temple; he was worshiping and presenting offerings, not organizing a crowd or causing a disturbance.

24:19 There are some Jews from the province of Asia, however, who ought to be here before you and bring charges, if they have anything against me (τινὲς δὲ ἀπὸ τῆς Ἀσίας Ἰουδαῖοι, οὓς ἔδει ἐπὶ σοῦ παρεῖναι καὶ κατηγορεῖν εἴ τι ἔχοιεν πρὸς ἐμέ). Paul's conclusion (*peroratio*) in vv. 19 – 21 emphasizes three points. First, Paul protests that the people who should be accusing him are Jews from the province of Asia. This is a major weakness of the case of Tertullus and the Sanhedrin. They cannot produce the Jews who were eyewitnesses to his presence in the temple, who accused him of teaching against the Jewish people and of desecrating the temple, starting the commotion that eventually led to his arrest (cf. 21:27 – 36).

If Paul is indeed guilty of subversive activities throughout the (Jewish) world, these Jews from another province — and there were only "some" (τινές) of them — must be present in these legal proceedings. They are the ones who should be

---

48. Bruce, *Book of Acts*, 445. Pervo, *Acts*, 599, points to Felix's expectation to receive money from Paul (v. 26) as an explanation for Luke's breaking his silence concerning the collection: "people who could afford to make generous contributions to the temple could also give concrete form to their gratitude

for the just decisions of local rulers."

49. Cf. Keith F. Nickle, *The Collection: A Study in Paul's Strategy* (Studies in Biblical Theology 48; London: SCM, 1966), 83 – 84, who points out that the Romans provided armed escorts for Jewish collections.

bringing charges, something they would do in the hypothetical case that they have anything against Paul. Their absence may indicate that they have withdrawn their charges — that Paul was teaching everywhere against the Jewish people (the charge that Ananias and the other Jerusalem officials had taken over), and the charge that Paul had desecrated the temple by bringing Greeks into the temple (21:27 – 28).

Paul hopes to achieve three goals with this statement. (1) He questions the credentials of Tertullus, Ananias, and the other members of the delegation who were not present when the commotion in the temple occurred, which led to his arrest. (2) He puts forward a sound technical objection:[50] accusers must face the accused in person during the legal proceedings that they have initiated. (3) He emphasizes again (cf. v. 13) that the charges against him cannot be proven. At the same time it should be noted that the protest regarding the absence of the original eyewitnesses is not the central point of Paul's legal strategy; he does not insist on redressing the procedural problem, but accepts the verdict of the Sanhedrin, as vv. 20 – 21 demonstrate.[51]

24:20 Or else let these men here tell what crime they had found when I stood before the Sanhedrin (ἢ αὐτοὶ οὗτοι εἰπάτωσαν τί εὗρον ἀδίκημα στάντος μου ἐπὶ τοῦ συνεδρίου). Second, Paul protests that there is no proof of a crime he might have committed in Jerusalem. Since the eyewitnesses of the original charges against Paul are absent, Paul invites Ananias the high priest and the other Jewish officials to introduce the accusation of an actual "crime" (ἀδίκημα) committed in Jerusalem. Paul summarizes the results of the hearing before the Sanhedrin (22:30 – 23:11), whose members had

not found any crime of which he was guilty and for which he would need to be punished.

This "invitation" to Ananias and others, expressed with third person plural imperative (εἰπάτωσαν), implies that all previous charges cannot be proven and that if they want the governor to convict him of a crime, they would have to come up with new charges. Paul insists that Ananias and the other Jewish officials must limit their charges to matters established (or not established) during the examination before the Sanhedrin that Claudius Lysias, the governor's commander in Jerusalem, had permitted. Since this hearing was the first time Paul had encountered the high priest Ananias and (presumably) the other Jewish officials present in Caesarea, he demands that they limit their role as accusers or witnesses to the events that transpired during the hearing in Jerusalem.

24:21 Unless it was this one declaration that I called out when I stood before them, "It is on account of the resurrection of the dead that I am on trial before you today" (ἢ περὶ μιᾶς ταύτης φωνῆς ἧς ἐκέκραξα ἐν αὐτοῖς ἑστὼς ὅτι περὶ ἀναστάσεως νεκρῶν ἐγὼ κρίνομαι σήμερον ἐφ᾽ ὑμῶν). Third, Paul asserts that there is only one possible charge that Ananias and other members of the Sanhedrin can bring: the single declaration that he uttered when he stood before them that he believed in the resurrection of the dead. The quotation in v. 21d-e reproduces 23:6; the omission of "hope" does not change the meaning, because belief in a future resurrection of the dead is always a hope, while the addition of "today" (σήμερον) emphasizes the face-to-face encounter of Paul and the Sanhedrin.

Paul insists, in other words, that his case involved not political but only Jewish religious

---

50. Cf. Winter, "Official Proceedings," 326. An accuser's failure to produce witnesses before court could be used by the defense to challenge the veracity of the charges.

51. Cf. Omerzu, *Prozess*, 449, who also points out that the

Sanhedrin may have had the right to appear as the official body that had the authority to make representations to the Roman governor, in particular in connection with sacrilegious acts against the temple (cf. ibid. 393 – 94).

questions, a point that agrees with the assessment of Claudius Lysias, the Roman commander in Jerusalem (23:29). Paul's legal strategy is to reduce his charges to a single theological charge. This is not simply a clever tactical move. Felix may have known that the Sanhedrin was divided over the issue of the reality of a future resurrection of the dead, and he may have to admit that he is not competent to render a judgment on such a question. Paul insists that all accusations against him are connected in a fundamental manner with his commitment to the "Way" (v. 14), i.e., to Jesus as Israel's crucified, risen, and exalted Messiah and Savior.

24:22 Then Felix, who was well-informed about the Way, adjourned the proceedings. "When Lysias the commander comes down," he said, "I will decide your case" (ἀνεβάλετο δὲ αὐτοὺς ὁ Φῆλιξ, ἀκριβέστερον εἰδὼς τὰ περὶ τῆς ὁδοῦ εἴπας· ὅταν Λυσίας ὁ χιλίαρχος καταβῇ, διαγνώσομαι τὰ καθ᾽ ὑμᾶς). The fifth incident of Luke's report about Paul's trial before Felix relates the governor's response to the speeches of the accusers (Tertullus) and of the defendant (Paul). The governor has three options: (1) to convict Paul of the serious crimes that Tertullus has accused him of, ordering his summary execution; (2) to release Paul and dismiss the case in view of the absence of eyewitnesses for the serious charge of sedition; (3) to adjourn the meeting in order to gather more facts before deciding the case. Felix chooses the third option. The text suggests two reasons for the adjournment.

(1) Felix is well-informed about "the Way" (see on 5:11; 9:2), i.e., about the movement of the followers of Jesus. This statement may imply that Felix is aware that Christians were not causing riots and presented no political problem for the government

of the province of Judea, a fact that would suggest that Tertullus's case is weak if not entirely spurious.[52] This does not mean, however, that Felix was legally required to release Paul. The proceedings of a *cognitio extra ordinem* give him ample discretion to gather further evidentiary material or to summon more witnesses.

The comment that Felix is "well-informed" about the Christian movement can be explained with reference not only to his wife Drusilla, who was Jewish (v. 24) and who would have been informed about Jesus' followers, but also with reference to Felix's political and administrative responsibilities in the province of Judea, which included the city of Jerusalem, where thousands of Jews had become followers of Jesus (cf. 21:20), meeting in public and in private as well as the capital Caesarea (21:8 – 9).[53] On a literary level, the comment shows Luke's readers that the favorable judgments of representatives of highest Roman officials about the Christians attesting their political innocuousness are grounded in fact.

(2) Felix promises a judicial decision after he has heard Claudius Lysias, his commander in Jerusalem. Lysias had communicated to Felix his evaluation of Paul's case as concerning Jewish religious matters that did not warrant his execution or imprisonment (23:29). Since Felix's concern had to be the maintenance of good relations with the Jewish leaders of his province, and since Tertullus's charges went beyond the points that Lysias had made in his letter to the governor, he wants to hear Lysias in person, presumably since he is (for Felix) the only independent eyewitness to what transpired in the temple courts at the time of Paul's arrest.

Luke does not report Lysias's appearance before Felix. Since it is implausible that such a meeting

---

52. Cf. Rapske, *Paul in Roman Custody*, 164; Omerzu, *Prozess*, 452.

53. There is no reason to doubt that "the historical Felix" had accurate (ἀκριβῶς) information about the Christian movement; cf. Dunn, *Beginning from Jerusalem*, 982, who argues that "an effective procurator would have agents and spies everywhere."

never took place, the reader has to assume either that the interview was of little help to the governor or, if Lysias confirmed Paul's innocence of the charges against him, Felix preferred to keep Paul in custody for the reasons mentioned in vv. 26 – 27. Felix does not want to acquit Paul because it could lead to political troubles.

Since the high priest had taken the trouble to travel from Jerusalem to Caesarea to accuse Paul of capital crimes, Felix would have to have good reasons for going against the powerbrokers of the province for whose order he was responsible. His immediate predecessor, Ventidius Cumanus, had been deposed and exiled precisely because he had failed to administer Judea in sympathetic cooperation with the Jewish officials.[54] Dismissing the case against Paul, throwing out the legal arguments of the highest representatives of Judea, was thus problematic, particularly when "Tertullus's opening remarks reminded him of the link between responsible administration of law and Jewish gratitude and passivity. Felix's awareness of the Jews' power to do him well or ill as he left office compelled him to do them the favour of leaving Paul incarcerated."[55]

At the same time, condemning Paul and ordering his summary execution was also problematic. Since Paul was a leader of the followers of Jesus whose base was in Jerusalem, the tensions in Judea may spread to new segments of the population. Moreover, since Paul had been active among their adherents in many cities outside of Judea, there was the prospect of potential unrest in other provinces, which, if traced back to his decision in the case against Paul, might harm his standing in the Roman imperial administration, particularly considering the fact that Paul was a Roman citizen. It was thus politically expedient to defer a decision in the case.

The fact that Paul is kept in custody confirms that the original charge that Paul had desecrated the temple by bringing pagans into the sacred enclosure (cf. 21:28) had been changed to the charge of fomenting disturbances in the context of an *attempted* desecration of the temple (24:6). This charge did not require the presence of the Jews from the province of Asia who had initially seized Paul, since the tumult in the temple courts was witnessed by a larger number of people, among them Jews from Jerusalem (cf. 21:31).[56]

24:23 Then he ordered the centurion to keep him under guard, but to let him have some freedom and not to prevent any of his friends from taking care of his needs (διαταξάμενος τῷ ἑκατοντάρχῃ τηρεῖσθαι αὐτὸν ἔχειν τε ἄνεσιν καὶ μηδένα κωλύειν τῶν ἰδίων αὐτοῦ ὑπηρετεῖν αὐτῷ). The last incident relates the terms of Paul's imprisonment in Caesarea. Felix issues an order on the the terms of Paul's custody. (1) He is to be kept under guard (τηρεῖσθαι).[57] The fact that a centurion (see on 10:1) is charged with guarding Paul rather than lower-ranking soldiers or the personnel running the prison attests to Felix's acknowledgment of the status of Paul, both as a leader of the movement of Jesus' followers and as a Roman citizen.

Paul's Roman citizenship had evidently not come up during the trial; however, since it had been mentioned in Lysias's letter to the governor (23:27), which would have been known to Paul as part of the trial documents, Paul could be confident that Felix knew about this. The governor evidently "wished Paul to be healthily preserved for

---

54. Josephus, *Ant.* 20.118 – 136.

55. Rapske, *Paul in Roman Custody*, 165; for the following see ibid., 165 – 66.

56. Cf. Omerzu, *Prozess*, 451.

57. For this verb (τηρέω) in sense of "retain in custody" see 12:5 – 6 (Peter in Jerusalem); 16:23 (Paul and Silas in Philippi), and later in 25:4, 21 (Paul in Caesarea).

the longer term from the predictable vagaries of military custody."[58]

(2) Paul is granted some freedom while in custody. In contrast to the first five days of Paul's custody in Caesarea, during which he was evidently placed under strict constraint (23:35), the terms of his custody are being relaxed. Felix orders the centurion to let Paul have some "freedom" (ἄνεσις).[59] Since it was expected that prisoners in military custody were manacled, "typically to their soldier-guards and especially when they were in open places," the lower level of vigilance given the relaxed terms of Paul's imprisonment "almost require Paul to be chained for proper security."[60] The place of Paul's custody was probably Herod's former palace.

Luke mentions two specific details of the relaxed terms of custody that Paul is granted. The centurion may not prevent Paul's friends (οἱ ἴδιοι; lit., "his own people," i.e., Christians) from visiting him. In view of 21:8 – 9 and 21:16, Luke surely wants his readers to think of the evangelist Philip and his four daughters as well as other Caesarean believers who had assisted Paul just a couple of weeks before his arrest. The governor expects Paul's friends to care for his basic needs in terms of physical sustenance. The verb "taking care of his needs" (ὑπηρετεῖν) denotes "to render service, be helpful" and describes in a prison context the provisions of food, clothing, and, perhaps (since Paul was a teacher and author) books and writing materials.

This arrangement may indicate that Felix intends to keep Paul in custody for an extended period of time. Since Paul's clothing suffered in the riot in the temple court (21:30 – 32) and in the Roman soldiers' preparation for his flogging (22:24 – 25), he probably required new garments. Since Paul is not in free or open custody (*custodia libera*) but in military custody (*custodia militaris*) — still an advantage compared to public custody (*custodia publica*) in an ordinary prison — it is not likely that Paul would be given access to the bathing facilities in Caesarea, and it is doubtful that he was permitted regular haircuts.[61]

24:24 Several days later Felix came with his wife, Drusilla, who was Jewish; he sent for Paul and heard him speak about faith in the Messiah Jesus (μετὰ δὲ ἡμέρας τινὰς παραγενόμενος ὁ Φῆλιξ σὺν Δρουσίλλῃ τῇ ἰδίᾳ γυναικὶ οὔσῃ Ἰουδαίᾳ μετεπέμψατο τὸν Παῦλον καὶ ἤκουσεν αὐτοῦ περὶ τῆς εἰς Χριστὸν Ἰησοῦν πίστεως). The second episode of this section about Paul's imprisonment in Caesarea during the governorship of Felix (vv. 24 – 27) begins with a report on the private conversations between Paul and Felix (vv. 24 – 26). A few days after the trial, Felix comes to visit Paul, accompanied by his wife, Drusilla.

Felix "sends" (μετεπέμψατο) for Paul because he wants to "hear" (ἤκουσεν) him speak. The aorist tenses here confirm that Luke is speaking of a specific event. While we do not know whether the motivation of receiving a bribe (v. 26) existed from the beginning, it is plausible that a Roman governor displays "a curiosity and intelligent interest in the new doctrine"[62] as presented by one of its main spokesmen. Formulated from the perspective of

---

58. Cf. Rapske, *Paul in Roman Custody*, 168; for the conditions of life in prison see ibid., 195 – 225, with evidence for "the debilitation, illness, suffering and death which were so often a part of prison life" (221).

59. The basic meaning of ἄνεσις is "loosening, relaxing" (LSJ) and denotes here the "relaxation of custodial control" (BDAG).

60. Rapske, *Paul in Roman Custody*, 169. Note that in 26:29 Paul appears before Festus and Agrippa in chains.

61. Cf. Rapske, *Paul in Roman Custody*, 171 – 72, 219.

62. William M. Ramsay, *The Church in the Roman Empire before A.D. 170* (orig. 1893; repr., Boston: Adamant, 2004), 133; Tajra, *Trial*, 131.

both Luke and Paul, the topic of the conversation is described as "faith in the Messiah Jesus."

While v. 25 specifies three topics of conversation, this comment reflects the main concern of any conversation that Paul would have with Gentiles (Felix) or Jews (Drusilla), fulfilling his calling given to him by Jesus on the road to Damascus: speaking about and leading people to come to faith in Jesus as Israel's Messiah and as the Savior of both Jews and Gentiles. This description indicates that Paul seeks to convert the governor and his wife to faith in Jesus (cf. v. 25) and demonstrates that Paul's testimony reaches the highest social levels.[63]

24:25 As Paul discussed righteousness, self-control, and the coming judgment, Felix became alarmed and said, "Leave for now. When I find an opportunity, I will send for you" (διαλεγομένου δὲ αὐτοῦ περὶ δικαιοσύνης καὶ ἐγκρατείας καὶ τοῦ κρίματος τοῦ μέλλοντος, ἔμφοβος γενόμενος ὁ Φῆλιξ ἀπεκρίθη· τὸ νῦν ἔχον πορεύου, καιρὸν δὲ μεταλαβὼν μετακαλέσομαί σε). Luke specifies three themes that Paul discusses with the governor in terms that would remind some of his readers of philosophical debates — terms, however, that described important realities in Jewish thought and in Paul's missionary proclamation.

"Righteousness" (δικαιοσύνη) suggests the double meaning of proper behavior in an ethical sense (Lat. *aequitas*) (10:35; 13:10) and justice in a forensic sense (Lat. *iustitia*), and the fulfillment of obligations placed on individuals by God, whose righteous judgment will reward those who practice righteousness and condemn those who behave unjustly (Cf. 17:31; Rom 3:5).

"Self-control" (ἐγκράτεια)[64] refers to a person's mastery of his or her pleasures and desires, which in Greek and Roman tradition can be achieved by self-discipline, but which in Jewish tradition requires God's power[65] and in Paul's teaching is the work of God's Spirit in the life of believers.[66]

The "coming judgment" (τὸ κρίμα τὸ μέλλον) is hardly a reference to the lawsuit and Felix's future decision or to the possibility that Felix may be required by the emperor to give an account of his judicial verdict in Paul's case. Rather, it refers more plausibly to the day of judgment, when God will either reward or condemn people for their behavior.[67]

After explaining Jesus' identity as the promised Savior, Paul challenges Felix and Drusilla in moral terms, confronting them with the need to evaluate their personal behavior, with the reality of God's judgment, and with the need to come to faith in Jesus, who alone can save from the guilt of past and present moral failures. Luke does not paint Paul "as a courageous philosopher who does not pull his punches"[68] but as an intelligent and courageous missionary, who speaks to the highest representative of the Roman Empire in terms that are understandable for a Roman trained in popular philosophy while speaking without ideological compromise about the day of judgment and about the need to come to faith in Jesus as Israel's Messiah.

Felix becomes "alarmed" (ἔμφοβος) when he hears Paul's explanation of the coming judgment,

---

63. Cf. Dunn, *Beginning from Jerusalem*, 982, and Bock, *Acts*, 695, respectively. Note that Luke omits from his gospel the private hearings between Herod Antipas — who had also "stolen" another man's wife — and John the Baptist (Mark 6:20), a narrative that also includes women (Herodias and her daughter), albeit with a much more sinister role (Mark 6:19, 20 – 25).

64. BDAG, s.v. ἐγκράτεια, "restraint of one's emotions, impulses, or desires, *self-control*." Cf. Aristotle, *Eth. nic.*

7.1145A – 1154B; Plato, *Resp.* 390B, 430C.

65. Cf. *Let. Aris.* 277 – 728.

66. Gal 5:23; cf. 1 Cor 7:9; 9:25; Titus 1:8; also 2 Pet 1:6.

67. Cf. Acts 17:31. Note the reference to the coming wrath of God in Paul's summary of his missionary proclamation in 1 Thess 1:9 – 10.

68. Pervo, *Acts*, 604.

given his rapacity, greed, and lust.[69] He adjourns the meeting, dismissing him "for now." He promises to find another "opportunity" (καιρός) to "send" for him. Felix is unwilling to commit to faith in Jesus. But further contacts with Paul are motivated not by the desire to receive further clarification about faith in Jesus and God's judgment but by opportunistic motives.

24:26 At the same time he hoped that Paul would give him money, and so he sent for him frequently and conversed with him (ἅμα καὶ ἐλπίζων ὅτι χρήματα δοθήσεται αὐτῷ ὑπὸ τοῦ Παύλου· διὸ καὶ πυκνότερον αὐτὸν μεταπεμπόμενος ὡμίλει αὐτῷ). Felix fulfills his promise to Paul. He sends for him frequently and "converses" with him. Luke does not comment on the content of the conversations. But the reference to money (χρήματα; cf. 8:18) suggests he may have spoken with Paul about his international contacts and the alms, i.e., the collection, he had taken to Jerusalem (cf. v. 17). Roman law, in particular the *Lex Iulia de pecuniis repetundis* of 59 BC, prohibited the taking of bribes,[70] but governors sometimes chose to ignore this law.

Josephus relates that Felix bribed the best friend of Jonathan the high priest to arrange for the *sicarii* to murder Jonathan.[71] Lucceius Albinus, Festus's successor as governor of Judea from AD 62 – 65, took bribes.[72] Felix evidently expects Paul to give him money to get a quicker trial or even a favorable verdict, assuming "that Paul was materially well off, or at least that Paul could gain access, as leader of an Empire-wide Jewish movement based in Jerusalem, to considerable financial resources."[73] Paul remains in custody for two years (v. 27) because of his principled resistance to the possibility of offering bribes, accepting the delay of the legal proceedings and the prevention of an early release.

24:27 After two years had passed, Felix was succeeded by Porcius Festus. Since he wanted to grant the Jews a favor, Felix left him in prison (διετίας δὲ πληρωθείσης ἔλαβεν διάδοχον ὁ Φῆλιξ Πόρκιον Φῆστον, θέλων τε χάριτα καταθέσθαι τοῖς Ἰουδαίοις ὁ Φῆλιξ κατέλιπε τὸν Παῦλον δεδεμένον). Luke concludes the episode by noting that Felix leaves Paul "in prison" (δεδεμένον; lit., "as a prisoner") for two years[74] because he wants to grant the Jews a "favor" (χάρις).[75] The long period of incarceration because of the official delaying tactic of Felix demonstrates the success of the strategy of the Jewish leaders to accuse Paul not of religious crimes but of the political crime of *seditio*, which was so serious that the governor could not easily dismiss it by releasing Paul.[76]

---

69. Cf. Steve Mason, *Josephus and the New Testament* (2nd ed.; Peabody, MA: Hendrickson, 2003), 177: "Paul's discussion of justice, self-control, and coming judgment seems to have been carefully tailored to the governor's situation … the narrative of Acts almost *assumes* knowledge of an account such as Josephus's" (emphasis Mason).

70. Cf. Olivia F. Robinson, *The Criminal Law of Ancient Rome* (Baltimore: Johns Hopkins Univ. Press, 1995), 81 – 82. The law forbade all enrichments by senatorial officials (with some exceptions; e.g., governors were allowed to accept money for building temples or monuments).

71. Josephus, *Ant.* 20.163. Luke's depiction of Felix expecting a bribe is thus "quite in character" (Dunn, *Beginning from Jerusalem*, 983).

72. Josephus, *J.W.* 2.273.

73. Rapske, *Paul in Roman Custody*, 167; for the next comment cf. ibid., 320.

74. The "two years" do not refer to a statute of limitations called the *biennium*, which required the termination of the legal case against Paul due to the nonappearance of Paul's accusers in Caesarea.

75. Cf. BDAG, s.v. χάρις 3, "practical application of goodwill, *(a sign of) favor, gracious deed/gift, benefaction*." The present tense of the causal participle "wanted" (θέλων) indicates that Luke refers not to a particular decision of Felix at the end of his tenure but to the entire period of the two years: Felix could have concluded the proceedings against Paul, but continued to delay a final verdict in order to please the Jews.

76. Cf. Omerzu, *Prozess*, 463.

It also demonstrates the depth of the hatred of the Jewish leaders in Jerusalem for Paul, who evidently continue to make representations to Felix concerning Paul. Thus, Paul's long incarceration confirms, by implication, his significance, whose continued imprisonment clearly has high currency in the eyes of the Jewish leadership.

Felix was recalled as governor of Judea in AD 59 when leaders of the Jewish community in Caesarea went to Rome accusing him of maladministration. This followed an incident in Caesarea where the Jews had claimed that Caesarea belonged to them, while the Greeks used the (pagan) temples that Herod had erected as proof that Caesarea was not a Jewish city. Felix ended the ensuing riots in the agora by sending in his troops, who killed many Jews, and Felix subsequently plundered their property. Both the Jewish and Greek communities of Caesarea sent their leaders to Rome. Felix was spared serious punishment by the emperor Nero only because Felix's influential brother Pallas pleaded for him.[77] If "the Jews" (οἱ Ἰουδαῖοι) are the Jewish leaders in Jerusalem, the circumstances of Felix's recall indicate, perhaps, that Felix's eagerness to curry favor with the Jews by leaving Paul in custody was successful. Felix was replaced by Porcius Festus, who was governor from AD 59–62.

Theology in Application

In light of the other Christians that Luke had been writing about, such as Peter and James or Barnabas and Philip, Luke's report about Paul's trial before Felix and about his subsequent two-year imprisonment in Caesarea focuses exclusively on Paul. For Luke, the expansion of the messianic movement of believers in Jesus as Israel's Savior beyond the Jewish communities to Gentiles was so much tied up with Paul's missionary work that he wants his readers to understand, beyond any doubt, how Paul fits into his story of Jesus and the fulfillment of God's promises in and through the new messianic community established in Jerusalem and then quickly expanded to many other cities of the Roman Empire.[78] This is why he does not pass over Paul's trial and imprisonment with a line or two,[79] but provides extensive reports on Paul's imprisonment in Caesarea. He wants his readers to see the answer to the question how Paul, who was not one of the Twelve, continued the work of Jesus and of the apostles.

Moreover, Luke wants his readers to understand the nature of the opposition to Paul in particular but also to the messianic movement of believers in Jesus more generally, both from the side of the Jewish authorities and from Roman officials. As Luke reports on the only true trial of Paul, with accusers and Paul each giving speeches and a judge merely adjourning the hearing, and on the years of custody in Caesarea, he illuminates Paul's commitment to the gospel and his integrity in terms of legal and financial matters. At the same time, the other characters — the high priest Ananias,

---

77. Josephus, J.W. 2.270; Ant. 20.182.

78. For this and the following comments see Johnson, Acts, 415.

79. Note the brief summary of Paul's ministry of one and a half years in Corinth in 18:11, and the brief summary of his two-year ministry in Ephesus in 19:10.

the lawyer Tertullus, the governor Felix — are not mere foils for his depiction of Paul, but protagonists in a struggle that has significance way beyond Judea and beyond the life of Paul, who will explain the gospel of Jesus Christ in Rome, the center of the empire. The following points are important.

Facing Dangerous Enemies

God's people may face dangerous enemies. The Jewish leadership of Jerusalem displays consistent hostility to Paul. The high priest Ananias and other representatives of the Jewish aristocracy evidently do not mind obeying the summons of Claudius Lysias, the Roman commander of the military garrison in Jerusalem, to appear in Caesarea within a few days of Paul's arrest and transfer to the "foreign" political capital of Judea (23:30; 24:1). They do not wait for a personal invitation from the governor, but travel from Jerusalem to Caesarea to confront Paul. In order to ensure they get their desired outcome — the summary execution of Paul — they hire a lawyer with the proper legal and rhetorical expertise to get results.

The appearance of Ananias the high priest, other members of the Jerusalem leadership, and a trained lawyer in Caesarea spells trouble for Paul. Their legal strategy is shrewd. Rather than accusing Paul of religious offenses, they focus on two political charges that, taken together, accuse Paul of sedition, a charge that no Roman governor can afford to dismiss, particularly in a province where insurrection and banditry were "the principal plague of the country" (Josephus, *J.W.* 2.271). The transposition of the accusation that Paul profaned the temple by taking a Greek into the sacred enclosure into the accusation of an attempted desecration of the temple renders a defense more difficult, as innocence of motivation is more arduous to prove. As Paul's life is at stake, the stakes have been raised both rhetorically and legally.

Christians learn from Luke's report that they may find themselves facing formidable enemies who want to harm them, who know what they are doing, and who do everything in their power to get what they want. God's presence in the messianic community of believers in Jesus does not exempt its members, particularly if they are leading missionaries and teachers, from facing dangerous (religious) enemies — sometimes from within the church — whose legal actions may result in imprisonment and even cost them their lives. A modern-day example is the involvement of leaders of the YMCA in Beijing in accusing Chinese Christian leaders such as Wang Mingdao (1900 – 1991).[80] The YMCA in China had become, in the spring of

---

80. In particular Wu Yaozong (Y. T. Wu), the head of the publications department of the YMCA in Shanghai. Cf. Thomas Alan Harvey, *Acquainted with Grief: Wang Mingdao's Stand for the Persecuted Church in China* (Grand Rapids: Brazos, 2002), 69 – 91. Philip L. Wickeri, *Reconstructing Christianity in China: K. H. Ting and the Chinese Church* (American Society of Missiology 41; Maryknoll, NY: Orbis, 2007), 119 – 21, describes how Ting Kuang-hsun (K. H. Ting), a former Anglican theologian and head of the Three-Self Patriotic Movement (TSPM), was at the center of the attacks against Wang Mingdao in the 1950s, leading to Wang's imprisonment for twenty years, and acknowledges that Wang's life, witness, and imprisonment "cast a shadow over the history of Christianity in that period" (121), but he fails to acknowledge that

1949, a springboard for China's communists in their efforts to control the Protestant churches.[81]

Defense with Legal Competence and Personal Integrity

Authentic witnesses defend themselves with legal competence and personal integrity. With hostile Jewish accusers who seek Paul's execution, a rhetorically trained lawyer who formulates dangerous charges and advances proofs that render a defense more difficult, and a corrupt and a cynical judge who cares more about his career and his personal well-being than about justice, Paul defends himself with competence and integrity. Paul knows his legal rights and puts them to good use (although not "effectively" in the sense that he achieves a not-guilty verdict and his release). He addresses Felix with the polite acknowledgment of his legal expertise as a governor of the province, surely well aware of the problems in Judea and the often less than adequate policies and behavior of Roman officials. He shrewdly argues that his accusers are not eyewitnesses to the events they use as the basis for their accusations; after all, they have not traveled "throughout the world" where he is supposed to have caused riots in the Jewish communities, nor were they present in the temple court when Jews from the province of Asia seized him. Their evidence is hearsay; they cannot prove their case.

The one event of which they were witnesses was the Sanhedrin's hearing where Paul spoke about the resurrection of the dead, a topic he is willing to address again. While Paul's enemies accuse him of being a public enemy of the Jewish people, Paul does not pay them back in kind, accusing them of being God's enemies. Later, when Felix appears willing to allow Paul to resolve the case against him by Paul's paying (presumably substantial) sums of money, he refuses to do so. As Luke describes Paul's experiences in the trial before Felix and during the two-year imprisonment in Caesarea, his readers learn once and for all that "he is not a charlatan but sincere, not a renegade from Judaism, but one faithful to the ancestral customs and beliefs, not a fomenter of unrest, but a prophetic witness to the resurrection, not a cowardly opportunist, but a loyal and obedient disciple whose path of suffering replicates that of Jesus himself."[82] Christians reading Luke's narrative are challenged to know their opponents and their agendas, to know their legal rights and the best way to use them, to argue their case with polite confidence and judicial competence, and to behave in a manner that is above reproach in all respects.

Ting bears personal responsibility for the suffering of Chinese leaders, in the context of the fact that both the theology and the politics of Ting and other Christians were in lockstep with the political demands of the Chinese Community Party.

81. David Aikman, *Jesus in Beijing: How Christianity Is Transforming China and Changing the Global Balance of Power* (Washington: Regnery, 2003), 55.

82. Johnson, *Acts*, 415; see ibid., 415 – 16, for some of the points in the next paragraph.

Theological Competence and Personal Courage

Authentic witnesses confess their faith in Jesus with theological competence and personal courage. Luke describes Paul as a faithful witness, speaking about the fulfillment of the Scriptures in Jesus Christ and about the resurrection of the dead. This is the real issue of the hostility of the Jewish leaders in Jerusalem: the conviction of Paul — and of Peter and James and the other apostles, as Luke has shown in his previous reports — that the movement of followers of Jesus ("the Way") represents the messianic people of God among whom and through whom God fulfills his promises made to the fathers and recorded in Israel's Scriptures (24:14). The accusation that he is a ringleader of the sect of the Nazarenes prompts Paul to confess, with great personal courage, that he indeed belongs to "the Way," which means believing in Jesus as Israel's Messiah and Savior.

Leading Others to Faith in Jesus

Authentic witnesses seek to lead others to faith in Jesus with intellectual competence and missionary zeal. Paul is now moving in the highest circles of the Roman Empire and the province of Judea, having the opportunity to speak before Ananias the high priest, other members of the Jewish aristocracy, Felix the governor, and his wife, Drusilla, the daughter of the last Jewish king. He consistently seeks to lead his conversation partners to faith in Jesus. This is true for his encounters with Felix, though not for the trial where Ananias and the Jerusalem leaders are his mortal enemies and where the only plausible strategy is a legal defense. But in his conversations with Felix, which are initiated by the governor, albeit with mixed motivations, Paul does not hold back, despite his chains. He seeks to bring the Roman governor of Judea to saving faith in Jesus.

If Luke's brief summary of Paul's main points — faith in Jesus the Messiah, righteousness, self-control, the coming judgment — is any indication, Paul combines, as he did in his address to the Areopagus Council in Athens (17:22 – 31), intellectual competence with a determined theological focus and missionary zeal. The topics of righteousness/justice and self-control are areas of philosophical discourse that Felix is familiar with and that Paul evidently is comfortable discussing as well. The topics of faith in Jesus as Israel's Messiah and of the coming judgment demonstrate that Luke presents Paul to his readers not as a Hellenistic philosopher but as a prophetic witness of Jesus, who speaks about God's fulfillment of his promises in sending Jesus into the world and about the need to come to faith in him as the one who saves from sin in view of the coming judgment, when God will raise the righteous and the unrighteous.

When Paul sees that Felix is alarmed about the coming judgment while he addresses the ethical consequences of behavior that is righteous or unrighteous, characterized by self-control or by selfish indulgence of passions, Paul risks the enmity of the governor, which could be deadly. Luke's readers learn here that authentic witnesses are willing to die for their faith in Jesus: because they have a clear conscience before God and before the people (cf. 24:16), because they are committed to faith in God and his revealed Word in Scripture (24:14), because they believe in Jesus as Israel's Messiah and Savior in the coming judgment (24:14, 24), and because they know that God will vindicate them as his people who are true to their calling as witnesses of Jesus.

Acts 25:1 – 26:32

Literary Context

The episode of Paul's imprisonment in Caesarea during the governorship of Porcius Festus is the last of three episodes about Paul's detention in Caesarea (24:1 – 26:32). This episode follows the two episodes in which Luke narrated Paul's trial before governor Antonius Felix (24:1 – 23) and his two-year imprisonment in Caesarea and his conversations with Felix (24:24 – 27). The entire section about Paul in Caesarea stands between the section on Paul in Jerusalem (21:18 – 23:35) and the section on Paul in Rome (27:1 – 28:31). These events took place in the summer of AD 59, when Porcius Festus replaced Antonius Felix as governor of Judea.

Main Idea

While the Jewish leadership continues to work for Paul's physical elimination, plotting another ambush and demanding his execution, and while the new governor acts quickly, decisively, and justly, though not understanding Paul's central beliefs, Paul demonstrates his loyalty to the state by expressing his willingness to be judged by the governor. He fights for his legal rights by appealing to the emperor and explains the gospel of Jesus Christ to the Jewish king Agrippa II. In his last major speech, Paul describes God as the Almighty who raises people from the dead, controls history, wants to save Jews and Gentiles, and helps people in need; and he describes Jesus as the resurrected Lord, who saves people from the consequences of their sins.

Translation

Acts 25:1 – 26:32

1a	Setting: time	Three days
b	Setting: event	after Festus had arrived in the province,
c	Action	**he went up from Caesarea to Jerusalem.**
2a	Character entrance	**The chief priests and**
b	Character entrance	**the leaders of the Jews**
c	Action	**gave him a report**
d	Content	concerning the charges against Paul.
e	Action	**They implored him**
3a	Entreaty	and **requested,**
b	Advantage	as a favor to them
c	Disadvantage	against Paul,
d	Content	that he have him transferred to Jerusalem.
e	Explanation	**They were planning an ambush**
f	Purpose	to kill him on the way.
4a	Response	**Festus replied**
b	Content	that Paul was being held
c	Geographical	at Caesarea and
d	Content	that he himself intended to go there
e	Time	shortly.
5a	Consequence	*"So,"*
b	Action: speech	**he said,**
c	Identification	*"let those of you who have authority*
d	Instruction	*come down*
e	Association	*with me,*
f	Condition	*and if there is anything wrong about the man,*
g	Instruction	*they can bring charges against him."*
6a	Time	After spending
b	Duration	not more than eight or ten days
c	Sphere	among them,
d	Action	**he went down to Caesarea.**
e	Setting: time	The next day
f	Action	**he took his seat on the judicial bench**
g	Action	and **ordered Paul to be brought before him.**
7a	Setting: time	When he arrived,
b	Character entrance	**the Jews**
c	Identification	who had come down from Jerusalem

d	Action	**stood around him**
e	Action	and **brought many serious charges against him,**
f	Description	which they could not prove.
8a	Reaction: speech	**Paul said in his defense,**
b	Negation	*"I have committed no offense*
c	Disadvantage	*against the law of the Jews,*
d	Disadvantage	*or against the temple,*
e	Disadvantage	*or against the emperor."*
9a	Setting: cause	Since Festus wanted to do the Jews a favor,
b	Action: speech	**he asked Paul,**
c	Question	*"Do you want to go up*
d	Place	*to Jerusalem*
e	Purpose	and *be tried there before me concerning these charges?"*
10a	Response: speech	**Paul answered,**
b	Assertion	*"I am now standing before the emperor's court,*
c	Place	*where I should be tried.*
d	Negation	*I have done no wrong to the Jews,*
e	Assertion	*as you know very well.*
11a	Condition	*If, however, I am in the wrong*
b	Condition	*and have committed something deserving death,*
c	Inference	*I do not refuse to die.*
d	Condition (contrast)	*But if there is nothing to their charges against me,*
e	Inference	*no one can hand me over to them.*
f	Petition: appeal	*I appeal to the emperor."*
12a	Time	After Festus had conferred with his council,
b	Response: speech	**he declared,**
c	Assertion	*"You have appealed to the emperor,*
d	Result	*to the emperor you will go."*
13a	Setting: time	After several days had passed,
b	Character entrance	**King Agrippa and**
c	Character entrance	**Bernice**
d	Event	**arrived at Caesarea**
e	Purpose	to pay their respects to Festus.
14a	Cause	Since they were staying there many days,
b	Action	**Festus discussed Paul's case before the king.**
c	Action: speech	**He said,**
d	Assertion	*"There is a man here*
e	Character description	*whom Felix left as a prisoner.*
15a	Report: Time	*When I was in Jerusalem,*
b	Protagonist	*the chief priests and*
c	Protagonist	*the elders of the Jews*
d	Action	*brought charges against him*
e	Demand	and *asked for a guilty verdict against him.*

Continued on next page.

Continued from previous page.

16a	Response	I told them
b	Content	that it was not the custom of the Romans
c	Action	to hand over anyone
d	Condition	before the accused had met the accusers
e	Manner	face-to-face
f	Condition	and before he had the opportunity
g	Purpose	to defend himself ⫷
		against the charge.

17a	Time	When they came back here with me,
b	Action	I did not postpone the case,
c	Action	*but* took my seat on the judicial bench
d	Time	the next day
e	Action	*and* ordered the man to be brought before me.

18a	Time	When his accusers stood up,
b	Action	they did not charge him with any of the crimes
c	Character thoughts	I had expected.
19a	Contra-expectation	Instead, they had certain points of disagreement with him
b	Content	about their own religion and
c	Content	about a certain Jesus,
d	Character description: identification	who had died
e	Contrast	but whom Paul asserted to ⫷ be alive.

20a	Cause	Since I was at a loss
b	Reference	concerning the investigation of these matters,
c	Action	I asked
d	Indirect question	if he would be willing to go to Jerusalem
e	Purpose	and stand trial there on these charges.

21a	Time	But when Paul appealed to be kept in custody
b	Purpose	for the decision of His Majesty the emperor,
c	Action: response	I ordered
d	Content	that he be kept in custody
e	Duration	until I could send him to the emperor."
22a	Response: speech	**Agrippa said to Festus,**
b	Request	"I would like to hear the man myself."
c	Response: speech	**He replied,**
d	Assertion	"Tomorrow you will hear him."

23a	Setting: time	The next day
b	Event	**Agrippa and**
c	Event	**Bernice came with great pageantry,**
d	Action	entering the audience hall
e	Association	with the military commanders and
f	Association	the most prominent men of the city.

g	Action	**Then Festus gave the order**
h	Action	**and Paul was brought in.**
24a	Action: speech	**Festus said,**
b	Address	"King Agrippa and
c		all here present with us,
d	Assertion	you see this man
e	Character description	about whom the entire Jewish community petitioned me
f	Geographical	both in Jerusalem
g	Geographical	and here,
h	Manner	shouting that he ought not to live any longer.
25a	Assertion	But I found
b	Content	that he had done nothing deserving death.
c	Time (cause)	When he appealed to His Majesty the emperor,
d	Decision	I decided to send him.
26a	Assertion	But I have nothing definite to write
b	Reference	to our sovereign about him.
c	Action (consequence)	Therefore I have brought him before all of you,
d	Sphere	and especially before you,
e	Address	King Agrippa,
f	Purpose	so that I may have something to write to our sovereign
g	Time	after we have examined him.
27a	Explanation	For it seems to me unreasonable
b	Action	to send a prisoner
c	Manner	without reporting the charges against him."
26:1a	Action: speech	**Agrippa said to Paul,**
b	Instruction (permission)	"You have permission to speak
c		for yourself."
d	Action	**Then Paul motioned with his hand**
e	Action: speech	**and began to defend himself.**
2a	Assertion	"I consider myself fortunate,
b	Address	King Agrippa,
c	Content	that I can defend myself
d	Time	today
e	Place	before you
f	Conflict	against all the accusations
g	Source	of the Jews,
3a	Cause	because you are especially familiar
b	Object (reference)	with all the customs and
c	Object	controversies
d	Source	of the Jewish people.
e	Entreaty	Therefore I beg you
f	Content	to listen to me
g	Manner	patiently.

Continued on next page.

Continued from previous page.

4a	Assertion	All the Jews know my way of life
b	Time	from my youth,
c	Description	the life which I spent
d	Time	from the beginning
e	Sphere	among my own people and
f	Place	in Jerusalem.
5a	Assertion	They have known me
b	Duration	for a long time,
c	Condition	if they are willing to testify,
d	Content (review of history)	that I have lived
e	Manner	according to the strictest sect of our religion
f	Manner	as a Pharisee.
6a	Assertion (explanation)	I now stand here on trial
b	Cause	on account of my hope
c	Sphere	in the promise
d	Agency	made by God
e	Object	to our ancestors,
7a	Description	a promise that our twelve tribes hope to attain
b	Circumstance	as they worship
c	Manner	with perseverance
d	Time	day and
e	Time	night.
f	Cause	It is because of this hope,
g	Address	King Agrippa,
h	Assertion	that I am accused by the Jews.
8a	Rhetorical question	Why should it be considered unbelievable
b	Agency	by any of you
c	Content	that God raises the dead?
9a	Review of history	I was convinced
b	Action	that I ought to do many things
c	Action	against the name of Jesus of Nazareth.
10a	Action	And that is what I did
b	Place	in Jerusalem;
c	Action	I locked up many of the saints
d	Place	in prison
e	Means	with the authority that I received
f	Source	from the chief priests,
g	Time	And when they were condemned to death,
h	Action	I cast my vote
i	Disadvantage	against them.
11a	Means	By punishing them
b	Time	often
c	Place	in all the synagogues,
d	Action	I tried to force them
e	Purpose	to blaspheme.

f	Action	*And* I was so furiously enraged at them
g	Result	that I pursued them
h	Place	even to foreign cities.
12a	Circumstance	Under these circumstances
b	Action: place	I went to Damascus
c	Means	with the authority and
d	Means	the commission
e	Source	of the chief priests.
13a	Time	At noon,
b	Place	as I was on the road,
c	Address	King Agrippa,
d	Event	I saw a light from heaven,
e	Comparison	brighter than the sun,
f	Sphere	shining around me and
g	Sphere	those who traveled with me.
14a	Event	We all fell to the ground,
b	Event	*and* I heard a voice saying to me
c	Means	in Hebrew,
d	Address	'Saul, Saul,
e	Interrogation	why do you persecute me?
f	Assertion: aphorism	It is hard for you to kick against the goads.'
15a	Response	*Then* I asked,
b	Question	'Who are you, Lord?'
c	Response	The Lord answered,
d	Identification	'I am Jesus,
e	Identification: expansion	whom you are persecuting.
16a	Command	Now get up
b	Command	*and* stand on your feet.
c	Explanation	I have appeared to you
d	Purpose	in order to appoint you as a servant and
e	Description	a witness
f	Object	of what you have seen of me and
g	Object	of what you will be shown.
17a	Promise	I will rescue you
b	Content	from your people and
c	Content	from the Gentiles,
d	Action	to whom I am sending you,
18a	Purpose	to open their eyes
b	Purpose	and to turn them from darkness to light and
c	Explanation	from the power of Satan to God,
d	Purpose	so that they may receive forgiveness of sins and
e	Explanation	a place among those who are sanctified
f	Means	by faith in me.'
19a	Address	*Therefore*, King Agrippa,
b	Negation	I was not disobedient
c	Object	to the heavenly vision,

Continued on next page.

Continued from previous page.

20a	Action	*but* proclaimed
b	Sequence: geographical	first to the people in Damascus,
c	Sequence: geographical	then to the people in Jerusalem and
d	Sphere: geographical	throughout Judea, and
e	Sequence: ethnic	then to the Gentiles
f	Instruction	that they should repent
g	Instruction	and turn to God
h	Instruction	and act in a manner consistent with their repentance.

21a	Explanation	That is why some Jews seized me
b	Place	in the temple
c	Action	*and* tried to kill me.

22a	Contrast	But to this day
b	Assertion	I have received help
c	Source	from God,
d	Assertion (consequence)	*and* so I stand here
e	Assertion	*and* testify to small and
f		great.
g	Assertion	I am saying nothing
h	Sphere	that goes beyond what the prophets and
i		Moses
j	Prophecy	said would take place:
23a	Prophecy: content	that the Messiah would suffer,
b	Prophecy: content	and that he would be the first to rise from the dead,
c	Purpose: geographical	to proclaim light both to his people and
d	Purpose: geographical	to the Gentiles."

24a	Time	When Paul defended himself with these words,
b	Reaction: speech	**Festus exclaimed,**
c	Exclamation	"You are out of your mind, Paul!
d	Exclamation	Your great learning is driving you insane!"
25a	Response: speech	**Paul replied,**
b	Negation	"I am not insane,
c	Address	most excellent Festus.
d	Assertion	What I am declaring is true and
e	Description	reasonable.
26a	Assertion	The king knows about these things,
b	Assertion	*and* I am speaking openly to him.
c	Assertion	I am certain
d	Content	that none of these things have escaped his notice,
e	Cause	for this did not take place in a corner.
27a	Address	King Agrippa,
b	Question	do you believe the prophets?
c	Assertion	I know that you believe."

28a	Response: speech	**Agrippa said to Paul,**
b	Question	"Do you think that
c	Time	in such a short time
d	Purpose	you can persuade me to become a Christian?"
29a	Response: speech	**Paul replied,**
b	Desire (prayer)	"I pray to God that,
c	Manner	whether in a short or
d	Alternative	long time,
e	Identification	not only you but
f	Generalization	all who are listening to me today,
h	Desire	may become what I am,
g	Contrast	except for these chains."
i		
30a	Action	**Then the king rose,**
b	Association	together with the governor and
c	Association	Bernice and
d	Association	the others who were sitting with them.
31a	Time	After they left the hall,
b	Action: speech	**they said to one another,**
c	Assertion	"This man is doing nothing
d	Consequence	that deserves the death sentence or
e		chains."
32a	Action: speech	**Agrippa said to Festus,**
b	Inference	"This man could have been released
c	Condition	if he had not appealed to the emperor."

Structure and Literary Form

Luke narrates the episode of Paul's imprisonment in Caesarea during the governorship of Porcius Festus (25:1 – 26:32) in three incidents. The first one relates events during the inaugural visit of the new governor in Jerusalem, where the chief priests and other members of the Jewish aristocracy reactivate the case against Paul (25:1 – 5). They ask the governor to transfer Paul from Caesarea to Jerusalem, planning to kill Paul in an ambush along the travel route. Festus's rejection of their petition is narrated in indirect speech, his summons to renew their case against Paul in Caesarea in direct speech.

The second incident relates trial proceedings in Caesarea (25:6 – 12) in six parts: the resumption of trial proceedings before Festus (v. 6), the charges of the Jewish leaders (v. 7), Paul's defense (v. 8), Festus's suggestion to relocate the trial from Caesarea to Jerusalem (v. 9), Paul's insistence to be tried in the Roman legal system and his appeal to the emperor (vv. 10 – 11), and Festus's decision to grant Paul's petition for a trial in Rome (v. 12). The charges of the Jewish leaders are narrated in indirect speech, Paul's defense in direct speech. Festus's suggestion to relocate the trial to Jerusalem is narrated in direct speech, as is Paul's negative reply; this leads into his appeal to be tried by the emperor in Rome, which Festus grants.

The third and longest incident reports the consultation of Festus and King Agrippa II (25:13 – 26:32). Luke narrates the arrival of Agrippa and Bernice (v. 13), an occasion that allows Festus to discuss Paul's case with the Jewish king (v. 14) and gives Luke the opportunity to include a lengthy speech of Festus (vv. 14 – 21). When Agrippa mentions his interest in meeting Paul (v. 22), the scene is set for Paul's hearing before Festus and Agrippa, which begins with the arrival of the notables and the summons of Paul the prisoner (v. 23). Both Festus (vv. 24 – 27) and Paul (26:2 – 23) give speeches. The incident culminates in a report of the reaction of Festus and Agrippa (vv. 24 – 32), who attest to Paul's innocence. Paul uses the opportunity of Agrippa's reaction to affirm that he indeed hopes he too will become a follower of Jesus (vv. 25 – 27).

Luke thus ends the Caesarea section of his narrative (24:1 – 26:32) on a high note, rather than with the discord of Paul's appeal to the emperor, which had become necessary when Festus's willingness to grant the Jewish authorities a favor had created a dangerous situation for Paul. Paul has another opportunity to describe his conversion to faith in Jesus, Israel's Messiah and Savior to exercise his calling as Jesus' witness among Jews and Gentiles by explaining the gospel to the Jewish king. He will leave Judea fulfilling his goal to go to Rome (cf. 19:21).

The episode is a *historical narrative* with chronological information (25:1, 6, 13, 23), geographical information (references to Jerusalem and to Caesarea in 25:1, 3, 4, 6, 7; to Damascus in 26:12, 20), and personal names (references to Paul, Festus, King Agrippa, Bernice, and Felix); the Jewish leaders are not mentioned by name (25:2, 5, 7). Luke includes *direct speech* of Festus (25:5, 9, 12, 14 – 21, 22, 24 – 27; 26:24, 31), Agrippa (25:22; 26:1, 28, 31 – 32), and Paul (25:8, 10 – 11; 26:2 – 23, 25 – 27, 29).

The first *speech of Festus* (25:14 – 21) identifies Paul as a prisoner (v. 14), reports on the hearing in Jerusalem (vv. 15 – 16), and then on the hearing in Caesarea (vv. 17 – 21). *Paul's speech* in 25:8, 10 – 11 during the trial proceedings in Caesarea before Festus (his eighth speech) summarizes his defense in two parts. (1) He defends himself against the charge of having committed offenses (v. 8). (2) When Festus suggests a relocation of the trial proceedings to Jerusalem (v. 9), Paul insists on being tried in the Roman legal system (vv. 10 – 11).

The second *speech of Festus* (25:24 – 27), in Paul's hearing before King Agrippa, has three parts. (1) After addressing Agrippa and all who are present (v. 24a-c), he reports on Paul's case (vv. 24d – 25). (2) Then he explains the purpose of the hearing (vv. 26 – 27), pointing to the need for definite charges in his letter to the emperor. (3) He expects that the hearing will provide clarification in order to report definite charges to the emperor.

Paul's second *speech*, in the hearing before Festus and Agrippa 26:2 – 23 (his ninth in Acts) consists of the traditional five parts of a speech.[1] (1) In his *exordium* (vv. 2 – 3) he expresses his gratefulness that he can defend himself before Agrippa and asks Agrippa to pay close attention to what he has to say. (2) Paul offers a lengthy statement of the facts of the case (*narratio*; vv. 4 – 18). (3) The proofs of Paul's innocence (*probatio*; vv. 19 – 20) are formulated with respect to Paul's obedience to Jesus' commission, his mission in Damascus, Jerusalem, Judea, and among the Gentiles, and his message, which is summarized in terms of repentance of sins, turning to God, and behavior consistent with devotion to God. (4) The refutation of the charges (*refutatio*; v. 21) is succinct, focusing on Paul's arrest in the temple as he was fulfilling his commission from God and on the attempt of the Jews to kill him. (5) The conclusion (*peroratio*; vv. 22 – 23) emphasizes Paul's acknowledgment of God's help and Paul's affirmation of his consistent testimony of his message about Jesus, the Savior and suffering and risen Messiah.

Exegetical Outline

→ **I. The Imprisonment in Caesarea during the Governorship of Porcius Festus (25:1 – 26:32)**

A. Festus's Inaugural Visit in Jerusalem (25:1 – 5)

1. Festus's arrival in the province of Judea (25:1a-b)
2. Festus's visit to Jerusalem (25:1c)
3. The Jewish leaders' accusations against Paul (25:2 – 3)
   a. Report concerning Paul (25:2a-d)
   b. Request that Paul be transferred to Jerusalem (25:2e – 3d)
   c. Plan to kill Paul in an ambush (25:3e-f)
4. Festus's decision to hear the case against Paul in Caesarea (25:4 – 5)

B. Trial Proceedings in Caesarea (25:6 – 12)

1. The resumption of trial proceedings against Paul (25:6)
   a. Festus's return from Jerusalem to Caesarea (25:6a-d)
   b. Festus's summons of Paul before the judicial bench (25:6e-g)
2. The Jewish leaders' charges (25:7)
   a. The charges (25:7a-e)
   b. The lack of proof (25:7f)
3. Paul's defense (25:8)
   a. He has not committed any offense against the Jewish law (25:8a-c)
   b. He has not desecrated the temple (25:8d)
   c. He has not committed any offense against the emperor (25:8e)

---

1. Cf. Winter, "Official Proceedings," 327 – 31. Note Kennedy, *Rhetorical Criticism*, 137, who comments on the rhetorical sophistication of the speech that "Paul has clearly had an opportunity to prepare his address in advance."

4. Festus's suggestion to relocate the trial to Jerusalem (25:9)

    a. Festus's desire to grant the Jews a favor (25:9a)

    b. Festus's suggestion that Paul stand trial in Jerusalem (25:9b-e)

5. Paul's petition to be tried by the emperor (25:10 – 11)

    a. Insistence that only a Roman court has jurisdiction in his case (25:10)

    b. Willingness to be executed for a crime deserving death (25:11a-c)

    c. Appeal to the emperor (25:11d-f)

6. Festus's decision to grant Paul's petition for a trial in Rome (25:12)

    a. Festus's conference with his counselors (25:12a)

    b. Festus's acceptance of Paul's appeal to the emperor (25:12b-d)

C. Festus's Consultation of King Agrippa II (25:13 – 26:32)

1. Agrippa's courtesy visit of the new governor (25:13)

2. Festus's discussion of Paul's case (25:14 – 21)

    a. The case of the prisoner Paul (25:14)

    b. Report of the Sanhedrin hearing in Jerusalem (25:15 – 16)

        i. The charges of the chief priests and elders against Paul (25:15a-d)

        ii. The demand of the chief priests and elders for a guilty verdict (25:15e)

        iii. Insistence that Roman law requires plaintiffs to confront defendants (25:16a-e)

        iv. Insistence that Roman law allows a defendant to defend himself (25:16f-g)

    c. Report of the trial in Caesarea (25:17 – 21)

        i. Prompt action concerning the case after his return to Caesarea (25:17)

        ii. Recognition that Paul was not accused of crimes punishable by the law (25:18)

        iii. Recognition that Paul was accused of religious offenses (25:19)

        iv. Offer to Paul that he stand trial in Jerusalem (25:20)

        v. Paul's insistence to stand trial before the emperor (25:21a-b)

        vi. Decision to keep Paul in custody until his transfer to Rome (25:21c-e)

3. Agrippa's desire to hear Paul (25:22)

4. The commencement of Paul's hearing (25:23)

    a. The entrance of Agrippa and Bernice in the audience hall (25:23a-d)

    b. The entrance of the military commanders and prominent citizens (25:23e-f)

    c. Festus's summons of Paul (25:23g-h)

5. Festus's speech (25:24 – 27)

    a. Address (25:24a-c)

    b. Report on Paul's case (25:24d – 25)

        i. The Jewish demand for a death sentence (25:24d-h)

        ii. The innocence of Paul (25:25a-b)

        iii. Paul's appeal to stand trial before the emperor (25:25c)

        iv. Decision to grant Paul's appeal (25:25d)

    c. Purpose of the hearing (25:26 – 27)

        i. The need for definite charges in his letter to the emperor (25:26a-b)

        ii. The expectation that the hearing will provide clarification (25:26c-g)

iii. The need to report definite charges to the emperor (25:27)

6. The permission for Paul to address the audience (26:1)

    a. Agrippa grants Paul the permission to speak (26:1a-c)

    b. Paul begins his address (26:1d-e)

7. Paul's speech (26:2 – 23)

    a. Introduction (*exordium*) (26:2 – 3)

        i. Paul's gratefulness that he can defend himself before Agrippa (26:2)

        ii. Agrippa's competence as an expert in Jewish affairs (26:3a-d)

        iii. Paul's plea that Agrippa pay close attention to what he has to say (26:3e-g)

    b. The facts of the case (*narratio*) (26:4 – 18)

        i. Paul's past as a Pharisaic Jew educated in Jerusalem (26:4 – 5)

        ii. The theological nature of the dispute with the Jews (26:6 – 8)

        iii. Paul's activity as a persecutor of the followers of Jesus of Nazareth (26:9 – 12)

        iv. Paul's encounter with Jesus on the road to Damascus (26:13 – 18)

    c. Proofs of Paul's innocence (*probatio*) (26:19 – 20)

        i. Paul's obedience to Jesus' commission (26:19)

        ii. Paul's mission in Damascus, Jerusalem, Judea, and among Gentiles (26:20a-e)

        iii. Paul's message (26:20f-h)

    d. Refutation of the charges (*refutatio*) (26:21)

        i. Paul's arrest in the temple while he was on a divine mission (26:21a-b)

        ii. The Jews' attempt to kill him (26:21c)

    e. Conclusion (*peroratio*) (26:22 – 23)

        i. Acknowledgment of God's help (26:22a-c)

        ii. Affirmation of his consistent witness, which agrees with Scripture (26:22d-j)

        iii. Affirmation of his message about Jesus, Israel's Messiah and Savior (26:23)

8. The reaction of Festus and Agrippa (26:24 – 32)

    a. Festus's reaction to Paul's discourse, declaring him mad (26:24)

    b. Paul's reaction (26:25 – 27)

        i. Affirmation of his sanity (26:25a-c)

        ii. Affirmation of his report's truthfulness and reasonableness (26:25d-e)

        iii. Attempt to claim King Agrippa as a witness for his truthfulness (26:26)

        iv. Challenge to King Agrippa concerning his faith in the prophets (26:27a-b)

        v. Assertion regarding Agrippa's faith (26:27c)

    c. Agrippa's reaction: Incredulity that Paul tries to make him a Christian (26:28)

    d. Paul's response: His hope that all who are present become Jesus' followers (26:29)

    e. The conclusion of the hearing (26:30 – 32)

        i. The departure of Festus, Agrippa, and Bernice (26:30)

        ii. Acknowledgment of Paul's innocence (26:31)

        iii. Agrippa's affirmation of Paul's innocence (26:32)

Explanation of the Text

25:1 Three days after Festus had arrived in the province, he went up from Caesarea to Jerusalem (Φῆστος οὖν ἐπιβὰς τῇ ἐπαρχείᾳ μετὰ τρεῖς ἡμέρας ἀνέβη εἰς Ἱεροσόλυμα ἀπὸ Καισαρείας). The arrival of the new governor, Porcius Festus, in Caesarea, the political capital of the province of Judea, was rapidly followed by an inaugural visit in Jerusalem. Jerusalem was the ancient capital of the region and the religious center of all the Jewish communities. If the new governor wanted to maintain good relations with the Jewish leadership, he had to show his respect and demonstrate his acknowledgment of their role in maintaining order and peace in Judea by meeting with them in Jerusalem as his first order of business. Note that Judea was not an independent province but belonged to the province of Syria, whose governors intervened in Judea if they deemed this necessary. Festus is portrayed in v. 1 as a competent governor who is well aware of his responsibilities and duties as the governor of a difficult province.

25:2 – 3 The chief priests and the leaders of the Jews gave him a report concerning the charges against Paul. They implored him and requested, as a favor to them against Paul, that he have him transferred to Jerusalem. They were planning an ambush to kill him on the way (ἐνεφάνισάν τε αὐτῷ οἱ ἀρχιερεῖς καὶ οἱ πρῶτοι τῶν Ἰουδαίων κατὰ τοῦ Παύλου καὶ παρεκάλουν αὐτὸν αἰτούμενοι χάριν κατ᾽ αὐτοῦ ὅπως μεταπέμψηται αὐτὸν εἰς Ἱερουσαλήμ, ἐνέδραν ποιοῦντες ἀνελεῖν αὐτὸν κατὰ τὴν ὁδόν). Festus's meeting with the Jewish leadership in Jerusalem presumably took place in the audience hall of Herod's luxurious palace[2] in the northwest corner of the city, which served as praetorium of the Roman governors when in Jerusalem. Festus met with the chief priests (see on 4:5), i.e., the highest representatives of the leading priestly families — probably including the high priest Ishmael son of Phiabi, who had just been appointed by Agrippa II in AD 59 near the end of Felix's term as governor[3] — and the "leaders" (οἱ πρῶτοι),[4] i.e., the highest representatives of the Jewish lay aristocracy.

During this meeting with the new governor, the Jewish leaders renewed the case against Paul. Luke specifies four actions of the Jewish leaders. (1) They "gave … a report concerning the charges" (ἐνεφάνισαν)[5] against Paul; i.e., they renewed their accusations against Paul (cf. 24:2 – 8, 9). (2) They "implored" (παρεκάλουν) the governor, making a strong request for their side of the case. (3) They "requested" (αἰτούμενοι) a favor,[6] that the new governor transfer Paul's case from Caesarea to Jerusalem. They know that if Festus grants them the favor of a Jerusalem trial, this will work against Paul.

(4) They "were planning" (ποιοῦντες) an ambush to take place during Paul's transfer on the road from Caesarea to Jerusalem. The Jewish leadership possibly wanted to exploit the inexperience of the

---

2. See the description in Josephus, *J.W.* 5.176 – 181. Cf. Netzer, *Architecture of Herod*, 129 – 32. The most impressive parts of the palace were two reception and banqueting halls.

3. Josephus, *Ant.* 20.179. Cf. VanderKam, *From Joshua to Caiaphas*, 463 – 75.

4. The same term is used in Luke 19:47 for members of the lay aristocracy in Jerusalem who were (presumably) members of the Sanhedrin. In Acts 25:15 the same group is described with the term "elders" (πρεσβύτεροι); cf. 4:5, 8, 23; 6:12.

5. BDAG, s.v. ἐμφανίζω 3, "to convey a formal report about a judicial matter, *present evidence, bring charges*," suggesting the translation "bring formal charges against someone." The term is also used in 24:1; 25:15; in 23:22 the verb means "provide information, *inform*."

6. Cf. BDAG, s.v. χάρις 3, "practical application of goodwill, *(a sign of) favor, gracious deed/gift, benefaction*." The connotation of χάρις in 25:3 is "political favor" (ibid. 3a); cf. 24:27; 25:9.

new governor and finish what they had planned to do two years earlier (23:12 – 15). The renewed efforts to obtain a verdict against Paul in a criminal trial and the revived plans for an ambush demonstrate the continued significance of Paul for the Jewish leadership in Jerusalem and the hostility of the Jewish leaders, who are willing to use extrajudicial measures for the physical elimination of Paul.

25:4 – 5 Festus replied that Paul was being held at Caesarea and that he himself intended to go there shortly. "So," he said, "let those of you who have authority come down with me, and if there is anything wrong about the man, they can bring charges against him" (ὁ μὲν οὖν Φῆστος ἀπεκρίθη τηρεῖσθαι τὸν Παῦλον εἰς Καισάρειαν, ἑαυτὸν δὲ μέλλειν ἐν τάχει ἐκπορεύεσθαι· οἱ οὖν ἐν ὑμῖν, φησίν, δυνατοὶ συγκαταβάντες εἴ τί ἐστιν ἐν τῷ ἀνδρὶ ἄτοπον κατηγορείτωσαν αὐτοῦ). Festus declines the Jewish leaders' request to transfer Paul to Jerusalem, for that would give the Jewish leaders a favor in a criminal trial;[7] it would involve a decision in a legal case without the presence of both accuser and defendant (cf. 23:35). Soon (in 25:9) Festus will give Paul a chance to comment on possibly relocating the trial proceedings to Jerusalem. By insisting that the Jewish accusers come to Caesarea, Festus demonstrates his administrative competency and integrity as well as the force of his authority as the governor of the province. Festus requests the Jewish leaders to appoint a delegation whose members have the authority to appear as Paul's accusers (κατηγορείτωσαν)[8] in the criminal trial.

The governor's integrity also shows in the formulation "if there is anything wrong about the man" (εἴ τί ἐστιν ἐν τῷ ἀνδρὶ ἄτοπον); this first class conditional allows for the possibility that the Jewish leaders may yet want to decide whether they are convinced that Paul has done something improper or wrong that demands official accusations in a trial. Festus implies that only accusations with proper reasons will be admitted. He may allude to the fact that Paul had insisted in the previous trial proceedings that the charges of the Jews could not be proved (24:13).[9] The term "wrong" (ἄτοπος) is a mild word for an alleged crime; Festus shows "proper legal caution"[10] as he does not prejudice his handling of Paul's case.

25:6 After spending not more than eight or ten days among them, he went down to Caesarea. The next day he took his seat on the judicial bench and ordered Paul to be brought before him (διατρίψας δὲ ἐν αὐτοῖς ἡμέρας οὐ πλείους ὀκτὼ ἢ δέκα, καταβὰς εἰς Καισάρειαν, τῇ ἐπαύριον καθίσας ἐπὶ τοῦ βήματος ἐκέλευσεν τὸν Παῦλον ἀχθῆναι). Luke begins his report on the trial proceedings in Caesarea (vv. 6 – 12) with a succinct description of the resumption of Paul's trial. The reference to "eight or ten days" reflects Luke's caution not to claim what he does not know for certain: he is not sure whether Festus stayed in Jerusalem for eight or ten more days. As the new governor, Festus would have wanted to get a good grasp of the Jewish institutions and traditions (such as the Sanhedrin, the temple, and the synagogues), to familiarize himself with the topography of the city, and to inspect the security arrangements in the city (e.g., by visiting the Antonia Fortress with its Roman garrison).

---

7. Cf. Omerzu, *Prozess*, 471 – 72, who goes on to point out that Festus's refusal to grant the Jewish leaders a favor clarifies that Paul's later appeal to the emperor was not due to deficiencies of the legal process.

8. For κατηγορέω in the sense of "bring legal charges" cf. 22:30; 24:2, 8, 13, 19; see also 25:11, 16; 28:19.

9. Cf. Omerzu, *Prozess*, 472.

10. Barrett, *Acts*, 1125; he also allows for the possibility that the term reflects Luke's desire "to show Paul in the best possible light." The term ἄτοπος is also used in Luke 23:41, which does not necessarily mean Luke's readers would recall the words of one of the two men who were crucified together with Jesus and who declared Jesus to be innocent.

On the day after his return to Caesarea, Festus "took his seat on the judicial bench" (καθίσας ἐπὶ τοῦ βήματος); i.e., he began the official trial proceedings in the legal case against Paul.[11] The governor then summons Paul, which implies that the Jewish leaders have indeed appointed a delegation that traveled with the governor from Jerusalem to Caesarea. Possibly they arrived earlier, during the time that Festus was busy in Jerusalem (cf. v. 7b-c, where the coming of the Jews from Jerusalem is not explicitly linked with the governor's travel). The fact that Festus summons Paul on the day after his arrival from Jerusalem suggests that he takes up Paul's case as the first item of business of his official functions as governor of the province of Judea. Clearly he wants to end this long-drawn-out case.

The judicial proceedings take place, perhaps, in the large hall of the Upper Palace in the governor's praetorium. We must assume that Festus has read the documents concerning Paul's case — both the letter of Claudius Lysias (23:26 – 30) and the transcript of the trial proceedings under his predecessor, Felix (see "In Depth: Reports of Court Proceedings," under "Structure and Literary Form" on 24:1 – 27).

25:7 When he arrived, the Jews who had come down from Jerusalem stood around him and brought many serious charges against him, which they could not prove (παραγενομένου δὲ αὐτοῦ περιέστησαν αὐτὸν οἱ ἀπὸ Ἱεροσολύμων καταβεβηκότες Ἰουδαῖοι πολλὰ καὶ βαρέα αἰτιώματα καταφέροντες ἃ οὐκ ἴσχυον ἀποδεῖξαι). The trial begins with the accusations of the Jewish leaders. Once Paul has entered the trial room, Festus asks the Jewish leaders from Jerusalem to proceed with their accusations. Luke does not specify their charges, but describes them as "many

serious charges," which is exactly what the accusations in the trial before Felix were; they presumably allege again that Paul is a public enemy of the Jewish people who causes riots as a ringleader of the Nazarenes, and that Paul has attempted to desecrate the temple (cf. 24:5 – 6).

The vivid description of the Jewish leaders standing around Paul as they make their accusations is probably meant to illustrate the dangerous situation in which Paul finds himself as a result of the charges against him. It is possible (but not certain, since Luke only summarizes in v. 7) that the Jewish leaders have decided to bring the charges in a "concerted and hence more forceful" manner, without the use of a professional rhetor.[12] Their legal strategy, which seemed to have lacked discipline and focus, backfired; in his later report to Agrippa, Festus expresses his surprise that the Jews "did not charge him with any of the crimes I had expected" (v. 18), leaving him with the impression that their case rested on Jewish religious questions and on questions related to Jesus, who had died but whom Paul asserted to be alive (v. 19). Thus, Festus is at a loss how to proceed in the investigation (v. 20). In v. 7 Luke comments that "they could not prove" (οὐκ ἴσχυον ἀποδεῖξαι) their charges. The imperfect tense of the verb ἴσχυον may suggest "continuous but unsuccessful attempts to prove."[13]

25:8 Paul said in his defense, "I have committed no offense against the law of the Jews, or against the temple, or against the emperor" (τοῦ Παύλου ἀπολογουμένου ὅτι οὔτε εἰς τὸν νόμον τῶν Ἰουδαίων οὔτε εἰς τὸ ἱερὸν οὔτε εἰς Καίσαρά τι ἥμαρτον). Luke relates Paul's defense in direct speech, which carries more weight than the charges of his accusers on account of its length. He defends

11. For βῆμα designating the dais or platform on which judges held tribunals, see 18:12, 16, 17; also 25:10, 17.

12. Rapske, *Paul in Roman Custody*, 184; see ibid. for the following comment.

13. Barrett, *Acts*, 1126, suggesting as translation: "They could not prove, however hard they tried."

himself against three charges, asserting he is innocent in each case.

(1) Paul asserts he has committed no offense[14] against the "law of the Jews" (νόμος τῶν Ἰουδαίων); i.e., he has not violated the Mosaic law. Paul had been accused of teaching against the Mosaic law in the temple court (21:28). He had defended himself against this charge by emphasizing his education and life according to the law (22:1 – 5) as a Pharisee (23:6), his belief in everything written in the Law and the Prophets (24:14), and his clear conscience before God and the people (24:16). Paul had not abandoned the Torah or encouraged other Jews to abandon the Torah, although he has modified the terms of admission to God's people for Gentile believers.

In the Sanhedrin hearing Paul had focused the dispute about his relationship with the law on the question of the resurrection of the dead (23:6), a connection that Claudius Lysias perceived when he described the controversy between Paul and the Sanhedrin as pertaining to questions regarding the law (23:29); this, of course, had caused a tumult in the Sanhedrin. In his trial before Felix, Paul had also asserted he was being accused only because of the question of the resurrection (24:20 – 21). The accusation that Paul had committed an offense against the Mosaic law had thus been effectively discredited during earlier trial proceedings. Moreover, the charge of having violated the Mosaic law concerned only the Jewish jurisdiction, a fact that Gallio, the governor in the province of Achaia, had clearly recognized (18:14 – 15).

(2) Paul asserts that he has committed no offense against the temple (τὸ ἱερόν). The charge that Paul desecrated the temple was made for the first time by Jews from the province of Asia, who claimed he

brought a Greek into the temple (21:28 – 29). The tumult that resulted from this charge led to the intervention of the Roman commander and to Paul's arrest. This charge was brought against Paul in the trial before Felix (24:6), albeit in a slightly different form: Paul was accused of having attempted to desecrate the temple, which was more difficult to disprove. Paul had countered this charge by insisting that his visit to the temple was peaceful, serving religious purposes, and that he was in a state of ritual purity when he was in the temple (24:12, 17 – 18). The charge of having desecrated the temple concerned both Jewish and Roman jurisdiction, which is probably the reason why this charge is mentioned in central position.[15]

(3) Paul asserts that he has not committed any offense "against the emperor" (εἰς Καίσαρα). The emperor at the time was Nero (AD 54 – 68). This seems to represent a new charge, unless Paul alludes to Claudius Lysias's initial thought that he was the Egyptian insurrectionist (21:38 – 39). The formulation in v. 8 seems to suggest that Paul defends himself against the charge of a *crimen maiestatis* (treason), which could be committed by Roman citizens or provincials "by the planned killing of a magistrate, by armed revolt or preparation for the same, by the liberation of prisoners or hostages, by the occupation of public and sacred buildings, or by co-operation with an enemy power."[16] Paul was (probably) accused of treason in Thessalonica, with a reference to the emperor as part of the charge (17:6 – 7), but Luke is hardly alluding to this episode in which Paul had been cleared. Paul probably alludes to the accusation that he has been fomenting riots, leveled against him by the Jewish leaders in the trial before Felix.

This corresponds to the serious (political)

---

14. The verb ἥμαρτον means here "transgress" in the sense of "do something legally wrong."

15. Omerzu, *Prozess*, 478.

16. C. Gizewski, "Majestas," *BNP*, 8:186. The punishment was the death penalty or the heaviest of other punishments.

charge of sedition (24:5). Even though the scope of Paul's seditious activities was described as being "among all the Jews," the geographical specification "throughout the world" raised the charge of sedition to a level where the governors of the Roman provinces, and in the city of Rome the emperor himself, would have to take action. And the combination with the accusation of being a "ringleader" (24:5) could very well be construed in terms of a *crimen maiestatis*, which constituted the most serious political charge.[17] Paul had asserted earlier that he was citizen of Tarsus and a Roman citizen, who had not broken Roman law (21:39; 22:25 – 28). And when he appeals to the emperor in the course of this trial (25:11), he places himself under the protection of the emperor, clearly implying that he has not done anything that would give him reason to be afraid of the emperor.

25:9 Since Festus wanted to do the Jews a favor, he asked Paul, "Do you want to go up to Jerusalem and be tried there before me concerning these charges?" (ὁ Φῆστος δὲ θέλων τοῖς Ἰουδαίοις χάριν καταθέσθαι ἀποκριθεὶς τῷ Παύλῳ εἶπεν· θέλεις εἰς Ἱεροσόλυμα ἀναβὰς ἐκεῖ περὶ τούτων κριθῆναι ἐπ᾿ ἐμοῦ;). After the speeches of the accusers (summarized in v. 7) and of the defendant (v. 8), Festus introduces the suggestion to relocate the juridicial proceedings to Jerusalem. He seems more impressed with the presence of the Jewish leaders of Jerusalem, whom he wants to do a favor, than with Paul and the fact of his Roman citizenship (which Luke does not mention here, but which must have been known to Festus; cf. 23:27 in Lysias's letter, which would have been part of the trial record).

If Festus merely wanted to change the venue

from Caesarea to Jerusalem to personally bring the trial to a conclusion, his suggestion would be perfectly legal. But Paul had been in the custody of the Roman legal system; he could be transferred to the jurisdiction of the Sanhedrin in Jerusalem only if he had first been acquitted at least of the political charges. Perhaps Festus wants to obtain a fuller consultation with the Jewish authorities, comparable with the consultation with the Jewish king Agrippa (cf. v. 26). But Paul does not know the reason for Festus's suggestion. His reaction in vv. 10 – 11 clearly indicates that he fears that Festus will transfer him to the jurisdiction of the Jewish authorities in Jerusalem. At the same time, the fact that Festus asks Paul for his agreement to the relocation of the trial indicates that the governor is following proper legal procedure. He evidently does not want to force Paul, Roman citizen that he is, to agree to be tried by the Jewish high court in Jerusalem.

25:10 Paul answered, "I am now standing before the emperor's court, where I should be tried. I have done no wrong to the Jews, as you know very well" (εἶπεν δὲ ὁ Παῦλος· ἐπὶ τοῦ βήματος Καίσαρος ἑστώς εἰμι, οὗ με δεῖ κρίνεσθαι. Ἰουδαίους οὐδὲν ἠδίκησα ὡς καὶ σὺ κάλλιον ἐπιγινώσκεις). Paul refuses to be taken to Jerusalem. His apprehension is understandable, given the continuous efforts of the Jewish leaders to obtain a summary execution from the governors Felix and Festus and given the plot to kill him in an ambush two years ago. Also, Paul may well have had information that they had renewed plans to have him killed when the Romans take him from his place of custody to the streets.

In view of this history, Paul cannot expect to

---

17. Cf. Omerzu, *Prozess*, 479, who agrees that the crime of instigating a riot can indirectly affect the *maiestas* of the emperor: the formulation in v. 8 functions perhaps as an escalation of the charge of sedition with the possibility of a charge

of *crimen maiestatis*; Luke probably intends his readers to be reminded of the charge of *crimen maiestatis* in Jesus' trial and as grounds of Jesus' execution.

receive a fair trial, a fair hearing, or even safe passage from Caesarea to Jerusalem, particularly since Festus's suggestion to relocate the trial was an open attempt to grant the Jews a favor. Paul's response to Festus's suggestion is the climax of Paul's trial in province of Judea, in that his appeal to the emperor removes him from the jurisdiction of the governor of Judea and from any jurisdiction of the Jews.[18]

Paul interprets Festus's suggestion to relocate the trial proceedings to Jerusalem not as an honest question regarding a change of venue. He seems to suspect that the governor wants to hand him over to the Jewish authorities. Thus Paul insists that he be tried by a duly constituted Roman court; he knows he has discredited the religious accusations of the Jewish leaders. Festus too knows, as a result of the trial proceedings over which he has been presiding, that Paul has "done nothing wrong" (οὐδὲν ἠδίκησα) to the Jews; i.e., he has not violated the Mosaic law (which is the offense that a Jewish court would indict him for). As a result, no Jewish court has jurisdiction over him. This means that "the emperor's court" (βῆμα Καίσαρος), i.e., the court duly constituted by the Roman governor who acts for the emperor, is the one venue where he must be tried. Paul can insist on being tried by a Roman court because he is a Roman citizen (see 16:37).

25:11 "If, however, I am in the wrong and have committed something deserving death, I do not refuse to die. But if there is nothing to their charges against me, no one can hand me over to them. I appeal to the emperor" (εἰ μὲν οὖν ἀδικῶ καὶ ἄξιον θανάτου πέπραχά τι, οὐ παραιτοῦμαι τὸ ἀποθανεῖν· εἰ δὲ οὐδέν ἐστιν ὧν οὗτοι κατηγοροῦσίν

μου, οὐδείς με δύναται αὐτοῖς χαρίσασθαι· Καίσαρα ἐπικαλοῦμαι). Paul evidently does not expect to be able to receive a fair verdict from Festus, even though the governor is responsible for his case as the emperor's representative. As a result, he appeals to the emperor, to be tried in the city of Rome. The statement "if there is nothing to their charges against me," formulated as a conditional clause (εἰ δὲ οὐδέν ἐστιν), implies that Paul acknowledges that if the charges of the Jewish leaders had been verified and proven, he could be handed over to the jurisdiction of the Jewish court in Jerusalem. He does "not refuse to die"; i.e., he is willing to be executed if his Jewish accusers prove that he is guilty and deserves the death sentence according to Jewish law.

Paul equates a transfer to the jurisdiction of the Sanhedrin with a death sentence. He insists that since none of their charges against him has been proven, no official can hand him over as a favor[19] to the Jewish authorities. Thus v. 11d-e formulates the legal consequence of v. 10d-e. While Festus, eager to grant the Jews a favor, conveniently "forgets" the principles of Roman law as they pertain to a Roman citizen, Paul asserts the validity of Roman law. Since Paul cannot be certain that Festus will follow Roman law, he appeals to the emperor in Rome.

The appeal to the emperor is succinctly formulated with two words (Καίσαρα ἐπικαλοῦμαι), which corresponds to the Latin phrase *Caesarem appello* ("I appeal to the emperor").[20] The available evidence confirms that it was possible in the first century to appeal directly to the emperor, to be tried in his imperial court, even before the trial

---

18. Cf. Omerzu, *Prozess*, 485; for the following comments cf. 485 – 87.

19. The verb χαρίσασθαι denotes here the "giving" of Paul to the Jewish authorities; cf. BDAG, s.v. χαρίζομαι 1, with reference to 25:11.

20. Cf. Plutarch, *Marc.* 2.4; *Ti. C. Gracch.* 16.1. The verb "appeal" (ἐπικαλέω) here is a legal technical term that denotes "a request put to a higher judicial authority for review of a decision in a lower court" (BDAG, s.v. ἐπικαλέω 3). Cf. 25:12, 25; 26:32; 28:19.

proceedings in a provincial court had concluded and a sentence had been rendered (see "In Depth: Appeal to the Emperor"). The possibility of a direct appeal to the emperor may have been connected with the fact that there was presumably no jury court in Judea to which his case might have been referred, which left the emperor, the only superior of the governor, as the judicial authority responsible for appeals.[21] The emperor in question was Nero, whose first five years in office (AD 54 – 59) were remembered with more fondness than his later years of megalomania. The cost of appeals had to be paid by the person making the appeal, including payment for transport and room and board.[22]

IN DEPTH: Appeal to the Emperor

In Republican Rome, there were two distinct forms of appeal: the *provocatio* as an appeal to the people, and the *appellatio* as an appeal to the tribune. The *provocatio* evidently served to limit the arbitrary use of the magistrates' authority and power to intervene (*coercitio*) when they judged that the public order had been violated (see on 16:23).[23] As regards the early imperial period, an older view[24] claims that the traditional form of the *provocatio*, which could be lodged *before* the trial, still existed in the first century, to be distinguished from the later *appellatio*, which takes place *after* the sentence of the judge. In view of the increasingly large number of Roman citizens in the provinces, the governors' rights were expanded to include trying citizens for statutory crimes (*ordo*) without *provocatio*. It is claimed that since the accusations against Paul did not fulfill the definitions of a statutory case that would have been tried as *cognitio extra ordinem*,[25] he had the right to an appeal. It has been established, however, that there is no evidence for an expansion of the rights of governors, nor is there evidence for a strict separation of statutory cases (*ordo*) and cases that belonged to the *cognitio extra ordinem*. Since the latter was not regulated by law, *extra ordinem* proceedings became the standard legal procedures in the provinces. The distinction between the earlier *provocatio* and the later *appellatio* had been largely abandoned.

The *appellatio* was a new legal action of the imperial period that came into

---

21. Cf. Jochen Bleicken, *Senatsgericht und Kaisergericht: Eine Studie zur Entwicklung des Prozessrechtes im frühen Prinzipat* (Göttingen: Vandenhoeck and Ruprecht, 1962), 179; Omerzu, *Prozess*, 107.

22. Cf. Tajra, *Trial*, 173; Rapske, *Paul in Roman Custody*, 55. See further on 27:3.

23. Jochen Bleicken, "Provocatio," in *Paulys Realency-clopädie der classischen Altertumswissenschaft*, vol. 23.2 (ed. G. Wissowa et al.; Stuttgart: Metzler, 1959), 2444 – 63.

24. Cf. Arnold H. M. Jones, "I Appeal Unto Caesar [1951]," in *Studies in Roman Government and Law* (orig. 1960; repr., Oxford: Blackwell, 1968), 51 – 65; Sherwin-White, *Roman Society*, 61 – 69. Most New Testament commentators rely on Sherwin-White.

25. Cf. C. G. Paulus, "Cognitio," *BNP*, 3:510: "the *cognitio extra ordinem* developed as a special type of court proceedings for legal situations which had previously not been actionable (entail, maintenance claims, etc.) in strict contrast ... to the conventional formula proceedings in civil lawsuits."

existence as a result of the authority and power of the emperor himself (*maius imperium*) and, more importantly, as the result of the delegated adjudication in the provinces and in the development and expansion of the *cognitio extra ordinem*, which became widespread in the imperial period. In the latter, the officials responsible for trials (such as provincial governors) were directly dependent on the *imperium* of the emperor, a fact that increased the emperor's importance and potential involvement in legal cases, in which he could not normally intervene (due to geographical distance). Initially the emperor's intervention seems rare. He apparently granted "extraordinary legal redress" when petitioned.[26] There is unambiguous evidence for the early imperial period that defendants could appeal directly to the emperor.[27] The case of Capito in AD 69 demonstrates that appeals could be made before the final verdict.[28]

The available evidence suggests that the *appellatio* was not fully regulated in the early imperial period. Since the *appellatio* constituted an appeal to the "original" *imperium* of the emperor, the latter could intervene at any point, even before the beginning of a trial (e.g., questioning an edict of the governor of the province). Thus, in contrast to later Roman law, the emperor's sentence rendered in response to an appeal was not necessarily the verdict of the high court superseding the verdict of a lower court; it could be the first verdict in the case. Paul's appeal to the emperor fits the historical reality of the possibility of *appellatio* in the first century, including Festus's consultation with his council and his prerogative to refuse the petition for an appeal.[29] The Roman character of the trial before the governor of Judea leaves no doubt that both Luke and his readers knew that Paul's status as a Roman citizen was the necessary prerequisite for his appeal to the emperor.[30]

25:12 **After Festus had conferred with his council, he declared, "You have appealed to the emperor, to the emperor you will go"** (τότε ὁ Φῆστος συλλαλήσας μετὰ τοῦ συμβουλίου ἀπεκρίθη· Καίσαρα ἐπικέκλησαι, ἐπὶ Καίσαρα πορεύσῃ). Festus was not required to grant Paul's appeal to the emperor.[31] This is why he confers with his "council," perhaps on the day after the trial proceedings

---

26. Bleicken, *Senatsgericht*, 137; Omerzu, *Prozess*, 106; see ibid. for the following observation.

27. Dio Cassius 59.8.5; Suetonius, *Nero* 17; Tacitus, *Ann.* 14.28.1; 16.8.3; see also *I. Cos* 26, an inscription that deals with the right of appeal (lines 3–5 read: "So then if the appeal to Augustus ([ἡ ἐκ]κλησις γείνεται) is made I must first scrutinize the charge." Cf. Horsley and Llewelyn, *New Docs*, 1:51.

28. Dio Cassius 64.2.3.

29. Omerzu, *Prozess*, 107–8, 489–91; for the following comment see ibid., 489.

30. There is no evidence that proves that governors were forced to grant the petition for an appeal to the emperor if lodged by a Roman citizen (contra Sherwin-White, *Roman Society*, 63–64; Barrett, *Acts*, 1131). See Wieslaw Litewski, "Die römische Appellation in Zivilsachen: Ein Abriss, I. Prinzipat," *ANRW* II.14 (1982): 60–96, 86–87; Omerzu, *Prozess*, 89, 100, 494.

31. Reasons for the rejection of an appeal included the legal status of the defendant, the contestation of a notification, formal errors, or nonobservance of certain deadlines. Cf. Litewski, "Appellation," 86, with reference to *Dig.* 49.5.6.

narrated in vv. 6 – 11. Luke portrays Festus again as the dutiful governor who consults his council, following procedure by examining the petition for an appeal.

Festus could release Paul since he knows that he has done nothing wrong (vv. 11, 25; cf. vv. 18 – 19). This, however, would be an inauspicious beginning of his term as governor of Judea; displeasing the Jewish leaders could threaten the stability of the province. Still, acceding to the demands of the Jewish authorities who demand Paul's execution would be risky, yet executing a Roman citizen at the request of Jewish accusers might create problems in Rome. Sending Paul to Rome to be tried in the imperial court was a solution that allowed Festus to extricate himself from a difficult situation. Festus could transfer Paul to Rome on his own initiative, but Paul's appeal to the emperor allows him to shift the "blame" (expected from the Jewish officials) for not sentencing Paul to Paul himself.

Festus announces his decision to grant Paul's appeal succinctly with five Greek words (Καίσαρα ἐπικέκλησαι, ἐπὶ Καίσαρα πορεύσῃ): "You have appealed to the emperor, to the emperor you will go." Festus's decision to grant Paul's petition of a trial in Rome immediately stops the current trial proceedings and effectively removes Paul from the sphere of influence of the Jewish authorities in the province of Judea. The hearing before the Jewish king Agrippa (25:23 – 26:23) does not change this new legal situation that Paul has been granted; that hearing merely serves to gather information that Festus can use in his letter to the emperor (v. 26).

25:13 After several days had passed, King Agrippa and Bernice arrived at Caesarea to pay their respects to Festus (ἡμερῶν δὲ διαγενομένων τινῶν Ἀγρίππας ὁ βασιλεὺς καὶ Βερνίκη κατήντησαν εἰς Καισάρειαν ἀσπασάμενοι τὸν Φῆστον). The third incident of Luke's report on the events connected with Paul's imprisonment in Caesarea when Festus was governor of Judea (25:1 – 26:32) relates Festus's consultation with King Agrippa (25:13 – 26:32). Since Festus needs to write a letter to the emperor (*littera dimissoria*; see on v. 26), explaining the circumstances of Paul's case and the reasons for granting Paul's appeal to be tried by the emperor, the courtesy visit of King Agrippa provides him with the perfect opportunity to obtain further information about the controversy between Paul and the Jewish authorities.

King Agrippa had ruled over areas in northern regions of Palestine since AD 50 and had been granted the authority over the temple in Jerusalem and over the appointment of the high priests. This close relationship with Jerusalem allowed him to intervene in the affairs of Judea and to present himself as representing the interests of all Jews. Agrippa II may have come to Caesarea not only to pay the new governor a courtesy visit,[32] but also to step into the trial proceedings against Paul, who had been arrested in the context of a tumult in the temple courts and who was being charged by the priestly aristocracy with the desecration of the temple.[33] If Agrippa had intended to intervene in the trial proceedings, he had arrived too late, since Paul's trial had just concluded with the prisoner's appeal to the emperor, which the governor had granted.

Bernice was Agrippa's sister, who lived with him in Caesarea Philippi and Rome. She was the older sister of Drusilla, the wife of Festus's predecessor, Felix. When Agrippa and Bernice met Paul in the summer of AD 59, the king was thirty-two years

---

32. Josephus, *Ant.* 20.189 – 196, describes Agrippa's good relationship with Festus.

33. Cf. Martin Hengel and Anna Maria Schwemer, *Jesus und das Judentum* (Geschichte des frühen Christentums Band I; Tübingen: Mohr Siebeck, 2007), 105.

old and his sister thirty-one years, while Paul may have been about sixty years old.

25:14 Since they were staying there many days, Festus discussed Paul's case before the king. He said, "There is a man here whom Felix left as a prisoner" (ὡς δὲ πλείους ἡμέρας διέτριβον ἐκεῖ, ὁ Φῆστος τῷ βασιλεῖ ἀνέθετο τὰ κατὰ τὸν Παῦλον λέγων· ἀνήρ τίς ἐστιν καταλελειμμένος ὑπὸ Φήλικος δέσμιος). Festus uses the opportunity of Agrippa's visit to consult with him concerning his prisoner Paul, whose trial had just concluded with Paul's appeal to the emperor. When Agrippa signaled he would stay for an extended period of time in Caesarea — perhaps in the praetorium, which used to be the palace of his great-grandfather, Herod — Festus decides to discuss the case of the Jewish authorities against Paul with Agrippa. The Jewish king was an expert in Jewish affairs because of his authority over the affairs of the temple in Jerusalem, and he was a friend of Rome, who had been educated in the imperial capital and who had been granted territories by the previous and the incumbent emperor (Claudius and Nero).

Festus's speech introduces the case of Paul with a succinct statement: his predecessor Felix left a particular man as "prisoner" (δέσμιος). This statement is probably not an implied criticism of Felix. The fact that he had not concluded the trial proceedings against Paul can be seen as a "bargaining chip" that he left behind for his successor, at the same time placing an "official question mark" to Paul's claims of innocence.[34]

Festus's subsequent report about his hearing in Jerusalem (vv. 15 – 16) recounts 25:1 – 5 and his report about Paul's trial in Caesarea recounts 25:6 – 12. Most of the material is identical; the differences highlight Festus's interest. It is natural for

a governor to describe his role in the affair in the best possible light.

25:15 When I was in Jerusalem, the chief priests and the elders of the Jews brought charges against him and asked for a guilty verdict against him (περὶ οὗ γενομένου μου εἰς Ἱεροσόλυμα ἐνεφάνισαν οἱ ἀρχιερεῖς καὶ οἱ πρεσβύτεροι τῶν Ἰουδαίων αἰτούμενοι κατ᾽ αὐτοῦ καταδίκην). Festus summarizes what transpired in the meeting that he had with the priestly and lay aristocracy of the Jews in Jerusalem. (1) He relates that they brought charges against Paul. The charges are not specified; Luke's readers know from 24:2 – 9 what they are.

(2) Festus reports that they demanded that he pronounce a "guilty verdict" (καταδίκη)[35] against Paul. While Luke reported the first action of the Jewish leaders in v. 2, he had omitted the request for a guilty verdict. The fact that in v. 3 Luke focused instead on their plan of an ambush in which Paul was to be killed during his transfer from Caesarea to Jerusalem, the guilty verdict mentioned in v. 15 implies the conviction of a crime that would require the death sentence. This is confirmed by Paul's statement in v. 11. Both the charge of desecration of the temple and the charge of fomenting riots (*seditio*) would qualify for such a verdict.

25:16 I told them that it was not the custom of the Romans to hand over anyone before the accused had met the accusers face-to-face and before he had the opportunity to defend himself against the charge (πρὸς οὓς ἀπεκρίθην ὅτι οὐκ ἔστιν ἔθος Ῥωμαίοις χαρίζεσθαί τινα ἄνθρωπον πρὶν ἢ ὁ κατηγορούμενος κατὰ πρόσωπον ἔχοι τοὺς κατηγόρους τόπον τε ἀπολογίας λάβοι περὶ τοῦ ἐγκλήματος). (3) Festus insisted to the Jewish authorities that he would uphold Roman law, here described as "the custom of the Romans," which

---

34. Rapske, *Paul in Roman Custody*, 321.
35. BDAG, s.v. καταδίκη, "condemnation, sentence of con-

demnation, conviction, guilty verdict." This noun occurs only here in the New Testament.

requires that plaintiffs confront the person(s) they accuse. By invoking custom as a source of law, "he was evoking a whole judicial use both ancient and standard."[36] The verb translated "to hand over anyone" (χαρίζεσθαί τινα ἄνθρωπον) denotes, with a dative object implied, "to make a present of any man *to anyone*."[37]

(4) Festus insists to Agrippa that he followed the principle that a defendant has the right to face his accusers and to defend himself against any charges. Roman jurisprudence insisted that accused and accusers "meet face-to-face" and that an accused person has the opportunity to "defend himself." The terms translated "defend" (ἀπολογία) and "charge" (ἔγκλημα; Lat. *crimen*) are technical legal terms. Festus insisted on Roman fairness (*aequitas Romana*), according to which anonymous denunciations were not tolerated and according to which charges could not be brought by representatives of the plaintiff. Luke omits Festus's insistence that Paul would be tried in Caesarea, rather than in Jerusalem as the Jewish authorities had requested (vv. 4 – 5).

25:17 When they came back here with me, I did not postpone the case, but took my seat on the judicial bench the next day and ordered the man to be brought before me (συνελθόντων οὖν αὐτῶν ἐνθάδε ἀναβολὴν μηδεμίαν ποιησάμενος τῇ ἑξῆς καθίσας ἐπὶ τοῦ βήματος ἐκέλευσα ἀχθῆναι τὸν ἄνδρα). In his report about the trial in Caesarea (vv. 17 – 21), Festus first emphasizes that he had taken prompt action, an emphasis highlighted by Luke with a series of aorists. On the day after his arrival in Caesarea, Festus took his seat on the judicial bench and ordered Paul to be brought before

himself, sitting as judge, and before the accusers. This review corresponds to vv. 6 – 7. The reference to a potential postponement,[38] which would have been his prerogative as a governor, emphasizes that he acted with prompt efficiency.

25:18 When his accusers stood up, they did not charge him with any of the crimes I had expected (περὶ οὗ σταθέντες οἱ κατήγοροι οὐδεμίαν αἰτίαν ἔφερον ὧν ἐγὼ ὑπενόουν πονηρῶν). Festus's description of the charges of Paul's accusers (the chief priests and other members of the Sanhedrin mentioned in v. 15) begins with a general reference to the charges. He informs Agrippa that he was surprised about these charges. He "had expected" (ὑπενόουν)[39] that they would accuse Paul of crimes (πονηρά), i.e., "evil deeds," which would justify the involvement of the highest Jewish officials in a legal case. But this is not what happened; they did not charge him with "any ... crime" (οὐδεμίαν αἰτίαν) that a Roman governor usually handles.

In v. 7 Luke had only referred to "serious charges" and commented that Paul's accusers could not prove those charges. Festus displays his impartiality. He is not partial to the authority of the chief priests and elders from Jerusalem. Rather, he carefully and objectively evaluated their charges and recognized that they were not serious political charges that would warrant a trial before the Roman governor. In the trial before Felix the charges of the Jewish leaders (24:5 – 7) were political, focused on fomenting riots (*seditio*). Perhaps the Jerusalem authorities tried a new legal strategy before Festus, deliberately moving the charges to religious questions and seeking the support of the governor on account of the decision that Julius Caesar had made in the time of Hyrcanus II:

---

36. Tajra, *Trial*, 155.

37. Barrett, *Acts*, 1137.

38. The term ἀναβολή ("postponement") is often used as a legal technical term; cf. the references in BDAG.

39. BDAG, s.v. ὑπονοέω defines, "to form an opinion or conjecture on the basis of slight evidence, *suspect, suppose*." Hemer, *Acts*, 131, interprets more positively in the sense of "of which I could take cognizance," suggesting that the expression reflects the legal formula *de quibus cognoscere volebam*.

Whatever high-priestly rights or other privileges exist in accordance with their laws, these he and his children shall possess by my command. If, during this period, any question will arise concerning the Jews' manner of life, it is my pleasure that the decision shall rest with them.[40]

25:19 Instead, they had certain points of disagreement with him about their own religion and about a certain Jesus, who had died but whom Paul asserted to be alive (ζητήματα δέ τινα περὶ τῆς ἰδίας δεισιδαιμονίας εἶχον πρὸς αὐτὸν καὶ περὶ τινος Ἰησοῦ τεθνηκότος ὃν ἔφασκεν ὁ Παῦλος ζῆν). Festus discovered that Paul was accused of religious offenses. He details two observations concerning the accusations of the Jewish authorities against Paul. (1) Their charges were related to "certain points of disagreement" concerning "their own religion" (περὶ τῆς ἰδίας δεισιδαιμονίας), i.e., the Jewish faith and cultic practice. The term "religion" (δεισιδαιμονία) means, here, not "superstition" (which would have been an insult to the Jewish king) but "religion" in terms of a particular system of cultic beliefs and practices. Paul certainly would have agreed with this assessment: what was at stake in the controversy with the Jewish leadership was not a criminal offense but his beliefs.

(2) Their charges concerned "a certain Jesus" (περὶ τινος Ἰησοῦ). In the discussion in court, the following facts stood out for Festus. The Jewish authorities insisted that Jesus "had died" (τεθνηκότος). The perfect tense of the participle indicates that they argued that Jesus' status was that of a man who had expired and who had been buried and who remained a dead man. Paul, however, asserted that this Jesus was "alive" (ζῆν). Since Paul did not dispute that Jesus had died, this means that he insisted that Jesus had been resurrected from the dead. Festus formulates the dispute concerning

Jesus not from a Jewish perspective, but from the perspective of a Roman pagan for whom talk about a "resurrection" of Jesus would be novel, if not incomprehensible. For him, the question is whether Jesus is dead or alive.

Even though he would have expressed the matter differently, Paul would have agreed with Festus's second point as well: the central issue that separated him from the Jewish authorities was the resurrection of Jesus (23:6), in which he believed because he had encountered Jesus on the road to Damascus (22:6 – 10; 24:15, 21; 26:12 – 18). Paul's belief in Jesus' resurrection committed him to acknowledge Jesus as Israel's Messiah, Savior, and Lord — convictions that had prompted him to persecute the followers of Jesus before his encounter with the risen Lord, and convictions that evidently motivated the Jewish authorities to seek to eliminate him as one of the "ringleaders" of Jesus' followers.

25:20 Since I was at a loss concerning the investigation of these matters, I asked if he would be willing to go to Jerusalem and stand trial there on these charges (ἀπορούμενος δὲ ἐγὼ τὴν περὶ τούτων ζήτησιν ἔλεγον εἰ βούλοιτο πορεύεσθαι εἰς Ἰεροσόλυμα κἀκεῖ κρίνεσθαι περὶ τούτων). The next point of Festus's report about Paul's trial was his offer to Paul to stand trial in Jerusalem. Festus tells Agrippa that the reason for this offer was his recognition that religious questions belonging to Jewish beliefs were outside of his expertise. He was "at a loss," which means he had doubts how he should handle the investigation (ζήτησις; Lat. *quaestio*, the controversial matter settled by judicial inquiry) of "these matters" related to Jesus' resurrection.

As a result Festus asked Paul whether he was willing to go to Jerusalem and "stand trial" (κρίνεσθαι) there "on these charges," i.e., regarding

---

40. Josephus, *Ant.* 14.195; see Fitzmyer, *Acts*, 751.

his belief that Jesus was alive. Since he portrays himself to Agrippa as the impartial governor and judge, he omits the fact that he wanted to grant the Jews a favor (v. 9) and that he hoped that Paul would accept his proposition.

25:21 "But when Paul appealed to be kept in custody for the decision of His Majesty the emperor, I ordered that he be kept in custody until I could send him to the emperor" (τοῦ δὲ Παύλου ἐπικαλεσαμένου τηρηθῆναι αὐτὸν εἰς τὴν τοῦ Σεβαστοῦ διάγνωσιν, ἐκέλευσα τηρεῖσθαι αὐτὸν ἕως οὗ ἀναπέμψω αὐτὸν πρὸς Καίσαρα). The final point of Festus's summary of Paul's Caesarea trial that had just been concluded reports Paul's insistence to stand trial before the emperor. While this statement summarizes vv. 10 – 11 in a generally adequate manner, it is true that Paul would have preferred that Festus act on his correct perception that the controversy was about Jewish religious questions and not about political insurrection, thus declaring him innocent and releasing him.[41] Paul did not exactly appeal "to be kept in custody" (τηρηθῆναι), although his appeal to the emperor implied, given his two-year custody in Caesarea, that he would be transferred to Rome as a prisoner.

The term "His Majesty" (ὁ Σεβαστός) is the Greek equivalent of the Latin term *Augustus*, meaning "worthy of reverence, revered," which is the title that the senate in Rome conferred on Gaius Julius Caesar Octavianus on January 16 in 27 BC when he became *Princeps*. The term became a title for the first emperor's successors. Nero's full name was Nero Claudius Caesar Augustus Germanicus. The term translated "decision" (διάγνωσις) is here a legal technical term that denotes "a judicial inquiry or investigation that culminates in a decision" (BDAG).

Festus concludes his report by relating his decision to keep Paul in custody until arrangements could be made to send him to the emperor (Καῖσαρ; see on 17:7; 25:8). The term translated as "send" (ἀναπέμψω) denotes the remission of a case (or person) to a higher court. In the context of his concern to highlight his competence as Roman governor, Festus portrays himself as protecting Paul against the hostility of the Jews. At the same time, Festus's statement here explains the assertion of Agrippa in 26:32 that Paul could have been released if he had not appealed to the emperor. The assertion was implausible in the early principate (no law prevented Festus from declaring Paul not guilty and releasing him, even after his appeal to the emperor); it is plausible if Agrippa refers to the fact that Paul's appeal only served the prolongation of his imprisonment.[42]

25:22 Agrippa said to Festus, "I would like to hear the man myself." He replied, "Tomorrow you will hear him" (Ἀγρίππας δὲ πρὸς τὸν Φῆστον· ἐβουλόμην καὶ αὐτὸς τοῦ ἀνθρώπου ἀκοῦσαι. αὔριον, φησίν, ἀκούσῃ αὐτοῦ). Agrippa understands Festus's report about Paul's case as an implicit suggestion to provide him with counsel concerning Paul's transfer to the imperial court in Rome (unless Festus asked Agrippa explicitly to help him draft a letter to the emperor, a proposition that he may have shifted to vv. 26 – 27 for reasons of dramatic effect).

The imperfect tense of the verb translated "I would like" (ἐβουλόμην) may indicate that Agrippa had been "wishing" for some time to hear Paul, having heard about his activities and the efforts of the Jewish authorities in Jerusalem to have him sentenced and executed. Given his authority over affairs of the temple and his control over who held the high priesthood, presumably Agrippa was informed about the criminal case against Paul, the alleged "ringleader" of the followers of Jesus. Fes-

---

41. Cf. Richard J. Cassidy, *Society and Politics in the Acts of the Apostles* (Maryknoll, NY: Orbis, 1987), 203.

42. Omerzu, *Prozess*, 489.

tus, wasting no time, promises a hearing on the following day. He knows that since his main duty was preserving order in the province and since he had only limited forces at his disposal, he must maintain good relations with the provincial upper classes and the important men of the region.

25:23 The next day Agrippa and Bernice came with great pageantry, entering the audience hall with the military commanders and the most prominent men of the city. Then Festus gave the order and Paul was brought in (τῇ οὖν ἐπαύριον ἐλθόντος τοῦ Ἀγρίππα καὶ τῆς Βερνίκης μετὰ πολλῆς φαντασίας καὶ εἰσελθόντων εἰς τὸ ἀκροατήριον σύν τε χιλιάρχοις καὶ ἀνδράσιν τοῖς κατ᾽ ἐξοχὴν τῆς πόλεως καὶ κελεύσαντος τοῦ Φήστου ἤχθη ὁ Παῦλος). Luke sets the scene of Paul's hearing with comments on the participants and the location of the hearing. The people present at Paul's final hearing in Judea include governor Festus, King Agrippa II, Queen Bernice,[43] the military commanders of the five cohorts of auxiliary units that the governor had at his disposal, and "the most prominent men" of the city, i.e., the members of the Greek and Jewish aristocracy of Caesarea.

Since the purpose of the hearing is to provide Agrippa with an opportunity to assess Paul's case in the criminal proceedings that are in the process of being transferred to the imperial court in the city of Rome, Luke focuses his narrative on Agrippa, both here in v. 23 and in 26:1. Agrippa and Bernice arrive with full regalia and retinue. The location of the hearing is the "audience hall" in Festus's praetorium, the former palace of Herod (see on

vv. 2 – 3).[44] The time and effort Luke spends on this scene serves to highlight the innocence of Paul and confirms the relevance of the gospel of Jesus, Israel's Messiah and Savior, for both Jews and Gentiles.

Luke's vivid description of the pageantry of the entry of the royal couple, the military commanders, and the political dignitaries, and of Festus's order to have Paul brought from his prison cell, prompts his readers to picture all eyes on Paul as he enters the audience hall. After the extended phrases describing all the guests, the words "Paul was brought in" (ἤχθη ὁ Παῦλος) stand out with "impressive simplicity."[45] The passive voice communicates Paul's status as a prisoner whose movements are controlled by those who hold him in custody. As his speech in 26:2 – 23 and his attempt to lead the king to faith in Jesus in 26:25 – 27, 29 demonstrate, Paul refuses to let his "social status" determine his actions.

25:24 Festus said, "King Agrippa and all here present with us, you see this man about whom the entire Jewish community petitioned me both in Jerusalem and here, shouting that he ought not to live any longer" (καί φησιν ὁ Φῆστος· Ἀγρίππα βασιλεῦ καὶ πάντες οἱ συμπαρόντες ἡμῖν ἄνδρες, θεωρεῖτε τοῦτον περὶ οὗ ἅπαν τὸ πλῆθος τῶν Ἰουδαίων ἐνέτυχόν μοι ἔν τε Ἰεροσολύμοις καὶ ἐνθάδε βοῶντες μὴ δεῖν αὐτὸν ζῆν μηκέτι). Festus begins with a brief speech (vv. 24 – 27), in which he explains the purpose of the hearing.[46] He requests the attention of "King Agrippa" and "all here present." The governor solicits advice regarding Paul's case and the letter he must write to the emperor,

---

43. Since Bernice played an active role in political matters (Josephus, *J.W.* 2.310 – 314, 333 – 334; *Life* 343, 355), her presence at Paul's examination by Festus is not surprising.

44. The translation of ἀκροατήριον as "hall of justice" (BDAG) suggests that the room in question always, and only, served as a room in which judicial proceedings took place. Such a room probably did not exist in the praetorium of a Roman governor; the tribunal (βῆμα) could be set up in differ-

ent locations, depending on the defendant and the importance of the trial. English versions generally translate "audience hall" (NET, NRSV, RSV), "audience room" (NIV, TNIV), or "auditorium" (NASB).

45. Barrett, *Acts*, 1146.

46. Soards, *Speeches*, 121, labels Festus's speech as "judicial rhetoric"; Padilla, *Speeches*, 229, finds identification as forensic, deliberative, or epideictic rhetoric unconvincing.

primarily from Agrippa but also from the military commanders and the Greek and Jewish notables in the hall. The phrase "you see this man" (θεωρεῖτε τοῦτον) implies a hand gesture of Festus in the direction of Paul; the reference to Paul with a mere demonstrative pronoun implies the low social status of Paul as prisoner.

(1) The first major part of Festus's address contains a report on Paul's case (vv. 24d–25). The governor first notes the Jewish demand of a death sentence. The phrase translated "the entire Jewish community" is hyperbolic, unless the term πλῆθος refers to the Jewish leadership rather than the Jewish people as a whole. The verb translated "[they] petitioned" (ἐνέτυχον) and the reference to the demand made both in Jerusalem and "here" (ἐνθάδε), i.e., in Caesarea, suggests the former option, while the verb "shouting" (βοῶντες) points to the latter,[47] which agrees with the circumstances of Paul's arrest in the temple court, where an excited crowd was shouting (κράζοντες), accusing Paul of having desecrated the temple and demanding his execution.

Perhaps Festus is deliberately ambiguous here. While he leaves no doubt that it was the Jewish authorities in Jerusalem who demanded Paul's execution, he implies — correctly — that there were many Jews who believed that Paul "ought not to live any longer." The position of μηκέτι ("any longer"), which intensifies the negation of the phrase μὴ δεῖν αὐτὸν ζῆν ("he ought not to live") underscores the vehemence of the Jewish demand for Paul's execution.

25:25 But I found that he had done nothing deserving death. When he appealed to His Majesty the emperor, I decided to send him (ἐγὼ δὲ κατελαβόμην μηδὲν ἄξιον αὐτὸν θανάτου

πεπραχέναι, αὐτοῦ δὲ τούτου ἐπικαλεσαμένου τὸν Σεβαστὸν ἔκρινα πέμπειν). (2) Festus points out that Paul seems to be innocent. During his examination of Paul's case he has "found" nothing that deserves the death sentence. This statement is the strongest assertion of Paul's innocence since the evaluation of Paul by Lysias, the commander of the Roman garrison in Jerusalem (23:29). It confirms that Paul's accusers indeed had argued for a death sentence.

(3) The governor relates Paul's appeal to stand trial before "His Majesty the emperor" (for Σεβαστός see v. 21). Festus explains neither the reason for Paul's appeal — avoiding the conclusion of the trial proceedings in Jerusalem, where the Jewish authorities are determined to make sure that he dies — nor his decision not to release Paul despite his firm opinion that Paul was innocent of charges demanding a death sentence. In both cases the demand for a death sentence comes from the Jewish authorities in Jerusalem. Agrippa knows this already (v. 20), and the military commanders and the local dignitaries surely knew about the position of the Jewish leadership in their case against the famous prisoner in custody in Caesarea for two years.

(4) Festus confirms that he made the decision to grant Paul's appeal to the emperor and to send him to Rome.

25:26–27 "But I have nothing definite to write to our sovereign about him. Therefore I have brought him before all of you, and especially before you, King Agrippa, so that I may have something to write to our sovereign after we have examined him. For it seems to me unreasonable to send a prisoner without reporting the charges against him" (περὶ οὗ ἀσφαλές τι γράψαι τῷ κυρίῳ οὐκ ἔχω, διὸ προήγαγον αὐτὸν ἐφ' ὑμῶν

---

47. In 17:6 the same verb described the excited shouts of Jews in Thessalonica denouncing Paul and Silas to the city authorities.

καὶ μάλιστα ἐπὶ σοῦ, βασιλεῦ Ἀγρίππα, ὅπως τῆς ἀνακρίσεως γενομένης σχῶ τί γράψω· ἄλογον γάρ μοι δοκεῖ πέμποντα δέσμιον μὴ καὶ τὰς κατ᾽ αὐτοῦ αἰτίας σημᾶναι).

The second part of Festus's address, which announces the purpose[48] of the hearing (vv. 26 – 27), has an A-B-A structure. The first and third points mention the need to explain definite charges in a letter that he must write to the emperor (vv. 26a-b/27). The governor's reference to his obligation to "have something to write to our sovereign" refers to the *littera dimissoria*, which the lower court had to present to the higher court.[49] The letter had to contain the following information: a notice that an appeal had been lodged; the name of the person lodging the appeal; the sentence that is being contested; the name and identity of the parties involved.

The *littera dimissoria* was a formal report that did not impact the substance of the case. The person lodging an appeal had to present the *libellus appellatorii* to the presiding judge of the higher court — to the emperor in the case of the imperial court — within a certain period of time, who would then decide on a date for the new trial. If the appellant failed to provide the higher court with the report, he forfeited his appeal. The issuance of *littera dimissoria* was the last legal action of the lower court. Festus knows that he has to report the specific charges against Paul (αἱ κατ᾽ αὐτοῦ αἰτίαι) in his report for the emperor, which he must send together with the prisoner.

The term translated as "sovereign" (κύριος) was one of the titles of the Roman emperors, emphasizing their authority as *princeps* in the empire. It is not merely "unreasonable" (ἄλογος) to fail to report the charges to the emperor; it was a legal ne-

cessity to issue a *libellus appellatorii* reporting the circumstances and details of the appeal.

The examination (ἀνάκρισις)[50] of Paul by Agrippa has the purpose of supplementing the information obtained in the trial (25:6 – 12) and to obtain "definite" (ἀσφαλές), i.e., assured information — facts that clarify the connection between the demand of the death sentence by the Jewish authorities, the refusal of the governor to release Paul despite the lack of political crimes that require a death sentence, and the prisoner's appeal to be tried by the emperor. It is especially on the first point that the Jewish king may be able to shed some light.

26:1 Agrippa said to Paul, "You have permission to speak for yourself." Then Paul motioned with his hand and began to defend himself (Ἀγρίππας δὲ πρὸς τὸν Παῦλον ἔφη· ἐπιτρέπεταί σοι περὶ σεαυτοῦ λέγειν. τότε ὁ Παῦλος ἐκτείνας τὴν χεῖρα ἀπελογεῖτο). Luke's account of Paul's hearing before Festus and Agrippa continues with a note that relates Agrippa's granting Paul permission to speak. The governor, who has arranged for the hearing, allows the Jewish king to initiate the examination of the prisoner. Paul is permitted to speak about himself, i.e., about his activities and his beliefs. It will become obvious that Paul cannot speak about himself without speaking about Jesus Christ.

Paul, who would have remained standing in front of the dignitaries since being led into the audience hall, "motioned with his hand" (ἐκτείνας τὴν χεῖρα; lit., "stretched out his hand"), one of the most common gestures recommended in the rhetorical handbooks. The verb "defend" (ἀπελογεῖτο) characterizes what follows as a forensic speech.

---

48. Note the inferential conjunction διό.

49. Cf. Litewski, "Appellation," 87 – 88; Omerzu, *Prozess*, 91; see ibid. for the following details. See on 23:25.

50. BDAG, s.v. ἀνάκρισις, "a judicial hearing, *investigation, hearing*." The term describes here "preparation of the matter

for trial" in a preliminary examination (LSJ, s.v. ἀνάκρισις II), i.e., of the trial before the imperial court in Rome. At the same time, the hearing concludes the trial proceedings held by the governor of Judea in Caesarea.

While Paul is not on trial, the examination with the purpose of writing a *littera dimissoria* was still a legal procedure in which the rhetorical recommendations for defensive speeches would be followed.[51]

26:2 – 3 "I consider myself fortunate, King Agrippa, that I can defend myself today before you against all the accusations of the Jews, because you are especially familiar with all the customs and controversies of the Jewish people. Therefore I beg you to listen to me patiently" (Περὶ πάντων ὧν ἐγκαλοῦμαι ὑπὸ Ἰουδαίων, βασιλεῦ Ἀγρίππα, ἥγημαι ἐμαυτὸν μακάριον ἐπὶ σοῦ μέλλων σήμερον ἀπολογεῖσθαι μάλιστα γνώστην ὄντα σε πάντων τῶν κατὰ Ἰουδαίους ἐθῶν τε καὶ ζητημάτων, διὸ δέομαι μακροθύμως ἀκοῦσαί μου). In his introduction, Paul briefly touches on all the subjects that the rhetorical handbooks mentioned as appropriate for the *exordium*: he comments on the judge, on himself, on the opponents, and on the case.[52]

Paul makes three points. (1) He expresses his gratefulness that he can defend himself before Agrippa. The address is simple: he acknowledges the person who is conducting the hearing as "King Agrippa," and he himself is the defendant (ἀπολογεῖσθαι; see on v. 1). His accusers (ἐγκαλοῦμαι; lit., "I am being accused")[53] are "the Jews." Moreover, he considers himself "fortunate" to be able to defend himself before the king. The desire to win the goodwill of Agrippa (*captatio benevolentiae*) continues in the next point.

(2) Paul compliments Agrippa's competence as an expert in Jewish affairs. He acknowledges that

Agrippa is "especially familiar" with Jewish affairs, specifying two areas in which Agrippa has expertise: "the customs" (τὰ ἔθη), i.e., the laws of the Jewish people, and the "controversies" (ζητήματα), i.e., the theological and legal disputes of the various Jewish groups. This point describes the legal case before Agrippa and will be developed more fully in the lengthy *narratio* that follows (vv. 4 – 18).

(3) The introduction ends with Paul's plea that Agrippa listen to him "patiently" (μακροθύμως), i.e., pay close attention to what he has to say, for he will speak at some length.

26:4 All the Jews know my way of life from my youth, the life which I spent from the beginning among my own people and in Jerusalem (τὴν μὲν οὖν βίωσίν μου τὴν ἐκ νεότητος τὴν ἀπ' ἀρχῆς γενομένην ἐν τῷ ἔθνει μου ἔν τε Ἱεροσολύμοις ἴσασι πάντες οἱ Ἰουδαῖοι). In the second part of his speech, the *narratio* (statement of the facts of the case), Paul describes his past as a devout Pharisaic Jew educated in Jerusalem (vv. 4 – 5), the theological nature of the dispute with the Jews (vv. 6 – 7), his activity as a persecutor of the followers of Jesus of Nazareth (vv. 9 – 12), and, in vivid detail, his encounter with Jesus on the road to Damascus (vv. 13 – 18).

Paul begins with the assertion that "all the Jews" — perhaps a reference to all the Jews of v. 2, i.e., the Jews who have been accusing him in Jerusalem and in Caesarea — know his "way of life" (βίωσις) since his youth. Paul's youth is linked either with his birth and initial upbringing in the Jewish community in Tarsus (assuming that τε distinguishes "my own people" from those in Jerusalem; cf. 22:3),[54]

---

51. Paul's speech is thus by no means "irrelevant in a Roman court of law" (Tajra, *Trial*, 163, followed by Witherington, *Acts*, 735). The primary audience is indeed Festus, who has to compose the *littera dimissoria* that Paul must take to Rome.

52. Cf. Quintilian, *Inst.* 4.1.6 – 11; Parsons, *Acts*, 338.

53. The present tense of the verb (ἐγκαλοῦμαι) implies recognition of the fact that the legal case that the Jews have brought against him has not yet been concluded.

54. GNB eliminates the difficulty that some see in relating the term "nation, people" (ἔθνος) to the Jewish community in Tarsus by translating "at first in my own country and then in Jerusalem" (e.g., Barrett, *Acts*, 1151). There is no reason, however, why ἔθνος cannot refer to the Jews in Tarsus; note the definition in BDAG, s.v. ἔθνος 1, "a body of persons united by kinship, culture, and common traditions."

or with both his early and later education in Jerusalem (assuming that τε means "including" or "actually"). Even if the Jewish community of Tarsus is distinguished from the Jews in Jerusalem, Paul's statement emphasizes that he lived "from the beginning" in Jerusalem, the center of the worldwide Jewish commonwealth (22:3; Gal 1:13 – 14).

26:5 They have known me for a long time, if they are willing to testify, that I have lived according to the strictest sect of our religion as a Pharisee (προγινώσκοντές με ἄνωθεν, ἐὰν θέλωσι μαρτυρεῖν, ὅτι κατὰ τὴν ἀκριβεστάτην αἵρεσιν τῆς ἡμετέρας θρησκείας ἔζησα Φαρισαῖος). Paul's second point is the assertion that the Jews who accuse him know very well that he was a member of the "conservative" Pharisaic party. His accusers "have known [him] for a long time [ἄνωθεν]"; this refers to his affiliation with students and teachers of the law when he was educated in Jerusalem thirty years ago, and to his association with members of the priestly aristocracy and with members of the Sanhedrin twenty-seven years earlier when he was involved in actions against the followers of Jesus in concert with the chief priests (cf. 22:5).

The conditional clause third class "if they are willing to testify" (ἐὰν θέλωσι μαρτυρεῖν) suggests that while some of his accusers know him personally, they are unwilling to admit their former association with him as well as their knowledge of the fact that Paul was a devout Jew. His accusers could testify that Paul lived as a Pharisee (cf. 23:6; Phil 3:4 – 6). The aorist tense of the verb translated "I have lived" (ἔζησα) refers, considering the context, to the past: he had lived as a Pharisee when his accusers knew him in Jerusalem.

Paul describes the Pharisees as "the strictest sect" (ἡ ἀκριβεστάτη αἵρεσις) of Judaism. The superlative of the adjective reflects Pharisaic self-understanding as believers who take God's will as revealed in the Law and the Prophets more seri-

ously than any other group; they study, apply, and teach the Scriptures with utmost devotion and sacrificial consistency. The term translated "religion" (θρησκεία) denotes "worship" with an emphasis on the cultic, ritual, and formal aspects of the faith and practice of the Pharisees.

26:6 I now stand here on trial on account of my hope in the promise made by God to our ancestors (καὶ νῦν ἐπ᾽ ἐλπίδι τῆς εἰς τοὺς πατέρας ἡμῶν ἐπαγγελίας γενομένης ὑπὸ τοῦ θεοῦ ἔστηκα κρινόμενος). After describing his past as a devout Jew, Paul switches to the present with "now" (καὶ νῦν). He describes the nature of the dispute with the Jews (v. 6 – 8). The substance of the charges that caused Paul to be on trial is differences of theological conviction. Paul singles out three points of disagreement that are at the root of the controversy.

(1) Paul stands before a court of law on account of the hope (ἐλπίς) of the "promise" (ἐπαγγελία) that God had made to "our ancestors" (v. 6), i.e., the patriarchs in particular and Israel more generally. For God's promises to the people of Israel, see 2:39; 13:23, 32. In v. 8 it will become clear that the hope that Paul refers to is the hope of the resurrection of the dead, a fact that Festus and Agrippa are well aware of (25:19) and that Paul had stressed both in the Sanhedrin hearing (23:6) and in the trial before governor Felix (24:15).

Both Paul's former affiliation with the Pharisees (who believe in the resurrection of the dead) and the connection between v. 8 ("God raises the dead") and v. 9 ("Jesus of Nazareth") indicates that the dispute is about Paul's conviction that Israel's hopes have become a reality in and through Jesus. Jesus was raised from the dead, through which God has fulfilled the promises he had made to the fathers — specifically, the promise of a Savior who would bring about "the authentic realization of the people of Israel as the children of the promise made to Abraham."[55] The scriptural basis for the hope in the resurrection of the dead and the restoration of Israel (see v. 7) are passages such as Isa 25:8; 26:19; Ezek 37:1 – 14; Dan 12:1 – 3; Hos 6:2.

26:7 A promise that our twelve tribes hope to attain as they worship with perseverance day and night. It is because of this hope, King Agrippa, that I am accused by the Jews (εἰς ἣν τὸ δωδεκάφυλον ἡμῶν ἐν ἐκτενείᾳ νύκτα καὶ ἡμέραν λατρεῦον ἐλπίζει καταντῆσαι, περὶ ἧς ἐλπίδος ἐγκαλοῦμαι ὑπὸ Ἰουδαίων, βασιλεῦ). (2) Paul asserts that the "promise" (ἐπαγγελία; note the relative pronoun ἥν) in whose present fulfillment he believes concerns the hope of "our twelve tribes," a term that signals the hope of Israel's eschatological regathering when the twelve tribes will live in peace and prosperity in the Promised Land. The Jews maintained this hope against political reality; there were Israelites belonging to Judah, Benjamin, and Levi (the priestly families) who lived in Judea, in Galilee, and in diaspora communities, and there were members of the northern tribes living in Samaria and somewhere abroad, but there was no people of Israel consisting of twelve tribes.[56]

Luke's readers know what Paul implies: the restoration of the people of Israel, symbolized by the figure twelve, has become a reality through the person and ministry of Jesus of Nazareth, who had chosen twelve apostles who would take the good news of the arrival of God's rule to Israel and to the nations.[57] As devout Jews worship God with perseverance day and night,[58] expecting the fulfillment of God's promises, Paul and his fellow believers in Jesus are convinced, and proclaim, that these promises *have* been fulfilled in and through Jesus, through whose life, death, resurrection, and exaltation he is establishing his rule. Paul repeats the basic point of contention, addressing King Agrippa again to underline the importance of his statement: "it is because of this hope" that he is accused by the Jewish authorities, i.e., the hope of the resurrection and the present fulfillment of God's promises.

26:8 Why should it be considered unbelievable by any of you that God raises the dead? (τί ἄπιστον κρίνεται παρ᾽ ὑμῖν εἰ ὁ θεὸς νεκροὺς ἐγείρει;). (3) Paul challenges Jews who believe in the resurrection to follow through on their conviction. Jews who accept the statement as true "that God raises the dead" should not accuse Paul of crimes and demand his execution. They should not deem "unbelievable" (ἄπιστον) that the almighty God can bring people who have died back to life. The context in v. 9 suggests that Paul is already thinking of the resurrection of Jesus (cf. v. 23). Jews who indeed accept that God raises the dead should not find it implausible that God brought Jesus back from the dead.

26:9 I was convinced that I ought to do many things against the name of Jesus of Nazareth (ἐγὼ μὲν οὖν ἔδοξα ἐμαυτῷ πρὸς τὸ ὄνομα Ἰησοῦ τοῦ Ναζωραίου δεῖν πολλὰ ἐναντία πρᾶξαι). After

---

55. Johnson, *Acts*, 432, with reference to Luke 1:55, 73; 3:8; 13:28; Acts 3:24 – 26; 7:1 – 8; 13:32 – 33.

56. On the twelve tribes in early Judaism cf. Fuller, *Restoration of Israel*, 154 – 56, with reference to *T. Levi* 10; 14; 16; 17; *T. Jud.* 23, and other passages; the community behind the War Scroll (1QM) understood its identity as "the people of the twelve tribes," with the implication of "a comprehensive claim *to the heritage and promise* of Israel's full re-gathering" (ibid., 455, emphasis Fuller's).

57. Cf. Johnson, *Acts*, 433, with reference to Luke 6:13; 8:1; 9:1, 12, 17; 22:30; Acts 1:15 – 26; 7:8. Luke included in the be-

ginning of his two-volume work the declaration of the priest Zechariah that the effect of God's visitation of the people in fulfillment of "the oath he swore to our father Abraham" was that they might "serve him without fear in holiness and righteousness before him all our days" (Luke 1:73 – 75).

58. The expression "day and night" (νύκτα καὶ ἡμέραν; lit., "night and day") probably does not refer to regular times of prayer in the temple, associated with the morning and evening sacrifice, but more generally to continuous worship that never stops.

speaking about his past upbringing (vv. 4–5) and about his present belief in the resurrection, which is the reason for the accusations against him (vv. 6–8), Paul reverts to speaking about the past. He now[59] reviews his involvement in the persecution of the followers of Jesus (vv. 9–12).

(1) Paul begins by describing the conviction that drove him to oppose Jesus' followers. He "was convinced" (ἔδοξα) that "many things" needed to be done in order to curb the activities of the followers of Jesus; in vv. 10–11 Paul will provide details. The combination of the explicit first person pronoun (ἐγώ) with the first person reflexive pronoun (ἐμαυτῷ) places a strong emphasis on the speaker. The term "the name" (τὸ ὄνομα) describes not only Jesus of Nazareth but also, and more specifically, the followers of Jesus and their activities (see on 2:38).[60] When he encountered Jesus on the road to Damascus, he learned that persecuting believers in Jesus was tantamount to persecuting Jesus himself (v. 14). Paul asserts that he regarded his actions aimed "against" Jesus' followers as an obligation.

26:10 And that is what I did in Jerusalem; I locked up many of the saints in prison with the authority that I received from the chief priests. And when they were condemned to death, I cast my vote against them (ὃ καὶ ἐποίησα ἐν Ἰεροσολύμοις, καὶ πολλούς τε τῶν ἁγίων ἐγὼ ἐν φυλακαῖς κατέκλεισα τὴν παρὰ τῶν ἀρχιερέων ἐξουσίαν λαβὼν ἀναιρουμένων τε αὐτῶν κατήνεγκα ψῆφον). (2) Paul informs King Agrippa about his active and energetic involvement in the measures of the Jewish authorities that aimed at crushing

Jews who believed in Jesus and who followed his teaching. The description is more concrete and Paul appears more virulent than in the reports in 9:1–3 and 22:4–5. He first focuses on his activities in Jerusalem. Two verbs in the aorist tense describe what he did: he "locked up" (κατέκλεισα) many Christians[61] in prison, and he "cast [his] vote against [κατήνεγκα] them" when they were condemned to death.

Paul acted with the "authority" (ἐξουσία) of the chief priests, which was expressed, at least on some occasions, in letters (9:1–2). The term translated as "vote" (ψῆφος) denotes "a pebble used in voting: a black one for conviction, a white one for acquittal" (BDAG). Paul's statement could refer to literal voting (implying that Paul was a member of the Sanhedrin), or it could function as "a metonymy for other forms of corporate approval."[62] The verb "condemned to death" implies participation in trials in which Christians were charged with capital offenses.

This statement has been taken to imply that Paul must have been a member of the Sanhedrin as an ordained rabbi.[63] While not impossible, this is unlikely because he was presumably too young in AD 30–31 for membership in the highest court. There were other courts in Jerusalem: the ruling body of each synagogue constituted a minor court of law (*beth din* or *sanhedrin*); however, the Jerusalem synagogues probably did not try capital cases, which was the prerogative of the supreme Sanhedrin. Perhaps Paul means to say that he was involved in death penalty cases as "one of the young

---

59. The expression μὲν οὖν takes up the narrative from v. 5 (Barrett, *Acts*, 1154), and at the same time it provides a transition from v. 8, building "on the implicit acknowledgment that it was Paul's previously finding it 'incredible' that God should have raised Jesus that accounted for his rage and hostility against the Messianists who claimed he had" (Johnson, *Acts*, 433).

60. Cf. 3:6, 16; 4:7, 12, 17–18; 9:14–16. On Ναζωραῖος (lit., "the Nazorean, the Nazarene") see 2:22; 3:6; 4:10; 6:14; 22:8; 24:5.

61. The Christians are called "saints" (ἅγιοι); see on 9:13. Paul speaks as a Christian.

62. Craig S. Keener, "Three Notes on Figurative Language," *JGRChJ* 5 (2008): 42–50, 46. Johnson, *Acts*, 434, suggests a wordplay: while some were stoning Stephen, throwing rocks, Paul cast his own pebble.

63. Cf. Jeremias, *Jerusalem*, 255 n. 34.

Pharisaic scribes in the Sanhedrin who helped in the interpretation of the Law."[64]

The death penalty could be carried out by the Sanhedrin only when the sanctity of the temple had been violated (see on 21:28). Other cases had to be referred to the Roman governor, who would have to be petitioned to confirm a death sentence of the Sanhedrin in a new trial (as in the case against Jesus). If we assume that such executions of Christians involving both trials before the Sanhedrin and the Roman governor would have been mentioned by Luke, this scenario is not likely. As a result of these difficulties, commentators understand Paul's statement as a generalizing reference to his involvement in the death of Stephen,[65] as a rhetorical statement for dramatic effect,[66] or as a metaphorical statement indicating that he sided with those who voted for the death penalty to be inflicted on followers of Jesus.[67]

When we consider the fact that the Jerusalem Christians met regularly in Solomon's Portico in the outer court of the temple (cf. 3:11; 5:12), that they regularly participated in the worship taking place in the Inner Enclosure of the temple (cf. 3:1), and that Paul wanted to be able to indict the Christians on a charge of blasphemy (v. 11), which was punished by death, it is not impossible to relate Paul's statement to accusations of breaches of the sanctity of the temple, which could have led to the death penalty. Note that Jesus, Stephen, and Paul were all accused of blaspheming against or desecrating the temple (Matt 26:60 – 61/Mark 14:57 – 58;[68] Acts 6:11, 13 – 14; 21:28).

Luke's report of Paul's account of his involvement in the execution of Christians may thus not merely represent folk memory but historical events.[69] The persecution affected a large number of Christians: many were thrown into prison, and many were executed. Luke relates in 7:60 only the death of Stephen (the execution of James [see 12:2] took place at a later date, when Agrippa I was king), but evidently more Christians were condemned to death.

26:11 By punishing them often in all the synagogues, I tried to force them to blaspheme. And I was so furiously enraged at them that I pursued them even to foreign cities (καὶ κατὰ πάσας τὰς συναγωγὰς πολλάκις τιμωρῶν αὐτοὺς ἠνάγκαζον βλασφημεῖν περισσῶς τε ἐμμαινόμενος αὐτοῖς ἐδίωκον ἕως καὶ εἰς τὰς ἔξω πόλεις). (3) Paul describes his involvement in synagogue punishments meted out to Christians. He visited all the Jerusalem synagogues (cf. 6:9) in which followers of Jesus worshiped.[70]

The basic meaning of the verb translated "punished" (τιμωρῶν) is "to be an avenger, to exact or seek to exact vengeance" (LSJ; cf. BDAG). Paul probably refers to flogging, particularly the forty lashes minus one (see on 4:21; 5:40; according to 2 Cor 11:24, he had received this punishment himself five times after he had become a Christian). This participle, whose present tense corresponds to the statement that he "often" inflicted punishments on Jesus' followers in the synagogues, is best taken as expressing means: he used punishments in order to "try to force" (ἠνάγκαζον)[71] or compel Christians "to blaspheme" (βλασφημεῖν; see on 6:11).

---

64. Witherington, *Acts*, 742.

65. Bruce, *Book of Acts*, 464.

66. Marshall, *Acts*, 393.

67. Fitzmyer, *Acts*, 758; Johnson, *Acts*, 434.

68. In the parallel account in Luke 22, the charge of Jesus wanting to destroy the temple is omitted.

69. Dunn, *Beginning from Jerusalem*, 338, asserts that Luke's language is "more soundly based than at first appears" when

compared with Gal 1:13, where Paul states that he persecuted the church "intensely," trying to destroy (ἐπόρθουν) the church.

70. According to 8:3 Paul also went from house to house arresting Christians. The statement in 26:11 adds a new detail.

71. The imperfect is conative, denoting a consistent effort that did not succeed: Paul *tried* to force Christians to blaspheme. Whether he was successful in this attempt is not stated by the text.

The use of this term in the charges against Stephen, who was accused of "speaking words against this holy place and against the law" (6:13), makes both Lev 24:11 – 16 and Exod 22:28 relevant. The former passage stipulates the death sentence for blasphemy against "the name of the LORD" while the latter passage prohibits "cursing a ruler of your people" (which could be interpreted as a reference to Moses). If Paul describes his actions from a Christian point of view, the blasphemies that he wanted Christians to utter by torturing them probably would involve cursing Jesus, i.e., renouncing him as Messiah.[72] If he describes his actions from the perspective of a Jewish zealot seeking to obtain indictments on the highest penalty possible, he may have tortured the Christians in the attempt to get them to utter a blasphemy against Israel's God, Israel's law, or God's people, or he tried to get Jesus' followers to say things about Jesus, perhaps his divine status, that would be regarded as blasphemy from a Jewish perspective.[73] The two interpretations are not necessarily mutually exclusive; the movement of Jesus' followers would be crushed either way, if these measures would have been universally successful.

(4) Paul mentions his pursuit of Christians to "foreign cities" outside of Judea. He describes his attitude in his actions concerning the followers of Jesus in terms of being "furiously enraged" (περισσῶς ἐμμαινόμενος). Note that in v. 25 Paul says to Festus that he is now, as a Christian, "true and reasonable," not insane (οὐ μαίνομαι; note the use of the root of the same verb). In 9:1 Luke had described Paul as "breathing threats and murder against the disciples of the Lord." His obsessive rage is given as the reason for taking the initiative to pursue Christians into cities outside of Judea (and Samaria and Galilee). In 9:2 and 22:5 only

Damascus is mentioned. Evidently Paul also traveled to other cities, presumably some east of Judea in Syria and Nabatea.

26:12 Under these circumstances I went to Damascus with the authority and the commission of the chief priests (ἐν οἷς πορευόμενος εἰς τὴν Δαμασκὸν μετ᾽ ἐξουσίας καὶ ἐπιτροπῆς τῆς τῶν ἀρχιερέων). After speaking about his past upbringing as a devout Jew (vv. 4 – 5), his belief in the resurrection of the dead as the cause of the accusations against him (vv. 6 – 8), and his fierce persecution of the church (vv. 9 – 12), Paul now describes his encounter with the risen Jesus (vv. 12 – 18). This event explains the particular shape of his belief in the resurrection of the dead as well as his dramatic change from persecuting Jesus' followers to proclaiming Jesus as Israel's crucified and risen Messiah and Savior.

(1) Paul first describes how he traveled to Damascus with the official support of the chief priests. The expression "under these circumstances" links the narrative that begins in v. 12 with the previous description of Paul's activities. His travels to foreign cities in the pursuit of Christians took him to Damascus with the "authority" (ἐξουσία) and "commission" (ἐπιτροπή) of the chief priests (v. 10; cf. 9:1 – 2). The first term describes the power that Paul had been given by the chief priests to arrest and punish Jewish believers in Jesus in the synagogues of Damascus, while the second term suggests that the chief priest had authorized him to carry out this assignment on their behalf.

26:13 At noon, as I was on the road, King Agrippa, I saw a light from heaven, brighter than the sun, shining around me and those who traveled with me (ἡμέρας μέσης κατὰ τὴν ὁδὸν εἶδον, βασιλεῦ, οὐρανόθεν ὑπὲρ τὴν λαμπρότητα

---

72. Cf. Tajra, *Trial*, 166. Pliny, *Ep. Tra.* 10.96.5, attempted to force Christians to reject Jesus (*maledicerent Christo*).

73. Peterson, *Acts*, 664; also Dunn, *Beginning from Jerusalem*, 989 n. 146.

τοῦ ἡλίου περιλάμψαν με φῶς καὶ τοὺς σὺν ἐμοὶ πορευομένους). (2) Paul describes the light and the voice from heaven that he heard while on the road to Damascus (vv. 13 – 14). This event was so significant that he remembered at what time it took place: "at noon" (cf. 22:6). All three accounts speak of a "light from heaven," but the description varies: in 9:3 Luke described a "light from heaven," in 22:6 "a great light," here a light "brighter than the sun," which highlights the supernatural origin of the phenomenon. The description of the light as one that "flashed around" in 9:3 and 22:6 is changed to "shining around" (περιλάμψαν), a term that emphasizes the constant glare of the supernatural light.

26:14 We all fell to the ground, and I heard a voice saying to me in Hebrew, "Saul, Saul, why do you persecute me? It is hard for you to kick against the goads" (πάντων τε καταπεσόντων ἡμῶν εἰς τὴν γῆν ἤκουσα φωνὴν λέγουσαν πρός με τῇ Ἑβραΐδι διαλέκτῳ· Σαοὺλ Σαούλ, τί με διώκεις; σκληρόν σοι πρὸς κέντρα λακτίζειν). The effect of the bright light caused Paul and his fellow travelers to fall to the ground (in 9:4 and 22:7 only Paul was described as falling to the ground). If this is not simply a stylistic variation, Luke emphasizes the witness that Paul's companions could provide concerning this event.

Blinded by the light and lying on the ground, perhaps face down, Paul heard a voice addressing him "in Hebrew" (see on 22:2; the reference to language, not included in the earlier accounts,[74] could be to Aramaic). The words spoken in the exchange between the heavenly voice and Paul are given in direct speech, a fact that emphasizes their significance for Paul. The question was so memorable that it is repeated verbatim in all three accounts (cf. 9:4; 22:7). The repetition of Paul's Jewish name highlights for Agrippa the significance of the communication from heaven. The question "Why do you persecute me?" identified the speaker with the cause that Paul had been attacking and suppressing. When Paul was told who the speaker was (v. 15), he was forced to acknowledge that he was persecuting not simply the followers of Jesus but Jesus himself, who was now speaking to him in the light of heavenly glory (see further on 9:4). The question challenged Paul's identity and activity as a persecutor of the believers in Jesus.

A new detail is the assertion by the voice from heaven that it was hard for Paul "to kick against the goads." A goad (κέντρον; κέντρα is plural) is "a pointed stick that serves the same purpose as a whip" or a cattle prod, used to drive horses, oxen, and other beasts of burden. The expression "kick against the goad" describes the struggle of a beast of burden (or riding animal) against the directions of the driver (or rider). As a proverbial expression it describes "futile and detrimental resistance to a stronger power, whether it be that of a god, of destiny, or of man."[75] This reference has been explained as Paul's attempt to clarify the implications of the question of the heavenly voice for his Greek-oriented audience. The heavenly voice told Paul not to resist God, who was directing him toward "the Way" to become a follower of Jesus.[76]

26:15 Then I asked, "Who are you, Lord?" The Lord answered, "I am Jesus, whom you are per-

---

74. The clarification may be included here in order to explain the reference to "Saul" when his listeners may have known him only as "Paul"; see Johnson, *Acts*, 435.

75. L. Schmid, "κέντρον," *TDNT*, 3:664. Cf. Euripides, *Bacch.* 794 – 795: "I would sacrifice to the god rather than kick against his goads in anger, a mortal against a god."

76. To interpret the "pricks" of the goad in terms of Paul's conscience, popularly often related to Paul's memory of his part in Stephen's death, is not plausible since Paul's references to his preconversion period do not indicate any pangs of conscience (cf. Acts 26:10 – 11; Gal 1:13 – 14; Phil 3:5 – 6).

secuting" (ἐγὼ δὲ εἶπα· τίς εἶ, κύριε; ὁ δὲ κύριος εἶπεν· ἐγώ εἰμι Ἰησοῦς ὃν σὺ διώκεις). (3) Paul relates the identification of the voice as the voice of Jesus. Paul's question is repeated verbatim from 9:5 and 22:8. The answer of the heavenly voice is also the same, apart from the addition of the identification "of Nazareth" added in 22:8. Paul's perplexed question makes sense both for a Jew like Agrippa and a pagan like Festus: heavenly revelations (or auditions) remain ambiguous if the person receiving the revelation does not know who is speaking. The fact that Jesus, whose followers Paul had been persecuting, identified himself as speaking from the reality of divine glory means that the Jew with the name Jesus who had been crucified by governor Pontius Pilate, on the instigation of the chief priests, is alive and shares God's glory and directs human affairs, at least in the case of Paul.

26:16 "Now get up and stand on your feet. I have appeared to you in order to appoint you as a servant and a witness of what you have seen of me and of what you will be shown" (ἀλλὰ ἀνάστηθι καὶ στῆθι ἐπὶ τοὺς πόδας σου· εἰς τοῦτο γὰρ ὤφθην σοι, προχειρίσασθαί σε ὑπηρέτην καὶ μάρτυρα ὧν τε εἶδές με ὧν τε ὀφθήσομαί σοι). (4) Paul describes his appointment by Jesus as his servant and witness (on Paul's call as Jesus' witness, see "In Depth: Paul's Missionary Work" in Literary Context on 13:1 – 12). In this account alone Paul received his missionary commission directly from Jesus on the road to Damascus; in 9:10 – 17 and 22:12 – 16 Paul was commissioned by Jesus through Ananias, a Jewish Christian in Damascus.[77]

This difference can be explained in various ways. (a) In 26:16 – 18 Paul telescopes events, omitting the involvement of Ananias altogether, be-

cause he wants to emphasize to King Agrippa that he has been divinely commissioned to proclaim the message for which he is being accused by the Jewish officials. (b) Paul provides in 26:16 – 18 the historically clearest report of his commission: according to his own words in Gal 1:1, 15 – 16, he did not receive his commission from human beings but directly from God; the words of Ananias in Acts 22:14 – 15 may allude to Paul's commission on the road to Damascus, whose significance Ananias explains to Paul, while the report concerning Ananias's involvement in 9:10 – 17 also does not speak of a commissioning of Paul by Ananias. Luke may have been saving this important detail of Paul's conversion and commission for maximum effect in Paul's speech before King Agrippa.[78]

In the previous accounts of his conversion, Paul was also ordered to "get up" (cf. 9:6; 22:10, 16). The charge to "stand on your feet," followed by divine instructions, echoes the call of Ezekiel, whom God sent to Israel (Ezek 2:1 – 4).[79] Jesus explains that the purpose of why he allowed himself to be "seen" (ὤφθην; see on 9:17) by Paul is Paul's appointment as his servant and witness. The verb translated "appoint" (προχειρίσασθαί; see on 3:20; 22:14) describes Paul's selection by the risen Lord Jesus for a specific task. Paul informs King Agrippa that he did not volunteer for his career as a preacher of Jesus Christ (as he had volunteered to persecute Jesus' followers); rather, his life's direction and purpose changed dramatically as a result of a commission given to him by Jesus, risen from the dead, whom he met on the road to Damascus.

Paul was commissioned to be Jesus' "servant" (ὑπηρέτης; see on 13:5), i.e., someone who helps and assists Jesus in what Jesus continues to do in the world (cf. 1:1). And he was commissioned to be

---

77. Since Paul omits in his account before Agrippa the role of Ananias, there is no need to include a reference to Paul's being blinded.

78. Charles W. Hedrick, "Paul's Conversion/Call: A Comparative Analysis of the Three Reports in Acts," *JBL* 100 (1981): 415 – 32, 427.

79. Cf. Marshall, "Acts," 599.

Jesus' "witness" (μάρτυς; cf. 1:8), joining the Twelve and other witnesses who spoke about their encounter with the risen Jesus of Nazareth and who took the good news of Jesus, Israel's Messiah and Savior, to the people living in Jerusalem and to the ends of the earth (cf. 1:8). The content of his witness was to communicate to others "what you have seen of me," i.e., the reality of Jesus risen from the dead, alive and active from heavenly glory as a "witness to his resurrection" (1:22); and to communicate "what you will be shown," i.e., further revelations of Jesus' reality conveying his will[80] and manifesting his power.[81]

26:17 "I will rescue you from your people and from the Gentiles, to whom I am sending you" (ἐξαιρούμενός σε ἐκ τοῦ λαοῦ καὶ ἐκ τῶν ἐθνῶν εἰς οὓς ἐγὼ ἀποστέλλω σε). (5) Paul relates Jesus' assurance of protection among Jews and Gentiles, a promise that underlines that his mission would be risky and dangerous. This is a new element in Luke's accounts of Paul's conversion, corresponding to the commission of the Twelve in Matt 28:18 – 20, who were promised the risen Lord's continued presence. The risen Lord promised that he would rescue (ἐξαιρούμενος)[82] Paul, i.e., deliver him, from dangerous situations that would arise among the Jewish people (λαός) and among the Gentiles (τὰ ἔθνη).

Jesus' promise echoes God's promise to Jeremiah, who was sent to the people of Israel despite his youth: "You shall go to all to whom I send you, and you shall speak whatever I command you. Do not be afraid of them, for I am with you to deliver you [ἐξαιρεῖσθαί σε], says the Lord" (Jer

1:7 – 8 LXX).[83] Luke's readers would remember that Paul had encountered dangers in Damascus (9:23 – 25), Jerusalem (9:29 – 30), Pisidian Antioch (13:50), Iconium (14:6), Lystra (14:19 – 20), Philippi (16:19 – 39), Thessalonica (17:5 – 9), Corinth (18:12 – 17), Ephesus (19:29 – 31), and most recently and repeatedly again in Jerusalem (21:27 – 36; 23:12 – 33).

Jesus sent Paul (ἀποστέλλω σε) to Jews and Gentiles. The relative pronoun (οὕς) would appear to refer only to the Gentiles. However, Luke has portrayed Paul since Acts 13 as a witness of Jesus both among Jews (in synagogues) and among Gentiles (both in the synagogues as God-fearers, and in the public lecture halls and marketplaces of the cities his visited). This makes it more plausible to interpret the masculine plural οὕς as taking up the masculine singular noun λαοῦ and the neuter plural noun ἐθνῶν. (a) If "your people" refers to Jews from whose opposition Paul is protected by the power of Jesus' promise, he is obviously threatened because he witnesses to them. (b) The images of turning to God and opening blind eyes in v. 18 are also used of Jews by Luke.[84] (c) According to v. 20 Paul's obedience to the divine commission takes him to Jerusalem and Judea, i.e., to Jews, and then also to the Gentiles (cf. Rom 15:16). (d) In v. 23 Paul speaks of the Messiah being proclaimed both to "his people" (the Jews) and to Gentiles.

26:18 "To open their eyes and to turn them from darkness to light and from the power of Satan to God, so that they may receive forgiveness of sins and a place among those who are sanctified by faith in me" (ἀνοῖξαι ὀφθαλμοὺς αὐτῶν, τοῦ

---

80. Cf. 16:7, 9 – 10; 18:9 – 10; 22:17 – 21; 23:11; 27:23 – 24; also 2 Cor 12:1 – 5.

81. Cf. 14:3; 15:12; 19:11; also Rom 15:19; 2 Cor 12:12. The future "seeing" that Paul will proclaim as Jesus' witness might also refer to the conversion of the nations.

82. The verb is used in this sense also in 7:10, 34; 12:11;

23:27. The present tense of the participle stands for future action.

83. Marshall, "Acts," 599, also points to 1 Chr 16:35 ("deliver us from the nations") since Paul is to be delivered both from the people (Israel) and from the nations (Gentiles).

84. Luke 1:16, 78 – 79; 4:18; Acts 13:47.

ἐπιστρέψαι ἀπὸ σκότους εἰς φῶς καὶ τῆς ἐξουσίας τοῦ σατανᾶ ἐπὶ τὸν θεόν, τοῦ λαβεῖν αὐτοὺς ἄφεσιν ἁμαρτιῶν καὶ κλῆρον ἐν τοῖς ἡγιασμένοις πίστει τῇ εἰς ἐμέ). (6) Paul describes for Agrippa the mission and message that he proclaims among Jews and Gentiles. The summary is structured with three infinitives.

(a) Jesus sends Paul to Jews and Gentiles "to open their eyes" (ἀνοῖξαι ὀφθαλμοὺς αὐτῶν) so that they see the reality of Jesus as crucified, risen, and exalted Messiah, Savior, and Lord who fulfills God's promises. This description echoes the mission of the Servant of the Lord in Isa 42:7, who was called by God, promised guidance and strength, and given the task "to open eyes that are blind" (ἀνοῖξαι ὀφθαλμοὺς τυφλῶν). Paul's missionary ministry is prophetic ministry through which God fulfills his promises.

(b) Jesus sends Paul to Jews and Gentiles "to turn them from darkness to light" (ἐπιστρέψαι ἀπὸ σκότους εἰς φῶς). This mission statement echoes Isa 42:6, where the Servant of the Lord is sent as "a light for the Gentiles" (φῶς ἐθνῶν), and Isa 42:16, where the Lord promises that he "will turn the darkness into light before them" (ποιήσω αὐτοῖς τὸ σκότος εἰς φῶς). In Isa 42:16, the turn from darkness to light is explained in ethical terms, where the next line reads: "and make the rough places smooth." Israel is promised a time when the people will walk on the straight path of the will of God.[85] Here, the turn from darkness to light is explained in cosmic terms: "from the power of Satan to God";

people are captive to Satan, but they can and will be liberated if they accept the witness of Jesus and thus return to God.[86] Luke's description of the ministry of Jesus and of the apostles, including that of Paul, gives numerous examples of the defeat of Satan and the power of his forces as God's rule (or kingdom) is proclaimed.[87]

(c) Jesus sends Paul to Jews and Gentiles so that they may "receive forgiveness of sins" (λαβεῖν αὐτοὺς ἄφεσιν ἁμαρτιῶν).[88] The sins that are forgiven are the sins of living in darkness instead of seeing and accepting the reality of God and his revelation, of serving Satan instead of God, and of refusing faith in Jesus. Forgiveness of sins is the result when people have their eyes opened, when they turn away from darkness, when they are liberated from the power of Satan, when they come into the light, when they return to God.

Jesus describes a second result of turning from darkness to light and from the power of Satan to God in terms of people receiving "a place among those who are sanctified by faith in me." The "place" (κλῆρος) or "lot" is a share in salvation of the people who have been cleansed from all impurities; i.e., it is a place in the community of God's people who enjoy fellowship with God (see 20:32). Forgiveness of sins and sanctification from impurity are effected by "faith in me" (πίστει τῇ εἰς ἐμέ), i.e., by faith in Jesus, the crucified, risen, and exalted Lord. Thus Paul's missionary commission ends with the emphasis that faith in Jesus is *the* way of sanctification and thus of salvation for all people.

---

85. Qumran texts divide humanity according to the Angel of Light and the Angel (1QS III, 13 – IV, 26) of Darkness into "sons of light" and "sons of darkness;" 1QS I, 9 – 10; 1QM I, 1.

86. On Satan (ὁ σατανᾶς) see on 5:3. Qumran texts contrast the "lot of Belial" with the "lot of God" (1QS II, 2, 5), with the world outside the covenant (of the Qumran people) being under the "dominion of Belial" (1QS I, 18, 23; II, 19; 1QM XIV, 9). In the Old Testament, Belial is connected with death and with the underworld (2 Sam 22:5; Ps 18:5) and is the one who

leads Israel astray from legitimate worship of Yahweh (Deut 13:13 – 15).

87. Cf. Luke 4:4, 8, 12; 10:18; 11:14 – 23; 13:16; Acts 5:1 – 11, 16; 8:7, 11, 20 – 23; 10:43; 13:38; 16:16 – 18; 19:12; see also Rom 8:38 – 39; 15:19; 1 Cor 12:28; 2 Cor 2:11; Col 1:13; with eschatological future outlook Rom 16:20. Note Eph 6:20; 1 Cor 4:20.

88. For the forgiveness of sins, see on 2:38. Cf. Luke 1:77; 3:3; 4:18; 5:20 – 21; 24:47; Acts 5:31; 10:43; 13:38.

These three infinitives describe three parts of the process and reality of conversion:[89]

- understanding[90] the reality of the darkness and the reality of light that make forgiveness of sin and purification from impurities possible through faith in Jesus
- change of direction from darkness to light, from Satan to God, from sin to forgiveness, from impurity to sanctification, from denial of Jesus' identity as Israel's Messiah and Savior to faith in Jesus, from alienation to an inheritance among the saints
- reception of the gift of the light of God's revelation, of the presence of God's power, of forgiveness of sins, of a place among the saints, of faith in Jesus.

26:19 – 20 Therefore, King Agrippa, I was not disobedient to the heavenly vision, but proclaimed first to the people in Damascus, then to the people in Jerusalem and throughout Judea, and then to the Gentiles that they should repent and turn to God and act in a manner consistent with their repentance (ὅθεν, βασιλεῦ Ἀγρίππα, οὐκ ἐγενόμην ἀπειθὴς τῇ οὐρανίῳ ὀπτασίᾳ ἀλλὰ τοῖς ἐν Δαμασκῷ πρῶτόν τε καὶ Ἱεροσολύμοις, πᾶσάν τε τὴν χώραν τῆς Ἰουδαίας καὶ τοῖς ἔθνεσιν ἀπήγγελλον μετανοεῖν καὶ ἐπιστρέφειν ἐπὶ τὸν θεόν, ἄξια τῆς μετανοίας ἔργα πράσσοντας). After the *exordium* (vv. 2 – 3) and the *narratio* (vv. 4 – 18), Paul provides the proofs (*probatio* or *confirmatio*) for his defense.[91] This new section is marked by another address of King Agrippa (cf. v. 2). Paul makes three points.

(1) He has been obedient to the commission given to him by Jesus, who appeared to him in the heavenly vision (οὐράνιος ὀπτασία).[92] His work and message are a response to a revelation from heaven, not an undertaking that he began or carried out on his own initiative. To be "disobedient" was not an option for a devout Jew and Pharisee who accepted God's revelation with consistent obedience. He had to obey the commission of "heaven," a term that served as circumlocution for "Yahweh" in Judaism.

(2) The proof of Paul's obedience is his work among Jews and Gentiles in the cities of various regions of the eastern Mediterranean world. Paul proclaimed the news of Jesus, Israel's Messiah and Savior, immediately after his encounter with Jesus on the road to Damascus twenty-eight years earlier. For Paul's proclamation of the gospel in Damascus see 9:20 – 22; for Jerusalem see 9:26 – 29 (cf. Rom 15:19); for Judea see perhaps 15:3;[93] for Paul's preaching among Gentiles see Luke's long narrative in Acts 13 – 20. The people in Damascus included both Jews (9:20 – 22) and perhaps Gentiles (who formed the majority of the population); the people in Jerusalem and in Judea are Jews; the ἔθνη are Gentiles. The description of Paul's initial mission in Damascus, Jerusalem, and Judea before going to the Gentiles corresponds to his missionary strategy of reaching "first … the Jew, then … the Gentile" (Rom 1:16) and to his hopes for the conversion of Israel once the fullness of the Gentiles has come to faith (Rom 11:11 – 15).

(3) Paul's message corresponds to the commission he had been given from heaven, which had spelled out the content of what he was to proclaim (v. 18). He has always proclaimed[94] that both Jews and Gentiles must repent (μετανοεῖν; see on 2:38),

---

89. Cf. Bock, *Acts*, 718.

90. Note the metaphors of open eyes and of light.

91. Winter, "*Captatio Benevolentiae*," 508 – 11.

92. BDAG, s.v. ὀπτασία 1, "an event of a transcendent character that impresses itself vividly on the mind, *a vision, celestial sight,* of that which a deity permits a human being to see, either of the deity personally or of something else usually hidden

from mortals." The term is used only here in Acts; but see Luke 1:22; 24:23; 2 Cor 12:1; cf. LXX Theodotion Dan 9:23; 10:1, 7 – 8; and LXX Esth 4:17; Mal 3:2.

93. Paul mentions in Gal 1:22; 1 Thess 2:14 that there were churches in Judea.

94. For the verb "proclaim" (ἀπαγγέλλω) see 4:23; 16:36.

"turn" (ἐπιστρέφειν; see on 3:19) to God, and "act" in their everyday lives in a manner consistent with repentance (see John the Baptist's preaching in Luke 3:8). In Rom 1:5 Paul explains that God has called him to bring about "obedience that comes from faith" (ὑπακοὴν πίστεως), i.e., submission to the lordship of Jesus Christ that begins in conversion and continues in a lifelong commitment to live out the consequences of faith.

26:21 That is why some Jews seized me in the temple and tried to kill me (ἕνεκα τούτων με Ἰουδαῖοι συλλαβόμενοι ὄντα ἐν τῷ ἱερῷ ἐπειρῶντο διαχειρίσασθαι). The brief *refutatio*[95] summarizes the proofs for Paul's innocence of the charges against him. Luke does not mention the accusation that Paul had desecrated the temple (cf. 24:18 – 19; 25:8), but focuses on his arrest in the temple and on the Jews' attempt to kill him. This reflects, for Luke, the central reason for Paul's arrest, namely, the desire of the Jewish leaders to eliminate Paul; this is the one factor that explains the developments in Paul's trial.

(1) Paul argues that his arrest in the temple took place as he was obediently fulfilling (vv. 19 – 20) the commission that God had given to him (vv. 16 – 18). The expression translated "that is why" refers back to Paul's description of his divine commission and especially of his preaching (vv. 18, 20). (2) Paul argues that Jews attempted to kill him after they had seized him in the temple, implying an illegal action that discredits their later accusations before the Roman court.

26:22 But to this day I have received help from God, and so I stand here and testify to small and great. I am saying nothing that goes beyond what the prophets and Moses said would take

place (ἐπικουρίας οὖν τυχὼν τῆς ἀπὸ τοῦ θεοῦ ἄχρι τῆς ἡμέρας ταύτης ἕστηκα μαρτυρόμενος μικρῷ τε καὶ μεγάλῳ οὐδὲν ἐκτὸς λέγων ὧν τε οἱ προφῆται ἐλάλησαν μελλόντων γίνεσθαι καὶ Μωϋσῆς). Paul's conclusion (*peroratio*) in vv. 22 – 23 begins with a plea for help, a characteristic of forensic speeches (the use of the verb τυγχάνω is standard). Instead of seeking help from Agrippa, however, Paul acknowledges God's help during the past twenty-eight years.

The fact that Paul has experienced the fulfillment of God's promise of protection during his work among the Jews and the Gentiles (v. 17) links the *peroratio* with the earlier parts of the speech. The fact of his protection "to this day," despite attempts on his life, authenticates his narrative of having received a commission from Jesus, confirms his proofs in which he emphasized his obedience to the divine commission, and secures his refutation of his accusers' charges who had attempted to assassinate him, an attempt that did not succeed because of the divine protection he has enjoyed.

The second point of Paul's conclusion affirms his consistent witness that agrees with Scripture. His message is unobjectionable. Paul stands before Agrippa, Festus, the military commanders, and the dignitaries of Caesarea giving witness[96] to "small and great," from the children to adults, from insignificant people to dignitaries, i.e., to all people without exception (cf. 8:10).[97] The testimony concerns the reality of Jesus, Israel's Messiah and Savior (cf. v. 23), whom Paul encountered on the road to Damascus and who had commissioned Paul as his servant and witness. Paul emphasizes that his witness of Jesus has been consistent with the Scriptures. He says "nothing that goes beyond what the prophets and Moses said would take place," i.e.

---

95. Winter, "Official Proceedings," 330.

96. The present tense of the participle (μαρτυρόμενος) emphasizes Paul's unceasing proclamation of the gospel since his conversion.

97. Cf. Heb 8:11; Rev 11:18; 13:16; 19:5, 18; 20:12.

what they predicted in terms of God's promises to Israel. In other words, Paul's proclamation is exactly what Scripture prophesied. This assertion is the basis of the subsequent exchange between Paul and King Agrippa.

Luke's readers would be reminded of numerous passages that make the same point,[98] of which two stand out. (1) In Luke 24:44 – 49 Jesus explained to his disciples after his resurrection that all the words he had spoken to them conveyed the fundamental point that "everything ... written" about him in the Law of Moses, the Prophets, and the Psalms must be fulfilled — in particular, the predictions relating to the Messiah, who would suffer and rise from the dead on the third day, and that in his name repentance and forgiveness of sins would be proclaimed in Jerusalem and to all nations. Jesus concluded by reminding the Twelve that they are "witnesses of these things," and by promising them the arrival of the power of the Holy Spirit.

(2) In Acts 3:19 – 25, Peter proclaimed in Solomon's Portico in the outer court of the temple to the assembled Jews the need to repent and to turn to God in order to receive forgiveness of sins, to experience the promised times of refreshing in connection with the promised coming of the Messiah, who is Jesus, as predicted by Moses and all the prophets, and to witness the fulfillment of the covenant given by God to Abraham that a time would come when all the families of the earth would be blessed.

26:23 "That the Messiah would suffer, and that he would be the first to rise from the dead, to proclaim light both to his people and to the Gentiles" (εἰ παθητὸς ὁ χριστός, εἰ πρῶτος ἐξ ἀναστάσεως νεκρῶν φῶς μέλλει καταγγέλλειν τῷ τε λαῷ καὶ τοῖς ἔθνεσιν). Paul ends his speech with a reaffirmation of his message about Jesus, Israel's Messiah and Savior. This statement summarizes the main points of Paul's witness, which concern the suffering (and death) of Jesus who is "the Messiah,"[99] the resurrection of Jesus as the first to rise from the dead,[100] and the proclamation of light to the Jewish people and to the Gentiles.

This statement, which echoes the mission of the Servant in Isaiah (Isa 42:6; 49:6; 60:1 – 3), depends on the identification of Jesus, who was crucified and whom Paul and the early Christians proclaim as Israel's Messiah, with the suffering Servant of Isa 53:1 – 9. And the statement depends on the interpretation of the vindication of the Servant in Isa 53:10 – 12, who sees his offspring, prolongs his days, causes the will of the Lord to prosper, sees light out of his anguish, and makes many righteous, in terms of the resurrection of the Messiah. The reference to light should remind Luke's readers of the words of Simeon in Luke 2:32, who said, with the newborn Jesus in his arms, that Jesus is God's salvation and "a light for revelation to the Gentiles, and the glory of your people Israel." Paul's mission is the mission of the Messiah. Paul's accusers, in reality, accuse the Messiah and oppose the Scriptures.

26:24 When Paul defended himself with these words, Festus exclaimed, "You are out of your mind, Paul! Your great learning is driving you insane!" (ταῦτα δὲ αὐτοῦ ἀπολογουμένου ὁ Φῆστος μεγάλῃ τῇ φωνῇ φησιν· μαίνῃ, Παῦλε· τὰ πολλά σε γράμματα εἰς μανίαν περιτρέπει). In the last section of Festus's consultation of King Agrippa II

---

98. Luke 16:29 – 31; 24:25, 27, 44; Acts 2:16; 3:18, 24; 10:43; 13:15, 27, 40; 15:15; 24:14.

99. See on 3:18; on Jesus as Messiah see on 2:31, 36.

100. Note 3:22 – 23: Moses is a witness to one coming who is a prophet like himself to whom everyone must listen. Cf.

1 Cor 15:20: "Christ has indeed been raised from the dead, the firstfruits of those who have fallen asleep;" similarly Col 1:18: "he is the beginning and the firstborn from among the dead, so that in everything he might have the supremacy." Cf. Rev 1:5.

(25:13 – 26:32), Luke narrates the reaction of Festus and Agrippa to Paul's speech (vv. 24 – 32). Festus apparently interrupts Paul's defense; the present tense of the genitive absolute (ἀπολογουμένου) suggests this is the case. Another indication that Paul is cut off is the reference to the loud voice (μεγάλη τῇ φωνῇ) in which Festus speaks. Since he has been the presiding judge in Paul's trial, and since Paul's hearing before Agrippa takes place at Festus's suggestion, it is the governor's prerogative to interrupt Paul.

Festus's response is narrated in direct speech, as is Agrippa's reaction (v. 28) and Paul's reaction to both (vv. 25 – 27) as well as the final evaluation of Paul's case by Festus and Agrippa (vv. 31 – 32). Festus, who for the first time addresses Paul with his name (Παῦλε; vocative), expresses his opinion of Paul with one single word: he is (lit.) "mad" (μαίνῃ), out of his mind, out of control, crazy. Festus explains Paul's madness as a result of his "great learning." His statement is sometimes understood in a positive sense: his remark is "not necessarily offensive" in the context of Plato's assertion that no one can be a true poet without μανία;[101] or the governor was "impressed with Paul's mode of argumentation."[102] The fact that Festus acknowledges Paul's intellectual erudition does not prove, however, that he is making a flattering remark. Paul's protest in v. 25 demonstrates that he does not regard the governor's assessment as a compliment.

For Festus, Paul's belief in the resurrection of Jesus, who had been crucified by one of his predecessors, defies logic. Paul's conviction that he has been sent by a heavenly voice to preach to Jews and Gentiles about light and darkness and forgiveness of sins flies in the face of common sense. Paul's

argument that his accusers oppose in reality not him but the promised Messiah, whose servant and witness he is, is a type of reasoning that he fails to grasp. Paul's bold affirmation of the beliefs he had preached for many years and which are the cause of his trouble, combined with his assertion that he stands under divine protection, is a type of conduct that he, Festus, cannot understand. Despite his learning, Paul must be "insane."

26:25 Paul replied, "I am not insane, most excellent Festus. What I am declaring is true and reasonable" (ὁ δὲ Παῦλος· οὐ μαίνομαι, φησίν, κράτιστε Φῆστε, ἀλλὰ ἀληθείας καὶ σωφροσύνης ῥήματα ἀποφθέγγομαι). Luke narrates Paul's reaction in five steps. (1) Paul affirms his sanity. He protests, albeit politely (note the address "most excellent Festus"), that the governor is wrong. He is "not insane" (οὐ μαίνομαι).

(2) Paul affirms the truthfulness and reasonableness of his report, for he is "declaring" (ἀποφθέγγομαι) a message that is sound and sober. He is speaking the (lit.) "words of truth" (ἀληθείας … ῥήματα), i.e., words that communicate truth (objective genitive); the report and the arguments of his defense agree with the facts. And he speaks (lit.) "words of reasonableness" (σωφροσύνης ῥήματα), i.e., words that are reasonable (subjective genitive); his treatment of the facts of his life and of his case agree with the rationality of human reason.[103]

26:26 The king knows about these things, and I am speaking openly to him. I am certain that none of these things have escaped his notice, for this did not take place in a corner (ἐπίσταται γὰρ περὶ τούτων ὁ βασιλεὺς πρὸς ὃν καὶ παρρησιαζόμενος λαλῶ, λανθάνειν γὰρ αὐτόν τι τούτων οὐ πείθομαι

---

101. Bruce, *Acts*, 505, with reference to Plato, *Phaedr.* 245A; he continues, "But anything in the nature of inspiration could not be treated seriously by a matter-of-fact Roman judge."

102. Fitzmyer, *Acts*, 763 – 64, who suggests that "Festus is concerned about Paul's mental stability."

103. Johnson, *Acts*, 439, comments that "it would be difficult to find a term more descriptive of the Greek philosophical ideal," with reference to Plato, *Resp.* 430E – 431B; *Symp.* 196C; Diogenes Laertius, *Vit. phil.* 3.91; 2 Macc 3:17; 4 Macc 1:3, 31; 5:23.

οὐθέν· οὐ γάρ ἐστιν ἐν γωνίᾳ πεπραγμένον τοῦτο). (3) Paul attempts to claim Agrippa as witness for his truthfulness. With courageous confidence, Paul turns to Agrippa. He speaks to the king "openly,"[104] i.e., with bold frankness and without fear. He begins with the assertion that Agrippa knows about "these things," because he is certain that none of them has escaped the king's notice.

The last phrase in v. 26 clarifies that "these things" refer to the ministry, death, and resurrection of Jesus as well as to the message that Jesus' followers proclaim and to the movement created by these events and message. These things did not take place "in a corner"; i.e., they were not done in private or in secret. Paul uses a Greek proverb[105] to emphasize that the events connected with Jesus of Nazareth and the activities of his followers were common knowledge and part of the historical record. Thus Paul, who is accused of being the "ringleader of the sect of the Nazarenes" (24:5), is not engaged in any subversive activities.

The emphasis on the public character of the events connected with Jesus and his followers is part of Luke's repeated concern to locate the history of Jesus and his followers in world history. The most explicit example is Luke 3:1 – 2, which dates the beginning of the Christian movement to the appearance of John the Baptist: "In the fifteenth year of the reign of Tiberius Caesar — when Pontius Pilate was governor of Judea, Herod tetrarch of Galilee, his brother Philip tetrarch of Iturea and Traconitis, and Lysanias tetrarch of Abilene — during the high-priesthood of Annas and Caiaphas, the word of God came to John son of Zechariah in the wilderness." Luke (and Paul) treats the arguments concerning Jesus' identity as Israel's Messiah and Savior and his death and resurrection as incontestable "because they are based on what is known to everyone, even if he presents these facts as the fulfillment of the prophetic Scriptures of old."[106]

26:27 "King Agrippa, do you believe the prophets? I know that you believe" (πιστεύεις, βασιλεῦ Ἀγρίππα, τοῖς προφήταις; οἶδα ὅτι πιστεύεις). (4) Paul now addresses Agrippa directly in an attempt to claim the king as his witness, a "dramatic masterstroke."[107] He asks the Jewish king, who believes the prophets, to reach the conclusion that what he has been saying is truthful. Paul suggests that Agrippa indeed "believes" (πιστεύεις); Paul probably means that he knows that Agrippa believes that the prophets foretold the coming of a Messiah.[108] Now Jesus' followers, as Paul has just explained, believe that the suffering, death, and resurrection of Jesus are the central part of God's plan of redemption, and they believe that Jesus is Israel's Messiah and Savior. Since these convictions are grounded in the Scriptures and foreseen by the prophets, whom Agrippa accepts, the king should believe in Jesus.

For Agrippa, the question poses a conundrum. If he refuses to confess belief in the prophets, he will lose his reputation as being loyal to the Jewish faith. If he confesses belief in the prophets, he will find himself in the awkward position of agreeing in public with the "ringleader of the sect of the Nazarenes," which could anticipate the follow-up question whether he then also accepts Jesus as the Messiah.

26:28 Agrippa said to Paul, "Do you think that in such a short time you can persuade me to become a Christian?" (ὁ δὲ Ἀγρίππας πρὸς τὸν Παῦλον· ἐν ὀλίγῳ με πείθεις Χριστιανὸν ποιῆσαι).

---

104. The present participle (παρρησιαζόμενος) indicates the manner in which Paul speaks to Agrippa. For παρρησιάζομαι ("express oneself freely, *speak freely, openly, fearlessly*," BDAG) cf. 9:27, 28; 13:46; 14:3; 18:26; 19:8.

105. Cf. Epictetus, *Diatr.* 2.12.17; Plato, *Gorg.* 485D; Plutarch, *Mor.* 777B.

106. Fitzmyer, *Acts*, 764.

107. Dunn, *Beginning from Jerusalem*, 991.

108. Marshall, *Acts*, 399.

Agrippa's reaction to Paul's challenge is an expression of incredulity concerning Paul's effort to make him a Christian. The meaning of the statement is contested. The most plausible interpretation of the prepositional phrase used here (ἐν ὀλίγῳ) is a temporal understanding: "in such a short time" (or instrumental: "with a little more time"). While it is not impossible that the tone of Agrippa's answer is ironic, Paul's response in v. 29 suggests that Agrippa may have been serious. Perhaps he stands between earnest consideration and irony.[109] This is perhaps best captured in the translation of Agrippa's response to Paul's question as a counter-question: "Do you think that in such a short time you can persuade me to become a Christian?" For the meaning of the term "Christian" (Χριστιανός) see on 11:26, where Luke stated that this term was used as a designation for the followers of Jesus for the first time in Antioch, the capital of the province of Syria, evidently coined by the Roman authorities as a label for a movement whose beliefs were focused on Jesus, who was believed to be the Messiah (Χριστός).

26:29 Paul replied, "I pray to God that, whether in a short or long time, not only you but all who are listening to me today, may become what I am, except for these chains" (ὁ δὲ Παῦλος· εὐξαίμην ἂν τῷ θεῷ καὶ ἐν ὀλίγῳ καὶ ἐν μεγάλῳ οὐ μόνον σὲ ἀλλὰ καὶ πάντας τοὺς ἀκούοντάς μου σήμερον γενέσθαι τοιούτους ὁποῖος καὶ ἐγώ εἰμι παρεκτὸς τῶν δεσμῶν τούτων). Paul's responds by expressing his hope that all who are present will become believers in Jesus. He formulates this hope with a potential optative in "I pray" (εὐξαίμην ἄν), i.e., with some reservation. Paul desires that Agrippa may

come to faith in Jesus as Israel's Messiah and Savior, and also "all" who are listening to the hearing, including governor Festus, his military commanders, and the dignitaries of Caesarea.

Paul does not care whether their conversion takes place in a short time or in a long time. He ends with the ironic, or perhaps humorous, comment that he does not wish, of course, that everybody in the audience becomes a prisoner like him. As Paul clarifies his statement with the comment "except for these chains," he probably holds up his chains for all to see.[110]

26:30 Then the king rose, together with the governor and Bernice and the others who were sitting with them (ἀνέστη τε ὁ βασιλεὺς καὶ ὁ ἡγεμὼν ἥ τε Βερνίκη καὶ οἱ συγκαθήμενοι αὐτοῖς). Luke's conclusion of the hearing (vv. 30 – 32) has three parts. He notes the departure of King Agrippa, Festus, Bernice, and "the others who were sitting with them" — the military commanders and the dignitaries of Caesarea (25:23). They rise from their seats, in the same order as they had entered the audience hall, to signify the conclusion of the hearing.

26:31 After they left the hall, they said to one another, "This man is doing nothing that deserves the death sentence or chains" (καὶ ἀναχωρήσαντες ἐλάλουν πρὸς ἀλλήλους λέγοντες ὅτι οὐδὲν θανάτου ἢ δεσμῶν ἄξιόν τι πράσσει ὁ ἄνθρωπος οὗτος). After the participants in the hearing retire from the audience hall, they converse about Paul's case. They pronounce Paul not guilty of charges that would demand his execution or prolonged imprisonment for further investigation. They conclude that Paul

---

109. Alfons Weiser, *Die Apostelgeschichte* (2 vols.; ÖTK 5; Gütersloh/Würzburg: Mohn/Echter, 1981 – 85), 655; Barrett, *Acts*, 1171.

110. Cf. Rapske, *Paul in Roman Custody*, 309, who points out that "his appearance before such an august body bound

with chains presents a picture of humiliation which Paul would be anxious to counteract," rejecting suggestions that Paul's reference to his chains was spoken in a lighter vein or intended as grim humor.

"is doing nothing [οὐδὲν … τι πράσσει][111] that deserves the death sentence or chains."

26:32 Agrippa said to Festus, "This man could have been released if he had not appealed to the emperor" (Ἀγρίππας δὲ τῷ Φήστῳ ἔφη· ἀπολελύσθαι ἐδύνατο ὁ ἄνθρωπος οὗτος εἰ μὴ ἐπεκέκλητο Καίσαρα). Luke ends by singling out King Agrippa's acknowledgment of Paul's innocence. In his evaluation of Paul's hearing that Festus had arranged, Agrippa informs the governor that Paul could have been acquitted, and he acknowledges that Paul "appealed" (ἐπεκέκλητο) to the emperor, agreeing with Festus's decision to grant Paul's petition to stand trial before the imperial court in Rome. This is the third declaration of Paul's innocence, after the assessment of Claudius Lysias, the Roman commander stationed in Jerusalem (23:29), and after the verdict of Porcius Festus (25:25).[112]

Agrippa's comment is problematic.[113] If he truly believes Paul is innocent and should be acquitted and released, and if he acknowledges that Paul's preaching is rooted in the Scriptures and has an essentially Jewish identity that does not threaten the political or social stability of the region, he could install a high priest in Jerusalem who would convince the chief priests and other members of the Sanhedrin to drop the charges against Paul. But he does not have full control over the affairs of the temple and over the aristocratic priestly families. Perhaps he thinks that working for Paul's release would make Agrippa look a Christian himself. Or he thinks that Paul is not important enough to take on the Jewish authorities in Jerusalem. At any rate, he does not secure Paul's release.

This is the judicial climax of Luke's narrative since 21:27. The highest political authorities of the region — the Roman governor of Judea, the Jewish king who controls the affairs of the temple, and presumably the military commanders and the Caesarean dignitaries — agree that Paul is not guilty since his case involves religious beliefs raised by the death and (alleged, from their point of view) resurrection of Jesus, but no political questions requiring capital punishment.

Festus had arranged for the hearing of Paul before the Jewish king Agrippa II, his military commanders, and other dignitaries, in order to clarify the case against Paul, so that he could formulate a summary of the charges and of the defense for inclusion in the *littera dimissoria* that he had to send with the prisoner to Rome. Paul's speech in 26:2 – 23 would have been included, in summary form, as written evidence in the case. The outcome of the hearing leaves Festus where he started. His earlier conclusion that Paul was innocent of serious charges demanding the death sentence or further imprisonment was confirmed as correct by Agrippa II and the other members of his *consilium*. The information that Festus had gathered and that would be part of the dossier that he had to send to the emperor included strong evidence exonerating Paul.

Festus's dilemma was that he did not want to release Paul because of the Jewish authorities' demand for a death sentence, while being convinced at the same time that Paul was not guilty of such serious charges. It is plausible that Festus included in the *littera dimissoria*, as justification for referring Paul's case to Rome, a description of the unrelenting opposition of the highest Jewish leaders in

---

111. The present tense of the verb (πράσσει) probably refers to Paul's entire life and beliefs; Barrett, *Acts*, 1173.

112. Johnson, *Acts*, 440, who sees a parallel with Jesus' trial, who was declared innocent three times by Pontius Pilate (Luke 23:4, 14, 22). Luke does not highlight such a parallel.

113. Omerzu, *Prozess*, 489, points out that Agrippa's declaration that Paul could have been released had he not appealed to the emperor is plausible only if it assumes that Paul's appeal was a measure designed to prolong the imprisonment.

Jerusalem against Paul, who demanded his execution, and a description of Paul's appeal by which he sought to avoid a trial in Jerusalem; "hence it would chronicle the legal and religio-political aspects of the case for the emperor or his agents in Rome."[114]

Theology in Application

Several important emphases of this episode have been discussed before, in particular the reality of sometimes fierce opposition to the Christian faith in general, and to individual Christians in particular.[115] This section emphasizes the following points.

Complex Situations Require Complex Responses

Paul faces the chief priests of Jerusalem and members of the nonpriestly aristocracy and their representatives, who demand his execution and whose opposition is so fierce that they are willing to assassinate him in an ambush. He faces the new governor of the province of Judea, Porcius Festus, who acts quickly, decisively, and justly, but who does not understand Paul's beliefs. And he faces the Jewish king Agrippa II, a descendant of Herod I, who at the time ruled over territories in southern Syria but who had control over the affairs of the temple in Jerusalem and who had the authority to appoint the high priests. Paul does not have a predetermined "plan" how to respond; he does not have cookie-cutter answers. Rather, he tailors his response to the various opponents and to the various situations in which he finds himself.

Christians are prepared to change "tactics" — legal or otherwise — if changed situations demand that they adapt. What does not change is the reason for their behavior: the reality of their identity as followers of Jesus, which safeguards their integrity as God's people; the authority of God, who gives courage; the power of God's Spirit, who assists them to use their intelligence, their rhetorical abilities, and their spiritual gifts; and the commitment to the church and to the divinely given mission to proclaim the gospel of Jesus Christ.

As regards his Jewish opponents, Paul is not willing to risk a guilty verdict in a Roman trial in Jerusalem or another assassination attempt if he were taken to Jerusalem. Thus, he extricates himself from Judea — after two years in prison in Caesarea — by appealing to stand trial before the imperial court in Rome. Christians do not risk their lives unnecessarily. If there are legal means by which they can save themselves, they will use them, particularly if this allows them to live and see another day when they can continue to preach the gospel.

---

114. Rapske, *Paul in Roman Custody*, 185.

115. See Theology in Application on 4:5 – 22; 6:8 – 7:1; 22:1 – 21; 23:23 – 35; 24:1 – 27.

Before Festus, Paul emphasizes his innocence of charges that would warrant the death penalty. He demonstrates his loyalty to the state by expressing his willingness to be judged by the governor. He fights for his legal rights by appealing to the emperor. He does not take on the governor for wanting to grant favors to the Jewish authorities in Jerusalem. He does not become cynical, rejecting the entire "justice system" of the Roman Empire. He is a realist and knows how Roman administrations in the provinces work and how Roman governors often secure the stability and peace in their province. He does what is necessary to "survive" Festus and his attempt to bring the trial to a close that has been dragging for two years.

Paul could insist on a fair trial before Festus, but he knows that given the fierce opposition of the Jewish leaders in Jerusalem, he may not stand a chance. So he cuts his losses and petitions for a transfer to Rome (where he will be a prisoner for another two years). Christians do not always insist on their legal rights, as this may hurt them in the long run. But they may decide to use legal means at their disposal in order to avoid serious damage to their situation and, more importantly, to safeguard the possibility of further witness for the gospel.

Before King Agrippa II, Paul explains the identity and significance of Jesus as Israel's crucified, risen, and exalted Messiah, who spoke to him from heavenly glory on the road to Damascus and who commissioned him to be his servant and witness among both Jews and Gentiles. Paul is bold enough to suggest to the king that he should become a follower of Jesus. Christians will use every opportunity to speak about Jesus. Their goal of leading people to faith in Jesus Christ may not always be overt, but when challenged they will readily admit that they indeed desire every person to become a believer in Jesus.

The Good News of Jesus Christ

The gospel was, is, and remains the good news of Jesus Christ. Paul's speech in chapter 26 before Agrippa (and Festus, the military commanders of Judea, and dignitaries of Caesarea) summarizes, for the last time in Acts, the message that he and all the other witnesses of Jesus have been proclaiming among Jews and Gentiles. The following emphases are important.

(1) *God* is the fundamental, central, and personal reality of the gospel. God has authority over life and death: he brings the dead back to life, as he has demonstrated in the resurrection of Jesus (26:8, 23). God has authority over history: he has fulfilled and is fulfilling the promises that he gave to the fathers (vv. 6 – 8). God has revealed himself and his will in Scripture: the events of Jesus' life, death, resurrection, and exaltation as well as the events of the activities of Jesus' witnesses in Jerusalem and among the nations are "authorized" by God as they fulfill Scripture (vv. 22 – 23, 26 – 27). God desires the salvation of all people, both Jews and Gentiles (vv. 17, 20, 23, 29). God demands the repentance and conversion of all people, both Jews and

Gentiles (vv. 18, 20, 29). God has the power to protect his people; they can rely on his help (vv. 17, 22).

(2) *Jesus Christ* is Lord. Paul's speech before Agrippa emphasizes that Jesus is the Lord who has come back from the dead and who directs God's people from the reality of divine glory (26:12 – 18). Whether this implies an anti-Rome nuance is disputed; it is not likely, at least not in Paul's hearing before Festus and Agrippa II. While Paul is willing to die for his faith in Jesus, whom he confesses as Israel's Messiah and Savior of the world, he is surely not risking death for political convictions. Whether Festus and Agrippa noticed the implicit anti-imperial thrust of the gospel in which God demands the repentance of all people without exception, and in which he promises the transformation of the lives of all people, also without exception, is another question.

But if the proclamation of Jesus as Lord of all brings Christians into conflict with political authorities, this is a risk they willingly accept. Jesus' life, death, resurrection, and exaltation are the central and unrelinquishable subjects of Christian witness (vv. 16 – 18, 26). The message of the church is not *primarily* about healing relationships, meeting human needs, or restoring confidence in life, but about Jesus Christ. This focus of the earliest witnesses is the reason why Roman authorities labeled them *Christianoi* (v. 28). Christians are people who believe, preach, and teach that Jesus is Israel's Messiah and the world's Savior. Paul emphasizes that the proclamation of the gospel to Jews and Gentiles is an integral part of the "event" of Jesus' reality (v. 23).

(3) *Salvation* is possible only through faith in Jesus, Israel's Messiah and the world's Savior (26:16 – 28, 22 – 23). Both Jews and Gentiles who do not believe in Jesus live in darkness; they do not have the ability to see God's solution to the problem of the human condition and the condition of the world. The inability to see means life under the control of God's enemy. The ability to see requires repentance, which involves turning away from sin and turning to the living God and submitting to his will. Life under the authority of the living God entails God's merciful pardon for those formerly subservient to Satan and for the sins committed in selfishness. It entails the ability to see and understand who Jesus is: the man from Nazareth who died and rose from the dead in fulfillment of God's promises given to the fathers and recorded by the prophets, the exalted Messiah of Israel, the Savior of all sinners.

40

Acts 27:1 – 28:15

Literary Context

The first section of Luke's account of Paul's imprisonment recounted Paul's arrest and imprisonment in Jerusalem (21:18 – 23:35), the second told of Paul's imprisonment and trials in Caesarea (24:1 – 26:32), and the third and last section narrates Paul's transfer to and imprisonment in Rome (27:1 – 28:31). The first episode of this last section reports Paul's transfer from Caesarea to Rome (27:1 – 28:15). Luke's report of the dramatic sea voyage to Italy links Caesarea and, by implication, Jerusalem, the capital of the Jewish people, with Rome, the capital of the empire.

After the back-and-forth drama of the judicial scenes of Acts 21 – 26, Luke's narrative now "becomes immersed in the slow details of cargoes and harbours, of wind directions and sails, dinghies and anchors, and finally drawn into the nightmare of storm and shipwreck" — content that "slows the narrative down and builds the tension."[1] While some see Paul's arrival in Rome as the fulfillment of the geographical movement of 1:8 from Jerusalem to "the ends of the earth," a view that may find some justification in the list of regions and nations provided in 2:9 – 11, where Rome is the farthest locality mentioned in the west, Luke's narrative of Paul's arrival in Rome "breathes an atmosphere which is progressively less, rather than more, exotic" as the reference to the last stages of the journey — Forum of Appius and the Three Taverns — have "almost an air of homecoming" and serve as a reminder that "from a Roman perspective, Rome was not the end but the centre of the earth, with a central milepost from which all the roads of the empire radiated out."[2]

1. Alexander, *Literary Context*, 212.
2. Ibid., 214.

Main Idea

In the long section depicting Paul's journey to Rome, Luke relates the perils of Paul's situation and emphasizes God's power at work in the world of dangerous natural and human forces, the faithfulness of God, who fulfills his promises, and the legitimization of Paul as God's witness who reaches Rome as intended and of his message as divinely authenticated good news for Jews and Gentiles.

Translation

Acts 27:1 – 28:15

27:1a	Setting: time	When it was decided
b	Content	that we would sail
c	Geographical	for Italy,
d	Event: protagonist	**Paul and**
e	Association	**some other prisoners**
f	Character entrance	**were handed over to a centurion**
g	Identification	named Julius
h	Character description	who commanded the Augustan Cohort.
2a	Action	**We boarded a ship from Adramyttium**
b	Description	that was about to sail
c	Geographical	to the ports along the coast of the ↵ province of Asia,
d	Action	**and we put out to sea,**
e	Association	accompanied by Aristarchus,
f	Identification	a Macedonian from Thessalonica.
3a	Setting: time	The next day
b	Action	**we put in**
c	Geographical	at Sidon,
d	Action	**and Julius treated Paul kindly**
e	Action	**and allowed him to go to his friends**
f	Purpose	to be cared for.
4a	Action	**From there we put out to sea**
b	Action	**and sailed under the lee of Cyprus,**
c	Cause	because the winds were against us.
5a	Time	After we had sailed across the sea
b	Geographical	off the coast of Cilicia and Pamphylia,
c	Action	**we landed at Myra in Lycia.**
6a	Action	**There the centurion found a ship**
b	Description: geographical	from Alexandria
c	Description: geographical	bound for Italy
d	Action	**and put us on board ship.**

Continued from previous page.

7a	Action	**We sailed**
b	Manner	slowly
c	Duration	for a number of days
d	Action: geographical	**and arrived off Cnidus**
e	Manner	only with difficulty.
f	Cause	Since the wind did not permit us to hold course,
g	Action	**we sailed under the lee of Crete off Salmone.**
8a	Action	**We sailed along the coast**
b	Manner	with difficulty
c	Action: geographical	**and came to a place called Kaloi Limenes**
d	Geographical	near the town of Lasea.
9a	Cause	Since much time had been lost
b	Cause	and navigation had now become dangerous,
c	Cause	because even the Day of Atonement ☌
		had gone by,
d	Action: speech	**Paul strongly urged them,**
10a	Address	*"Men,*
b	Prediction	*I see that the voyage will bring disaster and*
c	Prediction	*heavy loss,*
d	Object	*not only of the cargo and*
e	Object	*the ship*
f	Object	*but also of our own lives."*
11a	Action	**But the centurion listened to the advice of the captain and**
b	Association	**the owner of the ship**
c	Contrast	rather than to Paul's words.
12a	Cause	Since the harbor was not suitable
b	Purpose	for spending the winter,
c	Action	**the majority decided**
d	Content	that we should put out to sea from there,
e	Purpose	in the hope of being able to reach Phoenix
f	Object	and winter there;
g	Explanation	**this was a harbor of Crete**
h	Description: geographical	which faced both southwest and northwest.
13a	Cause/time	When a moderate south wind began to blow,
b	Characters' thoughts	**they thought**
c	Content	that they could carry out their plan.
d	Action	**They weighed anchor**
e	Action	**and sailed along the coast of Crete**
f	Place	close to the shore.
14a	Time	But soon afterward
b	Event	**a wind of hurricane force**
c	Identification	called the Northeaster
d	Event	**swept down from the island.**

15a	Cause	Since the ship was caught by the wind
b	Cause	and could not be turned into the wind,
c	Action	**we gave way to it**
d	Event	**and were driven along.**

16a	Time/geographical	As we ran under the lee of a little island
b	Identification	called Cauda,
c	Action	**we were scarcely able to get the lifeboat under control.**

17a	Time	After the men had hoisted it up,
b	Action	**they deployed supports**
c	Purpose	to undergird the ship.
d	Cause	Because they feared
e	Content	that they would run aground
f	Place	in the Syrtis,
g	Action	**they lowered the rigging**
h	Action	**and let the ship be driven along in this way.**
18a	Event	**We were pounded by the storm so violently that**
b	Time	on the next day
c	Action	they began to jettison the cargo.

19a	Time	On the third day
b	Action	**they threw the ship's rigging overboard**
c	Means	with their own hands.

20a	Time	When neither sun nor
b	List	stars
c	Event	appeared
d	Duration	for many days
e	Event	and rather bad weather pressed upon us,
f	Action	**we finally gave up all hope of being saved.**

21a	Cause	Since almost nobody wanted to eat,
b	Action	**Paul stood up**
c	Sphere	among them
d	Action: speech	**and said,**
e	Address	*"Men,*
f	Flashback	*you ought to have followed my advice*
g	Action	*and not have sailed from Crete,*
h	Consequence	*and thereby avoided this damage and*
	Consequence	*loss.*
22a	Entreaty	*I now urge you*
b	Exhortation	*to be confident,*
c	Cause/prediction	*because not a single one of you will be lost,*
d	Cause/prediction	*only the ship will be a loss.*

Continued on next page.

Continued from previous page.

23a	Explanation	*For* last night
b	Report: character entrance	an angel of the God
c	Identification	to whom I belong
d	Identification	and whom I serve
e	Event	stood before me,
24a	Action: speech	*and* said,
b	Exhortation	"Do not be afraid,
c	Address	Paul.
d	Prediction	You must stand trial
e	Place	before the emperor,
f	Promise	*and* indeed God has graciously given you the lives of all
g		who are sailing with you.
25a	Exhortation	*So* be confident,
b	Address	men,
c	Cause	*for* I have faith in God
d	Content	that it will happen
e	Manner	exactly as I have been told.
26	Prediction	*But* we must run aground on some island."
27a	Setting: time	On the fourteenth night
b	Event	**we were still driven across the Adriatic Sea,**
c	Time	when the sailors suspected
d	Time	about midnight
e	Geographical	that they were approaching land.
28a	Action	**They took soundings**
b	Action	*and* **found that the water was twenty fathoms deep.**
c	Time/geographical	After they had sailed a short distance farther,
d	Action	**they took soundings again**
e	Action	*and* **found that the water was fifteen fathoms deep.**
29a	Cause	Since they feared
b	Content	that we might run aground on the rocks,
c	Action	**they dropped four anchors**
d	Place	from the stern
e	Action	*and* **prayed for daylight.**
30a	Time	When the sailors tried to escape from the ship,
b	Means	lowering the lifeboat into the sea
c	Purpose	under the pretext of laying out anchors from the bow,
31a	Action: speech	**Paul said to the centurion and**
b	Association	**the soldiers,**
c	Condition	"Unless these men stay in the ship,
d	Inference	you cannot be saved."
32a	Action	**Then the soldiers cut the ropes**
b	Description	that held the lifeboat
c	Action	*and* **let it drift away.**

33a	Time	Just before dawn
b	Action	**Paul urged all of them**
c	Content	to take some food,
d	Action: speech	saying,
e	Assertion: time	*"Today is the fourteenth day*
f	Flashback	*that you have been in suspense*
g	Flashback	*and you have been continually without food,*
h	Flashback	*you have eaten nothing.*
34a	Exhortation	*Therefore I urge you*
b	Instruction	*to take some food,*
c	Purpose	*for it will help you to survive.*
d	Prediction	*Not one of you will lose a single hair from his head."*

35a	Time	After he said this,
b	Action	**he took bread**
c	Action	**and gave thanks to God**
d	Place	in front of them all,
e	Action	**and he broke it**
f	Action	**and began to eat.**
36a	Action	**They were all reassured**
b	Action	**and ate some food.**
37	Aside	**We were 276 persons on board.**

38a	Time	When they had eaten enough,
b	Action	**they lightened the ship**
c	Means	by throwing the wheat into the sea.

39a	Time	When daylight came,
b	Action	**they did not recognize the land.**
c	Action	**But they noticed a bay with a beach**
d	Place	on which they planned to run the ship ashore
e	Condition	if they could.
40a	Action	**They cast off the anchors**
b	Action	**and left them in the sea.**
c	Time: simultaneous	At the same time
d	Action	**they untied the pennants of the steering oars.**
e	Action	**Then they hoisted the foresail to the wind**
f	Action	**and headed for the beach.**
41a	Event	**But the ship struck a point**
b	Event	**and ran aground.**
c	Event	**The bow became jammed**
d	Event	**and remained immovable,**
e	Simultaneous	while the stern was breaking up
f	Means	through the force of the waves.
42a	Character's thoughts	**The soldiers' plan was to kill the prisoners**
b	Purpose	to prevent them from swimming away
c	Purpose	and escaping.

Continued on next page.

Continued from previous page.

43a	Character's thoughts	But **the centurion wanted to save Paul**
b	Action	and **kept them from carrying out their plan.**
c	Action	**He ordered those who could swim**
d	Command	to jump overboard first
e	Command	and get to land.
44a	Command	**The rest were to get there**
b	Means	on planks or
c	Means	on other pieces of the ship.
d	Event	And **so it happened that everyone was brought safely to land.**

28:1a	Setting: time	After we had reached safety,
b	Action	**we found out that the island was called Malta.**
2a	Event/character entrance	**The natives showed us unusual kindness.**
b	Action	**They built a fire**
c	Action	and **welcomed all of us**
d	Cause	because it was raining and
e		cold.
3a	Action	**Paul had collected a pile of brushwood**
b	Action	and **was putting it on the fire,**
c	Time	when a snake,
d	Cause	driven out by the heat,
e	Action	fastened itself on his hand.

4a	Time	When the natives saw the creature hanging from his hand,
b	Reaction: speech	**they said to each other,**
c	Assertion	*"This man must be a murderer.*
d	Cause: concession	*Because even though he has escaped from the sea,*
e	Contra-expectation	*Justice has not allowed him to live."*
5a	Action	But **Paul shook the snake off into the fire**
b	Action	and **suffered no ill effects.**
6a	Character's thoughts	**The people expected him**
b	Content	to swell up or
c	Content	suddenly drop to the ground dead.
d	Time	After they had waited a long time
e	Action	and saw nothing unusual happen to him,
f	Action	**they changed their minds**
g	Assertion (identification)	and **said that he was a god.**

7a	Description: geographical	**There was an estate nearby**
b	Character entrance	that belonged to the chief official of the island,
c	Identification	named Publius.
d	Action	**He welcomed us**
e	Action	and **kindly showed us hospitality**
f	Duration	for three days.

8a	Character entrance	**His father was sick in bed,**
b	Cause	suffering from fever and
c	Cause	dysentery.
d	Action	**Paul visited him and,**
e	Time	after he prayed for him,
f	Action	**he laid his hands on him**
g	Action	and **healed him.**
9a	Time	After this had happened,
b	Action	**the rest of the people on the island**
c	Description	who had illnesses
d	Action	**came**
e	Event	and **were cured.**
10a	Action	**They honored us**
b	Means	in many ways.
c	Time	When we were ready to sail,
d	Action	**they supplied us with all the provisions we needed.**
11a	Setting: time	After three months
b	Action	**we set sail**
c	Means	in a ship that had wintered in the island,
d	Description	an Alexandrian ship
e	Description	with the Dioscuri as its figurehead.
12a	Action: geographical	**We put in at Syracuse**
b	Action	and **stayed there**
c	Duration	for three days.
13a	Action	**Then we weighed anchor**
b	Action: geographical	and **arrived in Rhegium.**
c	Time	After one day
d	Event	**a south wind sprang up,**
e	Time	and on the second day
f	Action: geographical	**we came to Puteoli.**
14a	Event: character entrance	**There we found some believers**
b	Event	who invited us to stay with them
c	Duration	for seven days.
d		**And so we came to Rome.**
15a	Flashback	**The believers there had heard**
b	Content	that we were coming,
c	Action: geographical	and **they came as far as the Forum of Appius and**
d	Place	the Three Taverns
e	Purpose	to meet us.
f	Time	When Paul saw them,
g	Action	**he thanked God**
h	Action	and **took courage.**

Structure and Literary Form

The episode consists of five incidents, which take Paul the prisoner from Caesarea via Malta to Rome. The first two incidents relate the first stops of the ship setting out from Caesarea bound for ports in the province of Asia (27:1 – 8). The next, and longest, incident reports a dangerous storm and the shipwreck of the ship at Malta (27:9 – 44). The third incident narrates the winter layover of the ship's crew and passengers in Malta (28:1 – 6). The fourth incident relates the healing of the father of the Maltese officer Publius (28:7 – 10). The final incident brings the voyage to a close by relating Paul's arrival in Rome (28:11 – 15).

The historical value of the episode has been much debated. Some scholars read the episode against the background of popular novels of the Hellenistic period, particularly romances in which a sea voyage with storm and shipwreck is a regular feature,[3] and conclude that Luke gives his readers his version of such a story, defined by the conventions of the genre. Some suggest that the author has composed a "typical" account of a sea voyage, on the basis of sources, perhaps the story of Jonah and Homer's Odyssey,[4] into which he inserts Pauline speeches.[5] But a comparison of Acts 27 with ancient accounts of actual shipwrecks demonstrates the following: (1) Luke's narrative lacks fictional elements as well as literary motifs of the "storm at sea" tradition. (2) The description of the storm in 27:13 – 20 is prosaic even compared with the account of Plutarch and the reports of Arrianus and Aelius Aristides; the "drama" that is often mentioned is simply the precise observation of events and actions. (3) The route of the voyage in Acts 27 is realistic, as are the nautical details of the narrative.[6]

The question why Luke includes this long narrative of Paul's journey from Caesarea to Rome has received different answers. Some suggest that Luke was guided by literary models, but this is less than convincing. Even if parallels with literary/fictional stories of sea voyages and shipwrecks are acknowledged, they would explain the length of the narrative only if we assume that Luke's main goal was to entertain his readers, which is hardly plausible. There would have been a host of opportunities earlier in the book to include entertaining stories of dangers at sea and on the road. Coming after the extended narratives of Paul's arrest and imprisonment, Luke's readers are not looking for literary breathing space or comic relief so much as for an exposition on Paul's fate.[7]

3. Cf. the works of Chariton of Aphrodisias, Longus, Petronius, Achilleus Tatius, Heliodorus, Xenophon of Ephesus.

4. Cf. Dennis R. MacDonald, "The Shipwrecks of Odysseus and Paul," *NTS* 45 (1999): 88 – 107.

5. Cf. Haenchen, *Acts*, 710 – 11; recently Pervo, *Acts*, 647 – 48.

6. Marius Reiser, "Von Caesarea nach Malta: Literarischer Charakter und historische Glaubwürdigkeit von Act 27," in *Das Ende des Paulus: Historische, theologische und literaturgeschichtliche Aspekte* (ed. F. W. Horn; BZNW 106; Berlin: De Gruyter, 2001), 49 – 74, 61.

7. Johnson, *Acts*, 458, surmises that Luke wants to provide his readers with "narrative space" so that they have "time to assimilate what has happened to Paul and what will happen

The motif of demonstrating Paul's innocence, while certainly present, is hardly a major emphasis. Luke's readers know that Paul is innocent of the charges brought against him in Jerusalem and in Caesarea. A detailed story of Paul's surviving a shipwreck does not add substantially to what the readers already know. The report of Paul's behavior during the storm and shipwreck — warning the crew of impending disaster, encouraging the passengers to eat and not to despair, giving advice that saves the lives of crew and passengers, including the prisoners — confirms that Paul is an honest man (*homo honestus*), a man of high standing who is competent even in nautical matters. He is influential with various groups of people, receives the respect and recognition of the people with whom he has contact, and has words of advice and a message from the Lord that are vindicated.[8]

The report of the storm and shipwreck and the snake attack on Malta remind Luke's readers that Paul's life is indeed in danger. It reminds the readers that God's control over history includes the survival of Paul, who has been given the assurance that he will reach Rome to be a witness there (19:21; 23:11; 27:24). The long and detailed narrative shows that Paul's life is in the hands of God who is in control, protects his servant, and fulfills his promises.[9] It shows that Paul is a prophetic figure whose words convey God's assurance of survival and whose actions demonstrate the grace of God.[10]

The episode is a *historical narrative* of a storm, shipwreck, and survival, containing personal names (besides Paul: Julius, Aristarchus, Publius; 27:1, 2; 28:7), unnamed persons (the eyewitness of the "we" account [27:1 etc.]; the pilot and owner of the ship [27:11]; "friends" of Paul, i.e., fellow Christians, at Sidon [27:3]; believers in Puteoli [28:14]; believers from the city of Rome [28:15]), chronological information (27:3, 7, 9, 18, 19, 27, 33, 39; 28:11, 14), and detailed geographical and nautical information (see the commentary). The episode begins with a reference to a centurion serving in the Augustan Cohort named Julius (27:1) and ends with a reference to Roman believers meeting Paul as he approaches the city of Rome (28:15).

Three ships are involved in the journey: the ship from Adramyttium, which takes Paul from Caesarea to Myra (27:2 – 5); the Alexandrian ship, wrecked at Malta (27:6 – 44); and the Alexandrian ship that takes the survivors from Malta to Puteoli in Italy (28:11 – 13). The narrative includes a report of an *appearance of an angel* (27:23 – 24), a *prediction* (27:26), a *miracle story* (28:7 – 8: healing of Publius's father;[11]

---

to him" — in other words a "time of freedom" that allows the readers to comtemplate "the finality of Paul's condition and the inexorability of his future."

8. Cf. Michael Labahn, "Paulus — ein *homo honestus et iustus*: Das lukanische Paulusportrait von Act 27 – 28 im Lichte ausgewählter antiker Parallelen," in *Das Ende des Paulus: Historische, theologische und literaturgeschichtliche Aspekte* (ed. F. W. Horn; BZNW 106; Berlin: De Gruyter, 2001), 75 – 106. The

term *homo honestus* is from Cicero, *Fam.* 16.12, and is used by Labahn not in a technical sense.

9. Cf. Johnson, *Acts*, 458; Marshall, *Acts*, 401.

10. Cf. Peterson, *Acts*, 678.

11. Whether Paul's snake bite (28:3 – 6) is also a miracle story, which is often assumed, depends on whether the snake was a poisonous snake whose bite infallibly killed, which is far from certain; see on 28:3.

note that the miracles do not concern the storm or the shipwreck),[12] a *summary statement* about miracles (28:9), and *direct speech* of Paul (27:10, 21 – 26, 31, 33 – 34), and a *speech* by Malta's inhabitants (28:4).

Exegetical Outline

→ **I. The Sea Voyage to Italy (27:1 – 28:15)**

    A. The Journey from Caesarea to Myra in Lycia (27:1 – 5)

        1. The departure from Caesarea as a prisoner of the centurion Julius (27:1 – 2)

           a. The prisoner transport is put in the charge of the centurion Julius (27:1)

           b. Departure on a ship bound toward the coast of the province of Asia (27:2a-c)

           c. Paul's companions are Luke and Aristarchus (27:2d-f)

        2. The stopover in Sidon, where Paul is allowed to stay with believers (27:3)

        3. The journey past Cyprus to the coast of Asia Minor, reaching Myra (27:4 – 5)

    B. The Journey from Myra to Kaloi Limenes on Crete (27:6 – 8)

        1. The transfer to a ship from Alexandria bound for Italy (27:6)

        2. The journey past Cnidus to Crete, reaching Kaloi Limenes (27:7 – 8)

    C. The Storm and Shipwreck at Malta (27:9 – 44)

        1. Paul's advice to winter in Kaloi Limenes (27:9 – 10)

        2. The decision of the captain and shipowner to sail to Phoenix (27:11 – 13)

        3. The storm (27:14 – 26)

           a. The storm with hurricane-force winds (27:14 – 15)

           b. The hoisting on board of the ship's lifeboat (27:16)

           c. The reinforcement of the ship's hull (27:17a-c)

           d. The lowering of the rigging (27:17d-h)

           e. The jettisoning of the cargo and rigging (27:18 – 19)

           f. The abandonment of all hope of survival (27:20)

           g. Paul's address to the passengers (27:21 – 26)

               i. Reminder of his earlier advice not to continue the journey (27:21)

               ii. Assurance of survival of the passengers (27:22)

               iii. Reason for Paul's confidence: The appearance of an angel (27:23)

               iv. Promise of the angel that Paul and all on board will be saved (27:24)

               v. Confidence that the angel's promise will be fulfilled (27:25)

               vi. Assertion that the ship will run aground on an island (27:26)

        4. The shipwreck (27:27 – 44)

           a. The events of the fourteenth night (27:27 – 32)

           b. Paul's admonishment of crew and passengers to take food (27:33 – 38)

           c. The events after daybreak: The ship runs aground on a reef (27:39 – 41)

---

12. Cf. Johnson, *Acts*, 458, who emphasizes, "Paul does not pray to have the winds silenced or the winds stilled. He is *not* portrayed as a *theios aner* ('divine man') whose will can bend the forces of nature to his own."

Explanation of the Text

27:1 When it was decided that we would sail for Italy, Paul and some other prisoners were handed over to a centurion named Julius who commanded the Augustan Cohort (ὡς δὲ ἐκρίθη τοῦ ἀποπλεῖν ἡμᾶς εἰς τὴν Ἰταλίαν, παρεδίδουν τόν τε Παῦλον καί τινας ἑτέρους δεσμώτας ἑκατοντάρχῃ ὀνόματι Ἰουλίῳ σπείρης Σεβαστῆς). The first incident of Luke's report of Paul's journey to Rome records the journey of the first ship that the travelers use, which takes them from Caesarea to Myra on the southern coast of Asia Minor (vv. 1 – 5).

Luke begins with the departure from Caesarea (vv. 1 – 2). Since Paul's petition that his case be heard by the emperor in Rome had already been accepted by Festus (25:12; cf. 26:32), the decision in v. 1 refers to the practical arrangements for Paul's transfer to Rome: the appointment of the military escort of the prisoners, the time of departure, and the booking of passage on the ship. Luke resumes the we-narrative (left off in 21:18), which continues up to 28:16 (the arrival in Rome), implying his participation in the events as an eyewitness. This

means that besides Aristarchus (v. 2), Luke accompanies Paul on the voyage to Rome.

The verb "sail" (ἀποπλεῖν) is a technical nautical term denoting "to sail away, to sail off" (LSJ). The destination is "Italy." The city of Rome could hardly have been given as destination, since Rome itself had no harbor; the main port for reaching Rome by ship was Puteoli (150 miles [240 km.] southeast of Rome); Ostia at the mouth of the Tiber River (about 18 miles [30 km.] southwest of Rome) was developed as a new harbor at this time. The travel party is not able to use a ship traveling directly from Caesarea to Puteoli (or Ostia), so they use different ships, the last of which will eventually take them to an Italian port.

The transport of prisoners includes, besides Paul, "some other prisoners" (cf. v. 42). Since appeals to the emperor were rare and limited to Roman citizens, it must be assumed that these prisoners were convicted criminals being sent to Rome to be killed in gladiatorial games as part of the entertainment of the crowds. The implied plural subject of the verb "were handed over" (παρεδίδουν) refers to prison officials in the administration of Festus, the governor of Judea, who has organized the prisoner transport.

The officer in charge of the transport is a centurion (ἑκατοντάρχης; see on 10:1) whose name is Julius, evidently a Roman citizen. The "Augustan Cohort" seems to refer to a specific cohort, the *cohors Augusta* stationed in Syria during the first century. Julius would have carried the official documentation related to Paul's case (see "In Depth: Reports of Court Proceedings," in Structure and Literary Form on 24:1 – 27), including the *littera dimissoria*, which explained the circumstances of Paul's case and the reasons for granting Paul's appeal to be tried by the emperor (see on 25:13, 26). He is not in charge of the ship, only of the prisoners being taken to Rome.

27:2 We boarded a ship from Adramyttium that was about to sail to the ports along the coast of the province of Asia, and we put out to sea, accompanied by Aristarchus, a Macedonian from Thessalonica (ἐπιβάντες δὲ πλοίῳ Ἀδραμυττηνῷ μέλλοντι πλεῖν εἰς τοὺς κατὰ τὴν Ἀσίαν τόπους ἀνήχθημεν ὄντος σὺν ἡμῖν Ἀριστάρχου Μακεδόνος Θεσσαλονικέως). The two main verbs in the aorist tense describe the main actions of the departure: they "boarded" (ἐπιβάντες) a ship and they "put out to sea" (ἀνήχθημεν).[13]

The "ship from Adramyttium" was a trading ship that plied "the ports along the coast of the province of Asia" between Adramyttium, the ship's home port in western Asia Minor, traveling perhaps as far as Alexandria in Egypt. Apart from Luke, the author of the "we report" (cf. v. 1), Paul is also accompanied by Aristarchus, who has been mentioned in 19:29 (identified as a Macedonian)

and in 20:4 (identified as a Thessalonian). A prisoner could be accompanied by family members or friends, but this had to be allowed by the Roman officials.[14] The evidence of Col 4:10 and Phlm 24 shows that Aristarchus shared Paul's time of imprisonment in Rome.

The fact that Festus allows Luke and Aristarchus to accompany Paul attests to Paul's influence and status. Note the comment in v. 3 that Julius treats Paul kindly. Paul is probably in chains, although he seems to have been granted some dignity in transit. He is evidently kept above deck (vv. 10 – 11, 21 – 26, 30 – 36) and is able to obtain provisions from Christians in one of the ports of call along the way (v. 3).

27:3 The next day we put in at Sidon, and Julius treated Paul kindly and allowed him to go to his friends to be cared for (τῇ τε ἑτέρᾳ κατήχθημεν εἰς Σιδῶνα, φιλανθρώπως τε ὁ Ἰούλιος τῷ Παύλῳ χρησάμενος ἐπέτρεψεν πρὸς τοὺς φίλους πορευθέντι ἐπιμελείας τυχεῖν). The first port of call was Sidon, an ancient Phoenician seaport between Berytus and Tyre that owed its wealth to its glass and purple industry and to the significance of its harbor. The verb "put in" (κατήχθημεν) here is a nautical term describing the arrival of a ship in a port.

The centurion treats Paul "kindly" (φιλανθρώπως), a term probably to be understood here in the weaker sense of "humanely, with courtesy." He allows Paul to visit "his friends" (οἱ φίλοι), probably fellow Christians. Luke's comment in 11:19 suggests that a church in Sidon — evidently one of the Phoenician cities that the Jerusalem believers visited who had to flee after Stephen's execution — was established as early as AD 31/32. Note the reference to churches in Phoenician (and Samaritan) cities in 15:3. The Christians of Sidon

---

13. Both verbs (ἐπιβαίνω, ἀνάγω; see also 27:4, 12, 21; 28:11) are used here as technical nautical terms; cf. BDAG, s.v. ἐπιβαίνω 1; s.v. ἀνάγω 4.

14. Cf. Labahn, "Paulusportrait," 80 n. 15. Note Pliny, *Ep.* 3.16.7 – 9, for an example where the petition for companions was denied.

attend (τυχεῖν) to Paul's needs, probably providing food and clothing for the journey, although the transport and billeting of the prisoners, and the military escorts, were the responsibility of the centurion, which he would have carried out by means of requisition from the locals.[15]

27:4 From there we put out to sea and sailed under the lee of Cyprus, because the winds were against us (κἀκεῖθεν ἀναχθέντες ὑπεπλεύσαμεν τὴν Κύπρον διὰ τὸ τοὺς ἀνέμους εἶναι ἐναντίους). After an unspecified number of days, the ship with its passengers puts out to sea (ἀναχθέντες; see on v. 2) from Sidon and sails "under the lee" of Cyprus — that side of an island that protects the ship from the wind. The prevailing autumnal west winds force the ship to pass Cyprus on the eastern and northern side of the island. If the winds "against" the ship prevent the course that was originally planned, the most plausible port of call would have been Paphos on the south coast of Cyprus. Sailing between the northern coast of Cyprus and the southern coast of Asia Minor, the ship against the autumn winds "was assisted by local on-shore and off-shore breezes, and by the westerly trend of the currents along the south Anatolian coasts."[16]

27:5 After we had sailed across the sea off the coast of Cilicia and Pamphylia, we landed at Myra in Lycia (τό τε πέλαγος τὸ κατὰ τὴν Κιλικίαν καὶ Παμφυλίαν διαπλεύσαντες κατήλθομεν εἰς Μύρα τῆς Λυκίας). The ship lands at the port city of Myra. The verb translated "we had sailed across"

(διαπλεύσαντες) is a nautical term that denotes to "sail through a straight or gap" or "sail across" a particular sea. The verb "landed" (κατήλθομεν) is a nautical term that describes ships and their passengers who "come down" from the high seas and arrive in a port.

Myra was the customs port of the federation of Lycian cities and served, like Patara (cf. 21:1), as the principal port for the Alexandrian grain ships. The Western text includes the information that the voyage from Sidon to Myra took fifteen days; the addition is hardly original,[17] but it gives a plausible time for the journey in adverse conditions.

27:6 There the centurion found a ship from Alexandria bound for Italy and put us on board ship (κἀκεῖ εὑρὼν ὁ ἑκατοντάρχης πλοῖον Ἀλεξανδρῖνον πλέον εἰς τὴν Ἰταλίαν ἐνεβίβασεν ἡμᾶς εἰς αὐτό). The next incident relates the journey from Myra in Lycia to Fair Havens on Crete (vv. 6 – 8). Myra was the port where Julius could expect to find a ship sailing between Rome and the southern coast of Asia Minor, for many grain ships from Alexandria put in there, taking on board provisions after having crossed the Mediterranean.[18] Egypt provided a third of the grain that Rome needed annually. Many grain ships were owned privately. During the reign of Nero or shortly before, an "Alexandrian fleet" was formed — ships traveling in a single convoy.[19]

These ships followed one of two routes: a northerly route by way of Cyprus, Myra, Rhodes, or

---

15. Cf. Rapske, *Paul in Roman Custody*, 272; see Horsley and Llewelyn, *New Documents*, 1:36 – 45; 7:58 – 92.

16. Hemer, *Acts*, 133, who comments that "such considerations at least reflect experience of the climatic conditions of this voyage."

17. The addition is found in manuscripts 614. 2147 and in Latin and Syriac manuscripts; cf. Metzger, *Textual Commentary*, 440.

18. Most of Rome's grain came from Egypt. Under Augustus, 20 million *modii* of grain were annually imported from

Egypt to Rome (R. Sallares, "Grain Trade, Grain Import," *BNP*, 5:979). Under Claudius, shipowners were granted financial privileges if they made their vessels available for the transport of grain to the city of Rome (Suetonius, *Claud.* 18 – 19). For the following comment see Josephus, *J.W.* 2.386.

19. Seneca, *Ep.* 77.1; P. Oxy. XIV 1763; IG XIV 918. Cf. Lionel Casson, *Ships and Seamanship in the Ancient World* (orig. 1971; repr., Baltimore: Johns Hopkins Univ. Press, 1995), 297; for the following comment ibid.

Cnidus, south of Crete, Malta, and Messina; and a southerly route along the North African coast to Cyrene and from there to Italy. Leaving at the earliest possible date in the month of April, the voyage could take at least a month or two, sailing against the prevailing northwesterly winds (the return journey "downhill" could take as little as two or three weeks). Suetonius relates that the emperor Claudius "always gave scrupulous attention to the care of the city and the supply of grain," resorting "to every possible means to bring grain to Rome, even in the winter season" (*Claud.* 18).

If the turnaround in Rome and the reloading in Alexandria was quick enough, ships could squeeze in a second crossing before the season closed (cf. v. 9). The ship from Alexandria that the centurion Julius "found" was evidently a grain ship on its second crossing of the year, trying to reach Rome just before the onset of the winter season, when navigation on the Mediterranean was closed. The verb translated "put on board" (ἐνεβίβασεν) is used as a nautical term for embarking on a ship. The centurion puts on board Paul, his companions, and the other prisoners.

27:7 – 8 We sailed slowly for a number of days and arrived off Cnidus only with difficulty. Since the wind did not permit us to hold course, we sailed under the lee of Crete off Salmone. We sailed along the coast with difficulty and came to a place called Kaloi Limenes near the town of Lasea (ἐν ἱκαναῖς δὲ ἡμέραις βραδυπλοοῦντες καὶ μόλις γενόμενοι κατὰ τὴν Κνίδον, μὴ προσεῶντος ἡμᾶς τοῦ ἀνέμου ὑπεπλεύσαμεν τὴν Κρήτην κατὰ Σαλμώνην, μόλις τε παραλεγόμενοι αὐτὴν ἤλθομεν

εἰς τόπον τινὰ καλούμενον Καλοὺς λιμένας ᾧ ἐγγὺς πόλις ἦν Λασαία). The progress of the Alexandrian ship is narrated with three nautical terms: they "sailed slowly" (βραδυπλοοῦντες)[20] toward Cnidus, they "sailed under the lee" (ὑπεπλεύσαμεν; cf. v. 4) of Crete, and they "sailed along the coast" (παραλεγόμενοι).

Progress was slow. Their journey from Myra to Cnidus, a peninsula in Caria on the southwestern tip of Asia Minor straight west of Myra, was difficult because the ship sailed straight into the typical west-northwest wind.

The passage to Italy required the ship then to turn southwest toward Crete, the largest of the Greek islands with an east-west extension of 155 miles (250 km.) and a north-south extension of a maximum of 37 miles (60 km.), dominated by three large mountain ranges, with most of the towns and harbors on the gentle slopes of the north and east coasts. The northwesterly winds did not permit the ship to sail a straight course. It had to tack back and forth in order to make progress, traveling perhaps only 1½ to 2½ knots in the adverse conditions.[21] The normal route was to round the eastern cape of Crete and sail along the southern coast of the island. Salmone was the cape at the northeastern tip of Crete. There was a temple of Athene there, whose name may have been of Phoenician origin derived from a term describing a refuge from exposure to the wind.

The ship sailed along the southern coast of Crete, eventually arriving at a place called Kaloi Limenes (Καλοὶ λιμένες), usually translated as "Fair Havens,"[22] a settlement two kilometers west of Lasea, roughly 92 nautical miles (170 km.) west

---

20. The use of the unusual verb "to sail slowly" (βραδυπλοέω) "may reflect mounting impatience and anxiety at continuing delays if the wind force were greater than average, necessitating perhaps extensive tacking where they could not sail close enough into the wind" (Hemer, *Acts*, 134).

21. For sailing speeds and the difference between favorable winds (traveling east) and unfavorable winds (traveling west, as Paul's ship did), cf. Lionel Casson, "Speed under Sail of Ancient Ships," *TAPA* 82 (1951): 136 – 48; Casson, *Ships*, 291.

22. Cf. BDAG, s.v. Καλοὶ λιμένες. Archaeologists working on Crete refer to "Kaloi Limenes."

of Cape Salmone. A ship anchored at Fair Havens would be well protected from the sudden north winds that blew through the Asterousia Mountains to the north. The bay offered good anchorage — except from the southeast winds of winter, although offshore islands provide protection from the southwest. This settlement, which Luke calls "a place" (τόπος), was not large, nor was the town of Lasea, to whose territory the bay belonged. In v. 12 Kaloi Limenes is described as a place unsuitable for the grain ship and its crew and passengers to spend the winter.

27:9 – 10 Since much time had been lost and navigation had now become dangerous, because even the Day of Atonement had gone by, Paul strongly urged them, "Men, I see that the voyage will bring disaster and heavy loss, not only of the cargo and the ship but also of our own lives" (ἱκανοῦ δὲ χρόνου διαγενομένου καὶ ὄντος ἤδη ἐπισφαλοῦς τοῦ πλοὸς διὰ τὸ καὶ τὴν νηστείαν ἤδη παρεληλυθέναι παρῄνει ὁ Παῦλος λέγων αὐτοῖς· ἄνδρες, θεωρῶ ὅτι μετὰ ὕβρεως καὶ πολλῆς ζημίας οὐ μόνον τοῦ φορτίου καὶ τοῦ πλοίου ἀλλὰ καὶ τῶν ψυχῶν ἡμῶν μέλλειν ἔσεσθαι τὸν πλοῦν). Luke's report of the storm and shipwreck (vv. 9 – 44) begins with Paul's advice to the crew of the ship to winter in Kaloi Limenes.

While Luke does not indicate the purpose of putting into the bay of Kaloi Limenes, his report implies that the crew discussed whether they should continue the voyage. He notes that "much time" had been lost[23] and that navigation had become "dangerous" (ἐπισφαλής), i.e., unsafe and likely to cause a disaster. The term trans-

lated "navigation" (ὁ πλόος) is a nautical term. The adverb "now" (ἤδη), which can be translated "by this time," is specified by Luke in terms of the Day of Atonement, which had already "gone by" (παρεληλυθέναι). The perfect tense emphasizes the situation that pertained after "the fast" (ἡ νηστεία), i.e., the Day of Atonement celebrated on the 10th of Tishri, which in AD 59 fell on October 5.[24]

It is impossible to know whether Paul would have kept the traditional Jewish fast on the Day of Atonement. According to Vegetius, navigation on the Mediterranean was safe until September 14, uncertain until November 11, and "closed" from November 11 until March 10.[25] The term *mare clausum* ("closed sea") denotes the closure of navigation between November 11 and March 5 because of winter storms, fog, and overcast skies, which made navigation (by the sun and stars) nearly impossible.[26] Note that Luke mentions the invisibility of the sun and the stars in v. 20. According to (later) Jewish thinking, sea journeys were regarded unsafe after the Feast of Booths (Succoth), which took place five days after the Day of Atonement, which may suggest that the date given in v. 9 was between October 5 and 10.

Since it was past October 5 and since navigation had been slow and was becoming dangerous, Paul "strongly urged" the men in charge of the ship, who evidently had decided to set sail again, not to continue the voyage. That Paul intervenes in the crew's discussion about continuing the voyage is plausible in view of the fact that he was an experienced traveler and, besides the centurion Julius, possibly the only Roman citizen on board. The Sophist philosopher Aelius Aristides, who traveled

---

23. The verb διαγίνομαι denotes the passing or elapse of time (BDAG).

24. According to Lev 16.29 – 31, the Day of Atonement (Yom Kippur) was celebrated on the tenth day of the seventh month, later called the month of Tishri (from late September to the beginning of October). Cf. Hemer, *Acts*, 137 – 38, 270.

25. Vegetius, *De re militari* 4.39.

26. March 5 was the date of the festival Ploeaphesia (Lat. *navigium Isidis*), attested from the first century AD, which opened navigation. See Apuleius, *Metam.* 11.8 – 17, who describes the celebrations in Cenchreae, where the festival seems to have been connected with the Corinthian *Hybristica* festival.

as a sick man from Rome to Miletus in AD 144, warned the crew not to leave Patara shortly before the autumnal equinox (September 23) — advice that was not heeded, with a severe storm battering the ship after the departure from Patara.[27] Cicero advised his friend Tiro:

> I must again ask you not to be rash in your traveling. Sailors, I observe, make too much haste to increase their profits. Be cautious, my dear Tiro. You have a wide and dangerous sea to traverse. If you can, come with Mescinius. He is wont to be careful in his voyages. If not with him, come with a person of distinction, who will have influence with the captain.[28]

Luke relates Paul's advice in v. 10 in direct speech. After addressing the crew (ἄνδρες; "men"), Paul issues a warning, which is not presented as a prophecy or a prediction[29] but as a general warning of the dire consequence if the ship sets sail, reflecting common sense and prudence.[30] Paul perceives that continuing the voyage will bring "disaster" (ὕβρις)[31] and "heavy loss." Paul warns that the cargo, which the crew cares most about, is in danger, as well as the ship itself with its passengers.

27:11 But the centurion listened to the advice of the captain and the owner of the ship rather than to Paul's words (ὁ δὲ ἑκατοντάρχης τῷ κυβερνήτῃ καὶ τῷ ναυκλήρῳ μᾶλλον ἐπείθετο ἢ τοῖς ὑπὸ Παύλου λεγομένοις). Paul's advice is rejected. The centurion Julius may treat Paul kindly (v. 3), and he listens to his advice, but he does not follow it, which is hardly surprising given the fact that both the captain and the owner of the ship agree that the jour-

ney should continue. The "captain" (κυβερνήτης) is "a hired professional who had full authority over the running of the vessel and full command of its crew."[32] The "owner" (ναύκληρος) was "the man who had the use of a vessel, and thereby the possibility of exploiting it, whether through ownership or charter."[33] This man was the shipowner if the grain ship was private property; if it belonged to Rome's grain fleet, he probably would have been the person who chartered the ship for the Roman grain trade. The latter possibility has sometimes been taken to explain why the centurion, a commanding officer in the Roman army, seems to have made the final decision as regards the movements of the "government ship."[34]

One should note that Luke does not explicitly portray the centurion as having final authority over the vessel and the continuation of the journey. The decision related by Luke may not have been whether or not to sail, but whether he, his soldiers, and his prisoners would stay on board if the ship continued the journey.[35]

27:12 Since the harbor was not suitable for spending the winter, the majority decided that we should put out to sea from there, in the hope of being able to reach Phoenix and winter there; this was a harbor of Crete that faced both southwest and northwest (ἀνευθέτου δὲ τοῦ λιμένος ὑπάρχοντος πρὸς παραχειμασίαν οἱ πλείονες ἔθεντο βουλὴν ἀναχθῆναι ἐκεῖθεν, εἴ πως δύναιντο καταντήσαντες εἰς Φοίνικα παραχειμάσαι λιμένα τῆς Κρήτης βλέποντα κατὰ λίβα καὶ κατὰ χῶρον). The decision to continue the journey was made

---

27. Aelius Aristides, *Hieroi Logoi* 2.67 – 68; cf. Reiser, "Von Caesarea nach Malta," 57.

28. Cicero, *Fam.* 16.12; cf. Labahn, "Paulusportrait," 84 – 85.

29. Thus Barrett, *Acts*, 1189; Fitzmyer, *Acts*, 775.

30. Johnson, *Acts*, 447.

31. The term ὕβρις often denotes "insolence, arrogance" but denotes here "damage caused by use of force, fig. *hardship, disaster, damage* caused by the elements" (BDAG, s.v. ὕβρις 3).

32. Casson, *Ships*, 316; cf. BDAG, s.v. κυβερνήτης 1, "one who is responsible for the management of a ship, *shipmaster.*"

33. Casson, *Ships*, 315 n. 67. Cf. A. L. Connolly, in Horsley and Llewelyn, *New Documents*, 4:116.

34. Ramsay, *St. Paul the Traveller*, 261.

35. K. L. McKay, in Horsley and Llewelyn, *New Documents*, 4:117.

on the basis of the fact that the harbor of Kaloi Limenes was regarded as unsuitable for spending the winter months, perhaps because of the lack of amenities in the place and in the town of Lasea.

The "majority" (οἱ πλείονες) that made the decision to put out to sea again probably refers to the seamen responsible for the ship, i.e., the captain and the skipper mentioned in v. 11, over against Paul, who had advised staying put in Kaloi Limenes. The decision was made to put out to sea and reach Phoenix, about 40 nautical miles (75 km.) further west. Sailing close to the shore (v. 13) prolongs the distance. The crew knew that Phoenix was "a harbor of Crete" that faced both southwest and northwest. The topography of that harbor, in the western bay, has "two recessed beaches on the western flank of the headland facing northwest and southwest respectively."[36] This is where the captain and skipper of the ship hoped to winter (παραχειμάσαι; used for the second time in the verse).

27:13 When a moderate south wind began to blow, they thought that they could carry out their plan. They weighed anchor and sailed along the coast of Crete close to the shore (ὑποπνεύσαντος δὲ νότου δόξαντες τῆς προθέσεως κεκρατηκέναι, ἄραντες ἆσσον παρελέγοντο τὴν Κρήτην). When the northwesterly winds subsided and a "south wind" (νότος) began to blow gently, the captain and skipper believed that they could carry out their plan. Southerly winds were ideal for reaching Phoenix. They "weighed anchor," rounded Cape Matala about 4 miles (7 km.) to the west, coasted close to the coast of Crete, in a west-northwesterly direction across the Bay of Mesara, hoping to reach Phoenix in a day.

27:14 – 15 But soon afterward a wind of hurricane force called the Northeaster swept down from the island. Since the ship was caught by the wind and could not be turned into the wind, we gave way to it and were driven along (μετ' οὐ πολὺ δὲ ἔβαλεν κατ' αὐτῆς ἄνεμος τυφωνικὸς ὁ καλούμενος εὐρακύλων· συναρπασθέντος δὲ τοῦ πλοίου καὶ μὴ δυναμένου ἀντοφθαλμεῖν τῷ ἀνέμῳ ἐπιδόντες ἐφερόμεθα). Luke's account of the storm (vv. 14 – 38) begins with a description of the onset of the storm with hurricane-force winds. Mariners are well aware of the fact that south winds can suddenly change into a violent Northeaster. The ship evidently had just[37] rounded Cape Matala and was in the open bay when it was caught by winds sweeping down across the open plain of Mesara. The wind is described with three expressions: it "swept down" suddenly from the Ida Mountains of the island; it had "hurricane force"; it was called "the Northeaster" or Euraquilo (εὐρακύλων).[38]

Luke describes the consequences of the sudden onset of the Euraquilo. The ship was "caught by the wind," and since it blew so strongly the ship could not be "turned into the wind" (the verb ἀντοφθαλμεῖν is a nautical term describing the practice of putting the bow of a ship into the wind so that it sails against the force of the waves. As a result, the crew "gave way," i.e., surrendered the ship to the wind, so that the ship with crew and passengers was "driven along."

27:16 – 17 As we ran under the lee of a little island called Cauda, we were scarcely able to get

---

36. Hemer, *Acts*, 139, following Robert M. Ogilvie, "Phoenix," *JTS* 9 (1958): 308 – 14, 308 – 9.

37. The expression μετ' οὐ πολύ means "not long afterward" (BDAG, s.v. μετά B.2c).

38. Cf. BDAG, s.v. εὐρακύλων, "the northeast wind, Euraquilo, *the northeaster*." The fact that the sailors feared to be blown into the Syrtis (v. 17) confirms that the wind was a Northeaster. The name of the Northeaster has been confirmed

by the discovery at Thugga in proconsular Africa of a twelve-point wind rose that was 26 feet (8 m.) in diameter dating to the third century AD, incised in the pavement of the plaza between the marketplace and the temple of Mercurus; the wind rose uses only Latin names: between the north wind (*septentrio*) and the east wind (*vulturnus*) it lists the *aquilo* and the *euroaquilo* (CIL VIII 26652). In Greek wind roses, the equilavent of the *euroaquilo* is the καικίας.

the lifeboat under control. **After the men had hoisted it up, they deployed supports to undergird the ship. Because they feared that they would run aground in the Syrtis, they lowered the rigging and let the ship be driven along in this way** (νησίον δέ τι ὑποδραμόντες καλούμενον Καῦδα ἰσχύσαμεν μόλις περικρατεῖς γενέσθαι τῆς σκάφης, ἣν ἄραντες βοηθείαις ἐχρῶντο ὑποζωννύντες τὸ πλοῖον, φοβούμενοί τε μὴ εἰς τὴν Σύρτιν ἐκπέσωσιν, χαλάσαντες τὸ σκεῦος, οὕτως ἐφέροντο).

Luke relates three measures of the crew designed to offset the effects of the storm, undertaken when the ship was protected from the worst of the storm in the lee of the island named Cauda, which lies 30 nautical miles (55 km.) west-southwest of Cape Matala, precisely in the direction into which a square-rigged ship would be driven by a gale blowing from the northeast.[39] Cauda was indeed a "little island" (νησίον): the distance between the town of Kaudos on the north side of the island and Vatsiana in the south is only 4 miles (6 km.). The ship ran under the lee of Cauda, passing the island to the west.

The first emergency measure was securing the lifeboat. The crew hoisted it on board, which was usually towed astern. The effort to gain control of the ship's boat was hampered by the strong wind, the heavy seas, and the water in the boat, and could thus be achieved only with difficulty.

The second emergency measure strengthened the ship. The crew deployed "supports" (βοηθείαι), massive cables that were used to form a brace in order to "undergird" the ship. Luke describes the technique of frapping, in which "undergirds" are passed underneath the ship in order to reinforce the hull by securing planking that had come loose and was letting water into the ship. Some suggest that the cables ran under the hull horizontally (longitudinally) from bow to stern, anchored in a short loop that passed vertically about the stern;[40] others argue that the exterior cables ran vertically (transversely) around the bottom of the hull.[41]

The third measure aimed at changing the direction of the ship. The crew was afraid that the ship would drift into the Syrtis and run aground. The Syrtis is the Greater Syrtis (today the Gulf of Sidera), the eastern part of the coastal waters west of Cyrenaica between Berenice and Lepcis Magna in northern Africa. This gulf was "an extensive zone of shallows and quicksands" that "formed a notorious navigational hazard and inspired an obsessional fear constantly mentioned in first-century literature."[42]

The crew lowered all superfluous sail and rigging, retaining only a minimal storm sail with which to keep the ship steady. By lowering most of the sail and rigging, the crew would have been able to lay the ship "on a starboard tack, with its right side pointed into the wind, to make as much leeway as possible northward of the natural line of drift, and so away from the Syrtis."[43] If the crew did not take these precautions, the Northeaster would drive the ship across the open sea for 350 nautical miles (650 km.) straight toward the Syrtis within two or three days.[44]

---

39. Hemer, *Acts*, 142, who emphasizes that the island is "precisely placed, and correctly named." The spelling of the name of the island in the sources varies. The modern name is Gaudos/Gozzo.

40. John S. Morrison and Roderick T. Williams, *Greek Oared Ships, 900 – 322 B.C.* (Cambridge: Cambridge Univ. Press, 1968), 294 – 98, followed by Casson, *Ships*, 91 – 92, 211.

41. Hemer, *Acts*, 143 with n. 120.

42. Hemer, *Acts*, 144. Cf. Virgil, *Aen.* 1.11, 146; Tibullus 3.4.91; Propertius 2.9.33; Strabo, *Geogr.* 17.3.20.

43. Hemer, *Acts*, 144, following James Smith, *The Voyage and Shipwreck of St. Paul, with Dissertations on the Life and Writings of St. Luke, and the Ships and Navigation of the Ancients* (4th ed.; orig. 1848; repr., London: Longmans & Green, 1880), 110 – 11.

44. Cf. Casson, *Ships*, 282 – 88, with evidence that under favorable wind conditions, ancient ships averaged between 4 and 6 knots over open water. This answers the question of Barrett, *Acts*, 1196, whether the sailors would have feared this danger so soon.

27:18 – 19 We were pounded by the storm so violently that on the next day they began to jettison the cargo. On the third day they threw the ship's rigging overboard with their own hands (σφοδρῶς δὲ χειμαζομένων ἡμῶν τῇ ἑξῆς ἐκβολὴν ἐποιοῦντο καὶ τῇ τρίτῃ αὐτόχειρες τὴν σκευὴν τοῦ πλοίου ἔρριψαν). The violence of the storm made further measures necessary. The first person plural (ἡμῶν) focuses on the effect of the storm on the passengers. The crew lightened the ship twice (a third time in v. 38). On the day after leaving the lee of the island of Cauda, they began to jettison (ἐκβολὴν ἐποιοῦντο) the cargo. The imperfect of the verb is inceptive, denoting the beginning of the action (note that the wheat is jettisoned later).

On the third day after passing Cauda — i.e., on the day after they had jettisoned some of the cargo — the crew threw the ship's rigging overboard. The term "rigging" (σκευή)[45] means broadly "equipment" or gear, which may refer to anything on board not essential to survival.

27:20 When neither sun nor stars appeared for many days and rather bad weather pressed upon us, we finally gave up all hope of being saved (μήτε δὲ ἡλίου μήτε ἄστρων ἐπιφαινόντων ἐπὶ πλείονας ἡμέρας, χειμῶνός τε οὐκ ὀλίγου ἐπικειμένου, λοιπὸν περιῃρεῖτο ἐλπὶς πᾶσα τοῦ σῴζεσθαι ἡμᾶς). The crew and passengers of the ship gradually "gave up"[46] all hope of surviving the storm. The term translated "being saved" (σῴζεσθαι) here denotes being rescued from death. Neither sun nor stars appeared for many days, which made navigation impossible as the position of the ship could not be verified. Rather bad weather pressed upon them, and the storm did not let up for two weeks (cf.

v. 27). Despair may have descended on the crew "when they realized that they had probably missed Sicily and could never survive in the vain hope of reaching the Tunisian coast intact."[47]

27:21 Since almost nobody wanted to eat, Paul stood up among them and said, "Men, you ought to have followed my advice and not have sailed from Crete, and thereby avoided this damage and loss" (πολλῆς τε ἀσιτίας ὑπαρχούσης τότε σταθεὶς ὁ Παῦλος ἐν μέσῳ αὐτῶν εἶπεν· ἔδει μέν, ὦ ἄνδρες, πειθαρχήσαντάς μοι μὴ ἀνάγεσθαι ἀπὸ τῆς Κρήτης κερδῆσαί τε τὴν ὕβριν ταύτην καὶ τὴν ζημίαν). Luke ends his depiction of the severe storm that prompted crew and passengers to give up hope of survival with a speech by Paul (vv. 21 – 26), before narrating the shipwreck at Malta (vv. 27 – 44).

Luke introduces Paul's speech with a comment on the lack of appetite among crew and passengers — surely due to anxiety, seasickness, and the impossibility of cooking. Luke portrays Paul not as a "divine man" whose prayer stills the storm but, rather, as an experienced traveler whose advice should have been followed, and as a servant of God who is concerned about the welfare of the people on board the ship, who receives revelations from God, and who is able to inspire them with hope. The location at which Paul "stood up" is probably below deck. Luke does not indicate on which day of the ship's odyssey Paul told the crew and passengers about the appearance of the angel.

Paul begins his speech by establishing his competence as someone who has experience as a traveler (according to 2 Cor 11:25, he had been in shipwrecks three other times). He reminds the crew and passengers of his earlier intervention

---

45. Cf. NASB, NIV, NRSV, RSV, TNIV, translating as "tackle." James Smith, *Voyage and Shipwreck*, 114, suggests the main yard, which was very heavy, requiring the combined efforts of crew and passengers.

46. Note the imperfect tense of the verb περιῃρεῖτο. Here

λοιπόν is used adverbially of time: "finally" (BDAG, s.v. λοιπός 3aα).

47. Hemer, *Acts*, 145, following James Smith, *Voyage and Shipwreck*, 114 – 15.

when he warned them not to leave Kaloi Limenes (v. 10). They should have listened to his advice and not left the harbor on Crete. Had they done so, they would have avoided the damage to the ship and the loss of equipment (for ὕβρις and ζημία see v. 10). Paul's remarks should not be understood as those of a smart aleck who insists on having been right, but as establishing his credibility (*ethos*), which was a standard feature of speeches.[48]

27:22 I now urge you to be confident, because not a single one of you will be lost, only the ship will be a loss (καὶ τὰ νῦν παραινῶ ὑμᾶς εὐθυμεῖν· ἀποβολὴ γὰρ ψυχῆς οὐδεμία ἔσται ἐξ ὑμῶν πλὴν τοῦ πλοίου). In his first intervention, Paul had strongly urged the crew, in particular the captain and the skipper of the ship, not to leave the relative safety of Kaloi Limenes (v. 10); now he strongly urges the crew and passengers to be confident (εὐθυμεῖν), i.e., to regain their composure. The reason for his admonition is the announcement that there will be no loss of life of those on board; only the ship will be a loss. This prediction will come to pass (see vv. 41, 44). Paul does not correct an earlier prophecy of doom (which is read into v. 10). Rather, due to a revelation from God, he is in a position to assure the crew and passengers of their survival.

27:23 – 24 For last night an angel of the God to whom I belong and whom I serve stood before me, and said, "Do not be afraid, Paul. You must stand trial before the emperor, and indeed God has graciously given you the lives of all who are sailing with you" (παρέστη γάρ μοι ταύτῃ τῇ νυκτὶ τοῦ θεοῦ, οὗ εἰμι ἐγὼ ᾧ καὶ λατρεύω, ἄγγελος λέγων· μὴ φοβοῦ, Παῦλε, Καίσαρί σε δεῖ παραστῆναι, καὶ ἰδοὺ κεχάρισταί σοι ὁ θεὸς πάντας τοὺς πλέοντας μετὰ σοῦ). Paul's exhortation to be confident is grounded in a message from God relayed through an "angel of God," i.e., an angel whom God had sent the previous night. For angels see on 10:3; 12:7. The reference to the angel standing is a common feature of epiphanies.

Paul clarifies[49] for the benefit of the pagan crew and passengers, who would have known that Paul was a Jew, that he is the property (οὗ εἰμι ἐγώ, "whose I am") and the servant (ᾧ καὶ λατρεύω, "whom I serve") of the one true God. The pagan passengers might have expected help from the Dioscuri, deities called upon particularly in distress at sea "when their epiphany as a stellar constellation, possibly also by way of St. Elmo's fire, brought help,"[50] or from the Egyptian gods Isis and Serapis. Caught in terrible weather conditions that persisted for days on end without the possibility of navigation, the crew and passengers despaired of divine help and gave up hope (v. 20). Paul receives the assurance of rescue from the God of Israel.

In the dream vision, Paul receives an oracle of assurance.[51] The admonition "do not be afraid" (μὴ φοβοῦ) is followed by the direct address of the recipient of the divine assurance (i.e., Paul, vocative Παῦλε), followed by two reasons for the assurance. (1) It is God's will that he stands trial before the emperor in Rome. Since Paul had appealed to the emperor (25:12), a petition accepted by Festus, the Roman governor of Judea (25:21) who had

---

48. Correctly Pervo, *Acts*, 661 with n. 184, contra Bruce, *Acts*, 521, who makes Paul's remarks an issue of character (followed by Witherington, *Acts*, 768: Paul is not being portrayed as a perfect person; cf. Barrett, *Acts*, 1199: Paul's "I-told-you-so" approach was "unlikely to win him friends," wondering whether this is a mark of Lukan fiction).

49. The position of the relative clause between τοῦ θεοῦ and ἄγγελος gives it prominence.

50. T. Scheer, "Dioscuri I. Religion," *BNP*, 4:519. The Dioscuri appear also as helpers in distress (σωτῆρες) more generally, cf. Strabo, *Geogr.* 5.3.5. See further on 28:11.

51. Cf. Aune, *Prophecy*, 266 – 68, who argues that the form closely conforms to Old Testament and Jewish oracles of assurance, which consisted of three elements: (1) the phrase "fear not" (or equivalent); (2) designation of the addressee; (3) reason for the admonition.

eventually sent Paul off to Rome (27:1), he is now assured by God's messenger that he will indeed reach Rome and that his appearance before the imperial court is part of God's plan (note δεῖ; cf. 23:11).

(2) God "has graciously given" Paul (κεχάρισται) the favor of saving all on board the ship. The verb might imply that Paul had prayed for the rescue of his fellow travelers; while this implication is not certain, there is no doubt that the rescue of crew and passengers is due to the presence of Paul, whose protection by God is the cause of their deliverance.

27:25 – 26 "So be confident, men, for I have faith in God that it will happen exactly as I have been told. But we must run aground on some island" (διὸ εὐθυμεῖτε, ἄνδρες· πιστεύω γὰρ τῷ θεῷ ὅτι οὕτως ἔσται καθ᾽ ὃν τρόπον λελάληταί μοι. εἰς νῆσον δέ τινα δεῖ ἡμᾶς ἐκπεσεῖν). Paul formulates the conclusions (διό) from the angelic message with a word of encouragement (v. 25) and a prediction (v. 26). He commands the men on board the ship battered by the storm to "be confident" (εὐθυμεῖτε; cf. v. 22) because he believes that God will be true to his word: he will do exactly as he said he will do.

Paul then ends with a prediction.[52] The promised rescue pertains to the people on board, not to the ship, which will "run aground" on some island. To the west of Crete and south of Sicily, the direction of their drift, there are not many islands: Malta, Gaulos, and the tiny islands Lopadusa, Aethusa, and Cossyra. For the anxious passengers who have given up all hope of survival, to run aground on an island is certainly preferable to being in distress in high seas in the open sea (the cessation of the storm and docking in a safe harbor would be the preferred option). The island is identified in 28:1 as Malta.

27:27 – 28 On the fourteenth night we were still driven across the Adriatic Sea, when the sailors suspected about midnight that they were approaching land. They took soundings and found that the water was twenty fathoms deep. After they had sailed a short distance farther, they took soundings again and found that the water was fifteen fathoms deep (ὡς δὲ τεσσαρεσκαιδεκάτη νὺξ ἐγένετο διαφερομένων ἡμῶν ἐν τῷ Ἀδρίᾳ, κατὰ μέσον τῆς νυκτὸς ὑπενόουν οἱ ναῦται προσάγειν τινὰ αὐτοῖς χώραν. καὶ βολίσαντες εὗρον ὀργυιὰς εἴκοσι, βραχὺ δὲ διαστήσαντες καὶ πάλιν βολίσαντες εὗρον ὀργυιὰς δεκαπέντε). Luke begins his report of the shipwreck (vv. 27 – 44) with an account of events during the fourteenth night (vv. 27 – 32).

Since Luke seems to be counting the days since the ship left Kaloi Limenes (cf. vv. 18, 19), the fourteenth night marked the thirteenth day of drifting before the high winds of the storm, after the crew had lowered the rigging at the island of Cauda (vv. 16 – 17). It has been estimated that given a drift of 36.5 nautical miles (67.6 kilometers) in twenty-four hours, the ship would have drifted from Cauda to Malta — a distance of 476 nautical miles (882 km. or 584 statute miles) — in slightly over thirteen days. The term "Adriatic Sea" refers to the sea between Crete and Sicily.

As the ship was "driven" by the strong winds on the fourteenth night after leaving Kaloi Limenes on Crete, the sailors suspected around midnight that they were close to land. If the ship ran aground at the traditional site of St. Paul's Bay near Salmonetta Island (St. Paul's Islands), located in the northwestern part of the island of Malta, it would have been driven from the east past the rocky peninsula of Koura (Qawra) Point. The crew would have seen the breaking foam of the crashing waves on the rock.[53]

---

52. If the word translated as "must" (δεῖ) is interpreted in terms of God's sovereign will, v. 26 is a prophecy.

53. James Smith, *Voyage and Shipwreck*, 120 – 28; J. Michael Gilchrist, "The Historicity of Paul's Shipwreck," *JSNT* 61 (1996): 29 – 51, 50.

The sailors "took soundings" (βολίσαντες; a nautical term),[54] which dropped within a short distance from twenty fathoms (121 feet; 37 m.) to fifteen. A "fathom" (ὀργυιά) is the distance measured by a person's arms stretched out horizontally, usually reckoned at 1.85 meters (6 feet). These soundings correspond to the topography between Koura Point and St. Paul's Bay.

27:29 Since they feared that we might run aground on the rocks, they dropped four anchors from the stern and prayed for daylight (φοβούμενοί τε μή που κατὰ τραχεῖς τόπους ἐκπέσωμεν, ἐκ πρύμνης ῥίψαντες ἀγκύρας τέσσαρας ηὔχοντο ἡμέραν γενέσθαι). Realizing that they were rapidly approaching land but unable to see in the darkness, the sailors feared the ship would run aground (see on v. 17) on the rocks (κατὰ τραχεῖς τόπους; lit., "on rough, uneven places"). To prevent the ship from being dashed on the rocks and in order to await daylight, allowing them to safely put the ship on shore, the crew dropped "four anchors" from the stern.

This was an exceptional emergency measure — in the storm, the boat could not be turned around — intended to prevent "the immediate peril of letting the ship swing around broadside to the waves and of being smashed stern first on the rocks."[55] The prayers for daylight were motivated by the frightful prospect of running aground in heavy seas in complete darkness.

27:30 – 32 When the sailors tried to escape from the ship, lowering the lifeboat into the sea under the pretext of laying out anchors from the bow, Paul said to the centurion and the soldiers, "Un-less these men stay in the ship, you cannot be saved." Then the soldiers cut the ropes that held the lifeboat and let it drift away (τῶν δὲ ναυτῶν ζητούντων φυγεῖν ἐκ τοῦ πλοίου καὶ χαλασάντων τὴν σκάφην εἰς τὴν θάλασσαν προφάσει ὡς ἐκ πρῴρης ἀγκύρας μελλόντων ἐκτείνειν, εἶπεν ὁ Παῦλος τῷ ἑκατοντάρχῃ καὶ τοῖς στρατιώταις· ἐὰν μὴ οὗτοι μείνωσιν ἐν τῷ πλοίῳ, ὑμεῖς σωθῆναι οὐ δύνασθε. τότε ἀπέκοψαν οἱ στρατιῶται τὰ σχοινία τῆς σκάφης καὶ εἴασαν αὐτὴν ἐκπεσεῖν).

While it was still dark, the sailors sought to abandon the ship, which was prevented due to Paul's intervention. Their attempt to escape is motivated by the fear of drowning and shows a complete disregard for the life of the other passengers. Luke characterizes the sailors' actions as deceitful: they lowered the lifeboat into the sea "under the pretext" of laying out anchors from the bow. While it might indeed make sense to secure the ship's position in the line of the wind, there is no cogent reason to doubt that sailors have resorted to desperate, selfish, and dangerous measures in order to save their skin. They prefer the uncertain prospects of their desperate attempt to escape to trusting the predictions of Paul, which is hardly surprising.

Paul's intervention (v. 31), the third in Luke's account (cf. vv. 10, 21 – 26), warns of the consequences if the sailors are allowed to abandon the ship. He addresses the centurion and the soldiers (στρατιώταις; they are mentioned here for the first time). This warning, related in direct speech, connects the survival of the solders and the other passengers with the ship's crew staying on board. Although Paul may not have been concerned about his own survival because of the message of the

---

54. BDAG, s.v. βολίζω, "to use a weighted line to determine depth, *take soundings, heave the lead.*" Ancient sounding leads were either cone-shaped (one exemplar is 25.5 cm high, 3.5 cm across at the top, 6 cm across at the bottom, weighing 5 kg), pyramidal (one exemplar is 21 cm high and 8 cm at the base, weighing 4.3 kg), or bell-shaped (one exemplar is 10 cm high with a diameter of 7.5 cm at the top and 20 cm at the bottom, weighing 13.4 kg); the sounding leads had a hollow at the bottom that was filled with tallow or grease for bringing up samples of the sea bottom; Casson, *Ships*, 246 n. 85.

55. Hemer, *Acts*, 147; cf. James Smith, *Voyage and Shipwreck*, 133 – 34.

angel (v. 24b-e), he may have considered as condi-tional the divine assurance that all passengers and crew would survive (v. 24f-g).

The centurion accepts Paul's advice, perhaps be-cause he has been forced to acknowledge Paul's fore-sight and competence as a result of the events of the last two weeks (cf. v. 21) — surely out of self-preser-vation and the unwillingness to let the ship's crew get away, leaving the passengers on board to fend for themselves. He orders the soldiers to cut the ropes of the lifeboat, which was suspended over the side of the ship (v. 30), so that the boat fell into the sea and drifted away. While the soldiers thus prevented the crew from leaving, their action made it necessary to beach the ship. However, it is the soldiers who are thus responsible for the loss of the ship. Paul had not suggested that the lifeboat be sacrificed, which could have been used, after the end of the storm, to safely row crew and passengers ashore.

27:33 – 34 Just before dawn Paul urged all of them to take some food, saying, "Today is the fourteenth day that you have been in suspense and you have been continually without food, you have eaten nothing. Therefore I urge you to take some food, for it will help you to survive. Not one of you will lose a single hair from his head" (ἄχρι δὲ οὗ ἡμέρα ἤμελλεν γίνεσθαι, παρεκάλει ὁ Παῦλος ἅπαντας μεταλαβεῖν τροφῆς λέγων· τεσσαρεσκαιδεκάτην σήμερον ἡμέραν προσδοκῶντες ἄσιτοι διατελεῖτε μηθὲν προσλαβόμενοι. διὸ παρακαλῶ ὑμᾶς μεταλαβεῖν τροφῆς· τοῦτο γὰρ πρὸς τῆς ὑμετέρας σωτηρίας ὑπάρχει, οὐδενὸς γὰρ ὑμῶν θρὶξ ἀπὸ τῆς κεφαλῆς ἀπολεῖται). Paul's fourth intervention is connected with the lack of appetite mentioned in v. 21. Paul admon-

ishes "all of them" (crew, passengers, soldiers, and his companions) to take food. Luke carefully marks the sequence of events. They sensed that they were nearing land at midnight (v. 27); after establishing that they were indeed approaching land by sound-ings, they prayed for day to come (v. 29); now just before dawn (v. 33) Paul admonishes everybody to eat something (v. 39), especially since they can now see that the ship is in a bay with a sandy beach. Evidently nobody was able to sleep during that dra-matic night.

The imperfect tense of the verb translated "urged" (παρεκάλει) could be iterative; during this night, Paul repeatedly encouraged the people to eat something. Paul's calm demeanor is sometimes said to suggest to Luke's readers to view Paul as a true philosopher, who proves his mettle in a dan-gerous situation.[56] In view of Paul's sense of being guided by the almighty God, more likely they would have understood Paul's behavior as indicat-ing his complete trust in God.

Paul begins his address with a reference to the fact that crew and passengers have been "in sus-pense" for the fourteenth day. The subject of nour-ishment permeates this scene. Food is mentioned three times in v. 33 — Paul urges all "to take some food," and he reminds the crew and passengers that they "have been continually without food" and that they "have eaten nothing" (see also vv. 34, 35, 36, 38). Paul then "took bread" and "began to eat"; the crew and passengers "ate some food"; eventu-ally all "had eaten enough." Paul's concern that the people on board the ship take nourishment shows to Luke's readers that Paul can influence the fright-ened crew and passengers, who follow his advice (v. 36), and that Paul demonstrates social respon-sibility for his fellow travelers.[57]

---

56. Cf. Witherington, *Acts*, 772, with reference to Diogenes Laertius, *Vit. phil.* 2.71; Lucian, *Peregr.* 43 – 44; Johnson, *Acts*, 455, adds Homer, *Od.* 12.270 – 300; Lucian, *Tox.* 20; Epictetus, *Diatr.* 4.1.92; 4.1.174; Diogenes Laertius, *Vit. phil.* 2.130; 4.50; 6.74; 7.2; 9.68.

57. Cf. Labahn, "Paulusportrait," 88, who points to the fact that in Greco-Roman society the elites were actively concerned about the provision of food for the masses; cf. Isocrates, *Paneg.* 38; Augustus, *Res Gestae* 5.

Paul's advice to eat would have calmed the frayed nerves of the passengers, strengthened the crew for the task of putting the ship ashore, and given renewed hope and the will to live to both passengers and crew. The phrase translated "it will help you to survive" (πρὸς τῆς ὑμετέρας σωτηρίας) refers to the physical rescue of crew and passengers.[58] Paul repeats the promise of v. 22 that crew and passengers will be rescued, asserting that "not one of you" (οὐδενὸς ὑμῶν) will perish. Paul uses the image of the loss of a single hair from the head (θρὶξ ἀπὸ τῆς κεφαλῆς).[59] He conveys God's promise that they will all survive unscathed.

27:35 – 36 After he said this, he took bread and gave thanks to God in front of them all, and he broke it and began to eat. They were all reassured and ate some food (εἴπας δὲ ταῦτα καὶ λαβὼν ἄρτον εὐχαρίστησεν τῷ θεῷ ἐνώπιον πάντων καὶ κλάσας ἤρξατο ἐσθίειν. εὔθυμοι δὲ γενόμενοι πάντες καὶ αὐτοὶ προσελάβοντο τροφῆς). By taking bread, breaking it, and beginning to eat, Paul accentuates his admonition to take nourishment. By eating "in front of them all" (ἐνώπιον πάντων), he gives them an example. Luke describes Paul's action with four verbs (all in the aorist tense): he "took" (λαβών) bread, he "gave thanks" (εὐχαρίστησεν) to God, he "broke" (κλάσας) the bread, and he "began to eat" (ἤρξατο ἐσθίειν).

While the language may be reminiscent of the Lord's Supper (the Eucharist), the context leaves little doubt that Luke describes what Jews and Christians do when they eat (cf. 2:42, 46; 20:7, 11): they take the bread, and before breaking it into smaller pieces, they say "grace"; i.e., they thank God for the provision of food and nourishment.[60] The result of Paul's example is narrated succinctly (v. 36): the crew and passengers are "reassured" and take nourishment.

27:37 We were 276 persons on board (ἤμεθα δὲ αἱ πᾶσαι ψυχαὶ ἐν τῷ πλοίῳ διακόσιαι ἑβδομήκοντα ἕξ). The comment in v. 37 that there were 276 persons on board is not improbable.[61] The article before the adjective "all" (πᾶσαι) indicates that in the figure of 276 persons, all are included — crew with captain and skipper, and the passengers, including the soldiers and their prisoners. Josephus relates an experience, about four years after Paul's journey, where the ship he was traveling on from Palestine to Rome ran aground at the mouth of the Adriatic, forcing about 600 people to swim all night (*Life* 15).[62] The figure is given at this point in the context of the meal perhaps because it was necessary to count the people on board in preparation for the distribution of the available bread, or perhaps a roll call was made at this point at first light (vv. 33, 39), in view of "the likelihood of serious injuries or loss of crew overboard in the hazardous conditions of the last thirteen days."[63]

27:38 When they had eaten enough, they lightened the ship by throwing the wheat into the sea (κορεσθέντες δὲ τροφῆς ἐκούφιζον τὸ πλοῖον

---

58. The term σωτηρία, while used by Luke in the sense of spiritual deliverance and salvation (Luke 19:9; Acts 4:12; 13:26, 47; 16:17), here has the "secular" use of rescue and preservation in the context of the shipwreck; cf. W. Foerster, "σῴζω, σωτηρία," *TDNT*, 7:989; K. H. Schelkle, *EDNT*, 3:328.

59. Cf. 1 Sam 14:45; 2 Sam 14:11; 1 Kgs 1:52; Matt 10:30/ Luke 12:7; Luke 21:18.

60. Cf. Witherington, *Acts*, 772 – 73, for a critique of the sacramental interpretation.

61. Some manuscripts give smaller numbers: A has 275, manuscript 69 and Ephraem read 270, some Coptic manu-

scripts read 176, manuscript 522 reads 76, and B sa read "about 76." Cf. Metzger, *Textual Commentary*, 442. There is no reason to interpret the figure 276 as symbolical (276 is a triangular number, i.e., the sum of the digits from 1 to 23, written in triangular groups of dots).

62. Casson, *Ships*, 172 with n. 26, takes both figures at face value, suggesting that since the figure given in Acts 27:37 belongs to off-season sailing, the grain freighter carrying Paul "very likely could have accommodated more" than the 276 persons mentioned.

63. Dunn, *Acts*, 341.

ἐκβαλλόμενοι τὸν σῖτον εἰς τὴν θάλασσαν). After the crew had eaten, they prepared the ship for being put ashore. They lightened the ship (a third time, cf. vv. 18 – 19) by jettisoning the cargo, in the hope of running the ship up as high as possible on the beach in the bay. The decision to jettison the wheat, which was the cargo the ship was taking from Alexandria in Egypt (v. 6) to Italy, would have been made by the ship's captain, who was responsible for the safety of the cargo. This decision shows the precarious conditions at this point: the captain evidently came to the conclusion that if the ship founders on the rocks in the middle of the bay, few if any of the crew and passengers would survive the shipwreck. The fact that the wheat could be thrown into the sea indicates that it was transported in sacks, which could be thrown overboard.

27:39 When daylight came, they did not recognize the land. But they noticed a bay with a beach on which they planned to run the ship ashore if they could (ὅτε δὲ ἡμέρα ἐγένετο, τὴν γῆν οὐκ ἐπεγίνωσκον, κόλπον δέ τινα κατενόουν ἔχοντα αἰγιαλὸν εἰς ὃν ἐβουλεύοντο εἰ δύναιντο ἐξῶσαι τὸ πλοῖον). When daylight came and they were finally able to see their surroundings, they did not recognize the land. As there was no harbor in this region, the crew would not have been able to identify their location (the identification is given in 28:1). They noticed a bay[64] with a beach. They planned to run the ship up (ἐξῶσαι) on the beach.[65] The three imperfect tenses in the "not recognizing," the "noticing," and the "planning" probably indicate that to

Luke, these were "processes that were in progress as the sun rose."[66] The parenthesis "if they could" (εἰ δύναιντο), formulated with the optative, reveals the uncertainty of the crew as to what was likely to happen and suggests that the bay with the beach was not easily accessible.

27:40 They cast off the anchors and left them in the sea. At the same time they untied the pennants of the steering oars. Then they hoisted the foresail to the wind and headed for the beach (καὶ τὰς ἀγκύρας περιελόντες εἴων εἰς τὴν θάλασσαν, ἅμα ἀνέντες τὰς ζευκτηρίας τῶν πηδαλίων καὶ ἐπάραντες τὸν ἀρτέμωνα τῇ πνεούσῃ κατεῖχον εἰς τὸν αἰγιαλόν). The crew then attempts to carry out their plan with three actions performed simultaneously and aimed at putting the ship quickly under control.

(1) Some of the crew cast off the anchors; i.e., they cut the ropes that held the four anchors that had been lowered from the stern (v. 29), letting the anchors drop into the sea, as they were no longer needed. (2) Other members of the crew untie the pennants of the two side-rudders or steering oars,[67] lowering the rudders into the water. (3) They hoist the foresail to the wind. After lightening the ship and discarding the anchors, the crew prepares the ship for forward movement, attempting to nose it into the bay, using the foresail and the rudders for steering. Thus they head (κατεῖχον)[68] for the beach.

27:41 But the ship struck a point and ran aground. The bow became jammed and remained immovable, while the stern was breaking

---

64. The term κόλπος denotes "a part of the sea that indents a shoreline, *bay*" (BDAG, s.v. κόλπος 3); it occurs in this sense only here in the New Testament, but is frequent in Strabo's *Geography* (over 300 references).

65. Cf. BDAG, s.v. ἐξωθέω 2, "to run or drive ashore, *beach, run ashore;*" the verb is used here as a technical nautical term.

66. Culy and Parsons, *Acts*, 528.

67. The term ζευκτηρία denotes "something used to link things (usually two) together," i.e., "bands" or "ropes" that tied

the rudder; the technical nautical term in English is "pendant" or "pennant" (BDAG). The term πηδάλιον denotes the steering paddle, rudder, or steering oars (Lat. *gubernaculum*). Casson, *Ships*, 228 n. 17, comments on the action described in the expression ἀνέντες τὰς ζευκτηρίας τῶν πηδαλίων, that the pennants "must have been brought up tight when the vessel anchored" (ibid., 228 n. 17).

68. Cf. BDAG, s.v. κατέχω 7, "hold course," a technical nautical term.

up through the force of the waves (περιπεσόντες δὲ εἰς τόπον διθάλασσον ἐπέκειλαν τὴν ναῦν καὶ ἡ μὲν πρῷρα ἐρείσασα ἔμεινεν ἀσάλευτος, ἡ δὲ πρύμνα ἐλύετο ὑπὸ τῆς βίας τῶν κυμάτων). The crew's maneuvers are not successful. Drifting slowing across the bay in a westerly direction, the ship, instead of running up on the beach, suddenly runs aground on rocks.[69] The meaning of the expression translated as "point" (τόπος διθάλασσος) is disputed.[70] It means literally "a place with the sea on both sides" and denotes "a point (of land jutting out with water on both sides)."[71]

The bow of the ship becomes jammed, so much so that it remains immovable, while the stern breaks up (ἐλύετο)[72] as a result of the force of the waves. The imperfect tense of this verb is durative: the continued violent impact of the waves destroys the stern of the ship bit by bit. This has been explained by the conditions of the seabed on the east coast of Malta:

> The rocks of Malta disintegrate into very fine particles of sand and clay, which form mud in still water, but a tenacious clay where acted upon by surface water movements. So mud is found from below about three fathoms, which is about what a large ship would draw. Paul's ship was likely to have stuck in mud which quickly graduated into a shelving clay, where the forepart was held fast.[73]

27:42 The soldiers' plan was to kill the prisoners to prevent them from swimming away and **escaping** (τῶν δὲ στρατιωτῶν βουλὴ ἐγένετο ἵνα τοὺς δεσμώτας ἀποκτείνωσιν, μή τις ἐκκολυμβήσας διαφύγῃ). The soldiers plan to kill the prisoners, Paul included (cf. v. 43). They are afraid that when the crew and passengers of the ship swim ashore, the prisoners might escape by "swimming away" (ἐκκολυμβήσας; modal participle). Since the soldiers were responsible for the prisoners convicted of, and in the case of Paul charged with, capital offenses, their intention made sense from their perspective. According to Roman law, guards incurred the penalty that awaited any prisoner who escapes.[74]

27:43 – 44 But the centurion wanted to save Paul and kept them from carrying out their plan. He ordered those who could swim to jump overboard first and get to land. The rest were to get there on planks or on other pieces of the ship. And so it happened that everyone was brought safely to land (ὁ δὲ ἑκατοντάρχης βουλόμενος διασῶσαι τὸν Παῦλον ἐκώλυσεν αὐτοὺς τοῦ βουλήματος, ἐκέλευσέν τε τοὺς δυναμένους κολυμβᾶν ἀπορίψαντας πρώτους ἐπὶ τὴν γῆν ἐξιέναι καὶ τοὺς λοιποὺς οὓς μὲν ἐπὶ σανίσιν, οὓς δὲ ἐπί τινων τῶν ἀπὸ τοῦ πλοίου. καὶ οὕτως ἐγένετο πάντας διασωθῆναι ἐπὶ τὴν γῆν). Julius the centurion, who had been favorably disposed to Paul (v. 3), is determined to save Paul. After having rejected Paul's advice about leaving Kaloi Limenes (v. 11), he has experienced the consequences of the violent and persistent storm that was destroying

---

69. The verb ἐπικέλλω, "run aground," is a technical nautical term.

70. NJB, NLT, RSV, Barrett: "shoal"; ESV, NRSV: "reef"; NIV, TNIV, Barrett, Witherington: "sandbar"; GNB: "sandbank"; NASB: "reef where two seas meet"; NET: "a patch of crosscurrents." The interpretation in terms of a sandbar has been popular among commentators.

71. BDAG, s.v. διθάλασσος; LSJ II defines as "*between two seas, where two seas meet,* as is often the case off a headland." Cf. Richard J. Bauckham, "The Estate of Publius on Malta (Acts 28:7)," in *History and Exegesis* (FS E. E. Ellis; ed. S. W.

Son; New York: T&T Clark, 2006), 73 – 87, 78: "narrow strip of land with sea on both sides." The term "point" needs to be distinguished from "promontory" (ἀκρωτήριον), which refers to a high headland.

72. Cf. BDAG, s.v. λύω 3, "to reduce something by violence into its components, *destroy*."

73. Hemer, *Acts*, 151; cf. James Smith, *Voyage and Shipwreck*, 143 – 44.

74. Note the intention of the jailer in Philippi to kill himself when he feared that the prisoners had escaped (16:27).

the ship, and thus he probably remembers Paul's warning about people losing their lives if crew and passengers do not stay together (v. 31). As he had command authority over the soldiers, he is able to prevent the killing of the prisoners.

The centurion's orders about getting to shore would have been aimed at the soldiers and the prisoners, although common sense dictated that all the passengers followed these procedures as well. In order not to be hit by planks or other "pieces of the ship" thrown into the sea as flotation devices, those able to swim would jump first into the water, before those who could not swim. The sequence of the actions that brought the crew and passengers to safety was as follows: crew, passengers, and prisoners jumped overboard; they swam or floated on debris; they got to the mainland.

Luke ends his account of the shipwreck with the comment that the evacuation of the stranded ship is a total success: everyone (πάντας) comes safely to land. While Luke does not explicitly link the rescue of crew and passengers with God's sovereignty in v. 44, he has given several signals in the text (vv. 22 – 26, 31, 34) that emphasized to the readers that it was as a result of God's providence that despite the violent storm, despite the planned flight of the crew, and despite of the soldiers' intention to kill the prisoners, all people were saved.

28:1 After we had reached safety, we found out that the island was called Malta (καὶ διασωθέντες τότε ἐπέγνωμεν ὅτι Μελίτη ἡ νῆσος καλεῖται). The third incident of Luke's account of Paul's sea voyage from Caesarea to Italy relates the winter layover in Malta (28:1 – 6), a section in which Luke underlines features that we found in earlier descriptions

of Paul: he performs miracles, and he survives dangerous situations on his way to Rome. Luke begins by repeating the fact that crew and passengers of the stranded ship have reached safety (cf. 27:43, 44). Then he identifies the island on which the ship ran aground as Μελίτη, which is generally identified with Malta (Melite Africana).[75] The identity of the island was probably established once the passengers met the inhabitants of the island (v. 2).

28:2 The natives showed us unusual kindness. They built a fire and welcomed all of us because it was raining and cold (οἵ τε βάρβαροι παρεῖχον οὐ τὴν τυχοῦσαν φιλανθρωπίαν ἡμῖν, ἅψαντες γὰρ πυρὰν προσελάβοντο πάντας ἡμᾶς διὰ τὸν ὑετὸν τὸν ἐφεστῶτα καὶ διὰ τὸ ψῦχος). Luke connects the rescue of the ship's crew and passengers with the assistance provided by the inhabitants of the island. He calls them "natives" (βάρβαροι), a term often used by Greeks to describe people who do not speak the Greek language, who do not adhere to Greek cultural customs, or who are culturally inferior. Since the people of Malta were of Phoenician and Punic origin[76] and spoke a form of Punic, a development of Phoenician, the designation is apt. By the first century many of the inhabitants would have also spoken Greek and/or Latin, although perhaps not the villagers whom the castaways meet.

The term translated "kindness" (φιλανθρωπία) was understood in Stoic philosophy as "a kindly disposition in human interaction" and was regarded in Hellenistic culture as a "noble virtue" that characterizes the just person. It is a goodness of spirit that is expressed "especially as solicitude, in a willingness to serve, and in effective liberalities;

75. Others suggested identifications of Μελίτη with Mljet, called Μελίτη in antiquity (Melite Illyrica), located in the Adriatic Sea off the Dalmatian coast opposite Epidaurum and Stagnum and near Kefallinia (Cephallania), located off the west coast of Achaia in the Ionian Sea. For a critique see Brian M. Rapske, "Acts, Travel and Shipwreck," in *The Book of Acts in its*

Graeco-Roman Setting (ed. D. W. J. Gill and C. Gempf; Grand Rapids: Eerdmans, 1994), 1 – 47, 37 – 43.

76. Strabo, *Geogr.* 17.3.15 – 16. Punic inscriptions have been discovered on Malta. The early coins of Malta, minted soon after Roman occupation in 218 BC, bear a Punic legend.

it is a form of generosity" that included hospitality. The reference to the "unusual" kindness of the natives confirms that the term "natives" (βάρβαροι) has a linguistic rather than a cultural meaning. The inhabitants behaved as Greeks would behave, showing courtesy and generosity, while speaking a different language.

Their kindness is clear in that they "built" a fire, evidently in the open, probably close to the beach, so that the 276 crew and passengers could warm themselves, having arrived with clothes that were soaking wet from the rain and the swim to shore. The verbal phrase translated "it was raining" indicates rain had begun to fall, making the castaways "cold" and miserable and grateful for the fire.

28:3 Paul had collected a pile of brushwood and was putting it on the fire, when a snake, driven out by the heat, fastened itself on his hand (συστρέψαντος δὲ τοῦ Παύλου φρυγάνων τι πλῆθος καὶ ἐπιθέντος ἐπὶ τὴν πυράν, ἔχιδνα ἀπὸ τῆς θέρμης ἐξελθοῦσα καθῆψεν τῆς χειρὸς αὐτοῦ). The incident of Paul's encounter with a snake and the reaction of the islanders (vv. 3 – 6) underline Paul's innocence, who is protected by God's power. Paul is helping the islanders (v. 2) by gathering firewood and keeping the fire going. As he puts a bundle of brushwood on the fire, a snake is driven out of the pile of wood by the heat of the fire and takes hold of Paul's hand. The verb translated "fastened itself" (καθῆψεν) is the only finite verbal form in the verse and thus carries the emphasis: Paul is suddenly bitten by a snake that does not let go of his hand.

The term translated "snake" (ἔχιδνα) ordinarily suggests a poisonous snake, perhaps the *vipera* *ammodytes* or sandviper (BDAG).[77] Since there are no poisonous snakes on Malta today, some propose an alternate site for the shipwreck.[78] More plausible interpretations surmise that the nonpoisonous snake, possibly the *Coronella austriaca* (which looks like a viper and attaches itself to its victim as described by Luke) was regarded by the natives as poisonous, which accords with widespread popular belief in antiquity.[79] Alternately, poisonous snakes may have existed on Malta in antiquity; Malta "is a small, densely populated island territory whose original forest cover has gone."[80]

28:4 When the natives saw the creature hanging from his hand, they said to each other, "This man must be a murderer. Because even though he has escaped from the sea, Justice has not allowed him to live" (ὡς δὲ εἶδον οἱ βάρβαροι κρεμάμενον τὸ θηρίον ἐκ τῆς χειρὸς αὐτοῦ, πρὸς ἀλλήλους ἔλεγον· πάντως φονεύς ἐστιν ὁ ἄνθρωπος οὗτος ὃν διασωθέντα ἐκ τῆς θαλάσσης ἡ δίκη ζῆν οὐκ εἴασεν). Luke relates the natives' reaction to the snake, here described as a "creature" or "wild animal (θηρίον), attaching itself to Paul's hand; they infer that he is guilty of a serious crime — perhaps murder. Even though Paul has survived the storm and the shipwreck and thus escaped (διασωθέντα) drowning in the sea, he is punished by the snake. Justice does not allow Paul to live.

The term "Justice" (ἡ δίκη) probably refers not to justice as a general ethical or legal norm but to personified Justice (Δίκη), i.e., the goddess of justice, the favorite daughter of Zeus and Themis,[81] who "immediately reports to Zeus all the unrighteous deeds of mankind so that people will have to

77. The generic term for snakes in Greek is ὄφις.

78. Cf. Heinz Warnecke, *Die tatsächliche Romfahrt des Apostels Paulus* (SBS 127; Stuttgart: Katholisches Bibelwerk, 1987), 108 – 10.

79. Cf. Pliny, *Nat.* 8.85 – 86, who seems to share the belief that all snakes are venomous, seeking to avenge the killer of their spouses.

80. Hemer, *Acts*, 153. Cf. Bruce, *Book of Acts*, 498, who points to Ireland as an island that once had poisonous snakes but no longer does.

81. Themis is the personification of the divine order, of everything that is right and proper in nature and society.

pay for their crimes,"[82] and who, as companion of the gods of the underworld (the Erinyes, the "enforcers" of Dike), was "a mighty and relentless deity who wrathfully wielded the weapons of revenge." Greek mythology and art associated snakes, divine justice for murderers, and the Erinyes; and Dike is sometimes associated with the sea.[83]

28:5 – 6 But Paul shook the snake off into the fire and suffered no ill effects. The people expected him to swell up or suddenly drop to the ground dead. After they had waited a long time and saw nothing unusual happen to him, they changed their minds and said that he was a god (ὁ μὲν οὖν ἀποτινάξας τὸ θηρίον εἰς τὸ πῦρ ἔπαθεν οὐδὲν κακόν, οἱ δὲ προσεδόκων αὐτὸν μέλλειν πίμπρασθαι ἢ καταπίπτειν ἄφνω νεκρόν. ἐπὶ πολὺ δὲ αὐτῶν προσδοκώντων καὶ θεωρούντων μηδὲν ἄτοπον εἰς αὐτὸν γινόμενον μεταβαλόμενοι ἔλεγον αὐτὸν εἶναι θεόν). Between the natives' inference that Paul must be a murderer (v. 4) and their expectation that he will suddenly drop dead (v. 6), Luke relates Paul's reaction to their superstitious beliefs (v. 5). He shakes off the reptile from his hand and throws it into the fire. While the snake perishes in the fire, Paul does not suffer any harm. Whether this was a miracle depends on whether the snake was poisonous and on whether the bite of the snake always killed, both of which are uncertain. The expectation of the locals may have been due merely to superstitious beliefs rather than to knowledge of the effects of the bite of this particular snake.

The locals "expected" (προσεδόκων, imperfect tense) Paul to die from the snakebite, either by swelling up or by suddenly dropping to the ground. Luke emphasizes their expectation regarding Paul's fate with three present tense participles: they "waited" (προσδοκώντων) for a long time for

Paul to show symptoms indicative of Dike's vengeance but "saw" (θεωρούντων) nothing unusual "happening" (γινόμενον) to him. Thereupon they concluded that Paul is a god (εἶναι θεόν). In the context of pagan mythology, the logic is understandable: a person who survives both a shipwreck and a snakebite must be someone in whom divine power is revealed.

Luke's readers would be reminded of Jesus' promise in Luke 10:19: "I have given you authority to trample on snakes and scorpions and to overcome all the power of the enemy; nothing will harm you" (cf. Mark 16:17 – 18, a later addition to Mark's gospel). Paul is not concerned about the snakebite, because the Lord has assured him he will reach Rome (27:24). Unlike in Lystra, where Luke reports Paul as correcting the mistaken conclusion of the Lycaonians concerning the divine identity of Paul and Barnabas (14:8 – 18), he does not relate Paul's reaction to the Maltesians' assumption that Paul represents a divine epiphany.

28:7 There was an estate nearby that belonged to the chief official of the island, named Publius. He welcomed us and kindly showed us hospitality for three days (ἐν δὲ τοῖς περὶ τὸν τόπον ἐκεῖνον ὑπῆρχεν χωρία τῷ πρώτῳ τῆς νήσου ὀνόματι Ποπλίῳ, ὃς ἀναδεξάμενος ἡμᾶς τρεῖς ἡμέρας φιλοφρόνως ἐξένισεν). The fourth incident of this episode on Paul's voyage to Italy relates the healing of the father of Publius (vv. 7 – 10). The "chief official" of the island, whose name is given as Publius, welcomed the survivors of the shipwreck. The reference to "Publius," a Roman *praenomen*, is problematic only if we assume that he was a Roman citizen by birth, who would then be referred to by his *cognomen* (e.g., Gallio, cf. 18:12) or his *nomen* + *cognomen* (e.g., Porcius Festus, 24:27). If he was

---

82. P. W. van der Horst, "Dike," *DDD*, 251; cf. Hesiod, *Theog.* 901 – 3, *Op.* 213 – 285; Sophocles, *Aj.* 1390.

83. Cf. Kauppi, *Gods*, 108 – 12.

a non-Roman using the name Publius as his only Latin name and was later granted Roman citizenship (which can be assumed for the "chief official" of Malta), his existing Latin name would have become his *cognomen* while adding a *praenomen* and a *nomen*, which means that he would still have been known as Publius.[84]

Interpreted in the context of inscriptions that refer to a "first man" (πρώτῳ) in a region or province, Publius evidently was the highest official among the municipal offices of Malta. He would have spent most of his time in Melita, the capital of the island (mod. Mdina, Rabat) about 6 miles (10 km.) south of St. Paul's Bay, visiting his country estates from time to time and keeping tabs on his commercial interests. The site of the shipwreck would have been visible from the town, prompting Publius to investigate what had happened. Since one of his estates was nearby, he not only "welcomed" the survivors of the shipwreck but also "showed … hospitality."

The recipients of Publius's hospitality — "us" (ἡμᾶς) — included perhaps not all 276 survivors of the shipwreck but more specifically the centurion Julius (27:1) and his prisoners as well as Paul's travel companions. Following three days of (voluntary) hospitality by Publius in the villa of one of his estates, the Roman centurion probably requisitioned accommodation and provisions among the local population for himself and those traveling under this command.[85]

28:8 His father was sick in bed, suffering from fever and dysentery. Paul visited him and, after he prayed for him, he laid his hands on him and healed him (ἐγένετο δὲ τὸν πατέρα τοῦ Ποπλίου πυρετοῖς καὶ δυσεντερίῳ συνεχόμενον κατακεῖσθαι, πρὸς ὃν ὁ Παῦλος εἰσελθὼν καὶ προσευξάμενος ἐπιθεὶς τὰς χεῖρας αὐτῷ ἰάσατο αὐτόν). Luke does not provide chronological details regarding the time when the father of Publius was healed, but he leaves the impression that this happened early in the stay on Malta, perhaps right at the beginning. The condition of this man is described with two verbs in the present tense and two nouns: he was "sick in bed" because he was "suffering," having been afflicted by "fever and dysentery."

The ancient concept of fever (πυρετοί) was imprecise, as there was no accepted nomenclature or taxonomy. In modern terms, semitertian or epidemic fevers could be connected with malaria, typhoid, or typhus,[86] unless the fever was a symptom of the influenza.[87] Dysentery (δυσεντέριον) was accompanied by pain and colic, ulcerated intestines, and bloody stools.[88] As regards the combination of fever and dysentery, Hippocrates asserts, "dysenteries, if accompanied by fever, by variegated stools, or by inflammation of the liver, hypochondrium or belly, or if they are painful, or spoil the appetite or provoke thirst, are all troublesome, and whichever patient has most of these evils dies the soonest, whereas the one who has least of such things has the greatest chances of recovery."[89]

---

84. Cf. Bauckham, "Estate of Publius," 80. For the following comments see ibid., 81 – 86.

85. Cf. Rapske, *Paul in Roman Custody*, 273.

86. Paul F. Burke, "Malaria in the Greco-Roman World: A Historical and Epidemiological Survey," *ANRW* II.37.3 (1996): 2252 – 81, 2258.

87. Hemer, *Acts*, 153 – 54, refers to the so-called "Malta fever," whose causes were discovered in 1887, namely, an endemic microorganism called *Micrococcus melitensis*, which infected the milk of goats on Malta. This type of fever, if it existed in the first century, was certainly not the only kind of fever by which Maltese people could be afflicted. Craig S. Keener, "Fever and Dysentery in Acts 28:8 and Ancient Medicine," *BBR* 19 (2009): 393 – 402, 394 – 95, points out that Luke's audience would not have thought of a local Maltese disease but would have understood Luke's description in more general terms.

88. Keener, "Fever and Dysentery," 398, with reference to Hippocrates, *Aff.* 23.

89. Hippocrates, *Prorrh.* 2.22.

The father of Publius must have been of advanced age (the son was the "chief official" of Malta), which is relevant since several texts in the *Corpus Hippocraticum* state that young and elderly people are particularly afflicted by dysentery. Luke seems to want to make this connection between age, fever, and dysentery. The wind, cold, and rain mentioned in vv. 1 – 2 accord with the onset of dysentery:

> As for the seasons, if the winter be dry and northerly and the spring wet and southerly, of necessity occur in the summer acute fevers, eye diseases and dysentery, especially among women and those with moist constitutions ... in autumn occur most summer diseases, with quartans, irregular fevers, enlarged spleen, dropsy, consumption, strungury, lientery, dysentery, sciatica.[90]

Apart from medical treatment, the sick invoked the personified goddess Febris in an effort to ward off, or heal, fever attacks, or used charms and incantations against fever and fever demons.

Luke describes four actions of Paul. He "visited" the room in which the sick man lay in bed. He "prayed" for him, asking God to heal him. He "laid his hands" on him (ἐπιθεὶς τὰς χεῖρας),[91] touching his sick body and conveying God's blessing. He "healed" him so that the fever and dysentery left. The reference to Paul's praying suggests that Luke does not depict Paul as a "divine man" with the power to heal; rather, it is the power of God, to whom Paul prays, that heals Publius's father.

28:9 After this had happened, the rest of the people on the island who had illnesses came and were cured (τούτου δὲ γενομένου καὶ οἱ λοιποὶ οἱ ἐν τῇ νήσῳ ἔχοντες ἀσθενείας προσήρχοντο καὶ ἐθεραπεύοντο). The healing of Publius's father seems to have been the signal for other inhabitants of Malta who were sick to come to Paul for healing. The imperfect tense of the two verbs suggests that over the course of three months (v. 11), multiple healings occurred.

While the summary report of numerous healings underlines the effective power of God that became evident during Paul's stay on Malta, Luke does not link the miraculous healings with the proclamation of the gospel, the conversion of people, and the establishment of a church (as in 5:12 – 16; 19:11 – 12).[92] Since Paul asserts that God's commission to do missionary work among Gentiles (ἐν τοῖς ἔθνεσιν) sends him both to "Greeks" and to "non-Greeks" (Ἕλλησίν τε καὶ βαρβάροις; Rom 1:13 – 14), the reference to "natives" in vv. 2, 4 — the only place where the term βάρβαροι occurs in Acts — would have provided a logical opportunity to relate a missionary ministry of Paul among the Maltese population. While Luke's readers would certainly assume that Paul used every opening to preach the gospel, Luke's focus since 27:1 is on Paul's journey to Rome, not on opportunities for the proclamation of the gospel.

28:10 They honored us in many ways. When we were ready to sail, they supplied us with all the provisions we needed (οἳ καὶ πολλαῖς τιμαῖς ἐτίμησαν ἡμᾶς καὶ ἀναγομένοις ἐπέθεντο τὰ πρὸς τὰς χρείας). The many "honors" (τιμαί) with which the Maltese honored (ἐτίμησαν) "us" (Paul and his companions, including Luke) confirm the reality of the miracles taking place. Luke does not specify the nature of the honors, but the second part of the verse suggests that they consisted of "provi-

---

90. *Aphorismata* 3.11, 22; cf. *De aere aquis, locis* 3, 10.

91. This is the only passage in Acts where the laying on of hands is linked with prayer and healing. For the laying on of hands and healing, cf. Mark 5:23; 6:5; 8:23, 25; Acts 9:12, 17; cf. also James 5:13 – 14.

92. Johnson, *Acts*, 463, points to Luke 4:38 – 44; 6:17 – 20; 7:20 – 23; 9:1 – 11; Acts 3:12 – 16 for the connection between healing and the proclamation of the kingdom of God.

sions," probably beyond what would normally be expected, which the natives gave to them when they set sail at the end of winter. The Maltesians demonstrate their gratefulness by providing supplies for the journey.

28:11 After three months we set sail in a ship that had wintered in the island, an Alexandrian ship with the Dioscuri as its figurehead (μετὰ δὲ τρεῖς μῆνας ἀνήχθημεν ἐν πλοίῳ παρακεχειμακότι ἐν τῇ νήσῳ, Ἀλεξανδρίνῳ, παρασήμῳ Διοσκούροις). The fifth and final incident of Luke's account of Paul's journey to Rome relates the voyage from Malta to Rome (vv. 11 – 15). Luke first notes the length of the stay on Malta; after the ship had run aground, they stayed there for three months. In 27:9 Luke noted that Paul had warned the crew not to set sail from Kaloi Limenes some time after October 5; according to 27:27, the ship neared Malta fourteen days after the departure from Kaloi Limenes, i.e., in late October. The departure seems to have taken place in late January (or early February, if the early days of hospitality are not included in the three months). This is much earlier than March 10, which marked the reopening of navigation on the Mediterranean (see on 27:9), but Pliny asserts that spring opens the seas and that at the beginning of spring (on February 8) the west winds soften the winter sky.[93] Since the Alexandrian ship that had wintered in Malta was in all probability a grain ship, its skipper would have been in a hurry to leave early for Italy, hoping for "a rapid unloading and clearance at Ostia to catch up with the spring sailing schedule back to Alexandria."[94]

Luke adds the curious detail that the ship's figurehead was a representation of the Dioscuri carved on the bow, from which the ship took its name (the Dioscuri). The Dioscuri, the "sons of Zeus" (Διὸς κοῦροι), the twins of Leda, were known under different names in Greek mythology.[95] They were called upon as helpers in distress, particularly by seamen who regarded their epiphany as a stellar constellation (the Gemini Castor and Pollux) as a sign of help. Their cult was widespread, both in Greece and in Italy. Seen in the context of Paul's conviction that "gods made with hands are not gods" (19:26), the Dioscuri are mere wooden figures attached to the bow of the ship, not living beings capable of action, in contrast to the true and living God (cf. 14:15); they are "useless mythological brothers"[96] who "offered their protection to a ship that safely overwintered" on Malta while Paul was saved by the living God.[97]

28:12 – 13 We put in at Syracuse and stayed there for three days. Then we weighed anchor and arrived in Rhegium. After one day a south wind sprang up, and on the second day we came to Puteoli (καὶ καταχθέντες εἰς Συρακούσας ἐπεμείναμεν ἡμέρας τρεῖς, ὅθεν περιελόντες κατηντήσαμεν εἰς Ῥήγιον. καὶ μετὰ μίαν ἡμέραν ἐπιγενομένου νότου δευτεραῖοι ἤλθομεν εἰς Ποτιόλους). The first leg of the final voyage takes the Alexandrian ship on which Paul travels from Malta to Syracuse, a city on the east coast of Sicily, founded by the Corinthians in 733 BC, under Roman control since 211 BC; this was the center of the provincial government, retaining the beauty of earlier periods of prosperity in the fourth and third centuries BC, with one of the largest natural harbors in the Mediterranean.

93. Pliny, *Nat.* 2.47.122; cf. Hemer, *Acts*, 154.

94. Colin J. Hemer, "First Person Narrative in Acts 27 – 28," *TynBul* 36 (1985): 79 – 109, 94.

95. In Thebes: Amphion and Zethus; in Sparta: the Tindaridai. The names "Castor and Polydeuces" as well as their characters are thought to be of Indo-Germanic origin. The divine twins were eventually identified with the constellation of Gemini (Castor and Pollux). Cf. T. Scheer and A. Ley, "Dioscuri," *BNP*, 4:518 – 21.

96. F. Scott Spencer, *Acts* (Readings; Sheffield: Sheffield Academic Press, 1997), 263.

97. Kauppi, *Gods*, 116.

The expression translated "we put in" (καταχθέντες εἰς; see on 27:3) is used here as a nautical term for a ship that docks. The voyage from Malta to Syracuse was about 80 nautical miles (150 km.), which could be completed in a good day of sailing. The delay of three days in Syracuse is best explained by bad weather, "perhaps a north or northwest wind which would bar the passage of the Straits of Messina,"[98] only 7 miles (11 km.) wide near Rhegium.

The voyage from Syracuse to Rhegium at the southern entrance of the Straits of Messina, a distance of about 65 nautical miles (120 km.), could be completed in one day of sailing in favorable winds. The one-day delay was caused by adverse winds; when a south wind (νότος; cf. 27:13) began to blow, the ship was able to continue its journey. The voyage through the Straits of Messina and along the west coast of southern Italy to Puteoli, about 175 nautical miles (325 km.), was completed within two days.[99] It appears that in the late first century passengers disembarked at Puteoli and traveled overland to Rome, while the cargo of grain was taken to Portus, the new harbor at Ostia built by Claudius at the mouth of the Tiber River.

28:14 There we found some believers who invited us to stay with them for seven days. And so we came to Rome (οὗ εὑρόντες ἀδελφοὺς παρεκλήθημεν παρ᾿ αὐτοῖς ἐπιμεῖναι ἡμέρας ἑπτά· καὶ οὕτως εἰς τὴν Ῥώμην ἤλθαμεν). Luke reports that there was a Christian community in Puteoli. The term translated "believers" (ἀδελφοί; see on 1:16; 5:11) attested followers of Jesus in the city, which is not surprising given the cosmopolitan character of Puteoli and the evidence for resident aliens from Syria[100] and for a Jewish community. These believers invited Paul and his travel companions, Aristarchus (27:2) and Luke, to stay with them for seven days. The centurion, Julius, had treated Paul with courtesy and respect throughout the journey — allowing the believers in Sidon to care for Paul (27:3) and thwarting the soldiers' plan to kill all prisoners before the ship ran aground on Malta (27:43); he evidently allowed Paul to stay with his fellow believers in the city, no doubt making suitable arrangements to guard Paul.[101]

An alternative explanation assumes that since the centurion's responsibility for requisitioning travel and accommodation for his party amounted to a tension-filled and unhappy task, the sincere offer of hospitality from a Christian community, perhaps extended by a wealthy Christian patron, may have been attractive. It is not impossible that Julius, his soldiers, and all of his prisoners were accommodated by the Christian community in Puteoli. The seven-day duration of the stay there may be due to Julius's and his soldiers' need to replenish their equipment, damaged or lost in the shipwreck, or to the need to prepare for the overland journey ahead where billeting facilities would become increasingly scarce as the party drew closer to Rome, since Julius and his company of soldiers and prisoners were "non-priority" travelers.[102]

The second statement in v. 14 does not mark the party's arrival in Rome, which does not take place until v. 16. The adverb translated "so" (οὕτως) is anticipatory: "Here is the way we arrived in Rome."[103] Puteoli was about 150 miles (240 km.) southeast of Rome, a journey of about ten days.

---

98. Hemer, *Acts*, 154.

99. Cf. Casson, *Ships*, 284, assuming 1½ days with a speed of 5 knots.

100. Cf. N. H. Taylor, "Puteoli," *NIDB*, 4:692: "The origins of this church are unrecorded, but its existence in a major trading port at an early date is unremarkable."

101. Hemer, *Acts*, 156: "His guards would still have been answerable with their lives for his safety."

102. Rapske, *Paul in Roman Custody*, 275 – 76.

103. Johnson, *Acts*, 464, with reference to 1:11; 13:34, 47; 27:25.

28:15 The believers there had heard that we were coming, and they came as far as the Forum of Appius and the Three Taverns to meet us. When Paul saw them, he thanked God and took courage (κἀκεῖθεν οἱ ἀδελφοὶ ἀκούσαντες τὰ περὶ ἡμῶν ἦλθαν εἰς ἀπάντησιν ἡμῖν ἄχρι Ἀππίου φόρου καὶ Τριῶν ταβερνῶν, οὓς ἰδὼν ὁ Παῦλος εὐχαριστήσας τῷ θεῷ ἔλαβε θάρσος). Paul's arrival in Rome is prefaced by a reference to the Christian believers "there" (κἀκεῖθεν), i.e., in Rome. The fact that Luke does not describe the origins of the church in Rome, the capital of the empire, illustrates again the selective nature of his account of the life and ministry of the church in the first years and decades after Jesus' death and resurrection. Luke's attention is consistently focused on Peter and Paul, with the barest of details given for the work of people like Stephen and Philip and the unnamed believers who took the gospel to Antioch, the capital of the province of Syria. He had no room for reporting the origins of the church in the city of Rome (or in Damascus, Alexandria, Pergamon, Sardis, and other cities).[104]

The information that Paul was approaching the city of Rome was probably conveyed by the believers in Puteoli while Julius and his prisoners were delayed for seven days. When "the believers" (οἱ ἀδελφοί) in Rome heard that Paul's party was coming, they sent a delegation to meet him and his companions. Some Roman Christians traveled to the Forum of Appius, a market town on the Via Appia about 38 miles (62 km.) southeast of Rome. The place "Three Taverns" was a station on the Via Appia, about 30 miles (48 km.) southeast of Rome, a long day's journey from Rome, situated at the crossing of the road from Norba in the Lepinus Hills to Antium on the coast.

Luke describes the Roman Christians welcoming Paul. The fact that two parties of believers traveled a considerable distance to meet Paul's party shows that he was held in high regard in the Christian community in Rome, to whom Paul had written his long letter three years earlier. The encounter with the Roman believers encouraged Paul. He "thanked" (εὐχαριστήσας) God, presumably for his safe arrival in Rome, for the fulfillment of the prophecy that he would reach Rome and be a witness there (19:21; 23:11; 27:24), and perhaps for the assurance that the Roman Christians had understood his letter,[105] one goal of which was the preparation for his plan to proclaim the gospel in Spain.

Paul "took courage," confident that God had kept his promise and would continue to accomplish his will through his witness. He felt assured that the Christian community in Rome, rather than being ashamed of him and his status as a prisoner, showed physical solidarity and welcomed him officially.[106]

Theology in Application

The long section of Paul's journey to Rome emphasizes the power of God that is at work in the world of dangerous natural and human forces, the faithfulness of God who fulfills his promises, and the legitimization of God's witnesses, shown in the

---

104. Cf. Schnabel, *Early Christian Mission,* 2:800 – 815.

105. Hermann W. Beyer, *Die Apostelgeschichte* (NTD; Göttingen: Vandenhoeck & Ruprecht, 1959), 157, followed by Barrett, *Acts,* 1232.

106. Rapske, *Paul in Roman Custody,* 310, 387 – 86.

fact that Paul reaches Rome as intended and in his message as divinely authenticated good news for Jews and Gentiles.

The Power of God in Control of Events

Luke emphasizes the power of God that is at work in the world of dangerous natural and human forces. Through his depiction of the perils of the sea journey with the storm and the shipwreck and the snake attack, Luke may have wanted his readers to recognize the perils of their own situation as Christian believers surrounded by enemies both in Jewish synagogues and in pagan society. While we have no firm details about Luke's intended audience, the situation in the churches who would have read his work would hardly have been different from the situation of the Christians in Jerusalem and in the cities in which Paul had engaged in missionary work. While some people accepted the gospel and were converted to faith in Jesus, and while others were willing to have contact with the Christians, willing to listen to what they believed, others — both Jews and Gentiles — actively opposed their teaching, their meetings, and their presence.

Without resorting to a full-blown symbolic interpretation of Paul's journey to Jerusalem, for which Luke provides no impetus, the detailed description of the dangers of the sea would have reminded Luke's readers that their own existence as Christians may suddenly, although not unexpectedly, be threatened by forces they cannot control. While Paul's survival may have provided some encouragement to trust that God would guide them through difficult times, the fact that Paul had God's specific promise that he would arrive safely in Rome (19:21; 23:11; 27:24) would have suggested to Luke's readers that absent such a specific promise of protection and survival, they may not survive opposition and persecution unscathed. Note the examples of the Jerusalem apostles, who were beaten, and the example of Stephen and James, who were killed. Christians do not always survive storms at sea, or shipwrecks, or snakebites.

But Christians can rest assured that God's control over history, seen here in the survival of Paul, is a reality with which they can reckon in their own lives, knowing that God will surely fulfill his purposes — whether through rescue from life-threatening situations, through the ability to persevere in suffering, or through the provision of courage to face death. Paul knows that no matter what happens in the lives of believers who trust God and his Son Jesus Christ, they can rest assured that "in all things God works for the good of those who love him" (Rom 8:28).

The Faithfulness of God, Who Fulfills His Promises

God had given Paul the specific promise that he would reach Rome (19:21; 23:11; 27:24). Luke's report of Paul's journey from Jerusalem to Caesarea, which provided numerous opportunities for a fatal outcome, shows God fulfilling his promises given to Paul. While God does not always promise rescue and survival in dangerous situations, he always fulfills his promises. Luke's report of Paul's assurance to crew and passengers that they would not lose a single hair from their head (27:34) reminds the readers of the first volume that followers of Jesus must not fear those who kill the body but rather fear God, who has the authority to cast someone into Gehenna (hell), i.e., to fear the Judge rather than opponents of the gospel who have no real authority (Luke 12:5).[107] Christians do not need to worry about how exactly God will care for them. As God knows the needs of sparrows, he knows the needs of his people (Luke 12:7; cf. 21:18). As Paul asserts in 1 Cor 10:13, "No temptation has overtaken you except what is common to mankind. And God is faithful; he will not let you be tempted beyond what you can bear. But when you are tempted, he will also provide a way out so that you can endure it."

The Legitimization of God's Witnesses

Paul reaches Rome, and with him the message of Jesus as Israel's Messiah and Savior. The fact that Paul survives the severe storm, the attempt of the soldiers to kill all the prisoners, the shipwreck, and the snakebite underlines that he is God's legitimate, approved witness and that his message is the divinely authenticated good news for Jews and Gentiles. Paul's behavior during the storm and shipwreck confirms what Luke's readers already know: he is a competent, respected, and honest man, whose advice and help the crew and passengers eventually accepted.

Luke gives specific examples of how Paul lived out his own advice, given to the Galatian Christians a few years earlier, when he wrote: "Therefore, as we have opportunity, let us do good to all people, especially to those who belong to the family of believers" (Gal 6:10).[108] Paul's warning the crew of impending disaster, his encouragement to the passengers to eat and not despair, his advice that kept the crew on board and saved the lives of the passengers, including the prisoners, all confirm that Paul is God's witness who lives what he preaches. Christians show their true character in good times and in bad times, in "plain sailing" and in crisis situations, in peace and in persecution, in life and in death. They always live as God's people, full of faith in Jesus as the one true Savior and confident in the presence of the Holy Spirit, who gives them in all situations "love, joy, peace, forbearance, kindness, goodness, faithfulness, gentleness and self-control" (Gal 5:22 – 23).

---

107. Cf. Darrell L. Bock, *Luke* (BECNT; Grand Rapids: Baker, 1995 – 96), 1136.

108. Fernando, *Acts*, 618 – 22, speaks, under the heading "leadership in 'secular' situations," of Paul's example in terms of being agents of hope, acting with human wisdom, giving clear and appropriate testimony, a servant's lifestyle, and encouragement from fellow Christians.

Acts 28:16 – 31

Literary Context

The last episode of Luke's account of the life, ministry, and missionary expansion of the early church narrates Paul's life and ministry as a prisoner in Rome. This section concludes Luke's report of Paul's last visit to and arrest in Jerusalem (21:18 – 23:35), his trial and imprisonment in Caesarea (24:1 – 26:32), and his voyage to and imprisonment in Rome (27:1 – 28:31). The episode summarizes important themes not only of Acts but of the gospel of Luke as well, including God's faithfulness to his promises, the offer of the gift of repentance, the recalcitrance of the Jewish people, the move toward Gentiles, the restoration of an authentic people of God, the proclamation of the kingdom of God, and the teaching about Jesus as Israel's Messiah and Savior. Paul arrived in Rome in spring of AD 60 and was a prisoner in Rome at least until AD 62.

Main Idea

The gospel of Jesus Christ is the fulfillment of God's promises to Israel, whose offer of salvation is for everyone, Jew and Gentile alike. This gospel is the fundamental content of the teaching of the church and the unchanging task of Jesus' witnesses, whatever the challenges of their personal situation.

Translation

Acts 28:16 – 31

16a	Setting: time	When we entered in Rome,
b	Event	**Paul was allowed to live by himself,**
c	Association	with the soldier
d	Character description	who was guarding him.

17a	Setting: time	Three days later
b	Action	**he called together the leaders of the Jews.**

c	Time	When they had assembled,
d	Action: speech	**Paul said to them,**
e	Address	"Brothers,
f	Concession	although I have done nothing
g	Disadvantage	against our people or
h	Disadvantage	the customs of our fathers,
i	Contra-expectation	I was arrested
j	Action	*and* handed over
k	Agency	from Jerusalem
l	Object	to the Romans.
18a	Action	They examined me
b	Character's thoughts	*and* wanted to release me
c	Cause	because there was no basis for the death sentence
d	Reference	in my case.

19a	Cause	But because the Jews objected,
b	Consequence	I was compelled to appeal to the emperor,
c	Concession	even though I had no charge to bring against my own people.
20a	Explanation	*For* this reason I have asked to see you
b	Action	*and* speak with you.
c	Cause	It is because of the hope of Israel
d	Consequence	that I am bound with this chain."

21a	Response: speech	They replied,
b	Report	"We have not received any letters from Judea concerning you,
c	Source	and none of the brothers …
d	Character description	who have come from there
e	Action	… has reported or said anything ✍ bad about you.

22a	Desire	*But* we would like to hear from you
b	Content	what you think,
c	Cause	because we know about this party,
d	Description	which is opposed
e	Place	everywhere."

23a	Cause	As they had arranged a day to meet with Paul,
b	Action	**they came to the place**
c	Place	where he was staying
d	Measure	in even larger numbers.
e	Time	From morning until evening
f	Action	**he explained the matter to them,**
g	Means/content	witnessing to the kingdom of God,
h	Action	and **he tried to persuade them about Jesus**
i	Means/basis	from the Law of Moses and
j	Means/basis	the Prophets.
24a	Event	**Some were persuaded by what he said,**
b	Contrast	while others did not believe.
25a	Conflict	**They disagreed among themselves,**
b	Action	and **they began to leave**
c	Time: speech	after Paul had made one further statement:
d	Assertion	*"The Holy Spirit was right*
e	Time	*when he spoke to your ancestors*
f	Agency: quotation of OT	*through the prophet Isaiah,*
26a	Command	*'Go to this people*
b	Command	*and say,*
c	Prophecy	*You will indeed listen,*
d	Prophecy: negation	*but never understand,*
e	Prophecy	*and you will indeed look,*
f	Prophecy: negation	*but never see.*
27a	Cause	*For the mind of this people has become dull,*
b	Cause	*and their ears are hard of hearing,*
c	Cause	*and they have closed their eyes,*
d	Consequence	*so that they might not see with their eyes,*
e	Consequence	*hear with their ears,*
f	Consequence	*understand with their mind,*
g	Consequence	*and turn,*
h	Consequence	*and I would heal them.'* (Isa 6:9–10)
28a	Desire	*So I want you to know*
b	Assertion	*that this salvation of God has been sent*
c	Object	*to the Gentiles.*
d	Prediction	*They will listen!"*
30a	Event	**Paul lived**
b	Time	for two whole years there
c	Place	in his own rented place.
d	Action	**He welcomed all who came to him.**
31a	Action	**He proclaimed the kingdom of God**
b	Action	and **taught about the Lord Jesus Christ**
c	Manner	with all boldness and
d	Manner	without hindrance.

Structure and Literary Form

The episode is narrated in terms of four incidents. (1) Luke relates the conditions of Paul's imprisonment (28:16). (2) He describes Paul's first encounter with the Jews of Rome (vv. 17 – 22), which leads to a speech by Paul before the Jewish leaders of Rome (vv. 17 – 20) and a report of the reaction of the Jewish leaders. (3) Luke then reports Paul's second encounter with the Jews of Rome (vv. 23 – 28), during which he explains the gospel and gives his final speech (vv. 25 – 28). (4) Finally, Luke summarizes the ministry of the imprisoned Paul over the next two years (vv. 30 – 31). The question as to why Luke does not report the outcome of Paul's trial has been variously answered (see "In Depth: The Ending of Acts").

IN DEPTH: The Ending of Acts

The ending of Acts seems to be abrupt, particularly if seen in the light of Luke's long and detailed account of Paul's arrest in Jerusalem, his imprisonment and trial in Caesarea, and the journey to Rome (Acts 21 – 27). The following explanations have been given for this abrupt ending to Acts.[1]

(1) *Historical explanations*. Luke reports only what he observed as an eyewitness. He was not present when Paul was released from Roman captivity and traveled to Spain. Luke concludes Acts before Paul's trial in Rome took place. Luke concludes Acts either before Paul concluded his mission in Spain or during the persecution under Nero, omitting a reference to Paul's release from his (first) Roman custody in order to protect Paul. Luke died before he could conclude Acts. Luke ends Acts with only sparse information about Paul in Rome because he had no further information.

(2) *Theological-programmatic explanations*. Luke conveys the fulfillment of the program of Acts 1:8 in the proclamation of the gospel in the capital of the Roman Empire. Luke conveys the final turning away from the Jews and the turn toward the Gentiles. Luke did not want to equip the Christians for martyrdom (which Paul suffered); rather, he wanted to spare the church martyrdom, and thus he ends with good advice for Rome, namely, to allow the Christian message to be preached unhindered. Luke keeps quiet regarding the negative outcome of Paul's trial on account of his pro-Roman apologetics. Luke keeps silent

1. For the following summary cf. Heike Omerzu, "Das Schweigen des Lukas: Überlegungen zum offenen Ende der Apostelgeschichte," in *Das Ende des Paulus: Historische, theologische und literaturgeschichtliche Aspekte* (ed. F. W. Horn; BZNW 106; Berlin: De Gruyter, 2001), 127 – 56, 128 – 44; for shorter surveys see Stephen G. Wilson, *The Gentiles and the Gentile Mission in Luke-Acts* (SNTSMS 23; Cambridge: Cambridge Univ. Press, 1973), 233 – 36; Hemer, *Acts*, 383 – 87. For documentation see the electronic version of this commentary.

regarding the failure of the Jerusalem Jews to appear in Rome, resulting in the dismissal of the case against Paul, because this was disappointing as regards his Christian apologetic. Luke keeps silent about Paul's fate because he did not want to relate the (active or passive) complicity of the Roman church in the death of Paul. Luke keeps silent about Paul's execution (by decapitation) as he emphasizes Paul's innocence in the last chapters of Acts. Luke presents Paul as one like Jesus who is engaged in Jesus' mission, and thus establishes some continuity with the readers' Christian heritage going back to Paul, the Twelve, and Jesus, providing them with a pattern and program for world mission. Luke ends where he does because he wanted to stress the arrival of the word of the gospel to the highest levels of Rome.

(3) *Literary-rhetorical explanations*. Luke intended to write a third volume, which would have continued his account of Paul's ministry, but was prevented from doing so. Luke wrote a third volume, extant in the Pastoral Epistles. Luke wanted to turn the attention of his readers back to Jesus; the silence about Paul's martyrdom returns the reader to Jesus' passion, which means that the "absent ending" of Acts returns the reader to the beginning, i.e., the beginning of the gospel of Luke. Luke ends Acts the way he did in order to connect his readers with the mundane reality of their life and to remind them of the ongoing task of proclamation. Luke ends Acts with silence in order to challenge the readers to reconstruct for themselves the fate of Paul, whose death is anticipated earlier in Acts, who is divinely vindicated as innocent in the last chapters of Acts, and who, in the last scene of Acts, speaks as Israel's judge and as the ideal preacher who provides a model for the church in terms of the program of Acts 1:8.

Several of these explanations are plausible. The possibility that Luke concluded his account before Paul's trial in Rome took place should not be discounted.[2] Acts ends with the description of Paul's proclaiming the kingdom of God and teaching about the Lord Jesus Christ (28:31) — not as the fulfillment of the geographical program of Acts 1:8 (the city of Rome is not "the ends of the earth") but as the fulfillment of the commission that Jesus gave to his disciples to be his witnesses (Luke 5:10; Acts 1:8, 22, 25; 9:15). The final description of Paul's preaching and teaching reminds the readers of the fundamental tasks of proclaiming and explaining the gospel of Jesus Christ.

---

2. It should be noted that 20:25, 38 does not presuppose knowledge of Paul's death, nor does 23:11; 27:24 presuppose knowledge of a trial before the imperial court. Contra, e.g., Omerzu, "Schweigen," 129.

The episode is a *historical narrative*, with references to buildings (vv. 16, 23, 30), people (military guard, v. 16; the Jewish leaders of Rome, v. 17), chronological markers (vv. 17, 23, 30), dialogue (vv. 17 – 22, 23 – 25), explanation of legal matters (vv. 17 – 20), and explanation of the gospel (vv. 23, 30 – 31). *Direct speech* is used for a statement of the Jewish leaders in Rome (vv. 21 – 22), and particularly for Paul (vv. 17 – 20, 25 – 28). The episode ends with a *summary statement* about Paul's activity in Rome (vv. 30 – 31).

The *speech of Paul* in vv. 17d – 20 is Paul's twelfth speech, representing the summary of a judicial speech, explanation of the facts of the case (*narratio*; vv. 17f – 19d), and the summary of the case (*propositio*; v. 20). In the *narratio*, Paul (1) asserts his innocence, that he has done nothing against the Jewish people or their customs; (2) reports that the Roman officials acknowledged his innocence after they examined him; (3) explains how he was forced to appeal to the emperor when his opponents in Jerusalem continued to level charges against him. In the *propositio*, Paul emphasizes that the case against him is connected with "the hope of Israel," i.e., because of the resurrection of the dead (cf. 23:6) — in particular, his proclamation of the resurrection of Jesus, who is Israel's Messiah and Savior.

The *speech of Paul* in vv. 25c – 28, the last words of Paul related in direct speech by Luke, is a response to the unbelief of some of the Roman Jews who have heard his proclamation and explanation of the gospel (vv. 23 – 24). Paul first argues that there is a connection between Israel, which had always been obstinate, and those Jews in Rome who refused to accept Jesus as Savior. He goes on to substantiate this point by a long quotation from Isa 6:9 – 10. Third, he asserts that God has taken the initiative in sending his salvation to the Gentiles, who will listen to the message of Jesus Christ.

Exegetical Outline

→ **I. Paul as a Prisoner in Rome (28:16 – 31)**

    A. The Conditions of Paul's Imprisonment (28:16)

        1. Paul is allowed to stay in a rented apartment (28:16a-b)

        2. Paul is guarded by a soldier (28:16c-d)

    B. Paul's First Encounter with the Jews of Rome (28:17 – 22)

        1. Paul calls for the leaders of the Jewish community in Rome (28:17a-b)

        2. Meeting of the Jewish leaders with Paul (28:17c)

        3. Paul speaks to the Jewish leaders (28:17d – 20)

    a. Address (28:17d-e)

    b. The facts of the case (*narratio*) (28:17f – 19)

       i. Paul's innocence despite his arrest in Jerusalem (28:17f-l)

      ii. Paul's innocence as confirmed by examination of Roman officials (28:18)

     iii. The necessity of appealing to the emperor (28:19)

    c. Central charge: Paul's belief in the resurrection (*propositio*) (28:20)

  4. The reaction of the Roman Jews to Paul's proclamation (28:21 – 22)

    a. Assertion that the Jerusalem authorities have not sent instructions (28:21a-b)

    b. Assertion that Jews from Jerusalem have not accused Paul (28:21c-e)

    c. Willingness to hear from Paul concerning his teaching (28:22a-b)

    d. Willingness to clarify information concerning the Christians (28:22c-e)

C. Paul's Second Encounter with the Jews of Rome (28:23 – 28)

  1. The arrival of large numbers of Jews (28:23a-d)

  2. Paul's proclamation of the gospel (28:23e-j)

    a. Paul's teaching from morning until evening (28:23e-f)

    b. The content of Paul's teaching: The kingdom of God and Jesus (28:23g-h)

    c. The basis of Paul's teaching: The Law and the Prophets (28:23i-j)

  3. The reaction of the Roman Jews (28:24 – 25b)

    a. Conversion of some Jewish leaders (28:24a)

    b. Refusal to believe by Jewish leaders (28:24b)

    c. Disagreement among the Jewish leaders (28:25a)

    d. Conclusion of the meeting (28:25b)

  4. Paul's indictment of the Roman Jews (28:25c – 28)

    a. Israel and the unbelieving Jews in Rome (28:25c-f)

    b. Israel's refusal to accept God's word: Quotation of Isaiah 6:9 – 10 (28:26 – 27)

    c. God's initiative in sending his salvation to the Gentiles (28:28)

D. The Ministry of the Imprisoned Paul over the Next Two Years (28:30 – 31)

  1. Paul's imprisonment in Rome for the next two years (28:30a-c)

  2. Paul's welcome to visitors (28:30d)

  3. Paul's proclamation of the gospel (28:31)

    a. The proclamation of the kingdom of God (28:31a)

    b. The teaching about Jesus (28:31b)

    c. Paul's boldness (28:31c)

    d. Paul's freedom (28:31d)

Explanation of the Text

28:16 When we entered in Rome, Paul was allowed to live by himself, with the soldier who was guarding him (ὅτε δὲ εἰσήλθομεν εἰς Ῥώμην, ἐπετράπη τῷ Παύλῳ μένειν καθ᾽ ἑαυτὸν σὺν τῷ φυλάσσοντι αὐτὸν στρατιώτῃ). Luke begins his report of Paul's stay in Rome with a comment on Paul's arrival and on the conditions of his imprisonment. The main route into Rome from Puteoli, Capua, and the Forum of Appius was the *Via Appia*, which entered the capital at the Porta Capena, the southern gate in the old Servian wall on the slopes of the Caelian Hill. Paul "was allowed" (ἐπετράπη) to live by himself. The passive voice of the verb points to a Roman official who made this decision, after the centurion Julius presented Paul as a prisoner. It is plausible to assume that the lodgings in which "Paul was allowed to live by himself" were near the barracks of the Praetorian Guard (the *castra praetoria*).

The expression translated "by himself" refers not to solitary confinement in the barracks of the Praetorian Guard but to private lodgings.[3] The fact that Paul could receive visitors and that he rented the lodging where he stayed (vv. 23, 30) indicates that Paul was kept in a light form of military custody (*custodia militaris*), which was more lenient than the *custodia publica* in the *carcer* (the pretrial confinement in a municipal prison).[4]

Paul was guarded by a "soldier" (στρατιώτης) rather than a centurion or a larger contingent of soldiers, which suggests that the lighter custody was not due to Paul's social status as a Roman citizen but to the weakness of the case against him, as would have been evident from the *littera dimissoria* and the dossier that governor Festus would

have sent along (see on 25:26). The terms of Paul's custody included a chain (v. 20). The fact that the prisoner was bound by the wrist to the soldier who guarded him safeguarded the security of the prisoner against escape in light custody.

28:17 Three days later he called together the leaders of the Jews. When they had assembled, Paul said to them, "Brothers, although I have done nothing against our people or the customs of our fathers, I was arrested and handed over from Jerusalem to the Romans" (ἐγένετο δὲ μετὰ ἡμέρας τρεῖς συγκαλέσασθαι αὐτὸν τοὺς ὄντας τῶν Ἰουδαίων πρώτους· συνελθόντων δὲ αὐτῶν ἔλεγεν πρὸς αὐτούς· ἐγώ, ἄνδρες ἀδελφοί, οὐδὲν ἐναντίον ποιήσας τῷ λαῷ ἢ τοῖς ἔθεσι τοῖς πατρῴοις δέσμιος ἐξ Ἱεροσολύμων παρεδόθην εἰς τὰς χεῖρας τῶν Ῥωμαίων). Paul's first encounter with the Jews of Rome takes place three days after he had taken up residence in the lodging place in which the Roman authorities allowed him to stay.

The expression "leaders of the Jews" (οἱ ὄντες τῶν Ἰουδαίων πρῶτοι; lit., "those who were the first of the Jews," or perhaps "whose who held the title of 'the first of the Jews'")[5] most likely describes the leaders of the synagogues in Rome. If the group consisted of the presidents of each of the synagogues, this would have been a meeting of between ten and twenty people, including Paul and his companions and the leaders of the Christian congregations. Since there was apparently no overall leadership of the Roman synagogues, the invitation to meet with Paul was presumably taken to each synagogue leader individually. That Paul calls together the Jewish leaders of Rome is not surprising; he is preparing the ground for his later trial, con-

---

3. Cf. the Western text (614. 2147 it), which adds the phrase "outside the camp."

4. Cf. Tajra, *Trial*, 180; Rapske, *Paul in Roman Custody*, 182.

5. Cf. Barrett, *Acts*, 1237, interpreting ὁ ὤν as introducing "some technical phrase."

cerned "for the potential impact of the local Jewish communities upon the outcome of his trial."[6]

The question why Luke does not refer to or describe the Christians in Rome has been much debated. While some assume that Paul's reception by the Roman church(es) was less than enthusiastic, Luke suggests in Acts 28:14 – 15 that the Roman congregations demonstrated an eagerness to meet with Paul and help him. Luke continues in this final episode his focus on Paul's trial, in which the local Jewish leaders would be more helpful than the local Christians. This focus allows Luke to express again the identity of the followers of Jesus over against those Jews who refused to believe in the good news of Jesus as Israel's risen Messiah and Savior.

Luke's summary of Paul's speech before the Jewish leaders in vv. 17d – 20 summarizes the case against Paul. It can be compared with the review of Paul's arrest in the letter of Claudius Lysias (23:26 – 30) and with the recapitulation of the trial by Festus (25:14 – 21), in which the responsibility of the Roman authorities in Judea in Paul's appeal to the emperor is minimized. The issues in the case against Paul are not Roman officials but the Jewish leaders in Jerusalem.[7]

Paul addresses these leaders as "brothers," i.e., fellow Jews (ἄνδρες ἀδελφοί; cf. 23:1; see also on 1:16). He explains the facts of the case (*narratio*) with an assertion of his innocence. He has "done nothing" against the Jewish people (λαός) or against their ancestral "customs" (τὰ ἔθη τὰ πατρῷα),[8] including the Mosaic law. This would remind Luke's readers of earlier statements of Paul to the same effect (see 22:3; 23:6; 24:14 – 16; 26:4 – 8).

Yet, despite his innocence, he had been "arrested" and was "handed over from Jerusalem" into the hands of the Romans. According to 21:32 – 33 it was the Roman commander who took Paul, by force, out of the hands of the Jews and arrested him. But it was the charges of the Jews from the province of Asia and the Jewish crowds in the temple courts (21:21 – 31) who initiated the events leading to his imprisonment under the custody of the Roman authorities.

28:18 They examined me and wanted to release me because there was no basis for the death sentence in my case (οἵτινες ἀνακρίναντές με ἐβούλοντο ἀπολῦσαι διὰ τὸ μηδεμίαν αἰτίαν θανάτου ὑπάρχειν ἐν ἐμοί). The second assertion of the *narratio* is Paul's insistence that his innocence was confirmed by the Roman authorities. Luke summarizes Paul's Roman trial without specific reference to Claudius Lysias, the Roman commander of the garrison in Jerusalem, or to M. Antonius Felix or Porcius Festus, the Roman governors of Judea, who all had heard Paul's case (23:1 – 10; 24:1 – 23; 25:6 – 12; 25:13 – 26:23). Paul would have reported on these trials in some detail in his encounter with the Jewish leaders in Rome.

Luke reports Paul as saying that the Roman authorities "examined" (ἀνακρίναντες; see on 17:11; 24:8) him and that they "wanted to release" him because they had found no charge deserving "the death sentence" in the case against Paul. The Roman authorities who investigated Paul acknowledged his innocence.[9]

28:19 But because the Jews objected, I was compelled to appeal to the emperor, even though I

---

6. Rapske, *Paul in Roman Custody*, 330.

7. Cf. Omerzu, *Prozess*, 499, who adds that the suspected potential perversion of justice by Festus (25:10) is blanked out.

8. For λαός see 2:47; 3:23; 4:10; for τὰ ἔθη τὰ πατρῷα see 15:1; 21:21; 22:3; 24:14.

9. The previous accounts of Paul's trial did not explicitly

state that the Roman authorities "wanted" (ἐβούλοντο) to "release" (ἀπολῦσαι) Paul, but they did conclude that Paul had not done anything deserving death (23:29; 25:25; 26:31) or imprisonment (23:29; 26:31). Agrippa II had explicitly said Paul should be released (26:32). There is thus no contradiction to the earlier accounts.

had no charge to bring against my own people
(ἀντιλεγόντων δὲ τῶν Ἰουδαίων ἠναγκάσθην
ἐπικαλέσασθαι Καίσαρα οὐχ ὡς τοῦ ἔθνους μου
ἔχων τι κατηγορεῖν). The third assertion of the
narratio is Paul's explanation why he was forced
to appeal to the emperor. Even though the Roman
authorities established his innocence, he remained
in custody because the Jews objected to his release.
The present tense of the genitive absolute participle "objected" (ἀντιλεγόντων) indicates that the
Jews of Jerusalem repeatedly opposed the decision
(v. 18) of Roman officials to release Paul.[10] As a result Paul "was compelled" (ἠναγκάσθην) to appeal
to the emperor (see 25:11). Since Paul notes the
disagreement of the Jewish authorities in Jerusalem with the conclusions of the Roman authorities
in Jerusalem and Caesarea, he acknowledges they
had serious objections to Paul's claim of being loyal
to the Jews and faithful to the Mosaic law.

Paul clarifies the motivation for his appeal to
the emperor: not to bring charges against "my
own people; i.e., his appeal to the emperor does
not imply any disloyalty to the Jewish people. In
the upcoming trial before the imperial court, Paul
will appear as a defendant, not as a plaintiff against
the Jewish people. This statement may be intended
not only to explain the circumstances of his appeal
to be heard by the emperor, but it may also reveal
something of Paul's trial strategy: he does not intend to accuse the leaders of the Jewish people of
wrongdoing, "perhaps charging that his opponents
were guilty of malicious prosecution."[11]

Paul is probably confident that if he follows the

same legal strategy he used in Caesarea, focusing
on the resurrection of the dead, in particular the
resurrection of Jesus of Nazareth, the imperial
court will recognize, as Felix and Festus did, that
the dispute is not about political wrongdoing but
about religious controversies.[12] At the same time,
this would allow him to explain to gospel to the
highest representatives of the empire, if not to the
emperor himself.

**28:20 "For this reason I have asked to see you
and speak with you. It is because of the hope
of Israel that I am bound with this chain"** (διὰ
ταύτην οὖν τὴν αἰτίαν παρεκάλεσα ὑμᾶς ἰδεῖν καὶ
προσλαλῆσαι, ἕνεκεν γὰρ τῆς ἐλπίδος τοῦ Ἰσραὴλ
τὴν ἅλυσιν ταύτην περίκειμαι). Paul has asked the
leaders of the Jewish communities in Rome to see
him "for this reason." Since the phrase obviously
refers back to what Paul has said in vv. 17f – 19,
the term αἰτία can also be understood in terms of
"legal charges." The logic of the connection can be
described as follows: "It is because my appeal to
Caesar puts me in an ambiguous position, in which
I am at the same time defending myself against an
unwarranted attack from the Jewish side while I
am in truth maintaining all that is true and valuable in Judaism, that I must seize, or create, an opportunity of making clear to you exactly what the
facts are. I have been more than sufficiently misunderstood in Jerusalem, and I hope by seeing you
and speaking with you to be understood by you
and to be on good terms with you."[13]

Paul wanted to see the Jewish leaders in Rome

10. The addition of 614. 2147 sy[h*] (καὶ ἐπικραζόντων· αἶρε τὸν
εχθρὸν ἡμῶν, "and shouting, 'Away with our enemy!'") is reminiscent of Jesus' trial, which the original text does not include;
many interpreters see an allusion to Jesus' trial (e.g. Tannehill,
Acts, 346, who thinks that "the echoes of Jesus' trial reinforce
the portrait of Paul as a true follower of Jesus in facing the same
sort of rejection and suffering"), which is not certain, however.
Barrett, *Acts*, 1239, asserts that "here the Western text is not so
much introducing an anti-Jewish element into the text as filling

out connections that the shorter text implies but does not state."
11. Rapske, *Paul in Roman Custody*, 189.
12. Differently Witherington, *Acts*, 798, speaks of "the ultimate defense strategy … the threat of a countersuit," and points
to the fact that due to the expulsion of the Jews in AD 49 under
Claudius, only about a decade before Paul arrived in Rome,
"no doubt the Roman Jews did not want to get embroiled in
any such matter and risk incurring the animus of the emperor."
13. Barrett, *Acts*, 1240.

and speak with them about why he is bound "with this chain" (see on v. 16). Paul showed to the Jewish leaders of Rome the physical proof of his imprisonment, "perhaps raising his manacled hand" and thereby "challenging the Jews to interpret correctly the image he presents to them."[14]

The summary of the case (*propositio*) is expressed with four words: "the hope of Israel" (ἡ ἐλπὶς τοῦ Ἰσραήλ). Earlier Paul had insisted that the main contention between himself and his Jewish opponents was the resurrection — a hope of the Jewish people that Paul proclaims as having been fulfilled by the resurrection of Jesus of Nazareth, who was vindicated as Israel's messianic Savior. Luke's readers, who know about the scriptural promise of hope and resurrection (cf. 24:14–15; 26:6–8),[15] about the fulfillment of the promise in Jesus' resurrection (26:22–23),[16] and about the resurrection of Jesus as Messiah who is "the first to rise from the dead" (26:23),[17] connected the "hope of Israel" with the final resurrection of the dead and with the resurrection of Jesus, which is the key fulfillment of God's covenant promises.

The reference of the Jewish leaders in v. 22 to "this party" (ἡ αἵρεσις ταύτη) implies that Paul spoke about Jesus and about how the "hope of Israel" was connected with Jesus. For Paul, the hope of messianic salvation has been made a present reality by the resurrection of Jesus, who is the one through whom God is fulfilling his promises that constituted Israel's hope.

28:21 They replied, "We have not received any letters from Judea concerning you, and none of the brothers who have come from there has reported or said anything bad about you" (οἱ δὲ πρὸς αὐτὸν εἶπαν· ἡμεῖς οὔτε γράμματα περὶ σοῦ ἐδεξάμεθα ἀπὸ τῆς Ἰουδαίας οὔτε παραγενόμενός τις τῶν ἀδελφῶν ἀπήγγειλεν ἢ ἐλάλησέν τι περὶ σοῦ πονηρόν). Luke now relates the response of the leaders of the synagogues in Rome, which has four parts.

(1) The Jewish leaders assert that the authorities in Jerusalem have not sent any letters about Paul or his case. This may be less surprising than some commentators think. The envoys from Jerusalem might have traveled on a ship with more prudent captains than the ship the centurion Julius had chosen for the journey to Rome, so they could still be on their way to Rome.[18] Or, the Jewish authorities may have decided not to send representatives to Rome, content to know that Paul was still in Roman custody and willing to let the case go by default, "realizing that they had less hope of a conviction before the imperial court than before a provincial magistrate."[19] In view of the troubles of the Jewish community, which had been expelled from Rome on account of disturbances only a decade earlier (cf. 18:2), they may have decided to abandon the case, realizing that the accusation of a Roman citizen who had appealed to the emperor about questions of Jewish faith and practice would likely not succeed.

(2) The Jewish leaders assert that Jews ("brothers") who have come from Jerusalem to Rome have not accused Paul. Since the high priest and the Sanhedrin had been involved in Paul's trial (22:30–23:10; 24:1–9; 25:1–3), any embassy that the Jerusalem authorities would send to Rome to press charges against Paul before the imperial court would have to include, if not the high priest himself, at least prominent members of the

---

14. Rapske, *Paul in Roman Custody*, 181, the quotation ibid., 310.

15. Cf. Hos 6:1–3; Isa 25:8–9; 26:19; Ezek 37:1–14; Dan 12:1–3; 2 Macc 7:9, 11, 14, 36; *T. Jud.* 25:1, 3–5; *T. Benj.* 10:6–9.

16. Cf. Luke 24:21, 25–27, 44–47; Acts 2:25–28; 3:13, 15, 22–23; 13:23, 32–33.

17. Cf. Acts 4:2; 17:18.

18. Cf. Bruce, *Acts*, 539; Bruce, *Book of Acts*, 506.

19. Hemer, *Acts*, 157; cf. Witherington, *Acts*, 799.

high priestly families. The combination of the two verbs translated "reported" (ἀπήγγειλεν) and "said" (ἐλάλησεν) indicates that none of the Jews arriving from Jerusalem have brought any news whatsoever concerning Paul, which means that they have not heard anything "bad" (πονηρόν) about Paul.

The ignorance of the leaders of the synagogues in Rome concerning Paul can be explained by the expulsion of the Jews and the Jewish-Christian "troublemakers" from Rome a decade earlier, resulting in a situation where the newly returned Jews had little contact with the predominantly Gentile Christian congregations. Moreover, the lack of a central organization of the Roman synagogues allowed for some Jewish leaders to have more and other Jewish officials to have less information about affairs in Judea. Note too that Paul's case had been delayed in Caesarea for two years and was moved to Rome only recently, and Paul himself had arrived in Rome only a few days earlier, probably before most ships coming from the east arrived in Puteoli.

28:22 "But we would like to hear from you what you think, because we know about this party, which is opposed everywhere" (ἀξιοῦμεν δὲ παρὰ σοῦ ἀκοῦσαι ἃ φρονεῖς, περὶ μὲν γὰρ τῆς αἱρέσεως ταύτης γνωστὸν ἡμῖν ἐστιν ὅτι πανταχοῦ ἀντιλέγεται). (3) The Jewish leaders express their willingness to hear from Paul about his teaching. The phrase translated "what you think" refers to Paul's views concerning Jesus, as the next statement indicates.

(4) The Jewish leaders want to clarify information concerning the Christians. They know about the movement of the followers of Jesus, which they designate a "party" (αἵρεσις; see on 5:17). Since Luke has described both the Sadducees and the Pharisees as a αἵρεσις (5:17; 15:5; 26:5), the desig-

nation of the believers in Jesus with this term (cf. 24:5, 14) places the movement of Jesus' followers within first-century Judaism as one of several "parties, schools, or factions" among the Jewish people. Whatever the Roman Jews had heard about the Christians, they regarded them as a party within Judaism, with its distinctive interpretation of the Scriptures and of Jewish faith and practice.

The Roman Jews unwittingly testify to the wide appeal of the Jesus movement. It is present "everywhere." In other words, they have heard from many places and from numerous Jewish communities that people believe in Jesus as Israel's Messiah and Savior (*the* distinctive belief of the followers of Jesus). But they have also heard that wherever people join the party of the believers in Jesus, its beliefs and practices are "opposed" (ἀντιλέγεται; see on 13:45). The tumultuous disagreements concerning Jesus in the Jewish communities in Rome in AD 48/49[20] had been the most dramatic example of this opposition.

28:23 As they had arranged a day to meet with Paul, they came to the place where he was staying in even larger numbers. From morning until evening he explained the matter to them, witnessing to the kingdom of God, and he tried to persuade them about Jesus from the Law of Moses and the Prophets (ταξάμενοι δὲ αὐτῷ ἡμέραν ἦλθον πρὸς αὐτὸν εἰς τὴν ξενίαν πλείονες οἷς ἐξετίθετο διαμαρτυρόμενος τὴν βασιλείαν τοῦ θεοῦ, πείθων τε αὐτοὺς περὶ τοῦ Ἰησοῦ ἀπό τε τοῦ νόμου Μωϋσέως καὶ τῶν προφητῶν, ἀπὸ πρωῒ ἕως ἑσπέρας). Luke's description of Paul's second encounter with the Jews of Rome (vv. 23–28) begins with a comment on the arrival of "larger numbers" of Jews to hear Paul.

At the conclusion of Paul's first encounter with the Jews of Rome, they had arranged a day for a

---

20. Cf. 12:17; 17:7; 18:2; 28:17.

second meeting, which took place probably not long after the first meeting. Since the meeting is described as lasting the entire day, it is possible that it took place on a Sabbath day, when the Jews would have the time to meet with Paul for several hours, listening to the exposition of Scripture presented by a rabbinically trained believer in Jesus and discussing theological questions. Luke describes the events of the second meeting as follows.

(1) The Jews came "to the place where he was staying [εἰς τὴν ξενίαν]." The Greek noun ξενία describes the "lodgings" or the "place of residence"[21] that Paul, a prisoner under guard, was allowed to rent (vv. 16, 30).

(2) The Jews came "in even larger numbers" (πλείονες), or, if understood as an elative, "in considerable numbers." The reference could be to a larger number of Jewish leaders,[22] or more generally to a considerable number of Roman Jews interested in hearing Paul. The lodgings Paul rented were evidently large enough to accommodate a large number of people.

(3) Paul "explained" (ἐξετίθετο), "witnessed" (διαμαρτυρόμενος), and "tried to persuade" (πείθων) — terms Luke has used repeatedly to describe the process of the proclamation of the good news of Jesus as Israel's Messiah and Savior. The message about Jesus needs to be explained, since neither the significance of a crucified and risen Messiah nor the influx of uncircumcised Gentiles into the people of God was self-evident in Jewish tradition. The proclamation of Jesus as the risen and exalted Savior is supported by the eyewitness testimony of Paul, who encountered the risen Jesus on the road to Damascus. The people who listened to the explanation of the gospel had to be persuaded concerning the truth of Jesus' significance as Israel's Messiah and Savior, with arguments from Scripture[23] and from eyewitness testimony.

(4) The content of Paul's discourse is described with the phrase "the kingdom of God" (ἡ βασιλεία τοῦ θεοῦ) and with the name "Jesus" (Ἰησοῦς). The expression "kingdom of God" (see on 1:3, 6) is used here as a summary of the Christian message. The expression also summarizes the content of the preaching of Jesus[24] and of the Twelve and of Paul.[25] The reference to Jesus of Nazareth underlines the fundamental significance of Jesus for Paul's (and the apostles') understanding of God and of his rule (or kingdom), which is becoming a reality through the ministry, death, resurrection, and exaltation of Jesus, Israel's Messiah and Savior (1:6 – 11).

28:24 Some were persuaded by what he said, while others did not believe (καὶ οἱ μὲν ἐπείθοντο τοῖς λεγομένοις, οἱ δὲ ἠπίστουν). Luke notes the reaction of the Roman Jews in vv. 24 – 25b. Some Jews "were persuaded" by Paul's explanations, testimony, and arguments. The passive voice of the verb should be interpreted as a divine passive. While it was Paul's words that persuaded some of the Roman Jews, it was God who convinced them of the truth of the message about Jesus. When people come to faith in Jesus as Israel's Messiah and Savior, this is always God who opens "a door of faith" (14:27, with reference to Gentiles). The next statement clarifies that the Jews who were persuaded came to faith; i.e., they believed in Jesus as the messianic Savior through whom God has established his rule over Israel and the world of the Gentiles.

---

21. The older meaning "hospitality" is not intended here. Cf. BDAG, s.v. ξενία; C. Spicq, "ξενία κτλ.," *TLNT*, 2:559 – 60: the meaning "house or apartment, the place where friends or strangers are received" is the most common meaning in the papyri.

22. Cf. Johnson, *Acts*, 470.

23. Cf. Acts 13:27; 26:22; and the references to scriptural passages in the sermons of Paul (and of Peter).

24. Cf. Luke 4:43; 6:20; 7:28; 8:1; 9:11; 10:9 – 10; 11:20; 12:31 – 32; 13:29; 16:16; 17:20 – 21; 18:16 – 17, 25, 29; 19:11; 21:31; 22:30; 23:42; Acts 1:3.

25. Cf. Luke 9:2; 10:9 – 11; Acts 8:12; 14:22; 19:8; 20:25.

But other Jews "did not believe" (ἠπίστουν).[26] This divided response to the explanation of the gospel about Jesus is characteristic for the ministry of the Twelve and of Paul.[27]

28:25 They disagreed among themselves, and they began to leave after Paul had made one further statement: "The Holy Spirit was right when he spoke to your ancestors through the prophet Isaiah" (ἀσύμφωνοι δὲ ὄντες πρὸς ἀλλήλους ἀπελύοντο εἰπόντος τοῦ Παύλου ῥῆμα ἕν, ὅτι καλῶς τὸ πνεῦμα τὸ ἅγιον ἐλάλησεν διὰ Ἡσαΐου τοῦ προφήτου πρὸς τοὺς πατέρας ὑμῶν). The divided response of the Roman Jews prompts Paul to address the refusal of some Roman Jews to believe in Jesus as Israel's messianic Savior. This division is highlighted with an adjective (ἀσύμφωνοι; "in disagreement with") that denotes a lack of harmony.[28]

Since vv. 25c – 28 is best regarded as Paul's interpretation of the unbelief of a (large?) part of the Roman Jews to his explanation of the identity and significance of Jesus in connection with the arrival of God's kingdom, Luke's comment in v. 25a describes the reaction of the Roman Jews to Paul's proclamation of the gospel referenced in v. 23. As some Roman Jews are persuaded by Paul's arguments, accepting Jesus as Israel's Messiah and Savior, and as others dispute the validity of Paul's arguments and beliefs, the meeting comes to a close with a final statement by Paul in which he quotes Isa 6:9 – 10 as an explanation of the unbelief of some of the Jews. After Paul's final statement, related by Luke in direct speech, the people begin to leave.

Whether or not vv. 25c – 28 is the climax of Paul's preaching among the Jews, it is certainly a summary of Paul's past and present experiences regarding the response of the Jewish people to the proclamation of God's revelation in and through Jesus. Paul introduces the quotation from Isa 6:9 – 10 by referring to "the Holy Spirit," who inspired the words of Scripture — here particularly the words of Isaiah, which the prophet spoke (and wrote) as the words that God's Spirit spoke. The Holy Spirit addressed the "ancestors" (πατέρες; lit. "fathers") through Isaiah, and he continues to speak through his words to his people today. This is a straightforward expression of belief in the inspiration of the (Old Testament) Scriptures.

28:26 – 27 "Go to this people and say, You will indeed listen, but never understand, and you will indeed look, but never see. For the mind of this people has become dull, and their ears are hard of hearing, and they have closed their eyes, so that they might not see with their eyes, hear with their ears, understand with their mind, and turn, and I would heal them" (λέγων· πορεύθητι πρὸς τὸν λαὸν τοῦτον καὶ εἰπόν· ἀκοῇ ἀκούσετε καὶ οὐ μὴ συνῆτε καὶ βλέποντες βλέψετε καὶ οὐ μὴ ἴδητε· ἐπαχύνθη γὰρ ἡ καρδία τοῦ λαοῦ τούτου καὶ τοῖς ὠσὶν βαρέως ἤκουσαν καὶ τοὺς ὀφθαλμοὺς αὐτῶν ἐκάμμυσαν· μήποτε ἴδωσιν τοῖς ὀφθαλμοῖς καὶ τοῖς ὠσὶν ἀκούσωσιν καὶ τῇ καρδίᾳ συνῶσιν καὶ ἐπιστρέψωσιν, καὶ ἰάσομαι αὐτούς).

The quotation from Isa 6:9 and/or 10 also appears in Matt 13:13 – 15; Mark 4:12; Luke 8:10; John 12:39 – 40; Rom 11:8.[29] Paul quotes Isa 6:9 – 10 according to the LXX, with a slight change of word order in the introductory phrase "go to this people and say." The LXX is an accurate translation of the

---

26. The verb ἀπιστέω ("disbelieve, refuse to believe;" BDAG) is used here for the first and only time in Acts; cf. Luke 24:11.

27. Cf. 2:12 – 13; 4:1 – 4; 5:12 – 17; 6:8 – 14; 9:21 – 25; 13:42 – 45; 14:1 – 2; 17:1 – 5; 18:4, 12 – 17; 19:8 – 10. Cf. Johnson, *Acts*, 471.

28. Note the contrast to the harmony of the Jewish believers in Jesus, expressed with the term ὁμοθυμαδόν, cf. 1:14; 2:46; 4:24; 5:12.

29. Cf. Craig A. Evans, *To See and Not Perceive: Isaiah 6:9 – 10 in Early Jewish and Christian Interpretation* (JSOTSup 64; Sheffield: JSOT Press, 1989).

Hebrew original, with the following changes.[30] (1) The imperatives "keep listening, but do not comprehend" and "keep looking, but do not understand" (lit. trans.) are changed to emphatic future indicatives ("you will indeed listen, but never understand" and "you will indeed look, but never see"), which express what will happen. (2) The command that Isaiah is to make the people's heart dull ("make the mind of this people calloused") is changed to a statement of fact ("the mind of this people has become dull"), which seems to tone down the agent (Isaiah, Paul) of the hardening process.[31] (3) The passive voice "be healed" is changed to the future indicative ("I will/would heal them").

In the original context, Isaiah is in the Jerusalem temple, receiving in a vision the prophetic commission to go to the (Jewish) people as God's spokesman (Isa 6:1 – 13). God commands Isaiah to tell the people to go on behaving as apostates who hear God's word but who neither understand nor obey it. Their obduracy is so great that they will not escape judgment. It is only after God's judgment has run its course that there can be any hope of renewal (Isa 6:11 – 13).

Isaiah's task has been interpreted in different ways. The purpose of his preaching is to provide the Jewish people with further opportunities to reject God's message, and his preaching produces the effect that it predicts, which is hardening, judgment, and destruction.[32] Or, the formulation of Isaiah's call is ironic: his message is a warning for the Jewish people meant to encourage them to repent; if they continue to disobey God's word, as they

are presently doing, God will take away the opportunity and the ability to respond and repent.[33] Isaiah's further prophecies indicate that judgment is not God's final word for the Jewish people; the "holy seed" in 6:13 gives hope, perhaps a reference to the "shoot" out of the stem of Jesse (11:1), i.e., to the promise of the Messiah as "the guarantee of a future people over whom he will reign," and also a reference to the remnant of God's people "who will finally enjoy the promises."[34] In the LXX, the prophecy also sounds more like an announcement of judgment rather than a warning, although it was probably also meant to function as an appeal.

God commands Isaiah to deliver a message to the Jewish people (λαός). In the context of Acts 28:23 – 28, Paul asserts that God has given him the same mandate, which implies that the behavior of the people (living in rebellion against God) and their reaction to God's word (lack of understanding) has not changed since Isaiah's time. God's analysis of the behavior and situation of the Jewish people in the prophet's time — and now in Paul's time — is stark: they "listen, but never understand" (ἀκοῇ ἀκούσετε καὶ οὐ μὴ συνῆτε; lit., "with hearing you will hear and you will never understand"), and they "look, but never see" (βλέποντες βλέψετε καὶ οὐ μὴ ἴδητε; lit., "looking you will look and you will certainly not see").[35]

While the Jewish people are physically able to hear and see, spiritually they are deaf and blind. They are accused of listening without understanding and without responding to the word of God. The reinforced negation (οὐ μή), repeated twice,

---

30. Cf. Pao, *New Exodus*, 102 – 3; Gert J. Steyn, *Septuagint Quotations in the Context of the Petrine and Pauline Speeches of the Acta Apostolorum* (CBET 12; Kampen: Kok, 1995), 219 – 29; Marshall, "Acts," 600.

31. Cf. Pao, *New Exodus*, 102.

32. John N. Oswalt, *The Book of Isaiah* (2 vols.; NICOT; Grand Rapids: Eerdmans, 1986 – 98), 1:188, with reference to Otto Kaiser, *Isaiah 1 – 12: A Commentary* (OTL; London: SCM, 1972).

33. Cf. John Goldingay, *Isaiah* (New International Biblical Commentary 13; Peabody, MA: Hendrickson, 2001), 60 – 61.

34. J. Alec Motyer, *The Prophecy of Isaiah* (Downers Grove, IL: InterVarsity Press, 1993), 80, with reference to Isa 4:3; 43:5; 45:25; 53:10; 59:21; 65:9, 23; 66:22.

35. The cognate formulation (ἀκοῇ ἀκούσετε ... βλέποντες βλέψετε) intensifies the meaning of the statement.

"is the most decisive way of negating something in the future."[36] This analysis now also applies to those among the Roman Jews who have heard Paul explain the kingdom of God and its arrival in connection with Jesus, Israel's Messiah and Savior, but who are refusing to understand, accept, and believe; it does not apply to the Roman Jews who have responded positively and who have come to faith in Jesus (v. 24).

The indictment of the Jewish people continues in v. 27 (Isa 6:10). God, through the prophet, accuses the people of a condition described with three statements. (1) The Jewish people have minds (καρδία)[37] that have "become dull" (ἐπαχύνθη), i.e., impervious to the reality of God's words in which he reveals his will. (2) They have "ears"[38] that are "hard of hearing"; i.e., they do not understand the words that God is speaking through Isaiah, and now through Paul. (3) They have "eyes," but they "have closed" (ἐκάμμυσαν) them; they are hostile to God's word.

The purpose (μήποτε) and effect of Isaiah's proclamation of God's word is expressed with statements that correspond to the three statements of indictment (in reverse order): their eyes do not see, their ears do not hear, and their minds do not understand. As a result, they do not "turn" (ἐπιστρέψωσιν) to God; rather, they keep their distance from him and refuse to submit to his will, which explains why God does not "heal" them.[39] These purpose statements describe the purpose of God himself, "who brings inescapable judgment upon people who go on too long and too far in rejecting his message to them."[40] If the Roman Jews refuse to come to faith in Jesus as Israel's promised Messiah and Savior, this is their deliberate choice, a choice that results in God's judgment.

As in the original context of Isaiah, so for Paul this divine indictment of Israel's obstinacy is not God's final word, in the sense that from now on Jews are always unwilling and unable to repent and turn to God. The "all" (πάντες) who come to Paul (v. 30) and hear him explain the gospel of the Lord Jesus Christ (v. 31) surely include Roman Jews, some of whom would have accepted his message and come to faith in Jesus, as some of the Jewish leaders had done (v. 24).

This means that Luke did not intend the quotation from Isa 6:9 – 10 to be understood as Paul's parting shot to "the Jews" of whom he is washing his hands. The quotation explains once more that the mixed response to the proclamation of the gospel of Jesus Christ falls into "the national pattern of not believing and of reflecting hardheartedness."[41] As Isaiah continued to prophesy to his people, so Paul continues to proclaim the gospel to both Jews and Gentiles. Luke "understood Isaiah as indicating the course (and frustrations) of Paul's mission to his own and Isaiah's people, not as calling on him to end it in dismissive denunciation."[42]

28:28 "So I want you to know that this salvation of God has been sent to the Gentiles. They will

---

36. BDAG, s.v. μή; it can be translated as "never" (NET, NIV, NRSV, RSV, TNIV) or "certainly not."

37. In the context of the subsequent formulation "understand with the mind" (τῇ καρδίᾳ συνῶσιν), the term καρδία denotes the heart "as center and source of the whole inner life, with its thinking, feeling, and volition" (BDAG, s.v. καρδία 1b), here particularly in the sense of "inner awareness" (sense 1bβ), and is thus best translated as "mind" (GNB, Fitzmyer; most English translations have "heart").

38. The figurative reference to ears denotes "mental and spiritual understanding, *ear, hearing*" (BDAG, s.v. οὖς 2).

39. In Luke-Acts, "healing" is related to the proclamation of the kingdom of God and the restoration of Israel; cf. Luke 5:17; 6:18 – 19; 9:2, 11; 14:4; Acts 3:1 – 10; 9:34; 10:38; cf. Johnson, *Acts*, 472.

40. Marshall, "Acts," 601, modifying his earlier interpretation in terms of the purpose of the people (Marshall, *Acts*, 424: "This is a divine judgment upon them because they themselves have made their hearts impervious to the Word of God").

41. Bock, *Acts*, 755. See earlier 13:46 – 47; 18:5 – 6.

42. Dunn, *Beginning from Jerusalem*, 1006.

listen!" (γνωστὸν οὖν ἔστω ὑμῖν ὅτι τοῖς ἔθνεσιν ἀπεστάλη τοῦτο τὸ σωτήριον τοῦ θεοῦ· αὐτοὶ καὶ ἀκούσονται). Paul's declaration to the Jews of Rome — some of whom believe, others of whom do not believe in Jesus as Israel's messianic Savior — formulates the consequence of the national pattern of Israel's not believing God's word: the offer of salvation is now sent to the Gentiles. The reference to "this salvation" links salvation (see on 2:21, 40; 4:12) with Paul's teaching before these Jews about Jesus of Nazareth as the hope of Israel (v. 20), with the significance of Jesus for the reality of the kingdom of God and the fulfillment of God's promises in the Scriptures (v. 23), and with Jesus as Israel's Messiah and the risen, exalted Lord (v. 31).

This messianic salvation has been initiated by God and is granted to those who "will listen" (ἀκούσονται), i.e., who will accept the message about Jesus as the word of God, will repent, and will come to faith. The statement is perhaps an echo of Isa 40:5 ("all people will see [the salvation of God] together"), as Luke (Paul) sums up the universal scope of the salvation that God has made possible through sending Jesus Christ.

The turn to the Gentiles (τοῖς ἔθνεσιν) is the third such turn in Acts. When Paul turned to the Gentiles in Pisidian Antioch (13:46 – 47) and in Corinth (18:6), he did not give up on the Jews — not in these two cities, let alone in other cities. The statement alludes to Ps 67:2 (LXX 66:3), where God is asked to pour out his blessing on Israel "that we may know your way upon the earth, and among all nations your salvation [ἐν πᾶσιν ἔθνεσιν τὸ σωτήριόν σου; 'your salvation among all the nations].' The witness of Jesus, Israel's risen

and exalted Messiah and Lord sent by God to bring salvation, will be carried beyond the Jews of Rome to the Gentiles, indeed to "the ends of the earth" (1:8). Paul predicts that the Gentiles will listen to the gospel — although he knows from experience that just as not all Jews believed, not all Gentiles come to faith. But "God will gather a people for himself regardless of the Jewish response."[43]

28:30 Paul lived for two whole years there in his own rented place. He welcomed all who came to him (ἐνέμεινεν δὲ διετίαν ὅλην ἐν ἰδίῳ μισθώματι καὶ ἀπεδέχετο πάντας τοὺς εἰσπορευομένους πρὸς αὐτόν). Luke ends his two-volume work with a summary report about Paul's imprisonment in Rome. Paul welcomes all who want to see him and to whom he proclaims the gospel unhindered.[44] Paul is a prisoner in Rome for "two whole years," i.e., two full calendar years, likely to be reckoned from the time Paul arrived in Rome. During this time he "lived … in his own rented place." The Greek term μίσθωμα ("rented place") has been understood as (1) "at his own expense," indicating that Paul himself paid for his living costs in Rome, or as (2) "in his own rented place," highlighting the type of accommodation Paul was allowed to stay in as prisoner subject to light military custody. The second suggestion is more plausible: Paul lived in lodgings that he was able to rent.

The reference to the specific period of two years suggests a termination of some sort, either of Luke's conclusion of his two-volume project at this point, or Paul's release from prison, by default or acquittal (or, less likely, Paul's trial and death).[45] Arguments that according to Roman law, a prisoner had to be

---

43. Marshall, "Acts," 601; cf. Barrett, *Acts*, 1246. Note that the Western text and some manuscripts in the Byzantine tradition add here v. 29: "After he said this, the Jews left, arguing vigorously among themselves" (see Metzger, *Textual Commentary*, 444).

44. Many commentators suggest that Acts ends on a note of triumph (e.g., Barrett, *Acts*, 1246; Bock, *Acts*, 757). This is less evident than it seems: Luke records neither conversions nor the establishment of new churches.

45. For the ending of Acts see "In Depth: The Ending of Acts" in Structure and Literary Form on 28:16 – 31.

released if his accusers failed to appear within two years[46] have been effectively criticized as being relevant only for a much later period.[47] There is evidence for the custom of the emperor Claudius to render judgments against absent parties in legal trials including penalties for defaulting accusers,[48] although it should be noted that the purpose of this policy was to compel prosecutors to prosecute, not to legislate the release of defenders whose accusers failed to appear, and to curb vexatious prosecution by penalizing unsubstantiated allegations.[49]

Since Paul had a good case, his opponents in the Jerusalem hierarchy may have decided that winning a verdict against Paul in the imperial court was unlikely; so they may have accepted the less serious option of simply not appearing in Rome. Another possibility is that they may have counted on Jewish influence at Nero's court, through the empress Poppaea. However, since Nero was not as interested in the law courts as Claudius was, Paul's case might have been a routine matter for a judge such as the Prefect of the Praetorian Guard Sextus Afranius Burrus, who was honest. Some have suggested that Paul's trial had a favorable outcome for him, by acquittal or by default, just before Burrus's death in the spring of AD 62, before the succession of Ofonius Tigellinus to the position of prefect.[50]

The evidence that Paul reached Spain[51] — evidence that would require Paul's release from imprisonment in Rome — is limited to a comment by Clement of Rome and a line in the Muratorian Canon. Clement asserts in a letter written at the end of the first century that Paul "served as a herald in both the East and in the West; and he received the noble reputation for his faith. He taught righteousness to the whole world, and came to the limits of the West, bearing his witness before the rulers. And so he was set free from this world and transported up to the holy place, having become the greatest example of endurance" (*1 Clem.* 5:6–7). Slightly later, but more explicitly, the Muratorian Canon states:

> For the "most excellent Theophilus" Luke summarizes the several things that in his own presence have come to pass, as also by the omission of the passion of Peter he makes quite clear, and equally by (the omission) of the journey of Paul, who from the city [of Rome] proceeded to Spain.[52]

All in all, it appears that after a two-year imprisonment in Rome during which he wrote his letters to the Colossians and Ephesians, to Philemon, and to the Philippians, Paul was tried and acquitted (or released by default) in early AD 62.

Luke comments that Paul welcomed (ἀπεδέχετο), i.e., received, all who came to him. This includes Jews and Gentiles, whether believers or unbelievers, men and women, freeborn and slaves (such as Onesimus, who was converted while meeting the imprisoned Paul; Phlm 10). The insistence that Paul received all people confirms that the simple view of the gospel proceeding from Jews in Jerusalem to Gentiles in Rome is misleading: "Acts does not replace one form of particularism (Jews alone) with

---

46. Henry J. Cadbury, "Roman Law and the Trial of Paul," in *The Beginnings of Christianity, Part. I: The Acts of the Apostles,* vol. 5: *Additional Notes to the Commentary* (ed. K. Lake and H. J. Cadbury; London: Macmillan, 1933), 297–338, 319–38; cf. Tajra, *Trial,* 193–95.

47. Sherwin-White, *Roman Society,* 115–19, showed that the rule that Cadbury appealed to "does not make its appearance until AD 529" (ibid., 115 n. 4); cf. also Rapske, *Paul in Roman Custody,* 322–23; Omerzu, "Schweigen," 148–49.

48. Suetonius, *Claud.* 15.2; Dio Cassius 60.28.6.

49. Cf. Hemer, *Acts,* 392; cf. ibid. for the following points.

50. Cf. W. Eck, "Ofonius Tigellinus," *BNP,* 10:64–65, who notes that "the entire ancient tradition portrays him as the 'evil genius' behind all of Nero's crimes, e.g., the murder of Nero's wife Octavia and the Fire of Rome."

51. For Paul's plans to go to Spain see Rom 15:23–29.

52. Muratorian Canon, lines 35–39. Cf. Schnabel, *Early Christian Mission,* 2:1273–75.

another (Gentiles alone)."[53] Also, Paul's accessibility enabled him not only to be in contact with Christians and with unbelievers during the two years of his imprisonment (v. 31). It also facilitated the contact with coworkers and the dictation of letters to other churches.[54] Luke wants his readers to remember Paul "not as a martyr, or as a political apologist for Christianity, but as an evangelist who lived and died for the hope of Israel ... the story of Paul is cut short, but the story of the risen Jesus goes on."[55]

28:31 He proclaimed the kingdom of God and taught about the Lord Jesus Christ with all boldness and without hindrance (κηρύσσων τὴν βασιλείαν τοῦ θεοῦ καὶ διδάσκων τὰ περὶ τοῦ κυρίου Ἰησοῦ Χριστοῦ μετὰ πάσης παρρησίας ἀκωλύτως). Luke ends his report of Paul's ministry (since 13:1) and imprisonment (since 21:18) with a summary statement on Paul's proclamation of the gospel in Rome, which concludes his two-volume work. It also formulates Luke's main historical and theological concern: the connection between the kingdom of God and Jesus as Israel's Messiah and Lord of all, and the privilege and necessity of proclamation that communicates the significance of Jesus to all (v. 30), i.e., Jews and Gentiles.

(1) Luke summarizes the content of Paul's preaching with the expression "kingdom of God" (ἡ βασιλεία τοῦ θεοῦ; see on 1:3, 6; 28:23), which reflects God's revelation in Jesus as Israel's crucified, risen, and exalted Messiah and Lord and the Savior of all people, through whom both Jews and Gentiles find salvation and a new identity in the community of God's messianic people. Luke uses

the verb translated "proclaim" (κηρύσσω; see on 8:5) here for the last time.[56] Paul conveys the message about the intervention of God, who is fulfilling his promises with authority and with confidence, and with the expectation that the listeners will respond, absorb the meaning of the message, and follow the will of God being proclaimed.

(2) Luke summarizes Paul's preaching with reference to Jesus of Nazareth, who is the Messiah (Χριστός; see on 2:31, 36), fulfills God's promises, and is the risen and exalted "Lord" (κύριος; see on 2:36). This reality makes the proclamation of God's word effective. The message of the crucified and risen Jesus Christ was the consistent and effective content of the proclamation of the early church — the foundation of its faith and life that Paul the missionary had been laying (1 Cor 1:18 – 2:5; 3:10 – 11) and that he continued to establish in Rome.

Luke also uses the verb "teach" (διδάσκω; see on 2:42)[57] for the last time. Paul provides instruction concerning everything that is relevant for understanding the identity of Jesus as Messiah and Lord and concerning the significance of Jesus' life, death, resurrection, and exaltation. Paul instructed everyone who came to him (v. 30). At the same time, Luke provides an *inclusio* with the annunciation stories, where the birth of Jesus is announced as the messianic Son of David and Son of God who is born for Israel's liberation, in fulfillment of God's promises to Israel (Luke 1:32 – 33, 51 – 55, 68 – 71), and with the narrative of the birth of Jesus who arrives in the world in the context of Caesar Augustus's imperial reign (Luke 2:1 – 14). As Paul

---

53. Rosner, "Progress," 229.

54. Cf. Johnson, *Acts*, 473, who refers to Phil 2:19 – 20; 4:18; Col 4:7 – 17; 2 Tim 1:16 – 17; 4:9 – 13 for his point that "such accessibility makes the practical directives issued by Paul's captivity letters appear more plausible."

55. Anderson, *Jesus' Resurrection*, 286, with reference to Robert Garland, *The Greek Way of Death* (Ithaca, NY: Cornell Univ. Press, 1985), 65.

56. Luke 3:3; 4: 18,19, 44; 8:1, 39; 9:2; 12:3; 24:47; Acts 8:5; 9:20; 10:37, 42; 15:21; 19:13; 20:25.

57. The verb occurs 33 times in Luke-Acts, e.g. Luke 4:15, 31; 5:3, 17; Acts 1:1; 4:2, 18; 5:21, 25, 28; etc.; διδαχή ("teaching") occurs in Luke 4:32; Acts 2:42; 5:28; 13:12; 17:19; διδάσκαλος ("teacher") occurs 18 times in Luke-Acts, apart from Acts 13:1 always in Luke's gospel.

preaches the "kingdom of *God*" in Rome, the capital of the empire of Caesar, and as he proclaims Jesus Christ as *Lord*, Luke, probably deliberately,

> contrasts Jesus the Messianic king/lord to Caesar Augustus, and implicitly claims that Jesus is the true *kyrios* and *sōtēr*, the true bearer of the kingship of God, and that he will bring the true *pax* (peace) on earth, replacing the false *pax* brought by the military conquests of Caesar, a false *kyrios* and *sōtēr*.[58]

(3) Paul proclaimed and taught the gospel "with all boldness" (μετὰ πάσης παρρησίας). The noun translated as "boldness" (παρρησία; see on 4:13) could describe Paul's preaching and teaching as communication "that conceals nothing and passes over nothing" (outspokenness, frankness), as "openness to the public" before whom the preaching and teaching takes place, and as the "boldness and confidence" with which Paul continued his preaching ministry. Since Paul was a prisoner and thus in a situation exposed to insult and shame — for two years in Caesarea and for two years in Rome — the reference to παρρησία is God's gift that helps Paul "overcome the negative effects of his sufferings, but particularly the shame of his bonds."[59]

(4) Paul proclaimed and taught the gospel "without hindrance" (ἀκωλύτως), under the eyes of the soldiers guarding him (v. 16). Even though he was a prisoner, he could act like a free man. He met all who came, and he preached without restrictions. For Luke's readers, the general tolerance of Paul's activities in Rome was proof that Paul was innocent of the charges brought against him. Since Luke's readers were Christian believers, the last word of Luke's two-volume work means, more importantly, that the good news of God's kingdom, which is the gospel of Jesus Christ, cannot be hindered or restricted (cf. 2 Tim 2:9). Nothing could deter Paul from proclaiming the gospel and teaching about Jesus Christ. The good news continued to reach all people who were willing to listen — in Rome and beyond, to the ends of the earth.

Theology in Application

In the concluding section of his two-volume work about Jesus of Nazareth, God's promised Messiah, King, and Savior for both Jews and Gentiles, Luke emphasizes again that the gospel of Jesus Christ is the fulfillment of God's promises to Israel, that God's offer of salvation is for everyone, and that the gospel is the fundamental content of the proclamation and teaching of the church and the consistent and unchanging task of Jesus' witnesses.

The Gospel and God's Promises

Reporting on Paul's encounters with the Jewish leaders of Rome, Luke clarifies one last time that the content of Paul's preaching and teaching, as well as the reason for the opposition of Jews in Asia Minor and in Jerusalem that caused his arrest and imprisonment, is the "hope of Israel," i.e., his proclamation that God has fulfilled his

---

58. Seyoon Kim, *Christ and Caesar: The Gospel and the Roman Empire in the Writings of Paul and Luke* (Grand Rapids: Eerdmans, 2008), 80 – 81.

59. Rapske, *Paul in Roman Custody*, 311, with reference to Eph 6:19 – 20; Phil 1:20; 1 Thess 2:2; Phlm 8.

promises to Israel of messianic salvation and restoration in Jesus, Israel's Messiah and Savior. God's action in Jesus' birth, ministry, death, resurrection, and exaltation realized Israel's hope of a restored, authentic people of God living out God's promises given to Abraham, now empowered by the Holy Spirit, who has been given to all who believe in him and who submit to him as exalted Lord. The "things that have been fulfilled among us" (Luke 1:1) include in prominent position the reality that the good news of God's salvation has reached the Gentiles.

Luke has shown in Acts that the character of the church as God's people, consisting of Jewish believers and of an increasingly large number of Gentiles believers, is part of God's plan — a plan that does not entail the rejection of Israel. Jews have come in large numbers to faith in Jesus as Israel's Messiah and Savior — first in Jerusalem and then in every city in which the gospel has been preached, including Rome. The rejection of Jesus by the Jewish authorities in Jerusalem, who continued to oppose God's messianic salvation as they opposed the Twelve, then other believers such as Stephen, and then Paul, has led to their self-exclusion from God's people. God has been faithful to his promises, and the word of the good news about Jesus and the power of the Holy Spirit have been effective — among Jews and now increasingly among Gentiles.[60]

The church's authentic proclamation of the gospel speaks not merely about the salvation of individual sinners, but about God's plan of bringing salvation to a fallen world through his people Israel, extended in the days of the Messiah to the Gentiles from Jerusalem to the ends of the earth. The gospel is, in the first place, not about us but about God, not about our life but about God's kingdom, not about our needs but about God's grace, not about our priorities but about Jesus' accomplished work, not about our attempts to change but about the transforming power of the Holy Spirit. The gospel is the good news about God fulfilling his promises to Israel recorded in the Scriptures, about Jesus of Nazareth, who is God's promised Messiah, about God ushering in his kingdom through Jesus' ministry, death, and resurrection, about the exalted Jesus pouring out God's transforming Holy Spirit, about God restoring his people by bringing Jews and Gentiles to faith in Jesus, and about Jesus bringing salvation to sinners.

The Gospel and God's Universal Offer of Salvation

Paul proclaims the gospel to the Jews of the city of Rome, despite the strong and indeed ferocious opposition that he has experienced from Jews in the past, and despite the renewed rejection of his message by some of the Roman Jews. He welcomes

---

60. Cf. Johnson, *Acts*, 476, who emphasizes that as Luke has successfully demonstrated God's fidelity to his people and to his own word, "the ending of Acts is truly an opening to the continuing life of the messianic people, as it continues to preach the kingdom and teach the things concerning Jesus both boldly and without hindrance, knowing now that although increasingly Gentile in its growth, its roots are deep within the story of people to whom God's prophets have unfailingly been sent."

all who come to meet with him. The message of God's gracious offer of salvation through Jesus Christ is proclaimed to Jews and Gentiles alike, freeborn and slaves. Nobody is excluded.

At the same time Paul announces judgment for those who hear the gospel but refuse to understand, absorb, and respond to its claims. If Jews can become obdurate and incapable of responding to the gospel by coming to faith in Jesus, so can Gentiles. God's offer of salvation is not universal in the sense that all Jews and all Gentiles are unilaterally declared righteous. Those who by God's grace hear, understand, and respond to the gospel by believing in Jesus as Israel's Messiah and the Savior of all people receive God's salvation and eternal life.

The Gospel and Jesus' Witnesses

The final episode of Luke's two-volume work reports on Paul's ministry of preaching and teaching in Rome, both among the Jewish leaders and among all people, Gentiles included, who come to hear him. The mission of God was carried out first by Jesus among the Jews of Galilee as he proclaimed the dawn of God's messianic rule over his people. God's mission, entrusted by Jesus into the hands, the feet, and the mouth of his disciples, has now been carried out by the Twelve, then by other witnesses, sometimes unnamed, who carried the good news of God's salvation through Jesus from Jerusalem to Samaria, to cities on the Phoenician coast, and to Antioch, the capital of the province of Syria.

Then God's mission was carried out by Paul, commissioned by Jesus to preach before Jews and Gentiles, before ordinary people and before kings (9:15), who preached in numerous regions and countless cities in the eastern Mediterranean from Damascus in Syria, Jerusalem in Judea, Tarsus in Cilicia, in the cities of Galatia and Macedonia, in Athens and in Corinth in Achaia, in Ephesus in the province of Asia, and now in Rome. Paul's arrest and imprisonment do not hinder or curb the proclamation of the gospel. On the contrary, his imprisonment provides new opportunities to explain the gospel to more people, including Roman governors and the new Jewish king, and now to Jews and Gentiles in the capital of the empire.

Mission and evangelism are an integral part and a fundamental reality of the life and ministry of the church. As God has proven faithful to his promises, to his people, and to his word, so God's mission continues to be alive and effective as Jesus' witnesses proclaim the good news with boldness in the midst of suffering, without hindrance despite sometimes fierce opposition. His servants know that God himself, through the Lord Jesus Christ and the presence of the Holy Spirit, empowers their proclamation of the gospel as they go from Jerusalem to the ends of the earth and as they welcome all who come and listen to the good news of Jesus.

The Theology of Acts

Luke announces in his preface of his two-volume work that he is writing his report in order to confirm and consolidate the reliability and the assurance of the teaching communicated in the instruction received by Jesus' followers (Luke 1:4). In other words, Luke writes his gospel and Acts in order to contribute to the teaching going on in the churches established by the apostles and other missionaries. This concern is reflected in Acts 6:4, where prayer and preaching God's word about the Lord Jesus Christ is described as the priority of the apostles in Jerusalem.

Since early Christian teaching focused on the work of God in and through Jesus, Messiah and Savior, and since Acts is part of Luke's two-volume work, it is legitimate, indeed necessary, to analyze and describe the *theological* contribution of Acts, despite the fact that it is a historical narrative with a strong focus on two leaders of the early Christian movement.

While this closing section naturally focuses on Acts, a few key themes will be mentioned that the gospel of Luke and the book of Acts share in common. Several central themes were mentioned in the introduction (see "Luke's Two Volumes"): the centrality of God's purpose to bring salvation to all people through the life and mission of Jesus, God's messianic Son, and through the life and mission of his followers; and the connection between God's gift of salvation and the life of Jesus (gospel) and faith in Jesus (Acts). Other common themes include the role of the Holy Spirit (Luke 1:15, 35; 2:25; 3:16, 22; 4:1, 14, 18; Acts 2:1–4, 16–21, 33, 38; 4:31; 5:32; 8:15–17; 10:44–48); the role of Jerusalem as the city of salvation (Luke 2:22, 38; 9:31, 51; 18:31; 24:47; Acts 1:8; 6:7; 8:14) and as the city of rejection (Luke 13:33–34; 23:28; Acts 4:5–7, 18, 21; 9:13); the emphasis, from a Jewish perspective, on the marginalized or "outsiders" (the poor, women, Samaritans, a eunuch, the Gentiles); and the description of the gospel as "a light for revelation to the Gentiles" (Luke 2:32; Acts 13:47; see Isa 42:6; 49:6).

The theology of Acts has been described competently by a number of scholars.[1]

---

1. Cf. Robert F. O'Toole, *The Unity of Luke's Theology: An Analysis of Luke-Acts* (Wilmington: Glazier, 1984); Joseph A. Fitzmyer, *Luke the Theologian: Aspects of His Teaching* (New York: Paulist, 1989); Howard Clark Kee, *Good News to the Ends of the Earth: The Theology of Acts* (Philadelphia: Trinity Press International, 1990); Darrell L. Bock, "A Theology of Luke-Acts," in *A Biblical Theology of the New Testament* (ed. R. B. Zuck; Chicago: Moody, 1994), 87–166; Jervell, *Theology*;

While the reality of God, the continued initiatives of Jesus, and the power of the Holy Spirit are fundamental in Acts, we begin by reflecting on Christian origins and on the mission of the church.

Christian Origins

In Acts, Luke provides the churches with an account of Christian origins, beginning with Jesus (1:1 – 11) and continuing with the Twelve (1:15 – 26), led by Peter (2:1 – 6:7; 9:31 – 12:25), and with other preachers, such as Stephen (6:8 – 8:3), Philip (8:4 – 40), and Paul (13:1 – 28:31). The fact that Jews and Gentiles come to faith in Jesus despite continued and sometimes ferocious opposition is evidence of the continued work of Jesus in the ministry of his witnesses; this is also a confirmation of the reliability of the gospel that the missionaries and the teachers preach in the churches for which Acts was written.

The basis and the central content of early Christian preaching was the story of Jesus' life, death, and resurrection as the one who embodies the fulfillment of God's promises as Israel's Messiah and the Savior of the world.[2] What Jesus began to do in Galilee and in Jerusalem, he continues to do in the life and work of his followers (1:1). This is why the gospel of Luke and Acts belong together as the two sides of the same reality, connected in historical sequence. Jesus proclaimed the arrival of the kingdom of God, who is fulfilling his promises; Jesus' followers in Jerusalem experience the restoration of Israel as the Holy Spirit is poured out, as miracles happen, as thousands of Jewish people come to faith in Jesus as Israel's Messiah and Savior, and as Jesus' witnesses proclaim the good news of God's salvation in Jerusalem, in Judea, in Samaria, and in the regions of the eastern Mediterranean.

God's program to save the world, promised in the Scriptures for the last days, included the preaching of repentance and forgiveness of sins to all nations, beginning in Jerusalem (cf. Luke 24:47). In Acts, Luke shows how God's plan of salvation for the nations was fulfilled and how Gentiles were included among his people (15:14),[3] from Caesarea to Rome. The new movement emerged out of Jerusalem from Jewish believers in Jesus, and they came to incorporate Gentiles into the community of God's people. Luke assures Gentiles who have come to faith in Jesus that belonging to God's people as uncircumcised Gentiles is part of God's plan.

For many churches who were the first to read Luke's second volume, it described the origins of the Christian community in their city: Jerusalem (1:15; 2:41 – 47),

Barrett, *Acts*, 2:lxxxii-cx; Marshall and Peterson, eds., *Witness to the Gospel*; Petr Pokorný, *Theologie der lukanischen Schriften* (FRLANT 174; Göttingen: Vandenhoeck & Ruprecht, 1998); I. Howard Marshall, *New Testament Theology: Many Witnesses, One Gospel* (Downers Grove, IL: InterVarsity Press, 2004),

155 – 83; Thielman, *Theology*, 111 – 49; Bock, *Acts*, 32 – 42.

2. Acts 2:14 – 36; 2:37 – 40; 3:11 – 26; 4:5 – 22; 5:30 – 32; 13:16 – 41; 17:31; 23:6; 26:22 – 23; 28:20, 23.

3. Cf. Marshall, *New Testament Theology*, 155 – 56.

Caesarea (10:1 – 48), Antioch in Syria (11:19 – 26), Salamis on Cyprus (13:5), Paphos on Cyprus (13:6 – 12), Pisidian Antioch in Galatia (13:13 – 52), Iconium in Galatia (14:1 – 7), Lystra in Galatia (14:8 – 20), Derbe in Galatia (14:21), Perge in Pamphylia (14:24 – 25), Philippi in Macedonia (16:11 – 40), Thessalonica in Macedonia (17:1 – 9), Berea in Macedonia (17:10 – 15), Athens in Achaia (17:16 – 34), Corinth in Achaia (18:1 – 22), and Ephesus in the province of Asia (19:1 – 20:1, 17 – 38). Or it noted the existence of their church in the early years of the Christian movement: churches in Judea (5:16; 9:31), Samaria (8:25), Galilee (9:31), Damascus (9:1 – 2, 10, 19), Tyre (11:19; 21:3 – 4), Sidon (11:19; 27:3), Puteoli (28:13 – 14), and Rome (28:14 – 15). The fact that the New Testament canon contains not only descriptions of the life and ministry of Jesus and letters of various apostles, but also a "history book of the church" underlines that as God has revealed himself in the history of Israel (note the historical books from Genesis to Nehemiah), so he continues to reveal himself in the history of the life and work of Jesus' followers.

The fact that the ending of Acts is open (28:31) reflects that Luke was selective in what he included in Acts. There was much more missionary activity, and probably many more debates, than Luke reported in Acts. Even though Luke has provided a list of the Twelve (1:13) in connection with a description of their missionary commission (1:8, 21 – 22), his subsequent account focuses on the first twelve years of Peter's missionary ministry in Jerusalem, Samaria, the coastal plain, and Caesarea between AD 30 – 42. He provides no information on Peter's work during the next twenty-five years after his departure from Jerusalem (12:17) until his martyr's death in Rome. The reports of further missionaries of the early church, such as Stephen in Jerusalem, Philip in Samaria, and unnamed witnesses who reached the cities of the coastal plain, are brief. We receive no information about the work of John, James, Andrew, Philip, Thomas, Bartholomew, Matthew, James son of Alphaeus, Simon the Zealot, Judas son of James, and Matthias (1:23 – 26).

In the second part of Acts, Luke focuses on Paul's missionary work. Here, again, he reports selectively. He omits information about Paul's missionary work in Arabia and Syria/Cilicia during the first ten years after his conversion (between AD 32 – 42), concentrating on his activities between AD 42 – 57 in Syria, Cyprus, Galatia, Macedonia, Achaia, and the province of Asia, before relating his arrest and imprisonment between AD 57 – 62. While Luke's selectivity may be frustrating for historians of the early church, it probably would have been seen as an encouragement by Luke's readers: God is doing much more in the world than historians record or than what we are personally aware of. What counts is not what is recorded, but what congregations and their missionaries do in faithfulness to their calling as witnesses of Jesus, through God's grace and in the power of the Holy Spirit.

Mission

The narrative structure of Acts demonstrates that the theology of Acts is a theology of mission.[4] Immediately after the prologue, Luke relates Jesus' commission to his disciples to be his witnesses — to explain his life, death, resurrection, exaltation, and continued involvement in the affairs of his people — to the Jews living in Jerusalem, Judea, and Samaria, and to Jews and Gentiles living outside of the Holy Land to the ends of the earth (1:8). The congregations of Jesus' followers are missionary communities whose witnesses are empowered by the Spirit of God and who carry the message of Jesus Christ to the ends of the earth, helping Jews and Gentiles to find the salvation procured by Jesus Christ.[5]

The description of the missionary work of the early church focuses on the continued activity of Jesus in the proclamation of his witnesses. In the gospel, Luke related "all ... that Jesus began to do and to teach" (Acts 1:1), which means that Acts relates what Jesus continues to do and teach, now not only in Galilee and in Jerusalem, but in the whole world, through the witness of his disciples. The "heading" of Acts in 1:1, combined with the missionary commission of 1:8 and the ending of Acts in 28:31, which relates Paul's proclamation of the kingdom of God and teaching about the Lord Jesus Christ "with all boldness and without hindrance," communicates Luke's conviction that the missionary proclamation of Jesus as Israel's Messiah and Savior of the world is part and parcel of the nature of the church. The foundational character of the missionary identity of the church is emphasized in the election of Matthias in 1:15 – 26, who completes the Twelve as a witness of the life, death, and resurrection of Jesus (1:21 – 22).

The call narratives concerning the Twelve (Luke 5:1 – 11; cf. Acts 1:2) and Paul, whose missionary commission is reported three times (9:15 – 16; 22:14 – 15; cf. 26:16 – 18), emphasize the importance of the initiative of God and Jesus Christ in the calling of missionaries (who "left everything," as the Twelve did; cf. Luke 5:11). Paul's description of the gifts that God has given to the church through the Holy Spirit in 1 Cor 12:4 – 11 suggests that since these gifts, ministries, and activities are grouped together, and since apostleship is one among many ministries that do not seem to require a supernatural "direct address" by the risen Lord, the call narratives of the Twelve and of Paul should not be reduced to a principle (a missionary call is necessary) or to a rule (all missionaries must have been directly called by Jesus to full-time missionary ministry). The example of Barnabas confirms this: he was sent

4. I. Howard Marshall, *A Concise New Testament Theology* (Downers Grove, IL: InterVarsity Press, 2008), 55. Cf. Joel B. Green, "'Salvation to the End of the Earth' (Acts 13:47): God as the Saviour in the Acts of the Apostles," in *Witness to the Gospel* (ed. I. H. Marshall and D. Peterson), 83 – 106; Bolt, "Mission."

5. Cf. Andreas J. Köstenberger and Peter T. O'Brien, *Salvation to the Ends of the Earth: A Biblical Theology of Mission* (NSBT 11; Downers Grove, IL: InterVarsity Press, 2001), 157.

by the Jerusalem church to Antioch for the specific task of consolidating the work of missionaries who were already active in the city (11:22), while his later missionary activities are not linked with a specific divine call.[6]

Missionary work involves taking the gospel of Jesus Christ to people, cities, and regions where it has not yet been proclaimed. The apostles proclaim the good news of Jesus in Jerusalem (2:1 – 7:60), in Judea (2:14; 8:1; 9:32 – 43; 10:37), in Samaria (8:4 – 25), and in the regions beyond Palestine, reaching Ethiopians (8:26 – 39), Roman soldiers (10:1 – 11:18), Syrians (11:19 – 26), Cypriots (11:19; 13:4 – 12; 15:39), Phrygians (13:13 – 14:5), Lycaonians (14:6 – 20), Macedonians (16:11 – 17:12), Achaians (17:16 – 18:18), Ionians/Asians (18:19 – 20:1), Roman governors (13:12; 24:1 – 27; 25:1 – 26:32), a Jewish king (25:13 – 26:32), and Romans (28:17 – 31). Not all of these people believe, although thousands do.

Missionary work involves verbal proclamation of the gospel (see the speeches/ sermons of Peter and Paul); discussions and conversations with Jews and Gentiles (note the verb διαλέγομαι)[7] — dialogues with foreign officials (8:30 – 36), would-be believers (19:2 – 4), and philosophers (17:18 – 20, 32); sermons in public venues (2:14 – 36, 37 – 40, 46; 3:11 – 26; 14:15 – 18; 22:1 – 21) and in synagogues (13:5, 16 – 41; 14:1; 17:1, 10, 17; 18:4, 19, 26; 19:8); preaching and teaching in the marketplace (17:17) and in private houses (2:46; 18:7); and speeches before courts of law (4:5 – 22; 5:27 – 33; 25:13 – 26:32).

The missionary activity of the church leads to the salvation of individuals: Cornelius, the Ethiopian official, Saul/Paul, Sergius Paulus in Paphos, Lydia and the jailer in Philippi, Dionysius and Damaris in Athens, Crispus in Corinth, and hundreds, indeed thousands, of Jews and Gentiles between Jerusalem and Rome. The missionary work of the church leads to the establishment of congregations of communities of followers of Jesus.[8]

Such mission work brings reconciliation to divided communities. Many of the new Christian communities consisted of Jews and Gentiles. The problems that led to the Apostles' Council (15:1 – 33) were triggered precisely because the close fellowship of Jewish and Gentile believers in the church in Antioch had been a stumbling block for Jewish Christians, who insisted that Gentile believers must be circumcised and keep the law in its totality. The mission of the church, while not ignoring ethnic differences, overcomes traditional distinctions of insiders and outsiders; it addresses everyone with the gospel, welcoming all who are willing to listen (28:30).

---

6. Cf. Schnabel, *Paul the Missionary*, 382 – 88, for a fuller discussion of the calling of missionaries. See also A. Scott Moreau, Gary Corwin, and Gary B. McGee, *Introducing World Missions: A Biblical, Historical, and Practical Survey* (Grand Rapids: Baker Academic, 2003), 160 – 64.

7. Acts 17:2, 17; 18:4, 19; 19:8, 9; 20:7, 9; 24:12, 25.

8. Cf. Wolfgang Reinhardt, *Das Wachstum des Gottesvolkes* (Göttingen: Vandenhoeck & Ruprecht, 1995); Roger W. Gehring, *House Church and Mission: The Importance of Household Structures in Early Christianity* (Peabody, MA: Hendrickson, 2004).

Missionary work and church growth happen in the midst of opposition and persecution.[9] Peter and John and the rest of the Twelve are repeatedly imprisoned in Jerusalem by the Jewish authorities (4:1 – 4; 5:17 – 18) and by the Idumean king (12:3 – 19). Stephen is killed in Jerusalem (7:58 – 60). Jerusalem believers are imprisoned and tortured and leave the city (8:1 – 4). Believers in Damascus are threatened with persecution (9:1 – 2). James is killed in Jerusalem (12:2). Paul's life is threatened in Damascus (9:23 – 25), Jerusalem (9:29), Pisidian Antioch (13:50 – 51), Iconium (14:5 – 6), and Lystra (14:19). Paul and Silas are imprisoned by Roman officials in Philippi (16:19 – 24); they are persecuted by Jews and Gentiles in Thessalonica (17:5 – 10) and by Jews in Berea (17:13) and Corinth (18:12 – 13). Both the Twelve and Paul are accused by state authorities and defamed by both Jews and Gentiles.

In some places riots take place, as in the riot instigated by the silversmiths in Ephesus (19:23 – 40). Paul is imprisoned in Jerusalem, Caesarea, and Rome for a period of five years (21:27 – 28:31). The external pressure and persecution consolidate the theological identity of the Christian believers as followers of Jesus and as the community of God's people, helping them to correctly interpret the conflict with society, as the prayer of the Jerusalem church in 4:24 – 30 indicates. They realize that

> it is only from the center of the gospel that it is possible to recognize where it is worthwhile to fight and to suffer and where false fronts are set up. It is only by concentrating on their Kyrios that Christians can react to the controversies into which they are dragged in such a manner that the will of God becomes clearer for them and for their opponents.[10]

Followers of Jesus accept suffering for the sake of Jesus and for the sake of the gospel. This acceptance is specifically demonstrated in patient endurance,[11] in the refusal to strike back violently,[12] and in praying for the persecutors.[13]

God and His Purposes

God and his purpose form a major theme in Acts. Luke often highlights the necessity ("it must happen") of events linked with the origins and the expansion of the church.[14] God has foretold in the Scriptures the events that have now transpired.

---

9. Cf. Cunningham, *"Through Many Tribulations"*; Brian M. Rapske, "Opposition to the Plan of God and Persecution," in *Witness to the Gospel* (ed. I. H. Marshall and D. Peterson), 235 – 56.

10. Thomas Söding, "Widerspruch und Leidensnachfolge: Neutestamentliche Gemeinde im Konflikt mit der paganen Gesellschaft," *MTZ* 41 (1990): 137 – 56, 147.

11. Cf. Rom 12:12; 1 Cor 13:7; 1 Thess 1:3; 2 Thess 1:4; Heb 10:32, 36; Rev 1:9; 2:2, 3, 19; 3:10; 13:10; 14:12.

12. Matt 5:38 – 42/Luke 6:29 – 30; Mark 10:42 – 45/Matt 20:25 – 26/Luke 22:25 – 27.

13. Matt 5:44/Luke 6:28; Acts 7:60 (Stephen); cf. Rom 12:14; 1 Cor 4:12.

14. Cf. Charles H. Cosgrove, "The Divine ΔEI in Luke-Acts: Investigations into the Lukan Understanding of God's Providence," *NovT* 26 (1984): 168 – 90; John T. Squires, *The Plan of God in Luke-Acts* (SNTSMS 76; Cambridge: Cambridge Univ. Press, 1993); John T. Squires, "The Plan of God," in *Witness to the Gospel* (ed. I. H. Marshall and D. Peterson), 19 – 39.

The risen Jesus' instruction to the eleven disciples in 1:4 links the coming of the Holy Spirit, which would take place in Jerusalem, with the "promise of the Father." Having understood what Jesus was saying, Peter connects the gift of the Holy Spirit that he and the other followers of Jesus have just received with God's promise of the Holy Spirit, whom Jesus, now at the right hand of God, has poured out (2:33) and whom Jews and Gentiles alike can receive, as promised by God (2:39). Paul explains to the Jews and God-fearers in the synagogue of Pisidian Antioch that the coming of Jesus, who is Israel's Savior, is the fulfillment of God's promise (13:23). In the hearing before governor Festus and King Agrippa II, Paul asserts that he is opposed by the Jewish authorities in Jerusalem because of his conviction that the promise that God made to the fathers, a promise whose fulfillment the Jews were awaiting, has been fulfilled in Jesus, Israel's Messiah and Savior (26:6). Paul can use the phrase "the whole will of God" (20:27) as a summary of the gospel he proclaims.

God's initiative, mediated through Jesus, caused the coming of the Spirit (2:1 – 41), miracles in Jerusalem (3:1 – 10, 12 – 13, 16; 4:9), judgment over sinners (5:1 – 11), the conversion of Samaritans and Ethiopians (8:4 – 40), the conversion of Saul (9:1 – 19; 22:6 – 16; 26:9 – 18), the conversion of Cornelius (10:1 – 11:18; cf. 11:17), the move of Paul and Barnabas to new regions (13:2), the conversion of the Gentiles (15:7 – 8, 12), the missionary work of Paul (14:27; 19:11; 21:19), and the protection of Paul as he is taken to Rome (27:23 – 25). As God's initiatives are central for Luke, the responsibility of the human agents in Acts is "not responsibility in the sense of responsibility for planning events or deciding on strategies" but "the responsibility to be obedient to God."[15] It is no coincidence that the leaders of the church have to be pushed hard by God through a vision (10:9 – 16) and by divine intervention through the Holy Spirit (10:44 – 48) — and eventually (!) by argument (11:11 – 18) — to accept uncircumcised Gentiles as fellow believers. The inclusion of the Gentiles in the people of God is due to a new revelation by God (see also 15:7 – 11, 14).

God and the History of Salvation

The conviction that the recent events are part of God's plan of salvation laid out in Scripture conveys a history of salvation.[16] God's salvation is grounded in and caused by divine acts in history, such as Israel's exodus from Egypt.

God's salvation has now climactically been revealed in the life, death, resurrection, and ascension of Jesus the Messiah and Lord, so that both Jews and Gentiles

---

15. Beverly R. Gaventa, "Initiatives Divine and Human in the Lukan Story World," in *The Holy Spirit and Christian Origins* (FS J. D. G. Dunn; ed. G. N. Stanton, S. C. Barton., and B. W. Longenecker; Grand Rapids: Eerdmans, 2004), 79 – 89, 81.

16. Cf. Jacob Jervell, "Luke's Vision of Salvation History and Its Bearing on His Writing of History," in *History, Literature, and Society in the Book of Acts* (ed. B. Witherington; Cambridge: Cambridge Univ. Press, 1996); John Nolland, "Salvation-History and Eschatology," in *Witness to the Gospel* (ed. I. H. Marshall and D. Peterson), 63 – 81; Sellner, *Heil Gottes*.

are in *need of salvation*.[17] As regards the Jews, their need of salvation is implied in the rejection of Jesus by the Jewish leaders in Jerusalem; people share in this guilt unless they acknowledge Jesus as Messiah and Lord. As regards the Gentiles, they are ignorant of God, a fact, however, that does not provide them with an excuse; they need to repent of their idolatry, turn to the one true God, and believe in Jesus. God's saving activity in the past, as foretold in Scripture and as realized in and through Jesus Christ, implies that it continues into the future "in an ongoing history of Christian mission, of which Luke has reported only the first stage."[18] People are saved not through the preaching of preachers per se, but through God's acts in history for the salvation of people — a reality that is proclaimed by preachers who appeal to their listeners to accept the salvation that God has made possible through Jesus.

It is this conviction and this proclamation that prompt Jewish *accusations* that the followers of Jesus speak against God and the people (6:11; 21:28; 28:17). The Jewish leaders charge believers in Jesus that they are altering the Mosaic law (6:14; 21:21; cf. 25:8), are speaking against the temple (6:13), and are willing to defile it (21:28; cf. 25:8). Luke emphasizes that the life of the congregation of Jesus' followers and the mission of Jesus' witnesses among Jews and among Gentiles realize the anticipated *restoration of Israel* in terms of the *messianic people of God*. Believing in and following Jesus as Israel's Messiah and Savior and worshiping the God of Israel in the name of Jesus constitutes "times of refreshing" (3:20) and the rebuilding of the "fallen tent of David" (15:16).

The congregation (ἐκκλησία) or "church" of believers in Jesus as Israel's Messiah and Savior, including both Jews and Gentiles, is the *one people of God*. Luke shows throughout Acts that God is the "God of the people of Israel" (13:17), " the God of your ancestors/fathers" (3:13; 5:30; 7:32; 22:14; 24:14), and "the God of Abraham, Isaac, and Jacob" (3:13; 7:32) — the God who directed Israel's history (7:2 – 53; 13:17 – 25). Luke emphasizes that what happened in the life, death, resurrection, and exaltation of Jesus and in the life of the church and the missionary work of the witnesses was caused by the God of Israel. This means that Israel's history has become the history of the believing Gentiles, who have become members of God's people (λαός). When God reassures Paul, "there are many of my people in this city" (18:10), the term "people" (λαός) clearly refers *also* to Gentiles (note Paul's exit from the Corinthian Jews in 18:7 and his turn to the Gentiles in 18:6).

The anticipation in the Scriptures that in the last days the nations will come to Zion and worship the one true God has become a reality in this new period of the history of salvation. The fact that the gospel has reached Gentiles and that Gentiles are joining the people of God has been made possible by a new revelation by God,

---

17. Cf. Christoph W. Stenschke, "The Need for Salvation," in *Witness to the Gospel* (ed. I. H. Marshall and D. Peterson), 125 – 44; Stenschke, *Luke's Portrait of Gentiles*; also H.

Douglas Buckwalter, "The Divine Saviour," in *Witness to the Gospel* (ed. I. H. Marshall and D. Peterson), 107 – 23.

18. Marshall, *New Testament Theology*, 173.

who has removed the separation of Jews and Gentiles. This has modified the earlier revelation in the Scriptures about Israel as God's people and Gentiles as sinners, and about the necessity of circumcision and obedience to the food laws for membership in the people of God (10:9 – 16; 11:1 – 18; 15:7 – 11, 14).

God and His Revelation in the Scriptures

Since God's saving activity is the center of Israel's Scriptures, which foretold the coming and the work of Jesus, these Scriptures remain an integral part of the life and proclamation of the church. Luke repeatedly emphasizes that the plan of God to save Jews and Gentiles through Jesus the Messiah and thus to establish the community of the followers of Jesus and their missionary work has been foretold in the Scriptures.[19] This is why Paul asserts in his trial before governor Felix that he believes everything laid down by the Law or written in the Prophets (24:14). Luke includes numerous direct quotations of Scripture,[20] summary references to Scripture,[21] and recitals of scriptural narrative and allusions (7:2 – 53; 13:17 – 25).

For Luke, the Word of God in Scripture is "a word which has been and shall be spoken, since the word is always a prophetic word, a word also heard weekly in the synagogue."[22] There are numerous references to Moses,[23] various prophets,[24] and David,[25] who is himself a prophet and also the father of the Messiah (Luke 1:32; Acts 13:22), the risen and exalted messianic King (Acts 2:25 – 31, 36, with quotation and interpretation of Ps 16:8 – 11). Paul, in his sermon in the synagogue of Pisidian Antioch, interweaves historical survey from Scripture (13:17 – 25), scriptural quotations (13:33, 34, 35), and the message about Jesus as Israel's crucified, risen, and exalted Messiah and Savior (13:23, 26 – 33, 38 – 39), so that the gospel is indissolubly linked with the history of Israel.

The content of the Scriptures, focused on God's promises, is the suffering and death of the Messiah (3:18; 17:3; 26:22 – 23) and his resurrection and exaltation (3:21; 13:33 – 39; 17:3; 26:22 – 23; cf. Luke 24:26, 46); he grants forgiveness of sins (10:43) and is the coming judge (10:42). Luke repeatedly asserts that the Messiah witnessed to in Scripture can only be Jesus (3:18, 21; 10:42, 43; 17:3; 18:28; 26:22, 23). Scripture is not mysterious but clear and unambiguous. When it needs to be "opened" (8:31,

19. On Luke's use of the Old Testament Scriptures, cf. Bock, *Proclamation*; Darrell L. Bock, "Scripture and the Realisation of God's Promises," in *Witness to the Gospel* (ed. I. H. Marshall and D. Peterson), 41 – 62; Jervell, *Theology*, 61 – 75; Kenneth Duncan Litwak, *Echoes of Scripture in Luke-Acts: Telling the History of God's People Intertextually* (London: T&T Clark, 2005); Marshall, "Acts," 513 – 27.

20. Sometimes introduced with the phrase "it is written" (1:20; 7:42; 13:33; 15:15).

21. Acts 3:18, 24; 10:43; 17:3; 18:28; 24:14; 26:23.

22. Jervell, *Theology*, 63.

23. See Acts 3:22; 6:11; 7:20; 13:38; 15:1; 21:21; 26:22; 28:23.

24. See Acts 2:16 (Joel); 3:18; 8:28 (Isaiah); 10:43; 13:15; 15:15; 24:14; 26:22, 27; 28:23.

25. See Acts 1:16; 2:25, 29, 34; 4:25; 7:45; 13:22, 34, 36; 15:16.

35; 17:3), it is not in order to bring out hidden meanings but in order to apply its content to Jesus. This is of crucial importance, because "the messiahship of Jesus and the salvation of Israel are at stake when Scriptures are not understood."[26]

In addition to the use of Scripture in the context of statements about Jesus, the other main scriptural themes in Acts[27] are covenant and promise,[28] the mission of the community,[29] the inclusion of the Gentiles,[30] and the challenge and warning to Israel.[31]

Jesus, Israel's Messiah, Savior, and Lord

Acts is an account of the works of Jesus, the crucified, risen, and exalted Messiah and Savior of Israel (1:1).[32] For Luke, as for Peter and Paul, everything hangs on the God of Israel having raised Jesus.[33] Since both Peter and Paul have encountered Jesus after his crucifixion,[34] they proclaim that God has intervened and raised Jesus from the dead, vindicating him as Israel's Messiah and Savior who sits at God's right hand as Lord (2:29 – 36; 13:33 – 38). While Luke speaks of Jesus' "rising" from the dead (10:41; 17:3; intransitive ἀναστῆναι), he usually emphasizes God as the active subject in Jesus' resurrection, because it is God who raised the dead (26:8): "the God of our Fathers raised up Jesus" (5:30; cf. 3:15; 4:10; 10:41; 17:3; cf. active use of ἐγείρειν; and note the transitive ἀναστῆναι in 2:24, 32; 3:26; 13:33, 34; 17:31).

Since the life, death, resurrection, and exaltation of Jesus is the climactic intervention of God in the history of Israel, the preaching and teaching of the Jerusalem apostles and of Paul consistently focus on Jesus of Nazareth, who died, whom God raised from the dead, who has been exalted to God's right hand, and who is thus Israel's Messiah and Savior.[35] The selection of Matthias to replace Judas among the Twelve illustrates this focus: the task of the apostles is to be witnesses to the life, ministry, death, and resurrection of Jesus the Lord (1:21 – 22).

The central significance of Jesus is presented in Acts 2, a chapter that is programmatic for the Luke's second volume (as Luke 4 is programmatic for the gospel).[36] Peter interprets the coming of the Holy Spirit, who is the transforming presence of God among his people, not only as the fulfillment of Scripture but also, equally important, as the result of Jesus' resurrection, ascension, and exaltation as Lord of the

---

26. Jervell, *Theology*, 68.

27. Bock, "Scripture," 49 – 61; see also Evans, "Prophecy and Polemic," 209 – 10.

28. Cf. 2:16 – 39; 3:22 – 26; 13:13 – 41; 15:14 – 18; cf. Luke 1:54 – 55, 68 – 70.

29. Cf. 4:24 – 26; 13:47; 28:25 – 28.

30. Cf. 11:15 – 18; 13:47; 26:20, 23; cf. 1:8; Luke 2:32; 24:47.

31. Cf. 3:22 – 23; 4:25 – 26; 7:42 – 43, 49 – 50; 13:41; 28:26 – 27.

32. Cf. Barrett, *Acts*, 2:lxxxv.

33. Jervell, *Theology*, 32.

34. Peter: 1:3 – 8, 22; 2:32; 3:15; 5:32; 10:39 – 40; Paul; 9:4 – 6; 22:6 – 8; 26:13 – 18.

35. See the studies of Strauss, *Davidic Messiah*; H. Douglas Buckwalter, *The Character and Purpose of Luke's Christology* (SNTSMS 89; Cambridge: Cambridge Univ. Press, 1996).

36. Cf. Turner, *Power from on High*, 267 – 315.

Spirit (2:33). This means that the Spirit of God has become the Spirit of Jesus and that the promised restoration of Israel and the promised salvation for the Gentiles become a reality through the work of the Spirit, who does his saving work through the community of Jesus' followers empowered by the Spirit.[37] Thus the focus of the history of salvation has shifted from the Mosaic law to Jesus: following Jesus, believing in Jesus, and adhering to his teaching form "the necessary and sufficient condition of belonging to the Israel of fulfillment (3:22 – 23)."[38]

Describing Jesus' significance, Luke emphasizes his resurrection, ascension, glorification, granting the gift of God's Holy Spirit, and guiding and empowering his disciples as witnesses of the gospel. Jesus' death is not a focus of Luke's narrative in Acts; he does not use the preaching of the apostles to explain the purpose of Jesus' death. But Luke clearly knew about the saving significance of Jesus' death as an atonement for sins. In 20:28 Jesus' bloody death is described as the means by which God "acquired" the church as his people. The two main gifts of salvation for Luke are the forgiveness of sins and the gift of the Holy Spirit (2:36 – 40).

The titles used for Jesus in Acts are closer to Old Testament and Jewish thought than elsewhere in the New Testament.[39] Jesus is the "holy one" (ὁ ὅσιος; 2:27; 13, 35). He is the one who is dedicated to God and to his divine plan of salvation. Jesus is the "Righteous One" (ὁ δίκαιος; 3:14; 7:52; 22:14). Jesus is the one who fulfills the will of God. Jesus is God's "Servant" (ὁ παῖς; 3:13, 26; 4:27, 30). Jesus fulfills the task of the suffering Servant of Isaiah's Servant Songs. Jesus is the "Prophet" (ὁ προφήτης; 3:22, 7:37), the mouthpiece of God who launches the new era of salvation that the prophets of old had promised. Jesus is the Son of David. Although Luke does not use the title "son of David" (υἱὸς Δαυίδ) in Acts,[40] he portrays Jesus as David's son who fulfills the promise that David's kingdom would be restored to Israel (2:29 – 36; cf. 13:32, 34 – 37; 15:15 – 18) and who is thus King (17:7).

Jesus is the "Savior" (ὁ σωτήρ; 5:31; 13:23), the promised descendant of David who delivers God's people. Thus Jesus is the "Messiah" (ὁ χριστός), the Anointed One who fulfills God's promises for his people and thus brings salvation. "Messiah" is the most important title for Jesus in Acts.[41] The Jerusalem believers refer in their prayer to "your holy Servant Jesus, whom you have anointed [ἔχρισας]" (4:27). Peter, in his sermon before Cornelius and his friends, describes "how God anointed [ἔχρισεν] Jesus of Nazareth with the Holy Spirit and with power, how he traveled from place to place doing good and healing all who were in the power of the devil, because God was with him" (10:38).

---

37. On the background of the restoration of Israel in Isaiah's prophecies cf. Pao, *New Exodus*, 111 – 34.

38. Turner, "Sabbath," 120.

39. Cf. Jervell, *Apostelgeschichte*, 93 – 94; Fitzmyer, *Luke*, 1:197 – 219.

40. Cf. Luke 18:38 – 39; 20:41.

41. Twenty-five occurrences in Acts; cf. 2:31, 36, 38; 3:6, 18, 20; 4:10, 26; etc.; for Paul cf. 9:22; 16:18; 17:3; 18:5, 28; 24:24; 26:23; 28:31.

Most English translations, unfortunately, use the transliteration "Christ" for ὁ χριστός; since the Greek word ὁ χριστός renders the Hebrew *māšîaḥ*, a better transliteration in English is "Messiah," which would not be mistaken as a personal name. Whether χριστός functioned for some Christians as a name ("Jesus Christ," comparable to "M. Tullius Cicero"), or whether the term always retained its titular meaning ("Messiah"), Jewish Christians would never have forgotten the Hebrew origin of χριστός, which describes Jesus as the Savior whom Israel expected in the last days. For Luke (and Peter and Paul) Jesus is the one in whom God has fulfilled the promises given to God's people. Jesus is the Anointed One of Israel, God's agent who brings salvation, forgiveness of sins (2:38; 5:31; 10:43; 13:38 – 39; 26:18), the gift of the Holy Spirit (2:38), and eternal life (13:46, 48; cf. 11:18; also 3:15: Jesus is "the Author of Life").

Finally, Jesus is the "Lord" (ὁ κύριος),[42] a title that puts Jesus on the same level as Yahweh and expresses Jesus' authority over his followers.[43]

The Holy Spirit

Luke opens Acts with references to the Holy Spirit, which are significant since they come at the transition from the gospel (Luke 24:49) to the book of Acts (Acts 1:2, 5, 8), and at the transition from the ministry of Jesus to the ministry of the apostles.[44] The restoration of the kingdom of God to Israel (1:6) takes places as God grants the Holy Spirit through Jesus to Jesus' followers (1:4, 5, 8), who proclaim the good news as Jesus' witnesses from Jerusalem to the ends of the earth (1:8). As God had anointed Jesus of Nazareth with the Holy Spirit and thus with divine power, through which he healed and delivered people from the devil's oppression (10:38, which adds the explanatory phrase "because God was with him," a quality that is tied to the presence of God's Spirit), so the risen and exalted Jesus grants the Holy Spirit to his followers as the powerful and transforming presence of God.

The exalted Messiah receives and pours out the divine Spirit (2:33, 39). The coming of the Holy Spirit is a manifestation of the fulfillment of God's promises reiterated by John the Baptist and confirmed by Jesus. The presence of the Spirit is the tangible presence of God, whose reality has been manifested in Jesus' life, death, resurrection, and exaltation, whose power transforms the followers of Jesus and who empowers the apostles to be Jesus' witnesses from Jerusalem to the ends of the earth. Jesus' sta-

---

42. Acts 1:6, 21; 4:33; 7:59; 8:16, 26; 9:1, 27, 35, 42; 10:36; 11:20; 15:11, 26, 36; 16:31; 19:5, 13; 21:13; 22:8, 19; 23:11; 26:15; 28:31.

43. Fitzmyer, *Luke*, 1:204 – 5; Marshall, *New Testament Theology*, 175. Also Jervell, *Apostelgeschichte*, 96; Jervell, *Theology*, 29, wants to limit the meaning of the title to Jesus' rule over Israel.

44. On Luke's view on the Holy Spirit see Turner, *Power from on High*; idem, "Restoration"; also Max M. B. Turner, "The Spirit and Salvation in Luke-Acts," in *The Holy Spirit and Christian Origins* (FS James D. G. Dunn; ed. G. N. Stanton, S. C. Barton, and B. W. Longenecker; Grand Rapids: Eerdmans, 2004), 103 – 16; Jervell, *Theology*, 43 – 49.

tus as exalted messianic Savior who fulfills God's promises and pours out God's Spirit is intimately connected with the purposes of God, who is restoring Israel and who will grant salvation to the Gentiles. This connection can be seen in the fact that the first extended speech in Acts that explains the coming of the Holy Spirit as the Spirit of prophecy (2:14 – 36) leads straight into the first missionary sermon (2:38 – 40).

The Spirit is the "Holy Spirit" (thirty-nine times in Acts) and thus God's Spirit; once Luke speaks of "the Spirit of Jesus" (16:7). The Spirit is "the promise of the Father" (1:4), which has been granted through Jesus who pours out the Spirit on all who believe in him (2:17 – 18, 33; cf. 10:45 – 47): "Exalted to God's right hand, he has received from the Father the promised Holy Spirit, whom he has poured out" (2:33). Since this assertion explains the observable phenomena of wind, fire, and the speaking of unlearned languages, and since the Spirit is described as being active in the life and witness of the church, the Spirit is seen as a third form of divine activity.[45]

The Holy Spirit is repeatedly mentioned in Acts[46] as the transforming power of God bringing about the restoration of Israel, leading Jews in Jerusalem and from many regions to acknowledge Jesus as Israel's Messiah and divine Savior (cf. 2:9 – 11, 37 – 42). The Holy Spirit creates a community of people with diverse backgrounds, united in faith in Jesus as Savior and Lord — a community that includes Jews, Samaritans, Ethiopians, Romans, Syrians, Greeks, Galatians, Lycaonians, Macedonians, Achaians, and Asians who come to faith in Jesus.

The Spirit is the distinguishing characteristic of the believers in Jesus. He is God's gift to whose who repent and believe in Jesus as Israel's Messiah and Savior (2:38; 9:17; 13:52). Stephen is described as "a man full of faith and the Holy Spirit" (6:5; cf. 6:3, 10; 7:55). The believing Samaritans and the disciples of John the Baptist in Ephesus are bona fide believers only when they receive the Holy Spirit (8:15 – 17; 19:1 – 7). The converted Gentiles are bona fide believers and members of God's people because they have received the Holy Spirit (10:11 – 48; 11:15 – 18; 15:8). Saul's conversion entails receiving the Holy Spirit (9:17). The Spirit poured out by Jesus (2:4, 33, 38) grants wonders and signs done by the apostles (2:43) and made well-to-do believers willing to sell property to help needy Christians (2:44 – 45; cf. 4:32 – 37). Since the Holy Spirit, as the powerful and transforming presence of God, is guiding the church, deceit offends the Spirit, with serious consequences in the case of Ananias and Sapphira (5:3 – 4).[47]

Believers who have been granted the Spirit when they came to faith in Jesus are, on special occasions, "filled" with the Holy Spirit (4:8, 31; 6:3, 5; 7:55; 9:17; 11:24; 13:9, 52). The Holy Spirit directs the ministry of the church in Jerusalem

45. The phrase is from Barrett, *Acts*, 2:lxxxiv.

46. Cf. 4:8; 5:32; 6:3, 10; 7:51, 55; 8:29; 9:17, 31; 10:19, 44; 11:12, 24; 13:2, 4, 52; 15:8, 28; 16:6; 19:2, 21; 20:22; 21:4; 28:25.

47. It is thus incorrect when Barrett, *Acts*, 2:lxxxiv, claims that Luke "does not see the work of the Spirit in the moral renovation of human life."

(4:31; 15:28), of Peter (4:8; 10:19; 11:12), of Philip (8:29, 39), of Barnabas (11:24), of the church in Antioch (13:2), and of Paul (13:4, 9; 16:6, 7; 19:21; 20:22). The Holy Spirit appoints leaders in the local congregations (20:28) and speaks to the church through the Scriptures (1:16; 4:25; 28:25). The Holy Spirit grants invasive praise (2:4, connected with the supernatural ability to speak in unlearned languages; also 10:46; 19:6), words of prophecy (11:28; 20:23; 21:4, 11), and bold proclamation (4:31).[48] The Holy Spirit directs missionary initiatives (1:8; 13:4; 16:6, 7).

The Church

Believers in Jesus as Israel's royal Messiah and Savior are God's new people, to which all who repent belong; they believe in Jesus as Israel's exalted Messiah for the forgiveness of their sins, are immersed in water in the name of Jesus, and have received the Holy Spirit (2:38).[49] The church is God's people who experience the fulfillment of his promises, the restoration of Israel, and the incorporation of believing Gentiles. The church is God's people living between the death, resurrection, and exaltation of the Messiah Jesus, who has poured out the Spirit (1:2 – 5, 6 – 9), and the return of Jesus at the time of the "restoration of all things" (3:21).

In Acts, the church (ἐκκλησία) is, foremost, the local congregation of the believers in Jesus; it is the visible entity of those have come to faith in Jesus.[50] The first congregation was in Jerusalem. Subsequently congregations were established in Lydda, Joppa, Damascus, Samaria, Caesarea, Tyre, Sidon, Tarsus, Antioch, Salamis, Paphos, Pisidian Antioch, Iconium, Lystra, Derbe, Perge, Philippi, Thessalonica, Berea, Athens, Corinth, Ephesus, Troas, Miletus, Puteoli, and Rome. The individual churches came into existence through the preaching and teaching of the Twelve, Philip, Barnabas, Paul, and missionaries whose names Luke does not record.

As the first church, the congregation in Jerusalem plausibly served, for Luke, as a model for all other congregations. Acts 1 – 2 emphasizes the unity of the origins of the church in the one Lord (i.e., in the person, work, and commission of Jesus) and in the one Spirit (i.e., in the power of God's presence in the lives of Jesus' followers). This unity of origin is represented by a unity of place (the church of Jerusalem is *the* church in Acts 1 – 7) and a unity of practice of a community that lived and worshiped with "one heart and mind" (4:32).[51]

---

48. For "freedom of speech" in preaching see also 2:29; 4:13, 29; 9:27 – 28; 13:46; 14:3; 18:26; 26:26; 28:31.

49. On the church in Acts cf. David P. Seccombe, "The New People of God," in *Witness to the Gospel* (ed. I. H. Marshall and D. Peterson), 349 – 72; Peterson, "Worship of the New Community"; Loveday C. A. Alexander, "Community and Canon: Reflections on the Ecclesiology of Acts," in *Einheit der Kirche im Neuen Testament* (ed. A. A. Alexeev, C. Karakolis, and U.

Luz; WUNT 218; Tübingen: Mohr Siebeck, 2008), 45 – 78; Rowe, *World Upside Down*, 17 – 137.

50. On the church as a "narrative character" in Luke's second volume, see Richard P. Thompson, *Keeping the Church in Its Place: The Church as Narrative Character in Acts* (New York: T&T Clark, 2006).

51. Cf. Alexander, "Community and Canon," 54 – 57.

The large congregation in Jerusalem met in Solomon's Portico on the Temple Mount, and groups of believers met in private homes (2:46). The statement that they met "each day" means that every day some meeting of believers took place. There seems to have been minimal organization at the beginning: the Twelve, chosen by Jesus to be fishers of people as his witnesses (Luke 5:10; Acts 1:8), apparently oversaw the daily meetings and the distribution of money and food to the needy among the believers. When this arrangement led to difficulties, i.e., when Greek-speaking widows were neglected, the group of Seven was appointed to better organize this particular ministry (6:1 – 6).

The unity of practice is seen in the key characteristics of the meetings of believers: teaching, fellowship, breaking of bread, and prayers (2:42). (1) "Teaching" is one of the main terms that describe apostolic speech.[52] This teaching focused on Jesus, Israel's Messiah, Savior, and Lord, on God's new revelation through Jesus' death, resurrection, and exaltation, on the transforming presence of the Holy Spirit, on the integration of new believers into the new community of God's people, and on God's word revealed in the Scriptures, which are read, explained, and applied to the lives of the believers. It is because of their teaching that the Twelve provoke the opposition of the Jewish authorities in Jerusalem.[53]

(2) "Fellowship" means that the members of the messianic congregations are "one" because they have all accepted Jesus as Israel's messianic Savior and have received God's Spirit. The church is a fellowship because the believers meet at a particular place, listen to the same teaching, praise God, eat meals together, love each other, and share material resources with needy believers.[54]

(3) The "breaking of bread" includes sharing meals as an expression of belonging to the same family; it includes the remembrance and celebration of the death and resurrection of Jesus.

(4) Constant and joyful "prayers" characterize Christians because they acknowledge God's presence in their midst through the Spirit, his continual transforming of their lives, and his extending the scope of the church through Jesus' witnesses, whose ministry is often opposed and who thus need intercessory prayer.[55]

In addition to these four essentials, evangelism in the wider community and missionary work in other cities is an ecclesial reality for Luke. Peter proclaims the good news of Jesus in Jerusalem (3:11 – 26; 4:31), as do presumably the Twelve and Stephen (6:7 – 10). When the Jerusalem church hears that people in Samaria have come to faith, they send Peter and John (8:14); when they hear about conversions of Greeks and Syrians in Antioch, they send Barnabas (11:22). The church in Antioch

---

52. Cf. 11:26; 15:1, 35; 20:20; 21:21, 28. Cf. ibid., 58.

53. Cf. 4:2, 18; 5:21, 28, 42.

54. Cf. 4:32 – 34; 5:1 – 11. "Practical" fellowship is also seen in 6:1; 9:36 – 39; 11:29 – 30.

55. Cf. 3:1; 6:4; 10:9; 11:5; 16:25; 22:17; prayer for particular situations is mentioned in 1:14, 24; 6:6; 8:15; 9:40; 12:5, 12; 13:3; 14:23; 20:36; 21:5; 28:8.

sends Paul and Barnabas to initiate a new phase of missionary work in the cities of Cyprus and southern Galatia (13:1 – 4).

The evangelism of the congregations and the missionary expansion of the church indicate that the church in Acts was characterized by unity as well as by diversity.[56] The diversity of the church can be seen right at the beginning in Acts 1: Jesus commissioned twelve witnesses, not one — which points to an inherent diversity (even though Luke narrates the ministry of only one of the Twelve, i.e., Peter). In the subsequent chapters Luke depicts a diversity of leadership,[57] diversity of practice,[58] diversity of place,[59] and a diversity of mission.[60]

The believers in Jesus were called "Christians" (Χριστιανοί) for the first time in Antioch (11:26). This was apparently coined by the Roman authorities in the context of disturbances in the city resulting from the life and missionary work of the local believers, which incorporated an increasing number of believing Gentiles into the church; this fact established the public character of the local church and the ever-present potential for conflict.[61] Conflict resulted when, for example, Jewish believers in Jesus ate with uncircumcised Gentile believers who did not keep the food laws, abandoning the traditional apartheid required by Scripture (15:1 – 2, 6 – 29), and when Gentile believers no longer worshiped the gods of the Greco-Roman pantheon and thus abandoned their traditional customs (16:20 – 21; 19:23 – 28).

While the second occurrence of the term "Christian" (Χριστιανός; 26:28) is connected with the acknowledgment of the Jewish king Agrippa II that Paul was innocent of the charge of sedition (26:32), the conflict of the believers in the local congregations with both their Jewish and their Greek and Roman neighbors con-

---

56. Cf. Alexander, "Community and Canon," 59 – 67, for the following points.

57. Note the Seven (6:1 – 6), Stephen and Philip as preachers (6:8 – 15; 8:5 – 13), Barnabas (11:22 – 24), James (11:30; 12:17; 15:4 – 29), elders (11:30; 15:4, 22; cf. in Paul's mission, 14:23; 20:17), Saul/Paul (9:1 – 25), Paul and Barnabas (chs. 13 – 14), Paul (chs. 16 – 21), Judas and Silas (15:30 – 35), Paul and Silas (15:36 – 17:15). In view of the description of the Seven, put in charge of caring for widows, as "filled with the Spirit" (6:3; cf. 6:5, 10), it does not seem helpful to distinguish between the apostles as embodying the "itinerant charismatic strand in early Christianity" in contrast to the elders of the Jerusalem church as nonitinerant "community organizers" (Alexander, "Community and Canon," 73 with n. 71, following Gerd Theissen, *The Social Setting of Pauline Christianity: Essays on Corinth* [orig. 1982; repr., Philadelphia: Fortress, 2004], 27 – 76). The conclusion of Alexander, "Community and Canon, " 75, is helpful, with the caveat that instead of competition, we should more plausibly see cooperation, correlation, and supplementation: "What Luke presents ... is not a unilateral attempt to exert either 'top-down' or 'bottom-up' authority, but a genuine at-

tempt at mutual listening and discernment under the guidance of the Holy Spirit. The competing loci of authority as checks and balances on each other: old churches and new, charisma and order, global and local, testimony and tradition."

58. The pattern of repentance, baptism in the name of Jesus Christ, forgiveness of sins, and the gift of the Holy Spirit (2:38) is varied, at least in terms of the elements mentioned by Luke, in Samaria (8:12, 14 – 17, 18 – 19), on the road to Gaza (8:36 – 38), in Damascus (9:18; cf. 22:14 – 16), in Caesarea (10:44 – 48), and in Ephesus (19:4 – 5).

59. While Jerusalem is *the church* in Acts 1 – 8, it becomes *a church*, i.e., one of many local churches between Jerusalem and Rome.

60. Mission to Jews (Acts 1 – 7), mission to Samaritans and proselytes (?) (Acts 8), mission to God-fearers (10:1 – 11:18), mission to Gentiles (11:20; 13 – 21). In view of the missionary initiatives of the Jerusalem church, it is difficult to see how the church in Jerusalem can be described, in comparison with the church in Antioch, as "a much more static, centralized model of ἐκκλησία" (Alexander, "Community and Canon," 72).

61. Rowe, *World Upside Down*, 126 – 35.

tinued to create problems that led to ostracism, public accusations and defamation, eviction from the city, and the attempt to secure death sentences. These conflicts led to more severe persecutions, particularly in connection with the emperor cult, in subsequent centuries. Since the church is the community of people who believe that God has revealed himself in Jesus, Israel's Messiah and the only Savior, living out their convictions in the way they relate both to fellow believers, to contemporary culture, and to Greeks and Romans, such conflicts were inevitable. As followers of Jesus, they bore such sufferings willingly, "full of joy that they had been considered worthy to be insulted for the sake of the Name" (5:41).

Acts and the Church Today

The book of Acts is a narrative, not a systematic theology. This truism has immediate ramifications for the role of this text for the church. Even though the claim that Acts does not contain direct theological statements[62] is obviously wrong — one has to think only of Peter's declaration in 2:36 ("Therefore, let all the house of Israel know with certainty that God has made him both Lord and Messiah, this Jesus whom you crucified"), or of his statement in 4:12 ("Salvation can be found in no one else, because there is no other name in the whole world given to human beings through which we are to be saved") — it is obvious that Luke's main concern in Acts is not to provide a systematic presentation of the teaching of the early Christians. This raises the question of how to use Acts in the context of the teaching and preaching ministry of the church.

Since Acts is primarily a historical narrative, the question of normativity becomes an issue.[63] What was normal for the church in Jerusalem may not be taken by Luke to be the norm for the churches who read his work. The followers of Jesus in Jerusalem had all things in common (Acts 2:45; 4:32); does Luke regard this as a norm for all believers in all churches? The answer could be yes, if he indeed describes the life of the Jerusalem church as an ideal that all churches should emulate. Yet Luke could be merely providing a historical account of the first years of the Jerusalem church, which later became so poor that many believers needed financial assistance from other churches (Acts 11:27 – 30; cf. Gal 2:10).[64]

Since Luke does not treat the history of the early church as an entirely unique period of the history of salvation, it can be assumed that he was convinced that what God was doing through Jesus Christ and through the power of the Spirit, Christians in all churches should experience and be involved in. This is particularly true when

---

62. Cf. Jervell, *Apostelgeschichte*, 91.

63. Cf. I. Howard Marshall, *The Acts of the Apostles* (New Testament Guides; Sheffield: Sheffield Academic Press, 1992), 101 – 5; Fernando, *Acts*, 31 – 41; Witherington, *Acts*, 97 – 102.

64. Note Paul's collection for the believers in Jerusalem, 1 Cor 16:1 – 4; 2 Cor 8 – 9; Rom 15:25 – 28.

Luke's narrative provides not only a description of events but a piece of teaching. Thus, the missionary activity of the early Christians, grounded in Jesus' commission (Acts 1:8), surely is described as a mandate for all churches. Nevertheless, the specific actions of missionaries such as Peter and Paul are described without the necessary implication that, for example, Paul's focus on cities is a model for all missionary work — note that in his gospel, Luke repeatedly reports that Jesus visited villages,[65] an emphasis that we do not find in Acts.[66]

Another example is the miracles of Acts. The fact that miracles are mentioned in two of Luke's summaries (2:43; 5:12) indicates that Luke regards "signs and wonders" as paradigmatic for the church; they are a regular manifestation of God's presence in the church, which provokes awe among those who witness the miracles. Thus understood, it becomes obvious why the miracles in Acts function as a contrast with magic (13:6 – 12): "miracle is not about technique or influencing God but about God's sovereign activity in spreading the gospel."[67] Other functions of the miracles in Acts are the authentication of the gospel message (2:22; 4:10, 30), the establishment of a link with the salvation-history of the Old Testament (judgment among the people of God: Achan/Ananias and Sapphira, 5:1 – 11; the prophecy of Isa. 35:4 is fulfilled in the healing of lame men, 3:1 – 10; 14:8 – 18), and the point that the ministry of the apostles is parallel to the ministry of Jesus (note the exorcisms of demons, 5:16; 8:7; 16:16 – 24; 19:12, and the healings, 3:1 – 10; 9:32 – 35; 9:36 – 43; 14:8 – 18; 20:7 – 10; 28:7 – 10).

Since it is God who causes miracles to happen, not the apostles or Paul as "miracle workers," it is a moot point whether miracles should always, or at least ideally, accompany the proclamation of the gospel. It is God, not the missionary, evangelist, or the local church, who determines whether miracles happen. Christians believe God can work through miracles today, and they pray for the sick to be healed, as the risen and exalted Jesus Christ continues to have the power to heal the sick and to drive out demons. At the same time, Jesus' power did not prevent Peter from being thrown into prison (4:1; 5:18; 12:3), Stephen and James from being killed (7:58 – 60; 12:2), and Paul from being shipwrecked (27:13 – 44).

Teaching rather than description appears to be the main purpose of Luke's summary passages that outline the behavior and values of the Jerusalem church (Acts 2:43 – 47; 4:32 – 37). Elements of these summaries are implicitly used as criteria to evaluate the uneven distribution of food to the Greek-speaking widows in the Jerusalem church (Acts 6) — a story that indicates how Luke wanted his comments about having all things in common to be understood and applied.

65. Luke 5:17; 8:1; 9:6; 10:38; 13:22; 17:12.

66. Each of the cities of the Greco-Roman world often controlled dozens of villages; cf. Christof Schuler, *Ländliche Siedlungen und Gemeinden im hellenistischen und römischen Kleinasien* (Vestigia 50; München: Beck, 1998); cf. Douglas E.

Oakman, "The Countryside in Luke-Acts," in *The Social World of Luke-Acts: Models for Interpretation* (ed. J. H. Neyrey; Peabody, MA: Hendrickson, 1991), 151 – 79.

67. Peter H. Davids, "Miracles in Acts," *DLNT*, 750.

The main focus of the speeches of Acts surely reflects Luke's convictions about the pastoral and missionary proclamation of the church. The life, death, resurrection, and exaltation of Jesus; the presence and power of the Holy Spirit of God; the reality of the one true God as the Creator of the world to whom all people are responsible; the coming judgment; the resurrection of the dead; the necessity of repentance and of faith in Jesus Christ; the reality and necessity of missionary work—these are themes that are both fundamental and central. It is telling that questions of church government are few and far between.

The biographical focus of many passages in Acts suggests that Luke intends his readers to emulate the deeds of men like Peter, Philip, Barnabas, James, and Paul, and of women like Lydia and Priscilla. The negative example of Ananias and Sapphira, on the other hand, indicates that Luke's characters are not always ideals meant to be followed.

The hermeneutical process of applying the book of Acts in general and the missionary work of the early church in particular involves the following observations.[68] (1) A close reading of the text will produce more compelling results than a casual reading or a reading that treats the biblical text only as proof texts. Serious exegesis does not solve all problems of application, but the reading of Acts in the historical context of the Greco-Roman world of the first century, for example, will at least help the teacher and preacher to avoid mistakes caused, e.g., by an anachronistic understanding of the text.

(2) Luke tells the *story* of the life and the missionary work of the early church. Here we need to remember that the authority of Scripture is not only connected with its content but is also a function of its form. For example, the proverbs of the Old Testament are not divine promises for the individual believer. Similarly, the narratives of Acts should not be turned into rules or principles. The fact that Paul always visited the local synagogue first does not imply the missiological principle that evangelism by Christians today must always begin with outreach to the local Jewish community. Stories function not as rules but as *paradigms*, i.e., as models for the church. The fact that Paul's sermons before Jewish audiences are different in terms of structure, argumentative flow, and appeal to the Scriptures from his speeches before Gentile audiences is a paradigm for missionary preaching; the ethnic, religious, and social identity of the audience helps to shape the structure, content, and linguistic formulations of sermons.

(3) Some texts do formulate *principles*. This is obvious for Paul's letters. For example, in 1 Cor 14 he establishes the principle of intelligibility for what worshipers contribute during their weekly gathering—a principle that is formulated regarding the practice of speaking in unlearned languages, but that can also be applied to other

68. Cf. Schnabel, *Paul the Missionary*, 376–82. Cf. Richard B. Hays, *The Moral Vision of the New Testament: Community, Cross, New Creation. A Contemporary Introduction to New Testament Ethics* (New York: HarperCollins, 1996), 207–14, 291–98, who comments on the application of New Testament ethics to the ethical behavior of Christians today.

realities of the life and ministry of the church. In Acts, such principles are found particularly in Luke's summary passages.

(4) Some texts formulate *rules*, direct commandments or prohibitions of specific conduct. Jesus' promise and missionary commission ("you will receive power when the Holy Spirit comes upon you, and you will be my witnesses in Jerusalem and in all Judea and Samaria, even as far as the ends of the earth," 1:8) is an important example in Acts. Peter's answer to the question regarding the proper reaction to the life, death, resurrection, and exaltation of Jesus ("Repent, and be immersed, every one of you, in the name of Jesus the Messiah, on the basis of the forgiveness of sins, and you will receive the gift of the Holy Spirit," 2:38) also formulates a rule.

(5) The *symbolic world* of Acts provides fundamental categories through which we are to understand and interpret the history of salvation and the identity of the church. Examples from Acts are the following.[69] Jerusalem, mentioned sixty-one times in Acts, symbolizes the Jewish context of the origins and the identity of the church. The journey from Jerusalem to Judea, to Samaria, and to the ends of the earth (1:8) symbolizes the identity of the church as people on the move toward those who need salvation. The outward expansion of the church symbolizes the church as focused not on her own needs but on the world beyond.

The prisons that Luke mentions with astonishing frequency,[70] while literal for the apostles in Jerusalem and for Paul, are at the same time symbols both of the continuous opposition the church faces and of the open doors that God again and again provides. The arrests, hearings, trials, and defense, while again literal in the experience of the early church, are metaphors for the gospel that is being tried and defended. The numerous geographical terms and the many people and people groups whom Luke mentions in Acts symbolize the reality that the life and mission of the church are not focused on theory and discussion but on people and places. Noting the symbolic world of a work is not the same as allegorization. Analyzing words and motifs in the text as symbols must not lead to allegorizing the text in which an ever-expanding number of terms, objects, or persons mentioned in the text are given symbolical meanings while the historical content is disregarded.

When we read the texts of Acts with a view to preaching and teaching, we need to take care that we read not in one mode: only as rules, or only as principles, or only as paradigms, or only as symbols. We must also be careful not to use one mode of appeal to New Testament texts in order to override the emphasis of another mode. A principle such as the centrality of Jesus as the crucified Savior for the missionary message cannot be dodged by appealing to the paradigm of Paul's behavior as a missionary, who adapts his preaching to his audiences (e.g., 14:15 – 17; 17:22 – 31) and who becomes "all things to all people" (1 Cor 9:22).

---

69. Cf. Leland Ryken, James C. Wilhoit, and Tremper Longman, eds., *Dictionary of Biblical Imagery* (Downers Grove, IL: InterVarsity Press, 1998), 7 – 9 for the following comments.

70. Acts 4:3; 5:18; 8:3; 12:4, 6; 16:23; 22:4; 23:18; 24:27; 25:14, 27; 26:10; 27:1, 42.

Most of the texts in Acts are presented in the form of story, describing paradigmatically the life and the missionary work of the early church. Consequently, the Christian church that seeks to take the form of these texts seriously will be drawn to the *paradigmatic mode*. Luke's narrative is a fundamental resource for the life of the church and for the task of missions today. Repeated patterns of behavior often suggest a template for Christian behavior today. Divine approval, or disapproval, in the text for a particular conviction, experience, or behavior is a clue for the application of the text.

The picture that then emerges is complemented by the principles and the rules concerning the task of reaching people with the news of salvation through Jesus Christ, and by modes of discourse that we also find in Acts, and even more so in other New Testament texts.

Scripture Index

1 Corinthians

Other Ancient Literature Index

Philo

Rabbinic Literature

Early Christian Literature and Ancient Church

Subject Index

Author Index

Matthew

Grant R. Osborne

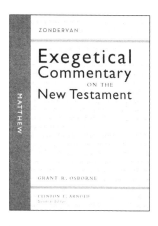

In this volume, Grant Osborne offers pastors, students, and teachers a focused resource for reading the first book of the New Testament. Through the use of graphic representations of translations, succinct summaries of main ideas, exegetical outlines, and other features, Osborne presents Matthew's gospel message with precision and accuracy. Because of this series' focus on the textual structure of the Scriptures, readers will better understand the literary elements of Matthew, comprehend the author's revolutionary goals, and ultimately discovering their vital claims upon the church today.

Luke

David E. Garland

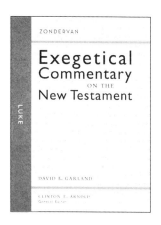

Luke sought to assure believers about the truth of the gospel (1:4) and to advance their understanding of God's ways in the world as revealed in Christ's ministry, death, and resurrection. Luke wrote as a historian, theologian, and pastor, and Garland's commentary strives to follow suit in assisting those who will preach and teach the text and those who seek to understand it better. The commentary presents a translation through a diagram that helps visualize the flow of thought, provides a summary of the central message of the passages, reveals how they function within the gospel, and offers an exegetical outline and verse-by-verse commentary that takes notice of Jewish and Greco-Roman background evidence that sheds light on the text. Christians interpret the Bible to make sense of their lived experience, and the commentary highlights theological emphases of each passage and applies them to the everyday struggles of faith and practice.

Available in stores and online!

Galatians

Thomas R. Schreiner

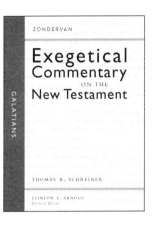

In this volume on Galatians, Thomas R. Schreiner presents a brief and lucid commentary for pastors, students, and laypeople, while also attending to questions that have arisen in light of the New Perspective on Paul. Schreiner, endorsing a Reformation reading of the text, reminds readers of Paul's chief concerns in writing the letter: justification by faith, the full divinity of Christ, freedom from the power of sin through the death and resurrection of Christ Jesus, and dependence on the Holy Spirit to live the Christian life. Schreiner argues that it is not enough to read Galatains with an academic lens; we must realize that these are issues of life and death, and we must let the gospel revive us.

Ephesians

Clinton E. Arnold

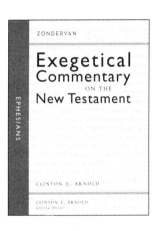

In this volume, Clinton Arnold (who is also the general editor for this series) offer pastors, students, and teachers four themes that emerge in Paul's epistle to the Ephesians: (1) the superior power of God over against spiritual powers; (2) the unity of Jews and Gentiles through Jesus Christ; (3) the encouragement for Gentile believers to live holy lives before God; and (4) the need for believers to be rooted in the knowledge of their new identity in Christ Jesus. Woven into Paul's theology is a refrain of praise and adoration to the glory of God that insists that such praise should also be our response. With attention to issues that continue to surface in today's church, this commentary offers pastors, students, and teachers a focused resource for reading Ephesians.

Available in stores and online!

ZONDERVAN®
.com

Colossians and Philemon

David W. Pao

In this commentary, David Pao explores Paul's presentation in Colossians of a robust Christology that depicts Christ as the fullness of Deity, who death and resurrection has brought about reconciliation with God. Christ is now Lord over every realm of existence. Thus, every aspect of our lives — in the world, in the church, in our homes, and in our personal lives — requires that we adopt a Christlike manner of living and reject patterns of behavior that characterized the old self. Moreover, our response to the lordship of Christ should lead us to a lifetime of worship and thanksgiving. Pao goes on to show how Paul's letter to Philemon is a personal application of these themes.

1 and 2 Thessalonians

Gary S. Shogren

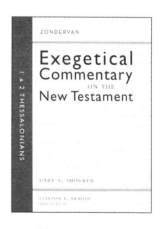

Gary S. Shogren, a missionary teacher at Semanario ESEPA of Costa Rica, explores the pastoral heart of the apostle Paul in 1 and 2 Thessalonians. Paul wrote these two letters to a church from which he had been torn away and was forbidden to return. He needed to instruct the believers in Thessalonica regarding the doctrine of the return of Christ and admonished them to stand firm since that day at hand.

Shogren's goal is that those who use this commentary will learn to imitate the apostle Paul by making themselves available to teach and train other believers, by taking an active role in personal evangelism, by participating in work projects that tangibly show Christ's love, and, above all, by praying for the advance of the gospel.

Available in stores and online!

James

Craig L. Blomberg
and Mariam J. Kamell

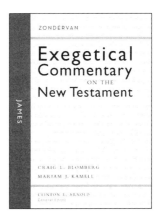

In their study of James, Craig L. Blomberg and Mariam J. Kamell introduce readers to three key themes that dominate the letter: (1) trials and temptations; (2) wisdom and speech, particularly with a view to obedience; and (3) wealth and poverty. Tying these together, however, is the motif of single-mindedness, a trait God consistently displays and one that therefore his people should increasingly display. Readers may be surprised to see how the famous passage on faith versus works actually emerges from the more central topic of wealth and poverty. Replete with insights and timely theological applications, this commentary provides pastors, church leaders, and those in the academy with a complete "one-stop" resource they need for this letter of James.

Available in stores and online!

We want to hear from you. Please send your comments about this book to us in care of zreview@zondervan.com. Thank you.